DICTIONARY OF CANADIAN BIOGRAPHY

DICTIONARY OF CANADIAN BIOGRAPHY
DICTIONNAIRE BIOGRAPHIQUE DU CANADA

FRANCESS G. HALPENNY GENERAL EDITOR

JEAN HAMELIN DIRECTEUR GÉNÉRAL ADJOINT

VOLUME VI

TORONTO

MARY P. BENTLEY supervisory editor JANE E. GRAHAM associate editor
HENRI PILON executive officer

ROBERT LOCHIEL FRASER, STUART R. J. SUTHERLAND
senior manuscript editors
CURTIS FAHEY manuscript editor

PHYLLIS CREIGHTON translations editor
SUSAN E. BÉLANGER bibliographies editor
DEBORAH MARSHALL editorial assistant

QUEBEC

HUGUETTE FILTEAU, MICHEL PAQUIN codirecteurs de la rédaction
THÉRÈSE P. LEMAY rédactrice-historienne principale

PAULETTE M. CHIASSON, CÉLINE CYR, CHRISTIANE DEMERS
FRANCE GALARNEAU, JAMES H. LAMBERT, JACQUELINE ROY
rédacteurs-historiens

SUZANNE ALLAIRE-POIRIER éditrice
MICHÈLE BRASSARD, MARIE-HÉLÈNE LÉVESQUE
auxiliaires de recherche

TRANSLATOR J. F. FLINN

UNIVERSITY OF TORONTO PRESS
LES PRESSES DE L'UNIVERSITÉ LAVAL

DICTIONARY

OF CANADIAN

BIOGRAPHY

VOLUME VI

1821 TO 1835

UNIVERSITY OF TORONTO PRESS

Toronto Buffalo London

©University of Toronto Press and
Les Presses de l'université Laval, 1987
Printed in Canada

ISBN 0-8020-3436-5 (regular edition)

Canadian Cataloguing in Publication Data
Main entry under title:

Dictionary of Canadian biography.

Added t.p. in English and French.
Issued also in French.
Contents: v.1. 1000–1700. – v.2. 1701–1740. – v.3. 1741–1770. –
v.4. 1771–1800. – v.5. 1801–1820. – v.6. 1821–1835. – v.8. 1851–1860. –
v.9. 1861–1870. – v.10. 1871–1880. – v.11. 1881–1890.
Includes bibliographies and indexes.
ISBN 0-8020-3142-0 (v.1)   ISBN 0-8020-3240-0 (v.2)
ISBN 0-8020-3314-8 (v.3)   ISBN 0-8020-3351-2 (v.4)
ISBN 0-8020-3398-9 (v.5)   ISBN 0-8020-3436-5 (v.6)
ISBN 0-8020-3422-5 (v.8)   ISBN 0-8020-3319-9 (v.9)
ISBN 0-8020-3287-7 (v.10)   ISBN 0-8020-3367-9 (v.11)
1. Canada – Biography
FC25.D52 1966   920'.071   C66-3974-5 rev.5
F1005.D49 1966

Contents

Introduction

VOLUME VI is the tenth volume of the *Dictionary of Canadian biography/Dictionnaire biographique du Canada* to be published. Volumes I–V appeared in 1966, 1969, 1974, 1979, and 1983, presenting persons who died or flourished between the years 1000 and 1820 (a separate *Index, volumes I to IV* was issued in 1981). Volume VI (1821–35) continues this progression, and will be followed in 1988 by Volume VII (1836–50). Volumes VIII–XI, encompassing persons who died or flourished 1851–90, have already been published, in 1985, 1976, 1972, and 1982 respectively. Volume XII (1891–1900), in preparation, will complete the 19th century.

The 283 contributors to volume VI, writing in either English or French, have provided 479 biographies ranging in length from fewer than 600 words to more than 10,000 words. They were invited to contribute because of their special knowledge of the period and of the persons who figured in it, and have been asked to write in accordance with the DCB/DBC's *Directives to contributors*. "Biographers should endeavour to provide a readable and stimulating treatment of their subject. Factual information should come from primary sources if possible. . . . The achievements of the subjects should be seen against the background of the period in which they lived and the events in which they participated." The contributors to volume VI bring to it also the benefit of new knowledge on both major and minor figures.

Finding aids for the biographies are provided in the cross-references within texts, the list of subjects of biographies, the nominal index, and special indexes of identifications and geographical locations. The General Bibliography, and the individual bibliographies, identify the principal sources contributors and DCB staff have consulted for the biographies.

Volume VI, like its neighbouring volumes, has themes which reflect both major events in Europe and North America and initiatives of the inhabitants of what is now Canada in response to expanding settlement and developing trade. These exterior and interior influences create patterns which have interesting similarities and differences across the six colonies of Newfoundland, Nova Scotia (with Cape Breton a colony for a time), Prince Edward Island, New Brunswick, Lower Canada, and Upper Canada. New Brunswick and Upper Canada, made provinces in 1784 and 1791, are still new colonies for the men and women of volume VI who come in numbers to build their future there. The west is the domain of the fur trade, with problems of settlement just emerging in the Red River colony.

The exterior influences are, as they were in volume V, largely those created by activities and conflicts of great powers: the American War of Independence, the revolution in France, Britain's battles with the forces of revolutionary France and of Napoleon, and the testing of British North America's existence in the War of 1812. These major events set thousands of people on the move, often as members of military forces but also as emigrants; the disruption of patterns of authority, of society, of trade they occasioned has pervasive consequences for individual lives. Volume VI, like volume V, thus chronicles many persons who moved north from the Thirteen Colonies because of the American revolution. It is concerned also with the effect of revolution in France upon loyalties and upon cultural and religious ties. Many of the British North Americans in the volume are both advantaged and disadvantaged by the fortunes of trade during the wars of Great Britain and France. Some are part of the migration northward from the United States after the loyalist move, or the waves of immigrants from overseas that began when the Napoleonic Wars ended and did not subside (in 1832, more than 51,000 people passed through the port of Quebec).

In the colonies a search for the stability which would enable people to maintain themselves and to benefit from society took many forms. It appears in the efforts to establish administrative and legal systems in the new colonies of New Brunswick and Upper Canada and to refine the exercise of law in others. In all colonies it lies behind the quest for office and patronage. It is part of the struggle by local assemblies to gain exclusive power to deal with pressing questions of finance and local improvements as they deem necessary and by cautious councils to restrain their claims. It underlies the debates over traditions of law and language and the practice of government in the province of Quebec and Lower Canada. Constant contentions over policies and regulations in the granting of land are evidence of how keen a preoccupation land was for the most modest farmer and the boldest entrepreneur. The quest for stability appears in the attempts to get officials in Britain to recognize that Newfoundland was no longer a seasonal base for a migratory fishery but the home of an increasing sedentary population. The expansionary activities of commerce within and trade without support the search, indeed largely help to give it success; the products of home – flour, potash, timber, ships, fish – move along the waterways to the east and over the Atlantic, and westward come manufactured wares, sugar and salt, textiles and spirits. The needs of commerce for a favourable environment are behind the proposals for better transportation by road and canal (the Danforth Road, the Lachine Canal), for banks (in Montreal, in Saint John, in Kingston), and for official regulations that would favour the growth of business.

Old and new inhabitants put forth efforts in the service of what they see as essential components of a society. Volume VI has much to say about those who introduce to new areas, and develop and defend in the old, the Roman Catholic faith and the tradition of the Church of England, and about the endeavours of dissenting groups seeking converts and also civil recognition. It tells of efforts to develop schools, the practice of medicine, and an independent, lively press. The craft traditions continue in Lower Canada, expressed in the making of trade or fine silver and in wood carving; François Baillairgé and Louis Quévillon are two great names. Music, literature, painting, in colonies still defining themselves, have as yet an incidental place, with here and there figures such as the naïve painter of the west, Peter Rindisbacher, or clear-sighted observers of the local scene such as authors John Reeves in Newfoundland, Andrew Brown in Nova Scotia, Robert-Anne d'Estimauville in Lower Canada, Alexander Walker among the Nootkas on the west coast, and with hints of poetry in Thomas Daniel Cowdell, satirist Samuel Denny Street, or Gaelic writer James Drummond MacGregor.

None of the many efforts to establish settlement and societies went forward without differences, even clashes of opinion. There were other serious disruptions: economic depressions because of slumps in world trade, the personal and physical damages of the War of 1812 and the testing of loyalties the war entailed, the sheer labour for women as for men of creating homes in newly opened territories. One of the most dramatic of the dislocations recorded in volume VI is in the great cholera epidemics. No fewer than 30 biographies are of those who died in 1832 or 1834 in the scourge which swept into the colonies with no respect for persons and which no one understood medically. François Romain, educator, is typical: stricken on an especially hot and humid 18 Aug. 1832 and rushed to burial in a new cemetery on the Plains of Abraham.

Dislocations of a different sort give a violent pattern to events in the west. Biographies in volume VI are greatly taken up with the bitter contest between the Hudson's Bay Company and the North West Company for control of the fur trade, especially in the far Athabasca country. The trade in furs and supplies is not confined, of course, to those two firms; there are a number of independents and some other companies. A few persons, from the age-old rivals Britain and Spain, appear on the Pacific northwest coast.

The activities of so many newcomers create situations to which representatives of the native peoples in volume VI, as in neighbouring volumes, must inevitably respond. The last of the Beothuks, stately Shawnadithit, is one. Experience of a different way of life, and often a different faith, is much of the story of Malecite Molly Ann Gell, of Mississauga Ogimauh-binaessih, of the Methodist Mohawk Thomas Davis, and of the important Mohawk chiefs Henry Tekarihogen and John Brant, both of whom fought in the War of 1812 for the British side and were concerned with mediation between the customs of the whites and the requirements of their people on the Grand River lands.

An introduction can only take a sample of the biographies that illustrate these themes – readers should consult the indexes for further leads into the volume. The world of business and trade is one place to start. The firms and agencies in the increasingly busy port cities of St John's, Halifax, Saint John, Quebec, and Montreal provide a prominent group. To these entry points came an impressive contingent of Scottish businessmen, usually linked, perhaps by family connections, with firms in Glasgow or Greenock. They quickly built up interests in the import-export trade or engaged in shipbuilding for it, and many consolidated their position with land or investments. They were often involved in politics especially when public affairs (such as a possible union of Upper and Lower Canada in 1822) related to the environment for business. Improved transportation, banks, and insurance were aids to their enterprises. Some were leading members of local St Andrew's or North British societies or took an interest in education, charitable endeavours, and immigrant societies. Success was not assured, of course, even for this canny group. But some retired with considerable wealth, a few to the Scotland none seems ever to have forgotten. Putting names to these figures brings up, for the Atlantic colonies, Alexander Brymer and Christopher Scott; in Lower Canada, for Quebec, John Goudie and John Mure, and for Montreal, John Fleming, John McKindlay, and John Richardson. Scottish business figures like them are also in Upper Canada: Thomas Clark of Queenston and Charles McDonald of Gananoque, Angus Mackintosh of Detroit and Sandwich.

There are others in the business world of volume VI, with different origins or locations but often similar concerns. Englishman John Cambridge exports timber from Prince

Edward Island. Laurent Quetton St George of York is a royalist *emigré* from France; John Janvrin and Charles Robin are Jerseymen in the Gulf of St Lawrence and on the Gaspé coast. To Newfoundland, Ireland contributed James MacBraire of Harbour Grace and Henry Shea of St John's; the West Country of England, George Garland of Trinity Bay. There are Jewish merchants David David of Montreal and Henry Joseph of Berthier-en-Haut. Natives of Lower Canada are Louis Gauvreau of Quebec and Pierre Guerout of the Richelieu valley. The loyalist immigration brings Munson Jarvis to Saint John.

The search for furs in the northwest becomes an increasingly tense, even violent, trade in the years covered by volume VI. The HBC, endeavouring to expand inland from Hudson and James bays, explores for new routes and sets up new posts but finds itself under the competitive eyes of the Nor'Westers. It has to adopt a "retrenching" system in the spring of 1810 as a way of husbanding men and resources. The settlement at Red River is caught in the middle of this rivalry, and the Nor'Westers, concerned over their supply lines, try to frighten officials and settlers alike. The HBC's activities may be followed in the biographies of Thomas Thomas for the James Bay area, of explorer and map-maker Peter Fidler in the Athabasca, and of William Tomison on the Saskatchewan; the NWC has Benjamin Joseph Frobisher and the powerful William McGillivray. The Red River troubles appear with Joseph Cadotte and William Bacheler Coltman, and especially with Miles Macdonell, governor of Assiniboia in 1811–17 who, unequipped by experience or character, has to cope with the privations of settlers and the pressures against their presence. The fur trade is not just a matter of two major companies in the northwest, however. Independents such as Charles Oakes Ermatinger and John Johnston trade from Detroit or Sault Ste Marie or Michilimackinac. Early in this area was Alexander Henry, who gave the trade an adventure classic with his *Travels* of 1809. The activities of other North American companies, most of them absorbed in the years before the great amalgamation of HBC and NWC in 1821, have a full example in John Richardson.

Biographies concerned with land and settlement are numerous. Many of the subjects are loyalists, who had often seen active service in the Revolutionary War. Gideon White immigrated to the enclave of loyalists at Shelburne, N.S. George Leonard established himself in Sussex Vale, N.B.; John Saunders, owner of an estate in Virginia, attempted another in New Brunswick, which remained wilderness though he rose to be chief justice. Samuel Gale and Gilbert Hyatt were among the Americans who struggled for validation of large grants in the Eastern Townships area. John Walden Meyers of Belleville and Joel Stone of Cornwall and Gananoque continue the story of loyalists in Upper Canada that runs through volumes V to VIII. But loyalist migration is only one context for careers based on land. Angus Macaulay experiences the frustrations of all those in Prince Edward Island caught up in "the land question." Étienne Hébert is one of the Acadians seeking secure homes after their wanderings. James Fulton on the Minas Basin represents the pre-loyalists of Nova Scotia. Archibald McMillan leads 400 emigrants during the Highland enclosures to settlement on the lower Ottawa. The Comte de Puisaye, royalist *emigré*, attempts a colony, ill fated, at Windham, Upper Canada; the claims of Robert Randal of Niagara and the Chaudière to land and installations become a classic case of prolonged litigation. A group of biographies for Lower Canada chronicle the fortunes of the seigneuries, many of them held by families known from the French régime, now living under a new allegiance: Aubert de

Gaspé, Chartier de Lotbinière, Godefroy de Tonnancour, Irumberry de Salaberry, Juchereau Duchesnay, Lambert Dumont, Saint-Ours, Taché, Taschereau. Pierre Casgrain, once a pedlar, and Jean Dessaulles, an agent, assume seigneurial responsibilities.

The administration of the colonies demanded a large group of governors and officials. Governors include some of the naval figures in Newfoundland in the early decades of the century, such as John Holloway and Sir Richard Goodwin Keats, whose terms coincided with tension about the island's future. The on-going conflicts of Cape Breton's administration appear with John Murray and Nicholas Nepean. George Stracey Smyth is tried by the special attitudes to the War of 1812 in the Atlantic colonies. A span of Lower Canada's history is provided with Sir Alured Clarke, who arrived for its creation in 1791, and Sir Francis Nathaniel Burton, who takes up the long-vexed question of government finances in the 1820s. Of special importance is Sir John Coape Sherbrooke, courageous soldier of empire, who after his arrival in Nova Scotia in 1811 meets with war emergencies and religious problems in a multiconfessional society, and later at Quebec, as governor-in-chief of British North America, steers a conciliatory course amid the Catholic clergy and the English and Canadian parties. Difficult to capture is the almost legendary Joseph Frederick Wallet DesBarres, famed cartographer, controversial lieutenant governor of Cape Breton and Prince Edward Island, initiator of complicated land disputes, and a man of unusual domestic habits.

Officials in the volume are both petty and important in several senses. Typical is the tenacious climber D'Arcy Boulton of Upper Canada. Many persons seek office as a source of power but to others public posts are a career in themselves: John Robinson, province treasurer of New Brunswick; Daniel Sutherland, deputy postmaster general of the Canadas; loyalist and tory Michael Wallace, provincial treasurer of Nova Scotia for 33 years. Loyalist John McGill, commissary in Newark and York and an executive councillor, experiences at the turn of the century the frustrations of civilian-military argument. In years marked by wars in North America and peace-time adjustments officials of the Indian Department such as Robert Dickson, Sir John Johnson, and Claude-Nicolas-Guillaume de Lorimier are important servants of the crown.

For colonies struggling to define and develop structures of government and justice, legal issues are inevitably important and lawyers often became participants in public affairs as assemblymen or as holders of office. Not all of those in high office are effective in the law, witness Thomas Tremlett in both Newfoundland and Prince Edward Island. Judicial figures from the early history of New Brunswick are John Murray Bliss and loyalists Jonathan Bliss, Thomas Wetmore, and especially Ward Chipman – promoter of the creation of the colony, solicitor general, assemblyman, judge, administrator. In Prince Edward Island the holding of legal or judicial office by such figures as William Johnston or Cæsar Colclough and Robert Gray becomes tangled by disputes with lieutenant governors over authority and land issues. Such disputes are particularly evidenced in the biography of lawyer James Bardin Palmer. Nova Scotian legal figures include Richard John Uniacke Sr, Irish pre-loyalist, solicitor and attorney general, advocate of freedom for the colonies' trade. Francis Maseres, well trained in law and made attorney general of the province of Quebec in 1766, addresses himself to study of the basis of law and government for the colony. Sir William Grant, acting briefly as attorney general, sets up in 1777 a judicial system for the province following the Quebec Act; a successor in high legal office in Lower Canada is James Monk of Halifax who, like lawyer Stephen Sewell of Montreal, is concerned about possible disaffection in the 1790s; he becomes a reforming chief justice, and as administrator in 1819–20 has to prepare for massive arrivals of destitute immigrants. Legal history for Upper Canada can be observed through William Osgoode, its first chief justice, who sets up a judicial system in 1792–94 with discriminating use of English models. Loyalist William Dummer Powell comes to seek his legal fortune in Quebec in 1779 and moves to a judgeship in Upper Canada in 1789, his rise in influence over long years at York taking him to the chief justiceship. A companion on the bench is William Campbell who comes to the colony in 1811 after an official career in turbulent Cape Breton. These two biographies provide new analysis of the conduct of criminal and treason cases in the critical early years of Upper Canada.

Politics provides a strong emphasis in the career of William Hersey Otis Haliburton, Windsor lawyer, who as an assemblyman 1806–24 serves ordinary Nova Scotians in his interventions about roads, schools, militia service, and dissenters' rights to marriages by licence. Another Windsor assemblyman, William Cottnam Tonge, always in conflict with the Council over spending, encourages a "country party." An impressive figure in Lower Canada is Quebec lawyer Pierre-Stanislas Bédard, "possessed by the demon of politics," who becomes a leader of the Canadian party after 1804, defining the ideology of the middle class to which he belongs, and advocating the supremacy of the assembly. Louis Bourdages, notary of the Richelieu, in 1831 introduces with Papineau a controversial bill on the *fabriques* designed to reduce the power of the parish priests. Many political issues may be studied through Robert Nichol of Niagara, the "clever little fellow" who prodded assemblymen first for the administration and after 1817 took up the cause of "the rights and privileges" of the house in the interest of ministerial responsibility.

A number of figures in education relate to the creation and operation in Lower Canada of the schools of the Royal Institution. Joseph Langley Mills is its secretary, Charles Desroches and William Nelson two of its teachers. Efforts in New Brunswick with schooling for Indians by Oliver Arnold and others meet with difficulties. Initiatives that have long-term results are those of Antoine Girouard with the Collège de Saint-Hyacinthe, Antoine-Bernardin Robert with the curriculum in the Petit Séminaire de Québec, James Durand of Hamilton pushing in the Upper Canadian Assembly for the Common Schools Act of 1816, François Romain of the Quebec Education Society helping to set up the town's first free public school in 1822.

Religious concerns are diverse. The activities of the Anglican church are reflected in the biographies of George Best coping in Fredericton with problems of a new colony; Robert Addison, a scholar in a young Upper Canada who sees its personal advantages in land; John Leigh facing the rigours of Newfoundland outports; Jacob Mountain, bishop of Quebec from 1793 to 1825, contending for church establishment against an inattentive government; Robert Stanser of Halifax living easily with other denominations. Among a number of Catholic *émigré* priests are François Lejamtel working with Acadians and Irish in Cape Breton and Jean-Henry-Auguste Roux, a Sulpician in Montreal. A powerful priest in the Maritimes was Highlander Angus Bernard MacEachern, struggling with lack of clergy, who lived to see civil emancipation in Prince Edward Island in 1830. Thomas Scallan of

Newfoundland faces the poverty of Irish immigrants in 1814–17 and the absence of official recognition of his church. Two significant figures are Joseph-Octave Plessis, priest and then bishop of the huge diocese of Quebec over a long span of its history, 1786–1825, carefully developing relations with the new government and the temporal and spiritual life of the church, and his successor for 1825–37, the conciliatory Archbishop Bernard-Claude Panet. The tracing of the parallel and interacting offices of these significant Anglican and Catholic priests offers a lengthy overview of both denominations.

The steady rise in Methodism is depicted in doughty pioneers of the faith, many of them itinerants, in the Maritimes and Upper Canada: Duncan M'Coll of New Brunswick; Wesleyan Methodist William Black of Nova Scotia, facing the effects of the New Light movement (which motivates John Payzant of Liverpool); William Losee in the Bay of Quinte; Henry Ryan, presiding elder in Upper and Lower Canada, from the American Methodist tradition but seeking an independent conference; Hester Ann Hubbard, teaching among the Mississauga Ojibwas. The doctrinal differences of the Presbyterians in Scotland are reflected in secessionist Robert Easton in Montreal, and the burgher/anti-burgher conflict affecting Hugh Graham and James Drummond MacGregor in their isolated service in Nova Scotia.

The professions appear also with medical figures, many of them military surgeons (including several Hessians of the anti-revolutionary army) who establish themselves in civil roles in the colonies. All doctors are concerned with standards of practice and the improvement of hospital care; health officers are confronted with waves of immigrants and epidemics of typhus, cholera, syphilis. John Frederick Gschwind in Halifax, William Caldwell in Montreal, and Charles-Norbert Perrault of Quebec (trained in Edinburgh as so many were) demonstrate these concerns. Journalists are an active group: Anthony Henry Holland and John Howe in Halifax; George Kilman Lugrin in Fredericton; Thomas Cary of Quebec; Hugh Christopher Thomson in Kingston, Francis Collins of York. A number of influential newspapers are the result. In a period of settlement surveyors are obviously in demand: Charles Morris copes with settling loyalists and veterans in the Maritimes, Roswell Mount with the immigrants of 1820–33 in the Western District of Upper Canada; DesBarres distinguishes himself in the charts that finally inform the *Atlantic Neptune*. The War of 1812 is the background for a great many of the military figures; in the group portrait are commanders Charles-Michel d'Irumberry de Salaberry, Henry Procter, and Francis de Rottenburg, officers such as Joseph-Maurice Lamothe, Adam Charles Muir, and Donald Macpherson, naval men George Benson Hall of the Provincial Marine and Sir John Borlase Warren on the Halifax station, privateer Joseph Barss out of Liverpool, and in Upper Canada, fighting along with the Indians, William Caldwell.

Like other volumes of the DCB, volume VI has its fair and full share of persons who escape easy classification and stand out for the difference they provide in the picture of a span of years. A random selection catches Jacques-Ladislas-Joseph de Calonne, abbot of France who as an *émigré* took up humble parish duties but was both celebrated preacher and ascetic; Mary Cannon, mistress of DesBarres and agent for his extensive properties in the Maritimes with little thanks; Michel-Eustache-Gaspard-Alain Chartier de Lotbinière, seigneur, whose eloquent 1793 address to the Lower Canadian assembly on the use of English and French in its debates was depicted in a famous portrait; Benjamin Chappell, suffering through dreadful first years on Prince Edward Island but establishing his craft as wheelwright in making over 600 spinning-wheels; Thomas Delvecchio, Italian innkeeper of Montreal who maintained a popular museum of natural history and curiosities; David Douglas, indefatigable botanist on the Pacific coast for whom the fir tree is named; Jean-Baptiste Duberger, surveyor and engraver, with his immense model of the Quebec defences which filled a ballroom; Charles French, a young York printer executed for his part in a street brawl; Robert Hood, naval officer and artist, stoical recorder of Sir John Franklin's disastrous first land expedition for which Tattannoeuck was a loyal Inuit guide; John Rodgers Jewitt, armourer, who as captive of the Nootkas shared and recorded their lives; Adam Kidd of Montreal, in his poem "The Huron Chief" mingling Irish nationalism and the style of Byron; Anne Powell, daughter of William Dummer Powell, pursuing John Beverley Robinson to her family's consternation and her own death; Grizelda Tonge, cherished as a fragile poetic promise for Nova Scotia, dead of tropical fever in her youth; Andrew Westbrook, flamboyant raider of the War of 1812, whom novelist John Richardson seized for fiction; Miller Worsley, captain of the *Nancy*, gallantly fighting off the Americans in 1814 at Nottawasaga Bay and Michilimackinac.

The efforts of the staff of the DCB/DBC in assembling these hundreds of texts for volume VI are another evidence of their skill, knowledge, and dedication. We wish to express our high appreciation.

FRANCESS G. HALPENNY

JEAN HAMELIN

Acknowledgements

THE *Dictionary of Canadian biography/Dictionnaire biographique du Canada* receives assistance, advice, and encouragement from many institutions and individuals. They cannot all be named nor can their kindness and support be adequately acknowledged.

The DCB/DBC, which owes its founding to the generosity of the late James Nicholson, has been sustained over the years by its parent institutions, the University of Toronto and the University of Toronto Press and the Université Laval and Les Presses de l'université Laval. Beginning in 1973 the Canada Council provided grants to the two university presses which made possible the continuation and acceleration of the DCB/DBC's publication program, and this assistance has been maintained and amplified by the Social Sciences and Humanities Research Council of Canada, created in 1978. We should like to give special thanks to the SSHRCC not only for its financial support but also for the encouragement it has given us as we strive to complete our volumes for the 19th century. We are grateful also for the financial assistance accorded us by the Université Laval.

Of the numerous individuals who assisted in the preparation of volume VI, we owe particular thanks to our contributors. In addition, we have had the benefit of special consultation with a number of persons, some of them also contributors. We should like to thank: Denise Bousquet, Susan Buggey, Brian Driscoll, Raymond Dumais, Micheline Fortin, Armand Gagné, Gilles Héon, H. T. Holman, Grace Hyam, Barry Hyman, Patricia Kennedy, Louis-Joseph Lépine, Allan J. MacDonald, Marianne McLean, Monique Mailloux, André Martineau, the late Keith Matthews, Pamela J. Miller, J. E. Rea, and Shirlee Anne Smith. We should like, in particular, to acknowledge with gratitude our debt to the late Phyllis R. Blakeley, whose friendship and support over many volumes will be sadly missed.

Throughout the preparation of volume VI we have enjoyed willing cooperation from libraries and archives in Canada and elsewhere. We are particularly grateful to the administrators and staffs of those institutions to which we have most frequently appealed. In addition to the Public Archives of Canada in Ottawa and the provincial archives in all the provinces, they are: in Manitoba, the Hudson's Bay Company Archives (Winnipeg); in New Brunswick, the New Brunswick Museum (Saint John) and the University of New Brunswick Library (Fredericton); in Ontario, the Kingston Public Library, the Metropolitan Toronto Library, the Queen's University Library (Kingston), the United Church Archives (Toronto), and the University of Toronto Library; in Quebec, the *archives civiles* and *judiciaires*, the Archives de l'archidiocèse de Québec, the Archives de l'université de Montréal, the Bibliothèque de l'Assemblée nationale (Québec), the Bibliothèque and Archives du Séminaire de Québec, the Bibliothèque générale de l'université Laval, the McCord Museum (Montreal), and the Montreal Business History Project. We should like to thank as well the staffs of the *archives départementales* and *municipales* in France, of the various record offices in the United Kingdom, and of the many archives, libraries, and historical societies in the United States who answered our numerous requests for information so kindly.

The editors of volume VI were helped in the preparation of the volume by colleagues in both offices. In Toronto, editorial and research assistance has been given by Charles Dougall, David Roberts, Catherine A. Waite, and Robert G. Wuetherick. Deborah Marshall provided invaluable editorial assistance and was in charge of the secretariat in Toronto, where secretarial and administrative services were provided by Joanne d'Abreau, Andrée Dubois, and Lina Peres. In Quebec, Marcelle Duquet, John Keyes, and Robert Tremblay aided the editors at one stage or another of volume VI. Jean-Pierre Asselin and Anne Rogier worked on the verification of translations. Pierrette Desrosiers was in charge of secretarial services, assisted by Suzanne East and Louise D. Barabé. We have also benefited from the advice of Jacques Chouinard of the Service des éditions des Presses de l'université Laval and also of the staff of the Office de la langue française as well as that of the Translation Bureau of the Department of the Secretary of State.

We should like to recognize the guidance and encouragement we have received from the two presses with which the DCB/DBC is associated, and in particular from Harald Bohne, H. C. Van Ierssel, Peter Scaggs, and Stephen Phillips at the University of Toronto Press and Marc Boucher and Jacques Beaulieu at Les Presses de l'université Laval.

DICTIONNAIRE BIOGRAPHIQUE DU CANADA   DICTIONARY OF CANADIAN BIOGRAPHY

Subjects of Biographies

ADDISON, Robert (1754–1829)
Agnew, Stair (d. 1821)
Ainse, Sarah (Montour; Maxwell; Willson)
  (d. *c.* 1823)
Amherst, Elizabeth Frances (Hale) (1774–1826)
Anspach, Lewis Amadeus (1770–1823)
Appleton, Thomas (fl. 1818–35)
April, Nance. *See* Shawnadithit
Arnold, Oliver (1755–1834)
Arnoldi, Phebe, named de Sainte-Angèle (Diehl)
  (1767–1825)
Atkinson, George (1777–1830)
Aubert de Gaspé, Pierre-Ignace (1758–1823)
Auld, William (fl. 1790–1830)
Auldjo, Alexander (1758–1821)
Aw-gee-nah (fl. 1771–1821)

BABY, James (1763–1833)
Badeaux, Joseph (1777–1835)
Baillairgé, François (1759–1830)
Bailly, Joseph (1774–1835)
Baker, Charles (1743–1835)
Barclay, John (1795–1826)
Barclay, Thomas Henry (1753–1830)
Barkley, Charles William (1759–1832)
Barss, Joseph (1776–1824)
Beckwith, Sir Thomas Sydney (1772–1831)
Bédard, Jean-Charles (1766–1825)
Bédard, Joseph-Isidore (1806–33)
Bédard, Pierre-Stanislas (1762–1829)
Bellet, François (1750–1827)
Beman, Elisha (1760–1821)
Berthelet, Pierre (1746–1830)
Best, George (d. 1829)
Bidwell, Barnabas (1763–1833)
Bigault d'Aubreville, Louis-Nicolas-Emmanuel de
  (fl. 1791–1828)
Black, John (d. 1823)
Black, William (1760–1834)
Blanchet, François (1776–1830)
Bland, John (fl. 1790–1825)
Bleakley, Josiah (d. 1822)
Bliss, John Murray (1771–1834)
Bliss, Jonathan (1742–1822)
Bond, Joseph Norman (1758–1830)
Bouc, Charles-Jean-Baptiste (1766–1832)
Boulton, D'Arcy (1759–1834)

Bourdages, Louis (1764–1835)
Bouthillier, Jean-Antoine (1782–1835)
Brant, John. *See* Tekarihogen
Brassard Deschenaux, Charles-Joseph (1752–1832)
Brauneis, John Chrisostomus (d. 1832)
Bro, Jean-Baptiste (1743–1824)
Brown, Andrew (1763–1834)
Brymer, Alexander (d. 1822)
Buell, William (1751–1832)
Burley, Cornelius Albertson (d. 1830)
Burns, John (d. 1822)
Burns, William (d. 1829)
Burton, Sir Francis Nathaniel (1766–1832)
Butler (Dight), John Butler (d. 1834)

CADOTTE, Joseph (fl. 1814–22)
Caldwell, William (d. 1822)
Caldwell, William (1782–1833)
Calonne, Jacques-Ladislas-Joseph de (1743–1822)
Cambridge, John (1748–1831)
Cameron, Æneas (d. 1822)
Cameron, John. *See* Ogimauh-binaessih
Campbell, Patrick (fl. *c.* 1765–1823)
Campbell, Sir William (1758–1834)
Cannon, John (d. 1833)
Cannon, Mary (d. 1827)
Carmichael, John Edward (d. 1828)
Cary, Thomas (1751–1823)
Casgrain, Pierre (1771–1828)
Chaboillez, Augustin (1773–1834)
Chaffey, Samuel (1793–1827)
Chamberlain, Theophilus (1737–1824)
Chappell, Benjamin (1740/41–1825)
Chartier de Lotbinière, Michel-Eustache-Gaspard-
  Alain (1748–1822)
Chaussegros de Léry, Louis-René (1762–1832)
Chenneque, Martin (d. 1825)
Chipman, Ward (1754–1824)
Ciquard, François (1754–1824)
Clark, Robert (1744–1823)
Clark, Thomas (d. 1835)
Clarke, Sir Alured (d. 1832)
Claus, William (1765–1826)
Clench, Ralfe (d. 1828)
Cobbett, William (1763–1835)
Cochran, William (d. 1833)
Cockrell, Richard (d. 1829)

Editorial Notes

Persons have been entered under family name rather than title, pseudonym, popular name, nickname, or name in religion. Where possible the form of the surname is based on the signature, although contemporary usage is taken into account. Common variant spellings are included in parenthesis.

In the case of French names, "La," "Le," "Du," "Des," and sometimes "De" are considered part of the name and are capitalized. When both parts of the name are capitalized in the signature, French style treats the family name as two words; however, with individuals who were integrated into an anglophone milieu, this rule of style has been applied only when it was confirmed by a signature. Compound names often appear: Charles-Michel d'IRUMBERRY de Salaberry; Nicolas-Eustache LAMBERT Dumont; cross-references are made in the text from the compounds to the main entry under the family name: from Salaberry to Irumberry and from Dumont to Lambert.

Where a signature was not available for a subject whose name began with Mc or Mac, the form Mac, followed by a capital letter, has been used. Scottish-born immigrants who were entitled under Scottish law to a territorial designation as part of their names appear with that designation included: Angus MACKINTOSH of Mackintosh, 26th Chief of Clan Chattan and 25th Chief of Clan Mackintosh. Scots for whom the designation was used merely as a convenient way of distinguishing one individual from another have the designation in parenthesis: Hugh McDONELL (Aberchalder). In all cases, appropriate cross-references are provided.

Married women and *religieuses* have been entered under their maiden names, with cross-references to the entries from their husbands' names or their names in religion: Hester Ann HUBBARD (Case); Marie-Anne-Louise TASCHEREAU, named de Saint-François-Xavier.

Indian names have presented a particular problem, since an Indian might be known by his own name (written in a variety of ways by people unfamiliar with Indian languages) and by a nickname or baptismal name. Moreover, by the late 18th century some Indian families, such as the Tomahs, were beginning to use family surnames in the European style. Indian names have been used when they could be found, and, because it is impossible to establish an original spelling for an Indian name, the form generally chosen is the one found in standard sources or the one linguists now regard as correct; variants are included in parenthesis: OGIMAUH-BINAESSIH (Okemapenesse, Wageezhegome, Wakeshogomy, Weggishgomin, John Cameron, Captain John). When Indians signed both an Indian name and a Europeanized one, as did TEKARIHOGEN (John Brant), they appear under the Indian name. Appropriate cross-references are included.

For reference works useful in establishing the names of persons not receiving biographies in the DCB/DBC, the reader is referred to section III of the General Bibliography.

The first time the name of a person who has a biography in volume VI appears in another biography his or her family name is printed in capitals and level small capitals: Ward CHIPMAN; Joseph-Octave PLESSIS.

An asterisk following a name indicates either that the person has a biography in a volume already published – Sir Isaac Brock*; Louis-Joseph Papineau* – or that he or she will receive a biography in a volume to be published – Jean-Jacques Lartigue*; Sir John A. Macdonald*. Birth and death (or floruit) dates for such persons are given in the index as an indication of the volume in which the biography will be found.

Place-names are generally given in the form used at the time of reference; where necessary, the modern name and/or the present name of the province, territory, state, or country in which the place is located have been included in parenthesis: York (Toronto), Norway House (Man.), Rutland (Vt), and Pressburg (Bratislava, Czechoslovakia). The English edition cites well-known place-names in their present-day English form: St Lawrence River, Montreal, Quebec,

Marseilles, Geneva. The *Encyclopædia Britannica* has been followed in determining whether place-names outside Canada have accepted English forms. Cities considered to be easily recognizable (such as London, Paris, Rome, and Boston) are not identified by country; within Canada, provincial capitals and several well-known cities (such as Montreal and Vancouver) are not identified by province.

Many sources have been used as guides to establish 18th- and early-19th-century place-names: Bouchette, *Topographical description of L.C.*; *Canadian Encyclopedia*; *Encyclopædia Britannica*; *Encyclopedia Canadiana*; HBRS (several volumes in this series have been helpful); "Historic forts and trading posts of the French regime and of the English fur trading companies," comp. Ernest Voorhis (mimeograph, Ottawa, 1930); Hormisdas Magnan, *Dictionnaire historique et géographique des paroisses, missions et municipalités de la province de Québec* (Arthabaska, Qué., 1925); *Place-names of N.S.*; *Places in Ont.* (Mika); Rayburn, *Geographical names of N.B.* and *Geographical names of P.E.I.*; P.-G. Roy, *Inv. concessions*; W. H. Smith, *Canada: past, present and future . . .* (2v., Toronto, [1852]; repr. Belleville, Ont., 1973–74); Walbran, *B.C. coast names*. For complete information about titles given in shortened form the reader is referred to the General Bibliography.

Modern Canadian names are based whenever possible on the Gazetteer of Canada series issued by the Canadian Permanent Committee on Geographical Names, Ottawa, on the *Canada gazetteer atlas* (n.p., 1980), and on the *Répertoire toponymique du Québec* (Québec, 1979) published by the Commission de toponymie and the supplements published in the *Gazette officielle du Québec*. For places outside Canada the following have been major sources of reference: *Bartholomew gazetteer of Britain*, comp. Oliver Mason ([Edinburgh, 1977]); Albert Dauzat et Charles Rostaing, *Dictionnaire étymologique des noms de lieux en France* (Paris, [1963]); *Dictionnaire universel des noms propres . . . le Petit Robert 2*, Paul Robert *et al.*, édit. (3ᵉ éd., Paris, 1977); *Grand Larousse encyclopédique*; *National Geographic atlas of the world*, ed. W. E. Garrett *et al.* (5th ed., Washington, 1981).

CONTEMPORARY USAGE

To avoid the anachronism of applying the terms "French Canadian" and "English Canadian" to the 18th and early 19th centuries, volume VI follows the contemporary practice of referring to the French-speaking inhabitants of the province of Quebec simply as "Canadians." Readers should be aware, however, that in the context of the fur trade the term "Canadian"

is used, as it was at the time, to refer to Montreal-based traders, whether French- or English-speaking.

Useful reference works for contemporary usage are *A dictionary of Canadianisms on historical principles*, ed. W. S. Avis *et al.* (Toronto, 1967) and *Dictionary of Newfoundland English*, ed. G. M. Story *et al.* (Toronto, [1982]).

QUOTATIONS

Quotations have been translated when the language of the original passage is different from that of the text of the biography. Readers of the DCB may consult the DBC for the original French of quotations that have been translated into English. When a passage in French is quoted from a work that has appeared in both languages, the published English version is generally used. The wording, spelling, punctuation, and capitalization of original quotations are not altered unless it is necessary to do so for meaning, in which case the changes are made within square brackets. A name appearing within square brackets has been substituted for the original in order to identify the person more precisely or to indicate that he/she has a biography within the volume or in another volume.

DATES

If, in spite of assiduous inquiry, it is impossible to uncover a subject's birth and death dates, only the dates of his/her active career are documented. In the introductory paragraphs and in the various indexes the outside dates of activity are presented as floruit (fl.) dates.

BIBLIOGRAPHIES

Each biography is followed by a bibliography. Sources frequently used by authors and editors are cited in shortened form in individual bibliographies; the General Bibliography (pp.827–58) gives these sources in full. Many abbreviations are used in the individual bibliographies, especially for archival sources; a list of these can be found on p.2 and p.826.

The individual bibliographies are generally arranged alphabetically according to the five sections of the General Bibliography: manuscript sources, printed primary sources (including a section on contemporary newspapers), reference works, studies and theses, and journals. Wherever possible, manuscript material is cited under the location of the original documents; the location of copies used by contributors is included in the citation. In general, the items in individual bibliographies are the sources listed by the contributors, but these items have often been supplemented by bibliographic investigation in the DCB/DBC offices. Any special bibliographical comments by contributors appear within square brackets.

TRANSLATION INTO ENGLISH (a note by the translator of French biographies)

The translation of French-language biographies in volume VI presented similar challenges to those faced in volume V. The existence in Quebec/Lower Canada of a British military establishment, a parliamentary system based on that in London, and a significant anglophone mercantile and entrepreneurial community resulted in the frequent use of English terms there; in translation these often had to be recognized under the French equivalents adopted in the province. The use of cognate terms or names in the two languages, particularly in the administrative and business worlds, which became fairly standard practice in the colony, normally caused little difficulty, as with the Union Company of Quebec/la Compagnie de l'Union de Québec, but required constant vigilance to discover the equivalent in the other language. The House of Assembly was officially bilingual and its statutes were a helpful source, as was the *Quebec Gazette/la Gazette de Québec*. A microfilm copy of the index to the commissions register (PAC, RG 68, General index, 1651–1841) was used frequently in establishing the English form for official appointments. The maintenance of the seigneurial system and French civil law assured the continuing use of many of the French terms found regularly in previous volumes. For some of the more unfamiliar terminology in property transactions, translation was attempted, as in "secured annuity" for *la rente constituée*, in order to give readers at least an idea of the nature of the obligation involved. *A dictionary of Canadianisms on historical principles*, ed. W. S. Avis *et al*. (Toronto, 1967), was again useful in decisions relating to translation. As in volume V the English originals of quotations in French biographies were used when available.

BIOGRAPHIES

List of Abbreviations

AAQ	Archives de l'archidiocèse de Québec	MAC-CD	Ministère des Affaires culturelles, Centre de documentation
AC	Archives civiles	MTL	Metropolitan Toronto Library
ACAM	Archives de la chancellerie de l'archevêché de Montréal	NLS	National Library of Scotland
		NMM	National Maritime Museum
ACC	Anglican Church of Canada	NWC	North West Company
AD	Archives départementales	*OH*	*Ontario History*
ADB	*Australian dictionary of biography*	PABC	Provincial Archives of British Columbia
ANQ	Archives nationales du Québec		
AO	Archives of Ontario	PAC	Public Archives of Canada
AP	Archives paroissiales	PAM	Provincial Archives of Manitoba
ASQ	Archives du séminaire de Québec	PANB	Provincial Archives of New Brunswick
ASSH	Archives du séminaire de Saint-Hyacinthe	PANL	Provincial Archives of Newfoundland and Labrador
ASSM	Archives du séminaire de Saint-Sulpice, Montréal	PANS	Public Archives of Nova Scotia
AUM	Archives de l'université de Montréal	PAPEI	Public Archives of Prince Edward Island
BCHQ	*British Columbia Historical Quarterly*	PRO	Public Record Office
BE	Bureau d'enregistrement	QUA	Queen's University Archives
BL	British Library	*RHAF*	*Revue d'histoire de l'Amérique française*
BRH	*Le Bulletin des recherches historiques*		
CCHA	Canadian Catholic Historical Association	RSC	Royal Society of Canada
		SGCF	Société généalogique canadienne-française
CHA	Canadian Historical Association		
CHR	*Canadian Historical Review*	*SH*	*Social History*
DAB	*Dictionary of American biography*	SPG	Society for the Propagation of the Gospel in Foreign Parts
DCB	*Dictionary of Canadian biography*		
DNB	*Dictionary of national biography*	SRO	Scottish Record Office
DOLQ	*Dictionnaire des œuvres littéraires du Québec*	UCC	United Church of Canada
		UNBL	University of New Brunswick Library
HBC	Hudson's Bay Company	USPG	United Society for the Propagation of the Gospel
HBCA	Hudson's Bay Company Archives		
HBRS	Hudson's Bay Record Society, *Publications*	UWOL	University of Western Ontario Library

Biographies

A

ABERCHALDER. *See* McDonell

ADDISON, ROBERT, Church of England clergyman; b. 6 June 1754 in Heversham, England, son of John Addison and Ellinor Parkinson; m. 24 Oct. 1780 Mary Atkinson in Cambridge, England, and they had four children, two of whom reached adulthood; m. secondly, probably after July 1807, Rebecca (Plummer?); d. 6 Oct. 1829 in Niagara (Niagara-on-the-Lake), Upper Canada.

Robert Addison attended Trinity College, Cambridge, where he received his BA in 1781 and his MA in 1785. He was ordained deacon in the Church of England on 11 March 1781 and served for a time as curate at Upwell. During the 1780s he was also employed as a tutor for students aspiring to university. By the late 1780s, however, his wife had developed some form of mental illness. Even without that disadvantage, his prospects in the church were not encouraging. At the end of the decade, therefore, possibly following his wife's death, he applied to the Society for the Propagation of the Gospel for a position as missionary. He was appointed to Newark (Niagara-on-the-Lake), Upper Canada. Addison spent the winter of 1791 at Quebec and arrived at his post in July 1792.

He had great expectations for life in Upper Canada. By the time he died some of them had been realized, but nothing was accomplished easily. When he arrived, Newark, although it was the colonial capital and a forwarding centre for the Laurentian fur trade, was no more than a small village. The adjacent agricultural land was sparsely populated and, at least until the 1820s, most of the people were Presbyterians or Congregationalists. In 1792 Addison was only the third Anglican missionary to be permanently settled in Upper Canada – the others were John Stuart* and John Langhorn* – and the only clergyman of any denomination in the Niagara region. He remained the sole Anglican clergyman west of Ernestown (Bath) until George Okill Stuart* arrived at York (Toronto) in 1801. Not only did Addison have primary responsibility for the whole of the Niagara peninsula but also, from the beginning, he was expected to minister to the Six Nations settlement on the banks of the Grand River. Until 1818, when he turned over this duty to

Ralph Leeming*, Addison made two visits to the settlement each year. He never learned the Mohawk language – relying instead upon Joseph Brant [Thayendanegea*] and John Norton as translators – but was as successful among them as could be expected.

Addison was a good preacher and, if not zealous, was at least assiduous in the performance of his duties. He was popular among his parishioners and was always able to report sizeable congregations. If people responded to him well enough on that level, however, there were other ways in which they were not so satisfactory. For example, it was 1809 before his congregation had built a church for him at Niagara, as Newark was then called. There was some consolation perhaps in the knowledge that when it was finally completed St Mark's was the finest church in the colony. But surely that made it all the more difficult for Addison to bear its fate: St Mark's was seized and eventually burned by American invaders in 1813. It was not restored until 1821 and stood without episcopal consecration until 1828, when Bishop Charles James Stewart* performed the ceremony.

Similarly, parochial response to Addison was something less than adequate on the matter of his remuneration. When they petitioned the SPG for a missionary in 1790, the citizens of Newark promised a glebe and a house and £100 a year for seven years. Addison made repeated attempts to obtain the money but in the end saw little of it. Prices were high in the isolated community and he suffered some deprivations, especially in the early years. In fact, in 1794 his financial difficulties induced him to seek permission from the SPG to relocate in Nova Scotia. But nothing came of the idea and toward the end of the decade Addison's position improved considerably. His salary from the SPG was augmented after 1796 by an annual allowance from the government. He also received a stipend as chaplain to the House of Assembly, a position he continued to hold even after the seat of government was transferred to York. Finally, he served as a military chaplain whenever the stationing of a regiment in the area provided an opportunity.

Taken all together, Addison's financial resources were adequate for his immediate needs. But there was still a difficulty – most of his income would end with

Addison

his death. Addison was 45 years old at the turn of the century and, at a time when longevity was for the very few, the possibility of leaving his family practically destitute was a source of considerable anxiety. That is probably why throughout his life in Upper Canada he was involved in financial ventures designed to build up an estate.

The most important of these secular activities was land speculation. Beginning in the mid 1790s, Addison displayed a keen interest in acquiring whatever land was available from the government. The records show that by the end of the War of 1812 he had received 27 grants scattered through seven townships in the Niagara area. He also purchased land – for example, 18,000 acres in Norwich Township and Dereham Township (Southwest Oxford Township) in 1800, and 13,000 acres in Nichol Township in 1826. By the late 1820s his total holdings were well in excess of 31,000 acres, making him one of the largest landholders in the colony. When the government attempted to collect high taxes on undeveloped land under legislation passed in 1824, Addison was ready to protect his investment. His name appeared at the head of a petition which opposed the legislation and which was presented to the house. He also joined with William Warren Baldwin*, Thomas CLARK, and William Dickson* in appearing before a committee of the assembly to argue forcibly against it.

If Addison's land speculation was successful, another of his enterprises was not. In 1798 he obtained from the government a lease on a salt spring in Louth Township, although apparently no formal contract was signed. Having no intention of producing salt himself, he spent some money improving the facility and in 1802 sublet it to one Solomon Moore. Problems developed in 1807, when the executor for the estate of Angus Macdonell* (Collachie), the saltworks' former operator, demanded compensation from Addison for improvements Macdonell had made. Three years later Moore submitted to the Executive Council a petition in which he asked that the spring be given to him and, presumably to strengthen his case, accused Addison of misrepresentation and extortion. In both instances the council proceeded in a brusque and peremptory manner against Addison. The dispute over compensation was eventually – after three years – decided in his favour, but in the contest with Moore, Addison protested his innocence in vain. He appeared personally before the council and presented testimony by Robert NICHOL and Thomas DICKSON denying the truth of Moore's allegations. The council, however, chose to believe Moore, and Addison was told that he had no claim on the spring. As it turned out, the spring was not granted to Moore; in fact, it never went into operation again. Addison made one more attempt to regain the property, but it came to nothing, and the accusations Moore had made against him were not cleared up.

Addison's expectations in the salt spring affair were unrealistic. It was naïve to think that he could maintain a hold on such a potentially valuable resource without a much more vigorous personal involvement than he was able to give. Nevertheless, the behaviour of the council was remarkable. Addison was, after all, a clergyman of the established church whose conduct had never been publicly criticized by military, civil, or religious authorities. Yet the council seemed prepared to believe the worst of him and, in the end, its treatment of him was unsympathetic, even hostile.

The probable reason is that during 1806 and 1807 Lieutenant Governor Francis Gore* came to see Addison as a dangerous radical. Gore was sure that there was an "intimate connection" between Addison and those critics of the administration led by judge Robert Thorpe*, William Weekes*, and Joseph Willcocks*. In the winter of 1806–7 Gore started to move against the anti-government faction and in the course of an investigation uncovered what he thought was evidence of Addison's complicity. Although the lieutenant governor was convinced, it seems highly unlikely that the connection ever existed.

The problem had all begun in the summer of 1806 when Brant attacked William CLAUS, head of the Indian Department in Upper Canada, in a speech given before an Indian council at Fort George (Niagara-on-the-Lake) which was attended by Thorpe, Weekes, and Addison. The latter's presence at the meeting was taken as evidence of his sympathy with the attack and with the views of the political opposition. But Addison had other, more plausible, reasons for attending. The council was held at Niagara, Addison had had a long association with Brant, and he was, after all, the established church's missionary to many of the Indians who were there. It seems likely that if he had had any subversive interest, it would have been that of a land speculator looking longingly at the Indians' territories.

There is no evidence linking Addison with the course pursued by Thorpe and his associates through the summer and early autumn of 1806. But in November he, along with Samuel Thompson, a merchant at Niagara, agreed to act as financial guarantors for Willcocks as sheriff of the Home District. By that time Willcocks was openly critical of the government and was, in fact, deeply involved in Thorpe's campaign for election to the assembly. In early 1807 Gore collected testimony from several witnesses bearing upon Willcocks's radicalism and transmitted it to London. References to Addison's agreement to guarantee Willcocks were included. Gore seems to have decided that Addison's connection with Willcocks was evidence of political sympathy. But that was simply guilt by association. An agreement which provided financial surety for a man whom Addison had known for years and which concerned only actions taken in his capacity as a government official is scarcely evidence of revolutionary intent. In fact, Addison had a very different evaluation of Willcocks. In a letter to Thorpe's wife, written in the summer of 1807, Addison expressed doubt over Willcocks's chance of success as a newspaper publisher and politician. Like all Irishmen, he said, Willcocks had no capacity for restraint. What he had to struggle against in his nature was "all the jealousy of power and all the malignity of rank Opposition." Those are not the words of a political sympathizer.

Addison did write on at least two occasions to the former surveyor general, Charles Burton Wyatt*, who left Upper Canada in 1807 to seek redress in Britain after he had been dismissed by Gore. But there is no evidence that Addison's letters expressed any radical sympathies and, in any case, Wyatt was not a central figure in the Thorpe group. Wyatt did regard himself as a friend of Addison and when he returned to England he went to considerable trouble to try to arrange a military chaplaincy for him at Niagara. But Addison did not return the friendship. In 1807 he described Wyatt as a man driven by the devil; later, he did not even bother to thank him for his efforts.

It seems clear, therefore, that Addison was not a silent partner of Thorpe, Weekes, and Willcocks during and after the summer of 1806. There remains a possibility, however, that he may have been more friendly with them earlier. If so, his friendship would have come as an outgrowth of his association with the group of Scottish merchants centred in Niagara. Dickson, Nichol, Clark, Robert Hamilton*, and their colleagues were Addison's parishioners, friends, and business associates. It has been shown recently that until 1806 the main feature of the political life of the Niagara peninsula was a conflict between these large-scale Laurentian traders on the one hand and government officials and representatives and small merchants on the other. Addison probably shared the political outlook of the Scottish merchants and, to the extent that he perceived the Thorpe group as critical of the existing government, he may have seen them as potential allies. By 1807, however, the strident radicalism of Thorpe and Willcocks was beginning to force a realignment of political groups in the Niagara area. The large merchants moved to a position of support for the lieutenant governor and his councils. Addison may have done the same.

In any event, Addison was politically suspect to Gore for years after 1806. In fact it was probably not until he demonstrated his loyalty in the War of 1812 that the earlier suspicions were forgotten. Addison's parish was in the most vulnerable part of Upper Canada, but he remained at his post throughout the war. He was present to officiate at the military funeral of Sir Isaac Brock*, he stood by helplessly while the

Americans burned the town, his church included, and he told the SPG that he had been "plundered made prisoner of war, & harrassed till he was dangerously ill." Before the conflict was over Addison had witnessed "almost all the sad scenes of Distress which a Country subject to the Ravages of War can suffer." As it came to a close, the part he had played began to receive public recognition. In 1814 the assembly unanimously voted him £100 in consideration of his work with the wounded soldiers of Fort George and the unfortunate inhabitants of the Niagara area. A year later he was chosen to distribute throughout the region money raised by the Loyal and Patriotic Society of Upper Canada for the relief of those who had suffered wartime damages.

Addison was probably the best-educated man in Upper Canada during his lifetime. When he came to the colony he brought with him a magnificent personal library of 17th- and 18th-century books. But he did not use them, at least not systematically. There was nothing in the new colonial environment to stimulate him and that, combined with a tendency to indolence, he admitted, resulted in only desultory reading and the lack of "excellence in anything." Nevertheless, he was able to contribute something to the educational history of the province. In 1815 he joined with John Strachan* in a report to the lieutenant governor proposing an organizational plan for public education in the colony. Part of it was accepted and formed the basis of the Common Schools Act of 1816. Strachan was so impressed by Addison's scholarly attainments as to confess that Addison was the only man in Upper Canada under whom he would be willing to serve in the university he hoped to see established. When the charter for King's College was issued in 1827, the office of president was vested in the archdeacon of York. But Strachan was willing to offer Addison the position of principal in the new institution. Addison had a momentary reverie in which he saw himself as the senior scholar enjoying the respect of young students. Quickly, however, he returned to reality: he was too old, he told Strachan, and his health was so poor that he would not live to see the university opened.

By the late 1820s Addison had been in Upper Canada nearly 40 years and had lived closer to the centre of colonial affairs than most men. His dedication to his church and his people was supplemented by considerable activity indicating acceptance and respectability. He sat on the Board for the General Superintendence of Education and was closely associated with the grammar school at Niagara; he was grand chaplain of the masonic lodge at Niagara, a member of Niagara's public library board, and had been, at least once, chairman of the district's Court of Quarter Sessions. Over the years he was instrumental in the building of churches at Grimsby, Chippawa, Queen-

Agnew

ston, Fort Erie, and St Catharines. By 1828 his health had failed to the point where he was unable to perform his duties as chaplain to the assembly. He never recovered, dying quietly in Niagara on 6 Oct. 1829. The sermon at his funeral was preached by Strachan.

H. E. TURNER

The author wishes to thank A. J. Stevenson of Ottawa for supplying genealogical information on the Addison family.

Information concerning Robert Addison's land holdings and transactions can be found at the AO in the crown land papers (RG 1), including the township papers (C-IV) for Niagara Township; in the nominal listings of the land record index and the index to land patents by district, 1790–1825 (RG 53, ser.2, 1: f.123); and in the microfilmed collection of Upper Canada land books and petitions (PAC, RG 1, L1 and L3).

Selections from his correspondence to the SPG appeared in "The Rev. Robert Addison: extracts from the reports and (manuscript) journals of the Society for the Propagation of the Gospel in Foreign Parts," ed. A. H. Young, *OH*, 19 (1922): 171–91, and one of his sermons was published under the title "An old time sermon" in Niagara Hist. Soc., [*Pub.*], no.5 (1899): 1–7.

AO, MS 35, letter-book, 1827–39, Strachan to Addison, 23 Jan. 1828; unbound papers, Addison to Strachan, 9 Feb. 1828; MS 88, C. B. Wyatt to W. W. Baldwin, 4 Dec. 1812. Niagara Hist. Soc. Museum (Niagara-on-the-Lake, Ont.), F-IV-1: 27 (mfm. at AO). PRO, CO 42/343: 104–17; 42/350: 212–91, 456–60, 478–82; 42/357: 254–93; 42/366: 204–7. "Journals of Legislative Assembly of U.C.," AO *Report*, 1912. *Statistical account of U.C.* (Gourlay; ed. Mealing; 1974), 189–93. Strachan, *Letter book* (Spragge), 75–79. *Town of York, 1793–1815* (Firth), 175–78. U.C., House of Assembly, *Journal*, 1828: 39–63, 92; app., "Report on several petitions, praying for an alteration in the law imposing certain taxes on uncultivated lands." *Valley of Six Nations* (Johnston). Joseph Willcocks, "The diary of Joseph Willcocks from Dec. 1, 1799, to Feb. 1, 1803," J. E. Middleton and Fred Landon, *The province of Ontario: a history, 1615–1927* (5v., Toronto, [1927–28]), 2: 1250–322. *Alumni Cantabrigienses* . . . , comp. John and J. A. Venn (2 pts. in 10v., Cambridge, Eng., 1922–54), pt.II, 1: 14. Armstrong, *Handbook of Upper Canadian chronology* (1967), 104. *Robert Addison's library: a short-title catalogue of the books brought to Upper Canada in 1792 by the first missionary sent out to the Niagara frontier by the Society for the Propagation of the Gospel*, comp. W. J. Cameron et al. (Hamilton, Ont., 1967).

Carnochan, *Hist. of Niagara*. Cowdell Gates, *Land policies of U.C.* Ernest Hawkins, *Annals of the diocese of Toronto* (London, 1848). David Thomas, "A history of Anglican beginnings in Niagara," *Religion and churches in the Niagara Peninsula: proceedings, fourth annual Niagara Peninsula History Conference, Brock University, 17–18 April, 1982*, ed. John Burtniak and W. B. Turner (St Catharines, Ont., 1982), 27–35. Wilson, *Enterprises of Robert Hamilton*. A. P. Addison, "Robert Addison, of Niagara," *Canadian Journal of Religious Thought* (Toronto), 1 (1924): 420–26. E. A. Brooks, "The little world of Robert Addison, first priest of Niagara (1792–1829)," Canadian Church Hist. Soc., *Journal* (Toronto), 4 (1960–62), no.1. Ernest Green, "The search for salt in Upper Canada," *OH*, 26 (1930): 406–31. A. H. Young, "The Rev. Robert Addison and St. Mark's Church," *OH*, 19 (1922): 158–70.

AGNEW, STAIR, landowner, politician, JP, and judge; b. in Virginia, likely on 19 Oct. 1757, son of the Reverend John Agnew and Teresa ——; m. Sophia Winifred ——, and they had at least eight children; d. 10 Oct. 1821, aged 63, at Monkton House, York County, N.B.

Stair Agnew was educated in Glasgow, and returned to Virginia in 1775, at the beginning of the revolution. He volunteered for service in the British forces and was made an ensign in the Queen's Loyal Virginia Regiment on 1 Dec. 1775; eight days later he participated in the action at Great Bridge, near Norfolk, the first major engagement of the revolutionary war in the colony. Commissioned a lieutenant in the Queen's American Rangers on 27 Nov. 1776, he was severely wounded at the battle of Brandywine, Pa, the following year. After his recovery he rejoined his unit as a captain. His father, also a staunch loyalist, became chaplain of the regiment in 1778. In 1781 both father and son were captured by a French squadron while on board the British frigate *Romulus*. They were imprisoned for the remainder of the war in Rhode Island, Saint-Domingue (Haiti), and France. On their return to Virginia they found that they were unwelcome and decided to go to England, where Stair would be married. Reduced on half pay in 1783, Stair was awarded an annual pension of £80 by the loyalist claims commission.

Dissatisfied in England, Agnew and his father had determined by 1789 to settle in British North America. Although they intended going to Quebec, they were persuaded by Benjamin Marston*, whom they met in London, to consider New Brunswick. They arrived at Saint John and after a visit to Fredericton decided to stay. The recipients of land grants along the Nashwaak River, they also purchased property, including 1,000 acres at the mouth of the Nashwaak bought from John Anderson, a pre-loyalist settler. In this location they attempted to build an estate they called Monkton. Patrick CAMPBELL, who visited the area in 1791, recorded Stair Agnew's "rising mansion house, which has the appearance of being a very handsome one." Situated opposite Fredericton, which provided a market for the Agnews' produce, the estate included mill sites and the right to operate ferries across the Nashwaak and Saint John rivers, privileges the family was to retain for many years.

Entering the political field in 1792, Stair Agnew was elected one of York County's representatives in the House of Assembly, and there became a spokesman for disgruntled landowners who opposed the restrictions that the British government had placed on land granting in 1790. When he was defeated in 1795, he contested the election on the grounds that the sheriff had struck off the results the names of a number of his voters. After an investigation he was awarded the seat the following year. Though his re-election in 1802 was challenged, an inquiry decided in his favour, and he retained his seat through four subsequent elections until his death in 1821. From 1799 to 1821 he also served as a justice of the peace and a judge of the Inferior Court of Common Pleas for York County.

Agnew was considered a conservative in politics, but he was a maverick and quite unpredictable in his behaviour. Many of his political decisions seem to have been based on personalities rather than on principles. For a time he joined James Glenie* in opposing Lieutenant Governor Thomas Carleton* and his supporters. In 1795 he criticized the government at a meeting in Van Horne's Tavern in Fredericton, claiming that the people of the province would be better off annexed to the United States than burdened with the existing restrictions on land granting and the shortage of labour that so hampered the efforts of gentlemen farmers. In the same year he supported Glenie's Declaratory Bill, the object of which was to limit the power of the lieutenant governor in council, and in 1797 he backed Glenie's attempt to have a vote of censure passed against Carleton. Within two years, however, he had deserted Glenie. Similarly, an alliance with Samuel Denny STREET, another thorn in the flesh of the government and a supporter of Glenie, did not last long, and the two men became bitter enemies.

By 1799 Agnew had made his peace with the government. In 1802 he was one of those who signed a petition requesting the removal of Caleb Jones* from the bench of magistrates for making disloyal remarks. Jones, like Agnew, was a slave owner and they had been friends in 1800 when both were involved in court cases testing the legality of slavery in New Brunswick. Agnew's political volte-face had been most apparent earlier in 1802 when a dispute arose between the assembly and the executive over the right to appoint the clerk of the house. Siding against Street, the assembly's choice for the position, and supported by Archibald McLEAN and others, Agnew was the member who – in the absence of the majority of assemblymen and on the order of the speaker, Amos Botsford* – struck Street's name from the revenue bill; the office thus passed to Dugald Campbell*, the lieutenant governor's appointee. Yet by 1818 Agnew had changed his position once more and was again opposing the administration, now headed by Lieutenant Governor George Stracey SMYTH. In 1821 he supported a bill, rejected by the Council, that would have allowed ministers of all faiths to perform marriages.

A controversial and often troublesome character, Agnew was motivated by his personal likes and dislikes. Nevertheless, throughout his many about-faces he remained popular in York County and the voters continued to elect him until the time of his death.

W. A. SPRAY

PANB, MC 1156, V: 16; RG 2, RS8, appointments and commissions, 2/1: 25; unarranged Executive Council docs., petition of the magistrates of the county of York, 14 Oct. 1802; RG 4, RS24, S5-P6, S10-P1; RG 10, RS108, Stair Agnew, 6 Dec. 1816 and two undated petitions. PRO, AO 12/56, 12/99–100; AO 13, bundles 33, 79. P. Campbell, *Travels in North America* (Langton and Ganong). *Revolutionary Virginia: the road to independence*, comp. W. J. Van Schreeven *et al.*, ed. R. L. Scribner *et al.* (7v. to date, [Charlottesville, Va.], 1973–   ). *Winslow papers* (Raymond). *New-Brunswick Royal Gazette*, 16 Oct. 1821. G.B., WO, *Army list*, 1783. "Roll of officers of the British American or loyalist corps," comp. W. O. Raymond, N.B. Hist. Soc., *Coll.*, 2 (1899–1905), no.5: 248. Sabine, *Biog. sketches of loyalists*. Hannay, *Hist. of N.B.*, 1: 256, 258, 273, 279, 296, 309–10, 348–49, 440. Lawrence, *Judges of N.B.* (Stockton and Raymond). MacNutt, *New Brunswick*. D. G. Bell, "Slavery and the judges of loyalist New Brunswick," *Univ. of New Brunswick Law Journal* (Saint John), 31 (1982): 9–42.

AHYONWAEGHS (Ahyouwaeghs). *See* TEKARI-HOGEN

AINSE (Hands), SARAH (Montour; Maxwell; Willson (Wilson)), trader; b. possibly as early as 1728 in the Thirteen Colonies or the Indian territory to the west; d. *c.* 1823 in Amherstburg, Upper Canada.

Trader, diplomatic courier, and vocal champion of her own legal rights, Sarah Ainse was well known around Detroit (Mich.) and the Western District of Upper Canada in the late 18th and early 19th centuries. Probably an Oneida, although she once claimed to be a Shawnee, she had been brought up on the Susquehanna River. Her exact name is not known but there is speculation that it may have been Hance, a name common among the Six Nations. She sometimes used her nickname, Sally. At 17 she became the second wife of Andrew (Henry) Montour, an Indian agent and interpreter, and lived with him in what is now Ohio, Pennsylvania, and New York. He fell into debt, perhaps as a result of her extravagance, and in the early 1750s he nearly went to prison. In 1755 or 1756 the family was split. Most of the children were placed with people in Philadelphia. Montour left Sarah and their son Nicholas*, who was baptized in Albany, N.Y., on 31 Oct. 1756, with her relations the Oneidas near the Mohawk River. Soon afterwards they gave her land near Fort Stanwix (Rome, N.Y.). Here she had become a trader by 1759. Within seven years she had expanded her activities westward to the

Ainse

north shore of Lake Erie and it seems she was trading to Michilimackinac (Mackinaw City, Mich.) by 1767. Because of the similarity of names it has often been thought that she was married to Joseph-Louis Ainsse*, the Michilimackinac interpreter, but it appears that when she was there she lived, for a while at least, with trader William Maxwell. During the American revolution she moved to the Detroit area. Thereafter she was rarely called Montour and was most usually known as Ainse.

Between 1775 and 1785 Sarah Ainse was an active trader in the Western District. In 1780, according to a list made by commandant Arent Schuyler DePeyster, two bateau loads of the merchandise ordered by the merchants of Detroit belonged to her. She accumulated large debts with merchants William Macomb, John Askin*, and Montague Tremblay. In 1781 her account with Tremblay was for £2,620, in 1783 she did business with Askin to the extent of almost £3,000, and in 1787 her account with Angus Mackintosh was for £685. She had become a person of property, owning two houses at Detroit, and the 1779 census records that she owned flour, cattle, horses, and four slaves. In May 1787 Sarah Ainse moved to the La Tranche (Thames) River and built a dwelling on the part of her property that later became lot 10, concession 1 of Dover East (Dover) Township. In 1788 she completed the purchase from local Indians of a 150-square-mile property which ran from the mouth of the river up to the forks where the city of Chatham now stands. During the 1780s she seems to have been the wife of John Willson, a trader. He took over responsibility in 1783 for her account with Askin.

In a petition of 1789 to Governor Lord Dorchester [Guy Carleton*], Sarah Ainse tried to get title to a portion of the land she had bought from the Indians. She claimed a parcel 300 acres in front by 33⅓ acres in depth. This property lay within the area purchased from the Indians for the British goverment by deputy Indian agent Alexander McKee* in 1790, but she repeatedly asserted, and her statements were confirmed by a number of Indian chiefs, including Egushwa*, that her lands were exempt from this treaty. Supported by Jean-Baptiste-Pierre Testard* Louvigny de Montigny, a member of the district land board present at the treaty negotiations, McKee denied that this exemption had been intended. McKee was himself a major landowner in the area, as were several members of the land board who denied Sarah her claim. Moreover, the land on the Thames was perceived as the most valuable in the district. Were the members of the board simply too inflexible to accept a sale made by Indians, since the institutionalized system disapproved of such sales to individuals? Was it simply that an Indian woman stood in the way of the speculative ventures of the local élite? Why was the word of 18 or 20 chiefs discounted? In June 1794, as a result of the influence and pressure of the superintendent general of Indian affairs, Sir John Johnson, and Mohawk chief Joseph Brant [Thayendanegea*], and of the outraged sense of justice of Lieutenant Governor John Graves Simcoe*, an order was given that she receive 1,673 acres. She now had clear title to 1.7 per cent of the amount for which she had originally petitioned, but the Executive Council nevertheless denied her claim in 1798! She received neither the land nor compensation.

While she was pursuing her land claim Sarah Ainse still carried on her trading. She successfully sued several people for small debts in 1792, and when the commanding officer at Detroit tried to prevent the sale of liquor to an Indian gathering at the Glaize (Defiance, Ohio), he complained that "Sally Ainse . . . availed herself of the general prohibition, and privately disposed of a sufficient quantity to keep an entire band drunk." She also acted as messenger and informant for Brant in the critical months after the defeat of the western Indians by Anthony Wayne's forces at the battle of Fallen Timbers (near Waterville, Ohio) in August 1794 [see Weyapiersenwah*]. Brant wanted to maintain Indian unity against the Americans and through Sarah Ainse sent messages to Egushwa and other leaders of the western tribes. "I am much afraid that your wampum and Speeches will be to little effect with the Indians," she advised Brant in February 1795, "as they are sneaking off to General Wayne every day." Her observation was entirely correct: that very month a preliminary agreement with the Americans was signed.

Records of Sarah Ainse's activities after the turn of the century are scant. In September 1806, when she purchased a quart of whisky from John Askin, she was still resident on her Thames River farm. ("I don't mean to ask payment," Askin noted on her account.) A woman of remarkable persistence, in January 1809 she petitioned Lieutenant Governor Francis Gore* about compensation for her land claim. At that date she was living in Amherstburg. Clinging to life as tenaciously as she had clung to her rights, she survived until about 1823. Agents for the executors of Richard Pattinson, to whom she had owed money, applied on 11 Feb. 1824 for authority to administer her estate.

A clearly exceptional person, Sarah Ainse was respected by native society and could function in white society. She had powerful friends and powerful opponents. The new order neither loved nor cowed her.

JOHN CLARKE

AO, Hiram Walker Hist. Museum coll., 20–138; RG 1, A-I-6: 303–4, 638–39. DPL, Burton Hist. Coll., Detroit notarial papers, 1737–95 (transcripts at PAC). PAC, RG 1, L3, 3: A4/45; 16: A misc., 1788–1843/17–23; L4, 1. "Board of land office, District of Hesse," AO *Report*, 1905. *Canada,*

Indian treaties and surrenders ... [1680–1906] (3v., Ottawa, 1891–1912; repr. Toronto, 1971), 1: 1–3. *Corr. of Hon. Peter Russell* (Cruikshank and Hunter). *Corr. of Lieut. Governor Simcoe* (Cruikshank). *John Askin papers* (Quaife). *Mich. Pioneer Coll.*, 10 (1886); 12 (1887); 19 (1891). *The papers of Sir William Johnson*, ed. James Sullivan *et al.* (14v., Albany, N.Y., 1921–65). "U.C. land book C," AO *Report*, 1931: 41–42. "U.C. land book D," AO *Report*, 1931: 147. F. C. Hamil, *The valley of the lower Thames, 1640 to 1850* (Toronto, 1951; repr. Toronto and Buffalo, N.Y., 1973). Louis Goulet, "Phases of the Sally Ainse dispute," Kent Hist. Soc., *Papers and Addresses* (Chatham, Ont.), [5] (1921): 92–95. F. C. Hamil, "Sally Ainse, fur trader," Algonquin Club, *Hist. Bull.* (Detroit), no.3 (1939).

AMHERST, ELIZABETH FRANCES (Hale),

water-colourist; b. 1774 in England, daughter of William Amherst, a British army officer, and Elizabeth Patterson; m. 3 April 1799 John Hale* in London, and they had four daughters and eight sons, including Jeffery* and Edward*; d. 18 June 1826 at Quebec.

Elizabeth Frances Amherst spent her childhood and adolescent years in England. In June 1799 her husband was appointed deputy paymaster general of the British troops stationed in the Canadas. She accompanied him to his posting at Quebec, and the young couple took up residence in the Upper Town. Through the years he accumulated titles and offices which assured him some prominence and a favourable place in society. Apart from occasional stays in England (particularly in 1812 and 1816), Elizabeth lived mainly at Quebec, first on Rue Saint-Louis, and then from 1818 on Rue des Carrières. The following year her husband purchased the seigneury of Sainte-Anne-De La Pérade, where the family spent the summer months.

In addition to attending to her family and social obligations, Elizabeth Hale took up drawing and painting in water-colours. The Public Archives of Canada has some of her works. The one best known is a water-colour depicting York (Toronto) in 1804, not long after it had been founded, which circulated widely as a print. As others have noted, it is quite possible that she copied the scene from a water-colour done on the spot by Edward WALSH in 1803, since there is no documentary evidence that she made a trip to York during this period. Another water-colour of hers, dating from 1805 and similar in treatment and dimensions to the previous one, shows the Île des Cèdres, on the St Lawrence above Montreal. There is a small sketchbook containing various wash and pen-and-ink landscapes that depict the surroundings in which the artist lived: the seigneury of Sainte-Anne-De La Pérade and its environs, Quebec, Sleepy Hollow (the Hales's residence at Sherbrooke), and Guisborough, England, where relatives of John Hale lived. The Public Archives also has a small wash drawing of a picturesque site at Deschambault and a variety of European scenes that are unsigned but are attributed to Mrs Hale. In addition, the Musée du Québec owns two signed water-colours dated 1823: the bridge over the Rivière du Sault à la Puce, and the St Lawrence off Pointe-aux-Trembles (Neuville).

Like the topographical artists of her time, whose style is indeed similar to hers, Elizabeth Hale liked to paint urban and rural landscapes in which she emphasized some interesting structure or natural feature such as a river or falls. As a rule, human figures are simplified and are of secondary importance in her work.

PIERRE B. LANDRY

ANQ-Q, CE1-61, 20 juin 1826. MAC-CD, Fonds Morisset, 2, dossier E. F. Amherst (Hale). PAC, MG 23, GII, 18; MG 55/30, no.51 (Lucy Hale Machin); Picture Division, Hale and Amherst coll. *Quebec Mercury*, 20 June 1826. W. M. E. Cooke, *W. H. Coverdale Collection of Canadiana: paintings, water-colours and drawings (Manoir Richelieu collection)* (Ottawa, 1983). J. R. Harper, *Early painters and engravers in Canada* ([Toronto], 1970). J. C. Webster, *Catalogue of the John Clarence Webster Canadiana collection, New Brunswick Museum* (2v., Saint John, N.B., 1946), 2: 353.

ANSPACH, LEWIS AMADEUS (baptized Louis-Amédée),

Church of England clergyman, schoolmaster, JP, and author; b. 22 April 1770 in Geneva (Switzerland), son of Jean-Louis Anspach and Jeanne-Marie Audibert; d. 1823 in London.

Lewis Amadeus Anspach was brought up in Geneva where his grandfather, the religious writer Isaac Salomon Anspach of the Palatinate, had settled. Lewis was educated at the Académie de Genève and studied classics, theology, and philosophy with the intention of entering the ministry of the Reformed Church. He left Geneva in December 1792 and travelled to England as tutor to the sons of a London merchant. In 1795 he retired from his tutorship and successfully applied to the bishop of London for ordination in the Church of England. His application had the support of the pastors of both the Swiss and the French Calvinist churches in London. He experienced no difficulty in moving from one denomination to another, and acted as curate of the parish of St Martin Orgar for £30 per annum, presumably eking out his income by teaching, until he received a better offer as a schoolmaster in Newfoundland.

The school to which Anspach engaged his services had its origin in the desire of some St John's merchants for a private school at which their children might receive an education superior to that otherwise available on the island. In December 1798 the group had informed Governor William WALDEGRAVE that they were prepared to subscribe some £273 for three years,

Anspach

and asked that he secure in England the services of a Church of England clergyman to superintend the institution, together with a master to instruct in the classics and a mistress to teach English, needlework, and French. Arriving in St John's on 13 Oct. 1799, Anspach was befriended by John Harries*, the missionary of the Society for the Propagation of the Gospel, who accepted his assistance in church, remarking that "in preaching his foreign accent was almost entirely lost." After disputes with the subscribers to the school, arising from the unwillingness of those with few children to pay a subscription equal to that of more prolific parents, and a consequent lawsuit which was settled in his favour, Anspach simply completed his contract as schoolmaster and then began a career as a missionary.

The SPG, disregarding a request from some inhabitants of Harbour Grace for the appointment of a Mr Dingle, presumably inclined to Methodism, appointed Anspach. Encouraged by Harries, he had applied, urging his "strict conformity with the Church which has honoured him by receiving him as a Minister." In the populous area of Conception Bay he busied himself as a missionary for the next ten years, and built schools at Harbour Grace, Bay Roberts, and Brigus. Since the time of Laurence Coughlan* the mission had been bitterly divided and the work of the church hindered by frequent squabbles between Methodist and Anglican. Under Anspach this situation eased and by 1810 he was exulting that "the sectarian spirit has in a very considerable degree given way to the spirit of unity, and there is no other Protestant Place of Worship." Because of his own very Protestant background, he may have appealed to a wider spectrum of belief than did more orthodox Anglican missionaries, and unlike most of them he did not complain of lack of local financial support. He could not "speak too highly of the kindness" he received "from every class of inhabitants . . . and of their attention to religious duties."

Anspach was also a justice of the peace in the Conception Bay area. Before his arrival there, he noted, the administration of justice had in fact been in the hands of one "magistrate of the old school," who had refused to institute the reforms in the court system brought in under Chief Justice John REEVES during the 1790s. Anspach seems to have been an efficient and thoughtful magistrate. He prepared *A summary of the laws of commerce and navigation, adapted to the present state, government, and trade of the island of Newfoundland*, which was published in London in 1809, and *A systematical review of the laws and regulations relating to the trade and fishery of Newfoundland*, which came out there the following year. A close and curious observer, he also compiled a mass of manuscript material, including a diary, relating to his experiences and reflections which he

"had some thought of arranging with a view to publication" when he returned to England.

Return to England he did towards the end of August 1812, but not to the Church of England. He was worried about the education of his children, and with some regret he accepted a position which his friends had secured for him, that of pastor at the principal French Reformed church, in Threadneedle Street, London. Huguenots had been in England since the time of the Reformation, maintaining a network of French-speaking churches of the Calvinist faith but keeping up friendly relations with the English church and king. Indeed, the ministers of the principal church were always in Anglican holy orders and licensed by the sovereign. It was a post of considerable importance and prestige. In it Anspach pursued a quiet and uneventful ministry until his retirement in 1821.

Meanwhile, he did not lose sight of his intention to publish his projected book on Newfoundland, and "determined silently to consign over the produce of my labours to a number of manuscripts . . . more immediately connected with the situations which I had held there, and which I had accumulated during the leisure hours that could be spared in the winter season, consistently with my public duties. I persevered in this determination." By the end of March 1818 the finished manuscript was communicated "to a literary friend," and it was published in London the following year as "printed for the author."

Anspach's *History of the island of Newfoundland* was the first general history of the country; and if the first ten chapters, based as they are on printed authorities now long outdated, are of little value today, the six concluding chapters, in which the author deals with a period that fell within his own knowledge, retain a continuing value. The work as a whole belongs to a genre (to which Sir Richard Henry Bonnycastle*'s 1842 study is also related) in which a general history culminates in descriptive chapters on natural history, climate and meteorology, natural productions, and the like. In Anspach's case, such set pieces are frequently informed by personal observation, and the work concludes with a highly original account "Of Character and Manners of the . . . Inhabitants of the Island of Newfoundland," which is nothing less than a pioneering essay on the social history of the region. Much of the theoretical background which Anspach brings to the subject is, as one would expect, classical, but he displays also a thoughtful reading of Montesquieu, and above all he presents a vivid and lively personal report. And if the point of view is often that of an establishmentarian to whom "the public mind" of St John's seemed "poisoned" by Thomas Paine's *Age of reason* and *Rights of man* (notwithstanding the refutation of those works by the bishop of Llandaff), Anspach's *History*, like the record of his varied service in Newfoundland, everywhere bears witness to his diligence, probity, and intelligence.

Anspach died in 1823, thus ending a career which had spanned two churches and two cultures. He was a product of the 18th-century religious climate, stressing the moral duties of religion and treating denominational differences lightly. Seeking in the colonial church a career which would have been difficult in England, he proved to be a major publicist for the island which he characteristically commended as having "unobserved and unknown . . . silently distributed subsistence to a considerable portion of the inhabitants, and particularly *of the poor* of both hemispheres."

FREDERICK JONES and G. M. STORY

Lewis Amadeus Anspach is the author of *A summary of the laws of commerce and navigation, adapted to the present state, government, and trade of the island of Newfoundland* (London, 1809); *A systematical review of the laws and regulations relating to the trade and fishery of Newfoundland* (London, 1810); and *A history of the island of Newfoundland, containing a description of the island, the banks, the fisheries, and trade of Newfoundland, and the coast of Labrador* (London, 1819). A German translation of this last work appeared under the title *Geschichte und beschreibung von Newfoundland . . .* (Weimar, [German Democratic Republic], 1822); and a second edition of the English was issued in London in 1827. One of his unpublished reports, preserved among the Duckworth papers at the PANL (P1/5), has been put out in mimeograph form by the archives as *Duckworth's Newfoundland; notes from a report to Governor Duckworth* (St John's, 1971).

Arch. de l'État (Genève, Suisse), État civil, Genève, reg. de baptêmes, 29 avril 1770. Guildhall Library (London), MS 10326/126 (Diocese of London, ordination papers, 1795). PANL, GN 2/1, 15–22. USPG, C/CAN/Nfl., 2, nos.181–98; Journal of SPG, 28–30. *Le livre du recteur de l'Académie de Genève (1559–1878)*, Sven Stelling-Michaud, édit. (3v. to date, Genève, 1959–), 2: 50. F.-A. Batisse, *Londres huguenot: sur les pas huguenots français à travers Londres* (Londres, 1978). R. H. Bonnycastle, *Newfoundland in 1842: a sequel to "The Canadas in 1841"* (2v., London, 1842). P. [A.] O'Flaherty, *The rock observed: studies in the literature of Newfoundland* (Toronto, 1979), 60–62. Charles Pedley, *The history of Newfoundland from the earliest times to the year 1860* (London, 1863), 169, 174, 185, 227, 266, 274. F. W. Rowe, *The development of education in Newfoundland* (Toronto, 1964), 51–62.

APPLETON, THOMAS, educator; b. in the East Riding of Yorkshire, England; fl. 1818–35.

Thomas Appleton is remembered chiefly for his role in a minor dispute that symbolized a much broader issue. In the early 1820s he became the central figure in a debate over how schooling in Upper Canada should be organized. Lieutenant Governor Sir Peregrine Maitland* and the Reverend John Strachan* favoured the spread of the national system, a network of monitorial schools controlled by the Church of England; reformers, on the other hand, supported the expansion of the system of non-denominational common schools inaugurated by the Common Schools Act of 1816. This debate was not resolved until the creation in the 1840s and 1850s of a non-sectarian, state-supported system of universal schooling under the supervision of Egerton Ryerson*.

A Yorkshire Methodist, Appleton came to Upper Canada in 1818. After teaching for a brief period in Scarborough and King townships, in February 1820 he took up a post at the York (Toronto) common school. His future was soon placed in jeopardy, however, by Maitland's plan to create national schools, which supposedly would play a key role in ensuring the loyalty of the populace. A few months after Appleton's move to York, Joseph Spragg*, whom Maitland had recruited in England with the object of turning the York school into a national school, arrived in the capital. Strachan, a member of the district board of education and a close ally of Maitland, now took the lead in trying to have Appleton replaced. Eventually Spragg was appointed to the York school for a five-month period and Appleton was given charge of a nearby common school in the "market square." Shortly afterwards, this arrangement was made permanent and Spragg's school was transformed into the Upper Canada Central School, the first of Maitland's planned series of national schools.

Here matters rested until mid 1821, when Appleton was abruptly denied his allowance for the previous six months on the grounds that the Central School had superseded the common school. The trustees of the common school, Jesse Ketchum*, Thomas David Morrison*, and Jordan Post*, petitioned Maitland and the district board on Appleton's behalf, but their appeals met with no success and they resigned in protest. In 1823 Appleton appealed to Maitland, who referred the matter to the recently created Board for the General Superintendence of Education. Strachan, as superintendent of the board, advised Maitland that Appleton's salary had been discontinued because, after the reduction of the common school fund in 1820, the district board had decided to support only one school in each township, and in York the presence of the Central School had made Appleton's school expendable. Maitland, according to Strachan, thought this argument "perfectly satisfactory" and no action was taken on Appleton's petition.

Despite his loss of salary, Appleton stayed on as a teacher at the common school, relying on the fees of his students. He continued petitioning, and in 1828 the House of Assembly established a select committee – composed of James Wilson, Robert RANDAL, John Rolph*, John MATTHEWS, and Thomas HORNOR – to investigate his charges of high-handedness on the part of the Executive Council. The reform members who dominated the committee saw an opportunity to expand what seemed a relatively routine case of unfair dismissal into a full-blown discussion of "family compact" policies. After all, the Central School had been established on the recommendation of the Executive Council but without the approval of the Colonial Office or the Upper Canada legislature. Moreover, some members suspected a deliberate attempt by Maitland, and perhaps Strachan as well, to set up through the national schools a system of Church of England schools which would rival the non-denominational common schools. From the outset, then, it was clear that the committee would take Appleton's side. After hearing several witnesses, including Appleton himself and Jesse Ketchum, the committee requested that the authorities pay Appleton the money owed him. It also announced that the Central School "is professedly adherent to the church of England – and, therefore, ought not to be supported by the revenues of a country struggling against ecclesiastical exclusion." Nothing came of the committee's report.

Appleton did not discourage easily and in April 1832 he appealed directly to the Colonial Office. Once more his efforts were in vain, for in 1833 Lord Goderich decided, after receiving information on the case from Lieutenant Governor Sir John Colborne*, that the affair did not warrant interference. Two years later William Lyon Mackenzie*'s committee on grievances considered another petition from Appleton, and resolved that the teacher was entitled to £85 4s. in compensation. It is not known whether this payment was ever made.

The details of Appleton's life in the 1820s and 1830s are obscure. In 1828 he was still teaching in York, and in 1835 Mackenzie described him as a resident of Toronto. His name, however, does not appear in city directories or assessment records for the 1830s; indeed, the name Thomas Appleton does not appear again in records of any kind until 1841, when a Thomas Appleton is listed as living in King Township. There is good circumstantial evidence to indicate that the Appleton of King Township was the same person as the subject of this biography. If so, Appleton lived a long and productive life. The Thomas Appleton of 1841, an English immigrant and New Connexion Methodist, moved into King Township that year. By 1851 he and his wife Elizabeth had three children, and Thomas with his son Tapple was operating a sawmill. At the time of the 1861 census Thomas was a widower and was residing with Teavill C. Appleton, probably a brother. He died in Aurora on 31 July 1866 at the home of his son-in-law, William Hartman, brother of Clear Grit politician Joseph Hartman*; he was then 82 years of age. That Appleton himself may have had ties with the reform party is indicated by a letter of 1841 from one T. Appleton – undoubtedly Thomas, his son Tapple, or Teavill – to Robert Baldwin*. In this letter, written from Whitchurch Township, Appleton asked Baldwin to fulfill "the promise you made me at the Husting."

Appleton was described as "a good teacher and a kind man, held in equally high esteem by the pupils and their parents." During the 1820s and 1830s his case had focused attention on the increasingly important question of who was going to control the evolving system of public schooling for the children of the masses. Was it to be the church or the state, the appointed executive or the elected legislative branch? In the Appleton case the assembly put itself on record as favouring state and legislative control, but the resolution of the issue required another two decades of debate.

J. Donald Wilson

AO, MS 451, York County, King Township cemetery records; RG 21, York County, King Township, assessment rolls, concession 2, lot 21, 1863, 1865–66. MTL, Robert Baldwin papers, Appleton to Baldwin, 18 Oct. 1841. PAC, RG 1, L1, 29: 10; L3, 7: A12/2; RG 5, A1: 24063–65, 33541–42; RG 7, G1, 69: 159–61; 70: 90–91, 328–30; RG 31, C1, 1851, 1861, King Township, concession 2, lot 21. PRO, CO 42/411: 210; 42/413: 208, 251; 42/414: 340–48. Univ. of Toronto Arch., A73-0015/001, 17 March 1830 (photocopy at AO). York North Registry Office (Newmarket, Ont.), Abstract index to deeds, King Township, concession 2, lot 21 (mfm. at AO). *Documentary history of education in Upper Canada from the passing of the Constitutional Act of 1791 to the close of Rev. Dr. Ryerson's administration of the Education Department in 1876*, ed. J. G. Hodgins (28v., Toronto, 1894–1910), 1–2, 4–5. J. R. Robertson, *Old Toronto: a selection of excerpts from "Landmarks of Toronto,"* ed. E. C. Kyte (Toronto, 1954). *Town of York, 1815–34* (Firth). U.C., House of Assembly, *App. to the journal*, 1835, 1, app.21: 81; 2, app.65: 19; *Journal*, 1828: 63, 66–67, 114; app., "Report on the petition of T. Appleton"; 1835: 204, 213, 232, 264. *Newmarket Era*, 3 Aug. 1866. R. R. Bonis, *A history of Scarborough* (Scarborough [Toronto], 1965). F. M. Quealey, "The administration of Sir Peregrine Maitland, lieutenant-governor of Upper Canada, 1818–1828" (PHD thesis, 2v., Univ. of Toronto, 1968). G. W. Spragge, "Monitorial schools in the Canadas, 1810–1845" (DPAED thesis, Univ. of Toronto, 1935). J. D. Wilson, "Foreign and local influences on popular education in Upper Canada, 1815–1844" (PHD thesis, Univ. of Western Ont., London, 1970). E. J. Hathaway, "Early schools of Toronto," *OH*, 23 (1926): 322–27. G. W. Spragge, "The Upper Canada Central School," *OH*, 32 (1937): 171–91.

APRIL, NANCE. *See* Shawnadithit

ARNOLD, OLIVER, teacher, Church of England clergyman, and JP; b. 15 Oct. 1755 in Mansfield, Conn., eldest child of Dr Nathan Arnold and Prudence

Denison; m. 9 Nov. 1786 Charlotte Hustice, *née* Wiggins, of New York, a loyalist widow, and they had seven children; d. 9 April 1834 in Sussex Vale (Sussex Corner), N.B.

Oliver Arnold was educated at Yale College, where he was a member of the class of 1776 (AM, 1792). His activities and whereabouts during the American revolution are unknown but he probably served in the British provincial forces. In 1783 he joined the loyalist migration to Parrtown, the future Saint John, N.B., and acted for a time as secretary to "The Directors of the Town at the Entrance of the River Saint John," who included George LEONARD, his future patron. After involvement in a number of land transactions in Saint John and vicinity and a brief residence in Long Reach, north of the city (where he married), Arnold secured, through Leonard's influence as a local commissioner for the New England Company, a position in 1787 as schoolmaster to the Indians at Sussex Vale, the location of Leonard's country seat to which Arnold removed.

The London-based New England Company, titled in full the Society for the Propagation of the Gospel in New England and the Parts Adjacent in America, transferred its program for educating, evangelizing, and apprenticing native people from New England to New Brunswick after the revolution. Relying on a local board of commissioners to hire and oversee the Indians' teachers and masters and to make provision for the natives' moral, spiritual, and economic welfare, the company employed Arnold as teacher until 1790, when he became its missionary. Although nominally he remained the instructor, he contracted out the teaching duties. His responsibilities for visiting, instructing, and reporting made him in effect the company's superintendent in Sussex Vale, where the enterprise was largely centred. He continued in this capacity until he was dismissed from the company's employment in 1824 following several years of mounting unease among its governors about the Indian policies being pursued on their behalf and at their considerable expense.

In the mean time, Arnold's involvement in Indian education and "civilization" became secondary to his other work as Anglican pastor to fellow refugees and new immigrants from Britain. He had been ordained in 1791 by Bishop Charles Inglis* on the basis of a title from the New England Company and given responsibility for the parish of Sussex, which then included three major settlements: Sussex Vale, where he continued to reside, Norton, and Hampton, respectively 20 and 33 miles distant from his church. After three years' pressure from the bishop and Leonard's gift of a 200-acre glebe, the Society for the Propagation of the Gospel agreed to designate Sussex Parish one of its missions in 1794. In receipt of a SPG stipend and a salary from the New Brunswick government,

Arnold continued to serve the settlements in his area until his death. The arrival of Elias Scovil in 1803 and James Cookson in 1818 as neighbouring missionaries eased his original duties for the SPG, but the opening of new settlements and Arnold's increasing infirmities led to the appointment of his son and successor Horatio Nelson Arnold as an assistant in 1829. Another son, Samuel Edwin, had also followed him into the church in New Brunswick in the 1820s.

Like other loyalist clergy in rural missions, Arnold experienced difficulties securing financial assistance from his congregations, whom he described in 1791 as "exceedingly poor," with "a very rugged country to subdue," and scarcely able to support their families, let alone a clergyman. He had to endure unfinished churches, sporadically maintained schools, and arduous travelling conditions in order to minister to his scattered flock. The burden of raising and educating his own family was not made any easier by the prevailing shortage of cash in New Brunswick and capriciously protested bills of exchange in London. The Nova Scotia diocese also suffered from inadequate supervision. Although Arnold referred specifically to problems relating to the ordination of his own sons, he spoke for all the clergy of the diocese when he lamented in 1823 the absence in England of Bishop Robert STANSER. Despite the pioneer hardships of the day, Arnold appears to have been one of the more energetic and adaptable clergymen of the loyalist era. Sussex Vale became the centre of an Arnold dynasty which contributed to the growth of a stable community. As a justice of the peace and a freemason, Oliver Arnold added secular and social prestige to his role as a well-loved pastor.

His success as a clergyman to people of his own kind stands in marked contrast to his notorious reputation as New England Company missionary to the Indians. That he benefited more from his position than the Indians did from his care seems unquestionable. He received a salary of £30 as missionary, increased to £50 in 1814; he gave the schoolmaster to the Indians only a portion of the money he was paid as instructor; he enjoyed premiums of £20 a year for each Indian apprentice whose indenture he undertook (between four and seven at a time); he lived in a house belonging to the company which he was ultimately able to buy on easy terms; his two eldest sons and other kin shared the remaining Indian indentures. The labour of the apprentices, certainly the second generation if not the first, represented a considerable boon in an agricultural community. Under the guise of apprenticeship, which Arnold considered necessary from infancy in order to wrest the Indians from the control of Catholic priests, the indentured children became virtual slaves to the leading families of Sussex Vale.

Arnold himself may not have been the worst of the masters. He apparently attempted to learn the Indians'

13

Arnoldi

language and train an Indian teacher or missionary, and he claimed that his settlement scheme for the predominantly Malecite people was as practicable as that projected by Walter Bromley* in the North American Indian Institution of 1814. But after the initial years of his involvement with the Indians, Arnold exhibited little enthusiasm for amelioration efforts. His description of the instruction of the Indians as an unpleasant task suggests that he may have been unsuited to the work. The financial rewards clearly afforded his incentive for persistence. John Coffin*, who became the salaried superintendent of the local New England Company board in 1807, may have been as financially involved as Arnold, but he still described the latter as "rapacious in the extreme," comparable more to "a mad dog – after his prey than a Clergyman in the habit of praying for things requisite and necessary." Whether out of a belief in Indian inferiority, financial self-interest, or despair of success, Arnold created the impression among colonists that the Indians were at best exploitable, at worst dispensable. The ignominious history of the New England Company enterprise at Sussex Vale portrayed in the reports of Walter Bromley (1822) and John West* (1825), commissioned by the company's governors in England, throws a revealing if unattractive light on the activities of this otherwise respectable white man.

JUDITH FINGARD

Guildhall Library (London), MSS 7920/1–2, 7954, 7956, 7970. N.B. Museum, Sussex Indian Academy papers. PAC, MG 23, D1, ser.1, 13. PANS, MG 1, 479, no.3: 206–59 (transcripts). USPG, C/CAN/NB, 1, nos.80–92; 4, no.521; Journal of SPG, 25–37. *Winslow papers* (Raymond). F. B. Dexter, *Biographical sketches of the graductes of Yale College, with annals of the college history* (6v., New York and New Haven, Conn., 1885–1912). "Roll of officers of the British American or loyalist corps," comp. W. O. Raymond, N.B. Hist. Soc., *Coll.*, 2 (1899–1905), no.5: 249. Leonard Allison, *The Rev. Oliver Arnold, first rector of Sussex, N.B., with some account of his life, his parish, and his successors, and the old Indian College* (Saint John, N.B., 1892). G. H. Lee, *An historical sketch of the first fifty years of the Church of England in the province of New Brunswick (1783–1833)* (Saint John, 1880). C. F. Pascoe, *Two hundred years of the S.P.G.* . . . (2v., London, 1901). Judith Fingard, "English humanitarianism and the colonial mind: Walter Bromley in Nova Scotia, 1813–25," *CHR*, 54 (1973): 123–51; "The New England Company and the New Brunswick Indians, 1786–1826: a comment on the colonial perversion of British benevolence," *Acadiensis* (Fredericton), 1 (1971–72), no.2: 29–42.

ARNOLDI, PHEBE (rebaptized **Apolline**), named **de Sainte-Angèle (Diehl)**, teacher, shopkeeper, and Ursuline; b. 22 May 1767 at Fort St Johns (Saint-Jean-sur-Richelieu, Que.), daughter of Peter Arnoldi, a soldier from Hesse (Federal Republic of Germany), and Philipina Maria (Phébé) Horn; d. 16 May 1825 in Trois-Rivières, Lower Canada.

Phebe Arnoldi was only 15 when her father forced her to marry John Justus Diehl on 22 Feb. 1783. Diehl was a German merchant at Quebec, 32 years old, with little money, a gloomy temperament, and an inflexible personality. The couple had one son, Peter, who was baptized on 4 June 1786. But by that time they were not getting on well together. Keen on making deals, Diehl was unsuccessful in business and became steadily gloomier. In 1787 Phebe sought shelter with her brother Michael*, a silversmith at Saint-Philippe-de-Laprairie, taking her son with her.

The Diehls were granted a legal separation on 15 Jan. 1789. Phebe obtained custody of her son, got back her furniture, jewellery, and clothes, but renounced the jointure of 1,000 *livres* provided for in her marriage contract. She then managed to assure herself of a modest income by giving English, French, and sewing lessons in Montreal. In November 1794 Michael put up the money for her to purchase a property on Rue Notre-Dame in Trois-Rivières. In return she agreed to keep him for the rest of his life.

Phebe opened a drapery store in Trois-Rivières, and in 1796 she bought another lot on Rue Notre-Dame. However, her enterprise was not doing well, and as a result in 1799 she made both properties over to her mother, who kept an inn at Trois-Rivières. She then wound up her business, assigned the income from it to her son, and entered the Ursuline convent in Trois-Rivières. Remaining there despite her mother's entreaties, she abjured Protestantism and was rebaptized Apolline on 3 May 1802. She took the habit three months later and on 6 Aug. 1804 made her profession. Now Apolline de Sainte-Angèle, she was assigned to teach the day pupils. Her new condition as a convert and her past as a businesswoman were to make community life in a semi-cloistered convent very difficult for her.

Apolline de Sainte-Angèle lost her brother Michael in 1807 and her mother the following year. In 1810 she became bursar of the community. But, suffering from dropsy and a liver ailment, she received permission in August 1813 to go to convalesce at the home of her brother Charles in Saint-Sulpice. After a few months she refused to return to Trois-Rivières. Pressure from vicar general François-Xavier Noiseux and the intervention of Bishop PLESSIS of Quebec were necessary to persuade her to return to the convent in January 1814. She died there on 16 May 1825 and was buried under the chancel of the convent chapel.

HERMANN PLANTE

ANQ-M, CE1-63, 22 mai 1767, 22 févr. 1783. *Les ursulines des Trois-Rivières*. Édouard Fabre Surveyer, "Une famille d'orfèvres," *BRH*, 46 (1940): 310–15; "Une ursuline d'origine allemande aux Trois-Rivières," *Le Canada français* (Québec), 2ᵉ sér., 28 (1940–41): 117–30.

ATKINSON, GEORGE (known as **Sneppy** until about 1790), fur trader and explorer; b. 15 March 1777 at Eastmain House (Eastmain, Que.), son of George Atkinson* and Necushin, an Indian woman; d. 25 Sept. 1830 at the Red River settlement (Man.).

The mixed-blood son of a Hudson's Bay Company trader, George Atkinson Jr became a formidable if not always tractable force in the affairs of the company on the Eastmain, the eastern coast of James and Hudson bays. Although he was baptized in England around 1790 and was sent there several times "to shake of a little of the Indian," as his father put it, he always retained his Indian connections and he contracted two country marriages with Indian women.

The period of Atkinson's service on the Eastmain was initially dominated by the HBC's efforts to meet the threat of competition from Canadian traders. His first experience of inland exploration seems to have been in the summer of 1793 when he accompanied an HBC party to the Canadian post at Lac Cheasquacheston (Lac au Goéland) by way of Lac Nemiscau. Later that year the 16-year-old caused a second expedition to be abandoned when he refused to take charge of a canoe after the accidental death of the steersman. In 1795 another effort to reach the post came to nothing because Atkinson and the Indians were "bad against it." As his superior, James Fogget, complained, "He delights always in the company of the Indians, and not in the Englishmens."

Indian skills were at a premium among company servants during the years when wartime demands had led to a drop in standards, and so Atkinson remained in the HBC's service in the Eastmain district, hunting and organizing transport. From 1803 to 1806 he was in charge of the post at Big River (La Grande Rivière), north of Eastmain Factory, where he competed in effective though sometimes unorthodox fashion against the North West Company. His salary increased steadily during this period, until by the season of 1805–6 he was earning £50 a year, plus bonuses. On his return from a visit to England in 1807 he was made a member of the council at Eastmain and again placed in charge of Big River, where he remained until the post closed in 1813. For his final three years there he also supervised the whale fishery along the coast to the north, although relations between him and other company traders and schooner masters were evidently difficult. As the London committee of the HBC wrote to his superior, Thomas THOMAS, in 1813, "We fear there may be some difficulty in establishing a cordiality between Atkinson and any European officers for long continuance."

The London committee had a more independent role in mind for Atkinson, in which, it was hoped, his contacts with the Indians would help rather than hinder the company's designs. He was to survey the Great and Little Whale rivers (Grand Rivière de la Baleine and Petite Rivière de la Baleine) in 1815, the beginning of the company's plan to explore "one part of the country after another" in an attempt to exploit new trading areas. Atkinson's insistence on hunting for his family delayed the survey until 1816, when he completed exploration of Great Whale River only. He proceeded about 350 miles by canoe as far as Lac Bienville and returned with a rough sketch of his route and a report that the river held out promise of neither trade nor provisions. In 1818 he embarked with a party of Indians on his second survey, striking inland from Richmond Gulf (Lac Guillaume-Delisle) along Deer River (Rivière au Caribou) to Clearwater Lake (Lac à l'Eau Claire) and then to the area of Upper Seal Lake (Petit Lac des Loups Marins). There or near by, he recorded on 22 July 1818 the first known observations of freshwater seals. At the beginning of August he met Indians who told him that the lakes at which he had by then arrived emptied into "the sea, on the other side of the continent." He had reached the height of land, but was forced back by the reluctance of his guide to go farther, and by sickness among the Indians. Again, his report was a depressing one – of a journey involving 50 portages to the height of land, of a barren country, and of few furs.

Atkinson's role as an inland explorer was subsequently taken over by HBC employee James Clouston. His hold over the Indians was illustrated by Clouston when he wrote in 1823 that the Indians believed Atkinson could kill them by his conjuring. Clouston also complained that Atkinson told the Indians they were being cheated by the HBC and that he encouraged them to demand higher prices for their furs. Atkinson became an increasing embarrassment to the company, and attempts were made to persuade him and his numerous family to move to the Red River settlement.

Atkinson performed one further service before retiring. His contribution to William Hendry's expedition of 1828 from the Eastmain to the Rivière Koksoak in the Ungava peninsula explains much of the journey's success. Hendry had no experience of inland travel, and although he complained of Atkinson's unpredictable behaviour, the mixed-blood's knowledge as guide and interpreter was invaluable. Soon after his return Atkinson moved to the Red River settlement, where he died in 1830. He left a widow and 14 children, 2 of them at least from his first marriage. Despite the problems which he caused his superiors and associates in the fur trade, Atkinson played a substantial part in securing the trade of the Indians in the Eastmain during a period of competition. His inland surveys of 1816 and 1818 were the

Aubert

precursors of more ambitious ventures which in the next 25 years were to open up Labrador.

GLYNDWR WILLIAMS

PAM, HBCA, G.1/40, G.1/42. *HBRS*, 24 (Davies and Johnson). Daniel Francis and Toby Morantz, *Partners in furs: a history of the fur trade in eastern James Bay, 1600–1870* (Kingston, Ont., and Montreal, 1983).

AUBERT DE GASPÉ, PIERRE-IGNACE, JP, seigneur, politician, and militia officer; b. 14 Aug. 1758 at Quebec, sixth child of Ignace-Philippe Aubert* de Gaspé and Marie-Anne Coulon de Villiers; m. there 28 Jan. 1786 Catherine Tarieu de Lanaudière, daughter of Charles-Louis Tarieu* de Lanaudière, and they had seven children, two of whom reached adulthood; d. 13 Feb. 1823 at Saint-Jean-Port-Joli, Lower Canada, and was buried two days later in the parish church.

Pierre-Ignace Aubert de Gaspé's early years were rather difficult. Born at the end of the French régime, he could not escape the misfortunes of his time. To begin with, he was deprived of the presence of his father, who was constantly obliged to be on active military service during the Seven Years' War. He also experienced material privations. Following the surrender of Montreal and the whole colony, his family, which had been ruined, was obliged to live in a water-mill near Rivière Trois-Saumons, at the western tip of the seigneury of Port-Joly. They remained there for about six years, until the houses burnt by the British in 1759 were rebuilt and a fresh start had been made in farming.

Aubert de Gaspé spent part of his childhood and adolescence at the manor-house on the seigneury of Port-Joly. He studied at the Petit Séminaire de Québec from 1769 till 1775. While still a student he readily responded to the call by Governor Guy Carleton* and Bishop Jean-Olivier Briand* of Quebec to take up arms against the American troops under Richard Montgomery* and Benedict Arnold*.

Upon reaching manhood Aubert de Gaspé mingled with the society of the Château Saint-Louis, the governor's residence; he had useful connections in political and military, as well as fashionable, circles, and he entered into the public life of his time. Around 1787 he received a commission as justice of the peace for the District of Quebec. The following year he signed a petition to the king opposing the creation of a house of assembly in the province.

Aubert de Gaspé was made a legislative councillor in 1812 on the recommendation of Chief Justice Jonathan Sewell* the previous year. An impressionable man who sometimes gave free rein to his emotions, he was remembered as a speaker prone to bombast but possessed of sound judgement. His son

Philippe-Joseph* described him as a "high Tory" and a "royalist" who preferred George III to Napoleon I. He also served the British crown in the militia; in 1814 he became colonel of the Saint-Jean-Port-Joli and Saint-Thomas militia battalions.

Upon his mother's death in 1789 Aubert de Gaspé became the fifth seigneur of Port-Joly. Like his father he took an interest in settlement and made a notable contribution to the development of his seigneurial lands. He is credited in particular with developing the third line of homesteads and building a mill to the east of it in 1819. In 1790 he had purchased Îlet-à-la-Peau, a seigneury with a frontage of half a league and a depth of two leagues.

Pierre-Ignace Aubert de Gaspé died at his manor-house on 13 Feb. 1823, leaving a will that 50 years later would result in the sale of almost all his property to people outside his family. This document seems linked with the financial difficulties that would soon cause his elder son, Philippe-Joseph, to lose his office as sheriff and go to prison for debt. Pierre-Ignace bequeathed half his seigneurial property to his wife. His son Antoine-Thomas received only the usufruct of one-third of the other half. Philippe-Joseph received the usufruct of the two-thirds portion, as well as of the seigneurial domain of Port-Joly, the manor-house, the mill and outbuildings, and the adjoining lands; the ownership of these properties went to the children of Philippe-Joseph and his wife, Susanne Allison. By 29 Jan. 1871, when Philippe-Joseph died, Antoine-Thomas was already dead, and the seigneuries of Port-Joly and Îlet-à-la-Peau passed to no fewer than 12 heirs. For reasons likely attributable to their number and their personalities, they decided to part with them. On 15 July 1872 the manor-house and seigneurial domain were sold; the following 22 February the family gave up the water-mill on Rivière Trois-Saumons. These sales marked the end of an important dynasty at Saint-Jean-Port-Joli. Pierre-Ignace, who was one of its most eminent figures, had succeeded in preventing a potential attachment of his seigneuries, but not in avoiding this unfortunate outcome.

JACQUES CASTONGUAY

AC, Montmagny, minutiers, L.-Z. Duval, 15 juill. 1872, 22 févr. 1873. ANQ-Q, CE1-1, 14 août 1758, 28 janv. 1786; CE2-18, 15 févr. 1823; CN2-12, 1er déc. 1820. ASQ, Fichier des anciens. *Quebec Gazette*, 13 Nov. 1788, 1 April 1813, 17 Feb. 1823. F.-J. Audet, "Les législateurs du Bas-Canada." "Papiers d'État – Bas-Canada," PAC *Rapport*, 1893: 52. P.-G. Roy, *Fils de Québec*, 2: 121–23; *Inv. concessions*, 3: 171. Turcotte, *Le Conseil législatif*. P.[-J.] Aubert de Gaspé, *Les anciens canadiens* (Québec, 1863); *The Canadians of old*, trans. G. M. Pennée (Québec, 1864); *Mémoires* (1866). H.-R. Casgrain, *Œuvres complètes* (3v., Québec, 1873–75), 2. Jacques Castonguay, *La seigneurie de Philippe Aubert de Gaspé, Saint-Jean-Port-Joli* (Montréal,

1977). [François Daniel], *Histoire des grandes familles françaises du Canada ou aperçu sur le chevalier Benoist et quelques familles contemporaines* (Montréal, 1867). P.-G. Roy, *La famille Aubert de Gaspé* (Lévis, Qué., 1907); *La famille Tarieu de Lanaudière* (Lévis, 1922).

AUBREVILLE, LOUIS-NICOLAS-EMMANUEL DE BIGAULT D'. *See* BIGAULT

AUDIVERT, *dit* **ROMAIN.** *See* ROMAIN

AUGUSTUS. *See* TATTANNOEUCK

AULD, WILLIAM, surgeon, fur trader, and JP; b. *c.* 1770, possibly in Edinburgh, Scotland; d. some time after November 1830, probably in Leith or Edinburgh.

William Auld may have studied medicine at the University of Edinburgh from 1785 to 1788, but he did not graduate. He began his career with the Hudson's Bay Company as a surgeon according to a contract signed in London on 27 May 1790, and he shipped for Fort Churchill (Churchill, Man.). Two years later Chief Factor Thomas Stayner described him as "not only skillful in his profession, but industrious, sober and of an amiable disposition." Like other surgeons hired by the HBC, he probably had more occasions to deal with furs than to call on his medical knowledge. His appointment as second at Fort Churchill in May 1793 recognized his contributions as a fur trader. On the conclusion of his first contract in 1795 the London committee of the HBC recalled him to England. The HBC re-engaged him as second, appointed him "Inland Trader," and dispatched him to Fort Churchill.

The shortage of personnel together with an inadequate amount of trade goods frustrated the attempts of traders such as Auld to mount an effective opposition to the North West Company, particularly in the Athabasca country. In 1797, during Stayner's absence in London for consultation with the company, Auld served as locum tenens. On Stayner's return the following year, the two visited the chief factor at York Factory (Man.), John Ballenden, in an unsuccessful effort to avoid competition between the two factories in pushing their respective enterprises into the interior. In the summer of 1799 Auld journeyed inland with instructions to establish new trading posts. Leaving William Linklater to build at Île-à-la-Crosse (Sask.), he travelled up the Beaver River to build at Green Lake. En route he encountered HBC surveyor Peter FIDLER, who was working under similar orders from York Factory, and insisted that Fidler continue up the Beaver River to locate at Lac la Biche (Alta). Aware of the importance of securing provisions from the Saskatchewan country for the HBC's penetration into the Athabasca, Auld journeyed overland to Edmonton House (near Fort Saskatchewan, Alta), arriving in January 1800, to consult with James Bird*. That summer he was back at Fort Churchill. He remained there, being promoted chief factor and surgeon in May 1802.

An injury Auld suffered in a fall led to a trip to England in 1804. The next year, however, he returned to Fort Churchill. Still frustrated in his continuing attempts to oppose the Nor'Westers, he left Thomas Topping in charge at the fort while he led an expedition, which included Fidler, to winter in 1808–9 at Clapham House on Reindeer Lake. There they met with determined opposition from Robert Henry* of the NWC. Convinced that more energetic and resolute measures would meet with success, Auld went to London in 1809 to persuade the HBC's governing committee to adopt his point of view and to make representations to the British government. Auld's personal quest was caught up in the "retrenching system" adopted in 1810 by the committee, whose membership had been altered significantly with the intervention of the Earl of Selkirk [Douglas*] and his brother-in-law, Andrew Wedderburn, in the company's affairs. The new scheme emphasized the reduction of expenses, the introduction of a profit-sharing program, and the reorganization of the fur trade into two departments, Northern and Southern. Auld returned to Rupert's Land as the superintendent of the Northern Department, which included the posts at York Factory and Fort Churchill as well as the Saskatchewan and Winnipeg districts. He would divide his time between York Factory and Fort Churchill. On 28 Nov. 1811 he was appointed justice of the peace for the Indian Territory.

Auld's closing years with the HBC emphasized his incompatibility with the "modern" management espoused by the committee. In addition to implementing the London committee's retrenching system Auld had to deal with the opposition it induced among long-serving employees. The mutiny at Brandon House (Man.) in February 1811 was the most noteworthy of a number of protests. Problems arising from the arrival of the first settlers for the Red River colony, the creation of which he had strongly opposed, further exacerbated his difficulties. Increasingly, Auld felt that the committee's policies and directives reflected ignorance of local circumstances and did not take into account the advice of knowledgeable experienced officers such as himself. The committee's "interference" undermined the challenge he could make to the NWC's hegemony.

In any characterization of Auld's administrative style, images of the Nor'Westers come to mind. Like them he was energetic, resolute, and to a degree impulsive, emphasizing individual responses to issues rather than sound structures and effective systems to achieve objectives. The problems attending the opposition of disgruntled employees and the advent of the

17

Auldjo

Selkirk settlers accentuated the differences between the new corporate managerial style of the committee and the traditional individualism exhibited in Auld's administration. Each side was disappointed with the other. It was no surprise when the committee accepted his resignation on 9 April 1814. Yet the value of his long experience was recognized when, on his return to London in the autumn of 1814, his services were contracted there for another year. Auld apparently gave written expression to his frustration with the committee in such a manner that a most acrimonious separation took place in December 1815. It would appear that he retired to Leith, Scotland.

Little is known of Auld's "country wife or wives." He had possibly as many as five children. Robert, Jane, and Mary appear in the parish records of the Anglican mission at the Red River settlement (Man.). William and Wilberforce have been identified as sons who left for England in 1820. The last letter to him from the company was addressed in care of an Edinburgh resident in November 1830.

J. E. FOSTER

Edinburgh Univ. Library, Special Coll. Dept., Medical matriculation records, 1785–88. PAC, MG 24, L3, 15; no.7217: 8980–82; no.7218: 9003–7; MG 25, G62. PAM, HBCA, A.5/9: 193; A.11/118; A.30/10; MG 7, B7, marriages, nos.65, 292. *HBRS*, 2 (Rich and Fleming); 26 (Johnson). *Quebec Gazette*, 19 Dec. 1811. Rich, *Hist. of HBC* (1958–59), vol.2.

AULDJO, ALEXANDER, businessman, militia officer, JP, and politician; b. 21 Oct. 1758 in Aberdeen, Scotland, son of John Auldjo, baker and manufacturer, and Margaret McKenzie; d. 21 May 1821 in London.

Alexander Auldjo arrived in Montreal about 1778. During the 1780s he invested considerable sums in the fur trade – some £3,000 in 1782 for example – stood security for fur traders, sold properties, and administered estates. In 1785 he was in partnership with William Maitland, and the following year they and Richard Dobie* bought a substantial quantity of wheat for export. By 1795 the firm of Auldjo and Maitland was dealing extensively in the sale of bills of exchange.

Auldjo and Maitland had expanded to become Auldjo, Maitland and Company by 1800. Supplied in part from London by Auldjo's younger brother John, it imported a wide variety of manufactured goods, which it sold in Lower Canada or forwarded to Upper Canadian storekeepers in return for flour and ashes. The Upper Canadian trade was not without difficulties. In 1800 preferential treatment given to cargo belonging to James and Andrew McGill and Company in the loading of government boats at the key port of Kingston put Auldjo, Maitland at a disadvantage. In

addition, as Thomas Cummings, a Chippawa merchant deeply indebted to Auldjo, Maitland, was warned in 1807: "Your goods are better on your Shelves than sold to doubtful people ye giving of inconsiderate credit has been ye ruin of many in your province, as well as in this." In order to turn to account rapidly changing market conditions, Auldjo, Maitland advised Cummings forcefully on what and when to buy and sell. The firm attended in the same business-like manner to the education of Cummings's children in Montreal. According to an Albany, N.Y., merchant, in 1803 Auldjo, Maitland was among the principal firms sending bateaux from Montreal to Upper Canada and exported merchandise worth some £36,000, making it, in his estimate, fifth among the city's exporters.

Auldjo invested heavily in real estate, notably in Upper Canada between 1797 and 1807; there he owned farm lots scattered throughout the province. (In 1829 his estate included 30 of these properties, totalling 5,450 acres.) In addition, he dealt occasionally in property at Montreal, owned land in Lower Canada, and apparently acted as the agent of individuals and groups in the Eastern Townships who were petitioning for grants.

Auldjo was already a leader among Montreal businessmen by the late 1780s. In January 1787 he was on a committee composed of the principal merchants of the city whose members testified before a committee of the Legislative Council on commerce and the police established by Lord Dorchester [Guy Carleton*] the previous year. The merchants demanded, among other things, a reorganization of the administration of justice, the introduction of a school system, a land registry office, and a bankruptcy law, as well as the building of a new prison in Montreal and the incorporation of the city; they also reiterated a long-standing demand for an elective assembly. The same year Auldjo was a captain in Montreal's British militia. He was a charter member of the Agriculture Society's Montreal branch in 1790, and that October joined with a number of leading firms and businessmen of the city to demand complete freedom of navigation in the fur-trade interior.

In the elections to the House of Assembly in 1792, Auldjo was defeated in Montreal West, but he won one of the riding's two seats in 1796. During his only term he strongly supported the English party, led in the house by two of the colony's most prominent merchants, John RICHARDSON and John Young*. Auldjo particularly pressed for improvements in transportation, especially to navigation on the upper St Lawrence; in 1805 he would be named a commissioner for the improvement of inland navigation between Montreal and Lachine. He was made a justice of the peace in Montreal in 1796 and a warden of Trinity House of Quebec four years later. Auldjo may have become better connected in the Montreal business community through his marriage on 21 Jan. 1804 in Portsoy, Scotland, to Ewereta Jane Richardson, who was probably John's sister; they were to have two sons and a daughter, but the latter died shortly after birth in 1808, along with her mother. Auldjo likely had informal business relations with Richardson.

In 1804 Auldjo was named the agent for the Canadas of the Phoenix Assurance Company of London, such an agency having been requested by merchants in Lower and Upper Canada. With a monopoly in the field, Auldjo at first was concerned only to increase the demand for insurance, determine premium rates, and make customers aware of their responsibility for policy renewals "in a country through which a regular post is not established" and the sending of renewal notices "cannot always be done with precision or certainty." The rates he calculated "on risks in the cities of Quebec and Montreal, where the houses in general are built of stone, and many fire proof"; premiums were higher for buildings "in the suburbs of those Cities and the other towns and villages of Lower Canada, as well as those of Upper Canada, which are mostly built of wood." In 1808, following upon a report by a Phoenix representative who had been sent to the colony and on orders from head office, Auldjo announced that Quebec's Lower Town was considered a fire-trap and thenceforth uninsurable. Indignant policy holders organized a lobby of the Phoenix head office by important London firms trading to Quebec. In July 1809 Auldjo advertised Phoenix's readiness "to revive their connections with the Lower-Town of Quebec to a certain extent, and under certain regulations." The company's reputation there had been dealt a serious blow, however; in April 1811 Auldjo was obliged to offer reduced premiums to Lower Town property owners, and in June he appointed an agent at Quebec to handle policy renewals. Later Phoenix would meet stiff competition by a locally organized company [see George GARDEN]. From 1807 Auldjo also represented the Pelican Life Insurance Company.

Like many prominent Montreal businessmen, Auldjo was a member of the Scotch Presbyterian Church (later known as St Gabriel Street Church); elected to its temporal committee in 1809 and 1810, he was vice-president the first year and president the second. He had continued active in the militia. By 1812 he was lieutenant-colonel of Montreal's 1st Militia Battalion, and on 6 July 1812 he was made lieutenant-colonel commanding the newly formed Montreal Militia Battalion. However, he resigned his commission on 25 Sept. 1813 and that year departed for Britain. He apparently took up residence in London.

In 1813 the partners in Auldjo, Maitland and Company were Auldjo himself, Maitland (who had been representing the firm in London since about the beginning of the century), and George Garden; within two years the firm had changed its name to Maitland, Garden, and Auldjo with the addition of Auldjo's nephew George Auldjo*, and it seems likely that Alexander Auldjo had retired. Clearly, however, Alexander continued to harbour an interest in Lower Canadian business affairs. At the behest of John Richardson in 1816, he hired an experienced Scottish road builder for the Montreal turnpike project, and three years later, after consulting with the renowned British canal engineer Thomas Telford, he engaged Thomas Burnett to design the Lachine Canal and supervise its construction. Meanwhile, in 1817 he and Maitland, on their own, had become two of only five London subscribers to the newly founded Bank of Montreal. Possibly active in the small London community of merchants formerly inhabiting Lower Canada, Auldjo was an intimate friend of one of them, Adam Lymburner*. Auldjo died in London in 1821, aged 62, and was buried in St George's Church, Bloomsbury.

GERALD J. J. TULCHINSKY

PAC, MG 11, [CO 42] Q, 30: 195–96; MG 23, GIII, 30; MG 24, D43; L3: 6601–2, 30528–33; MG 55/23, no.12 (Edward Watts); RG 1, L3ᴸ: 45–57, 65–113, 349, 518, 1306, 1537, 1664, 1681, 2115, 2440–50, 4461–66, 5058–73, 5132–35, 5146, 17736–89, 26831–59; RG 4, B28, 115; RG 43, CIII, 1, vol.2453, 26 July 1819; RG 68, General index, 1651–1841: 187, 211, 333–34, 339, 698. QUA, Auldjo papers, box 1, folder 1, John Richardson to J. B. Forsyth, 25 March 1829. *Docs. relating to constitutional hist., 1759–91* (Shortt and Doughty), 920. Douglas, *Lord Selkirk's diary* (White), 232. *Kingston before War of 1812* (Preston), 212. L.C., House of Assembly, *Journals*, 1805: 94–96; 1807: 100; *Statutes*, 1805, c.6. *Montreal Gazette*, 31 Jan. 1851. *Quebec Gazette*, 25 Oct. 1781; 27 June, 10 Oct. 1782; 7 Aug. 1783; 4 March, 15 July, 28 Oct. 1784; 3 Nov. 1785; 5 June, 11 Dec. 1788; 20 Aug., 12 Nov. 1789; 15 April, 28 Oct., 4 Nov. 1790; 16 June, 27 Oct. 1791; 31 May, 19 July 1792; 12 Sept., 3 Oct. 1793; 24 July, 11 Dec. 1794; 26 Feb. 1795; 26 Jan., 11 May 1797; 25 July, 19 Dec. 1799; 27 Nov. 1800; 11 March, 3 June 1802; 19, 26 July, 30 Aug. 1804; 16 May 1805; 9 Jan., 20, 27 March, 1 May, 23 Oct. 1806; 5, 26 Feb. 1807; 1 Sept., 29 Dec. 1808; 16 March, 6, 13 July 1809; 12 July 1810; 4 April, 4 July 1811; 4, 11 June, 9 July, 10, 17 Sept., 12 March 1818; 2 Nov. 1820; 16 July 1821; 13 June, 8, 15 Aug., 26 Sept. 1822; 4 Sept. 1837.

F.-J. Audet, *Les députés de Montréal*, 150–51. Massicotte, "Répertoire des engagements pour l'Ouest," ANQ *Rapport*, 1943–44: 410; 1945–46: 236, 291, 295, 318. *Officers of British forces in Canada* (Irving), 164–65. *Quebec almanac*, 1788: 52; 1791: 84. "State papers – L.C.," PAC *Report*, 1891: 141. R. Campbell, *Hist. of Scotch Presbyterian Church*, 99. Denison, *Canada's first bank*, 1: 92. Innis, *Fur trade in Canada* (1962), 184. Miquelon, "Baby family," 191–94. Paquet et Wallot, *Patronage et pouvoir dans le Bas-Canada*, 129. Phoenix Assurance Company Limited, *First in the field . . .* ([Toronto, 1954]). Robert Rumilly, *Histoire de Montréal* (5v., Montréal,

Aw-gee-nah

1970–74), 2: 83, 134. Tulchinsky, "Construction of first Lachine Canal," 39. E. A. Cruikshank, "A country merchant in Upper Canada, 1800–1812," *OH*, 25 (1929): 145–90. Hare, "L'Assemblée législative du Bas-Canada," *RHAF*, 27: 375. "L'honorable Adam Lymburner," *BRH*, 37 (1931): 558. Richard Lessard, "L'arrière-fief Hope," *BRH*, 33 (1927): 307. É.-Z. Massicotte, "Quelques maisons du vieux Montréal," *Cahiers des Dix*, 10 (1945): 260. P.-G. Roy, "La Trinity-House ou Maison de la Trinité à Québec," *BRH*, 24 (1918): 105–10.

AW-GEE-NAH (English Chief), Chipewyan chief; fl. 1771–1821.

Little is known of the family of the English Chief, but his relatives were said to rendezvous at Great Slave Lake (N.W.T.), which may have been his family locale. The Chipewyans, members of the Athapaskan linguistic family, inhabited the Arctic drainage lands to the west of Hudson Bay. The English Chief was with the "leading Indian" Matonabbee* when he guided Hudson's Bay Company explorer Samuel Hearne* to the Coppermine River in 1771. Following the death of Matonabbee and the smallpox epidemic of 1781–83, the English Chief assumed leadership of a band trekking to Fort Churchill (Churchill, Man.) to trade with the HBC. Shortly after North West Company partners began to arrive in the Athabasca country, around 1786, they persuaded the English Chief to act as middleman and carrier in the vicinity of Athabasca and Great Slave lakes.

Accompanied by two wives and his brother, the English Chief acted as guide, interpreter, and hunter for NWC explorer Alexander Mackenzie* on a journey from Fort Chipewyan (Alta) to the Arctic in 1789. During this voyage the English Chief was impressed by the prospects of carrying beaver pelts from the Beaver and Slavey tribes of the Liard–Mackenzie River region to NWC posts. He demonstrated to Mackenzie his working knowledge of the Slavey, Dogrib, and Beaver languages. Like Matonabbee, the English Chief showed no reluctance to plunder the weaker Hares and Dogribs, who were not kin and, more important, were intimidated by firearms. On his return the English Chief had sufficient prestige to fulfil the role of leader of a band of Yellowknife middlemen. From these foundations laid in 1790, the Yellowknives would act as carriers to the Dogribs, Beavers, Hares, and Kutchins until 1823, when the Dogribs rebelled against them. The English Chief himself operated in the upper Peace River area throughout the 1790s as provisioner to the NWC and was a carrier to the Beavers at least until 1821, the last reference to him in fur-trade records.

During the period 1805–14 the NWC had extended its posts to the more remote regions of the Mackenzie, Liard, and Peace rivers, reducing the need for middlemen such as the English Chief. After 1805 he apparently relocated in the area of Lake Athabasca and lower Peace River, alternately acting as carrier and as hunter at Fort Chipewyan for the NWC. By 1815 the Athabasca trade was undergoing severe dislocation. The Indians were affected by the decline of the large mammal populations in the Peace and Athabasca regions, and were withdrawing north to hunt the barren-ground caribou. Returns from posts on the lower Mackenzie River decreased because of the Indians' increased hostility towards the Nor'Westers, and the latter consequently retreated from those posts in 1815. A year later an HBC expedition to the Athabasca, led by John Clarke*, arrived in the region determined to counter the NWC's trading activities. The English Chief befriended the HBC by saving some expedition members who were starving in the Peace River area. By 1819 the HBC was firmly established at Lake Athabasca and, by supplying food to a starving brigade near Lake Athabasca and by acting as post hunter, the English Chief had ingratiated himself with George Simpson*, who was directing the HBC's Athabasca campaign from Fort Wedderburne (Alta).

The life of the English Chief was indicative of the changes occurring for the Athapaskan tribes attached to the fur trade between 1770 and 1820. He had followed the middleman Matonabbee and had led trading bands to Fort Churchill before European fur traders established themselves in the Athabasca; he had then acted as a carrier from NWC posts to the Indians in the recesses of the Arctic drainage lowlands. Later he also became a fort hunter for the HBC and an adviser to the company during a period when depletion of resources – particularly the buffalo, elk, and moose in the Peace River region – forced their rationalization. Specialized activities for Indians were then introduced in the fur trade, while strict conservation measures were employed by the HBC in the regions of the Peace and Athabasca rivers.

W. A. SLOAN

PAC, MG 19, C1, 51. PAM, HBCA, B.39/a/1–5; B.224/c/1: f.2d. *Les bourgeois de la Compagnie du Nord-Ouest* (Masson), vol.1. *HBRS*, 1 (Rich). Samuel Hearne, *A journey from Prince of Wales's Fort, in Hudson's Bay, to the northern ocean . . . in the years 1769, 1770, 1771 & 1772*, ed. R. [G.] Glover (new ed., Toronto, 1958). Mackenzie, *Journals and letters* (Lamb). W. A. Sloan, "Contact and enlightened co-operation: a history of the fur trade in the Arctic drainage lowlands, 1717–1821" (PHD thesis, Univ. of Manitoba, Winnipeg, 1985); "The native response to the extension of the European traders into the Athabasca and Mackenzie basin, 1770–1814," *CHR*, 60 (1979): 281–99.

B

BABY, JAMES (baptized **Jacques**), politician, office holder, judge, landowner, and militia officer; b. 25 Aug. 1763 in Detroit, son of Jacques Baby*, *dit* Dupéront, and Susanne Réaume (Rhéaume), *dit* La Croix; m. secondly 1802 Elizabeth Abbott, and they had five sons and one daughter; d. 19 Feb. 1833 at York (Toronto), Upper Canada.

An elder son of a prestigious family in the Detroit area, James Baby was educated in the province of Quebec under the supervision of his uncle François*. He also took lessons in fencing and dancing, activities esteemed as attributes of gentility. At the conclusion of his studies his father sent him on a European tour, during which Baby married an actress. Soon after, he was recalled by his father who effectively, if not legally, ended the union by providing her with a pension. Baby was then initiated into his father's commercial affairs and amassed considerable wealth.

Baby's family had been renowned for its loyalty to the crown since the conquest. After the division of the old province of Quebec in 1791 he became one of western Upper Canada's foremost office holders. Because of his loyalty and the need to represent the French community in the area, Lieutenant Governor John Graves Simcoe* named him in 1792 to the Executive and Legislative councils and the county lieutenancy of Kent. Surveyor General David William Smith* noted the probable influence of Baby's uncle with Lord Dorchester [Guy Carleton*]: "The Interest which brought the Young French Gentleman into the Councils, has prevailed in having him appointed Lord Lieutenant for the County of Kent, & that interest was not only planted previous to the Governments taking place, but seems to have taken exuberant Root in Quebec; where his [James's] Consequence, his Interest, his Property, & his Loyalty, seem to have been blazoned in lively tropes." Baby was also named to the first Heir and Devisee Commission and in January 1799 was, with Alexander Grant* and Thomas McKee*, temporarily appointed to the office of deputy superintendent general of Indian affairs.

When in 1793 Baby accepted an appointment from Simcoe as judge of the Surrogate Court for the Western District he noted: "The thought that I may be useful, particularly to our poor Canadians who have no other support here but me, makes me inclined to put up with everything, whatever my reluctance." The next year Baby and Richard G. England*, the commandant of Detroit, organized the local militia, many of whom were French Canadians; in part, Baby's role was to secure the loyalty of his people. During the crisis in Indian-American relations in 1794, Baby worked, again with England, to prepare the militia. Simcoe commended him for his efforts and put the 1st Kent Militia under his command. Following Jay's Treaty of November 1794, the Baby family abandoned considerable property in the Detroit region and moved to Sandwich (Windsor), where they built a residence and store.

Baby augmented his finances by acquiring large amounts of land in various parts of Upper Canada, through entitlement and by purchase. In the period from 1793 to 1800 he bought town lots in Sandwich, Newark (Niagara-on-the-Lake), and York where he also received 200 acres for a house appropriate to an executive councillor. In 1793 he secured 3,000 acres in his father's name, 1,200 acres for his mother, and 1,200 acres for each of his brothers – lands which were located in Yarmouth Township. Land records for 1805 indicate that Baby had 7,000 acres in Yarmouth which he had received as the transferee of these individuals, as well as 4,600 in Dorchester Township (North and South Dorchester townships), 246 acres in Harwich Township, and 180 acres in Malden Township. The same records reveal that, although he was entitled to 6,000 acres as an executive councillor, he was only to receive 5,300 because of possible conflicts with other claimants. In addition, he claimed small acreages in Aldborough and Sandwich townships and 1,500 acres in Dunwich Township; he surrendered his title to the latter in 1806.

At the outbreak of the War of 1812 Baby led the militia from Sandwich to Amherstburg. His own family was forced to flee when the invading American army entered Sandwich on 13 July and the Baby home was pillaged. He was with Major-General Henry Procter's force of regulars, militia, and Indians at the disastrous battle of Moraviantown on 5 Oct. 1813. Baby was taken prisoner but released shortly after. He had sustained considerable losses. The damage to his home alone was estimated at almost £600 and he was never compensated. His greatest loss in these years, however, was his second wife, who died during an epidemic of fever in the winter of 1812–13. Tired, ill, with young children, and stricken with grief, Baby retired to Quebec late in 1813 for rest and medical care.

In 1815 Baby was appointed inspector general and moved to York where, with his five sons, he built a home on an estate with 1,500 acres of uncultivated land. He attended to his administrative and political duties faithfully and only on rare occasions missed a meeting of the Executive Council. In the capital he enjoyed the friendship of John Strachan* (one of the executors of his estate), John Beverley Robinson*,

Badeaux

George Herchmer Markland*, and Thomas CLARK. Like Baby himself, they were members of the so-called "family compact." His conservatism, his traditional Roman Catholicism, which inculcated respect for authority, and his refusal to accept American democratic ideas made him a natural part of this group. In addition to the inspector generalship, Baby took on other tasks. He was one of the commissioners of forfeited estates charged with settling the property affairs of men such as Abraham MARKLE who had been traitors during the war. More important, early in 1823 he was appointed Upper Canada's arbitrator in the dispute over the sharing of customs revenues with Lower Canada. He was surprised and flattered. Writing to a friend, he exclaimed: "I have become a great man, no less than Arbitrator for Upper Canada. What think you of this, a Canadian from Upper Canada to settle matters embarrassed by Lower Canada." The arbitration was successful and ended an acutely difficult period in the province's financial history. By 1827 Baby's influence was diminishing. He had become largely dependent on his emoluments from office to support his family. Historian John Charles Dent* suggests this reliance compromised him politically. For instance, on one occasion, Baby voted against his conscience and with the administration on the issue of taxing wild lands.

While at York Baby continued to speculate in land. In 1830 he and ten other men, including his brother François*, were speculating in the Lake St Clair area of the Western District and encountering stiff opposition from Thomas Talbot*. Avoidance of taxation by speculators was a common occurrence in the early 19th century and Baby was no exception. On a large number of his properties he failed to pay his taxes and as a consequence stood to lose more than 9,000 acres. The law, however, allowed those in arrears to redeem their property and Baby did. In addition to his activity in the land market, he continued to receive land for his services to government. As a militia colonel he was allowed 1,200 acres, which he sought in Vespra Township. He died, however, before the transactions could be finalized, and 26 years later his only surviving executor (Strachan) was still involved in the legal ramifications.

At a period when pluralism of office was common, James Baby was an office holder *par excellence*; between 1792 and 1830 he held more than 115 appointments or commissions of varying degrees of importance. Gracious and distinguished, he was the epitome of a gentleman. He was an impressive figure – clean-shaven, tall, good-looking, and well proportioned – and possessed, according to his grandson, a "primitive simplicity" and a "moral beauty." Strachan eulogized him as "a Christian without guile, affable and polished in his manners, courteous in his conversation, dignified in his deportment, warm in his affections, steady in his friendships and unshaken in

his principles and the spring of all his actions was of the religious." A stalwart member of the Roman Catholic community, he played a key role in building York's first Catholic church, St Paul's. In his leisure he enjoyed fishing and gardening. His funeral was well attended, and shops and offices were closed in his honour. He was buried in St Paul's churchyard and later was reinterred at Sandwich.

JOHN CLARKE

Numerous references to Baby may be found in the following collections: AO, MS 498; Arch. of the Archdiocese of Toronto, M (Macdonell papers); PAC, RG 1, L1 and L3; RG 5, A1; RG 8, I (C ser.); and RG 68, General index, 1651–1841.

Corr. of Hon. Peter Russell (Cruikshank and Hunter). *Corr. of Lieut. Governor Simcoe* (Cruikshank). J. C. Dent, *The story of the Upper Canadian rebellion; largely derived from original sources and documents* (2v., Toronto, 1885), 1: 140, 215–18. *John Askin papers* (Quaife). Armstrong, *Handbook of Upper Canadian chronology* (1967). H. J. Morgan, *Sketches of celebrated Canadians*. [E. A.] Baby, Mme C.-E. Casgrain, *Mémoires de famille: l'honorable C.-E. Casgrain* (Rivière-Ouelle, Qué., 1891). W. L. Baby, *Souvenirs of the past, with illustrations: an instructive and amusing work, giving a correct account of the customs and habits of the pioneers of Canada . . .* (Windsor, Ont., 1896), 58–71. P.-B. Casgrain, *Mémorial des familles Casgrain, Baby et Perrault du Canada* (Québec, 1898). [A. J. Dooner, named] Brother Alfred, *Catholic pioneers in Upper Canada* (Toronto, 1947). Joseph Tassé, *Les Canadiens de l'Ouest* (4e éd., 2v., Montréal, 1882). F. H. Armstrong, "The oligarchy of the Western District of Upper Canada, 1788–1841," CHA *Hist. papers*, 1977: 87–102. John Clarke, "The role of political position and family and economic linkage in land speculation in the Western District of Upper Canada, 1788–1815," *Canadian Geographer* (Toronto), 19 (1975): 18–34.

BADEAUX, JOSEPH, militia officer, notary, landowner, JP, office holder, politician, and seigneur; b. 25 Sept. 1777 in Trois-Rivières, Que., son of Jean-Baptiste Badeaux* and Marguerite Bolvin, daughter of wood-carver Gilles Bolvin*; d. there 12 Sept. 1835.

Joseph Badeaux followed in his father's footsteps and took up the notarial profession. On 13 Nov. 1792 he began articling with his brother Antoine-Isidore, who was also a notary. He finished his clerkship on 1 Nov. 1797 but had to wait until he came of age to apply for a commission to practise. He was granted one on 1 Oct. 1798.

With this document in hand, Badeaux set up an office in Trois-Rivières. In 1799 he took Nicolas-Benjamin Doucet* as a student clerk. The following year, on 9 June, he married Marguerite Dumont in Trois-Rivières; she died in 1801 while giving birth to their first child. On 16 May 1802, at Quebec, Badeaux then married Geneviève Berthelot, daughter of

Michel-Amable Berthelot* Dartigny, a notary who served as a commissioner for the Jesuit estates, and sister of Amable Berthelot*, a young lawyer who had come to Trois-Rivières to practise law. The couple were to have at least 14 children. On 23 July 1800 Badeaux had become district agent for Trois-Rivières of the commission set up that year to manage the Jesuit estates after the death of Jean-Joseph Casot*, the last member of that order in the province; this post netted him 10 per cent of the sums collected. In May 1801 he had received a commission as president of meetings of inhabitants to regulate the common of Trois-Rivières.

Through the years Badeaux became one of the most prominent figures in Trois-Rivières. His many and various responsibilities furnish the proof: chief cantor, with "a voice that would have filled an enormous cathedral and that 'shattered the windows' of the parish church," justice of the peace for the district (his first commission dated 1803, the last 1833), collector for the *fabrique* (1804), churchwarden (1806), commissioner to receive the oath of allegiance (1812, 1833), sheriff (1813), commissioner for the improvement of internal communications (1815, 1817), member of the board of examiners of applicants to be inspectors of flour and meal (1818) and of a similar board for the posts of potash and pearl ash inspectors (1818, 1830), one of five commissioners appointed by the governor to supervise repairs to the church of Trois-Rivières (1818), and finally, commissioner for the building of churches and presbyteries (1819, 1820). On 18 Feb. 1823 Badeaux was named royal notary, a title that was largely honorary but none the less accorded him the exclusive privilege in Trois-Rivières of receiving contracts to which the king was a party; he was given a new commission on 11 Dec. 1830, after William IV's accession to the throne.

In addition, Badeaux rose through the militia: commissioned a lieutenant in 1798, he was promoted captain in the Trois-Rivières battalion of militia in February 1812 and served with that rank during the War of 1812; he was made a major in 1822. Badeaux was also active in politics. His first two terms as a member of the House of Assembly for Trois-Rivières, from 18 June 1808 till 1 March 1810, coincided with a tumultuous period in the parliamentary and political life of Lower Canada [*see* Sir James Henry Craig*]. Most of the ridings then had two members, and he was elected in 1808 with Ezekiel Hart*, who had been expelled from the assembly earlier that year because of his Jewish faith, and in 1809 with Mathew Bell* because Moses Hart*, who sought to succeed his brother, failed to get elected. According to the listing of members' affiliations published by the newspaper *Le Canadien* in October and November 1809, Badeaux sided with the "government party." Moreover, during the brief and single sessions that constituted the fifth and sixth parliaments, he almost always voted with the bloc in power and was one of the four

Canadians who opposed making judges ineligible to sit in the House of Assembly [*see* Sir James Henry Craig; Pierre-Amable De Bonne*]. Badeaux ran in the 1810 elections but was beaten by Bell and Thomas Coffin*. Six years later he was returned for Buckingham, which he represented until February 1820; he sat for Trois-Rivières again from July 1820 to July 1824, and finally for Yamaska from October 1830 to October 1834.

All these occupations, however, led Badeaux to neglect certain duties, notably that as agent for the Jesuit estates commission. In January 1823, while recognizing that Badeaux himself was highly respectable, the commissioners found themselves obliged, after several warnings, to relieve him of his office.

Concurrently with his professional life and public activities, Badeaux was involved personally in numerous financial matters. Landed property, such as town lots, lands, or seigneuries, drew his attention particularly. His most important purchase was probably that of half the seigneury of Courval, made in 1815. It seems that although he handled large sums, he often found himself in a difficult position financially. His business dealings with Moses Hart, for example, were often strained and gave rise to interminable lawsuits. In 1829 Badeaux was obliged to sell Hart his share in the seigneury.

Joseph Badeaux practised as a notary until his death in 1835, following a short illness, a few days before his 58th birthday. His funeral in Trois-Rivières was attended by a great many people, and he was buried in the parish church. "As a man of the law," *La Minerve* observed, "M. Badeaux had won the public's confidence; he stood out particularly through his willingness to oblige those of his fellows who found themselves in need."

RENALD LESSARD and JEAN PRINCE

Joseph Badeaux's minute-book, containing instruments notarized between 1798 and 1835, is available at ANQ-MBF, CN1-6.

ANQ-MBF, CE1-48, 26 sept. 1777, 9 juin 1800, 15 sept. 1835; CN1-19, 7 avril 1828, 9 nov. 1829, 30 juin 1832; CN1-32, 22 févr. 1815; CN1-35, 28 nov. 1814; CN1-77, 19 janv., 2 mars 1815; CN1-79, 25 mars, 7 juin 1800; 1er oct. 1805; 30 août 1815; 20 mai 1816; 21 juill. 1818. ANQ-Q, CE1-1, 16 mai 1802; CN1-147, 26 août 1817; CN1-262, 16 mai 1802; E21/77, 19; E21/81, 19 avril, 13 déc. 1822; 27 janv., 5 sept. 1823; E21/96; E21/97, 1er août 1800, 4 févr. 1823; E21/110, 14 déc. 1822; T6-1, 3: 2278–80. Arch. du séminaire de Trois-Rivières (Trois-Rivières, Qué.), 0009, KL3E3, nos.1–3; KL3E4, nos.4, 7–9; KL3E5, nos.1–2; KL3F2, no.11; KL3F3, no.3; LF5. PAC, RG 4, B8, 2: 355–63; RG 68, General index, 1651–1841: 61, 195–96, 224, 280, 282–83, 336–37, 341–42, 344, 351, 377, 575, 582–83, 628, 667. L.C., House of Assembly, *Journals*, 1814–16. *La Gazette de Québec*, 4 oct. 1798; 19 mai 1808; 2, 30 nov. 1809; 8 juin 1815; 4 avril 1816; 22 mai 1817; 25 juin 1818; 29 nov. 1819; 27 nov., 11 déc. 1820; 18 juill.

Baillairgé

1822; 24 févr. 1823; 16 sept. 1835. *La Minerve*, 17 sept. 1835.

F.-J. Audet, *Les députés des Trois-Rivières*, 5–11, 18, 33; "Les législateurs du Bas-Canada." Ivanhoë Caron, "Papiers Duvernay conservés aux Archives de la province de Québec," ANQ *Rapport*, 1926–27: 251, 368–69. Desjardins, *Guide parl.* "Papiers d'État – Bas-Canada," PAC *Rapport*, 1892: 162. *Quebec almanac*, 1810: 53; 1815: 103; 1820: 105; 1821: 129. "Références biographiques canadiennes," *BRH*, 49 (1943): 59–64. P.-G. Roy, *Inv. concessions*, 2: 75; 5: 118; "Shérifs de Trois-Rivières," *BRH*, 7 (1901): 356. *Jalons, paroisse de l'Immaculée-Conception, Trois-Rivières, 1678–1978* (s.l., 1978). J.-E. Roy, *Hist. du notariat*, 2: 47–49, 233. Benjamin Sulte, *Mélanges historiques . . .*, Gérard Malchelosse, édit. (21v., Montréal, 1918–34), 3: 100. *Les ursulines des Trois-Rivières*, 2: 514. "La famille Berthelot d'Artigny," *BRH*, 41 (1935): 16. Hare, "L'Assemblée législative du Bas-Canada," *RHAF*, 27: 381–84. Victor Morin, "La 'République canadienne' de 1838," *RHAF*, 2 (1948–49): 492. "Les notaires du roi," *BRH*, 32 (1926): 538–39. P.-G. Roy, "L'émancipation politique des Juifs au Canada," *BRH*, 11 (1905): 89–91.

BAILLAIRGÉ, FRANÇOIS, painter, sculptor, architect, and office holder; b. 21 Jan. 1759 at Quebec, son of Jean Baillairgé* and Marie-Louise Parent; m. there 9 Jan. 1787 Josephte Boutin, and they had six children, of whom only Thomas* reached adulthood; d. there 15 Sept. 1830.

When he was 14 François Baillairgé began his apprenticeship in woodworking, wood-carving, and architecture in his father's shop. He also had the benefit of advice from wood-carver Antoine Jacson*, his father's journeyman. Subsequently he took the mathematics courses given at the Petit Séminaire de Québec by priests Jean-Baptiste Lahaille* and Thomas-Laurent Bédard*.

In July 1778 Baillairgé left for Paris, on a trip likely made possible by Bédard. The priest even had the Séminaire des Missions Etrangères in Paris take on responsibility for his instruction. Thanks to this protection Baillairgé was given the status of a sponsored student when he entered the school of the Académie Royale de Peinture et de Sculpture on 21 Feb. 1779. As a result, he was exempted from the competitive system that decided standing in the school, where he probably came in contact with the best draftsmen and sculptors of the emerging neoclassical movement.

Baillairgé seems, however, to have been rather impervious to the rigorous character of this new style. He acquired much of his training outside the academy, in the studios that he frequented for private lessons. He studied sculpture, for example, with Jean-Baptiste Stouf, painting and drawing with a certain Julien, probably Simon Julien. He also assiduously followed courses in perspective and anatomy given respectively by Jacques-Sébastien Leclerc and Jean-Joseph Sue, a surgeon. He did not actually study architecture, but

some quick sketches and writings indicate that he visited numerous monuments in Paris, including the Palais des Tuileries and the church of Sainte-Geneviève (the Panthéon), Germain Soufflot's masterpiece.

Baillairgé left Paris on 8 March 1781, his training incomplete. As a painter he would never be able to overcome this handicap. But he had to return to Quebec because the superior of the Séminaire des Missions Étrangères feared, no doubt rightly, that "a long stay in Paris might perhaps become dangerous for him as for many others and dissuade him from returning to his country."

From September 1784 Baillairgé kept a diary in which he made notes on his professional and family life. At the time he described himself as a painter, sculptor, architect, and drawing-master. Undoubtedly his ambitions in the first of these fields were as great as his aspirations in the others, but inevitably he would have to reconsider his priorities.

Baillairgé was far from being an isolated painter, obliged to improvise crude equipment from local materials or guided by a provincial mentality. He made a point of assimilating and mastering the techniques of painting. He had access to virtually all the pigments and other products commonly used in Europe, or was in a position to prepare them himself by the latest formulas. Through the material at hand in his personal library, he was familiar with the methods of using the various substances.

Baillairgé's religious painting was done in greatest part from 1784 to 1786 and from 1794 to about 1806. During these years he turned out some 30 works whose titles or subjects are known. About 20 are still extant, counting those that can reasonably be attributed to him. Some seem to be quite original creations, but most were copied from engravings and earlier works. Baillairgé was also active as a portrait artist, miniaturist, painter of stage scenery, and decorator (of drums, *calèches*, and even apartments). In addition, he restored a number of paintings. But his involvement in these fields took second place to endeavours to complete the commissions he received from church officials.

None of the works from the years 1784–86 listed by title or subject in his diary has survived. But there is one painting still in existence that may have been commissioned, and indeed finished, before the diary was written: *Le martyre de Saint Denis* over the high altar of the church in Saint-Denis, on the Richelieu. Baillairgé completed a religious work, perhaps a St Louis, for the church of Saint-Louis at Kamouraska towards the end of November 1784. In 1785 he painted for the church of Saint-Jean, on Île d'Orléans, a St John the Baptist in the Desert (over the high altar) and a St Joseph (as well, probably, as a Nativity or a Holy Family). A composition that he called a "representation of saints Peter and Paul" was completed for the church of Saints-Pierre-et-Paul at Baie-Saint-Paul on 23 September of that year.

While he was executing these works Baillairgé's optimism and confidence were sorely tried. One order was cancelled, others had to be redone or required a great deal of effort. On 29 Sept. 1785 he published the following notice in the *Quebec Gazette*: "I the undersigned beg amateurs and experts in the art of painting to be so kind as to come to my studio on Rue Ste. Anne . . . to see and examine a picture done by me, portraying Saint Peter and Saint Paul. Being deprived in this country of the lessons needed to guide me in this art, I hope that the criticism and advice of experts will lead me to the perfection to which I aspire." The artist's discouragement would seem at last to have overcome his optimism. In one final burst of energy in 1787 he did a canvas depicting St Anne for a chapel in Notre-Dame cathedral at Quebec.

When Baillairgé again put his brush at the service of the church, in 1794, his ambition was tempered by the need to make a living. From then on he cut short the process of conception and execution by simplifying his subjects and systematically taking inspiration from engravings or old works. A few canvasses, however, are exceptions to this rule. One is the painting of St Francis of Sales, done in 1798 for the church of Saint-François on Île d'Orléans, which is generally considered his best canvas. It was undertaken at a time when the artist's reputation as an architect was firmly established. Worth study is the building in the background, which looks like the court-house at Quebec, an edifice Baillairgé designed in 1799. The bell tower on the building has some characteristics in common with that of the Quebec cathedral, which had been built by Jean Baillairgé. The painting demonstrates François's talent, giving proof of remarkable intelligence and skill. He made a raised tabernacle less intrusive by employing a perspective with two vanishing points, in this way reconciling the two points of view possible. The details and colouring are flawless. With this canvas, to which he had devoted 30 days and of which he was very proud, he allowed himself the luxury of pursuing his ideal of painting to the very limit of his ability.

Other works of lesser interest done during this second part of Baillairgé's career have a certain originality, stemming principally from the manner in which he combined and revised borrowed elements. *Le Sacré-Cœur* and *La Présentation de la Vierge*, which were done in 1795 for the church of Saint-Roch-des-Aulnaies, fall into this category. Despite a maudlin quality, the first of these canvasses is interesting since it follows closely the major themes of Eudist spirituality, which the Canadian church from the earliest days had disseminated.

Mention must be made of a beautiful *esquisse* portraying the Guardian Angel, done in water-colours and squared off in preparation for a work completed in 1802 for the church of Sainte-Famille on Île d'Orléans. The drawing reveals the manner in which he recreated his figures, even though they are borrowed from another source. From 1802 to 1806 he did a series of five works for this church, which vary in originality. At least three are copies, while another is the result of his method of borrowing and assembling. Thus the main figures of *Le miracle de saint Pierre* closely resemble a composition by Domenichino, and the architectural background corresponds exactly to that of an anonymous work held at the Hôtel-Dieu of Quebec. Despite its derivative nature, *La Résurrection du Christ*, which was painted in 1804 to fit into the same series, is one of Baillairgé's most ambitious works, particularly in its use of colour. The sketch for it, which was squared off, is still in existence. On the back of it the artist took care to describe the pigments and the way they were applied.

Baillairgé's other religious paintings are all copies. Among the compositions reproduced most often are two versions of an Immaculate Conception and three or four of an Education of the Virgin, which were copied from a work by Peter Paul Rubens. Also noteworthy is a *pietà* after Annibale Carracci, done for a chapel in the cathedral. Baillairgé completed a number of compositions on subjects for which the iconographical sources are unknown because the canvasses have disappeared. These include *Saint Michel terrassant le démon*, done in 1795 for the church of Saint-Louis at Lotbinière, *Saint Ambroise absolvant l'empereur Théodose*, painted in 1796 for the church of Saint-Ambroise (at Loretteville), *Saint Jean-Baptiste dans le désert*, done in 1800 for the church of Saint-Joachim, near Quebec, and *Saint Antoine*, reputedly painted in 1802 for the church of Sainte-Famille.

Despite his quite abundant production, Baillairgé failed to establish himself as a painter. That art had always been difficult and laborious for him. The gaps in his training and lack of practice had kept him from improving. His church clients, for their part, may have been disappointed with some of his pieces. None the less, because of the modernity and wide diffusion of his work, his influence is undeniable.

Baillairgé was to make a name for himself primarily as a wood-carver. On returning from Paris he worked in his father's shop. Between 1782 and 1785 he executed various furnishings such as the rectangular moulding designed to hold the altar frontal, the tabernacle, and the altar ornaments for the church of Saint-Joachim. The quality he achieved in these pieces prompted his father to propose larger ones for him, such as the design of the retable (the structure housing the altar) for the church of Notre-Dame-de-Bon-Secours at L'Islet.

Baillairgé

From his very first endeavours in wood-carving Baillairgé displayed his originality. For the tabernacle at Saint-Joachim he replaced the baroque idiom of arabesques and acanthus leaves with naturalistic designs of flora native to the country and easily recognizable. He went even further with the retable for L'Islet, conceiving not simply a piece of furniture but rather an interior decoration integrated into the architecture of the building. This decorative *ensemble* assumed a truly architectural dimension through the play of its component parts, which was designed to suggest a more structured space, with a series of arcades even creating the illusion of an ambulatory. He also executed at L'Islet his first large pieces of wood-carving: *Saint Modeste* and *Saint Abondance*. He undertook next two tabernacles for the parish of Saint-Laurent, on Île d'Orléans, which continued the tradition of Saint-Joachim, not only in form but also in decorative motifs. However, the naturalistic floral motifs are more numerous, and the starkly simple pinnacle sets the tabernacle off to greater advantage.

The interior decoration of the cathedral of Notre-Dame in Quebec, which was designed and executed between 1787 and 1793, is undoubtedly Baillairgé's largest project. Working as usual in collaboration with his father, he was responsible for planning the project and executing the carvings. It was a marvel of organization and went ahead briskly. In the first months Jean Baillairgé prepared and installed the panelling and the cornices on which all the carved work would fit. Then François carved and systematically set in place the winged angels which were to support the consoles of the baldachin, the decorations on the pedestals, the crown, the glory that topped the baldachin, the bishop's throne, the statues that stand on the cornice and the pedestals, and finally various adornments, including the large frame above the altar. This whole masterly *ensemble* is known only through photographs, since the cathedral was destroyed by fire in 1922. After this big project Baillairgé contented himself with doing the storiated carvings for the tabernacles in the church of Saint-Joseph at Maskinongé and the church of Saint-Roch-des-Aulnaies.

During this period Baillairgé seems to have freed himself from the constraints inherent in his materials and learned to be more flexible with his chisel. The figures, for example, were no longer carved in stiff frontal poses; the heads were presented in semi-profile, the drapery and folds of garments were more skilfully executed, giving proof of greater study, and the poses had acquired much more elegance. These statues marked the end of a period in the development of Baillairgé's style. He subsequently abandoned his attachment to the archaic, a change possibly related to his distancing himself from his father's production.

Not much of Baillairgé's work from the period 1793–1800 is still in existence. Through his diary, however, it is known that he was producing a great deal and that his clientele consisted largely of the local bourgeoisie and garrison officers. The high quality of the only two pieces extant, *L'Assomption de la Vierge* at Les Éboulements and a fragment of the *ensemble* in the church of Saint-Jean-Port-Joli, suggests that during this period Baillairgé was reaching his prime in technique and expression. For the years after 1800 records are scant but there is a good deal of evidence of Baillairgé's activity. He did not undertake any large pieces in the period 1800–15. He executed tabernacles (Pointe-aux-Trembles (Neuville), 1802; Saint-François at Beauceville, 1815); altars (Pointe-aux-Trembles, 1802; Sainte-Anne-de-la-Pocatière, 1804; Saint-Jean-Port-Joli, 1804, 1817); and chairs (Saint-Roch-des-Aulnaies, 1804; Saint-Ambroise, 1815–16; Baie-Saint-Paul, 1816, 1817). Between 1804 and 1810 he carved two large statues representing St Louis and St Flavian for the parish of Saint-Louis on Île aux Coudres, and a bas-relief of two angels in adoration for the parish of Saint-Laurent on Île d'Orléans (1808–9).

In 1815 Baillairgé took his son Thomas into his business. They would turn out three masterly *ensembles*: the baptistry for the parish of Saint-Ambroise, the interior decoration of Saint-Joachim church, and the retable in Saints-Pierre-et-Paul. All that now remains is the decoration in Saint-Joachim, where the design covered not only the bay of the chancel but also the entire building. The project came out of the meeting of the ideas of Jérôme Demers*, Thomas Baillairgé, and his father, François. Thomas was responsible for the work as a whole, François executed the carved portions. François's work presumably was completed in 1824, the year the carvings were probably gilded. Consequently he was able to devote himself until 1828 to carving the ornamentation and panels of the retable at Baie-Saint-Paul.

Baillairgé made good use of the means at hand to find inspiration. The inventory of his library drawn up in 1808 is revealing. Numerous treatises by famous architects are included. His openness of mind led him to consider everything – drawings, prints, paintings, as well as the treatises of less famous architects such as Jacques-François Blondel and Giacomo da Vignola. He adapted, modified, or copied models. For example, his portfolio, held in the Musée du Québec, contains drawings done from works by both famous and lesser-known artists, such as the head of a bearded man he copied from a drawing by René-Michel (Michel-Ange) Slodtz; he even carried attention to details to the point of reproducing the tear in the original. For the water-colour of the Guardian Angel, which is also held at the Musée du Québec, he took his inspiration freely from an engraving by Jean Couvay, *Angelus Custos*. *Le repentir de saint Pierre* combines elements of a St Augustine engraved in 1660 by

Claude Mellan and a 17th-century *canivet* (a devotional image with an ornamental border) representing the repentant St Peter. This work was later transformed into a Christ on the Mount of Olives for the door of the tabernacle in the Saint-Isidore chapel on Île aux Coudres. For the baldachin in the cathedral he took his inspiration in large measure from the baldachin designed by architect Ocnort and executed by Slodtz in the abbey of Saint-Germain-des-Prés in Paris. A large number of trophies done at Saint-Joachim were copied from a work by French architect Jean-Charles de La Fosse.

Despite these borrowings, in themselves inevitable and common practice, Baillairgé was capable of original work. Through his training, his culture, and his knowledge of the world he was able to renew the decorative idiom of a baroque that had run out of imagination, organizing space intelligently and arranging iconographical designs in an intelligible manner. In the course of his long career he left his mark on religious art in Quebec.

Along with his activities as a painter and woodcarver, Baillairgé was winning renown in the field of architecture. He did not leave many traces of a highly developed architectural practice. However, it appears that his work was more extensive than was imagined even a few years ago, for the simple reason that much of his architectural production is now known to have been created anonymously in accordance with the traditional practice by which the builder, rather than the designer, played the leading role. Thus more than the buildings he left, his part in the evolution of this traditional practice confers upon Baillairgé a place in the forefront of the history of Quebec architecture.

When Baillairgé returned to Quebec in August 1781, the town had several builders but only one, his father, had risen to the rank of architect, particularly through his skill in presenting his projects in drawings. By his painting and carving François made a name for himself as an artist right from the start; in this respect he differed completely from the craftsmen of the traditional school, whose work perpetuated forms inherited from the French régime. Since he had not been initiated into building methods, it was his drawing skill that enabled him to take up architecture.

Baillairgé first displayed his talent as an architect with his plans for the interior decoration of Notre-Dame-de-Bon-Secours church and the cathedral of Notre-Dame in Quebec, which proposed decorative formulas of a surprising novelty. He gained acceptance for them by evocative drawings of high quality, for example, the plan for the retable in the cathedral chancel. This plan established Baillairgé's reputation, and his talents would be called upon in specific circumstances: when new forms were needed and had to be put on paper for craftsmen, and when traditional formulas proved inadequate for a particular project.

Active at a time when architecture was being revitalized through contact with English influences, Baillairgé had to produce plans that would lay out for local workmen the main architectural features deriving from the new aesthetics he brought to his constructions. Examples of this process include the building of the court-house at Quebec (1799) and of the jail there (1807) and at Trois-Rivières (1815). Although he was inspired by English architect James Gibbs's work, *A book of architecture*, which the authorities must have recommended to him, Baillairgé nevertheless used principles of composition borrowed from Philibert De L'Orme's *Le premier tome de l'architecture*. Hence it can now be affirmed that in architecture, just as in the other areas of art, he created original works, refusing to adopt the common practice of mere imitation. Having a curious and inventive mind, Baillairgé, with the help of Joseph-François Perrault*, in 1807 developed a plan for a "pleasant house of detention" that more than any other early 19th-century example in Lower Canada embodied the utopian concept of architecture as an instrument of social change.

Baillairgé was also in demand for building projects which were on a smaller scale but which suggested a desire to break out of the standardized formulas offered by builders. For example, François-Joseph Cugnet* in 1788, Alexander Fraser in 1789, and Perrault around 1805 commissioned plans for houses from him. In all three instances it must be assumed that in appearance and interior arrangement the residences tended to diverge from the traditional approach which relied solely on the town house model developed around 1720–30 at Quebec. It is certain that when plans were required for a brewery at Beauport in 1791 and for the lunatic cells at the Hôpital Général in 1818, the particular needs of the two structures, and the inability of the traditional work force to produce architectural designs to meet them, brought Baillairgé into both projects.

Although he was essentially concerned with architectural form, Baillairgé would none the less develop expertise in the field of construction. In 1807, for example, he devised scale models of stone arches that were to make the Quebec jail solid and secure; similar considerations for stability and security prompted him in 1818 to favour plaster for decorating the arches in the cathedral instead of wood, which until then had generally been employed.

The fact that Baillairgé experimented with the volume and proportions of his buildings by constructing wooden scale models entitles him to the name of architect from the period 1805–10. Moreover he demonstrated remarkable versatility when in 1812, having been appointed treasurer for roads in the town of Quebec to replace his brother Pierre-Florent*, he undertook to do a series of drawings to guide the rebuilding of several streets in the town. The plans for

Baillairgé

the construction of Côte à Coton, which date from 1816, are works of art in their handling of the topography, while also being most appropriate for directing the work of excavating, filling, and paving.

Baillairgé's plans were intended for his clients, who under French civil law would have to deal with the builders themselves. In that respect he played no part in the actual construction, where there was then no place for the person who conceived the plans. Since the builder directed operations on the work site, it was he who most often claimed the title of architect, and he made very free use of plans supplied to him, if there were any. Although he was not involved in the practical side of building, Baillairgé would none the less try to influence it. Thus in the plans for the Congreganist chapel on Rue d'Auteuil delivered to Bishop Joseph-Octave PLESSIS in 1818, he proposed a completely new approach to architecture. Cut down drastically by the bishop, the project was truncated further by master mason Pierre Giroux, who tried to reduce it to what he was capable of doing. The existence of the drawing and the dispute it occasioned between the bishop and the builder nevertheless permitted some progress to be made (in the elevation of the façade, the form of the bell tower, the location and interior disposition of the sacristy). The architect played a similar role at Saint-Roch in 1811 and probably at Saint-Augustin in 1816: instead of the usual models he proposed new designs which in the end produced a synthesis of the established and the innovative.

In this context it is understandable that Baillairgé did not sign his plans: no one was ready to attribute a building to the author of the plan, especially since the finished construction, except in rare instances, bore little resemblance to it. Obviously the practice allowed builders to use these anonymous documents as they wished. Consequently, in the absence of specific circumstantial evidence several houses and churches that exhibit Baillairgé's concerns can only be attributed to him. Yet there may be a sizeable number of them, because quite evidently the taste for novelty and the search for excellence had quickly brought the works of this architect – who was the only one at Quebec until about 1820 except for British military engineers – into such prominence that they served as models for the traditional work force.

The buildings by Baillairgé that are still standing, such as the prisons at Quebec or Trois-Rivières, and his house on Rue Saint-François (Rue Ferland), are certainly important monuments. However, the numerous plans that he drafted are equally important, for they reveal the art of an architect who had a great influence on the renewal of traditional forms and practices. Since that renewal was based upon the traditional heritage, a debt is in a way owed to Baillairgé for having ensured the permanence of a

Quebec architecture by demonstrating firmly that it could evolve through contact with new ideas, beyond the decade of the 1820s, when numerous architects from England would try to establish their aesthetic standards and their type of architectural practice. But by that time his son Thomas had taken over, and his entire career would be devoted to articulating and applying the methods of architectural practice that his father had defined as the 19th century dawned.

François Baillairgé died at Quebec on 15 Sept. 1830. He was buried the following day in the presence of silversmith Laurent Amiot* and painter Joseph Légaré*, among others. As a painter, wood-carver, and architect he was a towering figure at the beginning of the 19th century, and some of his works unquestionably count among the masterpieces of older Quebec art.

DAVID KAREL, LUC NOPPEN, and
MAGELLA PARADIS

ANQ-Q, CE1-1, 21 janv. 1759, 9 janv. 1787, 16 sept. 1830; CN1-178, 30 mai 1808; P-398. AP, Saint-François-de-Sales (Neuville), Livres de comptes, II, 1802; Saint-Joachim, Livres de comptes, I, 1782, 1783, 1786; Saint-Laurent (Île d'Orléans), Livres de comptes, 1786–87, 1808–9; Saint-Pierre-et-Paul (Baie-Saint-Paul), Recueil de lettres et de notes; Saint-Roch-des-Aulnaies, Livres de comptes, 1804. Arch. de l'univ. Laval (Québec), 214/D.595. ASQ, Lettres, M, 161; Paroisses diverses, 85. MAC-CD, Fonds ministère des Affaires culturelles, photographies des œuvres de Baillairgé; Fonds Morisset, photographies des œuvres de Baillairgé; 2, dossier François Baillairgé, 1–3. Musée du Québec, Albums de Charles Baillairgé; Œuvre de François Baillairgé. *Quebec Gazette*, 29 Sept. 1785. M.-N. Boisclair, *Catalogue des œuvres peintes conservées au monastère des Augustines de l'Hôtel-Dieu de Québec* ([Québec], 1977). G.-F. Baillairgé, *Notices biographiques et généalogiques, famille Baillairgé . . .* (11 fascicules, Joliette, Qué., 1891–94). Benjamin Demers, *Notes sur la paroisse de St-François de la Beauce* (Québec, 1891). David Karel, "The teaching of drawing at the French Royal Academy of painting and sculpture from 1760 to 1793" (PHD thesis, Univ. of Chicago, 1974). David Karel et al., *François Baillairgé et son œuvre (1759–1830)* (Québec, 1975). Raymonde [Landry] Gauthier, *Les tabernacles anciens du Québec des XVIIe, XVIIIe et XIXe siècles* ([Québec], 1974). Alexis Mailloux, *Histoire de l'Île-aux-Coudres depuis son établissement jusqu'à nos jours, avec ses traditions, ses légendes, ses coutumes* (Montréal, 1879). Luc Noppen, *Notre-Dame de Québec, son architecture et son rayonnement (1647–1922)* (Québec, 1974); "Le renouveau architectural proposé par Thomas Baillairgé au Québec, de 1820 à 1850 (l'architecture néoclassique québécoise)" (thèse de PHD, univ. de Toulouse–Le Mirail, Toulouse, France, 1976). Luc Noppen et al., *Québec: trois siècles d'architecture* ([Montréal], 1979). Magella Paradis, "Étude stylistique de l'œuvre sculpté de François Baillairgé (1759–1830)" (thèse de PHD, univ. de Toulouse–Le Mirail, 1976). G.-F. Baillairgé, "Biographies canadiennes," *BRH*, 20 (1914): 348–51. Marius Barbeau, "Les Baillairgé: école de Québec en sculpture et en architec-

Bailly

ture," *Le Canada français* (Québec), 2ᵉ sér., 33 (1945–46): 243–55. Gérard Morisset, "Une dynastie d'artisans: les Baillairgé," *La Patrie* (Montréal), 13 août 1950: 18, 42, 46.

BAILLY, JOSEPH (baptized **Honoré-Gratien-Joseph Bailly de Messein**), fur trader; b. 7 April 1774 in Varennes (Que.), son of Michel Bailly de Messein and Geneviève Aubert de Gaspé; d. 21 Dec. 1835 in Porter County, Ind.

Joseph Bailly's father descended from the son of a noble French family who became an officer in the colonial regular troops. His father's brother, Charles-François Bailly* de Messein, became coadjutor bishop of Quebec. His mother, the daughter of Ignace-Philippe Aubert* de Gaspé, seigneur of Port-Joly, also belonged to prominent families.

By late 1796, just over a year after his father's death, Bailly was involved in the fur trade at Michilimackinac (Mackinac Island, Mich.). During the next few years he developed an impressive trading network, with posts on the Grand River and at St Joseph (Mich.), Kankakee (Ill.), and Wabash (Ind.). In 1802 he and Dominique ROUSSEAU, possessing licences to trade in American territory, sent a canoeload of goods to Grand Portage at the western end of Lake Superior, but their men were thwarted by Duncan McGillivray* of the North West Company, which occupied the fort there. A legal suit against McGillivray, brought before the Court of King's Bench in Montreal, was decided in favour of Bailly and Rousseau. This judgement may have been responsible for the North West Company's decision to move farther inland to an area definitely under British control. In the next two decades, using Michilimackinac as his headquarters, Bailly enlarged his trade network, often visiting Montreal and Detroit to purchase supplies.

Early in the War of 1812, Bailly, acting under the orders of Captain Charles Roberts*, transported goods from St Joseph Island (Ont.) to Michilimackinac. In March 1813 he was asked by Robert DICKSON, superintendent for the Indians of the western nations, to recruit Indian warriors for the British, a work he later claimed that he had accomplished with success, notably among the Miamis, Potawatomis, Ottawas, and Kickapoos. His efforts eventually attracted the attention of American troops, who plundered his post and detained him for three months before releasing him on parole. The British detachment that Lieutenant-Colonel Robert McDouall* had sent to search for Bailly brought him back to Michilimackinac and then, ironically, requisitioned a large part of his remaining trade goods. Bailly later claimed £978 in compensation for losses incurred in service to the British government, "to which he was attached as much by principle as by birth." Before the close of the war he commanded a party of Indians in three engagements against the Americans.

Around 1797, at Michilimackinac, Bailly had married, probably according to the custom of the country, Bead-way-way (baptized Angelique), daughter of trader Patrick McGulpin and an Ottawa woman. The couple had at least six children. Bailly and his wife separated before 1810. Family tradition reports that "she was a secret votary of the Spirit of Darkness." Bailly, a devout Roman Catholic, tried to convert her, without success. Around 1810 he married, according to the custom of the country, Marie Lefevre, daughter of a trader from the River Raisin, Mich., and an Ottawa woman; she had one child from a previous marriage. The couple would have five children. Both of his marriages gave Bailly additional influence and opportunity in his commercial ventures.

Elizabeth Therese Baird, an early settler on Mackinac Island, described Bailly as well educated, "not gentle, not coarse, but noisy . . . an exceptionally good-natured man, fond of entertaining his friends." In 1822 he moved his family to a post at the southern end of Lake Michigan, on the north side of the Calumet River near present-day Porter, Ind. His post was the only one on the strategic Detroit–Chicago road, an excellent trading location, where he also set up a chapel for the Indians and other travellers. He owned several thousand acres near by and was known for his hospitality and for his friendly family. By the late 1820s he had a second post, at Baton Rouge, La., which he visited for several months each year, sending skins and furs directly to France.

Bailly, his wife, and the children from each of their marriages received considerable money and land in Illinois and Indiana as a result of the Ottawa treaties of the early 1830s. In addition to his trading posts, Bailly was involved in other business affairs. He owned some shares in the steamboat *Michigan* sailing out of Detroit, and he plotted the town of Bailly near his post on the Calumet River, but it was never developed. After his death his personal estate was evaluated at $2,600. His children were well educated. Alexis, who had been sent to school in Montreal for a few years, became the American Fur Company agent at Mendota (Minn.) and was elected to the first Minnesota territorial legislature; in 1826 he married Lucie-Anne, daughter of fur trader Jean-Baptiste Faribault*. Another son was sent to the Baptist mission at nearby Niles, Mich., and the entire family used the extensive library that Joseph had accumulated, which included works of history, fiction, and poetry.

Joseph Bailly was one of several Canadians descended from prominent families who became important merchants in the western fur trade. He was also the foremost pioneer of northern Indiana.

DONALD CHAPUT

[Joseph Bailly's life was the inspiration for Julia Cooley

Baker

Altrocchi's interesting novel *Wolves against the moon* (New York, 1940), but it makes no mention of either his first wife or his son Alexis, and it depicts him as being in a constant struggle with the nasty "Maurice Rastel" [Pierre Rastel* de Rocheblave]. D.C.]

ANQ-M, CE1-10, 7 avril 1774. Chicago Hist. Soc., L. P. Brock, "Joseph Bailly de Messein, born – Quebec, Canada – 1774; died – Bailly Homestead, Indiana – 1835" (1922). Ind. State Library (Indianapolis), Ind. Division, Joseph Bailly MS coll. PAC, RG 8, I (C ser.), 88: 13–21. "The Mackinac register," ed. R. G. Thwaites, Wis., State Hist Soc., *Coll.*, 19 (1910): 110–11, 141. U.S., Congress, *Indian affairs: laws and treaties*, comp. and ed. C. J. Kappler (2v., Washington, 1904), 2: 353, 374, 405–6. G. A. Brennan, *The wonders of the dunes* (Indianapolis, 1923). F. R. Howe, *The story of a French homestead in the old northwest* (Columbus, Ohio, 1907). Otho Winger, *The Potawatomi Indians* (Elgin, Ill., 1939). E. C. Bailly, "The French-Canadian background of a Minnesota pioneer – Alexis Bailly," *BRH*, 55 (1949): 137–55; "Genealogy of the Bailly de Messein family in the United States," *BRH*, 56 (1950): 180–95; 57 (1951): 27–38, 77–100. "La famille Bailly de Messein," *BRH*, 23 (1917): 193–206, 225–39, 257–74. E. T. [Fisher] Baird, "Reminiscences of early days on Mackinac Island," Wis., State Hist. Soc., *Coll.*, 14 (1898): 17–64.

BAKER, CHARLES, surveyor, office holder, JP, and judge; b. 5 Oct. 1743 in Virginia, son of William Baker and his first wife, Susannah Rice; m. *c.* 1770 Ann Barron, daughter of Captain Edward Barron, apparently at Fort Cumberland (near Sackville, N.B.), and they had seven children; d. 10 Feb. 1835 in Amherst, N.S.

Educated at home by his father, who was "a good English scholar," Charles Baker is reputed to have attended the College of New Jersey, but this claim is not borne out by the available records. The family was apparently living in Pennsylvania in 1756. That year they moved to the "county town" of Carlisle because of Indian raids after Major-General Edward Braddock's defeat near Fort Duquesne (Pittsburgh, Pa) the previous year, and Baker's father was employed by Adam Hoops, an army victualler. Two years later Brigadier-General John Forbes* was building a road through the mountains for his army in order to attack Fort Duquesne and, Baker later related, "taking a fancy for my father and willing to assist him he entered me into the Service a dollar a day and Rations."

Baker is known to have arrived in the Chignecto region of Nova Scotia in 1765, but he probably had gone earlier as a surveyor to the Petitcodiac River (N.B.) because of his connection with Hoops, who along with Colonel Frederick Haldimand* was a grantee of the new township of Hopewell there. Family tradition relates that Baker's appearance in Nova Scotia resulted from his having fallen in love with Edward Barron's daughter at Quebec and followed the family to the Chignecto Isthmus, where Barron had received a grant of land. Upon his arrival

Baker was appointed a deputy surveyor, and for a time he was employed under Captain John Huston, the county surveyor. Some years later he reported to Surveyor General Charles Morris* that Huston had forced him to make boundary adjustments he knew to be incorrect. Baker also acted as intermediary between the proprietors and the inhabitants of the Petitcodiac settlements, and after Hoops's death his nephew made Baker agent for his properties in Hillsborough Township. Baker's residence at this period is unknown, although there is some suggestion he lived in Monckton Township.

Few details are available about Baker's activities during the American revolution. In August 1775 he reported at Halifax that New England rebels had cleared a road from the Saint John River to the Shepody region (N.B.) in preparation for an attack on Fort Cumberland. Opposition to the provincial government was marked in Cumberland County, but like his father-in-law Baker was undoubtedly loyal during Jonathan Eddy*'s invasion of Nova Scotia in 1776. After the war he was one of the deputy surveyors employed by Morris in settling loyalists. Between 1783 and 1785 he worked along the Petitcodiac, and in the Ramsheg (Wallace), Cobequid Road, Westchester, and River Philip regions of Cumberland County. Although Morris praised Baker's plans as "well executed" and "very prettily finished," he often remonstrated with him about his accounts. For example, Morris complained on 22 Feb. 1784 that "your method of making out accounts is the most extraordinary of any among fifty Deputies now employed, were they to follow your example the annual expense of surveying for Loyalist[s] would amount to at least Sixty thousand pound." Baker was indeed soon in financial difficulties since he owed more money to the men he hired to assist him than he was able to collect from the government, partially because the wages he paid seem to have been higher than the government allowance. To pay the debts contracted in "searching Out and Surveying the Lands for the West Chester Refugees" he was forced to sell the lands in Monckton and Hillsborough townships he had been granted in 1784.

By late 1785 Baker was making preparations to move to Amherst Township, and in 1788 he was granted 800 acres there, although he commented that "the land is but Indifferent." The centre of population for the township gradually concentrated at Amherst Corner (Amherst), where Baker had his property, and where he donated land for an Anglican churchyard and cemetery. On 22 July 1785 he had been appointed a justice of the peace for Cumberland County, and he also served as clerk of the Court of Quarter Sessions. Baker became a judge of the Inferior Court of Common Pleas for Amherst Township on 15 April 1802, and one for Cumberland County on 22 May

1810. Prior to May 1778 he had been appointed a registrar of probate, and succeeded his father-in-law in that position for the county on 22 Jan. 1799, most likely continuing to serve until 1831. At the same time he aided Joseph Frederick Wallet DESBARRES, who had granted him power of attorney in 1782 to manage his Memramcook (N.B.) and Petitcodiac properties, and during DesBarres's residence in Amherst after 1812 the two men, who seem to have been on good terms, discussed plans for DesBarres's lands.

In his letters to his son Edward, who was MHA for Amherst Township from 1806 to 1818, Baker showed an interest in public affairs, a fatherly moral tone, and strong religious convictions, counselling "Dear Neddy" that "the Eyes of the Publick are now on you, all your words and actions will be Strictly Scrutenized" not only by "your fellow men" but also by "your Heavenly Judge." In 1826 and 1833 Baker and his wife disposed of lands they owned in Cumberland County to their son William since they were incapable of managing them "by reason of old age and infirmity." In return William promised to provide "all such decent Cloathing washing firing and attendance as they may reasonably Require." On his death Baker was lauded in a long obituary in the *Novascotian, or Colonial Herald* as "a firm magistrate, [and] an honest and faithful public servant" who was distinguished by his "natural pleasantry of disposition." The funeral service was conducted by the Baptist minister Charles Tupper*, although Baker had been a member of the Church of England.

PHYLLIS R. BLAKELEY

PANS, MG 1, 106; MG 9, no.34: 15–16; no.45: 289; no.184: 25; RG 1, 168: 173, 472; 169: 124–25; 172: 86, 118, 143, 152, 211; 173: 33, 36, 43, 69–70, 131, 394, 448; 394: 33, 105, 147, 225; 395: 21, 40, 42, 70; RG 20A, 16, 1786, no.8; 20, 1788, no.6; 30, 1809, petition of Charles Baker; RG 20C, 86, nos.5–7, 37, 43, 50, 52; RG 34-309, P, 1. *Novascotian, or Colonial Herald*, 26 Feb. 1835. Esther Clark Wright, *The Petitcodiac: a study of the New Brunswick river and of the people who settled along it* (Sackville, N.B., 1945).

BARCLAY, JOHN, Church of Scotland clergyman and author; b. 9 July 1795 in Kettle (Kettlehill), Scotland, son of the Reverend Peter Barclay; he may have been engaged to be married at the time of his death, which occurred on 26 Sept. 1826 in Kingston, Upper Canada.

"Can you name any type in history more ridiculous than a Scotch Presbyterian?" So said Dr Dougald MacKenzie in Hugh MacLennan's novel *Each man's son.* "If you can't laugh at him," he added, "you'll be tempted to murder him." Whether or not MacLennan's sense of the inherent absurdities of the type is accurate, Scotch Presbyterians have had an impres-

sive impact upon Canadian history. When they first began to exert their burnished wills, the effect upon society could be inflammatory. This was the case when in 1825–26 John Barclay of St Andrew's Church in Kingston issued a clarion call for the rights of the Church of Scotland.

Barclay graduated from the University of Edinburgh, was licensed by the Church of Scotland, and, in response to an application from Kingston, was ordained to that charge by the Presbytery of Edinburgh on 26 Sept. 1821. Arriving in Kingston on 25 December, Barclay took over a new church and an eager congregation. He attended to the usual round of pastoral duties, became a secretary to the local Bible society, and supported local philanthropic and educational institutions. In May 1822 he notified Lieutenant Governor Sir Peregrine Maitland* of the church's intention to distinguish the government pew as was "the usual form in Scotch Churches." A dignity worthless in itself, Barclay argued, it none the less worked towards "promoting Subordination, good order, & good Morals, among a people."

The controversy that earned Barclay unmitigated hostility from Kingston's Anglican élite began as an attempt to solve the problem of limited cemetery space. Late in 1822 Barclay appealed to the rector of St George's Church, the Reverend George Okill Stuart*, for equal privileges in the lower burial ground. Stuart gave a peremptory refusal, claiming that other Protestant denominations could have access to the cemetery only if they followed Church of England burial services. This position was unacceptable to Barclay, who successfully negotiated an arrangement to share the upper burial ground with the Roman Catholics. But this proposal fell through and Barclay turned his attention again to the lower ground.

The conflict which ensued centred upon two incidents, the first on 27 Dec. 1824, the second on 8 April 1825. In the first, Barclay led a funeral procession to the burial ground, where it was met by Stuart. Fearing a "Collision," Barclay expressed the hope that Stuart would not interfere. Stuart, however, insisted on performing the service of the "English" church, and Barclay departed the scene lest his presence signify a sanction of the Anglican's actions. On 29 December Barclay asked Attorney General John Beverley Robinson* for his official opinion on the episode. Barclay contended that, since the Anglicans had no deed to the land, they possessed no exclusive right; hence, it should be open to all denominations. Robinson, replying early in January, lamented the dispute and offered his professional opinion that without a deed there was "no *legal right*." He allowed, however, that St George's might have a prescriptive claim to the ground and he urged the parties to negotiate. Citing Robinson's suggestion, Barclay made the offer on 7 February and, on the following day, Stuart refused.

Barclay

Barclay and his congregation immediately petitioned Maitland for redress.

Although his language was always proper and, to a degree, conciliatory, he was becoming increasingly resolute about the issue. The second incident, at another funeral on 8 April, made compromise impossible. This time Barclay ordered a locksmith to be at hand in the event the gates to the cemetery were locked; as it turned out, they were open. Once again Stuart joined the procession and this time Barclay remained. When Stuart began to read at the grave site, Barclay ordered the grave to be filled as quickly as possible. He did not attempt to read himself because the Presbyterian rites called for complete silence. Stuart pressed on: the two men did not exchange a word. Stuart was furious at the effrontery. Several days later, Presbyterians were refused interment in the grounds. Barclay regretted the "unpleasant Competition" but vowed that until the matter was resolved "those who may use any force to prevent my Congregation from getting admittance to bury their dead . . . must be responsible for all the evil that may result from it."

The chain of events that followed brought into the open a struggle for not only religious but national rights as well. To Stuart, the incident was "indecent, outrageous and profane." He reported to a church committee composed of Christopher Alexander Hagerman*, John Macaulay*, and Robert Stanton* that any invasion of the church's right "must be checked and restrained by legal support." The committee investigated the affair and the church's claim to the ground. Its report of 16 April dismissed the Presbyterians' "pretensions" and upheld St George's "entire and exclusive possession" of the cemetery. The report, together with supporting documents, was forwarded to the Executive Council.

The council met on 22 April. Except for James BABY, those present, John Strachan* among them, were Anglican. The cautious councillors recommended seeking an imperial decision while upholding, in the interim, the *status quo*, including the right of "dissenters" to interment conditional upon acceptance of Anglican burial rites. Barclay, who was in York (Toronto) awaiting the decision, was irate. He had reason to be. Whether the councillors were conscious of the fact or not, there was an Anglican bias to the documents upon which they made their decision. In his letter of 22 June referring the matter to Colonial Secretary Lord Bathurst, Maitland noted that the Presbyterians felt "aggrieved in being deprived of a privilege which appears never to have existed, nor till very lately to have been thought of."

On 16 August Barclay forwarded to the council affidavits casting doubt on the legitimacy of the Church of England's prescriptive claim to the cemetery. Further, he enclosed a petition to the king to resolve a dispute which had arisen "by the assumption of an exclusive control . . . by the Episcopal Church." The council's needless equation of Presbyterians with dissenters gave Barclay a different perspective on his church's situation within the colony. The Scotch Presbyterians, "residing in a *British*, not an *English* Colony," claimed "equal rights with the Episcopal Church by the Act of Union." The council met again on 3 November, considered the new evidence, and then reaffirmed its earlier conclusion. Towards the end of the month, the petition, as well as all new documents, were forwarded to London. When in late May 1826 Stuart learned that the imperial government had vindicated his conduct, he felt justified.

Barclay did not. He responded on 1 June with a pamphlet setting out his church's rights, "so long neglected, and . . . now so strongly opposed" by the Church of England. His case had legal and historical foundations. Both the Quebec Act of 1774 and the Constitutional Act of 1791 referred to a Protestant clergy. Thus, the Church of Scotland by virtue of its position as one of the established churches of Great Britain had "a legal birthright claim to part of the profits arising from the Clergy Reserves in Canada." Canada had been conquered by Great Britain, not England or Scotland; "therefore, any right, privilege and advantage, enjoyed by the Clergy of the Religion established in England ought equally to belong to the Clergy of the Religion established in Scotland." Incredulous that Scottish legislators and clergy had allowed these rights in the colonies to slip away "silently," he pointed to the transformation wrought in Scotland by state support: the "poor, ignorant, idle and wicked" became "comfortable, enlighten[ed], industrious, and moral." Anticipating Egerton Ryerson*, he questioned claims about the number of Anglicans in the population and dismissed the structure of Anglicanism: "the genius of Episcopacy is in opposition to the genius of the people."

Small wonder his "Scotch pamphlet," as it was called, elicited a torrent of Anglican abuse. Stanton denounced it as "dull, dirty & disgusting." It was vilified in the columns of the *Kingston Chronicle* and Stanton's *U.E. Loyalist*. It prompted several rejoinders in pamphlet form by Stanton, William Macaulay*, and Hagerman. John Macaulay thought that Barclay's work would have "the bad effect of stirring up new dissenters in our society – The worst of it is that the disaffected will rejoice to see divisions created among those who ought to live together in harmony." Behind the legal, constitutional, and historical discussions of the respective rights of the churches lay an ill-disguised Anglo-Anglican hubris. Stanton sneered, "Let the Scotch gentry learn to ask for *favors* respectfully, and they will fare better . . . but wilful men, must ha' their way."

Barclay's death – the result of a fever contracted

while returning from a visit to Scots in the London District – brought an end to the immediate affair; but the battle for Presbyterian rights, tied as it was to Scottish nationalism, continued long after his passing [*see* William Morris*].

ROBERT LOCHIEL FRASER

[The major primary sources for the burial-ground controversy are PAC, RG 1, E3, 42: 12–121, and PRO, CO 42/375: 222–69, 335–57. The Colonial Office's response is contained in PAC, RG 7, G1, 61: 344–63; 62: 42–44, 69–70. Anglican reaction to the affair, and in particular to Barclay's pamphlet, may be found in the *Kingston Chronicle*, 1825–26, and the *U.E. Loyalist* (York [Toronto]), 1826. The more private side of this reaction is found in the Macaulay papers (AO, MS 78), Strachan to Macaulay, 9, 30 May, 22 Aug. 1825; Stanton to Macaulay, 29 June, 3, 8, 15, 22 July, 5, 18 Aug., 1 Sept., 5 Oct. 1826, 20 Sept. 1827; and Robinson to Macaulay, 25 July 1826. Barclay's pamphlet, *A letter to the Right Honourable the Earl of Liverpool, K.G., first lord commissioner of the Treasury; relative to the rights of the Church of Scotland in British North America; from a Protestant of the Church of Scotland* (Kingston, [Ont.], 1826), provoked in response: *An apology for the Church of England in the Canadas, in answer to A letter to the Earl of Liverpool . . . by a Protestant of the Church of Scotland; by a Protestant of the established Church of England* (Kingston, 1826); *The exclusive right of the church to the clergy reserves defended: in a letter to the Right Honorable the Earl of Liverpool; being an answer to the letter of a Protestant of the Church of Scotland, to his lordship; by a Protestant* (Kingston, 1826); and *A letter to "A Protestant of the Church of Scotland"; by Misopseudes* (n.p., 1826).

Biographical information and other material relevant to Barclay's career may be found in the following: PAC, RG 5, A1: 28881–83, 28956–61, 30583–86, 30758–59, 38157–58, 38264–69, 39120–26, 39447–50, 40315–20, 41756–59, 41760–62, 41818–21, 42284–86, 42713–14, 139062–65; Ramsay, *Dalhousie journals* (Whitelaw), vol.3; *Kingston Chronicle*, various issues from 12 Dec. 1821 to 13 Oct. 1826; Scott *et al.*, *Fasti ecclesiæ scoticanæ*, 7: 625; Gregg, *Hist. of Presbyterian Church* (1885); A. B. Burt, "The Rev. John Barclay, M.A., the first Presbyterian minister settled in Kingston," *OH*, 16 (1918): 37–39; and R. A. Preston, "A clash in St. Paul's churchyard," *Historic Kingston*, no.5 (1956): 30–44. On the general issue of the coherence of church rights and Scottish nationalism, *see* H. J. Bridgman, "Three Scots Presbyterians in Upper Canada: a study in emigration, nationalism and religion" (PHD thesis, Queen's Univ., Kingston, 1978). Finally, the quotation from Hugh MacLennan is found in *Each man's son* (Toronto, 1971), 67. R.L.F.]

BARCLAY, THOMAS HENRY, lawyer, politician, militia officer, and office holder; b. 12 Oct. 1753 in New York City, eldest son of the Reverend Henry Barclay and Mary Rutgers; m. 2 Oct. 1775 Susan DeLancey in West Falls (New York City), and they had 12 children; d. 21 April 1830 in New York City.

Thomas Henry Barclay was one of the most illustrious loyalists to settle in Nova Scotia. His father was a prominent Anglican clergyman who served as rector of Trinity Church in New York City, and his mother was the daughter of a rich brewer of old New York Dutch descent. Barclay's marriage strengthened his ties to the colonial establishment, for the DeLanceys had long been among the most influential families in New York.

Barclay spent his early life in New York. After graduating from King's College (Columbia University) in 1772, he entered John Jay's law office as a student and was called to the bar in 1775. His legal career was soon interrupted by the outbreak of the American Revolutionary War. Towards the end of 1776 he joined the British forces in New York and in April 1777 was commissioned a captain in the Loyal American Regiment. Later that year he was promoted major in recognition of his gallant service at the capture of forts Clinton and Montgomery on the Hudson River. In 1780 he was named to command the newly formed Provincial Light Infantry. Barclay served with distinction throughout the war, taking part in action in New York, New Jersey, and the Carolinas. He was captured by the French in 1781 while carrying dispatches to Lord Cornwallis but soon obtained parole and returned to New York. At the end of the war he was one of a group of senior officers who explored the Saint John River (N.B.) to locate suitable land for the settlement of the provincial troops.

Barclay's estate in New York had been confiscated in 1776 and he was specifically named in the act of attainder passed by the New York legislature in October 1779. He had therefore little choice but to join the loyalist migration north. At first he contemplated settling in New Brunswick, but instead he established his family in Wilmot Township in the Annapolis valley of Nova Scotia, where he and brother officers of the Loyal American Regiment received extensive grants of land. By the late 1780s he had moved to the town of Annapolis Royal and resumed his law practice.

As befitted a man of his education and social standing, Barclay promptly entered politics. He and fellow loyalist David Seabury were returned for Annapolis County in the House of Assembly elections of 1785. A gifted orator, Barclay became a dominant figure in the sixth assembly, the first in which the loyalists were represented. He was soon at the centre of a controversy which pitted loyalist against pre-loyalist when Alexander Howe*, member of an old Nova Scotia family, petitioned against Seabury's election. Howe claimed that the sheriff of Annapolis County had shown partiality by permitting some of Seabury's supporters to vote while disallowing some of his own. The assembly's election committee, four of whose five members were pre-loyalists, found in Howe's favour and ordered the issuance of a new writ.

Barclay

In the subsequent by-election, Seabury was returned but his election was again challenged. The assembly concluded the debate by unseating Seabury and declaring Howe duly elected. Throughout the controversy, Barclay had supported his running mate and indeed had exacerbated the split between old and new settlers by exhorting Annapolis County loyalists to unite behind Seabury who, he claimed, had been unjustly deprived of his seat because of the assembly's partiality. His inflammatory letter became a divisive issue during the 1786 session when, despite opposition from loyalist assemblymen, the pre-loyalist majority passed a motion forcing Barclay to apologize for his allegations of favouritism.

The sixth assembly proved to be preoccupied by constitutional issues, reflecting the political maturity and ambition of many of the new loyalist assemblymen. Loyalist members, with Barclay prominent among them, engaged in a forceful campaign to enhance the assembly's role as the representative branch of the legislature. The most sustained conflict between assembly and Council arose over the administration of justice in the Supreme Court. Since the death of Chief Justice Bryan Finucane in 1785, the puisne judges, Isaac Deschamps* and James Brenton*, had constituted a full court. Complaints about their actions prompted investigation by the assembly during the 1787 session. The house concluded that the evidence warranted a thorough review of the charges by Lieutenant Governor John Parr*. His official report was not presented to the assembly until the 1789 session. In the mean time, the question emerged as the major controversy in the Halifax by-election of February 1788, in which Jonathan Sterns, one of the loyalist witnesses against the judges, opposed Charles Morris, a Haligonian closely allied with the official clique. Opinion was further enflamed when the Council issued its own report soon after the election, completely vindicating the conduct of fellow councillor Deschamps and Brenton, brother-in-law of a Council member. When Sterns and William Taylor, the other chief witness against the judges, retaliated with public letters in March detailing their charges, Deschamps disbarred them for contempt of court. The two sailed for England the next month to present their case to imperial officials, while from Halifax Parr denounced their mission and warned that their actions represented a direct challenge to the maintenance of British authority in Nova Scotia.

Although less dramatically phrased, Parr's official response to the assembly on 12 March 1789 was wholehearted in its support of the judges, concluding that the evidence did not justify the accusations against them. Barclay immediately moved that the lieutenant governor provide copies of the documents justifying the Council's exoneration of the judges. This challenge to the independence of the executive branch was defeated on a close vote of 14 to 13 and Parr's report declared satisfactory by an equally close vote of 15 to 14. The issue was by no means dead: two days later Isaac Wilkins moved to ask Parr to dismiss his councillors for their "evil and pernicious" advice on the disposition of the judges' case. In seconding the motion, Barclay read his fellow legislators a lesson in constitutional theory. He urged them to consider themselves the natural guardians of the rights of Nova Scotians, invested with the authority to review the conduct of the Council and indeed of the lieutenant governor himself. Many assemblymen who had previously supported the attack on the judges drew back from such radical arguments and Wilkins's motion went down to defeat by a vote of 21 to 8.

The assembly returned to the "judges' affair" with renewed vigour during the 1790 session. A formal inquiry was instituted with Barclay serving as chief prosecutor to prepare impeachment charges against Deschamps and Brenton. In the end seven of the thirteen charges were included in an address to the king in April praying that the judges be brought to trial. By the time the Privy Council's review of the case had been received in Halifax in August 1792, the passage of time and the efforts of a new chief justice, Thomas Andrew Lumisden Strange*, had alleviated much of the dissatisfaction with the Supreme Court. The report acquitted the judges of deliberate wrongdoing but admitted that they had at times acted incompetently, which indeed had been the substance of the assembly's complaints.

The question of the judges had dominated the assembly's deliberations, but in 1789 assemblymen had turned again to the contentious issue of election reform which they had considered during their first session in 1785. Assembly members were especially concerned to control the composition of the house by adjudicating contested elections and determining qualifications for both electors and candidates, rights exercised prior to the sixth assembly by the lieutenant governor and Council. On 31 March 1789 Barclay moved a two-part resolution asserting these rights and also barring office holders from membership in the assembly. The first clause passed with broad support but the proposal to exclude placemen was defeated through the opposition of members allied with the Halifax coterie. The next day, a special committee on electoral reform brought in a bill setting forth the assembly's sole right to determine all election questions. The measure retained use of a single poll in each constituency, however, and therefore did not benefit the back-country voters, who were often effectively disenfranchised since they could not travel to the central polling location. Many of the rural areas affected were represented by loyalists, and the loyalist members, supported by other country members, unsuccessfully opposed the bill, despite its similarity to Barclay's earlier resolution.

The active participation of Barclay and other loyalists in the assembly reflected their assumption that the legislature was the natural focus of public life. As well, it illustrated their determination not to be excluded from positions of influence and authority by the strongly established bureaucracy they encountered in Nova Scotia. The appointment of loyalist John Wentworth* as lieutenant governor in 1792 helped to ease a number of their frustrations. Like many loyalists, Barclay was at the centre of public life throughout the 1790s. He was elected to represent Annapolis Township in 1793 and was unanimously chosen speaker of the new assembly. Wentworth, who had earlier recommended Barclay to fill a vacant Council seat, realized that he now had a valuable ally as leader of the assembly. Indeed Barclay worked closely with the lieutenant governor in managing the assembly's participation in a program of retrenchment and increased taxes to rid the province of the heavy debts that jeopardized its financial position.

Barclay's military experience was also called upon during the 1790s. In 1793 he was named lieutenant-colonel of the new Royal Nova Scotia Regiment, which Wentworth was authorized to raise following the outbreak of war between France and Britain. Barclay, however, preferred to establish a volunteer regiment of infantry, cavalry, and artillery, drawn largely from the former provincial soldiers now settled in the Annapolis valley. Known as the Nova Scotia Legion, this force of 1,000 men was intended principally to defend the Bay of Fundy shore but was available for duty elsewhere in the province. Barclay was also appointed adjutant general of the militia in June 1793 and was instrumental in drawing up a new act that reorganized the poorly equipped and ill-trained corps.

Wentworth's esteem for Barclay's abilities and loyalty was reflected in his recommendation of the speaker as the British boundary commissioner under the terms of Jay's Treaty of 1794. The fifth article of this treaty sought to clarify the border between the United States and New Brunswick, described by the Treaty of Paris in 1783 as the St Croix River. The essential problem was to establish which of the two major rivers flowing into Passamaquoddy Bay was indeed Samuel de Champlain*'s St Croix. Negotiations ended successfully for the British in October 1798 with the western river, known locally as the Scoodic, being accepted as the St Croix, and with its source being agreed on as the northwest headwaters of its tributary the Chiputneticook.

Barclay returned to Nova Scotia late in 1798 with his reputation enhanced by the success of the negotiations. As a native American with fine legal and diplomatic skills, he had indeed been an excellent choice as commissioner, although much of the strength of the British position had been the result of the indefatigable work of agent Ward Chipman and his volunteer assistant Robert Pagan. The British government rewarded Barclay with appointment to the Nova Scotian Council early in 1799. During his sojourn in the United States, however, Barclay had decided his future lay not in Nova Scotia but with the imperial public service, and had solicited the post of consul general in New York to succeed the ageing Sir John Temple. He was appointed to the office in January 1799 following Temple's death. Although Barclay never returned to Nova Scotia, he remained in touch with the province and its concerns. He held extensive tracts of land in the Annapolis valley throughout his life and in fact late in 1800, when it was expected that Wentworth would be dismissed for his mismanagement of the maroons, rumours flew in Nova Scotia that Barclay was seeking the office of lieutenant governor.

At the outbreak of war between Britain and the United States in 1812, Barclay was recalled to London, but in November was appointed agent for British prisoners in the United States and returned to New York in April 1813. The end of the war again brought the problem of the international boundary to the forefront. The Treaty of Ghent made provision for commissions to continue the work of establishing the border between New Brunswick and the United States. Barclay's experience on the earlier commission and his position as consul general made him the clear choice as British commissioner. Once again, Ward Chipman served as the British agent. The new commissions dealt with two areas: ownership of the islands in Passamaquoddy Bay and extension of the border from the source of the St Croix north to the St Lawrence. The issue of the Passamaquoddy islands was settled late in 1817, following arguments from both sides as to which islands had been included in the ancient borders of Nova Scotia established by the Treaty of Utrecht. The decision was a satisfactory compromise: Britain received Deer Island, Campobello, and Grand Manan while the United States retained Moose Island, where the town of Eastport had grown up, as well as two small adjacent islands.

The inland border proved a vastly more difficult problem. For three years, the commission met trying to agree upon the location of the "highlands" which had been set as the northern point of the border. British negotiators aimed to preserve the vital overland route through Lac Témiscouata, Lower Canada, to the St Lawrence while the Americans bargained for as much of the valuable timber area as possible. When agreement could not be reached, the question was submitted to the king of the Netherlands for arbitration. His decision, released in 1831, was not accepted by both parties and the question remained a contentious issue until settled by the Webster–Ashburton Treaty of 1842.

Barkley

Participation in the second boundary commission was Barclay's final contribution to public life. Early in April 1822 he made the last of his four visits to Britain, taking with him documentation for the British case for presentation to the Foreign Office. After his return to New York, he moved to a country home on Manhattan Island where he lived the peaceful life of a retired gentleman. His health began to fail during the summer of 1829 and he died on 21 April 1830. He is buried in the churchyard of St Mark's Church in the Bowery.

Thomas Barclay played a significant part in the political development of Nova Scotia during the turbulent sessions of the sixth assembly. Educated in the political ferment of the old colonies in the years before the American revolution, many loyalists retained assumptions about the role of the assembly which underlay later constitutional struggles in the province. Barclay's speech urging impeachment of the Council gave forceful utterance to a concept steadfastly espoused in subsequent years: that the assembly was the colonial counterpart of the House of Commons. Similarly, the assembly's firm assertion of its inherent right to primacy in financial measures, set forth by Barclay during the 1790 session, was no less tenaciously upheld than it was to be by succeeding assemblies. For Barclay, as for many loyalist leaders, entry into the colonial establishment was to blunt his opposition to executive authority. Yet the stimulus they gave Nova Scotian political life helped give rise to later reform movements. In many respects, Barclay epitomizes the romantic ideal of the loyalist: a rich university-educated Anglican who had fought bravely for his king. On the other hand, he is also representative of the large body of loyalists of all classes and conditions for whom Nova Scotia was little more than a way station. Barclay's talents and background, however, placed him in the fortunate position of being able to return to his native land while still honourably serving the cause for which he had accepted exile.

JUDITH TULLOCH

Some of Thomas Henry Barclay's correspondence has been published under the title *Selections from the correspondence of Thomas Barclay, formerly British consul-general at New York*, ed. G. L. Rives (New York, 1894).

Maine Hist. Soc. (Portland), Thomas Barclay papers (mfm. at PANS). PANS, RG 1, 33, 51–52, 171, 301–2; RG 5, A, 2–3. PRO, CO 217/36–37, 217/60–70. N.S., House of Assembly, *Journal and proc.*, 1785–1800. "Poll book for the county of Annapolis, 1786," ed. Karen Forsyth, *Nova Scotia Hist. Rev.* (Halifax), 1 (1981), no.2: 106–24. *Directory of N.S. MLAs*. Sabine, *Biog. sketches of loyalists*, vol.1. J. M. Beck, *The government of Nova Scotia* (Toronto, 1957). A. C. Flick, *Loyalism in New York during the American revolution* (New York, 1901; repr. 1969). Neil MacKinnon, "The loyalist experience in Nova Scotia, 1783 to 1791" (PHD thesis, Queen's Univ., Kingston, Ont., 1975). Murdoch, *Hist. of N.S.*, vol.3. Margaret Ells, "Nova Scotian 'Sparks of liberty,'" *Dalhousie Rev.*, 16 (1936–37): 475–92. W. F. Ganong, "A monograph of the evolution of the boundaries of the province of New Brunswick," RSC *Trans.*, 2nd ser., 7 (1901), sect.II: 139–449. Neil MacKinnon, "This cursed republican spirit: the loyalists and Nova Scotia's sixth assembly," *Humanities Assoc. Rev.* (Kingston), 27 (1976): 129–42. R. D. and J. I. Tallman, "The diplomatic search for the St. Croix River, 1796–1798," *Acadiensis* (Fredericton), 1 (1971–72), no.2: 59–71.

BARKLEY, CHARLES WILLIAM, ship's captain and fur trader; b. 1759, son of Charles Barkley; d. 16 May 1832 in Hertford, England.

At age 11, Charles William Barkley went to sea with his father, commander of the East India Company's ship *Pacific*. After his first voyage Barkley sailed to the West Indies in the merchantman *Betsy* but returned to the eastern seas on seven subsequent voyages for the East India Company. Even though his father drowned while he was still a lad, Barkley rose rapidly in the company's service. In 1786 he left the company to take what was apparently his first command, the ship *Loudoun*, outfitted for a trading voyage along the northwest coast of America. At 400 tons, the *Loudoun*, owned by various supercargoes in China and several East India Company directors in England who together called themselves the Austrian East India Company, was the largest and finest vessel that had yet visited the coast. Barkley subscribed £3,000 of his own to the venture.

The *Loudoun* left the Thames on 6 Sept. 1786 and sailed first to Ostend (Belgium) where she picked up supplies. There her name was changed to the *Imperial Eagle* and she hoisted Austrian colours since British vessels were required to respect the monopoly rights of the East India Company. While at Ostend, Barkley met and on 27 Oct. 1786 married Frances Hornby Trevor, the 17-year-old daughter of the minister of the Protestant chapel at Ostend. On 24 November the *Imperial Eagle* sailed for the Pacific via Brazil and Cape Horn.

The vessel reached Nootka Sound (B.C.) the following June. Barkley and his wife met John Mackay*, who had been left there the previous summer by James Charles Stuart Strange* to learn Indian customs. Mackay taught Barkley much about the Indian traders and also about the geography of Vancouver Island and the waters to the south of it, thus giving him an advantage over rivals such as James Colnett*. Barkley traded extensively with the Indians at Nootka and Clayoquot sounds and at another very large sound to which he gave his own name. Late in July the *Imperial Eagle* sailed into an extensive water-way that Barkley immediately recognized as the long-sought-for strait said to have been discovered by Juan de Fuca*. On his chart he named it after Fuca. He was surprised to find this strait because Captain James Cook* had stated emphatically that it did not exist.

After the loss of some crewmen at an island he named Destruction Island (Wash.), Barkley left for Macao (near Canton, People's Republic of China), which he reached in December 1787, and there he sold his 800 furs on an overstocked market for 30,000 Spanish dollars. He sailed with a cargo for Mauritius and then to Calcutta where he hoped to outfit his vessel for the second of three projected voyages to the northwest coast. That project never materialized for the East India Company had discovered the threat to its monopoly. According to Mrs Barkley, her husband's partners, eager to dissociate themselves from the venture, ignored his contract, sold the *Imperial Eagle*, and handed his charts and instruments to John Meares*, who later claimed some of the captain's discoveries as his own. Barkley recovered £5,000 in a case settled out of court in Calcutta.

Between 1788 and 1791 Barkley commanded the *Princess Frederica*, sailing in the Indian Ocean. After being dissuaded by his brother from continuing in the lucrative Indian coastal trade, on 16 Aug. 1792 Barkley was again on the northwest coast, in command of the 80-ton brig *Halcyon*, which he had purchased in Calcutta. Barkley traded at Sitka Sound (Alaska) and then sailed for the Sandwich (Hawaiian) Islands, China, and eventually Mauritius.

Nothing is known of the latter years of Barkley's career but they were probably not prosperous. In her diary Mrs Barkley wrote at his death, "I lost my beloved husband – in his 73rd year – worn out more by care and sorrow than by years, as he had been blessed with a very strong constitution." Barkley also left two sons and two daughters. Three other children had predeceased him. Mrs Barkley, his companion on two circumnavigations of the world, died in 1845 and was buried near him.

Charles William Barkley's name, which has been variously spelled, is perpetuated in Barclay Street, Vancouver, and Barkley Sound.

BARRY M. GOUGH

PABC, AA20.5, H12B, *Halcyon, Princess Frederica*; L92, *Halcyon, Loudoun*; L92W, J. T. Walbran, "The cruise of the *Imperial Eagle*" (1936). "Documents relating to the mystery of Mrs Barkley's diary," ed. W. K. Lamb, *BCHQ*, 6 (1942): 49–59. Beth Hill, *The remarkable world of Frances Barkley: 1769–1845* (Sidney, B.C., 1978). W. K. Lamb, "The mystery of Mrs. Barkley's diary," *BCHQ*, 6: 31–47; "Notes on the Barkley family": 143–44. J. T. Walbran, "The cruise of the *Imperial Eagle*," *Victoria Colonist*, 3 March 1901.

BARSS, JOSEPH, ship's captain, privateer, and businessman; b. 21 Feb. 1776 in Liverpool, N.S., second of 14 children of Joseph Barss and Elizabeth Crowell; d. 3 Aug. 1824 near Kentville, N.S.

Joseph Barss's father had been brought from New England to the pioneer settlement at Liverpool as a boy, and established himself as one of the township's leaders and its representative in the House of Assembly. Joseph was at sea by the age of 14 as a member of his father's salmon-fishing crew on the Labrador coast. By 1797 he was master on one of his father's vessels; the next year he was second lieutenant aboard a large privateer, the *Charles Mary Wentworth*; and in October 1799 he was given command of a smaller one, the *Lord Spencer*. After one prize had been sent back from the West Indies, three of the *Lord Spencer*'s crew were injured in a brush with French privateers, and the vessel later ran afoul of a "Reaf of Rocks," the crew having to be rescued by a friendly privateer. Barss then cruised in a prize, with no recorded success. January 1801 saw him sailing from Liverpool as master of the privateer *Rover*. He found little prey abroad (peace was rumoured), but sent home three prizes before returning in May.

Privateering did not become lucrative again until the War of 1812, and so between 1801 and 1812 Barss sailed vessels in the Maritimes and New England coasting trade, including the *Eliza*, which he purchased from Simeon Perkins*. From July 1803 until March 1804 he and his sloop were in the West Indies, probably in government service and reportedly earning 1,500 dollars a month. Barss had marriage on his mind. He returned to Liverpool on 24 March, and on 12 April a bond was issued for his marriage to Olivia DeWolf, daughter of Elisha DeWolf, a prominent inhabitant of Horton Township. The couple settled in Liverpool, and Barss continued in the coastal trade, buying and selling for himself as well as others. He was also a member of a local group of underwriters which insured Liverpool vessels and cargoes.

On 28 June 1812 news of the war with the United States arrived in Liverpool by the *Liverpool Packet* from Halifax. This small, fast schooner, originally built for the African slave trade, had been bought by Enos Collins*, with three other Liverpool men, including Barss's brothers John* and James, as shareholders. Prior to the war she had been placed on the packet run between Halifax and Liverpool. By 22 August Lieutenant Governor Sir John Coape SHERBROOKE had granted authorization to "apprehend seize and take any Ship vessel or goods belonging to the said United States," even though he had not received any orders from Britain in this regard. In early September the *Liverpool Packet* was at sea, with Joseph Barss second in command. During her first voyage the command changed from John Freeman to Barss, probably because of a need for effective discipline, and he remained in control on subsequent cruises.

When in November Sherbrooke received an order-in-council allowing the seizure of American vessels, privateers headed for the American coast, and Barss's skill and the *Liverpool Packet*'s speed made him the leader of the pack. He concentrated his attacks around

Batoche

the approaches to Boston, particularly in the vicinity of the northern shore of Cape Cod, and his name became well known in New England ports, a high reward being offered for his capture. Thirty-three prizes taken under his command were disposed of before the Vice-Admiralty Court in Halifax. Although he boarded many more than that number, some were not worth sending back, some were protected by British safe-conduct passes, some that he did send back were lost in storms, and some were recaptured by American privateers.

On 11 June 1813 Barss found himself engaged with a heavily armed American privateer, the *Thomas* from Portsmouth, N.H., and was forced to surrender. Although the crew was soon returned to Nova Scotia in an exchange of prisoners, Barss was kept in Portsmouth in close confinement. Influential friends such as Collins and his business partner Joseph Allison petitioned Sherbrooke to intercede on his behalf, but Barss was not allowed to return home for many months, and then only on parole. Nevertheless, in 1814 he took the *Wolverine* (the former *Thomas*, captured in 1813) to the West Indies as an armed trader, returning to Liverpool on 20 August. According to a Boston newspaper account of 28 October reprinted in the *Acadian Recorder* of Halifax on 12 November, Barss had been recaptured, having "broke his parole sometime since," and had been imprisoned again. If so, he was back in Liverpool by March 1815, his health possibly injured through imprisonment and his seafaring life at an end. The earnings of the *Liverpool Packet* in 1812 for 18 vessels were £21,814, of which Barss probably received £1,000.

In 1817 Barss bought a farm near Kentville, close to his wife's relatives and away from the sea. There he lived with his still increasing family (there were nine children in all) until his death at the comparatively early age of 48.

CATHERINE PROSS

Liverpool, N.S., Simeon Perkins, diaries (transcripts at PANS). PANS, MG 1, 819, no.1; 825; MG 4, 77 (typescript). C. H. J. Snider, *Under the red jack: privateers of the Maritime provinces of Canada in the War of 1812* (Toronto, [1927?]), 17–52. T. H. Raddall, "Joseph Barss, Jr. – a famous privateer captain," *Liverpool Advance*, 26 July 1972: 3.

BATOCHE, JEAN-BAPTISTE LETENDRE, *dit.*
See LETENDRE

BEAUJEU, JACQUES-PHILIPPE SAVEUSE DE.
See SAVEUSE

BECKWITH, Sir THOMAS SYDNEY, army officer; b. 1772, third son of John Beckwith, army officer; m. Clementina Loughnan; one son and at least two daughters; d. 15 Jan. 1831 at Mahabaleshwar, India.

Thomas Sydney Beckwith first saw active service as a junior officer in India (1791–98). In 1800 he joined the Experimental Corps of Riflemen, which was known successively after 1802 as the 95th (Rifle) Regiment and the Rifle Brigade; he distinguished himself by his training of this unit and, as lieutenant-colonel from 1803, by his leadership of it. After participating in expeditions to Denmark (1801 and 1807) and Hanover (1806), he served with great credit in Spain and Portugal (1808–11). In 1810 he was appointed to the staff as a deputy quartermaster general, and in 1812 he became an assistant quartermaster general. On 29 May 1812 he was made a knight bachelor.

In January 1813, Britain being at war with the United States, Beckwith was named an assistant quartermaster general in North America. At the same time he was given command of the landing forces in an amphibious operation intended to harry the Chesapeake Bay area and reduce American pressure on the Canadas. The landings did not go smoothly and were of questionable value as a diversion, though Admiral Sir John Borlase WARREN claimed that they prevented 25,000 men from marching against the Canadas. The expedition was troubled by a command that was shared among Beckwith and admirals Warren and George Cockburn. Captain Charles James Napier, Beckwith's second in command, blamed this "republic of commanders" for a failed attack on Craney Island, Va. Napier felt that Beckwith had "wanted neither head, nor heart, nor hand for his business; but he was not free to do what he thought wise, and run sulky when required to do what he deemed silly. . . . He is certainly a very clever fellow, but a very odd fish." The expedition went to Halifax in September 1813.

Later that year Beckwith joined the staff in Lower Canada as quartermaster general; this post was of central importance during the final phases of the war. His department was responsible for the encampment, quartering, and movement of the army, duties that involved the collection of topographical and "secret" intelligence. In the Marquis of Wellington's European army the quartermaster general had become the principal staff officer and adviser, and in Canada also Beckwith was consulted on a wide range of problems.

In the autumn of 1814 Beckwith took part in Sir George Prevost*'s abortive attack on Plattsburgh, N.Y., the conduct of which strained relations between Prevost's staff and senior officers just arrived from Wellington's Peninsular army. Despite his reputation, Beckwith did not escape the censure of the newcomers; Major-General Frederick Philipse Robinson was particularly critical of his failure to obtain proper intelligence. The offensive of 1814 was, however, conducted on an unprecedented scale for Canadian operations, at a time when all military departments

38

had too few personnel, and lacked in particular staff having a thorough local knowledge; nor was responsibility for gathering secret intelligence clearly assigned.

Plattsburgh was Beckwith's last experience of active service. It did not damage his reputation; indeed in January 1815 he was awarded the KCB. Appointed colonel commandant of his old corps, now the Rifle Brigade, in 1827, he became commander-in-chief at Bombay two years later and attained the rank of lieutenant-general in 1830. He died of fever in January 1831. According to a contemporary he had been "one of the ablest out-post generals, and few officers knew so well how to make the most of a small force." Unfortunately his talents do not seem to have been put to the best use in North America.

GLENN A. STEPPLER

Gentleman's Magazine, July–December 1831: 83. William Napier, *The life and opinions of General Sir Charles James Napier* (4v., London, 1857), 1: 221. *Select British docs. of War of 1812* (Wood). *DNB*. Hitsman, *Incredible War of 1812*. Reginald Horsman, *The War of 1812* (London, 1969). J. K. Mahon, *The War of 1812* (Gainesville, Fla., 1972). G. A. Steppler, "A duty troublesome beyond measure: logistical considerations in the Canadian War of 1812" (MA thesis, McGill Univ., Montreal, 1974). S. G. P. Ward, *Wellington's headquarters; a study of the administrative problems in the Peninsula, 1809–1814* ([London], 1957).

BÉDARD, JEAN-CHARLES, Roman Catholic priest and Sulpician; b. 4 Nov. 1766 in Charlesbourg, Que., son of Pierre-Stanislas Bédard, a farmer, and Marie-Josephte Thibault; d. 2 July 1825 in Montreal.

Jean-Charles Bédard, the fourth of 13 children, belonged to a respectable family that gained distinction in the judiciary, church, and politics [see Pierre-Stanislas BÉDARD]. After finishing his studies at Quebec, he was ordained priest on 19 Dec. 1789. The next year, on the advice of Joseph-Octave PLESSIS, who was then secretary to the bishop of Quebec, he requested admission to the Séminaire de Saint-Sulpice in Montreal. He was made a member on 28 Sept. 1792 and spent the rest of his life there, serving as assistant bursar and bursar. Having also been named curate and master of rituals in the parish of Notre-Dame, he preached regularly and worked in close collaboration with Claude Poncin*, whose biography, as yet unpublished, he wrote. In addition he always took a lively interest in astronomy, physics, and mathematics.

During the final years of his life Bédard suffered greatly from the conflict between his Sulpician colleagues and Jean-Jacques Lartigue*, a Canadian Sulpician who had been appointed auxiliary bishop in Montreal on 21 Jan. 1821 by Archbishop Plessis of Quebec. Anxious to retain their influence in Montreal, the Sulpicians looked very unfavourably on the advent of an auxiliary bishop. When Lartigue took refuge in the Hôtel-Dieu of Montreal after the seminary expelled him in February 1821, Bédard was one of the few Sulpicians to visit him. He tried to intervene between the two sides but only brought upon himself the disapproval of his Sulpician superiors. Thus in June 1824, after much hesitation, he gave to Jean-Henry-Auguste ROUX, his superior, and to his colleagues a document entitled "Déclaration et observations . . . au sujet du gouvernement ecclésiastique du district de Montréal," in which he expressed his opposition to the measures taken by the seminary to block Bishop Lartigue's installation. He examined in turn what was "permitted," "fitting," and "useful" with regard to the ecclesiastical administration of the District of Montreal, refuting along the way objections raised by Augustin CHABOILLEZ, to whom he had previously sent two letters. The Sulpicians reacted strongly to their colleague's memoir; distressed, Roux protested his favourable sentiments towards Lartigue and Plessis. Both bishops approved of the step taken by Bédard, who in their view was sacrificing himself "for the good cause," was laying himself open to "many snubs," and was forcing "his naturally timid disposition to an extraordinary degree by asserting himself so openly" on their behalf. Plessis pressed to have the document, which in his view was excellent, brought to the attention of the authorities in Rome. Bédard agreed only after informing Roux. At the Séminaire de Saint-Sulpice in Paris it was held that in writing it Bédard had committed "a mistake that is inexcusable."

Overwrought by all these events, after making a final attempt in October 1824 to secure a reconciliation between Lartigue and the seminary, Jean-Charles Bédard died on 2 July 1825, "in as godly a manner as he had lived," according to Bishop Lartigue.

GILLES CHAUSSÉ

Jean-Charles Bédard is the author of "Déclaration et observations . . . au sujet du gouvernement ecclésiastique du district de Montréal." The manuscript is held at ASSM, 27, tiroir 90.

AAQ, 26 CP, VI: 109. ACAM, 901.137. ANQ-Q, CE1-7, 5 nov. 1766. Arch. du séminaire de Saint-Sulpice (Paris), Circulaires des supérieurs, I, Garnier Mollevault, 19 mars 1826; Saint-Sulpice, dossier III, no.12. ASSM, 24, dossiers 2–3; 27; 49, dossier 25. Allaire, *Dictionnaire*, 1: 36. [F.-M.] Bibaud, *Dictionnaire historique des hommes illustres du Canada et de l'Amérique* (Montréal, 1857). Gauthier, *Sulpitiana*, 168. Louis Bertrand, *Bibliothèque sulpicienne ou histoire littéraire de la Compagnie de Saint-Sulpice* (3v., Paris, 1900), 2: 62–63. Lemieux, *L'établissement de la première prov. eccl.*, 179–83. Édouard Fabre Surveyer, "Pierre-Stanislas Bédard (1734–1814) et sa famille," *BRH*, 59 (1953): 153–56. Léon Pouliot, "L'abbé Jean-Baptiste-Charles Bédard, p.s.s.," *BRH*, 44

Bédard

(1938): 172–73. P.-G. Roy, "Les sept frères Bédard," *BRH*, 44: 65–67.

BÉDARD, JOSEPH-ISIDORE, poet, lawyer, and politician; b. 9 Jan. 1806 at Quebec, third son of Pierre-Stanislas BÉDARD and Luce Lajus; d. unmarried 14 April 1833 in Paris.

Joseph-Isidore Bédard began studying at the Séminaire de Nicolet at the age of 10 and was a brilliant student. Up to the time he left in 1824 he went from one triumph to another, particularly in Latin. He was then articled to lawyer Georges-Barthélemi Faribault*.

Bédard was interested in poetry inspired by Canadian themes, and on 6 Aug. 1827 he published the first two stanzas of "Sol canadien! Terre chérie!" in the *Quebec Gazette* under the *nom de plume* Baptiste. Two years later he brought out a new version of this song in the same newspaper, which introduced it as the Canadians' first national anthem. Set to music by Théodore-Frédéric Molt*, for many years it was more popular with them than any other patriotic song. Bédard's poetry reveals the influence of his father's political ideas, and he himself thought it summed up well the feelings of the Canadians of the period, who, though suspected of lacking in loyalty, had respect for the British régime and abhorred the idea of annexation to the United States:

If Albion's beloved hand
Should cease one day to you protect,
Then stand alone, my own dear land,
And treat with scorn the stranger's aid.

This declaration of fidelity to Britain was, however, accompanied by a stern warning to fellow citizens hostile to liberty:

Respect the shielding hand o'er you
Of Albion, your worthy stay,
But bring to grief the spitefulness
Of foes within your bosom reared.

Bédard was called to the bar on 12 Oct. 1829. His diverse talents, jovial and caustic wit, ardent temperament, ease in speaking, and manly, pleasing voice, made him sought after in public meetings. A devoted citizen, he took his place in the swelling ranks of the temperance movement and advised his younger brother, François-Zoël, to "avoid bad company and join the temperance society."

On 6 Oct. 1830 Bédard was elected to the House of Assembly of Lower Canada for the riding of Saguenay. Young and eager, he was notable in the assembly for his independence of mind. In voting against the expulsions of Robert Christie*, member for Gaspé, he opposed the leaders of the Patriote party, Louis-Joseph Papineau* and Denis-Benjamin Viger*. Later he attacked Thomas Lee, who sat for Lower Town Quebec and who was seeking the support of youthful colleagues for an elective legislative council. "M. Lee has appealed to the young people about it," Bédard exclaimed, "but he did not express their feelings when he deplored the misfortune that our ancestors did not separate from Great Britain. Our forefathers acted wisely in not accepting the invitation from the United States. This province draws its entire strength from the metropolis." On several occasions he sat as chairman of the assembly's committee on grievances. It was probably at this period that he passed on information, in particular a biographical note on his father, to Isidore-Frédéric-Thomas Lebrun, who was preparing the *Tableau statistique et politique des deux Canadas* for publication.

In 1831 Bédard went to England with Viger, who had just been appointed the House of Assembly's agent there. They left Montreal on 9 May and reached Liverpool on 13 June. After visiting Ireland, Scotland, and France, Bédard stayed in London with François-Xavier Garneau*, who was then Viger's secretary. In Paris his time had been taken up with trips, amusements, gambling, theatre, and strolls along the boulevards and in public parks, but in London, in Garneau's company, he was more circumspect. Like young European liberals of the period 1815–30 he displayed Byronic moods and poses. In moments of loneliness, thoughts of death beset him; he surmounted them by seeking in them the meaning and mystery of life. He lamented the harshness of the human condition with its struggle between wanting and doing. On the other hand he maintained an objective view of reality. An inveterate optimist, capable of staunch friendship, he reached a certain wisdom: enjoy the present in moderation, be thankful for what has been given, open one's mind to the mystery of the future. In fact he yearned for the day when he would return to serve his country. Towards the end of September 1832, when he was about to come back to Lower Canada, he suddenly suffered a violent lung haemorrhage. On 20 November he informed Papineau, the speaker of the assembly, that he would not be able to attend the session then in progress. His condition worsened and on 14 April 1833, at the age of 27, he died in Paris; he was buried in Montmartre cemetery.

Joseph-Isidore Bédard sought and found his own authentic response to the many questions challenging him as a poet, citizen, member of a legislature, and human being. His thinking endured through "Sol canadien! Terre chérie!" which has been reprinted some 30 times in Canada and was included in a work published at London in 1830. In 1901 Narcisse-Eutrope Dionne* wrote a short biography of him, but afterwards he was virtually forgotten. Scholarly works now accord him a modest place. If it were not for his song, he might be remembered only as a romantic bohemian who died at an early age in a foreign country. His thought and poetry, which are still topical, ought to have new light shed on them. As a witness to a sombre period when French Canada was experiencing near desperate conditions culturally, Bédard exemplifies the daring young Canadian who, enamoured of his country and determined to improve its lot, hammered out a personal approach.

JEANNE D'ARC LORTIE

Joseph-Isidore Bédard is the author of the song *Sol canadien! Terre chérie!* which appeared under the pseudonym Baptiste in the *Quebec Gazette* of 6 Aug. 1827 before being published separately in Montreal in 1859. This is the version found in most of the collections of songs published from 1830 to the end of the century as well as in various journals. The song can be found in *L'Aurore des Canadas* (Montréal), 15 déc. 1840; *Le Canadien*, 1er juill. 1835, 4 juill. 1842; *Quebec Gazette*, 1 Jan. 1829; *La Minerve*, 8 juill. 1830, 13 juin 1833; *Le passe-tems ou nouveau recueil de chansons, romances, vaudevilles . . .* , Ludger Duvernay, édit. (Montréal, 1830), 142–43; [P.-J. de Sales Laterrière], *Political and historical account of Lower Canada; with remarks . . .* (London, 1830), 251; Joseph Laurin, *Le chansonnier canadien ou nouveau recueil de chansons* (Québec, 1838), 152–54; Joseph Roch-Lettoré, *L'écho de la chanson ou nouveau recueil de poésies, romances, vaudevilles* (Montréal, 1843), 37–38; *La lyre canadienne: répertoire des meilleures chansons et romances du jour*, [T.-F. Molt, compil.] (Québec, 1847), 95–96; *Le répertoire national, ou recueil de littérature canadienne*, James Huston, compil. (4v., Montréal, 1848–50), 1: 211–12, 236; *Nouvelle lyre canadienne ou chansonnier de tous les âges* (Montréal, 1858), 106–7; *Journal de l'Instruction publique* (Québec et Montréal), 3 (1859); [Alphonse Lusignan], *Recueil de chansons canadiennes et françaises* (Montréal, 1859), 341–42; *Canadiana* (Montreal), April 1890: 75.

ANQ-Q, CE1-1, 26 juill. 1796, 10 janv. 1806. PAC, MG 24, B1, 15: 182; 38: 779–82; 42: 2094–97; MG 30, D1, 4: 10–15; MG 53, 246. *La Minerve*, 9 mai 1831, 25 juin 1835. *Quebec Gazette*, 11 Oct. 1830. F.-J. Audet, "Les législateurs du Bas-Canada." F.-J. Audet et Fabre Surveyer, *Les députés au premier parl. du Bas-Canada*, 36–37. Desjardins, *Guide parl.*, 153. *DOLQ*, 1: 683. Réginald Hamel *et al.*, *Dictionnaire pratique des auteurs québécois* (Montréal, 1976), 45. H. J. Morgan, *Bibliotheca Canadensis*, 23. P.-G. Roy, *Les avocats de la région de Québec*, 26. Wallace, *Macmillan dict.* J.-G. Barthe, *Souvenirs d'un demi-siècle ou mémoires pour servir à l'histoire contemporaine* (Montréal, 1885). N.-E. Dionne, *Pierre Bédard et ses fils* (Québec, 1909), 221–40, 266–67. J.-A.-I. Douville, *Histoire du collège-séminaire de Nicolet, 1803–1903, avec les listes complètes des directeurs, professeurs et élèves de l'institution* (2v., Montréal, 1903), 2: 137. Edmond Lareau, *Histoire de la littérature canadienne* (Montréal, 1874), 65, 71. I.[-F.-T.] Lebrun, *Tableau statistique et politique des deux Canadas* (Paris, 1833). Jeanne d'Arc Lortie, *La poésie nationaliste au Canada français (1606–1867)* (Québec, 1975), 171–72; "Les origines de la poésie au Canada français," *Arch. des lettres canadiennes* (Montréal), 4 (1969): 11–49. Étienne Parent, "Pierre Bédard et ses deux fils," *Le Foyer domestique* (Ottawa), 1 (janvier–juin 1876): 32–35. Alain Pontaut, "Le drôle d'amour de nos 'notables' pour la France," *La Presse*, 12 août 1967: 19.

BÉDARD, PIERRE-STANISLAS, lawyer, politician, journalist, and judge; b. 13 Sept. 1762 in Charlesbourg (Que.), son of Pierre-Stanislas Bédard and Marie-Josephte Thibault; d. 26 April 1829 in Trois-Rivières, Lower Canada.

Pierre-Stanislas Bédard was the first to achieve fame in a family which had taken root in the St Lawrence valley by the 17th century. His ancestor Isaac Bédard, a master carpenter from the Aunis region in France, came to New France before 1660. For many years he wavered over the choice of a permanent place of residence. After living at Quebec, and then in the seigneury of Notre-Dame-des-Anges, he finally settled at Charlesbourg around 1670. The second generation of Bédards became a rural, peasant family. Needless to say, they were prolific: the 4 sons of Isaac's son Jacques had 39 children, 11.7 persons per family, when at the beginning of the 18th century the average in the whole colony was 9.2 to 9.4. In the following generation the elder Pierre-Stanislas raised 7 boys and 1 girl.

For 150 years the Bédards in growing numbers remained on this land at Charlesbourg near Quebec. Before 1800 only 8 of the 88 marriages they contracted – 9.09 per cent – involved spouses from outside the area. Partners were generally chosen from 60 of a possible 88 different families. The figures indicate the exceptional proliferation of family ties in such rural communities, which of course maintained economic links with the outside world and provided seasonal manpower for the fur trade, forestry, shipbuilding, and the king's corvées, but which demographically created rather closed worlds. This family network makes it easier to understand the key role played by certain clans in rural communities of the period.

At Charlesbourg the Bédards had over the years clearly managed to climb into the groups that were influential at the local level and often beyond it. Their social advancement became more apparent with the rise of the middle classes within society as a whole, and in particular when the numbers of professional men began to grow. On leaving the Petit Séminaire de Québec, where he had studied from 1777 until 1784, Pierre-Stanislas Bédard followed the trend, and after articling for a few years he was called to the bar on 6 Nov. 1790. His brothers Joseph and Thomas took the same route, becoming respectively a lawyer and a notary. (Three of his own sons would also become lawyers.) On 26 July 1796 Bédard took as his wife Luce Lajus, daughter of François Lajus*, a prominent Quebec surgeon. Like his brother Joseph, he allied himself with an old family. Joseph had married into a

Bédard

merchant family; Pierre-Stanislas's wife was a member of a professional family that already had links with the local gentry.

Bédard was not very taken with his chosen career. The study of law undoubtedly could interest him passionately, but daily practice was definitely contrary to his tastes and temperament. After a dozen years before the courts, he expressed great pessimism about the bar: "Ignorant lawyers, charlatans, are the only ones who can succeed." Already the father of two children, he had the feeling by 1802 that he could not make a decent living in his profession. The following year, having abandoned his practice, he did not know where to turn and felt he could not even apply for a post as a copyist because he wrote too badly. In 1804 he tried to borrow money, and then to sell his landed property. He felt ill and declared: "My illness is adorned with the name of nervous disorder, that's a polite way of saying I am crazy. I am not yet convinced that I am." To relieve his tension and forget his troubles he did algebraic problems. The record of these cogitations remains in a thick, handwritten notebook of 590 pages entitled "Notes de philosophie, mathématiques, chimie, physique, grammaire, politique et journal, 1798–1810," which demonstrates the range of his interests. In addition to disillusioned remarks on judges and attorneys it contains excerpts of varying length from the works of a score of contemporary philosophers. Among his reflections is one apparently arising from a central concern: "It is surprising that so many great algebraists have not found a way to attempt to carry their method over into the other sciences. . . . These other sciences are usually regarded as of another nature; it seems that for them there is another sort of truth, another sort of evidence, another sky, another sun."

In political life Bédard was to have an experience more in keeping with certain of his aspirations. By 1792 he had gained election as a member of the assembly for Northumberland, which at that time took in the Côte de Beaupré and some parishes on the north shore of the St Lawrence below Quebec. He was re-elected consistently in this rural riding until 1808. That year he was victorious in Lower Town Quebec, an achievement which he saw as a great step forward. In 1820, long after he had retired from politics, he reminisced about how "proud" he had been "of being elected in Lower Town," and how this event had "helped assuage my grief and show me that everything had not been bad." From 1810 to 1812, when he retired from politics, he represented Surrey. One of the earliest professional politicians in the colony, this man was – as Louis-Joseph Papineau* put it – "possessed by the demon of politics."

Bédard's rise as a political leader after 1804 was due, it seems, neither to an imposing appearance nor to a striking personality. He himself felt that he was ugly, awkward, and extremely timid. That he was acutely conscious of his weakness and great vulnerability, and that in consequence he led a fragile, threatened existence, might partly explain the enormous effort he made to negotiate a place for himself in the outside world that confronted him so harshly. Certainly by the time he had taken up the cudgels against the colonial government Bédard had on several occasions been frustrated by it and its officials, and these experiences had coloured his political action and ideas. In 1801, for example, he had met with a refusal when he requested the grant of Tring Township; he had in fact suffered the same fate as the other 115 candidates seeking that kind of political favour. In 1807 he had been deeply hurt by a reply from protonotary Joseph-François Perrault*, through whom he had asked for a commission as a militia officer; Perrault suggested that he conduct himself more moderately in politics, declaring, "You know that the government instructs us to recommend to it only influential, competent and talented officers." Bédard's hostility towards judge Pierre-Amable De Bonne* probably stemmed from two facts: De Bonne had previously run against him in Northumberland riding, and he had been Perrault's partner in founding the newspaper *Le Courier de Québec* at the end of 1806. Yet all these things do not suffice, any more than do his intellectual capacities, to account for Bédard's destiny as a politician and party leader.

This intelligent and hypersensitive man, who read books so voraciously that he sometimes felt nauseated, was not the most cultivated of the small inner circle of the new Canadian party. Men such as François BLANCHET, Jean-Thomas TASCHEREAU, Louis BOURDAGES, Denis-Benjamin Viger*, Joseph Papineau*, John Neilson*, and Andrew Stuart* were not his intellectual inferiors. Stuart, for example, quite frequently discussed the concepts of scholars such as Malthus, Jean-Charles-Léonard Sismonde de Sismondi, and Robert Owen, in this select group. In any case intellectual attainment was not the essential point; at the practical level, where an ideological system was being hammered out day by day, it was Bédard who remained the most sensitive, and consequently the most attentive to the interests, aspirations, and situation of the particular social class which in his view should by all rights function as a governing class and national élite. His conception of the French Canadian collectivity as a "nascent people" implied a French, Catholic nation dedicated mainly to agriculture, buttressed by the seigneurial system and the Coutume de Paris, and protected from the American danger by England and the British constitution. It was at this practical level, where awareness is of decisive importance, that Bédard's intervention appeared determinative in his circle after 1805. His transcendent role as the person who defined the political ideology and strategies of the French Canadian middle class best explains his rise as head of a party which at that time had its deepest roots in the region around Quebec. His links with English-speaking men such as John Neilson and Andrew and James* Stuart, whom he described as "friends of the Canadians," were also politically important. In addition, although it was very difficult to reconcile the ideas, interests, and ambitions of people from Quebec with those of Montrealers, Bédard was able to build bridges between the party activists from the two regions. There is no doubt that his belief in the virtues of the press as an instrument of political action was a significant factor in spreading his influence. His power, then, had a fragile personal base, but it rested on the cohesion of a group claiming to represent better than any other the aspirations of the French Canadian collectivity.

By 1791 Bédard had become an admirer of British institutions because, as he wrote in *Le Canadien* of 4 Nov. 1809, they allowed an apprenticeship to liberty, whereas under the monarchy of the *ancien régime* in France "the people counted for nothing, or less than nothing. A governor would have considered he was demeaning himself if he had let anyone contradict him in the slightest." In his view, the idea of liberty underlying the British constitution was not primarily democratic in nature; it was rather a concept of balance in the organization of political life: "We now enjoy a constitution under which everyone has his place, and in which a man is something. The people have their rights; the powers of a governor are laid down and he knows them; those in high places cannot go beyond the limits that the law sets on their authority. . . . Such a carefully determined balance exists between the people's rights and his that if he exceeds the limits the constitution has assigned him . . . the people have a sure and fair means of stopping him in his course." The vision of the British constitution that Bédard assimilated around 1791 and that he called to Governor Sir James Henry Craig*'s attention around 1809, was based on the then generally accepted theory of the balance of powers. Clarifying his thinking, Bédard added that the British constitution was "perhaps the only one under which the interests and rights of the various classes composing society are so carefully arranged, so wisely set off against one another and linked to one another as a whole, that they illuminate and sustain one another through the very conflict which results from the simultaneous exercise of the powers that are entrusted to [these classes]." Before 1800 he upheld this theory in the face of the danger presented to the society of Lower Canada by the French revolution and the intrigues of so-called French agents who had slipped into the colony. Under the circumstances the British constitution became to a greater degree an instrument of social harmony providing beneficial effects that extended from the governing classes to the masses. After the early part of the 19th century, however, his conception of constitutional equilibrium underwent considerable change.

This change stemmed from the development of a national awareness among the French Canadian middle classes. From Bédard's thought as expressed in his correspondence, his writings in *Le Canadien*, which had been founded in 1806, and the memoirs and petitions he formulated wholly or in part, emerges clearly the notion that the "nascent people" of which he spoke and the social class with which he identified himself were basically threatened not only from without but also from within the country. In a memorial of March 1806, addressed by the House of Assembly to the king objecting to the imposition of a land tax for the construction of jails, there were ideas which were new but which would often be set out by Bédard in *Le Canadien*. These focused on the pernicious role of the fur-based economy and of the merchants dominating it: "The Assembly respect this trade, however contrary it may be to the population of the country, and to the advancement of its Agriculture, on account of the benefits supposed to arise from it to the Empire in general; but did not conceive it necessary wholly to sacrifice to that trade the dearest interests of the country, particularly those of its population and Agriculture, which holds forth more certain grounds for its commerce and defence than the Fur Trade."

Bédard's thinking on these matters, and that of his immediate circle (especially Taschereau and Blanchet), was expressed, in condensed form, in a November 1814 address to the Prince Regent and an attached memoir. Bédard undoubtedly co-authored the address and wrote the initial draft of the memoir. Although he thus made a key contribution to these documents, they went through a process of discussion and development at the hands of the Canadian party's leaders and so also took on, to some degree, a representative character. As the memoir shows, at the outset of the 19th century Bédard maintained his faith in the British constitution and the principles on which it was founded, in particular that of the balance of powers, which simply transposed to the political sphere the balance of power within society. "We consider our present constitution as the one best fitted to create our happiness, and our greatest wish would be to be able to enjoy it in accord with the intention of *His Majesty and his parliament*," he wrote. During these crucial years, however, Bédard stood out from the majority of the assembly members and established himself as the leader of a fledgling political party whose ideology was in its formative stages. It was in the creation of an ideology and the establishment of its theoretical bases during the course of a struggle involving almost every group in society that Bédard played his chief role as leader, though even as a political organizer he was hardly

Bédard

flamboyant. He was convinced that the French Canadian problem and nationalism as they were emerging had an origin that was political before it was social. Discussing the 1791 constitution, which in principle, he suggested in the memorial, was supposed to translate the existing social forces into the sphere of power, he observed: "Unfortunately the manner in which it has until now been administered imparts to it an effect quite contrary to this intention." Without hesitation, although not without contradicting himself to some extent, he attributed the responsibility for these distortions to the inordinate influence of a racial and social minority.

The absolute power of the English-speaking minority was, in Bédard's view, manifest throughout the political system except in the House of Assembly, where the true representatives of the Canadian people dominated. The influence of talentless office holders, and of greedy merchants supported by their henchmen – Canadians who had sold out or were sycophants – and that of ordinary English-speaking people who were dependent upon them was so great that the governors themselves gave in to them and became the tools of a malevolent clique. In the memorial he explained: "A governor cannot have the English party, the party of the government, on his side without adopting all its ideas, prejudices, and plans against the Canadians. . . . There will be very few governors with enough abilities to fight against so many disadvantages and with lofty enough virtue to do what they believe to be their duty in the best interests of the mother country."

According to Bédard, the members of the English-speaking bourgeoisie, far from being content to manipulate the governors in areas where the latter had the actual or virtual power to make final decisions, also used them to see that their views prevailed in England. He claimed that the governors "cannot help acquiring in short order the same prejudices . . . which they no doubt pass on to the government of the mother country." In addition to using ordinary channels to malign the Canadians, the English-speaking minority thus used the king's representatives for the task. This was a theme to which Bédard frequently reverted during his political career, and even after becoming a judge, in order to demonstrate the frustrations of his middle-class compatriots and the humiliation weighing upon the Canadians as a people. He went so far as to state in the 1814 memoir that the English party "has an interest in having them thought disloyal; it has an interest in governing them in such a fashion as to make them appear that way, in such a fashion even as to make them so, in order that they will so appear." The constant intervention of the English oligarchy upset the constitutional balance and tended to shape social relations according to its aims.

Bédard's extraordinary sensitivity on the patronage question reflected an awareness in the group he represented of the socio-economic disparities between the two ethnic elements and of the significance of these disparities for both the Canadian élite and the ordinary people. The leader of the Canadian party did not hesitate to ascribe these disparities to the practices of a profoundly unjust political régime, one dominated by a minority that monopolized patronage and set itself up as the exclusive beneficiary of royal favours. "When we were given our constitution," he recalled in the memoir, "the long-time subjects (called English here, whatever nation they belong to) were in possession of government places. If a few Canadians were admitted to them, it was on their recommendation, and they were chosen from among those who were devoted to them. Since the constitution, things have gone on in the same way, the old subjects have continued in possession of the places and have become the government party; the channel for recommendations continues to be the same, and, as before, only a few Canadians, whose devotion was known, have been admitted to places."

Thus the instrument of patronage was supposed to have been manipulated in order to fashion Canadians into what it was desired they should be: inferior and disloyal. The satisfaction of patronage demands in the judiciary had also meant that confusion and even seeds of destruction had been introduced into national institutions, particularly into the Coutume de Paris. "Our property laws have fallen into oblivion so that we might have on the bench judges from [the government] party who knew nothing about them," Bédard declared in the 1814 memoir. For him, the result was that the old laws, rules of practice, and procedures had often been changed to make room for new laws not conforming to needs. Between one change and another the judicial system had been completely upset and the reign of the arbitrary had been permanently installed. The presence of judges in the House of Assembly and the Legislative and Executive councils had been but the logical consequence of these intrigues to enslave the Canadians.

The universal pursuit of "place" by the English-speaking oligarchy, according to Bédard, also helped account for the impotence of the House of Assembly, the organ of the majority of the population, which by force of circumstances had been relegated to an opposition role. It was not surprising in these conditions that ethnic divisions had increasingly polarized the political commitment of individuals and groups. Bédard maintained in the 1814 memoir that, before spreading through the population, nationalism had taken shape on the political scene: "The divisions in the House of Assembly become national, the English on one side forming the minority, with which the government is allied, and the Canadians on the other forming the majority, to which is attached the mass of the people; the heat of these national divisions *passes from the House of Assembly to the people*. The whole country is divided into two: the English government party on one side, the mass of the people on the other."

Bédard's thesis was designed to reveal the universal character of the offensive being waged by the English-speaking minority against the French Canadian nation and its institutions. The efforts by this group to reduce the House of Assembly to impotence had had no aim but to imbue the majority of the assembly, and needless to say the nation it represented, with the "sense of its own degradation." Bédard was even convinced that this strategy, dictated by racial hatred and the thirst for "place," bore within it the Machiavellian scheme of engulfing the French Canadian population by prompting American immigration on a massive scale. As he explained it, colonial officials had an interest in so doing since they had cornered the crown lands close to the United States and wanted to have them worked by settlers from the other side of the border to "get rid of the Canadians"; it was already a known fact that the Canadians needed these lands to survive as an agricultural nation. On the matter of this immigration, which constituted a threat to the French-speaking population, Bédard commented: "Thus *the English party is opposed to the Canadian party*, precisely on the point that concerns its life and its existence as a people."

Because he was aware of the peril that Americans represented from the military and demographic point of view and from the economic and cultural one as well, and because he was convinced the British government was not an accomplice of the colonial oligarchy then deceiving it, Bédard attributed great importance to the protective role of Great Britain and its institutions. "So long as the country remains under the rule of Great Britain," he asserted in the memoir, the Canadians "do not have the same dangers to fear; they do not have to fear that a population hostile to their religion will emigrate from the domains of the mother country; they have hope that their population will always be the largest in the country, and that with a constitution such as the one the mother country has granted them they will have the means of preserving their religion and all that is dear to them, provided that the mother country is willing to let them enjoy this constitution without its being used to make them odious." Finally, Bédard believed that the authorities in London and Canadians through attachment to their country had such similar interests that "engulfing the Canadian population by the American population would mean engulfing the mother country's domination over [them], and the loss by the Canadians, as a nascent people, of their political life would also mean the loss of political life by the whole country, as a British colony."

Bédard had the feeling that the Canadians were the victims of a "strange contradiction" between the principles on which the constitution was based and the use that had been made of it since 1791. In theory he did not reject the principle of the balance of power, but to resolve the contradiction he was denouncing, he was led during his struggle against the government to call the principle into question in concrete terms, to advocate the supremacy of legislative authority, and to advance the principle of ministerial responsibility.

Historians are not of one mind in their assessment of Bédard's role as party leader in formulating the theory of ministerial responsibility in the first decade of the 19th century. There is a historiographic tradition going back at least to Aileen Dunham that tends to minimize the contribution made by the leader of the Canadian party to the elaboration of that political theory, laying emphasis instead on Robert Baldwin*, one of the reform leaders in Upper Canada from the late 1820s. In support of her assertions Dunham uses several arguments that are not really convincing. She writes: "It would appear, therefore, that the theory of responsible government, as distinct from the practice, had not been worked out or clearly expressed in Great Britain much before the Reform Act. Were the colonists more clear-sighted than the mother country?" She also insists that existing racial divisions prevented the setting-up of political parties in Lower Canada, an indispensable condition, in her view, for the advent of ministerial responsibility. She is obliged, however, to recognize that very early the political leaders in Lower Canada had made use of the weapon of impeachment and had therefore posed the problem of the legal and personal responsibility of the governor's councillors to the representatives of the people. The main elements of this thesis are also taken up by Frank Hawkins Underhill* and Lawrence A. H. Smith. Then there is a group of historians who give exaggerated importance to Bédard's perspicacity in the development of the concept of ministerial responsibility. They often recognize the innovative character of the analyses made by the leader of the Canadian party, but imply that he had more or less falsely attributed to the English in their own country a theory that was not put in practice there until after 1830. These two interpretations put the emphasis on the personal qualities of the agent in history.

It is obvious that since he defended the interests and values of a social class within a threatened nation, it was to Bédard's advantage, with a view to obtaining power, to take up the question of ministerial responsibility, which had been under debate for a long time in England. Quoting constitutional expert Alpheus Todd*, historian Anthony Harold Birch notes: "The great principle of ministerial responsibility . . . is a natural consequence of the system of Parliamentary government which was introduced by the revolution of 1688." From 1780 to 1832 there evolved in England

Bédard

the concept of the legal and personal responsibility of the king's advisers which culminated in the notion of the ministers' collective responsibility before the House of Commons and the nation, rather than before the courts of justice. Thus the principle of the supremacy of the legislative authority was admitted. At the beginning of the 19th century Bédard had detected, to his advantage, the essential tendency of the British constitution at a time when it escaped the attention of most English politicians.

When Bédard was formulating his ideas on the nature of the British constitution, he did not deal with the question from the point of view of the legal and personal responsibility of the sovereign's councillors. He started from the principle that neither the king nor his representative could err. Subsequently, writing in *Le Canadien* of 31 Jan. 1807, he demonstrated the essential character of the "ministry" in the balance of powers within the constitution: "As if there could be an administration without a ministry. . . . It is even a maxim of our ministry that there is no ministry here and that it is the governor who runs everything. This maxim, which tends to make the king's representative responsible for all the ministers' advice is as unjust as [it is] unconstitutional in that it lays the king's representative open to the danger of losing the people's confidence through his ministers' errors." According to the leader of the Canadian party, who was an attentive reader of Sir William Blackstone, Jean-Louis De Lolme, and John Locke, the balance of power within the constitution must be decided by the principle of the supremacy of the legislative branch over the executive authority. On Blackstone and Locke he observed in *Le Canadien* of 3 June 1809: "They demonstrate that the executive authority does not have the right to exercise any censorship over the branches of the legislature; that the executive authority, as such, is subordinate to the legislative authority, and that, as it is one of the branches of the legislature, although first in rank and dignity, the other branches are in no way subordinate to it." If Bédard still believed in the balance of power as a theory, evidently that balance had to tilt towards the legislative authority. Otherwise how could one justify the responsibility of the "ministers" before the House of Assembly?

Naturally Bédard had to be prudent and avoid vigorous exchanges of views on ideas that called in question the governor's authority, the powers of the British minority, and even the authority of the home government over its colony in matters of interest to the province. Although initially a radical, he displayed more prudence with the passage of time, especially after his arrest in 1810, and also after his appointment as a judge in 1812. Bédard had been one of those who had most vehemently denounced judges' participation in party politics. The 1814 memoir, to which he made an important contribution, offers a suggestion: "If it is

just that the governors be acquainted with both parties and that they refuse to entertain accusations against the inhabitants of the country without giving them a hearing, it is just that the latter also have a formal means of receiving a hearing from members of council and *placemen* chosen from among them, and that those members of council *not be appointed on recommendations made through the regular channel.* . . . If the governor *had the authority* to call to the council the principal members of the majority in the House of Assembly, he would in that way have the means of hearing both parties." A little later the memoir again outlines this proposition: "If it were possible for a number of *places on the council or other places of honour and profit to be given those who have the greatest influence on the majority in the House of Assembly, for [those places] to depend entirely on their success in keeping themselves there, and for it to be known generally and with certainty that there would be no other way of obtaining them, there is* reason to assume that the two parties would swiftly come together in the House of Assembly, that [the present] division of the country so contrary to the government's aim would disappear both within and without the assembly."

Although the memoir stated that the governor should not feel bound by the advice so given and that the "ministry" would be composed of men from both parties, in truth the system recommended was designed to bind the members of the council to those in control of the assembly, and in the final analysis to the nation as the primary source of sovereignty. The basic assumption was that no governor could go against the wishes of the majority. To read what Bédard asserted in the prospectus for *Le Canadien*, published 13 Nov. 1806, about the liberty of the press is to understand the true significance of the 1814 memoir: "It is this liberty of the press that makes England's constitution fit to create the happiness of the peoples that are under its protection. . . . Under England's constitution the people enjoy the right to make themselves known through the liberty of the press, and by the free dissemination of its sentiments the whole nation becomes, as it were, privy councillor to the government." In *Le Canadien* of 24 Jan. 1807 he went further in his analysis, leaving little doubt about his real intentions: "The ministry must of necessity have the majority in the House of Commons. As soon as it loses the influence that provides it with [this majority] or its policies no longer seem sound, it is dismissed. It also sometimes happens that when the king wishes to know which of the two sets of policies, the ministry's or the opposition's, the nation wishes to adopt, he dissolves parliament. The nation then exercises its judgement by electing those whose plan of action and conduct it approves of. . . . The new ministry is formed in accordance with the nation's feeling as shown by the choice of the persons whose approach it adopts. That ministry is certain of being supported by the House of Commons and the nation, so long as it does not depart from its principles."

Bédard was not primarily seeking means to punish, but rather an overall solution to a political problem that in his view had been created by the manipulation of institutions for the benefit of a particular ethnic minority. That was why he was basically concerned with the fundamental aspect of ministerial responsibility: the collective responsibility of the governor's advisers before the House of Assembly and the people. To set in motion a new political dynamic, this time for the benefit of another social class representing the ethnic majority, was his primary aim. In the circumstances the reform he suggested was designed to effect a radical change in political and social power. It is therefore understandable that the legal aspect of ministerial responsibility had been of but secondary importance in his eyes. By contrast, in the period prior to 1830 when the Canadian party under James Stuart and Louis-Joseph Papineau displayed greater moderation in its demands for reform, there was frequent recourse to impeachment of the governor's advisers. It was only one of a number of means to assert the need for control of the executive by the assembly.

Bédard's political thinking was not only innovative; in the context of the times it contained a revolutionary aspect, because it implied calling into question the governor's role and the traditional relations between the mother country and the colony. In this perspective the idea of ministerial responsibility was the one that best served to focus all of his actions as party leader. His efforts in 1808 to have judges excluded from the assembly [see Pierre-Amable De Bonne], like his project in 1810 to get an appointed agent of the assembly in England so that a Canadian version of things might be conveyed to that country, also arose from concerns encompassing all of his political concepts. The Canadian party's proposal to the British government in 1810 that the assembly be allowed to take over responsibility for the colony's expenditures followed logically from this thinking; it also set off a long series of struggles which, as they developed, would, in the period when Papineau was leader, pose the problem of the responsibility of the executive before the assembly in a somewhat less radical and less defined fashion. The fears expressed by Governor Craig regarding the 1810 proposal were well founded, since Bédard sought to strengthen the assembly's ascendancy over the executive and the holders of office by ensuring its control of finances. Because he was well aware of what had been the practice in colonial New York, he was in a position to urge the leaders of the party who came after him to claim for the assembly the right to vote the civil list annually and in detail.

Bédard was not primarily a man of letters engaged mainly in developing quite abstract theories with no concrete relevance for the moment; he was the leader of a political party whose ideas tended to alter profoundly the balance between existing forces. In 1807 the insecurity created by the operation of Napoleon's "continental system" against England and the mounting tensions with the United States only served to heighten the hostility that Governor Craig already felt for those who might disturb the peace inside the colony. He gradually became convinced that the people running the Canadian party were little more than individuals of an inferior station who were either nationalists or demagogues and who were frustrated because they were unable to take over as many prestigious and lucrative positions as they aspired to. Not content merely to call them revolutionaries, he even accused them of being ready to play into the hands of France and the United States in such critical circumstances. Having come to this conclusion, in June 1808 he deprived Bédard, Jean-Antoine Panet*, Taschereau, Joseph Levasseur-Borgia*, and Blanchet of their militia commissions. He had been annoyed at the attitude taken by the leaders of the Canadian party on the issue of the ineligibility of judges to sit in the House of Assembly, and his indignation reached its peak when the majority of the assembly voted to exclude Ezekiel Hart*, the new member from Trois-Rivières, who was of the Jewish faith. In May 1809 Craig therefore dissolved the assembly and appealed to the electorate. He suffered a defeat, and was forced to repeat the same scenario in March 1810. On 17 March he had Charles LEFRANÇOIS, the printer of Le Canadien, arrested and his presses seized. Two days later those responsible for the newspaper, Bédard, Blanchet, and Taschereau, were also thrown into prison on charges of carrying on treasonable activities. In the summer of 1810 Blanchet and Taschereau were released because of ill health, but Bédard remained incarcerated. He demanded a formal trial or an unconditional discharge. He was finally released in March 1811. He expected to emerge from prison triumphant and thus to find his hold on the leadership of the Canadian party strengthened, but within the party, and particularly in Montreal, his rivals were seeing to it that little fuss was made over him. Bédard remembered this with bitterness until his dying day. In 1819 he declared: "Mr Papineau and Mr Viger are no real friends of mine." It was with this episode that his political career came to an end.

It became even less possible to patch up matters when the new governor, Sir George Prevost*, after weighing the various opinions in Lower Canadian society decided to rely upon the most representative groups and to isolate the elements considered extremist. Some of these – for example Herman Witsius Ryland* and Jacob MOUNTAIN – were simply exclud-

Bédard

ed from power. In addition Prevost made use of patronage to win over vocal and influential individuals or to neutralize them. Bédard fell into this category: in 1812 he was offered a judgeship on the Court of King's Bench at Trois-Rivières. The former head of the Canadian party, who had been inclined to call French-speaking persons placed in such a situation *chouayens* and to castigate them as "sycophants" and "vendus," considered his own situation to be different. He accepted the post, and in the end rationalized the whole affair, interpreting Prevost's gesture as reparation for unjust imprisonment. In 1817 he observed: "I regarded this offer as recognition on the part of the government of its error with regard to me; otherwise I should certainly never have accepted it and I should be ready to hand back the place if it had not been given me in this way." He was not as ready to give up his position as he said he was. A few years earlier a pamphlet antagonistic to him had made him so indignant that he had almost asked the governor to relieve him of his duties. He had gone so far indeed that, as he confided to John Neilson, "I have put my place so close to falling through my hands that I am almost obliged to ask for it again in order not to lose it."

At Trois-Rivières judge Bédard led an uncomfortable, restless existence filled with dramatic events, in sum an unhappy one. Even his relations with his fellow judges and lawyers were apparently stormy at times. At bottom he had never really left the world of politics. In 1814 he still revealed an inability to make a true break with the past: "I think that I made a very poor move in accepting the place I have here. It scarcely seems possible to me to hold on to one without being of everyone else's opinion. . . . I am ill at ease, torn between conflicting interests and duties; although I have a place I do not feel free to exempt myself from contributing to what is needed for the good of the country. For twopence I would give up my place to become again as I was. Poor, it is true, destitute, but happier; but I have creditors, I have a family, I am in sad straits." In time his commitment to politics became less direct and less open, but it remained none the less real. It was mainly through Neilson, his intellectual mentor, that he made known his views on the role of newspapers in political life, the problem of providing for the civil establishment, the rivalries within the Canadian party between Quebec and Montreal, and the importance of the townships given the surplus of population on the seigneuries. On one occasion, however, he leaped back into political activity: at the time of the proposed union of Upper and Lower Canada in 1822, a sense of the danger it represented led him to join in the opposition. He even agreed to chair the protest committee for the district of Trois-Rivières. He was delegated by the militants from his district to go to

England with Neilson and Papineau, but was unable to carry out the mission since he could not obtain leave from the governor. In 1828 he was again mentioned as one of the delegates of the Patriote party (the name applied to the Canadian party from 1826) to be sent to England.

Since 1810 the nationalist movement embodied in the Canadian party had continued to grow under the impact of economic, demographic, and social conditions. With time, however, the centre of the movement had shifted from the Quebec region to Montreal. This evolution had also been reflected in the party leadership. When a successor to Bédard had to be found after 1810, there was no lack of candidates: such men as Levasseur-Borgia, Blanchet, Taschereau, Bourdages, Pierre-Dominique Debartzch*, and Viger could all lay claim to the succession. But in the end adherents rallied around James Stuart, a "bon anglais" from Quebec who could be nothing but a transitional leader. Indeed a new leader was emerging in the period between 1815 and 1818 in the person of Papineau. Still young but fully aware of the fragility of his power, Papineau adopted some of Bédard's methods. To obtain solid support in the Quebec region and among the English-speaking population, he joined forces with Neilson and Andrew Stuart. For a decade or so, for all sorts of reasons, he was obliged to confine himself to limited goals. Hence the question of ministerial responsibility, which was considered too radical, was not put forward as such, and until 1828 Papineau restricted the struggle to the control of supplies.

Bédard, who was intelligent, talented, and sensitive to his own woes, was probably obsessed by an awareness of having failed politically and of having tasted the forbidden fruit of patronage, but he was even more weighed down by the torments of his family life. Quite soon after his marriage, disagreement had become a permanent feature of his home, which he described as "hell." He reproached his wife for being untidy, frivolous, and spendthrift, casting the entire responsibility for their chronic indebtedness upon her. The incompatibility between the two was, however, much deeper and more complex than it first appeared. On the one hand, feeling overwhelmed, Bédard asked: "Why must I be sacrificed to serving her as a vile instrument of a husband?" On the other hand, in the conviction that his wife did not accept "her condition as a woman," he wrote: "I reproach her for only one [fault], that of being rebellious to my wishes . . . [my] great error is that I am no longer able to control her." Their relations deteriorated to the point that around 1815 they were seriously considering a legal separation, although it never did come about. The permanent state of crisis naturally had repercussions on the children, who were forced to witness the constant strife. Bédard later gave an explanation of the difficulty he experienced with his sons: "I attribute it to the unfortunate circumstances of my household and to the greater affection the children have always had for their mother."

The Bédards had had four sons. Pierre-Hospice, born on 21 May 1797, became a lawyer in 1823 and moved to the United States permanently in 1828. Elzéar*, born on 24 July 1799, was called to the bar on 17 Aug. 1824, and then in 1832 entered the assembly as member for Montmorency; he became the first mayor of Quebec in 1833 and a judge in Montreal in 1836. JOSEPH-ISIDORE was born on 9 Jan. 1806; on 12 Oct. 1829 he too was admitted to the bar, and in 1830 he became member of the assembly for Saguenay. The youngest son, François-Zoël, born in 1812, was a lighthouse keeper at Pointe-des-Monts, where he learned the Montagnais language.

Pierre-Stanislas Bédard, whose name is closely linked with the birth of political parties in Lower Canada and of Quebec nationalism, was the first person in the British empire to formulate in a coherent manner the theory of ministerial responsibility. He died in Trois-Rivières on 26 April 1829. His wife outlived him and died on 20 Feb. 1831.

FERNAND OUELLET

[Pierre-Stanislas Bédard's "Notes de philosophie, mathématiques, chimie, physique, grammaire, politique et journal, 1798–1810" is at ASQ, MSS-M 241. The collections essential for understanding his career and personality include the Papineau family papers at ANQ-Q (P-417); the Viger–Verreau papers at ASQ (sér.O, 095–125; 0139–52); the Papineau family and Denis-Benjamin Viger papers at the PAC (MG 24, B2, and B6); and in particular the Neilson collection at PAC (MG 24, B1), which contains valuable correspondence by Bédard. The newspaper Le Canadien is an indispensable source on this leader of the first political party in Lower Canada, and Bédard also figures prominently in all textbooks. F.O.]

ANQ-Q, CE1-1, 26 juill. 1796; CE1-7, 14 sept. 1762. F.-J. Audet et Fabre Surveyer, Les députés au premier Parl. du Bas-Canada. Claude de Bonnault, "Le Canada militaire: état provisoire des officiers de milice de 1641 à 1760," ANQ Rapport, 1949–51: 263–527. David Gosselin, Dictionnaire généalogique des familles de Charlesbourg depuis la fondation de la paroisse jusqu'à nos jours (Québec, 1906). Henri Brun, La formation des institutions parlementaires québécoises, 1791–1838 (Québec, 1970). Caron, La colonisation de la prov. de Québec. N.-E. Dionne, Pierre Bédard et ses fils (Québec, 1909). A. L. Guay, "'La constitution anglaise' and 'the British constitution' as seen in the editorial thought of Le Canadien and the Quebec Mercury, 1804–1823" (MA thesis, Univ. of Ottawa, 1975). Ouellet, Bas-Canada; Éléments d'histoire sociale du Bas-Canada (Montréal, 1972); Hist. économique. Paquet et Wallot, Patronage et pouvoir dans le Bas-Canada. Taft Manning, Revolt of French Canada. Marcel Trudel, La population du Canada en 1663 (Montréal, 1973); Le terrier du Saint-Laurent en 1663 (Ottawa, 1973). Wallot, Un Québec qui bougeait. N.-E. Dionne, "Pierre

Bédard et son temps," RSC Trans., 2nd ser., 4 (1898), sect.I: 73–93. Arthur Maheux, "Pierre Stanislas Bédard, 1763–1829: philosophe et savant," RSC Trans., 3rd ser., 50 (1956), sect.I: 85–93. Fernand Ouellet, "Officiers de milice et structure sociale au Québec (1660–1815)," SH, 12 (1979): 37–66. L. A. H. Smith, "Le Canadien and the British constitution, 1806–1810," CHR, 38 (1957): 93–108.

BELLET, FRANÇOIS (baptized **Antoine-François**), ship's captain, militiaman, businessman, office holder, and politician; b. 2 Nov. 1750 at Quebec, son of François Bellet and Marie-Anne Réaume, widow of Jean-Baptiste Gadiou; d. there 19 Feb. 1827.

Trained as a navigator, François Bellet became engaged at an early age in the St Lawrence River coasting trade of his father, a native of the diocese of La Rochelle, France. They operated out of Lower Town Quebec, where by 1775 young Bellet had begun to acquire property. During the American invasion of the province in 1775–76 [see Benedict Arnold*; Richard Montgomery*] they served together in the Canadian militia at Quebec. At the same time Bellet's father gained a reputation for his daring exploits running gunpowder for the British on the St Lawrence. For the next two decades at least, father and son were active as navigators, probably in some loose association which enabled them to meet the heavy seasonal demands of such mercantile clients as George Allsopp* and William Grant* of Quebec. The younger Bellet was the owner and master of at least one vessel, the schooner Magdelaine, built at Bécancour in 1774. In the early 1800s he established a small mercantile business in Lower Town. He sold the Magdelaine in 1804 to Hypolithe Duvilleray, another navigator, and became more involved in the purchase, sale, and rental of farm and town properties in the Quebec area, particularly in Charlesbourg, where his father lived, and in the Montreal region, where he was often represented by the notary Louis Guy*. In 1804 he was granted lots in Somerset Township, Buckingham County.

Bellet's permanence of residence, and possibly the influence of his father, who lived until 1812, was a factor in his decision to seek public office. In 1804 in Lower Town and five years later in York County, north of Montreal, he ran without success for election to the Lower Canadian House of Assembly. In June 1805 he secured appointment as an assistant examiner of pilots for the port of Quebec, a position he would hold for 12 years. In the spring of 1810 he was elected to the assembly to represent York with Pierre Saint-Julien. A long-time friend of Joseph Papineau*, Pierre-Stanislas BÉDARD, and other lights in the Canadian party, Bellet spent much time electioneering in Quebec County, where Joseph-François Perrault*, and possibly Ralph Gray*, both candidates, bitterly resented "the activity of the Bellets, the Lageux, the

Bellet

Langlois, the *Le Blonds*, and the *Germains*, (known firebrands)." By March, when Governor Sir James Henry Craig* seized the party's newspaper, *Le Canadien*, Bellet had joined Bédard, Jacques Leblond, François BLANCHET, Joseph Levasseur-Borgia*, Thomas Lee, and François HUOT as co-proprietors of that journal's printing establishment, the Imprimerie Canadienne. Though *Le Canadien* would not resume publication for several years, Bellet retained his share in the press's other printing operations as one business interest among others.

Bellet's participation in politics on the side of the Canadian party did not prevent him from obtaining other appointments. In 1811, he became, with John MURE and John Hale*, a commissioner to obtain plans for new parliament buildings; in 1815 a commissioner along with Andrew Stuart* and the notary Félix Têtu for the repair of Quebec's jail and court-house; and in 1817 a warden of Trinity House of Quebec [*see* François Boucher*]. He also held non-governmental offices, serving as a warden of Notre-Dame cathedral and as an inspector for the Quebec Fire Society. In 1814 he subscribed to the Quebec Free School, a non-sectarian institution founded by Thaddeus Osgood*. Five years later he was a manager of the Quebec Dispensary, a benevolent medical centre [*see* Anthony von Iffland*], and in 1821 he was a subscriber to the Quebec Emigrants' Society. In the general election of 1814 Bellet had been returned to the assembly for Buckingham along with James Stuart*, who was succeeded by Louis BOURDAGES (1815–16) and Joseph BADEAUX (1816–20). For the next six years Bellet continued to support, in the house and in public addresses, the nationalistic positions of the Canadian party, increasingly led by Louis-Joseph Papineau*, on such issues as the control of civil expenditure and patronage.

Meanwhile, in 1811 Bellet had taken his clerk, Jean-Olivier Brunet, into partnership, forming François Bellet et Cie. Their agreement expired five years later, but they carried on for two more years as Bellet et Brunet. During this period Bellet's domestic life had not been without incident. His first wife, Cécile Flamme, whom he had married at Quebec on 12 July 1773, died in 1815, and his marriage in Beaumont on 15 Sept. 1817 at the age of 67 to his maid, Marie-Honoré Fournier, provoked a charivari, the mood of which – light and comical or bizarre and derisive – is not certain. On a dark night in October the Bellets were drawn to their door by four men with faces blackened. They carried lanterns suspended from long poles and an illuminated paper coffin, and the din they made upon a fife, a drum, and pots attracted a small gang of street urchins. According to one account, a member of the group, perched on the shoulders of two companions, delivered a mock funeral oration on Mme Bellet, and to calm the men Bellet gave them

100 *piastres* to let them drink to the newly-weds' health. According to a second account, efforts by soldiers to pacify the rowdy band failed, and the men promised to return "all winter" unless Bellet gave them 25 guineas for the poor, which he was "obliged" to hand over. Marie-Honoré died in August 1820.

That year, within months of his re-election in Buckingham, Bellet retired from both politics and Trinity House for reasons that are not clear, though his wife's death may have been a factor. He nevertheless remained active in business, and he continued to maintain mercantile connections in England and Scotland. His activities ranged from investment in the Quebec Bank and the Quebec Fire Assurance Company, through the renting out or sale of properties, to the provision of supplies for shipwrecked seamen on Anticosti Island. In 1820, possibly to facilitate his trade, he had bought a schooner from Antoine Mayrant, a mariner in Sainte-Anne-de-la-Pérade (La Pérade). Bellet's third marriage, in the chapel of the Hôpital Général at Quebec on 4 March 1822 to Mary Robinson, a widow, probably developed from his mercantile contacts; her former husband, Gavin Major Hamilton, had been a merchant at Quebec, and her brother Webb, to whom Bellet would rent property, still was. About 1823 Bellet moved to the *faubourg* Saint-Jean and appears to have withdrawn from business, though numerous sums were still owing to him, including more than £500 by Brunet, who may have purchased his stock.

By 1827 Bellet's health had given out. In early February Louis-Joseph Papineau found him "dangerously ill," and on the 19th he died in the Hôpital Général. Among the respectful witnesses at his burial in the hospital chapel two days later were Andrew Stuart and Papineau with his brother-in-law Jean DESSAULLES.

DAVID ROBERTS

ANQ-Q, CE1-1, 2 nov. 1750, 12 juill. 1773; CE1-93, 4 mars 1822, 21 févr. 1827; CN1-116, 8 août, 5 sept. 1820; 20 févr., 28 avril, 14 mai, 15, 18 juin, 6 août, 15 nov. 1821; 29 mars, 12 avril, 15 mai 1822; 22 avril, 12 mai 1823; 31 mars 1824; 1er mars 1825; 2 janv. 1826; CN1-178, 12 janv., 30 mars 1813; CN1-205, 8 févr. 1775; CN1-230, 13 févr. 1798, 20 déc. 1803, 31 mars 1804, 28 mai 1811. AUM, P 58, U, Bellet à Louis Guy, 20 mars, 15 déc. 1806; 19 sept. 1808; 30 juin 1809; Bellet à André Guy, 5, 25 nov. 1818. PAC, MG 23, GII, 3, vol.3, E. W. Gray to William Grant, 13 Nov. 1786; GIII, 1, vol.2: 41; MG 24, B2: 363–72; L3: 8126, 8167; MG 30, D1, 4: 268–73, 280, 282; RG 1, L3ᴸ: 1291, 2098, 2646, 20603–38; RG 4, A1: 26969–71, 35953–57; 144: 93–93a; 145: 86; 147: 176; 165: 124; RG 8, I (C ser.), 600: 173–74; 714: 120; RG 31, C1, 1825, Quebec: 1786; RG 42, E1, 1382: 6; RG 68, General index, 1651–1841: 5, 226, 272, 698. *American arch.* (Clarke and Force), 4th ser., 4: 854. "Blockade of Quebec in 1775–1776 by the American revolutionists (les Bastonnais)," ed. F. C. Würtele, Literary and Hist. Soc. of Quebec, *Hist. Docs.* (Quebec), 7th ser. (1905): 274. L.C., House of Assembly, *Journals*, 1814–20. Joseph Papineau, "Correspondance de Joseph Papineau (1793–1840)," Fernand Ouellet, édit., ANQ *Rapport*, 1951–53: 175. L.-J. Papineau, "Correspondance de Louis-Joseph Papineau (1820–1839)," Fernand Ouellet, édit., ANQ *Rapport*, 1953–55: 246. *Quebec Gazette*, 12 Dec. 1776; 1 April 1779; 3 Nov. 1785; 13 March 1788; 28 Jan. 1790; 10 July 1794; 12 March 1795; 11 Jan. 1798; 31 Jan., 21 March, 18 July 1799; 10 April 1800; 14 May 1801; 26 May 1803; 10 May, 14 June 1804; 27 June 1805; 12 June 1806; 9 April, 9 July 1807; 8, 22 Dec. 1808; 2 March, 8 June, 14 Sept., 19 Oct., 16 Nov. 1809; 5, 19, 26 April 1910; 11 April, 2, 23 May, 6 June, 11 July 1811; 19 March, 17 Sept. 1812; 30 Dec. 1813; 25 May, 22 June, 24 Aug., 19 Oct. 1815; 4 April, 9, 16 May 1816; 16 Jan., 12 June, 25 Sept. 1817; 8 Jan., 20 April, 21 May, 9 July, 31 Dec. 1818; 4 Feb., 13 May, 19 Aug., 2 Dec. 1819; 17 Jan., 20 March, 13, 20 April, 5 June, 21, 24 Aug. 1820; 16 April, 26 Nov. 1821; 21 April 1823.

Quebec almanac, 1820: 138. Geneviève G. Bastien *et al.*, *Inventaire des marchés de construction des archives civiles de Québec, 1800–1870* (3v., Ottawa, 1975), 1: no.426. Beaulieu et Hamelin, *La presse québécoise*, 1: 16. P.-V. Charland, "Notre-Dame de Québec: le nécrologe de la crypte ou les inhumations dans cette église depuis 1652," *BRH*, 20 (1914): 279. Desjardins, *Guide parl.*, 125, 144. *Mariages et nécrologe de Beaumont, 1692–1974*, Rosaire Saint-Pierre, compil. (Québec, 1975), 17. "Papiers d'État – Bas-Canada," PAC *Rapport*, 1896: 70. P.-G. Roy, *Fils de Québec*, 2: 88–89. Tanguay, *Dictionnaire*, 2: 212. N.-E. Dionne, *Pierre Bédard et ses fils* (Québec, 1909), 243. Lanctot, *Canada & American revolution*, 93. Ouellet, *Lower Canada*, 186. P.-G. Roy, *Les cimetières de Québec* (Lévis, Qué., 1941), 147; *Toutes petites choses du Régime anglais*, 1: 194–95, 224–26. Albertine Ferland-Angers, "La citadelle de Montréal (1658–1820)," *RHAF*, 3 (1949–50): 506. L. A. H. Smith, "*Le Canadien* and the British constitution, 1806–1810," *CHR*, 38 (1957): 94–95. Benjamin Sulte, "L'exploit du capitaine Bouchette," *BRH*, 5 (1899): 318. "Un charivari à Québec," *BRH*, 44 (1938): 242–43.

BEMAN, ELISHA, businessman, JP, and office holder; b. 1760 in New York; married and had four children; m. secondly 5 Sept. 1802 Esther Sayre, widow of Christopher Robinson*, and they had a daughter; d. 14 Oct. 1821 in Newmarket, Upper Canada.

Elisha Beman settled at York (Toronto), Upper Canada, in 1795. He opened a tavern and also ran a mercantile business supplying provisions and baked goods. Beman prospered and became one of the town's more substantial residents. During the late 1790s he was involved with several proposals which, had they materialized, would have taken him from York. First, as a result of the government's interest in improving communications along Yonge Street to Lake Simcoe and beyond, on 6 Oct. 1798 Beman applied to Administrator Peter Russell* for 1,000 acres of land. He proposed to settle at the northern end of the Toronto portage, or on the Severn River, where

he would then open an inn, clear land, and keep horses and cattle. He also offered to run a ferry on Lake Simcoe and, when settlement occurred, to build grist- and saw-mills. He thought the capital for development could be provided from the "fruits of his own Industry and the produce of the Sale of his property elsewhere." In response the Executive Council granted him a town lot in York and 1,000 acres, in recognition of "his great and arduous exertions in providing the town with provisions at a time when no other persons had attempted it." The following spring the councillors permitted him to buy another 1,000 acres at 6*d*. per acre. Secondly, Beman was associated briefly with Abel STEVENS in a project to establish an iron foundry in the Gananoque area. On 11 Feb. 1799 they outlined their proposal in a petition in which they noted that in order to satisfy the government of the scheme's soundness, Beman had been recruited as one having "an established Credit in Montreal and who being bred to the Business and having for a long time followed it in the Neighbouring States, serves in a twofold Capacity to empower them to commence the intended manufacture."

Beman acquired a number of local offices. He was elected town assessor and surveyor of highways in 1799 and was appointed a commissioner of dry measures on 17 Oct. 1801. In order that they "might Keep good rule and order in their respective houses," tavernkeepers such as Beman were appointed constables. He was a constable for York in 1801, the Home District in 1802, and Whitchurch Township in 1805. A greater mark of distinction was his first commission as justice of the peace for the Home District, issued on 5 April 1803; his last commission, after successive reappointments, was dated 13 March 1820.

Shortly after his second marriage in 1802, Beman and his family moved north to a house built by Peter Robinson* near the Holland River. He continued, however, to operate his business in York for some years. In 1803 he bought a lot with a mill (or he may, in fact, have built the mill that summer) on the site of present-day Newmarket; a year later he sold it to Joseph Hill, from whom he bought half of the adjoining lot on which stood a house, a mill, and a store. He moved to this lot and opened a business. In 1805 he added to this complex with the purchase of the adjacent farm lot. On 28 December he applied for a tavern licence but was refused. Subsequently, however, he built a distillery.

Beman's business seems to have prospered. He evidently shipped furs and potash for merchants such as Laurent QUETTON St George, distilled and milled grains in Newmarket for the local markets, and retailed goods obtained from wholesalers in York and Kingston. His son Eli Beman built a mill and hotel at Holland Landing and operated a ferry and boat on Lake Simcoe. Another son, Joel Beman, seems to

Berthelet

have worked on and been responsible for Beman's farms. Both Elisha and Eli were evidently close associates of Peter Robinson who was building a similar wholesale-retail enterprise in Newmarket and Holland Landing. An accusation has been made in the *History of the town of Newmarket* that Beman and Robinson were guilty of sharp business practice in their dealings with Joseph Hill. The records of the Court of Nisi Prius put a different light on Beman's enterprises, that his businesses were not always successful. Seven judgements were won by his creditors between 1804 and 1808 for an amount totalling more than £7,000.

Little is known of Beman's politics. He was, with Samuel Heron* and others, one of the principals protesting the impropriety of judge Henry Allcock*'s election to the House of Assembly in 1801. He was also a member of the Upper Canada Agricultural and Commercial Society which may have had an organizing role in the opposition centred around Joseph Willcocks*. That his political views were of a dubious nature, from the standpoint of government, is hinted at in a letter from his stepson John Beverley Robinson*, acting attorney general, written on 18 May 1814. Robinson was responding to Surveyor General Thomas RIDOUT's assertion that Beman, in his capacity as JP, was "not being sufficiently active, in checking seditious proceedings in his neighbourhood." Robinson acknowledged that "the observation is in my opinion just." He went on, however, to note that Beman, though "wanting in zeal, is not a seditious or troublesome character, and except in his political opinions, is a good and exemplary member of Society – and in many duties of his situation as a magistrate considerably useful."

Beman gradually gave up active involvement in business, transferring the responsibilities to his sons and devoting full attention to his farms. In the autumn of 1821 his health failed and possibly he suffered a stroke. On 7 October, "being weak in body but of sound and disposing mind and memory," he made his will, dividing his land among his children; he died a week later.

ROBERT E. SAUNDERS

AO, MS 4; MS 87; RG 22, ser.131, 1: ff.19–21. PAC, RG 1, L3, 446: S misc., 1783–1818/71; RG 5, A1: 8339–42; RG 68, General index, 1651–1841: 412, 416, 422, 430, 438. "Journals of Legislative Assembly of U.C.," AO *Report*, 1909: 183. "Political state of U.C.," PAC *Report*, 1892: 41–43. *Town of York, 1793–1815* (Firth). *Upper Canada Gazette*, 1793–1821. *History of the town of Newmarket* (n.p., [1968?]).

BERTHELET, PIERRE, merchant and landowner; b. 15 April 1746 in Saint-Laurent, near Montreal, son of François Berthelet and Anne Boullard; m. 24 July 1775 Françoise Meloche in Detroit, and they had one son; m. secondly 2 Feb. 1779 Marguerite Viger in Boucherville, Que., and they had 13 children; d. 2 Jan. 1830 in Montreal.

Some members of the Berthelet family carried the added name of Savoyard, probably because of the part of the diocese of Geneva in which the first Berthelet to come to the colony had been born. Although Pierre Berthelet is often referred to as a doctor, nothing has been found to confirm that he practised medicine or had any medical training. Another supposition is that he worked in the fur trade. What is certain is his presence at Detroit, where he bought some pieces of land. He left there around 1776 or 1777 to settle in the province of Quebec at Lachine. His son Henry stayed behind and spent his entire life in the United States.

In 1780 Berthelet termed himself a merchant-voyageur and was probably engaged in the fur trade. In 1784 he bought a property on Rue Saint-Paul in Montreal, and at this time stated that he was a merchant in business in the town. There is no detailed information about his activities, but in 1788, 1793, 1794, and 1803 he made some sizeable wheat sales. From 1801 he invested in real estate and lent money. More than a hundred instruments signed before a notary in connection with loans, leases, and transactions concerning buildings have been located.

Real estate seems to have quickly become Berthelet's main field of activity. According to journalist Hector Berthelot*, around 1820 he was supposed to have owned more than 100 buildings, which would make him the largest property owner in Montreal. Jacques Viger*'s work on Montreal real estate in 1825 makes it possible to establish that Berthelet was indeed the major landlord in the town. His 23 properties, some of which were very large, were located principally inside the limits of the old town and at Pointe-à-Callière. He had 61 tenants, who rented commercial as well as residential buildings. He owned one, for example, that was occupied by 43 people. At the time real estate was attractive for two reasons. Montreal's rapid growth in the first quarter of the 19th century probably contributed to a rise in rents and, as historian Louise Dechêne has shown, in this pre-industrial milieu the return on capital put into real estate made it a relatively attractive investment.

Berthelet had also specialized in renting out cast-iron stoves. According to Berthelot, he owned about 300 and leased them out for the winter. In 1824 Berthelet came to the aid of his son Henry, who was tangled up in speculations in Detroit, and he took over responsibility for a project to build a wharf and a market there. But in 1827 he retired, leaving management of his affairs to his wife and his son Antoine-Olivier*.

Little is known about Berthelet's family life. He seemed, however, to be concerned with assuring his

52

descendants' well-being. His second will, dated 1806 and modified in the years up to 1826 by a series of codicils, specified that his assets should pass to his grandchildren, and even to his great-grandchildren some day.

Pierre Berthelet's career illustrates the transition from the 18th-century economy, which was dominated by the fur trade, to that of the early 19th century, which was more diversified. He became a lender and invested in town properties, where the possibilities were multiplying as growth in general accelerated. In his career can also be seen a diversification linked to his age: when approaching 60, Berthelet chose a field of activity easier to manage, and thus profited doubly from the situation.

JEAN-CLAUDE ROBERT

ANQ-M, CE1-22, 2 févr. 1779; CE1-51, 5 janv. 1830; CN1-16, 28 sept. 1801; 3 mai 1803; 12 mai 1804; 10 avril, 17, 19 sept., 19 nov. 1805; 27, 30 janv., 8 févr., 13 avril, 14 juill., 6 août, 9 oct. 1806; 14 janv., 2 févr. 1807; 12 avril 1809; 5 févr. 1820; 10 janv., 6 sept. 1826; 12 mars 1827; CN1-74, 16 mai 1788; 10 avril, 4 mai 1789; 19 nov. 1790; 10 mai 1791; 28 févr. 1793; 7 juin, 26 sept., 13 déc. 1794; 30 juin, 27 nov. 1795; 23 févr., 17 mai, 8 sept. 1802; 26 janv., 22 mars, 28 mai 1803; 16 janv., 27 févr., 14–15 nov., 13, 27 déc. 1804; 4 janv., 13–14 mars, 1er, 4 juill. 1805; 19 oct. 1807; 19 sept. 1808; 15 mars, 15 avril 1809; 3 mars, 31 oct. 1810; CN1-134, 13 nov. 1815; 27 janv., 20, 23 févr., 29 mai, 15, 17 juin, 4 juill., 16 août, 13 sept., 7 oct., 15 nov., 4, 18 déc. 1816; 8, 11 janv., 3, 5, 7 févr., 16 mai, 1er juin, 7 juill., 16, 18 août 1817; 28 oct. 1819; CN1-158, 27 juin 1780; CN1-194, 10 janv. 1805; 23 juin, 22 oct. 1808; 4 mai 1811; 7 avril 1818; CN1-243, 11 août 1807, 3 oct. 1809; CN1-313, 17 sept. 1792, 22 oct. 1806; CN1-334, 5 juill. 1804; 15 avril, 1er mai, 29–30 oct., 26, 29 nov., 2 déc. 1805; 11 mars, 5, 12, 21 oct. 1806; 21 mars, 10, 30 avril 1807; 6, 20 août 1807; 17 janv. 1809; 22, 26 oct. 1811. ASQ, Fonds Viger–Verreau, carton 46, no.9. PAC, MG 29, C89. *Montréal en 1781 . . .* , Claude Perrault, édit. (Montréal, 1969). *La Minerve*, 4 janv. 1830. *Montreal Gazette*, 4 Jan. 1830. Le Jeune, *Dictionnaire*. Tanguay, *Dictionnaire*. Hector Berthelot, *Montréal, le bon vieux temps*, É.-Z. Massicotte, compil. (2v. en 1, Montréal, 1916). Robert Rumilly, *Histoire de Montréal* (5v., Montréal, 1970–74), vol.2. Louise Dechêne, "La rente du faubourg Saint-Roch à Québec, 1750–1850," *RHAF*, 34 (1980–81): 569–96. Édouard Fabre Surveyer, "Pierre Berthelet and his family (in Canada and in the United States)," RSC *Trans.*, 3rd ser., 37 (1943), sect.II: 57–76. P.-A. Linteau et J.-C. Robert, "Propriété foncière et société à Montréal: une hypothèse," *RHAF*, 28 (1974–75): 45–65. É.-Z. Massicotte, "Un philanthrope canadien-français, M. A.-O. Berthelet," *BRH*, 22 (1916): 183–85. Léon Trépanier, "Un philanthrope d'autrefois: Antoine-Olivier Berthelet," CCHA *Rapport*, 28 (1961): 19–25.

BEST, GEORGE, Church of England clergyman; b. 1793 or 1794 in England; m. 21 Aug. 1820, in Halifax, Elizabeth Stanser, second daughter of Robert STANSER, bishop of Nova Scotia, and they had three children; d. 2 May 1829 in Bath, England.

Little is known of George Best's early life. He was educated at Westminster School, London, and he also studied architecture, although he may not have received any formal training in the field. In June 1817, as a catechist or perhaps a deacon of the Church of England, he applied to work overseas as a missionary with the Society for the Propagation of the Gospel and by 30 Oct. 1818 had arrived in the parish of Granville in the Annapolis valley of Nova Scotia, where he served until 1823. He loved Granville and took a particular interest in the schools for black children.

In April 1823, on the death of the Reverend James Milne, the Anglican congregation of Fredericton recommended Best's appointment as rector there. He began his duties in July, and also acted as his father-in-law's ecclesiastical commissary in New Brunswick. In September he was ordained priest in the Cathedral of the Holy Trinity at Quebec by Bishop Jacob MOUNTAIN. His positions in Fredericton were not confirmed until after the arrival of Sir Howard Douglas* as lieutenant governor of the province in 1824.

Early in 1825 the diocese of Nova Scotia was divided into four archdeaconries and George Best was appointed the first archdeacon of New Brunswick. Thus he became responsible for the province's ecclesiastical affairs under the direction of John Inglis*, who had replaced Robert Stanser as bishop of Nova Scotia. Best's energy and enthusiasm in the performance of his duties are illustrated by a long report on the state of religion in the province which he prepared for Sir Howard Douglas in 1825. This study gives figures on population generally and on the number of souls and church buildings in each county. Using late returns which came in after the 1824 census had been published, Best estimated the population of New Brunswick at 79,176. There were 16 resident Anglican clergymen serving 26 churches. Only two of the clergymen, however, served in the eastern half of the province. Best was enthusiastic about the potential for "the Established Church," and his report points out areas where the condition of religion demanded improvements. More missionaries were required, and they should be "men of mild and humble dispositions, who will assimilate themselves with the people, amongst whom they may be sent and endeavour to unite themselves with their interests, and their hopes." Best's study shows a tolerant attitude towards most of the ministers of other denominations, with the exception of the Baptists. It also displays a marked respect for the people among whom he ministered. "The people of this Country who gain a livelihood by their manual labour, for of the lower order there are none," he wrote, "are in intellect and sagacity superior far to

Bidwell

those of the same stamp in the Mother Country – they are, for the most part, shrewd and intelligent, and, generally speaking, well versed in the Scriptures."

As archdeacon, Best travelled through the province supervising the clergy and schoolmasters. His "active and valuable superintendence" was appreciated by a great many people. Bishop Inglis, who in 1826 made the first Anglican episcopal visitation to New Brunswick in decades, was impressed by the schools for which Best was responsible and found them to be "generally well attended and well appointed." In describing the need for additional clergymen as "even greater than I had supposed," Inglis underlined one of his archdeacon's constant concerns. In February 1827 Best hired the Reverend George McCawley* as his curate and encouraged him to undertake missionary journeys to isolated areas of the province. He also promoted the building of "small temporary churches in remote districts."

George Best played a significant part in the construction of a new building to house the College of New Brunswick. In 1825 he was one of three people to submit architectural designs to the college council, which decided in October that John Elliott Woolford*'s plan was the most appealing. That December Sir Howard Douglas chose as the site of the new structure a lot owned by Best, who insisted on being paid £500 for his property. Best became a member of the board of the college in January 1826, and the following month he was appointed to determine "what ornamental parts" of Woolford's plan might "be dispensed without injury to the convenience and comfort of the interior." In March he formed a committee with William Franklin Odell* to choose "Stone or Brick as they may judge best," yet not to spend more than £12,000. The committee chose stone but cut costs by replacing the planned dome with a pediment.

In 1828 the College of New Brunswick was reconstituted as King's College, Fredericton. The royal charter issued at that time designated the archdeacon of the province as titular president of the institution. Best was not happy with the new honour. He protested that he was not a university man and was disturbed that he was being assigned significant responsibilities without being provided with an additional income; Fredericton, he complained, was an expensive place in which to live. Nevertheless, he prepared to assume his new duties, and asked the SPG to make some provision for scholarships.

George Best's dedication to his ministry made him an able leader of the Church of England in New Brunswick in the 1820s. Described by a contemporary as "full of genuine gentleness and unaffected piety," he seems to have had the ability to avoid confrontation, and his broadmindedness helped to ease tensions both within his own communion and between denominations. The Reverend Benjamin Gerrish Gray*, for example – a restless, temperamental exponent of broad-church principles – looked upon Best as a fellow spirit who also desired to bring evangelical Christians into the Anglican communion. Best's bishop was impressed by his activities. "The Archdeacon," Inglis wrote, "is sometimes a little hurried by his zeal, but he is notwithstanding a very worthy officer, and I have a very warm regard for him." Best was also on good terms with the administration and was friendly with Sir Howard and Lady Douglas from the time of their arrival in New Brunswick. Although it had already been arranged at the Colonial Office in England that the Reverend Frederick Coster should be transferred from Saint John to Fredericton, the lieutenant governor soon found Best to be "in every way so fit for the situation" that he insisted that he continue as rector of Fredericton. The clergyman was a great favourite with Lady Douglas and her younger children and may have shared their enthusiasm for drawing and gardening.

In April 1828 Best's request for a leave of absence to visit England was granted. He died at Bath in May 1829 and was buried in Claverton Down churchyard. The Reverend George Coster* succeeded him as archdeacon of New Brunswick.

CAROLYN A. YOUNG

PAC, MG 24, A3, 3; C43 (mfm.). PANB, MC 211, MS4/5/1; RG 7, RS75, A, 1828, George Best. PRO, CO 188/32, 188/39 (mfm. at PANB). UNBL, Dennis Harvey to [John Anderson], president of the Univ. of N.B., 11 Dec. 1976; C. McN. Steeves to secretary, SPG, 15 May 1945; UA, "Minute-book of the governors and trustees of the College of New Brunswick," 1800–28. USPG, C/CAN/NB, 4, folder 181; C/CAN/NS, 3, folder 16 (mfm. at PAC). *New-Brunswick Royal Gazette*, 21 Oct. 1823. G. H. Lee, *An historical sketch of the first fifty years of the Church of England in the province of New Brunswick (1783–1833)* (Saint John, N.B., 1880). J. D. Purdy, "The Church of England in New Brunswick during the colonial era, 1783–1860" (MA thesis, Univ. of N.B., Fredericton, 1954).

BIDWELL, BARNABAS, author, teacher, and politician; b. 23 Aug. 1763 in Tyringham, Mass., son of Adonijah Bidwell and Jemima Devotion; m. 21 Feb. 1793 Mary Gray (d. 1808), and they had a son and a daughter; d. 27 July 1833 in Kingston, Upper Canada.

Descended from Puritan divines on both sides of his family, Barnabas Bidwell attended Yale College, from which he was graduated in 1785. As an undergraduate he was a prize essayist and the author of two plays: "The modern mistake" and *The mercenary match: a tragedy*. The latter is distinguished, according to one biographer, "by the general smoothness of the blank verse and the occasional felicity of the phrasing – qualities seldom found in eighteenth-century American plays." Indeed, the play is considered by that biographer to be Bidwell's chief claim to fame. In any event, this serio-comic burlesque is of interest to the student of the author's later career as a party politician. The long speeches with which it is filled reveal something of Bidwell's early interest in polemics, and the play itself reveals a hostility to the idea of party he would later depart from.

Upon graduation Bidwell taught in a school for young ladies at New Haven until 1787, when he was appointed to a tutorship at Yale. In 1790 he unexpectedly resigned from this position to study law under judge Theodore Sedgwick of Stockbridge, Mass. Sedgwick, a prominent member of the House of Representatives and later a senator, was an important spokesman for the Federalist party. Bidwell, disappointed, according to historian Paul Goodman, at failing to secure a postmastership, joined the emerging Democratic-Republican party to become an arch-enemy of Sedgwick.

Admitted to the bar in 1791, Bidwell established a practice at Stockbridge. The same year he was appointed treasurer of Berkshire County, which the Republicans had just captured from the Federalists. From 1801 to 1805 he was a member of the Massachusetts Senate and from 1805 to 1807 he sat as a state representative in Congress. Re-elected in 1807, he resigned without taking his seat to become attorney general of Massachusetts. Honorary degrees of AM were conferred on him by Williams and Yale colleges, and in 1805 he was granted an LLD by Brown University. Then, in 1810, when he was being considered by President James Madison for appointment to the Supreme Court, discrepancies were found in his accounts as Berkshire treasurer. He fled in disgrace to Upper Canada.

In the House of Representatives, Bidwell had displaced John Randolph of Roanoke as administration leader and become the leading spokesman of President Thomas Jefferson. In this capacity, he successfully defended the president's policy of imposing economic sanctions in response to British violations of neutral rights at sea. He also directed the campaign to purchase Florida and was deeply involved in the movement to abolish the slave trade. Experience gained within the house, however, was less relevant to Bidwell's later career than that gained as a party organizer and a manipulator of public opinion at the grass roots.

Notable in this regard was the attention he paid to the partisan press. "The people must judge from impressions, communicated through Newspapers principally," he wrote to Aaron Burr. "The true explanations of controverted measures should be communicated and circulated. They should be uniform in all parts of the United States. . . . For this purpose there ought to be an authentic paper, from which Republican editors can take their texts." Notable too were his views, which he expounded as a pamphleteer, on the necessity of the War of American Independence, on the excellence of the written American constitution, and on history in general. His own party was identified with a native, patriotic, non-European republican tradition, that of his opponents with an alien, decadent, monarchical, British tradition. The unwritten British constitution and the political thought of Edmund Burke, which were admired in certain Federalist circles, were objects of determined attack. Also of interest is Bidwell's early use of the term "family compact." In Canada this expression later took on a strange life of its own to shape political and historical thinking for many decades. Bidwell's views, however, are perhaps chiefly noteworthy as genuine expressions of an early form of American nationalism. This nationalism was to be quite at odds with sentiment which yet prevailed in George III's remaining North American colonies.

In Upper Canada, to which Bidwell fled in 1810, the American revolution, at least at a rhetorical level, long continued to be fought. First settled by American tory refugees committed to the idea of a continuing united British empire, it had later filled up with other settlers from the United States. When differences developed between these two groups, or when opposition to government opened within either group, so too emerged the rhetoric of revolution and republicanism. In part, this language was perhaps due to prior ideological commitment, and certainly opposition to established institutions often gave birth to republican commitment. More largely, however, the rhetoric of republicanism was the only language of opposition with which most of these folk were at all familiar. None the less, when understood within the context of then very strained British-American relations and against the threat of invasion by American armies, this language gave rise to intense concern on the part of those who supported the established government. Thus when Bidwell, who settled near Kingston, involved himself in controversy, he became an object of suspicion. And, by reason of his acknowledged political and intellectual ability, he became much feared.

The occasion of his first involvement sprang from the publication of *A discourse on the character of King George the Third*. Written in 1810 by John Strachan*, a then obscure Cornwall schoolmaster, this pamphlet was primarily a refutation of George's republican traducers and a defence of British institutions against republican critics. Strachan also assailed philosophical assumptions which underlay the Declaration of Independence and contended that the practice of government in the United States fell far short of the republican ideal. Bidwell, writing under the pseudonym "A Friend of Peace," replied to Strachan in the

Bidwell

Kingston Gazette of 9 Oct. 1810. Touching not at all upon the question of British institutions, he concurred with Strachan's "encomium upon those conjugal and domestic virtues . . . so justly ascribed to His Majesty." Then he took issue with certain "uncandid and ill-timed" reflections upon the people and government of the United States, focusing upon a remark to the effect that, although Britain had lost the revolutionary war, she might be in a position to avenge herself against a hostile United States at the end of the current war in Europe. "From such an unprofitable, ruinous contest, without a prospect of gain," replied Bidwell, "good Lord deliver us! should be the prayer of our teachers and rulers, and all the people should say Amen." Strachan's clumsy attempt at instilling loyalty in the populace was thus represented as provocative of war.

In contrast to much of Bidwell's other polemic, the tone of this letter, although condescending, was moderate. But he soon became an object of fierce controversy in the columns of the *Gazette*, when his pseudonym was pierced. Then, on 11 March 1811, a committee announced the opening of an "Academical School" at Ernestown (Bath). This school was to offer a more practical education than the classically oriented, government-sponsored grammar school at Kingston. It was with horror that conservative circles in the latter town learned that the "experienced preceptor" of this new school was to be Barnabas Bidwell. That he was more than well qualified academically was unquestioned, but he stood indicted before the courts of Massachusetts for embezzlement and forgery. Moreover, he was, as one contemporary has noted, "a distinguished partizan of democracy in the most unqualified sense of the word" and he was therefore deemed quite unfit to shape tender Canadian minds. This latter consideration, however, may well have been his chief attraction for prominent radical leaders in Ernestown such as the Perrys [*see* Peter Perry*] who had long been at odds with leading Kingstonians. Certainly the Ernestown Academy was more important as a political symbol than as an institution of learning.

During the War of 1812 Bidwell, suspected of acting as an American agent, was compelled by local authorities to swear an oath of allegiance. How much truth lay behind these suspicions, it is now almost impossible to determine. It is perhaps significant, however, that they were shared by certain American opponents of the war. Soon after Brigadier-General William Hull's abortive campaign of 1812 a satire, *The wars of the gulls*, was published at New York. In this pamphlet "the Gulls," Madison and his friends, having decided that Upper Canada could be captured by proclamation alone, dispatch "Hull-gull," enjoining him in the event of failure to "call for advice upon their trusty ci-devant cabinateer Barnabas Bidwell,

and other confidential friends of the great Mo-gull [Madison] resident in that country." Bidwell, it appeared, had "made a generous sacrifice of his reputation at home" that he might reside with a better grace in an enemy country, there to make "gradual preparations for the reception of the victorious Proclamation, by teaching the illiterate natives how to read it when it should arrive." Although it would be absurd to suppose that Bidwell took up residence in the colony with any such purpose in mind, he may well have advised the American administration about the nature of Upper Canadian public opinion having regard to the probable reception of Hull's army and proclamation. The authors knew about Bidwell's teaching activities in Ernestown; they may have known more.

Little is known, however, of Bidwell's activities either during or immediately after the war. At some point he became a law clerk in the office of Daniel Washburn, a radical elected in 1818 to Robert Gourlay*'s Upper Canadian Convention of Friends to Enquiry. Bidwell himself seems to have taken little or no part in the Gourlay agitations, although he did give Gourlay his unpublished manuscript "Sketches of Upper Canada," which was later published as part of Gourlay's account of the province. In 1820 Washburn was disbarred for theft and Bidwell took over the management of his affairs.

This same year he stood for election to the assembly in the riding of Lennox and Addington where, it seems likely, the now-disgraced Washburn had intended to stand as a Gourlayite. Bidwell was not very successful. Heading the poll was Daniel Hagerman, who had led the opposition to Gourlay, with 521 votes. He was followed by two other conservatives, Samuel Casey and Isaac Fraser, with 309 and 192 votes. At the bottom of the poll were Bidwell with 162 votes and a Mr Detlor with 43. Then, in the summer of 1821, Hagerman died. In the ensuing November by-election two candidates divided the conservative vote and Bidwell was returned with a majority of 49.

At this point, the attorney general, John Beverley Robinson*, suggested to Bidwell's opponents that, if a certificate could be secured from the United States establishing that, as an American official, Bidwell had forever renounced allegiance to the king, he could be unseated. But, perhaps because of the complicating factor of the oath Bidwell had been compelled to swear during the war, his antagonists also obtained certificates pertaining to his alleged malversations in Massachusetts. Thus, within two weeks of his election the outcome was protested on *moral*, as well as *legal*, grounds.

This stratagem completely backfired. Bidwell had paid the moneys he owed to the county of Berkshire and he now counter-petitioned that, all criminal charges having been laid before the electors and explained to them, he be confirmed in his seat. His petition opened up a debate in the House of Assembly as to the proper judge of moral fitness of assemblymen – the house or the electors. At stake were not only the privileges of the electors but also the vexed question of setting a precedent which would open the way to a host of petitions against the alleged moral failings of other members. To the embarrassment of those members, all such petitions would have to be tried. These issues, however, were avoided when the assembly resolved that it could not enter into consideration of crimes alleged to have been committed in the United States.

Legal arguments were also produced, but these proved more perplexing than the moral ones. Bidwell's opponents sought to establish that the oath he had taken in 1812 had been sworn reluctantly; that first having attempted to take novel oaths of his own devising, he had indeed sworn according to the proper form but had afterwards declared this oath invalid since it was taken under duress. Bidwell's friends then sought to establish that the magistrate before whom this oath had been made, and upon whose affidavit the case against Bidwell rested, was a notorious liar. The evidence produced by both parties was more bewildering than germane to the matter at hand; for the law seems to have been on the side of Bidwell. He, after all, had taken the oath, and his motives in doing so were scarcely relevant.

There was other law, however, arising from the Constitutional Act of 1791, which was not on Bidwell's side. This imperial statute provided that "no Person shall be capable of voting at any Election of a Member to serve in . . . an Assembly . . . or of being elected at any such election who shall not be . . . a natural born Subject of His Majesty or a Subject of His Majesty having become such by the Conquest and cession of the Province of Canada." This provision had never been amended, and Bidwell fell into neither category. But neither did other members of the assembly and neither did vast numbers of voters who, having entered the province as post-loyalist American emigrants, had hitherto been deemed subjects erroneously. The law was quite clear, but to fall back upon it was to invite a political convulsion such as the province had never seen. Hence, when on 30 Nov. 1821 Jonas Jones* and Mahlon Burwell* moved that Bidwell, "not being naturalized by any British Act of Parliament, is an Alien, and is therefore incapable of being elected to serve in the Parliament of this Province," they were supported only by legal purists and blind tories. Their motion was defeated 12 to 20. But then, having declined either to enter into a consideration of Bidwell's American past or to declare him an alien, the assembly proceeded to find on 4 Jan. 1822 by a majority of one that "sufficient of the allegations" made by the petitioners had been proved in such a manner as to render his election void. What these allegations were, or just how they had been proved in view of the house's own resolutions, it was most difficult to discover. And although the assembly later passed a bill disqualifying from membership all persons who had taken an oath of abjuration against His Majesty's government, or had held office in the United States, or had committed serious felonies, the impression lingered that Bidwell's expulsion had resulted more from opportunism than from any dispassionate consideration of law and evidence.

By itself this notion would have had little impact outside of the region around Lennox and Addington. But another, entirely false impression, zealously propagated by Bidwell, also lingered. This was that he had been expelled as an alien by ruthless tory opponents bent upon depriving all other unnaturalized persons of their civil rights. This alien question, the influence of which lasted for years, was of key importance in winning popular support for an emerging provincial reform party [see Sir Peregrine Maitland*].

Bidwell himself never again stood for public office. He brought forward his son, Marshall Spring*, as a candidate in his place, acted as his close political adviser, and busied himself orchestrating the press. In due course Marshall became a most able member of the assembly and a leader of the reform party. But tory opponents long remained persuaded that the tactical mind behind both him and the section of the reformers he led was that of Barnabas.

Up until 1828 there was much truth in this belief; thereafter, however, rather less. In 1828 the alien question was politically resolved and Marshall began to cooperate closely with William Warren Baldwin*. A leading reformer but not a republican, Baldwin proposed to reform government by making it conform more closely with that practised at Westminster. Barnabas was undoubtedly angered and dismayed. This reaction was strongly conveyed by a letter printed in Hugh Christopher Thomson's *Upper Canada Herald* of 14 Oct. 1829 and almost certainly written by the elder Bidwell under the pseudonym X.

The letter was a bitterly sarcastic commentary upon another document, likely written *circa* 1806–7 by one Canadiensis, who was most probably judge Robert Thorpe*. As such, X's letter was an attack upon William Warren Baldwin who, in 1828, had advanced again Thorpe's mostly forgotten proposal of ministerial responsibility within the colony as a solution to Upper Canada's political difficulties and as a means of maintaining the connection with the mother country. Reminiscent of Bidwell's early pamphlets in which he assailed Edmund Burke's views, X's letter clearly emanated from the pen of an American-oriented, republican separatist. It was probably elicited from Bidwell when he discovered his own son was being drawn into a system he abominated.

Bidwell

When Bidwell died in 1833, he was remembered by an American friend, judge William P. Walker, as one who in "his intercourse with his neighbours . . . was peculiarly mild and conciliating, and *no man had fewer personal enemies, except from political considerations*." The emphasis is Walker's and his exception is a most important one; for the politics of conciliation were anathema to Bidwell. Partly for this reason, no reform politician in Upper Canada ever inspired as much political hatred as did he. Even his friends sometimes had reservations about the political means he employed. In a curious sermon preached at his funeral, for example, the Reverend J. Smith felt obliged to observe that, "whatever may be said of his mode of accomplishing his intentions, none will say that these were not of a most liberal description, and designed for the general good." Bidwell having departed this world of party conflict, Smith added, perhaps he "may have already viewed many transactions in a different light, and weighed his own and others conduct and motives in a different balance than he formerly did."

In assessing Bidwell's methods, the 19th-century American historian Richard Hildreth wrote of him as "timid indeed, but cunning, supple and sly." The more perceptive of his tory enemies in Upper Canada would not have agreed that he was timid, and they would have pointed to a rigidity of mind which they ascribed as much to his Puritan background as to his uncompromising republicanism. The views of most tories, however, were coloured by their belief that they were dealing with a thief and a traitor.

In both instances, they were mistaken. In 1810 Bidwell's estate had been attached for $10,000 as the amount of his indebtedness; but the final judgement of the Berkshire court against him, which he paid in 1817, amounted to only $330.64 damages and $63.18 costs. Since Bidwell seems to have been able to pay both amounts, he did not flee on that account. There is little reason, moreover, to doubt his assertion that, because his public offices required his presence elsewhere in the United States, he employed clerks to handle his duties in Berkshire, one of whom, dead at the time of financial exposure, had been responsible. He fled, he claimed, from fear of his political enemies who were exaggerating his personal responsibility and indebtedness. As for the charge that he was a traitor, it is clear that he remained an American patriot until the day of his death.

G. H. PATTERSON

[The main collection of Barnabas Bidwell papers is sect.I of the Bidwell family papers, Yale Univ. Library, MSS and Arch. Dept. (New Haven, Conn.), MG 79. These are more useful with regard to Bidwell's American career than for his Upper Canadian. They are, however, of considerable interest in the latter regard. They are perhaps most useful in revealing something of the pleasanter side of his character and his puritan values. There is a smaller collection of Bidwell papers in the MS Division of the Library of Congress (Washington). Most, if not all, of these, however, are also in the Yale collection. The Marshall Spring Bidwell papers at Yale (MG 79, sect.II) contain some letters from Barnabas, and also a collection about him which Marshall intended to use for a biography of his father. The entire Yale collection of Bidwell papers is available on microfilm at the AO (MS 761).

Letters from and about Bidwell are scattered through a number of Canadian collections. The most important of these is the Macaulay papers in the AO (MS 78). References to others may be found in Patterson, "Studies in elections in U.C."

Bidwell's American publications include *The mercenary match; a tragedy* (New Haven, [1784?]; repr. Chicago, 1925); *An oration on the death of Roger Newton, Jun'r . . .* (New Haven, [1789]); *An oration, delivered at the celebration of American independence, in Stockbridge, July, 1795* (Stockbridge, Mass., 1795); *The Susquehannah title stated and examined, in a series of numbers, first published in the "Western Star," and now re-published, in this form, for the benefit of the public in general, and all persons concerned in particular*, issued anonymously at Catskill, N.Y., in 1796 (this work was republished as "The Susquehannah title stated and examined," ed. J. P. Boyd, in Wyo. Hist. and Geological Soc., *Proc. and Coll.* (Wilkes-Barre, Pa.), 20 (1925–26): 103–243); *An address to the people of Massachusetts* (n.p., 1804); *An address to the people of Massachusetts; February 1805* (n.p., 1805); *A summary historical and political review of the revolution, the constitution and government of the United States: an oration, delivered at Sheffield, July 4th, 1805* (Pittsfield, Mass., 1805); and *The attorney general's report respecting claims for confiscated debts* (Boston, 1808).

None of Bidwell's Canadian writings were published under his own name. He has been identified, however, as the author of the "Sketches of Upper Canada written by an inhabitant" in *Statistical account of Upper Canada, compiled with a view to a grand system of emigration*, by R. [F.] Gourlay (2v., London, 1822; repr. East Ardsley, Eng., and New York, 1966), 1: 1–268. He is also said to have contributed letters to the *Kingston Gazette* on practical agriculture and political economy which were afterwards published in pamphlet form under the title *The prompter* (Kingston, [Ont.], 1821). G.H.P.

John Smith, *"Immortality," a sermon occasioned by the death of Barnabas Bidwell, esq.* (Kingston, 1833). John Strachan, *A discourse on the character of King George the Third, addressed to the inhabitants of British America* (Montreal, 1810). *The wars of the gulls; an historical romance, in three chapters* (New York, 1812). *Upper Canada Herald*, 1820–30. J. P. Boyd, "Reprint of *The Susquehannah title stated and examined*: foreword," and "Barnabas Bidwell, 1763–1833," Wyo. Hist. and Geological Soc., *Proc. and Coll.*, 20: 49–52 and 53–102. G. [H.] Patterson, "An enduring Canadian myth; the family compact and responsible government," *Journal of Canadian Studies* (Peterborough, Ont.), 12 (1977), no.2: 3–16; "Whiggery, nationality, and the Upper Canadian reform tradition," *CHR*, 56 (1975): 25–44. J. E. Rea, "Barnabas Bidwell: a note on the American years," *OH*, 60 (1968): 31–37. W. R. Riddell, "The Bidwell elections: a political episode in Upper Canada a century ago," *OH*, 21 (1924): 236–44.

BIGAULT D'AUBREVILLE, LOUIS-NICOLAS-EMMANUEL DE (he signed **Emmanuel d'Aubreville**), army officer and office holder; fl. 1791–1828.

Born into an ancient noble family of eastern France, Louis-Nicolas-Emmanuel de Bigault d'Aubreville fled in 1791 during the French revolution and joined the *émigré* army of the Prince de Condé. He served in it until 1799 when he entered the Swiss service as a cadet in the Salis-Marschlins Regiment. For a brief time after 1801 he was a recruiting agent for the British army on the Continent. He then served in De Watteville's Regiment, becoming quartermaster in 1807.

D'Aubreville arrived in Montreal with his regiment in June 1813. Britain being at war with the United States, his unit was immediately sent to reinforce British regulars in Upper Canada at Kingston, York (Toronto), and Niagara (Niagara-on-the-Lake). Once more d'Aubreville was pressed into service as a recruiter. His zeal and effectiveness earned him, on 25 May 1814, a captain's commission and command of a company in the Voltigeurs Canadiens, then stationed at Chambly, Lower Canada. In July 1815, at the close of the war, he was reduced on half pay.

Having brought his wife, Catherine Ribenzki, and several young children to Lower Canada, d'Aubreville settled with them in Montreal. A man of some education, he attempted to provide the same for at least three of his sons, who studied at the Petit Séminaire de Montréal at different times from 1813 to 1825. In January 1817 he was sued for slander by one François Aumur; d'Aubreville requested the lawyer and politician Michael O'Sullivan* to defend him, charging that his accuser was motivated by jealousy, "because he perceives that I have the honour to be well considered by all the honourable people of this city." He could ill afford the suit, his finances being then in a precarious state; indeed, in April a London firm of army clothiers, who had probably not been paid for making his uniform, had the sheriff of Montreal seize land owned by him in the *faubourg* Saint-Laurent to be sold at public auction.

D'Aubreville's fortunes improved in August 1818 when he was appointed, at a salary of £75, captain of the newly organized night-watch in Montreal, the equivalent of today's chief of police. Until then peace and security at night had been maintained to some extent by the police force of 25 to 30 men established by authorization from the Lower Canadian legislature in 1815. Lighting of the main thoroughfares had begun that year, but not until April 1818 was an act passed providing for a regular night-watch and lamp-lighters; the city was authorized to hire a foreman, or

captain, an assistant, and up to 24 men. D'Aubreville's first duty as captain was to select 18 men to serve as watchmen, and in the autumn he hired four blacks as lamplighters. The night-watch was considered a department of the police, and d'Aubreville worked under the supervision of the Committee of the Watch and Night Lights, composed of police magistrates and justices of the peace. Philippe-Joseph Aubert* de Gaspé recalled the importance of the watchmen in his *Mémoires*: "What a feeling of well-being, of comfort, of security one felt when these guards announced the hours of the night beneath our windows, when one heard them sing out: *Past one o'clock, and a star light morning*, or *a stormy morning*, &c. &c."

Operating out of the first police bureau, located in the former Recollet convent, d'Aubreville had an uneven career as captain of the watch. Having been reprimanded in 1823 by the watch committee, which had received complaints against him, he was dismissed in October 1827 along with his two lieutenants; on the testimony of three watchmen, Jean-Marie Mondelet*, a member of the committee, had charged them with drunkenness and neglect of duty. D'Aubreville publicly denied the charges but to no avail. Only the editor of the *Montreal Gazette* defended him. Peter McGill*, a justice of the peace, supported the decision of the watch committee in a letter to the *Montreal Gazette*, asserting that d'Aubreville and his two officers were "notorious for their unsteady habits and inattention to their duty." The editor of *La Minerve* was no less harsh. It is a measure of the increasing tension of the period that d'Aubreville's firing by the committee, which was composed exclusively of Canadians, enabled the editor of the *Montreal Gazette* to insinuate that it had been politically motivated. In 1828 d'Aubreville himself explained what he called the "capricious conduct" of the committee members as being the price he had paid for "his sincere and zealous attachment to the British Government." He suffered another humiliation fast on the heels of his dismissal when his 21-year-old son, Emmanuel-Xavier, was convicted along with a companion of rioting, forcibly entering the house of a young woman, and destroying her effects. Young d'Aubreville was fined £5 and had to go to prison for a month because his father was unable to pay the sum.

As a war veteran d'Aubreville had received 800 acres of land in Halifax Township in April 1821, but, working in Montreal, he had never taken up the grant. In 1828, unemployed and destitute, he applied for the patent on it, and he may have retired there with his wife and at least some of his six children. An exile from his country, having served in three different armies in numerous campaigns on two continents while earning the praise of his commanding officers, a man educated and not without ambition, d'Aubreville

Black

apparently was unable to adjust to civilian life and disappeared into historical obscurity.

ELINOR KYTE SENIOR

ANQ-M, CE1-51, 7 sept. 1814. AUM, P 58, U, Aubreville à O'Sullivan, 20 janv. 1817. Centre de documentation du Service de police de la Communauté urbaine de Montréal, Jean Turmel, "Premières structures et évolution de la police de Montréal, 1796–1909" (copie dactylographiée, Montréal, 1971), 1, 8, 11–12. PAC, MG 30, D1, 2: 476; RG 1, L3ᴸ: 17534; RG 8, I (C ser.), 715. *La Minerve*, 1ᵉʳ, 8, 19 nov. 1827. *Montreal Gazette*, 22, 29 Oct. 1827. *Quebec Gazette*, 21 Aug. 1817; 27 April, 25 June 1818. *Montreal directory*, 1819: 17. *Officers of British forces in Canada* (Irving), 106. Aubert de Gaspé, *Mémoires* (1930), 2: 81. E. H. Bovay, "Les deux régiments suisses au Canada (1813–1817)" (paper presented to the International Symposium of Military Historians, Ottawa, 1978). Maurault, *Le collège de Montréal* (Dansereau; 1967), 474. F.-J. Audet, "Bigault d'Aubreville," *BRH*, 37 (1931): 279–80. Ægidius Fauteux, "Bigault d'Aubreville," *BRH*, 37: 222–23. É.-Z. Massicotte, "Le guet à Montréal au xixᵉ siècle," *BRH*, 36 (1930): 68–70. Zed [——], "Question," *BRH*, 37: 91.

BLACK, JOHN, businessman, politician, and jp; b. *c.* 1764 in Aberdeen, Scotland; d. there 4 Sept. 1823.

Little is known of John Black's early life, but the Blacks of Aberdeen were a well-established mercantile family which as early as 1745 had interests in the manufacture of linen and woollens and in other local industries such as herring-salting and lime-burning. Black arrived at Saint John, N.B., in 1786 as an Admiralty agent, entrusted with the securing of masts and other choice timber, and as the representative of Blair and Glenie, a Scottish timber-trading firm that had moved its headquarters to London in order to tender for Admiralty contracts. He soon realized that the New Brunswick timber trade had good prospects and, sensing quickly that Saint John and Passamaquoddy Bay were potential entrepôts for a bilateral trade with the United States, and for trade involving the United States and New Brunswick on the one hand and the West Indies on the other, he established a mercantile house on his own account at Saint John in 1787. He later invited a number of his kin – a younger brother, William*, and two cousins – to join him in the venture.

Business in Saint John was dominated by Scots, the main commercial area being known as "Scotch Row" and McPherson's Tavern serving as the exchange. Black found many useful friends and contacts through these countrymen, especially through the brothers William* and Thomas Pagan, who imported largely from the Clyde and had extensive connections in the timber trade. Supplying the fisheries with salt imported from Scotland, and with rum, clothing, and provisions, soon became one of Black's main lines of business. It was the basis of yet another of his activities: the shipping of salted fish to the West Indies. This was a most lucrative undertaking if, in return, sugars and molasses could be obtained cheaply for shipment to Britain and a "triangular" trade thus constituted. Black was also, as early as 1790, acting as agent for several firms in other centres – notably for the Greenock shipbuilding firm of Scott and Company [*see* Christopher SCOTT], for the important Halifax merchant William Forsyth*, and for James Dunlop* of Montreal, Lower Canada's most enterprising trader. By 1792 he had built up a shipping fleet of at least nine vessels, which carried lumber and salted dried fish to the West Indies and timber both to Greenock and to Aberdeen, where his firm maintained a full-time representative for the handling and sale of the cargoes. He was thus a pioneer of the British North American timber trade, and by 1805 there were branches of his firm at Miramichi, Fredericton, St Andrews, and Montreal.

Another of Black's interests was the promotion of hemp-growing in New Brunswick. Britain, as the major sea power, needed cordage for her ships, and she was dependent on imports of hemp from Russia, which was becoming an expensive and unreliable source of supply. Black persuaded several farmers and estate-owners to cultivate the plant, financing the experiments himself, but they came to nothing. His other concerns flourished, however, and his role as importer especially brought him to the fore, large-scale shipments of woollens, ironware, iron stoves, bar iron, cordage, and gunpowder from Scotland finding ready, profitable sale. His West Indies trade developed as British conquests proceeded in that quarter after war was declared in 1793, and Trinidad and the Turks Islands were added to the destinations of his vessels.

Scottish merchants – and the Blacks, predominantly – headed the commercial life of Saint John. In 1798 they formed the St Andrew's Society, a combination of mercantile club and social and welfare society that resembled a chamber of commerce. Black was the first secretary of the society and later served two years as president. An entertaining and convivial man, with a strong business sense, he was the natural leader of this group. In 1793, along with Ward CHIPMAN, he had been elected member of the House of Assembly for Northumberland County, and he actively supported measures conducive to the improvement of commercial practice and the extension of the colony's trade. In 1802 he served as a justice of the peace.

By 1804 Black had extended his shipping and trading empire to Halifax. Two years later, attracted by the wartime boom, he moved there, entering into partnership with William Forsyth and building a fine mansion near Government House, reputedly of granite brought out in his own vessels from Aberdeen, the principal destination of his timber cargoes. By

1808 he was serving as secretary of the Committee of Trade, the executive arm of an organization of Halifax merchants known as the Commercial Society [see William SABATIER]. Their major goal was the reservation to colonial exporters of the West Indies fish trade and they had already had considerable success in bringing effective pressure to bear on the home government. In 1808, as secretary, he organized support for their objectives among Quebec merchants. In this initiative he worked through his Quebec agents, the prominent firm of Irvine [James IRVINE], McNaught and Company, part of the extensive network of contacts, all Scottish firms, which he had carefully built up in the North American colonies, the West Indies, England, Scotland, and the Mediterranean.

Black's views were not narrow or parochial. He urged that all the colonies, and all the merchants in their ports and trading centres, should have freedom to develop their business, and that both colonial and home governments should encourage this freedom and give bounties and concessions if needed. To achieve these ends Black and the trade committee, which was dominated by Scots, made submissions to the British government through the influential Viscount Melville, head of the tory interest in Scotland, former president of the Board of Control, and first lord of the Admiralty from 1812 to 1827. In 1813 Black was appointed to the Nova Scotia Council, where he stressed the importance of the West Indies trade, and urged that no concessions in the Newfoundland fisheries be given to either France or the United States in the event of a peace settlement being made. Black used his influence with Melville to press these points in London, to secure for Lower Canadian, Nova Scotian, and New Brunswick shipbuilders substantial contracts for the supply of naval vessels, and to obtain for British North American suppliers large Admiralty orders for colonial masts and timber. His success helped to boom the whole wartime economy of the Atlantic region and Lower Canada.

As in Saint John, Black was regarded in Halifax as a leading light of the city's large Scottish circle, serving as president of the North British Society in 1809. His intimates included John Young*, better known by his *nom de plume*, Agricola, who traded "on the line" at the captured port of Castine (Maine) during the War of 1812. There is good reason to believe that Black, like Christopher Scott and other respectable Nova Scotia and New Brunswick merchants, was deeply engaged in this lucrative, albeit illegal, branch of commerce and that Young was his agent. With the peace of 1814 the trade ceased, as did another of Black's wartime activities – the speculative purchase of prize ships and cargoes condemned by the Vice-Admiralty Court at Halifax. A racket had developed by which captured ships and their contents, not properly inspected

officially, could be knocked down at low prices to bidders who had inside information. Many naval officers, officials, and merchants were able to make large fortunes. Wartime trade, legal and illegal, and participation in prize-purchase and in privateering ventures all contributed to make the years 1806–14 the most active and profitable of Black's business career. The last nine years of his life saw the onset of the post-war slump, but his firm was sufficiently well established and well funded to weather it, mainly because the export timber trade to Britain continued to thrive until 1825. In 1820 and 1821 he took an interest in bank promotion schemes, and he was associated with Christopher Scott of St Andrews, and with other Scottish merchants of Halifax and Saint John, in steamboat ventures. Unfortunately, he did not live to see the success achieved in both these fields.

A staunch British patriot, Black had been notable in Saint John for illuminating his house to celebrate the victories of the Nile and Trafalgar. He was an active member of Trinity Church there, subscribing £450 for the purchase of an organ, which he brought out free of charge in one of his own vessels. He continued his membership after moving to Halifax, where he was active in church affairs and a generous donor to charities. In 1797 he had married Mary, widow of John McGeorge, a member for Saint John in New Brunswick's first house of assembly. She died two years later, and on 3 Feb. 1807 Black married Catherine Billopp, daughter of Christopher Billopp, a member of the New Brunswick Council. One daughter was born of the first union, and the second produced a son and a daughter; the younger daughter, Rosina Jane, became the wife of James Boyle Uniacke*.

Black's health began to decline after 1819, and before his death he had been travelling for some time in Great Britain in the hope of restoring it. He had been one of the most constructive and enterprising merchants in the Maritimes, commanding respect and attention from his contemporaries. His obituary in the *Acadian Recorder* noted his "integrity" as a businessman, and praised "his reserved and quiet manners," "the kindness of his heart," "the soundness of his understanding, and the independence of his mind."

DAVID S. MACMILLAN

Halifax County Court of Probate (Halifax), Wills, 4: ff.125–28 (mfm. at PANS). NLS, Dept. of MSS, MSS 3847–51. St Paul's Anglican Church (Halifax), Reg. of baptisms, 19 Jan. 1808, 11 Feb. 1810. *Acadian Recorder*, 25 Oct. 1823. *New-Brunswick Courier*, 12 July 1816. *Royal Gazette* (Saint John, N.B.), 1785–1806. *Annals, North British Society, Halifax, Nova Scotia, with portraits and biographical notes, 1768–1903*, comp. J. S. Macdonald ([3rd ed.], Halifax, 1905). *N.B. vital statistics, 1784–1815* (Johnson et al.). I. A. Jack, *History of St. Andrew's Society of St. John, N.B., Canada, 1798 to 1903* (Saint John, 1903).

Black

Lawrence, *Judges of N.B.* (Stockton and Raymond). Macmillan, "New men in action," *Canadian business hist.* (Macmillan), 44–103. J. R. Armstrong, "The Exchange Coffee House and St. John's first club," N.B. Hist. Soc., *Coll.*, 3 (1907–14), no.7: 60–78. G. F. Butler, "The early organisation and influence of Halifax merchants," N.S. Hist. Soc., *Coll.*, 25 (1942): 1–16.

BLACK, WILLIAM, Wesleyan Methodist minister; b. 10 Nov. 1760 in Huddersfield, England, the second of five children of William Black and Elizabeth Stocks; m. first 17 Feb. 1784 Mary Gay in Cumberland County, N.S., and they had five children; m. secondly 20 July 1828 Martha Calkin, a widow, in Liverpool, N.S.; three of his children by his first wife, Martin Gay*, William Anderson, and Samuel, became leading Halifax merchants; a daughter, Mary, also by his first wife, married the merchant and politician John Alexander Barry*; d. 8 Sept. 1834 in Halifax.

What William Black would have described as the earthly portion of his life began at Huddersfield, Yorkshire, in the family of William Black, a Scottish draper who had moved from Paisley some years earlier. As a boy he lived with his uncle at Otley, near Leeds: "Here I went to school; but was inattentive to my learning, and assiduous in wickedness; particularly fighting, quarrelling, lying, stealing, and disobedience to my uncle." Nevertheless, he acquired a good primary education which would serve him well in later years. In 1775 his family joined the stream of emigrants from Yorkshire who settled in the Chignecto Isthmus of Nova Scotia in the 1770s. William Black Sr acquired a farm near Amherst; the young William's formative years were spent helping his parents in their arduous tasks.

Black was evidently a sensitive child and from an early age he was tortured by the religious outlook of his parents, who like many others of their generation cherished the fear of damnation and the hope of the new birth. He frequently said to himself: "O that I were a toad, a serpent, or anything but what I am!" His mother urged "the necessity of the new birth," but he continued on his sinful course. In Nova Scotia, at first he "grew in wickedness . . . turning the grace of God into lasciviousness; spending whole nights together" playing cards and dancing. Fortuitously, however, Black's neighbours provided the setting in which he resolved the tension in his own personality between the demands of the spiritual and the pressure of the secular worlds.

Many of the Yorkshire families who came to Nova Scotia in the 1770s were Methodists or had been influenced by John Wesley's teaching. Since they had no minister, they, as did Methodists elsewhere, held informal religious services in their homes, which Black attended. At one of them his conscience was stirred: the exhortation "went like a dagger" to his heart. Subsequently he went about with hanging head "whilst streams of tears rolled down" his cheeks, and he grew so disconsolate that he wished for death. At last, in a lengthy meeting, probably in 1779, "it pleased the Lord to reveal His free grace" to him; his "guilt was removed" and "a sweet peace and gladness were diffused" through his soul. He returned home with his heart "full of love" and his mouth "full of praise," convinced that he had joined the company of those to whom God had directly offered his grace and assurance. Although he was later tempted to believe that he had been deceived, his temptations confirmed his faith "the more," for "always proportionable comforts followed them."

In common with many who experienced conversion in his own generation and later, Black was not content simply to enjoy his own spiritual well-being; he "longed vehemently that all should know the sweetness and preciousness of Christ." He had "a feeling sense of their unhappy condition, as strangers to the grace of God, and could scarcely refrain from weeping over them." But rather than weep for his fellow sinners, Black began "to pray and exhort at almost every meeting" and to accept invitations to hold services in his neighbourhood. He gave his first sermon in the spring of 1781 during a visit to the Petitcodiac settlements (N.B.). The earliest specific date in his journal is 13 Nov. 1781, when, having come of age, he was freed from obligations to his family and "set off again, to visit the poor, hardened people of Petitcodiac river." Tacitly, Black had decided to become an evangelical preacher; he never altered his course until the infirmities of old age brought his search for lost souls to an end.

From the outset, apparently, Black was determined to be not simply an itinerant evangelist but a Methodist preacher. At this stage he had had no direct contact with Wesley or any of his colleagues. His knowledge of theology and particularly of Wesley's teaching was limited, and his understanding of the polity and discipline of the Methodist connection was derived from the older lay Methodists in his community. Yet he appears to have understood that in Wesley's preaching and practice an insistence on the new birth through justification by faith was combined with an emphasis on disciplined Christian living, the goal of which was Christian perfection or holiness. Similarly, he was aware that the essential features of the system which Wesley had devised for propagating his beliefs and training his converts were the circuits, staffed by an itinerant ministry, and the societies and the classes led by lay members. As he travelled about Nova Scotia, Black organized societies on the Methodist pattern. Nevertheless, he was very conscious of his intellectual inadequacy and of his lack of familiarity with Methodism. Hence, late in 1782 he wrote to Wesley requesting to be admitted to Kingswood

School, which Wesley had established in England, and asking him to send missionaries to Nova Scotia. Wesley promised that he would try to secure volunteers to help Black and to make room for him in the school. As it turned out, Black abandoned his plan to enter Kingswood.

Despite his awareness of his own deficiencies, Black with singular courage adopted the whole of Nova Scotia as his circuit. He knew he was entering on a difficult path, but with characteristic evangelical optimism probably had not assessed the full complexity of the challenge he had accepted. In 1781 Nova Scotia had some 20,000 inhabitants living in a number of largely isolated communities. Communications by land were rudimentary; travel by ship on the treacherous seas and the tide-swept Bay of Fundy was the principal link between the settlements. Sixty per cent of the inhabitants were New Englanders, the remainder being a heterogeneous assortment of Scots, Irish, the Yorkshire settlers, Germans, and others. Black probably assumed that many shared the characteristics of residents of Halifax, which he found inhabited by "a stupid set of people" among whom Satan had "many faithful and steady servants." Likewise Black doubtless agreed with Wesley's conviction that the Methodist message contained the essence of Christianity and that the innate wickedness of individuals was the only real obstacle to the acceptance of the word Wesley and he proclaimed.

In reality, however, the nature of the religious climate of Nova Scotia and the willingness of various groups to heed Black's words were influenced strongly by the diverse social, cultural, and religious traditions in the colony. The Scots and Scots-Irish were laying already the foundations of a distinct Presbyterian tradition in Nova Scotia in which there would be little affinity with Methodist doctrine and polity. Official Halifax was identified primarily with the Church of England and the values of the secular establishment in British society, and was unlikely to take seriously a self-appointed and unqualified enthusiast. Apart from his fellow Yorkshiremen, Black could hope to appeal effectively only to the New England settlers, who were for the moment the majority, but whose response to his ministrations was likely to be distinctly ambivalent.

The former New Englanders who had established communities in the Annapolis valley and along the South Shore brought with them the New England religious tradition, whose principal features were Calvinist theology, a learned ministry, and a congregational polity. The Great Awakening earlier in the century had profoundly shaken the New England churches and had made them more receptive than in the past to evangelical preaching. When Black began his mission, the Yankee settlements in Nova Scotia were caught up in a powerful revival led by Henry

Alline*, a movement which was nurtured by his own charismatic appeal, the unsettling effect of the War of American Independence on Nova Scotia, and the memory of the Awakening.

Twelve years older than Black, Alline was at the height of his influence in 1781, and within three years of his death. He, like Black, had had a powerful conversion experience, a "New Birth," which he believed should be the "evangelical norm." Thus he had entered upon a whirlwind itinerancy through the New England settlements which stirred immense enthusiasm and undermined the already weak Congregational churches. Initially, Black welcomed Alline as one who preached the necessity of the new birth and rejected the Calvinist doctrines of predestination and election. However, Alline was a mystic who, as Baptist minister John Davis* later wrote, was "converted in a rapture; and everafter he sought to live in a rapture; and judged of his religious condition by his enjoyments and raptures." Some, unfortunately, misunderstood Alline's teaching that newborn souls are inseparable from God and that there is "a final Perseverance of the Saints." For him, this conviction implied a new form of holy living, akin to the Wesleyan doctrine of holiness, but for others it led to antinomianism. According to Black, some of Alline's followers "taught publicly that no believer could make shipwreck of his faith; that his soul never sinned, though he should lie or get drunk . . . it was his body only." Many "sucked in the poison, as if it had been the marrow of the Gospel," and sought to administer it to others.

In effect, Alline's powerful preaching created an emotional climate among the Nova Scotia Yankees which was receptive to Black's appeal; yet although it had weakened it had not destroyed the influence of the Calvinist tradition. To Black, moreover, it appeared to be a source of division and controversy which could and did lead to the disruption of infant Methodist societies. Wherever the antinomian note was sounded, it constituted a fundamental challenge to the Methodist doctrine of holiness. Clearly, Black and his followers could hope to make significant inroads among the New Englanders only by charismatic preaching and by securing an adequate supply of missionaries.

Black's concern about his own qualifications and the danger of New Light competition was reflected in his initial approach to Wesley in 1782. Wesley replied: "The Antinomian you mention [Alline] ought to be guarded against with all possible diligence; otherwise, he will do more harm in one year than he can do good in twenty . . . of Calvinism, mysticism and Antinomianism, have a care; for these are the bane of true religion." But he was unable to send missionaries who could help to close the "flood-gates of iniquity" opened by Alline's followers. Black's anxi-

Black

ety about the future of the Methodist cause in the face of the New Light threat was intensified in 1783 by an equally disturbing development – the loyalist migration to Nova Scotia.

Black set sail for Shelburne on 5 June 1783 to meet the loyalists who were arriving there. "Our hearts were made glad by the sight of some of our friends from New York," he said, but inwardly he must have realized that the numbers of the new settlers were so great as to alter radically the magnitude of his mission. Some 20,000 loyalists came to Nova Scotia, mostly from the middle and southern colonies. Their coming changed the ethnic and cultural profile of the region and led to the establishment of the new colony of New Brunswick. Although the loyalists were by no means submissive to authority, they reinforced the conservative elements in colonial society. The new loyalist-dominated oligarchies which emerged in Nova Scotia and New Brunswick strengthened the position of the Church of England and evinced a marked distaste for radical religious or political movements.

Confronted with an overwhelming increase in the number of unawakened souls and the powerful thrust of the New Light movement, Black again sought advice and assistance from Wesley. Wesley responded that he had no time to answer Alline's "miserable jargon" and that he had "no hope of his being convinced [of his errors] until death opens his eyes." He urged Black to form a direct connection with the Methodist societies in the United States and to secure preachers from them. Black, perhaps recognizing that with Alline's death in February 1784 the evangelical movement was without strong leadership, and probably encouraged by Methodist loyalists from New York, evidently had decided already to turn in that direction. On 15 Sept. 1784 he "set off to visit the States, intending to get some help from our brethren there, as I alone could not take care of all the societies."

While Black was contending with the obstacles to his mission, Wesley had decided to initiate the establishment of a new and separate Methodist church in the United States. To that end he had set apart Thomas Coke as general superintendent of the American societies and had dispatched him to the United States to implement his design. Black met Coke and Francis Asbury, the leading American preacher, in Philadelphia and was invited to attend the conference which began on 24 Dec. 1784 in Baltimore, Md. This meeting became the first general conference of the Methodist Episcopal Church, of which Coke and Asbury were elected general superintendents or bishops. The new church already had 15,000 members and 81 preachers, and would soon become recognized as one of the most powerful evangelical denominations in the new republic.

Black's plea for help, which was strongly supported by Coke, resulted in the appointment of two missionaries to Nova Scotia – Freeborn GARRETTSON and James Oliver Cromwell. This action marked the beginning of a relationship between the Methodists in the Maritime provinces and the American Methodists which lasted until 1799. Throughout this period the stations of the Maritime ministers were generally listed in the minutes of the conferences in the United States, but Nova Scotia was never accepted formally as a district of the Methodist Episcopal Church. The real link between the two groups was Coke, who acted in effect as superintendent of all Methodist missions overseas and consequently was unable to devote his full attention to the needs of any particular region. For its part, the church in the United States was faced with a growing demand for preachers to meet its own requirements and would have difficulty in securing volunteers to serve in what many considered to be an alien environment.

In the euphoric atmosphere of the Christmas conference, however, this development was not foreseen. Black must have been overjoyed to participate in the momentous gathering and to have an assurance that his struggling mission could count on the assistance of Coke and Asbury. Curiously, he did not hasten home with the good news; he preached in the United States until May and did not meet with Garrettson until July 1785.

Garrettson had arrived in Nova Scotia in February 1785, and he left the colony two years later to resume his influential career in the Methodist Episcopal Church. In the interval he travelled and spoke unceasingly, visiting the New England communities in the Annapolis valley and the towns along the South Shore. God "compensated" him for his intense labours, "for many precious souls were awakened and converted." He was opposed by the followers of Alline who were, he believed, "as deluded a people as I ever saw," but his preaching stirred revivals in Horton, Cornwallis, Barrington, and Liverpool, which he hoped would give the New Light sympathizers a "wonderful Stab."

The spirit of revival, which Garrettson, building on the foundations laid by Black and Alline, had engendered, offered a great opening for the extension of the Methodist community in Nova Scotia and the other colonies. Partly for this reason itinerants began in 1786 to hold regular informal conferences at which they assigned themselves to circuits. The numbers of members and preachers and the stations were reported to the British and American conferences. Black was normally stationed on the Halifax circuit, and in addition was constantly on the move, visiting the societies in Nova Scotia and making missionary trips to the Saint John valley, Newfoundland, and St John's (Prince Edward) Island. However, he had little opportunity or incentive to exercise leadership until May

1789, when the American conference ordained and appointed him general superintendent for eastern British North America. Although he did not consider himself qualified "for so important and weighty a charge," he accepted Coke's decision because he shared Wesley's hope that "the days of coldness and darkness are now past, and that the Sun of Righteousness is rising on Nova Scotia likewise."

In the next decade Black had no colleague with the stature of Garrettson and the number of preachers at his disposal fluctuated from year to year. The New York Conference of 1791 sent six relatively inexperienced volunteers to Nova Scotia, but only eight ministers attended the Nova Scotia conference of 1794. Black was designated by Coke in 1793 as superintendent of the missions in the West Indies, from which post he was rescued by the protests of his brethren. Not surprisingly, in 1792 Black had tentatively proposed formal annexation of the societies under his care to the Methodist Episcopal Church. He informed Asbury that "it is now a subject of consideration amongst us whether we ought not to put ourselves under the direction of the American bishops." He added, however: "It is objected that such an union would excite the jealousies of our Civil Governors: but in my opinion, if the preachers who might come from the United States should be prudent men, and let politics alone, there would be nothing to fear from that quarter." Nothing came of this initiative; the conference of 1795 demonstrated its independent spirit by publishing its minutes in which the basic structure and rules of the Methodist connection in Nova Scotia and New Brunswick were laid down.

Despite his incessant travelling, Black found time to correspond regularly with his brethren; his letters combined mundane matters, prudent counsel, and exhortations to "preach up, and press after entire holiness." With few exceptions, he was warmly received not only by Methodists but by Anglican clergy and other influential people. At Charlottetown in 1794 he was given the use of the parish church by Lieutenant Governor Edmund Fanning* and visited with the rector, the Reverend Theophilus DESBRISAY, for "it is my desire to cultivate a Christian friendship and all proper union with the ministers of the Church of England." His preaching was often highly effective; in 1791 at Blackhead in Newfoundland, "the Holy Ghost fell upon the people, both as a Spirit of bondage to fear, and as a Spirit of liberty and love." On leaving Newfoundland he wrote: "I never had so affecting a parting with any people before in my life." He "left them weeping as for an only son."

Nevertheless, Black must have felt in 1799 that he and his brethren had waged an inconclusive battle to establish Methodism firmly in the eastern colonies. At this point there were only six ministers in Nova Scotia and New Brunswick, among them Duncan M'COLL

and James Man*. The Saint John valley was largely neglected and its inhabitants were "deeply initiated into the mysteries of Antinomianism." Prince Edward Island had seen no Methodist minister since Black's brief visit in 1794. There were in the entire region about 850 Methodists, a meagre harvest, particularly in the light of the powerful impetus which Garrettson had given to the spirit of revival and Black's faithful itinerancy. Clearly, if Methodism was to survive and grow drastic measures had to be taken.

By 1799 it was evident that, although Coke was sympathetic to placing the societies in Nova Scotia under the jurisdiction of the Methodist Episcopal Church, he was unable or unwilling to persuade Asbury and his associates to accept this responsibility. Asbury necessarily gave priority to the immense demands of the burgeoning church of which he was the effective head. Black, for his part, must surely have recognized that his societies could not count upon the American connection for preachers. Unlike Asbury, he had failed to recruit a native ministry. Yearning as he did to become a circuit minister in England, he turned naturally to the British Wesleyan Conference for help. He sailed for England in the autumn of 1799.

Black attended the session of the British conference in 1800 and, with the support of Coke, secured the appointment of Joshua Marsden*, William Bennett*, and two other preachers to assist him in Nova Scotia. The arrival of Black and these missionaries in Halifax on 4 Oct. 1800 opened a new phase in his career and in the history of Methodism in the eastern colonies. Although the ministers would continue to meet for a time as a conference and to describe Black as president of that body, in fact he was chairman of the Nova Scotia District (which included all the Maritime colonies) of the British conference. After 1804 this district would come under the jurisdiction of the various missionary committees of the home conference which sought to impose order and uniformity on Coke's diverse missionary enterprises, particularly after his death in 1814. But, until Black's retirement in 1812, the authority of the conference was exercised very lightly over the Nova Scotia District. In fact, although men and money were provided, the parent conference was never able to supply sufficient assistance to meet its needs fully.

Black continued ostensibly to live and work as he had before, but for several years his course was marked by uncertainty. Although he was only 40, 20 years of incessant travelling and preaching in the primitive conditions of the period had aged him prematurely. His visit to England had strengthened his nostalgic determination to retire to that country. This desire was reinforced by a dispute in 1802 on the Halifax circuit, where Thomas Daniel COWDELL, a local lay preacher, and others accused Black of a long

Black

list of misdemeanours – in effect he had been there too long for some members of the society. In this crisis Coke admonished him: "What will you do in a circuit in England? They don't want you. Give up your great sphere of action, in which God has by a series of miracles placed you, if you dare; mind you will repent of it but once, if you retain the life of God." The leaders of the Halifax circuit, convinced that his departure would "ultimately give a fatal stab to the Itinerancy" in the district and the conference, pleaded with him to remain, but in 1802–3 he made plans to preach for a year in Boston and then leave for England, a project which did not come to fruition.

Black's hesitations were, however, not yet at an end. Much against his better judgement, he was persuaded by Coke in 1804 to prepare for a mission in Bermuda, but this plan was frustrated by local hostility. Two years later the missionary committee and Coke again proposed that Black become general superintendent of the West Indies missions. Black insisted that he was not qualified for a supervisory role in such a large and scattered mission. His fellow preachers successfully petitioned the British conference to leave him in Nova Scotia and include Newfoundland in his superintendency.

From 1806 to 1812 Black was free to concentrate on his duties in the Nova Scotia District. He was normally stationed on the Halifax circuit; he travelled regularly throughout the region preaching and counselling his colleagues; he presided at the district meetings; and he reported regularly on the condition of the societies. His detailed account of the state of the work in 1804 illustrates his knowledge of the several circuits and his concern for their spiritual welfare. The constant theme of this as of other reports was the shortage of preachers which had left many potential converts without attention and resulted in the loss of others to worldliness or the "do nothing scheme or Antinomian delusion." From time to time he was encouraged by revivals, but the fact that in 1812 only seven of eleven ministers attended the Nova Scotia conference and only 1,153 members were on the rolls must have been deeply discouraging for him.

In 1810 Black wrote: "My constitution for several years has been much shaken. The labours of thirty years have contributed to infirmities. . . . I am not able to perform the active services of a travelling preacher." The Nova Scotia conference of 1812 acceded to his request that he should become a supernumerary preacher, stationed at Halifax, and that the British conference should be asked to appoint William Bennett as superintendent of the district. To the committee in England Black commented: "All the help I can afford the Brethren I shall gladly give. My health is somewhat improved since the warm weather came in; but a little exertion is too much for me."

Throughout the remainder of his life, Black helped his brethren as he was able, becoming in the process a kind of senior statesman in British North American Methodism. In 1816, for example, Bennett and Black were caught up in the first phase of the dispute between the British conference and the Methodist Episcopal Church over control of the Methodist missions in Upper and Lower Canada. They attended the meeting of the General Conference in Baltimore and endeavoured to persuade their American colleagues to put the societies in the Canadas under the jurisdiction of the British conference. They pointed out that the annexation of the Canadas to the Nova Scotia District would facilitate the interchange of missionaries and that the relationship between the Methodist Episcopal Church and the societies in the Canadas was and would continue to be a source of political difficulty for the latter. The General Conference decided, however, not to give up its role in Upper and Lower Canada. Black would have no further involvement in this contentious issue. The part he had played was indicative of his affinity for Wesleyan Methodism and his lack of understanding of the differences between the climate of opinion in the Canadas and in the eastern colonies. It also possibly underlined his failure to appreciate the importance of developing a native Methodist ministry in all parts of British North America.

By 1819 Black's health was failing rapidly. For relief he journeyed again to the United States, and was greatly cheered by his visits to the flourishing Methodist community in the eastern states. He preached to Congress on the text "What is a man profited, if he gain the whole world and lose his own soul?" He found the idea of being laid aside "as a broken and useless vessel . . . not a little painful." He was unable, however, to attend the district meeting in 1823 because of his "growing infirmities." In 1826 he was present at the historic district meeting at which, on the orders of the missionary committee, the Nova Scotia District was divided into the districts of Nova Scotia and New Brunswick. After 1829 Black no longer preached or led classes. He died, probably of heart disease, in Halifax on 8 Sept. 1834, in the midst of a cholera epidemic.

The death of the man who was known affectionately as "Bishop" Black to Methodists and non-Methodists alike throughout Nova Scotia was an occasion of profound sadness in the Methodist community. The Reverend Richard Knight*, who had attended Black in his last days, delivered the memorial sermon; in the course of it "the emotions of his heart became irrepressible, his feelings approached to an overpowering agitation . . . the mournful sympathy was universal." Grief so deep, even in an age more given to tears than ours, was an eloquent testimony to the honour and esteem in which Black was held as "the

Father of Methodism" in Nova Scotia and New Brunswick. He had fought the good fight.

What kind of man was he and what was the impact of his words and works on his generation? He was of average height, and in old age somewhat corpulent. According to Samuel Leonard Shannon*, Black "always wore the well-known clerical hat; a black dress coat buttoned over a double-breasted vest, a white neckerchief, black small-clothes and well polished Hessian boots." He had "a round, rosy face, encircled with thin, white hair, a benevolent smile and a sweet voice." The amiable countenance bespoke the inner man. Black was a person of deep humility, remarkable fortitude, and great kindliness. Above all he evinced a single-minded devotion to the business of his life, which was "to save souls." His preaching was both fervent and constructive. As the Reverend Robert L. Lusher* put it, "The benignity of the divine character rather than the 'terrors of the Lord' – the pleasures and rewards of piety . . . were the topics on which he seemed most to delight to dwell." In his gentle way he sought to instil in his colleagues his own positive and humble concern for the rescue of lost souls. In fact, especially as an ecclesiastical administrator, Black had the defects of his qualities. He lacked the holy ruthlessness of Asbury and Wesley which accounted in part for their striking success as evangelists and religious leaders; hence his own achievements were more modest.

Indeed one might conclude that, although Black was greatly esteemed by his fellow Methodists, his life and works were of little historic import. After all, in 1827 only 7.6 per cent of the people of Nova Scotia were Methodists; 16 per cent were Baptists, and the Anglicans and Presbyterians greatly outnumbered both denominations. Alline's disciples, as one historian has claimed, had "beaten the Methodists and all other religious competitors in the Yankee heartland" of Nova Scotia. Ethnic and cultural ties had perhaps been more effective in shaping religious affiliation than evangelical rhetoric of any kind. Nevertheless, Black's career was perhaps more significant than the statistics indicate.

The religious community which Black founded was deeply evangelical, strongly resistant to enthusiasm, and committed to stern adherence to moral discipline as an essential step toward the goal of holiness. Although Black and his brethren were occasionally discriminated against by the local élites and the Church of England, they remained unworldly and demonstrated little concern for the social and political implications of their beliefs. Also, in contrast to churches in the United States and Upper Canada, which showed great skill in recruiting and training their own leaders, the Nova Scotia Methodists became dependent for their ministers first on the Methodist Episcopal Church and later on the British conference.

For the first four decades of the 19th century, the district was dominated by missionaries who had been formed in England, and these missionaries were slow to seek out candidates for ministry who had been born and educated in British North America. They laboured in an atmosphere of dependence, and consciously or unconsciously sought to maintain a close link with the British conference and to foster intimate political and cultural ties between Britain and the emerging colonial societies. In effect, although numerically small in Nova Scotia and New Brunswick, the Methodist community was not only the custodian of a balanced evangelical tradition but also one of the forces of religious and cultural continuity which helped to shape the distinctive empire-oriented sense of identity of pre-confederation Nova Scotia. That this was the case owed much to Black's initiative in putting the societies under the jurisdiction of the British conference.

Such an assessment would have been, however, largely incomprehensible to Black. He would have wished to be remembered affectionately as one who at great peril and at great cost to himself brought a new hope and assurance to thousands of people, many of whom were beginning anew in an alien and inhospitable land. What was true of Alline's followers was also true of Black's: their acceptance of his teaching whatever its merits or implications was a seminal fact in their lives and in the growth of their social and cultural traditions.

G. S. FRENCH

Black's autobiography, "The life of Mr. William Black, written by himself," appears in *The lives of early Methodist preachers, chiefly written by themselves*, ed. Thomas Jackson (4th ed., 6v., London, 1873–78), 5: 242–95.

School of Oriental and African Studies Library, Univ. of London, Methodist Missionary Soc. Arch., Wesleyan Methodist Missionary Soc., corr., North America (mfm. at UCC, Central Arch., Toronto). UCC-M, William Black papers; Duncan McColl papers. Methodist Episcopal Church, *Minutes of the Methodist conferences, annually held in America; from 1773 to 1813, inclusive* (New York, 1813). *The New Light letters and spiritual songs, 1778–1793*, ed. G. A. Rawlyk (Hantsport, N.S., 1983). "The papers of Daniel Fidler, Methodist missionary in Nova Scotia and New Brunswick, 1792–1798," ed. G. [S.] French, UCC, Committee on Arch., *Bull.* (Toronto), 12 (1959): 3–18; 13 (1960): 28–46. Perkins, *Diary, 1780–89* (Harvey and Fergusson); *1797–1803* (Fergusson). John Wesley, *The letters of the Rev. John Wesley . . .*, ed. John Telford (8v., London, 1931; repr. [1960]). Wesleyan Methodist Church, *Minutes of the conferences* (London), 2 (1799–1807). *Novascotian, or Colonial Herald*, 10 Sept. 1834. *N.S. vital statistics, 1769–1812* (Punch); *1813–22* (Punch); *1823–28* (Holder); *1829–34* (Holder and Hubley). E. A. Betts, *Bishop Black and his preachers* (2nd ed., Sackville, N.B., 1976). G. G. Findlay and W. W. Holdsworth, *History of the*

Black Harry

Wesleyan Methodist Missionary Society (5v., London, 1921–24), 1. G. [S.] French, *Parsons & politics: the rôle of the Wesleyan Methodists in Upper Canada and the Maritimes from 1780 to 1855* (Toronto, 1962). Matthew Richey, *A memoir of the late Rev. William Black, Wesleyan minister, Halifax, N.S., including an account of the rise and progress of Methodism in Nova Scotia . . .* (Halifax, 1839). T. W. Smith, *History of the Methodist Church within the territories embraced in the late conference of Eastern British America . . .* (2v., Halifax, 1877–90). Abel Stevens, *History of the Methodist Episcopal Church in the United States of America* (4v., New York, 1864–67), 2. Howard Trueman, *The Chignecto Isthmus and its first settlers* (Toronto, 1902; repr. Belleville, Ont., 1975). John Vickers, *Thomas Coke, apostle of Methodism* (London, 1969).

BLACK HARRY, HENRY FLOYD, known as. *See* FLOYD

BLANCHET, FRANÇOIS, author, physician, teacher, militia officer, businessman, seigneur, politician, office holder, and JP; b. 3 April 1776 in Saint-Pierre-de-la-Rivière-du-Sud, Que., son of Jean-Baptiste Blanchet, a farmer, and Marie-Geneviève Destroismaisons; m. 9 Sept. 1802 Catherine-Henriette Juchereau Duchesnay, and they had three daughters and a son; d. 24 June 1830 at Quebec.

François Blanchet studied at the Petit Séminaire de Québec from 1790 to 1794, and then did a period of medical training with James FISHER, who taught him English and put him in touch with the most influential people in local medical and political circles. In 1799, on the advice of Fisher and physician John Mervin NOOTH and thanks to the 8,000 *livres* he had inherited from his father the previous year, he went to New York to study at Columbia College. In addition to acquiring democratic ideas Blanchet, who was a serious, hard-working, and ambitious student, received the degree of Bachelor of Medicine, having presented a thesis entitled *Recherches sur la médecine ou l'application de la chimie à la médecine*, which was published in French at New York in 1800. Also interested in the natural sciences, particularly mineralogy and physics, he bought books on these subjects, and he contributed a few articles to the *New York Medical Repository*. In 1801 he was elected a member of the American Philosophical Society, to which he submitted two papers on the origins of light and of the aurora borealis.

Blanchet returned to Lower Canada early in the summer of 1801. After passing the examination set by the medical examiners for the district of Quebec, he was authorized on 1 July to practise physic and surgery in the province. A year later he married the daughter of the wealthy seigneur of Beauport, Antoine Juchereau* Duchesnay, and her dowry of 20,000 *livres* enabled him to open an office in a handsome house on Rue des Remparts within a few months. He began to give private lessons on "chemistry applied to medicine" at his home in 1804. The next year he rented his house and bought another on Rue des Pauvres (Côte du Palais), near the Hôtel-Dieu.

Blanchet was appointed surgeon in the 1st Battalion of Quebec's militia in 1805, in recognition of his merit. The next year, with Pierre-Stanislas BÉDARD, Jean-Thomas TASCHEREAU, Louis BOURDAGES, Joseph-Bernard PLANTÉ, and Joseph Levasseur-Borgia*, he founded *Le Canadien*. However, as an owner of this newspaper, which Governor Sir James Henry Craig* considered a seditious publication, Blanchet was dismissed from his post as surgeon on 14 June 1808. He was elected member for Hertford to the House of Assembly of Lower Canada the following year, held his seat until 29 Feb. 1816, regained it on 6 April 1818, and kept it until his death.

Although Blanchet had embarked upon a political career, he always remained closely associated with the world of medicine. During the War of 1812 Governor Sir George Prevost* appointed him superintendent of the militia hospitals in Lower Canada, a position he held until 1816 and was given again in 1823. He became a member of the medical staff and the management committee of the Emigrant Hospital the same year. In 1830 he was offered the superintendency of the hospital and the post of health officer of the port of Quebec. That year he also became one of the medical examiners for the district of Quebec.

Quebec medicine owes to Blanchet a good many of the reforms undertaken in the early 19th century. He was one of the early organizers of the profession in Lower Canada. For example, he tried to set up a medical association at Quebec in 1818 but the plans fell through. In 1826 he was one of the contributors to the first medical journal published in Canada, the *Quebec Medical Journal/Journal de médecine de Québec*, founded by François-Xavier TESSIER. In addition, from 1823 he had taken part in various endeavours to make the medical boards elective.

A pioneer in medical education, Blanchet was one of the first doctors to give private lessons and to try to set up a progressive, uniform system of medical teaching. As a member of the assembly, he championed various bills aimed at allowing hospital circles to offer students practical training. In 1823, with Anthony von Iffland*, he reopened the Quebec Dispensary, which provided instruction in anatomy, chemistry, medicine, and surgery. Two years later the Emigrant Hospital also had a practical program.

Blanchet played an important role in the development of public health measures in the Quebec region. In 1817 he was on a special committee to promote "inoculation with vaccine." The need to keep a vigilant eye on European immigrants and increase assistance to them also engaged his attention. He was in favour of strengthening the quarantine laws and of founding an isolation hospital. He fought in the house to promote the latter project, which took shape in 1816 with the establishment of the first immigrants' hospital on Île aux Ruaux. In 1823 he was a member of the first municipal sanitation committee of Quebec; it was responsible for finding the means to fight epidemics and to provide medical assistance to immigrants.

Blanchet was thus a prominent figure on the Quebec medical scene in the early 19th century. His role was attributable to three factors: he was well informed and aware of the measures beginning to be adopted in the United States in the field of medicine; he was one of the best-qualified doctors in the town, enjoying a reputation that gave his projects more credibility; and, as the senior physician in the assembly, he was usually called upon when an important bill had to be steered through the house.

Blanchet also had an active political career. His thinking was attuned to that of the Canadian party, for which he was, indeed, one of the main spokesmen. He was in favour of democratic institutions and of "a liberal constitution," as he put it. On the eve of the 1810 elections Governor Craig jailed him for sedition, along with the other owners of Le Canadien. Upon his release the following July he sold his proprietary rights in the newspaper. As a politician Blanchet was closely involved in various debates on making the administration of the colony more democratic, managing public funds, and settling the problem of supplies [see Sir Francis Nathaniel BURTON]. On several occasions in the period 1818–28 he spoke out in the house to demand that it acquire increased powers in these areas.

When a plan for union between Upper and Lower Canada, with ominous prospects for the Canadians, was put forward in 1822 and the colony found itself at an impasse on the supplies question, Blanchet addressed a memoir to London in 1824 entitled Appel au Parlement impérial et aux habitans des colonies angloises, dans l'Amérique du Nord, sur les prétentions exorbitantes du gouvernement exécutif et du Conseil législatif de la province du Bas-Canada. The pamphlet sought to publicize the Canadian party's main grievances against the Executive and Legislative councils. In addition to making some attacks on the "placemen and the people who want to dominate the majority," Blanchet demanded scrutiny of the Legislative Council journals by the House of Assembly, election of the members of that council, control by the assembly of the salaries of senior office holders, and ministerial responsibility. In order to establish better contact between London and the colony, Blanchet also made several attempts to secure appointment of a Canadian agent to reside in Great Britain, but when he brought a measure to a vote in 1825 it was rejected by the Legislative Council.

As for the economy, Blanchet was concerned to have inland communications developed. In 1811 he proposed the creation of a provincial post office. Then he was in charge of various bills concerning, among other things, improvement of land communications between Upper and Lower Canada and utilization of means to promote the circulation of goods and persons within Lower Canada, such as construction of roads and bridges, upgrading of port installations, and development of steam navigation on the St Lawrence River all the way to Halifax. In 1829 he chaired the committee that brought out Reports from the special committee on roads and other internal communications.

Blanchet was also sensitive to some of the problems being encountered in rural circles, particularly the shortage of lands. In 1829 he was asked by the house to present an address on this subject to the governor. Reporting that the system of granting crown lands by auction was inadequate, because settlers did not usually have the means to bid for these lands, he suggested that grants be made without charge.

Blanchet played a part as well in the rapid progress of education in Lower Canada. At the outset of the century various groups complained about the state of education, particularly in rural areas. There were almost no primary schools, and on the secondary level the classical colleges remained inaccessible to most of the population. There was a demand for more public institutions, and to finance them it was proposed that the required sums be drawn from the annuities and income from the Jesuit estates. In 1814 Blanchet brought forward a bill on elementary education in Lower Canada. The following year he was put on an assembly committee to inquire into the state of education and its progress since the promulgation of the Education Act of 1801.

Throughout his political career Blanchet sat on numerous committees set up by the house to further education. On many occasions he acted as spokesman in the assembly for various associations, such as the Quebec Education Society, the British and Canadian School Society of the District of Quebec, and the National and Free School at Quebec, when they requested funds to purchase schools or continue financing their establishments. He also had a hand in the advancement and encouragement of some projects of a scientific nature, such as the publication of Joseph Bouchette*'s topographical atlas, the enlarging of Pierre Chasseur*'s Canadian natural history collection, and the founding of an agricultural college in Lower Canada.

In addition to practising medicine and engaging in politics, Blanchet was a justice of the peace for the District of Quebec from 1815 to 1825, he chaired the citizens' meeting held on 21 Oct. 1817 to seek municipal incorporation for Quebec, and he joined the Agriculture Society in 1818.

Bland

Blanchet was also a landowner. In particular he managed to acquire the seigneury of Saint-Denis-De La Bouteillerie, which had belonged to his father-in-law. At the latter's death the Blanchets had inherited part of his lands. Blanchet then reconstituted the whole fief by buying the shares of his brothers-in-law. In addition he owned a piece of land on the Rivière Bécancour, another near Lac Saint-François in Tring Township, and a third on the Rivière Saint-Charles, as well as a bakery in the *faubourg* Saint-Roch and two houses in Upper Town.

François Blanchet died at Quebec on 24 June 1830, aged 54, and was buried three days later in the church of the parish where he was born. He was clearly a leading reformer of the medical world in Lower Canada and an informed critic of politics and society in the colony in the first part of the 19th century.

JACQUES BERNIER

François Blanchet is the author of *Recherches sur la médecine ou l'application de la chimie à la médecine* (New York, 1800); *Appel au Parlement impérial et aux habitans des colonies angloises, dans l'Amérique du Nord, sur les prétentions exorbitantes du gouvernement exécutif et du Conseil législatif de la province du Bas-Canada* (Québec, 1824); and *Reports from the special committee on roads and other internal communications* (Quebec, 1829).

ANQ-Q, CE2-6, 4 avril 1776, 27 juin 1830; CN1-178, 8 oct. 1798; CN1-230, 8 mai, 13 juill., 9, 11 oct. 1809. ASQ, Fichier des anciens. PAC, MG 24, B1; RG 4, A1, 20, 149, 219, 325, 328; RG 8, I (C ser.), 1218: 234; RG 9, I, A5, 4: 1. L.C., House of Assembly, *Journals*, February–May 1812, 1815–16, 1818, 1825–30. *Le Canadien*, 18 juin 1808. *La Minerve*, 28 juin 1830. *Quebec Gazette*, 5 March 1801; 13 Dec. 1804; 20 Nov. 1806; 13 April 1815; March 1816; 23 April, 20 May, 21 Dec. 1818; 7 Dec. 1820; 13 April, 5 July 1821; 28 Aug. 1823. F.-J. Audet, "Les législateurs du Bas-Canada." F.-M. Bibaud, *Le Panthéon canadien* (A. et V. Bibaud). Hare et Wallot, *Les imprimés dans le Bas-Canada. Officers of British forces in Canada* (Irving), 101. *Quebec almanac*, 1806–8, 1812–16, 1830. Wallace, *Macmillan dict.* Abbott, *Hist. of medicine*, 50. T.-P. Bédard, *Histoire de cinquante ans (1791–1841), annales parlementaires et politiques du Bas-Canada, depuis la Constitution jusqu'à l'Union* (Québec, 1869), 104, 237. F.-X. Chouinard et al., *La ville de Québec, histoire municipale* (4v., Québec, 1963–83), 2: 36–37. Ouellet, *Bas-Canada*, 16–18. P.-G. Roy, *La famille Juchereau Duchesnay* (Lévis, Qué., 1903), 275, 277–301. J.-P. Wallot, "Le Bas-Canada sous l'administration de sir James Craig (1807–1811)" (thèse de PHD, Univ. de Montréal, 1965). Jacques Bernier, "François Blanchet et le mouvement réformiste en médecine au début du XIXᵉ siècle," *RHAF*, 34 (1980–81): 223–44. "Les Blanchet," *BRH*, 38 (1932): 735–40.

BLAND, JOHN, JP, office holder, and judge; likely b. in Devon, England; m. Sarah (probably Bayley), and they had five sons and three daughters; d. in or after 1825.

John Bland became a magistrate at Bonavista, Nfld, in 1790, but it is almost certain that he had some commercial connection with Newfoundland, possibly as a clerk or an agent for a merchant firm, as early as 1780. One probability is that he was an employee there of Samuel White and Samuel Rolles, merchants of Poole, Dorset, England, who traded into Bonavista until 1797 when White died and Rolles sold his property, part of it to Bland. In any event, he did not live off his civil appointments since the offices of justice of the peace and collector of Greenwich Hospital fees yielded little if any regular stipend. At the time he acceded to the position of surrogate court judge in 1801 with an annual salary of £60, Bland was comfortably situated at Bonavista.

Bland is remembered mainly for the penetrating interest he took in the fate and welfare of the dwindling tribe of native Indians, the Beothuks. In fact, many of the details, opinions, and certainly myths that have been become entrenched in the literature on them originate from the letters he wrote on their behalf to the governors at St John's between 1797 and 1807. His description of their habits and their treatment by English fishermen and settlers establishes him as a reasonably well-informed authority. At the same time he was also largely a purveyor of second-hand information, myths, and rumour obtained from individuals with whom he came into contact. Bland was especially harsh in his condemnation of salmon fishermen and furriers in Notre Dame Bay for their role in alienating the Beothuks and, in particular, he accused fisherman John PEYTON of numerous atrocities. Bland also recounted the capture and fate of three individual Beothuks. One was a little girl (whom other sources call Oubee) who was abducted after her parents were killed, "carried to Trinity, and treated with great care and humanity by Mr. & Mrs. [Thomas] Stone, who took her with them to England, where she died." The two others were Tom June and John August. June, according to Bland, was taken as a boy; he lived among fishermen and frequently made visits to his people in the interior of the island. August was captured as an infant when he fell from the back of his mother, who was shot trying to escape her white assailants. The details of the August story are confirmed by other sources which also provide evidence that he lived and worked in servitude to a merchant firm at Catalina and was buried in the churchyard at Trinity in 1788.

Some of Bland's proposals to befriend the Beothuks and save the tribe from extinction were later to be put into action by the naval governor. He advocated in 1797 that the first step should be "to obtain possession of some of the Indians," preferably by using soldiers from the St John's garrison, as a means of establishing further communications. The soldiers, if stationed in the area, would also act "as a check upon the furriers and salmon catchers, who are the chief delinquents," he reasoned. In 1800 he again pressed for a military party to be dispatched to Exploits. Meanwhile, the number of Indians was dwindling rapidly and the only scheme supported by the governors was to reward furriers and woodsmen for capturing Indians, on the assumption that these captives when befriended could later serve as ambassadors to their people. The results, Bland observed, were only more violence and more alienation of the surviving members of the tribe. Finally, in 1810–11 Governor Sir John Thomas Duckworth* sent an expedition led by Lieutenant David Buchan* to search out the abode of the Beothuks and attempt a conciliation, along the lines of Bland's plan. The experiment failed, however, as did another similar venture by Buchan in 1820.

The several governors that Bland served during his term at Bonavista relied much on him to provide information on affairs in the area. During the summers of 1805 and 1806 Bland compiled a complete survey of properties in settlements around Bonavista Bay, which included names of occupants and owners and the nature of their respective claims or leases. This document, known as the "Register of Fishing Rooms," is an invaluable record of the early population and settlement in Bonavista Bay.

Another important document that came from Bland's pen was a letter to Governor James GAMBIER in 1802 about the seal fishery. To satisfy Gambier's curiosity on the nature of the sealing effort, Bland provided a detailed description of the several strategies employed and the technology used, as well as of the environmental conditions related to success and failure and of the various seal species. He observed that "this adventurous and perilous pursuit is prosecuted in two different ways." The first was a method using nets which was practised during the winter months and extended from Conception Bay to the Labrador coasts, with the northern ports generally more successful. The second method, which he claimed "has not been general longer than nine years," was a venture which employed large boats – "ice-skiffs, decked boats, or schooners." These boats sailed into the ice floes off the northeast coast about the middle of March and sometimes continued to hunt seals until June. The merchants at St John's, he noted, had followed the new method "with uncommon spirit."

Bland's letters reveal a forthright, decisive, and confident individual. He earned the confidence of the governors and established himself as a man of integrity and honesty in official circles. His contentious opinions also gained him strong enemies, especially among merchants and traders. Thus, when in 1802 he sought to become chief justice for Newfound-land, many of the stronger Poole merchants, some of whom had vested interests on the northeast coast and connections there with men such as Peyton, opposed his appointment, and the position went to Thomas TREMLETT. Bland had to wait some years before he got promoted to office in St John's and even then had to settle for high sheriff.

Although Bland's name has been mainly associated with a philanthropic movement related to the Beothuks, he also pressed for measures to promote the well-being of white settlers in Bonavista Bay and in Newfoundland generally. Upon receiving instructions to take the survey of properties in Bonavista Bay, he believed erroneously, as did most of the settlers, that government intended to raise a revenue from property taxes and leases. He suggested that "such is the general condition of the poorer class . . . of this quarter . . . that humanity must plead exemption on their part." Bland also argued in 1805 that the act of 1699 which governed the rights to fishing rooms had long since become obsolete and impractical to enforce. Even though he was aware that the colonization of Newfoundland was still a contentious question, as early as 1805 he advocated that the island should be invested with a house of assembly, some 27 years before it became a reality. As a source of revenue, he suggested: "Rum is perhaps the first article that might contribute towards so reasonable an end."

Over time his progressive and, for the period, radical political views were taken up by others such as William Carson* and Patrick Morris*. With his move to St John's in 1811 to take up his appointment as high sheriff, Bland received a stipend of more than £220, a comfortable house, and fees for various special duties. He became financially secure and entrenched in the establishment. Moreover, within the larger political and social circles of St John's, his stature was relatively less. It is uncertain whether he died in office, or took his retirement in St John's or elsewhere. His name, prominent in official documents and local newspapers until 1825, abruptly disappears thereafter. Most likely he left Newfoundland, since his death would have almost certainly been noted in the papers and referred to in official despatches had it occurred there. He was succeeded as high sheriff by David Buchan. A son, John Bayley Bland, was active in Newfoundland life until 1840.

W. GORDON HANDCOCK

PANL, GN 1/13/4, reg. of fishing rooms, Bonavista Bay, 1806; GN 2/1, 1790, 1801, 8 Aug. 1804, 18 July 1805, 1811–26; GN 2/2, 1 Sept. 1790; 20 Oct. 1797; 25 Aug. 1800; 18 Aug. 1804; 1 Aug. 1805; 8 June, 4 July, 9 Sept.

Bleakley

1806; 22 Sept. 1807; 16 Jan. 1826. PRO, CO 194/42–43. Howley, *Beothucks or Red Indians*. Prowse, *Hist. of Nfld.* (1895), 419–20. F. W. Rowe, *Extinction: the Beothuks of Newfoundland* (Toronto, 1977).

BLEAKLEY, JOSIAH, fur trader, office holder, and militia officer; b. *c.* 1754; d. 22 Jan. 1822 in Montreal.

Josiah Bleakley was established in the province of Quebec, and possibly engaged in the fur trade, by November 1774 when he signed a petition from British merchants there for the repeal of the Quebec Act. He was in London with another colonial merchant, James Finlay Sr, in April 1778; they had returned to the province by July when they took two bateau loads of merchandise from Montreal to Detroit. Bleakley's investment in the fur trade that year was about £1,250, which made him a small trader in comparison with James McGill*, who the same year invested more than £24,000.

In 1782 Bleakley accompanied two canoe loads of merchandise to the fur-trading community at Michilimackinac (Mackinac Island, Mich.). By April 1783 he had secured government positions as clerk and Indian storekeeper, in charge of dispensing presents to visiting Indians. He continued to trade as well, and that summer, with Finlay and John Gregory*, he took eight canoes with a cargo valued at £4,500 from Montreal to Michilimackinac. Despite the uncertainty of property holding at Michilimackinac, which was placed in American territory by the Treaty of Paris in 1783, Bleakley found the place to his liking; he purchased a house and lot in 1785 and enjoyed the fellowship of St John's Lodge No.15, the local masonic lodge. During 1787 he served as a director of a short-lived fur-trade association called the General Company of Lake Superior and the South, or the General Society [*see* Étienne-Charles Campion*]. Although he established a permanent residence in Montreal about this time, and in 1787 was elected to the Beaver Club, he continued to travel west frequently.

The upper Mississippi River had attracted Bleakley's attention as early as 1785–86 when he wintered there, possibly in the service of the General Society. In April 1793 he was at Prairie du Chien (Wis.). During the late 1790s he maintained trade connections with William Burnett at the mouth of the St Joseph River on Lake Michigan and Jacques Clamorgan, Loisel et Cie in St Louis (Mo.). In 1800 he was trading with Auguste Chouteau, also of St Louis, a tie he continued until at least 1809. Again at Prairie du Chien in 1806, he encountered the United States Army exploratory party under Zebulon Montgomery Pike. He doubtless eyed the soldiers apprehensively because, as a British trader, he was excluded from the rich lands along the Missouri River which the United States had recently purchased from France. He was one of the Montreal merchants who, in a memorial of 8 Nov. 1805, had protested this exclusion. In 1807 he was again in the west, trading in partnership with Jean-Baptiste-Toussaint Pothier*.

To meet the increasing American challenge to their trade in United States territory, a number of British and Canadian merchants, including Bleakley, had formed the Michilimackinac Company in late 1806 [*see* John Ogilvy*]. Bleakley was a negotiator for the new co-partnership in discussions with the North West Company that led to an agreement defining the boundary between their trading territories. In May 1808 he was in a brigade of eight bateaux belonging to the Michilimackinac Company when it was stopped and the bateaux seized by American customs officials at Niagara (near Youngstown), N.Y. Some of the partners journeyed to Washington to protest while Bleakley remained at Niagara to straighten out the affair. The year's trade was thrown into disarray. However, by 1810, and again in the following year, Bleakley was sending men to winter on the Mississippi, and in 1812 he appears to have been associated with Jacques Porlier.

The War of 1812 probably disrupted Bleakley's operations, but during 1814 he returned to the Mississippi country. In September he was back in Montreal dispatching a brigade of canoes with supplies to the British garrison at Michilimackinac. At the conclusion of the war British subjects were barred from trading on American territory, and Bleakley seems to have retired at that point. Over the years he had acquired a solid reputation and been called on as an arbitrator or given power of attorney by such important firms as Meldrum, Parke, and Miamis Company and James and Andrew McGill and Company. Thus John Askin's description of him in 1807 as "that poor simple man" is somewhat perplexing but may explain in part why he never attained the status of a magnate in the trade.

On 24 Feb. 1798 Bleakley had married at Quebec Margaret McCord, sister of Montreal merchant Thomas McCord, in a ceremony at which the fur-trade merchant John Forsyth* was a witness. In 1803 Bleakley became a lieutenant in the 1st Battalion of Montreal's militia; he retired at that rank in 1812 but became the battalion's paymaster two years later. By 1819 he was secretary and treasurer of the Montreal Fire Insurance Company. At the time of his death in 1822 he was living in a stone house on the corner of Notre-Dame and Saint-Claude streets next door to Forsyth. This and other properties were seized by the sheriff in March 1823 for sale at public auction at the suit of the merchant Henry McKenzie, but by Margaret's marriage contract she was guaranteed the first £1,000 from the proceeds of the sale. Apart from his widow, Bleakley left a daughter and two minor sons, the latter under the tutorship of Thomas THAIN.

DAVID A. ARMOUR

ANQ-M, CE1-63, 24 janv. 1822. ANQ-Q, CE1-66, 24 févr. 1798; CN1-256, 24 févr. 1798; CN1-262, 18 janv. 1805. Bayliss Public Library (Sault Ste Marie, Mich.), Misc. coll., diaries, journals, and fraternal records; Mackinac notarial records, 1806–18 (photocopies at DPL, Burton Hist. Coll.); Port Mackinac, records, 1802–8. Bentley Hist. Library, Univ. of Michigan (Ann Arbor), Mich. Hist. Coll., United States Bureau of Customs, District of Michilimackinac, impost book, 1802–8. Clarke Hist. Library, Central Michigan Univ. (Mount Pleasant), T. C. and F. R. Trelfa coll., 1, 4, 15, 23 July 1803; 19 June, 15 July 1804; 10 July 1806; 28 April, 21 May, 8 June 1807. DPL, Burton Hist. Coll., Thomas Williams papers, petty ledger, 1775–79. McGill Univ. Libraries, MS coll., CH138.S9, 2, 10, 16 July 1807. Mo. Hist. Soc. (St Louis), Chouteau coll.; Kenneth McKenzie papers, John Bleakley to Hammond Ogden, 22 Oct. 1845. PAC, MG 23, GIII, 26, no.101; RG 4, B28, 115, 20 July 1778, 14 Sept. 1782, 8 July 1783, 19 May 1790. St Ignace County Court House (St Ignace, Mich.), Reg. of the post of Michilimackinac, 26 Sept. 1785.

William Burnett, *Letter book of William Burnett, early fur trader in the land of four flags*, ed. W. M. Cunningham (n.p., 1967), 3, 13, 41–42, 71, 78, 117. *Cahokia records, 1778–1790*, ed. C. W. Alvord (Springfield, Ill., 1907), 522–25. *Docs. relating to constitutional hist., 1759–91* (Shortt and Doughty; 1918), 2: 591, 695. *Docs. relating to NWC* (Wallace), 224–29, 427. *John Askin papers* (Quaife), 2: 202, 216–17, 230, 569. *Mich. Pioneer Coll.*, 11 (1887): 356–57, 393–95; 12 (1887): 445; 13 (1888): 73–74; 15 (1890): 647–49; 25 (1894): 218–21, 250–58; 37 (1909–10): 560–61. Joseph Papineau, "Correspondance de Joseph Papineau (1793–1840)," Fernand Ouellet, édit., ANQ *Rapport*, 1951–53: 186–90. [Z. M.] Pike, "Pike's explorations in Minnesota," Minn. Hist. Soc., *Coll.* (St Paul), 1 (1872): 415. "Records of Niagara . . . ," ed. E. A. Cruikshank, Niagara Hist. Soc., [*Pub.*], no.42 (1931): 42–63, 70–79. Wis., State Hist. Soc., *Coll.*, 19 (1910): 275–76, 322–24. *Quebec Gazette*, 16 Oct. 1800, 19 Nov. 1812, 6 March 1823. Massicotte, "Répertoire des engagements pour l'Ouest," ANQ *Rapport*, 1944–45: 315. *Quebec almanac*, 1804: 47; 1805: 47; 1810: 58; 1811: 58; 1815: 91; 1820: 134. L. P. Kellogg, *The British régime in Wisconsin and the northwest* (Madison, Wis., 1935), 358–59. Miquelon, "Baby family," 189. J. F. Smith, *A panorama of masonic history: sesquicentennial of the Grand Lodge, Free and Accepted Masons of Michigan, 1826–1976* ([Detroit, 1976]).

BLISS, JOHN MURRAY, lawyer, militia officer, office holder, politician, colonial administrator, and judge; b. 22 Feb. 1771 in Massachusetts, the only child of Daniel Bliss and Isabella (Isabel) Murray; m. 7 Aug. 1797 Sarah Green Upham in Saint John, N.B., and they had two sons and four daughters; d. there 22 Aug. 1834.

The father of John Murray Bliss was a prominent Massachusetts lawyer and loyalist who immigrated to New Brunswick with his family after being appointed to the first provincial council in 1784. His mother's father was Colonel John Murray, another prominent lawyer, who had been appointed a councillor in Massachusetts though he was never sworn in. In 1797 Bliss married his first cousin Sarah Green Upham, the daughter of judge Joshua Upham*, another member of the New Brunswick Council, and in 1819 their son George Pidgeon Bliss married the daughter of Thomas WETMORE, the attorney general of New Brunswick. By the 1820s the Blisses, Murrays, Uphams, and Wetmores thus composed an interrelated network of loyalist families and the acknowledged patriarch of "this powerful family," as Lieutenant Governor Sir Howard Douglas* described it, was John Murray Bliss.

Bliss studied law in the offices of Jonathan Sewell* and Jonathan BLISS, was admitted to the bar in 1792, and began to practise in Fredericton. In 1794 he became judge advocate to the forces in New Brunswick, a post he was to hold for nearly 20 years. As a youth he was known for his hot temper and in 1800 he fought a duel with Samuel Denny STREET, both men escaping unharmed. Their dispute arose out of a court case and was in part a reflection of the intense rivalry among the members of an overcrowded bar for fame and fees. During the 1790s Bliss had been so despondent about his prospects that he had seriously considered returning to the United States, but he persevered and gradually built up an extensive practice. After his father died, Bliss acquired the family estate in Lincoln, N.B., and completed the construction of Belmont, said to be the finest house in the colony. In 1798 he had been placed in command of a militia company and when the militia was embodied in 1808 he served as a major; during the War of 1812 he was to act as provincial aide-de-camp to the administrator and commander of the forces, Major-General George Stracey SMYTH. He succeeded Ward CHIPMAN as solicitor general in 1809 and two years later he became clerk of the House of Assembly. In 1809 he ran unsuccessfully for a seat in the assembly, but he was subsequently returned in a by-election in York County and took his place in the house on 26 Jan. 1814. On 17 May 1816 he was raised to the Council and on 9 July, with some reluctance since he claimed to be earning £1,500 per annum in private practice, he became an assistant judge of the Supreme Court, filling the vacancy left by the death of Edward Winslow*. Because of the "delicate health" of Chief Justice Jonathan Bliss, the frequent absences of assistant judge Ward Chipman and later his son, Ward Chipman* Jr, and the refusal of Chief Justice John SAUNDERS to go on circuit, Bliss performed an unusually large share

Bliss

of the business of the Supreme Court over the next two decades.

From 21 Feb. 1824 until the arrival of Sir Howard Douglas on 28 August, Bliss also served as administrator of New Brunswick. His most controversial action was the dismissal of George Shore* from the offices of surveyor general, receiver general, and auditor general, and the appointment of his son George Pidgeon Bliss to those posts. Douglas was unable to confirm the appointment but to pacify the ex-administrator he persuaded the authorities in London to confer the position of receiver general on the younger Bliss. While Douglas remained in the colony he managed to maintain an uneasy balance of power and patronage between the older loyalist families and a rival faction which gravitated towards Thomas Baillie*, the powerful commissioner of crown lands whose appointment had greatly diminished the value of the office of receiver general. After Douglas departed in 1829, Bliss persuaded the Council to vote for a substantial reduction in Baillie's emoluments, but this recommendation was set aside by the British government. According to Douglas, Bliss had been "deeply *wounded* & mortified" by the decision of the Colonial Office to prohibit judges from acting as administrator, and during the 1830s he played a less active part in the political affairs of the colony, particularly after judges were excluded from the Council in 1831. In 1834 he applied for the position of chief justice but was turned down in favour of the younger Ward Chipman, who, although Bliss's junior on the bench, had greater influence in London. Later that year Bliss died while on a visit to Saint John; he was buried in Fredericton.

In its obituary the *New-Brunswick Courier* proclaimed that Bliss had been "revered and beloved" by the legal profession and that "the dignity of his demeanor and the distinguished urbanity of his manners" had "won . . . the regard of all who were brought into contact with him." Yet neither as a lawyer nor as a judge does he appear to have been above the ordinary. The only important trial he participated in as an attorney was the famous test case over slavery in 1800, during which he acted as one of the five counsel who unsuccessfully upheld its legality in New Brunswick [*see* Caleb Jones*]. He does not appear to have attracted students to his law office. As a judge he seems to have been somewhat less severe in the sentences he imposed than his colleagues, and on one occasion his leniency was "a general topic of conversation." He took an active part in community affairs in Fredericton, where he served at various times as a trustee of the College of New Brunswick, chairman of the local branch of the Society for Promoting Christian Knowledge, and president of the New-Brunswick Agricultural and Emigrant Society. Yet he owed his political influence not to his public service but to his

extensive connections among leading loyalist families. Since one of his sons had predeceased him and George Pidgeon Bliss died in 1836, his own family went into decline after his death.

PHILLIP BUCKNER

The genealogical information in this biography is taken from PANB, MC 1, L. D. Bliss, "Lines of descent in the ancestry of George Pidgeon Bliss and Sarah Armstrong" (mimeograph of typescript, 1975); MC 1156; and the *New-Brunswick Courier*, 23 Aug. 1834. There are scattered references to Bliss in the Sewell papers, PAC, MG 23, GII, 10, vol.3: 636–40, 762–69, 790–93; in the Douglas papers, PAC, MG 24, A3, 3: 45–47, 57, and 4: 32–33, 143–45, 288–90; and in PRO, CO 188/41: 125; CO 188/50: 4–8, 97; and CO 323/158: 226–27. There are also numerous references in the *New-Brunswick Royal Gazette*, especially 9 Feb. 1819, 16 Jan. 1821, 2 Sept. and 14 Oct. 1823, 24 Feb. 1824, and 20 June 1826, and in the *New-Brunswick Courier*, 11 Oct. 1823, 27 July 1827, and 3 May and 11 Oct. 1828. The only secondary sources of value are Lawrence, *Judges of N.B.* (Stockton and Raymond) and MacNutt, *New Brunswick*.

BLISS, JONATHAN, lawyer, office holder, politician, and judge; b. 1 Oct. 1742 in Springfield, Mass., fifth child of Luke Bliss and Mercy Ely; m. there 11 July 1790 Mary Worthington, and they had four sons; d. 1 Oct. 1822 in Fredericton.

Jonathan Bliss's forebears emigrated from England to Massachusetts in 1635 and one branch of the family established itself in Springfield, where Jonathan was born. Over the years the Blisses had acquired property and status in western Massachusetts, and at the age of 15 Jonathan was sent to join the sons of the colonial élite at Harvard College. A high-spirited youth who rejected the Puritan moral code, he was frequently involved in clashes with the college authorities. In 1761 he was rusticated for taking part in a disturbance, but he was readmitted in 1762, graduated with a BA in 1763, and subsequently received his MA for defending the proposition that "the Offspring of Slaves are not Born Slaves." Following graduation he studied law in Boston and Cambridge in the offices of Thomas Hutchinson and Edmund Trowbridge; in 1764 he began to practise in Wilbraham. Although later described by Joseph Wilson Lawrence* as "one of the leaders of the Massachusetts Bar," Bliss appears to have had an extremely limited local practice, and he played at best a minor role in the organization of the legal profession in the colony. He achieved greater notoriety as a politician. His father had sat in the Massachusetts General Court and in 1768 Jonathan was chosen to represent Springfield and Wilbraham. On 21 June 1768 Governor Francis Bernard asked the legislature to revoke a resolution protesting the Townshend duties. Because he voted with the minority of 17 rescinders on 30 June, Bliss was condemned in newspapers from Massachusetts to Virginia as one whose name would "be handed down with infamy."

The roots of Bliss's loyalism are not difficult to unravel. His family was moving up in society and, like many lawyers of his generation, Bliss looked to the crown for preferment. He had studied law in the offices of two prominent loyalists and he remained closely associated with Hutchinson, who as acting governor of Massachusetts appointed Bliss a justice of the peace on 9 May 1770 and as governor commissioned him a major in the militia on 23 April 1771. None the less, Bliss was not the stuff of which martyrs are made. He did not seek re-election to the General Court after 1768, and on 30 Aug. 1774, when the Springfield court-house was occupied by a large mob, he signed a pledge not to accept office under the coercive acts. He also signed a non-consumption agreement.

After the battle of Lexington, Bliss sailed for England with his close friend and fellow classmate at Harvard, Sampson Salter Blowers*, who had also studied with Hutchinson. In London Hutchinson used his influence with Lord North to secure Bliss a sinecure as solicitor to the Board of Customs. Many of the prominent loyalists who migrated to England were disillusioned by their years in exile but Bliss retained happy memories of the experience. As one of Hutchinson's protégés he moved in high society, and he participated in the various clubs formed by the New England loyalists. He travelled on holiday to the Continent, spent his summers in Bristol, and wintered in London. At the end of the war he could not return to Massachusetts, since he had been proscribed in 1778 and his property had been confiscated in 1781. When Blowers declined an appointment in 1784 as attorney general of the newly created province of New Brunswick, Bliss obtained the post through the influence of Sir William Pepperrell, the leader of the New England community in London.

On 2 Feb. 1785 Bliss received his warrant of appointment and set off for Parrtown (Saint John), where he assumed office on 16 May. As attorney general he was theoretically chief legal adviser to the government. In practice he was seldom consulted by Governor Thomas Carleton*, who relied for advice on the chief justice, George Duncan Ludlow*, and the solicitor general, Ward CHIPMAN. In 1786 Bliss admitted, "I have as little to do in the Government as an Attorney General can have." Yet he was not displeased with the limited role assigned to him since he disliked "the Labor of the Bar" and yearned to retire "to a Farm on the Kennebecasis." He conducted the major crown prosecutions during meetings of the Supreme Court but, because he rarely went on circuit, Chipman, the clerk of the crown on the circuits, prosecuted at the circuit courts. In view of the lucrative fees involved, however, Bliss vainly tried to prevent Chipman, as advocate general, from monopolizing prosecutions in the Vice-Admiralty Court. Although as attorney general Bliss was automatically at the head of the bar, he trained few students in his office and only two of any prominence, John Murray BLISS and William Botsford*. Since he avoided the circuit courts, his private practice was limited, and his clients were drawn exclusively from the older members of the loyalist élite. He acted as counsel for the plaintiff in the first ejectment suit in the colony and as one of the attorneys for his good friend Benedict Arnold* in the first trial for slander. In 1800 he was one of five lawyers who represented the owner, Caleb Jones*, in the trial of Nancy (Ann), a fugitive slave, and he delivered a lengthy defence of slavery. Despite his efforts the bench was divided and no decision was reached. In this case, as in many others, he was overshadowed by his more talented rival, Ward Chipman, who with Samuel Denny STREET acted for Nancy.

In 1785 Bliss and Chipman both ran for election to the first assembly as part of the government slate in Saint John County and City. They were opposed by a rival slate which would probably have coasted to victory if the sheriff had not closed the polls for a time after a minor riot and disallowed a number of votes cast for the opposition candidates. The loyalist-dominated assembly upheld the sheriff's decision, but because the election was contested Bliss was passed over for the position of speaker. During the session of 1786 the house, prompted by Bliss and Chipman, passed a bill restricting the rights of petitioners to the crown and the legislature, and Bliss eagerly prosecuted a number of his opponents for signing a "most seditious" petition, in order "to convince these Men that they will not be able to subvert this Government." Bliss frequently introduced government bills into the assembly and acted as spokesman for the administration. He consistently supported conservative measures, voting to re-enact the Nova Scotia law of 1758 establishing the Church of England as the official church, and opposing pay for assemblymen. Although he disagreed with Carleton's decision to move the seat of government to Fredericton, he held his tongue, but he did criticize the Supreme Court for not meeting in Saint John.

Increasingly disgruntled with a salary of £150 and fees which amounted to about £30 per annum, and disheartened as well by the "cursed cold Climate" of New Brunswick, he unsuccessfully applied for a position on the bench of Upper Canada in 1791. He had also been lonely for some time and in 1786, "weary of this cursed Celibacy," he had begun to search for a wife. His eventual choice was Mary Worthington, nearly 20 years his junior, whom he had known as a child in Springfield. Mary's father, John Worthington, was a wealthy and prominent lawyer and her sister was to marry Fisher Ames, one of the leading members of the Federalist party in the American Congress. In 1790 Bliss travelled to Springfield, where he and Mary were wed, and upon his return to Saint John he purchased the large house previously owned by Benedict Arnold. The marriage was a happy one and produced four sons: John Worthington in 1791, Lewis in 1792, William Blowers* in 1795, and Henry* in 1797.

Bliss was defeated when he ran for re-election to the New Brunswick assembly in 1793, but in 1795 he was again selected to represent Saint John County and City. Since the assembly was dominated by opponents of the government [see James Glenie*], Bliss usually found himself voting with the minority. The 1790s were difficult years both for New Brunswick and for Bliss personally since his income shrank, but his wife and boys, he wrote to Arnold, "make my Fire side happy even in this wretched country." Bliss was devastated by Mary's death on 17 April 1799. Partly for financial reasons he was compelled to send his younger sons, William and Henry, to live with Mary's relatives in Massachusetts and he became more and more an aloof figure. After 1802 he did not seek re-election to the assembly. In 1803 he resigned from the board of commissioners of the New England Company, on which he had served since 1787, because of a dispute with his colleagues. Acting on behalf of the commissioners for auditing the public accounts, in 1804 and 1805 he prosecuted the former deputy paymaster of contingencies, Edward Winslow*, with a degree of enthusiasm that seemed to Winslow's friends to border on vindictiveness. When a vacancy occurred on the provincial bench in 1807 Bliss did not apply for the post because the salary of a puisne judge was so low. But when the salaries of the judges were raised the following year and the office of chief justice became vacant, Bliss used all of his influence in London to secure the appointment. He was sworn into office on 28 June 1809 and on 7 July 1809 he assumed a seat on the provincial council. The following year he moved from Saint John to Fredericton; there he presided over the deliberations of the Supreme Court and the Council conscientiously, but with little enthusiasm, while his health rapidly declined. In 1819 he attempted to retire but neither the British government nor the assembly was prepared to grant him a pension and he clung to his office, although increasingly unable to perform the duties, until his death on 1 Oct. 1822. He was succeeded as chief justice by John SAUNDERS.

In 1796 Bliss had written to a friend that he had lived "too long" in England "to be content in this wretched corner of his Majesty's Dominions." New Brunswick was for Bliss, as it was for many of the loyalists whose careers had been shattered by the American revolution, a poor second choice. Some of the younger loyalists, such as Ward Chipman, were able to adjust to their adopted home but Bliss never made the transition. He had not participated in the partition movement which had created New Brunswick and, although out of necessity he accepted the office of attorney general and later the office of chief justice, he played only a minor role in establishing the legal and judicial institutions of the colony. He served two terms as a legislator but mainly acted as the voice of the executive. His commitment to the colony was limited and his contribution to its development minimal. After his death all three of his surviving children, Lewis, William Blowers, and Henry, left the colony for greener pastures.

PHILLIP BUCKNER

The best collection of Jonathan Bliss papers is found in the Bliss family papers (PANS, MG 1, 1595–1613), esp. vols.1601–8. There is a smaller collection in N.B. Museum, Benedict Arnold papers, packets 1 and 2, and a number of letters among the Winslow papers (UNBL, MG H2), most of which are printed in *Winslow papers* (Raymond). Some useful references occur in the Colonial Office files for New Brunswick, esp. PRO, CO 188/4 and 188/14–15. There are also many references to Bliss's activities in N.B., House of Assembly, *Journal*, 1786–1822, and scattered mentions among the newspapers of the period.

The most complete secondary source is I. E. McAfee, "Jonathan Bliss: a loyalist success story" (MA thesis, Univ. of Maine, Orono, 1973). The chapter on Bliss in Lawrence, *Judges of N.B.* (Stockton and Raymond) and the sketch in Shipton, *Sibley's Harvard graduates*, vol.15, are useful. There are also brief references to him in Carol Berkin, *Jonathan Sewall: odyssey of an American loyalist* (New York, 1974); Gorman Condon, "Envy of American states"; Jones, *Loyalists of Mass.*; MacNutt, *New Brunswick*; and M. B. Norton, *The British-Americans: the loyalist exiles in England, 1774–1789* (Boston and Toronto, 1972).

BONA, JOSEPH DUFOUR, *dit. See* DUFOUR

BOND, JOSEPH NORMAN, doctor, militia officer, office holder, JP, and judge; b. 28 May 1758 in Neston, Cheshire, England, eighth son of James Bond and his wife Mary; m. 5 May 1785 Elizabeth Bell in Shelburne, N.S., and they had 17 children; d. 15 March 1830 in Yarmouth, N.S.

Joseph Norman Bond was descended from a family of great antiquity in Cornwall. Like his father and grandfather, he was educated in medicine. After receiving his training in London, Bond left England about 1779 as surgeon and captain's clerk on a merchant ship bound for Jamaica. Soon after his arrival he sailed aboard a privateer to New York, where he joined the British army and was made a surgeon's mate. Bond was at the surrender at Yorktown, Va, on 19 Oct. 1781. For some time he administered medicine to troops made prisoner with John Burgoyne* and Lord Cornwallis. In the fall of 1783 he came to Shelburne, N.S., from New York in the loyalist exodus, and in 1786 was granted a water lot there.

In 1787 Bond moved from Shelburne to Yarmouth, where he embarked upon a long career of public service. For about 20 years he was the only regular physician in what is now Yarmouth County. In the spring of 1802 Bond received a small packet of cowpox vaccine from his brother Norman, a doctor in Bath, England, and proceeded to vaccinate an infant child against smallpox. This treatment is reputed to be the first use of cowpox vaccine in Canada, but it is difficult to corroborate the claim. There is evidence of its use at an earlier date by John Clinch* in Newfoundland and George Thomas Landmann* in Quebec. Nor was this likely the first application of the vaccine in Nova Scotia, for Simeon Perkins* makes apparent reference to its use at the end of 1800 in Liverpool.

Bond was an active member of the Yarmouth community and held a number of offices, both civil and military. In July 1796 he was commissioned captain of the Yarmouth Volunteer Artillery Company. The following year he became captain of the artillery company attached to the 2nd Battalion of the Shelburne County Militia Regiment, and about 1812 he was made lieutenant-colonel of the 4th (Yarmouth) Battalion of Militia. In 1787 he was appointed deputy collector of customs, assuming the position of collector in 1805 upon the death of Ranald McKinnon*. A devout Anglican, Bond was elected a churchwarden when the Church of England parish was organized in Yarmouth on 29 Sept. 1806. In addition, he was made justice of the peace for Yarmouth Township in December 1803, justice of the Inferior Court of Common Pleas for Yarmouth Township in May 1810, and commissioner of courts for the trial of summary actions for the district of Yarmouth in 1817. In 1819 he was appointed justice of the peace for Shelburne County.

During his career Bond was also engaged in a number of civic improvement projects. In May 1802 the Nova Scotia government appointed him the commissioner for building the Tusket River bridge, east of Yarmouth, which was completed the next year, and in April 1805 he became commissioner of sewers for Yarmouth. Early in 1811 he and some others formed an association known as the Yarmouth Lock and Canal Proprietors in order to construct locks which would connect Yarmouth Harbour with lakes in the interior of the township. Although a subscription of £500 was got up, the Council refused a grant of £200, and soon thereafter the proprietors were claiming that the expenses had already been double their

expectations. The enterprise was ultimately unsuccessful. In July of the same year Bond, together with the Reverend Ranna Cossit* and Samuel Sheldon Poole, became a trustee responsible for the construction of the Yarmouth Grammar School.

Upon his death Bond left all his possessions to his wife. The estate was a sizeable one, and included a homestead of 67 acres, various properties in Yarmouth including a house and wharf, and some 35 lots with an estimated extent of 3,000 acres. The will makes no reference to a medical library or laboratory (although Bond did own a microscope) but does mention a pianoforte, perhaps the spinet Bond is said to have introduced to Yarmouth in 1799. Bond was in addition an important creditor, holding various mortgages, bonds, and promissory notes. His largest debtor was his son-in-law George Bingay, a Yarmouth merchant, who held a mortgage of almost £600. Three of Bond's sons followed him in his profession, two practising as doctors in Yarmouth. His son James P. was appointed to the Legislative Council of Nova Scotia in 1837. A daughter married judge Thomas Ritchie*.

COLIN D. HOWELL

PANS, MG 4, 166, vol.1; RG 1, 172: 40, 57, 69, 131–32, 152; 173: 34, 41–42, 48, 92, 394, 413, 417, 449; 174: 210, 294, 338. Yarmouth County Court of Probate (Yarmouth, N.S.), Wills, 2: 34–35 (mfm. at PANS). Perkins, *Diary, 1804–12* (Fergusson). D. A. Campbell, *Pioneers of medicine in Nova Scotia* (Halifax, 1905). "Joseph Norman Bond," *Herald* (Yarmouth), 29 Dec. 1896: 2. K. A. MacKenzie, "Nineteenth century physicians in Nova Scotia," N.S. Hist. Soc., *Coll.*, 31 (1957): 119–29. T. H. Raddall, "Early medical practice in Nova Scotia," *Nova Scotia Medical Bull.* (Halifax), 23 (1944): 187–94.

BOUC, CHARLES-JEAN-BAPTISTE, merchant and politician; b. 25 Nov. 1766 in Terrebonne, Que., son of Louis Bouc, a merchant, and Marie-Angélique Comparé; d. there 30 Nov. 1832.

Charles-Jean-Baptiste Bouc belonged to a family from the rural petite bourgeoisie, a diligent class devoted to work, which was held in greater esteem than village craftsmen or farmers because of its education and wealth. After the conquest Charles-Jean-Baptiste's father had moved to Terrebonne and set up a small retail business that proved highly successful. Through hard work and self-denial Louis Bouc also became one of the major landowners in his parish. Charles-Jean-Baptiste spent his childhood in the demanding and difficult world of small business, which was at the mercy of circumstances, subject to anxiety and audacity, to great hopes and bitter disappointments. He quite evidently was marked by his experience.

Boulton

On 20 Sept. 1785, when he was 18, Bouc married Archange Lepage at Terrebonne; they were to have five children. By the terms of the marriage contract his father generously guaranteed him 10,000 *livres*. In so doing Louis was setting his hopes on his eldest son, who he anticipated would one day become an important local merchant. The young Bouc seized the opportunity to widen his field of endeavour and to join the small, privileged group of rural merchants. Initially he speculated in wheat and furs. Through his activities as a merchant he was also drawn into the world of finance. However, he remained a minor money-lender of the traditional type, putting out small sums to farmers and craftsmen in the region. His first financial successes occurred just when he also enjoyed a large increase in fortune: under his father's will, which had been signed on 26 May 1796, he inherited a number of farming implements, a great deal of livestock, and six properties that he was barred from selling or transferring during his lifetime.

Bouc's much improved circumstances made him an excellent candidate for the House of Assembly. In July 1796 he easily won the seat for Effingham. At first he was bursting with activity and took an interest in various problems in his riding. His political career therefore seemed full of promise and it was aided by his many local contacts. But two years after being elected he was involved in a fraudulent wheat deal. Tried in the Court of King's Bench, he was sentenced on 9 March 1799 to three months in prison and a fine of 20 *livres*, and was obliged to put up guarantees of good behaviour for three years. The Executive Council had some fear of him because he was considered a chief organizer of the assembly members for the Montreal area, and on the pretext of this fraud he was expelled from the house. Bouc was returned in the general elections of July 1800 but was ousted a second time, and then a third time at the beginning of 1801. Elected once more in April of that year, he was expelled a fourth time. He wanted to return to the assembly, but the house ended his political career in 1802 by passing a bill explicitly titled "An Act for disqualifying and restraining, *Charles Baptiste Bouc*, from being elected, and from Sitting and Voting as a Member of the House of Assembly."

Although deprived of his riding, Bouc nevertheless still had prestige in his milieu. He played an important role in parish institutions, as his active participation in meetings of the *fabrique* clearly shows. He thus used these institutions to help consolidate his leadership in the community. In 1805 he was even elected syndic for the parish and so was responsible for repairs to the church. His prominence in the church also confirmed his importance by comparison with other parishioners.

In 1807 Bouc was imprisoned for treasonable practices. Four years later he was again accused of fraud and theft and was sentenced to six months in jail. His social position and his fortune were drastically affected. His reputation was compromised. When he returned to Terrebonne early in 1812, it was to painful rebuffs, calumny, and scandalmongering. Disgraced, his name dragged through the mud, he had lost authority and prestige in the community. His downfall was accompanied by big financial problems that became increasingly serious. He had no choice but to retire to his land and to rent it. He managed only with difficulty to survive, being unable to pay his seigneurial dues regularly. After 1820 he was forced to sell some of his property to avoid bankruptcy.

His health undermined by these set-backs, Bouc died on 30 Nov. 1832, a deserted and ruined man. His burial in the cemetery rather than in the church was another tangible sign of his disgrace. The difficulties in settling his estate were not cleared up until two years later.

RICHARD CHABOT

ANQ-M, CE6-24, 25 nov. 1766, 20 sept. 1785, 3 déc. 1832; CN1-295, 18 sept. 1811; CN3-7, 17 sept. 1785; CN6-13, 5 avril 1800; CN6-17, 21 juin 1813, 15 sept. 1818; CN6-24, 20 oct. 1829, 9 nov. 1830, 22 avril 1835; CN6-27, 18 juin 1810, 10 avril 1814, 11 juill. 1816, 23 sept. 1820, 20 mars 1829; CN6-29, 26 mai 1796. AP, Saint-Louis (Terrebonne), Reg. de l'assemblée des marguilliers, 3 nov. 1805. Lionel Bertrand, "L'étrange aventure de Bouc, député de Terrebonne de 1796 à 1802," *Rev. de Terrebonne* (Terrebonne, Qué.), 16 déc. 1966: 37. Yvon Bock, "Charles-Baptiste Bouc, député de Terrebonne," *BRH*, 52 (1946): 259–65. Hare, "L'Assemblée législative du Bas-Canada," *RHAF*, 27: 377. P.-G. Roy, "Charles-Baptiste Bouc," *BRH*, 7 (1901): 53–55.

BOULTON, D'ARCY (baptized **George D'Arcy**), lawyer, office holder, politician, and judge; b. 20 May 1759 in Moulton, Lincolnshire, England, son of Henry Boulton and Mary Preston; m. 18 Dec. 1782 Elizabeth Forster in Bloomsbury (London), and they had six boys and two girls; d. 21 May 1834 in York (Toronto).

When in 1833 William Lyon Mackenzie* drew up his list of the "family compact," he began with the name D'Arcy Boulton. Next followed Boulton's four sons, like their father office holders all, then one son's brother-in-law, and finally the brother-in-law's brothers. By underscoring family connections and the monopoly of offices, Mackenzie imparted a literal aspect to the political label he helped popularize. That position in this catalogue of names did not correlate with actual political influence did not matter: a connection had been suggested in a formidable manner. Boulton's place – at the top – seems, at the very least, symbolically apt. In the early history of the province he was surely one of its quintessential placemen.

The second son of an old family of Lincolnshire gentry, D'Arcy Boulton followed the example of his elder brother, Henry, enrolling at the Middle Temple in 1788 to study law. Law, however, took a back seat to a business career and Boulton became a partner in the Woollen Yarn Company. The enterprise encountered difficulties and in 1793 the partners declared bankruptcy. Boulton was unabashed and wrote to his wife: "Set not your mind on riches lest you should be deceived. They have wings to fly away. . . . We can, thank God, be as happy with the necessaries of life as many discontented persons *cannot* be with all the possessions of their imaginations." Bankruptcy proceedings lasted several years and in the end Boulton's financial problems may have had a bearing on his decision to emigrate.

Boulton with his wife and two sons arrived in the United States about 1797 and seems to have settled in New York's Hudson River valley. The exact nature of Boulton's activity is not certain: one story has him starting up a school in Schenectady, another has him an assistant oarsman on a lumber raft operating on Lake Champlain. By the turn of the century, however, he had set his sights north of the St Lawrence River. He first appears on the assessment roll of Augusta Township in 1802. Several years later, he recounted his sentiments at this change of scene in *Sketch of his majesty's province of Upper Canada*: "English people, untainted by political speculations, are naturally attached to their own constitution. I confess, for my own part, that when I first . . . set my foot on British ground, after residing in the American states, I perceived sensations that were unexpected even to myself. I seemed at once to step home. I need not describe my feelings on this occasion; a true Englishman can well imagine them, and with respect to those that are not so, I am perfectly indifferent."

If Upper Canada offered Boulton a more congenial social and political climate, there were other, more tangible, advantages as well. In 1802 his petition for a land grant was approved and he received 200 acres for himself and an additional 200 acres for each of his children, then five in number. The following year, in response to a dearth of accredited lawyers, parliament empowered the lieutenant governor to authorize attorneys to practise by licence. Boulton and others were examined by Chief Justice Henry Allcock* and admitted to the bar in Easter Term 1803; later critics labelled them "heaven-descended." Not long afterwards Boulton began his upward climb on the ladder of official preferment. The initial rung was provided him by the death of Solicitor General Robert Isaac Dey Gray* in the wreck of the *Speedy* early in October 1804. The following February Boulton assumed Gray's position. Boulton also succeeded Gray in a by-election as the member for the riding of Stormont and Russell.

His next opportunity resulted from the suspension of judge Robert Thorpe* by Lieutenant Governor Francis Gore* in July 1807. In Thorpe's stead Boulton carried out the business of the Court of King's Bench on circuit. He did, however, suffer a setback when he was defeated in the general election of 1808 by John Brownell. A sympathetic commentator remarked: "I really could not have believed there was so much ingratitude in the human frame as his former clients have manifested towards him." Boulton may have suffered by association with an administration unpopular for its slow handling of land claims; he also may have had disgruntled legal customers.

Boulton, in fact, had his own problems in government circles. Gore had grown disenchanted with the legal acumen of both Boulton and Attorney General William Firth* – who differed in their legal opinions – and had begun instead to place his faith in the counsel of William Dummer POWELL, an associate judge of King's Bench. When, in the late summer of 1810, it appeared that Boulton had decided to seek the vacant judgeship (Thorpe had received another posting), Gore and Powell worked in tandem to bar his appointment. The matter, however, became academic after the frigate on which Boulton was bound for England to press for the appointment was captured on 22 Dec. 1810 by a French privateer. Boulton fought vigorously in the short-lived attempt to defend the ship; for his troubles he received a sabre slash across his forehead. He was detained for more than two years at Verdun, France, during which time he wrote letters to authorities in London in an attempt to secure his release. He also acted as the lawyer for the community of British prisoners. In this regard he exasperated his son Henry John Boulton* who declared, "My father's letters are always about business for he has numberless 'poor devils' to assist as clients."

By the spring of 1813 Boulton had obtained his parole and crossed the Channel. He had, however, to put aside his hopes for a judgeship since the post had been filled in 1811 by the appointment of William CAMPBELL. None the less, in August 1813 he obtained a leave of absence from his duties in Upper Canada as solicitor general to transact business "regarding my family affairs of the first importance to myself and my children." He was admitted to the English bar in May 1814, his lack of this credential having been cited by Gore and Powell in their campaign to keep him off the bench. That June, Firth, who had been dismissed as attorney general in 1812, advised William Warren Baldwin* that Boulton was lobbying for the vacant attorney generalship. In this endeavour Boulton proved successful, although his wish that Henry John succeed him as solicitor general was frustrated by the ascending star of John Beverley Robinson*. Boulton was appointed attorney general on 31 Dec. 1814; Robinson became solicitor general less than two months later.

Bourdages

Robinson, the brother-in-law of D'Arcy Boulton's eldest son and namesake, proved pivotal in a further reshuffling of places in the colonial administration which occurred three years later and which stemmed from a desire on the part of Gore and Powell to have a vigorous, young attorney general, namely Robinson. A chain reaction had been set in motion by Chief Justice Thomas SCOTT's retirement in 1816. He was replaced by Powell and the resulting vacancy on the bench was filled by Boulton, who was appointed on 12 Feb. 1818 and replaced as attorney general by Robinson. What ought to have been a fairly straightforward procedure was complicated by Boulton's attempt to make appointment conditional upon Henry John's succeeding Robinson as solicitor general. The ploy, however, did not work. Henry John was named acting solicitor general in 1818, but his commission as solicitor general, although backdated to 2 December of that year, was not issued until 1 March 1820.

By the mid 1820s the rigours of riding circuit had begun to impose too heavy a strain on Boulton; moreover, he had started to become deaf. In 1827, several months after his retirement, his wife died, and Boulton was expected to follow her shortly. Instead, he lived another seven years, dying one day after his 75th birthday at the Grange, the home of his son D'Arcy. His tenure on the Court of King's Bench coincided with Lieutenant Governor Sir Peregrine Maitland*'s administration, a period of conservative reaction. Boulton could be said to have expressed the spirit of his time and place, and hence was useful to reformers such as Mackenzie as a symbol of the province's grievances. "How is Justice Boulton's speeches and addresses like saying Mass?" queried Mackenzie. "Because nine-tenths of the audience don't understand their meaning." Henry Scadding* provides a more personal description, presenting Boulton as "an English gentleman of spare Wellington physique; like many of his descendants, a lover of horses and a spirited rider; a man of wit, too, and humour, fond of listening to and narrating anecdotes of the *ben trovato* class."

JOHN LOWNSBROUGH

D'Arcy Boulton's *Sketch of his majesty's province of Upper Canada*, originally issued in London in 1805, was republished in Toronto in 1961.

AO, MS 88, William Firth to W. W. Baldwin, 8 June 1813; MS 525, H. J. Boulton to D'Arcy Boulton, 11 Sept. 1811, 7 Jan. 1813; MS 537, John Small Jr. to Samuel Ridout, 28 June 1808; RG 21, United Counties of Leeds and Grenville, Augusta Township, assessment roll, 1802. Art Gallery of Ont. (Toronto), Boulton papers, D'Arcy Boulton to Elizabeth Boulton, 3 Sept. 1793; Boulton family tree; corr. from Lindsey & Holland County Library (Lincoln, Eng.), 9, 12 March, 6 Aug. 1973; corr. from Middle Temple Library (London), 20 March, 16 June 1973; 10 June 1980. MTL, [Alexander?] Card, "An account of the Boulton family of Toronto . . . ," 20 Jan. 1870; W. D. Powell papers, Mrs Powell to George Murray, 13 Feb. 1807; S. P. Jarvis to Powell, 1 Oct. 1827; Alexander Wood papers, business letter-books, II, Wood to James Macaulay, 3 April 1809. PAC, RG 1, E1, 47, 6 July 1802; RG 5, A1: 15645. PRO, CO 42/336: 128; 42/349: 169–70; 42/350: 306–7, 361; 42/351: 236–37; 42/354: 192, 214; 42/357: 361. "The Boulton letters," ed. Mrs Marsh, Women's Canadian Hist. Soc. of Toronto, *Trans.* (Toronto), no.18 (1918–19): 48. "Journals of Legislative Assembly of U.C.," AO *Report*, 1911: 61. U.C., *Statutes*, 1803, c.3. *Colonial Advocate*, 14 Oct. 1824, 18 May 1826, 20 Sept. 1833. Armstrong, *Handbook of Upper Canadian chronology* (1967). John Burke, *A genealogical and heraldic history of the commoners of Great Britain and Ireland enjoying territorial possessions or high official rank; but uninvested with heritable honours* (4v., London, 1833–38), 2: 377–78. John Lownsbrough, *The privileged few: the Grange & its people in nineteenth century Toronto* (Toronto, 1980). W. R. Riddell, *The bar and the courts of the province of Upper Canada, or Ontario* (Toronto, 1928), 53. Scadding, *Toronto of old* (Armstrong; 1966), 25. "Hon. G. S. Boulton," *Journal of Education* (Toronto), 22 (1869): 29.

BOURDAGES, LOUIS, sailor, farmer, landowner, politician, militia officer, notary, and office holder; b. 6 July 1764 in Jeune-Lorette (Loretteville), Que., son of Raymond Bourdages*, a surgeon and merchant, and Esther Leblanc; d. 20 Jan. 1835 in Saint-Denis on the Richelieu, Lower Canada.

During the winter of 1756–57 Raymond Bourdages left Acadia with his family to settle at L'Ancienne-Lorette (Que.); once there, he practised medicine and engaged in trade. In 1762 he established himself on Baie des Chaleurs, where he set up two trading posts. Like many other Acadian families in the area, the Bourdages found themselves in a precarious situation because they lacked capital, were exposed to pillaging by American privateers and raiding by the Indians, and were at the mercy of the British government, which refused to give formal recognition to title deeds. With a childhood spent in this setting of chronic uncertainty, Louis early became aware of the misfortunes of his people and learned to curse the British authorities.

In 1777 his parents sent him to study at the Petit Séminaire de Québec, where a whole new world opened before him. He owed much to his family background and his Acadian origins, but he would owe his intellectual training and religious education to the Petit Séminaire. He likely stood out through his love of study and his lively intelligence. At any rate he reputedly was gifted in mathematics and philosophy and at the end of his studies defended a thesis in those subjects. He was also interested in matters of public concern and made friends with fellow student Pierre-Stanislas BÉDARD.

Upon leaving the Petit Séminaire in 1784, Bourdages, who was bent on getting ahead and aware of his family's financial difficulties, wanted to make money quickly. He became interested, therefore, in trade and went to sea. Although he failed to make his fortune, voyages to Europe and the West Indies opened new horizons, broadening his field of knowledge. In 1787, after his father's death, he decided to settle for good in the province of Quebec. That year he petitioned Governor Lord Dorchester [Guy Carleton*], for legal recognition of his family's title to landed property on Baie des Chaleurs. Despite numerous letters and requests, the British government would not settle this question until 1825.

Since he had inherited nothing from his family and had no financial backing, Bourdages was reduced to his own resources. Nevertheless, he was thinking of getting married, and on 9 Oct. 1787 at Quebec he took as his wife Louise-Catherine Soupiran. The dowry, jointure, and preference legacy set out in the marriage contract make it clear that the couple both came from modest circumstances. Three years later, having been unsuccessful as a merchant at Quebec, Bourdages moved to Saint-Denis on the Richelieu. He may well have made this choice because several Acadian families had already settled there. At that time he was just a small farmer of no means and he had to support his family in precarious circumstances. In 1791 he bought some land that he farmed himself. Hardworking and tenacious, he took up selling firewood to the habitants in surrounding parishes. In 1799 he managed to buy another piece of land. In property assets, he already vied with a number of the landowners at Saint-Denis.

With his family's livelihood assured, Bourdages turned to the notarial profession. He began his clerkship in 1800 with notary Pierre-Paul Dutalmé and completed it with Christophe Michaud, both residents of Saint-Denis. During this period he farmed his land and carried out financial transactions that imply a degree of prosperity. Among other things he owned a stone house in the village and held nearly 200 *arpents* in the seigneury. On 8 Jan. 1805 he received his commission as a notary and fell heir to the clientele of his colleague Michaud, who had given up practice the preceding year.

As a landowner and rural notary Bourdages came to play an important role in his milieu. First he was appointed agent for the seigneury and he became trustee for the funds of several merchants. Having business relations with habitants, seigneurs, and merchants, and being active in parish life, he frequently held positions of a representative nature. In 1802 he was elected syndic of the parish to bring the church building to completion; he already exercised significant influence in the militia as adjutant. He may even be suspected of inflaming disputes with his parish priest. Not only had he been attending, as a leading

citizen, the meetings of the *fabrique* since the beginning of the century, which he had no right to do, but he also backed the habitants in their protests against the parish administration. Given their ways of thinking and their power in the parish, the curé and Bourdages were bound to clash on many fronts. None the less, because of his wealth in land, his education, and his family connections, Bourdages managed to reach the top rank in the community. His rise in society also was in keeping with the rise of the liberal professions in Canadian society in the early 19th century and the development of a liberal and nationalist ideology within that group.

Like many in these professions, Bourdages saw in the machinery of politics a powerful means for securing prestige and authority. On 6 Aug. 1804 he was elected to the House of Assembly for Richelieu, and he retained this seat until March 1814. His political career began at a time when the assembly was controlled by members in the liberal professions and by small Canadian businessmen. These new leaders were beginning to find their voice within an organized political group, the Canadian party. They became advocates of Canadian nationalism, denouncing the colonial rulers, in the shape of the governor and the largely English-speaking members of the councils. Like a number of assemblymen, Bourdages felt that this oligarchy jeopardized the interests of his group and was a threat to the Canadian collectivity. In this context he approved the Canadian party's strategy, which was to weaken the existing colonial political power by demanding administrative reforms and seeking the support of the parliament in London.

Bourdages, who was a skilful tactician and an eloquent, persuasive orator, quickly established himself as a seasoned parliamentarian. In 1806 he attracted his colleagues' attention by seconding the motion made by his leader, Pierre-Stanislas Bédard, condemning an article in the *Montreal Gazette* about the rather sarcastic toasts proposed by some Montreal merchants at a banquet presided over by Isaac Todd*. That year he helped found the newspaper *Le Canadien*. A year later he tried to get the house to vote an expense allowance to members from outside the town of Quebec. He early became identified with the interests of his constituents, presenting a number of petitions and bills about matters of local and regional concern. Aware of Bourdages's skill in debates and popularity in his riding, Bédard entrusted him with several important tasks in the house. In 1808 Bourdages sponsored a bill to make judges ineligible to sit in the assembly [see Pierre-Amable De Bonne*; Sir James Henry Craig*]. In reality this dispute over the eligibility of judges, along with the later one over supplies [see Sir Francis Nathaniel BURTON], marked the beginning of a struggle for the control of political power. Bourdages again supported Bédard when he

Bourdages

called for ministerial responsibility, and he brought forward a motion to this effect himself. He unquestionably played an important role within the Canadian party at that period. He had always backed Bédard's leadership and had generally felt a sense of solidarity with this first generation of Canadian assemblymen, who largely came from the Quebec region. When those responsible for *Le Canadien* – Bédard, François BLANCHET, and Jean-Thomas TASCHEREAU – were imprisoned in March 1810, Bourdages was without doubt the member who opposed most vigorously this drastic step taken by Governor Craig.

The War of 1812 led to a lessening of tension and a marked *rapprochement* between the executive and the leaders of the assembly. Bourdages sided with the British in the fight against the American invader. On 18 March 1812 he was promoted major in the Saint-Denis battalion of militia by Craig's successor, Governor Sir George Prevost*. The following year he replaced merchant Joseph Cartier as the battalion's lieutenant-colonel, though not without some unpleasantness. Bourdages, who displayed uncommon zeal and was inflexible with his men, soon came into conflict with some of the local leaders. Among other things he was accused of wanting to run the militia and of meddling in the affairs of others. In 1814 Prevost made him superintendent of post houses in the colony at an annual salary of £100.

In this narrow and compartmentalized society, everyone was anxious to protect his interests and coveted the favours enjoyed by his neighbour; hence feuds between cliques, private animosities, and personality conflicts all loomed large. In the general election of 1814 Pierre-Dominique Debartzch*, a legislative councillor who was the seigneur of Saint-Hyacinthe and was assured of support from the prominent local people, campaigned vigorously against Bourdages and managed to secure his defeat in Richelieu riding. Bourdages was humiliated and sought to revenge his honour. In January 1815 he persuaded the assembly to void the election by alleging numerous irregularities at the polls. This sort of fight sometimes turned Bourdages into the head of a clan that was regional in its outlook and in its chauvinism, primarily concerned with petty local annoyances and quite closed to the real matters at stake in the politics of the time. That year by-elections were called in Richelieu and Buckingham and he stacked the odds in his favour by running in both. He was again defeated in Richelieu but he won in Buckingham. Governor Prevost's departure precipitated another general election in March 1816. Bourdages was beaten once more and had to resign himself to quitting politics.

He took advantage of the opportunity to give more attention to his profession and his family. The bonds of fellowship uniting this petit bourgeois family were indeed exemplary. In his wife Bourdages had a well-informed and supportive companion. The children were also closely attached to the family group, and to its sense of power and prestige. The boys began classical studies at an early age, held important posts in the militia, and participated in the daily affairs of the parish. Some of the girls had already married well. Proud of his family and anxious to leave a substantial inheritance, Bourdages, who was now in his fifties, became a real estate promoter and speculator. He practised as a notary with equal zeal, entering in his minute-book an average of 120 acts a year. In 1819 the British government granted him 1,200 acres in Ely Township for his militia service. Not taking offence or backing out, he simply accepted the offer. Like others in the professions, he did not worry about the contradiction implied in fighting the Executive Council while accepting profitable posts and favours from the government. By now he was one of the largest landowners in the district.

In 1820 Bourdages again won election in Buckingham. At Quebec the quarrel over the civil list was the centre of debate in the assembly. Louis-Joseph Papineau* engaged in open conflict with Governor Lord Dalhousie [Ramsay*] and increasingly asserted himself as the new leader of the Canadian party. These matters certainly were of concern to Bourdages. Once more he showed himself to be stubborn and astute as a parliamentarian, seizing every chance to attack the executive and the English-speaking oligarchy. Yet he entered into the assembly's everyday business as usual; he sat on numerous committees and dealt with his riding's problems. In 1822 the proposed union of Upper and Lower Canada and the systematic opposition of the English-speaking merchants to seigneurial tenure again made the climate more difficult. Although the union bill fell through in Britain, the Canada Trade Act, which favoured the transfer of lands held in fief and roture into free and common socage, was passed. Bourdages reacted violently to this act of the British parliament. In 1824, even though he was not supported by Papineau and Denis-Benjamin Viger*, he put forward a motion to repeal the measure, but in vain.

In spite of everything, Bourdages was not against the development of capitalism in the colony; indeed he apparently favoured it in so far as it advantaged his own people. For example, he opposed the bill to develop a canal system on the St Lawrence, which was bound up with the interests of the British merchants, but he promoted a similar endeavour on the Rivière Chambly (Rivière L'Acadie), which would favour the regional interests of the Canadian bourgeoisie. It seems difficult under these circumstances to see him as a defender of a form of society that had existed under the *ancien régime*. All things considered, he agreed with the majority of his fellow members of the assembly, who talked of democracy and separation of church and state yet unhesitatingly defended the seigneurial system.

None the less the Canadian party did not present a united front at this time. The quarrels over Papineau's leadership, the numerous personality conflicts, and the old rivalry between Quebec and Montreal members of the assembly had the effect of weakening the party and openly encouraging dissidence. Bourdages clashed primarily with Papineau. Since he backed the members from the Quebec region, he found it hard to accept the idea that the party would be run by someone from Montreal. He very much wanted to take Papineau's place as speaker of the assembly, but he quickly realized that he did not have enough support in the house. In 1823, after Papineau left for London, with the help of others in the assembly he got the member for Upper Town Quebec, Joseph-Rémi Vallières* de Saint-Réal, elected speaker. Upon his return Papineau resumed the office and took care not to lay himself open to his enemies. He was aware of the danger that Bourdages and a few other members from the Quebec region represented and took advantage of the victory in the 1824 elections to strengthen his leadership and unite the party. In 1826 the Canadian party became the Patriote party. It rapidly consolidated its base and equipped itself with a party newspaper, *La Minerve*. Electoral victory in 1827 unequivocally established Papineau's leadership. In his self-confidence he reoriented the party's strategy and went beyond complaints concerning administrative matters to demand complete control of the budget by the assembly and an elective legislative council. Being confronted with the *fait accompli*, Bourdages and other members had no choice but to adjust rapidly to the new political realities.

In 1830 Bourdages, recently elected in Nicolet, threw his weight behind Papineau and his ideas. His unconditional support of the Patriote party was confirmed at every vote by roll call in the house. Like his leader, he attacked the clergy who openly opposed the Patriote cause. In 1831 he joined with Papineau to put forward a bill on the *fabriques* designed to reduce the powers of the curés in parish administration by giving to all property owners the right to be present at meetings held for the election of wardens and the presentation of financial statements. He had often battled with his priest, and he saw in the bill an excellent means for the local élite to intervene in parish matters. The political needs of the past few years also prompted him to bolder views on nationalism. He was amongst those who believed that the British parliament had deceived the House of Assembly and that revolution was inevitable. On this matter he had even more advanced ideas than Papineau. The cholera epidemic in the years 1832–34, the dramatic decline in the francophone population in the towns and the increasing numbers of anglophones, the poor harvests in the preceding years, and the repressive measures carried out by British troops following the by-election in Montreal West in 1832 [*see* Daniel TRACEY] intensified national animosities and incited the population to agitation and revolt.

As he neared 70, Louis Bourdages attracted notice more and more as a political radical. But, however bold he was, he never went beyond a prudent search for reform in the religious sphere and always maintained a strict respect for seigneurial property. He represented well a large section of the petite bourgeoisie of the period, which wanted to change the political system in the colony without upsetting the social structure. He carried out one of the last important acts of his political career when he helped develop and publicize the 92 Resolutions setting out the assembly's main grievances and requests.

Bourdages suffered an attack of apoplexy on 11 Jan. 1835 and, with the consolation of the last rites of the church, died on 20 January. In his will, which he had drawn up on 6 Aug. 1833, he left 7,142 *livres*, a considerable number of properties, and net assets of more than 100,000 *livres*. His stone dwelling was furnished elegantly and tastefully, with hangings, an antique china table service, and silver plate. His library contained nearly 100 volumes and suggests that he was attracted to philosophical thought, democratic ideas, and the business world.

RICHARD CHABOT

Louis Bourdages's minute-book, containing instruments notarized between 1805 and 1835, is held at the ANQ-M, CN2-11.

ANQ-M, CE2-12, 23 janv. 1835; CN1-134, 4 mars 1818; CN1-168, 19 nov. 1821, 30 sept. 1822; CN2-19, 22 mars 1822, 28 juill. 1827; CN2-27, 18 juill. 1799, 13 août 1801, 9 mai 1804, 29 juill. 1811, 18 mai 1819; CN2-56, 15 mars 1791; CN2-57, 7 déc. 1824. ANQ-Q, CE1-1, 9 oct. 1787; CN1-83, 6 oct. 1787. AP, Saint-Denis (Saint-Denis, sur le Richelieu), Cahier des délibérations de la fabrique, 1797–1845. ASQ, Fichier des anciens. ASSH, Fg-12, dossier 7, boîte 13. PAC, MG 24, B2. L.C., House of Assembly, *Journals*, 20 March 1815, 27 Jan. 1818. *Réponse à Testis sur les procédures d'une cour d'enquête, sur plainte du lieut. colonel Bourdages* . . . ([Montréal], 1816). F.-J. Audet, "Les législateurs du Bas-Canada." Desjardins, *Guide parl. Officers of British forces in Canada* (Irving). J.-B.-A. Allaire, *Histoire de la paroisse de Saint-Denis-sur-Richelieu (Canada)* (Saint-Hyacinthe, 1905). Maurice Grenier, "La chambre d'Assemblée du Bas-Canada, 1815–1837" (thèse de MA, univ. de Montréal, 1966). F.-J. Audet, "Louis Bourdages," RSC *Trans.*, 3rd ser., 18 (1924), sect.I: 73–101. Fernand Ouellet, "Papineau et la rivalité Québec–Montréal (1820–1840)," *RHAF*, 13 (1959–60): 311–27.

BOUTHILLIER, JEAN-ANTOINE, surveyor, journalist, author, translator, office holder, and JP; b.

Brant

17 June 1782 in Montreal, son of Pierre Bouthillier and Angélique Lemaire Saint-Germain; d. 12 Nov. 1835 in Beauport, Lower Canada.

Although Jean-Antoine Bouthillier made his career at Quebec, his family came from the Montreal region, contrary to assertions made in biographical notices. His father was a merchant and militia officer there. Business was probably fairly good since Jean-Antoine attended the Collège Saint-Raphaël from 1792 until 1800. He was a good student and several times was on the honours list at the end of the year. He undoubtedly benefited from the excellent teaching then being provided by Sulpicians Jean-Baptiste-Jacques Chicoisneau* and Antoine-Jacques HOUDET. After leaving the college he studied to become a surveyor, possibly with his uncle, Hyacinthe Lemaire Saint-Germain, who had been established in Montreal since 1792. He received his surveyor's licence in May 1804 and immediately settled at Quebec. But he received no government contracts for surveying and thus was forced to do various kinds of work.

From January 1807 until March 1808 Bouthillier was an editor of *Le Canadien*, which at that time was devoting a good deal of space to the question of the freedom of the press and to ripostes to the francophobe stance of the *Quebec Mercury* [see Thomas CARY]. Denis-Benjamin* and Jacques* Viger also contributed to the paper, and Jacques succeeded Bouthillier as an editor in November 1808. Bouthillier was hired immediately by the *Quebec Gazette* as translator with an annual salary of £100, and he held this post until February 1819. The proprietor, John Neilson*, must have had great confidence in him, since he chose him to run his printing shop while he was travelling in England from August 1816 till June 1817. In 1815 Bouthillier had been appointed a surveyor of the highways, roads, lanes, and bridges for the town and parish of Quebec. Four years later he left the *Quebec Gazette* and moved to Beauport. In 1828 he obtained the position of assistant clerk of the House of Assembly, an office coveted by Georges-Barthélemi Faribault*, William Phillips (the son of Samuel Phillips, a former clerk), and Édouard-Olivier Desbarats, who would have liked to succeed his father, PIERRE-ÉDOUARD. Bouthillier was also appointed justice of the peace at Beauport in 1830, and he retained his two offices until his death.

Bouthillier was the author of *Traité d'arithmétique pour l'usage des écoles*, which was brought out by Neilson in May 1809 and was the first textbook of its kind published in Lower Canada. It was used in schools for a long time and up until 1870 it was reissued by George-Édouard Desbarats*, Joseph and Octave* Crémazie, and Jean-Baptiste Rolland*. According to historian Léon Lortie, the book drew its inspiration from French authors and conveyed knowledge as sound as it was useful to young Canadians.

Bouthillier had a respectable career. His various functions earned him the title of esquire and real esteem in the town of Quebec, but they did not make him rich. When he died, he owned three properties and a house in Beauport, less than £300 in movables, and £350 in uncollected debts, but his liabilities exceeded £1,000. His library contained several dozen books, among them the works of Racine, Cicero, and Horace, mathematical dictionaries and Jean Saury's *Institutions mathématiques*, Joseph Bouchette*'s *Description topographique du Bas-Canada*, and translation dictionaries, as well as some bibles, a New Testament, and the *Imitation de Jésus-Christ*.

Jean-Antoine Bouthillier had married Claire Parent, a widow, on 20 Feb. 1808. The marriage was solemnized at Beauport, perhaps to avoid the charivari that might have followed such a union. The couple had at least three children, but all of them died before the age of ten. Claire Parent passed away three years before her husband.

CLAUDE GALARNEAU

ANQ-M, CE1-51, 17 juin 1782. ANQ-Q, CE1-5, 14 nov. 1835; CN1-255, 22 déc. 1835; P-193, 19. ASQ, Séminaire, 145, no.3. PAC, MG 24, B1, 183: 666–69. L.C., House of Assembly, *Journals*, 1827–30. *Le Canadien*, 1806–10. *Quebec Gazette*, 19 Jan. 1815. Beaulieu et Hamelin, *La presse québécoise*, vol.1. Hare et Wallot, *Les imprimés dans le Bas-Canada*. [L.-A. Huguet-Latour], *Annuaire de Ville-Marie, origine, utilité et progrès des institutions catholiques de Montréal* . . . (2v., Montréal, 1863–82). *Quebec almanac*, 1791–1835. P.-G. Roy, *Fils de Québec*, 3: 11–12. L.-P. Audet, *Le système scolaire*, vol.6. Léon Lortie, "La trame scientifique de l'histoire du Canada," *Pioneers of Canadian science*, ed. G. F. G. Stanley (Toronto, 1966). Maurault, *Le collège de Montréal* (Dansereau; 1967). M.-A. Bédard, "Le greffier de l'Assemblée législative du Bas-Canada: origine de la fonction," Bibliothèque de l'Assemblée nationale du Québec, *Bull.* (Québec), 12 (1982), nos.1–2: 35–58. Léon Lortie, "Les mathématiques de nos ancêtres," RSC *Trans.*, 3rd ser., 49 (1955), sect.i: 31–45; "Les sciences à Montréal et à Québec au XIXe siècle," *L'Action universitaire* (Montréal), 2 (1935–36), no.1: 46. "Le premier traité d'arithmétique (1809)," *BRH*, 46 (1940): 143–44.

BRANT, JOHN. *See* TEKARIHOGEN

BRASSARD DESCHENAUX, CHARLES-JOSEPH, Roman Catholic priest, vicar general, and seigneur; b. 3 Nov. 1752 at Quebec, eldest son of Joseph Brassard* Deschenaux, secretary to Intendant François Bigot*, and Madeleine Vallée; d. 9 July 1832 in L'Ancienne-Lorette, Lower Canada.

Charles-Joseph Brassard Deschenaux entered the Petit Séminaire de Québec in 1765, the year it reopened. The scarcity of clergy probably accounts for the fact that Brassard Deschenaux began studies leading to the priesthood in 1769, received the tonsure in 1771, and finished his classical program the following year. While pursuing his theological studies at the Grand Séminaire de Québec, he served as a regent at the Petit Séminaire in the second, third, and fourth forms. Having been ordained priest by Bishop Jean-Olivier Briand* on 21 Dec. 1776, along with Pierre Conefroy*, Charles-François Perrault, and Benjamin-Nicolas Maillou*, he subsequently undertook ministry in the parish of Saint-Pierre on Île d'Orléans and at the same time looked after the mission at Saint-Laurent. In 1778 he became parish priest of Saint-Étienne at Beaumont, which he left in 1782 for Notre-Dame-de-Foy at Sainte-Foy. Four years later he went to serve the parish of Notre-Dame-de-l'Annonciation at L'Ancienne-Lorette.

During his early years in L'Ancienne-Lorette Brassard Deschenaux had some difficulties with the churchwardens over the *fabrique*'s account-books, which one of his predecessors, Ignace Tinon-Desroches, had neglected in his old age. Then he had trouble persuading some parishioners to have a chimney built at the back of the church. As well, in the summer of 1792 the habitants on one of the concessions complained to the governor and the bishop that Brassard Deschenaux, alleging that it would be superstitious, refused to celebrate a mass to ward off the grasshoppers ruining their crops.

At his father's death on 16 Sept. 1793 Brassard Deschenaux, with his brothers and sisters, inherited the seigneuries of Neuville, Saint-Michel, and Livaudière, and part of Bélair and Beaumont. Managing this small fortune prevented him, as he told the bishop in a letter, from accepting the office of vicar general of Trois-Rivières. In 1809, however, he accepted this office for Quebec, being well aware that under Bishop Joseph-Octave PLESSIS "a vicar general has practically nothing to do."

Thus Brassard Deschenaux possessed landed property, farms, houses, and mills, a good parish charge, and his bishop's confidence. A just and kindly man, the parish priest gave all the income from his ecclesiastical offices away in alms. Every morning at 11:30 a hand-bell called the poor to a meal at the presbytery. As seigneur and vicar general he also knew how to maintain appearances. He had fine carriages and horses to take him to Sainte-Foy and Quebec, where he owned part of the house that had belonged to his father at 5 Rue des Pauvres (Côte du Palais). Every Thursday he received priests, members of the government, and other important people from Quebec and the surrounding region, as well as foreign visitors who were passing through.

Like Bishop Charles-François Bailly* de Messein, Brassard Deschenaux had built up a fine library for the period, comprising more than 800 titles and about 2,200 volumes. The sections devoted to *belles-lettres*, history, and geography were the best stocked. Diderot's *Encyclopédie* and the works of Buffon, Mably, Rousseau, and Voltaire were side by side with those of Bonald and Burke. Religion had its proper place, as did the sciences and arts. It was the library of a gentleman of the late 18th and early 19th centuries, who had numbered Félix Berey Des Essarts, Bailly de Messein, and Philippe-Jean-Louis DESJARDINS among his friends. With his death disappeared one of the last priests from the great families of the end of the French régime.

CLAUDE GALARNEAU

AAQ, 1 CB, V: 57; 61 CD, L'Ancienne-Lorette, 1: 4, 7–8, 10, 17a, 18, 22–23b, 31, 31c, 31f–g, 33e, 33h–i, 34–35; 60 CN, III: 148. ANQ-Q, CE1-1, 4 nov. 1752; CE1-2, 11 juill. 1832; P-232. AP, Notre-Dame-de-l'Annonciation (L'Ancienne-Lorette), Catalogue de la bibliothèque de C.-J. Brassard Deschenaux, 1817. ASQ, C 35: 246, 252, 292; Fichier des anciens; Lettres, M, 433; P, 103. Allaire, *Dictionnaire*, 1: 161. P.-G. Roy, *Fils de Québec*, 2: 102–3; *Inv. concessions*. Lionel Allard, *L'Ancienne-Lorette* (Ottawa, 1979). Lambert, "Joseph-Octave Plessis." Charles Trudelle, *Le frère Louis* (Lévis, Qué., 1898). P.-G. Roy, "Un curé bibliophile: l'abbé Deschenaux," *BRH*, 44 (1938): 193–98.

BRAUNEIS, JOHN CHRISOSTOMUS (baptized **Johann Chrysostomus**; he also signed **Jean**), musician, teacher, and merchant; baptized 29 March 1785 in Herrnsheim (Federal Republic of Germany), son of Franz Benedikt Brauneis, teacher, and Katharina ——; m. Christine Hudson, and they had at least three sons; d. 15 Sept. 1832 at Quebec.

John Chrisostomus Brauneis was a musician in the band of the 70th Foot and probably arrived at Quebec on 4 Nov. 1813 with his regiment. His son Jean-Chrysostome* was born the following January and baptized in Notre-Dame cathedral. Brauneis enjoyed some success teaching piano in the city but he had to give it up, probably in the summer of 1814 when the 70th departed for Cornwall, Upper Canada. By September 1818 he had left his regiment in Kingston and returned to Quebec; on the 17th he advertised in the *Quebec Gazette* as a piano teacher with residence on Rue Sainte-Famille.

In addition to teaching and performing (the wind instrument he played has not been identified), Brauneis composed music. On 27 Feb. 1819 his "Grand Overture of Quebec" was played by the band of the 60th Foot in a public hall as the governor-in-chief, Charles Lennox*, Duke of Richmond and Lennox, made his entrance; the composition was dedicated to the duke's daughter Lady Mary Lennox. Brauneis advertised in the *Quebec Gazette* copies of this piece and of one written in September 1819 in memory of the duke's death. Presumably the copies were pre-

Bro

pared by hand on demand; no printed or manuscript versions have come to light.

By August 1821 Brauneis had moved to Rue de la Fabrique where he taught piano, violin, flute, and flageolet in English and French. In June 1822 he was importing these instruments from London and offering them for sale; in addition he advertised clarinets and French horns, violin strings and bassoon and clarinet reeds, printed music and music paper. Five years later he applied for permission to operate a billiard hall. About 1830 he opened a music store on Rue Saint-Jean.

In 1831 Brauneis became master of a band formed under the patronage of Joseph-François Perrault*, lieutenant-colonel of a militia artillery battalion at Quebec. A music enthusiast who was independent of fortune, Perrault hoped to give his unit a band equal to those of the British regiments in garrison. He provided Brauneis with the best musicians in the town, including Michel-Charles Sauvageau*. The band was apparently busy during the five or six months it existed; a cholera epidemic that swept Quebec at the time may account for its premature demise and was possibly the cause of Brauneis's own death in 1832.

HELMUT KALLMANN

ANQ-Q, CE1-1, 27 janv. 1814, 17 sept. 1832. *Quebec Gazette*, 17 Sept. 1818; 8 March, 16 Sept. 1819; 13 Aug. 1821; 17 June 1822; 29 May, 9 June 1823. *Encyclopedia of music in Canada*, ed. Helmut Kallmann et al. (Toronto, 1981). *The service of British regiments in Canada and North America . . .*, comp. C. H. Stewart (Ottawa, 1962). Willy Amtmann, *La musique au Québec, 1600–1875*, Michelle Pharand, trad. (Montréal, 1976), 375–76. Helmut Kallmann, *A history of music in Canada, 1534–1914* (Toronto and London, 1960), 71. T.-L. Brassard et É.-Z. Massicotte, "Les deux musiciens Braunies," *BRH*, 41 (1935): 641–42. Nazaire LeVasseur, "Musique et musiciens à Québec: souvenirs d'un amateur," *La Musique* (Québec), 1 (1919): 75–76. P.-G. Roy, "À propos de musique: la première fanfare québécoise," *BRH*, 43 (1937): 353–54.

BRO, JEAN-BAPTISTE, Roman Catholic priest; b. 20 April 1743 in Rivière-aux-Canards (near Canard), N.S., son of Séraphin Bréaux and Brigitte Martin; d. 12 Jan. 1824 in Saint-Jacques-de-l'Achigan (Saint-Jacques), Lower Canada.

Deported from Nova Scotia like many other Acadians, Jean-Baptiste Bro and his family reached England in the spring of 1756 and were imprisoned. After the signing of the Treaty of Paris in 1763 they were taken to France through the good offices of the Duc de Nivernais. Bro, who was 20, arrived at Saint-Malo with his family aboard the frigate *Dorothée* on 21 May 1763. He settled in Saint-Suliac, and then after 1766 in Saint-Servan.

Bro studied philosophy at the Séminaire de Saint-Malo and then took theology at the Séminaire du Saint-Esprit in Paris. He received minor orders on 9 June 1770. The priesthood was conferred upon him at Quebec by Bishop Louis-Philippe Mariauchau* d'Esgly, in order to circumvent the British authorities' refusal to admit Catholic priests into the colony. His ordination took place in the chapel of the Séminaire de Québec on 15 Nov. 1772.

Bro is generally associated with Joseph-Mathurin Bourg*, his stepbrother. They were deported to the same places, followed the same courses of study, came to the colony together, and were ordained the same year. Both had a desire to devote themselves to their unfortunate compatriots in North America, who were dispersed among English-speaking Protestants. Bourg went to serve the Acadians scattered about Nova Scotia and the Gaspé, while in October 1773 Bro was given charge of the exiles who had come to L'Assomption from New England in the course of the previous dozen years. Between November 1773 and June 1774 Bro also served in the parishes of Notre-Dame in Montreal and Saint-François-d'Assise at Longue-Pointe. On 27 June 1774 he became assistant priest to Sulpician Jacques Degeay* at L'Assomption.

On 8 Nov. 1774 Bro was made parish priest of Saint-Jacques-de-l'Achigan. The parish prospered and in 1801 work was begun on a church. In 1804, however, the syndics, who had been elected by the parish to look after the financial arrangements, suddenly stopped the project alleging that they lacked money, and asked for a new division of expenses. The churchwardens decided to take legal action and called upon the services of Montreal lawyer Joseph Bédard. The syndics retained Stephen SEWELL. In April 1805 the Court of King's Bench, with the chief justice, James MONK, and judges Pierre-Louis Panet*, Isaac Ogden, and Arthur Davidson* sitting, ruled in favour of Bédard's clients and ordered the syndics to give an account of their administration. In August another lawsuit began, this time over the administration of the syndics, who won the case in October 1812. The church was finally completed in August of the following year.

No longer able to attend to his duties as parish priest, Jean-Baptiste Bro retired in October 1814 and went to live with a niece. He died on 12 Jan. 1824. A gentle, shrewd, and conciliatory man, he had been held in high esteem by his parishioners.

PIERRE-MAURICE HÉBERT

"L'abbé Joseph-Mathurin Bourg," Anselme Rhéaume, édit., *BRH*, 6 (1900): 263–67. Placide Gaudet, "Généalogie des Acadiens, avec documents," PAC *Rapport*, 1905, 2, IIIe partie: 336–44. Allaire, *Dictionnaire*, vol.1. Le Jeune, *Dictionnaire*, 2: 241–42. Bona Arsenault, *Histoire et généalogie des Acadiens* (2v., Québec, 1965), 1: 229, 255. H.-R. Casgrain, *Les Sulpiciens et les prêtres des Missions-*

Étrangères en Acadie (1676–1762) (Québec, 1897), 329; *Un pèlerinage au pays d'Évangéline* (2ᵉ éd., Québec, 1888), 277. [F.-X. Chagnon], *Annales religieuses et historiques de la paroisse de St-Jacques le Majeur . . .* (Montréal, 1872), 16–27. Albert David, *Les missionnaires du séminaire du Saint-Esprit à Québec et en Acadie au XVIIIᵉ siècle* (Mamers, France, 1926). *Dialogue entre un Acadien et un Canadien français . . .* (Québec, 1889). L.-U. Fontaine, *Voyage du sieur de Dièreville en Acadie* (Québec, 1885), 123–41. A.[-H.] Gosselin, *L'Église du Canada après la Conquête* (2v., Québec, 1916–17), 1: 309, 318–19; 2: 155–56, 316. François Lanoue, *Une nouvelle Acadie: Saint-Jacques-de-L'Achigan* (s.l., 1972). Émile Lauvrière, *Brève histoire tragique du peuple acadien, son martyre et sa résurrection* (Paris, 1947). Arthur Melançon, *Vie de l'abbé Bourg, premier prêtre acadien, missionnaire et grand-vicaire pour l'Acadie et la Baie-des-Chaleurs, 1744–1797* (Rimouski, Qué., 1921). [F.-E.] Rameau de Saint-Père, *Une colonie féodale en Amérique: l'Acadie (1604–1881)* (2v., Paris et Montréal, 1889), 2: 215–16, 251. Christian Roy, *Histoire de L'Assomption* (L'Assomption, Qué., 1967). Robert Rumilly, *Histoire des Acadiens* (2v., Montréal, 1955), 1: 497–99, 500–3, 528; 2: 568, 573, 586–88, 634, 638. Antoine Bernard, "L'abbé Bourg, premier prêtre acadien," *Le Devoir* (Montréal), 9 avril 1938: 8; "Mathurin Bourg," *Le Travailleur* (Worcester, Mass.), 28 nov. 1957: 1–2. É.-P. Chouinard, "Le premier prêtre acadien – l'abbé Joseph-Mathurin Bourg," *La Nouvelle-France* (Québec), 2 (1903): 310–17, 403–11. Éva Comeau, "L'abbé Joseph-Mathurin Bourg, curé de Carleton en 1773," *Rev. d'hist. de la Gaspésie* (Gaspé, Qué.), 9 (1971): 239–42. Albert David, "Les deux premiers prêtres acadiens," *BRH*, 35 (1929): 444–46. P.-M. Hébert, "Paroisses acadiennes du Québec," Soc. hist. acadienne, *Cahiers* (Moncton, N.-B.), 3 (1968–71): 357–61. Maréchal Nantel, "Une querelle de paroisse en 1805," *Cahiers des Dix*, 13 (1948): 249–68.

BROWN, ANDREW, Church of Scotland minister and author; b. 22 Aug. 1763 in Biggar, Scotland, son of Richard Brown and Isabella Forrest; m. 10 Sept. 1792 Daniel [*sic*] Cranstoun at Harvieston, Clackmannanshire, Scotland, and they had two children; m. secondly 2 March 1805 Mary Grant in Edinburgh; m. there thirdly 10 March 1830 Mary Pearson, *née* Ogilvie; d. 19 Feb. 1834 in Primrose Bank (Carrington), Scotland.

Son of a weaver, Andrew Brown grew up with the Industrial Revolution and the Scottish Enlightenment. A precocious child, he matriculated at the University of Glasgow in 1776, at the age of 13, and from then until he was licensed to preach by the Presbytery of Biggar in 1786 he studied at both Glasgow and the University of Edinburgh. In 1787, before he had received his divinity degree, he decided to leave Scotland to take up an appointment as minister of St Matthew's Church in Halifax. On the eve of his departure he wrote to a friend: "It is with no small reluctance I have consented to quit my native land and seek a station, perhaps a grave, in another Hemisphere. . . . A simple day [has] altered, as it were, the whole plan of life, given a new range to hope and fear and interwoven my destiny with that Destiny of Strangers and a foreign land."

Apart from a short visit to Britain in 1792, when he married his first wife, Brown spent almost eight years in Nova Scotia. Described by Bishop Charles Inglis* as "an ingenious young man from Scotland with amiable manners," he was a brilliant preacher and a leading figure in intellectual and social circles. His ministry has been called St Matthew's golden age, because it was during these years that the church rose to prominence. Brown did much to heal the breach between Congregationalists and Presbyterians, New Englanders and Scottish immigrants, in his congregation. He also attempted to deal with the divisions afflicting the Presbyterian cause in other parts of Nova Scotia, as his correspondence with the Reverend James Drummond MacGregor, the uncompromising anti-burgher minister in Pictou, reveals. The award of a DD to Brown in 1788 by the University of Edinburgh increased his stature in the colony. His connections in Halifax society were reflected in the fact that he served as chaplain both to the North British Society and to the military and naval forces.

Brown had been recommended for his position in Halifax by the famous Scottish historian William Robertson, who appears to have acted as an intellectual mentor to him and could have stimulated his interest in history. Although Brown worked hard in Nova Scotia as a minister of the Gospel, he spent much of his leisure in collecting and studying historical documents. In his research he also drew upon the recollections and observations of several of his contemporaries, including Brook Watson*, Isaac Deschamps*, and Hugh Graham. His association with the American historian Jeremy Belknap, the founder of the Massachusetts Historical Society (to which Brown was elected as a corresponding member in 1793), inspired him to embark on a full-length historical study. He may also have been influenced by the failure of the ageing Robertson to complete the North American part of his history of the New World. In any event, his original intention was to write a history of Nova Scotia; soon, however, his design broadened to include North America as a whole.

Brown's reputation as a scholar quickly spread beyond the boundaries of Nova Scotia. In 1791 he visited Philadelphia and met the famous physician Benjamin Rush, who called him "a man of genius, learning, observation"; it was on this visit that his friendship with Belknap began. He did not restrict his historical researches to documents available in British North America and the United States but worked, intermittently from 1792 onwards, on British official records in London. After he left Nova Scotia, he even paid visits to Paris in his relentless search for documents. Brown was a genuine scholar, with a gift

Brown

for narrative, a critical and comparative sense, and an international as well as national and local approach. Yet he never completed and published his history of North America, although he made three drafts of it. Through family neglect many of his papers were lost; what remain are distributed largely between the British Library in London and the Edinburgh University Library. Some of Brown's documents and his handling of them have been appreciated by historians of Canada, notably by John Bartlet Brebner*.

Conservative in temperament and critical of both the American and the French revolutions, Brown nevertheless displayed a pronounced sympathy with the oppressed, whether Acadians, Indians, or Scottish villagers whom economic and social pressures had "driven to the workshop or to the wilderness of a new world." As an historian of Nova Scotia, he differed from later writers such as Thomas Chandler Haliburton*, Beamish Murdoch*, and Duncan Campbell* in his warm view of the Acadians and in his sophisticated analysis of the deportation. For him, Acadia before the expulsion was a peaceful, idyllic society, a "Paradise Lost," and much of his manuscript history is a detailed discussion of Acadian life prior to 1755. He greatly admired Paul Mascarene*, the administrator of the colony in the 1740s, for his tactful and compassionate treatment of the Acadians; at one point in his account he wrote "I love Mascarene" in the margin. Acting governor Charles Lawrence*, in contrast, was subjected to harsh criticism for his role in the removal of the Acadians. Brown regarded the deportation as a cataclysm that could not be justified on any grounds, and he devoted considerable attention to the sufferings of the Acadians in the course of their exile. But he was not content to moralize. The conclusion he reached after poring over his documents was that the expulsion was the work not of Lawrence alone but of Lawrence working in unison with a Council controlled by Boston interests. This notion that New England played an important part in the tragedy of 1755 was later to find brilliant expression in Brebner's *New England's outpost*. Brebner also seems to have been influenced by Brown's treatment of the Acadian quest for neutrality in the years leading up to the expulsion. The theme of Acadian neutrality figures prominently in *New England's outpost*, and it was also used to illuminate a later period in Nova Scotian history in Brebner's classic study *The neutral Yankees of Nova Scotia*.

Brown returned to Scotland in 1795; as chance would have it, he travelled on the same vessel as Prince William Henry, whom he impressed so much that in 1801 the prince recommended Brown for a university chair. Minister of Lochmaben from 1795 to 1799, Brown went on to become minister of two Edinburgh churches: New Greyfriars from 1799 to 1800, and the High Kirk of St Giles (St Giles Cathedral) until his death in 1834. In 1813 he was appointed moderator of the Church of Scotland. With the help of the prince's recommendation, in 1801 he was made professor of rhetoric and *belles-lettres* at the University of Edinburgh. The appointment proved almost disastrous to the chair, presumably because, in addition to his professorship, Brown struggled with ill health and family problems, the demands of his Edinburgh congregation, and his history of North America, ever expanding under the weight of new material.

Brown had high standards as an historian. In a revealing remark made at the end of his discussion of the deportation, he noted that "the last sentence must be changed . . . I can make it better." Unfortunately, his pursuit of perfection resulted in a meagre list of publications: three sermons in Halifax, and two sermons and a slim tribute to an academic colleague in Edinburgh. Although not without interest as reflections of and commentaries on his times, these works do not do justice to one who might have succeeded William Robertson as historian of North America or have produced, before Haliburton in 1829, the first history of Nova Scotia.

GEORGE SHEPPERSON

Andrew Brown's published works include *A discourse delivered before the North-British Society, in Halifax, Nova-Scotia . . .* (Halifax, 1791); *A sermon, on the dangers and duties of the seafaring life; preached before the Protestant dissenting congregation, at Halifax . . .* (Boston, 1793); *The perils of the time, and the purposes for which they are appointed; a sermon . . .* (Halifax, 1795); *Love of country explained and illustrated; a sermon . . .* (Edinburgh, 1801); *The standard of excellence established in the Gospel; a sermon . . .* (Edinburgh, 1810); and *Notice of the life and character of Alexander Christison, A.M., late professor of humanity in the University of Edinburgh* (Edinburgh, 1820). In addition, his notes on "The Acadian French" were published in N.S. Hist. Soc., *Coll.*, 2 (1881): 129–60; and his correspondence with Jeremy Belknap is available in "The Belknap papers," Mass. Hist. Soc., *Coll.* (Boston), 6th ser., 4 (1891): 521–615. The main manuscript collections of Brown's papers are BL, Add. MSS 19071–76, and Edinburgh Univ. Library, Special Coll. Dept., Gen. 154–59.

BL, Add. MSS 19069–70. Dalhousie Univ. Arch. (Halifax), DAL, MS-1-1, C-1 (Dalhousie College, letter-book, 1818–20): 13–30. *The matriculation albums of the University of Glasgow from 1728 to 1858*, comp. W. I. Addison (Glasgow, 1913). Scott et al., *Fasti ecclesiæ scoticanæ*, vol.1. *The university portraits*, comp. D. T. Rice and Peter McIntyre (Edinburgh, 1957). W. P. Bell, *The "foreign Protestants" and the settlement of Nova Scotia . . .* (Toronto, 1961). J. B. Brebner, *The neutral Yankees of Nova Scotia, a marginal colony during the revolutionary years* (New York, 1937; repr. [1970]); *New England's outpost: Acadia before the conquest of Canada* (New York and London, 1927; repr. Hamden, Conn., 1965, and New York, [1973]). Alexander Grant, *The story of the University of Edinburgh during its first three hundred years* (2v., London, 1884). William

Hunter, *Biggar and the house of Fleming; an account of the Biggar district, archæological, historical, and biographical* (2nd ed., Edinburgh, 1867). Nancy McMahon, "Andrew Brown and the writing of Acadian history" (MA thesis, Queen's Univ., Kingston, Ont., 1981). George Shepperson, *Edinburgh and Canada: two Brown studies* (Edinburgh, 1985). J. B. Brebner, "The Brown MSS. and Longfellow," *CHR*, 17 (1936): 172–78; "Paul Mascarene of Annapolis Royal," *Dalhousie Rev.*, 8 (1928–29): 501–16. W. C. Murray, "History of St. Matthew's Church, Halifax, N.S.," *N.S. Hist. Soc., Coll.*, 16 (1912): 137–70.

BRYMER, ALEXANDER, agent, merchant, office holder, politician, JP, and militia officer; b. *c.* 1745 in Scotland, possibly in Dundee; m. 11 Jan. 1796 Harriet Dobson, *née* Parr, in Preston, Lancashire, England, and they had three sons; d. 27 Aug. 1822 in Ramsgate, England.

The pre-Halifax career of Alexander Brymer remains a little obscure. He emigrated to North America probably as a young man, and entered business as a merchant in Boston. From at least 1772 he was the agent, first in Boston, then in Halifax, for the London merchants Robert Grant and William Brymer, who held the navy victualling contract for North America. Grant had been a member of the Nova Scotia Council; Brymer (Alexander's uncle) was a wealthy and influential businessman who had been involved in North American commerce from soon after the fall of Quebec [*see* Daniel Bayne*]. On 2 Dec. 1775 Alexander was nominated agent to Grant and Brymer. He had been doing business in Halifax as early as 1771, but did not finally leave Boston until shortly before its evacuation by British forces in March 1776. He could not have delayed his departure much longer: he was being mentioned by name in rebel newspapers and had signed a loyal address to Governor Thomas Gage* in October 1775. He was proscribed by the Banishment Act of Massachusetts in 1778. At some time Brymer had been appointed co-agent for the disposal of vessels captured or impounded by the Royal Navy, a position he seems to have retained after arriving in Halifax. He must have been comparatively wealthy when he settled there, for in 1776 and 1777 his property was assessed at the third highest value in the town.

To be the agent for prizes condemned in the Vice-Admiralty Court was to participate in war profiteering at its potentially most lucrative. Of the 39 letters of agency registered at the court in Halifax between 1776 and 1781, 18 were held either by Brymer alone or by him in partnership. Brymer not only represented naval officers and privateersmen in court; he also owned at least one privateer himself, the 40-ton schooner *Halifax Bob*, a letter of marque for which was issued on 29 Jan. 1779. From February to May of that year *Halifax Bob* cruised in the West Indies, returning "with richly laden prizes." *Halifax Bob* was itself a prize; Brymer no doubt had been the agent for its condemnation and had purchased the vessel when it went to the auction block.

Brymer's first place of business in Halifax was the navy victualling office. In 1779, however, he acquired the valuable estate of the merchant Thomas Saul*. The property consisted of a wharf, storehouses, and a residence so striking that it had been nicknamed "Saul's Folly" (and became known as "Brymer's Palace"). The mansion stood at the corner of Hollis and Upper Water streets, and for many years after Brymer's departure was the premises of the Jerusalem Coffee House or Tavern. In the next decade or so Brymer expanded what had been Saul's holdings to accommodate the increasing volume of his overseas trade.

The American war had not yet ended when Brymer began to make his presence felt in the political life of Nova Scotia. In 1781 some friends in London had obtained a recommendation from Lord North, the leader of the government, that he be appointed to the Council. Brymer in due course received the appointment, a vacancy having occurred with the death of Charles Morris* late that year, and he was sworn in on 26 March 1782. He also collected nine commissions as justice of the peace for seven different counties, and was likewise *custos rotulorum* for Hants County. In 1791 and 1792 he served on a committee of the Council which supervised the embarkation of the free blacks for Sierra Leone [*see* Thomas Peters*; David George*]. Deputy paymaster general to the forces from about late 1791, he was appointed revenue commissioner and auditor of public accounts in 1793 and commissioner in charge of a fund for building roads and bridges in 1797.

In 1787 Brymer had leased the 2,400-acre estate of Winckworth Tonge* in Windsor Township, and five years later he succeeded Tonge as colonel of the Hants County militia. When in the autumn of 1793 Lieutenant Governor John Wentworth* summoned the county militias to Halifax to repel an expected French attack, a quota from Brymer's regiment marched among them. Writing to the home secretary on 9 November, Wentworth praised Brymer's "excellent example of attachment and zeal to His Majesty's service."

Alexander Brymer was a pillar of the North British Society of Halifax, which was for all practical purposes a Scottish mercantile brotherhood. He entered the society in 1777, was elected moderator in 1778, 1779, and 1780, and president in 1790, and purchased its first life membership in 1783. He belonged, moreover, to a "literary coterie" of members who met regularly to read and discuss papers on learned subjects. Prince Edward* Augustus himself used to attend these symposia. Brymer was also a loyal supporter of St Paul's Church. He served as churchwarden with Gregory Townsend from 1793 to

Buell

1797; in the former year he had had a vestry built at his own expense. When Brymer and Townsend retired, the congregation resolved unanimously that they be thanked for their "prudent and judicious arrangement of the funds . . . , [by which they] discharged a heavy debt."

Brymer retired to England in 1801, presumably because his uncle William had died in September 1800; he was the principal beneficiary of the estate. He attended his last Council meeting on 16 April 1801 and left ten days or so later, having been entrusted with the dispatches and accounts of Wentworth, who described him in a letter about the same time as "a Gentleman of great distinction and carefulness." Brymer resided first in London and then in Bath. He held 100-year leases on seven houses in Bedford Square in London, and had the gift of the living of Charlton Mackrell in Somerset. He invested substantially in consols and also owned some East India Company stock. His youngest son was high sheriff of Dorset in 1865.

Alexander Brymer was already a councillor by the time the influx of his fellow loyalists into Nova Scotia began in 1783. He became one of the inner circle of Governor John Parr*, whose widowed daughter he married, and his relations with Parr's successor, the quixotic Wentworth, were those of mutual respect and loyalty if not friendship. Appropriately, his successor on the Council was William Forsyth*, a Scottish merchant hardly less eminent than himself.

According to Simeon Perkins*, Brymer was "Very Clever & Genteel." His philanthropy, moreover, was legendary: Beamish Murdoch* tells in *A History of Nova-Scotia, or Acadie* the story of his interceding with a relentless creditor on behalf of the aged and impecunious Winckworth Tonge. Judge Alexander Croke* held him responsible for the success of Andrew Belcher*, Brymer having taken the young son of a former chief justice into his office. There is, however, a contradictory oral tradition, apparently deriving from some satirical verse no longer extant, according to which Brymer was "really a hard, grasping man." But the memory of him was still green in the 1860s when Murdoch composed this eulogy of him: "It is not always that the prudence and industry that elevate the commercial man to wealth are united with honor, humanity and generosity, as was the case with Mr. Brymer; but the instances where they are found in combination, merit permanent honor and distinction."

J. B. Cahill

Halifax County Registry of Deeds (Halifax), Deeds, 15: f.89; 16: f.203 *et seq.* (mfm. at PANS). PANS, MG 1, 250, docs.31–34; RG 1, 169; 171: 33, 136; 172: 51; 411, doc.7; 499. PRO, CO 217/37: 290; 217/55: 196; 217/64: 288; CO 218/25: 171; PROB 11/1662/508. John Clarkson, *Clarkson's mission to America, 1791–1792*, ed. and intro. C. B. Fergusson (Halifax, 1971). *Naval documents of the American revolution*, ed. W. B. Clarke and W. J. Morgan (8v. to date, Washington, 1964–   ), 1–3. Perkins, *Diary, 1766–80* (Innis); *1780–89* (Harvey and Fergusson); *1790–96* (Fergusson); *1797–1803* (Fergusson). *Annals, North British Society, Halifax, Nova Scotia, with portraits and biographical notes, 1768–1903*, comp. J. S. Macdonald ([3rd ed.], Halifax, 1905), 24, 27. [Although Macdonald's work is the traditional account of Brymer's life and career, it is based largely on hearsay and contains several demonstrable factual errors. J.B.C.] Murdoch, *Hist. of N.S.*, 3: 204–5.

BUELL, WILLIAM, miller, JP, and politician; b. 5 Oct. 1751 in Hebron (Marlborough), Conn., son of Timothy Buell and Mercy Peters; m. first 10 March 1782 Martha Naughton (Norton), and they had ten children; m. secondly 31 March 1827 Margaret Barnard, *née* Berkley, and they had one child; d. 8 Aug. 1832 in Brockville, Upper Canada.

William Buell was a member of a moderately influential family which lived for several generations in Hebron. In the early 1770s Timothy Buell moved to Fort Ann on the Hudson River in New York. When the American revolution broke out, he initially refused to take sides and, when his family was persecuted for his neutrality, he went to Charlotte (Washington) County on Lake Ontario. William Buell, a cooper like his father, supported the British and moved to Montreal shortly after the start of the revolution. He held the rank of assistant quartermaster in Major-General John Burgoyne*'s army when it surrendered at Saratoga (Schuylerville, N.Y.) on 17 Oct. 1777. Subsequently Buell joined Robert Rogers*'s King's Rangers, raised in 1779, as an ensign; he was later promoted lieutenant. During the war, he also served as a courier and was captured twice, although in both instances he escaped. The unit was disbanded in 1783 and Buell went on half pay.

Following the revolution, Buell was joined by the remainder of his family, then in New York, and located briefly at Lachine, Que. In 1784 he moved to Township No.8 (Elizabethtown) in western Quebec and claimed 505 acres on the bay shore where Brockville ultimately emerged. There he built the first house in the vicinity. That same year he was rejoined by members of his family; eventually his father, brothers, and sisters all owned land in the same area. Buell, in 1793, also added 1,200 acres of land, to which he was entitled for military service, in Oxford Township near present-day Kemptville.

William Buell farmed the land in the Brockville area and during the 1790s opened a mill. He also became involved in a series of quarrels with the families of Justus Sherwood and Daniel Jones, both settled in the same area and both competing for economic and political influence. The three families, easily the most prominent in the locality, could not even decide on a name for their community, which was usually known as Elizabethtown but was dubbed "Snarlington" because of the acrimonious debates. Finally, in 1812, the issue was resolved and the name Brockville was chosen.

William Buell was commissioned justice of the peace for the Luneburg District on 24 July 1788 and for the Midland District on 15 July 1796. In 1800 he was elected to the House of Assembly representing Leeds County. He did not attend the assembly frequently, however; he missed the sessions of 1802 and 1803 altogether, and arrived late and left early in 1804. His voting record tended to be against the administration, thereby starting a reform tendency that would be continued by later generations of Buells.

Buell contributed significantly to the development of early Brockville. About 1809 he opened the first school, taught by Joseph Pyle, in his home, where it remained for several years. In 1811 he subdivided his land and by 1820 most of the approximately 60 houses in Brockville were located on his property. Out of a sense of public duty and a desire to attract development near his holdings, Buell donated land for the court-house, and the Presbyterian, Baptist, Methodist, and Roman Catholic churches. In 1820 he built the first stone house in Brockville, an impressive home in the centre of the village.

In 1823 Buell helped his son William* to purchase the *Brockville Recorder*, a newspaper that became an important organ of reform in eastern Upper Canada, and a financial success for the family. During the 1820s he spent most of his time attending to his mill or working on a farm north of the village, owned by his son William. Rather remarkably he fathered his last child in 1828 when he was more than 75 years of age. He died from cholera during the epidemic of 1832.

IAN MACPHERSON

AO, MU 275, A. N. Buell, draft of inscription for monument to William Buell and his wife Martha Naughton, n.d. PAC, MG 24, B7; B75; RG 1, L3, 32: B5/44. *History of the Buell family in England, from the remotest times ascertainable from our ancient histories, and in America, from town, parish, church and family records*, comp. Albert Welles (New York, 1881). T. W. H. Leavitt, *History of Leeds and Grenville, Ontario, from 1749 to 1879* . . . (Brockville, Ont., 1879; repr. Belleville, Ont., 1972), 181, 196–97. Ruth McKenzie, *Leeds and Grenville: their first two hundred years* (Toronto and Montreal, 1967), 36–37, 114–15. Ian MacPherson, *Matters of loyalty: the Buells of Brockville, 1830–1850* (Belleville, 1981).

BURLEY (Burleigh), CORNELIUS ALBERTSON, blacksmith; b. *c.* 1804 in Upper Canada, son of William Burley; m. *c.* 1825 Sally King; m. secondly June 1829, while his first wife was still alive,

Margaret Beamer (Beemer) of Dumfries Township; hanged 19 Aug. 1830 in London, Upper Canada.

Although executions in Upper Canada were infrequent, those that did occur provided an extraordinary entertainment for pioneer society. From the standpoint of the law, moreover, the spectacle of the gallows produced a salutary impression on the public and, especially important, on the potential criminal. Yet the lesson could be reinforced. Upper Canada being an essentially religious society, it was felt to be necessary that the offender atone for his misdeeds, explain his immoral behaviour, and acknowledge his faith in Jesus Christ. Thus the gallows address usually took the form of a confession whereby all concerned could be assured that justice had been done. One of the best examples is the trial and execution of Cornelius Albertson Burley.

Burley's family settled in Beverley Township in 1827; Burley himself claimed to have been a blacksmith. His story begins in the late summer of 1829, when he killed a yoke of steers belonging to a Mr Lamb, presumably Henry Lamb*, and a warrant was issued for his arrest. Burley claimed that Lamb had defrauded him and, unable to get legal redress, he had exacted his own form of vengeance. He was arrested by a Gore District constable, Timothy Conklin Pomeroy, but escaped and fled to the farm of his uncle Henry Ribble (Ribbel) in Bayham Township. Accompanied by his wife, he arrived there late in August. He worked on the farm until Pomeroy arrived on the scene on 13 September. About 3 o'clock on the morning of 16 September Pomeroy was shot, and he died shortly thereafter.

Murder was not uncommon but the killing of a constable in execution of his duty was sensational and unsettling news. The *Gore Emporium* claimed that "a more foul, cold-blooded murder scarcely ever disgraced the annals of civilization." Residents of both the Gore and the London districts petitioned Lieutenant Governor Sir John Colborne*, complaining of the magistrates' "gross neglect of duty" in failing to apprehend the constable's murderer(s). After consulting with judge James Buchanan Macaulay*, who stressed the necessity of "the most prompt and diligent exertions" in order to satisfy the concern for "Public Justice," Colborne on 23 September mildly chided Mahlon Burwell*, a local magistrate, and the sheriff for not making an immediate report. In fact, Burwell was not to blame; the problem was dated information, the natural result of slow communication.

On 19 September a man fitting Burley's description but claiming to be William Ribble had been captured by settlers in Dunwich Township; he was taken to St Thomas. The same day Burwell and two other magistrates examined the prisoner, who then identified himself as Burley. He recounted his flight from justice in Gore, claiming his innocence. He also gave

Burley

his version of events leading up to Pomeroy's death, saying that when the constable and another man had appeared at Henry Ribble's farm on 14 September he had hidden in a field and then in the barn. Believing Pomeroy had spotted him, he fled the following night, taking with him his wife and a rifle that he obtained from the home of his cousin, Anthony Ribble. Burley stated that he knew nothing of the murder and did not hear a gunshot on the night in question. He had travelled about 50 miles before being arrested.

On 20 September the JPS arrived from Bayham with three witnesses in tow: Isaac D. White, Henry Ribble, and his son David. The information of the Ribbles cohered neatly. When Pomeroy's party appeared, Henry Ribble urged Burley to give himself up but he refused, saying that "if they got him they should take him dead." On the morning of Pomeroy's killing, Henry had been wakened by a shot. He claimed that about a half-hour after sunrise, Burley appeared with a rifle and claimed to have shot Pomeroy in the leg. White, a member of Pomeroy's group, followed the same sequence of events sketched by the Ribbles, but put them in a different context. The Ribbles had been uncooperative. Anthony Ribble told Pomeroy to leave his house quickly, "or he would have his blood spilt and that Damned quick." While searching Henry Ribble's house about 45 minutes before his death, Pomeroy had unsheathed his sword to guard himself. He was shot returning from Henry Ribble's and in close proximity to Anthony Ribble's, where White saw a light burning. White did not know who shot Pomeroy. On 21 September the JPS committed Burley to jail charged on the oaths of the three witnesses. He was "put in Irons" and sent to London to await trial. The following month an indictment was issued against Anthony Ribble as well and he, too, was held over for trial. In the spring of 1830 a number of prisoners – Ribble among them – escaped. Burley remained behind; he may have been chained to the floor. Ribble was soon recaptured.

The assizes opened on 12 Aug. 1830 with Chief Justice John Beverley Robinson* presiding. His associates from the local magistracy were Burwell and James Mitchell. The grand jury found a true bill against Burley on 16 August and his trial, separate from that of Ribble's, commenced the following day. Only three witnesses were called for the crown by Solicitor General Christopher Alexander Hagerman*. Burley was found guilty and Robinson sentenced him to be executed on the morning of the 19th. In his subsequent report Robinson noted that the "evidence was such as to place the guilt of the convict beyond doubt. . . . He fully confessed his guilt." The confession, however, had come after sentencing and not during the trial. The Reverend James Jackson* noted that it was made "about forty-one hours before his execution." Presumably, then, it had some impact upon Anthony

Ribble's trial on the 18th; he was acquitted. Burley's was the only capital conviction on the Western Circuit in which Robinson did not order a respite of execution, probably because of the confession.

Burley had been the object of the attention of local clergy during the assizes. Jackson saw him "every day but one" and claimed, "Never have I witnessed so great an instance of obduracy and insensibility." Eventually, however, the clergy's discussions with the prisoner "wrought a victory over his unfeeling heart; he burst into a flood of tears" and confessed. Prior to going to the scaffold he received the sacrament of baptism and the Eucharist from the local Anglican clergymen. Jackson copied down the confession and read it from the scaffold before a crowd of some 3,000. Another minister addressed the throng and concluded with a prayer, whereupon the trapdoor dropped. But, as often happened, the execution was botched. The rope broke and Burley fell to the ground. It was some time before another attempt could be made because the sheriff had to buy a new rope. Throughout Jackson claimed that Burley was composed and "seemed as if the world was lost from his view, and his whole mind was devotion, prayer, praise, singing, and thanksgiving." When all was again ready he walked to the scaffold "without any appearance of hesitation; but with the utmost composure, submitted to his fate."

Some historians have questioned how much Jackson's efforts influenced the act of confession and several have concluded that Burley was probably innocent and Anthony Ribble guilty of Pomeroy's murder. On the first matter, there was nothing unusual about clergy and magistrates urging a convict to confess for the good of his soul and for the benefit of society. With regard to the confession itself, Jackson says, simply, that he copied down Burley's statement; however, he no doubt added a literate quality that otherwise would have been absent. Whether Burley was guilty must remain, in the absence of further evidence, a moot point. It seems that the evidence was stacked against him. The source of the accusation was Henry Ribble who, Burwell noted, "candidly believes that Cornelius Burley was the man who shot Pomeroy." But as White declared, it was the Ribbles who had threatened Pomeroy. Moreover, the *Gore Emporium*'s report of the magistrates' investigation stated that the Ribbles' evidence "betrayed strong symptoms of guilt." In the end Burley's confession probably saved Anthony Ribble. "I am constrained to say," the confession read, "that he had no hand in the crime whatever, Neither had any other person."

Burley's confession was published in Bartemas FERGUSON's *Gore Balance*; Ferguson also printed 1,000 copies as handbills. As an example of its type, the confession is a model. Burley hoped it would "have a tendency to check the progress of evil, and prevent others from doing as I have done." He had been "wicked and thoughtless from my youth." He was raised without the benefits of education or religion and was unable to read or write. He wandered through the world "under the influence of depravity. . . . I was often found in the merry dance, & lost no opportunity of inducing thoughtless & unguarded females to leave the paths of innocence and virtue." He took upon himself all guilt for the act, noting, "I only suffer the penalty that is justly due to my crimes." He thanked the ministers who saved him and claimed, "In my great extremity I have gained a confidence that through the merits of Christ alone I will be saved, although the chief of sinners. . . . I now leave this world with the fullest confidence that my sins are washed away in the Blood of the Lamb."

But it was not quite the end. As the sentence stipulated, Burley's body was given to surgeons for dissection. According to one account, Orson Squire Fowler, later a noted American phrenologist, had visited Burley in his cell and reported on his phrenological character. After the dissection on 19 August, Fowler received the head and the following day used it for a public lecture. Before leaving London he sawed it in two and took the top part with him. He subsequently used it on his extensive American and European tours. The bottom portion was discovered in London in 1960 and is now on display in Eldon House, a local museum.

ROBERT LOCHIEL FRASER

AO, RG 21, Wentworth County, Beverly Township, assessment rolls, 1826–30; RG 22, ser.61, vol.5, 17 April 1830; ser.134, 5, London District, 1830. PAC, RG 1, L3, 148: Canada Company, 1829–44/12; RG 5, A1: 53500–96, 53728–51, 53876–78, 53902–4, 57699–700, 63038–39. Wentworth Land Registry Office (Hamilton, Ont.), Beverly Township, abstract index to deeds, concession 7, lot 6 (mfm. at AO). U.C., House of Assembly, *Journal*, 1831, app.: 29, 52–53; 1831–32, app.: 152, 161. *Canadian Freeman*, 16 Sept. 1830. *Gore Balance* (Hamilton), 3, 10 Sept. 1830. *Kingston Chronicle*, 3 Oct. 1829. *Upper Canada Gazette*, 1 Oct. 1829–14 Jan. 1830. *History of the county of Middlesex . . .* (Toronto and London, Ont., 1889; repr. with intro. D. [J.] Brock, Belleville, Ont., 1972), 120–21. [H.] O. Miller, *Gargoyles & gentlemen: a history of St Paul's Cathedral, London, Ontario, 1834–1964* (Toronto, 1966), 16–20; *Twenty mortal murders: bizarre murder cases from Canada's past* (Toronto, 1978), 35–44. M. B. Stern, *Heads & headlines: the phrenological Fowlers* (Norman, Okla., 1971), 15. D. J. Brock, "The confession: Burleigh's pre-hanging 'statement' mystery" and "That confession again: error leads to further probe, suggestion of Burley's innocence," *London Free Press*, 10 April 1971: 8M, and 24 April 1971: 8M. *London Advertiser*, 31 March 1886: 4. *London Free Press*, 26 Nov. 1885: 2.

BURNS, JOHN, Presbyterian minister and teacher; baptized 12 Feb. 1773 in the parish of Fenwick, Ayrshire, Scotland, eldest son of Thomas B. Burns, a farmer, and Ann Tod; m. Jane ——, and they had at least six children; buried 27 Feb. 1822 in Stamford (Niagara Falls), Upper Canada.

The details of John Burns's early life are few. He was educated at the University of Glasgow and the Secession Theological Hall, becoming a licentiate of the Associate Synod in 1803. According to some sources, Burns, having travelled by way of Pennsylvania, arrived in Upper Canada in 1804. By his own account, however, the date of his arrival in the Niagara District was 1805.

As early as 1792 a numerous and prosperous Presbyterian congregation had been in existence at Newark (Niagara-on-the-Lake). In subsequent years its members had difficulty in securing the services of a regular minister for their church, later known as St Andrew's. Their first minister, John Dun*, resigned in 1796 and their second, John YOUNG, held office briefly in 1802 before resigning because of alcoholism. Burns's association with the church began in 1805; he served as minister until 1811 and then again from 1816 to 1818, and presided over sessions of the elders as late as 1820. Like Dun, Burns also preached regularly at Stamford.

In 1805 St Andrew's agreed to pay its minister an additional stipend to instruct 13 pupils in Latin, Greek, and mathematics, but it is not known whether Burns began teaching at this time. Two years later the District School Act provided for the establishment of district grammar schools and a salary of £100 annually for the teacher selected by the district trustees. In Niagara (Niagara-on-the-Lake) the local trustees, including Robert Hamilton*, Robert KERR, and William Dickson*, selected Burns as the first teacher at the district school. He held this position from 1808 until his death, when he was succeeded by the Reverend Thomas Creen. Burns was said to have educated many youths who later achieved prominence, including William Hamilton Merritt* and his own son Robert Easton Burns*. In his report of 13 July 1821 Burns had 59 scholars under his instruction: 20 commencing English reading, 30 studying "English Reading, Writing, Arithmetic," and the remainder at various stages of Latin and Greek authors.

During the War of 1812 the Niagara frontier was open to the depredations of disaffected raiders [*see* Abraham MARKLE] and the movement of armies. Like so many others in the region, Burns suffered greatly. From the spring of 1813 the American army occupied Fort George (Niagara-on-the-Lake). Later the invaders took possession of Burns's home, described as "a Very Comfortable Dwelling." On one occasion he tried to recover his furniture but was prevented by American officers. On 27 August the Americans burned the Presbyterian church. Burns's house was near the defence works thrown up on the commons

Burns

and was destroyed some time before the retreating forces of Brigadier-General George McLure razed Niagara in December. Burns himself was taken prisoner and incarcerated, probably in New York state, for six months. During this time he was said to have preached every Sunday to the American garrison. With the war over Burns began the task of rebuilding his life and recouping his losses, which his wife later estimated at £275 provincial currency (she received £213 in compensation). He also distributed relief funds for the Loyal and Patriotic Society of Upper Canada and petitioned for land. He was granted 400 acres in 1819.

The most noteworthy aspect of Burns's career was the publication in 1814 of a sermon he preached at Stamford on 3 June as part of a public day of general thanksgiving for British victories over Napoleon. On such occasions the pulpit often became a political rostrum, and thus can offer insights into the political language of early Upper Canada. Burns's text was taken from Proverbs 24:21 – "My son, Fear thou the Lord and the King; and meddle not with them that are given to change." In many ways the sermon followed the by then commonplace themes of Edmund Burke's *Reflections on the revolution in France* . . . (London, 1790), which had begun the ideological attack on the French revolution, but it differed in some important respects. Whereas Burke had been careful to distinguish the legitimacy of the American revolution from the illegitimacy of the French, Burns made no such distinction. Mindful of Upper Canada's loyalist roots and fearful of France's North American republican ally, he saw the two revolutions as products of the same destructive spirit that threatened the world with democratic tumult and despotism. Within the framework of the struggle between counter-revolution and revolution, represented by Great Britain and France, Upper Canada became the besieged western bastion of royalism. This Upper Canadian extension of a mentality common to the British élite in the period was not unique to Burns. It was shared by figures as diverse as Isaac Brock*, John Beverley Robinson*, John Strachan*, and William Dummer POWELL.

Peculiar to Burns was the origin of his political language in 17th-century English royalist ideas about the divine nature of kingship. Burns claimed that "when a daring spirit of anarchy, and confusion seems to prevail through the world, it becomes the duty of every man, whose situation in life gives him the opportunity, to inculcate the lessons of obedience and subordination." He urged the fear of God as a "guard to the conscience in an evil time, and a noble preservative from the spreading infection and insinuating poison of prevailing or fashionable sins." Following on this theme he stressed that the king should be feared because "Kings are God's deputies, or viceregents here on earth." He decried modern doc-

trines "of investigating the origin of government, or defining the prerogative of princes, or stating the pretended unalienable rights of individuals," instead of submitting to the ordinances of kings for God's sake. Human institutions were consecrated with divine initiation and deserved therefore to be revered. Burns cited the Cromwellian and Roman revolutions as examples of events by which people had "gained only an accumulated load of misery and oppression." In Upper Canada it would be just to look for "expedients and defenders" only if liberty and property, guaranteed by the British constitution, were threatened. Finally, Burns echoed another common theme within the early 19th-century mentality – the belief in a providential dispensation preserving both Great Britain and Upper Canada from the revolutionary onslaught. He exhorted Upper Canadians to defend their country with a courage "founded on religion" and based upon personal piety.

Burns died of pleurisy in February 1822. For several years after his death the Niagara congregation saw a number of ministers come and go – a period of instability that ended with the appointment in 1829 of Robert McGill*. Burns seems to have been a reserved and scholarly man with a love of learning and books. Surely few scenes could have provided such delicious irony as that of the ferocious royalist preaching his lessons during his captivity to an American military garrison.

ROBERT LOCHIEL FRASER

John Burns is the author of *True patriotism; a sermon, preached in the Presbyterian Church in Stamford, Upper Canada, on the 3d day of June, 1814, being the day appointed by his honor the president, &c.&c.&c. of Upper Canada, for a provincial thanksgiving* (Montreal, 1814).

AO, MS 522; RG 22, ser.155. PAC, RG 1, E3, 100: 214–21; L1, 29: 178; L3, 42: B12/117; 68: B misc., 1793–1840/82; RG 5, A1: 3324–25, 26384–85, 29129–30, 30027–32; RG 19, 3741, E5(a), claim 66. [James Croil], *A historical and statistical report of the Presbyterian Church of Canada, in connection with the Church of Scotland, for the year 1866* (Montreal, 1867). *Documentary history of education in Upper Canada from the passing of the Constitutional Act of 1791 to the close of Rev. Dr. Ryerson's administration of the Education Department in 1876*, ed. J. G. Hodgins (28v., Toronto, 1894–1910), 1: 30, 60–61. "Early records of St. Mark's and St. Andrew's churches, Niagara," comp. Janet Carnochan, *OH*, 3 (1901): 72. *The matriculation albums of the University of Glasgow from 1728 to 1858*, comp. W. I. Addison (Glasgow, 1913), 152. Read, *Lives of the judges*, 294. Scott *et al.*, *Fasti ecclesiæ scoticanæ*, 7: 628. E. R. Arthur, *St Andrew's Church, Niagara-on-the-Lake* (Toronto, 1938), 27. Janet Carnochan, *Centennial, St Andrews, Niagara, 1794–1894* (Toronto, 1895), 20–24. Gregg, *Hist. of Presbyterian Church* (1885), 184. *An historical narrative of some important events in the life of First Church, St. Catharines, 1831–1931*, ed. J. A. Tuer (Toronto, [1931]), 3–4. *History of St. Andrew's Presbyteri-*

an Church, 1791–1975 ([Niagara-on-the-Lake, Ont., 1975]), 4–6. J. S. Moir, *Enduring witness: a history of the Presbyterian Church in Canada* ([Hamilton, Ont., 1974?]). S. F. Wise, "God's peculiar peoples," *The shield of Achilles: aspects of Canada in the Victorian age*, ed. W. L. Morton (Toronto and Montreal, 1968), 36–61; "Upper Canada and the conservative tradition," *Profiles of a province: studies in the history of Ontario* . . . (Toronto, 1967), 20–33. Janet Carnochan, "Early schools of Niagara," Niagara Hist. Soc., [*Pub.*], no.6 (1900): 35, and "Two frontier churches," no.7 (n.d.): 13–14, 23–24, 26. S. F. Wise, "Sermon literature and Canadian intellectual history," UCC, Committee on Arch., *Bull.* (Toronto), 18 (1965): 3–18.

BURNS, WILLIAM, businessman, militia officer, and politician; b. *c.* 1755 in Great Britain; d. unmarried 25 Sept. 1829 at Quebec.

William Burns set out from Great Britain about 1770, reputedly with his father, who may have been George Burns, a British army officer. His death at sea left William an orphan, but on arriving at Quebec he was taken in by John Melvin and made a clerk in the mercantile house of Melvin and Meredith Wills.

Distracted briefly by his role as a militiaman during the American invasion of 1775–76, Burns quickly gained experience in the mechanics of the Quebec trade, including marketing wheat (notably for Samuel Jacobs*), coordinating river transport for the firm's business, auctioneering (Melvin and Wills was appointed public vendue master for Quebec in 1778), and dealing with London suppliers and their agents. By August 1784 Burns had been brought in as a partner, the company becoming Melvin, Wills, and Burns. Following Wills's death, some time before mid 1787, the firm continued as Melvin and Burns. Melvin died in August 1791. The following month Burns himself became public vendue master, and by the spring of 1792 he had taken John William Woolsey* into partnership, forming Burns and Woolsey, auctioneers, commission merchants, and brokers.

During the period 1790–1808 Burns emerged as a major merchant and wholesaler. He was involved in all the profitable sectors of the economy and continued to diversify his investments. Interested in the hunting and fishing sector, he held shares in a company operating in Labrador and the lower St Lawrence region. To develop the Îles de Mingan and the seigneury of Saint-Paul he went into partnership with influential businessmen John RICHARDSON, Patrick Langan, Woolsey, and Mathew Lymburner. In addition he was in the lumber business with Woolsey and a number of other partners, and generally sold the product wholesale by auction. He also imported and exported dry goods. The firm of Burns and Woolsey sold, at wholesale and retail, foodstuffs, spirits from the British West Indies, European wines, books, household goods, and lottery tickets.

Besides being public vendue master Burns was a well-known and respected auctioneer, holding sales with Woolsey on the various wharfs in Lower Town. Large volumes of merchandise, even entire cargoes and ships, passed through their auction books, particularly during the port's restricted shipping season. In comparison with the busier ports of the Atlantic seaboard, the scale of trade at Quebec was small. This situation left most of the auction business to the port's major practitioners, Burns and John Jones*, and was reflected in the apparent absence of complaints from importers and shopkeepers against undercutting by auctioneers. As a result, and possibly because of Burns's expertise on the rostrum, auctioneering at Quebec remained unregulated; in 1805, and again a year later, Burns did request the intervention of the Executive Council, but only to fix commission rates for auctioneers.

Burns ended his partnership with Woolsey in 1806. He probably no longer needed the backing of a permanent partner, since he not only had been active in the firm of Burns and Woolsey but already was doing business on his own account. He seemed to be more successful alone than when working with Woolsey, who indeed later owed him sizeable sums. After the firm was dissolved Burns went into partnership with other merchants solely for specific transactions, such as the purchase by three people of a seigneury or a wood-lot.

Although he did not abandon trade, during the period 1810–30 Burns speculated heavily in real estate and land in Quebec itself and on the outskirts of the town. The massive scale of the capital he invested can readily be illustrated. On 20 Sept. 1824 Burns bought 26 pieces of land at a sheriff's auction. Less than 11 months later he sold them all to Mary Neilson, notary Thomas Lee's wife, who had contracted marriage "without community of property." But six months before making this sale Burns had been able to purchase 30 more lots in the *faubourg* Saint-Jean.

At the same time Burns was offering his services as a ship-broker and land agent. In 1813, for example, he acted for a John Scott of London in selling pieces of land to a merchant. Two years later he became the attorney for some heirs to the fief of Grosse-Île who wanted to sell it; he concluded the transaction with Quebec merchant Louis GAUVREAU, a member of the Lower Canadian House of Assembly. Since the early 1800s Burns had been publishing advertisements regularly in the *Quebec Gazette* inviting prospective buyers to auction sales of ships – presumably ships that had been attached. Burns gave up this enterprise in 1811, handing it over exclusively to his partner in this field, Robert Melvin, the son of the man who had introduced him to business.

Burns also handled the assets and business affairs of various individuals, generally wealthy, who readily

Burns

gave him power of attorney when they had to be out of the country. His competence and honesty were recognized by the merchants of the town and even beyond, for Burns also had close relations with business circles in England. He turned out to be a capitalist on a grand scale who, surprising though it may seem, lent vast sums to prominent English merchants and London firms. In 1808, for example, he advanced £6,000 (sterling) to a London firm so that it could build a ship. This sizeable amount shows that Burns was not afraid to take risks and that he had considerable funds at his disposal. In Lower Canada various leading merchants and other prominent people also owed him large sums. Among those who found themselves in this situation were Woolsey, with a debt amounting to £10,000 around 1816 and £24,000 in 1829, Noah Freer, one of the directors of the Quebec Bank, Chief Justice Jonathan Sewell*, whose daughter Eliza Jannet Sewell was a god-daughter of Burns, and Mathew Bell*, a legislative councillor who owed him £10,000 in 1829.

Burns's role as banker enabled him to make attractive profits through the six per cent annual interest paid him on the capital borrowed. It was also one of some social significance, since there were no banks in Lower Canada until 1817 and 1818. As a result, there was a need for capitalists with a sound financial base who had surplus funds to invest in the commercial endeavours of other big merchants, thus promoting the country's economic development.

From 1816 Burns, who was now elderly, began to slacken the pace of his activities. On 5 September of that year he announced in the *Quebec Gazette* his intention of retiring from business shortly. He none the less went on attending to his affairs. In 1817 he again announced that he was retiring, but one William Smith continued to run his wholesale and retail stores. In 1818 and 1819 Burns put his share holdings up for sale, including those in the Dorchester Bridge and the Union Hotel. From 1819 he lived principally on his private income, that is, the interest his many debtors paid on the considerable sums he had lent.

Burns, who had been promoted ensign in 1787 in the Quebec Battalion of British Militia, rose to become lieutenant-colonel of the town's 3rd Militia Battalion in 1812. Though only modestly interested in public office – he turned down a magistracy in 1809 – he was made a legislative councillor in January 1818, a position he held until his death. Council journals reveal him to have been an infrequent attender but an apparent supporter of John Richardson and the extreme wing of the English party. This appointment may be interpreted as a reward crowning a career in which he had always been faithful to Britain and had figured in the great expansion of commercial capitalism in Lower Canada.

Towards the end of his life Burns took up social concerns such as the Agriculture Society in the district of Quebec, of which he was a member. He contributed financially to the society and to various other organizations, and gave money for the erection of a monument to Edward* Augustus, Duke of Kent and Strathearn. The Honourable William Burns had most certainly been a model for the business world. He had, in fact, been one of the small number of important merchants living in Lower Canada during the late 18th and the early 19th century to leave a debt-free estate. His material circumstances identified him with an immensely rich group. The inventory done after his death shows that there was nothing in his house, from the walnut and rosewood furniture to the Japanese liqueur-stands, the calling-card trays imported from China, and the fine linen, that was not highly desirable and imported. In short, his possessions reflected the wealth he had accumulated in large-scale business over the years. Never having married and having no direct heirs, Burns left more than £33,000 to his close friends and to the members of the Melvin family. Even more unusual, in addition to forgiving Woolsey's debts, he left his former partner £5,000.

William Burns had started in trade as a penniless youth. The financial success he attained demonstrated that, as a merchant, he was remarkably aware of the commercial trends of his time.

GEORGE BERVIN and DAVID ROBERTS

ANQ-Q, CN1-16, 9 nov. 1808, 11 mai 1809, 20 nov. 1815, 17 juill. 1816; CN1-26, 19–20 oct. 1802, 6 juill. 1816; CN1-171, 5 juill. 1819; CN1-188, 20 oct. 1825, 30 sept. 1829, 15–16 avril 1830; CN1-197, 23 janv. 1822; CN1-230, 29 mai 1801; 4 juin 1803; 18 avril 1805; 6 mai 1807; 22 avril 1808; 31 janv. 1809; 8 avril 1812; 26 févr., 19 mai 1813; 16 août, 6 oct. 1817; 14 juin 1823; 25 avril 1825; CN1-262, 6 févr., 20 oct. 1804; 6 févr., 17 juin 1805; 5 oct. 1813; 10 oct. 1817. ASQ, Polygraphie, XXXVII, no.12. AUM, P 58, U, Burns to Simon McTavish, 22 Aug. 1803; Burns & Woolsey to McTavish, Frobisher & Company, 20 June 1796. PAC, MG 19, A2, ser.3, 22: 3068, 3072, 3080, 3087, 3095–96; MG 23, GII, 3, vols.3–6; GIII, 13, 2: 147–49; RG 1, L3ᴸ: 26628, 62808–9; RG 42, E1, 1380, 1382; RG 68, 2: 99; 3: 515; General index, 1651–1841. "Les dénombrements de Québec" (Plessis), ANQ *Rapport*, 1948–49: 35, 85, 135, 185. L.C., Legislative Council, *Journals*, 1818–29. *Quebec Gazette*, 26 July 1787; 25 Aug. 1791; 19 Jan., 15 March, 10 May, 21 June 1792; 19 Sept., 28 Nov., 19 Dec. 1793; 12 June 1794; 4 June, 13 Aug., 15 Oct. 1795; 23 Feb., 18 May, 19 Oct. 1797; 9 May, 6 June 1799; 10 Dec. 1801; 17 June 1802; 10 March, 26 May, 6 Oct. 1803; 3 May, 14 June 1804; 19 Sept., 31 Oct. 1805; 4 Dec. 1806; 19 March, 20 Aug., 24 Sept. 1807; 15 March 1810; 3 Jan. 1811; 19 March 1812; 8 April 1813; 5 Sept. 1816; 25 June 1818; 9 Aug., 22 Oct. 1821; 21 April 1823. F.-J. Audet, "Les législateurs du Bas-Canada." *Quebec almanac*, 1788, 1791, 1794, 1813–15, 1817, 1819–20. P.-G. Roy, *Inv. concessions*, 3: 201; 4: 189–90. "State papers – L.C.," PAC *Report*, 1892: 219, 237. Tremaine, *Biblio. of Canadian imprints*, 355. Turcotte, *Le Conseil législatif*, 85. Paquet et Wallot, *Patronage et pouvoir dans le Bas-Canada.* P.-G. Roy, *Toutes petites choses du Régime anglais,* 1: 252–54. George Bervin, "Environnement matériel et activités économiques des conseillers exécutifs et législatifs à Québec, 1810–1830," *Material Hist. Bull.* (Ottawa), 17 (1983), no.1: 45–62.

BURTON, Sir FRANCIS NATHANIEL, colonial administrator; b. 26 Dec. 1766 in London, younger twin son of Francis Pierpont Burton and Elizabeth Clements; m. 4 June 1801 Valentina Letitia Lawless, daughter of Nicholas Lawless, 1st Baron Cloncurry, and they had two sons and three daughters; d. 20 Jan. 1832 in Bath, England.

Francis Nathaniel Burton was elected to the Irish parliament in 1790 for County Clare, in which were located the family estates at Buncraggy, near Ennis. After the union with Great Britain, he sat at Westminster for the same constituency between 1801 and 1808. Perhaps as a reward for his championship of the union or in recognition of his family's prominence in local Irish politics, Burton was appointed lieutenant governor of Lower Canada on 29 Nov. 1808. For more than a decade thereafter he was content to remain in Britain and draw an income of £1,500 a year. By 1818 the provincial House of Assembly had become critical of salaries paid to absentees, but it took Colonial Secretary Lord Bathurst several years, the threat of discontinuing Burton's salary, and possibly the promise of a knighthood to persuade the diffident lieutenant governor to repair to Quebec. Finally, in 1822 – the year he was knighted – Burton left, arriving in the colony in June and bringing with him the unexpected news that a bill for the union of Lower and Upper Canada was under discussion in London.

A courtier through and through, by 1824 Burton had sufficiently ingratiated himself with the assembly to secure an increase of salary as some compensation for condescending to reside in the colony. "Every body is pleased with his manners," recorded Governor Lord Dalhousie [Ramsay*], who added with a generous confidence cruelly belied by later events, "indeed he is in all things so courtly & well bred that he must command the respect of the better classes of society, and prove to me a powerful support."

Burton's brief day of administrative glory dawned on 7 June 1824 when he took over the government of Lower Canada following Dalhousie's departure on leave to Britain. For some time past the assembly had been attempting to enlarge its power at the expense of the executive by the time-honoured expedient of seeking to appropriate all revenues raised in the colony. Hitherto the executive had preserved a degree of financial independence and administrative flexibility through its control of crown revenues derived from fees, licences, customs duties, fines, forfeitures, seigneurial dues, and the renting of government-owned properties. Rarely sufficient to meet expenses,

these sources of revenue were supplemented as necessary by recourse to the military chest and by the surreptitious "borrowing" of money from the revenues under the assembly's control. Until the assembly was prepared to vote a permanent civil list, guaranteeing adequate salaries to the leading officials, successive governors had had to fight not only to maintain the integrity of crown revenues but also to frame annual money bills in such a way that even tacit recognition was not made of the assembly's claim to appropriate them. Burton, perhaps feeling that he might further his career with a daring coup, summoned the legislature in hopes of inducing it to pass an appropriation bill that would cover the government's expenses for one year. He was thus anxious to avoid the disputes and deadlock that in recent times had characterized Dalhousie's discussions with the assembly on the matter.

Burton began by hammering out an agreement with the Canadian party, which dominated the assembly: the elected house would not assert its claim to crown revenues and Burton would not press the executive demand for a permanent civil list; in the bill that was drawn up crown and provincial revenues were lumped together and the government's estimates, after some reductions made by the assembly, were passed in early 1825 for a single year. The new bill had to be endorsed by the Legislative Council, which was normally adverse to any proposal issuing from the assembly. There Burton faced redoubtable opposition from John RICHARDSON, a leader of the English party, which generally controlled the council. The lieutenant governor enlisted the aid of two men who were political and religious enemies: a leader of the office holders, Herman Witsius Ryland*, who felt neglected politically by Dalhousie and wanted revenge, and the Roman Catholic archbishop of Quebec, Joseph-Octave PLESSIS, who owed Burton a political favour for his having accepted a bill that constituted a first step towards the civil erection of parishes. Ryland brought over the British office holders in the council, while Plessis managed to bring in for the vote the decrepit and habitual absentees among the Canadian members. Richardson was defeated handily.

Burton triumphantly reported to the Colonial Office his happy settlement of a protracted controversy. However, in London Dalhousie, who had anticipated that the legislature would not be summoned until he returned, at once condemned an arrangement that, although it avoided mention of disputed rights, in his view implicitly conceded the assembly's claim to control crown revenues. At first the Colonial Office endorsed Dalhousie's interpretation and censured Burton for disobeying instructions, but the lieutenant governor's denials that he had sacrificed the government's position, eventually supported by legal opinions from the chief justice of Lower Canada, Jonathan

Butler

Sewell*, and the British law officers of the crown, gradually had their effect. To Dalhousie's chagrin and annoyance, Bathurst came to place a more charitable construction on the settlement and to dismiss the governor's melodramatic assertion that the assembly had acted with animus and cunning. The colonial secretary may also have been mindful that Burton enjoyed royal favour because of the notorious friendship between Lady Conyngham, his sister-in-law, and George IV, who took it upon himself in 1827 to suggest that Burton be appointed governor of Jamaica, a recommendation that ministers politely ignored.

On Dalhousie's return in September 1825, Burton left Lower Canada on an indefinite leave of absence under something of a cloud, still arguing about his salary. A reluctant resident at Quebec, he appears to have been more intent on advancing his career and financial interests than on the constitutional issues at stake in the rumbustious politics of Lower Canada. Yet for years after his departure, Canadian politicians and church leaders hoped he would return at the head of government, a dream Burton may have shared since he retained sufficient interest in the colony's affairs to continue a correspondence with local politicians such as Denis-Benjamin Viger*, John Neilson*, and Louis-Joseph Papineau*. He did not come back, although he remained lieutenant governor until his death. Personable, gracious, and skilful with his ample Irish blarney, Burton could charm and flatter, but he had proved no match for the wily leaders of the assembly. There was much truth in Dalhousie's judgement, despite its undisguised partiality, that "Sir F. has shewn a very weak & very vain mind – he has courted popularity in every step & in every act of his short Administration." Again according to Dalhousie, the crafty local politicians had beaten him at his own game and, in the case of Bishop Plessis, left him "vexed and disappointed & humbugged."

Burton's administration, however short, had long-term consequences for Lower Canadian politics. It bequeathed to the hapless Dalhousie a bitter legacy since the formula worked out for presenting estimates had whetted the assembly's appetite for influencing appropriations and encouraged that body all the more to resist the governor's return to the old claims for a permanent civil list. The acute political crisis that resulted led to Dalhousie's recall in 1828; his successor as the head of government, Sir James Kempt*, was obliged in the end to have recourse to the Burton model and the Colonial Office to endorse it in 1831.

PETER BURROUGHS

BL, Add. mss 35729, 35734, 38751–52; Loan 57. PAC, MG 24, A64; B1, 4–6; B2, 1; B6, 1–2; MG 30, D1, 6: 669–78. PRO, CO 42/177–213; CO 43/25–26; CO 324/95. SRO, GD45 (mfm. at PAC). L.C., House of Assembly, *Journals*, 1818–27. *Bath & Cheltenham Gazette* (Bath, Eng.), 24 Jan. 1832. Wallace, *Macmillan dict.* Joshua Wilson, *A biographical index to the present House of Commons . . .* (London, [1806]). Taft Manning, *Revolt of French Canada*, 132–48.

BUTLER (Dight), JOHN BUTLER, office holder, merchant, militia officer, JP, politician, and landowner; b. *c.* 1760 in England, son of Joshua Dight and Elizabeth Butler; d. 2 July 1834 in Windsor, N.S.

John Butler Dight was a protégé of Joshua Mauger*, the London-based entrepreneur who dominated Nova Scotian public affairs in the later 18th century. Nephew to John Butler*, Mauger's chief Halifax associate during the 1760s and 1770s, young Dight came to Nova Scotia in 1773 and later obtained, through the influence of his uncle, a position in the commissariat at Fort Cumberland (near Sackville, N.B.). At the end of the 1770s, just before John Butler returned to England, Dight moved to Halifax, setting up as a general merchant and succeeding his uncle as agent victualler to the troops in Nova Scotia and Newfoundland. He also took over the administration of both his uncle's and Joshua Mauger's real-estate holdings in Nova Scotia. Over the next decade Dight consolidated his position in Halifax society, serving as a captain in the local militia, a vestryman of St Paul's Church, and a town magistrate. On 21 June 1788 he married Melinda Burgess Morden, daughter of the Board of Ordnance storekeeper in Halifax; the couple was to have two boys and five daughters. Furthermore, following an 18th-century tradition of absentee representation for outlying constituencies, Dight held a House of Assembly seat for Cumberland County from 1785 to 1793. As a legislator, his only controversial action came when he defended office holders in the existing oligarchy against attacks from the emerging loyalist caucus in the assembly during the "judges' affair" of the late 1780s [*see* Thomas Henry BARCLAY; James Brenton*].

The death of John Butler in 1791 fundamentally altered Dight's career. Named chief beneficiary of his uncle's estate, on condition that he adopt the surname Butler, Dight acquired land in England, along with additional Halifax waterfront property and a Hants County holding of almost a thousand acres. Moreover, he received an invitation to enter Nova Scotia's Council. Acceptance of the appointment had to be deferred, however, since complications connected with his uncle's estate obliged him to go to England, probably in 1791 or 1792. At the time he gave every indication of intending an early return. Letters were written boasting that Martock, his estate near Windsor, would become a model agricultural site, teaching colonials "to grow Wheat and Pease, make Butter, raise Pigs and Black Cattle, more ever than will be required for all the wants of His Majesty's Troops."

He also joined James Glenie* in lobbying against recruiting for provincial regiments in British North America lest an already limited labour supply be further depleted. As it happened, over a decade passed before Dight, now Butler, again saw Nova Scotia. Delays in part were caused by the need to organize his Somerset estate and manœuvre for additional government patronage. In July 1799 the latter activity resulted in his appointment as deputy commissary general for all of eastern British North America. The post probably had been secured through the assistance of Brook Watson*, Joshua Mauger's business associate and a leading figure in London politics. Butler, it might be noted, had earlier named his eldest son after Watson.

Butler probably would have returned to Nova Scotia about 1800 had not a controversy arisen over whether he would be allowed to take up his seat on the colony's Council. Although Lieutenant Governor Sir John Wentworth* had earlier recommended him for this position, he now challenged Butler's commission, arguing that he could not simultaneously serve under civil and military superiors. This allegation of a conflict of interest concealed Wentworth's more basic fear that Butler would jeopardize the loyalist-dominated placemanship system that had emerged during the 1790s. After protracted delay, the struggle was resolved in favour of Butler, thanks mainly to the intervention of Edward* Augustus, Duke of Kent, who had a high regard for his talents in the commissariat. Accordingly, Butler returned to Halifax and to a seat in the Council early in 1804.

The second phase of Butler's Nova Scotian career was highlighted by a close association with Alexander Croke*, who had become judge of the Vice-Admiralty Court in 1801. The two men, both English born, shared the view that colonials, such as Wentworth, should never be trusted with high office in the imperial establishment. They also cooperated in seeking to minimize the influence of the assembly in public affairs. Their pursuit of ultra-tory, high Anglican ideals had little impact, other than to cripple the fledgling King's College [see William COCHRAN], an institution that Butler served as treasurer to the board of governors, by their insistence that prospective students subscribe to the Thirty-Nine Articles of the Church of England.

Apart from his association with Croke, Butler played only a marginal role in community affairs. Eschewing a return to trade, he devoted his time to the commissariat and to his Martock property, which he used as a summer residence. Portraying himself as a champion of agricultural improvement, he eventually secured a 4,000-acre crown grant along the Hants County coastline. The grant was never taken up, however, since he left Halifax in 1811 to perform commissariat work for Lord Wellington during his Peninsular campaigns. By 1813 Butler seems to have gone on half pay, and at the end of the Napoleonic Wars he settled in England, spending most of his remaining years in Bath. He came to Halifax in 1833 to see to his real-estate investments, but although tradition has him spending the next 20 years in active retirement at Martock, he actually died there the following year. Credit for transforming the Martock property into a landscaping and architectural triumph should go to his second son, Colonel Edward Kent Strathearn Butler, who came to Nova Scotia after his father's death.

As in the case of Joshua Mauger, his uncle, and a succession of other 18th-century entrepreneurs, Butler possessed an expatriate mentality, regarding his colonial enterprise merely as preparation for eventual position and affluence in Britain. The opposition he encountered from Wentworth testified to the emergence of a new "nativist" élite, one that had become dominant in the affairs of Nova Scotia by the early 19th century.

D. A. SUTHERLAND

Halifax County Registry of Deeds (Halifax), Deeds, 72: f.389 (mfm. at PANS). Hants County Registry of Deeds (Windsor, N.S.), Deeds, book 6: 284; 25: 530 (mfm. at PANS). PANS, RG 1, 173: 81; 214, 25 April 1809 (transcripts); 414, no.17; RG 20A, 1, 1775: 21; 1776: 24; 1779: 41. PRO, CO 217/37: 266; 217/62: 337; 217/63: 313, 323; 217/70: 186, 209; 217/75: 146; 217/78: 86, 250; 217/79: 205; 217/84: 158; 217/88: 12, 16, 242. N.S., House of Assembly, *Journal and proc.*, 1785–93. *Nova-Scotia Royal Gazette*, 1 Oct. 1799, 13 Feb. 1810. *Directory of N.S. MLAs*, 100–1. Akins, *Hist. of Halifax City*, 104. J. B. Brebner, *The neutral Yankees of Nova Scotia, a marginal colony during the revolutionary years* (New York, 1937; repr. [1970]), 254, 268. R. V. Harris, *The Church of Saint Paul in Halifax, Nova Scotia: 1749–1949* (Toronto, 1949), 135. Murdoch, *Hist. of N.S.*, 3: 101. F. W. Vroom, *King's College: a chronicle, 1789–1939; collections and recollections* (Halifax, 1941), 17–18. *Novascotian*, 26 Jan. 1846. A. W. Wallace, "Martock: colonial architecture in the Maritimes, part iv," Royal Architectural Institute of Canada, *Journal* (Toronto), 10 (1933): 97–100.

C

CADOTTE (Cadot), JOSEPH, office holder, interpreter, and fur trader; fl. 1814–22.

It is probable that Joseph Cadotte was Métis and possible that he was related to Jean-Baptiste Cadot* of

Cadotte

Sault Ste Marie (Mich.). On 24 Oct. 1814 he was appointed lieutenant in the Indian Department of Upper Canada. He was employed as an interpreter under Lieutenant-Colonel Robert McDouall*, commandant of the British garrison at Michilimackinac (Mackinac Island, Mich.). In 1814 and early 1815 Cadotte was sent by his superior on various missions to the Indians of the Grand River. He returned to Michilimackinac from the last of these with 84 Indians intended to bolster the defences of the fort. They arrived on 3 May 1815, two days after the news of the signing of the Treaty of Ghent had been received. In October a British court of inquiry held at Drummond Island (Mich.) cleared him of charges made by the Americans that he had acted improperly while on the expedition, undertaken after the official end of the war. McDouall recommended that Cadotte be retained in the "peace establishment" of the Indian Department and described the interpreter as a young man "of education & respectability" who did credit to the department. How long after this Cadotte worked in the Indian Department is not known.

Cadotte's involvement with the North West Company seems to have begun in 1816 when he was charged with several drafts paid by the company to Sault Ste Marie fur trader John JOHNSTON. That August he was at the NWC post at Bas-de-la-Rivière (Fort Alexander, Man.), where a council of Métis from the Red River settlement was held under the direction of Archibald McLellan of the NWC. McLellan was interested in recapturing Fort William (Thunder Bay, Ont.) from Lord Selkirk [Douglas*], but most Métis at the council declined to participate. Some time in late August or early September McLellan led a scouting group, which included Cadotte, Cuthbert Grant*, and Charles de Reinhard, in a light canoe to Rainy Lake (Ont.) and Minnesota. On 11 September, during the expedition, Reinhard and a Métis named Mainville, under the direction of McLellan, killed an employee of Lord Selkirk, Owen Keveny*, who had been captured by McLellan in yet another incident in the conflict between the Hudson's Bay Company and the NWC. Cadotte did not participate directly in the murder. He had, however, berated one of the men who had charge of Keveny for not having allowed Keveny to be killed by an Indian who had offered to do the job. Later in the fall Cadotte was said to have the key to Keveny's trunk in his possession.

Around 26 September Cadotte went with McLellan and Grant to the NWC post of Fort Gibraltar (Winnipeg, Man.), where he probably spent the ensuing fall. Cadotte was there when Miles MACDONELL, governor of Assiniboia, and a party of soldiers captured the post on 10 Jan. 1817. At this point Macdonell knew nothing of Cadotte's involvement in the murder of Keveny. Perhaps in part through the influence of

Macdonell's interpreter, Louis Nolin, who may have been Cadotte's half-brother, Macdonell put Cadotte to work helping to make an inventory of the fort. While other Nor'Westers were held under lock and key, Cadotte was set at liberty within the fort. On 24 January he was allowed to visit the Métis, including his wife, then on the Qu'Appelle River. Macdonell sent with him a letter for Grant in an attempt to make peace with the Métis leader.

In the months that followed Grant, Cadotte, and other Métis made several trips from the Qu'Appelle to the Red River, attempting to obtain the release of McLellan and several others held by Macdonell. Throughout, Cadotte was always more violently inclined than Grant. He proposed attacking several HBC posts and in early March, after a second unsuccessful attempt to win McLellan's release, he instigated the killing of HBC cattle. According to NWC employee Frederick Damien Heurter, as the Métis set out to return to the Qu'Appelle, Cadotte proposed "to go to Pembina, and to kill a party of Lord Selkirk's people who were there, saying that they must not return home without striking a blow to maintain their warlike reputation." Grant led the group in turning down the proposal: "We are not barbarians."

Towards the end of March 1817 the earlier activities of Grant and Cadotte became known to Macdonell, who offered a reward for their capture. The support of the Métis prevented their being seized near Fort Gibraltar on June 21. Commissioner William Bacheler COLTMAN persuaded the two men to give themselves up on 27 August, apparently by assuring them that they would not be imprisoned if they went back with him to Montreal. The two men went east with Coltman, arriving in Montreal on 10 November. Despite the agitations of the HBC, Cadotte, like Grant, was not put in prison until his indictment in early March 1818 for participation in the murder of Keveny. Soon afterwards he was released "on recognizance" and by early June he was said to have gone to Sault Ste Marie. Neither Cadotte nor Grant was ever brought to trial. Reinhard did stand trial and was convicted, but was never executed.

In the fall of 1818 Cadotte was sent by the NWC as a clerk and interpreter to the post at Rainy Lake (later named Fort Frances, Ont.). The HBC traders found him to be an energetic opponent who was apparently successful in obtaining the furs of many Indians indebted to the HBC. Cadotte continued there until 1821, when he was dismissed after the merger of the NWC with the HBC. While at Rainy Lake in July 1821, Nicholas Garry*, sent by the HBC to implement the merger agreement, reported Cadotte as declaring "that he would shoot Mr [James Bird*] and myself. He went about in a state of intoxication with loaded pistols."

Cadotte left Rainy Lake for Sault Ste Marie, where he obtained the backing of John Johnston. In the fall he set out with three canoes of merchandise and 12 men. Leaving a small contingent at Lac des Mille Lacs (Ont.), he established himself at Crane Lake (Minn.) in November, in competition with the HBC post at Rainy Lake. Cadotte's HBC opponent, Roderick McKenzie Jr, referred to him as a "Hero of Romance," an object of fascination not only for the Ojibwas of the region, with whom it was said he had great influence, but also for many former Nor'Westers in HBC employ, several of whom attempted to desert to his side. According to McKenzie, one of Cadotte's various means of intimidating the HBC traders was to tell them that he was "an American subject . . . vested with authorities to seize all persons illegally trading within their territories together with whatever property may belong to them." He also threatened to set fire to the HBC mill and buildings and kill the company's cattle.

The report that two of Cadotte's men at Lac des Mille Lacs had been killed by Indians during the winter of 1821–22 caused the abandonment of the post. In the fall of 1822 Cadotte helped establish an American Fur Company post at Rainy Lake, in competition with the HBC. Nothing is known of him after that date.

BRUCE M. WHITE

PAC, MG 19, E1, ser.1, 13: 4964, 5065; 33: 12285–86, 12297; 45: 17185–86, 17189, 17193, 17207, 17212, 17229, 17231–32; 46: 17804, 17806; RG 8, I (C ser.), 258: 81, 86; 283–323; 688D: 130. PAM, HBCA, B.105/a/6: ff.17–18, 20; B.105/a/8: ff.2, 9, 25, 27; B.105/a/9–18; D.4/116: 29, 45–50; F.4/10: f.40; F.4/32: f.180. U.S., Congress, *American state papers . . . in relation to public lands*, ed. Walter Lowrie (5v., Washington, 1834), 5: 258, 262, 264, 267. John Halkett, *Statement respecting the Earl of Selkirk's settlement upon the Red River* . . . (London, 1817). *HBRS*, 2 (Rich and Fleming). John Tanner, *A narrative of the captivity and adventures of John Tanner* . . . , ed. Edwin James (New York, 1830). *Montreal Gazette*, 11 March 1818. Marcel Giraud, *Le Métis canadien; son rôle dans l'histoire des provinces de l'Ouest* (Paris, 1945). M. A. MacLeod and W. L. Morton, *Cuthbert Grant of Grantown; warden of the plains of Red River* (Toronto, 1963).

CALDWELL, WILLIAM, army and militia officer, merchant, JP, and Indian Department official; b. *c.* 1750 in County Fermanagh (Northern Ireland), probably the son of William Caldwell and his wife Rebecka; father of a mixed-blood son, Billy Caldwell*; m. 1783 Suzanne Baby, daughter of Jacques Baby*, *dit* Dupéront, and they had five sons and three daughters; d. 20 Feb. 1822 in Amherstburg, Upper Canada.

William Caldwell came to North America in 1773. He served as an officer in the campaign of 1774 waged by the governor of Virginia, Lord Dunmore, against the Indians of the Pennsylvania and Virginia frontier. With the outbreak of the American revolution, Caldwell fought in Dunmore's forces again, taking part in the storming of Norfolk, Va, early in 1776. Defeated, Dunmore had to withdraw his troops by sea to New York.

When Caldwell recovered from his wounds, he went to Fort Niagara (near Youngstown, N.Y.) and was appointed captain in Butler's Rangers [*see* John Butler*]. In the rangers' campaigns Caldwell was "a very active Partisan," according to the fort's commandant. He led, rather than ordered, his troops into battle and he demonstrated a ruthlessness that the Americans would remember. When the victory of George Rogers Clark at Vincennes (Ind.) in 1778 threatened the Detroit River frontier, Caldwell and some 50 select rangers were sent from Niagara, and thus his long association with the Detroit area began. In succeeding years he alternated between Detroit and Niagara, parrying each anticipated American thrust and on occasion driving deep into enemy territory. In 1782 he commanded the British forces in two of the most notorious victories of the war. In June his troops and their Indian allies defeated William Crawford's advancing columns on the upper Sandusky River (Ohio), and Crawford suffered horribly at the hands of his Indian captors. Then Caldwell led a force into Kentucky and in August dealt a devastating blow to the Americans at the battle of Blue Licks. At this point in the war, action shifted to the diplomatic front, and it was just as well for Caldwell because he and his rangers returned to Detroit hardly capable of taking the field again.

By the war's end Caldwell and several associates had decided to settle in the Detroit area. In early 1783 he and Indian Department officer Matthew Elliott* took up and began developing tracts of land on the east side of the Detroit River opposite Bois Blanc Island. Late in the year, having been joined by several other men with similar intentions, they began negotiations with local Indian chiefs for a grant of the land. Jacob Schieffelin, secretary of the Indian Department at Detroit, heard of their intentions and secretly attempted to obtain the lands for himself, but Governor Frederick Haldimand* upheld the claims of the Caldwell group. Recognizing the value of a quasi-military settlement on the Detroit frontier, he also ordered provisions and implements for as many former rangers as wished to settle in the area. The tract was surveyed and 19 river-front lots were laid out. Captains Henry Bird, Caldwell, Alexander McKee*, and Elliott received the largest ones nearest the site of the proposed fort; the lots downriver were assigned to other Indian Department officers and interpreters. Caldwell later added to his holdings by obtaining grants in Malden Township until he had a compact

Caldwell

estate of some 2,000 acres anchored by his river-front lot beside the rising community of Amherstburg.

Caldwell was less than successful in establishing the loyalists and disbanded rangers he had invited to come from Niagara and settle in the Detroit region. When they arrived, they found that all the lands along the river had been taken up. To remedy the situation Caldwell obtained from the Indians a parcel of land on the north shore of Lake Erie, which he called the New Settlement. The provisions promised by Haldimand failed to materialize in sufficient quantity, however, and little development occurred until the arrival in 1787 of Major Robert Mathews* as commandant at Detroit. Sensing Mathews's concern, Caldwell quickly turned over to him the land and a portion of the provisions and implements that had been sent out, and Mathews proceeded to oversee the settlement, which became the nucleus of Colchester and Gosfield townships. Caldwell has nevertheless been credited with the founding of the New Settlement and, indeed, in 1788 he was rewarded with a 3,000-acre tract of marsh at the mouth of the river, which was granted in the name of two of his sons.

As well as accumulating land, Caldwell engaged in commerce at Detroit and among the Indians south of Lake Erie. In partnership with Elliott, he established an agreement in 1784 with David Duncan and William Wilson of Pittsburgh, Pa, to obtain flour, cattle, bacon, and other provisions that were often scarce at Detroit. Increasingly fierce American competition for the Indians' business eventually brought the venture to grief. Rumours in early 1787 that Caldwell and Elliott were failing led Duncan and Wilson to request payment of their outstanding debts. Actually, they were not the largest creditors: more was owed to Detroit merchants Robert Ellice* and William and Alexander Macomb. Pressed by these local creditors, Caldwell and Elliott assigned their available assets to them, leaving the Pittsburgh suppliers wholly unsecured. Duncan and Wilson, in turn, effectively blocked Caldwell and Elliott from conducting further business. Their debts greatly exceeded their assets, and their creditors consequently suffered heavy losses, but Caldwell and Elliott escaped further penalty and retained their substantial landed properties. Caldwell continued to serve as a supplier of timber, corn, and teams to the garrison and to seek other provisioning contracts from the military and from fur-trading companies. On 28 July 1788 he was made a magistrate for the District of Hesse.

The decade of apparent peace following the treaty of 1783 was in reality a period of constant military alert along the Detroit frontier. The British remained in control of posts in American territory and continued to encourage the land claims and military activities of their Indian allies. Whether they would actively intervene on behalf of the Indians was an open question. When in 1794 a large American force under Anthony Wayne advanced towards the Miamis (Maumee) River, Richard G. England*, the commandant at Detroit, sent Caldwell and some 60 volunteers to reinforce Fort Miamis (Maumee, Ohio), while the militia was held in reserve. Near the fort on 20 August, at the battle of Fallen Timbers, Wayne routed the Indians, who retreated behind the cover of a rearguard action fought by the Wyandots and the white volunteers.

Not satisfied with the Indian lands obtained by their victory, the Americans soon renewed their pressure, and tension in the region once again increased. For Caldwell, as for Elliott and others of their old comrades-in-arms, neutrality was impossible. The Americans associated their names with border warfare and with atrocities committed by the Indians. In the fall of 1807 rumour had it that if war were declared, ten thousand Kentuckians would seize Amherstburg and execute Caldwell, Elliott, and all the members of the Indian Department. When in 1812 war did come Caldwell and four of his sons took up arms.

In the autumn of 1812 Colonel Henry PROCTER, who commanded on the Detroit frontier, conceived the idea of establishing a ranger force of the sort that had been so effective during the American revolution. Early in 1813 he received authorization to create such a special corps, to be commanded by William Caldwell. These men, known as the Western Rangers or Caldwell's Rangers, served in various actions south of Lake Erie that summer and when in the fall Procter decided that retreat from Amherstburg had become necessary, they accompanied him. Caldwell played his usual fearless role in the thick of the battle of Moraviantown in October. He and his rangers took up position beside their Indian allies and continued the battle long after the British regulars had surrendered or withdrawn.

Having escaped death or capture, Caldwell and his sons fought again as rangers at the battle of Longwood (near Thamesville) in March 1814. In May, Caldwell replaced Elliott as superintendent of Indians for the Western District. He then secured places for his sons William and Thomas in the Indian Department; Francis Xavier* continued in the rangers. Members of the Caldwell family fought together again at the battles of Chippawa and Lundy's Lane and at the siege of Fort Erie.

As Indian superintendent Caldwell was soon involved in a heated controversy between the deputy superintendent general, William CLAUS, and John NORTON, spokesman for the Six Nations of the Grand River, a major native force in the war. Norton's success and obvious popularity with the Indians had earned him the temporary confidence of military leaders, who ordered the Indian Department not to interfere with his leadership or disposition of presents.

Caldwell

Claus and other Indian department officers complained that although they operated under severe quotas and restraint, Norton lavished gifts and alcohol on his followers. When some 120 Ojibwas and Ottawas deserted Caldwell for Norton's camp, he took up the Indian Department's fight. He complained to the military authorities that Norton "debauched" the Shawnees, hogged stores, and followed a policy calculated to draw the western Indians from their officers. Norton's tactics, he feared, would damage the effectiveness of the Indians as a fighting force.

The termination of the war in December 1814 offered an excellent opportunity for commander-in-chief Sir Gordon Drummond* to end the feud while reducing the complement of the Indian service. Norton was pensioned off and eased out as graciously as circumstances would permit. Caldwell's dismissal took longer and was preceded by more bitterness. Indeed, his competency had already been questioned. Claus was disappointed with his leadership of the western Indians, and members of the Indian Department anonymously accused him of trying to establish his sons at their expense. Moreover, his belligerent views were out of harmony with Britain's post-war intentions towards the Americans.

With the war over, Caldwell's task was the dispersal and resettlement of the western Indians. The problem was immense because the Indians were near starvation and almost in open revolt by the latter stages of the conflict. The military, from Procter to the highest levels, sought to make scapegoats of them, and hence of the Indian Department, for their own failures in the war. Moreover, conflicts between Caldwell and Amherstburg's commandant, Reginald James, developed into a classic confrontation between a military seeking retrenchment and an Indian Department defending its prerogatives. Lamenting military interference in departmental affairs, Caldwell blamed James for lack of progress in the resettlement of the Indians and the planting of their crops, as well as for their general dissatisfaction. He charged him with violating Indian Department usage and with lack of communication. James, in turn, described Caldwell's charges as "without foundation . . . originating, I hope, in the imbecility of the Deputy Superintendent." He complained, as well, of Caldwell's insubordination and inability to keep private information confidential. Moreover he asserted that Caldwell had failed to explain properly to the Indians that under the terms of the treaty which had ended the war there had been strict limitations placed on their freedom to cross the border with the United States, and he therefore blamed Caldwell for the border troubles involving Indians that occurred. The feud between Caldwell and James reached its peak in October 1815. According to James, Caldwell called him a liar in public and demanded that all further communication between

them be conducted in writing. James suspended Caldwell on 21 October and replaced him with Billy Caldwell, who had collaborated against his father.

Aged and ailing, William Caldwell spent his last years restoring his property in Malden Township. His losses had been heavy – his wife died in 1812 and his home and barns were destroyed by vengeful Americans. Although he claimed compensation of some £2,600, his refusal to provide adequate evidence led a military claims board to reduce the sum by 50 per cent. He could, however, take some comfort in his successful petition to receive the half pay owing to him as a reduced ranger captain, which was finally granted in 1820.

Meanwhile, Caldwell continued his role as civic leader. Still a magistrate, in December 1817 he chaired a meeting in response to Robert Gourlay*'s inquiry about the state of Malden Township. The old loyalist and sole surviving founder of the township could not but have been pleased at the public recounting of the area's development. His ongoing interest in building up the community is evidenced in his efforts to have the court-house and jail transferred from Sandwich (Windsor) to Amherstburg and to establish Amherstburg as the district town of a divided Western District.

In January 1818 Caldwell drew up a will dividing his property among his legitimate children. A convert to Roman Catholicism, during his lifetime he had donated land for both the Anglican and the Catholic churches in Amherstburg. He died on 20 Feb. 1822. Writing after the action at Fallen Timbers, Lieutenant-Colonel England had called him a "very very odd but very gallant fellow."

L. L. KULISEK

AO, RG 22, ser.155. BL, Add. MSS 21761–65 (mfm. at PAC). Can., Parks Canada, Fort Malden National Hist. Park (Amherstburg, Ont.), Arch. coll., Caldwell family papers; Information files, Caldwell family. Essex Land Registry Office (Windsor, Ont.), Abstract index to deeds, Malden Township, vols.1–2 (mfm. at AO). PAC, RG 1, L1, 22: 714; 26: 248–52, 256–59, 298–99, 357; L3; RG 8, I (C ser.); RG 19, E5(a), 3728, claim 5. "Board of land office, District of Hesse," AO Report, 1905. "Campaigns of 1812–14: contemporary narratives by Captain W. H. Merritt, Colonel William Claus, Lieut.-Colonel Matthew Elliott and Captain John Norton," ed. E. [A.] Cruikshank, Niagara Hist. Soc., [Pub.], no.9 (1902): 3–20. Corr. of Hon. Peter Russell (Cruikshank and Hunter). Corr. of Lieut. Governor Simcoe (Cruikshank). Doc. hist. of campaign upon Niagara frontier (Cruikshank). John Askin papers (Quaife). Mich. Pioneer Coll. Select British docs. of War of 1812 (Wood). "Surveyors' letters, notes, instructions, etc., from 1788 to 1791," AO Report, 1905. Windsor border region (Lajeunesse). Commemorative biographical record of the county of Essex, Ontario, containing biographical sketches of prominent and representative citizens and many of the early settled

103

Caldwell

families (Toronto, 1905). Christian Denissen, *Genealogy of the French families of the Detroit River region, 1701–1911*, ed. H. F. Powell (2v., Detroit, 1976). *Officers of British forces in Canada* (Irving).

Katharine Buchanan, "A study of the William Caldwell involvement in the establishment of the Anglican and Roman Catholic churches in the town of Amherstburg, Ontario" (undergraduate essay, Univ. of Windsor, 1981). E. [A.] Cruikshank, *The story of Butler's Rangers and the settlement of Niagara* (Welland, Ont., 1893; repr. Owen Sound, Ont., 1975). Reginald Horsman, *Matthew Elliott, British Indian agent* (Detroit, 1964). Allen, "British Indian Dept.," *Canadian Hist. Sites*, no.14: 5–125. F. H. Armstrong, "The oligarchy of the Western District of Upper Canada, 1788–1841," CHA *Hist. papers*, 1977: 87–102. John Clarke, "Aspects of land acquisition in Essex County, Ontario, 1790–1900," and "Land and law in Essex County: Malden Township and the abstract index to deeds," *SH*, 11 (1978): 98–119 and 475–93; "The role of political position and family and economic linkage in land speculation in the Western District of Upper Canada, 1788–1815," *Canadian Geographer* (Toronto), 19 (1975): 18–34. Reginald Horsman, "American Indian policy in the old northwest, 1783–1812," *William and Mary Quarterly* (Williamsburg, Va.), 3rd ser., 18 (1961): 35–53. C. M. Johnston, "William Claus and John Norton: a struggle for power in old Ontario," *OH*, 57 (1965): 101–8. J. M. Sosin, "The use of Indians in the war of the American revolution: a re-assessment of responsibility," *CHR*, 46 (1965): 101–21. G. F. G. Stanley, "The Indians in the War of 1812," *CHR*, 31 (1950): 145–65.

CALDWELL, WILLIAM, physician, surgeon, army officer, and teacher; b. 14 May 1782 in Kilmarnock, Scotland, third son and fifth child of George Caldwell and Jean Wilson; m. 23 Jan. 1822 Jane Douglass Sweeney in Montreal, and they seem to have had no children; d. there 25 Jan. 1833.

William Caldwell received his medical education at the University of Edinburgh, attending three sessions from 1800 to 1803, but he did not receive an MD there. That degree he acquired later, on 24 Jan. 1817, by attestation from Marischal College, Aberdeen. After his studies at Edinburgh, he became a hospital mate in July 1804 and was made assistant surgeon to the 4th West India Regiment in December 1805. Promoted surgeon and attached to the Royal York Rangers in 1809, he was subsequently assigned to the 1st Foot and then to the 13th Light Dragoons. In 1813 he attained the rank of staff surgeon, serving that year and the next in the Peninsular War. He came to Lower Canada in the summer of 1815 and retired on half pay in December. After settling in St Andrews (Saint-André-Est), he moved to Montreal in 1817 and there was licensed by the medical examiners for the district on 25 June. He was living on Rue Saint-Jacques in 1819 when Montreal, with a population of about 20,000, counted 21 doctors. Within ten years he and Dr William Robertson* had the principal English practices in the city.

Two years after settling in Montreal Caldwell found himself a participant in a duel that has been described as one of the longest and fiercest ever fought in Canada. The controversy preceding it originated in a petition presented by John Molson* to the House of Assembly in January 1819, which drew attention to the lack of facilities for the sick in Montreal and requested financial aid to erect and endow a public hospital. The petition met with considerable opposition from those who feared that the installation would usurp the role played exclusively until then by the Hôtel-Dieu. The most vocal opponent was Michael O'Sullivan*, a member of the assembly. In a satirical and highly provocative speech, reported in detail in the local newspapers, O'Sullivan attacked the motives of those who advanced the proposal. One of these was Caldwell. In the exchange of correspondence that followed in the press, Caldwell did not confine himself to refuting O'Sullivan's arguments; he lost his temper and implied, in a letter published in the *Canadian Courant and Montreal Advertiser* on 10 April 1819, that O'Sullivan lacked courage. O'Sullivan promptly challenged Caldwell to a duel, which was fought the following day. As reported in the *Quebec Gazette* of the 15th, "Five shots were fired by each Gentleman; two of them have dangerously wounded Mr. O'Sullivan; Dr. Caldwell has received a shot in the arm, which is much shattered." Both men recovered, although O'Sullivan probably lived out his life in constant pain from a ball on the spine.

There is no evidence that the duel influenced the fate of the projected public hospital except perhaps by increasing bitterness and further diminishing the chances of financial support from the government. Nothing more was heard of the petition, and supporters of the plan fell back on the resources of the citizens of Montreal for funds to establish the Montreal General Hospital, which opened its doors on Rue Craig (Rue Saint-Antoine) in 1819 and then was moved to Rue Dorchester in 1822. Caldwell became one of the original medical officers. In 1823 a number of doctors from the hospital set up a medical school called the Montreal Medical Institution [see Andrew Fernando Holmes*], and Caldwell became instructor in the "Practice of Physic." According to one of his students, Aaron Hart David, he was "tall, erect and very gentleman-like, but he had a stern countenance, although of a very mild, amiable disposition, and was constantly doing good. He was keen in discernment, cool in judgment, sagacious in expedient, and kind in counsel, he was, in fact, a physician of the highest order." He was also an "impressive lecturer," but "from his severe cast of countenance most of the students were afraid to approach him."

In 1823 Caldwell was appointed an examiner of persons to be licensed in medicine in Lower Canada when Lord Dalhousie [Ramsay*] remodelled the examination board to consist only of medical officers of the Montreal General Hospital. Their right to teach and to license gave the staff of the hospital a virtual monopoly of entry into the medical profession, a situation that angered many other doctors in the city. When in 1831 a new law authorized licensed doctors in Montreal and Quebec to participate in the election of 12 members to a board of medical examiners for each district, Caldwell and his colleagues all suffered resounding defeats at Montreal.

Caldwell found himself involved in yet another controversy in the early 1830s. A pew-holder in the Scotch Presbyterian Church, later known as St Gabriel Street Church, he was a member of the temporal committee from 1830 to 1833. When the congregation divided over the choice of a minister, Edward Black* or Henry Esson*, Caldwell vigorously supported Esson. Violence occurred when Black's party took possession of the church, and Esson's people tried to gain admission by force. Prominent in the fray was Caldwell.

The Montreal Medical Institution had become the medical faculty of McGill College in 1829, whereupon Caldwell was appointed lecturer in, and later professor of, the principles and practice of medicine. However, his early death prevented him from playing a major role in the affairs of the college. In 1832 Lower Canada was racked with Asiatic cholera. It appeared in Montreal on 8 June and, according to Aaron Hart David, more than 4,000 of the city's 32,000 residents fell victim to the dread disease. After the first few weeks Caldwell, so fearless in defending his opinions before men, became frightened of cholera to such an extent that he sent David, his senior student, "to all and every one of his patients, no matter what the disease." David asserts that the intensity of Caldwell's terror produced the debility which, a few months later, resulted in gangrene of the lungs, but the hypothesis is scarcely credible. Whatever the cause of Caldwell's initial illness, his condition was worsened by typhus fever, which broke out in Montreal in the winter of 1832; four of his students died of it, as did Caldwell himself on 25 Jan. 1833.

EDWARD HORTON BENSLEY

[A portrait of William Caldwell painted by Andrew Dickson Patterson hangs in the McIntyre Medical Sciences Building at McGill Univ. (Montreal). It was done from a photograph of a portrait destroyed by fire in 1907; the identity of the original artist is not known. E.H.B.]

ANQ-M, CE1-125, 28 janv. 1833; CE1-126, 23 janv. 1822. Edinburgh Univ. Library, Special Coll. Dept., medical matriculation records, 1800–3. General Reg. Office (Edinburgh), Kilmarnock, reg. of births and baptisms, 26 May 1782. McGill Univ. Arch., Montreal Medical Instit. and McGill College Medical Faculty, minute-book, 1823–33. *Canadian Courant and Montreal Advertiser*, 10 April 1819. *Montreal Gazette*, 26 Jan. 1833. *Quebec Gazette*, 15 April 1819. *Fasti academiae Mariscallanae Aberdonensis: selections from the records of the Marischal College and University, [1593–1860]*, ed. P. J. Anderson and J. F. K. Johnstone (3v., Aberdeen, Scot., 1879–98), 2: 149. William Johnston, *Roll of commissioned officers in the medical service of the British army . . .* (Aberdeen, 1917).

Abbott, *Hist. of medicine*. R. Campbell, *Hist. of Scotch Presbyterian Church*. Ægidius Fauteux, *Le duel au Canada* (Montréal, 1934). R. P. Howard, *A sketch of the late G. W. Campbell . . . being the introductory address of the fiftieth session of the medical faculty of McGill University* (Montreal, 1882). M. E. [S.] Abbott, "Early American medical schools: the faculty of medicine of McGill University," *Surgery, Gynecology and Obstetrics* (Chicago), 60 (1935): 242–53. E. H. Bensley and B. R. Tunis, "The Caldwell–O'Sullivan duel: a prelude to the founding of the Montreal General Hospital," Canadian Medical Assoc., *Journal* (Toronto), 100 (1969): 1092–95. A. H. David, "Reminiscences connected with the medical profession in Montreal during the last fifty years," *Canada Medical Record* (Montreal), 11 (1882): 1–8. Édouard Desjardins, "Un duel résulta d'une polémique autour de l'Hôtel-Dieu et du Montreal General Hospital," *L'Union médicale du Canada* (Montréal), 100 (1971): 530–35. Sylvio Leblond, "La médecine dans la province de Québec avant 1847," *Cahiers des Dix*, 35 (1970): 69–95. B. R. Tunis, "Medical licensing in Lower Canada: the dispute over Canada's first medical degree," *CHR*, 55 (1974): 489–504.

CALONNE, JACQUES-LADISLAS-JOSEPH DE, Roman Catholic priest; b. 9 April 1743 in Douai, France, son of Louis-Joseph-Dominique de Calonne and Anne-Henriette de Franqueville; d. 16 Oct. 1822 in Trois-Rivières, Lower Canada.

In the 15th century the Calonnes were still an ordinary bourgeois family of limited means living in Tournai (Belgium). Through their interest in the law and the church, they began to rise in society. The titles of squire and knight appear successively within the family during the 17th century. Jacques-Ladislas-Joseph had a pampered childhood and a happy adolescence. In 1768, having finished classical studies and a law course, he became a counsellor in the *parlement* of Flanders, where his father served as president and his brother Charles-Alexandre also held a position.

The *parlements* were abolished in 1771 and although they were revived in 1774, Jacques-Ladislas-Joseph had in the mean time decided to enter the Grand Séminaire d'Arras, in France. The bishop of Arras did not think him well suited to the ecclesiastical state, considering him as frivolous as he was brilliant. Admittedly he was a talented young man, dignified in his bearing and movements, tactful and discreet in conversation, all qualities that constituted the gentleman and man of the world as much as the man of the church. In view of this, his father and the bishop of Arras sent him to the Sulpician seminary in Paris where no time was lost in setting him to the study of

Calonne

theology and Holy Scripture, with the result that he was ordained priest on 1 June 1776. He went to Cambrai, received a canonry, and became vicar general and official of the diocese. Some time later he declined the office of bishop, but when his brother, who had become controller general of Finance in 1783, that year obtained the abbey of Saint-Père in Melun for him he could not refuse, although he would have preferred the office of king's librarian.

As an abbot Calonne had an income only slightly smaller than that of a bishop, and fewer responsibilities. He took an interest in the financial management of his abbey. During this period he was often in Paris and Versailles, and frequented the court and literary circles there, becoming a friend of Beaumarchais and of the reformers' group. His brother, who had presented a plan for financial reforms, failed to obtain the support of the Assembly of Notables, fell into disgrace, and had to leave for England in 1787; Calonne went with him. When elections to the Estates General were called, they returned to France. Although Charles-Alexandre was declared ineligible, Jacques-Ladislas-Joseph was elected for the bailiwick of Melun. Late in July 1789 he was arrested, but he was released fairly quickly and emigrated to England, where he rejoined his brother. From then on he led a hectic life dedicated to the counter-revolution; he wrote and published the *Courier de l'Europe* (printed in Paris, Boulogne, and London), travelled to Prussia and Italy, and dealt with matters of law and finance for the army of the princes, in the space of a few years ruining himself to the extent that he was sued for debt.

In 1799 Calonne decided to leave with a small group of *emigrés* to develop lands his brother had received on Prince Edward Island that year. From the day he arrived, his main responsibility as a priest was for the Irish settlers; Amable Pichard* served the Acadians and Angus Bernard MacEachern the Scots. He engaged in exemplary missionary activity, visiting the settlements and the faithful, seeking to understand the needs of various ethnic groups; he even wrote to the bishop of Quebec, who had episcopal jurisdiction over him, that the Indians, as the original inhabitants, had a better claim than anyone else to the small island of Lennox in Malpeque Bay. He went without hesitation to New Brunswick to carry on a ministry. Despite some effort he did not succeed in attracting the Trappists to Prince Edward Island.

During his episcopal visit in the summer of 1803 Bishop Pierre Denaut* met Calonne at Richibucto and invited him to move to Quebec. But Calonne was obliged first to return to England and reach an understanding with his creditors, who had been harrying him since his brother's death the previous year. Thus he spent three years in Liverpool doing parish ministry while settling his affairs and waiting for permission from Lieutenant Governor Sir Robert Shore Milnes* to go to Lower Canada. The permission came in 1807, and in October he landed at Quebec. Bishop Joseph-Octave PLESSIS immediately named him spiritual director and chaplain of the Ursulines at Trois-Rivières, as well as priest in charge of the parish of La Visitation at Pointe-du-Lac.

Despite his 64 years Calonne enjoyed good health, and he carried a heavy load. At the Ursuline convent he looked after ministry to the nuns and novices, the boarding and day pupils, and also the sick, since the only hospital in the region was under its roof. Although he was the parish priest at Pointe-du-Lac, he rarely stayed in the presbytery. On Sundays, after saying mass in the convent he would travel by carriage to his parish nine miles away, and celebrate a second mass, preach, conduct the catechism class, and sing vespers. He did not give up his parish charge until ten years later. The priest who had once received generous prebends and had lived in the midst of splendour, gave the income from his tithes to the poor and bought wheat to be ground at his own expense for distribution to the neediest of his parishioners.

In addition to drawing local people to hear him, Calonne used to go to give sermons at the Séminaire de Nicolet, where the superior, Jean Raimbault*, was also an *émigré* priest. Bishop Plessis brought Calonne to Quebec every year to preach the novena of St Francis Xavier, one of the high devotional periods in the parish of Notre-Dame. He was indeed a preacher with great style, who combined his theological knowledge and his convictions with the most forceful rhetorical devices. When he spoke of the French revolution, he could not restrain himself but declaimed vehemently and even burst into sobs. He was held in equal esteem by French and English, Catholic and Protestant, clergy and prominent laymen; not surprisingly, he had great influence and converted some Protestants. An adviser to whom Bishop Plessis paid attention, he was also the spiritual director of a number of laymen and priests, who came from Quebec or Montreal to consult him. Yet Calonne remained in touch with the changing times in Lower Canada and Europe. He was, for example, one of the first to read Hugues-Félicité-Robert de La Mennais's *Essai sur l'indifférence en matière de religion*, published in 1817. In November 1819 he made use of this work in an article for the *Gazette des Trois-Rivières* that set off a polemic in the other newspapers over Joseph Lancaster*'s monitorial system of teaching, to which Calonne was violently opposed.

During the 15 years he spent in Lower Canada, Jacques-Ladislas-Joseph de Calonne led an ascetic life, fasting every day and wearing a hair shirt and chain belt. The nuns considered him a saint and believed they saw him in ecstasy in the chapel when he was praying there. On 11 Oct. 1822 the priests and prominent people of the Trois-Rivières region came to say farewell to him. He died five days later. He was remembered in oral tradition until the end of the century at Pointe-du-Lac. In 1962 an old Ursuline nun in Trois-Rivières still spoke of "our M. de Calonne," as if she had known him.

CLAUDE GALARNEAU

ANQ-MBF, CE1-48, 18 oct. 1822. ASQ, Doc. Faribault, no.209; Fonds Viger–Verreau, sér.O, 081: 24; 0297; Polygraphie, XXXIV: 9d. Francis Hall, *Travels in Canada, and the United States, in 1816 and 1817* (London, 1818). John Lambert, *Travels through Lower Canada, and the United States of North America, in the years 1806, 1807, and 1808* . . . (new ed., 2v., London, 1816). Caron, "Inv. de la corr. de Mgr Plessis," ANQ *Rapport*, 1927–28: 215–316. J.-G. Barthe, *Souvenirs d'un demi-siècle ou mémoires pour servir à l'histoire contemporaine* (Montréal, 1885). Dionne, *Les ecclésiastiques et les royalistes français*. Alexandre Dugré, *La Pointe-du-Lac* (Trois-Rivières, Qué., 1934). Galarneau, *La France devant l'opinion canadienne*. Robert Lacour-Gayet, *Calonne: financier, réformateur, contre-révolutionnaire, 1734–1802* (Paris, 1963). *Les ursulines des Trois-Rivières*, 2: 437–512. G. Du Chevrot, "M. de Calonne," *BRH*, 8 (1902): 283–85. Yvan Lamonde, "Classes sociales, classes scolaires: une polémique sur l'éducation en 1819–1820," CCHA *Sessions d'études*, 41 (1974): 43–59. Robert [Philippe] Sylvain, "Louis XVII vint-il en Amérique?" *Rev. de l'univ. Laval* (Québec), 3 (1948–49): 743–61.

CAMBRIDGE, JOHN, land agent and businessman; b. 13 Dec. 1748 in England; m. 16 Jan. 1775 Mary Winchester, and they had ten children, only four of whom reached maturity; d. 26 Dec. 1831 in Bristol, England.

Before his arrival on St John's (Prince Edward) Island in 1784, John Cambridge remains a shadowy figure in historical records. A Privy Council report of 1791 identifies him as being "formerly an obscure chairmaker in St. Martin's Lane" but there are indications that as early as 1777 he was associated with a group of merchants who planned to trade with and promote settlement on St John's Island. One of this group was the Quaker colonizer Robert Clark* and it may have been the religious link that brought the two men together. Cambridge was known on the Island as a Quaker, and he refused to take oaths in court on religious principles. Nevertheless, he was not connected with the Society of Friends. Indeed, he wrote in 1793 that although "in full belief of Friends principles" he was not "united to the Society." It is probable that he became a member after returning to England, for he was buried a Quaker.

Cambridge was named Clark's agent in 1783 and took up the appointment the following spring when he came out with his family to the Island. He was called upon in 1786 to defend his employer's interests against the Island establishment following an attempt to confirm Governor Walter Patterson*'s seizure in 1781 of part of Clark's property for non-payment of quitrents. In doing so Cambridge alienated some Island officials; the alienation was later to develop into bitterness and litigation.

John Cambridge was not content to act simply as Clark's agent. In 1785, with the backing of merchants in London, including his brother-in-law William Winchester, he began commercial activities of his own. He acquired property in the Murray Harbour district in the southeast part of the Island and four years later was able to report that he had built two large brigs, both of which were on trading voyages, one to the West Indies and the other to Portugal. The shipping registers indicate that he was also the owner of a number of smaller vessels. These craft, mostly schooners, kept up a trade with Newfoundland. He built a large sawmill at Murray Harbour and had houses there and in Charlottetown.

By 1788 Cambridge had formed a partnership with William Bowley, another Island resident. Bowley had purchased debts owed by Clark, and Cambridge in turn had a large bill for his wages and expenses as Clark's agent. Together they sued Clark and the court case, begun in 1789, developed into protracted litigation, with countersuits and appeals dragging the matter out until the end of the century. Even before the conclusion of the court battle Cambridge was able to gain control of Clark's assets and land, establishing himself as a substantial merchant.

His relations with members of the colonial administration were not good, however. He had supported Lieutenant Governor Edmund Fanning* against the doomed Patterson faction on Fanning's arrival in 1786 but this support, predicated on a quick resolution of the problem caused by Patterson's illegal expropriations, did not last long. Of lesser officials Cambridge became excessively intolerant. He was a strong-willed individual who, when he considered himself slighted, took full measures to obtain what he considered justice. In 1787 he carried a complaint against Isaac Swan, a petty Patterson supporter, to the governor and Council; in another incident two years later he was able to persuade that body to dismiss high sheriff Walter Berry for irregularities. He was less successful when he brought charges against the attorney general, Joseph Aplin* – a poor move, since Aplin was usually successful in the courts whatever the law. As a sharp merchant Cambridge was especially conscious of any apparent favour extended to his competitors and, when he learned that collector of customs William Townshend* was allowing use of the Îles de la Madeleine for the evasion of customs duties, he was quick to publicize the fact. In doing so he precipitated a struggle because Townshend retaliated by seizing several of Cambridge and Bowley's vessels for smuggling. The latter case dragged on for three years

Cambridge

with Cambridge complaining that he could not obtain justice in the Island courts. It was not until 1791 that the case was settled, but by then Cambridge's complaints had been broadened to include almost the entire government of the colony.

In concert with John Hill*, another Island merchant, Cambridge and Bowley in 1791 brought charges of malfeasance before the Privy Council in London against Townshend, Fanning, Aplin, and Chief Justice Peter Stewart*. Cambridge carried the complaints to England in a petition that he persuaded a number of the Island's absentee proprietors to sign. The general charge was that the officials had formed an illegal combination to rule the Island and oppress all who opposed them. A collection of lesser grievances, some going back to Patterson's time, included partiality in the courts, election irregularities, and petty harassment. Hill later stated that in presenting the charges Cambridge spent time on the politics of the colony and none on the facts of the case. Much of Cambridge's difficulty arose because 12 of the 18 signatories, including Bowley, withdrew their names before the charges were presented. Cambridge and Hill were the only resident proprietors whose names appeared on the document and both seemed prosperous in spite of their lack of favour with the officials. The shaky presentation was rebutted by Fanning's personal emissary, Robert GRAY, and the case was dismissed the following year.

By October 1792 word of the outcome had reached the Island and Cambridge's troubles began in earnest. The notice from London was made public and his support and credibility sank. He was summoned before the House of Assembly to explain allegations he had made concerning members of that body, and after an investigation the house ordered that "the false and malicious words . . . be burnt under the gallows by the sergeant-at-arms." The same year suits totalling £55,000 were launched against him and Bowley by the four officials on charges of malicious prosecution. Cambridge attempted to have the suits tried in Nova Scotia owing to the partiality of the Island courts. He received the lieutenant governor's permission to do so, but he was unable to raise the necessary securities in case the decision should go against him. The trials were therefore held on the Island before judges who had a financial interest in the outcome. After verdicts were found for Aplin and Townshend in 1793, Cambridge agreed to settle out of court for Fanning's and Stewart's expenses. Total damages recovered amounted to £2,480, and Cambridge later reported that with his own expenses the complaints to London had cost him more that £10,000. He was forced to spend a short time in jail before he could convince the four officials of his ability to pay.

Because making the settlement would quickly exhaust Cambridge's assets, the officials, who were more interested in payment than in revenge, agreed to assist him in recovering funds from Hill and Bowley. The latter were each asked to contribute one-third of the settlement, and when they refused legal action was brought against them. In 1793 suits prepared by Aplin were successful and resulted in executions against their property on the Island. Within days the property of Hill, who was absent from the Island, and the valuable Greenwich estate, belonging to Bowley and his children, were sold at auction by the sheriff and passed into Cambridge's hands; Bowley himself was forced to flee under cover of darkness to avoid imprisonment. Attempts at appeal were refused by the courts and the governor in council in 1794, and Bowley was forced to appeal to the king in council in 1796 to have the case reopened on the Island. Hill, too, had to bring an action in London against his former associate and was successful, but before he could move against Cambridge the latter's assets were placed in the hands of a trustee. Hill appears to have given up at this point but Bowley's action was not settled for almost 50 years. In length and complexity the case *Bowley* v. *Cambridge* rivalled the celebrated Jarndyce case in Charles Dickens's novel *Bleak house*, which was ended only when the total assets of the estate were swallowed up in legal fees.

Cambridge's legal problems were exacerbated by business reverses. In 1794 he lost the support of his backers in England and his few remaining assets were seized by creditors. His schooner *Endeavour* was taken that year by the French on a voyage to the West Indies and he was left with no capital to rebuild his business. The loss of his London backers was the low point of his career. Faced with a report that even William Winchester, his brother-in-law, had joined the creditors, he considered leaving the colony and going to the United States. However, on learning that Winchester had stood by him and that it had been the other partners who had taken the action, he and his wife resolved to stay on the Island. The lieutenant governor and principal officers gave him encouragement. In a letter to Alexander Ellice*, a Montreal merchant for whom Cambridge was agent, he reported that "the People in the Island in General are much attached to us, and lament our failure, and hope we shall get into business again." That he was able to do so was the result of a fortunate precaution. It appears that Cambridge had placed his affairs in the hands of a trustee "as the property of a bankrupt," but he may not have declared bankruptcy. At any rate the move was sufficient to relieve the pressure on his finances and he was able to begin again. He kept the secure base at Murray Harbour and returned to the shipping of lumber and livestock to Newfoundland.

The key factor in Cambridge's ability to rebuild lay

in the fact that he retained control of several large parcels of property, much of which he had obtained through lawsuits. He seems to have made an effort to bring settlers to his lands and thereby avoid the attacks of those who would escheat for non-payment of quitrents. With this base he was able to continue efforts at settlement and the lumber trade. His mills processed timber from his own land which he then sent to Newfoundland in his own ships. By 1801 he had won back the contract to supply the garrison with fuel and had a new vessel on the ways, the first in ten years. It was launched the following year and Cambridge wrote to his wife that the ship, after proceeding to Liverpool with a timber cargo, was to sail to Ireland for a load of Irish Protestants "in order to preserve our lands from forfeiture." Perhaps it was the renewed threat of escheat that prompted him in 1805 to sign with Charles Worrell* and William Townshend a memorial to Lieutenant Governor Joseph Frederick Wallet DesBarres citing the efforts of himself and other proprietors, including John MacDonald* of Glenaladale and Lord Selkirk [Douglas*], in settling people on their lands and contributing to the Island's prosperity. In 1806 Cambridge was commended by the assembly for his efforts in this regard.

It was the timber trade that brought Cambridge fortune, and this prosperity he shared with the rest of the colony. Initially the trade was part of the Gulf of St Lawrence commerce and most cargoes went to Newfoundland. Shipping to Britain was too expensive and there was often a long search for a return cargo. From 1803 until 1807 only about two cargoes a year went across the Atlantic from the Island as a whole. The situation began to change in 1807 when the Napoleonic blockade of ports on the Baltic Sea opened the British North American timber trade. The Island was well suited to fill the demand: because it had many small harbours where trees grew close to the water's edge, timber could be easily moved and loaded. In 1808, 41 vessels left the Island with shipments for Britain and the following year the number swelled to 78 despite what Cambridge termed "an uncommon bad season" with timber left behind because of deep snow. The trade brought manpower shortages to the colony and high prices. Oxen, usually raised for food, were employed in the woods and the provisioning of ships left food scarce. Sales to Newfoundland fell off dramatically.

Ships were a necessary element of the Cambridge operation and John lost no time building and acquiring them. From 1808 there was rarely a year when a new Cambridge vessel did not appear on the register and often there were several. When the timber trade stabilized after 1817 Cambridge remained successful by entering a new form of commerce, later followed by James Yeo*, which combined the exporting of timber with the building and marketing of vessels. In

1824 four ships were registered and twice that number in the following year. Many of these vessels were large, fully rigged ships in excess of 300 tons; the *Cambridge* (536 tons), launched in 1826, was one of the largest built on the Island. In his will, made in 1829, Cambridge instructed his sons that he had "found the most effectual way of getting my debts remitted . . . to be by building a ship annually and by loading her with timber" and disposing of both in the United Kingdom. Family correspondence reveals that in spite of prosperity the firm was never far from a financial crisis as dependence on credit was a necessary part of long-distance trade.

Other operations of the Cambridge firm also seemed to do well. In 1808 he boasted that his mill at Murray Harbour was perhaps the first in North America equipped with an 18-unit gang saw cutting 7,000 feet of deals a day. A new venture was the construction of a brewery at the Bird Island (Wrights) Creek mills near Charlottetown. Unfortunately it was not a success, in part because food shortages had raised the price of barley on the Island.

In 1808 Cambridge, whose family figured in all his business affairs, formed a partnership with his son Lemuel and his son-in-law George Wright*, son of Thomas Wright*, the surveyor general. Wright did not have the business sense of other members of the Cambridge family and the partnership was dissolved in 1813 when John took his other son, Artemas, into the company, now termed Cambridge and Sons. In the next few years control of the firm passed more and more to the sons, who were described by Lieutenant Governor Charles Douglass Smith* as "very fine young men & of the very best reputation."

With some stability in business and his sons in charge of the Island operation, Cambridge, at the urging of his wife, who had run the business whenever her husband was in England, decided to conduct the British end of the firm's transatlantic commerce. He apparently moved to Bristol in 1814 and did not return to the Island in his later years. By the time of his departure he seems to have made his peace with the colonial administration. He was nominated high sheriff in 1809 but declined, citing his Quaker beliefs, and his son Lemuel served instead. By 1813 he was noted as being an intimate friend of Chief Justice Cæsar Colclough.

When he died in 1831 at age 83 Cambridge held 102,000 acres on the Island, almost one-tenth of the total. In addition he and his family owned extensive mills, shipbuilding facilities, and stores, and the Cambridge estate was the home of at least 5,000 people, many of whom were tenants. There is no doubt that Cambridge was the greatest Island landowner of his day but his empire, like many others, was built on credit. The lands had been heavily mortgaged to provide capital for shipbuilding and expansion.

Cameron

Seven years after Cambridge's death Samuel Cunard* and others purchased the mortgage for £12,000 sterling and in 1841 gained possession of the entire estate. In the same year the Island's Court of Chancery finally decided *Bowley* v. *Cambridge*. After twice reaching the king in council, and following the death of both litigants, the case was resolved when the court divided Bowley's estate equally between the claimants.

John Cambridge was hardly a typical merchant of his time. His religious beliefs in great measure governed his actions even in commercial dealings. After losing the case brought by the four government officials he wrote in 1793, "It has been my diligent study to keep a Continual Void of offence towards God first and to give no just grounds of offence towards my fellow men." Yet he was a sharp merchant who used the courts as a weapon against all who dared oppose him, including attorneys who failed to win his cases. He exhibited tenacity in the face of odds that caused others to give up and return to England. The reports we have of him are mostly assessments made by his enemies and they exhibit a bitterness coming from close and protracted conflict. However, when his own letters and his actions are examined, Cambridge emerges as a man of principle in a society which had little regard for that quality.

H. T. HOLMAN

[John Cambridge is the author of *A description of the Island of St. John, in the Gulf of St. Laurence, North America . . . by a person many years resident there* (London, [1798?]) (*see* PRO, T 1/4144: 17–26); a copy of a subsequent edition, *A description of Prince Edward Island . . . by a person many years resident there* (London, 1805), is available at PANS.

Few of Cambridge's business papers survive, but those that do throw valuable light on business operations in the early nineteenth century. The PAPEI possesses two letter-books covering the period 1793–1801 and 1808–9, at Acc. 2984/4 and RG 6, Supreme Court, case papers, 1808–9, respectively. The former provides details of Cambridge's struggle with the colonial officers and the ensuing court battles; the latter is extremely useful for details of the timber trade on Prince Edward Island. A letter-book of Cambridge's wife, Mary, covering the period 1811–12 is found on pp.17–114 of a collection of Charles Wright papers owned by Mrs J. T. McIntyre of Calgary; photocopies are available at PAC, MG 24, B133. Additional letters from Cambridge to Alexander Ellice are found in the Ellice papers at the NLS, Dept. of MSS, MSS 15113–26, available on microfilm at the PAC, MG 24, A2.

Cambridge's affairs appear frequently in Colonial Office correspondence, with the following references being most useful: PRO, CO 226/9: 176; 226/10: 29, 135–37, 234, 238, 252–93; 226/11: 17; 226/12: 12, 27; 226/13: 21–45, 207, 218–19, 280–82, 377–78; 226/14; 226/15: 172; 226/16: 186 *et seq.*, 248; 226/17: 107–48; 226/18: 162–206; 226/19: 72–74, 204 *et seq.*, 233, 347, 352; 226/20: 106–8, 142; 226/21: 110; 226/23: 65–74; 226/27: 78–83; 226/28: 53, 220–22; 226/29: 67–71, 115; 226/30: 177–80; 226/34: 391–99; 226/39: 49–54, 260, 416–22; 226/42: 132; 226/47: 166. Minutes of the Island's Executive Council, found in PAPEI, RG 5, have references to Cambridge on the following dates: 12 April 1787; 15 Dec. 1788; 12, 16, 19–20, 23–24 March, 6, 27 April, 5 May 1789; 26 April, 17 July 1790; 7, 30 Oct. 1792; 23 Feb. 1793; 25 Oct. 1796; 6 Aug. 1799.

Details of ship ownership by members of the Cambridge family are found in PAC, RG 42, E1, 1658; PAPEI, RG 9, 2; and the *Prince Edward Island Register*, 3 Jan. 1826, 16 Jan. 1827, 29 Jan. 1828, 13 Jan. 1829, and 9 Feb. 1830. A significant amount of information concerning Cambridge is found in the Prince Edward Island court records (PAPEI, RG 6), which were examined for the entire period. This source is especially detailed for *Bowley* v. *Cambridge*, 1793–1841 (RG 6, Court of Chancery papers, box 1). Material regarding the Privy Council appeals in the case is at PRO, PC 1/64/B.30; 1/65/B.33, 35, and 38; and 1/66/B.40. These collections shed much light on Cambridge's litigious nature. Information concerning his land holdings is scattered throughout PAPEI, RG 16, land registry records. Cambridge's will is located in the Estates Division of the Supreme Court of P.E.I. (Charlottetown), liber 2: f.198.

Secondary sources which proved useful include: *Canada's smallest prov.* (Bolger), pp.37–94; Warburton, *Hist. of P.E.I.*, 255–65; and W. S. MacNutt, "Fanning's regime on Prince Edward Island," *Acadiensis* (Fredericton), 1 (1971–72), no.1: 37–53. H.T.H.]

PAPEI, Acc. 2984/4, Cambridge to [Flowden?], 28 Sept. 1793; Cambridge to B [William Winchester], [*c.* 1793]; Cambridge to Alexander Ellice, 26 Nov. 1794; RG 3, journals, 18 Dec. 1806; RG 6, Supreme Court, case papers, 1789, *Cambridge, Bowley & Co.* v. *Clark*; 1790, *Townshend* v. *the Adventure*; 1790, *Townshend* v. *the Elizabeth*; minutes; RG 16, land registry records, conveyance reg., liber 8: f.94; liber 49: f.203. Private arch., George Wright (Charlottetown), Cambridge family Bible. *Bristol Gazette, and Public Advertiser* (Bristol, Eng.), 29 Dec. 1831. *Bristol Mirror*, 31 Dec. 1831. *Felix Farley's Bristol Journal*, 31 Dec. 1831. *Royal Gazette* (Charlottetown), 28 Feb. 1832.

CAMERON, ÆNEAS, fur trader; b. *c.* 1757 in the parish of Kirkmichael (Grampian), Scotland; d. 8 Sept. 1822 in Montreal.

Æneas Cameron's father, Alexander, farmed a small holding, Inverchabet, and his mother, Grace Grant, was from nearby Glen Lochy. His mother's brothers, John and Francis Grant, were wealthy Jamaican planters. Through his maternal grandmother, Æneas was also related to the merchant and fur trader William Grant* "of Three Rivers."

In December 1786 Cameron, recently arrived in Jamaica from Quebec under the sponsorship of Richard Dobie*, wrote from Kingston to his uncle Francis at Montego Bay concerning his future plans. Whatever they were, Francis did not approve and proposed that Cameron consider "the planting line" in his service. Whether Cameron agreed or not, he was apparently dissatisfied with his situation, for in the spring of 1788 he was back in the province of Quebec and was engaged by Dobie as clerk for Fort Abitibi (near La Sarre, Que.). He probably owed his introduction to the fur trade to his Grant connections. Dobie, a prominent Montreal merchant and fur trader, had acquired the Timiskaming posts the previous year in partnership with James Grant*, who, like William Grant, was originally from Kirkmichael, although there is no evidence of a blood relationship. But William Grant and Dobie, long-time business associates and friends, may have been more closely connected through Dobie's son-in-law, John Grant, a former Timiskaming partner, who was almost certainly related to Cameron's uncles, the Jamaican Grants. Such ties, together with Cameron's superior education and business habits, demonstrated in his surviving letters and papers, would also account for the generosity of Dobie's terms: if Cameron decided to remain in the fur country and if James Grant were willing, Dobie would offer Cameron part of his own share in the posts.

Cameron remained at Fort Abitibi for several years but his hopes for a share were deferred when, in 1791, Dobie and Grant sold the Timiskaming posts to Grant, Campion and Company, of which William Grant was senior partner. About 1792 Cameron took charge of the post at Grand-Lac (Grand-Lac-Victoria) and in the autumn of 1793 of that at Fort Timiskaming (near Ville-Marie), replacing James Grant whose health would prevent him from spending another winter there. The following summer Cameron secured an interest in the business. In 1795 the posts were again sold, to McTavish, Frobisher and Company, the agents of the North West Company, and in offering Cameron a generous salary to manage them Simon McTavish* also promised him a share in the new agreement (due to take effect in 1799) as soon as an opening occurred. During the next three years, however, apparently because of a misunderstanding, Cameron was in dispute with the agents over both his salary and his expected partnership. He finally signed the agreement in October 1798.

In 1800 the NWC sent an overland expedition, headed by Alexander McDougall, to establish posts on James Bay in order to compete with the Hudson's Bay Company. As commander of the Timiskaming posts, Cameron was involved in the plans for the venture, but it is clear that he was not enthusiastic. In the summer of 1805 he went overland to the bay to assess the company's position there. Returning to the area by ship the following summer, he ordered that all the posts be abandoned, apparently because they were not economically viable and had failed in their original strategic mission of forcing the HBC to come to terms with the NWC. He was afterwards reported to have been censured by the NWC partners at Fort William (Thunder Bay, Ont.) for giving up the station at Moose Factory (Ont.) but there is no doubt that his decision was correct.

Although Cameron seems to have left Fort Timiskaming in 1804, he probably did not retire to Montreal until 1806, after his return from the bay. He became a member of the Beaver Club in 1807 and until 1812, although never a partner of McTavish, McGillivrays and Company, he served the firm in a financial capacity, probably in the accounting and supplying of the Timiskaming business. During the War of 1812 he was captain and paymaster of the Corps of Canadian Voyageurs raised by the Nor'Westers and in 1815 he sold his hundredth share as a retired partner and all his interests in the NWC to its agents for £11,000. He had never formally married but he had at least one Indian wife at Fort Timiskaming. Margaret, who became the wife of Chief Factor Allan McDonell*, was apparently his daughter.

During his last years Cameron lived at a boarding-house kept by Thomas Holmes, father of Benjamin* and Andrew Fernando*. A member of the Presbyterian St Gabriel Street Church, he was buried in its cemetery on 10 Sept. 1822. His will, made on 24 June 1818, left the bulk of his estate, after numerous legacies, to his nephew, Angus Cameron* of Timiskaming, a former partner in the NWC.

Evidence reveals Æneas Cameron to have been a proud and upright Highlander, concerned for his family and esteemed and loved by his Montreal friends. He also proved to be an excellent trader, and an astute and meticulous businessman. Under his command the Timiskaming posts, long a losing venture, were well on their way to becoming one of the Nor'Westers' most profitable departments, a position they were to retain under the HBC for almost 40 years.

ELAINE ALLAN MITCHELL

PAM, HBCA, E.41/1–3 (mfm. at AO). Docs. relating to NWC (Wallace). E. A. Mitchell, Fort Timiskaming and the fur trade (Toronto and Buffalo, N.Y., 1977). W. S. Wallace, The pedlars from Quebec and other papers on the Nor'Westers (Toronto, 1954).

CAMERON, JOHN. See OGIMAUH-BINAESSIH

CAMPBELL, PATRICK, author; fl. c. 1765–1823.

Patrick Campbell, like numerous others who wrote of their tours through North America during the late 18th and early 19th centuries, probably acquired his taste for travel while in the army, although it is not clear when and where he served. Undoubtedly of Scottish origin, he may have gained his knowledge of German during service on the Continent; he later claimed to have "fought in many parts of Europe [and] killed many men."

By the mid 1760s Campbell had taken up the

Campbell

apparently hereditary office of head forester of the royal forest of Mamlorn, near Achallader, Scotland. He occupied the post for just over seven years, leaving because of "a slight misunderstanding with the factor." Then, as he explained in 1792, "I betook myself to farming, traded a little by sea and land, by which I made out so well as now to be enabled to give up all business, and gratify a passion for travelling, and seeing as much of the world as my little finances will admit of."

Accompanied by his servant and his dog, Campbell sailed from Greenock, Scotland, for North America on 2 July 1791 in order to assess the possibilities various settlements offered to immigrating Highland Scots. The chronicle of his journey, *Travels in the interior inhabited parts of North America in the years 1791 and 1792*, published in Scotland in 1793, is one of the most important accounts of British North America in the late 18th century. Campbell arrived on 28 August in Saint John, N.B., and after a stay of several days proceeded by boat and on foot to Fredericton. He called on Lieutenant Governor Thomas Carleton* to enquire about the assistance the government could provide to immigrants and then travelled up the Nashwaak River, visiting settlements established by disbanded soldiers of the 42nd Foot. He reached the mouth of the Miramichi River, where he stayed with merchant James FRASER, before returning to Fredericton. His investigations then took him on a long and difficult journey up the Saint John River and through the Madawaska valley to the St Lawrence. His nephew Dugald Campbell* accompanied him for part of this trip. Quebec was "ill looking" and did not impress Campbell, who quickly went on by land to Montreal and from there to Kingston and Niagara (Niagara-on-the-Lake) on foot, by boat, and on horseback. After spending two days as a guest of Mohawk chief Joseph Brant [Thayendanegea*] at Grand River, he returned to Niagara. With David Ramsay* as a guide, he set off through upper New York State to New York City. There he boarded a vessel to return to Saint John, where he arrived on 12 May 1792. Until his departure for Scotland on 4 November, he continued to explore southern New Brunswick, including the area around Fredericton, east along the Kennebecasis River to Sussex Vale (Sussex Corner), where he visited George LEONARD, and St Andrews on the southwestern border.

Campbell presents his narrative in a clear, direct prose which only occasionally shows signs of having been hastily written. The importance of his work lies in his assessment of the prospects for settlers in North America. Over half of his account is devoted to New Brunswick, but he describes economic conditions all along his route, commenting on the advance of settlement, the various agricultural practices and returns that could be expected, as well as the progress of several other industries including shipbuilding, fishing, lumbering, and the fur trade. Like many other travellers, he stresses the success settlers could achieve by steady application and exertion, and draws attention to the abundance of natural resources in the New World. Deeply discontented with policies of the British government that he felt prevented Scotland from flourishing and promoted emigration, Campbell none the less encouraged his fellow countrymen to settle in British possessions and in his book enumerated the many advantages of these colonies over the United States. As a former forester, he took a great interest in wildlife, noting the existence of numerous species now extinct. Keen and curious as well as hardy and indefatigable, Campbell is usually accurate when he relies on his own observations. On occasions where he relates the stories told to him by others, his work is considerably less exact. Everywhere he went he endeared himself to leading members of society, and his friendly and personable manner probably accounted for much of the warm and generous hospitality he received. Although his descriptions of the people he encountered provide few glimpses into character, he presents interesting insights into their economic and social condition, information unavailable from other contemporary sources.

On 3 Dec. 1794, after his return to Scotland, Campbell was appointed a lieutenant in an independent company of foot which soon became part of the 116th Foot. He had little time to reap any benefit from his new commission since the 116th Foot was disbanded in 1795. While on half pay he was advanced to the rank of captain. He disappears from the army lists after 1823. No details are known of his personal life except that he had a son and a daughter. Although Campbell himself remains an elusive figure, his *Travels* is an important historical work, especially for New Brunswick, providing first-hand observations of the province less than a decade after its establishment.

PAULETTE M. CHIASSON

[The author would like to thank Stuart R. J. Sutherland for his assistance.

The full title of Patrick Campbell's narrative, which was published in Edinburgh in 1793, is *Travels in the interior inhabited parts of North America in the years 1791 and 1792; in which is given an account of the manners and customs of the Indians, and the present war between them and the fœderal states, the mode of life and system of farming among the new settlers of both Canadas, New York, New England, New Brunswick, and Nova Scotia; interspersed with anecdotes of people, observations on the soil, natural productions, and political situation of these countries*. A new edition, edited by Hugh Hornby Langton* and William Francis Ganong*, was published in Toronto in 1937; it contains the best commentary on Campbell's work and most of the biographical data known about him. P.M.C.]

Early travellers in the Canadas, 1791–1867, ed. and intro. G. M. Craig (Toronto, 1955). G.B., WO, *Army list, 1759–1824*. P. M. Chiasson, "Travellers in Nova Scotia, 1770–1860" (MA thesis, Queen's Univ., Kingston, Ont., 1981).

CAMPBELL, Sir WILLIAM, lawyer, office holder, JP, militia officer, politician, and judge; b. 2 Aug. 1758 in Caithness, Scotland, son of Alexander Campbell and Susannah Poole; m. 1 June 1785 Hannah Hadley in Guysborough, N.S., and they had two sons and four daughters – two of the latter married Robert Roberts Loring* and William Robertson*; d. 18 Jan. 1834 in York (Toronto), Upper Canada.

William Campbell was born into a branch of Clan Diarmid that migrated north to Caithness late in the 17th century. His paternal grandfather was a captain in the Royal Navy, and his father owned land at Houstry in the south of Caithness, the possible location of William's birth. He attended a grammar school at Thurso where classical languages were taught, and studied law briefly at Elgin before the death of his instructor ended his formal education. By then the American colonies had rebelled, and against the advice of his friends Campbell decided to enter the army. He became a volunteer in the 76th Foot, a Highland regiment in which one of his relatives was a soldier, and accompanied it to North America. Captured at Yorktown, Va, in 1781, he remained a prisoner for some time. Before the end of the war he was awarded a commission in a provincial regiment so that he could receive half pay.

Midway through 1784 Campbell appeared in Nova Scotia with a group of refugees arriving at Chedabucto Bay to settle. He received a water lot in the new town of Guysborough and other acreage, and married the daughter of a pre-loyalist inhabitant. Local tradition tells that when Campbell became discouraged by his prospects his neighbour Thomas Cutler* suggested that he study law with him. Records of admissions to the provincial bar for this period are not extant. Campbell seems to have begun practising as an attorney around 1785. A remote fishing village offered little business, and he had to keep a small shop in order to make ends meet. His training and occupation set him apart from his neighbours, and undoubtedly helped him acquire several township offices such as assessor, surveyor, and overseer of the poor. By the early 1790s he had also obtained the socially significant appointments of justice of the peace and captain of militia. In 1799 Campbell was acclaimed to the House of Assembly as one of the two representatives for Sydney County, and he remained a member until his seat was declared vacant for non-attendance in 1806. Although Campbell was an infrequent visitor to the house, he came to notice during 1803 when he was a vocal supporter of fellow assemblyman William

Cottnam TONGE. Lieutenant Governor Sir John Wentworth*, the chief critic of Tonge, commented that another figure had joined the "reprehensible opposition."

Campbell's parliamentary career occurred while he was a member of the government of the neighbouring colony of Cape Breton. His involvement there began in October 1799. The administrator, John MURRAY, had fallen out with Attorney General David Mathews*, and Mathews's supporter Archibald Charles DODD refused to be a party to any prosecution of him instigated by Murray. Since Mathews and Dodd were the only lawyers on the island, Murray needed independent legal support, and Campbell was evidently chosen because of his proximity to Sydney and his need for work. Murray appointed Campbell solicitor general and, because there was no provision for such an official, a subscription was raised on Campbell's behalf and Murray took him into his home. The death of James Miller, the superintendent of the coal mines, gave Murray the chance to appoint Campbell to that position, though at first he had to share its attractive salary with Miller's sister, Jane. Campbell was also named to the Executive Council, and after Mathews's dismissal as attorney general in November he began to act in his place. In February 1800 Murray assumed control of the mines from the lessees, Jonathan Tremain and Richard Stout*, with the result that Campbell had even more responsibility over the operations there.

Despite Campbell's favoured status, he clashed with Murray when the administrator began to take all responsibility for the mines and ignore his remonstrances. He thus abandoned Murray when Murray was disputing the leadership of the government with John DESPARD in the late summer of 1800. Despard's victory left Campbell in an influential position, and his advice about the mines was solicited by Despard. Campbell disparaged the system of government control, and his arguments in favour of private management persuaded Despard, who advertised in Halifax for bids. When this effort failed, he leased the mines to Campbell, whose offer was accepted over that of his only rivals, Tremain and Stout, and Campbell took possession on 24 Nov. 1801. He promptly proved lacking in the experience to run the mines alone and by January 1803 claimed that his losses had been so ruinous that he required an increase in prices, a reduction in the government duty payable on each chaldron, or a termination of the lease with suitable reimbursement. Despard refused all three alternatives, but Campbell kept up the pressure and avoided sinking the new pit that Despard requested on the grounds that additional workers would cost too much. The disastrous drop in coal shipments which resulted placed Despard in a difficult position, since the money from the duties was a badly needed source of revenue

Campbell

for Cape Breton. By early 1804 Despard realized his mistake in allowing a relatively unskilled lessee to run a resource of such value to the colony, and on 28 February he took control of the mines on behalf of the crown. Campbell surrendered the mining equipment and other stock only after Despard paid him £477 in compensation.

Campbell had arrived in Cape Breton poor and much in debt, a situation which had been eased by the salaries of superintendent and attorney general. He had taken the lease hoping that the profits would solve his financial worries, and his inexperience did not prepare him for his losses, which were harder to take because he had ceased to be superintendent. While lessee he purchased land extensively and started building the largest house in Sydney, perhaps in anticipation of the revenue from the mines. Thus when Despard proved unwilling to help he turned against the administrator, and by February 1804 the rift between the two men was irreparable. That spring Despard took the advice of the other members of the council and ordered that Campbell not be summoned to further meetings because his behaviour had become "so violent, so disrespectful and indecorous." However, Despard did not dismiss Campbell as councillor or attorney general.

In his anger at Despard, Campbell tried to have him replaced as military commander in Cape Breton, and when that attempt failed he aligned himself with Richard Collier Bernard DesBarres Marshall Gibbons. The son of the colony's first chief justice, Gibbons had a keen legal mind and a desire to see the island's non-representative government replaced by an elected house of assembly. To this end, about 1805 he began to attack the tax on imported rum inaugurated by Despard in 1801 as illegal because it had not been approved by an assembly, and he went so far as to declare that the same reason made all the colony's ordinances invalid. It is difficult to tell if Campbell supported Gibbons out of a desire for revenge against Despard or because of his genuine belief in Gibbons's views. He may even have put some of these notions into Gibbons's head. Certainly Campbell accepted the principle of reform and subscribed to Gibbons's ideas, although Chief Justice William Woodfall believed that he did not advance them "quite so daringly" as Gibbons. Around the beginning of 1806 he declared publicly that he would dispute the legality of ordinances passed by the council and refused to prosecute a ship's captain who had carried coal from Cape Breton without a permit on the grounds that the relevant ordinance was illegal. Only after repeated orders from Despard did he take the case to court.

In July 1807 Despard was replaced as administrator by Brigadier-General Nicholas NEPEAN. A weak man, Nepean quickly fell under the influence of Campbell, whom he summoned to council meetings and nominated mines superintendent. The previous superintendent, John Corbett Ritchie, who had been appointed by Despard, complained to London, and in April 1808 Lord Castlereagh, the colonial secretary, ordered Nepean to reappoint Ritchie and commented adversely on the selection of Campbell. During that spring Nepean made some sort of family connection with Ritchie, and bolstered by the fear of endangering his own position, he dismissed Campbell as superintendent in June. In a further attempt to stay in Cape Breton Nepean then turned on his erstwhile confidant, describing him as an "instigator of mischief" who had opposed him at every turn. Before his replacement as superintendent, Campbell had lived at the mines and had rented his Sydney house to Nepean. When in July he reminded Nepean that the lease had almost expired the administrator dismissed him as councillor and attorney general and refused to move. Now homeless as well as jobless, Campbell was forced to leave Cape Breton, which he did some time that year, and sail for England to obtain redress.

In London, Campbell pressed his "hard case" at the Colonial Office, obtaining in March 1810 the promise "that something should be done to remunerate me for the injustice I have experienced." He then spent an anxious 15 months while he awaited news as to what that something would be. Moreover, the certainty that "uncommon and underhand means" had been taken to impugn his character with colonial officials was cause for further unease. An obvious solution and one which Campbell favoured was his appointment to the vacancy on the Upper Canadian Court of King's Bench. The judgeship had been empty since Robert Thorpe*'s removal in 1807.

In Upper Canada Lieutenant Governor Francis Gore* was eager to fill the vacancy. He urged the Colonial Office in October 1810 either to send out a judge from England or to permit him to make a provisional appointment. By May 1811 Campbell had been informed that the position was his. Immediately Campbell pressed under-secretary Robert Peel for a document making it official, adding, "I trust . . . you will please to pardon any Seeming impatience in me when I inform you that I have been upwards of two years from my family and business, at a very heavy expence." Campbell received his official appointment on 31 July and arrived at York (Toronto) in November. "His intelligence and authority," President Isaac Brock* reported, "promise every thing that can be desired." The following March Campbell petitioned the Executive Council for land; he was granted a town lot in York and 1,200 acres.

Campbell joined on the bench Chief Justice Thomas SCOTT, a worn soul eager for retirement, and Mr Justice William Dummer POWELL, an able, experienced judge and skilled, ambitious courtier. He seems to have had little desire to win political distinction in

Upper Canada, and as a result his career there was blessedly free of the vexation and rancour that had accompanied it in Cape Breton. His was a judicial life with its own particular seasons. Four times a year the Court of King's Bench sat *en banc* at York to decide on appeal issues of law. The terms had been set by statute in 1797 and amended periodically. The court also heard and decided upon motions. Until 1826 it was accommodated in a "mean and ruinous . . . wooden Cottage" which Campbell said was "in such a state of irreparable decay and dilapidation, as to be unfit for human residence."

More taxing for the judges were the assizes held once a year in each administrative district. These assizes were combined and arranged into an eastern and western circuit. Held in the district capital, each of the assizes was presided over by a supreme court justice. Civil cases were argued before the judge alone, whereas in criminal cases he was accompanied on the bench by associate judges chosen from the local magistracy. With the establishment of new districts (three were erected between 1816 and 1821, making a total of 11), there was a corresponding increase in travel and judicial workload. Aside from the Home District assizes, which were usually held in April, the other districts were visited by the judges between the spring and fall. The judges split the duties of the assizes, often taking turns on the eastern and western circuits. In 1825 Campbell opened the western circuit in Sandwich (Windsor) on 1 August and finished at Niagara (Niagara-on-the-Lake) on 16 September.

Campbell found the criminal calendar more onerous although not usually as full as the civil one. For one thing, the decisions of the criminal court had a more direct bearing upon individual lives. For another, until 1835 there was no statutory provision for defence counsel (except in cases of treason), and the interlocutory role was fulfilled by the judge. In sentencing, the judge's discretion was usually circumscribed by statute, in which case it was necessary for him to advise the lieutenant governor if there was any legal cause for gubernatorial intervention and pardon. For all cases of capital conviction the presiding judge was expected – Lieutenant Governor Sir Peregrine Maitland* was particularly adamant on this point – to advise the lieutenant governor's secretary on the circumstances of the case. In these instances the judge's counsel was crucial but, more often than not, Campbell was loath to suggest extenuating legal circumstances. During his career on the bench from 1812 to his last assizes in 1827 Campbell presided over 382 criminal cases. His criminal calendar from 1812 to 1819 (excluding the special assizes at Ancaster in 1814) averaged 17.4 cases, whereas from 1820 to 1827 the average increased to 32.5. Most cases involved larceny (of varying degrees) and assault. Sentences normally combined imprisonment, fines,

and corporal punishment (whipping and the pillory). Fewer than 10 per cent of Campbell's criminal cases resulted in capital convictions; most of these prisoners received full or conditional pardons.

In Upper Canada, Campbell was noticed and appreciated from an early date. In April 1814 President Gordon Drummond*, the performance of his Executive Council hobbled by the deaths of Prideaux Selby* and Alexander Grant*, recommended to Colonial Secretary Lord Bathurst that additions be made to both the Legislative and the Executive councils. Anxious for two or three appointments, he lamented that the only "properly qualified" candidate was Campbell. Drummond nominated him for seats on both councils, believing that he would be "no small acquisition of Talent and information to these Boards." Nothing, however, came of the suggestion.

Campbell's first years on the bench were uneventful enough. The special assizes at Ancaster in the spring of 1814, towards the close of the war with the United States, was a judicial highlight in the colony's history, but Campbell's role was undistinguished. Six men appeared before him; five were convicted and one acquitted. Of the former, three were executed and two were pardoned. The purpose of the great show-trial was to overawe disaffection [*see* Jacob Overholser*]. To this end, the crucial decision was whom to execute and whom to pardon. The pre-eminent figure in this process was the acting attorney general, John Beverley Robinson*. Campbell was circumspect in suggesting grounds for clemency, although it is worth noting that both men he cited as possibilities for royal mercy received it.

Occasionally Campbell was baffled by popular reaction to convictions and the role it could play in determining a criminal's ultimate fate. In the case of Edward McSwiney*, tried before Campbell at Brockville in 1813 and convicted of murder, there was, he concluded, no legal cause for pardon. But McSwiney was a calculating, articulate fellow whose compelling apologia and declarations of pristine loyalty won him the support of local worthies and President Drummond. The eventual result was McSwiney's pardon. A second instance occurred at Niagara in September 1817 during the trial of Angelique Pilotte* for infanticide. Although she was convicted before Campbell on what he considered "clear and sufficient evidence," he none the less respited her execution because of overwhelming popular support for mercy. In the end, imperial authorities pardoned her conditionally but not before she had escaped.

Between 1818 and 1828 the administration of justice operated increasingly under the cloud of charges of partiality. A series of incidents from the trials of Robert Gourlay* in 1818 and 1819 to the dismissal of Mr Justice John Walpole Willis* in 1828 convinced many opponents of the administration that

Campbell

justice was not blind but cock-eyed. Perhaps more by luck than connivance Campbell drew assizes with non-contentious cases. He escaped Gourlay's censure because of his handling of the two acquittals in 1818; Gourlay had defended himself, and one observer, Miles MACDONELL, commented that "Judge Campbell gave him every latitude." Seven years later the jury's acquittal of Robert RANDAL on a charge of perjury saved Campbell from the public displeasure – in some quarters at least – that would have accompanied a sentence. Still, Campbell's summation in this case has been considered unfriendly to Randal, and Randal himself had in 1820 claimed that Campbell was implicated in the judicial conspiracy to deprive him of his rights. Yet it would seem that the tar did not stick. Indeed, Campbell's handling of William Lyon Mackenzie*'s suit for damages against the young toughs who had destroyed his types and press – the so-called type riot of 8 June 1826 – earned him a measure of approval from the Maitland administration's most vituperative critic.

On the bench, Campbell displayed a deep concern for constitutionality. In this respect he was not exceptional among his brother judges, but he certainly gave less cause for anyone to doubt his sentiments. The British constitution had acquired, he thought, "a state of perfection unrivalled in the annals of the world." Absolute monarchies depended on the "mere will" of an individual; republics, "on the wild caprice of a Mob." But the British constitution had been "tried by the only infallible test . . . that of the experience of mankind from the earliest ages of the world." Habeas corpus and trial by jury ("the Bulwark of British liberty") were its principal supports. Grand juries held a particular place in his affection as "the most Constitutional and effectual means of protection against the efforts of public oppression or private malice." Their "inquisitorial capacity" – a power progressively circumscribed in the latter half of the century – was indispensable to protecting the constitution. The "upright and impartial discharge" of justice under that constitution was "the greatest benefit that can be conferred on society."

Campbell was not without his prejudices. In an 1826 note to Major George Hillier*, Maitland's secretary, on the efficacy of banishing rather than executing two black men convicted of stealing sheep, Campbell stated his opinion that "Nine tenths of the Blacks in this place [York], and I believe in all other parts of the Province Subsist principally by theft." An observation the same year at Kingston that "men as lords of the creation have a right to inflict a little gentle castigation on our rebellious dames" occasioned both public notice in the press and private twittering among Kingston's female gentlefolk. Yet, if the latter remark was conventional, his views on rape were not. The crime was "under any circumstances . . . of an abhorrent nature." What concerned him was the tendency to call the character of the victim into disrepute during trials, "for the most common Prostitute is as much under the protection of the law, as the most virtuous woman, – and the violation of her person by force and against her will, is as much a crime." Campbell lamented a situation in which "instead of trying the criminal fact, our time and attention would be occupied to little purpose in ascertaining the exact degree of female chastity."

It was customary in Upper Canada for the superior court judges to apprise the executive of what had transpired on circuit; Campbell was punctilious in this regard. He took pains, for instance, to inform Hillier of anything that even hinted of contention during the assizes. In 1817 he hesitated forwarding a presentment from a grand jury to the lieutenant governor because it was "somewhat exceptionable both in matter and expression." However, lest he be blamed for withholding information of a public nature, he submitted the offending material for Hillier's judgement. His correspondence was almost exclusively routed through Hillier and its tone was scrupulously formal and correct. On one occasion in 1825, having already written more often than was usual and without receiving any replies from Hillier, Campbell began "to doubt the propriety of continuing to trouble you in this sort of demi official style."

Only rarely was the subject at hand other than formal reports of what had transpired on the circuits or the official business of the court. One instance concerned Campbell's memorial of 1817 on the insufficient salaries of puisne justices. He deemed £750 (sterling) "very inadequate to the rank and important duties and to that pecuniary independence so essential to the faithful and impartial discharge of those duties." The sum was payable in England and thus subject to income tax, agency fees, and other incidental charges as well as "a most enormous discount on Bills of Exchange, amounting sometimes to 25 p.Cent – making in the whole a loss of considerably more than a third part of their income." On the other hand, he argued, judges in Lower Canada were paid in the colony, clear of "all expenses, taxes, discounts, or other loss of deductions whatsoever." Moreover, in 1817 the lower province had two chief justices and seven puisne justices, whereas the upper province had but one chief justice – Powell having succeeded Scott, who retired in 1816 – and Campbell (the bench was not brought back to full strength until D'Arcy BOULTON's accession in 1818). The Upper Canadian justices, Campbell complained, "have to hold assizes at a greater number of Districts, and to perform Circuits of nearly double the extent . . . besides the usual Terms and Sittings." In short, he averred, the "personal fatigue privations and expences sustained" by Lower Canadian judges on circuit "bear no reasonable proportion to that which is unavoidably endured and paid by those of the Upper Province, owing to its' far greater extent, more recent settlement, and consequent less improved state in regard to roads, accommodations, and other local disadvantages." Forwarded to the Colonial Office with Gore's recommendation, Campbell's appeal was turned down by Bathurst.

More frequent in his official correspondence is discussion arising from a judge's role as intermediary between the executive and the district grand juries. Local matters concerning appointments of district officials and the state of the jail and court-house were the stuff of the grand jury recommendations. It was not unusual for Campbell to initiate inquiries as to the fitness of certain men for public appointment or more generally to cast a net for names to be added to the magistracy. In performing the latter responsibilities, Campbell exhibited his characteristic wariness, diligently probing for possible problems. "Nothing," he declared, "can be more repugnant to my sentiments than to be in any degree instrumental in recommending improper characters."

His official correspondence was mainly concerned with reports of the assizes, the number of capital convictions, the possibilities for pardon, and the nature of sentencing. There was a strained, almost apologetic, quality to Campbell's letters whenever a convict was beyond the reach of royal mercy. This letter of early 1825 is typical: "It is always matter of extreme regret to me when . . . I am unable to make such report as I know would be most gratifying to His Excellency's benevolent feelings without injury to the administration of public justice, – but in the present case it is out of my power to do so consistently with the trust and duties incident to my Situation." Usually Campbell would respite execution for a sufficient length of time to allow petitions and gubernatorial review. Often good character or respectable connections would be sufficient to mitigate punishment. In 1821, for instance, he recommended a soldier in the 68th Foot "as a fit object of mercy on account of the favorable character given of him by several witnesses." Campbell derived "much satisfaction" in this case from complying with the jury's recommendation of mercy, whereas in another case five years earlier it had been his "painful duty" to state that there were no mitigating circumstances. Where statutes allowed judicial discretion in sentencing, Campbell was usually prepared to be lenient. In these instances it was his practice to confer with the local justices chosen to sit with him on the bench for the particular assizes.

Evidence of imbecility or a simple nature was yet another reason for urging some commutation of sentence. Penitence on the part of the offender also induced Campbell to incline towards slighter punishment. He was not above a measure of judicial theatrics

to induce repentance where none was apparent. In 1825, at Vittoria, Ebenezer Allan was convicted of two separate capital offences, but even after the verdicts had been delivered "he evinced a lamentable degree of audacious turpitude and impenitence, ill suited to his Situation." Campbell, "in compassion for his immortal fate," scheduled the execution to follow a "short period" after the sentencing – a strategy which had "the desired effect on him, and indeed on all present." Afterwards, the sheriff reported that Allan "employs much time in prayer an act of devotion which I am told and verily believe he never before had recourse to."

Juries had a tendency to acquit – as Campbell said, "some justly so, – others perhaps by mistake, – but many more I regret to say from less justifiable causes not unfrequent in all small Communities." Campbell's concern, however, was the possible conviction of the innocent rather than the acquittal of the guilty. In the 1825 cases of King Hans Hawe and Elizabeth Maxwell, convicted of murdering the child of their illegitimate daughter, Campbell had urged "the Jury to lean strongly to a Verdict of Acquittal – but the Jury thought otherwise and it being their exclusive province to judge of the fact," he passed sentence. Yet he availed himself of his discretionary power under the particular statute, respited sentence, consulted his fellow judges, and pressed for royal mercy, which was ultimately granted.

Campbell was advancing in age when he took up his duties in Upper Canada. The fluctuating composition of the King's Bench often added to a burden which his health was increasingly unable to tolerate. Powell's leave of absence in 1822 increased Campbell's responsibilities as senior judge and divided an already onerous work-load between two judges. Under the strain Campbell's health faltered. On 23 March 1823 he conveyed to Maitland "my apprehensions that the increasing infirmities of age and ill health will ere long deprive me of the power of fulfilling the important duties of my situation." For the past two years he had been "afflicted with occasional attacks of fever and temporary suspension of the mental faculties to a certain extent." The condition, although "alarming," had been brought under control. The following year, after particularly gruelling assizes and the prospect of equally wearisome ones yet to come, Campbell sighed that, "if he has not had the three regular warnings by being deaf, lame and blind, [he] has almost daily very broad hints to the same effect."

Age and overwork were taking their toll. The prospect, however, of the imminent retirement of an increasingly cranky and possibly senile Powell held out the possibility of Campbell's elevation to the chief justiceship. Campbell applied for the position and Maitland, anxious to be rid of Powell, warmly recommended Campbell. Bathurst concurred and on

Campbell

17 Oct. 1825 Campbell became chief justice. As was customary, he also became president of the Executive Council and speaker of the Legislative Council. The emoluments of the chief justiceship and the councillorships brought a hefty increase in salary which Mackenzie claimed was Campbell's only motivation in accepting the appointments. In doing so, the argument ran, he abandoned his "whig principles" and became the creature of Robinson and John Strachan*. His support, for instance, of Robinson's attempt during the alien issue of 1825–26 to deprive a large number of inhabitants of their "civil rights" was cited as an example of Campbell's "apostasy."

The burden of his new duties quickly proved too much. Although Levius Peters Sherwood* had replaced Campbell as puisne justice, Boulton was now failing. During the summer of 1826, reporting "his faculties irretrievably gone," Boulton was determined to suspend all duties. Forced to compensate for his incapacity, Campbell all but collapsed under the strain. At Brockville in September 1826, Christopher Alexander Hagerman* claimed, the "poor old Chief Justice did every thing in his power to go through all the suits, but his health was not equal to the undertaking. . . . he was taken so ill while on the Bench, that he was obliged to leave it, and I really thought he would have expired when he got into one of the Jury rooms, he was seized with a sort of fit, which resembled Cholera Morbus."

Only an extraordinary effort by Campbell and Sherwood (also suffering illness) prevented the administration of justice from grinding to a halt in 1827. Campbell's first inclination was to press for two additional puisne judges in addition to a replacement for Boulton. His personal choice for a judgeship was James Buchanan Macaulay*, whom he considered without equal in the colony "and less extensively, and perhaps less exceptionably connected than some others, a matter of important consideration in selecting a Colonial Judge." After him he thought Jonas Jones* and Hagerman worthy. Campbell took his last assizes in 1827, sailing for England to recover his health the following year. His absence from the bench, by giving Willis the occasion to deny the constitutionality of the court in the absence of the chief justice, precipitated a major crisis. Campbell, however, was beyond the fray. His health did not recover sufficiently to enable him to resume his duties, and in 1829 he retired on a pension of £1,200. He was knighted on 29 April of the same year.

Historians have paid little attention to Campbell. His career in Nova Scotia practically never progressed beyond the boundaries of his county. Although more is known of his activities in Cape Breton, his role there has not been studied in any detail. His long career as a judge in Upper Canada has received only incidental mention. Thus conclusions appropriate to the whole of his career are difficult. Two tentative suggestions are, however, possible. On the one hand, there is, at least until 1825, an attachment to the "whig principles" mentioned by Mackenzie. Campbell's early support for Tonge and Gibbons may be of a piece with his legal constitutionalism. On the other hand, there is his persistent concern with the precariousness of his finances. The desire for an increased salary, as Mackenzie suspected, may have been the object which weighed most heavily in his decision first to seek and then to accept the chief justiceship in spite of illness and advanced age.

In Upper Canada his career was almost exclusively judicial, and his historical stature suffers by comparison with his predecessor as chief justice, Powell, and his successor, Robinson. Not the saccharine saint portrayed by David Breakenridge Read*, Campbell is equally undeserving of William Renwick Riddell*'s barbed comment: "Campbell was not a strong judge; he seldom pressed for a conviction, but when a conviction had been secured, he was generally ruthless and seldom recommended commutation." He did make one significant contribution to Canadian legal history, in 1822 at the trial in Sandwich of SHAWANAKISKIE. His questioning of an Indian's supposed immunity from prosecution for crimes committed by one Indian against another was upheld by imperial authorities. As a result, although the prisoner had escaped, the legality of his conviction had been confirmed and Indians were brought fully within the compass of the criminal law.

R. J. MORGAN and ROBERT LOCHIEL FRASER

[The main source of information about Campbell's Cape Breton career is PRO, CO 217/117–28. Other useful material can be found in PANS, MG 4, 109; RG 34-311, P, 1; N.S., House of Assembly, *Journal and proc.*, 1801–5; and R. J. Morgan's thesis, "Orphan outpost." R.J.M.

Campbell's gracious mansion in York is one of the few landmarks of that bygone era to have withstood the onslaught of progress. Purchased by the Sir William Campbell Foundation, it was moved in 1972 to a fitting site across the street from Osgoode Hall. It stands today, an 18th-century oasis in a 20th-century desert.

References to Campbell's career in Upper Canada are scattered through the numerous private manuscript collections and government record groups relating to the province. The most useful for this study have been AO, RG 22, ser.125, ser.133, and ser.134; and the Robinson papers in MS 4; PAC, RG 5, A1; RG 7; and PRO, CO 42. Among printed sources, William Renwick Riddell's review of decisions on the legal status of Indians in *Sero* v. *Gault* (1921), 50 O.L.R. 27, is valuable. The following newspapers were consulted: *Upper Canada Gazette*, 1821–27; *U.E. Loyalist* (York [Toronto]), 1826–28; *Kingston Chronicle*, 1819–33; *Chronicle & Gazette*, 1833–34; *Colonial Advocate*, 1824–33; *Advocate* (York; Toronto), 1833–34; and *Canadian Freeman*, 1825–34. Secondary sources are not especially helpful. Read's *Lives of the judges* is a bloodless, uneven account. W. R. Riddell's article "The Ancaster 'Bloody Assize' of 1814," *OH*, 20 (1923): 107–25, although focused on only a single event, contains an acid-etched depiction of Campbell. R.L.F.]

CANNON, JOHN, master mason, architect, businessman, militia officer, and politician; b. *c.* 1783 in St John's, fourth son of Edward Cannon*, master mason, and Helena Murphy; d. 19 Feb. 1833 at Quebec.

John Cannon's parents were Irish Catholics who had immigrated to Newfoundland by 1774; his father worked thereafter as a master mason on the fortifications and government buildings in St John's. During the war between Great Britain and France that broke out in 1793 the youthful John was a volunteer alongside his father.

In 1795 Edward established his family at Quebec, where he launched himself once more in the building trade, securing several major masonry contracts, including the Anglican Cathedral of the Holy Trinity (1799–1804), the Union Hotel (1805), and an addition to the parish church at Baie-Saint-Paul (1804–5). Edward engaged three sons, Ambrose (until his death in 1804), Laurence, and John (from 1800), as paid apprentices. In 1808 he formed the partnership of Edward Cannon and Sons with John and Laurence. This move was perhaps prompted by the securing that year of an important government contract for the masonry work on a new prison to be built on Rue Saint-Stanislas (1808–14) under the supervision of architect François BAILLAIRGÉ. By 1809 John had become the effective head of the firm as his father, who was about 70, gradually withdrew from business. Under John, in 1810 the company built a house for Nicolas-François MAILHOT (who a year later fitted it up for a hotel) and in 1813 another for the carpenter and joiner Charles Marié. Beginning in 1814 the Cannons undertook full-scale speculation with a purchase of vacant lands on Rue Saint-Louis, where they intended to erect two large houses for resale. One house was under construction when the family partnership dissolved after the deaths of Edward in 1814 and of Laurence the following year.

John carried on alone as a master mason, rapidly expanding his practice to become a contractor of masonry works. Indeed by 1825 he was calling himself an "architect and builder," although there is no indication that he had undergone any professional training. He participated in a number of major projects both for clients and on his own behalf. These included a building at the Hôpital Général from designs by his friend Baillairgé (1818), all the plaster-work for the interior of Notre-Dame cathedral, again with Baillairgé (1820–21), houses for rental on property he owned on Rue Saint-Denis (1822–23; 1831) and

masonry work for St Patrick's Church, designed by architect Thomas Baillairgé* (1831–32).

Cannon's practice was not an easy one, for he was frequently challenged in and out of court on the quality of his workmanship and on money matters. The plaster-work in Notre-Dame was discoloured; a house built for rental was in such an unfinished state that the tenant, Joseph Bouchette*, surveyor general of Lower Canada, took Cannon to arbitration; and plasterers and fellow Irishmen James Sharp (who had apprenticed with Cannon) and Michael Quigley successfully sued him for unpaid work at the Albion Hotel and his houses on Saint-Denis.

Cannon's persistent financial difficulties stemmed in part from the burden imposed upon him by the will of his mother, who had died in 1821, in part from the failure of clients such as Philippe-Joseph Aubert* de Gaspé to pay for their houses, but chiefly from his own property speculations. Most notable was the case of the Albion Hotel. In 1824 he purchased at sheriff's sale a property on Rue du Palais, paying the hefty sum of £3,000, which he raised through loans and mortgages. After fitting up the house and two wings as a hotel, he rented it to innkeeper Thomas Payne in December 1825. Cannon never recovered his investment.

Cannon was moderately active in the social and institutional life of Quebec. In 1813 he was an ensign in Quebec's 3rd Militia Battalion, and he rose to the rank of lieutenant by 1824. A contributor to the Quebec Fire Society since at least 1809, he was elected its president for the year 1818. From 1822 he was frequently weekly director of the Quebec Savings Bank. He was considered an expert in agriculture and was occasionally called upon to attend competitions held by the Agriculture Society, of which he was a committee member in 1823.

A personal friend of the Irish-born lieutenant governor of Lower Canada, Sir Francis Nathaniel BURTON, Cannon apparently became interested in politics in the early 1820s and seems to have acquired some popularity by openly opposing a project, begun in 1822, for the union of Upper and Lower Canada. In 1824 he was elected to the House of Assembly of Lower Canada for the constituency of Hampshire, a largely Canadian county. According to the newspaper *Le Canadien*, Cannon's principal base of support was "in the parish of Pointe aux Trembles [Neuville], where there is a very considerable stone trade," and where the notary and seigneurial agent François-Xavier Larue* campaigned on his behalf. His election was contested on the grounds that he had bribed some voters, threatened others with suits for debts, and opened "Houses of Public Entertainment." On St Patrick's Day 1826, in a sitting that lasted from early afternoon until 2:00 A.M., the assembly concluded that the Irishman had indeed furnished liquor to voters. His election was voided and he was expelled from the assembly. According to Louis-Joseph Papineau*, "although his expenditures were petty in comparison with the wrong committed in other elections, the House has given a just example of severity by nipping the evil in the bud." Larue ran in Cannon's place in a by-election held in March and April and was elected. Cannon himself was again returned for Hampshire in the elections of 1827; he sat until September 1830. In the assembly he proved to be an independent, while leaning towards the Canadian party. In December 1831 he was appointed by Lord Aylmer [Whitworth-Aylmer*] a trustee for the erection of the Marine Hospital at Quebec, and in February 1832 he twice acted as a property valuation expert commissioned by government.

Cannon played an important role in the social and religious organization of the Irish Catholics at Quebec. In 1817 he signed a petition to the bishop of Quebec, Joseph-Octave PLESSIS, requesting an English-language priest for the city, and seven years later he provided Simon Lawlor with the sacerdotal title, or financial guarantee against indebtedness, required of ecclesiastics before they could receive ordination. By October 1827 he was vice-president of a committee formed to ask Plessis's successor, Bernard-Claude PANET, for permission to build a church for English-speaking Catholics at Quebec. He was among five delegates who carried out arduous negotiations on the subject with the *fabrique* of Notre-Dame cathedral and was probably instrumental in having the Reverend Patrick McMahon* brought back to Quebec in 1828 to minister for the most part to the Irish Catholics. By 1831 Cannon had become president of the building committee. However, it was not until 7 July 1833, some five months after his death, that the first mass was celebrated in the new St Patrick's Church. In 1829 he had been elected president of a newly formed branch of the Society of the Friends of Ireland in Quebec, and in 1832 he was vice-president of the Quebec Mechanic's Institute, founded in 1830 to improve the skills of labourers and tradesmen, particularly English-speaking, most of whom were Irish.

On 9 Feb. 1808 Cannon had married Angèle Grihaut, *dit* Larivière, daughter of a Quebec tinsmith; they had four sons and one daughter. After Angèle's death, on 13 Feb. 1827 Cannon married Archange Baby, widow of Ralph Ross Lewen, town major of Quebec; no children from this marriage survived infancy. Cannon maintained a comfortable residence in Upper Town, first on Rue Buade and later on Rue Sainte-Geneviève. His interests were varied if his library of more than 280 volumes is any guide; it included architectural pattern books as well as histories, biographies, travel books, dictionaries, religious treatises, and poetry. His children were well educated; his daughter attended the Ursulines' school and three sons joined the professional class as a notary, a lawyer, and a priest.

Cannon died on 19 Feb. 1833 and was buried three days later in Sainte-Anne's chapel, Notre-Dame cathedral; those who signed his burial act (there were nearly as many Canadians as British) included Provincial Secretary Dominick Daly*, publisher and politician John Neilson*, educator Joseph-François Perrault*, judge Edward Bowen*, and lawyer William King McCord*. Although at his death Cannon held title to nine urban and five rural properties (including township lands in Lower Canada that his father had acquired at the turn of the century), he died a bankrupt, owing some £12,000 to a long list of creditors, of whom the most important were the executive councillor John Hale*, to whom he owed £1,400, the estates of François Baby* and Pierre de Sales* Laterrière, the Montreal Bank, and the Quebec Bank. More than £4,000 was known to be owed to Cannon, £1,500 by Aubert de Gaspé, and "Considerable Sums as arrears of Constituted Rents [life annuities]" were also thought due to his estate. However his heirs, finding the situation hopeless, signed the succession over to the creditors as being "more onerous than profitable."

CHRISTINA CAMERON

ANQ-Q, CE1-1, 9 févr. 1808, 13 févr. 1827, 22 févr. 1832; CN1-16, 29 avril 1814, 10 déc. 1820, 12 févr. 1827; CN1-26, 6 févr. 1808; CN1-188, 26 févr. 1833, 28 mai 1834, 22 sept. 1843; CN1-197, 1er févr. 1825; CN1-212, 6 mai 1823; CN1-230, 28 déc. 1804, 1er févr. 1825; CN1-253, 30 déc. 1820; 28 oct., 10 nov. 1823; 30 déc. 1825; 5 sept. 1832; CN1-285, 15 févr., 11 mai 1802; 3 août 1809; 2 déc. 1815. MAC-CD, Yves Laliberté et Luc Noppen, "L'Église Saint-Patrice de Québec." PAC, RG 1, L3L: 756, 2115, 30626–27, 61669. L.C., House of Assembly, *Journaux*, 1825: 25–27. L.-J. Papineau, "Correspondance de Louis-Joseph Papineau (1820–1839)," Fernand Ouellet, édit., ANQ *Rapport*, 1953–55: 223–24, 243–44. *Le Canadien*, 25 août 1824. *Quebec Gazette*, 14 Sept. 1809; 22 Feb. 1810; 19 March 1812; 19 Oct. 1815; 13 March 1817; 6 April 1818; 22 April, 25 Nov. 1819; 6 Jan., 5 June, 7 Sept. 1820; 15 March, 9 Aug. 1821; 5 Aug., 4 Nov. 1822; 27 Jan., 21 April, 19, 26 May, 28 July, 1 Sept., 13 Nov., 1 Dec. 1823; 8 Jan., 1 March, 29 April 1824; 30 March 1826; 29 Aug. 1831. *Quebec Mercury*, 16 April 1816.

F.-J. Audet, "Les législateurs du Bas-Canada." Geneviève G. Bastien *et al.*, *Inventaire des marchés de construction des archives civiles de Québec, 1800–1870* (3v., Ottawa, 1975), 1, nos.222, 554, 659, 1749; 2, nos.2198, 2577, 3369; 3, nos.3787, 4093. Desjardins, *Guide parl.*, 129. *Recensement de Québec, 1818* (Provost). *Quebec almanac*, 1814–27. Marianna O'Gallagher, *Saint-Patrice de Québec: la construction d'une église et l'implantation d'une paroisse*, Guy Doré, trad. (Québec, 1979), 10, 41–43, 48, 57, 60, 62, 70, 74, 81, 84–85. Robert Cannon, "Edward Cannon, 1739–1814," CCHA *Report*, 3 (1935–36): 11–22.

A. J. H. Richardson, "Guide to the architecturally and historically most significant buildings in the old city of Quebec with a biographical dictionary of architects and builders and illustrations," Assoc. for Preservation Technology, *Bull.* (Ottawa), 2 (1970), nos.3–4. F. C. Würtele, "The English cathedral of Quebec," Literary and Hist. Soc. of Quebec, *Trans.* (Quebec), new ser., 20 (1891): 63–132.

CANNON, MARY (Polly), estate manager; b. some time after 1751; d. 7 Oct. 1827 at her residence, Castle Frederick, in Falmouth, N.S.

Available evidence indicates that Mary Cannon came from one of the obscure Cannon families resident in Halifax during the 1750s. In 1764 she met Joseph Frederick Wallet DESBARRES, an army officer who was then just beginning an ambitious survey of the coast of Nova Scotia. By "great attention and . . . great persuasion" DesBarres induced Mary to become his housekeeper at Castle Frederick. Between 1764 and 1774 he "treated her . . . with great Affection and Tenderness and always placed the most unbounded Confidence" in her judgement. He also instructed Mary in the management of his extensive Nova Scotian properties, promising that they would ultimately become hers. In 1774 DesBarres returned to England, where he remained until his appointment in 1784 as lieutenant governor of Cape Breton. Mary continued to live in Falmouth, and she saw DesBarres perhaps twice more before his death in 1824. Five daughters and a son were born of their relationship.

In 1776 DesBarres appointed Mary his agent and attorney, with "full Power and Authority" over all his colonial properties, comprising nearly 80,000 acres in Falmouth, Tatamagouche, Minudie, Maccan-Nappan, and the Memramcook–Petitcodiac area of present-day New Brunswick. The legal document was vague, but his personal instructions to her were explicit and benevolent. Mary was to visit each estate regularly, noting the progress of settlement, the number of livestock, and the extent of agricultural improvements; she was also to arrange tenants' leases, collect rents, and forward all details to DesBarres. At first the arrangement worked well. In addition to her other duties, Mary paid many of DesBarres's bills, shipped commodities to him during the period 1784–87 when he was lieutenant governor of Cape Breton, and, with the assistance of Richard John UNIACKE (1753–1830), fought his land-hungry creditors in the courts. Her requests for reimbursement were fair and few.

After DesBarres left Cape Breton for England in 1787, he became increasingly eccentric concerning his colonial properties. He rarely answered letters, failed to forward necessary legal papers, and provided little instruction or advice. Meanwhile, pressure from his creditors forced the attachment of various estates, the value of which declined as crops failed and tenants ignored leases and rents. In 1794 DesBarres appointed John MacDonald* of Glenaladale to investigate the condition of the estates. MacDonald reported that, although the tenants respected "Mrs. Cannon," her management was lax; he cited in particular her leasing arrangements and the loss of livestock to creditors. He also noted that Mary, claiming to have been cast off by DesBarres, was openly involved with an Irish labourer. Fearing that she would sue DesBarres out of spite, MacDonald urged an immediate legal settlement with Mary.

Most of the responsibility for DesBarres's properties was subsequently shifted to sub-agents, one of whom was Amelia DesBarres, a daughter by Mary. In 1809 – four years after his return to British North America as lieutenant governor of Prince Edward Island – DesBarres sued Mary and sub-agent Wellwood WAUGH in Nova Scotia's Court of Chancery, charging general mismanagement and collusion over a lease at Tatamagouche. DesBarres claimed that because of her repeated failure to advise him of leases he had lost his most valuable tracts of land to tenants who paid little or nothing. The legal difficulty lay in whether Mary's power of attorney even permitted her to make leases. The court never reached a decision.

DesBarres showed peculiar logic and lack of foresight in granting Mary control over his properties in an age when women were ill educated for such duties. His perversity in failing to assist her and his later rancour against her merely add to the enigma of a distasteful personality. For her part, Mary was faced with a difficult task for a colonial woman and, as Helen MacDonald* of Glenaladale had done in similar but less demanding circumstances, she performed it with ability, determination, and loyalty. Although she reported meticulously to DesBarres at first, her actions became increasingly independent when he persisted in showing total indifference to the fate of his properties. Her partial failure resulted from the enormity of her responsibilities, the vagaries of colonial agriculture, and her tendency to be easily deceived. The ultimate survival of DesBarres's landholdings, virtually intact but financially crippled, was her great achievement.

Mary had little to show for her efforts, since DesBarres refused financial assistance to her and their children. In her last extant letter to him, written in 1806, she implored, "The thread of life is only brittle at best and neither you nor I may long be permitted to settle our long standing affairs. I have had a hard life and would wish peace on just terms for what remains." In 1819 DesBarres finally deeded the Castle Frederick estate to their four surviving children, but it had declined to a mere subsistence farm where the family resided in genteel poverty. Mary's final comment concerning the near-centenarian DesBarres in 1820 was that he was still "like Pharaoh of old, hardened to every request."

Captain John

Since her death, Mary Cannon has been remembered only as DesBarres's mistress; her extraordinary responsibilities, unusual talents, and powerful position, all marking her as a distinctly different woman for her time, have been entirely forgotten. As she once said, "I think my treatment but indifferent."

LOIS KERNAGHAN

Manuscript sources used in the preparation of this biography include the J. F. W. DesBarres papers (PAC, MG 23, F1), the Court of Chancery papers in PANS, RG 36, and the records of the courts of probate and registries of deeds for the following counties, all of which are available on microfilm at PANS: Cumberland (Amherst, N.S.), Halifax (Halifax), and Hants (Windsor, N.S.).

Acadian Recorder, 13 Oct. 1827. G. N. D. Evans, *Uncommon obdurate: the several public careers of J. F. W. DesBarres* (Toronto and Salem, Mass., 1969). J. C. Webster, *The life of Joseph Frederick Wallet Des Barres* (Shediac, N.B., 1933). Lois Kernaghan, "A man and his mistress: J. F. W. DesBarres and Mary Cannon," *Acadiensis* (Fredericton), 11 (1981–82), no.1: 23–42.

CAPTAIN JOHN. *See* OGIMAUH-BINAESSIH

CARMICHAEL, JOHN EDWARD, army officer and office holder; b. *c.* 1790, probably in Britain; m. 7 July 1814 Frederica Ubrica Charletta Catherina Smith, and they had two daughters and one son; d. 20 Nov. 1828 in Port Glasgow, Scotland.

On 13 Oct. 1808 John Edward Carmichael, whose background is totally obscure, joined the New Brunswick Fencibles (later the 104th Foot) as an ensign, and in 1810 he was promoted lieutenant. In 1813, while stationed in Charlottetown, he became private secretary to the lieutenant governor of Prince Edward Island, Charles Douglass Smith*. The next year he married one of Smith's four daughters. On 1 April 1816 he was appointed acting receiver general of quitrents, and it was probably shortly thereafter that he resigned his commission in the army. Smith, from the time of his arrival in the colony in July 1813, had insisted that quitrents ought to be collected, but owing to the absence of the receiver general, John STEWART, and the failure of the Colonial Office to issue precise instructions, no action had been taken. Early in 1818 Smith ordered Carmichael to demand payment and in six months Carmichael collected more quitrents than had been submitted in the preceding 26 years. But in May, the secretary of state for War and the Colonies, Lord Bathurst, who had received numerous protests from absentee proprietors, censured Smith for acting precipitately, before a new schedule of rates had been sent. Although Bathurst's dispatch established new rates, Carmichael did not seriously attempt to collect quitrents again until ordered to do so by Smith in 1822.

In November 1818 the House of Assembly criticized Smith for extracting quitrents illegally. On 15 December Carmichael added to his own unpopularity by attempting to enforce Smith's subsequent order to have the assembly adjourn against its wishes. According to one account, Carmichael shook his fist at the speaker, Angus MACAULAY, and declared that "if you sit in that Chair one minute longer . . . this House will be dissolved." The assembly ignored Carmichael and adjourned only when Smith himself intervened. Although Carmichael's overbearing manner won him few friends in the assembly, the next September Smith appointed him colonial secretary, registrar, and clerk of the Council upon the death of Thomas Desbrisay*. On 26 June 1822 Carmichael, following Smith's instructions, again issued a notice demanding the payment of quitrents. When it was ignored he reissued the notice in November and December, and in January and February he launched legal proceedings against two of the resident proprietors, Donald McDonald* and John Stewart, and a large number of the tenants in Kings County. In mid winter many of the latter travelled to Charlottetown where they sold their meagre possessions to pay their arrears, and Carmichael treated them with ill-disguised contempt.

Carmichael's actions set in motion a chain of events which led to Smith's recall in 1824 and his replacement by John Ready*. Charles Joseph Briscoe was appointed receiver general of quitrents by the British government and on 14 July 1824 he replaced Carmichael, whose provisional appointment had never been confirmed. Unfortunately for Carmichael, an investigation of his accounts revealed a deficit which he could not meet. Early next year the assembly, spurred on by John Stewart, who had been elected speaker of the new house, condemned Carmichael for enforcing quitrents "in an illegal, arbitrary and oppressive manner," and the attorney general, William JOHNSTON, who had recently been restored to that office after being dismissed by Smith, prosecuted Carmichael for the recovery of the fees he had earned as acting receiver general. Carmichael began to drink heavily in order, as he himself was to say, to "drown the recollection of the very . . . embarrassing dilemma into which he was plunged by the vindictive and vexatious proceedings against him." In October 1827 Ready reported that because of "constant and habitual Intoxication" Carmichael was not fit to continue in office, and in May 1828 dismissed him from his posts. Virtually destitute, Carmichael journeyed to London later that year to appeal for reinstatement or appointment to a lesser position. Although both Ready and the Colonial Office were sympathetic to his plight, he died of "brain fever" before any action could be taken. His brother-in-law, Ambrose Lane*, undertook to care for his widow and three children, who had been left unprovided for.

Carmichael was a man of limited talent who rose to high office through nepotism. He was not guilty of all the exaggerated charges laid against him and, as he legitimately claimed in his own defence, he was simply obeying Smith's orders. None the less, by the high-handed and arrogant way in which he implemented his instructions, he contributed not only to the widespread popular unrest on Prince Edward Island that Smith generated but also to his own disgrace.

PHILLIP BUCKNER

PRO, CO 226/31: 126–28; 226/32: 41, 150; 226/34: 15–23, 31–33; 226/35: 69, 255; 226/36: 237–38; 226/38: 137; 226/39: 126–27, 131, 141–42; 226/40: 113–14; 226/41: 93–94, 121–23, 421–54; 226/42: 194–95, 363–64; 226/43: 195–203; 226/44: 105–7; 226/45: 159–60, 173–74, 237–38, 303–23; 226/46: 37–38; CO 227/7: 69–73. St Paul's Anglican Church (Charlottetown), Reg. of baptisms, marriages, and burials (mfm. at PAPEI). *Petitions from Prince Edward Island . . .* (London, [1824]), 7–8, 27. P.E.I., House of Assembly, *Journal*, 21 March 1825. *Prince Edward Island Register*, 27 Jan. 1829. G.B., WO, *Army list*, 1809–17. Duncan Campbell, *History of Prince Edward Island* (Charlottetown, 1875; repr. Belleville, Ont., 1972), 66. *Canada's smallest prov.* (Bolger), 86–91. Frank MacKinnon, *The government of Prince Edward Island* (Toronto, 1951). W. A. Squires, *The 104th Regiment of Foot (the New Brunswick Regiment), 1803–1817* (Fredericton, 1962), 79, 188. *Islander* (Charlottetown), 27 Oct. 1848.

CARY, THOMAS, businessman, office holder, poet, lawyer, and newspaper editor; b. 1751 near Bristol, England; by his union with an unknown woman he had at least two sons, Thomas* and Joseph; m. 20 April 1795 Jane Oliver at Quebec, and they had no children; d. there 29 Jan. 1823.

Thomas Cary apparently spent his early years in England and likely received his education there. Little is known of his career prior to his arrival in the province of Quebec, except that he had been in the service of the East India Company, where he no doubt first learned about business. His duties in the company seem to have brought him into contact with Canadians, and this acquaintance may in part account for his coming to the colony. But the full explanation of why he left England remains unknown.

Contrary to the usual claim, Cary did not arrive in the province around 1787. By 1775 he was already living at L'Assomption, in the Montreal region, and was selling spirits. In September 1779 he was offering provisions for sale in the Quebec home of merchant Mathew Lymburner, with whom he lived. However, he was soon in a precarious financial position. In the summer of 1785, obviously much in debt and pressed by his financial backers, he had to stand by while a court ordered a public trustee to seize his business and sell it at auction. He found a job, probably the same year, as a clerk in a government office at an annual salary of £40.

In March 1789 at Quebec Cary published *Abram's Plains: a poem*, written in the style of the poet James Thomson whom he greatly admired. This rhymed poem of 568 lines describes the valley of the St Lawrence, the towns along its banks, and the people who lived there. With his love of poetry went a marked interest in theatre, particularly revealed by the fact that he acted in some of the plays produced at the Patagonian Theatre. When it first opened, he recited a poem of his own that defended theatre "with a view to its being put on as respectable a footing as possible."

In 1798 Cary became secretary to Governor Robert Prescott*. In the exercise of his new duties he was prompted to write an article on the disposal of crown lands which appeared in the *Extract of the minutes of Council* for 20 Sept. 1798, printed that autumn at the shop of Roger Lelièvre and Pierre-Édouard DESBARATS. Cary had had some differences with the members of the Executive Council, and through this piece he was making light of the slanderous comments about his administrative competence made by some members in a government report. Prescott, who was himself engaged in a dispute with the Executive Council about land grants, gave his backing to Cary and this did not please the councillors.

Some time before, Cary had set up a lending library on Rue Saint-Louis which opened on 14 Sept. 1797. The following day he issued a catalogue, printed in two separate runs of 300 and 1,000 copies by John Neilson*'s shop at a cost of £5 3s. 4d. The catalogue sold at 7½d. (no copy survives), and in it he listed the authors and titles to be found in the library, as well as its lending rules. Cary bought his stock of English books directly from London. But he apparently encountered many difficulties in obtaining French works since he had to put an advertisement in the *Quebec Gazette* offering to buy them from private individuals. In the summer of 1799 he went to Paris, evidently to bring back a shipment of French books. Subscribers to his library could borrow books for 20s. annually, 12s. semi-annually, 7s. 6d. quarterly, or 3s. monthly; this type of subscription ensured the venture's success. In order to satisfy his clientele and to increase it, Cary early in January 1798 opened a reading-room on the second floor carrying European, American, and local periodicals. He also had a small bookshop adjoining the library, stocked with books, office supplies, and mathematical instruments. Because of illness Cary had to hand over his lending library to his son Thomas on 18 April 1820.

Cary had lost or given up his job with the government shortly after Prescott was recalled to England on 10 April 1799. This was probably the reason he offered his services as legal counsel, particularly to look after matters concerning landed property. It seems that he was finally authorized to practise law in 1800. That year he ran for the House of Assembly in

Case

the riding of Quebec but was not elected. He apparently remained in practice for only a short time, since in the summer of 1801 he had 150 copies of a handbill printed in English and French at Neilson's shop to announce his new auctioneering and brokerage business. His auction room, first located on Rue Saint-Louis but moved to Rue Sainte-Anne in 1815, specialized in the sale of household furnishings and books. Although his own newspaper, the *Quebec Mercury*, began publication in 1805, Cary continued to advertise his auctions in the *Quebec Gazette*, which enjoyed a wider circulation than the *Mercury*. In April 1817 Cary went into partnership with his son Joseph and three years later retired, leaving him to manage the enterprise.

In the midst of this commercial activity, Cary had founded his newspaper, a weekly which was first issued on 5 Jan. 1805 and had its offices on Rue Saint-Louis. It had eight pages printed in three columns, more than half of them devoted to advertising, and it drew items from American and English papers. Although it relied heavily on foreign news, it did not neglect the local scene. It was printed in Desbarats's shop and cost a guinea a year. The paper became a bi-weekly on 14 May 1816, but its circulation remained geographically limited, since there were only seven agencies looking after its distribution in Upper and Lower Canada. However, Cary contacted some printers and journalists outside the country who served as agents for the sale of the paper in the United States, probably on a reciprocal basis. Supported by the conservative, English-speaking Quebec bourgeoisie, who sought to ensure the political and economic domination of the British, the *Mercury* featured business matters, kept readers informed of economic developments, discussed current social issues, and regularly attacked the House of Assembly with its Canadian majority. Cary, who was the editor, displayed a relentlessly anti-French attitude towards Canadians and thereby provoked the founding of *Le Canadien*, around which debate would polarize.

To meet the cost of printing the *Mercury* Cary had to seek other sources of revenue, since he did not own a printing-shop to supplement his income. Forced to carry on another occupation, he regularly advertised his services as an auctioneer. Contrary to the claims made by historian Antonio Drolet, he was never a printer. That Cary was his son Thomas, who took over the *Quebec Mercury* at his father's request in July 1819.

Decried by some historians, not so much for the stands he took in the *Mercury* as for his exaggerated anti-French attitude, extravagantly praised by some of his biographers, particularly for the breadth of his knowledge and his erudition, Thomas Cary remains a brilliant polemicist who defended his principles to the end. Though his name is remembered because of the extreme positions he adopted, it is his career in the book trade that stands out in his life.

DANIEL GAUVIN

Thomas Cary is the author of *Abram's Plains: a poem* (Quebec, 1789) and "A true extract . . . ," *Extract of the minutes of Council, of the 20th September, 1798; on the waste lands of the crown, being a continuation, of the extract, of the 11th of June last* (Quebec, 1798).

ANQ-Q, CE1-61, 20 avril 1795; CN1-25, 4 févr. 1783; CN1-178, 2 mars 1815; CN1-253, 20 févr. 1812, 7 juin 1817, 27 juill. 1824, 27 août 1829; CN1-256, 2 mai 1791. PAC, MG 24, B1, 64, 84, 143–44, 147. *Quebec Gazette*, 30 Sept. 1779–31 Jan. 1823. *Quebec Mercury*, 5 Jan. 1805–31 Jan. 1823. Beaulieu et Hamelin, *La presse québécoise*, vol.1. Hare et Wallot, *Les imprimés dans le Bas-Canada*. H. J. Morgan, *Bibliotheca Canadensis*; *Sketches of celebrated Canadians*, 156–57. "Papiers d'État – Bas-Canada," PAC *Rapport*, 1891: 171, 177–79. *Quebec directory*, 1822. P.-G. Roy, *Les avocats de la région de Québec*, 77. Tremaine, *Biblio. of Canadian imprints*, 271–72, 533–34. Wallace, *Macmillan dict.* Antonio Drolet, *Les bibliothèques canadiennes, 1604–1960* (Ottawa, 1965). Gilles Gallichan, "Bibliothèques et culture au Canada après la Conquête (1760–1800)" (mémoire de MA, univ. de Montréal, 1975). Réjean Lemoine, "Le marché du livre à Québec, 1764–1839" (thèse de MA, univ. Laval, Québec, 1981). *Literary history of Canada: Canadian literature in English*, ed. C. F. Klinck et al. (2nd ed., 3v., Toronto and Buffalo, N.Y., 1976). Horace Têtu, *Historique des journaux de Québec* (2e éd., Québec, 1889). Wallot, *Un Québec qui bougeait*. "La circulating library ou bibliothèque circulante de Cary," *BRH*, 42 (1936): 490. "Le théâtre Patagon à Québec," *BRH*, 42: 300–3.

CASE, HESTER ANN. *See* HUBBARD

CASGRAIN, PIERRE, businessman, JP, seigneur, and militia officer; b. 16 June 1771 at Quebec, son of Jean Casgrain and Marguerite Cazeau; d. 17 Nov. 1828 at Quebec and was buried four days later under the seigneur's pew in the church at Rivière-Ouelle, Lower Canada.

Pierre Casgrain left his father's house when he was about 12 or 13 to work for a fur trader who was operating in the northwest. Then, after spending some years as a pedlar, he settled down at Rivière-Ouelle, where on 27 July 1790 he married Marie-Marguerite Bonnenfant, the 14-year-old daughter of a local merchant. He opened a general store there but nothing is known of the conditions and the means that permitted him to set up his business.

In 1797 Casgrain established a general store at Kamouraska, entrusting it to François Perrault. For a ten per cent commission Perrault undertook to sell the goods that Casgrain would supply. On 12 Feb. 1798 Casgrain paid Quebec merchant James McCALLUM £200 for a huge house near the church in Rivière-Ouelle. Two days later he signed a partnership agreement with James and John McCallum. Casgrain, who held two-fifths of the shares in the enterprise, agreed to open a store in his new house and build two barns, one at Rivière-Ouelle, the other at Kamouraska, each to store at least 10,000 to 15,000 *minots* of wheat. Casgrain was also interested in fisheries and in 1802 he bought one such operation in the seigneury of Saint-Denis-De La Bouteillerie. A decade later he went into partnership with Amable Dionne*, a merchant at Kamouraska. The firm of Casgrain et Dionne, which dealt in dry and wet goods, was dissolved by mutual accord in 1818.

Casgrain's commercial activity led him to give credit to some of his customers, who were mostly farmers from Rivière-Ouelle. The amounts owing on recognizance normally varied from £10 to £85, were payable on a set date, and bore the legal interest rate of six per cent. Casgrain converted part of his liquid assets into landed property. In 1812 and 1813 he bought in succession the three parts of the seigneury of Rivière-Ouelle from the brothers Pierre, OLIVIER, and Michel Perrault for £12,000 altogether. Income from seigneurial dues, as well as rent from the saw- and flour-mills, the salmon and porpoise fisheries, the ferry across the Ouelle, and the lands on the domain, ensured him a comfortable living. Indeed, Casgrain apparently lived in fine style. When relatives or friends visited him, they were treated to sumptuous banquets. He had a number of servants devoted to the culinary arts: a pastry cook, assistant cook, head cook, and butler. In 1815 he received at his table the administrator, Sir Gordon Drummond*, and the coadjutor bishop, Bernard-Claude PANET.

Casgrain in February 1817 obtained from the House of Assembly the exclusive right to operate a toll lift-bridge over the Ouelle for a 50-year period. Contractor Jean-Baptiste Bédard* had been given the job of building the bridge, which was completed in October 1816. Casgrain's monopoly, however, aroused discontent among the habitants who had to pay the toll. In 1823 some of them decided to put up a makeshift bridge over the river, but the plan fell through after Casgrain threatened to sue them for £1,000.

In 1821 Casgrain formed a partnership with his son Pierre-Thomas to go into business. He invested £1,500 in the company, and profits were to be shared equally. The company, known as Pierre et Pierre-Thomas Casgrain, ceased to exist on 14 Sept. 1826.

In the absence of documents little is known about Casgrain's social life. He signed a declaration of loyalty to the British crown in 1794. Five years later he received a commission as justice of the peace for the District of Quebec which was renewed at regular intervals. He enlisted as an adjutant in the Rivière-Ouelle battalion of militia in 1812. From 1819 he participated in the meetings of the Agriculture Society

of the Quebec district. That year he was one of the shareholders in the Bank of Quebec.

Pierre Casgrain and his wife had 13 children, 6 of whom reached adulthood. Being well provided for with a dowry of £1,000, each of the daughters made a good marriage: Marie-Sophie married notary François Letellier de Saint-Just, Luce lawyer Philippe Panet*, and Marie-Justine doctor Charles Butler Maguire. When his wife died in 1825, Casgrain liquidated his personal possessions. The sale brought in more than £675, which was divided equally among the children. Casgrain died three years later at Marie-Sophie's home. He bequeathed to each of his daughters £1,500 and the shares he held in the porpoise fisheries. His eldest son, Pierre-Thomas, inherited the seigneury of Rivière-Ouelle, a few properties, and the store. Olivier-Eugène received the part of the seigneury of L'Islet bought by his father in 1815, and Charles-Eusèbe*'s inheritance comprised some pieces of land, annuity payments, and a property at Quebec.

SERGE GAGNON

ANQ-Q, CE1-1, 16 juin 1771; CE3-1, 27 juill. 1790, 21 nov. 1828; CN1-262, 12, 14 févr. 1798; CN3-17, 10 juin 1797; CN3-30, 5 déc. 1812; 2 mai, 7 nov., 2, 8 déc. 1813; 10 sept., 18, 28 déc. 1815; 2 mai 1819; 18 juill. 1820; 9 janv., 25 avril 1821; 6 mai 1823; 7 août 1825; 14 sept. 1826; 8 mars, 6 sept. 1827; CN3-55, 25 mai 1812. PAC, RG 68, General index, 1651–1841: 335, 338, 345, 347, 359. L.C., House of Assembly, *Journals*, 1814–17. *Quebec Gazette*, 24 July 1794; 8 April, 2, 9, 16 Aug., 18 Oct. 1819; 9 Aug. 1821. P.-G. Roy, *Fils de Québec*, 2: 155–56. P.-B. Casgrain, *Mémorial des familles Casgrain, Baby et Perrault du Canada* (Québec, 1898). P.-H. Hudon, *Rivière-Ouelle de la Bouteillerie; 3 siècles de vie* (Ottawa, 1972).

CAVANAGH. *See* KAVANAGH

CHABOILLEZ, AUGUSTIN, Roman Catholic priest and author; b. 1 Dec. 1773 in Montreal, the youngest of the six children of Louis-Joseph Chaboillez, a merchant-voyageur, and Angélique Baby-Chenneville; d. 28 Aug. 1834 in Longueuil, Lower Canada.

Augustin Chaboillez studied at the Collège Saint-Raphaël in Montreal from 1782 to 1788, and then taught in that institution until he was ordained on 4 Dec. 1796. The following year, on 8 September, Bishop Pierre Denaut* of Quebec chose him as his secretary and appointed him curate of the parish of Saint-Antoine at Longueuil. Chaboillez served in these capacities until 28 Oct. 1799, when he was replaced by Jean-Jacques Lartigue* and appointed parish priest of Sault-au-Récollet (Montreal North).

On 10 Feb. 1806 the new bishop of Quebec, Joseph-Octave PLESSIS, put Chaboillez in charge of the parish of Saint-Antoine. Although he was a

Chaboillez

conscientious administrator, Chaboillez had difficulties with parishioners on several occasions. In March 1810 one of them interrupted his sermon just as he was broaching the delicate question of apportioning the costs for rebuilding the parish church. Chaboillez was unimpressed and had the disturber put in jail. Twenty years later he did not hesitate to take a parishioner to court for refusing to pay the tithe.

On 4 July 1822 Chaboillez and three other priests – François-Joseph Deguise, Thomas Maguire*, and Antoine Bédard – formed an association to further the education and increase the numbers of the clergy. That summer he and parish priest François Pigeon* campaigned against the installation of Bishop Lartigue as auxiliary bishop in Montreal. Chaboillez considered Lartigue's appointment prejudicial to the Séminaire de Saint-Sulpice and its superior, Jean-Henry-Auguste ROUX, since the Sulpicians enjoyed full authority in spiritual affairs in the Montreal district. He further complained that Bishop Plessis had failed to respect the right of those most concerned in the matter to be consulted. On 18 Aug. 1823 Chaboillez published a pamphlet in Montreal entitled *Questions sur le gouvernement ecclésiastique du district de Montréal*; he had already taken the precaution of submitting it to lawyers Joseph Bédard, Benjamin Beaubien, and Michael O'Sullivan* to be sure it was consonant with civil and canon law.

The pamphlet, which was steeped in gallicanism, raised five questions in connection with the pastoral letter of 20 Feb. 1821 which had officially placed Bishop Lartigue in charge of the District of Montreal. Was Montreal legally and canonically an episcopal district? Was the bishop of Telmesse – Lartigue – the diocesan bishop of that district, or could he be? Was he entitled to claim the honours due the diocesan bishop? Would his powers continue after Bishop Plessis's death? Were the priests in the District of Montreal obliged to consider him their immediate superior? The pamphlet answered the first four questions in the negative and hedged on the fifth.

The reaction to Chaboillez's pamphlet was immediate: it provoked lively controversy among both priests and laity. Early in September the coadjutor, Bernard-Claude PANET, wrote to Plessis, "Mr. Chaboillez's publication is getting unprecedented circulation and is going to do immense harm. An effort is being made to refute it, and a remedy is urgently needed because the harm is considerable." Thus in October 1823, under the pseudonym P.-H. Bédard, Bishop Lartigue replied with his *Lettre à Mr. Chaboillez, curé de Longueuil*. At about the same time *Observations sur un écrit intitulé "Questions sur le gouvernement ecclésiastique du district de Montréal"*, which took Chaboillez to task for his gallicanism and liberalism, was brought out [*see* Louis-Marie Cadieux*]. For his part parish priest Charles-François Painchaud* wrote an "Exa-

men sommaire de deux pamphlets publiées en 1823 sur le gouvernement ecclésiastique du district de Montréal," which Plessis thought did not "take the aggressor sufficiently to task, nor perhaps deal tactfully enough with the refuter." The controversy continued in the newspapers, and then in February 1824 things became even more acrimonious with the publication of the *Réponse de messire Chaboillez, curé de Longueuil, à la lettre de P. H. Bédard*, for Chaboillez reiterated his adherence to gallican principles and stressed the state's right to intervene in religious matters. Moreover the governor, Lord Dalhousie [Ramsay*], had read both of his pamphlets "with pleasure and the greatest interest," and had promptly sent them to Lord Bathurst, the colonial secretary. This controversy came to an end in April 1824, at the express request of Bishop Plessis, after a formula of adherence to the papal brief of 1 Feb. 1820 which had made Lartigue auxiliary bishop in the District of Montreal had been signed by 54 of the 93 parish priests in the district.

Upon Plessis's death on 4 Dec. 1825, Lartigue feared that London would use the occasion to impose Chaboillez as coadjutor to the new archbishop, Bernard-Claude Panet. In fact, the parish priest of Longueuil was "too much in Rome's black books for the pope ever to give him bulls." Lartigue did not know that Dalhousie, upon seeing a portrait of Chaboillez at Quebec, had made a comment (recalled by *La Minerve* at the time of Chaboillez's death): "If this man had been in the army and had conducted himself there as he has towards his ecclesiastical superiors, he would long since have been cashiered." In January 1834 Chaboillez denied having taken part in the intrigues to prevent the issuing of bulls to Pierre-Flavien Turgeon* as the new coadjutor to Joseph Signay*, the archbishop of Quebec, and to have the parish priest of Saint-Laurent, Jean-Baptiste Saint-Germain*, replace him. It is true, however, that along with the priests of the Séminaire du Saint-Sulpice in Montreal, he had refused in December 1833 to sign the petition in favour of Turgeon which the clergy of the diocese of Quebec had sent to the pope.

Augustin Chaboillez died of cholera on 28 Aug. 1834. *La Minerve* laid stress upon "his talents and his generosity to the poor." His funeral was held on 29 August, and he was buried in the church at Longueuil.

GILLES CHAUSSÉ

Augustin Chaboillez is the author of *Questions sur le gouvernement ecclésiastique du district de Montréal* (Montréal, 1823) and *Réponse de messire Chaboillez, curé de Longueuil, à la lettre de P. H. Bédard; suivie de quelques remarques sur les observations imprimées aux Trois-Rivières* (Montréal, 1824).

ACAM, 780.034; 901.016. ANQ-M, CE1-12, 29 août 1834; CE1-51, 1er déc. 1773. ASSM, 24, 27. P.-H. Bédard

Chaffey

[J.-J. Lartigue], *Lettre à Mr. Chaboillez, curé de Longueuil, relativement à ses "Questions sur le gouvernement ecclésiastique du district de Montréal"* (Montréal, 1823). [L.-M. Cadieux et J.-O. Plessis], *Observations sur un écrit intitulé "Questions sur le gouvernement ecclésiastique du district de Montréal"* (Trois-Rivières, Qué., 1823). *La Minerve*, 1er sept. 1834. Allaire, *Dictionnaire*, 1: 106. F.-M. Bibaud, *Le Panthéon canadien* (A. et V. Bibaud; 1891), 51. Caron, "Inv. de la corr. de Mgr Denaut," ANQ *Rapport*, 1931–32: 134, 136, 162; "Inv. de la corr. de Mgr Plessis," 1927–28: 241; 1928–29: 166, 169, 173, 182; 1932–33: 188, 204, 214, 224. Chaussé, *Jean-Jacques Lartigue*. Alexandre Jodoin et J.-L. Vincent, *Histoire de Longueuil et de la famille de Longueuil ...* (Montréal, 1889). Lambert, "Joseph-Octave Plessis." Lemieux, *L'établissement de la première prov. eccl.*, 161–66, 174–83, 201–3, 217–18. Robert Rumilly, *Histoire de Longueuil* (Longueuil, Qué., 1974). É.-Z. Massicotte, "Les Chaboillez," *BRH*, 28 (1922): 184–88, 207–9, 241–42, 274–76, 311–13, 325–32, 355–59.

CHAFFEY, SAMUEL, businessman; b. 4 Feb. 1793 in Norton sub Hamdon, England, son of Benjamin Chaffey and Sarah ——; m. 25 Dec. 1821 Mary Ann Poole, originally from Somerset, and they had a son, Samuel Benjamin; d. 26 July 1827 at Chaffey's Mills (Chaffeys Locks), Upper Canada.

Samuel Chaffey was the fifth son of a Somerset wool-stapler and woollens manufacturer. The economic slump in England which followed the Napoleonic Wars was probably a factor in the immigration of Samuel and his brother Benjamin to Upper Canada in 1816. They settled for a time at the Perth military settlement, but about 1817 located in Brockville, where they entered mercantile trade as B. and S. Chaffey, set up a small distillery, and rented (under Benjamin's name) the nearby farm and mills of Daniel Jones Sr. While preparing these mills for operation, the Chaffeys were asked by settlers from the rear township of South Crosby to erect a mill there. The brothers agreed and in April 1820 Benjamin secured a lease to lot 17, concession 8, a clergy reserve lot with a suitable mill-seat. Construction began that summer under Samuel's direction.

The Chaffeys were in business at Brockville for about three years, dealing frequently with wholesalers and lumber merchants in Montreal and Quebec City. The firm soon was seriously indebted, principally to the estate of Daniel Jones. Benjamin fled to the United States in late 1820 to escape prosecution but Samuel remained behind to extricate their interests, in which effort he was not altogether successful. Creditors won judgements against him for £155 7s. 6d. in 1822 and for £186 9s. 2d. the following year; yet in 1827 the former partnership was still owed more than £1,060 on outstanding notes. Samuel nevertheless retained, in his brother's name, the interest in the mill-seat in South Crosby, where, by the time of Benjamin's flight, a sawmill had been partially erected.

About 1822 Samuel moved to the township, began farming, and pushed ahead with the construction of a large milling complex, which by 1827 contained the sawmill, a grist-mill, a distillery, and carding and fulling machinery. Although he had attempted with others in 1823 to have a road surveyed to Chaffey's Mills in South Crosby, there was no efficient system of roads or water-ways to serve this "barren and rocky country" and his products were probably consumed locally. Nevertheless, reports in 1829–30 of the annual income of the Chaffey enterprises by Mary Ann Chaffey (£205), Lieutenant-Colonel John By* (£300), and the township assessor (£457) revealed an operation of moderate value. John MACTAGGART, clerk of works on the Rideau Canal, estimated the total worth of this self-sufficient industrial hive to be at least £5,000.

In 1826 work had begun near Chaffey's Mills for a lock on the proposed Rideau canal. The site was one of the unhealthiest on the entire water-way because of the prevalence of malaria, known also as swamp fever or ague. Its symptoms were later described by Mactaggart: "They generally come on with an attack of bilious fever, dreadful vomiting, pains in the back and loins, general debility, loss of appetite. . . . After being in this state for eight or ten days, the yellow jaundice is likely to ensue, and then *fits* of trembling. . . . For two or three hours before they arrive, we feel so cold that nothing will warm us . . . and then the *shaking begins*. Our very bones ache, teeth chatter, and the ribs are sore, continuing thus in great agony. . . . This over, we find the malady has run one of its rounds, and start out of the bed in a feeble state." Many survived such attacks, but Samuel Chaffey did not – he died of the fever on 26 July 1827.

His widow and Benjamin Chaffey, who returned from the United States in 1828, contested the rights to the mill complex. Benjamin claimed ownership by virtue of the lease and his former partnership with Samuel, Mary Ann by possession and the claim that her husband had made the improvements. She was supported in her claim by two other immigrants from Somerset, John Rowswell, a neighbouring settler, and Benjamin Tett, her future brother-in-law. After much dispute, a compromise was announced in June 1829 and Mary Ann and Benjamin Chaffey submitted a joint payment on the lease. Meanwhile the mill-site had been incorporated into the plans for the canal in order to simplify its layout and to effect savings in construction costs. After negotiations with By similar to those he engaged in for other lands along the canal route, in October 1829 Mary Ann and Benjamin Chaffey assigned the lease and other lands in the township to By for £2,000. Over the next two years the mills were dismantled and replaced by a lock-station, named for Samuel Chaffey, which soon

127

Chamberlain

formed the nucleus of the present-day community of Chaffeys Locks.

DAVID ROBERTS

AO, MS 393, A-2-c(i), box 2, envelope 1; RG 1, C-IV, South Crosby Township, concession 8, lot 17; RG 21, United Counties of Leeds and Grenville, Elizabethtown Township, assessment rolls, 1816–21; South Crosby Township, census records, 1815–25; assessment rolls, 1816–30; RG 22, ser.131, 1: ff.82, 86; ser.176, 1: 156. Leeds Land Registry Office (Brockville, Ont.), Abstract index to deeds, South Crosby Township, vol.1 (mfm. at AO). PAC, RG 1, E3, 8: 12–18; L3, 108: C15/103; 146: C leases, 1819–36/157; RG 5, A1: 19743–44, 23611–14, 23857–58, 24073–75, 24082–85, 56945. QUA, Tett family papers. Somerset Record Office (Taunton, Eng.), South Petherton Independent (Congregational), reg. of baptisms, marriages, and burials. "Journals of Legislative Assembly of U.C.," AO *Report*, 1913: 298. John Mactaggart, *Three years in Canada: an account of the actual state of the country in 1826–7–8* ... (2v., London, 1829). "Parish register of Brockville and vicinity, 1814–1830," ed. H. R. Morgan, *OH*, 38 (1946): 83. Karen Price, "Construction history of the Rideau Canal" (National Hist. Parks and Sites Branch, Parks Canada, *Manuscript report*, no.193, Ottawa, 1976). *Sights and surveys: two diarists on the Rideau*, ed. Edwin Welch (Ottawa, 1979). J. A. Alexander, *The life of George Chaffey; a story of irrigation beginnings in California and Australia* (Melbourne, Australia, and London, 1928). *Hearth and heritage: history of Chaffey's Lock and area, 1800–1980*, comp. Laurel Fleming (Kingston, Ont., 1981). R. W. Passfield, *Building the Rideau Canal: a pictorial history* (Toronto, 1982).

CHAMBERLAIN, THEOPHILUS, soldier, JP, surveyor, and office holder; b. 20 or 27 Oct. 1737 in Northfield, Mass., fourth son of Ephraim Chamberlain and Anne Merriman; m. 15 May 1768, apparently in Danbury, Conn., Editha White, and they had two children; m. secondly 24 Dec. 1781 Lamira Humphraville, and they had eight children; d. 20 July 1824 in Preston, N.S.

It was a Chamberlain characteristic to answer the call of duty. Ephraim, a blacksmith, was killed during the New England expedition against Louisbourg, Île Royale (Cape Breton Island), in 1745. An uncle adopted the seven-year-old Theophilus and saw that he received an education. In the Seven Years' War the young man served with Burke's Rangers. Ingenious, determined, and physically fit though Chamberlain undoubtedly was, no one could have done all the things during the next few years which are ascribed to him by two divergent sources.

The accounts agree that the rangers joined the British at Fort William Henry (also called Fort George; now Lake George, N.Y.), where Chamberlain shared in fighting and reconnoitring. In one skirmish he was one of two survivors. After the fort fell to Montcalm* in August 1757 the Indian allies of the French seized part of the British garrison. At the end of a march to the Indian encampment at Montreal several prisoners, headed by Chamberlain, escaped into the town. He and a friend were sheltered by one of Montcalm's interpreters, a Northfield native. Dressed as women, the two were escorted to a nearby prison to prevent recapture, and then transferred to Quebec. From this point the accounts differ, but it seems likely that Chamberlain and a second Northfield man were exchanged for French prisoners. After his arrival in Halifax in October 1757 Chamberlain worked at an inn; by February 1758 he had saved enough for passage to Boston.

Joining his foster parents, who had moved to South Hadley, Mass., Chamberlain became foreman in his uncle's tannery. Within a few years he entered Yale College, graduating BA in 1765. After studying theology under the Reverend Eleazar Wheelock at Lebanon, Conn., he was ordained a Congregational minister on 29 April 1765, and with a fellow minister was immediately dispatched to the settlements of the Six Nations in New York. By September 1767, however, he was teaching in a private Latin school in Boston. He also served briefly as minister of a Presbyterian congregation in Worcester, Mass.

By this time, Chamberlain had become interested in the teachings of Robert Sandeman. In 1768 he was re-ordained as a Sandemanian bishop, married, and moved to Danbury, where he set up a clothing business. Sandemanianism laid stress upon personal salvation, and the Danbury group had an especially sensitive religious conscience and strong convictions on civil duties. Overt persecution began about 1770, when Chamberlain and others found themselves before the courts for ignoring warnings to leave town. Within months of their appearance in court most of the group had moved to New Haven, Conn. There Chamberlain established a dry-goods store, which he soon abandoned, and in 1772 he returned to teaching. Ill will among the townspeople and the onset of the revolution again made the Sandemanians' position difficult, since their faith required obedience to constituted authority. For their refusal to contribute to the war fund some, including Chamberlain, were imprisoned; they were then freed and allowed to go to British-controlled territory. Chamberlain and his family settled on a farm near Bedford Village, N.Y. In 1776 his infant son died, and in 1779 his wife. Two years later he remarried and by 1782 was teaching again, this time at a private school in New York City.

As the British occupation drew to a close, Chamberlain accepted a captain's commission in the city militia from Sir Guy Carleton* with responsibility for arranging the transfer to Halifax of a group of refugees. With his family and friends he reached there in the early fall of 1783. Almost at once he was commissioned a justice of the peace, named a deputy surveyor, appointed to lay out a new township east of Dartmouth, and made agent to distribute land within the area, which at that time boasted only a handful of stragglers from the Dartmouth settlement. The actual grant in December 1784 gave Chamberlain and 143 others, including loyalists, blacks, disbanded soldiers, and Germans, a "plantation" of 32,000 acres in Preston, his name for the new township. Chamberlain himself received one of two grants of 1,000 acres. In April 1785, 194 refugees arrived from St Augustine (Fla), and fresh grants in 1785 and 1786 accommodated them and other newcomers. An additional 35 settlers received 4,700 acres in December 1787.

As Preston grew, Chamberlain's duties increased. When some blacks complained about the quality of their lots or the fact that they had not received title, he replied that they had not paid his agent's fees or had been "too negligent to look after their own interests." Given official guidelines on lot sizes and his Sandemanian belief that responsibility was in direct proportion to proven will and ability to handle it, Chamberlain's land allocations were reasonably fair. Some Halifax residents never occupied their lots, and in January 1792 most of the blacks left for Sierra Leone [see Thomas Peters*; David George*]. Many soldiers sold or abandoned their grants, and Preston was thus left mainly to the Sandemanians, of whom Chamberlain was the acknowledged leader. As his large family grew up and married into the prominent Sandemanian families in Halifax, he subdivided his acreage or acquired new grants for some of his children in Preston.

In July 1796 about 550 maroons from Jamaica arrived at Halifax. These descendants of escaped slaves had warred with the Jamaican authorities for more than a year, and when the fighting ended in March 1796 they had been deported to Nova Scotia. There they were supported financially by the Jamaican government and were assigned superintendents. Although the maroons were not at first Chamberlain's responsibility, he oversaw the surveys and allocations of land purchased for them in Preston. For a time he also acted as schoolmaster, and in July 1797 he was requested to share some duties connected with their supervision. When he threatened to withhold rations the formerly unwilling maroons finally began to work their lands. On 9 July 1798 Chamberlain was named superintendent of the maroons, replacing Alexander Howe*. Using his former tactics he was able to get them to work, but found them as exasperating as they found life in Preston. From then until the removal of the maroons in August 1800 Chamberlain occupied Maroon Hall, built by Francis Green* and acquired by the Jamaican government as the superintendent's mansion.

Apart from French and American prisoners tempo-rarily resident there, few people moved into Preston in the following years. Vacant properties hampered development, especially the maintenance of roads, and Chamberlain in vain urged the escheat of these lands. After the War of 1812 he welcomed a government proposal to settle a group of freed slaves as a chance to fill empty lands, afford assistance in repairing roads, and supply needed labourers for the original settlers. The unoccupied lands were duly escheated, and in order to provide space for a reasonably compact settlement Chamberlain and some others relinquished part of their properties in exchange for acreage elsewhere. During the summer of 1815 Chamberlain laid out portions of the proposed lots, and in the fall he supervised the issue of provisions and the arrangements for the storage of supplies for the refugees. He continued to report on the progress of the new settlers until the end of 1816, when this last of his major public responsibilities ended.

Chamberlain's long career was many-sided. He was a pragmatist with principles: as circumstances or conscience required, he moved with little hesitation from one task to another, wasting no time on regret, salvaging what he could, seeking new solutions to old problems or taking on new challenges. His driving force was an inner tension resulting from a practical nature tempered with religious conviction and moral conscience. With Chamberlain, action followed decision: when he found Congregational tenets wanting he became a Sandemanian; when political beliefs ruled out rebellion he started a new life behind British lines. His loyalism was typical in that it was based on the political and social need for a duly constituted figure of authority irrespective of the figure itself. Yet his Sandemanianism insisted on individual independence, permitted no double standards, and saw time, education, and Christianity as the great equalizers. Honesty, work well done, thrift, and acceptance of responsibility brought their own rewards. It was men such as Chamberlain who set Nova Scotia on course; the brittle gaiety of government circles and the shadowy half-world of the Halifax waterfront were peripheral to real development, and he no doubt grew impatient with both.

Yet Chamberlain was on friendly terms with several lieutenant governors. Sir John Wentworth* in fact placed his natural son Edward Lowe in the old man's house and under his legal custody. His home life was irreproachable and he retained the loyalty of lifelong friends. Chamberlain's portrait reflects his mixture of human vanity and spiritual humility; his will, made at age 87, provides a deeper insight into his character. He greatly loved the countryside around his home, having given it his name and having left his mark upon it with his surveyor's instruments. Before he died on 20 July 1824, he asked to be buried in the small

Chappell

cemetery near the church built for the maroons atop a high hill in Preston.

GERTRUDE TRATT

Halifax County Court of Probate (Halifax), Estate papers, C51 (Theophilus Chamberlain) (mfm. at PANS). PANS, Biog., Theophilus Chamberlain, diary (mfm.); MG 1, 164C (typescript); 1184B (photocopies); 1619A (photocopies); RG 1, 419, no.41. *Nova-Scotia Royal Gazette*, 21 July 1824. *Loyalists in N.S.* (Gilroy). Richard Hildreth, *History of the United States of America* (6v., New York, 1848–71), 3. *Historical essays on the Atlantic provinces*, ed. G. A. Rawlyk (Toronto, 1967; repr. 1971). Murdoch, *Hist. of N.S.*, vol.3. Francis Parkman, *A half-century of conflict* (2v., Boston, 1892). [A. G.] Archibald, "Story of deportation of Negroes from Nova Scotia to Sierra Leone," N.S. Hist. Soc., *Coll.*, 7 (1891): 129–54. F. E. Crowell, "New Englanders in Nova Scotia . . . ," *Yarmouth Herald* (Yarmouth, N.S.), 11 Oct. 1932. J. N. Grant, "The 1821 emigration of black Nova Scotians to Trinidad," *N.S. Hist. Quarterly*, 2 (1972): 285–92. E. B. Harvey, "The Negro loyalists," *N.S. Hist. Quarterly*, 1 (1971): 181–202. "House linked with historic name," *Mail-Star* (Halifax), 8 Jan. 1954. "Living links with the past," *Halifax Herald*, 24 June 1897. "Portraits," N.S., Provincial Museum and Science Library, *Report* (Halifax), 1934–35: 30. C. StC. Stayner, "The Sandemanian loyalists," N.S. Hist. Soc., *Coll.*, 29 (1951): 62–123.

CHAPPELL, BENJAMIN, wheelwright and machinist, Methodist lay preacher, postmaster, politician, and diarist; b. 5 March 1740/41 (Old Style) in London, son of Richard and Rachel Chappell; d. 6 Jan. 1825 in Charlottetown.

Benjamin Chappell was trained as a wheelwright and machinist, and like many other young urban artisans of his time he was drawn to the preaching of the Wesley brothers, who were reinvigorating the Church of England with pietistic fervour. Chappell was particularly associated with John Wesley at Islington (London), and with his brother William Chappell became a lay evangelist. In April 1770 Wesley, writing in his journal of a visit to Inverness, Scotland, noted: "Benjamin and William Chappel, who had been here three months, were waiting for a vessel to return to London. They had met a few people every night to sing and pray together; and their behaviour, suitable to their profession, had removed much prejudice." In the summer of 1774 Chappell and his wife Elizabeth, whom he had married in February, left London aboard the snow *Elizabeth*, bound for the north shore of St John's (Prince Edward) Island. Chappell has left no record of his reasons for emigrating, but unemployment was heavy in 1774 among artisans, and the newly-weds may, like thousands of their fellow Britons, have hoped for a better future in land-rich North America. Moreover, the moving spirit behind the voyage of the *Elizabeth* was a Quaker

merchant named Robert Clark*, who had purchased Lot 21 on the Island in 1773 and thought of himself, according to Governor Walter Patterson*, as a "second Penn" who wished to found a settlement for the "recovering of sinners." Chappell, whose pietism always verged on the "inner light" of Quakerism, was probably attracted by a combination of spiritual and economic motives to join Clark's venture at New London.

Like most such well-meaning ventures, especially to jurisdictions as isolated as St John's Island, Clark's settlement was a disaster from the outset, despite a considerable expenditure of funds. He and his business partner Robert Campbell brought out a number of indentured servants, including Benjamin Chappell, who received their passage and provisioning in return for four years' service. Clark was able to wax rhapsodical about well-timbered land, available at "4d per Acre, for life, or 1s P^r acre free-hold." He is reported to have said that the wood could readily be sold to incoming ships and that "Sawyers were better paid for their labour, than in England, that the Rivers abounded with fish & the Country with game which were free for any one, that Deer & Turkeys were so plentiful that a person might shoot them some times from the Windows, & when at work in the woods might shoot enough to serve his family without loss of time – in short any man could live much more comfortable there, than in England." Although Clark's optimism about the abundance of natural resources was not without foundation, his expectations about the ease of their exploitation proved chimeric. Few of Clark's settlers had the skills and determination (backed by religious faith) of the Chappells; the Island lacked a commercial infrastructure to provide even the rudiments of life beyond the natural resources, which themselves were difficult to obtain during the cold, snow-filled, and ice-bound winters; and the naval privateering of the American rebellion ended any transatlantic timber trade.

There were 129 persons at the village of Elizabethtown (near Springbrook) when Benjamin Chappell made his first diary entry on 19 Jan. 1775. They were huddled together against the winter in a few hastily constructed log-houses. The Chappells shared their dwelling with "three gentlemen" and their cook-room with 17 people, including "eleven strangers." Timbering was made virtually impossible by the shortage of horses, hunting by the snow, fishing by the ice. Food was extremely difficult to obtain, and the people became restive. On 18 February Chappell recorded, "Very short of provisions. No rum, no bread, no meat, no beer, no sugar in the stores." He attempted to ration what little remained, but the settlers threatened to raid the storehouse. Occasional supplies drifted in from other settlements, particularly from David Lawson* at Covehead, but by the end of March a large party of

Chappell

men "outrageous through want of Provisions" formed a plan to "surprize Charleytown." The coming of spring sent folk to their gardens and made shellfish such as oysters available. Chappell and his wife considered leaving, but on 9 May "Concluded not to remove but to trust to God for food." The next winter, again hard, was complicated by the November shipwreck of the *Elizabeth*, which lost the supplies on board and merely added new mouths to the tiny settlement. Through all the suffering, which included the death of an infant Chappell in November 1775, Benjamin and Elizabeth worked, exhorted the people to trust in God, and believed.

Even before his indenture had expired, Chappell had begun working for acting governor Phillips Callbeck* – who had a market for timber in the military buildings and other public construction he was organizing at Charlottetown – and had spent some time in the little capital, which was clearly more prosperous than Elizabethtown. Chappell removed to Charlottetown in October 1778, leaving his family temporarily in Rustico. Economic opportunities were much greater in Charlottetown than on the north shore and, as a skilled mechanic and woodworker, Chappell found a variety of tasks to be done. He worked for a succession of governors on their mansions, built boats for leading inhabitants, and even turned his hand to such unusual projects as a saddle for parson Theophilus DESBRISAY. On 3 Dec. 1780 he agreed with Governor Patterson to take care of the town pump for £6 per year, and he served the parish for many years as churchwarden and overseer. He supervised the erection of the church spire and weathercock in 1801. Between outside employments, he laboured in his workshop, making almost anything the market would demand; he specialized in spinning-wheels, especially after 1800, eventually handcrafting more than 600 of them. In 1802 he was appointed deputy postmaster, apparently using a packet he owned with his brother William to transport the mail to the mainland. More sophisticated society required new gadgets, and after 1801 he built coaches and sleighs for several leading Charlottetown figures.

Chappell was elected to the third House of Assembly in 1779, but his diary makes clear that he was not interested in politics. Besides his craft and family, Chappell's chief concerns were spiritual and religious. In the absence of a clergyman of Methodist leanings he led prayer-meetings, and the first visit to the Island of a Methodist preacher, by William BLACK in 1783, was at his "earnest and repeated invitation." Black described him as "an eccentric but truly pious and upright man." John Wesley, with whom Chappell corresponded, recommended, "If you have no clergyman, see that you constantly meet together, and God will be where two or three are gathered together." Chappell formed a class at his home about this time.

Wesley also warned against the "broad, ranting Antinomianism" of Henry Alline*, suggested that the British government be petitioned about the sorry state of the Island, and advised that "it will be a difficult thing to find apprentices who will be willing to take so long a journey to a cold and uncomfortable place." It was as difficult to find clergymen as apprentices. A Quaker visitor to the Island in 1786 reported that the Chappells "haveing no Religious place of worship to go to seam to lament their situation with some others." Chappell held the small Methodist community of the "true genuine believing few" together against the "Rigged [rigid] Clamerous, Bigoted, disputing" many, supporting clergymen when they appeared, until the arrival of a substantial group of Methodists from Guernsey in 1806 firmly turned the tide and established the denomination on the Island.

If Chappell was a pious man, he was not a narrow sectarian or proselytizer. He corresponded with leaders of other denominations, including Presbyterian James Drummond MacGregor of Pictou, to whom he wrote, "It is my constant care not to wean any person from their own Church & peopel only pracktice helping them out of the Pit of Unbelief & Ignorance, and then send them amongst their own people to tell them what wonderous things God hath done for their Souls." Nor were his intellectual interests solely confined to the spiritual, for although "One Immortal Soul, is a greater Miracle than all the Inanamate Creation of God," he was interested in the latest developments in astronomy and science, difficult as it was to obtain such information on the Island.

Chappell's diary ends in 1817, probably because he ceased activity in his workshop, although he maintained the post office in his home until his death. Tradition suggests that he was somewhat irascible in his last years, but he died feebly singing with his last breath, "O love! how cheering is thy ray! All pain before thy presence flies." Chappell was that combination of skilled artisan and committed pietist which was so typical of 18th-century Methodism, and he more than anyone else made the spirit of John Wesley a reality on Prince Edward Island.

J. M. BUMSTED

Nantucket Hist. Assoc. Library and Research Center (Nantucket, Mass.), Nantucket Monthly Meeting of Friends papers coll., no.51, box 1, folder 1, John Townshend, journal (photocopy at PAPEI). PAPEI, Acc. 2277; Acc. 2575/8, memorial of Benjamin Chappell, 11 March 1788; RG 16, land registry records. P.E.I. Museum and Heritage Foundation (Charlottetown), File information concerning Benjamin Chappell. UCC-M, John McGregor papers, Chappell to McGregor, 1802. Thomas Curtis, "Voyage of Thos. Curtis," *Journeys to the Island of St. John or Prince Edward Island, 1775–1832*, ed. D. C. Harvey (Toronto, 1955). John Wesley, *The journal of the Rev. John Wesley . . . ,* ed.

Chartier

Nehemiah Curnock (8v., London, [1909–16]), 5: 364; *The letters of the Rev. John Wesley . . .*, ed. John Telford (8v., London, 1931; repr. [1960]), 7: 199–200, 385–86. *Prince Edward Island Register*, 8 Jan. 1825. J. T. Mellish, *Outlines of the history of Methodism in Charlottetown, Prince Edward Island . . .* (Charlottetown, 1888). Matthew Richey, *A memoir of the late Rev. William Black, Wesleyan minister, Halifax, N.S., including an account of the rise and progress of Methodism in Nova Scotia . . .* (Halifax, 1839). E. P. Thompson, *The making of the English working class* (London, 1963).

CHARTIER DE LOTBINIÈRE, MICHEL-EUSTACHE-GASPARD-ALAIN, army and militia officer, seigneur, JP, and politician; b. 31 Aug. 1748 at Quebec, son of Michel Chartier* de Lotbinière and Louise-Madeleine Chaussegros de Léry; d. 1 Jan. 1822 in Montreal and was buried 5 January in the church at Vaudreuil.

Michel-Eustache-Gaspard-Alain Chartier de Lotbinière was destined for a military career. During the siege of Quebec in 1759, when he had just turned 11, he became a cadet in the second artillery company, and when the French army was quartered in Montreal in 1760 he was breveted a second ensign. The conquest abruptly changed the course of his life. He accompanied his father to France in 1760 and there pursued studies with the aim of serving in the French cavalry. Reverses in the family fortunes obliged him to return to the province of Quebec, probably in 1763. He continued with his education for some years and in 1768 received a surveyor's commission. But through force of circumstance he was soon involved in managing his father's seigneuries. While in France his father had added to his seigneuries of Lotbinière and Alainville those of Vaudreuil, Rigaud, Rigaud De Vaudreuil (also known as Saint-François-de-la-Nouvelle-Beauce), Villechauve, and Hocquart. The purchases had saddled him with heavy debts, and in 1770 he was forced to sell his properties. Michel-Eustache-Gaspard-Alain was successful, however, in keeping much of the land in the family. With the financial help of his friend Charles-François Tarieu* de La Naudière he bought Lotbinière on 15 Feb. 1770, and then the seigneuries of Vaudreuil, Rigaud, and Rigaud De Vaudreuil on 14 Sept. 1771; in 1772 he sold Rigaud De Vaudreuil to Gaspard-Joseph Chaussegros* de Léry. Because of his immense properties, prestigious name, and family connections, Chartier de Lotbinière was now among the most influential Canadian seigneurs.

If Michel Chartier de Lotbinière could not adapt to the new political situation in the colony, his son, by contrast, offered many tokens of loyalty to the British crown and gradually earned the trust and protection of the colonial officials. A confidential remark in 1786 reveals his opportunism and his attitude towards the new régime: "I am destined to live with the English,"

he wrote to his father, "my welfare is in their control, I depend entirely upon them, consequently my policy is to adapt myself to circumstances." At the time of the American invasion in 1775 he was one of the first Canadian seigneurs to offer his services to Governor Guy Carleton*. He participated in the defence of Fort St Johns (Saint-Jean-sur-Richelieu) under François-Marie Picoté* de Belestre and Joseph-Dominique-Emmanuel Le Moyne* de Longueuil. Taken prisoner in November, he was removed to Albany, N.Y., and then to Bristol, Pa, and remained in captivity until December 1776. After an exchange of military prisoners he spent the winter of 1776–77 in New York, returning to Quebec the following spring. His services earned him a captaincy, and half pay which he would receive until his death. Having won Carleton's confidence, he was appointed justice of the peace for the district of Montreal in 1777. He obtained the rank of lieutenant-colonel of the Vaudreuil battalion of militia in 1794, and that of colonel in 1803; he retired from the militia in July 1818.

The first house of assembly of Lower Canada, constituted in 1792, contained a great many owners of seigneuries, one of whom was Chartier de Lotbinière. He was elected, with his brother-in-law Pierre Amable De Bonne*, for York, a riding that took in the seigneuries of Vaudreuil and Rigaud. His name is associated in a particular way with debates in the first session that sanctioned the use of French in the workings and records of the assembly. In a speech reported in the *Quebec Gazette* on 31 Jan. 1793, he asked for English and French to be given equal recognition in the house: "Since the majority of our constituents are placed in a special situation, we are obliged to depart from the ordinary rules and forced to ask for the use of a language which is not that of the empire; but, being as fair to others as we hope they will be to us, we should not want our language eventually to banish that of His Majesty's other subjects." In the painting that occupies a place of honour above the speaker's chair in the present-day Assemblée Nationale at Quebec, Charles Huot has depicted the house on the occasion of this speech. On 28 Jan. 1794 Chartier de Lotbinière was unanimously elected speaker, replacing Jean-Antoine Panet*, who had been appointed a judge of the Court of Common Pleas, and he held this office with dignity until the dissolution of the house in 1796. He then became a member of the Legislative Council and retained this office until his death.

On 13 Dec. 1770 he had married Josette Tonnancour, daughter of Louis-Joseph Godefroy* de Tonnancour, in Trois-Rivières; she died at Vaudreuil on 28 July 1799 leaving no children. On 15 Nov. 1802 he married Mary Charlotte Munro, daughter of John Munro*, a member of the Legislative Council of Upper Canada, and widow of Captain Paul Dennis.

They had six children but only three daughters survived their father. Marie-Louise-Josephte married Robert Unwin Harwood* in 1823 and inherited the seigneury of Vaudreuil. In 1821 Marie-Charlotte married William Bingham, the son of an American senator whom Chartier de Lotbinière had known during his captivity, and she received the seigneury of Rigaud as her share. Julie-Christine married Pierre-Gustave Joly in 1828 and inherited the seigneury of Lotbinière.

MARCEL HAMELIN

ANQ-Q, P-44, P-163, P-239, P-351, P1000-21-378. "Lettre de M. de Meloizes à l'hon. M. E. G. A. Chartier de Lotbinière," *BRH*, 52 (1946): 181–83. "Lettre de M. Fresnay Desmeloises à M. E. A. Charlier de Lotbinière," *BRH*, 52: 180–81. "Lettre de Mr. Juchereau Duchesneau à l'hon. M. E. G. A. Chartier de Lotbinière," *BRH*, 52: 184–85. "Lettres du marquis de Lotbinière à son fils," *BRH*, 49 (1943): 377–78. "Une lettre d'amour de M. de Lotbinière fils," *BRH*, 41 (1935): 632. Nicole de La Chevrotière, *Chartier de Lotbinière, Gaspard Alain, 1748–1822; Gaspard Alain Chartier de Lotbinière: correspondance* ([Québec, 1981]). C.-A. [de Lotbinière-]Harwood, *L'honorable M. E. G. A. Chartier de Lotbinière* (Montréal, 1910). Sylvette Nicolini-Maschino, "Michel Chartier de Lotbinière: l'action et la pensée d'un Canadien du 18ᵉ siècle" (thèse de PHD, univ. de Montréal, 1978). L.-L. Paradis, *Les annales de Lotbinière, 1672–1933* (Québec, 1933). Gérard Parizeau, *La seigneurie de Vaudreuil et ses notables au début du XIXᵉ siècle; essai sur le milieu* (Montréal, 1984). F.-J. Audet et Édouard Fabre Surveyer, "L'honorable M.-E.-G.-A. Chartier de Lotbinière," *La Presse*, 16 juill. 1927: 26–27. J.-J. Lefebvre, "Michel-Eustache-Gaspard-Alain Chartier de Lotbinière (1748–1822)," ANQ *Rapport*, 1951–53: 371–411. C.-A. de Lotbinière-Harwood, "L'honorable M. E.-G.-A. Chartier de Lotbinière," *BRH*, 40 (1934): 67–103.

CHATTAN, ANGUS MACKINTOSH OF MACKINTOSH, 26th Chief of Clan. *See* MACKINTOSH

CHAUSSEGROS DE LÉRY, LOUIS-RENÉ, seigneur, army and militia officer, office holder, JP, and politician; b. 13 Oct. 1762 in Paris, son of Gaspard-Joseph Chaussegros* de Léry and Louise Martel de Brouague; m. 20 May 1799 Madeleine-Charlotte Boucher de Boucherville, daughter of René-Amable Boucher* de Boucherville, a seigneur, at Boucherville, Lower Canada; d. there 28 Nov. 1832.

Finding it impossible to carve out a place for himself in France after the British conquest of New France, Gaspard-Joseph Chaussegros de Léry left Louis-René and another son with a nurse and returned to Canada in 1764. At Governor Guy Carleton*'s suggestion he tried to bring his children out, but it was not until June 1770 that Louis-René rejoined his parents at Quebec. They intended him to have a

military career, and in December 1774 on Carleton's advice his mother approached Viscount Townshend*, master general of the Board of Ordnance, hoping to obtain a lieutenancy in the artillery for her son. Unfortunately Louis-René could not become an officer because he lacked the practical knowledge required; in addition, according to Townshend, not being a Protestant constituted an insurmountable obstacle. When Mme Chaussegros de Léry informed Carleton, he was extremely annoyed and reportedly said that in the light of the revolutionary ferment in the American colonies he thought it a serious matter "for the Canadian nobility to discover it was prevented by religion from holding positions in the military." The young Chaussegros de Léry attended the Séminaire de Québec, where he finished his studies in August 1782, and in October his father approached the current governor, Frederick Haldimand*, seeking a place for him in the service of the government. But in vain. The next August, giving up hope of finding anything in Canada, Louis-René took the safe-conduct he had been given and went to try his luck in France.

Through prior arrangements with some relatives, Chaussegros de Léry entered upon a military career by joining the king's bodyguard on 8 Jan. 1784. According to his brother François-Joseph he was "a very promising lad who, with his readiness to learn, his agreeable nature, and his good looks, will turn out well." At age 26 he was a captain. The French revolution, however, jeopardized his future. In 1791 he emigrated to Germany with a good part of the nobility and fought the revolutionary movement with the forces of the king of Prussia. After the defeat at Valmy, France, on 20 Sept. 1792 he was discharged. In November he took refuge in Great Britain, at the home of an aunt. For two years he again had a difficult time trying to find a patron and a regiment that would take him in. He exchanged long letters with his brother Gaspard-Roch-George, who was also living in exile and was seeking employment. Neither had any thought of looking for help from François-Joseph, since he was in the enemy camp, having managed to rise in the revolutionary army. Faced with the failure of his endeavours in Europe, Louis-René decided to return to Lower Canada, where he had high hopes of being appointed an officer in the Royal Canadian Volunteer Regiment which Governor Carleton, by now Lord Dorchester, had been ordered to raise in February 1794.

To win the good graces of the government, Chaussegros de Léry hastened upon his return in June 1794 to join with 130 citizens of Quebec town in founding an association "for the express purpose of supporting the *Laws, Constitution and Government* of the Province of *Lower Canada.*" The group was taking up an initiative launched in Great Britain in December 1792 as a response to the revolutionary

Chenneque

agitation in France. But Louis-René did not get the post he coveted. It was not until after his father had died in 1797 and he himself had become head of the family that he received, on 25 Oct. 1798, the rank of captain in the 2nd battalion of the Royal Canadian Volunteer Regiment. His appointment met with some opposition from the British in the colony, particularly from Chief Justice William OSGOODE, who always considered him a French officer. In 1802 the regiment was disbanded.

From 1802 to 1812 the British authorities once more relegated the Canadian seigneurial gentry to the background as far as military matters were concerned. Chaussegros de Léry had no choice but to adapt to civilian life since, as he admitted in 1796, it was a bit late and it would be costly to "line up for a place" in a regular regiment of the British army. This time he was in a better situation and the transition was easier. His father's death and his connection by marriage with the Boucherville clan gave him greater access to seigneurial holdings. Furthermore, his father-in-law did everything in his power to leave him his post as *grand voyer* (chief road commissioner) in the district of Montreal; Chaussegros de Léry succeeded him on 7 April 1806 and held the post until his death. He was also appointed justice of the peace in the same district a year later. During the war of 1812 Chaussegros de Léry, who no longer felt drawn to military life, was content to remain in the Boucherville sedentary militia, receiving the rank of major in September 1812 and lieutenant-colonel in June 1813. On 9 Feb. 1818 he became a member of the Legislative Council, a privilege that on the death of his father he had sought unsuccessfully from Governor Robert Prescott*. In the course of his remaining years he received a number of commissions, particularly as justice of the peace in various districts.

With the exception of Charles-Étienne*, Louis-René's brother, the branch of the Chaussegros de Lérys in Canada were above all soldiers. So determined were they to satisfy their ambitions in this field, that they tried to make careers for themselves abroad to get around the British policy which after 1760 forbad them a real military career in their own country. Louis-René Chaussegros de Léry returned home only when driven out of France. It was in the end as a landowner that he gained stability, recognition by the British authorities, and some control of his destiny.

ROCH LEGAULT

ANQ-Q, CN1-230; P-40. PAC, RG 68, General index, 1651–1841. F.-J. Chaussegros de Léry, "Lettres du vicomte François-Joseph Chaussegros de Léry à sa famille," ANQ *Rapport*, 1933–34: 34–35, 39, 60. *Quebec Gazette*, 24 May 1792, 10 July 1794, 23 April 1807, 19 Nov. 1812, 10 June 1813. F.-J. Audet, "Les législateurs du Bas-Canada."

Officers of British forces in Canada (Irving), 100–1, 189. *Quebec almanac*, 1799: 98; 1801: 100; 1805: 53; 1810: 65; 1815: 102. P.-G. Roy, *Inventaire des papiers de Léry conservés aux Archives de la province de Québec* (3v., Québec, 1939–40), 2: 262; 3: 51, 57–59, 67–68, 165–66, 178–79, 187–90, 196–97, 208–9, 212, 227. Turcotte, *Le Conseil législatif*. Galarneau, *La France devant l'opinion canadienne (1760–1815)*, 173, 242–43, 287. Paquet et Wallot, *Patronage et pouvoir dans le Bas-Canada*, 40. P.-G. Roy, *La famille Chaussegros de Léry* (Lévis, Qué., 1934). L.-P. Desrosiers, "Montréal soulève la province," *Cahiers des Dix*, 8 (1943): 77–78, 80, 90. J.-J. Lefebvre, "Michel-Eustache-Gaspard-Alain Chartier de Lotbinière (1748–1822)," ANQ *Rapport*, 1951–53: 378, 382, 404–5. P.-G. Roy, "La famille Chaussegros de Léry," *BRH*, 40 (1934): 599–601; "Les grands voyers de la Nouvelle-France et leurs successeurs," *Cahiers des Dix*, 8: 228–29. "Les seigneuries de la famille de Léry," *BRH*, 40: 684–92.

CHENNEQUE, MARTIN (he also signed **Dechennequi** or **de Chennequi, Chennequy,** and **Chineque**), mariner, militiaman, trader, and shipowner; b. *c.* 1734, possibly in the parish of Saint-Pierre-d'Irube, France, son of Martin d'Echenic, carpenter, and Marie d'Urcudoy; m. first 24 June 1760 Susanne Rollete (d. 1764) at Quebec; m. there secondly 8 Feb. 1768 Marie-Louise Grenete (d. 1773), and they had a daughter and a son, Martin Chinic*; m. there thirdly 9 May 1774 Élizabeth Pelerin; he had other children, but by which marriage is uncertain; d. 11 Nov. 1825 in L'Ancienne-Lorette, Lower Canada.

Martin Chenneque, who was almost certainly not the "fearless Spanish sailor" portrayed by his grandson Charles-Paschal-Télesphore Chiniquy*, may have come to New France as a child. He mastered early the difficulties of navigating the lower St Lawrence River, where tides, strong currents, shifting shoals, and ice could be treacherous. By the late 1750s he was operating as a pilot there and in the Gulf of St Lawrence.

In September 1758, in the Baie de Gaspé, Chenneque was taken into service in the British squadron under Sir Charles Hardy*. The following year Chenneque, Augustin Raby*, and other pilots guided the fleet of Charles Saunders* to Quebec. Over the course of the next four years Chenneque piloted numerous naval vessels to and from the new British colony. Unlike Raby and Théodose-Matthieu Denys* de Vitré, Chenneque "declined," he later claimed, a pension for these services, "being then young and able to gain a Livelihood by his Industry."

During the 1760s Chenneque also piloted British merchantmen, and he was attached for several years to Samuel Johannes Holland*, surveying the gulf region. He did further service on naval vessels between 1774 and 1778, during the American revolution; in 1775 he was a member of the Canadian militia at Quebec. After 1778 he continued to be employed as a navigator, pilot, and captain "in the Service of His Majesty and the Trade." Since about 1769, when pilotage was first regulated by provincial ordinance, Chenneque had been an examiner of seamen seeking qualification as pilots. In 1786–87, at the request of the committee of the Legislative Council on commerce and police, Chenneque, James Frost*, and two others formulated detailed regulations for pilotage which would become the basis of an important regulatory ordinance in 1788. Chenneque also periodically sold goods and owned at least one vessel.

Chenneque appears to have worked as a pilot until some time after 1812. In 1803 he petitioned for land; he and his family received a grant of 2,000 acres in Acton Township two years later. A list of pilots in 1805 showed him to be the senior among 49 pilots licensed to work the St Lawrence between Quebec and the outermost piloting station at Île du Bic; of these, 14 lived at Quebec. On 12 June 1805 he was appointed assistant examiner of pilots at Trinity House of Quebec [see François Boucher*]. Seven years later he applied to its board for remuneration, but the board resolved that "his Services . . . have been but seldom necessary or required," that he had already received a grant, and that "should he be unable to exercise his profession as a Pilot, and his circumstances require assistance he will be entitled to an allowance from the Decayed Pilot funds." On 21 June 1822 he became a warden of Trinity House.

In 1823 Chenneque claimed to have lost to British warships two commercial vessels and cargoes, with which he had planned to outfit fur-trading and fishing operations. This and other misfortunes compelled him in April of that year to run up, once again, his petition of service to the crown, which included a long-forgotten promise of Major-General James Wolfe* to compensate him. He appears to have obtained some recompense, for at about the time of his death a contemporary affirmed that he "held a small government pension in reward of his past services in piloting the fleet that conveyed Wolfe's army to Quebec." The statement describes him as "a little sturdy old man."

Given the practical experience of Chenneque and other veteran mariners, criticism by Governor Lord Dalhousie [Ramsay*] two years later of the piloting community as unseamanlike was unjust, but his comments did come close to the mark in one respect: pilotage "might be an excellent depot or retreat for old British seamen, and several have attempted, but they have constantly been driven off by the Canadians, who consider it a field of their own, in which no stranger must enter."

DAVID ROBERTS

ANQ-Q, CE1-1, 24 juin 1760, 8 févr. 1768, 9 mai 1774; CE1-2, 14 nov. 1825; CN1-207, 6 févr. 1768, 8 mai 1774; CN1-251, 23 juin 1760. Arch. du monastère de l'Hôtel-Dieu de Québec, Reg. des malades, 1740–51: 22. Arch. municipales, Saint-Pierre-d'Irube (France), certificat de naissance de Jean d'Echenic, 1720; certificat de sépulture de Martin Etchenique, 1764. PAC, RG 1, L3^L: 16292, 29979–89; RG 8, I (C ser.), 600: 144–49; 1714: 14, 121; RG 42, ser.1, 183: 12; RG 68, General index, 1651–1841: 5, 698. Ports Canada Arch. (Quebec), Trinity House, Quebec, minute-books, 1: 15–21; 2: 130–31; sér. pilotage, certificat de pilotage de Martin Chinique, 25 juill. 1761; "List of pilots for and below the harbour of Quebec agreeable to seniority," [1811]. PRO, CO 42/50: 168, 179, 232–40 (mfm. at PAC). "Les dénombrements de Québec" (Plessis), ANQ Rapport, 1948–49: 28, 78, 126, 178.

John Knox. An historical journal of the campaigns in North America for the years 1757, 1758, 1759, and 1760 . . . , ed. A. G. Doughty (3v., Toronto, 1914–16; repr. New York, 1968). "Ordinances made for the province of Quebec by the governor and Council of the said province, from 1768 until 1791 . . . ," PAC Report, 1914–15: 10–14, 212–15, 233–34. Ramsay, Dalhousie journals (Whitelaw), 3: 162, 207–8. Quebec Gazette, 24 Aug. 1769, 17 July 1777, 1 Oct. 1789, 28 Jan. 1790, 31 March 1791, 21 March 1799, 14 June 1804, 27 June 1805, 2 July 1807, 16 Feb. 1815. Mariages de N.-D. de Québec (1621–1980), B. Pontbriand, compil. (7v., Québec, 1963–81), 1: 156. Quebec almanac, 1788: 56. P.-G. Roy, Inventaire des contrats de mariage du Régime français conservés aux Archives judiciaires de Québec (6v., Québec, 1937–38), 2: 35. Tanguay, Dictionnaire, 3: 52. International Maritime Pilots Assoc., Canadian pilotage: a profile (Quebec, 1982). [C.-P.-T.] Chiniquy, Fifty years in the Church of Rome (6th ed., Toronto, 1886), 12. Wilbrod Leclerc, "Canadian pilotage – past and present" (working paper, Univ. of Ottawa, 1982). P.-G. Roy, La ville de Québec sous le Régime français (2v., Québec, 1930), 2: 317–18; "La famille Chinic," BRH, 45 (1939): 207; "Les traîtres de 1759," Cahiers des Dix, 1 (1936): 48.

CHIPMAN, WARD, lawyer, office holder, JP, politician, judge, and colonial administrator; b. 30 July 1754 in Marblehead, Mass., sixth child of John Chipman and Elizabeth Brown; m. 24 Oct. 1786 Elizabeth Hazen, and they had one child, Ward*; d. 9 Feb. 1824 in Fredericton.

Ward Chipman was the scion of a distinguished Massachusetts family. His father was a fourth-generation and his mother a fifth-generation American. Both his paternal grandfather and his father had attended Harvard College and in 1766 Chipman began his studies there. Students were ranked on admission in the order of their social prominence, and in recognition of his standing Chipman was placed seventh in his class of 41 students. A precocious and studious youth, he was deferential to the college authorities and in 1769 was awarded a prize for his dedication to learning. In 1770, upon graduation, he was chosen to deliver a commencement address, which he gave, unusually, in the vernacular, and for his MA he prepared a discussion of the topic "An feuda talliata, juri naturali repugnet?" Under normal circumstances, as the eldest surviving son, he would have been assured of a promising career at the bar, since his father was a lawyer with an adequate if not overly lucrative practice. But in 1768 John Chipman had died while pleading a case in Falmouth Neck, Mass. (Portland, Maine), and Chipman became "the Guardian and hope" of his mother, four sisters, and a younger brother. John Chipman bequeathed to his son a small estate but little capital and Ward's "prospects were then truly distressing." Fortunately, John Chipman had been popular among his colleagues, and Jonathan Sewell, attorney general of Massachusetts and advocate general of the Vice-Admiralty Court in Boston, solicited contributions to an interest-free loan to enable Ward to complete his degree at Harvard.

After teaching school in Boston in 1770 and in Roxbury (Boston) in 1771, Chipman began to study law under the tutelage of Sewell and in the office of Daniel Leonard. In many law offices a clerk received little guidance or training, but Chipman was given a thorough grounding in the complicated legal procedures of the day and he read voraciously in Sewell's unusually extensive library. He lived in Sewell's home at Cambridge, where he tutored the latter's children in Latin. In 1775 he began to practise in the Vice-Admiralty Court and Sewell secured for him a position as clerk-solicitor in the Boston custom-house. With an income of £400 per annum and Sewell as his patron, Chipman confidently expected to rise "to the most lucrative and honorable situations" in Massachusetts.

The American revolution dealt a crushing blow to these expectations. Although many of his contemporaries at the colonial bar supported the patriot cause or at least equivocated, Chipman's loyalties were never seriously in doubt. The impecunious heir of a family on the fringe of the Massachusetts social élite, he did not have the benefit of an extensive estate nor did he have the capital to engage in trade; thus he had to depend on his profession and he looked to the crown for rapid advancement in it. Moreover, his mentor, Jonathan Sewell, to whom he felt "an attachment . . . as strong and real as that which arises from the ties of natural affection," was devoted to the loyalist cause and Chipman naturally followed his example. In September 1774 Sewell's home in Cambridge had been attacked by a "mob"; Chipman had participated in its defence and then retreated with the Sewell family to Boston. Early in 1775, while establishing himself in his profession there, he assisted Daniel Leonard in the preparation of a series of anti-revolutionary tracts which Leonard published under the pseudonym Massachusettensis. He remained in Boston after the Sewells left for England that year. On 14 Oct. 1775 he signed a loyal address to Governor Thomas Gage* and, when Boston was evacuated in March 1776, he travelled with the British army to Halifax and then to London, where Sewell's home had become the central gathering place for a growing number of New England refugees. Chipman participated in the activities of a club composed of the more prominent New England loyalists and was one of the inner circle allowed to call upon Thomas Hutchinson, the ex-governor of Massachusetts. None the less, he did not enjoy his exile. Before leaving Massachusetts he had signed the property which he had inherited over to his mother and sisters to prevent its confiscation and, despite Sewell's patronage and the friendship of John Wentworth*, the former governor of New Hampshire, he was unable to find official employment and went deeply into debt. In the summer of 1777 he therefore eagerly accepted a minor post in New York City as deputy to the muster master general of the loyalist forces, Edward Winslow*.

Chipman assumed his position in July 1777. Since Winslow was frequently absent for long periods of time, Chipman was placed in charge of preparing the muster-rolls for the loyalist regiments stationed in and around the city. Although he received only five shillings per diem initially, his duties continued to expand and his salary was increased to ten shillings. He was also admitted to the New York bar and allowed to engage in private practice. During his first court appearance he so impressed his employer, Samuel Jones, a prominent Long Island barrister, that Jones made him a partner in his firm. Because of the war, business in the Vice-Admiralty Court sky-rocketed and Chipman earned "great fees . . . for very little trouble." In April 1779 he was appointed registrar of the Vice-Admiralty Court of Rhode Island and he also served as paymaster to at least two provincial regiments. His income totalled nearly £500 per annum and he lived extravagantly. Despite periodic bouts of insecurity, he remained confident that "a cause as good as that of Government is, must finally prevail," and in the mean time was "determined to enjoy as highly as I can the sources of happiness" that were available.

Like many loyalists, Chipman became increasingly critical of the British conduct of the war and he was devastated by the terms of the peace treaty announced late in 1782. For a time he planned to "remain quietly in the line of my profession here" until he learned that loyalists were to be prohibited from practising at the bar in New York State. During 1783 his position as deputy muster master general was abolished, but he was given a military pension of £91 a year and in May was appointed by Sir Guy Carleton* as one of the commissioners to register claims for supplies furnished to the British army. Although the post carried no salary, Chipman hoped to "lay a foundation for some claim upon Government hereafter"; at the same time he decided to prepare for "asylum" in Nova Scotia by becoming "as large a Proprietor as my claims will admit." In July he was one of a group of 55 loyalists who signed a petition requesting grants of 5,000 acres of land apiece in Nova Scotia. When the petition of the 55 aroused a storm of protest from the rest of the loyalist community, Chipman withdrew his name, but he asked Edward Winslow to find him a desirable tract of land at the mouth of the Saint John River. In the autumn of 1783 Chipman made a farewell visit to his relatives in Massachusetts, whom he had not seen in nine years, and, delaying his departure "till the last embarkation," in December he sailed to Halifax and then to London.

Chipman arrived in England armed with letters of introduction from Sir Guy Carleton. He had had a number of important contacts in the coalition government of Charles James Fox and Lord North, but that administration had collapsed in December and Chipman had little influence with the new executive, headed by William Pitt. In March 1784 he submitted a memorial to the commissioners for loyalist claims, requesting compensation for the £400 per annum he had lost because he had been deprived "of the exercise of his Profession." His claim was eventually rejected since he had not been "in the settled enjoyment" of this income "at the Commencement of the Troubles." He also worked diligently, but in vain, for the dismissal of Governor John Parr* of Nova Scotia, who viewed with ill-disguised contempt the demand of the loyalists for preferential treatment in the distribution of jobs and land. Although Chipman's savings were rapidly depleted and he contemplated returning to Halifax to practise law, he persevered in his search for government employment in Nova Scotia and joined in the agitation for the partition of that province.

To some extent the partition movement was a natural and inevitable result of the settlement of more than 15,000 loyalists north of the Bay of Fundy, primarily along the Saint John River, and their growing disgruntlement with the government of Nova Scotia. But it was assisted by three men who played a particularly important role in organizing the partition lobby. Edward Winslow acted as the spearhead of the movement within Nova Scotia, Brigadier-General Henry Edward Fox, the brother of Charles James Fox, placed himself at the head of the lobby in Britain, and Ward Chipman acted as Fox's adviser and coordinated the activities of the loyalists in London and in Nova Scotia. In March 1784 the Privy Council committee for trade endorsed partition, and in June the Pitt government, which was looking for an economical means of finding employment for as many as possible of the loyalist supplicants, agreed to the creation of New Brunswick. With the stroke of a pen a myriad of new jobs was created. Ironically, despite the active part he had played in the agitation, Chipman was disappointed in the division of the spoils. Although he had aspired to be attorney general in the new govern-ment, Sir William Pepperrell, the leader of the New England community in London, secured that post for Sampson Salter Blowers* and, when the latter declined, for Jonathan BLISS. Largely through the influence of Sir Guy Carleton, Chipman was given the less desirable, and unpaid, position of solicitor general. In August 1784 he received his commission and the following month, "heartily sick" of England, he embarked with Thomas Carleton*, the newly appointed governor of New Brunswick, for "our Land of promise the New Canaan."

Despite the relatively humble post he occupied in the government of New Brunswick, Chipman was frequently called upon by Governor Carleton for legal advice, particularly from November 1784 to May 1785 when he served as acting attorney general until the arrival of Jonathan Bliss. One of Chipman's tasks was to prepare a charter for the city at the mouth of the Saint John River, which at his suggestion was named "St John" rather than St John's. Chipman chose as his model the charter for New York City, which allowed for the election of aldermen but gave the power of appointing civic officials to the crown, and in 1785 he was named in the charter as the first recorder of the city, a position he held until 1809. As recorder, he was automatically a justice of the peace for the county of Saint John and presided with the mayor in the Court of General Sessions of the Peace and in the Inferior Court of Common Pleas or Mayor's Court. In 1786 Chipman assisted Edward Winslow in drafting the provincial legal code and in establishing rules of procedure for the grand juries and the inferior courts. When the Supreme Court began to function in 1785, Chipman became clerk of the crown on the circuits and acted as crown prosecutor in most of the important criminal cases over the next quarter-century. Since persons charged with a capital offence were not allowed counsel, he was almost invariably successful in the cases he prosecuted. With the establishment of the Vice-Admiralty Court in 1785, Chipman also became advocate general and he initiated most prosecutions there, despite the objections of the attorney general, who unsuccessfully challenged his authority to do so. Although none of Chipman's multiple offices initially carried a salary, they generated fees and added to his prestige and predominance at the bar.

Chipman was one of nine lawyers who formed the New Brunswick bar in February 1785, and in May he opened an office in Saint John. Since lawyers rarely participated in criminal cases, except when acting for the crown, the bread and butter of a legal practice was disputes over land titles and money, the preparation of deeds and wills, and cases involving real or imagined insults to reputations. With his extensive contacts among the wealthier members of colonial society, who alone could afford the hefty legal fees in these transactions, Chipman inevitably attracted a large

Chipman

share of the business in Saint John, notably from the merchant community. Because of the haste with which the province had been settled, disputes over land were unusually common in the early years; Chipman acted as agent for a number of loyalists, particularly after he had successfully defended judge Isaac Allan against ejectment proceedings launched by the family of Bryan Finucane, the former chief justice of Nova Scotia, in a dispute over the ownership of Sugar Island, eight miles above Fredericton. One of the more prominent of Chipman's clients was Benedict Arnold*, on whose behalf he and Jonathan Bliss prosecuted in the first slander trial in New Brunswick. Chipman also acted as a real-estate manager and as a debt collector for merchants such as Gideon WHITE of Nova Scotia, and his clients were drawn from as far afield as Boston and New Jersey.

Because of his standing in the profession Chipman's office became a Mecca for students. In total, he prepared 13 students for entry to the bar. The first, Jonathan Sewell* Jr, became chief justice of Lower Canada and the last, Ward Chipman Jr, chief justice of New Brunswick. A number of the others, including Stephen SEWELL, William Botsford*, Charles Jeffery Peters*, Thomas WETMORE, and William Franklin Odell*, had distinguished legal careers. By the standards of the time Chipman's clerks received a rigorous training. His library was one of the most extensive in the colony and he bequeathed it to his son, who carried on the family tradition and prepared nine students for the bar. For nearly half a century the bench and the bar of New Brunswick were dominated by students trained by the Chipmans, and partly because of their influence New Brunswick had one of the best qualified bars in British North America.

Yet Chipman's influence was not an unmixed blessing. His approach to the law was extremely conservative and his students, particularly Ward Chipman Jr, inherited this characteristic. They were little influenced by the legal-reform movements of the period. In Massachusetts the complicated and antiquated system of common-law pleading was swept away after the revolution but changes there evoked no response in neighbouring New Brunswick. Even the movement for a reform of the criminal code in Britain had little impact. Both as a prosecutor and later as a judge, Chipman vigorously defended the existing code, which prescribed the death penalty for an enormous range of offences. The only reform that Chipman supported was a revision of the law affecting debtors. Because of the shortage of capital in the colony, he believed it was counter-productive to imprison debtors – at least respectable ones – and in 1807 he sponsored a bill which modified the law. But he never recommended its abolition for he was, like most of his contemporaries, determined to protect the rights of the property-owning class. In general,

Chipman was devoted, almost slavishly, to English precedents and models and he rejected as "rather fanciful" the idea that there could be a "common law in the colonies . . . repugnant to the Common law of England." Yet he was inconsistent in his commitment to extending English laws to the colony. He strongly supported the decision to adopt 1660 as the "reception" date for English statute law in New Brunswick, because the choice of this date precluded the application to the colony of subsequent laws limiting the power of the monarchy and thus placed more authority in the hands of the crown in New Brunswick than the crown possessed in Britain. Moreover, in 1805, when defending the right of the landowners of Saint John to exclusive access to the fisheries adjoining their land, Chipman declared that it was "absurd to apply the obsolete articles of Magna Charta and principles of the Common Law to this Country, whose settlement depends upon principles and practice diametrically opposite to them." Since one of the largest landowners was William Hazen*, his father-in-law, his inconsistency on that occasion is understandable.

The legal system, both conservative and harsh, was not popular in the colony, and Chipman contributed to its unpopularity by insisting upon a scale of fees that was excessively high. In 1787 Chief Justice George Duncan Ludlow* cut Chipman's fees as clerk of the circuits by nearly one half. In 1802 Chipman sought to have disallowed an act of the assembly which prohibited attorneys from accepting fees in cases where the sum contested was less than £5. In both instances Chipman defended the existing fees as essential for the maintenance of a "respectable" bar. In reality, as Ludlow recognized, the higher level of fees made the legal system accessible to only a tiny percentage of the population, limited the number of potential clients, and thus contributed to the ferocious competition among the members of the bar, which Chipman found "peculiarly unpleasant" and which in part accounted for the number of duels fought by members of the legal fraternity [see George Ludlow WETMORE]. The emphasis on respectability also ensured that the legal profession was a closed community drawn from the children of the wealthy and well connected. All of Chipman's students were the sons of prominent loyalists and, since no one who entered his office failed to be admitted to the Supreme Court as an attorney, one may assume that birth was more important than talent in becoming a lawyer. Chipman was not alone in defending a legal system that was relatively unresponsive to public opinion and a profession that was extremely unrepresentative of society at large, but he was one of the most vociferous and influential critics of reform.

Chipman's legal career was not, however, entirely devoid of acts of altruism. In 1800 he acted without payment as counsel for a black woman, Nancy (Ann), in a test case of the legality of slave-holding in New Brunswick. Virtually the whole of the loyalist legal establishment sympathized with slavery, and Chipman and his co-counsel, Samuel Denny STREET, who was something of an outsider, were opposed in court by Jonathan Bliss, Thomas Wetmore, John Murray BLISS, Charles Jeffery Peters, and William Botsford. Although Street was the driving force behind the case – it was he who had initiated the proceedings – and although the comparative importance of the two men in the conduct of the litigation is uncertain since Street's brief has not survived, there is no doubt that Chipman played a major role. After an exhaustive search of the Nova Scotian statutes, he realized that his case was weak, but he "carefully avoided mentioning" the law that undermined his position and prepared an 80-page brief which helped convince two of the four Supreme Court judges that slavery was illegal in New Brunswick. Since the bench was divided, no judgement was rendered and Nancy was returned to her master, Caleb Jones*. Slave-holding persisted in New Brunswick for at least another two decades because of the conservatism of the Supreme Court, but the legal uncertainty that the 1800 case prompted contributed to the withering away of slavery.

Historian David Bell has implied that Chipman's participation in this case was motivated by a desire to bring himself to the attention of the imperial authorities, and certainly his decision in 1805 to take the side of Stair AGNEW in another slavery case suggests that he was not a fanatical abolitionist. Nevertheless, there is no reason to doubt that in 1800 he joined with Street because he found slavery morally repugnant, and he had every right in later years to extol his work as a "volunteer for the rights of human nature." Following the War of 1812, when several hundred black refugees from the southern United States were accepted into New Brunswick, Chipman championed their cause. In 1816 he was responsible for the decision to grant licences of occupation to the refugees in the Loch Lomond area, about 12 miles from Saint John, and he urged in vain that the government should absorb the expenses of surveying the land upon which the blacks were to be settled. Yet this incident reveals the limits as well as the sincerity of Chipman's humanitarianism. He recommended that the blacks should be given 50-acre lots rather than the 200-acre lots normally given to white settlers. By arranging for their settlement on these terms he effectively created a subculture of poverty and a source of cheap domestic labour for the Saint John élite.

The same mixture of charitable intentions and ethnocentricity can be seen in Chipman's attitude to the native peoples of New Brunswick. In 1786 he was the prosecutor in a celebrated case in which two former soldiers were convicted of murdering an Indian, a case which established that crimes against native peoples would not go unpunished [see Pierre Benoît*]. After the London-based New England Company, a philanthropic organization dedicated to "civilizing" the Indians, had extended its operations to New Brunswick, Chipman was appointed to the local board of commissioners in 1795 and actively participated in its deliberations. In 1802 he was one of a number of dissident commissioners who expressed dissatisfaction with the slow progress of the company's program of assimilation, although he did not join the others when they submitted their resignations in 1803. After the board was reconstituted in 1806, Chipman became secretary-treasurer at a salary of £50 per annum and he supported the new policy, adopted in 1807, of attempting to segregate Indian children from their parents. Chipman can hardly be condemned for his insensitivity in approving such a policy, since it reflected contemporary attitudes, but he can legitimately be criticized for turning a blind eye to the incompetence and rapacity of Oliver ARNOLD, the Anglican minister in charge of the company's school at Sussex Vale (Sussex Corner), and to the failings of John Coffin*, the superintendent of the apprenticeship program, who exercised virtually no supervision over the whites to whom Indian children were apprenticed. In the long term the major beneficiaries of the company's activities, which were terminated in 1826, were Chipman and his colleagues who, as a modern historian has commented, regarded "the Company's funds as another source of English compensation for the deprivations" they had suffered as loyalists. Chipman was eager to accelerate the rate of assimilation, but he never seems to have taken seriously the desire of the company to bring the rudiments of European education and the benefits of the Protestant religion to the Indians.

Chipman's limited devotion to the religious objectives of the New England Company is hardly surprising. Although a member of the Church of England, he was no zealot. It is true that, as solicitor general, he was responsible for preparing the bill incorporating Trinity Church in Saint John in 1789 and that he was for many years a vestryman of the church; towards the end of his life, moreover, he agreed to give Trinity the land upon which to erect a new church in return for pews for himself and his family. He also supported the 1786 law establishing the Church of England in New Brunswick and opposed the bills introduced at virtually every session of the assembly to allow dissenting ministers to perform marriages. In 1822 he claimed that "the interests of the Church are daily gaining strength." In reality, however, like most of his contemporaries according to a modern historian, he accepted "the limited effectiveness of the Anglican Church with a curious indifference." He was prepared to see some government patronage extended to all the Protestant sects and to allow the more respectable

Chipman

dissenting ministers to receive commissions as justices of the peace and thus to perform civil marriages. Similarly, on questions of education, he was a moderate. He sat on the board of directors of the public grammar school in Saint John and, after 1820, on the board of trustees for the Madras schools, which, while run by the Church of England, were open to the children of dissenters. But this ambivalence did not extend to institutions of higher learning. In 1785 he was one of the original petitioners for the incorporation of a provincial college, and in 1786 he assisted Attorney General Bliss in preparing the charter, which was modelled upon that of Columbia College in New York and effectively restricted entry to those who belonged to the Church of England. After 1800 he served on the governing board of the College of New Brunswick and assisted in its fund-raising campaigns in Britain. Clearly Chipman was not prepared to compromise when the interests of the privileged class to which he belonged seemed to be at stake.

Chipman was nevertheless more tolerant toward dissenters than were the members of the loyalist gentry in Fredericton. His sympathy was in part determined by his marriage on 24 Oct. 1786 to Elizabeth Hazen, daughter of an important non-Anglican family. He at no time regretted this decision: in 1793 he wrote to a friend, "I never knew what real happiness was till I was married." Moreover, the union with Elizabeth brought a number of tangible advantages. Her father, one of the founders of the firm of Simonds, Hazen and White, which had been established at the mouth of the Saint John River prior to the revolution, was a member of the Council, a wealthy and influential merchant, and the owner of a large and valuable estate in and around Saint John. Chipman became William Hazen's solicitor and gradually acquired a substantial quantity of Hazen land, inherited in due course by Ward Chipman Jr, who was born on 10 July 1787.

Chipman's marriage consolidated his standing among the social élite. In Saint John, unlike Fredericton, the distinction between loyalist and non-loyalist was early blurred through intermarriage, and by virtue of his alliance with the Hazens Chipman became connected to a network of highly influential families in the colony, including the Murrays and the Botsfords. His own loyalist credentials were, of course, impeccable and he remained on friendly terms with key figures in the Fredericton élite, particularly Edward Winslow. But he was also willing to part company with them on such questions as where the Supreme Court should sit and whether slavery should be upheld in New Brunswick. Indeed, on the latter issue he found himself acting with Samuel Denny Street, the *bête noire* of the Fredericton establishment. Yet the provincial secretary, Jonathan Odell*, commented when Chipman

was named to the Council that the appointment "cannot fail to be considered by every member of the Council as a very valuable acquisition to that Board and the public."

Part of the reason for Chipman's ability to maintain good relations with the different factions of the New Brunswick élite was his immense charm. He could work with those with whom he disagreed politically, and he did not allow professional disappointments to destroy personal friendships. When Winslow was appointed a judge over his head, Chipman accepted the decision philosophically, and after Winslow's death he generously contributed to a fund to assist his three unmarried daughters, who had been left virtually destitute. Unlike Jonathan Bliss, who was once a close friend but who became so disillusioned with life in the backwoods of New Brunswick that he retreated into semi-seclusion, Chipman was noted for his hospitality. Following his marriage, he built one of the most impressive houses in Saint John. Decorated with English wallpaper and furnished lavishly, it became, in one historian's words, "the social center of the city for a century." Prince Edward* Augustus stayed with the Chipmans when he visited Saint John in 1794. Over time Chipman added to his estate and constructed an elaborate garden and a flourishing farm. He took his responsibilities as a gentleman farmer seriously. He imported seeds, experimented with crops, and was noted for his "fine potatoes," which he sold in New England. On 7 Oct. 1818 he was made an honorary member of the Massachusetts Society for Promoting Agriculture.

Although Chipman was dedicated to re-creating in New Brunswick the style of life of an English country gentleman, he was by no means opposed to commerce. He could not afford to be. Not only was he connected to the most prominent merchant family in Saint John but he depended for his livelihood upon the income generated by his legal practice and the merchants of Saint John were the only group in the city wealthy enough to avail themselves of his services. Indeed, since money invested in land brought a poor return and there was a need to diversify his holdings, Chipman himself became involved in commerce. During the 1780s he invested heavily in a flour-mill, which flourished for a time. From 1808 until 1820, as one of the members of the committee of correspondence with New Brunswick's agents in London, he was involved in a campaign which brought about changes in the navigation acts of considerable advantage to the merchant community in Saint John. In the 1820s he assisted in organizing the Bank of New Brunswick and he was one of the earliest and most prominent advocates of a canal between the Bay of Fundy and the Baie Verte.

Despite Chipman's social standing and his enthusiastic advocacy of the commercial interests of Saint

140

John, he was not a popular figure among ordinary citizens in the city. In 1785 he ran for the House of Assembly as one of a slate of six pro-government candidates in Saint John. The slate was composed entirely of prominent loyalists who had been given choice grants of land in the Upper Cove section of the city and was opposed by a rival slate from the Lower Cove section, who denounced the favouritism shown to the élite, resurrected bitter memories of the petition of the 55, and appealed to the electorate to reject office holders such as Chipman and Jonathan Bliss. Just when the Lower Cove candidates were virtually assured of election, a riot broke out between supporters of the two factions. The sheriff, William Sanford Oliver, closed the polls for a time, arrested a number of the Lower Cove supporters, including one of their candidates, and called in the military. In a post-election scrutiny he disallowed many of the votes cast for the Lower Cove slate and declared Chipman and his colleagues elected, a decision upheld by the governor and the loyalist-dominated assembly.

With Chipman and his friends at the helm, New Brunswick's first assembly proved extremely pliable to the wishes of the executive. Chipman was partly responsible for drafting the reply to the speech from the throne in 1786 and he helped to prepare the rules of procedure of the assembly. According to Edward Winslow, he was "as much distinguished in the midnight revels as in the noon-day debates." The only serious dispute in the assembly was over the payment of members, which Chipman opposed. In 1788 he divided the house 23 times on this question and thus incurred the displeasure of the majority of his fellow assemblymen who supported the measure and the future hostility of the liberal historian James Hannay*. Chipman also antagonized his constituents when he did not protest against the decision made in 1786 by Carleton, now lieutenant governor, to transfer the capital from Saint John to Fredericton. In private Chipman was doubtful of the wisdom of Carleton's action but he was not prepared to challenge the lieutenant governor's authority. He did, however, criticize the Supreme Court for holding all its sessions in Fredericton, partly because he believed that this procedure detrimentally affected his legal practice, and in 1791 he introduced a bill, subsequently rejected by the Council, to compel the Supreme Court to hold two of its sessions in Saint John.

Whatever support this bill may have won Chipman in Saint John was dissipated in the long dispute in which he supported the right of his father-in-law to a monopoly of the fisheries adjoining the latter's vast estates in Saint John. In February 1791 a measure granting owners exclusive access to the fisheries off their properties was passed in the assembly by one vote. All of the Saint John members, save Chipman, voted against the measure and all of the city magis-

trates, save Chipman, subsequently endorsed a petition objecting to the assembly's decision. After the bill became law, the city council obstructed Hazen's efforts to restrict access to the fisheries and appealed to the courts, where Chipman acted as Hazen's attorney. The matter was contested for many years and was not finally settled until 1830, when the Privy Council pronounced against the Hazen interests.

In the election of 1793 Chipman was soundly beaten in Saint John. Although he was returned for Northumberland County, he was unsuccessful when he sought "to get the Speaker's chair" and he criticized the majority in the assembly as "a set of fools or blackguards & quite under the influence of City Politics." Blaming his defeat in Saint John on the "lower Covers headed by [Elias Hardy*]," he tried, unsuccessfully in 1794 but successfully in 1795, to have Hardy dismissed as the common clerk of the city. In 1795 another general election was called and Chipman was again defeated in his bid to represent Saint John; this time he was left without a seat in the house. During the later 1790s, when the assembly and the executive were engaged in a bitter dispute over finances, Chipman was forced to watch from the sidelines. In 1793 he had petitioned for and had received a salary of £50 per annum for his work as solicitor general, but his salary went unpaid because of the refusal of the assembly to agree to the government's supply bill and he seethed with anger at the assembly's activities. His anger was fuelled by financial distress. The late 1780s and 1790s were not a prosperous period in New Brunswick and his legal practice withered. Chipman had spent money lavishly on his new house and in 1786 he lost "the little I had in the world" when one of his investments went sour. In 1790 he was severely disappointed when a vacant judgeship was not given to the attorney general, since if Jonathan Bliss had received the appointment, Chipman would have been next in line for the attorney generalship and for a subsequent opening on the bench. The following year he tried in vain to secure a judicial post in Upper Canada. By 1792 he had begun to "despair" of the future. Deprived of a political career after 1795 and tied to a law practice that consumed little of his time and generated insufficient income for his needs, Chipman became even more despondent.

Chipman was "regenerated," to use Winslow's word, by a stroke of unanticipated good fortune. The Treaty of Paris of 1783 had inadequately drawn the boundary between Nova Scotia and the District of Maine (then part of Massachusetts), and in 1794 the American and British governments agreed to establish a commission to resolve the territorial dispute that had resulted. In 1796 Chipman was selected as the British agent and for two years and nine months he devoted his very considerable talents to the task of preparing

Chipman

and advocating the British case. The primary task of the commission, on which Thomas Henry BARCLAY sat as the representative of Great Britain, was to decide the identity of the river defined as the St Croix in the treaty of 1783. The American agent, James Sullivan, argued that the Magaguadavic was the St Croix and based his case upon the map drawn by John Mitchell in 1755 and testimony from Indians in the area, but Chipman was able to cast doubt upon the accuracy of the Mitchell map and turn the evidence of the Indians to his own advantage. In his presentation to the commission, based upon extensive research into both French and English documents, Chipman marshalled irrefutable evidence to show that the Scoodic was the St Croix. Although he was unable to convince the commissioners that the southern branch of the Scoodic should be adopted in tracing the river to its source, he secured his major objective and earned high praise for his diligence and industry. During the meetings of the commission Chipman was able to make a "long promised visit" to old friends in Massachusetts and to renew contacts with his family there. Two of his sisters had married prominent Salem merchants and Chipman wisely invested a large proportion of the £960 per annum he had earned as agent in ships owned by his brothers-in-law, William Gray and Thomas Ward. By 1798 he was again on the road to solvency and he had been promised by his superiors in London that his services would "not be unrewarded."

The return to a relatively inactive life after 1798 was disillusioning. Chipman's legal practice in Saint John continued to occupy little of his time and he was "obliged to condescend to the most laborious drudgery of office in matters of the most trifling concern." In October 1802 he was again rebuffed when he ran for the assembly in Saint John and in 1804 he complained that he would never have settled in New Brunswick if he known how "unrewarding" life would be there. Chipman's complaints must be taken with a grain of salt. In 1801 he was able to purchase another substantial block of land in Saint John, his investments in Massachusetts continued to return a handsome profit, and his wine-cellar was the most extensive in the city. Chipman's difficulty was that he wished to enjoy a style of life vastly superior to that of his neighbours and out of line with his resources. By 1807 he was in such desperate financial straits that he was compelled to accept a small allowance from his sister, Elizabeth Gray. The Grays had boarded Ward Chipman Jr while he prepared for his entry to Harvard and they encouraged Chipman Sr to return to the United States. Chipman was not prepared to become an American citizen but in 1805, after a visit to his relatives the previous year, he unsuccessfully sought to become the British consul in Boston. In 1807 Edward Winslow obtained the vacancy on the New

Brunswick bench caused by the death of Isaac Allan, even though Thomas Carleton pointed out that it would be "an act of injustice to pass over" Chipman, because of his "superior Talents." Although Chipman had apparently disclaimed interest in the appointment because the annual salary of a puisne judge was only £300, he was clearly disappointed by Winslow's promotion, particularly since Winslow had no formal legal training and was not a member of the bar.

Chipman had been named to the Council on 6 Feb. 1806 and took his seat on 2 Feb. 1807. The appointment gave him a renewed sense of purpose and he took an active part in the deliberations of the Council, although except during the three-month presidency of Edward Winslow in 1808 he had limited influence with the various administrators and lieutenant governors of the colony. In 1808 two vacancies occurred on the bench with the deaths of George Duncan Ludlow and Joshua Upham*. Chipman was unable to secure the post of chief justice, which went to Jonathan Bliss, but he mustered all his influence in Britain to ensure that he, and not "the little Creeper," Samuel Denny Street, was given the other vacancy. Although the salary of a puisne judge had been raised to £500, Chipman claimed he would lose money by accepting the appointment, since he would have to resign his multiple offices and retire from private practice. None the less, eager to be relieved of "the slavish drudgery and *butchery*" of private practice and content with a modest but secure income "during the residue of my pilgrimage in this sequestered retirement on the *back side* of the Bay of Fundy," he accepted the post and took his place on the bench in 1809. One additional attraction of the appointment was that it enabled him to provide for Ward Chipman Jr, who succeeded his father as advocate general and clerk of the crown on the circuits and inherited his father's private practice. Chipman performed his judicial duties conscientiously and competently, but he did not contribute significantly to the evolution of provincial law. His primary concern was to insist upon the enforcement of the existing criminal code and he was known for his severity and rigidity.

Chipman did, however, earn a lasting place in New Brunswick history by his contributions to the settlement of the boundary dispute with the United States. The commission of 1796–98 had identified the Scoodic as the St Croix, but it had not resolved the ownership of a number of islands in Passamaquoddy Bay or settled the location of the boundary along the highlands north of the St Croix. The fourth and fifth articles of the Treaty of Ghent of 1814 provided for the establishment of commissions to settle these problems. On 12 July 1815 Chipman was again named the agent for Britain; Barclay was reappointed as the British commissioner. In preparing his case for the St Croix commission, Chipman had carefully laid the basis for establishing British ownership of the major islands in Passamaquoddy Bay and, although the British government eventually agreed to surrender several of the smaller islands to the United States, the Passamaquoddy Islands commission, which began its meetings at St Andrews in September 1816, upheld the British claim to Grand Manan, the most important of the islands in dispute. The commission dealing with the northern boundary between New Brunswick and the United States also began its hearings in September 1816. As early as 1796 Chipman had recognized that "by the most favorable decision we can obtain . . . our communication with Canada by the River St. John will be interrupted," and he had recommended then that Britain ought to obstruct the negotiations until the Americans were ready to agree to a settlement which would "preserve that communication unbroken." In 1816 Chipman implemented this policy. He successfully disguised the weakness of the British case in order to ensure that the commission would fail to reach agreement and would be forced to refer the dispute to a neutral umpire from whom Britain might anticipate "a favorable decision." With great skill Chipman prepared his arguments and largely because of his efforts the commission concluded its meetings in October 1821 without reaching an agreement. In 1830 the dispute was referred to the king of the Netherlands, who in 1831 recommended, as Chipman had predicted, a compromise settlement favourable to Britain. Although the American Senate refused to accept this recommendation, the dispute was eventually settled by the Webster–Ashburton commission in 1842, roughly upon the basis that Chipman had anticipated. A critical figure in preparing the British presentation to the king of the Netherlands and in the later negotiations was Ward Chipman Jr, who assisted his father as a co-agent after 1816.

Increasingly afflicted by gout, from which he had suffered intermittently since 1779, Chipman delegated the more onerous part of his duties as British agent to his son after 1817. Although he was antagonized by the conduct of Lieutenant Governor George Stracey SMYTH, who refused to distribute patronage exclusively to the older loyalist families, and although he signed a petition objecting to Smyth's decision to dismiss Henry Bliss* as clerk of the Supreme Court in 1822, Chipman did not play a particularly active role in politics at this time and he began to prepare for retirement. Early in 1823 he offered to resign from the bench if given a pension. In March 1823, however, Smyth died and, when the senior member of the Council, George LEONARD, declined to take on the administration and Christopher Billopp, the next in line, refused to come to Fredericton to take the oaths of office, Chipman was sworn in as president on 1 April 1823. Encouraged by a minority on the Council residing in Saint John, Billopp challenged the legality

of Chipman's appointment and issued a proclamation as administrator. Somewhat reluctantly, the British government allowed Chipman to continue in office, and he set out "to correct some of the abuses which have lately crept in, and place the public business in a train which will smooth the path of those who come after me." One of Chipman's first decisions was to suspend from office the surveyor general, Anthony Lockwood*, because of his "eccentric, outrageous and apparently insane conduct & behaviour." For more than a year Chipman held the reins of office and during that period he appointed a host of his relatives to minor offices, thus incurring the anger of those who had supported Smyth and expected preferment. Because the new lieutenant governor, Sir Howard Douglas*, had to postpone his arrival, Chipman was responsible for convening the assembly in January 1824. Ward Chipman Jr was elected speaker, and as a result Chipman's relationship with the assembly was cordial, even though he denied the members access to some of the government documents they requested. The burden of administering the government nevertheless proved too great for his health. He fell ill, and died on 9 Feb. 1824. He was succeeded as administrator by John Murray Bliss.

Upon Chipman's death the *New-Brunswick Royal Gazette* noted that he was "the last Survivor" of the loyalist office holders who had founded New Brunswick and praised "his able and zealous exertions at all times to promote the Interests of this Colony." Indeed, it is arguable that Chipman was the most influential of the founding fathers of New Brunswick. Although the pressure for the partition of Nova Scotia originated with others, Chipman played an active part in convincing the imperial government that partition was desirable. As one of Carleton's legal advisers and as a member of the first assembly, he played an important, if secondary, role in establishing the institutions of the new colony, particularly the municipal institutions of Saint John. Passionately devoted to the interests of the legal profession, he critically influenced its development and the legal system of the colony. In a host of areas he helped to shape the social institutions of New Brunswick and he was crucially important, through his work on the boundary commissions, in defining the territorial limits of the province.

Undeniably, Chipman's commitment to New Brunswick was the child of necessity. The "New Canaan" was a refuge for those loyalists, like Chipman, who had tied their careers in the Thirteen Colonies to the imperial connection and who had limited options after the United States won its independence. Chipman's attitude to the new American nation was ambivalent. Although he joined the loyalist exodus, he did not initially rule out the possibility of remaining in the land of his birth; he maintained strong ties with his relatives there; he visited New England whenever he had the opportunity; he invested a substantial proportion of his capital in American shipping; and he sent his son to Harvard. His attitude to Britain was similarly ambivalent. He was a supporter of the British cause, but he did not enjoy exile in the mother country in 1776–77 and 1784 and he was disillusioned by the imperial government's benign neglect of the North American colonies after the outbreak of the Napoleonic Wars. Moreover, "the Land of promise" did not live up to his hopes and expectations. Although he achieved greater financial success than most of his contemporaries and bequeathed to his son a substantial estate and a position of social prominence, Chipman's life was spent in a continuous struggle against insolvency. He was also discouraged by political developments in New Brunswick. During the constitutional crisis of the 1790s, he began to doubt whether the proper balance of power between the executive and the assembly could be preserved. On the occasion of a later conflict he lamented, "If there was one spark of spirit or discernment in their Constituents not one of them [those advocating the claims of the assembly] would ever be again chosen – but so capricious is the many headed monster, and so revolutionary the spirit of the present times, that the probability is that as ignorant as abandoned and wicked a set would be again returned."

Despite fits of despondency, Chipman continued to believe that, if properly governed, New Brunswick would become "one of the most valuable and important parts of His Majesty's North American Possessions." In 1824 he called upon the members of the legislature to remember that "we are the Survivors and Descendents" of those settlers who had created New Brunswick "as an Asylum for his [majesty's] faithful and loyal Subjects." Since Chipman's loyalty was based in large measure upon self-interest and he continued to view "Superior interest" as the key to promotion in his profession, one may view these protestations cynically. But over time Chipman's muted anti-Americanism and moderate conservatism hardened into an ideology of loyalism that profoundly influenced the provincial culture of New Brunswick. In a very real sense his greatest achievement was the role he played in passing on this ideology to the second-generation loyalist gentry, who continued to uphold "the principles of their Fathers."

PHILLIP BUCKNER

A diary by Chipman has been published under the title "Ward Chipman diary: a loyalist's return to New England in 1783," ed. J. B. Berry, Essex Insitute, *Hist. Coll.* (Salem, Mass.), 87 (1951): 211–41.

Maine Hist. Soc. (Portland), Thomas Barclay papers, Chipman to Smythe, 3 Dec. 1817. Mass. Hist. Soc. (Boston), T. W. Ward papers, Chipman to William Ward, 30 May 1816; Ward to Chipman, 19 Sept. 1822. N.B. Museum, Chipman, Ward, CB DOC., nos.8, 18; F66, no.20; W. F. Ganong coll., Ward Chipman to Thomas Carleton, 12 Aug. 1796, 26 Dec. 1798; Chipman to William Knox, 19 Oct. 1796, 1 Dec. 1798; Knox to Chipman, 2 Feb. 1797; H. T. Hazen coll.: Ward Chipman papers, Ward Chipman, notebook of law study under Daniel Leonard and Jonathan Sewell, Boston, 1774; corr. of Chipman to: Henry Appleton and Frederick Pigeon, 7 Nov. 1789; Stephen DeBlois, 18 May 1786; Sir Howard Douglas, 18 Dec. 1823; James Fraser, 30 Nov. 1803; William Gray, 22 June 1807; H. Hatch, 7 Jan. 1814; William Hazen, 3 June 1809; Thomas Paddock, 28 May 1823; Rev. Sherwood, 2 May 1822; Sir John Wentworth, 18 March 1816; Gideon White, 25 May 1786; corr. to Chipman from: Henry Bass, 16 April 1788; Jonathan Bliss, 8 Nov. 1810; William Botsford, 17, 20, 29 Oct. 1822; M. Brimmer, 18 Sept. 1822; Eliza Gray, January 1806; Joseph Gray, 9 Dec. 1787; William Gray, 28 Dec. 1787; John Hammell, 26 Nov. 1787; C. W. Hazen, 21 April 1806; Gideon White, various dates; Justus Wright, 6, 12 Dec. 1789; Hazen papers, court records, 1783–1806. PAC, MG 23, D1, ser.1, 2: 572–73; 6: 499–502; 7: 183–98; GII, 10, vol.2: 325–32, 357–64, 373–84, 393–98, 411–14, 452–57, 586–89; vol.3: 644–57, 762–69, 776–79, 790–93, 805–12, 831–34, 867–72, 943–46, 960–63, 1031–42, 1168–71; vol.4: 1373–76, 1708–11, 1865–68, 1878–81, 1889–92, 1903–6; vol.6: 2805–6, 2824–27. PANB, RG 2, RS6, A3, 27 March, 1 April 1823. PANS, MG 1, 164c, no.1; 1603, no.40. PRO, AO 12/11: 86–88; 12/61: 45; CO 188/29: 75–76; WO 42/59: 426. UNBL, MG H2, 5: 1: 9: 69; 11: 93; 14: 108.

N.B., House of Assembly, *Journal*, 1786, 1791; Legislative Council, *Journal* [1786–1830]. *Winslow papers* (Raymond). *New-Brunswick Royal Gazette*, 8 Aug. 1820, 20 Aug. 1822, 10 Feb. 1824. R. M. Chipman, "The Chipman lineage, particularly as in Essex County, Mass.," Essex Institute, *Hist. Coll.*, 11 (1871): 263–319. Jones, *Loyalists of Mass.* Shipton, *Sibley's Harvard graduates.* Stark, *Loyalists of Mass.* (1910). Carol Berkin, *Jonathan Sewall: odyssey of an American loyalist* (New York, 1974). Gorman Condon, "Envy of American states." Hannay, *Hist. of N.B.* Lawrence, *Judges of N.B.* (Stockton and Raymond). J. S. MacKinnon, "The development of local government in the city of Saint John, 1785–1795" (MA thesis, Univ. of N.B., Fredericton, 1968), 26–43, 137. MacNutt, *New Brunswick.* D. R. Moore, "John Saunders, 1754–1834: consummate loyalist" (MA thesis, Univ. of N.B., 1980). J. M. Murrin, "The legal transformation: the bench and bar of eighteenth-century Massachusetts," *Colonial America: essays in politics and social development*, ed. S. N. Katz (Boston, [1971]), 415–49. M. B. Norton, *The British-Americans: the loyalist exiles in England, 1774–1789* (Boston and Toronto, 1972). P. A. Ryder, "Ward Chipman, United Empire Loyalist" (MA thesis, Univ. of N.B., 1958). E. O. Tubrett, "The development of the New Brunswick court system, 1784–1803" (MA thesis, Univ. of N.B., 1967). R. W. Winks, *The blacks in Canada: a history* (London and New Haven, Conn., 1971).

Murray Barkley, "The loyalist tradition in New Brunswick: the growth and evolution of an historical myth, 1825–1914," *Acadiensis* (Fredericton), 4 (1974–75), no.2: 3–45. D. G. Bell, "Slavery and the judges of loyalist New Brunswick," *Univ. of New Brunswick Law Journal* (Saint

John), 31 (1982): 9–42. Kenneth Donovan, "The origin and establishment of the New Brunswick courts," N.B. Museum, *Journal* (Saint John), 1980: 57–64. Judith Fingard, "The New England Company and the New Brunswick Indians, 1786–1826: a comment on the colonial perversion of British benevolence," *Acadiensis* (Fredericton), 1 (1971–72), no.2: 29–42. W. F. Ganong, "A monograph of the evolution of the boundaries of the province of New Brunswick," RSC *Trans.*, 2nd ser., 7 (1901), sect.II: 139–449. Marion Gilroy, "The partition of Nova Scotia, 1784," *CHR*, 14 (1933): 375–91. Edward Gray, "Ward Chipman, loyalist," Mass. Hist. Soc., *Proc.* (Boston), 54 (1920–21): 331–53. R. W. Hale, "The forgotten Maine boundary commission," Mass. Hist. Soc., *Proc.*, 71 (1953–57): 147–55. D. R. Jack, "James White, late high sheriff of St. John," *Acadiensis* (Saint John), 3 (1903): 296–300. I. A. Jack, "The loyalists and slavery in New Brunswick," RSC *Trans.*, 2nd ser., 4 (1898), sect.II: 137–85. W. O. Raymond, "The fishery quarrel," *New Brunswick Magazine* (Saint John), 3 (July–September 1899): 57–70. W. A. Spray, "The settlement of the black refugees in New Brunswick, 1815–1836," *Acadiensis* (Fredericton), 6 (1976–77), no.2: 64–79. R. D. and J. I. Tallman, "The diplomatic search for the St. Croix River, 1796–1798," *Acadiensis*, 1 (1971–72), no.2: 59–71.

CIQUARD, FRANÇOIS (baptized **François Roussel**), Roman Catholic priest and Sulpician; b. 30 Aug. 1754 in Langlade, France, son of François Roussel Ciquard and Luce Gautier; d. 28 Sept. 1824 in Montreal.

François Ciquard, who came from a humble background, entered the well-known college run by the Jesuits at Billom in 1771; after six years of study there he took his theology at Clermont-Ferrand. To support himself he tutored a boy from the town. Drawn to an ideal of perfection, after some hesitation and a trip to Sept-Fons he entered the Sulpician seminary in Clermont on 30 Oct. 1779 and was ordained priest on 22 Dec. 1781. For a while he served as a curate, and then he asked to be allowed to join the Sulpicians. He arrived at the Séminaire de Saint-Sulpice in Paris in May 1782 and did his solitude (noviciate) there. During his stay he informed the superior, Jacques-André Émery, of his desire to serve in the mission field. When Étienne Montgolfier* sought recruits for the Séminaire de Saint-Sulpice in Montreal, Émery persuaded Ciquard to leave for the province of Quebec with Antoine Capel.

Since the royal instructions of 1764 did not allow French priests into the province, Ciquard went to England dressed as a layman, with a passport that termed him a merchant, and he finally reached Quebec on 21 May 1783. After a short visit with Bishop Jean-Olivier Briand*, Capel and Ciquard went to Montreal, where Montgolfier welcomed them with open arms as the first priests to arrive from France since the conquest. But Governor Frederick Haldimand*, who was opposed to the recruitment of clergy

through immigration, decided to expel them, even though a petition from parishioners in Montreal was presented by Jean-Baptiste-Amable Adhémar* and Pierre-François Mézière. Ciquard was arrested in Montreal on 19 June and put on board a ship at Quebec. As he was ill, he obtained permission to land temporarily at La Malbaie. He seized the chance to flee and returned to Montreal. Retaken and again arrested, he embarked at Bic on the frigate *Pandore* and reached Paris on 20 Sept. 1783.

Ciquard was appointed professor at the Séminaire de Bourges, and then bursar at the Petit Séminaire there. During the French revolution he took refuge in Orléans. Subsequently he agreed to join three other Sulpicians to assist the bishop of Baltimore, John Carroll. On 7 Oct. 1792 he arrived at Passamaquoddy Bay (Maine/N.B.), and Carroll entrusted him with the Abenaki mission at Penobscot (Castine, Maine). But when the American authorities refused to grant land to the missionaries and the Indians, they left the United States and in May 1794 sought asylum in New Brunswick, settling at Saint-Basile in the Madawaska region. Ciquard went to Quebec in June and was recognized by the British authorities there and in New Brunswick. He even received an annual allowance of £50 from Thomas Carleton*, the lieutenant governor of the latter colony.

Returning to New Brunswick, he began ministering to some Acadian families and Indians at Saint-Basile. Although he had been warmly welcomed, Ciquard recorded nevertheless that the Acadians did not fully respond to his exhortations and that the Indians did not want to work and disappeared during the winter. He paid a visit to Bishop Jean-François Hubert* in 1796 and then went to Montreal to see his former confrères again. In the summer of 1798 Bishop Carroll invited him to join Sulpician missionary Michel Levadoux at Detroit. After serving there for some months Ciquard left in May 1799. He returned to his flock in the Fredericton area and got on better with the Indians and the French-speaking parishioners than he had before. Despite his poverty he made donations to nuns in Lower Canada and to various charitable endeavours. In the summer of 1802 he went to Quebec again and met Bishop Pierre Denaut*. The following year Denaut put him in charge of the parish of Caraquet, N.B., but the priest there did not want to surrender his post. Ciquard, distressed by this experience, was transferred to Memramcook, replacing Thomas Power, who nevertheless continued to live in the parish. At first Ciquard gave his predecessor a third of his tithes; after Power's death in 1806 he was a little better off. He was already beginning to think of his retirement and wanted to return to the Sulpician seminary in either Montreal or Baltimore.

In August 1812 the bishop of Quebec, Joseph-Octave PLESSIS, put him in charge of the parish of

Clark

Saint-François-du-Lac and the Odanak mission, in Lower Canada. Ciquard, who had a good grasp of the Abenaki language and who had secured permission to take up residence in the province, chose to live in the presbytery at Odanak, judging that since the mission had been left without a priest for 30 years, it was in greater need of his presence. His material circumstances were precarious, but Ciquard was able to adapt to an ascetic régime. The division of time he was required to make between the mission and the parish earned him criticism from people at Saint-François-du-Lac. To prepare for his replacement at the mission Bishop Plessis appointed seminarist Jacques Paquin* as his assistant, so that Ciquard could teach him the Abenaki language. Paquin was ordained in 1814 and Plessis named him to the mission in October 1815.

Ciquard returned to the Séminaire de Saint-Sulpice, was admitted as a member of the community on 23 Oct. 1815, and was immediately made assistant priest in the parish of Notre-Dame in Montreal. He replaced Jean-Henry-Auguste Roux as chaplain to the sisters of the Congregation of Notre-Dame, and in addition he had the task of visiting and tending the sick in the neighbourhoods to the west of the parish. That year he also took on the chaplaincy of the Congrégation des Hommes de Ville-Marie, a Marian brotherhood active in the community, and after 1817 he held the chaplaincy of a women's organization in the parish, the Confrérie de la Sainte-Famille. He preached in church about ten times a year, including one or two sermons during the novena of St Francis Xavier. Although at times stilted and solemn, his style was none the less lively and agreeable.

François Ciquard thus had a busy old age. His presence and his pastoral activity were greatly appreciated by his fellow Sulpicians, most of whom were also French in origin. He was stricken suddenly with hemiplegia and died within two days, on 28 Sept. 1824; he was buried in the crypt under the chancel of Notre-Dame in Montreal.

BRUNO HAREL

François Ciquard's large collection of papers, which Sulpician Jean-Baptiste-Elizé Philpin de Rivières consulted for an unpublished biography, is at the Arch. of the U.S. Province of the Sulpician Order, St Mary's Seminary and Univ., Baltimore, Md., RG 52, Box 1: 581–676. Ciquard is the author of *Portrait d'un missionnaire apostolique* (Québec, 1810), the manuscript copy of which is at ASSM, 36, no.13.

AAQ, 22 A, V: 511; 1 CB, VI: 21–22; IX: 129; 71-31 CD, I: 192, 197, 202, 216; 7 CM, I: 8; 311 CN, III: 15, 18–22, 24, 27, 29–30, 32–42, 44–56, 58–63; IV: 7, 67; VI: 26; 26 CP, II: 111. AD, Puy-de-Dome (Clermont-Ferrand), État civil, Vic-le-Comte, 30 août 1754. ANQ-M, CE1-51, 30 sept. 1824. ASSM, 24, dossier 6; 25, dossier 2; 49, dossier 23. Allaire, *Dictionnaire*, 1: 124. *The Catholic encyclopedia*, ed. C. G. Herbermann et al. (15v., New York, 1912), 14: 329–32. Gauthier, *Sulpitiana*. Louis Bertrand, *Biblio-*

thèque sulpicienne ou histoire littéraire de la Compagnie de Saint-Sulpice (3v., Paris, 1900), 2: 60–62. [Pierre] Boisard, *La Compagnie de Saint-Sulpice; trois siècles d'histoire* (s.l.n.d.). T.-M. Charland, *Histoire de Saint-François-du-Lac* (Ottawa, 1942), 213–28. A.[-H.] Gosselin, *L'Église du Canada après la Conquête* (2v., Québec, 1916–17), 2: 192, 194–97. Laval Laurent, *Québec et l'Église aux États-Unis sous Mgr Briand et Mgr Plessis* (Montréal, 1945). J. W. Ruane, *The beginnings of the Society of St. Sulpice in the United States (1791–1829)* (Baltimore, 1935). "Le gouverneur Haldimand et les prêtres français," *BRH*, 12 (1906): 248–52. Olivier Maurault, "Le troisième centenaire de l'arrivée des sulpiciens à Montréal, 1657–1957," *CCHA Rapport*, 24 (1956–57): 55–63. Fernand Ouellet, "Mgr Plessis et la naissance d'une bourgeoisie canadienne (1797–1810)," *CCHA Rapport*, 23 (1955–56): 83–99.

CLARK (Clarke), ROBERT, master millwright, JP, and militia officer; b. 16 March 1744 in Quaker Hill, N.Y.; m. Isobel (Isabella) Ketchum of Long Island, N.Y., and they had five sons and one daughter; d. 17 Dec. 1823 in Ernestown Township, Upper Canada.

Before the American revolution Robert Clark was a carpenter, millwright, and farmer, first in Dutchess County and then in Albany County, N.Y. Although a member of the rebel militia for three weeks in 1776, he joined the Loyal Volunteers and saw service in Major-General John Burgoyne*'s army. After the surrender at Saratoga (Schuylerville) in October 1777, Clark escaped and, "Leaving his family Exposed to the Rage of the Enemy," made his way to the province of Quebec. There his skill as a millwright was recognized. By 1780 he was attached to a corps of artificers under the control of the engineers. In this capacity, he worked on projects at St Johns (Saint-Jean-sur-Richelieu) and Montreal; he was last mustered with Major Edward Jessup*'s Loyal Rangers in 1783.

On 22 Aug. 1783 Captain William TWISS, the commanding engineer in Quebec, ordered Clark to report to Lieutenant William Tinling, who was in charge of the engineers at Cataraqui (Kingston) in western Quebec. Clark became master millwright and supervisor responsible for building the saw- and gristmills at Kingston Mills in preparation for the impending influx of loyalists [see Michael Grass*]. Good millwrights were in great demand but the commandant at Cataraqui, Major John Ross*, although satisfied with the technical aspects of Clark's work, wished to replace him with Lieutenant David Brass of Butler's Rangers whom he considered a "remarkable genious" and "exceeding Good Mill-wright." Commenting to Governor Haldimand* about Clark's administration of the project in a letter written on 10 June 1784, Ross was mildly critical: "The Saw Mill is a very good one, but an expensive Job and taken much longer time building than what Mr. Brass ... told me was necessary. I believe the man employed on the occasion to be a very good artificer himself, but perhaps has not the influence or command over the workmen as Mr. Brass is said to have." Whether the judgement was fair or not, Ross cited the need to reduce costs and expedite construction and sent immediately for Brass. Whatever disappointment Clark may have felt was probably mitigated by his reunion with his family in that same year.

In 1782 Isobel Clark and her three sons had been driven from their farm in New York and they arrived at Quebec in the autumn of the following year. In his memoirs another, younger son recalled their plight: "They wintered at Sorel, where they all were afflicted with the small-pox, and being entirely among strangers, most of whom spoke a language not understood by them, they were compelled to endure more than the usual amount of suffering incident to the disease." After a separation of seven years the family came together again at Cataraqui. In 1785 Clark took his wife and children to Napanee where he was again employed by the government to build saw- and gristmills, which were completed by late 1786. Although he usually worked in either Napanee or Millhaven, Clark located along the lake front of Ernestown Township near Parrotts Bay. In 1791 and 1792 he made repairs to the Napanee mill complex and provided dimensions for a new mill. In fact, he may have built Richard Cartwright*'s mill at Napanee, erected in 1792. From 1789 until his death he attempted to secure title to a lot at Millhaven and build his own grist-mill; however, he was continually frustrated by the Executive Council.

Appointed a justice of the peace for the Mecklenburg District in 1788, Clark also served on the Court of Requests and was a captain in the 1st Addington Militia. He was a member of the second (Ernestown) Methodist class organized by William LOSEE; indeed, early Methodist meetings may have been held at his house. Moreover he was a subscriber to and the builder of the Ernestown or Parrotts Bay Chapel, on which construction began in May 1792. Clark was one of the judges at the second trial of the controversial Methodist itinerant preacher Charles Justin McCarty* on 13 July 1790; the court ordered McCarty deported, a verdict whose justice has been hotly debated by historians.

The early government mills located at both ends of the Cataraqui–Bay of Quinte settlement were a boon to pioneer development. Although Major Ross and Deputy Surveyor General John Collins* have received many of the laurels for laying the foundations of the new settlements, it took men such as Robert Clark to design and construct the mills so essential to a pioneer economy. Clark also contributed to the development of a society in the fledgling loyalist community.

LARRY TURNER

[In some sources Clark's career has been confused with that of James Clark*. This confusion is neatly dealt with in an unpublished paper available at the QUA, E. [O.] Clark Watson, "The families of Col. John C. Clark and Col. John Clark" (typescript, n.d.), which also includes a valuable summary of Robert Clark's life. L.T.]

AO, MS 768, A-1, P. M. Clark to Canniff, January 1868; MU 571; RG 22, ser.156, 1, administration book B (1821–33); RG 40, D-1, no.697. BL, Add. MSS 21786: 40–41, 92–95, 104–9, 126, 142; 21815: 59; 21827: 174, 319, 326. PAC, RG 1, L3, 89: C1/45; 99: C11/107; 108: C15/80; 118: C19/139; 126: C misc., 1785–95/171; 184: Ernestown Mills, 1804/1–10. PRO, AO 13, bundle 80; WO 28/4: 273, 281; 28/10, pt.II: 286, 317–18; pt.IV: 464 (mfm. at PAC). QUA, Parrot family papers, file 2, James Parrot, corr.; file 5, legal docs. "Grants of crown lands in U.C.," AO *Report*, 1929: 62. "United Empire Loyalists: enquiry into losses and services," AO *Report*, 1904: 474. E. [O.] Clark Watson, *Loyalist Clarks, Badgleys and allied families* . . . (2 pts. in 1v., Rutland, Vt., [1954]), pt.II. G. F. Playter, *The history of Methodism in Canada* . . . (Toronto, 1862). Egerton Ryerson, *The loyalists of America and their times: from 1620 to 1816* (2nd ed., 2v., Toronto and Montreal, 1880). T. W. Casey, "Napanee's first mills and their builder," *OH*, 6 (1905): 50–53. C. C. James, "The origin of Napanee," *OH*, 6: 47–49.

CLARK (Clarke), THOMAS, businessman, militia officer, JP, politician, and office holder; b. in Scotland, probably in Dumfriesshire, son of Samuel Clark; m. 30 March 1809 Mary Margaret Kerr, daughter of Robert KERR; they had no children; d. 6 Oct. 1835 in Niagara Falls, Upper Canada.

Thomas Clark arrived in Upper Canada in 1791 to work for his cousin Robert Hamilton*. The Queenston magnate was impressed with his young charge, reporting to Clark's father in 1792: "I have found him possessed of Attention & Assiduity in my Business, & I'm convinced that he has Abilities & Morals to Conduct with success his own, as soon as he shall find it convenient to embark on his own Account. No Country perhaps in the world furnishes better prospects for young men with Moderate Views than the one we are now in." In 1794, armed with his employer's recommendations, Clark travelled to Michilimackinac (Mackinac Island, Mich.) "to look around," but found the northwest fur trade, by that time in decline, not to his liking. Two years later he opened a shop at Queenston and shortly after formed a partnership with Samuel Street*. Hamilton, who held the contracts for portaging army and fur-trade goods around the falls at Niagara, assured the prosperity of the new partnership by sharing a portion of the contracts.

Early in 1799 Clark applied to the British military for permission to erect storage and portaging facilities along the Niagara River. The same year he built a wharf and storehouse at Queenston at the enormous cost of $3,000. He also owned similar facilities at

Clark

Chippawa and Fort Erie. At the end of the year Street left the partnership and in 1800 Clark founded a new firm, Thomas Clark and Company, with Robert NICHOL, another Old World acquaintance and member of Hamilton's network. The partners traded in flour and other commodities throughout 1802 and 1803 with John Askin* among others. On 22 Oct. 1803 Nichol announced to Askin that the enterprise "had not been beneficial" to either partner and had been dissolved; he and Clark had, however, parted as friends.

Clark's ventures in land speculation were modest by comparison with some by his relatives, notably Hamilton. In 1806 he purchased block 4 of the Six Nations' Grand River lands. He sold the southern part to Robert ADDISON in 1808 and the remainder during the 1830s. Before 1809 Clark had acquired 1,900 acres in the Niagara peninsula. In 1811 he bought block 1 in partnership with his cousin William Dickson*; five years later Clark formally transferred these lands to Dickson.

About 1808 or 1809 Clark entered a second partnership with Street. Abandoning the forwarding trade, the partners undertook large-scale flour-milling at complexes on the Niagara River: first the Falls Mills which Street had acquired in 1807 and later the Bridgewater Mills. After Hamilton's death in 1809, Clark, as an executor, assumed much of the responsibility for the financial well-being of the Hamilton children and the management of the estate. That same year he made an agreement with the Earl of Selkirk [Douglas*] to act as business agent for the ill-fated Baldoon settlement. Clark's biggest problem was rectifying the financial mismanagement of the chief agent, Alexander McDonell* (Collachie). By the time he took over in 1810, there was little he could do other than suggest selling livestock in hopes of recovering some of the investment.

The War of 1812 was an interruption in Clark's business affairs. Afterwards, in 1816, he observed of his cousin Robert DICKSON's activities: "[He] has made a great deal of noise & horror in the country . . . but has forgot the money – which is a much better standbye than either hard Knocks or Glory." Yet Clark himself, although always mindful of money, had, as lieutenant-colonel of the 2nd Lincoln Militia, served with distinction. One of the major militia commanders on the Niagara frontier, he saw action at Queenston Heights on 13 Oct. 1812 and again the following month at Frenchman Creek. On both occasions he was mentioned in dispatches. In June 1813 he was present for the American surrender at Beaver Dams (Thorold) and participated in the raids on Fort Schlosser (Niagara Falls), N.Y., and Black Rock (Buffalo) in July. Partly as a consequence of a slight wound received in the latter engagement, he left the province late in 1813 for Scotland, returning in mid 1814. After the war he was one of the commissioners for assessing war losses in the Niagara District. He was also one of the commissioners selected to erect a monument at Queenston Heights to Major-General Sir Isaac Brock*.

Clark and Street lost both their mills to the torches of the Americans in July 1814. Only the Falls Mills were later rebuilt, but the partners continued to dominate milling in the region. The profits were reinvested in stocks, debentures, and land. Moneylending, on both a small and a large scale, was one of their most profitable activities. In 1821, for instance, the firm loaned the government £20,000 to pay arrears due on the pensions for militia veterans of the war. In 1832 Receiver General John Henry Dunn* held two bonds in favour of Clark totalling £10,000. On his own, Clark was not a major speculator in lands; he seems to have owned about 5,000 acres but he held another 55,000 owned jointly with Street.

During his partnership with Street, Clark also conducted separate business ventures on his own behalf. For instance, he participated in a four-way, long-term agreement with John Jacob Astor of New York and some of his associates for the sale and shipment of flour. Sales were conducted in Montreal, New York, and Jamaica; Clark's share of the profits on one transaction was a substantial $15,500. He also continued his association with Selkirk, advising on and outfitting the expedition to Red River in 1816, and handling the disposition of Selkirk's Grand River lands.

Clark was a sceptical individual with a clear, if narrow, definition of his goals in life. Of politics he wrote, "Ever since my arrival in Upper Canada, I have had nothing but turmoil and trouble, that is, with public affairs . . . [politics is] a troublesome task without any emolument. It is an honourable trade, yet I wish I were quit of it, as I have many private concerns to attend to which are of more consequence to me." Unlike his partner, however, Clark was willing, albeit grudgingly, to take part in politics after the war. He had previously held minor offices: justice of the peace from 1800 and trustee of the district grammar school from 1808. As a reward for his military service and partially in recognition of his wealth and prominence, he became a member of the Legislative Council on 16 Nov. 1815. The council was an important bastion of large landholders and merchants and, not surprisingly, the major events of his political career frequently involved issues that could have affected his landholdings or business dealings.

One of the first issues of major dispute concerned the dissatisfaction of the Niagara élite with the government's decision to bar Americans from owning land. This measure was forcibly opposed by Clark and

William Dickson in the council and Nichol in the assembly. The issue was taken up by Robert Gourlay*, whose wife was a cousin of Clark's and who had come to the province in 1817 in an attempt to recoup his fortune. His hope of borrowing money from Clark was dashed by the latter's explanation that his wealth was tied up in land, the market for which had been depressed owing to the government's policy of excluding American settlers. Gourlay's address to resident landowners embodying 31 questions elicited a favourable response from Clark who in November 1817 added his name to the signatures of notables requesting a township meeting to prepare answers to Gourlay's questions. When, however, Gourlay fell from grace the following year as a result of his attacks upon the administration in his second address, Clark moved quickly to distance himself. On 20 April he read an address to the inhabitants of Stamford Township in which he attacked Gourlay as a malcontent who had misinterpreted his own complaints against the government (Gourlay had claimed that his second address had been not only inspired but also approved by Clark and Dickson).

A related concern was a dispute over policies on land taxation which followed shortly after the Gourlay agitation. Several attempts to tax the province's wild, or uncultivated, lands – usually held by speculators who were often non-residents of the district in which the lands were located – had been blocked by vested interests within the council. But in 1819, and again five years later, new acts, passed by the House of Assembly, supported by Lieutenant Governor Sir Peregrine Maitland*, and approved by Colonial Secretary Lord Bathurst, forced the council's compliance in the matter. Speculators such as Clark were to pay the taxes or they would lose their lands by public auction after arrears for eight years. When in 1828 the assembly considered revising the act, Clark and others lobbied furiously for relief. Appearing before a house committee, he argued adamantly that it was unfair to tax all land equally regardless of its value or location. In spite of such strenuous opposition, the act was not rescinded, although its terms were modified somewhat in deference to the critics. In 1830 the first sales of tax-delinquent lands occurred, and large speculators took advantage of yet another opportunity for investment; thus, contrary to the act's intent, the land was not brought under cultivation but was purchased by men such as Clark, Dickson, and Street.

Although Clark courted official disfavour by his persistent opposition to policies which he perceived as harmful to his commercial self-interest, such as tax on wild land, he performed useful public service in instances where his own welfare and government policy coincided. In 1821, for instance, he was appointed one of the commissioners to negotiate a new revenue-sharing agreement with Lower Canada. In council, he was most concerned with advancements in transportation. He understood, no doubt, that improvement of internal navigation between the upper and lower provinces would ultimately benefit merchants operating on a large scale. In 1818 he served with James Crooks* and others on the joint provincial committee studying the improvement of navigation along the St Lawrence River; the commissioners called for a system of locks and canals which would be equal in dimension to those of New York State. Several years later he served on the commission superintending the construction of a canal linking Burlington Bay (Hamilton Harbour) and Lake Ontario. In 1825 he chaired a meeting convened to defray the expense of a survey for the best canal route between Montreal and Prescott to admit lake-size vessels. He was also interested in schemes of a more local nature such as the Grand River Navigation Company and the Erie and Ontario Railroad.

Clark began his career in Upper Canada with nothing more than a family introduction to Robert Hamilton. His success in business stemmed from a combination of hard work, determination, and perseverance with foresight and solid business sense. These qualities made him one of the most important and wealthiest merchants in Upper Canada; upon his death, William Lyon Mackenzie* estimated the value of his estate at £100,000. Clark's correspondence indicates a continuing use of family networks through to the 1830s. On his estate overlooking the falls at Niagara, Clark lived as a gentleman in his 40-room house, Clark Hill (later the estate of Sir Harry Oakes*), with his wife and servants, and in his leisure he enjoyed playing cards with other members of Upper Canada's élite.

BRUCE A. PARKER and BRUCE G. WILSON

AO, MS 500. MTL, E. W. Banting coll., Samuel Street papers. PAC, MG 11, [CO 42] Q, 318: 499; MG 19, El; MG 23, K16; MG 24, I8, ser.I; I26; I137; RG 1, E3, 32; RG 8, I (C ser.), 272: 21–22. QUA, Richard Cartwright papers, letter-books, Cartwright to Clark and Street, 4 May 1798 (mfm. at AO). UWOL, Regional Coll., James Hamilton papers. "Additional correspondence of Robert Nichol," ed. E. A. Cruikshank, OH, 26 (1930): 45–51, 59. Doc. hist. of campaign upon Niagara frontier (Cruikshank), vols.1–3. R. F. Gourlay, The banished Briton and Neptunian: being a record of the life, writings, principles and projects of Robert Gourlay . . . (Boston, 1843); General introduction to "Statistical account of Upper Canada . . . ," in connection with a reform of the corn laws (London, 1822). John Askin papers (Quaife). "The journals of the Legislative Council of Upper Canada . . . ," AO Report, 1910, 1915. "The probated wills of men prominent in the public affairs of early Upper Canada," ed. A. F. Hunter, OH, 23 (1926): 328–59. Statistical account of U.C. (Gourlay). Valley of Six Nations

Clarke

(Johnston). *Gleaner, and Niagara Newspaper*, 1 May, 10, 24 Sept. 1824. *St. Catharines Journal, and Welland Canal, (Niagara District,) General Advertiser* (St Catharines, [Ont.]), 15 July 1841. Cowdell Gates, *Land policies of U.C.* E. A. Cruikshank, *A memoir of Colonel the Honourable James Kerby, his life in letters* (Welland, Ont., 1931), 12–16. Aileen Dunham, *Political unrest in Upper Canada, 1815–1836* (London, 1927; repr. Toronto, 1963). Wilson, *Enterprises of Robert Hamilton*. G. C. Patterson, "Land settlement in Upper Canada, 1783–1840," AO *Report*, 1920.

CLARKE, Sir ALURED, army officer and colonial administrator; b. *c.* 1745, possibly the son of Charles Clarke, baron of the Exchequer in England, and his second wife, Jane Mullins; d. unmarried 16 Sept. 1832 in Llangollen, Wales.

Alured Clarke obtained an ensigncy in the 50th Foot in 1759 and six years later became a captain in the 5th Foot. After being made major in the 54th Foot in 1771, he was promoted lieutenant-colonel in 1775. He proceeded with that regiment to New York the following year. In 1777 he assumed command of the 7th Foot, and he served with it until he became muster master general of the German troops in succession to John Burgoyne*; in 1782 he became a colonel. Between that year and 1790 he was lieutenant governor of Jamaica, where he enjoyed great popularity with the planters and earned the approbation of Home Secretary Lord Grenville. Having been raised to the rank of major-general, Clarke was promoted colonel of the 1st battalion, 60th Foot, in July 1791.

On 19 March 1790 Clarke had been appointed lieutenant governor of the province of Quebec in succession to Henry Hope*. He arrived at Quebec on 7 October and assumed his responsibilities the following day. On the departure of Governor Lord Dorchester [Guy Carleton*] for Britain in August 1791, Clarke took over command of the British forces in North America and the administration of what that month became the province of Lower Canada. His major task as civil administrator was to put into operation the provisions of the Constitutional Act of 1791, an undertaking that necessitated action by the local executive on a variety of administrative matters before the new legislature could be called into session.

The exact definition of geographical boundaries, not only between Lower and Upper Canada but also with the United States, presented Clarke with a tangled problem because of discrepancies in the wording of various instruments and instructions he received from London. Determining the boundary with the United States was a particularly sensitive issue, Anglo-American relations having remained delicate since Britain had decided to retain possession of certain posts on the American side of the Great Lakes, contrary to the terms of the peace treaty of 1783. Moreover, Indian tribes in the Ohio region, angered by Britain's promised cession of territory south of the lakes to the Americans, posed a constant threat to peace and stability on the frontier. Clarke could only attempt to avoid conflicts in the Indian territory; settling the disposition of the posts was a matter of diplomatic negotiation between the British and American governments and was finally decided in 1794 by Jay's Treaty.

Within Lower Canada, on the basis of general guidelines from London and perhaps the specific advice of local officials, Clarke issued a proclamation on 7 Feb. 1792 that laid down the terms for granting crown lands in the province. To attract settlers and reward loyalists, a maximum of 200 acres, to which the head of the administration might add up to 1,000 acres, was offered to each petitioner who would give assurances of cultivating the land, take an oath of loyalty, and pay the stipulated fees to officials. With such open-handed generosity, the land committee of the newly created Executive Council was soon deluged with claims, which took years to process, Clarke alone issuing warrants for the survey of 150 townships comprising some 7,000,000 acres. Large tracts of land would be monopolized by speculators and government officials through the system of township leaders and associates [*see* Samuel GALE] to the detriment of bona fide settlers and the province's economic development. Another source of inconvenience and controversy was the reservation of one-seventh of each township for the support of a Protestant clergy and an additional one-seventh as crown lands from which the local executive might eventually derive a revenue free from the assembly's control. More unwisely still for the future, Clarke's original plan of setting up both crown and clergy reserves as a single block in each township was rejected in London in favour of a scheme that would scatter them through the townships in 200-acre lots according to a chequered pattern and thus intersperse them even more inconveniently among grants to individuals.

Institutional adjustments to the new constitutional order involved reorganization of the courts of justice and establishment of an executive council, which would be a court of appeal among other things. As a preliminary to summoning the Lower Canadian legislature, Clarke issued a proclamation on 7 May 1792 that divided the colony into counties, cities, and boroughs, constituting electoral districts, and apportioned 50 representatives among them. With this potentially controversial issue settled to the general satisfaction of the colonists, provincial elections were held that year. In December Clarke proudly opened the first legislature of Lower Canada, which met in the bishop's palace at Quebec. Since he spoke no French, and many representatives no English, his address to the House of Assembly and the Legislative Council was repeated by a translator. Clarke's report on the functioning of the assembly to the new home secretary, Henry Dundas, described conditions that in general would plague its operations for years to come. "Upon the first meeting of the Legislature," he informed Dundas, "a Spirit of Jealousy and some animosity discovered itself," arising from the Canadians' fear that, although they held a comfortable majority, the British members would control the assembly and use it to change the laws and customs of the colony. The Canadians insisted on and obtained a high quorum of 34 to ensure that no bill would pass unless a majority of them accepted it. As well, they were determined that a Canadian must occupy the key post of speaker and voted Jean-Antoine Panet* into the chair. They also initially attempted to establish French as the enacting language, but ultimately all bills were passed in English; had a piece of legislation reached Clarke in French, he assured Dundas, he would have reserved sanction. Combined with the atmosphere of suspicion that reigned in the assembly, the high quorum effectively blocked the entire legislative process until the last month. Many members having departed in frustration to attend to their private concerns, it was feared that "the Session would close in a very unseemly manner," with virtually no legislation completed. The quorum was reduced and business conducted briskly until eight bills had been passed, including one granting Quakers exemption from militia service and from the oath of allegiance. By that time spring was so advanced that nothing could keep the remaining legislators away from their personal affairs, and Clarke prorogued the session on 9 May 1793.

The whirlwind end of session gave Clarke grounds for optimism: "The Canadian Members having, as they conceived, established their consequence" by demonstrating to the people that they could act together to control the assembly, and the British members having demonstrated moderation, "the invidious distinctions that at first appeared, had previous to the Prorogation, in great measure vanished; and . . . all the Members, New and Old Subjects, who remained in Town, dined together on the last day of the Session, and parted in the greatest harmony and good humour with each other." Consequently, although the amount of legislation passed had been meagre, Clarke considered "that as much has been done as could reasonably be expected" and was confident that the experience acquired by the members of the assembly would enable them to act more effectively in future.

Following Dorchester's return to Quebec in September 1793, Clarke gladly departed, probably in November, for England, where he had spent only some five months during the previous 20 years. Dundas had earlier expressed his "compleat satisfaction" with Clarke's service and promised "more

effectually to demonstrate the opinion I entertain of your merit." There had been talk of Clarke's being appointed governor of Jamaica, but he remained lieutenant governor of Lower Canada until 1795. Meanwhile, in 1794 he had transferred successively to the colonelcies of the 68th Foot and the 5th Foot. That year Dundas became secretary for war, and perhaps he kept his promise in 1795 when Clarke was chosen to command a body of reinforcements bound for India. He stopped en route to assist in the capture of the Dutch colony at the Cape of Good Hope (South Africa). In India he was promoted to the local rank of lieutenant-general in 1796 and received the full rank in January 1797. After being commander-in-chief of Madras, in 1797 he transferred to the same post in Bengal, where he also served as president and senior councillor; that year he was made a KB. In September he was appointed governor general of India, but he resigned in 1798 to become commander-in-chief of the British forces there, a position he held until 1801.

Back in England that year, Clarke transferred to the colonelcy of the 7th Foot in August, and in 1802 he rose to the rank of general; he was ultimately made field marshal in 1830. The promotion was a fitting, if belated, tribute to a professional soldier whose modest talents and courteous manner had enabled him to discharge the civil duties of a colonial administrator without either distinguishing or disgracing himself.

PETER BURROUGHS

PAC, MG 23, GII, 10, vol.3: 724–27, 732–37; MG 30, D1, 8: 359–83. PRO, CO 42/73–98; CO 43/16. *Corr. of Lieut. Governor Simcoe* (Cruikshank). *Docs. relating to constitutional hist., 1791–1818* (Doughty and McArthur), 54–82, 107–16. "Quelques prêtres français en exil au Canada," ANQ *Rapport*, 1966: 144, 158, 168. *Quebec Gazette*, 29 Aug., 8 Sept., 10, 24 Nov. 1791; 5 Jan., 9, 23 Feb., 1 March, 10, 17 May, 12 July, 16 Aug., 20 Sept., 18 Oct., 27 Dec. 1792; 24 Jan., 25 April, 2, 16 May, 31 Oct. 1793. *Times* (London), 20 Sept. 1832. *DNB*. G.B., WO, *Army list*, 1759–1832. Morgan, *Sketches of celebrated Canadians*, 113–14. Wallace, *Macmillan dict.* Caron, *La colonisation de la prov. de Quebec*, 2: 11–55. Christie, *Hist. of L.C.* (1848–55), vol.1.

CLAUS, WILLIAM, army and militia officer, Indian Department official, office holder, JP, and politician; b. 8 Sept. 1765 at Williamsburg (formerly Mount Johnson), near present-day Amsterdam, N.Y., son of Christian Daniel Claus* and Ann (Nancy) Johnson; m. 25 Feb. 1791 Catherine Jordan, daughter of Jacob Jordan*, and they had three sons and two daughters who survived to adulthood; d. 11 Nov. 1826 in Niagara (Niagara-on-the-Lake), Upper Canada.

A man of modest abilities, William Claus was fortunate to be born into a family of prominence, wealth, and influence. His maternal grandfather, Sir

Claus

William Johnson*, had vast estates in the Mohawk valley and was superintendent of northern Indians. His father held important positions in the Indian Department also. Claus's family had intended to give him a proper education in a New York City school but was prevented from doing so by the outbreak of civil war and rebellion in colonial America, which forced them to flee to the province of Quebec late in the spring of 1775.

Young Claus began his military service about 1777 by enlisting as a volunteer in the King's Royal Regiment of New York under the command of his uncle Sir John JOHNSON. In the summer of 1782 he apparently took part in a successful raid by Joseph Brant [Thayendanegea*] against the settlements at Fort Dayton (Herkimer, N.Y.) and nearby Fort Herkimer. By war's end, he was a lieutenant in the regiment. In October 1787 he obtained a lieutenancy in a regular British regiment, the 60th Foot, and in February 1795 was promoted captain.

As early as 1788 Sir John Johnson, who had become superintendent general of Indian affairs, had attempted to get Claus a position in the Indian Department. He recommended him for the office of deputy agent of the Six Nations in Canada, and former governor Haldimand* apparently lent his support, but Governor Lord Dorchester [Guy Carleton*] opposed the request because of Claus's youth. In 1795, following John Campbell*'s death, Johnson tried unsuccessfully to have Claus given charge of the Indians of Lower Canada. Finally, in 1796 the death of John Butler* opened a place that Johnson was able to obtain for Claus. He was named deputy superintendent of the Six Nations at Fort George (Niagara-on-the-Lake), a position which gave him responsibility for the Indians of the Grand River, among others.

Claus reached his post in October 1796 and immediately became involved in the conflict between Joseph Brant and the government over Brant's claim that the Six Nations of the Grand River had the right to sell off portions of their lands as they chose. Claus argued the government's case: that the Indians did not have full sovereignty over unceded land and that under the Royal Proclamation of 1763 the sale of Indian lands could be made only through the crown. Brant continued to press the matter with Upper Canadian authorities and in 1797 he forced Administrator Peter Russell* to recognize the validity of sales that had already been arranged. Claus was named one of the trustees to manage the proceeds for the Indians' benefit.

On 30 Sept. 1800 Claus took another step up in the Indian Department when he was appointed to succeed Alexander McKee* as deputy superintendent general for Upper Canada, a post he would hold until his death. He again found himself in conflict with Brant, who had not given up the idea of the Six Nations' right

to sell land and who in 1803 decided to go over the heads of the provincial authorities. Brant entrusted war chief John NORTON with attempting to obtain the agreement of the British government itself. Claus managed to get together a council (including, said Brant, a number of chiefs from the American side of the Niagara River) that disputed Norton's authority and claimed to have deposed Brant. Claus had a copy of the proceedings sent to London and thereby thwarted the mission.

The frontier with the United States was rather quiet during the early years of Claus's term, but the *Chesapeake* affair of 1807 [see Sir George Cranfield Berkeley*] brought fears of an American invasion and authorities encouraged resuscitation of the British-Indian alliance. Claus assembled Indian chiefs at key centres such as Fort George and Amherstburg to "consult privately" with them and to remind them of the "Artful and Clandestine manner in which the Americans [had] obtained possession of their lands." The policy was so successful that the tribes of the American northwest were too eager to engage the enemy and Lieutenant Governor Francis Gore* had to urge Claus to restrain them.

The United States finally declared war on Britain in June 1812, and throughout the conflict Claus performed his duties with efficiency and dignity. He had been appointed lieutenant of the county of Oxford in June 1802 and since then had been involved in militia matters. He was named colonel of the 1st Lincoln Militia in June 1812 and in July he was given command of British regulars and Upper Canadian militia at Fort George and Queenston Heights. Much of his time was devoted to stemming desertion. As well, he continually met in council with the Indians. In late May 1813 the Americans launched a major amphibious attack against Fort George. After a stout resistance, the defenders retreated towards Burlington Heights (Hamilton). Claus was said to have been the last officer to abandon the damaged fort, and he was with the forces that returned to it in December when the Americans withdrew.

By 1814 the toughest fight remaining for Claus was the continuation of his acrimonious feud with John Norton. Through his activities in the war, especially at the battle of Queenston Heights, Norton had gained favour with senior British authorities. In October 1813 a general order had been issued instructing the Indian Department to cooperate with any "Chief of Renown," such as Norton, who enjoyed the Indians' confidence. Then, in March 1814, Norton was given authority to dispense presents to the warriors fighting with him. Claus struggled to maintain the Indian Department's prerogatives, and much bitter correspondence ensued. The conclusion of the war and the subsequent pensioning-off of Norton diminished the scope for this rivalry, and by the early 1820s the young

John Brant [TEKARIHOGEN] replaced Norton as a principal spokesman for the Grand River Indians.

For Claus and the department, the post-war years were marked by a dramatic shift in British policy towards the native people of Upper Canada. In the new era of peace, the unhindered development of the province was urgently desired, and plans were put forward which would change the Indians from warriors to wards. Key elements in the strategy were the extinguishment of Indian land title and the location of Indians in specified villages or reserves. The first post-war decade witnessed seven major land cessions by the Ojibwas of Upper Canada, and Claus played a major role in negotiating them all. An agreement made at York (Toronto) with the Mississauga Ojibwas in February 1820 was typical, concluding with the assurance by Claus that "the whole proceeds of the surrenders . . . shall be applied towards educating your Children and instructing yourselves in the principles of the Christian religion" and that "a certain portion of the said Tract – will be set apart for your accommodation and that of your families, on which Huts will be erected as soon as possible."

As a result of the new non-military role of the Indian Department, Claus was obliged to spend much time in assisting the Indians to adapt to a new way of life and in attempting to obtain adequate funding for services the department supplied to them. He was precise and orderly; his determination sometimes caused him to clash with his superiors and at one point he was threatened with dismissal. He seems genuinely to have cared about the native people. "I trust in the end the Indians will not lose," he wrote to George IRONSIDE, "for I have trust in His Majesty's kind feelings and consideration for such faithful poor people."

Claus undertook a number of other responsibilities in addition to his work for the Indian Department. In 1812 he had been appointed to the Legislative Council, and after becoming an honorary member of the prestigious Executive Council in 1816 was made a full member in 1818. In 1816 he had been named, along with Thomas CLARK and others, to the commission that negotiated with Lower Canadian representatives about the division between the two provinces of the revenue from customs duties. He had been a justice of the peace since 1803. He was also a trustee for the Niagara public school and a commissioner of customs for the Niagara District.

Claus was a proud family man, and home life was important to him. His vegetable and flower gardens were among the best in the region and his orchards were renowned. Indeed, his meticulous records provide excellent information on horticulture in Upper Canada. After suffering from cancer of the lip for about five years, he died on 11 Nov. 1826 and was buried at Butler's Burying Ground outside the town.

ROBERT S. ALLEN

PAC, MG 19, F1; RG 8, I (C ser.), esp. vols.1203½–3½AA, 1700–3; RG 10, A2, 11–21; 10017–18. PRO, CO 42, esp. 42/136, 42/143, 42/321. "Anticipation of the War of 1812," PAC *Report*, 1896: 24–75. "Campaigns of 1812–14: contemporary narratives by Captain W. H. Merritt, Colonel William Claus, Lieut.-Colonel Matthew Elliott and Captain John Norton," ed. E. [A.] Cruikshank, Niagara Hist. Soc., [*Pub.*], no.9 (1902): 3–20. "Indian lands on the Grand River," PAC *Report*, 1896: 1–23. *Mich. Pioneer Coll.*, 20 (1892). Norton, *Journal* (Klinck and Talman). *Valley of Six Nations* (Johnston). "State papers," PAC *Report*, 1890: 207, 219. "State papers – U.C.," PAC *Report*, 1891: 105, 115, 136, 158, 181. M. W. Hamilton, *Sir William Johnson, colonial American, 1715–1763* (Port Washington, N.Y., and London, 1976). R. J. Surtees, "Indian land cessions in Upper Canada, 1815–1830," *As long as the sun shines and water flows: a reader in Canadian native studies*, ed. I. A. L. Getty and A. S. Lussier (Vancouver, 1983), 65–84. Isabel Thompson Kelsay, *Joseph Brant, 1743–1807: man of two worlds* (Syracuse, N.Y., 1984). Allen, "British Indian Dept.," *Canadian Hist. Sites*, no.14: 5–125. E. A. Cruikshank, "The King's Royal Regiment of New York," *OH*, 27 (1931): 320. Reginald Horsman, "British Indian policy in the northwest, 1807–1812," *Mississippi Valley Hist. Rev.* (Cedar Rapids, Iowa, and Lincoln, Nebr.), 45 (1958–59): 51–66. C. M. Johnston, "Joseph Brant, the Grand River lands and the northwest crisis," and "William Claus and John Norton: a struggle for power in old Ontario," *OH*, 55 (1963): 267–82, and 57 (1965): 101–8. J. McE. Murray, "John Norton," *OH*, 37 (1945): 7–16. G. F. G. Stanley, "The significance of the Six Nations participation in the War of 1812," *OH*, 55 (1963): 215–31.

CLENCH (Clinch), RALFE (Ralph, Rolfe), army officer, office holder, judge, militia officer, politician, and farmer; b. *c.* 1762 in Schenectady, N.Y., son of Robert Clench and Hannah Vernon; m. Elizabeth Johnson, granddaughter of Sir William Johnson*, and they had at least 12 children; d. 19 Jan. 1828 in Niagara (Niagara-on-the-Lake), Upper Canada.

After the outbreak of the American revolution Ralfe Clench joined the 53rd Foot as a cadet and served in John Burgoyne*'s campaign of 1777. He escaped the débâcle that befell Burgoyne's army and was detached as a volunteer in Captain Henry Bird's company of the 8th Foot. He probably participated in Bird's raids along the upper Ohio in 1779 and was described by the regimental commanding officer as a promising young man. For a short time he was a volunteer with John Butler*'s rangers and in April 1780 he was commissioned second lieutenant. Detailed to the company of William CALDWELL at Detroit, he distinguished himself in the defeat of American colonel William Crawford near present-day Upper Sandusky, Ohio, in 1782.

Cobbett

A first lieutenant by 1784, Clench was reduced on 24 June, and he settled at Niagara. His war service appears to have stood him in good stead with government. In 1790 he was appointed the first clerk of the Court of Common Pleas for the Nassau District. By 1800 he had garnered the offices of registrar of the Surrogate Court, clerk of the District Court, and clerk of the peace in the Niagara District. He received many other appointments during his life, including judge of the District, commissioner of the Heir and Devisee Commission, commissioner of customs for Upper Canada, and commissioner for the administration of oaths. He assiduously sought these offices for himself as well as others for his son, Joseph Brant Clench*. Before the War of 1812, he was probably the only office holder within the district whose chief source of income was office.

Clench was very much a social and political animal. By 1792 he was a captain and adjutant in the local militia, rising by 1804 to lieutenant-colonel; two years later he was promoted colonel of the 1st Lincoln Militia. He was clerk of Niagara Township from 1793 to 1807 and again in 1812. During this period, he held three other township offices. A charter member of Masonic Lodge No.19 from 1787, he later served as its secretary, and he also belonged to the Niagara Agricultural Society, the Niagara Library, the Turf Club, and the local Presbyterian church.

Clench was that combination of sophisticate and frontiersman often produced in early Upper Canada. The noted traveller Patrick CAMPBELL described him in 1792 as a "young man of liberal education," equally capable of entertaining company on an organ and of translating speeches into Iroquois. On the other hand, Clench could also amuse listeners with many strange and grisly stories of his war experiences. Campbell was fascinated by the tale told by Clench and Joseph Brant [Thayendanegea*] of the time when they "once brought boys, and a number of women and girls, prisoners to Detroit, and so served the whole settlement, which was much in the want of females."

Clench first seems to have engaged in political controversy in 1795 when he supported Isaac SWAYZE in a local agitation against the intended wording of land deeds. In 1800 Clench and Swayze emerged as the most active leaders of local opposition to the regional élite, which was dominated by Scottish merchants such as Robert Hamilton*. That year they were elected members of the House of Assembly for the riding of 2nd, 3rd and 4th Lincoln; they were re-elected in 1804. Together they proposed legislation championing the interests of small merchants, local office holders, loyalists, and farmers. Clench was initially attracted by the parliamentary opposition of Robert Thorpe* and Joseph Willcocks*, particularly by its demand that land be granted on more liberal terms. But as an office holder and hence essentially a member of the conservative establishment, Clench was careful on most issues not to align himself with the group. Its initiatives drove him to the defensive and consequently destroyed his political effectiveness. His subsequent career as the member for 2nd Lincoln in the sixth (1812–16) and seventh (1817–20) parliaments was much quieter, although he did emerge as a staunch opponent of Robert Fleming Gourlay*.

During the War of 1812, Clench fought at Queenston Heights and was mentioned in dispatches. In March 1813 he became assistant quartermaster general to the militia forces stationed at Niagara. Three months later he was captured by invading American forces, and he spent the duration of the war as a prisoner.

Clench kept a fine home in Niagara which burned, along with all his personal papers, in February 1820. His orchard, described as the largest and finest in Niagara and destroyed during the war, had consisted of 114 trees producing six types of peach and five kinds of plum, as well as quinces, apricots, and nectarines. His second home, built in the 1820s and still standing, is described by architectural historian Peter John Stokes as the "finest example of its type surviving."

BRUCE G. WILSON

AO, RG 21, Niagara County, 1812; Niagara Township, council minutes, 1793–1807, 1812; RG 22, ser.138, box 1, R. v. Isaac Swayze, 1795, affidavits of John Young et al., 16 March 1795. BL, Add. MSS 21761: 41–42; 21762: 70; 21765: 211; 21786: 100. PAC, MG 23, HI, 1, ser.3, 6: 3; ser.4, vol.5, packet A7: 65–66 (transcripts); RG 5, A1: 2054; RG 8, I (C ser.), 690: 125; 692: 268; RG 19, E5(a), 3745, claim 324; RG 68, General index, 1651–1841. PRO, WO 28/4: 13. P. Campbell, Travels in North America (Langton and Ganong), 165–72. Doc. hist. of campaign upon Niagara frontier (Cruikshank), 2: 15, 151. Farmers' Journal and Welland Canal Intelligencer (St Catharines, [Ont.]), 30 Jan. 1828. Gleaner, and Niagara Newspaper, 21 Jan. 1828. U.E. Loyalist (York [Toronto]), 2 Feb. 1828. Armstrong, Handbook of U.C. chronology (1985), 173, 186. Quebec almanac, 1790. Carnochan, Hist. of Niagara, 179, 184, 251. P. J. Stokes and Robert Montgomery, Old Niagara on the Lake (Toronto and Buffalo, N.Y., 1971), no.24. London Free Press and Daily Western Advertiser (London, [Ont.]), 23 Feb. 1857.

COBBETT, WILLIAM, soldier, controversialist, and author; b. 9 March 1763 in Farnham (Surrey), England, third son of George Cobbett and Ann Vincent; m. 5 Feb. 1792 Anne Reid in Woolwich (London), and they had seven children; d. 18 June 1835 in Ash (Surrey).

William Cobbett, the great English radical-tory polemicist, was of uncultured, modest, rural stock. Even as a young boy, however, he exhibited that capacity for rebellious self-education that characterized his entire life. An occasional runaway from the age of 14, he left home permanently on 6 May 1783, and on 4 Feb. 1784, after a few unhappy months as a lawyer's clerk in London, he enlisted at Chatham (Kent) in the 54th Foot. A dreary year of barrack life followed, but by the time he sailed from Gravesend in March 1785 for Halifax to join the body of his regiment he had been promoted corporal. He was to spend six years in the Maritimes, chiefly in New Brunswick, before returning home with his unit.

Once back in England, Cobbett obtained an honourable discharge and then brought charges of corruption against his former officers. Fearing retaliation he fled to France in 1792 and later that year he moved to the United States. After establishing a reputation as an outspoken anti-Jacobin and anti-Jefferson journalist he returned to England in 1800 following a conviction for libel against Benjamin Rush, a prominent physician. En route in June he stopped briefly at Halifax. Now a celebrity and hero to the loyalists, he was received by Edward* Augustus, the Duke of Kent.

In 1802 he founded the famous *Cobbett's Weekly Political Register*, a personal organ that he edited until his death. From 1810 until 1812 he was imprisoned at Newgate for libelling the government, and from 1817 until 1819 he was in the United States, again a fugitive from official persecution. In 1830 he published in London his best-known book, *Rural rides*, an unparalleled description of the English countryside in the early 19th century. From 1832 until his death in 1835 he was a member of parliament for Oldham.

The neglected Canadian years of the otherwise much studied Cobbett are important both for their influence on his distinguished later career and for the light they throw on the history of New Brunswick. The dearth of contemporary records unfortunately causes a reliance on Cobbett's subsequent, opinionated, and often contradictory writings. Even the chronology of his New Brunswick years is impossible to recount with complete accuracy. It was in July 1785 that he and the 54th sailed across the Bay of Fundy from Windsor, N.S. (where the regiment had been stationed) to Saint John. Cobbett was certainly quartered at Fort Howe in Saint John for some time, and he may have been among the troops called out to suppress an election riot in November [*see* Elias Hardy*]; he was to comment upon the election in later life. He probably moved permanently to Fredericton in July 1787.

Cobbett claimed a wide familiarity with "the able Yankee farmers" who comprised the bulk of the population of the new province of New Brunswick, and his experience with them shattered his view of the class structure. To his surprise he found "thousands of captains and colonels without soldiers, and of squires without stockings or shoes." At home he "had never thought of approaching a squire without a most

respectful bow: but, in this new world, though I was but a corporal, I often ordered a squire to bring me a glass of grog, and even to take care of my knapsack." More intimately, about July 1789, he became acquainted with an unnamed New England loyalist farmer, 40 miles from Fredericton, whose daughter he courted and almost married despite his engagement, while stationed at Fort Howe two years earlier, to his future wife, Anne Reid, the 13-year-old daughter of an artillery sergeant, Thomas Reid. Cobbett's later staunch Federalism and criticism of the American revolution can be partly attributed to his experience with the New Brunswick loyalists.

The loss in the Bay of Fundy, during the stormy 1785 crossing to New Brunswick, of Cobbett's well-thumbed copy of Jonathan Swift's *A tale of a tub* . . . , the book that had begun his intellectual awakening eight years earlier, did not dampen his passion for self-education. While rising within two years, through hard work and natural ability, to sergeant-major and by his own account virtually running the entire regiment, he also instructed everyone from the officers down in a new drill known as "Dundas's system," supervised the building of a large stone barrack in Fredericton, ghosted a royal commission report on New Brunswick (since lost), taught himself and several colleagues English grammar, studied geometry, and wrote the first of many textbooks, "Notebook on vulgar fractions" (which remains in manuscript form). When the 54th left New Brunswick, Lieutenant Governor Thomas Carleton* publicly commended Cobbett's military services.

His army experience launched Cobbett on his lifelong career as critic of the establishment, the class system, and corruption. Most of the officers, he claimed, were drunk, incompetent, and, even worse, venal. Aided by Corporal William Bestland, he searched the regimental records for evidence. The result of his naïve and unsuccessful attempt to bring charges against his superiors was his first published work, *The soldier's friend* . . . , an exposé printed in London in 1792. He had discovered his métier: crusading writing. He remained "the soldier's friend" and mounted an attack on flogging, which he had learned to hate in New Brunswick.

Cobbett's vocation as gardener and agriculturist was influenced by New Brunswick. "I have cultivated a garden at Frederickton," he declared. "I had as fine cabbages, turnips, and garden things of all the hardy sorts, as any man need wish to see. Indian Corn grew and ripened well." In Britain he strongly advocated the growing of turnips and maize, which in typically immodest fashion he called "Cobbett's corn." The 54th's goats began his boosting of the benefits of those self-sufficient animals. Cobbett enjoyed the New Brunswick scenery and such country pleasures as hunting, skating, and especially rambling – a sort of

Cochran

early "rural ride." Conversely, he always disliked commercial towns. With Saint John probably in mind he wrote, "I have always, from my very youth, disliked sea-ports."

Cobbett was never very consistent. For example, his descriptions of New Brunswick range from the rhapsodic – "some of these spots far surpass in rural beauty any other that my eyes ever beheld" – to the bleak – "that miserable country," "one great heap of rocks, covered with fir-trees." In his later years his criticisms of the North American colonies deepened because he hated the emigration there of English country folk. Throughout his voluminous writings he drew on his New Brunswick period for metaphors. Thus he used the hardships of the winter as a metaphor for the hardships caused in England by paper money.

Although Cobbett remains arguably the most important person who ever lived in New Brunswick, he is but a footnote in the history of the province. New Brunswick had more influence on him. His experiences there undoubtedly resulted in his discovery of his true calling, and until his death he used these experiences, and indeed his whole life, as raw material for his art, his writing, and his causes.

WALLACE BROWN

William Cobbett is the author of a large number of works, both published and unpublished. Two bibliographies of his published writings are available: M. L. Pearl, *William Cobbett: a bibliographical account of his life and times* (London, 1953), which also provides some information on the unpublished material, and P. W. Gaines, *William Cobbett and the United States, 1792–1835; a bibliography with notes and extracts* (Worcester, Mass., 1971). The following items, and editions, were used in the preparation of this sketch: *Advice to young men and (incidentally) to young women in the middle & higher ranks, in a series of letters . . .* (London, 1926); *The autobiography of William Cobbett: the progress of a plough-boy to a seat in parliament*, ed. William Reitzel (London, [1947]); *Cobbett's Weekly Political Reg.* (London), 1802–35; *Life and adventures of Peter Porcupine . . .*, ed. G. D. H. Cole (London, 1927; repr. Port Washington, N.Y., 1970); "Notebook on vulgar fractions . . . decimal fractions and geometry . . . , Fort Howe, 26 January 1789," an uncatalogued manuscript in Yale Univ. Library, Beinecke Rare Book and MS Library (New Haven, Conn.); *Rural rides . . . with economical and political observations . . .* (London, 1830); and *A year's residence in the United States of America . . .* (Fontwell, Eng., 1964).

D. G. Bell, *Early loyalist Saint John; the origin of New Brunswick politics, 1783–1786* (Fredericton, 1983). George Spater, *William Cobbett, the poor man's friend* (2v., Cambridge, Eng., 1982). Wallace Brown, "William Cobbett in the Maritimes," *Dalhousie Rev.*, 57 (1976–77): 448–61. Gerald Keith, "The legend of Jenny's Spring," N.B. Hist. Soc., *Coll.*, no.18 (1963): 48–54.

COCHRAN (Cochrane), WILLIAM, educator, editor, and Church of England clergyman; b. *c.* 1757 near Omagh (Northern Ireland), son of Andrew Cochrane, a "respectable farmer"; m. 30 Sept. 1785 Rebecca Cuppaidge in Philadelphia, and they had seven children; d. 4 Aug. 1833 in Windsor, N.S.

Much of the information on William Cochran's early life derives from an account which may or may not have been written by Cochran himself. According to this account, Cochran, who displayed "an avidity for knowledge" at an early age, was classically educated at a private grammar school in County Tyrone. He entered Trinity College, Dublin, in June 1776, and despite a "low conception of his own capacity" he was elected a scholar in 1779 and took his degree in 1780. During his later years at the college he developed doubts about divine revelation and renounced his previous intention of ordination in the Church of Ireland. In 1781 he took a position as tutor to the family of a country gentleman in County Galway. However, he was not to remain much longer in Ireland. The ideals of the American revolution aroused his strong sympathies, and at the close of the war in 1783 he found himself irresistibly drawn to the nascent republic, believing that "these rising states would be the abode of the greatest virtues and happiness that would be found on earth." Repelled by political conditions in Ireland, a country he still greatly loved, he emigrated to the United States in late 1783, landing at New Castle, Del., that November. (In the course of passage he changed the spelling of his name from Cochrane to Cochran.)

Determined to make his own way in his new home, Cochran had not brought with him any letters of recommendation. Still, he was confident about his prospects, feeling that "young states" were "like young women, rather favourable to adventurers." In the event, his confidence was justified. Quickly following on his arrival he was appointed chief assistant in the Academy of Philadelphia, a grammar school attached to the University of Pennsylvania. After a visit to New York in January 1784 he resigned his position in Philadelphia and moved to New York to open a grammar school there. At the end of that year he was appointed to Columbia College as professor of Greek and Latin. His conversations in 1787 with the college president, William Samuel Johnson, led to a revival of religious studies and belief. Finding that ordination in the United States would debar him from preferment within any Church of England jurisdiction, he decided to seek ordination in Nova Scotia and resigned his professorship. Disgust with the realities of life in the republic – he was especially revolted by the institution of slavery – contributed to this decision. He now realized that "the character of the human race remained the same even in this new regenerated hemisphere."

Cochran sailed for Halifax in October 1788 and upon arrival called upon Bishop Charles Inglis*. In

November, and again the following March, Inglis recommended Cochran to the Society for the Propagation of the Gospel as a suitable candidate for a mission. Terming Cochran "a great acquisition," he praised him as "a most amiable exemplary young man, very studious and an excellent scholar." Cochran was not inactive while awaiting the SPG's response. In June 1789 he was appointed headmaster of the newly established Halifax Grammar School – a rival to Inglis's favoured academy, already established in Windsor. The same month, with the support of Halifax printer John HOWE, Cochran brought out the first issue of his *Nova-Scotia Magazine and Comprehensive Review of Literature, Politics, and News*. In general it was composed of material taken from other publications, but the second issue, of August, contained the first of three articles on "A plan of liberal education for the youth of Nova-Scotia" evidently written by Cochran himself. In 1790 Cochran, shortly after his appointment as president of King's College, resigned as the magazine's editor. Two years later the *Nova-Scotia Magazine* ceased publication.

Cochran's appointment to the presidency of King's College began an association with that institution which was destined to last for more than 40 years. In 1788 the Nova Scotia legislature had provided a grant for the rent of a building in Windsor to house a grammar school. The next year the legislature passed an act for the establishment of a college, to bear the name of King's College, to be located in Windsor, and to be headed as president by a clergyman of the Church of England, removable only for misconduct or neglect of duty. To find the requisite president and professors, Inglis appealed to the archbishop of Canterbury, patron of the college. At a meeting of the board of governors on 12 Oct. 1789 the bishop reported that the archbishop had failed in his quest, and the board accordingly decided to offer the position of president to Cochran. Cochran agreed to accept the position, which was to be combined with the principalship of the grammar school. The next spring, when his engagement was due to take effect, he asked the board for a certificate of his appointment as president "during good behaviour," but nothing came of this request. Nevertheless, he moved to Windsor on 23 June 1790 and on 12 June of the following year he was ordained a Church of England clergyman. On 1 July 1791 he was invested as president of King's College.

It had been expected that the foundation of the college by statute would be speedily followed by the grant of a royal charter, but the outbreak of war between France and Britain postponed consideration of this matter. In the years of difficulty that followed, Cochran and his family lived in hardship at Windsor. Enrolments were small (between 1790 and 1803, according to John Inglis*, 18 students entered the

college annually), building proceeded slowly, and inflation depreciated his fixed income. And, to add to his chagrin, during the early 1800s his brother-in-law, the Reverend George Wright*, lived in comparative ease on increasingly lucrative remuneration as head of the Halifax Grammar School.

After a memorial of September 1801 from the governors of the college, a royal charter was issued in May 1802 and arrived in the province in September. It made no mention of the existing institution and gave plenary powers to the governors to draw up the necessary statutes. Three of the governors – Bishop Inglis, Chief Justice Sampson Salter Blowers*, and Alexander Croke*, the judge of the Vice-Admiralty Court and a graduate of Oxford – were appointed a drafting committee. On 3 May 1803 the committee presented its report to the board. One of the draft statutes required matriculants to subscribe to the Thirty-Nine Articles, thus creating an exclusively Anglican college in a multi-confessional society. Another stipulated that the president and professors should be educated at Oxford or Cambridge, or at Windsor under persons thus qualified. In July the governors approved the statutes. As for Cochran, he now learned that he was to be removed from the position he had held for 13 years. In August he addressed a memorial, supported by the bishop, to the archbishop of Canterbury. Apparently through ill health, the archbishop failed to make any decision upon it. Yet on 20 March 1804 he was in a condition to despatch a recommendation for the appointment of the Reverend Thomas Cox, a graduate of Oxford, as president. The governors approved, and upon Cox's arrival he was formally appointed to the presidency and elected a governor, Cochran becoming vice-president and retaining his professorship.

Late in October 1805 Cox died suddenly, Cochran resumed the duties of the presidency, and the governors had again to consider the question of a successor. At a meeting of the board on 22 Jan. 1806 Inglis and two other governors voted for Cochran, but Croke, who insisted that the president be an Oxford or Cambridge graduate, Lieutenant Governor Sir John Wentworth*, and Blowers voted against him. Cochran thus lost his second chance to become president. In September 1806 the archbishop of Canterbury recommended the Reverend Charles Porter*, another graduate of Oxford; he was duly appointed and installed in 1807, and his tenure outlasted Cochran's association with the college. Some years later, in 1814, Cochran's status was enhanced by his appointment, against the opposition of Croke, to the board of governors. From this position in the 1820s, he opposed all attempts to forge a union between King's and the non-sectarian Dalhousie College.

Plans to end the separate existence of King's College reflected widespread dissatisfaction in the

Cockrell

colony with the institution, dissatisfaction that had led not only to the founding of Dalhousie but also to the creation in 1816 of Pictou Academy by secessionist Presbyterians under the leadership of Thomas McCulloch*. With regard to King's College itself, it had languished since the passage of the statutes of 1803: in 1815 there were a mere 17 students in the college, and from 1820 to 1830 admissions averaged six annually. Lieutenant Governor Lord Dalhousie [Ramsay*] visited the college in 1817 and, after noting the small number of students, claimed that "the state of the building is ruinous; extremely exposed by its situation, every wind blows thro' it. The passage doors are torn off, the rooms of the students are open & neglected." As if these problems were not serious enough, relations between Porter and Cochran were greatly strained – with Porter disliked by the students as a severe disciplinarian, and Cochran much appreciated as a genial personality and entertaining instructor. Dalhousie at first was impressed with Cochran, describing him as "a man of singularly mild & amiable manner, with a talent for instructing & captivating the disposition of his pupils by easy & relaxed discipline." By 1819, however, the lieutenant governor could not conceal his disgust over the constant bickering between Porter and Cochran. "The President & Vice President," he wrote, "are at variance. They don't speak to each other. What the one does or says is opposed by the other. . . . I never in my life met so violent a hatred in private circumstances as these two Rev. Gentlemen bear to one another."

Cochran received two honorary degrees – an MA from Columbia in 1788 and a Doctor of Sacred Theology from Trinity College, Dublin, in 1802. In 1804 he joined Robert STANSER in a doctrinal dispute with Edmund Burke*, the Roman Catholic vicar general of Nova Scotia. Apart from his educational duties, with the support of the SPG Cochran served as minister to several settlements in the vicinity of Windsor, concentrating on Falmouth and Newport townships but also visiting the townships of Rawdon and Douglas on a frequent basis. Dissenters were prevalent in all these settlements – in 1792 Cochran complained that Newport and Falmouth were "miserably overrun by various sorts of Enthusiasts" – and nothing changed in this respect over the years.

In 1821 Cochran, on the advice of physicians, travelled to the United States "in the hopes of removing a serious complaint in his chest." The following year, though "far from well," he returned to Nova Scotia and resumed his duties as professor and clergyman. That age was beginning to take its toll was evident in his reports to the SPG, which became more sporadic and less detailed. In October 1831 he resigned his appointments in the college. He died in Windsor on 4 Aug. 1833 and was buried in the Old Parish Burying Ground. One of his sons, James

Cuppaidge*, was a prominent Anglican clergyman in Nova Scotia. Another, Andrew William*, served as civil secretary to three governors of Lower Canada – Sir George Prevost*, Sir John Coape SHERBROOKE, and Lord Dalhousie – and also sat on the Executive Council of that province.

C. P. WRIGHT

In addition to editing the *Nova-Scotia Magazine and Comprehensive Rev. of Literature, Politics, and News* (Halifax) for its first year – vols.1 (July–December 1789) and 2 (January–June 1790) – William Cochran wrote on a variety of subjects. The series of articles entitled "A plan of liberal education for the youth of Nova-Scotia, and the sister provinces in North-America," which appeared in the first volume of the *Nova-Scotia Magazine*, pp.105–6, 199–202, 364–66, seems to have been written by Cochran under the pseudonym "W." Other publications by Cochran include *A sermon preached in the church at Falmouth, Nova-Scotia, on Friday, the 10th of May, 1793 . . .* (Halifax, 1793); a textbook, *Brief rules of the Latin prosody, with explanatory notes, drawn up for the use of King's-College, Nova-Scotia* (Halifax, n.d.), a copy of which is in the library of the Univ. of King's College, Halifax; and "A journal of the thermometer, hygrometer, barometer, winds, and rain; kept at Windsor, Nova-Scotia," printed in the Royal Irish Academy, *Trans.* (Dublin), 9 (1803): 133–46.

Among the William Cochran papers at PANS are two volumes of notes for a history of Nova Scotia (MG 1, 223, nos.3–4), and a life of Cochran (MG 1, 223, no.1); whether the latter is autobiography or biography cannot be determined. The life has been published under the title "The memoirs of William Cochran, sometime professor in Columbia College, New York, and in King's College, Windsor, Nova Scotia," ed. M. H. Thomas, N.Y. Hist. Soc., *Quarterly* (New York), 38 (1954): 55–83.

Lambeth Palace Library (London), Moore papers, I: ff.96–115. PANS, MG 1, 223, no.2; 479–80 (transcripts). Univ. of King's College Library, Univ. of King's College, Board of Governors, minutes and proc., 1 (1781–1814)–2 (1815–35). USPG, Journal of SPG, 25–27, 29–32, 34–36, 38, 40–41. Ramsay, *Dalhousie journals* (Whitelaw), vol.1. T. B. Akins, *A brief account of the origin, endowment and progress of the University of King's College, Windsor, Nova Scotia* (Halifax, 1865). *Canadian education: a history*, ed. J. D. Wilson et al. ([Toronto], 1970). Judith Fingard, *The Anglican design in loyalist Nova Scotia, 1783–1816* (London, 1972). R. S. Harris, *A history of higher education in Canada, 1663–1960* (Toronto and Buffalo, N.Y., 1976). H. Y. Hind, *Sketches of the Old Parish Burying Ground of Windsor, Nova Scotia . . .* (Windsor, 1889); *The University of King's College, Windsor, Nova Scotia, 1790–1890* (New York, 1890). J. S. Moir, *The church in the British era: from the British conquest to confederation* (Toronto, 1972). F. W. Vroom, *King's College: a chronicle, 1789–1939; collections and recollections* (Halifax, 1941). A. G. Archibald, "Sir Alexander Croke," N.S. Hist. Soc., *Coll.*, 2 (1881): 110–28.

COCKRELL, RICHARD, author, educator, office holder, surveyor, editor, and publisher; b. 1769 or

1773 in Yorkshire, England, son of an officer of the East India Company; m. 1800 Mary Stewart, and they had three children; d. 7 July 1829 in Ancaster, Upper Canada.

Richard Cockrell came from a family with connections in the army and navy and in the East India Company. He attended school and college in England, graduating at 21, and then proceeded to the study of law and medicine, which he gave up some time in the early 1790s in order to visit North America. He went first to the United States but by 1795 was in Newark (Niagara-on-the-Lake), Upper Canada. On his arrival he seems to have been promoting some sort of colonization venture: in June 1795 he petitioned for a grant of land on the Thames River sufficient to accommodate 40 families. When the Executive Council turned down this petition, Cockrell and one Thomas Otway Page petitioned for a grant of 1,200 acres, apparently in the Newark area. The council responded with grants to Cockrell and Page of 200 acres each; Cockrell's was in Windham Township. For some reason, he did not take it up, probably because in 1796 he obtained a town lot in Newark.

Mainly as a result of his experiences in the United States, Cockrell published at Newark in 1795 a pamphlet entitled *Thoughts on the education of youth*. This is a remarkable document, the first piece of writing on educational theory and practice published in English in North America, preceding by 13 years the first such effort in the United States. Significantly, it was also the first non-governmental publication in Upper Canada, appearing after the publication of Lieutenant Governor John Graves Simcoe*'s speech at the opening of the first parliament and the laws passed by the first and second sessions of that parliament. Cockrell's *Thoughts* reveals modern views on such aspects of education as discipline and pedagogy, but one of his major concerns was the deplorable state of the teaching profession in Upper Canada. Referring to teachers as the "mushroom gentry," Cockrell lambasted them for having "neither abilities nor address to recommend them, scarce knowing B from a bull's foot." To improve this situation, Cockrell proposed adoption of the American practice of examining teachers before appointment, a practice not as widespread in the United States as he supposed. His advocacy of object-lesson learning and the use of spellers in reading instead of the Bible marks Cockrell as an educator well ahead of his time. His commendation of American educational practices foreshadowed an attitude in Canadian education that has continued to the present day.

In 1796 Cockrell opened a school in Newark, teaching writing, arithmetic, and bookkeeping. Although his name is now virtually unknown, he appears to have been one of the outstanding pioneer schoolteachers. Probably in 1797 he moved to Ancaster to

establish another school, which the most eminent teacher of the day, the Reverend John Strachan*, described as "an excellent mathematical school." Cockrell also taught school in Wellington Square (Burlington), Cobourg, York (Toronto), and then back at Niagara (Niagara-on-the-Lake); in 1817 he and another teacher, John Conner, were operating a common school in Grantham Township. Among his students in these schools were William Hamilton Merritt*, Allan Napier MacNab*, John Brant [TEK-ARIHOGEN], and members of the Butler, Crooks, and Bolton families.

After moving to Ancaster, Cockrell was made a deputy sheriff of the Home District, and thereupon applied for additional land "in Consideration of the office he holds." The council rejected his request, but in 1811 Cockrell did obtain a grant of 400 acres in Garafraxa Township, north of present-day Guelph. His success in obtaining a second grant was probably due to his career as a surveyor over the preceding decade. He had begun work as a private, unlicensed surveyor after his arrival in Ancaster – one source claims that he had moved to the settlement to survey the lands of John Baptist Rousseaux* St John – and in 1798 he had angered the administrator of the province, Peter Russell*, by conducting an unauthorized survey of the Six Nations lands on the Grand River. Fortunately for Cockrell, this crisis blew over, and in 1802 or thereabouts he was licensed as a deputy provincial surveyor. In the years that followed he conducted surveys in several townships, including Saltfleet, Grantham, and Niagara. As well, in June 1818 he published *Thoughts on the subject of land surveying* . . . , a book that included severe criticisms of the Surveyor General's Office.

In 1810 Cockrell was made a judge of the Newcastle District, but he does not appear to have taken up the appointment. He participated in the War of 1812 as an army surveyor, and according to a family tradition was present at the battle of Lundy's Lane in July 1814. At the close of the war he became founding editor of the *Spectator*, published by Amos McKenney at St Davids from 15 March 1816. In February 1817 the paper became known as the *Niagara Spectator*, and the following August its office was shifted to Niagara, where Bartemas FERGUSON became its publisher. In 1818 Cockrell moved to Dundas; there he and the powerful businessman Richard Hatt* founded the *Upper Canada Phoenix*, the first newspaper published in the province west of York. This newspaper probably ceased publication the next year, thereby bringing to an end Cockrell's journalistic career.

Little is known of Cockrell's politics. In the election of 1800 he was a candidate in the riding of Norfolk, Oxford and Middlesex but lost to Surveyor General David William Smith*; he later contested the election on the grounds that the returning officer,

Colclough

Thomas Welch*, had acted improperly. In ensuing years Cockrell remained free of any taint of political extremism. In 1801 and 1802 he apparently played a devious game with Asa DANFORTH, leading him to think that he supported plans for an invasion of Upper Canada from New York State but at the same time forwarding Danforth's incriminating letters to the provincial authorities. On the other hand, Cockrell does seem to have had reformist sympathies. In 1816 the *Spectator* embroiled itself in controversy by attacking the Loyal and Patriotic Society of Upper Canada, a body whose moving spirit was John Strachan, and the following year Cockrell was called before the bar of the House of Assembly for publishing in his paper an election address by James DURAND that had been harshly critical of the government. There is also little doubt that Cockrell was a supporter of Robert Gourlay*. To begin with, Cockrell was a close friend of Richard Hatt, himself a supporter of Gourlay in the early stages of his agitation, and Hatt's friends generally followed his lead on political matters. Furthermore, as late as June 1818 the *Phoenix* was diligently reporting on the township meetings that had been called in response to Gourlay's appeal.

Cockrell was a freemason – in 1796 and again in 1816 he served as grand secretary of the masonic lodge that met in Newark. As for his religion, a committee of the assembly in 1830 claimed that he was "believed to be a Presbyterian." An artistic man who dabbled in verse and excelled in painting and drawing, Cockrell is also said to have delighted in "speechifying, and song-singing assemblies." In appearance, he was described as "tall, with regular features, rather florid complexion, gray eyes, and a wealth of dark-brown billowy hair, which was tied at the back with a bow of black ribbon."

In 1829 Cockrell decided to return to England to secure for his children their inheritance, but he died on 7 July at Ancaster of a "sudden and severe illness." An obituary declared that he "was endowed by nature with talents far above mediocrity; and was highly and justly esteemed for many amiable qualities."

J. DONALD WILSON

Richard Cockrell's pamphlet *Thoughts on the education of youth* (Newark [Niagara-on-the-Lake, Ont.], 1795) has been reprinted by the Biblio. Soc. of Canada (Toronto, 1949).

AO, Pamphlet coll., 1935, no.65, Alicia Cockrell Robinson, "'The Upper Canada Phoenix' and 'The Niagara Spectator'" (photocopies, n.p., n.d.); RG 1, A-I-1, 23: 90–98; 55: 129; A-I-6: 2944, 3131, 3348, 4135, 5048, 5080, 5350, 5661, 5684. PAC, RG 1, L3, 89: C1/39, 116; 90: C2/11, 98; 98: C10/40; RG 5, A1: 659–61; 687–89, 758–62, 8821–22, 15359–60. "Ancaster parish records, 1830–1838," comp. John Miller, *OH*, 5 (1904): 163. *Documentary history of education in Upper Canada from the passing of the Constitutional Act of 1791 to the close of Rev. Dr. Ryerson's*

administration of the Education Department in 1876, ed. J. G. Hodgins (28v., Toronto, 1894–1910), 1. "Grants of crown lands in U.C.," AO *Report*, 1929: 103. Joseph Neef, *Sketch of a plan and method of education, founded on an analysis of the human faculties, and natural reason, suitable for the offspring of a free people, and for all rational beings* (Philadelphia, 1808). "U.C. land book B," AO *Report*, 1930: 33, 106. *Colonial Advocate*, 31 July 1828. *Farmers' Journal and Welland Canal Intelligencer* (St Catharines, [Ont.]), 22 July 1829. *Niagara Spectator* (Niagara [Niagara-on-the-Lake]), 1816–17. *Upper Canada Gazette*, 30 Nov. 1796. *Upper Canada Phoenix* (Dundas, [Ont.]), 16 June 1818. W. D. Reid, *The loyalists in Ontario: the sons and daughters of the American loyalists of Upper Canada* (Lambertville, N.J., 1973), 309. *Ancaster's heritage: a history of Ancaster Township* (Ancaster, Ont., 1973). J.-P. Wallot, *Intrigues françaises et américaines au Canada, 1800–1802* (Montréal, 1965). W. S. Wallace, "The periodical literature of Upper Canada," *CHR*, 12 (1931): 4–22.

COLCLOUGH, CÆSAR, judge; b. 1764 in County Wexford (Republic of Ireland); m. 24 Oct. 1804 Susan Leech, and they had two daughters who lived to adulthood; d. 10 Feb. 1822.

Cæsar Colclough was the eldest son of Adam Colclough of Duffrey Hall and Mary Anne Byrne of County Dublin. His family were influential members of the Irish Protestant gentry, and he strongly upheld the English government in its suppression of the Irish rebellions of 1798; he was left with a lifelong antipathy to any tendency towards "democracy" as well as with the gratitude of the authorities for his loyalty. Supported by powerful friends and patrons, including the Duke of Kent [Edward* Augustus], Lord Camden (lord lieutenant of Ireland in 1798), and Charles O'Hara (an Irish member of parliament), Colclough was appointed chief justice of Prince Edward Island on 1 Jan. 1805 at a salary of £500 per annum, to succeed fellow Irishman Robert Thorpe* who became a judge of the Court of King's Bench in Upper Canada. A qualified barrister-at-law, Colclough was expected to sort out legal practices on the Island, which were in considerable confusion because of local controversy and a rapid succession of ill-trained chief justices in the opening years of the 19th century.

The Duke of Kent himself supported Colclough's request to remain in Britain through the summer of 1806 to sort out his business affairs, and the new appointee did not arrive in Halifax until 25 Nov. 1806. He was not eager to make his way to the Island, particularly in view of the information he received from Charlottetown describing the Byzantine political and legal situation there. Moreover, Lieutenant Governor Sir John Wentworth* of Nova Scotia advised him that the sole way to remain uninvolved in Island politics – and therefore impartial – was to visit only when his court was in session. Furthermore, as a gregarious and hospitable man who enjoyed "good

160

company," Colclough found Halifax society quite agreeable. He began seeking an alternate appointment even before he had personally assumed his present one.

Finally offered a decent house to rent in Charlotte-town, Colclough arrived on the Island on 3 July 1807. His initial reaction was hardly favourable. The Island, he reported to Charles O'Hara, was populated largely by Scots Highlanders who for "Sloth, Filth & drun-kenness" surpassed any other race of men, and the head of government (Lieutenant Governor Joseph Frederick Wallet DesBarres) was an old Swiss soldier of fortune with "a good Heart & no Head," completely under the influence of a dishonest Irish attorney (James Bardin Palmer) acting as "Prime Minister." To his surprise, the new chief justice soon found congenial company among the Island's "better sorts," chiefly among those officials who had support-ed the previous lieutenant governor, Edmund Fan-ning*. He gradually became "reconciled to my Lot," although he and DesBarres – "a foolish dotard upwards of eighty years of age" – took an instant dislike to each other, no doubt facilitated by the ease with which the newcomer was taken into the camp of the opposition.

Despite an open lack of cooperation between DesBarres and Colclough, the chief justice succeeded in remaining out of major political controversy until 1809. It was possible for him to keep to his declaration that he would confine himself to judicial matters because the lieutenant governor seldom took impor-tant business to the Council, of which the chief justice was president. In the spring of 1809, however, actions on judicial matters involved him in open battle with DesBarres's supporters, organized as a society called the Loyal Electors. By this time the political divisions of the Island had taken definite shape: the Loyal Electors were attacking the proprietors in the name of the people, and the older popular party associated with Peter Stewart* and his family – denominated the "cabal" by its enemies and the "old party" by those sympathetic to it – was now on the defensive. DesBarres had for several years been urging the establishment of county courts of sessions, which would be presided over by justices of the peace, and he strongly backed for the posts supporters such as Angus Macaulay and William B. Haszard, although they lacked formal legal training. Colclough decided – on the strength, he insisted, of advice from Nova Scotia – to oppose any such decentralization of the administra-tion of justice, and he further irritated the DesBarres faction by nominating candidates for sheriff who were known enemies of the lieutenant governor and strong supporters of "property rights" on the Island.

The membership of the Loyal Electors, which met monthly at Bagnall's Tavern, grew over the summer of 1809. Its secretary, William Roubel, later wrote

that the organization was devoted to the consideration "of proper Measures, for the Introduction of upright independent Men, and persons of unimpeached Char-acters into the House of Assembly," in order to counteract the influence "possessed by a Set of persons (either personally or by their unprincipled Agents) engaged in monstrous Speculations in Land." Unfortunately, the leaders of the Loyal Electors, especially James Bardin Palmer, were not of "unim-peached Characters" themselves, many being land speculators prevented from "monstrous" operations only by their exclusion from power.

Early in 1810 Captain John MacDonald* of Glena-ladale passed on to the chief justice excerpts from the correspondence of Roubel (whom MacDonald else-where described as Palmer's "Chief Understrapper") with proprietor John Hill*. The passages were highly critical of Colclough's impartiality and expertise. Roubel, who was acting as attorney in many legal cases against men of the "old party," claimed that the chief justice was entirely too friendly with its mem-bers and favoured them in his court. There was a grain of truth in the charges, for Colclough was a convivial man who always gravitated towards "genteel" compa-ny, which in the context of the Island in 1810 meant the large landholders and officials. But no chief justice who resided on the Island could fail to be friendly with many of the litigants in his court, and it was probably unnecessary to pack juries to get ones favourable to his friends, since as landholders they usually had the law (if not justice) on their side. Nevertheless, Colclough was conscious of the delicacy of his position, asserting to his friend O'Hara that he was the only person on the Island of "no Party vices or Spleen to indulge," although admitting a willingness to accept an appoint-ment as chief justice of Newfoundland if he could obtain a salary of £1,000 per annum. "Our governor," he added, "is so indecisive in doing what is right & Positive in doing what is wrong."

The smouldering conflict between the Loyal Elec-tors and the "old party" burst into open flame in 1810, when Attorney General Peter Magowan* died. Des-Barres supported Palmer as Magowan's successor. Palmer's past record of questionable personal finan-cial dealings and evidence that he was stripping timber from land not belonging to him succeeded in persuad-ing the major proprietors in England that – as Lord Selkirk [Douglas*] trenchantly put it – Palmer was "so extremely objectionable in every respect" there ought to be "no possibility of his receiving any countenance from Government." Charles Stewart* got the appointment, and the Loyal Electors soon became a public political issue. The rumour began circulating in the spring of 1811 that a secret commit-tee had been organized "to control the affairs of the society." The leading members of the Loyal Electors sent DesBarres lengthy affidavits both denying the

Colclough

imputations of conspiracy and excoriating Stewart, Colclough, and the two assistant judges, Robert GRAY and James Curtis*. Learning of these affidavits, Colclough and his colleagues visited the lieutenant governor at his home in October 1811. According to their later accounts, Colclough told DesBarres that "as some of those affidavits contained matter libellous and highly defamatory of the administration of justice in this Island," he "trusted his Excellency, according to his own frequent declarations to that effect would suffer the Law to take its course." DesBarres replied, "God forbid he should not," and sent the visitors to his secretary with permission to examine the documents, apparently unaware of what would transpire.

What the justices did, of course, was to make copies of the documents and take them straight to Attorney General Charles Stewart. Stewart opined that such a "self created permanent political Body organized after the manner of Corporations and associated for the purpose of controlling the Representation of the people in the House of Assembly, as well as the appointment of Public Officers," which sought to "obtain possession of the whole power of the Government," was certainly inconsistent with the "Genius and Spirit of our Constitution." While to modern ears it may sound incredible to thus condemn what was, after all, merely a nascent political party, it must be remembered that the British political tradition had always been hostile to parties, as well as to quasi-political organizations, which were readily associated with rebellion. Stewart's opinions were fully shared by the British government, which was to offer no sympathy to the Loyal Electors of Prince Edward Island. More to the immediate point, whether the society was unconstitutional or not, the affidavits – particularly those of Angus Macaulay, William Roubel, and William Haszard – were clearly libellous, both in the sense of defaming personal reputations and in the larger sense of undermining the established institutions of government (an offence known at the time as seditious libel). Roubel had included a number of charges of bias and ignorance against the justices of the Supreme Court, and Macaulay had made unsubstantiated allegations against both the administration of justice and his previous employer, Lord Selkirk. Colclough permitted Stewart to file the affidavits in the Supreme Court late in October 1811, and when Roubel refused to apologize for his statements, the judges peremptorily struck his name from the roll of attorneys qualified to practise before the court. Informations for libel were filed against Haszard and Macaulay, but not acted upon immediately.

Relations between Colclough and DesBarres understandably continued to deteriorate, reaching a low point early in 1812. The chief justice described a final confrontation at the meeting of the Executive Council on 26 March: "The Governor after some very intemperate expressions threw himself back in his Chair and collecting all the foul Breath he could in his Mouth puffed it full in my face. With more temper than I thought I possessed, I coolly got up and said I could not remain to meet such Conduct, and as I was retiring, he in the most contumacious manner continued repeating, 'Good Morning to you, good Chief Justice, go home & study Law' – to which I only replied that I considered my knowledge of Law was at least equal to His Excellencys of Politeness." A few weeks later an election was held, in which the Loyal Electors increased their representation in the House of Assembly from five to seven, although William Roubel was defeated in Charlottetown. The election had been hard fought, and both John Frederick Holland* and Charles Stewart had been forced to retreat from the hustings by the popular hostility to them. Their defeat meant that the victorious "old party" was leaderless in the house, and while it attempted to regroup it sought to frustrate the opposition by boycotting the first session. Despite the absence of six members, the house carried on, dominated by Palmer and the Loyal Electors.

In answer to a request for information, DesBarres wrote to speaker Ralph Brecken that the Loyal Electors' affidavits had been given to the Supreme Court without his authorization. Acknowledging that the judges had called upon him and had been given permission to examine the documents, DesBarres insisted he "had not the most distant idea of the possibility of these Affidavits being applied to the purpose of carrying on any criminal prosecution against the persons who made them," for they were intended to support him against charges made in the Council. The lieutenant governor's statement was undoubtedly accurate, but his lack of understanding did not mean that the affidavits had been obtained through misrepresentation or that the judges' conduct had been "arbitrary, disrespectful and illegal," as the assembly's subsequent resolution (introduced by Angus Macaulay and passed by the rump house) insisted. Taking advantage of the resolution, DesBarres suspended Colclough on 30 Sept. 1812.

Meanwhile, the proprietors had met in London on 4 May 1812 to consider "the unfortunate and dangerous state" of the Island, and had appointed a committee consisting of Robert Montgomery, John Hill, and Lord Selkirk to present the situation to the British government. Their chief aim was to replace DesBarres, whom they represented as a man "sunk into absolute dotage and . . . completely under the guidance of an Adventurer of infamous character [James Bardin Palmer], under whose influence all the powers of Government are perverted to the worst of purposes, . . . [and who] has in many instances acted the part of an absolute swindler." Although these charges had considerable veracity, the characterization of the

Loyal Electors as a society of Americans disguised as loyalists who hoped for "an invasion of the Republican Americans" was hardly true or fair. Nevertheless, Colonial Secretary Lord Bathurst was impressed, and in August 1812 recalled DesBarres and stripped Palmer of his many offices.

By the beginning of 1813, when Attorney General Charles Stewart unexpectedly died, all the major participants in the crisis of 1811–12 except Colclough were gone from the Island. DesBarres, Palmer, and Roubel had left, the last threatening to bring charges of misconduct against Colclough. The acting administrator, William Townshend*, reinstated the chief justice in October 1812, but Colclough found much hostility remaining in Charlottetown. In April 1813 a notice was posted near his house accusing Colclough (who had recently freed two self-confessed murderers on legal technicalities) of being "The Friend and Protector of the Vilest of all Miscreants, even of Murderers, the shedders of Human Blood." This accusation upset his wife far more than had the Loyal Elector controversy and earlier complaints that Colclough had publicly beaten his manservant or had often been seen walking inebriated in the streets of Charlottetown. The family thus looked forward to an impending transfer to Newfoundland, the result of a British decision to exchange two unpopular chief justices [see Thomas TREMLETT]. The Colcloughs finally arrived at St John's in September 1813.

To his dismay, Colclough, who had expressed great dissatisfaction with his salary on Prince Edward Island, found that he had really been well off there. As Governor Sir Richard Goodwin KEATS put it in writing to London of Colclough's arrival, "House Rent, Fuel, Servants Wages, and all articles of Provisions (fish excepted) are more expensive at Saint Johns than any place I know." The chief justice found his legal business "heavy and multifarious," involving lay pleaders without legal training and much criminal work from the rowdy Irish community in the town. He complained bitterly that he was for the first time in his life forced to live "in seclusion from Society" for want of money, and he was also required to defend himself against the charges levelled in England by William Roubel, who had put together a 16-item bill of indictment. Fortunately for Colclough, Colonial Secretary Lord Bathurst rejected out of hand most of the charges and required explanations of only seven, most particularly Colclough's role in the affidavits business. Colclough's actions over the affidavits were perhaps the easiest item to defend, and he did so resoundingly.

Even after Colclough had successfully cleared himself in the eyes of the Colonial Office, his enemies circulated printed copies of the Roubel charges in Newfoundland without reference to their fate in London. This "most unjust and malicious Persecu-

tion" was added to the chief justice's financial worries and his heavy official responsibilities. These last were not inconsiderable, for in the absence of the governor (a naval officer usually only at St John's a few months in the year) the chief justice was the ranking British civil official, a position which Colclough perhaps took far too seriously. Never a friend of the people, he found the Irish rowdies of the town more than he could stomach, and began to see conspiracies and plots in the constant riots of St John's. After several relatively unsuccessful attempts to employ his position as chief magistrate to restore law and order, Colclough ultimately challenged the Irish poor by using the discovery of rabies on board a visiting ship as a pretext for ordering destroyed all dogs found at large in the town except those muzzled and hitched to sleds. Naturally this action led to a "threatening and seditious letter."

Colclough defended his stern measures by writing to the absent governor that from experience he knew "the Mildness & temporizing of Government in Ireland for years previous to 1798 fostered and matured that Rebellion." Governor Keats was himself disposed to blame the unruly behaviour of the populace on high wages and good spirits, but then, he did not live in St John's. Colclough's letters became increasingly hysterical, alternating fears of Irish Catholic plots with complaints about his salary, the continued persecution of him by Prince Edward Island enemies, and his deteriorating health. William Carson*, who attended the patient, certified that Colclough's nerves were completely shattered and he needed a break from his arduous responsibilities. He was finally granted leave of absence to return to Britain in the autumn of 1815. In London, Colclough kept up a barrage of visits and letters to the Colonial Office, first to get his salary increased, then to get his leave extended, then to retire from service at half pay, and finally to retire at a higher pension than the colonial secretary thought justified. He spent his last years in France and Ireland.

Cæsar Colclough's social pretensions and hostility to the Irish lower orders were legendary in his own country, producing a number of barbed anecdotes originally recounted in the Wexford region. Newfoundland historians have been equally disparaging, judge Daniel Woodley Prowse* labelling him an "absurd Don Pomposo" and "a very inefficient judge." The former charge was accurate enough, but the latter is decidedly unfair. During his two-year tenure in Newfoundland Colclough had dealt with 995 writs, 80 causes by memorial, and 97 probates. Few of these cases were straightforward, for the lay pleading then standard in the absence of trained lawyers forced the judge to treat each action individually and ponder carefully at great length; such procedures were unlikely to produce precedents or "lawyer's law." Moreover, if Colclough over-reacted to the turmoil of St

Collins

John's, he was the only major representative of British civil authority who witnessed it personally and had to deal with it. That fact, of course, says as much about official British attitudes to Newfoundland as about Cæsar Colclough.

J. M. Bumsted

National Library of Ireland (Dublin), Dept. of mss, ms 20287 (5) (O'Hara papers), Colclough to Charles O'Hara, 14 Aug., 9 Sept. 1807; 11 Nov. 1809; 5 Feb. 1810; 11 Jan., 18 Oct. 1812; 8 April 1813; 22 Feb. 1814. PAPEI, Acc. 2849/129–30. PRO, CO 194/54–58; CO 226/21–22, 226/24–26, 226/28–29. [J. B.] Burke, *Burke's Irish family records* (5th ed., London, 1976). Jonah Barrington, *Personal sketches of his own times* (3rd ed., 2v., London, 1869). Prowse, *Hist. of Nfld.* (1895). J. M. Bumsted, "The Loyal Electors of Prince Edward Island," *Island Magazine*, no.8 (1980): 8–14.

COLLINS, FRANCIS, journalist, printer, publisher, and office holder; b. *c.* 1799 in Newry (Northern Ireland); m. 1824 Ann Moore of Newry, and they had four children; d. 29 Aug. 1834 in Toronto.

After receiving what he said was a "tolerable" classical education in Newry, Francis Collins served an apprenticeship in Dublin as a printer and also learned to write shorthand. For a brief period he ran a whig opposition newspaper known as the *Ulster Recorder*, which, he claimed, was forced to shut down because of pressure exerted by Lord Castlereagh. He emigrated to Upper Canada in 1818 and obtained a grant of 100 acres near York (Toronto). Soon after his arrival he found employment with Robert Charles Horne*, the king's printer, as compositor on the *Upper Canada Gazette*. As well, in early 1821 he began reporting House of Assembly debates for the *Gazette*, as John Carey* was doing for the *Observer*. His stenographic reports were fuller and in general more accurate than any that had previously appeared in print. Yet he gave more extensive coverage to reform members than to tories, and on one occasion Attorney General John Beverley Robinson* protested in the house that Collins's report of a debate could not have been "more false, absurd, even ludicrous." Horne was reprimanded at the bar of the house and he apologized for the report in the *Gazette*, but he retained Collins, cautioning him to report impartially. "Trifling inaccuracies" Horne later blamed on the cramped quarters assigned to reporters in the gallery – what Collins called "the fiddlers' box in the cock-loft."

When Horne resigned as king's printer in 1821, Collins hoped to succeed him but was told that the office would be given to "no one but a gentleman," an affront he resented since he traced his ancestry to the ancient kings of Ireland. General satisfaction with his reportorial skill, however, led to his appointment for the 1821–22 session as official reporter to the legislature and also, at about this time, as court stenographer; the position as house reporter he seems to have held for five years. In July 1825 he established his own newspaper, the *Canadian Freeman*, and at once began attacking the administration of Lieutenant Governor Sir Peregrine Maitland* and his "reptile band" of tory advisers. He protested against the government's policy in the alien controversy [*see* John Rolph*] and published a pamphlet on the subject. He also took a firm stand for freedom of the press when a group of young tories raided William Lyon Mackenzie*'s printing-house in 1826, but he held no brief for Mackenzie himself as a man or as a politician. Indeed he expended an arsenal of insulting epithets on most of his fellow editors, whether reformers or tories.

In 1826, following the dismissal of Charles Fothergill* as king's printer, the chairman of the assembly's printing committee, Hugh Christopher Thomson, had solicited tenders for printing the journal of the house. Mackenzie got the contract by submitting a bid below the going rates, much to Collins's annoyance. "We shall have cheap journals this session!" commented Thomson. But when Mackenzie's press was destroyed by the rioters, he had to turn over the printing to Collins, though he retained his own imprint on the journal's title page. Collins lost the contract to Mackenzie again in 1827, partly because he could not resist heading his tender "Proposals for Printing 'Cheap Journals,'" a gibe at Thomson which did not amuse members of the assembly. Collins was cited for contempt of parliament and summoned to apologize at the bar of the house. In January 1828 a motion carried in the assembly to divide the printing of the house among Collins, Carey, and Mackenzie. The following year, while Collins was incarcerated for libel in the York jail, his press published the journals from 9 January to 20 March "by order of the House of Assembly."

Because of his attacks on the administration in the *Canadian Freeman*, the executive in 1826 had withheld payment of the stipend voted to him by the assembly for reporting the debates. But instead of restraining him, this action gave him another stick with which to beat the government. Maitland reacted by having Collins indicted on four counts of libel in the spring of 1828. When the editor appeared in court without counsel, he was allowed by judge John Walpole Willis* to make a preliminary statement and took the opportunity to attack Attorney General Robinson, who was prosecuting the case for the crown, for dereliction of duty. Robinson, said Collins, had failed to bring criminal charges against Henry John Boulton* and James Edward Small*, Samuel Peters Jarvis*'s seconds in the fatal duel he fought with John Ridout in 1817; he had also failed to prosecute the rioters who had destroyed Mackenzie's press. Against Robinson's protest, Willis instructed

Collins to lay this information before the grand jury. True bills were found. In the subsequent trials the seconds were acquitted and the rioters let off with a nominal fine. Willis then recommended that the libel charges against Collins be dropped "in order to quiet the public mind," but Robinson held them over until the fall assizes.

On Collins's second appearance in court in October 1828, he was defended by John Rolph and Robert Baldwin*. Three charges were withdrawn and on the fourth he was acquitted. Robinson then laid two new charges, one for a libel on himself, Collins having accused him of "native malignancy," the other for the journalist's disrespectful reference to judge Christopher Alexander Hagerman*. The presiding judge in the trial, Levius Peters Sherwood*, was temporarily absent from the bench when the jury brought in a verdict of guilty on the first count only. Hagerman, acting for Sherwood, instructed them to bring in a general verdict, which would cover his own case as well. The jury complied and Sherwood sentenced Collins to one year in jail, a fine of £50, and sureties of £600 for good behaviour for three years – a sentence widely condemned as out of all proportion to the offence.

At public meetings in York and in Hamilton on Collins's behalf, subscriptions were taken up and protests sent to Lieutenant Governor Sir John Colborne*. On 26 Nov. 1828 and again on 4 December Collins himself petitioned Colborne, who declined to take any action. The assembly then took up his cause and, with only three dissenting votes, passed a resolution asking that his sentence be remitted. When this appeal, too, failed to move Colborne, the assembly drew up a much stronger address to the king praying for royal clemency. The crown's response was positive and Collins was released in September 1829 after serving 45 weeks in jail, his fine and sureties remitted.

If his persecutors had sought to silence Collins by incarceration they had badly misjudged their man. From his jail cell he had continued to edit the *Freeman*, denouncing his opponents with scathing sarcasm in a series of "open letters." After his release he concentrated his editorial attacks mainly on Egerton Ryerson* and the Methodists, and on Mackenzie, whom he accused of republicanism. As a self-professed independent whig, he believed in reform on the British rather than the American model. When in 1831 Mackenzie was expelled from the assembly for libelling the house in the *Colonial Advocate*, many reformers counted on Collins once again to lead a crusade for liberty of the press. Instead, he branded the *Advocate* a seditious publication and commended the assembly for ousting a "despicable demagogue." When Mackenzie set about collecting "grievances," Collins retorted that there was no grievance a good

assembly could not remedy. In Maitland's administration, Collins contended, "there was much to blame and little to praise," in Sir John Colborne's "much to praise and little to censure." Accused of turning tory, Collins replied that he had joined with "the rankest Tories" to prostrate Mackenzie and his faction, but having accomplished this purpose he would continue to state his political opinions "without regard to sect or party." By 1833 Collins was in a benevolent mood towards his former tory antagonists, declaring in the *Freeman*: "It is very well known that 'the highest law officers of the crown' prosecuted the Freeman, at one time. . . . Well all that has been forgotten, we believe, on both sides, by the parties concerned, and mutual forgiveness extended."

During the last three years of his life, Collins became embroiled in a bitter public dispute with the Reverend William John O'Grady*, the Roman Catholic priest in York. Trouble first began when in July 1831 Collins's brother John had to sue O'Grady for recovery of debt. Reports of this case in the *Freeman* angered O'Grady, who then refused baptism to Collins's son. The feud might have subsided had not O'Grady, smarting under a reprimand from Bishop Alexander McDonell*, disputed McDonell's authority, claiming that he held his commission directly from Rome. Collins was the chief lay supporter of the bishop, and James King the principal ally of O'Grady. When Rome intervened in support of McDonell, O'Grady capitulated and, with King, established a radical reform journal, the *Canadian Correspondent*, which carried on a weekly vendetta with the *Freeman*.

But for Collins, time was running out. During the cholera epidemic of 1834 he visited Irish victims in the hospital. Late in August he himself contracted the disease and died soon afterwards. His wife and eldest daughter also succumbed, as did his brother and sister-in-law.

John Charles Dent* wrote of Collins that "his nationality was clearly indicated by his personal appearance, his features being rough-hewn and unmistakably Celtic; while his red hair and beard, usually not very well cared for, gave him an aspect of uncouth wildness." A complex and paradoxical character, he could be generous, humane, and forgiving, but too often indulged in crude polemics and personal abuse. Opposed to arbitrary power whether of the right or the left, he believed in constitutional reform within the framework of loyalty to the king and the British connection. In an obituary tribute that appeared in the *Patriot* on 29 Aug. 1834, Thomas Dalton* described him as a true liberal who cared "alike for the honor and dignity of the Crown and rights and welfare of the subject. . . . It is [questionable] if the Press of Upper Canada can now boast so robust an Advocate of Principle as was departed Francis Collins."

H. P. GUNDY

165

Coltman

Francis Collins is the author of *An abridged view of the alien question unmasked; by the editor of the "Canadian Freeman"* (York [Toronto], 1826).

AO, MS 78, J. B. Robinson to Macaulay, 4 March 1821; Hagerman to Macaulay, 11 March 1821; Robert Stanton to Macaulay, 14 Oct., 4 Nov. 1826; 14, 23 April, 10 Nov. 1828; MS 444, B-2-1, Ewen Macdonald to Aeneas Macdonald, 15 Oct. 1831. Arch. of the Archdiocese of Toronto, M (Macdonell papers), AB46.03; CC50.04, .06; CD06.02. MTL, W. D. Powell papers, S. P. Jarvis corr., Jarvis to Powell, 24 Aug., 28 Oct. 1828; 1 April 1829. PAC, RG 1, E3, 15: 1–19; L3, 101: C12/80; 103: C12/274. *Debates of the Legislative Assembly of United Canada, 1841–1867*, ed. Elizabeth Abbott [Nish] Gibbs (12v. in 25 to date, Montreal, 1970–   ), 1: xxix–xxx. J. C. Dent, *The story of the Upper Canadian rebellion: largely from original sources and documents* (2v., Toronto, 1885), 1. *Town of York, 1815–34* (Firth). U.C., House of Assembly, *App. to the journal*, 1835, no.21: 133–37. *Canadian Correspondent* (Toronto), 30 Aug., 6 Sept. 1834. *Canadian Freeman*, 1825–34. [A. J. Dooner, named] Brother Alfred, *Catholic pioneers in Upper Canada* (Toronto, 1947), 141–65. H. P. Gundy, "Liberty and licence of the press in Upper Canada," *His own man: essays in honour of Arthur Reginald Marsden Lower*, ed. W. H. Heick and Roger Graham (Montreal and London, 1974), 71–92. Charles Lindsey, *The life and times of Wm. Lyon Mackenzie* . . . (2v., Toronto, 1862; repr. 1971), 1. F. M. Quealey, "The administration of Sir Peregrine Maitland, lieutenant-governor of Upper Canada, 1818–1828" (PHD thesis, 2v., Univ. of Toronto, 1968). John Ward, *The Hansard chronicles: a celebration of the first hundred years of Hansard in Canada's Parliament* (Ottawa, 1980). Mary McLean, "Early parliamentary reporting in Upper Canada," *CHR*, 20 (1939): 378–91.

COLTMAN, WILLIAM BACHELER, businessman, JP, politician, and office holder; b. in England; d. 2 Jan. 1826 in London.

William Bacheler Coltman arrived at Quebec aboard the *Caroline* in early July 1799, but whether for the first time is uncertain. Possibly by May 1805, but definitely in January 1807, he was established as a merchant at Quebec. In the latter year he purchased the schooner *Sainte-Anne* from a Cap-Santé mariner for £500 and had a quay and warehouse built at the mouth of the Rivière Portneuf. By 1807 he was a partner with his brother John in John Coltman and Company, the Quebec branch of a copartnership which also included William Hamilton and Francis Ridsdale; the copartnership operated in Leeds (West Yorkshire), England, as Francis Ridsdale and Company and in London as Ridsdale, Hamilton, and Coltman. John Coltman and Company sold wines, rum, sugar, timber, Upper Canadian flour, maritime supplies, and crockery, acted as a shipping agent, and operated its own vessels. In 1808, on its behalf, William Bacheler negotiated with Deputy Commissary General John Craigie* two contracts worth a total of £10,400 to supply flour to the army.

The copartnership with Hamilton and Ridsdale gave the Coltmans access to substantial capital, on which they drew liberally. In May 1807 John Coltman and Company acquired by assignment from the merchant Mathew Macnider the remainder of a 50-year lease on the seigneury of Sainte-Croix and the barony of Portneuf, which Macnider had obtained from the Ursulines in 1801. The company established an important commercial enterprise on the Portneuf barony, where it operated a banal mill, insured for £2,000, and where either Macnider or the Coltmans erected a manor-house and a sawmill. Between 1807 and 1810 John Coltman and Company acquired 31 lots in Nelson Township, four in each of the seigneuries of Lavaltrie and La Noraye, and two in Cap-Santé, as well as a lease on a beach lot at Anse des Mères, Quebec, and roture holdings and leases on valuable beach and other lots in Portneuf and Sainte-Croix; among the buildings on the Portneuf and Sainte-Croix lands were houses, wharfs, storehouses, and workshops. On 31 Dec. 1811 the partnership with Hamilton and Ridsdale, including John Coltman and Company, was dissolved. The following year John, and presumably William Bacheler, formed with Edward Hale the partnership of Coltman and Hale, which took over the assets of John Coltman and Company and a debt of more than £7,500 to Hamilton and Ridsdale. Then disaster struck. In August, John was crushed by a piece of timber being loaded aboard a vessel at the Portneuf installation. In May 1813 Ridsdale and Hamilton declared bankruptcy, and in 1816 the purchasers of their estate, Adam Lymburner*, David Barry, and Benjamin Howard, pressed for at least partial payment of the debt owed by Coltman and Hale. A complicated series of legal procedures ensued, designed to maintain for Coltman and Hale legal title to their assets while they paid £4,254 off their debt. In 1820, operating from stores on Rue Saint-Paul in the Lower Town commercial district, the firm offered for sale Lower and Upper Canadian flour, Newfoundland biscuit, "Upper Country Pork," and a variety of iron products; it also offered to lease part of its premises and wharf. Coltman's prominence in the Quebec business community is reflected in his presidency of the Quebec branch of the Bank of Montreal in 1820 and 1821.

Coltman had been made a justice of the peace for the district of Quebec in January 1810. On 13 Jan. 1812 he was appointed to the Executive Council of Lower Canada. Three years later he received a nomination to the unsalaried position of commissioner for the management of the Jesuit estates, a position he held until at least 1824. He and his fellow commissioners faced a wide range of concerns in supervising lands of nearly 900,000 *arpents*. Besides receiving and accounting for revenues from the estates, the commissioners were encouraged to improve them in the hope that the income would eventually be appropriated for the general benefit of the province.

In October 1816 Governor Sir John Coape SHER-BROOKE gave Coltman and John Fletcher*, a Quebec lawyer, commissions of the peace for the Indian territory of the northwest. Shortly after, they each received a special commission to inquire into crimes resulting from the life-and-death struggle between the Hudson's Bay Company and the North West Company for hegemony in the fur trade. Violence had increased when the HBC allowed Lord Selkirk [Douglas*] to establish a colony of landless Scottish farmers on the Red River in 1812. In June 1816 it culminated in the deaths at Seven Oaks (Winnipeg) of the colony's governor, Robert Semple*, and some 20 settlers at the hands of a band of Métis under Cuthbert Grant*. In retaliation, Selkirk seized the NWC headquarters of Fort William (Thunder Bay, Ont.). It was these events, the conditions that led to them, and means of resolving the conflict that Coltman and Fletcher were to investigate. To reinforce their authority, they were given commissions of lieutenant-colonel and major respectively in the Indian Department. The choice of Coltman, who had legal training and a reputation for honesty and common sense, pleased both sides.

Having failed in an attempt to proceed to the northwest in 1816 because the season was too advanced, Coltman and Fletcher set out again in late spring 1817. They were armed with a dispatch from the colonial secretary, Lord Bathurst, ordering the arrest of Selkirk, cessation of hostilities, and restitution of captured property by both sides; they also carried a proclamation from the Prince Regent making public the government's desires. The commissioners were accompanied by a small detachment of troops. Fletcher remained at Fort William, and thenceforth Coltman conducted the work of the commission alone. He arrested Selkirk at the Red River settlement (Man.) and imposed on him bail of £6,000. Throughout the summer he worked 12 hours a day amassing evidence and taking depositions. After re-establishing a modicum of peace among the factions, he left for Lower Canada in the fall with Grant and Joseph CADOTTE, who were to be tried in Montreal; Selkirk made his own way to Upper Canada to stand trial on the charges against him.

In his proceedings Coltman appears to have sought a compromise rather than a rigorous imposition of the law, which might have provoked renewed violence. A contemporary described him as "a good-natured Laugh and Grow fat sort of person who had no wish but to reconcile and tranquillize all parties." Samuel Gale*, Selkirk's shrewd and able counsel from Montreal, wrote that Coltman "took it for granted that Government looked upon all parties in almost the same light . . . and like a good subject he has laboured

to fulfil what he conceived to be the wishes of the Government." The Selkirk party considered this approach unjust, but could only admire the commissioner's manner of proceeding. "Such is the man's bonhomie and good nature," Lady Selkirk acknowledged in December 1817, "that none of us can quite attribute bad intentions to him."

Coltman submitted his report on 30 June 1818. Although justifying to some extent the fears of the Selkirk party that NWC partners, particularly William McGILLIVRAY, had managed to influence Coltman, the report nevertheless testifies, by its thoroughness, accuracy, and relative impartiality, to a genuine striving on the part of its author to be objective and fair. Coltman had doubts about the legal basis for the establishment of the Red River settlement and the legality and morality of Selkirk's actions at Fort William; he also exposed sympathetically the arguments of the NWC that the colony represented a threat to its conduct of the fur trade. On the other hand, while condemning both protagonists for their recourse to violence, he particularly denounced the "system of intimidation and violence" employed by the NWC. Moreover, he acknowledged the sincerity of Selkirk's opinion that the NWC was behaving as an enemy of the government as well as of the Red River settlement and that the exigencies of the situation authorized proceedings otherwise unjustifiable. Coltman's commission and report had little immediate effect in discouraging violence in the northwest, but its conciliatory nature may have facilitated the union of the Hudson's Bay and North West companies three years later.

At Quebec Coltman enjoyed considerable social status. In 1811 he was elected to the managing committee of the Quebec Fire Society for Saint-Laurent ward. Four years later he was proposed as a member of a committee to promote the education, on non-sectarian principles, of the poor of Quebec [see Thaddeus Osgood*]. Having developed a special concern while in the northwest about the lack of education and religious instruction for the Métis and Indians, he supported efforts in 1818–19 by the Roman Catholic bishop of Quebec, Joseph-Octave PLESSIS, to establish a mission at Red River [see Joseph-Norbert Provencher*]. In 1819 he became a committee member of the Quebec Emigrants' Society. The following year he was elected to the committee of the Quebec branch of the Royal Humane Society of London for the Recovery of the Apparently Drowned or Dead, a society devoted to methods of resuscitation.

Coltman enjoyed an excellent reputation with the colonial executive. In January 1817 Sherbrooke recommended him for a seat in the Legislative Council, but the nomination was never received from London. In May 1819 he was appointed to the newly constitut-

Comingo

ed Board of Cullers [see Peter Patterson*], and five months later he was named chairman of the Board of Audit of the Public Accounts, a post with a salary of at least £400 per annum. His commission of the peace, which had been extended to the Western District of Upper Canada in 1816, was further extended throughout Lower Canada in 1821 and 1824.

Coltman's social and political prominence encouraged him to seek a seat in the House of Assembly in the elections of 1820. Defeated in Upper Town Quebec by Joseph-Rémi Vallières* de Saint-Réal, he tried again in Hampshire, but withdrew before the close of the poll in a bitter contest won by Charles Langevin of the Canadian party with the assistance of François HUOT. Coltman's position in the executive government, his interest (if not a continuing career) in commerce, and his skirmishes with the Canadian party all made him sympathetic to the movement that developed in 1822, chiefly among British merchants and office holders, for a legislative union of Lower and Upper Canada. At a meeting in November he was elected president of the Quebec branch of a provincial organization to promote this cause. He asserted forcefully that, as a consequence of the division of 1791, "a majority of the Legislature almost inevitably led astray by Party Spirit, have adopted measures tending to foster National Prejudices and distinctions, instead of such as should have tended to allay them and assimilate the whole People; thus for retaining the monopoly of power . . . they have perhaps unconsciously rejected as connected with British feeling and making part of the British Colonial System, the various advantages offered to the Public . . . by the adoption of the more liberal views of the Commercial Spirit." Coltman's arguments were representative of the movement's justifications for union. The project met immediate and stiff opposition led by the Canadian party and the Roman Catholic Church, but, although it had little chance of success from the outset, it was not finally abandoned until 1824. Coltman left for his native England on 3 November of the following year and died in London on 2 Jan. 1826.

In collaboration with ROY C. DALTON

William Bacheler Coltman is the author of "A general statement and report relative to the disturbances in the Indian Territories of British North America . . . ," 1818, a copy of which is in PAC, MG 19, E2. This document does not bear the signature of John Fletcher, Coltman's fellow commissioner. More extensive than a text in the Colonial Office correspondence (PAC, MG 11, [CO 42] Q, 148: 278–315, 551–66), it should also be compared with that printed in G.B., Parl., House of Commons paper, 1819, 18, no.584: 1–288, *Papers relating to the Red River settlement . . .* , which was reprinted in N.Dak., State Hist. Soc., *Coll.* (Fargo), 4 (1913): 451–653, as "Summary of evidence in the controversy between the Hudson's Bay Company and the North West Company."

ANQ-Q, CN1-16, 31 oct. 1816; CN1-262, 16, 23 janv. 1807; 22 mars, 25 mai 1808; 11 mai 1812; 14 févr., 2–3 mai 1817. PAC, MG 11, [CO 42] Q, 144–45, 147–48; RG 4, B46; RG 8, I (C ser.), 0: 1956; RG 68, General index, 1651–1841. SRO, GD45/3/86. *Documents relating to northwest missions, 1815–1827*, ed. G. L. Nute, (St Paul, Minn., 1942). *HBRS*, 1 (Rich), xx. *Quebec Gazette*, 11 July 1799; 24 Oct. 1805; 5 Nov. 1807; 25 Jan. 1810; 11 April 1811; 7 May 1812; 16 March, 13 April, 13 July, 21 Dec. 1815; 15, 22, 29 May, 25 July, 7, 14, 21 Nov., 19 Dec. 1816; 13 March, 13 Nov. 1817; 1 Jan., 26 Feb., 6, 9 Aug., 7 Dec. 1818; 20 May, 1 July, 2, 9, 12 Aug., 14 Oct., 23 Dec. 1819; 6, 30 March, 26 June, 23 Oct., 29 Dec. 1820; 21, 25 Nov., 2, 19 Dec. 1822. *Quebec almanac*, 1821–22. F.-J. Audet, "Les législateurs du Bas-Canada." Wallace, *Macmillan dict.* D. [G.] Creighton, *The empire of the St Lawrence* (Toronto, 1956). R. C. Dalton, *The Jesuits' estates question, 1760–1888: a study of the background for the agitation of 1889* (Toronto, 1968), 60–77. J. S. Galbraith, *The Hudson's Bay Company as an imperial factor, 1821–1869* ([Toronto], 1957). William Kingsford, *The history of Canada* (10v., Toronto and London, 1887–98). C. [B.] Martin, *Lord Selkirk's work in Canada* (Oxford, Eng., 1916). Morton, *Hist. of Canadian west* (Thomas; 1973). W. L. Morton, *Manitoba: a history* (Toronto, 1957). E. E. Rich, *The fur trade and the northwest to 1857* (Toronto, 1967).

COMINGO, JOSEPH BROWN, painter; b. 1784 in Lunenburg, N.S., eldest son of Romkes Comingo and Jane (Jeanne) Margaret Bailly; m. 6 Dec. 1812 Elizabeth Winslow Reynolds in Halifax, and they had three children; d. 1821 in Nassau, Bahamas.

As far as can be determined, Joseph Brown Comingo was the first professional painter born in Nova Scotia. The earliest known work by him is a portrait, painted around 1800, of his grandfather, the Reverend Bruin Romkes Comingo*. Although he may have received some instruction from John Thomson or another of the itinerant artists who worked in Halifax and conducted drawing academies before 1809, there is no record of his art studies. From 1808 until 1820, however, his work and movements are fairly well documented. In 1808 he was in Fredericton, working at John MacLeod's inn, where he painted "miniature watercolour portraits and family groups." Two years later he could be found on Grafton Street in Halifax painting oil portraits and "miniatures of different descriptions on ivory and fine wove paper," and also offering lessons in "drawing and painting, landscape, figures, flowers &c." at his lodgings. In 1811 he placed an advertisement in the *Halifax Journal* informing potential clients that they should "apply as early as possible as he intends to leave this town soon." For the next several years he appears to have travelled a good deal, practising his craft for short periods in Halifax, Saint John, Fredericton, Lunenburg, and Yarmouth. Around 1821 he went to Nassau in the Bahamas, where soon after his arrival he died at the age of 37.

Comingo seems to have been a fairly prolific artist, and a number of his paintings have survived. In 1812, while residing in Halifax, he painted a small water-colour portrait of Quartermaster George Mathew of the 99th Foot (this work was at one time incorrectly ascribed to Robert Field*). Two years later he painted a miniature of Thomas Henry Bailey, barrack master of Fort Anne at Annapolis Royal and son of the Reverend Jacob Bailey*. In the same year he produced a profile miniature on ivory of Andrew Crook-shank of Saint John, now in the New Brunswick Museum, as well as a water-colour "View of Saint John." While in Lunenburg in 1816 he painted a view of that town and its harbour, and the following year in Halifax he executed one of his finest miniatures – a portrait on ivory of Anne Henry (Murdoch). In 1817 he painted a "View of the Town of Yarmouth," now owned by the Public Archives of Nova Scotia. Just before leaving Nova Scotia he painted miniatures of two Yarmouth residents, Joseph and Mary Tooker. These miniatures were reproduced in a 1952 issue of *Antiques* magazine, which mistakenly claimed that they had been painted in Baltimore, Md.

Reflecting the influence of current neoclassical taste, Comingo's painting aspired to the elegant formality of the European "grand manner" style. Although affected by the accomplished portraits of Robert Field, Comingo's work expresses the naïve quality inherent in colonial painting. His characterizations show a reliance on line rather than modelling, on detail rather than generalization. Variety and experimentation in his work were limited by the conventions of miniature portrait painting. Only slight alterations in the posing or positioning of his sitters were allowed within the formula. Delicate drawing and transparent colour compensate for the lack of three-dimensionality in his images. Their charm and directness suggest Comingo's search for that combination of idealism and pragmatism so typical of early Canadian painting.

Comingo was survived by his wife Elizabeth, who died at Chester, N.S., in 1893 at the age of 100, and three children – Jane Catherine, Joseph, and Elizabeth Brown. Some confusion about the artist's later life has been caused by the existence of his uncle J. Brown Comingo, son of the Reverend Bruin Romkes Comingo and a schoolmaster in Lunenburg until the late 1860s.

DONALD C. MACKAY and SANDRA PAIKOWSKY

PANS, MG 4, 94–105; MG 100, 125, nos.17–17f (photocopies). *Halifax Journal*, 1 Oct., 1 Dec. 1810; 19 Aug. 1811. *New-Brunswick Courier*, 17 Aug. 1814. *New-Brunswick Royal Gazette*, 12 Sept. 1808, 17 June 1815. *Nova-Scotia Royal Gazette*, 9 Dec. 1812. J. R. Harper, *Early painters and engravers in Canada* ([Toronto], 1970). M. B. DesBrisay, *History of the county of Lunenberg* (2nd ed., Toronto, 1895). J. R. Harper, *Painting in Canada, a history* (Toronto and Quebec, 1966). Harry Piers, *Robert Field, portrait painter in oils, miniature and water-colours, and engraver* (New York, 1927). *200 years of art in Halifax; an exhibition prepared in honour of the bicentenary of the founding of the city of Halifax, N.S., 1749–1949* (Halifax, 1949). *Antiques* (New York), 62 (1952): 182. William Hazen, "The earliest painting of Saint John," N.B. Hist. Soc., *Coll.*, no.17 (1961): 97–101. D. C. Mackay, "Artists and their pictures," *Canadian Antiques Collector* (Toronto), 7 (1973), no.1: 81–86.

COUTLÉE, THÉRÈSE-GENEVIÈVE, superior of the Sisters of Charity of the Hôpital Général of Montreal; b. 23 Nov. 1742 in Montreal, eldest daughter of Louis Coutlée (Coutelais), *dit* Marcheterre, a day labourer, and Geneviève Labrosse; d. there 17 July 1821 at the Hôpital Général.

At the time she entered the Hôpital Général of Montreal on 14 Oct. 1762, Thérèse-Geneviève Coutlée had an enviable education for a young girl of that era. Mme d'Youville [Dufrost*] quickly noted the intellectual abilities of this particularly gifted candidate. Consequently, immediately after she had made her profession on 24 Oct. 1764 Sister Coutlée was initiated into the business matters of the house by Mme d'Youville, who entrusted her with the office of assistant bursar. She was soon put to the test, for on 18 May 1765 a fire utterly devastated the hospital. The patients and nuns took shelter in the Hôtel-Dieu or on the farm at Pointe-Saint-Charles (Montreal). Providing for the needs of the poor, who were now scattered, and watching over the rebuilding of the house proved a challenge that she met to everyone's satisfaction. On 9 June 1792, three days after the death of the superior, Marguerite-Thérèse Lemoine* Despins, Sister Coutlée was elected to succeed her; overwhelmed by the responsibility, she wept freely.

Mother Coutlée paid great attention to the needs of the poor, whose numbers were growing faster than were resources, and like her predecessor she endeavoured to collect the annuities that were held by the hospital in France and that were now devalued with disastrous consequences for Canadian religious communities. But the Hôpital Général was unable to obtain any revenues during her lifetime and so sustained heavy losses. To cope with insufficient income Mother Coutlée rented out part of the land adjoining the hospital on a long lease; then she developed or opened workshops to turn out embroidery, vestments, candles, wafers, wax products, book-binding, and gilding. She herself did some of this work, and artist Louis Dulongpré* chose to portray her with a piece of embroidery in her hands. Her participation was appreciated and helped keep the others in good spirits. During her term of office the nuns, who ate sparingly and had a great many other tasks to do, had to give up working in the fields.

Couvillon

The institution continued to be in an extremely precarious financial position, despite gifts from coadjutor bishop Pierre Denaut*, the gentlemen of the Séminaire de Saint-Sulpice, and the nuns of the Congregation of Notre-Dame and the Hôtel-Dieu. In 1795 Mother Coutlée asked Bishop Jean-François Hubert* about the advisability of leasing out two properties, one at Pointe-Saint-Charles, the other adjoining Côte à Baron. She even contemplated selling the seigneury of Châteauguay "if these deals [could] be of advantage to the poor." Bishop Hubert offered only one objection: the proposed rent was too low. Fortunately, in 1801 the House of Assembly agreed to provide an annual grant for the work with the insane and with foundlings. These sums helped put the finances of the hospital on a firmer basis, but Mother Coutlée's worries were by no means at an end. Too many young nuns were dying, and there was a dearth of workers for the tasks at hand. To improve the situation, in 1804 she set up an infirmary where sick nuns thenceforth received better care.

In 1814, in the midst of stubborn struggles to defend the interests of the underprivileged, Mother Coutlée reached the 50th anniversary of her religious profession, a memorable occasion for it was the first time a golden jubilee had been celebrated in the community. However, it was but a pause between two battles. To the superior's surprise, in 1818 the assembly voted £2,000 for the construction of accommodation for the insane on the Hôpital Général's land. The nuns could scarcely sustain their existing level of work, but Joseph-Octave PLESSIS, the bishop of Quebec, advised them to accept the assembly's grant so that they could meet the urgent financial needs of caring for foundlings and the insane [see George SELBY]. That year the town of Montreal made plans to continue Rue Saint-Pierre to the St Lawrence, an extension that would have cut the nuns' house in two. After clarifying the matter, the superior again benefited from episcopal counsel and support for the sisters' defence of the unfortunate. Moreover, Charles-Michel d'IRUMBERRY de Salaberry, a member of the Legislative Council, considered it an honour to take up this cause. In the end those managing the Hôpital Général gave up the work with the insane in 1844 because they could no longer house the patients adequately.

On 17 July 1821 Thérèse-Geneviève Coutlée died, commending to her sisters the precept of charity which she had herself received at Mme d'Youville's bedside.

LAURETTE DUCLOS

Arch. des Sœurs Grises (Montréal), Aliénés, historique; Ancien journal, I; Dossier de sœur Thérèse-Geneviève Coutlée; Maison mère, historique; Musée; Mémoire de sœur Julie Casgrain-Baby; Reg. des baptêmes et sépultures de l'Hôpital Général de Montréal; Reg. des minutes du Conseil général; Reg. des recettes et dépenses de l'Hôpital Général de Montréal. Allaire, *Dictionnaire*, vol.1. Gérard Brassard, *Armorial des évêques du Canada . . .* (Montréal, 1940). Gauthier, *Sulpitiana*. [É.-M. Faillon], *Vie de Mme d'Youville, fondatrice des Sœurs de la charité de Villemarie dans l'île de Montréal, en Canada* (Villemarie [Montréal], 1852). [Albina Fauteux et Clémentine Drouin], *L'Hôpital Général de Sœurs de la charité (Sœurs Grises) depuis sa fondation jusqu'à nos jours* (3v. parus, Montréal, 1916–).

COUVILLON. *See* QUÉVILLON

COWDELL, THOMAS DANIEL, merchant, Methodist lay preacher, author, and music teacher; b. 2 Oct. 1769 in London, son of Samuel Cowdell; d. 25 or 26 March 1833, possibly in Halifax.

Thomas Daniel Cowdell was born of an Irish mother and an English father who was a professional soldier. He grew up in London and there converted to Methodism in 1784. In 1789 he came to Halifax and subsequently married a Scots girl, Margaret, who bore him four sons and four daughters. During his time in Halifax he ran a small shop on Duke Street near the Theatre Royal, selling sweets, miscellaneous goods, and "Oddities." But though he was a shopkeeper by profession, his real interests lay in religion, poetry, and music.

While a member of the Methodist congregation in Halifax, Cowdell rose to the positions of class leader and lay preacher. He is remembered, however, less for his church work than for his quarrel with the Reverend William BLACK, the resident minister in Halifax from 1786 and founder of the Methodist movement in the Maritimes. From the spring of 1802 until early 1803, Cowdell took the lead in an attack on Black. Ostensibly, the problem was Black's failure to follow certain Methodist rules, particularly that requiring circuit preachers to change circuits every two years. But the main irritant seems to have been Black's desire to tear down the existing preacher's house in Halifax, which was almost paid for, and to build a new, larger residence. On 22 March 1802 seven of the Halifax class leaders expressed their dissatisfaction to Black in a letter. All except Cowdell quickly withdrew from the dispute. But Cowdell continued to press the matter and ultimately lost his "class papers" for "vulgar preaching and railing." His wife was also ejected from the congregation because it was supposed "she was the principal author of the letter." None the less, Cowdell turned up briefly as a lay preacher in Prince Edward Island between December 1805 and June 1806. His controversial career in the church perhaps accounts for the hostile attitude of Thomas Watson Smith, the historian of Maritime Methodism. Smith, describing Cowdell as a man whose "broad shoulders and short legs made him a frequent subject of remark," claimed that the preacher became "a prey to intemperate habits, which brought him to thorough degradation." No evidence has been found to substantiate this charge.

Cowdell's business affairs seem never to have gone particularly well. He was continually plagued with financial problems, and in December 1808, upon hearing that his maternal uncle had died, he decided to journey to Dublin to claim an inheritance. The trip lasted almost three years, during which Cowdell visited England, Ireland, Scotland, and Wales. But the object of the journey – the expected inheritance – appears to have eluded him. In order to support himself while abroad, he wrote and published a book of verse entitled *A poetical journal of a tour from British North America to England, Wales & Ireland* . . . , which was published in Dublin in 1809. Another version of this book was printed as *The Nova Scotia minstrel, written while on a tour from North America to Great Britain and Ireland* . . . in London in March 1811 to raise money for his return to Halifax.

Back in Halifax, Cowdell again turned to shopkeeping, but in addition opened a school for teaching "vocal music." He had long had a local reputation as an excellent violoncello player and had participated in Halifax concerts. While abroad, he apparently had added the study of voice to his musical interests; his singing voice was described as a "fine bass." However, Cowdell did not remain long in Halifax. In March 1815 his house and shop were sold at auction and he planned "to leave the Province as early as possible." A book entitled *A poetical account of the American campaigns of 1812 and 1813* . . . , published anonymously at Halifax in September 1815 under the signature of An Acadian, has been attributed to Cowdell. There is, however, no conclusive evidence of his authorship.

In 1815 Cowdell returned to Ireland, where two years later he once again printed, with further revisions, *The Nova Scotia minstrel*. After nine years abroad, he turned up in Saint John, N.B., in October 1824 to visit his children. They apparently had been left there with friends or relatives when Cowdell went to Dublin in 1815. In early 1825 he travelled to Halifax, where he published in 1826 a pamphlet entitled *An awful fact, or narrative of the most extraordinary instance of supernatural vision; or, the appearance of a late wife to her husband, in Halifax.* Nothing is known of Cowdell from 1825 until his death in 1833. One story, probably apocryphal, has it that on his deathbed Cowdell remarked to a Methodist minister attending him, "I weep, because I cannot weep."

Cowdell's significance in early 19th-century Maritime life rests on his poetical accomplishments. He claimed that his book of poetry was "the first Fruit of a distant Colony offered to its Parent Isle." Although not strictly accurate in his claim to precedence, he was in fact the first Maritime poet to publish and circulate a volume of verse in the British Isles. But he was certainly not the first Maritime poet, nor even the first published poet from that area. Indeed, in the history of Maritime poetry Cowdell belongs to a transitional period, coming after such poets as Henry Alline*, Jacob Bailey*, and Jonathan Odell*, whose works form the core of the 18th-century phase of Maritime verse. Together with the writings of poets such as Oliver Goldsmith* and the young Joseph Howe*, Cowdell's verse at times looks back to the 18th century and at times forward to the sentimental attitudes and lyric forms that dominate Maritime verse from the 1830s to the 1860s. This dichotomy is strikingly demonstrated in the differences between the 1809, 1811, and 1817 editions of his poetry. Aside from two lyrics, the 1809 edition is wholly comprised of relatively long descriptive and narrative verse, patterned on 18th-century models. In the 1811 edition, however, 24 songs and lyrics are introduced into the text at various points. The 1817 edition has more than 40 lyrics. Not only does Cowdell experiment in these lyrics with newer metric patterns, but their tone and spirit differ from his descriptive-narrative verse. In spite of some rewriting, the didactic objectivity of the descriptive-narrative sections contrasts sharply with the personalized, sentimental response to subject displayed in the lyrics.

It is difficult to estimate to what extent Cowdell recognized the dichotomy in his verse. As a poet, he never seriously attempted to reconcile this dichotomy in his aesthetic response to reality. Nor did he grow beyond it artistically; but then, he was one of the first in Maritime poetry to reflect it.

THOMAS B. VINCENT

An advertisement for Thomas Daniel Cowdell's 1826 pamphlet appeared in the *Acadian Recorder*, 11 March 1826, but no copies of it are now known to exist. In addition to the works discussed in this biography, he is the author of a number of poems published in local newspapers, including an untitled verse advertisement for his Halifax shop which appeared in the *Nova-Scotia Royal Gazette* on 15 July 1812; "The occasional address at the late concert for the benefit of the poor . . . ," *Nova-Scotia Royal Gazette*, 28 April 1813; and "An acrostic sonnet" and "The good ship Waterloo," both in the *New-Brunswick Courier*, 4 Dec. 1824.

The uncertainty over Cowdell's exact death date is due to the fact that it is given as 25 March in an obituary in the *New-Brunswick Courier*, 6 April 1833, and as 26 March in the *Novascotian, or Colonial Herald*'s obituary of 28 March 1833.

UCC-M, "Address to Mr. William Black, Methodist preacher, Halifax, Nova Scotia, on the subject of deviating from the minutes of the British Methodist Conference; by Thomas Roby, class leader in Halifax and signed by other leaders; with notes illustrative of the subject by Thomas Daniel Cowdell . . ." (Halifax, 1802; mfm. at PANS). *A*

Crawford

checklist of Canadian literature and background materials, 1628–1960, comp. R. E. Watters (2nd ed., Toronto, 1972). R. J. Long, *Nova Scotia authors and their work: a bibliography of the province* (East Orange, N.J., 1918). J. T. Mellish, *Outlines of the history of Methodism in Charlottetown, Prince Edward Island ...* (Charlottetown, 1888). T. W. Smith, *History of the Methodist Church within the territories embraced in the late conference of Eastern British America ...* (2v., Halifax, 1877–90).

CRAWFORD, ALEXANDER, Baptist preacher and author; b. 1786 in Argyllshire, Scotland; d. 13 May 1828 in Tryon, P.E.I.

Although born in Argyllshire, Alexander Crawford spent his early years on the Isle of Arran, where he became exposed to a breakaway Presbyterian sect led by Robert and James Alexander Haldane, which had both pietistic and revivalistic tendencies. Crawford subsequently attended an academy in Edinburgh organized by the Haldane brothers, and shortly thereafter became convinced of the scriptural unsoundness of infant baptism. He joined the tiny group in Scotland led by James Alexander Haldane, who in 1808 took his Edinburgh congregation into the Baptist fold. In 1809 Crawford married Jane MacLaren of Breadalbane and the couple emigrated to Nova Scotia, where he attempted to preach and exhort.

Nova Scotia was fertile territory both for itinerant preaching and for anti-paedobaptist principles, but the peculiar tenets of the Scotch Baptists led to much opposition to Crawford, especially among the clergy. Because of their Presbyterian origins, the Scotch Baptists tended to be extremely suspicious of sudden crisis conversions, which were at the heart of the Nova Scotia New Light–Baptist experience, and they were also exclusivist, opposing marriage with unbelievers and barring from fellowship any who married spouses not adhering to their tenets. Moreover, the Scotch Baptists refused to regard the Lord's Supper as a church ordinance, but instead permitted any small group of laymen to celebrate communion among themselves.

In 1811 Crawford came to Prince Edward Island, where there was a large Scottish population and few competing clergymen of any denomination. He was probably encouraged to migrate to the Island by John Scott, another Haldanite who had come in 1806 and was a lay exhorter there for many years. Crawford was much better educated than Scott and was both a compelling preacher (although some said overbearing in manner) and an energetic organizer. He may have taught briefly at Charlottetown, but soon spent his full efforts on religious activity. His first successes were on Lot 48, where he immersed eight believers. A great storm a few days later was blamed by Islanders on his temerity in "plunging" people rather than sprinkling them. Although he organized a church in the Three Rivers (Georgetown) region in 1812, he left the Island

briefly for Nova Scotia and returned permanently only in 1814, settling a year later at East Point through the support of two local people, both formally adherents of the Church of Scotland. Crawford remained based at East Point until his death; he organized a church but never became ordained, probably because he was unable to assemble an ordaining council. He did not associate with the Maritime Baptists, and for many years after his death the peculiar beliefs of the Island's Scotch Baptists remained a stumbling-block to union between the two groups.

James Douglas Haszard* of Charlottetown in 1827 printed a book written by Crawford the year before entitled *Believer immersion, as opposed to unbeliever sprinkling*, the first substantial religious publication on the Island or by an Island clergyman. It contained two lengthy doctrinal essays on the Abrahamic Covenant, and three polemic letters supporting the Baptist arguments of William Elder* of Nova Scotia, who had engaged in a lengthy controversy in print with Duncan Ross and James Munroe, both Presbyterian paedobaptists. In this work Crawford did not pursue the peculiarities of his brand of Baptist belief, but concentrated instead on the larger question of the scriptural justification for believer's baptism. He refused to accept the typological arguments which were used to find support for infant baptism in the Old Testament, particularly the commitment by God to the "seed" of Abraham. For Crawford, circumcision and baptism were quite distinct: "Circumcision is a cutting off the extreme point of the generating member. Baptism is the immersion of the body in water. They represent different things." Like all Baptists, he defied his opponents to find New Testament justification for the baptism of infants, and suggested that the practice entitled them to be regarded as church members although they were clearly too young to assume the responsibilities of membership. He accused the Presbyterians of a concept of "hereditary christianity" which was "ANTICALVINIST IN DISGUISE."

Believer immersion demonstrated Crawford's intellectual capabilities and may in part have been intended as a preliminary gesture of fellowship with Baptists off the Island. Unfortunately, he died soon after its publication. He was survived by his wife and eight children.

J. M. BUMSTED

Alexander Crawford is the author of *Believer immersion, as opposed to unbeliever sprinkling; in two essays: first on the Abrahamic covenant, second on Christian baptism; to which are added three letters to Mr. Ross of Pictou, containing strictures on his first letter to Mr. Elder of Annapolis* (Charlottetown, 1827).

Atlantic Baptist Hist. Coll., Acadia Univ. (Wolfville, N.S.), [W. H. Warren], "A century of Baptist history on Prince Edward Island." PAPEI, Acc. 3209/33 (photocopy).

P.E.I. Museum and Heritage Foundation (Charlottetown), File information concerning Alexander Crawford.

CROSSKILL (Croskill), JOHN, ship's captain and landowner; b. 1740 in Norwich, England, the son of a shipbuilder; m. *c*. 1785 Charlotte Fillis, daughter of Nova Scotia merchant John Fillis*, and they had seven children; m. secondly 1812 Frances Morrison, *née* Gidney; d. 23 May 1826 in Bridgetown, N.S.

Brought up by an aunt in London, John Crosskill was placed in the merchant navy, and rose to the rank of captain by the time he was 30. During the American Revolutionary War he was engaged in transporting German auxiliary troops to North America for the British army. After the peace he went to the West Indies, where he lived at Nassau in the Bahamas and Bridgetown in Barbados. While in the Bahamas he acquired property on Rum Cay, Andros, and New Providence islands, and also some vessels, two of which were lost in the hurricanes of September 1785 and August 1787. He claimed in a later memorial to have held the positions of justice of the peace and harbour-master during his stay at Nassau, but these appointments are not confirmed in the records. John Fillis, his father-in-law, died in 1792, and Crosskill brought his family to Halifax in June 1793 to receive a "small portion" left to his wife, the farm of Henley, 1,500 acres along the Annapolis River.

Although he remained in Nova Scotia, Crosskill had not decided whether he wished to settle permanently there. In February 1795, as he was about to set out in a sloop he owned on a trading voyage to the Bahamas, Lieutenant Governor John Wentworth* offered him the command of the *Earl of Moira*, a snow of 135 tons mounting 14 guns which had been built for the provincial service the year before. Crosskill readily accepted. In his own words, "I hesitated not to accept his offer; my Heart ever beat high in my Countrys cause, and in a station of that responsibility I had no doubt but I would do credit to myself, and be of service to my Country." Under the command of Crosskill, who was described by Beamish Murdoch* as "a skilled pilot," the *Earl of Moira* was employed in protecting the fisheries along the coast of Nova Scotia and in the Gulf of St Lawrence, convoying merchant vessels to Quebec, driving off smugglers, and watching for privateers. In August 1795, moreover, Wentworth reported that the vessel had been of great assistance to Lieutenant Governor Francis Le Maistre* in quelling disturbances between Indians and fishermen in Gaspé. Early in 1796 Wentworth issued Crosskill letters of marque. Thanks to the *Earl of Moira*'s light draught, privateers could be chased in shallow water; during the time Crosskill was in command he seized three ships. Wentworth consistently praised the captain's efforts, and in January 1796 even the Duke of Portland, secretary of state for

the Home Department, recognized that Crosskill's services had been "of great utility."

In June 1796 the *Earl of Moira* sailed for Boston, as usual carrying a complement of soldiers of the Royal Nova Scotia Regiment. While in Boston some of the soldiers deserted, and on the vessel's return to Halifax in July a military court of inquiry was held. On the 15th Crosskill was informed by Wentworth that, since the presence of soldiers on the *Earl of Moira* required that a commissioned officer be in charge, he was being relieved as the ship's commander. At the same time the lieutenant governor expressed his "full approbation" of Crosskill's conduct. Captain Jones Fawson of the Royal Nova Scotia Regiment replaced Crosskill the next day.

The reasons for Crosskill's dismissal remain somewhat obscure. Prince Edward* Augustus, commander of the forces in the Maritime provinces, was convinced that "the person from whose disobedience this Desertion has happened can not otherwise be punished than by being dismissed from the ship." But Crosskill was not on board when the desertion occurred. He had dismissed the second mate for his negligence in allowing the desertion, but the man was later reinstated. It is known, however, that the prince was displeased about Crosskill's having authority over the officers and soldiers on the vessel, and that there was friction between Crosskill and the army officers, whom he described as ill fitted for their positions. A family tradition holds that Crosskill disapproved of the prince's companion, Mme de Saint-Laurent [MONTGENET], and forbad his wife to attend social affairs where she would be present. Perhaps in reprisal for this affront, Edward Augustus had insisted that the captain be dismissed. Whatever the circumstances, Crosskill did not regain his position. In a memorial of 23 July 1796 he appealed for justice to the Duke of Portland, but without success.

Crosskill then retired to his wife's property on the Annapolis River. The site was at the head of navigation, and over the bridge erected there ran the road between Granville and Annapolis townships. Crosskill, seeing the advantages of the location, had long wanted to lay out a town site on the land, but after Charlotte's death in 1806 the property went to their children, and it was the autumn of 1821 before he could obtain a controlling interest. He then laid out the property in town lots, deeding the streets to the county for perpetual public use. Thereafter a community grew rapidly, developing as a centre for small vessels which exported the products of the surrounding region. In 1823 more than 100 vessels loaded there, and by 1828 Thomas Chandler Haliburton* could write that the village contained 3 churches, 25 houses, 12 stores, and 13 shops, and conveyed "an idea of comfort and thrift." At a dinner on 15 Feb. 1824 the name Bridgetown was proposed and adopted. Al-

Cull

though his children had been baptized in the Congregational-Presbyterian church of Mather's (St Matthew's) in Halifax, Crosskill gave a lot in Bridgetown to the Church of England in May 1825, and with his second wife subscribed £30 for the building of a church. His last public act seems to have been the christening of the first vessel to be launched in Bridgetown, on 16 October of the same year. At his death he left the bulk of his estate to his surviving children.

ETHEL A. CRATHORNE

PANS, MG 4, 46–47A. PRO, CO 217/67: 212–17 (mfm. at PANS). E. R. Coward, *Bridgetown, Nova Scotia: its history to 1900* ([Bridgetown], 1955), c.2. Murdoch, *Hist. of N.S.*, 3: 140. *Seasoned timbers* . . . (2v., Halifax, 1972–74), 1: 84–85. John Irvin, "History of Bridgetown . . . ," N.S. Hist. Soc., *Coll.*, 19 (1918): 31–51. J. F. Smith, "Crosskill vs Kent," *N.S. Hist. Quarterly* (Halifax), 2 (1972): 269–81; "John Fillis, MLA," 1 (1971): 307–23.

CULL, HENRY, businessman, seigneur, militia officer, inventor, and JP; b. 1753 in Dorset, England; d. 8 Jan. 1833 in North Hatley, Lower Canada.

Henry Cull was the youngest in a family of ten children, several of whom had careers in the Royal Navy. He was trained for business, and for some years he worked in a London concern. He then emigrated to North America. The date of his arrival at Quebec is unknown, but in 1784 the *Quebec Gazette* mentions that a consignment of assorted goods (fabrics, leather trunks, etc.) had arrived for Henry Cull, a merchant on Rue Saint-Pierre. The records of the Anglican church at Quebec also indicate that he was the father of an illegitimate child, Louis, baptized on 17 June 1787. From 1788 the transactions he signed in the presence of a notary and the advertisements he placed in the *Quebec Gazette* furnish evidence of sustained business activity. Among other things he acted as agent for Dickinson and Lloyd, a London firm involved in the manufacture of cotton goods.

Cull seems to have fitted well into the Quebec merchant group; with others he signed several petitions to promote the group's economic interests or to oppose various laws limiting their autonomy, while at the same time he swore fidelity to the Constitution of 1791. He also took part in the community life of Quebec, being an active member of the Fire Society, an ensign and then lieutenant in the Quebec Battalion of British Militia, and a juror, particularly in the famous trial of David McLane* for high treason in 1797. Moreover, he supported the creation there of a non-sectarian university, in which languages and sciences would be taught. Cull was also associated with the invention of a machine for hulling barley that he put into operation in his workshops in the *faubourg* Saint-Roch in 1796. His properties were valued that

year at £1,000; they consisted of a potash factory equipped with a mill and some kilns, a workshop for producing linseed oil, and a bakery, house, and stable.

In May 1798 Cull made a will bequeathing all his belongings to one of his natural sons, George Irwin, "aged about nine months and a half." At the same time he named William Vondenvelden* his executor, rented his properties in the *faubourg* Saint-Roch to Moses Hart*, a merchant from Trois-Rivières, and announced that he was leaving the colony. The next month he sailed for England, along with the clerk of the Executive Council, Herman Witsius Ryland*. But during the crossing the ship encountered the French privateer *Gironde*, and Cull was taken prisoner by Captain E. Cazalès. On 26 August Ryland, who had reached England, requested the British authorities to exchange Cull for some of the *Gironde*'s junior officers. Cull was released, spent some time in Great Britain, and then returned to Lower Canada.

In 1799, after bad business transactions in the Baie des Chaleurs region, Cull tried to set up a triangular trade with the West Indies and England in order to rebuild his fortune; he planned to sell wood and flour in exchange for rum and slaves. This undertaking, however, does not seem to have met with the success he had anticipated, since in 1801 Cull was short of liquid assets and had to sell the seigneury of Bic, which he had owned since 1791. After these failures he contemplated launching into land speculation, hoping to make more in a short time "than in ten years in the common routine of business with four times the sum."

Following the opening of the Eastern Townships to settlement in 1792, Cull saw an opportunity to carry out his plans. Together with Captain Ebenezer Hovey he formed an association of 33 members which on 25 March 1803 obtained a grant of 23,493 acres in the new township of Hatley. Cull received 1,200 acres through letters patent. In conformity with the system of township leader and associates [see Samuel GALE] he repurchased from some of his associates 1,000 of the 1,200 acres that had been granted each of them, paying the symbolic sum of 5 shillings. By 1805 he had increased his holdings to 4,200 acres. Cull thus became the owner of the fine lands along the Rivière Massawippi at its source and on Lac Tomifobi (Massawippi) at both ends, where North Hatley and Ayer's Cliff are now located. He seems, however, to have lacked discernment in choosing the site of his farm, which he laid out on the west side of the lake. According to chronicler Benjamin F. Hubbard, "the greater part of his farm proved to be wet and cold, and was the poorest land in the township." Clearly, Cull's priorities were not in agriculture. The numerous transactions recorded in the minute-book of notary William Ritchie, of Sherbrooke, as well as a holograph will dated 13 Aug.

174

1827, reveal that the Quebec merchant had become a land speculator.

Cull, who had owned 4,200 acres in Hatley Township, left only 1,200 to his heirs; thus he had sold five-sevenths of his original property. On the other hand, the known transactions show that he speculated on at least 5,500 acres in Hatley. His speculative activity was evidently on a large scale, particularly since it extended beyond Hatley. He also bequeathed 2,800 acres in Auckland Township and 1,400 in Tring Township to his children. These lands were less valuable: in 1857 the heirs sold the British American Land Company 1,600 acres in Auckland for a mere £40, whereas in 1835 they had received £50 from the company for 400 acres in Hatley. Although Cull was not, according to Jean-Chrysostome Langelier, one of the biggest landowners in the region, the North Hatley pioneer certainly profited from the golden age of land speculation in the Eastern Townships.

Cull took an active part in the community life of Hatley Township. He supported the Anglican mission at North Hatley and was one of the founders of the parish established in 1822 at Charleston (Hatley). He gave the settlers access to his personal library, 500 volumes of English literature and ancient and modern history. From 1807 he was a justice of the peace in the District of Montreal. On 2 April 1808 he was named lieutenant-colonel of the 3rd Townships Militia Battalion, which during the War of 1812 incorporated under its command the 14 companies from the townships of Stanstead, Hatley, and Barnston.

Henry Cull had married Elizabeth McMillan, who died on 1 Dec. 1814, and he was the father of six legitimate children born between 1803 and 1813. Of the four surviving him, three lived at Fairfax, Vt. Only George, who inherited his father's farm, ended his days in Canada. With the exception of his daughter, George's descendants also emigrated to the United States. The family's story thus gives some idea of the movement of people in the border regions of Canada even before the industrial era.

ANDRÉE DÉSILETS

ANQ-E, T11-501. ANQ-Q, CN1-256, 5 avril 1788; 5 janv., 9, 11 juill. 1792; 23 mai 1796; CN1-262, 30 mai 1798. BE, Stanstead (Stanstead Plain), Reg. B, 8, nos.2942–45, 2992, 2995; 10, no.47. EEC-Q, 26–29, 30b, 53. PAC, MG 23, GIII, 13. *Quebec Gazette*, 1784–1822. *Sherbrooke Gazette and Eastern Townships Advertiser* (Sherbrooke, Que.), 1832–57. *Illustrated atlas of Eastern Townships*. Langelier, *Liste des terrains concédés*, 15–17, 1013–14. Christie, *Hist. of L.C.* (1848–55), 1: 183. Albert Gravel, *Les Cantons de l'Est* ([Sherbrooke], 1938). B. F. Hubbard, *Forests and clearings; the history of Stanstead County, province of Quebec, with sketches of more than five hundred families*, ed. John Lawrence (Montreal, 1874; repr. 1963), 77–78, 284–85.

CULL, WILLIAM, fisherman, trapper, and lumberman; fl. 1792–1823 in Newfoundland.

William Cull belongs to a group of English pioneers who began exploiting resources in the inner reaches and river estuaries of Notre Dame Bay during the late 1700s. Though few in number compared to the migrants and settlers who engaged in the cod and seal fisheries at outer bay locations, these frontiersmen – furriers, salmoniers, and woodsmen – pushed into the domain of the native Beothuk Indians in the basins of the Exploits and Gander rivers and Indian Brook. The result for them has been a somewhat unenviable reputation in Newfoundland history. Their occupational pursuits entailed contact, competition, and conflict with the dwindling remnants of the island's ill-fated aboriginal Indians. They came to regard these natives as thieves of implements and food supplies, and consequently as a threat to survival. Some observers and writers have concluded that these fishermen-trappers waged a deliberate and systematic campaign to exterminate the Beothuks; others have maintained that factors such as European diseases were more prominent in their demise. That the settlers did commit numerous atrocities against the Beothuks and were, directly or indirectly, a prominent factor in their decline and eventual extinction, is admitted by all scholars and professional writers.

Like many of his contemporaries in Notre Dame Bay, Cull probably came from the vicinity of Poole in Dorset, England, although it is possible that he was a native Newfoundlander. In 1792 he worked for Harry Miller, trapping beaver and fox on Northern Arm Brook and Peters River which flow into the estuary of the Exploits. In 1796 he was employed as a furrier by John PEYTON, who also paid his passage on a visit to England. As the accounts of John Slade and Company – merchants of Poole with establishments at Fogo and Twillingate – attest, from 1797 onward Cull was an independent entrepreneur. He delivered to the Slades some sealskins and codfish, but mostly salmon and furs. Occasionally he cut and sold wood products, as in 1823 when he sold them an amount valued at £140.

Although he earned his livelihood chiefly on the mainland of Newfoundland, Cull had his principal residence in Barr'd Islands, a settlement on the north side of Fogo Island. When the Reverend John LEIGH, one of the first Anglican missionaries in the area, visited there in August 1821, William Cull and his wife Mary presented seven children for baptism. The records also show that five Cull adults, all from Barr'd Islands, were baptized, and that two other Cull nuclear families resided there.

It is in the context of documented English-Beothuk contacts for the period 1791–1823 that William Cull attracts special attention. Indeed his activities together with those of Peyton and others have been associated most prominently with the legends, myths, and

Cuvillon

controversies, as well as with the scholarly assessments, of the Beothuks. Cull's own place comes from his having captured four of the eight members of the tribe who fell into European hands between 1758 and 1829, and from his activities as an emissary and guide hired by Newfoundland governors to establish amicable relationships with the Beothuks during the early 1800s.

In 1792 George Christopher Pulling, a naval officer, made a survey of relations between the Beothuks and fishermen-furriers on the northeast coast. Among his informants was William Cull who stated that he had been disturbed by Indians while furring the previous spring. Cull did not openly admit to having harmed the natives but did say that on one occasion when two Indians were lurking around he would have shot at them if he had had the opportunity. Pulling's opinion was that Cull, like many of the other furriers, thought little of killing Indians.

The circumstances of Cull's capture of an Indian woman in 1803 are related in several different sources which vary somewhat in substance and opinion. One source claims that Cull seized the woman "when she was paddling in her canoe a short distance from the mainland for the purpose of getting birds' eggs from an island." Cull took his captive, described variously as a "young female," "about 50 years of age," and by Cull himself as "the old Indian woman," to St John's in order to collect the bounty which had for some years been offered "for capturing and establishing friendly relations" with the Indians. After she had spent some time in St John's where she was given presents, Cull was instructed to return her to her people whom it was hoped she could convince of the good intentions of the white people. Cull kept the woman at his home on Fogo Island for nearly a year but in August 1804 took her up the Exploits River "as far as we possibly could, for want of more strength; and there let her remain ten days. . . . When I returned," he stated, "the rest of the Indians had carried her off in the country." He also noted his desire to have little more to do with the Indians unless the government would ensure payment to hire men and expressed the common prejudice of white settlers in the area who "do not hold with civilizing the Indians."

In the fall of 1809 Cull was engaged by Governor John Holloway to lead a winter expedition into "Red Indian" (Beothuk) country. Setting out on 1 Jan. 1810, he was accompanied by six settlers from Notre Dame Bay and two Micmac Indians. They traversed the Exploits River, then frozen, and moved inland some 60 miles in four days, near to Red Indian Lake. The party found plenty of evidence of Beothuk activity: buildings, large fences for hunting deer, food supplies, and dressed furs. They caught a glimpse of two Indians, who eluded them and evidently spread an alarm to others in the vicinity, whereupon Cull decided to return, citing as reasons "want of bread and some difference of opinion among the party." The difference of opinion probably was rooted in a fear of ambush.

The following year Cull was appointed chief guide to an expedition arranged by Governor Sir John Thomas Duckworth* and headed by Lieutenant David Buchan*. The Buchan expedition was the most ambitious attempt ever made to establish contact with the Beothuks. Cull guided a party of 28 men, mostly armed marines, from the Bay of Exploits up the Exploits River over the route he had taken the year before and then some ten miles beyond. Near Red Indian Lake a part of the expedition surprised a group of Beothuks but events that followed resulted in the murder by the Indians of two members of Buchan's party. One scholar has suggested that Buchan erred by taking furriers such as Cull, "those inveterate enemies of the poor Red man."

Cull's capture of three Indian women in the spring of 1823, like his taking of a Beothuk 20 years earlier, occurred by chance. He and some of his men encountered an Indian man and an old woman. The woman gave herself up and several days later led Cull to where her two daughters – one 20, the other about 16 – were in a starving condition. Cull placed the three in charge of John Peyton Jr, a magistrate. All succumbed to tuberculosis, the third, Shawnadith-it, dying at St John's in 1829. She was the last known survivor of her people.

Like his early years Cull's later life is cloaked in some obscurity. He apparently died in Newfoundland some time in or after 1831 and left behind a large progeny.

W. Gordon Handcock

BL, Add. ms 38352. PANL, P7/A/6, 1796–1831. USPG, C/CAN/Nfl., 3, reg. of baptisms for the parish of Twillingate, Nfld., 1816–23 (copy at PANL). *Public Ledger*, June 1831. Howley, *Beothucks or Red Indians*. F. W. Rowe, *Extinction: the Beothuks of Newfoundland* (Toronto, 1977).

CUVILLON. *See* Quévillon

D

DANFORTH, ASA, colonizer and road builder; b. 29 June 1768 in Brookfield, Mass., son of Asa Danforth and Hannah Wheeler; m. there in 1789 Olive Langdon, and they had three daughters; d. in or after 1821.

Asa Danforth Sr moved with his family to New

York's Onondaga valley in 1788. Asa Danforth Jr returned to his birthplace the following year to marry and shortly afterwards settled with his bride at Salt Point, later Salina (Syracuse), N.Y., where he manufactured salt. His father was a prominent figure in the Onondaga area and was described in 1794 by Upper Canada's first lieutenant governor, John Graves Simcoe*, as "the most virulent enemy of Great Britain in that Country." Thus, it was somewhat surprising when young Danforth appeared in the province in 1797 seeking the favours of government.

In 1792 Simcoe had initiated a policy of entrusting whole townships to the exclusive control of colonizers in the hope of promoting rapid settlement. There apparently was a misunderstanding as to the benefits promised to the township promoters; they seem to have thought they had been promised an outright grant of their townships if they succeeded in establishing a certain number of new settlers. In fact they were only entitled to 1,200 acres of land and the right to settle people where they pleased. In any case, it soon became evident that the scheme was a failure. In May 1796 Simcoe proclaimed many of these townships forfeited for lack of settlement, and declared that those who claimed to have settled their townships must submit their proofs to the Executive Council on or before 1 June 1797. Danforth was, as he put it, "connected . . . in Settling" the townships of Haldimand, Hamilton, Percy, and Cramahe, and to demonstrate that the proprietors' obligations had been met in these townships he appeared before the council in 1797 to ask that some 205 settlers there be confirmed in possession of their lots.

Simcoe's successor, President Peter Russell*, had a more conciliatory approach to the proprietors than Simcoe. Thus, in July 1797 the unforfeited townships were reopened but the proprietors, Danforth included, were allowed 1,200 acres each if they became residents of the province. The council's decision fostered a good deal of discontent and under the leadership of William Berczy*, one of the most disappointed of the proprietors, caveats were being filed contesting the council's right to grant lands previously entrusted to proprietors. To protect their claims to the four townships, Danforth and his associates directed their attorney, William Weekes*, to join in filing caveats. Outraged, the council dismissed this action as "most improper and unfounded" and rescinded its recommendation that Danforth be granted 1,200 acres personally. Early in 1799 Danforth apologized, explaining that he was bound to people in the United States "to use every exertion that might be made" and that no "disrespect" had been intended. His apology was accepted and the council restored his personal grants. His problems, however, were not at an end. In 1798 two settlers who had been part of the colonization of the four townships com-

plained to the council that Danforth's name, rather than their own, had been entered against the lots which they had settled and improved. The council ordered an investigation and on the basis of the subsequent report (tabled in 1799) Danforth and his associates were accused of fraud and duplicity. As a result, all previous confirmations of lots in these townships were suspended; no new warrants for land were issued until 1 July 1800 and then only upon proof of actual improvement.

It is somewhat surprising therefore that, while this investigation was proceeding, the council on Russell's recommendation had contracted on 9 April 1799 with Danforth to open a road from York (Toronto) to the mouth of the Trent River. With causeways and bridges it was to be completed by 1 July 1800. Danforth was to be paid portions of what was owed him as the road progressed and was inspected, the balance upon completion. He did not receive his payments promptly, and was hampered by a shortage of capital. During a brief absence in the United States in March 1800, he was jailed as a debtor. Released, he returned to Upper Canada in May, sought and was allowed an extension, and completed the road on 18 December.

The council was not satisfied with his work. He received a partial payment but was told no further payments would be made until the road was properly finished. A bitter Danforth returned briefly to the United States where the pressure from his creditors had not abated. He claimed to have had several conversations with presidential candidate Aaron Burr. Danforth anticipated that a Republican triumph in the election would "afford something handsome to those who were draged from home by fair promises of Genl. Simcoe and the like . . . when the Executive Council saw that our Americans had made choice of the best lands in the Province they laid a plan to recind & take away the Lands theretofore granted and placed their own locations on the same." Danforth believed that Upper Canadian officials feared the likelihood of the eclipse of British power in North America but that "three-fourths of the common people would be happy of a Change." Back in the province in June 1801 he was hopeful of a favourable settlement on his claims for land and money. Disappointed yet again he left the province for good in January 1802.

Before departing Danforth laid plans for a meeting in Albany, N.Y., of disgruntled Upper Canadians. Among those he wished to include were Joseph Brant [Thayendanegea*], Ebenezer Allan*, and Silvester Tiffany*. The purpose was the overthrow of the provincial government. Several meetings apparently took place but nothing came of the plan. As late as 1806 Danforth saw a possibility for recovering land and money. In this instance Weekes's successful attack on Lieutenant Governor Peter Hunter*'s handling of public money was the source of his hope.

Darling

Danforth spent some years at Salina working his salt leases, constantly hampered by lack of capital and forced to borrow to finance necessary improvements. In 1811 he leased his salt privileges and equipment to his principal creditor, who eventually acquired outright ownership of the property as well. Last notice of Danforth dates from 1821. He was in New York City hiding from the sheriff. The road for which he is famous fared little better. Official reports of October 1802 were highly critical. Deficient from the outset, within a few years it had deteriorated and was largely unused.

LILLIAN F. GATES

PAC, RG 1, E3, 32: 37–43; RG 5, A1: 557–59. Syracuse Univ. Libraries, George Arents Research Library (Syracuse, N.Y.), Green family coll., Timothy Green papers. *Corr. of Hon. Peter Russell* (Cruikshank). Onondaga Hist. Soc., *Pub.* (Syracuse), 1913: 134–36; 1914: 168. "U.C. land book D," AO *Report*, 1931. *Danforth genealogy: Nicholas Danforth, of Framlingham, England, and Cambridge, N.E. (1589–1638) and William Danforth, of Newbury, Mass. (1640–1721) and their descendants*, comp. J. J. May (Boston, 1902). Canniff, *Hist. of the settlement of U.C.* J. V. H. Clark, *Onondaga, or reminiscences of earlier and later times . . .* (2v., Syracuse, 1849; repr. Millwood, N.Y., 1973), 2: 108, 139–40. Cowdell Gates, *Land policies of U.C.* George Geddes, *Report on the agriculture and industry of the county of Onondaga, state of New York . . . from the transactions of the N.Y. State Agricultural Society, 1859* (Albany, 1860). J.-P. Wallot, *Intrigues françaises et américaines au Canada, 1800–1802* (Montréal, 1965). C. J. Werner, *A history and description of the manufacture and mining of salt in New York State* (Huntington, N.Y., 1917), 28–29. L. F. [Cowdell] Gates, "Roads, rivals, and rebellion: the unknown story of Asa Danforth, Jr.," *OH*, 76 (1984): 233–54.

DARLING, JOHN, businessman and office holder; b. 23 March 1769 near Ridgefield, Conn., son of Joseph Darling and Mary Street; m. early in the 1790s Elizabeth Canby, widow of Samuel Birdsall, and they had six children; d. 23 Feb. 1825 in St Johns (St Johns West), Upper Canada.

After his father's death in 1780 and his mother's remarriage in 1786, John Darling entered a period of legal wardship. In 1789 he settled in the Niagara peninsula where he came under the influence of Benjamin Canby, a local entrepreneur. Darling boarded with Canby and his widowed sister Elizabeth Birdsall and, if not actually employed by Canby, was at least able to observe firsthand his numerous business activities in the 1790s. In 1792 Canby erected a sawmill on the Twelve Mile Creek in an area known as the Short Hills; this location was the future site of the village of St Johns. The following year he moved to Queenston and leased the ferry service to Lewiston, N.Y. In 1794 he operated a tannery and by mid 1795 had constructed a saw- and grist-mill above

the falls at Niagara. Selling his mills in 1799, Canby acquired the 19,000-acre Dochstader Tract in Haldimand County and went there to found the township and village of Canboro.

Darling's career is inseparable from the history of St Johns and the five township lots (each 100 acres in size) over which the village ultimately extended. Land records indicate that, although Darling eventually owned four lots outright and part of a fifth, the lots were not patented until after 1800. He received a patent to one in 1816 and had purchased 318 of the remaining 400 acres in 1813. In land petitions written in 1808 and 1809, he claimed, however, to have purchased 400 acres, which included at least three of the aforementioned lots, from Canby in 1790. Moreover, some of these petitions are supported by certificates from such local notables as Samuel Street* and Robert Hamilton*, attesting to the fact that Darling had built his various mills on these properties.

Certainly Darling brought youthful energy and experience to St Johns. He took over Canby's sawmill and by 1808 had built a grist-mill and a fulling-mill. Thereafter, he also operated a tannery. His next two initiatives set him apart from other pioneer businessmen and millers, and thrust St Johns for a time to the forefront of industrial development in the peninsula: by 1813 he had constructed a woollen factory and by 1817, and doubtless even earlier, he had established an iron foundry. Each initiative was significant in its own right; together they were unique. He also ran a butchery, selling mostly beef and pork; the pigs it slaughtered were probably his own and fed on mash from yet another Darling enterprise, a distillery. His businesses were well integrated: Darling's whiskey, for instance, was sold in barrels apparently made in his own cooperage. Darling offered settlers a range of agricultural services as well, including teaming, the rental of oxen and land for grazing, and the sale of hay, straw, and root crops. His retail store sold a wide range of goods from spades to tea and featured such innovations as the rental of glass panes. His customers were distributed through the peninsula eastwards from the Grand River in the southwest and Ancaster in the northwest. Existing records indicate that he was more an enterprising and practical man than an accomplished bookkeeper, but it is clear that by 1820 his total operation was well in place and, on the evidence, his business peaked in 1824.

John Darling was barely active in political and civic affairs; he held office only once, in 1815 as a township assessor. He was, as Samuel Street described him, a "sober, industrious, and useful Inhabitant." Remembered as a man of cheerful disposition, he was a freemason and a Presbyterian.

For a brief period Darling's enterprises exemplified the potential, and the limits, of harnessing waterpower for manufacturing purposes. In relative terms he made a significant contribution to the development of St Johns and the economy of the peninsula. As he himself said, he had built his milling complex "at a great expence when that part of the Country was a Wilderness, thereby inducing other Valuable Familys to settle in that Township." His death in the winter of 1825 was followed almost immediately by the fragmentation of his businesses. In a sense, his passing presaged the demise of St Johns as a leading pioneer industrial centre. In 1829 the Welland Canal bypassed the village and gave rise to more vigorous and lasting communities. When the railway also bypassed the area in the 1850s, St Johns went into eclipse and years later was deserted.

COLIN K. DUQUEMIN

John Darling's account-book is in the possession of John Smith of Limehouse, Ont.; a photocopy is available at St Johns Outdoor Studies Centre, Fonthill, Ont.

MTL, Samuel Birdsall, autobiography, 1862 (typescript, 1928) (copy at St Johns Outdoor Studies Centre). Niagara South Land Registry Office (Welland, Ont.), Thorold Township, deeds, lot 111, instrument no.690. "District of Nassau; letterbook no.2," AO *Report*, 1905: 334. "Grants of crown lands in U.C.," AO *Report*, 1929: 99, 138. Gwillim, *Diary of Mrs. Simcoe* (Robertson; 1911). "U.C. land book C," AO *Report*, 1930: 131. E. H. Darling, "John Darling of St. Johns, U.C., a pioneer industrialist and his day-book, 1768–1825," *OH*, 40 (1948): 53, 57, 61.

DAVID, DAVID, fur trader, businessman, and militia officer; b. 14 Oct. 1764 in Montreal, eldest son of Lazarus David and Phebe Samuel; d. there, unmarried, 30 Nov. 1824.

The first Jew born in the province of Quebec and son of one of the earliest English-speaking merchants to settle in Montreal after the conquest, David David grew up in the colony's small, interrelated, and closely knit Jewish community [*see* Jacob Raphael Cohen*]. His father had established an extensive trade and acquired large land-holdings in Montreal by the time of his death in 1776, and the following year the family donated the site on which Shearith Israel Synagogue, the first in the colony, was built; in 1778 they made a large donation towards the purchase of a cemetery. David's mother apparently fell on hard times, however, and by February 1780 she was struggling, as she wrote in a petition to Governor Frederick Haldimand*, to maintain five children "out of the profits of a small shop, her only support." Her difficulties evidently did not dispirit her. When Robert Hunter, son of one of the most prominent London merchants trading to the colony, took tea with her in 1785, he found her "really a very sensible clever old woman and very entertaining in her conversation. I never laughed more in my life than at the droll stories she told. . . . Her son showed us the synagogue, which is a very neat one for so small a congregation."

David received his early education in the province, and then went into trade, as did his brothers Samuel and Moses. He probably wintered in the west as an *engagé* or a trader and established links with traders of the North West Company; in 1817 he would be accepted into the prestigious Beaver Club, membership in which was limited to prominent merchants who had wintered at least once in the interior. By 1787 he was residing in Montreal at 15 Rue Notre-Dame, where he had a wholesale and retail store; there he sold teas, spices, groceries, hardware, dry goods, crockery, and glassware. Two years later he was importing wheat from Vermont through Quebec merchant John Samuel de Montmollin. For a short period from 1793 he was in partnership with his brother-in-law Myer Michaels, a fur trader. From David's shop they offered "a large and general assortment of Goods" and sent merchandise to Moses, who had established a fur-trade outlet at Detroit and later operated from Sandwich (Windsor, Ont.). After the dissolution of the partnership in 1795, David continued in the wheat trade, one of his suppliers being the merchant John Porteous, and the provisions business, in which he purchased powder and shot from James and Andrew McGill and Company [*see* James McGill*] in 1797 and 1798. He had a wide range of customers, including the military at William Henry (Sorel, Que.), Sir John JOHNSON, superintendent general of Indian affairs, whom he supplied with goods as late as 1817, and George Ermatinger, a merchant of Amherstburg, Upper Canada, whom he supplied in conjunction with Frederick William ERMATINGER. He may have engaged in brewing as well, since in 1797 he imported 1,000 pounds of hops from New Hampshire. Described as a man whose probity and punctuality brought him an ever-increasing share of the Montreal retail trade, he had achieved prosperity by 1804, when he was able to pay the high price of £999 for a house in the city. By August 1806 he was renting out two stone houses on Rue Notre-Dame.

David supported a number of economic demands made by the merchant community of Montreal. At the turn of the century he and his brother Samuel joined its petition to government for modification of customs regulations obliging ships bound for Montreal to put into Quebec for inspection. On 30 March 1805 he attended a dinner at Dillon's Hotel given by merchants to honour local members of the House of Assembly who had voted against a tax on commerce to finance construction of new jails. In April 1822 he was a charter member of the Committee of Trade, forerunner of the Montreal Board of Trade, formed to give merchants a stronger voice in government decisions on trade.

David's involvement in public affairs extended to concerns not exclusively mercantile but in which the merchant community played a leading role. In 1784 he

David

signed a petition for repeal of the Quebec Act and establishment of an elective assembly. Five years later he was the only Jew among the nearly 100 members of the congregation of Christ Church who petitioned for legal erection of the parish, and in 1814 he subscribed funds for the completion of the church [see Jehosaphat Mountain*]. A lieutenant in Montreal's 1st Battalion of militia by 1804, he became a captain in 1812, and the next year took part in the battle of Châteauguay under Lieutenant-Colonel Charles-Michel d'IRUM-BERRY de Salaberry; he was promoted major in 1821. He was one of the first life governors of the Montreal General Hospital, founded in 1819 [see William CALDWELL (1782–1833)], and three years later was the centre of attention for members of the Montreal medical profession who gathered at his home to watch young Robert Nelson* perform an operation on him. According to Thomas Storrow Brown*, David's open-handed charity led the poor to refer to him affectionately as "the big Jew against pomp," while "his conciliating and candid manners procured him the sincere respect and friendship of all his neighbours and acquaintances."

David may have run into financial difficulties by 1806, when he had the properties of two of his debtors seized and was a trustee of the bankrupt estate of Cuvillier, Aylwin, and Harkness, a Montreal firm. In 1809 a lot with two stone houses and other buildings belonging to David, Thomas Blackwood*, and James Dow was seized at the suit of James Finlay. Eight years later Thomas Andrew Turner had the sheriff seize David's residence on Rue Saint-Paul, a luxurious two-storey stone house, acquired from James Dunlop* or his estate, for which David still owed £2,675. David managed to keep the house, but in 1820 Turner had a lot and stone house belonging to him in the faubourg Sainte-Marie seized. Whatever the reality, David's outward appearances persuaded Thomas Storrow Brown in 1818 that he was one of Montreal's wealthiest and most respected citizens.

In his investments David placed himself in the vanguard of Montreal businessmen pioneering new strategies to enable the rising merchant community to undertake increasingly ambitious projects requiring huge amounts of capital and to reorient the city's economy to the growing province of Upper Canada. Thus in 1818 he became a director of the Bank of Montreal, founded the previous year, and held that post until 1824. In late 1818 he was among a group of 14 associates who petitioned the legislature for authorization to construct a canal past the Sainte-Marie current and Lachine rapids in order to facilitate water communications with Upper Canada [see François DESRIVIÈRES]. When, the following year, the Company of Proprietors of the Lachine Canal was capitalized at £150,000, David was one of seven partners empowered to sell the 3,000 shares of £50 each. He and his colleagues managed to sell only half the shares, however, and in 1821, despite significant government investment, the company failed and was taken over by a public commission. At the time David held 25 shares in it.

Since at least 1802 David, like many of his colleagues in business, had been engaging in property speculation. Indeed, between 1814 and 1823 his business activities seem to have been limited largely to property transactions, investments, and loans. At his death in 1824 his estate included four extensive properties in Montreal, which were sold for £8,807, and lots in the faubourgs Saint-Laurent and Saint-Antoine. Elsewhere in Lower Canada he owned a house in Trois-Rivières as well as land in the Yamaska area and in Aston, Sutton, and Ditton townships. In Upper Canada he owned lots in Charlotteville and Walsingham townships. In most cases, the properties had been purchased at a sheriff's sale or received in payment of debt. Money owed to David's estate totalled more than £67,000 and included £3,378 in Bank of England annuities and nearly £7,000 in Bank of Montreal stocks. Debts of more than £10,000 were owed by Inglis and Company of London and Samuel Gerrard*, while more than £2,000 was owed by each of the firms of Gillespie, Moffatt, and Finlay of London, Moffatt and Company, McGillivrays, Thain and Company, and Desrivières, Blackwood and Company [see François Desrivières; William FINLAY; William McGILLIVRAY]; even the fabrique of Notre-Dame owed £1,000. In 1825 the executors of David's estate were still trying to recover some £52,000 owed to it by the North West Company, which had been obliged to merge with the Hudson's Bay Company in 1821.

David had obviously lived in splendid style and led an active social life. His house was furnished in cherry and mahogany, decorated with paintings and engravings, and prepared, in terms of dishes, fine glassware, and cutlery, to receive large gatherings; the silver plate alone was worth £65. His personal property was valued at nearly £400, but the modest library of 135 volumes, which did not even merit a detailed inventory, was estimated to be worth only £7. David had apparently negotiated with success a perilous era, during which Montreal, through a more diversified economy, prepared its rise from the ruins of the NWC.

ELINOR KYTE SENIOR in collaboration with
JAMES H. LAMBERT

American Jewish Arch. (Cincinnati, Ohio), Samuel David, excerpts from a diary, 1801–49 (copy). ANQ-M, CN1-29, 4 Feb. 1789, 27 Sept. 1792, 1 March 1797 (copies at American Jewish Arch.). Arch. of the Shearith Israel Congregation (Montreal), Minute-book, 1778–80. BL, Add. MSS 21877:

125–28 (copies at PAC). McCord Museum, Beaver Club minute-book; "List of subscribers towards building the Protestant parish church, 1805–14"; McCord papers. PAC, MG 11, [CO 42] Q, 24: 14; MG 24, B4, 7: 366; I61, Fanny Joseph diary. *American Jewry: documents, eighteenth century* . . . , ed. J. R. Marcus (Cincinnati, 1959), 111, 113–14, 429–31. *Montreal Gazette*, 1 Dec. 1824. *Morning Courier* (Montreal), 11 Feb. 1836. *Quebec Gazette*, 7, 25 June 1787; 28 Oct. 1790; 19 July 1792; 21 Feb., 23 May 1793; 14, 21 Sept. 1795; 25 May 1797; 15 March 1798; 18 April, 25 July, 26 Dec. 1799; 3 March, 5 May 1803; 23, 30 Oct., 6 Nov. 1806; 22 June 1809; 15 Nov. 1810; 4 June 1812; 28 March, 1 Aug. 1816; 16 Oct. 1817; 7 Dec. 1818; 12 July 1819; 13 July, 31 Aug., 26 Oct., 23 Nov. 1820; 18 Jan., 24 May 1821; 25 July, 29 Aug., 31 Oct. 1822; 2 Jan., 13 Feb., 17 April 1823.

Officers of British forces in Canada (Irving), 165. *Quebec almanac*, 1805–24. F. W. Terrill, *A chronology of Montreal and of Canada from A.D. 1752 to A.D. 1893* . . . (Montreal, 1893). T. S. Brown, *Montreal fifty years ago* (Montreal, 1868), 20. Denison, *Canada's first bank*, 1: 122. Solomon Frank, *Two centuries in the life of a synagogue* (n.p., n.d.). *The Jew in Canada: a complete record of Canadian Jewry from the days of the French régime to the present time*, ed. A. D. Hart (Toronto, 1926), 24–26. B. G. Sack, *History of the Jews in Canada, from the earliest beginnings to the present day*, [trans. Ralph Novak] (Montreal, 1945). G. J. J. Tulchinsky, "The construction of the first Lachine Canal, 1815–1826" (MA thesis, McGill Univ., Montreal, 1960), 10, 36. E. I. Blaustein *et al.*, "Spanish and Portuguese Synagogue (Shearith Israel), Montreal, 1768–1968," Jewish Hist. Soc. of England, *Trans.* (London), 23 (1971): 111–41.

DAVIS, THOMAS. *See* TEHOWAGHERENGARAGHKWEN

DEBLOIS, SARAH (Deblois), merchant; b. 29 Dec. 1753 in Boston, daughter of Lewis Deblois and Elizabeth Jenkins; m. 25 Dec. 1771 George Deblois, and they had nine children; d. 25 Dec. 1827 in Halifax.

Sarah Deblois was of Huguenot stock. Her great-grandfather, Louis Deblois, settled in England around the time of the Glorious Revolution in 1688, and her grandfather, Stephen Deblois, was born and educated in Oxford. Stephen emigrated to New York City in September 1720 and then moved in 1728 to Boston, where he became the organist at King's Chapel. Stephen's two sons, Lewis and Gilbert, pursued successful careers as dealers in imported goods in Boston. However, by the mid 1770s their loyalty to the crown had made them highly unpopular and they left for England in 1777.

Sarah, Lewis's daughter, had in 1771 married George Deblois, her father's first cousin and an English immigrant who had established himself in Boston as a merchant. In 1774 the couple moved to Salem, but their stay there was short. Like Lewis and Gilbert Deblois, George was known for his loyalist principles, and in April 1775, having become "obnox-ious" to local patriots, he fled with Sarah to Halifax. Two years later they took up residence in New York City, where George became involved in a co-partnership with Sarah's family, importing and selling foreign goods. Along with his family, he returned to Halifax in 1781 to engage in a commission trade. During the next two decades he built up a prosperous business in general merchandise ranging from Irish linens and hats to locks, kettles, and soap. By the time of his death, his firm was importing £1,227 17s. 0d. worth of articles, a figure that was the second highest – the firm of Foreman and Grassie [*see* James Foreman*] boasted the highest figure – among 90 Halifax merchants. Not surprisingly, his success as a merchant enabled him to occupy a prominent position in Halifax society: in 1793 he became a justice of the peace, and at St Paul's Church he acted as a churchwarden from 1785–86 and as a vestryman in 1788, 1793, and 1797.

Sarah apparently assumed supervision of her husband's firm upon his death on 18 June 1799. The business continued under the name of George Deblois until 1801, when, for the first time, it was referred to as the store of "S. Deblois," selling imported dry goods and hardware. According to one source, Sarah, with her sons Stephen Wastie* and William Minet and her daughters Lydia and Ann Maria, sailed from Halifax on 8 May 1802 on the schooner *Mary* to make her home once again in Massachusetts. The next month the sons returned to Halifax but Sarah and daughters reportedly remained at Dedham. At Halifax the business continued in Sarah's name. At least twice yearly ships commissioned by the Deblois firm and other merchants brought back a wide assortment of goods from Britain and India, particularly dry goods such as "superfine navy blue, black and fashionable broad cloths and cassimeres . . . cambricks, lawns, plain and figured cottons, lutestring ribbons, etc." By 1805 there was greater emphasis on teas, particularly "Bohea Tea . . . likewise Hyson and Souchong Teas." In early 1808 Stephen Wastie Deblois seems to have taken control of the business, importing goods worth £1,324 from London on the *Britannia* and selling merchandise under the name "S. W. Deblois and Co." It is not known for certain in what year Sarah returned to Halifax but she died there (probably at the house of her son Stephen Wastie) on 25 Dec. 1827 at the age of 73.

The extent to which Sarah controlled her late husband's business is uncertain, but her short term as merchant was significant. Until the mid 19th century a woman merchant in Halifax was something of a novelty: the only other besides Sarah was Phebe Moody, who, like Sarah, assumed control of her deceased husband's affairs. Sarah of course came from a strongly mercantile background in an age when merchants formed an élite, serving as the leading laity of the more prestigious churches and monopolizing executive positions in various fraternal organizations. It is also important to note, however, that she was active at a time when economic conditions fluctuated and many merchants lost their businesses. In particular, the years 1805 and 1806 saw severe commercial stagnation, although they were followed by a marked recovery in 1807–8. Between 1800 and 1815, 117 individuals became merchants, but of the 159 merchants who were active at the peak of wartime prosperity, only 87 remained in business in 1822–23 at the conclusion of the post-war slump. One of the firms still in existence was S. W. Deblois and Company. It may be argued that the family business might not have continued even into the early years of the 19th century had it not been for the efforts of Sarah Deblois, woman merchant.

JULIE MORRIS and WENDY L. THORPE

Halifax County Court of Probate (Halifax), Estate papers, D33 (George Deblois); D34 (Sarah Deblois) (mfm. at PANS). Halifax County Registry of Deeds (Halifax), Index to deeds, 1; Deeds, 19–20 (mfm. at PANS). PANS, MG 5, 12–13; MG 9, no.109; RG 1, 444; RG 31, boxes 6–7 (1799–1808); RG 35A, 1, 1817, 1821–22; RG 39, C, 1809, box 94, *Sarah Deblois* v. *Augustus Fallack*; 1817, box 127, *Deblois et al.* v. *Church*; J, book 15, 1803–9, *Sarah Deblois* v. *Hugh Ritchie*. PRO, AO 13, bundles 25, 50 (mfm. at PANS). St Paul's Anglican Church (Halifax), Reg. of baptisms, marriages, and burials (mfm. at PANS). *Glimpses of Nova Scotia, 1807–24, as seen through the eyes of two Halifax merchants, a Wilmot clergyman and the clerk of the assembly of Nova Scotia*, ed. C. B. Fergusson (Halifax, 1957). "United Empire Loyalists: enquiry into losses and services," AO *Report*, 1904: 491–93. *Nova-Scotia Royal Gazette*, 1790–91; 1793; July 1799–17 Oct. 1810. W. E. Boggs, *The genealogical record of the Boggs family, the descendants of Ezekiel Boggs* (Halifax, 1916). A. W. H. Eaton, "Old Boston families, number one: the De Blois family," *New England Hist. and Geneal. Reg.* (Boston), 67 (1913): 6–23 (also published as a separate pamphlet, [Boston, 1913]). F. B. Fox, *Two Huguenot families: De Blois, Lucas* (Cambridge, Mass., 1949). Jones, *Loyalists of Mass.* Stark, *Loyalists of Mass.* (1910). D. A. Sutherland, "The merchants of Halifax, 1815–1850: a commercial class in pursuit of metropolitan status" (PHD thesis, Univ. of Toronto, 1975). G. F. Butler, "The early organisation and influence of Halifax merchants," N.S. Hist. Soc., *Coll.*, 25 (1942): 1–16. D. [A.] Sutherland, "Halifax merchants and the pursuit of development, 1783–1850," *CHR*, 59 (1978): 1–17.

DECARRIHOGA. *See* TEKARIHOGEN

DECHENNEQUI. *See* CHENNEQUE

DeGAUGREBEN (Gaugreben, Gaugräbe), FRIEDRICH (Frederick), army officer and military engineer; b. *c.* 1777, apparently in Germany;

d. 6 Jan. 1822 in Kassel (Federal Republic of Germany).

Apart from his military service with the British army, little is known of Friedrich DeGaugreben's life. A Roman Catholic, he became a second lieutenant in the engineer corps of the King's German Legion on 14 Nov. 1809, no doubt after receiving a grounding in the principles of military engineering. On 22 Feb. 1811 he was promoted lieutenant, and spent that year on the island of Jersey. In mid October of the following year he arrived at Quebec as part of the reinforcements for the troops in the Canadas, an unusual assignment since the King's German Legion itself served in Europe. DeGaugreben was soon on his way to Upper Canada, and early in 1813 was at Prescott, where Lieutenant-Colonel Ralph Henry Bruyeres*, commanding engineer in the Canadas, had directed him to erect a blockhouse. When Christopher Alexander Hagerman* passed by in November he noted that Fort Wellington, as the work had become known, was "a very deep mound of Earth thrown up enclosing a strong blockhouse said to be bomb proof," but claimed that since the fort had been "very badly constructed" by DeGaugreben, it was "falling to pieces very fast." DeGaugreben's duties were not, however, confined to construction. His commanding officer, the aggressive Lieutenant-Colonel George Richard John Macdonell*, mounted an attack on Ogdensburg, N.Y., on 22 Feb. 1813, and DeGaugreben took charge of a field piece, receiving Macdonell's commendation for his conduct.

By the end of that year DeGaugreben found himself on the Niagara frontier, where on 19 December he accompanied the troops in the successful assault on Fort Niagara (near Youngstown), N.Y. He remained at the fort improving the defences, but by March 1814 Major-General Phineas Riall*, commanding on the frontier, was complaining to Lieutenant-General Gordon Drummond*, "I shall get nothing done if [DeGaugreben] is to continue the head of the [engineer] Department here." DeGaugreben's inactivity seems to have been caused by an attack of ophthalmia, and in April Drummond sent him back to the less demanding post of Prescott. There DeGaugreben remained for the rest of the war. He seems to have been no favourite with the local inhabitants, who remembered with displeasure his allegedly severe treatment of farmers when martial law had been proclaimed by Major-General Francis de ROTTENBURG in November 1813 to enable the army to purchase food forcibly.

By mid 1815 DeGaugreben was in Lower Canada as commanding engineer of the Montreal district. At this time he penned two memoirs on the defence of the Canadas for the inspector general of fortifications of the Board of Ordnance, Lieutenant-General Gother MANN. In one he made the suggestion that a canal be constructed to link the Ottawa River and Lake

Ontario. It seems likely, however, that the first person to hit upon this idea had been Macdonell, who saw it as a more permanent means of ensuring Upper Canada's military communications. DeGaugreben appears to have given technical advice about routes and designs, but there is no evidence to support a case that the canal idea was his, and he did not accompany Macdonell and Reuben Sherwood, a captain in the intelligence department, on the initial surveys.

Nevertheless, when the military authorities sought to implement Macdonell's scheme, DeGaugreben, now a second captain (from 5 March 1814), was ordered by Rottenburg in January 1815 to make preliminary surveys for a canal at Lachine which would be the first part of a military water-way to Lake Ontario. Although the general complained that De-Gaugreben was doing too little, by May he had produced and submitted the first detailed plans of part of what became the Ottawa–Rideau canal system [see John By*]. If DeGaugreben did less than hoped for, it was perhaps because he saw no real military need for the Lachine canal, and also because the few engineers in the Canadas were overburdened by their duties in other departments, as DeGaugreben and captains Samuel Romilly and Matthew Charles Dixon pointed out to Mann in June. Their complaints helped persuade the Duke of Wellington, master general of the Ordnance, to reorganize the board, and the improved department's officers subsequently carried out many projects and services of great value to colonists in the Canadas.

DeGaugreben himself left Quebec late in 1815. The King's German Legion was ordered disbanded in December, and in April 1817 it was recorded that he had reached Hanover (Federal Republic of Germany) and had been placed on half pay. Unlike many of his fellows, DeGaugreben did not enter the newly constituted Hanoverian army. His career until his death is unknown.

G. K. RAUDZENS

PAC, RG 8, I (C ser.), 38. PRO, WO 17/1516–19; WO 55/860. *Select British docs. of War of 1812* (Wood), 2: 64; 3, pt.I: 98. *Montreal Gazette*, extra, 26 Feb. 1813. N. L. Beamish, *History of the King's German Legion* (2v., London, 1832–37), 2: 531. G. [K.] Raudzens, *The British Ordnance Department and Canada's canals, 1815–1855* (Waterloo, Ont., 1979), 20–25. B. H. Schwertfeger, *Geschichte der Königlich Deutschen Legion, 1803–1816* (2v., Hanover, [Federal Republic of Germany], 1907). G. [K.] Raudzens, "'Red George' Macdonell, military saviour of Upper Canada?" *OH*, 62 (1970): 199–212.

DEKARIHOKENH. *See* TEKARIHOGEN

DELEZENNE, MARIE-CATHERINE (Pélissier; Sales Laterrière), b. 26 March 1755 at Quebec, daughter (the third christened Marie-Catherine) of Ignace-François Delezenne*, a silversmith, and Marie-Catherine Janson, *dit* Lapalme; d. 3 May 1831 in Les Éboulements, Lower Canada, and was buried there three days later.

Marie-Catherine Delezenne is remembered because of her love affair with Pierre de Sales* Laterrière. She began seeing him after he moved to Quebec in 1771 and they quickly fell in love. Notwithstanding this attachment, and despite her "refusals, tears, wailings," Marie-Catherine at the age of 19 was forced to marry a 46-year-old widower, Christophe Pélissier*. Pélissier was a friend of her father, director of the Saint-Maurice ironworks, and "a very rich man, from whom [her parents] were hoping to receive substantial assistance." The marriage took place in secret at Bécancour on 8 March 1775, at night, with the connivance of the ecclesiastical authorities and of "people who had been bribed."

Marie-Catherine was immediately taken to the ironworks. Laterrière later told the story: "She nearly went mad there, not believing that she was married to Pélissier and not wishing to remain with him. The father and this husband tried by every means to calm her. Frightened, afraid of losing her, feeling that only my presence would do her good and that there was no other solution, Pélissier called me to the ironworks; that was how I got the job as inspector there. . . . Only my presence calmed her and made her put up with her misfortune, [or] at least kept her from causing some sort of scandal. If I got up at the crack of dawn, I invariably found her at the doorway; a kiss sealed our never-ending promises and resolves to love each other until death!" Pélissier's abrupt departure with the Americans on 7 June 1776 left the field open to the lovers: "We gave way to our inclination, and the fruit of so much love was a pregnancy that resulted in the birth of our dear Dorothée on 4 Jan. 1778." They took up residence at Bécancour, where they lived "a quiet and happy life." But because of her illegitimate birth Dorothée would not be baptized until she was 16.

In the summer of 1777 Pélissier, who was then in Lyons, had given orders for his wife to be sent to France. Naturally Marie-Catherine had refused to go. On the other hand, a power of attorney from her husband had enabled her to play a role in transferring the lease to the Saint-Maurice ironworks, which was shifted from Pélissier to Alexandre Dumas* through the agency of Ignace-François Delezenne. Pélissier came back to Quebec in the summer of 1778. While he was working with Laterrière on the accounts of the ironworks, some ruffians in his employ carried off Marie-Catherine, who was then confined to the home of silversmith François Ranvoyzé*. They tried to make her sign a statement that Laterrière had raped her. The document, they said, would set her free. In fact it would have enabled Pélissier to get her back as

Delezenne

his wife and to take legal action against Laterrière. Marie-Catherine, however, did not consent to signing this "foul" declaration. An astute woman, she succeeded in slipping away and reached Île de Bécancour. Under Pélissier's instructions her parents went after her. She escaped them by hiding in various places, including a secret room set up in a barn in among bundles of hay.

Pélissier went off again to Europe, empty-handed, in September 1778. On 1 November in the presence of witnesses Marie-Catherine and Laterrière signed what can be interpreted as a private marriage contract, a document they took the precaution of having recorded subsequently in the register of notary Charles-Louis Maillet, at the same time sending a copy to Marie-Catherine's parents. The stinging rejoinder took the form of a virtual excommunication pronounced by Bishop Jean-Olivier Briand* on 12 November. But this did not suffice to separate the "adulterous concubinaries." Pélissier started working on his friend Governor Frederick Haldimand*, mounting a skilful campaign to defame Laterrière by making him appear to have collaborated with the Americans, even though he was by his own account basically a royalist. Ignace-François Delezenne was also drawn into conspiring against Laterrière, using as a basis some false testimony proffered by Delezenne's son Michel-Mathieu. Laterrière was wrongfully charged with treason, imprisoned in March 1779, then stripped of his property by profiteers. Predictably, with her lover in prison Marie-Catherine was still being detained at her parents' home in July 1779. All her clothes had been seized along with Laterrière's belongings and had not yet been given back despite her complaints to Haldimand. Consequently it was impossible for her, "lacking them, to go out."

In the autumn of 1780 the conditions of Laterrière's detention improved, thanks to the "silver key" that "opens many doors." Marie-Catherine, who was living with her daughter in a house at Quebec purchased by her lover, was able to see him every day and even spend the night with him regularly. Therefore, though he was in prison, Laterrière succeeded in taking Marie-Catherine away from her parents, thus depriving them of the allowance being paid them by Pélissier. This situation prompted Delezenne and his wife to draw up a deed of disinheritance on 4 Nov. 1780. In it they declared that their daughter had "indulged in an excess of dreadful debauchery" and "prostituted herself in the vain hope of marriage with Jean-Pierre Laterrière"; that they "have done everything that nature and fatherly affection can suggest, . . . to the point of having the offer made her of returning to their home . . . ; that to urge her further to cease a life of vice they have even offered to take care of the child that their aforesaid daughter has had with the aforesaid Laterrière." Invoking the laws, ordi-

nances, and "nature itself," they therefore barred their daughter from all rights of succession.

In 1782 Laterrière was freed, on condition that he go into exile until peace had returned. He had only 24 hours to get ready. Whether through bad luck or by someone's design, Marie-Catherine was visiting her parents in Trois-Rivières at the time. Laterrière took refuge with Dorothée in Newfoundland. Marie-Catherine consequently had to wait until the spring of 1783 to be reunited with them at Quebec. Then, with her daughter and her brother Michel-Mathieu she went to live at Saint-Pierre-les-Becquets (Les Becquets), where she ran a small store, and where Laterrière came "to see her very often." He, Marie-Catherine, and Dorothée soon moved to Bécancour, and then from the spring of 1784 they lived for five years in Gentilly (Bécancour). In 1784 the Delezennes also moved to the same region, to Baie-du-Febvre (Baieville), just after renewing the deed disinheriting Marie-Catherine. Finally, faced with the unshakeable determination of the couple, they retreated from their stand. Mme Delezenne died in Laterrière's arms in November 1787, "happy," and he recalled, "commending to my care her daughter, her husband, and all her children." And when Laterrière went to Boston to study, Marie-Catherine went to live with her father on a property that he had just made over to her. The fond grandfather became so attached to his grandson Pierre-Jean that he "never left him for an instant," according to Laterrière's memoirs.

Shortly after Delezenne's death in 1790 Marie-Catherine settled in Trois-Rivières with Laterrière. They had to wait a number of years, however, before they could make their union legal, a step they were finally able to take at Quebec on 10 Oct. 1799, after obtaining Pélissier's death certificate. They could then enjoy a privileged rank in society befitting their improved fortunes. Their daughter Dorothée, however, made an unhappy marriage that ended in separation from bed and board, since "those who are in authority in this matter refuse to allow divorce in this country." One of their sons died in a tragic accident. Pierre de Sales Laterrière, who had become the seigneur of Les Éboulements, died at Quebec on 14 June 1815. Marie-Catherine survived him by many years; "after an illness lasting two years and two months," she died at Les Éboulements in 1831 at the age of 76. Since 1829 the entire seigneury had been in the hands of her son Marc-Pascal*.

It was only through her exceptional strength of character that Marie-Catherine Delezenne had been able to face and overcome the enormous social pressures exerted to make her, against feeling, taste, and personal choice, "return to the straight and narrow path." Her struggle was exemplary in this respect, and in it there was the germ of a fight for the recognition of the rights and liberties of women as full partners in

Canadian society. The role she played therefore confers upon her a prominent place in the defence of the ideals of personal liberty, tolerance, and respect for the fundamental rights of the individual.

ROBERT DEROME

The descendants of the Laterrière family possess a portrait of Marie-Catherine Delezenne as well as the manuscript copy of Pierre de Sales Laterrière's memoirs. The diploma he received in 1789 from Harvard College and his licence to practise medicine in the province of Quebec were given to the Arch. de l'univ. Laval by his great-grandson Edmond de Sales Laterrière, a notary at Les Éboulements (Que.). The deed of gift was notarized by Lavery Sirois of Quebec and three copies were issued. Sirois's minute-book was entrusted to his son, Joseph Sirois, a notary in Quebec.

AAQ, 12 A, G: f.21v; 20 A, I: 181; 210 A, VII: f.192. ANQ-MBF, CN1-5, 24 sept. 1778; 10 févr. 1779; 5 sept., 4 nov. 1780; 15 oct., 6 déc. 1783; 12 mars 1787; 27 sept. 1788; 16 sept. 1790; 5 févr., 26 nov. 1793; CN1-64, 11 juill. 1777; 12 févr., 22 juin, 6, 23 oct., 1er nov. 1778; 25 févr., 29 mars, 15 sept. 1779. ANQ-Q, CE1-1, 26 mars 1755, 10 oct. 1799; P-597. AP, Saint-Antoine-de-Padoue (Baieville, Qué.), Reg. des baptêmes, mariages et sépultures, 14 nov. 1787; 1er juill. 1789; 1er, 2 mai 1790; 25 mars 1792; 20 févr. 1794. Arch. de l'univ. Laval (Québec), 298/17. ASQ, C 36: 180; Séminaire, 70, no.62. BL, Add. MSS 21681/2, 21845 (copies at PAC). "Collection Haldimand," PAC Rapport, 1888: 984–88, 994. Pierre Du Calvet, Appel à la justice de l'État; ou recueil de lettres au roi, au prince de Galles, et aux ministres; avec une lettre à messieurs les Canadiens, . . . une lettre au général Haldimand lui-même; enfin, une dernière lettre à milord Sidney . . . (Londres, 1784), 151–52. Pierre de Sales Laterrière, Mémoires de Pierre de Sales Laterrière et de ses traverses, [Alfred Garneau, édit.] (Québec, 1873; réimpr. Ottawa, 1980). L'Observateur (Montréal), 21 mai 1831. Quebec Gazette, 6 Aug. 1778, 5 Jan. 1792. Caron, "Inv. de la corr. de Mgr Briand," ANQ Rapport, 1929–30: 119; "Inv. de la corr. de Mgr Denaut," 1931–32: 159; "Inv. de la corr. de Mgr Plessis," 1927–28: 277. P.-G. Roy, Inv. concessions, 3: 246. Tanguay, Dictionnaire. Yvon Thériault, "Inventaire sommaire des Archives du séminaire des Trois-Rivières," ANQ Rapport, 1961–64: 93. H.-R. Casgrain, La famille de Sales Laterrière (Québec, 1870). Robert Derome, "Delezenne, les orfèvres, l'orfèvrerie, 1740–1790" (thèse de MA, univ. de Montréal, 1974). Raymond Douville, Visages du vieux Trois-Rivières (Trois-Rivières, Qué., 1955). Benjamin Sulte, Mélanges historiques . . . , Gérard Malchelosse, édit. (21v., Montréal, 1918–34), 6: 147. Robert Derome, "Delezenne, le maître de Ranvoyzé," Vie des Arts (Montréal), 21 (1976), no.83: 56–58.

DELVECCHIO, THOMAS (Tommaso), innkeeper and founder of a natural history museum; b. 1758 on the shores of Lake Como in Italy, son of Pierre Delvecchio and Catherine Buti (Bufi); d. 5 May 1826 in Montreal.

Thomas Delvecchio and his brother Pierre (Pietro), along with the Bonacinas, Rusconis, Doneganis, and Rascos, were among the first Italians to settle in the province of Quebec. These families, which arrived in the late 18th century and for the most part came originally from Lombardy, were probably endowed with the business acumen commonly attributed to people from that region, since they soon carved out a place for themselves in Montreal in trade, the hotel business, and speculation in real estate.

The Delvecchio brothers made their mark in particular as inn- and tavern-keepers. The exact date and the circumstances of their arrival in the colony are not known, but when on 23 Jan. 1797, at Lavaltrie, Lower Canada, Thomas married Thérèse Chevalier, the 15-year-old daughter of innkeeper Michel Chevalier and Marguerite Brault, he gave his age as 38 and identified himself as an innkeeper and resident of Pointe-aux-Trembles (Montreal).

Delvecchio probably settled in Montreal shortly after his marriage. His first child was baptized there in the parish of Notre-Dame in 1799. In 1812 Delvecchio was running an inn on the Place du Vieux-Marché, now the Place Royale. This establishment, which was called the Auberge des Trois-Rois because its façade boasted a large clock with three figures that struck the hours, was one of the most popular in the town.

As a prosperous innkeeper Delvecchio was a respected member of the small Italian community in Montreal. In 1791 he was godfather to one of the children of merchant Carlo Rusconi. Upon Rusconi's death in 1796 and that of his wife a short time later, Delvecchio became the guardian of their four underage children, a responsibility that he is said to have carried out scrupulously. As another mark of his compatriots' esteem, in 1800 he was chosen, along with his brother, to serve as Giuseppe Donegani's executor.

At the end of 1822, perhaps to reinvigorate his establishment at a time when customers were being increasingly attracted to the new market on the Place Jacques-Cartier and reportedly deserting him, Delvecchio announced that he intended to set up a museum of natural curiosities. On 14 Aug. 1824, "after many efforts, expenses, and trips (again lately in the United States)," he announced the opening of the Museo Italiano at No.4, Place du Vieux-Marché. For a sum between 30 sols and one Spanish dollar, based on the number of persons, visitors could admire a large natural history collection of stuffed quadrupeds, amphibians, reptiles, birds, and fish. They could also see wax figures of a South American Indian family and some Philadelphia and Montreal beauties, as well as automatons, musical instruments, and many other curiosities, among them "a lamb with eight legs, a pig with two bodies in its lower part, four ears, and eight legs, and a ram's head with four horns." The museum premises were not spacious, but they were well laid out and music was played during the tours. Delvecchio was at pains to point out that nothing to be seen

Denison

there "is in the slightest degree contrary to morality or decency, so that the most religious persons . . . may see the curiosities without qualms. Smoking will not be permitted in the exhibition hall, and neither indecent speech nor indecent conduct will be allowed."

This sort of museum – devoted to the arts and sciences as well as to the most varied "curiosities," the most famous one in North America being Charles Willson Peale's in Philadelphia – probably appealed to the public. Although the first in Canada, Delvecchio's museum was not the only one for long. Soon after the Museo Italiano was inaugurated, Pierre Chasseur*'s natural history collection and the museum of the Literary and Historical Society of Quebec opened one after the other at Quebec. In 1827 the Natural History Society of Montreal inaugurated its museum.

The Museo Italiano does not appear to have made its founder rich. In a notice dated 20 Jan. 1826 Delvecchio announced that if the public showed no greater interest in it, he was going to close the museum and sell the collections at the start of the navigation season. Strangely enough, the *Montreal Herald* published this announcement again on 6 May 1826, the day after Delvecchio's death.

The inventory of Thomas Delvecchio's estate reveals that the innkeeper was reasonably well off. The assets in his house and museum were worth £1,115, and there was £361 in cash. He also owned a house on Rue Saint-Jacques and two lots on the Place du Vieux-Marché, one having a two-storey house with a vaulted cellar and a shed, the other a three-storey house and stable built in stone. In addition a total of £845 was owing him. The estate went to his wife and four daughters (the couple reportedly had had eight children). In a will drawn up the day before he died, Delvecchio bequeathed £500 to his daughter Marie-Christine in accordance with her marriage contract, and he gave instructions for a like amount to be paid to each of his daughters when they married. The rest of his assets went to his wife on condition that she not remarry. His son-in-law, Pierre-Cajetan Leblanc, took over running the museum, and in 1842 he was on Rue Saint-Paul, engaged as well in the grocery business. The collections of the Museo Italiano were ultimately dispersed in 1853.

RAYMOND DUCHESNE

ANQ-M, CE1-51, 8 mai 1826; CE5-6, 23 janv. 1797; CN1-134, 4 mai 1826, 7 févr. 1827. *La bibliothèque canadienne* (Montréal), 1 (1825): 53–55. *Canadian Spectator* (Montreal), 21 Aug. 1824. *Montreal Gazette*, 8 May 1826. *Montreal Herald*, 6, 10 May 1826. *Quebec Gazette*, 28 Oct. 1819. *Scribbler* (Montreal), 12 Dec. 1822. Giroux et al., *Inv. des marchés de construction des ANQ-M*, 1, nos.1093–95; 2, no.1334. Lebœuf, *Complément*, 3e sér.: 32. *Montreal directory*, 1842. W. H. Atherton, *Montreal, 1535–1914* (3v., Montreal and Vancouver, 1914), 2: 130–31. L.-P. Audet, *Le système scolaire*, 5: 283. J. I. Cooper, *Montreal, the story of three hundred years* (n.p., 1942), 63. Kathleen Jenkins, *Montreal, island city of the St Lawrence* (New York, 1966), 259. J.-C. Marsan, *Montréal en évolution: historique du développement de l'architecture et de l'environnement montréalais* (Montréal, 1974), 130, 135. Giosafat Mingarelli, *Gli Italiani di Montreal; note e profili* (Montreal, [1967]), 12–15. Robert Rumilly, *Histoire de Montréal* (5v., Montréal, 1970–74), 2: 134, 141, 164. A. V. Spada, *Les Italiens au Canada* (Ottawa et Montréal, 1969), 54, 62–64. P. G. Vangelisti, *Gli Italiani in Canada* (Montreal, 1956), 63–64. F.-J. Audet, "Les Donegani de Montréal," *BRH*, 47 (1941): 66–67. Raymond Duchesne, "Magasin de curiosités ou musée scientifique? Le Musée d'histoire naturelle de Pierre Chasseur à Québec (1824–1854)," *HSTC Bull.* (Thornhill, Ont.), 7 (1983): 60, 75. É.-Z. Massicotte, "Noms de rues, de localités, etc., à Montréal," *BRH*, 30 (1924): 175–77; "Scènes de rues à Montréal au siècle passé," *Cahiers des Dix*, 7 (1942): 279.

DENISON, AVERY, settler; b. *c.* 1775 at Stonington, Conn., son of Elisha Denison and Keturah Minor; d. 28 June 1826 near Trois-Rivières, Lower Canada, and was buried at Danville, Lower Canada.

Avery Denison's ancestors, who were probably Scandinavian-born, had settled in England, and some of them moved to the American colonies towards the end of the 17th century. Whether through attachment to the loyalist cause or desire to obtain cheap land, several members of the family petitioned for grants in the province of Quebec in 1789. According to a strong tradition in the family, Denison, who was just 21, crossed the border on 19 Feb. 1796, applied to the Lower Canadian authorities, and obtained a grant of 5,000 acres in Shipton Township. The story is rather implausible, since official documents make no mention of this large grant and, even more important, all transactions by the land committee of the Executive Council had been suspended in 1795. Moreover, Governor Robert Prescott*'s opposition to the system of township leaders and associates was to delay settlement of the non-seigneurial sector of Lower Canada for some years. Under this system a promoter would recruit a number of associates, who were granted 1,200 acres apiece in a given township; each of them would then hand over 1,000 acres to the township leader to reimburse him for the expenses of petitions, surveys, road-building, and the like. The speculators won out over Prescott. Thus Shipton Township, which at that time comprised the present Cleveland Township, was granted to Elmer Cushing on 4 Dec. 1801, partly to reward him for his role as an informer in David McLane*'s trial in 1797. Since Cushing was always short of money, it is quite possible he sold several lots to Denison even before the grant was official; this hypothesis would explain the absence of documentary evidence about the boundaries of Denison's properties and the way they were acquired. It is certain, however, that Denison owned a huge estate, much of which remained in his descendants' hands until recently, despite numerous transactions and squatters' encroachments.

Although the lands in Shipton were considered the best in that part of Buckingham County, it took unusual courage to push into the area in the late 18th century, through the woods, along water-ways, or on the few improvised trails. Denison spent several seasons clearing the land and building a log house, and then in 1801 brought Eunice Williams, whom he had married the previous year, from the United States; shortly after her arrival she gave birth to a son, Simeon Minor, and they subsequently had three more children, John Williams, Malvina, and Eunice.

Denison's homestead was well situated in the middle of the township near Leet Creek; it was on the 8th concession between lots 22 and 24, a few miles from the road that in 1809 was named after Governor Sir James Henry Craig*, and at an equal distance from the future villages of Richmond and Danville. In the first two decades of the 19th century Denison continued to develop his lands, raised cattle, and even ran a distillery which utilized his own potato crops. Around 1822 he turned over all his assets to his elder son, who had attained his majority but was then still unmarried; the reason for the transaction is unknown. On 28 June 1826 Denison apparently was returning on horseback from Quebec, where he had sold some cattle, when he was attacked by highwaymen and died near Trois-Rivières. His body was the first to be buried in the Protestant cemetery at Danville.

The mill Avery Denison had planned to build was put up by his son Simeon Minor and became the hub of a small village with a post office and an Anglican church. Although the village no longer exists, the site of Denison Mills bears vivid witness to this pioneer family's spirit of initiative and unrelenting labour. The mill, which has been carefully restored, was made a historic monument by the Quebec government on 20 Sept. 1973, as an example of loyalist architecture in the Eastern Townships.

MARIE-PAULE R. LaBRÈQUE

ANQ-E, CN1-27, 19 août 1826. ANQ-Q, ZC2-3, 1–4. PAC, MG 11, [CO 42] Q, 79–82; RG 1, L3ᴸ: 71987, 78413, 78480; RG 31, C1, 1825, Shipton Township. Elmer Cushing, *An appeal addressed to a candid public; and to the feelings of those whose upright sentiments and discerning minds, enable them to "weigh it in the balance of the sanctuary"* . . . (Stanstead, Que., 1826). Bouchette, *Topographical description of L.C.* Langelier, *Liste des terrains concédés*, 915–16. "Papiers d'État – Bas-Canada," PAC *Rapport*, 1891: 150–75. Denis Allaire et Danielle Bédard, *Le hameau Denison Mills* (Québec, 1977). Caron, *La colonisation de la prov. de Québec*, 2: 86, 120–21, 137, 182–83. Edward Cleveland, *A sketch of the early settlement and history of Shipton, Canada East* (Richmond, [Que.], 1858; repr. Sherbrooke, Que., 1964). Rodolphe Fournier, *Lieux et monuments historiques des Cantons de l'Est et des Bois-Francs* (Montréal, 1978). Hilda MacNaughton, *History of Denison's Mills, founded Feb. 19, 1796* (n.p., 1966). G. F. McGuigan, "Administration of land policy and the growth of corporate economic organization in Lower Canada, 1791–1809," CHA *Report*, 1963: 65–73. [Hilda MacNaughton], "History of Denison's Mills," Richmond County Hist. Soc., *Annals* (Richmond), 1 (1966): 100–5.

DENNIS, JOHN, shipbuilder; b. 1758 in Pennsylvania, son of Henry Dennis and Martha Lynn; m. 1781 Martha McLaney, a widow, in New York City, and they had five children; d. 25 Aug. 1832 in York (Toronto), Upper Canada.

The Dennises were a prosperous family of Philadelphia Quakers. During the American revolution Henry Dennis, a shipbuilder, sided with the British. Consequently, when the British evacuated Philadelphia in June 1778, the family fled to New York City where Henry and John Dennis found work refitting and re-equipping British ships. Dennis quickly tired, as he later put it, of "his Father's peaceable employment" and joined the British army. He saw action at the taking of St Lucia in December 1778, contracting a fever there which left him with a game left leg and thus rendered him "incapable of Hard service." He returned to New York and shipbuilding.

After his father's death in 1782, Dennis emigrated with his young family, eventually settling in New Brunswick. In 1795, when fire destroyed their property, Dennis moved to Alexandria, Va. The following year he was back in British territory, attracted to Upper Canada by Lieutenant Governor John Graves Simcoe*, who wanted him to build gunboats. Just west of York, at the mouth of the Humber River, Dennis established his stocks and turned out ships, among them the government schooner *Toronto*, which the *Upper Canada Gazette* deemed in 1799 "one of the handsomest vessels, of her size, that ever swam upon the Ontario."

Dennis's evident talents won him the position of master shipbuilder at the government dockyards in Kingston. Receiving the appointment in January 1803, he filled it for some ten years and, during his tenure, he built a number of naval vessels. In the summer of 1812, after war had broken out with the United States, he was transferred back to York to complete a ship under construction there. When the Americans seized the provincial capital in April 1813, they destroyed the ship. The Provincial Marine decided to close the vulnerable York yard and offered Dennis a post back at Kingston. He refused, however, because he did not wish to be subordinate to recently arrived Royal Navy personnel. He was dismissed from service.

DePeyster

Undeniably, Dennis's work had given satisfaction, but his talents were not of such a high order that he could dictate his rank. In fact, he had some blemishes on his record. Though he described himself as a "naturally diffident" person, he had had several confrontations with colleagues. In 1806, during an unseemly affair at Kingston involving missing material, he was criticized by a panel of inquiry for eagerly making unfounded charges against others. Later, at York, his bickering with a draftsman reached the ear of the commander-in-chief, Sir George Prevost*, who determined to "get rid" of him. Having been persuaded that Dennis was not at fault, Prevost relented in September 1813. Still, by this time, the builder had proven himself a difficult fellow, and there could not have been much hesitation among officials in releasing him. Dennis felt hard done by, and must have relished the opportunity soon afforded of reminding his ungrateful former employers of the value of his work. In 1814 the military approached Dennis, the only competent person available, to build gunboats at Penetanguishene. Though unemployed at the time, he declined the offer, explaining that skilled workmen would not be available there.

John Dennis spent the rest of his life at York, where he had acquired property. He continued building ships – out of financial necessity, he said in 1826. He took an active interest in local and provincial politics, aligning himself with the reformers and voting for Robert Baldwin* in the election of 1830. His long and useful life came to a close in the summer of 1832 when he fell victim to the cholera epidemic then ravaging the province. His grandson, John Stoughton Dennis*, was Canada's first surveyor general.

COLIN READ

AO, MU 1131, W. W. Duncan, "Narrative of the Skirving and Dennis families, by a descendant" (typescript, Toronto, 1967), Dennis family section. PAC, RG 1, L3, 149: D1/5; 151: D4/61, D5/20; 158: D15/4; 159, pt.i: D16/22; RG 8, I (C ser.), 84: 222, 228, 246, 254; 108: 72; 110: 32, 37–38; 732: 10. *Town of York, 1793–1815* (Firth), 88, 96, 147; *1815–34* (Firth), 128, 267.

DePEYSTER, ARENT SCHUYLER, army officer; b. 27 June 1736 in New York City, son of Pierre Guillaume DePeyster and Cornelia (Catherine?) Schuyler; cousin of Abraham De Peyster*; d. 26 Nov. 1822 near Dumfries, Scotland.

The second son of a prominent New York family, Arent Schuyler DePeyster was connected with the colonial aristocracy through both his father and his mother. At the age of 15 he sailed for London to further his education. Military life soon attracted him and on 13 April 1755 he obtained an ensign's commission in Major-General William Shirley's 50th Foot. On 10 June he was appointed lieutenant in Sir William Pepperrell*'s 51st Foot.

During the Seven Years' War young DePeyster served with his uncle Colonel Peter Schuyler* of New Jersey on the northern frontier of the colonies. He was probably caught up in the capitulation of Oswego (N.Y.) on 14 Aug. 1756 [see Louis-Joseph de Montcalm*], taken to France as a prisoner of war, and exchanged some time in 1757, as were the other officers of the 51st. In England, DePeyster transferred to the 8th Foot on 21 Sept. 1757 and he accompanied his regiment to Germany in 1760. After the war the 8th was stationed in Scotland, where DePeyster met and married Rebecca Blair, daughter of Robert Blair, later provost of Dumfries. They had a happy but childless marriage and were seldom separated. On 19 Sept. 1767 DePeyster was present at the funeral in New York City of his uncle Abraham DePeyster, treasurer of the province of New York.

On 16 May 1768 the 8th embarked from England for the province of Quebec. It was stationed in Montreal, where in October Captain-Lieutenant DePeyster (appointed 15 July 1767) served as a member of the court martial that tried Major Robert Rogers*. On 23 November DePeyster was promoted captain. His activities during the next six years of his life are not clear. He is known to have been on leave between September 1769 and the summer of 1770, was recruiting in Albany, N.Y., in May 1771, and on 1 June 1772 served as president of a court martial at Quebec, where he apparently spent most of his time.

Early in 1774, when the 8th was sent to replace the 10th Foot at the western garrisons, DePeyster was appointed commandant of Michilimackinac (Mackinaw City, Mich.). On 4 May the DePeysters left Quebec, arriving at Michilimackinac on 10 July. For the next five years this small, stockaded, fur-trading community at the juncture of lakes Huron and Michigan was their home. Soon after his arrival, DePeyster held a council with chiefs Nissowaquet* and Madjeckewiss*. Indian affairs dominated his stay in the west, and he had a remarkable ability to establish trust and rapport with a multitude of tribesmen. In the spring of 1775, with the help of intermediaries such as the trader Peter Pond*, he was able to hold a grand council at Michilimackinac which established a truce between the hereditary enemies the Sioux and Ojibwas. When the American revolution broke out it was imperative that the British retain the allegiance of the Indians of the Upper Lakes, who greatly outnumbered the British soldiers there. Working with the assistance of his interpreter, Joseph-Louis Ainsse*, and a former French officer, Charles-Michel Mouet* de Langlade, DePeyster was able to rally Indian war parties: in 1776 to assist in the recapture of Montreal, and in 1777 to join John Burgoyne*'s thrust into New York. As a reward for his achievements DePeyster was appointed major of the 8th on 6 May 1777.

The following year the American lieutenant-colonel George Rogers Clark put British authority in the west in serious jeopardy. During the summer of 1778 he swiftly captured Kaskaskia (Ill.), Cahokia (Ill.), and Vincennes (Ind.) in the Illinois country. Lieutenant Governor Henry Hamilton* of Detroit retook Vincennes in December 1778, but was himself captured by Clark on 25 Feb. 1779. DePeyster feared an American attack on Detroit, and subsequently one on Michilimackinac by way of Lake Michigan. In an effort to secure intelligence of American plans he purchased from his good friend John Askin* the sloop *Welcome*, which he sent up the lake. He also dispatched 20 soldiers and 200 Indians under Lieutenant Thomas Bennett to rally the Indians at Fort St Joseph (Niles, Mich.). A major council was held on 4 July in the Ottawa town of L'Arbre Croche (Cross Village, Mich.), and two days later DePeyster welcomed the prestigious Sioux chief Wahpasha (either Wahpasha* or his son) to Michilimackinac. Thanks to the truce of 1775, he was able to secure the temporary cooperation of the Sioux and Ojibwas in defending Michilimackinac.

Despite his accomplishments, DePeyster had been asking for a transfer from Michilimackinac, and when he received word that he was to be sent to Detroit he was delighted. The local merchants wished him well and commissioned an elegant silver punch-bowl as a token of appreciation. On 4 Oct. 1779 Lieutenant Governor Patrick Sinclair* arrived to take charge of the straits. Less than two weeks later the DePeysters departed aboard the *Welcome* for Detroit, where he assumed command on 1 November. DePeyster was immediately plunged into negotiations with the Indians. Although it was necessary to use Indian war parties to attack the American settlers in what is now Kentucky and to block American thrusts at Detroit, he repeatedly warned the warriors to avoid cruelty to prisoners. DePeyster himself treated humanely the wretched captives brought to Detroit and made many efforts to ransom prisoners held by the Indians.

As the war dragged on, DePeyster had many captives to worry about. In April 1780 he sent Captain Henry Bird and Captain Alexander McKee* to attack the Kentucky settlements; other parties took the war-path towards Vincennes and Fort Pitt (Pittsburgh, Pa). More than 2,000 Indians were organized and they brought in nearly 400 prisoners by the end of the summer. These successes notwithstanding, DePeyster, knowing his defences were in a deplorable state, was worried by persistent rumours of an American attack. The rumours proved true. In November a force under Colonel Augustin Mottin de La Balme from Cahokia advanced on Detroit, but warriors led by Michikinakoua* destroyed it near the Miamis Towns (Fort Wayne, Ind.). A wing of La Balme's expedition captured Fort St Joseph in December, and in February 1781 another group sacked the fort again.

Only the Indian allies stood between Detroit and the growing American presence in the Kentucky settlements. To keep them loyal demanded not only consummate tact but also costly presents. General Frederick Haldimand*, DePeyster's superior, bemoaned the flood of bills, but he trusted DePeyster's judgement that the expenditures were necessary. During 1781 Indian war parties continued to cross the Ohio River to raid into Kentucky. They brought back rumours that a band of Moravian Christian Delawares living in villages on the Muskingum (Tuscarawas) River (Ohio) were informing the Americans of the raiders' intentions. DePeyster had a number of the band's Moravian missionaries and some of the Indians brought to Detroit in October for interrogation. Satisfied that they were not hostile, he let them go, but invited them to settle near Detroit. In March 1782 many of the Delawares were massacred by vengeful Americans at Gnadenhutten (Ohio) [see Glikhikan*]. Only a remnant under David Zeisberger* was left to settle north of Detroit at New Gnadenhütten (Mount Clemens, Mich.). The vicious attack roused the Ohio valley Indians and when an American force under Colonel William Crawford probed into what is now Ohio in June 1782, it was cut off and Crawford was tortured to death. DePeyster was appalled, but attributed the barbarity to the Indians' anger over the attack on the Delawares.

By this time the war was winding down, and DePeyster was instructed by Haldimand to adopt a defensive posture. But sometimes a good offence is the best defence, and Captain William CALDWELL achieved a stunning victory over the cream of the Kentucky militia at the battle of Blue Licks in August 1782. DePeyster was concerned about whether he could stop the frontier war even if peace was declared. As long as the Americans raided across the Ohio River the Indians would never cease resisting. DePeyster encouraged the Indians not to attack, but his supplies had been cut back and he had few presents with which to influence them.

Word of peace arrived in Detroit on 6 May 1783 and Lieutenant-Colonel DePeyster (appointed in the army 20 Nov. 1782) immediately recalled the war parties and attempted to ransom all captives. The 492 prisoners held in Detroit were sent to Montreal to be repatriated. Though the peace treaty included Detroit in the new republic, no orders were given to evacuate the town. When the American Indian commissioners visited Detroit in July 1783 they were treated politely, but no commitments were made.

In November DePeyster received word that he had been appointed lieutenant-colonel of the 8th on 13 September and that he was being transferred to Fort Niagara (near Youngstown, N.Y.) to take command of the regiment. It was not until 30 May 1784 that he left for Niagara, where he assumed command on 5

DePeyster

June. Although suffering from ill health, during the summer he presided over the reduction of the regular and provincial troops stationed there. One of the four most senior officers in the province of Quebec, DePeyster was growing increasingly anxious to leave the frontier and return to the civilization of Quebec or Europe. While he waited, he listened to rumours of possible American attacks on Oswego and was instructed to fight if necessary to retain possession.

Finally, in the summer of 1785, the 8th sailed from Quebec and after only 25 days arrived in England, where DePeyster was given command of the garrison of Plymouth. While he was stationed there Lieutenant Isaac Brock* served under him, and Rebecca had an opportunity to dance with the Prince of Wales. In 1790 the 8th was transferred to Jersey, and in 1793 to Ireland. DePeyster's appointment as colonel in the army was made on 12 Oct. 1793. The following spring the regiment was sent to Flanders to confront the French but DePeyster, wracked by a violent illness, decided to leave the army. He sold his lieutenant-colonelcy to a connection of the lord lieutenant of Ireland, who ten years later had not yet paid for it. DePeyster retired to Dumfries, Rebecca's home, where they settled down at Mavis Grove, a pleasant country estate.

In 1795, when a French invasion appeared possible, the locals formed a volunteer unit called the Dumfries Volunteers, and DePeyster became its major commandant. One of his men was the poet Robert Burns, who penned "The Dumfries Volunteers" and an "Epistle to Colonel DePeyster." Sharing an interest in poetry, DePeyster and Burns were kindred spirits. However, their association was short since Burns died in July 1796.

During the following years DePeyster enjoyed his retirement, spending his time training the militia, corresponding with old friends, and worrying about the slowness of the government in paying some of his bills from 20 years before. Disturbed by the events of the Napoleonic Wars, he drafted many poems which, together with others from his period in the western posts, he finally published in 1813 under the title *Miscellanies, by an officer*. His health remained good in his old age, and he loved to play billiards and ride his large horse. When he died on 26 Nov. 1822 he was buried with full military honours in St Michael's churchyard, only a short distance from the grave of his friend Burns. His lifelong companion, Rebecca, died on 20 Feb. 1827.

DAVID A. ARMOUR

Arent Schuyler DePeyster is the author of a volume of poetry, *Miscellanies, by an officer* (Dumfries, Scot., 1813); a second edition, which adds some correspondence and speeches by DePeyster and others, was prepared and published by John Watts DePeyster (2v. in 1, New York, 1888).

A photograph of DePeyster's grave at Dumfries is reproduced in *"The Kingsman"; the Journal of the King's Regiment* (Liverpool), no.30 (July 1950): plate following p.6. A collection of his papers, including manuscript poetry and correspondence, also remains at Dumfries in the Ewart Library of the Dumfries and Galloway Regional Library Service. Other archival material relating to him is scattered amongst a variety of repositories in North America and Great Britain; this documentation includes numerous references in the Haldimand papers at the BL and in the Thomas Gage papers at the Clements Library (both detailed below); a letter from DePeyster to Sir John Caldwell, dated 14 Nov. 1785, in the Bagshawe muniments of the John Rylands Univ. Library (Manchester, Eng.), B3/37/48; a group of Indian artifacts collected by DePeyster and Caldwell in the King's Regiment coll. at the Merseyside County Museums (Liverpool); a collection of DePeyster family papers in the N.Y. Hist. Soc. (New York); the Durell Saumarez papers, photocopies of which are available at PAC, MG 23, K10; and PRO, AO 1, bundle 376, no.1, and WO 71/26: 371.

BL, Add. MSS 21763: 236, 291, 312, 316, 320, 344, 357; 21781: 9–18, 74–90, 293, 299, 315, 319, 321, 325, 328, 331, 335, 339, 341, 343, 345, 347–48, 351, 357, 361–63, 368, 370, 373–75, 379, 381–85, 387–89, 391, 395, 399, 404–5, 408, 410, 412, 414, 417–18; 21833: 101, 194, 202, 210. Clements Library, Thomas Gage papers, American ser., 81, Carleton to Gage, 29 Sept. 1768; 82, Gage to Jones, 5 Dec. 1768; 103, Bradstreet to Gage, 12 May 1771; 111, Jones to Gage (enclosure), 4 June 1772; 114, Jones to Gage, 24 Sept. 1772; 121, DePeyster to Gage, 16 June 1774; 123, Gage to DePeyster, 5 Oct. 1774; 128, DePeyster to Gage, 5, 14 May 1775; DePeyster to Maturin, 5 May 1775; 129, Gage to DePeyster, 20 May 1775; 130, DePeyster to Gage, 16 June 1775. Robert Burns, *Poetical works . . .* , ed. J. L. Robertson (London and New York, 1904; repr. 1950), 212–13. *John Askin papers* (Quaife), 1: 67, 72, 80, 83–84, 86, 90, 105, 108, 112, 118; 2: 171–74, 382–83, 407–8, 478–79. *Mich. Pioneer Coll.*, 9 (1886); 10 (1886); 11 (1887); 15 (1889); 19 (1891); 20 (1892). *Treason? at Michilimackinac: the proceedings of a general court martial held at Montreal in October 1768 for the trial of Major Robert Rogers*, ed. D. A. Armour (rev. ed., Mackinac Island, Mich., 1972), 9. *Wis., State Hist. Soc., Coll.*, 1 (1855); 3 (1857); 7 (1876); 8 (1879); 10 (1888); 11 (1888); 12 (1892); 18 (1908); 19 (1910). *New-York Gazette, and Weekly Mercury* (New York), 2 Aug. 1773.

D. A. Armour and K. R. Widder, *Michilimackinac: a handbook to the site* (Mackinac Island, 1980), 17. J. W. DePeyster, *St. Paul's Church, Red Hook, Duchess County, New York . . . Rose Hill . . . De Peyster family . . . ; by "Anchor" (*J. W. de P.*)* (New York, 1881). G.B., WO, *Army list*, 1760, 1768–69, 1782–84, 1794. D. A. Armour and K. R. Widder, *At the crossroads: Michilimackinac during the American revolution* (Mackinac Island, 1978). "An American DePeyster," *Dumfries and Galloway Saturday Standard* (Dumfries), 1 Nov. 1902. D. A. Armour, "A white beaver for the colonel," *Mich. Natural Resources* (Lansing), 42 (1973), no.4: 11–14. "Colonel Arent de Peister," *"The Kingsman": the Journal of the King's Regiment*, 3 (1931–33), no.2: 4–5. "Colonel Arent Schuyler DePeyster, the King's Regiment," *White Horse & Fleur de*

Lys (Altrincham, Eng.), 3 (1964): 370. "Colonel DePeyster," *Free Press* (Detroit), 4 Nov. 1894. "The three Caldwells," ed. David Boston, *White Horse & Fleur de Lys*, 3 (1964): 316–17.

DESBARATS, PIERRE-ÉDOUARD, merchant, translator, office holder, printer, landowner, militia officer, and JP; b. 7 Oct. 1764, son of Joseph Desbarats, a merchant, and Marie-Louise Crête; m. 24 Sept. 1798 Josette Voyer, daughter of notary Charles Voyer, at Quebec, and they had eight children; d. there 23 April 1828.

Some biographers have linked the long line of Desbarats who had been printers in Béarn since the mid 17th century with the Canadian line of printers. There is no documentary evidence, however, for a connection between the two families. Joseph Desbarats, who came from the region of Auch and was a wigmaker by trade, arrived in New France in 1756 with the Régiment de La Sarre as a servant. In 1760 he was authorized to settle at Trois-Rivières and to do business as a merchant. Pierre-Édouard spent nearly the first half of his life there and for a few years was in business like his father.

In 1794 Desbarats moved to Quebec and embarked upon a new career as a translator for the *Quebec Gazette*. He familiarized himself with the printer's trade in the shop of the proprietor, John Neilson*. In 1797, while retaining his post with the *Quebec Gazette*, he became the French translator for the House of Assembly, a task he carried out during parliamentary sessions until 1808.

On 14 May 1798 Desbarats and Roger Lelièvre were appointed official printers for the statutes of Lower Canada, succeeding William Vondenvelden*. On 23 May Vondenvelden sold them his business, the Nouvelle Imprimerie. Lelièvre retired on 16 Nov. 1799 and made over his share in the operation to Desbarats. Neilson became Desbarats's new partner on 19 May 1800, thus formalizing an arrangement made on 23 Oct. 1799. However, Neilson already owned a printing shop, and his name was never used publicly in connection with their firm.

During the early decades of the 19th century Desbarats's printing shop was the second largest at Quebec, Neilson's alone taking precedence. For a time the two firms were not in competition but rather complemented each other. Moreover, Desbarats continued to work as translator for Neilson's *Quebec Gazette* until 1808. A long-time partner of Thomas CARY Sr and Thomas Cary* Jr, he printed their newspaper, the *Quebec Mercury*. He also printed the *Courier de Québec* in 1807 and 1808 and *Le Vrai Canadien* in 1810 and 1811. These papers were vehicles of the English party and often violently opposed the claims of the Canadian party and its newspaper *Le Canadien*.

Since at that time printing runs were not large and circulation was limited, managing a press was often a hazardous undertaking. The steady supply of printing contracts that came to Desbarats because of his position as printer for the statutes and the public offices he had been given enabled him, however, to extricate himself from financial difficulties. Initially the French translator for the House of Assembly, he held the important post of deputy clerk for that body on a temporary basis in 1798 and then on permanent appointment from 1809 till his death.

On 10 July 1806 Desbarats, as township leader, was granted more than 11,000 acres in Frampton Township, through which ran the Rivière Etchemin. Most of the recipients of such huge, wooded, inaccessible domains gave little thought to their development, but Desbarats had his heart set on clearing and settling his lands, which lay to the west of the river. In 1817, as road and bridge commissioner for the counties of Dorchester, Devon, and part of Buckingham, he had a road built to link Frampton Township with the village of Sainte-Marie-de-la-Nouvelle-Beauce (Sainte-Marie). Later he built a sawmill and a grist-mill at his own expense. To fill his lands he recruited settlers mainly from among the Irish immigrants crowding into the port of Quebec. Although the roads were often impassable, he went regularly to visit the Frampton pioneers and took an interest in their well-being.

Desbarats owned several properties in the town of Quebec and the *faubourg* Saint-Jean. In 1819 he had master mason John Phillips build him an imposing three-storey house at the corner of Rue Sainte-Geneviève and Rue des Carrières, across from the governor's gardens and a few steps away from the Château Saint-Louis. His country house was located north of the town at Petite-Rivière-Saint-Charles. In 1796 he had bought a farm there which he rented out, while keeping for his own use a two-storey stone house near the Saint-Charles.

In the space of a few years Desbarats became an influential figure in the public service and in Quebec society. In April 1800 he was named secretary of the Fire Society. Two years later he received the same office on a committee set up to encourage the growing of hemp. Around 1810 he joined the militia as a captain in the town's 2nd Militia Battalion, and in April 1815 he was promoted major in the 1st Battalion of Saint-Vallier militia, of which he was lieutenant-colonel at the time of his death. Again in 1815 he received a commission as justice of the peace for the district of Quebec, which was renewed in 1821 and 1828. In 1824 he was a member of a committee set up to attend to the redevelopment and improvement of the Place d'Armes.

Desbarats's contemporaries remembered him as a distinguished and hospitable man – it was said that he always wore white tie and tails at dinner, whether he

DesBarres

had guests or not. His remarkable rise was accompanied by a gradual anglicizing of the family. Several of his children married into the English-speaking Quebec bourgeoisie. Louise-Sophie married Frederic Horatio Fisher, a doctor from London, Hélène and Sophie married the Quebec merchants George and Henry Pemberton. Charlotte-Louise became the wife of Dr Charles-Norbert PERRAULT, Joseph-François Perrault*'s son.

On 23 April 1828, at the age of 63, Desbarats passed away at his home in Petite-Rivière-Saint-Charles. The funeral service was conducted by Joseph Signay*, the coadjutor bishop, in the cathedral of Notre-Dame at Quebec. The cortège then crossed the St Lawrence and wended its way to Frampton Township by roads difficult at that season. In keeping with his last wishes he was buried in the local chapel, for which he had donated land in 1825. Although his family showed some reluctance, his remains were transferred from the chapel to the new parish church of Saint-Édouard around 1870. As founder and benefactor Desbarats was long remembered by the early settlers in Frampton; his son Édouard-Olivier was to continue developing the land there. The Desbarats name also became established in the difficult and precarious fields of printing and publishing. One after another through the 19th century, his son, grandson, and great-grandson – George-Paschal*, George-Édouard*, and William-Amable – headed the family printing firm. They carried on its work with distinction and were often innovators in the field.

JEAN-MARIE LEBEL in collaboration with
AILEEN DESBARATS

ANQ-MBF, CN1-5, 30 janv., 25 avril, 18 juin 1788; 28 mars, 24 avril 1794. ANQ-Q, CE1-1, 24 sept. 1798; CN1-16, 28 mai 1819; CN1-26, 29 avril, 26 sept. 1809; CN1-116, 9 janv. 1818; 15, 19 févr., 21 sept. 1821; 19 avril, 13 août, 6 sept., 11, 15 oct. 1822; 3, 21 févr., 9, 20 mai 1823; 26 sept. 1824; CN1-178, 27 févr. 1796; 26 avril 1797; 2 janv., 21 mars, 17, 22 sept., 5 déc. 1798; 24 janv., 30 mai 1800; 16 mars 1801; 2 févr., 2 mars, 2 avril, 3 mai 1802; 22 juin, 27 sept. 1803; 27 févr. 1805; 15 juill. 1809; 18 mai 1810; 22 févr., 7 mai 1811; 3 sept. 1814; 9 mai 1815; CN1-208, 7, 16 oct., 25 nov. 1820; 29 mai 1821; 13 août 1822; 20 mai, 3, 7, 13 oct. 1823; 5 août 1824; 10 juin, 16 sept. 1826; 1er oct. 1828; CN1-230, 30 avril 1794; 7 juin 1800; 6 juin 1801; 8 juill. 1802; 28 mai, 13 sept. 1806; 19 mars, 24 nov., 30 déc. 1807; 24 oct. 1808; 25 janv., 10 mars, 14 avril, 21 mai, 5, 22, 25 juin, 5 juill., 7 nov. 1810; 27 mai, 7 juill. 1812; 25 mai 1814; 6 déc. 1815; 19, 21 août, 6, 14 oct., 24 nov. 1817; 9 févr. 1818; 16, 24 juill., 30 oct. 1819; 9 août 1820; 4 mai 1821; 31 mai 1822; 26 mai, 10 juin 1824; CN1-253, 20 févr. 1812; 5 déc. 1823; 23 juill., 11 déc. 1824; 8 déc. 1826; CN1-262, 23 mai 1798, 16 nov. 1799, 7 juin 1800; CN1-284, 10 janv. 1794, 25 nov. 1819; ZQ6-45, 26 avril 1828. Arch. de la ville de Québec, Juges de paix, procès-verbaux des sessions spéciales relatives aux chemins et ponts, 1816–28. PAC, MG 24, B1, 1: 182–87; 2: 106–7; RG 68, General index, 1651–1841.

"Cahier des témoignages de liberté au mariage commancé le 15 avril 1757," ANQ Rapport, 1951–53: 115. "Les dénombrements de Québec" (Plessis), ANQ Rapport, 1948–49: 155, 213. "Recensement des habitants de la ville et gouvernement des Trois-Rivières tel qu'il a été pris au mois de septembre mil sept cent soixante," ANQ Rapport, 1946–47: 8. Quebec Gazette, 10 April 1800; 20, 29 May 1802; 3 April 1806; 27 April 1815. Quebec Mercury, 26 April 1798. Beaulieu et Hamelin, La presse québécoise, 1: 19, 23. Hare et Wallot, Les imprimés dans le Bas-Canada. Le Jeune, Dictionnaire, 1: 499–500. Officers of British forces in Canada (Irving), 143. Quebec almanac, 1796–1828. P.-G. Roy, Fils de Québec, 2: 130–32. Tremaine, Biblio. of Canadian imprints, 525, 528–29, 634, 664. Christina Cameron et Jean Trudel, Québec au temps de James Patterson Cockburn (Québec, 1976). Louis Lacaze, Les imprimeurs et les libraires en Béarn (1552–1883) (Pau, France, 1884). Yvan Lamonde et al., L'imprimé au Québec, aspects historiques (18e–20e siècles) (Québec, 1983), 98–99, 109–10, 276, 285. J.-E. Roy, Hist. de Lauzon, 4: 70–71; 5: 86–87. Henri Têtu, Histoire des familles Têtu, Bonenfant, Dionne et Perrault (Québec, 1898), 523–24. Claude Galarneau, "Les métiers du livre à Québec (1764–1859)," Cahiers des Dix, 43 (1983): 149–50, 159–60. Eugène Rouillard, "Les chefs de canton," BRH, 2 (1896): 183–85.

DeSBARRES, JOSEPH FREDERICK WALLET (baptized **Joseph-Frédéric Vallet Des Barres**), army officer, military engineer, surveyor, colonizer, and colonial administrator; b. November 1721, either in Basel, Switzerland, or in Paris, eldest of three children of Joseph-Léonard Vallet Des Barres and Anne-Catherine Cuvier; with Mary CANNON he had six children and with Martha Williams eleven; d. 27 Oct. 1824 in Halifax.

The many fields of interest of Joseph Frederick Wallet DesBarres have made him a unique figure in the early history of the Maritimes, and the length and vigour of his career still elicit admiration. A member of a Huguenot family that originated in the Montbéliard region of France, DesBarres received his initial schooling at Basel, where he obtained a thorough grounding in science and mathematics. In 1752 or 1753, under the patronage of the Duke of Cumberland, he entered the Royal Military Academy at Woolwich (London), England, and there immersed himself in the study of fortifications, surveying, and drafting. DesBarres broke his ties with Europe in 1756 when he left for North America to begin a military career as a lieutenant with the Royal Americans (62nd, later 60th, Foot). Within two years he was serving as an assistant engineer at the siege of Louisbourg, Île Royale (Cape Breton Island). His ability there impressed his superiors, and he was commissioned to prepare a chart of the St Lawrence River, which was used by James Wolfe*. His success led to further surveys in the Quebec area while he was participating in the campaigns of 1759 and 1760 as an assistant engineer, followed in 1761 by work on the Halifax defences under the supervision of John Henry Bastide*. The next year DesBarres acted as an assistant engineer at the recapture of St John's [see Charles-Henri-Louis d'Arsac* de Ternay], and after the French surrender carried out surveying tasks in Newfoundland in conjunction with James Cook*.

In October 1762 Commodore Richard Spry arrived in Halifax to become commander of the Royal Navy in North America. Soon afterwards he suggested to the Admiralty that a coastal survey of Nova Scotia would aid in settlement and improve "the safety of Navigation," and he recommended DesBarres, who had volunteered his services for the task. A year later, Spry's successor, Rear-Admiral Lord Colvill*, brought instructions from the Admiralty to have DesBarres make "accurate Surveys and Charts of the Coast and Harbours of Nova Scotia." This project was one of several approved about this time by the Board of Trade and by the Admiralty for the survey of parts of Britain's North American possessions, and it reflected the bias of its sponsor: whereas the board's main interest was in land surveys, the Admiralty was most concerned with sea-coasts and harbours. In part because of this divergence of interests, DesBarres was to have only limited contact with Samuel Johannes Holland*, who in 1764 began a survey of the northern colonies for the Board of Trade. DesBarres was undoubtedly happy with this arrangement since he resented Holland, perhaps because of the latter's seniority and better connections; indeed, he may have suggested the Nova Scotia survey to Spry in order to avoid working under Holland. DesBarres's tendency to think of new projects is illustrated by his suggestion at this time for the establishment of a corps of pioneers which would construct roads in Nova Scotia.

By May 1764 DesBarres had commenced the survey, which gave full rein to his surveying and artistic genius. Previous maps of inshore waters had been poor, inadequate in scale and unreliable in detail. Thanks to his painstaking methods, however, DesBarres was able to refine existing techniques of surveying and adapt others. Each summer he worked with a staff of assistants, usually numbering about 7, some 20 to 30 labourers, and small vessels detached from the naval establishment. During the winter he prepared rough drafts of the maps. The tortuous nature of the shore line was a major problem; DesBarres commented, "There is scarcely any known Shore so much intersected with Bays, Harbours and Creeks as this is, and the Offing of it is so full of Islands, Rocks and Shoals as are almost innumerable." In addition, conditions were sometimes harsh and occasionally dangerous – in 1767 he narrowly escaped drowning when landing on Sable Island.

Other problems were administrative in nature. In

1766 DesBarres and Colvill had a disagreement about the scope of the survey, Colvill believing that only the Atlantic coastline should be charted and DesBarres holding out for the entire coast followed by a review of all work undertaken before it was incorporated in "an accurate and perfect Map." DesBarres apparently carried his point with the Admiralty, but that body was not as accommodating about expenses. Initially only the cost of hiring a vessel was allowed, there were disputes over the wages of the labourers, and DesBarres's own expenditures were not fully reimbursed. Nevertheless, the survey continued steadily until its completion in 1773.

After returning to England in 1774, DesBarres toiled for some years to produce his charts and views in a finished form. They were eventually incorporated in *The Atlantic Neptune*, a large collection of charts and views produced by DesBarres. The *Neptune* was published by him on behalf of the Admiralty, and appeared between 1774 and 1784. It consists of four series of charts covering Nova Scotia, New England, the Gulf of St Lawrence including Cape Breton and St John's (Prince Edward) Island, and the coast south of New York, accompanied by "various views of the North American coast." Although DesBarres was indebted to Holland and his assistants for many surveys, a fact which he acknowledged, his own contribution is not negligible. Moreover, it is in their artistic quality that the charts and views especially shine, since their accuracy is combined with an aesthetic character that places DesBarres among the more notable of the century's minor artists. The *Neptune* does contain some inaccuracies, but these are probably accounted for by the fact that DesBarres had rushed production in response to the mounting pressure for publication, unrest in the Thirteen Colonies having created a demand for accurate naval charts. Nevertheless, DesBarres's charts served as standard guides for navigation until the work of Henry Wolsey Bayfield* and Peter Frederick Shortland* well into the 19th century.

While in Nova Scotia, DesBarres became convinced of the great potential of the Maritime colonies for settlement. He began to obtain land by grant or purchase, and eventually came to own property in the Tatamagouche region, Falmouth Township, and Cumberland County in Nova Scotia, as well as tracts between the Memramcook and Petitcodiac rivers in present-day New Brunswick. These acquisitions, which made him one of the greatest landowners in the Maritime colonies, were procured relatively cheaply, partly because he was friendly with Nova Scotian officials. The Tatamagouche grant, for example, came to him as the result of an association with Michael Francklin*, Richard Bulkeley*, Joseph Goreham*, and others. In addition, DesBarres looked after the interests of other Nova Scotian landowners

DesBarres

such as Frederick Haldimand*. DesBarres's dream was that rents would provide money for his chart-making activities, which were always in need of support. Some time before 1768 he built a headquarters in Falmouth Township known as Castle Frederick, and there worked on the surveys during the winters. When he returned to England he left his mistress Mary Cannon, whom he had met in 1764, in charge of the Castle and his estates. On her appointment as his agent in 1776 she was given power of attorney in land transactions, and was to consult him only for final decisions.

DesBarres began submitting bills for the *Neptune* in 1775, but the Admiralty decided that, given the high costs, parliamentary approval would be needed before payment could be made. This decision initiated proceedings that dragged on until 1794 and were never satisfactory to DesBarres. The confusion in his records – the result of an unusual arrangement whereby he was permitted to receive the profits from the sale of charts while working for the crown – makes them almost impossible to interpret. But in October 1782 the Admiralty reported favourably on his requests for compensation, thus vindicating his honesty and confirming the value of the *Neptune*.

Deeply involved with the war in North America and its aftermath, the government did not act on DesBarres's case immediately. However, the need to establish refuges for the loyalists came to DesBarres's assistance, since in May 1784 it was decided that Cape Breton would be separated from Nova Scotia and made an independent colony for that purpose. One of the few persons with an intimate knowledge of the island, DesBarres had been consulted when discussions about its future were under way, and he had been enthusiastic, claiming that the fisheries could be developed as they had been under French rule and that the coal mines could pay for the operation of the government. He was quick to make a case for his appointment as lieutenant governor in partial compensation for the 20 years spent on surveys and the *Neptune*, which he claimed had cost him money and military promotion (he had become a captain only in 1775). Thanks in part to his knowledge of the island, he received the appointment, his commission being dated 9 Aug. 1784. Governor John Parr* of Nova Scotia was supposed to exercise some supervision over him, but in practice DesBarres corresponded directly with London.

The new colony was not a particularly appealing place. Since its cession to Britain in 1763, Cape Breton had remained undeveloped because of indifference in Halifax and the unwillingness of the British government to see the island's coal compete with the home product on the North American market. As a result there were only about a thousand inhabitants, mainly Acadians and Micmacs, in scattered locations.

During 1783, however, Abraham Cornelius Cuyler*, a former mayor of Albany, N.Y., had begun to plan for the immigration of loyalists from Quebec, and 140 arrived in October 1784 at Louisbourg and St Peters. DesBarres had also been gathering settlers, mostly poor Englishmen and disbanded soldiers, and 129 persons landed from the *Blenheim* at Spanish Bay (Sydney Harbour) one month later. DesBarres's settlers were joined by some of Cuyler's group, and the lieutenant governor himself arrived at Spanish Bay on 7 Jan. 1785; by spring the colony's capital, named for the home secretary, Lord Sydney, had been founded. DesBarres laid out the town along typically Georgian lines, intending that it should have the advantage of controlled development. The proposal was unusual for its time, and a later commentator has claimed that, had it been fully carried through, it would have resulted in "the only imaginative planned project in 18th century Nova Scotia."

But while DesBarres shone as a planner, he failed in human relations. More accustomed to military discipline than to the compromise needed in civilian government, he rashly tried to impose his will on others and earned their enmity and opposition. The chief source of controversy was the shortage of supplies. It soon became evident that, thanks to a lack of planning in Halifax and Britain, there were inadequate provisions to support the settlers and garrison of Sydney. Moreover, when government supplies became available, they were allotted only to the troops and loyalists. The settlers sponsored by DesBarres were thus placed in an unenviable position. DesBarres claimed that as lieutenant governor he alone had the right to distribute these supplies, but Lieutenant-Colonel John Yorke, the garrison commander, insisted that he had been ordered to take charge of them. The acrimonious debate between the two men lasted from late 1785 well into the spring of 1786, and was accompanied by several confrontations between DesBarres's supporters and the troops. The tiny society of Sydney was divided by the dispute, which slackened to some extent when DesBarres obtained control over some supplies by seizing those he found in a ship wrecked off Arichat. Yorke had been willing to distribute supplies to the non-loyalist settlers, but DesBarres's refusal to compromise about control drove him to ally himself with members of the Executive Council who had already begun to rebel against DesBarres's strict control, notably Cuyler and Attorney General David Mathews*. Cuyler, Mathews, and others sent petitions to the British government condemning the conduct of DesBarres and his supporters such as Chief Justice Richard Gibbons* and demanding his recall.

Unfortunately for DesBarres, by the time the petitions reached London in the late summer of 1786 his position was less than secure. In April Lord

Sydney had reprimanded him for attempting to promote one of his favourite schemes, the establishment of a whale fishery, by encouraging whalers from Nantucket Island and Martha's Vineyard, Mass., to settle in Cape Breton. Sydney had reproved Parr for the same activity. He was also disturbed by DesBarres's failure to wait for instructions before entering into agreements with whalers, and his expenditure of money without prior approval on such items as barracks. The arrival of the petitions and supporting letters from Parr apparently decided Sydney to recall DesBarres to explain his conduct. In spite of DesBarres's sending Gibbons to London to present his case, Sydney ordered him to Britain in November 1786. Just under a year later DesBarres handed over power to his successor, William Macarmick*, and left Cape Breton.

There were several reasons for DesBarres's failure. Cape Breton had a low priority with British officials and there was no patience with disputes in a minor colony. Moreover, a conservative Home Department showed no imagination about cooperation in the implementation of DesBarres's far-reaching schemes. Then too, ambitious loyalists such as Cuyler and Mathews were unwilling to submit to DesBarres's control, and were prepared to use their influence in Britain. And lastly, Nova Scotian officials resented losing Cape Breton and were jealous of a contender for government support; they would hinder the development of the colony as much as possible.

DesBarres's career in Cape Breton complicated his claims for compensation even more, since he had been compelled to purchase £3,000 worth of supplies. To pay the bills, he had to pledge *Neptune* plates and mortgage some of his estates. For the next several years DesBarres's confusing financial records were examined, while he demanded every penny he felt was owed him in numerous lengthy petitions which reveal the singularity of purpose that characterized his whole life. The government agreed to pay some of the £43,000 that formed his total claim, but most of the amount was still outstanding when in 1794 his friend William Windham became secretary at war. Although not all of the *Neptune* claims were accepted, apparently because the plates were considered to be DesBarres's property and therefore profitable to him, most were approved. In addition, his expenses arising from Cape Breton were paid, and he was even granted half the salary of lieutenant governor from 1787 to 1793.

DesBarres was 72 in 1794 and the settlement of his claims should have spelled the happy end of a long career. It did not: he wanted recognition that his errors in Cape Breton had not been great enough to deny him another colonial appointment. He remained in England pressing his case and was not satisfied until May 1804, when at the age of 82 he was appointed

lieutenant governor of Prince Edward Island, to succeed Edmund Fanning*.

During Fanning's tenure the absentee landlords, who owned most of the land on the Island, had become suspicious of certain developments, notably the movement for escheat for non-fulfilment of obligations. Since the landlords feared that they had not exercised great influence on the administration of the Island, DesBarres was instructed by the British government to investigate the situation and make reforms, especially in the judicial system, which had been the subject of complaints from several quarters. DesBarres experienced great difficulty in reaching the Island, and it was not until July 1805 that he arrived in Charlottetown. He brought with him his tendency to propose imaginative plans but, tutored by the Cape Breton experience, showed greater tact and willingness to compromise.

DesBarres was concerned to discover the state of the Island's economy, and by the end of 1805 he had forwarded to London both a census and a detailed account of the crops and livestock in the colony. The relatively backward condition of the Island prompted him to attempt changes, and he planned to create a more prosperous future by erecting public buildings and improving communications. To accomplish his aims, he adapted the militia organization to fulfil the statute labour laws; by 1810 new roads were being opened and public buildings planned [*see* John Plaw*]. DesBarres also devoted much time to questions of defence, organizing the militia on a proper basis and trying to interest both local and British politicians in improving the Island's military position.

At the same time, the lieutenant governor was involved with a complex political situation. On his arrival DesBarres had found that Fanning's supporters dominated the public offices, and he was therefore forced to turn to one of the few unattached residents, James Bardin PALMER, for advice. Palmer's appointment to the Council and to a number of minor positions raised suspicions among the Fanningites, or "old party" as they were known, about his influence with DesBarres. Palmer was already in ill favour with them, and he became even more so in 1806 when he and some others founded the Loyal Electors, a society which opposed the "old party" and aimed at control of the House of Assembly.

The Loyal Electors and the "old party" maintained a strained relationship during the following years, one marked by increasing hostility on both sides. In 1810 matters came to a head when Attorney General Peter Magowan* died. DesBarres, who had hitherto been successful in staying out of political quarrels, recommended Palmer for the position, but the proprietors, led by Lord Selkirk [Douglas*], distrusted Palmer and succeeded the following year in having their candidate, Charles Stewart*, appointed. In 1811 as well

DesBarres

accusations were made that a secret committee had been formed to control the Loyal Electors. Members of the society refuted the charge in affidavits to DesBarres which were highly critical of Stewart, Chief Justice Cæsar COLCLOUGH, and two other judges. When the judges learned of the attacks they demanded and obtained permission from DesBarres to examine the affidavits, which they then used to start legal proceedings against some of the Loyal Electors.

After a fiercely contested assembly election in 1812 the Loyal Electors increased their representation. When the "old party" supporters boycotted the house in September, a rump composed mainly of Loyal Electors requested from DesBarres an explanation of his role in the affidavits affair. The lieutenant governor denied that he had authorized the use of the affidavits for legal proceedings, and the assembly thereupon condemned the judges' actions. Shortly thereafter DesBarres took the opportunity to suspend Colclough, with whom he had been on bad terms for some time.

But these events had been overtaken by others in Britain. The proprietors, alerted to the controversy by Colclough and others, had attacked DesBarres for being under the domination of Palmer and had attacked the Loyal Electors as sympathetic to the Americans. Lord Bathurst, the colonial secretary, was sympathetic to their arguments and in August 1812 recalled DesBarres; Palmer was stripped of his public offices. DesBarres was almost certainly not as heavily influenced by Palmer as was alleged, since he was percipient and headstrong enough not to be led by advisers. It seems likely that the Colonial Office, quite apart from the proprietors' lobbying, felt that in wartime a younger, more militarily active man was needed to replace one of 89.

After his supersession DesBarres left Prince Edward Island for Amherst, N.S., where he lived until he moved to Halifax in 1817. His vitality was far from exhausted, for he continued trying to prod the British government into paying more of his claims, and spent a great deal of time on his land problems. It is reputed that he celebrated his hundredth birthday by dancing on a table top in Halifax. There he died one month short of 103 and was buried beside Martha Williams.

Over many years his problems with his lands had grown more and more complicated, and they had become inextricably involved with his personal relationships. Mary Cannon had remained in charge of his estates and during his tenure in Cape Breton had sent timber and produce to Sydney. Their relationship deteriorated, however, after the arrival at Sydney late in 1785 of Martha Williams and two of her children by DesBarres. Williams, a native of Shrewsbury, England, is a shadowy figure. It is not known whether DesBarres had bothered to marry her before she arrived in North America, but thereafter he remained loyal to her and severed personal connections with Cannon, who continued to defend his land titles in the courts against creditors and against tenants increasingly seeking to own their own property.

During the years in Cape Breton and England DesBarres had had scant time for his estates. In 1794, however, when prospects brightened for the settlement of the *Neptune* and Cape Breton claims, he had taken a renewed interest in the properties. Claiming that he could not obtain information on them from Cannon, he appointed Captain John MacDonald* of Glenaladale as agent in her place. MacDonald discovered that Cannon had run up £4,000 worth of debts in DesBarres's name and feared that she would sue DesBarres for that amount; he also found out that she was having an affair with an Irish labourer at Castle Frederick. DesBarres acted coolly, remaining in England and ignoring the estates, but not making any provision for Cannon and their children. By about 1800 one of their daughters, Amelia, had taken charge of the estates; like all his children she was loyal to him and tried to enforce payment of rents.

When DesBarres was appointed to Prince Edward Island in 1804, he replaced Amelia with a son-in-law, James Chalmers. However, Chalmers's heavy-handed approach to collecting rents drove some lessees to sell out and move. By this time DesBarres had lost contact with agricultural and settlement conditions on his estates, and no manager could satisfy his final visions of landed wealth. Believing that Cannon had "fraudulently and corruptly betrayed [his] trust and confidence" in her management of his land, in 1809 he went so far as to take her to the Court of Chancery in Halifax, but the case was still unresolved at his death, when it was presumably closed without any decision. Meanwhile he was unable to divest himself of his land since disputes with tenants over land values had prevented prices from being set on his holdings. His children by Martha Williams inherited the problem, eventually squabbling among themselves and gaining little. Cannon and her family were totally excluded from his estate.

The long career of Joseph Frederick Wallet Des-Barres unfolded during the pioneer period of four Maritime colonies. There can be no dispute that his greatest contribution is the *Atlantic Neptune*, which stands as a landmark in Canadian cartographic achievement. His enthusiastic visions for Cape Breton were not realized and his impatience with government and opposition spelled failure to his efforts. In Prince Edward Island his administration was more successful and saw the formation of what has often been called the first political party in the colony. Difficulties over land resulted in a time-consuming waste of energy which soured his later years. DesBarres's private life was not altogether unusual in so far as colonial officials in the 18th century often had families on both sides of the ocean. However, it must be said that in his treatment of Mary Cannon and her family he showed callousness, ingratitude, and suspicion.

For himself he demanded complete justice, and he showed "Ingenuity and Contrivance" in obtaining it during the years of subtle battles over his *Neptune* and Cape Breton claims. His personality "never demonstrated an abundance of the pleasing traits," according to a recent biographer, Geraint Nantglyn Davies Evans, and could hardly have been agreeable. Yet his enthusiasm and sheer breadth of vision appealed to women, politicians, and officials alike. These characteristics brought DesBarres his successes but the attention to detail he showed as an artist brought a certain pettiness to his personal affairs and led to his failures.

R. J. MORGAN

The collection of plates which constitutes *The Atlantic Neptune, published for the use of the Royal Navy of Great Britain* was printed in London at various times between 1774 and 1784. The work is sometimes described as appearing in four editions, dated 1777, 1780, 1781, and 1784, but these dates apply only to the four versions of the main title page and not to the rest of the contents, which bear various dates and differ so widely from copy to copy that no two known sets are alike, and no definitive list of the variant plates is available despite considerable bibliographical investigation. The complexities of this publication are discussed at greater length in Evans's biography (cited below) and in Robert Lingel's article, "The Atlantic Neptune," New York Public Library, *Bull.*, 40 (1936): 571–603. A facsimile reprint of one of the copies bearing the 1780 title page has been published in four portfolios of unbound plates, Barre, Mass., 1966–68.

DesBarres is also the author of *Nautical remarks and observations on the coasts and harbours of Nova Scotia . . .* ([London?], 1778); *Surveys of North America, entitled: Atlantic Neptune . . .* (London, 1781), a partial catalogue and price list of the *Neptune* plates; *A statement submitted by Lieutenant Colonel Desbarres, for consideration; respecting his services . . . during the war of 1756; – the utility of his surveys . . . of the coasts and harbours of North America, intituled "The Atlantic Neptune" ; – and his proceedings . . . as lieutenant governor . . . of Cape Breton* (n.p., [1795]); and of *Letters to Lord ***** on "A caveat against emigration to America . . . "*, which was published anonymously in London in 1804.

BL, Add. MSS 21710, 21828, 37890 (copies at PAC). PAC, MG 11, [CO 217] Nova Scotia A, 106; Cape Breton A; [CO 220] Cape Breton B; MG 23, F1. [William Smith], *A caveat against emigration to America; with the state of the island of Cape Breton, from the year 1784 to the present year; and suggestions for the benefit of the British settlements in North America* (London, 1803). DNB. G. N. D. Evans, *Uncommon obdurate: the several public careers of J. F. W. DesBarres* (Toronto and Salem, Mass., 1969). R. J. Morgan, "Orphan outpost." J. C. Webster, *The life of Joseph Frederick Wallet Des Barres* (Shediac, N.B., 1933). Michael Hugo-Brunt, "The origin of colonial settlements in the Maritimes," *Plan Canada* (Toronto), 1 (1959–60): 102–4. Lois Kernaghan, "A man and his mistress: J. F. W. Des-

Barres and Mary Cannon," *Acadiensis* (Fredericton), 11 (1981–82), no.1: 23–42. R. [J.] Morgan, "Joseph Frederick Wallet DesBarres and the founding of Cape Breton colony," *Rev. de l'univ. d'Ottawa*, 39 (1969): 212–27. J. C. Webster, "Joseph Frederick Wallet Des Barres and *The Atlantic Neptune*," RSC *Trans.*, 3rd ser., 21 (1927), sect.II: 21–40.

DESBRISAY, THEOPHILUS, Church of England clergyman, JP, office holder, and politician; b. 9 Oct. 1754 in Thurles (Republic of Ireland), son of Thomas Desbrisay* and Ellen Landers (Landen); m. 1778 Margaret Stewart, daughter of Peter Stewart*, and they had six sons and seven daughters; d. 14 March 1823 in Prince Edward Island.

Theophilus Desbrisay's appointment as governor's chaplain for St John's (Prince Edward) Island was obtained for him in 1774 by his father, the lieutenant governor. A student at Trinity College, Dublin, Theophilus was already in deacon's orders. He was ordained to the priesthood by the bishop of Waterford on 3 July 1775, although he was not yet of canonical age, and he then set out for Charlottetown. In the Strait of Canso the vessel on which he was a passenger was captured by American privateers who had just plundered Charlottetown. Following his release, he arrived late in the year at the capital only to discover that there were no funds for his support and the £3,000 allocated by the crown in 1772 for construction of a church, court-house, and jail had been appropriated by Governor Walter Patterson* to pay government salaries.

Desbrisay found a berth on a man-of-war, which he served as chaplain for two years. In 1777 he was assured a stipend and he took up residence ashore. When the parish of Charlotte was created in 1781, Desbrisay became the first rector. Later he served as a justice of the peace and an overseer of roads. By 7 Oct. 1782 he had become a member of Council, but his resignation was accepted on 16 April 1784. Reappointed on 15 May 1787, he did not attend any meetings after 24 September, and it is possible that his disappearance from the record is connected with the reinstatement in October of Phillips Callbeck*, Thomas Wright*, and others, who had been suspended earlier in the year.

Desbrisay's ministry was complicated by his relationship through blood or marriage with many in his cure of souls. For example, he encountered both pastoral and familial difficulties when in the early 1780s Chief Justice Peter Stewart accused his wife, Mrs Desbrisay's stepmother, of having been "compromised" by Governor Patterson and expelled her from his bed and board.

From 1780 to 1801 Desbrisay made his home at Covehead, a rural retreat on the Island's north shore, saying that he considered Charlottetown "a wicked place" and himself "more retired and happy in the country." He came to town on weekends to conduct divine service and devoted the remainder of his time to his family and the cultivation of his garden, in the manner of an English squire-parson. Services were held in private residences or more commonly in a house which also functioned as the Cross Keys Tavern. When the bishop of Nova Scotia, Charles Inglis*, visited in 1789, he showed his disapproval of having worship conducted in "so very improper a place" by holding service in the house of former governor Patterson. He also upbraided the church-wardens and vestry for their failure to build a church; they in turn laid the blame on Patterson for his requisition of the moneys the crown had provided. However, Inglis was pleased with Desbrisay, whom he described as a "decent, sensible young man."

Following construction in 1800–1 of a church in Charlottetown, Desbrisay took up residence in town, where he remained until his death in 1823. He was reported to be "a man of liberal sentiments and of a benevolent disposition" who "faithfully reproved the prevailing sins in the highest as well as the lowest, even when his doing so gave great offence in high quarters, and among his own relatives." His theological position and understanding of his pastoral duties were said to be influenced by the Calvinist doctrines of his Scottish Presbyterian neighbours. If so, it was an influence reinforced by his own family history, for the Desbrisays were originally French Huguenots. In any case, he was irenic in his relationships with those whose religious loyalties differed from his own, particularly the Presbyterians, who shared the use of the church building. But the respect in which he was held was a minor factor in the fortunes of his church in the colony: the established church's identification with the absentee land proprietors, the Charlottetown élite, and the crown (which was expected to supply all its needs without effort on the part of its adherents), together with his own lack of enterprise in ministering to the religious needs of settlers in rural areas, meant a slow start for the Church of England in the colony. It did not begin to show signs of vigorous life until the 1840s.

ROBERT CRITCHLOW TUCK

Diocesan Church Soc. of P.E.I. Arch. (Charlottetown), Peter MacGowan, diary; Notes on the hist. of the Anglican Church in P.E.I., comp. T. R. Millman and Edgar MacNutt. PAPEI, RG 5, minutes, 1782, 1787. P.E.I. Museum and Heritage Foundation (Charlottetown), DesBrisay family notes. St Paul's Anglican Church (Charlottetown), Reg. of baptisms, marriages, and burials for the parish of Charlotte. *Prince Edward Island Register*, 12 Oct. 1824. "Completion of the correspondence and journals of the Right Reverend Charles and John Inglis, first and third bishops of Nova Scotia," PAC *Report*, 1913, 227–83. Frank MacKinnon, *The government of Prince Edward Island* (Toronto, 1951). T. R. Millman and A. R. Kelley, *Atlantic Canada to 1900; a*

history of the Anglican Church (Toronto, 1983). George Patterson, *Memoir of the Rev. James MacGregor, D.D. . . .* (Philadelphia, 1859). Percy Pope, "The Church of England in Prince Edward Island," *Past and present of Prince Edward Island . . .*, ed. D. A. MacKinnon and A. B. Warburton (Charlottetown, [1906]), 244–77. *Two hundred and fifty years young: our diocesan story, 1710–1960* (Halifax, 1960). Warburton, *Hist. of P.E.I.*

DESCHENAUX, CHARLES-JOSEPH BRASSARD. *See* BRASSARD

DESJARDINS, PETER (Pierre), businessman; b. 1775 in Nesle, France; d. unmarried 7 Sept. 1827 in Grimsby, Upper Canada.

A royalist refugee from the French revolution, Peter Desjardins emigrated from England in the spring of 1792 and arrived in Upper Canada that fall. He settled at Newark (Niagara-on-the-Lake), where he clerked for John MacKay, a minor local merchant. By 1802 he had left MacKay and Company, possibly because of a civil suit for debt which MacKay successfully brought against him in that year. Desjardins was described in the action as a yeoman, late of Saltfleet Township. The same year he became a clerk to James DURAND, the new owner of the Bridgewater Works near Chippawa. For a brief time he supervised Durand's enterprises in Norfolk County before moving to the Head of the Lake (the vicinity of present-day Hamilton Harbour), probably with Durand, in 1805. Desjardins took up residence in the village of Coote's Paradise (Dundas). Although Durand's son Charles Morrison later recalled that Desjardins had served his father until 1812, in 1808 Desjardins moved into the household of another of MacKay's former clerks, Richard Hatt*.

Hatt was one of the most successful and innovative businessmen in Upper Canada and a dominant figure at the Head of the Lake. When absent on his yearly trips to Montreal, Hatt left instructions with his wife that Desjardins should "let me know how things go on," adding, "if I have omitted any thing necessary to be done in my directions to Peter you will I am sure remind him of it." Desjardins evidently found working for Hatt to his liking: an anonymous account of his affairs noted that Desjardins was "without any ambition" and had "made up his mind to remain a bachelor." Indeed, Desjardins did not strike out on his own until after Hatt's death in 1819.

Desjardins is usually associated with the canal that bears his name. On 9 Aug. 1820 he petitioned the Executive Council for the lands necessary to connect Dundas to Burlington Bay (Hamilton Harbour) by canal. Whether the idea was his own or not will probably never be known. Certainly as Hatt's clerk he would have been only too aware of the difficulties of trans-shipment from the shallow marsh known as

Coote's Paradise into the bay. Access to the village was by way of this marsh, which was "choked up by Weeds and Sand Banks, more than half the Summer," and the winding Spencer Creek. In 1818 and 1819, probably on Hatt's behalf, Desjardins had cleared the creek, rendering it, temporarily, navigable from the marsh to Dundas. As a merchant shipping large quantities of flour from Dundas, he was vitally interested in the improvement of navigation, but he also stressed the "considerable advantage and benefit" of a canal to the public as a whole. This claim was supported by a resolution of the Court of Quarter Sessions of the Gore District, chaired by the major merchant James Crooks*, that the building of a canal would be "highly beneficial" to the region.

The timing of Desjardins's petition was propitious: canal-building in New York State, an economic depression, the concern for economic improvement so evident in the responses from townships across Upper Canada to Robert Gourlay*'s address to resident landowners, all had combined to turn the attention of the legislature and key government spokesmen such as John Beverley Robinson* and John Strachan* to the need for economic development on a provincial scale. Robinson, the most enthusiastic advocate of development among the provincial élite, visited the site of the Dundas canal in the fall of 1820. On 1 November he added a short note to Desjardins's petition stating his approval; later that day the council, chaired by Chief Justice William Dummer POWELL, approved the petition.

Desjardins borrowed £775 from the Hatt estate and began work; two years later he signed an agreement for digging a canal 12 feet wide at the top, 7 feet wide at the bottom, and $3\frac{1}{2}$ feet deep. In 1825 he petitioned the council for full title to the lands he had sought in his 1820 petition. Claiming to have expended "upwards" of £1,000 on the project, he submitted depositions to the effect that the canal was now navigable by sail (and without the use of poles) from the marsh to Dundas. The council found his documentation satisfactory and issued an order-in-council giving him full title to the land in question. Meanwhile, Desjardins and others, most notably the Lesslie family, had sought authorization from the legislature to incorporate a joint-stock company. A bill was soon passed and the Desjardins Canal Company was incorporated in January 1826. The act provided for management by five directors, a capital not to exceed £10,000 provincial currency, and 800 shares valued at £12 10s. apiece.

Within the Gore District, the old rivalry among localities for commercial supremacy had not abated; it had, however, narrowed to a struggle between Dundas and Hamilton. What the latter had lacked in initial commercial advantages had been counterbalanced by its selection in 1816 as the administrative capital of the district. Hostility to that decision by the other communities at the Head of the Lake did not abate quickly. When in 1825 a new court-house and jail were proposed for Hamilton, the residents of Dundas and Ancaster seized the opportunity as their last chance to urge reconsideration of the site of the capital. The canal had been used as an argument in favour of Dundas's pretensions to be the capital, but it was even more vital to the town's commercial pre-eminence. Since the summer of 1824 work had progressed on the Burlington Bay Canal [see James Gordon STRO-BRIDGE]. Without a parallel effort of equal dimensions linking Dundas directly to the bay and hence to the lake, Hamilton would quickly, and perhaps irrevocably, gain the upper hand.

In view of the advantages Dundas would acquire by the canal, Desjardins should have been able to marshal widespread local support. As it turned out, however, his plans met with considerable criticism and fatal opposition. Three points were at issue: the limited scope of the canal (it did not go beyond Dundas), its dimensions, and the fact that it was a private rather than a public venture. Everyone was concerned that the canal be able to handle lake shipping, as the Burlington Canal would be able to. The foremost political spokesman of Hamilton's interests, Speaker John Willson*, derided the usefulness of the canal. Most important, Crooks complained bitterly to William Lyon Mackenzie*, a friend and former business associate of Desjardins, that Desjardins's efforts to this point were worth little "to any Canal whether Public or Private." He preferred a public enterprise which could attain "the great advantage" yet recover the initial capital costs and eliminate the need for tolls except in the immediate future. Mackenzie, for his part, championed Dundas's cause and ridiculed Willson's arguments. Still, he shared Crooks's reservation about "a private company, as all monopolies, except the post-office, are hurtful." He reiterated Crooks's concerns in his editorial columns, noting that Desjardins might have spent less than £200 or as much as £1,000. In the long term, Mackenzie's support of Dundas and attack on the Burlington Canal backfired and contributed significantly to making Hamilton a tory and, later, a conservative bastion.

Local opposition focused on the benefits to Desjardins and the company. The act of incorporation provided for Desjardins's personal indemnification by allowing him stock worth half of the amount of his expenditures. As well, although the land Desjardins had been granted was worth less than £200, if the canal were finished the grant might fetch between £2,000 and £4,000. Crooks was particularly outraged by the ability of the company to set its own tolls. He suggested, however, that Desjardins "did not himself seek the advantage he has taken of the Public" but was put up to it by others. When in May 1826 Desjardins

Desjardins

tried to interest Crooks in canal shares, Crooks remained unmoved: "None of us about the Head of the Lake will take Stock: If he gets the work done without us good & well, but the Tolls will, nay must, necessarily be so high that we must continue the old channel by which to transport our produce to Markets, this not *too bad* when by judicious management the same advantages given to the Public would have made the Canal for Nothing!!!"

Desjardins tried to meet some of the criticism and rouse support in the Dundas area. In February 1826 he picked up Mackenzie's suggestion to build a canal joining Dundas to Lake Huron, but apparently nothing came of it. The failure to attract the support of merchants such as Crooks probably hastened an outcome which was, already, virtually inevitable. In the contest between Dundas and Hamilton, whichever centre possessed access for large ships would become the commercial emporium at the Head of the Lake. Hamilton obtained the advantage when the Burlington Bay Canal was opened on 1 July 1826. Meanwhile the Desjardins Canal languished. Mackenzie had indicated in early 1826 that navigation through to Dundas was rare; indeed, the canal was so dry in the summer he had been able to walk along it.

Desjardins needed funds desperately and on 25 Aug. 1827 he advertised his house and adjoining two acres for sale. A week later the company called on stockholders to make payments upon issued stock. Peter Desjardins was on a collecting tour when he died in a field at Grimsby while trying to catch and saddle his horse. A coroner's inquest ruled he had "died by the visitation of God." Described by George Gurnett*'s *Gore Gazette* as a "very excellent and public spirited individual" and by Mackenzie's *Colonial Advocate* as a man "generally esteemed" in the Gore District, Desjardins was buried in the churchyard of St Andrew's, the Anglican church in Grimsby. He died intestate. Because his only heirs were living in France and there were claims against his estate by creditors, most notably the Hatt estate, the settlement of his affairs was a complicated matter resolved only by an act of parliament in 1835.

That Desjardins was more than the tool of others is suggested by the effect of his death on the canal: work ceased and was not resumed until June 1830. Original funding had proved inadequate and debentures for £5,000, £7,000, and £5,000 were approved by the legislature in 1832, 1835, and 1837 respectively before the canal was finally opened officially on 16 Aug. 1837, 11 years after the Burlington Bay Canal. By now Hamilton had risen to prominence at the Head of the Lake, and the old dreams that had inspired the Desjardins Canal were in tatters. In 1839 the president of the company mentioned the many complaints from those interested in trade that lake shipping could not navigate the canal and thus imports and exports from

Dundas had to be trans-shipped – the very difficulty Desjardins had set out to remedy in 1820! Through the 1840s the canal was used only by scows and small vessels. The coming of the Great Western Railway to Hamilton in the 1850s [*see* Samuel Zimmerman*] buried Dundas's commercial hopes forever, and as for the Desjardins Canal itself, a railway bridge built over it in 1854 made it impossible for lake vessels to enter the marsh. By the late 19th century the canal had fallen into utter disuse. What historian John Charles Weaver has called Desjardins's folly became for most of the 20th century Dundas's revenge, an outlet for pollution into Hamilton Harbour.

ROBERT LOCHIEL FRASER

The AD, Somme (Amiens), has no record of the baptismal date of Peter Desjardins. The parish records of Nesle were destroyed during World War I.

AO, Hist. plaque descriptions, "The Desjardins canal," 28 Aug. 1967; MS 88, Desjardins to St George, 2 July 1808; MS 94, Richard Cockrell to Norton, 22 Oct. 1819; MS 516: 53–56, 101–2, 107, 342–45, 424–27; MU 1857, no.2305; MU 1860, no.2483; MU 2099, 1792, no.4; MU 2104, 1826, no.2; RG 1, A-I-6: 21738–40, 22176–78; vol.25, no.9; RG 22, ser.131, 1: f.106; ser.155. Dundas Hist. Soc. Museum (Dundas, Ont.), Richard Hatt folder, Richard Hatt to M. Hatt, 30 June 1808; W. L. Mackenzie folder, Mackenzie to Desjardins, 22 May 1822. Niagara Hist. Soc. Museum (Niagara-on-the-Lake, Ont.), F-I-10, I: 40 (mfm. at AO). PAC, RG 1, E3, 21: 2–4, 26–27, 75–88; L3, 105: C13/162; 150: D2/32; 155: D12/171, 173–74; 157: D14/138; RG 19, E5(a), 3747, claim 503. U.C., House of Assembly, *Journal*, 1825–26: 62, 77, 85; *The statutes of Upper Canada, to the time of the union* (2v., Toronto, [1843]), 2: 182–90, 1013–14. *Colonial Advocate*, 22, 29 Dec. 1825; 5 Jan. 1826; 13 Sept. 1827. *Gore Gazette, and Ancaster, Hamilton, Dundas and Flamborough Advertiser* (Ancaster, [Ont.]), 25 Aug., 1, 8 Sept. 1827. *Dictionary of Hamilton biography* (1v. to date, Hamilton, Ont., 1981–), biogs. of Peter Desjardins, James Durand, and Richard Hatt. Charles Durand, *Reminiscences of Charles Durand of Toronto, barrister* (Toronto, 1897), 73. R. L. Fraser, "Like Eden in her summer dress: gentry, economy, and society: Upper Canada, 1812–1840" (PHD thesis, Univ. of Toronto, 1979). *The history of the town of Dundas*, comp. T. H. Woodhouse (3v., [Dundas], 1965–68), 1: 31, 34, 41; 2: 35.

DESJARDINS, PHILIPPE-JEAN-LOUIS, Roman Catholic priest and vicar general; b. 6 June 1753 in Messas, France, son of Jacques Desjardins de Lapérière, a merchant, and Marie-Anne Baudet; d. 21 Oct. 1833 in Paris.

Philippe-Jean-Louis Desjardins did his classical studies at the Petit Séminaire de Meung-sur-Loire and quickly displayed remarkable intellectual ability. After receiving the tonsure at Orléans in 1772 he passed the entrance examinations to the Séminaire de Saint-Sulpice in Paris. For the next five years he devoted himself to study and devotional exercises. Having obtained his *baccalauréat* in philosophy in 1777, he finished his theology at the Séminaire Saint-Irénée in Lyons, where he was ordained priest on 20 December. He immediately became a canon at Bayeux. Four years later he was back in Paris to pursue studies for the licentiate and the doctorate, which he completed in 1783. Desjardins was already dedicating part of his income to the education in Paris of his younger brother Louis-Joseph Desjardins*, *dit* Desplantes. In 1788 Philippe-Jean-Louis was named dean of the chapter of Meung-sur-Loire and vicar general of Orléans. Then came the revolution and with it the Civil Constitution of the Clergy, which did away with ecclesiastical titles and benefices. Desjardins first withdrew to his parents' home in Messas and then went to Bayeux with Louis-Joseph, who had become a priest. At the time of the upheaval of August 1792 the Desjardins brothers did not want to get their hosts into trouble and decided to emigrate. In London Philippe-Jean-Louis met Jean-François de La Marche, the bishop of Saint-Pol-de-Léon, who happened to be engaged in recruiting priests for the Canadas.

The Canadian church had not been able to call upon French clergy since the conquest. With the arrival in England of some 8,000 priests fleeing the revolution, the situation changed and the door to the Canadas was opened [*see* Jean-François Hubert*]. Bishop de La Marche named Desjardins head of a mission to study the conditions for settling French priests, and possibly even *émigrés* generally, in Upper and Lower Canada. On 2 March 1793 Desjardins reached Quebec, via New York, with François-Josué de La Corne, Abbé Pierre Gazel, and Abbé Jean-André Raimbault. In order to prepare the way for some hundreds of his compatriots who were to go to Upper Canada, he got in touch with Lieutenant Governor John Graves Simcoe*, whom he met in July; this plan, however, met with little success.

More than 50 priests came to settle in Lower Canada, swelling the ranks of the Canadian clergy by a third. They ministered as curates or parish priests in 50 parishes, founded or taught in three classical colleges, and served as chaplains in the women's communities as well as in the missions in the east and west of Quebec diocese. The *émigré* priests, who were endowed with a superior education and exceptional intellectual and moral qualities, constituted for 60 years one of the most important pillars of French culture among the Canadians. These "confessors of the faith," as they were then known, more or less re-established the Canadian Catholic church, and it was revolutionary France that gave it this second wind!

Bishop Hubert sensibly kept Desjardins with him as an adviser; in September 1794 he appointed him vicar general, as well as chaplain to the nuns of the Hôtel-Dieu in Quebec and later to the Ursulines.

Desjardins lived at the Séminaire de Québec and from time to time taught theology at the Grand Séminaire. Responsibility for the congreganists of Notre-Dame parish was entrusted to him. He was often invited to preach retreats and sermons. The bishop of Quebec took him along on his pastoral visit to Acadia in 1795. His broad culture, his ease in conversation, and the warmth of his greeting made him well liked. Everyone wanted to have him to dinner, and high society sought him out. As he wrote to a friend who had remained in England, "All the eminent people anticipate our desires, render us homage, treat us as public figures." He was entertained at dinner by Prince Edward* Augustus, the old Canadian nobility of Rue des Remparts, and the good merchant families of Rue Buade and Rue de la Fabrique. With the Treaty of Amiens in 1802 he had to resign himself to returning to France, apparently because of serious health problems. Sir Robert Shore Milnes*, who feared the French like the plague, never forgave him for leaving and did not want to admit any more French priests. In all other quarters this man of rare distinction in manners and intellect left nothing but regrets behind him.

On returning to France Desjardins went to serve as parish priest at Meung-sur-Loire, and then as vicar general of Orléans; he soon came back to Paris as secretary to the papal legation, taking up residence at the Séminaire des Missions Étrangères. His smiling diplomacy enabled him to maintain harmony in his entourage, yet at the same time he had difficulty in refusing requests. Consequently in 1810 he wrote to Edward Augustus on behalf of an adventurer, and Napoleon's police intercepted the letter. Desjardins was arrested, tried, sentenced, and imprisoned, finally being put under house arrest in Italy, an exile that lasted nearly five years.

The restoration of the Bourbon monarchy brought Desjardins back to Paris and to various ministries and functions there. Until 1819 he was the priest in charge of the parish of the Missions Étrangères and at the same time he worked on the plan for a concordat with Rome. Then he busied himself with the Maison Saint-Michel, which had been founded for former women prisoners convicted under ordinary law who wanted to enter a religious order. The Comte de Frayssinous made him superior in the Paris convent of the Société du Sacré-Cœur de Jésus. Archdeacon of Sainte-Geneviève, and vicar general of Paris from 1819, Desjardins accompanied Bishop Hyacinthe-Louis de Quélen to Rome in 1825, advising him in his administrative and pastoral tasks. As a monarchist he was a friend of Abbé Charles-Dominique Nicolle, another vicar general. Having been spiritual director of the Ursulines of Quebec, he played the same role with the Duchesse de Berry after the duke's assassination, without neglecting his other duties to the two women's communities that he directed.

Despard

In spite of all his preoccupations Desjardins did not forget his family or his Canadian friends, as his correspondence with Bishop Joseph-Octave PLESSIS, his brother Louis-Joseph, Jean Raimbault*, Antoine-Bernardin ROBERT, and the Ursulines of Quebec abundantly demonstrates. He warmly welcomed Canadian bishops, priests, doctors, and merchants who came to Paris, and he endeavoured to lend them his assistance. For example, on several occasions he sent back books, engravings, and even minerals for Jérôme Demers*'s physics laboratory. He remained extremely grateful to those who had welcomed him and his *émigré* compatriots so generously. The better to prove it, he bought a collection of pictures, which has borne his name ever since, from a ruined Parisian banker who had himself purchased them from the state. These paintings by masters came from churches in Paris that had been pillaged during the revolution. Wishing to furnish the *objets d'art* so noticeably absent in Canadian churches, Desjardins sent out nearly 200 paintings, which arrived at Quebec in 1817.

The 1830 revolution forced Desjardins to go into hiding in the Maison Saint-Michel, and he lost a good many of his personal possessions when the archbishop's palace was sacked in 1831. That year he had a seizure that paralysed him permanently and on 21 Oct. 1833 he died of a stroke. A service was held at the Maison Saint-Michel, and a second one was celebrated at Notre-Dame, in the presence of the *chargé d'affaires* of the Holy See, a large number of bishops, and priests from parishes in the capital.

CLAUDE GALARNEAU

AAQ, 1 CB, VI: 131–71. AD, Loiret (Orléans), État civil, Messas, 9 juin 1753; Paris, État civil, Paris, 21 oct. 1833. Arch. du monastère des ursulines (Québec), Corr., 1815–33. Arch. du séminaire de Nicolet (Nicolet, Qué.), AO, Polygraphie, II: 64, 80; III: 21, 36; Séminaire, III, nos.40, 43, 54, 56; IV, no.25. ASQ, Lettres, T, 56, 56c. PAC, MG 11, [CO 42] Q, 93: 45; MG 23, GIV, 7. *La Minerve*, 13 févr. 1834. Allaire, *Dictionnaire*, 1: 164–65. [Catherine Burke, dite de Saint-Thomas], *Les ursulines de Québec, depuis leur établissement jusqu'à nos jours* (4v., Québec, 1863–66), 4. Dionne, *Les ecclésiastiques et les royalistes français*. Galarneau, *La France devant l'opinion canadienne (1760–1815)*. Lambert, "Joseph-Octave Plessis." Jacqueline Lefebvre, *L'abbé Philippe Desjardins, un grand ami du Canada, 1753–1833* (Québec, 1982). Jean Leflon, *Monsieur Emery* (2v., Paris, 1945–46). Gérard Morisset, *La peinture traditionnelle au Canada français* (Ottawa, 1960). J.-B.-A. Ferland, "L'abbé Philippe-Jean-Louis Desjardins," *BRH*, 5 (1899): 344–46. M. G. Hutt, "Abbé P.-J.-L. Desjardins and the scheme for the settlement of French priests in Canada, 1792–1802," *CHR*, 39 (1958): 93–124. "Les tableaux de M. l'abbé Desjardins," *BRH*, 6 (1900): 56–57.

DESPARD, JOHN, army officer and colonial administrator; b. 1745 in Ireland, fifth son of William Despard; m. Harriet Anne Hesketh, and they had one daughter; d. 3 Sept. 1829 at Swan Hill, Oswestry, England.

John Despard began his military career on 21 April 1760, when at the age of 15 he became an ensign in the 12th Foot. The following year he saw action in Germany at the battle of Vellinghausen, and on 12 May 1762 he purchased a lieutenancy. Placed on half pay at the peace in 1763, he exchanged into the 7th Foot on 1 Sept. 1768 and in 1773 came with the regiment to the province of Quebec. Returning to England in 1774 to recruit, he arrived back in Quebec in May 1775, and that November was part of the force in Fort St Johns (Saint-Jean-sur-Richelieu) that surrendered to Richard Montgomery*'s troops. After a prisoner exchange in December 1776, he was immediately sent to New York. On 25 March 1777 he was promoted captain-lieutenant, on 7 October captain, and he was at the capture of Fort Montgomery, N.Y., in the latter month. In May 1778 he was appointed major of the Volunteers of Ireland, a loyalist unit, and in December 1779 he sailed to South Carolina as deputy adjutant general of the army sent there. Present at the surrender of Charleston, S.C., in May 1780, he continued fighting under Lord Cornwallis in North and South Carolina and in Virginia until the British surrender at Yorktown, Va, in October 1781. He distinguished himself throughout this phase of his career, serving in 24 engagements and having two horses shot from under him.

On 13 June 1789 Despard was promoted major of the 7th, and on 13 July 1791 lieutenant-colonel. Joining the regiment at Quebec in 1793, he was ordered the following year by Prince Edward* Augustus, commander of the forces in the Maritime provinces and colonel of the 7th, to supervise recruitment for the regiment in England, a task he completed successfully. Despard returned to serve under the prince at Halifax in 1795, and on 21 June of the same year he was promoted colonel in the army. Edward Augustus seems to have developed great trust in Despard's abilities, and his promotions continued; in 1799 he was appointed, as a major-general (from 21 June 1798), to the military command of Dorset. His time in this position was brief, for while there he was approached by Edward Augustus, now Duke of Kent, and George III and offered the post of military commander (and therefore civil administrator) of the colony of Cape Breton. Despard accepted and in August 1799 was named to the staff of Nova Scotia.

Despard's first problem related to his appointment. The incumbent, Brigadier-General John MURRAY, was loath to resign the civil command, and when Despard arrived in Halifax in May 1800 he was advised by Lieutenant Governor Sir John Wentworth* of Nova Scotia that his commission entitled him to the military command only. Despard went to Sydney on 16 June and at first made no move to supplant Murray as administrator, but by August he had decided to challenge him and was demanding that Murray hand over the government. In September, Wentworth changed his views and informed Despard that as military commander he was *ex officio* civil administrator. This opinion prompted Despard to move. On 17 September he called a meeting of the colony's Executive Council to have himself proclaimed administrator, and simultaneously had the local militia assembled. Sydney was in a high state of excitement as both factions collected support, and a mob favourable to Murray gathered; violence was avoided only by the presence of the militia. Despard's show of force broke the resistance of Murray and his supporters on the council, headed by the Reverend Ranna Cossit*. They failed to attend the meeting and were eclipsed by Despard's adherents, led by Archibald Charles DODD.

With a hold on the reins of government and a supportive council, Despard moved to improve the colony's economy. In November 1801 he leased the coal mines to the acting attorney general, William CAMPBELL, but when he became dissatisfied with his work assumed control in the name of the crown in February 1804, appointing John Corbett Ritchie, a Halifax merchant, as superintendent. Under Ritchie's guidance the level of the mines was extended, a new pit was completed, and the wharf at the mines strengthened and lengthened to deeper water for the easier loading of large ships. These improvements greatly expanded coal production, which increased by almost 2,000 chaldrons from 1805 to 1807, and Sydney was now able to supply Halifax and Newfoundland with adequate amounts of coal.

At the beginning of Despard's term, however, the colony was in a tight financial situation, since a house of assembly did not exist and revenues could not therefore be raised. On the other hand, Despard reckoned that 10,000 gallons of rum were being imported each year; a tax of 1s. 3d. per gallon would result in over £600 of government income annually, which could lead to much-needed public improvements, in particular roads. Thus in December 1800 he presented the idea to the council, which agreed that such a tax could be imposed by local ordinance. The proposal was meanwhile submitted to the Treasury, and by convincing it that British taxpayers would have to bear the costs of improvements if the tax were disallowed Despard received approval in July 1801, although the measure was recognized as illegal.

At the same time, Despard addressed the land question. By forbidding grants after 1790 the British government had driven away potential settlers, while others had simply squatted, depriving the colony of revenue. Despard discovered that a great deal of land which had previously been granted to loyalists by Lieutenant Governor Joseph Frederick Wallet DES-BARRES, particularly 100,000 acres around the Mira River, had been either abandoned or never taken up. With the approval of the British government, in December 1801 he organized a court of escheat to seize such properties. In this way large quantities of land were made available for sale or lease.

The combination of a quiet political environment, local revenues, and available land could not have existed at a better time, since in early August 1801 the first boatload of Scots sailing directly to Cape Breton arrived in Sydney with 415 passengers. This influx began the great tide that was to transform Cape Breton into Canada's strongest Scottish enclave. Anxious for settlers, Despard offered them land and financial assistance. This quick action and successful land and financial policies were doubtless important factors in the continuing flow of Scottish settlers to Cape Breton. In five years the colony's population increased from 2,500 to nearly 5,000 and new settlements sprang up all along the coasts. In July 1803 approval was given for the construction of a new market-house in Sydney to accommodate the increasing amounts of local produce, new grist-mills appeared in several locations, and between 1801 and 1805 the number of vessels built in the colony increased by one-quarter, from 217 to 267.

As the population and economy began to change, the political situation followed suit, with the former self-seeking factionalism beginning to transform itself along ideological lines. This development was due to Richard Collier Bernard DesBarres Marshall Gibbons, son of the colony's former chief justice. He balked at the rum tax and by 1805 was calling for a house of assembly so that revenue could be legally collected. Gibbons became the spokesman for what had been Cossit's group, and at first was opposed by Dodd, now senior councillor, who felt that the colony was still too small to support the expense of an assembly. Despard himself showed little reaction to Gibbons's plans, concerned as he was with the material well-being of the colony, and probably banked on Gibbons's personal unpopularity to quell the movement, which had already been blunted by economic prosperity.

Gibbons continued to call for an assembly, and when Dodd was appointed chief justice in 1806 he too began to have qualms about the legality of the rum tax. As Dodd and Gibbons grew closer together, Despard decided to leave. Not only the political situation, but also his own health, and probably family matters in the wake of his brother's execution for treason in 1803, contributed to his decision to depart in July 1807.

The rest of Despard's life was spent in England in semi-retirement. Promotions came regularly: on 25 June 1808 he was appointed colonel of the 12th Royal Veteran Battalion, on 29 Dec. 1809 colonel of the 5th

Desrivières

West India Regiment, and on 4 June 1814 a general. The eventual cause of his death was "ulcerated intestines," a problem he had had while in Cape Breton.

To govern Cape Breton demanded patience, imagination, sympathy, and business and administrative abilities, qualities not usually associated with military men. John Despard displayed all these traits, which with his "mild and chearful . . . disposition" made him popular with British officials and the most able and successful of the island's colonial administrators.

R. J. MORGAN

PAC, MG 11, [CO 217] Nova Scotia A, 131. PANS, MG 1, 262B; RG 1, 53. PRO, CO 217/117–25. *Gentleman's Magazine*, July–December 1829: 369–70. *DNB. The royal military calendar, containing the service of every general officer in the British army, from the date of their first commission . . .* , ed. John Philippart (3v., London, 1815–[16]), 1: 129–30. R. J. Morgan, "Orphan outpost"; "Sydney's debt to John Despard: administrator of Cape Breton, 1800–1807," *Essays in Cape Breton history*, ed. B. D. Tennyson (Windsor, N.S., 1973), 24–34.

DESRIVIÈRES (Trottier Desrivières), FRANÇOIS (François-Amable, Francis) (baptized **Amable-François**), businessman, militia officer, office holder, and JP; b. 5 Oct. 1764 in Montreal, son of Amable Trottier Desrivières and Charlotte Guillimin; m. there 19 Sept. 1791 Marguerite-Thérèse Trottier Desrivières Beaubien, and they had two sons and two daughters; d. there 16 March 1830.

François Desrivières's father was a fur trader; he died in 1771, leaving his widow with two small boys. François's mother was a daughter of Guillaume Guillimin*, a successful lawyer. When François was 12 years old, Charlotte married the rising Scottish merchant James McGill*, and François later entered McGill's firm, Todd and McGill. About 1792 he became a partner in Todd, McGill and Company, which on the retirement of Isaac Todd* in 1797 became James and Andrew McGill and Company. By 1808 Desrivières was a property owner on Mont Royal, along with such prominent businessmen as McGill, Todd, Joseph Frobisher*, William McGILLIVRAY, and Pierre Foretier*. On 10 April 1810, following the dissolution of James and Andrew McGill and Company, Desrivières, Thomas Blackwood* (another partner in the McGill company), and Peter Harkness founded Desrivières, Blackwood and Company to continue the activities of the dissolved firm, including the fur trade in the southwest. Harkness retired in 1818 but the firm would continue operations until 1828 at least.

As his fortunes in business rose, Desrivières accumulated a number of government commissions, more valuable for the prestige they conferred than for any income they may have produced. An ensign in the British Militia of the Town and Banlieu of Montreal by 1790, he progressed through the ranks to become major in Montreal's first Militia Battalion on 26 March 1814. He was also justice of the peace from 1800, warden of Trinity House in Montreal from 1805, commissioner to administer oaths to officers of government in 1807, and commissioner for the relief of the insane and foundlings from 1813.

In December 1818 Desrivières joined 13 other prominent Montreal businessmen, including McGillivray, David DAVID, and John Forsyth*, in petitioning the Lower Canadian legislature for a bill authorizing them to dig a canal from Sainte-Marie current on the St Lawrence to Lachine. The scheme was audacious, inaugurating transportation as a new – and expensive – field of enterprise, and Desrivières's participation in it indicates that he was in the forefront of the Montreal business community. On 26 July 1819 the shareholders of the Company of Proprietors of the Lachine Canal met to choose eight members to act as a management committee; Desrivières, who held 25 shares, was among those elected. Thereafter the company's operations were conducted almost exclusively by the committee, chaired by John RICHARDSON, but the firm soon ran into financial difficulty. In January 1821 Desrivières, Richardson, and Thomas Gillespie petitioned the assembly for additional legislative and financial support (the government had already purchased shares worth £10,000). The assembly refused, and in May the company's assets were transferred to the province, which appointed ten commissioners, among them Desrivières, to oversee the project; construction began shortly thereafter. The firm's difficulties may have affected Desrivières's financial situation, for in August 1820 the sheriff of Montreal, on a court order obtained by Benjamin Beaubien, had seized property he possessed at Coteau-Saint-Louis for non-payment of debt.

In this period of possible financial strain, Desrivières engaged in a celebrated legal dispute in order to retain valuable property in his possession. In 1811 he and his nephew James McGill Desrivières had been named residuary legatees of James McGill's immense estate. Following McGill's death in 1813 François Desrivières had inherited £23,000 and extensive lands in Stanbridge Township. As residuary legatee, however, he stood to inherit yet more. McGill had left an estate called Burnside and an endowment of £10,000 to the Royal Institution for the Advancement of Learning for the establishment of a university, one college of which was to bear his name. Provisos were, first, that Mrs McGill and, after her, her son François would enjoy the usufruct of Burnside until the Royal Institution was ready to erect the college; secondly, that until the college was erected the endowment would be held by trustees; and, thirdly, that if the college were not erected by the tenth anniversary of McGill's death, Burnside and the endowment would revert to McGill's heirs, that is, to Desrivières and his nephew. Though in 1801 an act of the legislature had authorized a board of directors of the Royal Institution to administer public education in the colony, the board had still not been established at the time of McGill's death, and its members were not named until 1818 [see Joseph Langley MILLS]. In 1820 it was in a position to call upon the Desrivières to surrender the estate. This, however, they refused to do on the grounds that the Royal Institution had no funds with which to build a college and the government had given no undertaking to do so.

In 1820–21 the Royal Institution launched two suits against the Desrivières, one to obtain possession of Burnside and the other to receive the endowment. In 1821 it received a royal charter for McGill College and in court contended that as a result the college was "erected" in law, in fulfilment of the requirements of McGill's will. The legal battle was between a strict interpretation of the language of the bequest and a broader one apparently more consonant with the public interest. To demonstrate the strength of their case on the strictly legal interpretation of the bequest the Desrivières engaged as their senior counsel James Stuart*, who had written the will for McGill. In any case, Desrivières, as a Canadian and a convinced Roman Catholic – he was a churchwarden of Notre-Dame and in 1818 had been charged by Bishop Joseph-Octave PLESSIS with collecting donations for a mission in the Red River colony – did not have his stepfather's dedication to an English-language university as an object of public interest. Bishop Plessis was at the time boycotting the Royal Institution as not proper to administer the education of Roman Catholics. Since at least 1814 that body's monopoly of public education had been contested by the Canadian party as well, on the ground that it favoured the British population, and it was probably not a coincidence that the Desrivières also retained Louis-Joseph Papineau*, a leader of the Canadian party, as their attorney for a time.

The case was conducted in a period of considerable agitation over the possible union of Lower and Upper Canada, a plan opposed by both the Canadian party and Plessis, but strongly supported by the British commercial community of Montreal [see John Richardson]. The senior counsel for the Royal Institution, Stephen SEWELL, was himself an ardent unionist and prominent member of the English party. Although Desrivières was much too closely involved with the British merchants to support the Canadian party generally, he was sufficiently independent of them to oppose actively their cherished project of union, and in 1822 at a popular meeting in Montreal he was elected to an 18-man committee to find ways of defeating it. Given his attachment to certain Canadian and Roman Catholic causes, he was not widely condemned for maintaining an anti-social position in fighting the Royal Institution, even though personal considerations, including possible financial difficulties, were the primary factors guiding him in the litigation. Indeed, he continued to have excellent relations with the British community in Montreal: in 1821 he was promoted lieutenant-colonel in the 1st Battalion of Montreal militia, a unit dominated by the British élite; the same year he was elected by the Montreal business community to an 11-man committee to petition for the unrestricted opening of the British market to British North American flour and grain; and from 1824 to 1830 he was a governor of the Montreal General Hospital.

The Desrivières lost both suits in Montreal and then again on appeal in the colony. Subsequently they appealed to the Privy Council in England. The case relating to Burnside was finally settled in favour of the Royal Institution in 1828, while a decision in that relating to the endowment, also in favour of the Royal Institution, was delivered only in 1835. François Desrivières never learned of his last defeat; he had died five years earlier.

STANLEY B. FROST

ANQ-M, CE1-51, 5 oct. 1764, 19 sept. 1791, 18 mars 1830. McGill Univ. Arch., James and Andrew McGill journal, 1798–1813; Montreal General Hospital visiting governors' book, 1822–28; Alan Ridge, "Genealogy of Desrivières family, from 1764 to 20th century" (1966); Royal Instit. for the Advancement of Learning, papers relating to Desrivières V.R.I.A.L., 1820–37; Will of James McGill. McGill Univ. Libraries, ms coll., CH143.S13, CH145.S15. PAC, MG 30, D1, 10: 766–69; RG 43, CIII, 1, vol.2453; RG 68, General index, 1651–1841: 213, 215, 278, 282, 339, 349, 353, 633. Quebec Gazette, 19 July 1792; 25 July 1799; 16 May 1805; 23 April 1807; 6 July 1809; 3 May, 12 July 1810; 2 Sept. 1813; 28 March 1816; 23 Oct. 1817; 19 Jan., 24 Sept., 7 Dec. 1818; 7 June, 5 Aug. 1819; 25 May, 18 June, 10 Aug., 7 Sept., 12 Oct., 23 Nov. 1820; 24 May, 5, 28 June, 27 Aug., 23, 25 Oct. 1821; 13 Jan., 30 June 1823. Caron, "Inv. de la corr. de Mgr Hubert et de Mgr Bailly de Messein," ANQ Rapport, 1930–31: 250; "Inv. de la corr. de Mgr Plessis," 1928–29: 114. Massicotte, "Répertoire des engagements pour l'Ouest," ANQ Rapport, 1945–46: 315–16, 325. Quebec almanac, 1791: 45; 1796: 83; 1805: 46; 1815: 90. Thomas Chapais, Cours d'histoire du Canada (8v., Québec et Montréal, 1919–34; réimpr. Trois-Rivières, Qué., 1972), 3: 122. S. B. Frost, McGill University: for the advancement of learning (2v., Montreal, 1980–84). M. S. MacSporran, "James McGill: a critical biographical study" (MA thesis, McGill Univ., [1930]). G. J. J. Tulchinsky, "The construction of the first Lachine Canal, 1815–1826" (MA thesis, McGill Univ., 1960), 39, 48, 65. F.-J. Audet, "Montréal, l'université McGill et F.-A. Trottier Desrivières," La Presse, 9 sept. 1933: 26. J.-J. Lefebvre, "La vie sociale du grand Papineau," RHAF, 11 (1957–58): 479.

Desroches

DESROCHES, CHARLES, schoolteacher; b. in France, son of Charles Desroches and Anne Delestrade; fl. 1816–26.

Charles Desroches was educated in Paris and went to England at the time of the French revolution. He continued his studies there and joined the Royal Navy as an officer, serving for eight years. Perhaps it was in this capacity that he came to Lower Canada. He is believed to have been engaged in teaching at Pointe-aux-Trembles (Neuville) early in 1810. On 7 Oct. 1816 he married Nathalie Marcotte at Cap-Santé, and they were to have seven children.

At the outset of the 19th century Sainte-Famille at Cap-Santé was a flourishing parish. Covering a large area, it took in several villages, one of which was Portneuf. In 1816, 60 of the inhabitants of that village signed a petition requesting the opening of a Royal School there. Desroches was appointed the teacher in May 1817. According to regulations laid down by the three trustees responsible for the school and by Desroches himself, parents had to pay two shillings monthly for each child, in addition to supplying firewood. The school was open from Monday to Friday, winter and summer, from nine till noon and from one to four. The teacher had his holidays from 15 August to 15 September. Twice a year he was absent for three days in order to go to Quebec and pick up his salary. In 1817 Desroches was making £50 a year, but from 1819 he received no more than £45.

Reading, grammar, and arithmetic were the three main subjects taught at the school in Portneuf. Desroches enjoyed great freedom as a teacher. The method he used was the monitorial system developed by Joseph Lancaster* which was very popular at the time. The pupils were divided into sections, with one of their number who was more advanced as instructor. The Royal Institution for the Advancement of Learning left a great deal of latitude in the choice of books, and Desroches used everything he could lay his hands on. Taking his student body into account, he had to teach in English and French and give courses in religion for Catholics and for Protestants.

Although in historian Louis-Philippe Audet's view Desroches was one of the most dynamic schoolteachers of the period, the number of pupils attending his school decreased steadily, from 32 in 1820 to 16 in March 1822, and then to 14 in September. Therefore in October 1822 the trustees of Portneuf and Cap-Santé suggested that Desroches be transferred to Cap-Santé as a replacement for Charles Harper*, who had resigned from his post in April. Desroches expressed some interest, and apparently the parish priest of Cap-Santé, Félix Gatien*, consented to the arrangement. The governor gave his approval for the transfer; on 15 November the school at Portneuf closed.

Desroches began teaching at Cap-Santé in January

1823. At that time the school had 34 pupils. The trustees expressed their satisfaction, even though they regretted that Desroches could not teach the same subjects as Harper. One of them, George Waters Allsopp*, asked the secretary of the Royal Institution, Joseph Langley MILLS, for permission to hire an assistant to teach Latin, mathematics, and bookkeeping. In September the number of pupils rose to 48. In March 1824, 42 were attending Desroches's school; they were divided into five classes, with 9 pupils learning English and 33 French.

It became evident by 1825 that the problem which had occasioned the closing of the school at Portneuf was recurring. The number enrolled dropped to 25. Desroches, who was afraid of being blamed, wrote to Mills that he was doing his best but that as soon as the children could read their prayers, the parents took them out of school. He complained of Father Gatien's negative attitude and, fearing for his post, he reminded Mills that he had a family to support. Mills replied that he was not considering closing the school but that the parents should be made aware of this possibility. In March 1826 there were only 19 boys at the school, and Desroches, who had been very ill, was deeply discouraged. He asked for a transfer, and the Royal Institution agreed.

In November 1826 Charles Desroches went to Quebec to collect his salary. He did not return to Cap-Santé. He reportedly was seen in Montreal and New York, where he is thought to have tried to board a ship for England. His wife and seven children, the youngest of whom was barely six months old, were left in dire straits.

YVES FRENETTE

ANQ-Q, CC1, 11 mars 1829; CE1-8, 7 oct. 1816; CN1-28, 5 oct. 1816; 26 janv. 1818; 7 nov. 1825; 1er févr., 25 avril 1828; 1er juin 1829; CN1-157, 9 mars 1813. McGill Univ. Arch., Royal Instit. for the Advancement of Learning, letter-books, 1820–27. Private arch., Yves Frenette (Orono, Maine), Notes d'entrevue avec François Desroches, descendant de Charles Desroches et de Nathalie Marcotte, 29 juin 1982. L.-P. Audet, *Histoire de l'enseignement au Québec* (2v., Montréal et Toronto, 1971); *Le système scolaire*. Boulianne, "Royal Instit. for the Advancement of Learning." Félix Gatien *et al.*, *Histoire du Cap-Santé* (Québec, 1955). L.-P. Audet, "Deux écoles royales, 1814–36: Sainte-Marie de la Nouvelle-Beauce et Cap-Santé," RSC *Trans.*, 3rd ser., 50 (1956), sect.I: 7–24. R.-G. Boulianne, "The French Canadians and the schools of the Royal Institution for the Advancement of Learning, 1820–1829," *SH*, 5 (1972): 144–64.

DESSAULLES, JEAN, seigneurial agent, militia officer, seigneur, and politician; b. 1766 in Saint-François-du-Lac, Que., son of Jean-Pierre De Saulles and Marguerite Crevier Décheneaux; d. 20 June 1835 in Saint-Hyacinthe, Lower Canada.

Having "made up his mind to go to foreign lands," Jean Dessaulles's father obtained from the community of Fenin in Switzerland on 18 Dec. 1759 a letter certifying his place of birth and good character. According to family tradition, he was then a soldier and a Huguenot. He settled in the province of Quebec at the time of the conquest and became a merchant. His son Jean studied with the Sulpicians at the Collège Saint-Raphaël in Montreal from 1779 till 1781.

Around 1780 the Dessaulles removed to the seigneury of Saint-Hyacinthe, which was being managed by Marie-Anne Crevier Décheneaux, a sister of Mme De Saulles and widow of Jacques-Hyacinthe Simon, *dit* Delorme. Jean seems to have regarded his aunt as a second mother, even though his parents were still living. In adulthood he worked for her, possibly in charge of the sawmill, and certainly as a seigneurial agent for the years 1796–98. Until then Mme Delorme had turned for help to the parish priest of Saint-Mathieu, at Belœil, François-Xavier Noiseux, who from 1777 till 1783 also ministered to Saint-Hyacinthe.

Dessaulles bought a piece of land in 1795 and the following year obtained the grant of a lot in the village from Mme Delorme. On 7 Jan. 1799, at the church in Saint-Hyacinthe, he married Marguerite-Anne Waddens, daughter of the late Jean-Étienne Waddens*. In little more than two years he lost three children, and then in 1801 his wife as well.

Mme Delorme also died that year. As it turned out, her son Hyacinthe-Marie Delorme retained five-eighths of the seigneury, and three-eighths went to Pierre-Dominique Debartzch*, a grandson of Jacques-Hyacinthe Simon, *dit* Delorme, by a previous marriage. Dessaulles continued to act as seigneurial agent for his cousin Delorme, who was elected to the assembly for Richelieu in 1808. At the beginning of the War of 1812 Dessaulles was serving as major in the Saint-Hyacinthe battalion of militia, and on 26 March 1813 he took command of it, replacing Lieutenant-Colonel Delorme, who was ill. Having a premonition of death, Delorme, who was unmarried, settled his estate in 1814, excluding Debartzch and making Dessaulles the sole legatee and heir to all his rights and claims on the seigneury. Thus, just before he turned 50, Dessaulles came into possession of a large manor-house and numerous seigneurial rights. The sale at auction of his own goods and chattels demonstrated the transition to a new station.

Dessaulles was an active seigneur. He bought, sold, and granted lands. Notarial records show, for example, 200 land grants for the years 1826 and 1827 alone. He busied himself with building a road, a dam, and a sawmill. He surrendered rights on an island to allow the construction of a bridge, and on lots to be the sites of a market and a court-house. He was thoroughly familiar with the problems facing the *censitaires*, his

relations with them were straightforward, and he was regarded as fair-minded.

On 21 Feb. 1816, in Montreal, Dessaulles had married Marie-Rosalie Papineau, daughter of notary Joseph Papineau* and sister of Louis-Joseph*. That year he was elected to the assembly for Richelieu, which had been represented by Delorme and Louis BOURDAGES and which was within the Papineau family's sphere of influence. From 1830 to 1832 he represented Saint-Hyacinthe riding, which had been separated from Richelieu in 1829. Dessaulles did not attract as much attention in the assembly as did his brother-in-law Louis-Joseph or Bourdages, being less well educated and less inclined to speak than they, as well as more moderate. At the manor-house the young Mme Dessaulles was the soul of family and social life and took an interest in seigneurial matters. By 1820 her brother André-Augustin was given responsibility for arrears and land grants. For decades the Papineau and Dessaulles families were closely linked.

At the end of 1831 Dessaulles was invited to sit on the Legislative Council by Governor Lord Aylmer [Whitworth-Aylmer*], who hoped to meet the assembly's criticism of the council by appointing a number of prominent Canadians. Dessaulles intended to retain his freedom to criticize the council's place in the political structure, but he considered it "better that men friendly to the House of Assembly enter the council to effect a desirable reconciliation between the two bodies than to see them constantly embroiled in fights and opposition." He received his appointment early in 1832. Five months later Papineau, who was then leader of the Patriote party in the assembly and who favoured an elective legislative council, wrote Dessaulles a letter, apparently avoiding either congratulations or disapproval, which called upon him to resign his seat in the assembly quickly and to collaborate in finding a "patriotic, energetic, and national" candidate to run for it. Dessaulles's career in the council was in fact undistinguished, as were those of the other French-speaking members, who were absent most of the time during the years 1832–35.

Dessaulles's Huguenot ancestry on his father's side, his contacts with Antoine GIROUARD, the parish priest of Saint-Hyacinthe who founded the local classical college, and his marriage with the pious Marie-Rosalie Papineau lend interest to the matter of his attitude to religion and the clergy's influence. Dessaulles had known Girouard at the Collège Saint-Raphaël. As seigneurial agent he had been involved in the priest's purchase of the lot on which his classical college was to be built. On becoming the seigneur he abstained from exacting the annual payments from the institution. Girouard was godfather to his eldest son, Louis-Antoine*. Parish priest and seigneur worked together when new parishes were being created. In 1829 and 1830 both were chosen as trustees to

Dibblee

promote primary education and the establishment of schools at Saint-Hyacinthe. Whether all this was simply a matter of being good neighbours and having common interests or whether there was more to it can only be conjectured. However, it seems that the warmth in these relations with the clergy came more from the seigneur's wife than from the seigneur himself.

On 20 June 1835, after an illness that had lasted six months, Dessaulles died in the seigneurial manor-house. He was buried in the parish church. His widow lived until 1857. They had had five children, three of whom survived them: Louis-Antoine, who was well known as an influential member of the Parti Rouge and a political foe of the clergy; Rosalie, wife of Maurice Laframboise*, a politician who became a judge; and Georges-Casimir, who was a leading figure in business circles in Saint-Hyacinthe at the end of the 19th century and who became mayor and senator.

Two of Jean Dessaulles's granddaughters made their mark in Quebec letters and the feminist movements. In 1939 Caroline-Angélina*, only daughter of Louis-Antoine, published *Quatre-vingts ans de souvenirs*, a book recalling aspects of feminine activity at the outset of the 20th century. For some 15 years George-Casimir's daughter Henriette*, under the pseudonym Fadette, wrote an interesting literary column in Montreal's *Le Devoir*.

JEAN-PAUL BERNARD

ANQ-M, CE1-51, 21 févr. 1816; CE2-5, 7 janv. 1799, 23 juin 1835. Arch. de la Soc. d'hist. régionale de Saint-Hyacinthe (Saint-Hyacinthe, Qué.), sér.2, dossier 34.7; sér.16, dossier 10. ASSH, Fg-4, A-64; B, dossier 1: 239; dossier 2: 79–80. George Allsopp, "Lettre de George Allsopp à M. Dessaulles, député," *BRH*, 40 (1934): 319–20. F.-J. Audet, "Les législateurs du Bas-Canada." Desjardins, *Guide parl.* Turcotte, *Le Conseil législatif*, 19, 113. Suzanne Bédard, *Histoire de Rougemont* (Montréal, 1978). [C.-A. Dessaulles] Mme F.-L. Béique, *Quatre-vingts ans de souvenirs* (Montréal, [1939]), 120–30. C.-P. Choquette, *Histoire de la ville de Saint-Hyacinthe* (Saint-Hyacinthe, 1930). Henriette Dessaulles, *Fadette: journal d'Henriette Dessaulles, 1874/1880* (Montréal, 1971), 13–17, 285–89. Gérard Filteau, *Histoire des Patriotes* (3v., Montréal, 1938–39), 1: 199–201. Gérard Parizeau, *Les Dessaulles, seigneurs de Saint-Hyacinthe; chronique maskoutaine du XIXᵉ siècle* (Montréal, 1976). Taft Manning, *Revolt of French Canada*. Louise Voyer, *Saint-Hyacinthe: de la seigneurie à la ville québécoise* ([Montréal], 1980).

DIBBLEE, FREDERICK, schoolmaster, Church of England clergyman, and diarist; b. 9 Dec. 1753 in Stamford, Conn., third son of the Reverend Ebenezer Dibblee (Diblee) and Joanna Bates; m. Nancy Beach of Stratford, Conn., and they had seven sons and six daughters; d. 17 May 1826 in Woodstock, N.B.

Having served for some years as a Congregational preacher, Frederick Dibblee's father decided to embrace the Church of England and in 1745 became lay reader to the Anglican congregation in Stamford. After his ordination in England in 1748, he returned to Stamford, where he was to minister for 51 years. At the age of 18 Frederick entered King's College, New York. According to his father, he was "honor'd with a Degree" in May 1776, but the college records indicate that he left without graduating. On his return to Stamford he found it enveloped in the revolutionary struggle.

In 1775–76 the General Assembly of Connecticut passed increasingly harsh measures against tory sympathizers, and in November 1776 a number of loyalists from Stamford, including Frederick, were removed to Lebanon, in the eastern part of the state. In April, after he had been allowed home, Frederick's life was threatened and he fled to Long Island, where his brother Fyler had already taken refuge. There he engaged in trade in company with a Mr Jackson at Oyster Bay. Eventually he "acquired something considerable," in his father's words, and married a fellow refugee. Five times his business was raided by rebels, however, and the damages amounted to £1,200 or more. In November 1782 he and his wife were even stripped of their household goods and best clothes. Dibblee resolved to go to Nova Scotia with his brother Fyler and other loyalists in the spring fleet of 1783. Unable to settle his accounts in time, he was further delayed in moving there by his wife's pregnancy and then by his own illness with "a remitting fever." It was not until the following spring that he was able to leave.

Dibblee drew a lot in Parrtown (Saint John) in what was shortly to become the province of New Brunswick, but he settled in Kingston, where he became lay reader to the Anglican congregation. In 1787 he was sent to Woodstock Parish by the Society for the Propagation of the Gospel in New England and Parts Adjacent in America, commonly called the New England Company, to run a school for Indians. This school was one of a number established by the company, whose aim was to convert the Indians from Roman Catholicism and to teach them both the English language and a trade. His efforts met with moderate success. By 1790 he had built a log schoolhouse 26 feet by 22 feet and on 4 January of that year he had 22 students, adults as well as children. "They are Constant in their Attendance," he wrote, "and exceeding quick in receiving Instruction, five of them in Particular are amazing so, having made great Improvement both in Spelling and Writing." He enjoyed a salary of £30 as well as an allowance for boarding Indian boys and the occasional gratuity from the Society for the Propagation of the Gospel in Foreign Parts. According to Bishop Charles Inglis*, who visited in 1792, he was "much beloved by the Indians and respected by the Whites." By that time he had made some progress in the Indians' language, though reportedly hindered by "a necessary attention to his Farm, in order to subsist his family." Two years later, however, the New England Company decided to centralize its efforts at Sussex Vale (Sussex Corner) in the school under Oliver ARNOLD, and the other schools were closed.

The mainstay of Dibblee's livelihood after 1791 was his work as an Anglican minister. That fall he had travelled to Halifax, where he was ordained a deacon by Bishop Inglis in St Paul's Church, and on 19 August of the following year he was raised to the priesthood by Inglis in Trinity Church, Saint John. He was given the four large parishes of Prince William, Queensbury, Northampton, and Woodstock, the last being his chief station. In 1794 he was taken into the service of the SPG as an "Itinerant Missionary" at an annual salary of £50. He toured his parishes regularly at considerable personal hardship, and in 1820 added to his labours by going to visit the military settlements north of Woodstock, the first clergyman, he said, to do so. He was much respected by his parishioners for his energy and dedication. Despite the financial difficulties of the communities he served, churches were constructed. By 1805 Prince William had a rudimentary building, and in 1811 a church was completed at Woodstock at a cost of £150, though five years later the congregation was still working on its internal and external decoration. One in Queensbury was still not finished in 1820, however, and could be used only in the summer.

Dibblee's interest in education was constant and in his letters to the SPG he frequently requested aid for schools and schoolmasters and asked that books be sent out to them. By 1822 there were in his large district ten of the Madras, or National, schools promoted by Lieutenant Governor George Stracey SMYTH; they averaged about 40 students each. After his death the *New-Brunswick Royal Gazette* made special mention of Dibblee's concern, describing him as "a warm friend to every Institution which promised to be of publick utility, particularly the education of youth, to the furtherance of which most useful and momentous object, his efforts were unremitting and zealous to a degree seldom equalled." In recognition of his services the SPG awarded his widow a pension of £50.

Dibblee's legacy to education would extend far beyond his own pupils. He maintained a series of diaries from 1803 to 1825 which provide historians with a rich commentary on the agricultural and social conditions of the central Saint John River valley during the loyalist era. These diaries are stored in the archives of the New Brunswick Museum in Saint John.

DARREL BUTLER

ACC, Diocese of Fredericton Arch., "Inglis papers, 1787–1842," comp. W. O. Raymond, 99, 148, 150, 179–80 (photocopies at PANB). PANS, RG 1, 369, no.165 (Ebenezer Dibblee to Sir Guy Carleton, 31 Oct. 1783). USPG, Journal of SPG, 25–36, esp. 25: 415–17; 26: 70–71, 74, 215–16, 373–77; 27: 57–58; 29: 127–28; 31: 210–12; 32: 293–95; 33: 54–55; 34: 44–47; 36: 340–43. *Source materials relating to the New Brunswick Indian*, ed. W. D. Hamilton and W. A. Spray (Fredericton, 1976). *Winslow papers* (Raymond). *New-Brunswick Royal Gazette*, 30 May 1826. *Columbia University officers and alumni, 1754–1857*, comp. M. H. Thomas (New York, 1936). F. B. Dexter, *Biographical sketches of the graduates of Yale College, with annals of the college history* (6v., New York and New Haven, Conn., 1885–1912). E. B. Huntington, *History of Stamford, Connecticut . . .* (Stamford, 1868; repr. with corrections, Harrison, N.Y., 1979). G. H. Lee, *An historical sketch of the first fifty years of the Church of England in the province of New Brunswick (1783–1833)* (Saint John, N.B., 1880). K. F. C. MacNaughton, *The development of the theory and practice of education in New Brunswick, 1784–1900: a study in historical background*, ed. A. G. Bailey (Fredericton, 1947). Pascoe, *S.P.G.* W. O. Raymond, "The old Meductic fort," N.B. Hist. Soc., *Coll.*, 1 (1894–97), no.2: 221–72.

DICKSON, ROBERT, fur trader and Indian Department official; b. *c.* 1765 in Dumfries, Scotland, son of John Dickson, a merchant; m. 1797 To-to-win (Helen), and they had four children; d. 20 June 1823 on Drummond Island (Mich.).

Robert Dickson, in an official dispatch of July 1812, was described as "closely connected with the most respectable families" in Upper Canada. His brother William* was at that time a prominent lawyer and land speculator at Newark (Niagara-on-the-Lake); another brother, THOMAS, was a merchant, politician, and, during the War of 1812, militia officer. Robert and his brothers were cousins of Robert Hamilton*, a merchant established in the Niagara peninsula. Some time after the American revolution Robert was employed in the Niagara region by Hamilton's partner, Richard Cartwright*, in selling and shipping goods to the upper fur-trade posts and in managing accounts, especially those of ex-officers of Butler's Rangers, a disbanded loyalist corps. The young immigrant soon tired of this drab, routine life, and was pleased to be sent to Michilimackinac (Mackinac Island, Mich.) in July 1786 "to learn the art and mystery of commerce."

According to the dispatch of 1812 Dickson resided "for a number of years in the character of a mercantile Trader," primarily in the Spanish territory west of the Mississippi, and acquired an extensive knowledge of the distribution and customs of its numerous Indian tribes. In the spring of 1797 he strengthened his association with the Indians through his marriage to To-to-win, the daughter of an influential chief of the Wahpeton branch of the Santee Sioux. Soon afterwards he established a small fur-trading post along the

Dickson

upper St Peter (Minnesota) River at Lake Traverse, a traditional camping ground of the roving Sioux bands, and he gradually became one of the leading traders in an area now comprising southern Minnesota, Iowa, part of Wisconsin, and eastern South Dakota.

In August 1804 he formed a partnership with James Aird* and Allen C. Wilmot of Prairie du Chien (Wis.), which led to the establishment of the short-lived Robert Dickson and Company at Michilimackinac the following year. The firm was composed primarily of Canadian fur traders who hoped to protect their interests in the face of the growing restrictions placed on them by the American government as a result of Jay's Treaty (1794), the heavy customs duties imposed on their British goods, and the increased competition from American traders throughout the area south and west of Michilimackinac. Robert Dickson and Company was unable to overcome these problems and in 1807 it became part of the larger Michilimackinac Company [see John Ogilvy*], organized for similar reasons by some of the major Montreal partnerships. During the winter of 1810–11 Dickson and Aird were trading for the Michilimackinac Company above the Falls of St Anthony (Minneapolis, Minn.). But this company also bowed to increased pressure and in 1811 it was replaced by the South West Fur Company, in which the powerful American Fur Company under John Jacob Astor and the North West Company [see William McGillivray] held equal shares.

British and Canadian fur traders in the northwest such as Dickson became increasingly bitter over American encroachment on their trading territory and by early 1812, with war between Britain and the United States imminent, they were anxious to cooperate with any military plans which might produce British paramountcy in the region. There is no doubt of Dickson's own attachment to the British government. Motivated by these twin factors, he quickly responded to a "Confidential Communication" from Major-General Isaac Brock* which sought information on the loyalty of the Indians of the northwest and requested Dickson's assistance in recruiting "your friends" for the British cause. In his reply of 18 June, the day the United States declared war, Dickson reported that he had gathered about 250 to 300 "friends" whom he would lead immediately to St Joseph Island (Ont.), the nearest British military post.

Indeed, Dickson enjoyed a complete success in raising "His Majesty's Indian Allies." His influence was particularly significant during the first critical months of the war. On 17 July Dickson and John Askin Jr, storekeeper for the Indian Department at St Joseph Island, commanded about 400 Indians in the successful attack led by Captain Charles Roberts* against the American garrison at Michilimackinac. That victory secured for the British the support of the Indians of the Upper Lakes region, and the large number of warriors Dickson rallied to Brock's forces at Detroit played an important role in the capture of the fort and town the following month.

In the autumn of 1812 Dickson travelled to Montreal. There, fur merchants James McGill*, William McGillivray, and John Richardson highly recommended his efforts to Sir George Prevost*, lieutenant-general and governor-in-chief of British North America. As a result, Dickson was appointed agent and superintendent for the Indians of the western nations on 1 Jan. 1813, with a salary of £200 per year plus £300 for travel and expenses, to be paid out of the secret-service fund. He was given a high degree of autonomy, was permitted to hire five officers and fifteen interpreters, and was to report directly to the British military command. In addition, a claim for £1,875 he had incurred in distributing goods to the Indians the previous winter and spring was accepted in full by Prevost, "as compensation for the eminent services which he had rendered to His Majesty's government by his loyalty, zeal and exertions in bringing forward the Indians to aid in the capture of Michilimackinac and Detroit."

For the duration of the war Dickson continued to rally Indians to the British cause. He returned to the northwest early in 1813. That summer he brought about 1,400 Indians to Fort Malden (Amherstburg, Ont.); from this post a second siege of Fort Meigs (near Perrysburg, Ohio), directed by Major-General Henry Procter with the support of Shawnee chief Tecumseh*, was launched. The siege was unsuccessful, as was another – in which Dickson participated – at Fort Stephenson (Fremont, Ohio) at the end of July. He spent the next winter among the Indians trying to regain some of the influence lost after these failures. He served in the successful defence of Michilimackinac in August 1814. In September, under the direction of Miller Worsley, he and 200 Indians participated in the daring capture of the American schooners *Tigress* and *Scorpion*, which had blockaded Mackinac Island. He then travelled to Prairie du Chien, where he spent the winter of 1814–15 organizing support among the Indians of the region. He unfortunately became embroiled in a bitter feud with Andrew H. Bulger*, commandant at Fort McKay, over the distribution of gifts and the feeding of the various Indian bands. Dickson was accused of favouring the Sioux and of attempting to usurp the authority of the British military officers. As a result, he was ordered back to Michilimackinac in March 1815. The case was referred to London, and in a hearing at Quebec he was completely vindicated; he was rewarded for his services with the title of lieutenant-colonel and retired from the Indian Department with a pension.

The War of 1812 had ruined Dickson's fur-trade career. While on a brief visit to Scotland after the war, he applied, unsuccessfully, from Perth in June 1816 for the vacant position of superintendent of the Indian Department at Amherstburg. He subsequently returned to the northwest, where he remained popular with the Indian chiefs and warriors. A burly Scot, of full face, tall and commanding, Dickson had been referred to often in council by Indian spokesmen as the Red Head because of his flaming red hair and beard. In 1816–17 he became involved in a futile plan to provision the Red River colony of Lord Selkirk [Douglas*] with beef. He also worked on Selkirk's behalf to try to persuade Wisconsin settlers to move to Red River; the plan was abandoned when Selkirk died. Dickson continued to travel throughout the northwest, probably as a trader for Astor's American Fur Company. In 1818 he and Aird were trading on the upper Mississippi. He died unexpectedly at Drummond Island on 20 June 1823.

The contribution of Robert Dickson during the War of 1812 is too little known. His efforts in recruiting Indian allies and dispatching the warriors to theatres of active military operations were vital to the successful defence of the Canadas.

ROBERT S. ALLEN

AO, MS 35; MU 2102, 1816, no.11. McCord Museum, War of 1812, folder 6. PAC, MG 19, E5; F29; RG 8, I (C ser.), 1220. QUA, Richard Cartwright papers, letter-books, 1785–1802. Andrew Bulger, "The Bulger papers," Wis., State Hist. Soc., *Coll.*, 13 (1895): 10–153. "Dickson and Grignon papers – 1812–1815," ed. R. G. Thwaites, Wis., State Hist. Soc., *Coll.*, 11 (1888): 271–315. "Lawe and Grignon papers, 1794–1821," ed. L. C. Draper, Wis., State Hist. Soc., *Coll.*, 10 (1888): 90–141. *Select British docs. of War of 1812* (Wood). *DAB*. R. S. Allen, "Robert Dickson and the struggle for the 'old northwest,' 1783–1818" (BA thesis, Mount Allison Univ., Sackville, N.B., 1967). A. R. Gilpin, *The War of 1812 in the old northwest* (Toronto and East Lansing, Mich., 1958). L. A. Tohill, "Robert Dickson: a story of trade, war and diplomacy" (MA thesis, Univ. of Minnesota, Minneapolis, 1927). R. S. Allen, "British Indian Dept.," *Canadian Hist. Sites*, no.14: 5–125; "Canadians on the upper Mississippi: the capture and occupation of Prairie du Chien during the War of 1812," *Military Collector & Historian* (Washington), 31 (1979): 118–23. A. E. Bulger, "Events at Prairie du Chien previous to American occupation, 1814" and "Last days at Prairie du Chien," Wis., State Hist. Soc., *Coll.*, 13 (1895): 1–9 and 154–62. E. A. Cruikshank, "Robert Dickson, the Indian trader," Wis., State Hist. Soc., *Coll.*, 12 (1892): 133–53. Reginald Horsman, "British Indian policy in the northwest, 1807–1812," *Mississippi Valley Hist. Rev.* ([Cedar Rapids, Iowa]), 45 (1958–59): 51–66. G. F. G. Stanley, "British operations in the American north-west, 1812–15," Soc• for Army Hist. Research, *Journal* (London), 22 (1943–44): 91–106. L. A. Tohill, "Robert Dickson, British fur trader on the upper Mississippi," *N.Dak. Hist. Quarterly* (Bismark), 2 (1928): 5–49; 3 (1929): 83–128, 182–203.

DICKSON, THOMAS, merchant, office holder, JP, politician, and militia officer; baptized 19 Feb. 1775 in Dumfries, Scotland, son of John Dickson; m. first 17 Nov. 1799 Eliza Taylor, *née* Wilkinson, and they had one son; m. secondly 20 Sept. 1803 Archange Grant, daughter of Alexander Grant*, and they had two daughters; d. 22 Jan. 1825 in Queenston, Upper Canada.

John Dickson was a successful merchant and provost of Dumfries. After he suffered financial setbacks his sons Thomas, ROBERT, and William* left home to join their cousin, Robert Hamilton*, a wealthy Scots merchant established in what would soon become Upper Canada. Thomas Dickson arrived at Queenston in 1789 and, following an apprenticeship with Hamilton, opened a shop at Fort Erie in 1793. There he sold goods to the small garrison and received and forwarded goods on Lake Erie, mainly for the British military and the fur trade. By 1796 he had moved his shop to Queenston and he gradually built up a clientele which, by 1809, extended as far west as Long Point, on Lake Erie, and as far north as the Forty (Grimsby), on Lake Ontario. He also maintained a business connection with John Warren*, a prominent merchant at Fort Erie, to forward goods on the lakes. In 1801 Dickson received permission to build warehouses at Queenston, Chippawa, and Fort Erie; he does not, however, appear to have implemented his plan to start a portaging business. From 1804 he held the licence to operate a ferry from Queenston to Lewiston, N.Y.

Dickson's involvement in local society and politics was more limited than that of his brother William or of Robert Hamilton. He did hold local office. Following the dismissal of the deputy collector of customs at Queenston, Samuel Street*, Dickson assumed the post, on 28 March 1803. At the same time the port was removed from the control of the collector at Niagara (Niagara-on-the-Lake), Colin McNabb*. Dickson had served on the first Heir and Devisee Commission for the Niagara District and had been appointed justice of the peace on 30 June 1800: he served continuously in the latter capacity, receiving his last commission on 9 May 1823. After Hamilton's death in 1809 Dickson became chairman of the Court of Quarter Sessions.

In 1800 Dickson made his first foray into politics. He urged Thomas Welch*, a leading office holder in the London District, to support a favourite of the Niagara merchants, Surveyor General David William Smith*, who was running for election in Welch's area. In 1807 Dickson himself was persuaded to accept nomination, albeit rather reluctantly, for one of the Niagara seats in the House of Assembly. If he ran, he lost. He was elected to the sixth parliament in 1812 for the riding of 3rd Lincoln. Unfortunately the records for this parliament are only fragmentary. In the third session (February–March 1814) Dickson was absent for part of the time and barely emerges from the journals. He was, however, highly conspicuous in the fifth session (February–March 1816). He moved the formation of a committee to study the militia laws and sponsored a bill to appropriate money for militia purposes. His interests as a merchant figure in much of the legislation he promoted during this session. He introduced bills to amend the act for the speedy recovery of small debts, extend the jurisdiction of the Court of Requests (essentially a small claims court), and facilitate the circulation of army bills issued by the Lower Canadian government. On a broader scale, he brought forward bills to provide a sum for improving navigation on the St Lawrence River, to allow the lieutenant governor to designate additional ports of entry and appoint more collectors of customs, and to continue the provisional agreement with Lower Canada respecting customs duties at the port of Quebec. The latter two bills indicate a concern with augmenting government revenues and to that end he seconded bills placing additional duties both on ship and tavern licences and on licences for hawkers and pedlars. He introduced several pieces of legislation defraying the expenses of individuals serving in various non-remunerative public offices. He proposed bills to increase the salary of the speaker of the assembly and to provide salaries for judges in district courts, although he voted with the minority against wages for assemblymen. He sponsored an amendment to the school act of 1807, which was defeated, and he initiated measures extending the limits of the town of Niagara, regulating the police in Kingston, and empowering JPs to regulate the price of bread in several towns within the province. Finally, he opposed, unsuccessfully, further liberalization of the province's restrictive marriage laws.

Dickson's experiences during the War of 1812 were varied. On one occasion he barely eluded capture by the Americans at his Queenston home. In 1813 he moved to Thorold and made his will, "thinking it necessary in the present eventful times . . . in case of my death either in battle or otherwise." Dickson served with the 2nd Lincoln Militia; taking command of the regiment during the absence of Thomas CLARK, he was promoted lieutenant-colonel on 5 Jan. 1814. Under his leadership, the unit distinguished itself at the battle of Chippawa on 5 July 1814. Dickson was wounded slightly and mentioned in Major-General Phineas Riall*'s dispatches for his "most exemplary" conduct and great zeal. He was also active in a civil capacity. On 24 March 1814 he was appointed one of the commissioners to secure traitors within the Niagara District. It is worth noting that a few months earlier his previous action as a JP handling the case of Jacob Overholser*, an American-born farmer persecuted by some of his Upper Canadian neighbours and later tried for treason, indicates a humane and sympathetic magistrate. In the spring of 1814 Dickson sat as an associate judge at the special assizes held at Ancaster to try suspected traitors. Towards the end of the war, in August 1814, Administrator Gordon Drummond* used Dickson and Robert NICHOL to urge farmers in the peninsula to thresh their grain earlier than usual so that the troops could hold out until further supplies arrived. Dickson acted on behalf of the Loyal and Patriotic Society of Upper Canada, distributing money to individuals and families who had suffered during the war. Never a strong man, he spent his last years quietly.

BRUCE G. WILSON

AO, MS 198; RG 1, A-II-5, 1, Niagara District reports. General Reg. Office (Edinburgh), Dumfries, reg. of births and baptisms, 19 Feb. 1775. PAC, MG 19, F10, Robert Nichol to Walsh, 17 March 1807; RG 1, E3, 20: 155; E14, 8: 600–3, 615; RG 7, G16C, 3: 95–96; RG 8, I (C ser.), 272: 116–18; 684: 56; RG 68, General Index, 1651–1841: 30, 410, 416, 418, 425, 428, 437, 450. PRO, CO 42/471: 9. UWOL, Regional Coll., "Index compiled in 1950 to the ledger of Thomas Dickson, Queenstown, 1806–1809." "Early records of St. Mark's and St. Andrew's churches, Niagara," comp. Janet Carnochan, OH, 3 (1901): 17, 31, 55–56. John Askin papers (Quaife), 1: 542. "Journals of Legislative Assembly of U.C.," AO Report, 1912. Select British docs. of War of 1812 (Wood), 2: 114–17. Quebec almanac, 1801. Lois Darroch Milani, Robert Gourlay, gadfly: the biography of Robert (Fleming) Gourlay, 1778–1863, forerunner of the rebellion in Upper Canada, 1837 ([Thornhill, Ont., 1971?]), 140, 151, 170–71, 211. Wilson, Enterprises of Robert Hamilton. J. E. Kerr, "Sketch of the life of Hon. William Dickson," Niagara Hist. Soc., [Pub.], no.30 (1917): 19–20.

DIEHL, PHEBE. *See* ARNOLDI

DIGHT. *See* BUTLER

DODD (Dods), ARCHIBALD CHARLES, lawyer, office holder, politician, and judge; b. *c.* 1740–45, probably in Northumberland, England; buried 7 June 1831 in Sydney, N.S.

Local tradition in Cape Breton relates that Archibald Charles Dodd was born into a wealthy family and was raised at Tofthouse, Northumberland. He is moreover alleged to have lost his inheritance, an event which forced him to become a lawyer. In 1775 Dodd married a woman named Bridget, who, he later claimed, was a bigamist. She in turn stated that he had left her when her money was gone and that after she had refused his proposals for divorce they had agreed on his paying her an annual allowance. Between 1783 and 1787 Dodd worked in London as a lawyer, representing the interests of loyalists and negotiating to purchase army commissions for wealthy clients. During one such transaction for Captain Edward Pellew, later Viscount Exmouth, money was misappropriated, and though Dodd later claimed that he was innocent his reputation was probably hurt.

It was therefore to escape a clouded past that in 1787 Dodd arrived in Cape Breton, which three years earlier had been separated from Nova Scotia as a distinct colony. Since he was one of only two lawyers there (the other being Chief Justice Richard Gibbons*), he was immediately engaged by Lieutenant Governor Joseph Frederick Wallet DesBarres as acting clerk of the Executive Council, the governing body of the island. In 1788 Lieutenant Governor William Macarmick* appointed Dodd his private secretary, and on 8 July of the same year Dodd married Susannah Gibbons, daughter of Richard Gibbons; the couple were to have 11 children.

Dodd's acumen was revealed not only by his marriage, but also by his ability to adapt to shifting political alliances within the colony. One faction headed by the attorney general, David Mathews*, was opposed by another headed at different times by Gibbons and the Reverend Ranna Cossit*, and though Dodd was identified as a member of the latter body during DesBarres's term, he kept a low profile. Appointed to the council in 1789 by Macarmick, he was careful not to upset the unanimity which prevailed there once Mathews's faction had become predominant, and he therefore acquired the friendship of Mathews. The latter became administrator of the colony after Macarmick's departure in 1795 and made Dodd his private secretary. Then on 14 June 1797 Mathews appointed him first assistant judge of the Supreme Court, an act that apparently suspended Ingram Ball*, who had been serving as chief justice. That spring Dodd had become personally involved in the controversy between Mathews and his opponents. Angered by allegations from the wife of William McKinnon* that he had accused Cossit of robbery and sacrilege, in an uncharacteristic loss of control Dodd attacked the McKinnons in personal terms. McKinnon then challenged Dodd to a duel, which through Cossit's intervention failed to take place.

Dodd's importance waned when James Ogilvie* replaced Mathews as administrator in June 1798, since Ogilvie blamed Mathews for the colony's problems. Ogilvie used the McKinnon incident as an excuse to force Dodd's resignation from the council on 3 July, and that summer he was replaced as chief justice by Ball and William Smith*. The eclipse was only temporary, however, since Ogilvie was in Cape Breton for less than a year. His successor, John Murray, tried to end the factional quarrels by naming members of both groups to the council; thus Dodd received an appointment. Within a few months of Murray's arrival, however, Mathews was questioning his authority. Murray, a stern and exacting military figure, would brook no opposition and dismissed Mathews as attorney general. When Dodd attempted to defend Mathews he was dismissed from the council on the grounds that he had packed juries during his term as chief justice.

Two events in 1800 marked a turning-point in Dodd's fortunes: the death of Mathews and the arrival of John Despard. The former lessened the bitter factionalism that had affected the lives of many of the colony's officials, and Despard's term as administrator saw Dodd attain a position of importance. Not surprisingly, Dodd warmly supported Despard in his struggle to force Murray to hand over power, and after Murray was ousted he was rewarded with reappointment to the council. Dodd soon became Despard's confidant and received commissions as deputy surveyor of woods in 1803 and, at the death of William Woodfall in 1806, chief justice.

Soon after the last appointment, however, Dodd and Despard fell out over the legality of the tax on imported rum, which Despard had been allowed to levy by a Treasury decision of 1801. The tax was opposed by Richard Collier Bernard DesBarres Marshall Gibbons, son of the former chief justice, and by 1805 Gibbons was arguing that any tax was illegal unless approved by parliament or a local house of assembly. Gibbons's solution was to establish a house of assembly, which had not been set up when the colony was founded because of its small population. Dodd had at first opposed his brother-in-law, but as chief justice he seems to have become sympathetic to his arguments, and in 1806 the two men, hitherto enemies, became confidants. Despard's dislike of Gibbons caused his alienation from Dodd and in May 1807 he dismissed him from the council. He could not, however, circumvent Dodd's official appointment as chief justice by the British government, which had taken place the previous year.

Nicholas Nepean, who succeeded Despard in July 1807, soon reappointed Dodd to the council. Like Dodd, Nepean was convinced by Gibbons's arguments, and he let the tax lapse. But as Dodd settled in as chief justice he took a closer look at the legality of the tax and concluded that the crown did indeed have the right to impose a duty of this type in a colony such as Cape Breton unless otherwise directed by the House of Commons. He was also not as sympathetic to an assembly as he had been previously because he foresaw that his power would be diminished under a representative government, and he seems to have fallen out with Gibbons. Because Nepean and Gibbons had become allies, in 1812 Nepean dismissed Dodd from the council, on the pretext that his original distrust of Gibbons had been fostered by the chief justice. However, Dodd's stand kept him in good stead with Nepean's successor, Hugh Swayne*, who was not interested in constitutional niceties; after he arrived in January 1813 he promptly reinstated the rum tax and reappointed Dodd to the council.

Dorland

In 1812 Dodd's life had been disrupted when his past caught up with him. His first wife suddenly reappeared in England, charging that he had deserted her, and Lord Exmouth accused Dodd of having swindled him. Dodd refuted the charges, in which, he suspected, Nepean and Gibbons were involved, but Swayne was obliged to suspend him as chief justice. In July 1813 he went to England to answer Exmouth's accusation, and remained for three years. He maintained that he had lived in London for two years after Exmouth's money had disappeared, and though Exmouth had known of his presence he had not laid charges. Indeed, Dodd claimed, both his agent and Exmouth had professed their belief in his innocence. Exmouth failed to bring the case to court since he was on duty in the Mediterranean for most of the period. Lord Bathurst, the colonial secretary, therefore simply lifted Dodd's suspension. Dodd's first wife presented a petition in 1818, but nothing seems to have come of it.

Dodd returned to Cape Breton on 20 Aug. 1816 and was soon presiding over a dispute between the crown and the firm of Ritchie and Leaver, then operating the coal mines, over the company's refusal to pay taxes on rum, which it distributed to miners, on the grounds that the tax was unconstitutional. The case came before Dodd in November. Influenced by Gibbons's arguments in court, he returned to his earlier conclusion that the tax was illegal because the royal prerogative to tax the island had been surrendered in 1763. As a result of the grand jury's agreement, the tax was suspended, and the colony was left without funds. Gibbons and his followers insisted that an assembly be summoned to make the tax legal, but Dodd was opposed. His memory of disputes in the council dimmed, he predicted that in an assembly "inapplicable Topics" would be debated in an atmosphere of "passion and party discussion."

The chaos on Cape Breton had stimulated the British government into considering the reannexation of the island to Nova Scotia. With the occurrence of famine in the summer and fall of 1816, Henry Goulburn, under-secretary in the Colonial Office, advised Bathurst to avoid allowing a house of assembly because of the poor condition of the colony. In the mean time, following Dodd's decision Gibbons had maintained that all ordinances passed by the council were unconstitutional since no assembly had ever been called to pass them. Bathurst submitted this argument to the English law officers, and in April 1818 they reported that Gibbons's opinion was correct. Faced with this dilemma, Goulburn recommended that the colony be reannexed to Nova Scotia and that two members from Cape Breton be summoned to the Nova Scotia House of Assembly. Early in 1819 Lieutenant Governor George Robert Ainslie* was secretly informed of the decision to reannex, and

by the summer it had become common knowledge. Despite protests, on 16 Oct. 1820 Lieutenant Governor Sir James Kempt* of Nova Scotia proclaimed the end of the colony's existence in Sydney. Dodd himself was retired on full pension, a measure of the respect the Colonial Office and Halifax had for him. Although no longer employed, he continued to lead an active life, and died as the result of injuries received by a fall from his horse. On the day of his burial all businesses in Sydney were closed and ships in the harbour flew their flags at half-mast.

Dodd played a key role in the history of the colony of Cape Breton. In his long career he influenced the thinking of every lieutenant governor or administrator, and his decision as to the illegality of the rum tax led directly to the colony's reannexation to Nova Scotia. He and his family were very influential in Cape Breton society for over 150 years. His son, Edmund Murray Dodd*, was Sydney Township's first elected representative, became a leading tory MHA and executive councillor, and later served as a puisne judge of the Supreme Court of Nova Scotia. In turn, his son, Murray Dodd, became a Conservative MP for Sydney and then a judge before his death in 1905.

R. J. MORGAN

Beaton Institute of Cape Breton Studies, College of Cape Breton (Sydney, N.S.), A. C. Dodd papers; MG 13/4. PANS, MG 1, 262B, 263A. PRO, CO 217/115–36; CO 220/15. St George's Anglican Church (Sydney), Reg. of baptisms, marriages, and burials. C. B. Johnston, *Memories* (n.p., 1931). *Novascotian, or Colonial Herald,* 29 June 1831. R. J. Morgan, "Orphan outpost."

DORLAND, THOMAS, JP, politician, office holder, and militia officer; b. 1759 in Beekmans Precinct, Dutchess County, N.Y., son of Samuel Dorland; m. Alley Gow, and they had two sons and three daughters; d. 5 March 1832 in Adolphustown, Upper Canada.

Thomas Dorland was descended from Dutch Quakers who immigrated to North America in the mid 17th century and settled on Long Island, N.Y. His family was loyal during the American revolution, but only Thomas broke with the non-violent doctrines of the Quakers and fought. According to legend, he was captured by rebels and escaped; his slaves, although threatened, refused to reveal his hiding-place. Dorland was one of the many loyalist refugees who made his way to New York City. He served there with the Associated Loyalists until September 1783, when he left in a company led by Peter Van Alstine. After wintering in Quebec at Sorel [see Michael Grass*], Van Alstine's company moved on and arrived at Township No.4 (Adolphustown) along the Bay of Quinte in June 1784. A return of 5 October describes Dorland and a woman, presumably his wife, as being "housed on their land." The next few years were given over to the commonplace tasks of clearing land and raising a family.

Thomas's brother Philip was one of the dominant figures in the township. He was elected to the first parliament of Upper Canada but, being a Quaker, refused to take the requisite oath. Thomas, however, had been disowned by the Society of Friends for taking up arms and his public career was not hobbled by the same constraints. From 1793 he was elected to a variety of municipal offices: overseer of highways, pathmaster, assessor, and collector. By 1797 he had evidently been appointed a justice of the peace for the Midland District. His petition that year for 1,200 acres of land due to him as a magistrate was accepted by the Executive Council. Dorland was a regular participant in the meetings of the Court of Quarter Sessions.

In 1804 Dorland was elected to the House of Assembly for the riding of Lennox and Addington. The timing was important. Dorland came to York (Toronto) when opposition to Lieutenant Governor Peter Hunter*'s administrative reforms was acquiring a parliamentary focus. Led by David McGregor ROGERS and, after 1805, by William Weekes*, a small, fluctuating group of assemblymen used the house to air public grievances. Although never a major figure in the assembly, Dorland was active through the session of 1805. He supported attempts to revise the Assessment Act of 1803, to extend full civil and religious rights to dissenters, and to limit the salaries of public officials. The opposition found its stride during Alexander Grant*'s brief administration and, under the leadership of Robert Thorpe* and then of Joseph Willcocks*, grew in strength until the War of 1812. Branded by its detractors as a "party" – a contemporary synonym for faction – the group was, in fact, a loose coalition of interests coming together at times, often for disparate reasons, on matters of perceived common concern.

The loyalists had a profound sense of grievance because of many of Hunter's reforms, particularly the limitations placed on free land grants to loyalists and their descendants, and in 1807 Dorland and Allan MacLean* petitioned the Executive Council on behalf of local loyalist children. Thorpe hoped to make common cause with the loyalists and, according to Richard Cartwright*, actively courted loyalist assemblymen such as Dorland and Ebenezer WASHBURN. The appeal was successful; a Thorpe resolution to discuss the claims of loyalist and military claimants for land was defeated in March 1807 by only one vote. Cartwright considered men such as Dorland "simple folks" who were the "dupes of Mr. Thorpe in his attempts to create confusion."

The truth, however, was not so simple. Dorland was a man of independent bent. He actively supported attempts to assert the rights of the assembly and to use

the power of that institution to redress grievances. Yet he would not support the motion of 1 March 1805 by Weekes and Rogers to consider "the disquietude which prevails in the Province by reason of the administration of Public Offices." He was a moderate and his criticisms of government were never as all-encompassing as those of Weekes or his successors. Dorland's opposition bore strong hues of sectional interest and reflected the concerns of the small farmer and loyalist. He was, for instance, a persistent opponent of the District School Act of 1807. To his mind, it was "not useful to the District in general." What he meant by that remark is indicated by petitions he introduced in the house. "A few wealthy inhabitants, and those of the town of Kingston," the petitioners complained, "reap exclusively the benefit [of the district school]. . . . The institution, instead of aiding the middling and poorer class . . . casts money into the lap of the rich." When in March 1808 the house attempted to reorder the day's business to accommodate a third reading of an amendment to the School Act, Dorland, Rogers, and Peter Howard* walked out of the chamber to deny a quorum. Lieutenant Governor Francis Gore*, describing their conduct as "extraordinary" and their action as "unprecedented," stripped them of office. Dorland was left off the commission of the peace and was not restored to the magistracy until 1814. He was unabashed. Re-elected in 1808, he continued in much the same fashion as before. Still, his level of activity diminished, probably because of ill health. Through 1811 and 1812 he often supported Willcocks's initiatives against the administration but departed from the opposition group whenever he saw fit. Whether Dorland contested his riding in the election of 1812 is not known.

A long-standing officer in the 1st Lennox Militia, he was a captain during the War of 1812; in this capacity he was a member of the court that convicted Joseph Seely*. If nothing else, the war made clear to York officialdom the distinction between the discontented and the disaffected. Dorland was clearly one of the former. On 24 March 1814 he was appointed a high treason commissioner.

In the years following the war and until his death, Dorland was the epitome of the public-spirited subject. He was, with John Macaulay*, John Kirby*, and Thomas Markland*, one of the foremost JPs in the Midland District. He served regularly on the grand jury, often as its foreman, a role that gave him a further degree of public prominence. In the last few years of his life he was a perennial choice as one of the associate justices at the district assizes. He was a member of the Midland District Agricultural Society, a subscriber to the Brock monument, and the agent in Adolphustown for the *Kingston Chronicle*. In 1823 he was promoted major in the militia. From 1802 to 1824

Doucet

he operated the ferry from Adolphustown to Prince Edward County.

Dorland was said to own as many as 20 slaves. Supposedly called "Devil Tom," he was well known for his "eccentric and risky tricks." He does not seem to have been a man of strong religious conviction. Although his children were married by the Presbyterian clergyman Robert McDowall*, Dorland's only formal association with religion after his Quaker youth came late in life when he joined the Church of England. Gore and Cartwright were scandalized by Dorland's political behaviour, but John Beverley Robinson* and Macaulay remembered him differently. Robinson, commenting on Macaulay's address to the grand jury at Adolphustown after Dorland's death, noted: "You speak of our respected old friend Thomas Dorland having left a '*gap*' which will not be easily filled up – It is literally true however, for the present times do not seem to breed such men."

ROBERT LOCHIEL FRASER

AO, MS 78, J. B. Robinson to John Macaulay, 25 March 1833; MS 522, memoranda respecting the District School Bill, 5 March 1808; RG 22, ser.54, 1–2; ser.159, Thomas Dorland, 1833. BL, Add. MSS 21828: 68 (copy at PAC). Lennox and Addington County Museum (Napanee, Ont.), Lennox and Addington Hist. Soc. Coll., William Bell papers, p.357; T. W. Casey papers, pp.11728–29; Thomas Dorland, deed, 1807, p.31263; mortgage, 1831, p.31265. PAC, RG 1, E3, 27: 78, 83–85; L3, 104: C13/56; 150: D3/28, 68; 152: D8/46; 153: D9/21; 155: D12/175; 555: leases and licences of occupation, 1798–1838/18; RG 5, A1: 14037–39; RG 8, I (C ser.), 1203: 16, 31, 40; 1717: 24; RG 68, General index, 1651–1841: 124, 126, 128–29, 406, 411, 424, 432, 436, 441, 452, 467. QUA, Richard Cartwright papers, letter-books (transcripts at AO, 63, 252–61, 264–68). "Early municipal records of the Midland District," Ont., Bureau of Industries, *App. to the report* (Toronto), 1897: 4, 7–8, 13, 35–49, 60, 70–71. "Journals of Legislative Assembly of U.C.," AO *Report*, 1911; 1912: 1–97; 1914: 447–49. "McDowall marriage register," comp. [Robert] McDowall, *OH*, 1 (1899): 75, 84. "Political state of U.C.," PAC *Report*, 1892: 43. "U.C. land book C," AO *Report*, 1931: 22, 53. *Kingston Chronicle*, 4 May, 9 Sept. 1814; 19 Feb., 16 April 1819; 5 May 1820; 29 Aug. 1823; 22 Sept. 1826; 18 May 1827; 19 July 1828; 19 Sept., 31 Oct. 1829; 10 Sept. 1831; 10 March 1832. *Upper Canada Gazette*, 26 Feb., 2, 9 March 1808.

Armstrong, *Handbook of Upper Canadian chronology* (1967), 42. *Commemorative biographical record of Dutchess County, New York, containing biographical sketches of prominent and representative citizens, and of many of the early settled families* (Chicago, 1897), 99–100. *Death notices of Ont.* (Reid), 160. W. D. Reid, *The loyalists in Ontario: the sons and daughters of the American loyalists of Upper Canada* (Lambertville, N.J., 1973), 93. Canniff, *Hist. of the settlement of U.C.*, 210, 449, 453. Cowdell Gates, *Land policies of U.C.*, 77. A. G. Dorland, *Former days & Quaker ways* ([Picton, Ont.], 1965), 6–8; *A history of the Society of Friends (Quakers) in Canada* (Toronto, 1927), 51, 277. W. S. Herrington, *History of the county of Lennox and Addington* (Toronto, 1913; repr. Belleville, Ont., 1972), 139, 141, 145. Richard and Janet Lunn, *The county: the first hundred years in loyalist Prince Edward* (Picton, 1967), 117, 167, 171. Patterson, "Studies in elections in U.C.," 296, 307, 314, 335. G. E. Reaman, *The trail of the black walnut* (Toronto, 1957), 71. E. R. Stuart, "Jessup's Rangers as a factor in loyalist settlement," *Three hist. theses*, 102, 112, 137. Lennox and Addington Hist. Soc., *Papers and Records* (Napanee), 5 (1914): 60. A. C. Osborne, "Pioneer sketches and family reminiscences," *OH*, 21 (1924): 224. Larry Turner, "An early history of the Glenora Ferry," *County Magazine* (Bloomfield, Ont.), 2 (1980), no.17: 32–37, 50–64.

DOUCET, ANDRÉ, Roman Catholic priest; b. 30 Nov. 1782 in Trois-Rivières, Que., son of Jean Doucet and Magdeleine Mirau; d. 19 Dec. 1824 in Tracadie, N.S.

André Doucet was the fourth child in a family of 12. His father, a prosperous baker and mill owner of Acadian origin, was able to provide for the education of his numerous offspring: Nicolas-Benjamin* became a notary and André himself entered the Séminaire de Québec in 1797, destined for an ecclesiastical career. In 1804 Doucet became the subject of a jurisdictional dispute between Antoine-Bernardin ROBERT, superior of the seminary, who wanted to admit him as a member of the community, and Bishop Pierre Denaut* of Quebec, who, recognizing his superior abilities, wished to retain his services for the diocese. The seminary deferred to the bishop and, after his ordination on 1 Dec. 1805, Doucet was named one of the curates to assist Joseph-Octave PLESSIS, parish priest of Notre-Dame and Denaut's coadjutor bishop. On 9 Oct. 1807, to fill the vacancy caused by his own elevation as diocesan bishop, Plessis appointed the 24-year-old Doucet to Notre-Dame, one of the two most important parishes in the province. Plessis no doubt intended to groom his promising young protégé as his episcopal successor.

Doucet served as parish priest of Notre-Dame for the next seven years, to Plessis's entire satisfaction. He also maintained the reputation he had early acquired as the best preacher in Lower Canada. On 11 June 1809, before a crowded audience, he gave a sermon on "inward peace," and demonstrated his loyalty to the British crown by concluding that Lower Canadians had enjoyed outward peace for 50 years "under the influence of the most just and mildest government in the world." Doucet was appointed vicar general of the diocese on 23 Jan. 1813 and sat on a variety of secular bodies where he probably represented the Roman Catholic church. A subscriber to the Quebec Fire Society, he was a director of the Loyal and Patriotic Society of the Province of Lower Canada in 1813 and a member of a committee to prepare an address of thanks to Governor Sir George Prevost* the same year.

Yet all was not well with Doucet. By 1813 he had begun to request transfer to a mission. Plessis repeatedly encouraged him to remain at Notre-Dame, "for which ever way I look, I see no one for whom this position is better suited than you." But on 20 Oct. 1814 he accepted Doucet's resignation. Besides citing ill health, Doucet had indicated that he was unable to endure any longer the "fits of rage, quarrels, [and] insults" which, while not directed at him personally, had characterized the meetings of the *fabrique*. He was immediately named to the chapels of Notre-Dame-des-Anges in Quebec and Notre-Dame-de-Foy at Sainte-Foy and was made chaplain to the nuns of the Hôpital Général as well as to the poor.

Doucet was defended by Plessis against accusations from certain priests that he had lost his bishop's confidence. The following year, however, that confidence and Plessis's hopes of finding a successor in Doucet were shattered. In September 1815, while Plessis was in the Maritimes, Doucet made, "with the greatest secrecy, the preparations of a man who is not returning." He sold his belongings, paid off as many debts as he could (although some substantial ones apparently remained), and left for France via Nova Scotia and Cape Breton Island, where he stayed for some time with Laurence KAVANAGH, a well-known Irish Catholic merchant.

Rumours as to the reasons for Doucet's departure were deflected as much as possible by clergy in Quebec and Nova Scotia, who hoped for an explanation from him that would discourage talk of scandal. None was forthcoming and, according to Plessis, the Quebec clergy concluded that his flight "was the act of a deranged mind." In August 1816 Doucet wrote to Plessis from the Trappist monastery of Aiguebelle, near Montélimar, France, where he was finally beginning to enjoy "internal peace" and felt a call to join the order. Historians have claimed that, although talented, amiable, and intelligent, Doucet was not an able administrator. Possibly his numerous responsibilities at Quebec and the high expectations Plessis had of him were beyond his capabilities and physical strength. In leaving, he had perhaps sought to rid himself of a burden he could no longer bear, and to pursue his religious vocation in a manner better suited to his abilities. Some time in 1817, however, for unknown reasons, he changed his mind. After a noviciate of 10 months, accomplished, according to his Trappist superior, "with meticulousness and great spiritual edification," he left the monastery.

Doucet arrived in Halifax in November 1817, and indicated to Edmund Burke*, vicar apostolic of Nova Scotia, that he wished to work in the province's missions. Plessis approved. From his arrival until October 1819, Doucet ministered to the Catholics of Halifax, though he spoke only French, and to those of Chezzetcook, an Acadian community near by. He was then sent to the Acadian parish of Ste Anne at Ste Anne du Ruisseau, in southern Nova Scotia, as assistant to Jean-Mandé Sigogne*. His new position also included the mission at West Pubnico. In 1822 he founded the mission of Saint-Michel, at Bas-de-Tousquet (Wedgeport), and constructed its first church. Although in ill health, he completed his duties to Sigogne's "great satisfaction." Sigogne's report that Doucet was "liked and esteemed" by his parishioners is significant in view of the numerous complaints from missionaries that the Acadians of the Maritimes, who had been for many years without priests, often manifested their independence of the clergy and quarrelled with them.

For a few years Doucet seemed content in the isolation experienced by most Maritime clergy. He excused himself for not writing more often to Plessis: "The country in which I live offers literally nothing of interest for those who do not know it, and over three years would provide hardly enough material for a tolerable sentence." By late 1822 he began to express an interest in returning to Lower Canada. His brother Nicolas-Benjamin had pleaded with Plessis for his return so that he could repay his debts. The bishop was cautious in his replies: he would be glad to see his old friend and former confidant but Doucet could not expect to receive an important post immediately. In addition, the severe shortage of priests in Nova Scotia might make it impossible for him to leave. Whether Doucet chose not to return or was unable to do so is not known. In mid 1824 he was named to replace Father Vincent de Paul [Jacques Merle*] as parish priest at Tracadie. The parish, with missions at Pomquet and Havre Boucher, was probably an easier charge for the ailing priest. His pastorate there, however, lasted a brief six months. He became gravely ill in December and died within a few days, at age 42.

André Doucet was not typical of most Roman Catholic priests. He abandoned, for reasons which remain obscure, an exceptionally promising career in Lower Canada and ended his days in the isolation of the Acadian missions. Although he had lost the confidence of Plessis, he earned the respect of his Nova Scotian parishioners.

PAULETTE M. CHIASSON

AAQ, 210 A, IV, VIII–XII; 61 CD, Notre-Dame-de-Québec, I: 55, 58–59, 66; 7 CM, II; 312 CN, IV–VII. ANQ-MBF, CE1-48, 30 nov. 1782. ANQ-Q, CN1-230, 25 févr. 1811, 20 oct. 1814, 1er avril 1817; CN1-262, 10 oct. 1807. Arch. of the Archdiocese of Halifax, Edmund Burke papers (mfm. at PANS); St Anselm's Roman Catholic Church (West Chezzetcook, N.S.), reg. of baptisms, marriages, and burials (mfm. at PANS). ASQ, Fichier des anciens. *Quebec Gazette*, 1 Dec. 1808; 15 June, 14 Sept. 1809; 25 April 1811; 1–15 April, 30 Dec. 1813; 13 April 1815; 5 Feb. 1818; 4 March 1819; 24 Jan. 1825. C. J.

Douglas

d'Entremont, *Histoire de Wedgeport, Nouvelle-Écosse* (s.l., 1967). Johnston, *Hist. of Catholic Church in eastern N.S.* Lambert, "Joseph-Octave Plessis." Henri Têtu, "L'abbé André Doucet, curé de Québec, 1807–1814," *BRH*, 13 (1907): 3–22, 33–46.

DOUGLAS, DAVID, scientist; b. 25 June 1799 in Scone, Scotland, son of John Douglas, stonemason, and Jean Drummond; d. unmarried 12 July 1834 near Laupahoehoe, Hawaii.

David Douglas acquired his early education tramping the woods and fishing trout streams while skipping his classes at the parish school of Kinnoull, on the outskirts of Perth. From an early age he reared birds and collected plants. Not until he served an apprenticeship, from around 1811, in the gardens of the Earl of Mansfield at Scone did he develop a taste for books, in large part botany manuals. Following his engagement about 1818 as a gardener on the estate of Sir Robert Preston, near Dunfermline, he frequented Preston's extensive botanical library and became enamoured of exotic plants, for which Preston's gardens were renowned. Some two years later he was admitted to the infant Glasgow Royal Botanic Garden, where he became a star student of Professor William Jackson Hooker. On Hooker's recommendation he was engaged in 1823 by the Horticultural Society of London as a botanical collector.

That year the society sent Douglas to botanize in the northeastern United States. Authorized to go as far as Amherstburg, Upper Canada, he nevertheless proceeded to Sandwich (Windsor), passing through "The French Settlement" where, he noted, "the Fields are well cultivated . . . [and] attached to each house is a neat garden laid out and kept with taste." He remained at Sandwich from 18 to 22 September. On the 20th, during a trip into the countryside, his guide ran away with his money and coat while he was up a tree. Fortunately left with the hired horse and carriage, Douglas was, however, obliged to engage a driver to take him back to town, "the horse only understanding the French language, and I could not talk to him in his tongue." From Sandwich Douglas took a steamboat to Buffalo, N.Y., botanized on both sides of the Niagara River, and returned to New York via Queenston, Upper Canada, and Albany. He left for England on 12 December.

The many specimens Douglas brought back made his trip a publicly acclaimed success. After perfecting his knowledge of scientific and technical procedures in various fields, in July 1824 he was dispatched by the Horticultural Society, through the good offices of the Hudson's Bay Company, to the Pacific coast of North America. Based at Fort Vancouver (Vancouver, Wash.), he travelled extensively throughout the company's Columbia district, between northern California and the Columbia basin. In March 1827 he left with

the HBC's annual brigade to York Factory (Man.), where he was to take ship for England. In the Athabasca Pass he performed the remarkable task of climbing a mountain of 9,156 feet in five hours, alone and without equipment; he named it Mount Brown in honour of Robert Brown, a prominent botanist, and to a nearby peak he gave the name of Mount Hooker.

Douglas collected botanical and zoological specimens as he travelled. En route, he encountered two scientists of John Franklin*'s second Arctic expedition, Thomas DRUMMOND at Carlton House (near Batoche, Sask.) and John Richardson* at Cumberland House, and pronounced the collections of each "princely." Franklin himself took Douglas across Lake Winnipeg (Man.) to the mouth of the Winnipeg River. At the Red River settlement, where he remained for a month, Douglas formed "a small herbarium of 288 species." He arrived at York Factory on 28 August only to have his odyssey end on a tragic note: a "calumet eagle," given to him by Chief Factor John Rowand* at Fort Edmonton (Edmonton), had become tangled in its jess and was strangled. "What can give one more pain?" he wondered. "This animal I carried 2,000 miles and now lost him, I might say, at home." Douglas nearly lost his own life shortly after. Along with eight company men he, Drummond, and Edward Nicholas Kendall* and George Back*, who were also of Franklin's party, were sailing in a small boat from their ship to York Factory when they were caught in a violent storm and driven some 70 miles out into Hudson Bay. Their boat threatening to sink at any moment, soaked and frozen, without a compass and unable to see the shore or the stars, the group called on their combined experience and vigour to get themselves back to the ship, where they had been given up for dead. Douglas remained ill from the effects long after his arrival at Portsmouth, England, on 11 Oct. 1827.

Douglas's harvest of plants and seeds established a record for species introduced by an individual into Britain, the leading country in botanical research. The gardens of the Horticultural Society were overwhelmed, and recourse was had to private nurseries. Moreover, many of the species were considered valuable and were distributed among appropriate institutions. Douglas's discoveries were exhibited at meetings of the society and published in scientific periodicals. Almost the whole of his collection was described, along with those of Drummond and Richardson, in Hooker's *Flora Boreali-Americana* . . . (2v., London, 1840). Douglas had also sent and brought back zoological specimens, some of which were used by Richardson in his *Fauna Boreali-Americana* . . . (4 pts, London, 1829–37) and by James Wilson for his *Illustrations of zoology* . . . (Edinburgh and London, 1831). In addition, Douglas stated that he had brought back "several volumes of lunar, chronometrical, magnetical, meteorological and geographical observations, together with a volume of field sketches." At 29 he was a celebrity, and was admitted with honours to the Linnean, Zoological, and Geological societies of London. Consulted by the Colonial Office as to the boundary Britain should claim in the Oregon country, Douglas vigorously rejected American claims to the region and urged Britain to insist on the Columbia River as the most appropriate line west of the Rockies.

Another expedition to the American Pacific coast was organized for Douglas by the Horticultural Society in collaboration with the HBC. On 31 Oct. 1829 he left England for Fort Vancouver, where he arrived on 3 June 1830 to a warm welcome by the traders. His eyes, never strong, had deteriorated on his previous expedition because of blowing sand and brilliant snow and of glaring sun during the long sea voyage. As his eyesight dimmed he concentrated on his work, to the detriment of his safety; thus on one sortie he fell blindly into a ravine and lay in pain for five hours before being rescued. Yet a trader who accompanied him in the summer of 1830 noted: "I was much surprised to remark the quickness of sight he displayed in the discovery of any small object or plant on the ground over which we passed. When in the boats, he would frequently spring up abruptly in an excited manner, and with extended arms keep his finger pointed at a particular spot on the beach or shelving and precipitous rocks where some new or desirable plant had attracted his notice. This was the signal to put on shore, and we would then be amused with the agility of his leap to the land, and the scramble like that of a cat upon the rocks to the object he wished to obtain."

From 1830 to 1833 Douglas botanized from Puget Sound to Santa Barbara (Calif.) and in the Sandwich (Hawaiian) Islands. In March 1833, having completely lost the vision of his right eye, he set out to return to England through New Caledonia (B.C.) to Sitka (Alaska) and then across Siberia. Leaving the HBC's annual brigade at Fort Okanagan (Wash.), he went north to Fort Alexandria (Alexandria) on the Fraser River and from there to Stuart Lake. Unable to find a sure party of traders going to the coast, where he intended to embark for Sitka, he was obliged to go back down the Fraser. On 13 June his canoe shot over a cataract below Fort George (Prince George) and was lost; he and his guide were spun through a whirlpool, and disgorged onto the rocks. Douglas saved his astronomical journal, charts, and barometrical observations, a book of rough notes, and some instruments but lost his botanical notes and entire collection of some 400 species. Without food or clothes, he arrived back at Fort Vancouver in July, with his guide, on the verge of starvation and broken in spirit.

On 18 October Douglas left for the Sandwich Islands, arriving at Honolulu on 23 December. On 12 July 1834 he was taking a mountain trail in northern Hawaii when he disappeared. He was 35. His gored and trampled body was found at the bottom of a cattle trap occupied by an enraged bull. Mysterious circumstances surrounding the death have given rise to speculation about whether it was an accident, murder, or suicide.

Douglas's celebrity brought him in contact with the most prominent British scientists of his time. Yet he was, wrote the president of the Horticultural Society, Thomas Andrew Knight, "the shyest being almost that I ever saw." He was at ease, however, with his mentor, Hooker, to whom he wrote letters full of humour and charm, and among the fur traders at Fort Vancouver, where, trader George Barnston* recalled, he was "one of the happiest, heartiest mortals in our little society." To the Indians of the Columbia region he was "King George's Chief or the Grass Man," a vaguely menacing little magician capable of drinking boiling liquids ("an effervescent draught") and lighting his pipe with the sun (through a lens). He was as tough or as friendly with them as any trader, as skilful in shooting, and as capable of suffering hardship. But although he was comfortable among the traders – one of whom described him as a "sturdy little Scot; handsome rather; with head and face of fine Grecian mould" – he was not of their race and complained of being "molested out of my life by the men singing their boat-songs" as he tried to study while travelling by canoe. He had, indeed, little consideration for the HBC, which had greatly facilitated his work, describing it once to an astonished trader as "simply a mercenary corporation; there is not an officer in it with a soul above a beaver skin." The remark instantly earned Douglas an invitation to duel, which he heatedly accepted, but then, after some reflection, declined.

Douglas was more than a scientist who saw in nature only grist for the scientific mill. His eye "was alive to all that is picturesque," in the words of one contemporary, and his writings point to the inexhaustible variety and "great operations of nature" as manifestations of "an infinite intelligence and power in the Almighty hand." A man obsessed by the study of nature, he deplored a narrow-minded devotion to the pursuit of scientific truth as leading to "a condition little better than moral servitude." "We can travel through distant lands," he wrote, "and become acquainted with the complexions and the feelings and the characters of mankind, under every form of life; and in so doing this, if we be not most indocile pupils we must learn many lessons of kindness, and freedom of thought along with an appropriate knowledge of our immediate vocation."

The richness of Douglas's character, the variety of his skills, and his limitless enthusiasm, energy, and endurance enabled him to compress into a decade the accomplishment of a lifetime. An English colleague wrote: "If we only imagine the British gardens deprived of the plants introduced by Douglas, we shall find them but little further advanced in point of ornamental production than they were a century ago." At a time when some 92,000 species of plants were known the world over, Douglas had sent to Britain about 7,000 species, many of them new and native to what later became western Canada. His name has become a household word through the Douglas fir, the country's largest tree, but it is also attached to numerous smaller plants. Towards the end of the century George Mercer Dawson*, director of the Geological Survey of Canada, named an 11,000-foot peak northeast of Lake Louise (Alta) in honour of Douglas. A man who lived to search and died perhaps of curiosity, Douglas has been described by an historian of science as "one of our greatest and most successful exploring Botanists, to whom the world is deeply indebted," an opinion that no one would gainsay.

In collaboration with M. L. TYRWHITT-DRAKE

David Douglas is the author of *Journal kept by David Douglas during his travels in North America, 1823–1827* . . . , published in London in 1914 by the Royal Horticultural Society and reprinted in New York in 1959; he also wrote eight scientific papers, which are listed in appendix V of the *Journal*. The fullest study of Douglas is A. G. Harvey, *Douglas of the fir: a biography of David Douglas, botanist* (Cambridge, Mass., 1947), which includes a complete bibliography on Douglas up to 1946, as well as a portrait in pencil by a niece of the botanist. William Morwood, *Traveler in a vanished landscape: the life and times of David Douglas* (New York, 1973), is a speculative psychological study of Douglas which reaches the conclusion that his death, in mysterious circumstances, was suicide. The book has a bibliography of works published up to 1970.

Douglas's botanical specimens are housed at the British Museum, London, which acquired them from the Horticultural Society of London in 1856, at the Royal Botanic Gardens (London), and at the University of Cambridge. Zoological specimens are owned by the University of Glasgow, the Andersonian Institution, Glasgow, the Royal Scottish Museum, Edinburgh, and the Zoological Society of London.

PABC, Add. MSS 623. G. P. V. and H. B. Akrigg, *British Columbia chronicle, 1778–1846: adventurers by sea and land* (Vancouver, 1975), 230, 232–33, 235, 247–48, 306. Esther Fraser, *The Canadian Rockies: early travel and explorations* (Edmonton, 1969), 35, 135–38, 151, 154–55, 162, 165–66, 221. J. W. Eastham, "A note on Archibald Menzies and David Douglas, botanists," *BCHQ*, 12 (1948): 247–48.

DRAPEAU, MARIE-GENEVIÈVE. *See* NÖEL

DRUMMOND, ROBERT, businessman; b. 1791 at Huntly-wood, in the parish of Gordon, Berwickshire, Scotland, second son of Andrew Drummond and Jean Newton; m. 23 April 1819 Margaret Gentle of Perth, Upper Canada, and they had three sons and two daughters; d. 20 Aug. 1834 in Kingston, Upper Canada.

In 1817 Robert Drummond immigrated to British North America, settling in Montreal. He took up contracting work in Lower Canada, building a lock at Sainte-Anne's Rapids and a drawbridge at Île aux Noix. Drummond first came to the favourable notice of Lieutenant-Colonel John By*, superintending engineer of the Rideau Canal, as the principal designer of a bridge across the Ottawa River at the Chaudière Falls, spanning a cauldron known as the Big Kettle. Described as a "daring and magnificent undertaking" by the *Kingston Chronicle*, the bridge was completed by the end of 1828 and, though a perilous project, was finished without loss of life.

Drummond made his name as one of five main contractors on the Rideau Canal, the others being Andrew WHITE, Thomas McKay*, Thomas Phillips*, and John Redpath*. He himself was responsible for the construction of a dam and four locks at Kingston Mills, a lock and dam at Davis Mills, and a lock, dam, and waste-weir at Brewers Mills. Drummond and his family had moved from Bytown (Ottawa) to Kingston in January 1828, travelling in sleighs. The works at Kingston Mills were the third most extensive on the 126-mile line of the waterway. In common with other locations on the Rideau, Kingston Mills was an unhealthy spot, subject in the summer months to the ravages of the ague, since identified as a virulent form of malaria; it is estimated that about 500 men, mostly Irish immigrants, died along the line of the Cataraqui River, on which Kingston Mills was the biggest undertaking. Edward John Barker*, a contemporary observer, estimated that the dam and locks at Kingston Mills cost about £60,000.

Drummond lived during the week at Kingston Mills; he returned to Kingston on Saturday nights to spend Sundays with his family and was in the saddle at six o'clock on Monday mornings for his trip back to the works. An anonymous correspondent of the *Kingston Chronicle*, after touring the whole line of the canal in February 1830, reported that the works at Kingston Mills were in an advanced stage because of the pertinacity of Robert Drummond, who had overcome difficulties at the site which had "defeated Contractors not endowed with a due share of stern perseverance." In the course of blasting operations many workmen were killed through inexperience in handling charges, and Drummond himself narrowly missed injury or death. On a Saturday in February 1831 a 300-pound rock came through the side of a house within six feet of where he sat at dinner with a small company, but no one was hurt. Drummond, along with three other contractors, was honoured by Lieutenant-Colonel By for his signal services on the line of the canal. In August 1831 By presented him with an engraved and handcrafted silver cup, which carried an inscription acknowledging "the zeal displayed by him in the performance of his contracts" and By's "complete satisfaction" with his work.

Drummond was also a shipbuilder of note. At Kingston on 6 June 1829 he launched the first steamer to serve on the canal, the *Pumper*, so named because of its function in excavation work. The *Pumper*, 80 feet in length and 15 in the beam, was renamed the *Rideau* in May 1832, when it took on board By's gala party for an inaugural tour of the completed waterway from Kingston to Bytown. A leading entrepreneur in the carrying-trade, Drummond owned a line of steamers operating in the Montreal, Bytown, and Kingston service. Besides the *Rideau*, he built the *John By*, a 110-foot steamer of 200 tons, launched at Kingston in late November 1831 with the band of the 66th Foot in attendance (it began regular service the following fall). As well, he operated the steamer *Margaret*, the schooner *Lady of the Lake*, and a number of barges. Nor were his business interests restricted to shipbuilding and contracting. He and James Morton* were partners in a brewery, in late 1826 he joined Philemon Wright* and other businessmen in establishing the Hull Mining Company, and in 1832 he was made a director of the Commercial Bank of the Midland District. Had he lived longer, contemporaries expected that Drummond would have been elected to the legislature.

In 1832 Drummond left for Scotland to see his relatives in Edinburgh, and in January 1833 he accepted an invitation to visit By, now living in retirement at his country seat in Sussex. On this occasion By presented him with a personal memento, a silhouette portrait dated 1 Jan. 1833. He also offered his support for a contract on the Grenville Canal locks, but Drummond declined because of other commitments.

Robert Drummond did not long survive his return to Kingston, succumbing to a virulent cholera epidemic which carried him off in a matter of hours. He died on 20 Aug. 1834, at the age of 43, survived by his wife and his five children, ranging in age from 1 to 13. He was widely mourned. The *British Whig* carried a handsome obituary, concluding with the statement that his remains were followed to the grave "by every respectable person in the town." It is noteworthy that, in a sectarian age, the funeral procession for the Protestant Drummond was joined by the Roman Catholic bishop, Alexander McDonell*, in full canonicals. There can be no doubt of the respect and affection in which the man was held. Posterity remembers him as one of the early contractors in the upper province, as a pioneer in the steamship carrying-trade on the Rideau Canal, and as an important shipbuilder in the first days of steam navigation.

EDWARD F. BUSH

PAC, MG 29, A24; RG 1, L1, 35: 11; L3, 160: D18/5; RG 8, I (C ser.), 45: 23–24; 429: 187. E. J. Barker, *Observations on the Rideau Canal* (Kingston, [Ont.], 1834). John Mactaggart, *Three years in Canada: an account of the actual state of the country in 1826–7–8 . . .* (2v., London, 1829). *British Whig* (Kingston), 22 Aug. 1834. *Canadian Courant and Montreal Advertiser*, 24 June 1829. *Kingston Chronicle*, 1 May 1830. *Montreal Gazette*, 6 Dec. 1831. *Upper Canada Herald*, 23 Feb. 1831. *Archaeological historical symposium, October 2–3, 1982, Rideau Ferry, Ontario*, ed. F. C. L. Wyght (Lombardy, Ont., n.d.). E. F. Bush, *Commercial navigation on the Rideau Canal, 1832–1961* (Ottawa, 1981). R. [F.] Legget, *Rideau waterway* (rev. ed., Toronto and Buffalo, N.Y., 1972). A. H. D. Ross, *Ottawa, past and present* (Toronto, 1927).

DRUMMOND, THOMAS, naturalist; b. *c.* 1790 in Perthshire, Scotland; d. 1835, probably in March, in Havana, Cuba.

Thomas Drummond may have been attracted to botany by his elder brother James, director of the Cork botanic garden in Ireland and an associate of the Linnean Society of London in 1810. Thomas was trained in the Dog Hillock nursery garden near Forfar, which was owned by George Don, retired director of the Royal Botanic Garden in Edinburgh, and he took over ownership of the business on Don's death, about 1814. At this time he distributed collections of dried Scottish mosses entitled "Musci Scotici," and they attracted the attention of William Jackson Hooker, who would be appointed regius professor of botany at the University of Glasgow in 1820. Drummond's valuable information on plants was incorporated by Hooker in his *Flora Scotica* (London, 1821).

Hooker recommended Drummond as assistant naturalist to John Richardson* on Captain John Franklin*'s second expedition to the Arctic. After landing at New York in March 1825, the expedition advanced via Albany, Niagara Falls, and York (Toronto), then across lakes Huron and Superior to Fort William (Thunder Bay, Ont.), and finally on to Cumberland House (Sask.) with Drummond botanizing constantly en route. Drummond remained at Cumberland House to collect specimens while Franklin led the main party to the Arctic. From late August Drummond accompanied the Hudson's Bay Company's annual brigade to the Columbia River as far as "Upper House" (probably Henry House, Alta) on the Athabasca River, gathering plants according to an efficient schedule: "When the boats stopped to breakfast, I immediately went on shore with my vasculum, proceeding along the banks of the river, and making short excursions

Drummond

into the interior, taking care . . . to join the boats . . . at their encampment for the night. After supper, I commenced laying down the plants gathered in the day's excursion, changed and dried the papers of those collected previously . . . till daybreak, when the boats started. I then went on board and slept till the breakfast hour, when I landed and proceeded as before."

Drummond left the brigade in mid October 1825 and spent much of the winter in a hut built of spruce boughs on the Baptiste River, alone, without books, and subsisting on game he shot. The following spring, having met up with the annual brigade to York Factory (Man.), he was collecting mosses near Jasper House (Alta) when he encountered a large grizzly bear with young. "Growling and rearing herself on her hind feet . . . [she] advanced . . . to within the length of my gun from me," he recorded. "Judge of my alarm . . . when I found that my gun would not go off! The morning had been wet, and the damp had been communicated to the powder." At that juncture horsemen of the brigade arrived, and the bear made off. Thenceforth, Drummond rattled his vasculum to ward off bears. He botanized north of Jasper House until October 1826, when he accompanied the Columbia brigade across the Rockies, to determine the extent of changes in vegetation over the height of land. He returned immediately to winter at Edmonton House (Edmonton).

In the spring of 1827 Drummond travelled to Carlton House (near Batoche, Sask.); en route he and his companions "suffered much from snowblindness, . . . the dogs failed from want of food, we had to carry the baggage on our backs, and had nothing to eat for seven days." At Carlton House he encountered David DOUGLAS, probably an old botanical acquaintance. Douglas described his collection as "princely," and told how Drummond "liberally showed me a few of the plants in his possession – birds, animals etc., in the most unreserved manner," and even guided him to several habitats around the fort. In July Drummond accompanied Franklin's party to York Factory on Hudson Bay, whence they were to sail for England. Before departing, however, he and others were nearly lost when their small boat was swept by a gale some 70 miles out into the bay [see David Douglas]. The expedition reached Portsmouth, England, on 11 Oct. 1827.

The following year Drummond became curator of the Belfast botanic garden, where he assembled 50 two-volume copies of exsiccata of American mosses, entitled "Musci Americani." Hooker commented that "the whole . . . of North America has not been known to possess so many Mosses as Mr. Drummond [had] detected in this single journey." Drummond was elected an associate of the Linnean Society in 1830. From 1831 to 1834 he botanized in the southern United States, principally down the Mississippi val-

ley, around New Orleans, and in Texas. Though gravely ill with cholera, he dispatched from Texas hundreds of new specimens of plants and birds. After a brief stop in Florida, he sailed in 1835 to Havana and within weeks died there, probably of septicaemia.

Drummond was a quiet, intrepid, hard-working, and enthusiastic field naturalist, endowed, according to Richardson, with "an extreme quickness and acuteness of vision . . . [who] carried on under circumstances of domestic discomfort and difficulties, that would have quelled a meaner spirit." Hooker asserted that he had "accomplished enough, by his zeal and researches, to secure to himself a lasting name throughout the botanical world." Drummond's collection of several thousand herbaceous plants from the Prairies and Rocky Mountains, together with those of Douglas, Richardson, and Archibald Menzies*, formed the basis for Hooker's *Flora Boreali-Americana* . . . (2v., London, 1840). The insects, 150 birds, and 50 mammals collected by Drummond were used by Richardson in *Fauna Boreali-Americana* . . . (4 pts, London, 1829–37). Drummond's name is borne by about a dozen plant species (including *Potentilla drummondii* from the Rockies), the moss genus *Drummondia*, and one mammal, the pack-rat *Neotoma cinerea drummondii*, assigned by Richardson.

JUDITH F. M. HOENIGER

Thomas Drummond described his work in 1825–27 with Sir John Franklin's expedition in "Sketch of a journey to the Rocky Mountains and to the Columbia River in North America," *Botanical Miscellany* (London), 1 (1830): 95–96, 178–219. W. J. Hooker published a letter Drummond wrote in the Rockies dated 26 April 1826 in "Account of the expedition under Captain Franklin, and of the vegetation of North America, in extracts of letters from Dr Richardson, Mr Drummond, and Mr Douglas," *Edinburgh Journal of Science*, 6 (1827): 110–13. A portrait of Drummond executed by Sir Daniel MacNee is in the library of the Royal Botanic Gardens (London); it is reproduced in A. M. Coats, *The quest for plants: a history of the horticultural explorers* (London, 1969).

Royal Botanic Gardens, Director's corr., Thomas Drummond, II, XLIV, LXI–LXIII. W. J. Hooker, "Notice concerning Mr. Drummond's collections made chiefly in the southern and western parts of the United States," *Companion to the Botanical Magazine* (London), 1 (1835): 21–26, 39–49, 95–101, 170–77; 2 (1836): 60–64; "Notice concerning Mr. Drummond's collections, made in the southern and western parts of the United States," *Journal of Botany* (London), 1 (1834): 50–60, 183–201; "Obituary [Thomas Drummond]," *Gardener's Magazine, and Register of Rural and Domestic Improvement* (London), new ser., 1 (1835): 608. *DNB*. S. W. Geiser, *Naturalists of the frontier* (2nd ed., Dallas, Tex., 1948), 55–78. S. D. McKelvey, *Botanical exploration of the trans-Mississippi west, 1790–1850* (Jamaica Plain, Mass., 1955), 486–507. S. W. Geiser, "Naturalists of the frontier, Thomas Drummond," *Southwest Rev.* (Dallas), 15 (1930): 478–512.

DUBERGER, JEAN-BAPTISTE (he signed **John B.**, **Jean B.**, or **J. B. Duberger**), surveyor; b. 7 Feb. 1767 in Detroit, son of Jean-Baptiste Duberger, *dit* Sanschagrin, baker, and Louise Courtois; d. 19 Sept. 1821 in the parish of Saint-Thomas (Montmagny, Que.).

Son of a native of Vivonne, France, Jean-Baptiste Duberger showed early scholastic promise and was sent from Detroit to the Petit Séminaire de Québec, where he completed the last three years of the classical course between October 1785 and the summer of 1788. In June 1792 he secured temporary employment as a deputy land surveyor under Surveyor General Samuel Johannes Holland*. Two years later, under Samuel GALE, he drew the outline of a map of Lower Canada, and this work became a major element in the important topographical map of the province published in 1803 by William Vondenvelden* and Louis Charland*. Duberger received much valuable training with Holland, onto which was grafted an aesthetic taste derived from a circle of friends that included the artist and architect François BAILLAIRGÉ and the painters Louis Dulongpré* and William Berczy*. These influences are seen in the progress of his work from five relatively crude engravings, executed for a devotional book published in 1796, to later maps and plans which reflect remarkable precision and painstaking attention to detail and which are completed by elegant title cartouches and beautiful swags.

On 8 Jan. 1793 Duberger had married Geneviève Langlais; the two friends who witnessed his marriage contract were the lawyer Alexis Caron and Roger Lelièvre, who became a prominent notary in the city. Some time between 1795 and 1798 Duberger moved his small family out of the commercial bustle of Rue de la Canoterie in Lower Town to the quiet respectability of Rue Sainte-Ursule in Upper Town, where lived several men employed in military construction, including James THOMPSON. In 1794, following his work on land surveys, he had obtained another temporary position, as assistant draftsman with the Royal Engineers. He engraved a lead inscription plaque for the court-house in 1799, and he subsequently engraved another for the new Anglican cathedral, of which he also drew a plan and elevation in 1801. By his work as assistant draftsman, which lasted nine years, Duberger caught the attention of Colonel Gother MANN, the commanding engineer, and in June 1803, at the age of 36, he secured his first permanent employment, a position in the second class of the Corps of Royal Military Surveyors and Draftsmen in the Royal Engineers. His work was divided between surveying in the field and tending the drawing, or drafting, room adjacent to Porte Saint-Louis.

In 1804 Duberger completed a detailed plan of the city of Quebec and its defences to accompany a report from Mann on the state of the fortifications. At the same time Mann conceived the idea of having a scale model of Quebec constructed to assist the Board of Ordnance in planning major improvements to the defences of Britain's most important land station in North America. The task was confided to Duberger under the supervision and with the assistance of Captain John By*. Begun in November 1806 on the basis of the plan of 1804, the model was constructed on a scale of 25 feet to the inch. Through the long winter months of reduced activity, Duberger laboured on it by sections at home and transported each completed section to By's lodgings, a block west on Rue d'Auteuil, where the model was being mounted; to accommodate it By was obliged to knock down the walls separating four rooms. The model was completed at the end of 1807, but, according to By, when Governor Sir James Henry Craig* first saw it, he "expressed himself highly pleased with the correctness" and urged that the work be extended to include the strategic high ground on the Plains of Abraham. Duberger pushed on. By's lodgings being inadequate to contain the addition, the model was apparently moved to the ballroom of the Château Saint-Louis, and was duly completed in 1808.

Comprising 18 sections and measuring about 27 feet by 20 feet, the final work depicted the city from the Rivière Saint-Charles to the St Lawrence, and from Lower Town to the plains "as far as the spot where [James Wolfe*] died." The traveller John Lambert* described it as "beautiful" and its creator as "a self-taught genius." Others appreciated the model less; Duberger noted that it had raised the fears of a number of civilians who had been quietly appropriating crown property and who saw it as testimony of their stratagem. It had had to be completed almost in secret in order not to provoke open opposition to its being sent to England. Finally, in 1811, Craig dispatched it in By's care to the inspector general of fortifications.

Meanwhile Duberger had been accumulating misfortunes. In 1808 he requested a promotion to first class, and was supported by the commanding engineer, Lieutenant-Colonel Ralph Henry Bruyeres*, who observed that "he surveys and draws remarkably well" and that Craig wished to see rewarded "the great attention and assiduity he has shown . . . under the very increased labor and duty he has now to perform without any assistance whatever." But the promotion was not immediately forthcoming. In March 1810 Duberger's wife, Geneviève, was killed in a carriage accident, leaving him with six children. Their single-storey gabled stone house on Rue Sainte-Ursule, purchased in 1801, was sold for only £300 at auction by court order early in 1811. It was well furnished and even boasted a few luxuries such as a mahogany piano, seven pictures, and silverware. Duberger also

Duchesnay

had a small collection of some 20 books on mathematics and surveying. At the time he owned no other properties and was indebted for about £250, of which £100 was owed to James FISHER. On 27 May 1812 Duberger married Mary Plumby, with whom he would have at least three children. The marriage probably did not represent a social advancement since, although the daughter of a deceased "bourgeois," Mary could not sign her name. The following year Duberger was granted his promotion. The reversal of fortunes was short-lived, however; his health began to fail. Exposure to cold and wet weather while he was out on his surveys over the years had resulted in rheumatism and impaired eyesight, and though he now worked mostly indoors, he was frequently absent. In early 1815 he was in Montreal drawing plans for the Lachine Canal, and when he returned to Quebec about April he was gravely ill and transferred most of his work to his son Jean-Baptiste. In April 1817 a medical board found him "totally incapable of performing his professional duties, with little probability of recovery." He took temporary medical leave, but by October, recognizing that it would "scarcely be possible to draw or copy any Plans whatsoever," he retired from the service.

Irritated not a little by bad health, Duberger also suffered from injured pride at not having received proper recognition for his work. In April 1817 he complained to British military authorities that the map of Lower Canada published by Joseph Bouchette* in 1815 had been copied from one he himself had compiled for the use of the Royal Engineers' drawing room. At the same time he asserted that the model of Quebec had been taken to England without his concurrence, and that he believed "the merit of the work has been claimed by another." Concerning the model, his first charge was clearly false, since in 1807 he had feared that the work might not be sent to England, but there was much to substantiate his second accusation, for By had engineered the credit for the model to his own advantage.

Although Duberger retired in the bitterness of unrecognition, during his career he had established ties to the British authorities and population that ensured the future of at least some of his children: Jean-Baptiste had followed him into the Royal Engineers as surveyor-draftsman in 1812, and two daughters made excellent marriages with British inhabitants in 1817. None the less Duberger appears to have maintained his religious and social connections with the Canadian population. Although he may have lived for a time with a daughter and her English-speaking husband on the seigneury of Mount Murray, near La Malbaie, he spent most of his retirement years in the Canadian rural parish of Saint-Thomas. He was an extremely devoted father and from Saint-Thomas corresponded regularly with his daughters, in French.

In 1818, for example, he pressed one, "In the name of God let us know how you are and set me at ease," and closed with the assurance, "I am your father forever and sincere friend." That year he suffered a stroke that paralysed his right side, and he died in 1821 at Saint-Thomas.

BERNARD POTHIER

[Jean-Baptiste Duberger ultimately received the recognition denied him in his lifetime. The story of John By's injustice circulated freely at Quebec and over the years became much expanded and embellished at the hands of such writers as the French romantic Xavier Marmier in his *Lettres sur l'Amérique* (2v., Paris, [1851]), 1: 115–18. In recent years, however, Jean Ménard's *Xavier Marmier et le Canada, avec des documents inédits: relations franco-canadiennes au XIXe siècle* (Québec, 1967) and Bernard Pothier's *The Quebec model* (Ottawa, 1978), a critical study of both the history of the model and the genesis of the thorny legend that grew up around it, have contributed to a more accurate understanding of Duberger and his renowned work. In due course his model was set up at the Royal Military Repository, later the Rotunda Museum, Woolwich (London), where it remained on exhibit for nearly a century before being returned to Canada in 1908 – without the section depicting the Plains of Abraham which had been damaged in 1860 – as a gift to the Dominion. It was placed in the custody of the federal Archives Branch, later the PAC, in Ottawa, until the creation of the National Museums of Canada in 1967 when it devolved to the Canadian War Museum, Ottawa. In 1981 the work was transferred on permanent loan to Artillery Park, Quebec, where it was placed on display. Duberger's maps and sketches are in the National Map Coll. at the PAC. Five early engravings were printed in Amable Bonnefons, *Le petit livre de vie . . .* (Québec, 1796).

The present biography has been based in large part on *The Quebec model*, which contains a detailed and critical bibliography. The following sources may be added to those given therein. B.P.]

ANQ-Q, P-267. PAC, MG 23, K7, 3; RG 1, E1, 30: 71; E15, A, 277-1, 282. "Les dénombrements de Québec" (Plessis), ANQ *Rapport*, 1948–49: 87, 118, 169. *Quebec Gazette*, 17 Nov. 1785; 5 July 1798; 18 July 1799; 26 May 1803; 30 June 1808; 8 March, 27 Sept., 8 Nov. 1810; 31 Jan. 1811; 6 Nov., 18 Dec. 1817; 27 Sept. 1821. Jean Bruchési, "Le journal de François Baillairgé," *Cahiers des Dix*, 19 (1954): 120.

DUCHESNAY, ANTOINE-LOUIS JUCHEREAU. *See* JUCHEREAU

DUCHESNAY, JEAN-BAPTISTE JUCHEREAU. *See* JUCHEREAU

DUFOUR, *dit* Bona, JOSEPH (baptized **Joseph-Michel**), farmer, miller, seigneurial agent, politician, and militia officer; b. 7 Oct. 1744 in Petite-Rivière (Que.), son of Bonaventure Dufour and Élisabeth Tremblay; m. 2 Sept. 1771 Charlotte Tremblay at Île aux Coudres, Que., and they had four children; d. there 15 Dec. 1829.

Joseph Dufour, *dit* Bona, apparently remained with his parents until he married in 1771. He then went to live at Île aux Coudres, on some land inherited from his father-in-law. At this period the inhabitants of the island subsisted mainly by farming. Most of them also engaged in hunting *marsouins*, as beluga whales were then called. Hunting these small cetaceans, primarily sought for their oil, could sometimes be lucrative. To catch belugas the islanders formed groups of 10 to 15 men, each group being called a *pêche* (fishery). In 1778, following dissensions among various partners, the Séminaire de Québec, which was the seigneur of the island, had to strengthen the regulations in force. It limited the number of authorized *pêches* to four and appointed a leader to head each one, who was made responsible for seeing that the rules were respected. Dufour became the leader of the *pêche du large* (the offshore fishery) at this time, proof that he had rapidly acquired a degree of influence within the island community.

By 1781 Dufour had also become the largest *censitaire* on Île aux Coudres, with land holdings of 366 *arpents*, while the second largest had 300, and the others on average 120. Two or three years later the Séminaire de Québec chose Dufour to be one of the two millers on the island. He was free to do what he wanted with a portion of the grain ground, and could use for his own profit an extra share of water-side meadow besides the one already allotted to him as a *censitaire*. His various activities undoubtedly made him a tidy sum: between 1784 and 1790 he bought three more properties on the island, each for cash, in total laying out 3,000 *livres*.

In the summer of 1792 Dufour, who had recently been commissioned captain in the militia, was elected to the first Lower Canadian house of assembly for Northumberland riding, together with Pierre-Stanislas BÉDARD. During the two initial sessions he participated actively in the proceedings of the house and regularly voted with the Canadian party. He did, however, support the English party's request that laws be amended in order to improve the roads and bridges in Lower Canada. Dufour took no part in the next two sessions and did not run in the 1796 elections.

Dufour's withdrawal from political life may have been partly determined by events in his family life, because he lost his wife in 1792 and his eldest daughter in 1793, and so was left with two under-age daughters to look after. It is also possible that he had been disappointed by the focus of parliamentary proceedings, which were principally concerned with matters of a legal rather than a practical nature, such as the development of regulations for the house, the definition of its prerogatives, and the reorganization of the judicial system. Indeed, his withdrawal came after

he and a minority of his colleagues had unsuccessfully tried to prevent a debate on parliamentary privilege, occasioned by the arrest of member John Young*, that went on for several days. Some time earlier he himself had been the centre of a rather curious debate. The English party maintained that several Scottish officers garrisoned at Quebec were taller than Dufour, a claim the Canadian party disputed. To end the discussion the tallest Scottish officers were brought into the house for comparison with the member from Northumberland; when all had been measured, Dufour proved the tallest. The incident is amusing; none the less it illustrates the state of mind that at times moved the members of Lower Canada's first parliament.

Dufour subsequently turned his attention to farming and running the seminary's mill, while enjoying the benefits of greater social status. On 24 May 1794 he had been named lieutenant-colonel of the Baie-Saint-Paul battalion of militia and had thus become one of the rare persons of humble origin to hold this rank. In addition, the seminary increasingly relied on him to be its agent in dealings with the island residents. In October 1803, for example, Dufour was named leader of not one but all the *pêches* on the island. From time to time the seminary also commissioned him to convey its wishes to the islanders, to supervise the establishment of boundaries for its lands and the distribution of shore lots among the inhabitants, and even to settle disputes between individuals.

In 1804 Dufour and seigneur Malcolm Fraser* were among the chief initiators of a petition to the *grand voyer* (chief road commissioner), Gabriel-Elzéar Taschereau*, asking for a road to be opened between Saint-Joachim and Baie-Saint-Paul. The petitioners argued that the road would be as useful for the trade of Quebec town as for the development of agriculture in Northumberland County, since parishes on the north shore of the St Lawrence downstream from Saint-Joachim could be reached only by boat. Their request was well received, and in September 1806 Jean-Thomas TASCHEREAU laid out the route.

During the War of 1812 Dufour, as lieutenant-colonel of militia, had to intervene to quell a local mutiny. The militia in Lower Canada was raised in three stages, in May 1812, September 1812, and February 1813, the last levy being specifically for militia from the district of Quebec, to which the Baie-Saint-Paul battalion belonged. In March 1813 some militiamen from La Malbaie refused to answer the call to arms. They demanded that they be commanded by officers from their own area and be issued two outfits rather than one. By degrees, however, the mutineers surrendered of their own accord. On 2 April none the less Dufour had to order a detachment of 150 men to arrest the leaders of the movement, who in the end were imprisoned at Quebec.

Dugal

After these events Dufour, by then in his seventies, played a diminishing role, acting for the seminary only on rare occasions. He retained his lieutenant-colonelcy until July 1825, when he handed in his resignation. He died four years later leaving no male heir. His assets were bequeathed to one of his sons-in-law, Joseph Desgagnés.

Dufour is remembered chiefly because he was a member of the first parliament of Lower Canada. But the importance of such members of humble birth has generally been underestimated since historians have been more interested in its outstanding figures – men such as Jean-Antoine Panet*, Joseph Papineau*, Pierre-Amable De Bonne*, and John Richardson. Ontario historian Arthur Reginald Marsden Lower is a good illustration: "In the same assembly there was also a good 'sprinkling' of genuine men of the people, and with them we come to our last class division, the anonymous mass. . . . Another member [from this group] was Joseph Dufour. . . . Joseph, it appears, soon got too much of the grand company he had to keep at Quebec. . . . Under such stress, Joseph had the good sense not to stand a second time. He seems to have been a six-foot seven-inch innocent! Perhaps his height explains his election." Such a judgement says much about an author's preconceptions, for there is nothing in Dufour's career to corroborate it.

On the other hand the testimony of vicar general Alexis Mailloux* may at first glance seem suspect as almost a panegyric: "At Île aux Coudres there lived and died a sort of giant. . . . His name was Joseph Dufour. . . . Truly a man of peace, he laboured throughout his long life to maintain peace and unity among his fellow parishioners. Who can say how many disputes he settled, how many disagreements he smoothed over, how much acrimony he moderated." This testimony seems the more dubious in light of the fact that the vicar general's father, Amable Mailloux, was adopted as a child by Dufour and subsequently married one of his daughters. It none the less reflects Dufour's achievements more adequately than do Lower's cutting remarks. All things considered, the witness of contemporaries, even when sympathetically coloured, is sometimes more reliable than interpretations offered by some historians.

PIERRE DUFOUR

[A number of people named Joseph Dufour lived in the colony during the subject's lifetime. The following brief identifications are provided as an aid to researchers.

Joseph Dufour (fl. 1732–74), appointed royal bailiff on 25 May 1736 for the north shore of the St Lawrence around Beaupré and the Charlevoix region, was the subject's uncle; historians not infrequently confuse the two. One of his sons (and the subject's cousin), also named Joseph, was born at Petite-Rivière on 7 Oct. 1740. He seems to have settled around Kamouraska about 1770, and was killed by Indians in

1783 in New Brunswick. Joseph Dufour, *dit* Latour (fl. 1759–86), a carpenter living in Montreal in 1759 and in Lavaltrie in the 1780s, worked on the construction of a number of churches and other buildings. He was probably related to the Joseph Dufour of Montreal who signed up in 1797 as a voyageur for Todd, McGill and Company. The Joseph Dufour who was surveyor of roads at La Malbaie in 1807–8 may be the subject's cousin who was born 14 Sept. 1780 at Île aux Coudres. Finally, in the 1790s there was a Joseph Dufour living at Kamouraska and another at Madawaska. P.D.]

ANQ-Q, CE4-1, 11 févr. 1794; CE4-2, 2 sept. 1771, 3 juin 1774, 23 janv. 1788, 7 sept. 1792, 24 juill. 1793, 12 févr. 1798, 22 juin 1802, 16 déc. 1829; CN1-92, 23 sept. 1790; CN4-16, 5 nov. 1783, 25 mai 1784, 6 nov. 1786, 19 avril 1790, 18 juill. 1792. ASQ, C 36: 74, 146; C 37: 28, 33, 40, 85, 173–76, 187–88, 280, 304, 322; Lettres, S, 32–32b; S, carton 46: 8a–8b, 26, 26b–26c, 27a–27e; S-184a. PAC, MG 8, F131: 930–36; RG 8, I (C ser.), 704: 264; RG 9, I, A5, 4: 31. L.C., House of Assembly, *Journals*, 1793–95. "Le recensement du gouvernement de Québec en 1762," ANQ *Rapport*, 1925–26: 135. *Quebec Gazette*, 12 Feb. 1789, 22 Aug. 1793, 13 Feb. 1794. F.-J. Audet et Fabre Surveyer, *Les députés au premier parl. du Bas-Canada*. Bouchette, *Topographical description of L.C.* Desjardins, *Guide parl.*, 135. P.-G. Roy, *Inventaire des procès-verbaux des grands voyers conservés aux Archives de la province de Québec* (6v., Beauceville, Qué., 1923–32), 2: 28; 4: 74–75. Aubert de Gaspé, *Mémoires* (1971). Raymond Boily, *Le guide du voyageur à la Baie-Saint-Paul au XVIIIe siècle* (Montréal, 1979). F.-X.-E. Frenette, *Notes historiques sur la paroisse de St-Étienne de La Malbaie (Charlevoix)* (Chicoutimi, Qué., 1952). Robert Lavallée, *Petite histoire de Berthier* (La Pocatière, Qué., 1973). A. R. M. Lower, *Canadians in the making, a social history of Canada* (Don Mills [Toronto], 1958). Alexis Mailloux, *Histoire de l'Île-aux-Coudres depuis son établissement jusqu'à nos jours, avec ses traditions, ses légendes, ses coutumes* (Montréal, 1879); *Promenade autour de l'Île-aux-Coudres* (Sainte-Anne-de-la-Pocatière [La Pocatière], 1880). Paul Médéric [J.-P. Tremblay], *La Tremblaye millénaire* (Québec, 1975). Raynold Tremblay, *Un pays à bâtir, Saint-Urbain-en-Charlevoix* ([Québec], 1977). Hare, "L'Assemblée législative du Bas-Canada," *RHAF*, 27: 361–95. Alexis Mailloux, "Le colonel Joseph Dufour," *BRH*, 3 (1897): 157. P.-G. Roy, "Joseph Dufour," *BRH*, 7 (1901): 309.

DUGAL, OLIVIER (baptized **Charles-Olivier**), wood-carver; b. 4 Nov. 1796 in Saint-Michel, not far from Quebec, son of Louis Cotin (Cottin), *dit* Dugal, a tavern-keeper, and Madeleine Bernard; d. 5 May 1829 in Terrebonne, Lower Canada.

One of Olivier Dugal's ancestors was Dugal Cotin, who had come to settle in the Quebec region at the end of the 17th century. In the course of time his given name became the nickname and then the surname of his descendants. Olivier had at least two sisters and three brothers, among them François, two years his senior and also a wood-carver.

Olivier and François received their professional training in Louis QUÉVILLON's workshop, which was located in the vicinity of Montreal. Under Quévillon's guidance wood-carving, which at that time was focused on decorating church interiors, was taught according to a new aesthetic standard that combined elements drawn from well-known examples of decoration in the colony and from earlier European rococo styles. The Dugals must have been recruited by Quévillon some time between 1805 and 1814, during the visits he made to Saint-Michel to do work in the parish church. In the atelier, where there were a number of master wood-carvers, it was probably René Beauvais*, *dit* Saint-James, who taught them, judging by the close bonds that in subsequent years linked François to Saint-James.

While his older brother stayed to begin his career in the Montreal region, Olivier started out in the Quebec area. He must have followed Pierre Séguin, a colleague in Quévillon's workshop who had returned in 1815 to the area he came from. On 24 Feb. 1816 Dugal, Séguin, and Louis-Thomas Berlinguet formed a company to specialize in wood-working. On 8 June, however, Dugal left his partners, at the same time promising them that he would execute Séguin's design for the vaulting of the church of Saint-Augustin-de-Desmaures. The vaulting, which was of a type not widely employed by wood-carvers trained in Quévillon's workshop, was distinguished by alternating diamond-shaped and octagonal coffers in the chancel. This is the only piece of work by Olivier Dugal still extant.

Upon its completion he settled near his brother François at Terrebonne. In 1817 both of them were married there, François to Félicité-Zoë Séguin on 7 January, and 20-year-old Olivier to Marguerite-Hortense Limoges on 16 September. From then on Olivier's career as a wood-carver cannot be untangled from that of his brother, who, through the good offices of his former master Saint-James, had a successful career. In 1816 and again in 1823 Saint-James passed on to François his contracts for making liturgical furnishings and doing the interior decoration in the churches of Sainte-Thérèse-de-Blainville (Sainte-Thérèse) and La Présentation, near Saint-Hyacinthe. François worked for more than 9 years in the first place and for nearly 26 in the second. The decoration at La Présentation, the only extant example of his work in this field, gives evidence of Quévillon's artistic concepts in the pulpit and the churchwardens' pew and of the Baillairgés' ideas in the retable (the structure housing the altar) and the tabernacle; its vaulting displays the emerging neo-baroque style that would become fashionable in the second half of the 19th century. François also did similar works for the church of Saint-Benoît (Mirabel) in collaboration with his former master in 1824 and 1825, and for the church of Sainte-Rose (Laval) in the period 1828–32. Even though the records do not mention Olivier's presence on the sites, the number and scope of the works make it plausible to assume that he took part in creating them. In fact, in November 1828 the Dugals jointly bid for the contract to do the wood-carving in the new church of Notre-Dame in Montreal, but without success. The collaboration of the two brothers came to an end in 1829 with Olivier's untimely death at the age of 32. Subsequently François continued practising his craft in numerous churches of the Montreal region.

The few pieces of work by the Dugal brothers that have survived make it possible to appreciate not only their skill but also their openness to the diverse aesthetic currents in Quebec during the first half of the 19th century.

ANDRÉ LABERGE

AP, Saint-Louis (Terrebonne), Reg. des baptêmes, mariages et sépultures, 7 janv., 16 sept. 1817; 7 mai 1829; Saint-Michel, Reg. des baptêmes, mariages et sépultures, 1794, 5 nov. 1796. MAC-CD, Fonds Morisset, 2, dossiers François Dugal, Olivier Dugal, Pierre Séguin; 6, dossier Saint-Michel (de Bellechasse). *Quebec Gazette*, 14 May 1829. Lebœuf, *Complément*, 1re sér., 3: 46. *Mariages de la paroisse de St-Michel de Bellechasse (1693–1974)*, J. A. Turgeon, compil. (Montréal, 1975), 87–89. Tanguay, *Dictionnaire*, 1: 141; 3: 154. André Laberge, "L'ancienne église Notre-Dame de Montréal: l'évolution et l'influence de son architecture (1672–1830)" (thèse de MA, univ. Laval, Québec, 1982), 154–89, 218–19. Gérard Morisset, *Coup d'œil sur les arts en Nouvelle-France* (Québec, 1941), 36. Émile Vaillancourt, *Une maîtrise d'art en Canada (1800–1823)* (Montréal, 1920), 12, 16, 19, 28, 37.

DUGAS, JOSEPH, settler; b., probably in 1738, in Cobequid (near Truro), N.S., eldest child of Pierre Dugas and Isabelle Bourg; m. 1764 Marie-Josephte Robichaud in Annapolis Royal, N.S., and they had seven children; d. 26 Feb. 1823 in Anse des LeBlanc, N.S.

In 1751 Pierre Dugas and his family moved from Cobequid to Île Saint-Jean (Prince Edward Island). Along with other Acadians there, Pierre, his wife, and six children were victims of the deportation supervised by Colonel Lord Rollo* in 1758. Embarking on the *Tamerlane*, they reached Saint-Malo, France, on 16 Jan. 1759 and were later found at Saint-Servan. Young Joseph Dugas, however, does not appear among the children of Pierre and Isabelle who landed in France. Nor is he listed among the prisoners at Fort Cumberland (near Sackville, N.B.), Fort Edward (Windsor, N.S.), or Halifax.

According to one family tradition, Joseph had moved to Louisbourg, Île Royale (Cape Breton Island), at the age of 16, enrolled in the French militia there, and was wounded and taken prisoner at the fall of the fortress in 1758 to British forces under Jeffery Amherst*. The story continues that while in hospital Joseph was nearly poisoned but managed to survive;

Dumont

he then escaped and made his way to the Baie des Chaleurs, joining about 800 Acadians already settled in the region. This account may be true but its veracity is doubted by the Acadian historian Placide Gaudet*, who rather believes that Joseph's capture by British forces took place in October 1760 at the fall of Restigouche (Que.), the site of a large concentration of Acadian refugees [see Jean-François Bourdon* de Dombourg]. Gaudet's claim is supported by another Dugas family tradition, according to which Joseph lived at Restigouche, in the Miramichi region (N.B.), and in the vicinity of Fort Cumberland before moving to Pisiquid (Windsor, N.S.) and then to Annapolis Royal. Whatever the case, it is known for certain that after the Treaty of Paris in 1763 Joseph went to Annapolis Royal, where in 1764 he married Marie-Josephte Robichaud, daughter of Prudent Robichaud and Marie Richard. The Robichaud family had been among the Acadian prisoners at Fort Edward.

In 1764 the British government informed the authorities of Nova Scotia that Acadians willing to take the oath of allegiance could return to the colony. Three years later Lieutenant Governor Michael Francklin*, responding to the appeals of Acadians who had returned from exile, set aside lands for an Acadian settlement along St Mary's Bay. During the summer of 1768 this area, given the name of Clare, was surveyed by John Morrison, deputy provincial surveyor, and divided into lots. The lands surveyed later became known as the Bastarache Grant.

When in 1767 the government had announced its intention of creating a settlement along St Mary's Bay, Dugas had taken it upon himself to explore the territory from the mouth of the Sissiboo River to Chicaben (Church Point). In September 1768, accompanied by his wife and his four-year-old daughter, Isabelle, he again travelled to the bay and this time settled at a place later called Anse des LeBlanc. The following spring a large group of almost 100 Acadians joined Dugas in the region, and in the next few years still others arrived. Among the new settlers were Pierre Le Blanc*, Pierre Doucet*, and Amable Doucet*.

Dugas's wife had been pregnant at the time she and Joseph left for St Mary's Bay and, 20 days after their arrival, a baby boy was born and named Joseph. During that first year in the region the couple had to overcome the many difficulties of their isolated life in the wilderness, the nearest neighbour being some 50 miles away. The mere fact that they and their two children survived, depending only on their own resources, shows ability and initiative well above the ordinary. Perhaps Joseph's greatest accomplishment was in laying the foundation of the well-integrated subsistence economy by which the settlers of St Mary's Bay prospered even into the 20th century.

Following Joseph's example each settler skilfully combined the occupations of fisherman, farmer, lumberman, builder, and hunter.

Little else is known of Joseph Dugas and his family. On 8 Sept. 1769 Abbé Charles-François Bailly* de Messein celebrated the first mass in the present district of Clare in Dugas's rude dwelling at Anse des LeBlanc; the next priest to visit the area was Joseph-Mathurin Bourg* in 1774. Joseph Dugas the younger, the first Acadian born in Clare, settled at Grosses Coques; his house is still standing and bears a plaque commemorating both his birth and the establishment of Clare Township. A monument to Joseph Dugas the elder and his wife was erected in front of the Joseph Dugas School at Church Point. The inscription on the monument notes in part that "the courage of this couple, who faced and surmounted all the difficulties of survival by themselves, has inspired a feeling of pride among all the settlers who followed them."

J. ALPHONSE DEVEAU

Arch. de l'évêché de Bathurst (Bathurst, N.-B.), Caraquet, reg. des baptêmes, mariages et sépultures, 1768–73 (mfm. at Centre d'études acadiennes, Univ. de Moncton, N.-B.). Centre d'études acadiennes, Fonds Placide Gaudet, "Généalogies acadiennes," 1580 (mfm. at PAC); "Notes généalogiques sur les familles acadiennes, c. 1600–1900," dossier Dugas-3. PANS, MG 1, 258. Bona Arsenault, Histoire et généalogie des Acadiens (2v., Québec, 1965). Antoine Bernard, Histoire de la survivance acadienne, 1755–1935 (Montréal, 1935). P.-M. Dagnaud, Les Français du sud-ouest de la Nouvelle Écosse . . . (Besançon, France, 1905). Émile Lauvrière, La tragédie d'un peuple: histoire du peuple acadien de ses origines à nos jours (nouv. éd., 2v., Paris, [1924]). Arthur Melançon, Vie de l'abbé Bourg, premier prêtre acadien, missionnaire et grand-vicaire pour l'Acadie et la Baie-des-Chaleurs, 1744–1797 (Rimouski, Qué., 1921). I. W. Wilson, A geography and history of the county of Digby, Nova Scotia (Halifax, 1900; repr. Belleville, Ont., 1975). Placide Gaudet, "Mort de deux patriarches de la Baie-Ste-Marie," L'Évangéline (Weymouth Bridge, N.-É.), 31 mars 1892.

DUMONT, NICOLAS-EUSTACHE LAMBERT.
See LAMBERT

DURAND, JAMES,
businessman, politician, office holder, and militia officer; b. 1775 in Abergavenny, Wales, son of a British officer; m. first 1797 a woman whose name is unknown, and they had two sons and two daughters; m. secondly c. 1807 Kezia (Keziah) Morrison, a widow, and they had four sons; d. 22 March 1833 in Hamilton, Upper Canada.

James Durand arrived in British North America in 1802 as agent for Caldcleugh, Boyd, and Reid, a London mercantile house, to settle delinquent accounts. After a brief stay in Montreal, he turned his attention to the indebted partnership operating the Bridgewater Works near Chippawa, Upper Canada. Powered by the current above the falls at Niagara, this establishment included a sawmill, grist-mill, iron forge, ten outbuildings, and a tenement for labourers. Durand seized the operation, drew bills of exchange on his London masters, and initiated a lawsuit at York (Toronto) to hold mill master Robert RANDAL to an indenture with the works. Having put matters in order for his employers during the summer of 1802, in July 1804 Durand purchased the Bridgewater Works and considerable property along Chippawa Creek, as well as land in Ancaster and Delaware townships. To finance his acquisitions, he agreed to pay his employers £11,000 by instalments commencing in 1806 and concluding in 1811. Randal managed Bridgewater while Durand opened a trading depot near Long Point and arranged grain shipments to Bridgewater. For assistance he employed Peter DESJARDINS as clerk. In a short time Durand had established himself as an ambitious merchant.

He journeyed to England in 1804, returning to the store near Long Point with his wife and English hounds – Durand was a marksman, hunter, and dog fancier. In 1805 he moved to his newly purchased properties in lot 14, concession 3, Barton Township. From this site he continued until 1810 his extensive business with settlers in the Niagara and London districts. In 1809 he acquired a further acreage in lot 14 from Nathaniel Hughson and the following year the two men promoted their properties as the site for an administrative capital in the event a new district was established. About this time Durand's enterprises suffered from a depression in the produce market which forced merchants to sacrifice assets in order to collect hard currency to meet the demands of their Montreal and British creditors. His situation was exacerbated by competition with the Bridgewater Works from new grist-mills which had begun to operate in Norfolk County. As a consequence, he sold the works to Thomas CLARK and Samuel Street*, two of the leading financial magnates in the Niagara peninsula, in 1810. Durand maintained his store, some lands, and the Barton farm. The War of 1812, however, disrupted his remaining enterprises. Shipments were interrupted; the flow of American settlers, central to his lines of endeavour, stopped; settlers were unable to meet mortgage payments; and a few clients defected to the Americans leaving unsettled accounts.

Durand's experience of the war itself was a study in contrast. Major-General Isaac Brock* appears to have been entertained at his Barton farm while en route to Detroit in 1812. Durand, a loyal subject, served as captain of a flank company in the 5th Lincoln Militia and distinguished himself at the battle of Queenston

Heights. In 1814 he had to billet British troops on his farm and, like his neighbours, suffered considerable property damage, his losses amounting to £172. Perhaps more important to him was the abuse of civil liberties associated with the military presence. Criticism of the conduct of the regular army by anyone in the midst of what had become a military camp at Burlington Heights (Hamilton) implied risks. Durand was warned by John Willson*, a Saltfleet farmer and assemblyman, that "times were too dangerous for a man to open his mouth." None the less, Durand censured aspects of military conduct and when a local assemblyman, Abraham MARKLE, joined the Americans in 1813, Durand ran for his vacated seat, entering the assembly in February 1815. In the mean time he had sold his Barton lands to George Hamilton* for £1,750 and moved to a salt spring in the Trent River valley. The war had cut off the routine supply of salt – an essential preservative of meat – driving up the price. Durand, no doubt, had hopes of a successful enterprise.

Until 1820 Durand was a reform leader in the province who impressed his peers with his command of parliamentary precedents, his intimate knowledge of the colony, and his sharp tongue. In 1815 he denounced the imposition of martial law during the war and criticized the methods adopted for requisitioning supplies. By 1816 Durand had moved back to the Head of the Lake (the vicinity of present-day Hamilton Harbour), settling on a farm near Dundas. In 1816 he was a member of the committee on finance and the committee to draft a militia code. His greatest accomplishment, however, came as chairman of the committee on education. Its report, condemning the failure of the government to provide for the instruction of poorer inhabitants, led to the Common Schools Act of 1816. This reform, which annoyed John Strachan*, was largely the work of Durand. Efforts in support of economic development also made him an active local figure in 1816. He guided the bill establishing the Gore District through the house and acted as agent for Hamilton and Hughson to secure the designation of their plot as the site of the district town.

The new district presented Durand with opportunities for office. In April 1816 he became the registrar for Wentworth and Halton counties, a position offering intimate knowledge about land and business transactions. In May he took the oath of road commissioner and, as a self-interested merchant and land speculator, pressed for improvements to the roads in the area between Ancaster village and the Grand River. As foreman at a "Grand Inquest" held at Ancaster during January 1817, Durand criticized alleged disorder among the Indians which he considered a threat to the main road and to the general progress of contiguous settlements [see George Powlis*].

Durand was elected for the riding of Wentworth in February 1817. During the election he had attacked the conduct of wartime administrations and his opponent, John Willson. Durand took his seat on 25 February and on 1 March the assembly led by Robert NICHOL branded his election broadside (printed by Bartemas FERGUSON and published in the *Niagara Spectator* by Richard COCKRELL) a "scandalous and malicious libel." Three days later the assemblymen voted to jail him for the remainder of the session. Durand, however, absented himself and as a consequence on 7 March was held in contempt of the house and expelled. The previous day Nichol had introduced a petition from Richard Beasley* and other freeholders of Wentworth complaining that since Durand's name did not appear on the county assessment rolls he was ineligible to represent the riding. A writ for a new election was issued on 24 March; Durand, having established proper qualifications, was re-elected. In November 1817 he chaired a meeting held in Ancaster to collect information for Robert Gourlay*.

During the first parliamentary session of 1818, Durand recovered his position of leadership by defending the rights of the assembly against the pretensions of the Executive and the Legislative councils. As chairman of the public accounts committee, he investigated how annual grants from Great Britain had been spent; his conclusion was that they had not advanced the development of the colony but had lined the pockets of executive favourites. With regard to the Legislative Council, Durand led the house and council to a deadlock, claiming that, like the House of Commons, the House of Assembly could draft or revise money bills. His actions forced Administrator Samuel SMITH to prorogue the session.

The arrival of Lieutenant Governor Sir Peregrine Maitland* silenced Durand's reform activities. In part, Maitland's administration responded to concerns about inadequate internal development. Durand, for instance, sat on a committee to consider improvements to St Lawrence navigation; he chaired another recommending a canal to link lakes Ontario and Erie. Maitland, however, suppressed Gourlay's conventions, and Durand was sensitive to the denial of patronage and exclusion from land grants inflicted on Gourlay's supporters. Durand made his peace, presenting a motion in the assembly that a letter published by Gourlay in 1819 be deemed libellous. Then, in the election of 1820, he was defeated by George Hamilton; ten years later, Allan Napier MacNab* turned back an election challenge by Durand.

Durand's business affairs grew after 1820. He erected two sawmills on Fairchild Creek and secured 1,200 acres with timber stands. He also purchased land in Brantford, London, and Sarnia Township. In the late 1820s, along with his son-in-law Peter Hunter Hamilton and Peter Desjardins, he participated in the Desjardins Canal Company. Sons James and Charles Morrison enjoyed local reputations as reform spokesmen during the 1830s.

JOHN C. WEAVER

AO, RG 1, A-I-6: 4820–21. PAC, MG 24, B18, 14; RG 5, A1: 12784–85, 14336–39, 14957–64, 18473–74; RG 19, E5(a), 3732, claim 331. "Journals of Legislative Assembly of U.C.," AO *Report*, 1912: 177, 207–8, 210–16, 264, 292, 337–45; 1913: 3, 50, 73, 90, 170, 438–39, 550–52. Charles Durand, *Reminiscences of Charles Durand of Toronto, barrister* (Toronto, 1897), 9, 17–21, 45, 105–9, 143, 414. E. J. Hathaway, *Jesse Ketchum and his times: being a chronicle of the social life and public affairs of the province of Upper Canada during its first half century* (Toronto, 1929), 101–11. Adam Shortt, "The economic effect of the War of 1812 on Upper Canada," *The defended border: Upper Canada and the War of 1812 . . .* , ed. Morris Zaslow and W. B. Turner (Toronto, 1964), 299–300. E. A. Cruikshank, "A country merchant in Upper Canada, 1800–1812," *OH*, 25 (1929): 160–62; "A study of disaffection in Upper Canada in 1812–15," RSC *Trans.*, 3rd ser., 6 (1912), sect.II: 11–65. H. F. Gardiner, "The Hamiltons of Queenston, Kingston and Hamilton," *OH*, 8 (1909): 28–31.

DUVAL, CHARLES (baptized **Jean**, until 1795 at the latest he signed **Charle**), silversmith; b. 4 April 1758 at Quebec, son of Pierre Duval and Françoise-Élisabeth Panneton; his whereabouts are unknown after 1828.

In the autumn of 1775, when a census was taken of the English-speaking residents in the town of Quebec, Charles Duval was a 17-year-old apprentice living with George McClure (Maclure), his brother-in-law. It was likely in Quebec that he apprenticed as a silversmith, perhaps with Joseph Schindler* or Jean-Nicolas Amiot (who were witnesses at the marriage of his cousin Jacques Duval in 1769), but possibly with Joseph Lucas or Louis Huguet, *dit* Latour.

Duval was evidently well established as a silversmith in Montreal by 1783, since in that year he rented a stone house on Rue Saint-Jacques from silversmith Dominique ROUSSEAU, the payments to be made in "silver articles," such as "pins, large and small bracelets, crosses," at the rate of 700 "francs" for the rent, 480 "piastres worth 6 francs each" for wood, and 1,100 "livres" for "rolls for drawing silver" (an impressive tool employed in making such things as wire, mouldings, and tubes). Duval associated with silversmiths François Larsonneur, Pierre Foureur, *dit* Champagne, Louis and Pierre* Huguet, *dit* Latour; all of them, like Rousseau, were interested in the lucrative market in trade silver, which was being produced in quantity in Montreal to barter with the Indians for furs. On 6 Sept. 1795 Duval wed Magdelaine You, aged 37, the widow of Louis Huguet, *dit* Latour, with whom he had had a son six months earlier; the child died two weeks after being legitimized by their marriage. Duval was then 37, not 28 as stated in his marriage certificate. Through this union Duval became stepfather to Magdeleine Huguet, who married silversmith Jean-Baptiste-François-Xavier Dupéré, *dit* Champlain, in 1801.

Duval received his first orders for church silver the year he was married. He worked in turn for the *fabriques* of the parishes of Sainte-Anne-des-Plaines (1795) and Lachenaie (1798), making altar cruets; Notre-Dame in Montreal, doing various repairs (1800); and Vaudreuil, for which he crafted a chalice and a ciborium (1801). In 1798 he took Joseph Charbonneaux on as an apprentice for a period of ten and a half years. From 1801 to 1803 he lived on Rue Notre-Dame near Rousseau. In 1802 he took on a second apprentice, Charlemagne La Mothe, aged 6, who was to stay until he reached the age of 21. His business seems, therefore, to have been prosperous at that time.

In 1808 and 1810 Duval was living with his family at Saint-François-du-Lac, which was close to a trading factory. In 1818 he was at Trois-Rivières, where he contracted to make for Jean Lemaître Lottinville "twelve silver soup-spoons, each weighing twelve and a half shillings in the currency of the province," for a total amount of £10 10*s*. He apparently was still at Trois-Rivières in 1820, when he contracted to purchase a clock from Sophie Lemaître Lottinville, a woman who could transact business in her own right. Between 1817 and 1828 he executed various pieces for the *fabriques* of the surrounding parishes of Verchères, Bécancour, and Yamachiche. He was also present at the marriages of some friends and relatives at Saint-François-du-Lac, where his brother-in-law McClure had set up as a merchant. It may have been the same "Maclure" who in 1787 had received 66 *livres* 15 *sous* from the *fabrique* of Baie-du-Febvre (Baieville) "for a small silver ciborium." If so, the article, as yet not found, might have been made by Duval.

Only a small number of objects bearing Duval's mark are known. Nevertheless, almost all the church silver is of interest. In the chalice done for Verchères and the holy-water basin for Saint-François-du-Lac (both now in the Musée du Québec), for example, he gave evidence of creativity, an innate aesthetic sense, and even virtuosity, although his technique was somewhat naïve. He drew inspiration from the style of Ignace-François Delezenne*, who lived near Saint-François-du-Lac towards the end of his life. This influence may have been passed on to him by John Oakes, as well as through imitation. Few pieces of Duval's flatware and trade jewellery have been preserved, even though they must have been his main source of income. The diversity of his work well reflects the varied interests of society at that period.

ROBERT DEROME in collaboration with
MARY HENSHAW

[Marius Barbeau, in his *Maîtres artisans de chez nous* (Montréal, [1942]) and "Deux cents ans d'orfèvrerie chez nous," RSC *Trans.*, 3rd ser., 33 (1939), sect.ɪ: 183–92, gives two different death dates for Charles Duval, 1803 and 1843. It is my belief, however, that Duval probably died at or near Trois-Rivières shortly after 1828. His works have been located at Bécancour, Lachenaie, Montreal (in the École du Meuble), Quebec (at the Musée du Québec), Sainte-Anne-des-Plaines, Saint-François-du-Lac, Saint-Hubert, Vaudreuil, Verchères, and Yamachiche, as well as at the New Brunswick Museum. Others are held in the Henry Birks Collection of Silver at the National Gallery of Canada (Ottawa) and in the Louis Carrier and Gérard Morisset collections. R.D.]

ANQ-M, CE1-51, 7 janv. 1784; 12 déc. 1788; 21 mars, 6, 23 sept. 1795; 12 oct. 1801; CE3-8, 5 juill. 1808, 11 déc. 1810, 2 févr. 1818, 1819: f.19; CN1-74, 23–24 janv. 1788, 12 juin 1810; CN1-121, 19 déc. 1798, 12 mars 1801, 30 mars 1802; CN1-158, 11 août 1783, 24 oct. 1788; CN1-255, 13 mai 1794; CN1-269, 6 juin 1799. ANQ-MBF, CN1-32, 25 juill. 1822; CN1-79, 21 janv. 1818. ANQ-Q, CE1-1, 5 avril 1758, 3 avril 1769. AP, La Nativité-de-Notre-Dame (Bécancour), Livres de comptes, 1819: f.51v; 1827: f.66; 1828: f.68; Notre-Dame de Montréal, boîte 13, chemise 2, 18 janv., 5 mai 1800; Saint-Charles (Lachenaie), Livres de comptes, 1798: f.33; 19–20, 28, 30 août 1798; Sainte-Anne (Sainte-Anne-des-Plaines), Livres de comptes, 1795: f.14v; Sainte-Anne (Yamachiche), Livres de comptes, 1828: f.5; Saint-François-Xavier (Verchères), Livres de comptes, 1817: f.14b; Saint-Michel (Vaudreuil), Livres de comptes, 1801: ff.133, 137. Arch. des Religieuses hospitalières de Saint-Joseph (Montréal), Affaires temporelles de la communauté, comptabilité, 1799, 1801–10. MAC-CD, Fonds Morisset, 2, dossier Charles Duval. Tanguay, *Dictionnaire*, 3: 585; 7: 492. Robert Derome, "Delezenne, les orfèvres, l'orfèvrerie, 1740–1790" (thèse de MA, univ. de Montréal, 1974). J. E. Langdon, *Canadian silversmiths, 1700–1900* (Toronto, 1966). Ramsay Traquair, *The old silver of Quebec* (Toronto, 1940). Ramsay Traquair and G. A. Neilson, *The old church of St. Charles de Lachenaie* (Montreal, 1934). "Indian trade silver," N.B. Museum, *Art Bull.* (Saint John, N.B.), 6 (1961), no.1. É.-Z. Massicotte, "Dominique Rousseau, maître orfèvre et négociant en pelleteries," *BRH*, 49 (1943): 343. Gérard Morisset, "Bibelots et futilités," *La Patrie* (Montréal), 15 janv. 1950: 14–15; "L'orfèvrerie canadienne," *Technique* (Montréal), 22 (1947): 83–88.

E

EASTON, ROBERT, Presbyterian clergyman; baptized 15 Sept. 1773 in Selkirk, Scotland, eldest of four children born to William Easton, a gardener, and Nellie Thomson; d. 2 May 1831 in Montreal.

Easton

Robert Easton was a native of Hawick, near Selkirk, and he attended grammar school there. After moving on to the University of Edinburgh and graduating in 1793 from the seminary of the Associate Synod of Scotland at Selkirk, he was licensed by the Burgher Presbytery of Edinburgh; however, it was not until 2 Aug. 1798, following his acceptance of a call to Morpeth, England, that he was ordained to the ministry. He was recruited for service in America by the Reverend John Mason of New York, and in 1802 he resigned the charge of Morpeth and with Mason and five other young clergymen, one of whom was Robert Forrest, sailed to New York in September.

Easton undertook missionary duties in the United States before coming to Montreal in 1804 to minister to a congregation that Forrest had extracted from St Gabriel Street Church after losing his bid for its pulpit to James Somerville* in 1803. Having accepted a call to New York, Forrest had persuaded Easton to replace him in Montreal. Without a church, Easton's congregation worshipped in a room on Rue Notre-Dame. The members were largely Scottish Secessionists and American Presbyterians, for the most part "tradesmen and mechanics" according to James Leslie*, who added that his own congregation, St Gabriel Street Church, was attended "by the higher classes of the Presbyterian community." Under Easton the new congregation quickly elected a committee of managers and made plans to build a church. Two adjacent lots on Rue Saint-Pierre were bought; on one Easton laid the cornerstone for a church on 15 Oct. 1805. Given the high tension in relations between Britain and the United States, he took pains in a speech on that occasion to emphasize that his congregation was no less loyal to Britain than that of St Gabriel Street Church. At the same time, while deploring a decision of the Court of King's Bench at Quebec that refused civil registers to all but Anglican and Roman Catholic clergy [see Clark Bentom*], he urged forbearance on his congregation. In late 1806 or in 1807 the church, which became known as St Peter Street Church, was completed; of the £1,500 required to build it, £600 was collected by Easton in New York on condition that the institution would remain a Secession body.

In May 1808 Easton moved into the stone house that the congregation had acquired with the lot adjacent to the church. From his salary of £125, which was always in arrears, the committee of managers deducted £18 for rent. Easton soon brought to the manse a wife, Mary Beattie, who had moved with her family to Montreal from Salem, N.Y. Of the four children born to them, two would die in infancy.

The years 1808–18 were the most satisfying of Easton's career. The congregation finally obtained civil registers in 1815. It also prospered, and as a result Easton's salary doubled to £250 by 1818. In addition to serving his own congregation, he minis-

tered to Irish and Scottish Presbyterian immigrants passing through and to Presbyterians in settlements outside the city. He became better known; at least two of his sermons were published, one in 1815, the other, preached before the Female Benevolent Society of Montreal, in 1816. In the latter year he was appointed the Montreal agent for the British and Foreign Bible Society, and when an auxiliary was formed in the city in 1818 he became its first secretary.

Easton had attempted unsuccessfully in 1805 to connect St Peter Street Church with the Associate Synod of Scotland. In July 1817 another effort was made: Easton, William Smart*, the Secession Church minister at Brockville, Upper Canada, and William Bell* and William Taylor, two ministers recently arrived from Scotland who probably provided the initiative for the move, petitioned the Associate Synod for authorization to form a Canadian presbytery in connection with it. Before a response could be received, however, Smart launched the idea of an independent presbytery that would group all ministers in the Canadas whatever their affiliation to the various Scottish churches. In January 1818 Taylor, Smart, and Easton, who had become an enthusiastic supporter of the idea, met and formed the Presbytery of the Canadas, with Easton as moderator, in order to conduct an ordination. It was decided to hold another meeting in July in St Peter Street Church, to which all Presbyterian clergy would be invited, with the object of establishing a union on a more solid foundation. Bell, hoping for affiliation to the Associate Synod, had refused to attend the January meeting, but he was present in July. He had earlier found that Easton's "preaching was not reckoned evangelical" and had taken a personal dislike to him. "We soon learned," he recorded, "that Mr. Easton had taken all the business of the Presbytery into his own hands and had acted with all the authority of a bishop," and Easton continued to dominate the proceedings to Bell's great frustration. When the authorization to form a presbytery arrived from Scotland in the course of the proceedings, Easton feared it would compromise the independent organization and tried to suppress the news. Bell – and the press – learned of it, however, and a lively controversy ensued. Easton got his way, and the Presbytery of the Canadas was accepted.

In June 1818 the committee of managers of St Peter Street Church had reluctantly granted Easton a year's leave of absence in Britain on full salary to enable him to recover a declining health and attract ministers to the colony. He angered his congregation by remaining almost two years. In 1819–20, while he was still abroad, Bell had the Presbytery of the Canadas transformed into the Synod of the Canadas and seems to have insisted on the exclusion of Easton and his congregation; in any case, St Peter Street Church, probably unhappy with the assistance it was receiving, repudiated the synod in February 1820, thus cutting its ties with Canadian Presbyterian Secessionism, and forced its decision on Easton when he returned in the fall. Easton's influence with the congregation was diminished, and the break with Canadian Secessionism divided the church. When Easton offered his resignation in 1822 the congregation called John Burns, a Church of Scotland minister, to succeed him and resolved to establish its connection with that church. These decisions provoked the departure of the American minority, who had contributed to building the church on condition that the congregation remain a Secession body. The Americans founded the American Presbyterian Church, and St Peter's Street Church was renamed St Andrew's Church.

Easton turned increasingly to outside interests. Before leaving in 1818 he had proposed a revision of Britain's emigration policy to Sir John Coape SHERBROOKE and petitioned government for a land grant in Rawdon Township. After his return he was again appointed secretary of the Montreal auxiliary of the British and Foreign Bible Society and in 1822 he proposed to the Church Missionary Society, an Anglican body, the establishment of an Indian college in Lower Canada. He also pursued his application for a land grant, but without success.

With his eyesight deteriorating, Easton retired, on an annuity of £150, when John Burns finally arrived in 1824. Of Easton, Archibald Henderson, a Presbyterian minister who had arrived in Lower Canada in 1818, asserted that one could not long remain in his company "without perceiving him to be a complete visionary." Although his career had ended in failure, the division of the congregation he had nurtured produced two of Montreal's major Presbyterian churches.

ELIZABETH ANN KERR MCDOUGALL

Robert Easton is the author of *A sermon, delivered before the members of the Female Benevolent Society, in Montreal, September 8, 1816* (Montreal, 1816) and *Reasons for joy and praise, a sermon preached April 6, 1815, being the day of general thanksgiving for peace with the United States* (Montreal, 1815).

ANQ-M, CE1-125, 5 mai 1831. Arch. of the Mount Royal Cemetery Company (Outremont, Que.), Reg. of burials, May 1831. Church Missionary Soc. Arch. (London), C, C.1/M, Mission books (incoming letters), 28 Jan. 1822. Mount Royal Cemetery Company (Outremont), Tombstone of Robert Easton. PAC, RG 1, L3ᴸ: 79841. St Andrew's Presbyterian Church (Montreal), Minutes of the Church Committee, 1804–24. *Canadian Courant and Montreal Advertiser*, 22 Dec. 1821, 4 May 1831. *Montreal Gazette*, 21 Oct. 1805. W. M. Glasgow, *Cyclopedic manual of the United Presbyterian Church of North America* . . . (Pittsburgh, Pa., 1903). Hew Scott et al., *Fasti ecclesiæ scoticanæ: the succession of ministers in the Church of Scotland from the Reformation* (new ed., 9v. to date, Edinburgh, 1915–), 7. R. Campbell, *Hist. of Scotch Presbyterian Church*. William Gregg, *History of the Presbyterian Church in the Dominion of Canada* . . . (Toronto, 1885). E. A. [Kerr] McDougall, "The American element in the early Presbyterian Church in Montreal (1786–1824)" (MA thesis, McGill Univ., Montreal, 1965), 113–14, 152–53, 155; "The Presbyterian Church in western Lower Canada, 1815–1842" (PHD thesis, McGill Univ., 1969), 60–64, 307. William MacKelvie, *Annals and statistics of the United Presbyterian Church* . . . (Edinburgh, 1873). John McKerrow, *History of the Secession Church* (2v., Edinburgh, 1849), 2. Isabel [Murphy] Skelton, *A man austere: William Bell, parson and pioneer* (Toronto, 1947).

ELIZA Y REVENTA, FRANCISCO DE, naval officer and explorer; b. 1759 in El Puerto de Santa Maria, Spain; m. Saturnina Norberta Caamaño; d. 19 Feb. 1825 in Cadiz, Spain.

Francisco de Eliza y Reventa began his naval career as a marine guard in December 1773. He served in the Spanish expedition of 1775 against Algiers (Algeria) and in 1780 he was sent to America, where he later took part in the siege of Pensacola (Fla) during the War of American Independence. In 1789, as a senior warship lieutenant, he was dispatched to San Blas (Nayarit State, Mexico) with his brother-in-law Jacinto Caamaño and several other officers to bolster the Spanish naval presence on the Pacific coast. Since Eliza was the most senior officer available at San Blas, he was named in 1790 by Viceroy Count de Revilla Gigedo to command an expedition to reoccupy Nootka Sound (B.C.) in the wake of the crisis following the seizure of British merchant vessels the previous year by Esteban José Martínez*. Although Spain wanted no repetition of Martínez's aggressive actions without just cause, Eliza carried instructions to dislodge any foreigners found at Nootka. Besides occupying and fortifying the site, he was to collect data on the flora and fauna, conduct meteorological experiments, obtain mineral samples, and trade Mexican copper sheets for sea otter pelts. Just as important, he was to establish friendly relations with the Indians and study their society.

Commanding the vessels *Concepción*, *San Carlos*, and *Princess Royal* (renamed *Princesa Real*), Eliza arrived at Friendly Cove, in Nootka Sound, on 3 April 1790. Thus began a major effort to prove Spanish sovereignty. The expedition was accompanied by 76 soldiers of the 1st Free Company of Volunteers of Catalonia, commanded by Pedro de Alberni*. The seamen and soldiers constructed buildings, planted gardens, and built a small fort capable of repelling attack. Exploration was given first priority: on 4 May 1790 Eliza dispatched Salvador Fidalgo to visit the Russian posts in Alaska and on 31 May, Manuel Quimper was sent to examine Juan de Fuca Strait, which was believed to be the most likely entry to the fabled passage through the continent to the Atlantic. Although Eliza did everything possible to prepare

Eliza

the settlement for the long winter, it proved to be a difficult one. The Indians, remembering the murder of chief Callicum by the Spaniards the previous year, were not particularly friendly. Spanish efforts to obtain lumber led to a number of incidents and to the Spaniards' outright theft of planks from houses of Nootka Indians. On another occasion, five Indians were killed during an attempt to steal some casks. Despite these aggravations, Eliza was successful in improving relations with the people of chief Muquinna*. When British fur trader Captain Thomas Hudson and five men died in a shipwreck on their way to the Spanish settlement in October, Eliza was able to enlist the aid of Muquinna in searching for survivors and documents. On 4 Jan. 1791 British trader Captain James Colnett* arrived at Nootka Sound on the *Argonaut* and was assisted by Eliza in repairing his vessel. By then, the Spaniards had begun to suffer great privation. Lack of fresh food caused scurvy and the biscuit either rotted from the humidity or was consumed by hordes of rats. Nine men perished during the winter and by the spring Eliza had to send 32 soldiers and seamen, suffering from a variety of ailments including colds, rheumatic pains, and dysentery, by ship to California for recovery.

Viceroy Revilla Gigedo was not at all pleased with Eliza's rather laconic descriptions of life and conditions at Nootka Sound or by his apparent lack of scientific interest in the Indians. Information about the potential of the northern territory or about whether the Indians were being attracted to Catholicism was slow to arrive in Mexico City. The viceroy was further distressed when he learned that Eliza had given the Indians a large gift of copper sheets to search for the bodies of Hudson and the English sailors. The copper was intended to gauge the commercial potential of the sea otter trade. In Revilla Gigedo's opinion, a few trinkets and old scrap metal would do for gifts. In these complaints as well as in other criticisms of Eliza's policies, the bureaucrats reflected their total ignorance of frontier conditions. There had been little time at first to engage in scientific experiments and the Indians refused to trade for inferior goods when the British and American traders offered copper, weapons, and other desirable items.

In fact, Eliza did collect information during the quiet winter months and was able to present his superiors with a comprehensive view of the country, its inhabitants, and its potential usefulness to Spain. He was impressed by the Indians' canoes and their maritime skills. He described their methods of fishing and whaling and observed their ceremonies. Besides trading copper for sea otter pelts, Eliza began to purchase Indian children. By April 1791 he had bought eight boys and seven girls whom he believed he had spared from cannibal feasts. Like many other Spanish observers, he had nothing good to say about

the climate or the potential value of the northwest coast. In his view, Nootka Sound's only promise lay with the maritime fur trade, but he noted that otters were being depleted and the Indians were losing their interest in trade goods.

On 4 May 1791 Eliza, in command of the *San Carlos* and a small schooner reconstructed at Nootka and named, after his wife, the *Santa Saturnina*, set sail on a voyage of exploration. He visited chief Wikinanish* at Clayoquot Sound and then entered Juan de Fuca Strait. Although Eliza conducted fairly extensive explorations, described the agricultural potential of the region, and noted the influx of fresh water from the river now called the Fraser, he did not examine the nearby sound (Puget Sound, Wash.) or circumnavigate present-day Vancouver Island. He left these tasks and the greater honour to George Vancouver*, Dionisio Alcalá-Galiano*, and Cayetano Valdés y Flores Bazán. Some historians have criticized Eliza for not accomplishing more on this voyage, but the Indians were hostile and his crew was weakened from scurvy. More important, he could not take too many risks, knowing that he had to return to prepare the settlement at Nootka Sound for the next winter.

During the autumn of 1791 Eliza expressed fear that his men might not survive another winter with the few provisions that remained. Fortunately, the winter was not as bad as that of the previous year. Food supplies sent from Mexico were of better quality and the storage facilities afforded better protection from humidity and rats. The Indians were now frequent visitors to the settlement and Eliza was convinced that within a few years they would convert to Catholicism.

Successful at re-establishing the Spanish presence on the north Pacific coast, Eliza departed from Nootka Sound on 24 July 1792 and did not return. Although the settlement was in good condition when he left, he was anxious to return to Spain or to take up a less isolated post. His wife and children petitioned the ministry of Marine for his return, but Eliza was needed in Mexico. In 1793 he commanded an expedition to explore the California coast and from 1795 to 1801 he commanded the naval base at San Blas. Finally, he was transferred in 1803 to Cadiz, where he continued to serve in the navy. During the occupation of Spain by Napoleon, from 1808 to 1814, Eliza held a number of political posts at Cadiz.

CHRISTON I. ARCHER

Archivo General de Indias (Seville, Spain), Audiencia de México, legajo 1537. Archivo General de la Nación (Mexico City), Sección de Historia, vols.68–69. Museo Naval (Madrid), MS nos.575 bis, 2305. J. M. Moziño [Losada] Suárez de Figueroa, *Noticias de Nutka: an account of Nootka Sound in 1792*, trans. and ed. I. H. Wilson (Seattle, Wash., 1970). W. L. Cook, *Flood tide of empire: Spain and the Pacific northwest, 1543–1819* (New Haven, Conn., and

London, 1973). M. E. Thurman, *The naval department of San Blas; New Spain's bastion for Alta California and Nootka, 1767 to 1798* (Glendale, Calif., 1967). Javier de Ybarra y Bergé, *De California á Alaska: historia de un descubrimiento* (Madrid, 1945). C. I. Archer, "The transient presence: a re-appraisal of Spanish attitudes toward the northwest coast in the eighteenth century," *BC Studies* (Vancouver), no.18 (summer 1973): 3–32.

ENGLISH CHIEF. *See* Aw-gee-nah

ERB, ABRAHAM, miller; b. 12 July 1772 in Warwick Township, Pa, fourth son of Christian Erb and Maria Scherch; m. May 1804 Magdalena Erb in Lancaster County, Pa; d. 6 Sept. 1830 in Waterloo, Upper Canada.

The history of Waterloo County, Ontario, is much indebted to two Mennonite brothers, Abraham and John Erb, who in the early 19th century decided to leave Pennsylvania in search of new opportunity in the wilderness of Upper Canada. Both Abraham and John, as well as two other Erbs (a brother Jacob and a cousin Daniel), were founding members of the German Company, established in Lancaster County in 1803 to purchase a 60,000-acre tract of land in that part of Upper Canada later known as Waterloo County [*see* Samuel D. Betzner*]. In 1806 Abraham and a group of 48 other Mennonites left Pennsylvania for the German Company tract. Stopping briefly at the home of his elder brother John, who had immigrated a year earlier and founded the settlement of Preston (Cambridge), Abraham journeyed a dozen miles farther north.

The later emergence of the village of Waterloo was to occur within the confines of land held by Abraham Erb. He had acquired his land prior to his departure, having purchased a large tract from Jacob and Daniel Erb on 20 July 1805. His holdings of 900 acres included several watercourses, which provided water-power for mills. As early as 1808 he is recorded as having constructed a saw-mill. In 1816 he expanded his operation to include a grist-mill. It is reported that this mill and his brother John's in Preston were the only two in the region north of Dundas.

Abraham's role in the founding of Waterloo appears to have been important in two areas – early industry and pioneer education. With respect to industry, he was personally responsible for giving accommodation, training, or employment to a considerable number of Pennsylvania immigrants who found their way to his doorstep in the early part of the century. Among the prominent people who engaged themselves to work in some capacity in his enterprises were cooper Joseph Bauman and millers Jacob S. Shoemaker and Andrew Groff. That the grist-mill was a busy social gathering-place is shown by one account, according to which Erb had erected a large fireplace and installed a wooden floor and some rough furniture in the basement of the mill to accommodate farmers who would stay overnight (there were as yet no hotels in the area) while awaiting the conversion of their grain to grist.

The earliest program of education in this pioneer region received an impetus from Abraham Erb, who played a prominent role in the building of the first school in 1820. In his will, dated 3 Sept. 1829, he left a fund for the use of certain schools, to be administered by trustees appointed by the Mennonite Society of Waterloo Township, the interest to be used "for the benefit and education of the poor and needy children, and such as the trustees shall think proper."

The early growth of the village of Waterloo was slow, undoubtedly impeded by the fact that Abraham Erb did not wish to sell his property, preferring to keep it for his heirs. A major portion of the land and of his business enterprise went out of the family when, on 1 Sept. 1829, Erb sold his sawmill and flour-mill to Jacob C. Snider. A comparatively short but energetic career ended with Erb's death on 6 Sept. 1830. He and his wife Magdalena had had one child, who died at the age of seven; they also adopted two others, one of whom, Barnabas Devitt, became a successful miller in nearby Bridgeport (Kitchener). After Abraham's death Magdalena married Mennonite bishop Benjamin Eby*.

MICHAEL S. BIRD

AO, Hist. plaque descriptions, "John Erb, 1764–1832, founder of Preston," 20 June 1960. Waterloo Hist. Soc. (Kitchener, Ont.), Abraham Erb, day-book, 1822–26. *Valley of Six Nations* (Johnston). E. E. Eby, *A biographical history of Waterloo Township* . . . (2v., Berlin [Kitchener], Ont., 1895–96); repub. as E. E. Eby and J. B. Snyder, *A biographical history of early settlers and their descendants in Waterloo Township*, with *Supplement*, ed. E. D. Weber (Kitchener, 1971). L. J. Burkholder, *A brief history of the Mennonites in Ontario* (n.p., 1935). F. H. Epp, *Mennonites in Canada, 1786–1920: the history of a separate people* (Toronto, 1974). G. E. Reaman, *The trail of the black walnut* (Toronto, 1957). W. V. Uttley, *A history of Kitchener, Ontario* (Kitchener, 1937; repr. [Waterloo, Ont., 1975]). W. H. Breithaupt, "Waterloo County history," "The settlement of Waterloo County," and "First settlements of Pennsylvania Mennonites in Upper Canada," *OH*, 17 (1919): 43–47; 22 (1925): 14–17; and 23 (1926): 8–14; "Museum report," "Waterloo County millers," and "Historical notes on the Grand River," Waterloo Hist. Soc., *Annual report* (Waterloo), 1927: 381–84; 1928: 78–80; 1930: 219–29. I. C. Bricker, "The first settlement in central western Ontario," *OH*, 30 (1934): 58–65. Mabel Dunham, "A short history of the new city of Waterloo," Waterloo Hist. Soc., *Annual report* (Kitchener), 1947: 34–38. M. A. Johnston, "A brief history of elementary education in the city of Waterloo," Waterloo Hist. Soc., *Annual report*, 1965: 56–68. A. B. Sherk, "The Pennsylvania Germans in Waterloo County," *OH*, 7 (1906): 98–109. E. W. B. Snider, "Waterloo County forests and primitive economics," Water-

Ermatinger

loo Hist. Soc., *Annual report*, 1918: 14–36. C. W. Wells, "A historical sketch of the town of Waterloo, Ontario," Waterloo Hist. Soc., *Annual report*, 1928: 22–67.

ERMATINGER, CHARLES OAKES, fur trader, merchant, militia officer, and JP; b. 1 Feb. 1776 in Montreal, son of Lawrence Ermatinger*, merchant, and Jemima Oakes; d. there 4 Sept. 1833.

Charles Oakes Ermatinger apparently entered the fur trade as a clerk for the North West Company in 1795. He was working along the North Saskatchewan River in late 1798 when he and another trader became lost in the wilderness. Ermatinger found his way out after 16 days, but his companion never returned. In the summer of 1799 Ermatinger was in the area of Fond du Lac (Superior, Wis.) and, as Alexander Mackenzie* of the NWC suspected, working surreptitiously for John Ogilvy*, a leader in the fledgling New North West Company (sometimes called the XY Company). In July 1800, however, William McGILLIVRAY of the NWC rejoiced that "Ogilvy's haughty and imperious conduct" had induced Ermatinger to rejoin the older firm. Being more solid, it absorbed its rival in November 1804. By the agreement of union the NWC was authorized to designate three new wintering partners after the New North West Company had named six; thus in July 1805 Ermatinger and two other clerks were promised one share each in the enlarged concern, beginning with the outfit of 1808, "to stimulate them to continue their zeal & good conduct in the discharge of their duty." In 1806 he was a clerk in the Lake Ouinipique department under William McKAY.

In 1807 Ermatinger quit the NWC's service and, in return for £600, promised not to engage in trade detrimental to the firm for a period of seven years. Possibly as early as 1808, but apparently by 1810, he was established as an independent trader and merchant at Sault Ste Marie (Ont.) on the north, or British, side of the St Marys River; some years earlier he had been the NWC's agent at a post on the American side. His brother FREDERICK WILLIAM acted as his banker and outfitter in Montreal. During the War of 1812 Charles Oakes participated as a militia captain in the expedition led by Captain Charles Roberts* from Fort St Joseph (St Joseph Island, Ont.) which captured Michilimackinac (Mackinac Island, Mich.) from the Americans on 17 July 1812. By August 1814 Ermatinger had what Gabriel Franchère* described as "an attractive establishment," and had just completed a windmill, constructed "to encourage agriculture, for the inhabitants of Sault Ste Marie are not much addicted to work." Ermatinger himself grew wheat and other cereals. He enlarged his operations in 1819 by purchasing the interests of the merchant Jean-Baptiste NOLIN on the American side. About 1800 Ermatinger had married, according to the custom of

the country, a 15-year-old Ojibwa girl, Charlotte Cattoonaluté, with whom he had eight children by 1815; one boy was sent in 1817 to be educated in Trois-Rivières, Lower Canada, and another was sent the following year to Montreal, both under the care of Frederick William.

A man of some influence at the Sault, Ermatinger had been made a justice of the peace by 1816. After the massacre that June of Governor Robert Semple* and some 20 Red River settlers by a party of Métis friendly with the NWC, Lord Selkirk [Douglas*] asked Ermatinger and another justice of the peace, John Askin, to accompany him to Fort William (Thunder Bay, Ont.) in order to arrest the leaders of the company; both men declined, either out of fear of reprisals from the NWC or in the belief that Selkirk was acting irrationally. Ermatinger had, however, been forwarding supplies to Selkirk's Red River settlement (Man.) for some years, no doubt in the face of opposition from the NWC, and, despite Selkirk's evident disillusionment with him, the veteran trader continued to do so until at least 1821.

During this period Ermatinger constituted the only serious rival to John Jacob Astor's American Fur Company on United States territory around Sault Ste Marie. He displayed considerable ingenuity in circumventing restrictions placed by the Americans on British traders and goods; in 1817, for example, to trade British merchandise brought up from Montreal, he sold it to an American trader and then got himself employed as the trader's agent to work the south shore of Lake Superior and the country beyond Fond du Lac. But the American Fur Company ultimately persuaded United States authorities to revoke all licences previously granted to Ermatinger and his men, and by the end of 1819 he was obliged to limit his trade on American soil. Still, he continued for a number of years to annoy Astor's organization as a trader and to furnish British goods to other merchants in the region.

In 1822 Ermatinger's establishment in the American Sault Ste Marie (Mich.), probably at Nolin's former post, was expropriated by the military for the site of a fort, and only after a hard struggle did Ermatinger obtain compensation. He transferred operations there back to the British Sault and conducted trade around it, on Drummond Island (Mich.), and elsewhere. He built the first stone house in the area at the enormous cost of £2,000. The fur trader John Siveright* remarked in May 1823 that "Mr Ermatinger's New Elegant Mansion is quite an asset when all others are buildings indifferent in appearance . . . besides he has begun two stone towers on each side of the house, one for a Mill & the other as inn house, all being on a grand scale, & do much credit to his good taste." The house would become a centre of social life, but in 1823, Siveright noted, the deaths of three of Ermatinger's sons the previous summer and fall "prevented the usual Winter Amusement further than a game of Whist now and then."

Following the death of Frederick William in 1827, Ermatinger conceded his interests in the Lake Superior trade to the American Fur Company and, while retaining his establishment at the Sault, retired with his family to a farm at Longue-Pointe (Montreal). Late in 1829 he was sent by a group of Montreal merchants to London to settle their claims against the bankrupt firm of McGillivrays, Thain and Company, but the following year, when offered a commission as justice of the peace for the Montreal district, he was obliged to decline for reasons of health. On 6 Sept. 1832 he and Charlotte were married in Christ Church, Montreal. By that time they had had 13 children, four or five of whom had died in infancy; of the sons, Charles Oakes, the eldest, would inherit the establishment at Sault Ste Marie and become a cavalry officer in Montreal during the rebellions of 1837–38, and Frederick William* would become police superintendent of Montreal.

Ermatinger died on 4 Sept. 1833. He had acquired a reputation for his hospitality and jovial manner, particularly at Sault Ste Marie where he had encouraged the prosperity of the region by adding agriculture to trade. In his life he had witnessed the end of the independent fur trader and the arrival of an era when large corporations influenced decisively the economic life of the colonies.

MYRON MOMRYK

[Charles Oakes Ermatinger's stone house at Sault Ste Marie, Ont., is now a museum of local history and constitutes one of the few permanent reminders of the contribution made by the Ermatinger family to Canadian history. M.M.]

ANQ-M, CE1-63, 3 févr. 1776, 6 sept. 1832, 4 sept. 1833; CN1-185, 16 juill. 1807; CN1-187, 12 mai 1815, 18 avril 1828. Molson Company Arch. (Montreal), John Molson to Francis Perry, 6 Feb. 1830. PAC, MG 19, A2, ser.1, 1, 3; ser.3, 28, 32, 35, 184, 186, 192–93, 201–3; ser.4; E1, ser.1, 1–2 (copies); MG 23, GII, 3, vol.6, 21 Sept. 1810; RG 4, A1: 41531; vol.332: 50. *Docs. relating to NWC* (Wallace), 205, 220, 254, 438, 489. Gabriel Franchère, *Journal of a voyage on the north west coast of North America during the years 1811, 1812, 1813, and 1814*, trans. W. T. Lamb, intro. W. K. Lamb (Toronto, 1969), 185, 319–20. [James] Hargrave, *The Hargrave correspondence, 1821–1843*, ed. G. P. de T. Glazebrook (Toronto, 1938), 4, 6. *HBRS*, 2 (Rich and Fleming). Mackenzie, *Journals and letters* (Lamb), 478, 495. *Canadian Courant* (Montreal), 1807–34. *Montreal Gazette*, 1 March 1827, 5 Sept. 1833. E. H. Capp, *The story of Baw-a-ting, being the annals of Sault Sainte Marie* (Sault Ste Marie, 1904; repr. 1907). D. [S.] Lavender, *The fist in the wilderness* (Garden City, N.Y., 1964), 187, 268–69, 275, 298, 460, 462. C. [B.] Martin, *Lord Selkirk's work in Canada* (Toronto, 1916), 119. R. A. Pendergast, "The XY Company, 1798 to 1804" (PHD thesis, Univ. of Ottawa, 1957), 142. P. C. Phillips, *The fur trade* (2v., Norman, Okla., 1961), 2: 369. K. W. Porter,

John Jacob Astor, business man (2v., Cambridge, Mass., 1931; repr. New York, 1966), 2: 710. Sylvia Van Kirk, *"Many tender ties": women in fur-trade society in western Canada, 1670–1870* (Winnipeg, [1980]).

ERMATINGER, FREDERICK WILLIAM, militia officer, businessman, and office holder; b. *c.* 1769, son of Lawrence Ermatinger* and Jemima Oakes; d. unmarried 28 Feb. 1827 in Montreal.

Frederick William Ermatinger and his elder brother, Lawrence Edward, were sent by their father to England in 1778 for their education. At age ten Frederick William was learning a variety of mathematical exercises and calculations necessary for a career in business. However, when Ermatinger Sr experienced serious financial difficulties in the period 1780–83, both sons returned to Montreal. In 1783 Frederick William began performing a number of tasks for his uncle Edward William Gray*, sheriff of Montreal. After Gray was appointed colonel commandant of the British Militia of the Town and Banlieu of Montreal in 1787, he named Lawrence Edward his adjutant, but when the latter returned to England about 1795 Gray replaced him with Frederick William, who had entered the battalion the previous year; Frederick William remained adjutant until he left the militia with the rank of captain-lieutenant in 1811.

Gray was also a merchant and, being without children, he seems almost to have adopted Frederick William, assuming the direction of his nephew's apprenticeship in business and introduction into the Montreal business community. On 15 Sept. 1791 he announced his intention of taking Ermatinger into partnership in his import-export business. He gave his nephew a one-third share to begin on 1 May 1792, when the firm became Gray and Ermatinger. During the years 1792–94 Ermatinger visited England annually to establish business contacts there. Since Gray's position as sheriff employed most of his time and attention, he withdrew from active involvement in the company in October 1795, and Ermatinger continued the firm's operations of importing goods from Britain. Ermatinger struck out on his own into other fields of activity. In 1805 he was the treasurer of the Lachine turnpike. By 1806 he had acquired land in the seigneury of Ailleboust, his lot of 800 arpents fronting on the Rivière L'Assomption. In March of that year Sheriff Gray was obliged to seize his nephew's land at the suit of the seigneur, Pierre-Louis Panet*, but in October Panet conceded a tract to Ermatinger in the same seigneury. Ermatinger also had a farm at Saint-Constant. From 1808 to 1812 he was engaged in the potash trade.

In the 1790s and early 1800s Ermatinger began to participate in the institutional life of Montreal. He was a member of the Montreal Library from its inception as a joint stock association in May 1796 and its

Ermatinger

treasurer that year. In 1803 he was appointed treasurer of the committee to build a new church for the Anglican congregation [see Jehosaphat Mountain*], and from 1803 to 1805 he was treasurer of the Théâtre de Société [see Joseph Quesnel*]. In his later years he was a member of the Horticultural Society and the Agriculture Society. He was among the first directors and visiting governors of the Montreal General Hospital and a visitor and, from 1822 until 1826, member of the managing committee of the National School, a free school for poor children.

By the early 1800s Ermatinger had begun to receive government commissions. In May 1802 he was appointed secretary of the Board for the Encouragement of the Cultivation of Hemp, and in November 1807 he received a commission as treasurer and clerk to the commissioners for the erection of jails and court-houses. Two days after Gray's death on 22 Dec. 1810, Ermatinger succeeded his uncle as sheriff. Working out of his residence and office on Rue Saint-Vincent in the *faubourg* Saint-Laurent, he carried out duties that included the management of the city jail and payment of the public executioner. He received fees for cases brought before the magistrates, or justices of the peace.

Ermatinger had for some time been supplying goods to the fur trade and marketing furs. After his younger brother CHARLES OAKES established himself as an independent trader at Sault Ste Marie (Ont.) about 1808–10, Frederick William increasingly concentrated this aspect of his activities on his brother's business. He served as Charles Oakes's banker and paymaster, hired voyageurs, and acquired equipment, supplies, and trade goods, importing the latter from England or occasionally buying them in Montreal. The goods were shipped either over the Great Lakes or, if they were to be traded in the United States, as often as possible by an all-American route. Frederick William also acted as guardian to two of Charles Oakes's boys when they were sent east to receive their education.

At the same time as he was involved in that most traditional of Montreal's economic activities, the fur trade, Ermatinger was among the pioneers of new business directions. On 7 Aug. 1817 he was elected a director of the first banking institution in the Canadas, the Bank of Montreal, founded that year. He purchased shares in the bank in his own name and in the names of all members of his family. As a director he sat on a committee to find a location for the bank's operations. On his suggestion it chose a building belonging to Robert Armour*, but at the time in receivership, on Rue Saint-Paul. Although Ermatinger continued to serve as a director and committee member thereafter, he did so with no particular distinction until, beginning in January 1826, a factional struggle developed among the directors over the

introduction of changes in the bank's financial administration. The struggle was between the "old guard," led by John Forsyth*, Peter McGill*, and Samuel Gerrard*, and the "insurgents," led by George Moffatt* and James Leslie*. The equality of force of the protagonists gave the balance of power to a third group, the "neutrals" or "independents," prominent among whom were John Molson* Jr and Ermatinger. Molson, Ermatinger, and Horatio GATES produced compromises on occasion, but Moffat and Leslie were able to rally the neutrals and to triumph on 5 June in a shareholders meeting that adopted a new set of regulations for the administration of the bank. Possibly in an effort to heal the wounds, Ermatinger resigned as a director four days later to allow the entry of John Molson* Sr, who had not taken part in the conflict and who was shortly after elected president; however, when the younger Molson resigned his directorship later that month, Ermatinger was persuaded to rejoin the board. He was a director of the Montreal Savings Bank as well.

Ermatinger also expressed his interest in the commercial development of Montreal through participation in fledgling business organizations and investment in a number of new enterprises, particularly in transportation, which, with banking, was emerging as a major focus of activity. He subscribed to the Montreal News Room and Exchange, established in 1821, and the following year he was among the first members of the Committee of Trade. After buying 20 shares in the Montreal Fire Insurance Company in 1818, he purchased 20 the next year in the Company of Proprietors of the Lachine Canal. In 1823 he bought 100 shares of joint stock in a company manufacturing a steam tow-boat and two years later 10 in the Welland Canal Company. In October 1823 he had been one of 12 subscribers who announced their intention to seek authorization from the Lower Canadian legislature to establish a turnpike road from Montreal to Longue-Pointe (Montreal). He was also attracted to land, a traditional area of investment. In June 1825 he acted as chairman of a meeting to form the Lower Canada Land Company and to obtain for it the same privileges and rights as the Canada Company enjoyed in Upper Canada. A total of 49 persons subscribed £182,000 for 1,820 shares of stock, but the presentations made to the British government were not accepted. Ermatinger's investments got him into financial difficulties in 1820 and 1821 when a lot and house on the St Lawrence were seized at the suit of Samuel Gerrard for non-payment of debt; since Ermatinger himself was the sheriff, the seizure was conducted by the magistrate Jean-Marie Mondelet*.

Ermatinger died at age 58 of "an Astma complicated with dropsical complaints." Despite a long illness he had continued to exercise the duties of sheriff to the end. His obituaries in the *Montreal Gazette* and *La*

Minerve affirmed that he had led a regular, active life, was esteemed publicly and privately, and had fulfilled his responsibilities as sheriff with efficiency and conscientiousness. He was succeeded in that post by Louis Guy*. Since he had never married, Ermatinger left to brothers, sisters, nieces, and nephews an estate that included his house and office on Rue Saint-Vincent, a farm of 100 arpents at Longue-Pointe, other properties in the Montreal region, 138 shares of stock in the Bank of Montreal, and shares in other firms. In the course of his business career Ermatinger had helped found or was a member of many of the associations and enterprises that brought together the commercial establishment of Montreal in the early 19th century. He had thus played an active role in promoting the interests of a growing English-speaking business community that would become a dominant influence in the economic life of Canada.

MYRON MOMRYK

ANQ-M, CE1-63, 3 mars 1827; CL1; CN1-185, 25 août 1809. PAC, MG 19, A2, ser.1, 1: 370; ser.3, 28, 31, 35–38, 40–41, 186, 188, 208; ser.4, 1; MG 23, GII, 3, vols.3, 5–6; MG 28, III44, 1; MG 30, D1, 12; RG 1, L3ᴸ: 62162; RG 68, General index, 1651–1841. UWOL, Regional Coll., Ermatinger family papers, Edward Ermatinger papers. *Canadian Courant and Montreal Advertiser*, 6 July 1822. *La Minerve*, 1ᵉʳ mars 1827. *Montreal Gazette*, 1 March 1827. *Quebec Gazette*, 25 July 1799; 20 May 1802; 3 April 1806; 10 Dec. 1807; 10, 17 Jan., 16 May, 26 Dec. 1811; 23 July, 10 Sept. 1812; 21 Jan. 1813; 13 April, 17 Aug. 1815; 16 Feb., 1 Aug. 1816; 2 Jan. 1817; 12 Feb. 1818; 4 Feb., 27 May, 2 Sept. 1819; 12 Oct., 30 Nov. 1820; 21 Jan., 8, 15 Feb., 24 May, 22 Oct. 1821; 17 April, 13 Oct., 8 Dec. 1823; 19 Feb., 22 March 1824. *Quebec almanac*, 1795–1811. Boulianne, "Royal Instit. for the Advancement of Learning," 400. Denison, *Canada's first bank*, 1: 100, 236–37. *Hochelaga depicta . . .*, ed. Newton Bosworth (Montreal, 1839; repr., Toronto, 1974), 103, 128, 152. M. S. MacSporran, "James McGill: a critical biographical study" (MA thesis, McGill Univ., Montreal, [1930]). R. A. Pendergast, "The XY Company, 1798 to 1804" (PHD thesis, Univ. of Ottawa, 1957), 142.

ESTIMAUVILLE, JEAN-BAPTISTE-PHILIPPE-CHARLES D', army and militia officer, office holder, and JP; b. 21 May 1750 at Louisbourg, Île Royale (Cape Breton Island), son of Jean-Baptiste-Philippe d'Estimauville de Beaumouchel, an officer in the colonial regular troops, and Marie-Charlotte d'Ailleboust; m. 13 May 1782 Marie-Josephte Courreaud de La Coste in Montreal, and they had a son and two daughters; d. 12 May 1823 at Quebec.

Jean-Baptiste-Philippe-Charles d'Estimauville, who belonged to the military aristocracy, was born at Louisbourg shortly after the fortress had come into French hands again. In 1761, after the conquest, the d'Estimauville family emigrated to France. Jean-Baptiste-Philippe-Charles went to the province of Quebec in July 1776. He immediately volunteered to serve under René-Amable Boucher* de Boucherville in the military operations against Brigadier-General Benedict Arnold*'s army in the vicinity of Lake Champlain. From 1778 to 1783 he was a lieutenant in the 60th Foot. While posted at Yamaska and Saint-François-du-Lac he learned the language of the Abenakis, and with their backing he obtained from Governor Lord Dorchester [Guy Carleton*] in 1787 the post of resident Indian agent at Saint-François-du-Lac. That year he was appointed lieutenant-colonel of militia for the District of Trois-Rivières. He recruited a company of about a hundred men for the Royal Canadian Volunteer Regiment in 1796 and served in this regiment until it was disbanded in 1802. From 1804 he held the office of interpreter at Quebec for the Abenakis. He also took part in the War of 1812 as lieutenant-colonel of the Quebec and Beauport battalions of militia. In 1814 he was a member of a court martial at Fort Chambly. Two years later he received the rank of colonel in the Lower Canada militia; Governor Sir John Coape SHERBROOKE excused him, however, from taking command of the Beauport battalion "in consequence of his long service and the zeal he has always displayed."

While pursuing his military career, d'Estimauville also distinguished himself by carrying out the duties of *grand voyer* (chief road commissioner) for the District of Quebec, an important office. He had succeeded Pierre Marcoux* on 21 Nov. 1809, having faced stiff competition from some of the Canadian seigneurial and military élite, who coveted this prestigious post with its highly attractive remuneration. D'Estimauville had charge of 58 surveyors, and 275 overseers, of highways and bridges. Their responsibility was to supervise the construction and maintenance of roads in their own sectors. The chief commissioner or his deputy had to deal with citizens' requests and settle disputes. After the date and place of a hearing had been published, he would hear the interested parties, often visit the area in quesion, and then record his decision in a report. During d'Estimauville's term in office 248 reports were produced. They were a family undertaking, since more than half of them were written by his brother ROBERT-ANNE and by his son Jean-Baptiste-Philippe, both serving as deputies.

In 1794 Jean-Baptiste-Philippe-Charles d'Estimauville had obtained a commission as justice of the peace for the District of Quebec. Five years later a similar commission was accorded him for the District of Trois-Rivières. Widowed in 1821, he died at Quebec on 12 May 1823 and was buried two days later in the Cimetière des Picotés.

ROGER BARRETTE

Estimauville

ANQ-M, CE1-51, 13 mai 1782. ANQ-Q, CE1-1, 14 mai 1823; CN1-178, 29 sept. 1812. PAC, MG 24, L3: 18517–24 (copies); RG 8, I (C ser.), 228: 66; 254: 382; 1220: 353; RG 68, General index, 1651–1841. L.C., House of Assembly, *Journals*, 1828–29. *Quebec Gazette*, 15 May 1823. P.-G. Roy, *Inventaire des procès-verbaux des grands voyers conservés aux Archives de la province de Québec* (6v., Beauceville, Qué., 1923–32). F.-X. Chouinard *et al.*, *La ville de Québec, histoire municipale* (4v., Québec, 1963–83). Paquet et Wallot, *Patronage et pouvoir dans le Bas-Canada*. P.-G. Roy, *La famille d'Estimauville de Beaumouchel* (Lévis, Qué., 1903); "Le chevalier Robert-Anne d'Estimauville de Beaumouchel," *BRH*, 10 (1904): 112–16; "Les grands voyers de la Nouvelle-France et leurs successeurs," *Cahiers des Dix*, 8 (1943): 181–233. "Vieilles poésies," *BRH*, 11 (1905): 216.

ESTIMAUVILLE, ROBERT-ANNE D' (he signed **Chevalier Robert d'Estimauville**), office holder, surveyor, JP, editor, publisher, and author; b. 2 or 3 Dec. 1754 in Louisbourg, Île Royale (Cape Breton Island), fifth of 14 children born to Jean-Baptiste-Philippe d'Estimauville de Beaumouchel and Marie-Charlotte d'Ailleboust; d. 31 July 1831 at Quebec.

As a child in Louisbourg Robert-Anne d'Estimauville enjoyed the charmed life of a nobleman's son. He later recalled "parading the streets of my village with frizzled and powdered hair, my hat adorned with a white plume, a little sword hanging by my side, and a small gold headed cane in my hand." His family moved to France, where his nobility entitled him to be financially supported by the king (his father being of modest fortune) at the École Royale Militaire near Paris, "to become, without much caring whether it was my inclination or not, a Military hero." He served with distinction in the French army and appears to have been created Chevalier de Saint-Lazare et du Mont-Carmel. Visiting London in late 1779 and again in 1781, he became "intimately acquainted" with the theologian and political writer John Jebb and the author Thomas Holcroft, and was influenced by their radical political principles. Back in France, unpalatable conditions in his corps and "some disappointment in love" induced him to join the Prussian army under Frederick II. He returned to the French army in 1788. Though his fortune and retinue were slender, he found "all the doors, even those of palaces, open to me . . . on account of my inherited nobility." The following year France exploded into revolution, and d'Estimauville's happy prospects were "at once blasted." By January 1797 he was back in England where, already widowed, he married Martha Blythe; they had three children, all born there, the last in February 1803. It may have been at this time that d'Estimauville converted to Protestantism.

Apparently finding no satisfactory niche in England, in 1812 d'Estimauville moved his family to Quebec, where his brother JEAN-BAPTISTE-PHILIPPE-

CHARLES was *grand voyer* (chief road commissioner) for the district of Quebec. The following year Jean-Baptiste-Philippe-Charles appointed him his deputy in that position, and in December 1813 he was named by Governor Sir George Prevost* surveyor of streets and bridges at Quebec. He resigned the latter post in January 1815. He was fully occupied as his brother's deputy; from June 1813 to May 1817 he produced 59 of 77 official reports fixing routes all over the Quebec district and assigning to inhabitants the charge of construction, maintenance, or repair of roads and bridges. He also made annual tours of inspection. His competence was publicly questioned after he determined the route of a road from Saint-Joachim to Baie-Saint-Paul in the spring of 1815; in 1819 a committee of the House of Assembly pronounced the road "very ill placed" and censured d'Estimauville for negligence. He, however, had already resigned in October 1817.

In May 1817 d'Estimauville had obtained a commission as surveyor, and one year later he was made a deputy to Surveyor General Joseph Bouchette*. About September 1818, no doubt drawing on his intimate knowledge of the city and district of Quebec, he joined with François ROMAIN to open an agency office at Quebec; among other services the partners provided information to immigrants and travellers, found and placed servants, and rented or sold real estate. By then d'Estimauville was living in respectable circumstances on Rue Sainte-Famille, Upper Town; in 1821, however, his brother had a lot and house belonging to him seized by the sheriff. In July 1820 d'Estimauville had been named high constable of Quebec and in June 1821 he achieved revenge on the assembly by being reappointed deputy *grand voyer* for the district of Quebec. He again did most of the field work, producing 48 of 49 official reports from August 1821 to June 1823 when his brother, who had died, was succeeded by Thomas-Pierre-Joseph TASCHEREAU and Robert-Anne presumably lost the deputyship. In 1822 d'Estimauville had been named translator to the courts of King's Bench and Quarter Sessions. The following year he relinquished this position and that of high constable after being named gentleman usher of the Black Rod for the Legislative Council and justice of the peace.

By this time d'Estimauville had attained a certain prominence in Quebec society. In December 1813 he was made a member of a committee formed to prepare an address of political support for Prevost, who was under attack by the English party in the colony for his policy of conciliating the Canadians. In January 1815 d'Estimauville was appointed acting secretary of the Association for the Relief of the Poor. He became in 1819 secretary of a committee to raise a monument to the memory of Princess Charlotte Augusta of Wales, secretary of the Quebec Emigrants' Society, and secretary of the Quebec Harmonic Society, whose first public concert was held in the Union Hotel in January 1820. That year he was a member of the Frères Canadiens, lodge number 23 of Lower Canadian freemasons, as well as secretary of the Provincial Grand Lodge of Lower Canada and grand director of ceremonies. He was elected in 1821 to a committee, chaired by Joseph-François Perrault*, to frame the regulations of an association for the promotion of education. He was also a member of the Agriculture Society and the Quebec Fire Society. D'Estimauville's activities on these numerous voluntary committees testify to his interest in public matters and his several appointments as secretary to a penchant for writing. In late November 1816 Robert Christie*, proprietor of the *Quebec Telegraph*, hired him as the editor of that newspaper, but the two men had a falling out and d'Estimauville left before the end of the year.

By May 1821, then, d'Estimauville was secure as an office holder, experienced in the social life of the city, and seemingly unwilling to write under constraint by others. These conditions and d'Estimauville's European background make it almost certain that he was the founder of the *Enquirer*, a monthly publication established to communicate with those who had not studied English sufficiently to be able to read it with ease and pleasure. The editor identified himself only as C.D.E., but he was known to the writer Samuel Hull WILCOCKE as "a gentleman of French extraction, who, altho' his English is rather quaint, and has a Gallic twang, is no bad writer." Wilcocke added that the articles in the *Enquirer* bore "a strong stamp of originality"; the *Quebec directory* for 1822 described them as conducted on "chaste" principles. The journal's main themes were agriculture, education, and freemasonry, but in a series entitled "My own life" the editor often touched on political philosophy, denouncing the "new fangled doctrines" of the Enlightenment and the French revolution. The *Enquirer* was a financial failure and folded about May 1822.

Five years later, under the pseudonym Un Vrai Canadien, d'Estimauville published *Esquisse de la constitution britannique*, a pamphlet written to elucidate "the admirable constitution under which [the Canadians] have the happiness to live." He tacitly endorsed an argument of the Canadian party, and of its political theoretician Pierre-Stanislas BÉDARD, when he affirmed "that the often irregular functioning of colonial governments ought not to be attributed to individuals or to parties, but to the faulty construction of constitutional charters . . . and that the organization of the legislature can only be good when the elements that compose it are analogous to those that are part of the imperial legislature." The Canadian party maintained that in Lower Canada the House of Assembly, which it dominated, should have the same power over the public purse as had the House of Commons in Britain. D'Estimauville, however, sought to undermine this position by arguing that the British constitution was an organic product of a unique national history, and therefore unexportable in its entirety, and that, Britain being an imperial power, a constitution analogous to its own "cannot exist in any subordinate portion of the British empire." He concluded, nevertheless, that Lower Canada was just beginning to share in the advantages of the British constitution, and he urged the Canadians to hold fast to it.

The year after the *Esquisse* was published a select committee of the British House of Commons inquired into the worsening political crisis in Lower Canada under the administration of Governor Lord Dalhousie [Ramsay*], and its report, largely favourable to the views of the Canadian party, which was led by Louis-Joseph Papineau*, induced d'Estimauville to remark that Lower Canada was "a kind of political nondescript" for the committee members, who knew little about it. Hoping to influence the parliamentary discussion of the committee's report, in 1829 he published *Cursory view of the local, social, moral and political state of the colony of Lower-Canada*. The pamphlet was in part a lucid analysis of the colonial system. D'Estimauville asserted that political difficulties were inevitable in a colony both because of the "levelism" wrought by large-scale immigration and because of a contempt for constituted authority; this contempt was fostered by the familiarity of the population with its small colonial administration and by that administration's incapacity to deal quickly with emerging problems, obliged as it was to seek instructions from a distant, and often indifferent, imperial power. These problems were aggravated in the case of conquest because victors and vanquished had little in common and were divided by "a repulsive feeling proceeding from a wounded pride on the part of the conquered, and from a national prejudice on that of the conquerors." He stressed the role of patronage in creating bitterness, the conquered being invariably excluded from public situations, honours, and profits. To ensure social and political cohesion Britain ought to have deprived the Canadians of those customs and institutions that reminded them of their French heritage; if the English language and laws had been made mandatory, the Canadians would have had to obtain an English education. Because Britain had not taken this step there had resulted a "jumble of contradictory and clashing forms, languages, laws, usages, habits and interests" that could only create trouble. He surmised that the Canadians would uphold their distinctive social features as long as they were allowed to do so. British negligence and the propagation of French revolutionary ideas had provided "the most untoward circumstances" for the granting of a house of assembly in 1791, and it had become the forum for hostilities. But more than these circumstances were to blame for Lower Canada's political problems; its constitution was only a "counterfeit" of the British model. The governor was not the king, but the representative of imperial authority; he inevitably became a political figure because if he governed on the advice of his official advisers, all British, he was viewed as anti-Canadian, while if he avoided falling under their sway he was considered pro-Canadian. Neither was the Legislative Council a replica of the House of Lords; the councillors did not constitute a hereditary aristocracy which could mediate between monarch and commons. Rather they were drawn from "a population in which gradation in regard to independence and rank is almost imperceptible" and from the same social level as members of the assembly. However, until a true aristocracy could develop in the colony and constitute a hereditary upper house, it was imperative to maintain the existing appointed council since it was the only check on the assembly. The assembly most resembled its imperial counterpart, but it was controlled by a party that dominated rather than represented the Canadian people and it had somehow to be restrained; in this regard d'Estimauville approved the action of Governor Sir James Henry Craig* in seizing its newspaper, *Le Canadien*, in 1810.

In his various publications Robert-Anne d'Estimauville revealed a perception of the causes of Lower Canada's political ills that often resembled that of the Canadian party. But from that perception he provided a theoretical framework for some of the solutions proposed by the English party, much as Pierre-Stanislas Bédard did for its rival. The conservative-leaning Michel Bibaud*, who probably did not know d'Estimauville's identity, asserted that the author of the *Cursory view* had shown himself to be but a poor Canadian yet had stated many truths. D'Estimauville's writings are of interest for what they reveal of the social life and political views of a man of his position, for their keen observations on the problems of colonialism generally, and because of his surmises that the causes of French-English conflict would persist as long as the French-language population remained distinct.

BARBARA TEATERO

[Robert-Anne d'Estimauville wrote most of the articles which appeared in the *Enquirer*, a newspaper he also edited at Quebec from May 1821 to about May 1822 under the pseudonym C.D.E. In addition, he wrote two essays on political matters: *Esquisse de la constitution britannique, par un vrai canadien* (Québec, 1827), and *Cursory view of the local, social, moral and political state of the colony of Lower-Canada* (Quebec, 1829). The identification of d'Estimauville as C.D.E. was made by William Kaye Lamb. B.T.]

ANQ-Q, CE1-61, 8 août 1815. Bibliothèque nationale (Paris), MSS, Fr., 30470: f.263; 31352: ff.6–9. L.C., House of Assembly, *Journals*, 1819, app.I. *Recensement de Québec, 1818* (Provost), 248. *Quebec Gazette*, 9 Sept., 30 Dec. 1813; 19 Jan. 1815; 5 Sept. 1816; 2 Oct. 1817; 18 May 1818; 21 Jan., 5 Aug. 1819; 13 Jan., 14 Aug. 1820; 10 May, 4 June, 9 Aug. 1821; 29 July 1822; 21, 28 April, 12 May 1823. *Scribbler*, 18 Dec. 1823. *Quebec directory*, 1822. P.-G. Roy, *Inventaire des procès-verbaux des grands voyers conservés aux Archives de la province de Québec* (6v., Beauceville, Qué., 1923–32), 2: 51–66, 76–85. *A concise history of freemasonry in Canada*, comp. Osborne Sheppard (Hamilton, Ont., 1915), 101. Aubert de Gaspé, *Mémoires* (1885), 330. P.-G. Roy, *La famille d'Estimauville de Beaumouchel* (Lévis, Qué., 1903). Ivanhoë Caron, "Le 'Chemin des caps,'" *BRH*, 32 (1926): 23–41. P.-G. Roy, "Le chevalier Robert-Anne d'Estimauville de Beaumouchel," *BRH*, 10 (1904): 112–16.

ESTISSAC, FRANÇOIS-ALEXANDRE-FRÉDÉRIC DE LA ROCHEFOUCAULD, Duc de LA ROCHEFOUCAULD-LIANCOURT, Duc d'. *See* LA ROCHEFOUCAULD

ETTER, BENJAMIN, watchmaker, silversmith, office holder, militia officer, and shipowner; b. 1763 in Braintree, Mass., son of Peter Etter; m. first 19 May 1789 Mary Bessonett in Halifax; m. secondly there 8 Jan. 1798 Margaret Elizabeth Tidmarsh; m. thirdly there 14 March 1818 Sarah Holmes; d. there 23 Sept. 1827.

Benjamin Etter's father emigrated to the Thirteen Colonies from Bern, Switzerland, in 1737, settling first in Philadelphia and later, in 1752, in Braintree, where he earned his living as a weaver. Peter Etter remained loyal to the crown after the outbreak of the Revolutionary War, and with the evacuation of Boston in March 1776 he and his family of seven left Boston for Halifax in one of the transports carrying troops and civilian refugees. By 1780 Benjamin was working in Halifax as an apprentice with his elder brother Peter, a watchmaker. In 1784 he received a grant of 100 acres in Chester Township, but since he failed to improve the land it was escheated in 1811. Peter Jr, who had served at Fort Cumberland (near Sackville, N.B.) as a sergeant in Lieutenant-Colonel Joseph Goreham*'s Royal Fencible Americans during the abortive uprising of Jonathan Eddy* in 1776, left Halifax in 1787 to establish a business in Westmorland County, N.B. Benjamin was placed in charge of the Halifax shop but, as he had completed his apprenticeship, he soon began working independently as a watchmaker in a shop on Hollis Street.

In 1789 Etter was listed as one of the original subscribers to the *Nova-Scotia Magazine*, printed by John HOWE and edited by William COCHRAN. On 19 May of that year he married Mary Bessonett, the daughter of a watchmaker, and afterwards he took on Mary's brother Daniel as an apprentice. On 14 June

1794 he advertised in the Halifax *Weekly Chronicle* as a watchmaker and jeweller on George Street, but four years later a notice in the *Royal Gazette and the Nova-Scotia Advertiser*, describing him as a watchmaker, jeweller, and silversmith, announced that he had "removed to Lower Side of the Grand Parade, corner of Barrington and George Street, adjoining Mr. Richardson's" and listed an extensive stock of watches, jewellery, silver, military accoutrements, and many other imported goods for sale. By 1799 he was occupying Richardson's store as well, and on 1 October of that year he entered into a partnership with James Tidmarsh, brother of his second wife (the partnership was dissolved in 1803). In 1802 he took as an apprentice William Anderson Black, son of the Methodist preacher William BLACK.

Etter was a prominent figure in Halifax society. On 31 March 1795 he had been appointed clerk of the market, from 1796 to 1808 he was an officer in the Nova Scotia militia, and he served as an honorary aide-de-camp to Prince Edward* Augustus, commander of the forces in the Maritime provinces. He was evidently prosperous financially, for by 1800 he and James Woodill had purchased the armed brig *Earl of Dublin* and obtained her letters of marque as a privateer. Her first cruise proved successful and with his profits he joined William Duffus and others in buying the 135-ton armed schooner *General Bowyer*, a former American privateer, prize to the *Earl of Dublin*. With 14 guns and a crew of 80, the *General Bowyer* captured two schooners, the *Peggy* and the *Nancy*, the Spanish ship *Nostra Signora del Carmen*, and a quantity of specie including gold bullion, all in one profitable cruise "against H.M.'s enemies." It was probably because of the profits he made in privateering that Etter was financially comfortable enough to build in 1820–21 one of the finest houses in Halifax, Belle Vue, at the corner of North and Gottingen streets.

In the *Acadian Recorder* of 29 May 1813 Etter announced his retirement in favour of his son, Benjamin B. Etter, and Thomas Hosterman, silversmith, who continued the business until the partnership was dissolved in 1815. Benjamin Sr, who had had at least 19 children by his three wives, died on 23 Sept. 1827 and was buried in the cemetery of St Paul's Church, Halifax.

Etter advertised silver tea-services and other pieces in the round, but only sturdy "Old English" table and dessert spoons, sugar-tongs, and teaspoons with delicate bright-cut engraving are in public and private collections, struck with several variations of his marks, including B. Etter, B.E., H, HX, an anchor followed by N.S., and a lion passant. His spoons, evidently cut from rolled silver and beaten to form, are well proportioned and graceful, sometimes engraved with a feather-edge or chased. Several circular engraved watch-papers, removed from the backs of watches he repaired, have survived, but apparently no attempt has been made to identify any watches made by him.

DONALD C. MACKAY

Halifax County Court of Probate (Halifax), wills, 4: ff.223–25 (mfm. at PANS). PANS, MG 5, 12–13; MG 100, 139, no.24 (C. St C. Stayner, "The Etter family"); RG 1, 444, nos.47, 69. St Paul's Anglican Church (Halifax), Reg. of baptisms, marriages, and burials (mfm. at PANS). *Nova-Scotia Magazine* (Halifax), 1 (July–December 1789): iv. "United Empire Loyalists: enquiry into losses and services," AO *Report*, 1904: 686–87. *Acadian Recorder*, 29 May 1813, 29 Sept. 1827. *Royal Gazette and the Nova-Scotia Advertiser*, 6 Nov. 1798, 2 Oct. 1799. *Weekly Chronicle*, 14 June 1794. *Halifax almanac*, 1795–1815. Jones, *Loyalists of Mass.* J. E. Langdon, *American silversmiths in British North America, 1776–1800* (Toronto, 1970); *Canadian silversmiths & their marks, 1667–1867* (Lunenburg, Vt., 1960). *Loyalists in N.S.* (Gilroy). D. C. Mackay, *Silversmiths and related craftsmen of the Atlantic provinces* (Halifax, 1973). *N.-S. calendar*, 1795–1801, 1814–15. *N.S. directory*, 1864–69. Stark, *Loyalists of Mass.* (1907). Akins, *Hist. of Halifax City*. Harry Piers, *Master goldsmiths and silversmiths of Nova Scotia and their marks . . .*, ed. U. B. Thompson *et al.* (Halifax, 1948). Howard Trueman, *The Chignecto Isthmus and its first settlers* (Toronto, 1902; repr. Belleville, Ont., 1975). G. E. E. Nichols, "Notes on Nova Scotian privateers," N.S. Hist. Soc., *Coll.*, 13 (1908): 111–52.

EWER (Yore), THOMAS ANTHONY, Roman Catholic priest, Franciscan, and vicar general; b. *c.* 1750 in Dublin, son of John Ewer and his wife Catherine, and brother of William Yore (Ewer), later vicar general of Dublin; d. 5 Feb. 1833 in Harbour Grace, Nfld.

Thomas Anthony Ewer's parents "enjoyed a considerable degree of affluence" and could send him to a Latin school at an early age. Inclined towards religious life, Thomas eventually entered St Isidore's College, Rome, and was ordained a priest on 19 Jan. 1776. His next years were spent at Franciscan houses in Bohemia at Prague, and in France at Nimes and Avignon; for a time he was lecturer in philosophy at St Isidore's. In 1782 he returned to Dublin to become curate of Rathfarnham, and in 1787 he was made guardian of the friary of Clane, in County Kildare.

That same year, having volunteered for Newfoundland, Ewer was sent for by the prefect apostolic, James Louis O'Donel*. Upon arrival in 1789, he was appointed to the new parish of Ferryland. This was a difficult assignment, since Ewer was expected to counteract the activities of Patrick Power, also resident at Ferryland, one of several Irish priests in Newfoundland who had refused to recognize O'Donel's authority. Power had won support by reviving the

Ewer

Irish provincial quarrels of several years before and by suggesting that O'Donel, a Munsterman, was biased against priests from the province of Leinster.

As a Leinsterman, Ewer was the obvious choice to challenge Power, although he was hampered by his inability to speak Irish, the only language of most of his people. By the time of the new pastor's appointment Power had been suspended by several Leinster bishops and excommunicated by O'Donel. With prudence and patience (despite being accosted and threatened by Power during a service), Ewer was able to master the situation quickly. By 1790 Power's influence seemed to have waned, and he apparently left Ferryland shortly afterwards.

However, Ewer's troubles had not ended. Governor Mark Milbanke*, unlike his predecessors John Campbell and John Elliot, was hostile to Catholicism. Ewer's request in 1790 to construct a chapel at Ferryland was rejected summarily, with Milbanke using the occasion to threaten the restriction of church activities. The situation remained perilous until the arrival the next year of chief judge John REEVES, who was able to assure O'Donel that the Catholic Church in Newfoundland would not be harassed by the local authorities.

The danger of persecution removed, Ewer was free to attend to the needs of a large parish. In 1791 O'Donel sought an Irish-speaking priest for the Trepassey–St Mary's section, but without success, and Ferryland continued to include "near 2,500 people . . . in ten different harbours in the space of about seventy miles." By 1796 Ewer had completed an elegant chapel and house at Ferryland, built largely at his own expense. At Bay Bulls he had much success in bringing Anglicans to Roman Catholicism. In fact, so strongly Catholic did the entire district become that in 1796 the Anglican clergyman, Samuel Cole (with whom Ewer was on good terms), had to leave Ferryland for lack of support.

In 1806 Ewer exchanged parishes with Father Ambrose Fitzpatrick, moving from Ferryland to Harbour Grace (where he had temporarily served in 1800). There, too, Ewer showed himself to be an enterprising pastor. He is regarded as the founder, in 1814, of the Harbour Grace Benevolent Irish Society, a charitable association. In his time chapels were built throughout the parish – at Bay de Verde, Port de Grave, Carbonear, Harbour Main, Northern Bay, Cupids, and Brigus. The assistance of able curates from 1817 onwards, notably Nicholas Devereux from 1819 to 1830 and Dennis Makin from 1822 to 1832, meant that better service could be provided. Liberally supported, in the 1820s Ewer spent over £5,000 in erecting at Harbour Grace a new house and a magnificent wooden church, probably then the colony's largest building. No religious strife disturbed the area; indeed Lewis Amadeus ANSPACH, the Church of England

rector, once wrote that "no part of the world could possibly enjoy a greater degree of peace and tranquility."

In 1796 O'Donel had become Newfoundland's first bishop and vicar apostolic. Ewer, previously vice prefect, thereupon became vicar general, an appointment he held until his death. He thus administered the vicariate (usually from St John's) during several prolonged absences of the bishops, notably in 1796–97, 1811–12, 1815–16, and 1823–24. In this role Ewer handled the final negotiations with government in 1811 for a cemetery in St John's, the first grant of public land to the Catholic Church in Newfoundland. Similarly, in 1823–24 he shouldered much of the responsibility for organizing opposition to proposed marriage legislation [see Thomas SCALLAN].

Ewer actively supported various educational projects. In 1812 he was a leading proponent of a non-denominational Sunday school in St John's for poor children. He personally founded a school at Harbour Grace in 1814 and for 12 years supported it from his own pocket. In 1826 he had this school put on a more permanent footing as St Patrick's Free School, wherein there was to be "no distinction of clime, country or creed," with clergy of all denominations invited to care for their own charges. Ewer's great dream was to see a local seminary for the training of priests, to him an essential need if Newfoundland was to have a sufficient and stable clergy. He initiated such a project in 1817 but had to abandon it, probably because of the poverty of the times. (His will, however, provided a major bequest for the education of priests for Newfoundland.)

By 1830 Ewer's health was faltering, and three years later he died after a short, though painful, illness. His 44 years in Newfoundland had witnessed Roman Catholicism's growth from the religion of a barely tolerated minority to that of a powerful and well-organized majority. Ewer was an intelligent, effective, and dedicated church leader, who made his own substantial contribution to this progress, all the while retaining universal respect. An obituary spoke of his greatest quality as "the boundless benevolence of a truly catholic spirit." It was an apt summation.

RAYMOND J. LAHEY

AAQ, 210 A, I: 8; 30 CN, I. Arch. of the Archdiocese of Dublin, Troy papers, I–III. Arch. of the Archdiocese of St John's, Fleming papers; O'Donel papers; Scallan papers. Archivio della Propaganda Fide (Rome), Scritture riferite nei Congressi, America Antille, 2 (1761–89)–3 (1790–1819). Cathedral of the Immaculate Conception (Harbour Grace, Nfld.), Reg. of baptisms. PRO, ADM 80/121; CO 194/46, 194/49, 194/67, 194/78. USPG, C/CAN/Nfl., 1–3; X 145. M. A. Fleming, *Relazione della missione cattolica in Terranuova nell'America settentrionale* . . . (Rome, 1837). Patrick Morris, *Remarks on the state of society, religion,* morals, and education at Newfoundland ... (London, 1827). *Newfoundlander* (St John's), 28 Oct. 1829, 14 Feb. 1833. *Newfoundland Indicator* (St John's), 17 Feb., 18 May 1844. *Newfoundland Mercantile Journal*, 4 April 1822, 3 Nov. 1825, 6 July 1826. *Public Ledger*, 8 Feb., 1 March 1833. *Centenary volume, Benevolent Irish Society of St. John's, Newfoundland, 1806–1906* (Cork, [Republic of Ire., 1906?]). George Conroy, "The first bishop of Newfound-land," in his *Occasional sermons, addresses, and essays* (Dublin, 1884), 315–27. M. F. Howley, *Ecclesiastical history of Newfoundland* (Boston, 1888; repr. Belleville, Ont., 1979). "The old graveyards of St. John's," *The book of Newfoundland*, ed. J. R. Smallwood (6v., St John's, 1937–75), 5: 108–10. Philip O'Connell, "Dr. James Louis O'Donnell (1737–1811), first bishop of Newfoundland," *Irish Ecclesiastical Record* (Dublin), 103 (1965): 308–24.

F

FANNING, DAVID, loyalist partisan, politician, and author; b. 25 Oct. 1755 in the settlement of Birch (or Beech) Swamp, Amelia County, Va, son of David Fanning; m. April 1782 Sarah Carr, and they had three children; d. 14 March 1825 in Digby, N.S.

Although born in Virginia, David Fanning spent his early life in North Carolina. An eight-year-old orphan in July 1764, he was bound to Needham Bryan (Bryant), a county justice who provided for his education. In 1773, when Fanning was 18 and of legal age to leave his guardian, he moved to Raeburn's Creek in the western section of South Carolina, where he farmed and traded with the Indians.

At the time of the outbreak of civil war and rebellion in colonial America, Fanning was a company sergeant in the Upper Saluda militia of South Carolina, which was assembled in July 1775 "to see who was friends to the King and Government, and . . . who would Join the Rebellion." Because the up-country militia tended to support the royal cause, the Council of Safety in Charleston dispatched a mission to persuade these "loyal Americans" to think in terms of rebellion. Although peace between the factions was maintained for a time, it was shattered in November with the arrest by the rebels of a prominent loyalist and the rumour of a patriot scheme to "Bring the Indians Down into the Settlement where the Friends of Goverment Livd to murder all they Could." Under Major Joseph Robinson* the loyal militia, including Fanning, besieged the rebels at Ninety-Six, and on 22 November the latter "were forst to Surrender, and give up the Fort and Artillery." This success prompted a large-scale rebel invasion from both the Carolinas into the South Carolina up-country, which ended with the dispersal of the loyalist faction at Big Cane Brake in December. Having narrowly eluded capture, Fanning fled to the Cherokee Indians.

Fanning was now staunchly committed to the cause of the king. He was motivated, apparently, by the fact that he had been pillaged of his trade goods by a rebel group and because the patriots had broken their word of honour not to molest loyalists. His sympathies well known, he was made a prisoner by the rebels in January 1776 – the first of 14 incarcerations or captures over the next three years. Though on occa-sion released, he also brought off a number of daring escapes; however, ill treatment in prison and long months in hiding took their toll. By early 1779 his situation was miserable, and he described himself as looking "So much like a Rack of nothing But Skin and bones and my wounds had never been Drest and my Clothes all bloody." When he encountered a young girl with whom he was acquainted, she ran off in horror, saying that "I was Dead and that I then was a Sperit and Stunk yet." Tired, discouraged, and be-coming desperately ill, Fanning negotiated with the rebels, and received a conditional pardon. He conse-quently returned home and agreed in principle to remain neutral and to guide rebel units through the woods upon request.

The expedition of the royal forces to South Carolina in 1780, and the capture of Charleston on 12 May, renewed the hopes of the "loyal Americans" in the province, many of whom – Fanning among them – organized themselves into the "bloody scout" and assisted the regular and provincial troops over the next several months. During this campaign colonial Amer-icans fought each other in an increasingly brutal fashion. By the end of October, the loyalists had lost the initiative, however, and Fanning removed to North Carolina. There he occupied himself recruiting followers in anticipation of an advance north by Lord Cornwallis.

In February 1781 Cornwallis raised the royal standard at Hillsborough, N.C., and called for local support. Although he had informed the now popular and influential Fanning in January that he could not give him a command suitable to his standing, the zealous loyalist partisan continued to raise men for the royal cause. Yet all but about 50 of the 500 he recruited were sent home because of the almost total lack of arms and provisions. On 5 July Fanning was appointed by Major James Henry Craig* colonel of the loyal militia of Chatham and Randolph counties, N.C., and for several months he conducted raids "in the interior parts of N. Carolina," the civil war having continued unabated after Cornwallis's departure for Virginia in May. At Hillsborough, for example, Fanning led 1,220 loyal militia in a classic surprise attack early on 12 September, captured the rebel

Fanning

governor of North Carolina, and took more than 200 prisoners.

Fanning continued the struggle long after the surrender of Cornwallis at Yorktown in October 1781. By the spring of 1782, however, he had finally decided to "settle myself being weary of the disagreeable mode of Living I had Bourne with for some Considerable time." As a first step in attempting to establish a normal life, he married Sarah Carr, a 16-year-old woman from the settlement of Deep River in North Carolina. In June the two arrived at Charleston, which was overflowing with loyalist refugees, and in November, a month before the British evacuation of the city, they went with other loyal refugees to St Augustine, East Florida. Since by the terms of the Treaty of Paris the Floridas were returned to Spain, Fanning sought yet another new home. After a futile attempt to reach the Mississippi, he went to Nassau in the Bahamas and then to New Brunswick, where he arrived on 23 Sept. 1784.

By 1787 Fanning had acquired property in Kings County. He resided there until he moved, some time after 1790, to Kembles Manor in Queens County, where he farmed, operated a grist mill, and built a sawmill. During these years Fanning made diligent efforts to gain compensation for his services during the rebellion. Like those of most loyalists, the claim he presented to the loyalist claims commission, for £1,625 10s. 0d., was probably inflated, yet the commissioners' award of £60 seems ridiculously low for a man whose exertions in the British cause, they acknowledged, had been "very great and exemplary." It was in support of his claim for further compensation that Fanning wrote his *Narrative* (completed in 1790), which details "astonishing events" pertaining to his personal exploits during the civil war and rebellion years. After 1800 he managed to secure an annuity of £91 55s. 0d. for his military service.

From 1791 until January 1801 Fanning served in the House of Assembly for Kings County. His political career was modest and uneventful; among other things he was appointed chairman of the committee of the whole house in 1793, introduced a bill the next year concerning earmarks on animals for identification, and sat on a select committee which studied a bill he himself had put forward in 1798 to register all marriages, births, and deaths in the province. Until 1795 he supported the assembly on many of the issues that set the elected house and the executive at odds, including James Glenie*'s Declaratory Bill, but his political ambitions later led him to support the administration.

Unfortunately, Fanning had the distinction of being the first member of the New Brunswick assembly expelled for a felony conviction. In July 1800 he was accused of attempting to rape Sarah London, "fifteen and stout," who was described as "a talking bold person, but unimpeachable on the article of chastity." In a deposition before John Golding, a justice of the peace, Sarah stated that she had visited the Fanning house, found David Fanning alone, and refused his invitation to join him. He then, she reported, "dragged her into his house and . . . used his utmost efforts to have Carnal knowledge of her." Two days later she changed her story – and the charge – from attempted rape to rape. Tried in October before a court of oyer and terminer, Fanning was pronounced guilty, in spite of inconclusive and contradictory evidence; Chief Justice George Duncan Ludlow* sentenced him to death. Fanning believed that the jury had been prejudiced against him because of his personality, his war record which many felt had been brutal and cruel, and his political ambitions (he was actively attempting to replace Golding as a justice of the peace). With his assessment of the situation his lawyers, Thomas WETMORE and Charles Jeffery Peters*, largely agreed. The causes of the prejudice, in their view, were Fanning's "foolish Publication of transactions in which he was concerned during the American War . . . his rash conduct in many instances during his residence in the Province – and . . . an unfortunate violence of temper by means of which he has made many enemies who are glad to seize every opportunity of holding him forth in the most unfavorable light." Protesting his innocence and alleging a biased jury, Fanning appealed to Lieutenant Governor Thomas Carleton* for a pardon. It was granted, but Fanning was exiled from the province forever.

With the exception of a brief interlude at Annapolis Royal, Fanning spent the remainder of his life in the Digby area, where he eventually built a comfortable house and where he engaged in farming, fishing, and shipbuilding. All his petitions and letters to Thomas Carleton, Provincial Secretary Jonathan Odell*, and others requesting permission to return to New Brunswick to settle his business affairs were frustrated. He died in Digby on 14 March 1825. Tough, wiry, plagued for a time by scald-head or tetterworm, Fanning was a stubbornly determined man who was a zealous and often brilliantly effective loyalist military leader. He was not a gentle man nor was he that type of philosophical loyalist, exuding refinement and contentment, who sat out the war in relative comfort in New York, Charleston, or England. Fanning fought tenaciously, fiercely, and sometimes cruelly against his ex-friends and neighbours, and his successes made him unpopular with the privileged loyalist "nabobs" of New Brunswick. His inflexible, even brutal, resolution notwithstanding, his epitaph in the Trinity churchyard at Digby reads in part: "Humane, affable, gentle, and kind – A plain honest open moral mind."

ROBERT S. ALLEN

The original manuscript of David Fanning's narrative has been lost. An incomplete but apparently faithful transcription prepared around 1890 is preserved among the Fanning papers at the N.B. Museum and forms the basis of a modern edition entitled *The narrative of Col. David Fanning*, ed. L. S. Butler (Davidson, N.C., and Charleston, S.C., [1981]). The introduction of this work includes a detailed discussion of the journal's publication history, but mention should be made here of the first edition, a heavily edited version of the original manuscript entitled *The narrative of Colonel David Fanning, (a tory in the revolutionary war with Great Britain;) giving an account of his adventures in North Carolina, from 1775 to 1783 . . .* , intro. J. H. Wheeler, ed. T. H. Wynne (Richmond, Va., 1861), and of a subsequent Canadian edition, *Col. David Fanning's narrative . . .* , ed. A. W. Savary (Toronto, 1908), which is also heavily edited but valuable because it contains the only surviving version of the final portion of Fanning's account.

PANB, RG 2, RS8, crime, 3/1, David Fanning case, 1800–2. Private arch., Harold Denton (Digby, N.S.), Family Bible. PRO, AO 13, bundles 137–38; PRO 30/11/84: 31–32. Trinity Church Cemetery (Digby), Tombstone inscription. *Loyalists in East Florida, 1774 to 1775; the most important documents pertaining thereto*, ed. W. H. Siebert (2v., De Land, Fla., 1929; repr., intro. G. A. Billias, Boston, 1972). N.B., House of Assembly, *Journal*, 1791–1801. "United Empire Loyalists: enquiry into losses and services," AO *Report*, 1904. R. C. DeMond, *The loyalists in North Carolina during the American revolution* (Durham, N.C., 1940). [G.] C. Watterson Troxler, "The migration of Carolina and Georgia loyalists to Nova Scotia and New Brunswick" (PHD thesis, Univ. of N.C., Chapel Hill, 1974). J. L. Wright, *British St. Augustine* (St Augustine, Fla., 1975). G. D. Olson, "Loyalists and the American revolution: Thomas Brown and the South Carolina backcountry, 1775–1776," *S.C. Hist. Magazine* (Charleston), 68 (1967): 201–19; 69 (1968): 44–56. [G.] C. Watterson Troxler, "'To git out of a troublesome neighbourhood': David Fanning in New Brunswick," *N.C. Hist. Rev.* (Raleigh), 56 (1979): 343–65.

FERGUSON, BARTEMAS (Bartimus), newspaperman and printer; b. *c*. 1792 in Vermont; m. with at least five children; d. 19 Jan. 1832 in York (Toronto), Upper Canada.

Bartemas Ferguson first appeared on the Upper Canadian scene in 1817 working as a job printer in St Catharines. From this modest position he quickly became involved in politics. In February of that year he printed for James DURAND an election bill attacking Durand's opponent John Willson*; the bill also appeared in the *Niagara Spectator*, published by Amos McKenney and edited by Richard COCKRELL. Years later Ferguson noted acidly that Durand had refused to pay him for his three days and nights of "indefatigable labour."

In 1818 Ferguson moved to Niagara (Niagara-on-the-Lake), where by 6 August he was printer and publisher of the *Spectator*. Under McKenney, the *Spectator* had supported the agitation of Robert Gourlay*. Nothing changed under Ferguson; he, too,

obviously sympathized with Gourlay's efforts, for he continued the policy of printing the Scot's blasts against the government. This action was fraught with peril. Gourlay was already awaiting trial on two separate counts of seditious libel; moreover, his "Upper Canadian Convention of Friends to Enquiry" of early July had deeply alarmed the administration of Lieutenant Governor Sir Peregrine Maitland*. When on 3 Dec. 1818 the *Spectator* (by then published jointly with Benjamin Pawling*) printed Gourlay's article "Gagg'd-Gagg'd, by Jingo!," the stage was set for confrontation. Gourlay was ordered from the province and upon his refusal arrested. Ferguson was jailed overnight on 16 December and released the next day on a technicality.

Pawling, who had been charged with Ferguson, died on the very day his colleague was arrested. Ferguson now again assumed sole control of the *Spectator*. A committed Gourlayite, he continued unabashed in his support of the imprisoned Scot. On 1 July 1819 the paper carried Gourlay's "Address to the parliamentary representatives." A short time later the House of Assembly unanimously passed a motion calling upon Maitland to order the prosecution of the author and publisher. Ferguson was arrested on the night of 13 July. Undaunted by the experience of several days' imprisonment, he was confident of acquittal and depicted himself as the champion of a free press. Just before his trial he suffered a setback on another front: Amos McKenney obtained a judgement of £1,000 against him in civil court.

Ferguson appeared at the Niagara assizes on 19 August before Chief Justice William Dummer Powell on a charge of seditious libel. A special jury was picked and the case was prosecuted to a rapid conclusion by Attorney General John Beverley Robinson*. In spite of what was, in Robinson's opinion, "an able defence" by Ferguson's counsel, Ferguson was found guilty by what Gourlay called a "weak jury" and held over for sentencing until 8 November at York. There has been some confusion as to the identity of Ferguson's counsel. What seems most likely is that Bartholomew Crannell Beardsley* defended him at the trial and Thomas Taylor acted as his counsel at sentencing. In any case, the defence was unsuccessful and Ferguson was sentenced to a fine of £50 provincial currency, imprisonment for 18 months, and the pillory for one hour daily during the first month of incarceration. Moreover, at the expiration of his jail term, he would not be released until he had given £500 in sureties for his good behaviour over the next seven years. Through the intervention of Maitland, however, Ferguson escaped the pillory.

Ferguson's conviction was the turning-point in his life. He lost his paper; his family suffered; his health failed; and his spirit was broken. The stress proved too much to bear and, on 4 March 1820, he petitioned the

Ferguson

assembly in chastened tones to urge royal clemency for the remainder of his sentence, claiming that his punishment would "operate as an example to all others who may violate the laws of public decency." Satisfied of his contrition, the assembly, despite the opposition of Robert NICHOL, recommended a pardon and the administration concurred. Upon release, he was quick to take up his calling again and by 2 November, in partnership with one Davidson, was printer and publisher of the *Canadian Argus, and Niagara Spectator*, which soon failed.

Ferguson moved to Lewiston, N.Y., where by 6 July 1821 he was publishing the *Niagara Democrat*. Although no copies are extant, Ferguson's prospectus was reprinted in several Upper Canadian newspapers. Its politics, he declared, "will be purely democratic." Thomas DICKSON reported to the government that the paper was "circulated here . . . and libels some of the first characters in the province." Dickson wondered whether Ferguson should be arrested if he entered the province. In an 1822 report to the Colonial Office on Gourlay, Robinson damned the paper for traducing "every respectable person in the Province." How long Ferguson continued to publish the *Democrat* is not known.

In 1826 he appears at York, first on 2 February as one of the subscribers to a fund in support of Robert RANDAL, later managing the *Colonial Advocate* in William Lyon Mackenzie*'s absence. The following year he surfaces in York again as the unsuccessful defendant in a civil action for debt amounting to £412. Ferguson's love was newspapers and on 24 Jan. 1828, with Edward William McBRIDE as co-publisher, he put out the first issue of the *Niagara Herald*. Again the venture proved short-lived. A dispute with the paper's proprietor, John Crooks, led to Ferguson's ejection in late October 1829. As was usual when the Ferguson family found themselves in dire financial straits, Mrs Ferguson promptly opened a millinery and mantua shop.

This time, however, Ferguson's prospects looked more promising. The Hamilton region had lacked a paper since George Gurnett* moved to York in 1829. Encouraged by offers of financial support from several "patriotic individuals," Ferguson had moved to Hamilton by early November. The publication of the first issue of his *Gore Balance* on 12 Dec. 1829 heralded an era of vigorous newspaper publishing in Hamilton that was to last about 15 years. Like Ferguson's other efforts, however, the *Balance* did not last long. In spite of Ferguson's success in expanding the number of subscribers from fewer than 100 to more than 400, the paper ceased publication on 2 Dec. 1830 and was sold soon afterwards. The press and type were sold to the *Western Mercury*. In spite of its short duration and the problems that plagued its brief life, the *Balance* is notable because it captured the spirit of the emerging political culture of the boisterous entrepôt at the Head of the Lake (the vicinity of present-day Hamilton Harbour). The defining characteristic of local politics in Hamilton from the 1820s to the present has been an unbridled enthusiasm for economic development combined with only a passing concern for political reform. Ferguson was the first to give voice to this attitude, which later received classic expression in Robert Reid Smiley*'s *Hamilton Spectator*. At a time in the province's political history when an editor of a whiggish bent had any number of issues on which to lash the government, Ferguson all but abandoned the concerns of his youth. In part, this transformation can be explained by changes in the colony's political life. It also seems likely, however, that his brush with authority had made him extremely reluctant to tilt at government windmills. He now applauded the measures initiated by his old antagonist, John Beverley Robinson, to implement a provincial strategy for economic development. He also supported Willson and Allan Napier MacNab* and spared nothing in his mordant attacks on Egerton Ryerson* and Mackenzie.

Throughout 1831 Ferguson tried to collect the *Balance*'s outstanding accounts. Finally, in August, he published notice that unless debts were immediately paid he would resort to the courts. But he died on 19 Jan. 1832 in the hospital at York. Francis COLLINS, the editor of the *Canadian Freeman*, attributed Ferguson's death to disease that had its origins in his imprisonment. Rather than dwell on his later career, Collins chose to hallow the memory of the young Ferguson, the supporter of the Gourlayite convention, the champion of the liberty of the press, and the victim (like Collins himself) of the harsh laws of libel. Mackenzie concurred, depicting Ferguson as one who was crushed "when the iron hand of power fell upon him . . . ruined his prospects, and aided in injuring his constitution."

ROBERT LOCHIEL FRASER

AO, RG 22, ser.126, vol.9, 5, 8 Nov. 1819; ser.131, 1: ff.159, 168, 174; 2: ff.175–76; ser.134, 5: 4. PAC, RG 5, A1: 21671, 22096–97, 26593–95. PRO, CO 42/369: 162, 167. R. [F.] Gourlay, *General introduction to "Statistical account of Upper Canada . . . ," in connexion with a reform of the corn laws* (London, 1822), xii–xiii. "Journals of Legislative Assembly of U.C.," AO *Report*, 1913: 255–58. *Town of York, 1815–34* (Firth), 97–98. *Canadian Argus, and Niagara Spectator* (Niagara [Niagara-on-the-Lake], Ont.]), 6 Aug. 1818–2 Nov. 1820. *Canadian Freeman*, December 1829–January 1832. *Christian Guardian*, 25 Jan. 1832. *Colonial Advocate*, 10 June 1824, 20 Jan. 1832. *Gleaner, and Niagara Newspaper*, 24 Oct.–7 Nov. 1829. *Gore Balance* (Hamilton, [Ont.]), 12 Dec. 1829–2 Dec. 1830. *Kingston Chronicle*, 3 Sept. 1819, 6 July 1821. *Niagara Herald*, 24 Jan. 1828–September 1829. *Western Mercury* (Hamilton), 20 Jan. 1831–26 Jan. 1832. Lois Darroch Milani, *Robert Gourlay, gadfly: the biography of*

Robert (Fleming) Gourlay, 1778–1863, forerunner of the rebellion in Upper Canada, 1837 ([Thornhill, Ont., 1971?]), 184–85, 195–99, 206, 210, 212–13. W. R. Riddell, "The first law reporter in Upper Canada," Canadian Bar Assoc., *Proc.* (Toronto), 2 (1916): 139–40; "Robert (Fleming) Gourlay," *OH*, 14 (1916): 5–133. W. S. Wallace, "The periodical literature of Upper Canada," *CHR*, 12 (1931): 4–22.

FIDLER, PETER, fur trader, surveyor, explorer, and cartographer; b. 16 Aug. 1769 in Bolsover, England, son of James Fidler and Mary ——; m. autumn 1794 according to the custom of the country and formally on 14 Aug. 1821 at Norway House (Man.), Mary, a Swampy Cree, and they had 14 children; d. 17 Dec. 1822 at Dauphin Lake House (Man.).

In April 1788 at London, in the midst of a renewal of the rivalry between the Hudson's Bay Company and the North West Company for the fur trade of the northwest, Peter Fidler joined the HBC as a labourer and reached York Factory (Man.) later that year. He had certainly received some formal education: he was soon promoted from labourer to post journal writer because he was "in every way qualified for that station, being a good Scholar and Accountant." Moreover, he was regarded as "a sober steady young man." Within a year of his arrival he was sent inland as a writer, first to Manchester House (near Standard Hill, Sask.) and then to South Branch House (near Batoche). The HBC's confidence in Fidler was again demonstrated during the spring of 1790 when he was ordered to Cumberland House and given intensive instruction in surveying and astronomy by the esteemed Philip Turnor*, the first surveyor engaged by the company to work in the northwestern interior.

The summer provided Fidler with unusually good prospects for advancement, the result of an accident to another promising student of Turnor, David Thompson*. Incapacitated through an injury and partially blind, Thompson was unable to travel, and accepting a suggestion that Fidler would be "a useful assistant," Turnor took him on a journey "to the Northland." The purpose of the HBC expedition was to observe the nature and extent of the NWC's hold on the fur trade of the Athabasca country and, most important, to find a short, direct, and navigable water route from Hudson Bay to the Athabasca and Great Slave (N.W.T.) lakes – a northwest passage which would link the Atlantic to the Pacific. The novice Fidler evidently did not comprehend the wider implications of the expedition; he noted that "our sole motive for going to the Athapescow is for Mr. Turnor to survey those parts in order to settle some dubious points of Geography, as both Messrs [Samuel Hearne*] and [Peter Pond*] fixes those places in their respective maps far more to the westward than there is good reason to think them." In fact, Turnor's more accurate astronomical observations did place Lake Athabasca much nearer Hudson Bay, but the great western river linking east to west proved to be illusory.

Although the Athabasca expedition of 1790–92 was a disappointment for the HBC, the venture significantly improved Fidler's skills in surveying and map making as well as his knowledge of wilderness and Indian life. Turnor commented that his young assistant had become an astronomer, had written away for "Sextants, watches," and seemed "a likely person to succeed me." Fidler's robust nature and competence were not unnoticed; he was observed by Malchom Ross*, who had accompanied the expedition, to be "a very fit man for surveying in this quarter, as he can put up with any sort of living, that is in eating and drinking." Fidler spent mid January to mid April 1791 with Chipewyans north of Île-à-la-Crosse (Sask.) and after reaching the Athabasca country he furthered his expertise by accepting an invitation from local Chipewyans to winter among them. With no provisions or tent and with little clothing, shot, or powder, he passed the winter of 1791–92 with them in the area of Great Slave Lake. The following spring he returned "in good health" to Turnor's temporary Athabasca camp. He had managed the experience well. His sojourns with the Chipewyans had enabled him to acquire, in his own words, "a sufficiency of their Language to transact any business with them," an accomplishment that was to be particularly important for him and the HBC in the years ahead.

Fidler's enthusiasm, skill, and endurance were rewarded immediately. He was sent to the Saskatchewan River region in 1792 to assist the company in stabilizing and extending its new inland settlements along the upper reaches of the North Saskatchewan River. In part to trade and survey, but also to gain more knowledge of Indian life and manners, he undertook a winter journey from Buckingham House (near Lindberg, Alta) to the Rocky Mountains. He mapped much of the area to the southwest of the North Saskatchewan River as far as the foothills of the Rockies. In addition, he not only observed and recorded various aspects of Plains Indian life, but spent much of the winter of 1792–93 among the Peigans and managed to learn their language. Before returning to the Saskatchewan, he became the first European to trade with and describe the customs of the Kootenays.

The interest of the HBC in finding a short and direct water route to Lake Athabasca was demonstrated again in the summer of 1793 when Fidler was sent from York Factory on an expedition to the Seal River (Man.); no direct passage to Reindeer Lake via that river, north of the Churchill, was found. Following this attempt Fidler remained at York Factory for two years, performing routine duties. In the autumn of 1794 he married *à la façon du pays* a local Swampy Cree named Mary. Also during this period, he sent the first of several maps to the London committee of the HBC. Dated 1795 and illustrating the winter journey of 1792–93 to the foothills of the Rockies, it contributed to the cartographic knowledge of that part of North America. The London committee became annoyed that Fidler was shackled at the bay and wrote his immediate superiors that "for the future we direct him to proceed inland on discoveries." Thus, after travelling from Cumberland House to the upper reaches of the Assiniboine River, Fidler built Carlton House (near Kamsack, Sask.) in the autumn of 1795. There the fur trade rivalry was so intense that of five trading houses in the vicinity, two were actually HBC establishments competing with one another. The following summer he was in charge of Cumberland House.

Fidler spent the next winter at Buckingham House and in the spring of 1797 he journeyed to York Factory with 19 canoes and 2 boatloads of furs. He returned to Cumberland House in the autumn and remained there for the next two years, engaging in trade and acting as the writer. By 1799 the London committee had determined to push vigorously into the Athabasca country to compete more effectively against the NWC. Fidler left Cumberland House on 5 August and two weeks later, near Île-à-la-Crosse, caught up with William AULD, an HBC trader. Auld, leading an advance into the Athabasca from Churchill (Man.), and Fidler, under similar orders from York Factory, were both attempting to establish a chain of trading posts which could supply provisions for the HBC's penetration into the Athabasca. Deferring to Auld, Fidler agreed to travel farther south, along the Beaver River to Meadow Lake (Sask.), where he built Bolsover House, and then west to winter at Greenwich House (Alta), a post he established at Lac la Biche. The NWC reacted angrily to the HBC intrusion into the Athabasca watershed and "used every mean and rogish method" to force the HBC to retire. During the winter Fidler recorded that he was "constantly harassed by Canadian men," who tried to prevent the Indians from trading at the company post. He none the less experienced a good trading season and surveyed the route from Greenwich House to Lesser Slave Lake. But the expected sequel to the voyage to Lac la Biche, an HBC expedition to Lake Athabasca, failed to materialize. Instead, Fidler was sent to the South Saskatchewan River, where he established Chesterfield House (Sask.) in August 1800. This house survived only two trading seasons because of unrest among the various Indian tribes of the region.

By the summer of 1802 Fidler was back at York Factory; he remained only briefly at the bay before being ordered to lead an expedition to trade at Lake Athabasca. After a decade of HBC vacillation the struggle between the two companies for the richest beaver country in Rupert's Land was to begin in

earnest. Before departing, Fidler sent "some Maps and Papers" to the London committee. One map, dated 1801, purportedly showed for the first time the drainage network of the Missouri River, and provided new insights into the location and width of the western mountain system. Aaron Arrowsmith, the noted British cartographer and publisher, thought the map contributed significantly to geographical knowledge about "the face [of an area] until now unknown to Europeans." The map, based in part on one drawn by A-ca-oo-mah-ca-ye*, a Blackfoot chief whom Fidler had met at Chesterfield House, was quickly incorporated by Arrowsmith into the new maps he was to publish of North America.

Although the HBC had long desired another expedition to the Athabasca, there had been great difficulty in recruiting men for it because of the rough living conditions, isolation, danger, and staple diet of fish. There was optimism for this mission, particularly since the local Chipewyans had always been more favourably disposed to trade with the HBC. In mid September 1802 Fidler and 17 men, including Thomas Swain who was to establish a provision post on the Peace River, began the construction of Nottingham House on English Island in Lake Athabasca, less than a mile from the NWC post of Fort Chipewyan, which had been relocated on the northwest shore about 1800. For the next four hectic years, this small HBC post attempted to compete against the large and solidly entrenched NWC.

Throughout these years Fidler and his contingent were continually harassed by the NWC. The HBC traders and the employees of the New North West Company (sometimes called the XY Company), also established in the region, occasionally joined forces to oppose the NWC. But after the union of the NWC and the XY Company in 1804 Fidler faced a formidable opponent, especially in the person of the cruelly effective Samuel Black*, who arrived the following year. According to Fidler, the NWC used abusive tactics to intimidate him and his men. They destroyed a canoe, ripped up the garden, scared away game, and nearly burned down the post. "I suppose it was their intention to starve our people out." Black and his cohorts humbled the HBC men and, with little prospect of trade, Fidler became convinced that the competition was unfair and senseless. As a result, a loose "agreement" was made in which Fidler promised to quit the Athabasca for the following two years; in return the NWC agreed to provide Fidler and his men with provisions and pay 500 made beaver, roughly equivalent to the HBC credit in the Athabasca. The agreement was not honoured by either side, however, and the intimidation continued until June 1806 when a dispirited Fidler and the HBC contingent paddled out of the lake. For Fidler, the abandonment of the Athabasca was the nadir of his fur trade career.

In a final comment in the Nottingham House post journal he excused the adventure with a simple truth – "Too few to do anything for the Company."

Fidler reached York Factory in mid summer 1806. He rested briefly at the bay before being dispatched as postmaster to Cumberland House. The contrast between this post and the Athabasca was incredible; he even dined with the NWC "gentleman" at Christmas and all was friendliness and good cheer. The following summer, under orders from Auld and William Tomison, he explored the area around Reindeer Lake, another lake to the north which he named Wollaston Lake (Sask.), and as far as the eastern end of Lake Athabasca. He wintered at Swan Lake House (Man.), and surveyed and mapped much of the Lake Winnipeg–Red River region during the summer of 1808. In August he sent these and other maps and papers to England. He spent the following winter with Auld near Reindeer Lake. In 1810 he was rewarded for his long, dedicated, and valuable service: he was appointed surveyor, his salary was raised to £100 per year, and there was a suggestion that he would eventually be appointed chief trader with a share in profits.

The rewards bestowed on Fidler were part of the London committee's recently devised "retrenching system," which accentuated efficiency, economy, and individual initiative in combatting the NWC. As part of this program, Fidler was ordered to Île-à-la-Crosse in June 1810, but there the NWC, led by Black and Peter Skene Ogden*, so badgered Fidler and his men that they departed within a year. Tired and discouraged, Fidler was granted a one-year furlough in England. By late August 1812 he had returned to York Factory and was transferred to the Red River settlement (Man.), where the colonization scheme of Lord Selkirk [Douglas*] was in progress. To the NWC, the Red River colony was a direct threat to its transportation and canoe routes to the northwest, and to the buffalo hunting-grounds of the Métis, who provided the company with pemmican, the staple food of the fur trade. The colony was therefore to be opposed at any price. Fidler, newly appointed postmaster of Brandon House, escorted the second party of colonists to the settlement in autumn 1812. The following spring he began surveying property lots along the river using the river-lot system of Lower Canada. By June 1815, after the resignation of the colony's governor, Miles Macdonell, Fidler was temporarily in command. As a result of constant harassment by the Métis, led by Cuthbert Grant* and encouraged by the NWC, he signed, on 25 June 1815, a capitulation that ordered "all settlers to retire immediately from this river, no appearance of a colony to remain." Fidler and the colonists abandoned the settlement and fled to Jack River House (Man.). There they were met by Colin Robertson*, who returned with some of the settlers to

re-establish the colony. Fidler went on to York Factory, to be given the task of transporting the newly arrived governor of the HBC territories, Robert Semple*, and additional settlers, to Red River. He then went back to Brandon House, and from there continued to aid the struggling colony. The Métis retaliated in early June 1816, plundering Fidler's post. Two weeks later at Seven Oaks (Winnipeg), Semple and about 20 men were killed. The next year Selkirk re-established the colony once again, and Fidler resumed the surveying of property lots.

In September 1817 Fidler left the colony to return to the fur trade and from then until 1821 he lived an uneventful life as chief trader at the HBC posts of Brandon House and Dauphin Lake House. In failing health, he travelled in August 1821 to Norway House, where he was informed that he was soon to be pensioned, in large part because of the need to reduce surplus employees following the merger of the HBC and the NWC that year. Within a week of receiving the unhappy news, Fidler arranged for the baptism of his wife and some of his children, he and Mary were formally married, and he prepared his will. His retirement was postponed, however, and the ageing and sick Fidler returned to Dauphin Lake House with the nominal rank of a clerk at his old salary of £100 per year. In the York Factory list of servants for 1821–22 he was described as "a faithful and interested old Servant, now superannuated, has had a recent paraletic affection and his resolution quite gone, unfit for any charge." He lingered in this condition at Dauphin Lake House, where he died in 1822. For his family Fidler had possessed a genuine affection. He and Mary had had 14 children, of whom 11 were alive in 1822. His Indian wife had accompanied him on most of his journeys and postings, sharing the hardships and joys of a fur trader's life.

Throughout his long and remarkable career, Fidler was a serious, dedicated, and loyal servant of the HBC. His meticulous post journals, personal notebooks, and journey accounts reflect his zeal for writing and education. He was a conscientious student all his life, acquiring much of his knowledge in the northwest largely on his own initiative. His extensive collection of books reflected his desire to refine his professional skills as surveyor yet his inquisitive mind also probed into such subjects as algebra, meteorology, wild animals, and Indian customs and languages. His detailed post journals and notebooks provide a valuable record of life and adventures in the northwest during the era of fur-trade rivalry. As a result of his penchant for learning, however, Peter Fidler assumed a rather didactic manner, particularly in his later years at Red River, where he was considered something of an eccentric prig by the settlers.

Fidler's character was undoubtedly moulded by the ordeals and hardships he had endured in the compa-

Field

ny's service. Although distinguished, his career was marred by ill luck. At Nottingham House he found himself in a hopeless situation, faced with the harassment, intimidation, and overwhelming superiority in numbers of the NWC. He reacted in a controlled, practical, yet determined manner, and capitulated only when the Athabasca adventure was obviously lost; however, misfortune continued to dog his steps. Brandon House was sacked while he was master, and the colonists under his direction were chased from the Red River settlement; they were led back by the more aggressive Colin Robertson. What may seem to be failure in these incidents is excusable, yet Fidler appeared to lack dash and spirited leadership, with the result that he was not always fully supported by his followers in critical situations. His most significant and lasting contributions were not as a fur trader but as a surveyor and map maker. His meticulously drawn maps, which covered areas from Hudson Bay to Lake Athabasca and the Rocky Mountains, as well as his lot surveys at Red River, are testimonies to his dedication and competence.

ROBERT S. ALLEN

This text is based on the author's article "Peter Fidler and Nottingham House, Lake Athabasca, 1802–1806," *Hist. and Archaeology* (Ottawa), 69 (1983): 283–347, parts of which are reproduced by permission of the minister of Supply and Services Canada.

Peter Fidler is the author of "A journal of a journey with the Chepawyans or Northern Indians, to the Slave Lake, & to the east & west of the Slave River, in 1791 & 2," published in *Journals of Samuel Hearne and Philip Turnor*, ed. J. B. Tyrrell (Toronto, 1934; repr. New York, 1968).

PAC, MG 19, E1 (copies; mfm. at PAM). PAM, HBCA, B, D.4, D.5, E.3 (mfm. at PAC). David Thompson, *David Thompson's narrative, 1784–1812*, ed. R. [G.] Glover (new ed., Toronto, 1962). J. S. Galbraith, *The Hudson's Bay Company as an imperial factor, 1821–1869* ([Toronto], 1957). Innis, *Fur trade in Canada* (1962). J. G. MacGregor, *Peter Fidler: Canada's forgotten surveyor, 1769–1822* (Toronto and Montreal, 1966). A. J. Ray, *Indians in the fur trade: their role as trappers, hunters, and middlemen in the lands southwest of Hudson Bay, 1660–1870* (Toronto and Buffalo, N.Y., 1974). Rich, *Hist. of HBC* (1958–59), vol.2. D. W. Moodie and Barry Kaye, "The Ac ko mok ki map," *Beaver*, outfit 307 (spring 1977): 5–15. J. B. Tyrrell, "Peter Fidler, trader and surveyor, 1769 to 1822," RSC *Trans.*, 3rd ser., 7 (1913), sect.II: 117–27. W. S. Wallace, "Two curious fur-trade wills," *Beaver*, outfit 274 (June 1943): 34–37. Glyndwr Williams, "Highlights in the history of the first two hundred years of the Hudson's Bay Company," *Beaver*, outfit 301 (autumn 1970): 4–63.

FIELD, ELEAKIM, iron producer and founder; fl. 1831–35 in Upper Canada.

During the early 19th century there were numerous attempts to establish ironworks in Upper Canada, but capital costs were high and most projects failed. The expectation of profits, however, was a powerful lure and entrepreneurs, usually American, were often ready to take the risk. The Colborne Iron Works (also known as the Colborne Furnace) in Gosfield Township, Essex County, is a good example of a foundry and also of a rarer enterprise, a blast-furnace for smelting. Certain that the area abounded with iron ore of the first quality, Eleakim Field and Benjamin Parker Cahoon opened the Colborne works about 10 Oct. 1831. According to the local newspaper, the partners were "well acquainted with their business, having been for many years conducting works" in Ohio. They were convinced of the superiority of the local ore and confident that it could be worked to "much greater profit."

Colborne Iron Works was located a mile from the deposits of ore. By the fall of 1831 one blast-furnace was in operation and the works was producing from four to five tons of pig-iron daily. Because no suitable streams were located near by to operate a blower for the air blast, power for the furnace blower was produced by a 15-horsepower steam-engine. The necessity of using steam rather than water power added about $3,000 annually to the costs of production. Limestone, to aid in reduction of the iron ore, and sand for casting were available on the site. The furnace used about 500 bushels of charcoal daily, which was manufactured at the works using local timber; yearly requirements were estimated at approximately 200 acres of forest, and in return for timber, the partners offered to clear neighbours' property. A travel guide pointed to this feature of the operation as an inducement to potential settlers.

The complex, which was later described as "rude but extensive," consisted of a casting house (60 feet square), two dwelling houses, two bunkhouses, and a blacksmith's shop. It provided employment for 60 to 70 men; wages were said by the newspaper to be "liberal." Although no castings were made in the fall of 1831, sufficient pig-iron was produced to allow exports to York (Toronto) where, apparently, there was a great demand. On 1 March 1832 Field and Cahoon placed advertisements in Kingston, York, Hamilton, and Sandwich (Windsor) newspapers indicating their readiness to furnish pig-iron and, at the opening of navigation, castings. They claimed that their products – stoves and hollow-ware – were "manufactured from the first quality of Iron, and in workmanship that shall not be surpassed by any other manufactory in or out of the Province." Although there were Upper Canadian rivals for the provincial market, such as Joseph Van Norman*, it seems clear that the major competition was from American producers, particularly those who marketed in Buffalo, N.Y. The partners offered, they said, "a better article . . . at least as cheap as Buffalo prices" and hoped therefore to "keep so much capital in the Province."

The enterprise was, however, troubled by financial difficulties. As a result of two small judgements against the partners in January 1835, the sheriff seized their real and personal estate. On his own account, Field had lost a suit to a creditor for more than £444. Unable to give satisfaction he fled to the United States never, apparently, to be heard of again. On 2 February James Dougall*, a Sandwich merchant, won a judgement against the partners for £603 10s. 2d. The partnership was dissolved on 9 February and Cahoon assumed the debts. The works was sold and, after extensive repairs and additions, reopened in June, but the operation was in serious difficulty. Cahoon retained some equity in it, and perhaps served in a managerial capacity as well, until 1839 when he, too, fled south to escape creditors. Francis Xavier Caldwell*, who was liable for a portion of his debts, consequently suffered a severe financial blow. William Henry Smith*'s gazetteer of 1852 noted that the furnace "has ceased working for some time."

The career of most iron founders and smelters in Upper Canada was precarious. In 1835 Amos Horton, a Toronto founder, appeared before the House of Assembly's committee on trade. He urged barriers against American iron products, arguing the need for a protective tariff to nurture provincial iron manufacturers. He was, however, happy to rely on imports of American pig-iron, although he admitted "Gosfield Iron is the strongest I know of, I think it surpasses both the Scotch and Welsh pig iron, no.1." In contrast, blast-furnace operators wanted restrictions on both pig-iron and castings. Field and Cahoon had operated at a double disadvantage. As iron founders, they had to compete with cheaper American goods; as iron producers, they could not rely on the loyalty of their supposed natural customers, the Upper Canadian iron founders.

Successful and stable iron foundries were, however, not long in coming. James Bell Ewart* and Edward Gurney* were but a few of the men who established thriving operations in the 1830s and 1840s primarily in the Hamilton–Dundas area. Profitable and enduring iron and steel production would not come to Ontario until the Hamilton Blast Furnace Company [see John C. Milne*] opened in 1895.

CHRISTOPHER ANDREAE

AO, Hiram Walker Hist. Museum coll., 20–85; RG 1, A-I-6: 20848–49; A-II-2, 1: 10–11; RG 22, ser.131, 4: f.110. Hugh Murray, *An historical and descriptive account of British America . . .* (3v., Edinburgh, 1839). U.C., House of Assembly, *App. to the journal*, 1835, no.11, "The second report of the committee on trade," 3. *Canadian Emigrant, and Western District Commercial and General Advertiser* (Sandwich [Windsor, Ont.]), 23 Feb., 1 March 1832; 14, 21 Feb., 13 June 1835; 3 May 1836. *Illustrated historical atlas of the counties of Essex and Kent* (Toronto, 1880; repr. 1973). W. H. Smith, *Canada: past, present and future . . .* (2v., Toronto, [1852]; repr. Belleville, Ont., 1973–74), 1: 27. W. L. Baby, *Souvenirs of the past, with illustrations: an instructive and amusing work, giving a correct account of the customs and habits of the pioneers of Canada . . .* (Windsor, 1896), 121.

FINLAY, JACQUES-RAPHAËL (often referred to as **Jaco Finlay**), fur trader, guide, and interpreter; b. *c.* 1768, perhaps at Finlay's House (near Neepawin, Sask.), son of James Finlay and a Saulteaux; d. May 1828 at Spokane House (near Spokane, Wash.).

Jacques-Raphaël Finlay's father was a native of Scotland who wintered in the Indian country as a fur trader as early as 1766. Jaco had entered the service of the North West Company by 1798; in 1804 he was commissioned clerk for the newly reorganized company [*see* William McGILLIVRAY]. Two years later he was in charge of an outpost of Rocky Mountain House (Alta) on the Kootenay Plains. He became associated with explorer David Thompson*, who was searching for a suitable pass by which the NWC could traverse the Rockies in order to reach the Columbia River watershed. In 1806 Finlay crossed the pass later named after Joseph Howse* and he cut out a trail and built a canoe for Thompson the following year. Thompson crossed the pass in 1807 but found the trail virtually useless since it was too narrow for his loaded packhorses. The canoe, cached on the banks of the Columbia River near the mouth of the Blaeberry River (B.C.), was found to have been damaged. Finlay does not appear to have been with Thompson at this time, or when Thompson built Kootenae House near Lake Windermere, but he was hunting and trapping in the vicinity, possibly as a free trader.

By 1809 Finlay had penetrated to the Flathead River country of present-day northwestern Montana and northern Idaho and had commenced trading with the Flatheads. He acted as guide for Thompson when the explorer built Kullyspell House (Idaho) on Pend'Oreille Lake that October. The following year Thompson, on his return to Kootenae House, engaged Finlay as clerk and interpreter. Finlay appears to have been an excellent guide and interpreter and is described by Thompson as "a fine half breed." In the summer of 1810 Finlay, possibly with the assistance of Finan McDonald, built Spokane House at the junction of the Spokane and Little Spokane rivers. In 1819 he participated in the Snake River country expeditions south of the Columbia River, led by Nor'Wester Donald McKenzie*. At the union of the NWC and the Hudson's Bay Company in 1821 neither his name nor those of his sons appeared on the rolls of the HBC, which would seem to indicate that at that time he was probably a free trader and trapper. In mid October 1824 Finlay, the leader of a group of freemen who were watching the Shuswap (Salish) Indians near Jasper House (Alta) in order to intercept their furs

Finlay

before they reached the HBC posts, encountered George Simpson*, governor of the HBC in North America, then on his way to the Columbia district. Simpson deplored the hold the freemen had over the Indians and the fact that, as middlemen, they pushed up the prices of furs. He ordered that no further supplies be granted to freemen such as Finlay unless they stopped trading with the Indians. Perhaps in order to watch Finlay's activities, but probably also to benefit from his experience, Peter Skene Ogden*, referring to him as Keyachie Finlay, included him among the freemen and HBC servants who left the Flathead Post (Mont.) for the Snake River country in December 1824.

By 1826 the HBC had abandoned Spokane House but Finlay continued to live there. Scottish botanist David Douglas noted on 9 May 1826: "I had for my guides two young men, sons of a Mr. Jacques Raphael Finlay, a Canadian Sauteur, who is at present residing in the abandoned establishment of Spokane, in which direction I was going." And two days later: "Reached the old establishment at Spokane at eleven o'clock, where I was kindly received by Mr. Finlay." Finlay had been recommended to him as "a man of extensive information as to the appearance of the country, animals, and so on." Douglas further noted that Finlay spoke only French, the language of the NWC. He was the father of a large family.

ERIC J. HOLMGREN

David Douglas, *Journal kept by David Douglas during his travels in North America, 1823–1827* . . . (London, 1914; repr. New York, 1959). *HBRS*, 13 (Rich and Johnson). George Simpson, *Fur trade and empire: George Simpson's journal . . . 1824–25*, ed. Frederick Merk (new ed., Cambridge, Mass., 1968). David Thompson, *David Thompson's narrative, 1784–1812*, ed. R. [G.] Glover (new ed., Toronto, 1962). Morton, *Hist. of Canadian west* (Thomas; 1973). J. A. Meyers, "Jacques Raphael Finlay," *Wash. Hist. Quarterly* (Seattle), 10 (1919): 163–67.

FINLAY, WILLIAM, businessman and JP; d. unmarried 5 Dec. 1834 in Funchal, Madeira.

William Finlay was possibly a native of Kilmarnock, Scotland, or of Glasgow, where an uncle was a manufacturer. He may have been related to James Finlay Sr and Jr, early fur traders at Montreal, or to Hugh Finlay* at Quebec; Hugh named as his testamentary executor the Quebec merchant John MURE, who was a brother-in-law of William's Glasgow uncle. Whatever his immediate family relations, William was likely born into one of the wide connections in the forefront of what was known as the "Canada trade." Consisting principally of Hunters, Patersons, Parkers, Robertsons, and Dunlops in London, Glasgow, Kilmarnock, and Greenock, this group's old-country members were linked by business, family, and social ties among themselves and to many representatives in the British American colonies. The latter, often young relatives sent out to manage the colonial side of matters and including such future business leaders in the Canadas as James McGill*, Adam Lymburner*, James Dunlop*, and Robert Hamilton*, frequently worked with emigrants from the Edinburgh area, including Richard Dobie*, and with the little group of Grants from Strathaven and Glen Livet represented at Quebec by the merchant William Grant*. By 1800 major elements of this loosely tied, broad interest had formed into a copartnership that spanned the line of trade from London to the Great Lakes and included, in London, John Gillespie, who was related to the Patersons; in Montreal, the former Hunter correspondent William Parker, Samuel Gerrard*, an in-law of the Grants, and John Ogilvy*, who was linked to the Paterson and Robertson elements; and, at Quebec, another relative of the Patersons, John Mure. In the family-organized world of 18th-century Scottish business, being born into such a connection was a prime introduction to commerce.

Finlay arrived at Quebec possibly between 1798 and 1805; by 1808 he was working for Mure, and in 1816 he was first clerk in Mure's counting-house, which was then operating outside the copartnership but serving as an agent for Mure's former Montreal associates. Mure praised Finlay's "faithful Service and friendship" and made him guardian of at least one of his sons, whose "regard and affection" Finlay also gained. Finlay's long apprenticeship with Mure gave him a thorough grounding in the numerous aspects of trade in which Mure engaged, including the fur and timber trades, the import-export business, ship chartering, and property speculation. When Mure retired to Scotland in 1817 Finlay took over his firm and apparently brought it back into a copartnership with the Montrealers and Londoners, directing it first under the name Gerrard, Finlay and Company from 1817 and then as Gillespie, Finlay and Company from about 1822. Possibly in 1817 as well Finlay obtained one share in the copartnership's Montreal branch, Gerrard, Gillespie, Moffatt and Company; by 1 May 1819 he possessed two shares, and in 1821 he was negotiating to obtain Gerrard's interest. George Moffatt*, the dominant figure in the Montreal firm, was similarly a partner with Finlay in the Quebec concern.

Under Finlay the Quebec firm retired, to a large extent, from the fur trade; until 1826 at least, however, it continued to pass through Quebec a declining share of the outfits and correspondence between the London office and Frederick William ERMATINGER in Montreal, agent for his brother CHARLES OAKES in Sault Ste Marie (Ont.). As well, although Finlay's company was still exporting staves in 1819, an agency for British contractors furnishing masts to the Admiralty and participation through the copartnership in a large timber-cutting operation called the Canada Company were wound up. In 1827 Gillespie, Finlay offered for lease its beach at Anse des Mères and perhaps at the same time it disposed of its big storage ground for timber at Wolfe's Cove (Anse au Foulon) to the Gilmours [see Allan Gilmour*]. It does not seem to have owned sawmills.

Although Finlay withdrew his company from fur and timber, he kept it as active as had Mure in the local sale and export of flour, corn meal, and wood ashes as well as of pork from Upper Canada. He also brought in rum from New Brunswick, whisky from Upper Canada, Spanish and Madeira wines in quantity, West Indies rum and sugar, and Scotch spirits, in addition to groceries and hardware. For its shipments the firm had its own big wharf, Finlay's, by 1818, and it continued until 1832 at least to use part of the King's Wharf, held on lease.

Finlay engaged his company heavily in shipping. It had at least two vessels constructed, a 128-ton schooner in 1828 and a 430-ton ship in 1834, bought at least one, financed construction of a number of others (and in this manner had transferred to it no fewer than two ships, a barque, two brigs, and two schooners), and chartered craft for individual voyages. It frequently offered for freight or charter its own vessels or others for which it was agent, and its little fleet carried passengers to Britain or the West Indies. Finlay adapted to the steam age. In 1830 he became the first chairman of the Quebec and Halifax Steam Navigation Company, which had the steamship *Royal William* built in 1830–31. However, he was one of the many proprietors of the ship who sold out in the depression of 1832, before it made its pioneer transatlantic voyage [see Sir Samuel Cunard*]. Although Finlay had little direct interest in canals, a new field of enterprise in the colony, he provided introductions at Quebec for William Hamilton Merritt*, who came in 1827 seeking financial backing for the Welland Canal, potentially so useful for Gerrard, Gillespie, Moffatt and Company's trade with Upper Canada.

Finlay was more involved in another new field of investment for colonial businessmen, that of financial institutions. He was among a number of businessmen who had the Bank of Montreal incorporated in 1821 and with others obtained incorporation of the Quebec Bank the following year, but by 1831 neither he nor his firm had any more connection with the latter. In 1825 he was a director of a rival organization, the Quebec branch of the Bank of Montreal, Gerrard and Moffatt being powerful figures in its Montreal office. The same year he was a shareholder in the City Bank (of Montreal). During the 1820s he was often a weekly director of the Quebec Savings Bank. At the end of the decade he was an incorporator of, and a shareholder in, the Quebec Fire Assurance Company, and in the early 1830s his firm, like Gerrard, Gillespie, Moffatt and Company in Montreal, had the local agency for the big Phoenix Assurance Company of London. Land, a traditional area of investment, may also have attracted Finlay; he seems to have acquired property of his own, by purchase and foreclosure, in Lower and Upper Canada.

With a mix of business activities somewhat different from that of Mure's day, the Quebec firm seems to have continued to prosper under Finlay's direction despite the weak economy of the early and late 1820s and the depression of 1832. Since all the branches of the copartnership had the same partners, they probably all benefited from the prosperity of any one of them; thus Finlay's company must have been aided by Gerrard, Gillespie, Moffat and Company, which reaped the profits of Upper Canada's growth and was, along with Forsyth, Richardson and Company and Peter McGill and Company, one of the three great firms of Montreal. An indication of Gillespie, Finlay and Company's success is the construction on Finlay's Wharf in 1832 of two long three-storey stone warehouses, which, with several built at the time by other merchants, changed the scale of the Lower Town waterfront.

Finlay's wide interests and success earned for him a leading position in Quebec's business world. He served as chairman of the Committee of Trade from 1825 to 1833, and was an intelligent and well-informed – and often the first – witness before committees of the Lower Canadian House of Assembly investigating commercial matters such as Britain's corn and tariff acts of 1828. Politically and socially, Finlay was discreet. In 1822 he was elected to the Quebec committee, presided over by William Bacheler COLTMAN, of a provincial movement to promote the union of the Canadas, but he was much less active than William Walker, his counterpart at Quebec in the Ellice–Forsyth–Richardson transatlantic chain [see John RICHARDSON]. For some time Finlay resisted appointment as a justice of the peace, pleading the pressure of private business, but he finally accepted a commission in February 1828. He was long a trustee of the Quebec Library and occupied the same position in St Andrew's Church from 1830 until his death.

The fear of cholera in 1832 appeared to Samuel Neilson*, publisher of the *Quebec Gazette*, "to have overcome [Finlay's] physical & moral powers completely." Although he recovered fully from his fright, in late summer 1834, with his health deteriorating again, he made a will and then almost immediately left for the mild climate of Madeira. He did not last out the year, however. Neilson related that "women had had much to do with his illness," and in 1836 learned from Finlay's landlady at Funchal that during his last days he was "inconceivably fractious & hated women so much that he fairly interdicted her visiting him on any

Fisher

formula. He was strange mortal." However, a woman, Margaret Maloney, was the only individual not clearly of his family or business background to be remembered generously in his will. Against Neilson's account of the dying man should be set the ample evidence of his kindness and broadmindedness; among specific bequests totalling £14,000 were £100 to the poor of each of Quebec's seven principal congregations (Roman Catholic and Protestant), £200 to the Quebec Library, £1,000 to the Montreal General Hospital, and £1,000 to the city of Quebec for the improvement of streets and squares. The unestimated residue of the estate went to nephews. The bequest to the city was used to open a new, larger market-place on the waterfront, and in 1838 it was named Finlay Place in his honour.

A. J. H. RICHARDSON

ANQ-Q, CN1-16, 27 janv. 1809, 6 août 1817; CN1-188, 13 nov. 1826; CN1-197, 22 juill. 1816; 20, 22 oct., 7 nov. 1817; 3 juill. 1819; 12 févr. 1820; 2 oct. 1821; 27 févr. 1822; 5 janv., 23 mars, 15 avril, 13, 16, 23, 25 mai, 13 nov. 1826; 2 avril, 5 mai, 16, 30 oct., 13 déc. 1827; 4, 19 janv., 15 mai, 25 juin, 27 août, 6 oct. 1828; 10, 30 avril, 13 déc. 1829; 14 janv., 25 mai, 28 août, 3, 9 sept. 1830; 4 août, 2 déc. 1831; 4 avril, 10, 17, 29 mai 1832; 8 févr., 15 nov. 1833; 22 avril 1835; CN1-219, 18 mai 1832; CN1-230, 10 oct. 1804; CN1-253, 27 oct. 1813; P-219. Arch. judiciaires, Québec, Holograph will of William Finlay, 13 March 1835 (see P.-G. Roy, *Inv. testaments*, 3: 64). PAC, MG 19, B2, 1, 14 Aug. 1817, 6 July 1818; MG 23, GII, 3, vol.6; MG 24, B1, 5: 451–53; 16: 238; 18: 134–55; 36: 551; 187: 3824; L3: 8809–10, 8855–58, 8939–41, 8953–58, 9191–92, 9855; National Map Coll., H2/340-1845; RG 4, A1, 253: 54–55; 332: 25; 352: 132; RG 31, C1, 1831, Quebec. Private arch., A. J. H. Richardson (Ottawa), J. A. Paterson to Richardson, 22 May 1950. PRO, CO 42/275: 142 (mfm. at PAC). L.C., House of Assembly, *Journals*, 1828–29, apps.F, R; 1830, app.N; 1831, app.M; 1831–32, app.TT; 1832–33, apps.U, W; 1834, apps.Q, S; *Statutes*, 1821–22, c.26; 1826, c.11; 1828–29, c.58; 1830, c.15. G.B., Parl., House of Commons, *Report from the select committee on timber duties . . .* (London, 1835). *Statistical account of U.C.* (Gourlay), 463, 504. Wis., State Hist. Soc., *Coll.*, 4 (1857–58): 95.

Quebec Gazette, 26 June, 21 Aug., 27 Nov. 1817; 5, 12 Feb., 12 March, 2 July, 9 Nov. 1818; 11 Nov. 1819; 29 May, 23 Oct. 1820; 2 April, 24 May, 21, 28 June, 19 Nov. 1821; 6, 20 June, 4, 8, 11 July, 15 Aug., 24 Oct., 4 Nov., 2 Dec. 1822; 27 Jan., 10, 21 April, 19, 29 May, 9, 29 June, 4 Aug., 22 Sept. 1823; 9 March 1824; 7 Oct. 1828; 14 April 1829; 8 Feb. 1831; 21 April 1834. *Quebec almanac*, 1825–34. *Quebec directory*, 1826: 18, 20, 53, 95. George Gale, *Historic tales of old Quebec* (Quebec, 1923), 29. Ouellet, *Hist. économique*, 362–65. H. B. Timothy, *The Galts, a Canadian odyssey; John Galt, 1779–1839* (Toronto, 1977), 14–16, 50–51. G. J. J. Tulchinsky, *The river barons: Montreal businessmen and the growth of industry and transportation, 1837–53* (Toronto and Buffalo, N.Y., 1977). Archibald Campbell, "The *Royal William*, the pioneer of ocean steam navigation," Literary and Hist. Soc. of Quebec, *Trans.* (Quebec), new ser., 20 (1891): 29, 32–35, 41. O.-A. Coté, "La Chambre de commerce de Québec," *BRH*, 27 (1921): 26–28. "The *Royal William*, 1831–33," Literary and Hist. Soc. of Quebec, *Trans.*, new ser., 13 (1879). "William Finlay," *BRH*, 42 (1936): 733.

FISHER, Sir GEORGE BULTEEL, army officer and painter; b. 16 March 1764 in Peterborough, England, youngest of nine sons of John Fisher and Elizabeth Laurens; m. 7 May 1814 Elizabeth Rawlings in White Waltham, and they had one daughter; d. 8 March 1834 in Woolwich (London).

George Bulteel Fisher's family was a distinguished one. His eldest brother, John, followed in the footsteps of his father, an Anglican clergyman, graduating from Cambridge to pursue a career in the Church of England, which culminated in an appointment as bishop of Salisbury. Dubbed "the King's Fisher" on account of his friendship with George III, John was a well-known patron of artists, especially John Constable, and through him George developed an association with Constable. George, John, and their brother Benjamin were all competent amateur watercolourists; however, the first has received more notice. Their artistic bent may have been derived from their mother, a Huguenot heiress.

George, like Benjamin, followed a military career. He began his training, probably at about age 16, in the drawing room of the Tower of London, which focused on forming technical rather than tactical officers. Afterwards he attended the Royal Military Academy at Woolwich; he would have studied draftsmanship under Paul Sandby, chief drawing-master there from 1768 to 1796. In 1780 he and Benjamin were honorary exhibitors at the Royal Academy of Arts. Benjamin showed a view of Dominica and George one of the Isle of Wight, where their father was rector of Calbourne; the following year George showed another of the same island. Commissioned a second lieutenant in the Royal Artillery on 1 July 1782, Fisher was promoted first lieutenant on 28 May 1790 and that month was sent to Gibraltar.

Fisher departed from there in 1791 for Lower Canada, where, by his account, he "had the honour of attending" Prince Edward* Augustus. This appointment may have been obtained through the influence of his brother John, who had been the prince's tutor from 1780 to 1785. Fisher's travels to Gibraltar, Lower Canada, and the West Indies paralleled those of Edward Augustus from 1790 to 1794, and it may be that he was on the prince's staff for the same period. In April 1792 at Quebec Elizabeth Posthuma Simcoe [Gwillim*], wife of the recently appointed lieutenant governor of Upper Canada, John Graves Simcoe*, noted that she had seen some beautiful views of Windsor Castle drawn by Fisher for Edward Augustus and an oil painting of his which did not please her.

Later that month Fisher set out from Quebec to take some views of Niagara Falls, which he showed to the Simcoes on meeting them at Carleton Island (N.Y.) on his return.

Fisher left Lower Canada for the West Indies in 1794 and was present that year at the capture of Martinique, St Lucia, and Guadeloupe under Sir Charles Grey. He was promoted captain-lieutenant on 6 March 1795. Once back in England he arranged for John William Edy to engrave and publish *Six views of North America* (London, 1796) after his sketches. These finely executed aquatints were originally issued in pairs dated 10 May 1795, 1 Sept. 1795, and 1 Feb. 1796; a descriptive pamphlet dedicated to Edward Augustus was published in 1796 to accompany them. Edy, a painter as well as an engraver active from about 1780 to at least 1824, deserves as much credit as Fisher for their superb quality. According to the art historian Gerald E. Finlay, the elements of the Picturesque so evident in these prints influenced a profound and immediate change in the style of a prolific contemporary painter of the Canadian landscape, George Heriot*. Equally beautiful is a larger scale aquatint by Fisher and Edy entitled *View of the falls of Niagara, North America*, which was probably published between *c.* 1795 and 1800. One extant impression was personally coloured and inscribed by Fisher for General John Hale; the general's son John* had been aide-de-camp and military secretary to Edward Augustus at Quebec, where Fisher in all likelihood knew him. The duo of Fisher and Edy, presumably satisfied with the response to their North American prints, published six aquatints of Gibraltar scenes in 1796–97. In 1800 a Captain Fisher, believed to be George, exhibited a view of Niagara Falls at the Royal Academy of Arts. Eight years later Fisher made his last appearance there, exhibiting landscapes of Durham and Blackheath (London). He allegedly took views in Portugal with the panorama painter Robert Barker (d. 1806) for use in the latter's exhibition room on Leicester Square in London.

Having been promoted captain in 1801, major in 1806, and lieutenant-colonel on 28 June 1808, Fisher served in Portugal and Spain during the Peninsular War, beginning in March 1809. He assumed command of the Royal Artillery following the siege of Burgos, Spain, in the autumn of 1812; however, a misunderstanding with the Marquess of Wellington resulted in his return to England in July 1813. Fisher's successor, Lieutenant-Colonel Alexander Dickson, had only high praise for him and intimated that Wellington had acted with haste and injustice. Fisher, favourably impressed with the fine Portuguese scenery, about which he remarked to the painter Joseph Farington in 1810, painted several water-colours while there.

Fisher was an accomplished amateur artist in oil and water-colour who had the advantage of social contacts with professional artists, among whom were Constable, Farington, and possibly John Downman and Francis Towne. His penchant for lecturing about art impressed at least one subordinate officer in Portugal but failed to endear him to Constable, who confessed to being "tired of going to school." Ten years earlier, however, Constable had praised Fisher's North American drawings, and Fisher's importance to Canada is undoubtedly this artistic legacy.

Fisher was promoted brevet colonel on 4 June 1814, regimental colonel on 6 Nov. 1820, and major-general on 27 May 1825. He was made KB on 21 Sept. 1831 and a knight commander of the Hanoverian Order in 1833, and he was commandant of the Woolwich garrison from 10 Feb. 1827 until his death in 1834. He received a splendid military funeral and is buried at Old Charlton (London).

W. MARTHA E. COOKE

[George Bulteel Fisher is sometimes confused with his brother Benjamin, ultimately major-general in the Royal Engineers, in which he was active from 1771 until his death in 1814. The Fisher family nicknamed George "the Colonel" and Benjamin "the General." Benjamin was posted in Lower Canada from 1785 to about 1796 to report on and to take drawings of fortifications. In March 1792, while at Quebec, he lent Mrs Simcoe his portfolio of drawings taken in Dominica. The only known extant Canadian water-colour by him, formerly attributed to George, is of Baie-Saint-Paul, province of Quebec; it is signed and dated "B. Fisher/1787" and is in the PAC.

Impressions of the prints that make up *Six views of North America* are in the King George III Topographical Coll. in the Map Library of the BL, the PAC, the New York Public Library, and the Royal Ontario Museum, Toronto. The New York Public Library also owns a water-colour of a bridge, questionably identified as the Pont Déry, on the Rivière Jacques-Cartier and the Royal Ontario Museum owns one of the Great Falls of the Potomac in the Potomac River. Both are attributed to George; however, their attribution is under review. *Fall of Montmorenci*, plate number six of the *Six views*, is similar in subject to a water-colour, dated 1792, in the Victoria and Albert Museum, London. Impressions of the print of Niagara Falls, which are even rarer than the others, are in a private collection and in the PAC, which also owns water-colours of Canadian subjects by Fisher. A water-colour of Niagara Falls, attributed to Fisher but more likely a copy taken after an original drawing by him, fetched £1,485 at a London auction in 1983. Some of his European subjects are in the Victoria and Albert Museum and the British Museum in London, the Laing Art Gallery in Newcastle upon Tyne, the Leeds City Art Gallery, and the Whitworth Art Gallery in Manchester. Views of the Thames, Durham, Ireland, and Portugal were in dealers' hands in 1938 and 1965.

The author wishes to thank R. H. Hubbard, M. Allodi, J. T. Crosthwait, Lydia Foy, Douglas Schoenherr, and an anonymous private collector for their assistance. W.M.E.C.]

257

Fisher

AO, MS 517, 1: 46–48, 75. Berkshire Record Office (Reading, Eng.), Reg. of marriages for the parish of White Waltham, 7 May 1814. Northamptonshire Record Office (Northampton, Eng.), Reg. of baptisms for the parish of Peterborough, 6 April 1764. PRO, WO 76/360: 21. *John Constable's correspondence*, ed. R. B. Beckett (6v., Ipswich, Eng., 1962–68), 2: 115–16, 344; 6: 1–4, 10, 23, 25, 107–8, 134, 157, 166, 221. *Gentleman's Magazine*, January–June 1834: 656. William Swabey, *Diary of campaigns in the Peninsula, for the years 1811, 12, and 13 . . .* , ed. F. A. Whinyates (n.p., [1895]), 15–16. *United Service Journal and Naval and Military Magazine* (1834), no.1: 575. Mary Allodi, *Canadian watercolours and drawings in the Royal Ontario Museum* (2v., Toronto, 1974), no.743. *British watercolours in the Victoria and Albert Museum . . .* , comp. Lionel Lambourne and Jean Hamilton (London, 1980), 133. W. M. E. Cooke, *W. H. Coverdale Collection of Canadiana: paintings, water-colours and drawings (Manoir Richelieu collection)* (Ottawa, 1983), 220, 236–37. S. W. Fisher, *A dictionary of watercolour painters, 1750–1900* (London, 1972), 73, 79. M. H. Grant, *A dictionary of British landscape painters from the sixteenth to the early twentieth century* (Leigh-on-Sea, Eng., 1952), 68. Algernon Graves, *The Royal Academy of Arts . . .* (8v., London, 1905–6), 3: 115, 118. J. R. Harper, *Early painters and engravers in Canada* ([Toronto], 1970), 112. Laing Art Gallery and Museum, *Illustrated catalogue of the permanent collection of water colour drawings*, comp. C. B. Stevenson ([Newcastle upon Tyne, Eng., 1939]), 17. *List of officers of the Royal Regiment of Artillery from the year 1716 to the year 1899 . . .* , comp. John Kane and W. H. Askwith (4th ed., London, 1900), 19, 169. Parker Gallery, *A catalogue of views of the world* (London, 1973). *Quebec almanac*, 1792: 116; 1794: 80, 84–85; 1795: 70; 1796: 78. *Sigmund Samuel Collection, Canadiana and Americana*, comp. C. W. Jefferys (Toronto, [1948]), 121–22. I. N. P. Stokes and D. C. Haskell, *American historical prints . . .* (New York, 1933; repr. Detroit, 1974), 36, 40, 135–36. Ulrich Thieme and Felix Becker, *Allgemeines Lexikon der bildenden Künstler von der Antike bis zur Gegenwart . . .* (37v., Leipzig, German Democratic Republic, 1907–50), 10: 353; 12: 55. Victoria and Albert Museum, *Catalogue of watercolour paintings by British artists and foreigners working in Great Britain* (1v. and supp., London, 1927–51), 206–7; supp., 30.

R. B. Beckett, *John Constable and the Fishers* (London, 1952), 6, 13, 176, 241. G. E. Finley, *George Heriot: postmaster-painter of the Canadas* (Toronto, 1983), 49–51, 63–64, 89, 93. M. H. Grant, *A chronological history of the old English landscape painters (in oil) from the XVIth century to the XIXth century . . .* (new ed., 8v., Leigh-on-Sea, 1957–61), 7: 513. Martin Hardie, *Water-colour painting in Britain*, ed. Dudley Snelgrove et al. (3v., London, 1966–68), 3: 264–65, plate 272. I. O. Williams, *Early English watercolours, and some cognate drawings by artists born not later than 1785* (London, 1952; repr. Bath, Eng., 1970), 243–44, plate 398. "A newly discovered early English water-colour master," *Walker's Monthly* (London), no.125 (May 1938): 1; no.126 (June 1938): 1–2. Adrian Bury, "Soldier-artist," *Connoisseur* (London), 159 (May–August 1965), no.169: 47. Miriam Kramer, "United Kingdom news and views," *Canadian Collector* (Toronto), 18 (1983), no.5: 63.

FISHER, JAMES, surgeon, army officer, politician, and office holder; probably b. in Scotland; d. 26 June 1822 in Edinburgh.

Like many of his colleagues who would leave their mark on Canadian medical history, James Fisher came to the province of Quebec with the British forces sent out during the American revolution. He had been appointed a hospital mate for the military hospital at Quebec on 1 Feb. 1776 and on 25 Oct. 1778 was made a garrison mate at Quebec by Governor Frederick Haldimand*. His services apparently were well regarded, since on 12 Nov. 1783 he received the post of garrison surgeon following Adam Mabane*'s resignation.

In 1787 Fisher, like his colleague Charles Blake*, presented his views before a committee set up to investigate agriculture and suggest ways to increase the population. In his brief Fisher protested against the lack of regulations, which allowed anybody to take the title of doctor. He thought that a shortage of the disciples of Asclepius would be better for the health of the colonists than the proliferation of medical know-nothings. He was in favour of inoculation against the terrible ravages of smallpox. Finally, he proposed that medical boards be set up in the towns of Quebec and Montreal to conduct examinations and give doctors, surgeons, midwives, and apothecaries certificates to practise. In 1788 Governor Lord Dorchester [Guy Carleton*] promulgated a law on the practice of medicine that took these recommendations into consideration. From that year, Fisher was one of those who examined applicants for a medical licence.

Fisher's reputation grew steadily. He was in great demand and held several posts concurrently. In 1789 he became doctor to the Hôpital Général in Quebec. Two years later he went before a committee of the Legislative Council to give advice on the nature and extent of the Baie-Saint-Paul malady, as did his colleagues John Mervin NOOTH, George Longmore*, John Gould, and Philippe-Louis-François Badelard*. In 1795 he appeared before the House of Assembly with Nooth, Longmore, and Frédéric-Guillaume Oliva* to give his opinion on a bill to quarantine ships suspected of carrying a contagious disease. Then in 1800 the government selected him to treat the inhabitants of Nicolet, Bécancour, and Jeune-Lorette (Loretteville), who had been stricken with an infectious fever. The following year he was appointed commissioner for the relief of the insane and foundlings. He became physician to the Ursulines of Quebec in 1807. In 1812 Governor Sir George Prevost* offered to name him medical director for the military district of Montreal, but Fisher declined the post, pleading his age and infirmities. He recommended instead surgeon William Stewart, a suggestion that was accepted. Two years later Fisher was appointed commissioner for insane asylums.

Fleming

Fisher's numerous occupations seem to have been highly lucrative and enabled him to lend £8,000 to various people between 1783 and 1802. Several loans were made to master-craftsmen and merchants, most of them Canadians, but Fisher gave the biggest ones to his compatriots. He moved in fashionable circles and had close links with the leading figures in the colony. He lived on Rue des Remparts in Quebec at first, and then moved to Rue Sainte-Anne early in the 1790s. He belonged to the Fire Society from 1790 and in 1797 became a member of the board of the Quebec Library. In 1794, concerned about the activities of French emissaries who had come to preach the benefits of revolution, he joined some fellow citizens in signing a declaration of loyalty to the British crown. Lower Canadian politics did not leave him indifferent. In 1796 he stood as a candidate in Northumberland riding. On 20 July he was elected to the assembly, where he sat until 4 July 1800 and supported the English party.

Fisher retired from military service on half pay on 25 June 1815 and the following year returned to Scotland. He asked two medical colleagues, Joseph Painchaud* and Joseph Parant*, to look after his Canadian interests. When he left, the country lost one of its most eminent practitioners. Painchaud, who had known him well, said that he "was not a 'learned' man . . . but on the other hand he possessed great tact, good judgement, and an excellent memory, which, combined with experience, made him the greatest practitioner at Quebec." Fisher must have been a highly competent doctor, judging by the extent of his practice and the reputation earned by some of his pupils: Painchaud, Anthony von Iffland*, François BLANCHET, and John McLoughlin*.

GILLES JANSON

ANQ-Q, CN1-83, 8 août, 2 oct. 1783; 25 sept. 1786; 31 août, 5 sept. 1789; 16 juill. 1794; CN1-256, 12 août 1791, 11 janv. 1792, 1er mai 1795, 2 mai 1796, 2 mai 1797, 27 août 1798; CN1-284, 22 nov., 1er déc. 1787; 28 mars, 21 avril, 24 mai, 26 juin 1788; 1er mai, 1er juin, 25, 28 août, 10, 21, 23 sept., 2 oct. 1789; 1er, 5 mai, 19 juin, 5 août, 18 déc. 1790; 15 janv., 1er, 21, 26 oct. 1791; 22 oct., 26 déc. 1792; 12 févr., 6 sept., 31 déc. 1793; 2 mai, 26 juill., 20 août, 21 oct. 1794; 27 févr., 5 sept., 17 déc. 1795; 4, 8 janv., 17 févr., 8 avril, 13, 17 mai, 13–14, 27 juin, 22 sept., 12 nov. 1796; 6 janv., 30 mars, 24 juin, 23 sept., 24 nov. 1797; 11 juill., 6 août 1798; 25 mai, 12, 30 oct., 11 nov. 1799; 21 mai 1802; 5 avril 1803; CN1-285, 15 avril 1811. BL, Add. mss 21723: 10–12, 21, 56; 21734: 120–21; 21735: 86; 21739: 180–85; 21745: 15, 46, 82. PAC, MG 11, [CO 42] Q, 23: 29; 27-2: 524–54; RG 8, I (C ser.), 30: 57; 230: 144; 289–90; 372; 1168; 1170; 1218: 298, 322–23; 1220: 420. *Quebec Gazette*, 23 June 1785; 16 April 1789; 28 Jan. 1790; 26 Jan., 5 July 1792; 14 Feb., 13 June 1793; 13 Feb., 3 July 1794; 26 March 1795; 26 Jan., 9 Feb. 1797; 2 April 1801; 16 July 1806; 7 April 1808; 22 Feb. 1810; 21 Nov. 1811; 30 Dec. 1813; 12, 19 Oct. 1815; 12 July, 8 Aug. 1816. *Quebec almanac*, 1791, 1794, 1796–99, 1801–13, 1815–16. Abbott, *Hist. of medicine*. M.-J. et G. Ahern, *Notes pour l'hist. de la médecine*. [Catherine Burke, dite de Saint-Thomas], *Les ursulines de Québec, depuis leur établissement jusqu'à nos jours* (4v., Québec, 1863–66), 4: 622–24, 633. Sylvio Leblond, "Une conférence inédite du docteur Joseph Painchaud," *Trois siècles de médecine québécoise* (Québec, 1970), 56–65. "Les disparus," *BRH*, 32 (1926): 173.

FLEMING, JOHN, businessman, militia officer, JP, and author; b. c. 1786 in Aberdeenshire, Scotland, possibly in Aberdeen, eldest son of Daniel Fleming and Margaret McHardy; d. unmarried 30 July 1832 in Montreal.

John Fleming came from a relatively poor family. His father died when he was a boy, but he received the rudiments of a classical education from a shopkeeper-uncle, Charles McHardy. In 1803 he emigrated to Montreal, where he apprenticed with Logan and Watt, an import house formed in 1796 with links to Greenock, Scotland; his family was connected with the Logans. Logan and Watt was not involved in the fur trade, but it was probably active in the export of the new staples, wheat and timber. Hart Logan, Fleming's employer, was also a shipowner and shipbuilder; he launched John Molson*'s second steamship, the *Swiftsure*, in 1812.

In 1815 Logan and his brother William, a baker and landowner, returned to Britain. Fleming was left in control of William's Quebec assets jointly with William's son James and Fleming's cousin John Catenach. At the same time he acquired a one-quarter interest in Hart Logan and Company, created on the dissolution of Logan and Watt. Hart Logan, who held three-quarters' interest, settled in London, and his firm's British export activities appear to have been shifted from Greenock to that city and to Liverpool. By 1817 James Logan was also a partner. The company dealt in such usual Canadian export commodities as oak timber, pine staves, deals, ashes, wheat, and flour. By 1820 it appears to have concentrated its British and colonial imports on European wines and spirits and on rum, sugar, molasses, and coffee from Jamaica and the Leeward Islands. It also built and operated ocean-going sailing vessels and St Lawrence steamships. The firm relied in part on loans from William, which by 1831 totalled £6,117.

As head of one of Montreal's principal wholesale firms, Fleming rose in the business community. In 1822 he was elected to the Committee of Trade, and he served as its secretary from at least 1827 until 1829; a precursor of the Montreal Board of Trade, it provided a lobby for merchants' concerns. Fleming was a shareholder in the Welland Canal Company, chartered in 1824, and the following year he was among 12 Montreal merchants who, with a group of London businessmen, founded the Lower Canada Land Com-

259

Fleming

pany; Hart Logan was on the correspondence committee of the land company's London subscribers. In 1826 Fleming subscribed 25 of the company's 1,820 shares at £100 each. Two years later he and 76 other merchants petitioned the government for ownership of water lots in Montreal Harbour so that as owners of the adjoining lands they could build wharfs.

Fleming's rise in the business community had been confirmed in January 1826 by his election to the board of directors of the Bank of Montreal. Aged about 40, he was then the youngest director after John Molson* Jr. A struggle within the board pitted an old guard, led by the president, Samuel Gerrard*, against a younger generation, led by George Moffatt*, who sought a more formal administration of the bank's business. Fleming supported the Moffatt faction, which triumphed at a board meeting on 5 June 1826; the following day Fleming was elected vice-president. Though a supporter of Moffatt, he joined a majority of the board in opposing Moffatt's attempt to petition Simon McGillivray* into bankruptcy, a question related to the Moffatt–Gerrard dispute. Fleming occupied the vice-presidency until June 1830 when he became president, a full-time post, the demands of which became his major preoccupation. Under him the bank's involvement in foreign exchange grew and the practice of keeping considerable funds in New York for call loans was initiated. At the end of 1831, when the charter of the Bank of Canada expired, Fleming organized the absorption of that institution by the Bank of Montreal. During Fleming's short tenure as president, which lasted until his death, the Bank of Montreal more than doubled its "net profit on hand" to £31,482, and in 1832 it declared a bonus in addition to its dividend of seven per cent, distributing £30,000 to shareholders.

As Fleming's prominence in the business community increased he took on offices typically filled by its members. In May 1821 he was promoted lieutenant in the Montreal militia. Five years later he became a justice of the peace, but in 1830 he declined reappointment on grounds of business pressures. By 1827 he had been elected a life governor of the Montreal General Hospital. Since 1807 he had been an active member of the Scotch Presbyterian Church, later known as St Gabriel Street Church, which was favoured by the Scottish merchant community; in June 1831 his activism extended to occupying the church with other supporters of the Reverend Edward Black* when the congregation split over the choice of a minister [see William CALDWELL].

In addition to his business and social occupations, Fleming had strong cultural interests. He corresponded with Daniel Wilkie*, a Quebec scholar, and was a friend of Montreal educator Alexander Skakel*. In 1824 he published "An essay on the education and duties of a Canadian merchant," in which he asserted that English grammar, writing, arithmetic, and book-keeping were necessary but not sufficient elements in the education of a merchant; to those subjects must be added "mathematics including practical navigation to strengthen the mind," geography (including national customs) "to render it liberal," and the languages of the principal trading nations. At the same time he was sensitive to local needs and conditions. He was scandalized that "no school-book has yet been compiled" that would give a colonial boy "some correct notions of his native land," and felt that it was "expedient and necessary that a history and description of Canada should be published, expressly composed for the use of Canadian schools." Examples in the teaching of business subjects should be drawn from the Canadian scene, he asserted, and the student made "acquainted with the face of his Country, her climate, soil, productions and capabilities" in order better to ascertain the resources that would justify "extensive undertakings in trade or manufactures." He wrote French fluently, and his friend William Berczy*, who taught him Italian and German, good-naturedly dubbed him "Flemming l'Italien" or "Jean Flemmin," according to circumstances. Fleming felt as well that a knowledge of ancient languages was necessary for anyone wishing to write English properly, and he made Latin translations for amusement.

Fleming wrote patriotic poetry and songs, but his only known published verse is an ode entitled "On the birth day of His Majesty King George the Third," which won a gold medal offered by the Literary Society of Quebec in 1809. In it, referring to Lower Canada, he writes:

See! Industry and Plenty rise
And wealth and Commerce greet our eyes
And Science, teaching all these gifts to prize.
While like an Angel sent by Heav'n's command,
The brave SIR HENRY [Sir James Henry Craig*]
   guards the happy land.

Fleming's major published work, however, was polemic in the guise of history. *Some considerations on this question: whether the British government acted wisely in granting to Canada her present constitution?* was written under the pseudonym A British Settler. It appeared in 1810, the year that Governor Craig attacked the Canadian party, seizing *Le Canadien* (Quebec), a nationalist newspaper, and imprisoning for "treacherous practices" some 20 people, including assemblymen, connected with it. Fleming shared Craig's objective of assimilating the Canadians but felt, unlike Craig, that it would be best achieved through the functioning of British institutions – such as an elective assembly, to which the inhabitants of the colony had a right in any case as British subjects – rather than through a return to the

260

French colonial institutions of the Quebec Act. Indeed, in Fleming's view the British government ought rather to eliminate the last vestiges of the Quebec Act, and he felt that a reunion of the Canadas might create favourable conditions for doing so. His attitude towards the Canadians, patronizing rather than vilifying, was moderate for a British merchant of the time.

In 1813, as Britain and her colonies warred with the United States, Fleming published *The resources of the Canadas* under the pseudonym A Querist. A celebration of the colonies' human and physical resources and of the abilities of the commander-in-chief of the British forces, Governor Sir George Prevost*, the book was intended to counter the lack of support for the war effort that low militia enrolments were thought to reveal. Fleming's last and best-known work, *Political annals of Lower Canada*, was published by A British Settler in 1828. It was written at a time of political tension to influence opinion in Britain in favour of the Montreal merchants. Their proposal of 1822 to unite the Canadas as a means of promoting British immigration and assimilating the Canadian population had been thwarted in the British parliament [*see* Louis-Joseph Papineau*]. A polemic in the form of a chronological history from 1534, Fleming's book favoured revival of the union project. A more aggressive work than *Some considerations*, it contributed to the identification of Fleming as ideologically aligned with an increasingly alarmed "English commercial party," and provoked a response by Pierre-Jean de SALES Laterrière in *Political and historical account of Lower Canada; with remarks* (London, 1830); he wrote that Fleming's work was "as full of information as it is of prejudice against the French Canadians."

Over his lifetime Fleming amassed one of the largest personal libraries in Lower Canada, nearly 10,000 volumes, comprised of some 4,000 books and 145 periodical and newspaper titles; even the Montreal Library counted only 7–8,000 volumes in the 1830s. Fleming's library included rare books and titles in French, Italian, and Latin, but most works were contemporary and in English; the major subject areas were history (30 per cent) and *belles-lettres* (25 per cent). Among the periodicals was undoubtedly the *Canadian Review* (Montreal) of 1824–26, which he had helped to establish. Although he had reputedly wanted his library left to McGill College, it was auctioned off after he died intestate, of cholera, in 1832.

Fleming's early death has left him in somewhat undeserved historical obscurity. In most respects he was typical of Montreal businessmen of his era, although his poor origins gave him a slow start, compared with others, in his rise to prominence. A cultured man by the standard of his time, he was so more by taste and inclination than by achievement. That he has been remembered for his publications

more than for his business activities is an indication that competition was much keener in business than in literature within the British community in Lower Canada.

PETER DESLAURIERS

John Fleming is the author of "On the birth day of His Majesty King George the Third," published in *Séance de la Société littéraire de Québec, tenue samedi le 3e juin 1809* (Québec, 1809); *Some considerations on this question: whether the British government acted wisely in granting to Canada her present constitution? . . . by a British settler* (Montreal, 1810); *The resources of the Canadas . . . by a querist* (Quebec, 1813); "An essay on the education and duties of a Canadian merchant," *Canadian Rev. and Literary and Hist. Journal* (Montreal), 1 (1824): 73–80; and *Political annals of Lower Canada . . .* (Montreal, 1828).

ANQ-M, CN1-134, 6 mai 1820, 2 juin 1831; CN1-187, 28 janv., 11 oct., 22 nov. 1817; 27 mai 1820. McGill Univ. Arch., W. E. Logan papers, corr. of John Fleming. PAC, MG 30, D1, 12: 855–56; RG 1, L3^L: 45043–46, 62161–232; RG 4, A1, 332, no.47; RG 68, General index, 1651–1841: 358, 361. William Berczy, "William von Moll Berczy," ANQ *Rapport*, 1940–41: 39, 42, 64, 67, 71, 76, 92. [P.-J. de Sales Laterrière], *Political and historical account of Lower Canada; with remarks . . .* (London, 1830). *Canadian Courant and Montreal Advertiser*, 1 Aug. 1832. *Le Canadien*, 1er août 1832. *Montreal Gazette*, 31 July 1832. *Quebec Gazette*, 1 Aug., 14 Nov. 1816; 27 Nov. 1817; 14 Jan., 14 Oct. 1819; 7 Sept. 1820; 7 May, 27 Sept. 1821. *Canada, an encyclopædia of the country: the Canadian dominion considered in its historic relations, its natural resources, its material progress, and its national development*, ed. J. C. Hopkins (6v. and index, Toronto, 1898–1900), 4. Augustin Cuvillier and J. Cuvillier, *Catalogue of books comprising the library of the late John Fleming, esquire . . .* (Montreal, 1833). Philéas Gagnon, *Essai de bibliographie canadienne . . .* (2v., Québec et Montréal, 1895–1913; réimpr. Dubuque, Iowa, [1962]). Hare et Wallot, *Les imprimés dans le Bas-Canada*. H. J. Morgan, *Bibliotheca Canadensis*. F. W. Terrill, *A chronology of Montreal and of Canada from A.D. 1752 to A.D. 1893 . . .* (Montreal, 1893). Wallace, *Macmillan dict.* R. Campbell, *Hist. of Scotch Presbyterian Church.* Denison, *Canada's first bank.* Antonio Drolet, *Les bibliothèques canadiennes, 1604–1960* (Ottawa, 1965). T. G. Marquis, "English-Canadian literature," *Canada and its provinces; a history of the Canadian people and their institutions . . .*, ed. Adam Shortt and A. G. Doughty (23v., Toronto, 1913–17), 12: 493–589. Benjamin Sulte et al., *A history of Quebec, its resources and its people* (2v., Montreal, 1908). Wallot, *Un Québec qui bougeait.* Thomas Chapais, "Une séance littéraire à Québec en 1809," *Le Courrier du Canada* (Québec), 31 déc. 1890: 3.

FLOYD, HENRY, known as **Black Harry**; b. on the west coast of Africa; d. 5 Nov. 1830 in Brockville, Upper Canada.

Blacks were among Upper Canada's earliest settlers. The total numbers were small and the greatest concentrations were at Detroit and in the Niagara

Fraser

peninsula. Most blacks were ex-slaves who had received their freedom in return for military service during the American revolution; a small number were slaves, brought to the new land by loyalist masters. Occasionally a criminal trial such as that of Jack York* or a petition such as that of Richard Pierpoint* gives a glimpse of black lives in early Upper Canada. Most blacks in this period, however, never emerge from the historical shadows; quite simply, the conditions of their lives offered few opportunities for exposure. By 1830 circumstances had changed: increased migration from the American slave states combined with the growth of the anti-slavery movement to bring the black population into public view. The post-1830 period thus witnessed the rise of black leaders such as Paola Brown* in Hamilton.

There were few blacks in the loyalist settlements along the St Lawrence River. In 1808, for instance, the census of Elizabethtown (Brockville) revealed only 4 slaves in a total population of 1,643. Many years later, in 1868, Sheriff Adiel Sherwood* could remember only two or three slaves who had settled in the Johnstown District. There were also ex-slaves in towns such as Brockville, whose most noted black resident was Henry Floyd. Black Harry, as he was usually called, is known only from a lengthy obituary in William Buell*'s *Brockville Recorder*.

When he was quite young and still under the care of his parents, Floyd was captured by slavers and sold in the West Indies. He was later purchased by a Mr Floyd of New London, Conn., "from whom he absconded and came to Canada after its first settlement." The obituary refers to Floyd's presence at the burning of New London by Benedict Arnold* in September 1781. Floyd may have belonged to a loyalist corps, but there is no record of it. Nor did he apply for a grant of land in Upper Canada for which he would have been eligible as a loyalist. It is possible he had some connection with the Arnold family, since one of Benedict's sons had settled in Elizabethtown by 1808. How Floyd provided for himself is not known. He reached a great age; towards the end of his life he claimed to be almost 100. He was "for a long time supported by the benevolence of the gentlemen of Brockville."

For several reasons Black Harry was a distinctive individual in Brockville. He was "very highly tattooed both on his breast and on his face." Claiming to be the son of a native prince, he insisted that the tattooes were "evidence of his royal descent." More important, he was a pagan who refused to embrace Christianity. "Pious individuals," no doubt concerned about the state of his soul, attempted for a time to "instruct him in the nature of the true God" without success. Later in life, however, he "would listen with more attention and patience on subjects of this sort." Floyd's religion consisted of "some kind of incanta-

tions" and "some kind of orisons the meaning of which he [could] not himself seem to understand." Shortly before Floyd died, the local Presbyterian clergyman, William Smart*, delivered a sermon on the evils of slavery from the house in which the ex-slave lived. Smart was an ardent opponent of slavery and urged on his flock the "duty of commiseration to the unfortunate & afflicted."

Although his life was characterized by upheaval of the most profound sort, Floyd, like Pierpoint, still retained vestiges of, and an attachment to, the society into which he was born. Upper Canada was his haven; it never became his home.

ROBERT LOCHIEL FRASER

AO, RG 21, United Counties of Leeds and Grenville, Elizabethtown Township, census records, 1808. *Brockville Recorder, and the Eastern, Johnstown, and Bathurst Districts Advertiser* (Brockville, [Ont.]), 9 Nov. 1830. T. W. H. Leavitt, *History of Leeds and Grenville, Ontario, from 1749 to 1879* . . . (Brockville, 1879; repr. Belleville, Ont., 1972), 20–21. Ian MacPherson, *Matters of loyalty: the Buells of Brockville, 1830–1850* (Belleville, 1981), 98–99. J. W. St G. Walker, *A history of blacks in Canada* (Hull, Que., 1980).

FRASER (Frazer), JAMES, businessman, JP, judge, and politician; b. *c.* 1760 in Farraline, in the parish of Dores, Scotland, only son of Alexander Fraser and a Miss Cameron; m. 14 Oct. 1802 Rachel Otis DeWolf in Windsor, N.S., and they had eight children; d. there 14 Oct. 1822.

James Fraser was educated in Aberdeen, Scotland, and in 1780 came to Nova Scotia. Beginning "in humble circumstances," he soon built a small business in Halifax. Around 1785 he formed a partnership there with a fellow Scot, James Thom. They had commercial dealings with the local merchant William Forsyth* and his Scottish partners, James Hunter and George Robertson of Greenock, and with Allan, Kerr and Company, also of Greenock. Forsyth was interested in the salmon fishery in New Brunswick, and in 1785 Fraser and Thom went to the Miramichi region to establish a fishing enterprise for him. Along with George Worthington, who was a partner in their firm until 1808, they also set themselves up as merchants there and were soon supplying goods to many of the settlers on the river. Between 1785 and 1788 they imported to Miramichi goods worth £10,000, and between 1787 and 1789 they exported on Forsyth's behalf "more salmon than has ever been known before." They began building on Beaubears Island in 1787 and a year later they obtained title to part of it. By 1789 they had constructed a frame-house, two log-houses, and a store, valued in total at £430. In 1788 Fraser was also involved with Otho ROBICHAUX in the construction of a sawmill, which was apparently never completed.

262

In 1789 Forsyth entered into an agreement with the lumber merchant William Davidson*, who undertook to supply him with masts and spars. After Davidson's death the following year, Fraser and Thom took over his masting contract and were much more successful than Davidson had been. They were shortly employing a number of crews and more than 40 oxen in getting masts out. The firm expanded its activities and in 1792 the partners shipped their first cargoes of squared timber from Miramichi. They soon controlled virtually all the trade on the river and were shipping fish and timber to Halifax, Boston, the West Indies, and Scotland. They continued to build at Beaubears Island; by 1805 they owned the whole of the island and their property there was worth £1,500. Fraser and Thom were among the first to recognize the potential of New Brunswick as a shipbuilding centre. They brought shipwrights to Beaubears Island from the Clyde in Scotland and built ships which were either employed in their own trade or were sold in Halifax, Boston, and Kingston, Jamaica. Their first two vessels were launched some time before 1797, and the shipyard they established was in continuous use until 1873.

The long war with France caused temporary problems for the timber trade in the 1790s. In 1793 Fraser and Thom had 7,000 tons of timber cut, but during the next three years they were able to sell only 2,800 tons. Their masting contract with Forsyth ended in 1801; by then, however, the firm was so well established that the partners no longer depended heavily on this branch of their business operations. Although in 1792 they had been forced to mortgage some of their property at Beaubears Island and other locations to Forsyth for £3,800, they were able to pay this debt off by 1795. Their various business activities appear to have been profitable throughout the early 1790s, despite difficulties in disposing of their timber. In 1797, when the estate of William Davidson was sold, they acquired more than 14,000 acres of land, much of it unimproved but including Davidson's mill tract, mills, and other buildings, all for the sum of £450.

Fraser and Thom also expanded their activities in other regions. Unfortunately, since none of their firm's records have been found, it is not possible to document all their undertakings, but it is known that they had extensive fishing establishments and stores on the Gulf of St Lawrence and Northumberland Strait and at Antigonish and Arichat. After 1805 Fraser began spending more of his time in Halifax and he moved there about 1810, although he continued to visit Miramichi regularly. By that time he and Thom were both wealthy men, with a reputation for fair dealing with their employees and customers. Thom decided to retire from the business and in 1811 their partnership was officially dissolved. A year earlier Fraser had formed a new partnership with Alexander

Fraser, and in 1817 the firm was reorganized as James Fraser and Company with James Fraser, John Fraser, and Alexander Fraser as partners. This new house continued in operation in both New Brunswick and Nova Scotia until James Fraser's death.

Fraser had been a justice of the peace and justice of the Inferior Court of Common Pleas for Northumberland County from 1788. Defeated in his first bid to enter politics in 1791, he was successful four years later when he and Samuel Lee* were returned to the New Brunswick House of Assembly for Northumberland County. Fraser was re-elected in 1802, 1809, and 1816 and remained a member of the house until he was appointed to the Nova Scotia Council in 1818. His career in politics was not distinguished but he represented Northumberland County well and its inhabitants had continued to elect him after he moved to Nova Scotia. Fraser was an enterprising businessman who was successful in both provinces; at the time of his death he was a respected member of the Halifax business community.

W. A. SPRAY

Northumberland Land Registry Office (Newcastle, N.B.), Registry books, 1–24 (mfm. at PANB). N.S. Museum (Halifax), Museum accessions book, 1924, no.5509. PANB, MC 1156, XI: 32–33; RG 2, RS6, B2: 648, 688, 714; RS8, appointments and commissions, 2/1; RG 10, Northumberland County, petition nos.169, 208, 217, 235–36, 319, 481, 569, 777. PANS, MG 3, 150: 62, 82–85, 182. Robert Cooney, *A compendious history of the northern part of the province of New Brunswick and of the district of Gaspé, in Lower Canada* (Halifax, 1832; repub. Chatham, N.B., 1896). *Winslow papers* (Raymond). *Acadian Recorder*, 19 Oct. 1822. *New-Brunswick Royal Gazette*, 22 Oct. 1822. *Annals, North British Society, Halifax, Nova Scotia, with portraits and biographical notes, 1768–1903*, comp. J. S. Macdonald ([3rd ed.], Halifax, 1905), 101–2. Esther Clark Wright, *The Miramichi: a study of the New Brunswick river and of the people who settled along it* (Sackville, N.B., 1944). W. H. Davidson, *An account of the life of William Davidson, otherwise John Godsman, of Banffshire and Aberdeenshire in Scotland and Miramichi in British North America* (Saint John, N.B., 1947). Macmillan, "New men in action," *Canadian business hist.* (Macmillan), 72–100. Louise Manny, *Ships of Miramichi: a history of shipbuilding on the Miramichi River, New Brunswick, Canada, 1773–1919* (Saint John, 1960). Murdoch, *Hist. of N.S.*, 3: 416. C. H. Morris, "Early British settlers on the north shore," *Telegraph-Journal* (Saint John), 25 June 1926: 4.

FRASER, THOMAS, army officer, colonizer, landowner, JP, office holder, politician, and militia officer; b. 1749 in Strath Errick, Scotland, son of William Fraser; m. first Mary MacBean, and they had at least four sons and three daughters; m. secondly 7 Feb. 1795 Mary MacDonell; m. thirdly Cornelia Paterson, a widow, and daughter of John Munro*; d. 18 Oct. 1821 in Matilda Township, Upper Canada.

Fraser

The Fraser family emigrated about 1767 and by 1770 had settled in Tryon County, N.Y., as tenants of Sir William Johnson*. At the outbreak of the American Revolutionary War Thomas Fraser was operating the original Fraser tenant farm, his father and elder brother, William, having moved to a larger one. In May 1777 the brothers were captured by rebels while fleeing to Quebec with a company of men. Imprisoned at Albany, the Frasers and their men escaped custody in August and joined Major-General John Burgoyne*'s forces at Fort Edward. They were commissioned lieutenants and served until the British surrender at Saratoga (Schuylerville) the following month. They were later allowed to escape to Quebec.

In 1779 Thomas and William took command of the loyalist blockhouses on the Rivière Yamaska. They were responsible for scouting patrols sent to the American colonies and occasionally joined in these expeditions. While still serving on the Yamaska, in 1781 the Frasers were attached to the Loyal Rangers commanded by Edward Jessup*. In June 1782 Fraser became a captain in the unit. After the war Barrimore Matthew St Leger* described the brothers as "the most confidential and loyal among the King's Subjects." On the basis of this reputation, they were able to obtain a pension for their father shortly after his arrival in Quebec in 1780.

Fraser retired on half pay in 1783; the following year he settled in Township No.6 (Edwardsburgh) with his company of Loyal Rangers. By 1791 he had built a prosperous farm on the 700 acres he had received as a loyalist captain. When traveller Patrick CAMPBELL first saw the farm he observed, "It could be no Highlander that owned that place." He described it as having a "good house, but a still larger barn of two stories high, several office houses, barracks, or Dutch barns ... considerable flocks of Turkies, Geese, Ducks, and Fowls." Campbell, as it turned out, knew Fraser's wife from the Highlands and, after a conversation in Gaelic, was warmly welcomed. He claimed that the Fraser brothers had been Indian interpreters to Johnson "for some years prior to the rebellion" and commented that these "two gentlemen, whose father was but poor ... and unable to give them the necessary education ... when the rebellion broke out ... raised themselves to the rank of Captains, got money and education by it, and are now in very high esteem among all their acquaintances."

Fraser was interested in settlement and land acquisition and participated with other loyalists such as Richard Duncan*, Peter Drummond, and John Munro in several ventures. In 1789 Fraser and others were granted four acres in Edwardsburgh to build a sawmill. Four years later he appeared before the Executive Council on behalf of an association including Duncan, Drummond, and Munro. Claiming the support of influential men in Vermont, he hoped to draw settlers from that area to the new province of Upper Canada. Although the response to his request for land equivalent to 30 townships was deferred, Fraser and his associates were later granted seven townships. By 1796 Lieutenant Governor John Graves Simcoe* had begun to rescind the township grants. Fraser's group had not accomplished its objectives, although the partners claimed to have attracted several settlers and proposed to draw more from Scotland. In spite of this new proposal, the grant was revoked.

After 1800 Fraser became preoccupied with the accumulation of land. In 1804 the Earl of Selkirk [Douglas*] noted that Fraser "has a great extent (about 20,000 acres) of lands bought up at trifling prices many at 12$ per 100 acres from Soldiers etc after the disbanding of the troops – he & his brother Wm came from Mohawk R. very poor – have managed these affairs well." Selkirk's estimate seems to be exaggerated although there is no doubt that Fraser's holdings were extensive. By 1805 he himself claimed to own over 11,000 acres and at his death his estate included more than 15,000 acres.

During his life Fraser was a prominent office holder and politician. He served as a justice of the peace from 1786. In March 1792 he was appointed to the land board for Leeds and Grenville, becoming its president the following year. Fraser was the first sheriff of the Johnstown District, erected in 1800, and held the post until April 1803 when he was succeeded by his eldest son, William. In 1808 he became a road commissioner; four years later he was appointed a commissioner under the Sedition Act. Finally, in 1816, he was named to the Board of Militia Pensions for the Eastern District. From 1797 to 1800 he sat in the House of Assembly for Dundas County. A slave owner – he had at the time at least four slaves working on his farm – in 1798 he voted for Christopher Robinson*'s bill to extend the legal limits of slavery within the province. He ran again in 1800 but, according to Selkirk, "lost his popularity, & was not reelected." In 1808 he was elected with Alexander McDonell* (Collachie) for the riding of Glengarry. Fraser was an active member and a faithful supporter of the government.

After the outbreak of the War of 1812 Fraser, a lieutenant-colonel, commanded the 1st Dundas Militia and its flank companies stationed between Cornwall and Prescott. In February 1813 he commanded the militia at the capture of Ogdensburg, N.Y., by George Richard John Macdonell*. At the end of the war he moved his residence from Fraserfield, his farm in Edwardsburgh, to Matilda in Dundas County. Lieutenant Governor Francis Gore* recommended Fraser to a vacancy on the Legislative Council in May 1815; he took his seat that fall.

Fraser was eulogized in the *Kingston Chronicle* after his death as "long an upright, independent and impartial magistrate." His estate, spreading across three districts, was divided among his five living children and his original farm in Edwardsburgh was divided between John Fraser and Richard Duncan Fraser*, his two eldest surviving sons.

Catherine Shepard

AO, MS 107, reg. of baptisms, marriages, and burials: xliii, xlix, 24, 32; MS 520; MS 521; MU 2138, 1952, no.1; RG 1, A-I-l, 18: 17; RG 21, United Counties of Leeds and Grenville, Edwardsburg Township, assessment rolls, 1801–18; census records, 1800–25; RG 22, ser.16, box 1, Thomas Fraser, account as sheriff, 1802; box 2, Fraser, account as sheriff, 1806; ser.155, Cornelia Fraser; Thomas Fraser; ser.179, William Fraser, 1813; John Fraser, 1822. BL, Add. MSS 21741: 68; 21821: 121; 21826: 47; 21827: 98; 21828: 122; 21874: 161 (mfm. at AO). PAC, RG 1, L3, 149: D1/57; 185: F1/54; RG 5, A1: 2162, 3203–4, 6089–90, 27968–70. PRO, CO 42/68: 115–16; 42/320: 167; 42/356: 88; 42/373: 7. P. Campbell, Travels in North America (Langton and Ganong), 133, 135–36, 335. Douglas, Lord Selkirk's diary (White), 192. [E. P. Gwillim] Mrs J. G. Simcoe, Mrs. Simcoe's diary, ed. Mary Quayle Innis (Toronto and New York, 1965), 69. "Journals of Legislative Assembly of U.C.," AO Report, 1909: 71; 1912: 285–86. Public papers of George Clinton, first governor of New York, 1777–1795, 1801–1804 . . . , ed. Hugh Hastings and J. A. Holden (10v., New York and Albany, N.Y., 1899–1914), 6: 269. Strachan, Letter book (Spragge). Kingston Chronicle, 25 Oct. 1821. Armstrong, Handbook of Upper Canadian chronology (1967), 31, 43, 59, 62, 168, 214. Officers of British forces in Canada (Irving), 36, 46, 49, 258. Duncan Fraser, William Fraser, Senior, U.E., and his descendants in Fulton County, New York, and Grenville County, Ontario (Johnstown, N.Y., 1964). E. R. Stuart, "Jessup's Rangers as a factor in loyalist settlement," Three hist. theses, 45, 48, 111. E. A. Cruikshank, "An experiment in colonization in Upper Canada," OH, 25 (1929): 37, 40, 42. Duncan Fraser, "Sir John Johnson's rent roll of the Kingsborough patent," OH, 52 (1960): 186.

FRENCH, CHARLES, printer's assistant and convicted murderer; b. c. 1807 in Ireland, son of John French and his wife Jane; hanged 23 Oct. 1828 in York (Toronto), Upper Canada.

The son of a former corporal in an Irish fencible regiment, Charles French spent about four years learning the printing trade in York, first with Robert Charles Horne* and then with Charles Fothergill*. After working as a journeyman in William Lyon Mackenzie*'s office, he went to the United States before returning to York and serving as a surgeon's helper and later with Mackenzie again. In 1828 he was dismissed because of what Mackenzie regarded as his dissolute habits; afterwards he worked on the House of Assembly journals. A young man of respectable, if humble, parents, his only brush with notoriety occurred when he witnessed, while in Mackenzie's employ, the so-called type riot of 1826 in which Mackenzie's press was destroyed by a gang of young tories led by Samuel Peters Jarvis*.

Two years later French won a broader measure of notice when towards midnight on 4 June two small bands of youths collided violently in the streets of York; Edward Nowlan died at the hands of French, who gave himself up to the authorities. The incident provided a platform for journalist Francis Collins to bewail the increase of "vice and immorality" and point to possible remedies: more police, better street lighting, and a reformed House of Assembly. Mackenzie, with puritan gusto, expressed similar concerns. In 1828 muddy York had, by Mackenzie's reckoning, some 60 taverns or the like for a population of about 2,000. Along with theatres, these spots were the popular rendezvous points for many young people, including French. Here he enjoyed with his companions the town's limited pleasures, indifferent to, or unmindful of, his parents' displeasure. To them, these establishments were the haunts of "the gay and the dissolute – the idle and the profligate – the ruffian and woman of lost fame." Mackenzie damned them as "hotbeds of vice and infamy."

French was charged with murder, his companions James Pratt Goslin and William D. Forest with abetting. On 17 Oct. 1828 French was tried before judge Levius Peters Sherwood*. On the request of his counsel, Simon Ebenezer Washburn*, French's accomplices were to be tried separately the following week. After French's plea of innocence, Attorney General John Beverley Robinson* opened the case with a "simple history of the facts." On the fateful night, French was at the theatre, one of his favourite pastimes (on occasion he had even appeared in minor roles). Later, having borrowed a pistol, he shot Nowlan in the streets. The central question in the trial concerned French's motivation. Was the murder done in self-defence or with malice aforethought? Robinson tried to establish that French wanted revenge on Nowlan for a past indignity and that Nowlan's actions on the evening in question had not provoked French's violent action. In his cross-examination Washburn hinted at his line of defence: French was drunk and did not know what he was doing; Nowlan was a hot-tempered, swaggering ruffian.

Defence witnesses amplified Washburn's argument. Concerning Nowlan's reputation, which Robinson did not challenge, there was no doubt: Nowlan was a hard-drinking, "stout powerful man," "a noted bully" whose character was bad. On the other hand, French was a small, "very inoffensive young man," antagonized by a quarrelsome lout who had threatened him. Pre-trial publicity had underscored French's mental problems. Washburn's witnesses depicted him as simple-minded, given to fits of insanity, and at times suicidal. Robinson countered by drawing from Mackenzie the more qualified statement that French was not "entirely insane"; rather he was "not of as sound mind as others." Weak of intellect he may have

French

been, Robinson observed, but he knew right from wrong: his testimony, for instance, in the type riot trial had been accepted in court. Finally, French himself addressed the jury – rather inadvisedly, Collins thought, for the effect was to raise doubt about his supposed insanity.

The jury deliberated about an hour before finding French guilty. Sherwood then addressed the prisoner, noting that vice had led to his downfall and imploring him to seek mercy in the hereafter. "The blood of your victim," Sherwood emphasized, "demands retribution." French was sentenced to be hanged and then dissected on the 20th, but the judge respited execution until the 23rd in the event that the trials of Goslin and Forest had any bearing on French's case.

The trial had caused much excitement and generated a good deal of sympathy for French. Indeed, within hours of his conviction, some 1,100 men signed a petition urging royal clemency. After the acquittals of Goslin and Forest, Lieutenant Governor Sir Peregrine Maitland*, always punctilious about capital cases, required Sherwood to report on the possibility of clemency for French. The judge indicated that, although the accomplices' trials did not affect French, affidavits which had been sworn by them after their acquittals might. In particular, the new information challenged the crucial crown argument that Nowlan had not made a threatening gesture to French before he was shot. Sherwood concluded that "the Jury might have found French guilty of Manslaughter only." An emergency meeting of the Executive Council was convened at 5 A.M. on the 23rd: present were Maitland, James BABY, Peter Robinson*, and James Buchanan Macaulay*. Sherwood was questioned about the importance of the new evidence. He responded equivocally and attempted to shift the burden of the decision to the council. Prodded further about whether the affidavits warranted another respite and a recommendation for mercy, Sherwood replied affirmatively, reiterating, however, that it was not his decision. The council adjourned, directing him to compare Goslin's original deposition to the coroner with his later affidavit and to confer with judge Christopher Alexander Hagerman*. Sherwood found contradictions between the two documents and, for reasons known only to himself, considered the deposition to have "more credit." He thus sealed French's fate. Lacking legal cause for mercy, the council "felt it their painful but incumbent duty to advise His Excellency that the Law should be allowed to take its course." Maitland concurred.

At 2:30 P.M. on the same day, attended by clergymen Thomas Phillips and William Ryerson*, French was led to the gallows and executed. In the days previous he had spent much time with these men and the Reverend John Saltkill Carroll* preparing for his end with an equanimity that Carroll felt bordered on eagerness. He had prepared a gallows address which

was read by Ryerson and later published by Mackenzie. In it he upheld the justness of his conviction and sentence, blaming "bad company and drinking" for his unhappy fate. Urging the young to avoid vice and ruin, he enjoined them to accept the "wholesome restraints" of parental discipline "for their present as well as eternal good." After his death, a few perfunctory incisions were made upon his body in accordance with the sentence. He was then sewn up and given a "decent private funeral" in the Presbyterian burial-ground.

On the cultural level, the effect of French's case was the suspension of popular theatre in York for about five years. The political controversy attached to the case, then and since, stems from French's failure to gain a pardon. Carroll recalled that Nowlan was "a reputed bully for the 'Compact'" and that "there were too many and powerful influences in the Council against the prisoner's life." John Ross Robertson* believed that Robinson and John Strachan* had "refused" mercy. Mackenzie's biographer, Charles Lindsey*, was more explicit. French had been a "marked man" for testifying at the type trial. Nowlan, "as savage as a gorilla and twice as vicious," was the man "who undertook to execute vengeance."

Thus emerged the story that the "family compact" was unwilling to save one of Mackenzie's employees, a witness to the type riot and a victim of a tory bully-boy. As such, it is of a piece with the charges of partiality hurled by opposition critics against Maitland and Robinson. The main objects of the denunciation have long been familiar: the persecution of Robert RANDAL, the dismissal of judge John Walpole Willis*, and the so-called outrages against John MATTHEWS and William Forsyth*. French's execution ranks with such lesser-known incidents as the tarring and feathering of George Rolph and the trial of Michael Vincent [see John Willson*]. These incidents contributed to the erosion of public trust in the judicial system but, in French's case, surviving documents dissipate the air of villainy present in the popular account. There was no evident animus in Robinson's prosecution or in the council's deliberations. Everything seems to have been proper and above-board. Whether or not manslaughter would have been the more appropriate charge was a question requiring an assumption of judicial responsibility of which Sherwood was incapable [see George Powlis*].

ROBERT LOCHIEL FRASER

AO, MU 1864, no.2622; RG 22, ser.134, 5, Home District, 17 Oct. 1828. PAC, RG 1, E1, 28: 119–56; E3, 103a; L3, 189: F12/26; 192: F17/36; RG 5, B27, 1, Home District, 1 July 1828. Town of York, 1815–34 (Firth), 96–97. Canadian Freeman, 23–30 Oct. 1828. Colonial Advocate, 12 June, 23 Oct. 1828. J. S. Carroll, Salvation! O the joyful sound: the *selected writings of John Carroll*, ed. J. W. Grant (Toronto, 1967). Charles Lindsey, *The life and times of Wm. Lyon Mackenzie . . .* (2v., Toronto, 1862; repr. 1971), 1: 117–20. P. B. A. O'Neill, "A history of theatrical activity in Toronto, Canada: from its beginnings to 1858" (PHD thesis, 2v., Louisiana State Univ., Baton Rouge, 1973), 1: 38–39. *Robertson's landmarks of Toronto*, 3: 258. Scadding, *Toronto of old* (1873), 59.

FROBISHER, BENJAMIN JOSEPH, fur trader, politician, JP, and militia officer; b. 26 March 1782 in Montreal, second child of Joseph Frobisher* and Charlotte Jobert; d. 18 March 1821 at Quebec.

As was the custom among wealthy English-speaking families in the province of Quebec, Benjamin Joseph Frobisher was sent to England in 1791 to continue his studies. He was placed in the care of his uncle, Nathaniel Frobisher, who was instructed by the boy's father to "put Ben to some good school & to spare no expence for his education." In 1799, when he was 17, Benjamin Joseph went into the service of the North West Company and was sent to the west to do his apprenticeship in the fur trade. Within a few years he was promoted to the post of clerk in the English River department, which bordered on the Athabasca department.

In 1804 Frobisher was living at Quebec, where he called himself a merchant but appears to have been working as a clerk for a merchant who was probably connected with the NWC. There, in an Anglican ceremony on 6 February he married Isabella Grant, a young woman of about 18 who was the niece of Sir William GRANT, master of the rolls in England, and stepdaughter of the deputy commissary general, John Craigie*. That year Frobisher was elected to the House of Assembly for Montreal, the riding he represented until April 1808. He ran again in 1810, in Dorchester riding, but withdrew before the polling was over, having received fewer votes than his three opponents in a contest that John Caldwell* won. In 1805 Frobisher was a director of the Quebec Assembly, a social club, and from 1806 to 1812 he was a member of the Fire Society in Quebec. He received a commission as justice of the peace for the district of Trois-Rivières in July 1805, which was renewed in December 1811 and July 1815, and was given one for the district of Quebec in November 1815. He also served in the district of Trois-Rivières militia, first as captain (1810) for the parish of Sainte-Geneviève-de-Batiscan, then as major (1812) and lieutenant-colonel (1815) of the Sainte-Anne battalion. In addition he was given the office of paymaster of the battalion in April 1815. That year he became provincial aide-de-camp to Administrator Sir Gordon Drummond*, and from 1816 he carried out the same duties with the new governor, Sir John Coape SHERBROOKE.

Frobisher continued meanwhile to work for the NWC. His relations with the company were more like those of his uncle Thomas, the voyageur, than those of

his uncle Benjamin* or even his father. From his father's death in 1810 until 1814 the company paid Benjamin Joseph £500 a year for the share he had inherited, but he remained until the end of his life a minor employee, often travelling and working in the trading regions. In 1806, for example, he was Charles Chaboillez*'s clerk at Fort Dauphin (Man.); in 1812 he was at Fort Gibraltar (Winnipeg), on his way to Lake Athabasca.

Frobisher was engaged in the trade at the period when the fur economy was declining. Pressure from American competitors was steadily mounting and the struggle against the Hudson's Bay Company was becoming violent. Not only did a change in the HBC's trading strategies worry the NWC partners, but the establishment in 1812 of the Red River colony by Lord Selkirk [Douglas*], a major shareholder in the HBC, brought the two rival companies into a conflict that quickly took on the dimensions of a private war. Miles MACDONELL, who had been appointed governor of Assiniboia by the HBC, did not confine himself to helping the settlers get established when they began to arrive at the beginning of the autumn of 1812; he set in motion a strategy that undermined the system by which the NWC partners maintained their supply of provisions. In 1816 Colin Robertson*, an officer of the HBC, attacked and demolished Fort Gibraltar, and his men seized Fort Daer (Pembina, N.Dak.). The situation continued to worsen and led to the massacre at Seven Oaks on 19 June 1816 [*see* Cuthbert Grant*].

Frobisher became directly involved in the ongoing hostilities. In 1817 he was sent with a group of NWC employees to attack the HBC fort at Île-à-la-Crosse (Sask.); he challenged his adversaries to come out and fight, but to no avail. Two years later the new HBC governor, William Williams*, anxious to cut his rivals' communications, decided to seize Grand Rapids (Man.). It was the obvious target, since, according to Samuel Hull WILCOCKE, a writer in the service of the NWC, "the only practicable route to and from Athabasca and the northern departments of the fur trade . . . is through the northwestern outlet of Lake Winipeg, leading through Cedar or Bourbon Lake, to the River Saskatchewan. Between that lake and Lake Winipeg is the Grand Rapid." There, on 18 June 1819, the canoe transporting John Duncan Campbell and Frobisher was stopped. Frobisher was beaten because he protested against Williams's conduct and he suffered a severe head injury. Then he was taken with the other prisoners to York Factory, which he reached on 1 July. His detention under particularly harsh conditions lasted until 30 September, when he escaped with two other prisoners. In the account that Wilcocke gave of these events he claimed that Frobisher was forced through exhaustion to stop on the shores of Cedar Lake, where his body was found on 27 November. In reality Frobisher returned to Quebec, but his health had probably been undermined, because he died less than two years later at the house he lived in on Rue Mont-Carmel. He was buried on 21 March 1821, and on 24 April his wife renounced his estate in the name of their only child, James Joseph.

FERNAND OUELLET

ANQ-M, CE1-63, 31 mars 1782. ANQ-Q, CE1-61, 6 févr. 1804; CN1-230, 9 avril 1821; CN1-262, 6 févr. 1804. *Les bourgeois de la Compagnie du Nord-Ouest* (Masson), 1: 115–54; 2: 179–226. *Docs. relating to NWC* (Wallace), 300, 446. *Quebec Gazette*, 9 Feb. 1804; 10 Jan., 28 Nov. 1805; 12 June 1806; 2 July 1807; 21 Jan. 1808; 5, 12 April 1810; 26 Dec. 1811; 2 July 1812; 20 April, 26 June 1815; 18 July, 8 Aug. 1816; 9 Aug. 1819; 7 Jan. 1821. F.-J. Audet, *Les députés de Montréal*, 357–59; "Les législateurs du Bas-Canada." Desjardins, *Guide parl.*, 133. *Quebec almanac*, 1805: 15; 1810: 34, 53; 1815: 60, 104; 1820: 106. Wallace, *Macmillan dict.* Wilkins Campbell, *NWC* (1973), 32, 70, 198–253. W. S. Wallace, "Northwesters' quarrel," *Beaver*, outfit 278 (December 1947): 9.

FULTON, JAMES, JP, judge, militia officer, surveyor, and politician; b. 1739 in Belfast, son of John Fulton and Ann Boggs; m. 1 Nov. 1770 Margaret Campbell in Nova Scotia, and they had seven sons and eight daughters; d. 25 Sept. 1826 in Bass River, N.S.

Tradition records that James Fulton immigrated to New England around 1760, one of the thousands of Ulstermen to settle in the Thirteen Colonies since the early 18th century. After working as a surveyor for several years he moved to Nova Scotia, joining the migration of New Englanders drawn north by Governor Charles Lawrence*'s settlement proclamations of 1758 and 1759. Fulton is said to have arrived in Nova Scotia in 1765 and was certainly resident in Londonderry Township by August 1767, when he was appointed a justice of the peace for the district of Colchester. One of the original grantees of the township (then part of Halifax County), he established his home at Bass River. Fulton remained a prominent figure in the local community throughout his life. In addition to his commission as a justice of the peace, he was appointed a judge of the Inferior Court of Common Pleas for the district of Colchester in 1791, and in 1793 was commissioned a captain in the local militia regiment. He also made the first complete survey of Londonderry Township and its small villages.

Fulton's influential position in the Londonderry area was demonstrated in 1799 by his election to the House of Assembly. He joined with Edward Mortimer* of Pictou and William Cottnam TONGE of Halifax to contest the Halifax County seats previously held by powerful Halifax merchants allied with Lieutenant Governor Sir John Wentworth* and the Council. The chief election issue was the conflict between the interests of the town and those of the country: more precisely, Fulton declared, between the policies of Wentworth's friends, the "court party," and measures that would benefit the province as a whole. The "country" candidates ran a well-organized campaign, taking full advantage of their opponents' mistakes, while local committees, formed before the election had been called, rallied support throughout the constituency. Fulton in fact had been in Halifax when the assembly was dissolved and may have discussed strategy with Tonge at that time. Certainly he worked closely with Mortimer to consolidate support for the "country" ticket.

Their campaign strategy was a success: the "country party" took three of the four county seats. Fulton topped the poll in Onslow Township, where the four "court party" candidates could muster only 90 of the 1,600 votes cast. He placed second to Mortimer in Pictou and finished third of the four candidates elected. His record in the assembly illustrates, however, that cohesive political parties with effective discipline were still far in the future. Despite his close association with Tonge's opposition party, Fulton frequently voted with those usually considered the lieutenant governor's friends, even on questions that were a direct challenge to Wentworth's policies. He attended sessions regularly and served on numerous committees, especially those dealing with the construction of roads and bridges.

Fulton does not appear to have run in the 1806 election. He spent the remainder of his life in Bass River, a prosperous farmer and respected local official.

JUDITH TULLOCH

PANS, RG 1, 167, 169. UCC-M, James MacGregor papers, letters LXXIX–LXXXV. N.S., House of Assembly, *Journal and proc.*, 1800–6. *Colonial Patriot* (Pictou, N.S.), 6 Nov. 1830. *The Fulton family of Atlantic Canada; sponsored by the Fulton Family Associates* (Truro, N.S., 1979). Thomas Miller, *Historical and genealogical record of the first settlers of Colchester County . . .* (Halifax, 1873; repr. Belleville, Ont., 1972).

G

GALE, SAMUEL, surveyor, land claims agent, office holder, and notary; b. 14 Oct. 1747 in Kimpton, Hampshire, England; d. 27 June 1826 in Farnham, Lower Canada.

Samuel Gale came to America about 1770, apparently as a paymaster in the British army. Well-educated and trained as a surveyor, in 1772 he was appointed to the lucrative office of deputy surveyor general of New York. The same year he issued a prospectus of a work in preparation entitled "The complete surveyor," but it does not appear to have been published. On 25 June 1773 he married Rebecca, eldest daughter of Samuel Wells of Brattleboro (Vt). Gale began to survey disputed land grants in New Hampshire for New York speculators; they no doubt included William Smith*, prominent attorney and politician, for whom Wells was land agent. In March 1774 Gale was appointed clerk of the Inferior Court of Common Pleas for Cumberland County (Windham County, Vt), on which his father-in-law sat as a judge.

Gale was well positioned to profit from land speculation on the New York–New Hampshire border, but progress towards making his fortune ended abruptly in 1775. It was claimed that on 13 March he had played an inflammatory role in a pre-revolutionary scuffle in Westminster (Vt) during which two men taking part in an occupation of the Cumberland County court-house were killed. Gale was confined for three weeks by local whigs. After moving with his family to Long Island, N.Y., he was apprehended by the rebel military the following spring and jailed without charge in Connecticut for more than two months. Released by order of the New York Provincial Congress, he became cashier for the deputy paymaster general of the British army. In 1780 he switched to the position of itinerant paymaster in Virginia, the Carolinas, and Florida, and gave full satisfaction in the post.

After the war Gale pressed claim in London to a pension for loss of his professional income, but his case was weakened by his not having served in a military capacity; as well, his property, although confiscated, had not been sold, and he was thus prevented from proving its irrevocable loss. Gale attempted to strengthen his claim to an annuity by publishing *An essay on the nature and principles of public credit* (1784), a complicated treatise on means of gradually extinguishing Britain's public debt; it was followed by two additional volumes in 1785 and another in 1787. In 1785 he received a small temporary annuity of £40, apparently raised about 1788 to £100.

In 1791 Gale accepted an invitation to Quebec by William Smith, who had become chief justice of Lower Canada, and upon his arrival he became principal assistant to Surveyor General Samuel Johannes Holland*. His organization of the province's chaotic land records made possible the publication in 1795 of a map – the outline of which had been drawn under his supervision by Jean-Baptiste Duberger – displaying the grants issued during and after the French régime and the boundaries of surveyed townships. However, that year Lord Dorchester [Guy Carleton*] failed to support a recommendation by the Executive Council for a small raise in Gale's meagre stipend of 5s. a day, and Gale resigned in bitterness. Smith's successor, William Osgoode, asserted that Gale had been "the most able Surveyor and perhaps the most diligent Officer that ever was employed in Service of Government."

Gale threw himself into the task of defending the claims of those who had received warrants of survey after the townships were officially opened for settlement in 1792. Under Smith's chairmanship of the Executive Council's land committee, some 173 warrants were issued, largely to Americans, for the survey of townships. Smith argued that rapid settlement by Americans was the surest means of repairing the "rent" in the empire, and he persuaded the committee to accept a local version of the American system of leaders and associates for the granting of lands. As the system operated in Lower Canada, a group of petitioners would be granted up to an entire township, each associate compensating the group leader for the expenses of, among other things, surveying lots and building roads and mills, generally by turning over 1,000 acres of a maximum grant of 1,200 acres. The leaders were thus expected to become progenitors of a landed aristocracy. Many councillors objected to Smith's activities in land-granting as favouring his friends, such as Gale and the Wellses, and promoting union with the United States. Gale attempted to speed up the granting process by drafting "Chamber Surveys" rather than waiting for boundaries to be verified in the field, but bureaucratic delays and Smith's death in 1793 gradually brought it to a halt for the original petitioners.

In 1794 the land committee, under Hugh Finlay*, opened the township lands, even those already under warrant for survey, to new applications for grants. It argued that the original recipients of warrants were mere speculators and that, their warrants having expired, government was free to grant the townships to new petitioners; the latter were mainly Quebec officials and their merchant allies. Gale hinted at "some secret motive" on the part of councillors, and in fact Finlay was later revealed to have conspired to take over townships which American claimants had begun to develop. Gale's warning that civil unrest in border townships might follow the reopening of lands to new petitioners was answered by Finlay to the effect that American settlers, "with their pernicious principles," should not be allowed to settle in the province. The council itself introduced obstacles that frustrated even the most loyal and diligent of the original claimants. However, in the spring of 1796 Gale became private secretary to Dorchester's successor, Robert Prescott*, and he soon won the new head of the colony to his

Gambier

clients' side; two years later, on Prescott's recommendation, Home Secretary the Duke of Portland dispatched new regulations authorizing grants to the original claimants based on their investment and progress in promoting settlement. Officials at Quebec protested, and a public conflict developed between the Executive Council and Prescott. The governor's bitterest critic was Osgoode, whose estimation of Gale took a decided turn for the worse; the "Man of the Woods" was identified as "a Land Jobber" and "a disappointed Land Speculator" busily engaged in stirring up "the Liberty Boys of Vermont."

When Prescott was recalled in 1799 Gale accompanied him to England, where he remained for almost three years, lobbying on behalf of the original claimants to ten townships, among whom were Gilbert HYATT and John SAVAGE. On 5 Feb. 1800 he presented a lengthy petition documenting their progress in colonization. Finding it ignored, in the fall he had a shortened form printed for each privy councillor; it pointed out that of the hundreds of loyalists who had received orders in council for land prior to 1791, only ten or twelve had obtained title, and reiterated suspicions of the personal motives of the executive councillors in rejecting those petitioners of 1792 who had made substantial investments in good faith. In the spring of 1802 Gale's petition was finally rejected, although the Privy Council did agree that titles should be issued to settlers with location certificates dated prior to 1791. If Gale's mission had largely failed, his presence in London may well have stimulated the Executive Council to adopt a more generous policy towards his clients. Gale had probably had to cover most of his living expenses, but he had been promised a commission of five per cent on whatever his clients were granted, which presumably he collected.

Through Prescott, Gale, seven brothers-in-law, and two nephews had received in 1798 a total of 9,600 acres in Farnham Township. Although that township had been set aside for individual loyalist claimants, the Gale–Wells family grant had followed the pattern of the system of leaders and associates, the main difference being that the associates did not sign over the bulk of their allotments to Gale. Several in-laws, including Micah Townsend, Vermont's first secretary of state, eventually joined Gale at Farnham. There, on his estate in comfortable obscurity, Gale played the country squire, accumulating a fine library, and, it appears, acquiring the sobriquet of "Judge" although he was only a notary, commissioned in March 1800; he conducted a small practice from 1802 to 1819. Aside from championing settlers in the townships, who, being mostly Americans, resisted at the beginning of the War of 1812 enforcement of militia laws that would oblige them to fight relatives and former friends, Gale does not appear to have been active in public life. His son, Samuel*, became a judge and a wealthy landowner. Gale's death in 1826 followed by just six months that of his wife.

J. I. LITTLE

Samuel Gale is the author of *An essay on the nature and principles of public credit* (4v., London, 1784–87). In connection with his mission to London from 1799 to 1802 Gale published *The memorial and petition of the undersigned attorney for . . . applicants for grant of various tracts . . . of waste lands . . . in Lower Canada* (London, [1800]) and *Reply to the report of the Executive Council of the province of Lower Canada, upon the memorial of the undersigned attorney, to the lords of his majesty's most honourable Privy Council, of the 28th of November 1800 . . .* (London, 1802). William Berczy* did a portrait of the Gale family which included Samuel, and probably did one of Gale alone because Gale is said to have brought a copy to London in 1799. It is not known whether these portraits are extant. Gale's minute-book is held at ANQ-E, CN2-21.

Brome County Hist. Soc. Arch. (Knowlton, Que.), Samuel Gale papers; Samuel Willard papers (mfm. at PAC). McCord Museum, Samuel Gale papers, IV, 68. New York Public Library, MSS and Arch. Division, American loyalist transcripts, XI: 154–55; XLV: 293–94, 487–93. PAC, MG 11, [CO 42] Q, 57: 497–540; 74: 370–81; 80–82; 85: 311–12; 88: 51–53, 311; 89: 103; 90: 47–49, 98–212; MG 24, L3: 16175–76, 16182–83; RG 1, L3^L: 34672, 34745–48, 44176, 44184, 44189; RG 31, C1, 1825, Farnham, Richelieu: 740. PRO, CO 42/22: 203, 281–302, 350, 355–56, 418–20 (copies at PAC). "Reports respecting Vermont from the British Audit Office," Vt. Hist. Soc., *Proc.* (Montpelier), new ser., 1 (1930): 5–13. *State papers of Vermont*, ed. M. G. Nye (17v. to date, Montpelier, 1918–), 6: 25–27, 249–52. "Papiers d'État – Bas-Canada," PAC *Rapport*, 1891: 107–8, 115, 179; 1892: 164, 170, 173–75, 182, 186, 194–95. L.-R. Betcherman, "Genesis of an early Canadian painter: William von Moll Berczy," *Historical essays on Upper Canada*, ed. J. K. Johnson (Toronto, 1975), 286–301. Caron, *La colonisation de la prov. de Québec*, vol.2. C. M. Day, *Pioneers of the Eastern Townships . . .* (Montreal, 1863). B. H. Hall, *History of eastern Vermont from its earliest settlement to the close of the eighteenth century . . .* (New York, 1858). G. F. McGuigan, "Land policy and land disposal under tenure of free and common socage, Quebec and Lower Canada, 1763–1809 . . ." (3v., PHD thesis, Univ. Laval, Quebec, 1962). Neatby, *Quebec*, 209, 218. Ouellet, *Bas-Canada*, 37–38. E. M. Taylor, *History of Brome County, Quebec, from the date of grants of land therein to the present time; with some records of early families* (2v., Montreal, 1908–37), 2: 162–63. L. F. S. Upton, *The loyal whig: William Smith of New York & Quebec* (Toronto, 1969), 216. J. P. Noyes, "The Canadian loyalists and early settlers in the district of Bedford," Missisquoi County Hist. Soc., *Report* (Saint-Jean-sur-Richelieu, Que.), 3 (1908): 99–101.

GAMBIER, JAMES, 1st Baron GAMBIER, naval officer and governor of Newfoundland; b. 13 Oct. 1756 on the island of New Providence in the Bahamas, son of John Gambier, lieutenant governor of the Bahamas, and Deborah Stiles; m. July 1788 Louisa

Matthew (Mathew) in London; they had no children; d. 19 April 1833 at Ivor House in Buckinghamshire, England.

James Gambier's connection with the Royal Navy began at the age of 11, when his name was entered on the books of the *Yarmouth* guard-ship, commanded by his uncle James Gambier. On 12 Feb. 1777, when serving on the North American station, he was promoted lieutenant; the next year, while in command of the *Thunder* bomb, he was captured by the Comte d'Estaing's squadron. Soon exchanged, in October 1778 he was made post captain. Gambier was a friend of the Pitt family, and his advancement in the navy was apparently due to this relationship rather than to the extent of his experience at sea. From 7 March 1795 to 19 Feb. 1801 he sat as a lord of the Admiralty; meanwhile, he was promoted rear-admiral on 1 June 1795 and vice-admiral on 14 Feb. 1799.

In the spring of 1802, shortly after the Treaty of Amiens was signed, Gambier was appointed governor of Newfoundland to replace Sir Charles Morice Pole. The lull in the war gave him some time to concern himself with civil affairs on the island. In the navy he was noted for his piety and his strict views on morality. In Newfoundland he earned a reputation for assistance to schools and charitable institutions and for encouragement of the clergy. When William CULL brought a captive Beothuk woman to St John's, Gambier ordered that she be kindly treated, and she was later returned to her people.

Official British policy had always been that Newfoundland was not a colony, but rather an adjunct to the fishery. The result had been injustices towards local residents and a lack of revenue for necessary works on the island. In giving leases to some lands for grazing sheep and cattle, Gambier hoped to provide inhabitants with a measure of security of tenure while at the same time bringing in revenue for the government. Recognizing that the fishery itself had essentially changed from migratory to sedentary, he recommended that vacant properties along the shore reserved at no charge for fishermen from Britain should instead be leased to local people. The value of continuity in administration was evident to him and he proposed the appointment of a permanent secretary. In December 1803, towards the end of his term, Gambier summarized his views for Colonial Secretary Lord Hobart. "The present system of policy," he wrote, is "insufficient for effecting the happiness and good order of the community which is the chief end of all government. This I attribute to the want of *a power in the Island for framing laws for its internal regulation*, and for raising sums necessary to promote any measure of public utility." Thirty years were to pass before such a government was established.

In the latter half of his term Gambier had been obliged to turn his attention to defence, since war

resumed in June 1803. At that point the garrison at St John's consisted of 63 artillerymen. Brigadier-General John Skerrett* was authorized to raise a regiment of 1,000 men, but recruiting was difficult because it was banned during the fishing season. Gambier remained apprehensive about local defence throughout the time taken to enlist and train the force.

On 15 May 1804 Gambier was reappointed to the Admiralty, being succeeded in Newfoundland by Sir Erasmus Gower*. He was made admiral of the blue on 9 Nov. 1805 and commanded the fleet which in 1807 took possession of the Danish navy. This success was rewarded with a barony in November and command of the Channel fleet from the following spring until 1811. Gambier was named head of the British commission that negotiated peace with the Americans in 1814. Two other distinctions followed, the GCB on 7 June 1815 and promotion to admiral of the fleet on 22 July 1830. He died at his home, Ivor House, in 1833. Although his time in Newfoundland had been short, his career reflects that moral earnestness and desire for progress which gave rise in Britain to the great reform movements of his day.

FREDERIC F. THOMPSON

PRO, CO 194/43: 75, 171–78, 323. *Gentleman's Magazine*, 1788: 365. *Admiralty officials, 1660–1870*, comp. J. C. Sainty (London, 1975). G. E. Cokayne, *The complete peerage of England, Scotland, Ireland, Great Britain and the United Kingdom, extant, extinct, or dormant* (new ed., ed. Vicary Gibbs et al., 13v. in 14, London, 1910–59). DNB. G.B., ADM, *Navy list*, 1808. John Marshall, *Royal naval biography* . . . (4v. in 6 and 2v. supp., London, 1823–35), 1: 74–86. James Ralfe, *The naval biography of Great Britain* . . . (4v., London, 1828), 1: 82–90. Joseph Hatton and Moses Harvey, *Newfoundland, the oldest British colony; its history, its present condition, and its prospects in the future* (London, 1883). Howley, *Beothucks or Red Indians.* William James, *The naval history of Great Britain, from the declaration of war by France in 1793 to the accession of George IV* . . . (new ed., 6v., London, 1860), 4. G. W. L. Nicholson, *The fighting Newfoundlander; a history of the Royal Newfoundland Regiment* (St John's, [1964?]). Prowse, *Hist. of Nfld.* (1895), 375–77.

GARDEN, GEORGE, businessman, militia officer, politician, and JP; b. *c.* 1772 in Scotland; m. Euphemia Forbes, and they had two sons; d. 15 Oct. 1828 in Montreal.

George Garden reached Quebec from Glasgow in July 1793. In the first decade of the 19th century he occasionally executed wills and administered estates in Montreal; in 1806 property administered by him was seized for debt at the suit of Alexander AULDJO and William Maitland. By June 1812 Garden was a partner of both in Auldjo, Maitland and Company, a wholesaling firm in Montreal which sold imported goods to merchants in Upper Canada and exported

Garden

ashes, timber, and wheat. It became Maitland, Garden, and Auldjo after the departure for England of Alexander Auldjo in 1813 and the addition to its ranks of his nephew George Auldjo*. By 1815 the firm was the business agent for Lord Selkirk [Douglas*], with whom Garden and his wife became close friends; when, that spring, Selkirk feared that the settlement he had recently established on the Red River might be attacked by traders from the powerful North West Company of Montreal, Maitland, Garden, and Auldjo relayed to the administrator of Lower Canada, Sir Gordon Drummond*, his urgent requests for military aid. It appears that by 1822 Garden and George Auldjo were also partners in a firm called Garden, Auldjo and Company, with headquarters on Goudie's Wharf at Quebec.

By 1818 Garden had become, with Auldjo, an agent of the Phoenix Assurance Company of London, a fire insurance firm operating in the Canadas through a Montreal agency established in 1804 by Alexander Auldjo. In 1808 Phoenix had provoked the anger of merchants at Quebec by cancelling most policies in Lower Town on the ground that the area was a fire-trap. Reversal of the decision and improvements in service – including an offer in 1816 of policies of up to £10,000 in one risk, with immediate payment in the colony – apparently had not removed all rancour. That year a number of Quebec businessmen had founded the Quebec Fire Assurance Company and a bitter rivalry ensued. When in 1818 Phoenix decided to contest a claim at Quebec, Garden and Auldjo became embroiled in a lively dispute with the new company, which sought to profit by the decision. In September, faced with the establishment of yet another firm, the Montreal Fire Insurance Company [see Horatio GATES], Phoenix attempted to regain its monopoly in the field by authorizing Garden and Auldjo to undersell all competitors by ten per cent, except in the cases of mills and wooden buildings crowded together, upon which Garden and Auldjo had "constantly been large losers."

In 1817 Garden had become involved in launching another field of financial endeavour in Lower Canada, banking. With others, and on behalf of Maitland, Garden, and Auldjo, he had signed the articles of association of the Bank of Montreal and had petitioned for its incorporation. As a director from 1817 to 1826, and a vice-president from 1818 to 1822, he proved to be an energetic administrator. He was on a committee that chose a site for the bank on Rue Saint-Jacques; indeed, the bank's first building seems to have been modelled on Maitland, Garden, and Auldjo's austere Georgian edifice, constructed on Rue Saint-Paul according to plans by an English architect whom Garden had engaged. As well, Garden was a member of a committee that studied the possibilities of implanting the bank at Quebec [see Daniel SUTHER-

LAND] and in Upper Canada. He was also a director of the Montreal Savings Bank, founded in 1819.

Maitland, Garden, and Auldjo's interests in the Upper Canada trade stimulated Garden to work for improved communications with that colony and expanded markets for Upper Canadian produce. In May 1817 he received an appointment as a commissioner for improving and repairing the road from Montreal to Lachine, and in August 1818 another as a commissioner for improving communications between the Canadas on the St Lawrence and Ottawa rivers. The principal obstacle to water communications with Upper Canada being the Lachine rapids, a group of prominent Montreal businessmen, including Garden, formed the Company of Proprietors of the Lachine Canal, chartered in March 1819 [see François DESRIVIÈRES]. Following its failure in 1821 he was appointed to a commission authorized by the Lower Canadian legislature to complete the project, which ultimately took five years and cost £107,000. When financial backing from the House of Assembly ceased briefly in 1823, Garden and another commissioner, John RICHARDSON, drew on the Bank of Montreal for loans totalling £8,000. In August 1821 both men had been members of a committee of prominent merchants in the city formed to lobby the imperial government to open British and West Indian markets without restriction to wheat and flour from the Canadas, since the colonies' agriculture and commerce were "in such a state of depression and distress as threatens ruin to those engaged therein, if relief be not speedily obtained."

Garden's rising prominence in business was reflected socially. He was a founder of the Montreal Curling Club in 1807. From ensign in the British Militia of the Town and Banlieu of Montreal in 1799, he had risen by 1812 to captain in Montreal's 1st Militia Battalion, a British unit, and he served in that rank in 1812–13 with the Montreal Incorporated Volunteers. A leading member of the Scotch Presbyterian Church (later called St Gabriel Street Church), he served on its temporal committee – as president in 1812 – and was ordained an elder in 1819. He was a governor of the Montreal General Hospital, founded in 1819 [see William CALDWELL]. He represented Montreal West in the House of Assembly from 1820 to 1824, along with Louis-Joseph Papineau*, and often acted as a spokesman for business interests. A justice of the peace for Montreal from 28 June 1821, he was foreman of a grand jury that in May 1823 denounced interference in the administration of justice by the Executive Council. In the name of austerity, the council had been quietly reducing funds allotted to defray the expenses of witnesses in criminal trials and restricting jury duty to inhabitants of the city. In 1824 and 1827 Garden received commissions of oyer and terminer and general jail delivery.

In the early 1820s Maitland, Garden, and Auldjo, having borrowed heavily in Britain, found itself in increasing financial difficulty at a time when the British money market was tightening. About July 1825, in order to meet the demands of British creditors, it obtained from the Bank of Montreal, through the bank's president, Samuel Gerrard*, advances that in total far exceeded the limit of £10,000 per customer established by the bank's rules. As a result, Gerrard was accused of favouritism by a director of the bank, George Moffatt*, and the board divided into camps; Garden supported Gerrard. The resounding crash of Maitland, Garden, and Auldjo in 1825 [see George Auldjo] rocked a Montreal business community already weakened by economic depression and, combined with the subsequent failures of two other major firms, brought the removal of Gerrard as president of the Bank of Montreal.

Garden had gone to Britain in 1825; he had previously sojourned there in 1809–10 and 1821–22. In 1827 he returned to Montreal, probably to try to retrieve his personal condition through the renewal of his firm. He failed, and in October 1828 he died a ruined man at about age 56. The inventory of his estate, which showed assets of only £375 against debts of £698 11s. 11d., was a sad financial epitaph for one of Montreal's early commercial tycoons.

GERALD J. J. TULCHINSKY

ANQ-M, CN1-187, 16 mars 1829. PAC, RG 4, B46: 19–23, 31–32, 1400–4; RG 43, CIII, 1, vol.2453, 31 July 1819; RG 68, General index, 1651–1841: 96, 196, 212, 349. L.C., Statutes, 1820–21, c.6. Quebec Gazette, 23 July 1799; 22 Dec. 1803; 9 Jan. 1806; 4 June 1812; 22 May 1817; 25 June, 17 Sept., 5 Dec. 1818; 1 April 1819; 20 March, 20 April, 18 May, 3, 20 July, 2 Nov. 1820. Quebec almanac, 1800: 104; 1805: 47; 1815: 90. F.-J. Audet, Les députés de Montréal, 228–29. Caron, "Inv. de la corr. de Mgr Plessis," ANQ Rapport, 1927–28: 141. Officers of British forces in Canada (Irving), 164. R. Campbell, Hist. of Scotch Presbyterian Church, 318–19. Denison, Canada's first bank, 1: 72–73, 84–85, 103–4, 117–20, 122, 132, 161–63, 171, 188, 193, 207–8, 215, 219–20, 225, 228, 238. J. M. Gray, Lord Selkirk of Red River (Toronto, 1963), 122, 180, 195, 248–49. G. J. J. Tulchinsky, "The construction of the first Lachine Canal, 1815–1826" (MA thesis, McGill Univ., Montreal, 1960), 37.

GARLAND, GEORGE, merchant and JP; baptized 2 Aug. 1793 in Poole, Dorset, England, seventh son of George Garland, merchant of Poole, and Amy Lester, daughter of Benjamin Lester*; d. unmarried 20 Feb. 1833 in Stanley Green (Poole).

George Garland was eight years old when in 1802 his father inherited half of the immense Newfoundland trading estate of Benjamin Lester. Just three years later the Garland family fortunes surged upward again following the death without a male heir of

Lester's only son, Sir John, who had been his other chief heir. Now the whole Lester estate in Newfoundland and most of that in England devolved to the Garland family. This swift turn of events had a great impact upon the lives and careers of George Garland Jr, his five surviving brothers, and his two sisters.

Although the ascent of the Lester family to wealth and power in the affairs of Poole and Newfoundland can be traced back several generations from Benjamin Lester, the final stages of Lester's becoming the wealthiest and most influential of the Poole–Newfoundland merchants occurred towards the end of the 18th century. By the time of his death Lester owned the largest firm in the England–Newfoundland cod trade. His Newfoundland headquarters were at Trinity, but he also owned properties distributed between Bay de Verde and Fogo Island, and held other fishing and sealing stations on the coast of Labrador. Besides Trinity, permanent trading establishments manned by agents, clerks, shopkeepers, and artisans were maintained at Scilly Cove (Winterton), Bonavista, Barrow Harbour, Greenspond, Tickle Harbour (Bellevue), and Fogo. By 1806 all of these were owned and controlled by George Garland Sr.

The initial link between the Lester and Garland families was the marriage in 1779 of George Garland, the son of a yeoman farmer of East Lulworth, Dorset, to Amy Lester. Shortly after the marriage Garland, who had already embarked upon business with his brother and uncle in Poole and Southampton, became a salaried manager in Lester's Poole counting-house. This event turned his career in a new direction. He was soon managing most of the practical aspects of Lester's Newfoundland trade, on which account he travelled extensively both in England and on the Continent, buying supplies for transatlantic shipment and selling the incoming staples of salt cod, train oil, salmon, and other products. By the time he inherited a share of the trade and became a principal partner Garland was nearly 50, and in the process of raising a large family. Indeed, in 1802 he had four sons over 20 and the youngest child was only four. His age, the ages of his family, and his election to parliament for Poole in 1801 were probably the factors that prevented Garland from ever going to Newfoundland. In conducting his trade he thus came to rely upon his nephews and increasingly, as they grew older, upon his sons.

George Garland had an exceptional head for business and during the lucrative years of the Newfoundland trade at the time of the Napoleonic Wars, particularly between 1809 and 1815, he made substantial profits and added immensely to his estate. In 1817 he took his sons George Jr and John Bingley into partnership and two years later he was able to declare a profit of £15,000 despite a continuing post-war depression. In 1822 Garland relinquished control of

Garland

the firm to his two sons but remained involved until his death three years later. He left an estate greater than that of Benjamin Lester, and the Garlands became one of the largest landed families in Dorset during the 19th century.

Like his father-in-law, Garland laid careful plans for his succession. He paid close attention to the education of his children, and took special pains to place his sons in favourable situations. The eldest, Benjamin Lester, was sent to Trinity in 1797 "to see, hear, remark, learn and endeavour to understand everything and every body concerned in Grand Father's business." In 1805, in accordance with his grandfather's will, Benjamin Lester Garland changed his surname to Lester. He was elected to the House of Commons in 1809 and, much to the chagrin of his father, preferred politics and the social life in London to the career of a Poole merchant. After he had repeatedly refused his father's offers to make him a partner, the latter grudgingly provided him with a stipend out of the profits of the Newfoundland trade. Benjamin Lester Lester held his parliamentary seat until 1835, when he retired to travel. Unmarried, he died in Paris in 1838. Garland's second and third sons were twins, Joseph Gulston and Francis Penton. The former went into the Royal Navy and became a rear-admiral, while the latter managed a Poole iron and timber trade inherited from the Lesters. All the other sons were sent abroad and established in various branches of the cod trade. Lester went to work for a marketing company in Leghorn (Italy), where he died in 1798 at the age of 15, and the youngest, Augustus Lester, was in 1820 supplied £4,000 to become a partner in a Leghorn brokerage firm with Henry Lloyd Routh, son of Richard*. The two sons who contributed most to keep the Garland name associated with the Newfoundland fishery and trade were John Bingley and George Jr.

In 1807, 16-year-old John Bingley was sent by his father to the counting-house of the London firm of Hart and Robinson [see Marmaduke HART] to be "useful to his employers as well as himself to be instructed in a Counting House business." At about the same time 14-year-old George Jr was dispatched to Trinity to become acquainted with the fishery and trade under the direction of the firm's agent, David Durell. Durell was instructed to "treat him as your son, to keep him sober, deligent and attentive to his business . . . if possible bring him to write a good hand . . . overlook no faults." Garland carefully scrutinized reports on his son, which evidently were not always completely favourable. He was particularly disturbed that George was averse to visiting John Clinch*, the Trinity clergyman and doctor, for whom he himself had a high regard. But before he was sent to Trinity George Jr had developed certain character traits which his father felt suited him better for the Newfoundland

trade than some of his other sons. He was rough, somewhat unpolished, and very aggressive; thus when Durell made some uncomplimentary reports about him, Garland noted that "he may not be the worse for the Newfoundland Trade for which I intend him."

Young Garland spent five years in Trinity under Durell's tutelage, years when the firm flourished. Several of Lester's chief competitors in Trinity – John Jeffrey, Thomas Street*, and Samuel White, for example – withdrew from the Newfoundland trade between 1797 and 1809, and although another Poole firm owned by Robert Slade (brother of Thomas*) moved into Trinity in 1804 it was not sufficiently well established to challenge the Garland firm. Thus when the price of fish soared between 1809 and 1811 Garland, who had a virtual monopoly on trade both in Trinity Bay and on the northeast coast, reaped enormous profits. The firm also began to expand into the seal fishery, using schooners built in Newfoundland, and enlarged its supply trade with the growing resident population.

In 1812 Garland established a brokerage house in Lisbon and sent his son George to work there. George remained in Lisbon for seven years and returned to Trinity with John Bingley as partners in the firm of George Garland and Sons. The Garland brothers arrived in the brig *Brothers* on 9 June 1819 and the next day George left to inspect the Greenspond and Bonavista premises. During the rest of his Newfoundland residence, he functioned primarily as an "outside agent," making frequent trips to the out-harbour establishments and to St John's. Although in theory equal to John Bingley, George was clearly subordinate to his elder brother, who ran the counting-house in Trinity. In July 1819 Governor Charles Hamilton* visited Trinity and the Garlands were appointed two of the four justices of the peace for the district.

Until 1821 the brothers returned to Poole each winter. Evidently their father felt that they needed assistance in managing the trade, for in that year he sent out William Furnell from his Poole counting-house. Furnell and George Jr constantly plagued William Kelson (Robert Slade's agent) with their aggressiveness and intrigues, so much so that he wrote in frustration, "I wish both Furnell and G. G. Jr. would remain at home." At the same time Kelson confided that he respected John Bingley and had amicable relationships with him in settling wages, prices, and other trade matters.

Most of George Garland's sons ventured into politics at some stage of their career. John Bingley was elected as the first member for Trinity Bay in the Newfoundland House of Assembly of 1832 and served as the first speaker. Apart from his appointment as magistrate, however, a position which at the time usually went to the merchant's agent, George Jr had no such involvement. He served on a committee for the building of a new church at Trinity in 1820, but here again he was vice-president and his brother president.

Following the death of George Sr in 1825, the name of the firm was changed to include the names of the two heirs. George Jr left Newfoundland for the last time on 20 Sept. 1828. He seems to have been in ill health, for which reason he withdrew from the trade two years later. Still unmarried, he went to live at Stanley Green, a country estate near Poole previously owned by Benjamin Lester but purchased in 1823 for George and his unmarried sister Maria by their father. George died at Stanley Green on 20 Feb. 1833, aged 40. A memorial tablet subsequently placed in the Trinity mortuary chapel states it had been given by "the inhabitants of Trinity ... to be a Grateful Memorial of [George's] unostentatious munificence as a benefactor of this Church," but it was probably inscribed and paid for by his brothers.

When George Jr and John Bingley were taken into the Newfoundland trade in 1817, their father stated that their investment was £80,000, and when he relinquished control of the firm in 1822 he allowed them to share the profits after paying him an annual interest of four per cent, apparently on the amount of the investment. He retained personal title to his Newfoundland properties and ships but in his will left them in half shares to the brothers. At their father's death they shared a further £14,000 and the surplus capital in the Newfoundland trade; moreover, each received a country estate and numerous other assets.

As entrepreneurs, neither George Jr nor John Bingley exhibited the drive, pragmatism, or acumen of their father: possibly they were so independently wealthy that they lacked sufficient motivation. Indeed, they seemed more intent upon sustaining the Newfoundland trade as long as it was somewhat profitable rather than upon attempting to expand it. Throughout the 1820s they pursued a policy of achieving efficiency through concentration and economy, a policy advocated by their father in his declining years. The Garland fleet between 1827 and 1830 consisted of ten ocean-going vessels; when he assumed sole control in 1830 John Bingley quickly reduced the number to four. But although the Garlands were content to maintain the *status quo* and reduce their shipping and establishments, Robert Slade strove to expand, and by 1830 his firm was on an equal footing in Trinity Bay with theirs.

W. GORDON HANDCOCK

ACC, Diocese of Nfld. Arch. (St John's), St Paul's Church (Trinity), reg. of baptisms, marriages, and burials (mfm. at PANL). Dorset Record Office (Dorchester, Eng.), D365; P227/RE3–18. Nfld. Museum (St John's), W. G. Handcock, "The merchant families and entrepreneurs of Trinity in the nineteenth century" (report prepared for the Nfld. Dept. of Culture, Recreation, and Youth, typescript, St John's, 1981). PANL, GN 5/1/B/1, Trinity, minutes, 1805–25; estates, 1789–1816; GN 5/4/B/1, Trinity, 1775–1811, 1826–42; P7/A/6, Slade & Kelson, letters, Trinity, 1809–26. Trinity Hist. Soc. Arch., Slade–Kelson diaries, 1809–46 (photocopies at Maritime Hist. Group Arch., Memorial Univ. of Nfld., St John's). *DCB*, vol.5 (biog. of Benjamin Lester). Derek Beamish *et al.*, *Mansions and merchants of Poole and Dorset* (Poole, Eng., 1976).

GARRETTSON, FREEBORN, Methodist minister; b. 15 Aug. 1752 in Maryland near the mouth of the Susquehanna River, son of John Garrettson and Sarah Merriarter, *née* Hanson; m. 30 June 1793 Catharine Livingston in Rhinebeck, N.Y., and they had one daughter; d. 26 Sept. 1827 in New York City and was buried in Rhinebeck.

Freeborn Garrettson was a member of a wealthy Anglican family, but as a young man he fell under the influence of itinerant Methodist preachers. In 1775 he had a traumatic conversion experience – "my soul was exceeding happy," he later wrote, "that I seemed as if I wanted to take wings and fly to heaven." He freed his slaves, and in due course resolved to become a Methodist preacher. Beginning his ministerial work in 1776 as a preacher-on-trial, he itinerated widely for the next several years in Maryland and neighbouring states. As a pacifist, he wanted to have nothing to do with the American revolution, explaining that "it was contrary to my mind, and grievous to my conscience, to have any hand in shedding human blood," and he carefully pursued a policy of neutrality despite much persecution from the patriots. He was ordained a Methodist minister at a conference held in Baltimore in December 1784, the same conference that witnessed the creation of the Methodist Episcopal Church of the United States.

For more than 50 years Garrettson preached his evangelical Methodist gospel from North Carolina to Nova Scotia, being responsible for thousands of conversions. He was an indefatigable itinerant and a powerful preacher and committed to centralized control at the expense of congregational independence. Even though he spent only 26 months in Nova Scotia, it may be argued that next to Henry Alline*, Garrettson was the most gifted and influential preacher in 18th-century Nova Scotia. His coming to that province occurred immediately after his ordination. The 1784 conference, encouraged by John Wesley, Thomas Coke – Wesley's able lieutenant – and William BLACK, the leader of Nova Scotia Methodists, appointed Garrettson and James Oliver Cromwell as special missionaries to Nova Scotia. The death of Alline had created a religious vacuum in the province, and this fact, together with the arrival of many thousands of loyalists (some of whom were Methodists), seemed to provide an opportunity for the

Garrettson

Methodists to break the Allinite–New Light hegemony over much of the colony.

Garrettson and Cromwell sailed from New York for Halifax in the middle of February 1785. On his arrival Garrettson received offers of assistance from Governor John Parr* and the Reverend John Breynton*, the Anglican rector of St Paul's Church, and over the next few weeks he preached in Halifax in a house rented by Philip Marchinton*. In late March he set out on his first missionary tour. During his sojourn in the colony, Garrettson was to visit almost every settlement apart from Pictou. He was particularly successful in the Yankee-Allinite heartland stretching from Falmouth down the Annapolis valley to Granville and Yarmouth, and then up the southern shore to the Argyle district, Liverpool, and Chester. In this region he took advantage of the work done not only by Alline but also by Alline's supporters such as Thomas Handley Chipman and John PAYZANT. As well, Garrettson was able to build upon the evangelistic labours of Black in the Chignecto-Cumberland region and Halifax, and he also broke new missionary ground in the loyalist centre of Shelburne. One of the men he recruited to the Methodist standard, James Man*, was to have a long and distinguished ministerial career in Nova Scotia and New Brunswick.

Garrettson attracted large and enthusiastic audiences who were drawn by his charismatic personality to his emotional and pietistic message. Though he was sometimes violently attacked by disciples of Alline because of his criticism of aspects of Alline's theology, Garrettson was nevertheless able to trigger in 1785 and 1786 a major revival in the colony, which he referred to as "this visitation of the Spirit." The stress he placed on "Free Grace" and on the possibility of sanctification, as well as the warm fellowship provided by the "Class Meetings," appealed to those many Nova Scotians who wanted the old evangelical Christianity of Alline but not the antinomian excesses of some of Alline's followers.

"I have had a blessed winter among them," Garrettson reported to Wesley on 10 March 1787. "If the work continues much longer as it has done, the greater part of the people will be brought in." Yet, despite his optimism, Garrettson left Nova Scotia in April, never to return. He felt compelled to go back to his native land because, as he explained, "I was not clear that I had a call to leave the United States." When he left Nova Scotia, the Methodists were the fastest-growing religious group in the colony and on the verge of pushing the New Lights to the dark periphery of historical oblivion. Yet within two decades the Methodists had been overtaken by a burgeoning Baptist movement led by a remarkable group of young, dynamic preachers such as Harris Harding*, Joseph Dimock*, Theodore Seth Harding, and James and Edward* Manning, the first three of whom had been converted during the Garrettson revival. The talents of these Baptist preachers as well as other factors – Garrettson's departure from the colony, the absence of strong indigenous Methodist leadership, the poor quality of Methodist missionaries from Great Britain, and the decision of American Methodists to concentrate in the United States – significantly weakened the Methodist movement in Nova Scotia after 1786.

When Garrettson returned from Nova Scotia a plan was afoot, apparently devised by Wesley and supported by Francis Asbury of the United States, to have him appointed general superintendent of Methodist missions in British North America and the West Indies. For some reason, however, nothing came of this scheme. Instead Garrettson continued to labour as an itinerant preacher, and for many years he served as presiding elder of the New York District. He had an estate at Rhinebeck and used his considerable wealth, augmented further by his marriage into the Livingston family, to support the Methodist cause, particularly in New York state. Until his death in 1827, Garrettson remained an ardent critic of the "crying sin" of slavery and an enthusiastic and committed disciple of John Wesley.

GEORGE A. RAWLYK

Freeborn Garrettson's manuscript journal and other papers are in the Garrettson coll. at Drew Univ. Library (Madison, N.J.); photocopies of correspondence relating to British North America and a microfilm copy of the journal are available at the UCC-C. Various published editions of material from the journal have been produced; the following were consulted in the preparation of this biography: *The life of the Rev. Freeborn Garrettson; compiled from his printed and manuscript journals and other authentic documents*, comp. Nathan Bangs (4th ed., New York, 1838) and *American Methodist pioneer: the life and journals of the Rev. Freeborn Garrettson, 1752–1827*, ed. and intro. R. D. Simpson (Rutland, Vt., 1984). An autobiographical address delivered by Garrettson in 1826 before the New York Annual Conference appeared the following year under the title "Methodism in America," *Wesleyan-Methodist Magazine* (London), 50 (1827): 672–76, 740–45, 810–15.

The New Light letters and spiritual songs, 1778–1793, ed. G. A. Rawlyk (Hantsport, N.S., 1983). R. Reece, "Death of the Rev. Freeborn Garrettson," *Wesleyan-Methodist Magazine*, 50: 861. *DAB*. W. C. Barclay, *History of Methodist missions* (3v., New York, 1949–59), 1. S. D. Clark, *Church and sect in Canada* (Toronto, 1948). G. [S.] French, *Parsons & politics: the rôle of the Wesleyan Methodists in Upper Canada and the Maritimes from 1780 to 1855* (Toronto, 1962). J. T. Hughes, *An historical sketch of the life of Freeborn Garrettson, pioneer Methodist preacher* (Rhinebeck, N.Y., 1977). G. A. Rawlyk, "Freeborn Garrettson and Nova Scotia" (paper presented to the World Methodist Hist. Soc., Asbury Theological Seminary, Wilmore, Ky., 1984); *Ravished by the spirit: religious revivals, Baptists, and Henry Alline* (Kingston, Ont., and Montreal, 1984). Matthew Richey, *A memoir of the late Rev. William*

Black, Wesleyan minister, Halifax, N.S., including an account of the rise and progress of Methodism in Nova Scotia ... (Halifax, 1839). T. W. Smith, *History of the Methodist Church within the territories embraced in the late conference of Eastern British America* ... (2v., Halifax, 1877–90). Abel Stevens, *The women of Methodism* ... (New York, 1866). N. A. McNairn, "Mission to Nova Scotia," *Methodist Hist.* (Lake Junalaska, N.C.), 12 (1973–74), no.2: 3–18. W. J. Vesey, "Freeborn Garrettson: apostle to Nova Scotia," *Methodist Hist.*, 1 (1962–63), no.4: 27–30.

GASPÉ, PIERRE-IGNACE AUBERT DE. *See* AUBERT

GATES, HORATIO, businessman, office holder, JP, and politician; b. 30 Oct. 1777 in Barre, Mass., son of Benjamin Gates; m. 2 March 1814 Clarissa Adams in Highgate, Vt, and they had four children; d. 11 April 1834 in Montreal.

Horatio Gates was connected around 1802 with a number of merchants, the principal one being Abel Bellows, from Walpole, Mass. It seems clear that Gates acted as a middleman for marketing agricultural products from the regions of Vermont and New York that were oriented towards the St Lawrence valley, with Montreal as their natural centre. On 15 Dec. 1807 Bellows and Gates rented a store in Montreal on Rue Saint-Paul, the main business artery. Gates went into partnership in 1810 with Bellows, Cordis, and Jones, a Boston firm, under the name of Bellows, Gates and Company. Far from interrupting his activities, the War of 1812 gave him the opportunity to take part in a curious unauthorized trade. Faced with a sudden influx of military personnel into Upper Canada and Montreal, the British commissariat had difficulty finding all the provisions needed by the army; meat in particular was scarce, and prices were rising in the colonies. Disregarding prohibitions and backed by the military, Gates undertook to ensure that the troops had food by bringing in produce from Vermont and New York. Thanks to his network of American partners, he had no difficulty filling his orders. Historian Adam Shortt* relates that in the Kingston area of Upper Canada one of the men in charge of commissariat services was related to the officer commanding the American troops, and the two men were in constant contact by letter to share veiled information about this traffic and to organize, with every precaution, their sentries' rounds so the exchanges would not be disturbed.

The times were, indeed, exceptional. Gates, who had been born in the United States and was nŏt a British subject, could be suspected of disloyalty. At the beginning of the war Governor Sir George Prevost* had issued orders for all Americans living in the colonies to take the oath of allegiance. Gates had refused, not wanting to fight against his native land.

After some hesitation he took the oath at the end of 1813 or early in 1814; however, he obtained exemption from bearing arms against the United States. For him the dilemma was such that he apparently had even been ready in 1812 to sell his holdings and leave Lower Canada.

The war, and supplying the army, enabled Gates, like many other Montreal merchants, to do a profitable business. His personal fortunes were distinctly improved. In 1810 he was still a tenant; in 1816 in quick succession he bought a lot with two stone houses on Rue Notre-Dame and a piece of land on Rue de l'Hôpital. He lived in one of the two houses until his death. In the world of business his prestige grew. He regularly signed supply contracts with the commissariat; at one time or another he supplied almost all the garrisons below Quebec. During the war he sometimes collaborated with merchant Reuben Miles Whitney, and furnished fresh beef. In the 1820s it was chiefly pork and flour that Horatio Gates and Company supplied. Some contracts involved large quantities: the firm contracted to deliver 1,000 barrels of flour and 900 of pork in 1826, and 1,200 barrels of each the following year.

Gates went into partnership with a succession of merchants to do business at Quebec. In 1815, for example, the firm of John Jones Jr and Company was founded by Whitney, John Jones, and Gates, and it lasted until 1818. In 1830 Gates worked through the agency of Jones, Murray and Company. Quebec remained the principal port of entry until Montreal replaced it after 1830. But his principal enterprise remained the Montreal firm of Horatio Gates and Company, which consisted of Nathaniel Jones, Charles Bancroft, and himself. It had probably succeeded Horatio Gates and Nephew, a partnership of Gates and his nephew Nathaniel Jones, which was in existence in 1818.

Around 1815 Gates apparently was quite active as an importer. He advertised in Montreal newspapers that he sold tea, assorted fabrics, shawls, blankets, and even tables "of the best London make." He also had in stock pork, American butter, and tobacco, items that indicate the extent of his importing trade with the United States.

In the export sector Gates dealt particularly in potash, wheat and flour, pork, and staves in small quantities. In 1818 Horatio Gates and Company was in the forefront of Montreal exporters, and in 1825 it shipped the most potash, with 6,726 barrels. At that period potash was the first product from the clearing of land that could be converted into cash; made by leaching hardwood ash, it was indispensable for bleaching fabrics, and remained important until chemical methods were developed in the second half of the century. In 1832 Gates was still one of the major Montreal exporters; figures compiled from newspa-

Gates

pers suggest that he ranked fifth. In 1833 he apparently was still trading in potash, pork, beef, wheat, flour, and butter. His advertisements indicate that these products came from the United States as well as from the Canadas. In 1834 he dealt with Festus Clark, of Sackets Harbor, N.Y., from whom he bought a large quantity of pork.

Gates's commercial activities also extended, not unnaturally, to instruments of payment. In his dealings with the United States and Upper Canada, and probably in part with Lower Canada as well, he had become thoroughly acquainted with the principal methods of paying for trade goods, and he had developed a large network of correspondents. In 1815 he announced in one of his advertisements that he would continue, on a commission basis, to conduct transactions involving bank notes, cash, and bills of exchange. He added that he had on hand £10,000 in British government bills of exchange and £5,000 in private ones.

It was not surprising, therefore, that Gates helped found the Bank of Montreal. The want of a bank was being felt more and more by the mercantile community in Montreal. From the moment that the urban economy began to be less reliant on furs and more dependent on varied trade with the swiftly developing hinterland, institutions for settling matters of credit and permitting the exchange of bills of payment became indispensable. After an unsuccessful attempt in 1808, in which Gates may have participated, the Montreal merchants organized a private company in 1817 to found a bank.

Gates was a charter member, and with others was commissioned to assemble the capital for the Bank of Montreal. His position as agent for the New York bank of Prime, Ward, and Sands and his American contacts proved valuable, since he succeeded in finding takers for nearly 50 per cent of the shares in New York, Boston, and other parts of New England. This involvement shows the importance of American capital in the institution and of the strategic bridging role that Gates played. He served as a member of various committees of the bank, and as a director. He thus dealt with hiring personnel, renting the first premises, buying a lot, and constructing the first building. He was also president in 1826 and from 1832 until his death. In the period 1830–34 he worked with John FLEMING and Peter McGILL* at reorganizing the bank.

But Gates had further involvement in banking. In 1818, a year after the founding of the Bank of Montreal and while he was on some of its committees, he helped found the Bank of Canada. He signed the deed of partnership and was president from 1826 until 1831. According to Shortt, this bank was originally to specialize in trade with the United States, as the participation of Gates and of Montreal merchant Jacob

De Witt* suggests. Both banks received their charters from the government in 1822. From 1823 Gates worked on a merger of the two, which was effected in 1831. However, there was evidently still a need for another bank, since in 1835 De Witt went into partnership with Louis-Michel Viger* to found the Banque du Peuple.

Gates was also interested in communications and transportation. In the field of communications he was for several years engaged in making the general conditions of Canadian trade known in the United States through his correspondence and circulars. His reports, which furnished information on prices, crops, and inventories, were reprinted in a number of American and Canadian newspapers. But he did not confine himself to commercial matters. For example, at the time of the cholera epidemic in 1832 Horatio Gates and Company did not hide the seriousness of the situation and its repercussions on trade in Montreal, for the firm considered it a duty to warn correspondents of the imminent dangers. It also acted as an agency for supplying credit information on Montreal and Quebec businessmen, a function for which Gates was well placed. He was connected with the Bank of Montreal, and his own market activity put him in touch with anything of importance in trading in Montreal. A glance at contemporary notarial acts gives some idea of the impressive number of businessmen who had dealings with him. His importance in the commercial world is also attested by the role he played as public trustee in some major bankruptcies. For example, when the Montreal firm of Maitland, Garden, and Auldjo, which fell victim to the 1825 economic crisis, created a stir by going bankrupt in 1826 [see George Auldjo*], he was one of the trustees responsible for liquidating its debts.

By 1810 Gates had become interested in the port of Montreal, and with his partners unsuccessfully sought permission to build wharfs. Facing resistance from various quarters, he turned to shipping, a sector expanding rapidly with the introduction of the steamship. He participated in the shipping boom on the St Lawrence that began in 1815 and ended with the takeover of the entire sector by the Molson family in 1822. Gates was a shareholder in the ships *Telegraph* and *Car of Commerce*. His interest in transportation had also drawn him into a project to build a canal linking Saint-Jean (Saint-Jean-sur-Richelieu) with Longueuil or La Prairie. In 1826 he signed a petition to the House of Assembly for legislation to that effect. In 1828 the project was changed into a plan to build a railroad, and Gates was again among the promoters. Such an interest comes as no surprise, since Gates had long been involved in improvements to the route from Montreal to the American border.

Like many merchants Gates was active in real estate. In 1825 he owned property estimated to have brought in £320 a year, and this made him one of the major landlords in Montreal. When he died, he was sole owner of six building sites in the city. On occasion it was his commercial activities that had led him into land deals. Thus, when he had sought to build wharfs for the port of Montreal in 1810, he took care to buy a farm near by on the eastern edge of the town; when his initiative failed he rented the farm, and then sold it in 1820.

Because of his importance to the economy of Montreal Gates held various offices in bodies connected with the business world. He was on the board of examiners of applicants for the posts of inspectors of flour and meal and of pot- and pearl ash in Montreal. This responsibility was quite in keeping with the bases of his trade. He was also appointed warden of Trinity House, which was responsible for the administration of port activities, commissioner for the Lachine Canal, and commissioner for building the Montreal market. In 1822, when the merchant community felt a need to create an agency for itself, he took part in the movement and served on the board of directors of the Committee of Trade, the body that became the Montreal Board of Trade.

Gates never stood for election; he was always appointed to the offices he held. As a justice of the peace he helped administer Montreal. Before 1840 the city enjoyed no autonomy, and except for the years 1833 to 1836 when Jacques Viger* was mayor, it was managed by magistrates who formed a special court. In 1833 Gates was called to sit on the Legislative Council. Louis-Joseph Papineau* apparently had doubts about his loyalty. Obviously the confused situation in the years 1812–15 had not been forgotten in certain circles. In the 1820s, however, Gates seems to have played a conciliating role between Papineau's party and the Montreal merchants, persuading the two groups to work together to obtain municipal incorporation and greater autonomy for the port of Montreal. In 1823 he had given Papineau and John Neilson* a letter of recommendation to one of his London correspondents, when the two went to England as delegates to oppose the union of the Canadas that business circles were promoting. But Gates retained his loyalist sympathies, as his participation in the constitutional movement proves.

Through his religious, social, and cultural commitments Gates was thoroughly integrated into Montreal society. He was a member of St Gabriel Street Church from 1808 to 1813, and then became active in St Andrew's Church. Like many of the town's middle class he belonged to the Montreal Auxiliary Bible Society. He played a part in the founding of the Montreal General Hospital, and in 1820 he was one of its governors. He also devoted time to the House of Industry, of which he was a trustee in 1829. A freemason, he held several offices, including that of treasurer of the Provincial Grand Lodge of the District of Montreal and William Henry. He was a member of the committee appointed to set up the Theatre Royal, and in 1825 he acted as trustee. In 1828 he helped found the Mechanics' Institute of Montreal and in the 1820s also was president of the British and Canadian School Society of Montreal.

Gates's death, following a stroke, plunged the Montreal business community into mourning. His funeral on 14 April 1834 was attended by a large part of the bourgeoisie. During the service cannon were fired by two ships at minute intervals. *Le Canadien* reported that "a great many of the stores were closed, and his death seemed to have cast a veil of mourning over the whole of the city which was losing him." Shortly afterwards Bancroft, one of Gates's partners, died, leaving Nathaniel Jones alone at the head of Horatio Gates and Company. When Gates's estate was found, on inventory, to have sizeable liabilities, his widow renounced it for herself and her children. In July 1834 the firm proceeded to liquidation.

The career of Horatio Gates well illustrates the economic development of Montreal in the first third of the 19th century. Starting from a weak economic base, the urban middle class improved its commercial prospects by exploiting a developing hinterland, thereby transforming the small town into a hub for the trade of much of the St Lawrence basin. The Montreal merchants amassed fortunes for themselves, but they also strove to enhance the town's economic power. Gates had early grasped the importance for the mercantile community of setting up institutions and instruments that enabled business to function more efficiently.

JEAN-CLAUDE ROBERT

[Henry Griffin's notarial minute-book, kept at ANQ-M, CN1-187, is an indispensable source for a detailed analysis of Horatio Gates's activities. It contains nearly 150 instruments on various matters dated from 1815 to 1834, and after that date as a result of his estate.   J.-C.R.]

ANQ-M, CE1-125, 30 août 1816, 14 avril 1834, 26 avril 1842; CN1-7, 22 févr., 10 mars 1827; 14 juill. 1832; 6 mai, 24–25 juin, 12 juill. 1834; 23 févr. 1836; CN1-194, 15 déc. 1807; CN1-295, 13 mai 1822; 18, 20 juill., 10 oct., 29 déc. 1823; 15 juill., 29 oct. 1824; 28 mai, 8 juill. 1825; 16 sept., 11 nov. 1826; 10, 13 mars 1827. McGill Univ. Libraries, CH334.S294, CH341.S301. PAC, MG 24, B2; MG 30, D1: 730–52. *Election of the West Ward of the city of Montreal, 27 March 1810, from the poll books alphabetically arranged* (Montreal, n.d.). *Canadian Courant and Montreal Advertiser*, 23 April 1830, 15 June 1833. *Le Canadien*, 18 avril 1834. *La Minerve*, 14 avril 1834. *Montreal Gazette*, 1 June 1815, 4 Sept. 1822, 12 April 1834. *Montreal Herald*, 7 Jan., 4 Feb., 20, 27 May 1815. *Patriot* (Toronto), 2 May 1834. *Quebec Gazette*, 1 May 1818. J. D. Borthwick, *History and biographical gazetteer of Montreal to the year 1892* (Montreal, 1892). Desjardins, *Guide parl. Montreal almanack*, 1829–

Gaugreben

30. *Montreal directory*, 1820. *Quebec commercial list* (Quebec), 1818, 1825, 1832. F. W. Terrill, *A chronology of Montreal and of Canada from A.D. 1752 to A.D. 1893 . . .* (Montreal, 1893). Turcotte, *Le Conseil législatif*.

Baudoin Burger, *L'activité théâtrale au Québec (1765–1825)* (Montréal, 1974). R. Campbell, *Hist. of Scotch Presbyterian Church*. J. S. Chambers, *The conquest of cholera, America's greatest scourge* (New York, 1938). Christie, *Hist. of L.C.* E. A. Collard, *The Montreal Board of Trade, 1822–1972: a story* (Montreal, 1972). Denison, *Canada's first bank.* E. A. [Kerr] McDougall, "The American element in the early Presbyterian Church in Montreal (1786–1824)" (MA thesis, McGill Univ., Montreal, 1965). J.-C. Lamothe, *L'histoire de la corporation de la cité de Montréal depuis son origine jusqu'à nos jours* (Montréal, 1903). H. E. MacDermot, *A history of the Montreal General Hospital* (Montreal, 1950). Robert Rumilly, *Histoire de Montréal* (5v., Montréal, 1970–74), 2. L. J. Ste Croix, "The first incorporation of the city of Montreal, 1826–1836" (MA thesis, McGill Univ., 1971). G. J. J. Tulchinsky, *The river barons: Montreal businessmen and the growth of industry and transportation, 1837–53* (Toronto and Buffalo, N.Y., 1977). Alfred Dubuc, "Montréal et les débuts de la navigation à vapeur sur le Saint-Laurent," *Rev. d'hist. économique et sociale* (Paris), 45 (1967): 105–18. Adam Shortt, "Founders of Canadian banking: Horatio Gates, wholesale merchant, banker and legislator," Canadian Bankers' Assoc., *Journal* (Toronto), 30 (1922–23): 34–47.

GAUGREBEN (Gaugräbe). *See* DEGAUGREBEN

GAUVREAU, LOUIS, merchant, landowner, and politician; b. 11 May 1761 at Petite-Rivière-Saint-Charles, in the parish of Notre-Dame de Québec, son of Alexis Gauvreau and Marie-Anne Hamel; m. first 23 Feb. 1783 Marie-Louise Beleau at Quebec, and they had three children; m. there secondly 13 Sept. 1806 Josette Vanfelson, and they also had three children; d. there 16 Aug. 1822.

Louis Gauvreau was apparently not much drawn to the idea of becoming a farmer like his father, since he was quite young when he left the family farm at Petite-Rivière-Saint-Charles to go and live at Quebec. It is not known how much schooling he had received. However, from his signature, with its well-formed, legible letters, it can be assumed that he had had more than a primary education.

In his family life, Gauvreau was sorely tried by a painful series of deaths. Married at 21, he lost his wife in April 1805; she left three grieving children. In 1808, two years after he had remarried, his wife gave birth to a stillborn child. On 9 June 1813, at the age of 35, she died, as did the infant she had borne two days earlier. Then, in 1818 his only son, Édouard, who had been a lieutenant in the Royal Newfoundland Regiment, died.

Gauvreau was actively involved in the social concerns of the community. By the 1790s he was a member of the Quebec Fire Society, and in the period 1807–14 he is listed as a churchwarden of Notre-Dame at Quebec. At the turn of the century, having become a man of comfortable means, he was making regular financial contributions to charitable organizations. He gave money in 1817 for the construction of a road to link the Plains of Abraham with Cap-Rouge. He was now an important figure, and such generosity enabled him to cultivate his image as a politician eager to participate in community life. He was one of the town's social élite. His daughter Adélaïde married Claude Dénéchaud*, and Marie-Josephte-Reine, the only living child of his second marriage, married Sir Narcisse-Fortunat Belleau*.

In business Gauvreau was unquestionably a success. He was active in three sectors of the economy: wholesale and retail trade, real estate (both land and buildings), and banking. The evidence suggests that his trading activities had begun to expand at the outset of the 19th century. As late as 1799 he had to borrow £250 from two compatriots to finance his operations, one of the rare times that he incurred a debt. By 11 March 1800 he had paid off part of the loan, and on 19 March 1801 his creditors gave him a receipt in full.

Between the time of this borrowing and 1806 Gauvreau was remarkably successful with his general store in the *faubourg* Saint-Jean, which was a large one for the period, the inventory of his stock that year totalling more than £1,000. He had a large quantity of lumber warehoused and thus, on the eve of the boom in lumber and shipbuilding that began around 1807, he was already established in this promising sector. Lumber apparently made up a substantial part of his sales, for he occasionally obtained supplies of it from the United States. The large quantity he had on hand in storage suggests further that buyers could purchase it wholesale as well as retail.

In his general store Gauvreau sold local and imported goods of all kinds, such as stoves and shovels from the Saint-Maurice ironworks, and fabrics, hats, and gloves from England. Because of the size and variety of his stock, his customers came from all over the region, from Cap-Santé, Saint-Nicolas, Sainte-Marie-de-la-Nouvelle-Beauce (Sainte-Marie), Berthier (Berthier-sur-Mer), Sainte-Anne-de-la-Pocatière (La Pocatière), and Baie-Saint-Paul, for example, as well as from the town of Quebec and its suburbs. They included people from nearly all classes of society – farmers, blacksmiths, members of the professions such as notary Joseph-Bernard PLANTÉ, and, of course, several minor merchants.

Gauvreau may have either dealt directly with the trading houses in London, or used middlemen such as the major merchants and wholesalers at Quebec, who got their supplies from the large firms in England. It is difficult to make a categorical statement on this matter, but Gauvreau did owe sums on account with some British firms and merchants at Quebec, including Blackwood, Paterson and Company and one

Joshua Wharton. These accounts seem to indicate that he obtained his dry goods through the big local importers.

Probably to avoid putting all his capital into a single sector – a sign of a certain prudence – Gauvreau advanced fairly substantial sums to numerous individuals at Quebec. Their size shows that he was engaged in banking on a rather high level. His debtors came from among the leading citizens and big merchants as much as from the general population. For example, he lent John Caldwell* the large sum of £1,860 in 1812, and £3,250 in 1815; in the latter year he provided £350 to merchant Michel Borne. Between April and October 1817 he advanced £2,622 in all to various people from Quebec and the surrounding region. Since between 1804 and 1806 he had lent only £666, Gauvreau evidently had become a rich man, as well as a recognized and sought-after financier. Indeed, to put out so much money that was repaid over the relatively long periods of between one and two years, he had to have a great deal of capital at his disposal, especially to be able to go on investing in his business and real estate and continue living in a manner befitting his social station.

Although his real estate activities were on a smaller scale than his banking ones, nevertheless Gauvreau was actively involved in this sector. He received some income from renting two houses in Lower Town and a baker's shop in the *faubourg* Saint-Jean, for instance. He occasionally sold one of his properties, particularly in the early years of the century, probably in order to re-invest in his business or to make loans. This strategy enabled him to consolidate his position. When his fortune was firmly established, about the second decade of the century, he chose mainly to accumulate real estate and landed property, which was a way to hedge himself against the unforeseen. With this in mind, in 1815 he purchased the entire fief of Grosse-Île for £600 in cash; around 1800 he had owned a quarter of it, but he had made over his holding to his daughter Adélaïde in 1808. In 1817 he bought a small house in the *faubourg* Saint-Roch, probably for rental purposes. That year he acquired a major claim on the seigneury of Rivière-du-Sud by buying, through a deed of transfer, the debts of one of its owners, Jacques Couillard-Després, for £550.

Gauvreau resided in a magnificent two-storey stone house on Rue de la Montagne in Lower Town. In 1808 this family home was valued at £1,200, quite a large sum for a house at the period. Gauvreau lived, then, in a building symbolizing his extraordinary success in business. The course of his career was leading him logically towards the upper echelons of the mercantile community and, had he lived another ten years or so, he would probably have made the transition.

Having accumulated a fortune in business, Gauvreau decided to go into politics. He was 48 when in March 1810 he used the *Quebec Gazette* to campaign in the elections for the Lower Canadian House of Assembly to be held the following month. Successful in the riding of Quebec, and mindful of his image, he took time to express through this newspaper his thanks to the voters who had placed their confidence in him. He followed the same procedure in 1816 and 1820. Gauvreau sat continuously in the house from 1810 to 1822, the year of his death. At no time did his new office prevent him from carrying on commercial and financial activities.

Gauvreau's work in the assembly was marked by moderation and assiduity. He seems to have been on excellent terms with Louis-Joseph Papineau*. When the first session of the eighth parliament opened on 21 Jan. 1815 he seconded Thomas Lee's motion nominating Papineau for speaker of the house. In February, Lee brought a motion to grant a salary to the speaker, and Gauvreau again seconded it. He did, however, oppose a bill to pay the speaker of the Legislative Council.

Gauvreau did not vote consistently with his Canadian colleagues. Instead, he acted and voted according to his conscience and his concerns. In 1815 he came out in favour of applying English private law in the province as it was practised in England, but the proposal was rejected by a majority of the house. Again, in 1816 when Augustin Cuvillier* presented a petition from the Montreal merchants for a bank to be established, Gauvreau unreservedly supported Cuvillier's motion that it be sent to a house committee for study. The following year the Bank of Montreal was founded, and by 1818 it had set up a branch at Quebec. As a merchant cognizant of the current economic situation, in which there were forces moving towards the establishing of a banking system in Lower Canada, Gauvreau was in favour of founding a bank. But as a Quebec merchant he might have opposed setting up an establishment emanating from the Montreal business world. That he was not governed by regional considerations demonstrates his broadmindedness.

As a member of parliament Gauvreau sat on several committees set up to study various problems of a socio-economic nature. He was, for example, on the committee responsible for examining the "Accounts and Statements which accompanied the Message of His Excellency the Governor in Chief, respecting the distress of the Country Parishes," and on one set up to study a statute concerning police regulations. In addition, he frequently was involved in all the various stages dealing with bills put before the members of parliament. The constant presence in the house of a man who was engaged in numerous profitable activities outside its walls was a good thing. Even when he was very ill in 1822, the year he died, Gauvreau still found the energy to participate in the diverse endeavours of the assembly. It is thus easy to under-

Gell

stand why his electors put their trust in him for 12 years.

In the final analysis, Louis Gauvreau must be seen as the epitome of that part of the Canadian bourgeoisie which showed it could attain material success through commercial activity.

GEORGE BERVIN

ANQ-Q, CE1-1, 12 mai 1761; 13 sept. 1806; 26 janv. 1808; 9 févr. 1812; 7, 9 juin 1813; 19 août 1822; CN1-16, 30 mars, 10 nov. 1805; 10, 21 févr., 23 juin, 25 juill., 25 août, 1er, 20 sept., 29 oct., 19–20 nov. 1806; 8 mars, 1er avril 1808; 24 oct., 20 nov. 1815; CN1-49, 15 juin 1815; CN1-99, 23 nov. 1802; CN1-178, 15 mars 1799; 11 mars 1800; 19 mars, 11 avril 1801; CN1-205, 23 févr. 1783; CN1-212, 2 août 1822; CN1-230, 10 avril 1804, 12 sept. 1806; CN1-262, 24 mai 1807; 1er avril 1808; 18 juin 1812; 29 mai, 6 sept. 1815; 31 mars, 11, 21, 23 avril, 30 mai, 2, 4, 6, 9, 13–14, 20 juin, 2, 4, 7 juill., 6 sept., 9, 20 oct. 1817. L.C., House of Assembly, *Journaux*, 1815: 26–27, 57, 331, 492; 1816: 173; 1817: 169, 203, 217; 1818: 12; 1822, February. *Quebec Gazette*, 11 June 1795; 21 March 1799; 15 March, 5 April 1810; 14 March, 4 April 1816; 13 March 1817; 9 April 1818; 2, 16 March 1820; 19 April, 19 Aug. 1822. Desjardins, *Guide parl.* George Bervin, "Aperçu sur le commerce et le crédit à Québec, 1820–1830," *RHAF*, 36 (1982–83): 527–51. Henri Têtu, "L'abbé André Doucet, curé de Québec, 1807–1814," *BRH*, 13 (1907): 18.

GELL (Gill), MOLLY ANN (Thomas), Malecite apprenticed as a domestic servant; fl. 1807–22 in New Brunswick.

Soon after the founding of New Brunswick in 1784, the New England Company, a London-based missionary society, began to sponsor efforts to acculturate the Catholic Micmac and Malecite Indians of the province by placing their children in residential schools [*see* Frederick DIBBLEE]. After some 20 years, this plan was replaced by one for "educating and placing the Heathen Natives and their Children in English Families, in some Trade, Mystery or lawful calling." Indians were induced to apprentice their children to local whites for training, the boys as farmers and the girls as domestic servants. Each Indian who bound his children out received an annual allowance of three yards of coarse blue cloth, a blanket, and enough flannel for one shirt; there was also a weekly cash grant so long as the child was apprenticed. For each apprentice taken in, the company paid the master £20 a year in maintenance; he was to provide board, lodging, clothing, "proper Schooling," and instructions in the principles of the Protestant religion. The apprentice was to be faithful and obedient. The indentures were normally out when the apprentice reached 21.

Molly Ann Gell was one of the five children of Joseph Gell, whose wife died in the winter of 1807. Aged and infirm, he was unable to provide for his family and turned them over to the company for the clothing allowance and 2s. 6d. a week. Molly was sent to learn the mystery of domestic service in the household of the Reverend Oliver ARNOLD, master of the New England Company's school at Sussex Vale (Sussex Corner) and minister of the Society for the Propagation of the Gospel. Arnold had some half dozen apprentices at a time, for each of whom he received £20 a year. There were especial hazards for the female apprentices. On 6 Jan. 1809 Molly Ann Gell deposed before the magistrates that, returning from Saint John the previous July, she had met a stranger who "Carried her into the Bushes and Against her Will forced her to Comply with his Wishes." A son was born to her in February 1809, Joseph Solo Gill, who was taken on as an apprentice at birth by Arnold. Molly Ann Gell's indentures expired in 1811; years later she confessed that the father of the child was Arnold's son Joseph, who had seduced her in his father's house. This treatment of female apprentices was not uncommon. The illegitimate children were taken on as apprentices and so tended to make the program self-perpetuating. No fewer than 13 persons of the name of Gell, for example, appear on the apprenticeship lists.

Humanitarian Walter Bromley* of Nova Scotia was sent by the New England Company to investigate complaints in 1822. He found that the Indians were looked on as inferiors, "treated as Menial Servants and compelled to do every kind of drudgery." A 15-year-old boy did as much work as a hired hand who would have cost £25 a year. Some of the boys were given a little schooling, but the girls received none. Bromley condemned Arnold for squandering the company's funds on his dissolute relatives, and he found all the whites of Sussex Vale entirely unsuited to authority over anyone. As soon as their apprenticeships expired, the Indians rejoined the Catholic Church but, as a group, remained "a peculiar distinct people, shut out from all Society," fated to earn their living by begging. Following Bromley's report and a further one from the Reverend John West* in 1825, the New England Company withdrew its funds; the apprenticeship system lingered on until the last indentures expired.

In 1822 Molly Ann Gell was married to a black named Peter Thomas and lived near Sussex Vale. The couple had five children.

L. F. S. UPTON

Guildhall Library (London), MS 7954 (Copy minutes of meeting of the commissioners appointed by the Company for the Propagation of the Gospel in New England, 17 Oct. 1808). N.B. Museum, Sussex Indian Academy papers, docs. 11, 19, 42; Webster MS coll., packet 31, [Walter Bromley], "Report of the state of the Indians in New

Brunswick under the patronage of the New England Company, 14th August 1822." L. F. S. Upton, *Micmacs and colonists; Indian-white relations in the Maritimes, 1713–1867* (Vancouver, 1979). Judith Fingard, "The New England Company and the New Brunswick Indians, 1786–1826: a comment on the colonial perversion of British benevolence," *Acadiensis* (Fredericton), 1 (1971–72), no.2: 29–42.

GERRISH, MOSES, settler, JP, and office holder; b. 10 June 1744 in Byfield Parish, Newbury, Mass., son of Moses Gerrish and Mary Moody; m. 13 Oct. 1774 Ruth Ingalls in Andover, Mass.; d. 30 July 1830 off Grand Manan Island, N.B.

Moses Gerrish's loyalty to the British cause was constant. Forced to leave his home in Massachusetts during the American revolution, he found shelter under British protection in the District of Maine. When at the end of the war that territory was ceded to the United States, he was again forced to relocate. He settled on Grand Manan Island in the Bay of Fundy. For three decades it was uncertain to which of the former combatants, Great Britain or the United States, the Fundy islands belonged. In a letter of 20 Feb. 1817 to Ward CHIPMAN, the British government's agent before the boundary commissioners, Gerrish wrote, "As I am arrived so near to the close of life it would be a serious mortification to lose Grand Manan and be compelled by my Countrymen to move again, or live under their Government." In another statement he noted that, had there been any insinuation in 1783 that Grand Manan belonged to the United States, he would have withdrawn his petition for a grant of the island. He wanted no part of the republic, and much to his relief the island was ceded to the British crown later in 1817.

Gerrish had entered Harvard College in 1758, graduating as an AB with the class of 1762. He was a school teacher for several years in settlements along the upper Connecticut River, but at the beginning of the revolution he and a brother, Enoch, went to live on land owned by the family in Lancaster, Mass. Charged on 30 June 1777 with being "Dangerous persons to this and the other United States of America," they were arrested and their property was confiscated. A year later they were released on a technicality, but within two days an order was issued for their rearrest. Fortunately, the interval had given them time to escape. In October 1778 it was revealed that Moses had been active in passing counterfeit money printed by the British in New York in order to deflate local currency.

Gerrish next appears as an officer in the commissariat at Fort George (Castine, Maine), which had been built at the mouth of the Penobscot River in June 1779 by a British military expedition under Francis McLean*. He was soon involved in the successful defence of the post when it was besieged for 21 days by American forces in July and August. The ultimate aim in establishing the fort had been to create a British province, to be called New Ireland, that would extend from the Penobscot to the St Croix River and would serve as a haven for loyalist refugees [*see* John Caleff*]. However, under the terms of the treaty of peace, agreed to on 30 Nov. 1782 and signed on 3 Sept. 1783, the proposed province was included in United States territory. In the mean time, the Penobscot Associated Loyalists sent emissaries to survey the land just east of the St Croix, in Nova Scotia, and it was here they would settle. By January 1784 all of the loyalists, Gerrish among them, together with discharged soldiers, had been evacuated from the Penobscot area [*see* William Gallop*].

Although Gerrish obtained a shore lot on the mainland of what is now Charlotte County, he chose not to settle there. On 30 Dec. 1783 Governor John Parr* of Nova Scotia issued a licence to John JONES, Thomas Oxnard, Thomas Ross, Peter Jones, and Moses Gerrish "to occupy during pleasure the Island of Grand Manan and the small Islands adjacent in the fishery, with liberty of cutting frame Stuff and timber for building." Hoping to obtain a grant of Grand Manan, the licensees undertook to settle a certain number of families there, but they were to be unsuccessful in attracting the required quota and the original plan would not be realized. Gerrish and his colleagues arrived at the island on 6 May 1784, in the same year that New Brunswick became a separate province, and a permanent settlement was begun. Thomas Oxnard and Peter Jones never exercised their share in the licence of occupation, and in 1786 John Jones sold his interests to others. Ross was a sea captain, maintaining a commercial link to the mainland with his vessels and carrying on a shipping business in his own interests. Though his family was established on the island, he was away from home much of the time. Gerrish was left to manage the civil affairs of the young community.

Gerrish was appointed a justice of the peace. In that capacity he attended the Court of General Sessions in St Andrews, the shiretown of Charlotte County. He was named sub-collector of imperial customs for St Andrews as well and, although the speculation has not yet been substantiated, no doubt also served at the end of his life as deputy treasurer for collecting customs duties imposed by New Brunswick in its own right, it being a matter of convenience in 1830 to combine the two posts in the smaller ports of entry. Since, after its settlement, nearly four decades were to pass before there were resident clergy on Grand Manan, Gerrish also was made a commissioner for performing marriages.

Among other initiatives, Gerrish purchased a pair of moose in 1784 and brought them to the island, where they soon multiplied. In 1810, when they were in danger of extermination, the provincial legislature passed a law for their protection, one of the earliest game conservation acts on record in British North America. An unusual feature allowed only Gerrish, or those permitted by him, to hunt and kill these big game animals. The law was later allowed to lapse and by 1835, only five years following Gerrish's death, they had become extinct.

The development of the young community on Grand Manan was not without problems. The claims of the first settlers to individual land grants were not recognized until 1806 and, in the 22 years that had passed since the community was established, occupancy of lots by new settlers within the licence system had created a number of unfavourable situations. On occasion the founders were accused, unjustly, of speculation in land to which they held no regular title. Before 1817 the inhabitants of the island had also to cope with the uncertainty resulting from the disputed boundary with the United States.

Gerrish's house was located on Ross Island, next adjacent to the main island. In 1830, when he was returning home from the performance of a marriage ceremony at Seal Cove village, about four miles distant by water, his boat capsized and he was drowned. His body was recovered and he was buried in what is now an unmarked grave on Ross Island. His wife, Ruth, died in Massachusetts five years later. The couple had apparently been parted for almost 50 years, and it can only be presumed that their marriage, like so many others, had fallen victim to war and revolution.

Forty-six years of Gerrish's life had been devoted to obtaining settlers for Grand Manan and helping to build what is today a thriving fishing community. That he had been unusually gifted for his role is more than evident. One man who knew him well said, "He would spread more good sense on a sheet of paper than any person of my acquaintance." A later historian commented, "Life on Grand Manan must have had a peculiar charm for this solitary man, who could have filled with honour a much higher place in society." Gerrish's love for that magnificent island and his loyalty to Great Britain were what mattered most of all.

L. K. INGERSOLL

[It was long believed that Moses Gerrish was a bachelor. His marriage to Ruth Ingalls – the certificate may be found in Mass., Dept. of the State Secretary, Arch. Division (Boston) – was first noted in *The genealogy and history of the Ingalls family in America* . . . , comp. Charles Burleigh (Malden, Mass., 1903), 51, but the information did not find its way into biographical accounts of Gerrish. L.K.I.]

Winslow papers (Raymond). Sabine, *Biog. sketches of loyalists*. Shipton, *Sibley's Harvard graduates*. *International adjudications, ancient and modern: history and documents . . . modern series*, ed. J. B. Moore (6v., New York, 1929–33), 6. W. H. Siebert, *The exodus of the loyalists from*

Penobscot to Passamaquoddy (Columbus, Ohio, 1914). Jonas Howe, "Letters and documents relating to the history and settlement of the island of Grand Manan . . . ," N.B. Hist. Soc., *Coll.*, 1 (1894–97), no.3: 341–65.

GIBB, BENAIAH, businessman; b. 6 May 1755 in Northumberland County, England, of a Scottish family; m. first 3 Sept. 1790 Catherine Campbell in Montreal, and they had four sons and two daughters; m. there secondly 26 Dec. 1808 Eleanor Pastorius, daughter of Abraham Pastorius, and they had a son and a daughter; d. there 18 March 1826.

Benaiah Gibb was trained as a tailor in England and may have come from a family of craftsmen, since his brother set up a firm specializing in ready-made clothing in London. He immigrated to the province of Quebec as a young man in 1774. There are conflicting accounts of the beginnings of his career. According to some, Gibb settled in Montreal upon arrival and opened his first shop in 1775. Others claim that he came to Montreal to form a partnership with Peter McFarlane, who was in business there, and then succeeded him when he died.

The advertisements Gibb published show, however, that his progress in his trade was actually more complicated. From his arrival until the summer of 1784 Gibb seems to have worked alone, perhaps on his own account; at least part of that time he spent in Sorel. It was not until 19 Aug. 1784 that McFarlane and Gibb was founded, to specialize in making ready-to-wear clothes for men. The firm was dissolved on 1 Oct. 1790, and McFarlane retired, leaving the business to Gibb. McFarlane probably had a considerable influence on Gibb's career. They had more than just a business connection, for McFarlane lived in Gibb's home in his old age. Except for a brief partnership with Thomas Prior from 1795 to 1797, Gibb ran his establishment on his own until he retired in 1815. The firm of Gibb continued to serve the Montreal élite under the management, first of his sons Thomas, James Duncan, and Benaiah, and then of various other members of his family, throughout the 19th century.

An inventory taken in 1804 when Catherine Campbell, Gibb's first wife, died, tells much about the operations of the firm at the height of his career. At that time the shop and storeroom on Rue Notre-Dame contained an immense variety of fabrics and supplies for making men's clothes, valued at £1,392 9s. 11d. There were thousands of yards of fabric to be made into garments for every occasion: velvet, satin, woollens, India nankeen, cotton, flannel, as well as more than 100 pounds of thread, 40 pounds of beeswax, 800 dozen buttons, and also large quantities of lace, binding, silk galloon, silver braid, gold and silver frogs, and gold and silver epaulettes. Gibb's store also offered the public a limited choice of ready-made clothing and indispensable accessories, such as white silk stockings and kid or angora gloves. Unfortunately no estimate can be made from this single document of the number of apprentices and journeymen tailors who plied the needles, 18 pairs of scissors, and 4 pairs of shears that made up the stock of tools in the shop.

In 1804 the business seems to have been flourishing. There were assets of £8,820 17s. 11d., consisting of stock in the shop and storeroom and receivables (£7,428 8s., including £2,275 0s. 10d. in doubtful debts), and these greatly exceeded the £2,499 16s. 10d. in accumulated debts. The list of principal creditors reveals some aspects of the way the shop functioned. For a merchant tailor, cloth was the essential raw material and it represented the largest production cost. Gibb imported his cottons and woollens from Great Britain, mostly dealing direct with English companies. More than half his debts were reckoned in pounds sterling, and the chief creditor was the London firm of Edward and Thomas Sheppard. But sometimes Gibb bought goods put on sale by Montreal importers. Consequently the list of creditors also includes Parker, Gerrard, Ogilvy and Company, McTavish, Frobisher and Company, James and Andrew McGill and Company, and John and William Porteous.

The prosperity of Gibb's firm was due to his ability to respond to the demands of very special customers. Among them were numerous officers of the garrison. Gibb was tailor also to notaries (Louis Chaboillez*, John Gerbrand Beek, Jonathan Abraham Gray, Louis Guy*), seigneurs (Jean-Baptiste-Toussaint Pothier*, Jacques-Philippe SAVEUSE de Beaujeu, Jacob Jordan*), and merchant princes (Simon McTavish*, Joseph Frobisher*, William Maitland, George McBeath*, William McGILLIVRAY, George GARDEN, John Ogilvy*, Thomas Blackwood*).

Gibb's relations with the Montreal élite he served were complex. As a craftsman he was in another social class, but since he was at the top of that pyramid, he was one of the few to turn out luxury articles. In time his enterprise's prosperity enabled him to adopt a way of life quite different from that of his fellow craftsmen, which brought him closer to the Montreal bourgeoisie. By 1804 he owned a two-storey stone house inside the town ramparts, and a property at Près-de-Ville north of the *faubourg* Saint-Laurent that had fruit trees and a "China summer house." Gibb's other activities also contributed to his rise in society. He was active as a Presbyterian, in St Gabriel Street Church, serving for several years on the temporal committee, of which he was the vice-president in 1804. In 1820 he became a director of the Montreal Savings Bank.

By the time of his death in 1826 Gibb had become a wealthy Montrealer. The outstanding debts owed to his estate amounted to more than £25,482, whilst liabilities amounted to only £1,112. He had also increased considerably his investments in landed property in Montreal and elsewhere, particularly by acquiring numerous land grants in Ashton, Sutton, Elmsley, Ely, Eardley, and Clifton townships as well as in Roxborough Township in Upper Canada.

Benaiah Gibb's gradual integration into the Montreal bourgeoisie was confirmed by the careers and marriages of some of his children. His daughter Elizabeth married James Orkney, a merchant of the firm of J. and R. Orkney. The best known of his sons, also named Benaiah, consolidated the rise in society that had begun with his father. He attended to the firm while devoting himself to a passion for art. He took advantage of business trips to London to buy paintings by young artists "who were generally hard up [and] willing to sell at a reasonable price." His collection of 90 paintings and 8 bronzes, as well as a site on Rue Sherbrooke and a sum to be used for building a gallery, were bequeathed to the Art Association of Montreal. Thus the son of a merchant tailor played a fundamental role in the founding of an establishment that was closely connected with the Montreal bourgeoisie, the Montreal Museum of Fine Arts.

JOANNE BURGESS

[The author wishes to thank Mrs Mary Anne Poutanen, who shared the results of her research on Benaiah Gibb and the merchant tailors of Montreal. J.B.]
ANQ-M, CE1-63, 3 sept. 1790; CE1-126, 10 févr. 1796, 27 juin 1798, 29 avril 1800, 26 déc. 1808, 11 oct. 1813, 16 janv. 1817; CN1-121, 24 avril 1804; CN1-134, 15 févr. 1822; 28 juill. 1823; 14–15 mars, 12 avril 1826; 12 déc. 1828; CN1-185, 23 déc. 1808. McCord Museum, Gibb account-books, ledger P (1906–12); Kollmyer papers, 29 July 1795. PAC, MG 22, A9, 4: 38–39; MG 24, K61; L3: 25425, 26369–90. *Canadian Courant and Montreal Advertiser*, 1, 5 Nov. 1815. *Montreal Gazette*, 13, 27 Jan. 1791; 21 Aug. 1832. *Montreal Herald*, 29 April 1815. *Quebec Gazette*, 19 Aug. 1784; 9 July 1795; 29 June, 19 Aug. 1797. F. W. Terrill, *A chronology of Montreal and of Canada from A.D. 1752 to A.D. 1893 . . .* (Montreal, 1893). R. Campbell, *Hist. of Scotch Presbyterian Church*, 113–16.

GILKISON, WILLIAM, ship's captain and merchant; b. 9 March 1777 in Irvine, Scotland, son of David Gilkison and Mary Walker; m. 13 Jan. 1803 Isabella Grant, daughter of Commodore Alexander Grant*, and they had 11 sons; d. 23 April 1833 in Onondaga, Upper Canada.

Having received a liberal education, William Gilkison went to sea and served on a merchant vessel. The ship was captured by the French, and the young sailor was imprisoned for almost a year until he escaped on a second attempt. He emigrated to North America in 1796 and took command of a schooner owned by John

Jacob Astor and employed in the service of the North West Company. The ship sailed Lake Erie between Fort Erie and Detroit. After his marriage Gilkison, according to the family historian, assisted his father-in-law in the management of the Grant estate. By 1810 he was living at Elizabethtown (Brockville) and the following year moved to Prescott where he entered the forwarding business.

Prior to the outbreak of the War of 1812 Administrator Isaac Brock* drew up proposals for the defence of the province, one of which was to enquire "if he [Gilkison] will take a Naval Command." Gilkison did so. In August 1813 he was sent from Prescott to Ogdensburg, N.Y., to gather political information. He was with Joseph Wanton MORRISON at the battle of Crysler's Farm on 11 November. Several days later he bore a flag of truce to the defeated American army.

After the war Gilkison returned to Scotland to provide for the education of his sons. His wife died in 1826, several of his elder sons went back to Upper Canada, and his cousin, John Galt*, became superintendent of the Canada Company which commenced its operations in 1827. Increasingly, it would seem, Gilkison thought of returning to the colony. Finally, in March 1832 he came back, accompanied by Galt. Some of his children had settled in the Brantford area. Gilkison purchased a farm west of the town on the Grand River for £500, naming it Oak Bank after his home in Glasgow.

On 4 Sept. 1832 he bought the southwest half of Nichol Township, approximately 13,816 acres, from Thomas CLARK. By November a town site had been laid out which he named Elora. He began to make plans for this picturesque spot situated on the Grand River gorge, proposing mills and bridges as the basis for "a new City" and as a lure for future settlement, and journeying about the province to purchase supplies. In the spring of 1833 he stopped at the parsonage of Abram Nelles* where he was stricken with paralysis and died. Superintendence of the Elora project was carried on by his son David*, although William Gilkison's first plan had been to make another son, Jasper Tough*, the manager.

D. E. FITZPATRICK

AO, MS 497. Brant County Museum (Brantford, Ont.), Gilkison papers, William Gilkison corr. PAC, MG 24, I25. St John's (Sandwich) Anglican Church (Windsor, Ont.), Reg. of marriages, 13 Jan. 1803. UWOL, Regional Coll., William Gilkison papers, diary (transcript). J. R. Connon, "Elora" (n.p., 1930); repub. as The early history of Elora, Ontario, and vicinity, intro. Gerald Noonan (Waterloo, Ont., 1974). F. D. Reville, History of the county of Brant (2v., Brantford, 1920). Expositor (Brantford), 14 May 1948, 24 Jan. 1956. A. I. G. Gilkison, "Captain William Gilkison," OH, 8 (1907): 147–48. R. E. Mills, "Elora," Waterloo Hist. Soc., Annual report (Kitchener, Ont.), 1935: 164–68.

GILL. See GELL

GIROUARD, ANTOINE, Roman Catholic priest and educational administrator; b. 7 Oct. 1762 in Boucherville (Que.), son of Antoine Girouard and Marguerite Chaperon; d. 3 Aug. 1832 in Varennes, Lower Canada.

Antoine Girouard, whose father had died before he was born, was a good student, first at the Collège Saint-Raphaël in Montreal from 1773 to 1780, and then in theological studies at the Grand Séminaire de Québec. He was ordained priest by the bishop of Quebec, Louis-Philippe Mariauchau* d'Esgly, in the autumn of 1785. The bishop almost immediately sent him as a missionary to the Baie des Chaleurs region. This first ministry south of the bay brought him into contact with Acadian fishermen and Indians. In the autumn of 1790 he was named parish priest of Saint-Enfant-Jésus (in Montreal) and was given responsibility as well for Saint-François-d'Assise (also in Montreal).

In September 1805 Girouard became parish priest of Saint-Hyacinthe, replacing Pierre Picard. He was 42, and had some savings. The Saint-Hyacinthe region, where the Rivière Yamaska had been settled more recently than the shores of the St Lawrence and the Richelieu, was then entering a period of rapid development. Girouard's parish had been established in 1777 but had only acquired a resident curé in 1783; it was huge, extending to the upper reaches of the Yamaska and even into the Eastern Townships. A stone church had been built a few years earlier, to which Girouard would add a large presbytery.

But Girouard had other ideas in mind as well, specifically a plan to found a classical college. Existing institutions in Lower Canada were the Séminaire de Québec, the Collège Saint-Raphaël, and, since 1803, the Séminaire de Nicolet. The parish priest of Saint-Denis on the Richelieu, François Cherrier*, set up a boys' school with a boarding establishment in 1805, but it lasted only a few years. By 1809 Girouard was asking Bishop Joseph-Octave PLESSIS to send him a Latin teacher. Classes were held in the sacristy, and later in the parishioners' room in the presbytery. Girouard soon tried to persuade the bishop that a building should be put up. He believed the need existed, and he had the essential resources, the support of local seigneurs, and the access to voluntary labour for transporting materials. At first Plessis thought premature competition would be created with the Séminaire de Nicolet, which still had to secure the teachers, pupils, and conditions that would permit it to make ends meet. But Girouard insisted, wrote letter upon letter, particularly in 1810, and late that year Plessis gave in to his pleas. He was given permission to build, although he was to proceed gradually and bear in mind the establishment at Nicolet.

The site of the college, in the village of Saint-Hyacinthe, was given to Girouard in 1810 by seigneurs Hyacinthe-Marie Simon, *dit* Delorme, Pierre-Dominique Debartzch*, and Claude Dénéchaud*. In addition Girouard bought land which provided wood and hay and could one day be developed for the benefit of the college. For a few years the parish priest became an entrepreneur, buying materials and even overseeing work in progress. Sometimes he secured exemption from seigneurial dues. A few donations were obtained from priestly friends. He was able to buy cheaply the house that had been built by Picard, and he considered putting the pupils in it temporarily but had to rent it to the army during the War of 1812. Throughout this period the college was being built on plans drawn up by Abbé Pierre Conefroy*. It was completed in 1816 and comprised a main building 88 feet by 50 with three storeys, and two wings 24 feet square of the same height as the main building. In 1816 also, Girouard, who for some years had wanted to encourage the founding of a girls' boarding-school, welcomed into the Maison Picard the sisters of the Congregation of Notre-Dame, who opened a school in it in August.

In 1818 Girouard requested a principal be named for the classical college, and Joseph-Philippe Lefrançois was appointed the following year. Although freed from officially directing the institution, Girouard remained its owner, and since there was no bursar, he carried out most of the administrative tasks until 1826. The few grants given by the government were made out to him. In such matters as the appointment of teachers or disciplinary rules for the pupils, the principal and the founder were rather strictly subject to ecclesiastical authority. The general direction of the college was thus defined through a shifting balance among the bishop, the principal appointed by him, and Girouard. Girouard had several advantages: unlike the bishop, he had some experience of the local situation and unlike the principal he had a permanent position. There were six principals in succession in the period 1819–31.

The college had its ups and downs but nevertheless expanded. In 1822 it had about 50 boarders, as many day pupils, and a staff of nine teachers and regents. But when in 1824 authority over the parish and the Collège de Saint-Hyacinthe was transferred from Quebec to Montreal, at the time the diocese of Montreal was taking shape, Bishop Jean-Jacques Lartigue* asked the college to limit itself to teaching the lower forms. Girouard, who saw his project threatened just as it was growing rapidly, respectfully refused. The college first admitted pupils to every year of the classical program in 1826.

In his work as an educator Girouard thought he had "many enemies, even within the clergy," and at the same time "many friends, even among the laity" and "among those most enlightened." He was especially proud of being able to count on the financial and moral support of an association for improving educational opportunities in the Rivière Chambly area, which had been formed in 1821 on the initiative of Charles de SAINT-OURS; with 21 members, including Plessis, the organization over a period of eight years gave the Collège de Saint-Hyacinthe the funds to educate some 30 pupils. Its goal was to help "children of worthy habitants chosen and recommended by the parish priests" to become "either priests or well-educated citizens . . . two aims advantageous to the country."

As priest, Girouard was also in charge of a large parish. Although its territory had been reduced by the formation of three other separate parishes – Saint-Damase in 1817, Saint-Césaire in 1822, and Saint-Pie in 1828 – his parish had 3,792 inhabitants in 1831, 1,100 of them in the village itself. Girouard seems to have resigned himself to the creation of these new parishes. For example, in the case of Saint-Pie he was willing to contribute lands of which he was the owner, but he insisted on keeping a wooded property so its yield could be used by the college.

Girouard's relations with the family of Saint-Hyacinthe's seigneurs apparently were cordial. Before becoming seigneur in 1814, Jean DESSAULLES had been the seigneurial agent, and in this capacity he had dealt with the original gift of land for the college. In 1820, when writing to Joseph Papineau* in Montreal to order wine, Girouard suggested that it could be delivered to him through Dessaulles's good offices. The seigneur and the parish priest were among those elected in 1829 and 1830 under the Syndics Act to promote primary education in Lower Canada.

But Girouard's relations with important people in his parish were far from cordial when the question of the appointment of churchwardens had to be dealt with. According to his successor, from 1820 Girouard was under pressure to let the *habits à poches* (justices of the peace, notaries, doctors, merchants, and persons of independent means) attend the meeting held each year to decide who would replace the outgoing churchwarden. In December 1830 a lawsuit was even brought against him for having called a meeting of the churchwardens, both old and new, rather than one of prominent parishioners. The time had come for confrontation on the issue [*see* Louis BOURDAGES].

In 1823 Girouard had made a request to Governor Lord Dalhousie [Ramsay*] for the incorporation of the college, and to this end he had prepared a deed of conditional gift of his property to the future corporation. Bishop Plessis headed the list of members, whereas Bishop Lartigue's name was conspicuous by its absence. But the following year, at the request of Plessis, despite his own reservations Girouard had to replace the name of the principal, Jean-Baptiste Bélanger, with that of Lartigue, the superior of the

Godefroy

college, in the draft deed. Lartigue advised Édouard-Joseph Crevier, whom he appointed principal in 1825, to consult Girouard when necessary and to treat him with deference. With the next principal, Thomas Maguire*, Girouard's relations were rather bad. Throughout this period the question of the incorporation of the college dragged on.

In response to a suggestion from Bishop Lartigue, Girouard drew up his will in 1830, bequeathing the equivalent of 11,000 *livres* in money and vestments to the parish church. He named Lartigue, "not in his capacity as a bishop but as a private individual," sole legatee of all his personal and real estate. In May 1832 Girouard asked the bishop to relieve him of his parish charge, being "entirely confident that in appointing his successor the bishop will take into consideration the interests of his college, and even that on this point he will perhaps go so far as to deign to yield to the preferences of an old man who no longer has any thought but to desire what God desires." Girouard and his bursar expressed themselves in favour of Crevier, who was then priest of the parish of Saint-Luc, on the Rivière Richelieu, and who, after teaching philosophy at the Séminaire de Nicolet, had been principal of the Collège de Saint-Hyacinthe from 1825 till 1827, and then bursar of the institution and Girouard's curate for a while.

On the way back from a trip to Saint-Luc, Girouard went to visit his friend François-Joseph Deguise, the parish priest at Varennes; it was there that on 3 Aug. 1832 he died. At that time plans for enlarging the college were already under discussion. In keeping with Girouard's wish, Lartigue made over to the corporation of the college – legal status finally came in 1833 – all the assets from the founder's estate. Now firmly established and well endowed, the college was on its way to a sound future. As for the parish, Crevier would have to stand up to its prominent residents, and in particular many problems would be brought up over the rebuilding of the church. In Girouard's obituary in *La Minerve* of 9 Aug. 1832 Joseph-Sabin Raymond*, who had been a pupil at the Collège de Saint-Hyacinthe, rightly noted that death had just deprived "religion of a worthy minister, the country of a generous citizen, and education of a zealous advocate." On the day of the funeral "stores were closed, work sites shut down" in Saint-Hyacinthe.

Antoine Girouard in a way was representative of the rural priests of the period 1800–30, an age when the initiatives of the Catholic clergy in Lower Canada met with less outright opposition than in the subsequent period. But beyond this, the founding of the Collège de Saint-Hyacinthe was one of the bases for the development of the religious and educational institutions in that area. This development would contribute to the growth of the town, and, leaving its mark on Saint-Hyacinthe's specific character, would account for its important intellectual role in the 19th century. Girouard was remembered personally as a robust, active, determined, and unaffected man.

JEAN-PAUL BERNARD

ANQ-M, CE1-22, 7 oct. 1762. ASSH, Sect.A, sér.A. J.-S. Raymond, *Discours prononcé à la translation du corps de messire Girouard, au séminaire de St-Hyacinthe, le 17 juillet 1861* (Saint-Hyacinthe, Qué., 1861). *La Minerve*, 9 août 1832. Allaire, *Dictionnaire*, vol.1. Richard Chabot, *Le curé de campagne et la contestation locale au Québec (de 1791 aux troubles de 1837–38): la querelle des écoles, l'affaire des fabriques et le problème des insurrections de 1837–38* (Montréal, 1975). C.-P. Choquette, *Histoire du séminaire de Saint-Hyacinthe depuis sa fondation jusqu'à nos jours* (2v., Montréal, 1911–12). Jean Francœur, "Saint-Hyacinthe, esquisse de géographie urbaine" (thèse de MA, univ. de Montréal, 1954). P.-A. Saint-Pierre, *Messire Antoine Girouard* (Saint-Hyacinthe, 1938). É.-P. Chouinard, "L'abbé Joseph-Mathurin Bourg," *BRH*, 6 (1900): 8–20. Lionel Groulx, "Les fondateurs de nos collèges," *Rev. nationale* (Montréal), 11 (1929), no.12: 5–8; 12 (1930), no.1: 7–11.

GODEFROY DE TONNANCOUR, JOSEPH-MARIE (he signed **J. M. Tonnancour**), army and militia officer, JP, seigneur, office holder, and politician; b. 15 Aug. 1750 in Trois-Rivières (Que.), son of Louis-Joseph Godefroy* de Tonnancour and Louise Carrerot; m. 23 Aug. 1785 Marie-Catherine Pélissier in Yamaska, Que., and they had 15 children, including Léonard*; d. there 22 Nov. 1834.

The Godefroy de Tonnancour family had lived in the Trois-Rivières region from the town's earliest days, and they enjoyed a privileged position as merchants, seigneurs, and office holders. The much-coveted office of king's attorney in the Government of Trois-Rivières passed from Joseph-Marie's great-grandfather, Louis Godefroy de Normanville, to his grandfather, René Godefroy* de Tonnancour. His father, Louis-Joseph, who also held the office, was at the same time king's storekeeper, one of the richest merchants in Trois-Rivières, and owner of numerous fiefs. He lost his offices and part of his fortune following the conquest of New France by the British.

Joseph-Marie, a worthy son of a rich family, excelled as a student, first at the Petit Séminaire de Québec from 1765 till 1771, and subsequently in Paris at the Jesuit Collège Louis-le-Grand where he did his classical studies. He then went to England to attend the University of Oxford, and some sources even claim that he was the first Canadian to take courses there.

Tonnancour returned to the province of Quebec in 1775 and, like his father and his brother Charles-Antoine*, was caught up in the American War of Independence, which had just begun. That year he helped defend Fort St Johns (Saint-Jean-sur-Richelieu) when it was besieged by the Americans.

The garrison held out for 45 days before surrendering in early November. Tonnancour was made a prisoner and taken off to the American colonies. After being liberated in an exchange of captives in 1777, he remained in the army until hostilities ended with the signing of the Treaty of Paris in 1783. The following year he became colonel of the Trois-Rivières militia battalion, in which he served until 1831.

In 1784 Tonnancour went to live in the seigneury of Yamaska, which belonged to his father. When the latter died that year he inherited part of the fief, and after numerous transactions with his sisters and brothers he became its sole owner in 1787. According to one of his contemporaries, he apparently was held in the highest esteem as a seigneur. He was reputed to be a very humane man. There are also indications that he put his considerable knowledge and notable scientific mind at the service of the Yamaska townsfolk. For example, in the face of prejudice and superstition, he led a campaign for vaccination against smallpox of which several thousand people took advantage.

In 1788 Tonnancour, like a number of other seigneurs, signed a petition to the king opposing the constitutional reform being sought by the colony's merchant bourgeoisie. In the summer of 1792 he was elected to the Lower Canadian House of Assembly for Buckingham, along with the seigneur of Beauport, Antoine Juchereau* Duchesnay. He represented the riding until 1796 and voted with the Canadian party.

In 1784 Tonnancour had obtained a commission as justice of the peace for the district of Montreal. He received a similar commission for the district of Trois-Rivières in 1788, 1790, and 1799 and for the district of Quebec in 1794. In 1791 he sat as a judge under a commission of oyer and terminer and general jail delivery. In 1819 he, his brother-in-law Thomas Coffin*, Charles Thomas, and Joseph BADEAUX were appointed commissioners for the building of churches and presbyteries in the district of Trois-Rivières. Finally, he became commissioner of roads and bridges in 1831.

Tonnancour felt the constraints ensuing from the conquest and was unable to take up the lucrative commercial pursuits in which his family had engaged. This was the situation facing the seigneurial class, which continued to enjoy privileges it had acquired but could not capitalize on its patrimony. Such circumstances pointed to the decline of a class whose position was threatened by the dominance of the merchant bourgeoisie and the coming of the industrial era.

MARTIN ROCHEFORT

ANQ-M, CE3-5, 23 août 1785, 24 nov. 1834. ANQ-MBF, CE1-48, 16 août 1750. PAC, MG 24, I97; RG 68, General index, 1651–1841. L.C., House of Assembly, *Journals*, 1792, 1835. *Quebec Gazette*, 13 Nov. 1788, 8 July 1790, 4 June 1812, 26 Nov. 1819, 27 Dec. 1820, 5 Dec. 1822. F.-J. Audet, "Les législateurs du Bas-Canada." *Officers of British forces in Canada* (Irving). P.-G. Roy, *Inv. concessions*, 3: 264–65. *Hyamaska, Yamaska, Maska, 1727–1927* (s.l., 1977). P.-G. Roy, *La famille Godefroy de Tonnancour* (Lévis, Qué., 1904). F.-J. Audet et Édouard Fabre Surveyer, "J.-M. Godefroy de Tonnancour," *La Presse*, 5 nov. 1927: 57, 72.

GOGUEN. *See* GUEGUEN

GOUDIE, JOHN, shipbuilder, naval contractor, entrepreneur, militia officer, and JP; b. 15 Sept. 1775 in Kilmarnock, Scotland, son of John Goudie, a soldier, and Elizabeth Greenwood; m. 17 Nov. 1803 at Quebec Jane Black, daughter of a cooper, and they had six children; d. 14 Dec. 1824 at Quebec.

Having served his time either in Scotland or at John Black*'s shipyard at Quebec, John Goudie began his career as a shipwright in 1795 at the Detroit dockyard, where he assisted in the construction of a sloop for the Provincial Marine. By 1800 he was operating his own shipyard on the Rivière Saint-Charles in the *faubourg* Saint-Roch, Quebec, and had a 400-ton ship on the stocks. Like his neighbour John Munn*, he gradually assembled parcels of beach property as the opportunity arose; by 1812 his frontage stretched from Rue Grant to the Dorchester Bridge, and in 1820 he pushed its western boundary back 350 feet along to Rue du Prince-Édouard, or Rue des Chantiers-Goudie.

From 1800 to 1812, Goudie's most prolific period, he regularly built one-quarter of the production of Quebec-area yards, increasing his average annual output from 400 to 900 tons. Of the 24 vessels he constructed, 11 ships measured a respectable 400 tons or more. His ships were built for timber or general merchants, such as Henry Usborne* of London and Quebec or Rogerson, Hunter and Company of Greenock, Scotland. The smaller vessels were constructed for local owners, including Goudie, but were sold to British owners within a few years. Two exceptions were a small schooner ordered by Trinity House of Quebec [*see* François Boucher*] in 1806 and another by the quartermaster general in 1809.

These were busy and profitable years for Quebec shipbuilders. As Quebec's timber trade got under way, and the need for shipping increased, prices rose from £7 per ton in 1805 to as much as £14 in 1810. Repair and maintenance work increased as more vessels called at port, while the growth in river traffic, combined with a lack of navigational aids, produced more stranded vessels for salvage. Prizes condemned by the Vice-Admiralty Court often needed repairs. Goudie undertook work in all these areas, sometimes operating a repaired vessel on his own account or in partnership until a favourable sale was made. He built up a network of agents in the West Indies, Newfound-

Goudie

land, Labrador, and Britain. Goudie was perhaps the only shipbuilder at Quebec to set up a rope-walk.

In 1810 Goudie went into partnership with the merchant Henry Black to set up a sawmill at the Chute Montmorency near Quebec. Having purchased the land, they arranged with a millwright from Platts-burgh, N.Y., to build the mill and put a canal through the rock from the top of the falls to convey water to it. A dwelling house and smithy were also to be built, but the venture was abandoned in May 1811 for unknown reasons and sold to timber merchants Peter Patterson* and Henry Usborne for £3,000.

Meanwhile, war with the United States had become imminent, yet the British naval force on the Great Lakes, known as the Provincial Marine, was little more than an army transport service. After the Americans struck in 1812 Governor Sir George Prevost*, commander-in-chief in British North America, launched an emergency shipbuilding program; arrangements were made for the construction and operation of the fleet to be taken over by the British navy in May 1813. By then York (Toronto) had fallen, the Niagara peninsula was threatened, and Kingston was the only naval dockyard where vessels could safely be laid down. Prevost asked Goudie to go there and prepare a fleet for active duty, and Goudie left in June with a first contingent of 100 shipyard workers. He immediately began fitting out suitable merchant-men for service. He also laid down the 56-gun frigate *Prince Regent* and in October took over construction of the 36-gun frigate *Princess Charlotte* from the regular dockyard personnel; both were launched in April 1814. By then Goudie had contracted to build a three-decked, 112-gun ship, which would be by far the largest vessel that had been built on the lakes. Construction was completed in record time, and the *St Lawrence* was launched on 10 Sept. 1814 to a royal salute. Its imposing size and firepower kept the enemy in port on Lake Ontario until the end of the war [*see* Sir James Lucas Yeo*].

The launching of these vessels was a triumph for Goudie. Getting large numbers of workers to Kings-ton and keeping them there was in itself a challenge. The steamboat ride to Montreal presented no difficul-ty, but the journey was continued by bateaux, towed by the men over numerous and swift rapids. Though Goudie had taken the precaution of having the men dressed in army uniform to deter the enemy from attacking, this deception did not discourage the occasional sniper. In Kingston the difficulties were of a different nature. The higher wages received by Goudie's men caused friction with other dockyard workers. When their pay was late and local merchants refused to give credit, his men struck, and they used the occasion to demand an increase in the rum ration, too. Employees who walked out could not immediate-ly be replaced. Moreover, specialists such as sail-makers, glaziers, and block-makers were almost impossible to find. Finally difficulties in obtaining on short notice the huge quantities of timber required and in transporting supplies from Montreal tremendously complicated operations.

In the winter of 1814–15 Goudie received contracts for a 74-gun ship to be built at Kingston and for 2 frigates, 2 brigs, a provision vessel, and 11 gunboats to be built at Île-aux-Noix, Lower Canada. These contracts have to be considered a tribute to his organizational ability as well as to his skill in shipbuilding, but they were cancelled in March 1815, the war having ended; only the gunboats were com-pleted. Goudie received £13,000, one-third of the contract price. It is ironic that while he worked at Kingston, a boyhood friend, Henry Eckford, was building up the American navy across Lake Ontario at Sackets Harbor, N.Y.

After the war Goudie, then 40, took on a number of important projects with well-warranted self-confidence. In 1816 he built a deep-water wharf off Rue Saint-Pierre in Quebec's Lower Town. At the time it was considered hazardous to build, as Goudie did, out beyond what was known as "the bank," particularly because of the pressure of ice in winter, but Goudie was not daunted by public opinion, and his wharf, which was denounced as "Goudie's folly," stood the test of time. In 1817 he formed a partnership with four others, two of whom were Americans, to build a diving-bell, the purpose of which was to rid the harbour of lost anchors. Though a number of chains and anchors were brought up, a lack of experienced divers terminated operations.

Even as Goudie's wharf was building, so was the 86-foot *Lauzon*, the first steamboat built for ferry service on the St Lawrence. With a rudder at each end, it was launched from Goudie's yard in 1817 and registered in the names of Goudie and five others, including François Languedoc*. Prospective passen-gers were advised that the *Lauzon* would leave Goudie's wharf at 4 o'clock every morning for Pointe-Lévy (Lauzon and Lévis) and ply until dark, that canoes would replace it in winter, and that within weeks a commodious hotel would be completed close to the landing stage on the south shore, with stables for 150 horses. Regular ferry service began only in 1818. The *Lauzon* reduced the cost of crossing by one-half, and the results were significant, according to Philippe-Joseph Aubert* de Gaspé. The new ferry altered the habits of Quebec's inhabitants, for whom Pointe-Lévy and the south shore had been *terra incognita*. The poor, for example, saved their pennies for a Sunday excursion across the river, and farmers from the south shore were able to bring their produce to market at reduced costs. Not everyone found the ferry a bless-ing, however; competing canoe owners called the *Lauzon* "a damned English invention."

Goudie

Three other steamboats were laid down by Goudie. The 554-ton paddle-steamer *Quebec* was built in 1818 for the Quebec Steamboat Company, in which Goudie was a partner, to run between Quebec and Montreal. Two small vessels, the 52-ton *Experiment* and the 29-ton *Flying Fish*, were constructed in 1823. Meanwhile, confident of the future of steam, Goudie had sent his son James as an apprentice to the shipbuilder William Simons of Greenock; there James acquired the knowledge of steamship construction that enabled him to return to Quebec in 1830 to superintend construction of the *Royal William* [*see* George Black*]. In 1820 Goudie bought shares in the *Car of Commerce*, another steamboat on the Quebec–Montreal run, and two years later he became a shareholder in the St Lawrence Steamboat Company [*see* William Molson*], at which time his *Quebec* joined the company's fleet. Between 1816 and 1818 Goudie and a number of associates had laid the groundwork for a steamboat service linking Montreal to the United States, but their plan, which included the building of canals on the Rivière Richelieu, apparently did not come to fruition.

In 1818 Goudie opened at Quebec the first steam-powered mill in Canada. Both a flour-mill and a sawmill, it was run by a 48-horsepower engine and had a flywheel 27 feet in diameter and a chimney more than 100 feet high. Its three large boilers were brought from Glasgow on the deck of a ship and caused some amazement when Goudie had them plugged up and floated to his shipyard, iron then being generally thought not to float. Scottish engineers and workmen were imported with the machinery to set it up. The flouring department had 5 pairs of stones. The sawmill had 4 saw-gates, each with a gang of 22 saws, supplemented by 8 circular saws to make shingles and laths; it could cut, daily, 200 saw logs, which were ordered from Upper Canada and localities between Montreal and Quebec. The army wasted no time in contracting with Goudie, but shipyard sawyers perceived the mill to be a threat and, after several attempts, managed to burn it down on 10 May 1819. Goudie, whose loss was estimated at £10,000, was not intimidated, and the following year he opened an even larger mill, to which he added a nail-making department in 1821. It took determination to keep the mill running; Goudie had to contend not only with the sawyers but also with delays running to several months since replacement parts had to be imported from Scotland. When the sawmill was put on the market after Goudie's death, it found no takers.

Goudie's business ventures were not limited to shipbuilding, shipping, and milling. During the War of 1812, for instance, he had repaired and leased three buildings to the government and had undertaken work on a line of telegraphs on the St Lawrence below Quebec. In 1821 he contracted with the surveyor of highways, streets, lanes, and bridges of the city to make sewers along Rue Saint-Jean and elsewhere. The following year he and four associates acquired a 20-year lease at £1,200 per annum on the king's posts, formerly held by the North West Company, which had recently been absorbed by the Hudson's Bay Company. However, he is said to have referred to this partnership as the worst ship he ever sailed; the HBC conducted an illegal competition for furs from bases in neighbouring seigneuries. Goudie sold his interest in 1823 and was no doubt relieved when James McDouall bought out all the partners and took over the lease the following year. Goudie was also a shareholder in the Quebec Fire Assurance Company, founded about 1816, and a director of the Quebec Bank from 1818 and of the Quebec Savings Bank from 1821.

Goudie was active in a number of public bodies, including the Fire Society by 1805, the Quebec Emigrants' Society in 1819, and the Agriculture Society, of which he was one of only 35 honorary members in the colony in 1821. That year he was promoted lieutenant in Quebec's 2nd Militia Battalion, a Canadian unit in which he had been an ensign since the War of 1812 at least. In 1820 he had been commissioned a member of Trinity House of Quebec, and in 1822 he was given a commission of the peace for the district of Quebec. In October of the latter year he was elected to a committee, chaired by Ignace-Michel-Louis-Antoine d'IRUMBERRY de Salaberry, to oppose a projected legislative union of Lower and Upper Canada [*see* John RICHARDSON].

John Goudie had the dynamic qualities shared by many Scotsmen who emigrated to British North America, the West Indies, or elsewhere in the British empire. They knew how to adapt and improvise, and they made practical contributions to their adopted countries. Goudie's contribution to the British cause at Kingston, for example, is viewed by modern experts as an incredible achievement given the conditions under which he had to work. Frequently, arriving Scottish businessmen enjoyed the financial backing of associates at home, who were often related by blood or marriage. Goudie did not have that support; he was, as his son James proudly wrote, a self-made man. In almost all his ventures, Goudie followed the maxim that risks should be shared. His policy was particularly important in the relatively new field of steamboat ownership, where misfortune was frequent. The steam sawmill, however, seems to have held a special place in his heart; he kept it for himself. In a poem written in 1821 by a young lady leaving Quebec, there is a simple yet eloquent farewell to the "saw mills, steam engine, dear of Mr. Goudie."

EILEEN MARCIL

[John Goudie, the subject of this biography, is not to be

291

Governor Tomah

confused with his father, who is often mentioned in the sources as John Goudie Sr. The latter, who died in 1819, held the office of deputy surveyor of highways, streets, and bridges for Saint-Laurent Ward in 1797, and was constable in 1803.

Notarial minute-books at the ANQ-Q contain more than 250 acts involving John Goudie. They include contracts for the construction, repair, and sale of ships, agreements with workers and apprentices, sales and leases of property, financing arrangements, and the inventory done after Goudie's death. The instruments listed below relate specifically to this study. The *Quebec Gazette*, which was indexed for the period 1764–1824 at the PAC (mfm. copy at ANQ-Q), contains many references to Goudie, but only those directly related to the text are cited. The registers of the port of Quebec (mfm. at PAC) furnish various details on all the ships registered in Goudie's name; however, it proved impossible to identify the ships which were built but not registered by him. The Goudie family has photographs of a portrait of him.

The author wishes to thank the following members of the Goudie family for their assistance: Peggy Goudie (Bolenbaugh), Grace Goudie (Budway), Ainslie Goudie, Clarence Goudie, and Stuart Goudie.   E.M.]

ANQ-M, CN1-187, 4 févr. 1815. ANQ-Q, CE1-66, 17 nov. 1803, 19 déc. 1824; CN1-16, 24 juin, 31 oct. 1808; 15 avril 1809; 19 oct. 1810; 25 févr., 22 oct., 12 déc. 1811; 24 févr. 1812; 22 juin, 1er juill., 15 nov., 21 déc. 1813; 7 févr., 4 août 1816; 19 août, 13 déc. 1817; 22 sept. 1818; 23 nov. 1819; 28 avril 1820; CN1-49, 3 juill. 1810; 27 avril 1820; 26 juill., 2 août 1822; 8 sept. 1823; CN1-145, 15 nov. 1805; CN1-171, 18 avril 1806, 29 mars 1821, 10 janv. 1825; CN1-178, 23 août 1821; CN1-197, 6 juin 1818, 8 juill. 1825; CN1-253, 20 nov. 1813; 15 août, 17 oct. 1814; 12, 15 janv. 1815; CN1-285, 27 oct. 1800, 14 août 1801. Arch. de la ville de Québec, Doc. antérieurs à l'incorporation, procès-verbaux des sessions spéciales relatives aux chemins et ponts, 1: f.421. PAC, RG 1, L3ᴸ: 46682; RG 4, A1, 16 May 1820, 14 May 1822; RG 8, I (C ser.), 723: 43; 730: 182; 731: 32, 36–37, 60–61; 1281: 182; 1708: 60; RG 42, E1, 1382–83. PRO, ADM 106/1997, 28 Jan., 12 March 1815. Can., Secretary of State, *Report*, 1894. *Quebec Gazette*, 1 June 1803; 28 March 1805; 28 April, 29 Sept. 1814; 9 Nov. 1815; 17 March 1816; 1 May, 2 Oct. 1817; 5 March, 14 May, 3 Sept., 19 Nov., 28 Dec. 1818; 11 Jan., 15 Feb., 12 April 1819; 23 Oct. 1820; 2 April, 2 July, 2, 9 Aug. 1821; 17 Oct. 1822. *Quebec Mercury*, 22 June 1813, 12 May 1818, 11 May 1819, 8 June 1821, 18 Dec. 1824. *Quebec Morning Chronicle*, 24 Jan. 1883. *Recensement de Québec, 1818* (Provost), 68. Christina Cameron and Jean Trudel, *The drawings of James Cockburn; a visit through Quebec's past* (n.p., 1976). H. I. Chapelle, *The history of the American sailing navy: the ships and their development* (Norton, N.Y., 1949), 249. W. A. B. Douglas, *Gun fire on the lakes: the naval war of 1812–1814 on the Great Lakes and Lake Champlain* (Ottawa, 1977). R. A. Preston, "The fate of Kingston's warships," *Historic Kingston*, 1 (1951–52), no.5: 3–14. A. J. H. Richardson, "Indications for research in the history of wood-processing technology," *APT* (Ottawa), 6 (1974), no.3: 35–146.

GOVERNOR TOMAH, PIERRE TOMAH, known as. *See* TOMAH

GRACE, THOMAS, named **Father James**, Roman Catholic priest and Capuchin; b. December 1755 in Knocktopher (Republic of Ireland), son of Richard Grace and Elizabeth O'Neil; d. 2 March 1827 in Halifax.

Thomas Grace was educated at the Capuchin convent in Bar-sur-Aube, France, where he took the habit of the order on 25 July 1774. Following his ordination at Bordeaux in 1777, he returned to Ireland; he then served as a priest at Callan for several years, and possibly elsewhere in Ireland. In 1789 he was sent to be a missionary in Nova Scotia under the direction of the superintendent there, the Reverend James Jones*, another Capuchin. Travelling by way of Newfoundland, Grace reached Halifax early in 1790 and was appointed to the mission of St Mary's Bay.

The task of a missionary in Nova Scotia required a mixture of qualities almost too great to expect in one man. Since most Catholics in the colony lacked luxuries and had little money to spare, a priest either had to have outside support or be self-sufficient. But the resourcefulness necessary to survive meant more than learning how to provide for oneself without financial assistance from the faithful; it also meant being a jack of all trades, a tactful diplomat, and a skilled linguist. A Nova Scotian missionary had to be carpenter and cook, trail-blazer and oarsman, doctor and lawyer, friend to his flock and to others. He had to be true to his Catholicism yet not arouse the suspicion of the colonial authorities about "popery." He had to speak French to Acadians, Gaelic to Irish and Scots, English to some, perhaps Micmac to a few, and always remember his Latin for the mass. These demands called for a man of considerable bodily vigour, if not of great physical strength, a man of some presence and psychological stamina who could bear the solitude of being perhaps the only literate man for miles around, cut off for months from the intercourse of his peers. Those who had the fortitude, character, and faith might succeed and even thrive.

Unfortunately, Grace was misplaced. Jones described him as a holy and humble monk but an ineffective missionary, and claimed that he was too wrapped up in his breviary – a charge which probably meant that he preferred thought to action. On the whole, Jones's view of Grace would seem to be just. A reflective man quite unprepared for the shock of being set down amidst poor fishermen in a land of rock, Grace displeased his superiors by failing to erect the much-needed churches and rectories. In addition, he celebrated mass only on Sundays, and he even lacked the confidence to preach. Not that all his problems were of his own making. During his ministry in the St Mary's Bay region, the Acadians had little use for him since the last Irish priest among them, the Reverend William Phelan, had made off with a large amount of money they had collected to build a church. In 1791

Jones, thinking that Grace's difficulties in this mission were less the result of his own shortcomings than of Phelan's scandalous conduct, transferred the "simple and good" Capuchin to Memramcook, N.B., where he was to act as an assistant to Father Thomas-François Le Roux*.

Grace did not stay in New Brunswick long, however, for about 1792 he was assigned his own mission: the coastline of mainland Nova Scotia from Sheet Harbour to Liverpool. Here, again, Grace did what he could, but he was not aggressive enough to suit the hierarchy. He remained in his mission, serving mainly the settlements of Chezzetcook, Ketch Harbour, and Prospect, until the autumn of 1801, when he had what appears to have been a nervous breakdown. By November 1802, Edmund Burke*, the vicar general of Nova Scotia, was nearly at his wit's end as to what to do about Grace. Grace was then in Halifax living among poor people, and only after a direct order in 1805 from Joseph-Octave PLESSIS, the coadjutor bishop of Quebec, did he return to his charge.

When in 1815 Plessis, by then bishop, came to Grace's mission, he found fault with nearly everything connected with "this pitiable colony." In his journal he noted that Grace "has as yet no lodging of his own, and changes it every day, eating in the house of one inhabitant and sleeping in another. Until this year he had had no chapel, or rather he had none other than one of the dwellings." He went on: "How can one reform a man of this age, who has his habits formed so long, and Irish ones at that! who with the devotion of an excellent monk, is found isolated in a mission for which he was in no way prepared . . . who for ten years has worn only rags, because he believes himself too close to death to undertake to dress himself." Yet Plessis was kind enough to accept the fact that the old priest could not do his job. Grace was in good health for a few years afterwards, but he soon had to live in Halifax where the Reverend John Loughnan supported him and gave him the last rites in 1827. He was buried by the church in Ketch Harbour.

Grace's career and character raise questions about the level of his education and preparation, the sort of person he was, and his effect upon those he served. A simple and rather gullible man he may have been, but he did have three languages, English, French, and, of course, Latin. He had studied in France and would have been relatively well educated for the times. As to practical preparation, none of the early missionaries who came to Nova Scotia had prior experience of the conditions that would face them, or knowledge about how to cope with them. Grace was a genuinely humble man. He was happiest among poor working people, and he had the good sense to see the futility of squeezing support from people as hard pressed as his Irish fishermen. Not surprisingly, therefore, he seems to have been a beloved figure to many. At Ketch Harbour there is an old well called Father Grace's Well, because he had blessed it during a drought and it never went dry. Although there are few precise traditions about Grace, after his death people were quick to let visitors know that they had been part of "old Father Grace's circuit."

TERRENCE M. PUNCH

[The assistance of the director of the AD, Aube (Troyes), and the Right Reverend Gerald B. Murphy of Ketch Harbour, N.S., in providing additional information concerning Thomas Grace is gratefully acknowledged. T.M.P.]

AD, Aube, Couvent des capucins irlandais (Bar-sur-Aube), reg. des vêtures et professions, 24 sept. 1773, 25 juill. 1774. Arch. of the Archdiocese of Halifax, J. M. McCarthy papers, D-2 (Visitation of Bishop Denaut, 1803). Cyril Byrne, "The Maritime visits of Joseph-Octave Plessis," bishop of Quebec," N.S. Hist. Soc., Coll., 39 (1977): 23–47. [H.-R. Casgrain], Mémoire sur les missions de la Nouvelle-Écosse, du cap Breton et de l'île du Prince-Édouard de 1760 à 1820 . . . réponse aux "Memoirs of Bishop Burke" par Mgr O'Brien . . . (Québec, 1895), 42, 62–63, 66–69, 81. Johnston, Hist. of Catholic Church in eastern N.S. T. M. Punch, Some sons of Erin in Nova Scotia (Halifax, 1980). Père Pacifique [de Valigny] [H.-J.-L. Buisson], "Le premier missionnaire de langue anglaise en Nouvelle-Écosse," Soc. de géographie de Québec, Bull. (Québec), 26 (1932): 46–62.

GRAHAM, HUGH, Presbyterian minister; b. 16 Oct. 1758 in West Calder, Scotland, son of Hugh Graham and Agnes Allan; m. first c. 1785 Elizabeth —— in Scotland; m. secondly 1792 Elizabeth Whidden of Cornwallis, N.S., and they had five children who survived to adulthood; d. 7 April 1829 in Upper Stewiacke, N.S.

Since his father was a prosperous farmer, Hugh Graham was able to attend the University of Edinburgh. Upon graduating he studied theology under the Reverend John Brown of Theological Hall, Haddington, and in 1781 he received his licence from the Presbytery of Edinburgh as a minister in the Secession Church, the church in which his father had been an elder. His first call came from the congregation of South Shields, England, in 1785, but a second soon followed from the people of Cornwallis, N.S. The synod appointed him to the Nova Scotian post.

Graham arrived at Halifax in the summer of 1785. He stayed briefly there before joining his congregation in Cornwallis, where he delivered his first sermon on 29 August. Cornwallis had been initially settled by Acadians, who were replaced after the expulsion of 1755 by New Englanders [see Charles Lawrence*]. The first English-speaking minister in the settlement was the New England Congregational pastor Benajah Phelps, who served from 1765 to 1776. The evangelical New Lights followed Phelps, erecting a church in 1778 and maintaining a ministry under John PAYZANT from 1786 to 1793. The success of the New Lights, who opposed compulsory contributions from their congregations, was a source of continual frustration to Graham. His congregation was small, and he was not able to afford his own house until 1791. For a time he considered returning to Scotland, but decided against it.

On 2 Aug. 1786 Graham assisted three other Presbyterian clergymen, Daniel Cock of Truro, David Smith of Londonderry, and George Gillmore* of Windsor, in organizing the Associate Presbytery of Truro, the first such body in the colony. However, the 1747 division of the Secession Church in Scotland into burgher and anti-burgher factions carried over into Nova Scotia: in 1795 three anti-burgher ministers, James Drummond MacGregor, Duncan Ross, and John Brown, established the Associate Presbytery of Pictou in opposition to the Truro presbytery, whose ministers adhered to the church's burgher wing. Some years later, because of his position in the Truro presbytery (he had been chosen its clerk in 1795), Graham figured prominently in discussions aiming at a merger of the two presbyteries. Union was finally achieved on 3 July 1817, when the synod of the Presbyterian Church of Nova Scotia assembled in Truro. This was the first synod in British North America of the Presbyterian Church. The only ministers who remained separated from the new body were at Archibald Gray, the Church of Scotland minister at St Matthew's, Halifax, and Bruin Romkes Comingo*, the German Reformed pastor at Lunenburg.

Graham was never content at Cornwallis and, when in 1799 a call came from the united congregation of Stewiacke and Musquodoboit, he accepted. This area, split between Colchester and Halifax counties, had been settled in the 1780s by Irish and New England Presbyterians. Graham was attracted to it because of the religious homogeneity of its inhabitants and the promise of an annual stipend of £110. He was inducted on 27 Aug. 1800 and settled in Upper Stewiacke. As a result of rapid population growth, Stewiacke and Musquodoboit were divided into separate congregations in March 1815, with John Laidlaw assuming responsibility for Musquodoboit and Graham retaining Stewiacke.

Graham's lot in Nova Scotia was not an easy one. He had a tragic personal life, losing two wives (the first in 1786 after scarcely a year of marriage and the second in 1816) and several children. Travel was always a problem – on one occasion he walked upwards of 30 miles to preach at an isolated settlement – and contact with his fellow clergy was rare, something he had hoped would change with the move from Cornwallis to Upper Stewiacke. After taking charge of Stewiacke and Musquodoboit he had to contend with hostility from the anti-burghers of the area, and a few years passed before he gained the

respect and support of his entire flock. Still, life was better at Stewiacke, since he had land and the sons to work it.

Graham was called by Thomas Chandler Haliburton* one of the founders of Presbyterianism in Nova Scotia. His career is also important, however, because it typifies the struggle that confronted all ministers in pioneer Nova Scotia.

JAMES E. CANDOW

A sermon by Hugh Graham, "A warning to youth; or an address to the rising generation," is available in the *Christian Instructor, and Missionary Reg. of the Presbyterian Church of Nova Scotia* (Pictou, N.S.), 5 (1860): 5–13. References to another published work, possibly called *Two sermons entitled the relation and relative duties of the pastor and people, delivered at the admission of the Reverend John Waddel to the charge of the united congregations of Truro and Onslow* (Halifax, 1799), appear in a number of secondary sources, including Robertson's history of the Secession Church, cited below, and Tremaine, *Biblio. of Canadian imprints*. The sermons are also recorded under two different titles, along with an unpublished history of religion in Nova Scotia by Graham, in H. J. Morgan, *Bibliotheca Canadensis*. No copies of any of these works have been located.

PANS, MG 1, 332B; 742; RG 20A, 38, Hugh Graham, 1811. Univ. of King's College Library (Halifax), Israel Longworth, "A history of the county of Colchester" (2 pts., Truro, N.S., 1866–78; typescript at PANS). T. C. Haliburton, *An historical and statistical account of Nova-Scotia*, (2v., Halifax, 1829; repr. Belleville, Ont., 1973). *Weekly Chronicle*, 21 June 1816. J. M. Bumsted, *Henry Alline, 1748–1784* (Toronto, 1971). Gregg, *Hist. of Presbyterian Church* (1885; 1905). Alexander Maclean, *The story of the Kirk in Nova Scotia* (Pictou, N.S., 1911). Thomas Miller, *Historical and genealogical record of the first settlers of Colchester County ...* (Halifax, 1873; repr. Belleville, 1972). J. S. Moir, *Enduring witness: a history of the Presbyterian Church in Canada* ([Hamilton, Ont., 1974?]). George Patterson, *Memoir of the Rev. James MacGregor, D.D. ...* (Philadelphia, 1859). James Robertson, *History of the mission of the Secession Church to Nova Scotia and Prince Edward Island, from its commencement in 1765* (Edinburgh, 1847). *Stewiacke ...* (Truro, 1902; repr. Belleville, 1973). C. B. Fergusson, "The sesquicentennial of the first synod of the Presbyterian Church in Canada," *Dalhousie Rev.*, 48 (1968–69): 215–21.

GRANT, Sir WILLIAM, lawyer, militia officer, and office holder; b. 13 Oct. 1752 in Elchies, Scotland, son of James Grant, a farmer and customs collector; d. unmarried 23 May 1832 in Dawlish, England.

William Grant studied first at Elgin, Scotland, and subsequently at King's College in Aberdeen. Then he did Roman law for two years at the University of Leiden in the Netherlands. Admitted to Lincoln's Inn in London as a law student on 30 Jan. 1769, he was called to the bar on 3 Feb. 1774.

Grant arrived at Quebec in 1775. When the Americans invaded that year [see Benedict Arnold*; Richard Montgomery*], he participated in the defence of the town, taking command of a corps of volunteers. Following the departure for England in 1775 of the attorney general, Henry Kneller*, Grant was chosen to assume the post temporarily and on 10 May 1776 Governor Guy Carleton* appointed him to it officially. The right of appointment, however, rested with the crown. Consequently Carleton asked his lieutenant governor, Hector Theophilus Cramahé*, to write to Lord George Germain, the secretary of state for the American colonies, recommending Grant. In his letter of 18 Aug. 1776, Cramahé put forward Grant's great qualities and his knowledge of the French language and law. In the mean time Germain had chosen James MONK for the office. When he learned this in May 1777, Carleton could not conceal his dissatisfaction, particularly since the rebuff over Grant had been preceded by that over judge John Fraser, and thus was the second case of the sort to come up in a short period. On 23 May he wrote to Germain emphasizing that he had "turned out of their Employments two men of Abilities and good Character." Then he added: "I am at a loss to know, after the fate of these gentlemen, how I can even talk of rewarding those who have preserved their Loyalty without an Appearance of Mockery. Of this you may be assured that such things will occasion no small exultation among the King's enemies." Nevertheless, Grant's office had been lost to Monk.

During his brief term as attorney general Grant had drawn up three ordinances to give the province its first regular judicial system since the Quebec Act: the ordinance of 25 Feb. 1777 establishing civil courts in the province, another adopted the same day establishing procedures in these courts, and a third, of 4 March, setting up criminal courts. In drawing up these measures Grant took inspiration from a plan prepared by Chief Justice William Hey* before he left for England in 1775. By their terms the province was divided into the districts of Quebec and of Montreal, as it had been prior to the Quebec Act.

The judicial structure for dealing with criminal cases was not greatly altered. The only change was to give the limited powers of bailiffs to militia captains. Justices of the peace had always had broad powers of first instance deriving much more from their commission than from an ordinance. The Court of King's Bench remained a court of first instance, with full authority. There was again provision for convening assize courts.

By contrast, the judicial system for civil cases underwent major change. The Court of King's Bench ceased to have jurisdiction in this field. The Court of Common Pleas in each district became the only one to exercise complete authority in all civil suits of first instance. The same laws were to be applied in all courts; these consolidated the regulations laid down by the Quebec Act and the ordinances of the governor and the Legislative Council. The bailiffs' limited field of jurisdiction disappeared. There was no longer any provision for the appointment of judges to settle suits of minor importance. In respect of appeals the powers of the governor and the Legislative Council were widened. The decisions of the Court of Common Pleas of each district could be taken to the Court of Appeals, which was composed of the governor and the legislative councillors, in cases involving more than £10 sterling or "the taking or demanding any Duty payable to His Majesty, or to any Fee of Office or Annual Rents, or other such like Matter or Thing, where the Rights in future may be bound." Finally, decisions from this court could be appealed to the Privy Council in London in cases where more than £500 sterling was in dispute or "where the Rights in future may be bound." As for civil procedure, it was mixed, being partly French and partly English. In addition English rules of evidence were introduced in commercial matters.

On 25 Oct. 1778 Grant left Quebec and returned to Britain, where he was to have a remarkable career as a lawyer, politician, and judge. As legal counsel, he agreed in 1787 to undertake the defence in England of the judges of the Court of Common Pleas in the District of Quebec, who had been subjected to an investigation by Chief Justice William Smith* following charges brought against them by Monk.

In 1790 Grant was consulted by Prime Minister William Pitt about the reforms needed in the government of the province of Quebec, and he became a protégé of the famous politician. In June of that year he was elected to the House of Commons for the borough of Shaftesbury. The following year he took an energetic part in the discussion on the Constitutional Act. When he was called to serve as judge of the high court sessions at Carmarthen in 1793, he had to give up his seat in parliament. In February 1794 he was elected for the borough of Windsor, and that year he was appointed the queen's solicitor general.

From June 1796 till September 1812 Grant represented the Scottish county of Banffshire. Two years after this term in the house began, he accepted the office of chief justice of the district of Chester. He was appointed solicitor general in the Pitt government on 18 July 1799 and retained the office until Pitt's resignation in February 1801. In 1799 also he was knighted.

On 21 May 1801 Grant became a member of the Privy Council. Six days later he was appointed to the important office of master of the rolls, which he held until he retired on 23 Dec. 1817. He was elected rector of King's College, Aberdeen, in 1809. Grant died on 23 May 1832 at Dawlish. His decisions had strongly influenced the development of equity in English law.

Gray

Sir Samuel Romilly, the noted jurist, praised "his eminent qualities as a judge, his patience, his impartiality, his courtesy to the bar, his despatch, and the masterly style in which his judgments were pronounced."

JACQUES L'HEUREUX

PAC, MG 11, [CO 42] Q, 12: 173; 13: 160, 180; 14: 264; 19: 266; RG 4, B8, 28: 56. *Docs. relating to constitutional hist., 1759–91* (Shortt and Doughty; 1918). Quebec, Legislative Council, *Ordinances*, 1777, c.1, c.2, c.5. *Quebec Gazette*, 29 Oct. 1778. F.-J. Audet et Fabre Surveyer, *Les députés au premier parl. du Bas-Canada*, 231. *DNB*. A. W. P. Buchanan, *The bench and bar of Lower Canada down to 1850* (Montreal, 1925), 71, 73, 75. John Campbell, *The lives of the chief justices of England, from the Norman conquest till the death of Lord Tenterden* (5v., Long Island, N.Y, 1894–99), 4: 460. William Holdsworth, *A history of English law*, ed. A. L. Goodhart et al. (7th ed., 15v., London, 1956), 13: 278, 501, 578, 656–62. H. M. Neatby, *The administration of justice under the Quebec Act* (London and Minneapolis, Minn., [1937]), 31, 37–40, 259–60, 351; *Quebec*, 162–63. W. R. Riddell, *The bar and the courts of the province of Upper Canada or Ontario* (Toronto, 1928), 27. H. S. Smith, *The parliaments of England from 1715 to 1847*, ed. F. W. S. Craig (2nd ed., Chichester, Eng., 1973), 12, 91, 622–23.

GRAY, JOHN, businessman, militia officer, and JP; b. c. 1755 probably in London, son of John Gray; m. 19 March 1806 Mary Pullman in Montreal, and they had at least two children; d. 13 Sept. 1829 in Côte-Sainte-Catherine (Outremont), Lower Canada.

Some time before October 1781 John Gray followed his elder brother Edward William* to Montreal, where he doubtless benefited from Edward William's prominence in the city's business and public life. John began in the fur trade, and from 1782 to 1790 he invested modest sums (between £1,250 and £3,000) in the trade to Niagara (Niagara-on-the-Lake, Ont.), Detroit, and Michilimackinac (Mackinac Island, Mich.).

By the late 1780s a solid reputation enabled him to act as an attorney, a trustee for estates, and an executor of wills. He executed the will of a former attorney general, Alexander Gray, in June 1791, and by August he and John Lees* were attorneys for the London merchant Alexander Davison in liquidating the partnership of Davison and Lees. By 1793 he and the Quebec commercial partnership of Monro and Bell [see David MONRO] had become agents for Davison, to whom the British Treasury had awarded the coveted contract to supply the troops in Upper Canada. Working closely with the lieutenant governor of Upper Canada, John Graves Simcoe*, and through sub-contractors, Richard Cartwright* at Kingston, Robert Hamilton* at Niagara, and John Askin* and David Robertson at Detroit, Gray conducted a lucra-

tive provisions trade in that colony for a period of time. Meanwhile he built up a network of useful associates and diversified his commercial interests; by the early 1790s he was a dry-goods merchant, and in December 1798, with Henry Caldwell* and John Steel, he was operating a flour-mill at Caldwell's Manor, Lower Canada, an enterprise that doubtless had developed out of his activities in supplying flour to the troops in Upper Canada.

Probably in the summer of 1799 Gray quit dry goods for real estate. Properties he sold, likely on occasion as an agent for others, included fine houses in Montreal occupied at one time or another by such prominent figures as Alexander Mackenzie*, William McGILLIVRAY, and William Robertson*. He advertised for sale properties outside the city as well; among them were a 112-acre estate of his late friend Gabriel Christie* and farms, grist-mills, and sawmills as far away as the Yamachiche–Rivière-du-Loup (Louiseville) region, formerly belonging to George Davison*. In the developing colony of Upper Canada he acquired 1,443 acres around York (Toronto) from Samuel Heron* in 1803, 400 acres in Markham Township in 1807 from his friend William Berczy* in payment of a debt, and 1,000 acres in Norwich Township in 1809.

On 8 April 1801 Gray, two North West Company fur-trade merchants, Joseph Frobisher* and Daniel SUTHERLAND, the lawyer Stephen SEWELL, and Thomas Schieffelin had obtained a provincial charter to provide "good and wholesome water" for the inhabitants of Montreal. Given a 50-year monopoly on pipe distribution of water, the Company of Proprietors of the Montreal Water Works was capitalized at £8,000 (with authority to raise an additional £4,000 if required); individual shares were set at £100, provision being made that no one could own more than 20 per cent of them. Using a system based on gravitation and wooden pipes, the company brought water from a spring-fed pond behind Côte-des-Neiges (Montreal) to two cisterns in the city. It supplied subscribers on Rue Notre-Dame by 1805, and on other streets as work progressed. Trouble plagued operations from the beginning: in winter the wooden pipes froze and burst; in dry summers, such as that of 1806, the source failed, and the company was compelled to purchase another spring. The operation was offered for sale in April 1816, and three years later it was sold at a loss for £5,000 to a company under the direction of Thomas PORTEOUS.

Meanwhile, in 1817 Gray and 12 prominent Montreal businessmen launched another major project: the Bank of Montreal. Subscriptions having been solicited in May, on 7 August a meeting of the stockholders chose 13 directors, including Gray. At a meeting of the directors two days later, Gray was chosen president, apparently with votes controlled by the two rival fur trade firms, the North West Company and the Hudson's Bay Company. These firms probably wanted a president with a conciliatory personality and with first-hand experience in the fur trade but no ties to either one. During Gray's presidency branch agencies were established at Quebec in 1817–18 under Daniel Sutherland and in Upper Canada in 1818 at Kingston, under Thomas Markland*, and at York, Queenston, and Amherstburg; a permanent head office was constructed and opened in Montreal in 1818–19; procedures were begun that would lead to incorporation, sanctioned by royal charter in 1822; and a solid place was carved out for the bank in the commercial life of the Canadas.

Gray resigned as president of the bank in 1820. Ill health may have been the cause, or possibly personal business reverses apparently suffered in late 1818 and early 1819. Whatever the reason, it did not prevent him from beginning new business ventures. In October 1820 he announced his intention of seeking authorization to establish a market in the city, and in April 1822 he was among some 50 prominent businessmen who met under the presidency of John RICHARDSON and founded the Committee of Trade of Montreal. He continued to work in real estate; in January 1822 he paid John McKINDLAY £2,107 for about 27,000 acres in Lower and Upper Canada, and in late 1823 he advertised for sale the large estate of Alexander Allison, which included land in Upper Canada and the St Mary's Foundry in Montreal. Failing to sell the foundry, he purchased the apparatus, moved it to his property in Côte-Sainte-Catherine, and in August 1825 solicited orders for stoves, sawmill gearing, cranks, ploughs, and screws.

An extremely retiring man, Gray, unlike his brothers Edward William and Jonathan Abraham, played only a minor role in public life. Interested in education and science, he signed a petition in 1790 for a university in the colony and in 1805 was the host of the visiting Scottish botanist Francis Masson*. Although of Quaker origins, Gray was on a committee that welcomed Anglican bishop Charles Inglis* to Montreal in July 1789 and was a friend of Bishop Jacob MOUNTAIN. He was a member of the Anglican congregation of Christ Church but also held a pew in the Scotch Presbyterian Church, later known as St Gabriel Street Church. He contributed generously to the Montreal Fire Society and to a subscription opened in October 1799 to help defray the cost of Britain's war with France. During the War of 1812 he seems to have been a captain in the 5th Select Embodied Militia Battalion, the Chasseurs Canadiens, and the 3rd Select Embodied Militia Battalion successively. He was made a justice of the peace in June 1821 and received commissions of oyer and terminer and general jail delivery in June 1824 and April 1827.

On 13 Sept. 1829 Gray died at his residence at Côte-Sainte-Catherine, where he held large properties. His career reflects the evolution of Montreal's economy from one based largely on the fur trade and the import-export business to one of greater diversity, embracing public works, such as the Montreal Water Works, and the founding of financial institutions, such as the Bank of Montreal. Energetic and shrewd, he made good early use of family and government contacts to establish his fortune while maintaining a reputation for "the strictest integrity of character."

CARMAN MILLER

ANQ-M, CE1-63, 19 mars 1806; CE1-126, 19 sept. 1829; CN1-187, 12 janv. 1822. McCord Museum, J. S. McCord papers, personal finances, box 1, file 2, 10 March 1836. PAC, MG 24, I9, 14–17; RG 4, B28, 115; RG 68, General index, 1651–1841: 96, 349. L.C., *Statutes*, 1801, c.10; 1820–21, c.25. *Corr. of Lieut. Governor Simcoe* (Cruikshank), 1: 193, 300; 3: 298; 4: 342. *Montreal Gazette*, 9 Sept. 1789; 27 Feb., 25 Sept., 13 Dec. 1792; 24 Dec. 1798; 28 Jan., 12 May, 1 July 1799; 8 Dec. 1800; 26 Jan., 18 May, 24 Aug., 28 Sept. 1801; 14 June, 8 July 1802; 19 Jan. 1807; 7, 21 Sept. 1812; 20 Nov. 1823; 13 Aug. 1825. *Quebec Gazette*, 5 Sept. 1781; 15 March 1787; 2 May, 16 June 1789; 28 Oct., 4 Nov. 1790; 16 June, 18–19 Aug. 1791; 16 Feb., 1 Nov. 1792; 9 Aug. 1794; 9 April 1795; 25 July, 17 Dec. 1799; 21 Aug. 1800; 29 Jan. 1801; 13 June, 5 Oct. 1809; 21 Nov. 1811; 11 April 1816; 7, 14 Jan., 22, 29 April 1819; 19 June, 5 Oct., 14, 21 Dec. 1820; 5 June, 22, 25 Oct. 1821; 9 Jan. 1823; 13 Aug. 1825; 24 Sept. 1829. R. Campbell, *Hist. of Scotch Presbyterian Church*, 129. Denison, *Canada's first bank*, 1: 84, 86, 122, 132, 160–61, 427. Miquelon, "Baby family," 191, 194–95. Robert Rumilly, *Histoire de Montréal* (5v., Montréal, 1970–74), 2: 152. Alfred Sandham, *Ville-Marie, or, sketches of Montreal, past and present* (Montreal, 1870), 235. F. C. Smith, *The Montreal Water Works: its history compiled from the year 1800 to 1912* (Montreal, 1913), 13.

GRAY, ROBERT, office holder, politician, judge, and army and militia officer; b. c. 1747 near Glasgow; d. 12 Feb. 1828 in Charlottetown.

Like many Glasgow Scots, Robert Gray was employed in the American tobacco trade, and in 1771 he came out to Virginia as storekeeper and agent for a Glasgow tobacco merchant. Not surprisingly, when rebellion against Britain broke out in 1775, Gray supported the mother country and joined a volunteer corps raised by Governor Lord Dunmore. In 1777 he was appointed a captain in Colonel Edmund Fanning*'s King's American Regiment, being in charge of the defence works on Goat Island during the rebel siege of Rhode Island in 1778. He later served in the fierce guerrilla warfare of the Carolinas, and was commanding the British garrison at Georgetown, S.C., at the time hostilities ceased. Gray then retired on half pay of £86 per annum and came to Shelburne, N.S., on a commission to assist in the disbanding of loyalist soldiers there. His wartime commander Fanning was appointed lieutenant governor of St John's (Prince Edward) Island in 1786 and soon after invited Gray, whom he regarded as "a gentleman of superior merit and worth," to become (at £60 per year) his private secretary and "man of business." Gray arrived on the Island in 1787. Fanning appointed him to the Council, made him provincial treasurer, and gave him the unpaid post of assistant judge of the Supreme Court. He was also granted two town lots and two 12-acre pasture lots.

In 1790 Fanning sent Gray to England to lobby for new arrangements with the Island's absentee proprietors, and to obtain the office of receiver general of quitrents, a post also sought by John STEWART, who is said to have offered to pay Gray £80 per year if he would withdraw his candidacy, although the office paid only £50. Stewart's reputed bid was possible because the quitrents were never paid to the government, but, as Captain John MacDonald* of Glenaladale put it, went "to make a parcel of idle fellows live without work, and drink wine and debauch girls." Gray did not pursue his claim to the office (which Stewart obtained), but he was still in London when a group of proprietors pressed charges of malfeasance against the Island's major officers, including Fanning [see John CAMBRIDGE]. Gray mobilized support for the lieutenant governor among the proprietors and successfully argued his case before the Privy Council. Following his return to the Island in 1793, he gradually added a number of minor appointments, such as captain in the Island's fencible companies, colonel of militia, and paymaster of volunteers, to his portfolio of offices. Although Gray continued to support Fanning publicly, he privately complained of the lieutenant governor's close political association with the Stewart family, and gradually developed a reputation, unusual in Island politics, as an independent and unbiased official. His critics charged that he managed to remain free of factions by never doing anything.

Gray married Mary Burns (daughter of George Burns, an original proprietor) some time after 1793, and they had six children, including John Hamilton Gray*. He was active in organizing an agricultural society in Charlottetown in 1803, and especially after Fanning's retirement in 1804 devoted much of his time to reading and literary pursuits. From November 1802 to September 1803, and again from August 1804 to July 1807, he served as acting chief justice and over the remainder of his life he attempted to gain remuneration for this service, as well as a regular salary as assistant judge. Between 1806 and 1808 he assisted the Burns interests in settling a large number of Guernsey immigrants on the Island.

Despite his increasingly low profile, Gray was unable to keep completely out of political controversy. In 1811 William ROUBEL and other members of the Loyal Electors, an incipient political party, made charges against the Supreme Court that prompted Chief Justice Cæsar COLCLOUGH and the assistant judges to call on Lieutenant Governor Joseph Frederick Wallet DESBARRES, who had control of the affidavits containing the charges. Although no specific criticisms had been directed against Gray, he joined the delegation and his testimony about the lieutenant governor's reaction to their visit helped destroy DesBarres's credibility. Gray was no friend of the Loyal Electors, whom he called a "Club instituted for the avowed purpose of regulating and controlling the Government, and headed by two men without principle and without property." He sat on the Court of Chancery, which in 1816 prosecuted one of those two men, lawyer James Bardin PALMER, for professional and political misconduct. Under Thomas TREMLETT, Colclough's successor, Gray often found himself a minority of one when the court came to split decisions, and although he protested he never made his concerns a public issue. In later years he became quite infirm, and died in 1828 after a long illness.

J. M. BUMSTED

National Library of Ireland (Dublin), Dept. of MSS, MS 20287 (5) (O'Hara papers), J. F. W. DesBarres, printed letter, 25 Sept. 1812. PAC, MG 23, E5, 2. PAPEI, Acc. 2702/643; Acc. 2810/132a; Acc. 2849/116; Acc. 3355/1–2; RG 1, commission books, 72: 5, 51; RG 3, "Memorial & petition of Robert Gray," 28 Jan. 1825; RG 16, land registry records. P.E.I. Museum and Heritage Foundation (Charlottetown), File information concerning Robert Gray. PRO, CO 226/12, 226/18, 226/31, 226/39. SRO, GD293/2/78/2, 24. *Prince Edward Island Register*, 12, 26 Feb. 1828. *Royal Gazette and Miscellany of the Island of Saint John* (Charlottetown), 3 June 1793. J. M. Bumsted, "The Loyal Electors of Prince Edward Island," *Island Magazine*, no.8 (1980): 8–14.

GREEN, JAMES, army officer, office holder, businessman, and JP; b. *c.* 1751 in Sweden; d. 1 Feb. 1835 at Quebec.

"Not having a single Farthing left," James Green enlisted in the 62nd Foot in 1772. His abilities were soon recognized, and he had been promoted sergeant-major by 1776 when his regiment arrived at Quebec, then under siege by American rebels. In June, as Governor Guy Carleton* pursued the retreating Americans toward Montreal, Green saw action at Trois-Rivières, and in October he was in an engagement with Benedict Arnold*'s fleet on Lake Champlain. In 1777 he served on Major-General John Burgoyne*'s expedition into New York and was captured on 19 September during the battle of Freeman's Farm. After ten months as a prisoner at Hartford, Conn. (during which time he learned of his promotion to an ensigncy, dated 20 Sept. 1777), he was exchanged and joined the British garrison at New York. Sir Henry

Clinton, commander-in-chief in North America, gave him three appointments: barrack master for the "island of New York," deputy judge advocate for the city of New York, and paymaster for troops whose regiments were not then serving in the vicinity.

Green's appointment as deputy judge advocate proved of great value, for it gave him "an opportunity of acquiring genteel and general Acquaintaince with most officers in the Army – a thing so essentially necessary to a Young Officer, particularly to one under my circumstances, who had no one to recommend me, but such into whose good Graces I might be able to get by a constant perseverance in a Line of Good Conduct." He resigned all three appointments in September 1779 when, with the help of Charles Stuart, lieutenant-colonel of the 26th Foot, he purchased a lieutenancy in that regiment; he also received appointment as the regiment's adjutant, a post he held for 17 years. In December 1779 he and the other officers of the 26th were sent back to the British Isles on recruiting duty.

In 1787 Green returned to the province of Quebec with the 26th. He had married, and a son, WILLIAM, was born at Quebec in early October. By 1798 Green's household in Upper Town counted eight members. The following year his friend, the painter William Berczy*, whom he perhaps supported financially, did pen-and-ink sketches of his wife Maria, William, and a daughter.

Green had been promoted captain-lieutenant on 2 March 1791, but not until May 1795 did he succeed to the full captaincy of a company. In 1795 as well he was selected by Carleton, now Lord Dorchester, to be his military secretary. He continued to occupy the post under Carleton's successors as commander, and was in addition employed at York (Toronto) from 1799 as civil secretary by Lieutenant-General Peter Hunter*, who was also lieutenant governor of Upper Canada. Replaced in the latter position in 1806, Green returned to Quebec and remained military secretary under Colonel Isaac Brock*, commander of the forces. In this capacity he held a key position in the administration of the armed forces in the Canadas. His merit was acknowledged in his brevet promotions to major in January 1798 and to lieutenant-colonel in September 1803, following his confirmation as major in the 26th Foot that July. With the arrival of Lieutenant-General Sir James Henry Craig* as commander of the forces and governor in chief in October 1807, he was replaced as military secretary, though he was continued for a short while as assistant secretary. In view of Green's long service and great experience, in 1808 Craig offered him an appointment as acting deputy commissary general in place of John Craigie*, then under suspension for fraud and embezzlement. In his new position Green was acting head of the commissariat in the Canadas but, though he was strongly recommended by Craig to the Treasury, new regulations prevented confirmation of his appointment, and he was replaced in 1810.

With the loss of this post Green found himself in "uncommon hardship" and pressed for an appointment more suitable to his "situation in society." In April 1812 he obtained partial relief when he was made paymaster to a new provincial regiment, the Voltigeurs Canadiens [see Charles-Michel d'IRUMBERRY de Salaberry]. In June a lengthy period of strained relations between Britain and the United States finally resulted in war and in August Green resigned as paymaster to be named director of the newly established Army Bill Office. The chronic shortage of specie in the Canadas and the difficulty of obtaining a ready supply in time of war prompted the government to introduce a paper currency through the issue of army bills. These notes did much to alleviate the problems of war-time finance, and the good faith shown in their redemption weakened a long-standing prejudice in the population against paper money.

The Army Bill Office closed in December 1820, but Green's involvement in financial matters continued. In 1821 he was appointed a vice-president of the Quebec Savings Bank, in which he also served as treasurer; in November Green was given a vote of thanks "for his very strenuous and persevering services" in bringing the bank to "its present flourishing situation." One year later he became president, a position he still occupied in May 1824. Green also took an interest in land transactions. In 1802 he, his wife, and their three children each received 1,200 acres of land in Burford Township, which he offered for sale, along with 6,000 acres in Potton Township, in 1811. At some point he arranged the sale of Major-General Lauchlan Maclean's lands in Chatham Township on the Ottawa River.

From the humble station of a private soldier Green had risen not only to commissioned rank and some distinction in the army but also to a position of note in Lower Canadian society. A regular contributor to the Quebec Fire Society, he also subscribed to several charities assisting immigrants, most notably the Quebec Emigrants' Society. He received a commission of the peace in 1821 and another in 1828. At his death in 1835 at the home of his son-in-law John Stewart*, the *Quebec Mercury* summed up his career with the affirmation, "In all . . . capacities Mr. Green maintained a high character for integrity and assiduity, and for a most conscientious discharge of his official duties."

GLENN A. STEPPLER

ANQ-Q, CE1-61, 5 oct. 1787, 4 févr. 1835. PAC, MG 24, L3: 9706, 9712, 9737, 9739, 9781, 9838, 9856; RG 1, L3ᴸ: 48097–98, 48102–3, 48166–75, 48221–22, 48225, 48227;

Green

RG 8, I (C ser.), 0, 15, 112, 114, 223, 330, 703, 744, 1218, 1706; RG 68, General index, 1651–1841: 360, 640. William Berczy, "William von Moll Berczy," ANQ *Rapport*, 1940–41: 22, 30, 36–37. "Les dénombrements de Québec" (Plessis), ANQ *Rapport*, 1948–49: 124, 174. *Quebec Gazette*, 21 March 1799; 10 April 1800; 13 Jan. 1803; 12 June 1806; 2 July 1807; 30 June 1808; 14 Sept. 1809; 12 Sept. 1811; 19 March, 6 Aug. 1812; 25 Feb., 25 March, 15 April, 30 Dec. 1813; 12 Jan., 19 Oct. 1815; 4 May, 11 June, 7 Dec. 1818; 22 April 1819; 5 June, 23 Oct. 1820; 2, 16 April, 19, 26 Nov. 1821; 18 Nov. 1822; 19 May 1823; 17 May 1824. *Quebec Mercury*, 3 Feb. 1835. Langelier, *Liste des terrains concédés*, 1413, 1446, 1459, 1465. James Stevenson, *The War of 1812 in connection with the Army Bill Act* (Montreal, 1892).

GREEN, WILLIAM, lawyer, office holder, science enthusiast, and author; b. 5 Oct. 1787 at Quebec, son of James GREEN, an army officer, and Maria ——; m. there 27 May 1815 Elizabeth Irwin, and they had at least one son; d. there 15 June 1832.

William Green articled in the legal offices of Jonathan Sewell*, along with James Cartwright and Philippe-Joseph Aubert* de Gaspé. He studied there from 9 Aug. 1802 to 21 Aug. 1807, five years being the period then required before licensing as an advocate, barrister, attorney, and solicitor. He was called to the bar on 8 Nov. 1809, and practised his profession until 25 June 1812, when he was appointed clerk of the peace for the District of Quebec, conjointly with Joseph-François Perrault*. To this office he added that of English translator in the House of Assembly from 29 Dec. 1812, clerk of the crown on 22 March 1813, and law clerk for the assembly from 1 Dec. 1828.

On 15 April 1802 Green had acquired 1,200 acres in Barford Township, which belonged in part to members of his family. He is known to have made business arrangements with Pierre de Sales* Laterrière. In particular, on 11 April 1823 he signed an acknowledgement of debt for £150 in connection with purchases of furnishings and other objects. On that occasion he mortgaged his personal and real estate, including a property in the seigneury of Fossambault. He signed new recognizances on 12 May 1823 and 16 Aug. 1828 for £337 4s. 7d.

While carrying on his professional activities Green played an active role in Quebec intellectual circles. In 1814 he was one of the subscribers who made possible the opening of the Quebec Free School in a former theatre on the corner of Sainte-Anne and Des Jardins streets. He also displayed great interest in the sciences. When the Literary and Historical Society of Quebec was founded by Lord Dalhousie [Ramsay*] on 6 Jan. 1824, Green became a member of its first board, serving as recording secretary; five years later he held the offices of treasurer and secretary. At the time its museum was created he made several donations to it:

an arrowhead, a piece of Irish peat, and a sample of anthracite used in lithographing.

During the period 1829–33 Green published six memoirs in the *Transactions* of the Literary and Historical Society. One, entitled "Memoranda respecting colouring materials produced in Canada," attracted Lord Dalhousie's attention. Dalhousie sent it to the Society for the Encouragement of Arts, Manufactures, and Commerce in London, with some samples of colouring materials. This initiative was not wasted, since the society published Green's work and awarded him the Isis gold medal. Moreover, his good friend the painter Joseph Légaré* experimented with the root of the *Galium tinctorium* (dyer's yellow bedstraw) and he tried in his art a red lacquer extracted from the plant, finding this lacquer better and cheaper than that procured from Europe. The London society offered another medal to anyone who would send 40 pounds of the famous root in good condition. But there was no response because the reward was not commensurate with the work that it required, since the root, which runs underground, is no thicker than a thread. Green was also secretary of the Société pour l'Encouragement des Sciences et des Arts en Canada.

In 1832, when cholera was beginning to spread at Quebec, William Green succumbed to the disease and died on 15 June.

GINETTE BERNATCHEZ

William Green is the author of several articles published in the *Trans.* (Quebec) of the Literary and Hist. Soc. of Quebec: "Memoranda respecting colouring materials produced in Canada," 1 (1824–29): 43–46; "Notes on the country in the neighbourhood of the falls of Montmorency," 181–87; "Some observations upon the myrtus cerifera or myrtle-wax shrub," 231–39; "On some processes in use among the Huron Indians in dyeing," 2 (1830–31): 23–24; "Notes respecting certain textile substances in use among the North American Indians," 310–12; and "Pigments of Canada," 3 (1832–37): 191–92.

ANQ-Q, CE1-61, 5 oct. 1787, 27 mai 1815, 17 juin 1832. PAC, MG 8, F131: 1269–84, 1554–56; MG 23, GII, 10, vol.5: 2336–42; MG 30, D1, 14: 491–93; RG 4, B8, 18: 6599–604. *L'Institut* (Québec), 3 avril 1841. *Quebec Gazette*, 6 Nov. 1809, 6 April 1815, 18 June 1832. *Quebec Mercury*, 13 Nov. 1809, 11 April 1815. F.-J. Audet et P.-G. Roy, "Greffiers de la paix à Québec," *BRH*, 11 (1905): 247. F.-M. Bibaud, *Le Panthéon canadien* (A. et V. Bibaud; 1891). P.-G. Roy, *Les avocats de la région de Québec*, 207. Aubert de Gaspé, *Mémoires* (1866). Ginette Bernatchez, "La Société littéraire et historique de Québec (the Literary and Historical Society of Quebec), 1824–1890" (thèse de MA, univ. Laval, Québec, 1979), 20, 142–43. P.-G. Roy, *Toutes petites choses du Régime anglais* (2 sér., Québec, 1946), 1: 195, 251.

GREEN, WILLIAM, teacher and almanac writer; probably m. Sarah Cronk and had at least six children; fl. 1783–1833 in New Brunswick.

William Green arrived in Parrtown (Saint John, N.B.) in 1783 with the New York loyalists. By late 1788 he was advertising in the *Royal Gazette, and the New-Brunswick Advertiser* that for two guineas he would teach navigation in the house of Robert Wood, with a new method of finding latitude and longitude at sea. He also advertised the opening on 20 April 1789 of an "English School" where aspiring youths could be taught reading for 7*s*. 6*d*. a quarter and reading with "English GRAMMAR, and the proper accent" for 10*s*. Green's diversified curriculum included writing, arithmetic, bookkeeping, surveying, navigation, and map reading, all of these subjects being taught in a manner approved by the "principal Academies" of Great Britain and Ireland. A footnote to parents assured them that those giving him "a preference in the tutorage of their children, may depend on the strictest attention being paid to their natural genius, and their moral abilities."

By October 1791 Green was on Campobello Island as a schoolmaster for the Society for the Propagation of the Gospel, teaching only 12 scholars in his first year because of the severity of the winter and the scattered nature of the population. In both this endeavour and his application to the society to become a catechist, he was supported by David OWEN of Campobello Island, who recommended him to the SPG and provided him with a house and farm as well as a £10 supplement to his salary. The poorly defined financial arrangements made between Green and the society rebounded on him in 1792 when Charles Inglis*, bishop of Nova Scotia, conveyed to him London's decision that his salary (half-yearly) be £10 instead of the previous incumbent's £15. Green appealed this judgement in a letter to the society on 27 March 1792, arguing the necessity of SPG support in a situation where the poverty of the fishermen and the barrenness of the land made local assistance to the schoolmaster an impossibility. Nevertheless, Owen felt compelled to go to the people of Campobello to propose "certain methods to raise a small annual sum for the school in addition to the Society's Salary and [Green's] house and his farm." The islanders' response was a negative one, as Owen explained in a letter to the SPG on 16 June 1792, for "the settlers were dissatisfied with Green, and would neither do, nor promise anything for him; so that he does not, nor has taught school since Easter, but nevertheless says that he will draw for his pay, and will probably stay to receive this half year from the society, and then move away to the States, where he was formerly." Owen added, with some acerbity, that Green had "acted very indiscreetly, having every sense but common sense," had imposed upon Owen himself, and deserved "no countenance from any one, and has no claim to any pay from the Society." The society agreed to dismiss Green and not honour any draft for money. By

October 1792 the Reverend Samuel Andrews* of St Andrews had reported to the SPG, as had Inglis, that "Mr. Green, the Societies schoolmaster at Campo Bello has left the country, nor was there any School there, for some months before his Recess."

At some point prior to his teaching experience on Campobello, Green had arranged for the publication of *The British American almanack . . . for the year of our Lord God 1791* with John HOWE in Halifax. Beginning with a preface dated 28 April 1790 this publication included tables, calendars, riddles, doggerel, axioms, arithmetical questions, and advice to farmers. It reflected the author's personal wit in its epigrams and rhymes while at the same time providing navigational and astronomical calculations designed specifically for Maritime readers. The almanac closed with an advertisement for Green's school in Saint John in which he included a verse satire on indulgent mothers and fledgling schoolboys:

On education all our lives depend;
And few to that, too few, with care attend.
Soon as mama permits her darling joy
To quit her knee, and trusts at school her boy;
O, touch him not, whate'er he does is right,
His spirits tender, though his parts are bright.
Thus all the bad he can, he learns at school,
Does what he will, and grows a lusty fool.

It would appear that difficulties with the Saint John printers Christopher Sower* and John Ryan* had led Green to publish his almanac with Howe at his own expense. Throughout 1791 while teaching on Campobello, he seems to have been preparing a second almanac; this Sower and Ryan agreed to publish jointly as *The British American almanack . . . for the year of our Lord Christ 1792*. The almanac lacks the epigrammatic and witty tone of its predecessor, but it includes more practical information on the political offices, costs, and organization of New Brunswick society than does the 1791 edition.

Green, who reportedly spent some time in Nova Scotia after 1792, was apparently the William Green who moved to Grand Manan in 1803. In December 1806 he successfully applied for 200 acres on the island near Castalia. The following July he helped deputy surveyor Donald MacDonald survey sections of Grand Manan, and around 1811 he moved to Wood Island, off Grand Manan, to supervise the interests of its owner, William Ross. The 1821 census of Grand Manan shows Green and his wife with four children at home and two maintaining separate households. After Ross's death, Green acquired his rights to Wood Island. It is likely there that he himself is buried; he had died by March 1836.

Green's name on a petition concerning the fishery in 1833 and his reputed importation of the American hare

Greenfield

into Grand Manan both suggest his involvement with the island's development, but it is as a compiler of original almanacs and New Brunswick navigational tables that he is best remembered.

GWENDOLYN DAVIES

William Green is the author of *The British American almanack, and astronomical ephemeris of the motions of the sun, moon, planets and stars, for the year of our Lord God 1791* . . . (Halifax, 1791) and *The British American almanack, of the motions of the luminaries, for the year of our Lord Christ 1792* . . . ([Saint John, N.B., 1792?]).

Charlotte Land Registry Office (St Andrews, N.B.), Record books, 8, no.347; 11, no.301; Q: 24–25; S: 840. N.B. Museum, Green family, CB DOC. PAC, MG 17, B1, C/CAN/NS, I/12–I/12a, esp. I/12, folder 140; Ib/14, folder 168, no.286 (mfm.; copies at PANS); MG 23, D1, ser.1, 2, Saint John file, item 470, "Education for Young Gentlemen." PANB, RG 4, RS24, S30-M11 (copy at N.B. Museum); RG 10, RS108, William Green, 1806. USPG, Journal of SPG, 25: 35, 390; 26: 40–42. SPG, [*Annual report*] (London), 1792: 33. *Royal Gazette, and the New-Brunswick Advertiser*, 23 Dec. 1788; 13 Jan., 7 April 1789. *Saint John Gazette, and the Weekly Advertiser*, 16 Jan., 27 March, 3 April 1789. Tremaine, *Biblio. of Canadian imprints.* J. G. Lorimer, *History of islands & islets in the Bay of Fundy, Charlotte County, New Brunswick* . . . (St Stephen, N.B., 1876), 24, 30. J. R. Harper, "Christopher Sower, king's printer and loyalist," N.B. Hist. Soc., *Coll.*, no.14 (1955): 84–85; "Old New Brunswick almanacks," *Maritime Advocate and Busy East* (Sackville, N.B.), 44 (1953–54), no.8: 5–10. Keith Ingersoll, "Deserted Fundy island left to sheep, gulls," *Saint Croix Courier* (St Stephen), 23 Feb. 1961: 9, 12.

GREENFIELD. *See* MACDONELL

GREENWOOD, WILLIAM, mariner and farmer; b. *c.* 1750 in Virginia; m. first Grace Smith of Chatham, Mass., and they had two sons and two daughters; m. secondly Deborah Berry, *née* Bootman, and they had six sons and three daughters; d. 1824 in Port Saxon, N.S.

As a youth William Greenwood ran away from an unhappy home to Massachusetts, and sailed in vessels out of Cape Cod. In the early 1770s he came to Barrington, where his father-in-law, Solomon Smith, was a proprietor of the township. Barrington had been founded in the early 1760s, chiefly by fishermen from Cape Cod and Nantucket Island, Mass., and its inhabitants depended on trade with their former homes. As a master mariner, Greenwood sailed on coastal voyages to Halifax, fished along the shores, and traded his dried fish for provisions in the seaports of New England. With the outbreak of hostilities between Britain and her American colonies in 1775, these ports were closed to the Barrington settlers. The latter were, however, sympathetic to the struggle of their kinsmen for independence. They gave assistance

to distressed American seamen and escaped prisoners and, in doing so, revisited New England ports and were able to continue to trade with the rebellious colonies. Although fraught with danger because of possible reprisals from the provincial authorities, the opportunity was one the settlers valued, for wartime conditions meant that essential supplies were often lacking.

Greenwood himself first conveyed several stranded privateersmen to Massachusetts in the fall of 1777. He had shipped some fish at the same time in the hopes of purchasing corn for himself and his fellow settlers, and in consideration of his services he was granted permission to do so by the Massachusetts Council. In 1778 he repeated his voyage, returning to Barrington with his schooner laden with provisions, and he continued to sail to Massachusetts until 1782. Despite his aid to fellow Americans, Greenwood had his schooner *Sally* taken and his storehouse plundered by a privateer in 1779. The following year some escaped prisoners boarded his schooner *Flying Fish* (or *Peggy*) in Halifax Harbour and forced him to put to sea. Notwithstanding his protests of friendship, his captors set him and his crewman on an island after "stripping him of all his Cloaths and Robbing him of his Money." Because Greenwood was recognized as "a uniform friend to . . . the United States," the Massachusetts House of Representatives ordered the *Flying Fish* restored to him and permitted his return to Nova Scotia.

With the re-establishment of peace in North America, Greenwood turned his attention to the land. In 1785 he was granted 235 acres east of Barrington at Port Saxon, on the east side of Negro Harbour. There he cleared land for a farm, on which he raised horses, cattle, sheep, and pigs, and grew crops of vegetables and hay. On his property he built a sturdy house, some barns, a milk-house, a workshop, and a fish-house. Greenwood also kept the first inn on Negro Harbour, and his son William was the first ferryman on the east side of the harbour. But he did not neglect his earlier calling. He continued to sail in his schooner *Deborah*, and with William and others he owned the schooner *Ruby* and engaged in the carrying trade along the coast of Nova Scotia and to the New England states. Little was known about his private life other than that he was a Methodist. In his will, proved on 22 Nov. 1824, he bequeathed to his widow and children an estate valued at £203 1*s.* 9*d.*

MARION ROBERTSON

Annals of Yarmouth and Barrington (Nova Scotia) in the revolutionary war, compiled from original manuscripts, etc., contained in the office of the secretary of the Commonwealth, State House, Boston, Mass., comp. E. D. Poole (Yarmouth, 1899), 32–33, 39, 47, 51, 62–63, 75–80, 96,

129–31. Edwin Crowell, *A history of Barrington Township and vicinity ... 1604–1870* (Yarmouth, [1923]; repr. Belleville, Ont., 1973), 441, 485–86, 570, 573. Marion Robertson, "William Greenwood of the *Flying Fish* and the *Sally*," *Dalhousie Rev.*, 42 (1962–63): 209–17.

GSCHWIND (Gschwindt, Schwindt), JOHN (Johann) FREDERICK (Friedrich) TRAUGOTT, army and militia officer, physician, and office holder; b. *c.* 1748 in Oberdaubnitz, near Meissen, Saxony (German Democratic Republic); m. 3 Aug. 1782, probably in Halifax, Anna Fletcher, and they had at least one child; d. 2 Sept. 1827 in Halifax.

Nothing is known of John Frederick Traugott Gschwind's youth, but he may have obtained some medical training in early adulthood. In the mid 1770s he enlisted with the Hessian troops which were to be sent to North America in order to assist the British government in suppressing the colonial revolt. His unit, the Regiment von Stein (renamed von Seitz in 1778 and von Porbeck in 1783), was assembled at Hersfeld in Hesse (Federal Republic of Germany), from where it departed in May 1776. Five months later, having passed through Bremen (Federal Republic of Germany) and Portsmouth, England, the troops arrived in New York City, in the vicinity of which they remained during the next two years. In October 1778 Gschwind's regiment was transferred to Halifax. Gschwind is listed as a surgeon in the 3rd Company during the years 1780 to 1782, although he may have functioned as such prior to that time. When his regiment embarked for the return to Europe after the conclusion of the Treaty of Paris in 1783, Gschwind decided to stay behind.

One of his reasons for remaining in Nova Scotia must have been the fact that in 1782 he had taken a wife, Anna Fletcher, a widow slightly younger than he. She was to die in 1805, at the age of 55. Their daughter Anna married another military surgeon, Charles Alexander Simpson.

Gschwind succeeded in establishing himself in Nova Scotian society. In 1784 and 1788, as a reward for his wartime services, the provincial government issued to him land grants of 500 and 400 acres in Halifax County; the 500-acre grant was escheated in 1820. In Halifax itself, Gschwind and his family occupied a house at the corner of Duke and Grafton streets and worshipped at St Paul's Church. Gschwind also kept in close touch with the German community, becoming vice-president of the High German Society in 1789.

During his more than 40 years as a Halifax resident Gschwind made his living as a physician. His skill was recognized by his appointment in 1793 as surgeon of the 2nd Halifax Militia Regiment with the rank of adjutant, and even more so by his promotion in 1796 to the post of surgeon and physician general of the provincial militia. Around 1801 he was appointed assistant surgeon to the garrison, a position he held for 15 years. His military obligations, however, left some room for civilian activities. From 1799 he was health officer, with salary, "in and for the Port or Place" of Halifax. His primary task in this capacity was to prevent the spread of contagious diseases; in particular, he was responsible for the inspection of incoming ships and decisions concerning quarantine.

Little is known about Gschwind's life during the following two decades. In 1818 his appointment as health officer was renewed. Instead of a salary, however, he obtained only the promise of compensation through the House of Assembly for services rendered. This arrangement proved to be an unfortunate one. The job itself was unpleasant and hazardous enough for the ageing Gschwind, who had to row out to arriving ships in any kind of weather and expose himself to possible typhus or smallpox infection. Under the new terms of his appointment, he had to advance his own money for expenses such as boat-hire and fumigating materials, and the legislature proved slow in compensating him for his efforts. The numerous petitions he addressed to the house in order to seek his just reward testify to his frustrations. He held out, however, until 1825, when infirmity forced him to tender his resignation.

Gschwind's performance as a military surgeon may have been ordinary, but his career as a health officer – like the career of another Halifax physician, Matthias Francis Hoffmann* – shows the hesitant involvement of government in a sphere then mostly regarded as a private concern. The unsatisfactory nature of this involvement is clearly seen in the difficulties Gschwind experienced. Yet, living up to his physician's ethos, he clearly did the best he could under the circumstances. The esteem in which his fellow citizens held him is evidenced by the fact that when he died in 1827 it was the bishop's chaplain, the Reverend Edward Wix*, who delivered the funeral sermon. Gschwind was buried in St Paul's cemetery.

U. SAUTTER

PANS, RG 1, 171: 51, 71; 172: 47; 173: 414–15; 232: 29; RG 5, O, 41; P, 80; RG 20A, 43; RG 32, 135. PRO, WO 17/1516: 2v. St Paul's Anglican Church (Halifax), Reg. of burials, 1816–1954: 63 (mfm. at PANS). *Acadian Recorder*, 3 June 1815, 8 Sept. 1827. *Novascotian, or Colonial Herald*, 6 Sept. 1827. *Hessische Truppen im Amerikanischen Unabhängigkeitskrieg (HETRINA): Index nach Familiennamen*, comp. E. G. Franz et al. (5v., Marburg, Federal Republic of Germany, 1972–76), 4. *Loyalists in N.S.* (Gilroy). D. A. Campbell, *Pioneers of medicine in Nova Scotia* (Halifax, 1905). Max von Eelking, *Die deutschen Hülfstruppen im Nordamerikanischen Befreiungskriege, 1776 bis 1783* (2v., Hanover, [Federal Republic of Germany], 1863); also available in an abridged translation, *The German allied troops in the North American War of Independence, 1776–1783*, trans. and ed. J. G. Rosengarten (1v., Albany, N.Y., 1893). Ernst Kipping, *Die Truppen von Hessen-Kassel im Amerikanischen Unabhängigkeitskrieg, 1776–1783* (Darmstadt, Federal Republic of Germany, [1965]). E. J. Lowell, *The Hessians and the other German auxiliaries of Great Britain in the revolutionary war* (New York, 1884; repr. Port Washington, N.Y., 1965). M. H. L. Grant, "Historical sketches of hospitals and alms houses in Halifax, Nova Scotia, 1749–1859," *Nova Scotia Medical Bull.* (Halifax), 17 (1938): 294–304, 491–512.

GUEGUEN (Goguen), JOSEPH, servant, secretary, interpreter, translator, merchant, and JP; b. 2 May 1741 in Morlaix, France, son of Jacques Gueguen and Anne Hamonez; d. 28 Feb. 1825 in Cocagne, N.B.

Late in April 1753 Joseph Gueguen sailed for Acadia with Abbé Jean-Louis Le Loutre*. He became servant and secretary to his own maternal half-brother Jean Manach*, a missionary priest who also came from Morlaix. Accompanying Manach on his pastoral visits, Gueguen learned the Micmac language. He also had the opportunity to meet many Indian chiefs, colonial administrators, merchants, fur traders, and Acadian farmers.

At the time of the deportation in 1755 [*see* Charles Lawrence*], Gueguen went to Île Saint-Jean (Prince Edward Island) to escape the British. After a brief stay he boarded a schooner for Quebec. He reportedly entered the Petit Séminaire and studied there until 1758. In the summer of that year he returned to Acadia, joining Manach, the family of François Arsenault (his future father-in-law), and other Acadian friends at Baie des Ouines (Bay du Vin, N.B.). In July, after the fall of Louisbourg, Île Royale (Cape Breton Island), and Île Saint-Jean, the manhunt in Acadia began again with renewed vigour. Gueguen was among the 3,500 Acadian refugees who gathered in the Miramichi region and who endured famine and harsh living conditions.

In June 1759 vicar general Pierre Maillard* visited Manach at Miramichi and suggested to him and to the Acadians and Micmacs that they submit to the British. Consequently, at the end of January 1760 Gueguen and a good many Acadians went to Fort Cumberland (near Sackville, N.B.) and signed articles of submission. They were promptly imprisoned. As he was well thought of by the authorities and could speak English, French, and Micmac, Gueguen was made translator and interpreter; he was also put in charge of distributing rations to the prisoners in the fort. At the same time, in the absence of missionaries he carried out various priestly functions. In September he married Anne (Nanon) Arsenault; they were to have six children.

In 1765 Gueguen, who was still being held prisoner, refused to take the oath of allegiance to the crown. In the autumn, like many Acadians, he went to settle on the French islands of Saint-Pierre and Miquelon. But in the summer of 1767 the French government expelled the Acadians from its territory [*see* François-Gabriel d'Angeac*]. Gueguen bought a schooner with his father-in-law and sailed for Halifax, where he landed in October. He received official permission to settle at Cocagne, which he reached the following month.

Gueguen then opened a fur-trading establishment, and until the end of the 1770s he was the only Acadian to carry on this activity on such a large scale. He owned a store, warehouse, barn, and several other buildings, as well as a schooner with which he carried on trade and fished for cod. He also had a small wharf and 472 acres granted him in 1772. In the period from 1770 to 1790 Gueguen was, it seems, the most prosperous trader in Acadia. In 1818 he stated that the Micmacs still owed him £5,709 for goods he had supplied in the period before 1800.

Gueguen, whose wife had died in 1768, leaving him with four young children to look after, married a widow, Marie Quessy, and they had three children. After much bickering, however, she left Gueguen and her children and never came back. In a statement made before a justice of the peace she bluntly declared that she had often thought of murdering her husband. Gueguen tried to obtain a divorce, vainly approaching Bishop Jean-François Hubert* of Quebec in 1795 and 1796.

When the American revolution broke out Gueguen made a show of benevolent neutrality towards the rebels. It was probably on his farm that in September 1776 the rebel leader John Allan* met with the chiefs of the Nova Scotia Micmacs, and he himself acted as interpreter on that occasion. He advised the chiefs to remain neutral, however, and not take up arms against the British government. They heeded his advice. Gueguen's adoption of a definite position was not to the liking of the American rebels, and in the summer of 1778 they stole goods, money, and a schooner from him in reprisal.

Like Otho ROBICHAUX and Alexis Landry*, Gueguen was one of a council of elders that constituted a sort of parallel government in the years from 1784 to 1810. This council tried more or less successfully to resist oppression and sought to defend the interests of the Acadian farmers. Being an educated man, Gueguen was often consulted and was led to share in its work. In 1794 he became a justice of the peace, and he also acted as a surveyor, notary, and replacement for the priest. Some of the missionaries accused him of possessing dangerous books and hence giving insidious advice to people. Gueguen did have an impressive library, which he had in large part inherited from Manach. He also owned some linguistic works by Maillard of which he made use in preparing manuscripts in French and Micmac.

A year after Marie Quessy's death in 1807, Gueguen married a widow, Nanette Surette, at Cocagne, and they had four children. On 28 Feb. 1825 the "Sieur Joseph Gueguen, Esq.," "scholar" and "Doctor," passed away. By that time he was the last of the group that had founded Cocagne.

RÉGIS BRUN

AAQ, 210A, II: 277–80, 304–7; III: 142–44, 154–55, 166–69; 311 CN, V: 3, 5–6, 8a, 9, 11, 15, 29, 33; 312 CN, V: 2, 51. Centre d'études acadiennes, univ. de Moncton (Moncton, N.-B.), Fonds Macdonald–Stewart; Fonds Placide Gaudet, 1.55-3, 1.56-11. PAC, MG 11, [CO 42] Q, 71; MG 23, D1, ser.1, 13: 585–87, 611–15. PANB, RG 2, RS8, appointments and commissions; RG 10, RS108; RG 18, RS153. PANS, RG 1, 364, no.96; RG 20. UNBL, MG H2; MG H54. J. C. Pilling, *Bibliography of the Algonquian languages* (Washington, 1891). Régis Brun, *Pionnier de la nouvelle Acadie, Joseph Gueguen, 1741–1825* (Moncton, 1984). D.-F. Léger, *L'histoire de la paroisse St. Pierre de Cocagne, diocèse de St. Jean, N.-B.* (Moncton, 1920). Paul Surette, *Memramkouke, Petcoudiac et la reconstruction de l'Acadie, 1763–1806 . . .* (Moncton, 1981). J. C. Webster, *The forts of Chignecto: a study of the eighteenth century conflict between France and Great Britain in Acadia* ([Shediac, N.B.], 1930). Albert David, "L'apôtre des Micmacs," *Rev. de l'univ. d'Ottawa*, 5 (1935): 49–82, 425–52; 6 (1936): 22–40.

GUEROUT, PIERRE (baptized **Pierre-Guillaume**, but he rarely signed that way), businessman, JP, politician, office holder, and militia officer; b. 31 Aug. 1751 in the parish of Mille Ville, diocese of Rouen, France, son of Jacques Guerout and Judith Lévesque; d. 18 June 1830 at Saint-Denis, on the Richelieu, Lower Canada, and was buried 23 June 1830 at William Henry (Sorel).

Pierre Guerout was born into a Huguenot merchant family. He emigrated to Quebec about 1767 and apprenticed under his uncle François Lévesque* in the latter's business there. Presumably any formal education he may have received was completed in France, and any further training would have been under his uncle's supervision; clearly he was literate, but he may never have become bilingual. He volunteered for military service in 1775 in the same company as Pierre Marcoux* and the merchant Louis Marchand, and he saw action along with Jacques-Nicolas Perrault*, with whom he became close friends, when the Americans attacked Quebec on 30 December [see Benedict Arnold*; Richard Montgomery*]. After the demobilization of his regiment Guerout started his own business at Quebec. On 10 May 1779 he married 17-year-old Marie-Anne-Magdeleine Mayer, daughter of Quebec merchant Jean Mayer, and even though she was Roman Catholic, the ceremony was performed by David-François de Montmollin*, a Church of England clergyman.

By September 1783 Guerout had sold his property at Quebec and moved to Saint-Antoine-sur-Richelieu, where his appointment in April 1785 as a justice of the peace indicates that he quickly attained local prominence. The death in January 1787 of Lévesque, who, Guerout wrote to Perrault, "acted as my father for 20 years and proved his goodness to me on all occasions," was apparently the latest in a series of misfortunes which included the loss of an infant son, and the beginnings of which may have induced Guerout to leave Quebec. He requested Perrault to look into obtaining for him Lévesque's position as legislative councillor, but nothing came of the effort.

After Guerout moved across the Rivière Richelieu to Saint-Denis in 1787, misfortune continued to pursue him; two infant daughters died that year, and the death of his wife followed in early 1790. However, he rapidly became a prominent merchant, and one of the largest dealers in general goods in the Saint-Denis region, aided no doubt by contacts with the Quebec mercantile community; in 1790, for example, he was executor of the estate of a merchant of Saint-Antoine-sur-Richelieu along with Quebec businessmen Louis Marchand and Mathew Lymburner. Later, Guerout was given a power of attorney by Lymburner to collect a debt due to him by two residents of Saint-Marc. In 1790 he was a member of the Agriculture Society in the district of Montreal.

It was probably Guerout's local prominence that got him returned to the House of Assembly for Richelieu County in 1792 during the first elections held in Lower Canada. He attended only the first session; health or business considerations may account for his absence during the three succeeding sessions. He participated on committees and voted intermittently, in 1792 supporting the candidate of the Canadian members for the speakership, Jean-Antoine Panet*. On 13 May 1793 he married 24-year-old Josephte Maria Woolsey, a Roman Catholic, in the Presbyterian Scotch Church at Quebec. Her brother John William* was a merchant, and she was related to the merchant Louis Dunière* and to Pierre-Louis Panet*, both of whom were members of the assembly. Guerout may not have run for election again in 1796 and 1800; in 1804 he was defeated. By that time he was clearly supporting the Canadian party, and Louis Marchand wrote to one of its successful candidates, Jacques Cartier* of Saint-Antoine-sur-Richelieu, that the defeat would deprive the group of a potentially useful member. Marchand nevertheless felt that it had spared Guerout the financial sacrifice that elected businessmen inevitably made through the neglect of their personal affairs, for which there was no compensation by salary.

In fact, Guerout's financial situation seems to have been solid. In the years 1809 to 1812 at least, he was a supplier of wheat to the Batiscan Iron Work Company

His land sales and purchases, loans, investments, and speculations increased over the 20 years from about 1805. He could not have participated in many of these ventures without substantial surplus capital; in 1805, for example, he promoted local construction by financing the operations of a master carpenter from Saint-Ours, Pierre Cormier. In 1817 he was a shareholder in the Bank of Montreal. Two years later he and three other men planned to construct a toll-bridge over the rapids of the Richelieu near Chambly. In 1821 he bequeathed at least £500 to each of his seven surviving children, and the following year he advanced £1,500 to a daughter and her husband.

Guerout's business success was paralleled by, or perhaps tied up with, an ever-improving social status. In 1802 he had been appointed lieutenant-colonel of the Chambly battalion of militia, and in 1812 he was given command of the 2nd Battalion of Kent militia, but it is unlikely that he saw action during the war with the United States. In 1812 as well he received a commission to administer the oath of allegiance, although he did not hold it for long. Five years later he was made a commissioner for the improvement of internal communications; since he and the two other commissioners had responsibility for the state of the roads and of navigation on the Richelieu between William Henry and Chambly, Guerout had a strong voice in determining local economic development. Finally, in 1821 he was named a commissioner for the summary trial of small causes in Saint-Denis. Meanwhile family ties with the colonial élite were solidified by the marriages of two daughters, Julie in 1815 to Henry LeMesurier*, formerly deputy assistant commissary general, and Sophie in 1818 to Antoine-Narcisse Juchereau Duchesnay, son of ANTOINE-LOUIS, seigneur and executive councillor. Although all Guerout's children had been baptized Roman Catholics, both marriages were performed by Anglican clergymen; one other daughter and two sons became Anglicans, one of the sons, Narcisse, eventually being ordained a clergyman. One daughter remained Roman Catholic. Religion, therefore, does not seem to have presented a problem to Guerout and his family; Pierre held to his Protestantism, Josephte Maria to her Catholicism, and the children ultimately decided for themselves.

By the mid 1820s Guerout's health was in decline, and he does not seem to have conducted business after 1826. In the fall of 1827 an apoplectic attack destroyed his mental faculties and the following January his son Louis, who succeeded to the administration of his business, had him interdicted. At the time of his death Guerout was a substantial property holder with lands in Saint-Denis, Saint-Ours, Saint-Hyacinthe, La Présentation, Saint-Jude, and Saint-Césaire. It took 25 years of litigation to sort out the ownership of his properties and other legacies.

In his own lifetime Pierre Guerout had managed to capitalize on good business and political connections at Quebec to make himself a prominent, wealthy member of the Richelieu valley élite; he then extended his strong social and business links in the area back to the mercantile and political circles at Quebec and Montreal. In many ways he is representative of regionally important merchants and politicians, a relatively neglected yet significant historical group.

ALAN DEVER

AD, Seine-Maritime (Rouen), État civil, 31 août 1751. ANQ-M, CE3-1, 23 juin 1830; CN2-11, 1805–29; CN2-27, 1798–1812. ANQ-Q, CE1-61, 10 mai 1779; CE1-66, 13 mai 1793. AUM, P 58, U, Guerout à Perrault, 27 janv. 1784, 29 janv. 1787, 5 nov. 1792. McGill Univ. Libraries, MS coll., CH100.S118, CH308.S268, CH341.S301, CH344.S304, CH356.S1316, CH378.S338, CH379.S339–41, CH389.S353, CH395.OLS, CH423.OLS. PAC, MG 30, D1, 14; RG 68, General index, 1651–1841: 197, 282, 323, 327, 330, 334, 339, 350, 353, 357. L.C., House of Assembly, *Journals*, 1792–96. *Quebec Gazette*, 14 Jan. 1779; 8 Feb. 1781; 14, 28 Aug. 1783; 12 May 1785; 29 June 1786; 29 April 1790; 14 July 1791; 27 April 1797; 27 April, 12 Oct. 1809; 12 July 1812; 5 June, 3 July, 18 Sept. 1817; 6 July 1818; 19 Aug. 1819; 18 May, 31 Aug., 21 Dec. 1820; 22 Feb., 26 March, 9 April, 5, 9 July, 25 Oct. 1821; 13, 27 June, 15 Aug., 26 Sept. 1822; 16 Jan., 20 March, 1 May, 30 June 1823. "La milice canadienne-française à Québec en 1775," *BRH*, 11 (1905): 268. *Quebec almanac*, 1791: 82. J.-B.-A. Allaire, *Histoire de la paroisse de Saint-Denis-sur-Richelieu (Canada)* (Saint-Hyacinthe, Qué., 1905), 211. F.-J. Audet et Fabre Surveyer, *Les députés au premier parl. du Bas-Canada*, 258–73. Denison, *Canada's first bank*, 1: 104. Marthe Faribault-Beauregard, "Famille Guerout," SGCF *Mémoires*, 8 (1957): 97–105; "L'honorable François Lévesque, son neveu Pierre Guérout, et leurs descendants," SGCF *Mémoires*, 8: 13–30. Hare, "L'Assemblée législative du Bas-Canada," *RHAF*, 27: 372–73. J.-J. Lefebvre, "François Levêque (1732–1787), membre des Conseils législatif et exécutif," *BRH*, 59 (1953): 143–45. P.-A. Sévigny, "Le commerce du blé et la navigation dans le Bas-Richelieu avant 1849," *RHAF*, 38 (1984–85): 5–21.

H

HALE, ELIZABETH FRANCES. *See* AMHERST

HALIBURTON, WILLIAM HERSEY OTIS, lawyer, office holder, militia officer, politician, and judge; b. 3 Sept. 1767 in Windsor, N.S., son of William Haliburton and Susanna (Lusanna) Otis; m first 1794 Lucy Chandler Grant in Westmorland County, N.B., and they had one child, Thomas Chandler*; m. secondly 1803 Susanna Davis, *née* Francklin, daughter of Michael Francklin*, in Windsor; they had no children; d. there 7 July 1829, "after a most painful illness."

William and Susanna Haliburton, first cousins, were pre-loyalists who emigrated from Boston to Newport Township, N.S., in 1761 and settled on part of the 58,000 acres granted to a group including Edward Ellis, husband of William's stepmother. In comfortable circumstances, the Haliburtons brought with them two black servants and 18 months' provisions, but two years of pioneer farm life were hardship enough for them and in 1763 they moved to Windsor. There William studied and later practised law. Legend has it that the third of their ten children, William Hersey Otis, and his only child, Thomas Chandler, were born in the same house 20 miles apart, one of several explanations being that the original Haliburton house, built above the village of Avondale, was floated 20 miles down the Avon River to Windsor. But the story is evidently apocryphal since William Hersey Otis was not born until four years after the move to Windsor.

Of his early life little is known until he studied law in Halifax, apparently in the office of Jonathan Sterns. Returning to Windsor, he built up a comfortable law practice, acquired substantial holdings of land, and held such offices as clerk of the peace for Hants County in 1786, and second lieutenant, first lieutenant, and captain of militia in 1793, 1804, and 1820 respectively. From 1806 to 1824 he was a member of the House of Assembly, until 1811 for Windsor Township and afterwards for Hants County. If attendance at divisions is the criterion, he was the most faithful of all assemblymen over those 18 years.

Beamish Murdoch* was to single out Haliburton, Thomas Ritchie*, Simon Bradstreet Robie*, and Samuel George William Archibald* as natives of the province "working their way to distinction" by "dint of their own exertions" and exhibiting "statesmanlike ideas, a power of subtle reasoning and much eloquence" in the assembly. A more questionable judgement is that of Victor Lovitt Oakes Chittick who, in his biography of Thomas Chandler Haliburton, concludes that there can be "no doubt of W. H. O. Haliburton's complete acceptance of Tory principles, or of his undeviating adherence to them. They are proclaimed in his every act and utterance of which we have record." Seeming to support this opinion was the action of Lieutenant Governor Lord Dalhousie [Ramsay*] in appointing Haliburton and Archibald as the province's pioneer king's counsel in 1817 and passing over the more prestigious Robie – a move which, although described by Israel Longworth as "one of the unexplained mysteries" of the administration, was

clearly attributable to Dalhousie's dislike of Robie's seeming radicalism. Yet, if Chittick's picture serves his purpose in explaining the toryism of the son, it is nevertheless an outrageous caricature of the father drawn from a misinterpretation of scanty references in the assembly *Journal* and Murdoch's *History of Nova Scotia*. These materials, together with limited reports of the debates in the *Acadian Recorder* (Halifax) and the *Halifax Journal*, actually demonstrate that the father displayed the usual attitudes of the "country" assemblyman, though clearly better educated and more articulate, and that he was a highly pragmatic, common-sense person who, cautious and conservative in some respects, was highly enlightened and liberal in many others.

For Haliburton, a promoter of provincial development, the extension of common schools was "a favorite object," although in 1823 he rightly opposed their support by compulsory assessment as impracticable. He presented numerous bills to encourage the growing of bread-corn and the clearing of new lands; yet his intent was to assist not older farmers, who were "rich enough," but more recent settlers, as in 1818 when he proposed a bounty on bread-corn grown by them. He also advocated large outlays on roads and bridges, £50,000 in 1818, even if it meant that Government House, still in the course of construction, "stood still for a year or two – the making and repairing of roads and bridges were of much more consequence." More than once he showed his concern for the difficulties of ordinary Nova Scotians. He opposed the reform of the militia laws through consolidation of the regiments because it would "throw the burthen upon the poorer class of persons" by making it difficult for them to fulfil their obligations to drill. When property was being sacrificed at sheriffs' sales for want of money and complaints deluged the assembly, he proposed an issue of paper money by way of loan with adequate security.

Neither lieutenant governor nor Council nor the moneyed interests daunted him. When Lord Dalhousie's proposals for the militia seemed to be impolitic, he insisted that the representatives of the people not "flinch . . . from speaking their sentiments freely to his excellency." When Dalhousie wanted to put the main roads under the Council and the by-roads under the sessions and grand juries, he objected to the assembly giving up any of its hard-won prerogatives. When his fellow assemblymen suggested that the Council was certain to reject some proposal, he refused to anticipate what the other house might do and demanded that the assembly treat the matter as it thought proper. And when Halifax merchants sought to incorporate a bank, he frowned at their proposal to put a great deal of paper money into circulation and demanded that the bank be as useful to the public as to its stockholders.

Hall

Even Chittick admits that Haliburton's attitude towards marriage licences displayed nothing of toryism: in essence, his position was that dissenting ministers should have the power to solemnize marriage by licence, a monopoly then confined to ministers of the Church of England. Actually, Chittick measures Haliburton's "Tory devotion to the rights of property, the Church, and the King" by his resistance to debtor relief legislation, to support of a Presbyterian academy, and to the admission of a Catholic to the house without oath. Yet in 1823 Haliburton voted for the admission, first, of Catholic Laurence KAVANAGH and, later, of any Catholic without their taking the oaths against popery and transubstantiation. On Pictou Academy, he took the position that "we had not the means at present, of keeping up two Colleges in this country," but he was prepared to put the academy on the same footing as other academies, and he wanted elimination of the requirement that degree students at King's College subscribe to Anglican tenets [*see* William COCHRAN]. Admittedly, on the relief of insolvent debtors, he favoured the retention of a process "which took away body and goods" and, in view of the experience with relaxed legislation in Massachusetts, came out strongly for the creditor over the debtor. But even here he was reflecting prevailing attitudes rather than pronounced toryism.

Chittick also pictures Haliburton as growing more and more unpopular in an era in which a party of reform was increasingly challenging the Council's abuse of privilege. But he predates the appearance of such a party by more than a decade, and there is no evidence that Haliburton became unpopular until 1824. In that year all the lawyers in the assembly incurred popular disfavour by pressing successfully a measure which, though purportedly designed to improve the efficiency of the lower courts by introducing professional men to head them, had the effect of conferring "three easy chairs" on the "hungry profession." Haliburton denied that the lawyers were "capable of being biased in favor of their own interests," but he convinced no one, the more so as he was shortly made chief justice of the Inferior Court of Common Pleas and president or first justice of the Court of Quarter Sessions for the Middle Division (Lunenburg, Queens, Kings, and Hants counties), an office he held until his death five years later. Although he is not remembered for any particular case or decision, he enjoyed an excellent reputation both as lawyer and as judge.

For most of his legislative career Haliburton stood out, with three or four other members, as a leading participant in every significant debate. He differed markedly from his son, Thomas Chandler, who started out with much the same political stance as his father and became a thoroughgoing tory. In contrast, W. H. O. Haliburton, a conservative in some matters,

served for 18 successive years as a not illiberal, highly enlightened assemblyman.

J. MURRAY BECK

N.S., House of Assembly, *Journal and proc.*, 1806–24. *Acadian Recorder*, especially 1818–19. *Halifax Journal*, especially 1823–24. *Novascotian, or Colonial Herald*, 16 July 1829. "Descendants of William Haliburton and Lusanna (Otis) Haliburton," comp. R. L. Weis (mimeograph, Providence, R.I., 1962; copy at PANS). V. L. O. Chittick, *Thomas Chandler Haliburton ("Sam Slick"): a study in provincial toryism* (New York, 1924). [R. G. Haliburton], "A sketch of the life and times of Judge Haliburton," *Haliburton: a centenary chaplet* ... (Toronto, 1897), 13–40. Murdoch, *Hist. of N.S.*, vol.3.

HALL, GEORGE BENSON, naval officer, office holder, politician, JP, militia officer, and merchant; b. 1780 in Ireland; m. 1 Feb. 1806 Angelica Fortier in Amherstburg, Upper Canada, and they had four sons, including George Benson*, and one daughter; d. there 9 Jan. 1821.

During the French revolutionary wars George Benson Hall served in the Royal Navy for four years as a midshipman and occasionally as a master's mate. Following the Treaty of Amiens in 1802 he left the navy and signed on a merchant ship as chief mate. A voyage that year to Quebec ended abruptly when the vessel became stranded in the St Lawrence. In December 1802 he accepted an offer from the assistant quartermaster general, Captain William Robe, to serve as mate on the government yacht *Toronto* in Lake Ontario. A vacancy was created in April 1804 in the Provincial Marine by the death of an officer, and Hall became a lieutenant in command of the brig *General Hunter*, on Lake Erie. In October 1806, following another death, he was placed in command of the scow *Camden*, and by 1811 he was captain of the *Queen Charlotte*.

The Provincial Marine, which was administered by the quartermaster general's department, was intended to provide transportation for troops in both war and peace. As time passed, increasing attention was paid to its being used as a fighting force. The *Queen Charlotte* was thus constructed in 1809 with the intention of its being armed with guns and carronades in case of war. In peace-time, however, the vessels provided transportation for goods, including commercial cargo, on the Upper Lakes. This duty provided Hall with an opportunity to establish links with local merchants, especially John Askin* and his family. While Hall provided a vital service for the merchants, they in turn were occasionally able to provide him with needed supplies.

Prior to 1812 Hall gradually became a respected resident of Amherstburg. He acquired property in town, including a storehouse which was used by the

Provincial Marine. In February 1812 he also obtained six lots, or 1,200 acres, in Colchester (Colchester North and Colchester South) and Aldborough townships. His future thus seemed secure, particularly since he was regarded as the most efficient officer in the Provincial Marine on Lake Erie and perhaps in the entire branch.

That year Major-General Isaac Brock*, anticipating the outbreak of war, ordered the removal of Alexander Grant* as commodore of lakes Erie, Huron, and Michigan, and Hall was appointed in March in his stead. It was typical of the Provincial Marine, however, that when war broke out in July the *Queen Charlotte* was carrying commercial cargo, including a quantity of heavy-duty cloth for a merchant in Philadelphia. As commodore, Hall had to oversee the preparation of his vessels for military action. This included the positioning of guns and carronades on board the various vessels, as well as the integration of the newly arrived members of the Royal Newfoundland Regiment and the 41st Foot into the crews.

Hall's first major engagement came in August 1812 at the attack on Detroit when he was placed by Brock in charge of the batteries. Brock was satisfied with his conduct and he was awarded a medal for his service at Detroit after his death. Following the town's surrender, the Provincial Marine helped to transport the British troops to the Niagara frontier and to provide support for them. With the advent of winter Hall was authorized to go to Quebec to arrange for the sending of seamen, skilled carpenters, and essential supplies for both Lake Erie and Lake Ontario.

Because of his absence in Quebec, Hall did not take part in the engagement at Frenchtown (Monroe, Mich.) on 22 Jan. 1813. He was, however, in command of the Provincial Marine during the attack on Fort Meigs (near Perrysburg), Ohio, in May 1813, when again his performance received official approval. Even after experienced officers of the Royal Navy arrived and Lieutenant Robert Heriot Barclay* was given control of Lake Erie, Hall was confirmed in his command of the *Queen Charlotte* by Sir James Lucas Yeo*, commander of naval forces on the lakes. It would have been more satisfactory if the military had found some administrative position for Hall, because as soon as Barclay reached Lake Erie he used his position to take command of the *Queen Charlotte* on 9 July. Without any official position, Hall contented himself with waiting till the squadron was absent to go down to supervise the dockyard. Before Barclay would find a position for Hall, he insisted that the latter acknowledge that he would rank below all the officers of the Royal Navy. When Hall, who was as conscious of status as Barclay, insisted on being recognized as a junior commander, he was dismissed from the Provincial Marine on 15 August. He did not have sufficient influence to have his dismissal reversed, but he was promptly appointed superintendent of the dockyard and naval stores at Amherstburg with the same pay and allowances he had received as commodore. In addition, Barclay was given a pointed notice by Captain Noah Freer, the military secretary, that he had no authority to annul any appointment made by Governor Sir George Prevost*'s warrant.

Hall carried out his duties until the autumn when he and his family were forced to retreat from Amherstburg with the British forces [*see* Henry PROCTER]. With others from the Amherstburg dockyard, Hall arrived in Kingston in late October and was offered his choice of three positions. As he was still on full salary, he preferred to go to Quebec, where he probably expected that patrons such as Freer would find him an important post. He was indeed appointed on 24 Dec. 1813 as naval storekeeper at Montreal. However, he decided that "with the limited assistance that was to be afforded to him" he would not be able to carry out his duties properly and the appointment was cancelled on 24 Jan. 1814.

Without position or substantial income, Hall was in a critical financial state. His principal sources of revenue were a half-pay allowance, granted on 1 Oct. 1814, and prize money, awarded in 1815 for the capture of goods and vessels in 1812. Following the end of hostilities Hall returned to Amherstburg, where he quickly became the complete representative of the local élite. By using his pre-war connections, in 1816 he was elected to the House of Assembly as one of two members for Essex County. The same year he was appointed a magistrate, and on 21 Sept. 1818 he was commissioned major in the 1st Regiment of Essex militia. As an MHA until 1820, he devoted much of his time to local issues, including an attempt to move the county seat from Sandwich (Windsor) to Amherstburg. In Amherstburg he busied himself with trying to obtain the services of an Anglican minister and to have land titles confirmed for the occupants of town lots. Relying on his experiences as a naval storekeeper, he traded in hardware, and also supplied bricks and stone. But despite his political connections, Hall's financial position remained poor. In 1821, following his death, his widow was granted £25 per annum by the Treasury, but she remained in financial difficulty for the remainder of her life.

K. G. PRYKE

AO, Hiram Walker Hist. Museum coll., 20–107. PAC, RG 1, L3, 226A: H10/36; 228: H11/66; 252: H misc., 1797–1820/72; RG 8, I (C ser.), 76, 86, 678–79, 688A, 725, 729–31, 1202, 1220, 1224, 1726; RG 19, E5(a), 3728, claim 242. *John Askin papers* (Quaife). "List of vessels employed on British naval service on the Great Lakes, 1755–1875," comp. K. R. Macpherson, *OH*, 55 (1963): 173–79. W. A. B. Douglas, "The anatomy of naval incom-

Hamond

petence: the Provincial Marine in defence of Upper Canada before 1813," *OH*, 71 (1979): 3–25. C. P. Stacey, "The ships of the British squadron on Lake Ontario, 1812–14," *CHR*, 34 (1953): 311–23.

HAMOND, Sir ANDREW SNAPE, naval officer and colonial administrator; b. 17 Dec. 1738 in Blackheath (London), England, only son of Robert Hamond and Susannah Snape; m. first April 1763 Cecilia Sutherland; m. secondly 7 March 1779 Anne Graeme, and they had two children; d. 12 Sept. 1828 in Terrington Clement, England.

Andrew Snape Hamond entered the Royal Navy in 1753 and served during the Seven Years' War. Promoted post captain in 1770, he was present at most of the important naval actions of the American Revolutionary War up to 1780; in 1779 he was told "that scarce a dispatch had arrived from the active part of the War, that did not make mention of some creditable exploit in which [he] had been engaged against the Enemy." While in England in 1780 he was offered and accepted the posts of resident commissioner of the naval dockyard at Halifax and lieutenant governor of Nova Scotia, replacing Sir Richard Hughes*. Two years later he would be appointed to the naval command in the province as well.

Hamond and his family arrived in Halifax during the night of 29–30 July 1781; he was sworn into office on the 31st. That the highest priority of his administration would be defence was demonstrated on 29 August, when two American privateers raided Annapolis Royal [*see* John Ritchie*]. A more serious assault took place the next year by a squadron of privateers on Lunenburg [*see* John Creighton*]. When news of the second attack reached Halifax, Hamond sent a force to pursue the raiders. As commander-in-chief, he inspected the Halifax County militia in the autumn of 1781 and the outlying county militias the following spring. Apart from defensive measures, Hamond was most concerned to guarantee the supply of masts from the Saint John valley (N.B.) [*see* William Davidson*]. In this effort he was successful: the Indians of the region remained at peace.

The naval hospital at Halifax was in a bad state when Hamond arrived, and he soon "found it absolutely necessary to prepare for building an Hospital in the Spring." Tenders were called for in December 1781, and the new facility, which cost almost £8,000 and could accommodate 200 patients, was ready by the end of 1782. Its first physician was the Rhode Island loyalist John Halliburton.

Hamond's tenure as lieutenant governor coincided with the beginning of the loyalist migration from the American colonies, and a proposal for settling the Port Roseway (Shelburne) area was made to him in August 1782. Hamond approved the plan and promised his support, although he discouraged loyalists from trying

to come before the spring. Then he received unexpected news. On 8 July 1782 the home secretary had written to Hamond informing him that John Parr* had been appointed to succeed Francis Legge* as governor of Nova Scotia. Hamond was surprised and embittered, having accepted the office of lieutenant governor "on the strongest assurances of succeeding to the Government." Parr arrived when Hamond was absent and promptly moved into the governor's house, thus getting relations between the two men off to a bad start. Hamond quickly realized that the province could not contain both of them, and he resigned on 8 October. The pretext for Hamond's supersession was that the office of governor was incompatible with the duties for which he was so well qualified in time of war. The real reason, however, was that Parr's influence was stronger than Hamond's; in the new ministry in London Parr's patron, Lord Shelburne, was first home secretary and then prime minister.

The news of Hamond's resignation was greeted with surprise and genuine regret in the province. Five counties presented him with "addresses of approbation," and the Council voted him a grant of 10,000 acres at the mouth of the Kennebecasis River (N.B.). Hamond remained in Nova Scotia performing his naval duties until January 1783. After his return to England that year, he was awarded a baronetcy in consolation. In 1785 he became commander-in-chief on the Medway and at the Nore, and in 1793 a commissioner of the navy. By August 1794 he had become controller of the navy, and although he held this arduous and thankless job for 12 years, he was not really a success. Member of parliament for Ipswich between 1796 and 1806, he resigned on the death of William Pitt, whom he had supported. He was also an elder brother of Trinity House and a fellow of the Royal Society.

The Hamond family name attached itself to two locations in the town and county of Halifax. A road begun by Hamond "from the foot of the Block house hill to the North Farm" eventually became known as Lady Hammond Road. Moreover, in 1786 some 9,000 acres between Birch Cove and the head of St Margarets Bay were granted to 45 proprietors, who voted to call the settlement Hamond Plains. These were tokens of the high esteem in which Andrew Snape Hamond and his consort were held by the society over which they had presided for so short a time.

J. B. CAHILL

[Sir Andrew Snape Hamond's papers form volumes I–IX of the Hamond papers in the Univ. of Va. Library, Tracy W. McGregor Library (Charlottesville). A microfilm copy is available at the PANS. Volume I consists of Hamond's autobiography, "Heads of the life of Sir Andrew Snape Hamond, bart., written merely for the private information of his own family; as the narrative will shew; being of little interest to the world at large" (2 books), an edited version of which appeared under the title "The autobiography of Captain Sir Andrew Snape Hamond, bart., R.N., 1738–1828, covering the years 1738–1793," ed. W. H. Moomaw (MA thesis, Univ. of Va., 1953). The autobiography is the principal source of information about the life and career of Hamond prior to 1793 (it was composed *c.* 1815); unfortunately, as is stated in *Guide to the naval papers of Sir Andrew Snape Hamond, bart., 1766–1783, and Sir Graham Eden Hamond, bart., 1799–1825*, ed. P. P. Hoffman *et al.* (Charlottesville, 1966), 13, "little of his tenure in Nova Scotia is mentioned." J.B.C.]

PRO, ADM 1/490: 61–135; CO 42/51; CO 217/55: 197; 217/56: 40. *Gentleman's Magazine*, July–December 1828: 568–69. *DNB*.

HANDS. *See* AINSE

HART, MARMADUKE, merchant and shipowner; b. *c.* 1754, probably in England; in 1779 he and Hannah Tucker of St John's had an illegitimate son; m. January 1783 in St John's Susanna Winter, daughter of James Winter, a merchant of the town, and they had one son and one daughter; d. 3 Nov. 1829 in Mecklenburgh Square, London.

Marmaduke Hart may well have been of Devon or Dorset origin. He immigrated to Newfoundland in 1777 as an employee of James Winter, a resident merchant of modest trade. Through previous employment with Michael Gill of New England (and from 1748 of St John's), Winter had excellent connections in New England and Bermuda. By 1783 Hart was a full partner and continued in relative prosperity until 1789 when, by entering into partnership with William Isham Eppes, he took the step which made his fortune and eventually led to the creation of one of Newfoundland's largest mercantile firms, Hart and Eppes. Over the years, it underwent several name changes to reflect adjustments in the partnership.

Hart and Eppes was formed at an opportune time. St John's was growing in importance to the economy of Newfoundland, and the outport merchants, especially those in the West Indies trade, were finding it increasingly expedient to do some of their business through St John's rather than directly with foreign suppliers and markets. Until the American revolution, these merchants had sent to New England traders a grade of fish known as "west india fish" in exchange for rum, sugar, and molasses, products they used in turn along with fish in their trade, in their own ships, with European sources and outlets. The revolution, by placing the United States outside the British navigation system, broke this relationship and created a trading void which was gradually filled by resident merchants in St John's, and even more by the shipowners and traders of Bermuda who rapidly became prosperous as middle men in the Newfoundland–West Indies trade.

From the outset, Hart and Eppes acted as intermediaries between merchants in the West Indies and in the Newfoundland outports. However, the lucrative prospects soon led them into direct mercantile concerns, and by 1793 they owned two vessels and plied constantly between Newfoundland and Europe, operating out of Poole, Dorset. By the following year the company was collecting fish from planters on its own account, but its dealings were largely with other merchants rather than directly with fishermen. In this situation, the partners made themselves indispensable to many outport planters – especially those from Poole – not only through their Caribbean connections but also by acting as attorneys and spokesmen before the Newfoundland Supreme Court and the governors, and generally as sources of intelligence and means of communication.

By 1794 Hart had prospered sufficiently to allow him to spend most of his winters in England; until 1806 he leased substantial houses in Devon. During the summers, however, he resided in Newfoundland, except for a year or two when he nominally commanded one of the company's vessels engaged in the European trade. In 1797 Hart and Eppes received another windfall when they were contracted to supply the naval squadron with fresh provisions. The firm thus flourished in the war years when many of the Newfoundland merchants, primarily engaged in exporting fish to Europe, found themselves in grave difficulties. George Gaden of St John's, son of a Poole family which had been in the Newfoundland trade since the 1750s, became a partner in 1805. The union proved successful, the firm continued to prosper, and in 1808 Hart purchased a house and mercantile premises in London. At the end of the fishing season that year, he left the island permanently to establish himself as the senior partner in the new English house. About that time, John Bingley Garland, son of the prominent Poole merchant George Garland, was taken into the firm as an apprentice in London while his cousin, George Richard Robinson, was sent to direct affairs in St John's. In 1810 Robinson became a full partner.

Hart was able to exercise both political and commercial influence from London. The company's trade, especially to Europe, expanded greatly and, as one of the most prominent Newfoundland merchants, Hart increasingly served as spokesman for the interests of the whole industry. In 1811 he was appointed to act as "agent for the Trade of Newfoundland" and dealt with the British government on political and military issues of concern to the island and the fishery. In December of that year the composition of the firm again changed. George Gaden's widow was bought out. Eppes retired from active participation and Garland, deciding that he did not like his prospects, also gave up his ties. The company now consisted only

Hartshorne

of Hart and Robinson, although another promising young Devon man, Thomas Holdsworth Brooking*, joined the business to learn the Newfoundland side from Robinson. Garland returned as full partner in the 1820s.

The closing years of the Napoleonic Wars had been ones of great prosperity in the Newfoundland trade, and Hart and Robinson shared fully in the expansion. By 1815 the firm was among the largest in the Newfoundland trade and took on as apprentices many young members of old mercantile families such as the Gadens, Winters, and Scotts, who eventually would flourish in competition with Hart and Robinson.

In 1816 Robinson joined Hart in the London office. Under Brooking's management the company not only survived the devastating post-war slump which ruined many merchants but prospered. For example, between July and December of 1818, it acted as consignee for the import cargoes of 23 vessels, and exported fish and other produce in 29 more. Its network embraced almost every conceivable port of call in the Newfoundland trade, the inward cargoes coming from the United Kingdom, Europe, the Caribbean, and British North America.

In 1822 Hart retired from the business, which now became Robinson, Brooking and Company. He continued to take a paternal interest in Newfoundland, especially concerning himself with the formation and development of the Newfoundland School Society [see Samuel Codner*]. By now, the man who had started with nothing but a little education and some family connections had succeeded as far as a Newfoundland merchant could, short of acquiring a knighthood or a seat in parliament. The knighthood eluded him, although there is no evidence that he sought one. Nor did Hart emulate many other prosperous merchants by purchasing a country estate in the United Kingdom. His daughter Susannah had maintained the ties with England and Newfoundland. In 1807 she married Charles Augustus Tulk, a reform-minded politician who sat for Sudbury from 1820 to 1826 and the Newfoundland-connected constituency of Poole from 1835 to 1837.

Hart died in 1829 and for once an obituary, in the *Public Ledger*, amply summed up a career: "The integrity of his principles – his unremitted industry and punctuality, directed by his experienced judgement and discretion in all affairs of business – procured and secured to him, through life the confidence of an extensive circle of respectable and valuable correspondents: and, amidst the vicissitudes of a trade so fluctuating as one founded in the fisheries, these valuable qualities honourably raised him, from small beginnings to wealth and independency." Hart's main contribution to Newfoundland lay in the complex mercantile trade he created, and in the education and training of many younger men whose careers are

better known. Even more, perhaps, his life was an example of how a rather poor young man could attain wealth and social esteem in the English-speaking world of the early 19th century.

KEITH MATTHEWS

Most of the information on which this biography is based was drawn from the Gaden, Hart, and Robinson name files and other copies of records relating to the trade and fisheries of Newfoundland available at the Maritime Hist. Arch., Memorial Univ. of Nfld. (St John's).

Cathedral of St John the Baptist (Anglican) (St John's), Reg. of baptisms, marriages, and burials, 1779, 1783–84 (mfm. at PANL). Centre for Nfld. Studies, Memorial Univ. of Nfld. Library, "D'Alberti papers" (transcripts of corr. between the Colonial Office and the governor's office of Newfoundland, 1780–1825, from various PRO, CO files), comp. Amalia and Leonora D'Alberti (34v., typescript). Dorset Record Office (Dorchester, Eng.), D365, F2–10; F21, January 1808. Hunt, Roope & Co. (London), Robert Newman & Co., letter-books. Nfld. Public Library Services, Provincial Reference and Resource Library (St John's), Philip Saunders and Pierce Sweetman, letter-book (copy at PANL). PANL, GN 1/13/4, St John's, 1794–95; GN 2/2, 10 Aug. 1811; GN 5/2/A/1; P7/A/6; P7/A/53, letter-book, 1792. PRO, ADM 1/476; ADM 7/141; ADM 50/111; BT 1/28; CO 194/68; CO 324/7. G.B., Parl., House of Commons paper, 1817, no.436, *Report from Select Committee on Newfoundland Trade*. . . . *Felix Farley's Bristol Journal* (Bristol, Eng.), 1791. *London Chronicle*, 1791. *Morning Chronicle* (London), January 1792. *Newfoundland Mercantile Journal*, 1818; 1 Dec. 1822. *Public Ledger*, 11 Dec. 1829; November 1831. *Royal Gazette and Newfoundland Advertiser*, 30 Nov. 1809, 31 May 1810, 26 Dec. 1811, 9 Jan. 1812. *DNB* (biog. of C. A. Tulk). *The register of shipping* (London), 1792–1826.

HARTSHORNE, LAWRENCE, businessman, office holder, JP, and politician; b. 1 July 1755 in Black Point, N.J., son of John Hartshorne and Lucy Saltar; m. first 20 Jan. 1780 Elizabeth Ustick in New York City; m. secondly 2 Sept. 1802 Abigail Tremain in Halifax; d. 10 March 1822 in Dartmouth, N.S.

Born into a leading Quaker family in the Sandy Hook area of New Jersey, Lawrence Hartshorne had a career which developed as a by-product of the American revolution. Immunized from revolutionary sympathies because of his religion, as well as by the proximity of British military forces, young Lawrence moved in 1777 to nearby New York City, where he entered trade. Three years later he advanced his career and also compromised his political neutrality by becoming the son-in-law of William Ustick, a hardware merchant who had earlier antagonized the New York Sons of Liberty by violating the colonial boycott of British manufactures. Family and business links with the loyalist and British military establishment, forged during the war, prompted Hartshorne to join the loyalist exodus from New York in 1783.

Having successfully drawn upon his association with such notables as Sir Guy Carleton* to obtain grants to several thousand acres of land in Nova Scotia, Hartshorne decided to establish himself in Halifax as a hardware dealer, in partnership with Thomas Boggs, also a refugee from New Jersey. During the 1780s, Hartshorne became active in the cause of agricultural improvement, both as treasurer of a pioneering agricultural society in 1789 and as proprietor of a model farm located on the outskirts of Dartmouth. Popular among his peers, Hartshorne made his initial entry into public affairs in 1791, when he acted as chief assistant to John Clarkson in the project designed to transport Nova Scotian black loyalists to Sierra Leone [see Thomas Peters*; David George*]. Hartshorne appears to have been motivated by a Quaker-inspired concern for blacks and by a belief that their advancement could best be achieved with a return to Africa.

Hartshorne's rise to prominence was accomplished during the tenure of John Wentworth*, lieutenant governor of Nova Scotia between 1792 and 1808. A fellow loyalist, Wentworth made Hartshorne one of the favoured recipients of official patronage, bestowing on him such offices as seats on the magisterial bench, the local street commission, and the poor house commission. Having the ear of the lieutenant governor probably helped Hartshorne win election in the House of Assembly for Halifax County in 1793. Then in 1801, after having been defeated in the controversial general election of 1799 by "reformers" under the leadership of William Cottnam TONGE, Hartshorne was named to the Council. The appointment confirmed that he had become a member of the inner circle of the oligarchy. Indeed, an anonymous critic of the Wentworth régime, denouncing Hartshorne as a "cedevant quaker ironmonger," claimed that he exercised an influence second only to that of Michael WALLACE.

Wentworth's patronage was not confined to the allocation of office. In response to prompting from the lieutenant governor, Hartshorne formed a partnership with yet another loyalist, Jonathan Tremain, and around 1792 or so built a combined grist-mill and bakehouse on the Dartmouth side of Halifax Harbour (the site being chosen because of the availability of water power). This enterprise, which represented an investment of between £6,000 and £7,000, long ranked as the largest manufactory in Nova Scotia. Its success was largely dependent on the securing of military contracts for flour, and here the partners received decisive assistance from Wentworth. In addition, Wentworth encouraged Hartshorne to become involved with projects designed to establish a bank in Halifax and build a canal linking the town with the Bay of Fundy [see Isaac Hildrith*]. Following the outbreak of war with France in 1793, Wentworth,

thanks to his contacts in the Home Department, helped the firm of Boggs and Hartshorne secure military contracts and also named them as provisioning agents for Nova Scotia's Indian population. In yet a further gesture, he gave Hartshorne and the partnership of William Forsyth* and William Smith an exclusive lease to mine coal deposits in mainland Nova Scotia. Apart from the flour-mill and the military contracts, these ventures proved abortive, but their existence underscored Hartshorne's membership in Wentworth's entourage. As a reciprocal gesture, Hartshorne loaned money to the frequently hard pressed Wentworth family.

The one major controversy in Hartshorne's public career came in 1804, when he resigned from the Council to protest the appointment to that body of John Butler BUTLER, a commissariat official and military contractor. Butler's supposed offence had been to claim precedence over Hartshorne in the Council, but it is more likely that Hartshorne could not tolerate the presence of someone who had earlier outmanœuvred him in bidding for lucrative military flour contracts. Wentworth attempted to restore Hartshorne to the Council in 1807 but the appointment was never ratified by London. The episode, however, did little damage to Hartshorne's prospects. Even after Wentworth's fall in 1808, he continued to receive official perquisites; for example, in 1812 he was named to the commission in charge of issuing provincial paper money.

Through the first decade of the 19th century, Hartshorne remained active as a hardware merchant and flour miller. It is hard to assess the relative value of his business activities because of a lack of evidence. But he did not monopolize either the local or the provincial flour trade, competition from American imports remaining a constant problem for the milling operation. He also became a founder of the association that developed into the Halifax Fire Insurance Company. Despite losses through escheat, Hartshorne continued to hold over 17,000 acres in what is now Guysborough County, which he made at least some attempt to settle. As well, he retained an interest in agricultural improvement and emerged after the War of 1812 as a supporter of John Young*.

Some time after 1800, Hartshorne moved from Halifax to Dartmouth to take up residence in a large three-storey wooden mansion known as Poplar Hill. There, with his second wife, daughter of Jonathan Tremain, his business partner, he presided over a family of three sons and six daughters from both marriages, along with a younger cousin, Robert Hartshorne, who had come from Virginia to work in the family business. Securing the prospects of the next generation became the major theme of the last phase of Hartshorne's career. One step in this direction consisted of having the children baptized (some as adults) in

Hébert

the Church of England. As well, the family acquired a pew at St Paul's, the Anglican church in Halifax. A series of marriages ensued, with three of the children emulating their father's example by marrying into the Tremain family. Of the three sons, John died early, Lawrence succeeded his father as partner of Thomas Boggs, and Hugh trained as a lawyer. The Hartshorne family remained prominent in the business, political, and social life of the Nova Scotian capital into the middle years of the 19th century, acquiring special notoriety for the lavish entertaining conducted at their Dartmouth estate. In this way, Lawrence Hartshorne contributed to the often exaggerated claim that the loyalists left a lasting imprint on the character of British North America.

D. A. SUTHERLAND

Halifax County Court of Probate (Halifax), Estate papers, H48 (Lawrence Hartshorne) (mfm. at PANS). Halifax County Registry of Deeds (Halifax), Deeds, 33: f.145; 35: f.438 (mfm. at PANS). PANS, MG 9, no.218: 18, 26; RG 1, 54: f.150; 58, no.7; 173: f.169; 224, no.131; 287, no.171; 369, no.271; 430, no.446; 458, 3 Jan. 1817; RG 4, LC, 1, 14 March 1811; RG 20A, 5, 1784, 1796. PRO, CO 217/36: 144; 217/37: 266; 217/63: 242; 217/64: 5; 217/66: 215; 217/68: 207; 217/76: 222; 217/77: 108; 217/79: 23; 217/81: 354; 217/98: 99, 198. John Clarkson, *Clarkson's mission to America, 1791–1792*, ed. and intro. C. B. Fergusson (Halifax, 1971). N.S., *Acts*, 1801, c.5–6; House of Assembly, *Journal and proc.*, 11 June 1801, 2 March 1811. *Acadian Recorder*, 17 Oct. 1818, 20 March 1819. *Free Press* (Halifax), 12 March 1822. *Nova-Scotia Royal Gazette*, 19 Feb., 24 Dec. 1793; 18 March 1794; 16 Feb. 1796; 17 June 1800; 8 March 1808; 25 April 1809; 27 May 1812. *Directory of N.S. MLAs*. Sabine, *Biog. sketches of loyalists*. W. C. Abbott, *New York in the American revolution* (New York and London, 1929). A. H. Bill, *New Jersey and the Revolutionary War* (Princeton, N.J., 1964). R. M. Calhoon, *The loyalists in revolutionary America, 1760–1781* (New York, 1973). L. R. Gerlach, "New Jersey in the coming of the American revolution," *New Jersey in the American revolution: political and social conflict; papers presented at the first annual New Jersey History Symposium . . .* (Trenton, N.J., 1970), 8–20. J. P. Martin, *The story of Dartmouth* (Dartmouth, N.S., 1957). Murdoch, *Hist. of N.S.*, vol.3. J. E. Pomfret, *The province of East New Jersey, 1609–1702: the rebellious proprietary* (Princeton, 1962). Margaret Ells, "Governor Wentworth's patronage," N.S. Hist. Soc., *Coll.*, 25 (1942): 49–73.

HÉBERT, ÉTIENNE, farmer; b. 1736 in Grand Pré, N.S., son of Jean-Baptiste Hébert and Élisabeth Granger; d. 11 Jan. 1823 in Saint-Grégoire (Bécancour), Lower Canada.

Étienne Hébert belonged to the fourth generation of Héberts in Acadia. The deportation of the Acadians in 1755 [see Charles Lawrence*] separated him from his family at the age of 19. He was sent to Baltimore, in Maryland, which was almost the only American

colony to show sympathy for the unhappy people arriving from that persecuted land. The fact that many inhabitants of Maryland were Catholics who had been sheltered in England by Lord Baltimore and his brother, Leonard Calvert, may account for this response. The Acadians were left free to move about as they wished, settle permanently, or emigrate, even to New France.

Hébert was able to take advantage of this favourable attitude. Placed in the service of an army officer who quickly became his friend, he gradually acquired not only substantial savings but above all valuable experience; in particular, he learned how to make his way through great stretches of forest, and along lakes and rivers, as well as over portages known only to a few. With this experience, he could tackle the project that had been taking shape in his mind from the time he arrived in Maryland: to find his parents, three brothers, and four sisters. This was no mean task, since the policy of deportation had been in effect until 1762, increasing the ranks of the exiles, who in addition had been widely dispersed. Acadians were to be found in all the British colonies from Massachusetts to Georgia. Some had fled to Louisiana, others had been sent to England. The large number in Maryland were scattered in more than eight localities, all distant from one another. At some unknown point, Hébert succeeded in finding his father, mother, and brother Jean-Baptiste in that colony, at Georgetown. But no trace was to be found of the others.

Then in 1763 came the cession of New France and the complete impossibility of a return to Acadia. The interdiction was lifted the following year, but with the proviso that the Acadians take the oath of allegiance. In 1764 or 1765 Hébert made up his mind to "go up to Canada" where, it was said, the conquerors had provided the new British subjects with acceptable conditions of life. Having learned from sailors in Boston, where by 1764 he had gathered his rediscovered parents and brother, that Trois-Rivières was less than 100 leagues away, he set out on his own in that direction, with a compass, axe, musket, tinder-box, saucepan, and birchbark canoe. After many adventures he wound up among the Acadian refugees near Nicolet at Saint-Grégoire (then called Sainte-Marguerite). At first he was disappointed to find none of his family there; but having been advised to cross the St Lawrence to Petite Acadie, a row of concessions in Yamachiche where some Acadians were living, he had the great joy of finding his sisters Marguerite, Françoise, and Marie.

Since he felt sure that he could gather his family together in the region, he bought four adjoining properties in the upper part of the village of Saint-Grégoire. Soon after, he left for Boston, which he had chosen as the gathering point for his family and for many other exiles whom he had been asked to bring back. He organized veritable expeditions, assembling five to ten families to travel from Boston to the Trois-Rivières region overland or by ship. From the autumn of 1766 registers of births, marriages, and deaths attest to the arrival of a great many of these Acadian exiles. In 1767 he brought his parents and brother Jean-Baptiste. But exile and the rigours of the voyage proved fatal for his mother, who was buried at the age of 66 in Trois-Rivières on 3 Oct. 1767. Hébert was also successful in his search for his sister Anne and brothers Joseph and Honoré, so that by 1771 or even earlier the entire Hébert family was finally reunited.

In the course of his searches Hébert had also found Marie-Josephte Babin, a girl from his native region. She was 24 and he 33 when they were married at Trois-Rivières on 2 Oct. 1769. They were to have nine children. One son, Major Jean-Baptiste Hébert, was a farmer, builder (notably of the Séminaire de Nicolet), Patriote, and member of the House of Assembly. Their grandson Nicolas-Tolentin Hébert*, parish priest of Saint-Louis at Kamouraska, helped to colonize the Saguenay and Lac Saint-Jean regions, and Hébertville was named after him.

After his 15 years of wandering and searching, Étienne Hébert enjoyed what seems to have been a happy and uneventful life. He died on 11 Jan. 1823. As a person responsible for reconstituting a whole family that had been dispersed along the east coast of what is now the United States, a task considered impossible, Étienne Hébert belongs to the ranks of unrecognized heroes with whom the history of Acadia abounds. There are now more than a million and a half descendants of Acadian refugees from the years 1755–75 living in Quebec.

ADRIEN BERGERON

[Our knowledge of the Hébert family is drawn from several accounts which unfortunately were not committed to writing until after three generations of this Acadian family had lived in Quebec. Inevitably, although in broad outline these accounts furnish similar information, each group of the many Hébert descendants identifies the hero differently, as one or other of the four brothers. In addition to the oral tradition, there are a number of written accounts of varying quality. These materials were studied in conjunction with contemporary documents, in particular the score of lists of Acadian prisoners in New England recently located in the Archives nationales in Paris, the many parish registers of the old administrative district of Trois-Rivières covering both shores of the St Lawrence, the valuable notes on Acadia compiled by Mgr Louis Richard, and the Journal paroissial de Saint-Grégoire, at Bécancour. This extensive research led to the conclusion that it was Étienne who was responsible for the reunification of the Hébert family. A.B.]

Arch. du séminaire de Trois-Rivières (Trois-Rivières, Qué.), Louis Richard, "Notes sur l'arrivée des Acadiens dans le district de Trois-Rivières après 1755," cahier 3. J.-E.

Bellemare, *Histoire de Nicolet, 1669–1924* (Arthabaska, Qué., 1924), 144–47. Adrien Bergeron, *Le grand arrangement des Acadiens au Québec . . .* (8v., Montréal, 1981), 4: 103–23. H.-R. Casgrain, *Un pèlerinage au pays d'Évangéline* (2e éd., Québec, 1888), 273–75. F.-L. Desaulniers, *Les vieilles familles d'Yamachiche* (4v., Montréal, 1898–1908), 4: 71–83. Alfred Désilets, *Souvenirs d'un octogénaire* (Trois-Rivières, 1922), 58–70. C.-É. Mailhot, *Les Bois-Francs* (4v., Arthabaska, 1914–25), 3: 216–21, 279–80. P.-M. Hébert, "Jean-Baptiste Hébert, 1779–1863," *Les Cahiers nicolétains* (Nicolet, Qué.), 2 (1980): 67–89; 6 (1984): 128–29, 131; 7 (1985): 3–7; "Jean-Baptiste Hébert, 'Major,'" Soc. hist. acadienne, *Cahiers* (Moncton, N.-B.), 3 (1968–71): 168–73.

HÉBERT, JEAN-FRANÇOIS, Roman Catholic priest; b. 24 June 1763 in Saint-Pierre, Île d'Orléans, Que., son of François Hébert and Marie-Joseph Côté; d. 20 Aug. 1831 in Saint-Ours, Lower Canada.

Jean-François Hébert came from a family of farmers in modest circumstances. As is usual in a devout Christian milieu, he felt the call to the priesthood early in life. He attended the Petit Séminaire de Québec from 1777 till 1785, and then began theological studies. On 12 Oct. 1788 he was ordained by Bishop Jean-François Hubert*.

After serving briefly as curate at Saint-François on Île d'Orléans, where he replaced the ailing parish priest, François Le Guerne*, and then at Notre-Dame in Montreal, Hébert was appointed curé of Sainte-Thérèse (at Sainte-Thérèse) in September 1789. The presbytery was barely fit to live in, and a number of the habitants refused to pay their tithes. Evidently the new priest was not happy in this difficult parish and wanted to leave as quickly as possible. Although he urged Bishop Hubert to give him another charge, it was not until 1792 that he was sent to the parish of Immaculée-Conception in Saint-Ours. When he arrived there at the end of October, he was acutely aware that he had to act with tact and circumspection. In the coming years he was to meet the challenge, carrying out his priestly duties to his parishioners' satisfaction for the rest of his life.

Hébert, who was a man of the *ancien régime*, first concentrated on the maintenance and embellishment of the church, which he saw as visible signs of religious vitality in the parish. In 1793 he had the building repaired. Two years later he hired woodcarver Louis QUÉVILLON to decorate the tabernacles. From then on improvements and purchases were made regularly. He bought a silver-plated crucifix and candlesticks, fitted out the sacristy and had two chapels built, completed the collection of vestments, secured consecrated vessels of better quality, bought a new bell, had a rood loft constructed, and purchased several paintings.

Hébert was concerned about the spiritual life of his parishioners and undertook to visit them regularly,

Henry

even though many lived at quite a distance. This visiting brought rapport with the habitants, who discovered in him a man close to their worries and their way of life. Thus he succeeded in 1824 in setting up the devotion of First Fridays, an observance that prompted his flock to practise their religion fervently and take communion frequently. While deeply conscious of his spiritual duties, he also paid close attention to his own interests. In his correspondence with Bishop Joseph-Octave PLESSIS and later with Bishop Bernard-Claude PANET, the matter of tithes was frequently discussed. Hébert in addition was particular about his records and proud that they were well kept.

Plessis considered Hébert a steady, reliable person, respectful of the rules governing his state and obedient to his instructions. In recognition, he named him archdeacon in 1818 and delegated him to supervise the construction of the presbytery for the parish in Sorel. Similarly, in 1827 Archbishop Panet asked him to look into the prospects of creating the parish of Saint-Pie. Two years later, again at the archbishop's request, Hébert chaired an inquiry into the incorporation of Belœil under canon law. In 1830 and 1831 he received similar commissions for the parishes of Saint-Hugues and Saint-Denis.

Hébert's relations with the seigneur, Charles de SAINT-OURS, were marked by cordiality and good feeling. Their submission to the authority of the crown brought them even closer together. Both belonged to the association that had been created in 1794 to support British rule in Lower Canada. To Hébert's pleasure, Saint-Ours donated 600 *livres* to build the church cupola in 1805. Twelve years later he and Hébert both favoured the creation of a second parish in the seigneury.

For more than 30 years Hébert led an uneventful existence, one that kept him busy with work on the church, collecting tithes, keeping records, administering the parish, and carrying out his ministry. The only new direction he took in the latter part of his life was to become more interested in education. In 1830 he was one of the few parish priests who accepted the government grant provided under the 1829 schools act. But Panet soon pointed out to him that its terms kept parish priests from running the schools, which were to be administered by parish syndics. Respecting his superior's opinion, Hébert was nevertheless quick to explain his action. He reported that his authority was not threatened, since he had had himself appointed school chairman. The parish priest of Saint-Ours consequently remained in complete accordance with the ecclesiastical authority. His simple, quiet life held no surprises in store. On 18 July 1831, with the unanimous support of his parishioners, he sent a petition to Panet asking that the parish be incorporated under canon law. Unfortunately he was not able to

follow the progress of this initiative. On 15 Aug. 1831 he was stricken with apoplexy and five days later he passed away.

Jean-François Hébert stands in the tradition of the rural parish priest of the *ancien régime*, preoccupied with material and spiritual matters, entirely obedient to his bishop, and devoted primarily to administrative tasks. This attitude had led to certain conflicts with the rural community, which he had managed to attenuate by adroit and flexible manœuvring.

RICHARD CHABOT

ANQ-M, CE3-6, 1792–1831. ANQ-Q, CE1-12, 24 juin 1763. Arch. de la chancellerie de l'évêché de Saint-Hyacinthe (Saint-Hyacinthe, Qué.), XVII.C.39, 23 août 1792, 18 juill. 1831. Allaire, *Dictionnaire*. Caron, "Inv. de la corr. de Mgr Panet," ANQ *Rapport*, 1933–34; 1934–35; 1935–36. Azarie Couillard-Després, *Histoire de la seigneurie de Saint-Ours* (2v., Montréal, 1915–17), 2: 174–210.

HENRY (Hendrick). *See* TEKARIHOGEN

HENRY, ALEXANDER, fur trader, merchant, militia officer, JP, and author; b. August 1739, possibly the third son of Alexander Henry, a merchant of New Brunswick, N.J., and Elizabeth ——; d. 4 April 1824 in Montreal.

In 1760, at the age of 20, Alexander Henry was in charge of three loaded supply bateaux which were following Major-General Jeffery Amherst*'s advance along Lake Ontario to Montreal. Henry, a merchant working out of Albany, N.Y., made a lucrative but hazardous living supplying the British army.

When Montreal surrendered on 8 September and Canada became open to English traders, Henry immediately travelled to Albany to purchase merchandise. He sold the goods at Fort William Augustus (east of Prescott, Ont.) and in January 1761 pushed on towards Montreal. At Les Cèdres he met former fur trader Jean-Baptiste Leduc, who acquainted him with the possibilities of trading at Michilimackinac (Mackinaw City, Mich.) and around Lake Superior. After buying supplies in Albany that spring, Henry returned to Montreal and secured a fur-trade pass from Major-General Thomas Gage*. He was the second Englishman to do so, Henry Bostwick having preceded him by a few days.

Following the Ottawa River–Lake Nipissing–French River route, Henry proceeded to Michilimackinac with his guide and assistant, Étienne-Charles Campion*, arriving in early September 1761. Britain and France were still at war and France's Indian allies remained hostile to the British. Apprehensive about how he would be received, Henry disguised himself as a French trader, but the stratagem was unsuccessful. One of the war chiefs of the local Ojibwas, Minweweh*, soon learned of him; he and 60 warriors, "each with his tomahawk in one hand, and scalping-knife in the other," paid Henry a visit. After first threatening Henry, Minweweh offered friendship. Henry and the other English traders at the post, Ezekiel Solomons and James Stanley Goddard, were nevertheless relieved when British soldiers finally arrived to take over the fort from Charles-Michel Mouet* de Langlade.

During the winter of 1761–62 or the following spring a minor Ojibwa chief, Wawatam*, adopted Henry as a brother. In May Henry went to Sault Ste Marie (Mich.), where he met fur trader Jean-Baptiste Cadot*. His ability to get along well with both the French and the Indians greatly facilitated his trading activities. After a fire late in December destroyed the small fort at the Sault garrisoned by Lieutenant John Jamet*, Cadot and Henry in February brought Jamet through the deep snow to Michilimackinac. Returning to the Sault in the spring of 1763, Henry met Sir Robert Davers*, who was touring the Upper Lakes, and accompanied him back to Michilimackinac.

In the spring of 1763 the Ottawa chief Pontiac* launched an uprising of the Indian nations against the British posts in the northwest. On 2 June Ojibwa warriors led by Madjeckewiss* and Minweweh attacked the British garrison at Michilimackinac. Henry hid for a time in Mouet de Langlade's house, but was later discovered and captured. He was rescued by Wawatam and lived with the chief's family for nearly a year, following them on their seasonal moves to hunting or fishing territories. Late in April 1764 the band returned to Michilimackinac to trade their furs. When some Ojibwas from Saginaw Bay plotted to kill Henry, Wawatam permitted him to go to Sault Ste Marie to seek the protection of Cadot. Madjeckewiss then came to the Sault seeking Henry's life, but Cadot dissuaded him. When word was received that Sir William Johnson* was holding a peace conference at Fort Niagara (near Youngstown, N.Y.), the Ojibwas decided to attend and Henry joined them. But, eager to return to Michilimackinac in order to recover his property, Henry accompanied Colonel John Bradstreet*'s expedition from Niagara to Detroit and then joined Captain William Howard's troops, who reoccupied Michilimackinac on 22 September.

Early in 1765 Henry secured from Howard a licence to trade in the Lake Superior area and in July he formed a partnership with Cadot. While trading with the Indians, Henry occasionally represented Robert Rogers*, the new commandant at Michilimackinac. Henry would complain to Johnson that Rogers had not paid him for his efforts. In 1767–68 he wintered at Michipicoten (Michipicoten River, Ont.) and later in 1768 entered into a partnership headed by Alexander Baxter to mine silver found in copper ore on the shores of Lake Superior. In the winter of 1770 the mining

company built a sailing vessel at the Sault and used it to search for and transport copper. The scarcity of labour and the costs of transporting the ore made the venture unprofitable and the company wound up its affairs in 1774.

Fortunately, Henry had continued in the fur trade, and in 1775, eager to see some new country, he took four large and twelve small canoes into the territory northwest of Lake Superior. There he, Cadot, and other pedlars, including Peter Pond* and Joseph* and Thomas Frobisher, challenged the Hudson's Bay Company. On 14 Oct. 1775 the group stopped at Cumberland House (Sask.), where Matthew Cocking* recorded their arrival. After setting up a trading post on Beaver Lake (Amisk Lake), Henry set off in January to Fort des Prairies (Fort-à-la-Corne) on the Saskatchewan River in order to see the plains. Having satisfied his curiosity and secured some furs from the Assiniboins, he returned to Beaver Lake. In the early spring he went to the Churchill River, where he purchased 12,000 additional beaver skins from Chipewyans probably on their way to trade at Hudson Bay, and then returned to Beaver Lake and rounded up his furs. Some of the last packs were forcibly acquired from Robert Longmoor*, an HBC employee who traded nearby. Henry set off in July for Montreal, laden with prime furs. He gave the governor, Sir Guy Carleton*, a large map of the western region through which he had travelled.

His imagination captivated by the rich potential of the northwest, Henry sailed to England in the autumn of 1776 and presented to the HBC a proposal that he recruit Canadian canoeists to work for the company. Bearing a letter of introduction from former fur trader Luc de La Corne* to his brother Abbé Joseph-Marie de La Corne* de Chaptes, Henry crossed the English Channel to France, where the abbé introduced him to the young queen, Marie-Antoinette.

In the spring of 1777 Henry returned to British North America and in partnership with Jean-Baptiste Blondeau took a trading canoe to Michipicoten. That fall he sold his post there to Jean-Baptiste NOLIN. The following year, in partnership with John Chinn, he traded at Sault Ste Marie, working closely with Cadot. Henry travelled to England in the fall of 1778 and again in 1780. On 18 Oct. 1781, after returning to Montreal from his third and last visit to England, he sent to naturalist Sir Joseph Banks* a detailed plan for an expedition to find an overland route to the Pacific.

Henry settled in Montreal, where he became a general merchant, but he remained involved in the fur trade and made occasional trips to Detroit or Michilimackinac. In 1784 he seriously considered moving to Schenectady, N.Y., so that he could continue trading at Detroit and Michilimackinac, which had been given to the United States by the Treaty of Paris. When the British did not immediately evacuate the western

Henry

posts, Henry remained in Montreal. On 11 June 1785 he married a widow, Julia Ketson. Their eldest child, Julia, had been born in October 1780. Four sons, Alexander, William, Robert, and John, were born between 1782 and 1786. By the time of his marriage Henry had become a prominent merchant. In February 1785 he and 18 other traders who had been active in the northwest had founded the Beaver Club. The following spring he apparently suffered a severe financial set-back, perhaps as a result of unsettled economic conditions following the end of the American revolution and the intertribal warfare around the western Great Lakes [see Wahpasha*]. To recoup his losses, Henry again traded at Michilimackinac from 1785 to 1790. There, in the summer of 1788, he was a representative of the General Company of Lake Superior and the South (also known as the General Society) at a court of inquiry which examined charges of misusing government supplies levelled against the interpreter Joseph-Louis Ainsse*.

During the mid 1780s Henry encouraged a friend in New York, William Edgar, to enter the trade in furs with China. Fascinated by the prospects offered by the Pacific coast, Henry passed on his ideas, which he called "my favorite plan," to New York merchant John Jacob Astor. He introduced Astor into the Canadian trade and Astor was Henry's guest during his annual visits to Montreal. In the 1790s Henry and Astor assisted the North West Company in organizing shipments of furs to China [see Simon McTavish*].

Over the years Henry maintained close personal ties with John Askin*. During the mid 1790s they were involved in several unsuccessful land speculation schemes in northern Ohio. One of these, known as the Cuyahoga Purchase, came to naught when the Ohio Indians, from whom the land had been acquired, refused to bring forth their land claims at the Treaty of Greenville (1795) and the deeds which had been obtained by Henry and his associates, Askin, Patrick McNiff*, and others, were considered invalid. Henry moaned, "We have lost a fortune of at least one Million of Dollars."

On 14 Sept. 1792 Henry and his nephew Alexander Henry* the younger together obtained one share in the NWC for six years. In 1796 he sold his interest to William Hallowell but he continued to buy furs from traders and export them to England. When one of his uninsured shipments was captured by the French in 1801, he suffered a serious financial crisis. In order to repair his fortunes, Henry in 1802 became a commission merchant and auctioneer in partnership with William Lindsay. Plagued by ill health, he worked hard at a job he did not find satisfying. Yet, despite his reverses, he maintained a secure place in Montreal's mercantile society. He served as a captain in the militia and from 1794 to 1821 as justice of the peace, entertained leading merchants in his home, regularly

signed petitions and memorials, and attended parties. He was particularly active in the Beaver Club, reactivated in 1807, of which he was the senior member.

Henry sensed, however, that new men were taking over the fur trade and in 1809 he wrote to Askin, "There is only us four old friends [James McGill*, Isaac Todd*, Joseph Frobisher, and himself] alive, all the new North westards are a parcel of Boys and upstarts, who were not born in our time, and suposes they know much more of the Indian trade than any before them." To recapture his exciting past, he wrote a memoir of his life which he published in New York in 1809. *Travels and adventures in Canada and the Indian territories, between the years 1760 and 1776* has become an adventure classic and is still considered one of the best descriptions of Indian life at the time of Henry's travels.

During the latter years of his life, Alexander Henry continued to trade and in 1812 was appointed vendue master and auctioneer for the district of Montreal. He worked in partnership with his nephew Norman Bethune, who lived with him at 14 Rue Saint-Urbain. A middle-sized man, easy yet dignified, Henry had been called by the Indians "the handsome Englishman." At age 85 he died in Montreal, esteemed by all who knew him.

DAVID A. ARMOUR

Alexander Henry is the author of *Travels and adventures in Canada and the Indian territories, between the years 1760 and 1776* (New York, 1809). Several editions have appeared, including one prepared by James Bain (Boston, 1901) and another edited and introduced by M. M. Quaife (Chicago, 1921). Its first part was reprinted as *Attack at Michilimackinac . . .* , ed. D. A. Armour (Mackinac Island, Mich., 1971).

ANQ-M, CE1-63, 11 juin 1785. British Museum (Natural History) (London), Banks coll., DTC 2: 39–51 (copy). Clements Library, Thomas Gage papers. McCord Museum, J.-B. Blondeau, account-book; Beaver Club minute-book, 1807–27. Mo. Hist. Soc. (St Louis), Chouteau coll. MTL, North West Company papers, William Edgar papers, Alexander Henry to William Edgar, 11 Aug. 1784–22 Oct. 1787 (typescripts); Alfred Sandham coll., Alexander Henry to Forsyth & Taylor, 9 Dec. 1786. PAC, MG 19, A2, ser.1, 3; A4 (copies); RG 4, B28, 115. "Biographical sketch of the late Alexander Henry, esq.," *Canadian Magazine and Literary Repository* (Montreal), 2 (January–June 1824): 289–304, 385–97. *Docs. relating to NWC* (Wallace). *Documents relating to the colonial, revolutionary and post-revolutionary history of the state of New Jersey*, ed. W. A. Whitehead et al. (42v., Newark, N.J., 1880–1949). *John Askin papers* (Quaife). *Journals of Samuel Hearne and Philip Turnor*, ed. J. B. Tyrrell (Toronto, 1934; repr. New York, 1968). *Mich. Pioneer Coll. The papers of Sir William Johnson*, ed. James Sullivan et al. (14v., Albany, N.Y., 1921–65), 4–6, 12. [Robert] Rogers, "Rogers's Michillimackinac journal," ed. W. L. Clements, American Antiquarian Soc., *Proc.* (Worcester, Mass.), new ser., 28 (1918): 224–73. Wis., State Hist. Soc., *Coll.*, 3 (1857): 76–82; 19 (1910): 67–68, 238, 253–54, 280–85, 289–91, 309–10, 336–37, 372–74. Innis, *Fur trade in Canada* (1962). Morton, *Hist. of Canadian west* (Thomas; 1973). K. W. Porter, *John Jacob Astor, business man* (2v., Cambridge, Mass., 1931; repr. New York, 1966). J. U. Terrell, *Furs by Astor* (New York, 1963). Charles Lart, "Fur trade returns, 1767," *CHR*, 3 (1922): 351–58.

HILL, CHARLES, businessman, politician, judge, and JP; b. *c.* 1748 in Londonderry (Northern Ireland), son of Robert Hill; m. first Rebecca (Cochran?), and they had four children; m. secondly 18 Jan. 1800 Isabella Allan in Halifax, and they had one child; d. there 16 Aug. 1825.

The brothers Robert, Charles, and Patrick Hill were probably among the 300 Ulstermen whom Alexander McNutt* brought out from Londonderry to Halifax in the autumn of 1761. The three eventually settled at Upper Economy in the district of Colchester, where each was allotted 500 acres on 24 March 1768. Charles Hill was again in Halifax by 1776, where he was joined by his young nephew Robert. Hill was probably associated with the brothers Thomas and William Cochran, merchants of Halifax, from the very start of his business career; they had perhaps been responsible for his coming to the town in the first place. (The identity of his first wife as a member of the family can only be presumed.) In September 1778 Hill and Temple Stanyan Piers (father of Temple Foster*) entered partnership as auctioneers. The association lasted until Piers's premature death in July 1786, after which Hill continued alone.

By 1790 he was recognized as one of the four main auctioneers in the town. Houses, lots, general merchandise, and even black slaves were disposed of by Hill "At his Auction-Room" and elsewhere, but after the outbreak of war between Britain and France in 1793 a high proportion of his business began to be taken up with ships captured by British naval vessels and privateers. Several auctioneers were authorized by the Vice-Admiralty Court to deal with prizes, and they presumably received a fixed percentage of the sums realized. What is certain is that Hill became a rich man, one who was later reputed to have sold more condemned prizes than any other auctioneer on the continent. As a supplementary activity, from about 1790 Hill was established as a money-lender. Probably about the same time he was engaged in the lucrative West Indies trade, but this endeavour was subsidiary to his other interests. Thanks to his prominence, Hill was one of the directors of the stillborn Shubenacadie Canal Company in 1798 [*see* Isaac Hildrith*], and of the Fire Insurance Association of Halifax in 1809. After the latter became the Halifax Fire Insurance Company in 1819, Hill served as its president from 1820 to 1822.

Commercial success in due course led Hill into politics. He represented Amherst Township in the House of Assembly from 1786 to 1793 but, like Richard John UNIACKE Sr, Charles MORRIS, and other members of the mainly Irish oligarchy that had developed during the 1770s, he did not contest the election of the latter year. Hill remained out of politics during most of the ascendancy of the loyalists under the lieutenant governorship of Sir John Wentworth*. Unlike his friend Uniacke, however, Hill made his peace with Wentworth, who recognized his influence and importance by appointing him to the Council in 1807. Hill retained the position until his death. In 1809 he served *ex officio* as a judge of the Vice-Admiralty Court when it sat in special session for the trial of Edward Jordan, who had been accused of piracy. Hill also held various minor commissions, among them four as a justice of the peace.

At some time Hill had taken his nephew Robert into partnership, and in 1808 Hill's only surviving son, Charles Samuel, also became a partner in the firm, which thenceforth was known as Charles and Robert Hill and Company. Robert died in 1812 and Charles Samuel in 1816, and by 1822, when Hill was no longer taking an active part in business, the firm, now known as Charles Hill and Company, had failed. Charles John Hill, son of Robert, had taken over direction, but got into serious financial difficulties and eventually found himself in debtors' prison.

Commerce and politics aside, Hill was prominent in the Charitable Irish Society, of which he had been a founding member in 1786. He served as treasurer from 1786 to 1799, president in 1799 and from 1801 to 1803, and secretary in 1820 and 1821. With Uniacke he formed a committee to revise the society's constitution. At some time Hill was also a member of the Rockingham Club, a convivial institution founded by Wentworth in the 1790s and revived under Lieutenant Governor Lord Dalhousie [Ramsay*].

Hill's mansion on Hollis Street, with its distinctive Palladian window, survived until 1960. It was apparently the scene of many lavish entertainments, to one of which Uniacke is alleged to have borne a spinet on his shoulders. The ties between the Hill and Uniacke families were strengthened when Richard John UNIACKE Jr married Hill's only surviving daughter, Mary Ann, in 1821. On Hill's death the *Acadian Recorder* published a long obituary which stated in part that few individuals had possessed "the good-will and esteem of the public" as had Hill, and lauded his "honorable, candid and generous character." The tribute was a measure of the respect in which he was held, not only by the more liberal press but also by the community in which he had flourished and which he had served so long in both business and government. Hill's remains were interred in St Paul's cemetery, where the tomb can be seen today.

Hill

The last will and testament of Charles Hill is remarkable for the size of the estate, which amounted to over £113,000, mostly in mortgages on local property, private notes from Halifax merchants and tradesmen, and British and American stocks, and for the nature and variety of its bequests. Hill not only established a trust for each of the grandchildren of his late nephew Robert but he also left money to each of the major denominations in Halifax. In matters of religion he seems to have been both large-hearted and broad-minded, rare enough attitudes among Haligonians of his time and after.

J. B. Cahill

Halifax County Court of Probate (Halifax), Estate papers, H110 (Charles Hill) (mfm. at PANS). PANS, MG 1, 469C; MG 3, 154; 164–65; MG 4, 46–47A; MG 20, 65; RG 39, C, 1817, box 130, Hill, Charles, notes. St Paul's Anglican Church (Halifax), Reg. of baptisms, marriages, and burials (mfm. at PANS). *Acadian Recorder*, 20 Aug. 1825. *Directory of N.S. MLAs.* A. W. H. Eaton, *Families of Eaton–Sutherland, Layton–Hill* (New York, 1899), 15–16. Akins, *Hist. of Halifax City.* Marion Moore, "Hollis Street building once elegant residence," *Mail-Star* (Halifax), 24 Oct. 1960: 3.

HILL, HENRY AARON. *See* Kenwendeshon

HOBSON, BENJAMIN, teacher and JP; b. *c.* 1737; d. *c.* 1832 in New Carlisle, Lower Canada.

Benjamin Hobson apparently served in Major-General John Burgoyne*'s army during the American revolution. He then established himself at Quebec, opening a school in Lower Town in 1778. Subsequently he moved to Yamachiche, where he taught for some years.

In 1784 Hobson decided to settle in the Gaspé peninsula, as did a large group of loyalists. He sailed on 9 June 1784. He seems to have been married by then, but he did not take any children with him. He chose to live in New Carlisle, a village selected by the British government as an administrative centre and rallying point for the English-speaking population in the region. New Carlisle already had 22 families.

Two years after arriving in the Gaspé, Hobson founded a Protestant primary school. At that time the government paid him £37 10*s*. 0*d*. a year. In 1790 he was one of four Protestant teachers in the province receiving a salary from the government, his being the sum of £25 annually. The New Carlisle school was the first institution of its kind outside the large centres to be recognized in the province. Hobson taught in his own home, without receiving any compensation whatever for the use of his premises.

This situation lasted until 1801, when the act setting up the Royal Institution for the Advancement of Learning was proclaimed. The school in New Carlisle then became the responsibility of that body. Hobson's salary was increased to £45, and a house was found where he could teach his pupils. The parents in the locality, however, more or less took on the upkeep of the establishment, partly in money, partly in kind. The people of New Carlisle did not build a real school until 1821, when the secretary of the Royal Institution, Joseph Langley Mills, threatened in writing to have payment of Hobson's salary stopped, a step which would have meant the closing of the teaching establishment.

Little else is known of Benjamin Hobson's life. It seems that his entire career was spent in teaching. On 29 May 1811 he received a commission as justice of the peace for the District of Gaspé, and it was renewed in 1824. He had retired from his profession in 1822 at the request of the government, which granted him an annual pension of £30 in 1823. Seven years later when pensions were abolished by the government, protests were received from pensioners, but Hobson was not among them. It appears that he died in 1832.

Mario Mimeault

BL, Add. MSS 21822: 309; 21823: 161–63. PAC, RG 68, General index, 1651–1841: 341, 343, 356. Ivanhoë Caron, "Les maîtres d'écoles de l'Institution royale de 1801 à 1834," *BRH*, 47 (1941): 21–32. Patrice Gallant, *Les registres de la Gaspésie (1752–1850)* (6v., [Sayabec, Qué., 1968]). L.-P. Audet, *Histoire de l'enseignement au Québec* (2v., Montréal et Toronto, 1971); *Le système scolaire.* Boulianne, "Royal Instit. for the Advancement of Learning."

HODGSON, JOHN, fur trader; b. *c.* 1763 in the parish of St Margaret, Westminster (London), England; d. before 6 Nov. 1833, probably in Onslow Township, Lower Canada.

John Hodgson entered the Hudson's Bay Company as an apprentice in 1774. Like several other 18th-century HBC men, he had been educated at the charity school of the Grey Coat Hospital in London. He was first sent to Fort Albany (Ont.), where his duties were to include "Writing & Accounts" as well as surveying. He then spent some 18 years at Henley House (near the junction of the Albany and Kenogami rivers), as writer, as second under John McNab in 1781–82 and 1783–86, as summer master during McNab's absences, and finally as master from 1786 to 1793. Two notable interruptions occurred in this service: during the years 1778–81 Hodgson was at Fort Albany, from which place in 1780 he accompanied HBC surveyor Philip Turnor* on a summer trip to Gloucester House (Washi Lake); and from March to August 1783 he took charge of Severn House (Fort Severn) after the capture by the Comte de Lapérouse [Galaup*] of its master, William Falconer. In 1786, expressing pleasure at Hodgson's "good conduct at

Severn and general good behaviour," the HBC awarded him a gratuity of £10 and made him master at Henley House. Henley was an important outpost in the competition against the Canadian fur traders. It was a base for the company's efforts to reach lakes Nipigon and Wepiscuacaw (McKay), where the Canadians were carrying on an active trade. Hodgson oversaw the preparation of inland journals and maps covering areas as remote as Rainy Lake, thus assembling valuable information.

Hodgson spent 1793–94 in England. In 1794–95 and again from 1796 to 1800 he took charge of the post at Martin Falls. He served as second at Albany in 1795–96, replacing the deceased John Kipling. In 1800 he succeeded John McNab as chief factor in command of Albany, a position he held until 1810, with the exception of a year, 1807–8, spent in England. His service after his second English leave was characterized by failures and frustrations. Efforts in 1808 and 1809 to open trade at Lac Seul were foiled by North West Company rivals, "Mr. [John] Haldane[*] and a set of abandoned wretches who stick at nothing short of murder." The trade at Osnaburgh House, one of the posts under his jurisdiction, was damaged by the chronic drunkenness of its master, John Sutherland. In the fall of 1809 the HBC men at Eagle Lake had an altercation with the Nor'Westers which led to the death of NWC clerk Aeneas Macdonell. The Canadians seized some of the HBC servants involved in order to bring them to trial in Montreal.

Hodgson's difficulties with the Albany outposts were matched by his growing management problems at Albany itself and, in the summer of 1810, he received word of his dismissal and his replacement by Thomas VINCENT, after a long service which for the most part had been well regarded. The change was applauded by William AULD, superintendent of the Northern Department, who, noting "the long Absence of all Sense of Duty or Discipline" at Albany, considered Hodgson "a Beacon to the unwary and inconsiderate. Surely his desolate State will strike Terror into the Bosom of the most thoughtless. . . . Officers of all Ranks will see the Destiny that awaits the Indulgence of uncontrould Passions and the Freaks of a mischievous Caprice."

Rather than retire to England, Hodgson decided to settle on the Ottawa River with his wife, Caroline Goodwin (daughter of HBC officer Robert Goodwin and Mistigoose, an Indian), and several of their nine children. Reaching Fort Timiskaming (near Ville-Marie, Que.) on 27 Sept. 1812 in hunger and despair, he was assisted with supplies by Nor'Wester Donald McKay, and went on to Montreal where he purchased a farm in Onslow Township on the Ottawa near Lac des Chats for 22,000 *livres*. Several fur traders who travelled the Ottawa in later years remarked on the

Hodgsons, whose inelegant household belied their former high standing. In 1815 Colin Robertson*, upon Hodgson's informing him "that he was many years Governor at Albany," commented, "but really I think the upper works of his excellency is a little deranged." And former NWC clerk Ross Cox*, descending the Ottawa in September 1817, was disappointed that the former HBC officer could offer his half-starved guests nothing more than "a meal of potatoes and butter"; there was "nothing very attractive about this solitary settlement." The Hodgsons were still living at Lac des Chats in 1828, but John Hodgson was described as deceased in minutes of the London committee of the HBC for 6 Nov. 1833.

JENNIFER S. H. BROWN

PAC, Reference file 341-1 (letters between F.-J. Audet and Frederick Easton, Port Arthur, Ont., 4 Oct. 1934). PAM, HBCA, A.1/58: f.65; A.6/16: f.111; A.6/17: f.115; A.92/17/507, no.15706; B.3/a/112: f.5; B.3/a/117b: f.25; B.3/b/45, 46, 48a; B.86/a/39–40, 42, 44; B.135/a/110: f.13; D.4/15: f.125; D.5/2: f.219; D.5/3: f.267. Ross Cox, *Adventures on the Columbia River . . .* (2v., London, 1831). *HBRS*, 2 (Rich and Fleming). James Tate, "James Tate's journal, 1809–1812," *HBRS*, 30 (Williams), 98–101. *Journals of Samuel Hearne and Philip Turnor*, ed. J. B. Tyrrell (Toronto, 1934; repr. New York, 1968). J. S. H. Brown, *Strangers in blood: fur trade company families in Indian country* (Vancouver and London, 1980).

HOLLAND, ANTHONY HENRY, printer, editor, and businessman; b. 25 Nov. 1785 in Halifax, eldest son of Matthias (Matthew) Holland, a soldier from Hesse-Kassel (Federal Republic of Germany), and Margaret Appledore; m. 22 Dec. 1816 Eliza Merkel in Halifax, and they had three children; d. 10 Oct. 1830 near Halifax.

Little is known about Anthony Henry Holland's early years, but it is clear that he was given a sound basic education and that he was encouraged to develop independence, integrity, and a strong social conscience. The namesake and godson of Anthony Henry*, another German settler and the first king's printer of Nova Scotia, he probably served his printer's apprenticeship in Henry's office. While in his early twenties Holland spent some time in the United States, at first apparently as an employee of William W. Clapp, publisher of the *Gazette of Maine, Hancock and Washington Advertiser* in Buckstown (Bucksport, Maine). In April 1811 Clapp sold the paper to Holland, who managed it for a year. He then announced a one-month suspension and about the same time, it seems, returned to Halifax.

Within six months of the outbreak of war with the United States in June 1812 Holland issued a prospectus for a newspaper to be entitled the *Acadian Recorder*. When the paper appeared on 16 Jan. 1813 it

Holland

became the fourth in Halifax, its competitors being John Howe's *Nova-Scotia Royal Gazette*, William Minns's *Weekly Chronicle*, and John Howe Jr's *Halifax Journal*. Unlike the other three, which generally avoided politics and were conservative in outlook, the *Recorder* intended from the start that "rational and fair discussion of political principles, and candid investigation of the characters of public men and public measures will never be rejected," and under its young editor and publisher adopted a tone of moderate reform. Aided by public goodwill and wartime prosperity, the venture flourished under Holland's able and energetic leadership and rapidly became one of the most significent journals in the province.

Although the *Recorder* had appeared under the banner of reform, the political climate dictated that any criticisms of the governing powers had to be made cautiously. Holland believed strongly in moderation and rational accommodation as a solution to most problems and rarely let his emotions override his common sense. On at least one occasion, however, he antagonized authority. In February 1818 the *Recorder* printed a satirical piece on Edward Mortimer*, a Halifax County MHA. Mortimer promptly brought up the subject in the House of Assembly. Holland was forced to apologize and he was reprimanded by the speaker. Two years later he apparently printed a pamphlet by William Wilkie* which castigated the local magistrates and other government officials. When Wilkie was tried and sentenced to two years' imprisonment, the *Recorder* agreed with the other Halifax papers that the punishment was deserved. Evidently Holland had decided that Wilkie's cause could not be safely supported.

In spite of these problems, Holland was able to present some innovative features in the *Recorder*. In February 1817 it became the first paper to print the debates of the assembly on a regular basis. The following year it published a series of letters by Agricola (the pseudonym of John Young*) which aroused widespread interest with their criticisms of the state of farming in the province and their proposals for improvement. Then in 1821 it presented some satirical letters by Thomas McCulloch* on the reasons for Nova Scotia's backwardness. Both series were related to the postwar economic depression and the need for improvement of the province's prospects, a topic dear to Holland's heart. In his editorial columns he supported the Halifax merchant community, which feared the potentially damaging effect of free trade on Nova Scotia. Like many Nova Scotians he admired the British character, constitution, and sense of freedom but was sometimes critical of the country's leadership. In contrast, he distrusted the Americans and disliked republicanism, considering that the American idea of liberty bordered on licence and that their culture was inferior to that of Nova Scotia. In patriotic terms, however, Holland was probably more self-consciously Nova Scotian than either pro-British or anti-American. One of the original intentions of the *Recorder* was to make Nova Scotians proud of their heritage and potential and to publicize the beauties and resources of the colony abroad, and Holland never ceased to see a great future in agriculture, mining, and merchandising.

Besides his difficulties with authority, Holland had a long-standing feud with Edmund Ward*, the bellicose publisher of the conservative *Free Press*, founded in 1816. The two papers regularly abused one another in their editorial columns and the dispute turned violent when Ward was horsewhipped by John Young's son George Renny* in 1820 and the next year assaulted by Holland's brother Philip John. Although Ward was fined for libelling a *Recorder* contributor, he won his own suit against Philip John Holland, at which point a truce seems to have been called. In 1822 Holland added Philip John and a friend, Edward A. Moody, as partners, and two years later left the newspaper business to them. Philip John continued until 1836, when he sold the *Recorder* to Hugh William Blackadar* and John English. From 1814 Holland had also issued a yearly almanac, the *Nova-Scotia calendar*, which was carried on by his brother until 1832.

While operating the *Recorder*, Holland had decided to open a paper-mill when American suppliers were unable to meet his requirements for newsprint, and he continued to manage the mill after he had left publishing. The mill, the first in what is now Atlantic Canada, was in operation on Nine Mile River near Bedford Basin by 1819. It had two storeys, the upper one with its walls slatted in the manner of venetian blinds to permit the circulation of air to dry the paper. In addition to newsprint, Holland produced brown wrapping-paper to fill the needs of Halifax merchants. The local historian Thomas Beamish Akins* remembered that the newsprint was of poor quality, but the wrapping-paper was quite reasonable. Besides the mill, Holland was involved in a number of other business activities, about which little is known, including a lumbering business on Bedford Basin, a stationery store, and a snuff factory. He was also the owner of several rental properties in Halifax and on Bedford Basin and, like many others, possessed shares in the Shubenacadie Canal Company.

Gifted with above average intelligence and a "splendid physique," Anthony Henry Holland was a man of independent thought and action and of sound judgement. As a newspaper publisher he thought of himself as a reformer who respected authority but refused to be intimidated by it, and he seemed to know intuitively what was possible without compromising his ideals or principles. To ensure that the *Recorder* was first with the highly prized foreign news he would row out to intercept a news packet even on stormy nights, while his competitors waited at the dockside the next morning. As a businessman he was honest and financially astute, taking only calculated risks. Socially he was friendly and outgoing, fond of entertaining and interested in cultural affairs. Unfortunately, his career as an active and influential Nova Scotian was cut short. He died on 10 Oct. 1830 following a driving accident. He was buried near his parents and their German friends in the graveyard of the little Dutch church in Halifax.

GERTRUDE TRATT

Halifax County Court of Probate (Halifax), Estate files, H135 (A. H. Holland) (mfm. at PANS). PANS, Churches, St George's Anglican Church (Halifax), records of Dutch Church, reg. of baptisms, marriages, and burials; Map Coll., Shubenacadie, Grand Lake area, survey map, c. 1840; MG 5, 14; MG 9, no.1; no.41: 68; RG 20A, 48, 1813; 115, 1830. N.S., House of Assembly, *Journal and proc.*, 1818: 30–31, 38. *Acadian Recorder*, 12 Dec. 1812 (prospectus); 22 Oct., 4 Dec. 1814; 27 Oct. 1821; 16 Oct. 1829. *Sun* (Halifax), 2 Sept. 1845. *Weekly Chronicle*, 27 Dec. 1816. *Directory of N.S. MLAs*. *N.-S. calendar*, 1814–32. G. E. N. Tratt, *A survey and listing of Nova Scotia newspapers, 1752–1957, with particular reference to the period before 1867* (Halifax, 1979). George Mullane, *Footprints around and about Bedford Basin* (n.p., n.d.). Elsie Tolson, *The captain, the colonel and me: Bedford, N.S. since 1503* (Sackville, N.B., 1979). *Acadian Recorder*, 16 Jan. 1888, supp.: 3; 16 Feb. 1913. *Bedford-Sackville News* (Lower Sackville, N.S.), 25 Sept. 1974. *Chronicle* (Halifax), 16 Dec. 1929. R. V. Harris, "In and about Halifax – notes of earliest times," *Acadiensis* (Saint John, N.B.), 8 (1908): 23–28. D. C. Harvey, "Newspapers of Nova Scotia, 1840–1867," *CHR*, 26 (1945): 279–301. *Mail-Star* (Halifax), 27 Jan. 1963: 7. J. S. Martell, "The press of the Maritime provinces in the 1830's," *CHR*, 19 (1938): 24–49. N.S., Provincial Museum and Science Library, *Report* (Halifax), 1931–32.

HOLLOWAY, JOHN, naval officer and governor of Newfoundland; b. 15 Jan. 1743/44 (Old Style) in the parish of St Cuthbert, Wells, Somerset, England, son of Robert Holloway; m. c. 1781, in the West Indies, Miss Waldron (Walrond) of Antigua, and they had three daughters who reached adulthood; d. 26 June 1826 in Wells.

The son of an old and respectable family, John Holloway entered the Royal Navy in 1760 aboard the *Antelope*, and the next year made his first trip to Newfoundland with the newly appointed governor, Captain Thomas Graves*. He became a lieutenant on 19 Jan. 1771 and post captain in January 1780. During the American revolution and the long wars with France and Spain, he served with distinction. Horatio Nelson, a friend, called him "an honest, good man." On 14 Feb. 1799 Holloway was raised to rear-admiral,

and on 25 Oct. 1804 to vice-admiral. In 1807 he was appointed governor of Newfoundland.

In his administration Holloway broke with the policy developed by his immediate predecessors, James GAMBIER and Sir Erasmus Gower*, which recognized the fact of permanent settlement on the island. Instead, he returned to the restrictive views of Hugh Palliser* and Mark Milbanke*. He refused the use of land for cultivation and enforced rigid regulations designed to retain the shore for the transient fishing fleets from England. The times, however, were not with Holloway. An American embargo on the export of foodstuffs and some particularly severe winters made land cultivation important.

Holloway's views on the freedom of the press were similarly restrictive. The first publication of the St John's *Royal Gazette and Newfoundland Advertiser* on 27 Aug. 1807 brought a severe caution to publisher John Ryan*, forbidding the printing of "anything inflammatory against the Government of Great Britain or its dependencies" and warning him "never to give or suffer any opinion to be given upon the policy of other nations but to confine the paper solely for what was to the benefit of commerce, and the inhabitants of this Government and others trading with it."

Although the Royal Navy was the island's first line of defence, the inhabitants had a role to play. Holloway was not impressed with the potential value of the militia, officially named the Loyal Volunteers, which had been established in 1805; nevertheless, he encouraged the force's maintenance. Command of the Loyal Volunteers changed in October 1808, going to James MACBRAIRE. Holloway, modestly pleased, reported that MacBraire was "using every economy, at the same time preserving the utility and respectability of the Corps."

Holloway was distressed by the inhuman treatment of the Beothuks at the hands of fur traders and fishermen [*see* John BLAND]. He issued a proclamation on 30 July 1807 against it and also tried to stop the influx of Nova Scotia Micmacs, who were moving into the Beothuks' hunting-grounds. Holloway twice sent one of his officers to the Bay of Exploits and other parts of the island to communicate with the Beothuks, without success. Then he dispatched an expedition under William CULL. It, too, was a failure, and the ugly process of extermination continued.

During Holloway's tenure, in March 1809, the imperial government finally gave the courts of judicature in Newfoundland their permanence, a step which, if not by intent, at least in fact foreshadowed the granting of colonial status in 1832 [*see* Sir Thomas John Cochrane*]. The same act of 1809 also re-annexed the Labrador coast to Newfoundland's jurisdiction from that of Lower Canada.

Holloway left the island in October 1809 and the same month was promoted admiral of the blue. On 31

Holmes

July 1810 he was made admiral of the white. He died in his 80th year. Contemporary observers remarked on his "rigid honesty" and "blunt sincerity," and found him "brave without ostentation, independent without being assuming . . . a deserving naval commander."

FREDERIC F. THOMPSON

PRO, CO 194/46: 82; 194/47: 33, 45, 61, 82. Somerset Record Office (Taunton, Eng.), Wells St Cuthbert, reg. of baptisms, 18 Jan., 23 Feb. 1743/44. "Biographical memoir of John Holloway, esq., vice-admiral of the Red, governor of the island of Newfoundland, and commander in chief on that station," *Naval Chronicle* (London), 19 (January–June 1808): 353–73. *Nelson's letters to his wife, and other documents, 1785–1831*, ed. G. P. B. Naish ([London], 1958), 237. G.B., Admiralty, *The commissioned sea officers of the Royal Navy, 1660–1815*, [ed. D. B. Smith *et al.*] (3v., n.p., [1954]), 2; *Navy list*, 1811. John Marshall, *Royal naval biography . . .* (4v. in 6 and 2v. supp., London, 1823–35), 1: 101–10. R. H. Bonnycastle, *Newfoundland in 1842: a sequel to "The Canadas in 1841"* (2v., London, 1842), 1: 141–42. Joseph Hatton and Moses Harvey, *Newfoundland, the oldest British colony; its history, its present condition, and its prospects in the future* (London, 1883). Howley, *Beothucks or Red Indians*. G. W. L. Nicholson, *The fighting Newfoundlander; a history of the Royal Newfoundland Regiment* (St John's, [1964?]). James Ralfe, *The naval biography of Great Britain . . .* (4v., London, 1828), 2: 209–14.

HOLMES, ELKANAH, Baptist missionary; b. 22 Dec. 1744, probably in Canterbury, N.H.; m. first *c.* 1763 in New York City, and he and his wife had two sons and one daughter; m. secondly in Bedford, N.Y., and he and his wife had two sons; m. thirdly 26 June 1802 the widow of James Bingham in New York City; d. 17 Jan. 1832 in Bedford.

After a military career during which he took part in the British captures of Fort Carillon (near Ticonderoga, N.Y.) in 1759 and Havana, Cuba, in 1762, Elkanah Holmes was baptized around 1770 and ordained to the Baptist ministry about four years later. An ardent republican, he served in the American revolution as a chaplain and combatant with a New Jersey regiment. Following the war he held a number of pastorates, the last and most notable being on Staten Island, N.Y., where in 1786 he was instrumental in establishing the first Baptist church. In 1791 he was one of the founders and the first moderator of the New York Baptist Association. Six years later he published *A church covenant*, embodying a strict Calvinism and the principle of "close communion," for the use of Baptist churches.

In 1796 Holmes had told the association of his inclination to travel among the Indians of western New York, thus foreshadowing the missionary career for which he is chiefly remembered. In 1797 and 1798 he visited the bands of Oneida County and two years

later he was employed by the New York Missionary Society, a coalition of Baptists and Presbyterians, to open missions among the Indians east of the Niagara River. Establishing his residence at Tuscarora village near Lewiston, Holmes preached the Gospel to the Tuscaroras and Senecas, and for a time he seems to have enjoyed the support of Seneca chief Red Jacket [SHAKÓYE:WA:THA?]. Early in 1801 he visited the Grand River to solicit the advice of Joseph Brant [Thayendanegea*], whose interest proved to be mainly in placing Indian boys in missionary schools. This trip marked the first time an accredited Baptist minister from the United States had ventured into Upper Canada. During the early 1800s several Baptist associations in the United States were actively promoting the establishment of congregations in the province. Holmes's station near Lewiston became a regular stopping-point for their agents, and on several occasions he crossed the border with them to preach.

In 1807 Holmes was dismissed by his society, from which the Baptists had withdrawn the previous year. Having preached on occasion at Queenston, Upper Canada, he proceeded in 1808 to organize a small church there with support from the Baptist missionary societies of Massachusetts and New York. Until 1810 he was also the minister of a church in what is now Beamsville. Like fellow Baptist preacher Elijah Bentley* in York (Toronto), Holmes welcomed invading American troops in 1813, and on one occasion he entertained their officers. That December, when forced to retreat, their commanding officer sent a wagon for Holmes and his wife. The family reached safety, however, only after capture by British troops, a dramatic rescue by Lieutenant-Colonel Cyrenius Chapin, and another flight from Buffalo when it was burned by the British. Holmes remained in the Canandaigua area for several years, removing to Bedford in 1818 at the age of 74. From 1814 until his death in 1832 he held no regular charge but continued to preach in "destitute churches" and to encourage support for the missionary cause. The Queenston congregation did not survive his departure, although as late as 1817 he reported that much of his income was provided by Canadian friends.

Those who had visited Holmes at Tuscarora village reported with unanimous enthusiasm on his religious and educational program and on the response of the Indians to it. After he left it, however, the directors of the New York Baptist Missionary Society stated that, in view of his inability to speak an Indian language, the Tuscarora mission had never shown promise in proportion to its expense. Probably Holmes's chief importance before coming to Upper Canada was as a publicist within his denomination for Indian missions. For many years he carried on correspondence, duly reported to his association, with a variety of bands. Among these were the Iroquois of Caughnawaga

(Kahnawake), Lower Canada, who asked the Baptists for agricultural instructors while showing little interest in their beliefs.

Holmes had many qualities typical of self-educated frontier preachers of his time, notably strength of conviction, readiness for argument, and quaintness of manner. He also possessed qualities of leadership that led his fellows to place confidence in him. In 1814 he resolved to put politics behind him and thenceforth could seldom be drawn into controversy or even public appearance. According to a contemporary, William Leete Stone, Holmes looked "truly patriarchal" in his latter years. "His hair, long and white, fell down upon his shoulders; his manner was remarkably impressive, and his whole demeanor that of one who was ripe for heaven."

J. W. GRANT

[A snapshot print purported to be of a portrait of Holmes is in the collections of the American Baptist Hist. Soc. (Rochester, N.Y.). The portrait does not resemble a late description of Holmes, but could be from an earlier period.   J.W.G.]

A church covenant; including a summary of the fundamental doctrines of the Gospel, compiled by Elkanah Holmes, was published in New York in 1797. A subsequent edition, adopted by the First Baptist Church of Baltimore, Md., appeared there in 1818. Some of Holmes's correspondence has been published under the title "Letters of the Reverend Elkanah Holmes from Fort Niagara in 1800: his work among the Tuscaroras, the Senecas, and in Buffalo" in the Buffalo Hist. Soc., *Pub.*, 6 (1903): 187–205.

American Baptist Hist. Soc., Elkanah Holmes, personal papers. Canadian Baptist Arch., McMaster Divinity College (Hamilton, Ont.), First Baptist Church (Beamsville, Ont.), minute-books, 1807–32 (typescript). *Baptist annual reg.* (London), 3 (1798–1801): 369–76, 421–23. Buffalo Hist. Soc., *Pub.*, 6. *Mass. Baptist Missionary Magazine* (Boston), 1 (1803–8) and (1808–10). New York Baptist Assoc., *Minutes*, 1791–1839. *New York Missionary Magazine and Repository of Religious Intelligence* (New York), 1 (1800): 381–88. William Parkinson, *The funeral sermon of Elder Elkanah Holmes, preached in the meeting house of the First Baptist Church in the city of New-York, Lord's Day, Feb. 26, 1832* (New York, 1832). Deidamia Covell Brown, *Memoir of the late Rev. Lemuel Covell, missionary of the Tuscarora Indians and the province of Upper Canada . . .* (2v. in 1, Brandon, Vt., 1839). S. [E. H.] Ivison and Fred Rosser, *The Baptists in Upper and Lower Canada before 1820* (Toronto, 1956). W. L. Stone, *Life of Joseph Brant – Thayendanegea . . .* (2v., New York, 1838; repr. New York, 1969, and St Clair Shores, Mich., 1970), 2.

HOLMES, WILLIAM, surgeon, physician, army officer, landowner, office holder, and JP; b. *c.* 1766 in Stewartstown (Northern Ireland); d. 24 Feb. 1834 at Quebec.

William Holmes had acquired an education as a surgeon before 31 March 1787, when he purchased a commission in the medical department of the British army at the customary price of 400 guineas. As surgeon to the 5th Foot he was immediately stationed at Quebec. In 1790–91 he was in Detroit tending Indians, under Little Turtle [Michikinakoua*] and Blue Jacket [Weyapiersenwah*], wounded in battle against the Americans. Garrisoned next in Newark (Niagara-on-the-Lake), Upper Canada, he proposed to settle in the province; in 1792 he was granted 1,200 acres in Pickering Township, where he also purchased land, and in 1796 he was issued a town lot in Newark. His transfer to Quebec in 1796, where his regiment was drafted, and his appointment as surgeon to the forces in Lower Canada on 17 Jan. 1799 precluded his plans for settlement.

Following a trip to Europe, where he probably acquired a degree in medicine, Holmes took up his duties at Quebec in June 1799. As senior medical officer in the Canadas after the departure of John Mervin NOOTH in July, he ranked above James FISHER, garrison surgeon, and George Longmore*, apothecary to the forces and physician, each of whom boasted a longer service record. The three men were required to work closely together. Longmore found Holmes a skilled surgeon and was to seek his assistance in a difficult case in 1801. However, conflict arose between Holmes and Fisher in 1799 over management of a typhus epidemic among the forces. In December Fisher was sent to Montreal in "complete control of the medical proceedings" there, and his persistent refusal to report direct to Holmes led to the intervention of the Duke of Kent [Edward* Augustus], who confirmed Holmes's seniority; Holmes was "responsible for all medical staff in the country," Fisher for the garrison sick only. Tension recurred during the reduction of hospital staff in 1802–3 following the signature of the Treaty of Amiens between Britain and France; Fisher's position was secured, while Holmes's was eliminated by the appointment of James MACAULAY as senior hospital officer and surgeon to the forces for the Canadas. Holmes was placed on half pay in June 1803 but was returned to full pay in December 1804 as surgeon to the forces in both provinces.

Meanwhile, Holmes had established himself in civil practice at Quebec. From about 1799 he was associated with Longmore at the Hôtel-Dieu and with Fisher at the Hôpital Général. He was physician to the nuns at both hospitals. These posts were unpaid, but they carried prestige that was valuable in building up a clientele as, no doubt, did his position of deputy grand master of Lower Canadian freemasons from 1805 to 1810 at least.

Holmes had married "a native" of Lower Canada named Mary Ann, and they had settled with their four children in modest surroundings in Upper Town. They had two more children before she died in 1803. His marriage on 12 May 1807 to Margaret Macnider,

Holmes

widow of the merchant James Johnston*, brought property and financial security; through her, for instance (and perhaps through David Lynd*, for whose estate he acted as curator), he became a co-proprietor of the Dorchester Bridge. After the birth of a daughter in 1808, the family moved into the house "lately occupied by Mrs. Lynd [Jane Henry]."

His plans to remarry had precipitated Holmes's retirement from the army; rather than accept a posting to Upper Canada, he returned to half pay on 25 April 1807. He volunteered his services to Governor Sir George Prevost* on the outbreak of war in 1812, but his offer does not seem to have been taken up. At times, particularly after the war, his finances appear to have been shaken; in late 1812 and again five years later his property was seized by the sheriff for sale at auction, and in 1818 and 1819 he was obliged to inflict similar treatment on two of his debtors. Nevertheless, he had the resources to become a keen farmer and owned well-kept properties along Chemin Sainte-Foy and the road to Cap-Rouge. He was an active member of the Agriculture Society, in which his farmers were prize-winners. In addition to the rural holdings, he owned several town houses, which he leased, and other property in the city.

Meanwhile, Holmes's clientele increased in town and out. He and Fisher "shared the whole practice," according to the physician and surgeon Joseph Painchaud*. Holmes gave care at times to the sick and infirm at the Hôpital Général, and until 1825 he held exclusive responsibility for the sick poor admitted to the Hôtel-Dieu. In 1813 he was appointed an examiner of candidates for medical licences. Fisher's departure three years later opened new avenues; Holmes replaced him as physician to the Ursulines and as president in the Quebec district of the examiners of candidates for licences. In June 1817 he was appointed a member of the Vaccine Board, and in 1821 he became its vice-president. On 28 June 1821 he was commissioned a justice of the peace.

In November 1816 Holmes had been appointed a commissioner for the relief of the insane and foundlings at Quebec. The previous month William Hacket, who had replaced Fisher as doctor to the Hôpital Général, had reported to Governor Sir John Coape SHERBROOKE on the deplorable housing of the insane at that institution, and in January 1818 Holmes's testimony on the subject before a committee of the House of Assembly helped to secure funds immediately for additional accommodation and repairs and later for further improvements; in May he was appointed a trustee to oversee the work. Holmes attempted to introduce fresh air and exercise and to remove restraint in the treatment of the insane, as advocated by the French specialist and theorist Philippe Pinel, but continued overcrowding in the older cells undermined such care. In 1824 Holmes and Hacket,

responding to questionnaires of a special committee of the Legislative Council, endorsed the committee's opinion that "one Lunatic Asylum to serve the whole province" should be constructed. Although strongly supported by Lieutenant Governor Sir Francis Nathaniel BURTON, the recommendation was rejected by a special committee of the assembly chaired by François BLANCHET; inquiry by another committee of the lower house in January 1829 resulted in only minor improvements in accommodation. Known familiarly as the "Insane Physician," Holmes remained solely responsible for care of the insane and the only medical man on the commission for their relief, to which he was reappointed in 1830 and 1832.

Holmes's term as president of the Quebec examiners for medical licences coincided with a rapid increase in the size of the medical profession; between 1816 and 1831 more than 200 persons were admitted at Quebec and Montreal. This growth and the changing composition of the profession were accompanied by internal ethnic and political conflict. Examiners, who were appointed by the governor, were mainly British, and at Quebec before 1824 were entirely military, with the exception of Thomas Fargues*. Their decisions were arbitrary; moreover, by an act of 1788, military and British-educated candidates for licence could receive preferential treatment. After 1818 the boards came under increasing criticism in the assembly; a movement, led by Blanchet and later by Jacques LABRIE, sought to repeal the act of 1788 and to have the examiners elected by members of the profession. Perhaps realizing the potential for conflict in the appointment of examiners, Holmes had recommended vainly to Sherbrooke in 1816 that Blanchet be made one, and in 1820 he requested from Governor Lord Dalhousie [Ramsay*] an increase in their number. Meanwhile, candidates for licence sympathetic to the movement disputed decisions of the examiners, and Holmes's exclusive appointment at the Hôtel-Dieu was censured in the nationalist newspaper Le Canadien. On 31 March 1831 a new medical act provided for elective boards of examiners; in the elections that followed Holmes and his last remaining military colleague were defeated. Holmes, who under the act of 1788 had not required a licence to practise, was obliged to appear before the new Board of Examiners at Quebec, presided over by Joseph Painchaud. Requested to attend a meeting in October 1831, he resisted until April 1832.

By that time, Holmes had generally withdrawn from active practice. As early as 1821 the Ursulines, declaring him "too old," had asked for his replacement by Fargues. In 1825 Fargues became associated with him as consultant at the Hôtel-Dieu where, although Holmes retained his position as senior medical officer, much of his work was taken over by younger staff members. Holmes's son-in-law Sydney

Robert Bellingham* recalled that in 1824 he was "a tall gray-headed sixty-year old gentleman with small eyes and a slight north of Ireland brogue." By 1832, two years before his death, "the old doctor wore a loose dressing-gown and slippers, and spent the greater part of his day at the Garrison Library, not a stone's throw from his residence, where he provoked much fun amongst the officers by his free and easy costume."

According to Bellingham, Holmes had been generous and kind to his patients, had been well liked in the religious hospitals, and had frequently "declined payment for his advice and medicines." On the other hand Painchaud, a professional rival and political opponent, asserted that he had overcharged for country calls and had been hampered in his practice by a poor facility in French. Successful in his private practice, in his appointive positions Holmes represented the medical establishment and British military and executive authority in a period of professional and political conflict and change. Although thrown by his offices into the debates, being neither an intellectual nor an innovator he did not play a leading role. As the system of health care and the medical profession became increasingly entangled in the political struggle between the assembly and the executive branch in the Lower Canadian legislature, Holmes tended to draw apart. If he had been quick-tempered as a young man, in later years he seems to have mellowed, living quietly with his family, yet "ever-activated," as he had earlier declared, "by the faithful discharge of [his] duties." Prosaic in outlook, Holmes outlived his contemporaries, in many ways an 18th-century practitioner to the end.

BARBARA TUNIS

ANQ-Q, CE1-61, 7 nov. 1796, 12 mai 1807; CE1-66, 3 avril 1808, 28 févr. 1834. ASQ, Univ., sér.U, U-17, U-18. PAC, MG 24, B1, 1: 294; B25, 2: 8–16, 67, 72, 103; RG 1, E1, 19: 36; 22: 104; L3, 222A: H1/4; 224A: H4/104; L3ᴸ: 52692–720; RG 4, A1, 155: 78; 257: 157; B28, 48–52; RG 7, G15C, 24: 31, 274; 29: 190; RG 8, I (C ser.), 287: 72–73, 88–148, 195–96, 212; 288: 104–6, 149; 372: 59–60; RG 68, General index, 1651–1841. "Les dénombrements de Québec" (Plessis), ANQ Rapport, 1948–49: 161. "Early records of St. Mark's and St. Andrew's churches, Niagara," comp. Janet Carnochan, OH, 3 (1901): 11, 13. Journal de médecine de Québec, 1 (1826): 97. L.C., House of Assembly, Journaux, 1808: 136–40; 1818: 80; 1820–21: 202; 1825: 256–57, 374; 1826: 38, 178, 350; 1828–29: 290, 359–65, app.L; 1831: 263; Legislative Council, Journaux, 1823–24, app.I. Le Canadien, 11 nov. 1818. Quebec Daily Mercury, 25 Feb. 1834. Quebec Gazette, 13 June 1799; 27 Oct. 1803; 10 Jan. 1805; 25 Feb., 4 Aug. 1808; 9 July 1812; 13, 29 May 1817; 17 Oct. 1822; 13 Jan., 16 June, 20 Oct. 1823. E. H. Dahl et al., La ville de Québec, 1800–1850: un inventaire de cartes et plans (Ottawa, 1975). William Johnston, Roll of commissioned officers in the medical service of the British army . . . (Aberdeen, Scot., 1917).

Langelier, Liste des terrains concédés, 15. Quebec almanac, 1789, 1794–97, 1801–3, 1805–11, 1814–31. The service of British regiments in Canada and North America . . . , comp. C. H. Stewart (Ottawa, 1962), 90.

M.-J. et G. Ahern, Notes pour l'hist. de la médecine, 208, 309–10. Jacques Bernier, "Le corps médical québécois à la fin du XVIIIᵉ siècle," Health, disease and medicine; essays in Canadian history, ed. C. [G.] Roland ([Toronto], 1983). Neil Cantlie, A history of the Army Medical Department (2v., Edinburgh and London, 1974), 1: 172. D. G. Creighton, "The struggle for financial control in Lower Canada, 1818–1831," Constitutionalism and nationalism in Lower Canada, intro. Ramsay Cook (Toronto, 1969). Graham, Hist. of freemasonry, 141–43. Sylvio Leblond, "Une conférence inédite du docteur Joseph Painchaud," Trois siècles de médecine québécoise (Québec, 1970), 56–65. Lise Mathieu, "Étude de la législation sociale du Bas-Canada, 1760–1840" (thèse de MA, univ. Laval, Québec, 1953). Ouellet, Bas-Canada, 268–71, 311–15. P.-G. Roy, À travers l'histoire de l'Hôtel-Dieu de Québec (Lévis, Qué., 1939), 196. Jacques Bernier, "François Blanchet et le mouvement réformiste en médecine au début du XIXᵉ siècle," RHAF, 34 (1980–81): 223–44. Sylvio Leblond, "La médecine dans la province de Québec avant 1847," Cahiers des Dix, 35 (1970): 69–95. B. R. Tunis, "Medical education and medical licensing in Lower Canada: demographic factors, conflict, and social change," SH, 14 (1981): 67–91.

HOOD, ROBERT, naval officer, explorer, painter, and surveyor; b. c. 1797 probably in Portarlington (Republic of Ireland), second son of Richard Hood and Catherine Roe; d. unmarried 20 Oct. 1821 near Lake Providence (N.W.T.).

Robert Hood came from an Anglo-Irish family. His father, a scholar and clergyman of some scientific ability, was probably responsible for Hood's education. By 1803 the family was living in Bury St Edmunds, England, where Hood Sr had obtained a curacy.

On 5 Feb. 1809 Hood joined the Royal Navy as a first-class volunteer. He served successively in the Baltic, off the Iberian peninsula, in the Mediterranean, in the English Channel, in an attack on Algiers in August 1816, and briefly on the Cape of Good Hope station. He had risen to able-bodied seaman in October 1810 and to midshipman in September 1811. At his examination for a lieutenancy in October 1816 Hood presented private logs, containing numerous drawings and water-colours depicting incidents of naval life, which the examining officers declared "journals which we have never seen surpassed." Hood received a passing certificate but his promotion was not confirmed and he went on half pay.

Following the Napoleonic Wars the British Admiralty turned its efforts to the discovery of a passage between the Atlantic and Pacific oceans through the North American Arctic, and in May 1819 Hood was appointed midshipman on an expedition to be led by Lieutenant John Franklin* overland from Hudson

Hood

Bay. Its ultimate purpose was to chart the Arctic coast eastwards from the mouth of the Coppermine River (N.W.T.) to Chesterfield Inlet on Hudson Bay. Hood and George Back* were to take navigational, geographical, and meteorological observations, and make such "drawings of the land, of the natives, and of the various objects of natural history" as the second officer of the expedition, John Richardson*, might suggest.

The expedition suffered from poor planning, unforeseen difficulties, and sheer bad luck. The party arrived at York Factory (Man.) on 30 Aug. 1819, having failed en route to hire a sufficient number of boatmen in the Orkney Islands, Scotland. The Hudson's Bay Company, embroiled in bitter competition with the North West Company, was unable to make up the deficiency in men and boats, and consequently many supplies had to be left behind when the group, numbering 11, departed for Cumberland House (Sask.) on the Saskatchewan River, which it reached in October 1819.

Franklin and Back, with seaman John Hepburn*, advanced to Fort Chipewyan (Alta) on Lake Athabasca in January 1820. Hood and Richardson remained behind to study the natural history and native people around Cumberland House and to record meteorological observations. In a personal journal Hood noted that their cabin "proved rather too airy for this climate" and although they "kept the chimneys in a constant blaze . . . our pens and brushes were frozen to the paper." In late March and early April he made an expedition into the bush to obtain a drawing of a moose and to study the aurora borealis. "The miseries endured during the first journey of this nature are so great, that nothing could induce the sufferer to undertake a second, while under the influence of present pain," he observed. "He feels his frame crushed by unaccountable pressure, he drags a galling and stubborn weight at his feet, and his track is marked with blood. The dazzling scene around him affords no rest to his eye, no object to divert his attention from his own agonizing sensations. . . . But fortunately for him, no evil makes an impression so evanescent as pain. . . . The traveller soon forgets his sufferings, and at every future journey their recurrence is attended with diminished acuteness."

On 13 June 1820 Hood and Richardson set out to rejoin Franklin. In the Otter Rapids (Sask.) on the Missinippi (Churchill) River Hood risked his life in a futile attempt to save a canoe foreman who had been accidentally swept down. Hood did not record the incident, but Richardson did. From Fort Chipewyan the reunited expedition, reinforced by hired voyageurs and interpreters, advanced via Fort Providence (Old Fort Providence, N.W.T.) to Winter Lake, where, beginning in August 1820, it constructed Fort Enterprise. Back and Hood reconnoitred a route to the

Coppermine for the following spring. The two men fell in love with a 15-year-old Copper Indian girl named Greenstockings and, had not an alert Hepburn surreptitiously removed the charges from their guns, they would have fought a duel over her. The dispatch of Back to obtain crucial supplies at Fort Chipewyan, 1,100 miles distant, prevented further incidents. Hood painted a portrait of Greenstockings, who gave birth to a daughter by him. That winter Hood worked intensely on his drawings, paintings, and observations, in the process weakening his health through lack of air and exercise.

In June 1821 the expedition set out for the mouth of the Coppermine. It had for some time suffered from a severe shortage of provisions, a result of the rivalry between the HBC and the NWC, and continued to do so. From 18 July to 18 August the party of five Englishmen, eleven Canadians, two Indian hunters, and two Inuit (one of whom was TATTANNOEUCK) charted 675 miles of coastline never before seen by white men. Lack of food and the onset of winter forced it to halt at Point Turnagain on Dease Strait. Franklin chose to return to Fort Enterprise by way of Bathurst Inlet, the newly discovered Hood River, and the barren grounds, but this route proved far more difficult than could have been imagined. The trek over the barren grounds was made Indian file, the voyageurs taking turns at the head to break the snow, Hood in the gruelling second position directing their steps until, on 20 September, weakness forced him back. The group subsisted on small game and a lichen called rock-tripe, which unfortunately caused some, but especially Hood, to have diarrhoea. Hood had volunteered to perform the "invidious task," as Franklin put it, of issuing the food, and "always took the smallest portion." On 7 October Franklin, Back, and the stronger voyageurs were forced to leave behind several men, including Hood, who were too weak to keep up the pace. Two had already been abandoned, and presumably had died, on the 6th. By the 18th Hood was nearing death from exhaustion, dehydration, and starvation, but his life was evidently ended instead by an Iroquois voyageur, Michel Terohaute, who seems to have shot him in the head on the 20th after a violent quarrel. Terohaute was subsequently executed by Richardson, who later suspected him of cannibalism.

A devout Christian – he was reading Edward Bickersteth's *A Scripture help . . .* at the moment he died – Hood was conscientious, hard-working, honest, self-effacing, stoical, and possessed of an inquiring, philosophical mind and a wry sense of humour. He may have lacked the physical strength to endure the strenuous conditions under which the expedition laboured, but overwork and self-deprivation had also weakened his ability to survive. Had he lived he might have achieved the fame and knighthood that awaited his colleagues. As it was, news of his promotion to lieutenant on 1 Jan. 1821 reached Franklin's party some weeks after his death.

In all 11 men had died on this first overland expedition sent out by the Admiralty. The survivors, who included all the Englishmen except Hood, brought back valuable information on the northwest and Arctic regions. Previously uncharted portions of the continent were mapped with great precision, in large part thanks to Hood; with "extraordinary talent" and "a degree of zeal and accuracy that characterized all his pursuits," in Franklin's words, he had made surveys as the party advanced and "protracted the route every evening on a ruled map." He had been the first to conduct a careful magnetic survey of the northwest. Hood's journal constitutes a well-written record of the travels, work, and tribulations of the expedition from 23 May 1819 to 15 Sept. 1820. It describes the flora, fauna, and geography of the land, and records observations on the climate, magnetic phenomena, and aurora borealis. There are notes on the transportation, hunting, and fishing techniques of the inhabitants, and on the physique, customs, and ways of the Inuit, Métis, and Indians, particularly the Crees. The journal formed the basis for part of Franklin's *Narrative of a journey to the shores of the polar sea in the years 1819, 20, 21 and 22*, which was illustrated with eight engravings from Hood's drawings, including the portrait of Greenstockings. Feeling that Hood's observations on the aurora borealis presented "some new facts," Franklin reproduced them in full in a second edition.

Hood's paintings of wildlife, particularly birds, are among the best of their time. Five winter birds painted at Fort Cumberland were until then unknown to ornithologists, and had his paintings been published on their arrival in London and the species named, Hood would have been credited with priority in their discovery. His memory is perpetuated by a flower, *Phlox hoodii*, or moss phlox; a sedge, *Carex hoodii*; an animal, *Citellus tridecemlineatus hoodii*, or 13-striped ground squirrel; and a river, the Hood, taken by the expedition on its tragic return.

JIM BURANT

Robert Hood is the author of "Narrative of the proceedings of an expedition of discovery in North America under the command of Lieut. Franklin, R.N." A manuscript copy is held at PABC, AA20/H76, and a microfilm copy at the Glenbow-Alberta Institute. It was published as *To the Arctic by canoe, 1819–1821: the journal and paintings of Robert Hood, midshipman with Franklin*, ed. C. S. Houston (Montreal and London, 1974), with reproductions of a silhouette of Hood and several of his paintings. Chapters four and five of the journal had already appeared as "Some account of the Cree and other Indians, 1819," in *Alberta Hist. Rev.* (Edmonton), 15 (1967): 6–17.

Five engravings from sketches done by Hood in 1809, 1811, and 1812 aboard the *Melpomene* and *Imperieuse* were published in James Ralfe, *Naval chronology of Great Britain* . . . (London, 1820). The journals he kept on the *Imperieuse* and the *Spey* are in the possession of the Birch family of Surrey, B.C.

Many of Hood's sketches and water-colours have survived. They are mainly in private collections, and the greater part of them are still in the hands of his family. Six water-colours done during the Franklin expedition are held at the PAC and are reproduced in black and white in W. M. E. Cooke, *W. H. Coverdale Collection of Canadiana: paintings, water-colours and drawings (Manoir Richelieu collection)* (Ottawa, 1983).

J.-R. Bellot, *Memoirs of Lieutenant Joseph René Bellot . . . with his journal of a voyage in the polar seas, in search of Sir John Franklin*, [ed. Julien Lemer] (2v., London, 1855). John Franklin, *Narrative of a journey to the shores of the polar sea in the years 1819, 20, 21 and 22* . . . (London, 1823). *HBRS*, 1 (Rich). John Richardson, *Arctic ordeal: the journal of John Richardson, surgeon-naturalist with Franklin, 1820–1822*, ed. C. S. Houston (Kingston, Ont., and Montreal, 1984). G.B., ADM, *Navy list*, 1805–22. W. R. O'Byrne, *A naval biographical dictionary: comprising the life and services of every living officer in her majesty's navy* . . . (London, 1849). R. E. Johnson, *Sir John Richardson: Arctic explorer, natural historian, naval surgeon* (London, 1976). Paul Nanton, *Arctic breakthrough; Franklin's expeditions, 1819–1847* (Toronto and Vancouver, 1970). L. H. Neatby, *The search for Franklin* (Edmonton, 1970). *CHR*, 66 (1985): 588–89. A. G. E. Jones, "Lieutenant Robert Hood, R.N., 1797–1821," *Musk-Ox* (Saskatoon, Sask.), no.16 (1975): 67–68.

HOPPNER, HENRY PARKYNS, naval officer, explorer, and painter; b. 1795 in London, fourth of five children of John Hoppner and Phoebe Wright; d. unmarried 22 Dec. 1833 in Lisbon.

Henry Parkyns Hoppner was born into an artistically inclined family. His father was an eminent portraitist and his mother the daughter of a popular American sculptress, Patience Lovell Wright. In 1808 he joined the Royal Navy and, during the Napoleonic Wars and the War of 1812, he saw continuous service off northern Spain, in the English Channel, and on the east coast of the United States. Commissioned in September 1815, he was a junior lieutenant aboard the frigate *Alceste* in 1816 when it carried Lord Amherst on a diplomatic mission to China. After the *Alceste* was lost in the Strait of Gaspar (Selat Gelasa, Indonesia), Hoppner conveyed Amherst to Batavia (Djakarta) and then returned to relieve his comrades with the Indiaman *Lion*.

Hoppner's intrepidity on this occasion and the development of his artistic talents probably motivated his appointment on 18 Jan. 1818 as second in command to Lieutenant William Edward Parry* aboard the brig *Alexander* in an expedition led by John Ross* to Baffin Bay in search of a northwest passage. Having scientific as well as exploratory objectives,

Hornor

the party required one or two artists to make a pictorial record of the landscape, people, plants, and animals encountered; the voyage lasted seven months.

Subsequently, Hoppner participated in three voyages of exploration led by Parry himself. During the first, from May 1819 to October 1820, he was lieutenant on board the gun-brig *Griper*, while another artist, Frederick William Beechey*, was Parry's lieutenant aboard the *Hecla*, bomb. Hoppner and Beechey charted and surveyed in addition to drawing. During the winter, spent on the south coast of Melville Island, Hoppner was active in the ships' theatre company, one of the novelties introduced by Parry to relieve the tedium of wintering in the Arctic. On the return journey Hoppner sketched an Inuk encountered in Baffin Bay. Parry recorded of the man: "It required . . . some shew of authority, as well as some occasional rewards, to keep him quietly seated on a rock for a time sufficient for this purpose; the inclination they have to jump about, when much pleased, rendering it a penalty of no trifling nature for them to sit still for half an hour together."

On Parry's second expedition, from April 1821 to October 1823, Hoppner was lieutenant on board *Hecla*. In mid September 1821 he surveyed a large inlet adjoining Lyon Inlet, Melville Peninsula (N.W.T.), and Parry named it for him. He was active in the Royal Arctic Theatre, which helped the men while away two winters near the shores of Melville Peninsula. Having been promoted commander on 25 Jan. 1822, Hoppner was commanding officer of the *Fury*, bomb, when it accompanied *Hecla* on Parry's third expedition, which left England in May 1824. After wintering at Port Bowen on the east shore of Prince Regent Inlet, the ships encountered pressure from ice off Somerset Island in late July and early August 1825. *Fury* was driven aground, and, despite heroic efforts by Hoppner and his men, eventually had to be abandoned near Fury Point. The expedition immediately returned home on board *Hecla*. The requisite court martial attached "no blame whatever" to Hoppner for the loss of his ship. On 30 December he was promoted captain.

Already in poor health by the end of this voyage, Hoppner was unable to join Parry in the latter's attempt on the North Pole in 1827, and his application to accompany Ross in 1829 was rejected. Often severely ill thereafter, he died in Lisbon during a visit to southern Europe.

Hoppner was reportedly an "excellent officer and worthy man." In 1826 Parry had written of his "constant companion" in the exploration of the Arctic: "I feel every possible obligation for his steady and persevering zeal . . . and for his advice and assistance on every occasion." Hoppner's work illustrated some of Parry's published narratives, notably the *Journal of a third voyage for the discovery of a north-west passage*. Hoppner Inlet in Melville Peninsula, Cape Hoppner on Melville Island, and Hoppner Strait, between Winter Island and Melville Peninsula, all commemorate him.

CLIVE HOLLAND

G. F. Lyon, *The private journal of Captain G. F. Lyon, of H.M.S. "Hecla," during the recent voyage of discovery under Captain Parry* (new ed., London, 1825), 426–27, 435. W. E. Parry, *Journal of a voyage for the discovery of a north-west passage from the Atlantic to the Pacific; performed in the years 1819–20 . . .* (London, 1821); *Journal of a second voyage for the discovery of a north-west passage from the Atlantic to the Pacific; performed in the years 1821–22–23 . . .* (London, 1824); *Journal of a third voyage for the discovery of a north-west passage from the Atlantic to the Pacific; performed in the years 1824–25 . . .* (London, 1826). John Ross, *A voyage of discovery, made under the orders of the Admiralty, in his majesty's ships "Isabella" and "Alexander," for the purpose of exploring Baffin's Bay, and enquiring into the probability of a north-west passage* (London, 1819). *Times* (London), 1 Jan. 1834. C. R. Markham, *The Arctic navy list; or, a century of Arctic & Antarctic officers, 1773–1873; together with a list of officers of the 1875 expedition and of their services* (London, 1875). John Marshall, *Royal naval biography . . .* (4v. in 6 and 2v. supp., London, 1823–35), 3, pt.I: 279–80. William McKay and William Roberts, *John Hoppner, R.A.* (London, 1909).

HORNOR (Horner), THOMAS, colonizer, militia officer, JP, office holder, and politician; b. 17 March 1767 in Mansfield Township, Burlington County, N.J., eldest son of Isaac and Mary Hornor; m. 22 March 1801 Olive Baker in Oxford County, Upper Canada, and they had seven children; d. 4 Aug. 1834 in Burford Township, Upper Canada.

Raised in a prosperous family of New Jersey Quakers, Thomas Hornor received a good education at the College of New Jersey, now Princeton University – as befitted the nephew of one of its founders. During the summer of 1794 he and his cousin Thomas Watson Jr brought 20 settlers to Watsons (later Blenheim) Township in Upper Canada, a township grant made by the government the previous summer to Thomas Watson Sr and his associates. Having selected a mill site near the front of the township, Hornor brought from Albany, N.Y., in May 1795 the necessary men and materials to construct a sawmill. That year Abraham Iredell* surveyed a part of the township and Hornor completed the construction of the first sawmill, on lot 15, concession 1, along what became known as Hornor's (Horner) Creek. He then began to cut a road, six miles in length, through the township. In 1797 Administrator Peter Russell* rescinded many township grants, including Watson's; Hornor received 600 acres in Blenheim, exactly half the amount he had requested.

Some time after settling in Blenheim, Hornor was

apparently dismissed from the Society of Friends for becoming a freemason and joining the militia. He served as senior warden in Masonic Lodge No.11 in 1797 and, in March 1798, was appointed a captain in the Norfolk militia; he also became a member of the Church of England. The erection of the London District in 1800 brought Hornor a host of local offices: justice of the peace, commissioner of the Court of King's Bench, registrar for the counties of Oxford and Middlesex (on the recommendation of Samuel Ryerse*), and commissioner for administering the oath of allegiance to persons claiming possession of lands in the district. In 1802 William CLAUS was appointed lieutenant of Oxford County, the most powerful and important local office; initially he relied upon Benajah Mallory* as his unofficial deputy in militia matters, but by May 1803 Hornor, who was captain of the Blenheim company of the 1st Oxford Militia, had assumed this role. Resentful, Mallory sought the formal position, but in vain: Hornor was officially appointed in June 1806.

Over the next few years Hornor became entangled in the factionalism which characterized local politics. He was a natural target for the widespread resentment against district officials, particularly Ryerse and Thomas Welch*. On one occasion, Hornor and another magistrate were brought before the Court of Quarter Sessions on charges of being drunk on duty as JPs. On another occasion, in June 1804, Sheriff Joseph Ryerson allegedly informed Daniel McCall that Hornor and another were "principal Characters" in a "dangerous Conspiracy" to shoot "every good and loyal Subject" of the king. McCall, however, waited until June 1807 before swearing a deposition about the plot. Some time after January 1809 Hornor lost the deputy lieutenancy, probably as a result of these charges. To compound his misfortune, in 1809 his grist-mill, built in 1802, was destroyed by fire; it was never rebuilt.

At the outbreak of the War of 1812 the old suspicions of his loyalty had not died and he lost the long-coveted lieutenant-colonelcy of the 1st Oxford Militia to Henry Bostwick. Hornor was eager to demonstrate his loyalty and his opportunity came when in 1812 John NORTON mustered only a handful of the Six Nations Indians. Hornor immediately proceeded to the Grand River and used his influence to enlist some 75 Indians who travelled with him on foot to the Detroit area. The expedition, which was made entirely at Hornor's expense and for which he was never compensated, was dismissed before reaching its destination. In spite of this gesture of loyalty he was still unable to obtain a commission; early in 1813 he enlisted as a private and served as such until the end of the war. Following a militia reorganization in 1822, Hornor was finally commissioned colonel of the 1st Oxford.

In 1820 Hornor won the riding of Oxford by acclamation. Once in the House of Assembly he proved himself a reformer although an office holder, JP, and militia officer. He supported, for example, the right of both Bidwells, BARNABAS and Marshall Spring*, to sit in the house, the repeal of the Sedition Act of 1818, and the bill for the relief of Wesleyan Methodists. In the election of 1824, when the riding returned two members, Hornor topped a three-man poll and was joined in the assembly by Charles Ingersoll. Hornor was re-elected in 1828 but lost to Ingersoll and Charles Duncombe* in 1830. Although no longer a member of the assembly he expressed opposition to the expulsion of William Lyon Mackenzie* from the house in 1831.

Hornor continued to engage in farming in addition to his other endeavours. In March 1830 he secured the patent to a new and improved horse-powered threshing machine which he had co-invented. He died intestate in August 1834, a victim of the cholera epidemic; his estate was valued at more than £428 and he was survived by his wife and six of their seven children.

DANIEL J. BROCK

PAC, RG 1, L3, 224: H3/100; 230a: H13/36; 251a: H misc., 1797–1820/15; 523a: W5/19; 525a: W9/16. UWOL, Regional Coll., London District, Surrogate Court, estate files, 1800–39, no.250. *The Oxford gazetteer; containing a complete history of the county of Oxford from its first settlement . . .*, comp. T. S. Shenston (Hamilton, [Ont.], 1852; repr. Woodstock, Ont., 1968). *History of Princeton, 1795–1967*, [comp. Mrs W. H. Williamson and Evelyn Brown] ([Princeton, Ont., 1967]).

HOUDET, ANTOINE-JACQUES, Sulpician and teacher; b. 1 Dec. 1763 in Château-Gontier, France, son of Antoine Houdet, a locksmith, and Jacquine Houdet; d. 7 April 1826 in Montreal.

Antoine-Jacques Houdet, who came from a humble background, began his studies at the Séminaire d'Angers in 1783 and did the two-year philosophy program and four years of theology there. After being ordained priest on 27 Sept. 1788, he was appointed to teach philosophy at Angers, did his year of solitude (noviciate) at Issy-les-Moulineaux, near Paris, in 1789, and was admitted into the Society of Saint-Sulpice. He became a teacher of dogmatics at the Séminaire de Nantes in 1790. Having refused, like the other Sulpicians, to take the oath of loyalty to the Civil Constitution of the Clergy, he left Nantes for Bilbao, Spain, on 15 Sept. 1792. He spent three years in Spain, first at Estella and later in the diocese of Orense. In September 1795 he left Astorga for London, and then, armed with a letter of recommendation from the Duke of Portland, he sailed for New York, where he arrived on 31 December. He reached

Howe

Montreal on 19 Jan. 1796 after a trip made difficult by the severity of the winter.

In October Houdet received an appointment to teach at the Collège Saint-Raphaël. He began his career there just at the time when the director, Jean-Baptiste MARCHAND, was leaving. Jean-Baptiste-Jacques Chicoisneau*, the new director, and the other French Sulpicians, Claude Rivière, Jacques-Guillaume Roque*, and Houdet, brought to the college the new traditions and stricter requirements that established its importance as an educational institution. From 1796 until his death Houdet, who was not drawn to pastoral ministry and who preached only a few sermons a year in the parish church, devoted himself wholly to teaching. He taught Latin, French, mathematics, science, astronomy, and philosophy. With Rivière he prepared courses and published textbooks, and he also gave assistance in the bursar's office and the library.

At the Séminaire de Saint-Sulpice Houdet was a highly respected counsellor whose opinion was sought on controversial matters. The seminary was at odds with the bishop of Quebec, Joseph-Octave PLESSIS, and after 1820 with Jean-Jacques Lartigue*, his auxiliary bishop in Montreal. When Plessis asked the Sulpicians to establish a seminary in Montreal for training those seeking ordination, Houdet expressed his opposition to this proposal in a memoir. He thought that the Séminaire de Saint-Sulpice could do nothing more for the time being than train regents at the college. He also drew attention to the fact that there were only a limited number of candidates for the priesthood. In 1821 Houdet put forward a justification for the seminary's uncooperative attitude at the time of Bishop Lartigue's arrival in Montreal the year before. He explained the seminary's refusal to accommodate Lartigue in the community and to render him honours that were due only to a resident bishop. The discussions were prolonged and became acrimonious [see Augustin CHABOILLEZ]. In June 1824 Sulpician Jean-Charles BÉDARD, who was sympathetic to Lartigue, wrote a report which was sent to Rome. Houdet prepared a reply summarizing the quarrels with Plessis, Lartigue, and the latter's coadjutor, Bernard-Claude PANET, and refuting Bédard's arguments point by point. This 130-page text reflected Houdet's theological and social training. He was a priest who had come out of the *ancien régime* imbued with the importance of the acknowledged rights and privileges of the Catholic church of France, and he was convinced that their strict enforcement would ensure the greatness and stability of a divine institution recognized and supported by the state. At times Houdet's remarks dealt with utter trivialities, and the force of his argument was weakened by his dwelling upon them. There is no doubt that he was intensely caught up in this quarrel and that he summed up the views held by the majority of the members of the Séminaire de Saint-Sulpice in Montreal, most of whom were from France.

Antoine-Jacques Houdet's relatively robust health suddenly deteriorated in 1825; he suffered two paralytic strokes from which he only partially recovered. Stricken by a third one, he died on 7 April 1826. He was buried on 10 April under the chancel of Notre-Dame church.

BRUNO HAREL

Antoine-Jacques Houdet is the author of *Cours abrégé de rhétorique à l'usage du collège de Montréal* (Montréal, 1835) and *Cours abrégé de belles-lettres à l'usage du collège de Montréal* (Montréal, 1840). In collaboration with his colleague Claude Rivière he wrote two works both called *Grammaire françoise pour servir d'introduction à la grammaire latine* and both published at Montreal in 1811. The ASSM holds two unpublished dictionaries by Houdet, one French-Latin (133 pages) and the other Latin-French (198 pages.)

AAQ, 71-31 CD, II: 39a, 40. ACAM, 465.101, 816-1, 818-1, 829-3. ANQ-M, CE1-51, 10 avril 1826. Arch. de la Compagnie de Saint-Sulpice (Paris), Dossier 102, no.4. ASSM, 11, 21, 24, 27. Allaire, *Dictionnaire*, 1: 271. [L.-A. Huguet-Latour], *Annuaire de Ville-Marie, origine, utilité et progrès des institutions catholiques de Montréal* ... (2v., Montréal, 1863–82). Louis Bertrand, *Bibliothèque sulpicienne ou histoire littéraire de la Compagnie de Saint-Sulpice* (3v., Paris, 1900), 2: 65–66. [Pierre] Boisard, *La Compagnie de Saint-Sulpice; trois siècles d'histoire* (s.l.n.d.). Dionne, *Les ecclésiastiques et les royalistes français*. Maurault, *Le collège de Montréal* (Dansereau; 1967).

HOWE, JOHN, printer, newspaperman, JP, and office holder; b. 14 Oct. 1754 in Boston, son of Joseph Howe and Rebecca Hart; d. 29 Dec. 1835 in Halifax.

Member of a fifth-generation family in the Thirteen Colonies, John Howe was just "out of his time" as an apprentice printer when the American revolution began and, according to his son Joseph*, witnessed the Boston Tea Party in December 1773. Although he was not, as one writer states, the John Howe who acted as a spy for Lieutenant-General Thomas Gage* behind the rebel lines in 1775, he left no doubt about his unbending allegiance to the crown. Because of it, Margaret Draper, who had like political sympathies, made him a junior partner at age 20 in the *Massachusetts Gazette; and the Boston Weekly News-Letter*, of which she was publisher.

On the British evacuation of Boston in March 1776, Howe went to Halifax, but by January 1777 he was in Newport, R.I., publishing the *Newport Gazette* in support of the British cause. There, on 7 June 1778, he married 16-year-old Martha Minns, known for her beauty. When Newport was evacuated in October 1779, he moved to New York and later to Halifax, his home for his remaining 55 years. But he continued to love New England and especially Boston with "filial regard," and whenever he got sick in his later years, his family sent him there to recuperate: "He generally came back uncommonly well." Howe was the only male in his family to leave the old colonies at the time of the revolution, and his pronounced pro-British feelings did not stem from his devotion to the crown as such and especially not to King George III. What counted with him, as with many New England loyalists, was the British heritage, the contributions of Britons over the centuries to politics, the arts, science, and literature. He was determined never to relinquish his membership in a nation whose accomplishments he admired and idealized.

On 28 Dec. 1780 Howe began to publish a weekly newspaper, the *Halifax Journal*, which in that day "set a new standard of newspaper printing." He also did general printing, including pamphlets, sermons, and an almanac, and participated in one of British North America's earliest literary movements when, in 1789, he printed a monthly, the *Nova-Scotia Magazine and Comprehensive Review of Literature, Politics, and News*, edited during its first year by William COCHRAN. The next year Howe succeeded Cochran as the magazine's editor, but through lack of support it failed in March 1792. His first wife having died in 1790, on 25 Oct. 1798 he married Mary Austen, *née* Ede, who in 1804 gave birth to Joseph, the last of his eight children.

Although most loyalists expected to be well rewarded for their allegiance, John Howe declined to press his claims and not until 1801, almost by default, did he become king's printer and hence publisher of the *Nova-Scotia Royal Gazette*, succeeding Anthony Henry*. The returns from this office were hardly great, since prior to 1809 the yearly allowances were a meagre £140 and subsequently only £175. Even less rewarding was the deputy postmaster generalship of Nova Scotia, New Brunswick, and Prince Edward Island, the duties of which he assumed in 1803. Somehow he was induced to give the incumbent, John Brittain, supposedly about to die, £200 a year for the good will of the office. But Brittain lived another seven and a half years and during that time the net return of the office to John Howe, for all the effort he and his family put into it, was a loss of £75. Later Joseph Howe would point out that his father's heavy payment to Brittain "laid the foundation of debts and sources of perplexity which ran over half his life."

In 1807 acute tension developed between Britain and the United States [*see* Sir George Cranfield Berkeley*], and the following year Sir George Prevost*, the lieutenant governor of Nova Scotia, was instructed to "gain Intelligence" about the intentions of the American government. He sent "a respectable and intelligent Inhabitant of Halifax," John Howe, to the United States. During his first mission, between April and September 1808, Howe reported that little had been done to fortify New York City, that Fort Mifflin, near Philadelphia, was in "very indifferent repair," and that "as far as respects military preparations . . . there are none whatever." In November he was back to observe official Washington at the highest level for about two months. With David Montagu Erskine, the British ambassador, he called on President Thomas Jefferson and Secretary of State James Madison, and, like Erskine, concluded that Madison, almost certain to be the next president, would not engage in war if – as seemed improbable – he were left to himself. Unlike Erskine, however, he did not think that war was inevitable, although Nova Scotia would be following the safest course by preparing for it; certainly the colony need not fear an attack that winter.

For these services, Joseph Howe said ruefully, his father "never received a farthing." The son could not understand why a man of talent, who consorted with governors, ambassadors, and even a president, should be so self-effacing as his father. In the world of politics, for example, should he not occasionally have put his great talents to work in "hammering some of our great folks"? But John Howe remained a quiet, sedate man who rarely meddled in political matters and made no enemies, altogether unobtrusive and unambitious. Indirectly he helped maintain established authority in the first decade of the century when Lieutenant Governor Sir John Wentworth* made extraordinary uses of the prerogative, especially to counteract William Cottnam TONGE and his "country party." Until 1813 the Howe family had a complete monopoly of the Halifax press through John Howe, who controlled the *Halifax Journal* and the *Nova-Scotia Royal Gazette*, and his brother-in-law William MINNS, who owned the *Weekly Chronicle*, and they both shunned political controversy. When, in 1809, the House of Assembly asked Howe to print in the *Royal Gazette* its resolutions condemning Administrator Alexander Croke*'s rejection of the appropriation bill, he followed without question the administrator's directive not to honour the request.

Howe accepted things as they were, not because he was a tory in the usual sense of the term, or because he approved the actions of authoritarians such as Wentworth and Croke, but rather because he refused to become embroiled in the politics of what he thought would always be an imperfect world and imperfect people. Recognizing human imperfection for what it was, he thought "this the best of all possible worlds, and the people upon it the best of all possible people." Contributing to these beliefs was his Sandemanianism, highly puritanical in its content, to which he had become strongly attached while in Boston. In that city, according to Charles St C. Stayner, the Sandemanians consisted of "a devout group of dignified

Howe

business men . . . [who] seem to have been more concerned with leading Christian lives than with mixing in either religious or political discussions." Two of the Sandemanian tenets which Howe especially honoured were the "community of goods, by which each [member] considered the whole of his property liable to the call of the poor and of the church; and the unlawfulness of laying up treasures upon earth, by setting them apart for distant, future, and uncertain use."

Understandable, therefore, was his lack of concern with temporalities. Although associating daily with local leaders because of his offices, he was never part of Halifax society. Story-tellers have pictured two kinds of Haligonians: "the world of fashion on the one side, and the demi-monde of the waterfront on the other." But there was a third world, the New England puritans and their families, which scorned "the wild life at Government House and the depraved orgies of the dives in Barrack Street." To this third world John Howe belonged, and his early move from the centre of the city to a cottage two miles away on the Northwest Arm kept him all the more remote from the other worlds.

John Howe's determination to render the highest type of public service may be seen in his administering the post office without thought of personal gain. Under him, a historian of the post office has noted, it "never seemed, as it did in the Canadas, to be imposed on the province. From the beginning it was accepted for what it is: an agency indispensable to the varied activities of a civilized state." Howe worked closely with a committee of the legislature in considering applications for post offices and routes, and in determining the subsidies for those routes which produced only scant revenues. Since he put the provision of service first, he was not averse to winking at the procedures governing the operation of the post office, even going so far as to establish new offices and make new contracts without the approval of his superior, the postmaster general in Britain. But because he was held in universal respect and sought nothing for himself, he was always let off with the gentlest of warnings.

In 1818 Howe relinquished his two offices in favour of his son John and in his remaining 17 years busied himself with a variety of unpaid activities. Above all, he continued the philanthropic work for which he had long been known. During the War of 1812 he had rendered all sorts of kindnesses to the American prisoners incarcerated on Melville Island; he often brought "jail birds" to live with him until he could find employment for them; on Sunday afternoons, Bible in hand, he regularly ministered to the religious and other needs of the inmates of Bridewell, the house of correction.

Posterity knows him best, however, for his influence on his son Joseph, for whom he was "instructor, . . . play-fellow, almost . . . daily companion" for 30 years. The evidence suggests that Joseph was his favourite child, perhaps "because he was the son of his old age." In turn, Joseph had a respect for his father that he accorded no other man. To the end of his days his speeches and writings frequently referred to him in terms almost of reverence. From his father's influence came his unabashed admiration of the British heritage; his preference for simple, non-ritualistic religious practices; his willingness to perform public services without thought of financial gain; and his compassion for society's unfortunates. From his father, too, he got his knowledge of Shakespeare and the Bible which became a basic part of a well-stocked repertoire that he drew upon at will in his speeches and letters.

During Joseph's "rambles" throughout the province in the late 1820s and early 1830s, John Howe wrote extensively for his son's paper, the *Novascotian, or Colonial Herald*. Joseph encouraged his wife to let his father "launch out as much as he pleases. A few good paragraphs from him will cover my retreat famously." Occasionally there were difficulties and twice John was asked not to "crow too much on the side of the Russians . . . as our politics have been rather Turkish." For John Howe, who believed this "the best of all possible worlds," it was a traumatic experience to have his son Joseph "hammer some of our great folks" with whom he had always been on the friendliest of terms. While on a "ramble" in 1830, Joseph wrote worriedly to his wife telling her not to let his father or half-brother John put "a scrape of a pen" in the *Novascotian* which would retract something he had written against the Council during the celebrated "Brandy Dispute" [*see* Enos Collins*]. In 1832, when Joseph and his fellow grand jurors succeeded in having the inefficient William H. Cleaveland removed as clerk of licences, his father and John Jr were among the 11 magistrates who asked Lieutenant Governor Sir Peregrine Maitland* to restore their long-time acquaintance to office.

Curiously, it was in John Howe's capacity as justice of the peace that a situation arose in his last months which was altogether out of keeping with his past life. During Joseph's trial for libel in 1835 – a trial sparked by his attack on the Court of Quarter Sessions in its role as an instrument of local government – he exempted his father from his blanket criticism of the court (which included all the magistrates of Halifax County): "He never took a shilling of the fees to which he was entitled; he had nothing to do with their dirty accounts and paltry peculations." John Howe, thinking it was high time to expose his fellow magistrates for the way in which they were carrying out their civil responsibilities, "laughed till his sides shook" when his son was acquitted, and told him, "I knew you'd thrash them – I thought they had better let you alone." The outcome of the trial was the appointment of William Q. Sawers as *custos rotulorum* or first magistrate of the county, supposedly to effect reform in its judicial and administrative system. John Howe had had a confrontation with Sawers three years earlier, when, as senior magistrate of Halifax County, he presided over a case in which Sawers behaved altogether intemperately and made unfounded charges after his clients were found guilty; the result was that Sawers was forbidden to practise before the court until he made a public apology. In the light of this incident it is easy to understand Howe's surprise when in late March 1835 a letter-writer to the *Novascotian* credited Sawers with being the first to point out the ills in the judiciary. In the next issue 82-year-old John Howe, bursting with indignation, replied that Sawers, instead of being praised, should have been castigated for making in 1832 "a lawless and impudent attack, upon a Court which was fairly and impartially performing its duties."

The old man's action was astounding, coming as it did from one who had avoided partisan controversy like the plague during all his adult life and had seldom, if ever, written a letter to a newspaper. Perhaps it was because some deterioration was taking place in his mental processes. Always friendly with the poor, he had become obsessed with the idea that he ought to be devoting his remaining life to improving their condition and he was seeking to settle as many of them as possible on a large tract of land on the Dartmouth side of Halifax Harbour. To that end he had placed orders for ploughs, harrows, and spinning-wheels, and he would have incurred large obligations if the younger John Howe had not prevented those orders from being carried into effect.

Because there was nothing irrational in his father's letter, Joseph had let it be published, probably hoping it would escape rough treatment. But Sawers's friends took strong exception to the statement that "not many . . . have the least confidence" in him, and for the first time in his life John Howe was subjected to angry, bitter criticism. In the *Acadian Recorder* Nemo told him he had long been an encumbrance to the Court of Quarter Sessions, in which the younger members respected his age but pitied his imbecility; in the Halifax *Times* Investigator stated that his letter did not "manifest the disposition of a follower of the meek and lowly Lamb." For a time Joseph kept the peace, but eventually "I had . . . to take up my pen, and clear the decks of these scribblers which I did, giving Sawers some deserved hard knocks in return for those given to my father."

On a Sunday late in December 1835 John Howe presided over a Sandemanian service at the home of his friends, the Reeves, near Dartmouth. That night, still at the Reeves', he died in his sleep. To Joseph's

regret the only writing he left behind was a single religious tract. Although he might have written informatively about "a great number of people who were worth knowing . . . or became eminent for something," he did not; perhaps he thought it "unfair to preserve even friendly notices of his contemporaries." Modest above all, John Howe may well have been the most respected person in the Halifax of his day.

J. MURRAY BECK

A portrait by William Valentine* of John Howe which was handed down to Joseph and his wife Catherine Susan Ann, and then to their son Sydenham, is now in the collection of the N.B. Museum.

Harvard College Library, Houghton Library, Harvard Univ. (Cambridge, Mass.), MS Can. 58 (Joseph Howe papers) (mfm. at PANS). PAC, MG 30, D11, 1–2 (mfm. at PANS). PANS, MG 9, no.109: 132–33. *Novascotian, or Colonial Herald*, especially 1829–35. Akins, *Hist. of Halifax City*. J. M. Beck, *Joseph Howe* (2v., Kingston, Ont., and Montreal, 1982–83), 1. J. N. Grant, "John Howe, Senior: printer, publisher, postmaster, spy," *Eleven exiles: accounts of loyalists of the American revolution*, ed. P. R. Blakeley and J. N. Grant (Toronto and Charlottetown, 1982), 25–57. William Smith, *The history of the Post Office in British North America, 1639–1870* (Cambridge, Eng., 1920; repr. New York, 1973). J. N. Grant, "John Howe (1754–1835)," *United Empire Loyalists: loyalists of the American revolution*, ed. Mary Archibald (ser. of 9 leaflets, Toronto, [1978]). D. W. Parker, "Secret reports of John Howe, 1808 . . . ," *American Hist. Rev.* (New York and London), 17 (1911–12): 70–102, 332–54. T. M. Punch and A. E. Marble, "The family of John Howe, Halifax loyalist and king's printer," *N.S. Hist. Quarterly*, 6 (1976): 317–27. William Smith, "The early Post Office in Nova Scotia, 1775–1867," N.S. Hist. Soc., *Coll.*, 19 (1918): 53–73. C. St C. Stayner, "The Sandemanian loyalists," N.S. Hist. Soc., *Coll.*, 29 (1951): 62–123. J. J. Stewart, "Early journalism in Nova Scotia," N.S. Hist. Soc., *Coll.*, 6 (1888): 91–122.

HUBBARD, HESTER (Hetty) ANN (Case), teacher; b. *c.* 1796 and baptized 1816 in Granville, Mass.; d. 24 Sept. 1831 in Belleville, Upper Canada.

Hester Ann Hubbard was to be a member of the Methodist mission to the Mississauga Ojibwas of Grape Island, Bay of Quinte, which depended largely on the generosity of American friends. This generosity was fostered by William Case*, superintendent of Indian missions for the Canada Conference of the Methodist Episcopal Church, in several speaking tours of the leading cities in the northern states. In the spring of 1828 he made such a trip, accompanied by the Indian exhorter Peter Jacobs [Pahtahsega*], and as on other occasions probably also hoped to secure new labourers for the mission. He was successful on both counts, recruiting two new teachers, Hester Ann Hubbard and John B. Benham, along with Eliza

Huot

Barnes who had already taught at Grape Island in 1827. Of Miss Hubbard's previous career her obituary records only that she left behind "many endearments in New England."

Although she was said to have spoken to the Indians on the morrow of her arrival "with much energy and power," Hetty Hubbard concentrated her attention almost entirely upon the pupils of the "female School" at Grape Island. She rarely appeared before the public, and then only to display the academic, domestic, and musical skills of her charges. In her only composition to have survived, a letter written in late 1828, she described how the missionary group at Grape Island had formed a household to which four of her Indian pupils had been admitted. Case went on frequent missionary tours during this period, and one of those most often in his company was Eliza Barnes.

On 26 Feb. 1829 a missionary party set off on another foray to the United States. On 11 March the party divided, Case proceeding directly to New York City with the missionary Peter Jones* while Barnes and Hubbard visited friends and held meetings in their native New England. By 30 April they were reunited in New York City. Then, on the evening of 4 May, after a busy set of meetings at which he had been a speaker, the 40-year-old Case took a wife. Domesticity triumphed. Hetty Hubbard was the bride, Eliza Barnes the bridesmaid. The ceremony was performed by the Reverend Nathan Bangs*.

After a honeymoon spent furthering the missionary cause in western New York, the Cases seem to have enjoyed more than a year of happy and useful life together. The birth of a child, Eliza Jane, on 10 Aug. 1830 must have added to their bliss, although the busy father complained mildly of the attention it required. Mrs Case seems to have relinquished her school, for a Miss Skelton was engaged to introduce the Pestalozzi system.

In February 1831 Hetty Case and her daughter became seriously ill. Although both were later reported on the way to recovery, during the summer the mother took a distinct turn for the worse. After months of acute depression she died in September; on her deathbed she handed over her daughter to the Reverend Sylvester Hurlburt and his wife for adoption. Case described the loss of his wife as "irreparable." He did not slacken his missionary efforts, however, and on 28 Aug. 1833 he married Eliza Barnes.

Quaintly described by John Saltkill Carroll* as possessing a countenance and spirit "not unlike that of the Rev. John [William] Fletcher, of saintly memory," Hetty Case was an able though modest woman who felt called to a field of labour that proved to be beyond her strength. As her husband wrote, "She seemed worthy of a better death."

J. W. GRANT

No likeness of Hester Ann Hubbard has been found. The portrait of Mrs Case in the UCC-C is of Eliza Barnes.

Granville Public Library (Granville, Mass.), Congregational Church (Granville), reg. of baptisms, 1816. Methodist Episcopal Church in Canada, Missionary Soc., *Report* (York [Toronto]), 1829–31. "Selections from the papers of James Evans, missionary to the Indians," ed. Fred Landon, *OH*, 26 (1930): 474–91. *Christian Advocate and Journal, and Zion's Herald* (New York), 25 Jan., 18 April, 8 Aug., 24 Oct., 5 Dec. 1828; 6 March, 15 May 1829; 24 Oct. 1831. *Christian Guardian*, 13 Feb. 1830, 1 Oct. 1831, 28 June 1854, 13 Jan. 1858. "New York Evening Post, New York City . . . : marriages . . . ," comp. G. A. Barber (typescript, 23v., New York 1933–48; copy in New York Public Library, Local Hist. and Geneal. Division). J. [S.] Carroll, *Case and his cotemporaries . . .* (5v., Toronto, 1867–77), 3. Peter Jones, *Life and journals of Kah-ke-wa-quo-nā-by (Rev. Peter Jones), Wesleyan missionary*, [ed. Elizabeth Field and Enoch Wood] (Toronto, 1860).

HUOT, FRANÇOIS, merchant and politician; b. 23 Aug. 1756 in Sainte-Foy (Que.), son of François Huot and Marie Maheu; m. first 18 Jan. 1780 Marie-Charles Leblond in Sainte-Famille, Île d'Orléans; m. secondly 14 Jan. 1783 Marie-Louise Robitaille at Quebec; m. thirdly 10 Oct. 1801 Françoise Villers in Charlesbourg; d. 29 Jan. 1822 at Quebec.

The son of a farmer, François Huot is believed to have been a servant with the Lanaudière family for several years before setting up a small shop, probably at Quebec. Even though he could not sign his marriage certificate in 1780, he no doubt was intelligent and resourceful. On 18 March 1782 he rented a two-storey house on Rue des Pauvres (Côte du Palais), where it is likely he carried on a retail business in various items, including spirits, which he had been licensed to sell in 1781. Some years later he was in business on Rue Saint-Jean. In 1787 he was able to afford £1,000 for a two-storey stone house on Rue de la Fabrique in addition to another house behind it which stood on Rue Saint-Joseph (Rue Garneau). He made up the capital for the purchase through a loan of £500 from notary Michel Sauvageau to be repaid as an annuity. The house on Rue de la Fabrique was opposite the Place du Marché, one of the busiest shopping areas in Upper Town, and it served as his residence and place of business until the end of his career.

For the 1790s Huot may be considered a fairly large-scale retailer. He carried in stock a great variety of fabrics, particularly woollens and cottons, shoes, stockings, hats and gloves, assorted household items, hardware, stationery, and some foodstuffs. In 1796 his complete inventory was worth £785 wholesale. His principal suppliers were probably the large wholesalers James Tod* and John Blackwood*, to whom he then owed respectively £705 and £170 for goods furnished. Despite owing more than £1,400 overall, Huot was in good shape financially because his liabilities were easily covered by his personal assets, debts owing to him of £390, and merchandise in stock.

An active and ambitious man, Huot attracted attention through the role he played in public affairs and through his participation in a number of organizations. On 4 Nov. 1790 his name appeared on a petition calling upon the government to establish a non-sectarian university in the province [see Jean-François Hubert*], and the following year he was among those opposing a plan to change land tenure [see Thomas-Laurent Bédard*; William Smith*]. He also signed the declaration of loyalty to the new constitution in July 1794. Huot belonged to the Quebec District Agriculture Society in 1793, but he was more closely identified with the Fire Society, of which he was a member from 1795 till 1820 and a director in 1800 and 1806. In addition he served as a churchwarden of the parish of Notre-Dame from 1807 to 1814.

Huot ran in the 1796 elections for the Lower Canadian House of Assembly and was elected in Hampshire, along with Joseph-Bernard PLANTÉ. He was esteemed for his honesty and his administrative abilities, and he enjoyed the steady support of his constituents, who kept returning him. Consequently he sat in the assembly from 1796 to 1804 and from 1808 till his death. In 1804 he withdrew from the slate before polling closed, apparently to ensure the election of his fellow candidate Planté. A man with little education, Huot played a discreet role as a member of the assembly, but he did participate assiduously in its work and in general supported the Canadian party.

In October 1796, shortly after being first elected, Huot went into partnership for a year with a young Quebec merchant, Michel Clouet*, evidently to lighten his work as a merchant, but after that he decided to continue on his own. As the years went by, he widened the scope of his activities by investing in enterprises of public utility and in real estate. In 1801 he paid £41 for one of the 48 shares in the Dorchester bridge over the Rivière Saint-Charles [see David Lynd*]. In 1807 he signed a five-year lease that gave him the operating rights to this bridge in return for £350 annually and a commitment to maintain it. Huot was also a shareholder and promoter of the Union Company of Quebec, which had been created in 1805 to finance the purchase and fitting-up of the Union Hotel on Rue Sainte-Anne. In addition to his properties on Rue de la Fabrique and Rue Saint-Joseph, Huot owned a house on Rue Saint-Jean, in the faubourg of that name. In 1800 and 1810 he also bought two properties at Beauport, as well as another small piece of land at La Canardière.

Huot retired from business in the mid 1810s and devoted himself primarily to his work as an assemblyman. His small capital and the income from renting or selling his properties ensured him a comfortable standard of living. In 1823 the liquidation of his assets brought his heirs more than £5,000, which was largely distributed among his four sons, one of whom was Hector-Simon*.

François Huot's career well illustrates the position of the Canadian merchant class at the period. His prospects of becoming rich were determined by his role as an intermediary between the importer of British origin and the consumer. Although he achieved only a modest degree of success, it none the less permitted him to participate in public affairs and political life, which gave him some social distinction, alongside the seigneurial class and the members of the liberal professions.

PIERRE POULIN

ANQ-Q, CE1-1, 14 janv. 1783, 1er févr. 1822; CE1-7, 10 oct. 1801; CE1-11, 18 janv. 1780; CE1-20, 23 août 1756; CN1-26, 27 janv., 25 mai, 27 nov. 1802; 8 juill. 1803; CN1-83, 20 mai 1782; 26 nov. 1787; 4, 16, 18 janv. 1788; CN1-157, 9–11 juin 1796, 3 mars 1821; CN1-178, 9 févr. 1807, 12 mai 1813; CN1-230, 8 août 1792; 11 oct. 1796; 14 janv., 18 avril, 18 oct. 1797; 23 avril 1798; 21 févr., 13 nov. 1801; 21 janv. 1819; 15 févr. 1822; 13 mars 1823. L.C., Statutes, 1805, c.16. Quebec Gazette, 4 Nov. 1790; 24 March 1791; 11 April 1793; 10 July 1794; 11 June 1795; 26, 29 June 1797; 10 April 1800; 9, 16 Aug. 1804; 3 April 1806; 2, 30 Nov. 1809; 26 April 1810; 31 Aug. 1815; 28 March 1816; 9 Jan. 1817; 23 March 1820; 31 Jan. 1822; 31 July 1823. F.-J. Audet, "Les législateurs du Bas-Canada"; "François Huot," BRH, 37 (1931): 695–702. Hare, "L'Assemblée législative du Bas-Canada," RHAF, 27.

HYATT, GILBERT, township leader, office holder, and JP; b. c. 1761, probably in the colony of New York, son of Abraham Hyatt; m. Anna Canfield, likely in Arlington, Vt, and they had several children; d. 17 Sept. 1823 and was buried two days later in Sherbrooke, Lower Canada.

The Hyatt family, which originally came from England, took root in North America in the mid 17th century, settling mainly in the colony of New York. Abraham Hyatt was living in Schenectady when the American revolution broke out. He joined the loyalist side, and in 1777 he enlisted in Major-General John Burgoyne*'s army with his two sons, Gilbert and Cornelius. Both sons served with the King's Loyal Americans [see Edward Jessup*], in which Gilbert was a corporal. After Burgoyne's surrender at Saratoga the Hyatts may have gone to the province of Quebec, and then returned to the United States. Abraham Hyatt asserted that he took his entire family, including his wife, seven sons, and three daughters, to British territory in 1780, but there is proof that Gilbert was at Missisquoi Bay by 1778.

A number of the Hyatts' compatriots had taken refuge in the region around Lake Champlain and, relying on what the king was offering, hoped to obtain there both assistance and lands. Petitions were circu-

Hyatt

lated, and when the Treaty of Paris in 1783 sealed their exile the Hyatts signed them. Their requests met with a categorical refusal from Governor Frederick Haldimand*, who wanted to fortify the border and move the American refugees away from it. This decision was maintained, despite the newcomers' stubborn insistence. They were told to join their former officers at Sorel or St Johns (Saint-Jean-sur-Richelieu) and remove to the Bay of Quinte (Ont.) or Baie des Chaleurs; if they did not, their rations would be cut off on 10 May 1784 and their homes destroyed. Even when faced with these punitive sanctions, Hyatt remained near the Rivière de la Roche with the malcontents who persisted in claiming the right to stay where they were.

Despite the royal instructions there were as yet no well-defined procedures for granting lands or laying out the clergy and crown reserves, nor were the fees to be paid established. Not until the Constitutional Act was passed in 1791 and the lieutenant governor of Lower Canada, Alured CLARKE, had issued a proclamation on 7 Feb. 1792 concerning settlement on crown lands in Lower Canada, could requests for land grants again be submitted. On 29 March Hyatt sent in a petition soliciting Ascot Township for himself and 204 associates.

This was a judicious choice, because the township, located at the confluence of the Saint-François and Magog rivers, had considerable resources of waterpower and a large potential hinterland. The area was already known to travellers and surveyors, among them Hyatt's friends Jesse PENNOYER, Nathaniel Coffin*, and Joseph Kilborn. Authorization to survey the township was given on 20 June 1792 and the fee of £15 was paid. At the urging of Chief Justice William Smith*, Hyatt at once began developing the land he would subsequently be granted. After selling his property at Missisquoi Bay, he managed with the help of Josiah Sawyer, of Eaton Township, to cut a 40-mile road through the woods so that he could bring his family and other settlers to Ascot. There he built his first settlement, which by 1794 was already viable.

For ten years, however, Hyatt had to engage in lengthy and costly proceedings to secure his letters patent. To comply with the many changes in regulations he had to reduce the number of his associates to 40; he was then authorized to take the oath of allegiance in June 1795. The obstacles that the Executive Council put in the way of those trying to get title to land were a matter of serious concern to him, since he had spent more than £1,000 for surveys, construction of a mill, and the settling of some 30 families. He joined a pressure group formed at Missisquoi Bay and set about organizing an initial meeting with his friends on 28 Nov. 1797. A committee of five was constituted to draw up a memoir for Governor Robert Prescott*. Hyatt served on it and along with eight others signed the document in the

name of the representatives of 29 townships. Pennoyer was charged with taking it to Quebec, and the governor dispatched it to London. In addition to expressing their grievances, the petitioners intended to send an emissary to the king if they did not obtain justice; the authorities did not think much of this plan but it was carried out when Samuel GALE accompanied Governor Prescott to England upon his recall in 1799.

Hyatt went to Quebec on several occasions to plead his cause. On 24 Jan. 1800 he was there again and submitted a detailed report to Lieutenant Governor Robert Shore Milnes* on his family's record of service. At the same time the land committee of the Executive Council allowed his petition and authorized his receiving, along with each of his associates, 1,200 acres. Hyatt concluded a number of agreements with his associates determining how the lands would be distributed and what share would be ceded back to him. On 28 Jan. 1801 the land committee allocated part of Ascot Township to Hyatt and 30 of his associates, the applications of the other 10 having been turned down. Since only 13 of the grants were for the anticipated 1,200 acres, the share that Hyatt would receive was reduced. Much more generous grants, however, had been made to several of his friends and to people who did not deserve them. Hyatt did not take this blow well. In numerous memoirs he demanded better terms, without success. The letters patent, signed on 21 April 1803, confirmed the existing arrangements. Fearing that he would be ruined, Hyatt worked at developing his properties, particularly those at the mouth of the Magog. A village had begun to grow around his mills there, at a place called Lower Forks, which subsequently took the name of Hyatt's Mills, and then became Sherbrooke in 1818.

It is difficult to say exactly when Hyatt settled in the village, but in 1805 he sold the lands being cultivated for a good price. There is some evidence that a mill had been built in 1796 and that it was producing lumber in 1800. Blacksmith Felix Ward had his shop on one of Hyatt's plots in 1804, and other businesses were getting started. At that time there was no municipal or other organization, and local administration was in the hands of the justices of the peace; in 1806 Hyatt was appointed to that office. He took an interest in all facets of economic activity and called for the transport of goods on the Rivière Saint-François to be made safer. He did not cease his requests for new grants, but they did not prevent his appointment in 1808 as commissioner to administer the oath of allegiance to applicants for land in Ascot Township.

Hyatt was unable, however, to meet his financial obligations, and his creditor Ezekiel Hart* of Trois-Rivières had some of his land sold at auction on 31 Oct. 1808. He lost his valuable lots in the village through another sale by court order on 6 May 1811, and then another 1,000 acres on 9 March 1812, again because of debts to the Hart family. The properties sold in the village included a large distillery and a potash factory. By means of deals Hyatt's wife was able to buy back part of the lots, and around 1813 Hyatt was still considered by Joseph Bouchette* to be the principal landowner in Ascot Township, but he never recovered all his lost properties.

Hyatt attended to his family's affairs, for example settling the estate of his brother Charles, who died in 1818. According to an 1819 census his family were among the 54 residents of the village of Sherbrooke, the name Hyatt's Mills having disappeared. Newcomers from England were buying up the land and working to exclude American pioneers from public affairs. In 1815 Hyatt's name had even been taken off the list of justices of the peace. Hyatt's last transactions were connected with the final settlement of his father's estate in 1822 and the sale of properties to two of his sons, Galen and Charles, the following year. He died of a heart attack on 17 Sept. 1823 and was buried in his wife's presence according to the rites of the Church of England, to which he belonged.

Gilbert Hyatt had the qualities of a true pioneer and leader. In reserving for himself the site of Sherbrooke he had given proof of vision. His courage enabled him to found a settlement that he saw grow from a simple hamlet to become the chief town of a judicial district shortly before his death. Fortune and fame eluded him, but his name deserves to be remembered and to be better known.

MARIE-PAULE R. LaBRÈQUE

ANQ-E, CN1-24, 29 nov. 1822, 3 avril 1823; CN1-27, 5 juill. 1819; CN2-26, 17 nov. 1800, 23 juin 1804, 27 avril 1805, 19 août 1812. ANQ-Q, E18/101. Bishop's Univ. (Lennoxville, Que.), Special Coll., Savage papers. Brome County Hist. Soc. Arch. (Knowlton, Que.), Samuel Willard papers, corr.; Miscellaneous family papers, Shufelt file; Township papers, Eastern Townships. PAC, RG 1, L3^L: 2442, 3939, 4196, 4208, 4585, 4861, 5197, 80989; RG 4, A1. Private arch., M.-J. Daigneau (Sherbrooke, Qué.), Notes personnelles. Soc. d'hist. des Cantons-de-l'Est (Sherbrooke), P21, P32. "Collection Haldimand," PAC Rapport, 1886: 448, 464. Elmer Cushing, An appeal addressed to a candid public; and to the feelings of those whose upright sentiments and discerning minds, enable them to "weigh it in the balance of the sanctuary" . . . (Stanstead, Que., 1826). Docs. relating to constitutional hist., 1759–91 (Shortt and Doughty; 1918); 1791–1818 (Doughty and McArthur); 1819–28 (Doughty and Story). Pierre de Sales Laterrière, Mémoires de Pierre de Sales Laterrière et de ses traverses, [Alfred Garneau, édit.] (Québec, 1873; réimpr. Ottawa, 1980). The settlement of the United Empire Loyalists on the upper St Lawrence and Bay of Quinte in 1784; a documentary record, ed. E. A. Cruikshank (Toronto, 1934; repr. 1966). "United Empire Loyalists: enquiry into losses and services," AO Report, 1904: 936. Quebec Gazette, 18 July 1799; 30 June 1808; 18 April, 30 Oct., 26 Dec. 1811; 17 Sept. 1818. Annuaire du séminaire St. Charles-Borromée,

Sherbrooke, affilié à l'université Laval en 1878, année académique 1881–82 (Sherbrooke, 1882). Joseph Bouchette, Topographical description of L.C.; A topographical dictionary of the province of Lower Canada (London, 1832). C. P. de Volpi and P. H. Scowen, The Eastern Townships, a pictorial record; historical prints and illustrations of the Eastern Townships of the province of Quebec, Canada (Montreal, 1962). Illustrated atlas of Eastern Townships. Langelier, Liste des terrains concédés. Officers of British forces in Canada (Irving).

Raoul Blanchard, Le centre du Canada français, "province de Québec" (Montréal, 1947). Caron, La colonisation de la prov. de Québec. L. S. Channel, History of Compton County and sketches of the Eastern Townships, district of St. Francis, and Sherbrooke County (Cookshire, Que., 1896; repr. Belleville, Ont., 1975). Day, Hist. of Eastern Townships. L.-P. Demers, Sherbrooke, découvertes, légendes, documents, nos rues et leurs symboles ([Sherbrooke, 1969]). Andrée Désilets, Les noms de rues de Sherbrooke (1825–1980) (Québec, 1984). Lucien Ferland, Histoire de Compton (Compton, Qué., 1981). Rodolphe Fournier, Lieux et monuments historiques des Cantons de l'Est et des Bois-Francs (Montréal, 1978). Graham, Hist. of freemasonry. Albert Gravel, Les Cantons de l'Est ([Sherbrooke], 1938); Pages d'histoire régionale (24 cahiers, Sherbrooke, 1960–67), cahiers 7, 16, 24; Vade-mecum du Sherbrookois (Sherbrooke, 1962). D. W. Hoyt, A genealogical history of the Hoyt, Haight, and Hight families: with some account of the earlier Hyatt families, a list of the first settlers of Salisbury and Amesbury, Mass. . . . ([2nd ed.], Boston, 1871). [Cuthbert Jones et al.], A history of Saint Peter's parish, Sherbrooke, diocese of Quebec . . . (Lennoxville, 1947). D. A. McArthur, "British North America and the American revolutions, 1774–1791," The Cambridge history of the British empire (8v., Cambridge, Eng., 1929–59), 6: 173–200. G. F. McGuigan, "Land policy and land disposal under tenure of free and common socage, Quebec and Lower Canada, 1763–1809 . . ." (3v., PHD thesis, Univ. Laval, Quebec, 1962). J. N. McIlwraith, Sir Frederick Haldimand (Toronto, 1906). Jules Martel, "Histoire du système routier des Cantons de l'Est avant 1855" (thèse de MA, univ. d'Ottawa, 1960). Jean Mercier, L'Estrie (Sherbrooke, 1964). G. H. Montgomery, Missisquoi Bay (Philipsburg, Que.) (Granby, Que., 1950). Maurice O'Bready, De Ktiné à Sherbrooke; esquisse historique de Sherbrooke: des origines à 1954 (Sherbrooke, 1973). H. B. Shufelt, Nicholas Austin the Quaker and the township of Bolton (Knowlton, 1971). The storied province of Quebec; past and present, ed. William Wood et al. (5v., Toronto, 1931–32), 2. François Gougeon, "Gilbert Hyatt ne serait pas le véritable fondateur de Sherbrooke; l'histoire locale bouleversée!" La Tribune (Sherbrooke), 9 avril 1979: 3. Albert Gravel, "Gilbert Hyatt," Le Messager de Saint-Michel de Sherbrooke (Sherbrooke), 14 févr. 1937: 8; "Gilbert Hyatt, fondateur de Sherbrooke," Annales de Saint-Gérard (Sherbrooke), 13 (1938), no.4: 107. T. C. Lampee, "The Missisquoi loyalists," Vt. Hist. Soc., Proc. (Montpelier), 6 (1938–39): 81–139. J. P. Noyes, "The Canadian loyalists and early settlers in the district of Bedford," Missisquoi County Hist. Soc., Report (Saint-Jean-sur-Richelieu, Que.), 3 (1908): 90–107. W. H. Siebert, "The American loyalists in the eastern seigniories and townships of the province of Quebec," RSC Trans., 3rd ser., 7 (1913), sect.II: 3–41. La Tribune, 31 juill. 1937.

Ironside

IRONSIDE, GEORGE, Indian Department official and merchant; b. *c*. 1761 in Scotland; m. 1 April 1810 Vocemassussia (Isabella), a relative of the Prophet [Tenskwatawa*], in Sandwich (Windsor), Upper Canada; d. 31 May 1831 in Amherstburg, Upper Canada.

Although George Ironside was an accredited scholar, having received an AM from King's College, Aberdeen, on 22 Feb. 1781, like many contemporary Scots he emigrated to North America. By 1789 he was settled at the Miamis Towns (Fort Wayne, Ind.) as a clerk, likely in the employ of George Leith. His clerical duties gave him a sound training in commerce and accounting, while his participation in what one observer called the "Rascally Scrambling Trade" for pelts brought him into close contact with other traders, government officials, and the resident Shawnees. Ironside learned the Shawnees' language, took part in their councils, and spoke on their behalf. He was widely recognized as a convivial companion and sincere friend.

Life on the frontier was perilous. In 1790 Ironside barely escaped drowning in a canoe accident. Then a series of punitive American raids culminating in the decisive battle of Fallen Timbers ruined the trade along the Miamis (Maumee) River. However, Ironside's skills were a valuable asset. In 1795 he was appointed storekeeper and clerk to the Indian Department on the recommendation of Alexander McKee*, the deputy superintendent general of Indian affairs in Upper Canada, and was stationed at Amherstburg, headquarters for the Western District.

Ironside was saddled with a corrupt, illiterate superior in Matthew Elliott*, the district superintendent. As Elliott's clerk, he was drawn into the confrontation with garrison commander Hector McLean when the latter accused Elliott of misappropriating government stores. Elliott was dismissed in 1797; Ironside barely escaped the same fate by apologizing to McLean and agreeing to follow a more regular line of conduct. There is no evidence that Ironside was personally involved in peculation. In fact, he subsequently received a strong character reference from William CLAUS, McKee's successor, who noted that his "Character for integrity is unimpeached." Ironside later acted as superintendent of the Western District when Elliott, reinstated in 1808, was absent with leave.

During the period before the War of 1812 Ironside pursued his own business interests. His petitions for land resulted in grants totalling some 2,000 acres in the Western District. He also operated a successful forwarding business, supplying the local worthies and officers at Fort Amherstburg with a wide range of luxury items. As a freemason and a member of the community's Anglican congregation, St John's Church, Sandwich, Ironside fitted comfortably into the local oligarchy, enjoying a measure of wealth, status, and influence.

The outbreak of conflict in 1812 shattered this tranquil existence. The demands of war, particularly meeting the needs of the native allies who actively supported the British [*see* Tecumseh*], placed a heavy burden on the department. In 1813 Ironside was forced to join in the precipitous flight to Burlington Heights (Hamilton) when the Right Division under Henry PROCTER abandoned the Detroit frontier.

With the return of peace, the Indian Department was re-established at Amherstburg. Ironside became embroiled in the feuding within the department, siding with Billy Caldwell* who successfully conspired to wrest the local superintendency away from his father William CALDWELL. Although a loyal and effective official, Ironside did not have sufficient power or connections to override the claims of more powerful rivals when Billy Caldwell was dismissed in 1816. The superintendency went to John Askin Jr and Ironside was appointed clerk. (The more important position of storekeeper had disappeared about 1817 when the commissariat at the fort took over the management of Indian Department supplies.) Within three years Askin's health failed and Ironside was called upon to act and then to serve as the superintendent at Amherstburg. His appointment was dated 1 Jan. 1820.

For the remaining years of his career, Ironside provided sound, efficient, and honest administration of Indian affairs. He continued to be a pillar of the community, serving as an elder in the Amherstburg Presbyterian church after it was founded. In 1830 he requested permission to retire from the Indian Department. He was the father of two daughters and five sons, and the fact that he was allowed to pass on his position to his son George* is a measure of Ironside's stature in the organization. His career is typical of many functionaries of the department. He entered it through talent and affiliation with an important official – in his case, McKee. Many years of faithful service finally enabled him to secure a senior position.

DENNIS CARTER-EDWARDS

[The best source for Ironside's activities with the Indian Department is his extensive correspondence with departmental officials, now located in the DPL, Burton Hist. Coll., George Ironside papers. Also useful is the correspondence in PAC, RG 8, I (C ser.), especially 251: 129, and 1206: 159–271. Other aspects of his career are found in Aberdeen Univ. Library (Aberdeen, Scot.), Kings College and Univ., record of graduates, 22 Feb. 1781; AO, GS 848, Session records, May 1831 (mfm.); PAC, MG 23, GII, 17, ser.1, vol.25: 123–40; RG 1, L3, 254: I–J2/21; 257: I12/8; RG 19, E5(a), 3744, claim 271; and St John's (Sandwich) Anglican Church (Windsor, Ont.), Reg. of baptisms, marriages, and burials, 1802–27 (copies at PAC).

Secondary sources useful for this study are various. The author would like to acknowledge the work of Douglas Leighton, who presented a paper on Ironside at the Western District Hist. Conference of 1979 at the Univ. of Windsor. R. S. Allen's study, "British Indian Dept.," *Canadian Hist. Sites*, no.14: 5–125, is basic for anyone looking into this topic. Reginald Horsman, *Matthew Elliott, British Indian agent* (Detroit, 1964), covers the early period of the Indian Department at Amherstburg, including the McLean–Elliott affair. Two doctoral dissertations which are helpful for a study of the department are D. R. Farrell, "Detroit, 1783–1796: the last stages of the British fur trade in the old northwest" (PHD thesis, Univ. of Western Ont., London, 1968), and H. C. W. Goltz, "Tecumseh, the Prophet, and the rise of the Northwest Indian Confederation" (PHD thesis, Univ. of Western Ont., 1973). There is also the author's study of the British military garrison at Amherstburg, *Fort Malden: a structural narrative history, 1796–1976* (Can., National Hist. Parks and Sites Branch, *Manuscript report*, no.401, 2v., Ottawa, 1976).

Other sources used in this study are: [Henry Hay], "A narrative of life on the old frontier: Henry Hay's journal from Detroit to the [Miamis] River," ed. M. M. Quaife, Wis., State Hist. Soc., *Proc.* (Madison), 1914: 208–61; *John Askin papers* (Quaife); O. M. Spencer, *Narrative of Oliver M. Spencer; comprising an account of his captivity among the Mohawk Indians, in North America* (2nd ed., London, 1842); "U.C. land book B," AO *Report*, 1930: 23, 79; J. A. Clifton, "Captain Billy Caldwell: on the reconstruction of an abused identity" (typescript, n.d.; expanded version of a paper presented to a symposium on ethnogenesis on the Great Lakes frontier at the annual meeting of the American Hist. Assoc., Washington, 1976); and R. D. Edmunds, *The Shawnee Prophet* (Lincoln, Nebr., and London, 1983). D.C.-E.]

IRUMBERRY DE SALABERRY, CHARLES-MICHEL D', army and militia officer, politician, seigneur, office holder, and JP; b. 19 Nov. 1778 in Beauport, Que., eldest son of Ignace-Michel-Louis-Antoine d'IRUMBERRY de Salaberry and Françoise-Catherine Hertel de Saint-François; m. 13 May 1812 Marie-Anne-Julie Hertel de Rouville, daughter of Jean-Baptiste-Melchior Hertel* de Rouville, in Chambly, Lower Canada, and they had four sons and three daughters; d. there 27 Feb. 1829.

Charles-Michel d'Irumberry de Salaberry enlisted at the age of 14 as a volunteer in the 44th Foot. In 1794, through Prince Edward* Augustus, a family friend, he received an ensign's commission in a

battalion of the 60th Foot stationed in the West Indies. After his arrival on 28 July that year, he distinguished himself by his bravery in the invasions of the French colonies of Saint-Domingue, Guadeloupe, and Martinique. During this time the prince, having become commander of the military forces in the Maritime colonies, undertook to obtain a lieutenancy for him in his own regiment, the 7th Foot, which was stationed at Halifax. On learning that Salaberry had already been promoted to that rank in the 60th, where advancement was swifter, he asked for the appointment to the 7th to be cancelled and in the interim had him sent home to Lower Canada on leave.

Salaberry's readmission to the 60th came through too late for him to sail for the West Indies. After being shipwrecked on St John's (Prince Edward) Island he was detained at Halifax, in the prince's service. The prince initiated him into freemasonry, and on 2 Feb. 1797 Salaberry was installed as master of Royal Rose Lodge No.2. From March till the end of June he served as a lieutenant on the *Asia*, which was chasing Spanish ships. He returned to the West Indies at the beginning of July and was garrisoned in Jamaica. Although the prince recommended him several times for a captaincy, Salaberry, who did not have the means to buy the commission, had to wait until the end of 1799 to receive the rank of captain-lieutenant, without a company, in the 60th Foot. On 18 June 1803 he finally obtained a company in the 1st battalion.

In 1804 Salaberry asked the prince – now the Duke of Kent – to use his influence to get him sick leave; he arrived at Quebec on 24 October. On 26 June of the following year he sailed for England with his brothers Maurice-Roch and François-Louis, both of whom had been promoted lieutenant in the duke's regiment. The three were warmly received at home by Edward Augustus and his companion, Mme de Saint-Laurent [MONTGENET], and the duke immediately took steps to have Salaberry exchanged into a different regiment to spare him another tour of duty in the West Indies. In the mean time Edward got several weeks' leave for him, gave him lodging, invited him to supper every day, and let him use his box at the theatre.

Early in 1806 Salaberry was transferred to the 5th battalion of the 60th Foot, under Colonel Francis de ROTTENBURG. At the duke's request he conducted recruiting in Britain for the 1st Foot between July 1806 and March 1807. Major-General Sir George Prevost* created difficulties for him, but to the duke's great pleasure he none the less succeeded in enlisting more than 150 men. In August 1806 the youngest Salaberry brother, Édouard-Alphonse*, arrived in England. The Salaberrys met only a few times, however, since Maurice-Roch and François-Louis left for India on 18 April 1807. For his part, Charles-Michel was called to Ireland in August. In 1808 he was appointed brigade-major of the light infantry brigade commanded by

Irumberry

Rottenburg which in 1809 was dispatched to the Netherlands. Like a number of his comrades, Salaberry caught a contagious fever in that disastrous campaign and returned to England in October. He was transferred back to the 60th Foot, 1st battalion, and in June 1810 learned that he would soon be leaving for the Canadas. There, in the autumn, he became aide-de-camp to Major-General Rottenburg.

On 2 July 1811 Salaberry was promoted brevet major. Seven months later, with the international situation pointing to the imminence of war, he put forward a plan to set up a militia corps, the Voltigeurs Canadiens. In the circumstances Prevost, who had become governor-in-chief in October 1811, could only commend Salaberry, who had the influence, zeal, and energy to raise a corps of volunteers and turn it quickly into an efficient and competent unit. Salaberry began recruiting for this "Provincial Corps of Light Infantry" on 15 April 1812.

Obtaining experienced officers for the militia was not easy, since a man's absence from his regiment held up his promotion in the army. Furthermore, a militia officer was subordinate to an officer of the regular army holding the same rank – hence Salaberry's anger when Prevost commissioned him a lieutenant-colonel in the militia, effective 1 April 1812, instead of giving him an army rank. But on 29 Jan. 1813 Rottenburg informed him that he was to have a supervisory function in the Voltigeurs Canadiens with the rank of lieutenant-colonel in the army. When, contrary to expectations, this rank was not confirmed, Salaberry had to be satisfied with receiving that of lieutenant-colonel of the Voltigeurs Canadiens, on 25 March 1813. Confirmation that he had the same rank in the army did not come until July 1814. Although the militia was subordinate to the army, some army officers insisted upon being taken on in the Voltigeurs Canadiens. They did so for two reasons: the virtual certainty of the militia unit becoming a regular army unit and their rank being recognized, and the desire of some to retire from the army with a militia officer's salary added to their half pay. Salaberry was thus able to obtain several experienced officers.

At the beginning the recruitment of militiamen succeeded beyond all hopes, on account of the economic crisis, Salaberry's reputation, and the fact that the Select Embodied Militia had not yet been raised. Notwithstanding the claims sometimes made, exaggerated notions that Salaberry deserves all the credit for recruiting and that the unit was raised in two days are not tenable. In April 1812 the target was a corps of 500, but Prevost reduced the number to 350 in June, and to 300 the next month. In fact, financial circumstances did not permit the Voltigeurs Canadiens and the Glengarry Light Infantry Fencibles to be raised at the same time. With 264 men recruited in the first three weeks, enlistment promised to be easy. But

the harshness of military life apparently led many discouraged recruits to desert, for numbers dropped from 323 in June to 270 in October. Salaberry had difficulty mustering 438 men in March 1813. Nevertheless, at the battle of Châteauguay the following October the Voltigeurs Canadiens had 29 officers and 481 non-commissioned officers and men.

Salaberry was a strict and conscientious commander. His officers did not always possess the same qualities. Jacques Viger*, a captain who was later to retain his company through Salaberry's intervention, often regretted his commission, complaining of the severe discipline and the onerous financial charges that the officers had to assume. Salaberry's brother-in-law, Jean-Baptiste-René Hertel* de Rouville, who was also a captain in the Voltigeurs Canadiens, begged the adjutant general of militia to transfer him to another regiment because he found his commanding officer too demanding.

On 18 June 1812 the United States had declared war on Great Britain, and the Americans were making ready to invade the Canadas. To defend Lower Canada, in May the government had conscripted the men to form four battalions of Select Embodied Militia; a fifth was created in September, and another in February 1813. The sedentary militia took training and on occasion was called up. Besides the Voltigeurs Canadiens a number of voluntary militia units were raised, sometimes for brief periods. In November 1812 an attempted invasion near Lacolle brought the Voltigeurs Canadiens into action. On 27 November Salaberry was praised for his conduct in commanding the advance guard. But in July 1813 he learned that Prevost had sent the British government a dispatch on the events making no mention of his name and congratulating the adjutant general, Edward Baynes, and Major-General Rottenburg, who had taken no part in the action.

Early in August the Voltigeurs Canadiens covered the withdrawal of the British ships sent to burn the barracks in Swanton, Vt, two blockhouses at Champlain, N.Y., and the barracks and arsenal north of Plattsburgh. In October Salaberry was sent to Four Corners, near Châteauguay, with a handful of soldiers and some Indians to reconnoitre the enemy forces and attack. However, there were not enough men and the plan fell through.

Disappointed with the missions being given him, Salaberry wanted to leave the army. But then he was summoned to proceed in all haste from Châteauguay with his troops to the river of that name. The Americans were preparing to attack Montreal in order to cut off the British army in Upper Canada. On 21 October Major-General Wade Hampton crossed the border at the head of some 3,000 men and advanced up the Châteauguay towards Montreal, which he and Major-General James Wilkinson, who was coming down the St Lawrence from Sackets Harbor, N.Y., were to attack.

Having foreseen that the enemy would cross the Châteauguay at Allan's Corners, on the east bank, Salaberry had an abatis thrown up at the spot. There he placed about 250 of the Voltigeurs Canadiens, the sedentary militia, and the Canadian Fencibles, along with some Indians. He sent 50 men from the sedentary militia and from the 3rd battalion of the Select Embodied Militia across the river. A mile behind the abatis about 1,400 militiamen under Lieutenant-Colonel George Richard John Macdonell* were divided among four entrenchments one behind the other.

When he reached Ormstown, some miles from the abatis, Hampton split his troops; he sent about 1,000 men across the Châteauguay and himself advanced with 1,000 or so, leaving a like number in reserve at his encampment. The American troops did not manage to surprise Salaberry's militiamen. By shrewd tactics Salaberry had succeeded in creating the illusion that his force was much stronger than it actually was and thus discouraged the enemy. After about four hours of fighting on 26 October, Hampton ordered his troops to retreat. The Canadians remained at the abatis, ready to resume combat the following day. But Hampton, who had received orders to take up winter quarters in American territory, thought that his superior, Major-General Wilkinson, had called off the attack on Montreal, and he moved his troops back towards the United States. His actions were based on a misunderstanding, but having learned of Hampton's defeat and withdrawal, Wilkinson did not want to attack Montreal. The battle of Châteauguay therefore saved that town from a large-scale attack [see Joseph Wanton MORRISON].

Salaberry's superior, Major-General Abraham Ludwig Karl von Wattenwyl*, and Prevost arrived at the same time to observe the enemy's retreat. After the battle, relying on prisoners' estimates, the Canadians thought they had faced 6–7,000 Americans. In reality some 3,000 Americans had met about 1,700 Canadians. According to Prevost's report, written on the day itself, about 300 Canadians had opposed 7,500 Americans. From that time, the battle of Châteauguay took on a legendary character and became a source of popular pride: the Canadians, commanded by one of their own, had displayed their bravery, their military capacity, and their loyalty in repelling the Americans.

If people found reasons for pride in Prevost's general order, Salaberry saw in it an intention to cheat him of credit for the victory. Indeed, Prevost said that he himself had been present at the battle and gave Wattenwyl credit for the strategy employed. Humiliated and denied his rights, Salaberry made innumerable attempts to obtain recognition from the authorities and a promotion in the army. But confronted with the attitudes taken by Prevost and by the Lower Canadian

parliament, which in the absence of the governor's assent, did not dare give the usual expression of thanks, Salaberry, who was tired and ill, enquired at the end of 1813 about the terms for retirement from the army. He asked his father to moderate his ambitions for him: he could never become a general officer, because he was a Catholic and because advancement would require 10 or 12 years' more experience. In January 1814 he offered his commission to Frederick George Heriot* for £900. After finally receiving the thanks of the House of Assembly on 30 January and those of the Legislative Council on 25 February, he was still thinking of retiring when he learned on 3 March that Prevost was to recommend him for appointment as inspecting field officer of militia. This promotion promised monetary gain and interesting work. He left the Voltigeurs Canadiens with some regrets, and Heriot replaced him in his command.

In a letter of 15 March Prevost did indeed recommend Salaberry for appointment as inspecting field officer, but in a confidential report dated 13 May he disparaged him, accused him of negligence, and claimed that he had only been carrying out Wattenwyl's orders; in so doing he robbed him of any credit for the victory at Châteauguay. Salaberry had, then, good reason to be wary of Prevost's duplicity, and the appointment was not confirmed. Therefore, having carried out the duties for several months, he sent in his resignation. It was intercepted by the Duke of Kent, to the good fortune of Salaberry, who continued to receive an army lieutenant-colonel's pay. He retained his appointment as inspecting field officer, and also remained lieutenant-colonel of the Voltigeurs Canadiens, his service being interrupted by a 42-day stint on the court martial of Henry PROCTER. The war ended on 24 Dec. 1814, but the news did not reach the colony until the spring. The militia was demobilized in March 1815. Once the troops had been discharged, Salaberry turned his attention for several months to obtaining his own pay; he also took steps on behalf of the militiamen entitled to payments and the wounded who were to receive compensation.

In 1816 Salaberry received a medal commemorating the battle of Châteauguay. Then, on 5 June 1817, he learned that as result of a recommendation from Sir Gordon Drummond* and Macdonell's friendly intervention, he had been made a companion of the Order of the Bath. In December, Governor Sir John Coape SHERBROOKE recommended him to replace Jean-Baptiste-Melchior Hertel de Rouville, his father-in-law, on the Legislative Council. His appointment dated from December 1818, and he took his seat on 19 Feb. 1819. His father was already a member of the council and thus, for the first time, a father and son served together on it.

In 1814 Salaberry had gone to live in Chambly. In July the Hertel de Rouvilles gave the Salaberrys some

Irumberry

land near the military reserve. Then Salaberry's father handed over to him the 2,000 *livres* that his godfather, vicar general Charles-Régis Des Bergères de Rigauville, had bequeathed him. Salaberry therefore found himself in possession of a sizeable estate; he managed it conscientiously, claiming compensation for the depredations his lands had been subjected to during the war and bringing lawsuits against several of his neighbours and *censitaires* to establish the boundaries of his lands and full possession of them.

The death of Pierre-Amable De Bonne* in 1816 enabled Salaberry to add to his fortune, since his mother-in-law, Marie-Anne Hervieux, was a relative of the judge. Having conferred power of attorney on her son and son-in-law to get possession of De Bonne's estate, she handed the property over to them and to her daughter in March 1817. This gift was made not long before Jean-Baptiste-Melchior Hertel de Rouville's death on 30 Nov. 1817, which was followed by his wife's on 25 Jan. 1819. Management of their estate was entrusted to Salaberry. Salaberry's wife had inherited the fief of Saint-Mathias, and on 5 Nov. 1819 Salaberry bought the adjoining fief of Beaulac from William Yule. Salaberry's brother-in-law, who was in financial difficulties, sold him and his wife part of his inheritance, including the flour-mill at Saint-Mathias. In January 1818 Salaberry had bought the rights on the part of the king's domain located in the seigneury from Samuel Jacobs, who was the seigneur of part of Chambly. Finally, when Jacobs went bankrupt in 1825, he bought his land and so was able to extend his own property. He profited from his holdings and in addition lent money.

Salaberry was also interested in transportation. With his friend and neighbour Samuel Hatt and several merchants and private individuals from the Richelieu region he founded a company in October 1820 to build the steamship *De Salaberry*. It was launched on 3 Aug. 1821, to ply between Quebec, Montreal, and Chambly. On 12 June 1823 the ship burned off Cap-Rouge; six or seven people perished and an extremely valuable cargo was lost.

In 1815 Salaberry had been appointed a justice of the peace for the District of Quebec. He received a similar commission for the districts of Montreal, Trois-Rivières, and Saint-François in 1821, and for the district of Gaspé in 1824. On 14 May 1817 he had been given responsibility for improving communications in Devon County, being named commissioner of roads and bridges. Although he was an illustrious member of the Legislative Council, he was more conspicuous by his absence than by his participation. He supported the petition against the Union Bill of 1822, but in 1824 he wrote to Viger that he expected the union of Upper and Lower Canada to come about.

That year Viger, who had become a friend of his former commander, undertook to raise a subscription to have an engraving done of Salaberry, "whose name is already part of history." The engraver, Asher Brown Durand of New York, did the portrait from a miniature by New York artist Anson Dickinson.

Salaberry was a man of impetuous temperament – Rottenburg called him "my dear Gunpowder." He was also pleasant, straightforward, and warmhearted. Stricken by an attack of apoplexy while supping at Hatt's, he died on 27 Feb. 1829.

The name of Charles-Michel d'Irumberry de Salaberry was, however, not to be forgotten. His role in the battle of Châteauguay, much disputed even during his lifetime, would be viewed in many different ways as Lower Canadian society evolved. In the mid 19th century he was perceived as an experienced, courageous, intrepid soldier who enjoyed the confidence of his men. At the turn of the century English-speaking historians put greater emphasis on the roles played by Macdonell or Wattenwyl, but French-speaking ones defended Salaberry, stressing his valour and intrepidity and pointing out that he had had to make do with limited means furnished by pusillanimous superiors. In the early 1950s Salaberry was looked upon as the French Canadian who had given an outstanding demonstration of the courage of the race. In the decade that followed, the portrait of the hero was effaced by the image of a body of national militia including both English- and French-speaking men who side by side defended Canada. Finally, more recently Salaberry's victory has been attributed to a fruitful collaboration by various elements against a common enemy.

MICHELLE GUITARD

AAQ, 210 A, VIII. ANQ-M, CN1-16, 21 mars 1814; CN1-43, 16 mai, 6, 30 juill., 7, 23 sept. 1814; 4 oct., 9 nov., 24 déc. 1816; 10 janv. 1817; 29 juin 1818; 1er, 5 févr., 30 avril, 5 juill. 1819; 23 mai, 4, 18 juill., 4 oct. 1820; 23, 26 janv. 1822; CN1-123, 14 sept. 1816; 29 juill. 1817; 27 janv. 1818; 30 oct. 1820; 29 juin, 21 juill., 6 août 1821; 28 mars 1822; 26 mars, 3 juill. 1823; 2 févr. 1825; CN1-194, 13 mai 1812, 25 janv. 1814. ANQ-Q, CE1-5, 19 nov. 1778; CN1-212, 28 avril 1816; E21/12; P-289; P-417. ASQ, MSS, 74. National Arch. (Washington), RG 94. PAC, MG 24, B2; B16; G5; G8; G9; G45; L5; RG 1, E2, 3; L3L; RG 4, A2; B21; RG 8, I (C ser.); RG 9, I; II, A4; A5. W. F. Coffin, *1812, the war and its moral; a Canadian chronicle* (Montreal, 1864). William James, *A full and correct account of the military occurrences of the late war between Great Britain and the United States of America . . . (2v., London, 1818).* L.C., House of Assembly, *Journals*, 1819, app.O; Legislative Council, *Journals*, 1814, 1818, 1819; *Statutes*, 1793–1814. *The life of F.M., H.R.H. Edward, Duke of Kent, illustrated by his correspondence with the De Salaberry family, never before published, extending from 1791 to 1814,* ed. W. J. Anderson (Ottawa and Toronto, 1870). *Official letters of the military and naval officers of the United States, during the war with Great Britain in the years 1812, 13, 14, & 15 . . . ,* comp. John Brannan (Washington, 1823).

[James Reynolds], *Journal of an American prisoner at Fort Malden and Quebec in the War of 1812*, ed. G. M. Fairchild (Quebec, 1909). *Select British docs. of War of 1812* (Wood). *Montreal Gazette*, 9 Nov. 1813. *Quebec Mercury*, 1805–14. F.-M. Bibaud, *Le Panthéon canadien* (A. et V. Bibaud; 1891). L.-O. David, *Biographies et portraits* (Montréal, 1876), 59. *Montreal almanack*, 1829. H. J. Morgan, *Sketches of celebrated Canadians. Quebec almanac*, 1811–14.

Gilbert Auchinleck, *A history of the war between Great Britain and the United States of America, during the years 1812, 1813, and 1814* (Toronto, 1855). F. F. Beirne, *The War of 1812* (Hamden, Conn., 1965). H. L. Coles, *The war of 1812* (Chicago, 1965). L.-O. David, *Le héros de Châteauguay (C. M. de Salaberry)* (Montréal, 1883). *The defended border: Upper Canada and the War of 1812 . . .* , ed. Morris Zaslow and W. B. Turner (Toronto, 1964). Lucien Gagné, *Salaberry, 1778–1829* (thèse de PHD, univ. de Montréal, 1948). George Gale, *Historic tales of old Quebec* (Quebec, 1923). Mollie Gillen, *The prince and his lady: the love story of the Duke of Kent and Madame de St Laurent* (London, 1970; repr. Halifax, 1985). G. R. Gleig, *A sketch of the military history of Great Britain* (London, 1845). Michelle Guitard, *Histoire sociale des miliciens de la bataille de la Châteauguay* (Ottawa, 1983). J. T. Headley, *The second war with England* (New York, 1853). Hitsman, *Incredible War of 1812*. Reginald Horsman, *The causes of the War of 1812* (New York, 1972); *The War of 1812* (London, 1969). J. R. Jacobs, *Tarnished warrior, Major-General James Wilkinson* (New York, 1938). W. D. Lighthall, *An account of the battle of Chateauguay . . .* (Montreal, 1889). R. B. McAfee, *History of the late war in the western country . . .* (Lexington, Ky., 1816). A. T. Mahan, *Sea power in its relations to the War of 1812* (2v., London, 1905). J. K. Mahon, *The War of 1812* (Gainesville, Fla., 1972). Theodore Roosevelt, *The naval war of 1812, or the history of the United States Navy during the last war with Great Britain, to which is appended an account of the battle of New Orleans* (New York and London, 1882). Robert Rumilly, *Papineau et son temps* (2v., Montréal, 1977). Robert Sellar, *The U.S. campaign of 1813 to capture Montreal; Crysler, the decisive battle of the War of 1812* (Huntingdon, Que., 1913). G. A. Steppler, "A duty troublesome beyond measure: logistical considerations in the Canadian War of 1812" (MA thesis, McGill Univ., Montreal, 1974). Benjamin Sulte, *La bataille de Châteauguay* (Québec, 1899). Wallot, *Un Québec qui bougeait*. J. R. Western, *The English militia in the eighteenth century; the history of a political issue, 1660–1802* (London and Toronto, 1965). Samuel White, *History of the American troops, during the late war . . .* (Baltimore, Md., 1830). W. C. H. Wood, *The war with the United States; a chronicle of 1812* (Toronto, 1915). C.-M. Boissonnault, "Le Québec et la guerre de 1812," *Rev. de l'univ. Laval* (Québec), 5 (1950–51): 611–25. W. H. Goodman, "The origins of the War of 1812: a survey of changing interpretations," *Mississippi Valley Hist. Rev.* ([Cedar Rapids, Iowa]), 28 (1941–42): 171–86. Eric Jarvis, "Military land granting in Upper Canada following the War of 1812," *OH*, 67 (1975): 121–34. R. J. Koke, "The Britons who fought on the Canadian frontier; uniforms of the War of 1812," N.Y. Hist. Soc., *Quarterly* (New York), 45 (1961): 141–94. G. F. G. Stanley, "The Indians in the War of 1812," *CHR*, 31 (1950): 145–65.

IRUMBERRY DE SALABERRY, IGNACE-MICHEL-LOUIS-ANTOINE D', army and militia officer, seigneur, politician, JP, and office holder; b. 4 July 1752 in Beauport (Que.), son of Michel de Sallaberry*, a naval officer, and Madeleine-Louise Juchereau Duchesnay de Saint-Denis; m. 18 Feb. 1778 Françoise-Catherine Hertel de Saint-François in Montreal, and they had ten children, seven of whom reached adulthood; d. 22 March 1828 at Quebec.

After the Seven Years' War Michel de Sallaberry retired to France with his wife. Ignace-Michel-Louis-Antoine stayed in the colony and lived with his maternal aunt Marie-Thérèse Juchereau Duchesnay. He attended the Petit Séminaire de Québec from 1765 to 1769. When the Americans invaded in 1775 [*see* Benedict Arnold*; Richard Montgomery*], he volunteered his services to help defend Fort St Johns (Saint-Jean-sur-Richelieu). The garrison at the fort surrendered early in November. Salaberry, who had been wounded twice during the hostilities, was hospitalized at the Hôtel-Dieu in Montreal. In May 1777 he joined the forces of Major-General John Burgoyne*, which were defeated near Saratoga (Schuylerville, N.Y.) in October. At the end of the war in 1783, he was put on half pay.

Like a number of the seigneurial gentry, Salaberry signed a petition to the king in 1788 opposing the constitutional reforms being sought by the merchants of the colony. In 1791 he became a friend of George III's son, Prince Edward* Augustus, and through him he benefited greatly from the patronage of the colonial and imperial governments. In July 1792 he asked the prince and his mistress, Thérèse-Bernardine MONTGENET, known as Mme de Saint-Laurent, to be godparents to his youngest son, Édouard-Alphonse*. His three other sons also enjoyed royal favour, obtaining, for example, commissions in British army regiments.

Salaberry himself was made a justice of the peace for the district of Quebec in 1794, an appointment regularly renewed until 1821. He obtained the same office for the districts of Trois-Rivières and Saint-François in 1821, Gaspé in 1824, and Montreal in 1826 and 1828. In 1796 he was appointed major in the 1st battalion of the Royal Canadian Volunteer Regiment, which was disbanded in 1802. In January 1801 he was called upon to replace Louis-Joseph de Fleury Deschambault as deputy superintendent of the Saint-François Abenakis. Six years later he was appointed commissioner to receive the oath of allegiance and commissioner to build a new market and a new prison at Quebec. In 1808 he received the post of surveyor for the preservation of woods and timber for Lower Canada. His loyalty to the crown also brought him appointment to the Legislative Council in 1817.

When the first house of assembly had been constituted in the summer of 1792, Salaberry sought election in Dorchester and Quebec ridings and won in both. Having to choose between them, he decided in favour of Dorchester, which he represented with Gabriel-Elzéar Taschereau*. He left the Quebec seat to be filled by Michel-Amable Berthelot* Dartigny. In the election of a speaker, Salaberry voted for British merchant William Grant* rather than Jean-Antoine Panet*, a Canadian who in the event was elected. During the sessions he voted mostly with the English party.

Salaberry was defeated in the 1796 elections but ran again in 1804, this time in Lower Town Quebec. In the fourth parliament he joined the ranks of the Canadian party from the outset. It was certainly Salaberry's bill on the financing of prisons that caused the greatest division in the assembly. In his report he recommended that a new jail be built in every district at government expense, the cost of any one not to exceed £9,000 and the amount to be collected through taxes on imports. The report precipitated a severe crisis in the house, widening the split between the Canadians, who were in favour of the bill, and the British merchants, who opposed it fiercely, demanding that construction be financed by a land tax instead. Nevertheless, the bill received the assent of Lieutenant Governor Sir Robert Shore Milnes* in March 1805, after some stormy debates. Salaberry was defeated in his riding in 1808 but was successful in Huntingdon, which he represented until October 1809. He retired from elective politics that year after being defeated in Lower Town.

Being 60 did not prevent Salaberry from wanting to take part in the War of 1812. In May of that year he was appointed lieutenant-colonel of the 1st Select Embodied Militia Battalion, but after suffering a stroke he retired in October. He continued to serve in the militia as colonel of the 1st battalion of Quebec's militia. As for political interests, in October 1822 he chaired the Quebec committee formed to resist the proposed union of Upper and Lower Canada.

Salaberry died at Quebec on 22 March 1828, after a long illness. He was buried four days later in the parish church of Beauport. His sons Maurice-Roch and François-Louis had died while serving in India. Édouard-Alphonse was killed in a campaign in Spain. CHARLES-MICHEL inherited his father's estate, which he shared with his two unmarried sisters and his brother-in-law, Michel-Louis Juchereau* Duchesnay, the husband of the late Charlotte-Hermine-Louise-Catherine d'Irumberry de Salaberry. The estate comprised a two-storey stone house on Rue Sainte-Anne in the Upper Town of Quebec, two pieces of land in Godmanchester Township, 1,200 acres in Halifax Township, the seigneury of La Guillaudière, and a quarter of the seigneury of Beauport.

Ignace-Michel-Louis-Antoine d'Irumberry de Salaberry belonged to the seigneurial gentry who in an intelligent manner sought to enhance their social position and secure a certain standard of living through the patronage of the colonial and imperial governments. Salaberry's drawing-room became a favourite place for members of the seigneurial nobility, the clergy, and the government to meet. The paternalistic Salaberry tried to further careers, seeking out suitable jobs for his children and friends. He was often successful, particularly through the good offices of Prince Edward Augustus, with whom he was always on excellent terms.

CÉLINE CYR and MICHELLE GUITARD

ANQ-M, CE-51, 18 févr. 1778; P1000-4-461; P1000-44-877. ANQ-Q, CE1-5, 5 juill. 1752, 26 mars 1828; P-289; P1000-93-1906. ASQ, Fichier des anciens. PAC, MG 24, G45; RG 68, General index, 1651–1841. *The life of F.M., H.R.H. Edward, Duke of Kent, illustrated by his correspondence with the De Salaberry family, never before published, extending from 1791 to 1814*, ed. W. J. Anderson (Ottawa and Toronto, 1870). F.-J. Audet, "Les législateurs du Bas-Canada." F.-M. Bibaud, *Le Panthéon canadien* (A. et V. Bibaud; 1891). Desjardins, *Guide parl.* Le Jeune, *Dictionnaire. Officers of British forces in Canada* (Irving). *Quebec Gazette*, 20 Nov. 1788. Turcotte, *Le Conseil législatif.* Wallace, *Macmillan dict.* Jacqueline Lefebvre, *L'abbé Philippe Desjardins, un grand ami du Canada, 1753–1833* (Québec, 1982). Ouellet, *Bas-Canada.* P.-G. Roy, *La famille d'Irumberry de Salaberry* (Lévis, Qué., 1905). Wallot, *Un Québec qui bougeait.* F.[-J.] Audet et Édouard Fabre Surveyer, "Ignace-Michel-Louis-Ant. d'Irumberry de Salaberry," *La Presse*, 26 nov. 1927: 69. Hare, "L'Assemblée législative du Bas-Canada," *RHAF*, 27: 361–95.

IRVINE, JAMES, businessman, JP, militia officer, office holder, and politician; b. 1766 in England, son of Adam Irvine and Elizabeth Irvine; m. 13 July 1801 at Quebec Ann Pyke, eldest daughter of John George PYKE of Halifax, and they had two sons, one of whom died in infancy; d. 27 Sept. 1829 at Quebec.

James Irvine was part of the little Scottish colony at Quebec late in the 18th century. His father had settled there shortly after the conquest, and died in an accident in 1776. Like many of his compatriots James Irvine went into business, forming a partnership with John Munro to engage in retailing. The firm of Munro and Irvine was dissolved by mutual consent in October 1797, and while Munro continued his business activity, Irvine went to England. It was probably after his return to Quebec the following spring that he went into partnership with John McNaught to found Irvine, McNaught and Company, a firm specializing in the import and export trade, with offices on Rue Saint-Pierre in Lower Town. In 1809 James Leslie* became a partner.

Irvine, McNaught and Company was one of the

petitioners seeking repeal of the notorious act of 1805 for the construction of jails, one in the District of Quebec and the other in the District of Montreal. The dispute over how the prisons should be financed symbolized the struggle between Canadians and British for supremacy in Lower Canada and confirmed that there was a class of businessmen determined to take its interests in hand and make its demands heard even in England. The creation of the Quebec Committee of Trade in 1809 was not unconnected with this state of mind. Irvine was chairman of the committee from 1809 until 1822, and like the other members he had links with various sectors of the Lower Canadian economy. The Committee of Trade collaborated as well with several government services.

From 1805 to 1812 Irvine was warden of Trinity House of Quebec. In this capacity he was required to attend particularly to the mooring of ships, the building of wharfs and lighthouses, and the maintenance of the seaway. He could also make regulations concerning the safety of ships and recommend the admission of pilots. On 15 Aug. 1808 Governor Sir James Henry Craig* recommended to Lord Castlereagh, secretary of state for war and the colonies, that he be appointed to the Executive Council. Craig considered him a highly respectable merchant whose business experience would be of great value. Irvine sat from 17 Nov. 1808 to 1822, when he resigned. In June 1809 he stood as a candidate in the Lower Town riding for the House of Assembly. In a hotly contested election he was beaten by Pierre-Stanislas BÉDARD and John Jones*. He ran again the following year, however, and this time was successful in Upper Town; he sat until 22 March 1814. He ended his political career as a member of the Legislative Council, an office he held from 20 Feb. 1818 until his death.

In 1797 Irvine served on the jury in the Court of King's Bench in Quebec that found David McLane* guilty of plotting revolution. He moved in the narrow circle of those benefiting from government patronage. Between 1799 and 1828 he held commissions of the peace for the districts of Quebec, Montreal, Gaspé, Three Rivers, and St Francis. In 1809 he was appointed commissioner to receive the oath of allegiance from members of the legislature. Nine years later he was on the board of the Royal Institution for the Advancement of Learning. In 1822, in the absence of the chief justices of Montreal and Quebec, he became presiding judge of the Court of Appeal of the Executive Council. Lastly, in 1824 he was appointed an arbitrator for Lower Canada to take part in the apportioning of customs duties between Upper and Lower Canada.

Irvine also belonged to the Quebec Fire Society, and was its treasurer in 1800 and president in 1807. He was a member of the Agriculture Society in the District of Quebec, becoming its president in 1817. Irvine served in the militia as well. On 18 March 1812 he was promoted from lieutenant to captain in Quebec's 3rd Militia Battalion, and later, in March 1813, he was transferred to the Île d'Orléans battalion. He retired in 1822 with the rank of lieutenant-colonel.

Irvine owned a number of properties in both Upper and Lower Town Quebec. In particular he was the owner of several pieces of land between Rue Saint-Pierre and the St Lawrence, as well as of some lots on Rue Sainte-Ursule. He lived on an estate at Sainte-Foy that he had named Belmont House, and owned a house on Rue Saint-Louis at Quebec.

James Irvine died on 27 Sept. 1829; his widow outlived him, surviving until 1847. The career of his son John George would be as full as his own had been.

GINETTE BERNATCHEZ

ANQ-Q, CE1-61, 13 juill. 1801, 9 avril 1818, 1er oct. 1829. PAC, MG 30, D1, 16: 342; RG 68, General index, 1651–1841. *Quebec Gazette*, 4 Feb. 1790; 28 March 1793; 3 Aug., 5, 12 Oct. 1797; 10 April 1800; 29 March 1804; 12 Dec. 1805; 5 Feb. 1807; 6 April, 18 May, 8, 22 June, 26 Oct. 1809; 5, 26 April, 3 May 1810; 19 March, 23 July 1812; 8 April, 2 Sept. 1813; 29 May 1817; 12, 29 Nov. 1818; 6 Jan., 27 Nov. 1820. E. H. Dahl et al., *La ville de Québec, 1800–1850: un inventaire de cartes et plans* (Ottawa, 1975). Desjardins, *Guide parl.* P.-G. Roy, *Fils de Québec*; *Les juges de la prov. de Québec.* Turcotte, *Le Conseil législatif.* André Charbonneau et al., *Québec ville fortifiée, du XVIIe au XIXe siècle* (Québec, 1982). George Gale, *Historic tales of old Quebec* (Quebec, 1923). J. M. LeMoine, *Quebec past and present, a history of Quebec, 1608–1876* (Quebec, 1876); *Picturesque Quebec: a sequel to "Quebec past and present"* (Montreal, 1882). Fernand Ouellet, *Histoire de la Chambre de commerce de Québec, 1809–1959* (Québec, 1959). Wallot, *Un Québec qui bougeait.*

J

JAMES, THOMAS GRACE, named Father. *See* GRACE

JANVRIN, JOHN, businessman, politician, militia officer, and JP; b. 29 Aug. 1762 in St Brelade, Jersey, son of Brelade Janvrin, a merchant, and Elizabeth de Lecq; m. 16 Dec. 1799 Esther Elizabeth Filleul (1780–1864) in St Helier, and they had three sons and eight daughters; d. 22 Dec. 1835 in St Brelade.

John Janvrin belonged to the Valpy, *dit* Janvrin,

Janvrin

family that in 1826 received permission from British authorities to bear the name of Janvrin alone. This Jersey family had a long seagoing tradition. They were merchants, sailors, shipmasters, and shipowners, and some were trading with North America by the 17th century. In 1783, perhaps even a little earlier, two of John's brothers, acting as Philip and Francis Janvrin and Company, set up a fishing establishment at the Acadian village of Arichat on Isle Madame, south of Cape Breton Island. At the same time the Janvrins went into business on the Îles de la Madeleine, which also had an Acadian population. This maritime business, with which John would soon be associated, was carried on for a score of years. Around 1790 the brothers established themselves in the Gaspé region, on the bay of that name.

The youngest of the three, John was the only one who came to live on the North American continent, where he spent many years. He first managed the Isle Madame establishment, taking up residence there towards the end of the 1780s. He probably became the principal representative of Philip and Francis Janvrin and Company in North America. But shortly after settling in, he founded his own firm, John Janvrin and Company, and went into the fish and retail trade on Cape Breton. The October 1792 census listed him as a merchant connected with the Arichat fisheries. Later he operated a shipbuilding yard in Arichat and owned some merchant ships, in particular the cutter *Providence* in 1806.

On 17 March 1794 Janvrin was granted an island of about 1,500 acres just west of Isle Madame. He set up a fishing post there (Janvrin Harbour) and stayed for a while before returning to Arichat. Through the years he sold or rented to fishermen various small properties on the island, which was named Janvrin Island by his descendants. The government of Nova Scotia repossessed it around 1894.

On 16 May 1795 the lieutenant governor of Cape Breton, William Macarmick*, authorized John Janvrin and Company to occupy Bernard Island (a small island of some 40 acres located northeast of Isle Madame and near the village of D'Escousse) and to carry on a commercial undertaking, putting up buildings. Janvrin seems, however, to have paid little attention to this island. Early in the 1820s it was granted to a local fisherman, John Joyce, who laid claim to it on grounds that Janvrin had never settled there.

Following his brothers' example, or working with them, John Janvrin tried to run a fishery on the Îles de la Madeleine. In 1798 it involved only three fishermen. It was, in fact, Americans who took up almost the whole area. A few years later the fishery and Janvrin's storehouse were seized by the local seigneur, Isaac Coffin*.

Even though John was running his own firm and Philip and Francis soon arranged to have their own agents at Arichat, the three Janvrin brothers continued to do business together. John held a share in his brothers' company, and all three were shareholders or partners in a number of firms, particularly Jersey ones. In 1799 they were operating a trading vessel, the *Lottery*, and during the Napoleonic Wars they outfitted privateers. At that time there was also a firm called Janvrin and Durell, which operated a fishing station on the south shore of Newfoundland.

Of the Janvrin family ventures, the firm of Philip and Francis Janvrin and Company continued to be the most important. Around 1820 it was one of the main fishing companies on Cape Breton. It owned more than 600 acres, stores, warehouses, and wharfs at Arichat and Little Arichat (West Arichat) on Isle Madame and at Petit-de-Grat Island to the southeast. In the Gaspé it was second in size to the firm of Charles Robin and Company [see Charles ROBIN], in which the Janvrins also held shares. It was established at Grande Grave (Grande-Grève), Bassin (Havre) de Gaspé, Pointe-Saint-Pierre, and Île Bonaventure. In each of these places the company supplied the local fishermen, bought their cod, and through a credit system, kept them in a state of indebtedness which was profitable to it.

In the course of the many years he spent in the Cape Breton region John Janvrin held several important offices. For example, in the 1790s he sat on the island's Executive Council. For a long time he was also a lieutenant-colonel in the militia and a justice of the peace. He still returned regularly to Jersey, where in 1799 he married a young girl from a family of merchants. In 1800 he and his brothers were members of the local board of trade.

Around the period 1815–17 Janvrin returned to live on the island where he was born. From 1817 till 1820 he was even constable of St Brelade. While carrying on his various commercial activities, he became increasingly interested in banking and brokerage. This led to interests in London, and there is reference in correspondence to "John Janvrin & Co. of the city of London." He was also a partner in the London brokers DeLisle, Janvrin, and DeLisle.

In the 1820s John Janvrin handed management of the Cape Breton business over to his eldest son, John. On 22 Dec. 1835, at the age of 73, he died at St Brelade. In the years in between John Jr seems to have revived the family business. On 5 Feb. 1829 he had paid £1,200 for the facilities belonging to Philip and Francis Janvrin and Company at Arichat, where he went to live permanently, and in 1836 he was able to send two million pounds of cod to Brazil. As for the Janvrins' business in the Gaspé, it passed into the hands of Francis's grandson Frederick in 1837. Even though Frederick bought other properties, in the period 1841–55 he sold off all his company's fishing establishments on the Gaspé coast. As time went on, the Janvrin family began moving out of mercantile trade into banking and brokerage in London and on Jersey. Around the middle of the 19th century it concentrated its energies and capital in that sector of the economy.

MARC DESJARDINS

[The author would like to thank Roch Samson, Marguerite Syvret, and the late Keith Matthews for the large body of unpublished information which they kindly made available. This material remains in the possession of the author. M.D.]

BE, Gaspé (Percé), Reg. A, 1, no.37; B, 2, nos.836, 949, 1159. Beaton Institute of Cape Breton Studies, College of Cape Breton (Sydney, N.S.), Biog. file, Janvrin, "The family of Valpy dit Janvrin, Jersey" (1979). Can., Parks Canada, Hist. Research Division (Ottawa), André Lepage, "Histoire de la population et du peuplement de la péninsule de Forillon" (copie dactylographiée, Québec, 1978); Thérèse Savoie, "Historiques des établissements de pêche et compagnies du secteur de Grande Grave" (copie dactylographiée, Québec, 1978). Cape Breton County Registry of Deeds (Sydney), Deeds, 1 May 1794. PAC, MG 11, [CO 217] Cape Breton A, 10: 135; 40: 100–2, 105–6, 116, 162–64; 41: 8–28, 162; MG 23, GIII, 15; MG 24, D9: 154–64; RG 1, L3ᴸ: 39799, 54457, 54459, 54461, 81825; L7, 79: 77, 93, 153; RG 4, B49, 9 Dec. 1831, 5 Oct. 1842. PANS, RG 20A, 2, Janvrin, 1835; RG 20B, petitions, nos.1648, 1936–37, 2151. Private arch., Marc Desjardins (Québec), Marc Desjardins, "Un exemple de l'implantation du capital jersiais dans l'Est du Canada aux 18ᵉ et 19ᵉ siècles: les Janvrin." *Acadian Recorder*, 21 April 1821. *La Gazette de Jersey*, 21 févr. 1789. *Novascotian, or Colonial Herald*, 16 March 1836. *Quebec Gazette*, 12 Sept. 1811, 13 Aug. 1821. "State papers – Cape Breton," PAC *Rapport*, 1895: 87. Jules Bélanger et al., *Histoire de la Gaspésie* (Montréal, 1981). Clara Dennis, *Cape Breton over* (Toronto, 1942). W. G. Gosling, *Labrador: its discovery, exploration, and development* (London, 1910). H. A. Innis, *The cod fisheries; the history of an international economy* (Toronto, 1940). David Lee, *The Robins in Gaspé, 1766–1825* (Markham, Ont., 1984). R. E. Ommer, "From outpost to outport, the Jersey merchant triangle in the nineteenth century" (PHD thesis, McGill Univ., Montreal, 1978). A. C. Saunders, *Jersey in the 18th and 19th centuries . . .* (Jersey, 1930). M. G. Turk, *The quiet adventurers in Canada* (Detroit, 1979). Marc Desjardins et Yves Frenette, "Le pays de la morue; l'évolution des pêches en Gaspésie," *Gaspésie* (Gaspé, Qué.), 21 (1983): 14–24. David Lee, "La Gaspésie, 1760–1867," *Canadian Hist. Sites*, no.23 (1980): 117–92. Marguerite Syvret, "Jersey settlements in Gaspé," Soc. jersiaise, *Bull.* (Saint Helier, Jersey), 18 (1963): 281–95.

JARVIS, MUNSON, merchant and politician; b. 11 Oct. 1742 in Stamford, Conn., eldest son of Samuel Jarvis and Martha Seymour; m. 4 March 1770 Mary Arnold, and they had three sons and one daughter, the last two children born in Saint John, N.B.; d. 7 Oct. 1825 in Saint John.

Munson Jarvis was a silversmith working in Stamford when the American revolution began. He and his father, both "ardent Loyalists," were called before revolutionary committees several times in 1775 and 1776. Finally Munson was, in his own words, "condemned and advertised as inimical to the Liberty of America and an Obstinant Adherent to the Ministerial Cause." In August or September 1776 he escaped to Long Island, N.Y., where for some time he recruited for the Prince of Wales's American Regiment. He then set up in business in New York.

The end of the revolution in 1783 presented Jarvis with a dismal prospect. The death of his father on 1 Sept. 1780 was the beginning of a series of hardships that reached a climax with enforced evacuation to Saint John. He left behind real estate valued at £375 and other property worth almost £225, with little hope, it seemed, of compensation. Subsequently, however, the British government established the loyalist claims commission and Jarvis was able to submit an account of his losses. "The old proverb says half a loaf is better than no bread," he wrote ruefully on 25 Oct. 1787 to brother William* in Britain when consideration of his claim was delayed, "but in the present case if we could get a quarter we might think ourselves well off." He was nevertheless not one for regrets or going back. Some loyalists had returned to their former homes, but for Jarvis "generally speaking those that have gone back were a set of poor wretches. . . . Very few people of any consequence have left us." He continued to regard the revolution "as one of the blackest scenes of iniquity that ever was transacted. We have fought a good fight (temporal), if we have not overcome the thirteen United States, yet we overcome one of the great (I won't say good) allies, the devil and all his works." Eventually he was awarded £250 by the loyalist claims commission.

By the time he made this comment in 1788 Jarvis and his family were firmly established in New Brunswick. He had received lot no.87 in Parrtown (Saint John) when he arrived in the colony and on 20 April 1787 he had acquired no.17. Although not a member of the loyalist élite, he was far removed from the destitute. He sat as an alderman on the Common Council from its inception on 18 May 1785 until 20 April 1790. Defeated when he first stood for the provincial House of Assembly in 1789, he was successful in a by-election held in Saint John County and City in 1804 to replace the unseated Edward Sands. In the mean time he had become a pillar of Trinity Anglican Church, which he had helped to found and which he served first as a vestryman and later as a warden. On 24 May 1803 he placed his name fourth on the list of signatures that established Saint John's first social club at the Exchange Coffee House.

At the turn of the century Jarvis was among New Brunswick's leading entrepreneurs, contributing to

Jewitt

the remarkable growth that would make Saint John one of British North America's leading entrepôts. He had opened a hardware establishment shortly after arriving in the city in 1783, an astute move with so much development under way. Saint John and Fredericton as well as other towns and villages were being built, and the needs of the farmer, blacksmith, and lumberman also had to be met. By 1787 he was sending "Nails, Glass, Ayle and Paint" to Fredericton and receiving skins in return. When the building phase was ending he was quick to adjust. "Our merchants seem to be shifting the trade in quite a different line from what it has hitherto been," he wrote in 1788 to his brother William, "viz shipbuilding."

It was more than luck that drew Jarvis to the needs of shippers and the possibilities of trade. As early as 1783 he had purchased the brig *Lively* to facilitate his business ventures. Over the next three decades his company evolved a trading relationship that reached across the ocean to England, the West Indies, and the United States, and stretched into the interior of New Brunswick on the Saint John river system. His base was his establishment on South Market Wharf at the foot of King Street in Saint John. His brother Samuel, who had remained in Stamford, was his major American partner, while William, who in 1792 took up an appointment as secretary and registrar of Upper Canada, was his initial contact in England. The products that went through his warehouse were whatever the market demanded, including slaves. On 15 July 1797 he sold Abraham and Lucy to Abraham De Peyster* for £60.

Over the years Jarvis's company was expanded to include his two eldest sons. First Ralph Munson joined him in the firm of Munson Jarvis and Son, which was brought to an end in 1810, and later both Ralph and William were his partners in Munson Jarvis and Company, dissolved in 1812. At the time of his death he seems to have been in partnership with William only. His youngest son, Edward James*, studied law and in 1828 became chief justice of Prince Edward Island.

C. M. WALLACE

Conn. State Library (Hartford), Indexes, Barbour coll., Stamford vital records, 1: 59, 173–74; 2: 140. N.B. Museum, Jarvis family papers; Saint John, reg. of voters, 1785–1869. PANB, MC 1156. PRO, AO 12/2: 41; 12/109: 180/1412. *Canada's first city: Saint John; the charter of 1785 and Common Council proceedings under Mayor G. G. Ludlow, 1785–1795* (Saint John, N.B., 1962). *Loyalist settlements, 1783–1789: new evidence of Canadian loyalist claims*, comp. W. B. Antliff (Toronto, 1985). *Royal Gazette* (Saint John), 9 Oct. 1809, 22 June 1812. *New-Brunswick Courier*, 18 Feb. 1826. *The Jarvis family; or, the descendants of the first settlers of the name in Massachusetts and Long Island, and those who have more recently settled in other parts of the United States and British America*, comp.

G. A. Jarvis *et al.* (Hartford, Conn., 1879). Sabine, *Biog. sketches of loyalists*. J. W. Lawrence, *Foot-prints; or, incidents in early history of New Brunswick, 1783–1883* (Saint John, 1883); *Judges of N.B.* (Stockton and Raymond). MacNutt, *New Brunswick*. J. R. Armstrong, "The Exchange Coffee House and St. John's first club," N.B. Hist. Soc., *Coll.*, 3 (1907–14), no.7: 60–78.

JEWITT, JOHN RODGERS, armourer, blacksmith, and author; b. 21 May 1783 in Boston, England, son of Edward Jewitt; m. first c. 1804 a Nootka woman; m. secondly 25 Dec. 1809 Hester Jones in Boston, Mass., and they had several children; d. 7 Jan. 1821 in Hartford, Conn.

John Rodgers Jewitt was the son of a blacksmith from the small Lincolnshire town of Boston, which had traditional links with New England. He was educated in a local private academy and his father wished him to become a surgeon's apprentice, but Jewitt preferred the blacksmith's craft; his father consented eventually and accepted him as an apprentice in 1797. The following year the family moved to Kingston upon Hull, where the elder Jewitt worked in the shipyards.

In 1802 Captain John Salter, commanding the *Boston*, owned by the Amory brothers of Boston, Mass., arrived in Kingston upon Hull. The Jewitts worked for some weeks on his ship while Salter gathered merchandise from England and Holland for a fur-trading voyage to the northwest coast of North America. Salter engaged John Jewitt as armourer, to maintain firearms and also to make ironware for trade with the Indians. On 3 Sept. 1802 the *Boston* left British waters and on 12 March 1803 it cast anchor in Nootka Sound (Vancouver Island, B.C.).

Relations with the Nootkas, which at first seemed cordial, deteriorated when Salter insulted Muquinna*, a leading chief of the Nootkas summering at Yuquot. Muquinna decided to avenge himself for this and other slights his people had suffered at the hands of American and European captains such as James Hanna* and Esteban José Martínez*. On 22 March he and his men attacked the *Boston* and massacred the crew, with the exceptions of Jewitt and the sailmaker, John Thompson. Jewitt was spared by Muquinna on condition that he became the chief's armourer and smith; he pretended that the older Thompson was his father and successfully pleaded for his life.

Jewitt and Thompson remained in Muquinna's hands until the summer of 1805. They were theoretically slaves, but Jewitt eventually became a trusted retainer of Muquinna, and during periods of tension the two sailors acted as the chief's bodyguards. Certainly, their status as slaves was more relaxed than that of Indian captives, for they were evidently initiated, during a winter ceremonial, into a shaman society known as the Wolf Dancers, a privilege not usually granted to slaves, and during his second year of captivity Jewitt was married by Muquinna to the daughter of a chief from a neighbouring Nootka village. Undoubtedly Jewitt's metallurgical and Thompson's tailoring skills, together with Thompson's exploit of killing single-handed seven of Muquinna's enemies during a raid, gave the two captives a special place in the regard of the Nootkas.

Jewitt and Thompson shared the life of the Indians in every way, living in Muquinna's great 150-foot-long house, taking part in fishing and hunting expeditions, in raids on other villages, and in the potlatches and ceremonial bear feasts of the Nootkas. They were not allowed to accompany Muquinna on his whale hunt, but Jewitt manufactured the chief's harpoons, watched his ritual preparations for the hunt, and witnessed his return in triumph. He also contrived, with paper saved from the *Boston* and with homemade ink, to keep a journal of his life as a captive, in which he recorded not only the highlights but also what he later called "the dull uniformity that marks the savage life."

On 19 July 1805 the brig *Lydia*, commanded by Captain Samuel Hill, who had been told by a neighbouring chief of Jewitt's presence, arrived in Nootka Sound. By a ruse, Muquinna was persuaded to board the *Lydia*, where he was confined until Jewitt and Thompson were released. They stayed with Hill for the year that the *Lydia* remained on the coast, sailing with it and its cargo of furs to China in August 1806 and eventually reaching Boston, Mass., in June 1807.

Jewitt lost little time in publishing his journal, which appeared at Boston in 1807 as *A journal, kept at Nootka Sound*. A pamphlet of 48 pages, it seems to have attracted little attention until Richard Alsop, a merchant and author of Hartford, became aware of its existence about 1814 and got in touch with Jewitt, then living in Middletown, Conn. Out of their conversations, and out of Alsop's literary experience, emerged the fuller and more interesting *A narrative of the adventures and sufferings, of John R. Jewitt*, a production in the tradition of Daniel Defoe, published at Middletown in 1815. It remains a unique book, since it is one of the few accounts written from close and extended observation of the life of a Pacific Indian people before their society began to change radically under the influence of European contact.

Jewitt earned a brief and local fame through *A narrative*, which he hawked around New England on a handcart, entertaining his potential customers by singing "The poor armourer boy," a song which may have been composed by Alsop. He took part in the three performances, in Philadelphia in 1817, of *The armourer's escape; or, three years at Nootka*, a dramatic spectacle "Illuminated by Gas" and based on his book; he also performed "Nootkan" songs and

dances in a circus. His book was republished in New York and London and even translated into German; it continued to appear in various editions throughout the 19th century. But Jewitt himself sank out of fame, and died unregarded and poor in Hartford, not yet 38 years of age.

John Rodgers Jewitt spent little more than two years in present-day British Columbia, but he spent them in an unusual way, as a captive of the Nootkas. He, Thompson, and assistant ship's surgeon John Mackay*, who sojourned on the northwest coast during 1786–87, were the first Europeans to live for an extensive time among the Indians of the Pacific coast; Jewitt was the only one of the three to write an account of his experiences and observations.

GEORGE WOODCOCK

John Rodgers Jewitt is the author of *A journal, kept at Nootka Sound* . . . (Boston, 1807; new ed., ed. N. L. Dodge, 1931) and *A narrative of the adventures and sufferings, of John R. Jewitt, only survivor of the crew of the ship Boston, during a captivity of nearly three years among the savages of Nootka Sound* . . . (Middletown, Conn., 1815). The latter has appeared in a number of editions under various titles, and has been translated into German.

K. P. Harrington, *Richard Alsop, "a Hartford wit"* (Middletown, 1939). F. W. Howay, "Indian attacks upon maritime traders of the north-west coast, 1785–1805," *CHR*, 6 (1925): 287–309. E. S. Meany, "The later life of John R. Jewitt," *BCHQ*, 4 (1940): 143–61.

JOE, SYLVESTER (Joseph Sylvester or **Silvester), Micmac; fl. 1822 in Newfoundland.**

Sylvester Joe guided William Eppes Cormack* on his journey by foot across the island of Newfoundland in the autumn of 1822, the first such crossing by a white man. Cormack, although usually referring to him in his journal as "my Indian," gave his name as Joseph Sylvester or Silvester, but family and given names are often reversed by the Micmac Indians of Newfoundland. Since the surname Sylvester is unknown among them, whereas the surname Joe is of relatively high frequency, it is probable that the explorer was misled.

Cormack apparently formed the idea for his trip some time early in 1822. The coast of Newfoundland had long been known to Europeans, but the interior, which was rocky, mountainous, and covered with forests, lakes, and high barrens, was not. The Micmac people who had established themselves on the island in the 18th century were the only people apart from the Beothuk Indians, the aboriginal inhabitants in the northeast, who were familiar with the wilderness areas in the interior. In Sylvester Joe, Cormack obtained the services of "a noted hunter from the south-west coast of the Island," on whom he could rely as a guide. He would have had great difficulty finding his way and

John

indeed would probably not have survived without the skills of his Micmac companion.

The two men made a trial excursion of about 150 miles in July 1822, walking a circuit from St John's to Placentia and back. Then, on 30 August, they sailed for Trinity Bay. Having been landed on the east side, they set out on foot from a place close to the present town of Clarenville. They had to find their own way since, as Cormack said, "none of the inhabitants here or in the vicinity, as at other parts of Newfoundland, could give any information about the interior, never having been further from the salt water than in pursuit of animals for their furs, and for wood-stuff to build vessels and fishing boats."

By 10 September they had climbed out of the coastal forests and reached the interior where Cormack named Mount Sylvester after his Indian guide, a place name that survives to this day. The going was difficult, and a month later, on 10 October, Cormack commented that they had "for some time past felt severely the effects of continued excessive exertion, of wet, and of irregular supplies of food." At this point Sylvester Joe, who could see only hardships ahead and the possibility of encountering Beothuk Indians, proposed that they should turn due south to his home in Bay d'Espoir. Cormack, a truly eccentric individual, was determined to press on. Among his papers there is a contract written in the interior of Newfoundland and making promises of awards to Joe – including food supplies and a trip to Europe – provided he accompanied Cormack to St George's Bay, on the west coast.

On 12 October they met up with the Montagnais hunter James John and his Micmac wife at Meelpaeg Lake; since neither of them spoke either English or French, Joe served as an interpreter to explain their project, and to obtain information for continuing the journey. The travellers were told that there was another Micmac party "at the next large lake to the westward"; they fell in with this group on 18 October only after running into serious difficulties in stormy weather. Once again Joe interpreted, and they were told that they might reach St George's Bay in about ten days. Cormack, however, comments: "The Indian idea of a road is to Europeans little else than a probability of *reaching* a distant place *alive*; and I foresaw, from their report, much suffering before we could reach St. George's Bay." Indeed, 11 days later they fell in with another Micmac party, who informed them that they were still 60 miles from St George's. From this group they picked up a further guide, Gabriel by name, and they reached the sea coast at St George's early in November after a journey of incredible hardships that had occupied almost two months. Cormack himself remarked, "The toil and depredations were such that hired men, or followers of any class, would not have endured them."

Sylvester Joe wintered in St George's, to return to his friends and family in Bay d'Espoir the following spring. At this point he disappears from history, and no more is known of him.

JOHN HEWSON

[For a listing of the various forms in which Cormack's accounts of the journey appear, see the bibliography that accompanies his biography in *DCB*, vol.9. The most easily accessible account is the one printed in Howley, *Beothucks or Red Indians*. G. M. Story's "Guides to Newfoundland," *Newfoundland Quarterly* (St John's), 75 (1980), no.4: 17–23, makes a sensitive attempt to cross the barrier of culture and consider how Cormack's project must have appeared to his Micmac guide. F. G. Speck, *Beothuk and Micmac* (New York, 1922; repr. 1981), comments on the custom among Newfoundland Micmacs that has led to Sylvester Joe being known to historians as Joseph Sylvester. J.H.]

JOHN, CAPTAIN. See OGIMAUH-BINAESSIH

JOHNSON, Sir JOHN, army officer, Indian Department official, politician, landowner, and seigneur; b. 5 Nov. 1741 at Mount Johnson (near Amsterdam, N.Y.), the only son of William Johnson* (later Sir William) and Catherine Weissenberg (Wisenberg, Wysenberk); m. 29 June 1773 Mary Watts in New York City, and they had 11 children who survived to adulthood; d. 4 Jan. 1830 in Montreal.

John Johnson spent most of his childhood at Fort Johnson (near Amsterdam) on the Mohawk River. He received his formal education at home and sporadically at the College and Academy of Philadelphia from 1757 to 1760. At 13 he had served as a volunteer under the command of his father in the battle against the French at Lake George (Lac Saint-Sacrement); as a young man he accompanied him on expeditions to Niagara (near Youngstown, N.Y.) and Detroit. He attended most of Sir William's conferences with the Indians, including the one at Fort Stanwix (Rome), N.Y., in 1768 when a boundary between white and Indian territory was agreed upon. In 1764, during the aftermath of Pontiac*'s uprising, he acquitted himself satisfactorily when he led an Indian expedition into the Ohio country. He went on a two-year "grand tour" of the British Isles in 1765–67 and was knighted by George III in fulfilment of a promise made to Sir William.

Sir John Johnson came home a staunch supporter of his king, almost contemptuous of anyone who dared disagree with royal policy. He settled at Fort Johnson and took Clarissa Putman as his common-law wife, but in 1773 he yielded to his father's wish that he marry into the New York aristocracy. He brought his new wife, Mary Watts, to Fort Johnson and set Clarissa Putman aside, although he continued to support her and their two children. He did not, however, accede to his father's wish to groom him as the next superintendent of northern Indians, for he preferred the diversions of a country gentleman. In 1774, on Sir William's death, he moved to Johnson Hall (Johnstown), having inherited the baronetcy and close to 200,000 acres of land. He assumed responsibility for the numerous tenants and accepted the commission of major-general of the district militia.

During the early years of the American revolution Sir John and his brothers-in-law Christian Daniel Claus* and Guy Johnson* strove but failed to keep the Mohawk valley loyal. His brothers-in-law fled to the province of Quebec in 1775 and Sir John followed in the spring of 1776, narrowly escaping the military detachment sent to arrest him. Upon his arrival in Montreal he was commissioned to recruit the first battalion of the King's Royal Regiment of New York and in 1780 a second one. He participated in the ill-fated siege of Fort Stanwix in 1777 [see Barrimore Matthew St Leger*] and commanded the force which defeated the Americans at nearby Oriskany [see Kaieñ?kwaahtoñ*]. In 1780 he led raids into the Mohawk valley, laying waste the countryside and burning vast quantities of grain and flour intended for the use of the Continental Army.

In the first half of 1782 Sir John was appointed brigadier-general on the American establishment and, by a commission dated 14 March 1782, "Superintendent General and Inspector General of the Six Nations Indians and those in the Province of Quebec." During his long association with the Indians he never failed to champion their cause and to demonstrate his concern for their interests and rights. He was as well the defender and friend of the loyalists in the province. In 1784 Governor Frederick Haldimand* appointed him to supervise the settlement of loyalist refugees on the upper St Lawrence and the Bay of Quinte and, for many years after, these new settlers regarded him as their leader. In the winter of 1785 he presented a petition on their behalf to the king, praying that the new settlements might be separated from the rest of the province in order that they could enjoy freehold tenure of lands and English civil law. When Upper Canada was created in 1791, it was generally expected that Sir John would be named its first lieutenant governor.

Bitterly disappointed when the post went to John Graves Simcoe*, Johnson resolved to seek a place for himself elsewhere. He moved with his wife and children to London, where a stay of four years was sufficient to convince him that his abilities and contributions were quite unappreciated in England and that the Canadas offered the best opportunities after all for himself and his family. Accordingly, he moved back to Montreal in the fall of 1796. Shortly thereafter he was appointed to the Legislative Council

of Lower Canada; from 1786 to 1791 he had been a member of the same council for Quebec. He also resumed his duties as head of the Indian Department.

In the latter capacity, Johnson continued his efforts to provide the Indians with their needs and to serve as the guardian of their rights and interests, as well as to maintain an efficient and orderly department. As chief officer, he was not expected to make policy for the department's operation, but he volunteered his opinions when important issues arose. He "made strong opposition" in 1796 to the placing of the responsibility for Indian affairs in the hands of the civil authorities in the two Canadas; however, his advice went unheeded. He was not consulted when in 1815 the control of the department was once more assigned to the commander of the forces, but it seems certain that he approved of the move for he knew it "would give great satisfaction to the Indians." When in the early 1820s the British government considered the abolition of the practice of giving presents to the Indians, he made it known that he was emphatically opposed to the idea, and the presents continued.

During the years when the department was under military control, Johnson's influence depended on the pleasure of the commander of the forces and varied from one to another, being perhaps greatest with Haldimand and certainly least with Lord Dalhousie [Ramsay*], whose interference in the affairs of the department was limitless. Nevertheless, it was Sir John Johnson who was held responsible for the peace, contentment, and welfare of the Indians. When unrest appeared imminent among them, it was he who talked to the chiefs individually and held council with them collectively, dispelling their fears and suspicions. In the fall of 1782 at Niagara he convinced them that the king was not about to sacrifice their interests in peace negotiations with the United States. Again at Niagara in the summer of 1783 he succeeded in assuring them of something he did not himself believe, that the Americans would honour the boundary line agreed upon at Fort Stanwix in 1768; although on the occasion he knew he was feeding them with false hopes, he prevented them from embarking on a war that could only have brought disaster to themselves. In 1799, by visiting the posts of Upper Canada and conferring with the chiefs and warriors, he allayed the fears expressed by the governors of the two provinces of unrest among the native people. In the 1820s he carried on a bitter and protracted quarrel with Dalhousie over an unwise appointment the governor had made without consultation, and at the same time he tried to prevent construction workers on the Lachine Canal from stirring up trouble in the Indian village of Caughnawaga (Kahnawake).

Johnson also put a great deal of effort into the acquisition of property. Having renovated the palatial Château de Longueuil on Rue Saint-Paul in Montreal, he took up residence there late in 1798. Determined to recover at least the equivalent of what he had lost in New York, he became engrossed in the relentless pursuit of more real estate. He already owned a country residence in Lachine and another in the suburbs below Montreal; in Upper Canada he had a house on a large lot in Kingston, a property in Cornwall, and large tracts on Lake St Francis and the Raisin River, at Gananoque, and on Amherst Island; in addition, he had sundry smaller holdings in various parts of the Canadas. In 1795 he purchased the seigneury of Monnoir, roughly 84,000 acres, and a few years later the seigneury of Argenteuil, about 54,000 acres. Even so, he was not satisfied and all the rest of his life sought to augment his land holdings.

Johnson never lost his sentimental attachment to the valley of his youth. Although he built beautiful manor-houses at Monnoir and Argenteuil, the terrain surrounding the cone-shaped Mont Sainte-Thérèse (Mont Saint-Grégoire) on Monnoir reminded him of his homes in the Mohawk valley. He renamed the hill Mount Johnson, built a small house at its base, and lived there much of the time in the twilight of his life. Dalhousie described him as "very lively in countenance & speaks rapidly Very gentlemanlike manners, & with all that a kind of wildness, as if he wished to appear a character tinctured with the habits and the intercourse he has had with the Indian tribes." He died on 4 Jan. 1830 in Montreal. The military and masonic funeral, attended by 300 Indians as well as throngs of friends, relatives, acquaintances, and admirers, was colourful and impressive. The ancient Mohawk orator at the ceremony referred to him as the Indians' "friend and fellow warrior." His remains were conveyed to Mount Johnson for burial.

EARLE THOMAS

Portraits of Sir John Johnson can be found in the MTL, J. R. Robertson coll.; in Johnson Hall; and in the masonic temple on Rue Sherbrooke in Montreal.

BL, Add. MSS 21755: 13, 137, 258, 287; 21756: 1–2; 21818: 88, 90, 92, 95, 97, 126, 128, 152, 158, 162, 170 (transcripts at PAC). McGill Univ. Libraries, MS coll., CH104.S122. PAC, MG 11, [CO 42] Q, 14: 132–35; 62A, pt.II: 339; 77: 256–62; 336, pt.II: 337–49, 396–97, 402–4, 411–18, 430–36, 441–62, 465–66, 484–85; MG 19, F1, 1: 230–33; 3: 115–17, 143, 245–48; 5: 23–26; 14: 66, 75–78, 88–89, 92, 99–100, 104–5, 124–25; 15: 84, 108–15, 187–94, 250–53, 268–71; F2, 3; F6, Brant to Johnson, 20 March 1799; RG 1, L3^L: 2870–86, 2955–63, 54788–90; RG 10, A3, 493: 30523–24, 30583–85, 30679–83. PRO, AO 12/20: 324. *Corr. of Hon. Peter Russell* (Cruikshank and Hunter), vol.3. *The documentary history of the state of New York . . .*, ed. E. B. O'Callaghan (4v., Albany, 1849–51). *Documents relative to the colonial history of the state of New-York . . .*, ed. E. B. O'Callaghan and Berthold Fernow (15v., Albany, 1833–57). *The papers of Sir William Johnson*, ed. James Sullivan *et al.* (14v., Albany, 1921–65). Ramsay, *Dalhousie journals* (Whitelaw), 1: 147–48. *Mont-real Gazette*, 24 Dec. 1798, 11 Jan. 1830. *Quebec Gazette*, 15 Dec. 1774, 11 April 1793. Joseph Bouchette, *A topographical dictionary of the province of Lower Canada* (London, 1832).

Mary Archibald, "Sir John Johnson, knight of the revolution," *Eleven exiles: accounts of loyalists of the American revolution*, ed. P. R. Blakeley and J. N. Grant (Toronto and Charlottetown, 1982), 197–225. M. W. Hamilton, *Sir William Johnson, colonial American, 1715–1763* (Port Washington, N.Y., 1976). [John Johnson apparently believed he had been born in 1742, and gave his birth date as 5 November. Hamilton points out, however, that he was baptized on 7 Feb. 1741/42 and, supposing that Johnson was more likely to be wrong about the year of his birth than about the day, concludes that he was actually born in 1741. E.T.] Earle Thomas, "At home with Sir John Johnson" (paper delivered at the national convention of the United Empire Loyalists' Assoc., Kingston, Ont., 1984); "Sir John Johnson: loyal American knight," *The heroic age: loyalists in Montreal, 1775–1975* (Montreal, 1984). M. W. Hamilton, "An American knight in Britain; Sir John Johnson's tour, 1765–1767," *N.Y. Hist.* (Cooperstown, N.Y.), 42 (1961): 119–44. F. B. Risteen, "Children of Sir John Johnson and Lady Mary (Polly) Johnson, married at New York, June 30, 1773," *OH*, 63 (1971): 93–102; "Notes on Sir John Johnson's postwar activity, 1781–1800," *Loyalist Gazette* (Toronto), 13 (1975), no.2: 6–7; 14 (1976), no.1: 6–7. Earle Thomas, "Sir John Johnson and Kingston," *Historic Kingston*, 33 (1985): 56–68.

JOHNSTON, HUGH, businessman, politician, and JP; b. 4 Jan. 1756 in Morayshire, Scotland, son of William Johnston and Isabel Hepburn; m. first Ann Gilzean of Thornhill, Elgin, Scotland, and they had eight children, including Hugh*; m. secondly 1806 Margaret Thurburn of Banffshire, Scotland, and they had six children; d. 29 Nov. 1829 in Saint John, N.B.

Most sources repeat a local tradition that Hugh Johnston arrived in New Brunswick in 1784 or 1786 sailing his own vessel loaded with trade goods. Whatever the merits of this account, his rapid rise in the small provincial business community suggests that he was the offspring of a prosperous Scottish commercial family and that, like the Pagans and Rankins [*see* Robert PAGAN; Alexander Rankin*], he came as agent for Scottish interests. Johnston may have spent a few years in Maugerville but he soon established himself as a Saint John merchant. In 1789 he acquired a perpetual lease on a choice water lot near the North Market Wharf in Saint John Harbour; subsequently he built a wharf and formed the slip that was to bear his name for the next century. From this centre he organized an extensive business network which for 30 years was to play an important role in the commercial life of the province.

The structure of his firm reflected the changes in his family circumstances. Hugh Johnston became Hugh Johnston and Son in the early 19th century, and eventually Hugh Johnston and Company as one son passed out of the firm to form Crookshank and Johnston and the elder Johnston brought John Richard Partelow* into the partnership. Johnston's primary concern was the Caribbean market. His business centred on the supply of fish for slave consumption in the British West Indies. By 1796 he employed 11 vessels in the prosecution of this trade. Like most West Indies merchants Johnston engaged in a triangular commerce: he exchanged his fish and lumber for sugar and molasses, which were transported to Scotland and distilled into rum; much of the rum was brought back to Saint John, where most was sold on the regional market and the remainder exported to other North American centres. In addition, he was a significant importer and wholesaler of British hardware and dry goods.

Johnston was highly successful in these endeavours. By the early 19th century his was probably the most important New Brunswick firm engaged in the West Indies trade. In the post-1815 period his company exported more than 30,000 gallons of rum a year from New Brunswick to Quebec, and this figure would certainly represent only a fraction of the firm's total rum imports: typically three-quarters of those imports would be sold on the local market. Unlike most New Brunswick merchants, Johnston remained in the West Indies trade long after it had been superseded by the British timber trade. The firm of Hugh Johnston and Company was dissolved on 5 May 1827, two years before the death of its principal partner.

Not surprisingly, given his commercial success, Johnston participated in most of the activities designed to enhance the commercial and financial well-being of the port of Saint John. One sign of his influence was his appointment as a port warden of the harbour from 1816 until his death. An even more obvious sign was his role in the creation of the Bank of New Brunswick. He was one of the original petitioners for the bank and in the 1820 act of incorporation was named a director. This was an enviable position, one denied to some of the most prominent merchants in the province, and provides a clear demonstration of his standing in society. Among Johnston's other enthusiasms in later life was the new steamship technology. Although he was not among the two groups of entrepreneurs each of which in 1812 proposed to spend £2,000 on the building of a steamship and asked for a monopoly of the steam navigation of the Saint John River, Johnston was in correspondence with Robert Fulton in an effort to obtain advice on steamship construction. In 1816 he was one of the partners who built the *General Smyth*, which plied the river between Saint John and Fredericton. And shortly before his death he participated in the consortium which built the *Saint John*; she made the first steam crossing of the Bay of Fundy in 1827.

Johnston was a member of a Scottish circle in Saint John that included the most influential merchants in the province. Their earliest expression of community was the St Andrew's Society, formed in 1798. Among its officers were William Pagan*, the city's leading assemblyman, William Campbell, the long-time mayor and a member of the Council, and John BLACK, an important businessman. Johnston served as its president in 1813 and 1814. In common with other leading Presbyterian citizens of Saint John, Johnston found little difficulty in accommodating himself to the latitudinarianism of the loyalist Church of England establishment. He attended and held office in Trinity Church at various times between 1790 and 1814, and as late as 1815 he was one of the 36 New Brunswickers nominated for membership in the Society for Promoting Christian Knowledge. By the latter date, however, he had already made the decision to return to his original faith. In 1814 he, William Pagan, and five other prominent Scots were appointed a committee to erect a meeting-house "for the use of such of the inhabitants as are of the General Assembly of the Church of Scotland." Johnston and Pagan were both members of the legislature and their efforts yielded a provincial grant of £250 toward construction. The group procured a building lot in 1815, and in 1816, with the aid of Mayor William Campbell, acquired the grant of a city lot to be used for the benefit of the church. The Scotch Kirk (St Andrew's), the first Presbyterian church in New Brunswick, was completed in 1815. In the autumn of 1816 Johnston sailed to Scotland with authority from the new congregation to call a minister; his choice was the 26-year-old assistant minister at Aberdeen, George Burns.

It is difficult to assess the reasons for this late-blooming Scottish nationalism. The Presbyterians of Saint John had not been numerous but they were prosperous. There had been many gentle gibes levelled at their niggardliness and their failure to maintain their own institutions. The Saint John experience was repeated over the next decade in virtually every town in the province as Scots abandoned their adopted episcopalianism and re-embraced the Church of Scotland. Like so many of his co-religionists Johnston was a freemason, and he was a founder of St John's Lodge in 1802.

In contrast to many of his peers Johnston was not a man of public affairs. Given his status and wealth it was both expected and appropriate that he should occupy positions of honour and responsibility. Yet he did not undertake those responsibilities until well into middle age. Though most men of his class held the office of magistrate by 1800, Johnston did not assume that normal distinction until 1818. His first entry into public life occurred in 1802, when he won election to the House of Assembly as one of the four members for the constituency of Saint John County and City. He entered the legislature as a member of the populist group led by James Glenie*. The group, formed in the mid 1790s, was a coalition of various social, economic, and religious interests which had been largely excluded from the loyalist establishment. By insisting on the assembly's right to designate to whom the money raised by taxes should be paid, these dissidents had brought the political process to a standstill between 1795 and 1799 [see Glenie]. Although a compromise had been achieved and Lieutenant Governor Thomas Carleton* was able to gain effective control of the assembly, by 1802 the populists again dominated the house. After a controversy over the appointment of the clerk of the assembly [see Samuel Denny STREET; Dugald Campbell*], Carleton dissolved the legislature, counting on the loyalty cry to secure him a majority in the province at large.

The gamble succeeded. Johnston arrived in the assembly as one of only eight populists, or reformers as historian James Hannay* referred to them. The core of the group consisted of the Scots Presbyterians: Glenie from Sunbury, Robert Pagan from Charlotte, and William Pagan and Johnston from Saint John. Depending on the issue they could count on the support of four or five other members from Charlotte and Saint John. During the first session of the house Johnston, his compatriots, and four others unsuccessfully opposed a motion that the clerk of assembly should be appointed by the crown. This defeat was only the beginning of a series of disappointments for the group. A number of contested elections – usually between populists and government supporters – were brought before the house. Ward CHIPMAN's petition to invalidate Edward Sands's election in Saint John was upheld over Johnston's opposition. The petition of the populist Peter Fraser* to unseat his opponent in York was fruitless, as was that of Samuel Denny Street in Sunbury. The final humiliation for the group was the reappointment of William and Thomas Knox as provincial agents in London. They had previously been dismissed by the assembly for refusing to present a petition to the king's ministers protesting the lieutenant governor's position in the constitutional debates of 1795–98.

The bitterness of that first session did not persist. Carleton left for England in October 1803 and Glenie left in 1805. The new provincial administrator, Gabriel George Ludlow*, was not prepared to prolong the debates and until his death in 1808 the assembly rarely met and even more rarely discussed contentious issues of principle. After 1808 animosities revived somewhat. Re-elected to the assembly in 1809, 1816, and 1819, Johnston found himself in the opposition on most issues. On questions not involving constitutional prerogatives, he generally supported low duties, economy in government, and protection of property. Thus he opposed the 1813 imposition of an additional

tariff on rum to aid in the prosecution of the war, voted against a resolution of solicitude for the 104th Foot, opposed a motion to pay the cost of sleds for the 8th Foot's march to Quebec, rejected attempts of the Council to amend the militia bill, supported the bill to regulate the trade in plaster of Paris, and opposed the 1816 bill to regulate assessments in the province. On constitutional issues Johnston remained a parliament man. In 1816, arguing that it was unnecessary in time of peace, he and the Pagan brothers, and John Ward* and Stephen Humbert* from Saint John, alone opposed a resolution to continue wartime revenue bills for an additional year. Two years later the same group was defeated in its opposition to a meeting between the assembly and the Council to negotiate an appropriation bill for the public service. Johnston declined to contest the 1820 election. He may have continued to hold his appointment as a magistrate of Saint John County until his death.

Johnston died at his residence on the evening of 29 Nov. 1829 following a severe and lingering illness. He provided his wife with an annuity worth £100 a year to be paid so long as she remained his widow, and the sum of £200 and one-room's furniture to allow her to acquire lodgings. The remainder of his large estate was equally divided among his surviving three sons and four daughters.

T. W. ACHESON

PANB, MC 1156; RG 2, RS8, appointments and commissions; RG 4, RS24, S21-P5, S24-P17; RG 7, RS71, 1829, Hugh Johnston. N.B., House of Assembly, *Journal*, 1803–18. *Schedule of the real estate belonging to the mayor, aldermen and commonalty of the city of Saint John . . . January, 1842* (Saint John, N.B., 1849; copy at PANB). *New-Brunswick Courier*, 28 Jan. 1815; 8 April, 9 June 1827; 5 Dec. 1829. W. F. Bunting, *History of St. John's Lodge, F. & A.M. of Saint John, New Brunswick . . .* (Saint John, 1895). Hannay, *Hist. of N.B.* D. R. Jack, *History of Saint Andrew's Church, Saint John, N.B.* (Saint John, 1913). I. A. Jack, *History of St. Andrew's Society of St. John, N.B., Canada, 1798 to 1903* (Saint John, 1903). Macmillan, "New men in action," *Canadian business hist.* (Macmillan), 44–103. MacNutt, *New Brunswick*.

JOHNSTON, JOHN, fur trader and JP; b. 25 Aug. 1762, son of William Johnston of Portrush (Northern Ireland) and Elizabeth McNeil; d. 22 Sept. 1828 at Sault Ste Marie, Mich.

Born into the gentry, John Johnston was left fatherless in his seventh year. Nevertheless, he received a good education in literature and history. In 1778 or 1779 he went to Belfast to oversee the waterworks, which were part of his family's inheritance. In later years Johnston felt that at this period he had squandered his time and money and that his many hours spent reading "the trash of a circulating library" were wasted. He had to admit, however, that he had improved the waterworks' value. In 1789 he decided to go to the province of Quebec since it had become clear that the lease to the waterworks would not be renewed. With letters of recommendation to Governor Lord Dorchester [Guy Carleton*] from the president of the Privy Council committee for trade, Baron Hawkesbury, and from the influential merchant Brook Watson*, Johnston sailed in June 1790 on the *Clara* for New York. He landed on 25 August, took a sloop to Albany, and proceeded to Montreal.

By chance, in a Montreal coffee-house the young Irishman met an old acquaintance, Isaac Todd*'s nephew Andrew. Andrew Todd suggested that Johnston join the firm of Todd, McGill and Company, to which he was attached, in trading with the Indians via Michilimackinac (Mackinac Island, Mich.). Having greater hopes, Johnston declined and took a calèche to Quebec where he called on Lord Dorchester. The governor, however, had nothing to offer but a letter of introduction to Sir John JOHNSON, superintendent general of Indian affairs. After returning to Montreal late in the year, Johnston took lodgings at Varennes and spent the winter improving his French. Late in life he remembered the "urbanity and politeness" with which his stumbling phrases had been treated.

By May 1791 a trading trip to Michilimackinac with Andrew Todd looked attractive. Johnston arrived at Mackinac Island on the 16th, "a perfect spectacle of deformity" from mosquito bites. After the brisk summer business season was over, Todd fitted him out with a canoe and five voyageurs to winter among the Indians at La Pointe, on Lake Superior's southern shore near present-day Ashland, Wis. When he arrived in late September, he met Count Andriani, an Italian nobleman, taking observations to determine whether the earth was flattened at the poles. Johnston and his men built a small house on the Bad River (Wis.) and he began to learn the language and traditions of the Ojibwas. About the middle of November his men deserted him and he was left alone with one boy and two competing traders who resided near by. "It struck me," he recalled, "that my case, in many particulars, had a resemblance to that of Robinson Crusoe."

Always a hospitable person, Johnston befriended the elderly father of Wabojeeg (Waub Ojeeg), chief of the La Pointe Ojibwas. Eventually he asked to marry Wabojeeg's beautiful young daughter, Oshaguscod-awaqua. The chief replied that Johnston must promise never to forsake her as most whites forsook their Indian wives and that to show his good intentions he must wait a year. Johnston took his furs to Montreal and when he returned in the summer of 1792 he married Oshaguscodawaqua after the Indian custom. Later, at Fort St Joseph (St Joseph Island, Ont.), he married her again and gave her the name Susan. This

union forged for Johnston a firm trading alliance with the Ojibwas. Because he felt that his wife would never be happy in Ireland he abandoned any plans to return home.

Although Andrew Todd wanted him to settle in New Orleans, Johnston decided to establish himself at Sault Ste Marie in 1793 as an independent trader. The previous year he had secured a grant of land on the St Marys River near the place on the south bank where the old trader Jean-Baptiste Cadot* lived. Johnston was well liked by the Indians since he was courageous and helped them freely. He soon dominated the fur trade along the southern shore of Lake Superior and gradually became wealthy.

Johnston was in disposition "at once pious and cheerful." Cut off from the organized church he led his growing family in morning and evening prayers and read sermons on Sunday. From his small library he read history, divinity, and classics aloud to them. A sensitive man, he recorded his feelings in poetry which he shared occasionally with his friends. He wrote more than 2,000 lines but did not polish them for publication. Though she never spoke English, Susan was an excellent companion and taught their eight children a rich heritage of Indian lore and legends.

In 1804 Johnston's mother died and he inherited the family estate of Craige, near Coleraine, in Ireland. Initially he did not return to inspect his inheritance since he was so actively engaged in the fur trade, importing goods from London through John Jacob Astor in New York. Occasionally he travelled to Montreal, and he was elected a member of the Beaver Club there on 2 Jan. 1808. In 1809, however, he embarked at Quebec for Ireland accompanied by his nine-year-old daughter Jane (Obah-dahm-wawn-gezzhago-quay). After landing in Cork they visited Dublin and Jane was left with relatives in Wexford while Johnston tended to his affairs. His family and friends urged him to forsake the wilderness and accept a "civilized" marriage and position in Ireland. Refusing the offer, Johnston went to London, perhaps to secure entry of his sons Lewis Saurin and George into the army and navy. While there, he declined an invitation from Lord Selkirk [Douglas*] to head a planned settlement on the Red River. Instead he embarked from Liverpool in the middle of June 1810 and reached home with his daughter late in November. Having savoured the charms of civilization, Johnston made arrangements the following year to purchase an estate near Montreal with a view to becoming a gentleman farmer. He had never reconciled himself to the level of morality at which the North West Company and the Hudson's Bay Company conducted the fur trade. In the words of his son-in-law Henry Rowe Schoolcraft, he was "free and pointed in remarks against the rapacity with which they swept the

Johnston

spoils of the chace, often wrenched away with violence, and stained with blood."

Johnston's plans for moving were knocked awry by the events of the War of 1812. The south bank of the St Marys River had been designated part of the United States by the 1783 treaty; the Americans, however, had never occupied it although they took over Mackinac Island in 1796. Thus Johnston retained his loyalty to the crown and took part in Captain Charles Roberts*'s capture of the island on 17 July 1812. Shortly thereafter he returned to the Sault where he continued his trade. During the winters he would go to Montreal to sell his furs; at this time he usually dealt with merchant David DAVID. On 12 May 1814 he received a commission of the peace for the Indian Territory, which he held until 28 Oct. 1816.

In 1814 the Americans, having secured naval superiority on the Upper Lakes, sent ships to recapture Mackinac Island, and Johnston went to its defence. While he was on his way, an American force ascended the St Marys River, burning Fort St Joseph and the NWC post on the Canadian side at the Sault. Despite orders not to harm private property, on 24 July the American troops destroyed $40,000 worth of Johnston's goods. Within a few hours the fruits of 23 years of labour were wiped out. Unaware of what had happened, Johnston briefly took command at Michilimackinac while Lieutenant-Colonel Robert McDouall* led the forces that repulsed an American landing on the island. Soon after the beaten Americans sailed, Johnston returned to the Sault and surveyed his losses. Sustained by a deep faith in God's providence, he began rebuilding his shattered life. Late in the fall he went to Montreal to file his claim for compensation but, despite repeated requests stretching over many years and directed to both the British and the American governments, it was never paid. The British disallowed it because he lived on the American side of the line and the Americans refused to pay a British claim.

Following the war the boundary line was confirmed, and Johnston's property was indisputably in the United States. He never became a citizen, but he did not harbour resentment and was hospitable to the occupying forces. Although he preferred to operate as an independent trader, to rebuild his finances he associated himself with the American Fur Company and managed the post that took in the Sault and southern Lake Superior. In 1816 Congress passed laws that restricted the American fur trade to citizens of the United States; however, connections with an American firm permitted Johnston to continue operating. In the autumn of 1816 he went to Fort William (Thunder Bay, Ont.) on behalf of the NWC to present to Lord Selkirk that company's demand for the return of the fort, which Selkirk had seized. In an effort to broaden his trading base, in 1818 Johnston set up a

post on Drummond Island (Mich.), the site of the British garrison after Mackinac Island had to be abandoned at the end of the war.

Because of his financial distress, Johnston in 1819–20 went to Britain to press his claim for compensation and to sell his estate, Craige. While he was away, Governor Lewis Cass of Michigan Territory and a contingent of United States troops arrived at the Sault to treat with the Indians and purchase land for a fort. The Ojibwas were most belligerent, and only the diplomatic efforts of the respected Susan Johnston got them to accept the Stars and Stripes. Accompanying the expedition was Henry Rowe Schoolcraft, who returned as Indian agent in 1822 when troops came to build the fort. He boarded at the Johnston home and, being an avid scholar with broad ranging interests, soon became close friends with Johnston. In 1823 he married Jane Johnston.

By the mid 1820s Johnston's health was failing. He was respected, however, as the patriarch of the Sault and all passing dignitaries enjoyed his expansive hospitality. In 1826 Thomas Loraine McKenney of the United States Bureau of Indian Affairs toured the lakes and commented, "In his person, Mr. J. is neat; in his manners, affable and polite; in conversation intelligent. His language is always that of thought; and often strikingly graphic. He is always cheerful – even when he is afflicted most." In 1828 Johnston went to New York to confer with fur trader Ramsay Crooks* and John Jacob Astor. On 17 September he arrived back at the Sault in a state of collapse. He died on 22 September and was given a military burial two days later. Perhaps Lewis Cass best summed up Johnston's life: "He was really no common man. To preserve the manners of a perfect gentleman, and the intelligence of a well educated man, in the dreary wastes around him, and his seclusion from all society, but that of his own family, required a vigour and elasticity of mind rarely to be found."

DAVID A. ARMOUR

The Bayliss Public Library (Sault Ste Marie, Mich.) holds an oil portrait of John Johnston, said to have been painted by James Wilson in 1796.

Bayliss Public Library, George Johnston papers; Port Mackinac, records, April 1805; 19 June 1806; 29–30 June, 17, 25 July 1817. Bentley Hist. Library, Univ. of Mich. (Ann Arbor), Mich. Hist. Coll., U.S. Bureau of Customs, district of Michilimackinac, impost book, 29 Sept. 1802, 4 Oct. 1805, 23 June 1806, 12 Sept. 1808, 1 Oct. 1810, 10 Jan. 1811, 25 July 1816. DPL, Burton Hist. Coll., George Johnston papers. Library of Congress, MS Division (Washington), H. R. Schoolcraft papers, container no. 36 (General corr., unbound ser., 1826–29). McCord Museum, Beaver Club minute-book, 1807–27. PAC, RG 8, I (C. ser.), 91: 143–46; RG 10, A2, 26, Charles Gauthier, "Journal of the Indian Department," 29 June 1792; RG 68, General index, 1651–1841: 100, 325. Stuart House Museum of Astor Fur

Post (Mackinac Island, Mich.), American Fur Company, letter-book, 8 Oct., 5 Dec. 1821; 4 March, 30 April, 5 July, 17 Oct. 1822.

Les bourgeois de la Compagnie du Nord-Ouest (Masson), 2: 137–74. [Jacob] Brown, "Gen. Brown's inspection tour up the lakes in 1819," Buffalo Hist. Soc., *Pub.* (Buffalo, N.Y.), 24 (1920): 313–14. Joseph Delafield, *The unfortified boundary: a diary of the first survey of the Canadian boundary line from St. Regis to the Lake of the Woods . . .*, ed. Robert McElroy and Thomas Riggs (New York, 1943), 370–71. Gabriel Franchère, *Adventure at Astoria, 1810–1814*, trans. and ed. H. C. Franchère (Norman, Okla., 1967), 166–67. T. L. McKenney, *Sketches of a tour to the lakes, of the character and customs of the Chippeway Indians, and of the incidents connected with the treaty of Fond du Lac* (Baltimore, Md., 1827; repr. Minneapolis, Minn., 1959), 174, 181–211, 263, 265, 369, 381–82. *Mich. Pioneer Coll.*, 32 (1902): 304–53; 36 (1907): 53–100. H. R. Schoolcraft, *Personal memoirs of a residence of thirty years with the Indian tribes on the American frontiers, and brief notices of passing events, facts and opinions, A.D. 1812 to A.D. 1842* (Philadelphia, 1851). U.S., Congress, *American state papers . . . in relation to the public lands . . .*, ed. Walter Lowrie (5v., Washington, 1834), 4: 698–99, 701, 830, 832–41. *Detroit Gazette*, 23 Oct. 1828. J. M. Gray, *Lord Selkirk of Red River* (Toronto, 1963). Janet Lewis, *The invasion: a narrative of events concerning the Johnston family of St. Mary's* (New York, 1932). A. C. Osborne, "Old Penetanguishene: sketches of its pioneer, naval and military days," *Simcoe County pioneer papers* (6 nos., Barrie, Ont., 1908–17; repr., 6 nos. in 1v., Belleville, Ont., 1974), no.5: 47–48. W. W. Warren, *History of the Ojibway nation* (Minneapolis, 1957; repr. 1970).

JOHNSTON, WILLIAM, lawyer, office holder, and politician; b. probably in 1779 in Dumfriesshire, Scotland, son of George Johnston; m. Sarah Elizabeth ——, and they had three children; d. 18 May 1828 at his home, St Avards, in Charlottetown Royalty, P.E.I.

Between 1795 and 1798 William Johnston apprenticed as a law clerk in Edinburgh. Shortly thereafter he came under the wing of such substantial members of the Scottish aristocracy as Lord Selkirk [Douglas*], the Earl of Westmorland, and Viscount Melville. Melville, as keeper of His Majesty's signet in Scotland, commissioned Johnston writer to the signet on 27 Feb. 1805. All three of these patrons owned large tracts of land on Prince Edward Island. Finding it difficult to obtain an accurate accounting of their affairs, and likely concerned over recent reports of political unrest on the Island, they may well have been behind Johnston's decision to emigrate to the colony in the spring of 1812.

Upon his arrival Johnston settled in Charlottetown Royalty. The following year he enrolled as a barrister before the Supreme Court and officially took up duties as his patrons' local agent. As one of the fewer than a half dozen practising lawyers on the Island, he quickly attracted further agencies and briefs. Inevitably, he also attracted the animus of the one other talented lawyer then resident on the Island, James Bardin PALMER.

Johnston's and Palmer's professional animosity was exacerbated by Island politics. Palmer was the leader of a controversial political faction known as the Loyal Electors. Ostensibly organized to secure loyalist land claims, the Electors employed their populist rhetoric primarily to challenge the control exerted over Island affairs by what they called the "cabal" or "compact." Branded as levelling and Jacobin by their opponents, the Electors' activities – especially their strong showing at the election of April 1812 – distressed many proprietors. Johnston arrived determined, perhaps hired, to oppose the Electors. According to Palmer, he "had been but a very few days on the Island when he asserted in the public sheets that the House of Assembly then sitting was not a House but a Convention." The house unanimously resolved to prosecute Johnston for this slanderous suggestion of Jacobin sympathies, but before any action could be taken the proprietors secured the recall, in August 1812, of Lieutenant Governor Joseph Frederick Wallet DESBARRES, who had favoured the Electors. Interim administrator William Townshend*, a member of the "cabal," swiftly moved to dismiss Palmer and his friends from all public office. Fortunately for a "cabal" weakened by old age, illness, and death, Johnston was a new and reliable replacement for officials fallen victim to the house cleaning. In October Johnston found himself appointed registrar, and in November solicitor general. When Townshend gave him the office of attorney general in January 1813, following the death of Charles Stewart*, the administrator wrote to Earl Bathurst that he had reason to believe Johnston's appointment would "give satisfaction to the inhabitants of the Colony, as well as to the great proprietors in England." Significantly Lord Selkirk wrote twice to Bathurst recommending Johnston in similar terms.

When the new lieutenant governor, Charles Douglass Smith*, took up his duties on the Island in the summer of 1813, he accepted Townshend's appointments. In particular, Smith recognized that, with Palmer discredited, there was no local lawyer who could "with any propriety" be placed in competition with Johnston. This lack of alternative was to deprive Smith of legal counsel almost immediately, for Johnston fell ill and remained close to death throughout most of 1814 and 1815. When his health did improve in 1816, one of his first acts as attorney general was to obtain Palmer's removal from the roll of solicitors and barristers for malpractice. Pleased by his admission to the Council in February, revived by the apparent destruction of a foe, Johnston was ready to aid Smith in a program of escheat.

Prior to Smith's arrival, several attempts had been

Johnston

made to reinvest in the crown those lands belonging to proprietors who had failed to live up to the conditions of their grants. Each attempt stumbled before the power of proprietorial connections in London. It was Smith's hope to succeed where others had failed by instituting an escheat of only those lots for which there was no known proprietor. His initial target was Lot 55, and he set Johnston to secure the best legal advice on how to proceed. On the basis of precedents set in Nova Scotia, Johnston recommended in December 1817 that Smith constitute a commission of inquest independent of the Supreme Court justices. He also suggested adding the abandoned lots 15 and 52 to the targets. By February 1818 Smith had convened a commission, and the process of escheat appeared to be safely under way.

If Johnston felt he had finally gained a firm place in the running of the Island government, he underestimated the tenacity of Palmer and forgot the power of his original allies, the proprietors. Correctly anticipating that Smith's escheat of abandoned lands heralded wider proceedings, proprietors in Britain began to reconsider their support for the lieutenant governor. Palmer, in London in 1817, was able to have himself partially rehabilitated by playing on their fears. Indeed, he was able to wrest the power of attorney for the Melville and Westmorland estates away from Johnston. More ominous still was his comment in a letter to a client dated 22 July 1817: "I have a very pretty key to Master Johnston, which came from Scotland – you shall hear more by and by."

Palmer's key was the discovery that Johnston, like so many other agents for absentee proprietors, had failed to account to his clients for the management of their estates and had treated the revenue as his own. Palmer was possessed of evidence of one instance in which Johnston had collected a debt in a client's name and then pocketed the proceeds. He presented this evidence to Smith and the Council in February 1818. Johnston at first avoided giving a reply and, when pressed by Smith in May, impugned the source of the allegations, pleaded illness, and hid behind the pressures of public office. The Council was not convinced, and Smith seems to have been genuinely shocked. None the less, there was little the lieutenant governor could do: Palmer had not yet fully regained respectability and no other qualified candidate was at hand to fill Johnston's role.

Inevitably, personal and then political relations deteriorated between Smith and his attorney general. In January 1818 Johnston had been replaced as solicitor general and in September he was removed as registrar. However, he put his difficulties to good use. Belatedly realizing how deeply Smith's escheat had antagonized the absentee proprietors, he now suggested that his troubles with the lieutenant governor sprang from matters of policy, not scandal. Claiming

he had prosecuted the escheat only because Smith threatened to suspend him, he joined a resurgent "cabal" in opposition. Smith dismissed him from the Council in January 1819.

Clinging to his post of attorney general, Johnston was concerned by the growing *rapprochement* between Palmer and Smith, which was facilitated by Palmer's readmission to the Island bar early in 1819. With his office obviously threatened, Johnston requested sick-leave to visit Britain, which the lieutenant governor readily granted ("Pray keep him when you get him," Smith wrote to London). From the time he embarked in November 1819 until his return in December 1820, Johnston worked to mend his relations with the proprietors, to secure his position with British officials, and to undermine Smith's administration by circulating rumours of a wider escheat to come.

It was a fine double game Johnston was to play upon his return to the Island. He was recognized by Smith as one of the two or three leaders of the opposition on the Island; yet he avoided giving the lieutenant governor clear grounds to dismiss him by remaining in the background as a political strategist. Thus, while John STEWART and others organized a series of meetings which passed resolutions condemning Smith in the spring of 1823, Johnston was neither present at the meetings nor a signatory to their petitions. It was only in the autumn during the trial of the visible leaders of the petitioning campaign that Johnston openly committed himself to opposing Smith's "arbitrary power." Free then to replace Johnston with Palmer as attorney general, Smith did so, having told London in his letter of 11 December that this action would have "the very best political effect." But Johnston had judged his moment well, for the opposition to Smith was by then so widespread and well organized that before 1824 was out the lieutenant governor was sailing for home and Johnston was back in office as attorney general, having been named to the post as of 24 Nov. 1824 by Smith's replacement, John Ready*.

Johnston found himself something of a hero on the Island. In 1820 he had been elected *in absentia* as an MHA for Kings County (he was not sworn in before Smith dismissed the assembly in August), and in the general election of December 1824 he was returned by the same electors. When the assembly met in January 1825 it was clear that Johnston and his allies controlled the new house, and although John Stewart was picked as speaker, it was Johnston who led the majority. He also gained social respectability as a member of the Agricultural Society, vestryman of Charlottetown's Anglican church, St Paul's, and chairman of the Sons of St Andrew.

As a leader in the assembly Johnston pushed through a number of reform measures which were particularly beneficial to the local proprietors and middle-class merchants: bills were passed to support and promote a college, the fisheries, and the Agricultural Society. At the same time, having learned his lesson, Johnston was careful not to antagonize the absentee proprietors and he voted against a land assessment tax which they opposed. His most celebrated legislative accomplishment was his vigorous defence of the assembly's control over revenue against the inroads of the Council. Johnston's darker side was also present in the house, for even his friends had to admit that he was a "good hater." He led a series of investigations into the activities of Smith's supporters on the Island, paying particular attention to Palmer and making sure when his old foe won a by-election in 1827 that he was expelled from the house as "unworthy and unfit." Appropriately, Johnston died as he had lived, in the midst of a contest with Palmer – a court case again accusing Palmer of malpractice.

Talented, ambitious, and merciless, Johnston was a central figure in the politics of Prince Edward Island for almost two decades, and his early death left a gap not quickly filled. Although occasionally calculating to a fault, he was a skilful politician, and one of the few men who could lay claim to having got the better of James Bardin Palmer. That his quest for power incidentally benefited the Island has been overlooked, as indeed the era in which he operated has been neglected.

M. BROOK TAYLOR

PAPEI, Acc. 2367/33; Acc. 2849/25, 2849/69, 2849/90, 2849/106, 2849/117; RG 1, commission books, 1812–23; RG 6, Supreme Court, barristers' roll; RG 16, land registry records. PRO, CO 226/27: 35, 138, 188; 226/28: 8–9; 226/30: 12–33, 116; 226/31: 60, 72–77, 162; 226/32: 42; 226/34: 3–7, 57–77, 79, 83–85, 117–18, 158–59; 226/35: 3–5, 15, 267–68, 275, 304–42, 420–21, 424, 433–36; 226/36: 230–31, 233, 237–38, 244; 226/37: 109–10; 226/39: 11, 26, 153–58, 191–96, 414; 226/40: 58, 168. St Paul's Anglican Church (Charlottetown), Reg. of burials (mfm. at PAPEI). P.E.I., House of Assembly, *Journal*, 1825–28. *Prince Edward Island Gazette* (Charlottetown), 16 Feb. 1818. *Prince Edward Island Register*, 1, 15 Nov. 1823; 6, 27 March, 8, 18 May, 6, 27 Nov., 18 Dec. 1824; 20 Jan., 5 Feb., 31 March 1825; 2 Jan., 27 March, 17, 24 April, 8 May 1827; 25 March, 1, 15–29 April, 20 May 1828. Warburton, *Hist. of P.E.I.*, 310–11, 343. D. C. Harvey, "The Loyal Electors," RSC *Trans.*, 3rd ser., 24 (1930), sect.II: 101–10.

JOHNSTONE, WALTER, Sunday school teacher; b. in Dumfriesshire, Scotland, probably in the parish of Hutton on Dryfe and Corrie; fl. 1795–1824.

Little is known of Walter Johnstone apart from autobiographical references in his two published books, *A series of letters, descriptive of Prince Edward Island* (1822) and *Travels in Prince Edward Island, . . . in the years 1820–21* (1823). Brought up with a strict religious training and just enough common education to read his native tongue, the boy was taught the trade of shoemaker which he followed most of his life. Despite his humble station and limited education his religious fervour and commitment were such that he began, about 1795, to organize and teach Sunday schools in various parishes around his home. He married and began raising four sons, but his thoughts often turned to work as a foreign missionary outside Scotland, which was rapidly expanding such efforts in the opening years of the 19th century.

In 1816 the Sabbath School Union for Scotland was formed and around 1820 the Scottish Missionary Society opened a Dumfries and Galloway branch; the two foundings encouraged Johnstone to offer his services to the missionary society as a "hewer of wood and a drawer of water." It could not accept all those who applied for support, however, and it rejected Johnstone's overtures. Still anxious to help, he contemplated undertaking a missionary venture on his own account, but his wife understandably preferred that he remain at his trade and continue to support his family. Only when his master's business unexpectedly failed and "friends" (probably including the Reverend John Wightman, to whom his first published letters were addressed) offered to finance his efforts, did Johnstone decide to pursue his dream, choosing Prince Edward Island as his mission field.

The Island had long been a preferred destination for Scots emigrants (including many from Galloway), and it was known to have a substantial Scottish population in need of religious ministrations. Moreover, for both himself and his contemporaries in Scotland (who were experiencing unemployment and depressed economic conditions), Johnstone wished to explore the possibility of making a new life on the Island. He found a Dumfries brig preparing to depart for the Gulf of St Lawrence, and on 18 April 1820 he sailed with a number of emigrant passengers for Prince Edward Island.

Lacking both formal ordination and support from Scottish missionary agencies, Johnstone as a loyal member of the kirk did not intend to engage in preaching. His plan, the execution of which was begun on shipboard, was to create Sunday schools. In that day such schools commonly provided the rudiments of literacy while conveying moral precepts to the children of working-class parents. In the 18 months he spent on the Island, itinerating virtually from one end to the other dispensing books, tracts, and offers to set up schools, his efforts were scrupulously non-sectarian. Johnstone claimed that, with the aid of a published report from the Sabbath School Union, he had persuaded Lieutenant Governor Charles Douglass Smith* to approve his activities and patronize Sunday schools, and indeed during the summer of 1823 such a school was established in Charlottetown under

Smith's sponsorship. Johnstone spent much of his time with Gaelic-speaking Highlanders, including the settlers brought by the Earl of Selkirk [Douglas*], and regarded them as most in need of missionary assistance. But, despite his best efforts, he could not create any long-term employment for himself on the Island, and apparently decided he was too old to undertake the rigorous life of an agricultural pioneer. On his return to Scotland he received patronage from two "learned gentlemen" of Edinburgh, one helping him prepare his books for publication and the other supporting his family. At this time he was living at Maxwelltown, near Dumfries.

Johnstone's two books were intended to serve several purposes. He hoped to arouse his readers to provide financial support and encouragement for fellow Presbyterians on the Island. But into this plea was woven a careful and detailed report of Prince Edward Island, designed to appeal to people interested in reading about foreign parts and especially to those considering emigration to British North America. Johnstone was extremely enthusiastic about the Island as a destination for the younger industrious lower classes of Scotland who had some financial resources. It had "pure and healthful air, water of the very best quality . . . seldom a failing crop but when the cultivator has himself to blame for it" and a location "convenient for trading in all directions and none of the inland parts far from the shore." He was not only a shrewd observer but – despite his lack of formal education – an author highly sensitive to place and mood. Writing of fine June weather he remarked: "The sun, whose rays are more vertical than in Scotland, appears to have both more light and heat; the sky is generally so pure that the eye cannot discern the least vapour or cloud to intercept the sun's rays; and being without the least breath of wind to fan the opening leaf, the air is sultry and enervating in an astonishing degree." Some of his descriptions of Island scenes and locations remain classic.

Johnstone hoped to return to the Island. In 1824 he tried to obtain an appointment as superintendent of a monitorial school in the colony but he apparently was unsuccessful. None the less, he made a contribution to education. His concern over the absence of books there led him to collect nearly 400 volumes, mainly works suitable for Sunday schools, which he sent out in 1824. This "*free gift* to the Islanders" was handed over to a committee organized by prospective subscribers "for a Public Library in P.E.I.," meeting at the Wellington Hotel in Charlottetown on 9 July 1824. The committee sold the school-books at low cost and kept the remainder as the heart of a public lending library that was subsequently established. In his unspectacular way, Johnstone was thus instrumental in the advancement of learning on the Island.

J. M. BUMSTED

Walter Johnstone is the author of *A series of letters, descriptive of Prince Edward Island, in the Gulph of St. Laurence* . . . (Dumfries, Scot., 1822), and *Travels in Prince Edward Island, Gulf of St. Lawrence, North-America, in the years 1820–21* . . . (Edinburgh, 1823). The former was republished in full and the latter in part in *Journeys to the Island of St. John or Prince Edward Island, 1775–1832*, ed. D. C. Harvey (Toronto, 1955).

Sabbath School Union for Scotland, *Annual report* (Edinburgh), 1832. *Scottish Missionary Reg.* (Edinburgh), 1 (1820): 71. *Prince Edward Island Register*, 2 Aug. 1823; 3, 17 July 1824.

JONES, JOHN, surveyor; b. *c.* 1743; d. 16 Aug. 1823 in Augusta (Maine).

Prior to the signing of the Treaty of Paris between Great Britain and the United States in 1783, efforts were being made by the Penobscot Associated Loyalists in the District of Maine to move to a new home in Nova Scotia. Assisting their leaders in arranging the evacuation of several hundred settlers to a desirable site under British control was John Jones, an able land surveyor.

Jones is reported to have resided during his youth at Concord, Mass. He apparently acquired his skills as a surveyor with the Plymouth Company, an association of the proprietors of the Kennebec Purchase; by 1771 he had gone to the Kennebec region, where he conducted a number of surveys for the company. He made his residence at Hallowell. When the American revolution broke out, Jones chose to remain loyal to the British cause and subsequently he was imprisoned at Boston in 1778 or early 1779. Escaping in the spring of 1779, he made his way via Lake Champlain to Quebec and there was commissioned captain in a regiment commanded by Lieutenant-Colonel Robert Rogers*. Soon after, Jones was dispatched to Fort George (Castine, Maine), which elements of the 74th and 82nd regiments under Brigadier-General Francis McLean* had built as a preliminary to establishing a haven on the Penobscot River for loyalist refugees [see John Caleff*]. There he became notorious for leading small raiding parties against rebel settlements; at the head of his band of "Rangers," he marauded up and down the coastal areas. He was also employed in carrying dispatches to Quebec and Halifax.

Jones's talents as a surveyor must have been useful to Robert PAGAN, who after May 1780 was the highest ranking civilian leader at Fort George in charge of settling refugees along the Penobscot River. With the signing of the peace treaty in 1783 and the establishment of the St Croix River as the boundary between the United States and Nova Scotia, Pagan enlisted Jones to assist in preparing a town site and land grants at Passamaquoddy Bay (N.B.), just to the east of the St Croix. By August 1783, in concert with the loyalist agent William Gallop* and the surveyor Charles MORRIS, Jones had begun to lay out the town plat of St Andrews and adjoining parcels of land along the bay and river system. During the fall of that year Colonel John Allan*, the American superintendent of eastern Indians, captured Jones while he was surveying. Contending that the St Croix River mentioned in the treaty was farther east, Allan was attempting to stall any efforts by the Penobscot loyalists to settle and fortify the Passamaquoddy region. Jones succeeded in escaping, however, and managed to complete his surveys. In his role as surveyor Jones also suffered at the hands of the new settlers. The influx of refugees outpaced the efforts to complete the necessary work of surveying farmlands, especially as lots along the coast were taken up and others had to be found inland. Jones was often accused of favouritism, neglect, and out-right rudeness in dealing with both civilian and military refugees. In fairness, however, one must consider that during the period 1783–85 he was executing his duties virtually single-handed.

Jones was described as "small of stature, compactly built, and swarthy of complexion," and because of his colouring was sometimes referred to as "Black" or "Mahogany" Jones. Not much is known of his personal life in Charlotte County. He acquired a town lot in St Andrews and a garden lot at Waweig near by, but it is not certain where he decided to live. He appears not to have developed a 500-acre mill privi-lege he obtained at Waweig. In late 1783, along with Moses GERRISH and others, he received a licence to occupy Grand Manan Island; he disposed of his interest in this property three years later.

According to the Reverend Jacob Bailey*, a fellow Maine loyalist who had praised "his active and enterprising genius" during the revolution, Jones had lost "an ample estate" because of his loyalty. Perhaps wounded by his persecution at the hands of the Passamaquoddy settlers and frustrated by his inability to find a more lucrative and permanent position in the community than that offered by his surveying duties, he returned to the Kennebec region. He may have resettled there as early as 1793, when he compiled a map for the Plymouth Company. By 1809 he was living in Augusta and there he died 14 years later. He was survived only by his wife, Ruth Lee, originally of Concord; there had been no children of the marriage.

ROGER NASON

N.B., Dept. of Natural Resources, Lands Branch (Frederic-ton), Index to Nova Scotia grants, 1765–84; Land grant books. PANB, RG 2, RS6, B; RG 10, RS107, C4/1–4; RG 18, RS148, A1. PRO, AO 13, bundle 75. *Winslow papers* (Raymond). *Vital records of Augusta, Maine, to the year 1892*, ed. E. C. Conant (2v., [Auburn, Maine], 1933–34). J. H. Ahlin, *Maine Rubicon: downeast settlers during the American revolution* (Calais, Maine, 1966). W. S. Bartlet, *The frontier missionary: a memoir of the life of the Rev. Jacob Bailey, A.M., missionary at Pownalborough, Maine; Cornwallis and Annapolis, N.S.* (Boston, 1853). H. A. Davis, *An international community on the St. Croix, 1604–1930* (Orono, Maine, 1950). *Eastport and Passama-quoddy: a collection of historical and biographical sketch-es*, comp. W. H. Kilby (Eastport, Maine, 1888). Guy Murchie, *Saint Croix: the sentinel river* (New York, 1947). R. P. Nason, "Meritorious but distressed individuals: the Penobscot Loyalist Association and the settlement of the township of St. Andrews, New Brunswick, 1783–1821" (MA thesis, Univ. of N.B., Fredericton, 1982). Hunter Boyd, "Waweig," *Acadiensis* (Saint John, N.B.), 7 (1907): 274–83. Robert Fellows, "The loyalists and land settlement in New Brunswick, 1783–1790: a study in colonial administra-tion," *Canadian Archivist* ([Calgary]), 2 (1970–74), no.2: 5–15. R. H. Gardiner, "Jones's Eddy," Maine Hist. Soc. *Coll.* (Portland), 1st ser., 4 (1856): 41–48. W. H. Siebert, "The exodus of the loyalists from Penobscot and the loyalist settlements at Passamaquoddy," N.B. Hist. Soc., *Coll.*, 3 (1907–14), no.9: 485–529.

JONES, SOLOMON, physician, office holder, poli-tician, JP, judge, and militia officer; b. *c.* 1756 in New Jersey, youngest son of —— Jones and Sarah Dunham; m. Mary Tunnicliffe, daughter of a prominent New York landholder, and they had three daughters and four sons; d. 21 Sept. 1822 in what is now Maitland, Ont.

When Solomon Jones was a child the family moved from New Jersey to the Hudson River, settling near Fort Edward, N.Y., at the conclusion of the Seven Years' War. While his brothers were developing their prosperous farms, Solomon was studying medicine at Albany. The Joneses were ardent tories and, early in the American revolution, they joined with other loyalists in offering their services to the British commander at Crown Point, N.Y., Guy Carleton*. Solomon became a surgeon's mate in his brother Jonathan's company of the King's Loyal Americans, later called Jessup's Rangers. The Jones family took an active part in John Burgoyne*'s Saratoga cam-paign and were thus forced to flee north to British lines after the defeat in 1777. During the remainder of the war, Solomon was able to improve his medical skills by treating the loyalists at the various refugee camps as well as by serving in the field. He was also able to obtain further medical training at Montreal. At the end of the war, the loyalist corps were disbanded and given grants of land. Jones obtained 1,000 acres in Township No.7 (Augusta), in what was then western Quebec.

His immediate prospects were not encouraging. In 1783, shortly before going to settle on his land, he had terminated a joint business venture which he had tried with his brother Daniel, though to no success. In 1784 he petitioned Governor Frederick Haldimand*, noting that the province was "over run with Gentlemen of your Memoralists profession . . . and the small pay your Memoralist had during his seven years' servitude to His Majesty put it out of his power to have any Money beforehand." He asked that the governor "point out some Bread for him." While he was waiting, he had to endure the hardships suffered by loyalist settlers during these early years. However, his medical skill, unstinting generosity to those in need, and loyalty to the crown soon brought him recognition. In 1788 he was appointed surgeon to the local militia and by 1794 had become clerk to the district land board. He was made a justice of the peace in 1796 and the same year was elected to the Upper Canadian House of Assembly for the riding of Leeds and Frontenac. Although not a prominent political figure, he was a conscientious representative, patiently dealing with the petitions and claims of his constituents. At the end of his term as an assemblyman, he faced a turning-point in his career. In 1799 he applied, unsuccessfully, for the position of hospital mate at Kingston. However, later that year he was appointed a justice of the peace for the recently created Johnstown District and in 1800 he was sent a commission making him a judge of the District Court. He thereafter committed his talents and energies entirely to the needs of the region.

As a local official, Jones took an active part in the development of the community. From 1807 he served as trustee for the district grammar school. His own sons attended John Strachan*'s school in Cornwall, and Jones was thereby brought into an intimate and lasting relationship with the future bishop. The two men were instrumental in getting a regular parsonage for the area and having Anglican clergyman John Bethune* appointed its minister in 1814. They both felt that the Church of England, as an established church, helped support order and good government by promoting public morality and deference to duly constituted authority. Jones fully recognized the social obligations of his position and, he stated, made it his "particular object to set a good example to all within his influence of Loyalty, industry and perseverance in this province and has in his professional line been a sufferer in administering to the poor and needy settlers."

Jones's brief political career had brought him into close contact with the governing élite at York (Toronto). Using influential friends such as Richard Cartwright* of Kingston and William Dummer POWELL, he had the District Court clerk, Charles Jones*, dismissed and his own son Jonathan appointed in his place in late 1808 or early 1809. Strachan also lent his support, although in a private letter to Jones he delicately suggested that there might be something "unusual" in the clerk of the court being the judge's son. This minor bit of nepotism is indicative of Jones's rising position within the local oligarchy.

Another symbol of Jones's status was his fine residence, Homewood, built in 1800 by a master stonemason, Louis Brière (Brilliere) of Montreal. Apart from his own growing family, Jones was responsible for his mother as well as a female black slave whom he had purchased from his brother Daniel,

and a wayward nephew who had run into domestic troubles. As a firm but understanding parent, Solomon provided the necessary guidance for the boy. Jones kept in touch by regular correspondence with family members, providing them with news and financial support. His sister who had married a British officer and moved to England was particularly indebted to Jones for the sums of money he sent to her. With such a large household to support, Solomon was beset with financial worries and pressed by creditors in Montreal for payment of his overdue accounts. Still, he did his best to supply the available comforts to his family. His personal accounts contain frequent charges for tobacco, wines, and spirits along with occasional silks and laces. Solomon was also an accomplished fiddler and played the various reels and jigs which provided much of the loyalists' entertainment.

The declaration of war by the United States in 1812 posed a serious threat to all that Jones had worked for. In what was likely the first action of the war, early in July a detachment from the Grenville militia, which included Jones's son Dunham, conducted a surprise raid on a small fleet of American vessels sailing from Ogdensburg to Sackets Harbor, N.Y. This action was regretted by the senior militia officers who felt that the seizure of private property was to be discouraged. They delegated Solomon Jones to meet with the American commander at Ogdensburg. Following this meeting, the militia officers agreed that the goods should be returned and "all private property should be respected." However, Jones wanted a more active role in the war. He had held the rank of captain in the militia but had been obliged to give it up, probably in 1808, because of the demands of his medical practice. In March 1813 he was appointed surgeon to the garrison at Prescott. He also continued with his civil duties. In 1814 he was made a commissioner to detain persons suspected of treason. As the district representative of the Loyal and Patriotic Society of Upper Canada, Jones was able to help those left destitute by the war.

After the return of peace Jones continued to serve the Johnstown District despite his advancing years. In 1819 he was appointed to the land board. In addition to settling claims of local residents, he obtained substantial grants which were due him from the crown. However, he had little opportunity to develop his extensive holdings. By 1822 he was in poor health. A trip to take the waters at Saratoga Springs, near his boyhood home, proved unsuccessful. He returned to Homewood where he died on 21 September.

Jones's strong attachment to the Church of England, the governing élite, and the British connection are clear evidence of his tory outlook. His life was characterized by personal benevolence and he was held in high esteem by all classes. An obituary notice in the *Kingston Chronicle* aptly described him as "long an indefatigable physician, and a highly valuable member of the community." Jones lies buried in the Blue Church cemetery at Maitland beneath a simple stone marker.

DENNIS CARTER-EDWARDS

ACC, Diocese of Ont. Arch. (Kingston), St John's Church (Prescott, Ont.), reg. of burials, 13 Aug. 1821–6 Oct. 1890. ANQ-M, CN1-16, 6 mars 1800. AO, Map coll., C-5, Augusta Township, 1785–87; MS 520, notice of appointment to militia, 14 June 1788; Powell to Jones, 25 Oct. 1808; Jones to Powell, 25 Oct. 1808; Strachan to Jones, 19 Nov. 1808, 16 March 1812; officers of the Grenville militia, signed statement, 7 July 1812; G. O. Stuart to Jones, 8 March 1814; MS 816. BL, Add. MSS 21826; 21827: 298; 21875: 193 (transcripts at PAC). Grenville Land Registry Office (Prescott), Augusta Township, concession 1, lots 22–37, will of Solomon Jones, 1822. Ont. Heritage Foundation (Toronto), Heritage Trust Branch, E. M. Richards [McGaughey], "A report for the Heritage Trust: Homewood and the Jones family" (Toronto, 1977). PAC, RG 1, L3, 254: I–J3/33; RG 8, I (C ser.), 287: 65–66; RG 9, I, B1, 1, Peter Drummond to Lt.-Col. Shaw, 17 May 1808; RG 68, General index, 1651–1841. QUA, Jones family papers, esp. box 1, folder 11, corr. to Solomon Jones of: William Jarvis, 18 Feb. 1800; John Jones, 12 July 1803; John Strachan, 10 Oct. 1806; W. Halton, 13 March 1807; James Laing, 2 May 1808; folder 12, corr. to Jones of: E. Macdonell, 20 March 1813; John Bethune, 12 June 1814; circular, 24 March 1814; folder 13, Solomon Jones to his son, 23 July 1822; box 4, folder 35; dissolution of partnership, 30 Aug. 1788; folder 36, will of Solomon Jones, 20 Jan. 1800; box 15, Solomon Jones account-books. Loyal and Patriotic Soc. of U.C., *Report, with an appendix, and a list of subscribers and benefactors* (Montreal, 1817). *Kingston Chronicle*, 11 Oct. 1822. Dennis Carter-Edwards, "Solomon Jones: United Empire Loyalist" (typescript, n.p., n.d.; copy in Grenville County Hist. Soc., Prescott). Andrew Jones, "Reminiscences, or a biography of the Jones family" (typescript, 1904; copy in QUA, Jones family papers, box 1, folder 7). E. R. Stuart, "Jessup's Rangers as a factor in loyalist settlement," *Three hist. theses*. C. C. James, "The second legislature of Upper Canada – 1796–1800," RSC *Trans.*, 2nd ser., 9 (1903), sect.II: 167–68. E. M. Richards [McGaughey], "The Joneses of Brockville and the family compact," *OH*, 60 (1968): 169–84.

JOSEPH, HENRY (also known as **Harry**), businessman and militia officer; b. *c.* 1773 in England, son of Naphtali Joseph and of a sister of Aaron Hart*; d. 21 June 1832 in Berthier-en-Haut (Berthierville, Que.).

The Joseph family is thought to have emigrated from the Netherlands to England. About 1789 Henry and his older brothers Abraham and Judah immigrated to the province of Quebec at the suggestion of their uncle Aaron Hart, a prominent merchant in Trois-Rivières. Henry may have briefly joined the commissariat at William Henry (Sorel). However, he soon associated himself with his brothers, who had established themselves as commission merchants in Berthier-en-Haut, a strategic commercial site opposite the mouth of the Rivière Richelieu, a major artery of exchange with the United States. At Berthier-en-Haut on 28 Sept. 1803 Joseph married Rachel Solomons (Solomon), daughter of Levy Solomons*, a prominent Montreal merchant and fur trader who had died in 1792; they would have 12 children. Joseph gradually acquired considerable property in Berthier-en-Haut, including a large stone house from which he conducted business in association with his brother Judah, Abraham having gone to London as an agent for Moses Hart*. Henry and Judah were Hart's agents in Berthier, and to him they sold a wide range of goods including beer, nails, shoes, and hats. Another client was either Francis* or James Badgley, whose severe financial problems in 1803 threatened their own position.

During the War of 1812 Joseph saw service in the militia. After the war he broadened the scope and geographical range of his commercial activities. In the summer of 1815 he left Berthier-en-Haut to travel in the upper country. He furnished supplies and trade goods to fur traders in association with his brothers-in-law Benjamin Samuel Solomons (Solomon) and Jacob Franks* and brought furs down from the western posts in his own canoes for shipment to Britain. He chartered at least two vessels, the *Rachel* and the *Eweretta*, the latter of which acquired considerable popularity among the colony's most important businessmen as a cargo vessel and passenger carrier. One of the first merchants to charter Lower Canadian vessels directly to England and exclusively for the trade of the Canadas, he has been considered a founder of Canada's merchant marine. In 1817 he was among those who petitioned the House of Assembly for a charter for the Bank of Montreal.

By 1818 Henry and Judah seem to have been operating separately in Berthier-en-Haut. Henry maintained a store from which he supplied manufactured goods to the important agricultural market of the St Lawrence and Richelieu valleys. That year he offered for sale 13 pairs of French burr millstones, 4 querns for grinding malt and paint colours, cast-iron blocks, cast-steel mill picks, and "ANTI-ATTRITION, a Patent Composition for the use of steam Engines, Mills, Machinery, Carriages." The following year he advertised more than 200 French burr-stones.

By 1822, although still living in Berthier-en-Haut, he was a partner in Benjamin Samuel Solomon and Company, tobacco importers and manufacturers of Montreal. At the same time he evidently kept his hand in the fur business, for in December 1822 he announced in the *Quebec Gazette* that he was coming to Quebec with a large assortment of fur products of Montreal manufacture, including "Ladies Fur Bonnets consisting of Churchile [chinchilla], Seal, Sable,

Jourdain

Jenet and Martin Skins, likewise Muffs and Tippets to match, Gentlemen's Caps of Otter, Martin, Russia Cumer Seal Skin, Jenet, Fitch Skin do. with Gloves and Mitts to match, also a quantity of Cariole Robes of Racoon, Fisher, Fox and Buffalo." His various enterprises prospered, and in January 1825 he proposed purchasing a property in Montreal at a sheriff's sale for £3,000 if Moses Hart would spare him £1,000 or £2,000. Hart would not; nevertheless Joseph did buy a large property in Montreal on Place Près-de-Ville. By 1826 he was described as a resident of Montreal, but he still lived part of the time at Berthier-en-Haut, where he was captain and paymaster in the militia and where his eldest son, Samuel, ran the business. At an unknown date he established a branch at Quebec under the name of Henry Joseph and Company.

In 1830 Joseph retired to Montreal. He was a staunch Jew and became active in the city's Jewish community of fewer than 100 persons. While isolated in Berthier-en-Haut he had worked out a religious calendar that enabled his family to observe Jewish festivals and had learned the ritual killing of animals for food. With Rachel he had taught his children to be observant of the practices and laws of their religion.

In early October 1831, following the death of Benjamin Samuel Solomons, Joseph became tutor of Solomons's minor children and, it would seem, sole owner of the extensive tobacco factory and snuff import business on Rue La Gauchetière. In June 1832 Samuel Joseph contracted the dreaded cholera, which was wreaking havoc in Berthier-en-Haut. Henry rushed to be with him, but by the time he arrived his son had already died. Henry himself was struck down by the disease and died the next day at age 59. Father and son were immediately buried in the family garden but later reinterred in the cemetery of the Shearith Israel congregation in Montreal. Henry Joseph left his widow, four sons, and four daughters. After his death the business was briefly carried on by Rachel and a son, Jacob, who in honour of his father added the name Henry to his own. Henry's second surviving son, Abraham*, joined his older brother in partnership in 1837, but this arrangement was short-lived in reality, although it was not ended formally until 1859. In 1836 an inventory had been made of the community of property between Henry and Rachel. It indicates that Henry had probably left his family in good circumstances: the household effects were worth £532 and the stock-in-trade £3,650, while stocks and debentures totalled £900. All of Joseph's surviving children did well. His eldest daughter, Catharine, married Aaron Hart David, a prominent Montreal physician, and the youngest, Esther, married the Jewish religious leader Abraham de Sola*. Of the sons, Abraham married a granddaughter of Aaron Hart, Sophia David, and became a prominent mer-

chant, banker, and municipal politician at Quebec; Jesse became a leading industrialist and railway promoter; and the youngest, Gershom, who married a Frenchwoman, Céline Lyons, in California, became the first Jewish QC in Canada.

ANNETTE R. WOLFF

The *DCB/DBC* would like to thank Professor Robert Sweeny of the Montreal Business History Research Group for his assistance.

ANQ-M, CN1-7, 6, 25 avril 1836; CN1-134, 20 sept. 1822, 7 oct. 1825, 3 mars 1826; CN1-187, 3 oct. 1831. Arch. du séminaire de Trois-Rivières (Trois-Rivières, Qué.), 0009. AUM, P 58, U, J. and H. Joseph to James Reid, 22 March 1803, 10 June 1807, 8 Dec. 1808, 5 Dec. 1831. PAC, MG 24, I61. *Le Canadien*, 27 juin 1832. *Montreal Gazette*, 3 Oct. 1803. *Quebec Gazette*, 2 Sept. 1813; 17, 25 June 1819; 16 Dec. 1822. *The Jewish encyclopedia . . .*, ed. Isidore Singer (12v., New York and London, 1901–6), 7: 254. M. G. Brown, "Jewish foundations in Canada: the Jews, the French, and the English to 1914" (PHD thesis, State Univ. of New York at Buffalo, 1976), 87. *The Jew in Canada: a complete record of Canadian Jewry from the days of the French régime to the present time*, ed. A. D. Hart (Toronto and Montreal, 1926), 41. *History of the corporation of Spanish and Portuguese Jews "Shearith Israel" of Montreal, Canada* (n.p., [1918]). Martin Wolff, "The Jews of Canada," *American Jewish Year Book* (Philadelphia), 27 (1925–26): 154–229.

JOURDAIN (Jourdain, *dit* Labrosse), CHARLES, master mason and contractor; b. 8 May 1734 in Longue-Pointe (Montreal), son of Charles Jourdain, *dit* Labrosse, a tailor, and Marie-Joseph Aubuchon, *dit* L'Espérance; d. some time after 1823, probably at Quebec.

The Jourdain, *dit* Labrosse, family of the Montreal area was related to the Jourdains of Quebec, a family already active in the construction field when Charles came to set himself up there, probably after the conquest. He had spent his youth among craftsmen working in wood and stone; Paul-Raymond Jourdain*, *dit* Labrosse, a well-known wood-carver in the Montreal region, was his uncle.

As more building was being undertaken at Quebec in the early years of the British régime, mason Jourdain understandably thought it worth settling there; as well, in the Quebec region he was joining his cousins Augustin and Michel Jourdain, who were also masons. In 1818 the census of the town mentioned the presence in his house on Rue Saint-Jean of a woman named Henriette Jourdain, aged 28; presumably she was his niece, since no marriage contract involving Charles has been found.

From 1798 Jourdain signed many contracts with the new business élite for construction at Quebec. He apparently specialized in masonry for industrial buildings. For example, in 1800 he undertook for the firm of Lester and Morrogh the masonry of the Cape Diamond Brewery, which comprised a brewery 74 feet long, 64 feet wide, and 20 feet high, a shed 65 feet by 40 with two chimneys, and a store 26 feet square. In 1802 he also built the stone foundations, ovens, and chimneys for George Miller's bakery in the Saint-Roch district. His services were sought seven years later by Christian (Christianna) Ainslie, John Young*'s wife, to enlarge the malt-house at the St Roc Brewery, a contract being signed for £300. On 22 Feb. 1810 he undertook to put up an immense warehouse for merchant John MURE on Rue Saint-Pierre.

Although Jourdain did take on jobs for the *fabrique* of Notre-Dame de Québec and the Séminaire de Québec, his principal accomplishments were secular buildings. Thus, in 1815 he received a contract to enlarge the court-room of the Court of King's Bench in accordance with François BAILLAIRGÉ's plan; these alterations entailed two new wings including a vaulted cellar with windows. Under the contract Jourdain was to supply all the materials, including the stone which was to be taken from the quarries at Beauport. Payment was to be on the basis of £3 10s. a "toise" up to a maximum of £1,850. The work was completed in July 1816 and had required 674 "masons' days" at 7 shillings a day, 439 "labourers' days" at 5 shillings a day, and 336 loads of mortar at 8 shillings each.

Jourdain's competence had also been noted by Jean-Baptiste Bédard*, an important Quebec carpenter who had entrusted him in 1809 with building his house at the rate of "40 shillings per 'toise' of masonry work on the walls, the measurements being verified by Pierre-Florent Baillairgé[*]." Jourdain also acted as an expert for judging the quality of work in case of disputes, a common role for building craftsmen of recognized experience. The last mention found of him is dated 22 Dec. 1823, when the *Quebec Gazette* noted that he was a director of the Quebec Savings Bank.

It is difficult to evaluate Charles Jourdain's contribution to the stylistic evolution of buildings in his time. An examination of his career reveals that he only carried out the ideas of others at a period when the construction industry was making great strides as a result of the increase in Quebec's urban population and the growth of new districts and services. It is to architects and military engineers that one must look for creativity.

RAYMONDE GAUTHIER

ANQ-M, CE1-23, 9 mai 1734. ANQ-Q, CN1-16, 31 janv. 1807, 23 juin 1809, 22 févr. 1810, 17 oct. 1816; CN1-26, 5, 10 mars, 5 avril 1804; 23 mars, 27 avril, 21 juin 1805; 11 nov., 31 déc. 1806; 29 juill., 3 déc. 1807; 9 juin, 20 juill. 1808; 31 janv., 28 mars, 15 mai 1809; 5 oct. 1810; 15 juill., 1er août 1811; 10 juin, 6 oct. 1812; 10, 11 janv., 6 déc. 1814; 21 juill. 1815; 22 janv. 1816; 16 févr. 1819; CN1-171, 10 sept. 1818, 9 sept. 1820; CN1-178, 4 juin 1808, 24 avril 1809, 26 mai 1814; CN1-230, 27 juin 1800, 20 mai 1807, 11 mai 1812, 13 mai 1815, 16 mai 1817, 13 févr. 1823; CN1-253, 25 avril 1812, 29 sept. 1813, 26 juill. 1823, 5 mai 1826. AP, Notre-Dame de Québec, Cahiers des délibérations de la fabrique, 1777–1825: 234–37. ASQ, C 39: 21, 38, 41–43, 65, 82, 87, 113–14, 134, 155; Séminaire, 121, nos.403–10. *Quebec Gazette*, 10 July 1794, 14 May 1801, 19 March 1812, 22 Dec. 1823.

JUCHEREAU DUCHESNAY, ANTOINE-LOUIS, army and militia officer, politician, seigneur, office holder, and JP; b. 18 Feb. 1767 at Quebec, eldest son of Antoine Juchereau* Duchesnay and Julie-Louise Liénard de Beaujeu; half-brother of Jean-Baptiste JUCHEREAU Duchesnay; d. 17 Feb. 1825 in Beauport, Lower Canada.

Antoine-Louis Juchereau Duchesnay belonged to the sixth generation of a family resident in the colony since 1634. His great-grandfather, Nicolas Juchereau* de Saint-Denis, was ennobled in 1692. It was through Ignace*, the third child of Nicolas, that the Juchereau Duchesnay name was carried on. Ignace's uncle, Joseph Giffard, bequeathed him the seigneury of Beauport, which went by right to Antoine-Louis in 1806.

Juchereau Duchesnay studied at the Petit Séminaire de Québec from 1776 till 1785. In 1798 he joined the Royal Canadian Volunteer Regiment as a lieutenant. This regiment had been raised two years earlier to replace British troops needed elsewhere. Although it was disbanded in 1802, he evidently did not give up his military career, since on 21 Nov. 1809 he succeeded Pierre Marcoux* as assistant to the adjutant general of the Lower Canadian militia. It was no small task at the time to assemble and instil discipline into the militia. The general population did not always show much eagerness to respond to a call-up, and improvisation was apparently often the rule in the early military manœuvres. Juchereau Duchesnay, who had acquired the rank of lieutenant-colonel, received complaints on the matter from his subordinates, who in 1814 were quartered at Rivière-du-Loup with their men. No doubt he learned not to become discouraged by these problems, for on 24 Oct. 1816 he took command of the Beauport battalion of militia, following in the footsteps of his father, who had earlier held this post.

Concurrent with his military activity Juchereau Duchesnay was closely associated with the political life of Lower Canada. On 6 Aug. 1804 he was elected for Hampshire riding to the Lower Canadian House of Assembly. Six years later Governor Sir James Henry Craig* appointed him to the Legislative Council and he retained this office until his death. He became an honorary member of the Executive Council on 6 Jan. 1812, and then a regular member on 18 Jan. 1817.

367

Juchereau

Meanwhile, on 1 April 1813 the *Quebec Gazette* announced that he had been granted commissions of the peace for the districts of Quebec, Montreal, and Three Rivers.

In the course of his career Juchereau Duchesnay held various other commissions. On 29 April 1813 he replaced François Vassal* de Montviel as commissioner in charge of militia transport for the District of Quebec. Three years later he was appointed commissioner for the building of churches and presbyteries in the same district. In 1817, following the disastrous harvest of the previous year, he was made a commissioner to carry out a law for the relief of parishes in distress in Lower Canada, as well as commissioner for purchase of seed grain. In 1821 he was appointed to the board of trustees of the Royal Institution for the Advancement of Learning, which administered the public schools in Lower Canada [*see* Joseph Langley MILLS].

Juchereau Duchesnay's social background, his interest in public affairs, and the prestigious posts he held helped make him one of the important citizens of the Quebec region. His prominence in turn brought appointment to a committee that ran the public meeting held at Quebec on 14 Oct. 1822 to protest against a plan for union of the two Canadas [*see* Denis-Benjamin Viger*].

Juchereau Duchesnay died suddenly at the manorhouse in Beauport on 17 Feb. 1825, a day before his 58th birthday. In 1819 he had been a pallbearer at the funeral of the Duke of Richmond [Lennox*]. At his own funeral on 22 February most of the members of the Lower Canadian legislature were present in the Beauport church, when the archbishop of Quebec, Joseph-Octave PLESSIS, paid him a final tribute.

On 11 Feb. 1793 at Deschambault, Juchereau Duchesnay had married Marie-Louise Fleury de La Gorgendière, who was to die of cholera at Beauport on 2 July 1832. The couple had seven children – three sons and four daughters. The eldest, Antoine-Narcisse, followed his father's example and embarked upon a military career. He inherited the seigneury of Beauport but was obliged for financial reasons to sell it in 1844. Charles-Maurice and Elzéar-Henri* were both called to the bar but neither practised law for long. Charles-Maurice died at the age of 35, whilst Elzéar-Henri turned to agriculture and became a member of the Legislative Council and a senator. Only one of the couple's daughters, Louise-Sophie, reached adulthood and she married Bartholomew Conrad Augustus Gugy*.

GINETTE BERNATCHEZ

ANQ-Q, CE1-1, 19 févr. 1767; CE1-5, 22 févr. 1825; CE1-25, 11 févr. 1793; P1000-54-1047. "Lettres de no-

blesse de la famille Juchereau Duchesnay," *BRH*, 28 (1922): 137–41. *Quebec Gazette*, 12 Nov. 1812; 1 April, 20 May 1813; 24 Oct. 1816; 13 March, 10 April 1817. P.-G. Roy, *Les avocats de la région de Québec*, 145; *Fils de Québec*, 2: 137–39. Turcotte, *Le Conseil législatif*, 69–70, 85–86, 228. Thomas Chapais, *Cours d'histoire du Canada* (8v., Québec et Montréal, 1919–34; réimpr. Trois-Rivières, Qué., 1972), 3: 122–23. P.-G. Roy, *La famille Juchereau Duchesnay* (Lévis, Qué., 1903); "La seigneurie de Beauport," *BRH*, 9 (1903): 149–52.

JUCHEREAU DUCHESNAY, JEAN-BAPTISTE, army and militia officer, merchant, seigneur, and politician; b. 16 Feb. 1779 in Beauport, Que., son of Antoine Juchereau* Duchesnay and Catherine Dupré; m. 1 Sept. 1807 Eliza Jones at Quebec, and they had four children; d. there 13 Jan. 1833 and was buried two days later in the church at Beauport.

Jean-Baptiste Juchereau Duchesnay came from one of the richest families of the seigneurial aristocracy in the Quebec region. In 1792 he was placed as a boarder at Quebec, where for three years he attended the Petit Séminaire. He chose a military career, becoming in 1796 an ensign in the Royal Canadian Volunteer Regiment, under Lieutenant-Colonel Joseph-Dominique-Emmanuel Le Moyne* de Longueuil and his own godfather, Major Ignace-Michel-Louis-Antoine d'IRUMBERRY de Salaberry. He was promoted lieutenant, and like his half-brother ANTOINE-LOUIS served until the regiment was disbanded in 1802.

In March of that year Duchesnay borrowed £100 from lawyer Jean-Antoine Panet* and set himself up as a merchant at Lotbinière. However, he rejoined the army in 1805, being commissioned an ensign in the 60th Foot, a unit in which his brother Michel-Louis* also served. On the eve of his departure to join it he sent his illegitimate daughter, Marie-Anne, who was then aged four, to board with a family at Lotbinière. In 1806 he was promoted lieutenant in the same regiment.

During the War of 1812 Duchesnay served as a captain in the Voltigeurs Canadiens, under Charles-Michel d'IRUMBERRY de Salaberry. He distinguished himself on several occasions, particularly in the battle of Châteauguay on 26 Oct. 1813. The next day Governor Sir George Prevost* wrote a report in which he made a point of stressing Duchesnay's performance. Duchesnay was made a major on 25 Feb. 1814, and in July of the following year he was placed on half pay.

In March 1821 Duchesnay was named provincial aide-de-camp by Governor Lord Dalhousie [Ramsay*], an appointment bringing him the rank of lieutenant-colonel in the militia. Two years later he took command of the Saint-Jean-Port-Joli battalion of militia and in 1828 he was called on to serve as militia inspector. In April 1832 he was appointed to the Legislative Council. The following month he became a member of the Quebec Board of Health. But by then a cholera epidemic was raging, and to this malady Duchesnay succumbed on 13 Jan. 1833.

At his father's death in 1806 Jean-Baptiste Juchereau Duchesnay had inherited the use of the seigneury of Grande-Anse. He had, however, never taken up residence on the seigneurial domain, preferring to live at Quebec and entrust management of the fief to two brothers, Jean-Baptiste and Charles Taché. He rented out the communal mill and had a sawmill built which he subsequently also leased. By the terms of his father's will the seigneury was to go to Jean-Baptiste's male heirs, but all his children predeceased him. It thus came to be purchased by Amable Dionne*, a Kamouraska merchant.

CÉLINE CYR and MICHELLE GUITARD

ANQ-Q, CE1-5, 16 févr. 1779, 15 janv. 1833; CE1-66, 1er sept. 1807; CN1-16, 4 juin 1812; CN1-178, 9 mai 1812; 14 janv. 1815; 30 mars, 23 nov. 1819; CN1-262, 30 juill. 1804; 26, 29 oct. 1805; CN1-284, 15 mars 1802. ASQ, Fichier des anciens. PAC, RG 68, General index, 1651–1841. *Quebec Gazette*, 27 April 1812; 29 March, 7 June 1821; 28 April 1823. F.-J. Audet, "Les législateurs du Bas-Canada"; "Officiers canadiens dans l'armée anglaise," *BRH*, 29 (1923): 155–56. Le Jeune, *Dictionnaire. Officers of British forces in Canada* (Irving). Turcotte, *Le Conseil législatif*. Wallace, *Macmillan dict*. P.-G. Roy, *La famille Juchereau Duchesnay* (Lévis, Qué., 1903).

K

KAIN, WILLIAM, labourer and convicted murderer; b. 24 Nov. 1809 on the island of St Vincent; d. 6 Sept. 1830 in Kingston, Upper Canada.

The details of William Kain's life can be found in a short biography published just after his execution for murder. When he was three years old, he emigrated from St Vincent to Kingston with his hard-drinking father, who was serving in the 70th Foot; his mother, reportedly either French or West Indian, did not accompany them. In Kingston, William was educated at the regimental school until the age of 14, when his father was discharged. Of necessity, he went to work and was soon in constant demand for his great strength and skill at hunting, fishing, farming, and lumbering; he performed "miraculous feats, in chopping and clearing." Intelligent and articulate, he was also an ardent reader of the Bible and was instrumental in the building and running of his neighbourhood's Sunday school. Yet he sparked fear and dislike as well as respect in his community, for he suffered a fundamental ambivalence of character. He had unsteady work habits, moving restlessly from job to job. An excessive drinker, he formed the anti-temperance Buck Skin Society. He also earned a reputation for "unbridled passion" and for his close association with Kingston's criminals.

Towards the end of his adolescence Kain seemed to stabilize, labouring two years in Camden Township for John Rodolph Couche, a 40-year-old army pensioner. He even encouraged Couche to marry so as to free both men from domestic chores. Couche complied and wed 19-year-old Rebecca Smith of Richmond Township. Trouble began; Couche discovered that Rebecca had seduced Kain and he threatened to end the marriage. But Rebecca persisted in her adultery until June 1830 when Kain voluntarily left, returning briefly in August only to depart again after Couche refused to pay his wages and vowed to "take out his guts." On 15 August, infuriated by Couche's attitude and warning that he should never "enjoy the crop, or reap one sheaf," Kain returned and shot Couche five times.

Alerted by Rebecca, neighbours John and Samuel Foster apprehended Kain. His celebrated quarrel with Couche made him the obvious suspect. He was made to sit beside the corpse for several hours before being taken to the coroner in Kingston, William J. McKay. Kain freely confessed to the murder but pleaded self-defence, even castigating his neighbours for not having forced Couche to pay his wages.

At his trial on 3 September, Kain, defending himself, pleaded not guilty. The crown, represented by Attorney General Henry John Boulton*, called six witnesses, the defendant none. The jury required only five minutes to condemn Kain, despite his claims of being goaded by Couche's threats and refusal to pay him. He was then sentenced to hang three days later with his body to be given over to medical dissection. "The laws ought to punish and will punish," declared Judge James Buchanan Macaulay*, "as long as necessary, until the arm of violence shall be restrained." He characterized Kain's action as "heedless, malicious, vindictive, and bloodthirsty," and referred sarcastically to Kain's renowned strength: "One would almost suppose that some people believed their strength given to them, for no other purpose than to abuse it."

Kain heard Macaulay's address with outward indif-

Karrahogle

ference, even the admonition that he devote his final earthly days to achieving "a joyful immortality" by "weeping, by fasting and by prayer, by penitence and contrition." Yet the judge's advice or personal revelation revived Kain's latent religiosity, for he remained sleepless, praying, reading the Bible, and performing spiritual exercises with two ministers and his former Sunday school teachers. The evening before his death he was visited by Archdeacon George Okill Stuart*, and that same night he composed a scaffold address blaming alcohol, neglect of the Sabbath, and bad company for ruining his life "just in the prime." He died reciting the Lord's Prayer, apparently reconciled to his fate, repentant for the murder, confident of salvation. He was unswerving in his right to the wages he was owed by Couche, earmarking the money "to establish or support any school that may require it." Any other funds were to be used to erect a fence around his father's grave.

William Kain's life was brief, beginning and ending in bitterness. He died in profound disgrace, in front of "a large concourse" of curious spectators. Kain was equal to this occasion as to most others, couching his personal tragedy in terms of sin and erroneous judgment. Yet even his contemporaries sensed the hollowness of these explanations, and today it is difficult to penetrate the essence of the young man who was special and disturbing even to his obituary writers, and whose life embodies the age-old mysteries of the roots of criminality and violence.

ELIZABETH ABBOTT-GIBBS

AO, RG 22, ser.134, vol.5, 7 [i.e. 3] Sept. 1830. *The life of William Kain, who was executed at Kingston, Upper Canada, on the 6th day of September, 1830, for the murder of John Rodolph Couche* (Kingston, [Ont.], 1830). U.C., House of Assembly, *Journal*, 1831–32, app.: 150, 228. *Kingston Chronicle*, 4, 11 Sept. 1830. *Upper Canada Herald*, 8 Sept. 1830.

KARRAHOGLE. *See* TEKARIHOGEN

KAVANAGH (Cavanagh), LAURENCE (Lawrence), merchant, militia officer, politician, JP, and judge; b. 1764 in Cape Breton, probably at Louisbourg, second of three sons of Laurence Kavanagh and Margaret Farrell; m. by 1789 Félicité LeJeune, daughter of a merchant at Little Bras d'Or Passage (N.S.), and they had five sons and three daughters; d. 20 Aug. 1830 in St Peter's, N.S.

The Kavanaghs were one of the first English-speaking families to settle in Cape Breton after the fall of Louisbourg in 1758. Laurence Kavanagh's father immigrated to St John's, Nfld, from Waterford (Republic of Ireland) and by 1760 was living in Louisbourg, where he was supplying the British garrison. In 1774 he was killed in a shipwreck on his way to

Halifax, leaving his two sons, James and Laurence, a prosperous business. By 1777 the family had moved to St Peter's. Located on the narrow isthmus separating the Bras d'Or lakes from the Atlantic Ocean, the settlement was adjacent to the abundant fishery off Isle Madame and was an important centre of communications and commerce on Cape Breton. In order to increase business, James moved to Halifax, where he planned to centre operations, and left the 14-year-old Laurence in charge of their interests in Arichat, Main-à-Dieu, St Peter's, and even present-day New Brunswick. The young man showed much business acumen and shrewdly built the Cape Breton operation into a commercial success by supplying the needs of settlers from the Strait of Canso to the Margaree River, often by barter. In 1797 he and Richard Stout*, Sydney's wealthiest merchant, were described as "owning" three-quarters of Cape Breton's population. Although this claim cannot be substantiated, there is no doubt that Kavanagh and Stout must have controlled a large proportion of the island's commerce. When Bishop Joseph-Octave PLESSIS visited Cape Breton in 1815 he described Kavanagh's property as a "magnificent estate" and Kavanagh as a "rich Irish merchant, who had a thriving business." By that time Kavanagh was shipping barrels of fish as far as the Gulf of Mexico.

Kavanagh's wealth made him a powerful figure in southern Cape Breton, and his status was recognized by the provincial government in Sydney, which appointed him a captain of militia. Because of St Peter's distance from and poor communications with Sydney, Kavanagh was almost absolute ruler in his district. In 1811, when the colony's administrator, Nicholas NEPEAN, ordered a census, Kavanagh refused to divulge the extent of his holdings. Despite his importance, he was never appointed to the colony's Executive Council as were neighbouring merchants such as the Jerseyman John JANVRIN or the loyalist George Moore. No reason is known for this exclusion, though Cape Breton could have been following Nova Scotia's example of not permitting Roman Catholics to hold any but lesser offices. In keeping with his position, Kavanagh played the role of lord of the manor, welcoming visitors to the St Peter's area with boundless hospitality. Like Plessis, the Presbyterian minister James Drummond MACGREGOR was much impressed.

Cape Breton was reattached to Nova Scotia in October 1820, and in the elections to the House of Assembly held shortly thereafter Kavanagh became one of the two representatives from the island. His identification with the Acadians and Irish, his financial power, his status as patriarch of his area, and perhaps even his independence from the former rulers in Sydney assured his victory. A defeated candidate, Edmund Murray Dodd*, alleged that there had been

370

irregularities in the election, but his petition was dismissed by the assembly on 13 Feb. 1821. The house was dissolved on 3 March before Kavanagh took his seat.

The real obstacle to Kavanagh's admission, however, was his religion. Anyone wishing to hold a seat in the assembly had to take an oath against transubstantiation, a basic tenet of Roman Catholicism. Catholics had laboured under other disqualifications, but over the years the assembly had abolished them until only the transubstantiation oath remained. Lieutenant Governor Sir James Kempt* sensed that the mood of the province was now more liberal, and began to smooth Kavanagh's way. He informed the Colonial Office that no law expressly forbad Roman Catholics from holding legislative office and that he favoured the admission of Kavanagh. The colonial secretary, Lord Bathurst, replied that he would be prepared to allow Kavanagh to be admitted once he had presented himself to claim his seat.

When Kavanagh appeared early in the 1822 session he refused to take the oath against transubstantiation and was denied admission. After some bickering between assembly and Council the latter presented an address to the crown asking for the removal of the oath. Bathurst promptly replied that Kavanagh was to be allowed to take his seat without the oath. The resolution of the problem was deferred until 3 April 1823, when Kempt sent a message to the assembly reporting Bathurst's decision. A last-minute effort was launched by members from the overwhelmingly Protestant counties of Lunenburg and Cumberland and in the Annapolis valley to prevent Kavanagh's admission. But under the leadership of Richard John Uniacke Jr, Kavanagh's fellow representative from Cape Breton, assemblymen from Halifax, Queens, and Shelburne counties succeeded in having a motion passed which allowed Kavanagh to take his seat without the oath. It was also decided that the same privilege would be extended to all Roman Catholics who were duly elected.

Kavanagh served in the assembly until his death in 1830. His most memorable contribution was his survey of educational conditions in Cape Breton in 1824. Kavanagh's wide knowledge and the respect in which he was held on the island allowed him to paint the first accurate picture of the educational situation in this newly annexed part of Nova Scotia, and his report helped form the basis for the province's School Act of 1826. While sitting in the house, Kavanagh continued as justice of the peace and member of the Inferior Court of Common Pleas for Cape Breton County, positions which he had received at an unknown date.

Kavanagh's significance is both local and international. Locally, he was partly responsible for rebuilding the economy of southern Cape Breton after the fall of Louisbourg. His energy led him to become a key mover in the social and political development of that area and the first native Cape Bretoner to sit in the Nova Scotia assembly. His widest fame lies in his being the first English-speaking Roman Catholic to hold a seat in a legislature in the Atlantic provinces, six years before such a right was won in Britain. The fact that this landmark was achieved in Nova Scotia indicates both the political maturity of that colony and Kavanagh's perspicacity. His admission was accomplished with a minimum of acrimonious debate and a realization that laws against Roman Catholics were anachronistic. Kavanagh deserves credit for his great patience in allowing Kempt, the Colonial Office, and the legislature time to work out the delicate arrangements.

R. J. Morgan

PAC, MG 11, [CO 217] Cape Breton A, 8. PANS, RG 1, 64, doc.46. PRO, CO 217/113, 217/140. N.S., House of Assembly, *Journal and proc.*, 1821, 1823. *Free Press* (Halifax), 9 April 1823. *Directory of N.S. MLAs*. Johnston, *Hist. of Catholic Church in eastern N.S.*, vol.1. A. A. MacKenzie, *The Irish in Cape Breton* (Antigonish, N.S., 1979). T. M. Punch, *Some sons of Erin in Nova Scotia* (Halifax, 1980). D. J. Rankin, "Laurence Kavanaugh," CCHA *Report*, 8 (1940–41): 51–76; also issued as a separate pamphlet. Anthony Traboulsee, *Laurence Kavanagh, 1764– 1830: his life and times, including brief sketches of the history of Nova Scotia (Acadie) and Cape Breton Island (Isle Royale) . . .* (Glace Bay, N.S., 1962). [Only the appendices of these two works are of value. R.J.M.] *Journal of Education* (Halifax), 4th ser., 6 (1935).

KEATS, Sir RICHARD GOODWIN, naval officer and governor of Newfoundland; b. 16 Jan. 1757 in Chalton, Hampshire, England, son of Richard Keats, an Anglican clergyman, and his wife Elizabeth; m. 1820 Mary Hurt of Alderwasley, England; d. 5 April 1834 and was buried at Greenwich Hospital (London).

Richard Goodwin Keats joined the Royal Navy in 1770, and in 1776 served on the *Romney*, Governor John Montagu's flagship at Newfoundland. He was promoted lieutenant in 1777 and given his first command in 1789. Keats was a conspicuous figure in the naval history of England for the next two decades. Nelson described him as "a treasure to the service." In 1807 he was promoted rear-admiral, and in 1808, following a brilliant series of actions in Danish waters, he was made a knight of the Order of the Bath. He was promoted vice-admiral in 1811, but the following year, his health damaged, he resigned his command and returned to England. On 18 March 1813, he was appointed governor and commander-in-chief of the island of Newfoundland "and the Islands adjacent including the Islands of St. Pierre and Miquelon and all the Coast of Labrador from the River Saint John to Hudson's Streights the Island of Anticosti and all

Keats

other adjacent Islands the Islands of Madelaine excepted." He was sworn in at St John's on 1 June.

Keats would govern as a summer and autumn visitor for three years. This was the traditional pattern of gubernatorial rule in Newfoundland; but local problems were becoming too complex, the population – by now at least 70,000 – was increasing too rapidly, for the island to be administered as if it were merely a seasonal fishery. "If Newfoundland be not a Colony by Law, it is so in fact," Keats was assured by high sheriff John BLAND. The instructions given to Keats reflected a belated British recognition of the need for a new policy in at least one area: agriculture. He was authorized "to grant Leases of small Portions of Land to industrious Individuals for the purpose of Cultivation," taking care to charge an annual rent, either nominal or real, depending on the circumstances of the lessee. When he proceeded to act on this instruction, Keats found that most of the land suitable for farming had already been taken up by encroachments. "I have found but little Land within the neighbourhood of St. John's to dispose of," he told the colonial secretary. None the less, by the fall of 1813 he had granted 110 leases, on pieces of property up to four acres in size, all in the vicinity of St John's. (In the outports, removed from government, inhabitants had already enclosed the land they needed.) Keats recommended that all unauthorized landholders around St John's be permitted to rent their land on the same basis as the new leaseholders, and the Colonial Office, unwilling "to adopt any harsh measures," agreed.

This initiative did not end controversy over land tenure in Newfoundland, for the right to own property was still not recognized, and enclosures or buildings for uses other than fishing required the governor's permission. In August 1814 Irishman James Sweeney (who, according to Bland, had "hardly five words of English, and is perfectly unintelligible") had his house and other buildings on Bell Island, Conception Bay, razed to the ground by deputy sheriff John Mayne, when it was discovered that he had enclosed ground of "about forty or fifty acres" for farming despite a warning to confine himself to a smaller area. Mayne was following orders issued by Keats and surrogate David Buchan*. Similarly, Owen Kelly, who had cleared a ten- or twelve-acre farm on the same island, had his house demolished. These are arresting episodes, indicating that the grievances alluded to by reformers such as William Carson* were by no means imaginary. The legality of the governor's control over property was now also being questioned by the crown lawyers, who stated in 1814 that "Newfoundland being a settled Colony, the common law rights of English subjects apply . . . there, except in so far, as they have been altered or abridged by any peculiar laws or regulations applicable to Newfoundland." To Keats's credit, by the end of his term he recommended

that restraints on building ("a perpetual theme of inquietude at St. John's") be lifted within certain boundaries in the capital, and expressed doubt about the right of preventing building even on encroached land that was "clear of the Fisheries." He was also more inclined than his fussy predecessor, Sir John Thomas Duckworth*, to allow individuals to build houses. Yet he ultimately advised against any fundamental change in the system of governing Newfoundland.

Keats complained about the difficulty of governing Newfoundland, and especially about "the clamour of a Party for Colonization," but in fact he presided over the community at the end of a period of unprecedented prosperity. Many of the problems he encountered, or fancied, were produced by this buoyant economy. There was, for instance, great demand for land, and Keats was bothered by visitors to St John's from the outharbours pressing their claims to fishing rooms or disputing those of their neighbours. Thousands of Irishmen, attracted by high wages in the fishery, were streaming in, adding to the already volatile Hibernian component in the population. As the outports grew, it became apparent that more Anglican missionaries were needed. The "Dissenters and Catholics have benefited by our Indifference," Keats warned, having noted that the Catholic bishop, Patrick Lambert*, had "numerous priests" who were "too successful in making Proselytes." Reflected in Keats's correspondence are the signs of a bustling community: churches being built and missionaries requested, an application being made for the establishment of a second newspaper in St John's (which he tried unsuccessfully to prevent), tradesmen abandoning their "mechanical avocations" to take to the boats in the hopeful summer of 1814, the general hospital opening its doors, hundreds of ships moving in and out of port, and ideas percolating about the great timber resources on the Gander and Exploits rivers.

As the merchants well knew, this prosperity was due, in large part, to the exclusion of two traditional competitors, the French and, following the outbreak of the War of 1812, the Americans, from the Newfoundland fishery. In 1813 Keats supported a petition by the merchants requesting that neither the French nor the Americans be restored to their fishing rights on the return of peace, and the next year he wrote an elaborate plea of his own to keep the Americans out. These representations were not effective, and soon after the treaties with France in 1814 and 1815, and that with the United States in 1814, the Newfoundland fishery was once more international in character. Late in 1814 there were indications that the boom was coming to an end. In the spring of 1815 the wages offered were considerably lower than in the previous year; possibly as a consequence, there was unrest among the Irish in St John's that did not subside until May. By late 1815 the economy had worsened, and with nervous creditors demanding payment of debts there were 40 insolvencies between October and mid December. According to Keats, writing in November on his return from his last summer in Newfoundland, the arrival of 6,000 Irish immigrants in the summer of 1815 had "created some alarm in the minds of the peaceable Inhabitants" and might be "productive of some distress and additional expence to the district." Another grim sign of what lay ahead was a fire in St John's on 12 Feb. 1816, in which 120 houses were destroyed and many more damaged. As his successors Francis Pickmore* and Sir Charles Hamilton* would discover, Newfoundland had started on a slide into a serious post-war depression. Keats's term ended on 18 May 1816. He later became governor of the Greenwich Hospital for seamen, and was made an admiral in 1825.

The Bell Island episodes may show a vein of petty tyranny in Keats, but on the whole he was a moderate and conciliatory man who recognized that changes were taking place in Newfoundland society which needed attention.

PATRICK O'FLAHERTY

PANL, GN 2/1/A, 24–27. PRO, CO 194/54–57; CO 195/ 16–17. *Royal Gazette and Newfoundland Advertiser*, 1810– 18. *DNB*. James Ralfe, *The naval biography of Great Britain . . .* (4v., London, 1828), 2: 487–516. Prowse, *Hist. of Nfld.* (1895).

KENWENDESHON (Henry Aaron Hill), Mohawk, Church of England catechist, and translator; eldest son of Karonghyonte (David Hill); m. Christiana Brant, second child of Thayendanegea* (Joseph Brant), and they had at least three children; d. 1834 of cholera at the Grand River, Upper Canada.

The name Kenwendeshon, borne in the early 19th century by the subject of this biography, apparently belonged to the wolf clan of the Mohawks and meant "longer days." By that period Mohawks were well acquainted with white customs and some had begun to use family names in the manner of their neighbours. The Hills were among them; indeed, Henry Aaron Hill seems to have preferred his European name. When chief David Hill died about 1790, Joseph Brant attempted to have Henry Aaron succeed him, but Iroquois custom prevailed and the title passed in the female line instead. Nevertheless, Henry Aaron Hill was later regarded by some observers as a chief.

On visiting the Grand River in 1792, Patrick CAMPBELL described Hill as a young man "of very agreeable looks and mild manners," who had been "the best scholar" at Harvard. That university, however, has no record of his presence. Nevertheless, Hill was sometimes spoken of as doctor. During the War of 1812 he took part in the ambush of American forces on 24 June 1813 at Beaver Dams (Thorold) [see William Johnson Kerr*]. In November 1814 he was one of a small party which prevented a large American force from crossing the Grand River to attack Burlington Heights (Hamilton) from the rear. Called "a faithful Warrior on all occasions," Hill was wounded in the thigh and hand in this action.

By 1816 Hill was acting as interpreter at councils of the Six Nations and conducting services at the Mohawk chapel (which still stands in Brantford). He "touched his cheeks and forehead with a few spots of vermilion, in honour of Sunday; he wore a surplice, and preached at considerable length; but his delivery was unimpassioned, and monotonous in the extreme," according to traveller Francis Hall. St Paul's Church, as the chapel was named, was occasionally visited by the Church of England clergyman from Niagara (Niagara-on-the-Lake), and later from Ancaster. More usually an Indian catechist would read the prayers. Hill acted as reader and interpreter to Ralph Leeming* in 1821 and was described by Robert ADDISON the following year as catechist for the Society for the Propagation of the Gospel. The first resident Anglican clergyman at the Grand River, William Hough, was appointed in 1826. But the use of catechists continued, and in fact it was only in 1827 that Hill was officially designated a catechist for the SPG, at an annual salary of £20. He continued in the post when the interdenominational New England Company took over the mission in 1827.

Hough's appointment had been made partly in response to the establishment of a Methodist mission on the Grand in 1822. Indeed, it turned out to be the Methodists who encouraged Hill's program of translation. Joseph Brant's Gospel of St Mark had been appended to an SPG Mohawk prayer-book printed in 1787, and John NORTON's Gospel of St John had been published by the British and Foreign Bible Society in 1804. Despite adverse comments on the quality of the translation, Norton, encouraged by the SPG, resumed the work of completing the gospels, and he enlisted Hill's aid. But Norton was tiring of the task and thought that the Mohawks themselves would prefer English bibles. The American Bible Society discovered in 1823 that Hill, with the support of John Brant [TEKARIHOGEN], was already working on Luke, and proposed that he complete the four gospels. Missionary William Case* passed along reports that Hill was at times subject to intoxication, though some said he was reforming. Despite Case's qualms, Hill proved to be a diligent worker. His Luke appeared in 1828 (the title page says 1827, but the printer in New York, Azor Hoyt, had much trouble in setting the work). Three hundred and fifty copies were sent to the Methodist mission on the Grand and fifty to Lower Canada. The Church of England, holding aloof from association with dissenters in bible societies, made little use of the translations done by its catechist.

In turn, the American Bible Society's interest waned. The York Auxiliary Bible Society, formed in

Kerr

1828, saw that some Mohawk scriptures were already available and began work on Ojibwa translations instead. The continued publication of Mohawk scriptures was therefore undertaken by the Young Men's Bible Society of New York, an auxiliary to the Methodist Episcopal Church in the United States. Between 1831 and 1836 it sponsored translation of the rest of the New Testament, with the exception of 2 Corinthians. The bulk of the work was done by Hill, with corrections and completions (Hill died in 1834) by Brantford merchant John Aston Wilkes, Mohawk schoolmaster William Hess, and Elizabeth Kerr, *née* Brant. Hill's Isaiah, finished by Hess, was published by the American Bible Society in 1839, but that organization resisted pressure to proceed with the rest of the Old Testament. Hill was also the chief translator of a collection of psalms and hymns, which went through separate printings for its Methodist and Anglican users.

To some people, Henry Aaron Hill appeared to be more than he was: doctor, clergyman, chief. But on the title pages of his translations, his name was often missing. Although his work as a translator was little recognized in his own time or later, it was to him that the Mohawks owed the bulk of the scriptures and hymns in their own language.

RICHARD E. RUGGLE

For further publication details about the translations with which Henry Aaron Hill was involved, the reader is referred to J. C. Pilling, "Bibliography of the Iroquoian languages," Smithsonian Institution, Bureau of American Ethnology, *Bull.* (Washington), 6 (1888): 82–86.

AO, MS 500, H. A. Hill, deposition, 28 June 1830. P. Campbell, *Travels in North America* (Langton and Ganong). *Doc. hist. of campaign upon Niagara frontier* (Cruikshank), 2: 308–10. Francis Hall, *Travels in Canada, and the United States, in 1816 and 1817* (London, 1818). Norton, *Journal* (Klinck and Talman). "The Rev. Robert Addison: extracts from the reports and (manuscript) journals of the Society for the Propagation of the Gospel in Foreign Parts," ed. A. H. Young, *OH*, 19 (1922): 186–90. SPG, [*Annual report*] (London), 1827: 165–66; 1828: 189. *Valley of Six Nations* (Johnston). John West, *A journal of a mission to the Indians of the British provinces, of New Brunswick, and Nova Scotia, and the Mohawks, on the Ouse, or Grand River, Upper Canada* (London, 1827), 278. *Biblio. of Canadiana: first supp.* (Boyle and Colbeck). *Officers of British forces in Canada* (Irving), 220–21. R. E. Ruggle, "A house divided against itself: the denominational antagonisms of the Grand River missions" (papers presented at the meeting of the Canadian Soc. of Church Hist., London, Ont., 1978), 1–10.

KERR, ROBERT, doctor, Indian Department officer, judge, and office holder; b. *c.* 1755 in Scotland; m. Elizabeth Johnson, daughter of Sir William Johnson* and Mary Brant [Koñwatsiˀtsiaiéñni*], and they had three sons and two daughters; d. 25 Feb. 1824 in Albany, N.Y.

Little is known of Robert Kerr's youth, family, or education. He first comes to notice in North America serving as a hospital mate from 1776 to 1781. He was with John Burgoyne*'s expedition of 1777, when he was taken prisoner. Following his release he joined the 2nd battalion of the King's Royal Regiment of New York, and his zeal in service with this unit earned him the approbation of his superiors. After the war he settled in Cataraqui (Kingston, Ont.) and cared for the newly settled loyalists there, but by 1789 he had moved to the Niagara area, which was the scene of his activities for the remainder of his career.

Kerr was a prominent freemason, acting as deputy grand master of the Provincial Grand Lodge from 1797 to 1802 under William Jarvis*. During a rupture in Upper Canadian masonry which probably reflected the rivalry between York (Toronto), where Jarvis had moved, and Niagara (Niagara-on-the-Lake), Kerr was active in forming a schismatic provincial grand lodge at Niagara in 1803 and was its grand master from 1807 till his retirement in 1820. It would seem some tribute to Kerr's tact and diplomacy that he remained an honoured member of the combined grand lodge after 1822, when the schism was healed.

Kerr had become surgeon to the Indian Department in 1788, at a salary of £100 per annum, and he retained that position until at least 1820. He also attended the Royal Artillery at the fort, and marine, engineer, barracks, and commissary departments, and in the absence of the regimental surgeon performed his duties as well. In late 1789 or early 1790 Sir John JOHNSON, to whom he was related by marriage, proposed him as a member of the Executive Council of Upper Canada to Governor Lord Dorchester [Guy Carleton*], but he did not receive the appointment. Kerr did, however, hold many other public positions. He was judge of the Surrogate Court for the Niagara District from 1792 and was a member of the land board, commissioner of the peace, commissioner for administering the oath to half-pay officers, and trustee for public schools, all in that district. As well, he was a member of the Medical Board of Upper Canada from 1822, although he seems to have attended once only.

In addition to his many other duties, the doctor conducted a private practice of medicine. His bill for the care of William Jarvis's household indicates that, as was usual at the time, he relied largely on purging and bleeding. He also treated the family's horses. In 1794 he billed William Berczy* £70 for attending the German families at Queenston, and three years later he advertised, along with Dr James Muirhead, the availability of smallpox inoculation (free for the poor). He appears to have remained in active practice almost until the end of his life.

Kerr, although then well into his 50s, played a substantial role in the War of 1812. He was important enough to be a member of the formal entourage for the funeral of Sir Isaac Brock*. He lost a case of instruments in the American capture of Niagara on 27 May 1813, attended brigade-major John Baskerville Glegg at the British headquarters on Burlington Heights (Hamilton) the same year, and treated the wounded at the battle of Chippawa in 1814. His house and barn at Niagara had been burned by the Americans in 1813 and his claims for war losses amounted to £1,227. About the time of his death, in 1824, it was announced that claims were to be paid at the rate of 25 per cent; Kerr or his heirs would receive £306.

After peace returned Kerr had continued a full slate of activities in the Niagara area. In the autumn of 1823 he moved to Albany, N.Y., where he is said to have had many friends. He died there the following February at the age of 69 and was buried in the cemetery of St Peter's Episcopal Church. In Niagara he was remembered as a tall, well-built man who enjoyed sports. In fact, he was sometimes called "the boxing magistrate." His tombstone praised "his social habits and kindness of heart."

Like many others, Kerr had devoted time to the pursuit of land. In 1795 he stated that he owned 2,200 acres and believed he should get more. By 1797 he had grants totalling 2,856 acres, a relatively modest amount for the time. Kerr's daughter Mary Margaret married Niagara businessman Thomas CLARK; his son William Johnson Kerr* married Elizabeth Brant, daughter of Joseph [Thayendanegea*], thus strengthening the ties of the Kerrs with that prominent Mohawk family.

CHARLES G. ROLAND

Two portraits of Robert Kerr are located in the John Ross Robertson coll. of the MTL.

AO, RG 1, A-II-1, 1: 89. PAC, MG 23, HII, 6, vol.2: 377; MG 24, K2, 10: 158, 161–62; RG 1, L3, 268: K1/1–3, 7, 21, 24; K2/17, 23, 29; K4/8, 14, 20–22; 269: K5/29; L4, 6; RG 5, B1, 1; B6, 1, letter from Kerr, 15 May 1820; D1, 24: 183; RG 8, I (C ser.), 84: 206; 287: 9; 288: 10–11; 704: 305. Thomas Gilcrease Institute of American Hist. and Art (Tulsa, Okla.), John and Guy Johnston docs., p.84 (photocopies at PAC). *The battle of Queenston Heights . . .* , ed. John Symons (Toronto, 1859), 19. *The Talbot papers*, ed. J. H. Coyne (2v., Ottawa, 1908–9), 1: 187. Chadwick, *Ontarian families*, 1: 67. Jean Johnston, "Ancestry and descendants of Molly Brant," *OH*, 63 (1971): 86–92. *Officers of British forces in Canada* (Irving). William Canniff, *The medical profession in Upper Canada, 1783–1850 . . .* (Toronto, 1894; repr. 1980). Carnochan, *Hist. of Niagara*. J. R. Robertson, *The history of freemasonry in Canada from its introduction in 1749 . . .* (2v., Toronto, 1900). William Colgate, "Dr. Robert Kerr: an early practitioner of Upper Canada," Canadian Medical Assoc., *Journal* (Toronto), 64 (1951): 542–46.

KIDD, ADAM, poet; b. *c.* 1802 in Tullynagee (Northern Ireland), son of Alexander Kidd, a farmer; d. 6 July 1831 at Quebec.

Adam Kidd, according to his own account, was raised in a "straw-roofed cottage" on a farm in Tullynagee. At the "school of the good old Lawrence McGuckian" in nearby Moneymore he studied Latin and Greek, became enamoured of the poets Lord Byron and Thomas Moore, and determined to be either a Church of Ireland clergyman or a teacher. He came to feel, however, that his family lacked the influence to get him a job. It is uncertain whether he left for "America" in 1818–19 or worked for six years on his parents' farm "till the hopeless and sinking situation, of then oppressed Ireland, forced [him] to seek a scanty pittance in a foreign land."

By July 1824 Kidd was at Quebec supporting himself, possibly as a teacher, and being considered for the Anglican ministry by the Reverend George Jehoshaphat Mountain*, son of Jacob MOUNTAIN, bishop of Quebec. The Mountains, however, defended the refusal of the Church of England to allow Byron, who had died that year, to be buried in Westminster Abbey and thus earned Kidd's hatred for "whining cant." At the same time one of them decided that Kidd, possibly because of the "foolish wayward inclination" for an Indian girl suggested by a contemporary, was not a suitable candidate for ordination.

Late in 1824 Kidd began fashioning a career as a poet; signing himself Slievegallin, after a mountain near Tullynagee, he sent lyrics to several Lower Canadian newspapers, especially those with Irish connections. "To Miss M-G-" appeared in the *Quebec Mercury* on 30 Nov. 1824, and throughout the next three years Slievegallin contributed to that newspaper and to the *Canadian Courant, and Montreal Advertiser* and the *Canadian Spectator* of Montreal.

Possibly as a consequence of his alleged dalliance with the Indian girl, Kidd's concept of his role as a poet soon expanded from that of an Irish bard celebrating his homeland and lamenting its wrongs to that of a minstrel singing about the natural beauties of the Canadas and sighing over the plight of the North American Indians, particularly in the United States. He took notes from the travel accounts of Sir Alexander Mackenzie* and Alexander HENRY and from works by Cadwallader Colden, John Gottlieb Ernestus Hackenwelder (Heckewelder), and William Tudor. He travelled up the Ottawa River to Bytown (Ottawa), where he admired the Rideau Falls, and in 1828 toured along the St Lawrence River and Lake Ontario, where he canoed in the Thousand Islands and studied tree-frogs on the banks of the Moira River at Belleville. In 1828 too he seems to have journeyed in New York State and possibly to Philadelphia. By 1828–29 he had gathered enough information and inspiration to compose a long poem entitled "The Huron chief," set on the shores of lakes Erie and Huron – which he had not seen. He promoted his poem in Montreal early in 1829 for "half a crown . . . on subscription, and an

Kidd

equal sum on delivery." He also advertised in the *Irish Shield* of Philadelphia, to which he was a regular contributor and from which many poems by and to him were reprinted in Lower and Upper Canadian newspapers.

Kidd was living in Montreal, probably in late fall and early winter 1829–30, when he saw through the press what had become a volume incorporating "The Huron chief" and 40 "miscellaneous poems," including most of those already published in the serials. A piece entitled "To the Rev. Polyphemus," intended to ridicule the Mountains, was dropped at the last moment as "too satirical." *The Huron chief, and other poems* was dedicated in Montreal on 23 Jan. 1830; Kidd later claimed that it sold 1,500 copies, chiefly in the Canadas. It received generally favourable notices and reviews and was extracted in newspapers in the two colonies as well as in the *Irish Shield*. In March, for example, the *Montreal Gazette* greeted it as helping to fill a disgraceful literary void; a few months later, however, a correspondent to the same paper belittled the volume. It was, the writer alleged, plagiarized from Moore, but made up in "pure nonsense" what it lacked in originality. In a note to "The Huron chief" Kidd had criticized James Buchanan, British consul at New York, for pro-Americanism. Buchanan's sons, one of whom was Alexander Carlisle Buchanan*, scuffled with Kidd on a Montreal street; the poet had his "nose pulled" and "received severe chastisement," according to one account, but another, possibly by Kidd, claimed heroic withstanding of a "violent assault."

Through the summer and early fall of 1830 Kidd, preparing and probably selling subscriptions for a prose work on "the *Tales* and *Traditions* of the Indians," travelled in Upper Canada, where he may finally have seen the area he described in "The Huron chief." By late fall, however, he was "confined by sickness" in Kingston. The *Kingston Chronicle* published, among other pieces, "Farewell lovely Erin," a new poem, on 4 December and an article on SHAK-ÓYE:WA:THA? entitled "Red Jacket, the celebrated Indian chief" on 29 March 1831. About the latter date Kidd left for Quebec, from where he intended to embark on "a sea voyage for the recovery of his health." He died in the Hotel-Dieu on 6 July, however, and was buried from the Anglican Cathedral of the Holy Trinity on the 7th. *Le Canadien* noted that he had achieved "a certain reputation" as a poet.

Kidd's fame rests mostly on *The Huron chief, and other poems*. With an epigram from the legendary Ossian and a dedication to Moore, the title poem is a half-dramatic, half-lyrical narrative in language derived from Moore and Byron about the nobility of Indians and the savagery of white men, including Christian missionaries, dedicated to the Indians' destruction. It ends with an ambush by three Americans of an Indian band led by the chief Skenandow, during which

> SKENANDOW fell! – and calmly sleeps
> By ERIE's darkling groves of pine,
> Where gently now the wild grape creeps,
> As if to guard the holy shrine –
> Nor shall his name be e'er forgot –
> But future bards, in songs of grief,
> Will sadly tell of that lone spot,
> Where rests the noble HURON CHIEF!

Notes to the poem catalogue actual incidents of white cruelty to the Indians. Kidd, however, links his story of those wrongs directly to his own grievances against the Mountains and indirectly through language and form to his "oppressed Ireland." Thus the poem furnishes an example, interesting for psychological and sociological study, of the kind of projection that can occur when a disturbed personality seeks an objective correlative for its problems in what it perceives as hostilities and injustices suffered by people of another, alien culture.

MARY J. EDWARDS

Adam Kidd is the author of *The Huron chief, and other poems* (Montreal, 1830), as well as of poems and articles that appeared in the *Quebec Mercury, Canadian Courant and Montreal Advertiser, Canadian Spectator* (Montreal), *Irish Vindicator and Canada Advertiser* (Montreal), *Canadian Freeman* (York [Toronto]), *Kingston Chronicle*, and *Irish Shield* (Philadelphia).

ANQ-Q, CE1-61, 7 juill. 1831; P-239/57. *Canadian Courant and Montreal Advertiser*, 21 May, 6, 10 Aug. 1825; 22 Aug., 14 Nov. 1829; 13 March 1830; 13 July 1831. *Canadian Freeman*, 9, 16 Sept., 7 Oct. 1830; 7 April, 21 July 1831. *Canadian Spectator*, 2 July, 27 Aug., 10 Sept. 1825. *Le Canadien*, 6 juill. 1831. *Irish Shield*, 1829. *Irish Vindicator and Canada Advertiser*, 12 Dec. 1828; 2 June, 16 Oct. 1829; 23, 26 Feb., 1, 5, 12, 19, 29 March, 18 June 1830; 8 July 1831. *Kingston Chronicle*, 21 Aug., 4 Dec. 1830; 1 Jan., 18, 29 March, 16 July, 20 Aug. 1831. *Montreal Gazette*, 18 Jan., 4, 15 March, 7 June 1830; 9 July 1831. *Quebec Gazette*, 6 July 1831. *Quebec Mercury*, 30 Nov. 1824; 17 May, 23 Aug., 27 Sept. 1825; 20 June, 8 July 1826; 27 Feb. 1827; 31 July 1830; 7 July 1831. *Oxford companion to Canadian literature*, ed. William Toye (Toronto, 1983), 406–7. L. [M.] Lande, *Old lamps aglow; an appreciation of early Canadian poetry* (Montreal, 1957), 164–71. J. M. LeMoine, *Picturesque Quebec: a sequel to "Quebec past and present"* (Montreal, 1882), 332–33, 456–57. *Literary history of Canada: Canadian literature in English*, ed. C. F. Klinck *et al.* (2nd ed., 3v., Toronto and Buffalo, N.Y., 1976), 1: 144–46. M. L. MacDonald, "The literary life of English and French Montreal from 1817 to 1830 as seen through the periodicals of the time" (MA thesis, Carleton Univ., Ottawa, 1976), 69–71, 96–97; "Literature and society in the Canadas, 1830–1850" (PHD thesis, Carleton Univ., 1984), 433. D. M. R. Bentley, "From the hollow, blasted pine: centrifugal tendencies in Adam Kidd's *The Huron Chief,*" *Open Letter* (Toronto), nos.2–3 (1958): 233–56. C. F. Klinck, "Adam Kidd – an early Canadian poet," *Queen's Quarterly* (Kingston, Ont.), 65 (1958): 495–506.

KILBORN, CHARLES, farmer, mill owner, JP, office holder, and militia officer; b. 3 March 1758 in Litchfield, Conn.; m. February 1784 Margaret Young, and they had ten children; d. 20 June 1834 in Stanstead, Lower Canada, and was buried two days later.

Charles Kilborn's ancestor Thomas Kilborn left London on 15 April 1635 to go to Connecticut, where he settled at Weathersfield and founded a family. Nothing is known of Charles's childhood, but during the American revolution he was conscripted against his will into the American army. After participating in one campaign he joined the British forces, in which he reached the rank of captain. Taken prisoner in an engagement, he escaped and made his way on foot through the woods to the province of Quebec.

Like a number of his compatriots Kilborn settled in the Lake Champlain region near the border, at Caldwell's Manor, where he was married. In 1783 he had joined several groups organized to obtain lands, first in Hemmingford and then in what became the Eastern Townships. For that purpose he took the oath of allegiance on 5 May 1795 at Missisquoi Bay. Eventually, on 27 Sept. 1800, he obtained 1,200 acres in Stanstead Township as an associate of Isaac Ogden. Kilborn sold several pieces of land but kept some good lots on which he settled with his brother-in-law Andrew Young in 1803. They carried out a number of large-scale projects, building a dam near the falls on the Rivière Tomifobia and digging a canal to supply power for a flour- and a lumber mill, the first to be built in that part of the township. The land that was consequently surrounded by water acquired the name Rock Island. In 1804 Kilborn's family joined him there. He then added a carding- and fulling-mill and a plant to produce linseed oil. The site soon became known as Kilborn's Mills. At Jesse PENNOYER's suggestion Kilborn took up growing hemp, from which he made rope, but in 1811 the experiment ended for want of a market.

In 1803 Kilborn had been a charter member of Lively Stone Lodge No.22, a masonic lodge that brought together leading figures from both sides of the frontier. A meeting room was even built on the border, with an entrance on each side. About the same time Kilborn succeeded in capturing a notorious counterfeiter.

In response to popular demand in the Eastern Townships a militia corps was raised in 1805. When it was divided into six battalions in 1808, Kilborn was posted as major to the 3rd Townships Militia Battal-

ion, under Lieutenant-Colonel Henry CULL. But the War of 1812 would call for more onerous service. On 10 Jan. 1813, by order of Lieutenant-Colonel Sir John JOHNSON, the Frontier Light Infantry was created with 120 men recruited from the Eastern Townships militia and was assigned to the defence of the border. Kilborn shortly asked for a commission as captain in the new unit, and on 19 April he set off with a contingent for the military camp in La Prairie. On 13 August the Frontier Light Infantry was attached to the Voltigeurs Canadiens under the command of Charles-Michel d'IRUMBERRY de Salaberry, constituting its 9th and 10th companies at the end of the war. Kilborn served in various places, and after the battles of Lacolle and Odelltown he conducted the inquiries into the resulting damages. His active military career came to an end when the Voltigeurs Canadiens were demobilized on 24 March 1815, but he had to take steps to collect five months' pay and various expenses. In 1830 he was promoted lieutenant-colonel of the Stanstead militia battalion.

Kilborn had long been interested in education. Around 1800 there were already some schools in Stanstead Township, and in June 1809 Kilborn was appointed commissioner to build another school there. In 1817 the Royal Institution for the Advancement of Learning made him visitor of royal schools in the township. On 13 March 1821, as trustee, he accepted the gift of some land for educational purposes and made it over to the Royal Institution. For several years he continued to attend diligently to educational matters, at the same time running his mills and a big farming operation.

On 1 Aug. 1806 Kilborn had been made a justice of the peace for the district of Montreal, and this appointment was renewed in 1810, 1821, 1826, and 1828. He received a similar commission for the district of Trois-Rivières in 1805 and 1811, and for that of Saint-François in 1821. In September of that year he had been appointed commissioner for the summary trial of small causes.

Kilborn, who had left Rock Island, of which he is acknowledged to be the founder, passed away in 1834, after a full life, at Stanstead, in the large house he shared with one son and his family. In serving his chosen country he had devoted his energies to meeting the most pressing needs of a new community: land clearance, industry, education, and defence of the territory.

MARIE-PAULE R. LaBRÈQUE

ANQ-E, CE1-41, 22 juin 1834; CN2-26, 1803–19. PAC, MG 24, I11; RG 1, L3ᴸ: 32273, 59537; RG 4, A1; RG 9, I, A6; RG 68, General index, 1651–1841. Stanstead County Hist. Soc. Arch. (Beebe, Que.), Kilborn papers. *Docs. relating to constitutional hist., 1791–1818* (Doughty and McArthur). Bouchette, *Topographical description of L.C.*

Koenig

C. P. de Volpi and P. H. Scowen, *The Eastern Townships, a pictorial record; historical prints and illustrations of the Eastern Townships of the province of Quebec, Canada* (Montreal, 1962). *Illustrated atlas of Eastern Townships.* Langelier, *Liste des terrains concédés. Officers of British forces in Canada* (Irving). R. J. Ashton, *The life of Henry Ruiter, 1742–1819* ([Chicago], 1974). Boulianne, "Royal Instit. for the Advancement of Learning." Day, *Hist. of Eastern Townships.* Graham, *Hist. of freemasonry.* B. F. Hubbard, *Forests and clearings; the history of Stanstead County, province of Quebec, with sketches of more than five hundred families,* ed. John Lawrence (Montreal, 1874; repr. 1963). T. C. Lampee, "The Missisquoi loyalists," Vt. Hist. Soc., *Proc.* (Montpelier), 6 (1938–39): 81–139. *Sherbrooke Daily Record* (Sherbrooke, Que.), 10 April–16 July 1910. W. H. Siebert, "The American loyalists in the eastern seigniories and townships of the province of Quebec," RSC *Trans.,* 3rd ser., 7 (1913), sect.II: 3–41. Stanstead County Hist. Soc., *Journal* (Stanstead, Que.), 5 (1973); 7 (1977). W. S. Wallace, "The loyalist migration overland," N.Y. State Hist. Assoc., *Proc.,* 13 (1914): 159–67.

KOENIG (König, von König), EDMOND-VICTOR DE, Baron von KOENIG, army officer, physician, and teacher; b. 1753 in Osterwieck (German Democratic Republic), son of Edmund von König, Baron von König, and Louise-Émilie Rudolfi; m. first *c.* 1782 Marie-Louise Jean, probably at Quebec; m. secondly 24 May 1819 Marie-Céleste Guichard, *dit* Bourguignon, in Saint-Jean-Port-Joli, Lower Canada; d. 17 July 1833 in L'Islet, Lower Canada.

Edmond-Victor de Koenig belonged to an important Prussian family. His father was elector of the duchy of Brunswick and a cavalry colonel. Like two of his brothers, Edmond-Victor was led early to follow in his father's footsteps and take up a military career. He had joined the army by the age of 12 or 13. When the American colonies revolted in 1775, the British government had recourse to German troops. It was under these circumstances that Koenig arrived at Quebec in 1776 as a lieutenant in the forces under Major-General Friedrich Adolph Riedesel. During the war he suffered a gunshot wound in his right arm at Stillwater, N.Y. On 21 July 1783, when the war was over, he obtained his discharge from the army.

Realizing that there would be few opportunities for promotion in Europe, Koenig decided to settle at Quebec. For several months he tried without success to find a job, and finally, discouraged and at the end of his means, he considered returning to his native land. He changed his mind, however, and around 1786 decided to try his luck as a country doctor. It was in this period that he is believed to have renounced the Lutheran faith in favour of Catholicism. He stayed in the region of Saint-Roch-des-Aulnaies and Sainte-Anne-de-la-Pocatière (La Pocatière) for a time, and then settled for good at L'Islet.

Koenig was in an extremely precarious financial position. To support a family which by 1803 included eight children he had to go into debt. An inventory of his belongings that year shows the wretchedness of his situation. He owned no personal or landed property, had assets worth less than 2,000 *livres*, and debts totalling 1,650 *livres*. In 1799 Koenig tried to recover the inheritances that he had come into in Europe. Despite persistent efforts, he apparently received only part of the large sums bequeathed him. The matter had not been settled even by 1840, seven years after his death.

Koenig also sought help from the government on the basis of his service record but his efforts were fruitless until 1800, when he was granted 2,400 acres. A decade later, as a reward for his years in the army, Governor Sir James Henry Craig* had him appointed teacher at L'Islet in the school set up under the 1801 act that created the Royal Institution for the Advancement of Learning. This "small job" brought him £60 annually until 1822. After that he received a pension as a retired teacher until 10 Oct. 1831. Lack of funds then forced the Royal Institution to do away with this payment. An inquiry conducted in 1820 indicates how the school, which Koenig held in his home, operated. Teaching was free and in French, but the number of pupils nevertheless fluctuated constantly. The catechism was the subject to which greatest attention was given. As method, Koenig used the monitorial system developed by Joseph Lancaster*.

Like many of his compatriots Edmond-Victor de Koenig had quickly fitted into the French-speaking population. It is uncertain that he accomplished much, however. He lived in constant poverty. Moreover, his competence as a doctor and a schoolteacher is questionable. He was never licensed as a doctor, and his appointment as a teacher was a reward rather than a recognition of his talents. Moreover, he suffered the crowning blow for a schoolteacher: his own children did not even know how to sign their names. Their astonished European cousins found it difficult to conceive that things could have come to such a pass.

RENALD LESSARD

ANQ-Q, CE1-1, 22 sept. 1783, 17 janv. 1785; CE2-3, 1er févr. 1798, 4 sept. 1802, 19 juill. 1833; CE2-18, 24 mai 1819; CE2-25, 23 janv. 1786, 20 janv. 1787, 23 nov. 1793; CE3-12, 21 août 1786; 15 janv., 22 nov. 1788; 7 nov. 1790; CN1-188, 27 juill. 1827; CN1-224, 20 nov. 1789; CN1-230, 26 août 1816, 23–24 juill. 1817; CN2-7, 9 août 1799, 12–13 mai 1803; CN2-12, 17 janv. 1820, 26 juin 1830; CN2-48, 21 déc. 1818; 15 mai 1819; 7 févr., 26 mars 1821; 13 sept., 28 oct., 9 nov. 1822; 13 déc. 1825; 31 déc. 1827; 22 déc. 1828; 26 janv. 1829; 15 avril 1831; 28 févr. 1833; 5 août 1835; CN3-11, 12 nov. 1782. BL, Add. MSS 21735: 593; 21812: 200; 21879: 132. PAC, RG 1, L3L: 94259–62; RG 4, A3, 2; RG 31, C1, 1831, L'Islet. PRO, WO 17/1570 (mfm. at PAC). L.C., House of Assembly, *Journals,* 1810–11, app.B. L.-P. Audet, *Le système scolaire*, 3: 140; 4: 120, 126, 217, 252, 254, 258. Maurice Koenig, "La famille Koenig en Canada; un baron allemand allié à deux familles canadiennes-françaises," SGCF *Mémoires*, 16 (1965): 269–70. P.-G. Roy, "Le baron Edmond-Victor von Koenig," *BRH*, 23 (1917): 316–18.

L

LABADIE, LOUIS (from 1798 he signed **Louis-Généreux**), teacher; b. 18 May 1765 at Quebec, son of Pierre Labadie, a cooper, and Marie-Louise Paquet; d. 19 June 1824 in Verchères, Lower Canada.

According to an unsigned but presumably autobiographical account in *L'Aurore des Canadas* on 22 Aug. 1818, Louis Labadie learned the rudiments of teaching and practised this profession when he was barely past childhood. In 1776 he was teaching some ten youngsters; his father had given him permission to have the pupils in his home, and some Quebec merchants contributed the school supplies.

In 1778–79 Labadie studied at the Petit Séminaire de Québec. He divided his time between his classical studies and the teaching of reading and writing. But illness forced him to leave the institution, and on the recommendation of the bishop of Quebec, Jean-Olivier Briand*, he was put under the care of the parish priest of Beauport, Pierre-Simon Renaud, in the early 1780s. It was thought that he would regain his health in the country. Labadie undertook to teach there and in 1783 about 30 pupils were attending the school.

Labadie's health was still delicate. Consequently in 1785 Dr Philippe-Louis-François Badelard* prescribed salt-water baths for him. On a recommendation from the parish priest of Notre-Dame in Quebec, Auguste-David Hubert, Labadie went to live at Rivière-Ouelle. The local parish priest, Bernard-Claude PANET, found a house for him near the St Lawrence and gave him his meals at the presbytery. As payment Labadie conducted a parish school.

In 1787 Labadie was asked by the parish priest of Kamouraska, Joseph-Amable Trutault, to establish a school there. As his health had improved, he gave up his plan of returning to Quebec and accepted the offer. After a year or two he left for Quebec. A period of reflection settled what his diary termed his profession or vocation: teaching.

In 1789 Labadie met the parish priest of Berthier-en-Haut (Berthierville), Jean-Baptiste-Noël Pouget*, who suggested he take charge of a primary school there, a proposal to which he agreed. He taught in a house belonging to the *fabrique* and boarded in a parishioner's home. After teaching for five years at Berthier-en-Haut, and in the mean time refusing offers from the priests of Saint-Cuthbert and Trois-Rivières, he accepted an invitation from the priest of Verchères in 1794. He went to teach at Saint-Eustache in 1801, and then at Varennes four years later. He returned to Verchères in 1813 and remained there until his death.

This lay pioneer in primary teaching appears to have had exceptional pedagogical gifts. He certainly had little formal knowledge, much less than those who had studied at classical colleges. But he could read and write, even if his writing was full of grammatical errors and spelling mistakes. His extreme naïvety may have been an asset in enabling him to communicate with children, to whom he was close in spirit. He showed his pupils great affection, and they were attached to him. Not infrequently during the short summer holidays or around Easter, Labadie would take some pupils to Montreal or to visit acquaintances in a neighbouring parish. Several youths who left his school to attend the Séminaire de Nicolet or the Collège Saint-Raphaël in Montreal maintained more or less regular contact with him. Some of them – Ludger Duvernay*, for one – whose only stock of knowledge was what he had taught them, had a remarkable rise in society.

Labadie's curriculum was reduced to the bare bones: reading, writing, and arithmetic, to which was added a smattering of history, geography, and the catechism. His pedagogical methods were very much rule-of-thumb. "Friends of education" would supply books and paper. A curate would give pictures which the teacher distributed. Thanks to gifts of newspapers, the schoolchildren read the scarce periodicals of the time and when they went home passed the news on to their amazed parents. To vary his teaching format or simply to polish his pupils Labadie used to write addresses to prominent individuals on the occasion of their birthday or patron saint's day; the member of parliament, seigneur, parish priest, or curate would listen to the address, which was generally followed by a poem, a song, or some sort of play in verse.

Labadie exercised his profession in the shadow of the church. In the parishes where he agreed to teach he received a warm, if not a formal, welcome from the priest and the parishioners. In 1805 the priest of Varennes introduced him in his Sunday sermon noting, "I am expecting a great deal of the present

Labadie

schoolmaster, [in particular] that in his school he will maintain good order, which has never existed here. The first thing is to instruct the youth in religion and to make good Christians of them." On the first day of classes the priest celebrated high mass, with the *Veni Creator* and hymns sung by the pupils. For the occasion Labadie offered a prayer at the foot of the altar, asking God for the help needed to exercise his profession in a Christian manner.

On occasion Labadie prepared or officiated at religious ceremonies such as first communion, taking part through singing and readings. During his first stay at Verchères he collaborated in pastoral work to an even greater degree. He sought the office of sacristan and received from it the extra income he needed at the time. At that period, he was still a bachelor and lived somewhat like an assistant to the parish priest, who provided him with his meals at the presbytery.

In general Labadie's relations with the parish priests seem to have been marked by deference, submission, and a cooperative spirit. Nevertheless a major difference of opinion brought him into conflict with Pouget. In January 1792 Labadie had offered to give free instruction to the poor children of Berthier-en-Haut. This apparently displeased the churchwardens and the parish priest, who in May expelled him from the school, the premises of which belonged to the *fabrique*. Labadie promptly sued Pouget in the Court of Common Pleas at Montreal. Lawyer Robert Russell served as counsel for the dismissed schoolmaster. With the backing of Hugh Finlay*, who paid the rent for new premises, Labadie resumed teaching in Berthier-en-Haut. In June he announced in the press that he had 26 pupils, 5 of whom were being instructed free of charge.

The conflict between Labadie and Pouget was probably not based solely upon the principle of free schooling. It aroused controversy in Berthier-en-Haut. On the one hand, a certificate of good conduct given to the schoolmaster had 32 signatures. On the other, at the beginning of August the *Quebec Gazette* carried the reply from some 50 parishioners who sided with Pouget, the churchwardens being at the top of the list. In it they deplored Labadie's independent attitude towards the parish priest, an attitude which in the context of the period could easily be considered irreligious and scandalous. Labadie was supported by some prominent English-speaking Protestants. In addition to Finlay, his educational mission received the approval, if not the encouragement, of Samuel Neilson*, Chief Justice William Smith*, and Lieutenant Governor Alured CLARKE. Prince Edward* Augustus even declared himself patron of the school when he passed through Berthier-en-Haut in 1793. Nothing more was needed to show the teacher's loyalty to Great Britain and the holders of office in the colony during those years of open conflict between the

original mother country and the new one. Labadie had in fact published in the press some literary pieces in praise of the British. In 1798, banking on his exaggerated declarations of loyalty, he asked the civil secretary, Herman Witsius Ryland*, for "a position in the governmental secretariat or something equivalent, in order to retire from the wretched occupation of schoolmaster, which is a little too dependent on the whim [of the] clergy." Ryland made no reply, a silence that had the effect of dampening Labadie's enthusiasms, or rather of removing him from the sphere of politics. He penned the occasional couplet against Napoleon, but the passion had gone from them.

Labadie had such a good reputation that parish priests fought for his services. While teaching at Verchères he refused a considerable sum to go to L'Assomption. In 1801 he accepted an offer from the priest of Saint-Eustache which carried a tempting salary. From then on he had no more financial difficulties. Earlier, in 1795, he had thought it fitting to attach to his good wishes to the parishioners of Verchères a renewed plea: "I repeat today and beg you to be charitable enough to put a little stovewood in your carriages and throw [it] off at my door when you pass on your way to divine service." At that time, to make ends meet he had to act as sacristan and beg for his salary every year, going from door to door. By the turn of the century such embarrassing situations were part of the past. At Saint-Eustache he considered that he was "magnificently lodged" in a house with a parlour, a room for the school, and two bedrooms, as well as a room in which he installed his library. Nevertheless, although he received some extra income from two boarders, he took a less expensive house, and then in 1805 went to Varennes, where he received a better salary. The local parish priest set up a foundation which guaranteed the schoolmaster's salary and the upkeep of the school. Labadie was assured of a modest degree of comfort.

On 17 Feb. 1801 Louis Labadie had married Marie-Archange Charron. As the years passed Labadie and his kin were often afflicted with illness. When he was in his mid forties, he suffered from a canker on his nose which disfigured him. Then in 1811 his wife contracted a lung disease that forced them to sleep apart. When she was at the point of death, Labadie made a vow that if she recovered, they would forgo sexual relations. Vain promises? His wife died on 21 Jan. 1815 and six months later Labadie married Marie-Josephte Privée, a 47-year-old widow whom he described as a "small woman, but very sweet." To put an end to the whispering, and perhaps to forestall the possibility of a charivari, he had a high mass celebrated for his deceased wife three days before the wedding. On 24 July he was remarried, presumably with no open display of disapproval. The couple's happiness was short-lived, for Marie-Josephte fell seriously ill a few days after the wedding and died in January 1816. Shortly afterwards Labadie took as his third wife Louise-Zéphyrine Quintal, who gave birth prematurely on 8 March 1817 to a stillborn child. This succession of bereavements may have led Labadie to stop writing the diary that he had kept since 1794 and that has been used to reconstruct his life. It may be conjectured just as plausibly that the rest of the diary is no longer extant.

SERGE GAGNON

Louis Labadie's diary is kept at the ASQ (MSS, 74).

ANQ-M, CE1-26, 21 juin 1824; P1000-45-889. ANQ-Q, CE1-1, 19 mai 1765. ASQ, Fichier des anciens. *L'Aurore des Canadas* (Montréal), 22 août 1818. P.-G. Roy, *Fils de Québec*, 2: 134–37. Wallace, *Macmillan dict.* S.-A. Moreau, *Précis de l'histoire de la seigneurie, de la paroisse et du comté de Berthier, P.Q. (Canada)* (Berthierville, Qué., 1889). A.[-E.] Gosselin, "Louis Labadie ou le maître d'école patriotique, 1765–1824," RSC *Trans.*, 3rd ser., 7 (1913), sect.I: 97–123. Yves Tessier, "Ludger Duvernay et les débuts de la presse périodique aux Trois-Rivières," *RHAF*, 18 (1964–65): 387–404, 566–81.

LABRIE, JACQUES, journalist, physician, militia officer, educator, author, and politician; b. 4 Jan. 1784 in Saint-Charles, near Quebec, son of Jacques Nau, *dit* Labry, a farmer, and Marie-Louise Brousseau; d. 26 Oct. 1831 in Saint-Eustache, Lower Canada.

Like many of his generation, Jacques Labrie received an elementary education through the endeavours of the parish priest in his village. At 14 he entered the Petit Séminaire de Québec, where he proved a brilliant student. Having received his *baccalauréat* in 1804, he chose to prepare for a medical career and from 1804 to 1807 studied under François BLANCHET, one of the eminent doctors of the period. After this apprenticeship he completed his medical training with a year in Edinburgh.

While studying medicine, Labrie had also begun a career as a journalist. In the autumn of 1806 he was editor of the bi-weekly *Le Courier de Québec*, founded by Pierre-Amable De Bonne*. This newspaper had set out to defend the interests of the Canadians. It nevertheless denounced the Canadian party and its paper, *Le Canadien. Le Courier de Québec* reported political and literary news, both local and foreign, as well as research findings on the history of Canada. Labrie was the author of most of the articles. By this time he was an admirer of the British constitution and English liberalism, and he constantly flayed the despotism of the former French governors and France's neglect of her colony. Above all, Labrie demonstrated an uncommon interest in his country's past.

After *Le Courier de Québec* ceased publication in December 1808, Labrie devoted himself solely to the medical profession. He practised for some months in Montreal and then established his office in Saint-Eustache, where on 12 June 1809 he married Marie-Marguerite Gagnier, daughter of Pierre-Rémi Gagnier, the local notary. They had nine children but only three reached adulthood. During the War of 1812 he became surgeon to the 2nd Battalion of the Select Embodied Militia of Lower Canada.

In addition to professional activities, Labrie gave much of his energy to the cause of education. In 1821 he founded two schools in his parish, one for girls and the other for boys. Although he ran both, he clearly preferred the girls' establishment, which his eldest daughter, Zéphirine, attended, and he became its principal teacher. Labrie wrote history and geography manuals, and the school also gave courses in French, English, and mathematics. Built on a pleasant site at the junction of the Du Chêne and Des Mille Îles rivers, it had an excellent reputation but was obliged to close in 1828 because of a lack of funds. Labrie had supported it with his own money throughout its existence.

A devotee of the history of Lower Canada, an observer of its society, and a defender of the Canadians' rights, Labrie entered politics in 1827. In June he served as secretary for a general meeting held at Saint-Eustache. At that time he announced his intention of running for the House of Assembly in the constituency of York. He also severely criticized the administration of Governor Lord Dalhousie [Ramsay*] and his clique. In the elections held that summer one of Labrie's opponents was none other than Nicolas-Eustache LAMBERT DUMONT, seigneur of Mille-Îles, who was one of the members for York. The riding was hotly contested: voters had to force their way to the polling station. Labrie was elected along with Jean-Baptiste Lefebvre, and their opponents, Lambert-Dumont and John Simpson*, had to relinquish their seats.

In the autumn Labrie was busy persuading his compatriots to sign a petition that would be sent to London in 1828 with Denis-Benjamin Viger*, Augustin Cuvillier*, and John Neilson*. Labrie gave a particularly convincing speech at a meeting held in Vaudreuil on 27 Dec. 1827. The address, which was reported in *La Minerve* of 7 Jan. 1828, revealed that he still had confidence in British institutions; if the constitution of Lower Canada was being violated, then Dalhousie and his creatures on the Legislative Council were to blame. Historian Michel Bibaud* ranks this speech as one of the most inflammatory pieces of oratory in the years before the rebellion.

In the House of Assembly Labrie devoted his efforts to promoting the cause of education and the medical profession in Lower Canada. He was appointed to the medical board of examiners for the district of Montreal in 1831. In the autumn of that year he made a tour to inspect the schools in his riding. Fatigued by his travels, he came down with the pneumonia that was to prove fatal. On 26 October, feeling dangerously ill, he summoned his friend the notary Jean-Joseph Girouard* and indicated his intention of making a written declaration. Labrie delegated to Augustin-Norbert Morin*, a member of the assembly and a writer for the Patriote party, the task of completing a manuscript on the history of Canada which was his life's work. He then passed away at his home in Saint-Eustache.

Morin proved equal to the mission that his friend Labrie had entrusted to him. He studied the manuscript carefully, corrected it, and in November presented the house with a request for publication of the work, which was to comprise three or four volumes, each about 500 pages long. Labrie had commenced with the beginnings of New France and ended with the main events of the War of 1812. A house committee agreed to Morin's request, but the Legislative Council refused to publish the manuscript, citing the author's lack of objectivity. The councillors would consent only to buy it and deposit it with the Literary and Historical Society of Quebec. The assembly, however, refused to go along with the council's wish and decided to wait for better days to publish the work. In the mean time Morin deposited it in the library of his friend, the notary Girouard, in Saint-Benoît. There Labrie's history of Canada was destroyed by fire in 1837.

The value of Labrie's manuscript will never be known, but the author should surely be acclaimed as one of the great historians of French Canada. He was intensely interested in its history at a time when the subject was not even on the curriculum in the secondary schools. At that time the curious still had to turn to the work of Pierre-François-Xavier de Charlevoix*, who ended his account with the year 1731. Thus for the period from 1731 to 1812, Labrie was a pioneer. His correspondence with Jacques Viger* shows that he used original sources and carried his desire for accuracy to great lengths.

What attitude Labrie would have adopted in the rebellion of 1837–38 is an open question; he was an ardent supporter of Louis-Joseph Papineau* and father-in-law of Patriote leader Jean-Olivier Chénier*, who had married Zéphirine in 1831. It is certain that he remains one of the most illustrious representatives of the Patriote generation. Above all, he was passionately fond of the history of his land and dedicated all his leisure to it, a history that – symbolically – perished in the fire at Saint-Benoît.

BÉATRICE CHASSÉ

Jacques Labrie is the author of *Les premiers rudimens de la constitution britannique; traduits de l'anglais de M. Brooke; précédés d'un précis historique, et suivis d'observations sur la constitution du Bas-Canada, pour en donner l'histoire et en indiquer les principaux vices, avec un aperçu de quelques-uns des moyens probables d'y remédier; ouvrage utile à toutes sortes de personnes et principalement destiné à l'instruction politique de la jeunesse canadienne* (Montréal, 1827).

ANQ-M, CE6-11, 12 juin 1809, 29 oct. 1831; P1000-32-774; P1000-45-889. *Le Canadien*, 7 janv. 1832. *La Minerve*, 7 janv. 1828. *Quebec Gazette*, 14 June 1827. M.-J. et G. Ahern, *Notes pour l'hist. de la médecine*. Béatrice Chassé, "Le notaire Girouard, patriote et rebelle" (thèse de D. ès L., univ. Laval, Québec, 1974). A.[-H.] Gosselin, *Un bon patriote d'autrefois, le docteur Labrie* (3e éd., Québec, 1907). L.-J. Rodrigue, "Messire Jacques Paquin, curé de Saint-Eustache de la Rivière-du-Chêne (1821–1847)," CCHA *Rapport*, 31 (1964): 73–83.

LABROSSE, CHARLES JOURDAIN, *dit. See* JOURDAIN

LACOMBE, JACQUES TRULLIER, *dit. See* TRULLIER

LACROIX, HUBERT-JOSEPH (by 1802 he was known as **Joseph-Hubert**), merchant, JP, militia officer, politician, and seigneur; b. 5 May 1743 at Quebec, son of Hubert-Joseph de Lacroix* and Anne-Madeleine Dontaille; d. 15 July 1821 in Saint-Vincent-de-Paul (Laval), Lower Canada.

Hubert-Joseph Lacroix grew up in the family home in Lower Town Quebec, surrounded by merchants' establishments and navigators' homes. Lacroix's father, formerly a surgeon and botanist, had been a merchant for some time before his death in 1760. Young Hubert-Joseph was in business himself on Rue Saint-Jean in 1765 when, on 15 April, he married Françoise-Pélagie, daughter of another merchant in the city, François-Philippe Poncy. Lacroix did not lack money: as a wedding present his mother gave him an advance of 3,000 *livres* on his inheritance (one-third of which went into the community of property with Françoise-Pélagie) while Lacroix himself gave his wife a dower of 3,000 *livres*. His brothers Paul and Hubert were also merchants, the latter in the Vaudreuil area.

Lacroix may have participated as a militiaman in the defence of Quebec during the American invasion of the colony in 1775–76 [*see* Benedict Arnold*; Richard Montgomery*]. By 1776 he was established at Saint-Vincent-de-Paul. He engaged in the fur trade and in 1785 sent a modest expedition, valued at nearly £2,800, to Michilimackinac (Mackinac Island, Mich.) with Gabriel Cotté* standing security. In 1786, 1787, and 1788 he received trade passes for goods valued at £450, £1,000, and £500 with, as securities, himself, his brother Paul, François Le Guay, and Pierre-Joseph Gamelin*. In 1786 he stood security for an expedition by Gamelin valued at £1,500.

By the late 1780s Lacroix was forging a certain social standing for himself. In 1787, as an officer of militia, he was involved in what he called "an affair ... very important for the support of government authority": a dispute with Joseph Papineau*, who accused him of abuse of power in the enrolment of militiamen and whom Lacroix denounced as "the serpent in the fable" for Papineau's supposed ingratitude to government. Lacroix was made a justice of the peace in the district of Montreal in August 1791, and his commission was renewed several times. By 1795 he was a major in the Vaudreuil battalion of militia. In the 1780s he had opposed the movement in favour of constitutional reform, including the establishment of an elected house [see George Allsopp*], but he had accepted the assembly accorded by the Constitutional Act of 1791, and from 1792 to 1796 he sat for Effingham County. Early in 1793, along with most Canadian members, he voted for Jean-Antoine Panet* as speaker of the house, and voted six times out of seven with the Canadian party in the first two sessions. He missed the third and fourth sessions entirely. In 1796 he was elected for York County, and the following year he again supported Panet as speaker. He was even less assiduous than in the first parliament, however, voting only four times – always with the Canadian party – before dissolution of the legislature in 1800. Chronic absenteeism on the part of representatives from outside the town of Quebec was a serious obstacle to the efficient functioning of the early assembly; members were unpaid and had in addition to foot all their living expenses in the capital while their personal business back home went largely neglected.

Lacroix's social position was confirmed in 1802 by the marriage of his son Janvier-Domptail* with a niece of judge Louis-Charles Foucher in Notre-Dame church, Montreal, before several leading figures of the time, including judge Pierre-Louis Panet*. Both magistrates were adversaries of the Canadian party, and Lacroix's ties with its opponents were reinforced in 1806 when he became a seigneur. By the will of Marie-Anne-Thérèse Céloron de Blainville, widow of Jacques-Marie Nolan Lamarque, Lacroix inherited the seigneury of Blainville, formerly part of the seigneury of Mille-Îles. He had probably already been managing Blainville, since in 1804, at the request of Pierre Denaut*, bishop of Quebec, he had had a road built to link the third range of the seigneury to the church of Sainte-Thérèse in the first range. He had persisted with it despite strong opposition from the very habitants whose Sunday trip to mass was made

easier; they had been more concerned about the corvées and taxes it would cost them.

Lacroix's acquisition was a valuable one and, although remaining in Saint-Vincent-de-Paul, he exploited it fully. By 1815 Surveyor General Joseph Bouchette* had described the soil of Blainville as "for the most part good, rich, and productive" of all sorts of grains and of stands of beech, ash, maple, and oak. The seigneury was well watered by the Rivière Mascouche and its tributaries, which powered saw- and grist-mills. "By much the largest proportion of Blainville is conceded in lots of the usual extent," Bouchette had noted. "The greatest number of these are settled, and appear to be under a very beneficial system of management." In themselves the two major locations of settlement, the banks of the Mascouche and Saint-Jean (Mille Îles) rivers, formed "a valuable and highly improved property." Personal misfortune had, however, struck Lacroix in 1808, two years after he inherited the seigneury, when Françoise-Pélagie, with whom he had had five girls and four boys, died. On 9 Sept. 1811 the seigneur of Blainville married his sister-in-law, Louise Launière, in Saint-Vincent-de-Paul. His income was apparently modest at this time since by the marriage contract, which stipulated that there would be no community of property, he could promise his wife an annual pension of only £50 if she survived him.

For his military service in 1775–76 Lacroix had received a grant of land in 1802. The following year he was promoted lieutenant-colonel in the Île-Jésus battalion of militia, and four years later he was made colonel. In 1810 he denounced six of his officers for their attitude towards the government in the crisis that opposed Governor Sir James Henry Craig* and the newspaper Le Canadien. On 4 June 1812, on the eve of the war with the United States, when he was in his 70th year, he was made colonel commandant of the new Île-Jésus division, composed of the Île-Jésus battalion and two newly created ones, Terrebonne and Blainville. That month as well he received commissions for the trial of small causes and for the administration of oaths of allegiance at Saint-Vincent-de-Paul. He died there on 15 July 1821, "colonel of militia, seigneur of Blainville, good father, good husband, and useful citizen," according to the Quebec Gazette, and was buried in the parish church. The service was attended by at least five parish priests, as well as Roderick McKenzie* and Jean-Baptiste-Toussaint Pothier* among others.

As a seigneur and an honoured and respected member of the local élite, Lacroix, like Pierre GUE-ROUT and Jean-Baptiste RAYMOND, had realized the social aspiration of a numerous group of small merchants, Canadian and British, of his time. It was an aspiration they shared with more prominent colleagues, such as François Baby*, Joseph Drapeau*,

Lafontaine

Thomas Dunn*, and William Grant* of Quebec; only the scale differed.

W. STANFORD REID

ANQ-M, CE1-59, 1ᵉʳ févr. 1778. ANQ-Q, CE1-1, 5 mai 1743, 15 avril 1765; CN1-248, 13 avril 1765. PAC, RG 4, B28, 115; RG 68, General index, 1651–1841. "Le recensement de Québec, en 1744," ANQ Rapport, 1939–40: 134. Quebec Gazette, 13 Nov. 1788; 22 Jan. 1789; 20 Dec. 1792; 26 Jan. 1797; 20 May 1813; 14 Aug. 1817; 28 Sept., 14 Dec. 1820; 23 July 1821. F.-J. Audet, "Les législateurs du Bas-Canada." F.-J. Audet et Fabre Surveyer, Les députés au premier parl. du Bas-Canada, 291–98. Bouchette, Topographical description of L.C., 106–7. Officers of British forces in Canada (Irving), 177. Quebec almanac, 1791–1821. P.-G. Roy, Inv. concessions, 3: 276. Cahiers historiques: histoire de Sainte-Thérèse (Joliette, Qué., 1940), 71–74. Hare, "L'Assemblée législative du Bas-Canada," RHAF, 27: 371–72, 375. J.-J. Lefebvre, "Notes d'identité; le capitaine Pierre Matte (1774–1831)," BRH, 57 (1951): 166–67.

LAFONTAINE, dit Marion. See MARION

LAGUEUX, LOUIS, lawyer and politician; b. 20 Nov. 1793 at Quebec, son of Louis Lagueux and Louise Bégin; m. first there 9 July 1816 Rose-Louise Bergevin, dit Langevin, and they had a daughter who died soon after birth; m. secondly 3 Aug. 1820 at Chambly, Lower Canada, Josephte-Aurélie Mignault, who died three years later; d. 15 June 1832 at Quebec.

Louis Lagueux, who came from a wealthy family involved in business, did brilliantly in his studies at the Petit Séminaire de Québec from 1806 to 1814. He then went into law under the guidance of Joseph-Rémi Vallières* de Saint-Réal and was authorized to practise as a lawyer on 15 Dec. 1817. That year he went into business with William Grant, a shipwright; intending to trade with the British colonies in the West Indies, they jointly bought the Adeona, a 140-ton vessel. Unfortunately the two partners had to borrow £1,000 from Louis's father to repair and fit her out; when they were unable to repay the sum, Lagueux and Grant found themselves obliged on 28 Feb. 1818 to sell her to their creditor. After this experience Lagueux seems to have given up the idea of engaging in business. A few months later he headed a committee to help settlers in Dorchester County who had suffered damages from an unexpected flooding of the Rivière Beaurivage on 16 July 1818. He went to the scene of the disaster and on his return launched a public fund in aid of the victims.

In 1820 the voters of Dorchester, in a display of gratitude, elected Lagueux to the House of Assembly rather than Jean-Thomas TASCHEREAU. He represented his riding faithfully, retaining his seat until his death in 1832. In his early years as a member he took no major part in debates except to declare himself in favour of an 1821 bill incorporating the Bank of Quebec. He did, however, serve on the assembly's education committee, and in 1824 was chairman of a committee dealing with the Jesuit estates. On 17 Nov. 1823 he had also been appointed secretary of the Quebec Education Society [see Joseph-François Perrault*]. Early in 1825 he was named chairman of a committee to study a request from shipyard owners for a decrease in duties on materials imported for shipbuilding. After discussing the proposal the committee decided not to alter the tariffs. In 1827 Lagueux vigorously supported the bill to set up registry offices in Lower Canada.

That year, inspired by democratic principles and patriotism, he denounced the abuses of the régime in Lower Canada. As the head of a committee formed by voters of Quebec town, he objected to the composition of the Legislative Council and its dependence on the executive power; he also protested against the unduly high salaries paid through the civil list, the poor use of the monies voted by the assembly to promote progress in education, industry, and inland communications, the maladministration of public lands, the attempts by the imperial parliament to change the constitution without the knowledge of the province, and the laws affecting land tenure.

In 1830 Lagueux brought in a bill to secure municipal incorporation for Quebec. He spoke in the house for the last time in December 1831, during the stormy debates over the bill presented by Louis BOURDAGES giving all property owners the right to attend meetings of the fabriques and to take part in the discussions and voting. In accordance with the position taken by Louis-Joseph Papineau*, he supported the bill, stating that "those who are able to choose their [assembly] members are also capable of choosing churchwardens." But the Roman Catholic Church was against the proposed practice and the Legislative Council set the bill aside. The bishops did not change their stance until 1843.

The stand Lagueux took in the assembly might have caused him difficulties in the coming elections, but fate decided otherwise. He was one of the first victims of the cholera epidemic that broke out on 11 June 1832. He organized a meeting of Bourdages's supporters at his home on Rue Saint-Joseph (Rue Garneau) that day to discuss the question of meetings of the fabriques, but shortly afterwards he was stricken. He died on 15 June, a few hours after his former opponent, Jean-Thomas Taschereau. That day Le Canadien announced the death of Lagueux, "the second distinguished victim struck down by cholera," and paid tribute to him: "This gentleman had stood out at all times in the country's councils as a zealous and enlightened patriot, and his death is a loss for the general public."

YVON THÉRIAULT

Louis Lagueux is the author of a one-page tract entitled *Electors of Quebec submitting the present state of the province, and the abuses and grievances which prevail therein, and praying for relief and justice* (Quebec, 1827).

ANQ-M, CE1-39, 3 août 1820. ANQ-Q, CE1-1, 20 nov. 1793, 8 juill. 1816, 15 juin 1832; CN1-49, 1er mai 1832; CN1-116, 4, 28 févr., 9 oct. 1818; CN1-212, 6 juin 1823, 27 mars 1830; CN1-230, 8 juill. 1816; CN1-262, 7 juill. 1817. L.C., House of Assembly, *Journals*, 1820–32. *Le Canadien*, 15 juin, 6 juill. 1832. *Quebec Gazette*, 16, 27 July 1818; 15 March, 26 July 1821; 25 Nov. 1822; 13 Feb., 17, 24 Nov., 25 Dec. 1823; 22 July 1824. F.-J. Audet, "Les législateurs du Bas-Canada." P.-G. Roy, *Les avocats de la région de Québec*; *Fils de Québec*, 3: 54–55. Thomas Chapais, *Cours d'histoire du Canada* (8v., Québec et Montréal, 1919–34; réimpr. Trois-Rivières, Qué., 1972), 3: 188–89. J.-E. Roy, *Hist. de Lauzon*, 5: 261. "La famille Lagueux," *BRH*, 38 (1932): 577–79.

LAMBERT DUMONT, NICOLAS-EUSTACHE (also known as **Eustache-Nicolas**), militia officer, JP, seigneur, politician, office holder, and judge; b. 25 Sept. 1767 in Trois-Rivières, Que., son of Eustache-Louis Lambert Dumont and Marguerite-Angélique Boisseau; m. first 8 Sept. 1800 Marie-Narcisse Lemaire Saint-Germain, and they had at least three children; m. secondly 8 Nov. 1834 Sophie Ménéclier de Montrochon in Trois-Rivières; d. 25 April 1835 in Saint-Eustache, Lower Canada.

Nicolas-Eustache Lambert Dumont was born into a prominent and well-connected Canadian family. The Lambert Dumonts had been seigneurs of Mille-Îles since about 1743. Nicolas-Eustache's godfather, Nicolas Boisseau*, was formerly chief clerk of the Conseil Supérieur of New France. An aunt, Charlotte-Louise Lambert Dumont, had married Louis-Pierre Poulin* de Courval Cressé, seigneur of Courval, and, following his premature death, administered the seigneury of Nicolet, of which her husband was to have been the heir. Nicolas-Eustache's father was a lieutenant-colonel of militia.

Nicolas-Eustache followed in the family tradition. He was a major in the Vaudreuil battalion of militia by 1795. In 1796 and 1797 he had acquired from the Poulin de Courval Cressé family for 9,833 *livres* the seigneury of Île-à-la-Fourche, beside that of Nicolet. In 1799 he owned a farm, two lots, a sawmill, and a grist-mill in the seigneury of Mille-Îles and a house in its main village, Saint-Eustache. However, he was evidently in grave financial difficulty, since in 1799 Joseph Périnault* had the sheriff seize the Mille-Îles properties for public auction, and between 1800 and 1803 the seigneury of Île-à-la-Fourche was seized on no fewer than four occasions, each time at the suit of a different creditor, one of whom was François Vassal* de Montviel. From 1803 to 1827 at least Lambert Dumont would fight bitterly for recognition of the boundaries of Île-à-la-Fourche, contested by the colonial administration.

As befitted a man of his station, Lambert Dumont was active in public life. He was appointed a justice of the peace in 1800 and had reached the rank of lieutenant-colonel in the Vaudreuil militia by 1804. His political colours are probably indicated by his personal friendship with Louis-Charles Foucher, solicitor general of Lower Canada. In 1804 Lambert Dumont was elected along with John MURE to represent the county of York in the House of Assembly. Between 1805 and 1808 he voted 11 times with the minority English party, which supported the British colonial administration. Although he sided eight times with the Canadian party as well, it is doubtful whether he shared the nationalism of its members. In supporting, for example, this group's proposal to finance the construction of prisons through a tax on commerce (dominated by the British) – the alternative being a tax on land (owned mostly by Canadians) – Lambert Dumont likely voted as a seigneur. In the elections of 1808 he was defeated in York by the Canadian party's candidate, Jean-Joseph Trestler*, who was returned with Mure of the English party.

In 1807, following his father's death, Lambert Dumont had become co-seigneur of Mille-Îles with his sister Marie-Angélique, wife of Antoine Lefebvre de Bellefeuille. The seigneury, also known by the names Rivière-du-Chêne, Dumont, and Saint-Eustache, constituted but one-half of the original concession, the neighbouring seigneury of Blainville, owned by Hubert-Joseph LACROIX, having been detached in the first half of the 18th century. However, the inheritance also included a northern augmentation, conceded in 1750 and a virtual wilderness in 1807. Mille-Îles had excellent soil for grain, an important asset for a seigneur since wheat was a principal trade commodity in the early 19th century. From his residence in Saint-Eustache, Lambert Dumont, who had for some time been assisting his father in administering Mille-Îles, devoted much energy after 1807 to what was already a well-developed seigneury. Like his father, he hoped to open up the augmentation, and in 1810 he established a *pied-à-terre* at a promising site on the Rivière du Nord, to which he was able to attract a few settlers, including Casimir-Amable Testard* de Montigny. Despite Lambert Dumont's energetic supervision, however, the settlement, which he planned ultimately as an industrial centre, grew but slowly. Later, shifted slightly to the north, it formed the basis of Saint-Jérôme.

To encourage growth of the seigneury Lambert Dumont promoted education. He was the first to sign a petition in 1810 to have established in Saint-Eustache a school of the Royal Institution for the Advancement of Learning [*see* Joseph Langley MILLS], and on 3 September he was appointed one of three school commissioners. His support for a public school would

Lambert

not have pleased Roman Catholic bishop Joseph-Octave PLESSIS, a determined opponent of the Royal Institution, and in the end clerical influence aborted the project. By 1815 Surveyor General Joseph Bouchette* had painted an attractive picture of Mille-Îles. "The greatest part of this property is conceded, and most of the lots settled upon by an industrious tenantry. At the mouth of the Rivière du Chêne is the pleasant well built village of St. Eustache, containing from 80 to 90 houses, a handsome church, and parsonage-house." On the Rivière du Chêne and a number of smaller streams stood both saw- and grist-mills.

In order better to exploit the commercial potential of his seigneury Lambert Dumont sought to enlarge the market for its products by facilitating transportation to Montreal and its port. Apparently licensed as an engineer and surveyor, he made three attempts between 1809 and 1812 to obtain from the House of Assembly an act authorizing him to construct a toll-bridge over the Rivière Jésus (Rivière des Mille Îles), from the parish of Sainte-Thérèse-de-Blainville (Sainte-Thérèse) to Île Jésus. All failed, as did efforts to obtain an act authorizing construction of dams in the rapids where Lac des Deux Montagnes emptied into the Rivière Jésus between the seigneury of Mille-Îles and Île Jésus. In 1815 he again petitioned the assembly, this time through a member adhering to the Canadian party, Joseph Levasseur-Borgia*, for an act that would grant him the exclusive right to build bridges of wrought iron in the colony. Before a committee appointed to study Levasseur-Borgia's bill, Lambert Dumont explained that what would distinguish his from all iron bridges previously built would be the arches of wrought iron, and he proposed building a bridge over the Rivière Saint-Maurice as a prototype. The committee approved the bill, but it subsequently died in a committee of the whole house.

For all his activity, Lambert Dumont once more experienced financial difficulties in the years 1817–24. On two occasions, in 1817 and 1822, creditors again had the seigneury of Île-à-la Fourche seized for sale at public auction. In the latter year lots and buildings in the parishes of Saint-Martin and Saint-Laurent and in Saint-Eustache were seized at the suit of three merchants. In 1823 the seigneury of Mille-Îles itself was seized along with its two sawmills and three stone grist-mills, as was the augmentation with its sawmill and wooden grist-mill, and an island in the Rivière Jésus.

Nevertheless, Lambert Dumont maintained his prominence as a local public figure. Appointed lieutenant-colonel of the Rivière-du-Chêne battalion of militia in 1807, he held this rank until 1820 at least. In 1812 he received a commission of *dedimus potestatem*. Five years later the appointment of Lambert Dumont, Joseph Papineau*, and Philemon

Wright* as commissioners for the improvement of communications in the county of York provided all three with an opportunity to serve both public and private interests. The commissioners announced their concern to improve navigation of the Long Sault on the Ottawa River, of particular interest to Papineau and Wright, and communications between the mainland and Île Jésus, an interest Lambert Dumont had obviously inspired. No doubt hoping to benefit from the commission's support, in 1820, 1821, and 1823 Lambert Dumont petitioned the assembly to obtain the exclusive privilege for 50 years of constructing a toll-bridge from Saint-Eustache to Île Jésus. None of the petitions succeeded. However, by 1828 two bridges, perhaps built by him, spanned the Rivière du Chêne; in 1830 he obtained an act authorizing him to build a toll-bridge over the Rivière des Prairies from the parish of Saint-Martin to that of Saint-Laurent; and by 1837 three bridges, again possibly built by him, joined Saint-Eustache to Île Jésus. On 28 June 1821 he had received his last commission, that for the trial of small causes in York County.

In the increasingly tense political atmosphere after 1807 prominent public figures could with difficulty avoid political engagement; Lambert Dumont was not of a temperament even to try. After having been re-elected for York in 1814, he fought a close race with Jean-Baptiste Féré of the Canadian party in the elections of 1816 in the same riding, for which both were returned. Over the next 11 years Lambert Dumont undoubtedly supported the colonial administration in its struggles with the Canadian party, which, under the increasingly radical leadership of Louis-Joseph Papineau*, became known as the Patriote party from 1826. On 4 June 1827 a political meeting in Saint-Eustache passed 17 resolutions criticizing the administration of Governor Lord Dalhousie [Ramsay*]; Lambert Dumont denounced several prominent participants to the governor, who in consequence ordered their dismissal from the militia. Among them were Féré, William Henry Scott*, and Jacques LABRIE. Lambert Dumont, who by then commanded the militia in York, added insult to injury by his cavalier treatment of a number of officers dismissed from his command, and he participated enthusiastically in the newspaper war that resulted. In this heated atmosphere elections were contested in York in the summer of 1827. The other incumbent member, John Simpson*, withdrew from the fierce battle to reduce violence. In the end Lambert Dumont was defeated by Labrie and Jean-Baptiste Lefebvre, candidates of the Patriote party.

Yet, Lambert Dumont continued to exercise local leadership. In 1825 he donated land for a school to be built according to the *fabrique* schools law [see Joseph Langley Mills] and, when nothing was done, was responsible four years later for having syndics elected to establish a school in Saint-Eustache according to another schools act called the syndics act. In 1835 he granted eight *arpents* of land as the site of a church for the recently erected parish of Saint-Jérôme. With his old fighting spirit, he quarrelled with the Sulpicians, whom he accused of encroaching on the northwest part of the augmentation of Mille-Îles, and he continued to do battle politically with Papineau's followers in and around Saint-Eustache. To counter the latter's increasingly numerous and radical political assemblies, he held a pro-government meeting in Saint-Eustache in 1834 but saw it taken over by his opponents. Lambert Dumont, however, would not live to see the ultimate discomfiture of his enemies during the events of 1837 in the region [*see* Jean-Olivier Chénier*]; he died in 1835 and was buried in the parish church of Saint-Eustache.

Nicolas-Eustache Lambert Dumont was in many ways a figure representative of the seigneurial class on the local level, and even on the colonial level, in the early 19th century. He assumed that, by virtue of an honourable family heritage and his position as seigneur, he had a natural role of economic, social, and political leadership among the Canadians of his seigneuries second not even to that of the Roman Catholic Church. Thus, tied by his aspirations to the British colonial administration, which dispensed the offices of local leadership, and harassed by financial difficulties, he saw only as an enemy the upstart Canadian bourgeoisie of doctors, lawyers, notaries, and local merchants which, through an ideology that combined nationalism and alarming democratic notions, was relentlessly undermining the position of the seigneurs. Consequently, in the struggle between the British administration and the Canadian party, he threw the weight of his influence vehemently against those whom he saw as a threat, but to no avail; the day of the bourgeoisie had come in Saint-Eustache.

In collaboration with W. STANFORD REID

ANQ-Q, E-39. PAC, RG 1, L3^L: 3193–95, 38750–53, 38765–74, 7122–44; RG 4, A1, 182; RG 68, General index, 1651–1841: 196, 254, 281, 327, 330, 332, 334, 349, 357, 361, 374, 633. Private arch., A.-M. Loignon-Quesnel (Rigaud, Qué.), Yves Quesnel papers. L.C., House of Assembly, *Journals*, 29 Jan.–26 Feb. 1810. *Quebec Gazette*, 29 Aug. 1799; 10 April, 15 May 1800; 8 July 1802; 26 May 1803; 27 Dec. 1804; 2 June 1808; 20, 24 April 1809; 22 Feb., 12 July 1810; 5, 28 March, 28 Nov. 1811; 12, 19, 26 March, 14 May 1812; 2 March 1815; 11, 18 April 1816; 24 April, 29 May, 24 July, 28 Aug. 1817; 23 March 1818; 3 June 1819; 6, 20 April, 10, 17, 27 July, 21 Aug., 11 Dec. 1820; 5, 26 July, 25 Oct., 1 Nov. 1821; 1, 22 Aug., 19 Dec. 1822; 25 Sept., 18 Dec. 1823; 8 Jan., 1 April 1824. F.-J. Audet, "Les législateurs du Bas-Canada." Bouchette, *Topographical description of L.C.*, 106–7. Desjardins, *Guide parl. Officers of British forces in Canada* (Irving), 176. É.-J.[-A.] Auclair, *Saint-Jérôme de Terrebonne* (Saint-Jérôme, Qué., 1934), 43–44. Germain Cornez, *Une ville naquit: Saint-Jérôme (1821–1880)* (Saint-Jérôme, 1973), 10–13, 19, 35. Émile Dubois, *Le feu de la Rivière-du-Chêne; étude historique sur le mouvement insurrectionnel de 1837 au nord de Montréal* (Saint-Jérôme, 1937), 50–55. Hare, "L'Assemblée législative du Bas-Canada," *RHAF*, 27: 379. A. C. de L. Macdonald, "Notes sur la famille Lambert du Mont," *Rev. canadienne* (Montréal), 19 (1883): 633–40, 739–47.

LAMOTHE, JOSEPH-MAURICE (baptized **Maurice-Joseph**), fur trader, militia officer, and Indian Department official; b. 16 March 1781 in Montreal, only son of Joseph Lamothe and Catherine Blondeau; d. there 5 Feb. 1827.

Joseph-Maurice Lamothe's ancestors migrated to New France in the late 17th century and occupied civil and military positions. His father distinguished himself during the American Revolutionary War as a courier, carrying dispatches to Governor Guy Carleton* in 1775 while Quebec was besieged by American forces [*see* Benedict Arnold*; Richard Montgomery*]. From 1793 the elder Lamothe served with the Indian Department as an interpreter at Michilimackinac (Mackinac Island, Mich.) and then as resident agent at Lac-des-Deux-Montagnes (Oka), near Montreal.

Joseph-Maurice's maternal uncle was the fur trader Maurice-Régis Blondeau*, and it was doubtless through Blondeau's connections that in 1801 he obtained a posting as a clerk to Pierre Rastel* de Rocheblave in the New North West Company (sometimes known as the XY Company) [*see* John Ogilvy*]. Initially stationed at Grand Portage (near Grand Portage, Minn.) and Kaministiquia (Thunder Bay, Ont.), Lamothe travelled as far west as the Peace River country. Rivalry was acute between the New North West Company and its older, better established competitor, the North West Company. In 1803 a NWC trader assaulted Lamothe, who shot and killed him. Though never charged with a crime, and later exonerated of any blame, Lamothe worried about the affair for years. Among those who supported him morally during this difficult time were the fur trader John Haldane*, who dismissed the matter as a "rascally business," and Blondeau, on whose recommendation Lamothe returned to the Montreal area about 1807.

Lamothe's knowledge of Indians, gained in the western trade, and his father's influence with Sir John JOHNSON obtained for him, shortly after his arrival in Montreal, the post of assistant to his father, whom he ultimately succeeded as resident agent at Lac-des-Deux-Montagnes. His administrative diligence impressed Governor Sir James Henry Craig*; in 1810 Craig circulated a request for information on all Indian bands in the Canadas, and Lamothe was one of the few officials to reply fairly promptly. In early 1812, supported by Johnson, Lamothe petitioned Craig's successor, Sir George Prevost*, for the position of resident agent of the Indian Department at Montreal; the appointment and a posting in the department as captain "to the Indian Warriors" were made effective 25 March 1812. Lamothe was also commissioned a captain in Montreal's 3rd Militia Battalion on 8 April.

Early in the War of 1812 Lamothe and his Indians were attached to the Voltigeurs Canadiens under the command of Lieutenant-Colonel Charles-Michel d'IRUMBERRY de Salaberry and were used to gather intelligence on American troop movements. When Major-General Wade Hampton invaded Lower Canada in the autumn of 1813, Lamothe was directed to shadow his army and ascertain its probable route. The forces of Hampton and Salaberry clashed at Châteauguay on 26 Oct. 1813; Lamothe and his group of Abenakis, Algonkins, and Iroquois were deployed at the right front of the Canadian line, and were thus involved in some of the fiercest fighting. They acquitted themselves with distinction, and Lamothe received a personal commendation for his part in the battle and for his pursuit of the Americans during the two following days.

The British command had already considered sending Lamothe to the upper Great Lakes because of his familiarity with the region. Major-General Roger Hale Sheaffe*, commander of the troops in the Montreal district, was reluctant to let him go, claiming that "La Mothe is the only efficient officer here to act with the Indians and cannot well be spared." None the less, on 9 July 1814, he departed from Lachine in command of a brigade of canoes bound for Michilimackinac. In the northwest he again acquitted himself with distinction, performing what Johnson later termed "a very hazardous service . . . in an officerlike manner."

Paradoxically, Lamothe's absence in the northwest caused him to be missed when honours and awards were distributed to officers of the Indian Department after the war; worse still, he lost his captaincy. He petitioned for redress, supported by his superiors, and was eventually granted his proper seniority and allowances and restored to permanent rank in the department effective 25 Oct. 1816. He resumed his post at Montreal about that year and continued to serve the Indian Department efficiently. In 1824 he was involved in a survey of Algonkin and Mississauga Ojibwa claims in the Ottawa valley.

On 1 Feb. 1813 Lamothe had married Josette Laframboise in Montreal. They had five children, and his growing family may have contributed to financial difficulties that Lamothe apparently faced by 1823. A general order to purchase and wear the department's new green uniform with black facings and gold buttons may have been a factor as well. He died suddenly on 5 Feb. 1827 at age 45. His widow was granted a pension on the same basis as those provided to widows of regular army officers.

Lamothe's career had been a significant, if minor, one. As a fur trader he had gained a knowledge of native dialects and of the northwest that was greatly appreciated in the Indian Department; as a courageous and able officer he had contributed significantly to the British cause during the War of 1812; and as an efficient administrator he had strengthened the operations of the Indian Department in Lower Canada after the war. In addition, Lamothe's brief life has an aura of romantic adventure that adds to the interest of his story.

DOUGLAS LEIGHTON

ANQ-M, CE1-51, 16 mars 1781, 1er févr. 1813, 8 févr. 1827. PAC, MG 11, [CO 42] Q, 112: 273–83; MG 19, A12; RG 8, I (C ser.), 256: 135–36; 257: 316; 680: 54–56, 332; 1168: 294; 1218: 184; 1219: 126; 1224: 56–57; RG 10, A1, 487; A3, 488; 494; B3, 2368, file no.74316; 10019; RG 68, General index, 1651–1841: 349, 358. *Quebec Gazette*, 26 June, 14 Aug. 1817; 13, 20 Dec. 1821; 24 July, 4 Sept. 1823. *Officers of British forces in Canada* (Irving), 169, 214, 217. T.-M. Charland, *Histoire des Abénakis d'Odanak (1675–1937)* (Montréal, 1964), 324. Benjamin Sulte, *La bataille de Châteauguay* (Québec, 1899); *Histoire de la milice canadienne-française, 1760–1897* (Montréal, 1897). Léon Trépanier, "Guillaume Lamothe (1824–1911)," *Cahiers des Dix*, 29 (1964): 145.

LANDERGAN (Landrigan, Lanergan). *See* LUNDRIGAN

LA ROCHEFOUCAULD, FRANÇOIS-ALEXANDRE-FRÉDÉRIC DE, Duc de LA ROCHEFOUCAULD-LIANCOURT, Duc d'ESTISSAC, author; b. 11 Jan. 1747 in La Roche-Guyon, France, son of Louis-François-Armand de La Rochefoucauld de Roye, Duc d'Estissac, and Marie de La Rochefoucauld, known as Mlle de La Roche-Guyon; m. 10 Sept. 1764 Félicité-Sophie de Lannion, and they had three sons; d. 27 March 1827 in Paris.

When the French revolution began in 1789, François-Alexandre-Frédéric de La Rochefoucauld was elected to the National Constituent Assembly and served a term as its president. A liberal monarchist and confidant of King Louis XVI, he fled to England in 1792 and to Philadelphia in 1794. In May 1795 he embarked on a tour that covered much of the northern United States and Upper Canada. On 20 June, with five associates, he crossed the Niagara River to Fort Erie to be hospitably received by military officials who, the next day, took the party downriver to Fort Chippawa. After viewing Niagara Falls, on 22 June they travelled to Newark (Niagara-on-the-Lake), where they became the guests of Lieutenant Governor John Graves Simcoe*. Although Mrs Simcoe [Elizabeth Posthuma Gwillim*] described the Frenchmen as

Laterrière

"perfectly democratic and dirty," La Rochefoucauld was favourably impressed with his hosts. He witnessed a meeting of the colonial legislature and watched a band of Tuscarora Indians performing dances and playing lacrosse. Simcoe took him on a trip to Burlington Bay (Hamilton Harbour) while his associates visited York (Toronto).

On 10 July the party sailed for Kingston. Simcoe had told La Rochefoucauld that Governor Lord Dorchester [Guy Carleton*], because of concerns about French agents in Lower Canada [see David McLane*], had recently issued an order prohibiting foreigners from entering the colony. Although the duke had then persuaded Simcoe to write to Dorchester on his behalf, this effort came to nothing: on 22 July, while in Kingston, La Rochefoucauld learned that he would not be permitted to travel into Lower Canada. Insulted, the duke left immediately for Oswego, N.Y. In 1799 he returned to France, where his relationship with Bonapartist and Restoration governments was dignified but distant. In 1814 he entered the House of Peers, remaining a member of that body until his death; he also held several honorary posts from which he was dismissed in 1823 because of his liberal opinions. Much of his time was devoted to a model farm on his estate at Liancourt. As well, he maintained the tradition of the Enlightenment, playing the roles of writer and social reformer. His activities and publications were concerned with education, health, poverty, savings banks, and prisons.

The duke's account of his North American journey had been published in Paris, Hamburg (Federal Republic of Germany), and London in 1799. In Upper Canada he had been a meticulous observer. He saw Simcoe's political policies as "liberal and fair," and admired his plans for the settlement and development of the colony. Simcoe's anticipation of the construction of the Trent Canal, his preference for building the economy on agriculture rather than the fur trade, his ideas on defence, all favourably impressed the duke, who nevertheless saw obstacles to such projects; "the greatest of [these] consists in the Governor's determination to return to England at the expiration of five years. A plan of such vast magnitude . . . can be carried into execution by him only, who was able to conceive it." The duke wrote that Simcoe's hatred for the United States had led him to boast of the houses he had burned while campaigning during the American revolution. This statement produced a calm denial from Simcoe.

The lieutenant governor expected a considerable migration from the United States into Upper Canada, but the duke doubted that it would take place, partly because of the obstacles and limitations accompanying the granting of land titles, and partly because he thought that Simcoe overestimated the attachment of many Americans to the British monarchy. La Roche-

foucauld noted the scarcity of hired help; he also claimed that soldiers were sometimes employed by their officers in civilian tasks, and that desertion from the army to free land and financial independence in the United States was a common occurrence. He observed that Simcoe planned to check desertion by offering land to any soldiers who would recruit their own replacements, but he had heard that Lord Dorchester would not agree to this scheme. An anti-imperialist, La Rochefoucauld speculated that Britain's interest would best be served by rendering the Canadas independent.

Less controversial were the duke's reports on the geology, soil, climate, fauna, and flora of the colony. He observed the relations between the white and Indian peoples, and commented on the damaging effects of the use of alcohol. He described grist-mills, sawmills, defence works, and ships. In his narrative he included his impressions of life in Lower Canada based on information gleaned along the way and also on the journal of an associate who was allowed to visit there. He praised the hospitality of his hosts, but admitted that he never felt at home in British Upper Canada, where the anglophone community did not understand that even an *émigré* Frenchman would derive satisfaction from news of French rather than British victories in the European war. So comprehensive a report from an enlightened, cosmopolitan visitor is an invaluable historical document.

T. S. WEBSTER

La Rochefoucauld's account appeared as *Voyage dans les États-Unis d'Amérique, fait en 1795, 1796 et 1797* (8v., Paris, [1799]), and in a two-volume English version, *Travels through the United States of North America, the country of the Iroquois, and Upper Canada, in the years 1795, 1796, and 1797; with an authentic account of Lower Canada*, translated by Henry Neuman and published in London later the same year. A new edition of the section dealing with Upper Canada, based on Neuman's translation and incorporating contemporary comments and corrections by Sir David William Smith*, was prepared by William Renwick Riddell* and issued as "La Rochefoucault-Liancourt's travels in Canada, 1795 . . . ," AO *Report*, 1916.

Other works written by La Rochefoucauld are listed in *Biographie universelle* (Michaud et Desplaces) and *Nouvelle biographie générale . . .* , [J.-C.-F.] Hoefer, édit. (46v., Paris, 1852–66).

F.-A. [Aubert] de La Chesnaye-Desbois et —— Badier, *Dictionnaire de la noblesse . . .* (3e éd., 19v., 1863–76; réimpr., Nendeln, Liechtenstein, 1969). [A.-M.-E.-P.-B. Castellane, Marquis de Castellane], *Gentilshommes démocrates: le vicomte de Noailles, les deux La Rochefoucauld, Clermont-Tonnerre, le comte de Castellane, le comte de Virieu* (Paris, [1891]).

LATERRIÈRE, MARIE-CATHERINE DE SALES. *See* DELEZENNE

389

Laterrière

LATERRIÈRE, PIERRE-JEAN DE SALES. *See* SALES

LE BLANC, ÉTIENNE, merchant, landowner, JP, office holder, politician, and seigneur; baptized 13 Nov. 1759 in Champlain (Que.), son of Jean-Jacques Le Blanc and Marie Héon; m. there 10 May 1796 Josette Richerville, and they had at least one son; d. 11 July 1831 in Trois-Rivières, Lower Canada.

Étienne Le Blanc's parents were among a group of Acadian exiles who spent the winter of 1757–58 at Quebec. The circumstances were scarcely promising since they had to endure the rigours of the Seven Years' War. Many suffered from the severe famine, and by some accounts about 250 of them died of smallpox. A large number of the refugees fled Quebec and settled in the Bécancour region, which they had heard about in Acadia from the Abenakis and the missionaries. Jean-Jacques Le Blanc chose to settle at Champlain in 1758. He opened a small business which did so well that, when the time came, he was able to set his four sons up in good situations, in either farming or business.

Étienne Le Blanc was a merchant at Champlain in 1789. His business seems to have been rather prosperous, since he purchased numerous properties. On 21 April 1795, for example, he paid 700 *livres* for an eleventh of the seigneury of Champlain. In 1796, having obtained a licence, he married Josette Richerville, the under-age daughter of the seigneur of Dutort. The marriage contract stipulated that all the possessions and landed property belonging to the husband would remain his in his own right up to a total of 12,000 *livres*. The jointure was set at 3,000 *livres* and the preference legacy at 1,500 *livres*. On 4 Sept. 1824 Mme Le Blanc renounced community of property and it is thought that she took legal action against her husband for separation of property.

In 1801 Le Blanc moved to Trois-Rivières, where he continued to engage in business. He quickly adapted to his new setting. On 16 Aug. 1803 he was made a justice of the peace for the district, and his commission was renewed in 1805 and 1811. On 6 June 1808 he was appointed a commissioner for the relief of the insane and foundlings, as were Louis Gugy* and Charles Thomas. He was reappointed to this office in 1813, 1821, and 1825. In 1812 Le Blanc, with other residents of Trois-Rivières, sent a declaration to Governor Sir George Prevost* supporting Jewish merchant Benjamin Hart*, who was seeking a commission in the Trois-Rivières battalion of militia. Le Blanc was also a member of the Fire Society.

In 1811 Le Blanc had begun having difficulties with his brother Joseph, who launched an action against him in the Court of King's Bench concerning his lands. In June some of his properties were seized and put up for sale. Joseph apparently did not win his case,

and the disputed properties remained in Étienne's possession. Through various transactions Étienne went on building up a large landed estate. In 1816 he owned the seigneury of Dutort, part of the seigneury of Champlain, several pieces of land in Godefroy and Roquetaillade seigneuries, and a lot in Trois-Rivières. He seems to have devoted the last years of his life to managing his properties.

In 1814 Le Blanc had become a member of the House of Assembly of Lower Canada. Together with Joseph-Rémi Vallières* de Saint-Réal he represented the riding of Saint-Maurice until 1816. He was present in the house only irregularly and infrequently. A moderate, he wanted to retain the French laws that were in force and took a stand against the introduction of English private law.

SONIA CHASSÉ

ANQ-MBF, CE1-7, 13 nov. 1759, 10 mai 1796; CE1-48, 13 juill. 1831; CN1-56, 18 mars, 17, 21, 24 juin, 15 août, 13 oct. 1823; 4, 22 mars, 12 avril, 28 mai, 10 juin, 17 août 1824; 7 avril, 11, 21 juin, 20 juill., 12 sept., 12 déc. 1825; 4 févr., 27 juin, 16 sept., 27 nov. 1826; 29 août 1829; CN1-87, 11, 21 avril 1795; 11 avril, 7, 9 mai 1796. PAC, MG 24, B1, 170: 3960–73; RG 4, A1, 125; 128; RG 68, General index, 1651–1841. L.C., House of Assembly, *Journals*, 1815–16. *Montreal Gazette*, 23 July 1831. *Quebec Gazette*, 9 April 1789; 3 Jan. 1799; 11 June 1801; 30 June 1808; 2 Nov. 1809; 6 Dec. 1810; 27 June, 10 Oct., 26 Dec. 1811; 9 Jan. 1812; 2 Dec. 1813; 1 Aug., 21 Nov. 1816; 24 May, 27 Sept., 8 Oct., 6 Dec. 1821; 22 Aug., 31 Oct., 5 Dec. 1822; 20 July 1831. F.-J. Audet, *Les députés de Saint-Maurice (1808–1838) et de Champlain (1830–1838)* (Trois-Rivières, Qué., 1934). Bona Arsenault, *Histoire et généalogie des Acadiens* (éd. rév., 6v., [Montréal, 1978]), 3. Adrien Bergeron, *Le grand arrangement des Acadiens au Québec* . . . (8v., Montréal, 1981), 5. [Prosper Cloutier], *Histoire de la paroisse de Champlain* (2v., Trois-Rivières, 1915–17), 2. Maurice Grenier, "La chambre d'Assemblée du Bas-Canada, 1815–1837" (thèse de MA, univ. de Montréal, 1966). C.-É. Mailhot, *Les Bois-Francs* (4v., Arthabaska, Qué., 1914–25), 2.

LE COURTOIS, FRANÇOIS-GABRIEL, Roman Catholic priest and Eudist; b. 29 Aug. 1763 in Tirepied, France, son of Jacques Courtois and Marguerite Le Ménager; d. 18 May 1828 in Saint-Laurent, Île d'Orléans, Lower Canada.

François-Gabriel Le Courtois is believed to have begun his studies at the college run by the Eudists in Avranches, France. He joined the order in 1784 and continued his training at Valognes. Ordained priest at Bayeux on 21 Sept. 1787, he was admitted as a member of the community of the Congrégation de Jésus et Marie (Eudists) the following year. Then he taught the Philosophy program at the Collège de Valognes.

During the French revolution Le Courtois refused to

take the oath of allegiance to the Civil Constitution of the Clergy imposed by the National Constituent Assembly on 1 Oct. 1791. He went into exile in England in October 1792, joining some of his colleagues. Two years later, through the agency of Jean-François de La Marche, bishop of Saint-Pol-de-Léon, and at the request of Jean-François Hubert*, bishop of Quebec, Le Courtois was sent to Lower Canada. He reached Quebec in June 1794, along with abbés Louis-Joseph Desjardins*, *dit* Desplantes, Jean-Baptiste-Marie Castanet*, and Jean-Denis Daulé*.

After spending a few days at the Séminaire de Québec, Le Courtois was sent to minister to the parish of Saint-Philippe-et-Saint-Jacques at Saint-Vallier. On 18 September he was transferred to Saint-Nicolas, where his four years as priest proved fruitful. In 1798 Le Courtois asked for a larger charge. Hubert assigned him Rimouski, the king's trading posts, and the Montagnais mission. Ministry to this territory was no sinecure. Besides serving Rimouski, Le Courtois had to cover an area extending from Trois-Pistoles to Sainte-Anne-des-Monts on the south shore of the St Lawrence, as well as the Saguenay, Lac Saint-Jean, and the north shore. The distances were enormous and the means of transportation rudimentary – circumstances to dismay the most intrepid. In May 1799 Le Courtois signed his first entry in the parish registers at Tadoussac. The next year he journeyed beyond Natashquan, on the lower north shore, and there encountered Indians who in some instances had never seen a priest. Because he was unfamiliar with the language of the Montagnais and had difficulty communicating with them, he feared that on his missionary visits he would carry out his ministry badly. Like his predecessors, the Jesuit fathers, he also had to fight against the sale of spirits to the Indians.

In 1806 the bishop of Quebec, Joseph-Octave PLESSIS, put Le Courtois in charge of the parish of Saint-Étienne at La Malbaie. Le Courtois took up his post on 10 Jan. 1807. As the first resident priest in the parish, he made it his business to finish the church, which he subsequently continued decorating. All the gold needed for gilding was brought from France at his expense. He also furnished it with a huge lamp, a basin for holy water, a monstrance, and altar cruets, all in solid silver.

Despite appearances Le Courtois was delicate. By the time he came to the colony, he was suffering from serious disabilities. In 1808 Plessis asked him explicitly to seek medical treatment and to conserve his strength. He added that this kind of need "is what we, strong-willed men who always think we are above being ill, have difficulty understanding." Four years later he sent a deacon to spend the winter with Le Courtois and be initiated into ministry to the Indians.

Judging himself unable to minister to his parish

properly, Le Courtois asked Plessis in September 1822 to give him a smaller one. On condition that he visit the Indians in the Saguenay region from time to time, in November the archbishop assigned him the parish of Saint-Laurent, on Île d'Orleans. Le Courtois took up his task, but his zeal was quickly thwarted by his growing disabilities. He was forced to resign in 1827 and seek permission to live in the presbytery of Saint-Roch parish at Quebec. In the spring of 1828, in an effort to recover his failing health, he returned to Saint-Laurent to live in a parishioner's home. He died there on 18 May.

BASILE BABIN

AD, Manche (Saint-Lô), État civil, Tirepied, 29 août 1763. ANQ-Q, CE1-10, 21 mai 1828. Allaire, *Dictionnaire.* Caron, "Inv. de la corr. de Mgr Denaut," ANQ *Rapport,* 1931–32; "Inv. de la corr. de Mgr Hubert et de Mgr Bailly de Messein," 1930–31; "Inv. de la corr. de Mgr Panet," 1933–34; "Inv. de la corr. de Mgr Plessis," 1927–28; 1928–29. Arthur Buies, *Le Saguenay et la vallée du lac St. Jean* (Québec, 1880). Dionne, *Les ecclésiastiques et les royalistes français.* Charles Guay, *Chronique de Rimouski* (2v., Québec, 1873–74). J.-D. Michaud, *Le Bic, les étapes d'une paroisse* (2v., Québec, 1925–26). É.-T. Paquet, *Fragments de l'histoire religieuse et civile de la paroisse Saint-Nicolas* (Lévis, Qué., 1894). J.-E. Roy, *Hist. de Lauzon.* René Bélanger, "Les prêtres séculiers du diocèse de Québec, missionnaires au Domaine du roi et dans la seigneurie de Mingan, de 1769 à 1845," CCHA *Rapport,* 23 (1955–56): 13–23. Émile George, "À travers vingt-cinq années d'apostolat, les eudistes au Canada, 1896–1916," *Rev. acadienne* (Montréal), 1 (1917): 153–55. J.-C. Taché, "Forestiers et voyageurs; étude de mœurs," *Les Soirées canadiennes; recueil de littérature nationale* (Québec), 3 (1863): 125–28:

LEFRANÇOIS, CHARLES, printer and bookseller; b. probably in 1773 in L'Ange-Gardien, Que., son of Nicolas Lefrançois and Marie Vézina; m. 2 June 1801 Louise Ledroit, *dit* Perche, at Quebec; d. there 1 April 1829.

By the time Charles Lefrançois was born, his family had been settled in the parish of L'Ange-Gardien on the Côte de Beaupré for four generations. Unable to make a living on the family farm, which had been divided into small pieces through the generations, Charles Lefrançois moved to Quebec. He was residing in the *faubourg* Saint-Jean when on 12 May 1798 he was hired as an apprentice printer by Pierre-Édouard DESBARATS and Roger Lelièvre for their workshop. Two days later Desbarats and Lelièvre were officially appointed printers for the Lower Canadian statutes, and on 23 May they bought William Vondenvelden*'s Nouvelle Imprimerie.

To counteract the propaganda against Canadians being printed in the *Quebec Mercury* and to defend the interests of French-speaking members of the profes-

Leigh

sions, Pierre-Stanislas BÉDARD, with the backing of some compatriots, founded a newspaper, *Le Canadien*, which was launched on 22 Nov. 1806. Charles Roi (Roy) was its first printer. Some time in 1807 Lefrançois took over, printing the paper at the Imprimerie Canadienne on Rue Saint-François until 1810. That year, exasperated by criticism of his government, Governor Sir James Henry Craig* decided to muzzle *Le Canadien*. A warrant for the arrest of Lefrançois was signed by executive councillors Thomas Dunn*, François Baby*, and John Young*. On the afternoon of Saturday 17 March soldiers burst into the printing shop, thoroughly searched the premises, took possession of equipment, seized the editorial staff's papers, and took Lefrançois off to prison. The confiscated documents were deposited at the court-house in the presence of Ross Cuthbert*, a justice of the peace. In the days following, the owners and publishers of *Le Canadien*, Bédard, François BLANCHET, and Jean-Thomas TASCHEREAU, were incarcerated. Lefrançois was never brought before the courts and was not released until August.

In October he bought a two-storey stone house he had been renting since May 1809 on Rue Laval, a narrow street behind the Séminaire de Québec, to which he had to pay annual seigneurial dues. He opened a printing shop in this house, where he lived until his death, and over the years he added a bookstore and a bookbinding shop. In the second and third decades of the century new printing shops opened at Quebec, including the establishments of Flavien Vallerand, Charles Vallée, François Lemaître, George J. Wright, and William H. Shadgett, and competition became keen, even cutthroat. Thanks to his experience, Lefrançois was moderately successful in acquiring clients in a world largely dominated by two enterprises, the Neilsons' *Quebec Gazette*, which had been operating for more than half a century, and the Nouvelle Imprimerie, belonging to Desbarats and Thomas Cary* Jr. After 1810 Lefrançois did no more newspaper work but turned out books and pamphlets on his presses; most of these were devotional pieces, often destined for religious institutions or groups at Quebec such as the Grand Séminaire and the Ursuline community. He also did an imposing manual of criminal law by Joseph-François Perrault*.

Lefrançois was afflicted with a liver ailment as a result of his incarceration and he died at Quebec on 1 April 1829. With the consent of the parish priest, Antoine Bédard, a cousin of Pierre-Stanislas, he was buried three days later in the church of Charlesbourg, which was then under construction and is still standing. The printing shop was closed, but Lefrançois's widow made a living by keeping the bookstore open. The *Quebec Gazette* praised Lefrançois as "an honest, industrious, and useful citizen." At a time when printing was often the riskiest of trades, he had

survived for more than two decades. The extent to which he had shared and championed the political positions of *Le Canadien* remains a moot point. As a craftsman and professional above all, he simply set the texts of others and left no written work of his own. Events in 1810 showed that liberty of the press was still uncertain. Seeing their administrations openly criticized by certain papers and not knowing quite how to react, the governors sometimes attacked the printers themselves, putting them behind bars. Like Fleury Mesplet* before him and Ludger Duvernay* after, Lefrançois was both target and scapegoat.

JEAN-MARIE LEBEL

ANQ-Q, CE1-1, 2 juin 1801; CE1-7, 4 avril 1829; CN1-208, 20 janv. 1820, 2 oct. 1822; CN1-262, 12 mai 1798; 1er juin 1801; 21 oct. 1810; 3 nov. 1813; 12 janv., 18 oct. 1815. "Les dénombrements de Québec" (Plessis), ANQ *Rapport*, 1948–49: 163. *Recensement de Québec, en 1818* (Provost), 245. *Quebec Gazette*, 22 March 1810, 2 April 1829. Hare et Wallot, *Les imprimés dans le Bas-Canada*, 217, 229, 315, 352. *Quebec directory*, 1822. Raymond Gariépy, *Les terres de L'Ange-Gardien* (Québec, 1984), 602–3. J. [E.] Hare et J.-P. Wallot, "Les imprimés au Québec (1760–1820)," *L'imprimé au Québec: aspects historiques (18ᵉ–20ᵉ siècles)*, sous la direction d'Yvan Lamonde (Québec, 1983), 110–11. P.-G. Roy, *Toutes petites choses du Régime anglais*, 1: 232–33. Charles Trudelle, *Paroisse de Charlesbourg* (Québec, 1887), 198. N.-E. Dionne, "L'emprisonnement de Pierre Bédard," *BRH*, 6 (1900): 58, 60. Claude Galarneau, "Les métiers du livre à Québec (1764–1859)," *Cahiers des Dix*, 43 (1983): 148, 150, 154. J.-E. Roy, "L'imprimeur Charles Lefrançois," *BRH*, 2 (1896): 95. Charles Trudelle, "L'imprimeur Charles Lefrançois," *BRH*, 2: 126.

LEIGH, JOHN, Church of England minister, lexicographer, and JP; baptized 20 Feb. 1789 in the parish of St Decuman, England, son of Robert Leigh and Maria —; d. unmarried 17 Aug. 1823 in St John's.

John Leigh received his education at St Mary Hall, Oxford, and in 1813 he was ordained an Anglican priest at Wells, Somerset. Three years later the Society for the Propagation of the Gospel sent him to become its first missionary at Twillingate, off the northeast coast of Newfoundland. In March 1819 Leigh became involved with the native Beothuk Indians when the expedition led by John Peyton Jr returned from Red Indian Lake with one of their number, Demasduwit*. Leigh accompanied Demasduwit to St John's, and wrote to the SPG that he believed the society would wish to bend every effort "towards rescuing these poor Creatures from their miserable state." His was one of many humane voices urging an end to the hostilities between the white settlers and the Beothuks, and he was the first clergyman to express publicly an interest in evangelizing them.

To this end, in the summer of 1819 Leigh took

down a fairly extensive vocabulary from Demasduwit. Although there is some overlap with other vocabularies, for example that compiled by John Clinch*, over 200 of the 350 known words of Beothuk may be found in Leigh's notes. Leigh informed the SPG that he proposed to send the vocabulary of Beothuk, which "from the pronounciation [appears to be] somewhat similar to the Welsh language," but there is no record of its receipt in the SPG archives. What appears to have been the original, or at least its remnants, turned up in the possession of a Twillingate family in 1957. A copy of this document, made for John Peyton Jr, was the version published by Thomas George Biddle Lloyd in the *Journal* of the Anthropological Institute of Great Britain and Ireland in 1875 and subsequently by others. Another copy was made by a British naval officer, Hercules Robinson, at Harbour Grace in 1820, and was published by him in the *Journal* of the Geographical Society of London in 1834.

Leigh's health had been eroded by the harsh life on remote South Twillingate Island; in December 1818, for example, he had had scurvy. In the late summer of 1819 he accepted the offer of Commander David Buchan* to transport him to his new mission of Harbour Grace in view of his poor health and the unlikelihood of another vessel being available before winter. Leigh had been a magistrate at Twillingate and continued to be one, administering justice in a surrogate court with Buchan. In July 1820 public indignation was aroused when they ordered the public flogging of Philip Butler and James LUNDRIGAN for contempt of court. Buchan and Leigh were censured and the case was brought to the attention of the British government. As a result, in 1824 surrogate courts were eliminated and provision was made for the appointment of properly trained judges.

The Church of England in Newfoundland early in the 19th century was "entirely without episcopal ministrations" or any other form of church government, and in 1821 Bishop Robert STANSER of Nova Scotia appointed Leigh ecclesiastical commissary to supervise the island's missionaries. Despite his ill health, Leigh threw himself into his work with indefatigable zeal. He reported to the SPG that in 1822 he had journeyed "280 miles in decked vessels and 291 in *open* boats," and he spent the winter of 1822–23 in Bonavista because no other missionary was available. The strain told, and although still young he died on 17 Aug. 1823 after suffering a "severe and painful illness for nearly five weeks."

JOHN HEWSON

USPG, Journal of SPG. SPG, [*Annual report*] (London). John Hewson, *Beothuk vocabularies* (St John's, 1978). Howley, *Beothucks or Red Indians*. Pascoe, *S.P.G.*

LEJAMTEL, FRANÇOIS, Roman Catholic priest and Spiritan; b. 10 Nov. 1757 near Granville, France; d. 22 May 1835 in Bécancour, Lower Canada.

François Lejamtel studied at the Séminaire du Saint-Esprit in Paris and was ordained on 14 June 1783. In either 1786 or 1787 he was sent as a missionary to Saint-Pierre and Miquelon, and assumed responsibility for the parish of La Blouterie on Saint-Pierre. When ordered to take the oath to the Civil Constitution of the Clergy – termed by him an "iniquitous law" – he refused to do so and with another Spiritan priest, Jean-Baptiste Allain*, fled to the Îles de la Madeleine in August 1792. Shortly thereafter he went to Halifax and met with the superintendent of missions, the Reverend James Jones*. After taking the required oath of allegiance to George III of Great Britain as prescribed for Roman Catholics, Lejamtel was assigned to Arichat on Cape Breton Island.

Although installed as pastor of Arichat on 27 Sept. 1792 Lejamtel did not receive a land grant until 1803, and his efforts to establish parish boundaries met with delay. Another annoyance was the difficulty he encountered in gaining control of the Arichat church and presbytery. When Lejamtel arrived in the mission the title to the church property was still in the name of William Phelan, the previous missionary at Arichat, whom Jones had dismissed in April 1792. William Macarmick*, the lieutenant governor of Cape Breton, sympathized with Phelan and, fearing that Lejamtel would encourage disloyalty amongst the Acadians, allowed Phelan to keep the key to the Arichat church. In November 1792, after the heads of 111 Acadian families had petitioned on behalf of Lejamtel and Lejamtel himself had travelled to Sydney to present a certificate confirming that he had taken the oath of allegiance, Macarmick relented and authorized the French priest to take possession of the church. The presbytery, however, was another matter: as late as mid 1794 Lejamtel was complaining that the presbytery was occupied by tenants of Phelan.

Arichat at this time was a small but busy fishing and shipbuilding port and the logical centre for Lejamtel's missionary activities. From there he visited the Indians at Chapel Island, the Acadians at Chéticamp and Magré (Margaree) on the west coast of Cape Breton, as well as the Irish Catholics at Louisbourg and Little Bras d'Or. In 1799 he made his first visit to Sydney and was appalled at the lack of Christian morality in that settlement. Although he was too busy to minister to Sydney frequently and eventually had to stop visiting the area altogether, he did conduct an annual tour there from 1799 to 1811 (with the exception of 1802 and 1805). In addition to this large area in Cape Breton, Lejamtel was required to care for Tracadie on the eastern mainland and, whenever possible, to visit Acadian families at Tor Bay and

Leonard

Molasses Harbour (Port Felix) in present-day Guysborough County. Such districts were remote and travel to them was practically confined to the summer months when ships could easily navigate the rocky shoreline.

Throughout his missionary years Lejamtel kept his superiors informed of his progress. Describing his travels in a letter of 1800 to Joseph-Octave PLESSIS, the coadjutor bishop of Quebec, Lejamtel wrote: "The wheel is always turning. In this way, when I am asked if I am well, I reply that I have no time to be sick. However, when it is God's will, I will have to take the time. I sometimes feel fatigued, but I get my recreation in going from one place to another." Considering the extent of his territory and the difficulty of travelling, his efforts were highly impressive. During the first nine years of his pastorate on Cape Breton and in the period from 1808 to 1814 he was the only priest on the island, and the survival of the Roman Catholic faith there depended mainly on his exertions. In his lifetime he was highly respected by Catholics and Protestants for his learning and the zeal he demonstrated for those under his care. The Acadians and the Micmacs have good reason to remember Lejamtel for his efforts to bring them spiritual consolation under trying conditions.

Lejamtel's notable career as a missionary at Arichat ended in the summer of 1819, when he went to Lower Canada to become parish priest at Bécancour; he was succeeded in Arichat by the Reverend Rémi Gaulin*, later bishop of Kingston. He remained in Bécancour until his retirement on 1 Nov. 1833 and died there on 22 May 1835. An outstanding missionary of the Roman Catholic faith, Lejamtel was the last survivor of the Spiritans who had come to British North America because of the French revolution.

R. A. MacLean

AAQ, 312 CN, I, III, VI (copies at Arch. of the Diocese of Antigonish, N.S.). PANS, RG 20B, 1, 16 March 1803. T. C. Haliburton, *An historical and statistical account of Nova-Scotia* (2v., Halifax, 1829; repr. Belleville, Ont., 1973). J.-O. Plessis, "Journal de deux voyages apostoliques dans le golfe Saint-Laurent et les provinces d'en bas, en 1811 et 1812 ...," *Le Foyer canadien* (Québec), 3 (1865): 73–280; *Journal des visites pastorales de 1815 et 1816, par Monseigneur Joseph-Octave Plessis, évêque de Québec*, Henri Têtu, édit. (Québec, 1903). [R. J.] Uniacke, *Uniacke's sketches of Cape Breton and other papers relating to Cape Breton Island*, ed. C. B. Fergusson (Halifax, 1958). Allaire, *Dictionnaire*, vol. 1. Tanguay, *Répertoire* (1893). Richard Brown, *A history of the island of Cape Breton, with some account of the discovery and settlement of Canada, Nova Scotia, and Newfoundland* (London, 1869). Anselme Chiasson, *Chéticamp: histoire et traditions acadiennes* (Moncton, N.-B., 1961). Johnston, *Hist. of Catholic Church in eastern N.S.*, vol.1. R. J. Morgan, "Orphan outpost." C. W. Vernon, *Cape Breton, Canada, at the beginning of the twentieth century: a treatise of natural resources and development* (Toronto, 1903).

LEONARD, GEORGE, office holder, politician, militia officer, and agricultural improver; b. November 1742 in Plymouth, Mass., son of the Reverend Nathaniel Leonard and Priscilla Rogers; d. 1 April 1826 in Sussex Vale (Sussex Corner), N.B.

Of the fifth generation of his family to live in Massachusetts, George Leonard pursued a conventional existence until the American revolution. He established himself as a "corn and flour" merchant in Boston, clearing £800 annually before the war; he married Sarah Thatcher of Boston on 14 Oct. 1765 and began a family of ten children; and he apparently switched his religious affiliation from the Congregational Church of his father to the Anglican rite. Leonard asserted that he "opposed the riotous proceedings in Boston from the earliest period," and with his childhood friend and fellow loyalist Edward Winslow* he served under Lord Hugh Percy in the battle at Lexington in April 1775. From then until the end of the war and beyond, Leonard's fate was inextricably linked with the loyalist cause.

Leonard participated in the siege of Boston, serving in Abijah Willard*'s company, and in March 1776 was evacuated with the British troops to Halifax. That summer he was present at the British capture of New York City, and in the spring of 1778 he was with the troops in Rhode Island. His most conspicuous service in the war was his command of a small fleet of vessels which raided seacoast towns from southeastern Massachusetts to Long Island Sound in the summer of 1779. Leonard was able to organize this fleet himself, "having been so fortunate as to bring from Boston at the Evacuation . . . the greater part of his Property," the whole of which, "together with all the credit he could obtain," he "cheerfully devoted" to the venture. Winslow, Joshua Upham*, and other frustrated American loyalists, who had thought themselves condemned to be "idle Spectators of the Contest," were also employed in the coastal operations. The raids were a gratifying success, producing the capture of many small vessels, large quantities of livestock, and a number of persons; by mid September sales of the prizes had brought in more than £23,400. On the evacuation of Rhode Island in the fall of 1779, however, Leonard sold his fleet at a loss, "finding that these Vessels would be no longer of any use to Government."

In 1780 Leonard went to England in hopes of receiving compensation for his expenses and of obtaining a pension and other employment in the loyalist cause. There he impressed the secretary of state for the American colonies, Lord George Germain, with a proposal to establish a Board of Associated Loyalists in New York, which could organize

Leonard

additional loyalist offensive excursions on a large scale. The board was formed with Leonard and other loyalist worthies as directors, but the British commanders took little advantage of this new force. Then in 1782 Great Britain renounced all offensive measures, after the defeat at Yorktown, Va, the previous year, and that September the battle-hungry Leonard resigned from the board in disgust. The following month he was awarded a pension of £200 a year.

Like so many loyalists quartered in New York, Leonard resolved to move his family to "the asylum pointed out for the Kings Friends" in the northern British colonies. They arrived at the future Parrtown (Saint John) with the "spring fleet" in 1783 and Leonard was soon made a director of the town, charged with the distribution of town lots. He took this duty seriously; indeed, he seemed to consider himself a guardian of the new settlement whose views on its development must prevail. Leonard's energy and talent were valuable assets in the wilderness, but his self-righteousness antagonized many. When subsequent fleets arrived and the newcomers demanded a redistribution of water lots, which, they claimed, the directors had unfairly assigned to themselves and their friends, Leonard denounced such "Malcontents" and their lawyer, Elias Hardy*. In the spring of 1784 Governor John Parr* of Nova Scotia sent Chief Justice Bryan Finucane to mediate the dispute, and Leonard wildly accused Finucane of crediting "every idle report from Barbers and Grog shops." The chief justice redistributed some of the contested lots, but a hearing before the Nova Scotia Council cleared Leonard and his colleagues of any impropriety in the exercise of their duties. By the time the investigation was held, however, New Brunswick had been created as a separate province, and it may be that the judgement of Parr and his councillors was influenced by diplomatic considerations. Leonard's intense concern to establish the rule of "the Gentlemen" in the new settlements north of the Bay of Fundy had led him to work closely with Winslow and other loyalist officers in effecting the partition of Nova Scotia.

After its establishment in 1784, the new colony of New Brunswick engaged all of Leonard's imagination and loyalty. He spent the remaining 25 years of his active life trying to build up strong community institutions in the province and protect its trade from American competition. His appointment in 1786 to succeed Jonathan Binney* as superintendent of trade and fisheries at Canso, N.S., charged with enforcing the navigation acts against American smugglers, seemed highly appropriate for this loyalist merchant. Yet it was an impossible task. For neither the officers of the revenue nor the popular assemblies of Nova Scotia or New Brunswick would support Leonard's efforts. Visits to England and a constant stream of letters to imperial officials and his agent in London,

William Knox, expressed Leonard's fierce determination to suppress this "Illicit Trade" and make the colonies a "nursery of seamen" for the empire. In 1797 he did get his jurisdiction increased to include all of the Maritime provinces, and permission was granted to use armed vessels, but, although he had suggested that for reasons of economy the post of superintendent be combined with the lieutenant governorship of either Cape Breton or St John's (Prince Edward) Island, the higher position eluded him.

Leonard's zeal to enforce the navigation acts produced one of the great moments of comic opera in early New Brunswick history. At the turn of the century Great Britain was engaged in a mighty conflict with Napoleon and was therefore most anxious to maintain amicable relations with the United States. Oblivious to this larger concern, Leonard pursued his aggressive enforcement policy and in 1805 seized the American ship *Falmouth* for illegally trading in British waters. In the remarkable trial that followed the two British customs officers defended the *Falmouth*'s activities as having been sanctioned by informal agreement. Judge William Botsford* sought to mediate the dispute by condemning the *Falmouth*'s cargo but refusing to fine the ship's owners and at the same time reprimanding Leonard from the bench. Undeterred, Leonard advertised in the newspaper his determination to continue prosecuting smugglers "from the late revolted colonies," and his headstrong course was only halted after an outraged complaint from the British ambassador in Washington. Yet Leonard never conceded he had erred. His only crime, he told Winslow, was "too much zeal."

Zeal was indeed Leonard's merit and his undoing. His contributions to the settlement of New Brunswick were outstanding. While living in Saint John he served as an alderman and also as chamberlain and treasurer of the city. He was a member of the Council from 1790 to his death, a trustee of the college at Fredericton and of the academy in Saint John, a founder of the masonic lodge in Saint John, lieutenant colonel of the militia in Kings County, quartermaster of the provincial militia, a stalwart supporter of the New England Company's efforts to establish Indian schools in the province [see Oliver ARNOLD], and a benefactor of the Church of England. He tried to get a bishopric for New Brunswick and sought through his English friends to raise funds for a classical library. Yet many of his projects failed because of his contempt for popular politics and "the peasantry," as he termed them. The printer Christopher Sower* once provoked a fight with the much stronger Leonard in the belief it would advance his electoral prospects. And Leonard's inability to brook criticism over the management of the Indian school at Sussex Vale cost the support of Chief Justice George Duncan Ludlow* and other important officials. Few of Leonard's papers survive. Those that do display a man warm in friendship and generous in his enthusiasms. Among the small cadre of loyalists who governed New Brunswick in its early years, he seems to have been the most imprisoned by memories of his youth in Massachusetts and his wartime triumphs. He sought in New Brunswick to reproduce that earlier colonial society and reverse the verdict of the revolution.

Leonard's private pursuits proved more rewarding than his public life. Although he owned a substantial house in Saint John, his principal residence – likened by Bishop Charles Inglis* to a "European Villa" – was in Sussex Vale, an agricultural community 40 miles northeast of the city on the Kennebecasis River. This "pleasant valley" had earlier been marked off by the French as a site for seigneurial estates, and during the loyalist period it was praised repeatedly by travellers for its beauty, fertility, and abundance of fish, game, and wild fruit. Not only did Leonard make strenuous efforts to settle families and improve roads in the area, but he became the paternalistic benefactor of his neighbours, thanks in large part to the capital he had accumulated as a merchant in Boston, the compensation of almost £5,000 he received for his wartime losses, and the income of £200 he drew as superintendent of trade and fisheries. These sums enabled Leonard, according to Colonel Joseph Gubbins, to invest the remarkable amount of £8,000 in clearing and developing his lands at Sussex Vale.

In 1792 Patrick CAMPBELL reported enthusiastically on his ventures: "Mr. Lenard told me that he had a natural meadow of wild hay of vast extent, about two miles, of which he permitted the neighbouring inhabitants to carry off as much as they pleased; that he had pasture enough in his woods for several hundred head of cattle, of which he made no use whatever; that he had 200 Sheep, twenty Milk Cows with their followers, some Mares, Oxen, and Horses." Campbell was even more impressed by Leonard's willingness to let out such well-stocked lands to tenants on shares, with the profits to be divided equally after three years. To Campbell this method of proceeding seemed an ideal opportunity for an immigrant farmer who was intent upon "bettering his own condition." Twenty years later Gubbins singled out Leonard's far-sighted interest in agricultural improvements, particularly livestock breeding. Gubbins also noted that the collapse of land values in New Brunswick had more than halved the market value of Leonard's estate, but no one faulted Leonard's vision or his importance for the Sussex valley. He graced his efforts with a philanthropy reminiscent of the English squirearchy, making numerous gifts to local educational and religious projects, and with a personal style that was both "genteel and hospitable."

Leonard gradually retired from public life after 1809. A painful illness marked his final days and

when, on the death of Lieutenant Governor George Stracey SMYTH in 1823, he became eligible through seniority for the presidency of the Council he turned the post down owing to "my age and infirmities." He died in 1826, two months after the decease of his wife of 60 years. His son George Jr had drowned while on a hunting expedition in 1818. There were three other sons and six daughters.

ANN GORMAN CONDON

PAC, MG 23, D1, ser.1, 21: 43–112. PANS, MG 1, 480, 9–11 Aug. 1792 (transcripts). PRO, CO 188/9, Leonard to John King, 10 Sept. 1798; 188/10, Leonard to Duke of Portland, 1 Nov. 1800; 188/16, "Reports of officers of governments on duties and emoluments," 1810; PRO 30/55, no.5577. P. Campbell, *Travels in North America* (Langton and Ganong). G.B., Commission Appointed to Enquire into the Losses of American Loyalists, *American loyalists; transcript of the manuscript books and papers of the commission of enquiry into the losses and services of the American loyalists . . . preserved amongst the Audit Office records in the Public Record Office of England, 1783–1790 . . .* (60v., [London], 1898–1903), 14: 117–18, 136, 175; 28: 283. Gubbins, *N.B. journals* (Temperley). *Winslow papers* (Raymond). *DAB*. G.B., Hist. MSS Commission, *Report on American manuscripts in the Royal Institution of Great Britain*, [comp. B. F. Stevens, ed. H. J. Brown] (4v., London, 1904–9). Esther Clark Wright, *The loyalists of New Brunswick* (Fredericton, 1955; repr. Moncton, N.B., 1972, and Hantsport, N.S., 1981). Gorman Condon, "Envy of American states." MacNutt, *New Brunswick*. Judith Fingard, "The New England Company and the New Brunswick Indians, 1786–1826: a comment on the colonial perversion of British benevolence," *Acadiensis* (Fredericton), 1 (1971–72), no.2: 29–42.

LÉRY, LOUIS-RENÉ CHAUSSEGROS DE. *See* CHAUSSEGROS

LE SAULNIER, CANDIDE-MICHEL, Roman Catholic priest and Sulpician; b. 26 May 1758 in Doville, France, son of François Le Saulnier, a farmer, and Magdelainne Le Mouton; d. 4 Feb. 1830 in Montreal.

Candide-Michel Le Saulnier studied in the strictly gallican milieu of the faculty of theology in Paris. After five years he was ordained on 21 Sept. 1782 and was admitted as a member of the community of the Society of Saint-Sulpice. He then undertook a variety of tasks, including that of bursar at the Séminaire de Reims. He was still there when the revolution broke out in 1789. Following the example of his superior, Jacques-André Émery, and his confrères, he refused to take the oath of loyalty to the Civil Constitution of the Clergy. In the spring of 1791, when the bishops who had taken the oath were installed, he apparently thought of going into exile, as numerous non-juring priests were doing. Having obtained in July 1792 from the municipal offices in Rheims a passport for travelling within the country – a document which specified that he was 5 feet 2 inches tall, and had a round, full face, prominent forehead, well-shaped nose, grey eyes, light brown hair, medium-sized mouth, and round chin – Le Saulnier made his way out of France to Jersey. There he spent five months untouched by the hunt for non-juring priests being initiated in his homeland.

Le Saulnier left in 1793 for London, where nearly 3,000 French ecclesiastics had already sought refuge, and on arriving met Sulpician François-Emmanuel Bourret, who probably introduced him to the home secretary, Henry Dundas. Dundas gave him a letter of recommendation to the lieutenant governor of Lower Canada, Alured CLARKE, on 30 May 1793. On 15 July Le Saulnier landed at Quebec, where he was given a friendly reception; this response reflected a complete change in the British policy on the immigration of French subjects and it opened the door to the foreign recruits badly needed by the church in Lower Canada [see Jean-François Hubert*].

The Séminaire de Saint-Sulpice in Montreal immediately put Le Saulnier to work in the parish of Notre-Dame. He endeavoured to familiarize himself with his new surroundings and to learn English at the same time. The council of the seminary meanwhile pondered the delicate legal question of whether he should be made a member of the community as if he were not a Sulpician, in order to protect the seminary from any accusation of being organically united to the French society, or whether he should be taken in as a Sulpician joining colleagues in Montreal. It did not wish to risk weakening the position of the seminary in its dispute with the British government over seigneurial rights but, internally, the dominant place of French members in the institution was at stake. The council opted for the second solution. Le Saulnier swore the oath of loyalty to the king, and three months after his arrival he was received as a colleague, with the same rights and privileges, including that of receiving the fraternal kiss, and with the seniority he had enjoyed in France.

In mid November 1793 Le Saulnier became the fifteenth parish priest of Notre-Dame, replacing François-Xavier Latour-Dézery, the only Canadian ever to have held that charge. In view of Le Saulnier's experience, Bishop Hubert had thought of him rather for the office of bursar in the seminary. The Canadian-born Hubert would perhaps have preferred a Canadian Sulpician – Joseph Borneuf* in particular – as parish priest, because the recruiting of French priests into the Séminaire de Saint-Sulpice would cut short the newly begun process of Canadianizing this last bastion of French ecclesiastical power and would exacerbate a conflict between Canadian and French Sulpicians. The Canadian members saw the Montreal seminary as an important component of Canadian institutions and insisted that they had to be able to influence its policy. The French considered that even though the seminary was legally separate from the Paris one, it had to remain a French institution and by implication power had to be permanently consolidated in the hands of members of French origin. On arriving in Montreal, the French Sulpicians moved directly into senior positions. However non-committal he remained in his social relationships, Le Saulnier found himself siding with the French during the difficult period of integration that followed the arrival at the seminary of 11 new French Sulpicians in 1794. He likewise backed the seminary in the violent conflict it became engaged in with Bishop Jean-Jacques Lartigue* in 1821 over the issue of ecclesiastical authority in the District of Montreal [see Jean-Charles BÉDARD; Augustin CHABOILLEZ].

When the superior, Jean-Henry-Auguste ROUX, went to London in the summer of 1826 to settle the problem of the seminary's seigneurial rights, his departure provided the occasion for Le Saulnier to take charge of the seminary. He seemed to adopt a softer line. He re-established contact with Bishop Lartigue and reduced the tensions between Canadians and French within the institution. He even sided with the Canadians when a power struggle broke out in earnest between the two groups after Roux brought back from London in August 1828 an agreement that required the seminary to hand over some of its seigneurial rights to the British government in return for a fixed and perpetual annuity. It was during this difficult period that Le Saulnier, who was then ill and extremely weak, expressed his wish to be relieved of the parish charge and of all worldly concerns.

On the pastoral side, Le Saulnier had given his energies to administrative tasks and preaching, as well as to directing a team of assistant priests; these priests shared the work of visiting the various quarters of the town and caring for the 2–3,000 poor who lined up for food, shelter, money, and firewood. He thus had the opportunity to exhort the faithful to be loyal to the king at the time of the Napoleonic Wars and the American threat in 1812. In his ministry he recalled his parishioners to the religious view of the world and to an understanding of history as governed by a providence destining salvation for only the elect. From 1808 that ministry saw growing numbers of the faithful, beginning with those who were educated and active, gradually move away from religious obligations, so that by 1830 only 40 per cent of the people were still taking their Easter Communion. The chronic dearth of places of worship in the parish scarcely encouraged religious fervour. The parish church was already too small when Le Saulnier took charge in 1793. Not until 1823 was thought given to replacing it with the church building that still stands [see James O'DONNELL]. In

Letendre

1814 Le Saulnier had had chapels built at Saint-Henri-des-Tanneries (Saint-Henri, Montreal) and Côte-des-Neiges, and these were visited by a priest once a month.

Le Saulnier made quite an important contribution to cultural life in the Montreal region. Beginning in 1796 he set up with Philippe-Jean-Louis DESJARDINS in Quebec and Bourret in London an efficient network for bringing books to Montreal, with emphasis on devotional and religious works. He was also active in establishing primary schools outside the town, at Côte-des-Neiges, in the *faubourg* Saint-Antoine, at Saint-Henri-des-Tanneries, and in the *faubourg* Québec.

Less well known than his superior Roux, who was heavily involved in the political and economic scene, Le Saulnier left behind the memory of a pastor who was resourceful in administration, admired for truly classical eloquence, and endowed with a diplomacy particularly sought after throughout the internal and external crises that marked his career in Montreal. Late in the summer of 1829 he became completely paralysed and could communicate only with his eyes. At his funeral, Bishop Lartigue himself gave the absolution in the presence of an immense crowd of the faithful, a final token of respect for Le Saulnier's long ministry.

LOUIS ROUSSEAU

Arch. de la Compagnie de Saint-Sulpice (Paris), Dossiers 55, no.12; 67, no.10; 76, no.7; MSS 1208. ASSM, 9; 11; 16–18; 21; 24, dossier 2; 27–28; 49. "Quelques prêtres français en exil au Canada," ANQ *Rapport*, 1966: 141–90. Gauthier, *Sulpitiana*. Bernard Plongeron, *Conscience religieuse en révolution; regards sur l'historiographie religieuse de la Révolution française* (Paris, 1969). Louis Rousseau, *La prédication à Montréal de 1800 à 1830; approche religiologique* (Montréal, 1976).

LETENDRE, *dit* **Batoche, JEAN-BAPTISTE** (also known as **Okimawaskawikinam**), fur trader and farmer; b. 30 Aug. 1762 in Sorel (Que.), son of Jean-Baptiste Letendre (1736–1809) and Marie-Madeleine Cardin, *dit* Loiseau (1742–1808); m. *c.* 1785 *à la façon du pays* Josephte "Crise," a member of the Cree nation, in the northwest; d. in or after 1827, probably in St Boniface (Man.).

Jean-Baptiste Letendre, *dit* Batoche, came to the northwest in the 1780s. In 1785–86 he was employed by the North West Company in the Athabasca department as a "devant" or bowsman. He is listed as an interpreter in the region of Fort des Prairies (Fort-à-la-Corne, Sask.) in 1804. Marie-Anne Gaboury* and Jean-Baptiste Lagimonière*, who spent some time in the area in 1808, are reported to have met the Canadian Batoche and his Cree family. In 1810 Letendre or his son, who was also called Jean-Baptiste, was with the explorer David Thompson*. In his diary Thompson mentions that Letendre and his family arrived from the region near Beaverhill Lake (Alta), bringing a hundred or so beaver pelts. That year Letendre or his son went with Thompson to explore the Athabasca River as far as the Rockies but quit the expedition in January 1811 at the camp on the Canoe River (B.C.), a tributary of the Columbia.

In the 1810s and 1820s it appears that Letendre engaged in the fur trade on his own account as a "freeman," to use an expression common in the northwest. Alone or with his family he owned a trading post called Batoche at Muskootao Point, west of Fort-à-la-Corne on the north bank of the Saskatchewan. The Letendres also stayed for a time in the Red River colony (Man.) during this period. On 19 June 1816 one of their sons was killed in the engagement at Seven Oaks (Winnipeg), known in historical writings by the Métis and French of the west as La Grenouillère [*see* Cuthbert Grant*; Robert Semple*]. The NWC agreed to pay Mme Letendre compensation for this unfortunate accident because of the "good character her husband always bore."

Around 1825 the Letendres came from Rocky Mountain House (Alta), known by francophones as "poste de la montagne de Roches," to settle at St Boniface. On 6 June of that year Letendre's sons Jean-Baptiste and Louis (Louison) and his daughters Josephte and Angélique were married in religious ceremonies. In 1827 Letendre, his wife, and eight children were living on lot 906. Two of their sons occupied land near by with their families. Letendre was a well-to-do farmer, but he was keeping a family of 40. He owned seven horses, a herd of cattle, a canoe, and two carts. It is worth noting that he was farming 50 acres at a time when even the Catholic mission only cultivated 25.

No trace of Letendre has been found after 1827. He is not listed as head of a household or owner of a lot in the 1828 census, or in those that followed. His son Jean-Baptiste settled at Pembina (N.Dak.) around 1850. As for Louis, he made regular trips to the Fourche des Gros Ventres (as the South Saskatchewan River was known) and the post called La Montée on the North Saskatchewan. In 1849 he was one of the Métis who protested against the HBC's fur-trade monopoly, at the time of the Sayer affair [*see* Pierre-Guillaume Sayer*]. The Letendre family carried on business both on its own account and for the HBC in the area around Fort Carlton (Sask.) in the 1850s and 1860s and settled permanently in that region around 1870. In 1872 Jean-Baptiste's grandson François-Xavier founded the village of Batoche on the South Saskatchewan River. It was Batoche that became the centre of Métis resistance in 1885 and the Métis capital of the northwest.

DIANE PAULETTE PAYMENT

Arch. de la Soc. hist. de Saint-Boniface (Saint-Boniface, Man.), Dossier Marius Benoist; Dossier famille Letendre; Notes généal. de l'abbé Pierre Pictou sur la famille Letendre, dit Batoche. Arch. hist. oblates (Ottawa), Reg. de baptêmes de Lac-Sainte-Anne (Alberta), 1. Bureau of Indian Affairs (Belcourt, N.Dak.), Pembina reg. PAM, HBCA, D.4/7: ff.59, 160; E.5/1–9; E.24/3, 1825–26: 67; F.2/1; MG 7, D8. Saskatchewan Arch. Board (Regina), A. S. Morton, "Historical geography of Saskatchewan," 10, map. *Les bourgeois de la Compagnie du Nord-Ouest* (Masson), 1: 397. *New light on the early history of the greater northwest: the manuscript journals of Alexander Henry . . . and of David Thompson . . .*, ed. Elliott Coues (3v., New York, 1897; repr. 3v. in 2, Minneapolis, Minn., [1965]), 2. W.-J. Letendre, *Dictionnaire généalogique des Letendre d'Amérique (Canada & États-Unis)* (6v., Sherbrooke, Qué., 1981), 1: 15, 25. A.-G. Morice, *Dictionnaire historique des Canadiens et des Métis français de l'Ouest* (Québec et Montréal, 1908), 186. George Dugas, *La première canadienne du Nord-Ouest ou biographie de Marie-Anne Gaboury . . .* (Montréal, 1883), 48–49, 59. Marcel Giraud, *Le Métis canadien; son rôle dans l'histoire des provinces de l'Ouest* (Paris, 1945), 1047. Diane Payment, "Monsieur Batoche," Centre d'études franco-canadiennes de l'Ouest, *Bull.* (Saint-Boniface), no.10 (février 1982): 2–11; no.11 (mai 1982): 2–16; "Monsieur Batoche," *Saskatchewan Hist.* (Saskatoon, Sask.), 32 (1979): 81–103.

LEWIS, ASAHEL BRADLEY, journalist; b. 1804 or 1805 in Whitehall, N.Y., son of Barnabas Lewis and Amy Bradley; m. 9 April 1827 Alma Hopkins Freeman in St Thomas, Upper Canada, and they had at least three children; d. there 13 or 14 Oct. 1833.

The date of Asahel Bradley Lewis's arrival in Upper Canada is not known. At the time of his marriage in 1827 he was a "yeoman" living in Malahide Township. Later he edited the St Thomas *Liberal*, the organ of a so-called "Liberal" party, from its founding in September 1832 until his death the following year. In these few months the *Liberal* took advantage of changing reform politics at the provincial level to manipulate and organize local opinion perhaps more effectively, and certainly more originally, than had any other reform journal up to this time. Involved here was an attempt to unseat Mahlon Burwell* and Roswell MOUNT, representatives of Middlesex County in the House of Assembly, who were supported by Colonel Thomas Talbot*, the most formidable political figure in the county. Involved here too was an attempt to unite such factional, sectional, ethnic, and ideological opposition as already existed to these men with the object of establishing in place of Talbot's political machinery a new machine controlled by a group of not very popular American merchants. Based in St Thomas, this group was interested in improving Kettle Creek and its outlet into Lake Erie.

According to Lewis, the *Liberal* was financed by 50 local stockholders of Middlesex County. They were probably scattered throughout townships where early in 1832 meetings had been called by agents of the radical York Central Committee seeking signatures to petitions. Lewis acted as secretary at the first meeting, held on 4 February in Malahide. Here resolutions were passed condemning Burwell and Mount for supporting the expulsion of William Lyon Mackenzie* from the assembly and for their stands on reporting the proceedings of the house, the intestate estates bill, the libel bill, and the clergy reserves. These were all provincial, as distinguished from local, issues; as such, they are the first on record for Middlesex.

More important, however, a framework for permanent party organization was laid down. Thus Lewis and eight others were named to a Malahide subcommittee to convene meetings and act in concert with other township organizations. Out of all this emerged a county committee of three – Lewis, George Lawton, a radical Englishman from Yarmouth, and Lucius Bigelow, a St Thomas merchant of American origin. In September 1832 the *Liberal* began publication. The next month George Gurnett*, editor of the *Courier of Upper Canada* (York [Toronto]), charged that the *Liberal* was "*edited and owned* by four individuals at St Thomas who are lately from the United States" – he probably had in mind Lewis, Bigelow, and two other St Thomas merchants also of American origin, Josiah C. Goodhue and Bela Shaw. (It was in denying this claim that Lewis referred to stockholders around the county.) Lewis and the reformers associated with the paper were a dominant force behind the party they called not "Reform" but "Liberal," a label used nowhere else in Upper Canada.

The term is as significant as it is curious. It of course did not come from the British Liberal party, the father of which, William Ewart Gladstone, was then on the point of entering politics as a Tory. But it did come from Westminster, where in 1832 it meant a ministerialist too advanced to be called a Whig but not sufficiently advanced to be called a radical. Lewis and his friends were somewhat nativistic North American radical democrats who, hoping to shed their identification with American republicanism, represented themselves as standing in a tradition of moderate British reform.

In this they were prudent, if mendacious. From its origins the district had been torn by loyalist-republican conflict which had climaxed during the War of 1812. Just prior to that affray, Talbot had successfully contrived to elect Burwell in place of Benajah Mallory*, who soon turned traitor. Against the backdrop of this past history, a correspondent to the *Liberal*, expressing a view probably shared by Lewis and other like-minded reformers, argued that the homesick British immigrants now flooding the colony possessed "Liberal Principles and liberal

Liancourt

feelings." But "so nicely have the government and York gentry arranged matters, that they are able . . . effectually to smother all such sentiment." This argument displayed no understanding of immigrant psychology and vastly exaggerated the government's ability to bring official pressures to bear on such persons. The fact remains, however, that the *Liberal* bent itself to revivify reformist sentiment among Upper Canadian immigrants.

The success of the "quibbling Junto faction, who call themselves liberals" is suggested by the strength of the opposition organized by Colonel Talbot. The colonel's followers were numerous; some were also violent. "Ripstavers and Gallbursters" broke up the liberals' 4th of July celebrations of 1832, and an attempt to found a St Thomas political union was frustrated by "Loyal Guards" in January 1833. This same year the office of the *Liberal* was wrecked and its presses thrown down the hill on which it stood. Lewis, ill with typhus fever, rose from his sick-bed to view the damage. He then suffered a relapse and died, at the age of 28; an obituary in the Kingston *Chronicle & Gazette* gives the date of death as 13 Oct. 1833, but 14 October is the day given in another obituary in the *Christian Guardian*. In the election held the next year the liberal campaign was crowned with success, both Burwell and the other tory candidate, Joseph Brant Clench* of Muncey Town, being defeated by Elias Moore and Thomas Parke*.

G. H. PATTERSON

AO, MU 1128, Donald MacMillan, geneal. papers, biog. and geneal. notes on Amasa Lewis and family. "Register of baptisms, marriages, and deaths, at St. Thomas, U.C., commencing with the establishment of the mission in July, 1824," *OH*, 9 (1910): 164. *The Talbot papers*, ed. J. H. Coyne (2v., Ottawa, 1908–9). *Christian Guardian*, 15 Feb. 1832, 30 Oct. 1833. *Chronicle & Gazette*, 2 Nov. 1833. *Colonial Advocate*, 26 Oct. 1833. *Liberal* (St Thomas, [Ont.]), 25 Oct., 15, 29 Nov. 1832. *Illustrated historical atlas of the county of Elgin, Ont.* (Toronto, 1877; repr. Port Elgin, Ont., 1972). C. O. [Z.] Ermatinger, *The Talbot regime; or the first half century of the Talbot settlement* (St Thomas, 1904). Élie Halévy, *A history of the English people . . .*, trans. E. I. Watkin and D. A. Barker (6v., London, [1924]–34), 3. Patterson, "Studies in elections in U.C." C. [F.] Read, *The rising in western Upper Canada, 1837–8: the Duncombe revolt and after* (Toronto, 1982). Ian Mac-Pherson, "The *Liberal* of St. Thomas, Ontario, 1832–33," *Western Ontario Hist. Notes* ([London]), 21 (1965), no.1: 10–29.

LIANCOURT. *See* LA ROCHEFOUCAULD

LINDSAY, WILLIAM (usually he signed **William Lindsay Jr**), merchant, militia officer, office holder, and JP; b. *c.* 1761 in Great Britain, son of William Lindsay; d. 11 Jan. 1834 at Quebec, and was buried 14 January in Saint-Charles-Borromée parish at Charlesbourg, Lower Canada.

William Lindsay was about 12 when his father settled at Quebec around 1773. Lindsay Sr, a Scot, had been sent as a youth to London, where he had become a clerk with merchant Robert Hunter, and then a joint owner in the firm of Lawrie, Lindsay, and Thompson. At Quebec he went into partnership with a man named Brash. At the time of the American invasion of 1775–76 [*see* Benedict Arnold*; Richard Montgomery*], he enlisted in the militia, rising to the rank of lieutenant; during the siege of Quebec he kept a journal. In 1778 he and Adam Lymburner* were the Quebec agents of the London Underwriters, and in 1789 he was one of the original shareholders in the Dorchester Bridge [*see* David Lynd*]. In May 1797 he was appointed controller to audit the customs office accounts as well as customs collector at St Johns (Saint-Jean-sur-Richelieu), where he remained until his death in 1822.

William Jr went into partnership with merchant William McNider in February 1783 under the name Lindsay and McNider to open a retail store near the harbour, on Rue Saint-Pierre. Business seems to have been good, since on 17 June 1790 he married Marianne Melvin; they were to have four children. That year he became an ensign in the Quebec Battalion of British Militia and also performed the duties of adjutant with the rank of lieutenant, a rank to which he was in fact promoted around 1795. He was made a captain in the 3rd Battalion of the town's militia in 1805, and then major in 1812.

While continuing to carry on his dry and wet goods business, Lindsay entered the public service in 1792 as clerk assistant of the Lower Canadian House of Assembly. To these occupations were added those of justice of the peace for the district of Quebec in 1799 and secretary in 1805 of a joint stock company founded that year to provide the town with a fine hotel, the Union Company of Quebec, in which he also served as treasurer from 1813. He retained both offices in the enterprise until at least 1823. By a commission dated 6 Dec. 1805 he had been appointed clerk of Trinity House of Quebec [*see* François Boucher*] and later he also became its treasurer, receiving commissions in 1808 and 1830.

But Lindsay is known above all for his role in the assembly. Having been clerk assistant since 1792, on 7 Aug. 1808, because of "his experience and knowledge," he was commissioned clerk, replacing Samuel Phillips who was suffering from a "severe indisposition." He thus was the second person to hold that office in Lower Canada.

When the first session of the fifth parliament opened on 10 April 1809, Lindsay took up all his new duties. He received the oaths of allegiance of the members of the Legislative Council and the House of Assembly in the room reserved for the clerk, "commonly called the

Ward Robe." After presiding over the election of Jean-Antoine Panet* as speaker of the house, he was instructed to "revise and print the rules and regulations of the house." Thus began an arduous, and poorly paid, chapter in the life of Lindsay, under the orders of an assembly insistent on report after report. His tasks multiplied: purchasing items needed in the house, hiring workmen, superintending works, collecting debts, and paying accounts. Acording to historian Marc-André Bédard, in 1812 the clerk was no longer "a mere secretary to the house but had become in a way its administrator." That year Lindsay asked for a raise in salary but it was not granted until 1815 and then brought the added responsibility of printing bills. Because of this increase in workload, he had to hire some "extra writers" or part-time employees. A special committee on the contingent accounts also recommended the appointment of lawyer Robert Christie* as law clerk and he took up his duties on 26 Jan. 1816.

In 1818, after an inquiry, the special committee pronounced Lindsay's work satisfactory. The following year, however, there was stricter supervision. The assembly laid down rules for the working hours of its officials and extra writers. When the house was in session these were to be from 9 A.M. to 2 P.M., from 3 P.M. to 8 P.M., and after that until business for the day was finished. In addition the assembly insisted that the clerk furnish them with a list of the employees and their "respective duties" and salaries. On 26 March 1820 a special committee concluded that all the positions were necessary and gave a vote of confidence to Lindsay, whose role as manager and responsible official was thus confirmed.

But Lindsay's troubles were not over. In 1824 another special committee, set up to study the assembly's contingent accounts, recommended an overall reduction of 25 per cent in the salaries of all the "officials and writers," and also insisted upon the urgent need to enforce work schedules and prevent employees from attending to "any outside matters during their working hours." Lindsay was at odds with the committee over the translating (especially the translating into French) of the official journal of the House of Assembly and the salaries of those recording the proceedings. In 1828 the assembly passed a motion giving the clerk responsibility for "filling the empty positions in the house" but reserving the right to approve or reject appointments.

These administrative annoyances and the weight of his years severely taxed Lindsay's health. In November 1828 he had a medical certificate delivered to the speaker attesting that he had been "seriously ill at different times during the summer" and was now "confined to his room." Dr Joseph Morrin* gave it as his opinion that at his age (about 67) Lindsay needed "more rest, mentally and physically, than he has had up till now." Lindsay recommended his son William

Burns to the assembly as deputy clerk, a recommendation immediately accepted. On 30 Sept. 1829 young Lindsay officially succeeded his father, who passed away on 11 Jan. 1834, his age being recorded as 73.

William Lindsay, who had given unbroken service to the assembly since 1792, founded a veritable dynasty of clerks, for his son was succeeded in that office by his own son, also named William Burns, who held the post until confederation and then became the first clerk of the House of Commons in Ottawa, an office he retained until 1872. Pierre-Georges Roy* praised William Lindsay for having "always given satisfaction to [the] members of the House of Assembly, even though [they were] rather cantankerous and hard to serve."

YVON THÉRIAULT

[William Lindsay, clerk of the Lower Canadian House of Assembly, is wrongly credited in BRH, 45 (1939): 225–47, with the authorship of "Narrative of the invasion of Canada by the American provincials under Montgomery and Arnold . . . ," Canadian Rev. and Magazine (Montreal), no.4 (February 1826): 337–52, and no.5 (September 1826): 89–104. The journal, published 50 years after the American invasion, was in fact written by his father, William Lindsay, the customs collector at Saint-Jean, who died in 1822.

The text is in three parts. The first puts the invasion in the context of the Quebec Act and discusses the call issued by the Americans to the Canadians and their hesitation to invade the colony (1774–75). The middle section contains an account of the taking of forts Chambly and Saint-Jean (both in Quebec), and Ticonderoga (near Ticonderoga, N.Y.). The last part is an account of the capitulation of Montreal, and it concludes at the point when Arnold reaches the undefended town of Quebec.

Under the title of "Le siège de Québec en 1775–1776," the BRH for 1939 published extracts from the second part of the original text, selected to form a chronological montage of the period 6 Nov.–31 Dec. 1775, and similar extracts from the third part, covering the period up to May 1776. Official documents, such as the correspondence and views of General Montgomery, and the replies of Governor Guy Carleton*, are not altered in the BRH version, but the original account is sometimes cut. The biographical sketch accompanying this text confuses father and son, a fact made clear by the many details concerning the real author of the account that are given in the February 1826 article. Y.T.]

ANQ-Q, CE1-1, 14 janv. 1834; CE1-66, 17 juin 1790. PAC, RG 68, General index, 1651–1841: 74, 335, 348, 360, 654, 682. L.C., House of Assembly, Journals, 12 Feb., 25 March 1805; 1808: 23, 45; 1809: 23, 27, 49, 65; 1812; 1815–16; 1818–20; 1823–26; 1828. "Manifestes électoraux de 1792," BRH, 46 (1940): 99. Recensement de Québec, 1818 (Provost), 246. Quebec Gazette, index 1778–1823; 9 July 1778; 20 Feb. 1783; 6 May, 17 June 1790; 28 April 1791; 17 May 1792; 8 May 1794; 30 Jan., 10 April 1800; 26 Jan., 23 Aug. 1804; 18 April, 23 May, 12 Dec. 1805; 22 Sept. 1808; 10 Aug., 15 Dec. 1809; 23 April 1812; 28 Jan. 1813; 23 June, 25 Sept. 1823; 13 Jan. 1834. Officers of British forces in Canada (Irving), 145. "Les Presbytériens à Québec en 1802," BRH, 42 (1936): 728–29. Quebec almanac, 1791: 43–44; 1794: 88–89; 1796: 82–83; 1801:

Locie

102; 1805: 40–41; 1810: 49; 1815: 32; 1820: 82; 1821: 86. P.-G. Roy, *Les avocats de la région de Québec*, 280. M.-A. Bédard, "Le greffier de l'Assemblée législative du Bas-Canada: origine de la fonction" and "Le *Journal* et les autres documents publics à l'Assemblée législative du Bas-Canada" in Bibliothèque de l'Assemblée nationale du Québec, *Bull.* (Québec), 12 (1982), nos.1–2: 35–58, and no.3: 19–57, respectively. P.-G. Roy, "La Trinity-House ou Maison de la Trinité à Québec," *BRH*, 24 (1918): 110.

LOCIE. *See* LOSEE

LOEDEL, HENRY NICHOLAS CHRISTO-PHER, surgeon, army officer, doctor, apothecary, and landowner; b. *c.* 1754, probably in Hesse-Kassel (Federal Republic of Germany); m. 30 Jan. 1784 Marguerite Gamelin, daughter of Pierre-Joseph Gamelin* and Marie-Louise de Lorimier, in Montreal, and they had 12 children, 2 of whom died in infancy; d. 14 Jan. 1830 in Montreal.

Henry Nicholas Christopher Loedel arrived in the province of Quebec in 1776 as surgeon to a corps of German auxiliaries who had come to fight the Americans. After the 1783 Treaty of Paris put an end to the war between the American colonies and Great Britain, Loedel settled in Montreal.

On 1 Jan. 1784 Loedel went into partnership with one of the most eminent surgeons in Montreal, Charles Blake*, to practise medicine and engage in the pharmaceutical business. This partnership was frequently renewed, and also involved a number of real estate transactions. It proved highly profitable and probably was the basis for Loedel's comfortable circumstances. The shop where the two doctors prepared their medicines was in Loedel's home. They were assisted by youths to whom they taught surgery and pharmacy. Nothing is known about Loedel's medical training, but he was the first to obtain a licence from the medical examiners for the district of Montreal, who had been appointed under a statute of 30 April 1788 and one of whom was his friend Blake.

In 1799 Loedel offered his services in a serious typhus epidemic that was raging among the soldiers of the 41st Foot. For two months he fought to cure those affected. Finally he himself succumbed to the disease. It took four long months of convalescence before he could again attend to his affairs, and his health was permanently impaired. To these vicissitudes was added the difficulty he experienced in collecting his pay from the army. He complained bitterly about this matter in a letter to Governor Sir George Prevost* in 1813. In addition, he said, the rate of exchange deprived him of a third of his salary.

Loedel was prosperous enough to have two of his sons educated in England; Henry-Pierre and Pierre-Charles became doctors. The first was to be the co-founder of both the Montreal General Hospital and the Faculty of Medicine of McGill College. Before returning to Lower Canada he had given medical care to the Duke of Wellington's troops at Waterloo. The second son recounted later that he himself had been on board the *Bellerophon* when it carried Napoleon to St Helena.

Loedel seems to have had rather substantial real estate holdings. With Blake he owned a two-storey stone house on Rue de la Capitale near the Place du Marché; another one on Rue Notre-Dame; a property with a house, stone stable, orchard, and wood-lot that supplied his firewood, on Montreal Island south of the *faubourg* Québec; and a second very large piece of land at La Prairie on which there were two log houses and two stables. As well, Loedel lived in a splendid two-storey stone house with a storeroom and a cellar; he added a third storey in 1817 and put ten windows in on each storey. His wife had brought as her dowry a house on the corner of Rue Saint-Paul and Rue Saint-François-Xavier. In 1818 the government had granted him 600 acres in Godmanchester Township in recognition of his services as an officer.

A member of the upper middle class and a prominent doctor, Loedel died of an attack of apoplexy on 14 Jan. 1830. He had been ill for more than a year. In keeping with his express desire he was buried in his friend Blake's vault in the *faubourg* Sainte-Marie. Blake had been godfather to two of his children, to whom he bequeathed 800 acres in Upper Canada. After Loedel's death his widow went to live with their son Pierre-Charles.

GILLES JANSON

ANQ-M, CE1-51, 4 déc. 1784, 20 févr. 1786, 21 nov. 1792, 18 août 1794, 19 juin 1796, 3 mai 1798, 3 mars 1800, 19 janv. 1802, 12 sept. 1803; CE1-63, 30 janv. 1784, 14 janv. 1830; CN1-7, février, avril 1828; janvier, mai 1829; CN1-29, 30 janv. 1784; 7 févr. 1786; 30 avril 1787; 14 nov. 1788; 3 juin 1790; 23 sept. 1793; 16 mai 1794; 2 déc. 1795; 18 janv., 13 mars 1797; 5 févr. 1800; 29 mai 1802; 12 déc. 1803; CN1-134, 3 févr. 1817, 10 mars 1828; CN1-185, 17 avril 1802, 8 févr. 1803, 19 févr. 1807; CN1-187, 22 déc. 1814; CN1-189, 23 févr. 1785. AUM, P 58, G2, 1801–9. PAC, MG 11, [CO 42] Q, 16-2: 555–60; RG 4, B28, 47: 28–29; RG 8, I (C ser.), 187: 52–53; 206: 36–37; 207: 4–6. Abbott, *Hist. of medicine*. M.-J. et G. Ahern, *Notes pour l'hist. de la médecine*. J. J. Heagerty, *Four centuries of medical history in Canada and a sketch of the medical history of Newfoundland* (2v., Toronto, 1928). Louis Richard, "La famille Lœdel," *BRH*, 56 (1950): 78–89.

LORIMIER, CLAUDE-NICOLAS-GUILLAUME DE (known as **Guillaume, Chevalier de Lorimier**), militia officer, merchant, politician, and Indian Department official; b. 4 Sept. 1744 in Lachine (Que.), eighth child and fourth son of Claude-Nicolas de Lorimier* de La Rivière and Marie-Louise Lepallieur de Laferté; d. 7 June 1825 in Caughnawaga (Kahnawake), Lower Canada.

Claude-Nicolas-Guillaume de Lorimier boasted a prominent and prolific ancestry; born in a house once owned by the explorer René-Robert Cavelier* de La Salle, he was the third to bear his three Christian names. His father distinguished himself as an officer during the Seven Years' War, and in the last days of the French régime he himself was commissioned a junior officer despite his youth. When Montreal surrendered on 8 Sept. 1760 Lorimier's unit was near by on Île Sainte-Hélène.

After the war Claude-Nicolas-Guillaume may have been employed, like several members of his family, as an interpreter in the British Indian Department. He was running a wood-yard, however, when the American revolution broke out in 1775. With the threat of an American invasion that summer, he volunteered his services to Governor Guy Carleton*. In his first assignment, to enlist Indian volunteers at Caughnawaga, Lorimier met initially with only moderate success. In July and August he scouted American movements around Fort Ticonderoga (near Ticonderoga, N.Y.). When Major-General Philip John Schuyler, succeeded by Brigadier-General Richard Montgomery*, led an American expedition down the Richelieu valley in September, Lorimier, who that month fell under the command of Major John Campbell*, was employed in the defence of Fort St Johns (Saint-Jean-sur-Richelieu). On one occasion he and his brother Jean-Claude-Chamilly were instrumental in preventing an American landing on the west bank of the Richelieu near the fort. However, the surrender on 18 October of Fort Chambly to the north made the position of the St Johns garrison untenable, and Lorimier was sent through the American lines to inform Carleton. His attempt to return with arrangements for the withdrawal of the defenders was thwarted when, betrayed by an Indian, he narrowly escaped capture in an ambush just outside the fort. On 30 October Lorimier participated in an attempt by Carleton to land a relief force for St Johns at Longueuil; it was unsuccessful and on 3 November the garrison surrendered.

Lorimier remained in Montreal following the capture of the town by the Americans, but early in 1776 he ran foul of the commandant, Brigadier-General David Wooster, for urging militia officers not to surrender their British commissions. Ordered to prepare for departure to the American colonies, Lorimier was disguised and then spirited away in the dead of night by Louise Schuyler, a young Iroquois woman who had fallen in love with him. He went to Fort Oswegatchie (Ogdensburg, N.Y.), which was garrisoned by a company of the British 8th Foot under Captain George Forster. In the spring, after gathering Indians from the surrounding region and arranging

with Pierre Denaut*, parish priest at Les Cèdres, Quebec, for the caching of provisions, Lorimier led the advance party of Indians on an expedition towards Montreal composed of some 600 men, including several hundred Indians, under Forster. On 19 May the American garrison at Les Cèdres, commanded by Major Isaac Butterfield, surrendered after minimal resistance when Forster threatened to loose Lorimier's Indian force on it. Two days later Lorimier himself received the surrender of Major Henry Sherburne, ambushed with his relief detachment of 150 men by a mixed party of Indians and Canadians. Lorimier was instrumental in negotiating with Butterfield and Sherburne an exchange, extremely favourable to the British, of the roughly 500 American prisoners. Benedict Arnold* caught up with Forster on the 26th, but his initial attack was repelled with heavy losses, and he was forestalled from a second by news of the exchange agreement and threats from Lorimier's Indians to kill all the American prisoners. Arnold returned to Montreal with the released Americans; Forster, with Lorimier, retreated to Fort Oswegatchie.

Following the arrival of reinforcements from Britain in May and June 1776 the Americans hurriedly left the colony. That fall a struggle developed for the control of Lake Champlain, and in the naval battle of Valcour Island, N.Y., on 11 October Lorimier and a party of Indians brought Arnold's own vessel under withering fire from shore. In early 1777 he conducted a mixed party to scout American activities in the area of Crown Point and Fort George (Lake George), and in June he was part of Major-General John Burgoyne*'s expedition into New York. Wounded in the leg during the catastrophic diversion to Bennington (Vt), Lorimier made it back to Saratoga (Schuylerville, N.Y.), and was then evacuated to Montreal. Lorimier's departure having prompted the Indians from Caughnawaga to abandon Burgoyne's expedition, he was sent at once to Caughnawaga and Fort St Johns to persuade them to return. The trip aggravated his injury and nearly resulted in amputation of his leg.

Lorimier did not see action again until July 1780, when he was given *carte blanche* to lead a reconnaissance and raiding expedition into New York; a surprise attack on Fort Stanwix (Rome) netted 38 prisoners and 10 scalps. Shortly after his return he collapsed from exhaustion during a meeting at Quebec with the commander-in-chief and governor, Frederick Haldimand*; medical treatment almost finished him off. His participation in the war was over. In the course of his many adventures as a leader of the Indians, Lorimier had occasionally been disappointed by their seemingly erratic behaviour, but it was thanks to their aid at critical moments that he had cheated death and escaped capture.

On 26 June 1783 Lorimier married Louise Schuyler. The couple settled in Caughnawaga where Lori-

Losee

mier had been named resident agent of the Indian Department at the commencement of the war; in 1782 the department had been reorganized and placed under the superintendence of Sir John JOHNSON. Disaster struck Lorimier in 1790 when Louise died at age 36. They had had six children. On 23 March 1793 he married a daughter of the seigneur Joseph Brassard* Deschenaux, Marie-Madeleine-Claire Brassard Descheneaux, who in June became a part-owner of the seigneury of Beaumont; they would have two children. From 1792 to 1796 Lorimier represented Huntingdon in the Lower Canadian House of Assembly, but he voted on only four occasions, always in support of the Canadian party [see Jean-Antoine Panet*]. After the death of his second wife in January 1800, Lorimier married Sha8ennetsi (Anne Gregory) at Caughnawaga on 27 Feb. 1801; they would have four children.

On 22 Sept. 1812, following the outbreak of war with the United States, Lorimier was appointed resident captain to the Caughnawaga and other Iroquois Indians, and in October 1813, at age 69, he was present at the battle of Châteauguay [see Charles-Michel d'IRUMBERRY de Salaberry]. That year his eldest son, Guillaume-François, was killed at Crysler's Farm, Upper Canada, and his second, Jean-Baptiste*, was so badly wounded at Beaver Dams (Thorold) that he never completely recovered. When in August 1814 the government created the Embodied Indian Warriors, consisting of four companies from villages in the Montreal area, Lorimier was appointed deputy superintendent with the rank of major effective from 25 July, and he held the position even after the corps was reduced in 1815. His last years were spent quietly as resident agent in Caughnawaga. Known as Chevalier de Lorimier since at least 1783, he may have simply appropriated the title accorded his father in 1759; it was a common practice during the French régime for younger sons of the nobility to take the title of chevalier. The Patriote Chevalier de Lorimier* was a grandnephew.

A man of energy and endurance, Lorimier made the best of his brief hours of glory in a long career. His exploits during the American revolution and his meeting with Louise Schuyler – recorded with flair in a memoir entitled "Mes services pendant la guerre américaine" – contain the ingredients from which legends are created. His ability to serve – at different times – the kings of France and Britain was characteristic of the élite from which he sprang, and his quiet effectiveness as resident agent to the Indians was typical of a whole group of superintendents and agents, such as Joseph-Maurice LAMOTHE and Dominique Ducharme*, unjustly consigned to historical obscurity.

DOUGLAS LEIGHTON

Claude-Nicolas-Guillaume de Lorimier is the author of "Mes services pendant la guerre américaine," published in *Invasion du Canada*, [H.-A.-J.-B.] Verreau, édit. (Montréal, 1873), 245–98. This memoir was published in English as *At war with the Americans*, trans. and ed. Peter Aichinger (Victoria, B.C., n.d.).

PAC, MG 11, [CO 42] Q, 112: 283–93; MG 30, D1, 19; RG 8, I (C ser.), 1203½: 102; 6886: 101; RG 10, A3, 488: 28798; 496: 31508. Le Jeune, *Dictionnaire*, 2: 168. *Officers of British forces in Canada* (Irving), 215, 217–18. Lanctot, *Le Canada et la Révolution américaine*, 160–61. Benjamin Sulte, *Histoire de la milice canadienne-française, 1760–1897* (Montréal, 1897). F.-J. Audet et Édouard Fabre Surveyer, "Les députés au premier parlement du Bas-Canada: Claude-Nicolas-Guillaume de Lorimier," *La Presse*, 23 juill. 1927: 53, 60. Hare, "L'Assemblée législative du Bas-Canada," *RHAF*, 27: 372–73. Louvigny de Montigny, "Le Lorimier et le Montigny des Cèdres," *BRH*, 47 (1941): 33–47. É.-Z. Massicotte, "La famille de Lorimier," *BRH*, 21 (1915): 10–16, 33–45.

LOSEE (Loosey, Lossee, Locie), WILLIAM, Methodist minister; b. 30 June 1757, probably in Dutchess County, N.Y., son of John Losee and Elenor —; d. 16 Oct. 1832 in Hempstead, N.Y.

Descended from Dutch settlers, William Losee was a farmer in Beekmans Precinct, N.Y., at the outbreak of the American revolution. Though handicapped in one arm, variously described as "off close to the shoulder . . . short or withered," he was a bold horseman and served during the war in James DeLancey*'s Westchester Refugees, also known as DeLancey's "Cowboys," an unincorporated group of volunteers who foraged for the British garrison in New York City. Captured at some point by the rebels, Losee remained in prison until shortly before the end of the conflict. After the signing of the peace treaty in 1783 he sent a petition to the British commander-in-chief, Sir Guy Carleton*, in which he noted "that he is now Determined to Proceed to the Province of Nova Scotia to settle in that Country, that he is Reduced to Extreme Poverty and being a Cripple must unavoidably suffer unless some Assistance is given him from Government." Probably sailing for Nova Scotia with the June fleet, he settled with his unit on the Cobequid Road in Cumberland County, where two years later he received a grant of 250 acres.

There were already a number of Methodists in Cumberland County, mostly Yorkshire immigrants. Just when or where Losee espoused the Methodist cause is uncertain. One historian, quoting friends of Losee, says that in the summer of 1788 he had not yet "embraced religion." Nevertheless, in May 1789 Losee was examined and received as a travelling preacher of the Methodist Episcopal Church at its annual conference in New York City. Bishop Francis Asbury appointed him to open up a new area around Lake Champlain, but Losee remained in this district only a few months before obtaining permission to minister to the loyalists – among whom were some of his relatives – settled along the St Lawrence River. To this end, Asbury ordained him to deacon's orders on 13 Sept. 1789 in Baltimore.

That winter Losee crossed the border near New Johnstown (Cornwall) and preached among the people as far west as the Bay of Quinte. Soon after his arrival in the region he met John Stuart*, the Anglican missionary in Kingston. An unimpressed Stuart told Bishop Charles Inglis* that, like another preacher in the region, Charles Justin McCarty*, Losee carried a questionable recommendation – namely that he was formerly "a Man of very bad moral Character. But his Conversion is therefore the greater Miracle and he will be the better able to preach *experimental* Doctrine." As it turned out, thanks largely to Stuart's efforts, Losee was never able to gain a foothold in Kingston. Everywhere else, however, he enjoyed great success.

Losee was not the first Methodist preacher in the area, though he was the first who was regularly appointed. McCarty, an independent itinerant, and a local teacher named Lyons had preceded him but, being unauthorized, they could not form Methodist societies. In the fall of 1790 Losee returned to the United States with a widely subscribed petition asking the New York Conference to send a missionary to labour among the new townships along the northern shore of Lake Ontario. The conference concurred in the request and chose Losee for the job. In February 1791 he returned to his circuit and that month formed the first regularly organized Methodist classes in what is now Ontario, in the townships of Adolphustown and Ernestown; a third class was organized in Fredericks-burgh Township in early March. Appointed again by the 1791 conference to the same region, now officially known as the Kingston Circuit, Losee consolidated his gains and launched the building of two Methodist meeting-houses. The first, at Hay Bay in Adolphus-town, was completed in 1792 and still stands today, though in altered form. The second, in Ernestown, was never finished. In 1792 Losee reported 165 members.

This burgeoning mission field was divided into two circuits in 1792–93: Oswegatchie to the east of Kingston; Cataraqui to the west. Losee was assigned to the former, the Reverend Darius Dunham to the latter. On the Oswegatchie Circuit, Losee formed classes in the townships of Cornwall and Matilda, and he also served the class that had been meeting in Augusta Township since 1785 [see Barbara Ruckle*]. However, his work in Upper Canada was coming to an end. Apparently both he and Dunham set their affections on Elizabeth Detlor of Fredericksburgh. Her choice was made in favour of Dunham, whom she married. Overwhelmed, Losee returned to the United States, apparently in early 1795. A friend wrote of him: "I heartily pity Mr. Losee for withdrawing his

hand, he is now to be treated with patience and tenderness."

He stayed in Dutchess County for a couple of years and then came back to Upper Canada in 1797 to claim the free lands offered to loyalists. His petitions of that year won him 300 acres in Murray Township and two town lots in Kingston – all this in addition to 200 acres in Ernestown he had obtained earlier. By 1805 he had moved again to the United States, and by 1818 he had settled in Hempstead, N.Y., where he sold shellfish and preached whenever the occasion offered itself. There he married Mary Rushmore, *née* Carman. They did not have children of their own but he seems to have been close to his stepchildren.

In 1830 Losee made a last visit to see his friends on the Bay of Quinte and to sell his town lots in Kingston; the lots were purchased by the shipbuilder Henry Gildersleeve*. Methodist historian George Frederick Playter* has left us the following description of Losee at the time of his 1830 visit: "He was now a feeble old man, with spare features and his withered arm, but still walking in the way of the Lord. . . . His under jaw in speaking would fall a little, so that it was tied up while preaching. He would yet ride on horseback, resting his weight on the stirrups, and as he rode, he balanced himself with his one arm, his body violently shaking." Losee died on 16 Oct. 1832 and was buried in the preacher's plot beside the Hempstead Methodist church. In 1969 the grave was excavated for road-widening purposes, and his gravestone and that of his wife were removed to Ontario – to the cemetery beside his Hay Bay meeting-house.

Although he served in Upper Canada only about three years, Losee effectively laid the groundwork for what eventually became the largest Protestant denom-ination in Canada. John Saltkill Carroll* has said that as a preacher "he was impassioned, voluble, fearless, and denunciatory, cutting deep and closely, and praying to God to 'smite sinners!' He was, probably, more awakening than consolatory; and more of a John the Baptist, with a temporary, preparatory mission, than one adapted to build up a permanent cause." Carroll was not exaggerating when he wrote of Losee's fondness for divine "smiting" of sinners. On one occasion, according to Carroll, "an ignorant, wicked young man . . . was struck by the power of God while in the act of making derision in a re-ligious meeting, in answer to Losee's prayer, who, on seeing his misconduct, lifted his eyes and hands to heaven and cried out, 'Smite him, my God! My God, smite him!' He fell like a bullock under the stroke of the butcher's axe, and writhed on the floor in agony, until the Lord in mercy set his soul at liberty."

Losee was typical of those pioneer Methodist preachers who thundered at every door, a style well suited for the isolated, rural settlers with whom they

Lossing

identified. A generation honoured him as their "Father in the Gospel."

J. WILLIAM LAMB

ACC, Diocese of Ont. Arch. (Kingston), Group 11, John Stuart papers, Stuart to Inglis, 5 March 1790. PAC, RG 1, L3, 284: L3/58; 306: L misc., 1788–95/137. PANS, RG 20A, 8, no.51. PRO, PRO 30/55, no.7826 (transcript at PAC). *Abstracts of wills on file in the surrogate's office, city of New York* (17v., N.Y. Hist. Soc., *Coll.*, [ser.3], 25–41, New York, 1892–1908), 9: 259–60. *Kingston before War of 1812* (Preston). Canniff, *Hist. of the settlement of U.C.*, 286, 290–92. J. [S.] Carroll, *Case and his cotemporaries . . .* (5v., Toronto, 1867–77), 1: 7–14. Esther Clark Wright, *The loyalists of New Brunswick* (Fredericton, 1955; repr. Moncton, N.B., 1972, and Hantsport, N.S., 1981). W. S. Herrington, *History of the county of Lennox and Addington* (Toronto, 1913; repr. Belleville, Ont., 1972), 146–48. *The history of Dutchess County, New York*, ed. Frank Hasbrouck (Poughkeepsie, N.Y., 1909), 1: 51. Richard and Janet Lunn, *The county: the first hundred years in loyalist Prince Edward* (Picton, Ont., 1967), 151, 153, 157–58. A. G. Meacham, *A compendious history of the rise and progress of the Methodist Church, both in Europe and America . . .* (Hallowell, [Ont.], 1832), 449–52. G. F. Playter, *The history of Methodism in Canada . . .* (Toronto, 1862), 17–43. J. E. Sanderson, *The first century of Methodism in Canada* (2v., Toronto, 1908–10), 1: 27–31. J. W. Lamb, "William Losee: Ontario's pioneer Methodist missionary," UCC, Committee on Arch., *Bull.* (Toronto), 21 (1969–70): 28–47; repub. in pamphlet form (Adolphustown, Ont., 1974). F. F. Thompson, "A chapter of early Methodism in the Kingston area," *Historic Kingston*, no.6 (1957): 32–45.

LOSSING, PETER, colonizer, Quaker religious leader, and surveyor; b. 11 Oct. 1761 in Dutchess County, N.Y., son of Nicholas Lossing and Christina Woolweaver; m. first 15 Oct. 1781 Hannah Brill, and they had four sons and at least two daughters; m. secondly between 1799 and 1806 Catherine Delong, a widow whose married name had probably been Vanderburg, and they had one daughter; d. 23 April 1833 in Norwich Township, Oxford County, Upper Canada.

The ancestors of Peter Lossing were Dutch and had immigrated to the colony of New York in the mid 17th century; one of his nephews, Benson John Lossing, would become a well-known American historian. Lossing himself was probably a farmer and miller in New York, and he was also a member of the Oswego Monthly Meeting of the Society of Friends. In 1806 this body, claiming that Lossing "hath been neglectful in the attendance of Meetings & married a Woman out of the unity of friends, after being guilty of fornication with her," disowned him. It was not until 1810, on the eve of his departure for Upper Canada, that he acknowledged his errors and applied, successfully, for readmission to the society.

Lossing's decision to move to Upper Canada was inspired by his ambition to found an agricultural settlement as a method of advancing his fortunes. No large amounts of cheap land were then available in New York, and so Lossing and his brother-in-law Peter Delong looked to Upper Canada. In 1809 a relative of Lossing there, Thomas DORLAND of Adolphustown Township, secured an interview for them with William Chewett* and Thomas RIDOUT of the Surveyor General's Office. The administration liked the idea of a large settlement, and even Lieutenant Governor Francis Gore* discussed it with Lossing and Delong.

The two entrepreneurs were then introduced to William Willcocks*. In 1800 the government had sold large blocks of land in Norwich and Dereham (Southwest Oxford) townships in order to help finance the building of a road linking York (Toronto) with the mouth of the Trent River [see Asa DANFORTH]. Willcocks was one of the purchasers; the others included Peter Russell*, Robert Hamilton*, and clergymen Edmund Burke* and Robert ADDISON. By 1809 Willcocks was in debt and anxious to sell part of his holdings. In June 1810 Lossing and Delong agreed to buy from him 15,000 acres in Norwich for £1,875, the purchase price to be paid over a number of years as incoming settlers acquired lots. After reaching this agreement, Lossing and his brother-in-law returned to their homes, where they persuaded several people, mostly Quakers, to immigrate. In late 1810 the first settlers, led by Lossing and his family, arrived in Norwich, and over the next two years a considerable number followed. During the War of 1812 Norwich escaped the devastation inflicted on neighbouring communities by the enemy raiding parties of such men as Joseph Willcocks* and Andrew WESTBROOK. Following the war, and particularly during the 1820s, the settlement took firm root.

Lossing was for some years the leading figure among the settlers. Quaker religious services were begun in his home in 1811, and a school was started there in 1813. Later he gave land for a meeting-house. He also acted as a surveyor. In the 1790s Norwich Township had been surveyed first by Augustus Jones* and then by William Hambly, but the work had been done hastily and by 1811 a more complete survey was needed. When the government could not provide someone to undertake the job, Lossing volunteered. With an assistant whom he brought from the United States, Lossing, who had no training, surveyed the township and in the process dealt with the problems created by the original surveys.

Always shrewd, Lossing knew the importance of publicizing his loyalty: as soon as he had settled in the colony he told Gore of his distaste for American government – "pleasing in theory, but troublesome & frequently factious in execution" – and he reported then with satisfaction that previously disaffected people in the London District were discovering "their fears to have been illusory, and their grievances to be mostly imaginary." As a loyal settler and as a colonizer with genuine accomplishments to his credit, he was able to forge close links with government officials, including successive lieutenant governors up to the time of Sir John Colborne*. He often suggested measures to improve the moral and economic climate of the colony. From the beginning he was consulted on the eligibility of applicants for leases of clergy and crown reserves, and in most cases he had a hand in writing the applications. He also warned the government of squatters or timber thieves on crown land in Norwich township. In 1830 the first post office there was set up in his home.

Lossing constantly promoted the economic growth of Norwich and its vicinity. He attracted a miller to Norwich and aided the man to get started. When a local promoter, Hugh Webster, wished to create small holdings for poor people who could not afford larger properties, Lossing arranged the lease of a clergy reserve lot. He was an enthusiastic supporter of schemes to improve navigation on Otter Creek, which passed through Norwich, and on the Grand River. By introducing the industrialist George Tillson* to William Warren Baldwin*, trustee for Maria Willcocks, Lossing was instrumental in Tillson's acquisition of land in Dereham Township on which to build an ironworks.

Yet Lossing never lost sight of his own interests, and he was not above abusing the trust which his fellow settlers and the government placed in him. In his survey of Norwich his solution to the problems caused by earlier mistakes had been to create a gore, or triangle of land, adjacent to his own land. This gore cut access to the road on the third concession line. Lossing tried to have the gore declared crown land so that he could buy it and join it to his farm. When some settlers protested to the government, he took advantage of his connections in York, playing down the opposition to his scheme and the extent of improvements made in the gore by others. The result was a protracted struggle which did not end until 1835, two years after Lossing's death. At that time the lots on the first and second concessions were enlarged and the gore absorbed.

Lossing strongly supported the cause of temperance, criticizing as early as 1819 the "unnecessary multiplication of tipling houses" in the province. In politics he was a reformer, mainly because the reformers and especially Charles Duncombe* advocated temperance and improved education. His brand of moderate reformism was not shared by his eldest son. Solomon Lossing took over as spokesman for the Quaker community in Norwich after his father's death. In 1837 he recruited men to join the Duncombe rising.

RONALD J. STAGG

[Carson D. Bushell of Simcoe, Ont., was kind enough to make available genealogical data on the Lossing family. R.J.S.]
AO, Hist. plaque descriptions, "Historical plaque to be unveiled at Norwich," 26 June 1964; RG 1, A-I-6: 4646–48, 6573, 6655–56, 9394–96, 9437–38, 9975–76; C-IV, Norwich Township. Norwich and District Museum (Norwich, Ont.), Norwich Pioneer and Hist. Soc., geneal. coll., no.293; Stella Mott coll., nos.104, 117 (mfm. of Mott coll. at AO). PAC, RG 1, L3, 287a: L12/2; 289: L13/155; 290: L14/113; 305: L leases, 1801–1836/50; RG 5, A1: 4128–31, 5192–93, 20230–33. UWOL, Regional Coll., London District, Surrogate Court, estate files, 1800–39, no.219 (mfm. at AO). C. D. Bushell, *Gleanings by the Bushell* ([Norwich, 1984]). Brian Dawe, *"Old Oxford is wide awake": pioneer settlers and politicians in Oxford County, 1793–1853* (n.p., 1980). R. W. Macaulay, "The land dispute in Norwich Township in the London District of Upper Canada, 1811–1840" (MA thesis, Univ. of Toronto, 1982). [A. E. Poldon], *1810–1910, centenary souvenir, Norwich, Ont.* (Norwich, 1910). C. [F.] Read, *The rising in western Upper Canada, 1837–8: the Duncombe revolt and after* (Toronto, 1982). G. E. Reaman, *The trail of the black walnut* (Toronto, 1957). Max Rosenthal, "Early Oxford County post offices," *BNA Topics* (Toronto), 26 (1969): 204–6.

LOTBINIÈRE, MICHEL-EUSTACHE-GASPARD-ALAIN CHARTIER DE. *See* CHARTIER

LOVETT, PHINEAS, farmer, merchant, militia officer, office holder, JP, judge, and politician; b. 15 May 1745, probably in Milford, Mass., second child of Phineas Lovett and Beulah Morse; m. 6 April 1768 Abigail Thayer in Mendon, Mass., and they had 11 children; d. 17 June 1828 in Annapolis Royal, N.S.

Phineas Lovett came to Nova Scotia with the New England planters who settled on the fertile lands left vacant by the deportation of the Acadians. His father appears to have taken up land in Nova Scotia in 1760 and both father and son are listed among the grantees for Annapolis Township in October 1765. By 1770 Lovett was established on the substantial farm at Round Hill, Annapolis County, where he lived throughout his life.

Like many Nova Scotians of his day, Lovett was both farmer and merchant. He had a ship in the West Indian trade by the late 1780s, and in later years seems to have devoted more time to commerce than to agriculture. He took full advantage of the lucrative trading opportunities offered by the American embargo on British imports adopted in 1807. During the War of 1812, in fact, he spent so much time in New Brunswick trafficking across the American border that he was criticized for neglecting his public duties as a magistrate in Nova Scotia.

While in New England in 1775, possibly on a business voyage, Lovett encountered a rebel spy and came briefly to prominence by warning Nova Scotian authorities of invasion plans afoot in that hotbed of rebellion, Machias (Maine). While travelling from Salem, Mass., to Machias, Lovett was questioned about the strength of the forts at the Saint John River and at Annapolis Royal. He disclaimed any knowledge of their condition but on arrival at Machias was again quizzed about the probable reaction at Annapolis Royal to an American attack. Again Lovett pleaded ignorance. He observed that, since he had been away from home for some time, he had no idea of the public attitude towards the rebels' cause. On his return to Nova Scotia, Lovett travelled to Halifax to report the conversations to the Council. His actions, which aligned him squarely with government, were in contrast to the revolutionary sympathies held by many of his fellow New Englanders, including his own father. Fort Frederick (Saint John) at the mouth of the Saint John River was destroyed by the Machiasmen later that year, but the expected assault on Annapolis Royal did not occur until 1781 when two American privateers raided the town. Accounts of the attack alleged that the local militia had taken no steps to defend the town, a charge that Lovett, lieutenant-colonel of the regiment, vehemently denied. Lovett's personal courage was also impugned in local tradition that was still current a century later.

During his long life, Lovett held many public offices in Annapolis County. He served as high sheriff for the county in 1781 and 1782 and was named a justice of the peace in December 1794. In 1810 he was appointed a justice of the Inferior Court of Common Pleas. Lovett also served in the House of Assembly for several periods. In 1775 he was returned in a by-election to represent Annapolis Township. Like many country representatives before the introduction of a system of payment for assemblymen, Lovett did not attend regularly, and in November 1783 his seat was declared vacant for continued absence. He was again elected for Annapolis Township in 1799 but took little part in the political controversies of the turbulent eighth assembly [see William Cottnam TONGE], seldom serving on committees and almost invariably voting with the executive's supporters. He appears not to have contested the general election of 1806. Although he was returned for Annapolis County in a by-election held in 1808 after the death of the incumbent, his attendance was again irregular, probably because of his commercial pursuits.

Lovett exemplifies the many "country squires" who played a leading role in rural Nova Scotia in the 18th and 19th centuries. Such men sustained family traditions of public service at the local and the provincial level: both Lovett's father and his sons in turn served as assemblymen and magistrates. Similarly, the homes of the Lovetts provided a fitting stage for the entertainment of touring dignitaries; in Phineas Lovett's case, Prince Edward* Augusta's visits gave the added distinction of royalty. As merchants, farmers, or shipowners, the Lovetts were an integral part of the community they represented.

JUDITH TULLOCH

PANS, RG 1, 168–69, 171, 173, 189, 225, 278. PRO, CO 217/51. N.S., House of Assembly, *Journal and proc.*, 1775–83, 1800–11. *Nova-Scotia Gazette, and the Weekly Chronicle* (Halifax), 4 Sept., 2 Oct. 1781. W. A. Calnek, *History of the county of Annapolis, including old Port Royal and Acadia . . .* , ed. A. W. Savary (Toronto, 1897; repr. Belleville, Ont., 1972).

LUGRIN, GEORGE KILMAN, printer, office holder, and newspaperman; b. *c.* 1792 in Saint John, N.B., son of loyalist Peter Lugrin; m. there 5 Feb. 1815 Deborah Ann Smiler; d. 12 May 1835 in Fredericton.

By 1807 George Kilman Lugrin was a newsboy and apprentice printer in the Saint John office of Jacob S. Mott*, who the following year took over from John Ryan* both the post of king's printer and the publication of the *Royal Gazette, and New-Brunswick Advertiser*. One of Lugrin's early writings was a poem dated 1 Jan. 1808 in which "George as is usual with vendors of News, / Again wishes a Happy NEW YEAR." By 1813 he was a freeman of the city and a full-fledged printer with Mott.

The death of his employer in January 1814 was the occasion for several changes. Mott's wife, Ann, was denied permission to serve as king's printer because of her sex, and that spring Lugrin was appointed to the post, apparently on condition that the operation be moved to Fredericton, which had no newspaper at the time. In April he announced that he would begin publishing there as soon as his press and types had arrived from England and that, in the mean time, with the permission of the president of the Council, Martin Hunter*, he was appropriating a page of William Durant's *City Gazette* for the *New-Brunswick Royal Gazette*. It was not until 10 March 1815 that his journal, a combination of official government notices and general news, appeared in Fredericton. Having married a month earlier, Lugrin settled in the capital and established a newspaper tradition that was to last into the 20th century.

Lugrin was part of what has been called a "new generation in the printing fraternity," one separated from the issues that surrounded the founding of New Brunswick and from the politics of the loyalists. Their interests were centred on the province of the day. Foreign news continued to appear in their papers, but matters of local interest predominated, including provincial and municipal politics, the courts, economic activities, births, marriages, and deaths. The doyen of this group was Henry Chubb*, who had apprenticed under Mott with Lugrin. Lugrin's relationship with

Chubb was more than professional for Chubb married Jane Lugrin, a sister, in 1816.

As the newspapers turned their attention to local items, they frequently offended one sensitivity or another. Lugrin was to have an increasingly stormy tenure as king's printer and to be involved in several lawsuits, most connected with his business, though personal antagonisms often clouded the issues. One he brought against the aristocratic John Simcoe Saunders* in 1828 may have precipitated the loss of his office in 1829. Four years later, on 18 May 1833, he launched another paper, the Fredericton *Watchman*, which had as its motto: "Official oppression shall be exposed, and all the secret springs of government shall be closely inspected. A Watch shall be kept upon Public men, and Public measures shall receive censure or commendation as they may deserve, and the latter shall be fearlessly and independently dealt with." Lugrin aligned himself with Lemuel Allan Wilmot*, an impassioned reformer and government critic, who wrote several articles for the paper; however, the fear of official reprisal forced Lugrin to abandon him. By then a "lingering illness" had begun its work. He died on 12 May 1835 and with him the *Watchman*. He was 43.

The Lugrin family remained in newspapers into the following century. Charles S. Lugrin, his son, was publisher and editor of the Fredericton *Express* in 1863 and the *Colonial Farmer* from 1863 to 1877. Charles's son Charles Henry Lugrin* worked for several newspapers, founded the Fredericton *Herald* in 1882, and was editor of the Victoria, B.C., *Colonist* from 1897 to 1902.

C. M. WALLACE

N.B. Museum, G. J. Dibblee papers; Saint John, reg. of voters, 1785–1869. *City Gazette* (Saint John, N.B.), 18 April 1814. *New-Brunswick Courier*, 11 Feb. 1815, 16 May 1835. *Royal Gazette* (Fredericton), 10 March 1815–21 July 1829, 13 May 1835. J. R. Harper, *Historical directory of New Brunswick newspapers and periodicals* (Fredericton, 1961). H. J. Morgan, *The Canadian men and women of the time: a hand-book of Canadian biography of living characters* (2nd ed., Toronto, 1912). Hannay, *Hist. of N.B.* Lawrence, *Judges of N.B.* (Stockton and Raymond). MacNutt, *New Brunswick*.

LUNDRIGAN (Landergan, Landrigan, Lanergan), JAMES, fisherman; b. *c.* 1790 in Newfoundland, probably in Cupids; m. Sarah Morgan, and they had at least nine children; fl. 1818–30.

James Lundrigan was one of two central figures (the other was Philip Butler of Harbour Main) in a celebrated episode in Newfoundland history. A native-born Newfoundlander, he was a relative of Edward Lanergan, who in 1789 "cut and cleared" an extensive fishing room on the south side of Cupids in

Conception Bay. In 1818 Lundrigan, married and with a young family, contracted a debt of over £13 with the supplying firm of Graham McNicoll and Company, which was active in Conception Bay. In May 1819 an action for debt was brought against him by the firm in the surrogate court at Harbour Grace, and a decision was given in favour of the merchants, with costs. (The surrogates were, by this date, local notables, normally Anglican clergymen; they presided over legally constituted and movable courts of civil jurisdiction, and proceeded usually by summary conviction. In this case the surrogate was the Reverend Frederick Hamilton Carrington.) Judgement was by default, since Lundrigan himself did not appear in court. A constable then proceeded to Cupids and attached Lundrigan's room together with "a boat and craft"; these attachments were made for two executions, one against Lundrigan himself and another as security for James Hollahan, also of Cupids, who was apparently his fishing partner. Together the debts amounted to over £28. Lundrigan's property was sold to Donald Graham, a clerk in the employ of the creditor. After the sale an attempt was made to take possession of Lundrigan's house, but the fisherman was not at home and his wife threatened "to blow" a constable's "brains out." Whereupon the seizure of the property was deferred to another date.

A year later, on 5 July 1820, a surrogate court sitting at Port de Grave (or at Bareneed) summoned Lundrigan to appear before it, but he declined to attend. Constable William Keating later testified that Lundrigan "said he had no shoe to his foot and was nearly naked, and was ashamed to appear before gentlemen in the Courts. He was engaged at that time with two men in hauling a caplin sein, and said he was getting a little fish for the support of his wife and children, who had nothing besides to eat." On being told by another constable, Michael Kelly, that he would return with a party of marines to arrest him, Lundrigan replied (according to Kelly) that he wished them "a damn good time of it." His refusal was reported to the court, and a special warrant was issued to apprehend him. He was taken into custody late in the evening of 5 July, and was held on board the *Grasshopper*, commanded by one of the two surrogates presiding in the court, Commander David Buchan*, a veteran in the Newfoundland service.

The next morning Lundrigan was brought ashore at Port de Grave to appear before Buchan and a recently appointed surrogate, the Reverend John LEIGH, Anglican priest at Harbour Grace. Lundrigan seemed "much dejected." The warrant against him charged him with "divers contempt of court and resisting constables in the execution of their duty, and particularly for refusing and neglecting to attend" the court on the previous day. A summary conviction was made after Kelly's testimony, and Lundrigan was sentenced

Lundrigan

by Leigh (with Buchan concurring) to receive 36 lashes on the bare back. It was further ordered that Kelly, "with such assistance as he shall find necessary," take possession "this day" of Lundrigan's premises. The order meant, in effect, the immediate eviction of Lundrigan's wife and four young children.

Surgeon Richard Shea was called to attend the execution of the sentence, since Lundrigan "stated that he was subject to the falling sickness" (elsewhere called "fits," presumably epilepsy). He was taken from the court and tied by his wrists and legs to the shore of a flake. The boatswain's mate of the *Grasshopper* inflicted 14 lashes with a cat-o'-nine-tails, at which point Lundrigan fainted and Shea "desired the punishment to stop." The victim was cut down and taken into the house in which the court had sat, where, in Shea's words, "he appeared much convulsed." According to the court records, the remainder of the sentence was remitted on Lundrigan's "promising to deliver up the premises without further trouble."

A day later the same court sat in Harbour Main, and the Irish fisherman Philip Butler was sentenced to receive 36 lashes for contempt. He was given 12. When Butler's wife persisted in her refusal to vacate her home, which she claimed was her own property, the door was broken down and she and her children were evicted.

The treatment given to Butler and Lundrigan provoked deep outrage in Newfoundland and quickened the movement for reform. Hitherto that movement, though it had been a force on the island for a decade, had existed principally at the level of theoretical argument. William Carson* had railed against the surrogates and clamoured for a legislature, but in fact the old paternalistic system inherited from the 18th century had muddled on. The Butler and Lundrigan whippings gave Carson's cause momentum. An image of official tyranny over poor, helpless, out-harbour fishermen was provided to galvanize the public into recognition of the need for judicial and constitutional change. The fact that one of the fishermen was native and both were Roman Catholics added to the symbolic value of the event. So did the element of mercantile greed displayed in it, which Patrick Morris* in particular, now drawn for the first time into politics, was quick to seize on. The locally sensitive matter of right to property seemed also to be an aspect of the affair. Altogether, as the lawyer William Dawe perceived, "the moment was too favorable to be lost," and the reformers moved quickly to take advantage of it.

On 8 and 9 Nov. 1820, with the support of the reform party, Butler and Lundrigan made the extraordinary move of taking out actions of trespass for assault and false imprisonment against Buchan and Leigh in the Supreme Court of Newfoundland. Both claimed damages, Butler £500, Lundrigan £1,500. The chief justice, Sir Francis Forbes*, ruled that the cases hinged on a question of law, namely, whether or not the surrogate courts had the right to punish for contempt. He stated his view that they did have that right, and the jury in each case returned a verdict for the defendants, though not without expressing "abhorrence" at the "unmerciful and cruel punishment" given to Lundrigan. Forbes, too, strongly rebuked Leigh and Buchan for "a mode of proceeding which disuse had rendered obsolete in England; and which in every view of the present case, was particularly harsh and uncalled for." At the close of Lundrigan's case, the fisherman gave notice of an appeal against Forbes's decision to the Privy Council.

These were sensational events in the small trading and fishing port of St John's. And much more was to follow. Soon after the two fishermen lost their cases, a public meeting was called at which resolutions were passed expressing "*abhorrence* and *detestation*" for the scourging of Butler and Lundrigan and a determination to pursue legal and constitutional means "to have *the law repealed*, which it appears sanctions such arbitrary proceedings in the Surrogates." The committee struck to bring these and other resolutions into effect included Carson, Morris, the editor of the *Newfoundland Sentinel* newspaper, Lewis Kelly Ryan, and eight others. A powerfully worded petition was soon in preparation which linked the Butler and Lundrigan incidents to other grievances, including the lack of a house of assembly. Governor Sir Charles Hamilton* said in a dispatch that "it does not appear that any of the principal merchants even here have given their sanction to the petition," and although this was an unfair comment it was true that support for it was largely Catholic and Irish – an indication of who would carry the torch of reform in the decades ahead. Hamilton notwithstanding, in looking over the names one is struck by the prominence of those who now professed liberal opinion. Well within a year of the Port de Grave atrocity, this petition reached the king, the House of Lords, the House of Commons, and the colonial secretary, Earl Bathurst, who indicated to Hamilton that "alterations of existing laws" pertaining to Newfoundland would be forthcoming. (Bathurst also told the governor to caution the surrogates "against inflicting corporal punishment in the cases of a similar nature which they may be called upon to notice.") In effect, the aroused feeling over the treatment of the two fishermen began a process of agitation which led to the new laws for Newfoundland of 1824. Among other reforms, the surrogates were replaced by a system of circuit courts presided over by qualified judges. Nevertheless, it would take a further eight years of argument and petitioning by Carson and others to gain a local assembly.

Lundrigan's life after 1820 is obscure. The notice of

appeal to the Privy Council against the decision of the Supreme Court was not acted upon by the reformers once they realized they could make gains by political rather than judicial means. Unlike Butler, Lundrigan appears to have made no claims for redress from the governor. William Keating described him as "a quiet simple man – and if he had a little more spirit during his life time, it would have been better for him." This assessment may well have been a valid one. Lundrigan's property in Cupids was bought back for him by a penitent Leigh, who claimed "it was from the unfortunate circumstance of great misrepresentation" that his punishment had been ordered. In an unusual act in 1830, nine of Lundrigan's children were baptized as Roman Catholics in Harbour Grace, all on a single day. The event may hint at some family crisis, perhaps Lundrigan's illness. Local tradition holds that he remained unwell after the whipping and died while still a relatively young man. His wife, by contrast, lived to enjoy her old age.

PATRICK O'FLAHERTY

[The most extensive account of the Butler and Lundrigan incidents is in a pamphlet entitled *A report of certain proceedings of the inhabitants of the town of St. John, in the island of Newfoundland; with the view to obtain a reform of the laws, more particularly in the mode of their administration; and an independent legislature* (St John's, 1821). The relevant court records are available in the minutes of the Surrogate Court (GN 5/1/B/1, Harbour Grace, 1818–20) and the Supreme Court (GN 5/2/A/1, 1820–21), both at PANL, and in PRO, CO 194/64: 3–19 (see also 45–46, and 51–60). The legal context in which Forbes's decision to hear the cases of 8 and 9 Nov. 1820 was made may be studied in PANL, GN 2/1/A, vols.28–31; see in particular 31: 350–56. For information on Lundrigan and Cupids in 1817, see David Buchan, ledger listing inhabitants of Brigus, Cupids, etc., 1817, in Nfld. Public Library Services, Provincial Reference and Resource Library (St John's).

Information about Lundrigan's family is in the Cathedral of the Immaculate Conception (Harbour Grace), Reg. of baptisms, 21 Oct. 1830 (mfm. at PANL); see also PANL, Vital statistics, vols.34, 36A, for scattered references to his children. His fishing room is described in PANL, GN 1/13/4, plantation book, Conception Bay, *c.* 1805.

Little information from contemporary newspapers is available; however, see the *Newfoundland Mercantile Journal* for 23 Nov. 1820 and 5 July 1821. A wickedly ironical column directed at Leigh from the *Newfoundland Sentinel* (St John's), 28 Nov. 1821, is preserved in Leigh's file in PAC, MG 17, B1, C/CAN, Ia/19, folder 239, no.344 (mfm.), while the file as a whole provides insight into his character and helps to explain his response to Butler and Lundrigan.

Information about Lundrigan was also obtained from Newton Morgan and Edward-Vincent Chafe. P.O'F.]

M

M'ALPINE (McAlpine), JOHN, office holder, surveyor, and businessman; b. 1748 in the Highlands of Scotland, son of Peter M'Alpine and his first wife, Christian ——; m. first Jane ——; m. secondly 29 Jan. 1784 Rebecca Barss, *née* Gammon, in Liverpool, N.S.; m. thirdly 1790 Sarah Hills, *née* Caverly; m. fourthly 1796 Sarah Walker; there were two children from each marriage; d. 26 May 1827 in Halifax.

John M'Alpine's career had three phases. As a settler in upstate New York he found himself the victim of two sets of circumstances: the rivalry of New Hampshire and New York over the area where he was living, and the crisis of loyalty posed by the outbreak of the American revolution. As a man of 35 in Nova Scotia he was caught up in the conflict between pre-revolutionary settlers and loyalist newcomers. Finally, there was the older M'Alpine who made ends meet in Halifax by a fascinating range of activities.

M'Alpine's first North American homestead was situated on 600 acres bought from a Colonel Reid. Hardly had he arrived in 1773 when he was driven out by the Green Mountain Boys, who were asserting New Hampshire's right to the area east of Lake Champlain (now Vermont). M'Alpine retreated to a smaller farm near Crown Point (N.Y.). When the American revolution began he suffered the loss of his land, house, and stock, and became a refugee in Fort St Johns (Saint-Jean-sur-Richelieu) and Chambly, Que. After a period of procuring cattle for John Burgoyne*'s expedition in American territory, M'Alpine was captured. Once released, he was sent to Long Island, N.Y., where he was soon embroiled again with the Americans. Late in 1779 he returned to Scotland.

The following year M'Alpine published a memoir which recounted in vivid detail his adventures from 1773 to 1779. Although he spared none of his wrath in condemning the Americans as rebels and pillagers, his strictures on the British conduct of the war were telling. The British, he felt, had put "over much trust . . . in men who misled or betrayed our people, while our commanders distrusted and despised their loyal adherents and substantial friends."

The disgruntled M'Alpine appeared in 1783 at Shelburne, N.S., among the loyalist settlers, but quickly moved on to Liverpool, a more established

Macaulay

community. On 11 Feb. 1785 the loyalist claims commissioners heard M'Alpine's story, which included a claim for £5,000 in losses. They felt that he had no just demand for compensation, maintaining that his claim was "very improper" and "fraudulent," and "ought to be so reported to the Lords of the Treasury." On 28 Nov. 1786, however, Simeon Perkins* noted in his diary that "Capt. John McAlpine . . . is allowed £70 a Year on a Military list for Services in the Late war. . . . Three years pay will be due the 24th of Next month." Neither the rationale for M'Alpine's commission as captain nor the specific reason why the authorities changed their minds is known.

M'Alpine made his living at Liverpool by keeping a house of entertainment, operating a ferry, carrying supplies, repairing roads, and acting as deputy surveyor of the king's woods. At first his position and his marriage into the locally respected Barss family assured him of good relations in the town. Then in July 1789 he was appointed deputy naval officer for Queens County, with instructions to ensure that those fishing at Liverpool had the proper documents. M'Alpine attempted to execute his commission and stirred up the settlers of Liverpool against him. Within two months two naval vessels were sent from Halifax to search every ship in the harbour. Repeated requests for M'Alpine's dismissal were made by local inhabitants but without success.

Elkanah Freeman, an old settler and neighbour to M'Alpine, attempted to put pressure on him by fencing him off from the street. At least twice an angry mob assailed M'Alpine's premises, and the elder of his step-daughters, 17-year-old Hannah Barss, was remanded on bond to the county sessions on charges of taking down the pickets from Freeman's fence. In April 1790 the girl was relieved of the charges, but M'Alpine, like other deputy naval officers across the province, was discharged as part of the government's attempt to abate the widespread opposition to these officials. The death of M'Alpine's wife in May removed another tie to Liverpool, and by December he had left for Halifax. When his property was auctioned later, Elkanah Freeman bought it for only £28.

M'Alpine left Liverpool with nothing but his government pension, and his early years at Halifax reveal that he had to shift considerably to support himself and his dependents. An incomplete list of his activities includes selling horses and potatoes, road work, carrying supplies, money, and passengers, and acting as a drover, butcher, and undertaker. Between 1792 and 1795 he was a principal in five assault cases, and a key witness in a sixth, being sent to jail at least once until his fine could be paid.

By 1797 M'Alpine had erected Edward's Valley Inn, overlooking Bedford Basin near Halifax. This hostelry was much frequented during the time Prince Edward* Augustus was at Halifax and throughout the Napoleonic Wars. Part of the property was occupied by the military after the *Leopard* and *Chesapeake* incident in 1807 [*see* Sir George Cranfield Berkeley*], and a pentagonal blockhouse, Fort McAlpine, was built on it to guard the northern approaches to Halifax from an American attack. After the War of 1812, his lands were returned to M'Alpine. A fire destroyed his house in 1819 and he lived in his inn while a replacement was erected. He leased the inn to other operators during the 1820s. M'Alpine's declining years were quiet, and he served locally as an overseer of roads. At his death he was referred to as "an old and respectable inhabitant."

TERRENCE M. PUNCH

John M'Alpine is the author of *Genuine narratives, and concise memoirs of some of the most interesting exploits & singular adventures, of J. McAlpine . . .* , published at Greenock, Scot., in 1780. A subsequent edition was published (n.p., 1788), and a reprint of the 1780 version was issued at Greenock in 1883.

PANS, Places, Great Britain, half-pay officers, 1807–13 (mfm.); RG 1, 225, doc.69; RG 34-312, P, 7. Perkins, *Diary, 1780–89* (Harvey and Fergusson); *1790–96* (Fergusson). *Acadian Recorder*, 13 Oct. 1821. *Halifax Journal*, 16 Sept. 1811, 22 Feb. 1819. *Novascotian, or Colonial Herald*, 7 June 1837. *Royal Gazette and the Nova-Scotia Advertiser*, 26 March 1793, 19 July 1796, 15 May 1798. *Weekly Chronicle*, 19 Nov. 1791, 10 Oct. 1795. T. M. Punch, "Loyalists are stuffy, eh?" *N.S. Hist. Quarterly* (Halifax), 8 (1978): 319–43.

MACAULAY (McAulay), ANGUS (Æneas), schoolmaster, physician, Presbyterian lay preacher, and politician; b. 10 Dec. 1759 in Scotland, probably in the parish of Applecross, son of Æneas Macaulay, a Presbyterian minister, and Mary Macleod; m. February 1790 Mary Macdonald at Bornaskitaig, Scotland, and they had three daughters and three sons; d. 6 Dec. 1827 on Prince Edward Island.

Angus Macaulay was related to the well-known Macaulay family of London. After graduating with an AM from King's College, Aberdeen, in 1782, he probably attended Divinity Hall, Marischal College, in the same town from 1783 to 1785, and he was licensed to preach by the Syod of Glenelg upon the completion of his studies. Instead of taking up a pulpit, however, he accepted a position teaching school on Skye, and in 1789 became an estate agent for Lord Macdonald at Trotternish. In a successful effort to obtain a chaplaincy in the British army Macaulay recruited "22 hardy Highlanders" and marched to Edinburgh at their head to present them personally to Lord Adam Gordon, the commander in Scotland.

Although he appears to have been unable to find a permanent niche in his homeland, Macaulay's qualifications were ideally suited to the purposes of the Earl of Selkirk [Douglas*] when that worthy sought to enlist Highlanders for a proposed settlement in Upper Canada. He became Selkirk's principal agent in the recruitment of potential emigrants and met much opposition from the landholders in the western Hebrides over the autumn and winter of 1802–3. With Macaulay's assistance, Selkirk succeeded in signing up more than 800 Highlanders for his proposed settlement at present-day Sault Ste Marie, Ont., promising them inexpensive and even free transportation to Upper Canada, full provisioning while in transit, and land at reasonable prices. Tenants were to be provisioned on their land for two years and returned home at Selkirk's expense if not completely satisfied. Macaulay always insisted that his honour as well as his employer's was pledged to these commitments, which the earl was unable to implement when the British government at the last minute refused to sanction the scheme. In the spring of 1803 Selkirk did manage to gain grudging government support for a change of destination to Prince Edward Island, where he was able to obtain a number of unsettled lots at bargain prices. Macaulay was forced to renegotiate the original agreements but many of the emigrants refused to change destination and demanded the initial terms. He apparently promised that he as well as Selkirk would accompany the settlers to the Island. To add to his credentials, he applied for and was granted an MD degree from the University of Glasgow in 1803.

To his surprise and chagrin, Macaulay discovered that he was not to be rewarded for his recruiting efforts with the management of Selkirk's interests on Prince Edward Island, that plum being given to businessman James Williams*, who arrived on board the *Oughton* several weeks later than the *Dykes* and *Polly* in August of 1803. Macaulay thus disembarked as a former employee with a number of complaints against Selkirk, and his sense of grievance with his treatment was exacerbated by subsequent developments. A proud man with the sense of "honour" typical of the Highland tacksman class, Macaulay alienated both Selkirk and Williams. He stridently insisted that neither he nor the settlers were being treated in accordance with the initial promises. Although the accusation was perhaps technically true, Selkirk always felt that equivalents had been offered and no one forced to come against his will. Part of the problem, unfortunately, was that the earl did not remain long on Prince Edward Island to see that his commitments were carried out by Williams. Moreover, Macaulay quickly became persuaded that Selkirk had surrounded himself with sycophants and land speculators and was being exploited by the group of officials and landholders who ran the government of the Island. Inevitably he drifted into the ranks of the opponents of the "cabal" or "old party" as it came to

be called. The opposition centred at first around Edmund Fanning*'s successor as lieutenant governor, Joseph Frederick Wallet DesBarres, and DesBarres's principal adviser, James Bardin Palmer, although in 1806 it organized a society called the Loyal Electors which met monthly at Bagnall's Tavern to discuss public issues.

From the beginning of settlement, Angus Macaulay enjoyed a strong popular support among the Highlanders brought by Selkirk, serving them as schoolmaster, physician, and lay preacher. At his own expense he erected a chapel near his house (on the 1,100-acre lot on Point Prim granted him by Selkirk for his services), preaching regularly there in Gaelic and occasionally visiting other Gaelic-speaking Presbyterian districts on the Island; he also taught school at this "chapel of ease." Macaulay was thus easily elected to the House of Assembly in 1806 as a representative of Queens County. Soon afterwards he had his first serious encounter with the "old party," when he received from DesBarres a licence to practise law in the Supreme Court but was prevented from pleading by Attorney General Peter Magowan*, acting as a friend of the court, on the grounds that Macaulay lacked legal training and was a clergyman besides. The Highlander's response was that although he was not educated to the law, he understood Gaelic, an essential ingredient in legal dealings with the new arrivals. Only a few months later, early in 1807, Macaulay attempted to organize an exodus from the Island, where "industrious and Loyal Emigrants are paralyzed by indolent and monopolizing Land Proprietors of the uncultivated Wilderness in North America," but the authorities on Cape Breton displayed little enthusiasm for his schemes.

Over the next few years after 1807, Macaulay's public activities developed along two related fronts. One was vocal criticism of Selkirk and his agent James Williams, the other an increasingly closer relationship with the Loyal Electors, which he formally joined in 1809. By 1810, when Selkirk's dissatisfaction with Williams's performance as agent was reaching its height, the earl wrote to Captain John MacDonald* of Glenaladale that the rising troubles with Williams would undoubtedly bring into the picture Macaulay, "a character who cannot be unknown to you, tho you have probably not had the misfortune to know him as well as I do. His abilities are unquestionably great & he is also a man of great plausibility; but I have too certain experience, that no reliance can be placed on anything that he says: I have also seen in his conduct symptoms of a temper so diabolical, that in justice to human nature I can only describe them to a touch of mental derangement – which may perhaps account equally for his violence & his inconsistency." Captain John did not disabuse the earl of this opinion, writing independently at about the same time to Selkirk that

Macaulay

Macaulay was "officiously mischievous . . . on every occasion, railing, execrating, and incensing the populace against the Proprietors." Although many considered him "the Mad Dr. Macaulay," continued MacDonald, he was potentially a "first rate firebrand for kindling the Zeal of the Levellers," and at Loyal Elector meetings constantly abused Selkirk. Macaulay's discontents were added to by the fact that his crops had failed regularly so that he was forced to advertise some of his land for sale in 1811.

The year 1811 was a troubled one for Angus Macaulay, as it was for most of the Island's leading citizens. In August 1810 the lieutenant governor and council had ordered a new road opened to the Selkirk settlement, appointing Macaulay and James Williams as co-supervisors of the project. On Sunday 10 Feb. 1811 Williams ostentatiously posted an advertisement on the outside door of the chapel where Macaulay was preaching, charging that he had got an advance payment for the road from DesBarres "by unwarrantable means and under false pretenses," and had concealed the fact from Williams for months while refusing to pay the workmen under "frivolous & unjust pretexts."

Some months later, on 31 Aug. 1811, the *Weekly Recorder of Prince Edward Island* reported a speech to the Loyal Electors on the land question by William ROUBEL, secretary of the organization. Roubel had accused Selkirk of purchasing Island lots for a "mere trifle" and peopling them with Highlanders "at their own expense," charges supported by Macaulay in "a very animated and loyal Speech." Shortly thereafter, printer James Bagnall* advertised for sale a pamphlet by Macaulay answering claims in a London newspaper that new immigrants to the Island had been abandoned on a beach. The pamphlet itself has not survived, but Macaulay apparently distinguished between the generous treatment given the newcomers by the local population and their exploitation by the proprietors.

Macaulay also became involved in the "affidavits affair." In the late summer he and four other members of the Loyal Electors had sworn out affidavits bitterly critical of the administration of justice on the Island. Copies fell into the hands of Attorney General Charles Stewart*, who in October brought charges in the Island's Supreme Court that Macaulay had committed a "certain false wicked infamous and malicious libel" against Chief Justice Cæsar COLCLOUGH. The statement singled out as libellous Macaulay's allegation that the sheriff appointed by Colclough in 1810 (James Williams, although not named in the affidavit), "the Agent of a powerful Nobleman," had marched "at the Head of a prodigious number of Highlanders, composing no small Proportion of the Electors of this County, with Colours flying and Bagpipes playing to Influence the Elections" of 1806. The "Terror in the eyes" of some of them had revealed that they "from their Debts were obliged to Vote, as he the said Agent directed, though some of the People knew nothing about the Candidate, who lay upon his Death Bed, at the time." This statement probably had some basis in fact, but the criticisms made about Lord Selkirk elsewhere in the document were most unfair and probably actionable. In any event, the case against Macaulay was not proceeded with.

Legislative elections called in April 1812 were hard fought between the Loyal Electors and the "old party." William Roubel was routed in Charlottetown, but both Attorney General Charles Stewart and John Frederick Holland*, the leading spokesmen for the "cabal," were forced to withdraw from the hustings by public opposition. Although the "old party" elected a majority of the assembly – the Loyal Electors returning only 7 of 18 members, including Angus Macaulay – it was bereft of its leadership and chose to boycott the August–September 1812 session. As a result, the house was able to request that the lieutenant governor suspend Chief Justice Colclough for his part in the affidavits affair, which DesBarres did with alacrity and obvious relish. This action was the high point of the Loyal Electors' campaign against the "old party," for in response to information supplied by that party the proprietors at home forced the recall of DesBarres and the revocation of all James Bardin Palmer's many offices. The new lieutenant governor, Charles Douglass Smith*, who arrived in mid 1813, was no friend of private political organizations, and he quickly determined that the Electors were a dangerous confederacy who well deserved the attacks made upon them. Smith prorogued an unruly assembly in January 1814 and refused to meet it again for nearly four years, thus depriving critical gadflies such as Angus Macaulay of an official public platform for their views.

In a valedictory of sorts on his participation in the Loyal Electors, Macaulay in 1814 penned a lengthy letter of explanation and exculpation to his former employer Lord Selkirk, who had led the absentee proprietors against the society. The epistle was not in the least submissive, but it did attempt to explain Macaulay's actions; it also demonstrated his facility with the pen, showing him a worthy successor to fellow Highlander John MacDonald as an acerbic critic of Island foibles. Apologetically remarking that "a Cervantes or a Swift would make a valuable production from such materials as I have," Macaulay insisted that the "cabal" had hoodwinked the great while it "preyed equally like Peacham in Beggar's Opera upon the absent proprietors & industrious inhabitants." At the time of Selkirk's arrival, he continued, "the bulk of the inhabitants of the island consisted of entrapped Loyalists & illiterate Roman Catholic Highlanders, the latter mostly floating over the face of the country like Scythians, without money, bedcloaths, or permanent holdings for residence." Selkirk, he maintained, had been duped by the land speculators and had mistakenly chosen to support them. "The Kings Lands," Dr Macaulay insisted, "are every where else to be had in North America but [in] this monopolized wilderness," and he offered "to extricate the real Proprietors of whom you are one & [the] cultivating Inhabitants from the old system ruinous to both." Selkirk never answered this letter, and soon found himself embroiled in two legal actions brought by Macaulay, one dealing with alleged unfulfilled promises in 1803 and the other the "libellous" statement the earl had made about him in his 1810 private correspondence with Captain John Mac-Donald, which had somehow fallen into Macaulay's hands after Captain John's death.

When Lieutenant Governor Smith called for elections to a new assembly in 1818, Macaulay was returned from Queens County, and was active as speaker of the house in opposing Smith and his government. Elected again in 1820, Macaulay was once more chosen speaker when the house convened in July. This session was soon prorogued and Smith did not meet the assembly for the remainder of his term in office. Both sessions had witnessed scenes of open hostility between lieutenant governor and assembly, but Smith continued in office until he attempted in 1822 to collect quitrents which had been allowed to remain in arrears for some years. Led by John STEWART, the political élite of the Island turned upon him, and he was challenged at public meetings called in March 1823. Although Macaulay was easily returned to the assembly in 1824, he was resoundingly defeated in a contest for the speakership by the triumphant Stewart. This defeat marked the end of Macaulay's public career on the Island, although he continued his religious and medical ministrations until his death.

Regarded by most of his contemporaries as brilliant but unstable, Macaulay nevertheless stood by his people publicly and privately for more than a quarter of a century. Despite his rejection by Selkirk, Angus Macaulay had probably been the most consistent, honest, and useful agent the earl ever employed. Their incompatibility was a tragedy for the Highlanders of the Island.

J. M. BUMSTED

National Library of Ireland (Dublin), Dept. of MSS, MS 20287 (5) (O'Hara papers), Cæsar Colclough to Charles O'Hara, 18 Oct. 1812. PAC, MG 19, E1, ser.1, 39: 14977–15005; 50: 19123–44, 19153–56 (transcripts). PAPEI, Acc. 2534/24; Acc. 2849/129; RG 6, Supreme Court, case papers, 1811, King v. McAulay; 1812, King v. Williams. Private arch., Duke of Hamilton (Lennoxlove, Scot.), Hamilton muniments, Brown papers (National Reg. of Arch. (Scotland) (Edinburgh), Survey no.2177), bundle 1515, Macdonald of Boisdale to Robert Brown, 1 Dec. 1802; bundle 1516, James McDonald to Brown, 25 March 1803 (researchers wishing to consult papers should contact the National Reg. of Arch.). PRO, CO 226/22: 159–64; 226/42: 42. Douglas, Lord Selkirk's diary (White). Weekly Recorder of Prince Edward Island (Charlottetown), 31 Aug., 14 Sept., 2 Oct. 1811. Roll of alumni in arts of the University and King's College of Aberdeen, 1596–1860, ed. P. J. Anderson (Aberdeen, Scot., 1900). A roll of the graduates of the University of Glasgow from 31st December, 1727, to 31st December, 1897 with short biographical notes, comp. W. I. Addison (Glasgow, 1898). Scott et al., Fasti ecclesiæ scoticanæ, vol.7. J. M. MacLennan, From shore to shore, the life and times of the Rev. John MacLennan of Belfast, P.E.I. (Edinburgh, 1977). M. A. Macqueen, Hebridean pioneers (Winnipeg, 1957), 63–71; Skye pioneers and "the Island" ([Winnipeg, 1929]). J. M. Bumsted, "The Loyal Electors of Prince Edward Island," Island Magazine, no.8 (1980): 8–14; "Settlement by chance: Lord Selkirk and Prince Edward Island," CHR, 59 (1978): 170–88. D. C. Harvey, "The Loyal Electors," RSC Trans., 3rd ser., 24 (1930), sect.II: 101–10.

MACAULAY, JAMES, doctor, army officer, JP, and office holder; b. 1759 in Scotland; m. first 20 Nov. 1790 Elizabeth Tuck Hayter (d. 1809), and they had four sons and four daughters; m. secondly 10 Nov. 1817 Rachel Crookshank in York (Toronto); d. there 1 Jan. 1822.

James Macaulay joined the Queen's Rangers as surgeon's mate in 1779 and served with the regiment throughout the American revolution. He transferred to the 33rd Foot in 1785 and four years later was appointed surgeon of the New South Wales Regiment on the recommendation of his former commanding officer, John Graves Simcoe*. When Simcoe began planning his staff for the loyalist province of which he was to become lieutenant governor, he did not forget his "old Surgeon," whom he described as "a young man attached to his Profession, and of that docile, patient, and industrious turn . . . that will willingly direct itself to any pursuit." Macaulay was appointed surgeon on 1 Sept. 1791 and the following year accompanied Simcoe to Upper Canada.

Macaulay and his wife, a naval officer's daughter who had become close friends with Mrs Simcoe [Gwillim*], settled at Newark (Niagara-on-the-Lake), the provincial capital, and soon were prominent members of the local society. In 1795 the couple were among the victims of a scurrilous squib, purportedly written by the provincial secretary, William Jarvis*. By 1796 the family had moved to the new seat of government at York where Macaulay had been granted a town lot. An assiduous collector of land grants for himself and his family, before 1800 he had received 1,600 acres as part of his military allotment, a town lot in York and 1,200 acres for his wife, and 600 acres for each of his four children. But his most important acquisition was a 100-acre park lot north of

Macaulay

the town along Lot (Queen) Street west of Yonge Street; this area, on which he would later begin to lay out lots, became known as Macaulay Town and was absorbed into the city of Toronto in 1834.

At York, Macaulay took an active part in local affairs: he was appointed a justice of the peace in 1800, served as a commissioner to oversee the improvement of Yonge Street the following year, and with Chief Justice Henry Allcock*, the Reverend George Okill Stuart*, and others was on a committee planning the building of an Anglican church in 1803. That year, however, Macaulay was made senior hospital officer in the Canadas with the rank of surgeon to the forces, a post which required him to reside in Quebec. He managed to postpone his departure until September 1805, when he left York with "the prayers of a grateful community" and a "testimonial of regret" signed by its leading citizens.

Macaulay remained in charge of the medical department of Upper and Lower Canada until 1808 when he lost the post to William Somerville, the deputy inspector of hospitals on Governor Sir James Henry Craig*'s staff. In 1810 Macaulay petitioned to be appointed deputy inspector of hospitals but was judged unqualified for the position. He was named one of Lower Canada's medical examiners in December of that year along with Somerville, George Longmore*, and James FISHER and, after Somerville returned to England in 1811, again served as senior hospital officer. During the War of 1812 Macaulay helped to plan and establish military hospitals in Lower and Upper Canada. In May 1813 he served with Lieutenant-General Sir George Prevost* at the attack on Sackets Harbor, N.Y., and, following his appointment that July as deputy inspector of hospitals, was with Major-General Francis de ROTTENBURG on the Niagara peninsula. He was serving there at the end of the war and subsequently was stationed at Kingston until placed on half pay in February 1817.

That spring Macaulay returned to York, petitioned for the 1,000 acres to which he was entitled by his war services, and settled back into the medical circles of the town and the life of its local gentry. He served on the first Medical Board of Upper Canada with Christopher Widmer*, Grant Powell*, and William Lyons and acted as its senior medical officer from January 1819 until his death three years later. With James BABY, Peter Robinson*, and others, he was appointed to a commission formed in 1819 to deal with estates forfeited during the War of 1812, and he joined with other members of York's élite, including William Allan*, Thomas RIDOUT, and William Warren Baldwin*, in promoting the bank which was to be chartered as the Bank of Upper Canada.

James Macaulay's military career and land grants had brought him a comfortable existence and on his death he was able to leave to his children various land

holdings and to his widow £2,000 in Bank of England stock. By marriage the Macaulays were related to some of the most prominent families in Upper Canada. James's second wife was a sister of George Crookshank*, and his four daughters married Christopher Alexander Hagerman*, John William Gamble*, Peter Diehl, and John Solomon Cartwright* respectively. His eldest son, John Simcoe Macaulay*, was a captain in the Royal Engineers and a legislative councillor in Upper Canada from 1839 to 1841. Another son, James Buchanan Macaulay*, became chief justice of the Upper Canadian Court of Common Pleas.

GEOFFREY BILSON

Academy of Medicine (Toronto), MS 137. AO, MU 1095, Macaulay family. PAC, MG 23, H1, 3, vol.2: 38, 53–54, 77; RG 1, L1, 22: 238, 323; 25: 19; L3, 323A: Mc Misc., 1788–95/5; 328A: M2/258; 330: M4/121; 330A: M4/241; 333: M8/10; RG 5, B9, 61, 16 March 1819; RG 8, I (C ser.), 289: 12, 55–59, 63, 72, 87; 290: 299: 14, 21, 29; 680: 36, 236; 1015: 105; 1120: 205, 292; 1168: 33; 1171: 75; 1203½J: 13; 1218; 1709: 99; 1865: 93; RG 68, General index, 1651–1841. PRO, T 28/9, 24 Oct. 1811 (transcript at PAC). *Corr. of Lieut. Governor Simcoe* (Cruikshank). "Grants of crown lands in U.C.," AO *Report*, 1929: 49, 55, 76, 156, 159. Gwillim, *Diary of Mrs. Simcoe* (Robertson; 1911). "The probated wills of persons prominent in the public affairs of early Upper Canada: second collection," ed. A. F. Hunter, *OH*, 24 (1927): 402–6. *Town of York, 1793–1815* (Firth). "U.C. land book B," AO *Report*, 1930: 104. "U.C. land book C," AO *Report*, 1930: 141, 150; 1931: 18, 57. Chadwick, *Ontarian families. Commissioned officers in the medical services of the British army, 1660–1960*, comp. Alfred Peterkin *et al.* (2v., London, 1968), 1: 66. William Canniff, *The medical profession in Upper Canada, 1783–1850 . . .* (Toronto, 1894; repr. 1980). *Robertson's landmarks of Toronto*, 1: 177; 6: 326. F. N. G. Starr, "The passing of the surgeon," *Canadian Practitioner and Rev.* (Toronto), 26 (1901): 657–60.

MACAULAY, ZACHARY, sailor, merchant, seigneur, manager of the Saint-Maurice ironworks, JP, and militia officer; b. *c.* 1739; m. Genevieve Burrow, and they had three sons and three daughters; d. 18 April 1821 in Montreal.

Zachary Macaulay took part in the siege of Louisbourg, Île Royale (Cape Breton Island), in 1758 and in that of Quebec the following year as a midshipman on the *Princess of Orange*. Settled at Quebec by 1764, he bought a two-storey stone house on Rue du Sault-au-Matelot in Lower Town in 1765, where he opened a general store. Although James Cuthbert*, the seigneur of Berthier, had granted him an island in his seigneury, Macaulay continued to live at Quebec. In 1773 he joined a committee of local merchants chaired by William Grant* which sought constitutional reform. That year he went to London with Thomas

Walker* to press for a house of assembly. In 1774 he fought against the passage of the Quebec Act, which was unfavourable to the merchants' interests, and he subsequently agitated for its repeal [*see* Guy Carleton*].

In 1776 and 1780 Macaulay considered leaving the province but did not carry out his plans. However, in 1782 he decided to dispose of his property and put a notice in the *Quebec Gazette* offering for sale his house on Rue du Sault-au-Matelot, another on Rue Saint-Henri in Upper Town, and two pieces of land at Cap-Rouge, one bought in 1779 that had a house, barn, sawmill, and other buildings on it. The following year merchants James Dunlop* and John Wilson took legal action against him, and the Court of Common Pleas ordered the seizure of his property, which at that time included his two houses and the seigneuries of Rivière-de-la-Madeleine and Grande-Vallée-des-Monts. He retained possession of 120 *arpents* in the seigneury of Autray and another property of similar size in Berthier seigneury. But since Macaulay failed to pay the *cens et rentes* and clear his Berthier lands, Cuthbert threatened to re-incorporate them into the domain.

In 1785 Macaulay went to England, and on his return he settled in Yamachiche, a heavily wooded region from which he hoped to make money. Probably through his commercial activity, he came into contact with Mathew Bell*, who along with David MONRO and George Davison* was leasing the Saint-Maurice ironworks. Macaulay became manager of these works around 1794, the year that Bell sold him a piece of land in Trois-Rivières. From then on Macaulay seemed to be the guiding force behind the undertaking, and as superintendent or foreman he signed the contracts for hiring workmen and numerous notarized deeds connected with the running of the ironworks.

In 1797 Macaulay received a commission as justice of the peace in the district of Trois-Rivières, and it was periodically renewed until 1815. In 1798 he was a captain in the Saint-Maurice ironworks battalion of militia, and in July 1816 he was promoted major in the Trois-Rivières battalion. Little is known of his private life. On 2 Aug. 1796 he had signed a notarized declaration freeing his black slave Jenny, aged about 35. Three years later he was present as a witness and friend at Bell's wedding. He had, then, won the esteem of the man whom he had first known as his employer.

On 13 June 1821, two months after Macaulay's death, an inventory of his belongings was made. It reveals that he had been living in the main house at the ironworks and owned a few clothes, a watch, pencil, and chain, all of gold, two dozen silver spoons, and 21 books. The firm of Monro and Bell had owed him £2,645 1*s.* 2*d.* since 17 Jan. 1810 and his salary as manager of the ironworks since 31 Dec. 1817. That

Macaulay had accepted this situation shows his loyalty and attachment to the enterprise in which he had worked for 25 years. Since only a few things were found in his father's house, Henry Macaulay came directly into possession of them without having to evaluate and sell them.

MARIE-FRANCE FORTIER

ANQ-MBF, CN1-4, 2 août 1796, 17 sept. 1799; CN1-6, 13 juin 1821. ANQ-Q, CN1-205, 6 mai 1769, 28 déc. 1770, 6 déc. 1776, 21 déc. 1779, 26 janv. 1780, 24 avril 1780. PAC, RG 68, General index, 1651–1841. *Quebec Gazette*, 9 April, 12 Sept. 1776; 21 Sept. 1780; 8 Aug. 1782; 9 Jan. 1783; 4 May 1786; 11 July 1816. "Papiers d'État," PAC *Rapport*, 1890: 50, 56. *Quebec almanac*, 1798–1821. Benjamin Sulte, *Mélanges historiques* . . . , Gérard Malchelosse, édit. (21v., Montréal, 1918–34), 21: 42–46. Douglas Brymner, "Zachary Macaulay," *BRH*, 2 (1896): 172–73. Benjamin Sulte, "Zachary Macaulay," *Le Bien public* (Trois-Rivières, Qué.), 21 nov. 1918: 7. "Zachary Macaulay, père de lord Macaulay?" *BRH*, 52 (1946): 220–21.

MACBRAIRE, JAMES, agent, merchant, army and militia officer, office holder, and JP; b. 1757 in Londonderry (Northern Ireland); m. 29 March 1792 Elizabeth Bower in Bristol, England, and they had one son; he also had an illegitimate son with Mary Herald of Harbour Grace, Nfld; d. 24 March 1832 in Berwick-upon-Tweed, England.

Remembered mainly as a successful merchant and probably the greatest philanthropist of his generation in Newfoundland, James MacBraire was in his day distinguished for the unusual combination of attributes he demonstrated. He joined philanthropy and a genuine concern for the poor (especially the Irish poor) with a marked ability to win the trust of the island's officials and a genius for staying outside the political and social squabbles which affected Newfoundland during the first 30 years of the 19th century. In addition, he was a keen and grasping merchant who probably took out more writs for debt against the fishermen and small tradesmen with whom he dealt than any other merchant of his day. He thus died both rich and generally esteemed by all classes, proving that a Newfoundland merchant could be at once successful and popular. Few have managed to emulate him since.

During his lifetime MacBraire seemed to cultivate a certain mystery about his origins and early life, which were not typical of the average man of his class. His place of birth was singular, for northern Ireland had limited connections with the Newfoundland fisheries. MacBraire liked to be regarded as one who had risen from humble origins, although this picture may not be completely accurate. He apparently enlisted in the British army at the age of 18 and served for five years

MacBraire

during the American Revolutionary War before being discharged as a sergeant in 1780. He was then evidently apprenticed as a clerk to the firm of William Danson and Company of Bristol, which traded to Harbour Grace. MacBraire is said to have remained in their employ until 1786, when he purchased property in Harbour Grace. This story may be true, but if it is MacBraire did not acquire any immediate fortune or prominence. It is significant that when his name appears in records it is not as an independent merchant or trader but as the Newfoundland agent for the Bristol firm of Joseph Bower and Company.

On 29 March 1792 MacBraire married Elizabeth, only daughter of Joseph Bower; her father died shortly thereafter. Bower's son James should have been the principal inheritor of the fortune, but for some reason Elizabeth received the entire estate, which consisted mainly of vessels and a property in Harbour Grace. Almost certainly, therefore, MacBraire, far from acquiring wealth painfully, had acted in a traditional way by marrying his employer's daughter. There remains one mystery about MacBraire's early life, namely how in those localized and class-ridden times a poor young sergeant from Londonderry could have secured promising employment from a Bristol firm engaged in the Newfoundland trade. The one possible clue is the marriage in 1765 of a man named Macbraire, partner in an ironmonger's business, to a considerable heiress of Bristol. It is likely that this man was a kinsman of MacBraire and that his influence obtained James his entry into the commercial world of Newfoundland.

Whatever the true story, by 1793 MacBraire was established in a promising situation, but his prospects were probably comparatively modest. The Bower inheritance gave him a moderate capital and a small but solid trade in and around Harbour Grace. The area was relatively heavily populated, and thus the production of fish and the demand for supplies were substantial. For those reasons, however, competition was strong, probably more so than in any other part of Newfoundland, and chances for expansion were fairly slight. Moreover, the death of his father-in-law had left MacBraire without an "English house" essential in many aspects of the trade and placed him at a grave disadvantage when compared with other Conception Bay merchants. The most successful merchants of MacBraire's era did at least one but preferably all of three things: establish themselves in St John's, where communications with the outside world were far superior and trade could be carried on throughout Newfoundland; open up a business in some area of new settlement where the population was growing fast and established traders were either absent or slow to expand; and create through kinship or partnership a firm or branch in the United Kingdom, where the possibilities for international trading could be maximized.

MacBraire did all three, and by the time he left Newfoundland in 1817 had amassed a fortune of some £80,000. He found a base in the United Kingdom by entering into partnership with the firm of James Henderson and Company of Falkirk, Scotland. Just how MacBraire and Henderson met is not known, but Henderson's was a firm of shipowners and traders that apparently had vessels in the Newfoundland trade from the 1780s. Details of the partnership, which proved profitable for both parties, are unclear. However, there are indications that it began around 1796, and the partners certainly owned deep-sea vessels in the Newfoundland trade both jointly and separately. Probably the partnership affected only MacBraire's import and export trade and not his dealings in Newfoundland.

In 1795 MacBraire had been commissioned a captain in Thomas Skinner*'s Royal Newfoundland Fencible Regiment. Two years later he moved to St John's. He did not, apparently, begin by opening a fishery trade, but instead obtained an appointment as commissary to the naval hospital, a profitable but restricted position. In 1798 he brought his wife out from England and began to purchase property in and around St John's. His timing was excellent, for that year the Newfoundland trade was greatly depressed by the closure of almost all European markets, and many traders and merchants were insolvent. Soon MacBraire had purchased a wharf and store and he rapidly became an important merchant in the St John's region.

MacBraire's last and most successful step came around 1806 when he established a branch of his firm in Kings Cove, Bonavista Bay. To manage the business he brought out a fellow Irishman, Michael Murphy, who turned out to be a singularly able and trustworthy agent. Bonavista Bay had been fished and settled by Englishmen since the 17th century, but until the American revolution the population was confined mainly to Bonavista, Greenspond, and Salvage, and the inhabitants were supplied by the traders of Trinity in Trinity Bay. By 1806 the population of Bonavista Bay was increasing rapidly and many new coves and islands were being settled. MacBraire was able to tap this promising area by creating a permanent and year-round business at Kings Cove, and as the settlement grew his trade was bound to follow suit.

Bonavista Bay provided more than codfish, for it was a prime sealing area and possessed good quantities of prime timber which proved excellent for shipbuilding. By 1810 MacBraire's shipwrights had constructed ten vessels weighing between 30 and 140 tons, and in 1812 his production of codfish reached 15,000 quintals. From Kings Cove, MacBraire increasingly competed with the merchants of Fogo and Twillingate in supplying the trappers and fishermen of the Bay of Exploits region. By 1808 he had entered the Gander Bay salmon fishery.

Kings Cove eventually proved to be MacBraire's

most profitable and longest-lived business enterprise, but he seems hardly ever to have gone there, preferring the amenities of St John's. Between 1800 and 1804 he had disposed of his interests and trade in Harbour Grace, but he restlessly extended his fishery dealings down the Southern Shore and, by 1810, into Placentia Bay. By 1809 the insured value of Mac-Braire's premises in St John's was the third highest in the town. He had clearly established himself as one of the community's leading merchants and citizens, and this success inevitably propelled him into its social life.

MacBraire does not seem to have been active in any of the political or social squabbles that engaged the attention of most of the St John's élite during this period, and his equable character and obvious business acumen evidently won him the trust and regard of his fellow residents. Instead of quarrelling he used his energies and position constructively. In 1807 he played a leading part in the formation of the Society of Merchants, the forerunner of the present-day Board of Trade, and was elected its president, a position he held for most years until his departure from the island. MacBraire's work with the society brought him great esteem and recognition, but his role in the formation and development of the Benevolent Irish Society earned him the greatest applause and subsequent fame. By 1806 emigration to Newfoundland was building up rapidly, especially from southern Ireland, and much of this migration was into the larger centres such as St John's, which saw its population double in less than 20 years. The town was without a system of poor relief and was overcrowded and poverty-stricken, especially in the months between February and May when the landless poor, unemployed and with their earnings of the previous summer expended, faced acute distress and even starvation.

In this situation the more prosperous Irish residents combined to found the Benevolent Irish Society in 1806. Although the society was cordially supported by most of the middle-class Irish (and indeed in its early days by many English merchants and tradesmen), its creation and early leadership depended mainly upon Captain William Haly, a garrison officer, and MacBraire. Both were Protestant, but ecumenism flourished in Newfoundland during this era, and their work in the creation of the society was met with esteem and enthusiasm from all classes. In 1811 MacBraire assumed the presidency of the society from Haly, and in 1819 he was elected "perpetual president." Although there should be no disparagement of the real benevolence which MacBraire displayed in the society and in general (for example, in the distresses of 1817 he donated far more free meals to the poor than any other individual), his generosity did him no harm in his commercial dealings, which were overwhelmingly with Irish fishermen. His charity seems to have outweighed the effects of his hard commercial attitude towards the fishermen and his penchant for obtaining writs and foreclosing on mortgages in cases of debt.

In 1812 MacBraire was involved in his one disagreement with the authorities. It was a personal rather than a political matter. The outbreak of war with the United States caused Governor Sir John Thomas Duckworth* to reactivate a local militia in the form of the St John's Volunteer Rangers. As the most prominent merchant in the town and commander of the unit's predecessor, the Loyal Volunteers of St John's, MacBraire was asked to lead the rangers as captain commandant. Feeling no doubt that he deserved advancement from a rank he had already held, he demanded the grade of major. A temporary compromise was arranged and in 1813 the promotion came through.

By 1815, although he may not have realized it, MacBraire's greatest days were coming to an end. His business flourished and he continued as the acknowledged leader of St John's society, a position rounded out by his appointment that year as a justice of the peace for the town. This nomination was more unusual than might appear, for he was the only person not a government official to be appointed. The same year he served as an Anglican churchwarden. In 1817 MacBraire reached the age of 60. Although he had passed many winters in the United Kingdom, he had spent far more time in Newfoundland than most men of his wealth and prominence, and like them had always planned to retire and enjoy his declining years on an estate in the old country. On 10 July his partnership with James Henderson was dissolved, and he sailed for Scotland to the thunderous applause and tributes of St John's, and above all of the Irish community, which remembered him annually at the St Patrick's Day dinner.

After leaving Newfoundland, MacBraire leased out his St John's premises but retained and even expanded his business in Kings Cove. During the 1820s that trade produced 16–20,000 quintals of fish and 4–8,000 seals annually. By 1827 he had taken his old agent, Michael Murphy, into partnership. MacBraire played no part in the agitation for representative government during the 1820s but in 1830 was elected to serve on a committee of prominent Britons who presented a petition in favour of political reform to the home government. By then, however, his life was nearly over. In August 1831 Murphy died in Kings Cove, and the following March, MacBraire himself died. He thus passed from the scene before the British government permanently changed the Newfoundland he had known by introducing representative government. One doubts if he was upset at missing the innovation; charity not politics, and business not rhetoric, seem to have been his principles.

The Kings Cove business passed to his son John Joseph, who declined to visit Newfoundland and left

McBride

the concern in the hands of an agent. John Joseph was no businessman and by the time he died in 1839 the trade was a shadow of its former self. The property was left vacant until 1845, when a son of Michael Murphy took it over for his own use.

KEITH MATTHEWS

Professor Matthews died during the editing of the volume and did not leave a bibliography for the article. The DCB/DBC is grateful for the assistance of two members of the staff of Memorial Univ. of Nfld. (St John's), Roberta Thomas of the Maritime History Group and Professor John Mannion of the Department of Geography, in providing citations from which to construct a bibliography.

Hunt, Roope & Co. (London), Robert Newman & Co., journal, August 1796 (mfm. at Maritime Hist. Arch., Memorial Univ. of Nfld.). Maritime Hist. Arch., Conception Bay plantation books, 1804, 1806 (copies); MacBraire name file. PANL, GN 2/1/A, 13–15, 17, 19–21, 24; GN 5/1/B, Harbour Grace records, 1798, 1790, 1793, 1795; GN 5/2/A/1, 1798–1800, 1802–4, 1807–8; GN 5/2/B, 1827; James MacBraire file, box 1096; P1/5; P3/B/22. Phoenix Assurance Company Ltd. (London), Jenkin Jones, report to Matthew Wilson on St John's, 6 June 1809 (photocopy at PANL). PRO, ADM 50/111; BT 107 (copies at Maritime Hist. Arch.); CO 33/18, 33/23; CO 194/47, 194/54, 194/56; CO 199/18; WO 12/11020–23; WO 17/240. St Paul's Anglican Church (Harbour Grace, Nfld.), Conception Bay mission, reg. of baptisms, marriages, and burials, 7 Jan. 1778 (mfm. at PANL). *Felix Farley's Bristol Journal* (Bristol, Eng.), 25 May 1765. *Lloyd's List* (London), 1810. *Newfoundland Mercantile Journal*, 7 March, 11 April, 6, 8 June 1817; 25 Feb. 1819. *Royal Gazette and Newfoundland Advertiser*, 17 Feb. 1811; June 1813; 16 March, 31 Aug. 1815; 4, 17 March, 1, 8, 18 July 1817; 21 Sept. 1830; 16 Aug., 15 Nov. 1831; 1 May, 26 June 1832. *The register of shipping* (London), 1806–10. *Centenary volume, Benevolent Irish Society of St. John's, Newfoundland, 1806–1906* (Cork, [Republic of Ire., 1906?]). C. R. Fay, *Life and labour in Newfoundland* (Toronto, 1956), 168. J. W. McGrath, "James MacBraire, merchant and pioneer, 1795–1840," *Winning entries in the Newfoundland government sponsored competition for the encouragement of arts and letters, etc., 1970* (St. John's, [1970]). Prowse, *Hist. of Nfld.* (1895), 383.

McBRIDE, EDWARD WILLIAM, businessman, militia officer, printer, and politician; b. 1791 or 1792 in Niagara (Niagara-on-the-Lake), Upper Canada, son of Peter McBride and Mary Bradshaw; d. there 3 Sept. 1834.

Edward William McBride's father, an Irish Protestant, served in a British regiment during the American revolution. Some time after the war he apparently settled with other members of the family in the Niagara region; by the end of the century there were three McBrides, Peter, Edward, and James, listed as freeholders in the town of Niagara. In muster-rolls dating from the War of 1812, Edward William McBride first appears as sergeant and quartermaster of

the 3rd York Militia, and later he was promoted ensign in the 1st Regiment of Lincoln Militia. His services during the war were rewarded with land grants in York (Toronto) and Cramahe Township.

After the war McBride worked as an office assistant to king's printer John Cameron on the *York Gazette* and in late April 1815, with his employer ill, he began conducting the business himself. Cameron died on 26 November and from 9 December until 3 Feb. 1816 McBride is described on the *Gazette*'s masthead as the printer of the paper. He next appears in 1818 as an innkeeper at Niagara, where he occupied a "Large House." That year he was attracted to Robert Gourlay*'s movement for political reform. He was one of about a hundred residents of Niagara who in 1818 supported a petition to the Prince Regent which blamed the Legislative Council for the post-war depression in Upper Canada. McBride's involvement in politics increased after Gourlay's banishment in 1819. In 1824 he was elected to the House of Assembly for the new constituency of Niagara as a candidate against "small tyranny and oppression." His election was part of a wider reform victory in Lincoln County, where four of the five seats were won by reformers.

McBride's record in the House of Assembly shows him to have been a loyal reformer. He supported the reform position on the clergy reserves, the charter of King's College, and the alien question. He also voted for resolutions defending those connected with Gourlay's convention of 1818 and calling for the resignation of the chief justice from the Executive Council. Although not a leading figure in the house, he did sit on committees dealing with the case of Captain John MATTHEWS, the Welland Canal, and the alien question (he was one of two members given the task of drafting an address to the king on this subject).

It was the issue of the Welland Canal that got McBride into difficulty with Andrew Heron, publisher of the *Gleaner, and Niagara Newspaper*. Heron was devoted to retrenchment and he attacked McBride in the *Gleaner* for advocating government grants to projects such as the Welland Canal and, in the next breath, for not pressing the cause of a secondary canal to link Niagara with the new waterway. In one case, Heron's condemnation of McBride was justified. In 1828 McBride served as an arbitrator in a dispute between contractor James Gordon STROBRIDGE and the commissioners of the Burlington Bay Canal and, when the latter refused to abide by the settlement, he attacked them in print. He was particularly incensed that Attorney General John Beverley Robinson*, who had initiated arbitration of the dispute, had agreed to become the lawyer for the commissioners. Though McBride argued that he was motivated by principle and concern for the unpaid labourers employed on the canal, his conduct, as Heron pointed out, was contrary to his role as an arbitrator.

The platform from which McBride attacked the commissioners of the Burlington Bay Canal and the attorney general was the *Niagara Herald*. McBride and another friend of Gourlay, Bartemas FERGUSON, had undertaken publication of the paper for John Crooks. A reading of the few tattered issues of the *Herald* that survive provides an inkling of McBride's political ideas. In their first issue of 24 Jan. 1828, the publishers asserted "that the HERALD is not to be the *tool* of government nor the *dupe* of party. Its course shall be emphatically independent, neither courting nor wantonly insulting the powers that be, nor mingling with the scatter-brain'd politics of William Lyon Mackenzie[*]." Independent yes, but hardly non-partisan. The publishers expressed their dissatisfaction with the *status quo* and, with items such as a biography of the British free-trader William Huskisson, they sought to make reform respectable. With reference to the Burlington Canal episode, McBride wrote in the *Herald* in June 1828 that "a few more independent Judges, and a free and independent House of Assembly are the only remedies – and then the people of this beautiful Province will have the pleasure of seeing good and wholesome British Laws purely administered, and all this hitherto trifling pettifogging system entirely done away."

One month later McBride furnished an example of the inequities of justice in Upper Canada. In the 17 July 1828 issue of the *Herald* he reported to "the Electors of Lincoln" that "measures have been resorted to . . . in order completely to destroy my chance of being elected to the next House of Assembly." On the order of judge Levius Peters Sherwood*, the local sheriff had arrested McBride as guarantor for an indebted acquaintance who had jumped bail. McBride claimed that the debtor had been recaptured in the United States and that he himself had been summarily imprisoned so that he could not campaign for re-election. In the election that followed he was defeated.

McBride's defeat in 1828 can be partly credited to the anti-masonic movement. He had been treated by Andrew Heron as the spokesman for Niagara's free-masons. In 1826 hostility to the order reached fever pitch when Captain William Morgan of Utica, N.Y., was kidnapped and allegedly murdered for revealing the secrets of the order in a book entitled *Illustrations of masonry* . . . (Batavia, N.Y., 1826). An Albany newspaper reported that Morgan had been brought "blindfolded and tied" by the kidnappers to the house "of M—— a member of Parliament" en route to his supposed place of execution. McBride denounced the story as "utterly false" and offered to produce affidavits by himself "as well as that of my family, consisting of three persons" testifying to his innocence. McBride's denial was ignored and his name continued

to appear in anti-masonic literature as a party to the kidnapping and presumed murder.

A damaged reputation and political defeat were augmented by other misfortunes. For two years McBride advertised for payment from his debtors but, in 1827, his land and "elegant two storey Dwelling House" with outbuildings were seized to pay his own creditors. In 1829 a shop from which he sold liquor, dry goods, and lumber was taken over by his brother, a saddler. By that year as well McBride and Ferguson had lost control of the *Herald* and Ferguson went off to found another newspaper. McBride himself apparently remained in Niagara; he seems to have been a contributor to the local Presbyterian Church, St Andrew's, in 1830. He died in Niagara on 3 Sept. 1834, at the age of 42.

PETER N. MOOGK

PAC, RG 1, L3, 339: M11/320; RG 19, E5(a), 3740, claim 16. "Names only but much more," comp. Janet Carnochan, Niagara Hist. Soc., [*Pub.*], no.27 (n.d.): 13–17. U.C., House of Assembly, *Journal*, 1825–29. *Gleaner* (Niagara [Niagara-on-the-Lake, Ont.]), 1817–32. *Niagara Herald*, 1828–30. *York Gazette*, 29 April, 9 Sept., 9 Dec. 1815. *The anti-masonic almanack, for . . . 1828*, comp. Edward Giddins (Rochester, N.Y., 1827). Armstrong, *Handbook of Upper Canadian chronology* (1967). Chadwick, *Ontarian families*, 2: 92. *DAB* (biog. of William Morgan). *Death notices of Ont.* (Reid), 114. H. J. Morgan, *Sketches of celebrated Canadians*, 649–50. *Officers of British forces in Canada* (Irving). Carnochan, *Hist. of Niagara*, 123, 231–32. H. V. Nelles, "Loyalism and local power: the district of Niagara, 1792–1837," *OH*, 58 (1966): 99–114. W. S. Wallace, "The periodical literature of Upper Canada," *CHR*, 12 (1931): 15.

McCALL, DUNCAN, merchant, politician, JP, and militia officer; b. 18 Nov. 1769 in Basking Ridge, N.J., son of Donald (Donell) McCall (McColl) and Elsie Simpson; m. first Jemima Fairchild (d. 1798), and they had a son and a daughter; m. secondly Mary Lockwood, a widow, and they had a son; d. 25 Nov. 1832 in York (Toronto), Upper Canada.

Donald McCall came to North America from Scotland as a private in the 42nd Foot (Royal Highland Regiment) and transferred in 1762 to the 77th Foot (Montgomery's Highlanders). After the Seven Years' War he settled in New Jersey and raised a family. He saw service again during the American revolution. At the conclusion of that conflict he tried, briefly, to re-establish himself in New Jersey; he then moved to New Brunswick. Like other loyalists such as Samuel Ryerse* and Thomas Welch*, he became dissatisfied with life there; again like them, he was attracted by the possibilities offered in the new province of Upper Canada. On 26 June 1795 the colony's Executive Council approved the petition of McCall, his son John, and Patrick Haggarty for a tract of land on the

McCallum

north shore of Lake Erie "for the establishment of at least one hundred settlers" from New Jersey. McCall and his three sons, including Duncan, each received a grant of 600 acres. Every settler they brought with them was promised 200 acres. The family, with the exception of Duncan, arrived in 1796 and took up land in Charlotteville Township. He came the following year with a shipment of goods and merchandise from New York. For many years afterwards, Duncan McCall operated a store in the township; by 1816 he was farming as well, having 60 acres under cultivation.

The McCalls were a prominent local family in the Long Point region and became involved in the extreme factionalism that characterized the politics of the area prior to the War of 1812. John McCall, for instance, had supported Benajah Mallory* in his opposition to the office-holding élite symbolized by Ryerse and Welch. Welch dismissed him as an "abandoned Character . . . accustomed to escape from the penalties of the Law in New Jersey, where nothing less than *Grand Larceny* is laid to his Charge. . . . He is certainly a very bad Man." Early in 1810, when Duncan McCall was being considered for local office, Ryerse expressed concern to Chief Justice Thomas SCOTT. For one thing McCall was a trader who occasionally resided in the United States. For another and just as distressing, he had been seen in a tavern "deeply Engaged in a game of Chance (throwing Dice and pitching Dollars) which would Seem to indicate a partiality for low Company." McCall, needless to say, did not receive the appointment.

Duncan McCall made his mark at a later date as a politician. He was elected one of the two members for the riding of Norfolk in 1824, 1828, and 1830. The focus of his legislative activity was local. His major accomplishments included the rebuilding of the Vittoria jail and court-house after a fire in 1825 and the erection of a lighthouse on Long Point. His career witnessed the beginning of entrenched opposition in the assembly and an increase of political strife. He had close associations with opposition leaders such as John Rolph* and was an early subscriber to William Lyon Mackenzie*'s *Colonial Advocate*. Although issues such as the alien question [*see* Sir Peregrine Maitland*] touched him closely, he had an independent voting record, siding most often with members from neighbouring constituencies. In short, he reflected the major concern of legislators for material development in the areas they knew best. Asahel Bradley LEWIS's St Thomas *Liberal* considered him "always the firm, uncompromising and vigilant friend of equal laws, equal justice, and liberal opinions . . . the unyielding friend of the people, alike regardless of the frowns and smiles of the little York official."

An officer in the 1st Norfolk Militia, a justice of the peace (appointed in 1829), and a Presbyterian, Duncan McCall died in November 1832, having suffered from diarrhoea and fever for several days. The house was still in session. George Gurnett*'s *Courier of Upper Canada* (York) claimed he had been the oldest member in the assembly. He was survived by his wife and three children.

ELWOOD H. JONES

AO, MS 75, Thomas Welch to Russell, 31 Jan. 1805. Eva Brook Donly Museum (Simcoe, Ont.), Norfolk Hist. Soc. Coll., Walsh (Welch) papers. PAC, RG 4, B47, 3, naturalization reg., 1832; RG 5, A1: 4658–60; RG 68, General index, 1651–1841: 465. *Charlotteville Township assessments for the years 1808–1811*, ed. W. [R.] Yeager (Simcoe, 1976). *Corr. of Lieut. Governor Simcoe* (Cruikshank), 4: 31, 77. "Grants of crown lands in U.C.," AO *Report*, 1929: 101. *Pioneers of Charlotteville Township, Norfolk County, 1798–1816*, ed. W. [R.] Yeager (Simcoe, 1977). "The roster of Capt. John Reid's company of the 42nd Regiment of Foot, taken at Lake George Camp, 24th October 1758," ed. Mary McCall Middleton, *Ontario Reg.* (Lambertville, N.J.), 3 (1970): 223–30. *Transcript of the McCall–Fairchild cemetery*, ed. W. [R.] Yeager (Simcoe, 1978). *Colonial Advocate*, 18 Nov. 1830. *Liberal* (St Thomas, [Ont.]), 6 Dec. 1832, 10 Jan. 1833. *Death notices of Ont.* (Reid), 136. *Sources in McCall genealogy*, ed. W. [R.] Yeager (Simcoe, 1978). *Wills of the London District, 1800–1839: an abstract and index guide to the London District Surrogate Registry registers . . .*, ed. W. R. Yeager (Simcoe, 1979).

McCALLUM, JAMES, businessman, seigneur, office holder, and politician; b. *c.* 1762; m. Janet ——, and they had at least ten children; d. 19 Dec. 1825 at Quebec.

James McCallum was a master baker on Rue Saint-Pierre, in the commercial heart of Quebec, in 1794. That year he entered into an association with the brothers Philip and Nathaniel Lloyd to exploit the fisheries, hunting-grounds, and Indian trade of Labrador. McCallum, who seems to have had capital, was to purchase a boat, furnish supplies, and market the produce in return for a 50 per cent share in the profits. The partners had fallen out by March 1797 when McCallum, having failed to keep his side of the agreement, sold his interest to a rival firm, Lymburner and Crawford, for £622. The Lloyds took McCallum to court; they apparently obliged him in 1799 to dissolve his association with them at considerable cost, but the case dragged on for years.

McCallum's loss of interest in the Lloyd partnership stemmed from a desire to concentrate on the grain and flour trade of the south shore of the St Lawrence below Quebec. In 1796 he had become seigneur or co-seigneur of L'Islet-de-Bonsecours at a cost of £438, which he paid in cash. On his own and jointly with Pierre CASGRAIN of Rivière-Ouelle he began purchasing large quantities of barley for John

Young*'s brewery and distillery near Quebec. In February 1798 McCallum and John McCallum of St John's (Prince Edward) Island joined Casgrain in an association to trade and speculate in grain and other country products. In addition to advancing one-half of the operating capital, James was to build a storehouse in the parish of Saint-Roch-des-Aulnaies and manage operations at Quebec; Casgrain resided in Rivière-Ouelle and John probably in Saint-Roch-des-Aulnaies. In March, James McCallum and Casgrain also agreed to buy all their grain on the south shore jointly for seven years and to reserve the first 100,000 *minots* annually for Young, who had apparently undertaken to purchase in that region only through them.

In January 1801 McCallum entered another field of endeavour with the purchase from Young for £3,750 of two-thirds of St Andrew's Wharf, strategically located at Quebec; he acquired the remaining part at a sheriff's sale in March and built, at considerable expense, two large stone warehouses. The wharf was leased until 1805 successively to Henry Caldwell* and Monro and Bell [see David MONRO] for £500 per annum, but by 1812 it was bringing in £1,000 annually. McCallum continued to supply Young, whose firm of Young and Ainslie owed him nearly £3,000 by October 1803. Young paid for his grain partly in beer and spirits, which McCallum may have sold retail from a tavern on Rue Saint-Pierre and wholesale to such customers as Casgrain (who had agreed to buy only from him) and the merchant John Painter*.

McCallum also maintained grist-mills. In 1803 he leased the manorial mill of L'Islet-de-Bonsecours to the miller Archibald McCallum, probably a relative or clansman, in return for two-thirds of the wheat ground; nine years later he leased it to another miller for one-quarter of the profits and the right to have his grain ground at an advantageous price. In 1809 he had purchased at a sheriff's sale a large mill at Beauport formerly belonging to Young, and from 1813 at least he rented land around it from the seigneur of Beauport, Antoine-Louis JUCHEREAU Duchesnay, for the growing of grain. From the beginning he produced flour for use in his bakery, for sale locally, and for export; he transported it and wheat in vessels chartered from John GOUDIE and probably from others. In 1818 he was made an inspector of flour and meal at Quebec and two years later was an examiner of candidates for inspector.

By 1815 McCallum had formed James McCallum and Company with a son, John. The firm sold rum and Jamaica spirits, salt, oil, staves, peas, and grains. It received in April 1817 a contract worth £4,450 to supply government commissioners with seed grain for distribution to farmers who had suffered a disastrous harvest the previous fall.

In June 1813 McCallum had purchased the St Roc Brewery from Young's wife, Christian Ainslie, who was harassed by her husband's debts; the price agreed upon was £16,000 plus £2,177 for the stock on hand, all of which he had paid by September. He began immediately to make improvements; in the end they cost probably more than £1,000 and included a large wharf, which took five years to complete. He also hired a brewer at £150 per annum and a maltster at £90 and soon began importing hops from James Hunter and Company of Greenock, Scotland. He apparently manufactured containers for beer and spirits since in 1815 James McCallum and Company received contracts to supply the Transport Board with puncheons and hogsheads worth about £8,000. By the early 1820s the brewery was being operated by McCallum and Sons, composed of James and two sons, James and Duncan.

McCallum also engaged in property development. He bought a number of lots in Godmanchester Township in 1802 and leased 1,168 acres from the crown in Hemmingford four years later. In April 1810 he paid Anglican bishop Jacob MOUNTAIN £833 for about 4,000 acres that Mountain had just been granted in Sherrington Township. In June 1813 he acquired from Young some 7,200 acres in the same township for £1,672. His interest in Sherrington stemmed from its potential for immediate production of grain. Surveyor General Joseph Bouchette* had noted by 1815 that Sherrington was surrounded by established settlements, "and possessing within itself great inducements for settlers, it is likely to become in a few years a very fertile and valuable tract." In 1824, in order to avoid continued costly litigation with Canadians already settled on the lands when he acquired them, and in return for a promise by the government to concede the clergy reserves within their boundaries, McCallum had his Sherrington holdings converted to seigneurial tenure as the seigneuries of Saint-James and Saint-Normand. Some four years earlier he had bought 700 acres of unpatented land in Hinchinbrook Township from Bouchette.

In addition to developing rural property, McCallum rented out a number of houses in Lower Town Quebec, generally for commercial use. As a property owner he had been a member of the Fire Society and had occasionally served on its board. He was a stockholder in the Quebec Fire Assurance Company by 1819 and a director from 1820. This activity and his election in 1818 as a director of the newly formed Quebec Bank placed him in the vanguard of the Quebec business community.

McCallum appears to have been as aggressive in politics as in business. In 1817 he defeated John Neilson* in a by-election in Quebec County, where Beauport was located, but his victory was voided when Neilson was able to prove to the House of

McCallum

Assembly that McCallum had used bullies and bribery. Neilson was returned in early 1818. In the elections of March 1820 McCallum withdrew from the race in the riding of Devon, which included L'Islet-de-Bonsecours, after polling just four votes in two days, and he was defeated by Neilson and Louis GAUVREAU in Quebec County. His protest that the returning officer in Quebec County, Félix Têtu, had erroneously given a slight majority to Gauvreau was apparently rejected. McCallum succeeded, however, in getting elected for Lower Town Quebec in July. He represented that riding until 1824, when he was defeated by Thomas Ainslie Young*. He maintained that Young had employed corrupt tactics, but his claim was never fully studied by the assembly.

McCallum's rapid business expansion after 1800 was based increasingly on borrowed capital. With his acquisition of the St Roc Brewery and Sherrington lands in June 1813, however, he overextended himself. In 1814 he owed a Quebec blacksmith, David Douglas, £2,200; a year later he borrowed a total of £4,000 from John Painter, and in 1816 he obtained £4,000 from George Pozer* and £1,100 from a Quebec widow, Ann Purcell. By 1819 his debt to Douglas had soared to £15,000. The following year nearly £10,000 of this debt was in the hands of the Quebec Bank; impatient with McCallum's inability to make payments, in 1824 the bank obliged him to lease to it for five years McCallum's Wharf and two houses on Rue Saint-Pierre, the lease payments to be deducted from the debt. In 1822 McCallum and Sons was dissolved, and on 6 Oct. 1825 McCallum transferred all his properties to three sons in return for their promise to pay some £23,000 in debts to Painter's estate, François DESRIVIÈRES in Montreal, and Pozer, to whom he owed £18,000. At his death in December McCallum was insolvent, owing nearly £6,600 to the bank and £4,000 to Pozer.

James McCallum is representative of a part of the second generation of British businessmen at Quebec. Successors in the early 19th century to William Grant*, George Allsopp*, and Adam Lymburner*, members of this group included John Young, John MURE, and William BURNS and were generally Scots. They sought to benefit from the rapid development of Upper Canada, in large part through arrangements with merchants in Montreal, whose hinterland that colony formed. Yet their location more naturally led McCallum and merchants like him at Quebec to exploit the fisheries and fur trade of Labrador and the Gulf of St Lawrence as well as the rich agricultural lands of the south shore below Quebec, in the latter case through industries such as brewing, distilling, and flour milling. Brewing and distilling were, however, risky undertakings: Robert Lester*, Young, McCallum, and no doubt others found the internal market small, export markets non-existent, imported

wines and spirits strong competition, and the time needed for equipment repairs long because of a lack of skilled labour.

Quebec's principal economic asset being its port, the main activity of these merchants was the import-export trade with Britain and the West Indies, in which the Scottish merchants' home connections and support were especially strong. Despite the importance of the port, with the exception of Mure these merchants did not engage extensively in the timber trade, shipbuilding, or manufacturing as did such notable Quebec figures as John Goudie, Mathew Bell*, and Henry Usborne*. Merchants like McCallum also speculated in land, chiefly in the Eastern Townships, and invested in seigneuries and in urban – often commercial – property. After 1815, in part to avoid falling under the control of Montreal capital, they established financial institutions such as the Quebec Fire Assurance Company and the Quebec Bank [see George GARDEN; Daniel SUTHERLAND]. The great striving of these businessmen and others at Quebec did not always produce brilliant results, as McCallum's case demonstrates, but it did constitute the motive force in the commercial and agricultural development of Quebec and its hinterland in the early 19th century.

JAMES H. LAMBERT

ANQ-Q, CE1-66, 8 juin 1794, 14 juin 1795, 1er oct. 1797, 1er janv. 1799, 5 janv. 1800, 24 nov. 1805, 22 déc. 1825; CN1-16, 6 juin 1805; 31 déc. 1811; 8, 18 juin, 18 sept. 1813; 19 oct. 1814; CN1-49, 24 juin 1812; 16 nov. 1813; 3 mars, 28 avril, 3, 18 juill. 1814; 17 janv., 19 avril, 3, 15 mai, 15, 29 juin 1815; 17 juill. 1816; 5 sept. 1817; 8 mars, 8, 18 avril, 25 mai, 30 sept. 1818; 26 janv., 14 avril, 6 août, 16 nov. 1819; 13 mars 1820; 24 mai 1821; 13, 30 août 1822; 20 mai 1823, 21 févr. 1824; CN1-92, 10 oct. 1794; 16, 20 mars 1797; CN1-116, 8 mai, 10 juin 1822; 23 janv. 1824; CN1-147, 16 juill. 1803; CN1-178, 5 août 1817, 19 août 1818; CN1-197, 2 mai 1816, 5 janv. 1822; CN1-205, 28 nov. 1798; CN1-208, 12 avril, 4 oct. 1823; 18 juin 1825; 9 févr., 30 sept. 1827; CN1-230, 17 mars, 14 mai 1800; 30 juin 1803; 30 nov. 1809; 30 juin 1813; 22 avril, 1er oct. 1816; 26 avril 1817; 28 mars 1820; CN1-253, 6 oct. 1825; CN1-262, 12, 14 févr. 1798; 1er févr. 1799; 21, 26, 28 janv., 13, 25 mars, 8 juin, 21 août, 26 déc. 1801; 14 juill. 1804; 24 avril 1810; 24 août 1811; 18 févr., 20 mai, 2 déc. 1815; 16 avril 1816; 2 déc. 1818; 13–30 mars, 5–29 avril, 1er, 4, 6, 12, 15–16 mai, 15, 20 juill. 1820; CN1-285, 22 janv., 21 févr., 8 sept. 1801; 26 oct. 1802; 7 oct. 1803; 18 sept. 1804; 11 mars 1811; CN3-11, 12 avril 1796. PAC, MG 24, B1, 16: 86–95; RG 1, L3L: 62780, 62800–1, 62808, 62812, 62820–22, 62829, 62838, 62960, 63130–45, 63150–56. Joseph Bouchette, Topographical map of the province of Lower Canada . . . (London, 1815; repr. Montreal, 1980). "Les dénombrements de Québec" (Plessis), ANQ Rapport, 1948–49: 86. Quebec Gazette, 13 Feb. 1794; 18 June 1795; 23 March 1797; 5 April 1798; 21 March, 18 July 1799; 30 Sept. 1802; 14 June 1804; 5 April, 2 Aug. 1810; 19 Sept. 1811; 28 May 1812; 8 July, 30 Dec. 1813; 12 Jan., 4 Oct. 1815; 20

June, 25 July 1816; 13 March, 24 April, 14 July, 7 Aug. 1817; 8, 15, 19, 29 Jan., 12 March, 25 June, 10 Sept., 19 Nov. 1818; 19 April, 19 July, 11 Oct., 8 Nov., 2 Dec. 1819; 3, 24 Jan., 9, 13, 20 March, 17 April, 5, 19, 22, 26 June, 10 July, 21 Aug., 2 Oct., 11, 23 Dec. 1820; 19 March, 16 April, 16 June, 12 July, 27 Aug., 25 Oct., 26 Nov. 1821; 28 Oct., 19 Dec. 1822; 5 June, 3 July, 14, 21 Aug., 4, 11 Sept., 20 Oct. 1823; 1 April 1824. F.-J. Audet, "Les législateurs du Bas-Canada." Caron, "Inv. de la corr. de Mgr Plessis," ANQ *Rapport*, 1927–28: 219. E. H. Dahl *et al.*, *La ville de Québec, 1800–1850: un inventaire de cartes et plans* (Ottawa, 1975). Desjardins, *Guide parl.*, 137. "Les Presbytériens à Québec en 1802," *BRH*, 42 (1936): 728. *Quebec almanac*, 1821: 50. P.-G. Roy, *Inv. concessions*, 3: 103, 176; 5: 107. Ouellet, *Bas-Canada*, 310, 314. F.-J. Audet, "David Lynd, 1745–1802," *BRH*, 47 (1941): 89. Gérard Malchelosse, "Une seigneurie fantôme: Saint-Paul du Labrador," *Cahiers des Dix*, 10 (1945): 320–21. Victor Morin, "La féodalité a vécu," *Cahiers des Dix*, 6 (1941): 269–70.

McCARTHY (McCarty), JAMES OWEN (often known as **James Owen** or **Owens**), tailor and convicted murderer; b. *c.* 1794 in Ireland; m. Ann (Hannah) ——, and they had several children; d. 31 March 1835 in Hamilton, Upper Canada.

The emigration boom of the early 1830s added a new dimension to the social structure of the villages of Hamilton and Dundas – a large population of Irish Roman Catholics. Mired in poverty in what the local priest, John Cassidy, described as a "rude and toilsome mission," the Irish seemed particularly prone to the petty violence that characterized frontier towns. Indeed, from the 1830s to the 1850s, the face of such crime in the Gore District was Irish. For Cassidy, the "poverty and the vices" of his flock were a burden. In 1834 he was anxious about the forthcoming St Patrick's Day celebrations and spent "all the Lent" preaching "against their past drinking their riots and their ignorance." His efforts were to no avail. On 17 March 1834 a brawl erupted at a Dundas tavern in which "none were concerned but Irish Catholics." One man died of wounds suffered in the mayhem. Charged with wilful murder were John Rooney, a local innkeeper, and James Owen McCarthy.

McCarthy was a tailor who about 1821 was employed by R. Law and Company of London. Subsequently, he joined another establishment (reputedly tailors to George IV) as foreman. He then opened his own shop in Dublin, which he described as a "large and respectable" business with a select clientele. McCarthy left Ireland about 1832 and opened a store in New York City. Having "lost the whole of his effects by Fire," he moved with his family to Dundas in the fall of 1833. In jail awaiting trial, he wasted little time before seeking intercession on his behalf. On 26 March he wrote to Frederick Shaw, a former customer and one of the foremost Irish legislators, acquainting him with his situation, asserting his innocence, and begging Shaw to "use your influence with Mr Stanley [the Colonial Secretary] . . . that he might Intercede Immediately." Shaw forwarded the letter to Stanley, commending McCarthy as a "respectable well-Conducted Man." Stanley could hardly intervene in the manner suggested but he did forward the documents to Lieutenant Governor Sir John Colborne*, indicating his interest in the case.

Imperial interest was sufficient to ensure the keen attention of local authorities when McCarthy appeared before judge James Buchanan Macaulay* on 4 August, two days after Rooney had been found guilty in spite of the work of his defence counsel, Robert Baldwin Sullivan* and William Henry Draper*. Once testimony was concluded McCarthy addressed the jury with, as Macaulay noted, "great vehemence and gesticulation . . . and instead of manifesting any feelings of remorse or regret, rather exulted in his conduct as amply excusable." He was pronounced guilty, and Macaulay sentenced both men to be hanged. The judge, however, was a prudent man who was careful to act in accord with the "policy" of the legislature and the "Sense" of the bench with respect to capital convictions. Accordingly, he respited the sentences to allow opportunity for appeal and gubnatorial review.

The usually mute Irish Roman Catholics responded almost immediately to the plight of their countrymen, as did the local community at large. Cassidy, who had earlier dismissed McCarthy as a "loose character," forwarded a petition bearing 154 names, mainly Irish, which argued that both men were deserving of royal mercy since neither had acted with malice aforethought. The crime had been committed in the heat of temporary passions, "on a day when Irishmen are apt to indulge too freely in the intoxicating cup." John Law, a local worthy and representative of R. Law and Company, also came to McCarthy's defence. McCarthy's own petition for clemency cast his plight in the usual manner. A "stranger in the Country" whose wife and children would be left "destitute and friendless" upon his execution, he sought a pardon "that he may Strive to retain the good opinion of his fellow men, And have time to make his peace with his offended Maker." In spite of provocation, he maintained, nothing could have induced him "designedly to Shed the blood of his fellow man." His petition was supported by 307 men, including many of the prominent such as Allan Napier MacNab*.

Uppermost in the minds of McCarthy and his petitioners was the question of intent, for without premeditated design the appropriate charge was manslaughter. Macaulay had touched on this issue in his address to the jury and both his remarks and the jury's verdict were upheld by Chief Justice John Beverley Robinson*. Colborne, however, was not satisfied and he urged Macaulay to reflect further on the case. The judge, feeling "much repugnance to capital punish-

McCarthy

ments in cases not tainted with deliberate afore-thought," none the less held to his original conclusions and considered the question to be now one for the "Executive Govt." Colborne referred the matter to the Executive Council, chaired by John Strachan*. On its recommendation, which included respites for both executions, the question was referred in late August to the imperial government. In spite of Macaulay's repeated confirmation of the justness of the sentence, Colborne correctly ascribed to him "some doubts" as to whether manslaughter might not have been the more proper verdict. Imperial reservations about the inadequacy of the submitted documents notwithstanding, approval was given for conditional pardons. Before word of the pardons had reached the Gore District – it was sent from Toronto on 23 Jan. 1835 – Cassidy forwarded another petition from the Irish asking for commutation of the sentence. Dreading the personal consequences of attending the doomed men at their execution, he revealed a political awareness hitherto not evident in his community. He alluded to the burning of a Roman Catholic convent in the United States by an "American Mob," an incident that had occasioned a "Strong Sensation" among his parishioners. What had struck them was the acquittal of American incendiaries and the conviction of McCarthy and Rooney. Irish Roman Catholics were learning, Cassidy stated, the "Strict meaning of *Malice pretense*."

Before their pardon (including banishment) was due to take effect on 1 April, McCarthy and Rooney began complaining of the conditions of their confinement in what they described as an overcrowded, poorly ventilated, and unheated jail. McCarthy denounced the jailer's "Tyranical conduct . . . Such I think as Never disgraced the pages of history." Sheriff William Munson Jarvis tried to blunt the prisoner's charges by denigrating his character, noting that McCarthy's supposed wife (he claimed they had never been married) "has had Causes more than once to regret the Difference between his strength and hers" and that McCarthy himself was "very much addicted to Liquor." Jarvis hinted at the possibility of a plot to free McCarthy, who had himself vowed "to break Gaol or die in the attempt." He concluded that there had never been in the jail a "worse Character than Owen the Language he makes use of is enough to make any person shudder."

On 31 March 1835, one day before his release, McCarthy died "after a dispute with the Gaoler in which much violence took place." The official conclusion, by a coroner's jury, that he died of "an enlargement of the heart" touched off a further controversy. In late April McCarthy's wife presented a petition signed by some 1,200 people questioning the cause of her husband's "sudden and mysterious death" and wondering why "no action has been taken

against the gaoler and his assistants." In an editorial in the *Correspondent and Advocate*, William John O'Grady* juxtaposed the inquest, "the verdict of only twelve men," and the petition of 1,200. "To which should credence be given?" The jailer and his deputy were later absolved of criminal conduct by a grand jury. However, the state of the jails was a matter of both provincial and imperial concern, and McCarthy's death, probably by reason of the unusual imperial interest in his case and his demise, brought many of the problems to the fore. Two investigations concluded that the jails were greatly overcrowded and inadequately regulated. The second investigation, conducted by a committee of judges including Robinson and Macaulay, was the more important of the two; its report, tabled in the legislature on 22 Dec. 1835, urged the establishment of "more precise and satisfactory regulations than are at present provided." The result was a statute enacted in 1838 which attempted, with limited success, to bring district jails under a comprehensive system of provincial regulations.

ROBERT LOCHIEL FRASER

AO, RG 20, F-15, 1: f.4, nos.159–60; RG 22, ser.134, 6, Gore District, 2, 4 Aug. 1834. Arch. of the Archdiocese of Toronto, M (Macdonell papers), AB07.08, .010; AC04.01–2, .05; CA07.04 (mfm. at AO). MTL, Robert Baldwin papers, A73, no.66. PAC, RG 5, A1: 78467–70, 78485–86, 78581–86, 78809–12, 79032–61, 81634–35, 81666–68, 81792–802, 83032–34. PRO, CO 42/423: 89–91, 95–122; 42/427: 25–64. U.C., House of Assembly, *App. to the journal*, 1836, 1, no.44. *Correspondent and Advocate* (Toronto), 22 March 1834, 29 May 1835. J. C. Weaver, *Hamilton: an illustrated history* (Toronto, 1982). Michael Doucet and J. C. Weaver, "Town fathers and urban continuity: the roots of community power and physical form in Hamilton, Upper Canada, in the 1830s," *Urban Hist. Rev.* (Winnipeg), 13 (1984–85): 75–90.

McCARTHY, JEREMIAH, surveyor; b. *c*. 1758, son of Calahan McCarthy and Catherine O'Brian, of County Cork (Republic of Ireland); m. 5 June 1780 Marie-Magdelaine Dubergès in the parish of Saint-Thomas (in Montmagny), Que., and they had six children; d. 29 June 1828 in Saint-Hyacinthe, Lower Canada.

In the period from 29 Oct. 1777 to 26 Feb. 1778 Jeremiah McCarthy is mentioned four times on the inspection lists of the Prince of Wales's American Regiment, a loyalist unit recruited in New York State. By 6 Nov. 1779 he was living in the province of Quebec, at Saint-Thomas, and already owned a farm. However, the war was far from over, even if no military operations were taking place on the colony's soil. Great Britain was still maintaining large forces in the St Lawrence valley, which were stationed in a number of parishes for strategic purposes, and also so

426

that as many inhabitants as possible might contribute to the war effort. McCarthy billeted on his farm men from the German Anhalt-Zerbst regiment, which had arrived at Quebec late in May 1778 and was quartered at Saint-Thomas from 6 Nov. 1779 till 30 June 1780. He does not seem to have appreciated the experience much. On 21 July 1780 he applied to Governor Frederick Haldimand* for compensation, because his farmer's home had been used as a guardhouse and he had been obliged to lodge the family in his own residence. Late in December 1779 the commissariat, which had to buy, hold, and distribute the army's supplies and building materials, opened a storehouse at Saint-Thomas. McCarthy served in it as deputy commissary general from 24 Jan. 1781 until it closed in June 1783 as a result of reductions in the army's strength.

While working in the commissariat McCarthy had done some surveys, as the first report in his registry, dated 6 June 1781, shows. His career as a surveyor really began, however, in 1783. By 1792 he had surveyed the entire Côte-du-Sud area, which stretched from Lévis to Rivière-du-Loup and from the shores of the St Lawrence to the Appalachians. His clientele came mainly from the parishes of Kamouraska, L'Islet, Montmagny, Lévis, and Bellechasse. He went as far as the seigneury of Îlet-du-Portage in 1790 and, in another direction, the Beauce region in 1784. At that period a surveyor did various jobs: chain-measuring, marking boundaries, laying out lots, farms, and entire ranges of homesteads, establishing or confirming dividing lines between seigneurial or other properties, confirming surveys, and preparing reports and plans required as a result of a sale, court order, or division of an estate among heirs. A surveyor's career did not, however, bring the young Irishman living in a largely French-speaking region all the satisfactions he had anticipated. In a memoir sent to the Executive Council on 25 March 1784 he expressed great disappointment with a surveyor's living conditions. His low wages meant that he could not provide for his own subsistence by his professional activity. They had, he said, been set with the work done by "line drawers" in mind, rather than that of surveyors like himself who were competent to survey great stretches of land. He asked that his wages be doubled. Despite his claim to be superior to "common surveyors," McCarthy had to continue for several years with tasks he scorned. He was also afflicted with numerous health problems that confined him to the house for long periods. In 1786, for example, he was forced to remain inactive for more than a month. He told the acting deputy receiver general, Henry Caldwell*, in a letter dated 27 Nov. 1786 that his health was delicate and that he feared he would not long be able to do surveying.

McCarthy's requests for recognition of his competence were not in vain. He was asked to participate in the large-scale surveys initiated by the government to encourage settlement by loyalists and accelerate population growth. In 1785 and 1787 he and Edward Jessup surveyed Augusta Township (Ont.). He was more involved, however, in the surveying of Lower Canada. The terms of the Constitutional Act of 1791 concerning land holding and the method of land granting had spectacular results on settlement and proved a gift from heaven for surveyors. McCarthy was amongst those who benefited from the new system by surveying townships and participating in the determination of the limits of those lands granted on seigneurial tenure and in the establishment of the exact boundaries of regions to be developed. In 1792 he surveyed in turn Armagh, Stoneham, and Tewkesbury townships. That year he did a survey of the Rivière Chaudière as far as Lac Mégantic. In 1793 he established two base lines by exploring the entire area between the barony of Longueuil and the Chaudière and that between the Rivière Saint-François and the Yamaska up to Dunham Township. He also worked with other surveyors on the survey of the St Lawrence, which was begun in the winter of 1792 and continued in 1793, 1794, and 1795. This was not an easy task: the surveys of the river done in 1792 did not match, so the work had to be done over again the following year by McCarthy and Benjamin Ecuyer. Samuel GALE and Jean-Baptiste DUBERGER made use of their data to prepare a map in 1794 and 1795. The distances measured by McCarthy when he established the base lines turned out to be much less exact than anticipated, thus limiting the usefulness of Gale's and Duberger's map.

Administrative delays and political shilly-shallying over land distribution between 1795 and 1800 slowed surveying of the new townships considerably. Except for doing Milton and Granby townships in 1796, McCarthy worked almost exclusively for seigneurs and private individuals. Since moving to Quebec in 1791 he had acquired a good many clients in the neighbouring region, and he also continued to work occasionally on the Côte-du-Sud.

Around 1800, in compliance with regulations governing the granting of lands in the townships, requests for township surveys were handled through the Surveyor General's Office, and McCarthy benefited from this arrangement; in 1800 he surveyed Thetford Township, in 1801 those of Shenley, Simpson, Stoke, and Windsor, in 1802 Tring, Somerset, Newton, Nelson, Farnham, and Buckland, and in 1803 Aston. During the same period he confirmed the boundaries of several seigneuries.

Things began to go wrong for McCarthy at the time when Aston Township, adjacent to the seigneury of Nicolet, was being surveyed. On 18 June 1802 he had received instructions from the acting surveyor gener-

McCarthy

al, Joseph Bouchette*, to survey and subdivide the township; he was also told to confirm with the seigneurs concerned that the boundaries of their properties were clearly determined. Relying on the plan of Aston prepared by McCarthy, the seigneur of Nicolet, Pierre-Michel Cressé*, proceeded to develop two ranges of homesteads, with 120 lots, on land that was actually in the township. When Kenelm Conor Chandler* bought the seigneury in 1821, the matter was far from settled and it brought him into conflict with the land agent for the township. On the strength of some remarks Bouchette had made, which in effect invalidated McCarthy's survey as erroneous, inadmissible, and contrary to his instructions, the agent won the case around 1832.

The survey of Farnham Township and the seigneury of Saint-Hyacinthe, which McCarthy did in 1802, had even more serious consequences. It enabled the owners of the seigneury to recover 17,000 acres from the adjacent seigneuries, including Monnoir, which belonged to Sir John JOHNSON. Once more Bouchette showed his dissatisfaction with McCarthy's work, but that did not cause his report to be rejected.

From 1802 the correspondence between McCarthy and Bouchette reveals serious shortcomings on McCarthy's part, to the point that having reprimanded him in writing on 16 Dec. 1802, Bouchette was forced to summon him to Quebec on 30 May 1803. Bouchette had been discreet: he did not describe McCarthy's conduct but spoke of a "collection of letters" concerning him. He decided he would no longer use his services. McCarthy then saw his career begin to go downhill. He received fewer and fewer requests for surveys, and had to leave Lower Canada for the period 1806–14 to work in Upper Canada. Among the surveys he did there was one of the village of Williamstown, undertaken for Sir John Johnson in 1813.

McCarthy moved back to Quebec in 1814, but during the next two years practised in the seigneuries and parishes in the lower reaches of the St Lawrence, at Trois-Pistoles, L'Île Verte, Bic, and Rimouski. But he was suffering from alcoholism, which progressively made him unfit for his profession. He found refuge with Marie-Rosalie Papineau, Jean DESSAULLES's wife, at Saint-Hyacinthe, where he died on 29 June 1828.

If McCarthy's career as a surveyor ended rather lamentably, he was scarcely more successful in business. He was interested solely in real estate. In 1786 he and Duncan McDonald bought the seigneuries of Ristigouche and Port-Daniel in the Gaspé. But the sale was annulled that year, and ten years later the two seigneuries reverted to the crown. The Executive Council agreed to repay McCarthy the sum he had invested in the venture. In 1793 McCarthy made a request for Buckland Township in association with

Captain T. A. Wetherall. The matter dragged on, since Wetherall had not been able to secure the financing to develop the township, with the result that in 1800 McCarthy made a request for 1,200 acres in Barford Township for himself and his family. There is no indication that he ever received them.

McCarthy's contribution to teaching deserves mention. In 1789 he published an announcement in the *Quebec Gazette* that he would "teach a few young Gentlemen (not exceeding six at a time) . . . EUCLID's ELEMENTS or GEOMETRY, TRIGONOMETRY both Plain and Spherical, ALGEBRA, ASTRONOMY, CONICK SECTIONS, GEOGRAPHY, or the use of the GLOBES and MAPS, MENSURATION, GAUGING – GUNNERY, FORTIFICATION, ARCHITECTURE, DIALLING, MECHANICKS, NAVIGATION, SURVEYING in all its branches both in Theory and Practice." After moving to Quebec in 1791 he opened a school for mathematics in his home on Rue des Carrières. His courses, which were offered in French or English, helped train a considerable number of surveyors. He passed his knowledge on to his son Jeremiah, who was commissioned as a surveyor in 1797 and worked almost exclusively with him, and to the surveyor Louis Charland*.

Despite a most promising start, Jeremiah McCarthy's career appears to have been an unending series of failures. It is tempting to lay all the blame on alcoholism, where it may in part belong. The consequences of his surveying of Aston and Farnham townships, however, tarnished his reputation just as much, whether his surveys were accurate or not. If he had no luck with his efforts to become a seigneur or obtain land in the townships, there is no indication that he lost any sizeable sums in them. He seems to have had no backing among the governing classes, and what he obtained fell far short of his ambitions.

GILLES LANGELIER

The surveyor's reports of Jeremiah McCarthy for 1781–1817 are at ANQ-Q, CA1-45.

ANQ-Q, CE2-7, 5 juin, 13 sept. 1780; 22 oct. 1781; 29 déc. 1782; 10 nov. 1784; 7 avril 1786; 1er août 1787; CN1-92, 1er mars 1793; E21/357, 21 janv., 16 févr., 3 mai, 1er juill., 12 août, 7 oct. 1802; 5 sept. 1803; 20 août 1804; P-239: 72. BL, Add. MSS 21853: 36–37, 64–126; 21877: 124, 127–28. PAC, MG 9, D4, vol.8, sect.A7: 517 (mfm.); MG 23, GII, 10, vol.3: 916–24, 935–41; MG 30, D1, 20; National Map Coll., NMC-26878; NMC-57718; RG 1, L3ᴸ: 29331–445, 36132–68, 62080, 62103–8, 63521–31, 63554, 64102–14; RG 4, A1, 26: 8681–83; 62: 20007–8, 20011, 20015, 20019, 20024, 20028; RG 4, B33, 18; RG 8, I (C ser.), 1895: 1, 19, 25, 32. Québec, Ministère de l'Énergie et Ressources, Service d'arpentage, carnet d'arpenteur, A22, A22A, A22G, B33, F3B, M27A, N2, N6D, S10A, S17A, S24A, T8, T14, W16; Surveyor general office, letter-books, vol.2, 16 Dec. 1802, 30 May 1803. "Surveyors' letters, notes, instructions, etc., from 1788 to 1791," AO *Report*, 1905: 418–19. *Quebec Gazette*, 7 Aug. 1783, 5

Feb. 1789, 24 Nov. 1791, 16 March 1814, 7 July 1828. Maurice Saint-Yves, *Atlas de géographie historique du Canada* (Boucherville, Qué., 1982). Jules Bélanger *et al.*, *Histoire de la Gaspésie* (Montréal, 1981), 164. Caron, *La colonisation de la prov. de Québec*. C.-P. Choquette, *Histoire de la ville de Saint-Hyacinthe* (Saint-Hyacinthe, Qué., 1930), 86. V. E. DeMarce, *The settlement of former German auxiliary troops in Canada after the American revolution* (Arlington, Va., 1984).

M'COLL, DUNCAN, soldier and Methodist clergyman; b. 22 Aug. 1754 at Glastrein, parish of Appin, Scotland; m. 1784 Elizabeth Channal in Halifax; d. 17 Dec. 1830 in St Stephen (St Stephen–Milltown), N.B.

Duncan M'Coll was one of eleven children of Hugh M'Coll, a feuar of Glastrein. As a young man he entered a Glasgow commercial office but returned to Argyll after his apprenticeship and joined his father in business. Unfortunately their enterprise was a failure. After several setbacks the elder M'Coll was forced to sell the rights to Glastrein and another property, Carvin, both of which had been in the family for generations, and to retire on a modest income. At the age of 23 Duncan M'Coll faced a future of limited prospects. Fortunately the family had a number of military contacts. Among these was Colonel John Campbell of Barbreck, commanding officer of the 74th Foot (Argyll Highlanders), which was being raised for service in the American revolution. Barbreck enrolled the young man as a company pay sergeant late in 1777.

The following summer the 74th sailed to Halifax, N.S. In June 1779 M'Coll accompanied his regiment to the Penobscot River, where under Brigadier-General Francis McLean* he participated in the construction of Fort George (Castine, Maine) and in its defence against American attack in July and August. The next spring he was sent to New York as paymaster to the 2nd Grenadier Battalion. He remained in that city until the fall of 1781, when he accompanied his battalion to the relief of Lord Cornwallis in Virginia. The force was too late to save the British commander and retired to spend the winter at Jamaica, Long Island. While there M'Coll underwent a religious conversion, finding a "peace of soul," a freedom, and an ability to forgive which led him to abandon many of his old habits and friends. A member of the Episcopal Church in Scotland, M'Coll sought a spiritual catalyst within the Church of England but could not find it among the chaplains he knew. In the fall of 1783 he was discharged from the army and set off for Halifax on a refugee ship belonging to Philip Marchinton*. The ship was driven off course in a storm and eventually reached Bermuda, where the passengers spent the winter. Among them was a young refugee, Elizabeth Channal of Philadelphia, who had been disowned by her family for joining the

Methodist connection. Over the winter M'Coll was greatly influenced by the Bermudan Methodists who provided a framework and theological direction for his religious ardour.

In the spring of 1784 the vessel resumed its journey to Halifax, where M'Coll and Miss Channal were married. The newly-weds spent the next year in Halifax, the groom finding employment for a time with Marchinton. In 1785 they moved to the recently founded town of St Andrews, on Passamaquoddy Bay in New Brunswick, where many of the disbanded Argyll Highlanders had settled. M'Coll entered the employ of two army officers and took charge of their business in St Stephen Parish, some 20 miles up the St Croix River from St Andrews. St Stephen had been settled in 1784 by loyalist refugees and members of the British commissary corps whose first home in Nova Scotia, at Port Mouton, had been destroyed by forest fires. When M'Coll and his wife arrived in the spring of 1785 they found a wretched, lawless, and demoralized people, "a mixed multitude . . . from many parts of the world," living on the largesse of the British government, lacking any sense of community or purpose. In the absence of a clergyman the M'Colls began to hold prayer-meetings at their home in November 1785. On the first Sunday there were six persons present; on the second, more than sixty. Within two months a revival had broken out: in M'Coll's words, "some fell on their faces, some ran to the doors and windows, others adored the Lord." There were 21 converts in a matter of weeks and as the movement grew the following year M'Coll found himself more and more involved in pastoral work and less and less in his employment. He then severed his business connections, "called the believers together, and joined them together as near the Methodist plan as I knew and was able."

M'Coll brought his characteristic vigour and enthusiasm to the work. His early activities had been confined to the village area of St Stephen Parish, known as Saltwater, but after 1786 he began to proselytize in its rural districts (including the area that was to become St James Parish) and in the neighbouring parishes of St David and St Andrews. Between 1787 and 1795 he averaged a dozen converts a year and succeeded in bringing virtually all of the pre-loyalists as well as most of the less affluent loyalists of St Stephen into a single community and under a single discipline. By 1790 M'Coll was able to erect a chapel at Saltwater built entirely from the resources of the local Methodist community. Yet, despite his success in establishing the Methodist cause in southwestern New Brunswick, he had no status in the wider Methodist connection until 1792 and received financial support from neither the British Wesleyan Conference nor his impoverished parishioners. M'Coll not only maintained himself and his wife but, where

M'Coll

necessary, provided meeting-rooms, seats, and fuel from his own resources. As he noted in his journal, his property, which was managed by Mrs M'Coll, "was blest abundantly."

M'Coll began his ministry at a time when Maritime Methodism was just beginning to coalesce into an organized church. William BLACK founded the Nova Scotia District in 1786 and M'Coll became a member of it in 1792. That same year, as one of only two Methodist preachers in New Brunswick, he was given a circuit which included the societies at St Stephen, Saint John, and Fredericton. He held this appointment for two years. In 1797–98, as the only preacher in New Brunswick, he was given responsibility for the whole province. Meanwhile he had been summoned by Bishop Francis Asbury to a meeting of the Methodist Episcopal Conference at New London, Conn., where he was ordained on 22 July 1795. The return to St Stephen was the occasion of the second of the three great revivals which marked M'Coll's career. That of 1795–96 nearly doubled the membership of the existing societies and provided the impetus for a major missionary endeavour resulting in eight new societies. A similar expansion characterized the third revival, which occurred at the conclusion of the War of 1812. By 1816 M'Coll's circuit contained 15 per cent of the membership of the Nova Scotia District. The growth of the Methodist presence in Charlotte County is perhaps best illustrated in the baptisms of the period: before 1800 M'Coll baptized an average of 13 people a year; between 1815 and 1820 the figure increased to 52.

The third revival marked the end of M'Coll's missionary endeavours. By 1816 the 62-year-old cleric was serving 14 classes organized into 7 societies on a circuit more than 100 miles in length. The toll of 30 years of arduous circuit riding was compounded in the years between 1816 and 1819 by the deaths of virtually all of the remaining converts who had met in M'Coll's house in 1785, culminating in the death of Elizabeth M'Coll in March 1819. The loss of his wife devastated the childless missionary but he continued to minister to his large circuit until 1826, when the executive committee of the Wesleyan Methodist Missionary Society agreed to grant him a pension of £70 a year in return for clear title to all of the property on the St Stephen circuit. The next year an assistant missionary was sent to take the more distant societies in St David, St Andrews, and St Patrick parishes and thus allow M'Coll to concentrate his efforts in the St Stephen heartland of the circuit. In 1829 M'Coll retired from the active ministry. He died the following year at the age of 76.

M'Coll played an important role in defining community values and in moulding the popular culture of southwestern New Brunswick in the late 18th and early 19th centuries. In this he was unique among Maritime Methodist clergy, his influence stemming from the fact that he was not settled by the district on different circuits at three- or four-year intervals. Mrs M'Coll suffered two still births between 1784 and 1788, the second of which nearly took her life and left her a semi-invalid. This disability provided the conventional excuse for the couple to remain in St Stephen and M'Coll successfully resisted several attempts by the district to move him.

M'Coll had his greatest successes among the pre-loyalist and loyalist farmers and lumbermen of St Stephen, St David, and St James parishes. He was also the principal religious influence in the communities on the American side of the St Croix and for 20 years was able to prevent the building of any church in the Calais area. He was less successful in the town of St Andrews [see Samuel Andrews*] and had no impact on the merchant and official élite which dominated the political and social life of southwestern New Brunswick. Curiously, he particularly failed to have much impact on the Scottish groups in the county. For 20 years he made 24-mile trips every month to provide Gaelic services for the farmers on Scotch Ridge, but few became Methodists and M'Coll's long association with the community came to an abrupt end in 1821 when, during the course of a sermon, he attacked the Calvinist doctrines of the Westminster Shorter Catechism.

At the heart of M'Coll's religious philosophy was the concept of vital religion, which, like most late-18th-century evangelicals, he perceived as a series of positive responses on the part of each individual to the initiatives of the Holy Spirit, responses that would lead to conviction of sin, conversion, and spiritual rebirth. The new creature wrought by these experiences would manifest his rebirth in a changed life and conduct. This view of an active religion was reinforced by the Methodist doctrines of universality and holiness. The first of these affirmed that every individual is capable of receiving and accepting the grace of God (that the damnation of man was not the result of God's decree but of man's free choice); the second postulated that individuals are capable of knowing they have reached a state of grace. These doctrines posed a clear imperative to mission which drove M'Coll and other frontier preachers into the most inhospitable environments in their desire to offer the free gift of salvation to all people. Like his master, John Wesley, M'Coll always preached for conversion, although he was often distressed by some of the emotional responses that accompanied the process. And like all evangelicals he possessed that intensive introspection which viewed every act, no matter how trivial, as possessing a moral significance. In an often coarse and brutal frontier society, M'Coll drew the configurations of righteousness, demanded that his converts live within them, and worked incessantly toward the conversion of every individual in the community. His rules of conduct were not only spiritual guides but also recipes for survival in the harsh frontier environment.

Like most Methodists, M'Coll hesitated over the crucial question of whether he and his converts should remain in and remake the world or should be gathered out of the world into a society of the perfect. He never entirely abandoned the latter solution, but as his societies became numerically significant he came more and more to test his influence in the wider community. The mind of the man and his relationship with the community are perhaps best reflected in an incident he recorded in his journal. In 1796 or 1797 one of the weaker members of the St Stephen society married, and at the urging of some of his non-Methodist friends determined to cap the event with a dance – a euphemism for a two- or three-day-long drunken celebration with strong sexual overtones. M'Coll remonstrated with the man to no avail. On the Sunday following the celebration the groom and his friends were in the congregation when M'Coll directed his sermon against the miscreants: "He is in your hands, by exclusion from us; his blood now lieth upon you, as the blood of John the Baptist lay on Herod and his wicked family. Look ye well to it." The man apparently spent several difficult years before finally seeking and finding reconciliation with his Methodist brethren. And M'Coll noted with grim satisfaction, "For many years after this, I found none in the place who attempted to advocate dancing."

M'Coll's considerable authority stemmed from his flawless personal life – observers such as Archdeacon George Best, an Anglican, repeatedly commented that his character was beyond reproach – and from the dedication he brought to the task of evangelizing and protecting "his" community. His determination to maintain purity of worship led him to forbid even the taking of collections during services or at class meetings, and a disinterest in material things resulted in a ministry for which he received no remuneration before 1805. In the performance of what he perceived as vital duty M'Coll demonstrated great zeal and considerable courage. In 1786 he continued his services in defiance of the magistrates who threatened to prosecute him for his activities. On a number of occasions he went forth to do battle with various New Light, antinominian, and other itinerants who disturbed the peace of the St Croix valley. At the same time, M'Coll was no sectarian. His quarrel with the remnants of the New Light movement was theological: he perceived their emphasis as part of an antinomianism leading to violent emotional outbursts, whoredom, adultery, and family breakup, and finally to the abolition of all moral law. In most cases his concerns were broadly evangelical rather than specifically Methodist. He worked with Baptist preachers

who passed through the area, willingly surrendered control of his American classes to the Congregational minister who was brought to Calais in 1810, cooperated with the Church of England clergymen of Charlotte County, was a founder of the St Stephen branch of the British and Foreign Bible Society in 1819, and consistently supported the Bible Society in preference to the Wesleyan Methodist Missionary Society.

M'Coll's relations with the civil authorities were generally good. Although the small Methodist sect was initially persecuted by the St Stephen magistrates, M'Coll's military record and political conservatism soon persuaded the authorities that the social order was in little danger from such dissenters. M'Coll later used his record to good effect in obtaining for himself and other Methodists licences to preach from Lieutenant Governor Thomas Carleton*. M'Coll's birthplace, military credentials, and unquestioned loyalty were particular assets in the 1790s, when most of the preachers in the Nova Scotia District were Americans, and taken together may explain why the district conference left him in the sensitive border area for so many years, though his permanency was in clear violation of the Methodist discipline. Apart from his efforts to secure toleration of Methodist activities, M'Coll played little role in the civil life of the colony. In part this reflected the combination of pietism and social conservatism which marked his outlook; in part it stemmed from the low status of most early Methodists. M'Coll always accepted the distinction between church and chapel and never challenged the legal position of the Church of England. Even on the marriage debate, which began in the early 1820s, his journal is silent. And this despite the fact that he always lived in a community where Methodists greatly outnumbered adherents of the established church.

Only once, during the War of 1812, did M'Coll play a leading role in the public life of the colony. Since he almost certainly ministered to a clear majority of the population on both sides of the upper St Croix River valley, he had a particularly strong incentive to prevent the war from spreading into the community. Shortly after hostilities began, he initiated the formation of a committee drawn from leading citizens from both sides of the border which played an important role in maintaining peace in the region between 1812 and 1813. The situation became rather more serious in June 1813 with the arrival of American troops in Calais. M'Coll intervened with their commander, who attended his services, and later with the British commander, Sir Thomas Saumarez, both of whom agreed to a truce in the community. M'Coll continued services on both sides of the border throughout the war.

M'Coll's influence in southwest New Brunswick survived him. In 1785 he had entered a society in

McCord

which Methodism was virtually unknown. As late as 1861, 30 years after his death, more than 70 per cent of the native-born heads of households in St Stephen parish were Methodists. And when the Sons of Temperance entered New Brunswick in 1847 their first division, appropriately, was organized in M'Coll's St Stephen chapel.

T. W. ACHESON

Duncan M'Coll's journal was published in several parts under the title "Memoir of the Rev. Duncan M'Coll, late of Saint Stephen's, Charlotte County, New Brunswick" in the *British North American Wesleyan Methodist Magazine* (Saint John, N.B.), 1 (1840–41): 251–58, 291–302, 331–36, 411–15, 458–62, 491–98, 571–78, 611–18; 2 (1841–42): 5–11, 47–54, 121–29, 161–69, 201–11, 248–53, 452–56.

PAC, RG 31, C1, 1861, St Stephen Parish. PANB, MC 256, MS1/1 (Reg. of baptisms and burials, 1794–1848); 6/9 (Corr. with London Missionary Committee, 1828). UCC-M, Wesleyan Methodist Church, Nova Scotia District, minutes of the district meeting, 1816, 1826, especially 1 April 1826. E. A. Betts, *Bishop Black and his preachers* (2nd ed., Sackville, N.B., 1976). H. A. Davis, *An international community on the St. Croix, 1604–1930* (Orono, Maine, 1950). G. [S.] French, *Parsons & politics: the rôle of the Wesleyan Methodists in Upper Canada and the Maritimes from 1780 to 1855* (Toronto, 1962). D. W. Johnson, *History of Methodism in Eastern British America, including Nova Scotia, New Brunswick, Prince Edward Island, Newfoundland and Bermuda* . . . ([Sackville], n.d.). I. C. Knowlton, *Annals of Calais, Maine, and St. Stephen, New Brunswick* . . . (Calais, 1875; repr. St Stephen, [1977]). MacNutt, *New Brunswick*. Matthew Richey, *A memoir of the late Rev. William Black, Wesleyan minister, Halifax, N.S., including an account of the rise and progress of Methodism in Nova Scotia* . . . (Halifax, 1839). T. W. Smith, *History of the Methodist Church within the territories embraced in the late conference of Eastern British America* . . . (2v., Halifax, 1877–90). Robert Wilson, *Methodism in the Maritime provinces* (Halifax, 1893). A. B. Dickie, "St. James, N.B.," *Presbyterian Witness* (Halifax), 15 April 1916: 5.

McCORD, THOMAS, businessman, JP, militia officer, agricultural improver, politician, and office holder; b. 7 Feb. 1750 in County Antrim (Northern Ireland), tenth child and fifth son of John McCord and Margery Ellis; d. 5 Dec. 1824 in Montreal.

The McCords are believed to have been originally Mackays (Mac-Aoidh) of Argyllshire, Scotland, who emigrated to Antrim. Thomas McCord's father had settled at Quebec by 1764, and there he engaged in trade in association with James G. Hanna*, a watchmaker from Dublin and a relation by marriage, and eventually with his eldest son, John McCord. Thomas began operating as a merchant at Quebec and Montreal in 1770, and in March 1771 he secured a liquor licence for the latter place. He entered into partnership with George King in Montreal; although the dissolu-

tion of their association was announced in April 1779, the two men were still partners in 1785. In July 1787 McCord was the director of the Montreal Distillery Company, of which the merchant and seigneur Jacob Jordan* was a major backer. It operated two copper stills in a large stone building on Rue Saint-Sacrement between Saint-Nicolas and Saint-Pierre. In 1788 Jordan had the business seized for debt, and in January 1789 it was purchased at auction by a consortium of which McCord and King were members [*see* Isaac Todd*]. No more successful than its predecessors, the consortium dissolved the enterprise in 1794 and sold the property to Nicholas Montour* in October. Meanwhile, in February 1793 the partnership of King and McCord was again declared ended and its "neat and convenient Dwelling House and extensive Stores in Notre-Dame street" were offered for sale, but without result.

Like many Lower Canadian merchants of his time, McCord invested and speculated in land. On 23 July 1792 he obtained from the Hôtel-Dieu a 99-year lease on the Nazareth sub-fief next to the property of the Sisters of Charity of the Hôpital Général; because the rent of £25 per annum was paid to the poor of the Hôtel-Dieu, the farm which the sub-fief constituted was known as Grange des Pauvres. Between April 1793 and April 1803 he acquired leases on lots adjoining the sub-fief from the Congregation of Notre-Dame and the Sulpicians. McCord intended to develop the area and improve the farm. In 1795 he imported books on gardening, introduced raspberry, gooseberry, and currant roots from England, and experimented with numerous vegetable, spice, and flower seeds sent to him by his agent there, Jacques Terroux.

By the mid 1790s McCord had become a citizen of standing in Montreal. He had been admitted to St Andrew's Lodge No.2 of freemasons in 1778, and in 1780 he was appointed secretary of St Peter's Lodge No.4, of which he was master two years later; by 1788 he had become provincial grand secretary. In July of that year he was made a justice of the peace, an appointment renewed numerous times thereafter. A lieutenant in the British militia of Montreal by 1790, he held that rank probably until leaving the militia about 1802. In 1790 as well he was a director of the Agriculture Society. Two years later, as foreman of the grand jury, he criticized the slowness of the judicial process in the Court of King's Bench in Montreal and denounced the resulting confinement of prisoners "beyond a proper and necessary period for their being brought to trial." Since 1784 he had been signing petitions initiated by the merchant community requesting abrogation of the Quebec Act and the establishment, among other things, of a house of assembly. In the spring of 1792 he was one of some 20 prominent merchants who supported the nominations of James McGill*, John RICHARDSON, Joseph Frobisher*, and Alexander AULDJO as candidates in the two electoral ridings in the town for the first house of assembly. He was a member of the Montreal committee of the Association, a provincial organization founded in 1794 to support British government in the colony.

In early December 1796 McCord sailed for Ireland, partly in order to negotiate the sale of some Irish property and partly to oversee the Irish branch of his trade connections, which apparently included the firm of Houx and James Hanna and the merchant William Hanna of Newry (Northern Ireland). In November he had leased some of the Nazareth sub-fief and surrounding land to Daniel SUTHERLAND and Robert Griffin for 14 years at £110 per annum, and in May 1800 he rented the rest to Griffin for the same length of time at £45 a year. The negotiations were carried out for him by Patrick Langan, a personal friend and the husband of his niece. Although McCord had intended to stay in Ireland only one season, political troubles and eventually rebellion there adversely affected land sales, prolonging his residence until 1805. He had already fallen into financial difficulty before leaving Montreal and, despite the profit turned by his subleases, during his absence his business interests in that town continued to decline under Langan's management. King threatened to sue McCord for recovery of debt in 1799, and the following year both had their property on Rue Notre-Dame seized by the sheriff. McCord declared bankruptcy in December 1801. By October 1805 Langan had had the original lease to Grange des Pauvres seized by the sheriff, had purchased it himself at the subsequent auction, and had then sold it to Griffin.

McCord returned to Montreal to straighten out his affairs and quickly became established as a general merchant. He again suffered business reverses, which were probably aggravated by his indebtedness to the King estate. In 1807 he became agent for the seigneury of Villechauve, commonly called Beauharnois, where he took up temporary residence. In 1814 he recovered from Griffin the lease on the Nazareth sub-fief (then and subsequently known as Griffintown), and he eventually moved there. Still, he had numerous bad debts; between April 1816 and November 1818 he had the sheriff seize the properties of 12 of his debtors, and in 1820–21 five more saw their properties advertised for auction. In late 1822 or early 1823 he sought authorization from the legislature to build a market on land he was leasing, but he was apparently refused.

Virtually absent from the public scene during the period of his financial distress, McCord returned in 1809 to seek one of the two assembly seats for Montreal West and, running as an independent, came second with 288 votes to Denis-Benjamin Viger*, who obtained 343. In the short but contentious session that lasted until 1810 McCord voted solidly in support of Governor Sir James Henry Craig* and the English party. In the subsequent election he withdrew early in Montreal West when former supporters berated him for signing an address welcoming Craig to Montreal and then was defeated in Huntingdon. From 1816 to 1820 he sat as a member for Bedford.

In early 1810, as a senior justice of the peace and a police magistrate, McCord was joint chairman with Jean-Marie Mondelet* of the Court of Quarter Sessions at a time when new police regulations were promulgated and a police office established in the city. That April he delivered the charge to the grand jury and with Mondelet presided over the court's weekly sittings. At the urging of the Quebec Court of Quarter Sessions he instituted legal proceedings against Louis BOURDAGES of Saint-Denis, on the Richelieu, for distributing a tract that tended to undermine the credibility of the government and incite disaffection. In 1812, as a police magistrate, he led a contingent of British troops to Lachine to disperse a crowd that had gathered to free a number of habitants arrested for refusing to perform their militia duty. The situation deteriorated rapidly, shots were exchanged, and a Canadian was killed and another wounded in what proved to be the only serious incident of resistance to militia enrolment during the War of 1812. Six years later McCord was a prime mover behind a law passed by the assembly in April 1818 to establish a regular paid police force in Montreal; as a result, in August Louis-Nicolas-Emmanuel de BIGAULT d'Aubreville was hired to head a force of night watchmen and lamplighters. In connection with his work as police magistrate, McCord had prepared an index to provincial ordinances and statutes in 1815. Judge James Reid considered the work so valuable that he urged McCord to prepare a similar abstract of provincial criminal law for the benefit of the county magistrates.

In the years following his appointment as police magistrate McCord received a number of commissions: in 1811 to superintend the house of correction at Montreal, the following year to receive oaths of allegiance, in 1815 for the improvement of internal communications in the district of Montreal, three years later for effecting repairs to the court-house and prison and to act as a warden of the House of Industry, and in 1819 for building churches and parsonage houses. Some time before 1821 he was named a director of the Montreal Library. Most of these appointments were related to his duties as police magistrate and many were unpaid. Francis-Joseph Audet*'s harsh description of McCord, on the basis of these nominations, as a creature of government is unjustified, for others, French- and English-speaking, received the same commissions; few, however, took their responsibilities as seriously as McCord. The

McDonald

establishment of a house of industry, for example, had been a matter of personal commitment by McCord to an enlightened concept of prisoner rehabilitation. In 1815 he had refused an appointment as trustee of the projected house because the institution was being modelled on the English poor-house, for which he felt there was no need in the colony even were "the evils of the English system . . . not so apparent." Rather he insisted that it be designed "for the unfortunate objects coming out of the House of Correction, . . . who, altho willing to endeavour at reform and be industrious, are thrown back upon the World for want of a plan of trial." The esteem in which the citizens of Montreal held McCord is indicated by his nomination in November 1823 as chairman of a public meeting called to examine fire prevention and fire-fighting in the city and by his election during the meeting to a committee which would lobby to have the legislation overhauled and take over fire prevention and fire-fighting until a permanent body was established.

In 1824, many complaints having been received about the organization of the police in Montreal, McCord and Mondelet were removed as police magistrates and joint chairmen of the Court of Quarter Sessions in favour of Benjamin Delisle, appointed by Governor Lord Dalhousie [Ramsay*] high constable of the Montreal district and chairman of the Quarter Sessions. When McCord died of cancer in December, the editor of the *Montreal Gazette* wrote of his private virtues and charity to the poor, and, commenting on his public conduct, declared that "no honest or judicious man has ever ventured to accuse or even suspect him of malversation or neglect of duty." For many years a street in Griffintown bore McCord's name.

McCord had married Sarah Solomons (Solomon) in the parish church of Shoreditch (London) on 27 Nov. 1798. She was the daughter of the Montreal Jewish merchant Levy Solomons* and Louise Loubier, and by her mother's earlier liaison with the merchant Jacques Terroux* she was a half-sister of their son Jacques Terroux, McCord's London agent. By his marriage McCord had five children, of whom only two, John Samuel and William King*, survived; both became judges of the Superior Court of Lower Canada.

ELINOR KYTE SENIOR

ANQ-M, CN1-29, 31 juill. 1787; CN1-185, 29 nov. 1817, 26 mai 1818; CN1-187, 24 nov. 1814. AUM, P 58, U, McCord to Reid, 17 June 1796; 22 Sept. 1799; 7 Oct., 25 Nov. 1805; McCord to Loring, 2 March 1816; McCord to McDonald, 10 Oct. 1816. Centre de documentation du Service de police de la Communauté urbaine de Montréal, Jean Turmel, "Premières structures et évolution de la police de Montréal, 1796–1909" (copie dactylographiée, Montréal, 1971). McCord Museum, Thomas McCord papers, marriage certificate, Thomas McCord and Sarah Solomon,

27 Nov. 1798; Nazareth fief. PAC, MG 11, [CO 42] Q, 30: 140–41; MG 23, GIII, 8; MG 30, D1, 20: 611–19; RG 68, General index, 1651–1841. *Docs. relating to constitutional hist., 1819–28* (Doughty and Story), 22–23. *Montreal Gazette*, 24 May 1792; 30 Oct., 6, 13 Nov. 1809; 5, 12, 19 March, 9, 23, 30 April, 26 Nov. 1810; 15, 29 Nov. 1823; 29 May, 2, 5 June, 8 Dec. 1824. *Quebec Gazette*, 21 June 1764; 13 Oct. 1774; 15, 29 Oct. 1778; 15 April, 6 May 1779; 16 June, 3 Nov. 1785; 28 Feb., 4 Sept., 13 Nov., 11 Dec. 1788; 5 Feb. 1789; 28 Oct. 1790; 16 June 1791; 19 July, 13 Sept. 1792; 7 Feb., 11 April 1793; 17 July 1794; 1 Jan. 1795; 9 Oct. 1800; 7 April 1803; 6 July, 16, 30 Nov. 1809; 12 July 1810; 23 May, 26 Dec. 1811; 16 May, 8 June, 30 Nov. 1815; 11, 18 April, 1 Aug., 14, 21 Nov. 1816; 8 May, 5, 19 June, 27 Nov. 1817; 15, 22 Jan., 26 March, 6 April, 18, 28 May, 26 Nov. 1818; 21 Jan., 4 March, 19 April, 27 May, 28 Oct. 1819; 27 April, 8 June, 3, 10 Aug., 21 Sept., 5 Oct., 23, 27 Nov., 7 Dec. 1820; 4, 25 Jan., 1 March, 19 April, 31 May, 5, 12, 26 July, 2 Aug., 6, 20 Sept., 25 Oct., 19, 26 Nov. 1821; 15 Aug., 24 Oct., 5 Dec. 1822; 13 Feb., 10 April 1823; 31 May 1824.

F.-J. Audet, *Les députés de Montréal*, 196. J. D. Borthwick, *History and biographical gazetteer of Montreal to the year 1892* (Montreal, 1892). Desjardins, *Guide parl.*, 124, 135. Giroux *et al.*, *Inv. des marchés de construction des ANQ-M*, 1, nos.763–64, 896. *Montreal directory*, 1819. *Quebec almanac*, 1791–1804. R. Campbell, *Hist. of Scotch Presbyterian Church*, 149. Graham, *Hist. of freemasonry*, 50–51. Augustin Leduc, *Beauharnois; paroisse Saint-Clément; 1818–1819; histoire religieuse, histoire civile; fêtes du centenaire* (Ottawa, 1920), xv. A. J. B. Milbourne, *Freemasonry in the province of Quebec, 1759–1959* (n.p., 1960), 40. Hare, "L'Assemblée législative du Bas-Canada," *RHAF*, 27: 385. É.-Z. Massicotte, "Fief Nazareth-Griffintown quartier Sainte-Anne," *BRH*, 51 (1945): 73; "Les tribunaux de police de Montréal," 26 (1920): 180–83. J.-P. Wallot, "Une émeute à Lachine contre la 'conscription' (1812)," *RHAF*, 18 (1964–65): 133–35.

McDONALD, ALEXANDER, landowner, office holder, and militia officer; b. *c.* 1762 in Scotland; m. *c.* 1790 Grace McLean, and they had 13 children; d. 11 Dec. 1834 in Bartibog, N.B.

Little is known of Alexander McDonald's life before he settled on the Miramichi River, N.B., in 1784, and almost nothing at all of his birth and family. It is thought he was born in Argyllshire, probably at Ardnamurchan. Local tradition in New Brunswick says he was a tenant (tacksman) of the MacDonalds of Sleat, but this report seems unlikely since he was aged only about 15 when he joined the 76th Foot. Known as Macdonald's Highlanders, the regiment was raised to fight in the American revolution and it embarked for the Thirteen Colonies in 1779. After seeing service throughout the colonies, the unit became part of the British forces that surrendered at Yorktown, Va, in 1781. With the cessation of hostilities, in 1783, Macdonald's Highlanders were returned to Scotland to be disbanded. A portion of the regiment, including Alexander McDonald, was discharged at Shelburne, N.S.

The following year McDonald arrived on the Miramichi, probably some time during the summer. In 1788, and over the ensuing 30 years, he acquired by grant large tracts of land on both sides of the river. By 1818 he controlled approximately 1,400 acres. His partial interest in two islands near the mouth of the Miramichi allowed McDonald to participate in the salmon fishery. By all accounts, however, he took little part in lumbering and shipbuilding, the principal commercial pursuits of Northumberland County. His interests, beyond the fishery, were presumably largely agricultural. At the same time as his landholdings increased McDonald's status within the community rose. Beginning in 1791, when he was appointed town clerk for the Middle District, Southside, he was extremely active in parish government, serving in numerous capacities. He was reappointed a town clerk annually until 1798, and on various occasions up to 1824 acted as assessor, commissioner of roads, overseer of the poor, and school trustee. The large stone house he built at Bartibog, likely in the period 1815–20, illustrates his opinion of his raised position in society.

In 1799 McDonald was appointed captain commander in the 1st Battalion, Northumberland County militia. As a large landowner and minor public official he had the necessary income to support his militia activities; not only was he responsible for the yearly training exercises, but he had also to meet the costs of his uniform and accoutrements. In 1813 he became major commandant of the 1st Battalion, and it appears that around 1829 he was commissioned a lieutenant-colonel of the same unit. Militia service became a family tradition. At least three of his sons held militia commissions and their land was reportedly used as a parade-ground.

After 1824 McDonald ceased to hold any public office. Two years later, following the disastrous Miramichi fire of 1825, he sold large tracts of land to two of his children: on 2 March 1826, 140 acres to his son James and on 4 April, 800 acres to another son, Ronald. The expenses of building his stone house, advanced age, and the general devastation caused by the fire may have been too much for Alexander McDonald. After a short illness he died at Bartibog on 11 Dec. 1834.

McDonald's obituary said he was "universally respected" and that his memory would be "long cherished" along the Miramichi. An ambitious man, he involved himself in local political life and militia affairs. His failure, however, to involve himself in the most important economic activities of the area, precluded his becoming a greater political presence on the Miramichi or his having any lasting influence beyond the local sphere. Alexander McDonald arrived penniless, had great designs, but in the end left only a stone house as a symbol of his aspirations. The Province of New Brunswick has restored the McDonald house and surrounding lands as a historic park, in an attempt to illustrate the life of one of the first settlers in the Miramichi region and to tell the story of the early colonist's encounter with its vast resources and harsh realities.

DONALD P. LEMON

N.B., Dept. of Natural Resources, Lands Branch (Fredericton), Land grants, book 3, no.170; book 4, nos.326, 328, 340, 1042; book B, no.322; book F, nos.623, 625; book G, no.691. Northumberland Land Registry Office (Newcastle, N.B.), Registry books, 26, nos.163–64. PANB, MC 1, McDonald file; MC 216/66 ("Alexander MacDonald family disposition"); RG 1, RS559, C2a; E10–11; RG 10, RS108, Alexander McDonald, 1787; RG 18, RS153, A/1–4; B3/2–3. Gubbins, *N.B. journals* (Temperley). *Gleaner: and Northumberland Schediasma* (Miramichi, N.B.), 30 Dec. 1834. D. P. Lemon, "McDonald Farm Historic Park: critical path" (report, N.B., Hist. Resources Administration, Fredericton, 1978) (copy at PANB).

McDONALD, CHARLES, businessman, militia officer, JP, and office holder; b. 24 July 1784 in Blair Atholl, Scotland, third son of John McDonald and Amelia Cameron; m. 5 March 1811 Mary Stone, and they had three sons and two daughters; d. 7 Oct. 1826 in Gananoque, Upper Canada.

Charles McDonald's parents emigrated in or before 1787, settling in Athol, N.Y. During the late spring of 1809 McDonald arrived in Upper Canada to join two friends working at Gananoque for Thomas F. Howland, a timber merchant and local agent for Sir John JOHNSON. Howland employed McDonald as well and by September proposed taking him on as a partner. In spite of McDonald's favourable reception of the idea, it was apparently never put into effect. McDonald seems, however, to have continued working in the Gananoque area and in 1811 he married Mary, daughter of Joel STONE, a major landholder and merchant. By the outbreak of the War of 1812 McDonald had joined Stone's business and the two men were operating a prosperous enterprise in lumber and local retailing. McDonald made the annual rafting trips to Quebec in the summer while Stone remained behind, tending to local business and fulfilling his duties as collector of customs and justice of the peace.

During the war McDonald served as an ensign in Stone's regiment, the 2nd Leeds Militia. For the most part he spent these years quietly in Gananoque, although some historians credit him with building the blockhouses at Gananoque and Bridge (Chimney) Island. It was a period of general prosperity and the Stone–McDonald business proved no exception. In 1815 Stone seems to have retired, leasing his land on the west side of the Gananoque River to McDonald. That year McDonald set up a shop apart from his

McDonald

house and also planned a new sawmill as a replacement for Stone's old mill. In operation by 1816, the mill was later described by Robert Gourlay* as "a very superior kind, supposed to be the best in two provinces." In 1817 McDonald acquired the area's only grist-mill, presumably from Thomas Howland or his brother.

McDonald needed help with his expanding business and on 17 Jan. 1818 admitted his brother John* as a full partner in the company, now known as C. and J. McDonald. Another brother, Collin, joined at the same time; when he became a partner in 1825, the name of the firm was changed to C. and J. McDonald and Company. The business expanded steadily from 1818 through the 1820s. Its inventory of mercantile goods grew in both volume and variety while its inventory of lumber in Gananoque and Montreal doubled between 1819 and 1822. During this period a second sawmill was acquired upriver on the Gananoque. In addition the firm purchased lots in Leeds and Lansdowne (Front of and Rear of Leeds and Lansdowne) and Pittsburgh townships.

A major development was the acquisition in 1825 of Johnson's land on the east side of the river. This purchase gave the McDonalds control of all waterpower rights along the lower part of the Gananoque, thus making possible large-scale development of mills. With the extension of British tariff preferences to Canadian wheat and flour between 1825 and 1827, the McDonalds seized the opportunity to capitalize on the potential of the new trade. Heretofore lumbering had been the main thrust of the business but by December 1825 a new grist-mill was under construction. Plans were also under way for a new dam, an enlarged mill-race, and a new wharf. In operation by July 1826, the mill was, according to a local historian, the largest of its kind in the province. Charles McDonald did not, however, live to oversee its development; he died in October 1826.

McDonald's life centred almost exclusively on business. The militia, the magistracy (he was appointed in 1821), and trusteeship of the Gananoque school were his only other activities and these were minor and strictly local. He seems to have had scant interest in, or possibly little time for, politics although he signed and helped to draft local responses to Gourlay's famous questionnaire: they were, however, never returned to Gourlay. His personal life was somewhat tragic. Several children died in infancy and his wife suffered, as early as 1812, from what a family member described as "mental derangement at certain periods." By December 1821 she had been taken to New York City for treatment and she returned in July 1822 when her health had improved. She survived her husband, living until 1838, and continued to require some care for the remainder of her days. Only one of McDonald's three sons, William Stone, had a lasting connec-

tion with the firm; he joined it in 1833, became a partner the following year, and by 1851 had assumed control from his uncle John.

Charles McDonald left little to provide some measure of his character. At his funeral he was eulogized by William Smart*, the Presbyterian minister at Brockville, as a "kind husband and father, tender brother, warm friend and generous benefactor" as well as a "liberal contributor to the Sabbath and day school and public charities in the neighbourhood."

CATHERINE SHEPARD

AO, MS 519; MU 1760; RG 22, ser.179, Charles McDonald. PAC, MG 23, HII, 1, vols.2–4. *Kingston Chronicle*, 1825–26.

McDONALD, JOHN (known also as **McDonald le Borgne**), fur trader; b. 1770 at Munial Farm on Loch Hourn, Scotland, son of Angus Ban McDonald and Nelly McDonell; m. according to the custom of the country, Marie Poitras, a Métis, and they had at least six children; d. 27 Feb. 1828 near Kempenfeldt Bay, Upper Canada.

John McDonald's family immigrated in 1786 to the area which later became Glengarry County (Ont.). By 1791 he was a clerk at Lachine, Lower Canada, and in 1798 he became a wintering partner in the New North West Company (sometimes called the XY Company), which was formed as a rival to the North West Company. Around 1802 he was stationed in the Red River region, in opposition to his cousin, Nor'Wester John MacDonell*. When the two firms merged in November 1804 in Montreal, McDonald was one of six wintering partners of the XY Company, represented by Sir Alexander Mackenzie*, to be a party to the new agreement. Having wintered near the source of the Red River in 1804–5, he rendezvoused that spring at the mouth of the river for several days of "great amusement" with George Nelson* and other XY and NWC colleagues.

The tracing of McDonald's activities between 1805 and 1810 is complicated by the fact that he and Nor'Wester John McDonald* of Garth were at times in the same areas beyond Lake Winnipeg (Man.) and are mentioned without distinction in the sources. In 1806 both McDonalds were stationed in the Fort des Prairies department. McDonald le Borgne was evidently in charge of the Fort Dauphin department from 1808 to 1810, and for the next three years he managed the Swan River department, where his Hudson's Bay Company counterpart, Alexander Kennedy, found him a violent opponent and a "notorious scoundrel."

In August 1816 McDonald, Simon Fraser*, Alexander McKENZIE, and John McLoughlin* were among the NWC partners arrested at Fort William (Thunder Bay, Ont.) by Lord Selkirk [Douglas*]. They were charged with "Crimes of Treason and

Conspiracy and as accessary to the murder of Robert Semple[*] Esquire and to divers other Murders Robberies and Felonies committed in the Course of the Months of May and June [1816]" at the Red River settlement (Man.), and were brought to Montreal. In February 1818 the trial site was changed from Lower Canada to Upper Canada because the witnesses for the defence were all located in Upper Canada or the northwest. McDonald was subsequently acquitted at York (Toronto).

In 1821 McDonald became a chief factor in the HBC when the NWC merged with its old rival. In 1821–22 he had charge of the Upper Red River district, and from 1823 to 1827 he was based at Fort Alexander (Man.), managing the Winnipeg River district. In March 1827 "alarming accounts" began to circulate that McDonald was "at the last stage of life," and on 25 July the HBC governor, George Simpson*, reported to London that McDonald had been granted a furlough on account of "extreme ill health." McDonald, his wife, and their family settled in Upper Canada on an NWC land grant assigned to him by William McGillivray; it was situated on the Penetanguishene Road, near present-day Barrie on Kempenfeldt Bay. There he maintained an interest in fur-trade affairs, expressing pleasure at the Winnipeg River district returns for 1827, curiosity about the yields of his large plantings of wheat, barley, oats, peas, and potatoes at Fort Alexander, and hopes of returning to service.

By early February 1828, however, his "indisposition" was serious, aggravated by grief over the death of his wife following a miscarriage in January. On 2 March John Spencer, a retired fur trader and neighbour, reported that McDonald had died on 27 February, "depriving us of a gentleman that so many looked up to as calculated to inspire energy & emulation . . . in [this] infant settlement he was looked up to as nearly the father of the flock." Lady Franklin [Griffin*] later furnished a monument in the Church of England graveyard at Newmarket in recognition of McDonald's assistance to her husband, explorer Sir John Franklin*, during his overland journey of 1825.

John McDonald died intestate, and court negotiations about his estate continued for more than 20 years. The disputes involved McDonald's brothers James and Finan and their expenses and claims concerning not only his lands but also their care of his children during his fur trade service and – in the instance of Catherine, his youngest child – after his death. The conflict parallels tensions that arose among the kinsmen of numerous British Nor'Westers, including Samuel Black* and John Stuart*, as the heirs and the courts tried to limit and to define the claims of traders' native families.

JENNIFER S. H. BROWN

AO, MU 2197, instruments transmitting cases from Lower to Upper Canada, 7 Feb. 1818; MU 2201, no.2; RG 22, ser.155. MTL, George Nelson papers and journals. PAM, HBCA, A.36/9: ff.6–37; A.44/2: f.43; B.3/b/46: f.28; B.134/c/4: ff.313, 325; D.4/15: f.114; D.5/2: ff.353–54; D.5/3: ff.97, 128–29, 395. *Les bourgeois de la Compagnie du Nord-Ouest* (Masson). *Docs. relating to NWC* (Wallace). J. S. H. Brown, *Strangers in blood: fur trade company families in Indian country* (Vancouver and London, 1980). A. F. Hunter, *A history of Simcoe County* (2v., Barrie, Ont., 1900; repr. 1948), 1. W. S. Wallace, "Namesakes in the fur-trade," *CHR*, 13 (1932): 285–90.

MacDONELL, ALEXANDER, politician and office holder; b. *c.* 1774 in Inverness-shire, Scotland; m. Mary ——, and they had at least four daughters and four sons; fl. 1813–28.

Nothing is known of Alexander MacDonell's family or background. His experience as adjutant for the militia of Glengarry, Scotland, prompted him in 1813 to offer his services in a similar capacity to Lord Selkirk [Douglas*]. Impressed by his qualifications, Selkirk engaged MacDonell in January 1814 to recruit colonists in Scotland and accompany them to the Red River settlement (Man.). In June 1815 he embarked with the settlers and the new governor of Rupert's Land, Robert Semple*, arriving at York Factory in August. MacDonell intended to stay at Red River for a year and then return to Scotland for his family. Selkirk suggested that he might be employed as the colony's accountant, but Semple considered him too valuable for that post and on 5 Sept. 1815 appointed him temporary second-in-command to Colin Robertson* of the Hudson's Bay Company, whom he placed in charge of the settlement. After their arrival at Fort Douglas (Winnipeg) in November, Semple sent MacDonell and the settlers to winter at Fort Daer (Pembina, N.Dak.). There, early in January 1816, MacDonell was sworn in as councillor and high sheriff of Assiniboia. Semple had confidence in MacDonell's fitness for office, having reported to Selkirk that he possessed "firmness, prudence and conciliatory manners" and had earned the esteem of all. After returning to Fort Douglas in April, MacDonell witnessed the growing hostility between Semple and Robertson which resulted in Robertson's departure early in June. Semple then appointed MacDonell his second-in-command, and the charge of the colony thus fell to MacDonell after the governor's violent death at Seven Oaks (Winnipeg) on 19 June 1816 [see Cuthbert Grant*] at the height of the conflict between the HBC and the North West Company for control of the western fur trade.

Forced by the NWC to leave Fort Douglas a few days later, the settlers were taken by MacDonell to Jack River House, where they wintered. MacDonell re-established the colony in March 1817 and successfully guided it through two difficult years. Frost and

MacDonell

high winds almost destroyed the crops of 1817 and grasshoppers those of 1818. MacDonell carefully regulated the cultivation of crops and also kept the colony's expenses low. Some HBC officers complained about his management and implied that he was dishonest, but they were hostile to the colony anyway. According to Robertson, they protested because MacDonell's measures prevented them from overcharging the colony for supplies and making excessive profits. Selkirk did not believe the rumours impugning MacDonell's honesty and the settlers declared their satisfaction with him in a petition dated 2 Aug. 1819.

After his departure for Scotland in the fall of 1819 to see his family, MacDonell was appointed Selkirk's agent for the Red River colony on 24 Feb. 1820 and, following the earl's death, agent for Selkirk's executors in May. By June 1820 he was back in the colony, where he resumed his post as governor locum tenens. As agent, MacDonell was responsible for the regulation of the colony's economic affairs, with authority to distribute land, settle accounts, and recover debts on behalf of his employers. He was also to superintend Frederick Matthey, who was in charge of defence and public works, and William Laidlaw, manager of Hayfield, the first model farm. MacDonell was therefore responsible for establishing a stable economy and a sound administration. He accomplished neither task.

In the first place, he failed to stop illicit fur trading in accordance with the orders of George Simpson*, governor of the HBC's Northern Department. Moreover, he initially obstructed the efforts of John Pritchard* to establish the Buffalo Wool Company, though he later purchased shares in the venture. As far as his management was concerned, the settlers charged that only a favoured few received the supplies they requested, that their accounts were incorrectly kept, and that they were being cheated. The Indians, too, accused MacDonell of cheating them. MacDonell aggravated the situation by appointing to responsible positions friends and relatives who often proved dishonest and inept. A group of Swiss settlers, who spent the winter of 1821–22 at Fort Daer housed in ruins and faced with starvation, found that an appeal to MacDonell had no effect. Presbyterian Scots resented MacDonell's seeming indifference to their desire for a minister.

Although Selkirk had emphasized the importance of cooperation among the colony's officers, MacDonell accused Matthey of plotting against him and encouraged dissension between Matthey and Laidlaw. The Council of Assiniboia did not function during his tenure of office. Instead, he ran things as he wanted, alienating officers of the HBC and prominent settlers.

By September 1821 Simpson had concluded that MacDonell's mismanagement was hurting the colony and making it unattractive to respectable settlers. His investigations led him to conclude that the accusations

of dishonesty and favouritism were true and he corroborated settlers' charges of drunkenness and immorality. He also expressed disapproval of some of MacDonell's private financial transactions, such as his sale to the settlers, at a high profit to himself, of horses he had purchased, ostensibly for the colony. MacDonell was dismissed in March 1822 and Andrew H. Bulger* replaced him in June. Within two years of his return to the Red River settlement MacDonell had lost the confidence of his employers and the respect of the settlers; according to Red River historian Alexander Ross* he became known as the "grasshopper governor" because "he proved as great a destroyer within doors as the grasshoppers in the fields."

MacDonell was retained in the service of Selkirk's executors for one more year in the hope that his experience would be useful. He also served as councillor of Assiniboia under both Bulger and his successor, Robert Parker Pelly, and became a special constable on 21 Oct. 1823. But instead of working with the new administration, he encouraged dissension and cooperated with neither governor. He supported settlers in requests that challenged the authority of the HBC, using official documents he had kept to support his statements. Such actions convinced Simpson of the desirability of MacDonell's departure.

MacDonell appeared determined to remain in the colony. In 1822, with Pritchard and Robert Logan*, he applied, unsuccessfully, for permission to open a retail store. But his main interest was farming. He had received land from Selkirk in 1818 and his family had arrived in 1823. In 1824 he owned 2,576 acres, but by 1827 his holdings had declined to 36 acres. His losses perhaps resulted from the settlement of his account with Selkirk's executors, a process which thoroughly discredited him. MacDonell's demands were seen as exorbitant and fraudulent. His threats in 1824 to take his claim for board to court enraged Andrew Colvile, a director of the HBC, who declared that MacDonell was not to receive a deed to his land or have the right to sell it until he had settled his accounts. MacDonell was vulnerable because he had not applied for a deed, disliking the terms offered. As early as October 1824 he had been forced to recognize the sale of some of his land. In the end MacDonell had to settle on the executors' terms.

By 1824 Simpson considered MacDonell "disaffected," one of the most dangerous men in the colony, and inimical to the interests of Selkirk's executors. Simpson refused to associate with him or admit him to the society of HBC officers. This ostracism blocked all avenues to social prominence and influence. MacDonell's financial situation received another blow that year when he was denied credit at the company's store. By 1828 he had left. In

April of that year he was in York (Toronto), looking for a farm.

EDITH BURLEY

A transcript of Alexander MacDonell's journal is at PAC, MG 19, E1, ser.1: 17928–8177.

PAC, MG 19, E1, ser.1, vols.1–79 (mfm. at PAM); E11 (copies); MG 30, D1, 20: 636–43. PAM, HBCA, D.5/3: ff.196–97; E.5/1: ff.3d–4; E.8/6: ff.2–2d, 102–4d, 182–93; MG 2, C21, files 125, 150 (mfm.); C23, nos.7, 9, 36. *The Canadian north-west, its early development and legislative records; minutes of the councils of the Red River colony and the Northern Department of Rupert's Land*, ed. E. H. Oliver (2v., Ottawa, 1914–15), 1. Alexander Ross, *The Red River settlement: its rise, progress and present state; with some account of native races and its general history, to the present day* (London, 1856; repr. Minneapolis, Minn., 1957, and Edmonton, 1972). Morton, *Hist. of Canadian west* (Thomas; 1973).

MACDONELL, ARCHIBALD, office holder, JP, and militia officer; b. *c.* 1745, probably in the Scottish Highlands; d. 7 June 1830 in Mount Pleasant, Prince Edward County, Upper Canada.

Although it is known that an elder brother, Allan, emigrated to America in 1771, the timing of Archibald Macdonell's arrival is obscure. In any event he received land in Tryon County, N.Y., from Sir John JOHNSON, and later stated that he had not served in His Majesty's forces prior to 1775. In June of that year he was promised a commission in the Royal Highland Emigrants regiment then being raised to protect the king's interests [see Allan Maclean*]. He was one of three brothers who joined the British side. Archibald raised recruits for the regiment until January 1776 when his superior, Captain Macdonell, was taken prisoner. The captain left orders for him to take charge of the recruits and link up with Governor Guy Carleton*'s forces, which he did, according to his own testimony, "after much misery and difficulty, through the woods from Johnston [Johnstown, N.Y.] to Canada, and joined the Regiment in June 76." There he received a commission as ensign of the 1st Battalion Royal Highland Emigrants, which became the 84th Foot in 1778. For the remainder of the war, he served on the frontier of Quebec. He was promoted lieutenant in 1781.

In 1784 Macdonell was designated as a leader of the loyalist refugees settling west of Montreal. Thus he became involved in the attempt to found a loyal society in the wilderness by utilizing the connections and the hierarchy already present in the British and loyalist regiments. His duties were limited but important. He was responsible for the small, disparate group of settlers chosen to assemble in Township No.5, later called Marysburgh, which was the most westerly township above Cataraqui (Kingston). In the migration of 1784 these people were the leftovers, being attached to regiments other than the major units gathered in the region.

Marysburgh, now North and South Marysburgh townships, was to be Macdonell's home for the rest of his life. Essentially he continued to fill the role defined for him in 1784. He was the local representative in a network of authority centred first in Quebec, and after 1792 in Upper Canada, a network contingent on an intricate system of paternalism and personal patronage. Within this system Macdonell's scope was tightly circumscribed. Remote from the regional centre of Kingston, he had influence only in Prince Edward County. In 1800 he was appointed lieutenant of the county, its most prestigious position. This office, however, soon became obsolete in the evolution of regional government [see Hazelton Spencer*]. Instead Macdonell relied for his influence on his position as a large landowner, magistrate, and militia officer. An officer on half pay, he received more than 2,000 acres of land, mostly in Marysburgh, where he lived the life of a country squire. He was a justice of the peace, and between 1790 and 1818 appeared frequently at the meetings of the Court of Quarter Sessions, which comprised the local government of the Midland District. In 1797 he served as a member of the first Heir and Devisee Commission established to settle loyalist land claims. Finally, he was the senior officer of the militia in Prince Edward County from its inception until his death, a period of about 45 years. Like many loyalist officers, Macdonell emphasized service to the state as the basis of his leadership rather than involvement in commercial or industrial development. These pursuits, however, were the means of advancement for the men who began to challenge his power in the 1820s.

With the outbreak of war in 1812, Macdonell's influence had started to wane. He declared himself ready to serve again, but failed to win a commission in the 10th Royal Veteran Battalion, a regular British unit. Perhaps because of advancing age, he was not involved with the flank companies of militia from Prince Edward on active duty in Kingston. Instead he remained in Marysburgh in command of the sedentary militia, which was to be mobilized only in the event of an emergency. After the war, he was employed in 1816 as a commissioner for militia pensions. In 1820 he was an officer of the district agricultural society. Finally, in 1829 he resigned his commission in the militia. "Age and infirmities," he noted, "are the motives that have induced me to this step, worn out and not being able any longer to perform the necessary duties thereof." On 7 June 1830 he died, "much and justly regretted, by an extensive circle of friends," according to his obituary in the *Kingston Chronicle*. Macdonell apparently had no immediate family. The major beneficiaries of his will were his five nieces and a nephew. His passing marked a transition in leader-

Macdonell

ship from that based on landownership and military service to one stressing entrepreneurial initiative.

WILLIAM N. T. WYLIE

AO, RG 22, ser.159. BL, Add. MSS 21724: 38–39; 21734: 147; 21775: 274–75; 21822: 353; 21828: 100 (mfm. at PAC). PAC, MG 55/14, no.1 (loyalist claims and petitions); RG 1, E3, 27: 89; L1, 22: 237; 26: 230; 27: 29, 273; 28: 48, 263, 341, 540; L3, 327a: M1/221; 328: M2/179; 335a: M10/24, 29; RG 5, A1: 5437–38, 5444–46; RG 7, G16C, 1; RG 8, I (C ser.), 789: 90; 1035: 48; RG 9, I, B1, 1–15; B7, 1, 3, 10, 14. PRO, AO 12/109: 222; WO 28/8: 138 (mfm. at PAC). "Grants of crown lands in U.C.," AO *Report*, 1929. *The settlement of the United Empire Loyalists on the upper St Lawrence and Bay of Quinte in 1784; a documentary record*, ed. E. A. Cruikshank (Toronto, 1934; repr. 1966). "United Empire Loyalists: enquiry into losses and services," AO *Report*, 1904. "U.C. land book C," AO *Report*, 1930. "U.C. land book D," AO *Report*, 1931. *Chronicle & Gazette*, 27 July, 14 Sept. 1833; 16 Jan. 1836. *Kingston Chronicle*, 19 March, 2 July, 17 Dec. 1819; 21 Jan., 5 May 1820; 22 March 1822; 11 Aug. 1826; 18 July 1828; 12 June 1830; 8 Jan., 19 Feb. 1831. *Kingston Gazette*, 6 July, 7 Sept. 1816; 8 July, 14 Oct., 9 Dec. 1817. *Fighting men of a Highland Catholic Jacobite clan who fought in Canada to gain it for and preserve it to the crown, and for the honour of the name of Glengarry*, [comp. A. McL. Macdonell] ([Toronto, 1912]). *Pioneer life on the Bay of Quinte, including genealogies of old families and biographical sketches of representative citizens* (Toronto, 1904; repr. Belleville, Ont., 1972). K. M. Bindon, "Kingston: a social history, 1785–1830" (PHD thesis, Queen's Univ., Kingston, Ont., 1979), 467–68. H. C. Burleigh, *The loyalist regiments and the settlement of Prince Edward County, 1784* (Bloomfield, Ont., 1977). Canniff, *Hist. of the settlement of U.C.* Richard and Janet Lunn, *The county: the first hundred years in loyalist Prince Edward* (Picton, Ont., 1967). J. P. MacLean, *An historical account of the settlements of Scotch Highlanders in America prior to the peace of 1783 . . .* (Cleveland, Ohio, and Glasgow, 1900; repr. Baltimore, Md., 1968). E. A. Cruikshank, "The King's Royal Regiment of New York," *OH*, 27 (1931): 193–323.

MACDONELL, MILES, army officer, office holder, JP, and colonial administrator; b. *c.* 1767 in Inverness-shire, Scotland, son of John McDonell of Scothouse; m. three times and he had at least two sons and four daughters; d. 28 June 1828 in Pointe-Fortune, Upper Canada.

Details of Miles Macdonell's early life are sketchy. He was born into a distinguished Catholic family with a long military tradition. His father, known as "Spanish" John, had fought with distinction in the Spanish forces against the Austrians in the 1740s. In 1773, at the invitation of Sir William Johnson*, John, his family, and about 600 members of the Macdonell clan of Glengarry immigrated to North America and settled in the Mohawk valley of New York. At the outbreak of the American revolution the Macdonells rallied to the crown. Spanish John fought with Butler's Rangers and in 1783 he settled at St Andrews in present-day Stormont County (Ont.).

Miles had early shown an interest in the military and in 1782 was appointed ensign in the King's Royal Regiment of New York. He served with it until its reduction in 1784. Subsequently, he may have returned to Scotland and it was probably there that he married Isabella McDonell of Morar. By 1791 Macdonell, with his wife, had taken up farming in Osnabruck Township, Upper Canada. Three years later he was commissioned a lieutenant in the Royal Canadian Volunteer Regiment. In 1795 Spanish John wrote to Miles's brother John*, an employee of the North West Company, expressing the hope that this commission would "in some measure divert [Miles's] melancholly thoughts" about the death of his wife the previous year. She had left him with two sons and two daughters. Macdonell seems to have applied himself to his military career. Rising rapidly, he was promoted captain in 1796. Two years later he remarried, taking as his wife his second cousin Catherine (Kitty) McDonell of Collachie, sister of Angus* and Alexander* McDonell (Collachie). His family life continued, however, to be troubled by sorrow. Catherine died the following year; there were no children from the marriage. During this period Macdonell also dabbled in politics, seeking election as a member of the House of Assembly for Glengarry but, according to his father, he was thwarted by the "presbiterian faction."

From 1800 to 1802 Macdonell was stationed at Fort George (Niagara-on-the-Lake). When his regiment was disbanded in 1802, he returned to his farm and once more began to think of marriage. Through his third wife and distant cousin, Nancy (Anne) Macdonell, sister of Alexander MACDONELL (Greenfield) and John Macdonell* (Greenfield), Miles was further linked to prominent Scottish families in Upper Canada. (Nancy and one of their two daughters would predecease him.) Although he appears to have applied himself vigorously to improving his lands, which had been neglected by a tenant, Macdonell continued to covet a military career or other posts which would provide him with financial security. "Mere farming," he wrote in 1804, "will hardly support my family in the manner I would wish." He spared no expense in educating his children and as a result was often in debt. He frequently borrowed from his brother, drawing on John's account with the NWC, much to the displeasure of the company's agent, William McGILLIVRAY. From 1802 to 1811 he wrote numerous letters urging his friends and acquaintances to intervene to secure military positions, initially for himself and later for both himself and his son Donald Æneas*. In 1807 he was appointed registrar of the Court of Probate and, on the recommendation of his cousin, Alexander McDonell*, vicar general of Upper

Canada, was named sheriff of the Home District. An attempt to gain permission to raise a corps of Glengarry fencibles, in which he would hold a permanent paid position, was rebuffed by Lieutenant Governor Francis Gore* that same year. Preferment finally came in June 1811 when, through the efforts of Lord Selkirk [Douglas*], Macdonell was named by the governor and London committee of the Hudson's Bay Company first governor of Assiniboia. This appointment could hardly have been welcomed by Macdonell's family and friends, most of whom had a long association with the NWC. But for him, the position of governor and of agent for Selkirk held out the prospect of a regular salary, a large tract of land in the northwest which would be deeded to him, and four or five shares in a joint stock company to be formed at some future date. In short, it promised an end to his indebtedness.

Macdonell had first met his benefactor in Osnabruck Township in January 1804 when Selkirk was travelling through Upper Canada. Selkirk had been impressed by Macdonell, whom he found to be "very much a gentleman in manners & sentiments" and "so popular [among his neighbours] that he could get work done when nobody else could." Selkirk apparently either did not witness or was blind to Macdonell's less attractive character traits which included arrogance and vanity. As a consequence, their chance meeting led to an ongoing correspondence and attempts by Selkirk to secure a post for Macdonell. In a letter written in December 1809 Selkirk informed Macdonell that he had heard of an opening that would be "attended with permanent advantages." Undoubtedly, he was referring to his plans for the establishment of a colony on the Red River. His trip to North America in 1803–4 had been associated with the founding of settlements on Prince Edward Island and at Baldoon, Upper Canada. In 1804 he had hired Macdonell's second cousin and brother-in-law, Alexander McDonell (Collachie), to be his agent for Baldoon. By 1809 the greatest impediment to a colony in the northwest was the HBC's monopoly of Rupert's Land. Only with the company's sponsorship or at the very least, cooperation, could his plans be implemented.

Thus, inevitably, Selkirk's schemes became entangled with the politics of the fur trade and the aggressive competition between the HBC and the NWC. He began to purchase HBC stock in July 1808 and the following year his wife's brother, Andrew Wedderburn, and her cousin John Halkett* did the same, giving them a voice in the company's affairs. By 1810 the survival of the HBC depended upon a thorough reorganization of the company and its resources. The plan which was ultimately adopted was prepared and presented to the General Court of the HBC in March by Wedderburn. Called the "retrenching system," it aimed at streamlining the company's

operation, recruiting more "aggressive" servants, giving the officers a vested interest in the company's continued success by means of a profit-sharing plan, and supplying the inland posts with locally grown crops rather than expensive European produce. This scheme left the way open for the founding of a permanent colony within HBC territory, a colony that could become a source of both foodstuffs and servants. On 30 May Selkirk's proposal that he be given a grant of land on the Red River in return for a token payment and a promise to provide servants for the company was approved.

From the outset the Nor'Westers attempted to block the establishment of the colony. Although the Red River settlement was technically not a project of the HBC, but rather Selkirk's own, they saw it as a threat to the fur trade. The colony lay astride the major rivers that linked the fur country to the plains where pemmican, the staple of their diet, was procured. A more ominous threat than the disruption of the food supply was the Nor'Westers' belief that the colony was part of a coordinated plan organized by Selkirk and the HBC to establish a presence in the Athabasca country, the most important source of the NWC's profits. The colony could produce both the manpower and the supplies to support such an expansion. The urgency of vigorously opposing Selkirk's colony was underscored in a letter from Simon McGillivray* of the NWC to the wintering partners in April 1812: "He must be driven to abandon it, for his success would strike at the very existence of our Trade." The Nor'Westers' worst fears may have been confirmed when, on 15 June 1811, Macdonell was presented with his commission by Joseph Berens, deputy governor of the HBC. Even though Macdonell had earlier received detailed instructions from Selkirk for establishing the colony, the link between Macdonell, the colony, and the company appeared, once again, to be clearly demonstrated.

From the beginning the enterprise was plagued by bad luck, poor management, and the inability of Macdonell to win the loyalty and trust of the men put in his charge. Selkirk's intention in 1811 was to detach from a party of company recruits a few labourers who would prepare the groundwork for the arrival of settlers in 1812. Macdonell and William Hillier, a recently appointed officer of the company, were to meet the recruits at Stornoway, Scotland, and lead them to Hudson Bay. At the bay Macdonell was to select his men and lead them to the site of the proposed colony, Hillier was to take charge of those who were to remain as HBC employees. The two men's ships were delayed and they did not arrive at Stornoway until 17 July. There, more than 100 men recruited by the company's agents had been waiting since early June with little to occupy their time but drinking and grumbling about inadequate facilities and the pros-

Macdonell

pects of the voyage that lay ahead. Undoubtedly their discontent was fuelled by an article in the *Inverness Journal* written by McGillivray, which warned about the arduous voyage, extremes of climate, lack of food, and hostile Indians that awaited them. Macdonell did nothing to calm their fears. In fact, he handled the situation badly. When he discovered that Glaswegians had been recruited under different terms from some of the other employees, he attempted to reduce their wages. He also refused to fulfil promises made to other recruits with the result that many feared they would not be treated as promised. Some deserted, and the longer the men remained in port the more serious the problems became. These difficulties were exacerbated by customs officials who delayed the sailing even further while they minutely examined papers and cargo. When the ships finally sailed on 26 July 1811, it was the latest departure for Hudson Bay recorded up to that time.

The voyage, plagued by head winds, lasted 61 days, the longest on record. The ships' arrival on 24 September was so late in the season that the men would be unable to move inland until spring. Since such large numbers could not be accommodated at York Factory (Man.), the whole company, including Hillier's men, had to winter in log huts several miles up the Nelson River.

The winter was a troubled one. Food was in short supply and, despite his nomination as a justice of the peace for the Indian Territory in November 1811 to bolster his influence in the northwest, Macdonell continued to be bothered by his inability to establish authority over his men. They quarrelled among themselves and a mutiny had to be suppressed. Ice in the river prevented Macdonell's party from breaking camp until 22 June 1812. On 6 July he started up the Hayes River with 22 men who were to prepare the way for later settlers. The boats arrived at the junction of the Red and Assiniboine rivers on 30 August.

Over the next two and a half years Macdonell faced a series of challenges that would have taxed the ingenuity of a much more talented man. To establish a successful, self-sufficient colony on the Red River necessitated securing both the loyalty of the settlers and adequate supplies of food. It also required the fixing and maintaining of good relations with the local representatives of rival fur-trading companies, as well as with the Métis and Indian populations, who had reason to resent the colony. If the colony was to succeed, a deft hand in diplomacy was essential.

Initially Macdonell appeared to direct his efforts towards establishing cordial relations with the NWC. Alexander Macdonell (Greenfield), Miles's brother-in-law as well as cousin, was in command of Fort Gibraltar (Winnipeg), the NWC post. On 1 Sept. 1812 Miles and Hillier were invited to dine with the Nor'Westers and later Alexander placed two horses at

his cousin's displosal. In what he thought was the same spirit of cordiality, Miles invited Alexander and the NWC servants, as well as local Métis and Indians, to an impressive ceremony on 4 September, during which Selkirk's title to the colony was proclaimed amid the firing of guns and loud cheers.

Macdonell's party had arrived too late in the season to prepare houses, fields, and, most important, a harvest to feed both themselves and the settlers who were to follow. Consequently, he sent the bulk of his men south to winter near the HBC fort at Pembina (N.Dak.), within the Selkirk grant and close to the plains and ample supplies of buffalo meat. Staying behind with the remainder, Macdonell laid out the site for Fort Douglas (Winnipeg) and set to work clearing land and building houses, before joining his party at Pembina, where he built Fort Daer.

At Pembina, he continued his efforts to cultivate good relations with the Nor'Westers and with the Métis, whom he hired as hunters to run buffalo. He failed, however, to take as much care in his relations with the local representatives of the HBC. Within a few days of his arrival at Pembina, Macdonell had clashed with Hugh Heney, who was in charge of the post there, over purchases of meat he had made directly from the Métis. Although Macdonell had paid the prevailing rate, Heney objected that he was interfering with the company's trade. The resulting strained relations between the local officials of the company and the colony were only eased when Hillier took charge of the post.

The arrival at Pembina of the first contingent of actual settlers under the leadership of Owen Keveny* on 27 Oct. 1812 brought new problems. Houses were not ready to receive them and the settlers were sick. Hillier brought some of the women and children into the post where they could get better care and, with Macdonell, wrote to the outlying company posts requesting them to stockpile supplies of pemmican for the coming winter. Securing adequate amounts of food became the principal preoccupation of both the governor and the settlers. The winter of 1812–13 was especially difficult for all concerned and by spring the situation had worsened. Not only was food in short supply, in part because the Métis had refused to deliver meat for which they had been paid, but Miles Macdonell had received word that the Nor'Westers were attempting to stir up trouble among the native tribes. Moreover, John Dugald Cameron*, a NWC partner in charge of the Lake Winnipeg department, had arrived at Pembina and soon began fomenting discontent among the settlers, as well as persuading local employees of the NWC, including Alexander Macdonell (Greenfield), to oppose the colony. Cameron was operating on instructions from his superiors, but Miles Macdonell's own failings contributed to the opposition. Whenever the opportunity presented itself

Miles flaunted both his authority and Selkirk's title to the territory. In April 1813, convinced that even his brother-in-law had turned against him, Macdonell ordered all intercourse with the NWC to cease. The policy of conciliation was at an end.

A month later the settlers travelled north to begin building houses and planting crops. More provisions would be needed for new settlers expected towards the end of the summer. In July Macdonell journeyed to York Factory to meet the Kildonan settlers accompanied by Archibald McDonald* and to lead them back to the colony. He was disappointed. Fever on board ship and a diversion from York Factory to Fort Churchill (Churchill) meant that the settlers would have to winter on the bay. By 15 October Miles had arrived back in the colony only to find that the crops had failed and that it would again be necessary to send the settlers south to Pembina.

On 8 Jan. 1814, seeking to solve the colony's food problems once and for all, Macdonell issued a proclamation "which had been some time in contemplation." The proclamation prohibited the export of provisions of any kind from within the limits of Assiniboia without a special licence from the governor. From his point of view, the proclamation was essential to ensure an adequate supply of food for the settlers and to prevent future shortages. Only then could the colony hope to progress. From the point of view of the Nor'Westers and the Métis, the "pemmican proclamation," as it came to be known, was an open declaration of war. It interfered with the livelihood of the Métis, who supplied the pemmican, and it threatened the trade of the Nor'Westers, who relied upon the staple to feed their trading parties.

In the ensuing months the crisis escalated. The proclamation was sent to posts of both companies throughout Assiniboia and stocks of pemmican were expropriated. John Spencer was appointed sheriff and charged with enforcing the proclamation. Armed constables supported by artillery were stationed along the Red River to intercept and confiscate pemmican coming downriver. In retaliation, the Nor'Westers began to construct a blockhouse that would give them command of the river. By mid June, despite several attempts at negotiation, it seemed that a violent clash was imminent and unavoidable. Then, at the last moment, a compromise was worked out whereby Macdonell agreed to return pemmican stocks to the Nor'Westers in exchange for the promise of supplies for the following winter and a cessation of hostilities. The crisis had been averted, at least temporarily.

Throughout June and July 1814 Macdonell was exhausted and depressed. The pemmican war, Selkirk's criticism of his conduct of the colony's affairs, particularly its accounts, and the lack of support he had had from the HBC men, especially William AULD, superintendent of the Northern Department, all played on his mind. On 14 July he wrote to Selkirk asking that "your Lordship be not prevented by any delicacy to send a suitable person to take my place, as I find myself unequal to the task of reconciling so many different interests." He left for York Factory on 25 July to meet a new contingent of settlers. Soon after his arrival on 22 August he appears to have suffered a nervous breakdown. It could hardly have been a stable Macdonell who returned to the colony on 20 October. Once again he found himself at the centre of trouble. Spencer had been arrested by the Nor'Westers and Duncan Cameron*, in charge of the NWC's Red River department, had repudiated the June agreement. The next day, Macdonell ordered the Nor'Westers to quit Fort Gibraltar. Of course they did not and in remaining they were a constant reminder to the settlers of the ineffectiveness of their governor, who soon had to order some of them south once again because of food shortages.

Throughout the winter and the spring of 1815 the colony was subjected to harassing raids by the Métis and the intrigues of the Nor'Westers. By casting doubt on the legality of the Selkirk grant, creating fear of Indian attacks, and making invidious comparisons between the lot of settlers in Upper Canada and those in the west, Duncan Cameron tried to induce the colonists to leave. When he offered free passage to Upper Canada more than 40 settlers abandoned the colony in the spring of 1815. On 17 June, with the colony under threat of imminent attack, Macdonell surrendered himself to the representatives of the NWC in return for a promise that the settlers would not be harmed. On 25 June, however, in the face of constant harassment by the Métis, who were encouraged by the NWC, Peter FIDLER, the HBC surveyor temporarily in command of the colony, surrendered it and retired with the settlers to Jack River House. Macdonell was taken to Montreal by the Nor'Westers to stand trial for his "crimes," which included the "illegal" confiscation of pemmican. He was never brought to trial.

The colony's struggles did not end with Macdonell's surrender. Colin Robertson* persuaded some of the settlers at Jack River House to return and additional colonists arrived in August 1815 with Robert Semple*, newly appointed governor of the HBC territories. In the spring of 1816 Macdonell set out for the Red River. At Lake Winnipeg, he learned that the colony had once again been disrupted. He hurried back to warn Selkirk, whom he met at Sault Ste Marie (Ont.), that Semple and about 20 men had been killed at Seven Oaks (Winnipeg) on 19 June [see Cuthbert Grant*]. Accompanying Selkirk, Macdonell took part in the capture of Fort William (Thunder Bay, Ont.) on 13 August. William McGillivray and other partners of the NWC were arrested on charges of "aiding, abetting & instigating to the murders committed at Red River," and were sent to York (Toronto) for trial.

McDonell

The NWC's papers and all the furs at Fort William were seized. In October, claiming to be writing on behalf of NWC partner Daniel McKenzie, Macdonell sent a letter to Roderick McKenzie*, of the NWC's Nipigon department, in which he urged the wintering partners to abandon their ties to Montreal and send their furs out through Hudson Bay. In mid December Macdonell and some members of De Meuron's Regiment set out from Rainy Lake (Ont.) to reassume control of the colony. On 10 Jan. 1817 they captured Fort Douglas, then in the hands of the NWC. Macdonell spent a few months in the colony as governor, but returned to Montreal to take part in the trials. He never returned to the northwest.

Macdonell spent his final years in semi-retirement on his farm in Osnabruck Township. Much of his time was devoted to an unsuccessful attempt to recover from the Selkirk estate the payments he felt were due to him. These included £300 a year promised as salary, 50,000 acres of land, and shares in the joint-stock company. Unable to recover the moneys or to sell part of the extensive acreages he held in Upper Canada, he remained in debt throughout his life. He died on 28 June 1828 at his brother's farm at Pointe-Fortune and was buried at Rigaud, Lower Canada.

Historians have generally agreed that, despite the inherent difficulties of establishing a colony at the Red River amid the fierce competition between the fur-trading companies, Macdonell must bear some of the responsibility for the colony's initial failure. They have focused upon his character faults, his inability to inspire trust and loyalty among his people, his obstinacy, his arrogance, his unaccommodating temper, and his lack of staying power. It was these flaws, as well as his lack of shrewdness and diplomatic skill, that led to his failures. Either he never understood his situation, or worse, refused to come to grips with it. Nowhere is this better shown than in the decision to issue the pemmican proclamation. It was promulgated at a time when the colony was too weak to defend itself and it offered the NWC excellent propaganda against both the HBC and Lord Selkirk. His behaviour during those years suggests that he saw the colony as entirely separate from the fur trade but his point of view does not excuse an insensitivity that blinded him to the provocative nature of his actions. Through a similar blindness he alienated his own people, seeking out the company of "gentlemen" in preference to theirs. The result was that a successful colony could not be established until after the union of the two fur-trading companies, in 1821.

HERBERT J. MAYS

Miles Macdonell's papers are at PAC, MG 19, E4. A letter-book in this collection was published as "Selkirk settlement; letter book of Captain Miles Macdonell . . . ," PAC *Report*, 1886, clxxxvii–ccxxvi. Macdonell's journal is also at the PAC, in the Selkirk papers (MG 19, E1, copy at PAM, MG 2, A1: 16500–7599).

AO, MU 1780, A-1-1–A-1-4, A-1-6, A-2; RG 22, ser.155. PAC, MG 19, E1, E2 (copies at PAM). PAM, HBCA, A.6/18. *HBRS*, 2 (Rich and Fleming). Chadwick, *Ontario families*. Morton, *Hist. of Canadian west* (1939). J. M. Bumsted, "The affair at Stornoway, 1811," *Beaver*, outfit 312 (spring 1982): 53–58. J. G. Harkness, "Miles Macdonell," *OH*, 40 (1948): 77–83. A.-G. Morice, "A Canadian pioneer: Spanish John" and "Sidelights on the careers of Miles Macdonell and his brothers," *CHR*, 10 (1929): 212–35 and 308–32.

McDONELL (Aberchalder), HUGH, army and militia officer, land surveyor, politician, and office holder; b. *c.* 1760 at Aberchalder House, Scotland, son of Alexander McDonell of Aberchalder; m. first a Miss Hughes; m. secondly a Miss Ulich, daughter of the Danish consul in Algiers (Algeria), and they had two sons and eight daughters; d. 1833 in Florence (Italy).

In 1773 Hugh McDonell's father and his uncles John of Leek and Allan of Collachie led a major migration of Highlanders to North America, settling on Sir William Johnson*'s estate in the Mohawk valley of New York. In January 1776 McDonell, along with his father and uncles, was taken prisoner by Major-General Philip John Schuyler. He later escaped and returned to Johnstown. Having collected about 100 loyalists, he fled with them to Montreal in May 1777. There he joined the King's Royal Regiment of New York as an ensign; he was promoted lieutenant in 1781 and retired on half pay when the regiment was disbanded in 1783. The next year he joined his relatives in what was to become Upper Canada, taking up a 500-acre grant in Township No.1 (Charlottenburg). In 1788 he was appointed a deputy land surveyor. Until his retirement from the post in 1794 he plotted lot, concession, and township boundaries through the virgin forest of the Eastern District.

In 1792 McDonell and his brother John* were elected for Glengarry County to Upper Canada's first parliament, an indication of his family's local prominence. Perhaps it was as a politician that McDonell caught the eye of Lieutenant Governor John Graves Simcoe*. In June 1794, in spite of a modest military background, he was appointed the province's first adjutant general of militia. Later, through the influence of his brother John, he joined the Royal Canadian Volunteer Regiment as a captain. The disbandment of the volunteers in 1802 left him in near destitution, a state exacerbated by the government's failure to pay a portion of his salary. In 1803 he became lieutenant-colonel of the Glengarry militia, John then being the colonel.

McDonell journeyed to England in 1804. There

Robert Mathews*, former military secretary to Governor Frederick Haldimand*, attempted to find him a position: "a valuable officer is lost to himself and to the service, whose abilities [would be useful] either in a civil or a military capacity, particularly in Canada, where his knowledge of the French language, the customs and manners of the people, and of the interests of the Indian nation, might be turned to good account, while the services and sufferings of a very deserving officer would be rewarded." In London, McDonell sought the patronage of the Duke of Kent [Edward* Augustus], whom he had met while the duke was in British North America. Edward secured him an appointment as assistant commissary general at Gibraltar in 1805; five years later McDonell accompanied Lord Cochrane to Algiers and the following year he became consul general there, a position he held until 1820 when he retired to Florence.

ALLAN J. MacDONALD

AO, RG 1, A-I-1, 18: 37. PAC, RG 5, A1: 407–12. J. G. Harkness, *Stormont, Dundas and Glengarry: a history, 1784–1945* (Oshawa, Ont., 1946), 36–37. J. A. Macdonell, *Sketches illustrating the early settlement and history of Glengarry in Canada, relating principally to the Revolutionary War of 1775–83, the War of 1812–14 and the rebellion of 1837–8 . . .* (Montreal, 1893), 105–7, 112–13. "Hugh McDonell," Assoc. of Ont. Land Surveyors, *Annual report* (Toronto), 1922: 97–101.

MACDONELL (Greenfield), ALEXANDER, fur trader, politician, and office holder; b. 20 Nov. 1782 in Greenfield (Highland), Scotland, son of Alexander Macdonell of Greenfield and Janet Macdonell (Aberchalder); d. 23 Feb. 1835 in Toronto.

Alexander Macdonell immigrated to Upper Canada in 1792 with his family. His father, head of a cadet branch of the Macdonells of Glengarry, was a militant Highlander, renowned for his courtly manners, traditional dress, and skill in the forest. By his own account he became a clerk of the North West Company in 1803. In 1806 he was a clerk in the Monontagué department and in September 1809 he was posted to the Red River department. There he helped to welcome his brother-in-law and cousin Miles MACDONELL, who arrived in 1812 at the head of the advance party for the colony envisaged by Lord Selkirk [Douglas*]. Early relations between the cousins (and the conflicting interests they represented) were friendly and cooperative, although by April 1813 Miles had accused his kinsman of "insidious and treacherous conduct during the winter in endeavouring to swerve my people from their duty," charges which Alexander could quite legitimately deny.

Despite the breakdown of cordiality, open hostility between the colony and the NWC did not emerge until after Miles's notorious proclamation of January 1814 prohibiting the exportation of all provisions, including pemmican, the staple food of the Nor'Westers, and his subsequent successful attempts to enforce the embargo. Alexander and his senior colleagues, Duncan* and John Dugald* Cameron, initially failed to respond to the embargo with much vigour or enterprise, and were severely criticized by their superiors for their inaction. Alexander was upset by the censures, but he agreed that Miles's embargo should have been forcibly resisted. Alexander was made a partner of the NWC at its meeting in 1814 and, with Duncan Cameron, was placed in charge of the Red River department, perhaps on an implicit understanding that he would be more militant in future. For several years afterwards, with Cameron, he took the lead in organizing the resistance of the local freemen, mixed-bloods (particularly the Métis), and Indians to the Red River colony and, in a number of letters intercepted or captured by the HBC, expressed extreme views about the conflict between the contending forces. His words and actions led William Bacheler COLTMAN, whose report of 1818 on the events of the fur-trade war in the northwest was on the whole studiously fair-minded, to describe his conduct as one of "general violence," although Coltman was careful to note the conflicting testimony for most of the specific allegations made against Macdonell by Lord Selkirk and the HBC.

The contradictory evidence which characterizes the dispute makes it impossible to provide an unbiased account of Alexander's activities between 1814 and 1816, much less of his involvement in some of the more violent episodes. In general, it can be asserted that Alexander – along with Duncan Cameron – encouraged the early inhabitants of the region to fear and oppose the establishment of the colony. He probably helped to promote the articulation of a sense of aboriginal rights among the Métis and Indians; that he and Cameron invented the notion of these rights, as some sources suggest, is fairly dubious. Whether he bore direct responsibility for the violent means employed by the Métis is another matter, for he was not present during most of the incidents, and he did on more than one occasion express a desire to avoid the "shedding of blood," if possible. He certainly led the Métis in their successful seizure and dispersal of the settlement in the late spring of 1815, but these goals were achieved without the loss of life, although there was much intimidation.

Over the autumn of 1815 and the following winter he recruited a large part of the Métis force headed by Cuthbert Grant*. Macdonell led the Métis to Fort Qu'Appelle (Sask.), dashing about in military costume; yet he remained there until after the subsequent battle at Seven Oaks (Winnipeg) on 19 June 1816. Grant's men at Seven Oaks were under Macdonell's orders, but it was never proved that those orders directly provoked the killing of Robert Semple*, governor of the HBC territories, and about 20 men. Available evidence suggests that Seven Oaks was an inadvertent confrontation between antagonists who had been made extremely suspicious of each other's intentions. Less open to dispute than this conclusion are contemporary reports that Macdonell publicly rejoiced at its bloody outcome. Although he was one of those charged with responsibility for the murder of HBC employee Owen Keveny* in September 1816, Macdonell always maintained that the actual culprits, a Métis named Mainville and Charles de Reinhard, had acted on their own initiative.

Despite the many allegations against him, Macdonell was allowed by Coltman to escape westward in 1817, and he was never tried in any Canadian court for his actions. In 1819 *A narrative of transactions* appeared in London under his name; it attempted to exculpate him from the "calumnious libels" levelled against him. The work was probably at least partially ghost-written by Samuel Hull WILCOCKE, who was at the time the NWC's paid pamphleteer and who provided an unsigned preface to the work. Macdonell returned to Upper Canada in 1821, but by special order of Andrew Colvile of the HBC he was specifically omitted from the rosters of NWC men carried over after the merger of the two companies in that year.

In 1821, following in his family's tradition of involvement in the politics of Upper Canada, Macdonell was elected to the House of Assembly for Glengarry, a riding which his brothers John* and Donald* would also represent at various times between 1812 and 1841. He held the seat until 1824. Ten years later he successfully contested the riding of Prescott as a tory, but he died in February 1835 of consumption while attending the assembly. He had been sheriff of the Ottawa District since 1822.

J. M. BUMSTED

Alexander Macdonell (Greenfield) is the author of *A narrative of transactions in the Red River country, from the commencement of the operations of the Earl of Selkirk, till the summer of the year 1816* (London, 1819); it was probably written with the help of Samuel Hull Wilcocke.

PAC, MG 19, E1. PAM, HBCA, Nicholas Garry file. W. B. Coltman, "Summary of the evidence in the controversy between the Hudson's Bay Company and the North-West Company," N.Dak. State Hist. Soc., *Coll.* (Fargo), 4 (1913): 451–653. *Docs. relating to NWC* (Wallace). G.B., Colonial Office, *Papers relating to the Red River settlement* . . . (London, 1819). *HBRS*, 2 (Rich and Fleming). *Report of trials in the courts of Canada, relative to the destruction of the Earl of Selkirk's settlement on the Red River; with observations*, ed. Andrew Amos (London, 1820). *Correspondent and Advocate* (Toronto), 15 March 1835. *Patriot* (Toronto), 13 March 1835. J. A. Macdonell, *Sketches illustrating the early settlement and history of Glengarry in Canada, relating principally to the Revolutionary War of 1775–83, the War of 1812–14 and the rebellion of 1837–8* . . . (Montreal, 1893). M. A. MacLeod and W. L. Morton, *Cuthbert Grant of Grantown; warden of the plains of Red River* (Toronto, 1974). G. C. McMillan, "The struggle of the fur companies in the Red River region, 1811–1821" (MA thesis, Univ. of Manitoba, Winnipeg, 1955). C. [B.] Martin, *Lord Selkirk's work in Canada* (Toronto, 1916).

McDOUGALL, ALEXANDER, fur trader; b. 1759 or 1760, probably in Argyllshire, Scotland; d. 20 Nov. 1821 in Lachine, Lower Canada.

Alexander McDougall's introduction to the fur trade may have come about through his brother Duncan, who married a sister of Nor'Wester Angus SHAW. A lieutenant in the 84th Foot, Duncan was granted lands in Lower Canada after the revolution. Another brother, Donald, apparently settled in Upper Canada. The date on Alexander's Beaver Club medal, 1780, presumably commemorates his first winter in the Indian country. In 1788 he was a clerk at Fort Abitibi (near La Sarre, Que.) for Richard Dobie* and James Grant*. He remained there when the Timiskaming posts were sold to the firm of Grant, Campion and Company in 1791 and the following year he succeeded Æneas CAMERON as master at Fort Abitibi.

In the summer of 1795, dissatisfied with his prospects in the Timiskaming region and preferring the northwest, McDougall was in Montreal, where competition for his services, and perhaps Shaw's influence, led the North West Company to offer him a share in its new agreement. Until it should come into force in 1799, McDougall would return to Fort Abitibi for a year and go west the following three. In December 1795, however, McTavish, Frobisher and Company, agents for the Nor'Westers, bought the rights to the Timiskaming posts and McDougall spent the rest of his career there. On 26 Aug. 1799 he signed the new NWC agreement in Montreal.

McDougall was an enthusiastic advocate of opposing the Hudson's Bay Company in James Bay and in 1800 he headed an overland expedition to Moose Factory (Ont.) for the NWC, establishing his base on Hayes Island. When Cameron, head of the Timiskaming department, left Fort Timiskaming (near Ville-Marie, Que.) in 1804, McDougall succeeded him, using Fort Abitibi as his headquarters (except for the winter of 1806–7 which he spent at Fort Timiskaming) until he retired in 1816. Perhaps his decision to establish headquarters at Fort Abitibi was influenced by the strategic role of the fort: as a direct competitor with the HBC post on Lake Abitibi, occupied until 1812; as the Nor'Westers' key defence in the area against the HBC on the bay to the north; and as a guardian of the route south by the Ottawa River. On the other hand, it may have been a personal preference for remaining at his old station.

McDougall seems to have been typical of the early successful Scottish-Canadian traders, bold and impulsive, arrogant, ruthless, and determined in pushing the trade, yet friendly, hospitable, and helpful to his opponents at other times. After retiring, he settled on his farm at Lachine, where he died at the age of 61. He was buried on the estate, the funeral service being conducted by the Reverend James Somerville* of the Presbyterian St Gabriel Street Church. McDougall made two wills, the first on 23 Nov. 1812 and the second on 29 July 1820, the latter necessitated by the death in October 1818 of his principal heir, his nephew Duncan McDougall*, who had been a partner in John Jacob Astor's Pacific Fur Company and in the NWC.

McDougall divided his estate among the children of his daughter, Mary Charlotte McDougall, and her husband, Augustin Belisle of Deschambault; his brother Duncan's surviving children, including two daughters who lived with him; George, a natural son of his nephew Duncan; and the children of his brother Donald and his sister Sarah. Besides his watch and seals, McDougall's Beaver Club medal went to George, who later had it set in the bowl of a gold toddy ladle. McDougall's will did not mention his own sons, trappers and traders in Timiskaming, but the Louis McDougall who signed the treaty of 1906 between the Indians of Abitibi and the Canadian government was probably his grandson.

ELAINE ALLAN MITCHELL

PAM, HBCA, B.135/a, b; E.41 (mfm. at AO). *Docs. relating to NWC* (Wallace). *HBRS*, 17 (Rich). R. Campbell, *Hist. of Scotch Presbyterian Church*. J. A. Macdonell, *Sketches illustrating the early settlement and history of Glengarry in Canada, relating principally to the Revolutionary War of 1775–83, the War of 1812–14 and the rebellion of 1837–8 ...* (Montreal, 1893). E. A. Mitchell, *Fort Timiskaming and the fur trade* (Toronto and Buffalo, N.Y., 1977). H. G. Ryder, "The Beaver Club medal," *Canadian Antiques Collector* (Toronto), 3 (1968), no.4: 17–18.

MacEACHERN, ANGUS BERNARD (until 1822 he signed **MacEacharn**), Roman Catholic priest and bishop, office holder, and JP; b. 8 Feb. 1759 in Kinlochmoidart, Scotland, son of Hugh Bàn MacEachern and Mary MacDonald; d. 22 April 1835 in Canavoy, P.E.I.

The youngest child in a Highland family of middling circumstances, Angus Bernard MacEachern showed an early inclination towards the church. He became a protégé of Bishop Hugh MacDonald, vicar apostolic of the Highland District of Scotland, and, when his family joined the colonizing expedition of John MacDonald* of Glenaladale to St John's (Prince Edward) Island in 1772, 13-year-old Angus stayed behind to study for the priesthood in the secret Highland Catholic college at Buorblach (near Morar Station). In 1777 MacEachern entered the Royal Scots

College at Valladolid, Spain. He was ordained there on 20 Aug. 1787. Returning to Scotland, he spent three years as a missionary in the Inner Hebrides; then, with the reluctant consent of his vicar apostolic, Bishop Alexander Macdonald, MacEachern emigrated to St John's Island to join his family, in company with some 230 Scots settlers.

MacEachern arrived on the Island in August 1790, "a deserving young Clergyman full of zeal, and for abilities both natural and acquired, equal to the daily discharge of his respective functions," according to Bishop Macdonald's testimonial. At that point the colony had been five years without a resident priest, James MacDonald* having died in 1785. Granted faculties by Bishop Jean-François Hubert* of the diocese of Quebec, of which the Maritime district formed a part, and by James Jones*, superior of missions in the Maritime colonies, MacEachern assumed spiritual responsibility for the whole island. Almost immediately, his jurisdiction was enlarged to include Nova Scotia's gulf shore and Cape Breton Island. In the absence of any other Gaelic-speaking priest, MacEachern perforce ministered to those regions' Highland Catholic settlers from 1791 to 1793 and again from 1798 to 1802.

That beginning established the pattern for MacEachern's whole missionary career. Needed everywhere at once, he would endlessly criss-cross his pioneer missions from his headquarters, first on Savage Harbour and then at St Andrews. Although tolerated, his religion was still officially proscribed. Communication was poor. Travel by land and sea was at best difficult, at worst nearly impossible. And MacEachern's flock were numerous. On St John's Island alone his mission included over 2,000 Roman Catholics by 1798. Fluency in Gaelic, English, and (eventually) French enabled him to tend effectively his mainly Scots, Irish, and Acadian parishioners; a durable constitution helped him to weather the attendant physical hardships.

Two disputes punctuated the even, if arduous, tenor of MacEachern's early missionary labours. The first involved Glenaladale, the Island's leading Catholic layman. Objecting to the location and extravagance of a proposed church at St Andrews, Glenaladale had his tenants boycott both the project and the parish. While the laird had his brother, Father Augustine (Austin) MacDonald, perform mass on his estate at Tracadie (lots 35 and 36), MacEachern maintained a tactful silence and pushed ahead with his church. His protests unavailing, Glenaladale gradually abandoned the boycott. With his death in 1810 the issue, and the challenge to MacEachern's authority, disappeared.

The second incident emphasized the precariousness of the Catholic position in Prince Edward Island. In August 1813 the Island's new lieutenant governor, Charles Douglass Smith*, had MacEachern informed

MacEachern

that thenceforth all marriages performed without a government licence would be considered "null and void, and of no effect in law." Adding insult to injury, Smith dismissed the colony's two Catholic justices of the peace a short time later. MacEachern curbed his anger and simply ignored the government's directive, advising his bishop, Joseph-Octave PLESSIS, that if necessary he would send his people to Nova Scotia to be married "sooner than submit to a penny paper of such obnoxious dye." MacEachern's personal remonstrance to John Frederick Holland*, who had considerable influence with Smith, and perhaps more important, Plessis's quiet intervention with Governor-in-Chief Sir George Prevost*, resulted in the lieutenant governor's eventually denying any knowledge of the order. In keeping his opposition private, MacEachern made a graceful retreat possible for Smith. By 1819 MacEachern could report to Plessis: "Govr. Smith is not the same man he was. He is kind to me. And I am resolved to give his Excellency no cause of offense." He did not.

The extent of MacEachern's missionary labours underscored the chronic shortage of priests which plagued the Maritime district of the diocese of Quebec. But despite his frequent appeals to his bishop for clergy, little assistance could be tendered. Still hampered by disruptions which the British conquest had precipitated [see Jean-Olivier Briand*], the church in Quebec struggled to match a declining supply of clergy to a rising population. Uncertain status under British rule only compounded successive bishops' difficulties. Preoccupations at the core encouraged neglect of the extremities, and in seeking clerical reinforcements, missionaries in the outlying districts were left largely to their own devices.

In MacEachern's case, the resources were meagre. He found a measure of relief in 1799, when two French *emigré* priests, Jacques-Ladislas-Joseph de CALONNE and Amable Pichard*, came to Prince Edward Island. But what bishops of Quebec did occasionally give, they also took away. Both priests were transferred off the Island following Bishop Pierre Denaut*'s pastoral visit in 1803, and by 1808 MacEachern was again the sole Catholic missionary in the colony. A second pastoral visit, this in 1812 by Denaut's successor, Plessis, catalysed a long-standing scheme to provide a more permanent solution to the manpower problem. At Plessis's direction, the first two in a whole series of Catholic youths were dispatched to Lower Canada in the fall of 1812 to study for the priesthood at the seminaries there. For the short term, Plessis assigned Jean-Louis Beaubien to assist MacEachern on the Island.

By that time, however, the continuing want of clergy and the transparent inadequacy of administrative arrangements in the sprawling diocese of Quebec had convinced MacEachern of the need for its dismemberment. Beyond that, he appeared to share with other Celtic clergy in the see a sense of alienation from the Canadian hierarchy. When his associate, Edmund Burke*, vicar general of Nova Scotia, successfully petitioned Rome in 1816 for the erection of Nova Scotia into a vicariate apostolic responsible directly to the Holy See instead of to Quebec, he probably acted with MacEachern's foreknowledge and approval. More certainly, MacEachern took an active interest in the parallel campaign in 1817 of Alexander McDonell*, vicar general of Kingston, to carve two more vicariates out of the diocese of Quebec: one in Upper Canada, and another comprising New Brunswick, Prince Edward Island, and Cape Breton, with MacEachern its proposed vicar apostolic. For his part, Plessis preferred reorganization of the Quebec see into an ecclesiastical province with the creation of new suffragan dioceses.

MacEachern was in Upper Canada consulting with McDonell about future arrangements when word of the Holy See's decision was received early in 1819. Wary of offending the British government, which had endorsed McDonell's plan but might well discountenance that of Plessis, Rome compromised. Instead of independent vicariates, or even suffragan dioceses, the Holy See appointed vicars general with episcopal character, subject still to the bishop of Quebec. In his brief, dated 12 Jan. 1819, MacEachern was named titular bishop of Rosen, responsible for New Brunswick, Prince Edward Island, and the Îles de la Madeleine. By the time of his consecration at the church of Saint-Roch, Quebec, on 17 June 1821, Cape Breton, too, had been added to his charge.

MacEachern was clearly disappointed. To him, his elevation merely meant increased responsibility without enhanced authority. He made no protest initially, but as his problems multiplied during the 1820s, the ageing prelate's patience began to wear thin. Much to his chagrin, MacEachern received none of the emoluments usually attached to episcopal office. Nor was he accorded any financial compensation for the arduous pastoral visitations which now became necessary; "altho' money is as plenty with them [the archbishops of Quebec] as figs or apricots in Rome, I never received one shilling from the Diocese for my travelling expenses," he wrote to a friend in 1828. Too distant for close supervision, recalcitrant priests defied his authority or appealed over his head to Quebec. Summarizing his position in a letter to Archbishop Bernard-Claude PANET of Quebec in 1829, MacEachern would rail at "responsibility without authority, time lost to my flock, expenses without remuneration, a decision without effect."

Meanwhile, MacEachern became haunted by the necessity of ensuring a succession of clergy. Rising population continued to outstrip the supply of clergy without any promise of relief from Quebec. When, for example, Prince Edward Island's first native-born priest, Bernard Donald Macdonald*, was ordained in 1822, the colony's only Canadian priest was promptly allowed to return to Quebec. Thus, on Macdonald's return to the Island, MacEachern was forced to employ him among the Island Acadians, stirring resentment among the Scots Catholics who had paid for his education. Despite such setbacks, MacEachern had three native-born priests at work on the Island by 1830, and was able to restrict his own mission to the eastern third of the colony.

As his frustration with existing arrangements mounted, MacEachern's relationship with his diocesan superiors grew more strained. By 1825 he had come openly to interpret Quebec's historic neglect as more wilful indifference than a lack of resources. Already MacEachern had commissioned Alexander McDonell to plead his case for independence when the latter embarked for London and Rome in 1824 to seek Upper Canada's separation from the diocese of Quebec. McDonell met with partial success. The diocese of Kingston was erected, with himself as bishop, in 1826; but MacEachern's status remained unchanged. Despite London's ready agreement to his independence, Rome remained unconvinced.

Over the next four years MacEachern pursued a dual strategy. To Plessis's successor, Panet, and Panet's coadjutor, Joseph Signay*, he repeatedly stressed Quebec's present and traditional neglect, and the inadequacy of the current administrative structure. At the same time, he fought to convince the Holy See of the need for independence. Rome's objections were really those of Quebec. Though content to let the Maritime region shift for itself in obtaining clergy, the Quebec hierarchy remained anxious to retain ecclesiastical control over it. In answer to Quebec's objections that he lacked sufficient resources either to ensure a succession of clergy or to maintain himself with proper episcopal dignity, MacEachern periodically assessed his personal means, and those of his prospective diocesans, and brimmed with outward confidence that the governments of New Brunswick and Nova Scotia would bolster the £50 per annum pension which the Prince Edward Island House of Assembly had settled on him in 1825.

Another essential component in MacEachern's campaign for independence became his three-decade-old effort to establish a classical college for the preparation of prospective seminarians. Since 1794, when his Island Scots parishioners had purchased him a 200-acre farm at St Andrews to help support such an institution, MacEachern had contemplated a local college to foster a native clergy. But over the years lack of authority, or teachers, or funds had always conspired to defeat his plans. His efforts in concert with those of McDonell in Upper Canada and Burke in Nova Scotia had brought a regional seminary within

reach in 1819, but Burke's death the following year killed the project. After 1825 MacEachern revived the idea in cooperation with William Fraser*, Burke's eventual successor as vicar apostolic of Nova Scotia. By theoretically providing for a succession of clergy, the college would remove one key objection to independent diocesan status. But the school's continued deferral left MacEachern in an uncomfortable dilemma: needing the college to establish his credibility as a candidate for independence, yet needing episcopal authority to command the funds to establish the college.

Paralleling the elusive college's ecclesiastical significance was its political symbolism. The campaign on Prince Edward Island for Catholic emancipation began in earnest in 1825 with a petition to the assembly. An extensive debate in the local press followed in 1826, and a second, abortive petition in 1827. Through its additional function of educating Roman Catholic laymen, MacEachern seems to have intended the prospective college to demonstrate the Catholic population's resources, culture, and education – in short, its fitness for civil emancipation. With that in mind perhaps, he petitioned the Island legislature in the spring of 1829 for a grant in aid of a classical college. Intent on establishing its own non-denominational school, the assembly politely refused. In the end, both emancipation and independence would be achieved before MacEachern's college took form.

"The want of clergy in these countries is distressing, deplorable, and shameful in the extreme!!!" MacEachern wrote to his archbishop in May 1829. "And dreadful to reflect without any apparent chance of relief for years to come or ever from Canada. The thought is enough to distract a saint." Unknown to MacEachern, his deliverance was at hand. Responding at length to his persistence, the Holy See created the diocese of Charlottetown on 11 Aug. 1829, comprising Prince Edward Island, New Brunswick, and the Îles de la Madeleine. The 70-year-old MacEachern was named its bishop elect. There seemed, however, no end to delay and uncertainty. MacEachern's papal brief was lost en route from Rome, and a second arrived only on 14 Sept. 1830. Two months later, on 11 November, MacEachern took formal possession of his see in an elaborate ceremony at Charlottetown.

Independence proved not to be the panacea MacEachern had hoped. Indeed, experience partly justified Quebec's objections to the see's creation. Additional government pensions did not materialize. And, ironically, one of MacEachern's first acts as bishop of Charlottetown was to gain assurance that the Quebec whose neglect he had so criticized would continue to supply Canadian clergy to the Acadians of New Brunswick. A stable succession of clergy, in

MacEachern

fact, continued to be MacEachern's greatest concern. By 1830 the feeble trickle of missionaries from the similarly priest-poor Highland vicariate of Scotland had virtually dried up. Likewise, the tedious and expensive process of educating local boys at Lower Canadian seminaries had proved of limited success. In 1826 MacEachern had obtained two free places at the college of the Sacred Congregation of Propaganda in Rome, yet the long-term benefits would hardly begin to meet the diocese's manpower needs. A more immediately important step was taken on 30 Nov. 1831 when MacEachern and Bishop Fraser finally opened their regional college, at St Andrews in MacEachern's residence. Little more than a preparatory school, however, it provided no immediate answer to the pressing need for clergy.

Instead, as during the 1820s, MacEachern was forced to rely primarily on Irish ecclesiastics who, by various means, found their way into the Maritime region. Some, like William Dollard*, future bishop of New Brunswick, proved very reliable. Many others did not, and MacEachern's greatest episcopal headache continued to be enforcing ecclesiastical discipline.

MacEachern encountered his worst problems in New Brunswick. When his New Brunswick clergy and laity failed to support the St Andrew's College project, he established a second school at Gedaic (near Shediac). But the new college quickly foundered in a sea of mismanagement and non-support. The heart of disaffection in New Brunswick was, perhaps, Saint John, which had a history of disobedience to episcopal authority. MacEachern spent the winter of 1831 there investigating reports of irregular conduct on the part of its pastor, John Carroll, former administrator of the vicariate of Nova Scotia. The affair took on ugly ethnic overtones as Carroll roused the Irish congregation against their Scots bishop. Even on MacEachern's departure, after he had paid the debts owed Carroll by his parish and suspended his faculties, peace was not fully restored. Carroll eventually departed, but MacEachern had to content himself with, at best, sullen obedience from the Saint John laity.

No other major incident marred the remainder of MacEachern's brief episcopate. In 1833 he signed St Andrew's College over to a board of trustees (with himself as president). The following year he vacated his quarters there and moved into a new residence at Canavoy. Conscious of failing health, MacEachern took preliminary steps towards having a coadjutor named in the spring of 1835, favouring, as his personal choice, Bernard Donald Macdonald. Before further action could be taken on the matter, MacEachern was felled by a paralytic stroke in the midst of his Easter visit to the missions of Kings County, P.E.I. He died a few days later.

Angus Bernard MacEachern became one of the dominant figures on the Island during the early British colonial period. Sheer longevity – his career spanned five decades – only partly explains his stature. Another key was his own personality. A man of wit and good sense, he possessed shrewdness without cunning, dignity without pretension, and patience without passivity. To his people he was priest and doctor, teacher, lawyer, arbitrator, judge. Indulgent of, even as he was frustrated by, their reluctance to tithe themselves for his educational and ecclesiastical projects, MacEachern set an example that did much to reinforce a reliance on clerical leadership. His Canadian superiors deplored his unconcern for formality and ceremony, but that quality evidently appealed to his flock. "Father MacEachern is adored by his people," Father Jones reported to Bishop Hubert in 1792, shortly after MacEachern's arrival. During his pastoral visit 20 years later, Bishop Plessis recorded much the same sentiments: "The Scots and Acadians were equally pleased with his watchful care and attentiveness to duty . . . [he] is able to command universal respect." To his cherished Scots and the obedient Acadians, MacEachern returned that affection. Of the fractious, independent Irish he was less fond, and his complaints about the irregular Irish clergy with whom he was afflicted sparked accusations of prejudice. Nevertheless, MacEachern's open appeals to Irish bishops for clergy suggest that his objections were based less on nationality than on unhappy experience. In general, where MacEachern was best known his authority was most respected. His limited missionary contact with New Brunswick, for example, contributed to his continuing difficulties there.

The same charm and amiability that endeared MacEachern to his parishioners helped to foster the generally excellent relations with civil authorities which MacEachern exploited to win numerous small concessions for Roman Catholics. The Island government's respect was reflected in his pension "for meritorious service" in 1825, and the annuity awarded St Andrew's College beginning in 1834; its confidence, in his appointment as road commissioner in 1825 and justice of the peace in 1829. Although he did not lead the Maritime campaign for civil emancipation, MacEachern's stature undoubtedly smoothed its eventual passage on Prince Edward Island in April 1830. Growing up and labouring in an environment where exercise of his religion was dependent on official indulgence helped shape MacEachern's firm allegiance to the crown. By the same token, something more than respect for his personality lay behind officialdom's benevolence. "A succession of clergy, well attached to Gov.t," he reminded a British official in a letter of November 1827, "would train up their hearers as peaceable and useful subjects." Good relations served the interests of both parties.

With the Protestant population, too, MacEachern enjoyed generally cordial relations. He was personally popular with non-Catholics and he was careful not to arouse latent religious animosities; until ordered by his bishop in 1813, he even declined to wear clerical dress. As a result of his tact, Protestants did not perceive MacEachern as a threat. Reflecting this fact, Protestant laymen not only donated land for Catholic chapels, but also pledged money towards MacEachern's Catholic college. Against the background of a general relaxation of anti-Catholic sentiment during the period, MacEachern's efforts helped maintain relative religious harmony in his time.

MacEachern's missionary labours touched the whole Maritime region. And to it – excluding Nova Scotia – his most important contribution was, perhaps, ecclesiastical independence. His six-year episcopate was too short, however, to consolidate his achievement. Just as MacEachern always remained a missionary, so his diocese continued a missionary diocese. His greatest impact was on Prince Edward Island. During his 45-year pastorate there, the Roman Catholic population climbed from some 200 families, attending two places of worship, to roughly 15,000 people worshipping in eighteen churches or chapels. When he came to the colony, Roman Catholicism was an officially proscribed religion; at his death, virtually all disabilities had been removed. In ways both tangible and intangible, Angus Bernard MacEachern firmly established Roman Catholicism in Prince Edward Island. By the time of his death, he had already achieved heroic stature among his people; within years, he had passed into Island folklore.

G. EDWARD MACDONALD

AAQ, 310 CN, I (mfm. at Charlottetown Public Library). Arch. of Scots College (Pontifical) (Rome), Vicars Apostolic, corr. of A. B. MacEachern and William Fraser to Paul MacPherson and Angus MacDonald (transcripts at Arch. of the Diocese of Charlottetown). Arch. of the Diocese of Charlottetown, Box 1, item 1 ([A. B. Burke], "Notes on Bishop MacEachern" and "The Right Reverend Æneas B. MacEachern"); box 2; box 7. PAPEI, RG 16, land registry records, conveyance reg., liber 3: ff.47, 57; liber 32: f.452; liber 39: f.302. Supreme Court of P.E.I. (Charlottetown), Estates Division, liber 3: f.71 (will of Angus Bernard MacEachern) (mfm. at PAPEI). J.-O. Plessis, "Journal de deux voyages apostoliques dans le golfe Saint-Laurent et les provinces d'en bas, en 1811 et 1812 . . . ," *Le Foyer canadien* (Québec), 3 (1865): 73–280. *Prince Edward Island Register*, 27 Oct. 1825; 21 Feb.–6 June 1826; 3 April 1827; 17, 24 March, 30 June 1829. *Royal Gazette* (Charlottetown), 20 Dec. 1831; 22–29 Jan. 1833; 22 April 1834; 28 April 1835. F. W. P. Bolger, "The first bishop," *The Catholic Church in Prince Edward Island, 1720–1979*, ed. M. F. Hennessey (Charlottetown, 1979), 22–57. Johnston, *Hist. of Catholic Church in eastern N.S.* G. E. MacDonald, "'And Christ dwelt in the heart of his house': a history of St. Dunstan's University, 1855–1955" (PHD thesis, Queen's Univ., Kingston, Ont., 1984). J. C. Macmillan, *The early history of the Catholic Church in Prince Edward Island* (Quebec, 1905). James Morrison, "Roman Catholic Church . . . ," *Past and present of Prince Edward Island . . .* , ed. D. A. MacKinnon and A. B. Warburton (Charlottetown, [1906]), 277–95. [G.] E. MacDonald, "The good shepherd: Angus Bernard MacEachern, first bishop of Charlottetown," *Island Magazine*, no.16 (fall–winter 1984): 3–8. E. J. Mullally, "A sketch of the life and times of the Right Reverend Angus Bernard MacEachern, the first bishop of the Diocese of Charlottetown," CCHA *Report*, 13 (1945–46): 71–106. Terrence Murphy, "The emergence of Maritime Catholicism, 1781–1830," *Acadiensis* (Fredericton), 13 (1983–84), no.2: 29–49.

McGILL, JOHN, army officer, office holder, and politician; b. March 1752 in Auckland, Wigton, Scotland; m. Catherine Crookshank; no surviving issue; d. 31 Dec. 1834 in Toronto, Upper Canada.

John McGill emigrated to Virginia in 1773. When the American revolution began he joined the short-lived Loyal Virginians as a lieutenant, then late in 1777 transferred to the Queen's Rangers, in which corps he served as adjutant and was taken prisoner along with his commander, John Graves Simcoe*. He was promoted captain before the surrender at Yorktown, Va. After the war he settled in Parrtown (Saint John, N.B.), although he was perhaps at Quebec in 1788–89 as assistant to the commissary general. One of the first two captains proposed by Simcoe for the second Queen's Rangers in Upper Canada, he preferred the administrative post of military commissary. Setting out in February 1792 with Æneas Shaw* by the Témiscouata route to join Simcoe at Quebec, he accidentally injured his leg so badly that he periodically thereafter found it painful to walk or ride. He saw no regimental service in Upper Canada; when the Rangers mustered at Newark (Niagara-on-the-Lake) against an anticipated American invasion in September 1794, his duty was to escort Simcoe's family to safety at Quebec. Eventually, on 27 April 1805, he was appointed the last lieutenant of the county of York, remaining so until his death, but reforms accompanying a new militia act of 1808 virtually ended the military duties of that office.

The first military list of Upper Canada named him as commissary of stores and provisions at a captain's salary. Early in 1796 he combined that office with the new civilian post of provincial agent for purchases, his brother-in-law George Crookshank* becoming his deputy as commissary. In the intervening four years he was often frustrated by a jurisdictional quarrel between the civil authority of the lieutenant governor in Upper Canada and the military authority of the commander-in-chief at Quebec, a quarrel which also raised similar if lesser difficulties for the surveyor general and the deputy superintendent general of Indian affairs. McGill was held accountable to the

McGill

commissary general at Quebec, John Craigie*, although he and Simcoe had expected otherwise. Contracts to supply troops in the upper province were awarded over his head from Quebec, and he was ordered to limit his purchases to requisitions sent from there. Worse, his complaints about the profiteering of merchants and about irregularities in supplies from Lower Canada finally drew the rebuke from the commander-in-chief, Lord Dorchester [Carleton*], "that anything further on that head is unnecessary." Simcoe protested in vain that McGill was being reduced to "a public Accountant without Power." In order to perform his duties and to meet Simcoe's wishes, McGill regularly exceeded his authority as commissary: he continued at York (Toronto) the practice established at Newark of supplying civilians from military stores and he drew on the military budget for workmen and materials for civil works at York. The problem of jurisdiction was not solved merely by giving McGill civil authority. Administrator Peter Russell* was left with no instructions when Simcoe returned to England, and a new commander-in-chief, Robert Prescott*, thought in 1798 that military supplies could be bought without an Upper Canadian agent, "at less Expence to the Public, and with less trouble to myself." Since McGill was now a civil agent, Prescott cut off his military allowances and refused to accept many of the requisitions by which McGill continued to supply civilian contractors and settlers from military stores. The commander-in-chief did however make one concession: from late in 1798 he regularly sent McGill's military instructions through the lieutenant governor's office.

McGill had been disappointed in the hope that his new civil status would enable him to control the price and quantity of local supplies for the troops and government in Upper Canada. His reforms in purchasing, recommended by Simcoe but vetoed by Dorchester, were a failure when he finally introduced them in March 1796: merchants refused to make tenders on his terms, and farmers would not reveal how much wheat they had in store. The surplus of flour he managed to accumulate in a new depot at York was more than matched by a shortage – equal to the rations of 100 men for 236 days – produced at Niagara by the failure of local contractors. At Kingston Richard Cartwright*, "the only holder," set the price. Farmers there sold to the American rather than the provincial government. After the bad crops of 1796–97 McGill found Detroit merchants selling flour from Lower Canada to the United States army. Before local shortages eased in the following year, however, McGill was established as an energetic and efficient purchasing agent, as well as a careful public accountant. He even kept track of the minor indulgences he was ordered to make to his fellow officials at York, such as the issue of building materials to Shaw or the

use of government oxen by John Elmsley*. His civil appointment had in fact recognized the range of government business that he had already begun to conduct, especially the erection of public buildings at York and arrangements for the construction of Yonge and Dundas streets. Indeed, if the label "founder of York" were applied to the man who did most of the work, it would go to John McGill.

On 2 March 1796 McGill was appointed to the Executive Council along with the surveyor general, David William Smith*. Simcoe had begun recommending him more than two years earlier and in 1795 gave the pressing reason that there were too few councillors: "the sickness of a Single Member stops the whole Business of the Province." Since the receiver general, Peter Russell, was already a member, the effect was to put the heads of the three main executive departments together on the council for the first time, just when its business was rapidly increasing. McGill had to wait until 8 Oct. 1808 to become a regular salaried member, because the civil establishment allowed only five; but well before that he had risen above the status of Simcoe's most efficient protégé. Sensible, assiduous, and apparently indifferent to the animosities among his colleagues, he was by the end of 1801 a regular member of the council's standing committee. A new lieutenant governor, Peter Hunter*, had set up the committee to conduct business during his frequent absences, but even when in York he did not himself regularly attend the council. The committee therefore bore the brunt of routine business and of enforcing Hunter's measures for administrative reform. Although Chief Justice Henry Allcock* was no doubt its dominating personality, McGill seems to have been its work-horse, one of the "few Scotch instruments" on whom (according to Robert Thorpe*'s accusation) Hunter relied too much. With Allcock's departure in September 1804, the arrival of an able attorney general, Thomas Scott, in the following April, and Hunter's death four months later, the working style of the council changed. McGill remained a faithful attender for some years, but his influence and then his health declined. He resigned on 13 Aug. 1818.

He remained until his death on the Legislative Council, to which he had been appointed on 10 June 1797. He had been one of its officials, the master in chancery, since 22 May 1793 and did not relinquish that office until some time in 1803. He was a less regular attender on this council, at first perhaps because being agent for purchases often took him away from York.

On 1 July 1801 McGill exchanged the agency for a more sedentary but equally onerous post, the inspector generalship of public accounts. The office, which became the ministry of finance in 1859, was a new one, created at Hunter's instigation because the

McGill

province had no effective system of audit. Russell, the only auditor general ever commissioned for Upper Canada (10 Aug. 1794), had never developed the office. McGill's new post replaced it. Having set up a provincial system of audit and presided over it for nearly 12 years, McGill changed offices again. In his last administrative appointment, he took over the receiver generalship on an acting commission (5 Oct. 1813 to 2 Dec. 1819). He was succeeded, this time only briefly, by his brother-in-law George Crookshank. Beginning as the province's chief purchasing agent, he ended as its chief financial officer.

If McGill's duties were always unspectacular, their importance and their growth were in sharp contrast to his formal salary. When he made up his final accounts as agent for purchases, the Treasury had cleared bills from his office of more than £27,000 sterling. As acting receiver general he dispersed from £63,000 to £91,000 a year. The highest combination of stipends that he ever drew was £350 a year, with no share in land granting fees. Add that as agent for purchases and as inspector general until 1803 he had to be paid from contingency funds because his offices were not included in the civil establishment, that for 14 years he served as agent or as executive councillor with no salary, and that he never received a full commission as receiver general. The £200 pension he received in 1822 seems rather grudging recognition of vital services long and competently performed.

In the rewards anticipated by Upper Canadian officials, however, salary did not count for much. Land granting fees (to which McGill had access only when he became acting receiver general) might be of consequence. Social prestige and land were the main objects to which officials looked. McGill did not move in the highest society of York officialdom. No lieutenant governor after Simcoe, for example, is reported to have dined at his house. McGill lived among the "gentry" north of the town, but he visited with his wife's relations the Crookshanks and Macaulays or with other Scots such as the Beikies, none of them officials of his own rank and some of them merchants. His Presbyterianism seems to have been no disadvantage, although John Strachan* complained of it: it did not prevent him from joining Anglicans on a committee to sponsor a church at York. Nor did he dissent from the toryism of his fellow officials. The only public questions on which he recorded a strongly independent view were the size of a government grant for district grammar schools, on which he suggested spending up to £7,000 more than anyone else on the Executive Council, and a conflict of interest which he saw in borrowing by York magistrates under the Market Square Act. The skills he exercised on behalf of government were essentially those of a merchant and accountant, skills undervalued by officers with aristocratic pretensions. He continued to be known as "Commissary McGill" long after his seat on both councils entitled him to the prefix "Honourable."

Yet McGill prospered in Upper Canada. As a half-pay captain he was entitled to 3,000 acres of land and as an executive councillor to 5,000 more. Before he had taken up the second allowance the rule was changed, on 1 July 1799, to give councillors 6,000 acres "including former grants." His actual grants fell between the old and the new rules, at 7,509 acres. He can hardly be said to have abused the system, but he was adept at getting the most out of it. He obtained land in good locations, he exchanged bad lands for good, and he knew when to sell. He had 850 acres in York Township, including the 100-acre park lot where he usually lived. It was far enough from the town to be a refuge for the family when the Americans occupied York in 1813, but urban growth made it worth £12,000 when it was finally sold in 1855. Its value had been reckoned at £150 in 1799. He also had 400 acres in Scarborough, 1,000 in Whitby, 1,259 in Clarke (which he got in exchange for 1,000 acres in West Flamborough), and 3,000 in Oxford North townships. Except for the Oxford and some of the York lands, he had sold it all by 1831, mostly after 1817 and in lots of 200 acres.

He did not limit his financial skills to government service. He acted as agent to collect the fees of absent officials. In a province with no banking system, credit was arranged by personal notes, which were usually discounted on acceptance and were discounted less if presented or endorsed by someone known to be of substance. McGill was used enough to giving credit on this system to doubt the need for the Bank of Upper Canada in 1821. He nevertheless subscribed to its founding, "more than was perhaps prudent," he thought. His suspicions of the new credit system were confirmed when the bank refused a note he had endorsed in 1831. By then he was winding up his affairs. If he had not been "very ricth" in 1819, as his employee James Laidlaw thought, his will, dated 8 Nov. 1834, disposed of a considerable fortune in lands and investments. With no living children and his wife dead since 1819, he left his estate to Peter McCutcheon, his nephew, a Montreal merchant who had just become president of the Bank of Montreal. He made it a condition that McCutcheon assume the surname McGill*.

McGill could ensure that his name would be carried on, but not that his career would be remembered. The *Correspondent and Advocate* (Toronto) of 1 Jan. 1835 noted his death as that of "an old Pensioner on his Majesty's Government." Peter McGill's reply, though detailed, did not rescue his uncle from obscurity. John McGill may however have been as indifferent to fame as he was to high social position; the solid rewards he found in Upper Canada were surely those he valued most.

S. R. MEALING

453

McGillivray

[Beyond the brief notes in W. J. Rattray, *The Scot in British North America* (4v., Toronto, 1880–84), and Lorenzo Sabine, *The American loyalists, or biographical sketches of adherents to the British crown in the war of the revolution* . . . (Boston, 1847), there are no useful secondary accounts of McGill's career. His personal papers (MTL, John McGill papers, and a second group of his papers in the Henry Scadding coll.) relate chiefly to the conduct of his various offices. They supplement government departmental records, of which the most informative are PRO, CO 42, the minutes of the Executive Council of Upper Canada (PAC, RG 1, E1), and some Audit Office papers (PRO, AO 1, bundles 2038–40, and AO 2, bundle 142). Most of what is known about his personal life comes from scattered references in the papers of his contemporaries: the Samuel Peters Jarvis papers at the MTL; and, at the AO, the Crookshank–Lambert papers (MS 6), Macaulay papers (MS 78), Russell family papers (MS 75), and Simcoe papers (MS 517). The printed selections from the last two collections, *Corr. of Hon. Peter Russell* (Cruikshank and Hunter) and *Corr. of Lieut. Governor Simcoe* (Cruikshank), are helpful for his early career, as is Gwillim, *Diary of Mrs. Simcoe* (Robertson; 1934). Two other collections of documents, *Town of York, 1793–1815* and *1815–34* (Firth) and Strachan, *Letter book* (Spragge), are less rich but contain later material. An obituary notice by his nephew appeared in the *Patriot* (Toronto), 20 Jan. 1835. s.r.m.]

McGILLIVRAY, WILLIAM, fur trader, landowner, JP, office holder, politician, and militia officer; b. 1764 in Dunlichty, Scotland, son of Donald McGillivray and Anne McTavish, Simon McTavish*'s sister; m. first c. 1790 a mixed-blood woman named Susan *à la façon du pays*, and they had three sons and a daughter; m. secondly 22 Dec. 1800 Magdalen McDonald in London, and they had six children of whom four died in infancy; d. there 16 Oct. 1825.

William McGillivray came from a poor family unable to meet the costs of educating all six children. By unexpected good luck, his uncle Simon McTavish, who had been living in North America for 12 years, came to visit the family in 1776 and began a tradition by promising to finance secondary education for William and his brother Duncan*. For McTavish it was an investment, since in 1784 he brought William to Montreal and hired him to work for the North West Company at an annual salary of £100. At 20 William thus began the long and hard period of apprenticeship in the fur-trading business. The following year he was posted to the Red River department as a clerk, and in 1786, accompanied by proprietor Patrick Small, he reached the post at Île-à-la-Crosse (Sask.).

McGillivray spent the winter of 1786–87 at Snake Lake, where he had been given the task of setting up a trading post to compete with Gregory, MacLeod and Company [*see* John Gregory*; Normand MacLeod*]. He and Roderick McKenzie* served their respective companies by living without conflict and on good terms with each other. When they learned about the

murder of John Ross, a member in Gregory, MacLeod and Company and formerly a partner in the NWC, the two men hastily went to Grand Portage (near Grand Portage, Minn.). There they apparently played a role in the merger of the two companies in 1787, which was to McTavish's advantage.

There were some remarkable men in the NWC, among them Peter Pond* and Alexander Mackenzie*, both of whom felt the lure of the unexplored far west. Pond retired in 1788 after a chequered career; the following year Mackenzie travelled down the river that bears his name to the Arctic Ocean. Meanwhile McGillivray had returned to Île-à-la-Crosse, and in September 1789 he was trading at Rat River (Man.). The following year, on buying Pond's share for £800, he became a partner of the NWC and was promoted to the rank of proprietor with responsibility for the English (Churchill) River department. His headquarters were at Île-à-la-Crosse, where 80 men and about 40 Indian and Métis women lived. In 1791 he was given charge of the westernmost department, Athabasca, which would be extended to the Pacific by Mackenzie in 1793.

McGillivray was engaged in an experience that would eventually lead him to head the NWC, which was increasingly dominated by McTavish. On his return to Montreal in 1793, and before leaving for England and Scotland, he was made a partner in McTavish, Frobisher and Company [*see* Joseph Frobisher*], which managed the NWC and which at this time controlled the affairs of the larger firm. Specifically, with John Gregory he was to supervise the huge depot at Grand Portage. This promotion stirred the jealousy of the other partners, and certain proprietors spoke of nepotism. But these reactions did not impede McGillivray's advancement: when Alexander Mackenzie joined McTavish, Frobisher and Company in 1795, he simply became McGillivray's assistant at Grand Portage. After 1796 McGillivray continued to rise in the upper echelons of the company's management, and when Frobisher retired in 1798 McGillivray took his place. He was, it seems, involved in all the important matters: the establishment of an agency in New York; the activities of McTavish, Fraser and Company in London, a firm founded by McTavish in 1788 and managed by his cousin John Fraser; trade with China; the move from Grand Portage to Kaministiquia (Thunder Bay, Ont.) in 1803; relations with the Hudson's Bay Company; and the struggle with the New North West Company (sometimes called the XY Company) [*see* John RICHARDSON].

When McTavish died in July 1804, McGillivray became both executor of his uncle's will and his successor as head of the NWC. He took over at a period of intense competition in the fur sector. His immediate responsibility was to draw up the terms of an agreement putting an end to five years of rivalry with the XY Company which would serve as the basis for a coalition between the two groups. By the contract of 5 Nov. 1804 the NWC gave up 25 per cent of its shares to the XY Company. But despite being McGillivray's close friend, Alexander Mackenzie, who had bought into the New North West Company in 1800, was excluded from the new co-partnership because of his reputation as a trouble-maker in the fur trade.

The reorganization of McTavish, Frobisher and Company was also a delicate task, which McGillivray spread over the next two years. In December 1806, following Gregory's retirement, which came eight years after Frobisher's, he announced the new management structure of the firm, to be called McTavish, McGillivrays and Company. William and Duncan McGillivray, their brother-in-law Angus SHAW, and the two Hallowell brothers, James and William, all had places in it. These changes did not affect the status or the role in London of McTavish, Fraser and Company, into which McGillivray brought his younger brother Simon*. Nor were these the only problems to be resolved, since rivalry among the fur companies had been a factor contributing to the rise in salaries, numbers of salaried employees, and costs in general. Besides reducing manpower McGillivray made some decisions that brought into question various costly habits of the proprietors: the way they travelled, kept servants, and maintained their wives and children. Stricter control was imposed on the personal fur-trading of the *engagés*.

In fact the rise in operating costs and the fall in profits were chiefly linked to the intensified competition with the Americans and the HBC. Although the NWC had dealings with the American John Jacob Astor throughout the period when McGillivray ran the company, the rivalry between him and Astor became increasingly severe. The complexity of their relations was due first to the disruptions in the European market caused by the French revolution. McTavish had established a branch in New York in 1796 to enable the NWC to circumvent the East India Company's monopoly and send furs to the Chinese market. The NWC first chartered and then bought some ships, which were sailing under the American flag. In this undertaking, but only for a while, it had been necessary to collaborate with Astor, who was involved in the same commercial circuits. There was also cooperation with the Michilimackinac Company [*see* John Ogilvy*] and Astor's American Fur Company. But as rivalry with the American capitalist intensified, to retain his freedom of action McGillivray contemplated negotiating with the East India Company and setting up a trading post on the Pacific coast. David Thompson* in his explorations of 1810–11 sought to establish a direct line of communication with the Orient. But by the time Thompson reached the Pacific Ocean in July 1811, Astor's men, who had

come by sea, were already at the mouth of the Columbia River. For a good many years both Canadian and American vessels trading with the Orient, the *Isaac Todd*, the *Racoon*, the *Colonel Allan*, and the *Columbia*, had profitable runs. In time, however, the losses mounted. All in all, American pressure was applied to the Canadian company in a subtle but systematic fashion.

The rivalry with the HBC would gradually degenerate into a bitter, indeed violent, struggle. Year by year, the territorial expansion of the fur trade had revealed the superiority of the English company with regard to the cost of importing trade goods. McTavish had vainly tried by various means to resolve this problem, which was no closer to solution under McGillivray. The HBC in fact rejected the Nor'Westers' requests for the right to bring in goods via Hudson Bay. To force the English company's hand, McTavish had dispatched two expeditions; the one by land gained a foothold on Hayes Island (Ont.) in 1800 and the other by sea landed on Charlton Island (N.W.T.) in 1803. These very costly actions, which by 1806 had entailed the investment of more than £45,000, did not bring the desired results. Neither, it must be added, did the efforts to obtain a charter from the imperial government. There remained one final method, which was used several times, but to no effect: an attempt to purchase a majority of shares in the HBC.

After 1800 the fur trade had been conducted across a territory with quite well-known boundaries. The scarcity of beaver, which had become general, began to be a serious problem about 1810, and according to McGillivray it heightened the rivalry between the two companies. The HBC had already been forced to break with its traditional practice of waiting for the Indians to come to the bay and was seeking to establish posts wherever the Nor'Westers were located [*see* William TOMISON]. This change, along with other circumstances, contributed to increasing costs, particularly that of manpower, which had tripled. The two companies were affected by a drop in profits caused in part by inflation. The NWC was stronger on the ground but it suffered to a greater degree the consequences of external circumstances. The destruction of its post at Sault Ste Marie, Upper Canada, by the Americans during the War of 1812 [*see* John JOHNSTON] resulted in a net loss of at least £8,330. In addition, when settlers began arriving in 1812 at the colony established by Lord Selkirk [Douglas*], a shareholder in the HBC, on land granted by the company in 1811 at the junction of the Assiniboine and Red rivers, they met with an unfriendly reception from the NWC. The Nor'Westers considered the settlement a threat to the free transport of goods between their depot at Fort William (Thunder Bay, Ont.) and the fur-bearing Lake Athabasca region.

455

McGillivray

Selkirk's project served the interests of the HBC well.

McGillivray had no illusions about the consequences of Selkirk's dispatching the first settlers or about the conduct of the governor of the colony, Miles MACDONELL. He remarked that Selkirk "has thought proper lately to become the avowed rival of the North-West Company in the trade which they themselves have carried on for upwards of thirty years with credit to themselves. . . . In a fair commercial competition, we have no objection to enter the lists with his Lordship, but we cannot remain passive spectators to the violence used to plunder or destroy our property." The pemmican war, as the struggle for the free movement inland of pemmican from the Red River settlement was called, which had been declared by Macdonell and pursued by Colin Robertson* and Robert Semple*, Macdonell's successor as governor of the HBC's territories, finally resulted in the massacre of Seven Oaks (Winnipeg) on 19 June 1816 in which Semple and some 20 settlers were killed [see Cuthbert Grant*].

On learning of that event Lord Selkirk, who was on his way to Red River with a small force of regular soldiers and 90 mercenaries, headed for Fort William, and on 13 Aug. 1816 proceeded to arrest McGillivray and a number of proprietors, holding them responsible for the massacre. Then he seized the fort, confiscated for his own benefit furs belonging to the company, and put the goods stored in the warehouses under supervision. When he reached Montreal, McGillivray demanded to be released on bail, which was immediately granted. He complained to Governor Sir John Coape SHERBROOKE and asked him to issue orders for Fort William to be handed back. The various episodes of the pemmican war, whether in the west or in the law courts, certainly played a key role in the swift decline of the Montreal company after 1810. The actions taken by Selkirk and his men in some measure helped tip the balance towards the HBC, although that company's financial stability had been jeopardized by a debt of about £100,000 to the Bank of England.

The decline of the NWC had, however, begun well before Selkirk's intervention and was linked to many other factors. In a letter of 27 Dec. 1825 referring to some of them, Simon McGillivray emphasized that the richest and most talented partners had withdrawn and been replaced by men with no capital, less eager to work, and given to extravagant spending. There was also the problem of nepotism, which had gradually made inroads into the company: 14 members of the McTavish and McGillivray families, not including relatives by marriage, had been made members of it since 1800. The family had in time become a burden for the firm and had helped undermine the drive and morale of the staff.

It would take some time before McGillivray would accept the inevitability of the union between his company and the HBC. It was not until July 1821, four months after the agreement had been signed for the merger of the two companies, thenceforth to be known as the HBC, that he wrote to John Strachan*: "It would have been worse than folly, to have continued the contest further. We have made no submission – we met & negotiated on equal terms." The equality of which he spoke was, however, apparent, not real, since a couple of months after his death McTavish, McGillivrays and Company and McGillivrays, Thain and Company [see Thomas THAIN] were declared bankrupt.

McGillivray had also been interested in owning land on a grand scale. In 1802, at a time when agriculture was prosperous and the land was a source of profit, he had obtained the grant of 12,000 acres in Inverness Township, Lower Canada, a property he subsequently sold to Joseph Frobisher. In 1813 the government of Upper Canada made him a substantial land grant at Plantagenet. Finally, in 1817 he purchased the modest estate of Bhein Ghael, in Scotland.

McGillivray had an enviable position in Lower Canadian society. In 1795 he became a member of the select Beaver Club. Nine years later he obtained a commission as justice of the peace in the Indian Territories; he received a similar commission for the District of Quebec in 1815 and for the districts of Montreal and Three Rivers in 1821. In 1806 he was appointed commissioner for administering the oath of allegiance to half-pay officers. From June 1808 till October of the following year he represented Montreal West in the Lower Canadian House of Assembly, replacing John Richardson, who had been appointed to the Legislative Council. During the War of 1812 McGillivray obtained the rank of lieutenant-colonel in the Corps of Canadian Voyageurs, which was formed in October 1812 and disbanded in March of the following year. In 1814 he was appointed to the Legislative Council. Like many expatriate Scots living in Montreal, he was a member of the Scotch Presbyterian Church, later known as the St Gabriel Street Church.

William McGillivray died on 16 Oct. 1825 during a visit to London. In December his brother Simon wrote: "My Brother was considered a man of fortune; and he had been, in fact, originally the only capitalist amongst us." That sums up well the career of the man who started out with little, but with the encouragement of his uncle Simon McTavish climbed up through the ranks to become the principal director of the NWC; he achieved that position at the time when, although still powerful, the company was engaged in the struggle that led to merger with the HBC in 1821. In his will he had bequeathed his estate in Scotland to his daughters, Anne and Magdalen, children of his second marriage who also inherited £10,000 apiece. His sons, Simon and Joseph, the only surviving children of his first marriage, each received £2,000 as well as the lands in Plantagenet Township.

FERNAND OUELLET

PAC, RG 68, General index, 1651–1841. *Les bourgeois de la Compagnie du Nord-Ouest* (Masson). *Docs. relating to NWC* (Wallace). F.-J. Audet, *Les députés de Montréal*; "Les législateurs du Bas-Canada." Turcotte, *Le Conseil législatif.* Wallace, *Macmillan dict.* R. Campbell, *Hist. of Scotch Presbyterian Church.* Caron, *La colonisation de la prov. de Québec.* Innis, *Fur trade in Canada* (1956). E. A. Mitchell, *Fort Timiskaming and the fur trade* (Toronto and Buffalo, N.Y., 1977). E. E. Rich, *The fur trade and the northwest to 1857* (Toronto, 1967). Robert Rumilly, *La Compagnie du Nord-Ouest, une épopée montréalaise* (2v., Montréal, 1980). M. [E.] Wilkins Campbell, *McGillivray; lord of the northwest* (Toronto, 1962); *NWC* (1973); *Northwest to the sea; a biography of William McGillivray* (Toronto and Vancouver, 1975). Fernand Ouellet, "Dualité économique et changement technologique au Québec (1760–1790)," *SH*, 9 (1976): 256–96.

MacGREGOR (McGregor), JAMES DRUMMOND, Presbyterian minister, author, and composer; b. December 1759 in Portmore (St Fillans), parish of Comrie, Perthshire, Scotland, second son of James Drummond, farmer and weaver, and Janet Dochert (Dochart); m. 11 May 1796 Ann McKay in Halifax, and they had three sons and three daughters; m. secondly 25 Dec. 1811 in Pictou, N.S., Janet Gordon, widow of the Reverend Peter Gordon, Presbyterian missionary to Prince Edward Island, and niece of Archibald Bruce, minister of the General Associate Hall at Alloa, Scotland, and they had two daughters and one son; d. 3 March 1830 in Pictou.

James MacGregor's parents belonged to Clan Gregor, which was proscribed after the Highland rebellion of 1715. Upon resettlement elsewhere in the Highlands James's grandfather took the patronym Drummond of his protector, the Earl of Perth. Although James's father retained this name, his son resumed the ancient family name in the course of his university years. James was raised in the bosom of the Secession Church, so called because of its origin in Ebenezer Erskine's separation from the Church of Scotland in 1733, and within its strict anti-burgher wing, which rejected the burghers' oath required of civic officers. James's father is said to have been admitted to church communion by Erskine and to have been present when Erskine was expelled from his own church in 1740.

James himself was dedicated at baptism to the service of the Lord, a practice common among the Scottish peasantry. He attended grammar schools at Kinkell and Dunblane, and then studied at the University of Edinburgh, where he matriculated in 1779. From 1781 to 1784 he attended the General Associate Hall, the anti-burgher theological college, but was licensed before completing the five-year course. Like many students, James supported himself partly by teaching, for example at Glen Lednock, near Comrie, at Morebattle in southern Scotland, and in Argyll. The Secession Church had few Gaelic-speaking ministers and with his Highland ancestry James began learning the Gaelic language to become one. He made a study of the traditions of his native district, translated the Book of Proverbs into Gaelic, and taught school in the western Highlands. As a probationer he preached widely and some time in 1785 or 1786 was called to Craigdam in Aberdeenshire. The General Associate Synod would not allow him to accept the call. Instead, MacGregor was appointed to Nova Scotia.

In the fall of 1784 the people of Pictou had petitioned for a minister who would preach in both Gaelic and English. They sent their request through two residents of Greenock, Scotland, one of whom had been associated with Pictou from its founding. Upon receipt of the request by way of the Presbytery of Perth, MacGregor put himself in the hands of the synod. Although he had expected assignment to the Highlands, at a meeting on 4 May 1786 the synod unanimously appointed him to Pictou. Ordained by the Presbytery of Glasgow on 31 May, he sailed from Greenock on 3 June for Halifax, where he landed on 11 July.

Influenced by his own youthful intellectual prowess and the moulding of his mentors, MacGregor brought to Nova Scotia the cultural baggage of his Scottish education. He confronted immediately the fluid North American religious frontier. Within days of his arrival he was invited to join the Presbytery of Truro, then forming among the burgher ministers already settled in the province. The Reverend Daniel Cock of Truro, who had written the Pictou petition, assumed that the new arrival, whatever his Scottish affiliation, would unite with the presbytery in recognition of their common objective of sustaining Presbyterianism in Nova Scotia. MacGregor participated in the meetings and preached to the assembly, but was unable to reconcile himself to the presbytery's acceptance of Isaac Watts's psalms, its mode of electing elders, its acquiescence in doctrine which was imputed to be impure, and its insufficiently explicit adoption of the Westminster Confession. Cock knew, as MacGregor did not, that the settlers' alternatives to the ministrations of a few regularly ordained clergy lay in the occasional religious services provided by enthusiastic itinerants who were casual in both doctrine and church practices. Moreover, the Nova Scotian ministers saw the Scottish divisions within Presbyterianism, shaped by Scotland's relations of church and state, as irrelevant to Nova Scotia where there was neither a Presbyterian establishment nor a burghers' oath of office. MacGregor could not, however, in conscience join in presbytery with colleagues who were burghers, not anti-burghers. In his eyes, his affiliation with the

MacGregor

Presbytery of Glasgow precluded any other alliance, and he could not trespass upon the moral conviction that separated burghers and anti-burghers in his homeland. This intransigence left him isolated from religious brethren for nearly a decade.

MacGregor's firm adherence to anti-burgher principles also caused conflict with his parishioners' expectations. Upon arrival in Pictou, he found no town, no church, no school, and widely scattered settlers. He postponed celebration of the Lord's Supper for two years while he preached to his parishioners – each sermon four times, in English and in Gaelic at two separate stations – taught in their houses, and catechized them, for he had to assure himself of the sincerity of the celebrants before he admitted them to the communion table. Although his parishioners would gladly have had the burgher ministers join them in the sacrament, MacGregor could not bring himself to invite them. Similarly, he was concerned, in the absence of established congregations, about due ordination of elders, and he was relieved to find among his communicants three who had been regularly ordained in Scotland; he was thus able to form a session and ordain additional elders when required. His tenacity in baptizing only the children of sincere Christians caused the most criticism of his anti-burgher polity. In settlements deprived of religious ordinances, where other ministers regularly baptized upon the presentation of children regardless of parental adherence, MacGregor insisted upon the parents' knowledge of and commitment to Christian upbringing prior to the baptism.

MacGregor's early experiences in Nova Scotia confirmed his decision not to join the Presbytery of Truro. Sympathetic to the anti-slavery attitudes emerging in Britain, he put his convictions to practical use by applying £20 of the £27 he received for his first year's services toward purchasing the freedom of a slave girl from her Nova Scotian master, and he subsequently aided in the release of others. MacGregor extended this commitment when he confronted Cock, who was a slave owner, with the immorality of a Christian's enslaving God's children. The publication in Halifax in 1788 of MacGregor's rebuke to Cock, and the Reverend David Smith's reply on Cock's behalf, formalized MacGregor's split with the Presbytery of Truro.

MacGregor's conflict with the burgher ministers created tensions within the Presbyterian communities as well. Those discontented with local ministrations sought him out for occasional services, and MacGregor, in his fervour, appears to have encouraged them. In 1793 the Presbytery of Truro summoned him, but its failure to persuade him of the "groundlessness and wrongness of his separation" led to the promulgation of a public warning against him. Accusations in the same year, attributed to MacGregor, that Smith

neglected the proper teaching of his congregation at Londonderry were interpreted by the burghers as an attempt to lay the base for the introduction of an anti-burgher minister there, an event that occurred two years later when the Reverend John Brown was settled at Londonderry after Smith's death. In 1795 MacGregor received his first anti-burgher brethren, Brown and the Reverend Duncan Ross, and on 7 July formed with them the Associate Presbytery of Nova Scotia, more commonly known as the Associate Presbytery of Pictou. The congregational assignments to Ross and Brown were not, however, of MacGregor's choosing, despite his familiarity with local conditions, and it was not until 1801 that an amicable division of the Pictou settlements was arranged between Ross and MacGregor. The Presbytery of Truro sought communion of the two presbyteries, but, as in MacGregor's case, the initial period of the new ministers' residence was not opportune for approaching a closer union.

The driving force throughout MacGregor's life was his dedication to supplying the Gospel to those who did not have it. His acceptance of the posting to Nova Scotia exemplified this commitment. Arriving at Pictou, he found settlers who had lived there for up to 20 years with no religious services except occasional visits from itinerants of various denominations. His scattered parishioners were mostly Highlanders raised in the Church of Scotland and traditionally antagonistic to the Secession Church, but in time they became irrevocably bound to MacGregor. In 1791 immigration brought Roman Catholic Highlanders to Pictou, and MacGregor encouraged his flock to aid them. Within two years of arrival he set out on his first missionary journey – a duty he would perform regularly for more than 30 years through New Brunswick (Miramichi 1797, Saint John River 1805, Passamaquoddy Bay 1815), Prince Edward Island (1791, 1794, 1800, 1806), Cape Breton (1798, 1818), and from Amherst to Sherbrooke in Nova Scotia. In the religious environment of the frontier, he, like New Light, Methodist, Anglican, Roman Catholic, and other Presbyterian preachers, encountered settlements seeking religious services of whatever denomination they could obtain. Responding to this milieu as well as to his ordination instruction "to make Christians, not Seceders," MacGregor "resolved not to confine [his] visitations to Presbyterians, but to include all, of every denomination, who would make [him] welcome; for [he] viewed them as sheep without a shepherd."

Although Presbyterians were the largest religious group in the province and many sought Presbyterian leadership, there were few Presbyterian clergy in Nova Scotia. Upon arrival MacGregor was one of only five. Generally the Scottish churches of the 18th century lacked interest in pursuing missionary activities, and the absence of a missionary body such as the Anglican Society for the Propagation of the Gospel seriously hampered the extension of Presbyterianism. As a result MacGregor became a focal point of appeals to Scotland for ministers to settle in Maritime communities. His first letters home bespoke his isolation and entreated friends and synod appointees to join him in his labours; congregational petitions, beginning with that of Amherst in 1788, followed. The failure of both friends and synod nominees to come to Nova Scotia led to discouragement in settlements for which MacGregor had sought ministers. In his impassioned *Letter . . . to the General Associate Synod*, written in September 1792, he responded in a mixture of pleas of need, betrayed faith, and overt criticism of ministerial lukewarmness and selfishness. The arrival of Brown and Ross in 1795 broke MacGregor's isolation but did not restore his belief in Scottish capacity to supply North American demands.

If clergy sufficient to meet the region's religious wants could not be induced to come, other means of spreading the word could be pursued. MacGregor sought aid from the international religious bodies, of which his continuing correspondence with Scotland kept him aware and in which he took a most active personal interest. As early as 1807 he was in correspondence with the British and Foreign Bible Society and received from it the following year English and Gaelic bibles and testaments, for sale or free distribution at his discretion. He contributed to it financially and as a Gaelic scholar, and he also reviewed translations of English works to be published by the society. As secretary of the Pictou branch from 1813 to 1826, he collected and remitted contributions to aid in spreading the Gospel where it was little known; it is said that he was the branch. Alone in the province, his society remained unaffiliated with the Nova Scotia branch of the British and Foreign Bible Society. In part because of his personal commitment and in part because of the large Highland population in his region, MacGregor was also a keen member of the Gaelic School Society, founded in Edinburgh in 1811. It was active primarily in the Highlands, and MacGregor's involvement reflected his lifelong devotion to the people of his homeland and his continuing communication with Scottish religious and educational movements. He also organized local contributions to the London Society for Promoting Christianity among the Jews and to the Baptist mission in Burma. In Pictou he promoted Sunday schools – another British-initiated effort to give children a knowledge of the Bible – penny-a-week societies, and a domestic missionary society instituted by the Presbyterian Church of Nova Scotia.

In addition to translations of works from English to Gaelic, MacGregor wrote original works in Gaelic, primarily a series of spiritual songs published under the title *Dain a chomhnadh crabhuidh*. Inspired by the loneliness of the North American forests he traversed and by the works of such Scottish evangelical poets as Dugald Buchanan, which had been written to the tunes of familiar Highland songs, MacGregor completed about 25 long sacred poems. Their subjects are the central Christian doctrines such as faith, the Gospel, the Last Judgement, and the Resurrection, set forth simply not only for his Highland parishioners but also for the evangelizing of the Scottish North, where the tradition of reciting hymns for spiritual experience remained strong. MacGregor's study of the Scottish secular poets Duncan Ban MacIntyre and Alexander MacDonald in the course of preparing his poems and his choice of secular tunes raised aspersions on his religious principles in Pictou, but his *Dain* became widely renowned in the Highlands. MacGregor gave the copyright of his work to the Glasgow Tract Society on the condition that the society would be diligent in circulating it. At least seven editions were published between 1819 and 1870, but only one, that of 1861, in North America; both additional poems and excerpts from the *Dain* were published in later collections of Gaelic verse. On the basis of his poems MacGregor has been acclaimed "the apostle of Pictou" and the first Gaelic bard in Canada.

As MacGregor continued his work in Nova Scotia, he like other ministers moved from an initial adherence to Scottish denominationalism to a more ecumenical view of Presbyterianism. When the Presbytery of Pictou was formed, it followed the example of Truro and defined no doctrinal standards subordinate to the Westminster Confession, MacGregor having come to see in nine years the fruitlessness of seeking strict adherence to Scottish anti-burgher polity. As he explained to a colleague in Scotland, "You would see such a mixture of people here from different nations as throws the state of the church back as far as the days of John Knox." The contemplation of union among all Presbyterian ministers in the province by 1814 reflected this reality. The objectives of a union, as MacGregor saw them, were to provide a more extensive plan for perpetuating Presbyterianism, and especially to provide for training a native ministry. In 1816 the presbyteries of Pictou and Truro cooperated in sending to the St Marys River region two missionaries, of whom MacGregor was one. Although he was not a member of the committee appointed to define the terms of union, he was a strong supporter of the intent, and when the synod was formally created at Truro in July 1817 as the Presbyterian Church of Nova Scotia, he was chosen its first moderator. In a synod dominated by the Pictou ministers, MacGregor was active on a variety of committees from 1817 to 1825, including that discussing "ways and means for promoting religion," and he attended every synod meeting except the one prior to his death. MacGregor participated as

MacGregor

well in some informal attempts to obtain recognition of the Presbyterian Church of Nova Scotia by the Church of Scotland, but through Scottish denominational intransigence these came to naught.

The leading objective in forming the synod, in the eyes of the Pictou ministers, was to establish a college to train Nova Scotians for the Presbyterian ministry so that the church would no longer be reliant upon the meagre supply of clergymen from the Scottish synods. This concern was directly linked to the larger aim of providing Nova Scotian Presbyterians as well as dissenters with educational opportunities beyond those of the grammar school since religious tests, introduced in 1803, had effectively excluded non-Anglicans from King's College at Windsor, the only institute of higher learning in the province. MacGregor's life exemplifies the devoted relationship between education and religion that characterizes Scottish Presbyterianism, and he was an ardent supporter of this cause as well as of its obdurate promoter, the Reverend Thomas McCulloch*. In 1805, MacGregor was active in soliciting subscriptions for a society to support formation of an institution for training young men for the ministry. When the idea was renewed in 1814, he was again a leader in its promotion, and he was a trustee from Pictou Academy's initiation in 1815 until his death, the most generous subscriber to the academy after merchant Edward Mortimer*, and an active worker for its success. In support of the academy he preached, sought contributions, and occasionally penned some of the flood of appeals for recognition, legal status, books, and funds which were directed, starting in 1815, to the provincial government, the lieutenant governor, local congregations, newspapers, the Scottish synod, and such international bodies as the London Missionary Society. In one such appeal, prepared by McCulloch, University of Glasgow honorary degrees were sought for four warm political friends of Pictou Academy and for MacGregor; he was, as a result, awarded a DD in 1822.

In the 1820s the well-rooted Presbyterian Church of Nova Scotia and newly arrived Church of Scotland ministers clashed head-on in Pictou and in the wider provincial sphere over the local education and ordination of Presbyterian clergy. In the bitter struggle to protect Pictou Academy against the aspersions of the Church of Scotland and its missionary wing, the Glasgow Colonial Society, MacGregor's passionate adherence to the purposes of the institution in offering a college education and theological training for Nova Scotians was driven by his 40 years of appeals to Scotland for ministers to serve in the colony. In the wider scope of this strife, MacGregor was threatened with prosecution in 1825 by Church of Scotland stalwart the Reverend George Burns of Saint John, N.B., for having performed a marriage for a farmer 20

years earlier in contravention of the New Brunswick marriage law.

The politico-religious struggle over Pictou Academy that incited Nova Scotians from 1815 to the mid 1830s was the leading component of a larger movement in the province to establish the rights of non-Anglican denominations. The Presbyterian Church of Nova Scotia, steered by McCulloch, gave leadership in the endeavour. One focus of this activity was the Church of England's claim, as the established church, to its exclusive right to marry by licence, it alone having traditionally issued such papers. MacGregor had himself been married in Halifax in 1796 by licence rather than, as was required by ecclesiastical and civil law in Scotland, after the publication of banns, and he was severely criticized by his parishioners and ministerial brethren for such irregular procedure. In practice, marriage licences had been widely distributed for many years to ministers and justices of the peace, and as the right to their use became a principle with the Presbyterian Church of Nova Scotia, MacGregor also undoubtedly married by licence when so requested. In 1832 legislation was passed which allowed non-Anglican clergy to marry by licence.

Besides seeking legal status for interdenominational use of marriage licences, the Presbyterian Church of Nova Scotia undertook to bring all non-Anglican Protestants in the province into common communication. Beginning in 1819, its representatives sought cooperation with Methodist and Baptist preachers. MacGregor supported such collaboration, including the attempt to formalize common interests through a board, but he took little direct role in the promotion of the board except in 1825 during the absence in Scotland of McCulloch, who was its driving force.

The mid 1820s also saw discussion of another sort among non-Anglican Protestants. Beginning in 1822, Methodist, Baptist, and Presbyterian ministers in Nova Scotia carried on an active newspaper and pamphlet controversy over the rite of baptism, the point of disagreement being whether it should be performed by sprinkling or immersion. MacGregor had investigated this subject when still a theological student and had at that time favourably impressed a hearer by his preaching on it. He put the arguments in favour of paedobaptism to paper, possibly while he was still in Scotland, and circulated them privately during the Nova Scotian debate. He is said to have contributed to the treatise that appeared under Duncan Ross's name in 1825, but his own essay does not appear to have been published in his lifetime.

"A guide to baptism" was not MacGregor's first doctrinal work. In 1800 his "Essay on the duration and character of the millenial age of the church" had been published in the *Christian Magazine* (Edinburgh). "A defence of the religious imprecations and denunciations of God's wrath, contained in the Book of Psalms, against the enemies of the Gospel," also not published in MacGregor's lifetime, defended the use of the Old Testament Psalms in the face of prevalent criticism and preference for the hymns of Isaac Watts. MacGregor also wrote occasionally for the press, both on religious subjects such as the British and Foreign Bible Society and on broad topics such as improvements to transportation in the province.

While some Scottish congregations regarded a minister's farming and acquisition of land as indulgent worldliness, MacGregor's farming at Pictou was a necessity born out of the inability of his flock to pay regularly even the modest stipend he was promised. In 1799, for example, he received only £50, all in kind, currency being at times virtually unknown. When MacGregor married in 1796, he settled on the west side of the East River of Pictou. Two years later he bought 150 acres for £200, and in 1810 he obtained a confirming grant of the additional 450 acres he had improved. Unlike Anglican and some dissenting clergymen, MacGregor did not receive a glebe as the first permanent minister in the settlement, although Cock held such land at Truro and McCulloch obtained the glebe for Pictou town. On his land MacGregor reportedly built the first frame house on the East River and, as his family grew, the first brick house in eastern Nova Scotia, with bricks imported from Scotland. In farming for his family's subsistence he apparently used skills learned at his family home in Scotland.

MacGregor was a strong promoter of scientific agriculture in Nova Scotia. He was secretary of the East River, Pictou Agricultural Society throughout its existence from 1820 to 1825, and his regular reports to John Young*, secretary of the Central Board of Agriculture in Halifax, detail his experiments, such as the use of lime and coal ash to fertilize crops, and his successes in the form of prizes at the society's annual competitions for oats, turnips, barley, potatoes, wheat, lime, and the best ram. His labours provided a model for his neighbours, who were not experienced in agriculture and, as MacGregor explained, would adopt new schemes only when they had been proved effective. After the seeds sent by the Central Board turned out to be smutty, MacGregor advised Young of their deleterious impact on the society: membership had fallen away, and "some think the whole bustle about agriculture is a contrivance to pick poor people's pockets." Recognizing the potential of the society, however, MacGregor remarked, "No one knows how long we would have followed the example of our grandfathers, had we been left to continue on without a stimulus," and with its encouragement many improvements, including better equipment, were introduced. Nevertheless, only a small proportion of the farmers of the region were members of the society. In 1825, when the Central Board and its annual prizes to stimulate experiments and competition were abolished, MacGregor noted that agriculture in Pictou needed continued encouragement to keep it creeping forward. His own farming was soon to be drastically reduced by the sale of his land to Rundell, Bridge, and Rundell of London as part of the launching of the coal-mining operations of the General Mining Association in 1827. At the time of his death he owned only three cows, a horse, and a plough and cart.

MacGregor was one of the first Pictonians recorded to have found and used the coal under his property. A coal fire was burning in his house when he entertained the candidates for the 1799 provincial election, in which rural Nova Scotia made its first significant inroads on the Halifax-dominated House of Assembly. As minerals were a crown resource, MacGregor obtained a licence from Lieutenant Governor Sir John Wentworth* to mine the coal on his land. He was one of several Pictonians who heated their houses from such backyard operations and who were prosecuted in 1822 for raising coals from their lands in contravention of the monopolistic lease on coal mines held by Edward Mortimer's successors. About 1820 MacGregor experimented with burning hydrogen from the coal deposits for light in his house, but he was unable to establish an operating system because he could not afford the purifying apparatus and the piping necessary for safety and transmission.

MacGregor was a large man, six feet tall, and with a gift for conversation. In his mature years he was known for his patience, his tolerance, and his conciliatory manner, which contrasted with the fiery adherence to principle of his early years in Nova Scotia. His ardent Christian zeal remained unchanged, but found new expression. In 1824 a cancer was successfully removed from his lip, but in February 1828 he suffered a severe stroke which resulted in paralysis on his right side and some loss of memory. Another stroke, just over two years later, was fatal.

The surviving remains of MacGregor's autobiography and writings, published by a sympathetic editor, have made him renowned for undergoing hardships of Herculean proportions on the Nova Scotian frontier – the physical hazards and deprivations of his journeyings, the tribulations caused by his disputatious parishioners, and the "almost superhuman exertions" of his pastoral labours. He was the model clergyman depicted in McCulloch's novel *William and Melville*. The Anglican minister John Inglis* described him in 1811 as "a venerable man of great simplicity in manner, but well informed and very useful among his congregation who seem to respect him highly," and the *Novascotian, or Colonial Herald* of Halifax summed up at his death: "If he met a believer, he joined him as a traveller journeying on the same road,

461

McGregor

to the same country, and was happy that they had been brought together. If he found an unfortunate brother who needed consolation, he . . . administered to him the comfort of the Gospel."

SUSAN BUGGEY

[Miscellaneous doctrinal and evangelical works by Mac-Gregor, some of which were not published during his lifetime, are collected in *A few remains of the Rev. James MacGregor, D.D.*, edited by his grandson, the Reverend George Patterson* (Philadelphia, 1859). The collection also includes a number of previously published items, among them *Letter from the Reverend Mr. James M'Gregor, minister, at Pictou, Nova Scotia, to the General Associate Synod, April 30th, 1793*, which originally appeared at Paisley, Scotland, in 1793. In *Addresses at the celebration of the one hundred and fiftieth anniversary of the arrival in Nova Scotia of Rev. James Drummond MacGregor, D.D.*, by the Synod of the Maritime Provinces of the Presbyterian Church in Canada, ed. Frank Baird (Toronto, 1937), John Brown Maclean refers to unpublished Gaelic manuscripts in the possession of Alexander Maclean Sinclair at an unknown date after 1880, containing hymns, three-quarters of the Book of Psalms in metre, and secular songs. In the same work, Donald Maclean Sinclair refers to these manuscripts as also including the Confession of Faith.

A full list of editions of MacGregor's *Dain a chomhnadh crabhuidh* (the title varies slightly) has not been located. All the standard bibliographic sources contain incomplete lists. The following editions have been located: Glasgow, 1819 and 1825; Edinburgh, 1831; Glasgow, 1832; Edinburgh, [1847]; Pictou, 1861; and Edinburgh, 1870. Only some of these volumes have been personally examined; those held abroad have been reported to the author by the holding institutions. No confirmation has been found for the Glasgow, 1818 edition reported in H. J. Morgan, *Bibliotheca Canadensis*. Six additional poems by MacGregor appear in *Dain Spioradail*, edited by A. Maclean Sinclair (Edinburgh, 1880).

A great deal has been written about MacGregor. The vast majority of these writings are based on George Patterson's *Memoir of the Rev. James MacGregor, D.D.* . . . . (Philadelphia, 1859), and have not been included in this bibliography. s.b.]

PAC, MG 23, C6, ser.4, John Inglis, journal, 30 July 1811 (mfm.). PANS, MG 1, 332B; RG 8, 5, no.8, Pictou County; RG 20A, 35, 49. Pictou County Court of Probate (Pictou), Estate papers, no.158 (James MacGregor) (mfm. at PANS). Pictou County Registry of Deeds (Pictou), Index to deeds, vol.1 (1771–1840); Deeds, books 1B: 282–83; 11: 515–18; 12: 414 (mfm. at PANS). UCC-M, James Mac-Gregor papers; Presbyterian Church, Truro Presbytery, minutes, 1786–1830 (mfm. at PANS); Presbyterian Church of N.S. (United Secession), minutes of the Synod, vol.1, 1817–30. Univ. of Glasgow Arch., James MacGregor, records of education and awarding of honourary DD, 1822. *Novascotian, or Colonial Herald*, 10 March 1830. Susan Buggey, "Churchmen and dissenters: religious toleration in Nova Scotia, 1758–1835" (MA thesis, Dalhousie Univ., Halifax, 1981). John MacInnes, *The evangelical movement in the Highlands of Scotland, 1688 to 1800* (Aberdeen, Scot., 1951).

McGREGOR, JOHN, businessman, politician, office holder, and militia officer; b. *c.* 1751 in Scotland; he had five sons and two daughters, at least six of whom were borne by Martha Scott, whom he married in August 1815; d. 12 Feb. 1828 in Amherstburg, Upper Canada.

John McGregor emigrated from Scotland in 1784 to join his uncle Gregor McGregor in Detroit. He obtained property there and engaged in trade, being active in the Ohio region in 1794. It was not until October 1796, when he was granted 600 acres in Dover East (Dover) Township, that he acquired any property in Upper Canada. Following the British withdrawal from Detroit, he drew a lot in Sandwich. He subsequently received additional land there, as well as a lot in Amherstburg.

Soon after moving to Upper Canada, McGregor formed a partnership with his cousin James McGregor to engage in general trade. By 1800 John McGregor's trade had increased sufficiently for him to contract with John Askin* for a boat to bring down grain from the Thames River area. In 1801 he constructed the *Thames*, a keel of some 80 tons. As trade in grain increased, so did the need for milling facilities, which were inadequate in the area. Construction of a grist-mill at the forks of the Thames was begun by Thomas CLARK. Encountering financial difficulties, he borrowed money from McGregor to finish the job. Clark fell into arrears on his debt and in 1810 McGregor, who apparently had Clark jailed as a debtor, acquired his property as settlement. The mill itself, however, had been destroyed by flooding. McGregor constructed another mill on McGregor's Creek. Even though inadequate water levels meant that it could only operate for five months in every year and the product was probably of inferior quality, the mill became an important asset in McGregor's expanding trade.

Since he was one of the more prominent merchants and farmers it was not unexpected that in 1804 McGregor was returned to the House of Assembly for Kent County. He was re-elected in 1808 and again in 1812 but, in the latter instance, did not actually take his seat until 1816. As a member he took part in the general business of the house, serving on various delegations and occasionally chairing committees. Like other members he was keenly interested in roads and took seriously his duties as road commissioner for the Western District.

At the outbreak of war in 1812 McGregor was called out to serve in the militia. He had joined Askin's militia company as a private in 1791, and by 1812 was a lieutenant in the Loyal Kent Volunteers. An incident that year was only the beginning of his difficulties: invading American troops seized a large quantity of grain from McGregor's mill and two of his vessels, including the *Thames*. He was in Sandwich

462

when it was occupied by the Americans who quickly began to seize his supplies. Faced with the prospect of losing much of his property, McGregor agreed to sell them his stores. Before he received payment, the Americans withdrew to Detroit. Shortly after the capitulation of Brigadier-General William Hull, Major-General Isaac Brock*, at McGregor's instigation, threatened that Hull would be sent to Montreal as a prisoner unless McGregor was paid at once. Hull, however, would sign only a statement of account. This episode provided grounds for charges, raised in 1815, that McGregor had collaborated with the enemy.

McGregor also encountered problems with British troops. Members of the 41st Foot tore down two of his houses in Sandwich for firewood. Moreover, they damaged an orchard, two large stores which were used as a barracks, and a house in Amherstburg. His only property left unscathed was a house in Sandwich used as a residence by Major-General Henry PROCTER. McGregor also had difficulties arising from a contract he had accepted to provide 1,500 cords of firewood for the naval yard in Amherstburg. He sub-contracted the agreement to a farmer in Michigan but the British had to withdraw before the delivery could be accepted. McGregor later tried to recover the £100 which he paid as an advance but a court of arbitration ruled against him in 1822.

In September 1813, when the British began to retreat up the Thames, Indians burned McGregor's grist-mill and an adjacent sawmill to prevent them from falling into American hands. McGregor accompanied the retreat and, according to his own account, was captured by the enemy. Any captivity was of short duration, however, because on 15 Dec. 1813 McGregor and seven men participated in an attack by a combined force of militia on a small detachment of American soldiers in Raleigh Township. On 2 March he was ordered to Longwoods to provide a diversion covering the movement of some 200 Indians. He lost an arm in this engagement and was later awarded a year's salary as compensation. By 22 April his company was again active and about this time McGregor was promoted captain. Early in July 1814 he took part in the battle of Lundy's Lane. In October he was ordered to Chippawa and in November to Burford Township to intercept an American force. His unit was disbanded in March 1815.

McGregor was in poor health and this may have influenced his decision in August 1815 to marry Martha Scott, who had lived with him for a number of years. Financially he was in poor circumstances; much of his property had been destroyed and he had some debts with his Quebec suppliers. In the fall of 1815 he went to Montreal and Quebec where he attempted to obtain compensation for some of his losses and to straighten out his accounts. In December

he obtained £3,191 2s. 1d. (Halifax currency) for claims relating to his mill and properties in Amherstburg and Sandwich, and £1,317 7s. (Halifax currency) for claims relating to his business in Sandwich. He pressed for further compensation and in 1824 received additional payments. Five years later, however, his son and executor continued to demand payment for such items as crops that had been left in the field.

With the compensation McGregor partially re-established his trade and in 1818 he replaced the mill. He also took advantage of land grants for militia service to obtain 850 acres in Wallaceburg in 1817 and additional land in Chatham Township in 1820.

McGregor did not contest the general election of 1816 and took no further role in public life; he did, however, continue to serve in the militia. Plagued by ill health and beset by difficult financial problems, he gradually left the administration of his affairs to his sons. He died at the age of 77.

K. G. PRYKE

AO, Hiram Walker Hist. Museum coll., 20-151; MS 500; RG 1, A-I-6. Can., Parks Canada, Fort Malden National Hist. Park (Amherstburg, Ont.), Arch. coll., John and James McGregor, waste-book. DPL, Burton Hist. Coll., John Askin papers; Campau family papers; Labadie family papers. PAC, RG 1, E3, 100: 212–21; L3, 328: M2/59; RG 8, I (C ser.), 90: 57–58; 682: 47, 233; 688d; RG 9, I, B1, 6; B4, 1: 17–18; B7, 27, 32; RG 19, E5(a). *John Askin papers* (Quaife). *Death notices of Ont.* (Reid), 48. F. C. Hamil, *The valley of the lower Thames, 1640 to 1850* (Toronto, 1951; repr. Toronto and Buffalo, N.Y., 1973); "Early shipping and land transportation on the lower Thames," *OH*, 34 (1942): 48.

MACKAY, DONALD, fur trader and office holder; b. 1753 in Gordonbush, Scotland; d. 26 June 1833 in Barneys River, N.S.

When he entered the northwest fur trade in the spring of 1779 Donald Mackay's pugnacious character had already been formed by his service in the British army during the early campaigns of the American revolution. He left Montreal as the clerk of John Ross and, after several independent traders had combined forces at Grand Portage (near Grand Portage, Minn.), to form the North West Company [see Simon McTavish*] he became a clerk in the new organization. In September 1780 Ross and Mackay were trading at a post on the Assiniboine River above Portage la Prairie (Man.). From that post Mackay took four companions on an overland expedition to the Hidatsa villages on the upper Missouri River.

Mackay went back to Montreal at the end of 1781 to take a position as clerk in the Indian Department under Lieutenant-Colonel John Campbell*. In the spring of 1785 he returned to the fur trade, persuading Campbell to finance a trading expedition to the upper

McKay

Saskatchewan River. His independent venture encountered unrelenting resistance, constant intimidation, and direct physical attack from the NWC, which was trying to establish a trade monopoly. After nearly starving at Nepawi (Nipawin, Sask.) during the winter of 1785–86, Mackay pressed upriver the next summer to build an establishment on Pine Island (near Standard Hill, Sask.), close to where the Hudson's Bay Company's Manchester House would be built that autumn. Later he built an outpost even higher up the North Saskatchewan River to oppose the NWC under Edward Umfreville*. Mackay's pioneering efforts were defeated by intense competition, and lack of support from his Montreal suppliers caused him to return to Montreal in 1787. New backers in London proved even less determined and in 1789–90 Mackay was forced to sign on as a trader with Alexander Shaw in the Nipigon country. In the autumn of 1790, with his kinsman John McKay*, he travelled to Osnaburgh House (Ont.) on the Albany River to join the HBC.

The HBC was trying to push inland to oppose the NWC. Mackay presented a brilliant proposal to extend trade from Fort Albany to Portage de l'Isle (near the junction of the Winnipeg and English rivers) and on to Lake Winnipeg, and thus to cut into the heart of the NWC's vital supply route. Several exploratory voyages on the Albany River resulted in a map, drawn by him in 1791, which was probably used by British cartographer Aaron Arrowsmith. Mackay's activities culminated in 1793 with the establishment of Brandon House (Man.), from where the HBC interrupted the NWC's supply of pemmican and reopened the dormant trade with the Mandans. But his innovative and aggressive efforts reflected unfavourably upon the plodding HBC inland officers, who resented him and conspired to frustrate his plans. Forced into frequent voyages between Rupert's Land and London, Mackay was unable to continue his personal supervision of the extension of HBC trade. Jealous fellow officers managed to deny him the supplies, men, and equipment he needed to proceed inland from Osnaburgh House, and to cut off his correspondence with the London committee of the HBC. He and his family withdrew from the post and subsisted on fish during the winter of 1796–97. That spring he made the difficult canoe voyage to York Factory (Man.) accompanied only by his country wife, her sister, and his baby son. Mackay's abrasive personality found a cool reception at York Factory and he was again stranded, out of contact with his supporters on the London committee. The sobriquets Mad Mackay and Le Malin were given to him by rival Nor'Westers who thought him mad to oppose their overwhelming organization. In the swamps around York Factory Mackay was indeed driven dangerously close to nervous breakdown and suicide.

In 1799 Mackay returned to his home at Gordon-

bush and two or three years later converted his field notes into personal memoirs which recorded facts of considerable historical interest. He attempted to re-enter the northern fur trade in 1806–7, but was unable to adapt to conditions and returned to Scotland. According to family tradition, his country wife, the daughter of HBC officer James Sutherland*, was killed by angry Indians, leaving him with two sons, William and Donald. He and his Scottish wife, Mary McKenzie, had several children. In 1813 he assisted Lord Selkirk [Douglas*] in recruiting colonists for the Red River settlement (Man.), thus helping to implement his own plan to intercept the NWC on the Red River.

Mackay immigrated to Nova Scotia in 1822 with his Scottish wife and family and settled in present-day Pictou County. He was a colourful character and a subject of local folklore when he died in 1833. During his HBC service he had introduced his nephews Donald Sutherland and Donald McDonald to the fur trade and an incomplete count identifies 22 fighting Mackays in that business over a period of 130 years.

JOHN C. JACKSON

PAC, MG 19, E1 (copies); RG 10, A6, 474: 170439, 170447. PAM, HBCA, A.1/46: ff.146, 151; A.5/3: ff.109, 133d–34, 145, 149, 154; A.5/4: ff.80, 88d, 135, 153d, 158d; A.6/4: f.145; A.6/14: f.95; A.6/16: f.27; A.6/17: f.86; A.32/19: f.117; B.3/a/93b; B.3/a/100; B.3/b/28: ff.7d, 9, 13–14, 18, 23–23d, 32d; B.3/b/33: ff.17–19, 24d–27, 33–34; B.3/b/34: ff.13, 16–17d, 29d–31, 37d–38; B.22/a/1; B.42/a/132: f.7d; B.42/b/150: ff.1, 10, 15d, 17; B.49/a/16: f.109; B.121/a/1: ff.10, 50; B.121/a/2: ff.34, 38; B.155/a/4: f.30; B.155/a/7; B.155/a/12: ff.37d–40; B.239/a/101: ff.3, 8d, 21d, 60–61, 81; B.239/a/102: ff.60, 79; C.1/417: f.3; G.1/13: ff.1–28. Private arch., J. C. Jackson (Portland, Oreg.), J. C. Jackson, "The voyages of Mad Donald Mackay and the fight for the northwest fur trade, 1779 to 1807"; Kenneth Mackay (Barney's River, N.S.), Journal and other papers of Donald Mackay. PRO, WO 12/4250, 12/5637. [S. H. Wilcocke], *A narrative of occurrences in the Indian countries of North America . . .* (London, 1817; repr. East Ardsley, Eng., and New York, 1968). *Quebec Gazette*, 5 June, 17 Oct. 1788. *Eastern Chronicle* (New Glasgow, N.S.), 23 April, 9 July 1885; 9 Feb. 1886.

McKAY, WILLIAM, fur trader, militia officer, and Indian Department official; b. 1772, probably in the Mohawk valley of New York, son of Donald McKay and Elspeth (Elspy) Kennedy; d. 18 Aug. 1832 in Montreal and was buried in Mount Royal Cemetery.

William McKay's father fought as a non-commissioned officer at Quebec in 1759 and received a land grant in the Mohawk valley after the Seven Years' War. He and his family were United Empire Loyalists and eventually settled in the area that became Glengarry County, Upper Canada. Around

1790 McKay entered the service of the North West Company; it was probably at about the same time that his brother Alexander* joined the company. William initially traded along the Menominee River in the upper Mississippi valley, and subsequently at Portage la Prairie (Man.) and in the Lake Winnipeg area. His abilities were rewarded in 1796 when he was made a partner in the NWC. During the next 11 years McKay became well acquainted with the lands, Indian nations, and transportation routes of the northwest. He retired in 1807, a prominent partner in the company, and that year was admitted a member of the prestigious Beaver Club in Montreal.

While in the northwest McKay had married, according to the custom of the country, Josette Latour, but she probably remained in the northwest when he retired and she later became the country wife of NWC trader John Haldane*. On 15 Oct. 1808 at Montreal McKay married Eliza Davidson, daughter of the late Arthur Davidson*, a distinguished local judge. The couple would have two sons, one of whom survived infancy.

At the outbreak of the War of 1812 McKay was, in his own words, "one of the first men in Canada that turned out for its defence." In late June he journeyed from Montreal to St Joseph Island (Ont.) in a mere eight days carrying secret instructions from Major-General Isaac Brock* to Captain Charles Roberts*, commander of the British post on St Joseph Island. They authorized Roberts to use his own judgement in deciding whether to attack the Americans at Michilimackinac (Mackinac Island, Mich.), who were unaware that formal hostilities had commenced. The success of the British and the Indians [see Robert DICKSON] in forcing the surrender of the surprised garrison was in part due to the speed and secrecy with which McKay had accomplished his mission. Following his return to Montreal, McKay joined the Corps of Canadian Voyageurs and saw action at Lacolle in November 1812. In the spring of 1813 he was appointed captain in the 5th Select Embodied Militia Battalion of Lower Canada.

For McKay, as well as for other Montreal-based fur traders, the preservation of British hegemony in the northwest was of fundamental importance. The War of 1812 was an opportunity for such traders to grasp and to consolidate territory, especially on the upper Mississippi River, and thus extinguish American competition. McKay therefore devoted his knowledge and experience of transportation in the northwest to the dispatch of supplies and provisions to the British garrisons and "His Majesty's Indian Allies."

By early spring 1814 McKay's steadfast dedication had been rewarded by an appointment to command the Michigan Fencibles, a provincial corps raised at Michilimackinac the previous spring and composed mainly of "Canadians enlisted from the service of the Traders." According to Lieutenant-Colonel Robert McDouall*, commander at the post, the appointment was a wise decision since McKay was "very popular with [the Fencibles] & all the Canadians." In April McKay was made a brevet major. Late in June McDouall received news of the capture by the Americans of Prairie du Chien (Wis.). The occupation of that strategic post threatened British military control and Canadian fur-trade interests in the northwest. Thus, with the local rank of lieutenant-colonel and a determined force of Fencibles, voyageurs, and about 136 Indians, McKay was sent out in command of an expedition to retake Prairie du Chien.

En route McKay was reinforced at Green Bay by local militia, more voyageurs, and Indians. By the time he arrived at Prairie du Chien his contingent had swelled to 650 men, of whom, he noted, "120 were Michigan Fencibles Canadian Volunteers and Officers of the indian department the remainder were indians that proved to be perfectly useless." After two days of preliminary siege operations, McKay prepared hot shot for the cannon in order to set fire to the fort. Seeing that a serious assault was about to be made, the Americans capitulated. The victory of 19 July (the official surrender took place the following day) thrilled McKay and the fort was renamed in his honour. The Indians whom he had so recently maligned won a crushing victory on 21 and 22 July over an American relief column at the rapids on the Rock River. McKay suggested that it was "perhaps one of the most brilliant Actions faught by indians only since the Commencement of the war." These twin victories, coupled with the successful British defence of Michilimackinac in August, re-established and confirmed British superiority in the northwest until the late spring of 1815.

By autumn 1814 McKay had returned to his duties of conducting canoe loads of provisions and Indian presents from Montreal to Michilimackinac. He was appointed deputy superintendent and agent of the Indian Department at Michilimackinac on 25 December. In the spring of 1815 the official news of peace between Great Britain and the United States reached the northwest. Since the Treaty of Ghent dictated "the mutual restoration of all Forts," the British, Canadian, and Indian victories in the region seemed shallow indeed. McKay's painful duty as deputy superintendent was to advise the Indian tribes to cultivate a harmonious relationship with the Americans. At Drummond Island (Mich.), the new British post, he held a series of councils with the Indians throughout 1817 and 1818 and attempted to implement Britain's post-war Indian policy, which was to reduce "His Majesty's Indian Allies" from warriors to wards. The evolution of the reserve system in the Canadas had begun and McKay, who served as superintendent of Indian Affairs at Drummond Island from 1820 to

McKenzie

1828, was directly involved in overseeing the first stages in its development. He retained an affection for the Michigan Fencibles and made periodic attempts to obtain land grants for the disbanded soldiers.

William McKay became superintendent of the Indian Department for the district of Montreal in 1830, and continued in that post until he died of cholera in Montreal during the epidemic of 1832. Throughout his life, and especially during the War of 1812, he had exuded energy, enthusiasm, and dedication in supporting the British government and in defending and maintaining the prosperity of the Canadas.

ROBERT S. ALLEN

AO, MS 74, package 5, nos.6, 16. McCord Museum, William McKay papers; War of 1812, folder 10, military service of William McKay. PAC, MG 19, F29; MG 30, D1, 21: 143–52; RG 8, I (C ser.), 685, 1171. *Docs. relating to NWC* (Wallace). *Select British docs. of War of 1812* (Wood). *Officers of British forces in Canada* (Irving). R. Campbell, *Hist. of Scotch Presbyterian Church.* A. R. Gilpin, *The War of 1812 in the old northwest* (Toronto and East Lansing, Mich., 1958). Elizabeth Vincent, *Fort St. Joseph* (Can., National Hist. Parks and Sites Branch, *Manuscript Report*, no.335, Ottawa, 1978). Allen, "British Indian Dept.," *Canadian Hist. Sites*, no.14; "Canadians on the upper Mississippi: the capture and occupation of Prairie du Chien during the War of 1812," *Military Collector & Historian* (Washington), 31 (1979): 118–23. Douglas Brymner, "Capture of Fort M'Kay, Prairie du Chien, in 1814," Wis., State Hist. Soc., *Coll.*, 11 (1888): 254–70. B. L. Dunnigan, "The Michigan Fencibles," *Mich. Hist.* (Lansing), 57 (1973): 277–95.

McKENZIE, ALEXANDER, fur trader and militia officer; b. *c.* 1767, likely in Stornoway, Scotland; m., probably according to the custom of the country, Isabella Latour, and they had one son and one daughter; d. 23 July 1830 in Montreal.

Alexander McKenzie was the nephew of fur trader and explorer Alexander Mackenzie*, who referred to him as "my namesake," but so little information survives on the ramifications of the Mackenzie clan in the later 18th century that it is uncertain whose son he was. He may have come to North America with his family during the mass exodus of the Mackenzies from the Isle of Lewis in the hard economic times of the 1770s. Perhaps, like his uncle, he first settled in New York and after the War of American Independence went, like him, to Montreal. When he started trading in the environs of Detroit in 1790 he became associated with the Montreal firm of Forsyth, Richardson and Company [*see* John Forsyth*; John RICHARDSON], which operated in the area until 1796. After that date the British surrender of the western posts on the Great Lakes made fur trading in the region south and west of the lakes difficult for Canadian enterprises.

In 1793 Forsyth, Richardson and Company began trading north of Lake Superior in competition with the North West Company and in 1796, when McKenzie left the Detroit region, he gravitated to this area. He was one of the first six wintering partners in the New North West Company (sometimes called the XY Company), formed in November 1798 around the firms Forsyth, Richardson and Leith, Jameson and Company. NWC explorer David Thompson* encountered him with a brigade of New North West Company canoes on the North Saskatchewan River at Fort George (near Lindbergh, Alta) in September 1799, and a report from James Bird* noted that by mid October McKenzie and his men were building a post near Edmonton House (near Fort Saskatchewan). Though their relationship does not appear to have been close, McKenzie's presence may have helped induce his relative, now Sir Alexander, to acquire shares in the New North West Company by 1800; from 1802 it was sometimes known as Sir Alexander Mackenzie and Company. The company united in 1804 with the NWC, in which McKenzie continued his partnership.

From 1804 to 1808 McKenzie was in charge of the vital Athabasca department, where his high-handed manner earned him the title of "the Emperor," or sometimes "the Baron." In 1809 he commanded the NWC post at Pic (Ont.) on Lake Superior, and in 1811 became the company's agent at Fort William (Thunder Bay). At some point before 1814, McKenzie may have "cast off" his country wife; in that year she became the wife of NWC trader John McBean.

Up to now McKenzie had played no great part in the violence that had erupted between the NWC and the Hudson's Bay Company. But in 1815, during the crisis developing around the colony established by Lord Selkirk [Douglas*], he was sent as agent of the NWC to the Red River settlement (Man.) to hasten its destruction. It was he who persuaded Miles MACDONELL, governor of Assiniboia, to surrender that year and he helped to escort him to Fort William. For his complicity in this action, McKenzie was one of the NWC partners arrested by Selkirk at Fort William on 12 Aug. 1816. He and the others, among them John McDONALD, Simon Fraser*, John Siveright*, and John McLoughlin*, were tried at York (Toronto) in October 1818 on a variety of charges emerging out of the violence committed on the Red River, including the accusation of being accessories to the murder of Robert Semple*, governor of the HBC territories. They were acquitted after one of the most controversial series of trials in Canadian legal history.

From this time, McKenzie was no longer an active wintering partner of the NWC; when it merged with the HBC in 1821 he did not enter the new organization, though in the same year he was at Fort William as agent for McTavish, McGillivrays and Company. It is likely that during his remaining years in Montreal he retained an interest in the fur trade. He had been admitted a member of the Beaver Club in 1808. His standing in the community was shown by the fact that he became a major in the militia. He died in Montreal on 23 July 1830, having passed his life as a minor actor in historic events.

GEORGE WOODCOCK

Les bourgeois de la Compagnie du Nord-Ouest (Masson). *Docs. relating to NWC* (Wallace). *HBRS*, 26 (Johnson). Mackenzie, *Journals and letters* (Lamb). *New light on the early history of the greater northwest: the manuscript journals of Alexander Henry . . . and of David Thompson . . .*, ed. Elliott Coues (3v., New York, 1897; repr. 3v. in 2, Minneapolis, Minn., [1965]), 2. *Canadian Courant* (Montreal), 28 July 1830. Arthur Kittson, *"Berthier," yesterday & to-day* (Berthier, Que., 1953). Morton, *Hist. of Canadian west* (Thomas; 1973).

MACKENZIE, GEORGE, lawyer; b. 1795, probably in Dingwall, Scotland; m. 19 May 1829 Sarah Mackenzie in Ernestown (Bath), Upper Canada, the ceremony being performed by the Reverend John Machar*; they had no children; d. 4 Aug. 1834 in Kingston, Upper Canada.

George Mackenzie immigrated to British North America from Scotland before 1823. He settled at Kingston in the mid 1820s after a brief stay in Lower Canada and Ernestown. In 1828 he was called to the bar of the province and immediately went into private practice. Within a couple of years his practice was flourishing and he had staked out a prominent place for himself in Kingston society.

Along with other leading figures in the town, Mackenzie decried the monopoly of the Bank of Upper Canada and asserted the need for an independent bank in Kingston. At a public meeting there in January 1830, a committee was formed to draft rules and regulations for a Kingston bank and to petition the government for a charter; Mackenzie was secretary. A bill to charter the Kingston bank was soon after brought before the legislature, but it was defeated by the Legislative Council, most of whose members were directors and stockholders of the Bank of Upper Canada. Mackenzie persevered during the next year, speaking at public meetings on the advantages that would accrue to eastern Upper Canada from a Kingston bank, articulating the complaints of the growing non-tory commercial interest group to which he belonged, and galvanizing popular support behind a bank independent of the tory compact's control.

In February 1831 a second bill chartering the proposed bank passed the House of Assembly and was lost in the council, but the growing discontent over the Bank of Upper Canada's monopoly, combined with the assembly's refusal to pass a bill authorizing an increase in its stock, caused the supporters of the bank

in council to relent. In the fall session of 1831 a bill to charter the Commercial Bank of the Midland District was passed by the assembly and the council. Only the extreme radicals – who objected that the new bank would be fashioned too much in the image of the hated Bank of Upper Canada – and the extreme tories – who warned that the establishment of another bank would impair the credit of the Bank of Upper Canada – voted against it. The first president of the new bank was John Solomon Cartwright*; its first solicitor was Mackenzie.

Although obviously not a tory, Mackenzie did not sympathize with the reformers. In February 1832 he attended a reform meeting held in Fredericksburgh by assembly representatives Peter Perry* and Marshall Spring Bidwell*. He expressed his opposition to a resolution denouncing the Legislative Council and, chiding the reform members of the assembly, spoke long and effectively on the need for moderate reform without disloyalty to the crown. He then moved support for the government. Mackenzie later claimed that his motion had carried and that the meeting had been dissolved, but others, including the meeting's chairman and secretary, disputed his version of events.

Whatever happened, the fate of Mackenzie's resolution is not as important as the political ideas expressed in his two-and-a-half-hour speech. He disagreed with the expulsion of William Lyon Mackenzie* from the assembly and entered into a detailed account of the privileges of the legislature which did not follow the hard line of the tory party. Yet in phrases redolent of the tory spirit he dismissed Mackenzie as ill mannered and ill fitted to be a representative of his constituency. His moderate position regarding the clergy reserves steered directly and reasonably between the tory and reform camps. Most reformers by this time advocated the sale of the reserves, the endowment to be used to support secular education. John Strachan* and the high tories would have preferred little change in the existing situation. Mackenzie argued, as William Henry Draper* would advocate four years later, that the reserves should be used to support clergymen of all "respectable denominations." He disagreed with the more conservative elements in denying that the Church of England was or had ever been the established church in Upper Canada. The administration of Sir Peregrine Maitland*, he added, had done much that was injurious to various religious denominations, but he felt that Sir John Colborne*'s government "was on a conciliatory, moderate path."

As a lawyer Mackenzie was known to accept liberal causes, perhaps the most controversial of which was his defence of George Gurnett*, the editor of the *Courier of Upper Canada* (Toronto), who was alleged to have libelled tory John Elmsley* over the latter's conversion to Roman Catholicism. The case came before the Court of King's Bench in April 1834. Elmsley was able to retain five of the most renowned lawyers in Upper Canada – Draper, Marshall Spring Bidwell, Robert Baldwin Sullivan*, Allan Napier MacNab*, and Robert Baldwin*. Mackenzie, assisted by three other lawyers, represented the defendant and he alone spoke for the defence. After his four-and-a-half-hour speech, which was lauded throughout the Upper Canadian press as one of the most eloquent defences of freedom of the press ever voiced in the province, the jury returned a verdict for Gurnett. Mackenzie was the real victor, since his firm was now known throughout the province.

Mackenzie was a leader of the Scots community in Kingston: he was a member of the temperance society, the Emigration Society of the Midland District, and the bible society; he had been a lay commissioner at the Kingston convention of June 1831 which established the synod of the Presbyterian Church of Canada in connection with the Church of Scotland, and he often served as legal adviser to the church. He was actively associated with various committees important to the administration of town affairs, such as the committee to reform municipal government and another established in 1832 to alleviate the effects of the cholera epidemic. His name was put forward in 1834 as the Frontenac County candidate for election to the legislature, and he was widely supported throughout the campaign that summer as a moderate non-tory candidate. It seemed as though he would be elected, but his political career was cut off by his sudden death of cholera on 4 Aug. 1834.

In the early spring of 1830, 15-year-old John A. Macdonald* had been articled to Mackenzie as a student-at-law. For the next three formative years of his life he studied under Mackenzie and for most of that period boarded at the Mackenzie home. He gained his earliest understanding of the law and commerce under Mackenzie; he developed his first clientele and business contacts through him. In 1839 Macdonald became solicitor to the Commercial Bank of the Midland District, as Mackenzie had been, and on the verge of the public career denied to Mackenzie, Macdonald would also be a corporate lawyer and businessman, a moderate conservative whose fortunes and interests were tied to Kingston and to the commercial development of Upper Canada. At the time when Macdonald was articled to Mackenzie's law firm, the increasingly populous, clannish Scots community was infiltrating the positions of tory authority, was beginning to control commerce, and was laying the basis of a liberal-conservative faction whose stress on economic expansion would present an alternative to William Lyon Mackenzie's hope of establishing a rather traditional agrarian order. It was largely this same social and political group which

would coalesce and gain prominence as an emerging capitalist class in the late 1830s and 1840s. Then, it would be largely led politically by Macdonald, Mackenzie's former student.

WILLIAM TEATERO

Frontenac Land Registry Office (Kingston, Ont.), N21 (will of George Mackenzie). Law Soc. of U.C. (Toronto), Minutes, I. PAC, MG 26, A, 538. QUA, D. M. Gordon papers, general corr. Presbyterian Church of Canada in connection with the Church of Scotland, *Minutes of the convention of ministers and lay commissioners, at which the formation of a Canadian synod and presbyteries, in connection with the Church of Scotland, was determined on* (n.p., n.d.; copy in QUA, D. M. Gordon papers, box 20). *British Whig* (Kingston), 12 May 1832; 11 Feb., 1 April, 15 July 1834. *Brockville Recorder, and the Eastern, Johnstown, and Bathurst Districts Advertiser* (Brockville, [Ont.]), 18 April 1834. *Canadian Correspondent* (Toronto), 12 April 1834. *Chronicle & Gazette*, 1833–34, esp. 12 July 1834; 30 April 1836. *Colonial Advocate*, 1 March 1832. *Free Press* (Hallowell [Picton, Ont.]), 21 April 1834. *Kingston Chronicle*, 1819–33, esp. 8 Feb. 1822. *Kingston Spectator*, 17 April 1834. *Patriot* (Toronto), 11 April 1834. *Upper Canada Herald*, 6 Feb. 1832. D. [G.] Creighton, *John A. Macdonald, the young politician* (Toronto, 1952; repr. 1965). [A. M. Machar], *Memorials of the life and ministry of the Reverend John Machar, D.D., late minister of St. Andrew's Church, Kingston* (Toronto, 1873), 25, 38, 56. J. P. Macpherson, *Life of the Right Hon. Sir John A. Macdonald* (2v., Saint John, N.B., 1891), 86. W. R. Teatero, "'A dead and alive way never does': the pre-political world of John A. Macdonald" (MA thesis, Queen's Univ., Kingston, 1978). Adam Shortt, "The history of Canadian currency, banking and exchange . . . ," Canadian Bankers' Assoc., *Journal* (Toronto), 8 (1900–1): 227–43. C. L. Vaughan, "The Bank of Upper Canada in politics, 1817–1840," *OH*, 60 (1968): 185–204.

McKENZIE, HENRY, seigneurial agent, fur trader, merchant, JP, militia officer, and office holder; b. *c.* 1781 in Scotland, son of Alexander and Catherine Mackenzie; m. 1814 Ann Bethune, daughter of John Bethune* and sister of Angus*, in Montreal, and they had a son and a daughter; d. there 28 June 1832.

There were numerous McKenzies in the various categories of fur trader. Henry McKenzie, a lesser-known figure, was the brother of Roderick*, Donald*, and James*, and a cousin of Sir Alexander Mackenzie*. He came to Lower Canada as an immigrant shortly before 1800. Probably through the influence of Roderick, who was then a partner in the North West Company and would later become a partner in McTavish, Frobisher and Company, he was hired as a clerk at Grand Portage (near Grand Portage, Minn.).

In 1803 McKenzie settled not far from Montreal in the seigneury of Terrebonne, which belonged to Simon McTavish*, the chief partner in the NWC. A capitalist seigneur, McTavish had invested considerable sums to develop his fief. He ran a store as well as two extremely modern grist-mills, and he had had a bakery and a sawmill built. McKenzie probably helped him manage his seigneury, and so won his affection that McTavish left him £100 in his will. After McTavish's death in July 1804 McKenzie, as executor, ran the seigneury until his brother Roderick took possession of it. This transaction was, however, invalidated, and the property reverted to McTavish's heirs until 1832. It seems that throughout that period McKenzie continued to act as seigneurial agent. In this capacity he established contacts with grain dealers and exporters but did not sever his connection with the fur trade. Some of those he dealt with – Francis Badgley* and Peter Pangman*, for example – were retired fur traders. His association with Jacob Oldham and other fur traders in the region can be explained by the interdependence of the various sectors of the economy.

When in 1805 Alexander Mackenzie decided to retire to England, he entrusted management of his Canadian property to his cousin Henry. It may have been through his role as administrator of Sir Alexander Mackenzie and Company that Henry was again brought into close contact with the NWC. He moved in a circle of businessmen who maintained connections in Montreal and were involved in the important activities of the colony. It would come as no surprise if he had sought to ingratiate himself with William McGillivray, then the director of the NWC.

In November 1814 McKenzie purchased 2 of the 19 shares of McTavish, McGillivrays and Company which had just been reorganized by McGillivray. In so doing he became one of the partners of the Michilimackinac Company. The following year McGillivray put him in charge of public relations for the NWC, and in this capacity McKenzie saw to the preparation of rejoinders to the condemnation of the Nor'Westers' conduct by Lord Selkirk [Douglas*]. These began appearing in the *Montreal Herald* late in August 1816 under the pseudonym Mercator. They raised questions about the continued existence of the HBC and presented the NWC traders as the successors of the French explorers and fur traders.

McKenzie probably became a fairly important figure in the merchant community. He joined the Beaver Club in 1815, for example. His association with the NWC was anything but happy. Documents he made public in 1827 spoke about the emergence in 1816 of a conflict; the origins of the problem are unclear but it set him against the other partners and would explain the increasingly marginal role that he played in the company.

On 1 Aug. 1806 Henry McKenzie had obtained a commission as justice of the peace for the district of Montreal which was renewed a number of times. At the beginning of the War of 1812 he joined the Terrebonne battalion of militia as a major, and on 20 April 1814 he was promoted lieutenant-colonel. In 1824 he was appointed potash and pearl ash inspector and obtained a commission of oyer and terminer and general jail delivery. Like many Scottish expatriates in the Montreal region he was a member of the Scotch Presbyterian congregation, later known as the St Gabriel Street Church. He was on the congregation's temporal committee in 1816, 1817, and 1818, and served as its vice-chairman in 1819 and 1822, and chairman in 1823 and 1825.

FERNAND OUELLET

PAC, RG 68, General index, 1651–1841. *Docs. relating to NWC* (Wallace). *Officers of British forces in Canada* (Irving). R. Campbell, *Hist. of Scotch Presbyterian Church*. Innis, *Fur trade in Canada* (1956). Robert Rumilly, *La Compagnie du Nord-Ouest, une épopée montréalaise* (2v., Montréal, 1980). M. [E.] Wilkins Campbell, *Northwest to the sea; a biography of William McGillivray* (Toronto and Vancouver, 1975).

McKENZIE, JAMES, naval officer and steamboat captain; b. *c.* 1782 in Scotland; m. Catharine Milton, and they had three children; m. secondly Margaret Badden, and they had two children; d. 27 Aug. 1832 in Kingston, Upper Canada.

According to his own testimony, James McKenzie was "bred a seaman" and his earliest nautical experience was in the British merchant marine, which he entered as a boy around 1794. He served in the Royal Navy during the French revolutionary and Napoleonic wars, attaining the rank of master. In the spring of 1813, as part of the first Royal Navy contingent assigned to the defence of the Great Lakes, McKenzie accompanied Sir James Lucas Yeo* to Upper Canada. There he served in several roles during the war with the United States: in the gunboat service on Lake Ontario, as "master attendant" in the Kingston dockyard, and on board the *Wolfe* and *Prince Regent*. His exertions in the dockyard led Yeo to describe him as "a very worthy man and excellent officer" who had played an essential role in outfitting the expedition against Oswego, N.Y., in 1814.

At the conclusion of the war, McKenzie was reduced to half pay and returned to England, where he developed an interest in steam-engines and their marine applications. By 1817 he was back in Upper Canada and that year was appointed to the command of the steamboat *Frontenac*. The *Frontenac* was not the first steamboat in the Canadas; that honour goes to the *Accommodation*, constructed in Montreal in 1809 for John Molson*. Nor was the *Frontenac* the first steamboat on the Great Lakes – the American-built *Ontario* had begun operation on Lake Ontario in early 1817. The *Frontenac*, however, was the first Canadian-built steamboat on the lakes, its construc-

McKenzie

tion apparently instigated by military and naval authorities anxious to anticipate the Americans. The company that built her was composed of Kingston's leading businessmen, including John Kirby* and Thomas Markland*, and a shipwright involved in her construction, Henry Gildersleeve*, was to become one of the most active steamboat builders and promoters in Upper Canada. Designed to carry both passengers and freight, the *Frontenac* was described by the *Kingston Gazette* as "the best piece of naval architecture of the kind yet produced in America." It was launched at Bath on 7 Sept. 1816 and began its service between Kingston and Niagara (Niagara-on-the-Lake) the following June. In its ten-year career under the command of McKenzie, the *Frontenac* endured only one major accident, a well-publicized but relatively harmless grounding in the Thousand Islands.

Although McKenzie's critics could never fault him on his seamanship, questions were raised about his management of what proved an unprofitable business venture. McKenzie acted as the "confidential agent" of the *Frontenac*'s management committee, a role which did not protect him from the snide comments occasionally directed at the "immense salary" of both himself and his engineer. Moreover, John Strachan*, the owner of a partial share, complained bitterly that "no person here [York] ever knows any thing about her and it appears that she is entirely at the disposal of the Capt to go or come as he chooses." Others, however, shifted the blame below decks, claiming that the engineer "tyrannized" over McKenzie and determined the vessel's sailing times. When, after eight seasons, the *Frontenac* was sold to John* and Robert Hamilton of Queenston, McKenzie went to work for her new owners. Even after she was scrapped in 1827, McKenzie remained in Robert Hamilton's employ and assisted in the construction in 1828 of the *Alciope*, a much smaller vessel powered by the *Frontenac*'s machinery. He was captain of the *Alciope* for three seasons and probably part of a fourth. In 1831 Hamilton decided to install American-built high pressure equipment in the *Alciope* and McKenzie retired.

Throughout his career as Lake Ontario's premier steamboat captain, McKenzie had occasionally pursued entrepreneurial opportunities. His proposals to develop a place for outfitting and repairing vessels and for running a steam ferry between Kingston and Pittsburgh Township fell on deaf ears. After leaving active command, he became involved in the promotion of several other Upper Canadian steamers. He served on the building committee of the *John By*, which was eventually built under a contract obtained by Robert DRUMMOND, and he helped Colin Campbell Ferrie* and the other directors of the *Constitution* in negotiating terms for its construction. More important to McKenzie was the *Sir John Colborne*, the first steam vessel to run on Lake Simcoe. He had proposed

her construction, committed himself to taking 25 per cent of the stock, and arranged the delivery of her engine. None of these vessels were operating by the time of his death.

McKenzie's political interests never developed much beyond his commitment to the improvement of inland navigation. In the spring of 1828 he was appointed to the commission that built the first new lighthouse in a generation on the Upper Canadian side of Lake Ontario. Later that year, in the last provincial election of Sir Peregrine Maitland*'s administration, McKenzie ran as a conservative against Hugh Christopher THOMSON and Thomas Dalton* in the riding of Frontenac. On the hustings he asserted that "the Legislature may be regarded as the *steam-engine* of the vessel of the State" and argued that what the farmers of the riding wanted most were markets, good roads, and improved inland navigation. McKenzie placed last and, despite subsequent protests, the results stood.

By the time of his death in the cholera epidemic of 1832, McKenzie, although never claiming to be anything more than an indifferent farmer, had accumulated more than 3,500 acres of land (1,647 acres in Pittsburg Township alone), as well as town lots in Kingston and Niagara. On a personal level he was a well-read student of shipping and of engineering, his library being willed to one of his executors, John Macaulay*. Before McKenzie revealed his political leanings, he had been described in the *Colonial Advocate* as a "jolly" individual with "broad shoulders and triple chin." After his death, the relaxed hospitality of which the *Advocate* approved led others to comment on his wide circle of friends and acquaintances and the general respect in which he was held. One admirer went so far as to call him the "father of steam navigation in Upper Canada."

WALTER LEWIS

AO, MS 78, John Strachan to John Macaulay, 29 Nov. 1823; Macaulay, inventory of books [bequeathed by James McKenzie], 1832. RG 22, ser.155. PAC, MG 11, [CO 42] Q, 141, pt.II: 77–79; MG 24, I26, 4, John Hamilton to Robert Hamilton, 19 Jan. 1825; RG 1, L1, 28: 252, 254, 344, 368; 29: 148, 190; 301: 237, 278; L3, 338: M11/261, 281; 341: M12/165, 228; RG 5, A1: 26227–30; RG 8, I (C ser.), 126: 65–74, 101–2; 370: 114–17a; 730: 71–72; 731: 112–13. PRO, ADM 6/154; ADM 37/1021, 37/2347, 37/2490, 37/3818, 37/4498, 37/4686. John Howison, *Sketches of Upper Canada, domestic, local, and characteristic . . .* (Edinburgh and London, 1821; repr. [East Ardsley, Eng., and New York], 1965, and Toronto, 1970). *Town of York, 1815–34* (Firth). *Christian Guardian*, 5 Sept. 1832. *Colonial Advocate*, 18 May 1826. *Gleaner, and Niagara Newspaper*, 3 Sept. 1827. *Kingston Chronicle*, 14 Jan. 1825; 1 June 1827; 26 July, 2 Aug. 1828; 19 Aug. 1831. *Kingston Gazette*, 25 Nov. 1815; 6, 13 April, 14 Sept. 1816; 7 June, 20 Aug. 1817. *Upper Canada Gazette*, 14 Aug. 1817. *Upper Canada*

Herald, 27 May, 17 July 1828; 15–22 Dec. 1830; 29 Aug. 1832. *Western Mercury* (Hamilton, [Ont.]), 3 May 1832.

Canniff, *Hist. of the settlement of U.C.* W. A. B. Douglas, "The blessings of the land: naval officers in Upper Canada, 1815–1841," *Swords and covenants*, ed. Adrian Preston and Peter Dennis (London, 1976), 42–73. *Robertson's landmarks of Toronto*, 2: 699. Scadding, *Toronto of old* (1873). E. F. Bush, "The Canadian lighthouse," *Canadian Hist. Sites*, no.9 (1974): 61–62. E. A. Cruikshank, "Notes on the history of shipbuilding and navigation on Lake Ontario up to the time of the launching of the steamship *Frontenac*, at Ernesttown, Ontario, 7th September, 1816," *OH*, 23 (1926): 33–44. Walter Lewis, "John By," *Fresh-Water* (Kingston, Ont.), 1 (1986), no.1: 31–33. H. A. Musham, "Early Great Lakes steamships: the *Ontario* and the *Frontenac*," *American Neptune* (Salem, Mass.), 3 (1943): 333–44. R. A. Preston, "The history of the port of Kingston," *OH*, 46 (1954): 208–9.

McKINDLAY, JOHN, businessman, JP, and farmer; b. in Kilmarnock, Scotland, youngest son of Peter McKindlay, merchant; d. unmarried November 1833 in Cathkin Braes, Scotland.

John McKindlay served his apprenticeship as a clerk with Cunningham and Reid, West Indies traders in Glasgow and Greenock. In 1777 he established himself in Montreal, and the following year he invested £830 in the fur trade, a small sum compared with the largest that year of about £24,000, put up by James McGill*; ten years later McKindlay invested £4,550, the fifth largest amount advanced by an individual. He had already become one of the most important suppliers to the northwest trade by the early 1780s. Among his customers was Jean-Étienne Waddens*, and after Waddens was murdered in 1782 it was McKindlay who deposited a list of the trader's effects with a Montreal notary. McKindlay also stood security for traders, who needed guarantors of their good conduct in the Indian country in order to obtain a trading licence from government.

For a time, around 1784, McKindlay was in partnership with Étienne Dumeyniou, a French merchant in Montreal, and when Dumeyniou retired McKindlay took their clerk, William Parker, into partnership. McKindlay was also a general trader on his own account, and he did well as an importer specializing in textiles and liquor, mostly from Scotland; he had good contacts in Greenock, notably Allan, Kerr and Company, a principal Scottish firm in the trade to the colony. He was undoubtedly supplied from London by Robert Hunter, whose son Robert was hosted by McKindlay in Montreal in 1785. When Richard Dobie* mentioned to young Hunter that Montreal businessmen suffered much from fire, the latter noted "how well McKindlay has provided against it. His goods were in excellent order and his warehouses very complete." By the late 1780s a solid reputation enabled McKindlay to act as a curator of estates and business agent for merchants outside

Montreal as he did for Adam Lymburner*, a relative, in a property seizure in 1795. In the same period his own need to have properties seized for non-payment of debts owed to him may have involved him in land speculation in Montreal. He sold wholesale to rural merchants in the Montreal district, and at L'Assomption, where he was the principal supplier, and in 1792 all his customers but one were indebted to him.

It was also to collect a debt that McKindlay had the seigneury of Lac-Matapédia, owned by the rural merchant Jean-Baptiste RAYMOND, sold at sheriff's auction in 1797. When it was purchased by Patrick Langan, McKindlay acquired a one-third share, probably as payment of Raymond's debt. His dealings with Raymond reflect McKindlay's keen interest by the 1790s in the increasingly favourable prospects of Lower Canada as a grain-growing centre and a supplier of potash for markets in Britain and the West Indies. By 1795 he had begun to make large-scale purchases of those commodities, like his countryman and friend James Dunlop*. McKindlay employed agents to travel throughout the cultivated parts of the colony and buy up crops from country merchants, such as Raymond, and farmers. Among the agents were several young men, some of them his relations, brought out from Scotland on condition that they learn to speak French within a year. In 1796 McKindlay was negotiating with the Hôtel-Dieu of Montreal, either for the purchase of the sub-fief of Saint-Augustin or the lease of the farm there, but Bishop Jean-François Hubert* stopped the discussions.

McKindlay had probably achieved prosperity and a certain prominence by 1788, when he bought a two-storey stone house on Rue Notre-Dame. As a merchant he was led, like many of his colleagues, to become active in public affairs. From 1784 he signed numerous petitions for an elective assembly, which the merchants hoped to control in order to make the colony institutionally better adapted to commercial activity; when in 1792 elections were held to choose members of the first house of assembly, he was among some 20 of the city's most prominent businessmen supporting the nominations of merchants James McGill, John RICHARDSON, Joseph Frobisher*, and Alexander AULDJO in the city's two electoral districts. In 1786–87 he had been on a committee of Montreal merchants which reported to the Legislative Council on the state of commerce in the colony. In 1790 he was elected a director of the Agriculture Society in Montreal, newly formed to render colonial agriculture more commercial through the introduction of advanced techniques of cultivation and animal husbandry, an objective close to McKindlay's heart. The same year he took part in an unsuccessful campaign to secure the establishment of a custom-house at Montreal, and in November he was publicly thanked for his exertions by a group of his fellow merchants. In

McKindlay

December 1802 he was elected by an assembly of businessmen to a committee charged with pressuring London fire insurance companies operating in the city to lower their premiums.

McKindlay was also involved in public matters not directly related to commerce: in 1788 he was appointed a justice of the peace, two years later he supported the establishment of a non-sectarian university in the colony [see Jean-François Hubert], and in 1794 he was given a commission of oyer and terminer and general jail delivery. A leading light in the Scotch Presbyterian Church, in July 1803 he signed a call to James Somerville* in preference to Robert Forrest as the replacement for the congregation's disgraced minister, John YOUNG.

In March 1799 McKindlay had sold his establishment on Rue Notre-Dame for £1,500. He moved into a larger commercial establishment clustered around a two-storey stone house on Rue Saint-Paul. In addition to continuing his other activities, by June 1799 he had moved into the timber trade. According to Lord Selkirk [Douglas*], the estimated value of McKindlay's exports of all products in 1803 was £25,000, placing him among the city's ten largest exporters. By early 1804, however, he appears to have run into financial difficulties, caused in part by defaulting debtors, all Canadians and possibly retailers whom he supplied. In April 1804 he borrowed some £2,300 from Richard Dobie. About the same time he sold his business and returned to Scotland, apparently giving his friend Samuel Gerrard* power of attorney to handle his affairs in Montreal. However, the sale must have been annulled, because in April 1806 the establishment on Rue Saint-Paul was seized by the sheriff at the suit of Adam Lymburner; at that time it covered an entire city block, bounded by Saint-Paul, Saint-Denis, Sainte-Thérèse, and Saint-Vincent streets, in the centre of Montreal, "with a large commodious Dwelling House, two small houses, vaults, cellars, stores, and out houses, . . . the whole . . . well adapted for carrying on an extensive business." McKindlay apparently found the means to pay Lymburner, however, since the sale did not take place. In Scotland he lived for a time in considerable style in a mansion that he purchased at Cathkin Braes, on the outskirts of Glasgow, but by June 1806 he was established in Saltcoats. He acted as Dobie's attorney and from 1805 as an executor of the wills of Dobie and Andrew McGill, James's brother. In November 1811 he sold his Montreal business for £4,000 to Henderson, Armour and Company [see Robert Armour*].

Since at least 1796 McKindlay had been concentrating his efforts increasingly on land speculation in the Canadas. Between 1799 and 1826, but for the most part before 1806, he obtained numerous small grants in Upper Canada, totalling at least 14,000 acres scattered through 12 townships in the Ottawa and St

Lawrence valleys. In the period 1809–11 he received several extensive grants in Hinchinbrook and Hemmingford townships, Lower Canada, and in 1814 Governor Sir George Prevost* granted him 3,775 acres in Godmanchester Township, which, by the system of township leaders and associates [see Samuel GALE], may ultimately have brought him some 17,000 acres. He also bought land. On some of his properties he cut timber for export and fostered grain growing and dairy farming. He continued to promote new agricultural techniques in Lower Canada and encouraged the settlement of some of his lands by experienced immigrant farmers from Scotland and the north of England. On 12 Jan. 1822 McKindlay sold all his lands and land claims in the Canadas, except his share in the seigneury of Lac-Matapédia, to John GRAY of Montreal for £2,107. The lands in Upper Canada, then totalling around 15,000 acres, were by far the more valuable since Gray paid £1,707 for them; most of the remaining lands, comprising some 12,275 acres, were in Lower Canada.

By 1818 McKindlay had prospered sufficiently to purchase another estate at Cathkin Braes, and he moved there permanently in 1823, occasionally revisiting Lower Canada to oversee his affairs in the province. In Scotland he showed as much interest in agricultural improvement as he had in Lower Canada and tenanted his farms with men who employed advanced techniques of cattle breeding and the growing of turnips and other root crops for animal feed. He was highly regarded as a progressive landowner in circles that promoted agricultural shows and exhibitions. He invested in coal mines, shipping, and the timber trade with the Canadas. By the time of his death in 1833 he was considered a characteristic mercantile Scot who had done extremely well in the colonies.

DAVID S. MACMILLAN

ANQ-M, CN1-185, 29 janv. 1788; 29 juill. 1796; 1er déc. 1797; 20 mars 1799; 20 févr., 16 oct. 1800; 7, 27 mars 1803; 20 avril 1804; 7 nov. 1811; 25 avril 1812; CN1-187, 1er mai 1821, 12 janv. 1822. AUM, P 58, U, McKindlay to Gerrard, 2 June 1806, 31 March 1807. PAC, MG 11, [CO 42] Q, 30: 118–31; MG 24, I9, 14–17; I183, 38; MG 30, D1, 21: 173–82; RG 4, B28, 115, 1782, 1787; RG 68, General index, 1651–1841: 83, 327, 330, 332, 334. SRO, GD1/151. Douglas, Lord Selkirk's diary (White). "Inventaire des biens de feu Luc Lacorne de Saint-Luc," J.-J. Lefebvre, édit., ANQ Rapport, 1947–48: 66. Quebec Gazette, 16 June, 3 Nov. 1785; 26 July 1787; 7 Feb., 11 Dec. 1788; 10 Sept., 12 Nov. 1789; 28 Oct., 4 Nov. 1790; 16 June, 22 Dec. 1791; 19 July 1792; 23 July 1795; 23 March 1797; 20 June, 25 July, 31 Oct. 1799; 14 May 1801; 16 Feb., 31 May 1804; 7, 28 March, 21 Nov. 1805; 3 April, 1, 15 May 1806; 12 March 1812. Caron, "Inv. de la corr. de Mgr Hubert et de Mgr Bailly de Messein," ANQ Rapport, 1930–31: 344. Giroux et al., Inv. des marchés de construction des ANQ-M, 2, no.1478. Langelier, Liste des terrains concédés, 1653,

1663, 1667. *Quebec almanac*, 1791: 84. P.-G. Roy, *Inv. concessions*, 4: 85–86. R. Campbell, *Hist. of Scotch Presbyterian Church*. Miquelon, "Baby family," 189, 194. É.-Z. Massicotte, "L'honorable Gabriel Roy," *BRH*, 31 (1925): 347. Lise St-Georges, "Commerce, crédit et transactions foncières: pratiques de la communauté marchande du bourg de l'Assomption, 1748–1791," *RHAF*, 39 (1985–86): 323–43.

MACKINTOSH OF MACKINTOSH, ANGUS, 26th Chief of Clan CHATTAN and 25th Chief of Clan MACKINTOSH, businessman, JP, militia officer, and politician; b. 1755 at Castle Leathers, near Inverness, Scotland, son of Duncan Mackintosh of Castle Leathers and Agnes Dallas of Cantray; m. 17 June 1783, in Detroit, Mary Archange Baudry, *dit* Desbuttes, *dit* Saint-Martin, and they had 14 children; d. 25 Jan. 1833 at Daviot House, near Inverness.

Angus Mackintosh arrived in Detroit during the American revolution and in 1779 was a partner in Forsith, Dye, and Mackintosh. Unfortunately, his arrival coincided with the beginning of a severe downturn in the fur trade. This decline caused bitter competition within local commercial circles and in 1786, as a matter of survival, a number of prominent merchants including Mackintosh decided to cooperate in the formation of the Miamis Company [*see* John Askin*]. The project was abandoned after a few years, however, as unprofitable.

Mackintosh therefore turned to other activities to supplement his income. He became the North West Company's agent, first in Detroit and later at Sandwich (Windsor). In this capacity he assumed responsibility for its merchandise and pelts, and purchased provisions from local farmers. He continued to operate as an independent fur trader, maintaining his own *engagés* in the area southwest of Lake Erie. Like Askin, Mackintosh was chronically indebted to his Montreal suppliers. Shortly after the British evacuated Detroit in 1796, he purchased land on the south bank of the Detroit River. Here he built a small complex consisting of a store, wharf, and storehouse and a rambling frame residence, Moy House, which the family had moved into by 1799. Located just east of Sandwich, Moy was the centre of his commercial activities for the next three decades. As a merchant Mackintosh was vitally interested in shipping and several ships were built at Moy. It also became the home port for other vessels, such as the famous schooner *Nancy* [*see* Miller WORSLEY*].

Mackintosh speculated in land as well. He held extensive property in Detroit and Sandwich, on the Rouge and Raisin rivers in Michigan, in the Toledo and Sandusky areas of Ohio, and in Harwich township of the Western District. Acutely aware of the advantages of political connections, Mackintosh was one of the local merchants who supported the early

political fortunes of David William Smith*, and Smith's subsequent appointment to the post of surveyor general permitted Mackintosh in turn to assist his business friends in their land acquisitions. Occasionally, Mackintosh also sought help in land matters from his cousin Æneas Shaw*, an executive councillor.

In 1810 Mackintosh was appointed a justice of the peace. Five years later he became the paymaster to the 2nd Essex Militia. In 1820 he entered the Legislative Council. He was present during the debate over support for the Welland Canal Company and, as might be expected, supported its construction. Later, however, when the project encountered difficulties requiring repeated infusions of public monies, Mackintosh became disillusioned, doubting whether the canal would ever become operational [*see* William Hamilton Merritt*].

He experienced a deep personal loss on 10 July 1827 when his wife died. He left Moy the same year to return to Scotland, where he succeeded his late brother as the chief of Clan Mackintosh. He lived at Daviot House rather than Moy Hall, the traditional seat of the clan chieftains. After his death he was succeeded by his third son, who moved into Moy Hall in 1835.

Angus Mackintosh was a typical merchant of the period, whose activities, although impressive and diversified, were modest compared to those of Askin, Alexander Grant*, or William Robertson*. None the less, he was among that small group of entrepreneurs who left Detroit and contributed to the early commercial development of the Sandwich area and the Western District.

R. G. HOSKINS

AO, Hiram Walker Hist. Museum coll., 20-135, 20-138. Court of the Lord Lyon (Edinburgh), Public reg. of all arms and bearings in Scotland, 36: f.40. DPL, Burton Hist. Coll., Burton file E and M/929.2, Mackintosh family; Alexander Mackintosh papers, log-book of the schooner *Nancy*, 1813–14 (typescript); Mackintosh family papers. PAC, MG 19, A31. *Gentleman's Magazine*, January–June 1833: 478. *Windsor border region* (Lajeunesse). *Scotsman* (Edinburgh), 9 Feb. 1833. M. [E. Darroch] Mackintosh of Mackintosh, *The Clan Mackintosh and the Clan Chattan*, revised by Lachlan Mackintosh of Mackintosh (new ed., Loanhead, Scot., 1982), 60, 78. Christian Denissen, *Genealogy of the French families of the Detroit River region, 1701–1911*, ed. H. F. Powell (2v., Detroit, 1976), 2: 1072–73. D. R. Farrell, "Detroit, 1783–1796: the last stages of the British fur trade in the old northwest" (PHD thesis, Univ. of Western Ont., London, 1968). W. E. Stevens, "The northwest fur trade, 1763–1800," *Univ. of Ill. Studies in the Social Sciences* (Urbana), 14 (1926), no.3.

McLEAN, ARCHIBALD, JP, politician, and militia officer; b. *c.* 1753 on the Isle of Mull, Scotland, fourth son of Hector McLean of Torren (Torranbeg?) and Julia McLean; m. first Prudence French, daughter of

McLean

Captain James French of De Lancey's Brigade; m. secondly Susan Drummond, daughter of Donald Drummond of Poughkeepsie, N.Y., a brother to the laird of the McGregor estate of Balhaldie, near Stirling, Scotland; d. 18 Feb. 1830 in Nashwaak (Durham Bridge), N.B.

It is not known when Archibald McLean immigrated to America. On 1 Oct. 1777 he became an ensign in the New York Volunteers, one of the first of the loyalist regiments to be formed during the American revolution. He was promoted lieutenant in 1779 and captain in 1781, serving with distinction in a number of engagements, notably at the battle of Eutaw Springs, S.C. Placed on half pay in 1783, McLean went to New Brunswick with members of his disbanded regiment, choosing land on the Nashwaak River near his father-in-law, Captain French, and in close proximity to a number of Highland Scots, most of whom were disbanded soldiers of the 42nd Foot. Patrick CAMPBELL, who met McLean in 1791, spoke of the willingness with which all members of his wife's family worked together to clear the land and run their farm, usually without the help of servants. McLean almost certainly lived in this way in those early years, but despite the hard physical conditions of the frontier he and his friends tried to emulate the life-style and manners of the British gentry.

In 1793 McLean was elected one of York County's representatives in the House of Assembly where, in the long conflict between Lieutenant Governor Thomas Carleton* and James Glenie*, he was a firm supporter of the administration. In 1802, after the opposition members had left town, he figured prominently as one of those members of the rump who insisted on passing the revenue bill even though no quorum existed. Among the amendments made to the original bill was one which took the salary of clerk of the assembly away from Samuel Denny STREET, the assembly's choice for that position, and made it available to the lieutenant governor's candidate, Dugald Campbell*, McLean's brother-in-law. That autumn McLean was re-elected when York County returned four of Carleton's supporters in one of the bitterest elections in the history of the province. A justice of the peace, in October he joined six of his fellow magistrates in a petition praying that Caleb Jones* be removed from the bench for having conducted himself in a disloyal manner by expressing pro-American sentiments in his canvass of the voters. A solid majority of the members of the assembly elected in 1802 favoured the government. McLean became chairman of several important committees and was a leading figure in managing affairs in the sessions from 1803 to 1808. A bid by two unsuccessful candidates, Peter Fraser* and Duncan McLeod, to have the election in York declared invalid was turned down by the government majority in 1803. Both, however, were elected in 1809, at which time McLean retired from politics. It appears likely that the class feeling between the merchants and the "aristocrats," which was to continue as a prominent feature of Fredericton life, was influencing local politics by the beginning of the century.

Already an active militia officer, McLean was named, in December 1810, staff adjutant to Lieutenant-Colonel Joseph Gubbins, the inspecting field officer of the militia forces of New Brunswick. He accompanied Gubbins on extensive tours of the colony and was himself appointed to perform the duties of inspecting field officer when Gubbins left New Brunswick in 1816. He also served for a time as aide-de-camp to the lieutenant governor. As a justice of the peace for several decades, McLean almost certainly played a significant role in local affairs, but information on this aspect of his career is scant, for the records of York County have not survived. He was also a leading layman in the Church of England in the parish of St Marys.

McLean's career as an elected politician came to an end just 25 years after the founding of New Brunswick. Like Edward Winslow*, at whose funeral he was a pallbearer, he had a vision of a provincial society led by its gentry. Member of a family of Highland lordlings who from being the military leaders of a clan society became unquestioning supporters of the British social and political system, he upheld rural conservative values and looked upon government, in part, as a dispenser of benefits to the natural leaders of society. In common with many among the gentry, he found an outlet for his talents during the military interlude of the Napoleonic and 1812 wars. Afterwards, he was a member of the circle around the lieutenant governor and in the administration which rather unwillingly came to terms with the commercial and democratic spirit that accompanied the development of the timber trade.

Of the many half-pay loyalist officer gentry who came to the Nashwaak valley in the 1780s, only Archibald McLean came near to realizing the dream of establishing a landed family there. His two marriages produced four sons, of whom Allen commanded a unit of the New Brunswick militia and William served as sheriff of York County. Of his eight daughters, three, and possibly four, moved to Upper Canada; Salome's husband, James Scott Howard*, became postmaster of that colony. The other daughters married locally and lived near their parents. Three of the sons had prosperous farms on lands granted to their father and Captain French, and followed the tradition of landed gentry by serving as militia officers and local magistrates. Helped by timely inheritances from relatives in the West Indies and Scotland and by their own enterprise and good management, they retained their social position and prestige into the second half of the 19th century.

D. M. YOUNG

474

N.B. Museum, A33 (Notebook on the New York Volunteers and the King's American Regiment, [probably by Jonas Howe]); Webster MS coll., packet 117, item 1. PANB, MC 300, MS2/121; MC 315; MC 1156; RG 1, RS558, A1a, G. S. Smyth to Lieut.-Col. Addison, 26 March 1816; RG 2, RS8, unarranged Executive Council docs., petition of the magistrates of the county of York, 14 Oct. 1802; RG 4, RS24, S8-M9; RG 7, RS75, A, 1832, Archibald MacLean. P. Campbell, *Travels in North America* (Langton and Ganong). Creon [S. D. Street], *A statement of facts relative to the proceedings of the House of Assembly on Wednesday the third, and Thursday the fourth of March, 1802, at the close of the last session* ... ([Saint John, N.B.], 1802). Gubbins, *N.B. journals* (Temperley). N.B., House of Assembly, *Journal*, 1793–1808. *Winslow papers* (Raymond). *Royal Gazette* (Fredericton), 3 Jan. 1801, 26 Sept. 1808, 24 Feb. 1830. Chadwick, *Ontarian families*, 2: 190–91. *Commemorative biographical record of the county of York, Ontario* ... (Toronto, 1907), 277–78. Beckwith Maxwell, *Hist. of central N.B.* Esther Clark Wright, *The loyalists of New Brunswick* (Fredericton, 1955; repr. Moncton, N.B., 1972, and Hantsport, N.S., 1981). I. L. Hill, *Fredericton, New Brunswick, British North America* ([Fredericton?, 1968?]). Nashwaak Bicentennial Assoc., *And the river rolled on . . . : two hundred years on the Nashwaak* (Nashwaak Bridge, N.B., 1984).

McLEAN, NEIL, army and militia officer, office holder, politician, and judge; b. 1759 in Mingary, Scotland, son of John McLean and his wife Elizabeth; m. 1784 Isabella Macdonell, youngest daughter of John Macdonell of Leek, probably at New Johnstown (Cornwall, Ont.), and they had three sons – the most notable of whom was Archibald* – and five daughters; d. 3 Sept. 1832 in St Andrews, Upper Canada.

Neil McLean immigrated to North America as a young man. During the early years of the American revolution he joined the 1st battalion, Royal Highland Emigrants (84th Foot), commanded by Allan MacLean*, as an ensign. Promoted lieutenant, he went on half pay when the unit was disbanded in 1784 and, with other loyalist Highlanders, settled in Township No.2 (Cornwall). For his services he received a land grant of 2,000 acres. A leading Presbyterian and a Highland gentleman and officer, McLean was a pre-eminent figure in the local community, his importance being reflected primarily in his military service and office holding. In May 1796, for instance, he joined the 2nd battalion, Royal Canadian Volunteer Regiment, commanded by John McDonell* (Aberchalder), as a captain. When it was disbanded in 1802, McLean once again returned to the status of a half-pay officer. He was one of the first senior officers in the Stormont militia and rose to a colonelcy during the War of 1812.

McLean held a host of regional offices of varying degrees of importance: justice of the peace, district treasurer, sheriff, trustee of the district grammar school, road commissioner, judge of the surrogate court, chairman of the land board, inspector of shops, stills, and tavern licences, and commissioner to administer the oath of allegiance. The apex of his career in public office was his appointment in 1815, along with Thomas CLARK, Thomas FRASER, and William Dickson*, to the Legislative Council.

McLean was a founding member of the Highland Society of Canada, established at St Raphaels in November 1818 and dedicated to the goal of preserving "the language, martial spirit, dress, music and antiquities of the Ancient Caledonia." He served on the executive of the society for many years. McLean died in 1832 at his home after a long and painful illness; he was, apparently, the last surviving officer of the 84th.

ALLAN J. MacDONALD

[McLean's career is sometimes confused with that of Neil McLean*. A.J.MACD.]
AO, MU 1780, A-1-2, Miles Macdonell to John Macdonell, 9 May 1807; RG 1, C-I-1; RG 22, ser.47, 1. PAC, RG 5, A1: 2190–91, 7142–44, 19538–48. *Upper Canada Herald*, 12 Sept. 1832. Armstrong, *Handbook of Upper Canadian chronology* (1967), 30–32, 159–60. Read, *Lives of the judges*, 160. *York almanac*, 1826: 119, 121–22. J. G. Harkness, *Stormont, Dundas and Glengarry: a history, 1784–1945* (Oshawa, Ont., 1946), 104–5.

McMILLAN, ARCHIBALD, businessman, settlement promoter, settler, militia officer, office holder, and JP; b. 23 Feb. 1762 on Murlaggan farm, district of Lochaber, Scotland, son of Alexander McMillan, tacksman, and Margaret Cameron; m. 7 Dec. 1793 Isabella Gray in Fort William, Scotland, and they had 13 children, of whom at least two died in childhood; d. 19 June 1832 in Montreal.

Archibald McMillan's father was the head of the McMillans of Loch Arkaig, who had been tacksmen, or leaseholders, of the chiefs of Clan Cameron since the 14th century. In 1745 they participated in the Jacobite rising, and the following year they took part under Alexander McMillan in a famous charge of Clan Cameron which broke a British regiment at the battle of Culloden; Captain James Wolfe* remarked upon the pertinacity and courage of the Cameron–McMillan "tribe" on this occasion. As a youth Archibald was sent to London to learn commercial and clerical work with a firm trading to the East Indies. However, appalled by the violence of the no-popery riots caused by Lord George Gordon in 1780, and finding business life uncongenial, he returned to the Highlands. By 1798 he had succeeded his father as head of the McMillans of Loch Arkaig, and was, as tacksman of Murlaggan, looking after his small estate and its tenantry. Sensitive and intelligent, he felt keenly the distress that afflicted his poorer clansmen as a result of economic depression in that part of the Highlands, considerable increases in rents since the mid 1700s, and a growing tendency for landowners to

McMillan

introduce sheep on lands occupied by tenants. By 1802 he had decided to take a contingent of farmers to Lower Canada. On 3 July, with more than 400 of his people in three ships, he sailed from Fort William to Montreal, which was reached in September. During the crossing the passengers had been given poor quality subsistence, and at Montreal they were forbidden by the ships' captains to take with them what provisions they had saved. McMillan sued on their behalf and obtained favourable judgement from a tribunal of two Montreal merchants, James McGill* and John McKindlay.

Armed with letters of recommendation to the influential Simon McTavish*, McMillan may have worked for the North West Company for a time. In 1803 he set up as a general merchant in a modest commercial establishment on Rue Saint-Paul, bought in March for £560. He immediately acquired an agent at Quebec in fellow Highlander John Munro, and thereafter he established connections in Scotland, the West Indies, Albany, N.Y., and York (Toronto) where a friend from the Highlands, Duncan Cameron, was his agent by 1805. He became a member of the Scotch Presbyterian Church, later known as St Gabriel Street Church, and by 1804 he was on its governing committee.

Since many of the people McMillan had brought out spoke only Gaelic and knew no system of farming other than cattle-raising or the primitive agriculture known as crofting, he hoped to obtain a grant of land on which to settle them together, with the intention of recreating Highland society, without its abuses, under himself as laird. In August 1804, assisted by John Young*, a member of the land committee of the Executive Council and a friend of Munro, McMillan petitioned for land in Suffolk, Templeton, and Grenville townships on the Grand, or Ottawa, River but he soon ran into the bureaucratic delays that characterized the unwieldy land-granting system in the colony. Discouraged, and attracted by the blandishments of influential Upper Canadian Scots eager to increase the population of their localities and hence the market value of their holdings, many of McMillan's Highlanders left for Glengarry, Upper Canada, where they had relatives. "Our countrymen have a great aversion to go upon new lands," McMillan complained to a Highland acquaintance in 1805. "They are afraid to encounter fresh difficulties & they [hive?] together among their friends formerly settled in the country who encourage them as they find them useful in clearing their lands, without considering they are losing time for a bare subsistence." At least 80 of McMillan's associates promised to sell to him for from 5 to 15 shillings each their expected grants of 200 acres, according to the Lower Canadian system of township leaders and associates [see Samuel GALE]. In spite of the delays McMillan maintained his confidence in "the influence of Mr Young who has been uniformly friendly to the cause," and his patience was rewarded in 1807 with patents on 13,261 acres in Suffolk (which had been renamed Lochaber) Township and nearly one-half of Templeton Township. In October he was able to sell a lot of 200 acres in the first range of Lochaber for £50.

McMillan was an ardent promoter of immigration. To Highland acquaintances he vaunted the cheapness of living in the colony, where there were no taxes and the cost of establishment was moderate. In the immediate vicinity of Montreal, he wrote to one in 1805, "you can purchase a Farm with a suitable House offices Garden and Fences in compleat repair for 4 a £600 . . . , at the distance of 30 to 40 miles from this a Farm could be purchased for £150 a £200." He portrayed his own situation in glowing terms: he was able to educate his children conveniently; in business he was supported "by some of the first Characters" in Montreal, and there and at Quebec he commanded credit easily; Highland immigrants were "powering down every day in most astonishing numbers"; and even those who settled in Glengarry and Lancaster brought their produce to him in exchange for farm utensils and necessities. Initially he had conducted almost all his business in Gaelic, but by September 1803 he had acquired a sufficient number of French-speaking customers to have learned to "blaber pretty well upon Business in that language," which his little boys spoke better than English.

McMillan quickly diversified his business activities. He purchased imported goods with Upper Canadian produce and then sold his purchases in Montreal, York, and Quebec, where Munro was also sent agricultural and wood products from Upper Canada. If McMillan declined an invitation from Alexander McDonell*, Roman Catholic priest at Glengarry, to deal in potash and pearl ash from that settlement, he was ready by January 1805 to try the Newfoundland market in order to maximize the return on his expeditions to and from Europe by picking up fish en route. He was the Montreal agent for a Highlander merchant in Trois-Rivières, who obtained for McMillan a contract to furnish cloth for the making of military uniforms. He engaged in speculative ventures in the West Indies and purchased London bills in Montreal "to take advantage of the discount here & premium in New York and Boston." His banker, Alexander AULDJO, bought and sold stocks on the London market on his behalf.

By May 1807, however, according to McMillan, trade had become so flat that he was considering betaking himself "to the woods as my dernier resort." Costs in obtaining the patent on the lands in Lochaber and Templeton had obliged him to borrow from Munro. The latter was pressed to obtain for McMillan the patent on lands in Grenville, where McMillan intended to establish himself as a drawing card for settlers. Munro succeeded in January 1808, and McMillan began selling off stock-in-trade in Montreal and making frequent trips up the Ottawa to prepare the site of a homestead and mills. However, by summer he had perceived the immensity of his task and, abandoning hopes of immediate settlement on his land, had hired an agent for the Grenville project.

Returning to business, in September 1808 McMillan contemplated a "wild" gamble, the sending of a cargo of flour, fish, and other products to Cuba, the Floridas, and Spain or Portugal in order to open new channels of trade, "the old tract being so hackneyed that an honest man can hardly live by the gleanings of it." He formed a partnership with Alexander Cameron, and they opened a liquor and dry-goods establishment, called Cameron and McMillan, in leased premises in Montreal's lower town market. By late 1808 McMillan was preparing to send squared oak from Grenville, Norway pine, and staves to Munro, who owned a timber cove at Sillery; in February 1809 he sold 10,000 staves, worth £700, to one Quebec merchant.

Land settlement and development remained, none the less, an activity of interest to McMillan. In 1809 he, Cameron, and Simon Zelotes Watson, an associate at Quebec, proposed to draw Highlanders who had settled in the United States to Lower Canadian lands near the American border. The project was endorsed by the Executive Council and Watson was sent off to the United States with a sum of money. He disappeared. McMillan and Cameron tried once more, this time with the trustworthy Munro at Quebec; in the autumn they proposed first to Surveyor General Joseph Bouchette* and then to Governor Sir James Henry Craig* to settle Highlanders from Britain and the United States on a block of 150,000 acres south of the St Lawrence River at a rate of 300 settlers a year for five years. The government was to sell the land on easy terms to McMillan and Cameron, who, from profits on resale to immigrants, would build a road to Quebec. The scheme came to naught.

In 1809 McMillan increased his holdings in Grenville and Templeton through purchase and the lease of crown and clergy reserve lots. By November 1809 he had invested heavily in mills in Lochaber and was negotiating loans to build others in Templeton. He tried to attract settlers by adopting the tactics of his Upper Canadian competitors in development and by arguing that North West Company traders would purchase pork, flour, and butter along the Ottawa en route to the northwest. The following spring he sold his property on Rue Saint-Paul for £800, sublet the premises in the lower town market, and moved to Grenville.

McMillan soon found that profits could be made more quickly from lumbering than from farming. A tariff preference accorded by Britain to colonial lumber during the Napoleonic Wars made the timber trade highly lucrative, and a brief period of post-war prosperity maintained the boom [see Peter Patterson*]. McMillan's holdings were advantageous; Grenville and Lochaber were covered with pine and oak, both in demand for naval construction, and were veined with streams capable of carrying the logs to the Ottawa, while Templeton had beech, maple, basswood, pine, and some oak. In 1812 Christopher Idle, Brother and Company, a major London firm [see William Price*], ordered from McMillan 10,000 cubic feet of squared Norway pine, worth £400–£500. By 1816 he had seven sawmills and was employing many of his former crofters as lumberjacks and workers in the mills. In 1817 he formed an association with Thomas Noyes of Chatham Township; Noyes cut and rafted McMillan's timber, while McMillan delivered and sold it at Quebec. McMillan also established a general store in Grenville by 1821. His suppliers and backers, almost all in Montreal, included John* and Thomas Torrance, Gillespie, Moffatt and Company, the Bank of Montreal, and John Molson and Sons.

Devoted to lumbering, McMillan neglected settlement. In 1815 Surveyor General Bouchette praised the settlement efforts of the late Daniel Robertson* in Chatham, to the east of McMillan, and Philemon Wright* in Hull Township to the west, but he had no accolades for McMillan. In September 1821 the land committee of the Executive Council recommended to Governor Lord Dalhousie [Ramsay*] the escheating of all of McMillan's grants for which conditions of settlement had not been fulfilled. McMillan appealed to Dalhousie's Scottish blood, charging that Americans, wanting to reserve the valley for themselves, were painting a dismal picture of its agricultural possibilities to prospective Scottish farmers. He asked the influential William McGILLIVRAY to intervene with Dalhousie on behalf of "your Countrymen being kept in the back ground & deprived of their rights by designing Yankees who if encouraged will sooner or later be the ruin of this Country." On the back of McMillan's petition Dalhousie scratched that the Highlander was "a likely person to promote settlement, . . . [but] I do not think him a fit person to be employed or attended to in any manner whatever." Yet an extension was granted. In 1822 or 1823 McMillan lost his lease on the crown and clergy reserve lots for non-payment of rent. A new threat of escheat was blamed on "machinations" by Wright, who had established a timber enterprise in Hull Township and, McMillan complained, "has nothing so much at heart as to root me out of the River." Apprehending "the shamefull mortification of being foiled by such a vile person," he exhorted his son Alexander, in Montreal, to find a friend in government. Dalhousie was petitioned

McMillan

again, but in vain; the lands were escheated some time later.

By the early 1820s the lumber trade, too, had soured for McMillan. He had always been obliged to conduct it, like his other business activities, in the face of great transportation difficulties, stocks frequently being lost in the rapids of the Ottawa, but high prices generally in Britain had carried him through. However, a depression in the period 1819–22 irrevocably damaged his business. In 1825 he had debts "to a large amount," the result of having stood security for two sons "who have been unfortunate in the Lumber trade for 3 years back." Among his principal creditors were Horatio Gates and Company and James Ross of Montreal. Around 1827, in the midst of another depression, McMillan was forced out.

As a man of education, connections, and moderate wealth in a virtual wilderness, McMillan assumed a certain social leadership. In 1812 he was commissioned a major in the Argenteuil battalion of militia, largely composed of Lochaber emigrants. After war was declared with the United States that year, his unit marched rapidly to Pointe-Claire. It conducted successful raids in the Highland tradition, especially around Ogdensburg, N.Y., where much plunder, particularly horses and cattle, was carried off. McMillan was praised by the high command for his "activity and diligence" in these actions. In August 1816 he was appointed a commissioner for the erection of free schools in Chatham Township, and by 1819 he had been made deputy postmaster in the settlement of Grenville; he subsequently became postmaster. In February 1819 he was offered a commission of the peace, but he refused it. Seven months later he asked Munro to retrieve it; canal construction had introduced into the region "a motley population of 3 or 4 hundred military as well as civilians from Ireland & other quarters . . . [who] commit every species of fraud Impunits & I being next them suffer most." He had an abhorrence of litigation, however, and soon gained a reputation as a conciliatory magistrate.

A leader among the Presbyterians of the area, in December 1824 McMillan reported to the Reverend Henry Esson* of Montreal on the state of the denomination in the lower Ottawa valley. Earlier, he had led in petitioning the Lower Canadian government for a grant of land and money to encourage construction of a church and, when Dalhousie refused, had himself donated a lot. In 1827 the inhabitants of the seigneury of Petite-Nation decided to ask for a resident priest, and, at the request of Denis-Benjamin Papineau*, McMillan held a meeting of the Irish and Scottish Catholics of Grenville and Chatham townships at which it was agreed to help support the priest in return for his services. McMillan donated the land for a Catholic church. His own sizeable log house was known throughout the region as "the Old Abbey"

because of its isolated location in the woods by the Ottawa; it was nevertheless one of the best known social centres in the valley, and there travellers and visiting dignitaries were entertained with Highland hospitality.

Although a leader on the lower Ottawa, McMillan enjoyed little success in his relations with government, particularly with Lord Dalhousie, even though the governor was a Presbyterian and McMillan a strong supporter of the English party in the colony, on which Dalhousie depended politically. A Lowlander, Dalhousie may have shared the Scottish landowners' dislike for Highland emigration and hence harboured ill feeling for McMillan as a promoter of it. In the summer of 1827 McMillan campaigned strongly on behalf of Nicolas-Eustache LAMBERT Dumont and John Simpson*, the government candidates in a fiercely fought contest in York ultimately won by the opposition Canadian party. McMillan's chief rivals on the Ottawa, the Americans Philemon and Ruggles Wright Sr, exercised more influence than he in Montreal and Quebec. In 1825 he had complained to Simpson of the government's "Yankee fashion of appointing the commission persons" on the basis of petitions by people "generally republicans if not radicals without education or knowledge." In 1826–27 Ruggles Wright and Thomas Mears attempted to have McMillan fired as postmaster of Grenville, charging him with responsibility for the poor postal service between that place and Hull. McMillan blamed the Hull post office and the mail transport furnished by the only steamboat on the river, the *Union*, of which Mears was a proprietor. Mears had in fact probably learned of secret negotiations between McMillan and John Torrance of Montreal to launch a rival steamboat on the river and to wrest the mail contract from the owners of the *Union*. The affair ended with McMillan keeping his post but abandoning plans for a steamboat service.

By September 1827 the Wrights had won the war of attrition; McMillan acknowledged "an indolence which has become of late habitual," the result of having been "thwarted in . . . my land speculations" by a government favourite "jealous of my having secured some prominent situation on the River." In 1828 he retired from the 3rd Battalion of York Militia with the rank of major and from the postmastership at Grenville. He returned to Montreal that year in order to provide his younger children with a good education, and there he died of cholera in June 1832, three days before his son Alexander.

Archibald McMillan is outstanding as an example of a Highland leader who organized and brought a party of his people to the Canadas. Despite initial difficulties, most of the immigrants made a success of settlement, largely in Glengarry, where the 1852 census shows 545 McMillans, but also in Grenville and in Lochaber, where a township map of 1879 shows numerous farms held by families of that name. McMillan is also interesting because his correspondence documents abundantly the unceasing efforts of an ambitious Scot with a desire for adventure and a penchant for innovation to carve out his niche in Lower Canadian society using his Highland heritage and connections as his principal tools. Scandalized by the social injustice experienced by crofters in a homeland he nevertheless loved, he dreamt of transferring the basic structure of traditional Highland society to a land of unlimited potential for economic growth and of himself becoming a new world laird. The dream was never realized, yet the dreamer had not entirely failed. He had planted a seed, and the seed would grow; only the new plant was not a replica of the old stock.

JAMES H. LAMBERT and DAVID S. MACMILLAN

ANQ-M, CN1-185, 14 mars 1803; 1er mai 1804; 1er avril, 17 mai, 21 sept., 6 oct., 23 nov. 1807; 25 avril, 22 août, 1er oct. 1808; 11, 27 févr., 16, 31 mars, 18 nov., 1er déc. 1809; 2 févr., 1er mars 1810; 3, 17 avril 1811; 5 févr. 1812; CN1-187, 16 févr. 1810; 1er févr., 10 nov. 1821; 13 sept. 1824; 15 déc. 1827. PAC, MG 24, I183; RG 1, L3L: 569, 609, 780–87, 1317, 1320, 1548, 1552, 2126, 2131, 5415–20, 5428–31, 27147–59, 62446–61, 65065–68, 66477–733, 95134–58, 96506–13; RG 68, General index, 1651–1841: 263, 354, 362, 639. L.C., House of Assembly, *Journals*, 1823, app.T. Bouchette, *Topographical description of L.C.*, 248–51. Langelier, *Liste des terrains concédés*, 1650, 1672. R. Campbell, *Hist. of Scotch Presbyterian Church*, 233–34. Michel Chamberland, *Histoire de Notre-Dame des Sept-Douleurs de Grenville, P.Q.* (Montréal, 1931), 29, 38, 280, 284. Somerled MacMillan, *Bygone Lochaber historical and traditional* (Glasgow, 1971), 66–70; *The emigration of Lochaber Mac Millans to Canada in 1802* (Paisley, Scot., 1958). John Prebble, *The Highland clearances* (London, 1963); *Mutiny: Highland regiments in revolt, 1743–1804* (London, 1975). John Stewart of Ardvorlich, *The Camerons: a history of Clan Cameron* ([Glasgow], 1974).

MACPHERSON, DONALD, army officer; b. *c.* 1755 in Inverness-shire, Scotland; he may have married Elspeth Macpherson, and they had at least one child, Allan, "Laird of Napanee"; m. 23 Jan. 1795 Ann Shaw in the parish of Laggan, Inverness-shire, and they had three sons and six daughters; d. 25 Feb. 1829 in Kingston, Upper Canada.

Donald Macpherson's parentage and early life are surrounded by a haze of uncertainty, but the details of his military career are clear enough. In 1775, with the American revolution, Macpherson joined the 71st Foot. After receiving his first commission on 15 Jan. 1777 as a lieutenant with the 4th battalion of the New Jersey Volunteers, Macpherson served with this loyalist corps at Staten Island, N.Y., during 1777 and

most of 1778. However, he spent the greater part of the war with the 71st Foot, from August 1778 as an ensign with the 2nd battalion, and then from 19 Oct. 1779 as a lieutenant with the 1st battalion.

After returning to Scotland in 1783, Macpherson refused to lapse into half-pay obscurity. He seldom lost an opportunity to resume his career of soldiering. In 1794 he recruited at "considerable expense" a company for the Loyal Cheshire Regiment and in 1798 he assembled a company of clansmen called the Cluny Volunteers. On 9 July 1803 he received the rank of captain in the 92nd Foot, and on 1 Jan. 1805 that of major in the army. In January 1806 he was transferred to an old soldier battalion, the 9th Royal Veterans.

It was as a major of the 10th Royal Veteran Battalion that Macpherson was introduced to Canada. He arrived in Quebec with his family in 1807, and in 1809 was "honored with the Command" of the post at Kingston. Macpherson's pre-1812 administration at Kingston was uneventful, being characterized largely by a prodigious output of estimates for pointing, whitewashing, and carpentry, designed more to fortify the town against the weather than to repulse an enemy.

At the outbreak of the War of 1812, Macpherson decried the "critical" shortage of small ordnance and the disrepair of the barracks and public buildings at Kingston. The following year a line of fortified blockhouses and pickets changed the town's military face. Their construction was testimony not only to an emergency building program, but also to Macpherson's supervision and resolve to use "every exertion in my power . . . for the defence of this post."

Although it is generally believed that Macpherson spent the War of 1812 as commanding officer at Kingston, documentation proves otherwise. His daughter's recollections of bullets penetrating "the wooden walls of the pretty white cottage that then did duty as the commandant's residence" places Macpherson there during Commodore Isaac Chauncey's abortive attack of November 1812. However, by May 1813 Macpherson had transferred to Quebec, where he assumed command of the 10th. He was promoted lieutenant-colonel on 18 Nov. 1813. Although one of his children referred giddily to life in Quebec as "very gay, balls every other night," Macpherson's duties were seldom glamorous. His was the dull, desk-bound task of commanding a body of aged and infirm soldiers, certifying widows' pensions, recommending officers for promotion, and compiling returns of claims. He remained in Quebec until December 1816 to supervise the final departure of several detachments of his disbanded battalion for Europe.

When Macpherson, now reduced on full pay, returned to Kingston in 1817, he appeared to have all the props and pretensions of a prosperous, well-settled

Mactaggart

man. The "old Veteran officer," stocky in appearance and ruddy in complexion, had an air of substance about him. The government responded generously to his memorials for land, and he had ample grants situated in Kingston itself and in the townships of Eramosa, Nassagaweya, and Melbourne.

By 1820 Macpherson had retired to a property he nostalgically called Cluny, located in Pittsburgh Township near Kingston. But retirement was not synonymous with retreat. As part of a group of socially prominent Kingstonians, Macpherson lent his arm and pocket-book to a variety of civic and moral causes. He subscribed to the Kingston Compassionate Society (1817) and the Cataraqui Bridge Company (1826), acted as a director of the Kingston Boarding and Day School for Young Ladies (1826–28), and served as a representative for Pittsburgh and Wolfe Island in the agricultural society for the Midland District (1819–20). In 1822 he was ordained one of the founding elders of St Andrew's Presbyterian Church, Kingston, by the Reverend John BARCLAY.

Macpherson's devotion to clan and kinship was no less noteworthy. It was to his door and his patronage that his in-laws the Macdonalds came from Glasgow in the summer of 1820. The half-sister relationship between the colonel's wife, Ann Shaw, and Hugh Macdonald's wife, Helen Shaw, drew the families together. Tradition holds that as a schoolboy John A. Macdonald* was a frequent visitor to the Macpherson household, where he sampled his uncle's library and the "slices of pudding" set aside by Macpherson's youngest daughter.

Macpherson's civic activity waned during the last years of his life. As early as 1820, sobered by the "Certainty of Death," he prepared his will, outlining the disposition of his lands, army pension, and "Household furniture Plate Bed and Table Linen." By 1826 the local newspaper was advertising the sale of his "fine farm." Recurring bouts of "Fever and Ague" and rheumatism kept him convalescent. Macpherson died on 25 Feb. 1829, aged 74. "A large concourse of Inhabitants" witnessed his burial with military honours. In their silent prayers they acknowledged the passing of an "Officer and a Gentleman" who had spent 54 years "in the Service of His King and Country."

LAURIE C. C. STANLEY

[The author acknowledges the generous assistance of Professor Alan G. Macpherson and the Honourable George F. G. Stanley. In addition, private papers in the possession of Mrs Jean and Mrs Lisa Macpherson (Toronto) and Major J. P. C. Macpherson (Kingston, Ont.) were consulted in the preparation of this biography. L.C.C.S.]

ACC, Diocese of Ont. Arch. (Kingston), St George's Cathedral (Kingston), reg. of baptisms, 1812: 80. Allan Macpherson House (Napanee, Ont.), Dress sword inscription. AO, RG 1, A-I-6, 6; C-I-3, 20, 109; C-I-4, 4; C-IV,

Kingston (town), pp.2531–33; Pittsburgh Township, lot C front, pp.20–22; RG 22, ser.155; RG 53, ser.55, 4–16. Cataraqui Cemetery Company (Kingston), Reg. of burials, 1834–1940 (mfm. at Kingston Public Library); Tombstone inscription. General Reg. Office (Edinburgh), Laggan, reg. of baptisms, marriages, and burials. PAC, MG 26, A, 549: 258896–928; RG 1, L1, 14: 247–48; 28: 264, 317; L3, 273: K15/54n–q; 335A: M10/2–2a; 337A: M11/177–77a; 338: M11/ 237–37b; L3^L: 1585, 2167, 2387, 67053–80; RG 5, A1: 4891–92, 5699, 5701, 27325–26; RG 8, I (C ser.), 1–4, 6, 275, 548–49, 551–52, 554, 676, 688A, 789–90, 1168, 1203½H, 1218, 1707, 1858, 1860. PRO, WO 13/4376; WO 31, bundle 219. QUA, Frontenac County land reg. copy books, book C, F-145, instrument 315: 15–16; book J, F-249, instrument 146: 214. St Andrew's Presbyterian Church (Kingston), Memorial wall plaque; Reg. of baptisms, 1821–59; Reg. of marriages, 1822–57 (mfm. at QUA). St Andrew's Presbyterian Church (Quebec), Reg. of baptisms, marriages, and burials, 1770–1816 (mfm. at PAC). *Kingston before War of 1812* (Preston). David Stewart, *Sketches of the character, manners, and present state of the Highlanders of Scotland; with details of the military service of the Highland regiments* (2v., Edinburgh, 1822), 2. *Kingston Chronicle*, 1819–20, 1826–29. *Kingston Gazette*, 9 Dec. 1817. *Loyalist* (York [Toronto]), 14 March 1829. *Quebec Gazette*, 17 Sept. 1807, 9 March 1829. *Quebec Mercury*, 7 March 1829. *Star and Commercial Advertiser* (Quebec), 7 March 1829. G.B., WO, *Army list*, 1779–1817. D. [G.] Creighton, *John A. Macdonald, the young politician* (Toronto, 1952; repr. 1965). W. S. Herrington, *History of the county of Lennox and Addington* (Toronto, 1913; repr. Belleville, Ont., 1972). Mary Jukes, *New life in old houses* (Don Mills [Toronto], 1966). J. P. Macpherson, *Life of the Right Hon. Sir John A. Macdonald* (2v., Saint John, N.B., 1891); with reproduction of miniature of Donald Macpherson. A. G. Macpherson, "An old Highland parish register: survivals of clanship and social change in Laggan, Inverness-shire, 1775–1854, [part] II," *Scottish Studies* (Edinburgh), 12 (1968): 81–111. G. F. G. Stanley, "The Macpherson–Shaw–Macdonald connection in Kingston," *Historic Kingston*, no.13 (1965): 3–20. R. L. Way, "Soldiering at Fort Henry," *Canadian Geographical Journal* (Ottawa), 48 (January–June 1954): 178–99.

MACTAGGART, JOHN, engineer and author; b. 26 June 1791 near Plunton Castle in the parish of Borgue, Kirkcudbrightshire, Scotland; d. 8 Jan. 1830 at Torrs (near Kirkcudbright), Scotland.

According to his own account, John Mactaggart, the son of a Galloway farmer and one of 11 children, obtained his early education in "snatches" from tutors hired by his father on behalf of the local farmers and from reading and observing. When of an age to travel the four miles to Kirkcudbright, he attended the academy there as farm work allowed and evinced an exceptional aptitude for mathematics. After leaving the academy "with disgust" at the age of 13 and devoting himself to work on the farm, he developed an absorbing interest in the antiquities of his native countryside, recording his observations of social and natural phenomena for future publication.

In his 19th year Mactaggart entered the University of Edinburgh, where he attended his "favourite natural classes." However, he found that he had little further to learn in these subjects and, being uncomfortable with a structured education in any case, did not return for a second session but took to "wandering" through Scotland. Then, in a way as yet unknown, he "learned the engineering." Such training would normally have involved an indentureship of some kind with a practising civil engineer. He leaves few clues of this activity in his writings other than an allusion to working on John Rennie's celebrated Plymouth breakwater and the fact that it was Rennie's son who recommended him to Lieutenant-Colonel John By* for the post of clerk of works on the Rideau Canal project in 1826.

At some time in the 1820s Mactaggart moved to London where he taught "young gentlemen" mathematics and attempted unsuccessfully to establish a weekly newspaper called the *London Scotchman*, in partnership with two of his fellow-countrymen in the city, the poet Thomas Campbell and Lord Brougham. The year 1824 saw the publication of Mactaggart's *Gallovidian encyclopedia*, the fruit of his antiquarian zeal over many years. It was a substantial book comprising, in the author's words, "sketches of eccentric characters and curious places, with explanations of singular words, terms, and phrases, interspersed with poems, tales, anecdotes &c. and various other strange matters." It also included a good number of its author's own poems or, perhaps better, versifyings, and even more of verses current in the oral tradition of the south of Scotland. Unfortunately, one item in the book made what a local laird took to be aspersions on the character of his daughter, a beauty known locally as the "Star of Dungyle," and the laird brought pressure on Mactaggart to excise the offending passage. The book was withdrawn shortly after it appeared and was not reprinted until 1876, long after Mactaggart's death. The 1876 edition comprised a mere 250 copies and for long was a prized rarity. A reprint was produced in 1981.

On his arrival in Bytown (Ottawa), Upper Canada, in August 1826, Mactaggart was assigned to check the route recommended by Samuel Clowes for conducting the Rideau River into the Ottawa by canal. He then had to make a careful exploration and survey of the tract, eight miles long by four miles wide, embracing this region. The difficulties presented by dense forest, swamps, insects, and unexpected obstructions were prodigious and ultimately could only be overcome with the help of winter.

Not long after the completion of these duties, Mactaggart was ordered to finish the survey of the remaining 150 miles of waterway to Kingston, a task he performed in the months of June and July 1827, significantly observing that he "got back to the Ottawa alive." He revelled in his journeys, satisfying his appetite for social and natural history, and executed many incidental projects such as reporting on the Welland Canal (the design and construction of which he criticized severely), the Burlington Bay Canal, and the plans for a dockyard at Kingston. In the summer of 1827 he met William Dunlop* in "the wilds of Ancaster" as Dunlop was preparing to rendezvous with John Galt* at the site they had selected for the new town of Guelph. He later joined Dunlop and John Brant [TEKARIHOGEN] in an exploration of the Huron Tract and had much to say of the Canada Company's activities and policies.

Probably Mactaggart's most critical engineering assignment under By was the construction of a bridge over the Ottawa River at the Chaudière Falls. This bridge, called the Union Bridge because it linked the two Canadas, was completed by the end of 1828. "To build a *stone* bridge over one of the wildest rapids, and in the *depth* of a very severe winter" was, in Mactaggart's opinion, one of the most arduous of his undertakings in Upper Canada. The bridge had eight spans, the largest of which, of 200 feet, spanned the cauldron known as the Big Kettle. Mactaggart was only in part responsible for the design of the bridge; the principal designer appears to have been Robert DRUMMOND. Mactaggart's remarks on its completion were significantly guarded: "There it stands, and likely will for a length of time." It was, in fact, a remarkable feat of drystone construction, but it had a short life. A span was washed out in 1836 and the bridge was eventually replaced by a suspension bridge designed by Samuel Keefer*.

Soon after his arrival in Bytown, Mactaggart wrote several newspaper articles, one of which, in the *Montreal Herald*, posed a number of questions relating to the natural history and geography of British North America and to the fate of the explorer Samuel Hearne*. As a result of these articles, the Natural History Society of Montreal, founded shortly thereafter, elected Mactaggart to membership. He had already turned his geological interests to practical advantage by exploring for mineral deposits and by becoming, in late 1826, a founding member of the Hull Mining Company. This company had Philemon Wright* as its president and included among its other officers Alexander James Christie*, Thomas McKay*, John Redpath*, and Robert Drummond.

In the summer of 1828 there was an epidemic of fever among those employed on the swampy regions of the Rideau waterway. Mactaggart fell victim. Then he was dismissed from his post on the orders of Governor Sir James Kempt* for "being drunk on duty." There is no reason to believe that Mactaggart was more partial to the bottle than others of his culture and profession in these hard days. Indeed, he wrote in his youth that nature had given him a "frame of body"

Mailhot

that was a "sworn foe" to any fluid stronger than water. Nevertheless he became sufficiently discerning to praise "Craigdarroch . . . made after the Glenlivet mode" in Perth, Upper Canada, as "by far the most excellent spirit distilled in the country." Whatever indiscretion occurred was of less significance than the recommendations which Mactaggart, after his recovery from the fever, carried with him on his return to England in late 1828. By described Mactaggart in a letter to General Gother MANN, inspector general of fortifications, as "a man of strong natural abilities, well grounded in the practical part of his profession, and a zealous, hard-working man in the field." Bishop Alexander McDonell* was equally complimentary, informing the Colonial Office that Mactaggart was "perhaps the ablest practical engineer and geologist, and the properest person that has ever been in these Provinces for exploring the natural productions and latent resources of the country."

Within a year of his return to England, Mactaggart managed to complete and publish *Three years in Canada*. It is a remarkable record of social and scientific observations. In this book Mactaggart made it clear that he had no great esteem for the British and American settlers of the country; in an admittedly gloomy mood he suggested, probably half-seriously, that Britain should rid itself of colonists who were "as able a set of grumblers as you can meet with in the world." He was particularly censorious of the "gentry," the legal profession, and the "*low Irish*." The latter, who lived in squalid conditions, provided a large proportion of the labouring force on the Rideau Canal. Not unexpectedly he found the "Yankee" population of Upper Canada particularly lacking in warmth and colour, but the vitality and adaptability of the "Canadians" received his highest praise and the indigenous Indians his warm respect. The natural beauties of the Canadas, he thought, were "not to be matched in the world," and the potential wealth of the country gave a "consequence to Britain not to be sneered at." His vision of the country and its economic future included a canal system linking the town of Quebec with the Pacific coast.

No doubt the effects of Canada's "swamp fever" hastened Mactaggart's end. He died on 8 Jan. 1830 and was buried in Sandwich churchyard in his native Galloway. He was 38 years of age, with plans for a collection of voyageur songs, a history of the voyageurs, and a Canadian encyclopedia unfulfilled. He left behind an unfinished poem of more than 5,000 lines called "The engineer," which is now in the Stewartry Museum in Kirkcudbright.

Mactaggart emerges from his written work as an intelligent observer and passionate lover of life, a hard-headed but romantic Scot with all the contradictions these qualities imply. Alexander Trotter describes him in his *East Galloway sketches* as a "tall

handsome man of 6 feet 2 inches, and of stout figure, his proportions being majestic. He was fearless in asserting his opinions, hated duplicity, and his friendships were warm and lasting." Although he had an eye for a pretty face, he never married.

G. S. EMMERSON

John Mactaggart, *The Scottish Gallovidian encyclopedia; or, the original, antiquated, and natural curiosities of the south of Scotland . . .* (London, 1824; 2nd ed., 1876); repub. as *The Scottish Gallovidian encyclopedia; a new edition with a note on the author*, ed. L. L. Ardern (Perthshire, Scot., 1981); *Three years in Canada: an account of the actual state of the country in 1826–7–8; comprehending its resources, productions, improvements, and capabilities; and including sketches of the state of society, advice to emigrants, &c.* (2v., London, 1829).

PAC, RG 5, A1: 45081–100, 45388–89, 45890–91, 50823. Stewartry Museum (Kirkcudbright, Scot.), John Mactaggart, "The engineer." *Sights and surveys: two diarists on the Rideau*, ed. Edwin Welch (Ottawa, 1979). *DNB. The bards of Galloway: a collection of poems, songs, ballads, &c., by natives of Galloway*, ed. M. M. Harper (Dalbeattie, Scot., 1889). R. [F.] Legget, *John By, Lieutenant Colonel, Royal Engineers, 1779–1836: builder of the Rideau Canal; founder of Ottawa* (Ottawa, 1982); "The Rideau Canal and some of its builders," *Archaeological historical symposium, October 2–3, 1982, Rideau Ferry, Ontario*, ed. F. C. L. Wyght (Lombardy, Ont., n.d.), 127–36; *Rideau waterway* (Toronto, 1955). R. W. Passfield, *Building the Rideau canal: a pictorial history* (Toronto, 1982). Alexander Trotter, *East Galloway sketches; or, biographical, historical, and descriptive notices of Kirkcudbrightshire, chiefly in the nineteenth century* (Castle Douglas, Scot., 1901).

MAILHOT (Maillot, Malhiot), NICOLAS-FRANÇOIS, innkeeper; b. *c.* 1776 at Quebec, son of Joseph Maillot and Madeleine Levasseur; d. there 11 Feb. 1834.

At the time of his marriage, which was solemnized at Quebec on 10 Nov. 1801, Nicolas-François Mailhot was a servant in the town; he had no personal possessions and could not write his name. His wife, Marie-Marguerite Roussel, a maidservant from Saint-Michel, near Quebec, brought as her entire dowry a bed, bed-linen, and clothes. Four years later Mailhot was keeping a tavern on Rue Saint-Jean, in Upper Town. In 1812 he opened a luxurious hotel, which also served as a coffee-house and tavern, at no.40 of the same street. The three-storey stone hotel, which had been built in 1810 and 1811 by contractors JOHN, Laurence, and Edward* Cannon and carpenter Jean-Baptiste Chamberlain, cost more than £3,000.

In December 1818 Mailhot expanded his enterprise by putting up behind the hotel a house with public baths, a novelty that caused a sensation at the time. Frequented by the hotel's guests as well as by townspeople, it had three baths on the first floor and sitting-rooms and bedrooms on the second. Four years later Mailhot converted another house behind his hotel into an exhibition hall called the Royal Circus. In October 1824 a troupe under the management of William West and William Blanchard of Montreal began giving performances, putting on equestrian displays and a melodrama. The public paid from 1s. 6d. to 2s. 6d. to attend the various entertainments – theatre, ballet, opera, and acrobatics. The enterprise was not a success, however, and in the autumn of 1826 Mailhot turned the hall into a theatre, in which several companies performed. Plays by Shakespeare, Sheridan, and Sir Walter Scott, concerts, pantomimes, and equestrian displays were put on.

For 20 years Mailhot's hotel was one of the best of its kind at Quebec. It was famous for the way it was run, the quality of the various services it provided, and its table. Many notable events were held in it, particularly balls, banquets, shows, and concerts of classical music. The Quebec Education Society met there, and auctioneers used it to display and sell their merchandise. In the summer of 1831 the public could view the living skeleton Calvin Edson, the Canadian giant Modeste Mailhot, an exhibition of live snakes, and even a performing goat.

Despite this reputation, Mailhot had difficulty making his hotel and theatre pay. On many occasions he had to appear in court. He took action against insolvent clients and was himself sued by numerous suppliers whom he could not pay. In 1829 he put a notice in the *Quebec Mercury* stating his intention to retire from business and lease his enterprise, but the endeavour proved unsuccessful. It was announced in March 1832 that "this sound, comfortable, and elegant building known as 'Mailhot's Hotel'" and the bath house would be sold by the sheriff of the district of Quebec to meet his creditors' demands. Chief Justice Jonathan Sewell* acquired it for £3,025 in order to secure his debt. The sale followed that of the Royal Circus, which had taken place in September 1831 under similar circumstances.

Nicolas-François Mailhot probably retired to the property he had bought at Jeune-Lorette (Loretteville) in 1823. He died at Quebec on 11 Feb. 1834 and was buried two days later in the Cimetière des Picotés. By his marriage with Marie-Marguerite Roussel he had had three daughters and a son, Robert-Léonard, who became a lawyer and practised at Quebec.

CÉLINE CYR

ANQ-Q, CE1-1, 10 nov. 1801, 13 févr. 1834; CN1-178, 6 févr., 3 oct. 1810; 23 nov. 1811; 8 févr. 1814; 21 févr., 19 oct. 1815; 21 avril 1823; 22 juin 1824; CN1-230, 8 nov. 1801; T11-1/3553: 677; 3556: 249, 343, 506; 3563: 134, 1er févr. 1822; 3564: 336; 3567: 235; 3583: 1577; 3584: 1966, 2180, 2193, 2394. "Les dénombrements de Québec" (Plessis), ANQ *Rapport*, 1948–49: 204. *Le Canadien*, 24 oct. 1819; 16 mai, 20 juin 1821; 20 oct. 1824; 7, 14, 28 mai, 30 juin, 20 juill., 3, 6 août, 21 sept. 1831; 17 mars 1832. *Québec Gazette*, 19, 26 March 1812; 13 April 1815, 31 Dec. 1818. *Quebec Mercury*, 3 Feb. 1829. P.-G. Roy, *Les avocats de la région de Québec*. George Gale, *Historic tales of old Quebec* (Quebec, 1923). P.-G. Roy, "Le Cirque royal ou Théâtre royal (Royal Circus ou Royal Theatre)," *BRH*, 42 (1936): 641–66; "L'hôtel Malhiot, rue Saint-Jean, à Québec," *BRH*, 42: 449–52.

MALHERBE, FRANÇOIS, schoolteacher, merchant, and office holder; b. 21 March 1768 at Quebec, son (the second christened François) of François Malherbe, *dit* Champagne, a seaman, and Marie-Anne Margane de Lavaltrie; d. there 17 May 1832.

François Malherbe studied at the Petit Séminaire de Québec from 1781 to 1787. Tradition has it that he was a Recollet for a time, but there is no documentary evidence to support this claim. Some writers have suggested that he married Marie-Louise Thomas, *dit* Bigaouet, on 27 Oct. 1793, but in fact another man of the same name did, as the parents' names, and also François's 1801 marriage certificate, prove.

It is not known why Malherbe went to the south shore of the St Lawrence, but in any case he was teaching school at Saint-André, near Kamouraska, in 1799 and applied there for a licence to sell alcoholic beverages. Although no official explanation has been found, it appears that his plan was thwarted by the veto of the parish priest, whom the British authorities usually consulted in such matters.

On 13 Oct. 1801 Malherbe married Marie Chennequy, daughter of seaman Martin CHENNEQUE and sister of merchant Martin Chinic*. In the marriage contract signed on 12 October before Quebec notary Michel Berthelot, Malherbe declared that he resided at Saint-Jean-Port-Joli and was a merchant. But at the end of that year or in 1802 he moved again. Taking up residence at Rivière-Ouelle, he became the first teacher in a school opened under the legislation establishing the Royal Institution for the Advancement of Learning [*see* Joseph Langley MILLS]. Although the Catholic clergy generally considered the new school system a threat, the local parish priest, Bernard-Claude PANET, seems to have regarded Malherbe favourably, for according to the *Gazette de Québec* of 5 Aug. 1802 he employed "his enthusiasm, indeed his savings, to support a schoolmaster." The paper also noted that the schoolboys of Rivière-Ouelle, "under the direction of their worthy pastor, and aided by their schoolteacher," had given a warm welcome to the lieutenant governor of Lower Canada, Sir Robert Shore Milnes*, when he came to carry out the first general militia inspection. On that occasion Malherbe and nine pupils presented Milnes with an address, later termed extravagant by Louis-Philippe Audet and Pierre-Georges Roy*. The gesture, in which the other schoolboys joined, attracted attention, and the *Gazette de Québec* carried the full text of the address. The following year Malherbe turned his post over to John Johnston.

In March 1805 Malherbe was at Pointe-Lévy (Lauzon and Lévis), teaching 15 children. Because of the dearth of teachers there, the inhabitants were so happy to have him that they proposed moving him into the part of the presbytery reserved for the public and called the "salle des habitants." In addition he was to be provided with heating, and increased enrolment would bring him more income. The parish priest, Michel Masse, would not hear of it, being unprepared to welcome "a certain Sieur Malherbe and his family, with three turbulent and squalling children." Consequently Malherbe was forced to turn again to the Royal Institution.

Malherbe began teaching in the royal school at Pointe-Lévy in the spring of 1805, and on 1 July he was officially recognized by the government. At that time his salary was £60 a year. The journals of the House of Assembly show that he retained his post until 1820, when he was dismissed by the board of the Royal Institution for reasons unknown. In his final year he taught reading, writing, and arithmetic in French to 31 pupils, 14 of whom received free tuition. He was then receiving an annual salary of £54. Towards the end of his life, in 1829, he returned briefly to teaching at Pointe-Lévy. However, at the time of his death at Quebec in 1832 he was a bailiff. He was buried in the Cimetière des Picotés on 21 May.

François Malherbe had a puzzling life, full of ups and downs, interrupted by moves and by difficulties with clergy which were certainly not unrelated to his having turned to the Royal Institution. The vicissitudes he experienced, however, give a glimpse of life for a lay teacher at the outset of the 19th century in Lower Canada, at a time when the Catholic Church was preparing to tighten its hold on education, fearing to leave it in the hands of the secular and Protestant state.

NELSON MICHAUD

ANQ-Q, CE1-1, 10 janv. 1765, 21 mars 1768, 13 oct. 1801, 21 mai 1832; CN1-26, 12 oct. 1801. ASQ, Fichier des anciens. L.C., House of Assembly, *Journals*, 1807: 262; 1820–21, app.K. *Gazette de Québec*, 5 août 1802. Ivanhoë Caron, "Les maîtres d'écoles de l'Institution royale de 1808 à 1834," *BRH*, 47 (1941): 28. *Quebec almanac*, 1815: 124; 1820: 133. L.-P. Audet, *Le système scolaire*, 3: 136, 140, 149, 157; 4: 120, 127, 192–95, 217. P.-H. Hudon, *Rivière-Ouelle de la Bouteillerie; 3 siècles de vie* (Ottawa, 1972), 191. J.-E. Roy, *Hist. de Lauzon*, 3: 350–54; 4: 123. P.-G. Roy, *Toutes petites choses du Régime anglais*, 1: 124, 259–63. F.-J. Audet, "Les maîtres d'écoles de l'Institution royale," *BRH*, 28 (1922): 284. [——], "Francis Malherbe," *BRH*, 29 (1923): 57–58. "Le maître d'école François Malherbe," *BRH*, 44 (1938): 93–94. "Le maître d'école Malherbe," *BRH*, 51 (1945): 206–7. L.-J. Pelletier, "Quelques maîtres d'école de la rive sud," *BRH*, 49 (1943): 236. "Un triomphe de François Malherbe," *BRH*, 51: 207–8.

MANN, GOTHER, army officer and military engineer; b. 21 Dec. 1747 in Plumstead (London), England, second son of Cornelius Mann and Elizabeth Gother; m. 1767 Anne Wade, and they had eight children; d. 27 March 1830 in Lewisham (London), England.

Graduating from the Royal Military Academy at Woolwich (London) in 1763, Ensign Gother Mann was employed for the next 12 years on defence installations along the English coast. Commissioned lieutenant in 1771, he was posted to Dominica in the West Indies late in 1775 and while there was promoted captain in 1777. From 1779 to 1785 he served in Great Britain, reporting on defence arrangements on the east coast of England in 1781 at the request of Jeffery Amherst*, commander-in-chief of the British forces.

In 1785 Mann, then 38, was sent to the province of Quebec as captain and commanding engineer. As were his predecessor, William Twiss, and his successor, Ralph Henry Bruyeres*, who had accompanied him to Quebec, Mann was preoccupied with five principal items: the canals on the St Lawrence, the fortifications at Quebec, the defence of the routes into the province through the St Lawrence valley and the Richelieu valley, the possibility of war with the United States, and the more prosaic day-to-day duties of the engineers. In 1788 the governor, Lord Dorchester [Guy Carleton*], instructed Mann to conduct an extensive examination of military posts from Kingston (Ont.) to St Mary's (Sault Ste Marie, Ont.). The result was a detailed and useful 34-page appraisal of the posts, harbours, and navigable water routes. Although the report bears the signature of John Collins*, deputy surveyor general of Quebec, it is recognized as being the work of the commanding engineer. Mann delineated the decay that had set in since the conclusion of the American revolution, complaining of posts "improperly placed" and faultily constructed. He riddled his report with phrases such as "moulded away," "fallen down," "entirely rotten," and "all in ruins." Most of the bases he was instructed to inspect were actually on the American side of the border established by the Treaty of Paris (1783); the British continued to occupy the western posts until two years after the signing of Jay's Treaty in 1794.

Mann spent 1792–93 in the Netherlands, participating in various sieges of French forces. Promoted lieutenant-colonel late in 1793, he was ordered to return to Lower Canada to prepare defences at Quebec, since war with the United States seemed a possibility. Four years later he became a colonel. In 1800 he prepared a report on the state of the St Lawrence canals in which he referred to the locks as

Marchand

"very defective" and "much decayed." Understanding the vital importance of the canals in facilitating commercial and military movements, he suggested repairs and alterations, the latter necessitated by the larger craft involved and the decrease in water level since the construction of the locks had begun in 1779. At the turn of the century, British officials were also concerned with the possible impact of a proposed American canal from Lake Ontario to Albany, N.Y. The colonial secretary, Lord Hobart, suggested to Lieutenant-General Peter Hunter*, commander of the forces in the Canadas, that he select someone to look into the matter. Mann, whom Hobart described as "an officer of so much merit and experience . . . from whose professional abilities you will no doubt derive every possible assistance," was chosen. In 1803 Mann was promoted major-general and obtained permission to return to England where his family had remained. He left British North America in the spring of 1804.

During his two tours in the Canadas, Mann penned several reports on the necessity of a proper and permanent system of defence at Quebec. "When it is considered how greatly the safety and preservation of this part of His Majesty's Dominions depend on Quebec . . . too much attention cannot be paid to promote its strength and security." Although he recognized that a Canadian winter would offer a formidable obstacle to even a "strong, active and enterprising enemy," more defence than that was required for a military post "of consequence" such as Quebec, the "only hopefull resource in case of Invasion." Mann's recommendations for this defence system – the completion of the wall encircling the town, the construction of auxiliary defence works in front of the wall, the occupation of the Plains of Abraham, and the construction of a citadel at Cap Diamant – were not all carried out during his tenure, but would form the basis of any military construction at Quebec during the first half of the 19th century.

From August 1801 until his departure in 1804 Mann had been the second most senior officer in the Canadas. With strong support from Hunter, who left him in command of Lower Canada for periods of several months, he successfully petitioned for the salary of a brigadier because of his additional duties. He informed Hunter that the sum would make him "very comfortable."

After his return to Britain, Mann assumed various responsibilities as colonel commandant of the Royal Engineers, a commission he received in 1805. He obtained promotions: lieutenant-general in 1810 and inspector general of fortifications the following year. In these posts he continued his involvement with Canadian defences and communications, commenting on the construction of the citadel at Quebec and the attempt made by the Royal Engineers in the latter half of the 1820s to locate a navigable water route between Penetanguishene, Upper Canada, and the Ottawa River via Lake Simcoe. He also appointed engineer John By* to superintend construction of the Rideau Canal. In 1821 Mann was made a general and he was the senior officer in the engineers when he died at age 82.

JOHN C. KENDALL

PAC, MG 23, J10; MG 25, G235; RG 8, I (C ser.), 30, 38–39, 54, 61, 381–84, RG 8, II, 8–10. *Gentleman's Magazine*, January–June 1830: 477. *DNB*. "Papiers d'État," PAC *Rapport,* 1890: 301–3, 322. "Papiers d'État – Bas-Canada," PAC *Rapport*, 1891: 74, 152. André Charbonneau *et al.*, *Québec ville fortifiée, du XVIIe au XIXe siècle* (Québec, 1982). Whitworth Porter *et al.*, *History of the Corps of Royal Engineers* (9v. to date, London and Chatham, Eng., 1899– ; repr. vols.1–3, Chatham, 1951–54), 1.

MARAKLE (Marcle). *See* MARKLE

MARCHAND, JEAN-BAPTISTE, Roman Catholic priest and Sulpician; b. 25 Feb. 1760 in Verchères (Que.), son of Louis Marchand, a merchant, and Marie-Marguerite Boucher de Niverville; d. 14 April 1825 in Sandwich (Windsor), Upper Canada.

Jean-Baptiste Marchand belonged to a respectable family. Among his paternal uncles were Joseph, the seigneur of Saint-Charles-sur-Richelieu, Nicolas, an artillery officer killed in the siege of Quebec in 1759, and two secular priests, one of whom, Étienne*, was a vicar general. After studying at the Petit Séminaire de Québec from 1774 to 1784, Jean-Baptiste did his theology at the Grand Séminaire in the period 1784–86, and served at the same time as a study master at the Petit Séminaire. He was ordained priest by the bishop of Quebec, Louis-Philippe Mariauchau* d'Esgly, on 11 March 1786.

Attracted to the Séminaire de Saint-Sulpice, Marchand began his ministry in the church of Notre-Dame at Montreal in August 1786 and was received into the Sulpician community as a member on 21 Oct. 1788. In September 1789 Jean-Baptiste Curatteau* resigned from the Collège Saint-Raphaël, of which he was the principal, leaving to his successor the usufruct of all his assets invested in the province of Quebec. At the suggestion of Gabriel-Jean Brassier*, the bishop of Quebec's vicar general, the churchwardens of Notre-Dame, who owned the college, chose Marchand to succeed Curatteau.

He set about his task with enthusiasm, despite the difficulties and weaknesses of the institution: there were not many pupils (between 120 and 130), the teachers varied in competence, and the financial resources were limited. It took in both boarders (a fifth of the student body) and day pupils, offered elementary and secondary courses of study, and at the

Marchand

elementary level taught pupils in both French and English. Most of the teachers, called regents, were clerics lent by the bishop of Quebec and they received their moral and theological training from Marchand. Marchand was responsible for continuity at the college but often had his teachers removed by the bishop. Nevertheless, in 1790 he added the two-year Philosophy program, thus saving his pupils from having to go to Quebec to complete their studies. He also enjoyed the confidence of the bishop and the seminary authorities.

In 1794 the arrival in Lower Canada of French Sulpicians who had been driven out by the French revolution brought the college three new teachers. They were highly critical of the quality of the pupils and the requirements of the institution. After a period of tensions, which subsided in October 1795, Marchand wrote to Bishop Jean-François Hubert* of Quebec: "We have made concessions on both sides about how to act." The unity did not last, and in August 1796 Marchand resigned. From 1792 till 1794 he had also held the office of chaplain to the nuns of the Congrégation of Notre-Dame.

When François-Xavier Dufaux, the Sulpician missionary at l'Assomption-du-Détroit (later known as Sandwich), died, Hubert on 17 Oct. 1796 offered the parish charge of Notre-Dame-de-l'Assomption to the Séminaire de Saint-Sulpice. The superior, Gabriel-Jean Brassier, appointed Marchand to it. He arrived in his parish on Christmas night 1796. It stretched along the Detroit River from Lake St Clair to Lake Erie and extended about six miles inland. The presbytery had been built by Hubert, who had been the parish priest from 1781 to 1785, and the humble church had been completed in 1787. The congregation increased rapidly, and in 1816 numbered nearly 3,000. From the beginning Marchand won the trust of his people and was known for his zeal. There was, however, a good deal of dissension amongst the parishioners. In 1795 François Baby*, the deputy lieutenant of Essex County, had been granted a special pew in the church. After violent altercations with his fellow parishioners, who tried to prevent him from occupying it, Baby finally renounced his claim in 1797 in order to restore harmony. Another matter, which brought in question the titles to property held by the *fabrique*, was fraught with more serious consequences. A parishioner, François Pratt (Pratte), laid claim to almost all the *fabrique*'s land, which was then in use as a cemetery and had had several buildings erected on it. In 1801 Pratt fenced off the land and launched an action for damages, which he subsequently dropped. The question of the titles was not settled until 1806, when Pratt's rights to the property were confirmed. Marchand was left with his church and presbytery.

His duties took Marchand every six or eight weeks to the missions that he had founded shortly after his arrival, Saint-Jean-Baptiste at Amherstburg and Saint-Pierre-sur-la-Tranche (Prairie Siding) on the Thames River. He always promoted the establishment of schools and he brought in teachers, but the sparseness of the population was scarcely conducive to education. He maintained close relations with Michel Levadoux and Gabriel Richard, two Sulpicians at Detroit, and he even filled in for Richard when he was away from his parish in 1808–9. Marchand was also called upon to give him shelter. During the War of 1812, after the capture of Detroit by British forces, Richard, who had apparently expressed strong anti-British sentiments, was ordered on 21 May 1813 by Brigadier-General Henry PROCTER to go and live with Marchand pending his expulsion. Richard was supposed to suffer the same fate as some 30 inhabitants of Detroit who had already been sent to Quebec, but on 6 June he promised to refrain from further comments and thus could return to Detroit.

Marchand was twice visited by the bishop of Quebec. In June and July 1801 Bishop Pierre Denaut* stayed a month at Sandwich and confirmed 500 people. Denaut was accompanied by Abbé Félix Gatien*, who was to spend five years at Sandwich. In June 1816 Bishop Joseph-Octave PLESSIS made a pastoral visit, during which he could see for himself how heavy the parish priest's task was; in September he sent Marchand an assistant priest, Joseph Crevier, *dit* Bellerive, who would succeed him.

In July 1797 Jean-Baptiste Marchand had written to his bishop: "I am very happy here, as far as both temporal and spiritual matters are concerned." Later, in 1799, he thanked Jean-Henry-Auguste ROUX, the superior of the Séminaire de Saint-Sulpice, for not having suggested him for the parish charge of L'Assomption, near Montreal. After more than 26 years of ministry at Sandwich, however, his health began to fail in the spring of 1823. He died on 14 April 1825. In Hubert's words Marchand was "a man of character, gentle, kindly, who knew how to yield without cowardice, without weakness."

BRUNO HAREL

AAQ, 303 CD, I; II: 113; 71-31 CD, I: 129; 7 CM, V: 132, 137–38; 320 CN, IV: 3, 8, 10, 12, 14, 16, 18, 20, 22, 24, 26, 28, 34, 50, 62, 68, 70, 74, 83, 98–99, 102–7, 109, 144, 147, 150. ACAM, 901.137, 789–95. AO, Hiram Walker Hist. Museum coll., 20-135. ASSM, 10, dossier 2; dossier 3, no.30; dossier 4, no.24; 11, dossier 3, nos.19, 30; 14, dossier 1, nos.8, 11–12; dossier 2, no.21; 21; 24, dossier 6. PAC, MG 8, G8, 4–5. Allaire, *Dictionnaire*, 4: 45–46. Caron, "Inv. de la corr. de Mgr Hubert et de Mgr Bailly de Messein," ANQ *Rapport*, 1930–31. [L.-A. Huguet-Latour], *Annuaire de Ville-Marie, origine, utilité et progrès des institutions catholiques de Montréal . . .* (2v., Montréal, 1863–82). E. J. Lajeunesse, *Outline history of Assumption Parish* (n.p., [1967]). Maurault, *Le collège de Montréal* (Dansereau; 1967). George Paré, *The Catholic Church in*

Detroit, 1701–1888 (Detroit, 1951; repr. 1983). M. M. Connely, "Sandwich, Detroit and Gabriel Richard, 1798–1832," CCHA *Report*, 18 (1951): 25–37. D.-A. Gobeil, "Quelques curés de la première paroisse ontarienne de M. Hubert au curé A. MacDonell, Sandwich, 1781–1831," CCHA *Rapport*, 23 (1955–56): 101–16. Arthur Godbout, "La première paroisse de l'Ontario: L'Assomption de Sandwich," CCHA *Rapport*, 18 (1950–51): 39–53. J.-J. Lefebvre, "La descendance de Pierre Boucher (1617–1722), fondateur de Boucherville," SGCF *Mémoires*, 5 (1952–53): 80. É.-Z. Massicotte, "Une page de l'histoire du collège de Montréal," *BRH*, 23 (1917): 207–11. Henri Têtu, "Visite de Mgr Denaut au Détroit en 1801," *BRH*, 10 (1904): 97–106.

MARIE-ANNE DE SAINT-OLIVIER. *See* PAQUET

MARIE-ANNE-LOUISE DE SAINT-FRANÇOIS-XAVIER. *See* TASCHEREAU

MARIE DE L'INCARNATION, MARIE-CLOTILDE RAIZENNE, named. *See* RAIZENNE

MARION, SALOMON (baptized **Charles**, he was occasionally known as **Pierre-Charles-Salomon**; although he is named **Lafontaine**, *dit* **Marion**, on his marriage certificate and elsewhere is sometimes called **Marion,** *dit* **Lafontaine**, he signed Salomon Marion), gold- and silversmith and jeweller; b. 5 Feb. 1782 in Lachenaie, Que., son of Michel Marion and Marie-Charlotte Foisy; d. 31 Oct. 1830 in Montreal.

Salomon Marion was apprenticed to Pierre Huguet*, *dit* Latour, a Montreal merchant silversmith, in 1798. In Latour's large workshop he worked alongside silversmiths Faustin Gigeon, François Blache, and Paul Morand*. His contract was to end in February 1803, on his 21st birthday. In October 1804, when he rented a house on Rue du Saint-Sacrement in Montreal, he termed himself a master silversmith. In May of that year Marion had signed a one-year contract with merchant Dominique ROUSSEAU; he was to practise his craft and receive half the net profit, while Rousseau was to supply the shop and tools, and "sufficient silversmithing work to keep him employed." Given Rousseau's interest in the fur trade, presumably the objects made under this contract were mainly articles of trade silver.

That Marion's status was rising is indicated by the very different contract he concluded with his former master in June 1810. Marion was authorized to work at home, but only on "chains for lamps and censers and chain holders"; for the purposes of the contract he was to use Huguet's workshop with Huguet undertaking to supply "the silver, charcoal, and tools." The workmen required were the responsibility of Marion, who in addition was himself to work "regularly at least four days a week." Such were the terms on which he signed a one-year contract to make at least 27 major pieces of church silver, some elaborately decorated,

for 2,568 *livres*. Marion had already delivered several of the same sort of objects to Huguet even before the contract was signed. This fact probably explains why the document specifies in such detail all the steps and manufacturing techniques, prices, and working conditions. A clause giving Huguet exclusive rights clearly shows his hold on Marion, who "may not make in his home or have made there or elsewhere any piece of silver for the churches, for any other person whomsoever." It is thus easy to understand why a number of objects bearing the mark PH are so much like Marion's as to be mistaken for them.

In 1813 Marion became godfather to the eldest son of silversmith William Delisle, probably as the result of a friendship of some years' standing, if not of professional relations. In 1816 he published an advertisement in *Le Spectateur canadien* to inform "his friends and the public that he proposed to practise his silversmith's trade on a broader scale than previously, namely in all its branches." To the articles of church silver that he was already making he added "Items for the table in the best taste, jewellery, gilt ornaments, engravings, and a whole host of other articles." This advertising undoubtedly marked Marion's professional emancipation. He may well have been employing Hugh McQuarters, a clock and watch maker who in 1815 was living in his house. In any case, in 1817 his order book was sufficiently well filled for him to take on as an apprentice 12-year-old Hilaire Seguin, who helped him until he came of age. From 1818 the *fabriques* became regular customers of Marion's. Around this period he did the statue of the Virgin for the church of Verchères that is held in the National Gallery of Canada. The only surviving sculpture in the round by an early Canadian silversmith, it has a virtuosity and an aesthetic quality that make it an indisputable masterpiece of the colony's art.

In October 1817 Marion had married Sophie Lafrenière, a widow; silversmiths Joseph Normandeau and Paul Morand attended the ceremony. In 1819 he was present in turn at the wedding of silversmith Joseph Auclair, who was marrying Mme Marion's sister; silversmith Nathan Starns was there as well. That year Marion was given power of attorney for François Loran, "officer in the Indian Department, living at St-François," which was a busy centre for the production and exchange of trade silver. In 1822 he took on a new apprentice, 14-year-old Jean-Baptiste Guimont. His last apprentice, André-Zéphirin Grothé, son of silversmith Christian Grothé, was taken on in 1826 for a period of four years.

Marion's talent gained general recognition in 1826 with the publication in the *Canadian Spectator* of an article which remarked: "We recommend that those who are interested in the progress of the arts in this country, and particularly in the success of their compatriots in this field, visit the shop of Mr Marion, a silversmith in this town. There they will see a piece of his own creation that merits the attention of connoisseurs and that cannot fail to be admired by all persons of taste. It is a silver church lamp. Garlands of leaves, flowers, and fruit in relief form the decorations. Heads of winged angels conceal the first links of the chain that carries the lamp. The whole piece is most beautiful."

Marion died suddenly on 31 Oct. 1830. On several occasions in March and April 1831 Mme Marion published an advertisement in *La Minerve* announcing: "All orders for any church work or silverplate entrusted to her will be carried out as usual, and at very reasonable prices. She still has in hand a quantity of works of the specialty mentioned above and other pieces of silverware done by the late Mr Marion." She was, then, liquidating the stock in the shop. The question remains whether she really had new items made. If so, unless she practised the craft herself, she must have relied on the help of some silversmith, possibly André-Zéphirin Grothé, whose training was finished. His work had indeed been strongly influenced by his master's, yet was not of the same quality. Whatever transpired, Mme Marion moved, first to the home of Mme Millette and then to the house previously occupied by silversmith Joseph Normandeau. She remarried in 1832 and again in 1834. It is not known whether she then continued to carry on her silversmithing business. By her will drawn up in November 1830, she bequeathed to her sister, the wife of Joseph Auclair, all the silversmithing tools in her possession.

Salomon Marion's obituary in *La Minerve* suggests that he had had many close friendships: "His premature loss casts into mourning his numerous friends, who will long regret him." The *Quebec Gazette* of 4 Nov. 1830 made laudatory comments on his career: "He had acquired a deserved renown in his art." The numerous and splendid objects he had created reveal a productive and conscientious craftsman. His style shows an innate understanding of form, a refined sense of decoration, and a meticulous technique. His is the achievement of an aesthete and poet, comparable to that of François Ranvoyzé* in creativity and inspired craftsmanship. It unquestionably deserves to be better known.

ROBERT DEROME and JOSÉ MÉNARD

ANQ-M, CE1-51, 19 juin, 20 oct. 1817; 24 mai 1818; 28 juin 1819; 3 nov. 1830; 3 mars, 9 août 1832; CN1-121, 28 mai 1804; CN1-128, 30 mars 1795, 25 sept. 1797, 23 juill. 1798, 28 avril 1802; CN1-134, 20 janv. 1817, 6 sept. 1822, 7 juill. 1828, 23 nov. 1830, 18 mars 1834; CN1-243, 13 oct. 1804, 14 juin 1810, 3 sept. 1819; CN1-295, 16 août 1813, 9 févr. 1815; CN1-348, 6 nov. 1826. MAC-CD, Fonds Morisset, 2, dossier A.-Z. Grothé, Christian Grothé, Salomon Marion. *Canadian Spectator* (Montreal), 13, 27 May, 3, 10, 17, 24 June, 1, 8, 15, 29 July, 5, 12, 19, 26 Aug., 9 Sept. 1816; 31 July 1824; 10 June 1826. *La Minerve*, 1er nov. 1830; 10, 14, 17, 21, 28, 31 mars, 7 avril 1831. *Montreal Gazette*, 1 April 1811; 27 Nov., 4, 11 Dec. 1815. *Montreal directory*, 1819–20. Tanguay, *Dictionnaire*, 5: 517. Robert Derome, "Delezenne, les orfèvres, l'orfèvrerie, 1740–1790" (thèse de MA, univ. de Montréal, 1974); "Gérard Morisset et l'orfèvrerie," *À la découverte du patrimoine avec Gérard Morisset* (Québec, 1981), 205–20. Gérard Morisset, *Le Cap-Santé, ses églises et son trésor*, C. Beauregard et al., édit. (2e éd., Montréal, 1980); *Évolution d'une pièce d'argenterie* (Québec, 1943). Ramsay Traquair, *The old silver of Quebec* (Toronto, 1940). *Journal of Canadian Art Hist.* (Montreal), 5 (1980), no.1: 69–74. Jean Trudel, "Étude sur une statue en argent de Salomon Marion," National Gallery of Canada, *Bull.* (Ottawa), 21 (1973): 3–19.

MARKLE (Marakle, Marcle), ABRAHAM, businessman, politician, and army officer; b. 26 Oct. 1770 in Ulster County, N.Y.; m. Mrs Vrooman, a widow, and they had at least one son; m. secondly Catharine ——, and they had seven sons and two daughters; d. 26 March 1826 at his residence near Terre Haute, Ind.

Abraham Markle was of Dutch ancestry. By his own account he had four older brothers who served with John Butler*'s rangers and settled in the Niagara peninsula after the American revolution. That tie may explain Markle's brief residence in Newark (Niagara-on-the-Lake) in 1794; if so, it was not sufficiently strong to keep him there, and through the remainder of the decade and into the next he lived at various places in New York State. In 1801 he ran a hotel in Niagara (Niagara-on-the-Lake) in partnership with one of Robert Hamilton*'s sons; they also operated a local stage line for a short period. On 25 Jan. 1802 the partnership was dissolved with Markle taking control for several months before selling the operation to his former associate. By 1806 he was established in Ancaster as a distiller. In the first quarter of that year his distillery had the largest production in the Niagara District, outstripping even Richard Hatt*'s large complex, Dundas Mills.

Markle possessed a considerable measure of entrepreneurial flair, particularly for making deals. He headed the 15 shareholders of the Union Mill Company, which in 1809 purchased the milling complex of John Baptist Rousseaux* St John, and there is a possibility that the group had been running it as early as 1806. Like most businessmen of the period, Markle was an active speculator in land. He did not operate on the scale of investors such as Robert ADDISON, but his lots were always well chosen for their marketability. In 1808 he patented, and then sold, 200 acres in nearby Nelson Township; the following year he purchased 200 acres in Aldborough Township. By 1810 he had acquired 700 acres in Ancaster Township, 200 acres in Markham Township, and 400 acres in Nelson which he leased from the crown. His

Markle

portfolio was completed by the acquisition of a tavern licence in January 1813. As a businessman, if the records of the civil court are an indication, he managed to avoid the pitfalls which ruined Benajah Mallory* who, like Markle, would desert to the United States during the War of 1812. The court records reveal only one large judgement against Markle (for £200 in November 1806); his name does not appear again until February 1812 and then for a much smaller amount.

Markle's election to the House of Assembly for Saltfleet, Ancaster, and the west riding of York in June 1812 thrust him to the centre of provincial concerns. President Isaac Brock* had high hopes that this parliament would overcome the opposition led by Joseph Willcocks* and pass the emergency legislation he deemed crucial to wartime survival. Until this point, the only hint, and it is a veiled one at best, of Markle's political predisposition had been his refusal, reported in June 1811, to perform militia duty with the 5th Lincoln. The journals of the summer session of 1812 are no longer extant but the Niagara merchant William Hamilton Merritt* described Markle as one of Willcocks's "adherents." Three days after parliament met, Brock lamented a situation "critical, not from anything the enemy can do, but from the disposition of the people." Apparently led by Willcocks and Markle, the assembly spent, in Brock's words, eight days "in carrying a single measure of party – the repeal of the School Bill" – and in passing an act requiring public disclosure of treasonable practices before magistrates could commit suspects without bail. On the council's recommendation, Brock prorogued parliament. Lack of hard evidence precludes anything more than conjecture as to Markle's motives. There was nothing startlingly new about the presence of the opposition or its concerns; resistance to the executive arm of government had focused increasingly in the assembly, albeit with some interruptions, for a decade. Moreover, the Head of the Lake (the vicinity of present-day Hamilton Harbour) had already acquired a reputation for radicalism by the election of John Willson* in 1809. Markle obviously shared the broad concerns of the whig tradition, especially hostility to martial law and infringement of habeas corpus.

The opposition's behaviour in the second session (25 February to 13 March 1813) is somewhat mystifying. Merritt observed that Willcocks and "his party" had become loyal. Moreover, Brock's successor, Sir Roger Hale Sheaffe*, was so satisfied by the session that on 19 March he pronounced the death of the "cabal" within the house. The legislation passed was not especially controversial, and so perhaps there was less need for opposition. Besides, the military situation, after the victories at Detroit and Queenston Heights, was less desperate than the one faced by

Brock. However, in 1814 President Gordon Drummond* drew attention to the "malignant influence" of Willcocks and Markle in rejecting Sheaffe's call for a "suitable modification of the habeas corpus Act." Since the journals for this session are also missing, events in the house must remain obscure.

In the course of 1813, the climate of opinion with respect to the maintenance of civil law during wartime had begun to change. Nothing was more jarring than the actions of the disaffected such as Elijah Bentley* during the occupation of York (Toronto) in April 1813 and the Americans' subsequent push up the peninsula. In the aftermath, faith in due process faltered and collapsed: on 8 May "men of some standing and weight in this Society and holding real property to a great extent," men such as Thomas DICKSON and Robert NICHOL, emphasized to Brigadier-General John Vincent* that "self-defence" had become paramount; "recourse only to the civil laws . . . would be unavailing and . . . endanger our existence as a people and government." When on 6 June the British re-established their military presence with victory at Stoney Creek, fearful loyal subjects seized the opportunity to act against suspected traitors. A mere five days later Markle was ordered to appear before Vincent. Informed that "there were many Complaints lodged Against Me," Markle was sent to Kingston for detention on 17 June.

"Innocent & Unhappy," Markle immediately petitioned for release, proclaiming that it had been "Herriditary from My fore fathers to the Present age to be friends to the British Government." The charges against him he dismissed as "groundless," the fabrications of "My private Enemies." "Had I not suffered Myself to be Elected," Markle averred, "I should Never have been called disloyal or a traitor." Fearful for the safety of his family, "exposed to indians Who are Daily destroying the property of Our Neighbours," he was released. Some sources claim that Markle made his way back to Ancaster, but a militia return dated 22 June of those who had gone to the United States includes Markle. Yet late in November Merritt reported that Markle had "passed by the morning before, to join the enemy." What is certain is that by 12 Dec. 1813 he was a captain in the Company of Canadian Volunteers, formed by Willcocks after he had left for the United States. His enlistment was a coup for Willcocks, who described him as an assemblyman "possessing a Large property, and a very powerful influence."

The volunteers, dedicated to establishing a republic in British North America, fought mainly as guerrillas or scouts. Knowledge of the local territory and contacts among the population gave them an edge at this type of warfare. Moreover, they were eager to settle old scores and sought out unprotected civilian targets. The unit saw action during the burning of

489

Markle

Niagara in December 1813 and later at the British raids on Fort Schlosser (Niagara Falls), N.Y., and Lewiston. Markle was wounded "severely" during one of the latter engagements, but he recovered sufficiently to accompany a large American force which landed in Upper Canada at Dover (Port Dover) on 14 May 1814 and burned every building between the village and Turkey Point, including Robert Nichol's mills. Commissioned major on 19 April, Markle acted as liaison with Indians in New York before being stationed at Fort Erie until 31 August, when he moved to Albany. On 15 November Markle and another officer charged Benajah Mallory, Willcocks's successor as commander of the volunteers, with embezzlement and felonious conduct. Mallory was suspended and Markle assumed command of the unit. The following day he received permission to move his family "Estward . . . to procure a situation to settle them." When his unit was disbanded in March 1815, he seems to have been living at Batavia.

Markle's treason ranks on a scale with that of Willcocks and Mallory. Unfortunately, the lack of sources makes it difficult to judge the reason for his conduct. American historians tend to repeat the conclusions of the family historian that Markle, aided by his "Masonic connections," had fled official persecution in the courts and elsewhere, persecution that had resulted from his remarks "favorable to the annexation of Canada" by the United States. However, court minute-books do not reveal one single instance of official persecution of Markle. The only documented case of harassment, and it was not of an official nature, was his brief incarceration in June 1813. Mallory accused Markle of opportunism, suggesting that he "never Left Canada from Principle but from a narrow Escape from his Creditors." That may be, but there is no evidence either in court or forfeited-estate records to substantiate the allegation.

Unlike Ebenezer Allan*, Markle had remained loyal at the outbreak of war. It is possible that with so much to lose he wanted to await an outcome favourable to his interests. But in that case neutrality and not opposition would have been the prudent course in 1813. Crucial to an understanding of his treason, therefore, is its timing. Markle's successor in the assembly, James DURAND, decried the summer of 1813 as a period of military despotism. An echo of this view is found in an American newspaper's obituary for Markle. Opposing "the corruption and oppression practised upon the people," Markle, it said, "gave strong evidence that the spirits of those who had laid the basis of American Freedom, were very similar to his own." As for his treason, it was suggested that when the "civil law had been prostrated by martial despotism, the outrage and violence of the public functionaries toward him proved that the laws no longer afforded him protection, and consequently he

was absolved from any allegiance he could have owed that government."

Unlike his brothers, Markle had been too young for active involvement in the loyalist cause during the American revolution. Moreover, prior to 1801 he had spent almost his entire life in the United States. His political sympathies, then, were likely to have been democratic. Certainly in Upper Canada he shared the most radical tendencies in the opposition, those of Willcocks. Events during the summer of 1813 forced Willcocks to the logical extension of his beliefs, republicanism. They had a similar effect on Markle and Mallory. Convinced that civil rights had been extinguished, these three men saw no alternative but to cross the border – desperate times required desperate measures. It is, perhaps, significant that Markle's inn in Terre Haute, Ind., the Eagle and the Lion, carried a sign depicting a "sorely dejected British lion, fast losing its eyes under the attacks of a victorious eagle."

After the war Markle was alert to new opportunities for recouping his large personal losses. Indicted for treason on 24 May 1814 and convicted *in absentia*, in 1817 he was declared an outlaw and his lands vested in the crown. In December 1815 an acquaintance had estimated the value of his Upper Canadian holdings at $26,900. Small wonder that Markle participated in the lobbying of the American government which led in early 1816 to the passage of bounty legislation compensating volunteers. The bounty land acts of 1816 and 1817 entitled Markle to 800 acres in total. In June 1816 he applied for additional land in his own right and another 2,080 acres for others with himself as assignee; a month later he filed papers for 320 acres more. All these petitions were granted. He located his lands in Indiana's Wabash valley and on 19 Sept. 1816 became one of the five shareholders of the Terre Haute Land Company. The town of Terre Haute soon became the district capital for the newly organized Vigo County; Markle leapt at the possibility for investment. He owned several mills, a distillery and tavern, and land. He mortgaged his land to finance further expansion but overextended himself and by 1823 he faced foreclosure. At his death he had extensive property investments, mills, and shipping and manufacturing interests, but he was heavily in debt.

Markle was not a popular figure in Indiana. He frequently resorted to the civil courts to secure payment of debts. He himself was hauled before the criminal courts: in one instance on gambling charges and in another for assault and battery. When he ran for the post of lieutenant governor on 5 Aug. 1822 he received a mere two votes. Local American historians depict him as a large man, of great energy, quick-tempered, but often generous and warm-hearted. He loved horse-racing and enjoyed drinking. He died as a result of an apparent stroke, incurred while pulling up fence posts on his farm. A member of the local masonic lodge, he was buried with its full honours. Vilified in Upper Canadian history as a traitor, when remembered at all, he is viewed by Americans as a soldier in freedom's cause, a worthy inheritor of the revolutionary tradition.

ROBERT LOCHIEL FRASER

AO, MU 1368; MU 2555, receipts, 13 April 1801, 6 Jan. 1810; RG 1, A-IV, 16: 4; C-IV, Nelson Township, concession 3, lots 5, 11; RG 22, ser.131, 2: ff.3, 6, 16–17. BL, Add. MSS 21765: 392; 21826: 24; 21828: 92 (mfm. at PAC). Buffalo and Erie County Hist. Soc. (Buffalo, N.Y.), A419, A439, A558 (P. B. Porter papers). Elgin Land Registry Office (St Thomas, Ont.), Aldborough Township, alphabetical index to deeds, concession 2, lot 4; abstract index to deeds, vol.A: 40 (mfm. at AO). Halton Land Registry Office (Milton, Ont.), Nelson Township, abstract index to deeds, concession 1, lot 2 (mfm. at AO). National Arch. (Washington), RG 94; RG 107; War of 1812, U.S. Volunteers, Lt. Colonel Willcocks's detachment, compiled service record, Abraham Markle; bounty land claim, Abraham Markle. PAC, MG 11, [CO 42] Q, 121: 140–47; 315: 4–28; 318/1: 22–47; MG 24, B69 (photocopy); RG 1, L3, 287: L11/87; 328A: M2/228; 333: M8/30, 40; RG 5, A1: 6510–13, 6840–41, 6888–90, 9115–18, 9415–17, 10247–49, 12223–26, 12238–41, 12396–97, 13664–65, 15383–87, 16028–29, 16431–37. Vigo County Public Library (Terre Haute, Ind.), Markle family file. *Abstracts of wills on file in the surrogate's office, city of New York* (17v., N.Y. Hist. Soc., *Coll.*, [ser.3], 25–41, New York, 1892–1908), 7: 17; 12: 338; 13: 121; 14: 341. "Choose one knight with sword," ed. R. J. Powell, *Wentworth Bygones* (Hamilton, Ont.), no.3 (1962): 35–43. *Doc. hist. of campaign upon Niagara frontier* (Cruikshank), vols.1–2, 5, 7. "Indiana election returns, 1816–1851," comp. Dorothy Riker and Gayle Thornbrough, *Ind. Hist. Coll.* ([Indianapolis]), 40 (1960): 160. "Journals of Legislative Assembly of U.C.," AO *Report*, 1912: 111; 1914: 750. "Records of Niagara . . . ," ed. E. A. Cruikshank, Niagara Hist. Soc., [*Pub.*], no.42 (1931): 116–18. *Select British docs. of War of 1812* (Wood). *Niagara Herald* (Niagara [Niagara-on-the-Lake, Ont.]), 31 Jan. 1801; 13 Feb., 10 April, 2 May, 4 June 1802. *Spectator* (St Catharines, [Ont.]), 14 Feb. 1817. *Western Register and Terre-Haute Advertiser*, 31 March 1826. *Digested summary and alphabetical list of private claims which have been presented to the House of Representatives from the first to the thirty-first Congress . . .* (3v., Washington, 1853; repr. Baltimore, Md., 1970), 2: 378. *Ancaster's heritage: a history of Ancaster Township* (Ancaster, Ont., 1973), 20, 31, 33, 238, 253–54, 256–57, 262, 270–73. Carnochan, *Hist. of Niagara*, 116, 141. R. L. Fraser, "Politics at the Head of the Lake in the era of the War of 1812: the case of Abraham Markle," *Wentworth Bygones*, no.14 (1984): 18–27. D. E. Graves, "The Canadian Volunteers, 1813–1815," *Military Collector & Historian* (Washington), 31 (1979): 113–17. D. N. Lewis, "In memoriam – Major Abraham Markle," *Leaves of Thyme* (Terre Haute), November–December 1976: 4–5.

MASERES, FRANCIS, lawyer, office holder, and author; b. 15 Dec. 1731 in London, son of Peter Abraham Maseres, physician, and Magdalene du Pratt du Clareau; d. unmarried, and was buried 19 May 1824 in Reigate, England.

Francis Maseres excelled in law and mathematics as a student at Clare College, Cambridge, where he received a BA in 1752 and an MA three years later. Giving promise of a distinguished career in law, he was called to the bar in 1758, the year of his first publication, *A dissertation on the use of the negative sign in algebra. . . .* He proved unsuccessful in establishing a law practice, however, in part, it would seem, from a greater concern that justice – as he saw it – be done in a case than that his client win. Despite his mediocre record as a practising advocate, his reputation for integrity, his exceptional knowledge of the law, and his fluency in French (even if it was the French of the reign of Louis XIV) gave credible backing to his request to friends and acquaintances in 1766 that they secure for him the position of attorney general of Quebec, left vacant by the dismissal of George Suckling*. Among his friends were William Hey*, who had just been appointed Quebec's new chief justice, and Fowler Walker, London agent for the merchants in the colony. It was perhaps on the advice of Walker that Maseres was recommended by Charles Yorke, attorney general in the Whig administration of Lord Rockingham. In any case, his undoubted qualities marked his appointment, dated 4 March 1766, as one of the happier products of the patronage system.

Maseres immediately set to work studying every available document concerning the province of Quebec and conferred on several occasions with Hey and Guy Carleton*, the newly appointed lieutenant governor. The three were in substantial agreement on legal and constitutional matters, and Maseres was directed to prepare a pamphlet for circulation among important ministers. In it he seized particularly upon two related questions: the inadequacy of the Royal Proclamation of 1763 as a basis for law in the province of Quebec and the necessity for an act of the British parliament to define the laws, especially those concerning the methods by which revenue might be raised and the position of Roman Catholics in the province. The terms under which a house of assembly might be called (a major bone of contention in the colony between the merchants and Governor James Murray*) needed clarification, but Maseres indicated that he did not consider it expedient to call an assembly for some years.

Maseres sailed for Quebec on 23 June 1766. He found the St Lawrence River "noble" and the country "more beautiful than England itself." Quebec, however, was "very dirty, partly through the mischief done by the siege . . . and partly from the supineness

Maseres

and indolence of the French inhabitants which make them leave everything in a poor shabby condition." He observed that the British and Canadian inhabitants "agree together tolerably well and speak well of each other," but that the British were divided by great animosity [see George Allsopp*].

Maseres himself incurred the wrath of many British merchants soon after taking the oath of office on 26 Sept. 1766, when, in his first important case as attorney general, he argued that customs duties on rum were legal in the province. He cited precedents from the French régime and declared his belief that the British crown had assumed all the powers formerly exercised by the French king. This argument failed to convince a jury composed chiefly of British merchants. In March 1767, in another case, the jury chose to disregard his appeal to them and declared not guilty one of six men charged with assaulting the merchant Thomas Walker*; the result discouraged Maseres from trying the other five. A little more than a year after taking office Maseres again found himself in a controversy with many in the British merchant community for having affirmed that the English bankruptcy laws were in force in the colony; his views appeared in the *Quebec Gazette* in December 1767 and drew down on him a bitter, anonymous denunciation in the same newspaper, which he ascribed to George Suckling and Thomas Aylwin*, a Quebec merchant.

In large part Maseres's problems stemmed from the unpopularity of government positions that it was his task to defend. But his own inflexibility and weakness in judging character were clear contributing factors. He seized upon any evidence supporting his views and, for all his training in the law, showed a remarkable tendency to believe those who told him what he wanted to hear. In the Walker case, Maseres continued to reiterate his faith in a crown witness long after others believed the witness's testimony to be false, and he praised Walker's conduct in the face of widespread public disapprobation of the merchant. The frequent appearance before the courts of "the violent gentlemen of the army" disgusted Maseres, and he blamed their conduct on laxity in the administration of Governor Murray, whom he described as "a madman of parts."

Maseres's weakness in judging character was most evident in religious matters. Coming from a Huguenot family, he was eager to see Protestantism promoted in the colony. He advocated measures intended to favour conversion of the Canadians from Roman Catholicism, without overt persecution or proselytism, through the encouragement of priests prepared to espouse Protestantism and through a gradual weakening of the finances of the Catholic Church in the colony and of the authority of its bishop, Jean-Olivier Briand*. Consequently, he was always willing to hear and to repeat criticism of Briand, and for a long time

he assumed that the Huguenot Pierre Du Calvet* and Du Calvet's later associate, the ex-Jesuit Pierre-Joseph-Antoine Roubaud*, represented a general opinion in the colony. Almost alone, he was convinced of the worthiness of Leger-Jean-Baptiste-Noël Veyssière*, a former Recollet who wished to obtain an Anglican living, and of Veyssière's ability to persuade Canadian priests and laymen to follow his example in converting to Protestantism. Carleton took a different view, as did Maseres's friend and confidant, the Reverend John Brooke*, who, for supporting the governor, was accused by Maseres of "a low and foolish piece of flattery" and thenceforth deprived by the incensed attorney general of any further contact with him. Before long Carleton would note Maseres's "want of knowledge of the World, and his having conversed more with books than with Men."

Despite a growing concern over the limitations of Maseres's judgement and his religious views, the governor retained faith in his attorney general's ability to produce an effective plan for the administration of justice in the colony. After it became known at Quebec in March 1768 that the British government required the governor and council, with the assistance of the chief justice and the attorney general, to report on the judicial system and to present a draft ordinance covering proposed changes, Maseres was given the task of drawing up the report. It has often been claimed that until then Maseres had been ready to revive the entire body of French civil law, as Carleton desired, but that in the process of preparing his report he deviated from this course. However, his private correspondence before this time indicates frequent shifts in emphasis, as he grappled with the difficulties inherent in any proposal for the administration of justice. It was likely his realization of the complexity of French civil law and of its application in a society ethnically mixed and commercially tied to Britain rather than any sudden change of heart that produced the "Draught of an Intended Report."

Maseres devoted more than one-third of his document to an examination of the contradictory nature and sometimes dubious legality of each provision made for the government of Quebec since the capitulation. The wording of this section has given rise to speculation concerning Maseres's change of attitude during 1768, yet on close examination it becomes apparent that many of his statements are conditional; Maseres seems to have been determined to leave the decision to the British government, but to awake its ministers to an appreciation of past errors without overtly criticizing them or their predecessors in office.

After this lengthy introduction, Maseres presented his only concrete recommendations. He advocated essentially a return to the practice of the French régime in the administration of justice, a plan with which the governor would agree. However, the basic problem was not the machinery of justice but the uncertainty as to which law was in force, and here Maseres refused to commit himself. Instead, he outlined four possible solutions, stating the difficulties involved in each and leaving the reader to weigh the evidence. The proposals were: creating a code specifying every law, whatever its origin, that should prevail in Quebec; reviving the entire French legal system with a few English laws introduced by ordinance; introducing English law except for a few general exceptions in which French law should be followed; adapting the third plan so as to specify precisely what former customs were to be the law of the province. Maseres objected to both the second and the third plan because they would involve constant reference to French precedents and "keep up in the minds of the Canadians that reverence for the law and lawyers of Paris, and that consequential opinion of the happiness of being subject to the French government." He warned that the apparently easiest methods of dealing with the problem would be attended by the worst results.

Maseres seems to have considered that a code of laws combining English and French usages was the ideal solution, but the difficulties in preparing such a code had become obvious to him. When François-Joseph Cugnet* had prepared a digest of French laws, Maseres and Hey had taken four hours to master the first five pages, even with the author present to explain them. Yet Maseres concluded, "When I did understand it, I thought the several propositions neatly and accurately expressed." Presumably other lawyers could also be led to understand the digest, but a more serious problem could not be so easily resolved. Other Canadians disputed Cugnet's version of French law as it had operated in New France, and any effort to secure agreement on a code would have precipitated the reference to French precedents that Maseres sought to avoid.

Maseres presented his report to the governor in February 1769 and had it promptly rejected. Maurice Morgann*, who had arrived at Quebec the previous summer to convey the opinions of colonial officials back to London, denounced Maseres's work as "extreamly defective and improper" and declared that there was not a useful idea in it. This statement, obviously far too sweeping, may have reflected the governor's impatience with his attorney general's effort. Any administrator was likely to condemn a report that failed to provide a clear line of direction or to present proposals that could be immediately translated into the required ordinance. Hey and Morgann were then enjoined by Carleton to prepare material, and in September 1769 the governor dispatched to London over his signature a report that owed something to a variety of documents, including, it would seem, earlier work by Maseres on the character of the pre-conquest legal system. Both Hey and Maseres

sent written dissents from Carleton's report. In his comments Maseres expressed his views less equivocally. He recommended the formulation of a legal code and stated the opinion, contrary to the one he seemed to hold as recently as a few months before, that English law had been introduced into the province as a result of the conquest. But even in this most extreme statement of his views, Maseres made it clear that he considered it essential to retain, at least for the time being, all French laws pertaining to "the tenure, inheritance, dower, alienation, and incumbrance of landed property, and to the distribution of the effects of persons who died intestate."

The disagreement between Carleton and Maseres over the latter's report crowned the attorney general's increasing disillusionment with the colonial experience. Professionally, he had lost all his major cases in court, judicial reforms that he had projected were blocked by the grand juries or in council, and his carefully considered report on the laws and administration of justice had been rejected out of hand. He had not even the feeling of having made a significant contribution to improvement, which would, he remarked, "balance the disagreeable circumstances of living in a sort of banishment in this frozen kingdom of the Northwind." Within a year of his arrival at Quebec he had wanted to return to England. The colony lacked natural and social graces. "There are no downs to ride upon, no pleasant green lanes, no parks or forests or gentleman's seats to go and see, or gentlemen to visit at them," he complained. The land was covered either by commonplace farms or impenetrable woods. Intellectual life was non-existent, Catholicism ubiquitous. In the autumn of 1769 Carleton granted him a one-year leave of absence, but relations between the two men had so deteriorated that it was understood Maseres would not come back.

After his return to England, Maseres published several works dealing with Quebec. The first, *Draught of an act of parliament for settling the laws of the province of Quebec*, published in August 1772, proposed among other things the adoption for Quebec of a civil code compiled by Cugnet, Joseph-André-Mathurin Jacrau*, and Colomban-Sébastien Pressart* and known in the colony as the "Extrait des Messieurs." Cugnet violently opposed several aspects of Maseres's plan, and, offended by his attacks, Maseres published in August 1773 *Mémoire à la défense d'un plan d'acte de parlement pour l'établissement des loix de la province de Québec*, in which he refuted them systematically. Maseres had modified slightly an earlier version of his *Draught* so as to meet some of the objections of Cugnet and Michel Chartier* de Lotbinière, but he could not agree to the admission of Roman Catholics into the government of Quebec. His contention that he had Canadian support for his plan was based on an optimistic reading of a highly

Maseres

selective correspondence from persons who remained anonymous. In 1774 he was called as a witness before the committee of the House of Commons considering the Quebec Bill and, as spokesman in Britain for the colonial merchants, he unsuccessfully opposed many of Carleton's judicial and constitutional proposals. He made it clear to the merchants, however, that he remained unwilling to press for either the elective assembly they desired or the immediate uprooting of all French laws and customs. He urged them to support, for the time being at least, an enlarged legislative council, more independent of the governor, but still without the power to levy taxes. There seems little doubt that, from this time on, Maseres was able to exercise a certain restraint upon the demands of the British inhabitants.

Once the Quebec Bill became law, Maseres was the natural conduit through which petitions from British merchants in the colony for its abolition or amendment were transmitted to Westminster. For them he expressed concern over the absence of habeas corpus and trial by jury, and in 1775 he published *An account of the proceedings of the British, and other Protestant inhabitants, of the province of Quebeck, in North America, in order to obtain an house of assembly in that province*. He followed it in 1776 with *Additional papers concerning the province of Quebeck*, which included recommendations for effecting a reconciliation between Britain and her rebellious American colonies, consisting largely of concessions to the Americans' grievances. Among his proposals were repeal of the Quebec Act and its replacement by a new act confirming the boundaries set by the Royal Proclamation of 1763 and establishing in Quebec English law with specific exceptions, and, if possible, a Protestant house of assembly, elected by Protestants and Catholics. These proposals were repeated in *The Canadian freeholder*, published in three volumes between 1777 and 1779. In early 1784, along with Jean-Baptiste-Amable Adhémar*, Jean De Lisle*, Pierre Du Calvet, and William Dummer Powell*, he declared his support for a petition brought to London by Powell in which the British merchants of the colony called for a house of assembly. He also published the petition that year.

Governor Frederick Haldimand* fulminated against the influence Maseres wielded in London, not only in favour of the colonial merchants' reform movement, but also in favour of Du Calvet, who was there to obtain compensation for imprisonment by Haldimand on suspicion of treason. So strongly did Maseres believe in this case that he financed Du Calvet's lawsuits against Haldimand and the publication of two of Du Calvet's pamphlets. In addition, with the chief justice of Quebec, Peter Livius*, he is said to have drafted *The case of Peter Du Calvet*, which he published in March 1784. Du Calvet's

secretary, Pierre-Joseph-Antoine Roubaud, stated that in one meeting "Mr. Maseres explained himself in a tone of vehemence and agitation, which surprised me in an Englishman. There was none of the national phlegm; it was Gascon vivacity and quickness; in a word the most heated enthusiasm."

However much Haldimand protested Maseres's activities, he seemed prepared to accept him as chief justice at Quebec. If such a possibility existed it was removed when Maseres's old adversary Carleton, now Lord Dorchester, secured appointment to Quebec as governor-in-chief; with him came the new chief justice, William Smith*. In London Maseres continued to interest himself in the colony. It may have been he who in 1788 published *A review of the government and grievances of the province of Quebec*, although the author was more probably Adam Lymburner*; if the publication was Maseres's, he acknowledged in it more than he had previously done the influence of patriotic, or national, sentiment and social thought. The following year James Monk, who had been dismissed as attorney general of the colony for a virulent attack on its judges and judicial system, drew heavily on the *Review* in a pamphlet condemning the arbitrary nature of the administration of justice and of government in the colony. When some of the judges published a rebuttal in 1790, Maseres himself replied the same year in *Answer to an introduction to the observations made by the judges of the Court of Common Pleas*. It was his last new publication on Quebec affairs; probably the partial victory of the merchants represented by the Constitutional Act of 1791 removed the necessity for an agent in legal and constitutional matters. In 1809, however, he reprinted a number of his earlier publications in *Occasional essays on various subjects, chiefly political and historical*.

After his return to England Maseres had taken up rooms in the Inner Temple (where he had been admitted in 1750); in 1774 he had been made a bencher, in 1781 a reader, and the following year treasurer. He had become a fellow of the Royal Society in 1771 and cursitor baron of the exchequer in 1773 (a sinecure he held until his death). From 1780 to 1822 he was senior judge of the sheriff's court in London. A man of wealth who could pursue his special interests, he published widely on mathematics and optics, as well as on legal, religious, and historical questions, and financed the publication of many works by authors he deemed worthy of assistance. Much of his time each year was spent in chambers, and the remainder he passed at his country home in Reigate, where he died in May 1824.

Rather short physically, Maseres had always dressed in a fashion "uniformly plain and neat" and he retained to the last "the three-cornered hat, tye-wig, and ruffles" of the reign of George II. He was known, the *Gentleman's Magazine* remarked in 1824, for "the cheerfulness of his disposition, his inflexible integrity, the equanimity of his temper, [and] his sincere piety." Although he made no great mark on the legal profession and even joked of his lack of success as a lawyer before going to Quebec, few knew English law as well, "and in questions of great moment," noted the *Gentleman's Magazine*, "the members of both houses have frequently availed themselves of his judgement and superior information." Jeremy Bentham called him the most honest lawyer England ever knew.

Out of the controversies in which he engaged, Maseres acquired a reputation for anti-Catholic prejudice (presumably part of his Huguenot heritage) that has established him as an enemy of the Canadians and tended to enshrine his opponents as heroes. Carleton's declaration – "I very soon discovered his strong Antipathy to the Canadians, for no Reason, that I know of, except their being Roman Catholics" – has pursued Maseres down the centuries, but it does little to explain the changes in his views of a society in which Catholicism was a constant; and there is ample evidence that Maseres's concepts of law and society were no mere "rationalization of prejudice." According to a contemporary, he held "the most liberal views of toleration on religious opinions," yet the same writer affirmed that "the Baron was an Anti-Catholic." In a sense both these apparently contradictory statements are correct. It was Maseres's belief in freedom that led him to distrust the political power of the Roman Catholic Church, which he identified with illiberalism. While he would not exclude a deist or an atheist from public office, he would block accession to a Roman Catholic on the ground that it was a tenet of Catholicism not to tolerate heresy, and he felt that "who will not tolerate others ought not to be allowed to possess civil employments, which may gradually give them an influence in the state." But his refusal to countenance a place for Catholics in government did not prevent him from aiding them against their oppressors during the French revolution; a contemporary observed that "his house was open to the refugees from France, where were to be seen archbishops and bishops . . . driven from their homes by the atheistical bigotry of the time." At bottom, given Maseres's perception of Catholicism, his refusal to accept Catholic influence in government was in keeping with his whig political views and insistence on political liberty.

The historian William Stewart Wallace* found in Maseres's agency in London for the British colonial merchants before and during the American revolution his most significant contribution to Canadian history, for his "championship of the cause of the merchants of Quebec and Montreal was a safeguard and guarantee of the loyalty of a large part of them." It may be argued that his role was more negative and perhaps more important. At the same time as he distrusted Roman Catholicism in politics, he seems to have underrated the influence of religious faith on human actions and thus the tenacity with which the Canadians would consider their religion to be part of their identity. His views encouraged British merchants to maintain in their program of political and legal reforms anti-Catholic measures that at once intensified opposition to it in some Canadian circles and prevented Canadians otherwise disposed to support the program from joining in a common drive to achieve it. He thus contributed to delaying the entire constitutional and legal development of the colony. He looked for principles in politics that would approach the certainty he perceived in mathematics, but a search for universal values that transcended religion and nationality has earned him repeated denunciations by, in the words of historian Hilda Marion Neatby*, "nationalist romantics of the nineteenth century and nationalist zealots of the twentieth."

ELIZABETH ARTHUR

Francis Maseres was a prolific writer on mathematics and on legal and political subjects. His most important works relating to Quebec are: *Considerations on the expediency of procuring an act of parliament for the settlement of the province of Quebec* (London, 1766); *The trial of Daniel Disney, esq. . . .* (Quebec, 1767); *Considerations on the expediency of admitting representatives from the American colonies into the British House of Commons* (London, 1770); *Draught of an act of parliament for settling the laws of the province of Quebec* ([London, 1772]); *A draught of an act of parliament for tolerating the Roman Catholick religion in the province of Quebec, and for encouraging and introducing the Protestant religion into the said province, and for vesting the lands belonging to certain religious houses in the said province in the crown of the kingdom for the support of the civil government of the said province and for other purposes* ([London, 1772]); *Things necessary to be settled in the province of Quebec, either by the king's proclamation or order in council, or by act of parliament* ([London, 1772]); *Mémoire à la défense d'un plan d'acte de parlement pour l'établissement des loix de la province de Québec . . .* (Londres, 1773); *Réponse aux observations faites par Mr. François Joseph Cugnet, secrétaire du gouverneur & Conseil de la province de Québec pour la langue françoise, sur le plan d'acte de parlement pour l'établissement des lois de la ditte province . . .* ([Londres], 1773); *An account of the proceedings of the British, and other Protestant inhabitants, of the province of Quebeck, in North America, in order to obtain an house of assembly in that province* (London, 1775); *Additional papers concerning the province of Quebeck: being an appendix to the book entitled, "An account of the proceedings of the British, and other Protestant inhabitants, of the province of Quebeck, in North America, [in] order to obtain a house of assembly in that province"* (London, 1776); *The Canadian freeholder: in two dialogues between an Englishman and a Frenchman, settled in Canada, shewing the sentiments of the bulk of the freeholders of Canada concerning the late Quebeck-Act; with some*

Matthews

remarks on the Boston-Charter Act; and an attempt to shew the great expediency of immediately repealing both those acts of parliament, and of making some other useful regulations and concessions to his majesty's American subjects, as a ground for a reconciliation with the united colonies in America (3v., London, 1777–79); Observations and reflections, on an act passed in the year, 1774, for the settlement of the province of Quebec, intended to have been then printed for the use of the electors of Great Britain, but now first published (London, 1782); The case and claim of the American loyalists impartially stated and considered (London, 1783); The case of Peter Du Calvet, esq., of Montreal in the province of Quebeck; containing (amongst other things worth notice,) an account of the long and severe imprisonment he suffered in the said province . . . (London, 1784) [written in collaboration with Pierre Du Calvet and Peter Livius]; Questions sur lesquelles on souhaite de sçavoir les réponses de monsieur Adhémar et de monsieur De Lisle et d'autres habitants de la province de Québec (Londres, 1784); A review of the government and grievances of the province of Quebec, since the conquest of it by the British arms . . . (London, 1788); Answer to an introduction to the observations made by the judges of the Court of Common Pleas, for the district of Quebec, upon the oral and written testimony adduced upon the investigation, into the past administration of justice, ordered in consequence of an address of the Legislative Council, with remarks on the laws and government of Quebec (London, 1790); Occasional essays on various subjects, chiefly political and historical . . . (London, 1809). In addition, Maseres compiled A collection of several commissions, and other public instruments, proceeding from his majesty's royal authority, and other papers, relating to the state of the province in Quebec in North America, since the conquest of it by the British arms in 1760 (London, 1772; repr. [East Ardsley, Eng., and New York], 1966). His correspondence, with an introduction, notes, and appendices by William Stewart Wallace, was published as The Maseres letters, 1766–1768 (Toronto, 1919).

BL, Add. MSS 35915 (copies at PAC). Lambeth Palace Library (London), Fulham papers, I: ff.120–60. PRO, CO 42/20; 42/26–29. Docs. relating to constitutional hist., 1759–91 (Shortt and Doughty; 1918). Gentleman's Magazine, January–June 1824: 569–73. Reports on the laws of Quebec, 1767–1770, ed. W. P. M. Kennedy and Gustave Lanctot (Ottawa, 1931). William Smith, The diary and selected papers of Chief Justice William Smith, 1784–1793, ed. L. F. S. Upton (2v., Toronto, 1963–65), 1: 264; 2: 65, 67, 69, 77, 90, 145. DNB. A. L. Burt, The old province of Quebec (2v., Toronto, 1968), 1. John Mappin, "The political thought of Francis Maseres, attorney general of Canada, 1766–69" (MA thesis, McGill Univ., Montreal, 1968). Neatby, Quebec.

MATTHEWS, JOHN, politician; b. probably in England; d. 20 Aug. 1832, perhaps in England.

John Matthews's accounts of his youth hint at a genteel background. He claimed attendance at an English college in Paris and attended, some time after 1779, the Royal Military Academy, Woolwich (London). He served in the Royal Artillery for 27 years until his battalion's reduction in March 1819, when he

retired on a pension with the rank of captain. His period of active service was not continuous, though: at some point during the Napoleonic Wars he took up farming "to retrieve the reduced condition of my family," only to be ruined by the agricultural crisis that followed the peace. He then rejoined his battalion for the sake of pay until its disbandment 18 months later, when he emigrated to Canada.

Matthews reached Quebec shortly before the death of the governor-in-chief, the Duke of Richmond [Lennox*], in August 1819. He presented himself to Richmond's son-in-law Sir Peregrine Maitland*, lieutenant governor of Upper Canada, as an old friend of the duke's and claimed to have come out upon Richmond's promise to put him in charge of a planned military colony. He sought Maitland's aid in settling in Upper Canada and established himself temporarily near Queenston.

Maitland was willing to help, but Matthews proved hard to please and their relationship soon soured. The lieutenant governor successively recommended sites on Lake Simcoe and Rice Lake. Matthews refused these, while asking for an assortment of locations, all of which were either reserved or pre-empted. At last he was summoned before the Executive Countil and pressed to accept an 800-acre estate on the Thames River in Lobo Township.

Matthews, his family, and servants proceeded to Lobo in October 1820, forming a train of "nearly thirty persons . . . six waggons, one cart, twenty-four horses, a flock of sheep, and some cows." As soon as he arrived, he let the government know of his disappointment. He had sold his British properties at a loss of 1,000 guineas in order to speed to Richmond's side, and had been rewarded with stony oak-plains worth a dollar an acre. "This, Sir, certainly was not the sort of service the Duke proposed or intended to render me." He feared that Maitland's good intentions were thwarted by influences with which the lieutenant governor could not contend. This was the first murmur of a theme that was to become a staple of Matthews's political discourse.

Matthews now began to covet the estates of a neighbour, the magistrate Daniel Springer, whom he accused of enlarging his holdings by force and fraud. He dropped these charges when told that Springer's allegedly fraudulent claims had been certified by Thomas Talbot*, the aristocratic patriarch of the London District, but he continued to pursue the magistrate with charges of official and personal misconduct. A series of letters harped on Springer's indolence, drunkenness, rapacity, and deceit; on his reputed paternity of his associate in villainy, deputy surveyor Roswell MOUNT; and even, once, on the "unfortunate condition" of his eldest daughter (a misfortune to which Matthews, with daughters of his own, was no doubt especially sensitive).

Matthews also began feuding with the commissioners for forfeited estates and their secretary, James Buchanan Macaulay*, over two lots they had sold him. In one case they had given him a title-deed to a different lot from the one he claimed to have purchased; in the other they were simply unable to supply an adequate deed. In the second case Maitland supported Matthews, while chiding him for his insolence towards the commissioners. The lieutenant governor asked the commissioners to refund the purchase price, but to his chagrin they refused when advised by Solicitor General Henry John Boulton* that they had no legal power to do so. Boulton at once was added to Matthews's list of enemies, as was Attorney General John Beverley Robinson* for failing to take seriously the charges against Springer. "There is a jealous connexion of friendship, of family, and of interest throughout the province," Matthews told Maitland in 1822, "and under those circumstances every thing I say is misrepresented, and every thing I do is misconceived with a boldness truly astonishing." His calumniators were encouraged, he wrote, by the knowledge that he was not in Maitland's favour.

Matthews's denunciations of Springer, and his themes of oligarchic misrule and a local usurpation of power, found ready credence among those of his neighbours who felt similarly aggrieved. He made himself the spokesman of these malcontents, including even the local Indians, and enlarged his constituency by espousing the sectional interests of northern Middlesex County. At the general election of 1824 he and John Rolph* ousted the sitting members for Middlesex, Mahlon Burwell* and John Bostwick*, both of whom enjoyed the favour of Talbot. Talbot reported to Major George Hillier*, Maitland's civil secretary, that Matthews had been supported "by all the Old Country and Yankee Radicals."

A few months later, Talbot had to write to Hillier again. Matthews had taken witnesses to the London District assizes of September 1824 in order to complain of Springer to the grand jury. The resulting presentment apparently persuaded the government that an inquiry was desirable. Talbot advised that the inquiry be confided to three reliable men (whom he named) rather than to the district magistracy as a whole, since most of the magistrates would "lean to Matthews." Talbot urged Hillier to discuss his advice only with Maitland and Robinson, "as I am desirous of not appearing in these dirty works."

The incident for which Matthews is especially remembered happened on the last day of 1825. In the evening he was among a group of assemblymen who attended a theatrical performance by an American company. While the actors got ready, the musicians played popular airs, starting with "God Save the King!" and "Rule, Britannia!" Various members of the assembly competed in calling for a Jacobite song,

"Hail, Columbia!" and "Yankee Doodle." That day the assembly, agitated by Robinson's Naturalization Bill, had passed resolutions which humiliated the provincial government by rejecting the official view that post-loyalist American immigrants were aliens. One or two pro-government members took it in bad part when there was a call for "Yankee Doodle." A reformer's attempt to remove a tory's cap sparked a momentary scuffle, but the play then proceeded without further fuss.

It was a trifling incident and Matthews did not figure in it with special prominence. Three months later, however, he was officially apprised that Lord Dalhousie [Ramsay*], Richmond's successor as governor-in-chief, had read in the newspapers that Matthews and others "had in a riotous and outrageous manner called for the national tunes and songs of the United States . . . urging the audience then assembled to take off their hats, as is usual in the British dominions in honour of the national air of 'God Save the King.'" Finding these rumours "fully corroborated," Dalhousie intended to report the incident to the commander-in-chief of the army but wished to permit Matthews to transmit through Maitland "any explanations that may palliate (if possible) such report of his conduct."

Matthews protested that he had evidently been condemned unheard. There had been nothing "riotous or outrageous" about the incident; "it was all fun and frolic." The construction his traducers put upon it "must have originated in paltry political vexations, and in great baseness and malignity of Heart." He did acknowledge, though, that the political events of the day had coloured those of the evening. In forwarding Matthews's reply, Maitland seized on this admission to present Matthews's conduct in the worst light.

In September 1826 the Board of Ordnance ordered that Matthews should return to England by the first ship of the next season, and in the mean time go at once to Quebec. This order was transmitted to him from Quebec on 8 Dec. 1826, three days after the start of the new legislative session. The House of Assembly referred the affair to a select committee, which took evidence from almost every member of the theatre audience. Its report stressed the triviality of the incident, the impossibility that Dalhousie could have obtained "full corroboration" of misconduct that had not occurred, and the iniquity of condemning Matthews on the evidence of secret informers. It noted the impropriety of trying to place Matthews under arrest at Quebec during the parliamentary session.

Matthews's pension had been suspended, and it is commonly stated that he went to England in order to recover it and died there. In fact, it was restored without his going to England. Re-elected with Rolph in 1828 (after first declining to stand, because of ill health), he played his usual prominent role in the

Matthews

session of 1829 but seems to have missed that of 1830. When his wife died, in April 1830, he was reported to be in England, and he may have stayed there until his death.

Matthews was one of those post-war British immigrants to Upper Canada whose hostility to the provincial government was partly rooted in disappointment of their material expectations and a jealous contempt for the local élite. In the case of Matthews, a Unitarian, as in that of the Quaker Charles Fothergill*, religious heterodoxy played a part by fostering an aversion towards the narrow Anglican orthodoxy of the provincial establishment. Matthews has been dismissed as a self-deceiving egoist, often carried away by his own inflated rhetoric, a dissipated malingerer, an advocate of paternalistic social ideals which were old-fashioned, self-contradictory, and hopelessly utopian. There are grounds for believing that these judgements underestimate him. There is no evidence that he was more dissipated than others of his time and class. His ill health, which he traced in part to a fall from his waggon in 1820, was real enough to alarm his friends. Above all, he shows signs of too much intelligence to be written off as a political nitwit.

Matthews's was in fact a more complex personality than at first appears, and his paternalist rhetoric may at once represent a sincere commitment to the ideal and a satiric comment on society's failure to achieve it. One clue to his complexity is his outspoken Unitarianism – so inconsistent with his character as a simple old soldier – which inspired a fellow assemblyman to call him "the Reverend John Matthews." Another is his taste for subversive irony. When Maitland spurned his first charges against Springer, Matthews solemnly announced his conclusion that in future he should keep silent about abuses that were reported to him, "no matter how imperiously I should feel it my duty to expose them to His Excellency." When as an assemblyman he was invited by Maitland to dinner, he declined with the dry remark that his attendance could give pleasure to no one, but he punctiliously sent Lady Sarah Maitland (his old patron's daughter) a note regretting the circumstances that kept him from "once more paying my humble and most dutiful respects to your Ladyship." Even in the letter that was supposed to exonerate him from the charge of disgraceful conduct at the theatre, he characterized that day's resolutions on the alien question as a decision "that the King had thousands more of good and excellent subjects than many of his friends were willing to allow him." It was Matthews who presented Timothy Street's satirical petition against the Marmora Iron Works to the assembly in 1828, and he may well have had a hand in its composition.

Matthews's occasional invasions of the local Court of Requests in order to denounce the presiding magistrates suggest that his subversive instincts were allied with a politically effective sense of theatre. It is likely that this theatricality (somewhat compulsive perhaps, yet not entirely uncontrolled) pervaded his personality, and that his Falstaffian bombast and Shandean emotionalism were at least in part an affectation based on available cultural models. Matthews, in short, who owned a notable library, was more intelligent than he pretended, and his buffoonery was most likely the expression of an authentic English eccentricity rooted in social alienation.

Beneath the grease-paint, a courageous determination is evident in the relentlessness with which, in letter after letter to Maitland, he vilified enemies who enjoyed the lieutenant governor's confidence. "Captain Matthews is violent," observed William Lyon Mackenzie* in 1828, "but he is a tower of strength to the people in the Assembly." "Matthews political character is of the manly cast," commented a neutral observer, "for he has always acted as he said he would." Certainly Maitland and Talbot were not inclined to dismiss him as a clown. By subverting the established order in Middlesex he had proved himself one of the most dangerous men in the colony.

Here is the essential context for evaluating his treatment in 1826. It is inconceivable that the incident at the theatre came to Dalhousie's attention without the connivance of men close to Maitland. The two known informers against Matthews were John Beikie, clerk of the Executive Council, and Charles Richardson, a law student of Robinson's who was shortly to take part in the wrecking of Mackenzie's printing-shop. Beikie by his own admission had entered the theatre midway through the incident, and his account was completely superficial and disconnected. Richardson's was prejudiced against Matthews but could not disguise the trifling nature of the incident. Both men's extant reports were written by request. Although it is impossible to say whence the initiative came, Maitland made the most of the opportunity by his own disingenuous commentary on Matthews's letter of justification and by enclosing Beikie's and Richardson's tendentious remarks on it. Like the other vindictive blows struck at this time by the government and its supporters against leading critics, this one rebounded on its perpetrators by its effect on public opinion. Its petty vengefulness was typical of Maitland and his advisers, but it also hints at the danger they perceived in Matthews.

PAUL ROMNEY

[The main manuscript source for Matthews's career is PAC, RG 5, A1, 45–87 (volume 81 is devoted wholly to him); also relevant are RG 1, E3, 48a: 24–54, and RG 7, G16C. The chief printed primary source on the "affair" is U.C., House of Assembly, *Journal*, 1826–27, app.P. His political career can be traced in the *Journal*, 1825–29, the *Colonial Advocate*, 1824–29, the *Weekly Register* (York [Toronto]),

1823–24, and the *Gore Gazette, and Ancaster, Hamilton, Dundas and Flamborough Advertiser* (Ancaster, [Ont.]), April–June 1828.

Among secondary sources, Patterson, "Studies in elections in U.C.," 47–86, depicts Matthews's personality and importance in Middlesex politics; the flavour of the "affair" is best captured by J. C. Dent, *The story of the Upper Canadian rebellion; largely derived from original sources and documents* (2v., Toronto, 1885), 1: 144–50. Other useful sources are Craig, *Upper Canada*, 119–20, and Aileen Dunham, *Political unrest in Upper Canada, 1815–1836* (London, 1927; repr. Toronto, 1963), 108–9. P.R.]

MAXWELL, SARAH. *See* AINSE

MAYERS. *See* MEYERS

MECHTLER, GUILLAUME-JOSEPH (William), musician, music teacher, militia officer, and office holder; baptized 24 July 1764 in Brussels, son of Pierre-Paul Mechtler and Marie-Madeleine Moreau; m. 17 June 1793 Marie-Anne-Angélique Landrième in Montreal; d. there 13 Feb. 1833.

Guillaume-Joseph Mechtler may have appeared first in the province of Quebec with a theatre company. In April 1787 he was obliged to defer payment of an overdue debt to Montreal businessman and composer Joseph Quesnel* because his meagre income of about £2 a week with a troupe of actors was seized as soon as he received it in order to pay other debts. In July Mechtler advertised in the *Quebec Gazette* that, "having entirely quitted the business of the Theatre, he intends settling in this town, where he means to teach the VIOLIN and HARPSICHORD." By November his financial situation had not improved.

Perhaps it was his inability to make a decent living at Quebec that prompted Mechtler in September 1789 to announce in the *Montreal Gazette* that he had settled in Montreal as a music master and intended to take pupils in "FORTE PIANO, HARPSICHORD and VIOLIN." In 1790 he taught violin to Frederick William ERMATINGER for 15 shillings a month in February and 20 shillings a month thereafter. It was probably he who taught music to Rachel-Charlotte Frobisher, daughter of Montreal businessman Joseph Frobisher*; her manuscript music-book reveals that "Mr. M." had begun his lessons on 3 April 1793.

In July 1791 Mechtler had been appointed organist at Christ Church with a salary of £20 per annum, and one year later he had become co-organist with Jean-Louis Foureur, *dit* Champagne, at Notre-Dame church for about £20 a year; in 1800 he would apply to Notre-Dame for an increase of £10. A Mr Mechtler played a piano concerto by Leopold Antonín Koželuh at Philadelphia in January 1795 and performed there on the harp in April. It is doubtful whether a Montreal organist could have absented himself from his post for such a long period, and the Philadelphia

musician may have been a relative. As well, the Mrs Mechtler who sang in Halifax, New York ("lately from England"), and Boston in the early 1790s is unlikely to have been the wife of Guillaume-Joseph. On the other hand, it is reasonable to assume that the Mr Mechtler who performed a piano concerto in Montreal on 14 Sept. 1796 was Guillaume-Joseph. In addition to performing, Mechtler composed; in 1811 he received £48 for works of his own composition, presumably written for Notre-Dame church.

Mechtler's income as organist at Notre-Dame, music teacher, performer, and composer was evidently insufficient to live on, and he supplemented it with at least one other function, that of inspector of the hay market and stamper of weights and measures, a position he held from at least 1809 until his death. He had apparently joined the Montreal militia shortly after his arrival in the city and by 1813 he was quartermaster of the 5th Battalion of the Select Embodied Militia, which was reorganized in 1814 as the Chasseurs Canadiens.

Mechtler absented himself as organist of Notre-Dame for a time beginning in the summer of 1814, probably to perform military duty. When the *fabrique* of Notre-Dame could find no Catholic capable of replacing him, Bishop Joseph-Octave PLESSIS authorized hiring a Protestant (S. Brewer) on the ground that music on the organ during the mass was important to the Canadians, some of whom might otherwise attend Protestant services to hear the instrument played. His decision was strongly contested by the Sulpicians, who had the charge of the parish, and in September the case was sent to the Sacred Congregation of Propaganda in Rome for decision; it found in favour of Plessis in 1820. Meanwhile, Mechtler had resigned from the Chasseurs Canadiens in February 1815 and had received a new contract as organist in July at a salary of £60 a year (including the organ-blower's fee).

Mechtler returned to the sedentary militia in 1815 as a captain in the 2nd Battalion of Montreal's militia, a Canadian unit. About 1821 he rose to the rank of major, where he remained until, no longer qualifying as an officer under a new militia act in 1830, he offered to resign with a lieutenant-colonelcy. Although he may not have been continually dogged by financial worries, he had at least fallen on hard times again by late 1820 when 200 acres of land belonging to him in Hinchinbrook Township were seized by the sheriff of Montreal at the suit of a Montreal firm, J. J. and L. Henshaw. Many of Mechtler's business and professional activities as a musician would seem to have been conducted with the British population. His advertisements of 1787 and 1789 were in English only, although both the *Quebec Gazette* and the *Montreal Gazette* were bilingual newspapers. He called himself Guillaume-Joseph until at least the early 1800s, but in 1799 he signed William in an

Merrick

English context and by 1813 he was signing thus even to letters he wrote in French. Yet he maintained strong social ties with the Canadian community through the militia and Notre-Dame, where he remained organist until shortly before his death.

HELMUT KALLMANN

ANQ-M, CN1-121, 23 juill. 1792. AP, Notre-Dame de Montréal, Reg. des baptêmes, mariages et sépultures, 17 juin 1793, 15 févr. 1833; Reg. des délibérations du conseil de la fabrique, 22 juill. 1792. Arch. de l'Hôpital Général de Québec, R.-C. Frobisher, "Chants, textes anglais ou français." Arch. municipales, Bruxelles (Belgique), État civil, Sainte-Gudule, 24 juill. 1764. AUM, P 58, U, Mechtler à Quesnel, 24 avril, 22 nov. 1787; Mechtler à Guy, 4, 16 oct., 16 nov. 1813; 1er juin 1830. PAC, MG 19, A2, ser.3, 31: 71. *Montreal Gazette*, 3 Sept. 1789. *Quebec Gazette*, 12 July 1787, 25 July 1799, 16 Feb. 1815, 16 Nov. 1820, 22 Feb. 1821. *Encyclopedia of music in Canada*, ed. Helmut Kallmann et al. (Toronto, 1981). *Quebec almanac*, 1810–27. Willy Amtmann, *La musique au Québec, 1600–1875*, Michelle Pharand, trad. (Montréal, 1976), 296–97, 300–1. Helmut Kallmann, *A history of music in Canada, 1534–1914* (Toronto and London, 1960), 84. O. G. [T.] Sonneck, *Early concert-life in America (1731–1800)* (Leipzig, [German Democratic Republic], 1907), 141–42, 190, 292. "An account of Christ's Church in the city of Montreal, province of Lower-Canada," *Canadian Magazine and Literary Repository* (Montreal), 4 (January–June 1825): 217–24. Cécile Huot, "Musiciens belges au Québec," *Les Cahiers canadiens de musique* (Montréal), 8 (1974): 69–71. Helmut Kallmann, "From the archives: the *Montreal Gazette* on music from 1786 to 1797," *Canadian Music Journal* (Toronto), 6, no.3 (summer 1962): 7–8. O.[-M.-H.] Lapalice, "Les organistes et maîtres de musique à Notre-Dame de Montréal," *BRH*, 25 (1919): 245–46. "Souvenirs artistiques de Notre-Dame de Montréal," *Le Canada musical* (Montréal), 7 (1880): 135.

MERRICK, JOHN, artisan, merchant, and architect; b. *c.* 1756 in Halifax, third son of William Merrick and Ann Green; m. there 25 Aug. 1779 Sarah Boyer (Bayer); they had one son who died as an infant; d. 4 June 1829 in Horton, N.S.

John Merrick probably apprenticed in his father's firm, Merrick and Son, in the 1770s. By the mid 1790s he was one of three master painters in Halifax and had obtained provincial government contracts for painting and glazing. He would continue to obtain contracts for major building projects through the next three decades. From at least 1802 to 1812 Merrick also provided painting and glazing services to the Royal Navy's Halifax dockyard and supplies for the army's wartime building in the town. To private citizens he offered painting and glazing materials as well as "House, Sign, Carriage and Ornamental Painting, Gilding, Glazing, Varnishing, etc." Perhaps because his imperial contracts gave him the bills of exchange necessary for payment of his British suppliers, Mer-

rick was not pressed, like other Halifax merchants, to include the wide variety of goods that characterized local mercantile business in the Napoleonic era. In 1815 he took his nephews, William Parsons Merrick, an orphan whom he had raised, and Henry Boyer, into partnership as John Merrick and Company; in 1821, at age 65, he himself retired from the firm to a rural retreat in Horton.

Although Merrick achieved local prominence exceptional for an artisan, it is unlikely that his business as a painter and glazier accounted for his rising status. In the 1780s he had taken an initial interest in civic affairs and become active in St Matthew's Church (Presbyterian), perhaps through the influence of John Fillis*. In 1806 he was named one of three commissioners accountable to the legislature for erection of the county court-house, and five years later he was given a similar role for Province House, a building which, upon its completion in 1820, became the new home of the legislature and the courts. Merrick's importance was also reflected in his roles as a signatory of citizens' petitions, a subscriber to charitable funds, and an officer in the Philanthropic Society for Relief of Debtors (1812), the Halifax Fire Insurance Company (1819–20), and the Royal Acadian Society (1821). Although never a magistrate or militia officer, he, like other members of the Halifax gentry, had his portrait painted in oil by Robert Field*.

Merrick's renown lies in his association with the design of Province House, described by a modern writer as "the best example of Palladian architecture to be found in Canada." As early as 1809 his name was one of those suggested as "fit and proper persons . . . to prepare plans and estimates of a proper building," and in 1811, when the legislature approved a plan and elevation for the building, it clearly accepted the designs that Merrick presented and received them as his plans. Still, the attribution of the design is a difficult matter. If Merrick did in fact design Province House, it is curious that he is not known to have designed any other buildings. Tradition has associated his name with the Palladian-style St George's Round Church in Halifax [*see* George Wright*], but not generally as its designer. Nor have the several Palladian-style mansions built during the Napoleonic era for Nova Scotia's officials and gentry been credited to him. Furthermore, commentators as diverse as Thomas Beamish Akins*, Archibald McKellar MacMechan*, and Arthur W. Wallace have queried whether Merrick procured rather than drew the plans for Province House, a suggestion fuelled by a legislative committee's purchase in London in 1798–99 of "Plans Sections &c for the State House and Government House." In the end, the rough plans that Merrick presented in 1811 were selected by the legislators, apparently on the basis of size, over those prepared by Richard Scott, a well-established

Scottish-born builder who became responsible for the day-to-day construction of Province House. It was Scott who was named in the cornerstone as architect, a claim which was repeated in print during Merrick's lifetime and which he did not apparently refute.

Merrick may have been a "natural" architect, skilled in adapting the widely published Palladian designs to Nova Scotia's legislative building and perhaps other of the anonymously designed Palladian edifices in the province. Alternatively, he may have procured a design for Province House through his connections with the British army and navy or Prince Edward* Augustus. Either hypothesis implies skills on Merrick's part which contribute to explaining his rise in status after 1800 and his known association with Halifax buildings.

SUSAN BUGGEY

Kings County Court of Probate (Kentville, N.S.), Book 2: 315–17 (John Merrick) (mfm. at PANS). NMM, HAL, vols.1–5 (mfm. at PAC). PANS, Map Coll., 1.2.10.3., Halifax, 1811–19, Province House; MG 2, 611, no.22529; MG 4, 55, 68; MG 20, 214, no.132; RG 1, 140: 275; 228, nos.129–30; 287, docs.81, 122, 159, 170; 288, docs.26, 34, 36; 289, docs.28, 46, 51; 444, nos.47, 69; RG 5, A, 9, 13–22. PRO, WO 44/81: 81–120; WO 55/858: 321–32, 336–64 (mfm. at PAC). St Paul's Anglican Church (Halifax), Reg. of baptisms, marriages, and burials, copy of old marriage licences, 25 Aug. 1779 (mfm. at PANS). *Acadian Magazine* (Halifax), 1 (1826–27): 81. N.S., *Acts*, 1811, c.14; 1819, c.17. Perkins, *Diary, 1797–1803* (Fergusson), 270. *Free Press* (Halifax), 1 March 1821, 9 June 1829. *Nova-Scotia Royal Gazette*, 20 May 1783, 28 Oct. 1800, 6 March 1806, 21 Feb. 1809, 8 May 1810. *Weekly Chronicle*, 19 Nov. 1813; 19 May, 25 Aug. 1815; 12 Feb. 1819. *Halifax almanac*, 1806–9. Akins, *Hist. of Halifax City*, 127, 129, 148–49, 165, 271. Nathalie Clerk, *Palladian style in Canadian architecture* (Ottawa, 1984). A. [McK.] MacMechan, *The book of Ultima Thule* (Toronto, 1927), 145–56. E. A. Merrick Christian, "John Merrick, Esquire, 1756–1829, architect of Province House, Halifax, Nova Scotia" (mimeograph, n.p., 1983; copy at PANS). D. A. Sutherland, "The merchants of Halifax, 1815–1850: a commercial class in pursuit of metropolitan status" (PHD thesis, Univ. of Toronto, 1975). A. W. Wallace, *An album of drawings of early buildings in Nova Scotia* (Halifax, 1976). A. [G.] Archibald, "The Province Building," N.S. Hist. Soc., *Coll.*, 4 (1885): 247–58. J. D. Logan, "The architecture of Province House: the 'Adam' myth and the historic 'facts' which establish the right of John Merrick to be regarded as the designer of the home of Nova Scotia's General Assembly," *Novascotian, Nova Scotia's Farm and Home Journal* (Halifax), 4 May 1923: 22. "What the people say: the late John Merrick," *Morning Herald* (Halifax), 7 July 1881: 1.

MERRY, RALPH, businessman; b. 16 March 1753 in Lynn, Mass., son of Ralph Merry and Sarah Knower; d. 1825 at the Outlet (Magog), Lower Canada, and was buried there.

Ralph Merry's grandfather, also named Ralph, left London aboard his own ship and settled at Lynn towards the end of the 17th century. Merry was living at Providence, R.I., in 1783, and then in 1792 moved to St Johnsbury, Vt. Like many Americans he found the prospect of land in Lower Canada interesting, particularly after Lieutenant Governor Alured CLARKE's proclamation in 1792 concerning land grants in the townships and the publicity given the matter in American newspapers. On 7 March 1797 Merry, who had substantial means, obtained for $4,000 a proxy from William Powell in order to negotiate the grant of half of Acton Township, for which Powell was authorized to do the survey. In addition Merry represented a group seeking grants in Hatley Township. These applications were rejected by the land committee of the Executive Council in 1802, despite several favourable testimonials.

In 1799 Merry settled with his wife, Sarah Sylvester, and their eight children in Bolton Township, at a place then known as the Outlet; in 1855 the village that had developed there took the name of Magog. In the summer of 1800 he bought several lots for 2,000 Spanish dollars from Nicholas Austin, the Bolton Township leader. Two years later he purchased a huge tract in the same township from his brother Jonathan, and then in 1804 further enlarged his estate by acquiring several properties in the adjacent Hatley Township. Austin had already put the rapids on the Magog to good use by building an improvised sawmill and a grist-mill, and Merry improved and ran them. From 1808 he was in partnership with his son John S. In 1809 he put an ironworks into operation, but the venture was not successful because the iron ore found in the region was of poor quality. A carpenter's shop and a mill for carding and weaving wool proved more profitable. The first general store opened in 1820 with Merry's financial backing, and from 1823 it served as a stage-stop for the mail between Montreal and Stanstead. The establishment became a landmark in the region.

Merry did, however, suffer a number of severe set-backs; since the township lands were granted undivided, the title deeds of subsequent purchasers remained uncertain. He had to endure various lawsuits, and 2,300 acres of his property were sold by the sheriff in 1816. Tragedy cast a shadow over his family life. In May 1799 his 10-year-old son Benjamin lost his way in the forest and despite all the searches undertaken was never found. Another son, Ralph, suffered for a long time from the effects of an accident that occurred when he was working in the sawmill, and Merry had to take him to Boston for treatment. Finally, his wife died suddenly at the age of 57 on 8 Aug. 1814.

Merry's father had belonged to the Congregational Church, but Merry received Baptist ministers in his home, and one of them conducted his wife's funeral service. In the absence of religious and educational institutions the family setting had to provide moral and intellectual instruction. From 1818 his son Ralph served as a teacher, and the first school was built in 1824 near the comfortable family home erected in 1814 which is still standing.

Merry died at the age of 72, after a full life that had earned him the esteem of his fellow citizens. As a good family man he had helped his children establish themselves. He passed his courage and spirit of initiative on to his descendants, who followed in his footsteps and contributed to the rise of trade and industry.

MARIE-PAULE R. LaBRÈQUE

ANQ-M, CL1-2/3, 3 janv. 1817. PAC, RG 1, L3^L: 5171, 5225, 65519, 69514, 69521, 69523. Stanstead County Hist. Soc., Colby-Curtis Museum (Beebe, Que.), Journals of Ralph Merry, IV. *Quebec Gazette*, 29 Aug. 1816, 18 Sept. 1817. Bouchette, *Topographical description of L.C.*, 268. C. P. de Volpi and P. H. Scowen, *The Eastern Townships, a pictorial record; historical prints and illustrations of the Eastern Townships of the province of Quebec, Canada* (Montreal, 1962). *The Eastern Townships gazetteer and general business directory ...* (St Johns [Saint-Jean-sur-Richelieu], Que., 1867; repr. Sherbrooke, Que., 1967). *Illustrated atlas of Eastern Townships. Vital records of Lynn, Massachusetts, to the end of the year 1849 ...* (2v., Salem, Mass., 1905–6). Boulianne, "Royal Instit. for the Advancement of Learning." W. B. Bullock, *Beautiful waters devoted to the Memphremagog region ...* ([2nd ed.], Newport, Vt., 1926). Caron, *La colonisation de la prov. de Québec*, 2: 310, 312, 351. Day, *Hist. of Eastern Townships.* B. F. Hubbard, *Forests and clearings; the history of Stanstead County, province of Quebec, with sketches of more than five hundred families*, ed. John Lawrence (Montreal, 1874; repr. 1963). A. W. et P. L. Ling, *Souvenirs historiques* (Magog, Qué., 1936). Alexandre Paradis, *Histoire commerciale et industrielle de Magog, Qué.* (Magog, 1951). H. B. Shufelt, *Nicholas Austin the Quaker and the township of Bolton* (Knowlton, Que., 1971). *Stanstead County Historical Society centennial journal* (2v., n.p., 1965–67). Cyrus Thomas, *Contributions to the history of the Eastern Townships ...* (Montreal, 1866).

MESSEIN, HONORÉ-GRATIEN-JOSEPH BAILLY DE. *See* BAILLY, JOSEPH

MEYERS (Mayers, Mires, Myres), JOHN WALDEN (Walten, Walter) (baptized **Johannes Waltermyer**; sometimes known as **Hans Waltermeyer**), army and militia officer, businessman, JP, and office holder; b. 22 Jan. 1745/46 (Old Style) in Albany County, N.Y.; m. there c. 1765 Polly Kruger (Cruger), and they had seven children; m. secondly c. 1817, probably in Belleville, Upper Canada, Sophia Davy; d. 22 Nov. 1821 in Belleville.

John Walden Meyers was probably of German descent. At the outbreak of the American revolution, he was a farmer of modest means living with his family near Albany. His father decided to stand with the rebels, but in July 1777 Meyers himself set off to meet the army of Major-General John Burgoyne*, then advancing through upper New York. Tradition relates that on his trek Meyers was accompanied by his wife's brother and by a faithful dog which became so fatigued that Meyers had to carry it. When his brother-in-law commented on this dedication to the pet, Meyers informed him, in the German accent he never lost, "We may have to eat him yet." That is the earliest of the stories concerning Meyers, who became as much a legendary as an historical figure.

Upon joining Burgoyne's army, Meyers enrolled in the King's Loyal Americans. Absent on a recruiting assignment, he missed the battles that led to Burgoyne's surrender at Saratoga (Schuylerville, N.Y.) in October 1777. After this calamity for the British cause, Meyers made his way to New York City. During the next few years he continued to act as a recruiting agent, first for Colonel Gabriel George Ludlow* and later for Lieutenant-Colonel Robert Rogers*. His principal contribution to the British war effort, however, lay in the gathering of intelligence and in the carrying of dispatches through hostile territory.

On each hair-raising expedition Meyers managed to elude rebel troops while almost always returning to Fort St Johns (Saint-Jean-sur-Richelieu) with new recruits and prisoners. Some sources allege Meyers was so feared as an enemy agent that in New York state mothers warned their children that if they were not good Hans Waltermeyer would eat them. In August 1781 he was selected to conduct the principal attack on the house of prominent rebel Philip John Schuyler, the most memorable of his exploits, but Governor Frederick Haldimand*'s hope that the raiders would "procure Intelligence and ... carry off some of the most inveterate and active Leaders in the Rebellion" was disappointed. Still, although the raid was unsuccessful, Meyers's career in the army did not suffer. In June 1781 he had been authorized by Haldimand to raise an independent company. Unable to recruit sufficient men, he was given a commission as captain in Edward Jessup*'s Loyal Rangers on 13 May 1782. Meyers remained in this corps for the duration of the war. In 1782–83 he and his company did garrison duty in Quebec at Fort St Johns, Île aux Noix, and Rivière-aux-Chiens. He went on half pay when the rangers were disbanded in December 1783.

With the end of the war in 1783 the Meyers family was forced to launch a new life. Initially, along with other loyalist officers and soldiers, Meyers settled at Missisquoi Bay, at the northern tip of Lake Champlain. His family soon joined him in Quebec and resided in Yamachiche while Meyers readied a more permanent home at the bay. As it turned out, however, Meyers's plans conflicted with government policy. The authorities, fearing border incidents, did not want the loyalists to settle too close to the United States; Meyers and his comrades, for their part, were appalled at the prospect of relocating to the wilderness area west of the Ottawa River that had been set aside for the loyalist corps. The settlers insisted that only "Superior force" would drive them off their land, but the authorities prevailed in 1784. Having received permission to winter at Missisquoi Bay, Meyers moved in 1785 to the vicinity of Cataraqui (Kingston, Ont.). The following spring he resettled in what was to become Sidney Township and in 1790 he moved to nearby Thurlow Township, where he was to spend the rest of his life.

In the late 1780s the government was encouraging the construction of mills, and in January 1788 Meyers petitioned for a mill-site in Sidney Township in the hope of adding a saw- and grist-mill to his already flourishing farm. Although he was turned down, he seems to have purchased another site in Thurlow Township. By 1790 he had built the district's first dam and mill near the mouth of Meyers' Creek (Moira River). This fledgling industry formed the nucleus of a community that bore Meyers's name until it became known as Bellville (Belleville) in 1816. Soon Meyers began fur trading and, to the mill enterprises, added a distillery, an inn, and a number of vessels, including a small schooner that carried cargo to Montreal; among the people he did business with were Richard Cartwright* and David McGregor ROGERS. Within ten years of their arrival in the Bay of Quinte region the Meyers family moved into one of the first brick houses in Upper Canada – the bricks were produced on one of Meyers's farms. His achievements were the result of personal energy and the judicious use of capital provided by his half pay and by the money he received in compensation for war losses. When Meyers died he owned in excess of 3,000 acres of land and his estate was valued at more than £12,000. His claim to importance as an early Upper Canadian settler is enhanced by the fact that he served as a justice of the peace from 1788 until his death and as a captain of the Hastings County militia from 1798 to 1812. In 1800 he was appointed a commissioner for administering the oath of allegiance to new settlers in the Midland District, in 1802 he became first master of the local masonic lodge, and in 1820 he was made a vice-president of the Midland District Agricultural Society. Finally, he was one of the trustees responsible for the construction in 1820 of St Thomas Church, the first Anglican church in Belleville.

During the American revolution Meyers had renounced personal gain in the loyalist cause: on one occasion he asked his superiors for money only "sufficient to support me whilst here and on my journey," and on another he stated that "it is my Ambition to be serviceable." Despite his dedication to British rule and law, he was never blindly loyal. Always ready to combat injustice, he fought hard for the good land that he felt was his due, and even as an older man he associated, if only briefly, with the reform movement of Robert Gourlay*. He was one of those who drew up the report on Thurlow Township in response to Gourlay's questionnaire, and his son Jacob was the Sidney Township delegate to Gourlay's convention at York in 1818. Meyers had the normal human foibles – he quarrelled continuously with his business competitor James McNabb* – but, on balance, his actions reveal him as a man of admirable character. He freed his few slaves long before he was legally required to do so, and he enjoyed the confidence of the Mississauga Ojibwas, with whom he traded. The hospitality of his hilltop brick house was famous. What confirms the personal stature of John Walden Meyers more than anything else is one simple fact: he was so talked of in his own lifetime that even before he passed to his final rest he passed into the folklore where he lives today.

ROBERT J. M. SHIPLEY

AO, Hist. plaque descriptions, "Capt. John Walden Meyers, 1745–1821, founder of Belleville," 14 Aug. 1959; MS 768, G-5, William Canniff, notes on early settlement in Upper Canada; MU 1368. BL, Add. MSS 21723: 91, 118, 151, 187, 251; 21793: 293; 21794: 84; 21795: 62, 228; 21820: 42; 21821: 21, 30, 218, 283, 316, 319–20, 323, 328, 348, 389, 424, 429, 442; 21822: 25, 148, 190, 208, 210, 212, 214, 249, 252, 272, 276; 21823: 7, 101, 111, 114, 152; 21836: 225; 21837: 38, 42, 52, 158, 318; 21875: 69. Ont., Ministry of Citizenship and Culture, Heritage Administration Branch (Toronto), Hist. sect. research files. PAC, RG 1, L1, 22: 293; 26: 141; 28: 390, 551; 29: 28; L3, 338: M11/276; 376: M misc., pt.I, 1789–1803: 55; 377: M misc., pt.II, 1788–99: 117, 200, 202; 556: leases and licences of occupation, 1798–1840/82; RG 5, A1: 2080–85, 8186–99, 12305–12. Douglas, *Lord Selkirk's diary* (White), 178–80. *Kingston before War of 1812* (Preston). *Statistical account of U.C.* (Gourlay; ed. Mealing; 1974). "United Empire Loyalists: enquiry into losses and services," AO *Report*, 1904: 1050. "U.C. land book B," AO *Report*, 1930: 50, 52. "U.C. land book C," AO *Report*, 1931: 58, 71.

Kingston Chronicle, 8 Jan. 1819; 5 May, 9 June 1820; 5 Oct., 30 Nov. 1821. *Kingston Gazette*, 13 Nov. 1810. *Illustrated historical atlas of the counties of Hastings and Prince Edward, Ont.* (Toronto, 1878; repr. Belleville, Ont., 1972). *Pioneer life on the Bay of Quinte, including genealogies of old families and biographical sketches of representative citizens* (Toronto, 1904; repr. Belleville, 1972). Mary Beacock Fryer, *Loyalist spy: the experiences of Captain John Walden Meyers during the American revolution* (Brockville, Ont., 1974). G. E. Boyce, *Historic Hastings* (Belleville, 1967). Canniff, *Hist. of the settlement of U.C.* H. C. Mathews, *Frontier spies; the British secret service, northern department, during the Revolutionary War* (Myers, Fla., 1971). Nick and Helma Mika, *Mosaic of Belleville: an*

Miles

illustrated history of a city (Belleville, 1966). W. C. Mikel, *City of Belleville history* (Picton, Ont., 1943). E. A. Cruikshank, "Captain John Walden Meyers, loyalist pioneer," *OH*, 31 (1936): 11–55. Mary Quayle Innis, "The industrial development of Ontario, 1783–1820," *OH*, 32 (1937): 104–13.

MILES, ELIJAH, merchant, farmer, army and militia officer, politician, and magistrate; b. 16 Jan. 1753 in New Milford, Conn., son of Justus Miles and Hannah Olmstead; m. first 1779 Frances Cornwell of Hempstead, N.Y., and they had eight children; m. secondly 3 Aug. 1800 Elizabeth Harding of Maugerville, N.B., and they had two sons; d. 26 May 1831 in Maugerville.

Elijah Miles was educated at the public school in New Milford and at the outbreak of the American Revolutionary War was engaged in farming there. It is not known when he became a soldier but in 1776 he was serving as a captain in the 3rd battalion of De Lancey's Brigade, a loyalist unit; with the reorganization of the brigade in 1781 his battalion was renumbered the 2nd. Miles's elder brother Samuel avoided service with the rebels first by keeping out of the way and then by hiring a substitute before fleeing to Long Island in 1776. When the war ended, the two brothers went in 1783 with other provincial troops and loyalist refugees to the future colony of New Brunswick.

Samuel Miles was to settle in Saint John, where he set up as a merchant and later served as an alderman; Elijah established himself inland, becoming a storekeeper and farmer. As a member of the 2nd De Lancey's, Elijah drew land opposite Woodstock, so far up the Saint John River that, like most of the officers and men in the unit, he did not take advantage of the grant. Instead he obtained land by grant and purchase in the township of Maugerville, near Fredericton, an old settlement whose founders, Congregationalists from Massachusetts, had taken the American side during the war and now resented the loyalist intrusion [*see* Israel Perley*]. He became a vestryman when a Church of England congregation was organized in September 1784 and was one of those who, in their zeal to defend and promote what they regarded as the rights of an established church, contributed to political and social tensions in the community. Feelings ran particularly high during a dispute that arose in 1793 between Anglicans and dissenters over ownership of the meeting-house in nearby Sheffield, the dissenting minister there having joined the Church of England but kept possession of the parsonage that formed part of the meeting-house [*see* David Burpe*]. There were enough non-Anglicans in Sunbury County to ensure that one of the county's two representatives in the House of Assembly was drawn from their ranks and in 1789, when the voters elected the radical Scottish immigrant James Glenie*, a Presbyterian, a pattern was established of dividing the representation,

the other member at that time being a loyalist Anglican, William Hubbard. In 1795 the electors chose Glenie and Samuel Denny STREET, an Anglican but an ardent critic of the government.

From 1793 to 1802 Miles served as a captain in the King's New Brunswick Regiment, a unit recruited for local defence when the regular British troops were withdrawn on the outbreak of war with France. In 1802 he and William Hubbard came forward as government candidates in the most bitterly fought of all the early general elections in the colony. Glenie, in his address to the electors at the opening of the poll, compared Lieutenant Governor Thomas Carleton*'s despotism in New Brunswick to that of Henry VIII in England. During the poll Glenie and Street received the most votes but Sheriff Gabriel De Veber, after finding a number of voters to be ineligible as a result of a scrutiny, declared Glenie and Miles elected. Street's supporters appealed to the new House of Assembly, where a partisan majority favouring the government found no irregularity in the sheriff's conduct. Following the election a rancorous feud broke out between the rival groups, with charges and countercharges in the courts, including one from Miles "that Samuel D. Street on the 8th of October in 1802 in the Court House at Burton did assault and strike him with a large stick or distaff – at the same time made use of very aprobious language."

At the next election, in 1809, the successful candidates were Street and James TAYLOR, but by 1816 Miles had consolidated his position in the county and came at the top of the poll, with the support of 115 of the 207 voters. He was re-elected in 1819 and 1820, when there were no other Anglican candidates. Some of the old denominational animosities were softening. In 1816 the voters returned as their second representative William Wilmot, a Baptist lay preacher from an American loyalist family, their choice reflecting the success that communion was having in making converts in all sections of the population. About half of Wilmot's supporters also voted for Miles, but there is no evidence that Miles had any particular sympathy for the denomination in which his two youngest sons, Frederick William* and George, were later to become prominent members. He voted against an 1821 bill, favoured by the Baptists, "to authorize all Ministers of the Gospel licenced to preach, to solemnize Marriage," and in 1824 he supported the exclusion of Wilmot from the assembly on the grounds that, as a lay preacher, he was disqualified under the law prohibiting the election of religious teachers and ministers. He also voted against a motion to search the records for precedents on behalf of Wilmot; it was defeated by a majority of one.

In the assembly Miles consistently supported the government, so much so that in 1819 he was one of only four members who voted for a resolution upholding Lieutenant Governor George Stracey SMYTH's contention that the house should not question a duty of one shilling per ton on pine timber taken from crown lands. In Sunbury County he was one of the most active magistrates, performing a variety of administrative tasks, acting as a grammar-school trustee, and carrying out judicial duties as a justice of the Inferior Court of Common Pleas. For many years he also commanded the Sunbury battalion of the provincial militia, in which he held the rank of lieutenant-colonel.

In addition to being a storekeeper, Miles was a successful farmer and landowner. It is probable that he depended in part on slave labour. According to an early account, the first sexton of the Church of England in Maugerville was Miles's black slave, and George Harding, his father-in-law, bequeathed his slaves and hired servants to Elizabeth, Miles's second wife. In 1798 Miles prosecuted a black, John Windson, for burglary, then a capital offence. The jury acquitted the accused man but, of the money in Windson's possession, the court ordered Miles to take £2 15s., being satisfied that this sum belonged to him, and itself took the remaining pound to pay part of the fees of prosecution.

Miles appears to have borne a reputation for honour and integrity. He exemplifies the qualities that later admirers of American loyalists saw as typical of the younger men who ranked below the bureaucratic élite but were firm upholders of the principles of church establishment and strong executive authority. He was one of the practical "*gentlemen* of the American loyalists" who, as Patrick CAMPBELL, an early traveller, noted, "are all men brought up either to the law, or to some mercantile or mechanic business, or farming, to which they severally applied on their entering into this country, and make out in general very well."

D. M. YOUNG

ACC, Diocese of Fredericton Arch., Maugerville Parish Church (Maugerville, N.B.), vestry books (mfm. at PANB). N.B. Museum, Harding papers, folder 2; folder 3, item 2. PANB, MC 1, Miles file, genealogical chart; E. C. Wright, "Miles: pioneer families of New Brunswick" (newspaper clipping, no source or date); MC 211, MS4/5/13; MC 1156; RG 18, RS157, J2/1. P. Campbell, *Travels in North America* (Langton and Ganong). N.B., House of Assembly, *Journal*, 1803–27. *Royal Gazette* (Fredericton), 1 June 1831. G.B., WO, *Army list*, 1783. I. L. Hill, *Some loyalists and others* (Fredericton, 1976). PANB, "A new calendar of the papers of the House of Assembly of New Brunswick," comp. R. P. Nason et al. (3v., typescript, Fredericton, 1975–77). Beckwith Maxwell, *Hist. of central N.B.* I. E. Bill, *Fifty years with the Baptist ministers and churches of the Maritime provinces of Canada* (Saint John, N.B., 1880). Hannay, *Hist. of N.B.* Lawrence, *Judges of N.B.* (Stockton and Raymond). MacNutt, *New Brunswick. Maugerville, 1763–1963*, comp. I. L. Hill (Fredericton, 1963). W. D. Moore, "Sunbury County, 1760–1830" (MA thesis, Univ. of N.B., Fredericton, 1977). R. W. Colston, "Maugerville," *Weekly Herald* (Fredericton), 17 Sept. 1898; "Old Sunbury . . . ," *St. John Daily Sun* (Saint John), 9 Sept. 1898: 6–7.

MILLS, JOSEPH LANGLEY, clergyman of the Church of England, educator, and office holder; baptized 28 March 1788 in Deddington, England, son of Moses Mills and Sarah ——; m. 3 March 1817 Anna Cecilia Craigie, daughter of John Craigie*, at Quebec, and they had at least six children; d. there 13 Aug. 1832.

Joseph Langley Mills attended Magdalen College, Oxford, where he received his BA in 1809 and his MA three years later; he was a fellow of the college from 1810 to 1817. Commissioned a chaplain in the army on 12 Oct. 1812, he served in Portugal during the Peninsular War. He arrived in Lower Canada in August 1814 as a chaplain on the staff. After being stationed briefly at Fort Chambly, he was sent to Quebec later that year to relieve the Reverend Salter Jehosaphat Mountain as garrison chaplain. It seems to have been the practice for chaplains to assume other clerical duties in order to supplement their income and support the local clergy; thus in 1814 Mills succeeded George Jehoshaphat Mountain* as evening lecturer at the Cathedral of the Holy Trinity, a position which, for lack of a sufficient salary, could not otherwise attract a qualified clergyman. After the death of the Reverend George Jenkins, Mills was appointed senior chaplain to the forces in the Canadas on 30 Oct. 1821. The following year the BD and DD degrees were conferred on him by decree.

Like many of the clergymen of his time, Mills was a leading figure in the formation of local charitable and social institutions. In 1816 he appears to have been treasurer of a fund for the relief of soldiers wounded in the War of 1812 and of the widows and orphans of those killed. In July 1819 he, Jonathan Sewell*, George Jehoshaphat Mountain, Daniel Wilkie*, and the merchant Benjamin Tremain constituted a committee to study means of supporting distressed immigrants. On the 26th he was elected to the governing committee of the Quebec Emigrants' Society, established as a result of the study. The following year he was a founding member of the Quebec branch of the Royal Humane Society of London for the Recovery of the Apparently Drowned or Dead. Its object was to educate the public to determine whether persons were dead or merely unconscious and to instruct in methods of resuscitation; hitherto many had succumbed because given up for dead. About 1828 Mills helped collect funds for the erection of a monument (which still exists) to James Wolfe* and Louis-Joseph de Montcalm*; he also composed an inscription.

As garrison chaplain Mills had to attend to the schooling of the soldiers' children, and this task led to

Mills

a deep and lifelong commitment to education. In January 1816 he preached a sermon at the cathedral that brought in about £170 for the support of the "Female School" at Quebec. In March 1818 he was named secretary to the Quebec diocesan committee of the Society for Promoting Christian Knowledge, and as such was involved in the work of the Sunday schools and the founding of the National School, which operated on the Madras or Bell system [see John Baird*]. When Bishop Jacob MOUNTAIN accepted the principalship of the Royal Institution for the Advancement of Learning in December 1819, he nominated Mills to be its secretary, and the appointment was made on the 13th.

The Royal Institution, the first system of public education in Lower Canada, had been established in April 1801 by an act of the provincial legislature. The governor had the power to appoint the principal, trustees, and other officers of the body, and the Royal Institution was to run all schools in the colony with the exception of private schools, a restriction inserted in the act possibly at the insistence of the Roman Catholic coadjutor bishop of Quebec, Joseph-Octave PLESSIS. No school under the auspices of the Royal Institution could be built in any parish or township without its having been requested by a majority of the inhabitants; the cost of construction was then divided among all the residents. Beginning in 1801 several projects for funding the Royal Institution were proposed – including appropriation of the Sulpician estates and of monies from the Jesuit estates fund – but none was adopted. Indeed it was 1818 before a board of trustees was appointed. Until then only some 35 schools had received government funding by virtue of the act of 1801, and there had been no supervision over them. With the appointment of the board, regulations and procedures were promulgated, and Mills, as secretary, initiated a survey to establish the state of existing schools.

Mills virtually became the Royal Institution. He kept the board's minutes and records and interpreted and applied its policies. Since the board met infrequently, he had much autonomy in day-to-day administration. He maintained a constant correspondence with the commissioners of the institution, local officials who administered the establishment of schools, and the visitors, who inspected them, as well as with teachers, parents, and other clergymen. He received the visitors' semi-annual reports and conveyed their content to the board. In addition, after consultation with local leaders, he secured appointment of commissioners, visitors, and teachers, and the remuneration of the latter. He approved selection of sites and erection and maintenance of schoolhouses. With the cooperation of the visitors he authorized exemptions from fees of students in financial need. In almost every aspect of the institution's operations

people turned to him for solutions to problems, disputes, and crises. He undertook his numerous tasks wisely and was respected by all with whom he came into contact.

Despite Mills's efforts the Royal Institution met with only partial success. The British Protestant population, particularly in new settlements, readily accepted its schools, although the Methodists in the Eastern Townships did not always agree with its policies or follow its directives. The Roman Catholic clergy, however, strongly opposed it. From the beginning Plessis, who became bishop of Quebec in 1806, successfully discouraged establishment of its schools among Roman Catholics. The board appointed in 1819, being largely British and dominated by the Anglican clergymen Mountain and Mills, did not reassure Plessis by either its composition or its structure; indeed, although invited, he had refused to sit on it under the presidency of the Anglican bishop.

In this hostile climate, Mills administered with justice and humanity. He avoided religious and ethnic controversy and, with remarkable sensitivity and adaptability, tried to provide a system as acceptable to Canadians in the seigneuries as to British Protestants in the townships. The act of 1801 did not provide for ethnically or religiously distinct schools, but the policies of the board, in which Mills had great influence, were sufficiently flexible and liberal to enable Canadians to apply for Royal Institution schools without fear of entering an exclusively Anglo-Protestant system. Provisions were made for the separation of students during religious worship; there were regular inspections by local visitors, and if in Canadian parishes these posts were refused by the parish priests on Plessis's orders, they were ultimately filled by Canadian residents; only French-speaking Catholic teachers were appointed in Canadian areas, and then only with the consent of local authorities; and finally there was a separate list of textbooks for Canadian pupils. Thus sufficient local control existed to ensure that in Canadian regions the schools reflected the character of the population they served. Largely through Mills's unremitting efforts the Royal Institution grew slowly. The number of schools increased from 35 in 1818 to 55 in 1825, and then to a high of 84 four years later. But opposition by the Roman Catholic clergy was telling; from 1801 to 1829 only some 23 schools having a substantial number of French-speaking students were brought or established under the jurisdiction of the Royal Institution.

Mills's task, to make the Royal Institution the *de facto* public education system, would have been formidable under any circumstances, but increasing political tensions rendered it virtually impossible. The success of Plessis's boycott (continued by his successor, Bernard-Claude PANET) was not lost on Canadian representatives in the House of Assembly. Many had become opposed to a system of education under the control of the governor. Since at least 1814 the assembly, dominated by the Canadian party, had been struggling unsuccessfully with governors and councils to pass a new law that would establish a system of education more acceptable to the majority of the population. In 1824 it held an inquiry into the state of education before which Mills and other leading figures in Lower Canadian education testified. Mills affirmed that education advanced among Protestants thanks to the Royal Institution, but that it was stagnant among Catholics largely because of Plessis's boycott. The same year the assembly obtained royal sanction for what became known as the *fabrique* schools law, which enabled Catholics to finance the construction of schools from the funds of the parish *fabriques*; these bodies also administered the schools. Thus, while not financed by the state, a new semi-public system threatened the Royal Institution's dominance over education.

Mills had foreseen and tried to prevent such an eventuality. Before the assembly's committee of inquiry in 1824, he had invoked as a possible solution to the problem of Roman Catholic education a scheme that Governor Lord Dalhousie [Ramsay*] had been working out with Plessis, in the formulation of which he had been consulted. By this scheme a parallel Roman Catholic royal institution would have been formed. Mills, however, deplored the fact that the ultimate effect of this measure would be a further separation of Protestants and Catholics. The plan fell through in December when rejected by the colonial secretary, Lord Bathurst, for lack of funds; the colonial authorities were struggling with the assembly for control of provincial finances and had few resources, the assembly disposing of most of the colony's revenues. Mills supported more enthusiastically a revised plan worked out by Dalhousie on the one hand and Plessis and Panet on the other by which autonomous Protestant and Roman Catholic committees of a single royal institution would administer denominational schools. This system would have resembled the one adopted by the province of Quebec in 1869, whereby Catholic and Protestant committees coexisted within the Council of Public Instruction [*see* Louis Giard*]. However, by the time the new scheme was ready to be implemented in 1829, Mills found that provisions of the act of 1801 would not permit the necessary administrative adjustments. The assembly had to revise the act but did not do so. The act of 1824 having proved largely ineffective, it passed a bill in 1829 commonly called the syndics act in order to avoid having the education of Canadians come under the control of the governor through the Royal Institution. The financial generosity of the new act sounded the death knell of the Royal Institution as the system of public education in Lower Canada.

Mills also bore the brunt of a long legal battle begun in 1820 between the Royal Institution and the heirs of James McGill* over an estate and money left to it for the founding of a college to be named after McGill [*see* François DESRIVIÈRES]. Mills in fact was named the college's professor of moral philosophy, but the nomination was made solely for the cause of the institution's suit, to fulfil a requirement of McGill's will, and he was never active in the position. Despite these and his other efforts on behalf of the Royal Institution, Mills was never remunerated fully as its secretary. The colonial executive, because of its struggle with the assembly for financial autonomy, could not pay Mills's stipend of £100 per annum, while the assembly, having become opposed to the institution it had created, was not prepared to remunerate the secretary; in 1829, however, it paid £300 to Mills in an effort to close the matter. Mills claimed an additional £720, and that year he went to England to obtain it. At the same time he was authorized by Jacob Mountain's successor as Anglican bishop, Charles James Stewart*, to promote in government circles the division of the diocese of Quebec.

Mills returned to Quebec about May 1832, having failed to obtain his back pay. When he died that summer at age 44, he left his wife and family destitute; a request to the British government for support was granted only two years later. It was a sad end for someone who had given so much of himself to his church and to education in Lower Canada. Rather than being remembered as a pioneer and driving force in the development of public education in Lower Canada, he is recalled unjustly as a minor figure who administered an unpopular and controversial system that spanned, effectively, only a decade of operations. In fact, it was in part because of his efforts on behalf of the Royal Institution that others were spurred to lay the groundwork for a system of formal education for the Canadians.

RÉAL G. BOULIANNE

ANQ-Q, CE1-61, 15 août 1832. McGill Univ. Arch., Royal Instit. for the Advancement of Learning, incoming corr., 1807–56; letter-books, 1820–35. PAC, MG 17, B1, C/CAN/Que., IV/32; IV/34, folder 383 (mfm.); RG 8, I (C ser.), 0, 64–65, 67–68, 210–11, 213, 246, 1171, 1203½M, 1276, 1707, 1709; RG 68, General index, 1651–1841: 676. L.C., House of Assembly, *Journals*, 1816–33. *Quebec Gazette*, 18 Jan., 1 Feb., 18 April, 7 Nov. 1816; 5 March, 26 Nov., 7, 10 Dec. 1818; 22 April, 24 June, 1, 15 July, 2 Aug., 9, 16 Dec. 1819; 6 Jan., 16 March, 6, 27 April, 26 June, 23, 26 Oct. 1820; 22 Feb., 16 April, 12, 26 Nov. 1821; 6 Jan., 10 Feb. 1823. *Quebec almanac*, 1818–41. L.-P. Audet, *Le système scolaire*, vols.3–4. R. G. Boulianne, "The French Canadians under the Royal Institution for the Advancement of Learning, 1818–1829" (MA thesis, Univ. of Ottawa, 1964); "Royal Instit. for the Advancement of Learning." S. B. Frost, *McGill University: for the advancement of* learning (2v., Montreal, 1980–84). Cyrus Macmillan, *McGill and its story, 1821–1921* (London and Toronto, 1921). T. R. Millman, *Jacob Mountain; The life of the Right Reverend, the Honourable Charles James Stewart, D.D., Oxon., second Anglican bishop of Quebec* (London, Ont., 1953). G. W. Parmelee, "English education," *Canada and its provinces; a history of the Canadian people and their institutions . . .* , ed. Adam Shortt and A. G. Doughty (23v., Toronto, 1913–17), 16: 445–501. R. G. Boulianne, "The French Canadians and the schools of the Royal Institution for the Advancement of Learning, 1820–1829," *SH*, 5 (1972): 144–64. S. B. Frost, "A McGill personality: Joseph Langley Mills," *McGilliana, Bull. of the Hist. of McGill Project* (Montreal), no.1 (March 1976): 4–5. F. C. Würtele, "The English cathedral of Quebec," Literary and Hist. Soc. of Quebec, *Trans.*, new ser., 20 (1891): 63–132.

MINNS, WILLIAM, printer, publisher, merchant, and office holder; b. *c.* 1763 in Boston, son of William Minns and his wife Sarah; m. 29 Dec. 1798 Sophia Brown in Halifax, and they had one daughter, Sophia Ann; d. there 17 Jan. 1827.

William Minns was one of seven children born to a Boston doctor whose family had emigrated from Great Yarmouth, England, about 1735. During the evacuation of Boston in March 1776, young Minns and his sister Martha went to Newport, R.I., where she married the printer John HOWE. Apparently Minns's loyalist views offended his father; nevertheless, over the years he maintained contact with his Massachusetts relatives, and several of his Boston nieces lived with him in Halifax during the 1810s and 1820s.

Newport was evacuated by British forces in October 1779, and it seems to have been then that Minns left Rhode Island for Nova Scotia. By 1780, when John Howe began the *Halifax Journal*, Minns was probably an apprentice in his brother-in-law's Halifax printing shop. He soon established his own shop at George and Barrington streets, from which he first issued the *Weekly Chronicle* on 29 April 1786. Like the two other Halifax newspapers of the day, the *Journal* and Anthony Henry*'s *Nova-Scotia Gazette, and the Weekly Chronicle*, Minns's paper chiefly reprinted British and American news, although it also carried more detailed local news than the others. Its most notable local contribution was Joseph Howe*'s long poem "Melville Island" on 6 Jan. 1826.

By 1810 Minns was one of the principal retail merchants of Halifax, and was able to purchase the property on Barrington Street which adjoined his shop. It was in his shop that his friend Captain Philip Bowes Vere Broke* of the *Shannon* reportedly said, "Well, Minns, I'm going to Boston . . . to challenge the *Constitution*." When Minns advised caution, in the light of the *Guerrière*'s tragic encounter with the *Constitution* in August 1812, Broke replied that he would "trust more to boarding than to the calibre of his guns." In the event, the contest between the *Shannon*

and the *Constitution* never materialized, but another prize did fall to the British frigate: on 6 June 1813 the *Shannon* led the *Chesapeake* into Halifax Harbour.

Minns neither criticized the government nor engaged in acrimonious disputes, as did the newer Halifax papers of the 1810s, Anthony Henry HOLLAND's *Acadian Recorder* and Edmund Ward*'s *Free Press*. Yet, although a quiet man, he was active in community affairs. He was an actor in the theatre established in Halifax in 1789 and managed during its later years by Charles Stuart Powell*. In 1817 he was appointed a commissioner on the court for the trial of summary actions in Halifax County. By late 1826 he was in poor health and sold the *Chronicle* to his stepnephew Joseph Howe, who in partnership with James Spike* conducted it in 1827 as the *Acadian, and General Advertiser*. After Howe took over the *Novascotian, or Colonial Herald* in December 1827, Spike ran the *Acadian* as a tory organ until 1834.

Minns died in 1827 of an "ulcerous cancer of the throat," but he had retained his "superior powers of intellect" to the end. In an obituary notice the *Acadian Recorder* praised him as the "dispenser of comfort and delight." His estate had few claims against it and his family was well provided for. Sixty years later some Haligonians still remembered Minns as "a dignified, portly gentleman, with powdered wig, worsted hose, and silver shoe buckles," who "was always characterized by the courtesy and honor of a gentleman of the olden time."

GEORGE L. PARKER

PANS, MG 1, 574B. *Acadian Recorder*, 20 Jan. 1827. *Royal Gazette and the Nova-Scotia Advertiser*, 1 Jan. 1799. *A calendar of official correspondence and legislative papers, Nova Scotia, 1802–15*, comp. Margaret Ells (Halifax, 1936). *An historical directory of Nova Scotia newspapers and journals before confederation*, comp. T. B. Vincent (Kingston, Ont., 1977). Tremaine, *Biblio. of Canadian imprints*. Akins, *Hist. of Halifax City*. J. M. Beck, *Joseph Howe* (2v., Kingston and Montreal, 1982–83), 1. A. [McK.] MacMechan, *Old province tales* (Toronto, 1924), 188–90. W. S. MacNutt, *The Atlantic provinces: the emergence of colonial society, 1712–1857* (Toronto, 1965). J. S. Martell, "The press of the Maritime provinces in the 1830's," *CHR*, 19 (1938): 24–49. J. J. Stewart, "Early journalism in Nova Scotia," N.S. Hist. Soc., *Coll.*, 6 (1888): 91–122.

MIRES. See MEYERS

MITCHELL, DAVID, physician, office holder, fur trader, and JP; b. *c.* 1750 in Scotland, son of Andrew Mitchell, a manufacturer in Livingston, and Elizabeth Anderson; d. 7 Aug. 1832 in Penetanguishene, Upper Canada.

Nothing certain is known about David Mitchell's early life in Scotland, although the records of the

University of Edinburgh list a medical student of that name in 1770–71. In 1771 the David Mitchell of this biography took ship as a common sailor to the Thirteen Colonies, where he joined his uncle, a medical officer on the army staff at New York City. When his uncle was transferred to the West Indies in 1772, Mitchell was placed in charge of the New York hospital. In 1774 he was appointed surgeon's mate in the 8th Foot and later that year he accompanied a detachment of the 8th to Michilimackinac (Mackinaw City, Mich.). He was the only trained physician in the fortified trading community and the vast western wilderness of which it was the fur-trade centre.

In 1779 Lieutenant Governor Patrick Sinclair* took charge of the post, replacing Arent Schuyler DePeyster, and Mitchell was one of the few people with whom Sinclair, a fellow Scot, got along. This association broadened Mitchell's responsibilities. When Sinclair dismissed John Askin* as deputy commissary on 2 June 1780, Mitchell was given that position which he held for several years. Also in 1780 Sinclair, worried about a possible American attack on the weakly fortified post, decided to move the fort and the community to nearby Mackinac Island, and Mitchell's close connection with the lieutenant governor brought him several choice parcels of land there.

Meanwhile, rumours were circulating that the 8th Foot was to be transferred from Michilimackinac. Mitchell had married a vivacious girl of mixed blood, Elizabeth Bertrand, in July 1776. Unlike many whites who left their Indian families in the wilderness, he was deeply devoted to his wife and would not desert her. On Christmas Day 1780 he requested permission to resign when the regiment left. Permission was eventually granted and he gave up his appointment in 1783. Since the incoming regiment had no physician, however, he continued to serve for several years.

In 1781 the sloop *Welcome* had transported Mitchell's house timbers to Mackinac Island and he constructed a large, gambrel-roofed house on Market Street. The influx of men to build the new fort provided him with added opportunity for income. He received an allowance to attend to the Canadians employed on the works as well as to the Indians. To provide for himself when he resigned, Mitchell also began dabbling in trade. His wife's relatives gave him ready access to the native community and his business prospered. By the time he left the army he had built up a sizeable enterprise. Most of his contacts were along the eastern shore of Lake Michigan from L'Arbre Croche (Cross Village) to Traverse Bay (Grand Traverse Bay). By 1790 he was importing goods from Montreal and was considered one of the principal traders of the post. A freemason, he had helped found St John's Lodge No.15, which was chartered in 1782; active in civic affairs, he served as a justice of the peace and postmaster.

In July 1796, when the British garrison turned over Mackinac Island to the Americans in accordance with Jay's Treaty, Mitchell was so firmly established that he did not want to move to the new post on nearby St Joseph Island. Instead, he stayed on Mackinac, and as his sons David and Daniel came of age he involved them in his growing business network. Close contacts were kept with the traders on St Joseph, and Mitchell imported extensive amounts of goods from Montreal. In 1808 and 1809 the Mitchells worked in association with the Michilimackinac Company, in which a number of Montreal firms were involved [see John Ogilvy*].

Occasionally Mitchell went to Montreal on business and in 1806 he had witnessed the marriage there of David Jr to Maria, daughter of John Gregory*. At the invitation of his trading friends in Montreal, both David Mitchells joined the prestigious Beaver Club on 26 Jan. 1807. They attended from time to time until David Jr's death in 1809. On Mackinac Island Mitchell's home was one of the primary social centres for the 25 families who comprised frontier "high society." When the Reverend David Bacon came to Mackinac in 1802 in a futile effort to begin a Protestant mission, his wife spent considerable time at the Mitchells' attempting to learn the Ottawa language. She was frustrated, however, because their time was taken up by card parties for ladies and gentlemen twice a week, balls, dinners, and tea-parties. As members of the élite the Mitchells were concerned about the education of their children. The doctor had a large library, and they sent their sons to Montreal and their daughters to Europe for instruction.

By 1811 war between England and the United States appeared likely. Mitchell went to St Joseph Island and on 7 December rejoined the British army as a hospital mate. Living at St Joseph was his daughter Jessie, wife of the prosperous trader Lewis Crawford. Crawford was deeply involved in recruiting Indians for the British cause and Mitchell helped furnish supplies. When war was declared, Mitchell accompanied the British and Indian force under Captain Charles Roberts* that surprised and captured the garrison at Fort Michilimackinac in the first action of the war, on 17 July 1812. Mitchell had returned home in a most dramatic way.

Throughout the war Mitchell continued to serve as hospital mate on Mackinac. Occasionally he attended conferences with the Indians, and during the winter of 1813–14 he accompanied Robert Dickson's expedition to what is now Wisconsin. When in the summer of 1814 the Americans unsuccessfully attacked Mackinac Island, Elizabeth Mitchell actively recruited Indian allies for the British from her Ottawa relatives at L'Arbre Croche. As a token of appreciation, the authorities granted her an allowance of £50 a year for

Mitchell

two years. The Ojibwas also respected her highly. In November 1814 they presented her with a deed to Round Island, their traditional burying ground located half a mile southeast of Mackinac.

The Treaty of Ghent which ended the war confronted Dr Mitchell with a serious dilemma. Mackinac Island was returned to the Americans, whom he had grown to hate. A man of iron will, he decided to accompany the British forces when in July 1815 they moved to Drummond Island to build a new post. He secured an appointment as assistant surgeon in the Indian Department. Not willing to leave their extensive holdings on Mackinac unsecured, Elizabeth Mitchell stayed behind to manage their large hay farm, fishing enterprises, and fur-trade business.

Tension ran high in the months following the cessation of the war. The Indians, who had never been defeated, were indignant at the ending of hostilities. Elizabeth Mitchell's influence with them was resented bitterly by William Henry Puthuff, the newly appointed United States Indian agent on Mackinac. On 9 Sept. 1815 he posted a notice on the church door prohibiting her from holding conferences with the Indians. When "those unfortunate deluded People" continued to visit he threatened to arrest her. There followed a flurry of letters and recriminations between the British and American commandants at Drummond and Mackinac. Faced with being sent to Detroit for trial, she fled at night in a small canoe to join her husband.

Hostile feelings between the Americans and British cooled, and in 1816 or 1817 Elizabeth Mitchell returned to Mackinac. For the next ten years she spent most of her time on the island, where her home was still the centre of society, while the doctor remained on Drummond. At both locations they maintained retail stores, and the comings and goings of Elizabeth and their sons provided ample opportunities for trade and occasional smuggling. When son William came of age he became an American citizen and an active partner in his mother's fur-trade activities. Daniel, George, and Andrew resided on Drummond with their father. This family trade network was lucrative, and the Mackinac Island tax records for 1823 indicate that Mitchell was the island's third largest taxpayer.

On Drummond Island the ageing Dr Mitchell continued to attend conferences with the Indians and to minister to their medical needs. He also served as a justice of the peace. On 20 Feb. 1820 he presided at a double wedding when his son George married Harriet Ussher and his granddaughter Elizabeth Ann Hamilton married Captain Thomas Gummersall Anderson*. At about this time Mitchell was described as "built large and bony, with broad, rugged features, crowned with tangled masses of grizzled hair." Elizabeth visited him now and again, and died at Drummond Island on 26 Feb. 1827. On 18 April her son

Andrew sadly took her corpse back to Mackinac for burial.

The following year the British garrison was forced to leave the post because Drummond Island was determined to be within the boundaries of the young republic. Consequently Mitchell, who was nearly 80, had to move once again, this time to Penetanguishene in 1828. There, accompanied by Andrew and George, he built one of the first houses. Death found him on 7 Aug. 1832 – the result of cholera, according to family tradition. He was buried on his farm at Penetanguishene.

DAVID A. ARMOUR

ANQ-M, CE1-63, 14 oct. 1806. Bayliss Public Library (Sault Ste Marie, Mich.), Misc. coll., diaries, journals, and fraternal records, Mackinac notarial records, 1806–18 (photocopies at DPL, Burton Hist. Coll.); Port Mackinac, records, 1808; 25 June 1810; 28 July 1811. Bentley Hist. Library, Univ. of Mich. (Ann Arbor), Mich. Hist. Coll., U.S. Bureau of Customs, district of Michilimackinac, impost book, 1802–58. Clarke Hist. Library, Central Mich. Univ. (Mount Pleasant), American Fur Company papers, Charles Ermatinger to Samuel Abbott, 13 Oct. 1810; T. C. and F. R. Telfa coll., manifests, Mackinac, 1803–4, 1806, 1810. Clements Library, Thomas Duggan journal, 10 Sept. 1796, 19 Nov. 1799; W. S. Eveleth, "Map of the Island of Michilimackinac," c.1816; Thomas Gage papers, American ser., 121, Gage to Caldwell, 31 July 1774; 124, Caldwell to Gage, 24 Oct. 1774; Gage to Caldwell, 14 Nov. 1774; 126, Caldwell to Gage, 11 Feb. 1775. DPL, Burton Hist. Coll., Michael Dousman papers; Harrow family papers, Alexander Harrow, logbook of the armed sloop *Welcome*, 31 July 1780; 2, 9–10, 12 July 1781; James Henry, Mackinac Store journal and ledger, 1802–4; Robert McDouall, orderly book, Drummond Island, 1815; Map. coll., "Sketch of the situation of certain lotts in the village of Michilimackinac," n.d. (977.4m16/n.d./S627). Edinburgh Univ. Library, Special Coll. Dept., Medical matriculation records, 1770–71. McCord Museum, Beaver Club minute-book. Mackinac County Courthouse (St Ignace, Mich.), Reg. of the post of Michilimackinac, 35, 55, 69. Mackinac Island State Park Commission (Mackinac Island, Mich.), Photographs of the Mitchell house, c.1880s. Mich., Dept. of Natural Resources, Lands Division (Lansing), Private claims, nos. 110, 285–88, 707–8. PAC, RG 8, I (C ser.), 91: 33–37; 268: 157; 269: 179–84, 302–4, 510–11; 930: 53–56; RG 10, A2, 28: 16400; 30: 18127; 31: 18659–61, 18663, 18704; 32: 19106–15, 19118, 19131, 19143, 19160–61, 19172, 19221, 19226, 19236, 19243, 19824, 20002, 20073; A4, 51: 56727. Stuart House Museum of Astor Fur Post (Mackinac Island), American Fur Company, letter-book, 1820–23; retail store account-book, 1824–27. Wis., State Hist. Soc. (Madison), Consolidated returns of trade licences, 1 May 1790 (transcripts); J. D. Doty papers, "Memorandum of travels in northern Michigan and Wisconsin," 10 July–2 Aug. 1822, pp.218–20; M. L. Martin papers, 1 Sept. 1811; 19–20 June 1817.

J. J. Bigsby, *The shoe and canoe, or pictures of travel in the Canadas, illustrative of their scenery and of colonial life; with facts and opinions on emigration, state policy, and* other points of public interest . . . (2v., London, 1850). William Burnett, *Letter book of William Burnett, early fur trader in the land of four flags*, ed. W. M. Cunningham (n.p., 1967), 73. *John Askin papers* (Quaife). [G. T.] Landmann, *Adventures and recollections of Colonel Landmann, late of the Corps of Royal Engineers* (2v., London, 1852), 2: 78–79, 103. *Mich. Pioneer Coll.*, 9 (1886), 10 (1886), 11 (1887), 12 (1887), 15 (1889), 16 (1890), 19 (1891), 20 (1892), 23 (1893). *Michigan voyageurs: from the notary book of Samuel Abbott, Mackinac Island, 1807–1817*, ed. D. V. Russell (Detroit, 1982). "The migration of voyageurs from Drummond Island to Penetanguishene in 1828," comp. A. C. Osborne, *OH*, 3 (1901): 129–31, 139–40, 145, 148. U.S., Congress, *American state papers . . . in relation to the public lands . . .*, ed. Walter Lowrie (5v., Washington, 1834), 4: 820, 831. Wis., State Hist. Soc., *Coll.*, 3 (1857): 253; 9 (1882); 10 (1888); 11 (1888); 12 (1892); 14 (1898); 18 (1908); 19 (1910); 20 (1911). David Dobson, *Directory of Scottish settlers in North America, 1625–1825* (Baltimore, Md., 1985). "List of the Drummond Island voyageurs," comp. A. C. Osborne, *OH*, 3 (1901): 152–53, 157. *Officers of British forces in Canada* (Irving).

D. A. Armour and K. R. Widder, *At the crossroads: Michilimackinac during the American revolution* (Mackinac Island, 1978). Leonard Bacon, *Sketch of the Rev. David Bacon* (Boston, 1876), 46–47. J. E. and E. L. Bayliss, *Historic St. Joseph Island* (Cedar Rapids, Iowa, 1938). S. F. Cook, *Drummond Island: the story of the British occupation, 1815–1828* (Lansing, 1896). B. F. Emery, *Post cemetery, Drummond, Fort Collyer, 1815–1828* (Detroit, 1931). G. S. Hubbard, *The autobiography of Gurdon Saltonstall Hubbard . . .* (Chicago, 1911), 14–15, 21–22, 133. A. F. Hunter, *A history of Simcoe County* (2v., Barrie, Ont., 1909; repr. 1948), 2: 131. D. [S.] Lavender, *The fist in the wilderness* (Garden City, N.Y., 1964), 241–42. A. C. Osborne, "Old Penetanguishene: sketches of its pioneer, naval and military days," *Simcoe County pioneer papers* (6 nos., Barrie, 1908–17; repr., 6 nos. in 1v., Belleville, Ont., 1974), no.5. J. F. Smith, *A panorama of masonic history: sesquicentennial of the Grand Lodge, Free and Accepted Masons of Michigan, 1826–1976* ([Detroit?, 1976?]), 13. D. A. Armour, "David and Elizabeth: the Mitchell family of the straits of Mackinac," *Mich. Hist.* (Lansing), 64 (1980), no.4: 17–29; reprinted as *Mackinac Hist.* (Mackinac Island), 2 (1982), no.6. T. W. Blinn, "Some notes on early Michigan postal markings," *Mich. Hist.*, 32 (1948): 153–54.

MONK, Sir JAMES, lawyer, office holder, politician, and judge; b. 9 March 1745/46 (Old Style) in Boston, son of James Monk*, lawyer, and Ann Dering; d. 18 Nov. 1826 in Cheltenham, England.

James Monk grew up and received his education in Halifax. From 1761 to 1767 he studied law with his father, and on 10 March 1768 he was admitted to the bar. That year his father died, leaving a wife and five children in dire financial straits. As clerk of the crown in the Supreme Court and a beginning lawyer, James exerted "the Strictest Prudence" and a "stedy and unwear^d attention to business," in his mother's words, to provide most of the family's income. From 1771 to 1774 he studied law in London. In 1772 he was appointed solicitor general of Nova Scotia on the recommendation of Lord Hillsborough. While in London he married Elizabeth Adams, who was apparently well connected.

Monk took up his duties at Halifax on 8 Sept. 1774. Backed by the home secretary, Lord Dartmouth, he quickly won the confidence of Governor Francis Legge*, and by December he was also acting attorney general in place of William Nesbitt*. With Charles Morris* and others, Monk investigated deficiencies in the public accounts of a group of officials including former provincial treasurer Benjamin Green* and then prosecuted for recovery of missing funds. Monk was elected to the House of Assembly for Yarmouth in 1775 but was unseated in 1776 because of non-attendance. During the American revolution [*see* Jonathan Eddy*] he took a leading part in anti-revolutionary activity, founding the Association to crystallize loyalist sentiment.

Both as solicitor general and as attorney general Monk was unsalaried, and as an executor of Legge's policies he was unpopular in Nova Scotian official circles. In August 1776, therefore, Lord George Germain, secretary of state for the American Colonies, appointed him attorney general of the province of Quebec; he was commissioned at Quebec on 27 May 1777. Governor Sir Guy Carleton*, who disliked Germain's making colonial appointments and whose own candidate had been William GRANT, received Monk coolly. Carleton's attitude and his own development of a lucrative private practice among the colony's merchants pushed Monk into the English party in colonial politics [*see* George Allsopp*]. A friendship with Peter Livius* led to Monk's appointment in July 1778 as surrogate judge of the Vice-Admiralty Court, where Livius presided; he was to hold the position for ten years.

Monk avoided open conflict with Carleton, but he could not do so with Carleton's successor, Frederick Haldimand*, who did not appreciate the opposition Monk often found between policy and legality. In 1782 Haldimand resurrected the long dormant post of solicitor general and confided it to Jenkin Williams* in order to avoid having to call on Monk's services. Thus it was Williams who prosecuted merchants indebted to the state through John Cochrane [*see* James Dunlop*], and he won, thanks to a sympathetic judge in Adam Mabane*. Monk, a friend and creditor of Cochrane, had opposed the prosecution on legal grounds and saw in the large number of bankruptcies that resulted an economic and social vindication of his views. However, surmising (correctly) that Haldimand would seek his dismissal, he lamented to his wife in 1784: "If I act with Law & Constitution legal & political I am to be . . . ruined by a Governor – If I act against them I surely shall be ruined by Ministry who will screen their Govr under . . . my disgrace!"

Monk

Monk was saved two years later when Carleton, now Lord Dorchester, succeeded Haldimand. In 1787, in his private capacity, Monk acted as the attorney for the colony's merchants in opposing before the Legislative Council a bill sponsored by the French party to extend the use of French civil law in the province. During a 6½-hour speech Monk mercilessly attacked the administration of justice, particularly by the judges of the courts of common pleas, whom he accused of incompetence and, in Dorchester's words, "of granting by favor to one what they refused to another."

Dorchester ordered an inquiry presided over by Chief Justice William Smith*. Assisted by Isaac Ogden and Joseph Papineau*, Monk put the merchants' case; the judges, represented by lawyers Alexander Gray and Pierre-Amable De Bonne*, boycotted proceedings, claiming bias on Smith's part. Monk brought forth numerous witnesses, most of them disgruntled lawyers [see Arthur Davidson*] or merchants injured by the Cochrane decision. His main accusations were that the judges favoured some lawyers; operated without adequate rules of practice, thus introducing anarchy into judicial proceedings; failed to maintain court records properly, thus jeopardizing appeals; and, from lack of legal training, applied French or English law or even equity as it suited them, thus "assuming the powers of Legislators." Conscious that it was unwise to pillory judges, neither Smith nor Dorchester committed themselves; a great undigested mass of evidence was transferred hastily to London. In early 1789 astoundingly slim results came back: Monk was replaced as attorney general by Gray. The British government had agreed with a statement by one of the judges, Mabane, that it must support them or forfeit the people's confidence in the judiciary and in the government whose laws the judiciary upheld.

Monk went to England in late 1789 to recover his post. He enlisted the aid of influential colonial and imperial merchants, and the jurist Francis MASERES helped him publish *State of the present form of government of the province of Quebec*. In it Monk attacked the régime of the Quebec Act and asserted that proposing reform of the judiciary was not sedition: rather, "without any certain law" the colony was "in the worst state of civil society." However, he argued, effective judicial and constitutional reform was conditional on assimilation of Canadian to British norms. His efforts by this and other means to achieve reinstatement failed until 1792, after Gray died; Monk was named Gray's successor. From the experience Monk drew a bitter lesson, passed on to his brother George Henry in Nova Scotia: "Distinguish between your Gov^t and this at St James. . . . Never use uncommon ardor but where the . . . policy of St James is incontrovertibly clear. The . . . Tranquility of the colony is the object here, and no consideration should hazard that object with a politic Man."

Monk arrived back in Lower Canada in October 1792. In 1794 he and the new solicitor general, Jonathan Sewell*, investigated acts of civil disobedience, including a refusal by habitants at Charlesbourg to report for militia duty, which led to riots in May. Until then, Monk had on several occasions displayed repugnance for the abuse of legal authority; he would not tolerate civil disobedience, however. Drawing information from various sources, including an undercover agent, John Black*, he concluded that unrest was being created by French revolutionary and American subversives. To nip in the bud the development of a movement of resistance to British authority, Monk worked on several fronts. Judicially, he had a limited number of suspected ringleaders arrested – 50 to 100 between May and November 1794. Legislatively, he worked for passage of an alien bill the objects of which were to forbid unauthorized entry into the colony by foreigners, permit their summary deportation, suspend habeas corpus where treason was suspected, and outlaw seditious assemblies; once passed in 1794 it was effective in controlling the activities of emissaries. He also pushed for passage of a judicature bill, achieved the same year but reserved by Dorchester; Monk felt that, in part by strengthening the legal protection for *censitaires* from abusive practices by rapacious seigneurs, it would undermine a major source of social discontent. Finally, socially, he initiated the Association to promote loyalty to Britain; it changed the atmosphere in the colony, allowing Monk to arrest suspected agitators without provoking riots. Dorchester acknowledged officially the efficacy of Monk's measures, and Monk himself underlined to the Home Department his apparent success. In fact, a latent sympathy for the French, although exaggerated by Monk, existed among the habitants, and his policies prevented revolutionary activists from exploiting it fully.

It was Monk's ambition to attain the chief justiceship of Lower Canada. Although he had applied for it on Smith's death in 1793, it had gone to William OSGOODE. The judicature act, of which Monk had been the inspiration and chief promoter, among other things created three judicial districts: Quebec, Montreal, and Trois-Rivières. The first two were each to have a chief justice; Osgoode inherited the more prestigious and better paying position at Quebec, which was that of chief justice of Lower Canada, while Monk, on his performance in combating revolutionary ferment, won that at Montreal, with its salary of £900. Monk acquired as his residence in Montreal the estate of a former law associate, William Dummer POWELL, by having it auctioned for debt in 1795 and buying it himself. He already possessed a fine house on Rue Saint-Louis in Quebec, for which he had paid

£1,000 in 1784; he subsequently acquired several other prime properties on the street. In 1795 his Quebec house was razed by fire, but he replaced it with one even more impressive.

In Montreal, Monk set about reforming the administration of justice he had denounced in 1787, establishing, for instance, written grounds for decisions. Judicially, he sometimes supported, sometimes undermined, the use of French law and the legal position of the Roman Catholic Church. With respect to the latter, he opposed in policy as counterproductive Sewell's efforts to obtain control of the church through legal harassment. He took a controversial stand on slavery; the House of Assembly having proved unable to abolish it [see Pierre-Louis Panet*], Monk declared from the bench, contrary to fact, that slave ownership in the colony was unsupported in law and systematically dismissed all suits by owners against runaway slaves.

As a chief justice Monk held a seat on the Legislative and Executive councils, but he attended meetings only sporadically until Osgoode's departure in 1801 temporarily placed him in the speaker's chair of the former in January 1802. His opinions and actions over time had incurred the displeasure of successive administrators of the colony, and Lieutenant Governor Sir Robert Shore Milnes* pleaded with the Colonial Office for Osgoode's speedy replacement as chief justice at Quebec; that year John Elmsley* was appointed over Monk. Ever the opportunist, Monk sold his residence and other properties on Rue Saint-Louis to Elmsley for nearly £4,000. On Elmsley's death in 1805 Monk was again thwarted by Milnes; Elmsley was succeeded by Henry Allcock*. Monk's humiliation was complete when in 1808 his rival Sewell vaulted over him to replace Allcock on recommendations from the administrative oligarchy at Quebec. Subsequently Monk rather favoured Governor Sir James Henry Craig*'s stern conduct of the administration and privately pilloried Craig's successor, Sir George Prevost*, for his conciliatory approach to the nationalist Canadian party. Convinced during the War of 1812 that the Americans were weaker than they appeared to be, Monk was saddened by Prevost's defensive strategy. "We ought to have been Terribly great," he lamented; "we shall I fear moulder into a vegetative rejoicing at safety."

Meanwhile, Monk had continued his reform of the administration of justice in the Montreal district; in 1811 it culminated in the publication of rules of practice for his court. They were inspired by rules previously published by Sewell, following consultations with Monk and the other judges, for the Court of Appeals and the Court of King's Bench at Quebec. Monk's views and position made him a prime target for the Canadian party. In 1814, under the influence of James Stuart*, it used its majority in the House of Assembly to impeach him and Sewell for "exercizing a Legislative authority" by the establishment of rules of practice "subversive of the laws of this Province." Thus Monk found himself in Mabane's shoes 27 years after the inquiry of 1787. Recalling that unhappy experience, however, he had no doubt that the imperial government would clear them. In analysing the situation, with the realism that characterized his critical faculty, or in rebutting the charges, or in drawing up strategy, Monk played a major role in preparing their defence, although Sewell would present their case in England. He perceived that the Canadian party had erred politically; through their defence Sewell would be able to demonstrate its radical objectives and thus the folly of Prevost's conciliatory approach. The judges were readily absolved on all heads, but the policy of conciliation was not abandoned.

During Sewell's absence in England, Monk, when at Quebec, acted as speaker of the Legislative Council. Then, in September 1819, the unexpected death of the governor, the Duke of Richmond [Lennox*], placed him as the senior Protestant legislative councillor in the interim position of president of the colony, a position he filled with vigour and pragmatism until replaced by Sir Peregrine Maitland* in March 1820. Much concerned about the social and financial burden imposed on the inhabitants of Quebec by massive arrivals of destitute immigrants, Monk worked closely with the Quebec Emigrants' Society and colonial officials to prepare for the imminent wave of 1820. He urged Lord Bathurst at the Colonial Office to control and provision departing emigrants more effectively, sought authorization to spend public money on charitable assistance when private resources were overwhelmed, and initiated preparations to expedite the departure of immigrants from the town to lands prepared for them.

In June 1820 Monk took leave of absence as chief justice of the district of Montreal with the intention of retiring in England. His departure was lamented by Governor Lord Dalhousie [Ramsay*], who considered him among the "front rank, men really necessary here." In London in 1822 he was called upon, along with John Beverley Robinson* of Upper Canada and Charles Marshall, solicitor general of Lower Canada, to work on a bill to unite Lower and Upper Canada, a measure he felt was "urgently called for." His proposals were designed to encourage anglification of the colony, limitation of the growing pretensions of the assembly, and restriction of participation in the political process through the establishment of higher property qualifications for voting and election to office. Meanwhile, he had been seeking a pension of three-quarters of his salary. The assembly's refusal to accord him more than one-half, which he was ultimately constrained to accept by a chagrined Bathurst,

Monk

shocked the judges in the colony, who then sought conditions that would ensure them a satisfactory pension in the future. To compensate Monk for his loss, Bathurst, at Monk's own request, had him knighted; the ceremony took place on 27 April 1825.

Throughout his life Monk never lost the sense, acquired as a youth, of being the patriarch of his family. That his own marriage was childless was therefore a considerable disappointment to him. The marriage in fact was unhappy from the mid 1790s at least, and Monk's enjoyment of social life, in particular the company of women, scandalized the official oligarchy at Quebec. Monk exercised his sense of family responsibility on the numerous brood of his brother and closest confidant, George Henry, whose income was often unequal to the family's needs. Apart from a desire to prove himself, it was to support financially and to advance socially his Nova Scotia family that Monk strove for the head of his profession.

Monk saw particularly to the education of his nephews and nieces. As children they received gifts of grammars, dictionaries, and encyclopedias. As adolescents, they paraded to Quebec to complete their education under his vigilant eye. Some at least were placed for a time with a competent French or Canadian priest to learn French – "indispensable to prosperity in life" – and elements of a French classical education. Nephews were prepared for the law, government, or the military (Monk disdained business as a career); nieces for an advantageous marriage. Monk proposed to give them all a start in life, but all were expected to acquire the intellectual, psychological, and moral resources to succeed independent of patrons or husbands as the case might be. He inculcated into his nephews the necessity to "fulfill [honestly] the obligations, and conditions" of their offices or expect dismissal. He also insisted that their salaries were not to support "The table. The theatre. the Ladies, and the Bed," but to assist in "the protection of [the] Family."

Monk's closest relationship was with a niece, Elizabeth Ann, known as Eliza. He brought her up to be autonomous, well read, reflective, and feminine, lavished on her expensive clothes and jewellery, introduced her to society, and, on his retirement, took her as his companion to England, from where they made annual winter excursions to France and Italy. She demonstrated her independence by refusing an advantageous marriage that he had arranged and instead marrying an unemployed English half-pay officer whom she loved; a resigned Monk witnessed the marriage and subsequently supported the couple financially. Shortly before his death in 1826 Monk named Eliza his sole heir, thus freeing her financially from her husband and making her the head of the Monks. The legacy was substantial, consisting of landed properties (including an estate called Monkville near Windsor, N.S., and another of the same name in Montreal), interest-bearing loans, and stocks; the last alone were worth £18,668.

James Monk was despised by the Canadian party and misunderstood by the official oligarchy at Quebec. His independence of mind and seemingly scandalous behaviour, his often domineering nature and pretentious, confusing manner of expression effectively hid from many of his contemporaries a sharp critical faculty and strong devotion to family. Largely a self-made man, often frustrated by others professionally and privately, he was probably at times selfish, devious, haughty. He was certainly determined and persevering, and an unshakeable confidence in the correctness of his views and actions made him intolerant of opposition. His approach to life was defined in a letter to a nephew in 1819 – "You must learn to feel strength in your *own* Opinion & Judgment. And *reading*, study, knowledge and wisdom are the only means to attain it." Herein is the key to his relations with the Canadian party, the British oligarchy, and his family. In a society polarized around two parties, Monk was not a party man. His views often reflected those of the English party but not from any sense of solidarity on his part. His loyalties were, in order, to his brother's family and to Britain, and it was, he felt, through the full and responsible development of the individual that such loyalties could be rendered most fruitful.

JAMES H. LAMBERT

[The author wishes to thank Jacqueline Roy for her assistance in analysing the personality of James Monk. J.H.L.]

James Monk is the author of *State of the present form of government of the province of Quebec* . . . (London, 1789; 2nd ed., 1790) and *Bill présenté* . . . *au Conseil législatif intitulé "Acte qui assure plus efficacement aux créanciers les biens et effets des gens en commerce faisant faillite, et pour l'égale distribution de tels effets et biens"* (Québec, 1795). A portrait of Monk is in the McCord Museum; it is reproduced in P.-G. Roy, *Les juges de la prov. de Québec*, 382 (the photographic copy at the PAC comes from this source), in Raoul Roy, *Résistance indépendantiste, 1793–1798* (Montréal, 1973), 176, and in D. B. Webster et al., *Georgian Canada; conflict and culture, 1745–1820* (Toronto, 1984), 204.

AAQ, 22 A, VI: 338. ANQ-Q, CN1-25, 29 juill. 1784; CN1-224, 27 mars 1787; CN1-262, 3 janv. 1803. AUM, P 58, U, Monk to Reid, 10 Feb. 1803; 3 Nov. 1815; 12, 18, 27, 29 Feb., 15 Dec. 1816. BL, Add. MSS 21863: 1–16, 22–33, 42, 48–65, 71, 77, 85–87, 93, 97–98 (copies at PAC). MTL, W. D. Powell papers, B91. PAC, MG 11, [CO 42] Q, 28: 44; 42: 48–50; [CO 217] Nova Scotia A, 89: 127; 91: 189; 94: 230; 96: 115; MG 23, A6; GII, 10, vol.3: 1138, 1166, 1251; 4: 1616, 1621; 5: 2042–52, 2145, 2149, 2169, 2174, 2176, 2180, 2185–88, 2194–95, 2221–22, 2240, 2278, 2285–87, 2302–3, 2345–46, 2442, 2523, 2525, 2561–62, 2567–69, 2631; 6: 2886; 16: 8072–74; GII, 14, vol.2: 963, 966; 19; HI, 4, vol.2: 703; MG 24, B3, 3: 32; B10: 18–19; B16: 262, 594, 654, 766, 793a; MG 30, D1, 22:

14, 20, 30, 33–34, 94, 110–11, 124; MG 53, 191, 215, B37; RG 1, L3^L: 4225, 70683–96; RG 4, A1: 7350–51, 11755, 13735–37, 18284–86, 19097–98, 36943, 40364–68; RG 8, I (C ser.), 743: 137; RG 68, General index, 1651–1841. PANS, MG 100, 191, no.4; RG 1, 168: 368; 301, no.50; RG 5, A, 1b, no.13. PRO, CO 42/50: 109, 121–22, 348, 351–52; 42/52: 5, 49–50, 60–64, 71–89, 106–9, 129, 135–36, 212, 290, 378–82; 42/54: 118–47, 213–72, 280–309; 42/55–57; 42/97: 202–6, 229–35, 252–59; 42/99: 240, 298–304, 311, 314; 42/100: 4–21, 58–59, 103–6, 308–28, 345–55, 366–79, 384, 390–400; 42/101: 5–6, 9–11, 53–56; 42/104: 159–80; 42/111: 35, 57–58, 484–93; 42/113: 16–60, 83–89, 113–16, 121; 42/115: 5, 13–68, 165, 169–70, 227, 242, 275–79; 42/116: 33–43, 49–50, 59–61, 69, 75–85; 42/117: 10, 191, 275–81; 42/119: 9, 50, 79, 120–29, 136; 42/122: 112–39; 42/128: 136, 197–99, 204, 206; 42/129: 324–28, 460–64, 471–80; 42/131: 81–83, 100, 273–76, 337, 415; 42/182: 17, 137, 151, 167, 177, 222–40, 252–54, 267–75, 308; 42/185: 40, 56, 77–78, 375–76, 385; 42/186: 340–56; 42/189: 277, 362–68, 374–86, 397; 42/192: 288, 299, 304–8, 318, 320, 327; 42/193: 114–22, 144–56; 42/196: 222–27; 42/197: 396–402; 42/202: 325, 333–35, 341–47; 42/206: 291, 364–65, 379–85; 42/214: 7–16; 217/50: 117, 132; 217/51: 4, 190–202. "Les dénombrements de Québec" (Plessis), ANQ *Rapport*, 1948–49: 73, 122. *Docs. relating to constitutional hist., 1791–1818* (Doughty and McArthur), 113, 120–23, 418–21, 437–39, 455–82, 526–27; *1819–28* (Doughty and Story), 149–52, 284. L.C., House of Assembly, *Journals*, 1815: 584; 1816: 96–97, 214, 310, 338–44; *Proceedings in the assembly of Lower Canada on the rules of practice of the courts of justice and the impeachment of Jonathan Sewell and James Monk, esquires* (n.p., 1814); *Statutes*, 1793, c.6. William Osgoode, "Letters from the Honourable Chief Justice William Osgoode: a selection from his Canadian correspondence, 1791–1801," ed. William Colgate, *OH*, 46 (1954): 94–95, 151. Ramsay, *Dalhousie journals* (Whitelaw), 2: 59–60, 66, 125, 164, 196, 203. William Smith, *The diary and selected papers of Chief Justice William Smith, 1784–1793*, ed. L. F. S. Upton (2v., Toronto, 1963–65), 2: xxvii–xxix, xli, 150, 177–78. *Le Canadien*, 13, 20 déc. 1806; 7 mai 1808. *Quebec Gazette*, 23 April 1789; 18 Oct. 1792; 3 July 1794; 8, 15 Jan. 1795; 2 July 1800; 7 Jan. 1813; 30 March, 7 Dec. 1815; 29 Feb., 8 Aug. 1816; 27 Feb. 1817; 16, 23 Sept., 7, 14, 18 Oct., 11, 18, 29 Nov., 6, 16, 30 Dec. 1819; 13, 20, 31 Jan., 17, 24, 28 Feb., 6 March 1820; 5 March 1821; 20 Feb., 18 Dec. 1823. Caron, "Inv. de la corr. de Mgr Plessis," ANQ *Rapport*, 1932–33: 56. *Register of admissions to the Honourable Society of the Middle Temple . . .*, comp. H. A. C. Sturgess (3v., London, 1949), 1: 372. W. A. Shaw, *The knights of England* (2v., London, 1971), 1: 325.

Aubert de Gaspé, *Mémoires* (1885), 57, 325–26. L.-P. Audet, *Le système scolaire*, 3: 165, 177, 179–80, 235. Henri Brun, *La formation des institutions parlementaires québécoises, 1791–1838* (Québec, 1970), 63. R. P. Burns, "The English viewpoint on the proposed union of 1822 to unite the provinces of Upper and Lower Canada" (MA thesis, Univ. of Ottawa, 1966), 91–101, 153–54. A. L. Burt, *The old province of Québec* (2v., Toronto, 1968), 1: 248; 2: 31–32, 39, 40, 65, 117, 152–56, 187. Christie, *Hist. of L.C.* (1848–55), 1: 172–73; 2: 279–83; 6: 324–27. Galarneau, *La France devant l'opinion canadienne (1760–1815)*, 237–43,

247. F. M. Greenwood, "The development of a garrison mentality among the English in Lower Canada, 1793–1811" (PHD thesis, Univ. of B.C., Vancouver, 1970), 19, 23, 49–50, 123–25, 129. Lemieux, *L'établissement de la première prov. eccl.*, 116. Millman, *Jacob Mountain*, 21–22, 115, 174–75. Neatby, *Quebec*, 167, 214–15, 217. Ouellet, *Bas-Canada*, 137. Paquet et Wallot, *Patronage et pouvoir dans le Bas-Canada*, 68. Taft Manning, *Revolt of French Canada*, 106, 153–54, 160, 249. Marcel Trudel, *L'esclavage au Canada français: histoire et conditions de l'esclavage* (Québec, 1960), 141. L. F. S. Upton, *The loyal whig: William Smith of New York & Quebec* (Toronto, 1969), 180, 185, 208, 210. R. W. Winks, *The blacks in Canada: a history* (Montreal, 1971), 99–101. É.-Z. Massicotte, "Où naquit un vice-roi à Montréal?" *BRH*, 46 (1940): 9–12. W. R. Riddell, "A Philadelphia lawyer and early Lower Canada law," *CHR*, 9 (1928): 39–40. J.-P. Wallot, "Une émeute à Lachine contre la 'conscription' (1812)," *RHAF*, 18 (1964–65): 126–27.

MONRO (Munro), DAVID, merchant, ironmaster, militia officer, politician, office holder, JP, and seigneur; b. *c.* 1765 in Scotland; d. 3 Sept. 1834 in Bath, England.

Neither the date of David Monro's arrival at Quebec nor the reasons why he came are known. According to the *Quebec Gazette*, when the partnership between merchants Alexander Davison and John Lees* came to an end in August 1791, Monro was authorized to give discharges to the company's debtors. He had dealings at that time with another local merchant, Mathew Bell*, with whom he was to form the partnership of Monro and Bell. On 6 June 1793 the two partners joined George Davison*, the brother of Alexander, in purchasing from the latter the operating lease on the Saint-Maurice ironworks. In 1796, on his return from a stay in London, Monro resumed his endeavours, both at Quebec and at the ironworks, where he devoted his energies to adding to the properties owned by the enterprise. From then on he divided his time between Quebec and Trois-Rivières.

As a faithful subject, Monro in July 1794 had signed a declaration of loyalty to the constitution and government instituted in Lower Canada by Great Britain, and in 1797 he served on the jury at the trial of David McLane* for treason, a trial that caused much stir. In 1800 he became an ensign in the Quebec Battalion of British Militia; promoted first lieutenant before 1805 and captain on 18 March 1812, he reached the rank of major of the 4th Battalion of Quebec's militia in 1813. He was elected to the House of Assembly for Saint-Maurice, a riding that he and Michel Caron represented from 6 Aug. 1804 to 27 April 1808. In this fourth parliament, debates were increasingly bitter, particularly when the bills dealing with financing prisons and with ineligibility of judges to sit in the assembly [*see* Sir James Henry Craig*; Pierre-Amable De Bonne*] were presented. Monro voted with the English party. He did not stand for election in 1808, commenting that "the situation, I feel, would materially interfere with my future arrangements." In the period from 1805 he had been appointed to several offices: commissioner for building and repairing churches and presbyteries in Trois-Rivières (1805, 1818, 1820), justice of the peace for the district of Trois-Rivières (1805, 1811, 1815) and for the district of Quebec (1810), commissioner for receiving the oath of allegiance (1807, 1810, 1815, 1820).

Concurrently with these various functions, Monro played an active role in the merchant community of Quebec. He held shares in the Union Company of Quebec, an enterprise founded in 1805 to provide the town with a fine hotel, and in February 1806 he was appointed to its management committee. In March 1806 he was elected president of the Fire Society but declined the honour. On 21 Feb. 1809 he joined the town's leading merchants in founding the Quebec Committee of Trade and was put on a committee of seven, chaired by James IRVINE, to study proposals from the Halifax Committee of Trade. Monro had also strengthened his ties with the business community through his marriage, solemnized at Quebec on 5 March 1807; his wife, Catherine MacKenzie, aged 23, was the daughter of deceased Trois-Rivières merchant James Mackenzie, who had been a partner of William Grant* of Trois-Rivières, and the sister of Ann MacKenzie, who had married Mathew Bell in 1799. They were to have four children.

With George Davison's death in March 1799 Monro and Bell became the sole lessees of the Saint-Maurice ironworks. Under their direction the enterprise enjoyed a stability that promoted an intense development of activities, an increase in production, and some expansion. More than 20 buildings for industrial, residential, or service use were erected, and more than 300 men worked there. On 31 Dec. 1815 Monro withdrew from Monro and Bell and from the management of the ironworks. On 26 Oct. 1816 he handed his share over to Bell, on conditions drawn up before notary Joseph-Bernard PLANTÉ. Bell then went into partnership with John Stewart*, who had been in partnership with Monro and Bell until November 1806 under the name of John Stewart and Company. Collaboration between Monro and Bell was not ended, however; in May 1817 they bought Champlain seigneury for £2,520, and they also owned the banal rights on the seigneury of Rivière-du-Loup.

In 1817 David Monro refused Governor Sir John Coape SHERBROOKE's invitation to become a member of the Legislative Council, on grounds that he planned to leave the province as soon as possible for quite a long time. He was still at Quebec in 1818, but in 1821 he was in England, his return to Great Britain necessitating his replacement in an administrative

post. He died in Bath on 3 Sept. 1834. His will was registered at Quebec two years later and one of the beneficiaries was his former partner Mathew Bell.

MARIE-FRANCE FORTIER

ANQ-MBF, CN1-6, 1er avril 1807, 1er juill. 1817; CN1-32, 23 mai 1817. ANQ-Q, CE1-61, 5 mars 1807; CN1-171, 5 mars 1807; CN1-230, 26 oct. 1816; CN1-285, 1er juill. 1803. PAC, MG 23, A1, ser.3, 8: 56; RG 1, L3L: 3551–52; RG 4, A1: 18217–26, 36854–61; vol.175: 28; vol.178: 17; vol.193: 59; RG 68, General index, 1651–1841: 223–24, 279, 282, 337–38, 341–42, 344, 531, 543. "Les dénombrements de Québec" (Plessis), ANQ Rapport, 1948–49: 86, 135. John Lambert, Travels through Lower Canada, and the United States of North America, in the years 1806, 1807, and 1808 . . . (new ed., 2v., London, 1814), 1: 248. L.C., House of Assembly, Journals, 1805: 13. Quebec Gazette, 18 Aug. 1791; 6 April 1797; 8 May 1800; 6 Feb., 3, 10 April, 13 Nov. 1806; 12 May 1808. F.-J. Audet et Édouard Fabre Surveyer, Les députés de Saint-Maurice et de Buckinghamshire, 1792–1808 (Trois-Rivières, Qué., 1934), 37–38. Desjardins, Guide parl., 140. Officers of British forces in Canada (Irving), 145. "Les Presbytériens à Québec en 1802," BRH, 42 (1936): 728. Recensement de Québec, en 1818 (Provost), 91. Quebec almanac, 1801: 102; 1805: 41; 1810: 21, 34, 49; 1815: 46–47, 56, 60, 85; 1820: 44–45, 59, 83; 1821: 44–45, 60, 87. O.-A. Coté, "La Chambre de commerce de Québec," BRH, 27 (1921): 26–27. Hare, "L'Assemblée législative du Bas-Canada," RHAF, 27: 378–80. P.-G. Roy, "La première Chambre de commerce au Canada," BRH, 31 (1925): 394. A. St-L. [Trigge], "The two Kenelm Chandlers," BRH, 49 (1943): 112.

MONTGENET (Mongenet, Montgenêt), THÉRÈSE-BERNARDINE, Comtesse de MONTGENET, known as Mme de Saint-Laurent; b. 30 Sept. 1760 in Besançon, France, daughter of Jean-Claude Mongenet, a civil engineer, and Jeanne-Claude (Claudine) Pussot; d. unmarried and childless 8 Aug. 1830 in Paris.

In November 1790 Thérèse-Bernardine Montgenet, as Mlle de Saint-Laurent, agreed to join Prince Edward* Augustus, the fourth son of George III, then serving in Gibraltar. He had sent an intermediary to France to find "a young lady to be my companion and mistress of my house." She left her current lover – "a countryman of her own who calls himself the Marquiss de Permangle" – and became Mme de Saint-Laurent "with an hundred names and titles," among them Baronne de Fortisson, a title adopted, it seems, from an earlier lover. She charmed the prince, spurned a bribe to leave him, and accompanied him in the summer of 1791 to his military command in Quebec, beginning a 27-year liaison of great mutual happiness.

In January 1794 the prince left Quebec to join the British forces in Martinique. Madame went with him as far as St Johns (Saint-Jean-sur-Richelieu). He travelled to Boston to take ship; she continued to New York (followed by ribald American newspaper comment), and thence to Halifax and London. Edward, reaching Halifax in May, fretted until her return to him in August. For the next four years (the prince now military commander in the Maritime provinces) Madame was welcomed in Halifax as she had been in Quebec, except among "the proper ladies . . . [who] do not accept her socially," as a French visitor to the Lower Canadian capital had remarked. To John Wentworth*, lieutenant governor of Nova Scotia, she was "an elegant, well bred, pleasing sensible woman – far beyond most – I never yet saw a woman of such intrepid fortitude yet possessing the finest temper and refined manners." In Quebec she had made a lifelong friend of Ignace-Michel-Louis-Antoine d'IRUMBERRY de Salaberry and his family, and her letters to them reflect her gaiety and warmth.

In October 1798 Madame left for London with the prince, who needed treatment for a leg injury. He bought her a house in Knightsbridge, and set up a fund for her future security, which she thriftily invested. He returned to Halifax in September 1799 as Duke of Kent and commander of the forces in British North America, and Madame was hostess again in Prince's Lodge, the suburban retreat lent by Wentworth. She went with the duke on his provincial tours, and found a steadfast friend in the exiled Duc d'Orléans when he visited Halifax.

She made her sixth and last transatlantic crossing in August 1800 when the duke left the climatic rigours of North America forever. Over the next 16 years, including some ten months when the duke was governor and commander at Gibraltar, Madame created the "*quiet & peaceable* home" he valued. At his Ealing (London) estate, Castle Hill Lodge, or in his Kensington Palace suite, the duke's "beloved companion" arranged intimate dinners, welcomed friends, read in his extensive library, sewed ("she makes the whole of her cloaths herself"), or scribbled in her commonplace-book. Frequent visitors were the four Salaberry sons, delighted by her kindness and charm. She and the duke shepherded the youngest, Édouard-Alphonse* (their godson), through his studies and grieved over his death in April 1812 at Badajoz, Spain; he was the third of the brothers to die. Madame also followed with close interest the education at Ealing of Charles-Jean Mongenet, elder son of her brother Jean-Claude; the duke was godfather to Édouard, the younger son.

The duke's debts drove him in 1816 to live in less expensive Brussels. After tours in Germany and France, he joined Madame in Paris for 11 days of an 11-week reunion with her sister, Jeanne-Beatrix de Jansac, and two of their three brothers. She settled in Brussels with him in November, and happily acquired as protégé the young son of the duke's controller and friend, Frederick Augustus Wetherall*. Wetherall, in return, kept an eye on her nephew in England.

For some time the duke had been uneasily contemplating marriage as a way to clear his debts. The death in November 1817 of Princess Charlotte Augusta, second in line to the throne, increased pressure from friends, family, and London papers to marry and provide an heir. His letters to Wetherall showed his distress at losing "that excellent and beloved individual" with whom he was so happy: "*You may* judge how *my* heart sinks *within* me & *bleeds* at every mark of tenderness & affection she bestows on me."

They parted in Brussels in March 1818, she to return to Paris. Both behaved with impeccable dignity. She made no reproach. They corresponded: he worried about her, set up an annuity for her, sent friends to call. Louis XVIII gave her the title of Comtesse de Montgenet. She asked the duke only for Sir William Beechey's portrait of him: he sent it in care of the Duc d'Orléans.

In July 1818 Madame's sister died suddenly in the suite they shared in Paris, and her old lover the Marquis de Permangle helped to settle the estate. With the duke's death in January 1820 her annuity ceased, but he had provided for her well while he lived. His wife, respecting the duke's love for Madame, sent a personal message at once by her brother Prince Leopold of Saxe-Saalfeld-Coburg to the Duc d'Orléans, who took it to her and returned her reply.

Her nephews Charles-Benjamin and Charles-Jean Mongenet were present at her death in 1830. She had dictated personal bequests to her lawyer; her remaining assets went to her legal heirs, two surviving brothers and a nephew. Beechey's portrait of the duke she bequeathed to the Duc d'Orléans, who the day after her death acceded to the French throne as Louis-Philippe. The Duke of Kent having undertaken to support Madame for life, in 1837 Charles-Benjamin Mongenet petitioned Edward's daughter, Queen Victoria, for the rest of his aunt's annuity, which it is believed was paid.

Mme de Saint-Laurent had accepted her position with dignity and faultless behaviour, and had made no attempt to exercise influence in the duke's public life. She was buried from the Église de la Madeleine in her sister's grave in the Cimetière du Père-Lachaise, Paris; she had asked that the tombstone should read "Here lie two sisters united in life, whom death could not separate."

MOLLIE GILLEN

[In addition to a number of titles, Mme de Saint-Laurent went by a variety of given names: Alphonsine appears in the baptismal certificate of her godson; she herself signed her letters J. de St Laurent, the initial apparently standing for Julie, a name which also appears in her godson's baptismal certificate, though it was added apparently at a later date and in a hand other than that of the officiating priest; her will, however, was signed T.-B. de Montgenet. Many legends

Montour

have grown up around her – about her origins, the children she supposedly had with Edward, and her life after her separation from him; these myths have been put to rest in Mollie Gillen, *The prince and his lady: the love story of the Duke of Kent and Madame de St Laurent* (London, 1970; repr. Halifax, 1985). A codicil to Madame's will discovered too late for inclusion in the original edition of the book confirmed the assumption that Beechey's portrait of the duke was bequeathed by her to the Duc d'Orléans: Arch. de Paris, DQ⁷ 9162: f.103r, 5 mai 1825. M.G.]

MONTOUR, SARAH. *See* AINSE

MOREHOUSE, DANIEL, miller, soldier, militia officer, JP, and office holder; b. 26 Nov. 1758 in Weston, Fairfield County, Conn., son of Joseph Morehouse and Elizabeth Sullivan; m. 30 April 1783 Jane Gill in New York City, and they had one daughter and six sons; d. 20 Jan. 1835 in Queensbury Parish, N.B.

Fairfield County was an uneasy area in which to be living as the American revolution began to unfold. It had a larger number of tories than most other counties in Connecticut and was a centre of discontent for that state. The Morehouses, staunch Anglicans and loyalists, found themselves in difficult straits in the spring of 1775 after the General Assembly of Connecticut, which was dominated by whigs, passed harsh measures designed to suppress dissent. Daniel had been attending Yale College for a few months when the local committee of safety attempted to draft him into the patriot militia. His uncle paid a fine of £10 to prevent his arrest but after three months the rebels returned and confiscated a prized horse, a saddle, and a bridle. Enraged, Daniel left Connecticut and travelled to New York to join the British forces. He applied to Lieutenant-Colonel John Graves Simcoe* and served with the Queen's Rangers from at least 1778, first as a volunteer, and then as a sergeant. He later assumed the duties of sergeant-major and eventually became quartermaster. At the end of the war he received a half-pay pension of £40 annually.

On 18 Oct. 1783 Morehouse and his wife arrived by ship in Parrtown (Saint John, N.B.). They settled at Grimross (Gagetown) for a year until they received land in the Queen's Rangers' block in what became Queensbury Parish, about 25 miles upriver from St Anne's Point (Fredericton). Here Morehouse eventually acquired over 1,200 acres and built a grist-mill.

In 1791 Simcoe, as lieutenant governor of Upper Canada, was authorized to organize a new unit, also to be called the Queen's Rangers, for service in that colony. Æneas Shaw*, a former captain in the old Queen's Rangers and a neighbour of Morehouse, answered the call and persuaded Daniel to join him. Morehouse was recorded as a sergeant in 1792 but whether he went to Upper Canada is not clear. Certainly his service was brief. His military career

was revived late in 1807, when tensions over fishing rights in New Brunswick waters led to sabre-rattlings south of the border. Under the threat of a Yankee invasion down the Saint John River, the commander of the forces in the Atlantic region, Martin Hunter*, requested Administrator Gabriel George Ludlow* to call out the militia. John SAUNDERS, a former captain in the first Queen's Rangers and a prominent member of the New Brunswick bar, commanded the Volunteer Militia Rangers. Morehouse was made captain of one of its companies and proceeded upriver to the Meductic region to await the first Yankee charge. After serving from 25 January to 24 April 1808, with no incident occurring, the militia was disbanded. As a reward for his unchallenged bravery, Morehouse was made a justice of the peace for York County. He was to serve in this capacity until his death in 1835. War clouds again furthered his career in 1810. As the possibility of hostilities between Britain and the United States loomed larger, the New Brunswick government invigorated the militia with several new companies. These included the 2nd Battalion of York County militia, of which Morehouse was made major commandant. He would hold this post until his retirement on 2 April 1818.

On 11 March 1816 Morehouse was again pressed into service for his province. He was appointed one of three supervisors of "the Public Road leading from Fredericton to the Canada Line." Only he and Thomas Lee were active, it appears. They met in May and spent several weeks inspecting almost 60 miles of road, which they found to be in poor condition. They then supervised the building of eight bridges and the alteration of a considerable portion of the road. The total cost of construction was £3,055. This large undertaking created some resentment among local residents. Morehouse and Lee arbitrated minor disputes themselves but called juries for any important decisions, such as the amount of damages to be awarded for the rerouting of the road through the farm of the late chief justice, George Duncan Ludlow*.

With his resignation from the militia in 1818, Morehouse began to lead a more retiring way of life, though he retained his position as justice of the peace and occasionally served as a school trustee. His family was growing up and several of his sons left home to begin their own families. In 1829 his wife, Jane, died. Daniel outlived her by only six years. His final advice to his six surviving children was "that they sell and dispose of all the property I have left them as soon as they can dispose of it without making too great a sacrifice, and remove to another Country where their labour may yield them a better return." The frustration he was expressing was typical of the experience of many loyalists. As a young man he had had a promising future but his college education was terminated by the war. Although compensation for his service with the Queen's Rangers during the revolution included an annual pension and a large land grant in New Brunswick, a labour shortage made it difficult for him to clear his land. His prominence came, not from any stature as a large-scale farmer, but from the positions he was able to secure in the local administration and militia.

No pictorial record of Daniel Morehouse has yet been uncovered. The house that he built in 1812 has been restored at Kings Landing Historical Settlement in New Brunswick.

DARREL BUTLER

Lewis P. Fisher Public Library (Woodstock, N.B.), George Morehouse to John Morehouse, c. 1862–63 (typescript). N.B., Legislative Library (Fredericton), General account of the great road leading from Fredericton to the Canadas, February 1817. PAC, RG 8, I (C ser.), 1861: 43; 1862: 27; 1864: 10. PANB, RG 1, RS559, E9, 1808; RG 2, RS8, appointments and commissions, 13 May 1808; RG 4, RS24, S25-R6.9; RG 7, RS75, A, 1835, Daniel Morehouse. York Land Registry Office (Fredericton), Mortgage book 5, sect.D: 42–44; Record book A(1): 206, deed 151; 385, 391–92 (mfm. at PANB). *Corr. of Lieut. Governor Simcoe* (Cruikshank), 1: 111. *Winslow papers* (Raymond), 602–3. *New-Brunswick Royal Gazette*, 26 March 1810; 19 March, 14 May 1816. *N.-B. almanack*, 1829. C. J. Ingles, *The Queen's Rangers in the Revolutionary War*, ed. H. M. Jackson (n.p., 1956).

MORRIS, CHARLES, army and militia officer, surveyor, office holder, politician, and JP; b. 18 Nov. 1759 in Hopkinton, Mass., eldest son of Charles Morris* and Elizabeth Bond Leggett, and grandson of Charles Morris*, first surveyor general of Nova Scotia; m. 18 Nov. 1786 Charlotte Pernette, daughter of Colonel Joseph Pernette, in Halifax, and they had 15 children, including Frederick William*; d. there 17 Dec. 1831.

Charles Morris probably came to Halifax in 1760, when his parents apparently arrived. In March 1778 he was commissioned a lieutenant in the Loyal Nova Scotia Volunteers, a regiment raised in the province, and in September 1779 exchanged into the 70th Foot, then in Halifax. Promoted lieutenant on 6 March 1782, he was placed on half pay at the peace in 1783. Some time afterwards he was evidently appointed a deputy surveyor by his father, surveyor general of Nova Scotia, and began assisting him in his office, which was particularly busy because of the arrival of the loyalists. Morris was at the centre of things, occasionally assuming the duties of his gout-ridden father (whom he would succeed in 1802).

Early in 1788 Morris entered politics when he ran in the House of Assembly by-election for Halifax County caused by Sampson Salter Blowers*'s appointment to the Council. The contest was influenced by the controversial "judges' affair," which had begun a year

previously [*see* James Brenton*; Thomas Henry BARCLAY]: opposing Morris was the loyalist lawyer Jonathan Sterns, regarded as the chief accuser of the judges. The campaign was a violent one, a number of people being assaulted and one man dying of his injuries in riots which surrounded the election. When Morris won handily he was carried in triumph "on the shoulders of his fellow citizens . . . surrounded by an immense concourse of people, who filled the air with their repeated acclamations of joy." Morris declined to run in 1793, but re-entered the assembly in a by-election in 1797 and sat until 1806. Two years later he was appointed to the Council on the recommendation of Lieutenant Governor Sir George Prevost*, and continued to serve there until his death. In addition to being surveyor general, Morris was a captain (later major) in the Halifax militia, a justice of the peace, registrar of wills and probate from 1798, and from 1802 surrogate general of the court of probate and registrar of the Vice-Admiralty Court.

Morris's various offices kept him very busy, and he was also quite active in the assembly. On one occasion in 1800 he informed his father-in-law that he had been "so distracted with Business that half my time I know hardly which way to turn myself." His condition was undoubtedly aggravated by the fact that his family was then suffering from smallpox. Things were not much better in 1807, when Morris again complained to Pernette that "My Poor head is much affected with the complicated duties of my office, which I am afraid I shall not be long able to Discharge – the tearing and turbulent disposition of many unreasonable people in these levelling and turbulent times of Envy hatred and malice and all uncharitableness makes my office [very] obnoxious." Besides his difficulties as surveyor general, Morris encountered problems from his duties in the Vice-Admiralty Court. In 1805 actions taken against him in the High Court of Appeals in England for the refund of commissions of more than £1,200 put him to great expense before the case was settled in his favour.

After the War of 1812 Morris seemed more relaxed, although he was still busy. He worked hard to settle disbanded soldiers in the interior of the province and to develop a road between Halifax and Annapolis Royal which would serve the new settlements and give access to the resources of the area. Morris was also active in the Nova Scotia government's efforts to aid the Indian population. In 1815 he presented Lieutenant Governor Sir John Coape SHERBROOKE with a comprehensive report on Indian affairs. The report urged against making grants to individual Indians and recommended setting apart lands for their use "in such situations as they have been in the habit of frequenting." Morris also believed that moose and other animals could be reserved for the exclusive use of the Indians and that government could make arrange-

Morrison

ments for their handicrafts to bring a fixed price. As well, in 1820 he submitted a plan for suitable tracts for reservations.

As surveyor general, Morris was hampered throughout his career by the incompetence of many of his deputies and the difficulty of securing skilled, conscientious staff. In 1802 he criticized the "Blunders and inaccuracies" in one deputy's work, which would necessitate the resurveying of lands to rectify the mistakes, and four years later he upbraided another deputy for laying out crown lands without his direction or the order of the lieutenant governor. In 1814 he described a particularly questionable method of marking a boundary as "a standing and perpetual monument of disgrace to all concerned in that most shameful transaction." The problems in the department led Lieutenant Governor Lord Dalhousie [Ramsay*] to consider replacing him in 1819, but Dalhousie relented because he did not wish to ruin the family.

Between his offices and his extensive property investments (at his death £6,500 in land holdings and £1,139 in mortgages), Morris acquired considerable personal wealth. When he died in 1831 he left an estate variously estimated at from £8,000 to £9,000. He had a 900-acre country estate near Halifax, and a home in town comparable to those of such pillars of local society as Blowers and Michael WALLACE. Morris had also been president of the Charitable Irish Society in 1811 and 1816, and had participated in the Rockingham Club, a social institution founded by Sir John Wentworth* and revived by Dalhousie in 1818.

Although Morris's death attracted little attention, his career was noteworthy. Beset by family problems and plagued by the shortcomings of his staff, Morris in his writings gives the image of a harried functionary. However, he apparently managed to carry out his duties as surveyor general in a capable manner despite the difficulty of reconciling contentious land claims of individuals and of groups such as Acadians, Micmacs, and loyalists. In April 1831 he had been replaced by his son John Spry, who served until the office was merged with that of commissioner of crown lands in 1851. The Morris family thus held the position of surveyor general of Nova Scotia for its entire existence, a continuity of service rivalled only by that of the Wrights of Prince Edward Island.

DONALD F. CHARD

Halifax County Registry of Deeds (Halifax), Deeds (mfm. at PANS). PAC, MG 23, D4. PANS, MG 1, 192, no.19; 544; 794; 1206; MG 100, 112, folders 12–12.3; RG 1, 53, 169, 396B, 430–32; RG 35A, 1, no.3. N.S., House of Assembly, *Journal and proc.* PANS, Board of Trustees, *Report* (Halifax), 1937. Ramsay, *Dalhousie journals* (Whitelaw). *Novascotian, or Colonial Herald*, 21 Dec. 1831. *Nova-Scotia Royal Gazette*, 4 Feb. 1802. *Directory of N.S. MLAs.*

Akins, *Hist. of Halifax City*. E. A. Hutton, "The Micmac Indians of Nova Scotia to 1834" (MA thesis, Dalhousie Univ., Halifax, 1961). J. P. Martin, *The story of Dartmouth* (Dartmouth, N.S., 1957). Ethel Crathorne, "The Morris family – surveyors-general," *N.S. Hist. Quarterly*, 6 (1976): 203–15. Mrs G. R. [Dorothy] Evans, "The Annapolis road – its weakest link," N.S. Hist. Soc., *Coll.*, 38 (1973): 91–112. E. A. Hutton, "Indian affairs in Nova Scotia, 1760–1834," N.S. Hist. Soc., *Coll.*, 34 (1963): 33–54.

MORRISON, JOSEPH WANTON, army officer; b. 4 May 1783 in New York City, only son of John Morrison, deputy commissary general in North America, and Mary Wanton, who died two days later; m. 25 April 1809 Elizabeth Hester Marriott, daughter of the late Randolph Marriott of Worcester, England, and they had no children; d. 15 Feb. 1826 at sea.

Joseph Wanton Morrison entered the army as an ensign in the 83rd Foot in 1793 and was promoted to a lieutenancy in the 84th Foot the following year. However, at his young age he did not actually join either unit but was removed to an independent company and placed on half pay. His active career began in 1799 when he was appointed to the 17th Foot, serving with the 2nd battalion in the Netherlands, where he was wounded in the action at Egmond aan Zee on 2 Oct. 1799 [*see* Sir Isaac Brock*]. The regiment had returned to England by the end of November, and from April 1800 he was listed as one of its captains. The next month the 17th arrived on Minorca, where Morrison commanded a company on garrison duty until the Treaty of Amiens. After repatriation to Ireland in August 1802, the 2nd battalion was disbanded. He then received a brevet majority and was placed on the Irish half-pay list.

In 1804, following the renewal of hostilities between Britain and France, Morrison was appointed an inspecting officer of yeomanry in Ireland, and he transferred to the 2nd battalion, 89th Foot, in June 1805. In November 1809 he was promoted lieutenant-colonel in the 1st West India Regiment and immediately joined it in Trinidad. In July 1811 he exchanged back to the 89th Foot and the next year took the 2nd battalion to Halifax, arriving on 13 Oct. 1812. After wintering there, the battalion reached Quebec on 15 June 1813 and 19 days later marched to Kingston, Upper Canada. There Morrison spent the summer serving on courts martial, doing general garrison duties, and drilling his battalion, which was considered for an attack on Fort Niagara (near Youngstown), N.Y.

In the fall of 1813 American forces launched a two-pronged attack on Montreal. Major-General Wade Hampton advanced down the Chateauguay River from the south to meet Major-General James Wilkinson and Commodore Isaac Chauncey, who were moving down the St Lawrence from Sackets Harbor, N.Y. The threat prompted the commander-in-chief, Sir George Prevost*, to give Morrison his first field command, over a "corps of observation," with orders to follow Wilkinson as he descended the St Lawrence and to hinder his progress if possible. This was not an easy assignment because the invaders greatly outnumbered the British and colonial defenders. None the less, annoyed with Morrison's harassment, Wilkinson ordered Brigadier-General John Parker Boyd to land and defeat the pesky little British force nipping at their heels.

Unfortunately for the Americans, Morrison was able to fight the battle on ground of his own choosing, some 25 miles west of Cornwall – an essentially open stretch of about 700 yards on the property of John Crysler* between a wood and the river, from where he was supported by Commander William Howe Mulcaster's flotilla of gunboats, which had been accompanying him. Morrison was able to utilize the experience and discipline of his regulars by enticing the Americans into a set-piece battle in the European tradition. The individual sharpshooters of the enemy, who performed best when there was an abundance of cover, were at a disadvantage. Consequently, despite its own considerable losses, Morrison's "corps of observation" was able to inflict a stinging tactical defeat on Boyd's detachment, which outnumbered it by almost five to one. Combined with the reverse Hampton had suffered at Châteauguay 17 days earlier [see Charles-Michel d'IRUMBERRY de Salaberry], as well as the hesitancy and lack of accord among the American commanders, Morrison's victory of 11 November saved Montreal from attack that year. For his part Morrison received a gold medal, a sword from the merchants of Liverpool, England, and the thanks of the House of Assembly of Lower Canada.

Following the victory at Crysler's Farm, as the battle became known, Morrison served at Quebec, Montreal, Cornwall, Coteau-du-Lac, where he commanded the garrison and had charge of communications on that part of the St Lawrence, and Fort Wellington. It was from this last place that he and his battalion were ordered to proceed to Kingston at the end of June 1814 on the first stage of a journey that took them to the Niagara frontier in time for the battle of Lundy's Lane. At this action on 25 July Morrison and the 89th formed a key part of the centre of the defensive line as Lieutenant-General Gordon Drummond*'s troops successfully held the crest of the hill. Like the rest of the British force that day, the 89th performed brilliantly under a series of blistering American attacks. The lieutenant-colonel himself was wounded, "severely, not dangerously."

Although Morrison's wound forced him from the battlefield, it did not seriously incapacitate him. He remained with his battalion in the Canadas and in December 1814 sat as a member of Major-General Henry PROCTER's court martial in Montreal. The next year he returned with his battalion to Britain. However, in 1816 his wound had not healed enough to permit his joining the 1st battalion of his regiment in India and in April he went on half pay. On 12 Aug. 1819 Morrison received the brevet of colonel and in April 1821 returned to full-time service as a lieutenant-colonel in the 44th Foot, then in Ireland.

In June 1822 Morrison embarked with the 44th for India, arriving at Calcutta in November. From July 1823 he was with the 44th in Dinapore before returning to Calcutta. In July 1824 he was appointed brigadier-general with command of the southeastern division of the forces in India. It was in this capacity that he led the successful, though extremely unhealthy, expedition to Arakan against the Burmese. Like many of his men, Morrison took sick in this malarial area and, anticipating that a sea voyage would restore his health, decided to return home. Unfortunately, this brilliant officer, whose every command had been a success, "died at sea, on board the *Cara Brea Castle* on the 15th February, 1826."

Nothing is known of Morrison's private life and character. However, his army service illustrates how careful cultivation of a career by a zealous and capable officer could bring personal success and military glory. At his death it was regretted that the nation had prematurely lost the services of a good senior officer who was just beginning to realize his potential. With only brief stops in each, he had made important contributions to several parts of the empire, including the Canadas.

CARL CHRISTIE

PAC, RG 8, I (C ser.), 167: 21; 232: 142; 363: 87–92; 679: 480; 681–84; 1171; 1172: 54; 1203½H: 89; 1203½J: 125; 1203½K: 5, 56; 1203½L: 154, 171; 1203½R: 41, 95; 1222. *Annual reg.* (London), 1799–1827. *Doc. hist. of campaign upon Niagara frontier* (Cruikshank). *Select British docs. of War of 1812* (Wood). G.B., WO, *Army list*, 1793–1827. H. J. Morgan, *Sketches of celebrated Canadians*. J. W. Fortescue, *A history of the British army* (13v. in 14, London, 1899–1930), 9–11. *Historical record of the Forty-Fourth, or the East Essex Regiment*, comp. Thomas Carter (2nd ed., Chatham, Eng., 1887). Hitsman, *Incredible War of 1812*. G. F. G. Stanley, *The War of 1812: land operations* ([Toronto], 1983).

MOUNT, ROSWELL, surveyor, politician, militia officer, JP, and office holder; b. 1797 in Delaware Township, Upper Canada, the son of Moses Mount and Jane Burtch; m. *c.* 1820, he had one son and one daughter; d. 19 Jan. 1834 in York (Toronto).

Roswell Mount grew up in an isolated township with few educational opportunities, a disadvantage which, according to his obituary, he overcame "in a great degree" by applying his natural talents. He trained as a deputy surveyor under Mahlon Burwell*

Mount

and early in 1820 qualified to receive his licence. As Burwell's assistant and from about 1825 until 1833 on his own, Mount made surveys and laid out roads in several townships of the province's western districts. He also acquired land, both as a surveyor and by purchase, and showed more than a surveyor's interest in roads, development, and politics.

Mount was chosen as one of the two members for the riding of Middlesex in the general election of 1830. In a dull contest among three tories he held second spot in the polls behind Burwell. The *Christian Guardian* reported that during the first two sessions of the legislature he voted with the government on all important issues. It may be less than coincidence that in this period he rose from captain to colonel in the Middlesex militia and became a justice of the peace, a road commissioner, and, in 1832, crown land agent for the Western District. He had been known to the commissioner of lands, Peter Robinson*, since 1827 when they met in England while giving evidence before a parliamentary select committee on emigration.

Land agents normally encountered a range of problems in the performance of their duties but the peculiar circumstances of 1832 exacerbated the difficulties and increased their magnitude. That year over 51,000 immigrants arrived in Quebec, many bringing cholera with them. Harried agents having only vague instructions and acting, for the most part, on their own authority were forced to hurry the indigent and perhaps sickly immigrants through the towns and settle them on the land. Several hundred were sent to Kettle Creek (Port Stanley) and then on to Mount at Caradoc for location in Adelaide and Warwick, two completely uninhabited townships. Fear of cholera inhibited the local community from providing assistance or shelter. Thus, in a wet and difficult season, Mount became the only source of rations, wages, medical aid, and shelter. In July 1832 he assisted 400 immigrants, from Petworth in West Sussex; in August, another 800–1,000 newcomers arrived all at once; still others, according to a later memorial on Mount's behalf, "poured in on him week after week." Personally ambitious, he responded to all demands and ignored Robinson's warnings of the limits of the immigration fund. When autumn came Mount blithely delegated his authority to assistants and left for the parliamentary session at York.

Mount had allowed his local ambitions to colour his interpretation of his instructions. With larger responsibilities, Lieutenant Governor Sir John Colborne* faced the administrative implications of a totally unexpected expenditure which only came to his attention in the early months of 1833. Whereas a total of £5,000 had been allotted for the relief and settlement of immigrants in 1832, £13,286 had actually been spent, a staggering £7,588 by Mount. Robinson

immediately dispatched a more experienced agent, Alexander McDonell*, to investigate. His subsequent report allayed officialdom's worst fears. Mount had overspent, far more so than was necessary, but McDonell faulted him only for mismanagement resulting from inexperience. He had been badly used by local suppliers who had taken advantage of him and the situation, but there had been no "undue or intentional misconduct" by Mount's too numerous assistants or, by implication, Mount himself.

Colborne emphasized Mount's difficulties in his reports to the Colonial Office, noting the progress he himself had witnessed in Adelaide. Mount and his local supporters had already defended his efforts, pointing to the results. In 1833 Adelaide and Warwick had a population numbering more than 2,000. There were some 3,796 acres cleared, of which nearly one-third were cultivated, 53 miles of road, and the beginnings of a village. In fact, the benefits of Mount's expenditures had even spilled over into neighbouring townships. None the less, changes were forthcoming. Robinson, who had formerly left much to individual "discretion," warned all agents in May 1833 that expenditures could be incurred only with prior authorization. Unfortunately, too, Colborne was forced to reduce drastically the amount of aid available to immigrants for 1833.

Although Mount's agency seemed secure, the settlement of his accounts dragged on, to be completed only after his death. Robinson was understanding of Mount's alarm at the effect the delays would have on his personal credit. But Colborne and Anthony Bewden Hawke*, agent at York, were more struck by Mount's seeming arrogance and disregard of his superiors. All appeared unaware of Mount's ill health. By the summer of 1833 much of the work of the agency was beyond him; his sudden death at York in January 1834 came as a shock to officials.

Archdeacon John Strachan* conducted the funeral in St James' Church. Later Burwell appealed to Robinson for cash to pay the expenses. Mount had long operated at or beyond the limits of his resources, whether physical or financial. One obituary noted obliquely a "family difficulty" which had an "unfortunate influence upon his domestic and social relations." Mount's career demonstrated both the possibility of emerging from the backwoods to penetrate the York hierarchy and the stresses that might attend such ambition.

WENDY CAMERON

AO, MS 524; RG 1, A-I-4, 2; A-I-6: 6133, 11035, 11153, 11274. PAC, RG 5, A1: 70234, 70416, 70483, 70487, 70491, 70493, 70495, 70498, 70504, 71116, 72004, 74828. PRO, CO 42/414: 464; 42/415: 94, 118. *Canadian Emigrant, and Western District Advertiser* (Sandwich [Windsor, Ont.]), 1832–33; 1 Feb. 1834. *Christian Guardian*, 15 Feb.

1832. H. I. Cowan, *British emigration to British North America; the first hundred years* (rev. ed., Toronto, 1961). *History of the county of Middlesex . . .* (Toronto and London, Ont., 1889; repr. with intro. D. [J.] Brock, Belleville, Ont., 1972), 72, 187–89, 471. Patterson, "Studies in elections in U.C." Wendy [Stevenson] Cameron, "The Petworth emigration committee: Lord Egremont's assisted emigrations from Sussex to Upper Canada, 1832–37," *OH*, 65 (1973): 231–46.

MOUNTAIN, JACOB, clergyman of the Church of England, bishop, and politician; b. 1 Dec. 1749 in the parish of Thwaite All Saints, England, second son of Jacob Mountain and Ann Postle; d. 16 June 1825 at Quebec.

Tradition has it that Jacob Mountain's paternal ancestors were of Huguenot origin. The family was established near Norwich, England, by the middle of the 17th century, but at the time of the accidental death of Jacob Sr on the hunting field in 1752, the Mountains were living at West Rudham. They moved seven years later to Wymondham, Norfolk, home of Mrs Mountain's brother, and there Jacob and his elder brother, Jehosaphat*, attended the grammar school, as they subsequently did in Norwich where the family settled permanently. Jacob tried his hand at business but showed no aptitude for it and was sent to Scarning school near East Dereham. He became a favourite pupil of the master, the Reverend Robert Potter, an illustrious classical scholar. Mrs Mountain, who died in 1776, was careful with the education of her sons.

On 8 Oct. 1769 Jacob was admitted as a pensioner to Gonville and Caius College, Cambridge. He gained his BA (senior optime), was elected junior fellow of the college, and was ordained deacon by the bishop of Norwich, all in 1774. Three years later he took the degree of AM. (He received the honorary degree of DD when he was made a bishop in 1793.) He was ordained priest by the bishop of Peterborough, acting for the bishop of Norwich, on 17 Dec. 1780 in the chapel of Trinity College. On 18 Oct. 1783, in Little Bardfield, he married Elizabeth Mildred Wale Kentish; the couple would have seven children. On his marriage he relinquished his Cambridge fellowship and was appointed perpetual curate of St Andrew's Church, Norwich, a post he held for seven years. From 1788 to 1790 he was Caistor prebendary of Lincoln Cathedral, and from 1790 to 1793 examining chaplain to the bishop of Lincoln, George Pretyman, whose acquaintance he had made at Cambridge. He was also vicar of Buckden, Cambridgeshire, close by the bishop's palace, from 1790 to 1794, and for the same period he held in plurality the vicarage of Holbeach. Clearly a bright future awaited Mountain in the English church.

On 28 June 1793 Mountain was appointed to the newly created see of Quebec. Establishment of a bishop there had first been discussed shortly after the conquest, but no action was taken. In 1787 the diocese

of Nova Scotia was created and Quebec was placed under the jurisdiction of its bishop, Charles Inglis*. Four years later Lieutenant Governor John Graves Simcoe* of Upper Canada requested a bishop for his colony, but possibly on the insistence of the governor-in-chief of the colonies, Lord Dorchester [Guy Carleton*], the new see was located at Quebec and included Upper Canada. Candidates came forward, among them Philip Toosey* of Quebec, sponsored by Inglis, and Samuel Andrew Peters, backed by Simcoe. However, Mountain was successful after his name was drawn to the attention of Prime Minister William Pitt by Pretyman, who at Cambridge had been Pitt's tutor and mentor and had since become his intimate friend and chief adviser on ecclesiastical matters.

Mountain was consecrated bishop in the chapel of Lambeth Palace on 7 July 1793. It was quickly decided that all the family should accompany him to Lower Canada. Hence, when the frigate *Ranger* sailed from the Downs, its passengers were the bishop, his wife, and their four small children; Jehosaphat, with his wife and three children, including Salter Jehosaphat, who had just been made deacon; and the bishop's two maiden sisters. The group disembarked at Quebec on 1 November after a long voyage attended with discomfort and some danger from French corsairs.

The ecclesiastical situation in Mountain's huge diocese held elements both of encouragement and of warning. The policy of the British government, to establish the Church of England "both in Principles and Practice" in the colony and to induce the inhabitants "to embrace the Protestant Religion," had been stated in instructions to Governor James Murray* in 1763 and repeated to his successors. Protestant schools and provision for the support of schoolmasters and clergy by glebes were to have been the means of accomplishing these ends, but the small number of English-speaking Protestant inhabitants and the necessity of securing the loyalty of a population almost totally French-speaking and Roman Catholic had made it impossible to carry out the instructions. Beyond the placing at Quebec, Trois-Rivières, and Montreal in 1768 of Anglican clergy whose native tongue was French and the granting to them of government stipends [*see* David-François de Montmollin*], little had been done in the quarter century preceding Mountain's appointment. Indeed the position of the Roman Catholic Church had been strengthened by the Quebec Act of 1774 [*see* Jean-Olivier Briand*]. In 1791 the Constitutional Act decreed that a generous proportion of crown lands should be set apart for the support of a Protestant clergy, that parsonages, or rectories, should be erected, and that incumbents should be presented to them, but these provisions were still prospective in 1793.

In building the diocese of Quebec Mountain would try to transplant to Lower and Upper Canada ecclesi-

Mountain

astical traditions developed in England. For him the most important of these was the establishment of the Church of England as the state church in the colony. Such a measure, he felt, would heighten the status of the church and encourage dissenters and Roman Catholics to attach themselves to it, thus unifying the population under an institution that, by its very nature, was bound to support the government. And he understood correctly that establishment was the policy envisaged by the imperial authorities on his appointment.

In accordance with the British practice of having Anglican bishops sit in the House of Lords, Mountain's membership in the legislative councils of Upper and Lower Canada as lord bishop of Quebec had been arranged before he left England. Shortly after his arrival at Quebec, on the advice of local political figures such as Attorney General James MONK, he requested a seat on each executive council as well, they being the loci of real colonial influence on the provinces' administrators. Bureaucracy delayed his taking a seat in the Legislative and Executive councils of Lower Canada until 1795 and 1796 respectively (he did not attend sessions of either council in Upper Canada), but once he was installed the councils occupied much of his time and engaged him in manifold duties unrelated to his episcopal office, such as acting as a judge when the Executive Council sat as the Court of Appeals.

Although Mountain's political role resulted in part from traditional British practice, his decision to play it fully was determined rather by his belief that only through the councils could he hope to counter the influence on the colonial administration exercised by the Roman Catholic bishop because of the overwhelmingly Catholic population. Thus in the 1790s and early 1800s he used the weight of his council seats to block a proposal to facilitate the erection of Roman Catholic parishes; to support prohibition of entry into the colony of all refugees, including royalist clergy, from revolutionary France; and to encourage the government, although unsuccessfully, to take over the Sulpician estates [see Robert Prescott*].

Among the instructions that the governors had largely disregarded since the conquest was that concerning the exercise of the royal supremacy with respect to patronage, and no restrictions had been imposed on the Roman Catholic bishop in naming and placing his clergy. On the other hand, by section 39 of the Constitutional Act patronage in the Church of England was in the control of the governor. Mountain was therefore faced with the anomalous situation whereby as head of the church for which he claimed establishment he had less authority to place clergy than his Roman Catholic counterpart. His persistent and strong efforts to have a measure of control imposed on Roman Catholic appointments met with little success, however.

Mountain's relations with governors Dorchester and Robert Prescott were often strained. The governors found it undesirable to alter substantially the *modus vivendi* that existed between church and state, but what appeared to them as a policy of political realism was regarded by Mountain as dereliction of duty. When Dorchester was about to retire in 1794 Mountain wrote to Pretyman: "As a gentleman of some consideration in the country he has always treated me with great cordiality and attention; as a Bishop of the Church of England he has never shown the least wish to give me countenance or support." Mountain was in disagreement with Prescott over ecclesiastical policy to such an extent that it is quite likely he was among a group of executive councillors that succeeded in having the governor recalled over his land policy.

In seeking to impose restrictions on the power of the Roman Catholic church and bishop, Mountain found himself in agreement with the English party in the colony, led in the House of Assembly by John Young* and in the administration by Attorney General Jonathan Sewell* and Herman Witsius Ryland*, civil secretary and from 1796 clerk of the Executive Council. However, they did not fully share his ecclesiastical preoccupations, and there were, therefore, significant divergences of view. Even when they combined their efforts and, after Prescott's recall, enjoyed a sympathetic administrator in Lieutenant Governor Sir Robert Shore Milnes*, Mountain and his political allies had little effect on the position of the Roman Catholic bishop. When in 1806, following Milnes's departure, the administrator, Thomas Dunn*, accepted Joseph-Octave PLESSIS as successor to Bishop Pierre Denaut* without imposing limitations on his powers, Mountain bitterly declared that Dunn had "grievously disappointed my hopes & fatally thwarted my plans."

Mountain also used his council positions to promote the establishment of his own church. He considered that a practical first step would be the creation of parishes and the erection of rectories. Action, however, had to originate with the governor in council and was subject to much delay, which Mountain attributed to political timidity in the face of opposition from Canadian members of the Executive Council. Doubts raised by Sewell about the proper legal course to pursue were also a factor. Finally, on 7 June 1800, a council committee on ecclesiastical affairs pointed out the method to be followed, and Sewell advised the issuing of letters patent under the provincial seal. But no move was made. Crown lands had been set aside for the support of a Protestant clergy as provided for in the Constitutional Act, but their management by the administrator in council of each colony proved unsatisfactory, and as early as 1803 Mountain recommended that the clergy alone should handle them. Again, however, nothing was done. Neither was the bishop able to obtain the transfer from the governor to the church of the right to issue marriage licences.

Mountain felt that the prestige of the state church depended in large part on its appearance at Quebec, the capital of Lower Canada. But the congregation shared accommodation with the Roman Catholics, first in the Recollet chapel until it burned in 1796 and then in the Jesuit chapel. The church needed a cathedral "exclusively appropriated to our Worship," he had written to Home Secretary Henry Dundas in 1794. "That that worship should be performed only by permission of the Roman Catholic Bishop, and with that permission only once on the Sunday, that the Protestant Bishop should obtain a seat in the Church by the indulgence only of the Superior of the Franciscans; that our pure and reasonable service should only be performed within walls loaded with all the pageantry and meretricious ornament of Papish superstition, amid crucifixes, images, pictures of saints, altars, tapers and burning lamps, these Sir are circumstances which, while they shock and disgust the enlightened mind in the rational discharge of its duty, serve also strongly and publicly to mark a dependence of the Church of England, upon the Church of Rome." He had unaccustomed success; in 1799 the Colonial Office allotted money for the construction of a cathedral on the site of the Recollet chapel, and on 28 Aug. 1804 the Cathedral of the Holy Trinity, a shapely and spacious stone building, was consecrated; additions and repairs would bring the cost of the structure to £25,000.

Outside Quebec the church's situation in terms of buildings and clergy was modest. In Lower Canada a small wooden church had been built at William Henry (Sorel) before the bishop's arrival [see John Doty*]. At Trois-Rivières the former Recollet chapel, where the Anglicans had worshipped since 1768 [see Leger-Jean-Baptiste-Noël Veyssière*], was rearranged as a church in 1796. Christ Church in Montreal, the former Jesuit chapel, burned down in 1803, and the congregation began a new structure two years later under the ministry of Jehosaphat Mountain. The first Anglican church in what had become Upper Canada had been built for the Six Nations Indians at present-day Brantford in 1785. A church had been erected at Kingston through the efforts of the missionary and ecclesiastical commissary John Stuart*. In the nearby mission of Ernestown (Bath and region), served by John Langhorn*, three log churches had risen by 1793. At Newark (Niagara-on-the-Lake) the congregation met in the freemasons' hall in early years. By 1805 only five new missions had been opened: at York (Toronto), Cornwall, and Sandwich (Windsor) in Upper Canada and in the seigneury of Saint-Armand

and Chatham Township [see Richard Bradford*] in Lower Canada. As for the clergy, when Mountain arrived the diocese was served by only nine priests. The three ordained Mountains should have brought the number to 12, but of the three bilingual priests in Montreal, Quebec, and Trois-Rivières, who had failed to attract Canadians to the church and were old, two had been placed in semi-retirement by Bishop Inglis and the third was retired by Mountain. The nine effective priests were loyalists or English.

On his first tour of the diocese, in the summer of 1794, Mountain brought the few clergy together in Montreal for an official visitation and the delivery of the episcopal charge. One account of this journey, written for young relatives in Norwich, describes in detail the modes of travel by calèche, bateau, and king's ship as far west as Newark. A formal record, written for Dundas, told of the religious destitution of Upper Canada and made recommendations for improvement. On a second tour in 1799 the bishop revisited some missions and conducted confirmations. He saw York, the Upper Canadian capital, for the first time, although no clergyman was then settled there. On his third visitation, in 1803, he met with some encouragement, particularly at Cornwall, to which the recently ordained young Scot John Strachan* had just been appointed. He was prevented by contrary winds from journeying as far as Sandwich, where Richard POLLARD had been stationed in 1802, but at York he confirmed candidates prepared by George Okill Stuart*, whom he had ordained priest in 1801. On his return to Kingston he delivered an episcopal charge to the few Upper Canadian clergy assembled there. It was an earnest plea to them to be tolerant in relation to other Christians and blameless in their personal lives. He urged them to continue their studies and to avoid a cold, dry, lifeless kind of preaching.

In part to create conditions more favourable to the growth of his church, Mountain early addressed himself to a contentious political question, education, which in his view was eminently a concern of a state church. He also saw in it the means of establishing direct contact with the Canadian population, whose ignorance of English drew "a distinct line of demarcation" between them and the British. Writing to Dundas in 1794 and to Dorchester in 1795 he urged the setting up of grammar schools in each province and the placing of instructors in Lower Canadian towns and villages to teach English free of charge. His views were largely reflected in the act of 1801 that created the Royal Institution for the Advancement of Learning, to supervise schools functioning under the authority of the act. However, a clause providing for private schools largely enabled the Roman Catholic Church to prevent Royal Institution schools from becoming implanted among the Canadians, while failure to implement a recommendation of the Executive Coun-

Mountain

cil that land grants be made for the support of grammar and free parish schools, or other means of financing provided, hampered organization for many years [*see* Joseph Langley MILLS].

A number of reasons impelled Mountain, after nearly 12 years in Lower Canada, to plan a voyage to England. His sons Jacob Henry Brooke and George Jehoshaphat* had been tutored at Quebec by Matthew Smithers Feilde since late 1800, but their further education was a matter of family concern. Of greater weight, however, were the bishop's doubts about his own future and his failure to advance the establishment of his church. Three roads out of these difficulties presented themselves to his mind: translation to an English bishopric, partial retirement on a pension with a country living in England, or an improvement in his position in Lower Canada. The bishop and his family set sail early in August 1805 and arrived in England before mid September. The boys were placed under the tutorship of the Reverend Thomas Monro at Little Easton, where they remained until they both matriculated to Cambridge.

Despite much effort Mountain failed to obtain translation or partial retirement; consequently, he turned to promoting the establishment of his church. Bishop Plessis's London agent, François-Emmanuel Bourret, who feared Mountain's influence on the government, wrote to Plessis that Mountain "has unfortunately that advantage accorded by the conformity of principles and the interests of his religion. Add to that his presence, his bearing, his gracious manners, his property of being English, his title, his learning, his protectors etc." Mountain fared less well than Bourret apprehended, however. Although he had asked for the creation of parishes, the erection of rectories, the issuing of marriage licences by the church, funds to complete the cathedral, provision of a cathedral chapter, and the imposition of restraints on the Roman Catholic bishop, the only advantages he gained, apart from promises, were a rise in salary for six of his clergy and an extra £400 on his own in lieu of a see house. The struggle against Napoleon was of far greater concern to the government than the bishop's problems. As well, his agitation to control the Roman Catholic Church was unwelcome to a ministry that favoured Catholic emancipation in Ireland and tended, in Mountain's words, "to confound" the situation there with that in the colony. Political changes led to interminable delays; most notably the death of Pitt in 1806 shattered many of the bishop's hopes. He returned to Quebec in the summer of 1808; Jean-Baptiste Lahaille* of the Séminaire de Québec reassured Plessis that Mountain was "not much listened to by the present ministry."

Diocesan business was quickly resumed. The bishop set off on an episcopal tour in 1809 and reached Kingston but could not obtain transportation further.

On the return journey he paid his first visit to Saint-Armand, and was greatly heartened by the successful mission of Charles James Stewart*, who had settled there in 1807. The following year, accompanied by his children George Robert and Eliza, he was able to get a ship at Kingston but was driven back by contrary winds though in view of York and the light at Niagara (Niagara-on-the-Lake). He made his sixth and most adventurous visitation in 1813, amid war with the United States. His bateau was escorted by soldiers from Montreal to Kingston; there he was provided with a canoe manned by ten Indians and thus was spared the sickness that invariably attacked him on shipboard. At York he had his first sight of the new church and confirmed a large class prepared by the recently appointed incumbent, Strachan. After coasting Lake Ontario back to Kingston, where George Okill Stuart had succeeded his father, John, the bishop had a Canadian crew for the journey down the St Lawrence. A proposed trip to Saint-Armand was thwarted by an American invasion through that region, but the bishop was able to make the 450-mile ride from Quebec by way of Montreal in March 1814 and to confirm a combined class from Stewart's mission (then with two churches) and the adjoining one of Dunham under Charles Caleb Cotton*. For Mountain's visitation as far as Detroit in 1816 transportation from Montreal was in a large canoe of the North West Company. Lasting three months, the trip proved more satisfactory than Mountain had expected because "travelling with a canoe enabled me to see a great deal more of the country and of the people than I could otherwise have done." On his return he inspected the Lower Canadian missions near Missisquoi Bay and then crossed to the valley of the Rivière Saint-François, visiting Stanstead, Compton, Hatley, and Melbourne townships.

Considerable progress was made in the diocese after 1808, although only four new missions were opened before 1816. From the beginning of Mountain's episcopate most clergy had been paid a government stipend of £100, to which the Society for the Propagation of the Gospel added £50. From 1815 an annual parliamentary grant for North America was put at the disposal of the society, enabling it to pay its missionaries £200 a year. By his insistence that his clergy were inadequately paid the bishop had contributed to this happy outcome. Since the need for clergy was great and the supply from England meagre, beginning in 1815 the bishop obtained from the SPG an annual grant of £200 for the education of theological students. These young men were trained by senior clergy, including Strachan, who had proposed the scheme. The system proved to be a success, and 14 students received SPG scholarships before 1825. Meanwhile, management of the clergy reserves was improved by the setting up of a corporation in Lower

Canada in 1816 and in Upper Canada three years later. In the upper province, where the reserved lands were great in extent, the corporation, under the skilled direction of Strachan and with the support of Lieutenant Governor Peregrine Maitland*, transacted much business. The labours of the Lower Canada corporation were less exacting, but research was done on the length of leases. No marked increase in financial returns was made in either province for some years, however. A government proposal to sell the lands was under consideration in 1825.

Progress was also made in education. In 1813 James McGill* left a considerable bequest to the Royal Institution for the Advancement of Learning for the founding of a university to be named after him. To meet certain conditions of the bequest, trustees of the Royal Institution, which had remained a dead letter since 1801, were finally appointed in late 1818; Mountain was among them. On 4 Dec. 1819 the bishop became principal of the Royal Institution, and he immediately named Joseph Langley Mills to handle the administration as secretary. Mountain prepared a plan for the proposed university or college and played a part in obtaining a charter for it in 1821. Grammar schools, the establishment of which the bishop had proposed as early as 1794, were at last set up at Quebec, Montreal, and Kingston in 1816, the masters being clergy of his diocese. Two years later a primary school, called the National School, was set up in each of Quebec and Montreal by a diocesan committee of the Society for Promoting Christian Knowledge, formed at Quebec in 1818 at the bishop's prompting. These schools adopted the program of the National Society for Promoting the Education of the Poor in the Principles of the Established Church, founded in England in 1811, and employed the society's teaching method, called the Madras or Bell system, in which senior students were employed as monitors to teach younger children. Through its encouragement of religious education in the parishes, the diocesan committee of the SPCK also pioneered in the formation of Sunday schools.

Mountain continued to press colonial and imperial officials to reduce the authority of the Roman Catholic bishop and to give substance to the establishment of the Church of England. In Governor Sir James Henry Craig* he found a sympathetic interlocutor between 1808 and 1811, but Craig's enthusiasm was restrained by the Colonial Office. His successor, Sir George Prevost*, on the other hand, was committed to a policy of conciliating Canadian leaders, including Bishop Plessis, before and after war with the United States broke out. Like most of the English party, Mountain strongly opposed this policy: "From a vain hope of conciliating and an ill-founded fear of offending, we have given them [the Canadians] everything," he complained to Colonial Secretary Lord Bathurst. For his part, remarking that "the Head of our Church has far more disposition for Politics than Theology," Prevost informed Bathurst dryly that a refusal to endorse Mountain's ecclesiastical views had "added to my former disgrace with his Lordship for not yielding the Civil Administration to his supreme Judgement." As a result of this conflict, the bishop was almost certainly among the leaders of a secret cabal, based in the Executive Council, that contributed to having Prevost recalled in 1815. For his supposed role Mountain was sharply reprimanded by Bathurst.

His situation not having improved in the slightest, Mountain returned to England in 1816. He attempted again to resign or to receive translation but in these efforts he failed as before. He also failed to persuade government even to pronounce that his church was established. Although the war was over, the government's primary concern was political and social peace in the Canadas, not the adoption of policies that might lead to strife. Mountain's relations with Bathurst, like those with his predecessors, were difficult. The colonial secretary, while acknowledging the bishop to be "of considerable abilities," found him rigid and "of a very striving disposition." One advantage Mountain did gain was renewed government interest in the creation of parishes and the setting up of rectories within them. In this campaign he now had the aid of a strong committee of the SPG. Further delays occurred, but, between 1820 and 1823, 12 crown rectories were established by letters patent in Lower Canada. Although the bishop succeeded in getting the titles of his assistants, George Okill Stuart at York and George Jehoshaphat Mountain at Quebec, changed from official to archdeacon, he did not obtain a desired increase of £150 in their salary.

Mountain returned to Quebec in 1819, virtually acknowledging defeat for his dream of establishment. He knew that as a result of his persistent efforts to reduce the influence of Plessis, who had won the confidence of the British authorities for his loyalism during the War of 1812, he was suspected of intolerance by the Colonial Office. The limits he wished to have placed on the toleration of Catholicism were those roughly defined by "the Laws, and Constitution of this realm," which he believed permitted "freedom of religious *Worship* in the Colonies" but not "the promulgation of Doctrines" or the exercise of Roman Catholic "Principles of Church Government." British authorities, however, were quietly disregarding many of those restrictions.

In general Mountain's relations with the Catholic hierarchy were amicable. On his arrival in 1793 he had been greeted by the aged and retired Bishop Briand with words of welcome and the Gallic salutation of a kiss on both cheeks. Plessis described his relations with Mountain as "not of intimacy but of reciprocal

Mountain

propriety." But, because of Mountain's vigorous and open efforts to advance his church, he was long viewed with apprehension by the Roman Catholic hierarchy. Following his last and most discouraging trip to England, however, it saw him in another light. "The old bishop was what we needed, since there had to be one," wrote Plessis's successor, Bernard-Claude PANET, shortly after Mountain's death, "because in his last days he was very quiet and scarcely looked to make proselytes and what is better still, he no longer bothered with affairs and had practically no credit."

Mountain had also become increasingly aware of the challenge by Protestant denominations, particularly the Church of Scotland, to his cherished principle of Anglican establishment. It was to protect that principle that in 1803–4 he had had Clark Bentom*, an Independent minister, prosecuted for keeping parish registers. The right to hold registers, it was thought in Anglican and certain government circles, was restricted to the Anglican and Roman Catholic churches, and the court confirmed that view. As with the Catholics, so with the Protestants, Mountain argued, "they who do not choose to conform [to the establishment] lose perhaps some Civil advantages but are not thereby in the smallest degree restrained in the exercise of the public worship of God."

Because Mountain's approach to other denominations was institutional – he opposed church to church rather than faith to faith – he was little disposed to endorse proselytism and in this respect the traveller John Cosens Ogden remarked that "his moderation and discretion are very acceptable to all parties." His response to the proselytism of others reflected his perception that his was a state church; in 1813, for example, he suggested that, for having attempted to convert Anglicans, the Roman Catholic priest Charles French should be tried for high treason. Mountain was aware that in his conception of relations with non-Anglicans he was out of step with his era. To a close friend, James IRVINE, he described the times as "so strongly characterized by an unrestrained spirit of Conciliation & an inordinate desire of the praise of liberality" that from others he "might fear the imputation of extreme bigotry and narrowness of mind."

Mountain's last visitation, begun in June 1820, took him on the outward voyage to Montreal, Kingston, York, Fort Erie, Amherstburg, and Detroit. On the return journey the bishop confirmed in the Indian council house at Fort George (Niagara-on-the-Lake) since the church, damaged in the late war, had not been completely restored, in a schoolhouse at Grimsby, and in an interdenominational church in Barton Township. After holding a visitation of his clergy at York, he continued on to Hamilton (Cobourg), Ernestown, and Kingston, confirmed in the Brockville court-house, took a difficult diversion for a service in a Perth schoolhouse, and then descended the St Lawrence to Cornwall. Fourteen missions had been seen in the upper province. In Lower Canada he visited St Andrews (Saint-André-Est) and delivered his charge in Montreal to 14 clergy. Travel to other missions, ten in number, was postponed until February and March 1821. The only part of his great diocese that Mountain did not see was the Gaspé, where two missions had been established. George Jehoshaphat Mountain inspected them in 1824.

Growth in the population of the Canadas following the Napoleonic Wars led to a rapid extension of the church. In the last decade of Mountain's episcopate 35 new missions were founded, 19 of them in the upper province. In both Canadas Charles James Stewart did more than anyone to organize missions and raise money for church building. The secure though moderate stipends and the SPG's scholarships encouraged young men to train for the ministry and attracted clergy from England. Among those who began work in these years were Samuel Simpson Wood*, James Reid, and three pairs of brothers, Joseph* and William Abbott, Alexander Neil* and John* Bethune, and Ralph* and William Leeming. Apart from his brother Jehosaphat, his nephew Salter Jehosaphat, and his son George Jehoshaphat – the latter his father's steady support in all aspects of diocesan life – the only member of the clergy with whom the bishop was intimate was John Stuart. Significantly, it was the son of the former missionary, George Okill Stuart, who, in an address delivered before Mountain at York in July 1820, recalled occasions when "we have seen the Prelate descending into the Friend."

Mountain was an imposing man. In 1820 when one of the diocesan clergy first saw the bishop he confessed himself "struck with admiration at as perfect a specimen of the human form as I ever beheld; erect, standing above six feet, face what might be called handsome, eye mild yet penetrating, features well set and expression benevolent, limbs fully developed, and symmetry of the whole person complete." Mountain was then 70 years old. Before meeting the bishop Governor Lord Dalhousie [Ramsay*] had heard him spoken of as "a clever man, amiable in his outward manners but a lazy preacher, very haughty and imperious in society." When in 1820 Dalhousie heard a sermon by Mountain that pleased him, he described this "fine looking old Gentlemen" as "a Divine of exalted rank & of commanding abilities." With his background and training Mountain moved easily and graciously in society. Of his wife, Elizabeth, John Strachan recorded that she was "in her manners amiable and engaging – in her religion sincere active and cheerful – in charity unbounded, without regard to sect or nation." Through her letters to Elizabeth Pretyman Tomline written from 1793 to 1810 much can be learned of the home life of the Mountain family, of Mrs Mountain's care for her children, of the

528

bishop's many illnesses, of her continual concern for her husband and her sympathy with his problems.

Jacob Mountain died at Quebec on 16 June 1825 and was buried under the chancel of the cathedral he had built. He had never been able to overcome fully his English background and formation, and in 1823 after nearly 30 years as bishop of Quebec he had referred to his situation as "this long expatriation"; from it he had numerous times tried to extricate himself. His objective had been not so much to adapt the Church of England to the specific and differing circumstances in Lower and Upper Canada, but to bring the religious life of the colonies and particularly the relations between the churches and the state into conformity with the situation in England. This endeavour was impossible given conditions in the Canadas from 1793 to 1825. Dalhousie, a Scottish Presbyterian, despite his approval of Mountain's ability as a preacher, felt that the bishop carried "high church discipline too far for a colonial church," and Strachan felt that "his habits and manners were calculated rather for an English Bishop than the Missionary Bishop of Canada." Mountain gave to position, social dignity, and prestige, both institutional and personal, an importance that they perhaps did not merit in the North American context. His clergy, most of them sent from Great Britain by the SPG, were never numerous enough to minister effectively in all areas of their large mission stations and differed widely in ability. Some, because of strict adherence to church rubrics, were not able to attract to their services settlers without strong church loyalties. Others, because of their fear of religious "enthusiasm" – shared by the bishop – did not meet fully the emotional needs of a pioneer society. To all his clergy he held out high ideals for their conduct and spirituality, defending them in official correspondence, administering reproof and discipline in private as need arose. Jacob Mountain, despite his deficiencies, achieved much as a pioneer bishop, and even Strachan, recognizing the difficulties that Mountain had had to face, acknowledged what had been accomplished. Mountain could not realize a number of his dreams and did not live to see the realization of others, but in his long episcopate he fully earned the title given to him in his epitaph: "Founder of the Church of England in the Canadas."

THOMAS R. MILLMAN

Jacob Mountain is the author of *Poetical reveries* (London, 1777; repr. 1977); *A sermon preached at Quebec on Thursday, January 10th, 1799, being the day appointed for a general thanksgiving; . . . together with the form of a prayer drawn up upon the occasion* (Quebec, 1799); *A charge delivered to the clergy of the diocese of Quebec in August 1803* (Quebec, 1803); *The Holy Communion: a sermon preached in the cathedral of Quebec in the year 1804* ([Quebec, 1804]); *A sermon preached at the anniversary of the Royal Humane Society in Christ Church, Surrey, on Sunday, the 28th of March, 1819* (London, 1819); and *A charge delivered to the clergy of the diocese of Quebec in the year 1820* (Quebec, 1820). A journal of one of Mountain's pastoral visitations has been published: "From Quebec to Niagara in 1794; diary of Bishop Jacob Mountain," ed. A. R. Kelley, ANQ *Rapport*, 1959–60: 121–65. A portrait of Mountain done in 1778 by John Downman and kept at the PAC is reproduced in *Archivist* (Ottawa), 12, no.1 (January–February 1985): 19. Another portrait, by Henry Edridge, is the frontispiece of Millman, *Jacob Mountain*.

ACC-Q, 1–2, 16–24, 72–90, 106–10, 118, 123. ACC, Diocese of Montreal Arch. (Montreal), file C-11; Diocese of Ont. Arch. (Kingston, Ont.), Group 11, John Stuart papers. MTL, John Strachan papers. Norfolk Record Office (Norfolk, Eng.), T169A (copies at ACC, General Synod Arch., Toronto). PAC, MG 17, B1, C/CAN/Que., IV/32 (mfm.); RG 7, G1, 1–14; G15A; G15C. PRO, CO 42/94–175. Suffolk Record Office (Ipswich, Eng.), HA 119, 503/5, 540/1–5. USPG, Journal of SPG, 26–36. *Corr. of Hon. Peter Russell* (Cruikshank and Hunter). *Corr. of Lieut. Governor Simcoe* (Cruikshank). John Strachan, *A sermon, preached at York, Upper Canada, third of July 1825, on the death of the late lord bishop of Quebec* (Kingston, 1826). *Alumni Cantabrigienses . . .* , comp. John and J. A. Venn (2 pts. in 10v., Cambridge, Eng., 1922–54). *Biographical history of Gonville and Caius College . . .* , comp. John Venn *et al.* (5v., [Cambridge], 1897–1948), 2. A. R. Kelley, "Jacob Mountain, first lord bishop of Quebec: a summary of his correspondence and of papers related thereto for the years 1793 to 1799 . . . ," ANQ *Rapport*, 1942–43: 177–260. Philip Carrington, *The Anglican Church in Canada; a history* (Toronto, 1963). Christie, *Hist. of L.C.* Ernest Hawkins, *Annals of the diocese of Quebec* (London, 1849); *Annals of the diocese of Toronto* (London, 1848). Lambert, "Joseph-Octave Plessis." Cyrus Macmillan, *McGill and its story, 1821–1921* (London and Toronto, 1921). T. R. Millman, *A sketch of the life and work of the Right Reverend Jacob Mountain, D.D., first lord bishop of Quebec: a sermon preached on Sunday, October 31, 1943 in the Cathedral of the Holy Trinity . . .* ([Quebec, 1943]). A. S. H. Mountain, *Memoirs and letters of the late Colonel Armine S. H. Mountain, C.B., aide de camp to the queen and adjutant general of her majesty's forces in India*, ed. [C. A. Dundal] Mrs A. S. H. Mountain (London, 1857). A. W. Mountain, *A memoir of George Jehoshaphat Mountain, D.D., D.C.L., late bishop of Quebec . . .* (London and Montreal, 1866). C. F. Pascoe, *Two hundred years of the S.P.G. . . .* (2v., London, 1901). Henry Roe, *Story of the first hundred years of the diocese of Quebec . . .* (Quebec, 1893). [Frederic Rogers] Baron Blachford, *Some account of the legal development of the colonial episcopate* (London, 1883). "Memoir of the late bishop of Quebec," *Christian Sentinel and Anglo-Canadian Churchman's Magazine* (Montreal), 1 (1827): 5–17.

MUIR, ADAM CHARLES, army officer and settler; b. *c.* 1766 or *c.* 1770 in Scotland; m. 6 Aug. 1801 Mary Elizabeth Alexowina Bender in Montreal, and they had six sons and four daughters; d. 11 May 1829 in William Henry (Sorel), Lower Canada.

Partly because Adam Charles Muir began his

Muir

military career as a common soldier, little is certain in his background. He made his first appearance in British army records by enlisting on St Patrick's Day 1788 in the 41st Foot, which was then changing from a regiment of invalids to one of regulars. A deserving recruit could go far in such circumstances, and in five months Muir was a sergeant. On 30 July 1793 he was appointed adjutant, a position often given to worthy non-commissioned officers. His promotion to ensign soon afterwards made him a commissioned officer, and he advanced to lieutenant on 12 July 1794. His first active service took place during the campaigns of the mid 1790s in Saint-Domingue (Haiti).

The 41st came to the Canadas in 1799, and for more than a decade Muir made the rounds of the garrisons, spending most of his time at Amherstburg, Upper Canada, and obtaining a captaincy on 9 Feb. 1804. He was at Amherstburg in charge of the regimental detachment when war with the United States broke out in July 1812. As a senior officer of the only available regulars on the spot, he received command of several small expeditions during the summer and autumn. In the operations leading up to Major-General Isaac Brock*'s capture of Detroit on 16 August, Muir led British troops in skirmishes at Brownstown (near Trenton, Mich.) and Maguaga (Wyandotte, Mich.). Despite a wound received in the latter action, he was able to command the men of the 41st at the taking of Detroit. In September, Colonel Henry PROCTER, in charge on the Lake Erie frontier, sent Muir with some British troops and militia to accompany a large Indian force against Fort Wayne (Ind.). The expedition was intended to capture the fort and throw American preparations for a renewed offensive into confusion. At first things went well enough, but once scouts detected the unexpected approach of a large American army [see Sou-neh-hoo-way*], the enthusiasm of the Indians for the raid plummeted. Muir recognized that his plans were now futile, and as his allies drifted away he withdrew successfully to Detroit. He went back into action in January 1813 when the American advance guard was crushed at Frenchtown (Monroe, Mich.). During that year he was at the sieges of forts Meigs (near Perrysburg, Ohio) and Stephenson (Fremont, Ohio) as Procter vainly tried to halt the enemy's move on Detroit.

Thus far Muir had been one of the most active British officers on the Lake Erie frontier, if usually in a subordinate role. Procter had commended his behaviour on several occasions, but relations between the two men were cool. By the time the British and Indians began their retreat from Amherstburg in the fall of 1813 Muir, like several other officers of the 41st, was openly contemptuous of Procter's leadership. Just before the battle of Moraviantown in October, he said that Procter "ought to be hanged" for being away from the force. Captured in that disastrous

action, Muir spent some months in Kentucky in conditions vividly described by his friend and fellow captive John Richardson*. Meanwhile, Upper Canada from Amherstburg to Ancaster became a kind of no man's land open to forays by both armies. After his exchange in 1814 Muir was sent to the Grand River, where he took part in defending against American raids. Over the winter of 1814–15 he gave evidence at Procter's court martial.

The end of the war in 1815 left Muir with few prospects. Ranker-officers rarely attained field rank (although he did have a brevet majority, awarded on 4 June 1814), and the possession of a gold medal for his service at Detroit did little to help an ageing man who was trying to support his burgeoning family on a captain's pay. His luck got worse when he was in Dublin in September 1816, for his horse threw him and he suffered a badly dislocated thigh. Unable to move without crutches for several years and left permanently lame, he was forced to resign in 1818, and was granted an annual pension of £100. He returned to North America, where he took up land at St Andrews (Saint-André-Est), Lower Canada. There he was seen in August 1820 by Governor Lord Dalhousie [Ramsay*], who thought that he was trying hard to encourage settlement in the village. St Andrews prospered, but Muir evidently did not, for less than a year later his farm was advertised for sale, although it was not disposed of until 1827. His growing debts were burdensome enough to force his move to William Henry, where a military asylum for invalids was located. After a brief illness he died on 11 May 1829. His widow was hard pressed to make ends meet, and for some time thereafter addressed increasingly desperate petitions to the authorities. At least one of their sons, George Manly Muir, attained some distinction, as clerk of the Legislative Assembly of Quebec.

With the little personal detail available, it is practically impossible to assess Adam Charles Muir's character or life, and only through his military service can he be judged. That was of significant, if largely unrecognized, importance. Without the presence of experienced men such as Muir among the handful of British regulars who defended the Canadas for much of the War of 1812, the conflict might well have taken a different course.

STUART R. J. SUTHERLAND

PAC, RG 8, I (C ser.), 167: 21–22; 205; 206: 1, 18, 215–19; 676: 233–36; 677: 18–21, 97–99, 102–10, 163–65; 678: 261–70; 683: 135, 286–92; 907; 914: 106–8. PRO, WO 12/5406; WO 17/151, 17/1516–19; WO 27/98. *Doc. hist. of campaign upon Niagara frontier* (Cruikshank). Ramsay, *Dalhousie journals* (Whitelaw), 2: 34. [John] Richardson, *Richardson's War of 1812; with notes and a life of the author*, ed. A. C. Casselman (Toronto, 1902). G.B., WO, *Army list*, 1794–1819. D. A. N. Lomax, *A history of the* services of the 41st (the Welch) Regiment (now 1st Battalion the Welch Regiment), from its formation, in 1719, to 1895 (Devonport, Eng., 1899). Cyrus Thomas, History of the counties of Argenteuil, Que., and Prescott, Ont., from the earliest settlement to the present (Montreal, 1896; repr. Belleville, Ont., 1981).

MUNRO. See MONRO

MURE, JOHN, businessman, JP, militia officer, politician, and office holder; b. probably in the parish of Kilmarnock, Scotland; d. 17 Jan. 1823 in Glasgow.

John Mure was likely drawn to the province of Quebec through the network of Ayrshiremen and Lanarkshiremen active in trade there. John Porteous, his uncle and member of an Ayrshire family, had established himself in Montreal in the 1760s, and Porteous's cousin, John Paterson, was a partner in an early British firm at Quebec, Paterson and Grant. By 1782 Mure was in the province (evidently at Montreal), and by November 1788 he was apparently a clerk at Quebec for James Tod*, who had served with Paterson and Grant. Within a few years Mure began operating on his own account in the fur trade and as an importer.

The 1790s saw Mure move towards the front rank of merchants in the transatlantic trade as a period of unprecedented economic development, extending to 1815, began in Lower Canada and other British North American colonies. His business, conducted from stores on the Queen's Wharf in Lower Town, where he lived, was typical of import firms in its diversity. In addition to importing such products as salt by the shipload (mostly from Liverpool), wine, window glass, cordage, and "Scotch herrings," Mure auctioned wheat and sold dried cod from the Gaspé and flour from the Beauport mills of Antoine Juchereau* Duchesnay. As well, he performed numerous services arising from his contacts with other mercantile figures; he was, for example, a trustee or curator for the estates of many, including Jean Renaud* and Hugh Finlay*. In 1796, with Tod and two others, he acquired the fiefs of Grosse-Île and Granville, valued for their hay, timber, and nearness to porpoise and eel fisheries. On 11 Jan. 1798 Mure solidified his place among the colony's Scottish merchants when he married his cousin Margaret Porteous, daughter of John. The marriage, conducted by Presbyterian minister Alexander Spark, was witnessed by merchants James McGill* (a friend of the Porteous family), John Blackwood*, and Isaac Todd*. The union ended tragically; Margaret died in 1799, and their child died in infancy.

Between 1795 and about 1799, again facilitated by Ayrshire connections, Mure entered into an extended partnership that had developed from the founding in the former year of the Montreal firm of Parker, Gerrard, and Ogilvy. In 1800 the partners were William Parker (a Kilmarnock native), Samuel Gerrard*, John Ogilvy*, John and George* Gillespie, Thomas Yeoward, and Mure. Functioning through companies or offices in London, Quebec (where Mure directed business), Montreal, and Michilimackinac (Mackinac Island, Mich.), the copartners engaged in the fur trade, furnished goods to traders such as Robert DICKSON, operated a transatlantic shipping service, and supplied merchants in Detroit, Queenston, and Kingston, among them Thomas CLARK and Richard Cartwright*. Though none of the firms composing the copartnership was in itself formidable, together they formed an enormously strong organization, the most closely knit after the Hudson's Bay Company and the North West Company. Between 1799 and 1803, for example, Parker, Gerrard, Ogilvy and Company and Mure combined were the leading exporters of potash from Lower Canada, far outranking James Dunlop* and James IRVINE.

Mure's involvement in the fur trade was ultimately influenced by factors beyond his control. In July 1800 he, Ogilvy, Alexander Mackenzie*, James Leith*, and others had formed a partnership within the New North West Company (sometimes called the XY Company), recently organized to compete with the NWC. At first obligated by Ogilvy, who had taken the initiative in the arrangement without consulting them, Gerrard, George Gillespie, and Yeoward withdrew from it in October. Mure believed Ogilvy had had "no alternative but to form the connection he did or sacrifice almost the whole of the adventure" he had sent to the northwest. Despite this division of interest Parker, Gerrard, Ogilvy and Company became a supplier to the Ogilvy–Mackenzie group. Indeed, in October 1803 the copartnership was reorganized principally to bring in Mackenzie and thus strengthen its involvement in the fur trade. Subsequently, however, according to Robert Gillespie*, a clerk in the Montreal firm, "that branch of business became ruinous owing to the political state of . . . Europe where a great part of the furs from Canada were consumed." Mure also suffered as a shareholder in the New North West Company, which was affected not only by the blockage of European ports but also by ruinous competition in the northwest. On 5 Nov. 1804 the company, unable to sustain its losses any longer, was taken as a copartner into the NWC. Within a week, the partners in the New North West Company divided among themselves their shares in the restructured NWC; Mure held three shares in common with Ogilvy. The copartnership underwent further reorganization in 1807, at which time Mure's firm became known as John Mure and Company.

More profitable than the fur trade was Mure's engagement in the burgeoning timber and shipping trades at Quebec. In 1802 and 1807 he leased nearby

Mure

Anse des Mères from the Ursulines for timber storage. Beginning in June 1804 he joined successively with merchant Henry Usborne* and the firms of Blackwood, Paterson and Company and Monro and Bell to arrange terms for the use by themselves and rental to others of the coves between Anse des Mères and Pointe-à-Pizeau. By spring 1806 he had formed a partnership with James Hare Jolliffe to export timber and lumber. Within a year the partners became agents for the London wine and stave merchants Scott, Idle and Company, a major contractor to the Admiralty for colonial masts, spars, and staves. That company's contract and the agency of Mure and Jolliffe were challenged by competitors; chief among them was Usborne, who attempted to prevent local shipbuilders from "engaging" with Mure and Jolliffe. The timber and spars of the agents became the targets of thieves and saboteurs, but Mure and Jolliffe were no less aggressive in dealing with their rivals.

Between 1807 and 1813 the partners bought timber and planks from subcontractors at Plattsburgh and Peru, N.Y., and in Upper Canada at Kingston and York (Toronto), as well as from John Crysler* and Joel STONE along the upper St Lawrence. The firm's cutting was frequently indiscriminate, drawing unheeded complaints from resident spokesmen such as the Reverend Alexander McDonell* in Glengarry. In 1809 the combined timber operations of Mure and Jolliffe, John Mure and Company, and the London firm of Linthorne and Jolliffe necessitated their joint lease of virtually all the coves at Quebec. Their timber and lumber filled many vessels, and the ballast on incoming ships, usually salt, was sold by Mure. His association with Jolliffe ended when the latter and Benjamin Linthorne went bankrupt about 1813; Mure, Peter Patterson*, and James Henderson became trustees of the company's affairs.

At Quebec Mure held a commanding position as head of the transatlantic shipping operations of the major partnerships in which he was involved. Between 1800 and 1811 he acquired at least 16 schooners, brigs, and ships, many built or rebuilt for him by such notable shipbuilders as Alexander Munn* and John GOUDIE. Of these vessels, the "remarkable fine, fast sailing, staunch, new copper fastened ship" *Fame* was small in comparison to the mammoth merchantmen of the East India Company, but at 876 tons it dwarfed most vessels anchoring at Quebec. Those recording fast crossings advertised the apparent efficiency of Mure's operations; in April 1801 he heralded the crossing of the *Nancy* from Liverpool in just 28 days as the "shortest passage ever known from Great Britain." Within three weeks the *Nancy* was ready to return on one of the two round trips (spring and fall) that were then typical of shipping between North America and Britain.

Central to Mure's business was his integration of operations. He often supplied the timbers and planks for shipbuilding, and he operated a shipyard near the Dorchester Bridge. Several vessels were registered by Mure and associates in the Canada trade, including Jolliffe, Linthorne, Christopher and Jonathan Idle, and Mure's copartners at London and Montreal. All members of the Parker, Gerrard, Ogilvy group had access to vessels owned by Mure alone and to the flotilla he represented as an agent. The connection between the fur trade and shipbuilding, long suspected by historians, is illustrated by the 474-ton *Olive Branch*, constructed by Mure alone in 1809 to transport to London what was still the most valuable export per shipload from the colony: furs. Congestion on his wharf during the short shipping season, vessels arriving from or leaving for the Caribbean or Britain (occasionally armed or in convoys during the Napoleonic Wars), disputes with customs officers, extensive advertising, waterfront auctions, military provisioning – all were aspects of Mure's broad mercantile interest.

Mure took other steps to solidify his commercial base at Quebec. In 1809 he secured from the government a 21-year lease to the King's Wharf on Rue Champlain. This large dock and storage facility became his principal premises; the wharf was later shared with Irvine, McNaught and Company [see James Irvine]. The following year, using a loan of £2,095 from merchant Étienne-Claude Lagueux, Mure made an enormously profitable purchase: the southwest part of the burgeoning *faubourg* Saint-Roch. It was acquired from John RICHARDSON, a close friend of Mure and executor of William Grant*. Mure created 166 lots, from which he drew rental income of nearly £590 a year by 1823. In 1811 he donated land in Saint-Roch for a Roman Catholic church.

Mure's extensive business associations were undoubtedly a significant factor in his success at Quebec, where he became increasingly prominent commercially and publicly. In March 1799 he was elected president of the Fire Society and in June appointed a justice of the peace. George Thomas Landmann*, a British military engineer, described him as "an active magistrate, and a persevering man, exceedingly sanguine, a stout, square-shouldered, good-looking Scotchman, and quite a gentleman; he was a little vain of his abilities" as a magistrate. In 1800 Mure became an ensign in the Quebec Battalion of British Militia. That year as well he contested the general election for the riding of Gaspé but was soundly beaten by William Vondenvelden*. Four years later he tested his popularity in Lower Town Quebec only to face a "torrent of undue influence" and be squeezed out as the second member by merchant John Young*. According to one observer, Mure's "inordinate love of fame" cost him election; most of his support came from Canadian voters rather than British. Within weeks, however, he secured a seat for the Ottawa valley riding of York. Meanwhile, in 1802 he had gained a place on the Board of Pilots at Quebec and the following year had become a commissioner for regulating navigation on the St Lawrence. Between 1807 and 1811 he was acting coroner for the district of Quebec. In 1809 he, James Irvine, John Jones*, and other leading merchants of the city launched the Quebec Committee of Trade to promote their interests in imperial markets.

In the assembly Mure became a prominent representative of mercantile interests in debates and committees on commercial matters ranging from regulation of the timber trade to desertion by seamen from the merchant marine. In 1805–6 he fought for the financing of new prisons from a tax on land rather than on imports, a position supported in London by his copartner Sir Alexander Mackenzie, Gillespie, Parker and Company. After Young and Richardson retired from the assembly in 1808, Mure emerged as the leading spokesman there of the English party, which supported Governor Sir James Henry Craig* against the Canadian party. Sensitized by the Napoleonic Wars and the "threatening" prospect of Lower Canada falling prey to a foreign power, he opposed attempts by the nationalist assembly to obtain control of civil expenditures. As well, he supported in 1809 the eligibility of the Jew Ezekiel Hart* to sit in the house and in February 1810 reversed his stand on judges running as candidates when he sided with Pierre-Amable De Bonne*.

In the election of 1810, after at first declining to run, Mure won a seat along with Pierre Bruneau* in Lower Town. He represented it for four years, parrying with Canadian party spokesmen over civil expenditures, militia matters, the threat of war with the United States, and, in the wartime session of 1812–13, the prickly question of martial law. On 6 Jan. 1812, on the recommendation of Governor Sir George Prevost*, he had been made an honorary member of the Executive Council; he became a full member, with voting privileges, on 26 June. In 1811 he had been named a commissioner for erecting a jail and a court-house at Quebec and for obtaining plans for a new parliament building.

Mure participated in the War of 1812 both as a militia officer and as a merchant. In March 1812 he had been promoted captain in Quebec's 3rd Militia Battalion. The next year he became major in the Île d'Orléans battalion of militia and then in the 6th Select Embodied Militia Battalion. As a senior officer with commercial experience, he sat on a board formed in August 1812 to establish an office for supervising the government's issue of army bills [see James GREEN], which he and others had recommended to Prevost as a supplementary currency. These bills stimulated the province's economy, and Mure privately handled large volumes of them. After the war, in 1816, he supported formation of a bank to alleviate the shortage of currency resulting from termination of the bills scheme and to handle the unprecedented need for investment capital created by the timber trade and other rapidly expanding sectors of the economy. Mure was also among the early promoters of the Quebec Exchange, founded that year to facilitate the collection of commercial information and the transaction of business; in May 1817 he was one of its vice-presidents.

Mure devoted much energy after 1814 to educational concerns, such as the Book Society Committee, which donated books to schools. In the spring of 1815 he vigorously supported establishment of a non-sectarian school by the Committee for Promoting the Education of the Poor in Upper and Lower Canada, an initiative of the Reverend Thaddeus Osgood*, and he soon became president of its Lower Canadian branch, which succeeded in opening a school at Quebec by mid May. In 1815 Mure also became a commissioner for managing the Jesuit estates, revenues from which were used to support education. The following year he was appointed a commissioner for the construction and repair of churches in the district of Quebec.

The war and post-war years marked a number of major departures in Mure's business affairs. In May 1812 John Mure and Company had withdrawn from partnership in the Parker, Gerrard, Ogilvy group, in part perhaps because of severe reverses sustained by the copartnership in the fur trade. The war and the complexity of the copartnership's operations delayed until at least the fall of 1814 the disposal at Quebec and London of its assets, including ships, timber and lumber, land, and buildings, as well as debts owed to it. In October 1814 Mure informed Gerrard, "I am very anxious to have my own matters under my sole controul"; this preoccupation led him to purchase Ogilvy's half of their interest in the NWC (sold with his half in 1832 by his heirs to Edward Ellice*) and to reorganize the business of John Mure and Company. Mure nevertheless maintained some association with his former partners, apart from the wind-up of affairs; in October 1814 he was still in a position to advise Gerrard on the deployment of partners. In contrast to his importing activity, which he maintained at a time of inflationary increase in the value of imports, Mure took steps to reduce his firm's involvement in the fur trade. Though still a shareholder in the NWC, he was also a shipping agent for Lord Selkirk [Douglas*] and corresponded with him over the conflict that developed from 1814 between the NWC and the HBC in the Red River colony. Mure recommended to Selkirk sale of the HBC's trading rights or lease of its whole trade to the NWC. The latter proposal, however, would have necessitated recognition of the HBC charter by the NWC, a move Mure knew his associates were "not inclined to make." In May 1816 Selkirk dismissed

Mure

Mure's suggestions as "totally & radically inadmissable." The disagreement apparently did not rupture their business relationship.

In late 1815, during a period of significant economic malaise in Lower Canada, Mure took steps to lease out his shipyard and timber-yard. In February 1817 he offered for lease a newly constructed store, located on the King's Wharf; with a capacity of 30,000 bushels, it was one of the largest on the waterfront. Between then and August he dissolved John Mure and Company, granted power of attorney on his personal affairs and those of Mure and Jolliffe to William FINLAY (his first clerk and a cousin of Mure's nephew William Steel), and announced his intention to sail for Britain on 10 August.

The time was propitious in other respects for Mure to retire after some 35 years in Lower Canada. In November 1816 his daughter, Charlotte, whom he had had with a mistress, Louise Picard, had married another Quebec merchant, François-Xavier Pinguet. Some arrangement seemed possible for the guardianship of Mure's sons, James and William, from a liaison with Marie-Anne Chasseur. Mure had evidently enjoyed a style of life befitting a gentleman; it took three days to auction off effects that included mahogany furniture, silverware, more than 300 books, engravings, guns, fishing gear, silver spurs and gold epaulettes, choice wines, and a London-built curricle (among other carriages). Politically, he was leaving the colony at a time of relative tranquillity [see Sir John Coape SHERBROOKE].

Settled in Glasgow, Mure retained an interest in Lower Canada and corresponded with other members of the mercantile community in Britain who had Canadian backgrounds. Between 1818 and his death he initiated more than 14 sheriff's sales at Quebec to recover debts, most of them from Canadians. When, in 1819, St Andrew's Church at Quebec sought a successor to Spark, Mure and John Greenshields were delegated to find one; they presented James Harkness and provided money to facilitate resumption of services. In 1820, evidently at Selkirk's request, Mure agreed to help Colin Robertson*, an employee of the HBC, extricate himself from debt.

At Mure's death, in Glasgow in 1823, his residence was located 16 miles southwest at Dalserf House. Among the effects auctioned there in March were some 2,400 bottles of wine. Mure bequeathed more than £10,150, most of it to relatives and family, including his daughter and sons, the latter under the care of William Finlay at Quebec; annuities were provided for Louise Picard and Marie-Anne Chasseur.

DAVID ROBERTS

ANQ-M, CN1-187, 28 août 1816; CN1-269, 8 oct. 1795; CN1-290, 19 juin 1782, 20 déc. 1784, no.1913. ANQ-Q,

CE1-66, 11 janv. 1798, 19 mars 1799; CN1-16, 31 août, 25 sept., 13 oct., 12, 26, 28 nov. 1807; 23, 30 juill. 1808; 18 janv., 28 avril, 17 oct. 1809; 22 févr., 11 sept. 1810; 6 mars, 8 avril, 11 mai, 27 juill., 29 nov., 18 déc. 1811; 31 janv. 1817; 15 août, 20 oct. 1823; CN1-26, 8 avril 1808, 2 mai 1810; CN1-49, 26, 28 nov. 1814; CN1-178, 10 avril 1804; CN1-197, 22 juill. 1816; CN1-230, 27 avril 1802, 20 sept. 1807. Arch. judiciaires, Québec, Holograph will of John Mure, 13 Nov. 1823 (see P.-G. Roy, Inv. testaments, 3: 102). ASQ, Lettres, Z, 41; Polygraphie, XXV, no.19H. AUM, P 58, U, Mure to Gerrard, 6 Nov. 1800. NLS, Dept. of MSS 15125: f.41; 15126: f.163; 15182: 120–21. PAC, MG 19, A2, ser.3, 173; E1, ser.1, 6: 1993–95, 2074–75; 7: 2184–86, 2227–30; 8: 2811–14; 15: 4860–61 (copies); MG 23, HII, 1, vol.1: 36–37; MG 24, B1, 2: 425–26; 20: 77–85; 188: 3818–22, 3824, 3826; D8: 189–90; L3: 7482–83, 7504–5, 7512–13, 7519–22, 8107–8, 8127, 8847–51, 8853–59, 8910–12, 8928, 8930–41, 8953–59, 8960–67, 8972–73, 25039–40, 25718–25; MG 30, D1, 22: 656–81; MG 55/24, no.40 (William Hutchison); RG 1, L3L: 172, 572, 580, 649–51, 705, 2765–66, 3002, 3019, 33742–951, 37580–86, 72641–57, 72772–91, 88985–9016, 92039–76, 95851–52; RG 4, A1: 21707–11, 21733, 24515, 24812–13, 30322, 32890–92, 35083, 35715, 37252, 38558, 39612, 41030–32, 41101–3, 41850; vol.144: 195–202; vol.167: 85; B17, 41, 25 March 1820; B46, 2: 667–69; RG 5, A1: 2872–75, 3657–58, 3770–73, 3901–2; RG 8, I (C ser.), 14, 110, 114, 115E–15F, 117, 279–80, 329–30, 363, 372, 388–89, 599, 688E, 704, 909, 1061, 1203½, 1220, 1223–24, 1695, 1717; RG 9, I, A5, 2: 171; RG 42, E1, 1381–82; RG 68, General index, 1651–1841: 59, 70, 161, 223–24, 226, 259, 271, 278, 280, 336, 338, 344–46, 348, 351–52, 543, 637. PRO, CO 42/100, 42/130, 42/135, 42/140, 42/142–43, 42/148, 42/153, 42/180. QUA, Richard Cartwright papers, letter-book, 1799–1802.

Les bourgeois de la Compagnie du Nord-Ouest (Masson), vol.1. "Les dénombrements de Québec" (Plessis), ANQ Rapport, 1948–49: 136, 173, 180. HBRS, 2 (Rich and Fleming). L.C., House of Assembly, Journals, 1805–17. Mackenzie, Journals and letters (Lamb), 37, 39–40. [John Maude], Visit to the falls of Niagara in 1800 (London, 1826), 191, 208. Select British docs. of War of 1812 (Wood), 1: 195, 227–31. Glasgow Herald, 24 Jan., 7 March 1823. Quebec Gazette, 1791–1824. Caron, "Inv. de la corr. de Mgr Plessis," ANQ Rapport, 1932–33: 76–77. Desjardins, Guide parl., 30, 137, 144. Doris Drolet Dubé et Marthe Lacombe, Inventaire des marchés de construction des Archives nationales à Québec, XVIIe et XVIIIe siècles (Ottawa, 1977), no.1616. Officers of British forces in Canada (Irving), 135, 145, 147. P.-G. Roy, Inv. concessions, 1: 222–23. A. R. M. Lower, Great Britain's woodyard; British America and the timber trade, 1763–1867 (Montreal and London, 1973). Ouellet, Bas-Canada; Hist. économique. James Paterson, History of the county of Ayr: with a genealogical account of the families of Ayrshire (2v., Edinburgh, 1847–52), 1: 297; 2: 182, 361. R. A. Pendergast, "The XY Company, 1798 to 1804" (PHD thesis, Univ. of Ottawa, 1957). [J.] B. Porteous, The Porteous story: a Scottish border family from 1439 A.D. (1v. to date, Montreal, 1980–). Narcisse Rosa, La construction des navires à Québec et ses environs; grèves et naufrages (Québec, 1897; réimpr. Montréal, 1973). P.-G. Roy, Toutes *petites choses du Régime anglais*, 1: 203–5. *The trade winds: a study of British overseas trade during the French wars, 1793–1815*, ed. C. N. Parkinson (London, 1948). F.-J. Audet, "Les députés de la vallée d'Ottawa, 1792–1867," CHA *Report*, 1935: 5–23. O.-A. Coté, "La Chambre de commerce de Québec," *BRH*, 27 (1921): 26–27. Louise Dechêne, "La rente du faubourg Saint-Roch à Québec, 1750–1850," *RHAF*, 34 (1980–81): 569–96. "La famille Mure," *BRH*, 41 (1935): 63–64. R. H. Fleming, "The origin of 'Sir Alexander Mackenzie and Company,'" *CHR*, 9 (1928): 137–55. Hare, "L'Assemblée législative du Bas-Canada," *RHAF*, 27: 361–95.

MURRAY, JOHN, army officer and colonial administrator; b. *c*. 1739 in Ireland; m. Mary Pasco, and they had at least two sons; d. 4 May 1824 in Paris.

John Murray entered the British army on 6 March 1760 as an ensign and served in different parts of the world, becoming a brigadier-general in 1796. Two years later he came to Nova Scotia to serve under Prince Edward* Augustus, commander of the forces in the Maritime provinces. Murray never took to Halifax society, and his "haughty and despotic" temperament did not sit well with the local élite. He alienated himself from the prince by suggesting that the king might be displeased if Edward took his companion Mme de Saint-Laurent [MONTGENET] to London, and angered Lieutenant Governor Sir John Wentworth* by blocking him in his attempt to improve his own land at government expense. Consequently both men were pleased when early in 1799 Murray, as a senior officer in the Atlantic region, was appointed to administer Cape Breton, a colony from which Lieutenant-General James Ogilvie* had been begging to be allowed to retire.

Before leaving Halifax in June, Murray was given all the lurid details of the political quarrelling in Cape Breton. The contending parties, both trying to gain the ear of the colony's ruler, were headed by the Reverend Ranna Cossit* and Attorney General David Mathews*. When Murray arrived in Cape Breton on the 21st he was particularly suspicious of Mathews, about whom he had been warned in Halifax. But in an effort to follow the non-partisan path of the absentee lieutenant governor, William Macarmick*, he appointed his Executive Council from both parties. Mathews made it practically impossible to maintain this balance. When in July Murray attempted to conciliate the two sides by giving a dinner for the council, Mathews refused to dine with his political foes, and relations between the two men started to deteriorate.

Given Murray's impetuous nature, Mathews's dismissal from office seemed a certainty. However, Murray could not indulge his wishes since he was under the surveillance of his enemies in Halifax. He felt certain that they would be delighted by Mathews's disaffection and indeed that they were promoting it.

He thus decided to build up as much support as possible in Sydney before moving against Mathews. In turn, Cossit and his supporters saw the situation as an opportunity to gain Murray's favour and destroy Mathews. Murray was correct in his supposition about his enemies, for even as he reached Sydney negotiations were under way between Edward Augustus and Major-General John DESPARD for his replacement as military commander, and by the fall rumours had reached Sydney of Murray's impending removal. The Cossit faction began passing petitions asking that Murray be kept in Cape Breton; the opposing group drew up another resolution disclaiming support for the petitions.

Now sure of some backing, Murray decided to destroy Mathews's power. He had also sought approval from the Home Department for dismissing Mathews and a dispatch giving it was sent by the home secretary, the Duke of Portland, in October 1799. In November he dismissed Mathews as attorney general, appointed William CAMPBELL in his place, and a month later had the council agree to Mathews's removal from that body. Mathews would not give in without a fight and contended that Murray had no legal authority since his mandamus was made out to Thomas Murray, a clerical error which Murray had already noted to the Home Department. Murray was in no mood to argue and also dismissed Mathews's followers, who included secretary William McKinnon*, councillor Archibald Charles DODD, and joint chief justice Ingram Ball*.

While Murray was contending with his political enemies, he was still able to devote time to colonial improvements. Soon after he arrived he used the 150 troops brought by Ogilvie to complete a road from Sydney to the northwest arm of Sydney Harbour. He also improved the road from Sydney to the Mira River, and began construction of a new barracks, a government house, a brewery, and a market-house.

Murray's main achievement, however, lay in increasing the production of coal. He wanted a new pit dug at the mines since he felt that the existing one would soon run out of coal. The lessees of the mines, Jonathan Tremain and Richard Stout*, claimed that there was still plenty of coal, but Murray mistrusted their assessment and thought that the partners would let their lease expire and force the government to pay the cost of opening a new pit. He concluded that the government should assume control, but realized that this scheme would be expensive and therefore bargained with Tremain and Stout, offering to sink a new pit if they would renew their lease. In October 1799, as the contract was about to be signed, James Miller, the superintendent of mines, died. Murray was loath to let Tremain and Stout run the mines without Miller's supervision and allowed the lease to lapse. Stout meanwhile mercilessly stripped the pit. Murray, placing the mines under crown control, appointed Campbell superintendent to work with Miller's sister, Jane, a woman with good business sense and knowledge of mining. A new pit was opened without delay, and by the summer of 1800 this pit and a new pier had resulted in increased shipments of coal. Murray also made the first important innovation in the treatment of the miners when he began paying them in cash at regular intervals. The change broke Tremain and Stout's economic hold on the miners, who had previously had to take their wages in supplies.

In the mean time, Murray's position as administrator was becoming less secure. Though he had apparently broken the back of Mathews's party, its members were feeding the Duke of Kent [Edward Augustus] and Wentworth with any information that might lead to Murray's dismissal. Acting on this information, in March 1800 the duke charged Murray with naming military officers to the council. Murray admitted to the truth of the charge but pointed out that past lieutenant governors and administrators had done so because of a lack of qualified civilian candidates, and that he was only following a precedent. Since the defence was unanswerable, the duke decided not to press the point, and sent Despard, who had received a letter of appointment for assuming the military command, to take over control.

Murray had feared that he would be replaced, and he was not willing to surrender power easily. Since Ogilvie's time it had been assumed that the military commander would also have civil authority, and Murray used the wording of Despard's letter of appointment to retain the civil office after the latter's arrival in June 1800. Despard was confused and on advice from Wentworth bided his time. Early in September Wentworth became convinced that the person commanding the forces was *ex officio* civilian chief as well, and he advised Despard to prepare to take over.

Since Murray would not leave office peacefully, the dispute was settled by brute force. Despard had the advantage since he controlled the military and also because the captain of the militia was a son of Richard Stout, who was opposed to Murray. On 17 September Despard convened a meeting of the council to have himself proclaimed administrator. Murray was still popular because of the improvements he had effected, and a mob gathered at the governor's quarters. The militia was called out to prevent a riot. Murray was helpless: the presence of the troops and militia kept his followers from the meeting, and he could only send William Smith* to England in a fruitless effort to explain his case. Despard took no action but let him linger until the end of June 1801.

Murray's career after Cape Breton is unknown, although it has been claimed that he was a prisoner in Napoleon's France for 12 years. He was promoted by seniority to major-general on 25 Sept. 1803, to lieutenant-general on 25 Oct. 1809, and to general on 12 Aug. 1819. At the time of his death he was living in Paris.

The fate of John Murray provides a perfect example of the effect that the hopeless state of Cape Breton before 1800 had on careers. Though enthusiastic and well-intentioned, he was prey to warring factions, the ineptitude of the Home Department, and the interference of Nova Scotia in Cape Breton's affairs. Despite these obstructions, he managed to destroy the power of David Mathews and lay the groundwork for improvements which would be built upon by his successors.

R. J. MORGAN

PAC, MG 11, [CO 217] Nova Scotia A, 131. PRO, CO 217/117–18. [William Smith], *A caveat against emigration to America; with the state of the island of Cape Breton, from the year 1784 to the present year; and suggestions for the benefit of the British settlements in North America* (London, 1803). *The royal military calendar, containing the service of every general officer in the British army, from the date of their first commission . . .* , ed. John Philippart (3v., London, 1815–[16]), 1. R. J. Morgan, "Orphan outpost."

MYRES. *See* MEYERS

N

NANCY. *See* SHAWNADITHIT

NELSON, WILLIAM, teacher; b. 1750 in Newsham (North Yorkshire), England, son of George Nelson; d. 10 June 1834 in William Henry (Sorel, Que.).

William Nelson began teaching school in his native Yorkshire at age 16. Ten years later he moved to London and taught there until May 1781 when he emigrated to the province of Quebec. He later wrote that there were "but Two teachers worthy of the name" when he arrived, one at Quebec, the other at Montreal. Nelson settled at Trois-Rivières, then a busy centre of loyalist immigration, and opened a school there. He offered to board students and to teach them English, French, Latin, Greek, writing, bookkeeping, mathematics, geography, and navigation.

On 24 May 1785 at Sorel Nelson married Jane Dies, the 18-year-old daughter of a tory loyalist from Catskill, N.Y. Two years later he petitioned the grand jury at Montreal, "setting forth his desire of removing his school from Three Rivers to Montreal provided he should meet with proper encouragement." The jury recommended that he be granted "the bounty allowed by Government for a school master," a motion approved by Lord Dorchester [Guy Carleton*]. By 1790 Nelson had opened a school in Montreal; in the following year he had 48 students and in 1792, 32. He remained in Montreal only until 1794, when he moved his family to a farm he had acquired south of William Henry. There he held school in his house, boarding students and teaching the same subjects he had offered at Trois-Rivières. His pupils were mainly the children of British officers stationed at the military post. In addition he had, in his own words, "four, often even five scholars of poor Canadian parentage, whom he instructed from principles of consideration, say compassion – say for Nothing!" He also taught his own children, three of whom became medical doctors; Wolfred* and Robert* would later gain prominence in the political struggles of Lower Canada. The eldest son, George*, became a fur trader.

The life of a country schoolmaster was a struggle to feed his family. By Nelson's account, only "delusive hopes continually presenting themselves of new and further encouragement of better times" kept him at his work. In 1801, with his family numbering five boys and three girls, he petitioned the lieutenant governor, Sir Robert Shore Milnes*, for assistance. He was accorded a salary of £60 per annum "as an inducement not to leave William Henry." The grant was generous and it gave Nelson, and his family, a security which he had not known in the 20 years he had been teaching in Lower Canada.

In 1821, however, his peaceful life was shattered by a series of events initiated by Aaron Allen, a wealthy local merchant. In that year the Royal Institution for the Advancement of Learning determined to establish a schoolhouse in William Henry, which would be administered on the institution's behalf by local visitors, of whom Allen became one. Nelson – in his 70s and set in his ways – was appointed the teacher but he disapproved of removing the school from his own house and disliked being accountable to others for the first time in his career. When the visitors decided in 1822 to prevent Nelson from charging fees, he complained bitterly and threatened to resign. A few days later, Allen's son-in-law applied for the post. He did not, however, meet with the approval of another visitor, the Reverend John Jackson*, who considered Nelson "old but effective." Nelson continued to teach but refused to acknowledge the authority of the institution. In 1823, when the visitors imposed 35 free pupils on him, he dismissed these students. On 7 Jan.

1824, following the receipt of "a mortifying and authoritative" directive from the Reverend Joseph Langley MILLS, secretary of the institution, who considered Nelson's salary of £60 per annum a sinecure, Nelson resigned or, as he put it, "liberated himself" from the institution. Allen's son, Edward Carter, succeeded him.

William Nelson continued to teach at home and to charge his pupils a small fee of one dollar per month; without his salary, however, he encountered increasing difficulties as the years passed. In 1831, after almost 65 years as a teacher, he sent a petition to the governor, Lord Aylmer [Whitworth-Aylmer*], requesting a pension for his services. "Fifty years, and upwards," he wrote, "of the best of his existence he has sacrificed in this Province, in the diffusion of Education . . . on terms hardly superior to the wages of common agricultural labourers." His request was not granted. He died two and a half years later at his home, and was buried in the Protestant cemetery in William Henry.

JOHN BESWARICK THOMPSON

PAC, MG 24, B34, 2: 17; RG 4, A1, 369: 73–74; RG 8, I (C ser.), 634: 90. *Quebec Gazette*, 16 May 1784, 30 June 1785, 19 Feb. 1795. A. R. Kelley, "Church and state papers for the years 1787 to 1791, being a compendium of documents relating to the establishment of certain churches in the province of Quebec," ANQ *Rapport*, 1953–55: 117. *Quebec almanac*, 1791–92. L.-P. Audet, *Le système scolaire*, vols.2–4. J. D. Borthwick, *History of the Montreal prison from A.D. 1784 to A.D. 1886 . . .* (Montreal, 1886). Boulianne, "Royal Instit. for the Advancement of Learning." É.-Z. Massicotte, "Les premières écoles anglaises à Montréal," *BRH*, 46 (1940): 169–70.

NEPEAN, NICHOLAS, army officer and colonial administrator; baptized 9 Nov. 1757 in Saltash, England, youngest of three sons of Nicholas Nepean and Margaret Jones; m. 21 April 1784 Johanna Francisca Carolina Wedikind in Stoke Damerel (Plymouth), England, and they had at least three sons; d. 18 Dec. 1823 in Newton Abbot, England.

Nicholas Nepean began his military career on 15 Dec. 1776 as a second lieutenant in the Royal Marines. After service afloat and in New South Wales (Australia), Gibraltar, and Britain he became a brigadier-general in 1804. On 17 March 1807 he was appointed administrator of Cape Breton, a position he probably owed to the fact that he was the brother of Sir Evan Nepean, who had held various posts in the British government.

Nepean's career had not prepared him for the challenges in Cape Breton. The colony did not have a house of assembly, and hence had limped along without locally raised revenue until John DESPARD's term as administrator. In 1801 Despard had inaugurat-

Nepean

ed a tax on imported rum, of doubtful legality, in order to provide for even the simplest amenities. However, the money had gone to help settle the vanguard of the great Scottish migration to Cape Breton, which began in 1801. The resulting increase in population added fuel to the arguments of Richard Collier Bernard DesBarres Marshall Gibbons, son of a former chief justice, for an assembly. Then there were the coal mines, a potentially lucrative source of revenue which the meagre resources of public and private enterprise had failed to develop effectively.

An added handicap for Nepean was his personality. When he arrived in Sydney on 2 July 1807, he could not be persuaded by Despard to discuss the colony's situation. Despard declared that Nepean was "as I am informed by several who know him well a remarkably indolent Man, and unfortunately for himself too easily imposed upon by artful and designing Men." Despard's ill feeling may have been reciprocated, since from the outset Nepean seemed to gravitate towards his predecessor's enemies such as William CAMPBELL and Gibbons. He first fell under the influence of Campbell, reappointing him mines superintendent. However, Campbell was not regarded with much favour in Whitehall and in April 1808 Nepean was ordered to cancel his appointment. Before long Gibbons acquired influence over the administrator, and Nepean named him acting attorney general when he broke with Campbell in the summer of 1808. Nepean also replaced a number of Despard's nominees in the Executive Council.

When word of these seemingly arbitrary dismissals reached London, anger flared. Sir Evan Nepean tried to defend Nicholas by describing the Cape Bretoners as a "troublesome, turbulent set of people," but could not prevent his being warned in April 1809 to mend his ways or suffer dismissal.

Nepean reacted characteristically, reinstating a few officials. He retained Gibbons as his chief confidant, even though Gibbons had continued to call for an assembly, an institution Nepean considered "dangerous." In December 1810, however, Gibbons frightened Nepean when he persuaded the grand jury to petition for an assembly. Nepean dismissed him, but was swayed enough by his arguments to bring the matter before the council, which promptly opposed an assembly.

By the spring of 1812 Nepean seems to have come around to Gibbons's way of thinking, and appointed him to the council. Nepean then suspended the rum tax and asked the council to approve the calling of an assembly. Such was Gibbons's influence that this time his ideas were accepted. In order to strengthen his hand with the British authorities, Nepean allowed Gibbons to propose that a poll be taken of the colonists' views on an assembly. The emergency created by the outbreak of the war with the United

States in June and the consequent need for immediate revenue persuaded Nepean to forgo the poll and write in October to Lord Bathurst, the newly appointed colonial secretary, justifying the need for an assembly. However, Bathurst had already decided to replace Nepean by Hugh Swayne*, who arrived in Sydney on New Year's Day 1813.

It was Nepean's fate to leave other problems unsettled. Though the Napoleonic Wars and the American Embargo Act of 1807 had resulted in increased economic activity in Nova Scotia and New Brunswick, they affected Cape Breton only indirectly. Her ships were too small to take part in the growing transatlantic and Caribbean trade that the larger colonies enjoyed, but she could ship her goods to those provinces and participate in the economic growth of the region. However, increased trade meant increased inflation: for example, between 1807 and 1808 the price of flour went up by 100 per cent. To stop this trend Nepean allowed the importation of American food-stuffs and forbad the export of food or cattle, but prices continued to rise. Moreover, the attraction of prosperity in Halifax and Saint John and the growing demand for sailors drew away miners, many of whom had been Newfoundland fishermen. Inflation and a scarcity of labour drove up miners' wages and also production costs, and in 1808 John Corbett Ritchie, the mines superintendent, asked that the price of a chaldron of coal be raised from 16 to 20 shillings.

Nepean had also to face the poor state of the mines, which were still suffering from Campbell's mismanagement. Production was lagging just when the increasing number of troops in Halifax had created a demand for coal. To solve the problems of high wages and low production, Nepean put 30 of the New Brunswick Fencibles stationed in Sydney to work in the mines. The output of coal rose until the summer of 1811, when Lieutenant-General Sir George Prevost*, the lieutenant governor of Nova Scotia, ordered the troops to stop working, perhaps because he hoped to open the Pictou coalfields in his own colony. In frustration, Nepean leased the mines to the Halifax merchants Jonathan and John Tremain, but allowed the lease to expire after they asked for an increase in the price of coal. Negotiations were proceeding with another merchant when Nepean's term ended.

Nepean does not appear to have been employed after his return to England. While in Cape Breton he was promoted major-general, and on 4 June 1814 he became a lieutenant-general.

Nicholas Nepean's previous career and personality did not equip him to tackle the economic and political problems of Cape Breton. He failed to deal effectively with political questions and vacillated when faced by opposing forces. His lack of experience with economics prevented him from coping with the long-range

538

development of the island. On the other hand, rising inflation, economic competition from Nova Scotia, and the growing movement for an assembly were beyond his control, and indicated that a change in the colony's situation was necessary.

R. J. MORGAN

PAC, RG 8, I (C ser.), 366: 133–37. PANS, RG 1, 58, doc.88. PRO, CO 217/125: 76–77, 95, 97–98, 171–73, 178–79; 217/126: 16–20, 25–27, 34–36; 217/127: 5–6, 14; 217/128: 35; 217/129: 37–38; 217/130: 30–36; CO 220/15: 6–7, 103–4, 136, 142–45, 150–51, 172–73. *ADB. Burke's peerage* (1893), 1024. *The royal military calendar, containing the service of every general officer in the British army, from the date of their first commission . . .*, ed. John Philippart (3v., London, 1815–[16]), 1: 285–86.

NICHOL, ROBERT, mariner, businessman, JP, militia officer, office holder, politician, and judge; b. *c.* 1780 in Scotland, possibly in Dumfries; m. 21 Dec. 1811 Theresa Wright in Niagara (Niagara-on-the-Lake), Upper Canada, and they had two sons and two daughters; d. 3 May 1824 at Queenston Heights, Upper Canada.

Scant references survive for Robert Nichol's earliest years. He had, by his own account, some education although not as much care was "bestowed" on it as he would have liked. A career at sea came to an abrupt end at Montreal in 1792. "Badly used by his Captain," Nichol left the ship and made his way to Upper Canada. Like Thomas CLARK and the Dickson brothers, William* and THOMAS – all acquaintances, perhaps relatives, of Nichol – Bob (as they called him) found a niche in the trading empire of Robert Hamilton*. By August 1792 Nichol had taken up residence in Hamilton's Queenston home and was working as a sailor on one of his vessels.

Nichol worked his way up and through the extended Hamilton network, first as Thomas Dickson's clerk at Fort Erie in 1794. The following year he moved to Detroit where, on 18 September, he signed a three-year indenture as John Askin*'s clerk. Toward the end of 1798 he returned to Queenston. For a time he traded in his own right but by February 1800 he was working with Clark, whose partnership with Samuel Street* had recently dissolved. Plans for his own establishment at Fort Erie were set aside upon Clark's offer of a partnership.

Although he never wholly confronted the fact, Nichol was temperamentally unsuited to commercial life. His composition was, he wrote, "more of the Epicurean than Stoic." Unlike Clark, a Scottish Uriah Heep, Nichol required more spiritual nourishment than came from a bowl of porridge and a hard day's work. The forwarding trade was heaviest in spring, summer, and fall, and the opening of a Lower Canadian market for flour in 1800 added to the

pressure. Winter brought temporary relief, but with little leisure and few unmarried women in the neighbourhood, life was never easy. Nichol bemoaned his fate: "Solitude is to me a most insupportable State, & was it not for the few Books I possess, & now and then a visit from Some friends, I should die of Ennui." Under the weight of his responsibilities, his correspondence suffered. "I cannot collect or arrange my Ideas – in fact I am sometimes almost in a downright lethargy."

In 1802 Clark visited Scotland, leaving Nichol in "constant attendance" to the business. An additional strain was the "present unsettled State of the Country" and "the very unfavorable prospects for the future." By mid September Nichol, overtaken by melancholy and "seized with a kind of languor," began to consider "a happier Clime where the little talents I possess may be more useful to me than they are likely to be here." When, however, on 22 Oct. 1803, he wrote to Askin informing him of the dissolution of his partnership with Clark, it was from Fort Erie where he had set up as a forwarder, determined to "embrace every Object that may appear profitable."

The role of skinflint came naturally to Clark but not to Nichol. As conditions worsened through 1804 and 1805, he was forced to adopt a manner not to his liking. Hard pressed by his creditors and anxious to maintain his lines of credit, he had to deal bluntly with the accounts of his friend and former employer, John Askin. The relationship with Askin had been warm and friendly in spite of, as Nichol observed, the difference in age. But Askin's seeming casualness in resolving his account with Nichol proved more than the friendship could bear; by July 1806 their long and amicable correspondence had come to a halt.

The one bright spot amid his economic woes from 1804 to 1805 was Nichol's acquaintance with Isaac Brock*, apparently begun on the latter's visits to Fort George (Niagara-on-the-Lake). To some, such as James FitzGibbon* who served under Brock, it was a surprising relationship. Nichol, he recalled many years later, was a "mean looking little Scotchman, who squinted very much," and kept a "Retail Store of Small Consideration" at Fort Erie. In part it seems (and later events bear this interpretation out) that Brock recognized talents in Nichol which could be extremely useful. Indeed, Nichol was asked to prepare a "Sketch of Upper Canada, showing its resources in men, provisions, Horses &c." FitzGibbon saw this document in 1813 "and by that time every statement was proved to be most accurate and Valuable."

It is not surprising that Nichol followed other merchants, notably Clark and Richard Hatt*, in moving from the forwarding trade into processing, locating himself by 1808 in Woodhouse Township. The following year he finished renovating a grist-mill, which after repairs in the winter of 1813–14 was

Nichol

capable of producing 200 pounds of flour weekly. The mill, however, was only the centre of a complex including a sawmill, a distillery with three stills, a large barn, a house, a residence for workmen, a coopery, and a flour store. Supply of the British garrisons at Fort Erie and Fort George was an important part of his business; between 1805 and 1811 he billed the commissariat for more than £2,800 worth of flour and pork. The years up to the War of 1812 seem to have been as prosperous for Nichol – his annual profit was £750 – as they were busy. The debilitating lassitude of spirit that had plagued him seems to have lifted. For one thing, local non-commercial events captured his interest; he became entangled in the factionalism so characteristic of the London District [see Benajah Mallory*]. In addition, the looming crisis in relations with the United States acquired personal meaning when on 21 May 1808 the Americans seized 17 vessels belonging to Canadian traders, including 8 of Nichol's own. He duly reported the affair to Brock, noting also American troop movements at Detroit and Michilimackinac (Mackinac Island, Mich.).

In his private life Nichol was determined to end the lamentable want of female companionship. He was, according to one of the *grandes dames* of York (Toronto), Mrs Anne Powell [Murray*], "*almost unobjectionable.*" He was a "wealthy young *Merchant Miller,*" but Nichol's "long & earnest suit" of her daughter ANNE had been rebuffed owing to Anne's "sincere repugnance to the Man." A hitherto unknown equipoise came with his 1811 marriage to Theresa Wright. The "happy pair" set off for Nichol's home, occasioning Mary Boyles Powell to comment: "Poor thing I dont think she has much prospect of happiness shut up in the woods all her life."

In the 18 months or so preceding the outbreak of war, Nichol became a prominent actor on the provincial stage. His behaviour was a study in contrasts. The relationship between him and Lieutenant Governor Francis Gore* was constrained by the necessity of tact on his part. But Gore's leave of absence and Brock's assumption of the presidency of the administration removed that sort of control upon Nichol's increasingly vain and abrasive personality. An early supporter of the Niagara area's mercantile élite, Nichol evinced scant sympathy for its opponents. Even under the threat of war the political opposition, led by Joseph Willcocks*, proved more and more successful in thwarting executive initiative. Its actions prompted Nichol to crusade against, as Brock expressed it, "the machinations of a licentious faction" in his neighbourhood. The "essential good" he performed "in opposing the democratic measures of a Mr. Willcocks and his vile coadjutors" earned him, according to Brock, their enmity. Retaliation came in 1811 in the form of an assembly investigation, initiated by Willcocks,

into Nichol's handling of public funds as a road commissioner.

The house's conclusion that Nichol had abused his trust elicited a vigorous defence of his integrity in which he blamed the affair on "Party purposes." This slur on the assembly's motives resulted in a motion by David McGregor ROGERS charging Nichol with contempt and ordering his arrest. Forced to go to York in late February 1812 to explain himself, Nichol was incautious enough to remark that the assembly had exceeded its privileges. He promptly found himself confronted by two counts of contempt. Convicted and jailed, Nichol immediately applied for a writ of habeas corpus, which was granted by Chief Justice Thomas SCOTT, and launched a suit for damages against the speaker of the house, Samuel Street*. Brock had entered the fray, denouncing the assembly for its assumption of "inordinate power" and its "palpable injustice" to Nichol. The imbroglio resulting from Scott's decision was quickly assuming the proportions of a major confrontation between the executive, the judiciary, and the assembly, but it was averted by the continuing deterioration in relations with the United States.

In early 1812 Brock had failed, almost utterly, to wring from an uncooperative assembly the measures he deemed necessary for the impending conflict. But he had managed an amendment to the Militia Act permitting him to reorganize the militia. The Norfolk unit was divided into two regiments; Nichol became lieutenant-colonel of the 2nd Norfolk. In the best of times this would have been a controversial appointment given Nichol's bad temper and eager participation in political factionalism. In unsettled times the results were predictable. Soon rumours were spread that, in his capacity as commanding officer, Nichol had cast aspersions on the loyalty of American settlers in Upper Canada. In spite of assertions to the contrary, the damage was probably done. Meanwhile, Nichol ran roughshod over the regiment, which he considered "has been little better than a legalised Mob – the Officers without respectability without intelligence, and without Authority – and the men without any idea of Subordination." In defence of his authority and his character he instigated a fistful of charges against his officers. An election victory in June 1812 in Norfolk gave his enemies a larger target but strengthened his own grip on events. Like Attorney General John Macdonell* (Greenfield), he had probably entered politics at Brock's behest and almost certainly with his connivance. With two of the ablest men in the province managing the administration's interests in the house, there was at least the hope that the contumacious opposition could be brought to heel.

Nichol found his stride in the political-military world in which he was now moving. It did not take much inveigling on Brock's part to overcome his reasonable fear that "permanent" military employment would "Ruin" him. At stake was the post of quartermaster general of militia. His objections to acceptance allayed by Brock's contention that he "was the only Inhabitant . . . at all adequate to the Situation," Nichol left management of his enterprises to an employee and took up his new responsibilities on 27 June 1812. For the next three years, he was absorbed by military affairs to an extent unequalled by any other colonial. His immediate task was to clothe, quarter, and feed the province's militia but, in fact, his activities ranged from staff work to field duty, from the militia to British regulars, and from Upper to Lower Canada. After the war he reckoned he had been "personally engaged" with the enemy "upwards of thirty times."

At the outset Brock charged him with moving British forces to the threatened western frontier. Transport was a formidable problem which Nichol solved by pressing everything available, both civil and military, into service. In August he led 400 men to Detroit, where he was an enthusiastic supporter of Brock's audacious plan of attack. Indeed, his knowledge of the area proved invaluable to Brock, who recognized Nichol's services in both general orders and dispatches. The following month he acted as Brock's personal emissary to Governor Sir George Prevost*. During his absence Brock was killed at Queenston Heights. The province lost its commander, Nichol lost his patron. Returning to the province in November, he acquitted himself well in action on no fewer than three occasions that month. More important, perhaps, was his role – he claimed to have been "principally instrumental" – "in preventing the evacuation of Fort Erie . . . at a time when the moral effect . . . would have accelerated the ruin of the King's affairs in Upper Canada."

The burdens and pressing minutiae of his office plagued him. His running battles with the deputy commissary general, Edward Couche, whom he saw as an obstructionist, could be resolved satisfactorily only by the intervention of Brock's successor, Sir Roger Hale Sheaffe*. On one occasion Nichol exploded to his friend Thomas Talbot*, "Couche should be hanged." On 18 Dec. 1812 he complained that for more than a month he had not had "time even to see my own wife. . . . If I dont soon get leave to resign . . . I believe I shall go crazy." He did not, however: he cursed his fate out of momentary exasperation, not out of despair.

Meanwhile, there was a legislative session in the new year to prepare for, to say nothing of spring campaigning. The resumption of fighting with the American advance up the Niagara peninsula added the hardships of a field officer to the duties of staff officer and drew him as well into the councils of war. On 27 May 1813 he had his horse killed under him while acting as aide-de-camp during the American attack on Fort George. It was his counsel, he later insisted, that persuaded Brigadier-General John Vincent* to retreat to Burlington Heights (Hamilton) rather than Fort Erie. The decision to remain there rather than move farther eastward also, he claimed, stemmed from his suasion with senior officers. The wisdom of the withdrawal from Fort George was borne out by later events, particularly Lieutenant-Colonel John Harvey*'s successful attack upon the Americans at Stoney Creek in early June. Nichol's own summary of these events remains credible: "By this movement the Centre Division was placed in a strong and eligible position, its supplies were secured, and its communications with the right and left were completely re-established."

During the summer of 1813 Nichol was called upon to replace temporarily the wounded quartermaster general of the Centre Division. He was with Lieutenant-Colonel Cecil Bisshopp*'s force which raided Black Rock (Buffalo) on 11 July. Two months later he was ordered to open a new supply route from Burlington Heights to Major-General Henry PROCTER's force at Amherstburg. He did so successfully, returning to Burlington after Procter's defeat on 5 October at Moraviantown rendered the communication line unnecessary. The following month Nichol raised serious objections to Vincent's decision to retire with his force towards Kingston. The matter was referred to a council of senior officers who sided with Nichol. December witnessed the arrival of a successor to Vincent, Major-General Phineas Riall*, and a new commander, Lieutenant-General Gordon Drummond*. Nichol was highly recommended to both men. Drummond deliberated with him and Sir James Lucas Yeo* on the possibility of a winter campaign in the west, and in January 1814 Nichol prepared a logistical plan for such an operation.

February and March of 1814 were given over to a critical legislative session, dominated by Nichol. While managing the government's business in the daily sessions of the assembly, he also undertook a reorganization of the quartermaster general's department. In May, at Drummond's request, he drew up comprehensive plans for naval depots at Turkey Point and Penetanguishene. Nichol was again in the field during several engagements in August. On the 19th a serious shortage of flour threatened British forces in the Niagara peninsula. Drummond authorized Nichol and Thomas Dickson to use "their personal influence and exertions" to rectify the situation. Nichol later recalled that "in less than fourteen days all fears of want were removed." He remained on full service in his various capacities until March 1815. Then, although he lost both his pay and his allowance, he was required to spend another 90 days with the militia board of claims.

Nichol

For three years Nichol had worked tirelessly under the most taxing of conditions. But peace did not bring the laurels which he obviously deserved. The sparing amount of praise could be tolerated, the lack of financial compensation could not. On 14 May 1814 American marauders led by Abraham MARKLE had burned his home and enterprises, and his total losses were estimated at a staggering £6,684 (provincial currency). That October he had forwarded a claim to Colonial Secretary Lord Bathurst, but the home government was ill equipped to institute plans for immediate, large-scale compensation. In several other petitions and letters he depicted his plight: he had been "thrown upon the world – with his business lost – His Fortune ruined – & the means *he had possessed* of supporting His Family . . . destroyed." The omission of his name from the list of recipients for the Detroit medal was a blow as grievous as it was insulting.

Nichol marshalled numerous attestations of his service in "high and responsible" situations, including one from Drummond. Gore, whose assistance he solicited in 1816, wrote to Bathurst, "I can be no Judge of his Military Merits, . . . but I can speak to his general Talents, Zeal, and Ability in the Legislature, and am assured by competent Judges, that the same Qualifications were conspicuous in the Field, and in the conduct of the important Department of Quartermaster General." Disappointed at not receiving redress, Nichol went to England in June 1817 to petition Bathurst personally. He had "done More" than John NORTON, "who has got *Army Rank & a Pension.*" His services had been "More important" than those of Robert DICKSON, "who has got an order for lands and a Pension." Under the circumstances – "I have Sacrificed More to my publick duty and lost More from the War than all of them put together" – he was entitled to his opinion that the imperial government's award of a pension of £200 was niggardly.

By the war's end Nichol had, however, attained heights equalled by only a few in the colony. In addition to pursuing his military service and his business career, he had held a number of offices including municipal tax collector at Niagara (1802), justice of the peace (from 1806), and the usual commissions associated with the war years. His most impressive contribution to Upper Canadian society – his political career – had just begun. The legislative journals for the sessions of 1812, 1813, and 1815 are missing but the surviving ones for 1814 and 1816 attest to his pre-eminence during the sixth parliament (1812–16).

These two sessions were among the most controversial in Upper Canada's history, largely owing to the sullied reputation they acquired in William Lyon Mackenzie*'s published retrospect of 1833 upon the province's political past. In both sessions Nichol acted as the government's house leader, performing the task in a manner surpassed, if at all, only by John Beverley Robinson* in the 1820s. The role was probably self-appointed although a degree of consultation with the executive would have been essential to ensure a harmony of interest. The thrust of the 1814 session was defence and "every Strong Measure . . . was brought forward and Carried through," Nichol wrote, "*by Me.*" Under his guidance, procedural motions, amendments, and bills were moved through the assembly with dispatch. The cooperation sought by successive administrations in 1812 and 1813 and denied by the opposition led by Willcocks and Markle was at last won. Nichol had no sympathy with constitutional niceties when the province was in peril: on 22 Feb. 1814 he introduced, without any apparent qualms, the bill suspending habeas corpus. The old opposition, bereft of its leadership (Willcocks and Markle had gone over to the enemy), withered before the tough-minded Nichol; John Willson* cast the only dissenting vote. For Mackenzie the removal "of the last barrier between civil rule and military despotism" was Nichol's way of repaying the favours he owed the executive, a sorry chapter, he thought, in the history of civil liberties.

Of the 1816 session, perhaps the most renowned in reform lore, Mackenzie wrote that it had "Scarce a single redeeming feature." Notorious in his view for the assembly's fawning subservience to the executive, the session passed without serious incident or unfavourable comment by contemporaries. Gore certainly had good reason to be satisfied with Nichol's efforts: a civil list bill providing a permanent grant of £2,500, provision for a provincial agent in London and a provincial aide-de-camp, and the creation of a committee on inland navigation. With respect to the civil list bill, Nichol's motives were as self-serving as they were ingratiating; he did not hesitate to suggest to Colonial Office officials in 1817 that his compensation could be provided for "from that fund."

The opening of the seventh parliament (1817–20) – Nichol had been re-elected in Norfolk in 1816 – witnessed a striking reversal in his attitude towards the administration and Gore in particular. On the first day, 4 Feb. 1817, he gave dramatic notice of the change with a motion demanding that the lieutenant governor recognize "the rights and privileges of this House as amply as they are enjoyed by the House of Commons in Great Britain." Just how serious his opposition would become was not apparent until the end of the session. In a manner by then commonplace in popular assemblies, Nichol seized upon Gore's call for aid in defraying the costs of government to instigate a more general inquiry into the state of the province. Under his leadership the assembly went into a committee of the whole. Nichol introduced resolutions which, among other things, vilified the crown and clergy reserves as "insurmountable obstacles to the forming of a well-connected Settlement." A particularly contentious point was the policy of restricting immigration, especially from the United States. On 7 April, two days after Nichol had undertaken his sweeping attack upon the administration and imperial policy, an appalled Gore prorogued the assembly.

It was easy to question Nichol's motives. Mackenzie never quite believed in his sincerity, dismissing the action of this "mean sycophant" as "pretended" opposition. Gore reduced his conduct to a personal level; Nichol's "Apostacy" stemmed from "indignation" at not having received a Detroit medal and from Gore's refusal to provide "any special interference" on behalf of Nichol's war claims. There was, to be sure, a personal element to Nichol's new political direction. But, after all, there was nothing either new or unusual about his conduct. Private disappointments had a way of taking public – and moreover political – turns. This was the case with Willcocks, Mallory, and Robert RANDAL. And in each of these instances the transformation represented more than just an opportunity to vent, publicly, private spleen. Rather the personal experience entailed an altered perspective on the political vista. In the heat of debate contemporaries would throw up the seeming hypocrisy in Nichol's transformation from government to opposition man. But the decision never gave him any embarrassment and a mind as powerful as his was not blind to inconsistency. His explanation was simple: "When that character [Gore] insulted the House, and violated the Constitution, he felt it his duty to reprobate him and his corrupt advisers."

In so doing Nichol became the critical link between the pre-war and wartime opposition, which had been disgraced by the stigma of treason, and the opposition of the 1820s, associated principally with William Warren Baldwin*, John Rolph*, and Marshall Spring Bidwell*. Too little attention has been paid by historians to Nichol's role in legitimizing parliamentary opposition. Because of his ability, his earlier pro-administration stance, and his impeccable loyalty during the war, he could not, like Barnabas BIDWELL, be dismissed by opponents as a closet republican. In criticizing the administration, he adopted the traditional whiggish language of the 18th century. Ministerial responsibility had become an everyday notion in Great Britain by the 1760s. For far too long it has been assumed that in Upper Canada this idea was the exclusive property of the Baldwins and Robert Thorpe*, and that it derived from their Irish ancestors. When Nichol moved from being the administration's manager in the assembly to its principal opponent, he was sufficiently familiar with whig language to use it as the most appropriate justification for displacing irresponsible ministers and unpopular governors without being insurrectionary by attacking the crown.

The power of Nichol's opposition is apparent in John Strachan*'s delicacy and tact in attempting to persuade him from it. The rector of York tried unsuccessfully to mediate between Gore and Nichol in 1817. When Nichol returned from England with his pension the following year, Strachan reported rumours that Nichol had tried to "ingratiate himself" with the new lieutenant governor, Sir Peregrine Maitland*. But other rumours were also afloat, that Nichol would move a vote of censure against Gore and a motion asserting parliament's right to control land granting. Again Strachan intervened; this time, however, the fears were unfounded and Nichol confined his energies in 1819 to war relief, public accounts, and revenue-sharing agreements with Lower Canada, as well as to more political topics such as the prosecution of Robert Gourlay* and Bartemas FERGUSON for libel. His reputation, however, had been made. Maitland wondered aloud to the Colonial Office whether Nichol's pension was compatible with his opposition to government. In 1821 Governor-in-Chief Lord Dalhousie [Ramsay*] denounced him in his diary as "a violent opposition member."

It is difficult to determine Nichol's mental and emotional state from 1817 until his death. Certainly he was bitter about his difficulty with respect to his war losses and he had reason to be. His moods seemed to oscillate in a manner reminiscent of his first years as a merchant on his own. Always vain, he was even more wary of slights, real or imagined. Gore, he was sure, had in 1817 made "very unfavorable representations of My Conduct" to Bathurst; it was not true. On 2 March 1818 provincial agent William Halton wrote to a friend that "I have seen the Great Colonel Nichol once, & wished to have shewn him every Civilty in my Power, but he has cut me entirely & wont even answer my notes."

In Upper Canadian parlance, a "great man" was a figure of the first importance and, according to the Montreal merchant Isaac Todd*, Nichol had reached that status in the fall of 1812. But increasingly he became the butt of gibes juxtaposing stature with overweening pretensions. Even friends indulged in gentle mocking: Thomas Clark observed to a Scottish friend in 1818, "I learn you have seen our little Great man, Col. Nichol. He no doubt took plenty of your wine and gave you *talk* in proportion. He is a clever little fellow but excessively vain." Halton's dismissal of him as a "very mischievous unprincipled puppy" throwing "impediments in the way of public business" may be taken for what it is, the bleating of a courtier. Yet his labelling Nichol the "Demosthenes of Long Point" was, for all its jeering tone, not far from the mark as a comment on the man's oratorical powers.

Nichol's two major concerns from 1817 on were the constitution and the economy. For instance, he led over the course of several sessions the assault on the "obnoxious" Sedition Act of 1804, which had been used to expel Gourlay from the colony. He zealously guarded the privileges and prerogatives of the assembly; in his view, the speaker should have sufficient income "as would make him independent of any favours from government and would keep him free of all improper influence." He favoured the reporting of the debates but demanded controls which would "preserve the purity and dignity of the house, and the privilege of Parliament." During the depression of 1819–21 he derided the bloated civil list, excessive government pensions, and a rather useless provincial agent (the basic legislation for all of which he had introduced in 1816). He favoured a general retrenchment, with available money going not to courtiers but to those who deserved it, such as militiamen "who were dragged from their homes to be mutilated in defending their country for 6d. a day."

In 1820, during a stinging attack on the administration of the Common Schools Act of 1816, Nichol delivered a clear exposition of the doctrine of ministerial responsibility; in fact, he resurrected it single-handed from the disrepute in which it had been left by the pre-war opposition. According to a report of the debate in the *Kingston Chronicle*, he had "no intention of charging the head of the Government with malpractices, it was his advisers who were the responsible characters. He never would identify the Governor with the Executive – he had no intention to charge His Majesty, or the Prince Regent, with any such conduct; every person under them [however] was responsible. The king could do no wrong but wicked ministers lost their heads, and wicked and corrupt Governors were brought to trial. He had not the slightest intention to cast reflections upon the present Governor, whose conduct merited approbation – it was the base and wicked Executive, and the late Governor Gore." Small wonder an astonished James DURAND wondered that a man "who had passed fine eulogies on the characters of the Executive four or five years ago, should now attribute to it everything that was corrupt, wicked and unjust."

The opening of the eighth parliament in 1821 presented Nichol with a formidable challenge in the presence of Robinson in the assembly. Undaunted, Nichol gave notice of a bill "for securing the independence of the Commons House of Assembly." Little had changed: he pressed home the attack on the Sedition Act, assessment laws, and government revenues and expenditures. The attempt to unseat Barnabas Bidwell would, he thought, "violate the constitution," and preserving the constitution was more important than removing an immoral member. Although his opponents occasionally found a particular argument or stance absurd, they recognized his ability and formidable intellect. These gifts, combined with his oratorical skills and sporadic bursts of energy, made him more than a match for Robinson. "Without that little animal," Robinson moaned, "all would certainly be harmony."

For the administration, Nichol was at his most productive when dealing with his second great interest, the economy. Commercial depression, the strangulation of government finances as a result of the collapse of the revenue-sharing agreement with Lower Canada, and the lack of internal development gave a bleak cast to the future. With the province on the verge of bankruptcy, Nichol became a ruthless advocate of retrenchment, particularly in government offices. In 1821 he chaired the select committee on internal resources, struck at Baldwin's insistence, to examine the agricultural depression and collapse of British markets. Tabled on 31 March and printed on 4 April, this important report, the first of its kind in the province, provided a framework for the sort of provincial economic development espoused by men such as John Macaulay*. In the report, timber and furs were neglected in favour of wheat and flour production and a commercial strategy aimed at giving these products preferred entry to British and West Indian markets. More important, Nichol, who wrote the report, recommended "permanent measures" for relieving the stricken economy, especially the "improvement of our inland navigation . . . on an extensive scale, a scale commensurate with the increasing power and rapidly accumulating commercial resources of the Province." Unobstructed navigation from Lake Erie to the ocean was the ultimate goal. Robinson considered the report "comprehensive," and urged Macaulay to use the columns of the *Kingston Chronicle* to commend it.

One of its far-reaching consequences was the establishment of a commission on the improvement of internal navigation. This body, which began its work in the spring of 1821, would have been a natural appointment for Nichol. He declined it, however, with the "utmost regret." His finances were on the verge of "collapse, so much so that he had accepted a position to settle the affairs of Robert Hamilton's estate and was totally preoccupied by that duty. Early in 1822, however, he preferred his services and was appointed a commissioner on 25 February. Nichol threw himself into the effort, making a singular contribution to the commission.

Late that year he came out in support of the British government's plan for a union of the Canadas. This measure offered, he thought, the "only constitutional remedy" to the upper province's economic plight. Unlike most of the project's advocates, he was alive to the political need to preserve the parliamentary rights contained in the Constitutional Act of 1791. He exclaimed that "Money in comparison with constitutional right was a dross," and hoped that the assemblymen would not "barter their liberty for a mess of pottage."

Nichol never recovered from his war losses – the award of £4,202 10s. for his claim came too late; it was only announced a month after his death. The milling complex was rebuilt (some of it in his lifetime) but the loss of income was a permanent blow to his fortunes and probably to his emotional state as well. In March 1824 he was reduced to imploring Maitland for the petty appointment of surrogate judge of the Niagara District. The government complied. But the job which he hoped would be his salvation would in fact be his end. On 3 May 1824 Nichol left his residence at Stamford (Niagara Falls) – he had moved there by 1821 – to travel to Niagara on the business of the court. As he was returning late that night his horse and wagon went over the precipice below Queenston Heights. "A more ghastly spectacle could not well be conceived," one witness testified to the coroner's jury, the foreman of which was Mackenzie, who thought that Nichol was drunk at the time. The jury ruled out the possibility of foul play. Nichol was buried three days later in the Hamilton burying ground at Queenston in an unmarked grave. The funeral oration was delivered by Robert ADDISON, who eulogized Nichol as a man whose "general acquaintance with the usages of Parliament, with commerce, and the policy of nations, gave him a weight which few possessed; nor will we soon see his like again."

It is difficult to gauge the ability of a man in another time but there is no doubt Nichol had few peers. In a commemorative ceremony at Vittoria, with full masonic honours, Rolph extolled Nichol as a tribune of the people, "alive to every encroachment upon public liberty and the zealous advocate of religious freedom." Strachan was dumbfounded: "Poor Nichols dreadful fate shocked me exceedingly and his death at this time I consider a public loss he was returning to a better feeling and it was in our power to have made him useful – he had good parts and at times great industry and if his judgment was deficient yet it was easy to set it in many things right." Robinson could "scarcely persuade myself he has ceased to *be* – and that all his Canal projects and other speculations supported . . . by piles of papers & volume of calculations are cut off short." The most compelling testimony was written by Robinson in 1846. Nichol was a "singular little man – [who] squinted horribly . . . & had but a slender portion of personal beauty . . . He was really an extraordinary person – naturally eloquent – possessing a prodigious memory – [and] great spirit. . . . He had foibles enough too poor fellow, among which was the most egregious vanity, which however impelled him . . . to do many useful and brilliant things. . . . he became the leader of the opposition & gave infinite trouble – to no one more than to myself . . . but his good qualities out-numbered his faults."

ROBERT LOCHIEL FRASER

[Robert Nichol has been poorly served by historians. When he is mentioned at all, references have almost always been incidental. The first serious notice of him was E. A. Cruikshank*'s "A sketch of the public life and services of Robert Nichol, a member of the Legislative Assembly and quartermaster general of the militia of Upper Canada," *OH*, 19 (1922): 10–18. More comfortable with printing documents than with analysing them, Cruikshank prepared two compilations, "Some letters of Robert Nichol," *OH*, 20 (1923): 41–74, and "Additional correspondence of Robert Nichol," *OH*, 26 (1930): 37–96, which remain the starting-point for historical inquiry.

To date, no collection of private papers has come to light. References of varying degrees of importance are found scattered through many manuscript and record groups for the period. The most pertinent to this study are the following: at the AO, the Macaulay papers (MS 78) for 1821 to 1824; the Rolph papers (MS 533), ser.D; the F. B. Tupper papers (MU 3027); and Nichol's will in RG 22, ser.155. Although fewer references are to be found in the James Givins and W. D. Powell papers at the MTL, they are quite interesting. The collections of the Norfolk Hist. Soc. at the Eva Brook Donly Museum in Simcoe, Ont. (mfm. at PAC and AO), contain several mentions of Nichol, but, in general, they are disappointing. Much richer, indeed fundamental, for his career are the government records at the PAC. Here, RG 1, L3; RG 5, A1; RG 8, I (C ser.); RG 9, I; RG 19, E5(a), 3747, claim 509; and RG 68 are the most important; the Clark(e) family papers (MG 24, B130) are also worth consulting. PRO, CO 42 is essential. For Nichol's early career the John Askin papers in the DPL, Burton Hist. Coll., are without equal. Much of this material has been published in the *John Askin papers* (Quaife).

Of published primary materials, next in importance are the "Journals of Legislative Assembly of U.C." for 1814 to 1824, in AO *Report*, 1912–14. Heretofore unused for Nichol's political career are the newspaper reports of the assembly debates. Newspapers consulted for this as well as other aspects of his career include: *Colonial Advocate*, 1824–33; *Gleaner, and Niagara Newspaper*, 1824; *Gore Gazette, and Ancaster, Hamilton, Dundas and Flamborough Advertiser* (Ancaster, [Ont.]), 25 Aug. 1827; *Kingston Chronicle*, 1819–24; *Kingston Gazette*, 1816–18; *Niagara Herald* (Niagara [Niagara-on-the-Lake, Ont.]), 6 March 1802; *Upper Canada Guardian; or, Freeman's Journal* (Niagara), available issues; and *Weekly Register* (York [Toronto]), 1823. Strachan's *Letter book* (Spragge) is useful. *Docs. relating to constitutional hist., 1791–1818* (Doughty and McArthur), 425–27, and *1819–28* (Doughty and Story), 1–5, 159–60, highlight Nichol's political forays of constitutional interest. Other references may be found in *1812 Woodhouse Township census, with related documents (1814–1836)* . . . , ed. W. R. Yeager (2nd ed., Simcoe, 1978), 4; Ramsay, *Dalhousie journals* (Whitelaw), 2: 74; and "Claims for losses, 1812–15," PAC *Report*, 1897, note B: 47–56.

Bruce G. Wilson's study, *Enterprises of Robert Hamilton*, is the best work on the political-economic world in which Nichol first found his niche. R. L. Fraser, "Like Eden in her summer dress: gentry, economy, and society in Upper Canada, 1812–1840" (PHD thesis, Univ. of Toronto, 1979), places Nichol's critical report on internal resources within the framework of an emerging strategy for provincial economic development and assesses its importance to that strategy. For the 18th-century background of Nichol's constitutionalism, John Brewer's *Party ideology and popular politics at the accession of George III* (Cambridge, Eng., 1976) is required reading, particularly the chapter on ministerial responsibility. A useful discussion of that concept and of responsible government in the context of Lower Canada and the career of Pierre-Stanislas BÉDARD is J. L. Finlay, "The state of a reputation: Bédard as a constitutionalist," *Journal of Canadian Studies* (Peterborough, Ont.), 20 (1985–86), no.4: 60–76. R.L.F.]

NOËL, MARIE-GENEVIÈVE (Drapeau), seigneur and landowner; b. 13 Jan. 1766 in Saint-Antoine-de-Tilly, Que., daughter of Jean-Baptiste Noël, a seigneur, and Geneviève Dussaut; d. 17 Nov. 1829 at Quebec.

Marie-Geneviève Noël was only 16 when on 14 Oct. 1782 at Saint-Antoine-de-Tilly she married Joseph Drapeau*, a man 14 years her senior. He lost no time in carving an enviable place for himself in the business world at Quebec, becoming a merchant, shipbuilder, and major landowner, and at his death on 3 Nov. 1810 he left a sizeable estate to his wife. In particular she came into possession of a considerable fortune in land: the seigneuries of Lessard, Nicolas-Rioux, Rimouski, Mitis, Pachot, Sainte-Claire, Rivière-du-Gouffre, and half of Île-d'Orléans, and numerous other rural and urban land and properties, as well as two shipbuilding yards, one at Quebec, the other at Baie-Saint-Paul. The 44-year-old heiress was obliged to respect the clauses in her husband's will which required that the estate be kept undivided and which specifically forbad any request for an inventory or deed of sharing.

Unlike the status of a married woman, who at the time had only restricted rights since she was subject to her husband's authority, status as a widow conferred numerous possibilities. Indeed, the Coutume de Paris, which was in force in the colony, gave a widow the same rights as a male who was of age. Henceforth Marie-Geneviève Drapeau could manage her properties without any man being able to exercise authority over her.

Mme Drapeau decided to give up the retail business and the shipbuilding. In January 1811 she considered leasing the roomy house where she lived on Rue du Sault-au-Matelot, with its cellar, attic, bakehouse, sheds, stables, and wharf; she found a taker for it in February of the following year. In December 1815 she leased it again, this time to merchant Rémi Quirouet, who paid her an annual rent of £250. Three years later she concluded a large transaction with Quebec merchant Benjamin Tremain, whom she let have seven lots in Lower Town for £3,530. She reinvested her capital in four properties in the *faubourg* Saint-Jean, where she went to live. Cautious and sensible, she invested in real estate and did not hesitate to go to court to uphold her rights. In 1819, for example, she learned that part of the lot her husband had bought from the nuns of the Hôtel-Dieu in 1803 was to be sold by order of the government, to the prejudice of the owner, for the extension of Rue Saint-Paul. The lot was subsequently sold by the crown to another individual, John Bell, in November 1820, despite her protests. She therefore brought an action and, although she never knew the outcome, it was settled in favour of her heirs in 1832.

As her husband had done, Marie-Geneviève Drapeau entrusted management of the seigneuries to notaries or stewards. Her brothers-in-law Louis Bélair at Baie-Saint-Paul and Augustin Trudel at Rimouski also continued working for her as seigneurial agents. However, she ran her share in the seigneury of Île-d'Orléans herself, attending to such matters as leasing the mills. In 1816 she entrusted administration of Rivière-du-Gouffre and Île-d'Orléans to her daughter Luce-Gertrude. Then in 1827 she gave Luce-Gertrude power of attorney, with full authority to administer the entire seigneurial patrimony owned by the Drapeau family. None the less Marie-Geneviève Drapeau remained attentive to the management of the real estate. For example, it was she who leased out the fisheries at Rivière-du-Gouffre, granted leases for cutting wood on Mitis to William Price*, and negotiated with Pierre Tremblay the terms for building a flour-mill at Baie-Saint-Paul.

In October 1829 Mme Drapeau, being in poor health, drew up a will leaving her property to her six daughters, to be divided equally among them. She died the following month and was buried on 20 November in Notre-Dame cathedral at Quebec in the presence of Joseph-François Perrault*, Amable Berthelot*, Etienne-Claude Lagueux, and Michel Clouet*, among others. Her daughters continued to manage the family fortune and apparently discharged their task in an intelligent manner.

CÉLINE CYR

ANQ-Q, CE1-1, 20 nov. 1829; CE1-94, 30 janv. 1766, 14 oct. 1782; CN1-16, 12 nov. 1822; 31 mai, 21 oct. 1824; CN1-116, 22 sept. 1820; 5 juill., 27 sept. 1827; 25 janv., 21 nov. 1828; CN1-178, 19 févr., 28 avril 1812; 13 août 1814; 22 déc. 1815; 7 oct. 1816; CN1-230, 28 févr., 6 mai, 8 juill. 1811; 16 août 1815; 5 mai 1818; 23 mai 1822; P1000-32-592. *Quebec Gazette*, 10 Jan., 6 June 1811; 19 Oct., 2 Nov. 1815; 6 March 1817; 4, 11 March 1819. Bouchette, *Topographical description of L.C.* P.-G. Roy, *Inv. concessions.* J. W. M., "Notes sur les seigneuries du district de Rimouski," *BRH*, 17 (1911): 237–46, 257–67, 312–20, 331–38, 353–68.

NOLIN, JEAN-BAPTISTE, fur trader and militia officer; b. *c.* 1742; d. August 1826 in St Boniface (Man.).

Nolin

Jean-Baptiste Nolin first came to prominence in 1777 when in partnership with Venance Lemaire, *dit* Saint-Germain, he purchased the trading post at Michipicoten (Michipicoten River, Ont.) from Alexander HENRY the elder for 15,000 *livres*. The partners employed four or five men there for the next three years. Because the American revolution disrupted shipments of trade goods from Montreal, the business was only moderately successful. By 1781 Nolin had given up the post and gone to Michilimackinac (Mackinac Island, Mich.). For several years he travelled between Michilimackinac and Sault Ste Marie (Mich.), finally settling at the Sault by the late 1780s.

During the next 30 years Nolin and fur trader John JOHNSTON dominated the economic and social life of the Sault, gateway to the upper country. Nolin was the agent there for the North West Company, acting as middleman for shipments from Montreal, and providing salted fish for voyageurs and for settlers at Michilimackinac and Detroit. In 1806 the Michilimackinac Company [*see* John Ogilvy*] took over the NWC's role of furnishing Nolin with trade goods and Nolin probably acted as its agent. In the early 1790s NWC clerk John McDonald* of Garth, visiting the Sault, referred to Nolin and Johnston as "the principal persons here." Like Johnston, Nolin married an Ojibwa. His wife, Marie-Angélique, was the daughter of voyageur Joseph-Victor Couvret and Marie-Charlotte, a Sault Ojibwa. Some of the Métis offspring of both the Nolin and Johnston families were educated in Montreal. In 1794, through the influence of his wife, Nolin acquired a large strip of land at Sault Ste Marie, adjacent to the rear of the old fort built in 1752 by Louis Legardeur* de Repentigny.

During the War of 1812 the population at the Sault followed the example of most traders and Indians in the *pays d'en haut* by siding with the British. Johnston, Nolin, and Charles Oakes ERMATINGER were appointed militia captains. Because of illness, Nolin did not participate in the assault led by Captain Charles Roberts* on the American post at Michilimackinac in July 1812, but two of his sons went along in command of Ojibwa warriors. In reports of the action, Augustin Nolin was praised for keeping order among the Indians.

Gabriel Franchère* visited the Sault in the summer of 1814 and mentioned that both Johnston and Nolin lived on the south, or American side, of the St Marys River. Nolin had at that time three sons and three daughters; one of the girls was "passably pretty." Franchère was impressed with Nolin's home, furniture, and other marks of prosperity. Ermatinger lived on the north side of the river, in a house belonging to Nolin.

Lord Selkirk [Douglas*] met Nolin at the Sault in 1816, and for some years afterwards urged him and his family to move to the Red River settlement (Man.). Nolin's son Louis served as interpreter at Red River from 1815 to 1817, and by 1818 he and his brother Augustin, now both there, reported to Lord Selkirk that their father was considering the idea. Selkirk wrote to Alexander MACDONELL, administrator of the colony, that "such a Settler must be a great acquisition" and he went far beyond his normal practices, showering the Nolin family with inducements. Jean-Baptiste would be given a "free hand" in setting up a trading post, and several Nolins were promised land grants, including a home "as close to the church as possible." Before leaving for England in November 1818, Selkirk wrote to fur trader Robert DICKSON, stating that Nolin's decision to move to Red River was firm. "I am particularly desirous that he should meet with no impediment in conveying in so fine a lot of daughters, who may help to fix some of our Meurons more firmly to the soil of R.R."

Nolin sold his Sault interests to Ermatinger and in 1819 moved his family to the Selkirk colony, to the post at Pembina (N.Dak.). Selkirk died in 1820, but his promises to the Nolin family were honoured. Jean-Baptiste and Augustin received their land grants, and Louis again served as interpreter. When a resolution of respect for the late Earl of Selkirk was passed at Fort Daer (Pembina) early in 1821, Jean-Baptiste and Augustin Nolin were among the notables who signed.

By 1823 events had altered life in the Red River settlement. The NWC had become part of the Hudson's Bay Company in 1821, bringing an end to their ruinous quarrels. John Halkett*, administrator of the Selkirk estate, closed the HBC post at Pembina, now in United States territory, in order to concentrate the settlers on British land to the north and to protect them from the Sioux. Most of the Métis at Pembina, including the Nolin family, moved north to St Boniface.

In August 1826 Francis Heron, an HBC employee at Fort Garry (Winnipeg), reported that "Old Nolin is at length become a *lodger* with the Bishop." For the past few years, Roman Catholic bishop Joseph-Norbert Provencher* had urged Nolin's daughter Angélique to become a teacher of the local Métis, but Nolin was opposed. In a letter to Archbishop Joseph-Octave PLESSIS of Quebec in early 1826 Provencher explained Nolin's resistance: "He has all sorts of petty excuses, but above all he does not wish that his daughter be a servant. It is certainly not the status that I wish to give her."

Having resisted to the end, Nolin died at Provencher's home in August 1826 and was buried on 23 August; his age was given as 84. With Nolin out of the way, Provencher's hopes became reality. In 1829 the first school for girls in western Canada was opened at St Boniface, with Angélique and Marguerite Nolin as teachers. The students were mostly daughters of French and Cree or Ojibwa parents.

Nooth

The Nolin family was prominent on the Red River frontier in economic, political, and educational activities. One of Jean-Baptiste's grandsons, Charles Nolin*, was a power in the Red River troubles of 1869–70, but disagreed with Metis leader Louis Riel* over the use of violence during the North-West rebellion of 1885.

DONALD CHAPUT

DPL, Burton Hist. Coll., William Woodbridge papers. PAC, MG 19, E1, ser.1, 15, 22, 78. *Les bourgeois de la Compagnie du Nord-Ouest* (Masson). [James] Hargrave, *The Hargrave correspondence, 1821–1843*, ed. G. P. de T. Glazebrook (Toronto, 1938). *HBRS*, 2 (Rich and Fleming). *Journals of Samuel Hearne and Philip Turnor*, ed. J. B. Tyrrell (Toronto, 1934; repr. New York, 1968). "The Mackinac register," ed. R. G. Thwaites, Wis., State Hist. Soc., *Coll.*, 18 (1908): 476; 19 (1910): 53. U.S., Congress, *American state papers: documents, legislative and executive, of the Congress of the United States* . . . (38v. in 10 groups, Washington, 1832–61), group 8, vol.5: 255–56. A.-G. Morice, *Dictionnaire historique des Canadiens et des Métis français de l'Ouest* (Québec et Montréal, 1908); *Histoire de l'Église catholique dans l'Ouest canadien, du lac Supérieur au Pacifique (1659–1905)* (3v., Winnipeg et Montréal, 1912). A. [E. S.] Martin, *The Hudson's Bay Company's land tenures and the occupation of Assiniboia by Lord Selkirk's settlers, with a list of grantees under the earl and the company* (London, 1898). Télesphore Saint-Pierre, *Histoire des Canadiens du Michigan et du comté d'Essex, Ontario* (Montréal, 1895). Joseph Tassé, *Les Canadiens de l'Ouest* (2v., Montréal, 1878). Donald Chaput, "The 'Misses Nolin' of Red River," *Beaver*, outfit 306 (winter 1975): 14–17.

NOOTH, JOHN MERVIN, physician, army officer, and scientist; baptized 5 Sept. 1737 in Sturminster Newton, England, eldest son of Henry Nooth, apothecary, and Bridget Mervin; appears to have married twice, the second time to Elizabeth ——, and he had two sons and at least one daughter; d. 3 May 1828 in Bath, England.

John Mervin Nooth entered the University of Edinburgh in 1762 or 1763 and graduated MD in 1766; his thesis was a study of rickets. His family clearly was well-to-do, and in 1769–70 Nooth was able to follow the fashionable custom of spending a year touring the Continent. He evidently pursued scientific studies thereafter, since he was elected to the Royal Society of London on 13 March 1774, having been nominated by Benjamin Franklin and the anatomist William Hunter among others, and was admitted 11 days later. He had previously communicated a note to the society on an improved construction of an electrical machine. In 1775 he published in the society's *Philosophical Transactions* his most important contribution to science, "The description of an apparatus for impregnating water with fixed air." Fixed air was the 18th-century term for carbon dioxide. This paper caused a dispute between Nooth and the celebrated scientist Joseph Priestley over the design of Priestley's pioneering apparatus in the field, but Priestley himself eventually acknowledged the superiority of Nooth's device. Nooth's apparatus was widely employed for some decades to produce fixed air, which among many uses was highly regarded as a therapeutic agent. His suggestion that his method would permit the production of artificial spring waters, thus saving patients the expense of visiting distant spas, proved unsuccessful in practice, but it presaged the now ubiquitous carbonated beverage industry.

In October 1775, after the outbreak of the American revolution, Nooth was appointed both physician extraordinary and purveyor in the medical service of the British army in North America; he took up his posts at New York in the autumn. This combination of positions was unusual and suggests an influential patron. On 10 April 1779 he became superintendent general of hospitals for the British forces in North America. The medical department was racked with discord, and Nooth's position of high responsibility was intended to allow him to overcome difficulties, which he had some success in accomplishing. He held the post until 1783 when, the revolution over, he left America with the last units of the British army; he went on half pay on 6 Feb. 1784. In London by April 1784, Nooth invented an instrument for the giving of artificial respiration. A contemporary medical writer described the inventor as "a gentleman distinguished as much for liberality as genius, to whom the Arts are indebted for several valuable inventions, which are commonly attributed to others."

Nooth was placed on full pay some time in 1788 and in late summer was sent to Quebec as superintendent general of hospitals. He acquired the reputation of a superior physician, and was sought out by such distinguished patients as Governor Lord Dorchester [Guy Carleton*], Lieutenant Governor John Graves Simcoe* of Upper Canada, and Prince Edward* Augustus, the future Duke of Kent and Strathearn. Indeed Edward, who was in Halifax, had Nooth sent there in 1798 expressly to treat him for a severe leg injury sustained in a fall from a horse, because "Nooth is I believe justly considered the first professional man on this continent." Nooth helped to investigate the Baie-Saint-Paul malady, which was creating serious health problems in the 1780s [see James Bowman*]. He concurred in the general opinion of local physicians that the disease was probably a variant of syphilis and devised remedies that were thought to be helpful by contemporary authorities. In 1795 he testified before the Lower Canadian House of Assembly about the importation of contagious diseases into the colony on ocean vessels. His interest in medical discovery and the trust he inspired in others are indicated by his involvement in an agreement between one of his colleagues, Dr George Longmore*, and the Roman Catholic priest Pierre-Joseph Compain*, by which Longmore acquired a secret cure for cankers.

In addition to his official duties as the senior army medical officer in Canada and his activities as a practitioner, Nooth pursued numerous scientific interests. In the summer of 1792 he was visited for three days by the French botanist André Michaux*, who was on an expedition to Lower Canada; Michaux was impressed by a number of his inventions. Nooth was a regular correspondent of Sir Joseph Banks*, to whom he sent samples of many indigenous plants, including *Zizania aquatica* (wild rice). He made meteorological studies, examined mineral springs, and pointed out variations in the position of the magnetic pole.

Nooth also had a strong interest in the economic, social, and political situation in Lower Canada and wrote at length about it to Banks. He worried about the spread of revolutionary principles by the Americans, "who lately have taken upon them the kind office of debauching the good people of the Colony who are & I am sorry to say it, too much disposed to listen to those diabolical doctrines which have been lately propagated by the French Nation." He thus approved both the passage of an alien act to clear the colony of "French Emissaries" and the exemplary execution of David McLane* in 1797, which together "have greatly check'd the spirit of Democracy amongst us." He chafed at the want of economic development despite the colony's natural advantages and a healthy climate, unrivalled in the United States. "If this country was inhabited by an intelligent set of people," he fumed, "it would very soon become important." In 1790 he was a director of the Agriculture Society of Quebec, which had been founded the previous year to promote the commercialization of the colony's agriculture through the introduction of the most recent scientific practices in crop cultivation and animal husbandry. He reproached the Canadians for not exploiting the Labrador fisheries more fully and conducted experiments to find an improved method of extracting oil from white porpoise blubber. On the other hand he praised the Canadians for leaving no part of a carcass unused and declared their method of soap manufacture far superior to European practices.

Land granting, immigration, and settlement were also among Nooth's preoccupations. He approved Simcoe's policy of opening wide to Americans the door of Upper Canada and expected that the resulting immigrants would "greatly increase the internal Strength of this Country" and counterbalance the disaffected Canadians. In Lower Canada he was strongly critical of the Executive Council in its dispute with Governor Robert Prescott* over land-granting policy. He argued that the council's refusal to issue patents on land already applied for, and in some cases

occupied, was causing financial stress to *bona fide* colonizers, such as William Berczy*, a personal friend, whom he would be instrumental in having released from debtor's prison in 1799. As a participant in the war against the Americans from 1775 to 1783, Nooth was himself entitled to a grant of crown land in Lower Canada. He made numerous proposals for other grants individually and in company with associates. In November 1802, as a leader according to the system of township leaders and associates [see Samuel Gale*], he received a patent on 23,100 acres of land in Thetford Township. He also owned land in William Henry (Sorel).

In 1790 Nooth had purchased two adjoining lots on Rue Saint-Louis, Quebec, and he established his residence on them. Five years later his household counted three Protestants and four Roman Catholics, the latter probably servants. From 1797 Nooth mysteriously became increasingly ill, and in 1799 he requested permission to return to England. In July he sold his house to John Hale* for £1,500, a price that indicates he had been living in some luxury. He left Quebec at the end of the month and took up residence on Quebec Street, London. Soon after, he coughed up a lead bullet; it had apparently lain in a glass of wine that he had hurriedly finished off and had become lodged in his bronchial tree. Following his recovery, Nooth was physician to the Duke of Kent's household from 1800 until the duke's death in 1820. Nooth went to Gibraltar about 1804; three years later he was placed on half pay and returned to England. He maintained scientific contact with Lower Canada for some time through correspondence with Jean-Baptiste Lahaille*, professor at the Séminaire de Québec. Nooth died at Bath, where he had been living probably since at least 1819, and was buried in the rural parish of Bathampton on 10 May 1828.

Nooth's apparatus of 1775 remained in common use through most of his lifetime and was still on sale in pharmacies in the mid 19th century. Thousands were exported from Britain. In December 1846 the chemist Peter Squire made of its bottom chamber the essential part of a vaporizer he invented to administer ether in one of the first operations to employ general anaesthesia.

CHARLES G. ROLAND

In addition to his doctoral thesis, "Tentamen medicum inaugurale de rachidite . . . ," submitted in 1766 to the University of Edinburgh, John Mervin Nooth wrote at least two articles: "The description of an apparatus for impregnating water with fixed air; and of the manner of conducting that process," Royal Soc. of London, *Philosophical Trans.* (London), 65 (1775): 59–66; and "Case of a disease of the chest from a leaden shot accidentally passing through the glottis into the trachea," Soc. for the Improvement of Medical and Chirurgical Knowledge, *Trans.* (London), 3

Norton

(1812): 1–6. Nooth's letters to Sir Joseph Banks, which are held at the Bibliothèque de la Ville de Montréal, Salle Gagnon, were edited and published by Jacques Rousseau in *Le Naturaliste canadien* (Québec), 58 (1931): 139–47, 170–77, as "Lettres du Dr J. M. Nooth à Sir Joseph Banks." William Berczy did a portrait of Nooth but its location is unknown.

ANQ-Q, CN1-83, 16 avril 1790; CN1-256, 13, 21 juill. 1799. AUM, P 58, U, Nooth to [Berczy], 5 Dec. 1799. PAC, RG 1, L3^L: 2455–58; RG 8, I (C ser.), 279. PRO, PROB 11/1742/371; WO 7/96. Somerset Record Office (Taunton, Eng.), Bathampton, Reg. of burials, 10 May 1828. William Berczy, "William von Moll Berczy," ANQ *Rapport*, 1940–41: 23. *Corr. of Lieut. Governor Simcoe* (Cruikshank), 1: 159. "Les dénombrements de Québec" (Plessis), ANQ *Rapport*, 1948–49: 22, 72, 122. "Le duc de Kent: à quelle date faut-il assigner son départ définitif du Canada?" Montarville Boucher de La Bruère, édit., *BRH*, 25 (1919): 367–76. Gwillim, *Diary of Mrs Simcoe* (Robertson; 1911). L.C., House of Assembly, *Journals*, 1823, app.T. André Michaux, "Portions of the journal of André Michaux, botanist, written during his travels in the United States and Canada, 1785 to 1796 . . . ," ed. C. S. Sargent, American Philosophical Soc., *Proc.* (Philadelphia), 26 (1889): 72. Joseph Priestley, *Experiments and observations on different kinds of air* (3v., London, 1774–77), 2: 265–76. William Smith, *The diary and selected papers of Chief Justice William Smith, 1784–1793*, ed. L. F. S. Upton (2v., Toronto, 1963–65), 1: 46. F. X. Swediaur, *Practical observations on the more obstinate and inveterate venereal complaints; to which are added, an account of a new venereal disease which has lately appeared in Canada, and a pharmacopœia syphilitica . . .* (3rd ed., Edinburgh, 1788). Isaac Weld, *Travels through the states of North America, and the provinces of Upper and Lower Canada, during the years 1795, 1796, and 1797* (4th ed., 2v., London, 1807), 1: 384. *Bath Chronicle* (Bath, Eng.), 8 May 1828. *Quebec Gazette*, 16 Oct. 1788, 15 Aug. 1799. William Johnston, *Roll of commissioned officers in the medical service of the British army . . .* (Aberdeen, Scot., 1917), 47. John Andre, *William Berczy, co-founder of Toronto; a sketch* ([Toronto, 1967]), 53. Gabriel Nadeau, "Un savant anglais à Québec à la fin du XVIIIe siècle: le docteur John-Mervin Nooth," *L'Union médicale du Canada* (Montréal), 74 (1945): 49–74. P.-G. Roy, "Une vieille maison de Québec, le commissariat," *BRH*, 48 (1942): 362–64. David Zuck, "Dr Nooth and his apparatus; the role of carbon dioxide in medicine in the late eighteenth century," *British Journal of Anæsthesia* (London), 50 (1978): 393–405.

NORTON, JOHN (Snipe, Teyoninhokarawen), schoolmaster, Indian Department interpreter, Mohawk chief, army officer, and author; b. probably in Scotland, the son of a Scottish mother named Anderson and a Cherokee father named Norton; fl. 1784–1825.

The date of John Norton's birth is not known. His father had come from the Cherokee nation, "having been taken, a boy, from Kuwoki, when that village was burnt by the English," according to one report. His mother was an Anderson who was probably living near Dunfermline, Scotland, when their son John was born. It is also probable that the son received his education in a good school in Dunfermline, and in a print shop, perhaps his father's. The letters, speeches, and journal which John composed later show that he had had good training in the writing of English.

He came to Canada as a private soldier. The muster rolls of the 65th Foot record his enlistment at Mullingar (Republic of Ireland) early in 1784. He arrived in the province of Quebec with the regiment in the following year and accompanied it to Fort Niagara (near Youngstown, N.Y.) in 1787. There he deserted. In 1788 he received his discharge.

Norton then appears, in the records of the Society for the Propagation of the Gospel, as a schoolmaster in the Mohawk settlement established by John Deserontyon* at the Bay of Quinte. Norton found "teaching school too tedious, and confinement . . . more than he could bear," recalled one acquaintance, adding that "he associated with the young Indians in all their diversions." Norton resigned in 1791.

He next went to the old northwest to become a fur trader, employed by John Askin* of Detroit, evidently from 1791 until 1795. After Anthony Wayne's defeat of the western Indians at the battle of Fallen Timbers in 1794, Norton returned to the Upper Canadian side and became an interpreter in the Indian Department at Niagara.

Captain Joseph Brant [Thayendanegea*] soon drew Norton into his own service as an interpreter, made him an emissary, and adopted him as a "nephew," deputy, and successor. Norton resigned from the Indian Department and began living at Onondaga on the Grand River. His appointment as Teyoninhokarawen, a rank as a chieftain for diplomacy and leadership in war, came in 1799. It did not make him a hereditary chief; it gave him, as Joseph Brant's rank also did, a challenged, but strong, position between the chiefs and the Indian Department. Norton was soon acting in what he called "a public capacity without incurring blame" when he defended the cause of the Six Nations. He was, however, rejected by some of the chiefs when the Indian Department under William CLAUS, the deputy superintendent general of Indian affairs in Upper Canada, actively opposed, through channels of Upper Canadian officialdom, Norton's claims to speak for the Grand River Indians.

In the early 1800s Norton and Brant revived claims on behalf of the Six Nations for deeds to Grand River lands. After the American revolution the Six Nations had been invited to settle in what became Upper Canada on a vast tract of land. But the extent of the lands and the nature of the title had soon been called into question. Brant insisted that the grant allowed the Indians to sell off portions of land to white settlers. Officials in Upper Canada maintained that the Royal Proclamation of 1763 denied the validity of such purchases by white people. Not all the Grand River

Iroquois agreed with Brant on this matter. Free certified ownership by Indians was the issue.

Brant decided to go over the heads of Upper Canadian officials and to appeal to the Privy Council of Britain. With considerable secrecy, he sent Norton to plead the case in London. Norton was, in fact, eager to go because he wished to enlist in the British army for service in the war which had been declared against France. He set out for Britain in February 1804. His hopes for enlistment failed, and his mission to the government brought only disappointment when Claus through Lieutenant Governor Francis Gore* informed the British that some councils of the Six Nations had denied Norton's authority and that Norton was disreputable and unworthy.

Norton's trip from 1804 to 1806, nevertheless, was a personal triumph, for his character and potential were recognized by leaders of the evangelical missionary movement which was active at this time. His closest friends were members of the Society of Friends: the scientist William Allen and the Philadelphia-born brewer Robert Barclay. Through Barclay, Norton became associated on friendly terms with the members of the famous "Clapham sect," who founded the British and Foreign Bible Society in 1804, the year of Norton's arrival in Britain.

These parliamentarians and philanthropists were vigorously working for abolition of the slave trade and for the extension of Christian missions. They converted Norton, the discouraged political petitioner, to their humanitarian cause, sought his advice regarding the condition of North American Indians, and employed him as a translator. Indeed, the first application of the new bible society's funds for printing a portion of the Scriptures in a foreign language went to Norton's translation of the Gospel of St John into Mohawk. Two thousand copies were printed in English and Mohawk, but his introductory address to his own people was not published because the society's rules forbad supplements to the text. He was entrusted with 500 copies for circulation in the Canadas.

His friends sent him home in style: passage on a frigate of the Royal Navy was arranged for him by high-ranking officers in that service. He was now a changed man, having found an honourable place in missionary work, and a vocation in correspondence with his English friends, especially with Robert Barclay and his family, with the Reverend John Owen of the bible society, and with the Duke of Northumberland (a friend of Joseph Brant). The letters from abroad contained plans for the improvement of the Grand River community in agriculture, industry, education, religion, sobriety, and morality.

Discouraged by his failure to obtain deeds, when he returned to the Grand River Norton found conditions at home even more depressing. Joseph Brant was losing his strength, and his son John [TEKARIHOGEN] was still a youth. Norton's constructive service as Teyoninhokarawen was urgently needed, but he was constantly thwarted by the opposition of the Indian Department under Claus, Lieutenant Governor Gore, and some civil chiefs in council. Those antagonistic to Norton saw his idealism as hypocrisy, his claims for Indian ownership of land as greed, his loyalty to Britain as treachery, and his whole attitude as a threat to privilege. Humanitarian projects had to be postponed. Personal attacks upon him increased and he wished to retire.

On 9 April 1809 Norton set out from the Grand River to make a journey which would take him a thousand miles through Ohio, Kentucky, and Tennessee to the land of the Cherokees. He had several plans. He wished to trace his father's family and find relatives, and to make an inquiry into "the situation of our brethren the Cherokees." Relatives were, indeed, there to be visited. He was accepted as a Cherokee, and given every opportunity to make a careful study of all aspects of the "situation." Then he set out for Upper Canada by way of the Shawnee country. He arrived at his home on the Grand River in June 1810.

Depressed by conditions there, he soon had thoughts about leaving again, this time "to the westward." The prospect of war between Britain and the United States kept him in the colony. The proposed journal of his travels to the American south had to be set aside.

Throughout the campaign in 1812, the first year of the war, he assembled and commanded fighting men of the Six Nations and other tribes, the parties varying in size with conditions and necessities along the Niagara frontier. His leadership in the great victory at Queenston Heights was the high point in his military career. Norton's own account is vivid and inimitable.

His brilliant tactical decision to take a "circuit" meant an ascent of the escarpment at a considerable distance along the road west of Queenston, and a climb easier than that attempted by Major-General Isaac Brock* on the cliff close to the Niagara River. The woods on the right flank of the American force moving westward along the heights were precisely what Norton and his Indians needed for cover as they pinned down the enemy's advance until Major-General Roger Hale Sheaffe* and his troops came up to sweep the Americans off the heights. Reinforcements from Chippawa also arrived.

Sheaffe mentioned in his dispatches "the judicious position which Norton and the Indians with him had taken." One week after the battle, on 20 October, Sheaffe honoured Norton by appointing him "to the Rank of Captain of the Confederate Indians" – the same rank that Joseph Brant had held during the American revolution. Sir George Prevost*, governor-in-chief of British North America, congratulated

Norton

Norton upon his courage and perseverance, with advice "to keep up and increase the numbers of a description of Force so truly formidable to their Enemies and so capable of sustaining the good cause in which we are engaged."

In the campaigns of 1813 Norton was active again. He and a hundred Indians were at Fort George (Niagara-on-the-Lake) when the Americans attacked late in May, and they took part in the subsequent British withdrawal to Burlington Heights (Hamilton). After the American thrust was stopped at Stoney Creek on 6 June, Norton and some warriors pursued the retreating enemy. He was not with the Indians who fought at the important battle of Beaver Dams, but he participated in skirmishes during the remainder of the summer. His power was at a high point, for the wartime situation had enabled him to shake off much of the Indian Department's authority. Major-General Francis de ROTTENBURG recommended that Norton be given discretionary control over the allotment of presents to those who served with him; but he also remarked: "All my endeavours to reconcile . . . [Claus] and Norton are in vain, the latter is certainly a great intriguer, but is a fighting man – and may do a great deal of mischief if not supported." Early in 1814 Norton was called to Quebec by Sir George Prevost for consultation on the role of Indian support. Prevost confirmed Norton in the rank given him by Sheaffe. Indian Department officers were forbidden to interfere with Norton in his dealings with the Grand River Indians.

In the campaigns of 1814 Norton was at the head of some 200 Iroquois at the battle of Chippawa on 5 July. Although they did not play an important part in the action, they suffered their heaviest casualties of the war, and some seriously considered the proposal instigated by the American Iroquois leader Red Jacket [SHAKÓYE:WA:THA?] that the Iroquois fighting on both sides should withdraw from the war.

Norton himself remained on the frontier. His generosity with presents was such that Indians of other nations, including the Prophet [Tenskwatawa*], had joined him, but at least a few Iroquois remained with him after Chippawa. He was at the head of a fighting force at the battle of Lundy's Lane in late July and at the unsuccessful British assault on Fort Erie in mid August. After the Treaty of Ghent in December, he retired from fighting and was granted a pension of £200 per annum. He kept on supporting the claims of Indian war veterans for losses incurred in the campaigns.

During 1813, while the war was on, he was married at Niagara by the Reverend Robert ADDISON to an attractive and talented girl named Karighwaycagh (Catherine), said to have been a Delaware. She was about 16. Norton must have been about 50 and had at least one son by a previous marriage to an Iroquois woman. In 1815 he and Catherine, along with John (Tehonakaraa), one of his sons, went to visit Britain. Catherine and the boy were enrolled in a school at Dunfermline, Scotland, and she proved to be "a very keen student." She was befriended by the Duchess of Northumberland, who had her portrait painted by an Edinburgh artist. Norton spent some of his time in England with Barclay, Owen, and the Duke of Northumberland – the good friends of his 1804–6 visit.

These men became the recipients of a long manuscript journal. In its first section, Norton's trip of 1809–10 to the American south was described for the benefit of interested friends in England. He recorded in great detail what he had seen in the Cherokee country, and heard from the lips of the leaders of that nation. His notes had eventually covered Cherokee geography, history of warfare, traditions, mythology, customs, social conditions, and sport. The second section was devoted to a somewhat bookish history of the original five Iroquois nations, whom Norton correctly believed to be related to the Cherokees. Under Joseph Brant he had been well taught regarding Iroquoian lore, but he found it useful to prepare for the journal by consulting "the accredited Memoirs of the neighbouring Europeans." Among his sources were Cadwallader Colden's history of the Iroquois and George Heriot*'s history of Canada. Anthropologist William Nelson Fenton has suggested that Norton probably had "some contact with savants" in London or Edinburgh. The final section, an eye-witness account of various actions in the War of 1812, is the most personal, but carefully factual, part of the work.

Norton and his wife returned from Britain to Upper Canada in 1816. He had received a commission as a brevet major in the British army, but he was unofficially called Colonel Norton. He became the owner of a large farm overlooking the Grand River at Sims Locks, south of present-day Brantford, and he "improved" his lands, setting an example in agriculture for the Grand River community. Occasionally he gave parish assistance to Robert Addison, and he translated the Gospel of St Matthew into Mohawk – an effort which caused him to leave the work on other gospels to an assistant, Henry Aaron Hill [KENWENDESHON]. Debts kept on worrying him. The old traveller and warrior became restive; he toyed with plans to visit his Cherokee relatives in the south.

In 1823, believing that Catherine had been guilty of sexual misconduct, Norton ordered off his farm a young Indian named Big Arrow (Joe Crawford). This intruder demanded a duel; he died of a wound accidentally inflicted in a scuffle. Norton volunteered to stand trial. The charge was murder, but he behaved honourably, refusing to use his own "best defence," which would have exposed Catherine publicly to shame. He was convicted of manslaughter and fined

£25. Catherine wrote a pathetic letter, begging forgiveness, but he would not see her again. He settled a share of his pension upon her and then left for the territory of Arkansas. A friend received a letter from him in February 1824, stating that he might be away three years. Catherine, meanwhile, had left the Grand River to live at Fairfield (near Thamesville). She died there on 16 Jan. 1827.

The *Colonial Advocate* of 9 March 1826 reported that a friend of Norton had received at least one letter from him, written from Laredo (then in Mexico) "in November last." Norton had then "expected to come home." There is no evidence to show that he ever returned to the Grand River. As late as 4 Sept. 1851, a nephew and reputed heir-at-law stated to a lawyer that he was prepared "to prove [Norton's death] in the month of October 1831." No proof has been found.

CARL F. KLINCK

[John Norton's journal was dedicated to the Duke of Northumberland, in whose splendid library at Alnwick Castle (Alnwick, Eng.) the manuscript was preserved in a fair copy (evidently not in Norton's own handwriting), bound in two volumes. The amanuensis was probably "A. W.," a friend who signed a table of contents (and who may have been Adam Wilson of Edinburgh, a cousin of Norton). The manuscript had passed through the hands of Robert Barclay and John Owen during plans for publication, which then proved abortive for reasons of cost. Although completed shortly after the War of 1812, it remained unpublished for more than 150 years, until the Champlain Society brought it out under the title *The journal of Major John Norton, 1816*, ed. C. F. Klinck and J. J. Talman (Toronto, 1970). Most of the documentation for this biography of Norton can be found in the acknowledgements, footnotes, and introduction to the Champlain Society volume.

A portrait of Norton by Thomas Phillips is located in Syon House, London. C.F.K.]

Valley of Six Nations (Johnston). *Handbook of Indians of Canada* (Hodge), 224–26. J. P. Brown, *Old frontiers; the story of the Cherokee Indians from earliest times to the date of their removal to the west, 1838* (Kingsport, Tenn., 1938; repr. New York, 1971). E. C. Woodley, *The Bible in Canada; [the story of the British and Foreign Bible Society in Canada]* (Toronto, [1953]), 44–50. W. N. Fenton, "Cherokee and Iroquois connections revisited," *Journal of Cherokee Studies* (Cherokee, N.C.), 3 (1978): 239–49. Ray Fogelson, "Major John Norton as ethnologist," *Journal of Cherokee Studies*, 3: 250–55. C. F. Klinck, "New light on John Norton," RSC *Trans.*, 4th ser., 4 (1966), sect.II: 167–77. J. McE. Murray, "John Norton," *OH*, 37 (1945): 7–16.

O

ODIVERT, *dit* **ROMAIN.** *See* ROMAIN

O'DONNELL, JAMES, architect; b. 1774 in County Wexford (Republic of Ireland); d. unmarried 28 Jan. 1830 in Montreal.

James O'Donnell came from a family of substantial landowners. After receiving an elementary education, he left for Dublin, where he bound himself as an apprentice, probably to the famous Irish architect Francis Johnston. No trace of his stay in Dublin has been found except for the plans that he drew for a mausoleum in 1798. He is believed to have subsequently travelled all over Europe, with the exception of France, to study some of the finest architectural structures. In 1812 he took up residence in New York, where he successfully practised as an architect. His major works in that city were the Bloomingdale Asylum (1818–21), the Fulton Street Market (1821–22), and Christ Church (1822–23). O'Donnell took his inspiration for the last building from the neo-Gothic style, which he favoured throughout his career.

With this experience in large-scale projects O'Donnell had become a highly regarded architect in North America. He had already been elected to the American Academy of Fine Arts in New York in 1817. His reputation must have come to the attention of the churchwardens of the parish of Notre-Dame in Montreal, who were planning to build a large new church accommodating 8–9,000 people. In September 1823 the church's building committee, headed by parish priest Candide-Michel LE SAULNIER, recommended sending for O'Donnell. Upon his arrival in Montreal O'Donnell made detailed sketches, and on 17 October his plans were accepted. During the winter of 1823–24 he prepared the definitive plans in his New York studio. The building, 150 feet by 258, was to include two huge towers 196 feet in height. O'Donnell designed the church in neo-Gothic style because he thought it best suited to Canadian materials and workmen, and to the climate. According to contemporary statements the church was to be larger than any other building on the North American continent; it was to have walls of cut stone five feet thick, and a floor supported by 42 pillars three feet in diameter on which would rest trunks of oak trees split in two. In view of the colossal size of the building, provision was made for a system of ducts for hot air, which would be

O'Donnell

supplied by steam boilers in the basement. In November 1823 contractor John Redpath* was chosen to supply the cut stone, which came from the Tanneries quarry in Griffintown (Montreal). Statute labour by residents of various Montreal Island parishes was used to transport the stone.

In May 1824 O'Donnell moved to Montreal to take charge of the site and provide the working drawings needed for construction to begin. According to the terms of his contract he was to receive annual fees of £375 for four years. He is believed to have provided a hundred or more plans and drawings to guide the contractors. In June 1824 the *fabrique* of Notre-Dame also called upon Gabriel Lamontagne, a master mason, to act as chief contractor and supervise the execution of the work according to the standards laid down by O'Donnell; this post had been turned down by the young Quebec architect Thomas Baillairgé*, who disliked the neo-Gothic style intended for Notre-Dame.

The foundations were laid and the outside walls erected in the years 1823–26; during the period 1827–29 the interior structure and the finishings were completed. At the height of the summer season about 250 workmen (building craftsmen, day labourers, and carters) were employed on the site under the supervision of five foremen. In general the carpenters, joiners, and masons earned 5s. a day, whereas the day labourers received 2s. 6d. The workmen in the militia gangs received no remuneration. Despite the impressive numbers of workers during peak periods, O'Donnell often complained that he did not always have at his disposal the 45 masons and 45 labourers he had requested. Lack of funds also made it necessary on several occasions to lay off the workmen. In 1827 the *fabrique* of Notre-Dame had to resign itself to borrowing £22,000 at 6 per cent interest, despite income from donations, collections, and land levies. The walls of the church were finished that year at a cost of £18,000 just for the stone, and work was begun on the roof, which entailed an expenditure of £3,000 for tin plate imported from England.

As the building progressed, relations between employer and workmen steadily deteriorated because O'Donnell's attitude hardened. In 1827 he had forced the chief contractor, Lamontagne, to make the gangs work longer hours and to see that schedules were respected. Pressed to meet delivery dates, O'Donnell blamed the Canadian workmen for their lack of discipline: "Not a man of them appears the least interested in the building all they care for is to get their pay, and to do as little work for it as they can. They are determined too, to slight the work, and do it their own way whenever my back [is] turned." Confronted with the resistance of the Montreal carpenters, who were then fighting for a 10-hour day, O'Donnell had asked the contractors, one of whom was Jacob Cox, to

prevent the workmen from damaging materials and to forbid any joint action or gathering. This situation of conflict may perhaps be explained by the hypothesis that collective (or even social) organization of work, with its concomitant division of labour, brings with it increased exploitation of the work force.

The church was dedicated none the less on 15 July 1829 in the presence of a great many political and religious dignitaries. It had proved impossible, however, to complete the two front towers designed by O'Donnell, and it was not until 1841 that the *fabrique* entrusted their construction to architect John Ostell*. In 1832 the cost of building the church totalled £47,446, fifteen per cent more than originally estimated. The plans of the building later served as a model for other parish churches. In addition to this architectural legacy O'Donnell's work influenced a whole generation of Montreal architects in the 19th century, for example Victor Bourgeau*, Pierre-Louis Morin, John Wells, and John Ostell.

O'Donnell left other buildings worthy of mention. Having refused to take part in the project for a workhouse in Montreal despite the urgings of Lord Dalhousie [Ramsay*], he had contracted in 1824 to provide the plans for a new church on Rue Saint-Jacques commissioned by the American Presbyterian Church. Two years later he agreed to draw the plans for the premises of the British and Canadian School Society of Montreal. This two-storey building with an octagonal dome could accommodate 275 pupils.

For some years James O'Donnell had suffered from oedema, and from July 1829 his condition worsened. In November he dictated his will; at that point he decided to convert from Protestantism to Catholicism, probably as a result of pressure from the Sulpicians. He passed away shortly afterwards, on 28 Jan. 1830. A man of aristocratic manners and unlimited faith in science, he is said by art historians to have grasped and resolved structural problems very well. O'Donnell was fortunate in being able to prove himself at a time when the architect's function was beginning to emerge, bringing with it a division between conception and execution in the construction industry.

ROBERT TREMBLAY

[This biography draws a good deal on Olivier Maurault*'s *La paroisse: histoire de l'église Notre-Dame de Montréal* (2e éd., Montréal, 1957), 43–104, and especially on the more recent study by F. [K. B. S.] Toker, *The church of Notre-Dame in Montreal: an architectural history* (Montreal and London, 1970), which contains a thorough examination of James O'Donnell's career. The key records relating to him are at AP, Notre-Dame de Montréal, Reg. des délibérations du conseil de la fabrique, 1823–29, which contains 21 letters and 173 sketches by O'Donnell. R.T.]

ANQ-Q, CE1-51, 1er févr. 1830; CN1-134, 14 nov. 1829. *Le Canadien*, 29 oct. 1823. *La Minerve*, 9, 16 juill. 1829.

Montreal Gazette, 12 June, 4 Sept. 1824; 4 Feb. 1830. *Scribbler* (Montreal), 13, 24 June 1824. Charles Lipton, *Histoire du syndicalisme au Canada et au Québec, 1827–1859*, Michel van Schendel, trad. (Montréal, 1976). Luc Noppen, *Les églises du Québec (1600–1850)* (Québec, 1977). F. [K. B. S.] Toker, "James O'Donnell: an Irish Georgian in America," Soc. of Architectural Historians, *Journal* (Philadelphia), 29 (1970): 132–43.

OGIMAUH-BINAESSIH (Okemapenesse, meaning "chief little bird"; **Wageezhegome, Wakeshogomy, Weggishgomin**, meaning "who is like the day"; **John Cameron, Captain John**), Mississauga Ojibwa chief, member of the eagle clan, and farmer; b. May 1764 at the Credit River (Ont.); d. 30 Sept. 1828 at the Credit Mission (Mississauga), Upper Canada.

As a young man Wageezhegome witnessed the destruction of his people's way of life. The arrival in what is now southern Ontario of thousands of white settlers after the American revolution quickly led to the surrender of much of the Mississaugas' hunting territory and the loss of their fishing grounds. Close contact with the whites also introduced a series of epidemics, such as smallpox, against which the Indians had no immunity. In the 1790s the new diseases carried away more than 150 of the 500 members of the Credit River band at the western end of Lake Ontario. As the Mississaugas' old society collapsed, many simply sold whatever furs they trapped, or fish they caught, for the white man's firewater. Almost alone among his people Wageezhegome chose to follow a different path.

Recognizing that the world of his youth was gone forever, the young warrior earnestly sought to adjust to the society of the white people around him. From David Ramsay*, the notorious Indian-killer and fur trader, he learned some English and acquired a rudimentary idea of how to farm. He attended a school and even adopted the name of John Cameron, an Indian Department official, as his English name. Finally the energetic Wageezhegome built himself a comfortable log cabin on the Credit River flats, where he raised some Indian corn and potatoes. As if to symbolize his transformation he also discarded his Indian costume of breechcloth and leggings, and began wearing store-bought trousers.

The Mississaugas respected him, selecting their "westernized" tribesman in August 1805 to succeed his father as one of the band's two chiefs. It was presumably then that he received the title Ogimauh-binaessih, although even after this date his other name continued to be used. With the band's other "principal men and women" he signed the surrenders of 1805, 1818, and 1820 by which the Mississaugas, unable to resist white settlement any longer, ceded their remaining lands on the northwestern shore of Lake Ontario and retained only a small tract on the Credit River. There Ogimauh-binaessih continued to live in his log cabin and to farm, while his fellow tribesmen dwelt in wigwams and tried to support themselves by fishing and hunting and by making baskets and brooms to sell to the white people.

When Peter Jones* arrived at the Credit in late 1824, Ogimauh-binaessih gave the native Methodist missionary his full support. Over a decade earlier he had allowed himself to be baptized, and since that time, he confessed to Jones, "I have again and again wished that the good white christians might come and plant the christian religion amongst us, and teach us the right way we should go." A recently contracted family tie also drew him toward the Methodists. Shortly before Jones's arrival the 60-year-old chief had married Wechikiwekapawiqua (baptized Catharine Cameron), the missionary's 17-year-old half-sister.

After Jones's visit Ogimauh-binaessih travelled some 60 miles westward to the new community of Methodist Indians at Davisville, on the Grand River just north of present-day Brantford, where Thomas Davis [TEHOWAGHERENGARAGHKWEN] had invited them to settle. There the chief pitched his tent beside the mission house and immediately enrolled his young wife in the Methodist school. The following spring he returned briefly to the Credit, in Peter Jones's words, "to advise the pagan Indians to forsake their evil ways . . . to leave off drinking the fire-water and to try to serve the Lord." Many accompanied him back to Davisville.

When in 1826 the Christian Mississaugas on the Grand moved back to the Credit River to found a model native agricultural settlement, the vigorous Ogimauh-binaessih helped as much as possible. He read passages from the Bible to his tribesmen, served as an assistant class leader in the church, and aided Peter and his brother John* in teaching farming techniques.

At the Credit Mission Ogimauh-binaessih's daughter, Charlotte, was born on 24 Feb. 1828. Later that year the respected chief suddenly became ill and he died on 30 September. Peter Jones, who succeeded him as chief, later recalled that he had said shortly before dying, "I thank the Lord that I have lived to see all my people serve the Great Spirit." Ogimauh-binaessih was a dedicated modernizer or, to use the term frequently employed by the Department of Indian Affairs and the Christian churches later in the 19th century, a very "progressive" Indian.

DONALD B. SMITH

[The author would like to thank Basil Johnston of the Royal Ontario Museum (Toronto) for his advice on Ojibwa names. D.B.S.]

UCC, Central Arch. (Toronto), Credit Mission, record-book. *Canada, Indian treaties and surrenders . . .* [1680–

O'Hara

1906] (3v., Ottawa, 1891–1912; repr. Toronto, 1971), 1: 35, 48, 53–54. Peter Jones, *History of the Ojebway Indians; with especial reference to their conversion to Christianity* . . . , [ed. Elizabeth Field] (London, 1861); *Life and journals of Kah-ke-wa-quo-nā-by (Rev. Peter Jones), Wesleyan missionary*, [ed. Elizabeth Field and Enoch Wood] (Toronto, 1860). D. B. Smith, "The Mississauga, Peter Jones, and the white man: the Algonkians' adjustment to Europeans on the north shore of Lake Ontario to 1860" (PHD thesis, Univ. of Toronto, 1975).

O'HARA, EDWARD, merchant, politician, JP, office holder, and army officer; b. *c.* 1767 in Gaspé, Que., son of Felix O'Hara* and Martha McCormick; m. 10 May 1796 Elizabeth Cameron at Quebec; d. 24 June 1833 in London or its environs.

Edward O'Hara came from one of the first English-speaking families to settle in the Gaspé and likely spent his childhood and adolescent years in his native village. Moving to Quebec in the 1780s, he went into partnership with merchant Robert Woolsey. The firm of Woolsey and O'Hara, whose shop was on the Place du Marché (Place Notre-Dame) in Lower Town, specialized in fabrics, shoes, and clothing. The partnership was dissolved by mutual consent in June 1790, and the business was put up for sale by auctioneer John Jones* the following month. The partners delegated Simon Fraser and John Young* to look after debts owed to them.

On 10 July 1792 O'Hara was elected to the House of Assembly of Lower Canada for the riding of Gaspé. He won the seat with three votes of a total of five. His disappointed opponent, George Longmore*, had not appreciated the manœuvres of Jersey merchant Charles ROBIN, who worked to see that people like O'Hara, sympathetic to his company's interests, were elected. He put pressure on the masters of fishing rooms and the fishermen working for him, who had to vote by a show of hands. With this intimidation, it is not surprising that Gaspé electors failed to exercise their right to vote. The irregularities resulted in three petitions being brought to the house to have the election contested, two from voters and one from Dr Longmore. They were all denied for want of evidence. Bringing witnesses to Quebec would have cost too much.

As an assemblyman O'Hara concerned himself with the grievances of the loyalists who on emigrating to the Gaspé coast sought land there. In March 1793, for example, he passed on to the governor 25 requests for land grants in the Gaspé, which were favourably received. As he was well integrated into his community, O'Hara was commissioned a justice of the peace for the Gaspé District on 13 Oct. 1795. The following year he was appointed *grand voyer* (chief road commissioner) for the district, but he did not have many roads to inspect. Despite the objections to which his election had given rise, he was returned in 1796,

defeating his sole opponent by four votes to one. He sat until 4 June 1800, although he does not seem to have attended the sessions of 1798, 1799, or 1800.

O'Hara gave up politics in 1800 and joined the British army. A lieutenant in the 7th Foot at first, in 1803 he received a commission as captain in the York Rangers through the influence of the Duke of Kent [Edward* Augustus]. In 1805 he was transferred to the 1st Foot, and the following year to the 46th. He was promoted major in the York Light Infantry Volunteers on 12 April 1807. Appointed lieutenant-colonel of his regiment on 3 June 1813, he served in the 63rd Foot from 19 Dec. 1816. In addition to seeing service in India, O'Hara took part in the capture of Guadeloupe in 1810. Five years later he received a medal commemorating that victory and was made a companion of the Order of the Bath. He took his retirement on 16 May 1822.

RÉGINALD DAY

ANQ-Q, CE1-61, 10 mai 1796; CN1-256, 16 juin 1790; CN1-262, 26 juin 1797. PAC, MG 24, F86; RG 68, General index, 1651–1841. *Quebec Gazette*, 19 June, 9 Oct. 1788; 17 Dec. 1789; 17, 24 June 1790; 15 Oct. 1795; 18 March 1802; 28 Aug. 1806. F.-J. Audet, "Les législateurs du Bas-Canada." Desjardins, *Guide parl.* Jules Bélanger et al., *Histoire de la Gaspésie* (Montréal, 1981). C.-E. Roy, *Percé, sa nature, son histoire* (Percé, Qué., 1947). C.-E. Roy et Lucien Brault, *Gaspé depuis Cartier* (Québec, 1934). F.-J. Audet et Édouard Fabre Surveyer, "Les députés au premier parlement du Bas-Canada: Edward O'Hara," *La Presse*, 27 août 1927: 53, 63. Réginald Day, "Il y a deux siècles: les O'Hara à Gaspé," *Rev. d'hist. de la Gaspésie* (Gaspé, Qué.), 9 (1971): 342–97; 10 (1972): 31–35.

OKEMAPENESSE. *See* OGIMAUH-BINAESSIH

OKIMAWASKAWIKINAM. *See* LETENDRE, *dit* BATOCHE, JEAN-BAPTISTE

ORKNEY, JAMES, clock and watch maker, merchant, gold- and silversmith, and seigneur; b. 1760 in Scotland; m. 3 July 1790 Jane Hanna, daughter of James G. Hanna*, at Quebec in a Presbyterian service, and they had eight children; d. there 24 Jan. 1832.

It cannot be determined whether James Orkney received his clock and watch maker's training in his native country or acquired it at Quebec; his links with James G. Hanna, who was himself a clock and watch maker, argue that he could at least have completed his training with him. Whatever the case, an advertisement that Orkney published on 26 July 1787 in the *Quebec Gazette* is the first indication of his presence and activity in the colony; in it he invited the public to visit his business, located in front of the post office, where he had clocks, gold and silver watches, and a great variety of jewellery for sale.

In 1790 Orkney ran a prosperous business at 13 Rue de la Montagne. Two years later he had a journeyman by the name of François Lécuyer, who presumably helped him make clocks and watches. Orkney's next-door neighbour at this time was a gold- and silversmith, Louis Robitaille, and two others, Laurent Amiot* and Michel Forton*, lived a few doors away on the same street. As a clock and watch maker, Orkney already knew how to work with metals, and proximity to these men probably had something to do with his becoming interested in the silversmith's craft.

Orkney was primarily a merchant, whose shop offered a great variety of articles. He carried table silver – mainly flatware – in solid silver or metal plated with silver, as well as wedding rings, brooches, seals, and watches, which he could clean or repair when necessary. He also sold lead pencils, purses, and cut glass. In short, Orkney ran a store in which almost any luxury article could be found, along with articles of everyday use. Like Hanna, he imported movements for grandfather clocks which he fitted into cases made in the colony. He travelled to England twice, probably on business. On 21 May 1812 he came back from Liverpool; four years later he returned from London, landing at Quebec.

In addition to matters connected with his business, Orkney is known to have engaged in a certain number of other transactions. On 21 Jan. 1802, for example, he bought from Marie-Avine de Montigny, Pierre Trottier Desrivières's widow, half of a lot on Rue Mont-Carmel, as well as the usufruct of the other half; he sold the whole thing to Malcolm Fraser* on 9 Aug. 1806. On 25 Aug. 1808 he rented to Lieutenant-Colonel Edward Baynes for five years a two-storey stone house with outbuildings on Rue des Carrières. On 25 June 1813 he bought a lot at Sainte-Anne-de-la-Pocatière (La Pocatière) from silversmith Joseph Sasseville.

Orkney took an interest in the life of the community. In 1791 he joined other Quebec merchants in signing a petition against a bill "respecting Guardians and Curators." He repeatedly subscribed to the Quebec Fire Society. His name also occasionally appears on letters of appreciation or welcome to governors and distinguished visitors. In 1795 he and six other gold- and silversmiths petitioned to be exempted from a law on forge fires [see Michel Forton]. Two years later, in July 1797, he served on the jury in the trial of David McLane* for high treason. In October 1802 he joined the other Presbyterians in the capital in signing a petition for a site there on which to put up a church.

On 1 Jan. 1818 Orkney gave public notice that he had decided to liquidate his business; he still had a great many articles of all kinds, for instance at least 25 grandfather clocks. After retiring he bought the modest seigneury of Île-aux-Ruaux, near the Île d'Orléans in 1823; he even hired a workman for a little more than nine months to do various jobs on the new property. Orkney died at Quebec on 24 Jan. 1832. Since his wife had predeceased him, in August 1817, he left everything to his son Alexander, who lived with him.

Examples of James Orkney's work as a watch and clock maker are still held in several private collections and in various museums, particularly the Musée du Québec and the Royal Ontario Museum, both of which own fine grandfather clocks. Unfortunately his production as a gold- and silversmith is little known; there is, however, in the Musée du Québec a rare piece bearing Orkney's stamp – IO in a rectangle – alongside Joseph Sasseville's stamp, a proof that the two artists had worked together.

RENÉ VILLENEUVE

ANQ-M, CN1-121; CN1-134, 9 mai 1817; P-35/10, N-O-32, 28 avril 1808; N-O-33, 31 déc. 1811; N-O-34, 3 juill. 1816. ANQ-Q, CE1-66, 1790–92, 1794, 1798, 1800, 1804, 1806, 1810; CN1-26, 23 août 1808; CN1-49, 25 juin 1813, 25 déc. 1817; CN1-208, 14 mai 1831; CN1-212, 20 sept. 1823; CN1-230, 9 août 1806. MAC-CD, Fonds Morisset, 2, dossier James Orkney. "Les dénombrements de Québec" (Plessis), ANQ Rapport, 1948–49: 23, 26–27. Le Canadien, 25 janv. 1832. Montreal Gazette, 26 May, 6 Aug. 1817. Quebec Gazette, 26 July 1787; 16 June 1791; 5 Dec. 1793; 13 Feb. 1794; 3 Aug. 1797; 21 March, 18 July 1799; 21 May 1812; 23 May 1816; 1 Jan. 1818; 25 Jan. 1832. "Les Presbytériens à Québec en 1802," BRH, 42 (1936): 728. Quebec directory, 1790. "Les seigneuries des RR. PP. jésuites," BRH, 41 (1935): 509.

OSGOODE, WILLIAM, judge and politician; b. March 1754 in London, only son of William Osgood; d. there 17 Jan. 1824.

The elder Osgood (his son added the "e" after 1781) was a Leeds hosier who moved to London and left an estate of about £20,000 when he died in 1767. A friend and patron of John Wesley, he sent William to the Methodist school at Kingswood, near Bath, for a classical education. Osgoode then attended Christ Church College, Oxford (BA 1772, MA 1777), entered Lincoln's Inn in 1773 and, after a year in France, was called to the English bar on 11 Nov. 1779. In that year he published *Remarks on the law of descent*, a critique of Sir William Blackstone's *Commentaries on the laws of England*. He did not practise in the circuit courts, either because a hesitation in his speech made him an ineffective barrister or because he was not dependent on his fees as a lawyer. He appears to have accepted no common-law briefs, but gained a reputation as a draftsman in the courts of equity. There is no evidence to support the family tradition that he was an intimate of William Pitt; and the story that he was a natural son of George II is without foundation or plausibility.

Osgoode

He had enough influence in Whitehall to be appointed first chief justice of Upper Canada (31 Dec. 1791), with an undertaking that he could expect to succeed the ailing William Smith* in the same post at Quebec. It was as his nominee that John White* became attorney general for the upper province. Although Osgoode failed in an attempt to nominate his own replacement in Upper Canada in 1794 when he moved to Quebec, he retained the good opinion of successive secretaries of state for the colonies until 1801; and he was to keep up a frankly partisan commentary on his fellow officials at Quebec in private correspondence with the under-secretary, John King.

In Upper Canada, too, Osgoode won friends. Richard Cartwright*'s first impression of him as "a very worthy and respectable man" appears to have survived their differences over the law of marriage and the formation of the courts. Osgoode's disapproval of William Dummer POWELL, because he was not an English lawyer, was merely part of his generally condescending attitude towards colonials. His good manners, good looks, and kindliness – at Quebec he took in White's two sons for a time after their father's death – made him popular. He got on especially well with the new lieutenant governor, John Graves Simcoe*, whom he joined at Quebec (2 June 1792) on his way to Upper Canada. He lived with the Simcoes at Newark (Niagara-on-the-Lake) until almost the end of the year. He wrote periodically to Mrs Simcoe [Elizabeth Posthuma Gwillim*] long after leaving the province, just as he continued to advise Peter Russell* when the latter became administrator. Two years after Osgoode's departure for Lower Canada in 1794, Simcoe still found his absence "most severely oppressive."

The two agreed on most questions, including their mistrust of merchants as monopolists; but Osgoode never had Simcoe's commitment to the province, and his toryism was more rigid. His hostility to Americans was unqualified: he thought New York "the very Nest & Hotbed of Turbulence and Disaffection." In spite of his Methodist upbringing, he was ambitious for the effective establishment of the Church of England in both provinces and with Bishop Jacob MOUNTAIN was to regret that it had no legal claim to the tithe in Lower Canada. Notwithstanding his own origins (about which in later life he was secretive), he was sometimes more an aristocrat than a lawyer: he sympathized with duelling if it was conducted with proper restraint and he secured the acquittal of a duellist at Kingston who had been obliged to kill a persistent opponent. Passing through Montreal in July 1792 he was surprised to find that women could vote and that "the Returning Officer was an Englishman which makes it more Extraordinary."

In his application of English legal models to Upper Canada, Osgoode was in some ways discriminating. He gave attention before leaving England to "the different Arrangements it may be needful to make in attempting to simplify and adapt the Artificial practice & proceedings of English Jurisprudence to the circumstances of an infant Colony." It was, however, from English lawyers that he sought advice. His concern was not with frontier conditions but with the unreformed procedure of the English common-law courts. He was an accomplished equity lawyer in a period when the Court of Chancery and the equity jurisdiction of the Court of Exchequer had done far more than parliament to reform the law; he thought those courts of equity more just in their law and more reasonable in their procedure than the common law courts of common pleas and king's bench; and he did not mean to introduce into Upper Canada what he regarded as anachronisms in England. In drafting his first provincial statute, therefore, an act in 1792 to adopt English civil law, he retained the simple writ of summons and the proceedings already in use in Quebec after 1763. The act did not adopt the English bankruptcy or poor laws, nor the law relating to ecclesiastical rights and duties. He may have been in favour of limiting imprisonment for debt to cases of fraudulent evasion, although the change was not included in the act.

Never a finicky lawyer, he did not think it necessary to legislate the adoption of English criminal law, the proclamation of 7 Oct. 1763 having done so in general terms. He considered it enough to adopt recent English extensions of the right of trial by jury. His successor, John Elmsley*, would think differently in 1800. Similarly, he was of the opinion that simple letters of declaration issued with title deeds were enough to ensure the legality of land grants made before 1791. Although he had set three as a quorum for the Executive Council, he and Russell sometimes conducted its business alone. The greatest compromise that he accepted in Upper Canada, however, was forced upon him by the House of Assembly on the initiative of Cartwright. Osgoode's marriage bill of 1793, intended merely to validate existing marriages, was amended to allow justices of the peace to perform marriages whenever there were fewer than five Anglican clergymen in a district, none of them within 18 miles. Illiberal as those terms were for a province with a minority of Anglicans, a barrage of complaints against them did not force a change until 1831. In practice they allowed what amounted to civil marriage so long as the Anglican form of service was followed.

The Judicature Act of 1794 was the legislation by which Osgoode most hoped to set his mark on the province. It abolished the district courts of common pleas set up in 1788, replacing them with a single court of king's bench as the superior court for the whole province. An accompanying bill set up new district courts to settle contract disputes, not involving land titles, of from 40s. to £15. An earlier act had on the assembly's initiative empowered any two justices of the peace to hear cases involving less than 5s. A court of probate with district branches (surrogate courts) had also been introduced to settle the inheritance of estates. There was no provincial court of common pleas and no court of chancery.

The Judicature Act had a difficult passage through the Legislative Council, where it was attacked as too elaborate, centralized, and expensive for a province still thinly settled, and also because it put the chief justice in the position of hearing appeals from his own decisions. It was, however, as simple an arrangement as Osgoode and Simcoe would consent to. Its excessive centralization was mitigated from 1797, when the writs necessary to begin an action in king's bench could be obtained from a district rather than the provincial capital. In the short run at least it was a visionary scheme: even its central establishment – the chief justice, two puisne judges, an attorney general, a solicitor general, two sheriffs, and a clerk of the crown and pleas – could not be staffed by trained lawyers. Besides Osgoode and White, Powell and Walter Roe* of Detroit were the only lawyers in the province. Nevertheless, Osgoode's measures did regularize and extend the jurisdiction of the untrained justices of the peace and district magistrates who settled most of the legal disputes in the province.

These were Osgoode's main pieces of legislation during his two years in Upper Canada, the acts to abolish slavery and organize the legal profession being the work of White. But Osgoode was also a member of both the Executive Council (sworn in 9 July 1792) and the Legislative Council (sworn in 12 July 1792 and speaker from 10 September). He was the only member to attend all the meetings of both bodies over the next two years. In the Legislative Council he was in effect manager of government business, its chief defender against the opposition of Cartwright and Robert Hamilton*. Although his commission as chief justice at Quebec was issued on 24 Feb. 1794, he remained in the upper province for the next summer's meeting of the legislature.

He arrived at Quebec on 27 July, barely three weeks after his last meeting of the Executive Council at Newark. He was again a member of both councils (sworn in 19 Sept. 1794), and again speaker of the Legislative Council. He began his unhappy career at Quebec by chairing the Executive Council's committee on land grants. He had the misfortune to deal with two governors, Lord Dorchester [Guy Carleton*] and Robert Prescott*, who had grown old and irascible, but he himself became a prickly and vindictive character. Simcoe did not help matters with Dorchester by offering Osgoode as his spokesman on two disputed questions, the lease of the Six Nations' lands [see Thayendanegea*] and the provisioning of troops. It was, however, with Prescott that Osgoode came to an open and bitter quarrel.

The land grants of Lower Canada were in confusion from lax administration, lack of surveys, and the

prevalence of unauthorized settlement. The Executive Council's solution was merely to rescind township grants not already confirmed and to regrant the land. Prescott thought this too favourable to land speculators, among whom he included members of the council; his new regulations recognized actual settlement and even pending applications if they had been properly recorded; the rest of the lands were to be put up for sale. These regulations had been approved by the secretary of state, the Duke of Portland, when Prescott asked the Executive Council to advise him on their publication. The council's report of 20 June 1798, drafted by Osgoode, objected both to publication and to the regulations. Prescott then published them with the council's objections and with a foreword, highly critical of the council, by the disappointed land applicant William Berczy*. Osgoode was outraged by the publication, with its attack on his character by the "miserable Alien" Berczy, and perhaps most of all by the resulting personal incivilities. "How it will be relished at Home," he wrote prophetically, "remains to be seen." Prescott, at odds with most of his subordinates, was recalled to explain his conduct and never returned.

Robert Shore Milnes*, who came out in June 1799 as lieutenant governor, found Osgoode little easier to deal with. In May 1800 the chief justice demanded the dismissal of Pierre-Amable De Bonne* from the bench for adultery, absenteeism, and faulty court procedure. Unwilling to stir up further bitterness by a public inquiry, Milnes refused. When in 1801 the assembly passed an act to remit arrears of *lods et ventes* on crown lands, Osgoode objected: it was, he wrote, "an established rule as well of decency as of policy" that such concessions ought to be made by the crown, not the legislature. The assembly's request for a return of crown property held *en roture* seemed to him an unwarrantable interference with the royal prerogative; and he made it a grievance that the Executive Council was not forced by the secretary of state to record his protest in its minutes. He had already offered to resign on condition of receiving an £800 pension. When that was confirmed, he left Quebec in the summer of 1801, his resignation taking effect on 1 May 1802.

At Quebec Osgoode seems never to have been the charming and indefatigably industrious public servant that he was in the upper province. Prescott never accused him of being a land speculator, only of being vain and idle enough to act as the speculators' stalking-horse on the Executive Council. Since Osgoode received grants totalling nearly 12,000 acres, the governor might have gone farther in his accusations. Osgoode's disapproval extended beyond his colleagues on the bench and in the councils. He did maintain good relations to the end with Bishop Mountain, but almost the only other living things to win his approval in Lower Canada were the horses,

Otetiani

"the best little Creatures in the Universe." Although he had shrunk from the first sight of the black cap among his judicial robes, he even became a harsh judge. He had no choice in July 1797 about condemning David McLane* to death, nor about decreeing life imprisonment for McLane's merely foolish accomplice, Charles Frichet; but he did not recommend mercy for either of them, and poor Frichet's sentence was remitted without his advice. Milnes wrote that Osgoode would not be content except as "the sole adviser to government." Certainly Osgoode never again enjoyed so large a share of confidence as Simcoe had given him, and never worked as well without it.

Back in London Osgoode lived fashionably in apartments formerly occupied by the Duke of York, but he did not receive another judicial appointment. He was able to return to his interest in procedural reform as a member of the royal commissions on the courts of law which eventually led in 1832 to the Uniformity of Process Act. Osgoode Hall, first built in 1829–32 as the headquarters of the Law Society of Upper Canada, was named after him. His portrait by George Theodore Berthon* hangs there.

S. R. MEALING

[The main collection of Osgoode's papers is at the Law Soc. of U.C. (Toronto) (mfm. at AO). There are also letters from and about him in the papers of John Graves Simcoe (locations appear in his biography in DCB, vol.5), and Peter Russell (AO and MTL), and a few in those of Samuel Peters Jarvis (AO and MTL) and William Dummer Powell (AO, MTL, and PAC).

Osgoode was an assiduous but not a chatty correspondent. His letters, except for those to Jacob Mountain (in the Bishopthorpe papers at the ACC-Q) and to his cousin Ellen Copley (in an original collection of Osgoode correspondence at the AO, MU 3705), do not give much news of himself or what he was doing. Apart from his formal protests – a habit he developed late in life – they are, however, the main evidence for his opinions on questions of public policy and on his colleagues.

Some of Osgoode's letters from Upper Canada have been printed: "Letters from the Honourable Chief Justice William Osgoode: a selection from his Canadian correspondence, 1791–1801," ed. William Colgate, OH, 46 (1954): 77–95 and 149–68; "Three letters of William Osgoode, first chief justice of Upper Canada," ed. A. R. M. Lower, OH, 57 (1965): 181–87. See also the printed Corr. of Hon. Peter Russell (Cruikshank and Hunter) and Corr. of Lieut. Governor Simcoe (Cruikshank); Gwillim, Diary of Mrs. Simcoe (Robertson; 1934); Life and letters of the late Hon. Richard Cartwright . . . , ed. C. E. Cartwright (Toronto and Sydney, Australia, 1876); Town of York, 1793–1815 (Firth); the calendars of the "State papers – L.C." and "State papers – U.C.," both in PAC Report, 1891; "Lower Canada in 1800," PAC Report, 1892: 9–15; and L.C., Executive Council, Extract from the minutes of council, containing his majesty's late regulations relative to the waste lands of the crown . . . (Quebec, 1798), which has an introduction signed by William Berczy*, although Osgoode suspected that it had been written by Prescott's secretary, Samuel GALE.

Assessments of Osgoode, except for that in the DNB, are apt to consider his career in only one province: F.-J. Audet, Les juges en chef de la province de Québec, 1764–1924 (Québec, 1927) and Read, Lives of the judges. William Renwick Riddell*, though hardly wider in scope, was better informed. See his "William Osgoode – first chief justice of Upper Canada, 1792–1794," Canadian Law Times (Toronto), 41 (1921): 278–98 and 345–58; "The law of marriage in Upper Canada," CHR, 2 (1921): 226–48; his review of Corr. of Lieut. Governor Simcoe in CHR, 4 (1923): 323; The life of John Graves Simcoe, first lieutenant governor of the province of Upper Canada, 1792–96 (Toronto, [1926]); and The bar and the courts of the province of Upper Canada or Ontario (Toronto, 1928). S.R.M.]

OTETIANI. See SHAKÓYE:WA:THA?

OWEN, DAVID, landowner, JP, judge, and politician; baptized 16 Sept. 1754 in the parish of Berriew, Wales, son of Owen Owen and Anne Davies; d. 10 Dec. 1829 on Campobello Island, N.B.

Born into an old Welsh family which would distinguish itself in the law and the Royal Navy, David Owen chose a career in the church. After attending the free grammar school in Warrington (Cheshire), England, where his uncle Edward Owen was headmaster and rector of the parish, he entered Trinity College, Cambridge, on 23 Oct. 1772. He obtained his BA in 1777, achieving distinction as senior wrangler, was made a fellow of the college two years later, and was awarded his master's degree in 1780. Ordained a deacon in the Church of England in 1778, he served as a chaplain in the Royal Navy the following year. He advanced to the priesthood in June 1787.

As a lad of 13, with his brothers Arthur Davies, who was later knighted, and William, a future KC, Owen had been named as a grantee of Passamaquoddy Outer Island (Campobello Island, N.B.), a property of more than 10,000 acres. His uncle Captain William Owen* was to have been accorded the island for exemplary service in the Royal Navy but, because there was an arbitrary limit of 3,000 acres on grants to officers of his rank, he had been obliged to have his three nephews included in the document bestowing title to the land. In 1770, with 38 colonists, Captain Owen arrived at the grant, which he immediately renamed Campobello, and began establishing a permanent settlement. He left a year later, however, returned to active service, and died in 1778 at Madras (India). The little colony was then supervised by resident agents until 1787, when David Owen came out to represent the family interests. In addition to the three brothers, the owners now included two cousins: the sons of Captain Owen, Edward Campbell Rich and William Fitz William*, both of whom would later become admirals in the Royal Navy.

David, who never married, soon had the affairs of the island under wise management. For 42 years he lived as nearly as possible the life of a country squire, on what was a semi-feudal estate, winning the respect and on occasion the affection of his tenants. He had difficulty initially with the settlers at Wilsons Beach, three families from New England who had located on the island some time before 1770. Owen argued that they were "tenants," but in 1790 the courts ruled in favour of their claims of right by possession and thus created the only freehold property on the island not owned by the Welsh grantees. Appointed a justice of the peace and a judge, Owen attended the Court of General Sessions and the Inferior Court of Common Pleas at the shiretown of St Andrews, some miles distant on the mainland of Charlotte County. In 1795 he was elected a member of the House of Assembly. A scholarly man, he kept a journal and was the author of a number of manuscripts. Little of what he wrote ever appeared in print, but he did contribute articles, mostly dealing with British history and theology, to the *Eastport Sentinel*, published at Eastport, Maine, just across Passamaquoddy Bay from Campobello.

Towards the end of the War of 1812, in July 1814, the British captured Moose Island, on which Eastport is located, and held it for four years. The chief naval officer in charge until 1815, Sir Thomas Masterman Hardy of Trafalgar fame, had been a friend of Owen's in pre-Campobello days, and the two met frequently at the Owen estate. Moose Island, like Campobello and adjacent islands, was the subject of a territorial dispute between Great Britain and the United States that was not settled until a boundary commission established by the Treaty of Ghent (1814) completed its work late in 1817. Campobello, having been granted in 1767 and occupied by British subjects since 1770, retained its status against American claims, as did the island of Grand Manan [*see* Moses GERRISH].

Owen was described to the historian William Francis Ganong* as "a very stout though not tall man, white-haired and clean shaven," a memory of the proprietor's later years. His portrait in the public library at Welshpool, on Campobello, shows a younger man clad in academic dress, a likeness of some four decades earlier. He had given up his place with the clergy in order to take over the affairs of the island. Judging from his petitions to government and other evidence, he apparently believed that the royal grant of Campobello bestowed unique and personal rights transcending ordinary title to land. Removed from the mainland, he saw no wrong in free trade with the United States, just a stone's throw away, and was often found to encourage this kind of enterprise. The historian William Stewart MacNutt* pictured him as irascible and argumentative, quite in contrast to what might have been presumed from his background as an academic and man of the church.

Owen was not happy when St Andrews became the shiretown of Charlotte County shortly after the separation of New Brunswick from Nova Scotia and, weary of travelling there for official and commercial matters, he attempted in 1822 to create his own separate county. In a memorial to the king he asked that the parishes of Grand Manan, West Isles (Deer Island and several smaller islands), and Campobello be set apart from Charlotte County and that the shiretown for the new entity be at Welshpool. Though clearly expressed and logically argued, the petition was not acted upon, a rebuff that no doubt added to the disgruntlement of the ageing proprietor.

On 8 Sept. 1829 Owen prepared and signed his will, to which a codicil was added on 12 November. Within a month he was dead. In accordance with a last request, his body was taken across the Atlantic to the old home in Wales and there, in 1830, interred in the family vault.

L. K. INGERSOLL

Grand Manan Museum (Grand Harbour, N.B.), Petition of David Owen, owner and proprietor of the town or parish of Campobello in the county of Charlotte, 20 July 1822 (typescript). National Library of Wales (Aberystwyth), Berriew parish, reg. of baptisms, marriages, and burials, 16 Sept. 1754. NMM, RUSI/NM/137 a & b (List of chaplains in the Royal Navy, 1626–1916, by A. G. Kealy). N.B. Museum, F86, item 61; "New Brunswick scrapbook," no.1: 52 (W. F. Ganong, "Early settlers of Quoddy Bay & vicinity"). William Owen, "The journal of Captain William Owen, R.N., during his residence on Campobello in 1770–71 . . . ," ed. W. F. Ganong, N.B. Hist. Soc., *Coll.*, 1 (1894–97), no.2: 193–220. *New-Brunswick Courier*, 26 Dec. 1829. *Alumni Cantabrigienses . . .* , comp. John and J. A. Venn (2 pts. in 10v., Cambridge, Eng., 1922–54), pt.II, 4: 610. John and J. B. Burke, *A genealogical and heraldic dictionary of the landed gentry of Great Britain & Ireland* (3v., London, 1849). Olive Mitchell Magowan, "The Owens of Glensevern[: part I]," *Saint Croix Courier* (St Stephen, N.B.), 5 Oct. 1977: 22. [C. B.] G. Wells, "David Owen of Campobello, New Brunswick," *Acadiensis* (Saint John, N.B.), 1 (1901): 21–27.

OWEN (Owens), JAMES. *See* McCARTHY, JAMES OWEN

P

PAGAN, ROBERT, businessman, politician, JP, judge, and militia officer; b. 16 Nov. 1750 in Glasgow, third son of William Pagan and Margaret Maxwell; m. Miriam Pote, daughter of Jeremiah Pote,

Pagan

and they had no children; d. 23 Nov. 1821 in St Andrews, N.B.

Robert Pagan emigrated to North America in 1768 or 1769 and was established by his father, a prominent sugar refiner of Glasgow, in the expanding timber and shipbuilding trade of Falmouth Neck, Mass. (Portland, Maine). In partnership with the firm of Lee, Tucker and Company of Greenock, Scotland, Robert undertook to gain a firm position in the lucrative West Indies trade, where his elder brother William* had already been apprenticed. Robert expanded his contacts in the business world through another brother, John, who capitalized on the promotion of Scottish immigration to North America. This brother had formed a partnership with Governor William Franklin of New Jersey and the Reverend John Witherspoon, later president of the College of New Jersey, to entice settlers to Boston and Philadelphia in the 1760s. In 1773, under the title of the Philadelphia Company, the same associates and others organized the *Hector* expedition to Pictou, N.S. [*see* John Harris*]. Through these family and financial connections Robert Pagan developed one of the largest businesses in general merchandise and shipbuilding in Falmouth during the first half of the 1770s. The youngest Pagan brother, Thomas, joined him there in 1775.

In October 1775, however, the community of Falmouth felt the first impact of open hostilities in the American conflict. Upon orders from the commander-in-chief of the North American station, Vice-Admiral Samuel Graves, who was responding to rebel activity in the area, Captain Henry Mowat bombarded the harbour front and laid waste many of its commercial establishments. The property of loyalists as well as non-loyalists was destroyed, including the business premises of Robert Pagan, Jeremiah Pote, his father-in-law, and Thomas Wyer, his brother-in-law. By February 1776 the threats from rebel committees in Falmouth against suspected tory sympathizers forced Pagan and his family to flee to the West Indies. A year later, however, Robert and Thomas were reunited with their brother William, who was then engaged in trade at New York.

Prompted by the announcement that a haven for loyalists would be established at the mouth of the Penobscot River, the three brothers soon decided to base their commercial operations there, under the protection of the British garrison at Fort George (Castine, Maine). Leaving his wife behind until proper accommodation could be found for her, Robert Pagan moved to the Penobscot in December 1780. Over the next few years he and his brothers acquired a lumberyard, built two sawmills, and operated two stores. Their firm, Robert Pagan and Company, also had an interest in ships and shipbuilding. Some of the vessels the brothers constructed were sent to Britain with timber cargoes and sold there, and at least one of

their fleet was engaged in privateering. Thirty-six ships of which the Pagans were sole or principal owners were lost by capture during the time they spent at New York and Penobscot.

Robert Pagan's standing in the community is reflected by his appointment as a magistrate in June 1781 and by his replacement of John Caleff*, who left for England in 1780, as inspector and commissary, the highest non-military posts at Fort George. Unfortunately, however, the future of the settlement was cut short by diplomatic deliberations among Great Britain, France, and the American states. It was obvious by the beginning of 1783 that the Penobscot River was not to become, as loyalists had hoped, the new boundary between the United States and British North America. Instead, the peace treaty of that year would designate the St Croix River as the borderline. In anticipation of an evacuation Pagan and his brothers gathered intelligence through their wide-ranging commercial connections in Nova Scotia on possible sites for a new home. The conclusion was that the peninsula nearest the St Croix River was the most desirable location for a settlement, particularly in view of its advantages for the West Indies trade and its unlimited hinterland. Robert Pagan became the main spokesman for the Penobscot Associated Loyalists. Along with brother William, William Gallop*, and others he arranged for their removal to Passamaquoddy Bay, where he also superintended the allocation of grants. Not surprisingly Governor John Parr* of Nova Scotia appointed him one of the first magistrates for the Passamaquoddy district, his fellow justices of the peace being William Pagan, Pote, Wyer, and Gallop.

During the ensuing decade Robert Pagan came to be the life-blood of the new community, named St Andrews in 1786. Backed by an international network stretching from Glasgow, Greenock, and London to the West Indies, New York, and Quebec, based primarily on family ties, he established himself firmly as the most prominent merchant in the Passamaquoddy region. Under the business style of Robert Pagan and Company, he engaged in the timber trade, mill operations, shipbuilding, the fishery, and wholesaling and retailing. In 1792 alone he built several seagoing vessels for the West Indies trade and a fine ship of 400 tons, large by the standard of the times, for the transatlantic and Caribbean trade. All of these vessels were constructed of black birch, which Pagan and his shipwrights were among the first to prove an effective and durable material for ship construction. He also established, with his brother William, a packet service from St Andrews to Saint John. In spite of competition from American ports, Pagan's lumbering operations prospered. During the course of them he and his brothers were accused by the deputy surveyor of the king's woods, James Glenie*, of taking timber from lands reserved to the crown but the charge, if there was any truth in it, was not followed up. Pagan was the principal source of financial backing for many of his fellow settlers and was thus able to orchestrate the economic development of the Passamaquoddy region. So successful was he in his shipbuilding and timber operations, it seemed in the 1790s that St Andrews would surpass Saint John as New Brunswick's chief port and commercial centre. "To his activity and enterprising spirit," Patrick CAMPBELL noted in commenting on the town, "his country is indebted for this colony."

Pagan also came to dominate the public life of the Passamaquoddy area. In 1785 he was elected to the House of Assembly for Charlotte County, a seat he held until 1819. With the support of his brother William and several leading merchants of Saint John, especially William Black*, he was able to introduce major pieces of legislation beneficial to the economic growth of the county and of the province generally, such as the act to encourage immigration in 1803. In committee he drafted legislation relating to fisheries, roads, mills, revenue, customs, trade, and communication. Despite their differences with James Glenie, both brothers found themselves making common cause with their aggressive fellow countryman against the administration of Lieutenant Governor Thomas Carleton*. Reaffirmed as a justice of the peace in 1785, Robert Pagan became as well a judge of the Inferior Court of Common Pleas for Charlotte County. From 1787 to about 1808 he was colonel commandant of the Charlotte County militia. A member of the Friendly Society in St Andrews, founded by the Reverend Samuel Andrews*, he was, along with another Scots merchant, Christopher SCOTT, a principal supporter of the town's Greenock (Presbyterian) Church, for the building of which he donated £100. In 1816, at least, he was a trustee of the local grammar school.

Robert Pagan performed an important service for New Brunswick during the discussions in 1796–98 to determine its border with the District of Maine. At that time he assisted Ward CHIPMAN, who was responsible for arguing the British case before the boundary commissioners. Indeed, it was the excavations conducted by Pagan and surveyor Thomas Wright* in 1797 that to a large extent settled the issue. Their discovery of the remains of buildings erected by Pierre Du Gua* de Monts and Samuel de Champlain* in 1604 determined which of three rivers known as the St Croix was the St Croix intended in early documents.

By 1815 Pagan was one of the 12 wealthiest men in the province, and in 1820, along with John ROBINSON and others, he became a founding member and shareholder of the Bank of New Brunswick. The scarcity of timber and shipping in Britain during the Napoleonic Wars and the ability of New Brunswick merchants to trade "on the Line" during the War of 1812 had brought large profits. However, a combina-

tion of factors had already begun to undermine St Andrews's rapidly acquired commercial prominence. Greater competition from the Americans in the West Indies trade, the loss of a major portion of the hinterland behind the town to a crown reserve, and the rise of St Stephen (St Stephen-Milltown) as a rival in shipping and commerce all eroded the influence of the town and its representatives. Pagan may also have suffered financially from the collapse of other businesses within the family empire. Although his estate was estimated to be worth some £20,000 at his death, it was reduced by a series of court judgements over the next 35 years to near bankruptcy. Pagan's sense of responsibility toward his community is shown in a statement he made on his deathbed. "No person," he stipulated, "[is to] be imprisoned on account of any Monies he owes to my Estate, and I would Rather Lose the amount than take such a Step during my life time."

DAVID S. MACMILLAN and ROGER NASON

Charlotte County Hist. Soc. Arch. (St Andrews, N.B.), Mowat papers. Charlotte Land Registry Office (St Andrews), Record books. N.B. Museum, G.B., Army, 74th Regiment, order-book, 1784 (transcript). PANB, RG 7, RS63; RG 18, RS148, A1. PRO, A0 12/11: 71–72; 12/61: 71; 12/109: 246/1695; AO 13, bundles 51, 93. SRO, RS54. P. Campbell, *Travels in North America* (Langton and Ganong). "United Empire Loyalists: enquiry into losses and services," *AO Report*, 1904. *New-Brunswick Royal Gazette*, 11 Dec. 1821. Jones, *Loyalists of Mass.* Sabine, *Biog. sketches of loyalists.* C. A. Armour and Thomas Lackey, *Sailing ships of the Maritimes . . . 1750–1925* (Toronto and Montreal, 1975). M. N. Cockburn, *A history of Greenock Church, St. Andrews, New Brunswick, from 1821 to 1906* (n.p., 1906). I. C. C. Graham, *Colonists from Scotland: emigration to North America, 1707–1783* (Ithaca, N.Y., 1956; repr. Port Washington, N.Y., and London, 1972). MacNutt, *New Brunswick.* R. P. Nason, "Meritorious but distressed individuals: the Penobscot Loyalist Association and the settlement of the township of St. Andrews, New Brunswick, 1783–1821" (MA thesis, Univ. of N.B., Fredericton, 1982). R. W. Sloan, "New Ireland: loyalists in eastern Maine during the American revolution" (PHD thesis, Mich. State Univ., East Lansing, 1971). D. R. Jack, "Robert and Miriam Pagan," *Acadiensis* (Saint John, N.B.), 2 (1902): 279–87. W. H. Siebert, "The exodus of the loyalists from Penobscot and the loyalist settlements at Passamaquoddy," N.B. Hist. Soc., *Coll.*, 3 (1907–14), no.9: 485–529. R. D. and J. I. Tallman, "The diplomatic search for the St. Croix River, 1796–1798," *Acadiensis* (Fredericton), 1 (1971–72), no.2: 59–71.

PAINE, WILLIAM, physician, office holder, and politician; b. 5 June 1750 in Worcester, Mass., son of Timothy Paine and Sarah Chandler; m. 23 Sept. 1773 Lois Orne of Salem, Mass., and they had six children; d. 19 April 1833 in Worcester.

Born into the prominent Paine–Chandler family, William Paine acquired his lifelong interest in the arts

Paine

and sciences as a young man at Harvard College. After graduating in 1768, he took up the study of medicine with the eminent Dr Edward Augustus Holyoke of Salem, and in 1771 he began his practice in Worcester, where he later brought his bride.

Although Paine apparently remained aloof from pre-revolutionary political debate, in favour of his studies, he was led by increasing disturbances to sign a protest on 20 June 1774 "against all riotous, disorderly, and seditious practices," especially against the "dark and pernicious proceedings" of the committees of correspondence. The town meeting rejected the protest and censured the signatories, forcing men such as Paine to make an unequivocal political stand, the determinant of which in his case lay more in the social and political position of his family, with its interest in maintaining the *status quo*, than in any ideological conviction. To avoid persecution, Paine sailed for England in 1774 to pursue medical studies, and in November 1775 he received an MD from Marischal College in Aberdeen, Scotland. Subsequently, he served until 1781 as apothecary to the British forces in the Carolinas, Rhode Island, and New York. Commissioned a physician in 1782, he was shortly thereafter ordered to Halifax, N.S. The following year, with the conclusion of peace, he was placed on half pay. Since he had forfeited his personal estate in 1779, Paine and his family joined the stream of refugees seeking new homes in British North America.

More fortunate than the majority of exiles, Paine received substantial grants of land in the Passamaquoddy Bay area of New Brunswick, as well as his half pay, and was awarded by the loyalist claims commission £300 on his claim of £1,440. He settled with his wife and three small children on Letete (Fryes) Island, with the initial optimism typical of so many loyalists: "My lands are certainly well located. . . . The island will soon be a place of consequence, and ultimately the principal Port in British North America." Within a year, however, he had moved to Saint John in search of greater opportunities. Entering political life immediately, he was appointed an alderman of the new city in 1785, elected to the first House of Assembly for Charlotte County that same year, and named clerk of the assembly in 1786; in 1785 he succeeded Benjamin Marston* in the salaried position of deputy to John Wentworth*, surveyor general of the king's woods, a post he filled conscientiously.

In spite of his extensive landholdings and various sources of income, Paine felt increasingly frustrated in his new home: "I am almost discouraged, and find it absolutely impossible for me with all the Industry, & Œconomy I am master of, to live upon my half pay & profession." He and his wife were also deeply concerned over the lack of educational opportunities for their children, which led him in 1785 to join others in petitioning Governor Thomas Carleton* for "an Academy or School of Liberal Arts and Sciences." In 1787 Paine visited the United States in order to attend to financial affairs (unresolved since his pre-revolutionary days), and in spite of his avowed intentions to return to New Brunswick he remained in Massachusetts. He resettled his wife and children first in Salem, and then in the family home at Worcester in 1793. Besides achieving financial prosperity, he attained a position of distinction in the new republic: he became an honorary member of the Massachusetts Medical Society and a fellow of the American Academy of Arts and Sciences, received an honorary MD from Harvard College, and was a founding member of the American Antiquarian Society, to name only the most prestigious of his connections. His assimilation into the United States was completed on 14 July 1812 when he became an American citizen. He died at the age of 82, on 19 April 1833.

Paine remains an intriguing loyalist figure because of his uncommon decision to return permanently to his native home, where he not only achieved social acceptance but acquired wealth, honour, and dignity as well. Although the reasons for such complete acceptance of a former renegade on the part of Paine's neighbours, especially in a society that demanded outward consensus, remain largely conjectural, the most probable explanation lies in his own personality. His apparent lack of strong ideological bias, his academic nature, and his professional desirability all helped to ease his return to his original home.

CAROL ANNE JANZEN

William Paine's papers are held by the American Antiquarian Soc. (Worcester, Mass.) and are available on microfilm at the UNBL. The major part of the collection consists of business and legal documents, and day-books concerning Paine's farm in Worcester following his return there in 1787; however, there are also some letters and journals which reveal something of the man himself. Some of his correspondence was published as William Paine, "Letters of William Paine, 1769," Mass. Hist. Soc., *Proc.* (Boston), 59 (1925–26): 422–24; he is also the author of *An address to the members of the American Antiquarian Society, pronounced in King's Chapel, Boston, on their third anniversary, October 12, 1815* (Worcester, 1815).

PANS, MG 1, 939–40. UNBL, MG H2. "Worcester town records," Worcester Soc. of Antiquity, *Coll.* (Worcester), 5 (1883). *Massachusetts Gazette, and the Boston Weekly News-Letter* (Boston), 30 June 1774. *Massachusetts Spy* (Boston), 30 Sept. 1773. *Commissioned officers in the medical services of the British army, 1660–1960*, comp. Alfred Peterkin *et al.* (2v., London, 1968). Jones, *Loyalists of Mass.* Shipton, *Sibley's Harvard graduates.* Stark, *Loyalists of Mass.* (1907). *Worcester births, marriages, and deaths,* comp. F. P. Rice (Worcester, 1894). Esther Clark Wright, *The loyalists of New Brunswick* (Fredericton, 1955; repr. Moncton, N.B., 1972, and Hantsport, N.S., 1981). G. E. Francis, *Notes on the life and character of Dr. William*

Paine (Worcester, 1900). Lawrence, *Judges of N.B.* (Stockton and Raymond). MacNutt, *New Brunswick.* Louisa Dresser, "Worcester silversmiths and the examples of their work in the collections of the museum," Worcester Art Museum, *Annual* (Worcester), 1 (1935–36): 49–57. J. W. Lawrence, "The medical men of St. John in its first half century," N.B. Hist. Soc., *Coll.*, 1 (1894–97), no.3: 273–305. W. S. MacNutt, "New England's tory neighbors," Colonial Soc. of Mass., *Trans.* (Boston), 43 (1956–63): 345–61. W. H. Siebert, "The exodus of the loyalists from Penobscot and the loyalist settlements at Passamaquoddy," N.B. Hist. Soc., *Coll.*, 3 (1907–14), no.9: 485–529. E. O. P. Sturgis, "A sketch of the children of Dr. William Paine," Worcester Soc. of Antiquity, *Proc.* (Worcester), 20 (1904): 129–42. James Vroom, "Dr. William Paine," *Saint Croix Courier* (St Stephen, N.B.), 29 June 1893: 1.

PALMER, JAMES BARDIN, land agent, lawyer, office holder, and politician; b. *c.* 1771, younger son of Joseph Palmer and Susanna Bardin of Dublin; m. 22 Dec. 1803, in Charlottetown, Millicent Jones of London, and they had 12 children; d. 3 March 1833 in Charlottetown.

James Bardin Palmer's father was an ironmonger but both James and his elder brother became lawyers. James clerked to Benjamin Johnson of the Irish bar and was admitted as a solicitor in Chancery in 1791. By 1795 he was practising in the courts of King's Bench and Common Pleas, but he left Dublin for London before 1800. Enemies later charged that during his time in London he was reduced to "an advertising place broker, army agent, officer in the Devon militia, Clerk in the Lottery Office, and sometime a prisoner in the King's Bench." That there was a measure of truth to the charge is evidenced by Palmer's admission that he had "failed in his circumstances" before coming to Prince Edward Island as a land agent. He arrived in August 1802 as the agent of the Reverend Raphael Walsh of Dublin, half-brother of Benjamin Johnson.

The Walsh estate on Prince Edward Island was the whole of Lot 11, in the western part of the colony. The 20,000-acre township was one of the poorest on the Island, being mostly bog, but Palmer undertook expensive schemes for opening it up and attracting tenants. His efforts did not meet with success, and when Walsh refused to honour bills, his agent found himself in financial difficulties. It was not until 1807 that the matter was settled, following a visit to Ireland by Palmer who later stated that the affair had cost him £1,000.

Palmer had apparently not intended to practise law on Prince Edward Island, but after arriving there he decided that the opportunity was too great to be missed. There were only three practising attorneys in the courts – Joseph Robinson*, Peter Magowan*, and Charles Stewart* – and all of them were allied to the faction led by Lieutenant Governor Edmund Fanning* and Chief Justice Peter Stewart*; indeed, Charles Stewart was son of the chief justice. Palmer was admitted to the bar in November 1802 and immediately found employment in pressing actions for those opposed to Fanning and the Stewarts, such as James Montgomery and merchant John Hill*. Palmer's vigour and his legal knowledge and experience led to success in the courts, but his manner inflamed passions in the community, and within a year he had earned the reputation of being "an unpopular character and a man detested by the Governor," in the words of merchant Alexander Rea (Rae). The pattern of creating bitter enemies through legal activity became characteristic of Palmer's relations with almost all of those with whom he dealt in the colony.

Following the arrival of Lieutenant Governor Joseph Frederick Wallet DESBARRES in 1805, Palmer was thrust into a position of political importance. Evidently DesBarres was soon aware of the conflict in the colony for he wrote shortly after his arrival: "The one party seems to contend for a Democratical Institution, the other for an Aristocratical one, surely some measure may be devised and adopted for keeping in perfect consonance with our excellent Constitution, a due proportion of Aristocracy and Democracy in this island." He determined that many of the problems in the administration stemmed from deficiencies in the legal system and stressed the need for a lawyer on the Council. Unfortunately for the "perfect consonance," the lawyer he chose was Palmer, whom he appointed in June 1806. Palmer immediately involved the administration in a dispute with the Stewart faction by demanding an accounting of the quitrent fund from Charles Stewart. Stewart took the position that, having been appointed to the Treasury in London, he was accountable only to that office and he refused Palmer's demand. Intervention by DesBarres failed to resolve the dispute, and Palmer was unable to push the matter further because he lacked public support. He blamed this lack on promises made by the Fanning group – the "grand political bubble the escheat" – and he acknowledged that even the elected House of Assembly was opposed to DesBarres.

Palmer resigned from the Council in October 1806 and successfully ran for one of the Charlottetown seats in the general election held late that year. He sat during a short session in 1806 but was absent from the colony in 1808 during the second session. In October 1809 he was once again called to the Council. Palmer made himself indispensable to DesBarres and gathered a wide range of posts and positions including those of adjutant general of the militia, inspector of public accounts, master and registrar in Chancery, and inspector of roads. In the last post especially, Palmer displayed an enthusiasm for planning and building that was difficult to reconcile with the economic state

Palmer

of the colony but that met with the approbation of the lieutenant governor. In 1810 DesBarres's insistence on written responses to his proposal for major changes in the administration of public works brought the factions on the Council into sharp disagreement, with Chief Justice Cæsar COLCLOUGH opposing Palmer and DesBarres.

The 1806 election which had brought Palmer to the assembly had also seen the first appearance of a political group with which he became closely associated. The Society of Loyal Electors probably made its debut during the campaign, although Palmer later stated that it had not been formed until after he was a member of the house. It certainly played little role in the election, and its importance has been overstressed by historians, owing to a controversy five years later which was to provide exposure and examination it would not otherwise have received. Certainly, Palmer and four others elected in 1806 formed a more cohesive opposition group than was usual in the assembly but in 1809, perhaps expecting more lucrative political appointments, Palmer resigned from the house. He was then named to the Council.

Palmer's political opponents were alarmed at the influence he enjoyed with DesBarres. Colclough described him as a person "of some talent and more impudence" who had taken "possession" of the lieutenant governor, bending his thoughts and convincing him that the officers of the government were his opponents. The efforts of the two sides crystallized with the struggle for the attorney generalship which followed the death of Peter Magowan in June 1810. DesBarres supported Palmer for the office, while Colclough and the "old party" sought the appointment of Charles Stewart. In a detailed letter to the Colonial Office DesBarres recommended Palmer as successor. He was critical of other members of the legal profession on the Island and dismissed Stewart's qualifications lightly. His comments did not reach sympathetic ears, for the absentee proprietors in London, influenced by reports from their own sources on the Island, had been at work. Lord Selkirk [Douglas*] wrote to Lord Liverpool early in 1811 that Palmer was "so extremely objectionable in every respect." Under orders from London, Stewart's appointment was registered in November 1811.

Despite this personal set-back for Palmer, the Loyal Electors had made gains. By 1809 the society had attracted to its membership powerful individuals such as Angus MACAULAY, leader of the settlers brought out by Selkirk, and William ROUBEL, a London lawyer who had been induced to come to the Island by John Hill. The influence of the Electors was increased with the founding of the *Weekly Recorder of Prince Edward Island* in 1810 by James Bagnall*, himself a member of the society since its organization. William B. Haszard and William Hyde successfully fought by-elections under the banner of the Electors the same year, but the results were overturned because of irregularities.

The Loyal Electors came under public scrutiny as the result of charges directed against Palmer rather than against the organization itself. The opening shots were fired in April 1811 by Thomas Marsh and John Frederick Holland*, who swore affidavits that Palmer had proposed a secret committee to manage the affairs of the society. The charge amounted to an accusation of subversion and disloyalty. Marsh was then engaged in a lengthy suit with Palmer over the ownership of some 10,000 acres, and Holland had been openly opposed to Palmer since the latter gained the lieutenant governor's ear. Palmer's response to the charge was supported by four affidavits from members of the Loyal Electors which denied allegations of secrecy and disloyalty. These responses also contained detailed complaints against Colclough, Stewart, and the colony's unpaid judges, James Curtis* and Robert GRAY. Although the original complaint and the responses had been made to the lieutenant governor, word of their contents soon reached Colclough's ears and in October he obtained copies. Instead of treating them as evidence in the case against Palmer, he allowed them to be the basis of libel actions against Macaulay and Haszard and a charge of contempt against Roubel. Roubel refused to submit to questions put to him by the attorney general, and on 7 Nov. 1811 Colclough ordered his name struck from the roll of barristers for the contempt and for "threatening to exhibit charges against the Chief Justice at the Secretary of State's office." A public meeting called in support of Roubel met with such approval that the actions against Macaulay and Haszard were not proceeded with.

The Loyal Electors had a chance to test their support amongst the electorate when DesBarres called a general election in April 1812. Palmer again resigned from the Council to run and was again successful. The Loyal Electors increased their membership from five to seven in the 18-seat house. In September, a month after the house began sitting, a number of other members including James Curtis, Charles Worrell*, and Fade Goff* chose not to appear, and the Loyal Electors gained effective control of the assembly. The house then investigated the events surrounding the use made of the affidavits; instead of placing the blame on the lieutenant governor for releasing the information, it resolved that Colclough had obtained and used the documents illegally and it sought his dismissal. Armed with this support, DesBarres suspended the chief justice a few days later, on 30 September.

Meanwhile on the other side of the Atlantic, the proprietors' lobby was bringing pressure on the Colonial Office and in August DesBarres had been stripped of his post and the Island's administration given to William Townshend*. After the arrival in October of the dispatches Palmer was removed from the many minor positions he had collected under DesBarres. Late in the year he went to England in an effort to clear his name and regain some of the government posts he had lost.

Within a year all the leading characters of the drama except for Palmer had left the stage. DesBarres was banished to retirement, and Colclough to Newfoundland. Attorney General Charles Stewart died. Of the new protagonists, Stewart's successor, William JOHNSTON, became one of Palmer's bitterest enemies, and the new chief justice, Thomas TREMLETT, fell under Palmer's control. The new lieutenant governor, Charles Douglass Smith*, arrived already prejudiced against Palmer. Smith had been ordered to keep an open mind and to steer clear of party affiliation, but he was well aware of the charges against Palmer and the Loyal Electors because of correspondence he had received from individuals such as John Hill who had interests on the Island. Palmer's supporters failed to gain the ear of the lieutenant governor and Smith soon wrote that he was completely in agreement with the reports critical of Palmer.

While in England Palmer prepared a lengthy and detailed defence of his actions and badgered Lord Bathurst and other Colonial Office officials to review the affair. He met with limited success. On his return to the colony late in 1813 he found Tremlett installed in office, and it was not long before the chief justice and the lieutenant governor were at odds. Tremlett, untrained, quickly became dependent on the skill and experience of Palmer. Palmer, as usual, plainly benefited from the relationship, for by mid 1814 Smith was complaining that it "would not be safe to suffer any question of Property to be tried in the Supreme Court against Palmer, *with him* any man may be sure of success." The lieutenant governor also noted that Tremlett had arranged sittings of the court to allow Palmer to carry on a law practice in Pictou, N.S.

Despite the growing association of Tremlett and Palmer, Smith had greater problems. The corruption and petty politics of the colony were soon evident, and he complained that he was in charge of an administration where the chief justice would not do his duty, the attorney general was so ill he could not, two members of the Council were dying, another was living so far away he could not attend, and a fourth suffered from "political indisposition"; moreover, the militia was insubordinate. Smith continued to see the machinations of the Loyal Electors behind his problems and in 1815 linked them with the freemasons but, in fact, with the 1812 election the Loyal Electors had ceased to have any political importance in the colony.

Palmer meanwhile seemed unable to resist making further trouble through his legal practice. While he was in England in 1813 he was contacted by the creditors of John Hill concerning the fraudulent concealment of assets by Hill at the time of his bankruptcy in 1807. When Palmer returned to the Island he set out to prove the allegations. Hill, alarmed by Palmer's efforts, combined with Johnston to bring eight charges of professional and political misconduct against him, some of which predated his first arrival on the Island. They were brought in the Court of Chancery, where Smith presided as chancellor, rather than in the Supreme Court. Refused time to prepare a defence, Palmer was struck off the roll of barristers on 14 Nov. 1816. His request to appeal to the king in council was turned down by Smith and within two months Palmer was on his way to England seeking to have the matter reviewed and the decision overturned. At the time he considered leaving the Island for good and practising in the appeal court for the colonies, a forum with which he was becoming quite familiar. While in England, however, he was able to secure the support of some of the Island's absentee proprietors and he returned to the colony late in 1817 or early in 1818 as agent for Lord Westmorland and Lord Melville.

The appointment brought him into further confrontation with Attorney General Johnston, who had been Westmorland's and Melville's agent. Palmer had previously been critical of Johnston's Scottish training and complained that he was "unacquainted with the law, or at least the practice of English courts." The two frequently clashed in the courts and whether it was Palmer's skill or his influence over Tremlett, Johnston was rarely successful. Palmer now charged that Johnston had not accounted for funds relating to the Westmorland estate and in February 1818 took the complaint to Smith and the Council. Johnston's defence was couched in personal terms and referred to the "implacable animosity" that Palmer bore towards him. The Council decided it was not expedient at the time to suspend Johnston, but early in 1819 the lieutenant governor reported the "political necessity" of his having asked both Johnston and his ally Holland to resign as councillors. Palmer was reinstated on the roll of barristers in January 1819. A report on the affair by the law officer to the Colonial Office in August indicated that although Palmer was not beyond reproach he was not guilty of any offence warranting disbarment. For a few years Palmer steered clear of deep involvement in the colony's politics, although he did unsuccessfully seek a seat in the assembly in 1824, as he had done in 1818. Smith's escheat of two townships in 1818 had alarmed the proprietors and it united the forces that he had been alienating since his arrival in the colony. Palmer, writing to Roubel, noted with apparent satisfaction that there was "a Cabal against Smith very like that against our old friend his predecessor."

By 1823 Smith's unpopularity had resulted in a

Palmer

series of public meetings asking for his recall. When the proceedings were published that fall in the *Prince Edward Island Register*, he brought charges in the Court of Chancery for contempt and libel. Palmer was instructed to bring the charges but this move by Smith does not signal a reconciliation between the two so much as it does the extent of Smith's isolation in the community. Johnston was reported to be supporting the faction led by John STEWART, who escaped to England with the complaints against Smith. The lieutenant governor asked that Johnston be removed as attorney general and in April 1824 he named Palmer to the post. The appointment remained temporary despite Palmer's attempts to disassociate himself from the charges made against Smith. Less than two weeks after Smith's departure in November, the newly appointed lieutenant governor, John Ready*, reappointed Johnston to the post. Johnston and Palmer remained bitter antagonists until the death of the former four years later.

Shortly after his first arrival on the Island Palmer had been engaged by merchant John CAMBRIDGE and for many years had kept the case of *Bowley* v. *Cambridge* before the courts in both Prince Edward Island and England. His complex legal stratagems resulted in high costs for the litigants, especially when the arcane practice before the Court of Chancery (Palmer's specialty) was employed. In 1823 Palmer, in collecting arrears of rent on the estate which was the subject of the litigation, had ruined several tenant farmers. The proceedings were reviewed by the House of Assembly in 1825 as part of an attack on the officers of the Court of Chancery. The assembly saw Palmer's actions as having only one purpose, "to obtain illegal fees by illegal courses," and asked Lieutenant Governor Ready to institute an inquiry into Palmer's conduct. Palmer arrogantly refused to have anything to do with the inquiry and questioned the authority of the house even to consider his activities as a solicitor. Ready had the charges investigated by judge Brenton Halliburton* of Nova Scotia but the case dragged on without action being taken. When in 1827 the assembly formed its own committee to look into the matter Palmer once again refused cooperation. Later in that year he was elected in a by-election but when the house sat in the spring of 1828 it ruled that because of the Chancery actions Palmer was "unworthy and unfit" to take his seat and refused him admission. A court action based on the charges was dismissed the same year owing to want of prosecution.

Palmer had run in nearly every election and by-election held in the colony since his arrival, and by the late 1820s his electoral ambition was becoming something of a joke. Following his defeat in the by-election held because of the assembly's refusal to let him sit, it was noted by James Douglas Haszard*, publisher of the *Prince Edward Island Register*, that

Palmer's political life "had had its alloted time upon the earth, and it melted away like a lump of fetid grease, leaving nothing behind but the smell." Haszard was premature in his judgement, for Palmer fought by-elections in 1829 and again in 1830, unsuccessfully.

After his expulsion from the assembly in 1828 Palmer and others sought to establish a new newspaper on "loyal, patriotic and impartial principles." They advertised in Nova Scotia for a printer but it was James Bagnall of Charlottetown who brought out the *Phenix*. Palmer used the paper as a public forum to refute the charges against him, to seek re-election, and to press for all the reforms he felt were necessary in the colony, ranging from improvements in agriculture to changes in the courts. The newspaper had too much of the strident tone of Palmer to meet with success and fell back among the ashes in August 1828 after 15 issues.

Palmer continued to be active in the courts until his death, apparently from a stroke, in 1833. Since Charles Stewart's death in 1813 he had been senior member of the colony's bar, and many of the barristers and solicitors practising had been trained in his office. Among these were two of his sons, Henry and Edward*. In an obituary in the *Royal Gazette* Haszard praised his legal skills and noted that "to recapitulate the principal incidents of his public life during his thirty years' residence in this Colony, would be to write the history of the Island during that period, for in almost all public transactions, until latterly, he bore a part, either in supporting or opposing them."

The principal incidents of Palmer's public life have overshadowed the very real contributions he made to the law on Prince Edward Island. In addition to being the leading lawyer in the colony, he practised in Nova Scotia and possibly in New Brunswick. He wrote in 1813 that "an independent lawyer is the subject of perpetual alarm in P.E.Id.," and perhaps this independence is the key to the extreme reactions that he provoked. He was no doubt an individual of unsavoury characteristics who took every advantage he could either for himself or for his clients, but there are few criticisms of his professional ability. He had a deep interest in the evolution of the courts of the Island and was himself responsible for several important changes. He wrote the rules for the Court of Chancery and through his own successful practice made that court of equity a force to balance the shortcomings and political connections of judges and court officials of the Island's Supreme Court. He was instrumental in the colony's acquisition of a law library to remedy the situation described by DesBarres: "One hundred pounds would purchase in England a better selection of Law Books, than the joint stock of all the Judges and Lawyers in this Island would exhibit." He was not successful in all his efforts to improve legal services, however. From the time of his arrival he sought to ensure greater access to the law for those who lived some distance from the capital. He urged the establishment of courts of quarter sessions in places other than Charlottetown, but at his death the system remained unchanged, and it was not until the following year that county sittings of the Supreme Court were finally held.

James Bardin Palmer's 30 years on Prince Edward Island gave rise to a litany of complaint which for the most part has been uncritically accepted by historians. Yet few of the complainants could be regarded as disinterested and most had suffered as a result of Palmer's legal skills. Annoying and petty as Palmer could be, he was possessed of an obstinate determination. He successfully defended himself against all of the major complaints which were brought in his lifetime but in so doing usually created more enemies. It is fortunate that he was so good a lawyer, for he was often his own best client.

H. T. HOLMAN

James Bardin Palmer from time to time made announcements in the press concerning planned publications, but it appears that only one work was actually published, *The fruits of reflection; or, second thoughts are best: a little tract relating to Prince Edward Island* (Pictou, N.S., 1827). There are two Palmer collections at the PAPEI: the Palmer family papers (Acc. 2849), which include copies of his outgoing correspondence as well as other material, and the Palmer papers in the Smith–Alley collection, Acc. 2702/216–18, 221, 223, 236–38, 242, 319, 334, 346, 459–60, 833–34, 836–41, 843–51, 853–56, 858.

PAPEI, Acc. 2702/428, 430, 432, 437–41, 446, 463–65; Acc. 2810/25–26, 2810/138, 2810/145, 2810/154, 2810/171–72, 2810/174, 2810/182b–c; RG 1, letter-books, 54–56; RG 5, minutes, 1805–29; RG 6, Court of Chancery, minute-books, 1808–30; docket-books, 1802–10; prothonotary account-book, 1820–27; Supreme Court, case papers, 1802–25; minutes, 1802–27. PRO, CO 226/18: 33, 56, 70, 72, 82, 117, 134, 139, 166, 188, 198, 241; 226/19: 176, 202, 217, 221; 226/20: 15, 17, 43, 112–13; 226/21: 237; 226/22: 159, 182, 198, 221; 226/24: 74; 226/25: 11, 35, 80; 226/26: 15, 39; 226/28: 3, 8, 24, 53, 61, 137; 226/29: 19, 67, 115, 118, 153; 226/30: 7, 17; 226/31: 5, 12, 63, 72, 182, 243; 226/32: 251, 268, 270, 272, 304, 308, 311; 226/33: 41; 226/34: 57, 61, 347, 351; 226/35: 69, 303; 226/39: 264, 414; 226/40: 58, 160, 333; 226/43: 257; 226/45: 50, 52, 58, 64, 68, 175, 389 (mfm. at PAPEI). SRO, GD293/2/17. St Paul's Anglican Church (Charlottetown), Reg. of marriages, 22 Dec. 1803 (mfm. at PAPEI). P.E.I., House of Assembly, *Journal*, 1802–30.

Phenix (Charlottetown), 21–28 April, 5–19 May, 16 June, 7 July, 20 Aug. 1828. *Prince Edward Island Gazette* (Charlottetown), 5 Nov. 1818, 1 Aug. 1820, 13 April 1822. *Prince Edward Island Register*, 6–13 Sept., 11, 25 Oct., 1, 15 Nov., 20 Dec. 1823; 24 Jan., 6 March, 29 Dec. 1824; 22 April, 1 July 1825; 28 Feb. 1826; 20 Feb.–6 March, 15 May, 7 Aug., 13 Nov. 1827; 28 Feb., 7–13, 25 March, 1–15 April, 20 May, 24 June 1828; 16 June, 14 July, 3 Nov. 1829; 16 March, 22 June 1830. *Royal Gazette* (Charlottetown), 5 March 1833. *Royal Herald* (Charlottetown), 19 Jan., 21 Nov. 1805. *Weekly Recorder of Prince Edward Island* (Charlottetown), 23 Oct. 1810; 9 Feb., 3, 16 April, 18 July, 31 Aug., 2, 15, 26 Oct., 16 Nov. 1811; 28 March 1812; 12 June 1813. *Canada's smallest prov.* (Bolger), 75–99. G. N. D. Evans, *Uncommon obdurate: the several public careers of J. F. W. DesBarres* (Toronto and Salem, Mass., 1969), 79–94. Frank MacKinnon, *The government of Prince Edward Island* (Toronto, 1951), 53–56. Warburton, *Hist. of P.E.I.*, 291–361, 431–39. J. M. Bumsted, "The Loyal Electors of Prince Edward Island," *Island Magazine*, no.8 (1980): 8–14. D. C. Harvey, "The Loyal Electors," RSC *Trans.*, 3rd ser., 24 (1930), sect.II: 101–10.

PANET, BERNARD-CLAUDE, Roman Catholic priest and archbishop; b. 9 Jan. 1753 at Quebec, son of Jean-Claude Panet*, a notary, and Marie-Louise Barolet; d. there 14 Feb. 1833 at the Hôtel-Dieu and was buried four days later in the cathedral of Notre-Dame.

Bernard-Claude Panet came from a family of 14 children, among them Jean-Antoine*, who became the first speaker of the Lower Canadian House of Assembly, and JACQUES, who was parish priest at L'Islet from 1779 to 1829. He received his entire education at the Petit Séminaire and the Grand Séminaire de Québec. Ordained priest by Bishop Jean-Olivier Briand* on 25 Oct. 1778, he taught the sixth form (Rhetoric) and the final two years of the classical program (Philosophy) at the Petit Séminaire from 1777 till 1780. One of his pupils was Joseph-Octave PLESSIS.

In the autumn of 1780 Panet was chosen to minister to the parishes of Batiscan and Champlain. The following year he became parish priest of Notre-Dame-de-Liesse, at Rivière-Ouelle, a progressive parish that was, however, being undermined by strife. The authority of its previous curé, Jean-Louis-Laurent Parent, had always been hotly disputed, particularly during the American invasion in 1775, and in 1780 some people had even called upon him to leave. Bishop Briand had not given in to the rebellious parishioners, but after Parent's death in March 1781 he had to find a successor who could settle things down. Panet was "by nature kind and affable, pious, zealous, and charitable," as his biographer Mgr Henri Têtu* noted, and by displaying great patience and diplomacy he restored harmony. A practical and methodical man, he administered the parish in an exemplary manner. He also showed himself to be extremely charitable, feeding poor children who attended catechism and people who came from some distance to the church and had to wait around for vespers. He never refused to give alms, even to strangers.

In 1792 he secured general agreement from his parishioners to erect a new church; he was named treasurer and chief supervisor of the project. The building was completed in 1794, but for some years he continued working on its decoration, giving contracts to such craftsmen as Louis Dulongpré*, François BAILLAIRGÉ, and Louis QUÉVILLON. He uniformly bought consecrated vessels of great value. Being particularly interested in teaching, Panet had a convent built in 1807 and there, two years later, he installed the sisters of the Congregation of Notre-Dame. He had the *fabrique* establish an elementary school in 1824. He was also interested in agriculture and settlement and set an example by joining the Agriculture Society in the district of Quebec in 1791 and serving as a patron for the Société Auxiliaire d'Agriculture de Sainte-Anne de la Grande-Anse.

Panet's influence soon spread beyond his parish. The bishop of Quebec chose him as his delegate in the region between Quebec and Rimouski, particularly for the delicate missions that inquiries about building a presbytery (at Kamouraska, for example) or a church (at Trois-Pistoles, among other places) often proved to be. His wisdom and sense of fairness were generally recognized. This reputation did not escape the notice of his superiors. Plessis, who had been named bishop of Quebec in 1806, asked to have Panet as his coadjutor because, as he noted in a letter to Rome, he was "the best qualified in terms of piety, talents, and reputation," and "highly thought of by his flock, which he has constantly edified by his regular life and his conscientious attention to preaching and the duties of holy ministry."

On 12 July 1806, with the approval of the authorities in Great Britain and Rome, Panet was chosen as bishop of Saldae *in partibus infidelium* and coadjutor to the bishop of Quebec. He was consecrated by Plessis on 19 August of the following year. Plessis proposed to establish Panet in the Séminaire de Saint-Sulpice in Montreal, but the superior, Jean-Henry-Auguste ROUX, twice resisted this step, fearing that his authority would be overshadowed and his independence diminished. Panet was happy to remain the curé at Rivière-Ouelle, where besides ministering to a large parish with 1,400 communicants in 1804 and 2,000 in 1826 he assumed the duties associated with his new title. These tasks obliged him to be absent from his parish more often, and to participate on a regular basis in the rather brilliant social life of the colony at this period.

As coadjutor Panet continued to preside over various inquiries and to settle virtually all the parish problems in the region below Quebec, which he duly reported to his bishop in voluminous correspondence. His main task, however, was making pastoral visits to various areas, including the north shore of the St Lawrence. In the Montreal region from 1814 he was accompanied by the Sulpician Jean-Jacques Lartigue*.

During Plessis's stay in Europe in 1819–20 Panet moved to Quebec and ran the archdiocese in accordance with the instructions left by his superior, who had been named archbishop in 1819. On all occasions the coadjutor had been Plessis's chief counsellor. For example, when Plessis wanted to publish a new catechism, Panet encouraged him by acknowledging that "the shorter Quebec catechism could be greatly improved," and sent some observations that he had conveyed to the parish priests in his district, and later some remarks on the text that Plessis had prepared; when a debate arose between Plessis and certain Sulpicians following publication of the new *Petit catéchisme du diocèse de Québec* in 1815, the coadjutor took the bishop's side, even while criticizing some expressions and turns of phrase as faulty. This example illustrates well how Panet saw his role as coadjutor: a judicious counsellor for his superior, whom he supported while retaining the right to his own ideas.

When Plessis died in December 1825, the 72-year-old Panet became archbishop of Quebec. There was apprehension in certain quarters, particularly in Montreal, about what attitude the new incumbent would take. Would this "quiet man" with the conciliatory spirit not let himself be outwitted by the skilful manœuvring of the government or the subtle arguments of the Sulpicians? He quickly made known, however, his desire to follow in the footsteps of his predecessor and to leave things as he had found them, "without changing anything in any way." The Sulpicians were the first to discover that these were not idle words. In December 1825 their superior, Roux, who had come to put out feelers and suggest certain arrangements, met with the reply from the new archbishop that he would adopt the same position as Plessis had held. When Lartigue, who had become the auxiliary in Montreal to the archbishop of Quebec on 21 Jan. 1821, encountered difficulties with his former colleagues in the Séminaire de Saint-Sulpice, Panet fully backed him and unhesitatingly censured the Sulpicians' conduct severely. Similarly, when the Sulpicians proposed to the British government that part of their property be exchanged for an income in perpetuity [*see* Jean-Henry-Auguste Roux], Panet joined Lartigue in denouncing this "despoliation of the Canadian church's property," and together they eventually succeeded in getting Rome and London to reject the agreement that the Sulpicians obtained in 1827. In March 1830 Rome temporarily suspended the permission previously granted to Roux to alienate the seminary's property, and in October the British government decided against carrying out the arrangements that had been made with the Sulpicians. Finally, while restraining his impetuous auxiliary somewhat, Panet supported him steadfastly in his efforts to create a diocese in Montreal. He showed the same firmness in dealing with the rest of his clergy. To ensure respect for some of his decisions, in particular changes in parish charges, he did not hesitate to be stern, even though his naturally kind character made him lean to indulgence. He was sometimes accused of being autocratic, but there is every indication that he was able to gather around him a council of wise men whom he consulted on all important questions.

Panet's relations with the governmental authorities were marked with prudence and apprehension. Unlike Bishop Lartigue, who preached independence with regard to the state, Panet did not dare to undertake anything without the government's approval, and he often put off actions that could cause a conflict with the Executive Council. To justify this course, he always referred to the attitude that Plessis had adopted.

Education for the young was one of Panet's main concerns during his term. He supported the Collège de Sainte-Anne-de-la-Pocatière and especially the Séminaire de Nicolet with both his influence and his money. For a time he hoped for the establishment of a Roman Catholic committee of the Royal Institution for the Advancement of Learning, but in its absence he was instrumental in obtaining grants through an act of 1829 to build schools and support various colleges, academies, and convents in Lower Canada. In 1829 he also completed his predecessor's work on the catechism, publishing the *Grand catéchisme à l'usage du diocèse de Québec*.

Several other matters took up Panet's attention: a bill expanding the role of the *fabriques* [*see* Louis BOURDAGES], which through his efforts was blocked by the Legislative Council; the problem of the civil erection of parishes, which was finally settled in 1831; the cholera epidemic which struck Quebec and Montreal in 1832. These concerns and his advanced age impelled him to offer his resignation in order that his powers might pass to his coadjutor, Bishop Joseph Signay*. Rome refused it twice, in the autumn of 1831 and in January 1832, although allowing him to delegate some of his authority. But as his strength was declining rapidly, Panet entrusted administration of the archdiocese to Signay on 13 Oct. 1832 and retired to the Hôtel-Dieu in Quebec the following month. There, on 14 Feb. 1833, he died, leaving behind the memory, as Signay said, of "tender piety, unfailing gentleness, compassionate charity towards others, constant zeal for the salvation of his flock." Mgr Têtu emphasized that "his modest talents, his rare good sense" had been sufficient to ensure that he would not be eclipsed by his illustrious predecessor.

NIVE VOISINE

AAQ, 20 A, IV; 210 A, VIII–XIV; 24 CP, I–IV. ANQ-Q, CE1-1, 10 janv. 1753, 18 févr. 1833. Arch. du séminaire de Nicolet (Nicolet, Qué.), Séminaire, I: 21. ASQ, Polygraphie, XIV: 7A. [J.-O. Plessis], *Le petit catéchisme du diocèse de Québec, approuvé et autorisé* (Québec, 1815). "Testament de Mgr Panet, évêque de Québec," *BRH*, 51 (1945): 203–5. Allaire, *Dictionnaire*. Caron, "Inv. de la corr. de Mgr Panet," ANQ *Rapport*, 1933–34; 1934–35; 1935–36. Henri Têtu, *Notices biographiques; les évêques de Québec* (Québec, 1889; réimpr. en 4v., Québec et Tours, France, 1930). Raymond Brodeur, "Identité culturelle et identité religieuse, étude d'un cas: *Le petit catéchisme du diocèse de Québec, approuvé et autorisé par Mgr J. O. Plessis, Québec, le 1er avril 1815*" (2v., thèse de PHD, univ. de Paris-Sorbonne, 1982). Chaussé, *Jean-Jacques Lartigue*. P.-H. Hudon, *Rivière-Ouelle de la Bouteillerie; 3 siècles de vie* (Ottawa, 1972). Lambert, "Joseph-Octave Plessis." Lemieux, *L'établissement de la première prov. eccl.* [M.-E. Perreault] Mme E. Croff, *Nos ancêtres à l'œuvre à la Rivière-Ouelle* (Montréal, 1931). Ivanhoë Caron, "La mort de Mgr Panet racontée par Mgr Signay," *BRH*, 44 (1938): 7–8.

PANET, JACQUES, Roman Catholic priest; b. 14 Feb. 1754 at Quebec, son of Jean-Claude Panet*, a notary, and Marie-Louise Barolet; d. 23 May 1834 in L'Islet, Lower Canada, and was buried under the step of the high altar in the parish church.

Like his brother BERNARD-CLAUDE, Jacques Panet chose to become a priest. He was ordained by Bishop Jean-Olivier Briand* on 29 May 1779 and in October was named parish priest of Notre-Dame-de-Bon-Secours at L'Islet, which he served until his retirement on 7 Oct. 1829. To be priest of the same parish for 50 years might well suggest an unusual career as an ecclesiastic. This irremovable *curé* had in fact refused a new appointment to Saint-Thomas (at Montmagny) in 1798. Twenty years later his parishioners at L'Islet presented Bishop Joseph-Octave PLESSIS with a demand that he be moved, maintaining that he was no longer capable of doing his job. The bishop assigned a curate to the controversial incumbent. Almost immediately Panet began quarrelling with his assistant, and dismissed him. Despite offers from the bishop and grumbling from the parishioners, Panet remained in office.

Panet certainly had more bookish education than most people. In 1810 his library contained 150 volumes. His sermons and correspondence give proof of his exceptional knowledge of theological, moral, and legal matters. The other side of this eccentric figure was not so engaging. He not only failed to get along with his curate, but also was often on bad terms with his flock, when he was not quarrelling with his bishop. On one occasion Plessis reproached him for not always having scrupulously respected the requirements of civil law concerning the consent of parents or guardians to the marriage of minors. Another time, Panet's strict interpretation of the canonical condemnation of lending at interest prompted him to question the law. Referring to the permissibility of usury under civil law he declared, "As for obviously unjust laws, there is no power capable of making me respect them, though it had me burned or chopped up alive like minced meat." The legal grounds he found for his opinions are wonderfully elucidated in a discussion he had with Plessis about tithes.

Since he had charge of a densely populated parish, Panet had a large income. Every year he hired a sailing ship to take the product of his tithes to Quebec for sale. When potato growing was on the rise and the wheat crop decreased, he sent Plessis two long treatises to convince him that in his parish the tithe applied to potatoes. He was prepared to state under oath that Bishop Briand had reached a decision favourable to him on the matter. And what if his parishioners planted potatoes as a way to avoid the tithe? A refusal to support his claims would force him to institute legal proceedings. Plessis reminded his correspondent that the courts had dismissed a suit brought by the parish priest of Saint-Philippe-de-Laprairie for the same claim in 1809. A contestation of tithes in 1817, which originated among the people, received the bishop's support; in a letter of 27 Jan. 1818 Plessis told Panet, "Your incumbent churchwarden has asked me if he had to pay the tithe on potatoes; I have replied that he does not."

Whether through mystical ecstasy or a whim, a few days after this reply from Plessis, Panet informed him that he had been "electrified for many years" by the Holy Trinity. In a letter dated 8 Jan. 1825 Panet stated explicitly that he had been "electrified for eighteen years, nine months, and two days." He noted in his diary that he considered himself "exhausted by the work of the holy ministry and much more still by the adoration that I am even obliged to render often every day and even every night . . . to the eternal Trinity." There is every reason to believe he was in the grip of a phantasm born of a desire to escape from the traumatizing constraints of reality. Panet first reported his supernatural secrets following the disputes about tithes and the parishioners' request at the same time for his recall. In his diary he laid emphasis on his mystical ecstasies in the middle of an argument designed to refute those who had accused him of lining his own pockets. Panet explained that all his life he had deprived himself in order to distribute what he possessed to the poor, to relatives, and to the *fabrique*. He mentioned specifically that while parish priest he had given the *fabrique* some 3,000 *livres*, not to mention the consecrated vessels in gold that he had bequeathed to the parish – a chalice, ciborium, and monstrance executed by François Ranvoyzé* and paid for from 1810 to 1812 out of his own money. The old, retired priest was upset that he was known as stingy and was shocked that "priests who are rich and Catholic buy gold watches, gold snuff-boxes," but not consecrated vessels fashioned from the precious metal.

The Panet rock, rising out of the St Lawrence off L'Islet, recalls the name of Jacques Panet; it is there that he is said to have exorcised a young girl guilty of having sold her soul to the devil.

SERGE GAGNON

AAQ, 210 A. ANQ-Q, CE2-3, 26 mai 1834; P-197. Arch. de l'évêché de Sainte-Anne-de-la-Pocatière (La Pocatière, Qué.), L'Islet, I. Allaire, *Dictionnaire*, vol.1. P.-G. Roy, *Fils de Québec*, 2: 112–14. Léon Bélanger, *L'Islet, 1677–1977* (s.l., 1977). Fernand Ouellet, *Éléments d'histoire sociale du Bas-Canada* (Montréal, 1972). P.-G. Roy, *La famille Panet* (Lévis, Qué., 1906), 30–31. Léon Trépanier, *On veut savoir* (4v., Montréal, 1960–62), 1: 92–94.

PAQUET, MARIE-ANNE, named **de Saint-Olivier**, Ursuline and superior; b. 27 Sept. 1755 at Quebec, daughter of Jean-Baptiste Paquet, a blacksmith, and Élisabeth Choret (Chauret); d. 25 Jan. 1831 in Trois-Rivières, Lower Canada.

Marie-Anne Paquet entered the Ursulines' noviciate at Trois-Rivières on 12 March 1772. The choice of this convent, rather than the one at Quebec, may have been influenced by the fact that an aunt on her father's side had been a nun there since 1756. In 1789 Marie-Anne de Saint-Olivier held the post of depositary, and three years later that of zelatrice, the person responsible for the sisters in attendance at the turning box in the convent. Elected discreet (counsellor) in 1795, she became assistant to the superior three years later. In 1804 she was elected superior, and her first term was extended to 10 May 1811. She held the office again from 1814 until 1820, then from 1823 until 1829, and in between she was assigned to directing the novices.

Marie-Anne de Saint-Olivier deserves mention in the historical record not only for her personal qualities and the offices she held, but also because of the major event marking her early years as superior, the fire that completely destroyed the convent on the evening of 2 Oct. 1806. The flames spread swiftly from the chapel tower where the fire had started, and in less than three hours the building, which was more than a century old, collapsed. Of the 20 nuns living in it, 16 were taken into the Ursuline convent at Quebec. Marie-Anne de Saint-Olivier remained on the scene with three companions, living in the little building intended to serve as a bakehouse, which the flames had not reached. Under the direction of vicar general François-Xavier Noiseux, who was parish priest of Trois-Rivières, and through the generosity of parishioners and clergy, the Ursuline convent was rebuilt by the spring of 1808. Bishop Joseph-Octave PLESSIS of Quebec also extended his benevolent protection to the nuns in their time of trial.

During her years as superior Marie-Anne de Saint-Olivier was faced with great problems caused by lack of resources, and she applied herself to finding remedies. But after the fire in 1806 she demonstrated more concern for re-establishing the spiritual foundations of the convent and restoring the discipline of the rule, particularly cloistering, a goal in which she was strongly supported by Abbé Jacques-Ladislas-Joseph de CALONNE. In 1808 apostolic works resumed in the convent. The government entrusted the care of the insane to the sisters and six cells were allocated to their patients. The hospital, which had 12 beds, was opened again in January 1809. The main field of work, education, had not been interrupted, the day-school having been saved from the fire. The boarding-school re-opened on 20 November; 18 boarders and 4 day-boarders were added to the 60 day-pupils. In 1817 the noviciate, which was already flourishing, took in four Irish girls who after the completion of their training founded a convent in Boston. Five years later four Ursulines left Lower Canada for New Orleans.

As much because of her marked gifts for administration and spiritual direction as through her devotion and her composure under difficult circumstances, Marie-Anne de Saint-Olivier was able to win the favour of her companions, the confidence of her ecclesiastical superiors, and the support of the people of Trois-Rivières.

MARGUERITE JEAN

ANQ-Q, CE1-1, 27 sept. 1755. Arch. du monastère des ursulines (Trois-Rivières, Qué.), Adélina Bois de Saint-Ignace, "Chronique du monastère, 1830–1870"; Lettres des évêques aux ursulines, 1807–59; Liste des supérieurs, des confesseurs et des supérieures du monastère, 1835. *Les ursulines des Trois-Rivières*.

PAYZANT, JOHN, New Light Congregational minister and tanner; b. 17 Oct. 1749 in Jersey, third son of Louis Payzant and his second wife Marie-Anne Noguet (Nazette); m. 1774 Mary Alline, and they had eight sons and one daughter; d. 10 April 1834 in Liverpool, N.S.

John Payzant's Huguenot parents fled to Jersey to escape religious persecution in France. In mid 1753 they came to Nova Scotia "to make a fortune," as Payzant noted in his journal, the source of much information about his life. His father started a trading establishment on Coveys Island near Lunenburg. In May 1756 Louis Payzant was killed by Indians, who took his wife and their four children to the mission of the Jesuit Charles Germain* at Aukpaque, near present-day Fredericton. She was sent to Quebec without her children, two of whom were retained by the Indians for adoption; John was probably one of these, since he did learn an Indian language. Thanks to the intervention of the bishop of Quebec, Henri-Marie Dubreil* de Pontbriand, the family was reunited at Quebec in the spring of 1757, John's education

being undertaken at the Jesuit college. After the capture of Quebec in 1759, the family returned to Nova Scotia and Marie-Anne Payzant received a grant in Falmouth Township adjoining that of the Alline family. John's education was continued by a fellow Huguenot, John James Juhan, who had married his sister, and he obtained a grounding in Latin, Greek, and possibly Hebrew. This training later served, he stated, as an "introduction to my Preaching for at that time for men to preach without Learning was looked upon that they did that they were not master of."

The mental turmoil of worshipping as a Protestant after his time in Quebec and of adjusting to life in Falmouth "contributed to bring Serious thoughts" into Payzant's mind. Hoping "to compose" himself and live "a more Retired life," he decided to marry and settle down, choosing as his wife Mary, the sister of Henry Alline*. However, in the winter of 1774–75 his anxiety revived. He discussed his troubles with Alline, and found his peace in the Lord one week after Alline had done so, on 2 April 1775. Alline's mysticism and asceticism were to have little influence on Payzant, but he did believe with Alline that the essence of Christianity was spiritual rebirth through a personal religious experience. He did not share Alline's indifference to church rules, and he was to wage a long struggle to maintain order in the disputing New Light churches.

Neither Alline nor Payzant had any formal theological training, and Payzant was hesitant about engaging in preaching. He nevertheless began in 1778. He seems to have felt no need to be ordained, and it was not until 1786 that he was "set apart" and became minister of the Horton and Cornwallis New Light church. For the next six years he laboured in this church, increasing its membership from 30 to 130 while itinerating throughout the townships settled by New Englanders. He strove to keep the congregation together as disputes between paedobaptists and anti-paedobaptists became endemic. These quarrels were compounded by an outbreak of antinomianism at Horton in 1791, which spread to other New Light churches. Payzant opposed the antinomians, or "new dispensationers," as he termed them, but, exhausted by the struggle, in 1793 he accepted an invitation from Congregationalists and New Lights in Liverpool.

The New Lights in Nova Scotia either had formed separate churches or had sown such confusion within existing Congregational churches that these churches had been dissolved. In Liverpool, however, Payzant was requested to bring about a reconciliation between the majority of the Congregationalists and the New Lights, and the group which resulted was able to take over the town meeting-house. Payzant's training and his financial independence, conferred by the tannery he ran, made him one of the "first characters" of the community. Indeed, about 1804 he was approached to

Pélissier

be Simeon Perkins*'s successor as *custos rotulorum* but replied that the commission he had from God was the only one he wanted.

From Liverpool Payzant continued his efforts to bring order and organization to the scattered and quarrelling New Light churches in the colony, which were facing an increasing threat from the Baptists. Payzant believed in "open communion" churches, where the form of baptism was no bar to membership, whereas the Baptists were adherents of the "close communion" principle, which recognized only adult baptism. In 1797 Payzant took the lead in calling a conference to form an association of the New Light clergy to bring some discipline to the movement. However, inroads continued to be made by the Baptists, led by Thomas Handley Chipman, nominally a New Light. The association met again in 1798 as the Congregational and Baptist Association. Payzant did not attend the 1799 session because of a dispute in Liverpool with Harris Harding* over which of them would be minister there. The 1800 meeting was decisive since all the ministers attending, except Payzant, were now Baptists, although their congregations generally contained only a minority of that denomination. Chipman attempted to persuade Payzant to support "close communion" churches, but he refused, and after a spirited defence of "open communion" he withdrew. His church remained open to Baptist preachers, even though they used every means to try to oust him. Up to his last sermon, preached on Easter Sunday 1834 when he was 84, Payzant remained faithful to the indigenous sect inspired by Alline. Although lacking Alline's charisma, he had attempted to provide leadership and organization to the New Light movement, and in that sense he can be called Alline's successor.

B. C. CUTHBERTSON

Payzant's journal has been published as *The journal of the Reverend John Payzant (1749–1834)*, ed. B. C. Cuthbertson (Hantsport, N.S., 1981); the original is in PANS, MG 1, 1189A.

Atlantic Baptist Hist. Coll., Acadia Univ. (Wolfville, N.S.), Cornwallis, N.S., Congregational (Newlight) Church, records; Joseph Dimock, diary, 1796–1845; Fragment of letter announcing formation of a yearly conference, 1797; E. M. Saunders, "The trials, the patience, the firmness, and 'splendid isolation' of Rev. John Payzant" (typescript, n.d.). PANS, MG 1, 1185–89A. *The Payzant and allied Jess and Juhan families in North America*, comp. M. M. Payzant (Wollaston, Mass., [1970]).

PÉLISSIER, MARIE-CATHERINE. *See* DELEZENNE

PENNOYER, JESSE, surveyor, office holder, JP, mill owner, farmer, and militia officer; b. 16 April 1760 in Amenia, N.Y., son of Joseph Pennoyer, a Methodist minister, and Lucy Crippen; m. Martha Ferguson, and they had 12 children; d. 1 Dec. 1825 in Waterville, Lower Canada, and was buried at East Hatley (Hatley).

Jesse Pennoyer received a good education. In the American revolution he and his family supported the rebel side; on 1 Jan. 1777 he enlisted in the 4th New York Regiment, and he was discharged three years later. Why and when he changed countries and allegiances is not known, but in 1788 he was in the province of Quebec, where he received a surveyor's commission.

Pennoyer was first employed by Thomas Dunn* on his seigneury of Saint-Armand, near Missisquoi Bay, and then was sent by the deputy surveyor general to what would become Upper Canada. He was to survey the district set aside for the loyalists, lay out a road from Cornwall to Kingston, and then mark the boundaries of the new townships, among them Oxford, on the Rideau River.

The opening of the Eastern Townships to settlement brought Pennoyer back to Lower Canada, where in 1792 he was assigned the task of surveying the lower reaches of the Rivière Saint-François. It was at this time that he picked up a controversial account of the expedition Robert Rogers* had led against the Abenaki village of Saint-François-de-Sales (Odanak) in 1759 and of a combat near the subsequent site of Sherbrooke. The surveyor general commissioned him to survey and subdivide several townships around lakes Champlain and Memphrémagog, including those of Dunham, Sutton, Potton, and Barnston. Pennoyer was aware of the attractions of the region and asked for the grant of Compton Township to himself and his colleagues Nathaniel Coffin* and Joseph Kilborn, who, like him, had been received into the masonic lodge Select Surveyors No. 9 on 13 March 1793. On 10 Oct. 1794 he was appointed commissioner to select recipients for lands at Missisquoi Bay, a duty he carried out diligently, but with no scruples about attending to his own interests.

In 1797 Pennoyer was appointed a justice of the peace for the district of Montreal, a commission renewed in 1799 and 1810. He received a similar one for the district of Trois-Rivières in 1811, 1815, and 1821. In August 1797, after David McLane* had been convicted of treason and executed, Pennoyer wrote to Dunn about others associated with McLane. Having gone to Vermont with Coffin to investigate Ira Allen's intentions, in September he informed Governor Robert Prescott* that Allen was trying to send 20,000 weapons to Lower Canada.

Shortly afterwards Pennoyer supported the group of malcontents who had met at Missisquoi Bay to protest against the government's delay in making land grants. He helped prepare a strongly worded memoir that he

Pennoyer

handed to Governor Prescott in December after signing it along with his friends Gilbert HYATT and Samuel WILLARD.

On 31 Aug. 1802 Pennoyer and his 20 associates each received 1,200 acres in Compton Township. Having sold his properties in Saint-Armand seigneury, where he had been living, Pennoyer settled near the falls named after him and built mills on lands there that he busied himself clearing. From then on he worked indefatigably for the region's development and called numerous meetings to ask for roads to the Rivière Chaudière and the United States, as well as along the Saint-François. In 1807 he submitted a plan for a road from the Connecticut River to Ireland Township, which he had surveyed. This plan was taken up again by Governor Lord Gosford [Acheson*], and between 1838 and 1843 a road was built that bore his name.

The region's other needs did not escape Pennoyer's attention. In 1805 he took a memoir to Quebec asking for law courts, registry offices, parliamentary representation, and the establishment of a Protestant clergy. In 1806 he had tried to grow hemp, and in 1809 the government granted him a salary of £200, plus £100 to defray the cost of promoting and growing a crop for five years. There was, however, no market for it, and the War of 1812 brought an end to an experiment that had proved ruinous for him.

Pennoyer held the rank of captain in the Eastern Townships militia, which had been organized in 1805 by Sir John JOHNSON. In 1808 he was posted to the 5th Townships Militia Battalion and in 1812 he became its commanding officer. This appointment was no sinecure, since his men were scattered over a distance of a hundred miles or so, and he devoted his energies to it. Although he was promoted major early in 1813, his authority was not always sufficient to rally the men, who were eager to defend their own fields but not much disposed to join the force quartered at La Prairie. Johnson was furious when he learned that his orders were being called in question, and on several occasions Pennoyer had to apologize or give explanations for his men's conduct. His military career came to an end in 1821. He continued to practise as a surveyor, and on 23 Dec. 1824 he signed a survey of the village of Sherbrooke.

Pennoyer had been greatly affected by the death of his eldest son, John, in 1820, and that of his wife two years later. Having been ill for a short time, he died on 1 Dec. 1825, in the presence of his large family; he was mourned by many friends. Possessed of a strong personality and uncommon vision, he had wielded great influence in his milieu. Through his efforts and his perseverance he had contributed to the advancement of his adopted country.

MARIE-PAULE R. LABRÈQUE

ANQ-E, CE1-41, 1820, 21 oct. 1822; CN2-26, 1799–1808. Bishop's Univ. (Lennoxville, Que.), Special Coll., Savage papers. Brome County Hist. Soc. Arch. (Knowlton, Que.), Miscellaneous family papers, Savage file, Shufelt file; Township papers, Eastern Townships. Compton County Hist. Soc. Arch. (Martinville, Que.), Scrap-book. Missisquoi County Hist. Soc. Arch. (Stanbridge East, Que.), Edward Struthers, "Caldwell Manor today's Clarenceville and Noyan" (typewritten copy, 1960); Ruiter day-books. PAC, MG 11, [CO 42] Q, 110: 42–47; MG 23, GII, 27; MG 24, B3; I11; RG 1, L3ᴸ: 2442, 2487, 3866–67, 3884, 4584; RG 4, A1; RG 68, General index, 1651–1841. Private arch., M.-P. LaBrèque (Acton Vale, Que.), Notes d'entrevue avec M.-J. Daigneau, M. W. Laberee, Marion Phelps. "Book of official instructions to the land surveyors of Upper Canada," AO Report, 1905: 386. Docs. relating to constitutional hist., 1791–1818 (Doughty and McArthur). Documents relative to the colonial history of the state of New York . . . , ed. E. B. O'Callaghan and Berthold Fernow (15v., Albany, 1853–87). Henry Taylor, Journal of a tour from Montreal, thro' Berthier and Sorel, to the Eastern Townships of Granby, Stanstead, Compton, Sherbrooke, Melbourne, &c., &c., to Port St. Francis (Quebec, 1840). British Colonist and St. Francis Gazette (Stanstead, Que.), 15 Dec. 1825. F.-J. Audet, "Les législateurs du Bas-Canada." F.-J. Audet et Édouard Fabre Surveyer, Les députés de Saint-Maurice et de Buckinghamshire, 1792–1808 (Trois-Rivières, Qué., 1934). Bouchette, Topographical description of L.C. Langelier, Liste des terrains concédés. Men of today in the Eastern Townships, intro. V. E. Morrill, comp. E. G. Pierce (Sherbrooke, Que., [1917]). Officers of British forces in Canada (Irving). "Papiers d'État – Bas-Canada," PAC Rapport, 1891: 155, 159–60.

R. J. Ashton, The life of Henry Ruiter, 1742–1819 ([Chicago], 1974). Caron, La colonisation de la prov. de Québec. L. S. Channel, History of Compton County and sketches of the Eastern Townships, district of St. Francis, and Sherbrooke County (Cookshire, Que., 1896; repr. Belleville, Ont., 1975). Day, Hist. of Eastern Townships. Stanislas Drapeau, Études sur les développements de la colonisation du Bas-Canada depuis dix ans (1851–1861) (Québec, 1863). Louis Gentilcore and Kate Donkin, Land surveys of southern Ontario; an introduction and index to the field note books of the Ontario land surveyors, 1784–1859 (Toronto, 1973). Graham, Hist. of freemasonry. Albert Gravel, Les Cantons de l'Est ([Sherbrooke], 1938); Pages d'histoire régionale (24 cahiers, Sherbrooke, 1960–67), 2: 15–16. Histoire de Waterville ([Waterville, Qué., 1976]). Histoire de Compton . . . (s.l., 1981). B. F. Hubbard, Forests and clearings; the history of Stanstead County, province of Quebec, with sketches of more than five hundred families, ed. John Lawrence (Montreal, 1874; repr. 1963). G. F. McGuigan, "Land policy and land disposal under tenure of free and common socage, Quebec and Lower Canada, 1763–1809 . . ." (3v., PHD thesis, Univ. Laval, Quebec, 1962). Jules Martel, "Histoire du système routier des Cantons de l'Est avant 1855" (thèse de MA, univ. d'Ottawa, 1960). G. H. Montgomery, Missisquoi Bay (Philipsburg, Que.) (Granby, Que., 1950). Maurice O'Bready, De Ktiné à Sherbrooke; esquisse historique de Sherbrooke: des origines à 1954 (Sherbrooke, 1973). H. B. Shufelt, Nicholas Austin the Quaker and the township of Bolton

Perrault

(Knowlton, 1971). *The storied province of Quebec; past and present*, ed. William Wood *et al*. (5v., Toronto, 1931–32), 2: 922–72. D. W. Thomson, *Men and meridians; the history of surveying and mapping in Canada* (3v., Ottawa, 1966–69). Vincent O'Brien, "The United Empire Loyalists," Stanstead County Hist. Soc., *Journal* (Stanstead), 4 (1971): 28–31. *Sherbrooke Daily Record*, 10 April–16 July 1910, 13 Jan. 1970. *La Tribune* (Sherbrooke), 31 juill. 1937.

PERRAULT, CHARLES-NORBERT, physician, surgeon, militia officer, JP, and office holder; b. 16 April 1793 in Montreal, son of Joseph-François Perrault* and Ursule Macarty; d. 16 June 1832 at Quebec.

Charles-Norbert Perrault was the sixth of 10 or possibly 12 children. Shortly before his birth his father found himself in desperate financial straits: "Would to God," he wrote to his uncle François Baby* on 22 Oct. 1792, "I could get a [position] to help me keep my large family! Without a profession or employment I find the times very hard." The year 1795 saw the end of these difficulties, and the family came to live at Quebec; however, Mme Perrault died there in April 1800.

Charles-Norbert was the son of a man devoted to the cause of education and he studied at the Petit Séminaire de Québec from 1806 till 1810; then, in 1814, he went to Edinburgh to study medicine and surgery. During his stay overseas he had the opportunity to observe the progress made in medical services and assistance in Great Britain, to exchange ideas, and to plan projects. His conversations with his friend and compatriot Anthony von Iffland* proved particularly fruitful in this regard.

Possessed of a diploma as a doctor of medicine and proud of his membership in the Royal Medical Society of Edinburgh, Perrault returned to his native land. Soon after, in July 1818, he received his licence to practise medicine in Lower Canada. With Iffland, who had also come back, Perrault put forward a scheme dear to both the young doctors: to found "in the City of *Quebec*, a Dispensary, on the Plan of those in *Europe*, for the relief of the indigent sick," where medical instruction would also be given. At a meeting in that city on 1 Sept. 1818 Perrault delivered a long speech advocating such an establishment. Three months later the Quebec Dispensary was officially opened. In the course of a year several hundred sick people were treated and courses in medicine, surgery, physiology, anatomy, and obstetrics were given. Despite initial enthusiasm and the undeniable usefulness of the dispensary, it closed in January 1820 for lack of funds. A public campaign had brought in less than £100, and though several requests had been made to the House of Assembly, no aid had been granted.

The assembly's refusal to back the initiative of Perrault and Iffland stemmed in part from the estab-

lishment of the Quebec Emigrants' Society, founded in July 1819 to help immigrants, which undoubtedly had reduced the number of patients treated at the dispensary. But the prime cause of their failure was the lack of support for the undertaking from influential people. The dispensary was an innovation put forward by dynamic young doctors who were not yet out of their twenties, but were possessed of training in many respects superior to that of older physicians, who in turn insisted upon the value of their experience; thus the new institution was likely to arouse misgivings, distrust, and indeed outright opposition. The desire of these young doctors to reform medical practice in Lower Canada came as much from humanitarian motives as from the wish to make a place for themselves in society. The medical élite, which included well-known Canadians such as François BLANCHET and Joseph Painchaud* in addition to British military personnel, thus felt threatened and appeared reticent to support Perrault and Iffland. As an assemblyman, Blanchet in particular could have backed the requests for aid made to the house, but he did nothing.

The set-back did not, however, prevent Perrault from becoming a prominent doctor. His status was enhanced by his marriage at Quebec on 12 Oct. 1819 with Charlotte-Louise, a daughter of Pierre-Édouard DESBARATS; she had received a good education with the Ursulines, was an amateur musician, and above all came from a respectable family. In 1822 he was appointed surgeon to the Île d'Orléans battalion of militia, and two years later he was transferred to Quebec's 1st Militia Battalion. He received a commission as justice of the peace in May 1824. By that year at the latest he was also on the medical staff of the Emigrant Hospital, and in June he was made one of the medical examiners for the district of Quebec, an indication of his steadily growing reputation for they were responsible for admissions to the medical profession.

Since he was still anxious to participate in reforming medical practice in the colony, Perrault contributed to the *Quebec Medical Journal*, the first Canadian journal of medicine, which had been launched by his colleague François-Xavier TESSIER in January 1826. That year he became vice-president of the Quebec Medical Society, which had just been founded, and two years later he succeeded Dr Joseph Morrin* as president. It was in this capacity that he read a paper to his colleagues on the Baie-Saint-Paul disease in December 1829. The text, which had been prepared from information supplied by Morrin, is a good summary of medical knowledge about the illness at the time. In 1831 the medical society protested against the method of selecting medical examiners in force under an act of 1788, since it favoured British doctors, especially military ones. In 1825, for example, of the seven district of Quebec examiners only Perrault was Canadian. When this injustice was exposed, the society got agreement that the choice of examiners would no longer be left to the governor's discretion but would be determined by majority vote at a general meeting of the doctors. On 18 July 1831 Perrault was unanimously elected secretary for three years of the new body, the Board of Examiners.

In accordance with the act passed on 25 Feb. 1832 to prevent cholera from entering the province or to minimize its effects, Perrault was appointed resident physician, along with Joseph Parant*, on 1 March, and then health commissioner with Parant and Morrin on 7 March. The measures taken by the commissioners and the board of health that had been set up were, however, insufficient to keep cholera out. The epidemic raged in Lower Canada from June until mid October and caused about 8,000 deaths. Perrault himself was stricken and died on 16 June 1832, at the age of 39, "a victim of his devotion to duty"; he was buried the same day. At the time there reputedly was a rumour that he had been "buried too quickly, having given himself a large dose of opium," a treatment which according to Dr Olivier Robitaille* was common during the epidemic. As his wife had died in 1830, Perrault left three orphaned daughters, who were taken in by his father Joseph-François.

Charles-Norbert Perrault was a scholar, as his library demonstrates. At the time of his death it comprised 359 volumes, mostly on medical matters. Perrault also owned a barometer, a hygrometer, and a telescope. By 1821 at the latest he had become interested in meteorology, and a number of his readings are still extant. Despite the failure of the dispensary he was able to make an enviable place for himself among his colleagues and was one of the leaders seeking to reform medicine in Lower Canada. His professional success had not, however, kept him from running into financial difficulties throughout his life. In 1832 he did not own any property, and he had a personal estate of £330. Moneys owed him amounted to £165, but he owed £3,254, including £3,113 to his father.

RENALD LESSARD

ANQ-M, CE1-51, 17 avril 1793. ANQ-Q, CC1, 27 juin 1832; CE1-1, 12 oct. 1819; CN1-16, 11 oct. 1819; CN1-81, 3, 24 juill. 1832; CN1-178, 2 sept. 1828; CN1-208, 28 août 1826, 15 oct. 1829, 1er avril 1830; CN1-230, 18 juin 1817; CN1-253, 31 août 1826; E18/51; P-232/2: 1–15; T11-1/608, no.865; 3556: 801; 3558: 179–80, 217–18; ZQ6-52, 25 févr. 1830. ASQ, MSS, 20; Univ., sér.U, U-18, 4–5. PAC, MG 24, I38; RG 4, B28, 49: 645–46; RG 68, General index, 1651–1841: 65, 271, 360, 641, 656. L.C., House of Assembly, *Journaux*, 1819: 49; 1825, app.I; *Statutes*, 1831–32, c.16. *Quebec Medical Journal*, 1 (1826): 61–62; 2 (1827): 114. *Le Canadien*, 30 déc. 1818; 13, 20 juill. 1831; 10 mars, 2 mai, 18 juin, 29 oct. 1832. *Quebec Gazette*, 30 July, 3 Sept. 1818; 19 April, 15 July, 4 Nov. 1819; 24 Jan. 1820; 18 July 1822; 6 May 1824. *Quebec almanac*, 1823; 1825. C.-M. Boissonnault, *Histoire de la faculté de médecine de Laval* (Québec, 1953), 88–96. P.-B. Casgrain, *Mémorial des familles Casgrain, Baby et Perrault du Canada* (Québec, 1898), 180, 186–87. Jolois, *J.-F. Perrault*. Henri Têtu, *Histoire des familles Têtu, Bonenfant, Dionne et Perrault* (Québec, 1898), 592–93. Jacques Bernier, "François Blanchet et le mouvement réformiste en médecine au début du XIXe siècle," *RHAF*, 34 (1980–81): 223–44. Geoffrey Bilson, "The first epidemic of Asiatic cholera in Lower Canada, 1832," *Medical Hist.* (London), 21 (1977): 411–33. Ignotus [Thomas Chapais], "La profession médicale au Canada," *BRH*, 12 (1906): 142–50. Victor Morin, "L'évolution de la médecine au Canada français," *Cahiers des Dix*, 25 (1960): 74–75.

PERRAULT, OLIVIER (baptized **Jean-Olivier**), lawyer, office holder, militia officer, politician, judge, and seigneur; b. 21 July 1773 at Quebec, son of Jacques Perrault*, known as Perrault *l'aîné*, and Charlotte Boucher de Boucherville; m. 17 Sept. 1804 Marie-Louise Taschereau, daughter of Gabriel-Elzéar Taschereau*, a member of the Legislative Council, in Sainte-Marie-de-la-Nouvelle-Beauce (Sainte-Marie), Lower Canada, and they had eight children; d. 19 March 1827 at Quebec and was buried three days later in Sainte-Marie-de-la-Nouvelle-Beauce.

Olivier Perrault was one of 11 children. After studying at the Petit Séminaire de Québec he articled as a law student and was authorized on 1 Oct. 1799 to practise as an advocate, barrister, attorney, and solicitor. Two years later he was appointed secretary of a committee created to apply the act for the relief from all indebtedness to the government of people in arrears with *lods et ventes* on crown lands.

In June 1808 Perrault was named clerk of the land roll and inspector general of the royal domain, but shortly afterwards he resigned to allow Joseph-Bernard PLANTÉ, who had previously been dismissed from the office, to resume it. On 28 September he became advocate general of Lower Canada. A few days earlier Governor Sir James Henry Craig* had advised the colonial secretary, Lord Castlereagh, of the appointment, adding that it was "little more than nominal" and would flatter Canadian lawyers.

Eager to try his luck in politics, Perrault ran for election in Northumberland riding in 1810. He was defeated, however, probably because of his thinly veiled support for Craig's decision to jail the principal leaders of the Canadian party that year. Indeed, Perrault had maintained that in Pierre-Stanislas Bédard's case the courts were justified in withdrawing his parliamentary privileges and right of recourse to habeas corpus, given the charge of sedition that was pending.

In January 1812 Perrault was appointed by order in council an honorary member of the Executive Coun-

Peters

cil, and he retained this office until his death. He received the rank of major in the Île d'Orléans battalion of militia on 5 April, but on 24 October resigned his commission; later he was made a lieutenant-colonel in the Lower Canadian militia.

Perrault became a judge of the Court of King's Bench for the District of Quebec on 22 May 1812, replacing Pierre-Amable De Bonne*. On 26 Feb. 1814 he signed the memoir from the judges of Lower Canada supporting their colleagues Jonathan Sewell* and James MONK, whom the assembly considered ineligible to sit in the Legislative Council because they were judges. From 28 Jan. 1818 until his death he was a member of that council. Appointed speaker on 10 March 1823, he held office until 22 Jan. 1827, when he was replaced by James Kerr*. During his term, Perrault came out in 1824 in favour of the independence of judges from the executive authority, asking that they hold office on the basis of good conduct rather than at pleasure. He was a member that year of a council committee that rejected an assembly bill to force the seigneurs to make grants from their lands.

At the time of his death Olivier Perrault was living in Maison Kent on Rue Saint-Louis, which he had bought from Pierre Brehaut*'s estate in 1819. In the course of his career Perrault had built up a sizeable fortune in landed property. In 1809, for example, he had built a house on Place d'Armes, and two years later he advertised some properties for sale at Trois-Rivières. In the 1820s he had built three large houses on Rue Haldimand and another on Rue Saint-Denis. In addition he owned the seigneury of Sainte-Marie in 1821. Like many other members of the Legislative Council, Perrault enjoyed financial security.

JACQUES L'HEUREUX

ANQ-Q, CE1-1, 22 juill. 1773; CN1-80, 10 sept. 1823; CN1-208, 1ᵉʳ déc. 1825; CN1-212, 11 sept., 2 déc. 1823; CN1-284, 24 mai 1809. AP, Sainte-Marie, reg. des baptêmes, mariages et sépultures, 17 sept. 1804, 22 mars 1827. PAC, MG 11, [CO 42] Q, 107: 337; 114: 199; 117-2: 246; 119: 149; RG 4, B8, 17: 6392–93; 28: 129; RG 7, G1, 3: 167. *Docs. relating to constitutional hist., 1791–1818* (Doughty and McArthur); *1819–1828* (Doughty and Story). *Select British docs. of War of 1812* (Wood). *Quebec Gazette*, 3 Oct. 1799; 20 Sept. 1804; 6 Oct. 1808; 19 April 1810; 21 Feb. 1811; 23 April, 28 May, 19 Nov. 1812; 1 April 1813; 17 May 1821. F.-J. Audet, "Les législateurs du Bas-Canada." *Officers of British forces in Canada* (Irving). *Quebec almanac*, 1815: 73; 1820: 79. P.-G. Roy, *Les avocats de la région de Québec*; *Fils de Québec*, 2: 166–68; *Les juges de la prov. de Québec*. Turcotte, *Le Conseil législatif*. P.-G. Roy, "L'hon. Jean-Baptiste-Olivier Perrault," *BRH*, 8 (1902): 33–36.

PETERS, WILLIAM BIRDSEYE, office holder, army officer, lawyer, and journalist; b. 5 June 1774 in Hebron (Marlborough), Conn., only child of the Reverend Samuel Andrew Peters and his third wife, Mary Birdseye; m. 4 May 1796 Polly (Patty) Marvin Jarvis of Stamford, Conn., and they had nine children, seven surviving infancy; d. 4 June 1822 in Mobile, Ala.

William Birdseye Peters was descended on both sides from Puritans who settled in New England in the 1630s. His mother died a few days after his birth; his father was the Church of England minister in Hebron. In September 1774 Samuel Peters's strong tory views forced him to flee, first to Boston and then to England, leaving his baby son with the boy's maternal grandparents in Stratford, Conn. William lived with the Birdseyes until he was 14, studying under nearby Congregational and Episcopal ministers. He then joined his father in London, and in 1789 went to school in Arras, France, where he remained for three terms. He matriculated into Trinity College, Oxford, on 12 Oct. 1792; in that year also he was a law student at the Inner Temple. Growing concern was felt for his health, and in the summer of 1793 he was sent to North America to recuperate.

Although his half-sister, Hannah Peters*, had married William Jarvis*, secretary and registrar of Upper Canada, and was living in Newark (Niagara-on-the-Lake), Peters's first visit to the province was a brief one in 1794. Instead of returning to England to complete his education, he stayed in the United States, mainly in Connecticut, renewing acquaintance with relatives and friends. Hannah urged him to settle in Upper Canada, and in 1796 he married an American niece of William Jarvis, and moved to Newark.

In the beginning Peters had many advantages. Lieutenant Governor John Graves Simcoe*, who had tried unsuccessfully to have Peters's father become the first bishop of Upper Canada, appointed him assistant secretary and registrar of the province on 3 May 1796, and on 26 May licensed him to practise law. A grant of 1,200 acres was recommended on 25 July, and on 26 December he was commissioned an ensign in the Queen's Rangers. In addition, both he and his father were on the United Empire Loyalist list, and the Jarvises believed that other government appointments would be forthcoming.

Peters thus began his career in Upper Canada with a sound footing in three professions – the civil service, the law, and the army. Although multiple appointments were not uncommon in 18th-century Upper Canada, Peters encountered problems after Simcoe's departure. Chief Justice John Elmsley* refused to permit him to practise law because he was an army officer, and Major David Shank of the Queen's Rangers thought that he could not hold his government position while on active service, despite the precedent of David William Smith*. Peters, however, was not ordered to join his regiment until the secretary's office was moved to York (Toronto) in 1798. In Newark he worked under Jarvis, who complained that he was lazy and uncooperative; Peters wrote that the Jarvises expected him to be "*their Slave*" and that he was paid too little and too irregularly. Peters was unsuccessful in obtaining other government appointments, in his opinion because the Jarvises had no political influence, and also because he himself was a "Yankee." In 1799 Peters and his father were struck off the United Empire Loyalist list, because Samuel Peters had never come to Upper Canada.

While in Newark, Peters spent much time with the American officers at Fort Niagara (near Youngstown, N.Y.). From them he learned of opportunities for advancement in the American army, and in 1798 he applied for a commission to the American secretary of war. Shortly afterwards he moved to York and reported for duty to Lieutenant-Colonel Shank, who told him that promotion was likely within the British army. Peters therefore cancelled his American application, but Jarvis discovered it and sent a copy to Shank, according to Peters because he thought he had to sacrifice Peters to save himself. To the loyalist Jarvis, Peters was guilty of treason, but Peters claimed that he had merely breached military etiquette in not informing his commanding officer of his intentions. His explanation satisfied Shank, who did nothing further.

After this episode, Peters's relations with the Jarvises were strained. In York he served with the rangers until the regiment was disbanded on 25 Oct. 1802, when he retired on half pay. No longer an active army officer, he applied for admission to the Law Society of Upper Canada in Easter Term, 1803, and was called to the bar. On 16 June 1803, however, he moved to New York, where he established a dry goods store under the name William B. Peters and Company, with money borrowed from relatives and $2,000 won by his wife in a lottery. In two years he had lost everything and was $11,000 in debt. By 1808 he was a discharged bankrupt in Connecticut, living on the Birdseye estate with no means of support.

In 1807 Hannah Jarvis had advised against his return to Upper Canada, since "he is supposed to be in the opposition, he becoming a subject to the United States." In 1810, however, Peters settled in Niagara (Niagara-on-the-Lake) to practise law. Hannah hoped that he would "have the discretion to be Nutral," but he had no discretion and was soon writing for Joseph Willcocks*'s radical newspaper, the *Upper Canada Guardian; or, Freeman's Journal.* Through his friend the Reverend Robert ADDISON, he applied for the position of clerk in the projected Gore District in February 1812, but the new district was not established until after the War of 1812.

When war was declared, Peters immediately moved his law office to York and his household to John Mills Jackson*'s home three miles up Yonge Street. From the beginning his loyalty was suspect. After the capture of York by the Americans in April 1813, the acting attorney general, John Beverley Robinson*, was instructed to lay charges against him for providing information to the enemy, but sufficient evidence could not be found.

Peters was in serious trouble again after the second occupation of York. When the Americans marched in on 31 July 1813 "he met them with Expressions of Joy and shook hands with a number of the enemys officers and men." According to a second witness, Peters often said that the Americans would conquer the country, and was pleased at the prospect. The committee of information, consisting of five prominent York citizens, believed that suspicions of Peters were justified, and that "from his Information and talents he is capable of doing much mischief." Although he was possibly guilty of sedition, there was no evidence of actual aid to the enemy, and so no charges were laid. Preparations were being made for a great show trial of traitors – the "Bloody Assize" held at Ancaster in May–June 1814. Peters was defence lawyer for at least five of those accused of high treason; of these, two were acquitted, the sentence of one was commuted, and two were executed.

After the war Peters returned to Niagara to practise law. In 1816 he moved to Thorold and then to Hamilton, where he was the first lawyer in the new Gore District. By November 1819 he was back in Niagara, where he maintained a legal practice and succeeded Bartemas FERGUSON as publisher of the *Niagara Spectator.* Ferguson, a critic of the government, had been convicted of libel the previous August; Peters changed the newspaper's name to the *Canadian Argus, and Niagara Spectator* and published it until some time in 1820 when Ferguson, having been released, resumed his connection with the paper. That autumn Peters went to New York and briefly practised law. On 27 December he sailed for Mobile, Ala, where he died of yellow fever. His son, Samuel Jarvis Peters, became a prominent merchant, developer, banker, and politician in New Orleans.

Peters was one of the few gentlemen in Upper Canada popularly accused of treason. He never understood that Upper Canada was not part of the United States, and obviously felt no particular allegiance to either government. Basically an unsuccessful opportunist, he moved back and forth across a border he did not perceive. Despite his advantages, he was a failure in both countries.

EDITH G. FIRTH

AO, MS 787; MU 1368; MU 2316; RG 22, ser.134, 4: 153–71. MTL, [E. Æ. Jarvis], "History of the Jarvis family" (typescript, [19 —?]); William Jarvis papers. PAC, MG 23, HI, 3; RG 1, L1, 22; L3; RG 5, A1, esp. vol.16. PRO,

Peyton

WO 42/62: 5. Univ. of Guelph Library, Arch. Coll. (Guelph, Ont.), J. MacI. Duff coll., Samuel Peters papers. *Corr. of Hon. Peter Russell* (Cruikshank and Hunter). *Corr. of Lieut. Governor Simcoe* (Cruikshank). "Grants of crown lands in U.C.," AO *Report*, 1929. "Letters from the Secretary of Upper Canada and Mrs. Jarvis, to her father, the Rev. Samuel Peters, D.D.," ed. A. H. Young, Women's Canadian Hist. Soc. of Toronto, *Trans.*, no.23 (1922–23): 11–63. Samuel Peters, *A history of the Rev. Hugh Peters, A.M.* ... (New York, 1807), 109–22. *Town of York, 1793–1815* (Firth). "U.C. land book B," AO *Report*, 1930. "U.C. land book C," AO *Report*, 1930–31. *York, Upper Canada: minutes of town meetings and lists of inhabitants, 1797–1823*, ed. Christine Mosser (Toronto, 1984).

Canadian Argus, and Niagara Spectator (Niagara [Niagara-on-the-Lake, Ont.]), 1820. *Niagara Spectator* (St Catharines, [Ont.]; Niagara), 1817–19. *Spectator* (St Davids [Niagara-on-the-Lake]; St Catharines), 1816–17. *Upper Canada Gazette*, 1796–1820. *Upper Canada Guardian; or, Freeman's Journal* (Niagara), 1808–10. *Alumni Oxonienses; the members of the University of Oxford, 1715–1886* ..., comp. Joseph Foster (4v., Oxford and London, 1888), 3: 1102. Armstrong, *Handbook of Upper Canadian chronology* (1967). G.B., WO, *Army list*, 1796–1822. *The Jarvis family; or, the descendants of the first settlers of the name in Massachusetts and Long Island, and those who have more recently settled in other parts of the United States and British America*, comp. G. A. Jarvis *et al.* (Hartford, Conn., 1879). *Jones's New-York mercantile and general directory, for the year ... 1805–6* ..., comp. J. F. Jones (New York, [1805]). *Longworth's American almanac, New-York register, and city-directory* ... (New York), 1803–11, 1820–21. W. R. Riddell, *The bar and the courts of the province of Upper Canada, or Ontario* (Toronto, 1928); *The legal profession in Upper Canada in its early periods* (Toronto, 1916). W. B. Sprague, *Annals of the American pulpit* ... (9v., New York, 1857–59), 5: 191–200. E. A. Cruikshank, "A study of disaffection in Upper Canada in 1812–15," RSC *Trans.*, 3rd ser., 6 (1912), sect.II: 11–65. G. C. H. Kernion, "Samuel Jarvis Peters, the man who made New Orleans of to-day and became a national personality," La. Hist. Soc., *Pub.* (New Orleans), 7 (1913–14): 62–96. A. H. Young, "'Bishop' Peters," *OH*, 27 (1931): 583–623.

PEYTON, JOHN, fisherman and trapper; b. 1749 in Christchurch (Dorset), England; m. 12 Dec. 1788 Ann Galton of Wimborne Minster, England, and they had a daughter and a son; d. 1829 in Exploits, Nfld.

John Peyton arrived in Newfoundland as a youth, resided for a while in Fogo, and once travelled on the coast of Labrador. By 1781 he was residing, at least during winters, at Lower Sandy Point, in the Bay of Exploits, a locality which lay along one of the main migration routes of the Beothuks. Here he was engaged in salmon catching and the fur trade in partnership with Harry Miller. A few years later, Peyton struck out on his own and seems to have had some degree of success. In summer, he likely resided at Exploits, on the more northerly of the two Exploits Islands; in winter, he probably continued to live at Lower Sandy Point. He owned his own schooner, and references to him in the papers of several merchants represent him as an independent and successful trader.

Although Peyton was but one of many fishermen and furriers who had contact with the Beothuks, he was among the most prominent. Allegations and circumstantial evidence in a number of different sources suggest that Peyton behaved brutally towards them. An inquiry conducted by naval officer George Christopher Pulling in 1792 produced much testimony that hints at his activities. Evidently Peyton participated in several excursions into Beothuk territory in the 1780s and 1790s, each bent upon reprisal for various thefts of goods. Peyton's behaviour and reputation incensed John BLAND, the magistrate of Bonavista who took a great interest in the Beothuks. In 1797 Bland claimed that Peyton had "rendered himself infamous for his persecution of the Indians" and that "the stories told of this man would shock humanity to relate." He recommended that Peyton be expelled from the Bay of Exploits.

Bland also noted that Peyton was then residing near Poole, in Dorset, evidently conducting his Newfoundland trade through hired hands. Indeed, until 1812 Peyton maintained his family in England. In that year, both his daughter and his wife having died suddenly, he decided to bring his 19-year-old son John to Newfoundland and take him into partnership. Young Peyton had, like his father, been raised in Christchurch, and he was educated at Wimborne Minster Boys School. He had served three years at Somerset House in London as a junior clerk. In 1818 he was appointed justice of the peace for northern Newfoundland by Governor Sir Charles Hamilton*. His early career entailed some contact with the Beothuks but on a more positive level than that of his father. Nevertheless, confusion in the facts and details of the lives of the two Peytons has often resulted in the younger being tarnished with a reputation earned by his father.

The last expedition to the Beothuks that John Peyton Sr took part in was led by John Jr, who in 1818 had represented to Governor Hamilton that he had suffered extensive injury to his fishing establishments occasioned by the pilfering Beothuks over a four-year period. The governor empowered him to search for his stolen property and to capture one of the Indians in order to gain an envoy who might later serve to establish friendly relations. Accordingly, in March 1819 the Peytons and some men struck inland. They came upon three wigwams and about a dozen Indians. A woman, Demasduwit*, was captured, and there was a scuffle between the elder Peyton and an Indian man which ended with the Indian being shot.

There may be some irony in the fact that the last known Beothuk, SHAWNADITHIT, and John Peyton Sr lived under the same roof during the last few years of their lives. Shawnadithit was captured by William CULL, an erstwhile servant of Peyton Sr, in 1823. She was given into the care of Peyton Jr and became a servant in the Peyton household at Exploits for five years. John Peyton Sr died in 1829, aged about 80 years. John Jr spent most of his later years in Twillingate. He died in 1879 and was interred in the family plot at Exploits.

W. GORDON HANDCOCK

BL, Add. MS 38352: ff.1–44. Dorset Record Office (Dorchester, Eng.), D365, F2–3, F8–10; P227/RE3–18. Hampshire Record Office (Winchester, Eng.), Christchurch parish records, 1682–1804 (transcripts at Maritime Hist. Arch., Memorial Univ. of Nfld., St John's). PANL, P5/25; P7/A/6. G.B., Parl., House of Commons papers, 1793, no.4393, *First report from the committee appointed to enquire into the state of trade to Newfoundland*; no.4407, *Second report. . . .* C. R. Fay, *Life and labour in Newfoundland* (Toronto, 1956). Howley, *Beothucks or Red Indians*. Prowse, *Hist. of Nfld.* (1895), 385. F. W. Rowe, *Extinction: the Beothuks of Newfoundland* (Toronto, 1977).

PHEBE DE SAINTE-ANGÈLE. *See* ARNOLDI

PHILIPPON, JOSEPH-ANTOINE, teacher, militia officer, and merchant; b. 19 March 1789 at Quebec, son of Yves Philippon, *dit* Picard, a shipwright, and Marie-Louise Faucher; m. 11 Aug. 1817 Claire Taschereau, illegitimate daughter of Thomas-Pierre-Joseph TASCHEREAU, àt Sainte-Marie-de-la-Nouvelle-Beauce (Sainte-Marie), Lower Canada; buried there 4 June 1832.

On 8 April 1801 the lieutenant governor of Lower Canada, Sir Robert Shore Milnes*, gave assent to the act setting up the Royal Institution for the Advancement of Learning. The legislation, which provided the governor with wide powers in the field of education, was received coldly by the Catholic clergy. At Sainte-Marie-de-la-Nouvelle-Beauce the parish priest, Antoine Villade, would probably not have agreed to the creation of a royal school if prominent individuals had not intervened. On 4 March 1814 Jean-Thomas TASCHEREAU and Olivier PERRAULT presented a petition to Governor Sir George Prevost* for such a school. Four days later the request was granted; Joseph-Antoine Philippon is believed to have started teaching on 11 March.

Philippon received an annual salary of £54. It is thought that he lived in the presbytery until he was married and that he gave his lessons in a house belonging to Father Villade and then at his own house, which was near the parish church. In 1820 he was teaching English, French, writing, and arithmetic to 25 schoolboys. At that time there were only a few families in the village, and they, like the clergy, were not all in favour of the royal schools. This may partially explain the small number of pupils. The secretary of the Royal Institution, Joseph Langley

MILLS, nevertheless demanded that a school be built, and it was put up in 1823. Three years later Philippon's salary was reduced to £30 a year on the ground that the school was "being held irregularly." Philippon tried to defend himself by citing the severity of the winter, the distance of pupils from the school, and the topography of the parish as reasons for the absenteeism. But a few months later Mills announced that the establishment would soon be shut and offered Philippon a teaching post at Terrebonne, which he refused. The school finally closed on 12 Jan. 1828.

Because of his education and initiative Philippon had become an important person who was held in esteem in the parish. After his marriage his father-in-law had given him a house. Subsequently Philippon bought 120 *arpents* of land. While teaching he had been at the same time engaging in trade and serving in the local militia. On 2 Jan. 1818 he was commissioned captain and ten years later he held the rank of major. In 1821 he became secretary of the Société d'Agriculture de la Nouvelle-Beauce, which had been founded that year. In this capacity he had to prepare reports on agricultural exhibitions and competitions which were held at Sainte-Marie-de-la-Nouvelle-Beauce.

Joseph-Antoine Philippon drowned in the Rivière Chaudière, but the circumstances surrounding his death are not recorded. Following an inquest, his body was buried at Sainte-Marie-de-la-Nouvelle-Beauce on 4 June 1832. After this tragedy Philippon's family, which included several children, moved away to other parishes in the vicinity.

HONORIUS PROVOST

ANQ-Q, CE1-1, 19 mars 1789; ZQ6-45, 11 août 1817, 4 juin 1832. Boulianne, "Royal Instit. for the Advancement of Learning." Provost, *Sainte-Marie; hist. civile*; *Sainte-Marie; hist. religieuse*. L.-P. Audet, *Le système scolaire*; "Deux écoles royales, 1814–36: Sainte-Marie de la Nouvelle-Beauce et Cap-Santé," RSC *Trans.*, 3rd ser., 50 (1956), sect.I: 7–24.

PICOTTE, LOUIS, fur trader, farmer, businessman, and politician; baptized 4 May 1780 at Rivière-du-Loup (Louiseville), Que., son of Jean-Baptiste Picotte, a farmer, and Hélène Jarlais (Desjarlais); m. there 25 Sept. 1810 Archange Déjarlais; d. there 7 May 1827.

The son of an Acadian refugee, Louis Picotte seems to have received a good education, judging by his excellent penmanship. On 26 Jan. 1802 he signed on as a voyageur with McTavish, Frobisher and Company. On returning from the northwest in 1806 or shortly before, Picotte settled down in the village where he was born, and for 1,000 *livres* (600 of it in cash) bought a piece of land 3 *arpents* by 40. He also had help from his father, who on 4 June 1807 "out of kindness" gave him a property at Rivière-du-Loup

Pierre

measuring 80 feet by 130. Two years later the sale of this land brought him a little more than 5,000 *livres*.

Being in a financially sound position, Picotte was able on several occasions to lend small sums of money to habitants in his community. In November 1809, branching out beyond agriculture, he hired a number of people to work in the lumber camps on the Cataraqui River in Upper Canada. That month he rented out his land for a year. In late 1813 or early 1814 he moved to Trois-Rivières, where he concentrated on setting up a butcher's shop. On 18 Aug. 1814 butcher Joseph Chauret made an agreement to slaughter and dress for market all the animals Picotte sent him. On 27 August Joseph Pagé undertook to melt the fat, deliver it in cakes, and reduce the residue to soap. On 2 Feb. 1815 François Morel, a Nicolet farmer, agreed to deliver between 13,000 and 15,000 pounds of beef to him. Picotte also acted for the Quebec wholesale butchers Anthony Anderson and Charles Smith.

Picotte returned to Rivière-du-Loup in the spring of 1815. He continued to lend money and to hire men for lumbering. He also saw to the production of several thousand planks for George Kerr, a Quebec merchant, and at the same time attended to a retail business and his lands.

On 11 April 1820 Picotte was sworn in as member of the Lower Canadian House of Assembly for Saint-Maurice; he represented this riding until 6 July 1824, working on many committees. In 1822 he opposed the projected union of the two Canadas. He did not seek a second term, probably for health reasons.

Picotte apparently was not without a sense of humour. Historian Benjamin Sulte* recounts that one day in the assembly, when speaker Joseph-Rémi Vallières* de Saint-Réal was presiding, Picotte asked a question on which he had to render a decision. Given to irony and fluent in several languages, Vallières de Saint-Réal tried to ridicule Picotte by a string of quotations in Spanish, Greek, and Latin. Picotte was not impressed and replied sharply in Inuktitut, Cree, and Algonkin, to the great amusement of those present, who were unaccustomed to such linguistic virtuosity.

Picotte died in 1827 at the age of 47. His personal estate was small: he left no cash and had no debts owing to him. But he did own two properties and three pieces of land at or near Rivière-du-Loup. On the other hand he owed 9,426 *livres*, including 8,048 to Anderson and Smith.

Born in the country, Louis Picotte had always stayed in close touch with his origins. Farming had remained a constant interest, as his ownership of various pieces of land and the award of a first prize to him by the Trois-Rivières agricultural society in 1821 show. The parish priest of Rivière-du-Loup made no mistake when he tersely noted on Picotte's death certificate, "during his lifetime a farmer in this parish."

RENALD LESSARD

ANQ-M, CN1-74, 26 janv. 1802. ANQ-MBF, CE1-15, 4 mai 1780, 25 sept. 1810, 8 mai 1827; CN1-6, 2 mars 1815; CN1-8, 18 août 1818, 19 mars 1819, 20 oct. 1821, 20 juill. 1827; CN1-32, 18, 27 août 1814; 2 févr. 1815; 28 oct. 1818; CN1-38, 27 sept. 1806; 3 mars, 4 juin 1807; 27 avril, 1er juin, 25 juill., 16 sept., 14, 18, 20 nov. 1809; 25 juin, 21 sept. 1810; 3 déc. 1811; 14 mai 1813; CN1-77, 5 nov. 1811; 8 sept., 10 oct. 1812; 29 mai, 20 juin, 10 juill. 1815; 8 janv., 30 mars, 31 mai 1816. *Quebec Gazette*, 16 March, 13 April, 26 June 1820; 1 March 1821; 5 Dec. 1822; 22 Jan. 1824. F.-J. Audet, *Les députés de Saint-Maurice (1808–1838) et de Champlain (1830–1838)* (Trois-Rivières, Qué., 1934). Germain Lesage, *Histoire de Louiseville, 1665–1960* (Louiseville, Qué., 1961).

PIERRE, TOMA. *See* TOMAH, PIERRE

PILKINGTON, ROBERT, army officer, military engineer, artist, and landowner; b. 7 Nov. 1765 in Chelsfield (London), England, son of Robert Pilkington and Grace ——; m. 15 Oct. 1810 in Devizes, England, Hannah Tylee, daughter of John Tylee, and they had two sons, one of whom died in infancy, and four daughters; d. 6 July 1834 in London.

Robert Pilkington attended the Royal Military Academy at Woolwich (London), and was commissioned a second lieutenant in the Royal Artillery on 27 Aug. 1787. He transferred to the Royal Engineers on 5 June 1789 and embarked for Quebec in July 1790. The first references to him at Newark (Niagara-on-the-Lake), Upper Canada, appear in October 1792. On 16 Jan. 1793 he was promoted first lieutenant.

Pilkington's engineering skills were much in demand, at first in and around Newark but then at York (Toronto) and other parts of the province; in fact, the work took more time than Lieutenant Governor John Graves Simcoe* could really spare. In addition to his responsibility for barracks, blockhouses, and defensive works, he was consulted on a variety of matters relating to everything from civilian improvements to coastal defences. For example, he was responsible for repairs to the Six Nations' church on the Grand River after it was struck by lightning in 1797, and the same year he built an addition to Upper Canada's first legislative building at York. In 1799 and 1800 he designed and constructed York's first government house, a one-storey frame structure which stood until 1813, when it was destroyed in the explosion of the adjacent powder magazine. Not all the engineer's projects were of obvious public importance. In June 1796 Mrs Simcoe [Elizabeth Posthuma Gwillim*] recorded: "Mr. Pilkington has erected a temporary room adjoining our house for the ballroom tonight."

Pilkington also served the function of semi-official cartographer. On 20 Sept. 1793 Simcoe forwarded the young engineer's sketch-map of York harbour to George III, and four days later included him in the group travelling by canoe from Humber Bay on Lake Ontario to Georgian Bay. Pilkington drew maps of the waterways along the route and painted several scenes observed during the trip, most notably on the Severn River. It was a difficult journey, a consideration in Simcoe's decision to build Yonge Street from York to Lake Simcoe. In March 1794 Pilkington accompanied Simcoe to Detroit and to the Miamis (Maumee) River. He prepared an improved map of the western Lake Erie region and sketched the Miamis River area, where he also remained behind to rebuild Fort Miamis (Maumee, Ohio). This job lasted almost until winter but was considered an essential encouragement to the Indians because the United States claimed the territory.

Pilkington was active in the embryonic social life of the young colony and seems, in particular, to have become a friend of Mrs Simcoe. In her diary she mentions riding with him and more than once she admits to copying his sketches. Pilkington was also a friend of John White*, Upper Canada's first attorney general. They often visited one another and attended social events together. After White's mortal wounding in his duel with John SMALL on 3 Jan. 1800, Pilkington broke the news to White's brother-in-law and patron, Samuel Shepherd, the English jurist. His offer to assume responsibility for White's two sons was not accepted as they returned to England to be raised by their mother under Shepherd's general supervision.

On 3 June 1797 Pilkington was promoted captain-lieutenant and on 18 April 1801 captain. In the fall of 1802 he returned to England, where he spent the next few years in the Southern District and at the government gunpowder factory at Waltham Abbey. On 24 June 1809 he was promoted lieutenant-colonel and a month later embarked for the only real military action of his career, as part of the notorious Walcheren expedition sent by the moribund Portland administration in a vain attempt to capture Antwerp (Belgium). Pilkington was part of its only small success, the siege and capture of the second-rate fortress town of Flushing (Vlissingen, Netherlands), and later he was praised for his work in commanding a mixed force of artificers, sailors, and civilians which destroyed the naval facilities, arsenal, and sea defences there. After a brief stay at Woolwich in 1810 Pilkington was posted to Weedon to oversee large-scale Board of Ordnance construction. He served as commanding engineer in the Northwestern District between 1815 and 1818 and at Gibraltar from 1818 to 1830. In the

mean time he was promoted colonel in the engineers on 1 Dec. 1815 and major-general in the army on 27 May 1825. He became a colonel commandant of the engineers on 28 March 1830 and inspector general of fortifications on 24 Oct. 1832.

Despite the fact that he never returned, Pilkington maintained an interest in Upper Canada. He enjoyed entertaining friends from his Upper Canadian years during their infrequent trips to Britain. He watched over his Upper Canadian land and sought ways of attracting settlers. In 1811 he proposed raising a corps of Highland emigrants to be enticed to Upper Canada by the use of land grants. In addition to about 2,000 acres in York, Newark, and Grantham Township, he had managed to acquire 15,000 acres on the Grand River from Joseph Brant [Thayendanegea*]. Ironically, despite the physical facilities he designed, constructed, and maintained throughout the province, which demonstrated the importance of the military engineer in Canada's colonial history, Pilkington's largest and most lasting contribution to Upper Canada may well be Pilkington Township, the land he got from the Six Nations. Unfortunately this was not totally a positive legacy. "The Major," as he was known in the Grand River area, enticed settlers from Northamptonshire and Warwickshire to immigrate to these lands. Problems arose for the gullible pioneers when they arrived after a long and difficult journey to discover that the region was completely undeveloped. Worse still, as the years passed many had disputes over the title to their property. Most died cursing Pilkington for the impossible position in which he had placed them. For all his positive contributions as a military engineer, he will always be remembered by some people for his sins as an absentee landlord with grandiose ideas.

CARL CHRISTIE

PAC, MG 23, HI, 5, vols.1–2; RG 1, E3, 61; E14, 8, 11; L3, 400: P1/1, 35; P2/38, 83; 400A: P4/1; 402: P9/29; 418: P misc., 1775–95/128; 419: P leases, 1798–1818/10; RG 8, I (C ser.), 102, 106–7, 223, 405, 512, 546–47, 597, 724; RG 10, A1, 2, 789; A2, 9; B3, 4733. *Corr. of Lieut. Governor Simcoe* (Cruikshank). Gwillim, *Diary of Mrs. Simcoe* (Robertson; 1911). Alexander Macdonell, "Diary of Gov. Simcoe's journey from Humber Bay to Matchetache Bay, 1793," Canadian Institute, *Trans.* (Toronto), 1 (1889–90): 128–39. *DNB*. G.B., WO, *Army list*, 1789–1835. *Roll of officers of the Corps of Royal Engineers from 1660 to 1898 . . .*, ed. R. F. Edwards (Chatham, Eng., 1898). E. [R.] Arthur, *Toronto: no mean city* (2nd ed., Toronto, 1974). B. M. Dunham, *Grand River* (Toronto, 1945). Marcus Van Steen, *Governor Simcoe and his lady* (Toronto and London, 1968).

PINSONAUT, PAUL-THÉOPHILE, notary, militia officer, businessman, and JP; b. 10 March 1780 in La Prairie, Que., son of Thomas Pinsonnault, a

Plamondon

merchant, and Euphrasie Artaud; m. there 17 Aug. 1807 Clotilde Raymond, daughter of Jean-Baptiste RAYMOND, and they had 11 children; d. 27 May 1832 in La Tortue (Saint-Mathieu), Lower Canada, and was buried in the church of Saint-Philippe.

In 1796 Paul-Théophile Pinsonaut was doing his clerkship in the office of notary Jean-Marie Mondelet*. He received his commission as a notary in 1801 and drew up documents first in La Prairie and then in La Tortue, where by 1814 he had signed some 3,000 acts. He took up residence, possibly the year he was married, in the house where his wife had been born, a dwelling built at La Tortue by his father-in-law and eventually known as the Manoir Pinsonaut.

Pinsonaut took part in the War of 1812. In October 1812 as a militia captain Pinsonaut was put in charge of organizing the Chasseurs de Saint-Philippe, a unit in the Châteauguay élite company. He served for two years. According to a family tradition, he was at the battle of Châteauguay in October 1813 under Charles-Michel d'IRUMBERRY de Salaberry.

When the war was over Pinsonaut by degrees gave up the notarial profession to go into business; in the period 1814–28 he signed only about 300 acts. In October 1817 his father-in-law handed over to him and his wife, as an advancement, a property of about 63 acres, two other pieces of land, and two potashéries valued at 12,000 *livres*; he had already given them 5,800 *livres*. Pinsonaut had become an important businessman. He went into lumber and potash production, developed his lands intensively, and invested in real estate. When he died, he owned some 800 acres in the seigneury of La Salle.

Pinsonaut served as a justice of the peace for the District of Montreal from 1821, acted as agent for the neighbouring seigneurs, and became a lieutenant-colonel in the militia in 1830; he had achieved success. In his manor-house he lived in the style of the upper middle class. A tutor from France, who had fled during the revolution, resided near the house and attended to the children's education. They also went to the Petit Séminaire de Montréal or else to Mme Trudeau's boarding-school in Montreal, which occupied the former Recollet friary and offered painting, music, dancing, and riding lessons. Wealth did not, however, shield the family from misfortune. On 1 May 1832 Pinsonaut buried his second son, who was only 19. Some three weeks later he caught the malady that led to his own death.

Two of Pinsonaut's daughters entered religious orders: Marie-Adélaïde joined the Ursulines in Trois-Rivières; Marie-Honorine-Euphémie became a member of the Sisters of Charity of the Hôpital Général in Montreal and in 1840 was a founding member of the Hôtel-Dieu at Saint-Hyacinthe. His son Pierre-Adolphe Pinsoneault*, a Sulpician who had been ordained priest in France, became the first bishop of London in Upper Canada. Jacques-Alfred, a lawyer and seigneur of Léry, continued developing his father's properties and in 1851 set up an experimental farm.

JEAN-JACQUES LEFEBVRE

Paul-Théophile Pinsonaut's minute-book, containing instruments notarized between 1801 and 1828, is held at ANQ-M, CN1-327.

ANQ-M, CE1-2, 10 mars 1780, 17 août 1807; CE1-54, 30 mai 1832. PAC, RG 68, General index, 1651–1841. *Officers of British forces in Canada* (Irving). Henri Masson, *Joseph Masson, dernier seigneur de Terrebonne, 1791–1847* (Montréal, 1972). J.-J. Lefebvre, "Jean-Baptiste Raymond (1757–1825), député de Huntingdon (Laprairie), 1800–1808," *BRH*, 58 (1952): 59–72; "Manoir Pinsoneault ou maison Raymond?" *BRH*, 58: 173–75. É.-Z. Massicotte, "Paul-Théophile Pinsonault, ses ascendants et ses descendants," *BRH*, 34 (1928): 207–20.

PLAMONDON, LOUIS, author, lawyer, militia officer, and office holder; b. 29 April 1785 in L'Ancienne-Lorette, Que., son of Joseph Plamondon, a farmer and miller, and Louise Robitaille; m. 30 Sept. 1811 Rosalie Amiot, daughter of Jean-Nicolas Amiot, a silversmith, at Quebec, and they had one daughter; d. 1 Jan. 1828 in Saint-Ambroise (Loretteville), Lower Canada, where he was buried four days later.

When he was six, Louis Plamondon was taken in charge by Charles-Joseph BRASSARD Deschenaux, parish priest of Notre-Dame-de-l'Annonciation in L'Ancienne-Lorette. He spent his childhood at the presbytery, where he came in contact with priests, members of the colony's administration, and important people of the Quebec region whom the parish priest regularly entertained. He learned to read and write, and was allowed to browse at leisure in his benefactor's imposing library, which contained about 2,200 volumes.

Plamondon studied at the Petit Séminaire de Québec from 1797 to 1804. He chose the priesthood as his vocation, perhaps under Brassard Deschenaux's influence; on 16 Jan. 1803 he received the tonsure, but in the end he went into law. Beginning in 1805, he was articled first to lawyer James Kerr*, then to James SHEPHERD, and lastly to Andrew Stuart*. During his legal studies he published a 64-page booklet entitled *Almanach des dames pour l'année 1807, par un jeune Canadien*; this work in verse and prose was dedicated to Rosalie Amiot. He also was one of the founders of the Literary Society of Quebec and served as its secretary under the presidency of François ROMAIN. In this capacity he was called upon to award a silver medal to John FLEMING, the winner of a literary competition organized by the society in 1809. For the occasion Plamondon delivered a laudatory speech on

King George III's reign, making frequent allusions to the political situation in Lower Canada which was marked at the time by great tension between Governor Sir James Henry Craig* and the Canadian party.

Plamondon was licensed as an advocate, barrister, attorney, and solicitor on 1 Aug. 1811, and he devoted his time primarily to the practice of his profession. His clients were drawn in large part from the farmers and artisans of the Quebec region, although he sometimes served as attorney for people residing in the District of Montreal. Since there is no list of the briefs he took, it is difficult to make an exact estimate of his income; presumably he made at least £500 a year.

In addition to arguing in court Plamondon trained young men in the law. Among others, Joseph Bouchette*'s son Samuel-Louis and John Hale*'s son Bernard, as well as Thomas Cushing Aylwin*, articled in his office. In 1826 he undertook to give free weekly lectures in law. According to the *Quebec Gazette* of 6 November, the first lecture, which dealt with the definition of law and the history of procedure, "exhibited great judgment and research, and it was delivered with the ease that gentle[man] so much possesses." That year Plamondon succeeded the late Joseph-Bernard PLANTÉ as inspector general of the royal domain and clerk of the land roll for Lower Canada, and to a degree abandoned legal work.

In addition to his professional concerns Plamondon was actively involved in his community. He served in the militia during the War of 1812. At first a captain in the Quebec Volunteers, he became a lieutenant in the town's 2nd Militia Battalion, and ended the war in the 6th Select Embodied Militia Battalion of Lower Canada. In September 1818 he was put in charge of collecting donations for the establishment of a dispensary at Quebec. He also served as a director of the Quebec Assembly, a social organization that arranged dinners and parties, and he was one of the few French-speaking members of the Quebec Library. In 1821 he helped found the Quebec Education Society, which began its work amidst the endeavours of the government, clergy, and the most influential members of the rising local bourgeoisie to set up a school system in Lower Canada [*see* Joseph-François Perrault*].

Louis Plamondon died on 1 Jan. 1828 reputedly from the effects of his excesses as a *bon vivant*. His colleagues Andrew Stuart, George Vanfelson*, Louis LAGUEUX, Joseph-Rémi Vallières* de Saint-Réal, André-Rémi Hamel*, and Georges-Barthélemi Faribault* were present at his interment in the parish of Saint-Ambroise. His wife renounced the joint estate, which was "more burdensome than profitable," and had to surrender more than £2,600 in bonds to cover the mortgage for their house on Rue Saint-Louis. His daughter, Rosalie-Louise-Geneviève, who married Montreal merchant John Anthony Donegani* in 1830, also renounced her father's estate, contenting

herself with her mother's jointure. Plamondon was remembered personally as intelligent, witty, and given to incisive, mordant repartee.

CÉLINE CYR

Louis Plamondon is the author of *Almanach des dames pour l'année 1807, par un jeune Canadien* (Québec, [1806]) and of a discourse which appeared in *Séance de la Société littéraire de Québec, tenue samedi, le 3e juin, 1809* (Québec, 1809).

ANQ-Q, CE1-1, 30 sept. 1811; CE1-2, 29 avril 1785; CE1-28, 5 janv. 1828; CN1-178, 2 avril 1827, 20 juin 1828; CN1-208, 12 févr., 20 juill., 18 déc. 1820; 14 avril 1821; 31 janv., 11 sept. 1822; 22 janv., 29 avril, 20, 28 mai 1823; P1000-81–1672. ASQ, Fichier des anciens. *Quebec Gazette*, 13 April 1809; 14 Sept., 10 Dec. 1818; 15 June 1820; 10 May 1821; 6 Nov. 1826; 3 Jan. 1828. Caron, "Inv. de la corr. de Mgr Denaut," ANQ *Rapport*, 1931–32: 201. Hare et Wallot, *Les imprimés dans le Bas-Canada. Officers of British forces in Canada* (Irving). P.-G. Roy, *Les avocats de la région de Québec.* Aubert de Gaspé, *Mémoires* (1866). Antonio Drolet, *Les bibliothèques canadiennes, 1604–1960* (Ottawa, 1965). Galarneau, *La France devant l'opinion canadienne (1760–1815).* Jolois, *J.-F. Perrault.* J.-E. Roy, *Hist. du notariat*, 2: 366–67, 369. Alfred Duclos De Celles, "Louis Plamondon," *BRH*, 8 (1902): 242–44. J.-J. Lefebvre, "La vie sociale du grand Papineau," *RHAF*, 11 (1957–58): 474.

PLANTÉ, JOSEPH-BERNARD, notary, politician, militia officer, office holder, and JP; b. 19 Dec. 1768 in Pointe-aux-Trembles (Neuville), Que., son of Dominique-Bernard Planté, a notary, and Marie-Josephte Faucher; m. 20 May 1794 Marie-Louise Berthelot at Quebec, and they had six children; d. there 13 Feb. 1826 and was buried three days later at Sainte-Foy, Lower Canada.

Joseph-Bernard Planté attended the Petit Séminaire de Québec and then began his notarial training in the office of Jean-Antoine Panet*, continuing it with Olivier PERRAULT. He received his commission on 11 Nov. 1788 and practised as a notary until his death. He had a large clientele: his minute-book contains 9,693 acts.

On 20 July 1796 Planté was elected to the House of Assembly for Hampshire, which he represented with François HUOT. In the July 1804 elections he won that riding, along with Antoine-Louis JUCHEREAU Duchesnay, after Huot withdrew in his favour. Planté was elected for Kent on 18 June 1808, as was Louis-Joseph Papineau*, and he retained the seat until 2 Oct. 1809. He was an assiduous and active member, belonged to numerous committees of the house, and primarily supported the Canadian party.

At the time he was engaged in political activity, Planté, who had signed the declaration of loyalty to the British crown in 1794, benefited from government patronage. On 1 June 1801, for example, like John

Plessis

Craigie*, Michel-Amable Berthelot* Dartigny, James FISHER, and George Longmore*, he became a commissioner for the relief of the insane and foundlings, and his commission was renewed in 1804, 1808, and 1814. In 1802 he replaced Philippe-François Rastel de Rocheblave as clerk of the land roll, and the following year he was appointed inspector general of the royal domain. In 1808 he lost the last two posts as a result of differences with Governor Sir James Henry Craig*, who reproached him for having taken part in the founding of the newspaper *Le Canadien*. Having renounced his affiliation with *Le Canadien* and made due apology, he was reinstated in these offices. In 1810 he obtained a commission as justice of the peace for the district of Quebec. Five years later he was made responsible for receiving the oath of allegiance from members of the Legislative Council. In 1815 he was appointed commissioner to oversee the demolition of the old market at Quebec. On 11 May 1818 he was entrusted with supervising new construction and repairs at the Hôpital Général in Quebec.

In addition to his numerous professional occupations Planté was a member of the town's Fire Society from 1795. He held the rank of captain and was adjutant in the militia as of 10 May 1797. On 20 May 1809 he became a major, and on 16 April 1812 he was promoted lieutenant-colonel of Quebec's 1st Militia Battalion, subsequently serving as lieutenant-colonel of the 4th Battalion. He became a member of the board of directors of the Union Company of Quebec in 1806. Seven years later he was induced to serve as secretary of the Quebec section of the Loyal and Patriotic Society of the Province of Lower Canada. Vice-president of the Agriculture Society in the district of Quebec in 1817, he held the office of president from 1818 to 1821. In 1818 he was elected vice-president of the Quebec Fire Assurance Company, and in 1821 he exercised the same function for the Quebec Savings Bank. That year he was elected to the first board of the Quebec Education Society, which had been founded by a group of citizens under the leadership of Joseph-François Perrault*.

Planté died suddenly on 13 Feb. 1826. His close friend, Pierre-Stanislas BÉDARD, was to observe that "the cares and anxieties which he assumed in [all his] affairs and of which I have been a witness certainly contributed . . . to weakening him physically. He was a noble soul in a frail body."

MICHEL VERRETTE

Joseph-Bernard Planté's minute-book, containing instruments for the period 1788–1826, is at ANQ-Q, CN1-230.

ANQ-Q, CE1-1, 20 mai 1794; CE1-15, 19 déc. 1768; CE1-20, 16 févr. 1826. PAC, RG 68, General index, 1651–1841. L.C., House of Assembly, *Journals*, 1796–1809. *Quebec Gazette*, 26 Nov. 1793; 10 July 1794; 18 June 1795; 6 Feb. 1806; 5 Feb. 1807; 29 May 1817; 6, 12, 23 April 1818; 13 April, 26 Oct. 1820; 2, 16 April, 10 May 1821. Desjardins, *Guide parl.* Hare et Wallot, *Les imprimés dans le Bas-Canada. Officers of British forces in Canada* (Irving), 150. Jolois, *J.-F. Perrault.* Wallot, *Un Québec qui bougeait.* F.-J. Audet, "François Huot," *BRH*, 37 (1931): 695–702; "Joseph-Bernard Planté, étude historique et biographie," *RSC Trans.*, 3rd ser., 27 (1933), sect.I: 133–59. P.-G. Roy, "La famille Planté," *BRH*, 40 (1934): 193–96.

PLESSIS, JOSEPH-OCTAVE (baptized **Joseph**), priest of the Roman Catholic Church, archbishop, politician, and author; b. 3 March 1763 in Montreal, son of Joseph-Amable Plessy, *dit* Bélair, and Marie-Louise Mennard; d. 4 Dec. 1825 at Quebec.

Joseph-Octave Plessis was born a little more than three weeks after the Treaty of Paris confirmed the British conquest of New France. His paternal ancestors had moved to the colony from Metz, France, at the beginning of the 18th century. In 1713 Jean-Louis Plessy*, *dit* Bélair, married Marie-Anne Petit Boismorel, and nearly 40 years later, in 1752, their 17th child, Joseph-Amable, married Marie-Louise Mennard. Joseph-Amable was a blacksmith, with a forge near Montreal, and his prosperity was ensured after the conquest by the increased demand for iron products resulting from another British invasion, that of merchants in the fur trade.

The seventh of eighteen children raised in a home both happy and religious, Joseph-Octave acquired confidence in his manifest abilities. At the Sulpician primary school he had little difficulty with the curriculum of reading, writing, arithmetic, and the catechism. After just one year he was sent to a small Latin school operated by Jean-Baptiste Curatteau*, parish priest at Longue-Pointe (Montreal). In the spring of 1773 he was confirmed by Bishop Jean-Olivier Briand*. That year Curatteau's school was moved into the city and became the Collège Saint-Raphaël. Plessis easily mastered his subjects, winning several prizes, and in 1777 or 1778 he completed his sixth year (Rhetoric) at the college.

In the autumn of 1778, with the aid of a bursary, Plessis entered the Petit Séminaire de Québec. By its rigorism and emphasis on the practice of the priesthood, the program of studies instilled in Plessis a moral austerity and a preference for practical concerns over intellectual discussion. As always, he accomplished his studies with ease. He also demonstrated leadership qualities; received into the Congrégation de la Bienheureuse-Vierge-Marie-Immaculée in October 1778, he was elected prefect, the highest student position in the fraternity, in April 1780.

Plessis completed his classical course around July 1780; the following month he was tonsured by Briand and assigned as a teaching assistant to the Collège Saint-Raphaël. He enjoyed teaching, but in the fall of 1783, on the advice of vicars general Henri-François Gravé* de La Rive and Étienne Montgolfier*, Briand called him back to Quebec to fill the position of secretary, usually reserved for the most promising young priests because it provided an excellent training in diocesan administration. While in this office, which he would occupy for some 15 years, Plessis was first influenced by Briand to the point of adopting not only the bishop's principles, but also his tastes and manners. On 11 March 1786 he was ordained a priest by Briand's successor, Louis-Philippe Mariauchau* d'Esgly.

During springs and summers from 1787 to 1792 Plessis accompanied d'Esgly's coadjutor and successor, Jean-François Hubert*, on the pastoral visit of the diocese. He acquired much experience in hearing confessions and preaching, a feeling for rural parishes and people, and a solid grasp of the problems and workings of parish administration. Hubert succeeded d'Esgly in 1788 and from the new bishop, who was less authoritarian than Briand, Plessis learned a more psychologically oriented approach to the direction of clergy and people.

On 31 May 1792, following the advice of Gravé, Hubert appointed Plessis to the cure of Notre-Dame at Quebec, the most important in the diocese along with Notre-Dame in Montreal, while keeping him as diocesan secretary. The parish embraced the entire town, with its population of 7,200. To obtain the information required to organize realistically the social and spiritual life of Notre-Dame, Plessis conducted a census that year and then repeated the operation in 1795, 1798, and 1805 to keep himself abreast of the town's evolution. These censuses confirmed the growth of two working-class suburbs, Saint-Roch and Saint-Jean. Plessis devoted pastoral attention particularly to the former, where growth was more rapid and poverty more grinding, eventually building a church, a convent, and a college there.

Quebec was the scene of a proliferation of drunkenness, brawls, robbery, and prostitution, encouraged by the absence of effective law enforcement and stimulated by the presence of soldiers and of sailors and raftsmen released from the isolation of months at sea or in the bush. From his pulpit Plessis denounced the moral state of the town. "His action was animated and his sermon impressive," noted Elizabeth Posthuma Simcoe [Gwillim*] on one occasion. Although passionate enough, his discourses were nevertheless directed to the head rather than the heart. To foster the spirituality of his congregation, Plessis reinvigorated the Confrérie de la Sainte-Famille and introduced the 40-hours devotion at Pentecost. He ministered to the Irish, hitherto neglected, but laboriously for he never quite mastered English pronunciation. His pastoral work, however, was concentrated on the religious education of the young, particularly in Saint-Roch, and he established new catechism classes and an elementary school. The most intelligent boys were

directed to the Petit Séminaire de Québec, in hopes that some would become priests. Plessis also mobilized community support for victims of social disasters. He was unremittingly occupied; his day began around 4:00 A.M. and ended about midnight.

As secretary Plessis acquired a reputation as the power behind Hubert. Some priests began addressing themselves to him for solutions to their problems; others resented his influence. Hubert being ill at ease in society, Plessis played a prominent role as intermediary between him and the politicians. Plessis thus established working relations with such influential men as Chief Justice William OSGOODE, Anglican bishop Jacob MOUNTAIN, Solicitor General Jonathan Sewell*, Civil Secretary Herman Witsius Ryland*, and the merchant-politicians Thomas Dunn* and William Grant*. These relations were reinforced by his active support of the British government during the French revolution; in 1794, for example, his funeral panegyric upon Briand vaunting the merits of British rule and denouncing the atheism and bloodiness of the revolution left a favourable impression in official circles.

In 1797 Hubert retired in favour of Pierre Denaut*. Plessis was the hierarchy's choice as Denaut's coadjutor, and his candidacy was supported by Osgoode and Ryland. Governor Robert Prescott* accepted him and then resisted pressure by Prince Edward* Augustus, who promoted another priest. Disruptions in the Vatican administration caused by the revolution and the death of the pope delayed signature of Plessis's bulls until 26 April 1800; he was finally consecrated bishop of Canathe on 21 Jan. 1801. Denaut remained in his parish of Longueuil, leaving to Plessis the district of Quebec and relations with government, subject to his approval. It was fortunate the two were good friends because this singular arrangement produced angry moments between them. "Strongminded" by nature, in the words of Gravé, and experienced in diocesan administration, Plessis at times bore his subordination with impatience. Slow communications occasionally prevented his consulting Denaut adequately on major matters, as in December 1798 and January 1799 after Prescott had ordered a day of thanksgiving to celebrate Admiral Horatio Nelson's victory in the battle of the Nile. Following an unsatisfactory correspondence with Denaut, Plessis found himself obliged, without further consulting the bishop, to replace a relatively bland pastoral letter by Denaut announcing the event with one of his own drafting better calculated to answer "the enthusiasm at headquarters."

Fear that French emissaries were stirring up revolution in Lower Canada [see David McLane*] made even French emigré priests suspect to the British. In 1798–99 Plessis had to lobby for acceptance of the emigré Jean-Henry-Auguste ROUX as superior of the

587

Plessis

Sulpicians in Montreal. This necessity to court government in internal matters pointed up the bishop of Quebec's lack of legal status and the extent to which he was dependent on government goodwill and his force of persuasion rather than on guarantees of law in the management of church affairs. The bishop's decisions regarding the erection or division of parishes, for example, could be contested either legally or politically. Plessis attempted to regulate this problem in 1797 when Thomas Coffin* introduced into the House of Assembly a bill to erect a parish that Denaut did not want created. Plessis hoped to transform this specific bill into a general law establishing procedures for the erection of parishes such that canonical erection must precede civil recognition. He obtained Ryland's support but failed to overcome opposition by Sewell and Osgoode.

The major elements determining Plessis's role as coadjutor – Denaut's absence from Quebec, British suspicion of everything French, and the bishop's want of legal status – came together under the lieutenant governorship of Sir Robert Shore Milnes*. Alarmed that the executive had little social – and hence political – influence with the Canadian population, Milnes, drawing on Osgoode, Mountain, Ryland, and Sewell, produced a comprehensive plan to increase it. Among other measures the plan prescribed bringing the Roman Catholic Church under executive control in order to capitalize on its social influence. In return Milnes offered legal recognition. To obtain Denaut's consent to the proposed restrictions, in April and May 1805 Sewell engaged Plessis in a series of negotiations from which nominations to cures and the erection of parishes emerged as principal points of contention. Plessis was prepared to give ground on both but Denaut was not, and the bishop's accusations of imprudence on Plessis's part angered the coadjutor. The church was in a crisis, he insisted; it was losing the external authority needed to support its spiritual mission. He eventually prevailed on Denaut to ask the king for recognition, but the petition Denaut sent in July 1805 was a mere shadow of the one that Plessis had envisaged and had hoped would result in a veritable charter of the church's rights. It was never answered.

Denaut's death in January 1806 offered the government an opportunity to obtain the control it wanted in return for continuing the episcopal succession. Plessis upset all calculations, however, when he persuaded the administrator, Thomas Dunn, to accept him as bishop and Bernard-Claude PANET as coadjutor without conditions. Panet was older than Plessis, but in choosing him Plessis had bought time to groom a younger priest, such as André DOUCET or Pierre-Flavien Turgeon*, as his ultimate successor.

By 1806 long-term developments within the clergy had given Plessis more authority over it than his predecessors had had. Canadianization, which had accelerated since the conquest, had made the clergy more homogeneous and amenable to a Canadian bishop, and its predominantly urban, middle-class origins corresponded to Plessis's own. The disappearance of the Jesuits and Recollets [see Jean-Joseph Casot*; Louis Demers*] had reduced the number of priests not under the bishop's immediate authority. The elimination as forces in the colonial church of the chapter at Quebec [see Charles-Ange Collet*] and of the Séminaire des Missions Étrangères and the Séminaire de Saint-Sulpice in Paris [see Henri-François Gravé de La Rive; Jean-Henry-Auguste Roux] had further concentrated authority in the bishop, as had the disruption of the Vatican administration by political and military turbulence in Europe. Although Plessis would have preferred better communications with Rome, his strong position vis-à-vis the clergy suited his authoritative and decisive temperament.

The bishop's most urgent problem was an acute shortage within that clergy. Pleas for relief by overworked parish priests, he wrote to one, "are breaking my heart." Through short-term measures he reduced the physical toll on his clergy, even though their work load continued to increase. He attempted to import French priests, but was prevented from doing so by a British ban until 1813 and thereafter by a shortage of clerics in France. At the same time he sought to increase local recruitment, never a priority with his predecessors. Few Canadian boys received a secondary education, however, and most who did opted for a less restrictive life in the professions. To augment the numbers of candidates for orders Plessis virtually froze the parish complement, despite its low level, and put all additions to the clergy into secondary teaching, hoping that from an increased number of students would come an increased number of vocations. He immediately encountered opposition from the Séminaire de Québec. It claimed that, as a branch of the Séminaire des Missions Étrangères in Paris, it enjoyed a certain independence of the bishop, a pretension that Plessis would not tolerate in such a crucial institution. He took up residence in the Séminaire de Québec in 1806 partly to improve relations, but mainly to affirm the episcopal presence. He succeeded on both these counts; however, in a third objective, to improve substantially the quality of theological training given to his clergy, until then largely dispensed in the Grand Séminaire, he considered himself unsuccessful.

To remedy this state of affairs, in 1811 Plessis offered to make Saint-Sulpice in Montreal, whose program of theological education he admired, a diocesan seminary. As coadjutor he had established excellent relations with its superior, Roux, but several disagreements arose between them after Plessis became bishop. A branch of Saint-Sulpice in Paris, the Montreal community was determined to maintain its long-standing independence of Quebec, preserve its French character at the expense of recruitment of Canadians, and protect its dominance over Montreal's religious life by minimizing episcopal influence in it. In 1807 an attempt by Plessis to settle Panet in the area had been thwarted by Roux. Four years later Plessis's offer to make Saint-Sulpice a diocesan seminary was seen as a Trojan horse and politely declined.

Saint-Sulpice also opposed Plessis's development of a seminary at Nicolet. The stagnation of recruitment in Montreal and Quebec had determined him to tap the area between them; a seminary at Nicolet would do so and would preserve students from the temptations of city life. He bought the property from Denaut's heir [see Pierre-Michel Cressé*], persuaded a reluctant Jean Raimbault* to become superior, obtained through bequests part of the library of Pierre-Joseph Compain* and the whole of that of François Cherrier* for the college, financed building expansions, purchased land endowments, and offered prize volumes. In return he exacted episcopal control of administration and teaching.

About 1817 Plessis began endorsing rural classical colleges elsewhere as well. That year he drafted the rules for the Collège de Saint-Hyacinthe, established by Antoine Girouard, and thereafter he found directors and sought letters patent for it. He also gave encouragement to Pierre-Marie Mignault* at Chambly and Charles-Joseph Ducharme* at Sainte-Thérèse-de-Blainville (Sainte-Thérèse). He attempted to recruit from the working class at Quebec by founding a college in the *faubourg* Saint-Roch in 1818. However, staffing the new colleges with young ecclesiastics drew criticism from parish priests deprived of assistants and from Roux, who argued that it dispersed meagre teaching personnel and hindered the raising of standards in theological education. Plessis also encouraged institutions founded to finance theological studies and personally sponsored needy students. However, the results of all these labours only became evident in the 1830s when recruitment began to match population growth.

Plessis exercised considerable influence on the formation of his recruits through surveillance of their studies and through ecclesiastical lectures at Quebec and Nicolet. He instilled in most strong faith, rigorous morality, discipline, and humility, underlining that the last quality was judicious in a period of democratic effervescence. He demanded individual self-abnegation but vaunted the clergy as "this elected race . . . this royal priesthood, this holy nation."

With his priests Plessis sought to establish a personal association. Alexander McDonell*, in Upper Canada, looked on him in 1820 as "my mainstay, my guide and support, for you have always behaved towards me since I have had the happiness of living under your jurisdiction, rather like a father and a

friend than a superior." Naturally gregarious, Plessis regaled clerical gatherings with expertly told stories drawn from wide reading and from an endless stream of humorous incidents experienced during pastoral visits and a voyage to Europe in 1819–20. He scrutinized the moral and psychological make-up of each priest and tailored his counsel and orders in consequence. He addressed the problems that most worried them. Isolation was one; all were exhorted to write to him frequently. From far-off Prince Edward Island Angus Bernard MacEachern noted, "Your grace who has more to do than any other person in Canada, is the only one who writes to me." When unjustly attacked by parishioners, his clergy could depend on his support; he remained faithful to a reassurance given in 1800 while coadjutor to one beleaguered priest: "You have a conscience and principles. That is all you need with me." Drawing on a vast knowledge of his diocese, Plessis was able to provide practical advice for the handling of difficult situations, an assistance invaluable to young priests in their first charge. To older clergy who feared exhaustion, he could offer only solicitude and a little humour: "There are enough priests dying prematurely left and right without your getting involved," he wrote to one.

In Plessis's efforts to promote clerical *esprit de corps*, the Société Ecclésiastique Saint-Michel, a clerical mutual aid association that he had helped launch in 1799, played a significant role, even though possibly one-half of the clergy remained outside it. The society enabled Plessis to provide pensions to incapacitated members. Having been named president for life in 1801, he shrewdly managed the board of directors to obtain from the society's funds capital to finance projects that he wished to forward, such as clerical education; however, his control and use of the society were contested by a few priests, particularly Charles-François Painchaud*.

In handling his clergy Plessis was flexible, in response to his times. "Let us order only in those cases where it is entirely indispensable," he advised his auxiliary Jean-Jacques Lartigue* in 1824. "Everywhere else let us avoid any expression that smacks of domination. We belong to an age of pride in which the command is odious." No task of clerical management was more difficult than moving priests around in order to maximize their usefulness. Graduate seminarians, imbued with Plessis's ideals of self-abnegation and obedience, were prime candidates for the thankless Maritime missions. With the established clergy, who generally resisted any move not considered a promotion, he employed reason, flattery, appeals to sense of duty or personal advantage, even moral bribery as the case required; only as a last resort did he order. The placing of clergy was for Plessis the most important element in the administration of his diocese, and he gave close consideration to matching priests with parishes and clerical neighbours. His determination to keep a free hand as well as a constant preoccupation with maintaining episcopal authority rendered him nearly impervious to demands by parishes and priests for changes in his plans. The colonial government rarely intervened in nominations to parishes despite endless projects and threats to take them over.

It was most often in matters of discipline that Plessis was prepared to use authority, for he believed that the clergy's influence depended on its assiduity and moral credibility. He insisted that priests not visit outside their parishes except with good reason and preferably only with permission. To combat the resulting isolation, he attempted to organize spiritual retreats, but the clergy had little time to attend them. On their own, often witnesses to depressing human situations, their authority increasingly contested by liberal professional members of their congregations, some priests sought comfort in the bottle or a sympathetic woman. In such cases, and they were not common, Plessis demonstrated a combination of toughness and understanding. If exhortation to reform failed of effect, he would suspend the priest and send him as an assistant to a reliable colleague; rarely was a priest defrocked.

In directing his clergy and governing his diocese Plessis was a careful as well as decisive administrator. The diocesan secretariat expanded to such an extent during his episcopacy that in 1820 a three-storey building had to be erected to house it. Lacking a chapter, the bishop frequently consulted his vicars general, who had limited powers within fairly large districts, before making major decisions. He also consulted the archpriests, who had minor powers over a small number of parishes, and in special cases the ordinary clergy whose work would be affected by a given decision. According to Painchaud, he particularly consulted younger priests because, trained under his eye, they shared his views. But it was Plessis still who decided, and in most cases he personally executed the decision; in 1809 a reluctant Charles-Joseph BRASSARD Deschenaux accepted appointment as vicar general, consoled only by his knowledge that, "with a bishop like you, a vicar general has practically nothing to do."

Plessis's disinclination to delegate authority (at least prior to the division of his diocese in 1820) was criticized by a few priests, such as Painchaud. In part, it sprang from a desire to facilitate standardization of practices over his vast jurisdiction. He counted on his young priests to promote this uniformity; in 1813 he announced a common fee schedule for services throughout the diocese, but to avoid clashing with entrenched clerical interests where opposition to it arose, he generally introduced it on the accession of a young priest to the cure.

Despite his efforts to establish bonds with his clergy, Plessis's position as bishop inevitably separat-ed him to some extent from them. The geographical perspective of most Canadians in the early 19th century was restricted to the St Lawrence valley and their social concerns centred on preserving their culture. The lower clergy shared this outlook. As bishop of a diocese that extended from the Atlantic to beyond the Red River, and with responsibility for Catholics of all nationalities, Plessis had broader perspectives. He was criticized in Lower Canada for his pastoral visits outside the colony and for expenses incurred in educating missionaries to work there. Seminarians resented his insistence on their learning English. While he sought an entente cordiale with the British, some Lower Canadian clergy cautiously approved the nationalist Canadian party. However, by his prestige, experience, and character, Plessis forged in the clergy of Lower Canada an *esprit de corps* and sense of purpose it had previously lacked.

Since the early 1700s the clergy had seen its moral and social influence in the colony diminish. After the conquest its authority was no longer founded on civil law. Its influence was further weakened by commercial and military expansion at Quebec and Montreal and by secular and democratic tendencies issuing from the Enlightenment and the American and French revolutions. Enlightenment philosophy appealed particularly to the seigneurial class and the emerging bourgeoisie. The legal fraternity was further alienated from the church by professional functions involving the taking of interest – preparation by notaries of legal obligations, lending of money by tutors and administrators of estates, decisions by judges condemning debtors – which could entail refusal of the sacraments to its members. Aware that the taking of interest was a vital activity in the Lower Canadian economy but unable to find an acceptable theological justification for it, Plessis on the one hand instructed priests not to preach on the subject, inquire about it at the confessional, or demand restitution, but on the other ordered them to apply the required penalties when the taking of interest was brought to their attention. He suggested unobjectionable means of making money from money, such as purchasing life annuities; however, he also accepted the issue of interest-bearing army bills during the War of 1812.

With the Canadian bourgeoisie Plessis also faced the question of the leadership of the Canadians. Through the Canadian party the nationalist bourgeoisie proclaimed itself the sole defender of the rights of the Canadians against British oppression. Plessis's analysis of the social and political problems facing the Canadians did not differ substantially from that, for example, of Louis-Joseph Papineau*, a leader of the Canadian party, but his proposed remedies did. Whereas Papineau became increasingly democratic and belligerent, Plessis sought to influence British policy from within. Yet, despite his disagreements with the bourgeoisie, Plessis employed his talent for social relations to maintain a personal bridge to the leadership of the Canadian party, and principally to Papineau, whose wife, Julie Bruneau, was an unconditional admirer of the bishop. In any case his church remained influential in the life of the bourgeoisie. The Canadian party considered it a traditional Canadian institution, and Papineau could write of Plessis: "While reproaching him for his political errors, we appreciate what he has accomplished for the ecclesiastical institution over which he presides." In literature, explicitly anticlerical Voltairism declined, while religious works were a leading category of books produced. Newspaper editors, including Henry-Antoine Mézière*, so outspoken in the 1790s, were rarely disrespectful. Canadian theatre, dependent on middle-class support, experienced a hazardous existence owing in part to clerical opposition. Even in politics the church commanded respect. After Thomas Lee pronounced a vigorously anticlerical speech in the assembly in 1814, another leader of the Canadian party, Pierre-Stanislas BÉDARD, considered that he had "acted very thoughtlessly, and ought to make every effort to undo his error"; Lee was defeated in 1816. If the professional bourgeoisie was largely recalcitrant in spiritual matters, Plessis noted in 1807 that respect for the faith characterized the country merchants, and in 1821 Jean-Jacques Lartigue informed him that in Montreal, "as everywhere else, the people of the middle class are the most submissive and the most attached to religion and to their ecclesiastical superiors." Lartigue's middle class was probably composed of artisans and shopkeepers.

That Plessis was personally respected by the rural inhabitants seems beyond question, and the working class of Saint-Roch venerated him. His direct contact with the habitants was generally limited to his pastoral visits; he was, consequently, assiduous in performing them. They were veritable missions, with Plessis stopping in each parish for several days to preach, examine parish accounts, observe the conduct of priest and parishioners, and note the existence of religious fraternities and the presence of Protestants. His sermons were often successfully improvised on the spot to address the specific problems of the locality.

The attitude of the habitants and the workers towards the church and the clergy generally, while largely respectful, was not one of docile submission. In April 1808, for example, an act had to be passed (subsequently renewed annually) "to provide for the maintenance of good order on Sundays and Holidays." In December 1810, noting that the feast days of parish patrons had become "days of blasphemies and battles," Plessis ordered that a single Sunday would thenceforth be set aside as the feast day of all parishes. Such problems may have been created by roisterous minorities and rowdies. But parishioners did often divide into opposing camps over the manner of distributing pews, the projected location of a church building, the creation of new parishes, and even certain temporal powers of the priest in parish administration. These conflicts nevertheless reveal the importance of institutional religious life to the Canadians; they would fight passionately over forms and methods but rarely over fundamentals of faith. Nor did apparent recalcitrance necessarily indicate defection. "The church [of Saint-Esprit] is not finished, the grounds are not completely paid for, there is no presbytery, and of more than 200 inhabitants, only 53 have paid the tithe of 1808," Plessis noted that year. "Yet [the parishioners] ask for a parish priest." The habitants' religion might be superficial, conformist, and superstitious; but it was firmly anchored in their national and social life.

The morality of his people was a matter of concern to Plessis. In the towns of Montreal, Quebec, and Trois-Rivières moral standards possibly declined as prosperity and population increased. But in the rural parishes, according to John Lambert*, the inhabitants were "universally modest in their behaviour: the women from natural causes, the men from custom." At Quebec the workers of Saint-Roch were a consolation to Plessis. Shortly after becoming bishop he acknowledged that there was "a pretty good foundation of faith and religion" in the colony, particularly in comparison with Europe. At the same time he addressed himself to what he saw as a growing moral problem, though publicly he might exaggerate the extent of immorality and religious indifference to dramatize a real need for reform. His perception of the problem reflected in part a hardening of his own views over time. In 1800 he denounced "a literal adhesion to moral principles, which always have a certain latitude and which ought to bend according to circumstances of time and place." By 1823, however, he was writing: "Immorality follows so closely the negligence of certain precautions that there would be great imprudence in accusing of rigidity the laws prescribing them, and . . . these laws, like morality of which they are the shield, ought never . . . to be considered variable according to the circumstances of time and place." This increasing moral conservatism gave rise to a discreet but determined crusade. Paintings in churches were made more decorous. Reasons were required for granting marriage dispensations where there had been pre-marital sex, a requirement that had been abandoned by Plessis's predecessors. War was waged on drunkenness and alcoholism. The clergy were exhorted to denounce party-going, dancing, and improper dress with greater insistence. But Plessis was a realist and armed himself with patience; in the end probably nothing was more modest than the extent of his success.

Plessis

To stimulate spiritual life in the parishes, Plessis encouraged the establishment of religious associations, as he had done at Quebec. Ultimately, however, he depended on the clergy to make the church's influence felt, and in a lecture to seminarians he offered his vision of relations between laity and clergy: "Consider the world divided into two sorts of people, one needing teaching, the other charged with providing it; one famished, the other charged with feeding them; one searching for the way to salvation, the other charged with leading them to it; one afflicted, the other charged with consoling them; one filled with doubts and fears, the other charged with enlightening and reassuring them; one sick, the other charged with treating and healing them." Such a view left ample room for clerical despotism, but Plessis, in the interest of preserving respect for the clergy, endeavoured to prevent its development. Unlike some of his clergy, he saw the priests' financial dependence on their parishioners not as a nuisance but as a check on abuse of authority, and he defended the parishioners' right to protest even in court. Insensitive expenditures on grandiose projects of construction or decoration in times of crop failure incensed him; in 1806 he warned one priest to abandon plans for a new presbytery or have his church interdicted. He advised use of sanctions against fractious parishioners only when persuasion had failed. The church's uncertain legal status persuaded him to take parishioners to court only when victory was almost certain. On the other hand Plessis might threaten with interdiction or removal of their priest parishes that did not respect their pastor. Given the prevailing shortage of clerics, this threat was effective in achieving limited objectives, but it was less so in changing attitudes.

Plessis was aware nevertheless that long-term tenure of a parish enabled a priest to establish his authority and a bond of trust with his parishioners, and during his episcopacy 65 to 80 per cent of the clergy, depending on the period, remained in the same parish for more than ten years and 45 to 53 per cent for more than 20 years. He insisted that his clergy attend energetically to the social welfare of their parishioners. In times of agricultural distress the habitants looked to their priest for prayers and assistance, the latter being organized on a parish, district, or diocesan level according to the extent of the crisis. Only when the church's resources were overwhelmed was the state called on to contribute, and even then Plessis and the clergy directed operations. For Plessis this social agency demonstrated to the people the clergy's concern and ability to meet their needs.

With Protestants Plessis's relations were in some respects less arduous than those with his flock. Although the Enlightenment ideal of toleration had few adherents in Lower Canada – and Plessis was not among them – religious conflicts rarely scarred the period of his episcopacy. Plessis applied the conciliatory policy initiated by Briand, which consisted principally of religious separation. He refused government proposals to share churches with the Anglicans and stiffened rejection of mixed marriages. The marriage of two Catholics before a Protestant minister was considered null, and Plessis negotiated agreements with Mountain, with Presbyterian minister Alexander Spark*, and with Governor Sir George Prevost* (regarding marriage licences) that eliminated most avenues within the colony for such marriages. Enough remained, however, to compromise his efforts to restrain the granting of marriage dispensations, too freely accorded by his predecessors, he believed; disappointed couples threatened to go to a willing Protestant minister or to the United States.

Plessis was guarded in promoting proselytism. "My system is simply to not harass Protestants to bring them to true faith," he observed in 1809, "but if it only requires saying a few appropriate words to them to get them on the right road . . . that is an easy matter, which, without compromising a priest, can contribute in the highest degree to the glory of God and the honour of his church." He opposed proselytism by nuns in the hospitals; however, especially after the War of 1812, he cautiously encouraged production of indigenous controversialist literature by Jean-Baptiste Boucher*, Jackson John Richard*, and Stephen Burroughs. More commonly he imported English works, considered less likely to offend government susceptibilities.

At the same time Plessis took measures to counter Protestant proselytism, of which the most fervent practitioners were Methodists. Rural clergy harassed itinerant ministers and colporteurs and pressured, spiritually and socially, curious parishioners. Priests bought up tracts and Bibles or seized them from recipients and burned them. By 1816, however, Plessis had become convinced that he must produce his own edition of the New Testament to oppose that of the Methodists "and to shut the mouths of Protestants who complain unceasingly that we are concealing knowledge of the Scriptures from the faithful." After overcoming opposition from the Sulpicians and indifference on the part of Lartigue, enlisted to work on the manuscript, Plessis had his project defeated in 1825 by Rome's refusal to authorize publication. Protestant proselytism was in any case an unqualified failure. Most Canadians associated Protestantism with the conqueror; as Lartigue observed, they preferred impiety or even atheism. But in the discomfiture of Protestant proselytism the vigilance of the clergy and their ability to circumscribe all efforts by proselytizers cannot be discounted. The attempts of Jacob Mountain to attract Canadians to the Church of England by diminishing the prestige of the Roman Catholic bishop while raising that of the Anglican were equally unsuccessful. Before the War of 1812 Britain dared not alienate the vast majority of the colony's population by yielding to Mountain's importunities, and after the war it was obliged to recognize its debt to Plessis, whose loyalty had been ostentatious.

Although Protestantism made no gains, Plessis noted that "the inevitable relations of Catholics with the Protestants occasion a *rapprochement* of opinion that significantly alters the purity of the faith and causes some concern for the future." Catholic discipline regarding fasting, for example, had to be relaxed where Protestants were numerous. Progeny of mixed marriages, even when supposedly Catholics, formed "a species of bastard Christians who fall into disbelief." On the other hand Plessis used the Protestant threat to justify his insistence on renewed vigour in clerical education and pastoral work.

A focus for Plessis's concerns about growing secularism and the Protestant presence was primary education. It was universally acknowledged to be in a lamentable state, but there was no agreement over the type of person it should form: a good Catholic, a good Protestant, a good nationalist, or a good loyalist. An act adopted in 1801 to establish a public education system under the aegis of the Royal Institution for the Advancement of Learning [*see* Joseph Langley MILLS] soon proved unacceptable to the Canadian party and to Plessis. The bishop instituted a boycott of Royal Institution schools which the Canadians' indifference toward formal education made impressively effective. When in 1816 and again in 1818 he was offered a seat on the board of trustees of the Royal Institution, under Mountain's presidency, he refused. He was determined to have Catholic children educated in a system under the control of the Catholic bishop. Thus he strongly promoted Catholic primary education, in part to refute charges that his boycott of the Royal Institution was intended to maintain obscurantism among the Canadians, in part to provide students for the increasing number of colleges, but mainly because he still believed, as he had when parish priest of Notre-Dame, that the future of the church depended on educating children in the faith. He personally founded more schools in Saint-Roch and prodded his priests to establish them in their parishes. Those trained under his influence, such as Painchaud, Mignault, Ducharme, Turgeon, Thomas Maguire*, Jean-Baptiste Kelly*, Pierre-Antoine TABEAU, Narcisse-Charles Fortier*, and Jean-Baptiste-Antoine Ferland*, caught his sense of urgency, but most others did not. In 1815 Plessis revised the shorter catechism to better adapt it for rural children, who, he asserted, had perhaps "less disposition than [those] anywhere else in the world to seize things intellectual."

From 1814 Plessis supported a drive by the Canadian party to obtain a new education act. Progress was hindered by the determination of Lord Bathurst,

colonial secretary, to use the issue as a lever with which to pry concessions from the Canadian party over the control of government finances [*see* Sir Francis Nathaniel BURTON]. In 1824, the *fabrique* law, which permitted the financing of schools from the funds of the parish *fabriques*, was finally carried. Last-minute revisions to it obtained by Plessis ensured that the clergy, not its rival for control of the education of Canadians, the liberal bourgeoisie, would dominate the system. But Plessis's efforts to obtain government financing through the establishment of a Roman Catholic royal institution were unsuccessful. As well, since most clergy preferred to expend funds from the *fabriques* on construction or decoration of churches or presbyteries, the *fabrique* law ultimately was a failure and was replaced in 1829. In obtaining it, however, Plessis had demonstrated his strength.

Indeed the close relations of Plessis and his clergy with the Canadian lower class, the failure of Protestant proselytism, and the effectiveness of Plessis's boycott of the Royal Institution all reinforced a Protestant impression of the bishop and his priests as powerful forces in Canadian society. Protestants saw in the Canadians' love of the externals of religion – such as the numerous large churches and the elaborate, colourful processions of the host – an indication of profound devotion to the church. In auricular confession and the Canadians' ignorance of the principles of the Reformation they discerned powerful factors favouring clerical domination. Their perception of priestly power was further strengthened by the Canadians' tenacious attachment to their language and customs and by the stereotypes of them held by the British as a result of the religious, social, and geographic segregation of the two groups. Mountain wrote that such was the ignorance of the Canadians and the influence of the bishop that Plessis might be called "the Pope of Canada."

It was not unreasonable in the early 19th century to assume that religious power conferred social and political influence. Most of the British did, and then sought means to deal with the implications. Mountain wanted to sap the Catholic clergy's influence; Sewell advised harnessing it to the service of the state; John Lambert argued that government had to conciliate the clergy by granting the widest possible toleration. Plessis's policies were framed to promote the third view. Whatever the reality of clerical influence, the perception of it by government officials was of great concern to him. When addressing them he repeatedly invoked the vision of a clergy cherished by the faithful and prepared to use its influence in favour of government if left free to do so and supported by the authorities.

After having initially encouraged Milnes to obtain a favourable reply to Denaut's petition of 1805 for civil recognition of the bishop, Plessis, by the summer of

1806, was sharing fully his predecessor's fears that government might impose controls in return. He quietly abandoned the petition. At the same time efforts by Milnes, Mountain, and Ryland to have the home government adopt various restrictions all failed. Perhaps the most serious threats to Plessis's position were Sewell's affirmations that the church had no legal status in the colony. However, Sewell's victories in court on that ground [see Joseph-Laurent Bertrand*], when not reversed later, produced equivocal results politically. "The impression that these assertions make on the minds of Catholics is not at all disadvantageous to their religion," Plessis noted. "They are, on the contrary, irritated and encouraged to maintain it." The nationalists rushed to the defence of the church; colonial administrators and officials in Britain feared to exploit the gains. In February 1810, after more than two years under the administration of a governor strongly suspicious of the clergy, Sir James Henry Craig*, Plessis could reassure one of his priests that, "notwithstanding all the inconveniences that the holy ministry experiences here, we are . . . in a country . . . where there is more faith, and where the ecclesiastical offices are exposed to fewer difficulties" than anywhere in the world.

Plessis viewed with apprehension, however, intensification of the conflict between Craig and the assembly, the latter backed by the newspaper Le Canadien. He feared most the consequences for his church of a crisis that pitted the faithful against the established authorities, whom he felt duty-bound to support. He was obliged by law to have his priests read a proclamation by Craig justifying the governor's seizure of Le Canadien and imprisonment of its founders and printer in March 1810, but he was not cowed by Craig. A little more than a year later, maintaining that the British government would "consider that nineteen-twentieths of the inhabitants of the country are Catholics" and would not risk "setting the province on fire," he resisted both tempting offers and threats made by Craig in a series of heated discussions the object of which was to induce him either to resign his office or to give up some of his powers. The failure of a mission to England by Ryland to achieve Craig's objective of emasculating the bishop's authority proved Plessis right; the British government feared the creation in Lower Canada of a situation similar to that in Ireland.

Under Craig's successor, Sir George Prevost, Plessis was able to abandon the policy followed by preceding bishops of passive resistance to government encroachment on episcopal powers and go on the offensive in seeking legal sanction for episcopal authority. Needing Canadian support for prosecution of an imminent war with the United States, Prevost looked to the two most influential Canadian leaders, Papineau and Plessis. The bishop was asked to indicate what he felt would be necessary to place his office on a respectable footing. Plessis brushed aside warnings to caution by a suspicious Roux. The times invited audacity: "The governor is good. . . . The decided protection that the Catholics of Ireland receive from all Protestants of the realm, the dispositions recently manifested by lords Castlereagh, Grey, and Grenville, . . . the alarm that the success of French arms gives Great Britain, the desire to preserve Canada for England at a time when the United States seems to want to invade it; all this combines to inspire some hope from an attempt that we might later regret not having made." In May 1812 he petitioned, among other things, for civil recognition of the bishop and coadjutor. During the War of 1812 he was indefatigable in manifesting his loyalty and that of the clergy. For several reasons Canadian support of the British was assured from the outset; Plessis's loyalty was thus approved not only by the authorities but also by the people. In 1813 the government expressed its satisfaction by increasing the bishop's salary to £1,000.

Prevost was recalled before Plessis's petition of 1812 could be answered. In Prevost's successor, Sir John Coape SHERBROOKE, Plessis found another ally, and indeed a personal friend. Sherbrooke saw in the bishop a man of immense knowledge of the land and its people and a potential adviser. More important, in July 1816 he had received formal instructions from Bathurst to conciliate Plessis. Roman Catholics, Bathurst told Sherbrooke, "form a great majority of the Population and their influence in the House of Assembly must be predominant. . . . Our great object must be not to let the demagogues make the Roman Catholics the instruments of mischief . . . and for this purpose you will I hope be able to establish a good understanding with the Roman Catholic Bishop. The power which he has over the clergy is very great, and must therefore be very great also through the Clergy over the people . . . and there is no so effectual (I believe no effectual) way of conciliating the Roman Catholic laity, as by the clergy. There will be no indisposition here to attend to their Interests and wishes even tho' this should be unfavourable to the Protestants." Bathurst's dispatch marked the triumph of a decade of diplomacy by Plessis. In 1817 he was named to the Legislative Council; the mandamus of appointment constituted legal recognition of himself as bishop of Quebec. Admitted to the council in February 1818, he found himself at the head of a phantom contingent of Catholics, since his coreligionists rarely attended. He himself was present at about 60 per cent of council meetings, where he was generally discreet but became active when discussions embraced religious, educational, or social matters.

Meanwhile, Plessis had become increasingly preoccupied with another major problem: the ungovernable size of his diocese. His concern for Catholics outside Lower Canada cannot be questioned. He sent them missionaries whenever possible, and, lacking priests of his own, opened the doors of the Séminaire de Québec to their sons who aspired to the priesthood, often helping to finance their studies [*see* Ronald Macdonald*]. He was generous and intelligent in his counsel to missionaries and was no less sparing of his energies and time; in 1811, 1812, and 1815 he had visited the Catholics of the Maritimes, assessing the religious situation there, preaching, and organizing religious life. In a journal he took notes on the region's geography, history, demography, and economic activities. He remarked, with a perspicacious, often critical, if not entirely unbiased eye (he was clearly a metropolitan visitor to the hinterland), the social and moral life of the Acadian, Scottish, and Indian Catholics. At Paspébiac, headquarters of the Gaspé fishing operations of Charles ROBIN, he observed that "the inhabitants . . . are kinds of serfs, entirely dependent" on the Robins because kept hopelessly indebted to them. On Prince Edward Island he found "the most perfect harmony" reigning between the 3,750 Acadians and 250 Scots; but no intermarriage occurred, each group seeking to "hold on to the customs and manners of its nation." He was struck by the apathy of the Micmacs of New Brunswick, "for they see the English establish themselves among them, pillage their lands, steal their hay, take over their salmon fishing, without making any effort to obtain justice." Conditions during these voyages were often difficult. Aboard ship he was invariably seasick; on land the poverty of most Catholics often made meals and accommodation repulsive. At Sydney Mines, on Cape Breton Island, he reluctantly celebrated mass in a stable loft in intense heat that raised a nauseating odour from the horse stalls below. His reactions to these inconveniences were humorous or compassionate but never disdainful. A pastoral visit to Upper Canada in 1816 was altogether less trying; his most disagreeable experience was getting caught in a horde of American tourists at Niagara Falls.

Such visits, however, could not compensate for the absence of regular and immediate episcopal direction. Although Plessis accorded great latitude to his vicars general, Alexander McDonell in Upper Canada, Edmund Burke* in Nova Scotia, and Angus Bernard MacEachern on Prince Edward Island, geographical distance and the growth of the Catholic population, largely the result of Irish and Scottish immigration, required subdivision of the diocese to provide organized, constant, and effective ecclesiastical administration. In addition, although by 1818 he had barely initiated missionary activity in the northwest [*see* Joseph-Norbert Provencher*], he believed that the region's isolation would call for a bishop there immediately.

After he had become bishop in 1806, Plessis had made several unsuccessful attempts to obtain subdivision of his diocese. Then in 1817 London and Rome agreed to the creation of vicariates apostolic for Nova Scotia, Upper Canada, and Prince Edward Island; that for Nova Scotia was established immediately with Burke at its head. The formation of small, isolated vicariates apostolic, each dependent directly on Rome, offended Plessis's sense of organization and his appreciation of institutional power; in his view the British government would divide and rule. He preferred an ecclesiastical province, with an archbishop at Quebec and suffragan bishops in the Red River colony, Upper Canada, Montreal, Nova Scotia, and Prince Edward Island, in order to facilitate planning and concerted action. Influenced by Plessis's views, Rome abandoned the remainder of the agreement with London. On 12 Jan. 1819, without having consulted the bishop further, Rome elevated him to archbishop of Quebec, but, rather than ordinary suffragan bishops, it created suffragan and auxiliary episcopal vicars general for Upper Canada and Prince Edward Island, appointing McDonell to the former post and MacEachern to the latter. Rome's arrangement, moreover, did not include Montreal and Red River, which Plessis intended for Jean-Jacques Lartigue and Joseph-Norbert Provencher respectively. Furthermore, it had not been discussed with the imperial authorities. Before word of the new plan reached Quebec, Plessis had left for London to promote his own scheme; he heard word of his elevation only after his arrival in England in early August 1819. Offended by Rome's unilateral action, Bathurst, with whom Plessis had anticipated difficult negotiations in any case, was even less disposed to consider the archbishop's proposal for a regular ecclesiastical province. Only Plessis's persuasiveness obtained from the colonial secretary a vague acquiescence in his using McDonell, MacEachern, Lartigue, and Provencher as assistants with whatever powers the archbishop chose to confer on them.

Plessis also negotiated with Bathurst the disposition of the Sulpician estates, threatened with government expropriation, even though responsibility for protecting them belonged to the Sulpicians' representative, Lartigue, who accompanied him. Ryland noted that the Sulpicians were "aware of the advantage they will derive from the presence of this Personage [Plessis] in England, where he will possess the means of making a splendid appearance, and they flatter themselves, with reason, that his subtlety and Talents, and sanctimonious Professions of Loyalty which have already contributed so much to their advantage on this side . . . cannot fail on the other." An imminent seizure of the estates was averted largely through Plessis's intervention with Bathurst, but their ultimate disposition was not settled.

From London Plessis proceeded through France

Plessis

and Italy towards Rome. Wherever he stopped he sought out the archbishop, bishop, or parish priest to enquire about the state of religion locally while touring the church or cathedral. He observed the physical and human landscape, customs, and economic activities. Ever pragmatic, in the Papal States he criticized past popes and cardinals for their inattention to public utilities, even reproaching them for lavishing money on works of art and on monuments (be they to Catholicism) at the expense of agriculture, commerce, and public health. He was often scandalized by nudity in European painting and sculpture, the more so in works on religious themes used in church decoration. Yet he was sensitive to the power of religious architecture and art for edification: the grandeur and beauty of Lower Canadian churches were sources of pride to him, and he struggled to improve the quality of religious painting in his diocese. Thus, from 1817 he had vigorously urged religious communities and parish priests to purchase items from a magnificent collection of European works sent to Lower Canada from France by Philippe-Jean-Louis DESJARDINS.

Rome awed Plessis with its centuries of Catholic history, but his voyage was one of business, not a pilgrimage. He was not a spiritual ultramontane. As a seminarian he had been bathed in gallican influences, and these had later been reinforced in the 1790s by his particularly close relations with the French *émigré* priests whom Hubert had brought to the colony and who still looked on Plessis as their patron. Only circumstances dictated his adoption of views later characterized as ultramontane. Living under a Protestant government obliged him to emphasize the church's autonomy from the state. The presence of Protestantism evoked the argument that the pope, guided by tradition, was the standard authority for interpretation of the Scriptures; the Protestants, it was argued, had no standard. His penchant for a unified, hierarchical administration made attractive to him the vision of a powerful pope at the head of the church.

Plessis's primary objectives in Rome were to obtain agreement to the concession he had extracted from Bathurst and to prod the Vatican into negotiating with London the establishment of a regular ecclesiastical province. According to his agent in Rome, Robert Gradwell, this "clever sensible man . . . went a good John Bull way to work, which forced several to bestir themselves, who were well enough inclined to take their own time." Plessis dismissed Cardinal Francesco Fontana, prefect of the Sacred Congregation of Propaganda, as "an old woman, and no man of business." On the other hand he admired and imitated Cardinal Ercole Consalvi, the master diplomat of the Congress of Vienna; despite Plessis's aggressiveness, Gradwell remarked, "there is not in Rome one bishop who stands higher in general estimation." Although even Plessis could not overcome Vatican inertia on

most matters, he did obtain bulls for Lartigue and Provencher as episcopal vicars general, like McDonell and MacEachern, and indulgences and other religious privileges with which to stimulate the spiritual ardour of the Canadians. He had been granted three audiences with Pope Pius VII and had received appointments as count and assistant to the pontifical throne.

In February 1820 Plessis left for London. In Paris he had an interview with Louis XVIII that left him pessimistic about a restoration of religion in France. In London by May, he obtained authorization to bring 4 French priests to Lower Canada; he had requested 12. To Bathurst he complained, among other things, of the prejudice against Canadians in appointments to colonial offices. He personally presented papal greetings to George IV. In June he left for New York where, at Pius's request, he inquired into dissensions in the American church. On 7 August he was in Montreal, and, after a triumphal descent down the St Lawrence, he arrived at Quebec on the 14th to a tumultuous welcome.

Plessis found that since his departure confrontation between the Canadian party and the colonial administration had been renewed under the Duke of Richmond [Lennox*] and his successor as governor, Lord Dalhousie [Ramsay*]. In the Legislative Council he adopted an independent course between Dalhousie and the Canadian party while seeking to consolidate his recent gains. But political polarization made independent conduct suspect to Dalhousie, who came to consider the bishop a hidden source of opposition. Moreover, in the eyes of both Richmond and Dalhousie, the end of the war had freed government from the need to maintain Plessis's support, and they transmitted the feeling to Bathurst. "The horizon is darkening," Plessis wrote to one priest. "Those who come after me will have more difficulties than I. . . . Never mind, they will get out of them if they know how to tack. If determined to confront authority they will gain nothing. I adopt more and more every day this system, and frankly, it has not served me badly." He tacked toward the Canadian party. In March 1821 he voted in council against a resolution requiring approval of the civil list in its entirety for the life of the king, a measure long rejected by the Canadian party. In 1822–24 he joined with that group in opposing a bill to unite Lower and Upper Canada, one clause of which required government assent to clerical appointments. The clergy's opposition was a primary factor in scuttling the bill.

The backing of the leaders of the Canadian party was useful to Plessis when, after 1821, the elevation of Lartigue to the rank of Plessis's suffragan at Montreal was contested by the Sulpicians. They correctly surmised that Lartigue would challenge their spiritual hegemony in the city and region. Plessis requested Rome's support and then sought to keep the conflict under control until his position was confirmed. Discreetly, he built up support for Lartigue; Papineau and Denis-Benjamin Viger* were persuaded that a bishop at Montreal must be seen as an honour for the Canadian people. Lartigue's connections to prominent Montreal families ensured material support for construction of his church of Saint-Jacques, while Plessis cunningly delayed a rival Sulpician project to enlarge the church of Notre-Dame. Merely keeping the nervous, authoritarian Lartigue from either resigning in discouragement or, by his aggressiveness, escalating the struggle to a major conflict was an achievement. Plessis controlled matters until August 1823 when Augustin CHABOILLEZ, parish priest at Longueuil, published a diatribe on Lartigue's appointment. Rapid sales induced the bishop to authorize a reply by Lartigue, who, however, was so biting that he merely hardened opposition. Plessis took a firm hand in drafting a more moderate response by Louis-Marie Cadieux*, parish priest at Trois-Rivières, but vetoed publication of a proposed response by Painchaud because it did not support Lartigue and episcopal authority sufficiently. When an unrepentent Chaboillez came back with an even more incendiary pamphlet, Plessis ordered a halt to the war of words. Meanwhile, Propaganda had been neutralized by a deluge of memoranda from the Sulpicians and their allies.

Plessis got little support from the government, which might have refuted one of Chaboillez's major arguments, namely that the Montreal arrangement had not been authorized by the Colonial Office. The bishop's pursuit of an independent line in the council continued to embitter Dalhousie. In 1824 Plessis allied himself with the Canadian party to obtain passage of the *fabrique* law; however, without legal recognition many parishes could not benefit from it, and all Plessis's efforts to obtain such recognition failed while Dalhousie was in the colony. When Dalhousie went to England on leave that year, Plessis exploited the more favourable attitude of Lieutenant Governor Sir Francis Nathaniel Burton to have the parish of Sainte-Claire erected by letters patent capable of serving as a model. In return Plessis ensured support in council for a compromise on government finances worked out by Burton with the Canadian party. Dalhousie, who denounced Burton's move as a sell-out of the colonial executive's financial independence, never forgave Plessis for his role in it. By then, however, the governor's goal of eventually bringing the bishop under state direction had become virtually unattainable. When in July 1824 he proposed making another attempt to obtain control of clerical nominations, Bathurst responded that "it is now too late to rescue that authority which has been permitted to slide from us. At least the endeavour to rescue it would be

attended with a struggle that might counteract for a very long period any good effect to be obtained by its resumption." Plessis's flirtations with the Canadian party were, nevertheless, merely opportunistic. Each saw the other as an enemy ideologically and as a social rival. In council Plessis's votes on other points of government finances angered the nationalists. Polarization left no tenable ground between Dalhousie and Papineau; Plessis came under fire from both camps.

By the early 1820s, however, the bishop had more pressing concerns. Overwork and asceticism had undermined a robust constitution. As early as January 1810 he had had a combined office and hospital room built at the Hôpital Général for his exclusive use. From 1816 fevers and rheumatism or phlebitis in his legs and feet drove him to it with increasing frequency. Force of character overcame the pain when necessary – "I have decided," he wrote to Jean Raimbault in 1817, "to consider my sickness henceforth as a mere indisposition; that makes me more mobile and gives me greater freedom" – but in the spring and summer of 1825 his health deteriorated alarmingly, and fear grew that Dalhousie or the Sulpicians would be able to impose on Panet, who would succeed Plessis, a coadjutor of their choice. Efforts by Plessis to have Lartigue replace Panet as coadjutor were blocked by Dalhousie. However, from his hospital bed in late November 1825 Plessis persuaded Dalhousie to accept as candidates for coadjutor to Panet Pierre-Flavien Turgeon and Jérôme Demers*; Plessis did not like the latter but proposed him as a favourite with the clergy. His succession apparently ensured, a few days later he chatted easily with his physician, Thomas Fargues*, when suddenly Fargues observed that, "without a sigh or convulsive motion whatever, his eyes closed, his arm dropped on his chair, his head sunk on his breast and he silently ceased to breath."

Plessis was displayed at the Hôpital Général, after which he was taken by 40 pallbearers, led by clergy and an honour guard of the 79th Foot, through thronged streets to the Hôtel-Dieu. On 7 December shops closed at 9:30 before Plessis was taken for burial in the cathedral of Notre-Dame; as he had requested, his heart was placed in the church of Saint-Roch. Had he died more than ten miles from the cathedral, he had specified in his will, his body was to have been buried in the nearest parish church. Attending the burial ceremony, Dalhousie coolly observed the consternation of the population and the "very deep . . . distress evinced by many of the Priests both young and old."

Among those who mourned the bishop's death was a student at the Petit Séminaire de Québec, and later biographer of Plessis, Louis-Édouard Bois*. Plessis, he wrote, was "a little below the average height, but very corpulent. He had a wide forehead and a large head, and all facial features in good proportion. . . .

Plessis

He had a little beard and black hair, but always powdered white." It was found that Plessis's personal effects were inextricably mixed in with church property that he held in trust; in any case all his bequests were to religious institutions or to priests. His intimate friends, among them Antoine Girouard, Jean Raimbault, Philippe-Jean-Louis Desjardins, Pierre-Flavien Turgeon, and Thomas Maguire, were all priests.

French-Canadian historiography has portrayed Plessis and his clergy in light of the prevailing ideology. For most 19th- and early 20th-century writers, such as Bois, products of a clerically dominated society, Plessis was the first ultramontane bishop of Quebec. Recent historians, writing in a secular era, have seen him as struggling with a society under the influence of liberalism, nationalism, and secularism, forces which dominate their own times. In fact Plessis was not an ultramontane, and the great mass of Canadians remained strongly attached to their church, clergy, and religion, although the last was a popular version rather than authorized Catholicism. But the American and French revolutions had challenged the church's concept of a divinely ordered society. Plessis's predecessors had offered passive resistance to the forces contesting the church's place in the life of the colony: the colonial government, Protestantism, and liberal-democratic ideas. Plessis planned and carried out a counter-attack. It consisted, on the one hand, of ensuring the church's structural soundness – increasing the number of clergy, obtaining legal recognition, and seeking creation of an ecclesiastical province – and, on the other, of concentrating pastoral efforts on education and moral reform. He had the strength of character to sustain a long struggle and the adaptability to exploit favourable circumstances and wait out unfavourable ones – to tack – in order to advance his cause. His victories were, it is true, often semi-defeats: civil recognition was limited to him personally, the division of his diocese was far from the ecclesiastical province that he had envisaged, increase in clerical recruitment was frustratingly slow, the *fabrique* schools law was revoked after his death, and, although the shorter catechism was revised, the mooted adoption and revision of a greater catechism had been abandoned. Yet these were but laborious beginnings typical of major movements. This little, round, affable ascetic with an iron will and a big heart inspired in the younger clergy by force of example a sense of direction and dedication that their elders had lacked. He gave them a mighty push, which would carry them through the troubled 1830s and install them at the head of their society after leaders of the movement for secularism, liberalism, and nationalism, refusing to tack, took their forces to destruction on the rocks of rebellion in 1837–38.

JAMES H. LAMBERT

[Two of Joseph-Octave Plessis's sermons were published during his lifetime: *Discours à l'occasion de la victoire remportée par les forces navales de sa majesté britannique dans la Mediterranée le 1 et 2 août 1798, sur la flotte françoise prononcé dans l'église cathédrale de Québec le 10 janvier 1799 . . .* (Québec, 1799) and *Sermon prêché par l'évêque catholique de Québec dans sa cathédrale le IVe dimanche du Carême, 1er avril 1810 . . .* (Québec, 1810). Two others appeared in the 20th century: "L'oraison funèbre de Mgr Briand," *BRH*, 11 (1905): 321–38, 353–58, and "Sermon prêché à la cathédrale de Québec . . . à l'occasion de la paix américaine . . . le jeudi, 6 avril 1815," *BRH*, 35 (1929): 161–72. The Quebec censuses Plessis compiled as a parish priest are in ANQ *Rapport*, 1948–49: 1–250, as "Les dénombrements de Québec." The journals of the trips he took outside Lower Canada were also published after his death. Those for 1811 and 1812 appear as "Journal de deux voyages apostoliques dans le golfe Saint-Laurent et les provinces d'en bas, en 1811 et 1812 . . ." in *Le Foyer canadien*, 3 (1865): 73–280. The journal of the 1811 trip was reprinted under the same title in *Rev. d'hist. de la Gaspésie* (Gaspé, Qué.), 6 (1968): 23–43, 91–115. The journals of three visits to the Maritimes appear in *Soc. hist. acadienne, Cahiers* (Moncton, N.-B.), 11 (1980), as "Le journal des visites pastorales en Acadie de Mgr Joseph-Octave Plessis, 1811, 1812, 1815," with an introduction and notes by Anselme Chiasson. The journal of his 1815 trip, along with that of his visit to Upper Canada in 1816, was brought out by Henri Têtu* as *Journal des visites pastorales de 1815 et 1816, par Monseigneur Joseph-Octave Plessis, évêque de Québec* (Québec, 1903). In 1903 Têtu also published *Journal d'un voyage en Europe par Mgr Joseph-Octave Plessis, évêque de Québec, 1819–1820* (Québec).

Plessis's pastoral letters were published in volume 3 of *Mandements, lettres pastorales et circulaires des évêques de Québec*, Henri Têtu et C.-O. Gagnon, édit. (18v. parus, Québec, 1887–). For an inventory of Plessis's correspondence, *see* Ivanhoë Caron, "Inv. de la corr. de Mgr Plessis," ANQ *Rapport*, 1927–28: 215–315; 1928–29: 89–208; 1932–33: 1–244. His correspondence with American bishops, edited by L. St G. Lindsay, appears in American Catholic Hist. Soc. of Philadelphia, *Records* (Philadelphia), 18 (1907): 8–43, 182–89, 282–305, 435–67; 22 (1911): 268–85. Plessis should be considered the real author of *Le petit catéchisme du diocèse de Québec, approuvé et autorisé* (Québec, 1815; nouv. éd. 1816, 1819), and the co-author of *Observations sur un écrit intitulé "Questions sur le gouvernement ecclésiastique du district de Montréal"* (Trois-Rivières, Qué., 1823), the first draft of which was done by Louis-Marie Cadieux, to whom the work is generally attributed.

No collection of Plessis papers has survived except for a small one at AAQ, 31-11 A. However, numerous archival collections concern him specifically and the most important are listed below. AAQ, 20 A, I–VII; 210 A, II–XII; 22 A, V–VI; 1 CB, I–X; CD, Diocèse de Québec, I–VIII; 69 CD, VI–VIII; 515 CD, I–II; A–B; 6 CE, I; 7 CM, I–VI; 10 CM, III; 90 CM, I–II, IV; 60 CN, I–VII; A; 310 CN, I; 311 CN, I–II; 312 CN, I–VII; 320 CN, I, III–VII; Séries TC, TF. ACAM, 901.013; 901.036; RCD, XXXVIII; RLL, I–IV. AP, Notre-Dame de Québec, sér.1, MS 71–76. Arch. du séminaire de Nicolet (Nicolet, Qué.), AO, Séminaire III, nos.37, 58; Lettres de Mgr J.-O. Plessis à M. Raimbault.

Arch. of the Archbishop's House (London), IC, 56–57; ID, A-55; Gradwell papers, B-3, B-30, E-7, E-8; Poynter papers, VI B1, B2. Archivio della Propaganda Fide (Rome), Scritture riferite nei Congressi, America Settentrionale, 2 (1792–1830); Lettere della Sacra Congregazione e Biglietti di Monsignore Segretario, 297–307 (mfm. at PAC). ASQ, MSS, 205, 218–19, 257; MSS-M, 102, 978; Polygraphie, XI, 19; Séminaire, 253. ASSH, Sect. A, sér.A, 1.1, 4–1. ASSM, 21, cartons 45–46. PAC, MG 24, J4. PRO, CO 42/108–211 (mfm. at PAC).

There are a fair number of studies dealing with the Roman Catholic Church and the religious situation in the colony during the period 1790–1825. The most significant are: Noël Baillargeon, *Le séminaire de Québec de 1760 à 1800* (Québec, 1981); Raymond Brodeur, "Identité culturelle et identité religieuse, étude d'un cas: 'Le petit catéchisme du diocèse de Québec, approuvé et autorisé par Mgr J. O. Plessis, Québec, le 1er avril 1815'" (2v., thèse de PHD, univ. de Paris-Sorbonne, 1982); Richard Chabot, *Le curé de campagne et la contestation locale au Québec (de 1791 aux troubles de 1837–38): la querelle des écoles, l'affaire des fabriques et le problème des insurrections de 1837–38* (Montréal, 1975); Chaussé, *Jean-Jacques Lartigue*; Maurice Fleurent, "L'éducation morale au petit séminaire de Québec, 1668–1857" (thèse de PHD, univ. Laval, Québec, 1977); Serge Gagnon and Louise Lebel-Gagnon, "Le milieu d'origine du clergé québécois, 1775–1840: mythes et réalités," *RHAF*, 37 (1983–84): 373–97; Claude Galarneau, *Les collèges classiques au Canada français (1620–1970)* (Montréal, 1978); L.-E. Hamelin, "Évolution numérique séculaire du clergé catholique dans le Québec," *Recherches sociographiques* (Québec), 2 (1961): 189–241; Laval Laurent, *Québec et l'Église aux États-Unis sous Mgr Briand et Mgr Plessis* (Montréal, 1945); Lemieux, *L'établissement de la première prov. eccl.*; J. S. Moir, *The church in the British era: from the British conquest to confederation* (Toronto, 1972); Fernard Ouellet, "L'enseignement primaire: responsabilité des Églises ou de l'État (1801–1836)," *Recherches sociographiques*, 2: 171–87, and "Mgr Plessis et la naissance d'une bourgeoisie canadienne," CCHA *Rapport*, 23 (1955–56): 83–99; Fernand Porter, *L'institution catéchistique au Canada; deux siècles de formation religieuse, 1633–1833* (Montréal, 1949); Louis Rousseau, *La prédication à Montréal de 1800 à 1830: approche religiologique* (Montréal, 1976); Marcel Trudel, "La servitude de l'Église catholique du Canada français sous le Régime anglais," CCHA *Rapport*, 30 (1963): 11–33; and the following by J.-P. Wallot: "L'Église canadienne et les laïcs au début du XIXe siècle," *Le laïc dans l'Église canadienne-française de 1830 à nos jours* (Montréal, 1972): 87–91; "The Lower-Canadian clergy and the reign of terror (1810)," CCHA *Study Sessions*, 40 (1973): 53–60; "Pluralisme au Québec au début du XIXe siècle" in *Le pluralisme: symposium interdisciplinaire*, Irenée Beaubien *et al.*, édit. (Montréal, 1974), 57–65; and *Un Québec qui bougeait*, 183–224.

Funeral sermons constitute the earliest biographical accounts of Plessis. The most significant of these was Jean Raimbault's, published as "Oraison funèbre de Monseigneur J. O. Plessis, évêque de Québec, mort le 4 décembre 1825" in *L'Écho du cabinet de lecture paroissial* (Montréal), 2 (1860): 6–11. A biographical sketch, "Notice sur la vie de feu Monseigneur J. O. Plessis, évêque de Québec," *La Bibliothèque canadienne* (Montréal), 5 (1827): 89–96, was followed by "Notice biographique sur Mgr. J. O. Plessis," which appears in *Mélanges religieux* (Montréal), 2 (1841): 363–66, 381–84, 396–98. In 1863 Jean-Baptiste-Antoine Ferland, once a protégé of Plessis and then his secretary, published in *Le Foyer canadien* (Québec), 1: 70–318, under the title "Notice biographique sur Monseigneur Joseph Octave Plessis, évêque de Québec," a biographical account that is still useful and interesting. A translated version by T. B. French came out at Quebec the following year as *Biographical notice of Joseph-Octave Plessis, bishop of Quebec*; the account was published once more in French in 1878 as *Mgr Joseph-Octave Plessis, évêque de Québec* (Quebec). In the mean time, Louis-Édouard Bois wrote in 1872 a biography that is of interest mainly because it portrays Plessis as an ultramontane; it has not been published and is at ASN, AP-G, L.-É. Bois, Succession, XVII, nos.19–30. Between 1872 and 1883 Laurent-Olivier David* published three biographical sketches of Plessis that are of historiographic interest; the first is infused with liberal ideology, but the series demonstrates an interesting evolution in interpretation. Like Bois and David, Henri Têtu is heavily indebted to Ferland for his presentation of Plessis's career and character in *Notices biographiques; les évêques de Québec* (Québec, 1889; réimpr. en 4v., Québec et Tours, France, 1930), 436–525. Indeed, it was only with Ivanhoë Caron* that the study of Plessis's life went beyond Ferland's work and was undertaken in scholarly fashion. At his death in 1941 Caron left a massive, unfinished manuscript biography (AAQ, Sér.T, papiers Ivanhoë Caron, 3). The first five chapters of this work were published as "Mgr Joseph-Octave Plessis" in *Le Canada français* (Québec), 2e sér., 27 (1939–40): 193–214, 309–20, 826–41; 28 (1940–41): 71–96, 180–95, 274–92, 784–96, 1029–36. Caron also published four well-researched articles in RSC *Trans.*: "La nomination de Mgr Joseph-Octave Plessis, évêque de Québec, au Conseil législatif de Québec," 3rd ser., 27 (1933), sect.I: 1–32; "Monseigneur Joseph-Octave Plessis, archevêque de Québec, et les premiers évêques catholiques des États-Unis," 3rd ser., 28 (1934), sect.I: 119–38; "Monseigneur Joseph-Octave Plessis: sa famille," 3rd ser., 31 (1937), sect.I: 97–117; and "Monseigneur Joseph-Octave Plessis, curé de Notre-Dame de Québec (1792–1805)," 3rd ser., 32 (1938), sect.I: 21–40. No further biographical study of Plessis appeared until the completion of the author's thesis "Joseph-Octave Plessis," which includes a full bibliography up to 1979.

The 27 known portraits of Plessis were studied by Lucille Rouleau Ross in her 1983 MA thesis for Concordia Univ. (Montreal), "Les versions connues du portrait de Monseigneur Joseph-Octave Plessis (1763–1825) et la conjoncture des attributions pictorales au début du XIXe siècle." J.H.L.]

POLLARD, RICHARD, merchant, office holder, judge, JP, and Church of England clergyman; b. 1 Jan. 1753 in London; d. 6 Nov. 1824 in Sandwich (Windsor), Upper Canada.

Born into a "respectable family," Richard Pollard attended grammar school in England and was then trained in law and business, probably being articled to a firm of solicitors. Edward Pollard, either Richard's

Pollard

father or older brother, settled at Niagara (near Youngstown, N.Y.) in the 1760s, and Richard himself arrived in the province of Quebec in the spring of 1775. During the American invasion of Quebec in 1775–76 [*see* Benedict Arnold*; Richard Montgomery*] Pollard took up arms to repel the invaders, and later, "with much difficulty," made his way to New York and boarded a ship for England. Arriving at the end of May 1776, he immediately petitioned the British government to permit him to export "gunpowder, arms and ball" to Quebec since these articles were urgently needed there. It is not known whether this request was granted; however, in 1777 he was back in the colony, setting up as an Indian trader at Cataraqui (Kingston, Ont.) and Niagara. He also performed legal work in Montreal, where much of his time was spent. In 1780 he began his association with freemasonry, joining St Peter's Lodge No.4 in Montreal. He held various offices in the lodge over the next six years.

In February 1782 Pollard was trading with the Indians at the British settlement of Detroit. The following year he took out a licence for trading there in partnership with William Mason. He had accumulated enough money by 1784 to buy a tract of land at Petite Côte (Windsor) on the south side of the Detroit River near present-day Amherstburg, Ont. In 1787 merchant Laurent Durocher complained about "the Mackinac Company" (the General Company of Lake Superior and the South), a fur-trading organization based at Michilimackinac (Mackinac Island, Mich.), and "that young fool Pollard" associated with it.

Durocher's remark notwithstanding, Pollard was by then a prominent figure among the merchants of Detroit and the surrounding region. When on 16 July 1792 Lieutenant Governor John Graves Simcoe* introduced a new system of counties for Upper Canada, Pollard became sheriff of Essex and Kent counties. He acted as returning officer in the 1792 election which saw David William Smith* returned for the riding of Suffolk and Essex. In September 1794 he was appointed registrar of deeds for Essex and Kent counties, and he held this post until his death. In that year as well he became registrar of the Surrogate Court, surrendering this position on becoming a judge of that court on 29 Aug. 1801, another position the versatile Pollard held for life. He also served during the course of his life as postmaster, justice of the peace, member of the land board of the Western District, and trustee of the district school.

These offices brought Pollard little wealth; indeed, the records of his business accounts throughout his life were to show him in continuing debt. Only on 8 May 1797 did Administrator Peter Russell* and the Executive Council grant him a salary of £50 sterling per annum, with arrears from 1792, for the shrievalty. By 1796, when the Detroit territory passed to the control of the United States and government offices moved to Sandwich, Pollard had managed to purchase or had been granted various other lands on the south side of the Detroit River. But his debts were such that he was soon forced to sell at a time when land prices were falling.

Pollard's resources were further drained by his decision to undertake clerical duties that involved him in the toils of a missionary clergyman's life. In the late 1790s Peter Russell and Jacob Mountain, bishop of Quebec, were looking for "a discreet good Clergyman at Sandwich" who would combat republicanism, Methodism, and other evils threatening law and order, as well as perform marriages for the new settlers. Pollard was an obvious candidate for holy orders since he had conducted Church of England services in Detroit as a layman since the early 1790s and at Sandwich in the government offices building from 1796. Chief Justice John Elmsley* wrote to Lieutenant Governor Peter Hunter* that Pollard knew Latin, read much, and "seems in no degree deficient in those branches of knowledge which every Man who lives much in the World ought to possess." He would be "a very useful" parish priest and, even if Mountain considered Pollard "deficient in literary attainment," Hunter should stress to him "the other qualifications of which he possesses so large a share." Some people were relieved by Pollard's plans for a new career. Isaac Todd*, Montreal merchant, told John Askin* that Pollard was "twenty times fitter for a clergyman than a sheriff." Alexander Henry, an old trading friend of Pollard, thought he "may make a tolerable parson – anything for an honest livelihood."

Equipped with many "very satisfactory testimonials," Pollard was ordained deacon in Quebec by Bishop Mountain on 20 March 1802; two years later, on 2 June 1804, he would become a priest at the first ordination held in the new Cathedral of the Holy Trinity in Quebec. After entering the diaconate in 1802 Pollard was appointed chaplain to the garrison at Amherstburg and resident minister at Sandwich. Journeying back to Sandwich that year, Pollard stopped at Kingston to visit the Reverend John Stuart*, who was amused when the new deacon stumbled in his efforts to speak in a manner befitting his office: "When a sudden Oath escaped, he immediately checked himself for it, saying that, although not strictly clerical, he had a sort of Dispensation till he actually arrived at his Cure; after which he must not indulge himself in the use of such strong Expressions." Back in Sandwich, Pollard relinquished the post of sheriff to his friend William Hands, who six years later would also assume Pollard's post as registrar of Kent, Essex, and Suffolk counties.

As a clergyman, Pollard set himself the task of "raising the clerical Character to its proper Pitch" through conscientious exertion. Confronted with stark

Pollard

conditions he complained to Askin in October 1804, after being ill, that he had no church wardens, no assistance at communion services, no stove, and no servant to be hired at any price. In 1805 Pollard had recovered his health enough to begin making missionary visits to Detroit, something he did more or less regularly until 1821, initiating work which led to the formation of the diocese of Michigan. In 1806 he set about raising money to build St John's Church at Sandwich; this log building, the first church west of Niagara (Niagara-on-the-Lake), was in use by 1807. Until 1810 Pollard continued to serve, without remuneration, as chaplain to the garrison at Amherstburg. Because of the cost of travel and the three days' absence from Sandwich, he was limited to performing services on a monthly basis and visiting the troops in emergencies.

The war of 1812 brought Pollard great hardship. In September 1813 Major-General William Henry Harrison's Kentucky militia burned the church at Sandwich. As chaplain Pollard accompanied the men of the 41st Foot in their retreat along the Thames River. Taken prisoner at the battle of Moraviantown in October 1813, he was soon returned to Sandwich. He stayed there until February 1814, when he was allowed by the American commander to journey to York (Toronto). He conducted services in a Lutheran church at York and also in Ancaster and in Barton Township (Hamilton) before taking temporary charge – as a replacement for John Langhorn* – of the townships of Ernestown and Fredericksburgh in June 1814. By June 1815 Pollard was back at Sandwich. His church remained in cinders, his furniture was gone, and his house was beyond repair. In 1816 he received a gratuity of £100 from the Society for the Propagation of the Gospel for losses "by fire and the enemy," and the following year was granted another £50 by the SPG for building churches at Sandwich, Amherstburg, Chatham, and Colchester. In 1817 as well, despite attacks of fever, he made a circuit of 240 miles visiting these places, taking services, preaching, and leaving "useful sermons at the houses where I staid." He agitated to have some of the clergy reserves sold off to help meet the building costs of his new churches, and later to provide for a new parsonage which his parishioners had neglected in their zeal for putting up the church at Sandwich. In succession the four churches were opened, aided by generous donations from himself: on 12 Dec. 1819 the brick church at Amherstburg; on 11 June 1820 St John's Church, Sandwich; in October 1820 the church at Chatham; and by January 1821 the stone church at Colchester, covered in but not yet finished inside. Pollard visited Amherstburg until 1822 when Romaine Rolph, recently become a priest, was able to continue without assistance. He also regularly visited his new church at Chatham.

Richard Pollard's exertions in his Gilbert and Sullivan combination of roles taxed both his finances and his health. When he died on 6 Nov. 1824 his finances were in disarray. His sister-in-law Ann Pollard, writing from England to his executor William Hands, commiserated with him on the unpleasantness of settling Richard's concerns, "the state of which *did not surprize me.*" Pollard was remembered for the personal and pastoral qualities that he brought to his work in the church and in local government, two areas of endeavour which were interlinked in the informality of the frontier. "He was charitable, kind and humane, to all who acquainted him with their griefs and sufferings."

CHRISTOPHER HEADON

Especially important in the preparation of this biography was A. H. Young's article "The Revd. Richard Pollard, 1752–1824," *OH*, 25 (1929): 455–80.

ACC, General Synod Arch. (Toronto), M73-3, Stuart–Addison letter, 1811. AO, Hiram Walker Hist. Museum coll., 20-108, William Hands corr., Pollard to Hands, 1820; Ann Pollard to Hands, 26 Jan. 1825; C. J. Stewart to Hands, 17 June 1825; 20-135, no.86; 20-186; 20-245; 20-265; Hist. plaque descriptions, "St. John's Anglican Church, Windsor," 12 Sept. 1965; MS 75, Pollard to John White, 25 Oct. 1797; MS 606, ser.A: 115–18; RG 1, A-I-6: 1695–96; RG 22, ser.155. MTL, John Elmsley letter-book, Elmsley to Peter Hunter, 18 Sept. 1801; Richard Pollard, commission as registrar of the Surrogate Court of the Western District of U.C., signed by Peter Hunter, 1800; W. D. Powell papers, B32: 52; Sir George Prevost papers, "memorial-book," 1. PAC, MG 19, F16: 19–20; RG 1, E3, 13: 148; 60: 207–8; RG 5, A1: 4370–72, 5071–74, 19818–20, 20613–14, 21371–72, 28283–89, 34736–77 (mfm. at AO); RG 8, I (C ser.), 63: 86; 64: 67, 96; 65: 189. PRO, CO 388/62, no.81. St John's (Sandwich) Anglican Church (Windsor, Ont.), Reg. of baptisms, marriages, and burials, vol.2 (mfm. at AO). USPG, C/CAN/folder 441. *Anglican registers, 1787–1814: Rev. John Langhorn, rector of Ernestown, Upper Canada,* ed. C. L. R. Wanamaker and Mildred Parliament Wanamaker (Kingston, Ont., 1980). *Canadian Magazine and Literary Repository* (Montreal), 3 (July–December 1824): 573. *Corr. of Hon. Peter Russell* (Cruikshank and Hunter), vol.2. *John Askin papers* (Quaife). *Mich. Pioneer Coll.*, 10 (1886)–11 (1887); 13 (1888). "Petitions for grants of land, 1792–6," ed. E. A. Cruikshank, *OH*, 24 (1927): 107. *Windsor border region* (Lajeunesse). *Detroit Gazette*, 12 Nov. 1824. *Montreal Gazette*, 4 Dec. 1824. *Weekly Register* (York [Toronto]), 2 Dec. 1824 (supp.). Armstrong, *Handbook of Upper Canadian chronology* (1967). "State papers – U.C.," PAC *Report*, 1892: 289. John Clarke, "A geographical analysis of colonial settlement in the Western District of Upper Canada, 1788–1850" (PHD thesis, Univ. of Western Ont., London, 1970). R. M. Fuller, *Windsor heritage* ([Windsor, 1972]). F. C. Hamil, *The valley of the lower Thames, 1640 to 1850* (Toronto, 1951; repr. Toronto and Buffalo, N.Y., 1973). Millman, *Jacob Mountain*. W. R. Riddell, *The legal profession in Upper Canada in its early periods* (Toronto, 1916). *The township of Sandwich (past and present)* . . . , ed. Frederick Neal

Porteous

(Windsor, 1909), 179–91. H. P. Westgate, *St. John's Church, Sandwich, Windsor, Ontario, 1802–1952: the beginnings of the Anglican Church in the Western District; a goodly heritage* (2nd ed., [Windsor, 1952]). Wilson, *Enterprises of Robert Hamilton*. R. S. Woods, *First centennial of the Anglican Church in the county of Essex, with special reference to the history and work of St. John's Church, Sandwich* (n.p., 1903). F. H. Armstrong, "The oligarchy of the Western District of Upper Canada, 1788–1841," *CHA Hist. papers*, 1977: 87–102. Francis Cleary, "Notes on the early history of the county of Essex," *OH*, 6 (1905): 66–75. T. R. Millman, "Pioneer clergy of the Diocese of Huron: Richard Pollard," *Huron Church News* (London, Ont.), 1 March 1953: 10.

PORTEOUS, THOMAS, businessman, JP, politician, militia officer, and office holder; b. 8 Dec. 1765, probably in the province of Quebec; m. 20 Dec. 1786 Olivia Everest in Addison (Vt); d. 20 Feb. 1830 in Montreal.

A grain merchant, Thomas Porteous was the proprietor of Île Bourdon, near Montreal, where he resided, profiting from the island's advantageous geographic location for commercial transactions in the "Château fort" of the North West Company. With a fleet of bacs, bateaux, and canoes, Porteous operated a ferry service between Lachenaie and Montreal Island. About 1790 he opened a commercial establishment near the church of Sainte-Rose on Île Jésus. Four years later he began trading in wheat in the village of Terrebonne. Already prosperous by 1800, in that year he offered £20,000 for the seigneury of Terrebonne, renowned for its production of wheat and flour. In 1805 he opened a store and potashery opposite the church in Sainte-Thérèse-de-Blainville (Sainte-Thérèse).

In 1804 Porteous was elected to the House of Assembly for Effingham County. Although often absent, he usually voted with the small merchant party, led by John RICHARDSON, and took a special interest in the improvement of water transportation. In the legislature he lost no opportunity to promote his own commercial interests. To attract people from Montreal to Île Bourdon and make the island a commercial entrepôt, he sought and obtained provincial legislation permitting him to construct two wooden, two-tracked toll-bridges, one between the island and the mainland over the Rivière des Prairies, the other, a drawbridge, joining the island and Montreal at Bout-de-l'Île. Although the bridges were built at Porteous's expense, the act regulated tolls and forbad for a period of 50 years the construction of other bridges or the operation of ferries between Montreal Island and the mainland within three miles of the bridges. The opening of the first bridge was announced on 28 Oct. 1805, and the second was opened the following year. Both, however, were carried away by ice in the spring of 1807, and in 1808 Porteous was authorized to reconstruct the bridges as well as to build a third, this one from Île Bourdon to Repentigny. To facilitate traffic Porteous had manufactured, in Birmingham, England, metal tokens bearing inscriptions in French. In 1809 he and the firm of McKenzie, Oldham and Company set up a courier service twice weekly between Terrebonne and Montreal.

Prior to the War of 1812 Porteous had, at least on occasion, supplied large quantities of firewood to the military. During the war he received a government contract to supply the troops "throughout the country." It was probably at this time that he established himself as a general merchant on Rue Notre-Dame, Montreal, and thereafter he assumed a prominent place in the city's commercial life. In 1816 he and John Porteous were agents for the Saint-Maurice ironworks, selling bar iron and manufactured products such as cooking utensils, stoves, castings, tools, and mill machinery; they also imported English iron and steel. Two years later Thomas acquired shares in the *Telegraph*, a steamboat constructed for the Montreal–Quebec run, and in March 1821 he purchased a further interest jointly with Horatio GATES. The vessel was sold in June 1822 to the recently formed St Lawrence Steamboat Company controlled by the Molson family [*see* William Molson*]. Given his experience with water transportation and his mercantile interests it is not surprising that Porteous became a principal promoter of the Lachine Canal. In 1819 he was among the incorporators of the Company of Proprietors of the Lachine Canal [*see* François DESRIVIÈRES] and became one of its directors. After it was taken over by the government he was appointed one of its ten commissioners.

Porteous also played an important part in the early direction of the Bank of Montreal, a strong supporter of the canal. He was among the petitioners for the bank's incorporation, held shares, and served as a director from 1818 to 1823 and in 1826–27. In 1826 he supported George Moffatt*'s faction in its successful efforts to unseat the president, Samuel Gerrard*, and reform the bank's financial administration. One of the institution's largest debtors was Simon McGillivray*, who, it was charged, had received favoured treatment from Gerrard, to whom McGillivray was also indebted for a large sum. McGillivray offered a settlement to his creditors, but Porteous, placed on a bank committee to study the proposal, found it unsatisfactory, and supported Moffatt in an unsuccessful bid to force McGillivray into bankruptcy with a view to obtaining a more equitable return. In 1819 Porteous was elected a vice-president of the Montreal Savings Bank.

That year Porteous undertook another ambitious project: he formed a firm which for £5,000 bought the financially troubled Company of Proprietors of the Montreal Water Works [*see* John GRAY]. Ownership in the waterworks was divided into 40 shares, held in equal numbers by Porteous, his wife, their two eldest sons, and a son-in-law. Porteous, as president, visited the Glasgow waterworks. After his return the new company completely renovated Montreal's water supply system at a cost of some £40,000: its wooden pipes were replaced by four-inch iron ones; the wooden cisterns were changed for 240,000-gallon, lead-lined containers; and the spring-fed, gravitation system was replaced by a steam-powered pumping plant that drew water from the St Lawrence (at a point, as it turned out, insufficiently removed from sewage outlets). Baths were also installed. Despite these renovations, the waterworks remained only marginally profitable, and it was sold in 1832 by the executors of Porteous's estate for £60,000.

Porteous also made a significant contribution to the civic and religious life of the Montreal district. He was made a justice of the peace in 1800 and a commissioner to try small claims in the seigneury of Terrebonne in 1809. Appointed a major in the Blainville battalion of militia in 1812, and in 1826 promoted lieutenant-colonel in the 3rd Battalion of Effingham militia, he served for a time as cornet in the "Montreal Cavalry" (possibly the Royal Montreal Troop of Cavalry, raised and disbanded in November 1813). In 1817 he was among seven men selected at a public meeting to petition the legislature for the incorporation of Montreal, primarily to provide a better police service. The following year he became president of the Fire Engine Company, a volunteer body charged with protecting the city from fire. He was also a director of the Montreal Agriculture Society, of which he was president in 1820. In 1824 he was appointed a commissioner to examine applicants for the post of inspector of pot and pearl ashes, and in 1824 and 1827 he served on grand juries for the Court of King's Bench. He contributed to the Scotch Presbyterian Church, later known as St Gabriel Street Church, while still a resident of Île Bourdon, and in 1819 he was elected an elder (a position he retained until his death) and a member of the temporal committee, of which he was vice-president in 1820.

In 1816, before leaving on a voyage to England, Porteous willed to his wife the usufruct of his property and the annual income from a trust fund of £5,000. Upon her death the estate was to be divided equally among his seven children, with the exception that any unmarried daughter was to receive an additional £200. In February 1820 he announced his imminent retirement and offered for sale several "very valuable and extensive Commercial Establishments." Among them were "those well-known premises . . . in Terrebonne . . . in which he so long resided," comprising a large house, two stores together capable of holding 60,000 bushels of grain, a coach-house, a stable, and other buildings, all of stone, and a large productive garden:

it was "one of the first situations for a country Merchant in the District." He also offered for sale a contiguous smaller property with a stone house and gardens, a farm between Terrebonne and Lachenaie, and the properties in Sainte-Rose (where he had recently built a stone house) and Sainte-Thérèse-de-Blainville. The property in Sainte-Thérèse-de-Blainville included a large stone house, built in 1813–14 "of the best materials, . . . [and] laid out in a . . . superior style, according to a plan furnished by Mr. John Try[*]"; it also contained a potashery capable of producing 280 barrels a season and a 30-acre farm "in a high state of cultivation." Porteous kept his residence on Rue Notre-Dame in Montreal. The estate he left on his death in 1830 can be assumed to have been substantial.

CARMAN MILLER

ANQ-M, CE1-126, 23 févr. 1830; CM1, 5 mars 1830. AUM, P 58, U, Porteous to Jordan, 26 March 1800. PAC, RG 68, General index, 1651–1841. L.C., House of Assembly, *Journaux*, 1805: 118, 144, 171, 194–97; 1808: 176, 212; *Report of the special committee, to whom was referred that part of his excellency's speech which referred to the organization of the militia . . .* (Quebec, 1829); *Statutes*, 1805, c.14; 1808, c.23–24; 1819, c.6; 1821–22, c.25. *This was Montreal in 1814, 1815, 1816 and 1817 . . .*, comp. L. M. Wilson ([Montreal], 1960), 126–27. *Montreal Gazette*, 28 Oct. 1805, 19 Nov. 1817, 9 June 1819. *Quebec Gazette*, 25 July 1799; 27 Dec. 1804; 10 Jan. 1805; 23 Oct. 1806; 3, 17 March, 7 April 1808; 5 Jan., 4 May, 19 Oct. 1809; 29 Nov. 1817; 7, 28 Dec. 1818; 12 July, 5 Aug., 6 Sept. 1819; 16, 30 March 1820; 26 March, 5, 18 June, 25 Oct. 1821; 6 Nov. 1823; 29 March 1824; 4 March 1830. Audet, "Les législateurs du Bas-Canada." J. D. Borthwick, *History and biographical gazetteer of Montreal to the year 1892* (Montreal, 1892). *Montreal directory*, 1819. *Quebec almanac*, 1801: 79; 1815: 96; 1821: 110. R. Campbell, *Hist. of Scotch Presbyterian Church*. Denison, *Canada's first bank*. F. C. Smith, *The Montreal Water Works; its history compiled from the year 1800 to 1912* (Montreal, 1913), 14. Tulchinsky, "Construction of first Lachine Canal," 43, 65. F.-J. Audet, "Des hommes d'action à la tête de Montréal il y a 100 ans," *La Presse*, 4 nov. 1933: 30. Hare, "L'Assemblée législative du Bas-Canada," *RHAF*, 27: 379. Victor Morin, "L'art de la numismatique au Canada," *Cahiers des Dix*, 17 (1952): 78–79.

POWELL, ANNE, gentlewoman; b. 10 March 1787 in Montreal, sixth child and second daughter of William Dummer POWELL and Anne Murray*; d. 22 April 1822 at sea.

Anne Powell, daughter of a prominent jurist, belonged to one of the most prestigious families in York (Toronto). She was well travelled for the times and had lived with her mother's family in New York. In 1811 she studied in Montreal with the intention of obtaining a teacher's certificate. Before the outbreak of the War of 1812 she returned to York and indulged her desire to teach by becoming the tutor of her two orphaned nieces. Despite her expensive education, Anne's mother considered that she "requires knowledge" still. After the capture of York in April 1813, Anne devoted herself to tending the convalescent soldiers who were quartered with the Powells.

Anne's first romantic involvement had occurred in 1807, when she was courted by the French adventurer Laurent QUETTON St George. Her mother had dismissed his presumptuous suit. Later it became apparent that she was, in Dr John Strachan*'s words, "distracted after" a charming young lawyer, John Beverley Robinson*. Robinson had performed creditably during the war and had gained the post of acting attorney general as a result of the influence of judge Powell. It was unlikely that the ambitious Robinson would discourage familiarity with his benefactor's daughter. When Robinson decided to further himself by attending the English Inns of Court, Anne found a way to follow him: in 1816, the year her father was seeking the chief justiceship, she travelled with him to England. Upon her arrival she again took up with the young lawyer, who gallantly escorted her about London.

Yet, unknown to her, Robinson had developed a passionate attraction to an English girl, Emma Walker. This lady delivered an ultimatum to Robinson. If he wished their courtship to continue, he had best advise Miss Powell that he was no longer a free man. He complied, and also informed Powell, now chief justice, that he was engaged to another. The individual most annoyed by this announcement was the rector of York, John Strachan, who wrote to Robinson to ascertain whether he was "under any engagements directly or indirectly to Miss Powell." Admittedly, Robinson was not "eligible." His stepfather, Elisha BEMAN, was, after all, a tavern-keeper. Yet everyone in York had taken the marriage of John and Anne for granted. It appeared that ability counted for more than status in weighing the desirability of marriages among York's gentry. But although Robinson's marriage to Emma may have disappointed the Powells, it did not diminish their affection for him. Anne herself hoped that "nothing will ever interrupt the friendly intercourse between the families."

Anne remained in England with her relatives until her stubborn disposition and disregard of the expenses to which she put others made her an unwelcome burden. It was not long after her return, in the summer of 1819, that her parents began to question her sanity. She displayed a bitter hatred for them, a suspicion of her sisters, and a tyrannical domination over her nieces. The orphans came so much under her sway that she flew into a rage when her sister merely attempted to take them for a walk. Perhaps her most embarrassing eccentricity was her continuing infatuation with John Robinson. She sent him correspon-

dence which his brother William Benjamin* described to Samuel Peters Jarvis*, Anne's brother-in-law, as "some of the D—ndest letters you ever saw." Anne considered Emma Robinson to be possessed of a "romantic history" and hardly a fit companion for her beloved John. For her part, Emma routinely burned Anne's letters and refused to admit her to the Robinson house.

Her most bizarre behaviour occurred during the winter of 1822 when Robinson, now attorney general and leader of the government in the House of Assembly, was dispatched to England to negotiate a customs dispute with Lower Canada. At the end of January 1822, just as the Robinsons were about to leave York, Anne called on the attorney general and begged to be allowed to accompany him. He positively refused. Anne's brother Grant* and even Dr Strachan tried to reason with her. At last, her mother, although scandalized by Anne's "want of feminine indeed of decent feeling," sanctioned her departure. In deference to the attorney general, however, Mrs Powell promised him a 48-hour head start, and to that end had Anne locked into her bedroom. However, once Anne learned of her beloved's departure, she escaped, without either money or luggage, and chartered a sleigh in pursuit. Mrs Powell, considering Anne's motive "derogatory to feminine decency – it can be viewed in no other light," collapsed in despair at the "scandalous part she has acted." One of her daughter's letters after this episode she described as "a tissue of unladylike observations, or rather details of a systematic persecution, in which she perseveres convinced that she is acting the part of a Christian . . . they are so unlike the style of a delicate or sane woman."

As Emma was ill it was necessary for the Robinsons to make frequent stops; Anne quickly managed to catch up with them and accompanied them to New York City. Once there, Robinson approached his ship's captain and explained to him that under no circumstances was Anne Powell to be permitted on the vessel. Consequently, she was compelled to take a later ship, the *Albion*. This packet was caught in a violent gale off the south coast of Ireland and was wrecked off the Old Head of Kinsale. Anne Powell's body was washed ashore and was identified by a brooch which had been given to her by her father. The chief justice, who was in England at the time, had been infuriated by his daughter's perverse conduct. After learning of the disaster, he interviewed the surviving crewmen and arranged for her burial.

Charles Fothergill*'s *Weekly Register* reported the wreck of the *Albion* in lurid detail, but, tactfully, it only mentioned in passing Anne's presence on the ship. Nevertheless, Anne's mad infatuation had made the family, as Mrs Powell put it, the subject of gossip "from the Government House to Forests Stable" and hastened the decline of its prestige. The object of her obsession was held at least partly to blame and there was now an open rupture between the Powells and the Robinsons. Anne's eccentric conduct and tragic death contributed to the declining influence and weakened mental state of William Dummer Powell, although his career was already on the wane for other reasons. For Robinson the incident was socially awkward, possibly even embarrassing, but little else. As he was well established in government, neither the event itself nor the break with the Powells affected his career in the slightest.

PATRICK BRODE

AO, MS 4, Emma Walker to J. B. Robinson, June 1816; John Strachan to Robinson, 30 Sept. 1816; MS 787, Anne Powell to Mrs Powell, 6 Sept. 1818; W. B. Robinson to S. P. Jarvis, 28 Jan. 1822; Eliza Powell to M. B. Jarvis, 12 June 1822; S. P. Jarvis to M. B. Jarvis, 21 Nov. 1823. MTL, W. D. Powell papers, Mrs Powell to G. W. Murray, 4 Sept. 1807, 16 May 1811, 4 April 1812, 25 Feb. 1822. *Weekly Register* (York [Toronto]), 13 June 1822.

POWELL, WILLIAM DUMMER, lawyer, judge, office holder, politician, and author; b. 5 Nov. 1755 in Boston, eldest son of John Powell and Janet Grant; m. 3 Oct. 1775 Anne Murray*, and they had nine children; d. 6 Sept. 1834 in Toronto.

William Dummer Powell was descended on both sides of his family from 17th-century emigrants to Massachusetts from England. His maternal grandfather, William Dummer, had been lieutenant governor of the colony; his paternal grandfather, John Powell, had come out as Dummer's secretary. His father, also named John Powell, was a prosperous Boston merchant, the holder for three decades before the American revolution of a naval victualling contract. The Powells had been Anglicans and royalists, the Dummers Presbyterians and parliamentarians. By an agreement between his parents, the second John Powell was brought up in the Church of England, but his two younger brothers were raised as Congregationalists. Even before the declaration of American independence the family was also politically divided, John being a declared loyalist and his brothers rebels.

By that time William Dummer Powell had completed his formal education and was trying to decide on a career. After three years at the Boston Free Grammar School he had been sent to an Anglican school in Tunbridge (Royal Tunbridge Wells), Kent, for four years and then to Rotterdam, where for two years he studied French and Dutch. At the age of 16 he had then returned to England for a year, where he "cultivated the good graces of the ladies more than any other pursuit," until concern for his father's health recalled him to Boston in 1772. By his own later admission he had been a far from assiduous student: fluency in French, an enthusiasm for cricket, and a continuing taste for the Latin classics seem to have been the main results of his schooling. The Powell view of what constituted frivolity was, however, severe; his letters to his parents reveal a rather priggish young man, serious if not especially studious. He already showed the intense concern for social position that was to characterize him all his life, reacting vehemently to an inaccurate report circulated at the Tunbridge school of his father's insolvency.

Back in Boston, his father's bout of rheumatic fever over, Powell set about looking for commercial opportunities. His father proved unwilling to give him a share of the naval victualling contract. A plan to go into business with his mother's relatives in London having come to nothing, he visited Montreal in the summer of 1773 and Pennsylvania and New York in the next year. In the winters he studied law under the attorney general of Massachusetts, Jonathan Sewell (Sewall), but his object was to prepare himself for public life, not for a legal career. In 1774 Powell hoped to go into business in New York, where anti-imperial sentiment was less widespread than in Boston; but his journey there was interrupted by the death from smallpox of his mother, to whom his attachment was very strong. Returning to Boston, he threw himself into politics as one of the organizers of a declaration of loyal citizens against the revolutionary party (19 April 1775). He served in arms, although apparently not in action, as a volunteer with the British garrison. With open rebellion approaching and his opposition to it established beyond any chance of compromise, he decided to leave North America. He also met Anne Murray, the daughter of a Scottish physician, who had come to live with relatives in Boston. They were married just before leaving for England in October 1775 and settled near her family at Norwich.

His father followed within a year, taking up residence at Ludlow in Shropshire, the county from which his family had come. He continued to support his son, but his ability to do so was now diminished, mostly because a West Indian plantation in which he had invested heavily went bankrupt. A part of his Boston estates was confiscated on 30 April 1779 under an act of that year classifying him as an absentee rather than a traitor; but the confiscated part, inventoried at £902 1s. 2d., went to his rebel brother William, who had advanced him £1,000 when he left Boston. Under a later Massachusetts act of 1784 absentees were allowed to reclaim their property. It was to be a lifelong grievance of William Dummer Powell that he was never able to recover all his father's estate under the terms of that act, but it seems that most of the elder Powell's real property in America was retained in spite of his loyalism. It was nevertheless clear that the son would have to find a career to support his growing family.

He was unsuccessful in his competition with other

Powell

loyalists for a government appointment, and a second scheme for going into business with a relative of his mother's (this time in Jamaica) failed. He therefore decided upon the practice of law. By May 1779 he had kept the necessary terms at the Middle Temple. Unable then to afford the fees, he did not arrange his formal call to the English bar until 2 Feb. 1784. Yet another of his mother's relatives, William GRANT, the former attorney general of Quebec, recommended that province; and Powell arrived at Quebec in August 1779.

He obtained a licence to practise, but was disappointed in his hopes of patronage from the governor, Frederick Haldimand*. On the advice of the attorney general, James MONK, and the deputy commissary general, Isaac Winslow Clarke (a fellow Bostonian loyalist who later married his sister Anne), he went into private practice in Montreal. It proved a happy decision. Montreal was a growing commercial centre of some 15,000 people where there were not yet half a dozen lawyers. Powell did well enough to bring out his family, to acquire a house on Mount Royal, to command the highest fees at the Montreal bar, and perhaps even to dispense with his father's assistance.

Yet he was soon dissatisfied in Montreal. Paradoxically, part of the reason was his success at the bar. His first client was Pierre Du Calvet*, charged with a libel against the judges of the Court of Common Pleas in Montreal. Du Calvet, displeased at an earlier judgement by the court, had published a letter critical of the judges and had beaten one of them, John Fraser, who had attacked him. Although warned by Monk that any lawyer who took the libel case would earn the resentment of the whole bench and of the governor as well, Powell defended Du Calvet and persuaded the jury to acquit him. In January 1780 he scored another triumph, this time before a court of quarter sessions without a jury. He was able to show that an old English statute on which Haldimand had relied to prosecute grain merchants for price-fixing had been repealed. Powell was willing to defy popular as well as official disapproval – he undertook prosecutions for refusals to transport military stores under the law of corvée – but his successes branded him as an opponent of the administration. That did not prevent his being retained on government as well as on commercial cases, but it was a role which his toryism made uncomfortable.

He was, however, convinced that government and the administration of justice under the Quebec Act of 1774 were arbitrary, in particular that English law relating to juries and the writ of habeas corpus must be introduced. He claimed later to have been silent himself and to have "inculcated silence and subordination in others," but his views were well enough known to make him one of the delegates who sailed from Quebec on 25 Oct. 1783 with a petition against the Quebec Act. Nothing immediate came of the petition, but on his way back from England Powell spent almost a year in Boston. He attempted to recover the confiscated part of his father's property. He agreed to manage the estates of his rebel uncle Jeremiah Powell for a time and he even hoped that, with the American war over, he could return to Boston without renouncing his British allegiance. The failure of his attempt, the disappointment of his hope, and the death of his uncle sent him back to Montreal early in 1785.

There he not only recovered his position at the bar, he found that most of the sources of his earlier discontent had been removed. An ordinance of 29 April 1784 had introduced habeas corpus, and another of 21 April 1785 soon adopted the general common law right to jury trials in civil cases. Perhaps best of all, Haldimand had gone. Sir Guy Carleton*, now Lord Dorchester, arrived in October 1786 for his second term as governor of Quebec; and under him Powell at last found official favour. He must be said to have earned it. In 1787 he served without remuneration as one of two commissioners sent to report on the dissatisfaction of loyalists settled on the upper St Lawrence, who were worried about the tenure of their lands. This commission recommended the 200-acre bonus for settlers who had made improvements to their land that became known as "Lord Dorchester's bounty." Powell wrote the commission's report for a similar investigation of the seigneury of Sorel. He was on a commission to settle claims for freight charges against up-country traders who had used government vessels during the war. Finally, he led the board of inquiry into claims against the Quebec merchant John Cochrane, who had supplied specie to the army during the war and was accused of profiteering on bills of exchange. The board recommended dismissing the claims and found the court proceedings that had been taken against Cochrane improper. Powell therefore encountered the renewed hostility of the judges involved, Adam Mabane* and John Fraser. Mabane accused Powell of having taken an oath of allegiance to the American government, but he was not believed. Powell was granted the "few Acres of land" (in fact 3,000 acres) that Mabane was trying to deny him. Successful though his return to Montreal was, he could hardly look for a judicial appointment there.

The whole upper part of the province, which was to become Upper Canada in 1791, was still included in the district of Montreal. Except for justices of the peace, any two of whom could hear actions for debt up to £5, its only civil jurisdiction was the Montreal Court of Common Pleas. The St Lawrence loyalist settlers had petitioned for a separate province in 1785, and Montreal merchants in the next year made concerted complaints about the lack of courts in the interior. Dorchester opposed a separate province, but on 24 July 1788 he did create four new districts, each with a court of common pleas. The most westerly of them was Hesse (renamed the Western District from 15 Oct. 1792). Three judges were appointed for it, all residents of Detroit; Jacques Baby*, *dit* Dupéront, and William Robertson* were merchants, and Alexander McKee* was an officer in the Indian Department. All three joined in the inhabitants' petition for a trained lawyer, following no other profession and not connected with trade. Powell, with his experience of up-country cases in Montreal, was an obvious choice. On 2 Feb. 1789 he was appointed first judge, and as it turned out the sole judge, of common pleas at Detroit. The stipend of £500 (sterling) probably exceeded his Montreal income. In retrospect, Powell claimed to have accepted the position "with the latent but confident expectation" of getting the chief legal appointment when a new province was created. At the time, it may have been enough that the court of Hesse, because the fur trade required it to have jurisdiction over acts outside its district (ordinance of 30 April 1789), was from a lawyer's perspective the most important of the new courts.

Detroit was a rough town of about 4,000 people, the smallest and most remote place in which Powell had ever lived. He was to spend nearly all the rest of his life in smaller towns; York (Toronto) had not yet reached half that size when he retired there in 1825. Detroit was picturesque, and the officers of the garrison provided a society that Powell's wife and sister Anne found agreeable, but the Powells were not happy there for long. He made no particular enemies through his court, which sat at L'Assomption (Sandwich) because Detroit itself was on American soil. He instituted simple procedure and dispensed quick justice, perhaps aided by the fact that he never called a jury. But he was also on the land board (7 Aug. 1789 to October 1792), where his refusal to recognize irregular purchases from the Indians and his faithful attendance –he missed only 5 of 53 meetings – made him a threat to the military and Indian Department officers who were unused to interference, especially from a newcomer. Powell's life was threatened, his wife and children frightened by mock Indian ambushes, and his loyalty questioned. In October 1791 his wife took the family to England to keep them safe and to put the two eldest boys in school. Finally two officers, in what may have been intended as a cruel joke, forged a treasonable letter from Powell to the American secretary of war, Henry Knox.

By then Powell had other reasons for alarm. Upper Canada had been made a separate province, but Dorchester's advice had been ignored in choosing the officials of its government. His choice for lieutenant governor, the loyalist Sir John JOHNSON, had been passed over. Their combined support for Powell did not get him the post of chief justice which he coveted, nor even a place on the Legislative and Executive councils. His authority as a judge of common pleas

was extended beyond the Hesse District to cover the whole province (31 Dec. 1791), but his new masters were strangers with whom he had no influence. In February he went to Quebec to meet the new lieutenant governor, John Graves Simcoe*, and to disavow the forged letter. Their first acquaintance was reassuring to both of them, and he returned to his duties at Detroit. In the fall he went on leave to England, carrying Simcoe's guarded endorsement that "the behaviour and conduct of Mr. Powell, as far as lies within my knowledge, has been in every respect such as becomes the station He holds." He got similar assurance from the home secretary, Henry Dundas.

He remained an outsider under the new administration. The chief justice, William OSGOODE, who had none of Powell's experience of legal practice, of the bench, or of the province, did not consult him in reorganizing the courts. The new scheme replaced the district courts by a central court of king's bench having criminal as well as civil jurisdiction. Before this judges like Powell had only limited criminal jurisdiction, supplied by temporary commissions of oyer and terminer and of general jail delivery. Powell was commissioned puisne judge of king's bench on 9 July 1794. He first presided on the following 6 October at Newark (Niagara-on-the-Lake), his wider jurisdiction having released him from Detroit. Since the only other regular judge of the court was the often absent chief justice, Powell bore the brunt of its work from the beginning, as he did for the rest of his career.

Except for the location of the capital at York, Powell did not object to the policies of Simcoe's administration: his criticism of district land boards had already foreshadowed the grounds on which Simcoe abolished them, and he was an enthusiast for the plan of endowing the Church of England by leasing the clergy reserves. Yet he resented the young Englishmen set over him, was ostentatiously patient about the disappointment of his ambitions, and referred rather too often to "the long and unimpeached discharge of my Duty as the first Magistrate of this new Colony before its Seperation from Lower Canada." He was right in questioning the legality of land grants made before 1791, but he did so in conjunction with the malcontent Niagara magnate Robert Hamilton*, leaving the provincial attorney general, John White*, to find out about it after the law officers in Westminster had given their opinion. Without the substance of opposition, he deliberately gave the appearance of it: knowing of Simcoe's antipathy towards the governor at Quebec, he named his home at Newark "Mount Dorchester." When Osgoode left the province, Powell was again passed over, Simcoe urging a chief justice who was "an *English* Lawyer." There were private grounds for bitterness, too: the sale of Powell's house in Montreal to Monk led to a long squabble, and Mrs Powell's attempts to collect a Boston inheritance got

Powell

her little except a quarrel with her brother, George Murray.

Powell's patience was to be tried further. His friend Peter Russell*, who administered the government after Simcoe's departure, lacked the influence to be his patron; Powell acted as chief justice for over two years, only to see the appointment go to John Elmsley*. His claims were not entirely unrecognized: another lobbying trip to England, obtained by a threat of resignation, won him half the chief justice's salary, if that post was vacant, in addition to an increase in his own. This increase more than doubled his income whenever he was alone on the bench to £1,300 (sterling), although nearly half of that was taken up by the expense of making six district circuits a year. He had considerable political sense, as he showed in attempting to compose the quarrels of William Jarvis*, provincial secretary, with his colleagues. He advised David William Smith*, elected to the first assembly for the riding of Suffolk and Essex, that he could not expect French Canadian votes but could win without them. His advice against prosecuting the son of Joseph Brant [Thayendanegea*] for murder (3 Jan. 1797) was based on political considerations, although he did at that time think that Indians in their own villages were independent of the courts. On the first Heir and Devisee Commission from 1797 he showed the assiduity, grasp of detail, and concern for fairness that made him a good if unimaginative administrator.

He thought of himself as a man of principle, willing for its sake to risk the displeasure of authority, but his principles were apt to be most in evidence when his own interests or his partisan feelings were involved. When he called attention to the justice of loyalists' claims to special importance in Upper Canada, he added his own claims to advancement. He pointed out, in the long wrangle among officials over land fees, that Jarvis's share did not cover his costs; Jarvis was a friend, whose eldest son Samuel Peters* was to be Powell's business agent and to marry his youngest daughter, Mary Boyles. When Lieutenant Governor Peter Hunter* put government during his frequent absences in the hands of a committee of the Executive Council, Powell insisted on the possible illegality of the arrangement; he had just been ignored again for a seat on the council, and offended by Hunter's supersession of Russell. He felt himself to be "without Patronage in Europe," as he wrote Dorchester, "in a species of disgrace here, where my local Information and Zeal for the Service were an unpardonable libel on the new Government."

He continued to memorialize Whitehall on his merits and on the improvements to provincial legislation that he would have advised if asked. Before his ambition could be fulfilled, he had still to outlast two more immigrant chief justices: Henry Allcock* and Thomas Scott. He got along well enough with the latter to borrow $400 from him in July 1806 during the most melodramatic of his personal crises. His fourth son, Jeremiah, having joined a quixotic and farcical attempt to assist rebellion in the Spanish colony of Venezuela, lay in the notoriously fever-ridden prison of Omoa, near Cartagena (Colombia), sentenced to ten years' hard labour. Powell took six months' leave of absence to lobby in Boston, New York, Philadelphia, London, and Madrid for his son's release. Jeremiah was set free in 1807, only to die at sea the following year. Powell's success reveals that his connections outside Upper Canada were more extensive and effective than he admitted – they ranged from the Duke of Kent [Edward* Augustus] to the godmother of the son of the Spanish minister to the United States – and his grief did not prevent him from pressing his own case while in London. The deaths of his favourite sister Anne in childbirth at Montreal in 1792, of his infant daughter Anne in 1783, of his second son William Dummer in 1803, and of his youngest child Thomas William at school in Kingston in 1804 had been more tragic, but they had not drained his energies and finances as had Jeremiah's escapade. He returned to York, worn out, in October 1807. He and his wife were now touchier and more status-conscious than ever, jealous of their claims to precedence in York society and ready to feel slighted at the formal manners of a new lieutenant governor, Francis Gore*. Mrs Powell was insulted in September 1807 at the prospect of having a wealthy York merchant, Laurent QUETTON St George, as a son-in-law. She ignored her husband's requests and risked Gore's displeasure in refusing to cooperate in his attempt to rehabilitate Mrs John Small in York society.

In fact Gore's arrival marked a turn in Powell's fortunes. He declined the lieutenant governor's first offer of a seat on the executive council, because it would have been unpaid; but a regular salaried place came open and he was sworn in on 8 March 1808. He remained stiffly independent, offending Gore by his decision on 15 July 1809, upheld on appeal to the imperial law officers, that David McGregor ROGERS could not be dismissed as registrar of deeds because of his opposition in the House of Assembly. Gore however returned to the opinion he had expressed in the preceding March, that Powell was "a Gentleman who has discharged the duties of his important office with probity and honour for upwards of twenty years and whose local knowledge particularly fits him" to be an executive councillor. The council, with two assiduous and competent members in Powell and John McGill, now made progress with its backlog of business, Powell undertaking a simplification of the confused process by which land patents were issued. His credit rose steadily, and he soon had the satisfaction of being petitioned by such magnates as Richard Cartwright* and such prominent immigrants as John

Strachan* to use his influence with the lieutenant governor.

That influence was exaggerated in popular conception at the time, as it was by the later reform critics Robert Gourlay*, Francis COLLINS, and William Lyon Mackenzie*. It also appears greater and more personal in retrospect than it really was, because the later correspondence between Gore and Powell reached a level of cordiality exceptional in Powell's life. The two agreed that the subordinate officers of government should be men with experience of the province, but whereas that was a matter of practical common sense for Gore, for Powell it was a desire to "retain the Honors of the [legal] profession amongst ourselves." Powell could obtain the appointment of his eldest son John as clerk of the Legislative Council (19 Feb. 1807) in succession to James Clark*, but not that of his protégé John Macdonell* (Greenfield) as attorney general. It was Isaac Brock*, administrator of the province during Gore's absence, who agreed to Macdonell's appointment and who recommended that Powell's third son, Grant*, be made principal of the Court of Probate (April 1813). Powell drafted Brock's celebrated reply of 22 July 1812 in response to Brigadier-General William Hull's proclamation issued at Detroit. In Powell's view at the time, Brock and later Sir George Murray* (administrator from 25 April to 30 June 1815) relied on his advice as much as Gore had done.

The decade up to 1818 saw the height of Powell's career. Although in 1797 he had sworn never to settle his family at York, he now had an impressive house, Caer Howell, with another 100 acres in York Township and 5,000 more throughout the province. He assumed the obligations marking the status of which he, and still more his wife, were jealously proud; always complaining of the expense, he duly subscribed to building funds for a fire hall (1802) and for St James' Church (1803), and was director of the subscription library (1814), the Loyal and Patriotic Society of Upper Canada (1812), and the Society for the Relief of Strangers in Distress (1817). As his wife was to write in 1819, "in an aristocratical Government, expences must be incurred according to the station held." York was for him no longer, as he had called it in 1797, the seat of "the little policy of a remote Colony," it was his home. His family ties to Boston had been cut well before the War of 1812 and he was committed to York, where most of his success and all of his prospects lay.

After the war came, he resolutely stayed at York during its occupation by American troops. He ran no military risk – "Our principal distress," he wrote in 1815, "arose from the incredible Expense of living enhanced by the demands for the Army" – but he did keep British commanders informed of enemy movements and he sent regular reports on the state of the occupied town to the commander-in-chief, Sir George Prevost*. Less flamboyantly but just as firmly as Strachan, he insisted that the American commander maintain order and protect property against looting, whether by his own troops or by the civilians whom Powell thought chiefly responsible. The old charges of American sympathies, last raised briefly in 1807, were now totally implausible. By the end of the war, with Chief Justice Scott gravely ill and Gore returned from leave, Powell's ascendancy on the bench and his influence in council were unquestioned. He was appointed to commissions to hear charges of treason (11 April 1814) and claims for wartime losses (21 Dec. 1815). The assembly granted him £1,000 for his continued work on the Heir and Devisee Commission. When Scott became unable to chair the Legislative Council, Powell felt strong enough to drive a mean bargain. He accepted a seat on the council and its speakership on condition that Scott resign them at once, giving up the salary. When commissioned (21 March 1816) Powell took no salary, but he recovered the arrears two years later. And at last he received the post to which he had felt himself entitled 25 years before and in which he had so often acted: on 1 Oct. 1816 he was commissioned chief justice of Upper Canada.

The war and his own success resolved some complications in his toryism. He no longer had reason to be jealous of appointees from England, and his self-consciousness as an American loyalist was no longer defensive. His old sense of grievance and of colonial inferiority persisted only in the retention of personal animosities: memories of Haldimand, Simcoe, Osgoode, Elmsley, Hunter, and Allcock were an irritant all his life. He was incurably, perhaps deliberately, provincial in dress, manners, and speech – he bought his clothes in Boston, when at home gobbled food with his fingers, and his voice never lost its Yankee twang – but these had become assertions of his independent character, not obstacles to his success. He remained convinced that Upper Canada was by right destined to be a special loyalist province and that most of the refugees from New York in 1784 would have come to it if imperial delays in arranging their reception had not left their establishment in New Brunswick "too far effected to think of removal."

Upper Canada had become his country, with the imperial connection its essential support. The dangers that he saw to it arose not from imperial neglect or American aggression but from a spirit of democratic opposition and the pretensions of the legislative assembly. Much as he had disapproved of Robert Thorpe*'s combining his judgeship with political opposition in 1807, he had seen the main danger of Gore's early critics as lying in the popularity of Joseph Willcocks*'s newspaper, the *Upper Canada Guardian; or, Freeman's Journal*. He was worried enough

Powell

by the radicalism of John Mills Jackson*'s *A view of the political situation of the province of Upper Canada . . .* (London, 1809) to annotate his copy for a reply. The reply actually published, however, *Letters, from an American loyalist* (Halifax, 1810), was written not by Powell, as Robert Thorpe supposed, but by Cartwright. The assembly's claim to the sole initiative in introducing money bills had seemed to him a threat to the Legislative Council long before he took a seat on the latter, and he had denied the lower house's right to examine administrative expenditures even when it was asserted against the lieutenant governor he most actively disliked, Hunter. The assembly's final clash with Gore in April 1817, although it was led by Robert NICHOL, a land speculator whose interests coincided with his own, was for him evidence that the province was facing the same danger of democratic subversion that had driven him from Boston.

Perhaps he had simply been a malcontent for so long that he needed an object of disapproval. At any rate, from early in 1817 the references in his correspondence to the society of Upper Canada were increasingly gloomy. Having undertaken to raise his granddaughter Anne Murray Powell at York, he shared his wife's concern that "there can in this place be no distinction of classes," and that the young lady might therefore acquire plebian manners. It was probably as much a source of comfort as of concern for the Powells to find after the election of 1828 that "the majority of the lower House are too *low* to render association pleasant," but he had a growing sense that the province was departing from its original loyalist design. In 1822, by a passionate appeal to the "true British and Loyal" origins of the province, he secured the rejection of an assembly motion to restore the original name of Toronto to the town of York. When the town was at last incorporated as the city of Toronto in 1834, he recorded his objections to "the wild and Terrific Sound of TORONTO entailing upon its miserable Inhabitants the annual Curse of a popular Election to power to call forth all the bad passions of human nature." His disapproval of popular elections might have been mitigated if he had lived to see his grandson John chosen alderman in Toronto in 1837 and mayor of the city, 1838–40.

His appointment as chief justice and his reputation as the most experienced member of the provincial administration did not end his capacity for making enemies. His neighbour in York, John Strachan, conceded in 1816 that Powell's "knowledge of this Province (and perhaps of the Lower) exceeds that of any man living," but he was offended that Powell's displacement of Scott was "not conducted with delicacy." The two soon disagreed over plans to endow the Church of England in the province. It was Powell's early view that the term "Protestant clergy"

in the Constitutional Act of 1791 did not confine the clergy reserves to the Church of England. He changed his mind some time before February 1828, when he sent to the secretary of state, William Huskisson, a pamphlet *On clergy reserves* objecting to Presbyterian claims to a share of the revenue from them. He held to the opinion that the reserves had been intended as a substitute for tithes, which Strachan hoped to introduce. Apart from any question of their legality, Powell thought that it would be impractical to attempt the collection of tithes. It was hard enough to find tenants for the clergy reserves, because settlers with so much land open to them required "very strong baits to spend their labour on another's soil." By May 1817 Strachan had relegated Powell to being only "Perhaps" an adherent to the Church of England, although Powell's daughters were teaching in his Sunday school, and was regretting that Powell would be "a little indifferent or inclined towards opposition but would be afraid to come forward boldly" in the Legislative Council against Strachan's plans for the clergy reserves.

Apart from disagreements on policy, they were both jealously ambitious men; if Strachan resented Powell's greater influence, Powell resented Strachan's pretensions. They were also rivals over which of them could claim to be the patron of John Beverley Robinson*, Strachan's pupil who with Powell's support had risen to be acting attorney general (1812–14) and solicitor general (13 Feb. 1815). Powell helped Robinson to get two and a half years' leave to study law in England, but Robinson returned with London connections of his own that secured his appointment as attorney general (11 Feb. 1818) and left him little need of either Strachan's or Powell's favour. He also returned with an English wife, dashing the hopes of Powell's daughter ANNE. As attorney general he soon found that Powell was not an easily managed judge. A new lieutenant governor, Sir Peregrine Maitland*, found the same. The two parted company over a plan to tax unimproved lands. Maitland wanted legislation to make an existing tax effective. Powell objected to bringing the assembly into a matter that belonged to the courts and the administration. Maitland thought him pedantic, opinionated, and self-interested, while he thought Maitland neglectful of the royal prerogative and indifferent to local experience. In 1821 Powell was humiliated in the Legislative Council, which replaced him with Robinson as a commissioner to seek imperial help in settling the division of customs duties with Lower Canada. Powell, bitter at being displaced by his own protégé, believed that Robinson and Strachan had conspired against him; but it is more likely that his irascibility had simply offended too many people and would have made him a bad commissioner. There was worse to come: his daughter Anne, still enamoured of Robinson, defied her parents to follow him when he went to England as commissioner and was drowned in the wreck of the ship *Albion* (22 April 1822).

Powell's primary loyalty was always to the principles of English common law, not to the provincial administration of Upper Canada. The pettiness, the ungenerous spirit of calculation, and the tendency to store up resentment which characterized his pursuit of office contrasted with his joviality and concern for defendants on the bench. His judicial humour was merely conventional: to a divided jury in a murder trial he explained that he could neither half hang the defendant nor hang half of him, so that the verdict amounted to acquittal. His faith in jury trials did not involve a high opinion of jurors' ability to understand the law or even to distinguish the relevant facts in a case. His instructions to juries left little doubt as to which witnesses he himself found credible or what verdict he expected. When the slave Jack York* was tried for burglary in September 1800, Powell cautioned the jury emphatically against the self-interest of York's owner, James Girty, as a defence witness. York was convicted, and Powell sentenced him to death. A month earlier, he had pronounced the same sentence on William Newberry, the son of a loyalist, after his conviction on the same charge. If the two cases were parallel in law, however, Powell did not think that the practical results ought to be the same. He expected the letter of the law to be tempered with mercy; but mercy was properly a matter of prerogative discretion, not for the sympathy of juries. York, whose owner was connected with the Indian Department officers with whom Powell had clashed at Detroit, would have hanged if he had not managed to escape from jail; but Powell recommended to the lieutenant governor that Newberry's sentence be reduced. In a less dramatic case in August 1810, having charged the jury to convict a Methodist minister of illegally solemnizing marriages, he recommended a pardon.

Powell opposed the suspension of habeas corpus and the declaration of martial law during the War of 1812 and disliked the resort to special commissions on treason charges, because he thought that the regular course of the common law should not be interrupted for the sake of administrative expediency. In June 1814 he took turns with Chief Justice Scott and Mr Justice William CAMPBELL in presiding over treason trials at the Ancaster assizes. He charged the jury to convict only 7 of the 50 defendants whose cases came before him *in absentia*, despite his personal belief that they all deserved punishment. He presided over 6 of the 18 trials at which prisoners appeared to plead not guilty. His harsh view of what constituted a treasonable act, uncompromisingly conveyed to the jury, resulted in the conviction of the luckless Jacob Overholser*. Three others, against whom there was

an abundance of evidence, were also convicted. Yet, of the four prisoners acquitted at Ancaster, two, Robert Troup and Jesse Holly, were tried when Powell was presiding; and his summaries of the evidence clearly anticipated their acquittal. He was, however, unwilling to extend anything beyond strict justice to traitors: unlike the other two judges, he made no recommendations for mercy.

In the years after he attained the post of chief justice, Powell's crankiness began to show itself on the bench. He had long felt that the rules of his court were inconveniently restricted by statute; his original procedures, after having been changed to a more elaborate English model by Elmsley, had been partly restored by the assembly in 1797, in an act "ill comprehended by the Law makers . . . almost compelling the Court to evade by Shifts, Anomalies and Inconsistencies which could not be reconciled." He responded by an increasing, and to many it seemed an increasingly partisan, tendency to raise technicalities in the law, some of them of doubtful application. In August 1819, charging the jurors in an action for damages (*Randal* v. *Phelps*), he was said by the plaintiff Robert RANDAL to have threatened them with a writ of attaint – a writ unused for more than 100 years – if they did not follow his own preference for the defendant. He told the grand jury at Sandwich (Windsor) in 1821 that Indians, although subject by common law to the regular courts, might be exempt from their jurisdiction by treaty. The next year this remark became the basis for the defence in the murder trial of SHAWANAKISKIE, whose conviction was therefore not confirmed until after reference to the imperial law officers four years later. In October 1823 the trial for infanticide of a servant girl, Mary THOMPSON, showed how far Powell had retreated into technicalities. The jury in convicting her recommended clemency, and Powell himself felt sympathy for her, but her pathetic circumstances were not enough to make him recommend a pardon. It was only after finding that some of the evidence he had allowed against her would not have been admissible in contemporary English practice that he changed his mind. Growing finicky about the letter of the law did not prevent him, near the end of his career, from becoming a little vague about the limits of his authority. In 1823 he refused to support the nomination as commissioner for war claims of Alexander Wood*, to whose morals he objected. When Wood was appointed anyway on Strachan's recommendation, Powell as chief justice refused to swear him in. Wood successfully sued him for £120 damages. Powell tried to set aside the judgement by a bill of exceptions, which would have required Maitland to have acted as a judge in equity. Even when this dubious and obscure device failed, he refused to pay; and the debt was forgiven after his death.

His descent with advancing age into pedantic

crankiness was not surprising in one who had always been so self-consciously insistent on the independence of the bench. Perhaps the only concession to administrative expediency that he ever made as a judge was to refrain in the winter of 1791–92 from questioning the continued legality of his Quebec commission after Upper Canada was proclaimed a separate province. In 1818 he caused inconvenience to the provincial administration in a series of decisions arising from the quarrels of the Earl of Selkirk [Douglas*] in the Red River colony, some of which produced law suits in the courts of Upper Canada. To the chagrin of Robinson, he rejected charges of conspiracy against Selkirk; and to the outrage of Strachan he threw out most of the charges that Selkirk had brought against his opponents. In the most spectacular of his trials, however, Powell found himself trapped by the law into unwilling cooperation in a course of action that he thought unnecessary at best. He thoroughly disapproved of Robert Gourlay and recommended that land grants should be withheld from those who attended Gourlay's convention at York in July 1818, but he repeatedly advised that there were no legal grounds for prosecuting Gourlay's attacks on the administration of the province. When such grounds were found under the Sedition Act of 1804 and persisted in by Robinson in spite of Gourlay's obviously incapacitating illness, Powell had no choice but to pronounce a sentence of banishment.

Most of his cases, however, were mundane. He was uncompromising in the belief not only that convicted debtors should be imprisoned but that those accused of debt should be held in jail for trial. A survey of the province's 11 district jails in 1827 showed them to have a capacity of 298 cells, 264 of them occupied. Of the prisoners, 159 were being held for debt, and only 29 for felonies. In his last years on the bench he defied both the assembly and the councils by insisting that even legislators were not immune from arrest for debt. By 1824 his judicial duties had become as wearisome to Powell as his administrative work, and he planned to retire from the bench when he reached the age of 70 in November 1825.

He had made too many enemies to be left to a peaceful retirement. On 24 Oct. 1824 Mackenzie published a letter in the *Colonial Advocate* signed A Spanish Freeholder, which in the course of attacking the York élite lampooned Powell as "Cardinal Alberoni, Lord Chief Justice of His Imperial Majesty of Spain." It revived the old charges of his American sympathies at Detroit, alleged that he had obtained the chief justiceship in return for the harshness of his sentences at the Ancaster assizes, and condemned his behaviour on the bench in a case not named, but clearly that of Singleton Gardiner in 1822–23. Gardiner, a Middlesex farmer politically at odds with two local tory magistrates, Mahlon Burwell* and Leslie

Patterson, had brought a suit against them. Powell doubted that he had a good legal case, but by referring it to a jury he publicized the magistrates' abuse of their authority. He had acted correctly, but probably also with malice: Burwell in the assembly had promoted Robinson's appointment as commissioner in 1821, and he was the lieutenant of Thomas Talbot*, towards whom Powell's enmity went back to Gore's administration. The Spanish freeholder was probably Burwell's younger brother, Adam Hood Burwell*. Before it was printed in Mackenzie's paper, his letter received an approving notice, hinting broadly that it referred to Powell, in Charles Fothergill*'s *Weekly Register*. The letter soon received an equally intemperate reply in a pamphlet, *The answer to the awful libel of the Spanish freeholder, against the Cardinal Alberoni*, published under the pseudonym Diego ([York, 1824]).

Although Diego's pamphlet has been attributed to Powell and to his son-in-law Samuel Peters Jarvis, it is far more likely to have been the work of John Rolph*, Jarvis's law partner and the recent victor over Mahlon Burwell in the election of 1824. Even before the pamphlet appeared, however, Powell's temper had led him into indiscretions that neither Maitland nor the councils had the slightest disposition to forgive. Refusing to be content with the grudging apology that Maitland had exacted from Fothergill, the angry old judge prepared two pamphlets of his own: *Correspondence and remarks, elicited by a malignant libel, signed "a Spanish freeholder"* and *Spanish freeholder, app.A*. They had little to do with the recent libel: the first rehearsed his grievances against Maitland and his secretary, George Hillier*; the second was addressed to his quarrel with Robinson in 1821; and both printed correspondence meant to be private. Beginning as the victim in the affair, he had turned himself in the eyes of the York administration into the chief offender. On 28 Jan. 1825 the Executive Council reported that he had laid himself open to the legal charge of repeating a libel, had abused the lieutenant governor's confidence, and had exposed "measures of Government to public contempt and reprehension." This rebuke was the more bitter because its author was John Strachan, the other two councillors present being the quiescent James BABY and the aged Samuel SMITH. And although Strachan was by this time more an instrument of the lieutenant governor than an influence upon him, he felt secure enough to add that the chief justice had been sulking ever since Robinson's appointment as attorney general. Maitland refused to speak to Powell again except in the presence of a witness.

Powell was obliged to resign from the Executive Council in September 1825. He remained a legislative councillor until his death, but had to yield the speakership to William Campbell, who also succeeded him as chief justice (17 Oct. 1825). The secretary of state, Lord Bathurst, allowed Powell a pension of £1,000 (sterling) a year, in spite of the Executive Council's advice that he was "unworthy of such a favour." After almost three years in England, securing his pension and justifying his conduct, he returned in 1829 to spend his last years at York. He took no further part in public affairs, except to publish his correspondence with Maitland over the Wood affair.

No one else had put such sustained effort and such shrewd intelligence into the government of Upper Canada. In the history of the province, only Allcock in Hunter's administration and Robinson in Maitland's had greater influence than Powell. Strachan and Christopher Alexander Hagerman* may have approached it, but only briefly. Powell had achieved prosperity and seen his surviving children comfortably established. Yet he was pessimistic about the state of the province, with reform politics rising in the House of Assembly, and he had been without real friends in the administration ever since Gore's departure. Gourlay had well nicknamed him "Pawkie," for his awkwardness in personal relationships never left him. As his health declined, so did his mental powers, obviously enough to give malicious satisfaction to his erstwhile allies, Robinson and Strachan. He reviewed the quarrels of his life, writing self-justifying memoranda on them, and publishing a rather maudlin outline of his life, *Story of a refugee* (York, 1833). In the end, all his formal successes brought him little pleasure and little faith in the future of his adopted province.

S. R. MEALING

[Powell's autobiographical writings became increasingly unreliable as he grew older, but he kept a great deal of his correspondence. The main collection of his papers in the MTL, with a smaller collection in the PAC (MG 23, HI, 4), richly documents his life. He appears at his worst in the pamphlets *Correspondence and remarks, elicited by a malignant libel, signed "a Spanish freeholder," in Upper Canada, 14th October, 1824* ([York (Toronto), 1824]?), *Spanish freeholder, app.A* ([York, 1824]?), *[A letter from W. D. Powell, chief justice, to Sir Peregrine Maitland, Lieutenant-Governor of Upper Canada, regarding the appointment of Alexander Wood as a commissioner for the investigation of claims . . .]* ([York, 1831]?), and *Story of a refugee* (York, 1833). He was the object of much comment by his contemporaries at York; some of it survives, especially in the papers of John Strachan (AO, MS 35, and MTL), John Beverley Robinson (AO, MS 4), and Samuel Peters Jarvis (AO, MS 787, and MTL). The most valuable printed collections of documents are Strachan's *Letter book* (Spragge); *Town of York, 1793–1815* (Firth) and *1815–34* (Firth); and *Corr. of Lieut. Governor Simcoe* (Cruikshank). The AO *Report* for 1917 prints the records of Powell's district court as "Upper Canada, District of Hesse; record of the Court of Common Pleas, L'Assomption, 1789." The reports for

1910 and 1915 print "The journals of the Legislative Council of Upper Canada. . . ."

The life of William Dummer Powell, first judge at Detroit and fifth chief justice of Upper Canada (Lansing, Mich., 1924) by William Renwick Riddell*, although not the author's best work, remains the only useful biography of Powell. Riddell has also described the working of his courts in "Practice of Court of Common Pleas of the District of Hesse," RSC *Trans.*, 3rd ser., 7 (1913), sect.II: 43–56, and in "The early courts of the province," *Canadian Law Times* (Toronto), 35 (1915): 879–90. His review of Powell's decisions on the status of Indians is in *Sero* v. *Gault* (1921), 50 O.L.R. 27. See also his article "The Ancaster 'Bloody Assize' of 1814," *OH*, 20 (1923): 107–25; Alison Ewart and Julia Jarvis, "The personnel of the family compact, 1791–1841," *CHR*, 7 (1926): 209–21; R. E. Saunders, "What was the family compact?" *OH*, 49 (1957): 165–78; G. M. Gressley, "Lord Selkirk and the Canadian courts," *N.Dak. Hist.* (Bismarck), 24 (1957): 89–105; S. F. Wise, "Upper Canada and the conservative tradition," *Profiles of a province: studies in the history of Ontario . . .* (Toronto, 1967), 20–33, and "Conservatism and political development: the Canadian case," *South Atlantic Quarterly* (Durham, N.C.), 69 (1970): 226–43; Terry Cook, "John Beverley Robinson and the conservative blueprint for the Upper Canadian community," *OH*, 64 (1972): 79–94; R. J. Burns, "God's chosen people: the origins of Toronto society, 1791–1818," CHA *Hist. papers*, 1973: 213–28; K. M. J. McKenna, "Anne Powell and the early York elite," *"None was ever better . . .": the loyalist settlement of Ontario; proceedings of the annual meeting of the Ontario Historical Society, Cornwall, June 1984*, ed. S. F. Wise *et al.* (Cornwall, Ont., 1984), 31–43; and Paul Romney, "The Spanish freeholder imbroglio of 1824: inter-elite and intra-elite rivalry in Upper Canada," *OH*, 76 (1984): 32–47. S.R.M.]

POWER, JOHN, Roman Catholic priest and Franciscan; b. in the province of Munster (Republic of Ireland), probably in County Tipperary or County Waterford; d. between 14 June and 12 Sept. 1823 at Twenty Mile Pond (Windsor Lake), near St John's.

John Power, a Franciscan priest in Ireland, was guardian (superior) of the convents of that order in Bantry from 1785 to 1787 and in Clonmel from 1787 to 1797, and it is quite possible, but not certain, that he was the Franciscan priest who later resided in Newfoundland. This John Power came to Newfoundland from Ireland, apparently in 1808. He did so without the required ecclesiastical permissions and without the approval of Bishop Patrick Lambert*, the vicar apostolic of Newfoundland. Despite these irregularities, Lambert may have made use temporarily of Power's services. The priest's name appears as that of a Catholic clergyman at St John's on the government's list of Newfoundland clergy for 1810.

However, on 8 June 1812 Lambert suspended "the Reverend, or rather Irreverend Father John Power" from all his priestly functions, for "conduct *unpriestly, immoral* and *scandalously criminal.*" The specific charge was that the priest had formed a liaison with a

Pownall

woman who followed him to St John's from Bonavista or one of the other northern harbours. Power accepted his suspension "with an ill-grace," and in 1813 Governor Sir Richard Goodwin KEATS sought to have him quietly removed from Newfoundland. A close working relationship then existed between the Catholic bishops and the Newfoundland administration, and his disfavour with the bishop automatically made Power suspect. Although Keats had no evidence that Power was disloyal to the crown, he feared the priest's influence, describing him as "of manners plausible and taking with the Lower Classes." Keats even used the case to seek to have the British government take measures that would prevent any priest from emigrating to Newfoundland without the formal approval of the Roman Catholic bishop. However, no action was taken by the government on that suggestion or on the request to have Power removed.

Throughout this period, both fish prices and wages had been high, and Irish immigration substantial. In the spring of 1815, however, with the end of the Napoleonic Wars, the market became depressed. Nevertheless, swayed by reports of the booming fishery of previous years, thousands of Irish immigrants, many of them passengers on overcrowded vessels and near starvation, still streamed into St John's. They faced only disappointment, with massive unemployment and wages far below those of the past year. The workers formed into rival county gangs, with secret oaths to be true to each other and compacts not to hire out to merchants or planters at less than agreed wages. As had happened in the early 1780s, quarrels soon broke out between factions from Leinster and Munster, the two Irish provinces mainly represented among the immigrants. In St John's there were regular fights and disturbances along provincial lines, with the Leinster gangs – Wexford "Yellow-bellies" and Kilkenny "Doonanes" – pitted against those from the province of Munster – Waterford "Whey-bellies," Tipperary "Clear-airs," and the less numerous Cork "Dadyeens."

The quarrels were heightened by the dispute between Lambert and Power. Lambert's suspension of Power had offended many of the Irish from Munster, who continued to pay the priest, one of their own, "every demonstration of Respect and attention." Although at least half the Newfoundland Irish came from Munster, Lambert and almost all his clergy were Leinstermen from County Wexford; this gave further offence. In 1815 these factors created a body of support for Power and undermined the bishop's preaching against the oath-taking and fighting. The troubles continued until the early summer, but they appear to have subsided thereafter. The incipient unionism was a complete failure. The "combinations" against the merchants collapsed, and servants were obliged to accept what work there was at half the wages of the year before.

Although not a great deal is known of Power's activities in subsequent years, his troubles continued under Lambert's successor, Thomas SCALLAN. In 1820 Power went secretly to Labrador and, despite his suspension, celebrated mass there. On 29 October Scallan, who felt that the priest had been "generally in a state of rebellion against his ordinary" and who had previously given him a canonical warning, publicly excommunicated him. In his explanation to Rome, the bishop accused Power also of being prone to drinking, of having taken another priest to court in a dispute over a debt, and of having struck a priest who was saying mass. In his turn, Power soon afterwards sued the bishop himself in the Supreme Court, claiming that Scallan had deprived him of certain funds due to him. Chief Justice Francis Forbes* and a jury, however, found in the bishop's favour.

By 1822 Scallan could refer to Power as an "old reprobate" and note that he had few followers. He lived at Twenty Mile Pond, where he supported himself by using his house as a tavern, selling spirits to travellers. His death took place while Scallan was absent from Newfoundland, but the bishop was informed upon his return that Power had died "truly penitent" for his past deeds.

Almost all that is known of John Power comes from his opponents, and the picture that emerges is consequently one-sided. He must have been a talented man. In his prime he held great sway with the public, and even in the midst of the troubles of 1815 Chief Justice Cæsar COLCLOUGH noted that "some very respectable people speak very favourably of him." Power's differences with Lambert and Scallan partially reflect the social and economic pressures brought about by the wave of Irish immigration between 1810 and 1816, as well as the faction-fighting which constantly plagued the Newfoundland Irish in the late 18th and early 19th centuries. Perhaps in other circumstances Power's role might have been considerably different.

RAYMOND J. LAHEY

AAQ, 30 CN. Arch. of the Archdiocese of St John's, Lambert papers, suspension of John Power, 8 June 1812. Archivio della Propaganda Fide (Rome), Scritture riferite nei Congressi, America Settentrionale, 2 (1792–1830): ff.350–51. PRO, ADM 80/151: 16–19; CO 194/49: 119; 194/55: 233 et seq.; 194/56: 24, 26, 45–46, 51–52, 105–13, 173–75, 179–80, 211. Liber Dubliniensis: chapter documents of the Irish Franciscans, 1719–1875, ed. Anselm Faulkner (Killiney, Republic of Ire., 1978). Newfoundland Mercantile Journal, 29 Nov. 1821. M. F. Howley, Ecclesiastical history of Newfoundland (Boston, 1888; repr. Belleville, Ont., 1979).

POWNALL, Sir GEORGE, office holder, politician, and JP; b. 1755 in Lincolnshire, England, son of John Pownall; d. 17 Oct. 1834 in England.

George Pownall came from a ruling class background. His uncle, Colonel Thomas Pownall, held important posts in the colonies and from 1767 to 1780 was a member of the House of Commons. His father was, among other things, under-secretary of state for the American Colonies from 1768 to 1776 and so had great influence on one of the secretaries, Lord Dartmouth. He probably was largely responsible for George's rapid rise in the higher ranks of the colonial administration. Thus, on 7 April 1775 when he was just 20 George was entrusted by Dartmouth with the senior offices of secretary and registrar of the province of Quebec. These posts entailed considerable responsibility. The civil secretary had to prepare all official documents, including proclamations, under the direction of the governor acting on his own or in concert with the Legislative Council. Moreover it was the civil secretary who was responsible for the government's official correspondence and the issuing of letters patent and various commissions. Pownall arrived at Quebec on 15 June 1775 along with Chief Justice William Hey*. On 7 August Governor Guy Carleton* appointed him to the Legislative Council, of which he remained a member until his death. He was also the first person to serve as clerk of the council, being replaced in that office by Jenkin Williams* early in 1777.

In the summer of 1783 Pownall was granted a year's leave of absence to return to England. He was back in the province in June 1784 and soon after was chosen by Governor Frederick Haldimand* for the "privy council," a body of legislative councillors who belonged to the French party and had the governor's confidence. But after Haldimand left, Pownall sided with the English party, which represented the interests of the British merchants, sought to have English laws apply in civil and commercial matters, as well as criminal ones, and stood against the French party led by Adam Mabane*. The question of excluding the public from the deliberations of the Legislative Council, a subject of serious disagreement among its members, illustrates his attitude. The issue first arose at a meeting on 22 Jan. 1786, when 16 people asked permission to attend the debates. Henry Caldwell* immediately made a motion to that effect, but it was rejected by 10 to 8, with all the French-speaking members of the council voting against it. On 25 January Pownall registered a protest against the exclusion of observers, alleging that all British subjects had the right, on due request, to attend the debates of a body passing the laws to which they would be subject. The convention that legislative councillors were obliged by their oath to deliberate in camera no longer held, he added, and it was imperative for the suspicions fostered in the public mind by secrecy to be dispelled. In 1789 one official, Alexander Fraser, listed Pownall in a confidential dispatch to London as being among the councillors allied with

Chief Justice William Smith*, the leader of the English party.

On 6 Nov. 1786 four Legislative Council committees were set up by Governor Carleton (now Lord Dorchester) to inform the imperial government about the colony's administration and help it determine the best type of government to establish. Pownall was named to the committee on internal and external commerce and police regulations along with John Collins*, Edward Harrison*, William Grant*, and François Lévesque*. From 12 July 1788 till 31 Aug. 1789 he sat as a judge under a commission of oyer and terminer and general jail delivery. In July 1788 he received the first of a long series of commissions of the peace. He was also empowered to receive oaths, a function renewed in 1791 and 1793. Pownall was one of the founding members of the Agriculture Society in the district of Quebec in 1789. The following year, and again in 1802 and 1803, he was made an Admiralty commissioner for the trial of certain offences committed at sea. On 26 Dec. 1791, the day the Constitutional Act came into effect, his authority as secretary and registrar of Lower Canada was confirmed. As he had left for England on 14 August, Hugh Finlay* assumed the duties temporarily. In October 1795 Pownall received another leave, and in 1796 he was made a knight of the Order of the Bath. In November 1799 he was appointed commissioner, along with four other Anglicans, for the erection of a metropolitan church at Quebec, an appointment renewed in July 1803.

Sir George Pownall went back to England that year. There he came into possession of an estate in Norfolk bequeathed him by his uncle Thomas, who died in 1805. But he did not seek permission for retirement until 24 March 1807. The Colonial Office acceded to his request and granted him an annual pension of £300. Thomas Amyot succeeded him that year as provincial secretary and registrar.

CHRISTINE VEILLEUX

PAC, RG 68, General index, 1651–1841. *Docs. relating to constitutional hist., 1759–91* (Shortt and Doughty, 1918); *1791–1818* (Doughty and McArthur), 72. *Papers and letters on agriculture, recommended to the attention of the Canadian farmers, by the Agricultural Society in Canada* (Quebec, 1790), 3. *Papiers et lettres sur l'agriculture recommandés à l'attention des cultivateurs canadiens par la Société d'agriculture en Canada* (La Pocatière, Qué., 1882), 10. *Quebec Gazette*, 30 July 1783, 17 June 1784, 18 Aug. 1791, 9 June 1796. [F.-]M. Bibaud, *Mémorial des honneurs étrangers conférés à des Canadiens ou domiciliés de la Puissance du Canada* (Montréal, 1885), 18. *DAB* (biog. of Thomas Pownall). André Desjardins, "Guide de consultation des archives de la période britannique (anciennes séries QBC) conservés au Centre d'archives de Québec" (typescript, Québec, 1985). Desjardins, *Guide parl.* "Papiers d'État," PAC *Rapport*, 1890: 143–44, 208, 241, 250, 277. "Papiers d'État – Bas-Canada," PAC *Rapport*, 1891: 120, 123, 198.

Pritchard

Quebec almanac, 1788, 1791, 1794–1808, 1811–33. Turcotte, *Le Conseil législatif*. A. [C.] Valentine, *The British establishment, 1760–1784* . . . (2v., Norman, Okla., 1970), 716–17. Wallace, *Macmillan dict.* A. L. Burt, *The old province of Quebec* (2v., Toronto, 1968), 2: 129, 139. Millman, *Jacob Mountain*, 87. F.-J. Audet, "Les législateurs de la province de Québec, 1764–1791," *BRH*, 31 (1925): 489–90; "Oyer and terminer and general gaol delivery," *BRH*, 39 (1933): 216–19. F. B. Wickwire, "John Pownall and British colonial policy," *William and Mary Quarterly* (Williamsburg, Va.), 2nd ser., 20 (1963): 543–54.

PRITCHARD, AZARIAH, army and militia officer, spy, colonizer, entrepreneur, seigneur, and JP; probably b. in Connecticut, son of James Pritchard; d. *c.* 1830, likely in New Richmond, Lower Canada.

At the outbreak of the American revolution in 1775 Azariah Pritchard was a miller living in Derby, Conn. Remaining loyal to the crown, the following year he helped 160 loyalists cross the rebel lines to reach Long Island, N.Y. He was accused of transmitting information to the British but was acquitted by a military tribunal in 1777. He decided to flee to the province of Quebec with his wife and three children, and acted as a frontier guide in the Lake Champlain region. As a result of this decision 600 acres of land he owned along the Connecticut River were reportedly confiscated, together with his properties at Derby and a ship he had fitted out.

In 1779 Pritchard was serving as a captain in the King's Rangers [*see* Robert Rogers*]. Stationed at Fort St· Johns (Saint-Jean-sur-Richelieu), he was immediately put into service as a secret agent. He successfully carried out many missions into Connecticut and Vermont and did counter-espionage work within Quebec up to the time of his retirement from the army in 1784. During his years of service Pritchard often attracted suspicion for activities that he was thought to have carried on. He was accused of having traded illegally in beef with Vermont and of bringing counterfeit money into the province in 1782, and then of having trafficked in tea in the upper Lake Champlain region and of dishonestly acquiring lands on Missisquoi Bay in 1783. These accusations, which had no sound basis, were refuted in every instance.

Once the revolution was over, the British authorities contemplated demobilizing their troops and settling them on lands suitable for farming. Pritchard scoured the Yamamiche region near Trois-Rivières for settlers willing to establish themselves on Baie des Chaleurs. On 9 June 1784, after the troops had been discharged, 315 people sailed for that destination. The snow *Liberty*, with Pritchard and his family aboard, reached Bonaventure on 27 June. Since the good land was already occupied by Acadians, 77 of the new arrivals, including Pritchard, proceeded to the nearby site of Paspébiac. Lots were immediately marked out.

Clearly a man of enterprising spirit, Pritchard made an application on 18 August to build a grist-mill on the Rivière Caplan in order to help the new settlers at Paspébiac. He also began lumbering. Subsequently he made a number of applications for land grants, built a sawmill in the vicinity, and finally settled at New Richmond. The Pritchard family was well off financially and began to accumulate offices. Azariah became a captain in the Richmond Township battalion of militia around 1792 and a justice of the peace for the Gaspé District in 1811. His son Azariah was commissioned an ensign in the same battalion, and was appointed master culler and measurer of building timber in 1810.

In the mean time Pritchard's career was at risk because of new suspicions. Specific charges of selling forged certificates of British citizenship and of trafficking in false papers of registry for trade to the Mediterranean were brought against him in June 1790. These dealings in counterfeit documents were supposed to have gone on for two years and to have spread as far as Virginia. Pritchard collaborated closely in the investigation; despite this, a warrant was issued for his arrest. At the end of the trial held at New Carlisle in July 1790 he was acquitted by the jury and he was thanked by Lord Dorchester [Guy Carleton*] for his zeal in uncovering these fraudulent practices.

In 1801 Azariah Pritchard acquired the seigneury of Le Bic through an exchange. In doing so he was expanding his lumbering venture. In 1822 he parted with this property in return for building lots in the town of Quebec. During his last years he let his son take over his affairs in the Gaspé.

MARIO MIMEAULT

ANQ-Q, CN1-99, 13 nov. 1810; CN1-285, 27 juin 1801, 18 oct. 1822. BL, Add. MSS 21820: 68–69; 21821: 33–35; 21822: 58–59, 68–69, 200–4; 21828: 30–35; 21838: 71–81; 21862: 195. *Quebec Gazette*, 11 July 1793, 24 May 1810, 6 June 1811. "Papiers d'État," PAC *Rapport*, 1890: 265, 267, 281–86, 288. *Quebec almanac*, 1792–97. P.-G. Roy, *Inv. concessions*, 3: 156. *Le centenaire de la paroisse de New-Richmond, 1860–1960* (s.l., 1960). Lanctot, *Le Canada et la Révolution américaine*. J.-D. Michaud, *Le Bic, les étapes d'une paroisse* (2v., Québec, 1925–26). W. H. Siebert, "The loyalist settlements on the Gaspé peninsula," RSC *Trans.*, 3rd ser., 8 (1914), sect.II: 399–405.

PROCTER (Proctor), HENRY, army officer; b. *c.* 1763 in Ireland, eldest son of Richard Procter and Anne Gregory; m. 1792 Elizabeth Cockburn in Kilkenny (Republic of Ireland), and they had one son and four daughters; d. 31 Oct. 1822 in Bath, England.

The son of a British army surgeon who was at the battle of Bunker Hill, Henry Procter entered the 43rd Foot as an ensign on 5 April 1781. He obtained a lieutenancy that December, and served around New

York in the closing stages of the War of American Independence. A captain from November 1792 and a major from May 1795, he exchanged into the 41st Foot as a lieutenant-colonel on 9 Oct. 1800 and joined the regiment in Lower Canada two years later. His record as a commanding officer was praised by his superiors, including Major-General Isaac Brock*, who in 1811 ascribed the excellent condition of the 41st to the "indefatigable industry" of Procter.

After the outbreak of hostilities with the United States in the summer of 1812 Brock sent Procter, by then a colonel, to take command at Amherstburg, Upper Canada, which was threatened by an American army from Detroit. In August Procter took steps to cut communications between Detroit and the Ohio settlements. The resulting skirmishes at Brownstown (near Trenton, Mich.) and Maguaga (Wyandotte, Mich.) isolated the Detroit garrison and contributed substantially to its capitulation on the 16th to forces led by Brock. Procter remained as commander on the Detroit frontier after Brock's departure, and in September he sent an expedition under Captain Adam Charles MUIR against Fort Wayne (Ind.). By the end of the year an American army under Brigadier-General William Henry Harrison was en route to Detroit. On 19 Jan. 1813 Procter received news that its advance guard had occupied Frenchtown (Monroe, Mich.) on the River Raisin. He immediately launched an expedition which attacked and forced the surrender of the advance guard. As a consequence Procter was appointed brigadier-general (he would be promoted major-general in June) and the House of Assembly of Upper Canada passed a vote of thanks. On the other hand, he was accused by the Americans of failing to prevent the murder of some prisoners by his Indian allies after the battle.

Harrison had retreated upon hearing the news of Frenchtown, but by May 1813 he had established himself on the Maumee River at Fort Meigs (near Perrysburg), Ohio. Conscious of his own inferiority in numbers, Procter decided to attack the fort before American reinforcements could arrive. A relief column was successfully ambushed on the 5th, but Procter was unable to take the fort itself and withdrew on the 9th. Two months later, in response to Indian demands, he made a second and equally abortive attempt on Fort Meigs before thrusting at Fort Stephenson (Fremont), Ohio, on the Sandusky River. The failure of the latter assault cost the British many casualties.

The losses were especially unfortunate in view of the lack of adequate reinforcements and supplies, a result of the low priority of the Detroit frontier and the long and uncertain lines of communication. More important, these deficiencies also affected the British squadron on Lake Erie under Robert Heriot Barclay*, and the outcome of the campaign of 1813 on the Detroit frontier hinged on control of the lake, where by the summer the Americans were completing their own squadron. Procter was well aware of the situation, and he and Barclay proposed an attack on the American naval base of Presque Isle (Erie), Pa. Major-General John Vincent* was willing to send the necessary forces from the Niagara peninsula, but when Major-General Francis de ROTTENBURG assumed command he refused any aid.

The lack of sufficient troops and supplies continued to plague Procter during the summer, and Barclay's defeat in the battle of Lake Erie in September gave the Americans total command of the lake. Procter had little chance of halting the expected invasion without substantial reinforcements, which could no longer be sent to him. A withdrawal would, however, be difficult, for it would risk a rupture with the Indians, who were still anxious to attack the Americans [see Tecumseh*]. Such a break would not only result in the loss of allies who had been extremely valuable but might also expose all the settlements west of the Niagara frontier to attack by the disgruntled Indians as well as the Americans.

Procter planned to withdraw up the Thames valley, thus extending the enemy lines of communication and keeping his own forces well away from Lake Erie. The retreat from Amherstburg and Sandwich (Windsor) began on 27 September, those stores which could not be transported being destroyed. On 5 October, however, the pursuing Americans caught up at present-day Thamesville, and in the ensuing battle of Moraviantown Tecumseh was killed and the British troops were captured or scattered. Procter with a few survivors fled the scene and continued the retreat to Ancaster.

Controversy about the retreat and the battle began almost as soon as the fighting ended. Procter's staff adjutant of militia, John Christopher Reiffenstein*, who had left the action before his commander, spread the most alarming and exaggerated reports of the battle and Procter's conduct. Rottenburg and Lieutenant-General Sir George Prevost*, the commander of the forces, attempted to dissociate themselves from any responsibility for the defeat, though it is clear that hunger, fatigue, and lack of supplies had left the British troops in no condition to fight successfully even under inspired leadership. It remains a fact, however, that Procter's leadership was less than inspired.

Because of the defeat, Prevost refused to employ Procter elsewhere. For various reasons it was not until December 1814 that a court martial in Montreal began hearings. Procter faced five charges: first, that he did not begin his retreat sufficiently soon; second, that he allowed the retreat to be slowed by taking too much baggage, some of it personal; third, that he did not take appropriate measures to prevent supplies and ammunition from falling into enemy hands; fourth, that he neglected to fortify adequately positions along the Thames, in particular at the forks of the river (Chatham); fifth, that he made poor dispositions to meet the enemy at Moraviantown and failed to rally and encourage his troops and Indian allies at and after the battle. The court found him innocent of the first charge and guilty or partially guilty of the others, sentencing him to be reprimanded publicly and suspended from rank and pay for six months. When reviewed by the British judge advocate general and the Prince Regent, the findings of the court were confirmed on all but the second charge, on which grounds for conviction were found wanting. The sentence was reduced to a simple reprimand, but this was still sufficient to ruin Procter's career. He nevertheless remained in the Canadas until the fall of 1815, when he returned to England to live the remainder of his life in semi-retirement.

In Canadian historical writing Procter has almost always been condemned as a failure, not only for his final defeat but also for his actions on the Sandusky, Maumee, and Raisin rivers. John Mackay Hitsman, for example, concluded that of British generals "only Procter managed to blunder consistently." Often, though not in Hitsman's case, the censure seems to derive mainly from John Richardson*'s vitriolic criticism, which was apparently caused by Procter's failure to praise sufficiently Richardson's role in the fighting on the Maumee River. Certainly his conduct prior to the withdrawal from the Detroit frontier in September 1813 is beyond reproach. Moreover, relatively few accounts take enough note of the difficulties under which Procter operated, or of the fact that the charges against him were so general that it was obvious he would be found guilty on some. Perhaps the most charitable as well as the most accurate judgement has been made by Pierre Berton, who claims that "to the Americans he remains a monster, to the Canadians a coward. He is neither – merely a victim of circumstances, a brave officer but weak, capable enough except in moments of stress, a man of modest pretensions, unable to make the quantum leap that distinguishes the outstanding leader from the run-of-the-mill."

A. M. J. HYATT

PRO, WO 91/9–10. *Defence of Major General Proctor, tried at Montreal by a general court martial upon charges affecting his character as a soldier . . .* (Montreal, 1842). *Doc. hist. of campaign upon Niagara frontier* (Cruikshank). *Documents relating to the invasion of Canada and the surrender of Detroit, 1812*, ed. E. A. Cruikshank (Ottawa, 1912). [John] Richardson, *Richardson's War of 1812; with notes and a life of the author*, ed. A. C. Casselman (Toronto, 1902). *Select British docs. of War of 1812* (Wood). [J.] B. Burke, *A genealogical and heraldic history of the landed gentry of Great Britain* (12th ed., London, 1914). G.B.,

WO, *Army list*, 1781–1816. *Officers of British forces in Canada* (Irving). *The royal military calendar, containing the service of every general officer in the British army, from the date of their first commission . . .* , ed. John Philippart (3v., London, 1815–[16]). Pierre Berton, *Flames across the border, 1813–1814* (Toronto, 1980). Hitsman, *Incredible War of 1812*. Reginald Horsman, *The War of 1812* (London, 1969). D. A. N. Lomax, *A history of the services of the 41st (the Welch) Regiment (now 1st Battalion the Welch Regiment), from its formation, in 1719, to 1895* (Devonport, Eng., 1899). E. A. Cruikshank, "Harrison and Procter; the River Raisin," RSC *Trans.*, 3rd ser., 4 (1910), sect.II: 119–67. [C. O. Z.] Ermatinger, "The retreat of Proctor and Tecumseh," *OH*, 17 (1919): 11–21.

PUISAYE, JOSEPH-GENEVIÈVE DE, Comte de PUISAYE, Marquis de Brécourt, Marquis de Ménilles, colonizer and author; b. 6 March 1755 in Mortagne-au-Perche, France, son of André-Louis-Charles de Puisaye, Marquis de La Coudrelle, a high judicial officer, and Marthe-Françoise Bibron (Biberon) de Corméry; d. 13 Dec. 1827 near Hammersmith (London), England.

As a fourth and youngest son, Joseph-Geneviève de Puisaye was destined for the church to preserve the patrimony for his elder brothers and sister. He received the tonsure at the age of seven. Educated by a tutor until he was nine, he was then sent to the Collège de Laval, the Collège de Sées, and the Séminaire de Saint-Sulpice in Paris. The seminary's superior saw that this 17-year-old had no religious vocation and encouraged him to seek a worldly calling.

Following his father and brothers, Puisaye went into the army in 1773, but it gave him no experience of warfare. Through his maternal grandmother, he obtained a second lieutenant's commission in a cavalry regiment on the German frontier in February 1775. Since the regiment was at reduced strength, he was free to read and travel. He was summoned from this indolent life when his grandmother obtained the promise of a dragoon company for him. He did become a supernumerary captain in the Régiment de Lanan in 1779, but the company did not exist. Disillusioned with peace-time soldiering, he retired to Mortagne-au-Perche in 1781–82.

The next five years, he wrote, were "the happiest of my life," for his birthplace contained "all the delights of an agreeable and select society." Advised not to resign from the army without the cross of the Order of Saint-Louis, he bought a colonelcy and an honorary position in the king's household guard to qualify for this award. On 19 June 1788 he married Louise Le Sesne, the sole heir of the Marquis de Ménilles; "this marriage," he admitted, "put me into possession of a truly fine estate," at Pacy-sur-Eure in Normandy. Although he had other properties, he divided his time between this estate and Paris. Despite his professed dislike of public affairs, he helped draft the *cahier de doléance* of the Perche nobility and he was selected in 1789 to represent them in the Estates General. His family had a traditional pre-eminence in that province's nobility.

Puisaye was surprisingly liberal: he favoured a constitutional monarchy without the destruction of social ranks and allied himself with the Girondins. After the first session of the National Constituent Assembly, he stopped attending and he was not re-elected in 1792. His reformist politics and ambition had allowed him to become commander of the national guard in the Evreux district in 1790. When in 1793 the Jacobins in the National Convention proscribed the Girondins, Puisaye turned against the revolution; this late conversion made other, more conservative, counter-revolutionaries distrust him.

Puisaye was commanding the advance guard of a Norman army of federalists and royalists when it was surprised and scattered in July 1793; his nearby estate was sacked. He escaped to the forest of Pertre in Brittany where he tried to weld the anarchistic Chouans into a disciplined anti-Jacobin army. His ambition was both noble and selfish: to rally all insurgents under his leadership. By chance, he intercepted dispatches from England addressed to leaders of the royalist forces and he replied to them himself. His proposals so impressed the British government that it supported him with arms and money. As a constitutional monarchist, Puisaye was more acceptable than other French royalists. In another act of bravado, he initiated manifestos calling on the government troops to desert and the population to rebel. To arrange a royalist landing by sea that was to spark a general insurrection, Puisaye went to London in 1794.

His plan failed catastrophically. In June 1795 the Royal Navy landed 6,000 royalist troops at the Baie de Quiberon in southwest Brittany. Recognized by the British as commander, Puisaye found that the French princes had given command of the royalist regiments equipped by Britain to the cautious Comte d'Hervilly. Under a divided leadership, the royalist and Chouan allies did not act decisively. They were soon confined to the narrow Quiberon peninsula and then driven back to the water's edge. Thousands drowned trying to reach the British ships and those who surrendered were shot. Puisaye had already boarded a ship, ostensibly to save the official correspondence.

The count landed once more in Brittany in September 1795 to unite the remaining Chouans. Their factionalism and willingness to make peace with the republican government caused him to return to England, where he met a hostile and equally divided French community in exile. He was unjustly blamed for the Quiberon disaster and for being a coward. Puisaye believed that only a Bourbon prince's presence in France could revive the royalist forces there. When he organized a collective appeal to the Comte

d'Artois in December 1797 to provide that leadership as promised, a curt refusal was sent back and Puisaye's resignation as lieutenant-general in the king's armies was accepted.

Since 1793 there had been proposals to resettle exiled French royalists in the Canadas, where *émigré* priests had found a refuge [*see* Philippe-Jean-Louis Desjardins]. One French officer wrote of a common desire "to go and enjoy in Canada a less impure air than that of Europe . . . [and] to add to the number of Great Britain's faithful subjects." The British government was intimidated by the cost of aiding a mass migration until Puisaye and his associates presented a scheme that promised repayment of public expenses while converting those who were a burden to public and private charity in England into productive, self-supporting colonists who would help defend British North America. The plan would also "place decided Royalists in a country where Republican principles and Republican customs are become leading features."

Forty-one persons under Puisaye sailed from England in the summer of 1798 to lead the way for an expected migration of thousands of "French loyalists." They were to receive the same land grants and aid given to the American loyalists. With Puisaye were Major-General René-Augustin de Chalus, Comte de Chalus; Colonel Jean-Louis de Chalus, Vicomte de Chalus; Colonel Jean-Baptiste Coster, *dit* Coster de Saint-Victor; Colonel Jean de Beaupoil, Marquis de Saint-Aulaire; and Lieutenant-Colonel Laurent Quetton St George, among others. Most were veterans of the Breton army. When the main party reached Kingston in late October, their final destination in Upper Canada was unknown. The refugees wanted to settle apart from the established French-speaking population. As William Windham, the British secretary at war, explained, "considering themselves as of a purer description than the indiscriminate class of emigrants and being in some measure known to each other, they wish not to be mixed with those whose principles they are less sure of and whose future conduct might bring reproach upon the Colony." The administrator of Upper Canada, Peter Russell*, chose a site in Markham and Vaughan townships, equidistant from the French-speaking settlements on the Detroit River and in Lower Canada. Fifteen miles north of York (Toronto), the *émigrés* could be closely supervised and they would protect the little capital from a northern attack while at the same time extending Yonge Street to Lake Simcoe. The exiles were well armed and would have been formed into a regiment, had they been more numerous. Legislative councillor Richard Cartwright* recommended Puisaye as one who "brings with him a large Property" and whose colonists "will be a valuable Accession to the higher & anti-democratical Society of this Prov-

Puisaye

ince." Bishop Pierre Denaut* of Quebec hoped that the newcomers would strengthen the position of the Roman Catholic Church in Upper Canada.

Leaving the others in winter quarters at Kingston, Puisaye hurried on to York to confer with officials and he then took soldiers from his party to the designated site to clear the land and build shelters amid the snow. The settlement, near present-day Richmond Hill, was named Windham after the secretary at war who had befriended the *émigrés*. Eighteen homes were framed by February 1799 and more colonists proceeded to Windham. The hardships, privation, and isolation of pioneer life sapped their morale. They were a costly distance from York and roads were often impassable. Puisaye set off, the colonial government was told in March, to acquire a place at the head of Lake Ontario, near the mouth of "a little river capable of bearing a *bateau* to reach our establishment." This was to be an entrepôt for Windham, it was said, but Puisaye failed to obtain a government building at Burlington Beach (Hamilton) for the purpose. He bought an American loyalist's farm near Niagara (Niagara-on-the-Lake) and negotiated with Joseph Brant [Thayendanegea*] and the Mississauga Ojibwas for a large shoreline tract near Burlington Bay (Hamilton Harbour). Puisaye seemed to be looking for a more accessible and congenial location for the entire colony.

A few of the aristocrats at Kingston and Windham were discontented. They had expected estates upon which others would do the hard work. Of the 25 soldiers and servants brought from England as labourers, two drowned at Quebec and seven deserted. They were replaced by eight adults with a dozen children, hired in Lower Canada. Puisaye was helped by a manservant, a soldier, his young housekeeper Mrs Susanna Smithers, whom he had secretly married in 1797 (his first wife having died two years before), and her brother William Kent. Most of the *émigrés* could not afford to pay for servants.

A government agent was disturbed by the situation in May 1799. "The Emigrés do not seem to be united; the Gen'l. de Puisay, after having made great exertions in the winter to have Huts erected and Land cleared, has purchased for himself a House near Niagara seemingly intending to provide for himself a settlement and to have his followers to shift for themselves," reported Isaac Winslow Clarke. Windham was then inhabited by "only the Viscount de Chalus and six other officers with about a dozen Privates," as well as a score of Canadian servants. Coster de Saint-Victor reproached Puisaye for his promises of collective labour and military appointments for the officers; "not being educated to work the land, it would be impossible for me to obtain my living from it," he wrote. Saint-Aulaire also felt deceived. "This military unit in which I might find emoluments, these Breton peasants whose arms were to aid me are only a fantastic hope," he complained to Governor Robert Prescott*. Suspecting the count of maligning him, Saint-Aulaire wrote a long, defamatory memorial about Puisaye and his assumed mistress, Mrs Smithers. These two malcontents, Coster de Saint-Victor and Saint-Aulaire, returned to England. Some of the refugees settled in Lower Canada, a few drifted into commerce, and one shot himself. By June 1802 just sixteen, including two children born in Canada, remained at Windham. The agricultural colony continued to decline over several years and the anticipated influx of French exiles never came, although a few more individuals arrived.

After the spring of 1799 Puisaye lived at Niagara with a few of the emigrants. He still regarded himself as the head of the Windham settlement, where he owned land, and he sent supplies and lent money to the colonists. At Niagara he supervised improvements to his farm, planned a windmill, dabbled in trade, and composed his memoirs. He acquired a second farm and had a house built at York. The British government had already supplied the exiles with transportation, land, seed-grain, farm implements, and rations, yet Puisaye petitioned for a food allowance for his servants and for more land. He claimed that he had spent his own money to establish Windham and, in May 1802, he set out for England to obtain financial restitution, to publish his memoirs, and, possibly, to find some new position of authority. At New York he gave Quetton St George money to buy goods for a shop that the lieutenant-colonel and Captain Ambroise de Farcy were setting up in Puisaye's farmhouse near Niagara. William Kent later returned to manage the Niagara farm and the count's other Canadian properties.

From 1803 to 1808 Puisaye published his memoirs in six volumes, based on a voluminous collection of papers now in the British Library. In vindicating his military reputation, he disparaged others, including the Comte d'Avaray, confidant of Louis XVIII. Puisaye was not welcome in France after the restoration of the monarchy in 1814 and did not visit it, even to see his daughter, Joséphine. "I have had a small number of friends," he wrote, and "a much larger number of enemies." In 1806 he reported that "I have now retired to the countryside, fifteen miles from the capital [London], in a little cottage that I bought, where I lead almost the same sort of life as at Niagara, amid my chickens and cows – seeing, by chance, a few friends who . . . are sometimes good enough to come and share my solitude." He did not publicly acknowledge Susanna Smithers as his wife. His explanation in 1816 was that "though we are married those nineteen years, she does not bear my name, as my Circumstances Do not afford the means of Maintaining her according [to] her real Rank in Life." Considering his pride in his own ancestry, it is probable that he was ashamed of her humble origins. Despite his poor health, his pen was always active in writing to friends, in upholding his reputation, in seeking recovery of debts from other *émigrés*, and in petitioning the government for confirmation of his land grants and for compensation for the use of and damage to his properties during the War of 1812.

When the *Gentleman's Magazine* reported his death in 1827 "at Blythe-house, near Hammersmith, after a long and painful illness," Puisaye was described as "tall, well-formed, and graceful; his face was handsome, . . . and his eyes beamed with intelligence and spirit." The journal added that he "was well read, brought his knowledge to bear with facility and effect upon any subject, reasoned with force and precision, and spoke with a fluent and polished eloquence, which he often enlivened with flashes of playful or pointed wit." His persuasiveness, bravery, and energy had served the royalist cause well. Like many of the exiled French aristocracy, he was inordinately jealous of his rank and authority. When his failures and grandiose ambitions brought hostile comments, he became paranoid and used calumny and intrigue to destroy his critics. It was this sort of rivalry and backbiting that undermined French royalist undertakings, whether in France or in Canada.

PETER N. MOOGK

Joseph-Geneviève de Puisaye is the author of *Mémoires du comte Joseph de Puisaye . . . qui pourront servir à l'histoire du parti royaliste françois durant la dernière révolution* (6v., Londres, 1803–8); proclamations and other official publications issued in France under his name are listed in the *British Museum general catalogue* and the *Catalogue général des livres imprimés de la Bibliothèque nationale* (231v., Paris, 1897–1981).

A chalk portrait of the Comte de Puisaye and a watercolour painting of his home in Niagara are in the John Ross Robertson Canadian Hist. Coll. at the MTL.

AAQ, 20 A, I: 12–14; 210 A, IV: 10–11, 18–19, 42, 78. ANQ-Q, P-40/8: 476–80; P-289. AO, MS 88, Hamilton to St George, 8 Aug. 1808. Arch. du Ministère des Armées (Paris), Service d'hist. de l'Armée, classement généraux armées royales de l'intérieur concernant le général J.-G. de Puisaye. BL, Add. MSS 8075, 104: 1–120 (transcript at PAC). MTL, Laurent Quetton de St George papers; St George papers, sect.II; D. W. Smith papers, A11: 103–8; B5: 211–12, 221–22; B7: 353–56; B8: 159–60. Niagara North Land Registry Office (St Catharines, Ont.), Niagara Town and Township, abstract index to deeds, 1: 146v–47v. PAC, MG 11, [CO 42] Q, 57, pt.II: 372–73, 389–408; 140, pt.II: 393–94; 285: 465; 286: 478; 310: 289–90; 316: 217–22; 321: 172; 324: 423–24; MG 24, A6, letter-books, 1799–1805: 57–58, 89–91, 119, 139–40 (transcripts); RG 1, E14, 8: 579–80; L1, 22: 247, 330–1; 26: 21 (mfm. at AO); L3, 204: G5/52; RG 5, A1: 662–63; RG 8, I (C ser.), 14: 135–36; 77: 130–31; 106: 142–43; 515: 164; 556: 88, 90; 619: 4–151 [This source is invaluable. P.N.M.]; 620: 4–9, 34–62, 66–72, 81–84, 99–106, 109–10, 119–24, 140–41; 744: 39–40; RG 19, E5(a), 3732, claim 21; 3742, claim 173; 3745, claim 369. QUA, Richard Cartwright papers, letter-books, Cartwright introducing Puisaye to D. W. Smith, 4 Nov. 1798 (transcripts at AO). *Corr. of Hon. Peter Russell* (Cruikshank and Hunter), vols.2–3. "French royalists in Upper Canada," PAC *Report*, 1888: 73–87. *Gentleman's Magazine*, July–December 1827: 639–40. James Green, "Lettre de James Green au comte de Puisaye," *BRH*, 40 (1934): 644. *Inventaire des papiers de Léry conservés aux Archives de la province de Québec*, P.-G. Roy, édit. (3v., Québec, 1939–40). "Minutes of the Court of General Quarter Sessions of the Peace for the Home District, 13th March, 1800, to 28th December, 1811," AO *Report*, 1932: 3–4.

Caron, "Inv. de la corr. de Mgr Denaut," ANQ *Rapport*, 1931–32: 153–54, 157, 161, 181; "Inv. de la corr. de Mgr Plessis," ANQ *Rapport*, 1927–28: 218. *Landmarks of Canada; what art has done for Canadian history . . .* (2v., Toronto, 1917–21; repr. in 1v., 1967), nos.1214–15, 1305. Dionne, *Les ecclésiastiques et les royalistes français*. Maurice Hutt, *Chouannerie and counter-revolution: Puisaye, the princes, and the British government in the 1790s* (2v., Cambridge, Eng., and New York, 1983). L. E. Textor, *A colony of émigrés in Canada, 1798–1816* ([Toronto, 1905]). *Vendéens et chouans* (2v., Paris, 1980–81). Janet Carnochan, "The Count de Puisaye: a forgotten page of Canadian history," Niagara Hist. Soc., [*Pub.*], no.15 (2nd ed., 1913): 23–40. [A. J. Dooner, named] Brother Alfred, "The Windham or 'Oak Ridges' settlement of French royalist refugees in York County, Upper Canada, 1798," CCHA *Report*, 7 (1939–40): 11–26. Mrs Balmer [E. S.] Neilly, "The colony of French émigrés in York County, Ontario – 1798," Women's Canadian Hist. Soc. of Toronto, *Trans.*, no.25 (1924–25): 11–30. G. C. Patterson, "Land settlement in Upper Canada, 1783–1840," AO *Report*, 1920. P.-G. Roy, "Le nom Vallière de Saint-Réal était-il authentique?" *BRH*, 29 (1923): 164–67. Télesphore Saint-Pierre, "Le comte Joseph de Puisaye," *BRH*, 3 (1897): 146–48. Philippe Siguret, "Le comte de Puisaye . . . : épisode de la chouannerie dans le Perche," *Cahiers percherons* (Paris), no.17 (1963): 3–26 [An excellent article. P.N.M.].

PYKE, JOHN GEORGE, businessman, office holder, JP, militia officer, and politician; b. *c.* 1743 in England, son of John Pyke and Ann Scroope; m. 27 Aug. 1772 Elizabeth Allan, a sister of John Allan*, in Halifax, and they had 13 children, 9 of whom survived to adulthood; d. there 3 Sept. 1828.

The seven-year-old John George Pyke arrived in Nova Scotia with his parents in August 1750. In later years it was claimed that his father had arrived in 1749 with the settlers brought by Colonel Edward Cornwallis* to establish the town of Halifax, but there is no record of him in the passenger lists for that year. Almost certainly, John Pyke arrived on the *Alderney*, whose passengers became the first inhabitants of Dartmouth. Tragedy struck the family soon afterwards: in May 1751 John Pyke was killed by the Micmacs during a raid on the Dartmouth settlement, leaving the young John George and his mother in difficult circumstances. Fortunately, Ann Pyke remarried within two months of John's death. Her new husband was Richard Wenman*, soon to become a prominent figure in Halifax. Thanks to this match,

Quetton

John George came to maturity in comfortable circumstances.

Following the lead of his stepfather, Pyke established himself as a merchant. By 1773 he had built a wharf near the foot of Prince Street to carry on trade. Though it cannot be proved, it is almost certain that Richard Wenman provided his stepson with capital to establish himself in business. In any event, Pyke's position improved considerably when he inherited Wenman's properties, which included a brewery, in 1781. He retained ownership of the brewery until his death, and it likely provided a major portion of his income.

By the outbreak of the American Revolutionary War the young Pyke was a rising member of the circle of merchants, officials, and churchmen that held a tight grip on the affairs of Halifax. He was also increasingly influential as a politician. In 1779 he was elected as an MHA for Halifax County, a seat he was to retain until 1799. He was later to serve as MHA for Halifax Township from 1799 to 1800 and from 1802 to 1818. His political views were ardently conservative, and he fitted comfortably into the select group of pre-revolutionary Nova Scotians who sought to maintain their influence against loyal late comers. Beamish Murdoch* praised the "ready powers of debate" displayed by Pyke, Charles HILL, and others in the assembly of 1789–90.

Active as well in the municipal affairs of Halifax, Pyke was probably best known to the inhabitants of the town as magistrate in charge of the new police department, but he also served as a fire warden, roads commissioner, commissioner for the jail, and *custos rotulorum*. Militia, church, and charitable activities occupied a substantial portion of his time. He rose to the rank of colonel of the 1st Halifax Militia Regiment, and as an Anglican was a member of the congregation at St Paul's Church. He was also active in the Charitable Irish Society, occupying the presidency in 1808. Freemasonry was another of Pyke's enthusiasms. He was grand master of the masonic order from 1784 to 1785, and served another term as grand master from 1810 to 1820.

From the period immediately before the Revolutionary War to the time of his death in 1828, Pyke was a central figure in the growth of Halifax. He was in many ways typical of the men with connections of office, commerce, and church who led the development of the town. He left his heirs not only a substantial estate, but a very considerable record of service to his town and province. One of Pyke's daughters, Ann, married James IRVINE, a prominent Lower Canadian merchant and politician; one of his sons, George*, became a judge on the Court of King's Bench in Lower Canada.

Pyke's obituary notice in the *Novascotian, or Colonial Herald* claimed that "in the discharge of his Magisterial powers, great firmness, the utmost prudence, and the kindest forbearance marked his conduct. – He was always generous to the poor, and the lives of few individuals exhibited more genuine traits of benevolence." In his *History of Halifax City* Thomas Beamish Akins* gives us a picture of Pyke in office. "Old Colonel Pyke," Akins wrote, "presided as Chief Magistrate for many years, and was usually to be seen in the little police office in drab knee breeches with gray yarn stockings and snuff colored coat."

ANDREW ROBB

Halifax County Court of Probate (Halifax), Estate papers, P97 (J. G. Pyke) (mfm. at PANS). N.S., Dept. of Lands and Forests (Halifax), Crown land grants, general index, 1730–1937 (mfm. at PANS). PANS, MG 100, 211, no.416; RG 1, 35 (transcripts); 163. *Acadian Recorder*, 1818, 1828. *Nova-Scotia Gazette, and the Weekly Chronicle* (Halifax), 1781. *Novascotian, or Colonial Herald*, 4 Sept. 1828. *Royal Gazette and the Nova-Scotia Advertiser*, 1792. *Directory of N.S. MLAs*. Akins, *Hist. of Halifax City*. W. S. Bartlet, *The frontier missionary: a memoir of the life of the Rev. Jacob Bailey, A.M., missionary at Pownalborough, Maine; Cornwallis and Annapolis, N.S.* (Boston, 1853). A. W. H. Eaton, *The history of Kings County, Nova Scotia . . .* (Salem, Mass., 1910; repr. Belleville, Ont., 1972). "Masonic grand masters of the jurisdiction of Nova Scotia, 1738–1965," comp. E. T. Bliss (typescript, n.p., 1965; copy at PANS). T. M. Punch, "The Halifax connection, 1749–1848: a century of oligarchy in Nova Scotia" (MA thesis, St Mary's Univ., Halifax, 1972). D. A. Sutherland, "The merchants of Halifax, 1815–1850: a commercial class in pursuit of metropolitan status" (PHD thesis, Univ. of Toronto, 1975). G. A. White, *Halifax and its business . . .* (Halifax, 1876). *Acadian Recorder*, 12 Jan. 1918: 1.

Q

QUETTON ST GEORGE, LAURENT (born **Laurent Quet** though the family also used Quetton, adopted the surname St George in England in 1796 and signed Quetton St George thereafter, until his return to France in 1816, when he began to sign **Quetton de St Georges**), merchant and landowner; b. 4 June 1771 in Vérargues, near Montpellier, France, son of Jean and Catherine Quet; m. May 1819 Adèle de Barbeyrac, and they had a son; with Marguerite Vallière, daughter of a blacksmith at the Windham settlement north of York (Toronto), he had a son and a daughter; d. 8 June 1821 in Orléans, France.

It was the French revolution that launched the odyssey which transformed Laurent Quet into Quetton de St Georges. By 1789 he had begun mercantile training, but his family was so strongly Roman Catholic and royalist that it was soon swept up by events. Counter-revolutionary currents were strong and varied in the Hérault region, but a relatively small number of people chose or were forced to emigrate. His father and a brother were imprisoned, and in October 1791 Laurent and another brother, Étienne, decided to go into exile. Making their way to the Rhineland, they joined the Légion de Mirabeau in December as volunteers and saw action in Breisgau and Alsace; Étienne was killed in December 1793. In 1794–95, Laurent was a volunteer with the Légion de Béon in Holland, and in March 1795 he joined the royalist army of Brittany as sub-lieutenant in a cavalry regiment. Like Joseph-Geneviève de PUISAYE, he was a member of the invasion force that launched the disastrous and futile landing in June 1795 at the Baie de Quiberon in southwest Brittany. Fortunate to escape capture and almost certain execution, Laurent made his way back to England. Here, as the Comte de Chalus later attested, he and some fellow royalists adopted new surnames "to remove their families from the glory of the republic." He chose St George, it is said, because he had first arrived in England on St George's Day. On 1 April 1796 he was promoted major with the substantive rank of lieutenant-colonel in the royalist infantry. Probably in June 1796, but perhaps in 1798, he was inducted as a knight of Saint-Louis.

What to do with the royalist *émigrés* in England was a topic of increasing discussion. One scheme was put forward successfully by Puisaye, who arranged with British authorities a grant of land for a French military colony in Upper Canada. A group less suited to found a frontier agricultural community would be hard to imagine. St George, one of the 14 officers, was younger than most of them and from a less aristocratic background. He alone would succeed in the New World. The party arrived at Quebec in late 1798 and St George was among those who moved to the Windham settlement early in the spring of 1799. For the next two or three years, he engaged in the fur trade with nearby Indians. Evidence of his characteristically thorough preparation can be found in an extensive notebook that he kept of the Mississauga Ojibwas' vocabulary. He apparently traded in the Lake Simcoe region and had, for a time, a base at Lake Couchiching. It was a mobile and arduous existence but from it he emerged with connections to some of the most important fur merchants in North America, including John Jacob Astor in New York, and McTavish, McGillivray and Company and James and Andrew McGill and Company in Montreal.

In 1802, when Puisaye made plans to return to England, St George and a fellow officer, Ambroise de Farcy, decided to open a store in Puisaye's house near Niagara (Niagara-on-the-Lake). Puisaye would one day claim to have made possible St George's first steps up the commercial ladder, but this assertion exaggerated greatly his role in St George's specifically commercial career. By late July, St George and Farcy were advertising their wares. Almost immediately, St George moved to York to open a retail store. In 1803 he broke with Farcy, and until 1815 he was sole owner of Quetton St George and Company.

Like other Upper Canadian merchants of the time, St George was a generalist, handling every kind of imported goods and local produce as well as providing credit and other financial services. He dealt extensively with Montreal merchants and imported some items, notably tea, from New York. Soon he added branches to his operation, opening in 1806 at Kingston (with Augustin Boiton de Fougères, another royalist officer, in charge until 1810 and Hugh Christopher THOMSON thereafter), at Niagara (with Charles Fortier in charge until 1808), at Amherstburg late in 1807 (under the firm name of Boucherville and McDonell), and at the head of Lake Ontario in 1808, first near and then at Dundas (soon under Hector S. MacKay). All but the last were not only commercially promising communities but also centres of the province's small British garrison. Although the business operated mainly in English, it was possible for St George to correspond initially with all but the Dundas store in French. Within a few years furs had become at most a sideline; David DAVID, one of his leading Montreal connections, advised him in 1808 "either abandon that traid, or take more care of your Furs." He now handled as much flour and potash as fur and most of his payments were made in bills of exchange or cash. MacKay, at Dundas, also operated a distillery and a potashery. The firm's 1810 imports, worth at least £10,000 (Halifax currency), indicate that it was one of the most substantial businesses in the province. To operate so far-flung a network, St George had to travel and correspond extensively, to choose his clerks well, and to delegate effectively. It was quite unusual for a merchant so remote from major centres to be able to deal on an independent basis with as wide a range of suppliers as St George did, and this fact amply demonstrates his ability and reputation.

The expansion of his enterprises was accomplished despite St George's beginning on his own without partners and with little personal capital. By 1802, however, he had acquired the nearest substitute for capital, credit. His success at linking himself to the fur-trading network nicely illustrates how it was adjusting to the growth of settlement agriculture in Upper Canada. One key aspect of his rise was his decision to move from Niagara to York. There he and two other merchants, Alexander Wood* and William Allan*, became the dominant commercial figures for an entire generation.

Quetton

St George quickly established ties with the provincial government and especially the British army. He was never fully accepted by York's local élite, perhaps in part because so many of its members (William Jarvis*, for example) owed him money they could not afford to pay. One indication of this lack of acceptance was the Powell family's rejection of his "presumption" in wishing to propose marriage to their daughter ANNE in 1807. Though his prose style increasingly revealed only occasional gallicisms and spelling eccentricities, he spoke an imperfect English, if his own account is to be believed, and was thus marked as an outsider. His speech did not, however, affect his links to the garrison's officers, with whom he found much in common, as his very amicable correspondence, conducted in French, with Major William Halton, Lieutenant Governor Francis Gore*'s private secretary, reveals. His closest friend was likewise a slight outsider by the local élite's standards, Dr William Warren Baldwin*. St George was a good companion and had a widely acknowledged eye for a "petite fillette." Mrs Baldwin described him cheerfully as "a Frenchman still, a flatterer," and Dr Baldwin jestingly spoke of him as "almost entirely one of Epicureus's herd – with eating, drinking and frivolity." Since the army itself was a major spender and the provincial government also drew much of its money through the military chest at Quebec, St George's friendships with men who ran the garrison gave him access to the largest source of extra-provincial exchange. In effect, he provided financial services to the commissariat and other local branches of the forces, which regularly drew funds through him. As Robert Hamilton* had earlier done at Niagara, St George could use this exchange to sustain his payments and thus keep his credit high.

Risk-taking was essential to success, as an 1808 episode illustrates. St George ordered a large shipment of tea and other goods from New York City, then barred by the American government from export. With the help of a local man in "the Smugling Business," his clerk, Green Despard, tied up a Lewiston deputy sheriff and succeeded in bringing the goods across the Niagara River. St George had his share of unwise ventures, of bad debts, and of clerks who absconded, turned to drink, or otherwise proved unequal to the demands of business. Nevertheless, he was an effective manager of credit and of men. He was tested, for example, by his royalist officer colleagues, both as employees and customers, for they seem to have become somewhat jealous of his success and willing to presume upon old loyalties. While maintaining ties with them, he still controlled his losses from the actions of a Boiton or the credit given a Farcy or Chalus. He fiercely resisted what he saw as unwarranted claims by Puisaye. Though this seems not to have been an objective, he came to own a good deal of the land they had claimed as ex-officers. His relationship to employees had a military touch, as if they were junior officers and other ranks. His clerks were "young gentlemen" and his "sense of their fidelity" demanded his loyalty to them. In 1808–9 he defended one of his clerks, at considerable cost, in a legal case and refused to compromise. "You must permit me to withhold comployance with a proposition that should tend to impeach my honor and humanity and the entegrity of those in my employment."

With the War of 1812, increased military expenditures and the liquidity given to the provincial economy by the government issue of army bills further enhanced St George's ability to sell his goods profitably and to collect sums owing. Although he lost £2,000 by enemy action, he was undoubtedly able to compensate in other ways. His greatest problem was securing, at prices that were not prohibitively high, further goods to sell. He was financially able to order many goods direct from Great Britain, which he visited early in 1815. On his return to Upper Canada that spring he formed a partnership with John Spread Baldwin (William Warren's brother) and Jules-Maurice Quesnel*, two of his most trusted clerks, to run the business until the end of 1819. Planning an extended visit to France, he left York in May with a testimonial to his "honor and integrity" by York's society. Napoleon's return from Elba delayed his plans and he took the occasion to pass some agreeable months mainly at Quebec, where he apparently became engaged to a Mlle Baby. Still single, however, he set sail for England and France in November 1815.

He anticipated an early return to Upper Canada and continued to speak of business in his correspondence with friends there, though he soon lost touch with details. At a time of sharp deflation that undercut the value of lands and inventory and squeezed debtors mercilessly, Quesnel, John Spread Baldwin, and Dr Baldwin did a remarkable job of releasing capital from St George's assets in Upper Canada without crippling the ongoing business. Quetton St George and Company continued until December 1819, at which time St George's capital in it was still valued at £4,000. Thereafter, the firm was known as Baldwin and Quesnel.

Apart from his house and his share of the firm, St George also had substantial land holdings, evidently accumulated with a view to long-term returns. Management of all these assets could have been very costly, and it is testimony to both Baldwins' friendship, judgement, and honesty that St George did so well from them. How much money he extracted from Upper Canada is difficult to determine exactly, but it must have been no less than £20,000 (Halifax currency), quite enough to transform him into a landed

French gentleman. He acquired the domain of Engaran, near Montpellier, and invested at least 120,000 francs in French national debt securities.

After his marriage in 1819 St George revised his will, eliminating bequests to those with whom he had been associated in the Canadas, but leaving 50,000 francs to his natural daughter, now in a convent school in France. His natural son, working in Montreal, was not mentioned. It was not St George's French estate but rather his Upper Canadian lands (which still totalled 26,000 acres in 1831 when his title, in jeopardy because of his alien status, was finally confirmed by the Upper Canadian legislature) that became the basis for his legitimate son Henry's landed estate, Glen Lonely. Henry kept in touch with the Baldwins, then moved to the province in 1847 and became a naturalized British subject in 1849.

Quetton St George's career is unique, made so by his ability to function in France, in *émigré* society, and in frontier Upper Canada; by his rapid rise in rank in the army; by his success in trading alike with York gentlemen, frontier farmers, and Indians; by his courage in the face of physical danger and economic risk; and by his ultimate creation of himself as a royalist French country gentleman. Yet that career also illustrates the adaptability and resourcefulness needed by men who were caught up in the large events of his time and the elements involved in the business development of early Upper Canada. In his fashion, moreover, St George was a loyalist in Upper Canada himself. As he once wrote, "Revolution deprived me of my motherland, hence I will have the same devotion to the [land] that adopted me."

DOUGLAS MCCALLA

ANQ-Q, P-222. AO, MS 88. MTL, W. W. Baldwin papers, A90–91, B109–10; Laurent Quetton de St George papers; Quetton de St George papers, sect.II. T.-[R.]-V. [Boucher] de Boucherville, *A merchant's clerk in Upper Canada; the journal of Thomas Verchères de Boucherville, 1804–1811*, trans. with intro. by W. S. Wallace (Toronto, 1935).*Town of York, 1793–1815* (Firth); *1815–34* (Firth). Dionne, *Les ecclésiastiques et les royalistes français*, 127–65. Donald Greer, *The incidence of the emigration during the French revolution* (Cambridge, Mass., 1951; repr. Gloucester, Mass., 1966). Scadding, *Toronto of old* (Armstrong; 1966), 129–31. L. E. Textor, *A colony of émigrés in Canada, 1798–1816* ([Toronto], 1905]). T. W. Acheson, "John Baldwin: portrait of a colonial entrepreneur," *OH*, 61 (1969): 153–66; "The nature and structure of York commerce in the 1820s," *CHR*, 50 (1969): 406–28. R. J. Burns, "God's chosen people: the origins of Toronto society, 1793–1818," CHA *Hist. papers*, 1973: 213–28. Douglas McCalla, "The 'Loyalist' economy of Upper Canada, 1784–1806," *SH*, 16 (1983): 279–304.

QUÉVILLON, LOUIS (occasionally **Couvillon** or **Cuvillon**, but he always signed Louis Quévillon), woodworker, wood-carver, and contractor; b. 14 Oct. 1749 at Saint-Vincent-de-Paul (Laval, Que.), fourth of the eight children of Jean-Baptiste Quévillon and Marie-Anne Cadieux; d. there unmarried 9 March 1823.

Louis Quévillon's father, a habitant and militia captain of Saint-Vincent-de-Paul, died on 10 Dec. 1754. On 24 May 1756 his mother married François Chabot, a habitant from the same village. In her marriage contract she bound her second husband to look after the children of her first marriage. Louis was then six. He must have learned to read and write at an early age. Undoubtedly he did his apprenticeship in woodworking with a master carpenter during the 1760s. In this he was following in the footsteps of his older brother, Jean-Baptiste, himself a master joiner.

Quévillon began his career in woodworking at Saint-Vincent-de-Paul in the early 1770s. Around 1787 he was residing in Saint-Eustache. In 1790 he was back at Saint-Vincent-de-Paul, and six years later he was living at Belœil. Subsequently he settled down permanently at Saint-Vincent-de-Paul. Little is known about his activity before 1790. He shingled roofs and made window frames, doors, and chests of drawers. According to a newspaper of the period he learned wood-carving on his own, with the support and encouragement of some parish priests.

Early in the 1790s Quévillon began decoration of churches in the area around Saint-Vincent-de-Paul, at Sault-au-Récollet (Montreal North), and at Rivière-des-Prairies (Montreal). In the period between 1792 and 1800 he did work on the south shore of the St Lawrence, at Belœil, Saint-Ours, Saint-Marc, Saint-Mathias, and Varennes, carving tabernacles, the bases of altars, pulpits, and candlesticks. At Varennes he produced a retable (the structure housing the altar), his first large-scale creation. In 1798–99 he did various small pieces for the parishes in the north part of Montreal Island, at Saint-Laurent, Rivière-des-Prairies, and Sault-au-Récollet.

Between 1800 and 1805 Quévillon contracted to do large decorative works in the parishes of Nicolet, Verchères, Boucherville, Lanoraie, Vaudreuil, and Saint-Denis on the Richelieu. He also attempted at that time to break into the market in the Quebec region; he undertook projects at Saint-Henri-de-Lauzon (Saint-Henri), Saint-Michel, Rivière-Ouelle, and Sainte-Anne-de-la-Pocatière (La Pocatière). The volume of his production suggests that he collaborated with another wood-carver. It is probable that Joseph Pépin* was his apprentice; they had known each other at least since 1791, when they were both living in Saint-Vincent-de-Paul, and in 1803 Pépin was doing wood-carving with Quévillon at Boucherville. No partnership agreement between the two wood-carvers for that period has been found, however.

From 1805 to 1810 Quévillon did wood-carving,

Raby

gilding, silvering, and painting for the churches at Sainte-Thérèse-de-Blainville (Sainte-Thérèse), Rigaud, Lachenaie, Saint-Hyacinthe, Belœil, Saint-Eustache, Sainte-Anne-des-Plaines, Saint-Laurent on Île d'Orléans, L'Assomption, Cap-Santé, Saint-Jean-Baptiste-de-Rouville, Soulanges (Les Cèdres), and the parish of Notre-Dame in Montreal. Later his collaboration with Pépin became more evident; they worked together at Belœil and Soulanges. Amable Charron* worked with Quévillon between 1808 and 1812, as did Urbain Desrochers* at Saint-Michel in 1809.

Between 1810 and 1815 Quévillon undertook wood-carvings to decorate the parish churches of Sainte-Rose (Laval), Longueuil, Saint-Cuthbert, and Terrebonne. René Beauvais*, dit Saint-James, apparently began to collaborate with Quévillon at that time. Charron and others also joined him for the wood-carvings at Saint-Michel and Saint-Martin (Laval). In 1812 Paul Rollin* and Quévillon were working as partners.

On 3 Feb. 1815 Quévillon formed a partnership with Pépin, Beauvais, dit Saint-James, and Rollin. They contracted for the wood-carving at Pointe-Claire, which was taken in hand by André Achim after the dissolution of their association. Pieces contracted for prior to their partnership were carried out independently. Accordingly Quévillon did carvings in the parishes where he had made previous agreements, and among other things he did the relievo for the Stations of the Cross at the mission of Lac-des-Deux-Montagnes (Oka). The four worked together on the carvings for the church in Varennes. Their association was dissolved in January 1817 and Quévillon then joined with Beauvais, dit Saint-James. Subsequently he worked in the churches at Repentigny, Chambly, Verchères, Saint-Martin, and on Île Dupas. With Beauvais, dit Saint-James, he did carving, gilding, and painting in the churches of Saint-Eustache and Sainte-Geneviève.

Throughout his career Quévillon had many apprentices, undertaking to teach them the woodworker's and wood-carver's craft and to provide them with board and lodging. Around 1815, for example, the workshop was employing some 15 people, whose tasks were undoubtedly well defined. The number of parishes in which Quévillon did carving is impressive, about 40. His works and those from his shop were numerous, but many have been lost in fires. His retable in the church of Verchères can still be viewed, as can a few pieces of church furniture in the Musée du Québec, the museum of the Collège Saint-Laurent, the Montreal Museum of Fine Arts, and the National Gallery.

Louis Quévillon standardized the different elements in his wood-carvings. He created a process of mass production. His gift lay in making maximum use of the apprentices and journeymen in his shop and thus in successfully utilizing specialized but inexpensive labour. Quévillon displayed no great originality in his production. Over and over again he used motifs and forms that had been created by Philippe Liébert*. But unlike Liébert he emphasized quantity of output and in the space of 20 years flooded the market in the Montreal region. In his workshop he established the standards for 19th-century religious wood-carving.

NICOLE CLOUTIER

ANQ-M, CE1-4, 14 oct. 1749; CE1-22, 14 févr. 1803; CE1-59, 10 déc. 1754, 24 mai 1756, 15 juill. 1791, 30 oct. 1808, 11 mars 1823; CN1-16, 19 sept. 1812; CN1-47, 4 mars 1790; CN1-68, 12 févr. 1817; CN1-96, 19 juin 1808; 19 févr., 13 juill. 1812; 2 sept. 1816; 25 janv., 17 avril, 10 oct. 1817; 15 févr. 1820; 14 oct. 1822; CN1-98, 25 juill. 1744; 19 mai, 10 juin 1756; CN1-108, 17 mars 1745; CN1-121, 14 mai 1810; CN1-136, 30 avril 1809; CN1-158, 28 juin 1774; CN1-167, 25 mai 1801; CN1-273, 5 mai 1810, 1er févr. 1811; CN1-295, 14 juill. 1796; CN1-317, 5 mars 1820; CN1-334, 3 févr. 1815; CN1-383, 14 juill. 1816; CN1-391, 6 sept. 1819, 11 oct. 1820; CN3-2, 11 juill. 1818, 12 févr. 1820; CN3-7, 29 déc. 1770; CN3-11, 16 févr. 1787, 28 déc. 1806. ANQ-MBF, CN1-6, 12 oct. 1800; CN1-31, 9 févr. 1803; CN1-79, 26 avril 1816. ANQ-Q, CN3-17, 4 août 1805, 4 août 1806. MAC-CD, Fonds Morisset, 2, dossier Louis Quévillon. F.-M. Bibaud, Le Panthéon canadien (A. et V. Bibaud; 1891). [L.-A. Huguet-Latour], Annuaire de Ville-Marie, origine, utilité et progrès des institutions catholiques de Montréal . . . (2v., Montréal, 1863–82). Émile Vaillancourt, Une maîtrise d'art en Canada (1800–1823) (Montréal, 1920). Gérard Morisset, "Louis Quévillon, fondateur de l'école des Ecorres, 1749–1823," La Patrie (Montréal), 2 oct. 1949: 112. Émile Vaillancourt, "La maîtrise des Ecorres: l'œuvre de Louis Quévillon," La Presse, 24 déc. 1926: 19.

R

RABY, AUGUSTIN-JÉRÔME, militia officer, pilot, and politician; b. 10 Nov. 1745 at Quebec, son of Augustin Raby* and Françoise Delisle; m. there first 16 Sept. 1771 Catherine Chauveaux; m. there secondly 22 Nov. 1784 Marie-Gillette Turgeon; two daughters and one son were born of these marriages; d. 20 Sept. 1822 at Quebec.

Augustin-Jérôme Raby received a primary education and embarked upon a mariner's career, likely by becoming an apprentice to his father, who was well

Raizenne

known in the 18th century as a leading local figure in the shipping world. Until 1780 little trace of his career has been found; he received his licence as a St Lawrence pilot in the 1780s, and worked as one until he was appointed superintendent of St Lawrence pilots on 31 March 1797. In 1805 the governor reconfirmed him in his post and made him an officer of Trinity House at Quebec.

Founded that year, Trinity House was entrusted with important responsibilities related to maritime concerns in Lower Canada: supervision of pilotage, administration of port and marine facilities, and improvement of navigation on the St Lawrence. Raby drew up plans to facilitate shipping through construction of a lighthouse on Île Verte, which was built by Edward Cannon* in 1808, and the placing of various buoys and markers at the most dangerous spots between Saint-Roch-des-Aulnaies and Quebec. In supervising the work of the pilots, who were bound by numerous rules and a multitude of regulations, he had to see that offenders were fined or suspended in punishment, and to recommend new candidates for the pilot's licence. As a means of ensuring the quality of work, a pilot, each time he took a ship in or out, had to draw up a report to be submitted to the authorities by the captain or master.

Raby's last years as superintendent of pilots were very difficult. The minutes of Trinity House several times mention that he could no longer carry out his duties effectively because of his advanced age and precarious health and that several people were taking advantage of the situation to contravene the rules and regulations. Trinity House, which recognized his long years of devotion to duty, wanted him to retain the privileges that went with the function, but at the same time wanted to shield him from responsibilities increasingly onerous for a man who was ill and quite old. In 1821 it accepted Robert Young's offer to assume all the duties of the superintendent of pilots without charge, on condition that Trinity House guarantee him the post and its privileges upon Raby's death.

Raby had been active in Quebec society. He joined the militia and took part as a lieutenant in the defence of the town when it was besieged during the American revolution. Being concerned about educational problems, he signed the petition in 1790 requesting that a university be founded in the province. He became a member of the Fire Society in 1795, and of the Agriculture Society in 1821. In 1807 his fellow Catholics recognized his social status by appointing him a churchwarden of the parish of Notre-Dame, an office he held until 1814. Raby also took an interest in political life. He was elected to the House of Assembly for Lower Town Quebec in 1796, and four years later he ran in Upper Town, defeating William Grant*. He sat in the assembly until 1804 and at first supported the Canadian party. But in the third parlia-

ment (1801–4) he was one of the five Canadians who were sympathetic to the English party.

ROCH LAUZIER

ANQ-Q, CE1-1, 10 nov. 1745, 16 sept. 1771, 22 nov. 1784, 23 sept. 1822. Ports Canada Arch. (Quebec), Trinity House, Quebec, minute-books, IV. "Les dénombrements de Québec" (Plessis), ANQ Rapport, 1948–49. Quebec Gazette, 4 Nov. 1790; 25 June 1795; 30 March, 31 May 1797; 9 Aug. 1821. F.-J. Audet, "Les législateurs du Bas-Canada." Desjardins, Guide parl. Le Jeune, Dictionnaire. Tanguay, Dictionnaire. "Les disparus," BRH, 32 (1926): 362. Hare, "L'Assemblée législative du Bas-Canada," RHAF, 27: 361–95. P.-G. Roy, "Le pilote Raby," BRH, 13 (1907): 124–26.

RADSTOCK, WILLIAM WALDEGRAVE, 1st Baron. See WALDEGRAVE

RAIZENNE (Rézine), MARIE-CLOTILDE, named **Marie de l'Incarnation,** member of the Sisters of Charity of the Hôpital Général of Montreal (Grey Nuns), founder of the Congrégation de l'Enfant-Jésus, and educator; b. 12 April 1766 at Lac-des-Deux-Montagnes (Oka), Que., daughter of Jean-Baptiste-Jérôme Raizenne, farmer, and Marie-Charlotte Sabourin; d. 21 Aug. 1829 in Sandwich (Windsor), Upper Canada.

Marie-Clotilde Raizenne's paternal grandparents, Josiah Rising and Abigail Nims, and her maternal grandmother, Sara Enneson (Anson), were captured as children by Indians during raids into New England and were raised by them in the Montreal area [see Marie Raizenne*, named Saint-Ignace]. Marie-Clotilde herself grew up in a pious, orderly Quebec family in which seven of the ten children were to have vocations in the church. She attended the mission school at Lac-des-Deux-Montagnes for three years, and may have learned Mohawk. On 14 Feb. 1785 she entered the Grey Nuns at the Hôpital Général of Montreal. Appointed sacristan, Sister Raizenne displayed promise as an administrator and a gift for needlework. She became treasurer, and in 1811 was placed in charge of the men's wing. On 23 Feb. 1821 she was elected assistant to the superior. She was accustomed to copy into notebooks prayers, references to family events, and items of the Grey Nuns' history. One of these notebooks was later used to locate the grave of the community's founder, Marie-Marguerite d'Youville [Dufrost* de Lajemmerais].

In 1822 Bishop Alexander McDonell*, looking for nuns to operate a school for young girls in Upper Canada, extended an invitation to the Grey Nuns. This invitation, which the community declined, changed the course of Sister Raizenne's life. She became determined to go to Upper Canada herself and overcame difficulties raised by relatives, the views

627

Randal

held in her religious community, and even the reservations of members of the hierarchy. On 8 March 1828 Bishop Bernard-Claude PANET released her from obligations to the Grey Nuns so that she might found the Congrégation de l'Enfant-Jésus. Bishop McDonell had originally intended that Sister Raizenne's school should be located in Kingston, but by May 1828, "taking into consideration her being a Canadian speaking the French language and several other circumstances," he had concluded that the Western District would be more appropriate. Illness delayed McDonell's final authorization of the school; it was not until 9 Oct. 1828 that the 62-year-old sister, accompanied by two nieces and by Della McCord, left Montreal for McDonell's residence in St Raphaels, Upper Canada, where she put on her new religious habit and took the name Marie de l'Incarnation.

Uncertainty arising from McDonell's illness had also slowed preparations in the Western District for her coming, but the letter she wrote to Lieutenant Governor Sir John Colborne* on 17 Dec. 1828 gave no hint of the confusion attending her unannounced arrival at Amherstburg and subsequent move to Sandwich. McDonell was optimistic about the future of the enterprise, telling François Baby* that it would succeed if obstacles were not placed in its way "by the people themselves." For a time it seemed that his expectation was to be fulfilled. On 14 July 1829 Raizenne wrote to Bishop Panet that 50 children attended the school, the postulants had received the habit, and several candidates would enter the congregation when the convent was completed. But only five weeks later, on 21 Aug. 1829, she died after a short illness. She was buried beneath the parish church but on 24 Sept. 1850 her remains were transferred to the present Assumption Church.

The talents and tenacity of the congregation's founder, combined with her family background and experience as a Grey Nun, might have overcome pioneer difficulties in Sandwich. Without her leadership the novices dispersed after a few years, leaving Raizenne as the first and only member of the Congrégation de l'Enfant-Jésus.

ROBERT J. SCOLLARD

AAQ, 210 A, X: 374; 320 CN, IV: 177. ACAM, RC, I: f.160; RLL, IV: 319–20, 322, 325, 398, 408, 415; V: 139, 143. Arch. de la Compagnie de Jésus, prov. du Canada français (Saint-Jérôme, Qué.), 4072, Pierre Point, report for 1850 (copy at Assumption Church, Windsor, Ont.). Arch. des Sœurs Grises (Montréal), J. P. Macdonald à Sœur Raizenne, 24 avril, 3 juin 1828; Nécrologe, no.48; M.-C. Raizenne, cahier; formule des vœux, 14 févr. 1787; Reg. de vêture et profession, no.29. Arch. of the Archdiocese of Kingston (Kingston, Ont.), AI (Alexander Macdonell papers, corr.), 23 May 1828–20 June 1832 (transcripts at AO). Arch. of the Archdiocese of Toronto, M (Macdonell papers), AB03.03, 09.02, 20.05–6, 45.02; AC21.03–5, 22.03; CA04.01–2. ASSM, 21, Joseph Crevier à Macdonell, 25 août 1829; Macdonell à Roux, 12 sept. 1829. Assumption Church, Reg. of burials, 22 Aug. 1829. Private arch., Joseph Finn (Chatham, Ont.), R. H. Dignan, "History of the Diocese of London" (photocopy at Arch. of the Diocese of London (London, Ont.)). Dictionnaire national des Canadiens français (1608–1760) (3v., Montréal, 1965). Tanguay, Dictionnaire. [É.-M. Faillon], Vie de la sœur Bourgeoys, fondatrice de la Congrégation de Notre-Dame de Villemarie en Canada, suivie de l'histoire de cet institut jusqu'à ce jour (2v., Villemarie [Montréal], 1853); Vie de Mme d'Youville, fondatrice des Sœurs de la Charité de Villemarie dans l'île de Montréal, en Canada (Villemarie, 1852). [Albina Fauteux et Clémentine Drouin], L'Hôpital Général des Sœurs de la charité (Sœurs Grises) depuis sa fondation jusqu'à nos jours (3v. parus, Montréal, 1916–?), 1–2. [Guillemine Raizenne, named] Sœur Saint-Jean l'Évangéliste, Notes historiques sur la famille Raizenne . . . ([Ottawa], 1932). E. J. Lajeunesse, "The coming of the first nun to Upper Canada," CCHA Report, 22 (1955): 27–37.

RANDAL, ROBERT (before about 1809 he signed **Randall**), businessman and politician; b. c. 1766 probably in Harford County, Md; probably unmarried, he had a daughter by Deborah Pettit; d. 2 May 1834 at Gravelly Bay, Niagara District, Upper Canada.

Some secondary sources make Robert Randal a Virginian, but the earliest and best evidence traces him to Harford County in northeastern Maryland. Little is known of him before 1795, when he achieved notoriety as the first person cited for contempt for trying to bribe members of the United States Congress. In September 1795, Randal and two Vermonters had joined seven Detroit merchants, including John Askin* and William Robertson*, in a partnership to buy the lower Michigan peninsula, now to be open for American settlers, from the United States government. The associates planned to sell their scheme not only by bribing federal legislators with shares in the land but also by urging that, because Major-General Anthony Wayne had not effectually cowed the Indians in the battle of Fallen Timbers, the influence of the Detroit merchants with them was needed to persuade them to surrender their territory.

Randal and his American associates set about lobbying congressmen, Randal indiscreetly enough to be cited for contempt. Apart from the attempted bribery, several legislators took offence at Randal's private claims that 30 or 40 congressmen had already joined in and only a few more were needed. Randal claimed in his defence that he had not thought his proposals improper since the scheme would benefit the public, and complaisant legislators were not to receive any special consideration but merely to take part in the purchase on the same terms as the partners. His punishment was confined to a reprimand and a few days in custody.

When he visited Upper Canada in 1795, Randal had had other business dealings. Lieutenant Governor John Graves Simcoe* had recently granted John

McGILL and Benjamin Canby a 999-year lease of a prime four-acre mill seat on the Niagara River, where they had built a grist-mill and a sawmill. In October, Randal concluded a provisional agreement with Canby to buy a one-third share in this concern. The agreement lapsed, but Randal's interest in the site did not. In November 1798 he reappeared in Upper Canada and petitioned for a 999-year lease of a riparian tract, immediately north of the McGill–Canby grant, on which to erect an iron foundry. He also asked for an adequate wood-lot, the right to mine ore near by, and a 12-year monopoly of iron manufacture to compensate him for his investment.

At the time of the bribery scandal in 1795, Randal was said to have recently been "insolvent." Now, however, he produced letters of credit to the amount of £1,950 (Halifax currency) and assured the Executive Council that "General Christie" (perhaps General Gabriel Christie* of Montreal) would extend him credit to any amount. He presented letters of introduction including one from Robert Hamilton*, the preeminent Niagara merchant, which stated that Randal possessed "very respectable recommendations" from some of Hamilton's friends in New York. The council turned down Randal's first petition, but when he persisted they authorized him to proceed on the understanding that he would receive the desired lease once he had fulfilled his undertaking to make iron on the site. Randal then contracted to buy the adjoining mills from McGill and Canby's successors in the lease, Elijah Phelps and David Ramsay, as well as 1,200 acres in Wainfleet Township which they owned in fee simple. By these transactions, Randal constructed the cross on which he was to suffer for the rest of his life and inaugurated a train of events that was to make him, in the eyes of many Upper Canadians, the colony's foremost martyr to puissant greed.

Randal erected his forge and began making iron, but he soon ran into financial difficulties. In June 1800 he signed two-thirds of the business over to his Montreal suppliers, Nathaniel Burton and James Maitland McCulloch, in liquidation of a debt of £1,600. In 1802 Burton and McCulloch commissioned Randal to buy and grind enough wheat to ship 6,000 barrels of flour to England, flour which Randal later claimed was the first ever manufactured in Upper Canada for the European market. The speculation was either the ruin of their fortunes or a vain effort to recoup them; either way, by June 1802 Burton and McCulloch were bankrupt. They disposed of their interest in the Bridgewater Works (as Randal had named it) to their British creditors, Caldcleugh, Boyd, and Reid, who sent out James DURAND as their agent to assume control of the property.

A subsequent series of transactions in October 1802 left Randal as a one-third partner in the concern, with Durand holding the other two-thirds as agent for Caldcleugh, Boyd, and Reid. For some months

Randal continued to manage the property, but in August 1803 he went east, leaving it in the hands of Durand and their clerk, Samuel Street*. He bought land on the American side of the St Lawrence River, opposite Cornwall, erecting a tannery and potash works and setting up a ferry. In the summer of 1804 he established a mercantile concern at Cornwall. By his own later account, he undertook all these enterprises virtually on a whim, because he had some spare cash and nothing to do.

From the start, Randal encountered difficulty in receiving the payments due to him from Durand, who bought out his principals in 1804 and took Street into partnership. In 1806 Randal suffered a serious blow when Phelps, who had never surrendered the legal title, resumed possession of the property by ejectment, of which Durand kept Randal in ignorance. Phelps then let the property to Street. It is unclear whether Street and Durand were still partners, or whether any of these transactions constituted a collusive endeavour to dispossess Randal; but it was Durand from whom Street and his new partner, Thomas CLARK, were later to claim title by an instrument of 1810.

Far off in Cornwall, Randal was unable to protect his interests. By 1806 he was in debt to the amount of £3,000. He spent the second half of 1807 determinedly dodging the writs of his creditors (mostly Montreal merchants) while nagging them to grant him an amnesty that would let him proceed about his business without fear of arrest. Despite the initial obduracy of the merchant Samuel David (whom Randal accused of "a Jewish persecution," citing Shylock's persistent demand for his pound of flesh), the amnesty was obtained in April 1808.

Randal's scheme to recoup his fortunes entailed building an ironworks on a superb site he hoped to acquire by grant from the crown at the Chaudière Falls on the Ottawa River. These works were to be supplied from "an inexhaustible iron bank, a mountain of the richest & best quality rock ore," which he had acquired by grant across the river in Hull Township, Lower Canada (for which purpose he claimed to have left the Niagara area in 1803). His hopes were dashed in March 1809 when, just after he had finally acquired the Chaudière property, he was arrested for debt in Montreal. For the next six and a half years he languished in prison at the mercy of whichever of his creditors was to blame. He and his friends always claimed that his oppressor was Thomas Clark. After Clark and Street had forced Durand to sell them the major interest in the Bridgewater property in 1810, Clark visited Randal in prison in 1812 to press him to dispose of his share. While in Montreal, he sued Randal for a debt owed to the concern. Randal always claimed that this was an accounting transaction, but as an incarcerated debtor he was unable to defend himself. A note in his papers records one man's testimony that he had heard Clark and two others exulting at having Randal in their power; and it is additional, circumstantial evidence of Clark's responsibility that Randal was released only in October 1815, just after Clark had procured the Executive Council's fulfilment of an order of the imperial government to grant him the freehold of the Bridgewater site, which until then had been alienated only by lease.

Upon his release, Randal returned to the Niagara area, bent on resuming the Bridgewater property and asserting his right to the expected government compensation for damages in the recent war with the United States. His legal counsel was Attorney General D'Arcy BOULTON, whom he had employed when at Cornwall. Randal's first step was to institute an action for damages against Phelps for failing to transfer the legal title to his half of the property as provided by their contract of 1799. Randal could already produce evidence of legal title to Ramsay's half, and he apparently hoped that a successful action against Phelps, affirming his title in equity to the other half, would sustain a petition to the government to void as improvident the freehold grant to Clark, on the grounds that Clark had procured it by falsely representing himself to be the lawful tenant under the lease of 1794.

At the Niagara District Assizes of 1816, Randal won his case and nominal damages, the actual amount to be determined later by arbitration; but his opponents refused to agree to an impartial arbitrator and the matter came to trial again the following year. This time Phelps produced new evidence. In pressing their claim to the Bridgewater freehold, Clark and Street had asserted that the original deed of lease to McGill and Canby had been burnt during a fire in 1806. Now it was brought forward, endorsed with an instrument dated June 1801 by which Phelps and Ramsay had purportedly transferred the lease to Burton and McCulloch. Phelps claimed he had done this at Randal's behest in fulfilment of their contract of 1799, and he supported his claim by the testimony of two local notables, Robert NICHOL and William Dickson*, that Randal had been present and consenting at the time of the transfer. If valid, this instrument constituted grounds for the argument that Randal had renounced all title to the premises in 1801, and the one-third share he claimed under his agreement with Durand in October 1802 was a new interest which he had later forfeited by failing to fulfil the agreement. Phelps's claim was absurd on the face of it, however, since Randal (who always denied the validity of the instrument) could have transferred the lease by his own hand had he wished. Randal was also able to produce verbal testimony of McCulloch's denial that he and Burton had ever possessed title to the property. The jury awarded Randal £10,000 in damages, but the

Court of King's Bench ordered a new trial on the grounds that the award was excessive.

Before the assizes in 1818 D'Arcy Boulton was elevated to the King's Bench and his son, acting solicitor general Henry John Boulton*, took over Randal's cause. By now the Boultons had a substantial unpaid bill against their client, who was penniless until he could successfully assert his claim to the property in dispute. The younger Boulton refused to act unless Randal gave him a note of hand for £25 and security for a further £100. After Randal had given him the note and a mortgage on a lot he owned, Boulton went into court; but the presiding judge was his father, who refused to hear the case on the grounds that he had formerly acted in it. The action was held over for another year. Randal and his friends always claimed that H. J. Boulton must have known, or at least guessed, that his father would refuse to hear the case, though the solicitor general denied it.

Before the assizes of 1819, Randal's debt to Boulton fell due. He could not pay it, and Boulton instituted proceedings against him in the Home District. Randal heard nothing further after the initial notice and assumed, he later claimed, that Boulton had not proceeded to trial. In fact, he had done so and obtained judgement without Randal's knowledge. In doing so he broke at least three rules of the Court of King's Bench and unfairly exploited another rule, possibly promulgated *ultra vires*, which allowed a creditor to proceed to judgement without notifying the debtor when the latter lived outside the district in which the action was brought. To satisfy this judgement, Boulton attached the whole of Randal's 1,000-acre property at the Chaudière Falls. In 1820 it was sold for £449: far more than the amount of Randal's debt, but only a tiny fraction of its actual value, which was becoming known as a result of the area's recent opening to settlement. The purchasers were John Le Breton*, a half-pay army officer who had tried in 1819 to buy a piece of it from Randal, and Levius Peters Sherwood*, a Brockville notable who became in 1825 a judge of the King's Bench. When Randal learned of the sale, in January 1821, he instituted an appeal in *Boulton* v. *Randal*. The case was of such a nature that Alexander Stewart, Randal's attorney and a self-proclaimed "old Tory," later said of it that "a more rascally proceeding never disgraced the administration of justice in any country"; nevertheless, Randal's appeal was in vain. It is noteworthy that, while Randal may not have heard of the *sale* before 1821, he had heard of the judgement (though he later denied it) by December 1819. Perhaps, not imagining it would cause him such loss, he had preferred at the time to let the matter go by default. It is more likely, however, that he had simply become disenchanted with the legal process; for in December 1819 the breach with Boulton had just brought about the ruin of all his hopes.

In August of that year *Randal* v. *Phelps* had come on at the Niagara District Assizes for the fourth year in a row. The plaintiff, bereft of counsel, was forced to conduct his own case; Attorney General John Beverley Robinson* represented the defendant. The result of so unequal a contest was a foregone conclusion: the same evidence that had failed Phelps in 1817 now sufficed to secure a verdict in his favour. By Randal's own account, however, this result was achieved only with the help of an extraordinary act of oppression by the presiding judge, Chief Justice William Dummer POWELL. In a letter written soon afterwards, Randal asserted that Powell had threatened the jury with a writ of attaint if they found for the plaintiff (i.e., against the evidence as Powell interpreted it). This procedure had fallen into desuetude in England by the end of the 17th century. At the same assizes, Randal was successfully sued by Clark on the judgement he had won in Montreal in 1812. This decision was to lead to a sheriff's sale of Randal's 1,200-acre estate in Wainfleet, which Clark himself bought for the derisory price of £40.

Until now, Randal had evinced little interest in Upper Canadian politics, and such evidence as exists suggests that his predilections in American politics were conservative. Now it appeared that his experiences had radicalized him. A letter to an unidentified friend reveals, though incoherently, his disaffection. "Every coercive measure has been taken and admited on the part of Powell and Cambell [William CAMPBELL] to restrain my legal and equitable rights, to arme Clark, in withholding from me, my property. These are dispotic days; a sort of Mock Military, or tantalized Civil Government, a good deal like the Executive Religion in this Province. . . . I have now been a Victim to its influence for Ten Years." He accused the judges of intending to restrict his movements by exposing him to arrest for debt, and blamed the Executive Council for making an improvident grant of the Bridgewater freehold when Clark had clearly deluded the imperial government into believing that he and Street were the rightful tenants. He swore he would take revenge on the judges and Robinson by pursuing their impeachment in the provincial legislature, on Durand by suing him for breach of contract, and on Durand, Phelps, Clark, Street, Dickson, and Nichol by presenting them for perjury at the next Niagara Assizes.

Randal did none of these things. Instead, in July 1820, he stood in the riding of 4th Lincoln for the House of Assembly. In his election address he appealed to the popular dislike of aristocracy, favouritism, and patronage, assailed abuses in the administration of justice, and asserted the importance of electing men who would not become "puppets to executive influence." (This last declaration was a thrust against his opponent Isaac SWAYZE, MHA for

Lincoln in the last legislature, who had instituted the proceedings leading to Robert Gourlay*'s expulsion under the Sedition Act the previous year.) Observing that "it is private injuries that produce public grievances," he called for "an equal distribution of Justice" and "a liberal dispensation of rights." Upper Canada's constitution was mild and its laws just, but both were perverted by a "Maniac interest; that knows no bounds but the crush of its own weight." Randal, by now a popular hero, won easily. He was to remain MHA for Lincoln until his death.

In a series of initiatives taken during 1824, Randal continued his personal quest for justice against Clark, Street, and Boulton with the help of the brilliant young advocate, John Rolph*. An action for ejectment against Clark and Street failed because Randal could show a legal title to only the Ramsay half of the property. A second attempt to reopen *Boulton* v. *Randal* foundered because it had already been appealed in vain; a final attempt to do so never came to a decision, because both D'Arcy Boulton and his successor on the bench, Sherwood, were interested parties.

Randal also sought satisfaction by petitions to both the executive and the legislature. The governor-in-chief, Lord Dalhousie [Ramsay*], was sympathetic to his case concerning the Chaudière property, because the Lower Canadian government had been anxious to buy part of it at the very moment of the shrieval sale and he believed that Captain Le Breton had bid for it in that knowledge. Petitioning in 1822, when the proposed union of Upper and Lower Canada was a leading political question, Randal noted that the property (which lies immediately west of today's downtown Ottawa) was the most central site for the capital of the united province. In 1828, when the founding of Bytown at last nerved Sherwood to test his title by an action of ejectment against Randal's tenants, Dalhousie ordered Robinson to defend the case, but he found an excuse to refuse. With Chief Justice Campbell absent in England, John Walpole Willis* just dismissed from the bench, and judge Sherwood an interested party, the case was heard by the then puisne justice Christopher Alexander Hagerman*, who found for Sherwood at the assizes in August and then, a few months later, dismissed the appeal against his own errors in the Court of King's Bench. Randal's petitions to the lieutenant governor in council and the imperial government, seeking avoidance of the Chaudière sale and annulment of the Bridgewater freehold as an improvident grant, also failed. Those to the assembly evoked a swingeing denunciation of H. J. Boulton's conduct but no practical benefit. Since Randal's quest for justice was hampered by the colony's lack of an equity tribunal, the assembly passed bills in 1828 and 1830 erecting a court of chancery for the special purpose of inquiring

Randal

into his wrongs, but both bills failed in the Legislative Council.

Nevertheless, Randal's persistence made him a popular hero and led his enemies in the Niagara area to make another, and this time ill-judged, effort to crush him in the courts. In swearing to his qualification for parliamentary office at the general election of 1824, he claimed ownership of all the properties of which they had despoiled him. His defiance provoked Samuel Street and William Johnson Kerr* to present him for perjury at the Niagara Assizes of 1825. The trial was notable for Rolph's brilliant defence of Randal. After discrediting the prosecution by forcing Clark to confess to his attempts to coerce Randal in prison in Montreal in 1812 (a confession which threw doubt on Clark's claim to have been the lawful tenant of the Bridgewater property from 1810 on), Rolph closed with a speech which implicated the entire judicial establishment in Randal's persecution and secured his client's acquittal despite Chief Justice Campbell's hostile summing-up.

Two years later, Randal enjoyed a more devastating triumph over his enemies. In 1827 the provincial legislature passed an act to confer political and civil rights on all those residents of Upper Canada (the majority of those of North American origin and some foreign military settlers) who had been adjudged aliens by virtue of the English court case *Thomas* v. *Acklam* (1824). The terms of this legislation had been dictated by the Colonial Office and were highly obnoxious to many whom it affected. A petition for its disallowance was got up, and the steering committee, which included Jesse Ketchum*, appointed Randal to present the request to the imperial government and parliament. He was courteously received by the colonial secretary, Lord Goderich, and the parliamentary undersecretary, Robert John Wilmot-Horton, and returned with their promise that the colonial government would be instructed to bring in acceptable legislation. If this was not passed at the next session of the provincial legislature, it would be enacted at Westminster.

The success of Randal's mission was a staggering shock to the Upper Canadian political establishment. True, the petitioners had been lucky, in that one of the objectionable clauses – that which made naturalization conditional on the beneficiary's abjuration of his former allegiance – was now unacceptable to the British government for reasons of high policy. Nevertheless, the courteous treatment accorded Randal, whom they particularly despised, and his evident influence on the thinking of the imperial authorities, left Lieutenant Governor Sir Peregrine Maitland* and his advisers feeling betrayed (even though Goderich stated publicly that it was not they, but the Colonial Office, who were responsible for the legislation of 1827).

Randal's vendetta with the Niagara area élite persisted. Aided by the vagaries of imperial policy, he managed to postpone payment of most of the war losses compensation for the Bridgewater property to Clark and Street until 1833. This delay was despite the fact that, nine years earlier, Maitland had assigned the task of adjudicating the conflicting claims to their counsel, Attorney General Robinson, who had found in his clients' favour. As the general election of 1828 approached, Randal was threatened that, if by subterfuge he had managed to retain or acquire enough real estate to qualify for re-election, it would be attached by his creditors as soon as he identified it in his qualification oath. None the less, he was returned both in 1828 and in 1830.

It is unclear if these continuing feuds had any bearing on Randal's attitude towards the question of public financial aid to the Welland Canal Company. Until 1830, he consistently opposed such aid. In that year, he voted with the minority against a bill which authorized £25,000 in aid to the canal and appointed him as commissioner to report on the state of the works to the government. He reported very favourably on the future utility of the canal as an artery in the Laurentian trade system and in 1831 supported a measure authorizing a further £50,000 in aid. The measure might be unpopular in the old Niagara River commercial centres of Niagara (Niagara-on-the-Lake), Queenston, St Davids, and Waterloo, he observed, but it would benefit many more people than it harmed. Randal's explanation for his volte-face in 1831 was consistent with his support for the union of Upper and Lower Canada in 1822.

Despite his public prominence, Randal continued all but destitute till his dying day. He had no visible means of support but his salary as MHA during the short parliamentary session and, during the navigation season only, a small stipend as toll collector on the Welland Canal at Port Colborne. It is likely that his friends and fellow radical assemblymen William Lyon Mackenzie*, John Johnston Lefferty*, and Thomas HORNOR helped him with money: all three are named as beneficiaries in his will, along with the impecunious Montrealers who had succoured him during his long incarceration. Jesse Ketchum, named as an executor along with Mackenzie, Lefferty, Hornor and Willis, may also have helped.

An appreciation of Randal's historical importance must start with an assessment of his personality. His role in the Michigan bribery scandal, his deportment towards his creditors in 1807–8, and his contradiction by so many leading Niagara-area personalities in the Bridgewater litigation might suggest that he was merely an unscrupulous trickster who deserved his bleak destiny; yet his career of almost unrelieved failure forbids so glib a judgement. Under closer scrutiny he appears more like a naïve optimist, even a starry-eyed visionary – a simple, amiable man, apt to be deceived by men more designing than he. Yet this is also, perhaps, too superficial a view. There was, conceivably, a self-deceiving quality to his optimism. So often was he gulled and cast down, and so tenacious was his defiance in adversity, that one suspects him of having laid himself open to such disasters by an unconscious masochistic impulse to failure. In this he resembles another opposition politician of the 1820s, Charles Fothergill*.

Randal's apparent innocence and amiability, and his defiance in adversity, all contributed to his political importance, which lay chiefly in his symbolic role as martyr *par excellence* to the avarice and oppression of the "family compact" and its regional affiliates. His experience seemed to typify that of the pioneer farmer, struggling to make a living in a milieu in which both the legal system and the terms of trade favoured the merchant capitalist. To these Bible-drenched pioneers, Randal's story of spoliation by legal process was that of Naboth's vineyard; but it was also their story, and his persistent (and ultimately political) struggle for justice set them an example. Randal also fitted the period's conventional, "sentim-entalist" stereotype of injured innocence, and he was presented in that light by advocates such as Rolph and Mackenzie: a sort of Vicar of Wakefield, a man – as he was described by his contemporaries – of "romantic history and eminent worth," "long accustomed to persecution – the child of misfortune, and the com-panion of troubles," at one time "dressed in a dark-green suit that had long since been threadbare," at another "*literally* clothed with the approbation of his constituents." Nothing did more than his suffer-ings to discredit the legal profession and the adminis-tration of justice: H. J. Boulton was so unpopular because of them that Maitland opposed his application to be made a judge in 1825 and Lieutenant Governor Sir John Colborne* was dubious about making him attorney general in 1829.

It is paradoxical that Randal, this energetic and tenacious adventurer, should have played such an essentially passive role in public life; yet his political career was of a piece with it. Mackenzie remarked in his obituary that "few who have sat in the House have given as many good votes as Mr. R.," but "if he ever spoke for five minutes I don't recollect it." Mackenzie is said to have taken up politics under Randal's influence, and he made the cause of Randal and his heirs his own until his dying day. Randal, for his part, persuaded Mackenzie to move the *Colonial Advocate* to York (Toronto) in 1824 and promoted his election to the assembly in 1828. Randal probably owed his selection as the "Aliens'" ambassador in 1827 to Mackenzie and Ketchum, since both men had played leading parts the previous year in a fund-raising campaign to help him travel to London to pursue his case against Clark and Street (he tried in 1827 but was rebuffed by the British government).

Randal's correspondence in London with the Colo-nial Office shows an uncharacteristic polish which may reflect the counsel of his chief adviser there, the Scottish radical, Joseph Hume. The success of his mission entitles it to be considered as the first of the three great blows the imperial authorities delivered to the Upper Canadian political establishment during the colony's last years, the others being Mackenzie's reception in 1832, which led to the dismissal of H. J. Boulton and Hagerman as attorney general and solici-tor general respectively, and the decision in 1839 to unite Upper and Lower Canada.

PAUL ROMNEY

[The two major collections of Randal's papers are in series A-4 of the Mackenzie–Lindsey papers at the AO (MU 1915–17) and in volumes 13–14 of the William Lyon Mackenzie papers at the PAC (MG 24, B18); individual items are also intermingled with Mackenzie's own papers. Randal's ar-raignment before the House of Representatives is docu-mented in U.S., Congress, *Debates and proc.* (Washington), 1795–96: cols.166–244, and in William Cobbett, *Porcu-pine's works; containing various writings and selections, exhibiting a faithful picture of the United States of America* . . . (12v., London, 1801), 3: 43–55. The Bridgewater scandal is discussed in PRO, CO 42/373: 26–65; 42/374: 75–82; 42/375: 144–86; 42/376: 33–35, 401–8; the Chau-dière scandal in U.C., House of Assembly, *Journal*, 1828, app., "Report on the petition of Robert Randal, Esquire," and in Can., Prov. of, Legislative Assembly, *App. to the journals*, 1852–53, app.SSSS. Randal's report on the Welland Canal is in U.C., House of Assembly, *Journal*, 1831, app.: 182–95.

Regarding Randal's trial for perjury, see *A faithful report of the trial and acquittal of Robert Randall, Esq., a member of the Commons House of Assembly in Upper Canada, accused of perjury, and tried at Niagara, on Wednesday the 7th of September, 1825; from stenographic notes by Francis Collins* . . . (York [Toronto], 1825). His correspondence with the Colonial Office on the alien question in 1827 is printed in the *Colonial Advocate*, 6, 27 Sept. 1827. Major newspaper sources for his career are the *Colonial Advocate*, 14 March–7 April 1825, the *Examiner* (Toronto), 21 Aug. 1850, and *Mackenzie's Weekly Message* (Toronto), 18 May 1854.

The main secondary source for Randal's career is Paul Romney, *Mr Attorney: the attorney general for Ontario in court, cabinet, and legislature, 1791–1899* (Toronto, 1986), esp. c.3; see also H. P. Hill, *Robert Randall and the Le Breton Flats: an account of the early legal and political controversies respecting the ownership of a large portion of the present city of Ottawa* (Ottawa, 1919). P.R.]

PAC, RG 1, E3. *John Askin papers* (Quaife). U.C., House of Assembly, *App. to the journal*, 1836, 3, no.76.

RANVOYZÉ, ÉTIENNE, notary, militia officer, JP, office holder, and politician; b. 10 March 1776 at Quebec, son of François Ranvoyzé* and Marie-Vénérande Pelerin; m. 6 March 1802 Françoise Fillion in Jeune-Lorette (Loretteville), Lower Canada; d. 9 Aug. 1826 in Trois-Rivières, Lower Canada.

Raymond

Étienne Ranvoyzé was the fourth of ten children. Through his work as a silversmith his father assured the family of some security, and he was on good terms socially with the Quebec bourgeoisie and clergy. It is therefore not surprising that in 1790 Étienne went to study at the Petit Séminaire de Québec, where he remained until 1795. His brothers Louis and François-Ignace also attended this institution.

Étienne was attracted to law and trained with notary Jean-Marie Mondelet*. On 11 April 1799 he received his commission as a notary public. He went into partnership with his teacher for a time and practised at Saint-Marc and William Henry (Sorel). Around 1801 he settled in Trois-Rivières and, while carrying on his profession, he became interested in public affairs.

During the War of 1812 Ranvoyzé served in the Canadian militia. He was commissioned a lieutenant in the 3rd Select Embodied Militia Battalion on 25 May 1812 and served under Lieutenant-Colonel James Cuthbert*. On 25 March 1813 he was promoted captain, and on 26 October he took part in the battle of Châteauguay under Charles-Michel d'IRUMBERRY de Salaberry. He came under fire again on 11 Sept. 1814 at the battle of Plattsburgh. He remained on active service until at least the beginning of 1815, at which time he left the militia.

Peace having been restored, Ranvoyzé returned to his notarial practice in Trois-Rivières. Since he had neglected his clientele for some years, he had to rely on the prestige he had won on the battlefield, as well as on patronage. He received a commission as justice of the peace on 8 July 1815. On 2 October he was recommended for the post of clerk and treasurer of the commission set up to oversee the building of a prison in Trois-Rivières. In the general election of 1816 he served as returning officer for the riding of Trois-Rivières. These offices apparently did not bring in enough money to save him from serious financial difficulties in 1817. That year Louis Gugy*, the sheriff of Trois-Rivières, seized part of Ranvoyzé's assets, consisting of a property on Rue Notre-Dame. In 1818 Ranvoyzé was secretary to the municipal corporation of the town.

In March 1819, probably counting on the popularity he enjoyed from his numerous administrative posts, his prestige as a former military man, and a growing practice, Ranvoyzé ran in a by-election in the riding of Saint-Maurice against Pierre Bureau*, a Trois-Rivières merchant. Despite the encouragement and promises of numerous supporters, Ranvoyzé was defeated; he then unsuccessfully contested the election results. In 1820 he ran in Trois-Rivières, but again his hopes were dashed, since Joseph BADEAUX won.

When a general election was held in July and August 1824 Ranvoyzé again stood as a candidate there, with Amable Berthelot* as his running-mate. This time his constituents did not deny him their support and he won. Ranvoyzé would not disappoint the voters who had finally given him their trust. He took his role seriously and participated in no fewer than 15 select committees during the 1825 and 1826 sessions. As a member of the Canadian party, which was then predominant in the assembly, he voted regularly with the majority, although at the opening of the first session he had voted with the English party against the election of Louis-Joseph Papineau* as speaker.

Étienne Ranvoyzé died in Trois-Rivières on 9 Aug. 1826 and was buried there two days later. Active until the end, in less than 30 years he had carved out a reputation and an important place for himself in his adopted town. He energetically combined professional commitments as a notary with duties as a magistrate, and after a few tries attained the highest office for someone from his milieu, member of the Lower Canadian House of Assembly.

YVES BEAUREGARD

Étienne Ranvoyzé's minute-book, containing instruments notarized between 1799 and 1826, is held at ANQ-MBF, CN1-79.

ANQ-MBF, CE1-48, 25 nov. 1802, 11 août 1826. ANQ-Q, CE1-1, 11 mars 1776; CE1-28, 6 mars 1802. ASQ, Fichier des anciens. L.C., House of Assembly, *Journals*, 1817, app.H; 1819: 206. *Le Canadien*, 16 juin 1819; 15 mars, 26 juill. 1820; 11, 25 août 1824. *La Gazette des Trois-Rivières* (Trois-Rivières, [Qué.]), 16 juin 1818; 12 janv., 16 févr., 20 avril 1819; 4 juill., 8 août 1820. *Quebec Gazette*, 18 April 1799, 9 Jan. 1817, 19 March 1818, 10 Aug. 1826. F.-J. Audet, *Les députés des Trois-Rivières*. Ivanhoë Caron, "Papiers Duvernay conservés aux Archives de la province de Québec," ANQ *Rapport*, 1926–27: 148–49, 151. *Officers of British forces in Canada* (Irving). Fernand Ouellet, "Inventaire de la saberdache de Jacques Viger," ANQ *Rapport*, 1955–57: 131. *Quebec almanac*, 1815–16, 1822. Maurice Grenier, "La chambre d'Assemblée du Bas-Canada, 1815–1837" (thèse de MA, univ. de Montréal, 1966). J.-E. Roy, *Hist. du notariat*, 2: 233.

RAYMOND, JEAN-BAPTISTE, businessman, seigneur, politician, JP, office holder, and militia officer; b. 6 Dec. 1757 in Saint-Roch-des-Aulnaies (Que.), only surviving child of Jean-Baptiste-Moyse de Rémond and Marie-Françoise Damours de Louvières; d. 19 March 1825 in La Prairie, Lower Canada.

Jean-Baptiste Raymond's parents may have been Huguenots, but Jean-Baptiste was necessarily baptized Roman Catholic, Protestantism being officially banned in New France. Raymond evidently received some education, since he was literate; he was probably unilingual. Possibly at the age of 12, he left for the upper country, where, according to a descendant,

Henri Masson, "he had to endure great suffering and was riddled with injuries."

Raymond came back east in 1783, and on 6 Sept. 1784 he married Marie-Clotilde Girardin, daughter of the Montreal merchant Charles-François Girardin. By then Raymond was established as a merchant at La Tortue (Saint-Mathieu), a settlement he had founded in the parish of Saint-Philippe-de-Laprairie. His commercial activities seem to have been diversified. Initially, he was involved in a dry-goods business, selling manufactured and household wares in return for payment in specie or in kind, probably wheat. In 1785 he owed £400 to the firm of King and McCord [see Thomas McCord] and 11,500 *livres* to a merchant and personal friend, Charles Larrivé, both of Montreal, for goods purchased on credit; the debts took six years to repay. Yet, by the mid 1790s, Raymond was extending substantial credit in the La Prairie–La Tortue region. In 1796 he participated in a speculative venture envisaging the sale of gunpowder in the United States. He appears, however, to have over-extended himself. In June 1796 he sold the seigneury of Lac-Matapédia (left to him, along with a lot in Quebec, by his mother) to Patrick Langan for £700, of which £250 was to be paid to John McKindlay, a Montreal merchant, for liquidation of a debt. Yet in early 1797 McKindlay obtained judgement against Raymond for non-payment. The sale to Langan was annulled and the seigneury seized by the sheriff of Quebec and offered at auction on 26 September; Langan repurchased it, and McKindlay acquired one undivided third of the property from Langan, probably as payment of Raymond's debt.

Raymond seems to have bounced back quickly. In 1801 he purchased a lot in La Prairie, and soon after, perhaps because of actual or expected growth in his commercial interests, he moved his family from La Tortue to the town. Between 1805 and 1810 he took his son Jean-Moïse* into partnership in the dry-goods business, and Jean-Baptiste Raymond et Fils became one of the most prosperous commercial establishments of the region. By this time Raymond was crippled and chronically ill, possibly as a result of the injuries he had sustained as a fur trader, and he began to depend heavily on his son to run the business. The firm became involved in sawmills and potash processing in the first decades of the 19th century and probably dealt widely in wheat. Complementing Raymond's mercantile activities were extensive real-estate acquisitions; from 1810 he concentrated his property holdings in and around La Prairie, where he eventually rivalled the notary Edme Henry* as the largest property owner. In 1814 he was able to give Jean-Moïse, as an advance on his inheritance, a house, store, and warehouse in La Prairie, all of stone and valued at £750. Three years later his daughter Clotilde and her husband, Paul-Théophile PINSO-NAUT, received in a similar manner land and also two potasheries worth 12,000 *livres*. In 1818, when another daughter, Marie-Geneviève-Sophie, married the young and ambitious merchant Joseph Masson*, Masson was congratulated by his Scottish associate, Hugh Robertson: "On the whole I feel convinced that you could not have found a more prudent connection, as Mr Raymond is a good worthy man and highly respectable; it therefore meets my warmest approbation."

Raymond had already achieved local prominence by 1800, when he was elected along with Joseph-François Perrault* to the House of Assembly for Huntingdon County, replacing Joseph Périnault*. Four years later he was re-elected, his fellow deputy being Sir Alexander Mackenzie*. His attendance in the assembly was sporadic, however; his participation on committees related to trade reflected his expertise and interest, but it seems that personal business affairs remained his preoccupation. Indicative of his local prominence were his commission of the peace, received in August 1803 and renewed in November 1812, and his appointment to a commission for the improvement of internal communications for Huntingdon in 1817. In 1812 he was made a captain in Boucherville's 1st Militia Battalion. When in 1822 opposition to a planned union of Lower and Upper Canada was organized in the lower province by the Canadian party, Raymond was elected chairman, and Jean-Moïse secretary, of a meeting held in Huntingdon to protest the project.

Of the 17 children born to Raymond and his wife only seven – a boy and six girls – survived into adolescence. Marriage into the colonial élite, Canadian and British, was the rule: all the daughters married professionals or merchants. Raymond died in 1825 and, as befitted a man of his standing in La Prairie, he was buried in the parish church. His widow married Edme Henry three years later.

Jean-Baptiste Raymond's business activities, family connections, and public roles, which place him among the petite bourgeoisie of Lower Canada, follow patterns common to local, pre-industrial élites everywhere. Studies of other members of this class may reveal a good deal of the social and economic history of the colony and indeed of pre-industrial Canada generally.

ALAN DEVER

ANQ-M, CE1-51, 6 sept. 1784; CE1-54, 22 mars 1825; CN1-47, 1791–94; CN1-74, 1796; CN1-107, 1811–17; CN1-128, 1785; CN1-134, 1821–28; CN1-200, 1795–1800; CN1-327, 1805–21. AP, Saint-Roch-des-Aulnaies, reg. des baptêmes, mariages et sépultures, 7 déc. 1757. PAC, RG 68, General index, 1651–1841: 196, 633. L.C., House of Assembly, *Journals*, 1801–8. Can., Prov. of,

Red Jacket

Legislative Assembly, *App. to the journals*, 1843, app.F. *Quebec Gazette*, 23 March 1797; 24 July 1800; 27 Dec. 1804; 26 March, 8 Oct., 12 Nov. 1812; 22 May, 3 July 1817; 10 Sept., 22 Oct. 1818; 7 Jan., 1 July, 23 Dec. 1819; 3 Oct. 1822; 9, 16 Jan. 1823. Desjardins, *Guide parl.*, 130. *Inventaire des actes notariés du village de Laprairie, 1670–1860*, Michel Aubin, compil. (s.l., 1975). *Mariages de Laprairie (N.-D.-de-la Prairie-de-la Madeleine), 1670–1968*, Irénée Jetté et Benoît Pontbriand, compil. (Québec, 1970), 232–34. *Officers of British forces in Canada* (Irving), 190. P.-G. Roy, *Inv. concessions*, 4: 85–86. Henri Masson, *Joseph Masson, dernier seigneur de Terrebonne, 1791–1847* (Montréal, 1972). J.-D. Michaud, *Notes historiques sur la vallée de la Matapédia* (Val-Brillant, Qué., 1922), 137. L.-P. Desrosiers, "Montréal soulève la province," *Cahiers des Dix*, 8 (1943): 85. Hare, "L'Assemblée législative du Bas-Canada," *RHAF*, 27: 376, 379. J.-J. Lefebvre, "Jean-Baptiste Raymond (1757–1825), député de Huntingdon (Laprairie), 1800–1808," *BRH*, 58 (1952): 59–72.

RED JACKET. *See* SHAKÓYE:WA:THAˀ

REEVES, JOHN, judge and author; b. 20 Nov. 1752 in London, son of John Reeves; d. there unmarried 7 Aug. 1829.

Schooled at Eton College, John Reeves was denied a fellowship at King's College, Cambridge, but matriculated at Merton College, Oxford, on 31 Oct. 1771. He obtained his BA in 1775 and on 11 November was elected Michel scholar of Queen's College, Oxford. He became a fellow of Queen's on 8 Oct. 1777, qualifying for an MA the next year. In 1780 Reeves was made a commissioner of bankrupts, having been called to the bar via the Middle Temple the previous year. In 1779 too he had begun his career as a prolific author of works on legal, political, and constitutional questions. Legal adviser to the Privy Council committee for trade from 1787, he was elected a fellow of the Royal Society three years later.

In 1791 Reeves stepped out of the conventional life of his profession when he became a judge in Newfoundland. The circumstances of his nomination were complex. In 1787 a decision of the Court of Quarter Sessions in Devon, England, had challenged the legality of the system of civil justice on the island [*see* Richard Hutchings*]. As a result, prospective litigants were unable to obtain hearings on the island, a difficulty compounded by a severe set-back in the fishery late that year. In 1789 Governor Mark Milbanke* established a court of common pleas, but his authority to do so was denied by the English law officers. Finally, in 1791 remedial legislation was passed by parliament. The act 31 Geo.III, c.29, created "a court of civil jurisdiction" to determine "all pleas of debt, account, contracts respecting personal property, and all trespasses committed against the person or goods and chattels" in Newfoundland "and islands and parts adjacent, or on the banks" off

Newfoundland. The court was to consist of a "chief judge," appointed by the king, and two assessors, appointed by the governor. During the governor's residence it would also have exclusive jurisdiction in disputes about the wages of seamen or fishermen. In the governor's absence such disputes could be heard, as before, in the court of session mentioned in 15 Geo.III, c.31. The act was to take effect on 10 June 1791 and continue for one year, "and unto the end of the then next session of Parliament."

Reeves arrived in Newfoundland as chief judge on 10 Sept. 1791. The assessors were Aaron Graham*, secretary to successive governors, and D'Ewes Coke, the controller of customs. Between then and 31 October, 138 writs were issued. Reeves left for home on 1 November, and reports on his work went to Henry Dundas, the home secretary, and the Privy Council committee for trade. Noting that the influence of the court had been confined to the St John's area, Reeves proposed several reforms, the most important of which was the establishment of a permanent supreme court with both civil and criminal jurisdiction. The existing courts of session would work in concert with this new court by trying petty offences, "especially those arising from disputes over wages." Reeves also called for the granting of legal status to the courts held in the outports by naval officers.

An act incorporating these suggestions received royal assent on 15 June 1792, despite vigorous opposition from West Country interests. By its terms a supreme court with full authority in all civil and criminal cases was to be established. In criminal matters the court was to follow English law, and in civil cases English law "as far as the same can be applied to suits and complaints" arising in Newfoundland. Presiding over the court would be a chief justice, appointed by the king, with officers appointed by the chief justice. The act also empowered the governor, with the advice of the chief justice, to institute civil courts called surrogate courts in different parts of the island as required. These were also to determine cases according to English law. In civil cases in both courts defendants could claim trial by jury if "the cause of action" exceeded £10. Judgements by the surrogate courts for sums exceeding £40 could be appealed to the Supreme Court, those by the Supreme Court for sums exceeding £100 to the king in council. The court of civil jurisdiction established in 1791 was to function until the opening of the new court, which would have the same life as its predecessor.

Reeves returned to Newfoundland as chief justice on 3 Sept. 1792. Besides holding court in St John's, he "made a Circuit round to Conception Bay and Trinity Bay" and visited Ferryland. His staff consisted of a single clerk, but he had the "voluntary Assistance" of Coke. By 30 October, when he left for home, he had issued 120 writs. While in Newfoundland Reeves recommended to Dundas that a system of justice like that created by the 1792 act be made permanent, and on his return to England he devoted himself whole-heartedly to this cause. In February 1793 he was given a public forum for his views when the House of Commons appointed a committee to inquire into the state of the trade to Newfoundland.

On appearing before the committee, Reeves was permitted to read a paper which examined both the history and the existing state of Newfoundland. In particular, he was concerned to rebut the evidence of Peter Ougier* and William Newman, Devon merchants opposed to the judicial changes. Reeves attributed their attitude and that of their supporters in the West Country to the disreputable activities of merchants' agents in Newfoundland, who would resist the administration of justice in order "to draw as few Bills" as possible on their principals. "A certain Class" of West Country merchants had "invariably set themselves against every Attempt to introduce Order and Justice" to Newfoundland, looking upon the island as their own property. Their purpose had been "to secure their private Interests . . . independent of any Competition from other Traders, and of any Inspection." Their policy had been embodied in slogans such as "No Residents" and "A free Fishery carried on from Great Britain," but the freedom they had sought was that "of being free of all Rule and Order themselves, in the Enjoyment of an exclusive Monopoly, and at Liberty to exercise a Dominion over the Boatkeepers and poor Inhabitants, whom they kept in perpetual Thraldom." Reeves strongly recommended the continuance of the court system, and argued that it could be improved by the establishment of a court to function in the absence of the chief justice and surrogates for the recovery of debts and for the determination of any sort of cause. The personnel of this court, from which there should be right of appeal to the Supreme Court, might be "no other than the very Persons who sat in the Court of Common Pleas." Newfoundland needed "the Control and the Protection of Magistracy and Officers, like the rest of the King's Dominions," in short "something more of a resident Government."

Reeves also commented on the nature of landholding in Newfoundland, noting that the ownership of "Three Fourths of the Ground . . . used and possessed in the Island" could not be traced to any "Grant or . . . Thing to shew for the original Possession." Title by occupancy alone was especially the case in the outports, "where being removed from the Eye of Government, they make Inclosures, and carve for themselves almost as they please." He recommended that the crown should receive from landholders "some Acknowledgment by way of Quit Rent."

His judicial advice at least was sympathetically heard, for on 17 June 1793 royal assent was given to an act which continued the system he had inaugurated.

Reeves's successor as chief justice was D'Ewes Coke.

In April 1793 Reeves completed his famous *History of the government of the island of Newfoundland*, the first comprehensive account of the island's past. In keeping with his own experience, he focused on "the struggles and vicissitudes of two contending interests. – The *planters* and *inhabitants* on the one hand, who, being settled there, needed the protection of a government and police, with the administration of justice: and the *adventurers* and *merchants* on the other; who, originally carrying on the fishery from this country, and visiting that island only for the season, needed no such protection for themselves, and had various reasons for preventing its being afforded to the others." The dialectic thus posed was to be examined over and over again in the historiography of Newfoundland. In 1978 Keith Matthews argued that Reeves's work, the "first published identification of the West Country merchants with villainy," had "been read and broadly accepted by every recent historian."

On 22 March 1794 Dundas recommended to the Treasury that Reeves be paid £500 for each period of his service in Newfoundland. In 1795 the ultra-royalist Reeves published anonymously in London a pamphlet entitled *Thoughts on the English government; addressed to the quiet good sense of the people of England; in a series of letters; letter the first*. This work exaggerated the power of the monarch in the constitution at the expense of parliament and juries. He was charged with libel on this account – an unusual fate for a conservative spokesman – but was acquitted the following year. In 1800 Reeves was appointed king's printer and in 1824 elected a bencher of the Inns of Court. He died a wealthy bachelor and was buried in the Temple Church (St Mary's) on 17 Aug. 1829.

PETER NEARY

John Reeves is the author of *History of the government of the island of Newfoundland . . .* (London, 1793; repr. New York and East Ardsley, Eng., 1967).

G.B., Parl., House of Commons, *Journals* (London), 46 (1790–91)–48 (1792–93); House of Commons papers, 1793, no.4393, *First report from the committee appointed to enquire into the state of trade to Newfoundland*; no.4407, *Second report . . .* ; no.4438, *Third report. . . . DNB. The Eton College register, 1753–1790*, ed. R. A. Austen-Leigh (Eton, Eng., 1921). C. R. Fay, *Life and labour in Newfoundland* (Toronto, 1956). A. H. McLintock, *The establishment of constitutional government in Newfoundland, 1783–1832: a study of retarded colonisation* (London and Toronto, 1941). Keith Matthews, *Lectures on the history of Newfoundland: 1500–1830* (St John's, 1973). Prowse, *Hist. of Nfld.* (1895). Keith Matthews, "Historical fence building: a critique of the historiography of Newfoundland," *Newfoundland Quarterly* (St John's), 74 (1978–79), no.1: 21–30.

REVENTA, FRANCISCO DE ELIZA Y. *See* ELIZA

Rézine

RÉZINE. *See* RAIZENNE

RICHARDSON, JAMES, naval officer, mariner, miller, and merchant; b. *c.* 1759 near Horncastle, England; m. prior to 1789 Sarah Bryant, *née* Ashmore, and they had at least three children; m. secondly 14 Aug. 1809 Mary Louisa McDonnell in Kingston, Upper Canada; d. 20 Sept. 1832 in Presqu'ile Point, Upper Canada.

For three years during the American revolution, James Richardson was a naval quartermaster in the West Indies. In 1782 his ship, the *Ramillies*, sailing to England in Commander Thomas Graves*'s squadron, sustained heavy damage in a gale and had to be destroyed. Taken aboard a merchant vessel, he was subsequently captured by an American frigate and imprisoned in France. In 1785 he was appointed a second lieutenant in the Provincial Marine on Lake Ontario, where he served for the next few years. After the regulations prohibiting private vessels on the lower lakes were revoked in 1787, Richard Cartwright* hired Richardson to superintend construction of, and later to command, the *Lady Dorchester*. The joint enterprise of Cartwright, Robert Hamilton*, and Todd, McGill and Company of Montreal, she was launched in 1789 and thenceforth carried furs and supplies between Kingston and Niagara (Niagara-on-the-Lake), principally for the North West Company. Richardson appears to have taken up residence in Kingston when work began on the *Lady Dorchester*. He remained captain of the vessel until 1793.

That same year Richardson and a number of partners, including the firms of Crooks and Company and Auldjo and Maitland, agreed to challenge the monopoly on Lake Ontario of Richardson's former employers. Cartwright, though he respected Richardson's qualities as a seaman, claimed that the captain "has made himself so universally abnoxious that I shall not be very sorry to get rid of him." While Cartwright did his best to impede construction of the rival vessel, Richardson went to Montreal during the winter of 1794 to make what Cartwright called "insidious Attempts" to get a piece of the NWC's business. Although he was unsuccessful, he and his partners nevertheless launched the *Kingston Packet* in 1795. Subsequently, Richardson took advantage of his status as part-owner of the *Packet* and as an ex-officer of the Provincial Marine to launch a succession of petitions for land, most of which were granted. The land he obtained included sites on the Kingston waterfront, in York (Toronto), and in Newcastle (Presqu'ile Point).

After the wreck of the *Packet*, probably in 1801, Richardson's career temporarily took a new tack. By the early 1800s he was importing goods from the United States and appears to have begun operating as a merchant and miller. His failure at these trades prompted a reconciliation with Cartwright in 1807, and the captain assumed command of Cartwright's sloop *Elizabeth*. Later he took charge of the larger *Governor Simcoe*, owned by many of the men originally associated with the *Lady Dorchester*.

It was at the helm of the *Simcoe* that Richardson served in the early stages of the War of 1812. On the eve of the battle of Queenston Heights on 13 Oct. 1812 he delivered a shipment of gunpowder to Niagara and afterwards returned to York with prisoners and the news of Major-General Sir Isaac Brock*'s death. Scarcely a month later, the *Simcoe* ran past the American fleet into Kingston. Though skilfully piloted, she had been struck by American shot and virtually sank at the wharf. When, in the spring of 1813, the *Simcoe* was absorbed into Commodore Sir James Lucas Yeo*'s fleet, Richardson signed on as a master. He was discharged that fall.

After his discharge Richardson quickly reestablished himself as a Kingston merchant, setting up a partnership with his son-in-law, James Lyons. Before he closed his Kingston business affairs in 1818 Richardson had run this shop on his own and in partnership with his son Robert. At some point in the immediate post-war years he moved from Kingston to the neighbourhood of Presqu'ile Point. There he began to develop the property he had accumulated 20 years earlier. By July 1816 he was advertising for sale a wharf and large store at his waterfront site in Cramahe Township. His son James* was collector of customs at Presqu'ile (he went on to become a Methodist bishop), and James Lyons became the local MHA in 1824.

But before retiring to the life of country squire, Richardson once again took up command of a vessel. On 9 May 1818, less than a year after the *Frontenac* (the first Canadian-built steamboat on the Great Lakes) began running on Lake Ontario [*see* James MCKENZIE], the *Charlotte* took to the waters of the upper St Lawrence and the Bay of Quinte. For her first few voyages Richardson was at the helm. He did not complete the first season, however, perhaps because of a debilitating stroke he is known to have suffered about this time.

Richardson had been a generous benefactor and controversial churchwarden of the Church of England congregation in Kingston. When, in 1795, he proposed the rather radical step of abolishing pew rentals, the Reverend John Stuart* was incensed, describing Richardson as a "little blustering Sea Captain" and "a turbulent ambitious man . . . willing to try his Power & Influence." Turbulent and ambitious Richardson certainly was, with a mean streak for good measure. Twice he was found guilty of assault by the Midland District assizes. Yet Cartwright, a year after being "rid of him," described his replacements as "destitute in a great measure of that Energy, or perhaps Violence of Temper, which enabled [Richardson] to get the Duty better done by the People under him." From the introduction of private enterprise on the lower lakes to the first years of steam, these qualities made Richardson one of the most successful, though certainly not loved, captains on Lake Ontario.

WALTER LEWIS

AO, MU 500, Richard Cartwright, letter-book, 1793–96; MU 2099, 1795, no.10 (advertisement from *Quebec Times*, date not available). Northumberland East Land Registry Office (Colborne, Ont.), Brighton Township, abstract index to deeds, broken concession, lot 1; concession 1, lot 1 (mfm. at AO). PAC, RG 1, L3, 423: R1/30, 59; R3/5, 32, 60; 424: R4/14; 425: R7/22; 446: R misc., 1793–1840/37; RG 8, I (C ser.), 723: 27, 144–46; 740: 15; 741: 5; RG 16, A1, 133. QUA, Richard Cartwright papers, letter-books, 1798–1801 (transcripts at AO). James Crooks, "Recollections of the War of 1812," Women's Canadian Hist. Soc. of Toronto, *Trans.* (Toronto), no.13 (1913–14): 16. "District of Mecklenburg (Kingston): Court of Common Pleas," AO *Report*, 1917: 192. *Kingston before War of 1812* (Preston). *Parish reg. of Kingston* (Young). James Richardson [Jr], "Incidents in the early history of the settlements in the vicinity of Lake Ontario," Women's Canadian Hist. Soc. of Toronto, *Trans.*, no.15 (1915–16): 13–38. "U.C. land book C," AO *Report*, 1931: 64. *Christian Guardian*, 26 Sept. 1832. *Kingston Gazette*, 17 Nov. 1812; 4 Dec. 1813; 18 March, 20 July 1816; 27 Nov. 1817; 12 May 1818. *Montreal Gazette*, 12 Oct. 1795. *Quebec Gazette*, 26 Feb. 1795. *Upper Canada Gazette*, 19 June 1817. *Legislators and legislatures of Ontario: a reference guide*, comp. Debra Forman (3v., [Toronto, 1984]), 1. K. M. Bindon, "Kingston: a social history, 1785–1830" (PHD thesis, Queen's Univ., Kingston, Ont., 1979). Canniff, *Hist. of the settlement of U.C. Centennial of the incorporation of the village of Brighton, 1859–1959* (n.p., n.d.). Scadding, *Toronto of old* (1873). C. P. Stacey, "The defence of Upper Canada, 1812," *The defended border: Upper Canada and the War of 1812 . . .*, ed. Morris Zaslow and W. B. Turner (Toronto, 1964), 11–20. W. M. Tobey, *The history of Brighton, Ontario*, ed. W. M. Sprung and Barbara Nyland ([Kingston], 1975). Thomas Webster, *Life of Rev. James Richardson, a bishop of the Methodist Episcopal Church in Canada* (Toronto, 1876). Wilson, *Enterprises of Robert Hamilton*. E. A. Cruikshank, "Notes on the history of shipbuilding and navigation on Lake Ontario up to the time of the launching of the steamship *Frontenac*, at Ernesttown, Ontario, 7th September, 1816," *OH*, 23 (1926): 33–44. C. P. Stacey, "The ships of the British squadron on Lake Ontario, 1812–14," *CHR*, 34 (1953): 311–23.

RICHARDSON, JOHN, businessman, politician, JP, office holder, and militia officer; b. *c.* 1754 in Portsoy, Scotland, son of John Richardson and a daughter of George Phyn; m. 12 Dec. 1794 Sarah Ann Grant, a niece of William Grant*, and they had seven children; d. 18 May 1831 in Montreal.

John Richardson studied arts at King's College, Aberdeen, Scotland, before becoming apprenticed in 1774, through family connections, to the successful Scottish fur-trading partnership of Phyn, Ellice and Company, then with headquarters at Schenectady, N.Y. After his arrival in May, deteriorating relations between the American colonies and Britain forced the firm to reorganize. Richardson's uncle James Phyn established a supply house in London, and two years later Phyn's partner Alexander Ellice* shifted the main base of North American operations to Montreal. Early in the American revolution Richardson was taken into the employ of John Porteous, a former partner in Phyn, Ellice and a main supplier of the British troops in New York and Philadelphia. In 1779 Richardson was employed as captain of marines on the privateer *Vengeance*, principally owned by Porteous, but in which Richardson had shares. The letters he wrote during the ship's first cruise evince one of Richardson's dominant traits, an aggressive confidence in himself and those he considered his mates. "Let us only see a Vessel and we are not afraid but we will soon come up with her," he boasted. The letters also describe exhilarating adventure, the duplicity of prize crews, and above all the dangers and confusion of privateering. On 21 May 1779 the British naval vessel *Renown*, paying no attention to the British flag on *Vengeance*, fired five or six broadsides into her, wounding several of the crew, some mortally, and severely damaging the hull. Even after identity was positively established, the captain of *Renown* expressed no regret and left a dismasted *Vengeance* to its fate, a "wanton and unprovoked cruelty," Richardson wrote, "unworthy of a Briton."

By August 1780 Richardson had established a shop in Charleston, S.C., in association with Porteous and Phyn, Ellice and Company of London, to whom he exported indigo, rice, and tobacco. His letters from Charleston reveal a diligent mind, already attuned to accounting and very shrewd on matters of supply and demand in consumer goods ranging from fashionable cocked hats and artificial flowers to saddles. The letters also express hatred of disloyalty, an attitude Richardson would reveal time and again in Lower Canada.

After the peace in 1783, Richardson was again employed by Phyn, Ellice interests in New York and Schenectady. In 1787 he was sent to Montreal to help his cousin John Forsyth* reorganize Robert Ellice and Company, the successor to Alexander Ellice and Company. The firm had greatly overextended its operations south of Detroit and Michilimackinac (Mackinac Island, Mich.) and its principal partner, Robert Ellice*, was ailing. In the years 1787–89 Richardson divided his time between Montreal and the west. In the city he learned the details of the firm's business: the Montreal–southwest fur trade, speculation in bills of exchange, the collection from the government and payment to the recipients of loyalist

Richardson

compensations, and the forwarding of supplies to loyalist and military settlements in Upper Canada. In the west he supervised and reported on the trade – which was sadly depressed – and oversaw construction of the company's schooner, *Nancy*, designed for use on lakes Huron and Michigan. When Robert Ellice died in 1790 Richardson was made a partner in the reorganized firm, called Forsyth, Richardson and Company. Although the cousins were determined to avoid the costly excesses of Robert Ellice, they were far from stodgy. In the next few years their firm expanded the forwarding trade, particularly to Kingston and York (Toronto), increased investment in shipping on the Great Lakes, became a minor shareholder in the North West Company, and was involved in the unsuccessful Montreal Distillery Company [*see* Thomas McCORD], which ceased operation in 1794. One of Richardson's most imaginative initiatives was an attempt, through Forsyth, Richardson and in conjunction with Todd, McGill and Company of Montreal [*see* Isaac Todd*] and Phyn, Ellices, and Inglis of London, to found a bank in 1792. The Canada Banking Company was designed as a bank of note issue and of discount and deposit; it might have fulfilled a need stemming from the scarcity, variety, and unreliability of specie in circulation, but it proved premature. In this period, as later, Forsyth, Richardson was also active in lobbying local and imperial governments for political changes in the interest of commerce. For example, in 1791–92 it joined with other fur-trading concerns in opposing the evacuation of western military posts on American territory held by the British since the end of the revolution, a campaign which may have influenced retention of the posts until 1796.

From the outset of his residence in Montreal, Richardson identified with the merchants' movement for an elected assembly and the introduction of English commercial laws [*see* George Allsopp*; William Grant]. In 1787 he lamented that government obstructed the way of mercantile men at every turn when it "ought to acknowledge commerce as its basis, & the accommodation of the Merchant as one principal means of promoting the national prosperity." In March 1791 he joined colleagues from the colony and interested London merchants to petition against the bill that became the Constitutional Act. Examined at the bar of the House of Commons, he opposed the division of the colony on which the bill was based and the retention of French civil law, which favoured debtors over creditors, in the province of Lower Canada.

Although disappointed by the new constitution, Richardson stood in 1792 in the first general election held under it. He and Joseph Frobisher* were elected for Montreal East with "a great majority," having been supported by leading British merchants and Canadians such as Thomas McCord and Joseph Papineau*. He immediately assumed a role of leadership among the merchants in the House of Assembly. In February 1793, during an acrimonious debate over the language of legislation, he moved that the English alone should be the legal text of statutes. Ever forthright, he read his elaborate paper of justification only in English and bluntly stated that the "dearest interests" of the Canadians would be fostered if they would but accept a "gradual assimilation of sentiment" to the ways of His Majesty's old subjects. His intervention kept the political pot boiling for some weeks. Ultimately he succeeded; the governor was later instructed to assent only to the English version of bills, including those on civil law, for which the assembly had decreed that French would prevail. Richardson proved to be a member of prodigious energy in such matters as proposing and amending bills, drafting addresses to the governor, negotiating with the Legislative Council, improving the rules governing debate, and – ironically in view of subsequent events – asserting the assembly's exclusive privilege to initiate money bills. He was also highly effective; bills presented by him which became law dealt with the negotiability of promissory notes, the importation of potash from the United States, the rating of gold coins, the prevention of fraud by *engagés*, the regulation of registers of civil status, and the publication of statutes.

Richardson's experience in the assembly left him frustrated, nevertheless. The Canadians, he wrote to Alexander Ellice during the first session, caucused out of doors on all questions, and trying to change their minds was "like talking to the Waves of the Sea." There was a faction among them, he felt certain, which was "infected with the detestable principles now prevalent in France." Nothing could possibly be "so irksome as the situation of the English members . . . doomed to the necessity of combating the absurdities of the majority, without a hope of success." He did not stand for election in either 1796 or 1800.

From the outbreak of war with revolutionary France, Richardson exerted himself to the utmost in the interest of security. It was he who proposed the assembly's unanimous address to Lieutenant Governor Alured CLARKE of April 1793, which promised total cooperation and characterized the execution of Louis XVI as "the most atrocious Act which ever disgraced society." In 1794 he contributed important amendments to the Militia and Alien acts, the latter of which temporarily suspended habeas corpus, and was active on the Montreal committee of the Association, founded that year to support British rule. In October 1796, at the height of riots in Montreal over a new road act, Richardson was among a number of justices of the peace chosen to replace magistrates deemed by

Governor Robert Prescott* to have been too timorous in dealing with the rioters.

During late 1796 and in 1797 Richardson acted as the chief of Lower Canadian counter-intelligence, intercepting correspondence, having suspected traitors examined, and directing a string of informers from Montreal to the American border. He learned that the French minister to the United States was sending "emissaries" into Lower Canada to assess the attitudes of the habitants towards France, examine the colony's defences, and establish a fifth column to support a naval invasion projected for the summer or fall of 1797. The evidence Richardson compiled was used to arrest three Montrealers on charges of treason in February 1797 (they were later acquitted), to justify the Better Preservation Act, again suspending habeas corpus, which Attorney General Jonathan Sewell* successfully piloted through the legislature, and to build the crown's case against David McLane*, executed for treason in July 1797. Although sceptical of his informers' more grotesque tales, Richardson, like most of the governing élite, greatly exaggerated the danger: the Road Act riots, he thought, had been an attempt at insurrection fomented by emissaries; the French would send a fleet with up to 30,000 troops and find active support among the habitants and among disloyal politicians such as Joseph Papineau and Jean-Antoine Panet*, the leaders of a party of "Sans Culottes" in the assembly. In February 1797 Richardson urged a declaration of martial law as the only action that would adequately protect people of property from "all the horrors of assassination." When in July 1801 government officials learned that the Vermont adventurer Ira Allen had established a secret society in Montreal, Richardson was put in charge of the investigation; it resulted in the arrest of some of the ringleaders and proof that the society's aim had been to proliferate branches in the Canadas in order to provide support for an invasion from Vermont. Richardson was also an ensign in the British Militia of the Town and Banlieu of Montreal from 1794, and took the lead in establishing in 1801 a volunteer armed association, which carefully watched strangers, drilled, and in October patrolled the streets of Montreal at night.

About the turn of the century Richardson's business interests were reaching a critical point. With the exhaustion of prime beaver south of the Great Lakes and problems stemming from American tariff duties and settlement already evident, Forsyth, Richardson and Company had begun trading extensively in the northwest in opposition to, among others, the NWC, which it had left by 1798. That year, in order to sustain the intense competition that developed particularly with the NWC, Forsyth, Richardson, together with Phyn, Ellices, and Inglis, the Detroit firm of Leith, Jameson and Company, and six wintering partners,

founded the copartnership of the New North West Company, also called after 1799 the XY Company or the New Company. In 1800 the copartnership received an injection of capital and expertise when the famous explorer Alexander Mackenzie* and two partners in the successful Montreal firm of Parker, Gerrard, and Ogilvy – John Ogilvy* and John MURE – joined its ranks; from 1802 it was occasionally known as Sir Alexander Mackenzie and Company. Competition with the NWC became economic warfare, dividing British Montreal into two camps. From 1799 to 1804 the New North West Company tripled its investment in the annual outfit from about £8,000 to almost £25,000. By the latter year, it had secured about one-third of the northwest trade, and its share was growing.

The competition, however, was ruinous: massive quantities of trade rum demoralized the Indians, and costs spiralled, while the exchange value of trade goods plunged. As Edward Ellice*, Alexander's son, later commented, the only question was which company was losing most heavily. Crimes such as bribery of employees and theft of trade goods were commonplace. Indians were induced to pillage or fire on rival canoes. In one instance a clerk of the New North West Company shot to death an opposition clerk, but when he was brought to trial in Montreal in 1802 it was discovered that no court in British North America had jurisdiction over felonies committed in the Indian country. Reporting on the situation at the request of Lieutenant Governor Sir Robert Shore Milnes* of Lower Canada, Richardson concluded that if jurisdiction was not conferred on Canadian courts, force might well come to prevail over justice in the northwest, in which case "the Fur Trade must in the end be annihilated." Milnes urged Richardson's recommendation on the colonial secretary, Lord Hobart, as did Mackenzie. The result was an imperial act in 1803 giving jurisdiction for crimes in the Indian country to the courts of Lower Canada (and in some circumstances to those of Upper Canada) and giving the head of the administration of the lower province power to appoint magistrates in the interior. With competition driving both companies towards bankruptcy and the wintering partners fearing for their lives, amalgamation was arranged in 1804, the New North West Company acquiring one-quarter of the shares in a reorganized NWC.

Meanwhile, thanks no doubt to the diversity of its interests and the solidity of its London backers, Forsyth, Richardson was doing well. In 1803 a merchant from Albany, N.Y., estimated the value of its exports at £40,000, placing it third in Montreal after the NWC (£150,000) and Parker, Gerrard, Ogilvy and Company (£85,000). The importance of Upper Canada and the northwest to its operations is evident: that year it seems to have sent up the St Lawrence as many bateaux as the NWC.

At Milnes's insistence, a reluctant Richardson again stood for election in 1804. He won a seat for Montreal West and once more took the lead among the English representatives. In 1805 he became embroiled in a controversy over whether the building of jails should be financed by land taxation – as Richardson had pledged during the election – or by duties imposed on imports, the burden of which would fall mainly on the northwest fur trade. The following year he was prominent in futile attempts by the mercantile contingent in the assembly to have the Gaols Act disallowed and to prevent the majority from ordering the arrest for libel or contempt of Isaac Todd and newspaper editors Thomas Cary and Edward Edwards*, who had all denounced the act in ironic terms. In 1807 and 1808 he fought unsuccessfully for measures designed to promote immigration into the Eastern Townships and improve agricultural production and against passage by the assembly of a bill to render judges ineligible for election. Despite an ever-worsening political polarization, Richardson had some successes: his bills for regulating river pilots, improving the Montreal–Lachine road, and funding the improvement of navigation on the St Lawrence, among others, reached the statute books.

In April 1808 Richardson spoke at length in support of a bill he had introduced for incorporation of a "Bank of Lower-Canada." Although flawed to modern eyes by its adherence to the commodity theory of money value, the speech was nevertheless a stunning performance. With marvellous lucidity he traced the evolution of paper money, expounded the general principles of banking, and laid to rest numerous objections. He explained how short-term discounting worked, why the issuance of bank notes had to exceed specie holdings, why bank failures would be uncommon, and how counterfeiting could be severely curtailed. A brilliant stroke was his explanation of a seeming paradox: that corporate banks of limited liability but regulated as to investments and the issuing of notes were safer than private banks of unlimited liability. Richardson's speech and the bill were printed for public edification. Although the bill fell victim to prorogation of the legislature, both contributed greatly to gradual public acceptance of paper money and banking during the next decade.

Richardson's controversial stands in the assembly alienated the Canadian voters in Montreal West, and he was defeated in the election of 1808. He was not silenced politically, however, for he had been appointed an honorary executive councillor in December 1804 and had taken his seat on 25 Nov. 1805. As he had arranged with Milnes, he attended council meetings only when in Quebec for the legislative session or on business, but he was available for committee work

in Montreal. During the session of 1808 he was designated by Governor Sir James Henry Craig* official messenger from the Executive Council to the assembly on matters affecting the royal prerogative, a prestigious nomination previously accorded to John Young* and James McGill*. In December 1811 Richardson became a regular member of the council, and he held his seat until his death. As an executive councillor he was a particularly influential adviser of hard-line governors such as Craig and Lord Dalhousie [Ramsay*], but he was consulted much less by the conciliatory Sir George Prevost* and Sir James Kempt*. Among Richardson's duties was that of judge when the Executive Council sat as the Court of Appeals. Although a layman, he had a sound grasp of legal principles and could absorb legal detail quickly. In 1821 he delivered a council judgement that only clergymen of the "established" churches – Roman Catholic, Anglican, and Presbyterian – were empowered to keep official registers of baptisms, marriages, and burials, a restrictive decision later rectified by a number of provincial statutes.

During the war against Napoleonic France, Richardson again immersed himself in myriad aspects of the colony's security. In 1803 informers were set to work in Lower Canada and American border towns to ferret out the doings of emissaries. Rumours emanating from Paris that the colony would be attacked were reported by Richardson. A visit by Jérôme Bonaparte to the United States was carefully charted, and a suspicious fire in Montreal investigated. In 1804 Richardson drafted a bill to reward those who apprehended army deserters; it was presented by McGill and enacted. At Milnes's urging Richardson used secret-service money to turn Jacques Rousse – an expatriate Canadian who in 1793–94 had spied for the French minister to the United States – into an effective double agent.

By 1804 Richardson had come to believe that American foreign policy, dictated by France, was building towards war with Great Britain, and that secret clauses in the Louisiana Purchase treaty had promised the United States French military assistance should it attack the Canadas. These assessments, conveyed periodically to Civil Secretary Herman Witsius Ryland* and no doubt to other government officials, probably helped to shape the extremely pessimistic view of security taken at the Château Saint-Louis. After 1807 Richardson seems to have been less active in intelligence, although in 1809 he acted as the channel of secret communication from John Henry*, a spy used by Craig to explore the possibilities of New England separatism in case of war. In 1810, during Craig's so-called Reign of Terror (thoroughly approved of by Richardson), he was an active member of a committee formed from the Montreal members of the Executive Council which arrested three supporters of the Canadian party on suspicion of treason, examined numerous witnesses, and concluded (on thin evidence) that a Napoleonic plot aimed at "preparing the general mind" for insurrection had been narrowly thwarted.

In the decade after his final retirement from electoral politics, Richardson devoted much attention to problems of Lower Canadian merchants. In May 1810 he was chairman of an apparently short-lived Montreal committee of trade, probably formed, like one at Quebec the previous year [see John Jones*], to pressure the British government for improved conditions of trade, including better protection from American competition. Richardson was the Montreal head of a colonial lobby from 1809 to 1812 which persuaded the British parliament to prohibit inland importation from the United States of foreign products such as cottons and teas, although it failed to have American produce barred from the West Indies. More threatening to his personal interests were the growing assertion by the United States of jurisdiction over the southwest fur trade and the American government's discrimination against British traders in favour of John Jacob Astor's American Fur Company. Faced with high tariffs, seizures, embargoes, and other attempted exclusions, Montreal traders to the southwest – of whom Richardson and William McGillivray were the principals – had joined together in the Michilimackinac Company in 1806 [see John Ogilvy]. In 1810–11 Richardson and McGillivray reluctantly but realistically negotiated an amalgamation with Astor. The resulting agreement of January 1811 formed the South West Fur Company and gave Astor a 50 per cent interest with Forsyth, Richardson, and McTavish, McGillivrays and Company sharing the other half as the Montreal Michilimackinac Company; later the NWC purchased one-third of the interest of the Montreal firm. It was the British firms in the South West Fur Company which, through Richardson, gave Governor Prevost, commander-in-chief of the British forces, his first news of the American declaration of war in June 1812, a war the British and Canadian traders had looked forward to in hopes that the British abandonment of the southwest by treaty in 1783 and 1794 and militarily in 1796 could be permanently reversed.

Richardson and McGillivray exercised considerable influence on events in the west during the war. The enthusiastic support given by the agents, *engagés*, and dependent Indians of their companies enabled a small British force under Charles Roberts* to seize Fort Michilimackinac on 17 July 1812. The two men personally persuaded Prevost of the political and economic value of the southwest trade and of the fort's strategic importance for securing it. On their eulogistic recommendation and that of James McGill, Prevost commissioned the trader-adventurer Robert

DICKSON to raise an Indian force; it played a part in the successful defence of the fort under Robert McDouall* in August 1814. The chagrin of the two traders knew no bounds when it was learned that the peace negotiators had restored Michilimackinac to the Americans, and their legalistic interpretation of the Treaty of Ghent – a special pleading for delay – did not avail. Worse followed. In 1816 Congress closed the Indian trade to non-Americans. The next year, in a buyer's market, Richardson and his colleagues sold their South West Fur Company shares to Astor and withdrew from the southwest trade.

On the domestic front during the war Richardson served in the Montreal Incorporated Volunteers and attended to routine duties as executive councillor. He watched with dismay as Prevost cultivated the support of the Canadian party at the expense of those who had had Craig's ear. In 1814 Prevost reluctantly accepted the assembly's impeachment of chief justices James MONK and Jonathan Sewell for, among other things, having promulgated "unconstitutional" rules of practice. Although certain that Prevost's policy of conciliating the Canadian party was encouraging "the turbulent and revolutionary demagogues, who at present sway the Assembly," Richardson successfully countered Sewell's suggestion that the governor be attacked publicly. An open collision between Prevost and his Executive Council, which, as the colony's Court of Appeals, supported the chief justices, "would curtail our means of defense . . . even in Military operations," he asserted. He preferred "postponing such an extremity, to a more convenient season." Richardson also asserted that the assembly's impeachment of the chief justices alone should not be accepted, since they had had assistance in drafting the rules. "Every individual of every Court, is implicated," he argued. "Let us stand or fall together!" Finally, Sewell should abandon his idea of using legalistic grounds to avoid a hearing before the Privy Council in London; rather the best hope for the security of the colony lay in exploiting "the intemperance of those anarchists" in the Canadian party. The exposing by Sewell of their "cloven foot" would likely force ministers to repress them – if Richardson had his way, by "taking away the Representative part of the constitution." Richardson's counsel on these and other matters was followed; Sewell and Monk were acquitted, though no constitutional repression was undertaken by the British parliament.

Tradition has assigned to Richardson authorship of a famous series of letters signed Veritas, which appeared in the *Montreal Herald* in April–June 1815 and later in pamphlet form. They unmercifully attacked the character and generalship of Prevost, described in one as an officer who had the "extraordinary fatality of either never attempting an active operation, or thinking of it only when the time for practical execution was past." Although a plausible case can be made for the attribution to Richardson – especially since the letters were published only after the war – there is little direct proof, save the recollection 58 years later of a man who in 1815 had been a clerk in Forsyth, Richardson. Indeed, Prevost suspected Solicitor General Stephen SEWELL to have been the author.

Following the war Richardson's business interests underwent readjustment. His declining involvement in the fur trade dwindled further with the amalgamation of the Hudson's Bay Company and the NWC in 1821. He had until then played a prominent role in defending the interests of the NWC in its struggle with Lord Selkirk [Douglas*] over the establishment and maintenance of Selkirk's Red River settlement. Forsyth, Richardson and Company intensified its export of the newer staples such as grain and timber, while its interest in developing to the maximum its Upper Canadian trade is evident from Richardson's fundamental role in the construction of the Lachine Canal. Long an advocate of such a water-way, on 26 July 1819 he was elected chairman of a committee charged by the newly formed Company of Proprietors of the Lachine Canal [see François DESRIVIÈRES] with overseeing its construction. The company quickly ran into trouble, and in 1821 the colonial legislature took over its assets and appointed a commission to complete the project. On 17 July as chairman of the commission Richardson turned the first sod, and construction began. When the legislature momentarily ceased financing the project, advances were obtained from the Bank of Montreal on the personal security of Richardson and George GARDEN. Work was virtually completed in 1825.

Richardson and his company remained leading lobbyists. In August 1821 Richardson was named by a meeting of Montreal merchants to a committee to press for the removal of all restrictions on Lower Canadian wheat and flour in British and West Indian markets as a means of relieving the "state of depression and distress" that threatened them with ruin. The following year in Montreal he presided over the founding meeting of the Committee of Trade, successor to the committee of 1810; Thomas Blackwood* was elected chairman. In 1823–24 Forsyth, Richardson headed the list of mercantile houses which successfully sought reduction of the excise on tobacco imported into Great Britain from Upper Canada. Through John Inglis, a partner in the Ellice firm in London and a director of the East India Company, Forsyth, Richardson became in 1824 sole agents in the Canadas for the sale of East India Company teas, a lucrative contract it retained until after Richardson's death. In this period Richardson was also much occupied, as Edward Ellice's Montreal agent, with overseeing the management of the huge and rapidly

developing seigneury of Villechauve, commonly known as Beauharnois. His strenuous efforts to enable Ellice to convert the seigneury to freehold tenure under the Canada Trade Act failed in the Executive Council in 1823 for legal reasons, but Ellice was later able to effect his aim under the Canada Tenures Act of 1825. Among Richardson's many business involvements in the post-war period was his appointment as a director of the Montreal Fire Insurance Company in the early 1820s.

Richardson's most absorbing concern, however, was finance. In 1817, spurred by the success of the army bills during the war [see James GREEN], nine merchants, among them Richardson, signed articles of association and invited stock subscriptions to form the Bank of Montreal, the first permanent bank in British North America and the progenitor of Canada's chartered banking system. The guiding spirit was Richardson's. His speech of 1808 was widely quoted by the bank's supporters, he was chairman of the founding committee, and the articles, based largely on the charter of the First Bank of the United States, reflected his ideas. Although never a director, Richardson took a close interest as a shareholder in the bank's affairs for the remainder of his life. On his instance the outer front wall of the bank's first building, constructed in 1819 on Rue Saint-Jacques, displayed four much admired terra-cotta plaques from Coade of London depicting agriculture, arts and crafts, commerce, and navigation. That year, at the Colonial Office, he personally negotiated for royal assent to incorporation, which was finally granted in 1822. Richardson was unanimously elected to chair a critical stockholders' meeting of 5 June 1826 at which a developing confrontation between a young guard among the directors under George Moffatt* and the older fur traders – Richardson, Forsyth, and Samuel Gerrard*, president of the bank – came to a head. Gerrard was deposed as president, but Richardson, with the largest single voting block of shares and proxies, was able to save him from further humiliation and enable him to remain as a director, thus preserving the bank's unity. Richardson was a director of the Montreal Savings Bank, and in 1826 Forsyth, Richardson was appointed financial agent to manage the surplus funds of the receiver general of Upper Canada, a task it performed with profit and integrity into the 1840s.

Having declined earlier offers of a seat on the Legislative Council, Richardson accepted appointment to the upper house in 1816. There he supported all the mercantile and conservative causes with consistency and pugnacity. In 1821 he had the council pass a series of provocative resolutions which, going well beyond the pretensions of the House of Lords in matters of public finance, attempted to dictate to the assembly the form of its appropriation bills. The next year Richardson speculated in a council speech that a secret caucus of the Canadian party, redolent of the Committee of Public Safety in revolutionary France, might be planning to depose Governor Lord Dalhousie. The assembly called on the council to censure him and on the governor to dismiss him; both demands were rejected as threats to freedom of debate in the council. Throughout the 1820s he led those councillors – usually the majority – who were adamantly opposed to the assembly's claim to appropriate crown revenues. In 1825, however, he stood almost alone in protesting passage by the council of a money bill negotiated with the assembly by Lieutenant Governor Sir Francis Nathaniel BURTON, and in 1829 he led a minority attack on a similar bill worked out by Governor Sir James Kempt.

Richardson took a particularly active interest in a proposal in 1822 to unite the Canadas. As unrivalled dean of the colony's business community, he chaired a public pro-union meeting in Montreal and gave a lengthy speech. Besides solving a long-standing and contentious problem of dividing import duties between Upper and Lower Canada, he said, union would enable Lower Canadian merchants to escape thraldom to the Canadian majority in the assembly, who were "anti-commercial in habits." Not one to mince words, he told the crowd that the fundamental issue was whether they and their posterity would "become foreigners in a British land" or "the inhabitants of foreign origin . . . become british," which could only be to the great benefit of the Canadians. Led by Richardson, six members of the Legislative Council protested its decision on 23 Jan. 1823 to oppose union. That night he wrote to Edward Ellice with ammunition for use against Louis-Joseph Papineau* and John Neilson*, who were being sent to London by the Canadian party to oppose union. He pointed out, for example, that Papineau's weakness lay in his overweening self-esteem, that Neilson was so much a "Republican" as to have been obliged once to seek refuge in the United States, and that even Pierre-Stanislas BÉDARD, jailed in 1810 by Craig for attempted insurrection, had been contemplated as a delegate. These and further efforts by Richardson and Ellice were of no avail; the project was thwarted in the face of massive Canadian opposition.

Richardson was extremely active in public life. He was a charter member of the Montreal branch of the Agriculture Society in 1790. From 1793 to 1828 he was regularly appointed a Lower Canadian commissioner to negotiate a division of import duties with Upper Canada. In 1799 he was nominated treasurer to build a new court-house in Montreal and took a leading role in raising money for the imperial war effort. In the years 1802–7 he was successively named to commissions to demolish the city's crumbling fortifications and design new street plans, to build a

prison and a market house, to improve the Montreal–Lachine road, and to erect a monument to Lord Nelson. He headed a commission in 1815 to attract subscriptions for the families of soldiers killed or wounded at Waterloo, and in 1827 he was a leading promoter of subscriptions for a monument at Quebec to James Wolfe* and Louis-Joseph de Montcalm*. Richardson was appointed a trustee of the Royal Institution for the Advancement of Learning [see Joseph Langley MILLS] in 1818 and was a moving force behind the foundation and early financing of the Montreal General Hospital, established in 1819 [see William CALDWELL (1782–1833)]; he was the first president of the hospital after its incorporation in 1823. Among the many complicated estates that he helped settle was that of James McGill, a gruelling and thankless task except that it resulted in the beginnings of a university for his beloved city [see François Desrivières].

During the legislative session of 1831 a weary Richardson was at his post, protesting against whig conciliation, combating Papineau's manœuvres to achieve control of the legislature for the Patriote party, as the Canadian party had become known, and fretting about backsliders on the Legislative Council, of which he became speaker on 4 February. He opposed, though unsuccessfully, the incorporation of Montreal, until then governed by appointed justices of the peace, for fear that through elections its administration would fall into the hands of the Patriote party. To Ellice he wrote of the Canadians as "spoilt children," liberated by the British conquest, but trying to turn the tables on their "too generous emancipators." He urged that there was "too much British Capital . . . at stake, to be handed over to Canadian Legislative management" and was outraged that the country which gave the "Law to Europe" might "be dictated to, by the descendants of Frenchmen." Parliament should intervene to smash Papineau and his fellows. At the end of the session Richardson presented resolutions against the assembly's attempts to obtain repeal of the Canada Tenures Act. According to a sympathetic executive councillor, Andrew William Cochran*, "his feelings were deeply wounded by the desertion or coldhearted support" of former allies: "'Amidst the faithless, faithful only he.'" On returning home he took to his bed, Cochran wrote, lamented the treachery of his erstwhile political friends, and seemed "to give up hope and care for life."

John Richardson died on 18 May 1831. Flags on the ships in harbour were flown at half-mast until the state funeral at Christ Church, where a plaque was dedicated to his memory. The English-language newspapers were full of deserved eulogies to him as a man of integrity in matters financial and political and one of the city's greatest builders. A new wing of the Montreal General Hospital was constructed the fol-

Richardson

lowing year as a permanent memorial to him. But even in death Richardson roused intense passions. Papineau pointedly had not attended the funeral, while *Le Canadien* and *La Minerve* reminded readers that Richardson had been the leader in Lower Canada of that party, called tory in England and ultra-royalist in France, which denied the people their just rights and by its excesses had recently turned Europe into a vast theatre of war and revolution.

Richardson's interests went well beyond commerce and local politics. His aesthetic sense, like that of the British upper class in Montreal as a whole, was evident. The military surgeon John Jeremiah Bigsby* remarked that "at an evening party at Mr Richardson's the appointments and service were admirable, the dress, manners, and conversation of the guests in excellent taste." His wide-ranging curiosity led him to the presidency of the Natural History Society of Montreal, founded in 1827. He was well read in ancient and modern history, law, economics, and British poetry. The many comments on British, American, and European politics found in his letters are usually acute, if somewhat alarmist. Adam Smith was his preferred economist, but he was no unqualified believer in *laissez-faire*, as the provision in his bank proposal of 1808 for government participation and his continual lobbying for state assistance indicate. Byron was his favourite poet, but he did not admire the man or his politics. Edmund Burke governed his constitutional thinking on Lower Canada, but in 1831 he thought a moderate reform of parliament justified, a seeming paradox which Edward Ellice and Lord Durham [Lambton*] would have thoroughly understood. Like many upper-class Montreal Scots, he was a member of and generous patron to both the Presbyterian and the Anglican churches. In personality, he had much of the "state and distance" he so admired in Craig and which went well with his considerable height and majestic bearing. He was a man who wished to live by principles, and this desire often led to undue rigidity. He had the instincts of an outstanding team-player, although prone at times to define personally the true interests of the team. These instincts gave him superabundant energy and generated fierce and often selfless loyalties. Tragically, those who opposed his team, particularly Canadians, whose will to survive he could not fathom, whose loyalty to the Empire he could not accept, became enemies in his mind, which he spoke all too openly. Richardson did a great deal of good, but a great deal of harm also.

F. MURRAY GREENWOOD

John Richardson may be the author of *The letters of Veritas, re-published from the "Montreal Herald"; containing a succinct narrative of the military administration of Sir George Prevost, during his command in the Canadas . . .* (Montreal, 1815).

AUM, P58, U, Richardson to Grant, 16 Aug., 25 Oct. 1819; Richardson to Gerrard, 22 April 1828; Richardson and Gregory to McIntosh, 18 Oct. 1830. NLS, Dept. of MSS, MSS 15113–15, 15126, 15139 (mfm. at PAC). PAC, MG 11, [CO 42] Q, 86–87, 107–9, 118, 132, 157, 161, 166, 168, 293; MG 23, GII, 10, vols.3, 5; 17, ser.1, vols.3, 9–10, 13–14, 16; GIII, 7 (transcripts); RG 1, E1: 29–36; RG 4, A1: 10262–44628; vols.141–47; RG 7, G1, 3: 259–69; 13: 42; RG 68, General index, 1651–1841. PRO, CO 42/127. SRO, GD45/3 (mfm. at PAC). "L'association loyale de Montréal," ANQ *Rapport*, 1948–49: 257–73. "A British privateer in the American Revolution," ed. H. R. Howland, *American Hist. Rev.* (New York), 7 (1901–2): 286–303. L. A. [Call Whitworth-Aylmer, Baronness] Aylmer, "Recollections of Canada, 1831," ANQ *Rapport*, 1934–35: 305. *Corr. of Lieut. Governor Simcoe* (Cruikshank). "Courts of justice for the Indian country," PAC *Report*, 1892: 136–46. *Docs. relating to constitutional hist., 1759–91* (Shortt and Doughty; 1918); *1791–1818* (Doughty and McArthur); *1819–28* (Doughty and Story). Douglas, *Lord Selkirk's diary* (White). L.C., House of Assembly, *Journals*, 1792–1815; Legislative Council, *Journals*, 1816–31; *Statutes*, 1793–1831. Mackenzie, *Journals and letters* (Lamb). L.-J. Papineau, "Correspondance de Louis-Joseph Papineau (1820–1839)," Fernand Ouellet, édit., ANQ *Rapport*, 1953–55: 191–442. *Reports of cases argued and determined in the courts of King's Bench and in the provincial Court of Appeals of Lower Canada, with a few of the more important cases in the Court of Vice Admiralty . . .*, comp. G. O. Stuart (Quebec, 1834). John Richardson, "The John Richardson letters," ed. E. A. Cruikshank, *OH*, 6 (1905): 20–36. *Le Canadien*, 1806–10, 28 May 1831. *La Minerve*, 21 févr., 6, 9 juin 1831. *Montreal Gazette*, 1787–1815; 1821–22; 28 May, 4, 11 June 1831. *Montreal Herald*, 1811–15. *Quebec Gazette*, 7 Aug. 1788; 26 May 1791; 21 June 1792; 21 Feb. 1793; 17 July, 11, 25 Dec. 1794; 5 Nov. 1801; 31 March 1803; 5 July, 27 Dec. 1804; 14 Nov. 1805; 2 Jan., 23 Oct. 1806; 2, 9 July, 12 Nov. 1807; 3 March, 12 May, 1 Sept., 24 Nov., 22 Dec. 1808; 1 June, 6 June, 30 Nov., 14 Dec. 1809; 4 Jan., 8, 29 March, 12 April, 17 May 1810; 18, 25 April, 16 May, 27 June, 18 July 1811; 28 May 1812; 28 May, 2 Sept. 1813; 11, 25 July, 28 Nov. 1816; 9 Jan., 22 May, 26 June, 2 Oct. 1817; 29 Jan. 1818; 18 Feb., 14 June, 5 Aug. 1819; 6 Jan., 27 April 1820; 12 April, 18 June, 25 July, 27 Aug., 22 Oct. 1821; 27 Nov. 1823. *Quebec Mercury*, 2 Feb. 1805, 2 May 1808. *Quebec almanac*, 1791: 84; 1796: 83. *Roll of alumni in arts of the University and King's College of Aberdeen, 1596–1860*, ed. P. J. Anderson (Aberdeen, Scot., 1900).

F. D. Adams, *A history of Christ Church Cathedral, Montreal* (Montreal, 1941). F.-J. Audet, *Les députés de Montréal*. A. L. Burt, *The United States, Great Britain and British North America from the revolution to the establishment of peace after the War of 1812* (Toronto and New Haven, Conn., 1940). R. Campbell, *Hist. of Scotch Presbyterian Church*. Christie, *Hist. of L.C.* (1848–55), vols.1–3. D. [G.] Creighton, *The empire of the St Lawrence* (Toronto, 1956). G. C. Davidson, *The North West Company* (Berkeley, Calif., 1918; repr. New York, 1967). Denison, *Canada's first bank*. F. M. Greenwood, "The development of a garrison mentality among the English in Lower Canada,

1793–1811" (PHD thesis, Univ. of B.C., Vancouver, 1970). *Hochelaga depicta . . .*, ed. Newton Bosworth, (Montreal, 1839; repr. Toronto, 1974). Innis, *Fur trade in Canada* (1970). H. E. MacDermot, *A history of the Montreal General Hospital* (Montreal, 1950). R. C. McIvor, *Canadian monetary, banking and fiscal development* (Toronto, 1958). Ouellet, *Hist. économique*; *Lower Canada*. R. A. Pendergast, "The XY Company, 1798–1804" (PHD thesis, Univ. of Ottawa, 1957). K. W. Porter, *John Jacob Astor, business man* (2v., Cambridge, Mass., 1931; repr. New York, 1966). Robert Rumilly, *La Compagnie du Nord-Ouest, une épopée montréalaise* (2v., Montréal, 1980); *Histoire de Montréal* (5v., Montréal, 1970–74), 2. Taft Manning, *Revolt of French Canada*. Tulchinsky, "Construction of first Lachine Canal." M. S. Wade, *Mackenzie of Canada: the life and adventures of Alexander Mackenzie, discoverer* (Edinburgh and London, 1927). J.-P. Wallot, *Intrigues françaises et américaines au Canada, 1800–1802* (Montréal, 1965). M. [E.] Wilkins Campbell, *McGillivray, lord of the northwest* (Toronto, 1962); *NWC* (1973). R. H. Fleming, "The origin of Sir Alexander Mackenzie and Company," *CHR*, 9 (1928): 137–55; "Phyn, Ellice and Company of Schenectady," *Contributions to Canadian Economics* (Toronto), 4 (1932): 7–41. J. W. Pratt, "Fur trade strategy and the American left flank in the War of 1812," *American Hist. Rev.* (New York), 40 (1935): 246–73. Henry Scadding, "Some Canadian noms-de-plume identified; with samples of the writing to which they are appended," *Canadian Journal* (Toronto), new ser., 15 (1876–78): 332–41. Adam Shortt, "The Hon. John Richardson," *Canadian Bankers' Assoc., Journal* (Toronto), 29 (1921–22): 17–27. W. S. Wallace, "Forsyth, Richardson and Company in the fur trade," *RSC Trans.*, 3rd ser., 34 (1940), sect.II: 187–94.

RIDOUT, THOMAS, office holder; b. 17 March 1754 in Sherborne, Dorset, England, son of George Ridout; m. first *c.* 1776 Isabella ——, and they had one son, Samuel Smith*; m. secondly 26 May 1789 Mary Campbell, and they had seven sons, including George* and Thomas Gibbs*, and five daughters; d. 8 Feb. 1829 in York (Toronto), Upper Canada.

In 1774 Thomas Ridout emigrated to Maryland where an elder brother, already established as a government official at Annapolis, financed his entry into the carrying trade with the West Indies and France. By concentrating upon his commercial affairs, Thomas seems to have avoided the crisis of conscience posed by the revolution to many Americans, especially recent arrivals from Britain. At the end of the revolutionary war, during which he had continued his Atlantic trading activities, he was viewed as a friend and supporter of the new American nation.

In 1787, however, Ridout took a journey westward that would change his future and his allegiance. He set out in December 1787 for the new settlement of Kentucky. His ostensible purpose was to collect some business debts, but he also carried letters of introduction, one from no less a personage than George Washington, indicating that he went "to explore and perhaps to settle" there. His original plans, whatever they were, collapsed when he and a small band of travellers were captured by Shawnee Indians in March 1788 on the Ohio River. Unlike several of his companions Ridout escaped death and, after three months' captivity, was taken to British-held Detroit and freedom.

By mid July Ridout was at Montreal. He arrived there just as Lord Dorchester [Guy Carleton*] was erecting four new judicial districts in western Quebec. The possibility of establishing a separate western colony was being discussed and Ridout may have been influenced to stay by the positive reception he was accorded and by the chance of employment in the new jurisdiction. In May 1789 he married the daughter of a loyalist and by the end of the year was contemplating permanent residence in British North America. In 1792 he obtained a position in the commissariat and with his young family moved to Newark (Niagara-on-the-Lake) to join the new administration being set up there by Upper Canada's first lieutenant governor, John Graves Simcoe*.

In 1793 Ridout entered the surveyor general's office as first clerk. Despite this modest beginning and competition from deputy surveyor general William Chewett*, who was better trained and more professionally active, Ridout soon rose in the department. He and Chewett acted jointly as surveyors general in 1799, 1802, and 1807 during the absences of the regular incumbents. In the latter year Ridout succeeded in avoiding involvement in the dispute between Lieutenant Governor Francis Gore* and Surveyor General Charles Burton Wyatt*. Gore suspended Wyatt and, albeit temporarily, Ridout's eldest son, a deputy provincial surveyor. In the fall of 1809, after two years of acting as joint department head, Ridout travelled to England with Gore's support to lobby for the surveyor generalship. He was successful and officially received the appointment in September 1810, retaining the post until his death.

Ridout's rising stature in the young society is probably better mirrored in his activities outside the department. He was made registrar of York County in 1796, a year before moving to the new capital, sergeant-at-arms to the House of Assembly in 1798, and clerk of the peace for the Home District in 1800.

Ridout was elected in 1812 to the assembly for the East Riding of York and Simcoe, defeating Joseph Shepard* who, in Ridout's words, represented the "Democratic Faction" and was supported by Joseph Willcocks*. Ridout did not run in 1816 and his son George, a moderate loosely aligned with William Warren Baldwin*, lost the seat to Peter Robinson*. Ridout did not campaign for office again but he was called to the Legislative Council in 1825 and served until his death.

Rindisbacher

Ridout was rather old to take an active role in the War of 1812 but he supported his sons in their various endeavours and himself became a director of the Loyal and Patriotic Society of Upper Canada. A decade later he was appointed to the board established to review claims for war losses. In 1822 he became a member of the Clergy Reserves Corporation and in 1827 he was appointed to the original board of King's College (University of Toronto), thus joining initiatives of John Strachan* on behalf of the Church of England.

Ridout worked assiduously to establish himself in the new colony. By dint of perseverance and steady application he secured a niche for himself and his family, especially sons George and Thomas Gibbs, in the developing administration and society of Upper Canada. Though he saw himself as a man of independent mind, a characteristic more frequently displayed by his offspring, he was in reality one of many middle and minor functionaries upon whose steady support and conservative views rested the growing power of the colonial oligarchy which has come to be known as the "family compact."

ROBERT J. BURNS

AO, MS 537. Loyal and Patriotic Soc. of U.C., *Report, with an appendix, and a list of subscribers and benefactors* (Montreal, 1817), 42–43. *Ten years of Upper Canada in peace and war, 1805–1815; being the Ridout letters*, ed. Matilda [Ridout] Edgar (Toronto, 1890). Armstrong, *Handbook of Upper Canadian chronology* (1967), 24–25, 34, 105, 148, 164. Cowdell Gates, *Land policies of U.C.* Craig, *Upper Canada*, 12, 133–34.

RINDISBACHER, PETER, painter; b. 12 April 1806 in Eggiwil, Switzerland, second son of Pierre Rindisbacher and Barbara (Barbe) Ann Wyss; d. 12 or 13 August 1834 in St Louis, Mo.

Peter Rindisbacher's family were German-speaking Lutherans. His father was a middle-class farmer who began to work as a veterinarian in 1806. Peter sketched continuously from a very early age, and was encouraged and supervised by his parents. In 1818 he briefly received instruction in landscape painting from Jakob Samuel Weibel, a Bernese school miniaturist who left a strong imprint on his protégé's style. Peter's other interest was the army; he had been a volunteer drummer boy in a Bern company of grenadiers at the age of ten.

Peter's father was a restless man. Thus when Captain Rudolph von May, an officer in De Meuron's Regiment, visited Bern to recruit settlers on behalf of Lord Selkirk [Douglas*] for the Red River settlement (Man.) and described the colony's agricultural prospects in fabulous terms, he was seduced. On 30 May 1821 he and his family left Dordrecht, Netherlands, with a contingent of more than 160 emigrants, mostly Swiss, aboard the *Lord Wellington*, bound for York Factory (Man.) on Hudson Bay.

The passage was difficult. En route the *Lord Wellington* met up with the Hudson's Bay Company ships *Prince of Wales* and *Eddystone* and HMS *Hecla* and *Fury* of Commander William Edward Parry*'s expedition in search of the northwest passage. Fifteen-year-old Peter sketched the ships, their dramatic encounters with icebergs, and the Inuit who came to trade with them. The party arrived at York Factory on 17 August. Shortly after, having to leave behind a large part of their supplies and belongings for want of boats, the Swiss set out on the gruelling, dangerous trip via Norway House to Fort Douglas (Winnipeg), the seat of the colony's government, which was reached in November just before freeze-up. On the way Rindisbacher depicted HBC posts, Indians, and the party's struggles over portages and up rivers. At Fort Douglas the exhausted Swiss learned that no preparations had been made for their reception, and that they would have to survive the winter on their meagre supplies and what they could forage. At the end of the winter Governor George Simpson* described their situation as "the most distressing scene of starvation that can well be conceived."

In 1822 Pierre Rindisbacher built a house and began to farm. Peter supplemented the family income with earnings as a clerk at the HBC store in Fort Garry and from the sale of paintings. From 1823 James Hargrave*, a company clerk there, received orders for him from traders and officials delighted with his colourful and accurate depiction of life in the northwest, which they would keep as souvenirs or send home to relatives. Peter built up a repertoire of popular subjects; the original works were done in pen-and-ink, and from them copies were traced and finished in water-colour. In November 1824 George Barnston* at York Factory requested of Hargrave a number of works on Plains Indians and the buffalo, "in which I think the young lad excells." Submitting another order in 1826, he told Hargrave to let Rindisbacher "put his own price on the Drawings for he is a conscientious lad, I believe."

In 1823 the interim governor of Assiniboia, Andrew H. Bulger*, had commissioned from young Rindisbacher a series of six water-colours depicting Bulger travelling by various conveyances and meeting with Indian delegations. Robert Parker Pelly, Bulger's successor, saw copies of the series and ordered a set, which he took with him to England in 1825. There he had oil copies made, depicting himself in Bulger's place; from them coloured lithographs were produced and sold as sets in Britain, where John Franklin*'s expeditions were creating a market for them, and in the northwest, where "Pelly's picture books" also sold well. Rindisbacher received neither credit for his originals nor remuneration from the sales. Similarly, the Reverend John West*, Anglican missionary at the Red River settlement, took six views to London and had them published as lithographs in 1825 or 1826; the lithographs credited West rather than Rindisbacher as the artist.

The young painter's subjects included the Métis, company officials, and settlement life, but Rindisbacher was especially inspired by (and commissioned to paint) the exotic, colourful, and dramatic life of the Indians. Bulger allegedly arranged a winter expedition to give him the opportunity to sketch a buffalo hunt. Only a few paintings, however, document the increasingly desperate plight of Rindisbacher's own people. For the most part artisans, they were totally unfit to face the privations of a farming life at Red River. Man-made and natural disasters mocked their clumsy efforts to eke out a living. They began trickling south. In the spring of 1826 a devastating flood combined with an infestation of grub-worms discouraged the remaining die-hards, among them Pierre Rindisbacher. With his family and other Swiss settlers he left Red River on 11 July 1826 and settled at a place called Gratiot's Grove (near Darlington, Wis.).

Peter continued to paint Indian views, adding to his repertoire, but he also expanded his range of subjects to include miniature portraits of friends and local citizens. He visited St Louis in June 1829, and then travelled to Prairie du Chien (Wis.) to record a treaty-making ceremony and to do studies of Sauk and Fox Indians. By year's end he was living in St Louis, making miniatures in pencil, crayon, and water-colour. He had never lost his interest in the military life and both in the Red River settlement and on the American prairies was constantly in the company of soldiers; in St Louis he became a volunteer in the St Louis Grays. Army officers, through their contacts with the American social élite, brought their young painter friend to the notice of the buying public. In local newspapers the officers vaunted him as possessing "a genius as fruitful, and an imagination as vivid as the scenes amongst which he has dwelt" and asserted that "these will enable him, in cultivating his fine talents, to throw aside the threadbare subjects of the schools, and give to the world themes as fresh as the soil upon which he was bred; – glowing as the newness of nature; and picturesque as a combination of bold scenery, with bolder man and manners, will afford." His friends sent scenes to the *American Turf Register and Sporting Magazine*, which published them in its pages. But the promise of success was cut short in 1834 when Rindisbacher died, possibly of cholera, at the age of 28. He seems to have been married and to have had two children.

Peter Rindisbacher's success in his own time was based on the novelty of his subjects, the accuracy with which he depicted them, and the engaging quality of his style. Earlier paintings are naïve in execution, but his later Red River work is painted in clear harmonious colours and his subjects, spaced out in a tableau and bathed in a quiet, luminous light, have a serene quality. They remain somewhat wooden, however, and it was not until after 1826 that, through the use of sweeping lines, a more sombre restricted palette, and an almost metallic crispness of execution, he fully captured the spirit of his subjects. Constant improvement in his rendering of muscle structure may reflect his father's knowledge of anatomy; it certainly reflects the development of his style. As an admirer observed in December 1829, "There is a living and moving effect in the swell and contraction he gives to the muscular appearance of his figures, that evinces much observation, judgement, and skill."

Largely unknown until the 1940s, Peter Rindisbacher has come to occupy an important place in the history of Canadian art. Although he was of European origin, his youth and lack of formal training enabled him to develop a style rooted in the land of his adoption. He was the first resident professional artist west of the Great Lakes and superior in draftsmanship and feeling for his subjects to his closest American contemporary, the better-known George Catlin. He ranks among that group of celebrated artists of the west, including Catlin, John Mix Stanley, and Paul Kane*, whose principal interest was the recording of Indian life. Rindisbacher's close observation of detail combined with his growing ability to capture the spirit of his subjects and their land make him a valuable witness to his times and place, to be appreciated as much by historians, anthropologists, and geographers for the informational value of his work as by connoisseurs of art for the distinctive, evolving, authentic quality of his paintings.

In collaboration with J. RUSSELL HARPER

Through the promotional efforts of his fellow officers, the newly found popularity of Peter Rindisbacher lasted for a few years after his death. His works were published, usually by lithographic techniques, in J. O. Lewis, *Aboriginal portfolio: a collection of portraits of the most celebrated chiefs of the North American Indians* (Philadelphia, 1835–36); T. L. McKenney and James Hall, *History of the Indian tribes of North America with biographical sketches and anecdotes of the principal chiefs* (3v., Philadelphia, 1836–44); Augustus Murray, *Travels in North America during 1834, 1835, & 1836* (London, 1839); and *American Turf Register and Sporting Magazine* (Baltimore), 11 (1840): 495–96. From 1933, when historian Grace Lee Nute began rekindling interest in Rindisbacher, reproductions of his work have been used to illustrate a good many publications on Canadian and American art, on the Arctic and the West, as well as on the Indians.

E. H. Bovay, *Le Canada et les Suisses, 1604–1974* (Fribourg, Switzerland, 1976), lists 187 works by Rindisbacher and names the last known holder of each. In Canada,

Robert

his works are held mainly at the PAC, the Glenbow-Alberta Institute, Calgary, and the PAM. A self-portrait by Rindisbacher painted in 1833–34 is reproduced in Bovay and in A. M. Josephy, *The artist was a young man: the life story of Peter Rindisbacher* (Fort Worth, Tex., 1970), which has a complete bibliography on Rindisbacher.

Lauperswil Registry Office (Lauperswil, Switzerland), Reg. of baptisms for the commune of Lauperswil, 1806. J. R. Harper, *Painting in Canada, a history* (Toronto and Quebec, 1966). F. [J.] Lindegger, *Bruder des roten Mannes; das abenteuerliche leben und einmalige Werk des Indianermalers Peter Rindisbacher (1806–1834)* (Aare, Switzerland, 1983). Barry Lord, *The history of painting in Canada: toward a people's art* (Toronto, 1974). Karl Meuli, "Scythia Vergiliana: ethnographisches, archäologisches und mythologisches zu Vergils Georgica," *Beiträge zur Volkskunde* (Basel, Switzerland, 1960), 140–75. *Painters in a new land: from Annapolis Royal to the Klondike*, ed. Michael Bell (Toronto, 1973). F. J. Lindegger, "Wie der Eggiwiler Peter Rindisbacher zum Indianermaler wurde," *Berner Nachrichten* (Bern, Switzerland), 24, 29 Aug. 1978. J. F. McDermott, "Further notes on Peter Rindisbacher," *Art Quarterly* (Detroit), 26 (1963): 73–76.

ROBERT, ANTOINE-BERNARDIN (baptized **Antoine**), Roman Catholic priest, professor, educational administrator, and vicar general; b. 7 Feb. 1757 in La Prairie (Que.), son of Pierre Robert, *dit* Lapommeraie, and Marie Paquet; d. 11 Jan. 1826 at the Hôpital Général of Quebec and was buried two days later in the chapel of the Séminaire de Québec.

Antoine-Bernardin Robert studied first at the Collège Saint-Raphaël in Montreal from 1769 to 1775, and then continued at the Séminaire de Quebec until his ordination by Bishop Jean-Olivier Briand* on 20 Oct. 1782. Following a practice necessitated by the scarcity of teachers, the seminary called upon his services in 1780, even though he was still only a student. Starting as regent of the third form (Method), Robert followed his pupils all the way up through the sixth form (Rhetoric).

After serving as prefect of studies at the Petit Séminaire for two years, Robert felt the need to take stock of his situation, and at his request the bishop of Quebec, Louis-Philippe Mariauchau* d'Esgly, appointed him parish priest of Berthier (Berthier-sur-Mer) in 1786. But parish ministry did not suit his temperament, and in March of the following year he asked to return to the seminary. The bishop replied, "Your letter can only enhance the high opinion I already had of you[.] I very gladly consent to your leaving the charge of the parish of Berthier to go to the seminary, being quite convinced that you will be very useful there in training persons capable of teaching and edifying the people of my diocese."

Robert was admitted as a member of the community of the Séminaire de Québec on 13 Aug. 1787, along with Edmund Burke*, and both joined the seminary's council on 22 November. He again became prefect of

studies at the Petit Séminaire and in 1790 succeeded Burke in the philosophy and mathematics classes. Appointed bursar in the seminary early in May 1795, on the 30th Robert was elected superior and he held the two offices alternately until 1816. Despite the deplorable state of his health he took on the direction of the Petit Séminaire for a final term from 1817 till 1820, and he ended his career as first assistant to the superior. He had also been made vicar general to Bishop Joseph-Octave Plessis, who had honoured him with this office on 13 Jan. 1813.

Robert had a profound influence on the Petit Séminaire de Québec, particularly on the quality of the teaching. He apparently introduced the curriculum of the royal military schools that had been founded in France in 1776, as well as the manuals prepared for them by Charles Batteux, a disciple of the noted educationalist Charles Rollin. Under the title "Plan d'éducation du séminaire de Québec" he left a detailed description of this program as applied to the first- and second-year classes (Latin Elements and Belles-Lettres) in 1790. In these forms the pupils learned to master Latin step by step through studying grammar, literary appreciation, translation, composition, and versification. Each professor dictated his lectures, which were in Latin but contained abundant quotations from the best French writers of the 17th and 18th centuries. During his term as superior Robert applied himself, with the help of his confrères Jérôme Demers* and Antoine Parant*, to filling gaps in the 1790 program by introducing such new subjects as French grammar, English, history, and geography.

Robert above all had a scientific bent. His obituary in the *Quebec Gazette* on 12 Jan. 1826 observed: "Endowed with a great genius for the exact sciences, M. Robert directed his talents with brilliant success to the different branches of Philosophy and mathematics which he taught in this institution." His numerous manuscript treatises and his collections of notes attest to the breadth of his knowledge and to his predilection for astronomy. The value of his courses may legitimately be judged by the memorable oral defence presented in public on 30 April 1792. Five of his pupils had the honour of defending 63 propositions in mathematics and physics in the presence of Prince Edward* Augustus, Lieutenant Governor Alured Clarke of Lower Canada, Lieutenant Governor John Graves Simcoe* of Upper Canada, garrison officers, and a large number of eminent people. The students rose to the occasion. On 3 May the *Quebec Gazette* drew attention to "the satisfactory manner in which these young Gentlemen" answered all the questions put to them, after only eight months' work, at that.

Antoine-Bernardin Robert was the worthy successor to his colleagues Thomas-Laurent Bédard*, Charles Chauveaux, and Edmund Burke. The four educators merit recognition for having endowed the

Petit Séminaire de Québec with a genuine course in pure and applied mathematics as early as the 18th century. When new duties forced Robert to give up the office of professor, the teaching of scientific subjects at Quebec was only slightly inferior to that in the best schools in France.

NOËL BAILLARGEON

AAQ, 12 A; 210 A. ANQ-M, CE1-2, 8 févr. 1757. ASQ, MSS, 7, 12, 13, 432; MSS-M, 134, 148, 151, 185; Polygraphie, XXXVIII; Séminaire, 3, no.5a; 5, no.67; 92, nos.2–6, 8; 178, no.2; Séminaire de Québec, thèses, 1775–1815. Quebec Gazette, 3 May 1792, 12 Jan. 1826. Le séminaire de Québec: documents et biographies, Honorius Provost, édit. (Québec, 1964). Tanguay, Répertoire (1893). Claude Galarneau, Les collèges classiques au Canada français (1620–1970) (Montréal, 1978). Marc Lebel et al., Aspects de l'enseignement au petit séminaire de Québec (1765–1945) (Québec, 1968).

ROBICHAUX, OTHO (he also signed **Robichaud**), farmer, merchant, JP, militia officer, and office holder; b: 29 April 1742 in Annapolis Royal, N.S., son of Louis Robichaux* and Jeanne Bourgeois; d. 19 Dec. 1824 in Neguac, N.B.

Although Otho Robichaux's father enjoyed good relations with the British authorities at Annapolis Royal, the family was not spared the grief of deportation in 1755. They were, however, allowed to choose their place of exile and were sent to Massachusetts, where they resided first in Boston and then in Cambridge. In later years Otho would be among those who contributed information for Andrew BROWN's study of the deportation. While in New England, he attended English schools. The family moved in good circles; among their acquaintances were Edward Winslow* and the prominent Vassalls of Cambridge.

In 1775, at the outbreak of the American revolution, the Robichaux family, whose sympathies were with the loyalists, removed to Quebec. There Otho made contact with a number of Acadians from the Miramichi region of what was to become New Brunswick; they no doubt persuaded him to settle in that area. His personal savings, supplemented by an inheritance from his father, enabled him to purchase from Pierre Loubert (Loubère) on 28 May 1781 the rights to and improvements on a piece of land at Neguac. Loubert for many years had been engaged in trade with the Indian and Acadian inhabitants of the region. The improvements consisted of a house, barn, store, and bakehouse. Robichaux began farming and set up in business, operating a retail store, dealing in local products, and involving himself in the lumber trade. Among the local merchants with whom he had business relations were James FRASER, Francis Peabody*, and Richard Simonds*. He also exchanged goods with Charles ROBIN of Paspébiac, for whom he

seems to have acted as agent. Over the years he was to acquire a number of properties in the Miramichi area.

On 18 Aug. 1789 Robichaux, until then a bachelor, was married by Father Antoine GIROUARD to Marie-Louise Thibodeau (Thibaudeau), the 15-year-old daughter of Alexis Thibodeau and Marguerite Dupuis of Bay du Vin; the couple were to have twelve children, eight girls and four boys. For some reason, the marriage was the cause of dissension between Otho and his siblings. "My difficulties and my sorrows began when you got married," his sister Vénérande* once wrote. "You have around you people who overwhelm you," she commented on another occasion; "I thought that when you married you were taking only a wife, but it happens that you have married an entire family." Robichaux nevertheless maintained a fairly amicable relationship with his sisters at Quebec, particularly Vénérande, with whom he corresponded regularly. She often acted as her brother's agent, settling bills, pursuing debtors, and forwarding merchandise to him.

Robichaux came to occupy a position of considerable prominence in the Miramichi area. In 1788 he was asked by James Fraser to join in an application for courts of justice to be established in Northumberland County. Six years later, no doubt on the recommendation of Winslow, Robichaux became a justice of the peace, as did his fellow Acadian Joseph GUEGUEN of Cocagne. Among other positions he occupied at the county and parish levels were those of overseer of the poor, school trustee, and road commissioner. In addition he acted as assessor of rates; thus, when a jail and court-house for the county was being erected in 1791, it fell to him to apportion among the inhabitants the sum assessed on the district of Neguac. Active in the militia as well, he held the rank of captain from 1 Jan. 1799. He also served as a churchwarden and, according to oral tradition, acted as a sort of lay priest in the absence of a missionary, presiding at prayer meetings, baptizing children, and receiving the vows of couples who wished to marry.

A headstrong man, Robichaux was involved in many disputes with neighbours over the ownership of land and occasionally confronted the clergy, with whose opinions on temporal matters his own views were often at variance. In government circles his influence was recognized and his opinion valued. It was through him that the administration communicated with the Acadian residents of the Miramichi region, and few measures affecting them were passed without his having been consulted.

CEDRIC L. HAINES

Arch. de l'évêché de Bathurst (Bathurst, N.-B.), Papiers Robichaud. Centre d'études acadiennes, univ. de Moncton (Moncton, N.-B.), Fonds Placide Gaudet, 1.31-13A, 1.87-

Robin

1–5. PANB, RG 1, RS559, E10–11; RG 2, RS8, oaths, 2/1; Otho Robichaux *et al.* to Thomas Peters, 22 Aug. 1819; RG 18, RS153, A1–4. *Collection de documents inédits sur le Canada et l'Amérique*, [H.-R. Casgrain, édit.] (3v., Québec, 1888–90), 2: 94–95. Placide Gaudet, "Acadian genealogy and notes," PAC *Report*, 1905, 2, pt.III. "Vers le passé: la famille Robichaud, lettres d'une proscrite acadienne, de 1755, à son frère," *Le Moniteur acadien* (Shédiac, N.-B.), 26 juill. 1887: 2; 29 juill. 1887: 2; 2 août 1887: 1; 5 août 1887: 1; 9 août 1887: 1. *Winslow papers* (Raymond). Donat Robichaud, *Les Robichaud: histoire et généalogie* (Bathurst, [1967]).

ROBIN, CHARLES, businessman, judge, and JP; baptized 30 Oct. 1743 in St Brelade, Jersey, son of Philippe Robin and Anne Dauvergne, shopkeepers; d. unmarried 10 June 1824 in St Aubin, Jersey.

Although Charles Robin and his elder brothers, Philip and John, were orphaned when Charles was about 11, they all managed to acquire a good education. Philip married the daughter of the seigneur of Noirmont and subsequently filled important civil offices on Jersey. John and Charles, however, turned to the North American fisheries, in which their uncles had been occupied for many years. By 1763 John was a ship's captain engaged in the Newfoundland cod fisheries. Charles was never master of a ship, but he became well versed in nautical matters. In 1765 the three brothers joined James Pipon de Noirmont, Philip's brother-in-law, and Thomas Pipon de La Moye, John's future brother-in-law, to form Robin, Pipon and Company. That year the firm sent a brig to reconnoitre the fisheries of Cape Breton Island, and in 1766 Charles investigated the former French fisheries on Baie des Chaleurs. Having found abundant fish and excellent beaches for dry-curing on the Gaspé shore, he returned the following year to fish and to trade for timber and furs with the Acadians and Indians around Paspébiac (Qué.).

Since the conquest Baie des Chaleurs had become a site of fierce competition among Nova Scotians and New Englanders, and also Quebec merchants, such as Jacques Terroux* and William Smith, agent for the firm of Moore and Finlay [*see* Hugh Finlay*]; the losses suffered had been high. In 1768 Robin returned to Baie des Chaleurs with two vessels, only to have them seized and sold with their cargoes by customs officials who had been informed by some of Robin's competitors that he had not complied with a seldom enforced act obliging Channel Islanders to clear their vessels from England. The outcry provoked by Robin, Pipon and Company led to repeal of the act the following year, but the young firm received only about £250 compensation for its staggering loss of £2,700 sterling.

Robin had a dogged faith in the trade from Baie des Chaleurs even though, one after another, his competitors abandoned it. The limitless supply of cod easily found a market in Catholic Europe; by the 1770s he was shipping several thousand quintals (112 pounds each) of dried cod to Portugal and Spain, as well as small amounts of salmon, furs, cod oil, and wood to England and Quebec. In exchange for these products he imported goods for sale to fishermen and salt for curing. About 1770 a separate firm, Robin and Company, was formed to exploit the Cape Breton fisheries, and John was put in charge; Charles had an interest in it. By that year he was resident agent for Robin, Pipon at Paspébiac, where he set up his headquarters and built flakes for curing. Another establishment was subsequently built at Percé. Initially Charles dealt only with local fishermen (mostly Acadian), but in 1774 he and John brought more than 100 exiled Acadians to settle on Baie des Chaleurs and Cape Breton Island [*see* Jean-Baptiste Robichaux*]. They also brought over Jersey workers to remedy a chronic shortage of manpower, the principal problem faced by fishing merchants operating in the region.

The patient building up of the Robin enterprise was almost completely undone early in the American revolution. In 1776 John Paul Jones destroyed most of John's operation on Cape Breton. Two years later American privateers came to Paspébiac, captured one of Charles's ships, which they loaded with fish and furs, and plundered and burned his stores; Robin was captured momentarily but escaped into the woods. He returned to Jersey and served for the duration of the revolutionary war as an officer in the militia, which in 1781 helped to repel an attempted invasion by the French. Charles estimated the Robins' direct losses from the revolution at £6,000, exclusive of those resulting from their inability to trade.

Robin returned to Baie des Chaleurs in 1783 as a partner in a new firm, Charles Robin and Company. He held about one-eighth of the shares in the business, most of the remainder being owned by members of the Robin and Pipon families. He also held a one-quarter interest in the Philip Robin Company, which took over the assets of Robin and Company on Cape Breton Island; they were placed under a hired manager since John Robin remained in Jersey. Charles immediately rebuilt the stores, wharfs, and living quarters at Paspébiac.

Although the capital resources at Robin's disposal were perhaps no greater than those of the dozen new energetic competitors he faced, he ultimately won a near monopoly of trade in the region through a combination of experience, cunning, good contacts, hard work, and careful planning. From experience Robin knew the locations of the best fishing grounds and drying beaches. He had also acquired a perceptive understanding of the Acadian fishermen and, as a Jerseyman, he spoke and wrote their language. As well, in travels in his early years he had made useful contacts with important international fish buyers.

Robin's cunning use of a truck system of credit provided the company with long-term stability in exports. Cash was seldom used; rather Robin credited the year's catch against the equipment, merchandise, provisions, and salt that he had advanced to the fishermen. Once hooked by credit, the fishermen found it virtually impossible to escape their indebtedness, and Robin was ensured of a dependable labour force. The system also allowed Robin to obtain dried cod at a price no higher than the amount the fishermen needed to live on.

Also important in ensuring Robin's success after 1783 were his contacts. Philip handled the European end of the business reliably and kept him supplied. With Francis Janvrin, a Jersey-based operator on Baie de Gaspé and a minority shareholder in Charles Robin and Company, he forged an agreement of non-competition for fish and of mutual service in the carrying of supplies and mail. Aware of the value of political influence, Robin obtained the support of local officials, particularly in efforts to acquire and retain the beaches and woodlots necessary to a large-scale fishing operation. In 1784 he persuaded the lieutenant governor of the Gaspé, Nicholas Cox*, not to grant land immediately around Paspébiac to some 400 loyalists, and the following year he gained title to some of it for his firm. In the winter of 1787 Robin walked to Quebec to advise the provincial government on the cod fisheries; with the support of Cox, then deeply in debt to Robin's company, the government passed an ordinance in 1788 that benefited the firm in several ways, particularly by making it impossible for others to acquire large beach properties. Cox's successor, Francis Le Maistre*, was a Jerseyman and friend of the Robin family, but poor health prevented his being of material assistance. The seat for Gaspé in the Lower Canadian House of Assembly was held by Edward O'HARA, a man sympathetic to Charles Robin and Company and for whom Robin campaigned actively. Robin himself held a number of posts of considerable importance locally: he was a judge of the Court of Common Pleas around 1788–92, justice of the peace from 1788, and a member of the land board for the district of Gaspé from 1789. The last position gave him a say in the examination of requests for land grants and the issuing of location tickets. Although Robin's influence resulted in the opening of a seasonal customs office at New Carlisle, near Paspébiac, he was unable to obtain bounties on exports or exemption from duties on imported goods, benefits enjoyed by the fishing industry in other colonies. Still, he was content to be protected by his allies from adverse government action; neglect of the district of Gaspé by the government at Quebec enabled him to build a monopoly unhindered.

Robin worked hard to exploit his opportunities. With the exception of his business trip to Quebec in 1787, he resided uninterruptedly on Baie des Chaleurs from 1783 to 1802. He lived a frugal, orderly existence, never married, and had few interests beyond his business. He was the principal policymaker in Charles Robin and Company and the general manager of its day-to-day operations. This authority to make on-the-spot decisions allowed him to exploit the Gaspé fisheries more successfully than his competitors, most of whom were based in London or Quebec. In 1793, for example, he was in a position to seize the opportunity of purchasing the seigneury of Grande-Rivière, which had a good beach close to rich fishing grounds; it became Robin's third major post after nearby Paspébiac and Percé.

Planning, at which Robin excelled, was conservative. Risky ventures were avoided and high profits were not considered imperative; it was deemed more important to maintain a slow, steady growth in exports and a reputation among European importers for reliable delivery of good quality fish. Increasingly Robin specialized in dry-cured cod, forgoing diversification into timber, furs, mackerel, or salt-cured cod. No innovator of techniques of production or marketing, he laboured to make conventional methods function efficiently. He sought, however, to build a self-sufficient, vertically integrated business. Most fish was obtained in trade from local fishermen but some was caught by the company's own employees; their catch was cured on company beaches by men brought in every summer from the Quebec area. Company ships also took the fish to market and brought in most supplies. In the 1790s Robin established a shipyard at Paspébiac; in addition to shallops and small coastal schooners, every two years the yard turned out a vessel of about 200 tons especially designed to carry fish to Europe. As a result of integration and the truck system of credit Robin gained a near monopoly of dried codfish exported from the north shore of Baie des Chaleurs. His success may be attributed in part to his caution; in the organization of his fishing operations and his relations with the fishermen Robin to a large extent carried over, with refinements to increase profits, practices employed by Jersey concerns before him and by French traders in the Gaspé prior to the conquest.

The combination of these many factors also enabled Robin to ride out the French revolutionary war, which finished off his remaining competitors. In May 1794, however, the French navy captured three of his ships en route for Paspébiac with supplies and merchandise. That autumn another, carrying 4,900 quintals of dried fish, was taken off Spain. The war brought a shortage of shipping (which the Paspébiac shipyard alleviated for him) and impaired his ability to get cargoes to market in the season of greatest demand. Eventually the war closed Robin's most important outlets, Spain and Portugal, but he was able to forge temporary ones

Robinson

in New England and Lower Canada. Indeed Robin was able to maintain his exports at pre-war levels, seldom sending less than 13,000 quintals a year.

Robin retired to Jersey in 1802, when it was thought that the war had been ended by the Treaty of Amiens. By then Charles Robin and Company owned five ships, a large establishment at Paspébiac – including the shipyard, a small farm, wharfs, stages, store-houses, and lodgings for about 100 employees – a subsidiary post at Percé, and the seigneury of Grande-Rivière; the size of the company's profits is not known. Robin's chief investment in the firm had been his life rather than his money. As a manager he had received a modest annual salary of £150, and in 1800 he estimated the value of his shares to be about £2,250; he did not leave a large estate on his death in 1824. His goal in life had been the continuance of the firm that bore his name, and to that end he had trained his nephew Philip Robin since 1783 and tutored another, James Robin, for a number of years. Philip took over as manager of operations on Baie des Chaleurs in 1803 and James as director in Jersey about 1808. Charles had trained them well, and his goal was attained: the firm dominated the economy of Baie des Chaleurs for another century.

DAVID LEE

A detailed bibliography for Charles Robin may be found in David Lee, *The Robins in Gaspé, 1766–1825* (Markham, Ont., 1984). The following sources and studies are of particular interest: Judicial Greffier (St Helier, Jersey), Judicial greffe probate registry 1819, 4: 378. PAC, MG 23, GIII, 24; MG 28, III18; RG 68, General index, 1651–1841: 276, 324, 534. Jules Bélanger *et al.*, *Histoire de la Gaspésie* (Montréal, 1981). R. E. Ommer, "From outpost to outport: the Jersey merchant triangle in the nineteenth century" (PHD thesis, McGill Univ., Montreal, 1978). David Lee, "La Gaspésie, 1760–1867," *Canadian Hist. Sites*, no.23 (1980). A. G. Le Gros, "Charles Robin on the Gaspé coast," *Rev. d'hist. de la Gaspésie* (Gaspé, Qué.), 2 (1964): 33–43, 93–102, 141–51; 3 (1965): 39–45, 77–84, 148–55; 4 (1966): 195–204. Mario Mimeault, "La continuité de l'emprise des compagnies de pêche françaises et jersiaises sur les pêcheurs au XVIIIe siècle: le cas de la compagnie Robin," *SH*, 18 (1985): 59–74.

ROBINSON, JOHN, businessman, office holder, and politician; b. 1762 in the Highlands (Hudson Hills), near New York City, third son of Beverley Robinson and Susanna Philipse, and grandson of John Robinson, former president of the Council and administrator of Virginia; m. 1787 Elizabeth Ludlow, second daughter of George Duncan Ludlow*, chief justice of New Brunswick; d. 8 Oct. 1828 in Saint John, N.B.

A son of one of the most distinguished supporters of the British cause in New York, John Robinson was born to wealth and position and he remained a member of the loyalist aristocracy, which was to dominate the social and political life of New Brunswick during its first half-century. His education by private tutors on his father's estates in New York was interrupted by the American revolution, during which, at the age of 15, he enlisted in the Loyal Americans, the regiment raised and commanded by his father. By 1781 he had survived the battle of Kings Mountain and achieved the rank of lieutenant. He retired on half pay at the conclusion of the war and, after a brief stay in the Annapolis region of Nova Scotia, settled in the Saint John River valley, likely in 1786.

The central fact in Robinson's life and career was his membership in the Robinson family. His father was not only a wealthy loyalist refugee, he was a figure invested with great authority in his own lifetime, and around him much of the loyalist myth would gather. Each of his sons achieved distinction, the older ones in New Brunswick, the younger in the British army. John Robinson would eventually find himself at the centre of a network of relationships that comprehended most of the loyalist establishment of New Brunswick. His own marriage in 1787 made him a member of the Ludlow family; those of his brothers, children, nieces, and nephews would link him to the Barclays, Paddocks, Wetmores, Parkers, Hazens, Botsfords, Simondses, Millidges, and Jarvises.

It was from his father that John Robinson's influence in New Brunswick at first derived. Although resident in England, Beverley Robinson was a member of the New Brunswick Council from 1784 until his death in 1792. In 1789 he was joined in this position by his eldest son, Beverley – former lieutenant-colonel of the Loyal American Regiment – who retained the office until 1816. During the years when his family was represented on the Council John Robinson was named to several prestigious and lucrative posts.

Shortly after his arrival in New Brunswick Robinson was created sheriff of Queens County, a high honour for a man not yet 26 years of age; from this early period he also held for a time the office of deputy adjutant-general of militia. Within a few years he had abandoned the ideal of a country gentleman's life and joined the powerful commercial élite of the city of Saint John, setting up there as a general merchant. He became a popular figure in the city and was returned to the House of Assembly in 1802 at a general election which, despite the success of James Glenie*, was considered a defeat for the radicals and a triumph for the friends of Lieutenant Governor Thomas Carleton*. Robinson did not stand in the elections of 1809 but he was again returned to the house in a by-election held the following year. Although he was viewed as a political moderate, he generally supported the official party in the key issues of the period. His loyalty to the executive was rewarded with the office of acting deputy paymaster general of the forces during the War of 1812. Following the death of Amos Botsford*, Robinson was unanimously elected to the speakership of the assembly at its 1813 session. Three years later he resigned his seat in order to accept the office of province treasurer following the death of William Hazen. The province treasurer was responsible for receiving the revenues from the provincial customs and for the issue and payment of warrants authorized by the legislature through its appropriations bills. The office was in the gift of the lieutenant governor (whose office at the time of Robinson's appointment was filled by an administrator, George Stracey SMYTH) but, in contrast to those of the great offices of the crown, its salary and fees were set by the assembly. Robinson received £500 a year for his services as the province's chief financial officer. He appears to have given up his mercantile concerns shortly after his appointment.

In May 1816, three months after he had accepted the office of treasurer, Robinson was appointed mayor of Saint John by his benefactor, Smyth. The new office possessed a wide-ranging authority. The mayor alone determined who should be admitted as freemen of the city and who should receive tavern and other city licences; the Mayor's Court constituted the Inferior Court of Common Pleas for the city; the mayor served as chief executive officer for both the county and city governments of Saint John. The fees of office received for every warrant, certificate, and licence issued, and for every case heard, exceeded the salary that Robinson received from the treasurer's office. He was an able mayor and enjoyed considerable support from the merchant community.

On 6 March 1818 Smyth completed the trinity of honours which he conferred on Robinson by calling him to the Council. Robinson thus became the third member of his immediate family to hold the highest office in the gift of the crown in New Brunswick. As a councillor he certainly participated in the discussions over crown lands which led to the imposition of timber duties and the subsequent constitutional debate over the casual revenues [see Smyth]. But his most important role was that of spokesman for interests advocating the creation of the Bank of New Brunswick in 1819. At the first stockholders meeting on 12 June 1820 Robinson was elected to the board of directors. That same day the directors promoted him to the presidency of the new institution. As province treasurer, Robinson was by far the bank's most important customer and his election may be seen as the confluence of government and great merchant interests.

Indeed, perhaps the most interesting aspect of John Robinson's career is the light it sheds on the relationship between government and business in loyalist New Brunswick and the questions it raises concerning the widely accepted view that the competing aspirations of the official and merchant communities formed the central political dynamic of the period. For Robinson neatly encompassed both traditions, as well as the military element that characterized loyalist society.

Robinson was a member of the Church of England and a supporter of the Society for Promoting Christian Knowledge. His seven children all made good marriages, three of the sons to daughters of Thomas Millidge* and Sarah Simonds (daughter of James SIMONDS). Four sons followed their father into public life. Beverley became treasurer of New Brunswick; George Duncan was elected assemblyman for Saint John; Daniel Ludlow became a barrister, and served as assemblyman for York County and registrar of the Court of Chancery; John Morris, also a barrister, became registrar of the Vice-Admiralty Court and master in Chancery.

Robinson retired from the Council of New Brunswick in 1826. He held the offices of mayor and province treasurer until his death on 8 Oct. 1828.

T. W. ACHESON

PANB, MC 1156, IV: 34. *Winslow papers* (Raymond). *New-Brunswick Courier*, 1811–12; 28 Jan. 1815; 15 March 1817; 11 Oct. 1828. Sabine, *Biog. sketches of loyalists.* Hannay, *Hist. of N.B.* Lawrence, *Judges of N.B.* (Stockton and Raymond).

ROGERS, DAVID McGREGOR, farmer, office holder, politician, JP, merchant, and militia officer; b. 23 Nov. 1772 in Londonderry (Vt), son of James Rogers and Margaret McGregor; m. first 6 Jan. 1802 Sarah Playter in York (Toronto), and they had two sons and two daughters; m. secondly 1811 Elizabeth Playter (they had no children); d. 18 July 1824 at his residence in Haldimand Township, Upper Canada.

David McGregor Rogers possessed, as he was fond of pointing out, a distinguished name. His uncle Robert Rogers* was the famous ranger leader during the Seven Years' War; his father and two other uncles also fought in that conflict. During the American revolution, his father was major commandant of the 2nd Battalion, King's Rangers. In 1784 James Rogers settled, with his family and corps, in Township No.3 (Fredericksburgh) of western Quebec. In 1789 young Rogers received 200 acres of land in Sophiasburg Township, Prince Edward County. By the following spring he was labouring on his farm with "ten times as much work to do as I can get thro' with[.] I have

Rogers

not time to read or write, or pursue any other amusement[.] I work all day cook my own Victuals &c."

Rogers's background was sufficiently prestigious that he obtained a small office, clerk of the local land board, which he lost when the boards were abolished in 1794. He was interested in politics, notifying his brother in 1795 that he expected the nomination for the riding of Prince Edward in the next election: "I hardly know whether to accept or Refuse the Offer. One thing I am resolved not to be set up unless I am pretty sure of a Majority." He was returned for the riding in the 1796 election. The following year, despite his status as an assemblyman, he failed to win for his father's heirs the land grants to which, he argued, his uncle Robert had been entitled. The Executive Council declared, not unreasonably, that Robert Rogers had never settled in the province and therefore had no claim to lands.

In 1800 Rogers moved to a farm in Cramahe Township. There he lived alone "as usual," but he noted that "the care of my cattle prevents me from being from home much and with my books I never want company." Life was not easy: "I have too much business entirely for pleasure or profit, Cooking Farmer & merchant is too much business for one. . . . It is a hard strugle to get along." His sister visited him from time to time and the addition of a housekeeper promised to make daily life a little less rigorous. His official duties added to his responsibilities. In 1800 he was re-elected to the assembly, this time for the riding of Hastings and Northumberland; he was to continue representing Northumberland County until 1816, and again from 1820 until his death in 1824. He also served as registrar for the county (1799), major in the county militia (1801), clerk of the peace for the newly erected Newcastle District (1802), registrar of the district Surrogate Court (1802), and clerk of the district Court of Quarter Sessions (1802).

By 1806 Rogers had moved yet again, establishing himself in Haldimand Township. Reasonably prosperous, from 1815 he usually had about 1,000 acres or more of wild land and anywhere from 30 to 100 acres under cultivation. He was a major figure in the Newcastle District and, as befitted one of that stature, garnered more offices: justice of the peace (1813–21), high treason commissioner (1814), alien act commissioner (1817), commissioner of inquiry into forfeited lands (1818), and member of the reconstituted land board (1819).

His real mark was made in the arena of politics where his uncompromising concern with proper procedure, correct form, and the rights and prerogatives of the House of Assembly earned him notoriety, if not prominence. Notable in his early career had been his opposition in 1798 to Christopher Robinson*'s bill that would have allowed immigrants to bring their slaves into Upper Canada. More typical was his clash in May 1801 with Mr Justice Henry Allcock* over the crown's right to dismiss at pleasure an official holding office by patent. At issue were the limits of the crown's prerogative, a subject of increasing dispute during Lieutenant Governor Peter Hunter*'s administration. As an obdurate champion of the assembly, Rogers established himself as a leading member of the incipient opposition. Development of the rhetoric of opposition fell to others, especially William Weekes* and Robert Thorpe*. Their criticisms, particularly of the Executive Council and senior officials, attracted the support of many assemblymen stung by the so-called administrative reforms of Hunter's government. Rogers introduced Weekes to the house after his election in 1805 and subsequently seconded his motion to "consider the disquietude which prevails . . . by reason of the administration of Public Offices." Rogers was more sporadic in his support of Thorpe but worked closely with the *bête noire* of the government, Joseph Willcocks*.

Weekes's motion, although defeated, had been a dramatic assertion of the assembly's powers which would not be forgotten. In early March 1808 Rogers spearheaded an attack, largely by loyalist assemblymen, upon an attempt to remove a statutory time limit on the District School Act. When on 5 March the daily order of business was changed to allow quick passage of the amendment, Rogers denounced the step as "contrary to all rules of proceeding," a "dangerous innovation," and "a measure so injurious . . . to the Privilidge of the People." Rules, he insisted, "once formed should be cautiously disposed of and strictly adhered to." In the company of Thomas DORLAND and Peter Howard* he retired from the house, depriving it of a quorum for business. The disruption was more apparent than real. But what it symbolized – collective action – aroused the fury of Lieutenant Governor Francis Gore*, who stripped Rogers of his offices; the other two culprits were dropped from the magistracy.

Gore's action set the stage for further confrontation since Rogers, echoing his arguments in the contest with Allcock in 1801 and believing that he held office independent of the crown's pleasure, refused to give up his books as registrar. The government sought a mandamus ordering him to surrender them and, in the ensuing battle before the Court of King's Bench, Rogers defended himself. Chief Justice Thomas SCOTT and Mr Justice William Dummer POWELL rejected the arguments of Attorney General William Firth* and Solicitor General D'Arcy BOULTON that a great injustice had been done to the "ancient" royal prerogative and decided not to issue a mandamus. Firth and Boulton feared that the decision "will produce much harmful tendency . . . in shaking ye Royal Prerogative thro'out ye Province, within mens minds, especially among ye disaffected." The issue was referred by Gore to the imperial law officers, who upheld the decision of the lower court. Rogers had been vindicated.

Rogers's war work in various commissions, particularly during President Gordon Drummond*'s tenure, brought him another office in 1815: he was appointed deputy superintendent of locations, charged with settling ex-soldiers. Gore, on his return to Upper Canada, was outraged: "He is one of those persons who render themselves conspicuous by a long Course of Opposition to the Colonial Administration; and whom it has been deemed prudent to pacify – a policy in a Colony like this extremely doubtful." Rogers blamed Surveyor General Thomas RIDOUT for repeated delays and continual frustration in his work. Although Gore objected to the disrespectful tone of Rogers's complaints, Rogers received the support of Drummond, now commander of the troops in the Canadas, and Governor-in-Chief Sir John Coape SHERBROOKE. But, in characteristic manner, Rogers was simply doing his job the way he thought it should be done, with due attention to procedure, form, and division of responsibilities. Wherever there was ambiguity, he sought clarification in clear and simple terms. The same blunt manner and punctilious approach were evident in his chairmanship of the land board and the Court of Quarter Sessions; there, too, they invariably resulted in misunderstanding and innuendo.

Rogers's political star fell during the sixth parliament (1812–16). With Willcocks out of the way, the house was dominated by Robert NICHOL, the most effective manager of government business to date. In the 1814 session Rogers either acquiesced in the most contentious legislation, or was absent from the house. During the much maligned session of 1816, he was generally inconspicuous except for his attempt to put a time limit on the civil list bill. Rogers stood for election again in 1820 and won. His health, however, was failing. On one occasion in 1821 he was so ill he could barely write. He was a man of the past, speaking but rarely and then only by way of peripheral comment on the debate at hand. He voted for the repeal of the Sedition Act of 1804, which had been used to expel Robert Gourlay* from the province. He supported and worked with Barnabas BIDWELL, seconding, for instance, Bidwell's assault of December 1821 on primogeniture in cases of persons dying intestate; Rogers "wished to support the constitution of this country, but he did not want that kind of Aristocracy here which deprived younger children of a subsistence."

In his discovery of Upper Canada's political past, William Lyon Mackenzie* largely overlooked Rogers. Even had he paid more attention to him, Rogers would not have fitted neatly into Mackenzie's ministerialist/independent dichotomy. Some historians have singled out Rogers as representing a "liberal" or American strain within loyalism, while disagreeing on the significance of that strain. Drawing upon traditions and occasionally language which had strong roots in the transatlantic world of whiggery, Rogers represented a brand of loyalism that emphasized the king's prerogatives and the subject's rights brought together in constitutional equilibrium. When he retired from the magistracy in 1821, he thought others would prove more productive but "more zealously attatched to the British Constitution or more careful not willingly to encroach on the Prerogative of the crown or the Priviledges of their fellow subjects they cannot be." Missing from Rogers's political world was the aristocratic emphasis of a Richard Cartwright*. And, perhaps, it is more to Rogers than to him that one ought to look for the exemplar of the loyalist tradition in Upper Canada.

ROBERT LOCHIEL FRASER

AO, MS 522; RG 21, United Counties of Northumberland and Durham, Cramahe Township, assessment rolls, 1806–23; census records, 1803–5; Haldimand Township, census records, 1809–23; RG 22, ser.125, 2: 118, 131, 142, 147–48; ser.155. BL, Add. MSS 21828: 46, 74 (transcripts at PAC). MTL, W. D. Powell papers, B32: 113; D. McG. Rogers, "Statement of the services of David M. Rogers and of his family during the French-Indian war and the American revolution, made as a protest against his recent dismissal from public office as a result of his actions in the House of Assembly" (1808). PAC, RG 1, E14, 11: 269–70, 272–73; L3, 423: R3/17, 20; 424: R4/50; 426: R8/53; 428: R11/108–9; 445: R leases, 1798–1820/22, 32; 446: R misc., 1793–1846/9; RG 5, A1, 7–54; RG 8, I (C ser.), 84: 264–66; 370: 121–24; 621: 47; 688B: 89; 688C: 13; 1717: 70; RG 68, General index, 1651–1841: 191, 194, 245, 422–23, 431, 442, 451, 537. PRO, CO 42/349: 102–4, 169–82. QUA, Richard Cartwright papers, letter-books (transcripts at AO, 289–93). *Corr. of Hon. Peter Russell* (Cruikshank and Hunter), 3: 257. *Doc. hist. of campaign upon Niagara frontier* (Cruikshank), 9: 253. "Grants of crown lands in U.C.," AO *Report*, 1928–29. "Journals of Legislative Assembly of U.C.," AO *Report*, 1911–14. W. L. Mackenzie, *The legislative black list, of Upper Canada; or official corruption and hypocrisy unmasked* (York [Toronto], 1828), 7, 9. "Minutes of the Court of General Quarter Sessions of the Peace for the Home District, 13th March, 1800, to 28th December, 1811," AO *Report*, 1932: 7–8. "Petitions for grants of land in Upper Canada; second series, 1796–99," ed. E. A. Cruikshank, *OH*, 26 (1930): 292–93. "Political state of U.C.," PAC *Report*, 1892: 43. *Select British docs. of War of 1812* (Wood), 2: 85–86. "Settlements and surveys," PAC *Report*, 1891, note A: 5, 11. "U.C. land book C" and "U.C. land book D," AO *Report*, 1931. *Kingston Chronicle*, 25 March, 4 June 1819; 21 Dec. 1821; 11 Jan., 1 March 1822. *Niagara Herald* (Niagara [Niagara-on-the-Lake, Ont.]), 6–13 June 1801. *Upper Canada Gazette*, 5 Aug. 1824. *York Gazette*, 16

Romain

March, 1 April 1808. Chadwick, *Ontarian families*, 10–11. *Death notices of Ont.* (Reid), 30, 33. W. D. Reid, *The loyalists in Ontario: the sons and daughters of the American loyalists of Upper Canada* (Lambertville, N.J., 1973), 253. Patterson, "Studies in elections in U.C." *Robertson's landmarks of Toronto*, 3: 395.

ROMAIN (Audivert, *dit* Romain; Odivert, *dit* Romain), FRANÇOIS, office holder and militia officer; b. 7 Jan. 1768 at Quebec, son of François Audivert, *dit* Romain, and Anne Ledroit, *dit* Perche; m. there 15 Sept. 1789 Agathe Debigaré, *dit* Lebasque; d. there 18 Aug. 1832.

François Romain belonged to the third generation of a family whose forebear had come from Italy to New France early in the 18th century. After studies at the Petit Séminaire de Québec, which he cut short in 1786, he worked with his father as keeper of the Quebec Library, an institution founded in 1779 by Governor Frederick Haldimand*. In 1792, when the province's first house of assembly was convened, François Romain and his father undertook to set up a library for it. They may thus be considered the first Canadians to have exercised the profession of librarian in Lower Canada. The library apparently enjoyed a degree of popularity with the legislators, for a report of 1802 from an assembly committee suggested "arrangements. . . in regard to the Books imported for the use of this House." The official responsible for the legislative library was the clerk, William LINDSAY; from 1810 to 1816 Romain's name was on the civil list with the modest title of door-keeper at the former bishop's palace, which was being rented by the assembly. In 1809, however, when he assumed the office of president of the Literary Society of Quebec, he was called librarian.

During the War of 1812 Romain was made quartermaster of the town's 1st Militia Battalion; the following year he was promoted lieutenant. In 1818 he quit his position as librarian and formed a general agency at Quebec in partnership with surveyor Robert-Anne d'ESTIMAUVILLE. According to an announcement in the *Quebec Gazette* on 3 September, the agency offered immigrants and travellers information on Canada; it also placed servants and sold or rented houses. The business does not seem to have been successful, since d'Estimauville left his partner on 2 June 1821 to become assistant to his brother, Jean-Baptiste-Philippe-Charles d'ESTIMAUVILLE, the *grand voyer* (chief road commissioner) for the District of Quebec. As for Romain, he went back to his post as librarian.

From 1821 it is hard to distinguish Romain's career from that of his son François, a lawyer at Quebec from 1822 to 1832. Despite the identity of names, it seems logical, in view of his previous experience, to identify the elder François as the one who was the pioneer in the field of education. It would then have been he who on 7 May 1821 was a member of the founding committee of the Quebec Education Society and who a year later, with its president Joseph-François Perrault*, organized the first free public school at Quebec.

In May 1825, Romain became president of the society following the departure of Perrault, whose liberalism in matters of religion made Bishop Jean-Jacques Lartigue* deeply anxious. Romain was to retain the title of president until his death. In 1829, as a result of pressure from him, the assembly voted the society £483 "to pay the debts incurred and for the support of the school." Romain appeared before the assembly's special committee on education on 10 Feb. 1830 and explained that the society could no longer meet the demands on it and that a school with a capacity for more than 600 children was needed. The society had already bought land and was having a new building erected on Rue des Glacis in the *faubourg* Saint-Jean. Romain maintained that the high demand resulted from the fact that it was "the only truly Catholic free school at Quebec, although the Education Society admits all children, without reference to their faith."

The plan for a new school was accepted by the assembly committee, which recommended grants be made to the society. On 15 March 1831 one of the committee members, Hector-Simon Huot*, was questioned by his colleagues about a petition that Romain had just presented on behalf of the society. Huot reminded them that the society, of which he was the secretary, had received £1,182 from the assembly in addition to an annual contribution of £142. Huot drew upon Romain's report to stress that in 1831 the society's schools had a total of 402 pupils (230 in the French section and 172 in the English). Since August 1830 classes had been held in a new building. Making an assessment of François Romain's work as president, Huot noted that 918 pupils (618 in the French section and 300 in the English) had attended the schools since May 1826.

Romain then gave the committee an "estimate of probable expenses" for the year 1831–32. The budget of £401 included £250 for the two schoolmasters' salaries, £30 for paper and textbooks, £20 for heating, £15 for repairs, and even £3 for insurance. The request for funds was granted, prior to the passage of a new act in 1832 providing for a comprehensive budget for education in Lower Canada, an objective pursued for 11 years as much by Perrault the liberal, as by Romain the conservative.

For these two pioneers 1832 consequently marked the culmination of a long period of struggle for the advancement of education. A series of painful events, however, cast a shadow over this final phase of

Romain's career. His old friend and former partner, Robert-Anne d'Estimauville, died on 31 July 1831. Then on 11 Feb. 1832 his only son François passed away.

François Romain himself succumbed during the great cholera epidemic of 1832. On 20 August the *Quebec Gazette* reported that a fortnight earlier there had been a fresh outbreak at Quebec as a result of temperatures ranging from 65 to 80 degrees Fahrenheit accompanied by high humidity. The newspaper mentioned specifically that more than 2,000 people had perished since the beginning of the epidemic in June. According to the daily record of "the awfull visitation," 18 August with 33 deaths was the darkest day. Such were the ravages that the authorities were obliged to open a new cemetery on the Plains of Abraham for the residents of Upper Town. It was there that François Romain was hastily buried on 18 Aug. 1832, the day he died.

YVON THÉRIAULT

ANQ-Q, CE1-1, 7 janv. 1768; 15 sept. 1789; 11 févr., 18 août 1832; P-239. L.C., House of Assembly, *Journals*, 1823–31. *Quebec Gazette*, 6 March 1794, 24 Dec. 1799, 11 Dec. 1800, 8 Feb. 1810, 3 Sept. 1818, 10 May 1822, 20 Aug. 1832. Hare et Wallot, *Les imprimés dans le Bas-Canada*, 197. *Officers of British forces in Canada* (Irving). L.-P. Audet, *Le système scolaire*, 5: 33–34. Bernard Dufebvre [Émile Castonguay], *Journal d'un bourgeois de Québec* (Québec, [1960]), 83. Gilles Gallichan, *La biblio-thèque de la Législature de Québec, 1802–1977* (Québec, 1977), 3–4; "Bibliothèques et culture au Canada après la Conquête (1760–1800)" (thèse de MA, univ. de Montréal, 1975), 102–3. Jolois, *J.-F. Perrault*, 99–113, 131–34, 234, 240. André Labarrère-Paulé, *Les instituteurs laïques au Canada français, 1836–1900* (Québec, 1965), 7–8, 90–91. I.[-F.-T.] Lebrun, *Tableau statistique et politique des deux Canadas* (Paris, 1833), 180. P.-G. Roy, "Quatre générations de Romain," *BRH*, 34 (1928): 552–55.

ROSS, DUNCAN, Presbyterian minister, farmer, educator, office holder, and author; b. *c.* 1770 in the parish of Tarbat, Ross-shire, Scotland; m. 28 Sept. 1796 Isabella Creelman probably in Stewiacke, N.S.; d. 25 Oct. 1834 in West River (Durham), N.S.

At an early period the Ross family moved to Alyth, Forfarshire. Duncan Ross followed the usual paths for one entering the ministry of the anti-burgher Presbyterians, taking some courses at the University of Edinburgh and graduating from the theological hall of the General Associate Synod at Whitburn. He was ordained on 20 Jan. 1795 by the Presbytery of Forfar.

While students, Ross and John Brown had been moved by an appeal in 1792 from the Reverend James Drummond MACGREGOR, the Presbyterian minister in Pictou, N.S., stressing the colony's need of ministers.

In response, they made a secret pact to emigrate there. This fact became known to the synod and upon graduation both men were posted to Nova Scotia. Sailing for New York in the spring of 1795, they landed on 27 May and then made their way to Halifax.

Ross preached his first sermon in Londonderry, performed his first marriage on 29 June 1795 at Chiganois (Belmont) in Colchester County, and then proceeded to Pictou where on 7 July he, Brown, and MacGregor formed the Associate Presbytery of Nova Scotia, more commonly known as the Associate Presbytery of Pictou. Soon afterwards Ross was given charge of the congregation along the West River, MacGregor took responsibility for the East River, and Brown was assigned to Londonderry. In the years that followed Ross had many calls for his services. In addition to his duties on West River, he preached regularly in Pictou; he was the first minister to preach at Sheet Harbour; and at Stewiacke, 60 miles from Pictou, he gave 13 sermons a year between 1796 and 1800; he also preached at Amherst, 100 miles from Pictou, and ministered at various communities in Prince Edward Island.

In Pictou County Ross was an active and leading figure. Because of the low, infrequent, and uncertain pay of the ministry, Ross turned to farming to support his large family. He erected a threshing mill on his farm at West River and was elected president of the first agricultural society in the rural sections of the province on 1 Jan. 1817. On 16 April 1813 he helped found the first bible society in the county. He played a leading role in the temperance movement, aiding in the organization of the second temperance society in British North America in January 1828 and advocating the cause in the press and from the pulpit. He was a founding trustee of Thomas McCulloch*'s controversial academy at Pictou. As well, he privately tutored students of the Pictou Academy in Hebrew and Greek and later served as a commissioner for the inspection of schools in Pictou County.

Ross also subscribed to and circulated among his parishioners the *Boston Recorder*, the first religious newspaper on the continent. He was an active supporter of tariffs against American goods in order that the local agricultural industry might develop, and he contributed a lengthy series of articles to the *Acadian Recorder*, under the pen-name Solomon Wisewood, commenting upon many of the problems facing colonial Nova Scotia.

Despite Ross's quiet manner, disagreement and discord were his constant companions. Because of MacGregor's popularity, it was fully six years before Ross was grudgingly accepted by his West River congregation. Harmony prevailed for some time afterwards, but around 1816 a blistering sermon in which Ross ridiculed belief in witches and fairies resulted in the desertion of part of his flock. The

Rottenburg

arrival in the West River area in 1817 of the zealous and fiery minister Norman McLeod* brought two further years of congregational upheavals, and in the next decade the county witnessed a serious rift between secessionist Presbyterians and adherents of the Church of Scotland, the latter led by the Reverend Donald Allan Fraser*. Only in the later years of Ross's ministry did a modicum of peace settle over his charge.

Ross has long stood in the shadow of his two friends and contemporaries, MacGregor and McCulloch. Ross probably had the most difficult challenge of the three, but the flood of Presbyterian ministers from Pictou County, among them two of Ross's sons and five of his grandsons, attests to the thoroughness of his ministry. The secret of his success, perhaps, was that he possessed a capacity to adapt to change. It was Ross who convinced MacGregor that they should purchase horses in order to increase their effectiveness as missionaries. It was he who first married and established a homestead, shortly to be followed by Mac-Gregor. He stood steadfastly by McCulloch during the battles over Pictou Academy, continuing to tutor students when remuneration was most unlikely, and his views on education were both informed and far-sighted.

In stature Ross was below middle height and tended in later years to corpulence. Long, flowing white hair lent him an aura of venerability. He was blessed with sound health and a rugged constitution. His was not a forceful manner, and this, coupled with a weak voice and a hesitant command of Gaelic, tended to detract from his preaching. Most contemporaries spoke of him as hard-working, earnest, and sincere, and although his sermons lacked "fire," all agreed that he possessed an excellent, dry sense of humour. One suspects that McCulloch's *Letters of Mephibosheth Stepsure* (Halifax, 1860) reflects some of Ross's humour. His writings reveal his personality to its best advantage. They are forceful and logically constructed, displaying an intelligent and ordered mind. His pamphlet *Righteousness and peace, the fruits of the Gospel* is a moving and eloquent affirmation of the Christian belief in life after death.

In mid October 1834 Ross assisted at the ordination of Alexander McKenzie, a graduate of Pictou Academy; a week later he died of cancer of the bowels. Apparently no newspaper carried a report of his passing. He and his wife Isabella, who died in 1845, had nine sons and six daughters; one of their sons, James*, became principal of Dalhousie College.

ALLAN C. DUNLOP

Publications by Duncan Ross include *Righteousness and peace, the fruits of the Gospel; or, the relation of the Christian experience and triumphant death of Jane Cam-*

eron, in a letter addressed to the Rev. James McGregor, D.D. (Pictou, N.S., 1824), *Baptism considered in its subjects and mode: in three letters, to the Reverend William Elder . . .* (Pictou, 1825), *Strictures on a publication entitled "Believer immersion, as opposed to unbeliever sprinkling," in two letters addressed to Alexander Crawford* (Pictou, 1828), and *A reply to a pamphlet lately published, signed X; or, reasons for denying that Christ, by his death, purchased common benefits for his people* (Pictou, 1832). A portrait of Ross appears in J. P. MacPhie, *Pictonians at home and abroad: sketches of professional men and women of Pictou County; its history and institutions* (Boston, 1914).

PANS, MG 1, 742, no.xii; MG 4, James Presbyterian Church (New Glasgow, N.S.), reg. of baptisms, marriages, and burials, 28 Sept. 1796 (mfm.). *Acadian Recorder*, 1826–27. Gregg, *Hist. of Presbyterian Church* (1885), 184. Gordon Haliburton, "The Tattrie family of River John (1752–1952) . . ." (typescript, Newport, N.S., 1953; copy at PANS). George Patterson, *A history of the county of Pictou, Nova Scotia* (Montreal, 1877); *Memoir of the Rev. James MacGregor, D.D. . . .* (Philadelphia, 1859). James Robertson, *History of the mission of the Secession Church to Nova Scotia and Prince Edward Island, from its commencement in 1765* (Edinburgh, 1847).

ROTTENBURG, FRANCIS (Franz) DE, Baron de ROTTENBURG, army officer and colonial administrator; b. 4 or 8 Nov. 1757 in Gdańsk, Poland, son of Franz Gottfried Rottenburg, a prominent merchant and landowner of that city, and Anne-Marie Brunatti; m. 4 Jan. 1802 Juliana Wilhelmina Carolina von Orelli, daughter of Johann Ulrich von Orelli, a Neapolitan general, in Pressburg (Bratislava, Czechoslovakia), and they had one son, George Frederick*, and one daughter; d. 24 April 1832 in Portsmouth, England.

It is very likely that Francis de Rottenburg received a good education in view of his background and his later career as a military writer, but how he spent his early years is not known. He entered military service fairly late, being commissioned a second lieutenant in the Régiment de La Marck of the French army on 1 March 1782. Promoted lieutenant in 1785, he resigned in September 1791, probably because of developments in the French revolution, and returned to Poland. There he commanded a battalion of infantry in Tadeusz Kościuszko's unsuccessful uprising against foreign rule, and was wounded at the battle of Praga in 1794.

On 25 Dec. 1795 Rottenburg joined the British army as a major in Hompesch's Hussars, a foreign-manned unit then being raised. The next year he was promoted lieutenant-colonel and helped to raise Hompesch's Light Infantry. When that regiment was absorbed into the 60th Foot in the spring of 1798 Rottenburg became a lieutenant-colonel in the 5th battalion, the first in the British army to be armed entirely with rifles and trained for skirmishing. He commanded the battalion during the Irish rebellion

660

and was present at the taking of Surinam in August 1799.

About this time Rottenburg compiled a series of instructions on the training of light troops. Originally written in German, the instructions were translated into English and published by the War Office in 1798 as *Regulations for the exercise of riflemen and light infantry*. A number of other editions followed, and the book was used by Sir John Moore in training his Light Division. Rottenburg's effect on military thinking suggests that he was an officer of higher than average acuity with a concern for thorough training uncommon among British officers. Moreover, he appears to have been a popular commanding officer who kept his men well controlled. In 1805 he was promoted colonel, and in 1808 he became commander of a brigade of light infantry stationed in Kent, England. The next year he commanded the light troops in the expedition under Lord Chatham to Walcheren, Netherlands.

Rottenburg had been appointed a brigadier-general on the North American staff as early as April 1808, but he did not arrive at Quebec until the late summer of 1810, by which time he had been promoted major-general. In July 1812, just after the outbreak of war with the United States, he was placed in command of the Montreal district. The responsibility was a heavy one, for Montreal was second only to Quebec in importance to the defence of the Canadas, and it was dangerously close to the American border. In 1813 Rottenburg's duties increased when he assumed command of the administration and the troops in Lower Canada on two separate but brief occasions during the absence of Governor Sir George Prevost*. On 19 June Rottenburg replaced Major-General Sir Roger Hale Sheaffe* as administrator and commander of the forces in Upper Canada, and he held these positions until the arrival of Lieutenant-General Gordon Drummond* in December.

The increasing strains of war severely tested Rottenburg in both his civil and his military roles while he was in Upper Canada, and it cannot be said that he was conspicuously successful in either. On 28 June he forbad the distilling of rye in order to save food, an indication of the seriousness of the supply situation. Generally, however, he showed little interest and no initiative in civil matters – Chief Justice William Dummer POWELL later commented that he avoided "all civil duties as much as possible" – and left a large measure of decision making in the hands of the Executive Council.

In Upper Canada, Rottenburg's military decisions consistently demonstrated his tendency to caution and careful thought before action. During the summer of 1813, Major-General Henry PROCTER, commanding on the Detroit frontier, proposed an attack on the American naval base on Lake Erie at Presque Isle

(Erie), Pa. However, Rottenburg discouraged the idea and refused to provide the forces necessary to carry it out. On the Niagara frontier, Rottenburg ordered raids against American outposts and confined the enemy as much as possible to the vicinity of Fort George (Niagara-on-the-Lake), where the Americans had retreated following their defeat at the battle of Stoney Creek early in June [*see* Sir John Harvey*]. Prevost, Rottenburg, and Major-General John Vincent* were all present with the forces in front of Fort George in August, but the war in the peninsula had reached a virtual stalemate.

The defeat of Robert Heriot Barclay* in the naval battle of Lake Erie in September was a set-back to British plans, but Rottenburg did not see any need for Procter to retreat precipitately from his position at Amherstburg. Early in October Rottenburg learned that an American attack was planned on Kingston, and he moved his headquarters there, leaving Vincent in command on the Niagara peninsula. On the 9th Vincent learned of Procter's defeat in the battle of Moraviantown, and he retreated to Burlington Heights (Hamilton) lest he be cut off by American forces from the west. Rottenburg expected and indeed ordered Vincent to retire on York (Toronto) and then Kingston, but by 1 November he had changed his mind. Possibly influenced by Vincent, Procter, and others, he decided to retain the position at Burlington Heights with an eye to reoccupying the Niagara peninsula. Rottenburg was still at Kingston when an American army under Major-General James Wilkinson moved down the St Lawrence towards Montreal. He implemented Prevost's instructions by sending Lieutenant-Colonel Joseph Wanton MORRISON in pursuit, and Morrison was able to defeat part of the enemy command at Crysler's Farm on 11 November.

Then followed the most controversial act of Rottenburg's career in Upper Canada, the imposition of martial law in the Eastern and Johnstown districts to force farmers to sell supplies to the army. Although he was criticized both by individuals and by the House of Assembly, his action was probably justified, since he was not an officer who gave way to unreasonable fears. Drummond repealed the proclamation in January 1814, but three months later was compelled to impose it on the entire colony for the same reasons.

The arrival of Drummond and Major-General Phineas Riall*, both younger and experienced staff officers, allowed Rottenburg and Vincent to be withdrawn from Upper Canada. The possibility of using Rottenburg in Germany was discussed, but he was retained in the Canadas, partly because Vincent went home in ill health and partly because Prevost regarded him as a reliable subordinate. In Lower Canada, Rottenburg commanded forces on the south side of the St Lawrence at Montreal. In September 1814, when Prevost invaded the United States, he put Rottenburg

Roubel

in command of three brigades, thus making him in effect second in command. However, Rottenburg played no conspicuous role in the battle at Plattsburgh, and perhaps for this reason in part he escaped the barrage of criticism that descended on Prevost for the failure of the expedition. From 7 October to 3 November he again acted as administrator and commander of the forces in Lower Canada during Prevost's absence. In December, Rottenburg was among several staff officers recalled to Britain because they were no longer needed in the Canadas, and he left Quebec in July 1815. Before his departure he served as president of Procter's court martial. He apparently resided in England until his death, and accumulated various rewards: knight commander of the Royal Hanoverian Order in 1817, knight bachelor on 12 Feb. 1818, and lieutenant-general on 12 Aug. 1819.

Rottenburg was a competent and knowledgeable officer who demonstrated cautious and unimaginative leadership, and his outstanding qualities in the Canadas were perhaps reliability and imperturbability. Prevost recognized these assets by sending him to Upper Canada at a difficult and dangerous period in the war, and by giving him a command during the Plattsburgh campaign of 1814.

W. B. TURNER

[It remains unknown how and when Francis de Rottenburg obtained the title of baron, by which he was generally known while in the British army. He likely did not inherit it, but whether he was created a baron in France or in Poland or whether he simply assumed the title cannot be determined. W.B.T.]

Rottenburg has been identified as the author of *Regulations for the exercise of riflemen and light infantry, and instructions for their conduct in the field* (London, 1798, and subsequent editions), published by the War Office from a German original, in Richard Glover, *Peninsular preparation: the reform of the British army, 1795–1809* (Cambridge, Eng., 1963), 127–28.

AO, MS 520, Samuel Sherwood to Jones, 11 Feb. 1814. Arch. du Ministère des Armées (Paris), Service hist. de l'Armée, Y^c, 442. MTL, W. D. Powell papers, B31. PAC, MG 24, F78; RG 8, I (C ser.), 226: 50; 227: 18, 86; 230: 28–29; 231: 213; 550; 677: 240–42, 248–51; 679: 64–69, 148–50, 386; 1168: 191; 1170: 102, 231, 266; 1171: 346; 1203½H: 23; 1203½K: 35; 1203½L: 161, 240; 1218; 1219: 115–19, 279; 1220: 408–10; 1221: 179–80, 188; 1227: 50; 1706. Státny Oblastný Archiv v Bratislave (Bratislava, Czechoslovakia), Roman Catholic parish of St Martin, Bratislava, reg. of marriages, 4 Jan. 1802. Wojewódzkie Archiwum Państwowe w Gdańsku (Gdańsk, Poland), symbol 280/169: 147–48, 159; symbol 300, 60/6: 972. *Doc. hist. of campaign upon Niagara frontier* (Cruikshank), 6: 181–84, 206–7, 243–44; 7: 62–66, 138, 140–42, 148–49, 192; 8: 57–61, 68–69, 79–80, 88–90, 101–2, 117–18, 125, 226–29, 251. *Select British docs. of War of 1812* (Wood), 2: 253–54. John Strachan, *The John Strachan letter book, 1812–1834*, ed. G. W. Spragge (Toronto, 1946), 51–52. *Quebec Gazette*, 6 Sept. 1810, 24 June 1813, 3 Aug. 1815. G.B., WO, *Army list*, 1796–1832. H. J. Morgan, *Sketches of celebrated Canadians*. *Officers of British forces in Canada* (Irving). Wallace, *Macmillan dict.* L. W. G. Butler and S. W. Hare, *The annals of the King's Royal Rifle Corps* . . . (5v., London, 1913–32), 2: 12–15. J. W. Fortescue, *A history of the British army* (13v. in 14, London, 1899–1930), 7: 56, 67–68, 71. Hitsman, *Incredible War of 1812*. N. W. Wallace, *A regimental chronicle and list of officers of the 60th, or King's Royal Rifle Corps, formerly the 62nd, or the Royal American Regiment of Foot* (London, 1879), 291. Soc. for Army Hist. Research, *Journal* (London), 10 (1931): 237.

ROUBEL, WILLIAM, lawyer and politician; b. *c.* 1775, probably in England; d. in or after 1834, probably also in England.

William Roubel was the son of P. Roubel of London. Educated at Westminster School, he was "regularly bred" to the law, and admitted an attorney at the Court of King's Bench, Westminster, in November 1801. His practice did not flourish, however. Disappointed in hopes of inheriting the family property and feeling the "Want of Capital," he answered an advertisement from John Hill*, a proprietor of land on Prince Edward Island, for an attorney to supervise his properties. Arriving on the Island in June 1808, the newcomer inevitably found most of his legal employment among the local opponents of the colony's leading men, and soon gravitated in the direction of the Society of Loyal Electors, a nascent political party led by James Bardin PALMER, which he formally joined in June 1809.

By his own admission Roubel felt himself superior to those "whose knowledge Study and practice in the Law, had been confined" to the Island, an attitude which undoubtedly won him few friends among the entrenched interests there. His letters to John Hill in England were full of criticism of the legal administration and support for the pretensions of Palmer. The unguarded remarks to Hill would come back to haunt Roubel. Hill apparently quoted Roubel's strictures on the legal situation in correspondence with Captain John MacDonald* of Glenaladale, who on 28 Feb. 1810 turned excerpts over to the Island's chief justice, Cæsar COLCLOUGH.

Following the death of Attorney General Peter Magowan* in June, Roubel solicited the post through his father. But Charles Stewart*, backed by the proprietors, eventually got the job instead, although Lieutenant Governor Joseph Frederick Wallet DES-BARRES had written favourably of Roubel. Roubel settled for being returned to the House of Assembly for Charlottetown Royalty in a by-election, and was chosen secretary of the Loyal Electors.

In 1811 the controversy between the "old party," led by Charles Stewart, and the Loyal Electors moved into high gear. That spring Roubel was forced by Colclough to apologize publicly for the remarks he had made to Hill. This humiliation did not chasten Roubel, but made him even more outspoken. A few months later, in August, he delivered a lengthy speech to the Loyal Electors which excoriated the absentee proprietors, particularly the Earl of Selkirk [Douglas*]. Shortly thereafter Roubel prepared one of five affidavits for DesBarres justifying the activities of the Loyal Electors. He insisted upon the society's loyalty to the crown. The Loyal Electors were devoted, he wrote, to the consideration "of proper Measures, for the Introduction of upright independent Men, and persons of unimpeached Characters into the House of Assembly, with a view of counteracting a dangerous Influence . . . possessed by a Set of persons (either personally or by their unprincipled Agents) engaged in monstrous Speculations in Land, to the infinite discouragement of the active and industrious Settler, and consequent Check to the Settlement and prosperity of this Island." He went on to accuse Charles Stewart of attempting his ruin by means "as extraordinary and unprecedented as illegal, and unconstitutional," and claimed he could prove these allegations unless certain documents not in his possession had been "improperly destroyed." Roubel also complained that the Island's judges were too involved in party politics, singling out James Curtis* (an unpaid assistant judge of the Supreme Court) as a man who "constantly interferes with Elections in this Island."

Colclough and his colleagues Curtis and Robert GRAY obtained copies of Roubel's statement and the other affidavits from DesBarres's secretary, and Charles Stewart filed them in the Supreme Court in its October 1811 session. When Roubel refused to apologize for his remarks about the judges, the court accused him of contempt and struck his name from the list of attorneys qualified to practise before it. In the elections of April 1812 Roubel was defeated in Charlottetown Royalty, and later claimed that barrack master John Frederick Holland* had flooded the polls with soldiers. Further troubles ensued. His efforts to replace Stewart as solicitor general failed. In August 1812 he was attacked by Captain George Shore* of the 104th Foot, apparently as a result of the allegations he had made about the polling in April. Soon afterward he headed for Nova Scotia on his way back to England, threatening to bring charges of misconduct against Colclough and the other judges of the Supreme Court.

At the Colonial Office in 1813, Roubel did his best to substantiate his accusations of "a total defect of the administration of Justice in Prince Edward Island," and made a nuisance of himself by demanding many old documents from a reluctant colonial secretary. The result was a lengthy list of charges against Colclough (most of which the Colonial Office instantly dismissed as frivolous) and a shorter list against Gray and Curtis. In the end Roubel could make no better case against Curtis than to resurrect old accusations of perjury made in 1784 and heard by the Privy Council in 1792. Unable to persuade the British government of the legitimacy of his complaints (the

colonial secretary refused to allow his charges to be taken to the Privy Council or to restore him to the attorneys' roll on the Island), he was ultimately reduced to circulating printed copies of his complaint against Colclough in Newfoundland, where the chief justice had been transferred. Roubel apparently never returned to British North America. In 1817 he was again practising as a solicitor in London, and he continued to do so in obscurity until the mid 1830s.

J. M. BUMSTED

PAC, MG 19, E1, ser.1, 39: 14981–15005 (transcripts); MG 24, B133: 34–38. PRO, CO 194/55; CO 226/25–29. *Weekly Recorder of Prince Edward Island* (Charlottetown), 31 Aug. 1811. *Johnstone's London commercial guide & street directory . . .* (London, 1817). *Pigot & Co.'s national and provincial commercial directory, 1832–4* (London, 1832).

ROUSSEAU, DOMINIQUE, silversmith, fur trader, businessman, and militia officer; b. 9 Nov. 1755 at Quebec, son of Louis-Alexandre Rousseau, *dit* Beausoleil, a merchant, and his second wife, Marie-Joseph Chabot; d. 27 Feb. 1825 following a stroke, in Montreal.

Although Dominique Rousseau had a complex and diversified life, documentary sources make it possible to sketch the stages of his career. From 1776 to 1790 he was mainly called silversmith. The subsequent importance of his commercial activities is reflected in the designations *négociant* (1784–1815), *bourgeois* (1799–1806), *marchand* (1806–15), *marchand voyageur* (1816–21), and *commerçant* (1821–25). But he was equally an agricultural producer, potash manufacturer, militia captain (1802), and then major (1812), as well as a landowner with large holdings. He was called *écuyer* (esquire) from 1801.

Rousseau started out at Quebec, where he learned the silversmith's craft, probably in a group around Joseph Schindler* in which he met his friend Louis Huguet, *dit* Latour. He went to Montreal, as did Huguet, and may have worked there for fur merchant François Cazeau*; Cazeau was present at his marriage with Charlotte Foureur on 30 Jan. 1776. Rousseau lived at Grondines (Saint-Charles-des-Grondines), where his family made its home by 1779, but returned to Montreal in June 1780, several months after his father's death. The next year he moved into a house on Rue Saint-Jacques bought from his father-in-law Louis Foureur*, *dit* Champagne. His business prospered rapidly. In 1781 he rented a pew in the church of Notre-Dame and lent 1,175 *livres*, without interest, "in gold of Spanish currency," to his brother-in-law silversmith Pierre Foureur, *dit* Champagne, who may have apprenticed with Rousseau. But in 1783 he stopped practising his craft when he rented his house to silversmith Charles DUVAL. The rent was to be paid

Rousseau

in articles of trade silver which Rousseau was to market.

In the spring of 1784 Rousseau was in business as a merchant at Saint-Philippe-de-Laprairie. He bought at least six properties there, and lived in an apartment that he kept for himself in one of the houses he leased out. He worked his lands through several farmers, to whom he supplied farm implements and animals, and he marketed their meat, dairy products, vegetables, hay, and wheat. He was so successful that in 1789 he sold three of his farms for £900, more than triple what he had paid for them. He had moved back to Montreal in May 1787, but only for a year. From 1788 to 1791 he lived at Longueuil, where he called himself a merchant and silversmith. In 1792 he took up permanent residence on Rue Notre-Dame, across from the Recollets, in a house once owned by the Foureur, *dit* Champagne, family that his mother-in-law had made over to him the previous year. He immediately became keeper of the keys for the fire pumps in his ward.

From 1793 to 1795 Rousseau worked on Rue Saint-François-Xavier. To turn out in short order 12,000 pairs of drop ear-rings commissioned by François Bouthillier, he had the help of silversmiths Henry Polonceaux, Sigmund Hiltne, John Oakes, Nathan Starns, and Christian Grothé. Grothé indeed supplied Rousseau until 1801, even going into partnership with Charles-David Bohle for a year. Rousseau carried out this undertaking with great ingenuity. One of his properties at Saint-Philippe-de-Laprairie was used as a guarantee and changed hands several times, while Starns's salary was paid in kind, in the form of a draw-bench. A number of documents provide copious information about the price of items and salaries. A further detail illustrates the stiff competition in the field: a model "wrapped in a sealed paper" was not handed over to Grothé until the contract had been signed in the presence of a notary.

In 1796 Rousseau again became a merchant, moved into a house on Rue Saint-Paul, and sublet one of the two stores in it; the common passageway was also put at the disposal of sellers of "small items." Rousseau himself carried a variety of retail merchandise. In addition he went into partnership with his brother François and Jean-Baptiste-Toussaint Pothier* in March 1797 to set up a potashery at Deschambault. Pothier soon withdrew, but Rousseau had the necessary buildings put up and began production in the summer. In May 1798 he hired a "master potashmaker" for "as long as there is work."

The summer of 1798 marked a turning-point in Rousseau's career. He sold "merchandise, silver articles, and clothing" worth 16,223 *livres* 15 *sols* to Pierre-Gabriel Cotté, which he contracted to deliver at Michilimackinac (Mackinac Island, Mich.) and consign to Pothier. Rousseau became a *bourgeois* and hired voyageurs. He enjoyed the favour of Joseph

Lamothe, a captain in the Indian Department who made him long-term loans, interest-free, totalling 24,200 *livres* (£1,008 6s. 8d.). In the period from 1799 to 1809 Rousseau employed up to about 60 *engagés*, including some 50 winterers, and fitted out as many as seven canoes a year. Among the *engagés* the trades of baker, tailor, cooper, miller, and carpenter were represented. Rousseau had two clerks at Michilimackinac from 1802 to 1805, and three from 1805 till 1808, and he himself went there every summer. His winterers generally located in the south, in the regions then called the Illinois country, the Upper and Lower Mississippi, the Grand River (Mich.), and Detroit. But in 1802 in association with Joseph BAILLY he tried to establish himself at Grand Portage (near Grand Portage, Minn.). The 10-man crew under clerk Paul Hervieux included a guide, François Rastoulle, six voyageurs, a baker, and a winterer. But the powerful North West Company, jealous of territory it considered its exclusive property, attacked the expedition.

The dispute, which went on for some time, started in July 1802, mainly between Duncan McGillivray* and Hervieux. Simon McTavish*, Archibald Norman McLeod*, and Rastoulle also had a part in it. The NWC sought to prevent the expedition from putting up its tents and trading on sites cleared by the company. Hervieux produced the licence issued to his *bourgeois* by the American government and disputed the NWC's claims to a monopoly on trade. In a fit of anger and with a torrent of insults, McGillivray slashed one of the tents and mocked the expedition by setting fire to another. Then the NWC forbad its *engagés*, under pain of punishment, to trade with Hervieux. As a result Hervieux could only sell a quarter of his goods (half of which were dry goods and the rest wet); from the cargo, valued at £840, he had been expecting a profit of £2,500 to £3,000.

In October Rousseau and Bailly sued McGillivray in the Court of King's Bench. The examination of 16 witnesses was postponed until March 1803. A number of voyageurs testified for the plaintiffs, but so did merchants such as Thomas Forsyth, Maurice-Régis Blondeau*, Jean-Baptiste Tabeau, and Daniel SUTHERLAND. Hervieux admitted that in selling his merchandise more cheaply than his competitors he had been conducting a price war. Other testimony disclosed that he had been aiming in particular at Joseph Lecuyer, a merchant associated with the NWC who mainly sold liquor. Rousseau had himself stated, in the presence of Henry McKENZIE at Michilimackinac, that he had sent a canoe to Grand Portage in an attempt to force down the NWC prices and that he would persist until he reached his objective. McKenzie, who had arrived at Grand Portage before Hervieux, had warned his employers, and they had decided to thwart Hervieux.

The court ordered McGillivray to pay damages of

£500 plus court costs. Lord Selkirk [Douglas*] remarked that the sum "could not possibly indemnify [Rousseau] for the profit which he had reason to expect, and was a mere trifle to the North-West Company, in comparison with the benefit of maintaining their monopoly, and of deterring others from attempting a similar interference." It was a great moral victory, however, since by the case the NWC had lost legal recognition of its monopoly rights. Historian Grace Lee Nute concluded that it was this case that prompted the NWC to establish itself on British territory at Fort William (Thunder Bay, Ont.).

In 1806 Rousseau tried a new tactic against the NWC. In addition to the 47 winterers established south of Michilimackinac, he sent an expedition northwestwards led by François Hénault, dit Delorme, one of his voyageurs. However, the NWC got wind of the venture and detailed a few men under orders of Alexander MacKay* to "keep an eye" on them. Delorme prudently went from Grand Portage to Rainy Lake over American territory, taking a route that had been abandoned by the NWC since the events of 1802. But MacKay's party blocked their passage by cutting down trees, forcing Delorme to abandon his goods on the spot. This time the dispute would be settled out of court.

On 10 Dec. 1806 an agreement was reached between Rousseau and the agents of the Michilimackinac Company [see John Ogilvy*], that is to say Jean-Baptiste-Toussaint Pothier, Josiah BLEAKLEY, Jacques Giasson, George Gillespie*, and David Mitchell Jr. Rousseau promised to respect the limits of trading areas agreed to by that company and the NWC, not to engage in business dealings with the Indians but only with whites, and not to have any other separate interests. In return Rousseau was granted a retail store at Michilimackinac, enjoying a monopoly except for one other store which belonged to the Michilimackinac Company. The value of goods supplied annually by the company was not to exceed £2,000 unless by mutual agreement. In the event of failure to respect the agreement the offender would have to pay a fine of £1,000 to the injured party. The accord was ratified for a 10-year period, as was the one concluded that month by the NWC and the Michilimackinac Company.

On 12 Jan. 1807 Rousseau signed another agreement, this time with WILLIAM and Duncan McGillivray, William Hallowell, Roderick McKenzie*, John Ogilvy, and Thomas THAIN, to "put an amicable end to all contentious issues" arising from the confrontation between MacKay and Delorme. Rousseau was to receive £600, and in return the NWC would be allowed to recover the merchandise left behind by Delorme "at the place called Portage de l'Orignal." In the spring Rousseau fitted out only one very small expedition. On 6 July at Michilimackinac he signed a private agreement terminating his contract with the Michilimackinac Company. But there is every reason to believe that he continued none the less to work for it until it was taken over in 1811 by John Jacob Astor's South West Fur Company. Indeed, in the inventory of Rousseau's estate done after his death the notary recorded 68 documents concerning the Michilimackinac Company, which suggests that commercial operations had continued on a large scale.

In October 1807 Rousseau owed £3,208 to David DAVID and £1,500 to William and Andrew* Porteous for various goods that he had bought for trading. His creditors recognized Rousseau's honesty and integrity: his failure to repay them did not stem from negligence and had to be attributed "to the present state of commerce in this province." Rousseau actually owned furs worth £850, which were later sold in England. Several people also owed him sums totalling 76,284 livres (£3,178 10s.). Robert DICKSON and his company owed the largest amounts, 31,624 livres and 5,800 livres. In 1804 Rousseau had in fact entrusted to Dickson the management of all his belongings and business affairs in Upper Canada and the United States, "whether in his trading with the Indians or otherwise." Before leaving for Michilimackinac in the spring of 1808 Rousseau delegated his attorney, David David, to attend a meeting of the creditors of Dickson, who was represented in Montreal by James McGill*. That summer he had a three-storey warehouse with a deep cellar and a kitchen built on Rue Notre-Dame at a cost of £400. Rousseau set up his headquarters in it, but did not give up his trips to the pays d'en haut.

He returned to the fur business in 1811, as soon as the Michilimackinac Company was liquidated. Unfortunately the pelts stored in one of his warehouses on the Place des Commissaires were stolen. In March 1813 he supplied furs to dealer Joseph Lemoine, Gabriel Franchère*'s relative. He went back into business with Jean-Baptiste-Toussaint Pothier, who furnished him with goods worth £707. Despite the uncertainty engendered by the war with the Americans he sent four canoes to Michilimackinac in the spring. Seeing that the route was open, he went into partnership with Michel Lacroix to send a second, last-minute expedition at the end of August; it consisted of two winterers, one hired for two years. In December he signed a partnership agreement with Paul-Joseph Lacroix. The collaboration was profitable and lasted until after Rousseau's death since Lacroix, his loyal partner, was his principal executor.

In making the final inventory the notary recorded a number of documents relating to Rousseau's dealings with the two Lacroixs: 54 concerned Michel and 121 Paul-Joseph. From 1814 to 1819 Michel traded for Rousseau at "Haokia or Saint Louis" (the vicinity of St Louis, Mo.) and York (Toronto) with, among others, John Baptiste Jacobs, Joseph CADOTTE, and Duncan Cameron*. In 1823 Rousseau delegated his

Rousseau

attorney Pierre Cabané to go to St Louis and settle all debts owing him with the executors or administrators of Michel Lacroix and John Hays. During the same period Rousseau hired some voyageurs in partnership with Paul-Joseph and others for the firm of Berthelotte et Rollette. He also employed merchant-voyageurs from Lac-des-Deux-Montagnes (Oka) such as Bernard and Louis Lyons and François-Benjamin Pillet, whose pelts he alone stored and marketed. The contract that he signed with Pillet on 31 July 1823 gives copious, detailed information about Rousseau's business and the market prices then prevalent.

In the course of his career Rousseau invested in numerous pieces of landed property. He rarely mortgaged them, preferring to pay for them quickly. Only occasionally did he sell any, choosing instead to rent and improve them. In addition to those already mentioned he bought an impressive store on Rue Saint-Paul in 1803, as well as several lots and properties in the *faubourg* Sainte-Marie; he had at least one house built there, as well as a splendid store in 1820. In 1811 he was granted four pieces of land at Hemmingford which he gave to Marie-Anne Rousseau, the wife of his friend John (Jean-Baptiste) Delisle, in 1823. In 1814 he paid £2,250 for a fine property on Rue Notre-Dame that he rented to several merchants for £200 a year. In 1820 he bought some land in the seigneury of Léry, at Blairfindie (L'Acadie), which he immediately gave to one of his wife's adopted daughters. Throughout his life he regularly lent large sums to various people, and he frequently used his administrative talents as an attorney.

A biographical account of Rousseau would be incomplete without mention of his unusual marital situation. His relations with Charlotte Foureur remain unclear. He did not live with her over a long period because he had a regular female companion, Jean Cook, with whom in the years 1796–1811 he had five children, all unacknowledged publicly for a while. From 1803 Rousseau recognized them, gave them his name, and made them his heirs and their mother his usufructuary. Thereafter they lived in the *faubourg* Sainte-Marie, near Rousseau's other properties. Rousseau was alleged to have fathered two other children baptized at Michilimackinac in 1821, who were born of different mothers. In fact, it was his son, also called Dominique, who was the father of one mixed-blood girl and later the godfather of another. Charlotte Foureur for her part adopted two girls whom she had raised from childhood.

Rousseau's desire to bequeath his property to his illegitimate children became a veritable obsession. He drew up some ten wills, at least four of them in the last two years of his life. But the bequest made in 1812 was very unusual. Rousseau and his wife conjointly gave two properties to the five children, and to their mother as usufructuary. Nevertheless, after her husband's death Charlotte Foureur frustrated his wishes in part,

by exercising the rights and covenants consented to in her marriage contract. The saga furnishes some interesting information on those to whom Rousseau was close. For example, the choice of executors he made reveals that he had special ties with the following: Charles Dézéry Latour in 1788; Thomas Forsyth in 1803; Étienne Nivard Saint-Dizier from 1808 to 1812; Joseph-Maurice LAMOTHE, François Toupin, and John Delisle from 1816 to 1823; Henry Bellefeuille in 1824; then, in the last wills, Joseph Masson* and Paul-Joseph Lacroix.

The inventory of Rousseau's goods after his death and the sale that followed show beyond any doubt that he had an opulent style of life; he had several domestic servants. He owned a dinner service for 60, and had enough food and drink to get him through a siege. The silverware was valued at £46 2s., and he left a credit balance of £880. Only part of the library was inventoried. Rousseau's main interests can, however, be determined from it: nature, law, finance, and the fur trade. The sale of his belongings brought in £286; his partner Paul-Joseph Lacroix bought 2,227 drop ear-rings.

Rousseau had begun his career as a master silversmith, but had soon turned his natural talents as a merchant to selling first silver-work and then all sorts of goods, and he wound up trading in furs. Because of the nature of his double career he had a privileged position in the marketing of trade silver, which reached a peak of production coinciding exactly with Rousseau's career and the extraordinary epic of the NWC. His career as a silversmith was, indeed, devoted exclusively to this specialty. But sooner than make the articles himself, he called upon the services of various professional colleagues. Of these Salomon MARION seems to have had a privileged position. No example of this proto-industrial production has been preserved, and no mark has yet been attributed to Rousseau. It should be noted, however, that one contemporary silversmith at Detroit, Dominique Réopelle, had the same initials.

Dominique Rousseau's main activity, in truth, was trading in furs. His career gives insight into an economic situation pitting French-speaking merchants, on unequal terms, against monopolies held by English-speaking merchants marshalled in powerful companies. At the time of Rousseau's assaults on the NWC some hint of nationalism could be sensed in his claims to part of that lucrative market. The support he received in his lawsuit in 1802–3 and the agreements binding him to a number of French-speaking traders indicate there was a certain cohesion in this milieu, which has a history thus far neglected.

ROBERT DEROME

[I wish to thank three students, José Ménard, Joanne Chagnon, and the late Mary Henshaw, who worked closely with me in researching Dominique Rousseau and in amassing the abundant material available on him. This biography is based on computerized analysis of a vast number of notarized instruments and of other archival material. A useful source is Grace Lee Nute's "A British legal case and old Grand Portage," *Minn. Hist.* (St Paul), 21 (1940): 117–48; it provides a number of leads and a well-documented analysis, as well as a full transcript of the evidence heard in court on 21–23 March 1803 in the action launched by Rousseau and Bailly against McGillivray. The present account gives only a brief summary of the wealth of data in this material which, among other things, discloses a great many details about market practices in the fur trade. The short biography by Édouard-Zotique Massicotte*, "Dominique Rousseau, maître orfèvre et négociant en pelleteries," *BRH*, 49 (1943): 342–48, offers only a pale reflection of Rousseau's career; it is marred by several inaccuracies, but it does provide information not repeated in this biography. The interpretations in Lord Selkirk's *A sketch of the British fur trade in North America, with observations relative to the North-west company of Montreal* (London, 1816) must be used with caution, because they were part of his campaign to discredit the North West Company. Further study of the Michilimackinac Company might shed more light on the role Rousseau played in it. R.D.]

ANQ-M, CE1-51, 22, 30 janv. 1776; 24 janv. 1780; 14 oct. 1787; CN1-16, 7 déc. 1813; CN1-33, 8 mai 1824; CN1-47, 20 févr. 1797; CN1-74, 30 juill. 1796; 2 mars 1797; 16 mai, 13 août, 19 sept., 15 déc. 1798; 16, 19, 25, 31 janv., 4–5, 11 févr., 8, 27 mars, 12 avril, 7 mai 1799; 4, 9, 15, 27 janv., 13, 19, 21–22 févr. 1800; 17, 24, 30 janv., 7, 13, 19–20, 24, 26 févr., 28 mars, 1er avril 1801; 26 sept. 1804; 19 nov., 10 déc. 1806; 14 févr., 20 avril 1810; 16 mai 1811; 24 févr. 1813; CN1-120, 21 janv. 1776, 10 mars 1779, 20 janv. 1780; CN1-121, 6 juill. 1789; 8 janv., 2, 6 nov., 3 déc. 1793; 18 mai, 22 sept. 1795; 11 avril 1797; 12 mars, 31 oct., 1er, 21, 30 déc. 1801; 22, 28, 30 janv., 2, 8–10, 12, 26 févr., 3, 5, 11, 19–20 mars, 3, 6, 9, 13, 15–16, 21, 23, 27, 30 avril, 6 mai, 27 sept., 6 nov., 2, 9, 13–15, 20, 22, 28, 31 déc. 1802; 3, 7, 24, 27 janv., 3–4 févr., 16, 29 mars, 22, 25 avril, 4, 10, 12 mai, 26, 31 oct., 26, 28–29 nov., 1er, 9, 14, 16, 20, 27–28 déc. 1803; 3, 16, 18 janv., 18, 20 févr., 10, 13, 16, 24, 30–31 mars, 20, 27, 30 avril, 22, 28 mai, 26 sept., 7 nov., 28–29 déc. 1804; 11–12, 16–18, 21 janv., 4, 8–9, 12, 14, 25 févr., 26–28 mars, 1er, 5–6, 8, 11, 15, 17–19, 24, 26, 29 avril, 17 mai, 5 juin, 9 nov., 21, 30 déc. 1805; 3, 13, 23 janv., 1er, 3, 6–8 févr., 15, 18, 20 mars, 3, 5, 11, 14–15, 17, 22, 24, 30 avril, 1 mai, 23, 26 sept., 21 nov., 23–24, 26 déc. 1806; 10, 12, 24 janv., 5, 15–16, 24 oct., 29 déc. 1807; 19 avril, 5, 9 mai, 28 sept. 1808; 8, 18 mars, 2 oct., 5 déc. 1809; 17 mars, 10, 30 avril 1810; 20 févr., 3, 26 oct. 1811; 4 janv., 15, 19–20 juin 1812; 6, 8, 18–19, 27 mars, 12, 17, 26, 28 avril, 1, 15, 22 mai, 21, 23 août 1813; CN1-126, 16 mai 1811; 20 févr., 9 mars, 2, 9 sept. 1814; 3 janv., 13 févr., 14 août 1815; 20 févr., 15, 24, 29–30 mai, 31 déc. 1816; 2 mai 1817; 16 févr., 22, 30 mai, 3 oct. 1818; 6 avril 1819; 22 mars 1820; CN1-128, 6 févr., 19 sept. 1788; 16 oct., 13 nov. 1789; 5 juill., 10 août 1790; 12 mars 1791; 9 déc. 1793; 20 mars 1798; 4 janv., 12 sept. 1800; CN1-134, 27 mars 1817; 16 nov., 3 déc. 1819; 11 févr., 13 mars 1820; 3, 7 févr., 12 juill., 3 août 1821; 16 janv., 30 mars, 22 avril, 7 juill., 22 août 1822; 21, 27 janv., 24 févr., 11 mars, 22 avril, 6 juin, 4 août 1823; 13 févr., 3 nov., 4, 11 déc. 1824; 22 janv., 21, 30 mars, 7, 20 avril, 7, 23 mai, 7 oct. 1825; 4 juill. 1826; 31 janv., 23 juill. 1827; 30 avril 1832; 26 janv. 1833; CN1-158, 9 juill. 1775, 28 janv. 1776, 6 avril 1780, 24 déc. 1781, 11 août 1783, 27 févr. 1787; CN1-185, 22 oct. 1805; CN1-194, 7 mai 1801, 4 déc. 1810; CN1-229, 17 mai 1784; 7 mai 1785; 7 juin, 4 août, 25 nov. 1786; CN1-243, 2, 5 sept. 1814; CN1-295, 29 août, 2 sept. 1814; 20 janv., 2 févr., 2 oct., 25 nov. 1815; CN1-313, 16 févr. 1786, 11 avril 1792, 5 avril 1808, 4 avril 1809; CN1-334, 11 mars 1806, 2 sept. 1814, 2 oct. 1815; CN1-348, 25 avril 1826; T-10, 77, 1–2, 5, 7, 20 oct. 1802; 21–23 mars 1803. AP, Notre-Dame de Montréal, boîte 1756, 3 janv. 1781. AUM, P 58, P2/105, 20 avril 1802. MAC-CD, Fonds Morisset, 2, Dossier Dominique Rousseau. Private arch., Robert Derome (Montreal), Robert Derome, "Les migrations d'orfèvres au Québec (1760–1790)."

Montreal Gazette, 1 March 1792; 9 July 1804; 4 Nov. 1811–3 Feb. 1812; 31 Aug. 1812; 5 Oct. 1812–26 Jan. 1813; 10 Jan.–15 Aug. 1821; 5 March 1825; 1, 5, 19, 26 Feb., 5 March, 5 April, 6 Aug. 1827. Marthe Faribault-Beauregard, *La population des forts français d'Amérique (XVIIIe siècle)* . . . (1v. paru, Montréal, 1982). Massicotte, "Répertoire des engagements pour l'Ouest," ANQ *Rapport*, 1943–44. *Montreal directory*, 1819. *Quebec almanac*, 1807–13. Tanguay, *Dictionnaire*, vol.7. Robert Derome, "Delezenne, les orfèvres, l'orfèvrerie, 1740–1790" (thèse de MA, univ. de Montréal, 1974). R. A. C. Fox, *Quebec and related silver at the Detroit Institute of Arts* (Detroit, 1978). J. E. Langdon, *Canadian silversmiths, 1700–1900* (Toronto, 1966).

ROUX, JEAN-HENRY-AUGUSTE, priest, Sulpician, seminary administrator, and vicar general; b. 5 Feb. 1760 in Marseilles, France, son of Jean-Baptiste Roux, a doctor, and Françoise-Élizabeth Durand; d. 7 April 1831 in Montreal.

Jean-Henry-Auguste Roux scarcely knew his father, who owned immense plantations in Martinique and usually lived there in the town of Fort-Royal (Fort-de-France). At the end of brilliant classical studies in Corrèze, France, Roux entered the Séminaire d'Avignon on 20 Oct. 1779, and there on 5 June 1784 he was ordained priest. Having immediately been admitted as a member to the community of the Society of Saint-Sulpice, he taught moral theology at the Séminaire de Saint-Sulpice in Paris and gave several lectures that attracted notice. Early in 1791 he went to continue his teaching career at the Séminaire du Puy, at the same time becoming vicar general to the bishop of Le Puy, Marie-Joseph de Galard, on 15 January.

That summer, when the Constituent Assembly was setting up a state church that was clearly schismatic, Roux fled to the canton of Valais in Switzerland with his bishop, who had refused to take the oath of loyalty to the Civil Constitution of the Clergy. Roux had informed his father of this step, and on 26 Nov. 1791 had been invited by him to come and live with the family in Martinique. There was no doubt some notion that he might get a parish charge in that distant colony or even be named apostolic prefect. When Dr Roux

Roux

died the following year, Jean-Henry-Auguste refused an invitation from his elder brother, who inherited the largest share of the property, to join him.

The year 1794 marked the beginning of Roux's career in Lower Canada. The previous year, the superior of the seminary in Montreal, Gabriel-Jean Brassier*, had taken advantage of the British government's new disposition not to object to French Sulpicians being admitted to the colony and had requested recruits. In response, the assistant to Jacques-André Émery, the superior general of Saint-Sulpice who was then in prison, selected four former directors and eight young priests. At the head of the group was vicar general Roux, to whom Émery's assistant gave a religious rule of life to be followed during the voyage. The group of 11 Sulpicians – illness forced one to withdraw – left Switzerland at the end of April 1794 and reached Montreal on 12 September.

Thanks to his vast fund of knowledge and his dominant personality, Roux quickly became the recognized head of his colleagues. He was named bursar of the seminary upon arrival and quickly restored its financial position, retrieving it from a precarious state. Then in October 1798 he succeeded Brassier as superior. On 6 Sept. 1797 Bishop Pierre Denaut*, who had a high regard for him and took pleasure in calling him his "diocesan oracle," had appointed him vicar general of the district of Montreal. Roux soon became the "universal adviser of the whole colony." It was said that "every day one could see heading towards the seminary a curious crowd of consultants from every class, coming to beseech him for the help, [given] free of charge, of his beneficent understanding." Bishop Denaut, and then Bishop Joseph-Octave Plessis, both former pupils of the Sulpicians, more than once turned to him for his judicious counsel. It was Roux who on 15 May 1812 would prepare for Governor Sir George Prevost* a remarkable memorandum on the treatment to be accorded the bishop of Quebec. In it he spoke of the privileged circumstances of that bishop under the French régime. In concluding he stated that "the episcopate in this country needs, therefore, to be visibly recognized with the title of bishop," and he asked that Plessis be given official recognition by the civil authorities.

Since the Paris seminary had made over all its property in the colony to the Montreal seminary in April 1764, the Canadian institution had had complete financial autonomy. In spiritual matters, however, Montreal was still responsible to Paris. From 1792 until 1815 the hostility between Great Britain and France made communications between the two institutions extremely difficult. In February 1815, following the end of the war, they were restored and would not be further interrupted while Roux was superior. Fully cognizant of Roux's administrative talents, the superior general of Saint-Sulpice, Antoine de Pouget

Duclaux, contemplated appointing him one of his 12 assistants in 1817 and in 1818. Considering his presence in Lower Canada indispensable at a time when the seminary's position was being questioned by London, Roux declined the invitation. He remained none the less one of the advisers of the superior general who were most heeded. At the same time his seminary was giving important financial support to the one in Paris, as well as to the one in Baltimore.

Defending Saint-Sulpice's property against the claims of the British government was always a major concern for Roux. After the conquest the Sulpicians' property titles were regularly disputed, both by the civil authorities and by a number of well-known jurists who maintained that their lands were public property. In the spring of 1819 the question was again raised in the Legislative Council and commented upon at length in the newspapers. Roux, who since 1816 had also been engaged in lawsuits over seigneurial rights with Montreal merchants John Fleming and Thomas Porteous, had to submit the dispute to the governor, the Duke of Richmond [Lennox*]. In July 1819 Roux, writing to Jean-Baptiste Thavenet*, the Sulpicians' agent in Rome, said the governor had informed him that "it was useless to discuss once more a matter that had already been decided by the officers of the crown (in 1789 and 1811)," and had offered to pay the Sulpicians an allowance in perpetuity in return for giving up their rights. On this occasion Roux prepared a memoir for the governor that created "a great stir in the country"; he then decided to send Sulpician Jean-Jacques Lartigue* to clarify the situation in London. Lartigue's mission did not bring the results anticipated. The firmness displayed in this cause by the superior had, however, forced the British government to give up its plan. In June 1826 Roux left for England with Sulpician Jackson John Richard* to negotiate a final solution in the matter of the seminary's property. In October 1827 the discussions between Roux and Lord Bathurst, the colonial secretary, ended in an agreement by which the Sulpicians would yield part of their seigneurial rights in return for a fixed perpetual annuity. The agreement roused a strong reaction among the Canadians and the episcopate, which regarded that solution as a veritable spoliation of the patrimony. Rome had given permission to the Sulpicians to alienate their seigneurial property but, since the property initially belonged to the church, had retained the right to inspect agreements. Hence in March 1830 the Sacred Congregation of Propaganda temporarily suspended the permission previously granted.

The delicate, indeed precarious situation of the Séminaire de Montréal in the matter of recognition of its rights strongly influenced the feelings of loyalty which Roux unfailingly displayed to the British authorities. In July 1812, at the time of the riots marking the anti-conscription crisis at Lachine and

Pointe-Claire, he firmly declared his attachment to the crown. The superior would maintain this attitude consistently and would, moreover, be held in high regard by the British government, which considered the seminary the "headquarters" and "bulwark of loyalty." This behaviour inevitably stirred up some discontent and bitterness among the people and in the Canadian press.

Since their arrival in Montreal in 1657 the Sulpicians had always enjoyed a prestige and authority that the bishops of Quebec had never challenged. The welcome that Bishop Jean-François Hubert* of Quebec, and his future coadjutor, Mgr Denaut, had extended to the group of 11 in 1794 had only given further proof of the esteem that the Montreal institution enjoyed in high places. As for Bishop Plessis, although Thavenet suggested that he had intended to "lay hands on the Séminaire de Montréal" from 1807, when he had sought to introduce his coadjutor, Bernard-Claude PANET, into it, he was sincerely attached to the seminary and its superior. Plessis's decision at the beginning of 1821 to install Lartigue as an auxiliary bishop in Montreal, was, however, to bring him into direct conflict with Roux, even though he had taken care to choose one of the Sulpicians for the appointment. Jealous of the prerogatives of his house, Roux never accepted the presence in Montreal of an auxiliary bishop; such a person could only serve to diminish "the influence of the seminary and that of its superior, who previously governed the district." He found it unacceptable that this bishop was a Canadian, who would inevitably apply pressure to the Montreal institution to induce it to adapt more fully to the Canadian reality.

It is from this viewpoint that an explanation must be sought both for Lartigue's exclusion from the Séminaire de Montréal in 1821 and for the differences that were to set him against Roux, in particular when the new parish church was being built. Roux's attempts to recruit French priests in France on his trip to Europe in 1826, as well as the discrimination constantly practised against the Canadian Sulpicians within the seminary, were prompted by the same desire to retain its predominantly French character. The appointment in 1829 of the American Sulpician Jackson John Richard, and then of the French Sulpician Claude Fay as parish priest of Notre-Dame in Montreal to replace Candide-Michel LE SAULNIER, who was ill, and the election in 1830 of the Frenchman Joseph-Vincent Quiblier* as vice-superior of the seminary to succeed Roux, who was unable to continue in his charge, give evidence of Saint-Sulpice's firm intention to keep the Canadians out of the important offices in the house.

Jean-Henry-Auguste Roux died of a cerebral haemorrhage on 7 April 1831. Over the space of a year he had "suffered several attacks that had gone to his head and weakened his mind to the point that he no longer uttered anything coherent." His funeral on 11 April was widely attended. Joseph Papineau* paid him a final tribute: "The most illustrious Messire Roux was endowed with a deep, universal learning, as solid in civil as in canon law, of such enlightenment that while he lived he was consulted from all parts of Canada, by laity and clergy alike, and to the greatest profit." As well, he was to leave several written works on law and spirituality. With his death the superior general of the Sulpicians in Paris, Antoine Garnier, observed that Montreal had lost "a great administrator, an eloquent preacher, an astute theologian, a renowned canonist and legal expert."

GILLES CHAUSSÉ

Jean-Henry-Auguste Roux is the author of *Mémoire pour le séminaire de Montréal* (s.l., 1820).

ACAM, 901.029, 901.136, 901.137. ANQ-M, CE1-51, 11 avril 1831. Arch. de la Compagnie de Saint-Sulpice (Paris), Dossiers 75, nos.1–20; 112–14; mss 1214; Circulaire des supérieurs de Saint-Sulpice à l'occasion de la mort des prêtres de cette compagnie, I, 29 mai 1831. ASSM, 1bis; 21, cartons, 23, 24. Allaire, *Dictionnaire*, vol.1. F.-M. Bibaud, *Le Panthéon canadien* (A. et V. Bibaud; 1891), 252–54. Gauthier, *Sulpitiana*. Louis Bertrand, *Bibliothèque sulpicienne ou histoire littéraire de la Compagnie de Saint-Sulpice* (3v., Paris, 1900), 1: 124–31, 270–94. [Pierre] Boisard, *La Compagnie de Saint-Sulpice; trois siècles d'histoire* (s.l.n.d.). Chaussé, *Jean-Jacques Lartigue.* Dionne, *Les ecclésiastiques et les royalistes français.* Lemieux, *L'établissement de la première prov. eccl.*

RUSSELL, ELIZABETH, gentlewoman and diarist; b. 26 Dec. 1754 in Gibraltar, only surviving child of Richard Russell and his second wife, Dorothy Harrison; d. unmarried 19 Feb. 1822 in York (Toronto), Upper Canada.

When Elizabeth Russell was born, her Irish father was a captain in the 14th Foot; nine months later he was cashiered because of an unsavoury imbroglio involving a woman and a fellow officer. Disgraced, friendless, knowing only army life, Richard Russell was eventually appointed naval officer at Harwich, England. Mrs Russell's mental stability was shaken by her husband's misfortunes; for a number of years prior to her death in 1779 she was violently insane, and was cared for by her daughter. Elizabeth grew up with little education, in an atmosphere darkened by her mother's insanity and her father's debts, extravagance, ill health, and lawsuits.

After his court martial, Richard Russell had quarrelled with many people, including his only legitimate son, Peter*, Elizabeth's half-brother. It was not until 1771 that Peter visited Harwich. Elizabeth was charmed with her unknown, unmarried brother, who was more than 20 years older than she was, while Peter was delighted to help with advice, instruction, and encouragement. He returned from the American colonies in 1782, and after their father's death in 1786

Ryan

he and Elizabeth lived together in Ipswich; they were to be a devoted couple for the rest of their lives.

In 1791 Peter Russell was appointed receiver general of Upper Canada, and on 1 April 1792 the Russells left England with Chief Justice William OSGOODE and Attorney General John White*, who remained their closest friends in their early years in Upper Canada. With them also was Mary Fleming, whom Peter had brought back from America and placed in Elizabeth's charge. Born in 1779 at Peter's house in New York, she was probably his illegitimate daughter. The Russells settled in the temporary capital, Newark (Niagara-on-the-Lake), where Mary died of tuberculosis on 20 Jan. 1797. Elizabeth was very ill after Mary's death, and was still grieving when she moved to the new capital, York, on 3 November.

From 1796 until 1799, when Peter was administrator of the province, the Russells entertained officially, but both obviously preferred a quiet life, particularly when Peter's health deteriorated several years before his death in 1808. Their closest friends in this period were the family of their first cousin, William Willcocks*, especially his son-in-law, William Warren Baldwin*. A more distant cousin, Joseph Willcocks*, lived with them from 1800 to 1802, but because he tried to court Elizabeth he was cast forth from the house and from favour.

After Peter's death, Elizabeth, in poor health, faced settling his official accounts and managing the Russell estate. Baldwin helped with the business and an operation for dropsy in 1811 brought physical relief, but her spirits never recovered from Peter's death. During the War of 1812 her dejection became mental illness. In December 1814 the Baldwin family moved into her house, where she died in 1822. Peter had left Elizabeth his entire estate, including thousands of acres of land; by her will she left almost all this property to William Willcocks's two surviving daughters, Margaret Phœbe (wife of William Warren Baldwin) and Maria, who died unmarried. The vast Russell estate thus passed eventually to the Baldwin family.

Elizabeth Russell was unlike most of the other upper class women of her day in Upper Canada because she was older, not as well educated, and unmarried. Although she was always desperately homesick for England, she would never leave her brother, and indignantly rejected several proposals of marriage in York. She could be remarkably silly, but she could also be surprisingly shrewd. In her letters and diary she has left a detailed picture of one woman's life in early Upper Canada.

EDITH G. FIRTH

AO, MS 75; MS 88. MTL, W. W. Baldwin papers; Elizabeth Russell papers; Peter Russell papers. PAC, MG 23, HI, 5; HII, 7 (photocopies); MG 24, C1. Univ. of Guelph Library, Arch. Coll. (Guelph, Ont.), J. MacI. Duff coll.,

Samuel Peters papers. *Town of York, 1793–1815* (Firth). A. S. Thompson, *Spadina: a story of old Toronto* (Toronto, 1975).

RYAN, HENRY, Methodist minister; b. 22 April 1775 in Massachusetts; m. 30 Nov. 1794 Huldah Laird (Lord), and they had at least three children; d. 2 Sept. 1833 in Gainsborough, near Grimsby, Upper Canada.

Henry Ryan presumably had an Irish background and he may have been originally a Roman Catholic. Evidently he had some education, and the fact that in later life he maintained a farm may indicate that he came from rural Massachusetts. The circumstances of his conversion and his decision to become a Methodist are not known. By the 1790s he was a local preacher and in 1800 he was received on trial by the New York Conference of the Methodist Episcopal Church. From 1800 to 1805 he served on circuits in Vermont and New York; he was received in full connection and ordained elder in 1804, and in 1805 was appointed with William Case* to the Bay of Quinte circuit in the Upper Canada District, which was then part of the New York Conference.

Ryan was the kind of man who in the small Upper Canadian community was bound to become legendary. According to a contemporary, "he was well nigh six feet in height, of large, symmetrical proportions, with prodigious muscular developments, and without doubt one of the strongest men of his age. . . . His voice excelled, for power and compass, all that I ever heard from human organs." His energy, determination, and pugnacity were commensurate with his physical characteristics and doubtless account for the popular belief that he had been a boxer in his youth. He was a powerful preacher and would become a vigorous, albeit overbearing, administrator. Elijah Hedding, later a Methodist Episcopal bishop, described him in the first phase of his career as "a man of great love for the cause of Christ, and of great zeal in his work as a minister. He was a brave Irishman – a man who laboured as if the judgment thunders were to follow on each sermon." His customary exhortation was "Drive on, brother! drive on! Drive the devil out of the country! Drive him into the lake and drown him!" For many years Ryan drove himself and his brethren fervently to bring converts into the Methodist fold and to extend the range of Methodist influence.

During his first five years in Upper Canada, Ryan served for two years on the Bay of Quinte circuit; in 1807 he was stationed on the Long Point circuit, and in 1808 and 1809 he was on the adjacent Niagara circuit, where he acquired a farm which became his home. In company with William Case and Nathan Bangs*, who would play important roles in the evolution of Canadian Methodism, he held the first camp meeting in Upper Canada in September 1805. This largely attended gathering on the shore of Hay Bay was characterized by intense religious excitement. At the Sunday morning love-feast "the power of the Spirit was manifested throughout the whole encampment and almost every tent was a scene of prayer." Bangs recalled that the "parting scene" was "indescribable. The preachers . . . hung upon each other's necks, weeping and yet rejoicing. . . . As the hosts marched off in different directions the songs of victory rolled along the highways. Great was the good that followed." By such means, of which Ryan was an enthusiastic proponent, Methodism became firmly entrenched in the loyalist and post-loyalist settlements which extended from Cornwall to Detroit.

In 1810 the Genesee Conference, encompassing the districts in western New York and Upper Canada, was established. Ryan was appointed presiding elder of the Upper Canada District, which at that point reported a membership of 2,603; he was to remain a presiding elder, in different districts, until 1824. In that capacity he had to attend four quarterly meetings annually in each circuit in his district. To do so, he must have travelled about 4,000 miles each year. Since the quarterly meetings were "great religious festivals" as well as occasions for regulating the work, the presiding elder was expected in each case to preach, to administer the sacraments, and to foster the spirit of revival. At this time, says the Reverend John Saltkill Carroll*, Ryan was "the right man in the right place. He had zeal, enterprise, courage, system, industry, and that rough and ready kind of talent which was then more effective than any other. Moreover, he had authority by which to control others." He knew "how to melt the people into tenderness, while he addressed them, with floods of tears. He was communicative and lively in private conversation." He also had a strong feeling for the ludicrous aspects of daily life which endeared him to many. His religious commitment and his devotion to duty evidently earned for him the respect of the bishops as well as the people; hence his many years as a presiding elder.

The War of 1812 led to a serious disruption of the Methodist enterprise in the Canadas. Just prior to its outbreak Ryan was reappointed presiding elder of the Upper Canada District and Bangs became presiding elder of the Lower Canada District. However, Bangs and other American preachers did not venture across the border; others in the Canadas evidently gave up their circuits. Appparently, Ryan had become a British subject or was regarded as such; in any event, he demonstrated his commitment to the Methodist cause in the Canadas by accepting full responsibility for it throughout the years of war. His activities and the condition of the societies in Upper Canada during the conflict are not well documented. He seems to have convened annual meetings of the ministers and travelled throughout the district in his role as a presiding elder. He added to his modest income, and presumably demonstrated his political sympathies, by

transporting stores by wagon or sleigh from Montreal to the western part of the colony. He and his colleagues were reunited with their American brethren at the 1815 session of the Genesee Conference. At that time Case became presiding elder of the Upper Canada District; Ryan was appointed to the Lower Canada District, which extended eastward from the vicinity of Prescott to Quebec, and was elected a delegate to the General Conference which was to meet in 1816.

The re-establishment of the jurisdiction of the Methodist Episcopal Church in Canada in 1815 and the subsequent growth of the societies, especially in Upper Canada, obscured significant changes in Canadian conditions which would have profound consequences for the future of Methodism and Ryan's own career. Before the war, although most members of the governing élite were hostile to the United States, Upper Canada was in many respects a sector of the expanding American frontier. The colony emerged from the conflict, however, with a new sense of identity, of which a major component was a virulent suspicion of American ways and values. The flood of American settlers into Upper Canada did not resume; conversely, from 1815 onward the colony absorbed increasing numbers of immigrants from the United Kingdom. The diverse traditions and loyalties of these immigrants helped to create a climate of opinion which was pro-British and which did not differentiate between native Upper Canadians or those such as Ryan who had become committed to the colony, and those who were really identified politically and culturally with the United States.

As a religious body governed by and part of an American institution, and as one whose theology and practice were tainted by enthusiasm and promoted by allegedly uneducated and self-appointed agitators masquerading as ministers of the Gospel, the Methodist societies in the Canadas were bound to become suspect in a community whose leaders cultivated anti-American and conservative opinion. As it happened, however, the attack on Canadian Methodism would be initiated not by the local élite but by the British Wesleyan Conference. In 1814 the Wesleyan Missionary Committee, responding to complaints by Lower Canadian Methodists about the political attitudes of their American ministers, began a mission in the Canadas with the appointment of the Reverend John Bass Strong to Quebec. Strong apparently took over the Montreal society too, and in the following year the Genesee Conference's appointee there was prevented from preaching in the chapel by the local leaders and Strong. In 1815 as well William Bennett*, superintendent of the missions in eastern British America, conducted an investigation of the religious condition of the Canadas.

Ryan visited Montreal as presiding elder in September 1815, having learned already that Bennett had

Ryan

toured the Ottawa circuit. Following a sharp confrontation with Richard Williams*, the newly arrived Wesleyan missionary, he was admitted to the Montreal chapel and recommended that the question of jurisdiction and responsibility be referred to the British and American conferences. His proposal fell on deaf ears: "The chapel," he later wrote in a letter to the British conference, "sounded with outcrys from one and another I am a true Britton." He continued: "If national lines are agoing to be the bounds of our feloship, the Upper Province will be wrested from us likewise." But, he contended: "Who has ever proved any of us to be rebels? . . . Can it be proved that any of us has not been conscientious in praying for Kings and all that are in authority? . . . Therefore Manhood *Religion Justice Mercy Truth and* Every Thing that is *sacred* cals aloud for you to step forward in the real characters of men that fear God and call your Preachers immediately out of Canada."

Beset with this strong advice and the equally firm counsel of Bennett and William BLACK of Nova Scotia that the Canadas should be supplied with Wesleyan missionaries, the committee urged Bishop Francis Asbury of the Methodist Episcopal Church of the United States to give up the stations in Lower Canada, where "the general habits and prejudices [of the people] are in favour of English preachers." Black and Bennett were requested to attend the American General Conference in 1816 as representatives of the British conference. The General Conference, having heard the Wesleyan delegates and the views of Case and Ryan, concluded that it could not give up any of the societies in the Canadas "to the superintendence of the British Connexion." Predictably, this decision was not accepted by the missionary committee; missionaries were now sent not only to Lower Canada but also to Kingston, Cornwall, Stamford (Niagara Falls), and York (Toronto), thereby engendering bitter rivalry between the American and British preachers and their respective adherents in which Ryan, reappointed as presiding elder in Upper Canada in 1816, played a leading part.

The British missionaries alleged, doubtless correctly, that many parts of Upper Canada were destitute of religious services and that there was in fact room for all. They contended as well that the Methodist Episcopal itinerants were religiously and politically unsuitable, and indeed a danger to the well-being of Upper Canada. The latter were "so ignorant, & enthusiastic as to render their discourses ridiculous in the ears of respectable and well informed People. Much of their religion consists in a great noise at the house of God, & then all is over till their next meeting." Moreover, the preachers were disloyal as well as enthusiastic. Even William Case, a mild-mannered and apolitical minister, was said to be "a Bitter and Bold Enemy to this Government."

Several of the circuits in the Canadas, undoubtedly with Ryan's encouragement, prepared forceful protests to the committee. "Why," asked the leaders of the Yonge Street and Ancaster circuits, "should we cast off our preachers that God has owned in the Salvation of our Souls and be to a vast expence in fetching over Preachers from England barely because they were Brittish born?" Some of the signatories to the petitions noted pointedly that they were militia officers or justices of the peace. When Ryan forwarded these documents to London, he emphasized that the British missionaries could not go anywhere in Upper Canada without interfering with the Canadian brethren. Later, at the request of the Niagara and Ancaster Quarterly Meeting conferences, he published a manifesto entitled *To the Methodists in Upper Canada:-District.* "It must be something very singular," he wrote, "that has caused those men [the Wesleyan missionaries] to swarm out of England . . . and express by their practice, a desire to croud themselves upon the people in the Canadas, where a large majority of the Methodists are in pointed opposition to their procedure." He asserted, "Some of them have been childish enough to threaten our Preachers with the displeasure of government. . . . I suppose they did not know that we have as good right here as they. Government has proved us, and that in a very trying time." The Wesleyans, he believed, were not really accountable to the British Conference and were principally interested in preaching to the prosperous in settled areas. "If the missionaries deny what is here laid to their charge, proof will decide against them. Should any of them undertake to answer this by way of burlesque, I shall treat their arguments as they treat the people in the back settlements – pass them at a distance."

The missionary committee did instruct its representatives in 1819 to avoid conflict and competition with their American brethren, but its words were not heeded. A year later, however, on the initiative of the General Conference in the United States, the British conference agreed to divide the work in the Canadas; the General Conference was to have responsibility for Upper Canada, and the British Conference for Lower Canada. The Wesleyan missionaries were warned pointedly that "our objects are purely Spiritual and our American brethren and ourselves are one body of Christians, sprung from a common stock, holding the same doctrines, enforcing the same discipline and striving in common to spread the light of true religion through the world." This admirable injunction was met by robust protests from Wesleyan sympathizers in Upper Canada and, contrary to the understanding, Kingston was retained as a Wesleyan outpost in that colony.

Despite and perhaps because of the unsettling presence of the British missionaries, the Methodist cause gained strength in the post-war years. New itinerants were recruited and the 1817 meeting of the

Genesee Conference in Elizabethtown (Brockville) sparked a widespread revival in Upper Canada. In 1816 there had been some 2,500 members in the two Canadas; by 1820 there were more than 5,000, an increase certainly attributable in part to the labours of Ryan and Case, the two presiding elders in that period. Numerical increase, the clash with the Wesleyans, the evident affinity between some prominent laymen in the eastern circuits and the British missionaries, and the strong commitment of men such as Ryan to Upper Canada contributed to the emergence of a significant proposal – that Upper Canada should become a separate conference. Behind this suggestion lay possibly the notion of an independent Canadian Methodism, which at the very least would help to overcome the widespread belief that the Methodists were a subversive group.

Ryan and Case were among the Genesee Conference delegates at the session of the General Conference held in Baltimore in May 1820. The General Conference concluded in response to petitions from Upper Canada that it would not be expedient for the present to establish a separate Canadian conference. The conference's bishops were authorized, however, to take this step before 1824, provided it was acceptable to the Genesee Conference. The discipline was altered as well, to state that "all Christian ministers" are "subject to the supreme authority of the country where they may reside and [are] to use all laudable means to enjoin obedience to the *powers that be.*" In so doing, the conference undoubtedly hoped to weaken the Wesleyans' allegations about the political allegiance of its ministers and societies.

This meeting also witnessed an intense debate over an issue that would have a marked bearing on Ryan's role in Upper Canadian Methodism. The polity of the Methodist Episcopal Church entrusted legislative authority to the regional and general conferences, membership in which was entirely clerical; administrative authority was assigned to the episcopate, whose members were elected and set apart by the General Conference. The most visible and important aspect of the bishops' role was their right to preside at the meetings of the regional annual conferences and in that setting to appoint presiding elders and to station the ministers on their circuits, decisions against which there was no appeal. Although the church was in this respect a clerical oligarchy, the laity were not without influence. The preaching of the itinerants was supplemented by the work of local preachers, exhorters, and class leaders; the first were often granted ordination, a change in status which did not involve the right to vote in a conference. In addition, presiding elders, travelling local preachers, exhorters, class leaders, and stewards participated regularly in quarterly meetings, which in practice had a measure of consultative authority.

Almost from the outset, however, the Methodist Episcopal Church experienced tension between the bishops and the travelling ministers and between the conferences and the lay members. By 1820, this tension had taken the form of a demand for the election of presiding elders by the regional conferences, which would broaden soon into an agitation for the election of lay members of the regional and general conferences. At the 1820 General Conference there was a vigorous debate between the ailing senior bishop, William McKendree, and the ministers on the subject of the elective eldership. McKendree lost the initial battle but subsequently persuaded a majority of the annual conferences not to approve this change. The General Conference of 1820 also approved the holding of district conferences of local preachers as a means of placating lay and local interests, and thus inadvertently provided a forum for wide-ranging discussion of the democratization of the Methodist Episcopal polity.

What part, if any, Ryan took in the debate at the 1820 General Conference is not known. He was appointed subsequently as presiding elder of the Lower Canada District, and in 1821, 1822, and 1823 of the Bay of Quinte District, which embraced the circuits from Port Hope to the Lower Canada border. In 1822 the Genesee Conference received a resolution, two of whose signatories were close associates of Ryan, urging the prompt establishment of a Canada conference. At its 1823 session the Genesee Conference, knowing that the issue of the elective presiding eldership would be debated at the General Conference in 1824, decided not to elect Case and Ryan, who were interested parties, as delegates to that body.

Although Bishop Enoch George, the presiding officer at the Genesee Conference of 1823, had demonstrated his confidence in Ryan by reappointing him as presiding elder of the Bay of Quinte District, Ryan, either out of pique or conviction, apparently decided to become the champion of Canadian Methodist independence. At the conclusion of the conference session in 1823 he called an informal meeting of his brethren at which he argued that the demand for an elective eldership would split the church and that the Canadian people would not approve it. Subsequently, he organized a so-called convention at Hallowell (Picton), in the heart of his district, at which a petition to the General Conference urging the establishment of an independent Canadian conference was approved. Ryan, Case, and David Breakenridge, an ultra-conservative local preacher from the Prescott area, were appointed as unofficial delegates to the General Conference.

The General Conference met in Baltimore in May 1824. It did not entertain Ryan's petition, because he had not been chosen properly and was accompanied by a layman. In the end, the conference rejected lay representation and thereby precipitated the establishment of the Methodist Protestant Church in the United States. To allay unrest in Upper Canada the General Conference decided to establish a conference there, albeit one which would remain under its authority. It also asked the British conference to adhere to the terms of the 1820 agreement.

Evidently enraged at the conference's failure to establish a totally independent Canadian conference, Ryan called a second convention of local preachers at Elizabethtown in June 1824; for some reason, he himself was not present at the gathering. In the printed and signed proclamation which was issued by the members, the General Conference was condemned for not taking seriously the earlier petition for independence. The signatories asked: "Does reason or religion require us to submit to them [the General Conference] and thereby expose ourselves to ruin. Doth not the word of God require us to yield to the wishes of the Government we are under as far as we can, without weakening grace or wounding conscience? It certainly does." Thus they had decided to establish an independent body to be called the Wesleyan Methodist Episcopal Canadian Church and had renounced the jurisdiction of the American and British conferences. The new church was to be governed by the discipline of the Methodist Episcopal Church as defined in 1820, with certain exceptions. The convention urged the itinerants in Upper Canada to meet, elect a president, and assume control of the new church, and indicated that if they did not accept the new scheme the local preachers would take charge of the societies for the present.

This manifesto surely reflected Ryan's commitment to independence for Upper Canadian Methodism, his opposition to lay representation, and his willingness to promote the cause of the local preachers. The unrest among the latter may have stemmed from lay dissatisfaction with the Methodist polity; probably it was indicative that the Methodist Episcopal Church had created a source of tension in its ranks in allowing some local preachers to become ordained without granting them the full rights of the travelling ministry. In addition, Ryan and his supporters may have been honestly concerned to overcome the hostility of the local government toward the Methodists as an allegedly foreign body, and have believed that the church was moving too slowly in this matter. In any event, his campaign elicited a favourable response, especially in the circuits of his district, and persuaded the bishops that they must attempt to counter it through an official visitation in Upper Canada.

Bishop Hedding, Bishop George, and Nathan Bangs travelled throughout much of the colony in the summer of 1824 explaining the actions of the General Conference. Apparently they persuaded the ministers and the societies that they had little ground for complaint. When Ryan belatedly met George and Case, he expressed regret for his actions. At the ensuing meeting of the Canada Conference, in Hallowell, the bishops sought to restore peace to the church. Predictably, Ryan was not reappointed presiding elder; he thus ended his 14-year career in that capacity. He was assigned instead to a new missionary circuit, extending from the vicinity of Niagara (Niagara-on-the-Lake) to the upper reaches of the Grand River – an arrangement which would enable him to live on his own farm.

The deterioration of the relationship between Ryan and the Canada Conference is delineated exhaustively in the conference's records, but the nature of the forces at work is not wholly clear. The 1825 session of the conference was the scene of a bitter personal dispute between Ryan and the presiding elder, Thomas Madden, which was compounded by the charge that Ryan had neglected his own field and visited others. He was censured mildly, and in response he requested, and was granted, superannuated status. In the ensuing year Ryan travelled widely, ostensibly to promote the cause of independence for the Canada Conference. He was widely credited as the author of an anonymous pamphlet in which the conference was accused of dealing improperly with the Madden affair and of promoting the selfish interests of the preachers. The conference of 1826, in which Ryan had at least some covert support, took no action in his case and he was continued as a superannuated minister.

At this stage, support for the establishment of an independent conference in Upper Canada was growing, and there was reason to believe that the parent church would not stand in the way. Ryan, however, knowing that a formal decision could not be taken until the General Conference of 1828, insisted that as loyal British subjects the Canadian Methodists could not remain under a foreign ecclesiastical body. The preachers, he asserted, were ambitious and proud, the church was worldly and no longer committed to revivals, and the bishops were hypocrites with no real interest in protecting the rights of the people. These and other charges were embodied in an anonymous pamphlet entitled *A lover of truth*, which Ryan was generally believed to have written and circulated.

At the 1827 conference Ryan was charged with being the author of *A lover of truth* by William Case. Ryan admitted having publicly read the pamphlet in various places, but alleged that his object was to warn the people against it. The conference, charitably, acquitted him; he then renounced its authority. Apparently, the bishop and others attempted to dissuade him from leaving the church. In the end he seems to have departed violently, proclaiming his intention to implement the decision taken at the Elizabethtown convention in 1824.

The conference of 1827 was not put off its course by

its protracted deliberations on Ryan's case. A petition requesting the establishment of an independent Canadian conference was prepared, and the delegates to the next session of the General Conference were instructed to seek approval of the Canadian proposal. Despite the opposition of Bangs and others, the General Conference which met in May 1828 authorized the Canada Conference to constitute itself as a separate body in fraternal association with the Methodist Episcopal Church. Changes were made in the discipline which strengthened the position of the laity in the conference, a move presumably designed to conciliate the democratic element in the societies.

Ryan had been present in the wings at the Canada Conference session, but was not placated by what occurred. Shortly after the meeting he summoned two conventions at Copetown and Hallowell, ostensibly to hear his grievances against the conference. He insisted that he would abide by the decisions of these irregularly constituted assemblies. In preparation for the gatherings he published another pamphlet in which he asserted that "some of the preachers are fond of the bottle," a comment which led the conference to criticize "effusions of spleen." At a preparatory meeting in Kingston, he stated: "I have declared that I would never head a party, but I have never said I would not *preach* for a party. I now perceive there will be a division and *I will go with my friends.*"

The conventions were held in Copetown and Hallowell in December 1828 and January 1829. John* and Egerton* Ryerson attended the former, which continued for eight days. In the end those present decided unanimously that the conference of 1827 had dealt fairly with Ryan's charges. The second, at which Egerton Ryerson again represented the conference, lasted for nine days. Initially, Ryerson said, the majority of the members "turned their backs" to him, but gradually they were won around by his arguments. Once again, the group "decided in the strongest language, and unanimously, against Mr. Ryan's statements and proceedings." Undeterred by these set-backs, Ryan continued to agitate in many circuits through 1829, and in at least one case forcibly gained entry into a Methodist Episcopal chapel for a meeting at which resolutions in his favour were passed. Subsequently he held another convention composed principally of laymen and local preachers at which the Canadian Wesleyan Methodist Church was founded. Despite his earlier protestations against changes in the Methodist Episcopal polity, provision was made in the new body for lay representation in the annual conferences and an elective presidency.

Initially, the secession met with modest success, in part because Ryan had no hesitation in taking over the pulpits of his former brethren. After Ryan's death in 1833 the Reverend James Jackson* assumed the leadership of the church, which by 1835 had 21

ministers, 2,481 members, and 13 circuits. In 1841, however, the Canadian Wesleyan Methodist Church united with a British body, the Methodist New Connexion Conference, and the legacy of Ryan became the responsibility of this relatively small denomination. It was the New Connexion Conference which in 1855 initiated the erection of a monument to "the late venerable Elder Ryan, the founder of the system of lay representation in Canada."

Clearly, in the first phase of his career, Ryan's aggressive, authoritarian personality and methods made him an effective minister and administrator; without him, Upper Canadian Methodism might have grown more slowly. Moreover, unlike many of his brethren who moved easily between Upper Canada and the United States and who ultimately chose to remain with the parent church, Ryan became fully identified with the Canadian connection. In the 1820s, as in the previous decade, he was moved by concern for the growth of the Methodist Episcopal community in Upper Canada and was seemingly convinced that its continuing prospects depended upon the securing of independent status. This assessment was shared by the majority of the preachers and probably by many in the societies.

Ryan's conflict with his brethren and his decision to establish a new Methodist body in which laymen would have a stronger voice than in the Methodist Episcopal Church was not wholly over the issue of independence or the respective rights of clergy and laity. Rather, it may be that Ryan was responding to the impact of important changes in Upper Canadian Methodism and society. In the 1820s new leaders were emerging in the conference, particularly the Ryerson brothers, James Richardson*, and Anson Green*. Ryan may well have sensed that he was about to be pushed aside, in much the same way that William Case would be by the Ryersons in 1832. His complaints about the "great corruptions" in the church, the decline of the spirit of revival, the immodest attire of his presiding elder's family, and the studious habits of young ministers indicated an awareness that Upper Canada was becoming a more settled and more cultured community. In this society men such as Ryan, with limited education and a simplistic religious outlook, would not be as influential as they had been in the past. The resulting frustration and alienation, exacerbated no doubt by thwarted ambition, help to account for Ryan's actions.

Ryan did not live to a ripe old age, but in the last decade of his life he appeared old and bitter. His brethren may have portrayed him in a highly partisan light, but it is difficult to believe that he was other than devious and wilfully destructive. Their conviction, as Carroll put it, that he spoke "perverse things" to "draw away disciples" after him is understandable. Nevertheless, although he was reprehended, his achievements were rightly remembered by the Methodists of Upper Canada. His zeal, his courage, and his administrative skill contributed significantly to the growth of Methodism in the pioneer phase of the colony and thereby helped to create one of the principal elements in the religious culture of that society.

G. S. FRENCH

Ryan's tombstone gives 4 Aug. 1833 as his date of death. However, the newspaper obituaries agree that he died in September: the *Hallowell Free Press* (Hallowell [Picton, Ont.]) of 16 Sept. 1833 says that he died on 2 September, and the *Niagara Gleaner* (Niagara [Niagara-on-the-Lake, Ont.]) of 14 Sept. 1833, while not giving a precise date, says that it is "stopping the presses" to announce Ryan's death.

School of Oriental and African Studies Library, Univ. of London, Methodist Missionary Soc. Arch., Wesleyan Methodist Missionary Soc., corr., North America (mfm. at UCC, Central Arch., Toronto). Canadian Wesleyan Methodist Church, *Minutes of the annual conference* (Hamilton, [Ont.]), 1841. Canadian Wesleyan Methodist New Connexion Church, *Minutes of the annual conference* (Toronto), 1855. Methodist Episcopal Church, *Minutes of the Methodist conferences, annually held in America; from 1773 to 1813, inclusive* (New York, 1813); Canada Conference, *Proceedings of the Canada Conference in the case of Henry Ryan . . .* (Kingston, [Ont.], 1829). Wesleyan Methodist Church in Canada, *The minutes of the annual conferences . . . from 1824 to 1845 . . .* (Toronto, 1846). "Loyalist and pioneer families of West Lincoln, 1783–1833," comp. R. J. Powell, *Annals of the Forty* (Grimsby, Ont.), no.8 (1957). W. C. Barclay, *History of Methodist missions* (3v., New York, 1949–59), 1. J. E. Carlson Brown, "Jennie Fowler Willing (1834–1916): Methodist churchwoman and reformer" (PHD thesis, Boston Univ., 1983). J. [S.] Carroll, *Case and his cotemporaries . . .* (5v., Toronto, 1867–77), 1–3; *Past and present, or a description of persons and events connected with Canadian Methodism for the last forty years . . .* (Toronto, 1860). D. W. Clark, *Life and times of Rev. Elijah Hedding, D.D., late senior bishop of the Methodist Episcopal Church* (New York, 1856). G. [S.] French, *Parsons & politics: the rôle of the Wesleyan Methodists in Upper Canada and the Maritimes from 1780 to 1855* (Toronto, 1962). Anson Green, *The life and times of the Rev. Anson Green, D.D. . . .* (Toronto, 1877). A. E. Kewley, "The trial of Henry Ryan" (typescript, n.d.; photocopy at UCC, Central Arch.). G. F. Playter, *The history of Methodism in Canada . . .* (Toronto, 1862). Egerton Ryerson, *Canadian Methodism; its epochs and characteristics* (Toronto, 1882). J. E. Sanderson, *The first century of Methodism in Canada* (2v., Toronto, 1908–10). Gordon Schroeder, "Henry Ryan: arrogant demagogue or Canadian churchman?" (MA thesis, Univ. of Toronto, 1977). C. B. Sissons, *Egerton Ryerson: his life and letters* (2v., Toronto, 1937–47), 1. Thomas Webster, *History of the Methodist Episcopal Church in Canada* (Hamilton, 1870).

S

SABATIER, WILLIAM, office holder, merchant, JP, and lobbyist; baptized 10 May 1753 in London, son of Jean Sabatier and Susanne Pouget; m. 26 Oct. 1785 in Halifax Margaret (Peggy) Hutchinson; they had no children; d. 22 Sept. 1826 in Devonport (Plymouth), England.

In 1817 Lord Dalhousie [Ramsay*], then lieutenant governor of Nova Scotia, said of William Sabatier: "I think him very intelligent, inquisitive, and instructing on the history and commerce of this part of the New World. Here [in Halifax] he is considered a meddling 'Busy Body' in all concerns whether public or private." The subject of this assessment, a "tall, rather coarse featured, and deeply pock-marked" individual, had been born into the family of a Huguenot silk weaver. As a young man, Sabatier immigrated to Maryland, where he combined trade with commercial farming. Following the outbreak of the American revolution, he took refuge as a loyalist in New York City and secured employment with the British commissariat. Official duties brought him to Halifax in the early 1780s and he returned in 1785, establishing himself as a dealer in whale oil, the raw material being supplied by fishermen recently removed from Nantucket Island, Mass., to Dartmouth, N.S., thanks to encouragement from Governor John Parr*. That same year, he married the 19-year-old daughter of a local lawyer and former high office holder in colonial Massachusetts. Sabatier remained on the move over the next few years, spending time at Philadelphia, New York, and London, before settling down in Halifax at the end of the 1790s. By this time, the provincial whale fishery had collapsed, leaving Sabatier with no explicit occupation, but the income from British investments, combined with local family connections, assured him a position of prominence within the loyalist-dominated oligarchy taking shape in Halifax during the ascendancy of Lieutenant Governor John Wentworth*.

After 1800, Sabatier's business interests were concentrated on real estate. Acting in partnership with his brother-in-law, Foster Hutchinson Jr, he acquired 8,000 acres, including Joseph Scott*'s estate, at the head of Bedford Basin, where he built an impressive summer residence out of Norwegian oak and took up farming, experimenting with such crops as hemp and fruit. As well, Sabatier joined a number of Halifax notables who in 1803 obtained a crown land grant of some 8,500 acres on the St Marys River, territory rich in timber and with potential for settlement. Official influence further assisted Sabatier in the accumulation of public offices: trustee of the Halifax Grammar School in 1802, justice of the peace and chairman of the Halifax Poor House Commission in 1803, and sheriff of Halifax County in 1814. Sabatier also sought election to the House of Assembly in 1811, but lost out to more popular members of the oligarchy.

The most prominent aspect of Sabatier's Nova Scotian career involved his participation in the Halifax Committee of Trade. Organized in 1804 as the executive arm of the larger Halifax Commercial Society (later known as the Society for the Encouragement of Trade, Agriculture and the Fisheries), the committee functioned continuously over the next 15 years, lobbying on behalf of the local merchant community. Sabatier's familiarity with business and official circles in London, as well as his personal withdrawal from trade (obviating any conflict of interest), were qualifications which enabled him to secure election as chairman of the committee. He retained the position throughout his remaining years in Nova Scotia.

Sabatier's committee was dedicated to the promotion of colonial resource development, within an orthodox mercantilist design. British North America, its members claimed, had immense potential which could be realized if Britain would just secure local merchants from foreign competition. Exclude Americans from the northern cod fishery and from the West Indies carrying trade and, the committee predicted, British North America would rapidly become a new New England, acting as a supply base and market for imperial interests. Corollary measures sought by the committee included the establishment of protected markets in Britain for colonial produce, permission to exploit Nova Scotian coal deposits, the relaxation of restraints on colonial trade with Europe, the incorporation of a bank in Halifax, and aid in construction of a canal linking Halifax with the Bay of Fundy. The committee's case, reiterated in petition after petition, was gathered together by Sabatier into a 75-page pamphlet entitled *A letter to the Right Honorable Frederick J. Robinson ... on the subject of the proposed duties on colonial timber*, which he published privately in London in 1821, three years after his return to Britain.

The Committee of Trade often played a controversial role in provincial public affairs. Although no one disagreed with the broad outline of the merchants' development program, many did question it in terms of detail and priority. Most notably, farm spokesmen demanded tariffs to curtail the entry of cheap American foodstuffs into Nova Scotia. Merchant opinion opposed such tariffs, arguing that the effect would be to increase costs in the fishery, thereby compromising provincial efforts to capture the British Caribbean market. Controversy also erupted over committee initiatives toward the suppression of smuggling, the introduction of fish bounties, the appointment of a provincial agent in Britain, and the establishment of a chartered bank. Alignments often became obscure, but basically the committee found itself embroiled in the underlying conflict of interests between Halifax and the outport settlements. Sabatier possessed enough diplomacy to maintain generally friendly relations with the assembly and, from time to time, he secured grants to assist with the committee's work. Privately, however, he denounced the assemblymen for being "narrow, contracted, unsteady and selfish." Moreover, he castigated the mass of farmers, who dominated the electorate, as being "the most prejudiced of human beings."

These local quarrels ultimately proved to be of less significance than the opposition which the Committee of Trade encountered in London. Mercantilist assumptions fell rapidly out of favour in post-Napoleonic Britain. After 1815 the committee was on the defensive and found itself either overruled or ignored. That ineffectualness, combined with the onset of hard times and Sabatier's removal, probably accounts for the committee's collapse about 1820. Within the context of metropolitan society, Sabatier had become an anachronism by the time of his death. His ideals persisted, however, within the Halifax merchant community. These colonial entrepreneurs remained defiant opponents of free trade into the 1850s. Thus, in the end, Sabatier, the expatriate "Busy Body," embodied values that were quintessentially Haligonian.

D. A. SUTHERLAND

William Sabatier is the author of *A treatise on poverty, its consequences, and the remedy* (London, 1797) and *A letter to the Right Honorable Frederick J. Robinson . . . on the subject of the proposed duties on colonial timber, and on some other colonial subjects . . .* (London, 1821); the anonymously published *Hints toward promoting the health and cleanliness of the city of New-York* (New York, 1802) has been attributed to him.

Halifax County Registry of Deeds (Halifax), Deeds, 35: f.684; 36: f.179. PANS, MG 1, 1845, no.5; RG 1, 172: ff.122, 131; 173: f.274; 224, no.154; 225, no.20; 226, nos.74–75, 79; 287, no.171; 288, nos.55–56; 303, nos.68, 73; 304, nos.14, 61, 66, 79; RG 32, 135, 26 Oct. 1785. PRO, CO 217/79: 217, 243; 217/84: 57, 144, 146; 217/88: 3; 217/91: 141. N.S., House of Assembly, *Journal and proc.*, 1790, 1803. *Acadian Recorder*, 11 Nov. 1815, 28 Feb. 1818, 21 Aug. 1819, 25 Nov. 1826. *Nova-Scotia Royal Gazette*, 21 Feb. 1786, 17 Aug. 1790, 16 April 1799, 9 Feb. 1804, 11–18 Sept. 1811, 6 May 1812. *Weekly Chronicle*, 15 Feb. 1811. Murdoch, *Hist. of N.S.*, 3: 172. G. F. Butler, "The early organisation and influence of Halifax merchants," N.S. Hist. Soc., *Coll.*, 25 (1942): 1–16. C. B. Fergusson, "William Sabatier – public spirited citizen or meddling busybody," *N.S. Hist. Quarterly*, 5 (1975):

Sagoyewatha

203–30. N.S., Provincial Museum and Science Library, *Report* (Halifax), 1934–35: 43.

SAGOYEWATHA. *See* SHAKÓYE:WA:THAˀ

SAINT-AUBIN, JOSEPH-THOMAS (the name usually appears as simply **Joseph Tomah, Toma, Tomer**, or **Tomma**), Malecite captain; fl. 1776–1821 in Maine, New Brunswick, and Quebec; d. 16 May 1821.

During the American Revolutionary War, an alliance with the Malecites was solicited by both Americans and British, and Joseph-Thomas Saint-Aubin played a minor role in events. The extent to which his choice of strategy reflected his private interests, a desire to support his brother Ambroise* (the second in command among the Malecites and the strongest adherent to the American cause), or more general concerns cannot be determined. Years younger than his eminent brother, he must have viewed the conflict partly as a means of enhancing his status as a warrior in the eyes of his fellows. He was one of 16 Indians who fought in Jonathan Eddy*'s unsuccessful attack on the British at Fort Cumberland (near Sackville, N.B.) in November 1776. The following summer the main body of Malecites went to the aid of rebel forces at Machias (Maine), and Joseph-Thomas was among them. In the summer of 1778 he was a member of a small, trustworthy party under Nicholas Hawawes (Awanwest) which John Allan*, American superintendent of eastern Indians, sent to destroy Fort Howe (Saint John, N.B.). This venture did not succeed, but the party plundered a British vessel and killed the cattle of several settlers thought to be British supporters.

In September 1778 a conference was held at Menagouèche, near Fort Howe, between the British and the Malecites and Micmacs [*see* Nicholas Akomápis*]. It culminated in the Indians' taking an oath of allegiance. Joseph-Thomas Saint-Aubin is not listed as having attended but he may have been there. Later that fall he came to the fort on friendly terms, as did Hawawes and seven families who no longer aligned themselves with Ambroise Saint-Aubin.

Joseph-Thomas's participation in the war likely contributed to his recognition by the Malecites as a captain. The origin of this title and its significance among the Malecites are not entirely clear. The captain's authority may have derived initially from the whites, but the concept appears well integrated into Wabanaki culture by the 19th century. According to one study, the role of the *geptins* among the Passamaquoddies became "to defend and guard their chief and . . . spill their blood for him, in case of need and in defense of the tribe. All the women and children and disabled persons . . . were under the care of the *geptins*." Malecite usage was probably similar. In 1817 Saint-Aubin, likely in his capacity as a captain, appeared as one of four sureties in defence of Piol Zusup (Pierre-Joseph?), a Penobscot on trial in Castine (Maine) for having killed a white man the previous year. Two of the other sureties were Penobscots and the third was a Passamaquoddy captain.

A year later Joseph-Thomas Saint-Aubin, "Indian chief," appears in a document of 4 Aug. 1818, when he complained to Surveyor General George Shore* about trespassing by whites on the Tobique Indian Reserve. Such encroachment was a great problem for Indians, and because of the colonial government's unwillingness to enforce their rights they lost much of the land that had been set aside for them [*see* John Julien*].

Little is known of Saint-Aubin's family. In a list of Indians in the service of the United States, Allan records his presence along with a son Joseph, two women, and six children in Passamaquoddy territory on 28 July 1780. A "Joseph Tomah," almost certainly the subject of this biography, along with his wife and one child visited the Reverend Frederick DIBBLEE's school for Indians at Meductic (near present-day Meductic), N.B., in 1788 or 1789.

The death of "Joseph Tomas St. Aubin (Malecite)" on 16 May 1821 appears in the registers of the church at L'Isle-Verte, Lower Canada, in an entry of 16 June. His wife must have predeceased him since none is listed; nor are any children recorded. His age, said to have been 96, is likely exaggerated, but he could well have been in his eighties. The name Saint-Aubin (or sometimes Bear) appears in the baptismal records for the Malecite communities of Quebec beginning in 1830. Although the name Bear is at present associated with the Tobique Reserve in New Brunswick, in the 19th century the family apparently moved freely between the communities on the Saint John River and those of Quebec.

VINCENT O. ERICKSON

[The identity of Joseph-Thomas Saint-Aubin has been obscured by the fact that his surname does not usually appear in documents and that the name Thomas (variously spelled) was itself evolving as a surname among the Malecites. Michael Francklin*, superintendent of Indian affairs for Nova Scotia, mistakenly claimed that Joseph-Thomas was the son of Pierre Tomah*, supreme sachem of the tribe. F. G. Speck and W. S. Hadlock, "A report on tribal boundaries and hunting areas of the Malecite Indian of New Brunswick," *American Anthropologist* (Menasha, Wis.), new ser., 48 (1946): 355–74, mistakenly identifies Captain Jo Tomer with the Captain Tomah of Kingsclear (N.B.) whose traditional hunting territory was around the Chiputneticook Lakes (Maine/N.B.) and who died around 1890. However, the comments of John Allan (printed in *Military operations in eastern Maine and Nova Scotia during the revolution, chiefly compiled from the journals and letters of Colonel John Allan . . .*, ed. Frederic Kidder (Albany, N.Y., 1867)) and the registers of the Isle-Verte church (AP, Saint-Jean-Baptiste (Isle-Verte), Reg. des baptêmes, mariages et sépultures, 16 juin 1821) lead to the conclusion that the subject of this biography was the brother of Ambroise Saint-Aubin. v.o.e.]

PANB, RG 2, RS7, 40. *Kulóskap the master and other Algonkin poems*, trans. C. G. Leland and J. D. Prince (New York and London, 1902). W. O. Raymond, *The River St. John: its physical features, legends and history from 1604 to 1784* ([2nd ed.], ed. J. C. Webster, Sackville, N.B., 1943; repr. 1950). W. D. Williamson, *The history of the state of Maine; from its first discovery, A.D. 1602, to the separation, A.D. 1820, inclusive* (2v., Hallowell, Maine, 1832; repr. Freeport, Maine, [1966?]). W. H. Mechling, "The Malecite Indians, with notes on the Micmacs," *Anthropologica* (Ottawa), 7 (1958). W. O. Raymond, "The Revolutionary War: part played by the St. John River Indians," "Exodus of the Maliseets, A.D. 1777," "Franklin versus Allan," and "The great defection," in *Dispatch* (Woodstock, N.B.), 3, 17, 24 April and 1 May 1895; "The old Meductic fort," N.B. Hist. Soc., *Coll.*, 1 (1894–97), no.2: 221–72.

ST GEORGE (de St Georges), LAURENT QUETTON. *See* QUETTON

SAINT-LAURENT, THÉRÈSE-BERNARDINE MONTGENET, Comtesse de MONTGENET, known as Mme de. *See* MONTGENET

SAINT-OURS, CHARLES DE (baptized **Roch-Louis**), militia and army officer, seigneur, and politician; b. 24 Aug. 1753 at Quebec, youngest son of Pierre-Roch de Saint-Ours, an officer in the colonial regular troops, and Charlotte Deschamps de Boishébert; d. 11 Nov. 1834 in Saint-Ours, Lower Canada.

Charles de Saint-Ours, a distinguished representative of the old aristocracy that stayed on in the colony after the conquest, had a brilliant military career that has sometimes, however, been attributed to his ready cooperation with the British authorities. He was only 22 when the American War of Independence broke out in 1775. The previous year he had been made a major in the militia, and he soon took part in his first military exploit, joining a volunteer corps raised to defend Fort St John's (Saint-Jean-sur-Richelieu). After its surrender he was taken as a prisoner to the American colonies.

On 26 June 1777, having returned to the province of Quebec, Saint-Ours was commissioned a lieutenant in one of three companies of Canadian volunteers which were raised to accompany British armies on an offensive into New York State that year. On 11 December he became aide-de-camp to Governor Sir Guy Carleton*, an office he also held under Frederick Haldimand* and again under Carleton (by then Lord Dorchester). He was promoted captain-lieutenant in the 84th Foot in 1783 and was placed on half pay later in the year. Saint-Ours was one of four aides-de-camp to Prince William Henry, later William IV, during his stay in the province in 1787. He was appointed lieutenant-colonel of the Chambly battalion of militia in 1790, promoted brevet major in the regular army

four years later, and then made captain in the 60th Foot on 2 Dec. 1795. He was placed on the half pay of the 132nd Foot in 1796. At the outbreak of the War of 1812 he was colonel of the Saint-Ours battalion of militia. He was profoundly shocked at the attitude taken by some of the local residents at the time of the Lachine riot against conscription and he strongly condemned it. Garrisoned with his battalion at William Henry (Sorel) until it was demobilized on 26 Nov. 1812, he was recalled in October 1813. He was then stationed at Chambly, where he remained until the end of the war.

Saint-Ours had travelled in Europe in 1785. He had gone with his cousin, Charles-Louis Tarieu* de Lanaudière, and was received first at the British court, where George III showed the highest regard for him. In France he was admitted into the presence of Louis XVI and the royal family, a visit he fondly remembered, particularly after the revolution. Moving on to Prussia, he learned that Frederick II was to review the army. He requested permission to attend and was sent a signed note from the king, giving his assent. He kept the note all his life and enjoyed showing it to his acquaintances as a memento of one of his happiest experiences.

In 1782 Saint-Ours had inherited part of the seigneuries of Saint-Ours, L'Assomption, and Deschaillons. From then on he had two concerns: to reconstitute Saint-Ours, and to build on it a manor-house that he would make the centre of his endeavours as a seigneur. He took more than 30 years to achieve his first goal, obtaining his brother Charles-Quinson's right on 2 July 1790, his sister Jeanne-Geneviève's on 4 March 1806, and his brother Paul-Roch's on 18 March 1812. But it was actually not until 12 Oct. 1827 that he brought the project to completion, by using his status as attorney for the heirs of his uncle Jacques-Philippe de Saint-Ours to sell their share to his son François-Roch. Some 12 years later François-Roch would reunite with the main fief the part owned by the heirs to the seigneury of Contrecœur. In an area between the St Lawrence and the king's highway, about two *arpents* north of the parish church, Charles had constituted a domain of about 20 *arpents* by exchanging and buying pieces of land already granted to *censitaires*, and on it the construction of a manor-house was begun in 1792. Graceful avenues, lawns, and flower-beds were laid out, and the whole estate was planted with trees and flowers of various sorts, so that it was known locally as a "little paradise on earth." The attraction of the estate for Montreal and Quebec society became legendary, as did the glittering parties held there. Saint-Ours actively concerned himself with the development of his seigneury. In the period 1781–1827 he made more than 400 land grants, and while engaged in opening roads and building bridges to promote trade in grain, he also took part in establishing Saint-Jude parish in 1822, where his flourishing lumbering enterprises were located.

Like his brother Paul-Roch, Saint-Ours was appointed to the Legislative Council, on which he sat from 2 Dec. 1808 until his death. He spent the final years of his life promoting education. In 1821 he had supported Antoine GIROUARD, the founder of the Collège de Saint-Hyacinthe, by putting his library at the service of the teachers, and by founding an association for improving educational opportunities in the Rivière Chambly area. This organization sought to recruit gifted children and assure them board and tuition for an eight-year period. It lasted until 1829 and paid out some $4,500 to the pupils, a number of whom came from Saint-Ours where the seigneur encouraged the building of schools.

Charles de Saint-Ours was blessed with good health and remained active until his death on 11 Nov. 1834. He was buried three days later in the parish church. He and Josette Murray probably were married in 1792, and they had three children: Josette, who married Pierre-Dominique Debartzch*, Charles-Pierre, and François-Roch. The Patriotes, in particular Jean-Joseph Girouard*, have represented François-Roch as "the *bête noire* of the prisoners," "the old bear of a sheriff" who was detested by those held captive. As for Mme de Saint-Ours, she died in 1840 and was buried beside her husband in the parish church.

SERGE COURVILLE

ANQ-Q, CE1-1, 24 août 1753; CE3-6, 14 nov. 1834. PAC, MG 23, GII, 6; RG 31, C1, 1825, 1831, Richelieu. *La Minerve*, 13 août 1832. *Quebec Gazette*, 16 Aug. 1787; 5 May 1791; 17 July 1794; 15 Aug. 1811; 21 Nov. 1816; 6 Jan. 1820; 5 April, 7 June 1821. F.-J. Audet, "Les législateurs du Bas-Canada." Bouchette, *Topographical description of L.C.* Le Jeune, *Dictionnaire*, 2: 600. *Officers of British forces in Canada* (Irving). Tanguay, *Dictionnaire*, 3: 402. Turcotte, *Le Conseil législatif*. F.-J. Audet, *Contrecœur; famille, seigneurie, paroisse, village* (Montréal, 1940). Béatrice Chassé, "Le notaire Girouard, patriote et rebelle" (thèse de D. ès L., univ. Laval, Québec, 1974). C.-P. Choquette, *Histoire du séminaire de Saint-Hyacinthe depuis sa fondation jusqu'à nos jours* (2v., Montréal, 1911–12). Azarie Couillard-Després, *Histoire de la seigneurie de Saint-Ours* (2v., Montréal, 1915–17).

SALABERRY, CHARLES-MICHEL D'IRUMBERRY DE. *See* IRUMBERRY

SALABERRY, IGNACE-MICHEL-LOUIS-ANTOINE D'IRUMBERRY DE. *See* IRUMBERRY

SALES LATERRIÈRE, MARIE-CATHERINE DE. *See* DELEZENNE

SALES LATERRIÈRE, PIERRE-JEAN DE, doctor, militia officer, JP, and author; b. 1 July 1789 in Baie-du-Febvre (Baieville), Que., elder son

of Pierre de Sales* Laterrière and Marie-Catherine DELEZENNE; m. 16 Aug. 1815 Mary Ann Bulmer in London, and they had at least five children; d. 15 Dec. 1834 in Les Éboulements, Lower Canada.

Pierre-Jean de Sales Laterrière spent his childhood in Baie-du-Febvre. His father, anxious to assure the children of a good education, decided in 1799 to move to Quebec; he opened an apothecary's shop there and continued to practise medicine. Laterrière entered the Petit Séminaire de Québec, where his schoolmates included Philippe-Joseph Aubert* de Gaspé, with whom he became close friends, Louis-Joseph Papineau*, and Joseph Painchaud*. Upon completing his studies in 1807 Laterrière began an apprenticeship in medicine with his father. From July 1807 to June 1808, while the latter was travelling in Europe, Laterrière ran the shop by himself. Shortly after his father came back he in turn went off to England. He studied medicine at St Thomas's Hospital in London under a famous surgeon, Astley Paston Cooper. Admitted to membership in the Royal College of Surgeons in 1809, he did a period of training in a military hospital at Ramsgate.

On his return to Quebec in 1810 Laterrière took over his father's shop and clientele. Early in 1812 he went into partnership with his younger brother Marc-Pascal*, who had returned from studying medicine in the United States. At that time there were, other than Laterrière, few if any surgeons from Lower Canada with experience of military hospitals. Consequently on 24 April 1812 he was appointed surgeon to the Voltigeurs Canadiens, commanded by Charles-Michel d'IRUMBERRY de Salaberry. Laterrière, who was quite well off, rented a house near Fort Chambly, where his regiment was quartered; he even bought a horse for Captain Jacques Viger*, who was unable to meet such an expense. Laterrière remained with his regiment until 6 Oct. 1814. At that time he received a letter from his father requesting that he go to France and settle some family business there. Laterrière immediately applied for a six-month leave of absence and, assuming it would be granted, returned to Quebec with the intention of sailing for Europe. His request was turned down; Laterrière then tried to appeal to the governor, but in vain. Consequently he resigned from his posting with the Voltigeurs Canadiens early in November and left for France, where he was supposed to collect a large inheritance bequeathed to his father.

When Laterrière reached Bordeaux early in 1815, war was raging again following Napoleon's return from Elba. Being a British subject, Laterrière took Henry-Antoine Mézière*'s advice and fled to London to wait for normal times. On 24 July he wrote to Marc-Pascal: "I have just added another 10,000 sterling to our common fortune, not counting the advantages that will result." He was referring to the dowry that his young bride would bring him. On the eve of his marriage he wrote to his brother: "Tomorrow at nine is the day my bondage begins . . . I have considered my prospects and necessity alone has forced me to it." She "is not beautiful at all," he added, "but she is witty and I am persuaded that she will make me happy, because she loves me totally."

Having learned shortly afterwards of his father's death, Laterrière decided to return to Lower Canada. But first he took steps to be readmitted as an officer in the Voltigeurs Canadiens and so be eligible for half pay. Despite letters of recommendation in his favour from Lieutenant-Colonel Salaberry and Major Jean-Baptiste JUCHEREAU Duchesnay, and even though his regiment had not taken part in any engagements after he had left it, he met with refusal upon refusal.

On returning to Quebec in June 1816 Laterrière divided his father's estate with his brother. He kept the properties at Quebec for himself, and Marc-Pascal received the seigneury of Les Éboulements. Then Laterrière opened a new apothecary's shop in Upper Town at Quebec and started practising medicine again. As one of a group of Canadian doctors in the town he played a prominent role during the next six years. In 1818 he joined Charles-Norbert PERRAULT, Anthony von Iffland*, and other doctors in founding the Quebec Dispensary to provide free treatment for the needy and to offer the first courses in medicine at Quebec. Furthermore, in the spring of 1820 Laterrière was chosen to serve on the founding committee of a Quebec branch of the Royal Humane Society of London for the Recovery of the Apparently Drowned or Dead.

Laterrière also involved himself in social and political concerns. In 1819, with his medical colleagues Augustin Mercier, Joseph Morrin*, and Perrault, he became a director of the Quebec Fire Society. In the general elections held the following year he ran in Northumberland, but when four days of voting left him trailing the other candidates, Étienne-Claude Lagueux and Philippe Panet*, he withdrew. Then in 1821 he was appointed a justice of the peace for the district of Quebec. Along with these activities Laterrière engaged in numerous business ventures. He bought a number of properties in the town and its suburbs for rental or resale. With a group of partners he also invested in building and operating a toll-bridge over the Rivière Chaudière at Sainte-Marie-de-la-Nouvelle-Beauce (Sainte-Marie). In 1821, along with Joseph-Rémi Vallières* de Saint-Réal and others, Laterrière took over managing the assets of Joseph Bouchette*, who was at that time buying and selling properties on his own account and for others.

In the spring of 1823 Laterrière left for London to see his father-in-law, who was seriously ill. The following year, after the latter's death, he received a £3,000 annuity as an inheritance. He then bought a property in Middlesex, taking up residence there with his family. He started on a second, though short-lived, career in England. From then on, in fact, Laterrière devoted himself to managing the large fortune left by his father-in-law. He used his frequent periods of leisure especially to make numerous trips to Europe and North America. He also began to move in reform political circles and became a close friend of John Arthur Roebuck*, who would later serve as London agent of the Lower Canadian House of Assembly. Laterrière received Canadian delegates to the capital and supplied them with information, and he kept a close eye on proposed British legislative measures that could affect Lower Canada. With a view to making people in England aware of the trying situation his compatriots had been placed in by the imperial government, Laterrière in 1830 published his *Political and historical account of Lower Canada; with remarks . . .* , signing himself A Canadian. And Canadian Laterrière remained until the day he died. Despite his almost princely style of living, he never lost a deep longing for his native land; on several occasions he even tried to return there for good, but his wife was against the idea. In 1827 he applied unsuccessfully to Robert John Wilmot-Horton in the Colonial Office for the grant of a seigneury on the north shore of the St Lawrence east of the Saguenay, offering to invest the capital to settle about 200 young people who were prepared to go there. A short time later he also considered buying the seigneury of Deschambault. In fact, Laterrière never did return to live in Lower Canada. He died, a victim of diabetes, while on a visit to Les Éboulements in 1834.

In November 1835, less than a year after his death, Pierre-Jean de Sales Laterrière was the subject of a duel with pistols between his brother and lawyer Elzéar Bédard*, following Bédard's mention in court of an instance in which Pierre-Jean had practised usury. It was probably one of the last duels to take place at Quebec. Laterrière, however, left more than a controversial memory. His friend Aubert de Gaspé praised him in moving terms in his *Mémoires*. Contemporaries remembered him as a brilliant doctor, despite the brevity of his career. Even in October 1846, at a banquet following a general meeting of the doctors in Lower Canada, Joseph Painchaud called to mind Laterrière's talents and achievements.

PIERRE DUFOUR

ANQ-Q, CE4-4, 18 déc. 1834; CN1-171, 19 juin 1816. Arch. de l'univ. Laval (Québec), 298/17. PAC, MG 8, F131; MG 11, [CO 42] Q, 135, 140, 214; MG 24, A19, 3; RG 4, A1, 160, 162; RG 8, I (C ser.), 168, 202, 600, 796–97, 1218; RG 9, I, A5, 4. Joseph Papineau, "Correspondance de Joseph Papineau (1793–1840)," Fernand Ouellet, édit., ANQ *Rapport*, 1951–53: 165–299. [P.-J. de Sales Laterrière], *Political and historical account of Lower Canada; with remarks . . .* (London, 1830). Pierre de Sales Laterrière, *Mémoires de Pierre de Sales Laterrière et de ses traverses*, [Alfred Garneau, édit.] (Québec, 1873; réimpr. Ottawa, 1980). *Quebec Gazette*, 19 Sept., 17 Oct. 1816; 9,

Sargent

23, 30 Jan., 18 Sept. 1817; 12 March, 28 Dec. 1818; 4 Jan., 11, 15 March, 19, 22 April 1819; 10, 26 June, 23 Oct., 30 Nov. 1820; 18 Jan. 1821. Caron, "Inv. de la corr. de Mgr Signay," ANQ *Rapport*, 1936–37: 123–330. Philéas Gagnon, *Essai de bibliographie canadienne* . . . (2v., Québec et Montréal, 1895–1913; réimpr. Dubuque, Iowa, [1962]). Fernand Ouellet, "Inventaire de la Saberdache de Jacques Viger," ANQ *Rapport*, 1955–57: 33–176. P.-G. Roy, *Inventaire des procès-verbaux des grands voyers conservés aux Archives de la province de Québec* (6v., Beauceville, Qué., 1923–32). Yvon Thériault, "Inventaire sommaire des archives du séminaire des Trois-Rivières," ANQ *Rapport*, 1961–64: 71–134. Turcotte, *Le Conseil législatif*. P.[-J.] Aubert de Gaspé, *Les anciens Canadiens* (Québec, 1863); *Mémoires* (1866). H.-R. Casgrain, *La famille de Sales Laterrière* (Québec, 1870). F.-X. Chouinard *et al.*, *La ville de Québec, histoire municipale* (4v., Québec, 1963–83). Albert Lesage et H. E. MacDermot, *Le Collège des médecins et chirurgiens de la province de Québec, 1847–1947* (Montréal, 1947). Michelle Guitard, *Histoire sociale des miliciens de la bataille de la Châteauguay* (Ottawa, 1983). Albert Jobin, *Histoire de Québec* (Québec, 1947). Jacques Bernier, "François Blanchet et le mouvement réformiste en médecine au début du XIXᵉ siècle," *RHAF*, 34 (1980–81): 223–44. "Les disparus," *BRH*, 32 (1926): 690; 34 (1928): 739. Ignotus [Thomas Chapais], "La profession médicale au Canada," *BRH*, 12 (1906): 142–50. Sylvio Leblond, "La médecine dans la province de Québec avant 1847," *Cahiers des Dix*, 35 (1970): 69–95. Gérard Malchelosse, "Mémoires romancés," *Cahiers des Dix*, 25 (1960): 103–44. Gérard Parizeau, "Joseph Bouchette: l'homme et le haut fonctionnaire," RSC *Trans.*, 4th ser., 9 (1971), sect.ɪ: 95–126. B. R. Tunis, "Medical education and medical licensing in Lower Canada: demographic factors, conflict, and social change," *SH*, 14 (1981): 67–91.

SARGENT, JOHN, businessman, JP, judge, politician, and militia officer; b. late 1750 in Salem, Mass., second son of Epes Sargent and his second wife, Catherine Winthrop, a descendant of Governor John Winthrop of the Massachusetts Bay Colony; m. 1784 Margaret Barnard, *née* Whitney, in Boston, and they had three sons and one daughter; d. 23 or 24 Jan. 1824 in Barrington, N.S.

John Sargent was a member of a family prominent in Salem. His father was a noted merchant trading to the West Indies, and John joined the family business. In 1772 he was appointed by Governor Thomas Hutchinson as ensign to a company of militia. He was the first person in Salem to sign an address of welcome to Governor Thomas Gage* on his arrival in June 1774, and this act marked him for persecution by the patriots. Forced to flee to Boston in February 1775, in November he became a first lieutenant in the Loyal American Associates, a loyalist corps formed for the defence of the town. With the evacuation of Boston in March 1776 he went with the troops to Halifax and then sailed for England, where he received an allowance of £100 as a distressed loyalist.

On his return to North America in 1777 Sargent was appointed an ensign in Edmund Fanning*'s King's American Regiment, and on 25 July 1779 a lieutenant. By 1781 he was at Beaufort, S.C., as an assistant commissary, and at a later date went to Charleston, S.C., where he remained until its evacuation in December 1782. In the mean time he had been formally expelled from Massachusetts by the Banishment Act of 1778.

The King's American Regiment was disbanded at the close of the war, and Sargent went on half pay. He then came to Barrington, a settlement founded in the early 1760s by New England immigrants mainly from Massachusetts. There he purchased several lots, acquired a sturdy oak frame-house, a store, and a wharf, and built a fish-house, all to re-establish himself as a merchant and shipowner. In his schooners *Lucy* and *Argo* he exported fish and imported barrels of bread, flour, and Indian corn from New York and Boston; from Jamaica and other West Indian islands came puncheons of rum, sugar, and molasses. He is also known to have possessed the fishing vessels *Sally* and *Lilly*. Owner of a sawmill, in 1792 Sargent built a grist-mill near the Barrington River at a cost of nearly £300. He had some dealings with Simeon Perkins* of Liverpool, who recorded in June 1811 that when Sargent came to call he looked "very Smart & Healthy."

Sargent made a marked contribution to the political and military life of Barrington Township and Shelburne County. In 1784 he was appointed a justice of the peace for Queens County, and after Shelburne County was split off in 1785 he became one for Barrington Township. In 1813 he was made a justice of the Inferior Court of Common Pleas for the county. Sargent was elected by acclamation to the House of Assembly for Barrington Township in 1793, and held the position until his retirement in 1818, when he was succeeded by his son William Browne. His two other sons, John and Winthrop, also sat in the assembly at various times. As a militia officer, Sargent rose to high rank; in 1814 he was lieutenant-colonel of the 12th (Barrington) Battalion of Militia. A firm supporter of the Methodist church, Sargent passed his beliefs on to his children. At his death he was known and respected as a man of upright character and a public-spirited citizen.

MARION ROBERTSON

Shelburne County Court of Probate (Shelburne, N.S.), Estate papers, A232 (John Sargent) (mfm. at PANS). Methodist Burial Ground (Barrington, N.S.), Tombstone inscriptions. PANS, MG 1, 797B; 1130; MG 4, 141, Barrington, Methodist reg. of baptisms and marriages, 1790–1822 (typescript); Places: Shelburne County, Court of General Sessions records, 28 March 1786 (mfm.). RG 1, 169: 101. PRO, AO 12/105: 82 (mfm. at PAC); HO 76/1–2 (mfm. at Dalhousie Univ. Arch., Halifax). "United Empire Loyalists: enquiry into losses and services," AO *Report*,

1904: 638. *Epes Sargent of Gloucester and his descendants*, ed. Emma Worcester Sargent and C. S. Sargent (Boston and New York, 1923), 6, 307–9. Stark, *Loyalists of Mass.* (1910), 137–38. Edwin Crowell, *A history of Barrington Township and vicinity . . . 1604–1870* (Yarmouth, N.S., [1923]; repr. Belleville, Ont., 1973), 113, 292, 297, 364, 445. Murdoch, *Hist. of N.S.* A. E. Marble and T. M. Punch, "Sir J. S. D. Thompson: a prime minister's family connections," *N.S. Hist. Quarterly*, 7 (1977): 377–88.

SAUNDERS, JOHN, judge and politician; b. 1 June 1754 in Princess Anne County (Virginia Beach), Va, son of Jonathan Saunders and Elizabeth ——; m. 16 Feb. 1790, in London, Arianna Margaretta Jekyll Chalmers, daughter of James Chalmers, former commander of the Maryland Loyalists; d. 24 May 1834 in Fredericton.

Originally from England, the Saunders family was well established in Virginia by the mid 18th century. In the 1760s Jonathan Saunders had an estate there of 1,200 acres and a fine brick house, "the best in the County." When he died in 1765, his wife managed the property until her own death four years later. At that time Jacob Ellegood, who in 1768 had married John Saunders's eldest sister, Mary, became guardian of the younger children. John attended the College of Philadelphia from 1769 to 1772 and returned home without a degree to study law. In 1775 he assumed control of the Saunders estate.

When the American Revolutionary War broke out, loyalists were in a minority in Virginia, especially among the aristocracy. Saunders, a young man with a large estate, might have been expected to side with the rebels but he did not, and there are several reasons for his decision to remain loyal. Although a member of the planter élite, he also had ties with the commercial community, which formed the chief loyalist support in Virginia; for years the Saunders estate had supplied merchants with white-oak timber for European markets. But if Saunders's loyalism was in part motivated by economic considerations, far more important in determining his stand were his upbringing and the influence of his family. In later life he claimed that he had been taught from infancy "to fear *God* and honor the *King*," and these tenets were reinforced by the staunch loyalism of his brother-in-law and former guardian.

Efforts had been made by friends and acquaintances to win Saunders's support for the attempt to secure colonial rights but he refused to compromise himself. He would not endorse the Continental Association of October 1774, which called for the breaking of commercial ties with Great Britain, since he felt it was illegal. Pressured by friends to sign, he eventually did, but added a large "No" after his name. As a result he was denounced and ostracized. Saunders showed in this controversy not only the respect for law and order

that would mark his later years but also his strong conservatism, his loyalty to the crown, and his personal courage.

After the success of Governor Lord Dunmore in a minor skirmish with the Virginia militia in November 1775, many loyalists declared themselves openly. Later that year the Queen's Loyal Virginia Regiment was formed with Ellegood as commander; Saunders served as a captain, having raised a troop of cavalry at his own expense. A number of the "loyalists" in this unit were to desert the cause when Lord Dunmore abandoned the colony in August 1776, but not Saunders. He went with Dunmore to New York and his property in Virginia was subsequently confiscated by the rebels.

When the remnants of the Queen's Loyal Virginia Regiment were incorporated into the Queen's American Rangers, Saunders became an infantry captain. In his first engagement with this unit, the battle of Brandywine, Pa, on 11 Sept. 1777, he showed his bravery and was severely wounded. Five months later he was able to rejoin his regiment, now known as the Queen's Rangers and commanded by Major John Graves Simcoe*. Saunders became a cavalry instructor and in August 1780 the commander of a cavalry troop. Detached from his unit in October, he was sent to Virginia and then to South Carolina, where he was involved in operations around Dorchester and Charleston. For a time he was in command at Georgetown before being recalled to New York in 1782.

Although Saunders was a good soldier, his military career was marred by an incident that took place at Dorchester in 1781. After one bloody skirmish he ordered the execution of a prisoner. His action was, another loyalist wrote, "the most *disgraceful* thing I ever heard of a British Officer," but it does not appear to have damaged his reputation with other officers, especially Simcoe. Nevertheless, it does seem very much out of character, given Saunders's respect for law and order. Simcoe, who described his subordinate as "an officer of great address and determination," later lamented that Saunders had not kept a journal during the war to relate the "series of gallant and active services" that had characterized his "boldness and prudence." Saunders sailed for England in November 1782 and the respect and friendship of his commanding officer were to aid him in London.

Saunders had lost much in supporting the crown. His property in Virginia had been sold and he filed a claim with the loyalist claims commissioners for over £5,000. They allowed him an annual pension of £40 at first and then in 1789 gave him the sum of £4,850. These awards, combined with his salary as a half-pay captain, made him a fairly wealthy man. With his future reasonably secure, in January 1784 he entered the Inns of Court to study at the Middle Temple. He hoped eventually to acquire a government position.

He also hoped to build a great estate somewhere to compensate for the one he had lost in Virginia. That he did so in New Brunswick was in part the result of Jacob Ellegood's decision to settle there. Saunders visited his brother-in-law in 1788 and made his first purchases of land in the colony. At the time property was cheap since many disbanded soldiers were willing to sell their rights to land so that they could move elsewhere. Saunders was able to purchase many of these claims and he also submitted his own application for a large grant. To re-estabish a position such as he had occupied in Virginia, however, Saunders needed more than land. If he were to have authority and social status in New Brunswick, he needed a government position. He returned to England late in 1788 and on 6 Feb. 1789 was admitted to the bar. Now he was at least qualified for a legal career.

Saunders must also have felt the time was ripe to choose a wife. On 16 Feb. 1790 he married Arianna Margaretta Jekyll Chalmers, one of the five marriageable daughters of a distinguished Maryland loyalist. The union was to increase his wealth since his father-in-law gave him a cash settlement of £5,000 and provided his wife with a life annuity of £300.

A month after his marriage Saunders was appointed a judge of the Supreme Court of New Brunswick. His advancement was probably due to the influence of Simcoe, who was promised the lieutenant governorship of Upper Canada that same year. Saunders was now in a position to return to New Brunswick. Leaving his wife, who was expecting a child, he sailed for Saint John in July 1790. She and their baby daughter, who was the mother's namesake, joined him the next year. Another daughter, Eliza, would be born in 1794 and a son, John Simcoe*, in 1795. Saunders's first house was in Fredericton, but his real love was to be the home he built in 1795 at the Barony, his estate near the mouth of the Pokiok Stream in Prince William Parish, about 40 miles from Fredericton. It was almost identical to the one he had lost in Virginia except that it was constructed of wood rather than brick.

In attempting to achieve status in New Brunswick, Saunders was not content with his judicial functions. In February 1791 he stood for election to the House of Assembly as a member for York County. In putting himself forward he may have intended to compensate for the fact that all the other judges of the Supreme Court sat on the Council while he did not. With his election he became the only member of the court ever to hold a seat in the house. The historian James Hannay* claims that this "raid" into the assembly was a bold move in keeping with his character. Saunders remained in the house only until 1792 and was not a candidate in the elections of the following year. While he was a member, one hotly debated issue concerned the power of the Supreme Court and the place of its

meetings. From 1785 the inferior courts had shared with the Supreme Court jurisdiction in cases involving up to £50, and plaintiffs could ask that their cases be heard by the superior court. The Supreme Court, however, held only four sessions a year and always in Fredericton. Since travelling was difficult and the expenses of the judges were not paid, they showed a great reluctance even to consider the possibility of holding sessions in other parts of the province. Those who had cases before the Supreme Court consequently had to travel to Fredericton or employ lawyers there to represent them. This inconvenience led the assembly to pass a bill in 1792 calling for the court to meet twice a year in Saint John and giving the inferior courts exclusive jurisdiction in cases involving up to £10. Saunders opposed the measure in the assembly and the Council threw out the bill. Such actions soon earned him and the other judges a reputation for being enemies of popular causes. A bill enlarging the jurisdiction of the inferior courts was finally passed in 1795.

Saunders achieved full recognition as a member of the loyalist élite in May 1793 when he was made a member of the Council. He took this appointment seriously as he did anything connected with duty and responsibility. He was one of those who from 1795 to 1798 voted to throw out the appropriation bills, since he was opposed to paying the members of the assembly, and he thus contributed to a legislative impasse that brought the government virtually to a halt [see James Glenie*]. Saunders regularly attended meetings of the Council and, against the wishes of his family, continued to do so until just before his death. He expected an honourable course of action from his fellow councillors and his own conduct seems to have been above reproach. For this reason in 1802, when there was a question of corruption in the Council, he introduced a motion calling for an investigation. The matter had arisen as the result of charges by a Westmorland County assemblyman that members of the Council had offered him government preferment if he would vote the way they wished in the house. Saunders's motion was unsuccessful, but it revealed his strong concern that everyone should act within the law.

Saunders appears to have had only a moderate influence in the structure of power in the province. His position must have been evident to him in 1808 on the death of Chief Justice George Duncan Ludlow*. Since his friend and patron Simcoe had died, he had to rely on Lieutenant Governor Thomas Carleton* for support in his attempt to attain the highest judicial office. His brother-in-law Alexander Jekyll Chalmers tried to persuade Carleton, then in England, to back Saunders's petition, but the lieutenant governor, who as one of his supporters admitted "had a natural dislike of exerting himself to serve any one," claimed he could do nothing. The administrator of the province, Major-

General Martin Hunter*, helped kill any chance Saunders may have had by recommending Jonathan Bliss or Ward Chipman, with Saunders only a "fair candidate" since he was not very experienced at law before he became a judge. The office went the following year to Bliss, and Saunders, who was 55, must have been bitterly disappointed; it looked as if he had missed his one chance of ever becoming chief justice.

In 1808 Saunders's military abilities had been recognized when there was a threat of war with the United States. A lieutenant-colonel in the militia from 1797, he was placed in command of the units around Fredericton. Administrator Edward Winslow* paid tribute to "the unremitted exertions" and "steady perseverance" of Saunders and his officers: "A corps has been formed and disciplined which, had the threatened hostilities taken place, could not have failed to render essential service in defending the Country."

Saunders seems to have kept alive the dream of establishing a landed aristocracy in New Brunswick longer than most members of the loyalist élite. After his first purchases he had continued to buy land, hoping that it would increase in value as the province developed. At the Barony he took possession of over 5,000 acres, although he did not get a clear title to this estate until 1819. He also owned 3,000 acres in another tract and 2,300 in different lots at various places. He was continually buying property in Fredericton and along the Saint John River and he became one of the largest, if not the largest, landowner in the province. To build up his estate he hoped to attract tenants but he was not very successful, and indeed much of his land remained worthless. In 1811 Lieutenant-Colonel Joseph Gubbins noted that "his house stands in the midst of a wilderness of his own creation, without a neighbour or a practicable road, and his cleared lands are growing again up into forest."

In 1790 the granting of free land had been restricted by the British government in the hope that crown lands could be sold, a policy that tended to keep immigrants out and drive others from the province. Saunders profited to some extent from the restriction by buying land from those who left. After land grants were reinstituted in 1807, the population of the province steadily increased. Saunders was instrumental in the formation of the Fredericton Emigrant Society in 1819, served as its president from 1821 to 1829, and was still an active member in 1833. He was also involved in the formation of the New-Brunswick Agricultural and Emigrant Society in 1825 and was its first president. He dropped out the next year, however, possibly because of his dislike for Thomas Baillie*, one of the leaders in the organization.

Believing that an education in England was prefer-able to one in the colonies or in the United States, Saunders sent both his son and his elder daughter there. In the case of his son, whom he supported through school, university, and law studies, he came to regret his decision, since John Simcoe developed attitudes towards New Brunswick which his father did not share, acquiring, Saunders later wrote, "habits and prejudices perhaps impossible . . . to overcome." John Simcoe became contemptuous of the province and disinclined "to degrade my prospects . . . by practising in such a miserable place." He was also scornful of his father's success, claiming that it was his own ambition "to mount to the top of the top of the [tree] but it must be the summit of the lofty oak . . . not the summit of the lowly shrub whose branch is incapable of support." He later compared his father's advancement with that of the Lower Canadian judge Jonathan Sewell*, who "after an active career retires to the highest post of honor with more than two thousand a year"; Saunders himself would retire "with four hundred & fifty still obliged 'to bow the knee & the neck'" to Lieutenant Governor George Stracey Smyth.

John Simcoe also felt that the family estate was rather pretentious. In 1821 he sarcastically commented that he was pleased to hear "the Barony was again about to shine forth with that brightness which so justly becomes the respected family mansion of the Saunders." "When I last saw it," he noted, "it was with difficulty the foundation could be supported with props." Saunders was still maintaining his discontented son when the latter was in his thirties, but to his father's relief John Simcoe returned permanently to New Brunswick in 1830. He eventually had a successful career in government.

Saunders's eldest daughter, Ariana Margaretta Jekyll, had married Captain George Shore* in 1815. She and her husband cultivated the friendship of Lieutenant Governor Smyth and by 1822 Shore was acting at times both as his private secretary and as his aide-de-camp. This relationship may have helped Saunders realize his own ambition. In 1822 he was appointed chief justice of New Brunswick on the death of Jonathan Bliss. Smyth's dislike for Ward Chipman, the other candidate for the position, undoubtedly also contributed to his success.

At the time of his appointment Saunders was 68 years old. He had lived to see many changes in New Brunswick, few of which met with his approval. Therefore he was apprehensive when Sir Howard Douglas* was appointed lieutenant governor. "He appears to be a man of business thus far," he wrote in September 1824, "but the time to try him will be when the legislature meets." "I have never," he continued, "been altogether pleased with the line of conduct of any of his predecessors – they have been generally too conceding to the lower house and not sufficiently firm

Saunders

but at the same time conciliating and moreover not sufficiently acquainted with the principles of our constitution." These comments are another clear indication of Saunders's conservative tendencies and his distrust of the assembly.

Much of the political controversy of the 1820s centred on Thomas Baillie, who was appointed commissioner of crown lands in 1824 and whose arrogance made him many enemies. Saunders disliked him from the beginning, perhaps in part because he also took over as surveyor general, replacing George Shore who was temporarily filling the office. The chief justice viewed Baillie's appointment as a threat to the established New Brunswick families. "It is a matter of some surprise here," he wrote to his son, "that so young a man . . . should have offices bestowed upon him, the income of which . . . would comfortably provide for at least 8 of our young men whose education and rank in this society certainly entitle them to expect some of the passing benefits of the Government." The chief justice felt that the colonial secretary had conferred more power on both Douglas and Baillie "than is either constitutional or advantageous for the King or the Colony." To Saunders's alarm, the Colonial Office appeared to be pushing New Brunswick towards more independence. He therefore opposed a proposal in 1825 that the salaries of those on the civil list be paid out of assembly funds, believing with Douglas that implementation of such a plan would reduce the status of the executive by making its members financially dependent on the assembly and that the connections between mother country and colony would thus be weakened. Similarly he opposed proposals in Britain for removing the preferential duties on colonial timber.

That Baillie became quite friendly with John S. Saunders and George Shore must have annoyed the chief justice. However, Baillie's relationship with Shore did not continue and from the late 1820s they were to find themselves on opposite sides in all crucial votes in the Council. The friendship with John S. Saunders was of longer duration and, possibly because of it, the latter was appointed to the Executive Council in 1833. Any resentment John Saunders may have felt over his son's associations was exacerbated by the fact that the appointment was a personal humiliation for him. The Council had been divided in 1832 and there were now two bodies, the Executive Council and the less prestigious Legislative Council. When the new councillors were announced the following year, Baillie and John S. Saunders were members of the Executive Council, while John Saunders, as chief justice, was to lead the Legislative Council (of which his son was also a member). Although these appointments were consistent with the policy followed in other colonies, Saunders felt he had been demoted and slighted. He was the more discomfited

because Sir Archibald Campbell* gave Baillie precedence over the older members of the Executive Council and thus the right to assume the administration of the province in the lieutenant governor's absence; Saunders was one of those who protested to the Colonial Office. The matter was eventually resolved when the senior military officer in the province was designated to act as administrator.

Saunders in 1833 was no doubt already smarting because two years earlier he had been obliged by the commissioner of crown lands to pay for a town lot in Fredericton on which he had not fulfilled the terms of his grant. Baillie further annoyed him by encouraging Irish immigration. Saunders was not pleased with the influx of Irish settlers since on the whole they were poor, uneducated, and unskilled and they did not make good tenants. Many were Roman Catholics and Saunders was a firm supporter of the Church of England, serving as a warden and vestryman of Christ Church in Fredericton and a churchwarden in Prince William as well. He opposed the bill for the relief of Roman Catholics which was passed in 1830. Modelled on a British act, it allowed Roman Catholics to hold civil and military offices and to sit in the House of Assembly. Saunders felt that concessions might have been necessary in Britain but were not in New Brunswick since "the Roman Catholics in this colony have not made any complaints, or attempted to show that they are in any manner oppressed or aggrieved by the present laws." In truth, he disliked change of any kind. Describing him as "a Tory of the old school, on whose dull mind the progress of the world made no impression," Hannay states that as a councillor "he opposed all reforms until he came to be looked upon with contempt, even by those who had formerly been with him on the side of obstruction."

Like many of the refugee "gentlemen" who first administered New Brunswick, Saunders was dedicated to maintaining the imperial connection and to perpetuating in the colony the authority of the loyalist élite. Since the loyalists' position rested on the pensions, land grants, and offices they had received from the imperial government, they viewed any weakening of ties with Britain as not only undesirable in itself but as a threat to their pre-eminence, the more inexpedient because both the colonial economy and the province's defence were dependent on the mother country. In Saunders's eyes, the removal of British regiments from the province, the opening of the West Indies trade to the Americans, the plans to alter the preferential duties on New Brunswick timber, and the restriction on land granting in 1790 all jeopardized the established order. Similarly, within the colony, any diminution of the executive authority or granting of power to outsiders seemed to endanger his way of life. Since most of those who shared his view were dead by the 1830s, Saunders stood out as a reactionary to the new figures struggling for political power in the province. His son learned to adjust to and work within a changing society but Saunders either could not or would not.

For all his conservatism, and though he came from a slave-owning family, Saunders for some reason opposed slavery, and his attitude was in marked contrast to the view of many leading loyalists in New Brunswick. In 1800 he had been one of two Supreme Court judges who ruled against the master in a well-known test case on the legality of slavery in the province [see Caleb Jones*]; the bench was equally divided, however, and no judgement was rendered. Saunders later changed his mind about the legality of slavery – as became clear in a second case in 1805 – but there is no evidence to suggest that he ever supported the institution. His stand in 1805 appears to have been based solely on the belief that slavery was legal under the existing laws.

Saunders tried a number of interesting cases in New Brunswick, including one in 1808 involving deserters accused of murdering a man who had attempted to apprehend them. In 1822 he went to Miramichi to preside over the trial of a number of rioters, a case that involved some 59 sentences. That same year he also tried two men charged with murder as the result of a duel [see George Ludlow WETMORE]. Saunders's address to the jury on this occasion was a strange one: although everyone knew full well who was involved in the duel, Saunders claimed that the prosecution's case was based on presumption and that in such instances "character is a great weight." Hannay has suggested that if this address is any indication of the legal knowledge of the judges at the time, then it was probably not of the best. The man charged with firing the fatal shot, George Frederick Street*, was a member of a prominent family and for that reason Saunders felt he should be acquitted, as he indeed was. The whole affair seems to diminish Saunders's reputation as a strong supporter of law and order. With him, it appears, status in society was an important consideration in cases involving the law.

When the 50th anniversary of the coming of the loyalists was celebrated in Saint John in 1833, about 200 people attended the ceremony. Among those invited was Saunders. He was unable to be present but he sent a letter which was read at the dinner. In it he attempted to sum up his philosophy of life: "He was taught from his earliest infancy to fear *God* and *honor* the *King*, which he has made the two great objects of his life hitherto – And which, with the blessing of *God*, he will persevere in, till he shall be called to sleep with those, whose inflexible fidelity made them, at every hazard and sacrifice, to stand firm in their allegiance to their *King*, and in support of the glorious constitution under which they were born." As much committed to the old ways at the end of his life as he

had been in 1774, Saunders was not happy with what he saw around him. That his baronial estate was still very much a wilderness was a personal disappointment; moreover, he was at odds with the new social and political order typified by Baillie and seemingly illustrated by his own eclipse in the council changes. Nevertheless, he continued to do his duty as chief justice until a few days before his death. He was buried with full military honours and his funeral was attended by members of the assembly, the Executive and Legislative councils, the lieutenant governor, members of the bar, and students and professors of King's College.

Saunders's obituary described him as a man of "sound judgment" and "the highest integrity of purpose," "a disciple of the old school . . . unwavering in his political principles." These were admirable qualities. However, he was also inflexible and unwilling to change, and his letters show little evidence of wit or sense of humour. His wife appears to have been an efficient lady of strong character. When John S. Saunders was concerned that his father might leave the management of his lands to himself and George Shore, he was told, "It is not my intention to trouble either of you upon that account as I am quite certain that she would be more capable of managing her affairs herself than both of you put together." Saunders and his wife had formed no strong ties with other prominent loyalist families in New Brunswick; with one exception, all their children and grandchildren married partners from outside the province.

After his father's death John Simcoe gradually disposed of some of the family's land, but the Barony was not put on the market until after his own death in 1878. It had remained, as Moses Henry Perley* commented, "a waste howling wilderness" more properly entitled a "barren, eh!" – a symbol of the frustrated hopes of the loyalist élite. Its sale brought to an end John Saunders's dream of a landed estate that would be the base for the establishment of his family forever. If he had never quite regained the status he had lost in Virginia, he had none the less made a place for himself in his new home. As he himself once said, "I shall always wish to be of some importance in the society where I might live." He was certainly that in New Brunswick.

W. A. SPRAY

[The most useful sources for this biography were the Saunders papers at UNBL (MG H11) and Diana Ruth Moore's MA thesis, "John Saunders, 1754–1834: consummate loyalist" (Univ. of N.B., Fredericton, 1980). W.A.S.]

PANB, MC 1156, V: 81; RG 10, RS108, John Saunders, 1792, 1818. PRO, AO 12/54, 12/100, 12/109; AO 13, bundles 33, 79. UNBL, MG H2, 7: 44, 69, 121; 8: 6, 13; 13: 74; 14: 7, 63–65, 87, 93, 97, 124; 15: 5–6, 14, 19, 78. Gubbins, *N.B. journals* (Temperley). *Loyalist narratives*

Savage

from Upper Canada, ed. J. J. Talman (Toronto, 1946). N.B., Legislative Council, *Journal* [1786–1830], 27 Feb. 1830. [M. H. Perley], "Scenery on the St. John – reflections – Woodstock," *New-Brunswick Courier*, 29 Sept. 1832: 2. *Revolutionary Virginia: the road to independence*, comp. W. J. Van Schreeven et al., ed. R. L. Scribner et al. (7v. to date, [Charlottesville, Va.], 1973–   ). J. G. Simcoe, *Simcoe's military journal* (Toronto, 1962). *Winslow papers* (Raymond). *Gleaner: and Northumberland Schediasma* (Miramichi, N.B.), 3 June 1833. *New-Brunswick Courier*, 25 May 1833. *Royal Gazette* (Fredericton), 28 May, 4 June 1834. I. L. Hill, *Some loyalists and others* (Fredericton, 1976). E. A. Jones, *American members of the Inns of Court* (London, 1924). C. F. McIntosh, "Genealogy: Saunders–Princess Anne County, Virginia," *Va. Magazine of Hist. and Biog.* (Richmond), 32 (1924): 92–96. Sabine, *Biog. sketches of loyalists*.

Beckwith Maxwell, *Hist. of central N.B.* Sheila Carr, "John Saunders: Virginia loyalist" (graduate essay, Univ. of N.B., Fredericton, 1970). Esther Clark Wright, *The St. John River and its tributaries* (n.p., 1966). Kenneth Donovan, "The military career of a Virginia loyalist: Captain John Saunders, 1774–1782" (graduate essay, Univ. of N.B., 1972). Hannay, *Hist. of N.B.* Douglas How, *The 8th Hussars: a history of the regiment* ([Sussex, N.B.], 1964). C. J. Ingles, *The Queen's Rangers in the Revolutionary War*, ed. H. M. Jackson (n.p., 1956). Lawrence, *Judges of N.B.* (Stockton and Raymond). MacNutt, *New Brunswick*. E. A. Jones, "A letter regarding the Queen's Rangers," *Va. Magazine of Hist. and Biog.*, 30 (1922): 368–76.

SAVAGE, JOHN, land developer, militia officer, and JP; b. 1740 in Ireland; m. Ann Pratt, probably in Spencertown, N.Y., and they had seven children; d. 27 Sept. 1826 in West Shefford (Bromont), Lower Canada, and was buried there two days later.

The Savage family is believed to have arrived in North America in the latter half of the 18th century. They may have come with a contingent originally from the Palatinate (Federal Republic of Germany) which had taken refuge in Ireland; part of this group had emigrated to the Hudson valley and settled around Albany, N.Y. Before the American revolution the Savages owned land at Spencertown, where they had become quite influential.

In 1775 John Savage refused command of the local company of the Continental Army, despite pressure from fellow citizens and two of his brothers-in-law. As a result he was considered to be an enemy, was ordered to put up a guarantee, and then was imprisoned. Being daring and resourceful, he succeeded in escaping after several attempts and reached New York, where in 1776 he obtained a commission as a lieutenant in the Loyal Rangers. He was captured again, narrowly missed being hanged, and was incarcerated for several months. After being freed, he served in the British army as a spy during the summer of 1782. His zeal in the missions he carried out in the states of New York and Vermont earned him the highest praise. However, republican hostility forced

him to secure his family's safety. Bearing a safe conduct, Savage and his family, with his brother James, left Crown Point, N.Y., and sought refuge in the province of Quebec in October 1783. Savage applied for lands east of Lake Champlain.

The Allen brothers, who commanded the Green Mountain Boys, were then trying to attract loyalists to Vermont, claiming that in so doing they were promoting the annexation of Vermont to Quebec. Savage had served as an intermediary between the Allens and the military authorities in Quebec, and he supported this plan with the assent of some senior officers, despite the opposition of Governor Frederick Haldimand*, who did not favour settlement near the American border. In 1784 and for some years thereafter, Savage was living at Alburgh, south of the border, on what had been the seigneury of Foucault. The Allens, however, became supporters of Congress, and tried to make him take the oath of allegiance in 1791. Along with a number of other loyalists, he was forced to move to Caldwell's Manor, a property in Lower Canada belonging to Henry Caldwell*.

On 16 July 1792 Savage petitioned for the grant of Shefford Township. Like most of those signing petitions, he completed the many formalities at great expense: securing permission for a survey, drawing up a list of associates, taking various steps with the commissioners, as well as making several trips to Quebec, Chambly, and Missisquoi Bay. Once he had taken the oath of allegiance in 1792, he busied himself opening up roads and completing the survey of the township, always at his own expense and even though he had no title to the land. His family had to make do with a log cabin, and in the first winter he lost nearly all his livestock. Quarrels between Governor Robert Prescott* and the Executive Council were to paralyse land granting for some years. Tired of parading his service record and demanding fair compensation for his losses during the American revolution, he joined other dissatisfied people, among them Samuel WILLARD, in sending an agent to London to plead their cause. In February 1800 Samuel GALE presented a report on their behalf, which caused some commotion in high places at Quebec. On 10 Feb. 1801 the letters patent for Shefford Township were formally granted; Savage and his 38 associates, a group including his son John and three of his sons-in-law, were then able to divide up about 34,000 acres. To ensure financing for his undertaking Savage had engaged in real estate transactions even before the official grant was made, and he continued to make deals afterwards.

In 1805 Savage received a captain's commission in the 2nd battalion of the Eastern Townships Militia. The following year he obtained a commission as justice of the peace for the district of Montreal, which was renewed in 1810 and 1821. His home was long the scene of the principal events in the township; even religious services were held there. Anglican minister Charles James Stewart* came to Shefford in 1808 and met Savage and his family. Later he never failed to visit him when making pastoral rounds, and he held Savage in high esteem.

Despite his 72 years Savage wanted to play a part in the War of 1812. When on 10 Jan. 1813 Lieutenant-Colonel Sir John JOHNSON created the Frontier Light Infantry, Savage obtained a captain's commission in the regiment. On 13 August the Frontier Light Infantry was attached to the Voltigeurs Canadiens, under Charles-Michel d'IRUMBERRY de Salaberry; it formed the 9th and 10th companies in that regiment at the end of the war.

By then, Shefford Township had a population of about 500. There were still no roads, despite efforts by Savage, who had cleared the first path from Missisquoi Bay in 1792. In 1799 he turned his attention to the construction of a road to Montreal through Dorchester (Saint-Jean-sur-Richelieu) or the seigneury of Saint-Hyacinthe. Government grants would allow the construction of real roads, which Savage supervised, around 1816.

The establishing of regular religious services and the building of a church meant a great deal to Savage. Early in 1818 he told Stewart of his plan, and on 14 Oct. 1819 he gave him four acres near his home for a church, as well as 800 acres worth £200. Savage, who by then was 80, supervised the construction of the church in the summer of 1820, and he supplemented with his own money the small grant from the Anglican diocese. Perhaps he was too generous, since on 20 March 1824 he was taken to court by Saint-Hyacinthe merchant Joseph Cartier, who as his supplier since 1801 was claiming £42 from him. Savage could only give him two heifers in payment, and on 4 July 1825 two of his lots were seized by the sheriff and sold.

Like a true patriarch John Savage passed away in the midst of his family, a son and five daughters, their spouses, and 47 grandchildren all born in Shefford Township. Savage had identified himself with this corner of the country which he had made his own by enterprise and perseverance. He had never swerved from his path, and his name remains associated with a lasting work.

MARIE-PAULE R. LaBRÈQUE

ACC-Q, 69, 103–5, 124. ANQ-E, CE2-42, 20 sept. 1826; CN2-26, 1800–26. Bishop's Univ. (Lennoxville, Que.), Special Coll., Savage papers. Brome County Hist. Soc. Arch. (Knowlton, Que.), Township papers; Miscellaneous family papers, Savage file; Samuel Willard papers. PAC, MG 11, [CO 42] Q, 110: 42–47; MG 23, GIII, 12; RG 1, L3L; RG 4, A1; RG 8, I (C ser.); RG 9, I, A1; RG 68, General index, 1651–1841. "Collection Haldimand," PAC *Rapport*, 1888: 765, 879, 881, 889, 897. Bouchette, *Topographical description of L.C. Illustrated atlas of East-ern Townships*. A. R. Kelley, "The Quebec Diocesan Archives: a description of the collection of historical records of the Church of England in the diocese of Quebec," ANQ *Rapport*, 1946–47: 179–298. Langelier, *Liste des terrains concédés. Officers of British forces in Canada* (Irving).

Caron, *La colonisation de la prov. de Québec.* C. P. Choquette, *Histoire de la ville de Saint-Hyacinthe* (Saint-Hyacinthe, Qué., 1930). C. M. Day, *Hist. of Eastern Townships*; *Pioneers of the Eastern Townships . . .* (Montreal, 1863). *The loyalists of the Eastern Townships of Quebec, 1783–84: 1983–84, bi-centennial* (Stanbridge East, Que., 1984). Albert Gravel, *Pages d'histoire régionale* (24 cahiers, Sherbrooke, Qué., 1960–67), 20. G. F. McGuigan, "Land policy and land disposal under tenure of free and common socage, Quebec and Lower Canada, 1763–1809 . . ." (PHD thesis, Univ. Laval, Quebec, 1962). J. N. McIlwraith, *Sir Frederick Haldimand* (Toronto, 1906). Jules Martel, "Histoire du système routier des Cantons de l'Est avant 1855" (thèse de MA, univ. d'Ottawa, 1960). T. R. Millman, *The life of the Right Reverend, the Honourable Charles James Stewart, D.D., Oxon., second Anglican bishop of Quebec* (London, Ont., 1953). G. H. Montgomery, *Missisquoi Bay (Philipsburg, Que.)* (Granby, Que., 1950). H. B. Shufelt, *Nicholas Austin the Quaker and the township of Bolton* (Knowlton, 1971). *The storied province of Quebec; past and present*, ed. William Wood et al. (5v., Toronto, 1931–32), 2: 922–72. Cyrus Thomas, *Histoire de Shefford*, Ovila Fournier, trad. (Île-Perrot, Qué., 1973). W. B. Tucker, *The romance of the Palatine millers: a tale of Palatine Irish-Americans and United Empire Loyalists* (Montreal, 1929). *Un siècle d'histoire, les bâtisseurs de Granby, 1859–1959* ([Granby, 1959]). M. O. Vaudry, *A sketch of the life of Captain John Savage, J.P., first settler in Shefford County, 1792 . . .* (n.p., n.d.). Kathryn Burgess, "The journal of John Savage," *Chatham Courier* (Chatham, N.Y.), 4 March 1976. Claude Desrosiers, "Un aperçu des habitudes de consommation de la clientèle de Joseph Cartier, marchand général à Saint-Hyacinthe à la fin du XVIIIe siècle," CHA *Historical Papers*, 1984: 51–110. J. P. Noyes, "The Canadian loyalists and early settlers in the district of Bedford," Missisquoi County Hist. Soc., *Report* (Saint-Jean-sur-Richelieu, Que.), 3 (1908): 90–107; "The Missisquoi German or Dutch," Missisquoi County Hist. Soc., *Report*, 2 (1907): 31–35. W. H. Siebert, "The American loyalists in the eastern seigniories and townships of the province of Quebec," RSC *Trans.*, 3rd ser., 7 (1913), sect.III: 3–41.

SAVEUSE DE BEAUJEU, JACQUES-PHILIPPE, office holder, seigneur, militia officer, and politician; baptized 5 May 1772 on Île aux Grues, Que., son of Louis Liénard* de Beaujeu de Villemonde and Geneviève Le Moyne de Longueuil; d. 19 June 1832 in Montreal and was buried in the church of Soulanges (Les Cèdres), Lower Canada.

Jacques-Philippe Saveuse de Beaujeu belonged to a noble family that had a long military tradition. His grandfather, Louis Liénard* de Beaujeu, as well as his father and his uncle Daniel-Hyacinthe-Marie Liénard* de Beaujeu had chosen military careers, in which they had distinguished themselves. Jacques-Philippe broke with the family tradition and in 1794 assumed the office of protonotary of the Court of King's Bench for the district of Montreal.

On 3 Nov. 1802 at Vaudreuil, Saveuse de Beaujeu married Catherine, daughter of Gaspard-Joseph Chaussegros* de Léry. Through this marriage he extended his connections with official circles. The bride's cousin, Michel-Eustache-Gaspard-Alain CHARTIER de Lotbinière, the widow of Michel Chartier* de Lotbinière, Louise-Madeleine Chaussegros de Léry, and the groom's uncle, Joseph-Dominique-Emmanuel Le Moyne* de Longueuil, had been present at the signing of the marriage contract the previous day. Saveuse de Beaujeu signed the document in a beautiful hand, as was the fashion of the period, using only his surname and the family's territorial designation. He put 24,000 *livres* into the community of property; his wife brought a dowry consisting essentially of rights to her parents' estate. The jointure, a sizeable one for the period, was set at 10,000 *livres*.

On 12 June of that year Saveuse de Beaujeu renounced his father's estate, which was too encumbered with debt. In 1807, however, he came into a large inheritance from his maternal uncle, Joseph-Dominique-Emmanuel Le Moyne de Longueuil, who had died without an immediate heir. The estate was a considerable one: a manor-house, the seigneuries of Soulanges and Nouvelle-Longueuil, mills, 160 *arpents* in the barony of Longueuil, part of Newton Township, moneys owing in excess of 23,600 *livres*, and assets in cash estimated at £245. His sole obligation in return for this inheritance was to guarantee his two sisters, Élisabeth-Geneviève and Adèle, one-fifth of the income from the seigneuries for the rest of their lives.

Saveuse de Beaujeu, who was a captain in Montreal's 2nd Militia Battalion, served during the War of 1812. In 1813 he resigned from his office as protonotary. He was elected to the House of Assembly of Lower Canada for Montreal East in 1814, but he did little more than pass through the assembly, since he left it in February 1816. In 1823, at the height of the Canadian party's struggle with the administration over supplies, he refused an appointment to the Legislative Council.

In 1828, through an attorney, Saveuse de Beaujeu sought a delay in rendering fealty and homage, a duty required of him as a seigneur. He was in Europe at the time, probably staying with his brother, Charles-François. On his return to Lower Canada the following year he went to Quebec in order to renew his oath of fealty and give the particulars of his property titles.

Saveuse de Beaujeu agreed in April 1830, despite protests from the Canadian party, to join the Legislative Council, on which his brother-in-law, Louis-René CHAUSSEGROS de Léry, already sat. On 1

October of the following year he drew up his will, making his wife heir to his personal estate, his cash and moneys owing him. He bequeathed his real estate and seigneurial income to his son Georges-René*; to his daughter Catherine-Charlotte he left a secured annuity of £360. In 1832 Saveuse de Beaujeu succumbed to the cholera that was then raging in Lower Canada.

JEAN-JACQUES LEFEBVRE

ANQ-M, CE1-50, 3 nov. 1802; CE1-51, 19 juin 1832; CN1-74, 12 juin 1802, 21 nov. 1806; CN1-117, 2 nov. 1802. F.-J. Audet, *Les députés de Montréal*. Langelier, *Liste des terrains concédés*, 1073. Le Jeune, *Dictionnaire*. *Officers of British forces in Canada* (Irving), 167. Turcotte, *Le Conseil législatif*. [François Daniel], *Histoire des grandes familles françaises du Canada ou aperçu sur le chevalier Benoist et quelques familles contemporaines* (Montréal, 1867). Alphonse Gauthier, "Études généalogiques: la famille de Georges-René Saveuse de Beaujeu (1810–1865)," SGCF *Mémoires*, 6 (1954–55): 197–208.

SCALLAN, THOMAS (the name is sometimes written **Scallon**), Roman Catholic priest, Franciscan, and vicar apostolic; b. *c.* 1766 in Churchtown, County Wexford (Republic of Ireland); d. 28 May 1830 in St John's.

At an early age Thomas Scallan, who came of a respectable family, was placed under the care of his uncle, the Reverend Thomas Scallan, at the Franciscan convent in Wexford, where he received a classical education. In 1786 he entered St Isidore's College, Rome, to complete his studies for the priesthood. He remained there as lecturer in philosophy until 1794, when he returned to the Wexford friary. There he worked as a professor of classics with Father Patrick Lambert* in the Franciscan Academy, a preparatory seminary for candidates for the priesthood. For some years Scallan was principal of this institution, apparently highly regarded, and from 1802 to 1805 he served additionally as guardian (superior) of the Wexford convent and definitor (disciplinarian) of the Franciscan order in the province of Leinster.

Scallan remained at Wexford until 1812, when Lambert, now vicar apostolic of Newfoundland, secured his assistance as curate in St John's. In 1814 Lambert's ill health led him to recommend Scallan as his successor, and in this connection the two travelled to Ireland in the autumn of 1815. On 26 Jan. 1816 Scallan was named titular bishop of Drago and coadjutor to Lambert with the right of succession, and on 1 May he was consecrated in the parish church in Wexford. Later that year Scallan returned to Newfoundland. When Lambert, who had remained in Ireland, died on 23 September, Scallan automatically became vicar apostolic of Newfoundland (although formal notice of his predecessor's death did not reach him until the following spring).

Major difficulties immediately confronted Scallan. Attracted by high wages in the booming fishery, thousands of Irish had immigrated to Newfoundland between 1811 and 1816, increasing the Catholic population to some 21,000, double that of five years earlier, and now half the total population. However, by 1816 the economy had suffered a sharp reversal and destitution was widespread. In St John's alone during the winter of 1816–17, 1,800 people were on relief and, like others who were better off, Scallan daily fed ten of the poor at his own table. Violence and crime abounded, and upon the Catholic priests fell a major responsibility for the enforcement of law and order.

The bishop had to provide additional clergy for the increased population, a task made difficult by the prevailing poverty. Nevertheless in 1817 he ordained Nicholas Devereux to the priesthood, the first such event to take place in Newfoundland. By that year, too, Scallan had established a new parish at Kings Cove, Bonavista Bay, and had assigned assistants to the parishes of Harbour Grace and Placentia. There were then ten priests on the island, as many as he felt could be supported adequately. Although Scallan tried to maintain this strength throughout his episcopate (he left that number at his death), he did so only with difficulty. Those clergy he did have, however, were usually regarded as "pious, learned and liberal." They were also active men, travelling constantly and usually covering extensive territories. William Herron*, for example, the curate of Placentia, resided at Burin and from there cared for the inhabitants along the whole south coast of the island, including the Micmacs of St George's Bay. Scallan's priests were energetic, too, in continuing to make numerous converts among the English settlers of Newfoundland, especially in Placentia and St Mary's bays, and to some extent along the north coast.

Still, it was not easy to secure clergy of quality. Over the years Scallan had to dismiss two priests for drunkenness and immorality, and one left Newfoundland after his nephew was hanged for murder. He also had problems with the rebellious priest John POWER. When Power, who had been suspended in 1812 by Lambert, dared in 1820 to celebrate mass in Labrador, Scallan publicly excommunicated him and denounced him as "a rock of scandal and a stumbling block to the faithful." In retaliation, Power brought a lawsuit against the bishop alleging financial loss as a result of his dismissal. It was unsuccessful. By then Power had few followers; he died in 1823, apparently reconciled to the church.

From the beginning of his episcopate Scallan maintained a close relationship with Bishop Joseph-Octave PLESSIS of Quebec. As in Lambert's time, each bishop appointed the other his vicar general, an act that would be repeated in 1826 with Plessis's successor, Bernard-Claude PANET; Scallan regularly corresponded with Plessis and then Panet regarding the affairs of the North American church. Their collaboration was especially useful in providing for the Catholics in Labrador. As early as 1814 Plessis had suggested to Rome that Labrador and Anticosti Island be detached from the diocese of Quebec and joined to the vicariate of Newfoundland, because they had been under the civil government of Newfoundland since 1809, and Plessis felt they could be better served from there. Scallan formally agreed to this change in 1819, and on 1 Feb. 1820 a papal decree was issued transferring to the vicariate of Newfoundland Anticosti and the territory of Labrador north of the St John River (Rivière Saint-Jean, Que.). Scallan had already used his faculties as vicar general of Quebec to send a priest to the coast of Labrador in the summer of 1818, and from 1821 he seems to have sent missionaries there annually for the fishing season. Since he had nobody qualified to care for the Montagnais and Naskapis, both Plessis and Panet, at Scallan's request, continued to send priests to these native groups.

On 25 March 1823 Scallan suffered a stroke which temporarily left his right side paralysed. Having recovered sufficiently by June to follow his physician's advice to go to a warmer climate, he sailed for New York, leaving his vicar general, Thomas Anthony EWER, in charge of the mission. The bishop spent the next several months on the continent, chiefly in New York City and Washington, D.C., but also visiting fellow bishops in Baltimore, Philadelphia, and Boston. On his voyage home he spent three weeks at Halifax. Nova Scotia had been without a resident bishop since the death of Edmund Burke* in 1820, and Scallan confirmed nearly 600 people in Halifax. He returned to Newfoundland in September, his health restored, but his doctors cautioned him against wintering in a cold climate and in November he departed again, this time for Italy.

Scallan spent the winter of 1823–24 in Rome, concerning himself principally with the affairs of Nova Scotia. He obtained special faculties for Father John Carroll, then administering the colony's vicariate, and made urgent representations that Father Denis Lyons, an Irishman, be named bishop. (Lyons did not accept the appointment in 1824, and later that year William Fraser* was nominated to fill the position.) The spring and summer of 1824 Scallan passed in England and Ireland, and he returned to Newfoundland only in September. By this time his health had greatly improved, although he was never again completely well. A further journey for health reasons was made in 1826 to the spa at Cheltenham, England.

A notable feature of Scallan's espiscopate was the excellent, perhaps unparalleled, relationship in Newfoundland between Catholics and Protestants. "It was

Scallan

a boast," wrote an observer, "that one neighbour scarcely knew the religious sentiments of the other." This harmony, which later events proved to have been fragile, owed much to Scallan's personal outlook. He allowed his clergy to attend non-Catholic funerals, and on several significant occasions from 1818 onwards the bishop himself attended services in the Anglican church vested "in his suta rocket cross and cap." He was one of the first to pay a formal call on the Anglican bishop of Nova Scotia, John Inglis*, when Inglis visited Newfoundland in 1827. Scallan's great desire, said Governor Thomas John Cochrane*, "was to live in peace and harmony with the members of every religious denomination."

Scallan also enjoyed an excellent personal relationship with Cochrane and with the previous governor, Sir Charles Hamilton*, a relationship maintained despite the fact that Scallan, unlike his predecessors and his successor, never received a government salary. Although, with Hamilton's staunch support, he applied for a salary in 1819 and again in 1823, the British government chose to ignore the requests. Thereafter Scallan apparently decided not to pursue the matter, possibly preferring to retain his independent status.

Notwithstanding his conciliatory disposition, Scallan could be firm in upholding Catholic rights. In 1817 Governor Francis Pickmore* had introduced the first Newfoundland Marriage Act in an effort to prohibit the celebration of marriages by Methodist and Congregational clergy, but before doing so he felt obliged to assure Scallan that the traditional right of Catholic priests to solemnize marriages would be fully protected. The resulting act was vague and served only to anger dissenters who saw in it a tendency "to establish popery and to persecute Protestantism." Consequently the question was reopened in 1823. The draft of the new legislation included clauses that would permit both dissenting ministers and Catholic priests to perform marriages, but only when it would not be "convenient" to obtain a Church of England clergyman. When the draft reached Newfoundland from the Colonial Office, Catholics were outraged. Scallan led a massive protest against the proposed condition, claiming it was unjust and vexatious, and in petitions to the king, the Colonial Office, and the House of Commons, the Catholics of Newfoundland denounced it as "the most degrading and distressing infliction that could be laid upon them." Supported by Governor Hamilton, these representations carried great weight in London, and they ensured that the Newfoundland Marriage Act of 1824 left Roman Catholic priests on an equal footing with the Anglican clergy. The Catholics' only remaining objection to the act was the registration fee it introduced. Although Newfoundland Catholics had shown that they were a group whose interests could not be ignored, the net result of the two acts was to arouse sectarian controversy and to leave particularly embittered the growing body of Methodists, who in the final version of the law were still excluded.

Bishop Scallan was also concerned about the education of Roman Catholic children. He apparently endorsed the principle of schools open to pupils of all persuasions with religious instruction given separately outside school hours. He certainly supported the non-denominational St John's Charity School, which was organized along such lines. He approved, too, in 1826, the foundation on the same basis of the Benevolent Irish Society's Orphan Asylum Schools at St John's, even though the student body was almost entirely Catholic, and a similar school at Harbour Grace. However, when the Newfoundland School Society, an organization based in Britain and dominated by low church Anglicans such as Samuel Codner*, began to provide schools on the island in September 1824, Scallan invoked a Vatican prohibition against Bible society schools to ban the attendance of Catholic children at the new establishments. He seems to have feared, probably correctly, that despite protestations of non-sectarianism these schools were really aimed at proselytism. Substantial government assistance went to both the Newfoundland School Society and the Society for the Propagation of the Gospel, while the Orphan Asylum Schools, the largest in the colony, had to be maintained solely from voluntary subscriptions. This situation irritated its supporters throughout the remainder of Scallan's episcopate. Several applications to London for public funds, and even Governor Hamilton's endorsement, failed to obtain any consideration.

The most contentious issues of Scallan's time, however, were undoubtedly Catholic membership on the Council of Newfoundland and Catholic emancipation generally. The Council, an appointed body, was created by instructions included in Cochrane's commission as governor, as a half-measure toward local government. At its first session, in October 1825, the military commander in Newfoundland, Lieutenant-Colonel Thomas K. Burke, whose position entitled him to membership, took the oaths of office and allegiance but as a Catholic refused the oath of supremacy and the declaration against transubstantiation. Cochrane felt that these could be dispensed with, as in Lower Canada, but the justices present doubted the legality of this procedure and Burke was not seated. The governor immediately made it clear to Colonial Secretary Lord Bathurst that Burke's exclusion from Council could only give offence to the Roman Catholic majority in Newfoundland. In fact, Cochrane obviously intended to constitute a representative body, for within a few months he officially proposed for membership both Scallan, as "Catholic Bishop of Newfoundland," and Patrick Morris*, a leading Catholic merchant. Cochrane described Scallan as "entitled to this distinction from the rank he holds in the Catholic Church . . . as from his private character, which is marked by great liberality of principle, and moderation of conduct." He was not unmindful either that the bishop's influence would command Roman Catholic support for the Council and its decisions.

Bathurst himself had sought to omit the oath of supremacy and the declaration when the Newfoundland commission was in preparation, but it had been the opinion of the English attorney general that, Lower Canada notwithstanding, the constitution prevented the framing of a commission without these requirements. In any case they were now included, and Bathurst felt unable to submit to the king the names of the Catholic nominees. Although the proposal of Scallan and Morris for membership was never general knowledge, Burke's exclusion sparked Catholic resentment, and public agitation was prevented only by the bishop himself, who feared that it would destroy the religious harmony of the colony. Nevertheless, behind the scenes, Morris, apparently with Scallan's support, sent the governor a memorial asking that Newfoundland's Catholics be accorded the same rights and privileges enjoyed by their brethren in other colonies. Despite Cochrane's endorsement of this position, London took no action, and locally the composition of the Council remained a divisive factor.

Pressure for redress of these grievances may have been reduced by the growing expectation of passage of a Catholic relief bill for British subjects generally. Such legislation received royal assent on 13 April 1829, and upon receipt of the news in Newfoundland Scallan declared 21 May a day of public thanksgiving. In St John's and other major towns throughout the island bands, parades, and special church services evidenced the pleasure of Catholics that the penal restrictions of centuries had been lifted. However, their joy was short-lived; by December the colony's attorney general, James Simms*, and the Supreme Court of Newfoundland had concluded that the relief bill was inoperative there. Newfoundland Catholics were informed that the acts of parliament which in 1825 were held to make it necessary that the governor's commission include religious disqualifications for Catholics, did not, after all, apply to Newfoundland. Thus, neither did their repeal. The only legal basis for the disabilities was Cochrane's commission. Issued under royal prerogative, it could not be altered by any act of parliament, not even the new Catholic Relief Act. Newfoundland, with a Roman Catholic majority, was now the only British colony still officially under the old penal laws. Understandably, its Catholics entertained "angry and highly irritated feelings" and, as a result of massive protest meetings at Catholic churches, strongly worded petitions were

forwarded to the British parliament. Although Cochrane and Chief Justice Richard Alexander Tucker* insisted that the matter required urgent attention, London was again indecisive, and Catholic emancipation did not finally come to Newfoundland until the proclamation of representative government and the calling of the first elections on 26 August 1832. In the mean time a new and major source of religious grievance had been allowed to develop.

The last years of his life saw Scallan suffer greatly from physical and mental infirmity. By 1827 his nervous condition had improved somewhat, but his bodily health was failing. In that year he applied to Rome for a coadjutor with the right of succession, submitting as his *terna* the names of Michael Anthony Fleming*, James Sinnott, and Timothy Browne*, all priests of the Newfoundland mission. Fleming had been his curate in St John's since 1823 and, despite what Fleming referred to as "our repeated differences" over religious instruction at the Orphan Asylum Schools, lay control of church repair funds, and attendance at non-Catholic services, he was Scallan's first choice as his successor. Bishop Panet was consulted by Rome, but although he made a favourable comment on Sinnott, who had studied at Quebec, he disqualified himself as having insufficient knowledge. Fleming was formally appointed coadjutor bishop in 1829, and Scallan had the honour of performing the first episcopal consecration in Newfoundland on 28 October of that year. By then Scallan had become almost incapable of fulfilling his duties. "My nerves are a good deal out of order," he wrote; "formerly I could write in straight lines, and tolerably well, but now it is quite otherwise." His mind clear to the end, however, he finally succumbed to his illness on 28 May 1830. He was buried in the yard of the old chapel, but his remains were transferred to the new cathedral in 1850.

Scallan's death was an occasion of real grief for the Newfoundland people. Shops closed; ships' flags flew at half-mast. Scallan was buried as he had lived, with Bishop Fleming and Frederick Hamilton Carrington, the Anglican rector of St John's, standing side by side as chief mourners, with Methodist and Anglican clergy joining Catholic priests in the procession, and with 7,000 persons "of every religious persuasion" taking part in the funeral. He was a beloved bishop, whose piety, kindness, and intelligence had won him universal respect, and who had guided his church wisely through a difficult period. Fleming, no sycophant, called Scallan "the most zealous prelate that ever sat, or perhaps ever will sit, in the episcopal chair of Newfoundland." It was perhaps to his greatest credit that, while he could be adamant in defence of essential Catholic interests, yet he sought always to live in harmony with others. An obituary in the St John's *Newfoundlander* seemed

Schank

to sum up his qualities when it noted: "With his various accomplishments, he combined a lofty zeal for the advancement of religion, wholly free, however, from that bias of intolerance which is some times found in minds deeply imbued with religious feelings." In his latter years his illness obviously hampered him as a bishop and public leader. This was unfortunate, perhaps the more so for one naturally moderate. It must remain a matter for speculation whether in the eventful years from 1825 to 1830 more forceful approaches by the bishop himself might have prodded the government into action concerning Catholic rights, thereby defusing that sense of injustice so central to the bitter sectarian strife which followed his death.

Scallan's ecumenical spirit occasioned considerable controversy. Indeed, Michael Francis Howley*, who attributed such ecumenism to a mental weakness, stated flatly in his *Ecclesiastical history of Newfoundland* that Scallan was censured by Rome, but as the censure arrived only when he was near death, it was never communicated to him. Indeed, this story became a popular myth, encouraged by the striking and unusual monument of Scallan by the Irish sculptor John Hogan in the Cathedral of St John the Baptist in St John's, which had been commissioned by Fleming. It depicts Scallan on his deathbed receiving the last sacraments from his successor and was held to show his reconciliation with the church. However, no evidence of a censure exists either in the Vatican archives or in those of the archdiocese, and Fleming failed to mention it in reporting Scallan's death to Rome. In fact, the earliest foundation for the story seems to be an account of Scallan's activities found in Fleming's *Relazione della missione cattolica in Terranuova*, which was coupled with a general reference to censures imposed during the Reformation on Catholics who frequented heretical services. In times less tolerant than his own, Scallan's ecumenism had likely become an embarrassment which had somehow to be accounted for.

RAYMOND J. LAHEY

[An authentic portrait of Bishop Scallan was in the possession of the Franciscan house in Wexford at the time of the writing of Father Paul, *Wexford friary: a short account of the history and traditions of the Franciscan friary of Wexford* ([Wexford, Republic of Ire.?, 1949]). That portrait (and several others belonging to the house) cannot now be located. It is reproduced in Father Paul's book, but the quality of the reproduction is poor. Another original portrait of Scallan appears in both the *Centenary volume, Benevolent Irish Society of St John's, Newfoundland, 1806–1906* (Cork, [Republic of Ire., 1906?]) and *The centenary of the Basilica-Cathedral of St. John the Baptist, St. John's, Newfoundland, 1855–1955*, ed. P. J. Kennedy ([St John's], n.d.). It is quite possible that this second portrait was also in the possession of the Wexford friary. Its present whereabouts are unknown. R.J.L.]

AAQ, 12 A, K; 210 A, VIII, X, XIII; 10 CM, III–IV; 30 CN, I. Arch. of the Archdiocese of St John's, Scallan papers. Archivio della Propaganda Fide (Rome), Scritture riferite nei Congressi, America Settentrionale, 2 (1792–1830). PRO, CO 194/51, 194/55, 194/59–62, 194/66–76, 194/78, 194/80–81, 194/83, 194/87, 194/92; CO 195/17–18. USPG, C/CAN/Nfl., 3–4; C/CAN/NS, 9. "Documents relating to Wexford friary and parish," comp. Pádraig Ó Súilleabháin, *Collectanea Hibernica* (Dublin and London), 8 (1965): 126–27. M. A. Fleming, "Bishop Fleming to the Very Rev. Mr. Spratt, of Dublin . . . , Sept. 24, 1834," *Catholic Magazine and Rev.* (Birmingham, Eng.), 6 (1835): v–xii; *Relazione della missione cattolica in Terranuova nell'America settentrionale . . .* (Rome, 1837). Patrick Morris, *Remarks on the state of society, religion, morals, and education at Newfoundland . . .* (London, 1827). Newfoundland School Soc., [*Annual report*] (London), 1826–27; *Proposals for instituting a society for the establishment and support of schools in Newfoundland* (London, [1824]). James Sabine, *A view of the moral state of Newfoundland; with a particular reference to the present state of religious toleration in the island* (Boston, 1818). *Newfoundlander* (St John's), 27 Nov. 1828; 14, 28 May, 29 Oct., 31 Dec. 1829; 28 Jan., 3, 10 June 1830; 30 Aug. 1832. *Newfoundland Mercantile Journal*, 11 April 1817; 3 March 1818; 16 Sept. 1824; 5, 18 Jan., 5 Oct. 1826. *Public Ledger*, 22 May, 5 June 1829; 11 June 1830. M. F. Howley, *Ecclesiastical history of Newfoundland* (Boston, 1888; repr. Belleville, Ont., 1979). Johnston, *Hist. of Catholic Church in eastern N.S.* J. T. Mullock, *The Cathedral of St John's, Newfoundland, with an account of its consecration . . .* (Dublin, 1856). Paul O'Neill, *The story of St. John's, Newfoundland* (2v., Erin, Ont., 1975–76).

SCHANK (Schanck, Shank), JOHN, naval officer; b. *c.* 1740 in Scotland, son of Alexander Schank of Castlerig, Fifeshire, and Mary Burnet (Burnett); m. first Mrs Fitzgerald, a widow, and they had a daughter; m. secondly Margaret Grant, sister of Sir William GRANT; d. 6 Feb. 1823 in Dawlish, England.

John Schank entered the Royal Navy as an able seaman on the store-ship *Duke* in 1757 after the onset of the Seven Years' War, having sailed as a boy and young man in the merchant service. He next spent four years in the newly built *Shrewsbury* (74 guns) under Captain Hugh Palliser*. Rated a midshipman in 1761, he served under Captain Charles Douglas* as a midshipman and master's mate in the *Tweed* (32 guns) and later the *Emerald* (32 guns), and then went to the *Princess Amelia* (80 guns) and the *Asia* (64 guns). Schank passed the examination for lieutenant on 10 Jan. 1766 but did not win promotion until 2 Jan. 1776. Four months later he took charge of the *Canceaux* and sailed to Quebec, where he was attached to the squadron under Douglas that had just raised the siege of the town by the Americans [*see* Benedict Arnold*; Richard Montgomery*].

The rivers and lakes of the province of Quebec

694

played a vital role in military operations. In 1775 Montgomery had advanced by way of Lake Champlain and the Richelieu and St Lawrence rivers, not only threatening Quebec but also blocking the only practical route for supplying posts such as Niagara (near Youngstown, N.Y.), Detroit, and Michilimackinac (Mackinaw City, Mich.) on the Great Lakes. Governor Guy Carleton* drove the invaders back in 1776 and created a British naval presence on Lake Champlain, having recaptured Île aux Noix on the Richelieu and established a dockyard there. Schank's "infinite merit" earned him command of that establishment, where he supervised the unprecedentedly speedy construction of a flotilla which included the 300-ton ship *Inflexible*. Schank then commanded *Inflexible* in the British force under Commander Thomas Pringle that destroyed the American squadron led by Benedict Arnold.

In 1777 Schank built several floating bridges for John Burgoyne*'s ill-fated expedition and then at Carleton's request stayed in North America to become commissioner of the lakes. Normally such a position would have been filled by a post-captain, appointed by the Admiralty and reporting directly to the Navy Board in London. Carleton, however, insisted that the Admiralty's jurisdiction did not extend to inland waters. He needed professional support to administer his growing, and vastly dispersed, naval force, but wanted no interference from the British naval establishment. Not surprisingly, because the Royal Navy was very thinly spread when France formed an alliance with the Americans early in 1778, the Admiralty offered no objection to the secondment of an officer of lieutenant's rank to Carleton's marine department.

Schank's commission, signed by Carleton on 28 June 1778, was unequivocal in its delegation of authority, appointing him "Commissioner of all His Majesty's Naval Yards or Docks upon the Lakes, with power to controul and direct the construction repair and equipment of all vessels in the yards and docks aforesaid." Schank evidently insisted on these terms to protect and enhance his career. "I will esteem your Commissions," he told Carleton, "the same as if they were from the Lords of Admiralty," and he entrusted future preferment to his powerful new patron. When Captain Lord John Augustus Hervey, commanding naval forces at Quebec in 1779, asked for Schank's release, Carleton's successor, Frederick Haldimand*, replied, "It would not be reasonable to deprive him of the chance of succeeding in his Profession, expressly reserved to him, and for which he has been recommended to me by the First Lord of the Admiralty."

Haldimand permitted Schank to run the marine department, so far as circumstances permitted, along Admiralty lines. With three separate commands, on Lake Champlain, Lake Ontario, and lakes Erie, Huron, and Michigan, Haldimand and Schank leaned heavily on the Royal Navy for seamen, but for the most part depended on provincials to serve as shipwrights, artificers, and ships' officers. An effort was made to give a share of responsibility to Canadians, and several of them, including Jean-Baptiste Bouchette* in 1777, were awarded commissions and served on Lake Ontario. This framework of operations, consolidated under Schank's direction, governed the system by which the Provincial Marine would defend and develop inland navigation until the War of 1812. Schank's devotion to duty and his innovative adaptation of armed vessels for lake service was recognized when Haldimand exerted the necessary influence in the Admiralty to secure promotion for his protégé, to commander on 4 April 1780 and post-captain on 15 Aug. 1783.

Schank went home in 1784 and was placed on half pay. He directed his energies to an invention he had experimented with in 1774, a sliding keel that operated on the principle of a modern centre-board. The Navy Board in 1791 approved the construction of some vessels with this device, and it became standard on many small warships, including the survey brig *Lady Nelson*, which sailed around the world. In 1794 John Graves Simcoe* asked for Schank's services in Upper Canada, but he was in demand elsewhere as an agent of transports. From 1795 to 1801 he served as one of the commissioners of the Transport Board and, profiting from his experience in the province of Quebec, superintended great improvements to coast defences in England.

Failing eyesight forced Schank out of active employment in 1802, but he rose steadily in the flag list, being promoted rear-admiral of the blue on 9 Nov. 1805 and admiral of the blue on 19 July 1821. He died at his home in Dawlish, Devon, on 6 Feb. 1823 and was survived by his wife. His daughter, Margaret, who had married Schank's cousin and protégé Captain John Wight, had died in 1812. A fellow of the Royal Society, Schank was known as "Old Purchase" from his invention of a cot which could be raised and lowered by its occupant with ropes and pulleys.

In 1786 Schank had received the freedom of the city of Edinburgh "in testimony of the good services done to his King and Country as Captain and Senior Officer and Commissioner of H.M. Fleet on the lakes and rivers in Canada." By the end of his days, as one epitaph declares, he had "by his ability zeal and integrity raised himself to the highest rank in his profession and closed an honourable life after a service of sixty years."

W. A. B. DOUGLAS

BL, Add. MSS 21712, 21720, 21745, 21800–3, 21805 (mfm. at PAC). Can., Parks Canada, Hist. Research Division

Schwindt

(Ottawa), Carol MacLeod, "The tap of the garrison drum: the Marine Service in British North America, 1775–1813" (1983). McCord Museum, John Schank, letter-book, 1778–80. MTL, James Andrews corr., 1779. NMM, Pitcairn Jones, notes on sea officers; MID/1/164 (Schank to Middleton, 26 Feb. 1791); PNS/4 (letters relating to building of HMS *Wolverine*, sloop); RUSI/NM/13 ("A list of HM armed vessels upon the Canadian Lakes, St Lawrence & Provincial Service," 1780); RUSI/NM/86 (1) ("Description of a model of a frigate with three sliding keels, suggested by Captain Schank to the Duke of Northumberland," n.d.). PAC, MG 23, HI, 1, ser.3 (transcripts); RG 8, I (C ser.), 722A. PRO, ADM 1/2486; ADM 12/55/59. *Corr. of Lieut. Governor Simcoe* (Cruikshank). *Naval documents of the American revolution*, ed. W. B. Clarke and W. J. Morgan (8v. to date, Washington, 1964–ं), 6–8. *Biographie universelle* (Michaud et Desplaces). *DNB. Genealogical memoranda, relating to the family of Schank, or Shank of Casterig, in the county of Fife, N.B.* (London, 1885). G.B., Admiralty, *The commissioned sea officers of the Royal Navy, 1660–1815*, [ed. D. B. Smith et al.] (3v., n.p., [1954]). John Marshall, *Royal naval biography* . . . (4v. in 6 and 2v. supp., London, 1823–35), 1: 324–32.

[Secondary sources make very few references to Schank. The items mentioned here, except for my article, are simply standard works covering events connected with his life. W.A.B.D.] G. A. Cuthbertson, *Freshwater: a history and a narrative of the Great Lakes* (Toronto, 1931). R. McC. Hatch, *Thrust for Canada: the American attempt on Quebec in 1775–1776* (Boston, 1979). Neatby, *Quebec*. W. M. Wallace, *Traitorous hero; the life and fortunes of Benedict Arnold* (New York, [1954]). C. [L.] Ward, *The war of the revolution*, ed. J. R. Alden (2v., New York, 1952). W. A. B. Douglas, "The anatomy of naval incompetence: the Provincial Marine in defence of Upper Canada before 1813," *OH*, 71 (1979): 3–25.

SCHWINDT. *See* GSCHWIND

SCOTT, CHRISTOPHER, businessman and ship's captain; b. *c.* 1762 in Greenock, Scotland; d. 29 July 1833 in London.

Christopher Scott was the third and youngest son of William Scott, head of the old Clyde shipbuilding firm of Scott and Company. Scott Sr died in 1769 and his elder sons greatly extended the firm's activity, moving into the construction of large West-Indiamen, smaller ships for the Nova Scotia trade, and naval frigates; they were also to pioneer the building of steamships. Christopher served an apprenticeship as a mariner in the company's vessels and as a ship-designer and master builder in its yards.

In the wartime years of the late 1790s, as a result of heavy losses of merchant ships to French privateers, vessels were at a premium in Great Britain, and in January 1799 Christopher Scott was sent out to New Brunswick to establish a yard and thus take advantage of the colony's unlimited supplies of building timber, increasingly scarce and expensive in Scotland. He sailed from Greenock with two of the firm's ships; on board were 50 skilled craftsmen, including carpenters, blacksmiths, caulkers, and shipwrights, and a complete crew for the first vessel to be built. Cordage, copper nails and sheathing, iron fittings, and all the tools and machinery for a shipyard were also taken out – an early example in the modern western world of the complete transfer of an industrial installation. In addition, a large quantity of trade goods – woollens and linens – was carried, for much of New Brunswick's commerce was conducted by barter. Scott reached Saint John in March 1799 and by July had three sizeable vessels under construction. Soon after his arrival he met a local builder, William Barlow, whom he described as "a natural-born exponent of our art, with an eye for the practical use of his native timbers which makes it essential that we employ him." A fruitful working partnership between Scott and Barlow resulted, and the yard prospered.

As the demand in Britain for vessels accelerated, the home partners constantly urged Scott to lay down as many keels as possible and also to purchase any new ships he could obtain from other builders. In defiance of the British embargo on the export of copper fittings imposed in 1799, the Scotts smuggled out large quantities to Saint John. Further skilled craftsmen were sent out by the Greenock firm, as well as complete crews, from commanders to cabin-boys, for the new ships. In the years 1799–1804 some 25 vessels were constructed, most of them for immediate sale in London, Liverpool, and the West Indies, to whose ports they were dispatched with highly profitable cargoes of timber. The building of ships as a speculation was a practice that had begun on the Clyde in slack times in the 1760s. The Scotts now introduced it to the colonies, and made handsome gains from it. In 1804 the Scott yards were employing more than 400 workers.

The Scotts were early influenced by the ideas of Robert Seppings, a contemporary British naval architect, and quickly adopted his method of shipbuilding. It involved a heavy construction for the lower part of the vessel, using a much greater quantity of heavy timbers as cross-ties and reinforced lower ribs, so that the keel and the basic structure were "almost a solid bed of timber." The method made for a much sturdier, though more expensive, vessel and, when linked with Barlow's plans for vessels with sharper lines, produced ships which were at once fine-lined and solid, a much desired combination. No better vessels were produced in Saint John in the early years of the 19th century than those built by Scott and Barlow in conjunction. By 1804 the home partners were stating explicitly that all new vessels be constructed under Barlow's direction. These ships helped obtain for New Brunswick the high reputation as a shipbuilding centre that it enjoyed for the next century. Up to this time, vessels built in the colonies had tended to be regarded in Britain as rather second-rate in sturdiness and sea-going capacity. Scott and Barlow between them changed this estimate.

By 1801 Scott had embarked on the purchasing and exporting of timber on an even larger scale, and on general trading as well, collecting cargoes of potash, beech, pine, and black birch (much in demand for furniture-making) from various parts of New Brunswick and shipping them to Britain. Most of these goods came down the Saint John River and were paid for in rum from the Greenock distilleries and in soft goods, ironware, and other Scottish exports.

In 1803 Scott launched into shipowning on his own account, designing and constructing several small, but extremely well-built, brigs for operation on the Atlantic run, to take advantage of rapidly escalating freight rates. As a qualified master mariner he commanded one of these, the *Mary*, on two highly profitable voyages to the Clyde with timber, but in May 1805 she was taken and sunk by a French privateer off the island of Barra in the Outer Hebrides. Fortunately the *Mary* was insured, and Scott was able to purchase a large new vessel, the *Wilson*, in Liverpool, for which he immediately took out letters of marque as a privateer. No captures are recorded in his name. From 1805 to 1809 he captained voyages in his own ships, transporting timber cargoes to Britain and to Jamaica and other West Indian islands, occasionally spending periods of several months ashore to supervise his mercantile affairs.

Scott pursued his timber and shipbuilding activities successfully from Saint John until 1810, when he moved to St Andrews to take advantage of the lucrative trading which had opened up with the imposition in 1807 of the United States' "embargo" and "non-intercourse" policies against Great Britain and her colonies. He quickly became a leading citizen of the town, building a large warehouse where he stored silks, muslins, fine linens and cottons, and elegant furniture from Scotland. These he traded illegally, "on the line" along the coast of Maine and Passamaquoddy Bay, in return for tobacco, cotton, flour, and other American produce which he re-exported at a handsome profit to Britain. It was a dangerous enterprise, condemned by both the American government and, after 1812, the New Brunswick authorities, and further complicated by the presence of freebooting Americans who robbed traders and preyed on coastal shipping. Scott nevertheless succeeded in maintaining this trade and he amassed a considerable fortune from it. In addition, he speculated in "bargains" among the prize ships and cargoes auctioned off at Halifax.

When war broke out in 1812, Scott provided money for the construction of the fine "Block-house" or fort which still stands at St Andrews, and in 1822 he paid for the completion of the town's wooden Greenock (Presbyterian) Church, employing architects in Scotland and Scottish craftsmen from his Saint John shipyard. It is still there, an outstanding example of a fine "colonial" church, and bears on its tower a wooden representation of the oak tree, the device both of Greenock and of the firm of Scott. By 1820 Scott was regarded as one of the richest men in New Brunswick, with his extensive shipyard in Saint John, a mansion in St Andrews, town lots in both locations, a landed estate on the banks of the Saint John River, several farms around St Andrews, and two estates in his native Scotland. In addition, he owned eight vessels, held shares in steamships (with John BLACK and others), was part-owner of ships in the West Indies trade and numerous fishing boats, and was associated with partnerships engaged in flour- and grain-milling. His collection of silver plate and valuable furniture was extensive.

In April 1820, seeing the crippling lack of credit and cash in the colony, Scott, along with John ROBINSON and other businessmen, took a leading part in founding the Bank of New Brunswick. There was a pressing need to provide loan-capital to enable local timber-merchants to compete with large-scale operators such as the Glasgow-based and dominating firm of Pollok, Gilmour and Company [*see* Alexander Rankin*], and the new bank was founded on "the Scotch Commercial principle" of cash credits (bank loans given without collateral security on the basis of the borrower's reputation and obvious means). Of the 20 original directors, 9 were Scots traders, and Scott was pre-eminent among them as a shareholder. Two years later, in 1822, he took the leading part in establishing yet another bank on the "Scotch principle," the Charlotte County Bank, with its headquarters in his own town of St Andrews. Scott was listed as second among its promoters and directors, 25 in all, of whom 15 were Scots traders and businessmen. The bank was a success, but its first minute-book shows only too clearly that it faced enormous difficulties in its early years. By 1825 economic depression had affected the colony. The demand for New Brunswick–built ships fell away to nothing, there was a timber-glut on the British market, and mercantile houses in Saint John collapsed. Yet the two banks in which Scott was involved rode out the crisis and by 1828 had reached the point where profits were beginning to be made.

Scott was regarded by his Greenock kin as something of an "adventurer." He never married, but his will mentions "my reputed illegitimate son," William Scott, to whom he left a considerable part of his fortune. He died on 29 July 1833 in England, having played a leading part in the development of New Brunswick's shipbuilding industry and trade.

DAVID S. MACMILLAN

N.B. Museum, Christopher Scott papers; F86, will of

Scott

Christopher Scott. Univ. of Glasgow Arch., GD 319/
11/1–3. *N.S. vital statistics, 1829–34* (Holder and Hubley).
Esther Clark Wright, *The Saint John River* (Toronto, 1949).
M. N. Cockburn, *A history of Greenock Church, St. An-
drews, New Brunswick, from 1821 to 1906* (n.p., 1906).
Macmillan, "New men in action," *Canadian business hist.*
(Macmillan), 44–103. *Two centuries of shipbuilding by the
Scotts at Greenock* (2nd ed., London, 1920). Daniel Weir,
History of the town of Greenock (Greenock, Scot., and
London, 1829). D. S. Macmillan, "Shipbuilding in New
Brunswick ..." and "Christopher Scott: smuggler, priva-
teer, and financier," *Canadian Banker* (Toronto), 77 (1970),
no.1: 34–36, and 78 (1971), no.3: 23–26.

SCOTT, THOMAS, office holder, judge, and politician; baptized 18 Oct. 1746 in the parish of King-
oldrum, Scotland, son of the Reverend Thomas Scott;
d. 29 July 1824 in York (Toronto), Upper Canada.

Aspiring to a position in the British gentry, Thomas
Scott first sought to follow in his father's footsteps by
training for the ministry of the established Church of
Scotland. When he failed to obtain a posting, he
became a tutor in the house of Sir John Riddell in the
south of Scotland; in later years he became the
Riddells' benefactor. From an early age he also
assumed responsibility for the support of his younger
brother, William. These commitments were to intensify his career-long quest for financial security.

In 1788 he journeyed south to Lincoln's Inn in
London to study law and was called to the bar in 1793.
Unable to establish himself comfortably in Britain, in
1800 he accepted the appointment of attorney general
of Upper Canada, which came with a promise of
eventual preferment for the chief justiceship. He was
already in his 55th year. In Upper Canada Scott sought
to make himself indispensable to Lieutenant Governor
Peter Hunter*, who had supported his appointment.
Besides attending to his legal duties, Scott plunged
into an exhausting round of political activities, becoming second in influence only to Henry Allcock*,
the chief justice after 1802. Both men supported
Hunter's policy of rushing the preparation of land
patents to remove the confusion regarding land title in
the province. The program increased their income
from fees, but antagonized many settlers struggling to
meet the costs of establishing new farms. The strain of
Scott's duties probably contributed to the ill health
which plagued his later career.

In 1805 the attorney general was appointed to the
Executive Council and reached the height of his
political influence. With Hunter dead and a figurehead
– Alexander Grant* – in control of the government,
Scott and John McGill, the inspector general, blocked the aspirations of rival officials and briefly became
the colony's most powerful politicians. Scott was now
expected to exercise political skills which he did not
possess in abundance. Opposition to the government's
land policy was growing in the assembly. Yet acting

on Scott's advice, Grant attempted to usurp financial
appropriations which were rightly within the control
of the elected body, thus furnishing an opening to the
opposition. The situation was exacerbated by the
rivalry of Scott and Robert Thorpe*, a judge of the
Court of King's Bench, for the position of chief
justice, now vacant with the transfer of Allcock to
Lower Canada. Thorpe sought to attract attention by
joining the critics of the administration, but this move
only led to his dismissal.

In 1806 Scott was made a member of the Legislative
Council and finally received the appointment of chief
justice. Almost immediately he attempted to minimize
further responsibilities. He refused to be considered
for promotion to chief justice of Lower Canada on the
grounds that "at my time of life, it is too arduous an
undertaking for me to attempt." Although expected to
serve as the lieutenant governor's major adviser, he
declined further involvement in provincial politics.
Describing Scott's contributions on matters of state as
"water gruel," the new head of government, Francis
Gore*, turned to William Dummer POWELL, another
judge of the King's Bench, as his chief adviser. In
1811 Scott applied for a pension to enable him to retire
in dignity. Unsuccessful in obtaining it, he was forced
to remain the leading judicial officer of the province
during its years of greatest turmoil.

The War of 1812 marked a crisis of authority for the
ruling gentry. They doubted the loyalty of the colony's largely American-born population. In vain the
leading officials advocated the selective suspension of
civil liberties and the imposition of martial law; they
were blocked until 1814 by members of the assembly
such as Abraham MARKLE who were reluctant to
antagonize their constituents. As a distinguished
resident of York, Scott played a modest role in
encouraging order, but was easily outshone by more
energetic men such as Powell and the Reverend John
Strachan*. Scott filled a similar function during the
trials of 1814 which were intended to reassert the
authority of the state. The strategy of the government
was to manipulate the provisions of the law to strike a
balance of terror and mercy. Consequently, while the
courts convicted 15 persons, including Jacob Overholser*, of treason, only 8 were executed, the sentences of the remainder being commuted to banishment.
Scott supported these decisions, but the initiative
came from others, especially Attorney General John
Beverley Robinson*.

In 1816 the chief justice finally received the pension
he needed for retirement. He spent his last years
quietly in York where he died in 1824. Ever loyal to
his personal commitments, he left an estate sufficient
to support his brother in Scotland for the rest of his
life. In his public career, however, Scott had been less
successful. While his judicial opinions had been
competent, he showed little liking for the wider

responsibilities expected of legal officers in this period. His failings were partly the product of old age and uncertain health. Yet, his record was similar to that of many administrators who were drawn to this remote colony during its first generations of existence.

WILLIAM N. T. WYLIE

AO, RG 22, ser.125, 1–2; ser.134, 1–2; ser.155. MTL, William Allan papers, Thomas Scott papers; D. W. Smith papers, B8, Scott to Smith, 20 Oct. 1803, 10 March 1804. PAC, MG 11, [CO 42] Q, 298, pt.I: 2, 25; 300: 226; 303: 155; 308, pt.I: 68; 311, pt.I: 57–59; 312, pt.I: 34, 151, 153; 313, pt.II: 518; 316: 281; 318, pt.I: 133, 137; 319: 106–7; 320: 191–94; MG 24, A6, civil letter-book, 42; RG 1, E1, 47–50; L1, 22: 665, 803; 23: 278; 24: 69, 285, 308; 26: 185; L3, 452: S5/55, 93; 453: S7/40; 455: S9/82; 464A: S15/88; 490: S leases/49; RG 5, A1: 8326–28, 8729–33, 8805–7. "Political state of U.C.," PAC *Report*, 1892. *Town of York, 1793–1815* (Firth); *1815–34* (Firth). Read, *Lives of the judges.* Cowdell Gates, *Land policies of U.C.* W. R. Riddell, *The bar and the courts of the province of Upper Canada or Ontario* (Toronto, 1928); *The legal profession in Upper Canada in its early periods* (Toronto, 1916). J. B. Walton, "An end to all order: a study of Upper Canadian Conservative response to opposition, 1805–1810" (MA thesis, Queen's Univ., Kingston, Ont., 1977). W. N. T. Wylie, "Instruments of commerce and authority: the civil courts in Upper Canada, 1789–1812," *Essays in the history of Canadian law*, ed. D. H. Flaherty (2v., [Toronto], 1981–83), 2: 3–48. W. R. Riddell, "Thomas Scott, the second attorney-general of Upper Canada," *OH*, 20 (1923): 126–44.

SELBY, GEORGE, physician, surgeon, office holder, militia officer, and seigneur; baptized 14 Feb. 1760 in Stanton, England, son of George Selby and Ann Robson; m. 24 Aug. 1785 Marie-Josèphe Dunbar in Montreal; d. there 15 May 1835.

Armed with his diploma as a medical doctor from the University of Edinburgh, George Selby emigrated to the province of Quebec around 1782 and settled in Montreal. Despite his youth, in August of that year he obtained the post of chief surgeon at the Hôpital Général, which Louis-Nicolas Landriaux* had held for 16 years. On 5 September, following a request from the grand jury of Montreal, he, along with his colleagues Charles Blake*, Jean-Baptiste Jobert, and Robert Sym, signed a report on the Baie-Saint-Paul malady [see Philippe-Louis-François Badelard*]. The authors of the report proclaimed in tones of alarm the rapid spread of the disease and its disastrous consequences. They thought that they were dealing with syphilis, and recommended that a committee of the most eminent doctors and of people familiar with the internal organization of the colony study the means most suitable to bring the disease under control. Their suggestion was not, however, taken up.

In 1785 Selby was again associated with the struggle against the illness. In April, in accordance with new measures taken by Lieutenant Governor Henry Hamilton*, Dr James Bowman* of Quebec was officially delegated to visit all the parishes in the province and distribute remedies and advice through the clergy. Bowman immediately entered into correspondence with some of his English-speaking colleagues, including Selby. Selby communicated his observations to him on 21 April. He recognized that the disease was a venereal one and maintained that calomel, a mercury-based preparation, had proven the most effective remedy. That month, at Hamilton's request, Bowman charged Selby with seeing that no voyageur leaving for the *pays d'en haut* was a carrier. On 8 September he asked him to treat those affected in Montreal. A list dated 23 April 1786 reveals that Selby reportedly had treated and cured 94 people. He asked the government for £213 for the cures and for examining the voyageurs. Despite his numerous representations, he seems never to have received the money.

The several offices that Selby held simultaneously indicate the excellent reputation he enjoyed. He became in turn one of the first medical examiners for the District of Montreal (1788) [see Charles Blake], commissioner for the care of the insane and foundlings (1801), doctor of the Hôtel-Dieu in Montreal (1807), and surgeon to Montreal's 1st Militia Battalion (1812). He was also doctor of the Montreal prison from at least 1829.

Selby threw himself wholeheartedly into all these responsibilities. In 1818, for example, he opposed a £2,000 grant that the government was offering the nuns of the Hôpital Général to build more cells for the insane and carry out other repairs [see Thérèse-Geneviève COUTLÉE; William HOLMES]. According to Selby, locking up this kind of patient in tiny and often insalubrious cells "serves only to rid the Public of a nuisance, but is noways beneficial to the victims of that horrid disease." He noted that the primary aim of the Hôpital Général was to provide care for the aged and infirm and for foundlings, not to serve as a lunatic asylum. Asylums, he stated, "ought not to be prisons, nor hospitals for bodily disease"; rather, what was needed was "a house of a peculiar structure, with three or four acres of adjacent ground . . . for the attainment of regular and efficient treatment."

Selby led a comfortable life in Montreal and was in easy circumstances. In 1785, when he married Marie-Josèphe Dunbar, a daughter of Major William Dunbar, granddaughter of Joseph Fleury* Deschambault, and niece of William Grant*, he was already able to guarantee her a jointure of 48,000 *livres*. In 1789 he paid £400 for a stone house on Rue Saint-Paul which he made his permanent residence, and in 1791 he hired a manservant. In 1806 he was owed £925 by the joint estate of Marie-Charles-Joseph Le Moyne* de Lon-

Sewell

gueuil, Baronne de Longueuil, and her husband David Alexander Grant, who had just died. In addition to his house in Montreal, at his death in 1835 Selby owned some land on the road to Lachine three miles from Montreal, and he had also been co-owner of the seigneury of La Salle since 1829. By the terms of his will the usufruct of his estate was left to Marguerite, the daughter of François Baby* and widow of his only son, William Dunbar Selby, who had also been a doctor but had died in 1829.

George Selby was a respected citizen and one of the most eminent doctors in Montreal. Among his acquaintances and clients were such prominent people as Benjamin Frobisher*, who was his intimate friend, Bishop Pierre Denaut*, and Simon McTavish*, the leading businessman in the province during the second half of the 18th century. In 1804 McTavish had bequeathed £700 to him and his son. "In the 50 years he had practised in this country," *La Minerve* commented at the time of his death, "he had acquired and retained an outstanding reputation in his profession, and his personal qualities were appreciated by all who knew him."

RENALD LESSARD

ANQ-M, CE1-12, 5 août 1787; CE1-51, 24 août 1785, 18 mai 1835; CM1, 27 mai 1835; CN1-29, 5 oct. 1791; CN1-74, 8 mars 1804; CN1-128, 15 avril 1789; CN1-194, 4–5 janv. 1802; CN1-290, 23 août 1785. AUM, P 58, Q1/76. Northumberland Record Office (Newcastle upon Tyne, Eng.), Reg. of baptisms for the parish of Longhorsley, 14 Feb. 1760. PAC, MG 11, [CO 42] Q, 47: 326–28; 66: 368–71; RG 1, E1, 14: 263; L3L: 85943–46; RG 4, A1: 10994–95; A3, 2, pt.I, no.D.202; 3, no.72; B43, 1: 483–86; 2: 761–75. *Docs. relating to constitutional hist., 1759–91* (Shortt and Doughty; 1918), 2: 742–52. L.C., House of Assembly, *Journals*, 1816–35; Legislative Council, *Journals*, 1824, app.D, no.4. *La Minerve*, 18 mai 1835. *Montreal Gazette*, 8 Aug. 1803; 30 Oct. 1809; 25 May 1812; 5, 16 May 1835. *Quebec Gazette*, 4 Aug. 1803, 2 Sept. 1813. Giroux *et al.*, *Inv. des marchés de construction des ANQ-M*, 2, no.1483. *Quebec almanac*, 1791, 1812–13. Abbott, *Hist. of medicine*, 77. Renald Lessard, "Le mal de la baie Saint-Paul, la société et les autorités coloniales, 1775–1791" (thèse de MA, univ. Laval, Québec, 1983). J.-J. Lefebvre et Édouard Desjardins, "Le docteur George Selby, médecin de l'Hôtel-Dieu de 1807 à 1829, et sa famille," *L'Union médicale du Canada* (Montréal), 100 (1971): 1592–94.

SEWELL (Sewall), STEPHEN, lawyer, landowner, militia officer, office holder, and politician; b. *c.* 25 May 1770 in Cambridge, Mass., son of Jonathan Sewell (Sewall) and Esther Quincy; m. 18 June 1801 Jane Caldwell in Montreal, and they had at least six children; d. there 21 June 1832.

The younger son of a prominent loyalist who was the last British attorney general of Massachusetts,

Stephen Sewall was only five when his family emigrated to England at the beginning of the War of American Independence. In 1778 the Sewalls – the name was at some point changed to Sewell – settled in Bristol, where Stephen attended grammar school and at home absorbed his parents' fear of democracy and their fervent desire that he and his elder brother, Jonathan*, recoup what the family had lost in America.

In 1787 Stephen and his parents recrossed the ocean to join Jonathan, who had earlier immigrated to Saint John, N.B. Stephen followed his brother into the legal office of Ward CHIPMAN, and was called to the New Brunswick bar in 1791. Like Jonathan before him, he decided – later that year – to seek his fortune in the larger colony of Lower Canada, whose governor was Lord Dorchester [Guy Carleton*], patron of the loyalists. This decision evinced a permanent character trait: the desire to model his career after that of his elder brother. To the latter he had confessed in 1790, "It has been always my ambition to follow as nearly in your footsteps as I was capable and beleive me it always will be."

After obtaining his commission as a lawyer on 16 Dec. 1791, Sewell established himself in Montreal and began the pursuit of clients, who would soon include many of the leading merchants and wealthier seigneurs. By 1805 he had one of the most flourishing practices in the city, and from it he reputedly drew between £600 and £800 a year. He was less fortunate in his many business investments, among them the Company of Proprietors of the Montreal Water Works [*see* John GRAY], at least one high-risk venture to the West Indies in 1816–17, and extensive speculation in real estate in Lower Canada; he acquired 1,000 acres of land in Grenville Township in 1797, was granted 3,200 acres in Hemmingford Township in 1811, and owned land in Montreal.

Sewell was a staunch adherent of the English party in Lower Canada, and his most notable enthusiasm was ferreting out spies and revolutionaries. Like many others of his party during the wars against revolutionary France, he was convinced that at the appearance of even the smallest French force the Canadians would rise in arms and massacre the British minority. In the aftermath of riots against militia service in 1794 he was one of the organizers of cartridge making and other preparations to defend Montreal against what proved to be a phantom horde of armed habitants. During disturbances protesting the road act of 1796 Sewell believed the story of Montreal tavern-keeper Elmer Cushing that Citizen Pierre-Auguste Adet, the French minister to the United States, had come in person to Montreal to hatch a "plan for the extirpation of the English." With more reason he accepted his informer's claim that one of Adet's agents had attempted to recruit a fifth column. Sewell hurried

Cushing down to Quebec to see his brother, then attorney general. Promised an entire township for his evidence, Cushing swore a deposition describing the activities of the agent, David McLane*. McLane was arrested in the capital in May 1797, convicted of treason in July, and on the 21st of that month hanged, beheaded, and disembowelled as an example to others.

Sewell remained nervous and alert throughout the Napoleonic period. In 1801 he convinced himself that the parish priests north of Montreal were conspiring to aid a leader of the Canadian party in the House of Assembly, Joseph Papineau*, in his determination "to [be] a Buoniparte in this province." A series of fires in the city during the summer of 1803 was put down to the "great design which the Emissaries of France have on this Country," Sewell having earlier decided that Napoleon would "make every possible Exertion to land troops in the Province" and that "the Canadians will join them in numbers." "Heaven only knows," he concluded, "if we do not stand On the brink of destruction." In 1801, and again during a political crisis in 1810 [see Sir James Henry Craig*], he employed a Canadian informer to report on disloyalty among the captains of militia. Sewell himself joined Montreal's 1st Militia Battalion, a British unit, as an ensign about 1803; he became a captain in 1812. An attempt in 1814 by Canadian lawyers to establish an advocates' society – which Sewell helped to abort – was characteristically interpreted as the work of "Jacobins." Sewell made sure that Jonathan and, through him, the governor were kept informed of his activities, for visible loyalty was a common route to the government posts he coveted.

Sewell's longstanding efforts, and those of his brother, who became chief justice in 1808, succeeded the following year when he was named by Governor Craig to replace James Stuart*, recently dismissed for political unreliability, as solicitor general of Lower Canada; the office was worth about £1,700 a year in salary and fees. In November 1809 Sewell won a seat in the House of Assembly for Huntingdon County along with a leader of the Canadian party, Jean-Antoine Panet*. The contest had been hotly disputed: after 15 days of polling Panet obtained 897 votes to Sewell's 895, and the loser, Augustin Cuvillier*, protested Sewell's election in February 1810. However, Craig dissolved the legislature on 1 March, and in the subsequent elections Sewell was returned along with Joseph Papineau in Montreal East, Stuart being a defeated candidate. Like many others of his circle, Sewell thought Craig's imprisonment of certain Canadian political leaders in March – the so-called Reign of Terror – an heroic and infinitely wise act of statesmanship, but he was soon disappointed to learn that the imperial authority had quietly repudiated any further aggressive actions, including enforcement of

claims to royal supremacy over the Roman Catholic Church and a proposed suspension of the constitution. As usual Sewell and his friends proved to be more imperialist than the imperial government.

In 1811 Craig was replaced by Sir George Prevost*, who, requiring the support of the population as war with the United States loomed, adopted a conciliatory policy towards Canadian leaders. Sewell and his colleagues in the English party were outraged by the resulting deprivation of influence and patronage they suffered. They responded in part with a series of vitriolic letters to the Montreal Herald in 1814–15 attacking Prevost's civil and military administration. The most damning letters, signed Veritas, attributed the British retreats from Sackets Harbor, N.Y., in 1813 and Plattsburgh in 1814 to cowardice and stupidity on Prevost's part. Suspicious, despite Sewell's denials that he had authored the letters, the governor cleverly ordered him to prosecute the printer and the editor of the Montreal Herald for criminal libel. The editor, Mungo Kay, thereupon revealed that Sewell had written and brought to him in great secrecy an unsigned article entitled "Particulars of the late disastrous affair on Lake Champlain," which was published shortly after the Plattsburgh débâcle. Sewell admitted authorship but asserted that the piece was simply a review of the facts. Although the article was less explicitly critical than the polemics of Veritas, its conclusion left little doubt about what the writer thought of Prevost's strategy. "A few minutes more would have given up the fortifications . . . into our hands, and every American must have fallen, or been made prisoner," he wrote. Instead, "it was thought necessary to check the ardor of the troops" and control of the lake was lost. Sewell was suspended from office immediately, and in July 1816 he was dismissed by Governor Sir John Coape Sherbrooke following a report on the matter by the Executive Council.

Thereafter a great deal of Sewell's energy was expended in seeking rehabilitation. The chief justice operated under a standing injunction to work for his brother's interest whenever an office remotely suitable became vacant and to work fast, since, as Stephen put it in 1825, "there is no time ever to be lost in looking after Appointments." Jonathan pleaded with Governor Lord Dalhousie [Ramsay*] to restore the office of solicitor general to his brother, but to no avail. Nor could he, despite repeated attempts, satisfy Stephen's most cherished ambition, which was to follow him to the bench. The chief justice seems, however, to have been able to influence the granting of some minor posts and honours. In any case Sewell was named secretary to boundary commissioner John Ogilvy* (1817), a warden of the House of Industry in Montreal (1818), a commissioner for the repair of the Montreal prison

(1819), and a commissioner for the construction of the Lachine Canal (1821).

As secretary to Ogilvy, Sewell kept a journal of the boundary commission's work between May and September 1817 along the St Lawrence River from Saint-Régis to Cornwall, Upper Canada. In it he recorded meteorological observations and commented on geological structures, soil conditions, flora, and fauna. He also had a clear eye for revealing details of social life. Thus he remarked that Highland settlers made poor farmers but good militiamen, that it was the women who ran the farms – "in fact they are the supports of their husbands and families" – and that their daughters furnished Montreal with servants. He saw that "the manners of the St Regis Indians are fast changing to European their dress resembles the Canadians." Although the immigrants who passed by in bateau loads on the St Lawrence on their way to Upper Canada were not dressed in rags, there was an "appearance of great want amongst them," and he noted that "they frequently lament having quitted their own country." Their plight touched him, and he found it "a subject of great regret that Government in times of such extreme pressure should have deemed it proper to deprive the new settlers of their rations." He was also highly attentive to economic trends as trade with Upper Canada expanded and the machine age dawned in the colonies. Thus, he observed that Lower Canadian villages such as Vaudreuil, Les Cèdres, and Coteau-du-Lac could be developed around mills and factories using water-driven machinery, and that transportation procedures could be made more efficient on the heavily used section of the St Lawrence between Cornwall and Montreal.

In Montreal Sewell was active in community affairs. Early in the century he served on a committee for the erection of Christ Church [see Jehosaphat Mountain*]. In 1820 he acted as the senior attorney of the Royal Institution for the Advancement of Learning to negotiate the transfer from James McGill*'s estate of the Burnside property on which McGill College was to be built [see François Desrivières]. He was a principal founder seven years later of the Natural History Society of Montreal, of which he became president. In 1828 he was among the founders of a lawyers' library, which became the Advocates' Library and Law Institute of Montreal in 1830 and ultimately the Montreal bar library; he also served as the library's first president.

As a lawyer Sewell could not equal his brother's ability to go quickly to the nub of a complicated legal problem or to ground a conclusion in general principle as well as precedent. He was able, however, to weigh both sides of a case intelligently; he prepared thoroughly and was well read in both the common and the civil law systems. Sherbrooke's unfavourable opinion of Sewell's capacities at the time of his dismissal can

probably be discounted; the lawyer's clientele suggests high competence, and La Minerve, which was hardly sympathetic politically, observed after his death that his "knowledge of law made him one of our leading jurists." In 1827 Dalhousie had appointed him a king's counsel. His talent as a lawyer and his loyalty were much in demand in the spring of 1832 following an election riot in Montreal West during which regular troops had fired on a crowd, killing three Canadians [see Daniel Tracey]. He acted as legal adviser to the commanding officers, Lieutenant-Colonel Alexander Fisher MacIntosh and Captain Henry Temple, and in his capacity as king's counsel and doyen of the Montreal bar he later assisted in the deliberations of the Court of King's Bench that resulted in the freeing of the two officers, an outcome ardently desired by Governor Lord Aylmer [Whitworth-Aylmer*].

Sewell had less than three weeks to congratulate himself and imagine the favours soon to flow from government. In the early morning of 21 June he was struck down by cholera, and he died a few hours later. He left a comfortable home as well as moveable property valued at nearly £600. The library of more than 900 volumes alone was worth £215. His properties included a farm and lot in the seigneury of Prairie-de-la-Madeleine and 3,400 acres of township lands. However, unfortunate investments had continued to sink him in financial difficulties, and after 1817 he had avoided bankruptcy only through the generosity of his brother; in October 1832 his debts totalled £7,256, of which nearly £3,000 was owed to Jonathan. The estate was insolvent; his widow, Jane, and their six children, of whom two were minors, were obliged to renounce it.

F. Murray Greenwood

Stephen Sewell is the author of "Particulars of the late disastrous affair on Lake Champlain," published in the Montreal Herald, 17 Sept. 1814. He may also have written The letters of Veritas, re-published from the "Montreal Herald"; containing a succinct narrative of the military administration of Sir George Prevost, during his command in the Canadas . . . (Montreal, 1815), but this pamphlet may have been the work of John Richardson, as Henry Scadding* asserts in "Some Canadian noms-de-plume identified: with samples of the writings to which they are appended," Canadian Journal (Toronto), new ser., 15 (1876–78): 332–41.

ACC-Q, 72–79. ANQ-M, CE1-63, 18 juin 1801, 21 juin 1831; CN1-187, 27 oct. 1832. McGill Univ. Libraries, ms coll., CH1O.S46 (copies at PAC). PAC, MG 11, [CO 42] Q, 131: 173–83; 137: 44–47; MG 23, GII, 10, vols.2–7; MG 24, B169; RG 4, A1: 20706–8, 21772–76; RG 68, General index, 1651–1841: 272. L.C., House of Assembly, Journals, 1809–14; 1822–23, app.T; 1832–33, app.M. Natural Hist. Soc. of Montreal, Annual report (Montreal), 1828–32. Reports of cases argued and determined in the courts of King's Bench and in the provincial Court of

Appeals of Lower Canada, with a few of the more important cases in the Court of Vice Admiralty . . . , comp. G. O. Stuart (Quebec, 1834). Jonathan Sewall, "Letters of Jonathan Sewall," Mass. Hist. Soc., *Proc.* (Boston), 10 (1896): 407–27. *La Minerve*, 22 juin 1832. *Montreal Gazette*, 1791–1832. *Quebec Gazette*, 12 Jan. 1792; 18 Nov. 1802; 12 June, 6 Nov. 1806; 22 June, 23, 30 Nov. 1809; 15 Feb., 5, 12, 26 April 1810; 12 March, 19 Nov. 1812; 30 Nov. 1815; 28 May 1818; 7 Jan., 11 March, 27 May 1819; 10 May, 19 July, 2 Aug., 13, 27 Dec. 1821. F.-J. Audet, *Les députés de Montréal*, 81–83. *Quebec almanac*, 1804: 47; 1810: 58; 1820: 91; 1821–27. L.-P. Audet, *Le système scolaire*, 3: 239–43. Carol Berkin, *Jonathan Sewall: odyssey of an American loyalist* (New York, 1974). A. W. P. Buchanan, *The bench and bar of Lower Canada down to 1850* (Montreal, 1925), 76–77. F. M. Greenwood, "The development of a garrison mentality among the English in Lower Canada, 1793–1811" (PHD thesis, Univ. of B.C., Vancouver, 1970). *Hochelaga depicta . . .* , ed. Newton Bosworth (Montreal, 1839; repr. Toronto, 1974). Taft Manning, *Revolt of French Canada*, 105, 378–83.

SHAKÓYE:WA:THA? (Sagoyewatha, Otetiani, Red Jacket), Seneca chief and orator; b. *c.* 1750 in what is now New York State; d. 20 Jan. 1830 on the Buffalo Creek Reservation (Buffalo), N.Y. Although it has usually been translated as "he keeps them awake," the name Shakóye:wa:tha? means "he makes them look for it in vain" according to Wallace L. Chafe's translation of modern Seneca.

Red Jacket was born at either Canoga or Ganundasaga (near Geneva, N.Y.). He was a member of the wolf clan through his mother, Ahweyneyonh. His father, possibly a Cayuga, died when he was young. Married at least twice, Red Jacket had ten or more children with his first wife, although none survived him. He gained fame as a crusty, egotistical, but marvellously articulate spokesman for the values of Iroquois culture when it was under assault by whites and white institutions in the first third of the 19th century. Although his reputation was built largely in the United States, the famous orator was not without impact on Upper Canada and its native population. This brief sketch of his life concentrates on those of his achievements which are particularly relevant to Canada, and thus ignores some of his most eloquent speeches. It should be emphasized, however, that these orations often spoke truths of Indian-white relationships that transcend the border. "Your forefathers crossed the great water and landed on this island [North America]," he told white listeners. "Their numbers were small. . . . They asked for a small seat. We took pity on them, granted their request; and they sat down amongst us. We gave them corn and meat; they gave us poison in return."

As a young man of ability, Red Jacket (then known as Otetiani) attracted the attention of British officers during the American revolution. They employed him as a messenger and gave him the scarlet coat that provided him with his English name. He was with the Indian-loyalist forces at the battles of Oriskany, Wyoming, and Newtown, and at the raid on the Schoharie region [*see* Kaieñ?kwaahtoñ*; Thayendanegea*]. Despite the standing he enjoyed among the British military, presumably because of his intellect, Red Jacket earned a less than distinguished reputation as a warrior. He fled from the field at Oriskany. While on the Cherry Valley campaign he complained of the lateness of the season and returned home without seeing action. Another time he exhibited a bloody axe, only to have it revealed he had killed a cow, not a rebel. In later years Red Jacket found himself taunted by Joseph Brant [Thayendanegea] and others for his lack of courage.

Following the war, Red Jacket rapidly rose to prominence as a speaker in the numerous councils that established peace between the Senecas and the new United States. At this time the Senecas residing in New York and the Iroquois then at the Grand River (Ont.) became enmeshed in the power play involving Britain, the United States, and the native peoples of the Ohio valley and upper Great Lakes over control of the region west and north of the Ohio River [*see* Thayendanegea]. Neither the Senecas nor the Grand River Iroquois wished to join the western Indians as allies although both groups were sympathetic to their claims. An increasingly pro-American stand on the part of the Senecas soured their relationship with the Grand River people, and it is reported that Red Jacket even advocated that the Senecas go to war against the Mohawks of the Grand when a lacrosse game between the two groups ended in violence in 1794.

The enmity that had developed between the ambitious Red Jacket and the influential Brant during the 1790s had further consequences a decade later. Brant became involved in a dispute with the Upper Canadian Indian Department under William CLAUS and the government of the colony over the nature of the title to the Six Nations' lands on the Grand River. With Red Jacket's support, Claus and the anti-Brant faction of the Grand River Iroquois convened a council of Iroquois from both sides of the border at Niagara (Niagara-on-the-Lake) in 1805. Here war chief Brant and his allies were removed from office. Brant successfully challenged the legitimacy of this move and retained his position for the remaining two years of his life. Deposing chiefs was a typical move in the factional politics that dominated Iroquois reserves in the early 19th century. In 1827 the Seneca Christian faction deposed Red Jacket himself from the position of chief he had held for three decades. Like Brant, Red Jacket reasserted his right to office.

When the War of 1812 broke out, each side looked to the Iroquois communities within its borders as a source of manpower. The great Seneca prophet

Shank

Skanyadariyoh (Handsome Lake) preached neutrality, but others felt differently. The oratory of Red Jacket helped sway the New York Iroquois to the American cause. A council declared war on Upper and Lower Canada.

In the summer of 1813 Red Jacket, past his 60th year, took the field as a principal chief. The Senecas joined the American invasion of Upper Canada that year, and he was in an engagement on 17 Aug. 1813 at Fort George (Niagara-on-the-Lake), during which the Indians fought with "great bravery and activity." The Americans crossed the border again the next summer, with 500 Senecas accompanying them. Red Jacket fought at the battle of Chippawa on 5 July 1814, where among the British and Canadian forces were 200 Grand River Iroquois. Iroquois casualties were heavy on both sides at Chippawa. The wisdom of fighting a white man's war was questioned. At Red Jacket's instigation, a delegation of New York Iroquois met their Grand River brethren in mid July to discuss the withdrawal of the Iroquois from the war.

Red Jacket returned to Buffalo Creek where he followed a relentlessly conservative course. He resisted the growing white influence among his people. When a Seneca was tried for executing a witch in 1821, Red Jacket took the stand in his defence. In 1824 he even managed to expel white missionaries from the Seneca reservations for a short period. He argued that Christian missionaries could better labour to improve their own race. "Go, then, and teach the whites," he told one. "Select, for example, the people of Buffalo. We will be spectators, and remain silent. Improve their morals and refine their habits – make them less disposed to cheat Indians. . . . Let us know the tree by the blossoms, and the blossoms by the fruit. When this shall be made clear to our minds we may be more willing to listen to you. But until then we must be allowed to follow the religion of our ancestors." When his second wife became a Christian he left her, although they were later reconciled. It is reported that his dying request was: "Be sure that my grave be not made by a white man; let them not pursue me there!" He now lies in Forest Lawn cemetery, Buffalo, in a grave dug by whites.

THOMAS S. ABLER

Wis., State Hist. Soc. (Madison), Draper MSS, ser.S. W. F. Chafe, *Handbook of the Seneca language* (Albany, N.Y., 1963). T. L. McKenney and James Hall, *The Indian tribes of North America, with biographical sketches and anecdotes of the principal chiefs*, new ed., ed. F. W. Hodge and D. I. Bushnell (3v., Edinburgh, 1933–34; repr. St Clair Shores, Mich., 1976), 1: 5–32. W. L. Stone, *The life and times of Sa-go-ye-wat-ha, or Red Jacket, by the late William L. Stone; with a memoir of the author by his son* (Albany, 1866); *Life of Joseph Brant – Thayendanegea . . .* (2v., New York, 1838; repr. New York, 1969, and St Clair Shores, 1970). H. S. Manley, "Red Jacket's last campaign, and an extended bibliographical and biographical note," *N.Y. Hist.* (Cooperstown, N.Y.), 31 (1950): 149–68. A. C. Parker, "The Senecas in the War of 1812," *N.Y. State Hist. Assoc., Proc.* (n.p.), 15 (1916): 78–90; "The unknown mother of Red Jacket," *N.Y. Hist.* 24 (1943): 525–33. G. F. G. Stanley, "The significance of the Six Nations participation in the War of 1812," *OH*, 55 (1963): 215–31.

SHANK. *See* SCHANK

SHAW, ANGUS, fur trader, politician, militia officer, and JP; b. in Scotland; m. an Indian woman according to the custom of the country; m. secondly 30 Nov. 1802 Marjory McGillivray, sister of WILLIAM, Simon*, and Duncan* McGillivray and niece of Simon McTavish*, at Christ Church in Montreal; m. thirdly October 1823 Julia Agnes Rickman in Milford, Conn.; he is known to have had three children: Anna, baptized on 17 Oct. 1797 at age nine in the Scotch Presbyterian Church in Montreal, William, b. 29 May 1802 and baptized in Christ Church on 4 November, and Isabella, born of his last marriage; d. 19 July 1832 in New Brunswick, N.J.

Angus Shaw came from Scotland, most likely from the region between the Isle of Islay, where his sister Marion lived, and Inverness. When and where his career as a fur trader began cannot be determined. He seems to have had close ties with Roderick McKenzie*, whom he called "my dear Rory." By 1789 he was working for the North West Company. That year he built a post at Moose Hill Lake (Moose Lake, Alta, northwest of Muriel Lake), where operations involved a score of men and four canoes. Three years later he established Fort George (near Lindbergh), on the North Saskatchewan River. This major trading post employed more than 100 men and more than 15 canoes. In 1795 Shaw had Fort Augustus (Fort Saskatchewan) built farther up the river. As a wintering partner with Donald McTavish* in the English River department, he established a post at Lac la Biche in 1799, and from there sent 20 men to build another at the mouth of the Slave River. During these years Shaw was caught up in fierce rivalry with the Hudson's Bay Company and its employees, who included William TOMISON.

In 1802 Shaw was moved to another theatre of operations. The NWC put him in charge of the king's posts, which it had just leased. He was to live at Quebec and make an annual visit to the posts, located on the lower north shore of the St Lawrence and on the Saguenay. By the following year the NWC clearly wanted to intensify competition with the HBC and perhaps bring it around to conceding the right of passage through Hudson Bay. Shaw led an expedition of five canoes up to James Bay by an inland route to meet the *Eddystone*, a ship dispatched from Great Britain. Three posts were built on the south shore of the bay, on Charlton Island and at the mouths of the Moose and Eastmain rivers, but they were abandoned three years later. In July 1806 the company gave Shaw an assistant, James MacKenzie*, who was to winter at the king's posts, but in 1808 it decided to outfit them from Montreal and not appoint a replacement for Shaw at Quebec. During these years Shaw had helped and encouraged the Catholic missionaries at the posts for which he was responsible.

He had been admitted to the Beaver Club in 1796, and was a member of the Beef-Steak Club or Barons' Club at Quebec and of the Canada Club in London. He had also served as member for Effingham in the House of Assembly of Lower Canada from April 1802 to June 1804.

Shaw had been promoted wintering partner in the NWC in 1792, with 2 out of 46 shares, but he gave these up in 1808. Two years earlier McTavish, Frobisher and Company had been reorganized as McTavish, McGillivrays and Company, and Shaw had been taken in as a partner. Thus he was an NWC agent and in this capacity he went to Fort William (Thunder Bay, Ont.) in 1810, 1811, and 1812 at least. He also acted as justice of the peace for the Indian Territory from 1810 to 1816. He seems to have participated in the capture of Michilimackinac (Mackinac Island, Mich.) from the Americans in the summer of 1812, and on 3 October he was appointed major in the Corps of Canadian Voyageurs. On 1 Nov. 1814 McTavish, McGillivrays and Company of Montreal was again reorganized; Shaw no longer had any part in it, having transferred his shares to the firm the preceding May, but through a separate agreement he continued to receive the income from 2 of the 19 shares in the company. William McGillivray had apparently been disappointed by his brother-in-law's administrative abilities. The partners may also have thought that Shaw would be much more useful if he went back into service. John McDonald* of Garth considered him "an excellent trader, a man who managed his men and the Indians well."

"Le Chat," as he was nicknamed, took an active part in the final phase of the struggle between the two giants of the fur trade. In 1815 he was at Red River (Man.), where he seems to have helped break up the colony. For this reason in March 1816 Lord Selkirk [Douglas*] ordered Colin Robertson* to arrest him. In 1818–19 Shaw was in the Athabasca region. In the course of his return trip to Fort William in the spring, he was again arrested, this time at Grand Rapids (Man.) by HBC governor William Williams*. Because he threatened to come back and spread bloodshed and terror throughout the country once released, Williams decided to keep him prisoner. He had him transferred to York Factory and from there to London, where he was set free. His wife Marjory came to join him; she died on 27 March 1820.

After the amalgamation of the two great rivals in 1821 Shaw retired. He seems to have gone to live in the United States, where he was out of reach of the lawsuits arising from the bad state of McTavish, McGillivrays and Company's affairs. He died there of a "pulmonary complaint" in 1832. In the absence of an exact inventory it is difficult to put a value on his fortune, and the wills that he made in 1799 and 1810 are no longer in the Montreal notaries' minute-books. One thing is certain: he was anything but poor. At his death, he held shares in the Bank of Montreal and the HBC and owned properties in Montreal, at Quebec, and in the United States. In August 1832 George McDougall was appointed trustee of his estate, which was the object of suits for a number of years. In 1905 one of Marion Shaw's descendants was still investigating it.

GRATIEN ALLAIRE

ANQ-M, CC1, 3 août 1832; CE1-63, 4, 30 nov. 1802; CE1-126, 17 oct. 1797; CN1-29, 25 mars 1799, 29 nov. 1802, 18 mai 1810; CN1-185, 16 mars 1810. AO, MU 2117, 1872, no.3. McCord Museum, Beaver Club minute-book. PAC, MG 30, D1, 27. Univ. of Toronto, Thomas Fisher Rare Book Library, MS coll. 30 (J. N. Wallace). *Les bourgeois de la Compagnie du Nord-Ouest* (Masson). *Docs. relating to NWC* (Wallace). Simon Fraser, *The letters and journals of Simon Fraser, 1806–1808*, ed. W. K. Lamb (Toronto, 1960). *HBRS*, 1 (Rich); *HBRS*, 2 (Rich and Fleming), 20, 23, 72, 75, 85, 92–93, 284–89; *HBRS*, 24 (Davies and Johnson), 293, 305; *HBRS*, 26 (Johnson), xxx, lxix, 9, 12, 57, 59, 65, 216–17; *HBRS*, 30 (Williams). *Journals of Samuel Hearne and Philip Turnor*, ed. J. B. Tyrrell (Toronto, 1934; repr. New York, 1968), 358, 361, 364. *Select British docs. of War of 1812* (Wood). *Montreal Gazette*, 14 May 1810, 31 July 1832. *Quebec Gazette*, 10 May 1810. "Calendar of the Dalhousie papers," PAC *Report*, 1938: 3. Caron, "Inv. de la corr. de Mgr Plessis," ANQ *Rapport*, 1927–28: 232, 236, 243, 251. "General list of partners, clerks & interpreters who winter in the North West Company's service, with the dates and nature of their respective engagements," PAC *Report*, 1939: 53–56. É.-J.[-A.] Auclair, *Saint-Jérôme de Terrebonne* (Saint-Jérôme, Qué., 1934), 32. J. S. H. Brown, *Strangers in blood: fur trade company families in Indian country* (Vancouver and London, 1980), 99–100, 173. W. S. Wallace, *The pedlars from Quebec and other papers on the Nor'Westers* (Toronto, 1954). Wallot, *Un Québec qui bougeait*, 58. M. [E.] Wilkins Campbell, *McGillivray, lord of the northwest* (Toronto, 1962); *NWC* (1957). Jean Bruchési, "George Heriot, peintre, historien et maître de poste," *Cahiers des Dix*, 10 (1945): 204. L. J. Burpee, "The Beaver Club," CHA *Report*, 1924: 73. É.-Z. Massicotte, "Une rencontre de bourgeois du Nord-Ouest," *BRH*, 36 (1930): 717–18. Victor Morin, "Clubs et sociétés notoires d'autrefois," *Cahiers des Dix*, 13 (1948): 130.

SHAWANAKISKIE, Ottawa and convicted murderer; m. with at least one child; fl. 1813–26 in Upper Canada.

Shawnadithit

In 1813 Shawanakiskie fled from Amherstburg, Upper Canada, with Major-General Henry PROCTER's army when it retreated to the head of Lake Ontario. In the fall of 1821 he killed an Indian woman in the streets of Amherstburg. No details of the case survive, except for a reference to an "atrocious" and "heinous" crime. On 27 October he was lodged in jail at Sandwich (Windsor), pending his trial, which took place in August 1822 before Mr Justice William CAMPBELL. The case was prosecuted by Christopher Alexander Hagerman*, acting counsel for the crown on the Western circuit. The proceedings, according to Shawanakiskie in a later petition, were conducted solely in English, with no attempt to translate them into his native tongue. George IRONSIDE, Indian Department superintendent at Amherstburg, testified, despite threats from the accused against his family. Widely known as a violent individual, Shawanakiskie, according to a statement by Ironside, had "half scalped" a marine stationed at Amherstburg, allegedly murdered an old woman of his tribe, and killed his sister by cutting her throat. Shawanakiskie's counsel, probably William Horton, argued that in the matter at hand the accused had only avenged the murder of a parent, a custom sanctioned by native law. He further stated that the exercise of native laws and customs was guaranteed by treaty, thus rendering Indians immune from legal proceedings in such circumstances. None the less, Shawanakiskie was found guilty – the case, according to Campbell, having been "fully proved" – and sentenced to death.

Campbell, however, was uncertain about the terms of the supposed treaty and delayed the execution to permit time for Lieutenant Governor Sir Peregrine Maitland* to "ascertain upon what authority such opinion is founded." Maitland referred the question to Chief Justice William Dummer POWELL, whose reply was inconclusive. He then submitted the whole matter to the colonial secretary, Lord Bathurst, who in turn passed it on to the Home Department. Before acting, the home secretary, Robert Peel, requested any information in the colony regarding the existence of such a treaty. Thus in August 1823 Bathurst wrote to Maitland informing him that the contentious legal question was back on his desk. At stake was an important legal issue for both the Indian and the white communities, namely the applicability of English criminal law in cases involving Indians only. Of more immediate concern to local residents living in unsettled areas near the reserve, however, was the question of protecting themselves and their families.

It took over two years to check through the Indian Department's records. Finally, in November 1825 Maitland reported that "after the most diligent Search . . . there appears to exist no treaty that can give color to the idea that an Indian is not to be considered as amenable to the law for offences committed against another Indian within His Majesty's Dominions." Armed with this information, officials at the Home Department quickly concluded that there was nothing to prevent the law from taking its course. Yet because of the possibility of extenuating circumstances of which Maitland alone would be aware, the warrant issued for Shawanakiskie's execution included a proviso that the lieutenant governor could commute the sentence to transportation for life.

There is no evidence that Shawanakiskie received such a conditional pardon. Given his character and the threats to Ironside, it seems likely that he was executed at the Sandwich jail, probably in 1826. The legacy of his case was the resolution of a vexing legal question. Thereafter, as in the case of George Powlis*, an Indian could gain a pardon only on the grounds of legal cause and not by right of immunity.

DENNIS CARTER-EDWARDS

PAC, RG 7, G1, 60: 156; 62: 32–41. PRO, CO 42/370: 25–27, 33, 36, 41–42; 42/371: 35; 42/375: 309. "Accounts for 1823," AO *Report*, 1914: 708, 715.

SHAWNADITHIT (Nancy, Nance April), Beothuk; b. *c.* 1801, daughter of Doodebewshet; d. 6 June 1829 in St John's.

Shawnadithit was the last known survivor of the Beothuks or Red Indians, the aboriginals of Newfoundland. A member of one of their small and rapidly dwindling family groups, she was the niece of Demasduwit*'s husband, Nonosbawsut. As a child and young girl she witnessed several of the final documented encounters between her people and expeditions dispatched or authorized by the British and colonial officials to establish friendly relations; as herself a captive, she was the source of much of what is known about the customs, language, and last days of her people.

In January 1811 she was present at the meeting on the shore of Red Indian Lake with Lieutenant David Buchan* and his party which ended in tragic misunderstanding. In the summer of 1818 she was with the Indians who pilfered John Peyton Jr's salmon boat and cargo at Lower Sandy Point, on the Bay of Exploits. She observed the capture of Demasduwit and the killing of Nonosbawsut by Peyton's party in March 1819 and witnessed the return by Buchan of her aunt's body to the deserted encampment at Red Indian Lake in February 1820. In the spring of 1823 Shawnadithit, her sister, and their mother, Doodebewshet, in a weakened and starving condition, were taken by the furrier William CULL at Badger Bay, her father falling through the ice and drowning after a desperate attempt at rescue. Cull brought the three women to magistrate Peyton's establishment at Exploits, on the more northerly of the two Exploits Islands, and Peyton himself sailed with them to St John's by schooner in June. It was quickly decided by Buchan, acting in the absence but with the authority of the governor, Vice-Admiral Sir Charles Hamilton*, that the women should be returned to their people with presents as speedily as possible; and in July Peyton left them at the mouth of Charles Brook with provisions and a small boat to make their way back to any survivors of their group. Unsuccessful, the three later returned on foot to the coast; the mother and sister, desperately ill, died within a few days of one another, and Shawnadithit was taken into Peyton's household.

For the ensuing five years, Shawnadithit remained with his household at Exploits (not, as sometimes assumed, at Twillingate to which he removed at a later date); she seems to have been kindly treated. With the founding of the Boeothick Institution by prominent citizens of St John's and Twillingate, supported by interested patrons outside Newfoundland, she was brought to St John's under the auspices of that organization in September 1828. There she resided with the president of the institution, William Eppes Cormack*, the peripatetic explorer, merchant, and philanthropist. It is to her that we owe much of the data written down by Cormack: she is one of the prime witnesses to the Beothuk language, the customs of her people, and the events and general condition of the tribe in the final years when their numbers had fallen to perhaps less than a score. She was gifted with pencil and sketch-book, and her drawings (frequently reproduced) are especially valuable. Moreover, as the last of her people, Shawnadithit has naturally figured largely in popular accounts, the steady stream of which shows little sign of either abating or improving.

Insight into the historical truth about the Beothuks and their relationship with Europeans must start with the recognition that this small branch of the Algonkian people probably numbered less than 2,000 when they were first encountered in the 16th and 17th centuries. They were hunters and fishers who depended largely upon the caribou of the interior in winter, and the fish and marine mammals of the coast in the warmer months. Aside from an account of their tentative meeting with John Guy*'s colonists in 1612, little is known about their relations with Europeans until the last half of the 18th century. Before that time, the Beothuks seldom caught the attention of record-keeping white men, for the Europeans who went to Newfoundland did so to fish, not to convert Indians to Christianity, or to enlist their support in colonial wars, or to trade with them for furs. Indeed, the Beothuks were unusual among the native peoples in North America in that it was not always necessary for them to exchange furs or skins for highly valued manufactured goods. Newfoundland was a fishing colony above all else, and this fact meant that the seasonally vacant premises of migratory English fishermen were a rich source of iron tools, canvas sails, and the like. By the latter part of the 18th century, however, an increasingly permanent English resident fishery made it difficult to carry out this sort of pilferage without retaliation.

There is little doubt that such retaliation, both justified and otherwise, did contribute to the eventual extinction of these unfortunate people. Yet a more important factor was the growth of a white population along the coast which denied the Beothuks easy access to the marine resources upon which they were seasonally dependent. Archaeological work has suggested that by the end of the 18th century the Beothuks had been forced to rely too much upon the resources of the interior, a difficult place to live, especially without firearms. If the Beothuks were malnourished as a result of enforced dependence upon the meagre wildlife of the island's interior, they would have been that much more vulnerable to European diseases, the great killers of all New World peoples. It is quite possible that this susceptibility, more than any other factor, was responsible for their doom. Indeed, historian Leslie Francis Stokes Upton has calculated that if the Beothuks experienced anything like the population decline suffered by native groups elsewhere, their extinction could be explained solely as a result of loss through disease.

It was, however, the vivid accounts of fishermen and furriers murdering Indians, not the natives' slow deaths from hunger and sickness, that finally attracted the attention of white authorities. In keeping with the growing humanitarian spirit of that age, a succession of Newfoundland governors, beginning in the 1760s with Hugh Palliser*, attempted to end attacks on Beothuks and establish friendly relations with them. None of these efforts proved successful. The most promising of them, Lieutenant John Cartwright's expedition to the Beothuks in 1768, in which his brother George Cartwright* was a participant, produced much information about their abandoned camps, but Cartwright met no Indians on his journey up the Exploits River. Unfortunately for generations of future historians, Cartwright also brought back rumours that Micmacs from Nova Scotia were slaughtering Beothuks on a grand scale. There may have been occasional hostile encounters between Micmac trappers and Beothuk hunters, but the overwhelming weight of evidence suggests that, for the most part, they avoided each other. This, of course, was not the case with the Beothuks and the white population of the northern bays. In the face of official proclamations forbidding harassment of the Indians, fishermen and furriers continued to shoot Beothuks, and Beothuks continued to steal from European settlements and even to kill the occasional unwary white man.

This pattern continued in the 19th century with the additional development of a number of officially

Shawnadithit

sponsored or encouraged attempts to acquire Beothuk captives who would, it was hoped in St John's, be employed as mediators between the two races. In 1803 the policy produced one captive, a nameless Beothuk woman brought back to St John's by William Cull. Governor James GAMBIER gave her presents and entrusted Cull with sending her back to her people, but as far as is known, this effort had no effect on Indian-white relations. Subsequent Newfoundland governors also attempted to make peaceful contact with the elusive Beothuks, but it had become difficult, even dangerous, to approach these people who by then had had several centuries of experience with ill-intentioned white men.

The most nearly successful of these attempts occurred in the winter of 1810–11 when David Buchan and a small number of marines and settlers were sent up the Exploits River to Red Indian Lake by Governor John Thomas Duckworth*. Astonishingly, Buchan's men succeeded in surprising a small camp of Beothuks, but he erred terribly in leaving two of his marines with the Indians while he went back down the river to retrieve presents which he had left behind. When he returned he found the headless corpses of his men, inexplicably killed by the now vanished Indians.

There were no reprisals for these murders. Indeed, Duckworth's successor, Sir Richard Goodwin KEATS, restated his predecessor's warning that mistreatment of the Indians would be punished to the fullest extent of the law. The Beothuks did need protection, of course, but in defence of the fishermen and furriers, it should be noted that these men had ample cause to see the Beothuks, not as heroic remnants of a persecuted people, but as dangerous thieves whose persistent forays threatened the lives and property of honest people. For their part, the Beothuks were caught in a cruel dilemma. In common with almost all Indians they had grown dependent upon European materials, especially iron from which they fashioned spears, harpoon blades, arrowheads, and the like. Yet, to acquire these things they had to steal and this activity inevitably provoked reprisals such as that carried out by Peyton in March 1819 after he had lost £150 worth of gear.

It is now known that when Demasduwit was seized on that raid there were perhaps fewer than a score of Beothuks left alive, and fewer still by the time that Shawnadithit was taken. They had been the victims of white society, to be sure, but they had not been – as so many irresponsible writers have alleged – hunted for sport and massacred in large numbers. They died because they were few in number to begin with, because they had no resistance to European diseases, and because Newfoundland was a fishing colony which, almost by definition, lacked enough of the sort of white men who wanted or needed to keep Indians alive. By 1827, when the Boeothick Institution was

formed by Cormack and his handful of contemporaries, it was too late.

Shawnadithit remained in Cormack's care until his departure from Newfoundland early in 1829; she was then transferred to the care of the attorney general, James Simms*. Her health, precarious for a number of years, continued to deteriorate, and she was seen a good deal during this period by William Carson*, who tended her in her last illness. She succumbed to pulmonary consumption on 6 June 1829 and was buried two days later in the military and naval cemetery on the south side of St John's river-head, a site subsequently lost sight of but approximately fixed by the unearthing of the remains of several military personnel under and adjacent to the Southside Road in November 1979. Carson's description of her is brief but vivid. It was enclosed in a tin case with "the scull and scalp of Nancy Beothic Red Indian Female," dispatched in November 1830 to the Royal College of Physicians of London, together with "answers to a series of sixteen questions": "She was tall, and majestic, mild and tractable, but characteristically proud and cautious." A monument to her memory stands somewhat to the east of the general site of her burial.

RALPH T. PASTORE and G. M. STORY

[The principal sources for our knowledge of Shawnadithit and her people are printed in Howley, *Beothucks or Red Indians*, to which few documentary additions have since been made. In addition to important contemporary letters and manuscripts (many of which are preserved in the collections of the PANL), Howley printed a number of miscellaneous accounts that are of some value. The Pulling Manuscript (BL, Add. MSS 38352: ff.1–44) contains valuable information about relations between settlers and Indians *c.* 1792. William Carson's letter is at the PANL, GN 2/2, 17 Nov. 1830: 325–28. Recent archaeological work is of the utmost importance; secondary sources include: Helen Devereux, "Five archaeological sites in Newfoundland: a description," a report prepared for the former Nfld. Dept. of Provincial Affairs, now the Hist. Resources Division of the Department of Culture, Recreation, and Youth (2v., St John's, 1969), and on file with the Nfld. Museum in St John's; John Hewson, *Beothuk vocabularies* (St John's, 1978); R. J. LeBlanc, "The Wigwam Brook site and the historic Beothuk Indians" (MA thesis, Memorial Univ. of Nfld., St John's, 1973); Don Locke, *Beothuck artifacts* (St John's, 1974); Ingeborg Marshall, "An unpublished map made by John Cartwright between 1768 and 1773 showing Beothuck Indian settlements and artifacts and allowing a new population estimate," *Ethnohistory* (Tucson, Ariz.), 24 (1977): 223–49; R. T. Pastore, "Newfoundland Micmacs: a history of their traditional life," Nfld. Hist. Soc., *Pamphlet* ([St John's]), no.5 (1978); F. W. Rowe, *Extinction: the Beothuks of Newfoundland* (Toronto, 1977); Peter Such, *Vanished peoples: the archaic Dorset & Beothuk people of Newfoundland* (Toronto, 1978); J. A. Tuck, *Newfoundland and Labrador prehistory* (Ottawa, 1976); and L. F. S. Upton, "The extermination of the Beothucks of Newfoundland," *CHR*, 58 (1977): 133–53.

Both Shawnadithit and her aunt Demasduwit, or figures suggested by them, have been used in the fiction and poetry inspired by the Beothuks. The earliest work of this kind is the novel *Ottawah, the last chief of the Red Indians of Newfoundland; a romance*, published anonymously in parts in London in 1848, but attributed in later editions to Sir Charles Augustus Murray (*see* E. J. Devereux, "The Beothuk Indians of Newfoundland in fact and fiction," *Dalhousie Rev.*, 50 (1970–71): 350–62). George Webber*'s long poem, *The last of the aborigines: a poem founded in facts*, was published in St John's in 1851; there is an edition with introduction and notes by E. J. Devereux in *Canadian Poetry* (London, Ont.), no.2 (spring–summer 1978): 74–98. Recent contributions to this continuing literature include Peter Such's novel *Riverrun* (Toronto, 1973) and Sid Stephen's *Beothuck poems* ([Ottawa], 1976).

The most authoritative discussion of the interrelated portraits of Shawnadithit and Demasduwit is by Ingeborg Marshall, "The miniature portrait of Mary March," *Newfoundland Quarterly* (St John's), 73 (1977), no.3: 4–7, supplemented by Christian Hardy and Ingeborg Marshall, "A new portrait of Mary March," *Newfoundland Quarterly*, 76 (1980), no.1: 25–28. There is a modern portrait by Helen Shepherd (1951) displayed in the Nfld. Museum. R.T.P. and G.M.S.]

SHEA, HENRY, accountant, mercantile agent, merchant, and militia officer; b. *c.* 1767 in or near Carrick on Suir (Republic of Ireland); m. 20 Nov. 1800 Eleanor Ryan in St John's, and they had seven sons and three daughters; d. there 29 Oct. 1830.

Henry Shea probably arrived at St John's in 1784. Little is known of his background in County Tipperary beyond the tradition that he came from a respectable family and that he ran away from home. In 1786 he commenced work as a clerk, most likely for Nathaniel Philips, a New Englander who had settled in St John's around 1774 and had built up a substantial mercantile trade. Shea entered this service at a time when the St John's merchant community had begun its long and effective drive to engross the island's trade. Philips shared in the expansion, building up his extensive supply trade in St John's and along the populous east coast and shipping fish from these places. The late 18th century also witnessed a rapid growth of Irish participation in the fishery, especially in St John's and the districts near by. Like most Protestant merchants Philips hired Catholic Irish agents and accountants to help handle the trade with the Irish. Partly through employees such as Shea from major centres of Irish migration, Philips established a considerable Irish clientele in St John's, Conception Bay, and the southern half of the Avalon peninsula. Shea's lengthy term as an accountant thus afforded ample opportunity for him to learn the complex operations of the cod trade, develop business contacts, and accumulate enough savings to launch an independent mercantile career.

Probably the most significant step in Shea's slow transition was his marriage to the daughter of Timothy Ryan, merchant, which took place in 1800, two years after the death of Philips and the dissolution of his house. Ryan, like Shea a Tipperary man, had been resident in St John's some three decades and with his sons, particularly Patrick, had established a considerable trade. Ryan and Sons conducted an extensive supply business in St John's and contiguous districts, as well as in Placentia Bay, notably Burin where the firm Ryan and Morris was established in 1802 following the marriage of Geoffrey Morris of Tipperary to another Ryan daughter. The firms shipped fish back to the British Isles and to the Iberian peninsula. For much of the remainder of his life Henry Shea was intimately involved in this family enterprise, but he also traded on his own account and accepted commissions from other houses. By the fall of 1801 he apparently had a store of his own in St John's, had correspondents in the town of Placentia, had commenced obtaining writs, and was listed among the merchants and principal inhabitants expressing concern over the absence of a chief justice to settle disputes during the winter. It was, however, a modest trade. Shea did import goods on his own account and received small cash payments from the local authorities for arranging or providing passages home for some distressed Irish, but there is no evidence, for example, that he ever owned a ship or even a share in one. By comparison with other merchants, he obtained few writs and they were usually for small sums involving local Irish shopkeepers, artisans, and fishermen.

In the fall of 1810 Shea announced a formal partnership with Ryan and Sons of St John's to be called Henry Shea and Company. The Ryans stressed that this new firm was separate from their existing house in St John's, implying that Shea and Company would trade on its own account. Shea joined the Ryans at a propitious time, when their enterprise was expanding rapidly in response to rising demand and prices for fish in the European markets. It is difficult to determine precisely the business arrangements between Henry Shea and his in-laws but he did play a major role in the Ryans' St John's operations. Patrick Ryan's untimely death in 1814, at the peak of the company's trade, almost certainly meant that Shea succeeded as operating manager of Ryan and Sons in St John's under Timothy, whose other son, Joseph, remained with the firm's branch in Liverpool, England. Shea continued to trade, however, on his own account. Between 1811 and 1816, for example, he shipped over £800 of supplies, particularly butter but also pork, wine, nets, nails, and stationery, to Burin and he advertised foodstuffs for auction at his St John's store.

In February 1817 the Ryans' house in Liverpool

was declared bankrupt, a victim of the depression in the cod economy after the war, and three months later the parent house in St John's collapsed. The company was owed more than £18,000 and Henry Shea was appointed agent to assist the trustees collect debts, pay creditors, and sell off the insolvent estate. This latter task proved difficult because of the depression, and the problem was compounded by fires in the fall which also destroyed Shea's part of the premises. He commenced rebuilding and in the spring of 1819 advised "his friends and the public in general that his shop, stores and warehouse in the premises lately held by Ryan & Sons, Water St., are now nearly completed. He will import all kinds of goods to sell on commission by private or public sales." Sales did ensue as trade recovered and supplies arrived at Shea's premises from Waterford, New Ross, Dublin, Liverpool, and the North American mainland. The Ryans' transatlantic business also resumed. There was no significant change in the deployment of principal personnel: Joseph Ryan remained in Liverpool, Geoffrey Morris in Burin, and Henry Shea with his son John in St John's where he worked closely with the ageing Timothy Ryan. The business had little of its former vigour and finally collapsed with the demise of Timothy Ryan in 1830. Shea's own trade was also precarious after the mild recovery in the early 1820s. Its vulnerability was exposed in 1823 when he was declared insolvent because apparently he was unable to pay a small debt. Trustees were appointed but Shea recovered and, with his son John, continued his modest business to the end.

Despite his long and not very successful struggle to gain prominence as a merchant, Henry Shea was one of the most respected residents in St John's. This was true not only among Catholics but also among the Protestant community, local officials, and the governor. His long residence in the town and understanding of its character, his loyalty, and his integrity resulted in recognition in a world where economic circumstance and ethno-religious origins usually defined social rank. Shea was one of only a handful of Catholic Irish empanelled to serve on the grand jury of Newfoundland's Supreme Court in the first decade of the century. He served also on petty and special juries and as an expert witness, sometimes in precedent-setting or important cases relating to property rights, shipping, and the customs of trade. His talents were sought as an arbitrator, as an assessor of property or goods, and as trustee, executor, or administrator of estates.

Shea's popularity among local authorities, civil and military, led in 1806 to an appointment as lieutenant in one of the five companies of the Loyal Volunteers of St John's, two-thirds of whose ordinary members were Irish Catholics. He was the first Irish Catholic to be awarded this rank and two years later was promoted

captain; he held the position until 1812, when he resigned and was replaced by Patrick Ryan. Shea was distinguished by another appointment early in 1806 when he was elected secretary of the newly founded Benevolent Irish Society. The society was established to alleviate distress amongst the Irish poor whose numbers were increasing in St John's and who, in the absence of any regular form of official aid, frequently needed support. Membership was open to males of Irish birth or descent. Catholics comprised around 90 per cent of the original body but the mass of Catholic Irish were regarded with suspicion, at least by the government authorities, and partly to meet that concern members of the society's executive and one of two special committees were drawn overwhelmingly from the upper ranks of the military and from the small Protestant Irish community. Shea's selection as the only Catholic on the executive reflected his general acceptability to all parties. He held the secretaryship until 1814 when he was promoted vice-president; from the departure in 1817 of the president, James MacBraire, until the selection of Patrick Morris* as president in 1823, Shea acted as chairman. He then resigned the vice-presidency and was toasted at the annual dinner as "the oldest and best servant of the Institution." His allegiance continued and in the following year he delivered the St Patrick's Day address to 118 members in the president's absence.

The final 15 years of Henry Shea's life was a period of considerable economic difficulty in Newfoundland and witnessed the growth of public protest and the politicization of the island's woes. As the migratory fishery faded and residency increased, the need to reform an archaic system of government became more and more evident and was articulated especially by a growing middle class in St John's. In 1811, for example, the government decided to lease the ancient and outmoded "fishing ships' rooms" in St John's for private development. These lands, long used as commons, were perceived locally as public property and at a meeting in November of the principal inhabitants, which Shea attended, it was proposed that the substantial income derived from the leases be used for municipal improvements and services. The suggestions fell on deaf ears. Shea was also involved, both as expert witness and as special juror, in a case brought by the government against John Ryan, a St John's tailor-merchant, in 1813. Ryan had rented part of a ship's room in 1811 and proceeded to build substantial premises there that encroached, the government claimed, on public space. Ryan won the ensuing case but Chief Justice Thomas Tremlett overturned the jury verdict and then advertised the property for sale. Ryan protested vigorously and mustered substantial local support. He was sued by the crown for libel but a special jury, of which Shea was a member, acquitted him of all charges.

The most significant advance in the struggle for reform was prompted by a blatant miscarriage of justice in 1819–20 involving two Irish planters from Conception Bay, James LUNDRIGAN and Philip Butler. Both men were in debt to merchants and, after they resisted efforts to confiscate their properties, were flogged. A committee was formed in November 1820 under the chairmanship of Patrick Morris and a memorial sent to London expressing shock at the treatment of the planters. While proclaiming total loyalty, the committee, composed of eight Catholic Irish merchants including Henry Shea, four Englishmen, and a Scot, William Carson*, vowed to pursue every legal and constitutional means in their power to initiate judicial reform. A second memorial signed by 180 inhabitants, the vast majority Irish, at a public meeting in St John's in late December complained about various practices of the surrogate courts and raised the question of a local legislature. Official reaction was cool, and so in 1822 the committee members prepared a more detailed account of Newfoundland's difficulties and suggested some solutions. The fishery could be lucrative, they claimed, but large English houses took away the profits and did not re-invest locally; civil servants and surrogates also took their money away and over £30,000 was remitted annually to Britain in rents from St John's alone; this amount itself would support a local legislature. They urged the encouragement of farming, the construction of roads, and more government support for the cod fishery. This seminal statement on reform in Newfoundland did draw some response from London, but its proposals were deemed inadequate by another public meeting in November 1823 at St John's. A fresh set of requests was submitted by an expanded committee dominated for the first time by Protestant merchants. These proposals resulted in some important juridical reforms in 1824.

Although Henry Shea was consistently a member of the committees, he was overshadowed by the youthful, vigorous, and successful Morris, who emerged as the clear leader of the Irish community. Shea had smaller financial resources than Morris, perhaps did not have the literary skills, was ageing, and was politically moderate in a period when class and sectarian feelings were on the rise. His political philosophy is probably best expressed in the prospectus submitted to the governor for the *Newfoundlander*, a paper established by his son and mercantile partner, John, in 1827. The paper was "to be conducted on liberal principles, the object being to unite in the bonds of social harmony all classes of British subjects. With Religion, when unmixed with Politics, no matter of what sect or denomination its votaries may be, the Newfoundlander shall never meddle." These aims accorded by and large with the views of the Catholic hierarchy, from James Louis O'Donel*, who had

arrived in St John's at about the same time as Henry Shea, to the ecumenical Bishop Thomas SCALLAN, as well as with the opinions of much of the Catholic middle class and liberal Protestants.

Shea was a loyal supporter of the Catholic Church. He was one of 18 Irish laymen petitioning in 1794 to have O'Donel made bishop and vicar apostolic, and he acted as joint executor with O'Donel's successor, Patrick Lambert*, of wills where substantial cash or property was bequeathed to the church; he managed the finances involved in constructing an extension to the chapel and worked closely with the clergy in the affairs of the Benevolent Irish Society.

Henry Shea was an immigrant in a port and town dominated by newcomers. Many came from in and around Carrick on Suir, after Waterford and New Ross the leading centre of Irish migration to Newfoundland. One of the striking features of Shea's social and economic life was the close link he gradually forged with people from southeast Tipperary. Names of godparents in the St John's parish registers indicate his social connections with leading Tipperary families in Newfoundland – the Ryans, Morrises, Meaghers, Murphys, Gleesons, and O'Donels – and business records also reveal ties with Tipperary people. A number of them made him trustee or executor of their estates.

Shea's popularity endured to the end. "We have seldom heard such universal regret expressed for any person's death as for Mr. Shea's" began the obituary in the St John's *Royal Gazette and Newfoundland Advertiser*. "His kind and pleasing manners made him deservedly a favourite with all classes of the community." In a eulogy Stephen Lawlor, fellow merchant, fellow member of the original Benevolent Irish Society and now its president, described his friend as "kind, unaffected, generous, sincere, patriotic," with a heart that was "truly Irish." His funeral was honoured by a slow march through the streets and a day of general mourning. It was reported as the largest funeral for a private person in St John's since the death of Patrick Ryan.

Shea founded one of the most talented and respected families in 19th-century Newfoundland. Joseph, the eldest son, qualified as a medical doctor in Britain and returned to practise in St John's, where he married a daughter of William Carson. John inherited his father's trade and was active in the community until he moved to Cork (Republic of Ireland) in 1837. William Richard*, Henry, Ambrose*, and Edward Dalton* remained in St John's as publishers of the *Newfoundlander* and made a major contribution to the colony's political and literary life.

JOHN MANNION

Basilica of St John the Baptist (Roman Catholic) (St John's),

Shepherd

St John's parish, reg. of baptisms, marriages, and burials (mfm. at PANL). Benevolent Irish Soc. (St John's), Minutes, 1822, 1824 (mfm. at PANL). Maritime Hist. Arch., Memorial Univ. of Nfld. (St John's), Nathaniel Philips name file. NMM, WYN, 30 Aug. 1800 (mfm. at PANL). PANL, GN 2/1, 12, 14–16, 19–20, 24, 31–32; GN 2/2, 1827–32; GN 2/39/A, 1795, St John's; GN 5/1/A/4, 1801–3, 1821–25; GN 5/1/C/1, Burin, 1806, 1820; GN 5/2/A/1, 1798–1830; GN 5/2/A/9, 1798, 1802–26; GN 5/2/A/10, 1832; P1/5/4/10, 51; P/1/5/11/38; P7/A/6, Fogo Island misc., 1798; P7/A/18, letter-book and ledger; P7/A/48, letter-book, August 1809. PRO, ADM 1/475: 11–12; CO 194/21, 194/23, 194/36, 194/42–43, 194/45, 194/50–51, pt.II, 194/59, 194/64, 194/66, 194/68–69, 194/71. Public Record Office of Northern Ireland (Belfast), D 2935/5 (Edward Kough, letter-book), Kough to John Bland, n.d. Patrick Morris, *Remarks on the state of society, religion, morals, and education at Newfoundland . . .* (London, 1827). *Newfoundlander* (St John's), 1828–40. *Newfoundland Mercantile Journal*, 1817–24. *Newfoundland Patriot* (St John's), 6 Oct. 1835, 15 March 1836. *Public Ledger*, 1824–44. *Royal Gazette and Newfoundland Advertiser*, 1810–32. *Times and General Commercial Gazette* (St John's), 30 Oct. 1833; 23, 30 March 1836. *Centenary volume, Benevolent Irish Society of St. John's, Newfoundland, 1806–1906* (Cork, [Republic of Ire., 1906?]). M. F. Howley, *Ecclesiastical history of Newfoundland* (Boston, 1888; repr. Belleville, Ont., 1979). Prowse, *Hist. of Nfld.* (1895).

SHEPHERD, JAMES, militia officer and office holder; b. *c.* 1730; d. unmarried 10 Jan. 1822 at Quebec.

James Shepherd's origins and early career remain unknown. By his own statement, he served in the British army at Louisbourg, Île Royale (Cape Breton Island) in 1758. Six years later he signed a petition from the Quebec merchants who were demanding the recall of Governor James Murray*. On 13 Jan. 1765 he was commissioned clerk in the Court of Oyer and Terminer. He was appointed clerk of the peace for the district of Quebec on 13 May and he was also licensed as a notary, although he does not seem to have taken up that profession. Then on 6 August he received a commission as protonotary and chief clerk of the Court of King's Bench. Shepherd was appointed sheriff of the district of Quebec by Governor Sir Guy Carleton* on 31 July 1776. In 1788 he was a lieutenant in the Quebec Battalion of British Militia. He was promoted captain, and then major, but retired from the militia before the War of 1812.

In November 1793, after notary Jean-Antoine Panet* had signed a summons, Shepherd as sheriff ordered the arrest of John Young*, the member of the assembly for Lower Town, who was being sued for debt by a hardware merchant. At Young's urging, the assembly asserted that its members, like those of the British parliament, enjoyed immunity, and Shepherd, who was accused of having breached constitutional privileges, had to apologize to Young. As sheriff,

Shepherd on 16 April 1800 proceeded with the seizure of the Jesuit estates after the death of Jean-Joseph Casot*, the last member of the order in Lower Canada. The government thus entered into possession of the Jesuit properties, seigneuries, and belongings. However, Shepherd handed over the church ornaments, consecrated vessels, and paintings to the cathedral of Quebec. On 20 July 1812 he sent a report to Governor Sir George Prevost* with his resignation as sheriff and court clerk on grounds of precarious health and infirmities. He asked that upon resigning his two offices he be allowed to retain his two salaries, which amounted to £220 annually.

Shortly before his death Shepherd revoked the power of attorney held by his clerk, Charles Farrain, and gave it to Marguerite Poulliot, his servant, granting her authority to manage his assets. The will that he drew up on 9 Jan. 1822 named her executrix and sole legatee. He died the next day at his home on Rue Saint-Louis at Quebec.

The inventory of James Shepherd's possessions shows that he was well off, cultured, and in all likelihood bilingual. His estate consisted of a stone house on Rue Saint-Louis, debts owing to him estimated at £508 14*s.* 3*d.*, and liabilities amounting to £112 12*s.* 9*d.*; he had also deposited £16,000 in the Bank of England. He owned a guitar and a library of about 265 volumes, and he maintained a large garden.

FRANCE B. SIROIS

ANQ-Q, CE1-61, 14 janv. 1822; CN1-212, 17 déc. 1821, 21 janv. 1822. Arch. judiciaires, Québec, Holograph will of James Shepherd, 21 janv. 1822 (*see* P.-G. Roy, *Inv. testaments*, 3: 134). PAC, RG 4, B8, 1: 89; RG 68, 2: 19. *Docs. relating to constitutional hist., 1759–91* (Shortt and Doughty; 1918); *1791–1818* (Doughty and McArthur); *1819–28* (Doughty and Story). *Quebec Gazette*, 3, 31 Jan. 1822. J. M. LeMoine, *Quebec past and present, a history of Quebec, 1608–1876* (Quebec, 1876). "Les 'dépouilles' du père jésuite Cazot," *BRH*, 26 (1920): 286–88. J.-E. Roy, "La liste du mobilier qui fut saisi en 1800 par le shérif de Québec, à la mort du père jésuite Cazot," *Rev. canadienne* (Montréal), 25 (1889): 271–82. P.-G. Roy, "Les shérifs de Québec," *BRH*, 40 (1934): 433–46.

SHERBROOKE, Sir JOHN COAPE, army officer and colonial administrator; baptized 29 April 1764 in Arnold, Nottinghamshire, England, son of William Sherbrooke (Coape) and Sarah Sherbrooke; m. 24 Aug. 1811 Katherine (Katherina) Pyndar at Areley Kings, England, and they had no children; d. 14 Feb. 1830 in Calverton, Nottinghamshire, and was buried in nearby Oxton.

Born into the landed gentry, John Coape Sherbrooke began his career in the British army on 7 Dec. 1780, when he was appointed an ensign in the 4th Foot. He was promoted lieutenant on 22 Dec. 1781 and in March 1783 became a captain in the 85th Foot, but the regiment was disbanded later that year. On 23 June 1784 he obtained a company in the 33rd Foot, then serving in Nova Scotia. While Sherbrooke was stationed at Sydney, Cape Breton, in 1784–85, a strange incident occurred: he and Lieutenant George Wynyard thought they saw the ghost of Wynyard's brother, who, they later heard, had died in England at that very moment.

In 1786 the 33rd returned to England and an uneventful period intervened in Sherbrooke's military career until war broke out between Britain and revolutionary France. Promoted major on 30 Sept. 1793 and lieutenant-colonel on 24 May 1794, Sherbrooke travelled with his regiment that July to Ostend to join the Duke of York's army in the Flanders campaign. Returning home in 1795, the 33rd was ordered to sail with an expeditionary force to the West Indies but storms drove the ships back to England. In April 1796 Sherbrooke embarked with his regiment for India, landing at Calcutta the following February. Raised to the rank of colonel in the army on 1 Jan. 1798, he took part in the Mysore War of 1799, including the siege of Seringapatam. He suffered such persistent ill health during his time in India that he was forced in January 1800 to return to England, where he was placed on half pay in 1802. With the resumption of war with France he took command in July 1803 of the 4th Battalion of Reserve, stationed at Norman Cross.

On 1 Jan. 1805 Sherbrooke was promoted major-general and in June was sent to Sicily, where in February 1807 he became commander of the Sicilian Regiment. With French forces active in southern Italy and the Mediterranean, his energies were largely devoted to diplomatic activities and confounding the intrigues of the court at Palermo, which he did with adroitness and resolution. In May 1807 he went on a diplomatic mission to Egypt. A fellow army officer, Henry Edward Bunbury, has left a vivid description of the fiery, pugnacious Sherbrooke at this time. When he arrived in Sicily, "the brigade he commanded winced a little under the sharpness of his discipline, while they revenged themselves by comical stories of his rough sayings and impetuous temper. . . . A short, square, hardy little man, with a countenance that told at once the determined fortitude of his nature. Without genius, without education, hot as pepper, and rough in his language, but with a warm heart and generous feelings; true, straight forward, scorning finesse and craft and meanness, and giving vent to his detestation with boiling eagerness, and in the plainest terms. As an officer, full of energy, rousing others to exertion, and indefatigable in his own person." During the first half of 1808 he assumed temporary command of all British troops in Sicily until, relieved by Sir John Stuart, he went home on leave in June.

Transferring to the 68th Foot in May 1809, Sherbrooke served in the Peninsular campaign, with the local rank of lieutenant-general, as second in command to Arthur Wellesley, who later commented that "Sherbrooke was a very good officer, but the most passionate man I think I ever knew." In acknowledgement of his exploits in the battles of Oporto and Talavera he was made a KCB in September 1809. Again experiencing poor health, he was forced in May 1810 to return to England and recuperate at Cheltenham. On 4 June 1811 he was promoted full lieutenant-general and the following month appointed lieutenant governor of Nova Scotia, his commission being dated 19 August. Taking time to get married, he left Portsmouth on 8 September with his new wife and her sister and arrived at Halifax on 16 October to assume his gubernatorial duties and his responsibilities as commander of the forces in the Atlantic provinces.

The five years of Sherbrooke's administration were dominated by war with the United States, which broke out in June 1812, and matters relating to the colony's defence. With dilapidated fortifications and limited military resources, the needs of the Canadas being more urgent, he could do little to secure the scattered, vulnerable outports against the threat of invasion or the ravages of American privateers beyond mounting guns at harbour entrances and placing the militia in a state of readiness. For the rest, he had to rely on naval protection as British ships patrolled the seas and later blockaded the American coast, occasionally clashing with enemy men-of-war as in the celebrated engagement of the *Shannon*, commanded by Philip Bowes Vere Broke*, and the *Chesapeake* in June 1813. For the dual purposes of security and commerce Sherbrooke issued proclamations declaring a friendly disposition towards the adjacent New England states, where the outbreak of war was highly unpopular, and a willingness to continue trading with them by means of licences, a mutually convenient arrangement extensively supplemented by more clandestine operations throughout the war. Despite his initial anxieties about the shortage of specie and provisions, the war proved to be profitable for Nova Scotia. Sherbrooke's calculated commercial policy, which stimulated the free exchange of goods with New England, turned the Atlantic provinces into a thriving entrepôt for international trade. This lively commercial activity, the opportunities for privateering and smuggling, the increased demand for timber, and the enlarged expenditure of the commissariat all gave an artificial fillip to the Nova Scotian economy which, predictably, did not long outlast the return to peace in 1815.

The uneasy but lucrative state of commercial cooperation and military neutrality which existed between the Maritime colonies and New England was transfigured in 1814. Adopting a more belligerent posture in North America with the defeat of Napoleon

Sherbrooke

in Europe, the British government instructed Sherbrooke to guarantee winter communications with the Canadas and to put pressure on the United States government by occupying part of present-day Maine. Deciding to strike at the long-disputed borderland between Passamaquoddy Bay and the Penobscot River, Sherbrooke led an expeditionary force that August which successfully landed at Castine and proceeded to subdue the entire region between the Penobscot and the St Croix. Having arranged for the civil administration and commercial regulation of this British enclave, he returned to Halifax, after an absence of less than four weeks, to resume the more mundane responsibilities of a war now entering its closing stages: accommodating American and French prisoners on Melville Island, distributing to the Indians presents of damaged provisions and worn-out blankets from the Board of Ordnance store, and procrastinating over the settlement of refugee blacks on land grants. The eight-month occupation of Castine yielded customs revenues which were subsequently used to finance a military library in Halifax and found Dalhousie College. To express local feelings of pride and triumph engendered by the war the Nova Scotia House of Assembly voted Sherbrooke £1,000 for the purchase of a piece of plate.

Sherbrooke's unexpected talents as a civil administrator, later so evident in Lower Canada, were revealed in his pragmatic approach to religious affairs in Nova Scotia. As a practising Anglican, he appreciated the value of an established church for promoting the loyalty and welfare of the inhabitants. He found with regret that in a community largely peopled by dissenters "the established Religion is very far from being in a flourishing state at present." Like Bishop Charles Inglis*, he felt that part of the Anglican malaise could be attributed to the inadequacy of clerical incomes. The financial problem, however, was easier to identify than remedy. Sherbrooke was unable to persuade the provincial assembly, dominated by dissenters, to make provision for the Church of England even when he offered, as an incentive to generosity, a suspension of the threatened collection of quitrents owed on land grants. While looking to the imperial authorities for remedial action, he could do no more than continue the practice of allocating to the church small sums from the arms and accoutrements fund, generated by a duty on distilled liquors, and set aside lands as a potential endowment for a dean and chapter and for glebes and schools, a belated and wholly unsuccessful attempt to emulate the clergy reserves in the Canadas.

Sherbrooke's concern for the welfare of the Church of England was coupled with a candid recognition of the need for a latitudinarian and placatory approach to matters of religion in a multiconfessional society. Expecting in 1812 that a new bishop would soon have

to be appointed to succeed the ailing Inglis, Sherbrooke advised the colonial secretary that Nova Scotia required "a person of great coolness, moderation & good sense to soothe & conciliate rather than irritate & disgust the dissenters which might disturb the peace of the country and at the same time it demands firmness to support the Established religion." None of the local aspirants seemed to him suitably qualified, and he took a positive aversion to the assertive high churchmanship of John Inglis*, whose father wanted him to be acknowledged his successor. Both instinct and expediency led Sherbrooke to favour broad churchmanship and inter-denominational cooperation. His independence of mind and aloofness from religious and political factionalism were well regarded by Nova Scotians, and his successor, Lord Dalhousie [Ramsay*], was urged by members of the legislature to pursue the same line of conduct.

On 10 April 1816 Sherbrooke was commissioned governor-in-chief of British North America. Leaving Halifax on 27 June, he arrived at Quebec to assume his new responsibilities on 12 July. He did so in the aftermath of the American war and of bitter party strife. The previous governor, Sir George Prevost*, who had been under attack from the English party for his handling of military operations during the war and for his appeasement of the Canadians, had been recalled the previous year. For its part, the Canadian party had launched impeachment proceedings in the Lower Canadian assembly against the two chief justices, Jonathan Sewell* and James MONK. Sherbrooke was determined from the outset not to become embroiled in partisan politics but to steer a neutral, conciliatory course with the aid of personal suasion and fair dealing. Fully conscious of the need to secure and retain the colonial secretary's approval for his strategy, he was at first placed in a dilemma by Earl Bathurst's well-meaning but unrealistic instructions that he should cultivate the goodwill of Bishop Joseph-Octave PLESSIS and the Catholic clergy and, at the same time, work closely with Sewell, a leader of the English party, now returned in triumph to Quebec after his vindication by the Privy Council. Sherbrooke pointed out the impossibility of reconciling these two objectives. He described the deep-rooted loathing of Sewell that prevailed among the Canadians, and particularly among the Catholic clergy who blamed him for the colony's ills. This might be an unreasoning prejudice, deliberately cultivated by "designing demagogues," but its existence had to be recognized and accommodated if political harmony was to be restored. Sherbrooke would support Sewell and try to propitiate the leaders of the English party, but he believed that a conciliatory policy depended in large measure for its success on his establishing a good understanding with the Roman Catholic bishop.

From the time of their first meeting, in Halifax in

1815, Sherbrooke and Plessis had begun to develop a mutual sympathy and respect which soon ripened into close private friendship and professional cooperation. To cement and capitalize on this personal accord for the benefit of the local government and the imperial relationship, and to gain the confidence of the Catholic clergy and people, Sherbrooke revived a proposal that Plessis should be appointed to the Legislative Council under the title of Roman Catholic bishop of Quebec. Use of this designation caused anxious deliberations in Quebec, London, and Rome, raising as it did sensitive issues of religion, protocol, and law, including an apparent incongruity with the king's supremacy and the royal instructions. Eventually Sherbrooke short-circuited these legal quibbles by summoning Plessis to the council in 1818, an initiative readily accepted by Bathurst, who was keen to acknowledge by this singular distinction the services rendered by the Catholic clergy during the war. Under the governor's careful management, this appointment secured the local executive a valuable political ally as well as a closer link with the French-speaking inhabitants of the province.

Sherbrooke was able to supplement his understanding with Plessis by winning the support of Louis-Joseph Papineau*, the young and as yet impressionable speaker of the legislative assembly, who was eager to enhance the prestige of his position and guarantee his income. Sherbrooke arranged for the speaker's salary of £1,000 a year, originally granted for the duration of the war, to be made permanent, and he purchased the concurrence of the Legislative Council by paying Sewell the same stipend as speaker of the upper house. Through candour and courtesy Sherbrooke managed to establish a cordial, even paternal, relationship with the French Canadian politician who was later to become the scourge of governors less astute and accommodating in their conduct.

Sherbrooke capitalized on his good understanding with the speaker of the assembly when he turned to unravel the colony's chaotic financial affairs and secured an amicable agreement over the voting of supplies in 1818, a rare achievement for a governor of Lower Canada. Since the days of Lord Dorchester [Guy Carleton*] the executive had sought to avoid a full disclosure of the civil list, as well as an increase in the assembly's financial powers, by presenting the annual estimates in a severely truncated fashion and requesting the legislature to vote money to cover what was only a proportion of the government's expenditure. The balance had been supplied chiefly from customs duties levied under the Quebec Revenue Act of 1774 and from other crown revenues not subject to appropriation by the legislature. As the manifold expenses of administering a large province had grown, however, especially during the War of 1812, it had become customary to meet the annual deficit by

resorting to a British military account known as "army extraordinaries," a seemingly limitless fund not yet subject to parliamentary scrutiny, which routinely covered a host of items neither military nor extraordinary. A further complication facing Sherbrooke had arisen from the practice, begun by Governor Sir James Henry Craig* when he rejected the assembly's offer to negotiate a civil list in 1810 and extended by Prevost during the American war, of borrowing covertly from the provincial treasury the accumulating proceeds of local revenue acts, with the intention that the money would eventually be repaid. This appropriation of funds was referred to as a "debt" owed by Britain to the colony, but none of the imperial authorities had apparently known about it until Sherbrooke's revelations in 1817, when the accumulated total stood at £120,000.

To introduce some regularity into financial procedures and eliminate both the past "debt" and future deficits, Sherbrooke suggested in 1818 seeking an accommodation with the assembly. This would involve annual consideration of the budget by the legislature and the voting of adequate supplies for the ordinary expenditure of the province, but would stop short of recognizing the assembly's right to control all forms of revenue. Once he had obtained the colonial secretary's approval for this negotiation in the interests of imperial retrenchment, Sherbrooke was prepared to include in the estimate all items, however inexplicable, except clerical salaries, which Plessis was as anxious to omit as the Anglican bishop, Jacob MOUNTAIN. Compared with past and future controversies over financial control, the discussion in 1818 was pursued by both houses of the legislature with remarkable speed and unanimity. The assembly protested moderately against the payment of salaries to absentee office holders and Sherbrooke recommended to Bathurst that such items should be eliminated from future estimates. Because of this objection and the governor's inopportune illness, the assembly did not frame its vote in the shape of a regular appropriation bill but presented instead an address authorizing the governor to draw on unappropriated revenues to meet his budgetary deficit. This loose procedure was ill judged: a golden opportunity to establish a precedent for future supply bills was lost and financial appropriation again became a perennial bone of contention between governors and assemblies who were not on cordial terms.

Sherbrooke's health had not been robust since his arrival in Lower Canada. During 1817 he complained that the disabilities contracted in India were aggravated by the severe winter climate and advised Bathurst that he would be obliged to resign his commission the following year, even though he regretted the frequent changes of governor and for himself rued the loss of income which premature retirement would entail. On

Short

6 Feb. 1818 he suffered a severe paralytic stroke and at once resigned, recommending Dalhousie as his successor. On 30 July he handed over the administration instead to the Duke of Richmond [Lennox*], Bathurst's brother-in-law, and the following month he left for England. With his health partially recovered and sustained by visits to the spas of Cheltenham and Bath, Sherbrooke lived quietly in the English countryside at Calverton. From time to time he was visited there by Canadians, including Plessis in 1819, and he corresponded with colonists and British government officials about Canadian affairs, such as the abortive bill for a reunion of the provinces in 1822, until his death in 1830.

It might seem surprising that a military man of violent temper and indifferent health should have achieved such remarkable success in making the constitution of Lower Canada work harmoniously and in winning the confidence and respect of colonists of all parties. Appointed to a colonial governorship at the age of 46 as a reward for military services, Sherbrooke proceeded to display in that civilian capacity unexpected gifts as an astute diplomat and conciliator. Though instinctively conservative, he was no reactionary and his thoroughly pragmatic approach to colonial politics enabled him to preserve a sense of proportion and detachment. He was encumbered neither by strong prejudices nor by undue sensitivity about official prerogatives or personal honour, which so vitiated the conduct of governors like Dalhousie. The secret of Sherbrooke's success lay in a declared determination to combat factionalism and adopt a neutral stance, allied with the necessary independence of mind to pursue these objectives unswervingly and the engaging frankness of manner to convince all kinds of men of his probity and even-handedness. It would be impossible, Herman Witsius Ryland* avowed in January 1817, "to see a more amicable, upright and honorable Man, and I feel persuaded that his manly Candour, firmness and good sense will ensure Respect, & Compliance with his Views from the major part of the Assembly." Circumstances also favoured Sherbrooke. Not only did he receive full approval as well as a free hand from the colonial secretary, but he managed to establish a friendly rapport with leading political and religious figures in the province, such as Papineau and Plessis, whose interests and inclination made them at that particular moment receptive to such overtures. Through force of character and shrewd management Sherbrooke secured a lull in the politics of confrontation in Lower Canada. In so doing he attained for himself the rare distinction of being a senior military officer in the Wellingtonian army whose reputation was enhanced when he became a colonial administrator.

PETER BURROUGHS

A portrait of Sherbrooke painted by Robert Field* is in the possession of the Halifax Club.

Nottinghamshire Record Office (Nottingham, Eng.), Reg. of baptisms for the parish of Arnold, 29 April 1764. PAC, MG 23, GII, 10, vol.5; MG 24, A57 (mfm.); B3, 3–4. PANS, MG 100, 152, no.1; RG 1, 62–63, 111–11A. PRO, CO 42/166–79; CO 43/23–25; CO 217/88–98; CO 218/28–29. H. [E.] Bunbury, *Narratives of some passages in the great war with France, from 1799 to 1810* (London, 1854). *Gentleman's Magazine*, January–June 1830: 558–59. L.C., House of Assembly, *Journals*, 1816–18. N.S., House of Assembly, *Journal and proc.*, 1811–16. P. H. [Stanhope], 5th Earl Stanhope, *Notes of conversations with the Duke of Wellington, 1831–1851* (London, 1888; repr. New York, 1973). *Halifax Journal*, 19 April 1830. Cornelius Brown, *Lives of Nottinghamshire worthies . . .* (London, 1882), 326–27. *DNB*. G.B., WO, *Army list*, 1780–1830. H. J. Morgan, *Sketches of celebrated Canadians*. Wallace, *Macmillan dict*. Christie, *Hist. of L.C.* (1848–55), vol.2. Judith Fingard, *The Anglican design in loyalist Nova Scotia, 1783–1816* (London, 1972). Lambert, "Joseph-Octave Plessis." W. S. MacNutt, *The Atlantic provinces: the emergence of colonial society, 1712–1857* (Toronto, 1965). A. P. Martin, *Life and letters of the Right Honourable Robert Lowe, Viscount Sherbrooke . . . with a memoir of Sir John Coape Sherbrooke . . .* (2v., London, 1893). Murdoch, *Hist. of N.S.* Ouellet, *Economic and social hist. of Que.*; *Lower Canada* (Claxton). Taft Manning, *Revolt of French Canada*. *Evening Mail* (Halifax), 11 Nov. 1896. D. C. Harvey, "The Halifax–Castine expedition," *Dalhousie Rev.*, 18 (1938–39): 207–13. Helen Taft Manning, "The civil list of Lower Canada," *CHR*, 24 (1943): 24–47.

SHORT, ROBERT QUIRK, Church of England clergyman; b. *c.* 1759 at Withycombe Hall, Somerset, England, son of John Short; d. 31 Jan. 1827 in Trois-Rivières, Lower Canada

Robert Quirk Short entered the University of Oxford in 1778 and was ordained a deacon in the Church of England in 1783 and a priest on 30 Sept. 1787. He served as a curate in the diocese of Bath and Wells, where he apparently gave satisfaction. He married Mary Wood, and by 1796 they had seven children. That spring the Shorts emigrated to New York, but plans to purchase land there failed and in the fall they moved to Kingston, Upper Canada.

In March 1798 Short wrote to the bishop of Quebec, Jacob MOUNTAIN, requesting a pastoral charge in the diocese. Mountain was not impressed by the letter, concluding that Short was a man who lacked both education and sense, qualities the bishop prized in clergymen. He decided to await references from England and asked his commissary in Upper Canada, John Stuart*, to observe Short. Stuart concluded that Short's quick temper and harsh language made him unsuitable for appointment. Meanwhile, Short, who had been preaching and practising medicine in Kingston, had fallen into desperate financial straits, and by the autumn of 1799 he could afford neither food nor fuel. Mountain provided some firewood and sent a personal gift of ten pounds. In November his pity for the Short family and his difficulty in obtaining qualified priests from England led him to accept Short as a missionary. The Society for the Propagation of the Gospel, which would have to pay part of the salary, objected on the basis of Stuart's opinion that Short was unsuitable, but Mountain's need for priests prevailed.

Short was dispatched with a stipend of £200 to Saint-Armand, a seigneury along the Rivière Richelieu which had experienced significant English-speaking settlement after the American revolution. His stay was brief; in 1801 he was appointed with the same stipend to Trois-Rivières, in succession to Jehosaphat Mountain*. Short depicted to the bishop a small, struggling Anglican community of which fewer than 20 adults regularly attended Sunday services, held in the former Recollet chapel. Fifteen years after his appointment he reported that the congregation was still unable to contribute "a single farthing" to his living. In 1820 it was yet without chalice or flagon, and could afford to build neither a church nor a parsonage. There was no glebe land and there had been no donations for the poor. Short also served as chaplain to the troops garrisoned in the town.

Stuart's reservations about Short were confirmed to some extent at Trois-Rivières. Several conflicts with his parishioners reached the ears of the bishop; the parish clerk complained of Short's refusal to bury a dissenter's child, and one member of the congregation described the curate's fees as "extortion," bringing down on Short a severe reprimand from Mountain. Archdeacon George Jehoshaphat Mountain* reproached Short for the success of the Methodists in Trois-Rivières. On the other hand, according to the historian Benjamin Sulte* several inhabitants of the town later recalled Short's being "well-informed, obliging, a good conversationalist, active, and a man of the world," a social favourite of the leading families of Trois-Rivières, including the Antrobuses, the Bells, and the Harts. Indeed Short promoted the election of Ezekiel Hart* to the House of Assembly in 1807, and in 1811 he came to the defence of Benjamin Hart*, whom Colonel Thomas Coffin* wished to exclude from the militia, ostensibly on the ground of his Jewish religion. Short accepted good-naturedly the decoration of his old horse with paint and odd accoutrements by the town's young men, led by Charles Richard Ogden*. Somewhat of an eccentric, a quality that did not endear him to his bishop, Short once convened his friends for a demonstration of flight in a machine of his invention, during which he narrowly escaped severe injury.

On 15 Aug. 1823 Trois-Rivières was erected by letters patent into a parish, and Short was appointed its rector. That year the government provided funds for the conversion of the Recollet chapel into a church and for the purchase of a parsonage, consisting of that part

of the Recollet monastery being used as a court-house and jail. In the fall of 1823 Short moved into what had been the jail, and in 1826 the renovated chapel was opened for services. Short's last eight years were troubled by illness, and on several occasions the parish requested an assistant, which it finally received in November 1826 in the person of Francis Evans*. Short died in 1827 at age 68 and was succeeded as rector by Samuel Simpson Wood*; Evans assumed the charge of the parish until Wood's induction in 1829.

ROBIN B. BURNS

ACC-Q, 70; 74, 23 July 1801; 87, 15 April, 21 Oct. 1806; 107: 1. ANQ-MBF, CE1-50, 3 févr. 1827. Montreal Gazette, 5 Feb. 1827. Quebec Gazette, 25 April 1816. A. E. E. Legge, The Anglican Church in Three Rivers, Quebec, 1768–1956 ([Russell, Ont.], 1956). T. R. Millman, Jacob Mountain; The life of the Right Reverend, the Honourable Charles James Stewart, D.D., Oxon., second Anglican bishop of Quebec (London, Ont., 1953). Benjamin Sulte, Mélanges historiques . . . , ed. Gérard Malchelosse (21v., Montréal, 1918–34), 21: 56–61.

SILVESTER, JOSEPH. See JOE, SYLVESTER

SIMONDS, JAMES, businessman, JP, judge, office holder, and politician; b. 10 Dec. 1735 in Haverhill, Mass., son of Nathan Simonds and Sarah Hazen; m. 9 Nov. 1767 Hannah Peabody, and they had 14 children including Charles* and Richard*; d. 20 Feb. 1831 in Portland (Saint John), N.B.

James Simonds was one of the many younger sons of Massachusetts freeholders who came of age in the mid 18th century just as the supply of arable virgin land in the western part of the colony was becoming depleted. Divided among several heirs the Simonds patrimony could provide an adequate living for none. Following service in the Seven Years' War, during which he participated in James Abercromby*'s assault on Fort Carillon (near Ticonderoga, N.Y.) in 1758, Simonds determined to move to Nova Scotia in response to Governor Charles Lawrence*'s invitation. After careful examination of potential areas of settlement, he chose land at the mouth of the Saint John River in an area soon to be known as Portland Point. Promised by the government that a 5,000-acre grant would be forthcoming, Simonds, his brother Richard, and Captain Francis Peabody moved to the new location in 1762. It is difficult to imagine an economically more advantageous grant in the colony. The estuary provided a sheltered deep-water harbour containing one of the finest salmon and alewife fisheries on the Atlantic coast. The limestone outcrop at Portland offered the possibility of an extensive supply of lime. On the east side of the harbour was a 2,000-acre salt-marsh capable of providing an im-

Simonds

mense supply of hay. The Saint John valley itself, embracing some 26,000 square miles, was home to the Malecite Indians, who maintained a modest trade in furs with European factors.

Simonds came to Portland Point with the intention of becoming a businessman rather than a farmer. He began by exploiting the fishery and shipping the product to his cousin William Hazen*, a small merchant of Newburyport, Mass. Recognizing the commercial possibilities of the Saint John area and needing capital to exploit them, Simonds and Hazen formed a partnership with a kinsman, Samuel Blodget, a substantial Boston merchant engaged in the West Indies trade. Ownership of the new firm was split four ways: Simonds, Hazen, and Blodget each received a quarter share; the remaining quarter was divided among Richard Simonds, James White (another of Hazen's cousins), and Robert Peaslie (Hazen's brother-in-law). The three junior partners joined Simonds on the Saint John while Hazen handled the distribution of goods in Massachusetts and Blodget remained the sedentary partner. In February 1764 Simonds received from the Nova Scotia government a licence to occupy the lands at Portland Point together with a licence to carry on fishing and to burn lime. On 1 March the new partnership came into effect. Subsequently the firm was to obtain large grants at the mouth of the river.

Simonds and White brought 30 men to Portland in 1764, including lime burners, fishermen, coopers, and other tradesmen needed for the prosecution of the several businesses in which they were soon involved. Simonds was an aggressive entrepreneur: he created trading arrangements with his own employees, the garrison at nearby Fort Frederick, the Saint John valley Indians, and the New England settlers at Maugerville, in addition to maintaining an extensive trade in fish, furs, lime, and lumber products with Massachusetts. Between 1764 and 1774 the firm employed 17 vessels in its service, and Simonds dispatched to his partners some £30,000 worth of furs and fish, 2,540 hogsheads of lime, 1,171 barrels of castor, and many thousands of clapboards and barrel staves. In 1764 the partners joined the Saint John River Society, also known as the Canada Company, which included such influential figures as Governor Thomas Hutchinson of Massachusetts and Colonel Frederick Haldimand*, and through this means shared proprietorship of an additional 400,000 acres of land in the Saint John valley [see Beamsley Perkins Glasier*].

In 1765 Richard Simonds was killed by Indians, Peaslie left the partnership, and Hazen associated Leonard Jarvis in his share of the company. The following year Hazen and Jarvis bought out Blodget for £2,215. The firm was then reorganized. Under a new arrangement in 1767 Hazen and Jarvis acquired a

half interest in the firm, Simonds received a third, and James White was left with the remainder. In addition, all of the lands held individually by the partners in Nova Scotia, with the exception of Simonds's grant at Maugerville, were made part of the firm. That same year Simonds married Francis Peabody's daughter Hannah and by this act further strengthened his connection to James White, who had married Hannah's sister. He had bought Peabody's house at Portland Point in 1766 and he was to live there until 1778.

As the oldest resident and principal landowner in the area Simonds came to play a significant civil role in the Saint John valley in the late 1760s. Most of the garrison was withdrawn from Fort Frederick in 1768 and Simonds was left in charge of the few remaining soldiers with responsibility for maintaining the peace. At different times he occupied the offices of magistrate, judge of probate, registrar of deeds, and deputy collector of customs for Sunbury County, which embraced most of the territory that later became New Brunswick. In 1773 he was elected to the Nova Scotia House of Assembly in the place of Israel Perley*. He took his seat in October 1774 and continued to represent the county until 1782.

The firm's decline began with the onset of the American revolution. Hazen came to Portland in 1775 and, Leonard Jarvis having left the company, Samuel Jarvis was engaged to transact the Massachusetts side of the business. Jarvis soon had difficulty filling orders for the Saint John and the Portland partners began to trade directly with the West Indies. Fort Frederick was attacked and taken by the rebels that summer, and in September Simonds sailed to Windsor, N.S., seeking help from the government but to no avail. In May 1776 the Maugerville settlers issued a statement of support for the revolution [see Seth Noble*]; when it was circulated in the Saint John valley, Simonds, Hazen, and White refused to sign it. Some months later Jonathan Eddy* came through Portland on his way to attack Fort Cumberland (near Sackville, N.B.), and in 1777 John Allan* arrested Hazen and White during his unsuccessful expedition to the Saint John. By 1778 all trade was at a standstill. Simonds decided to abandon the business. He moved inland to his farm at Lower Maugerville (Sheffield) and took no further part in the firm. In 1780 he offered to sell to Hazen and White his interest in all of the lands at the river's mouth. Given the uncertainties of the time, the partners refused the offer.

Hazen and White proceeded to establish contacts with business and political interests in Halifax, Michael Francklin* among them, and were soon involved in the masting trade. As the war drew to its end and the transfer of the loyal refugees and regiments to Nova Scotia appeared imminent, the two active partners turned their attention once again to Portland.

James White displaced Simonds as deputy collector of customs, and Hazen became commissary to the garrison. The partners' lands at Portland comprised two large grants which they believed included all the land north of what became Union Street, Saint John, to the Kennebecasis River, east to the Great Marsh, and south to Red Head, as well as the Portland Point and Indiantown areas in the west. Prior to 1778 the partners had fulfilled the conditions of their grants by building roads, grist-mills, and wharfs and by attracting 30 families of settlers. When Hazen and White had the land surveyed in 1784 it was discovered that most of the Great Marsh lay outside the grants. Hazen and White then induced an old Seven Years' War officer, Lieutenant William Graves, to file on the marsh as part of his military service grant. Using their influence with Halifax officials, the two partners procured the grant for Graves, who in return for a small commission conveyed the land to them.

The loyalists' arrival in 1783 transformed what had been a wilderness settlement of 30 or 40 families and a small British garrison into the commercial hub around which the new colony of New Brunswick was structured. While perhaps 15,000 or 20,000 loyalists passed through Saint John in 1783–84, the resident population probably comprised about 5,000 people, mostly settled in the area that became the city of Saint John in 1785. The firm of Simonds, Hazen, and White controlled the north shore of the inner harbour of Saint John, and the Portland Point buildings, mills, and wharfs became the most valuable assets in the colony. Since the company's lands restricted the main city to a 600-acre peninsula, the partners anticipated reaping a rich reward by setting up streets in neighbouring Portland and selling town lots to loyalists. Having acquired control of the Great Marsh, Hazen and White, in 1785, attempted to purchase all rights in the firm from Simonds for £3,000. He refused the offer and the following year asked for a settlement of the affairs of the company. There was no response from the other partners and Simonds wrote again outlining nine proposals for the division. Among other things he suggested that he receive one-third of the lands and rents belonging to the firm as well as all buildings which he had constructed. Negotiations broke down over Simonds's claim to a share in the Great Marsh under the terms of the partnership agreement of 1767. Attempts by William Pagan* and others to arbitrate this particular dispute broke down in 1791 and the case was argued in the Court of Chancery between 1808 and 1810, when Hazen and White were forced to pay Simonds £1,312. Apart from this issue the division of the firm's assets had been accomplished without difficulty. Each partner gained exclusive title to large grants of land. Simonds and Hazen were the major beneficiaries and after 1800 the two men lived on the rents received from their extensive urban and subur-

ban holdings. Through no act of their own, Simonds and Hazen had been transformed from minor New England traders to wealthy landed gentry in a new British colony.

Simonds and his wife had 14 living children between 1768 and 1792, a number of them born in Maugerville. The family's exile in the interior of the province for some years was an important element in determining its status and the role it came to play in a loyalist-dominated society. Hazen, operating among the leading loyalists of Saint John after 1783, shortly began the process of contracting advantageous alliances through the marriage of his young adult children with prominent loyalists. He became a member of the Council for New Brunswick and the Hazens rapidly moved to the heart of the loyalist functionary aristocracy. In the case of the Simonds family the process was delayed by a full generation. When the Simonds children married, early in the 19th century, they took young second-generation loyalists as their consorts.

Yet, this later social integration is deceiving. The loyalist arrival was, if anything, a more difficult transformation for Simonds than the revolution. He had lived in the isolation of Portland Point and Maugerville for more than 20 years and had few connections and no influence with a new social and political order that had its metropolitan focus in England rather than New England. Though he had repudiated the rebel cause, Simonds now found that he had much more in common with the "old inhabitants" than with the high-status victims of the war. Indicative of this community of feeling was his continued residence at Maugerville. In 1785, in the first elections for the New Brunswick House of Assembly, he ran in Sunbury County on behalf of the old inhabitants. He was defeated by the loyalist ticket. He moved to Saint John a few years later and in 1795 was elected to the assembly for Saint John County and City. There he supported the popular opposition to the Council, headed by James Glenie*, and participated in the movement to secure the assembly's control of appropriations. The radicals were able to withhold the vote of supply between 1795 and 1799. In the end, Lieutenant Governor Thomas Carleton* and the Council agreed to demands that appropriation be contained in the supply bill and that the appropriation name the persons to perform the service and the remuneration allowed. James Simonds was a House of Commons man; though he never took a position as extreme as that of Glenie, he none the less remained in opposition throughout his career in the assembly. He retired from public life in 1802. The disfavour in which he was held by the élite was reflected in the fact that he held no public office in the gift of the New Brunswick government until his appointment to the magistracy in 1816 when he was 80.

Simonds lived to a great age. There is little evidence

Simpson

of his involvement in the business life of Saint John after 1810 – it seems that the family's affairs were handled by his eldest son, Charles – but his interests continued to prosper and his property to appreciate with the growth of the city. Though it is difficult to evaluate suburban and commercial real estate which was never sold, it is very possible that the Haverhill pioneer's estate was worth $1,000,000 at the time of his death.

T. W. ACHESON

[The most valuable source for the study of Simonds's life and career to 1785 is the collection of letters written by Simonds and White while at Saint John between 1764 and 1785 and published as "Letters written at Saint John by James Simonds, A.D. 1764–1785," "Selections from the papers and correspondence of James White, esquire, A.D. 1762–1783," and "The James White papers continued, A.D. 1781–1788," ed. W. O. Raymond, N.B. Hist. Soc., *Coll.*, 1 (1894–97), no.2: 160–86; no.3: 306–40; and 2 (1899–1905), no.4: 30–72. Material on the activities of the Simonds, Hazen, and White firm is also found in the Hazen family papers and the James White papers at the N.B. Museum. There is a fine study of Simonds's business activities by R. C. Campbell, "Simonds, Hazen and White: a study of a New Brunswick firm in the commercial world of the eighteenth century" (MA thesis, Univ. of N.B., Saint John, 1970). Other accounts are found in W. O. Raymond's *The River Saint John: its physical features, legends and history from 1604 to 1784*, ed. J. C. Webster ([2nd ed.], Sackville, N.B., 1943; repr. 1950) and in his articles on "Incidents in the early history of St. John," *Acadiensis* (Saint John), 1 (1901): 82–86, 151–56. T.W.A.]

SIMPSON, ÆMILIUS, hydrographer, surveyor, fur trader, and ship's captain; b. 27 July 1792 in Dingwall, Scotland, son of Alexander Simpson and Emilia MacIntosh; d. unmarried 2 Sept. 1831 in Fort Simpson, on the Nass River (B.C.).

Son of the Dingwall parish schoolmaster and a farmer's daughter who died soon after his birth, Æmilius Simpson was both a schoolfellow and a family connection of George Simpson*, whose aunt Mary Simpson was to become Æmilius's stepmother in 1807. Æmilius entered the Royal Navy on 13 April 1806 as a volunteer first class and served throughout the Napoleonic Wars, receiving his lieutenant's commission on 2 March 1815. Post-war retrenchment cut short his career; on 5 Dec. 1816 he was placed on half pay and went back to Dingwall, where for ten years he chafed under "the exclusion . . . from active employment in the service . . . he idolized." His young stepbrother, Alexander Simpson*, remembered him as "naturally irascible" but "a man of warm affections." He formed a connection with Margaret McLennan, and in 1821 they had a son, baptized Horatio Nelson, the sole beneficiary named in his will.

Early in 1826 George Simpson, now governor of the Hudson's Bay Company territories in North America, offered Æmilius a post as hydrographer and surveyor. The Admiralty granted Æmilius a three years' leave of absence and the appointment was made on 1 March 1826. Four days later the two Simpsons sailed from Liverpool for New York, continuing from there via Montreal to Upper Fort Garry (Winnipeg). Æmilius's first assignment was to check the boundary, the 49th parallel, at Pembina (N.Dak.), in order to prevent HBC fur traders from encroaching on American territory. He confirmed the survey made in 1823 by Major Stephen Harriman Long for the American Department of War.

On 25 June 1826 Æmilius was appointed hydrographer and clerk in the Columbia district. His specific task was to take command of the vessel being sent out from England to carry on the coastal trade which the governor had determined to develop. Leaving York Factory (Man.) with the autumn brigade on 14 July 1826, he made a detailed survey of his route and reached Fort Vancouver (Vancouver, Wash.) on 2 November. He then supervised work on two vessels already under construction on the Columbia River and charted the river from Cape Disappointment to Fort Vancouver. On 8 June 1827 he assumed command of the newly arrived *Cadboro*; in the course of supplying transportation and protection for the land party that established Fort Langley (B.C.) in the summer of 1827 [see James McMillan*] he made the first hydrographic chart of the lower Fraser River.

For several years Simpson traded along the coast from Sitka (Alaska) to Monterey, Calif., and in the Sandwich (Hawaiian) Islands. In October 1829 he was appointed superintendent of the marine department of the HBC, occupying what Governor Simpson later called "the most dangerous post in the Service." In August 1830 he selected the site for a fort on the Nass River, "the grand mart of the Coast both for Sea Otters and Land Skins" – a hazardous enterprise which the governor thought "necessary for the Salvation of our interior Trade in the event of our being excluded from the Columbia." Promoted chief trader and given command of the *Dryad*, Simpson spent the summer of 1831 helping chief trader Peter Skene Ogden* to establish the fort on the Nass. He then went farther north on a "very successful" trading cruise; illness forced his return to the fort, named after him, and on 2 Sept. 1831 he died of "his old enemy, the liver complaint." He was buried outside the stockade, but when in 1834 the establishment was moved to a more convenient site (present-day Port Simpson, B.C.), his remains were reinterred there.

During his four-year sojourn on the Pacific coast Simpson had not been "over popular" in the HBC service: he owed his appointments directly to the governor, he did his best to maintain in a frontier setting the "tight discipline" of a British man-of-war, and in contrast with other HBC captains he appeared "excessively the gentleman." His courage and his efficiency as a seaman and fur trader were never questioned. Governor Simpson had always had "a very great respect for his character & high opinion of his worth" and privately called him "as good a little fellow as ever breathed, honourable, above board and to the point. He may be a disciplinarian but it was very necessary among the Vagabonds he had to deal with. The Drunken wretched creature [Thomas] Sinclair [first mate of the *Cadboro*] could afford him no support, he was therefore under the necessity of doing all the dirty work of cuffing & thunking himself."

A well-established local tradition, substantially confirmed by contemporary evidence, maintains that the cultivation of apples and grapes in the Columbia River valley originated with this Scottish exile from the Royal Navy, who won chief factor John McLoughlin*'s "Respect and Esteem" by his "Gentlemanlike conduct and zealous discharge of his duty."

DOROTHY BLAKEY SMITH

General Reg. Office (Edinburgh), Dingwall, reg. of births and baptisms, 22 Oct. 1821. PABC, AB20, L2. PAM, HBCA, A.36/12: ff.35, 35d. PRO, ADM 1/3155: 24; ADM 9/174/5056. *HBRS*, 3 (Fleming); *HBRS*, 4 (Rich). Alexander Simpson, *The life and travels of Thomas Simpson, the Arctic discoverer* (London, 1845). George Simpson, "The 'Character book' of Governor George Simpson, 1832," *HBRS*, 30 (Williams), 151–236. Walbran, *B.C. coast names*. G. P. V. and H. B. Akrigg, *British Columbia chronicle, 1778–1846: adventures by sea and land* (Vancouver, 1975). H. H. Bancroft, *History of British Columbia, 1792–1887* (San Francisco, 1887). J. A. Hussey, *The history of Fort Vancouver and its physical structure* (Tacoma, Wash., 1957). *Wash. Hist. Quarterly* (Seattle), 1 (1906): 265; 2 (1907): 42–43.

SMALL, JOHN, office holder, JP, and militia officer; baptized 27 Aug. 1746 in Cirencester, England, eldest son of Joseph Small, a haberdasher, and Mary Atwell; m. Elizabeth Goldsmith, and they had five sons; d. 18 July 1831 in York (Toronto), Upper Canada.

Appointed clerk of the Executive Council of Upper Canada on 12 Sept. 1792 through the influence of Home Secretary Henry Dundas, John Small was sworn in at Newark (Niagara-on-the-Lake) on 18 May 1793. The lieutenant governor, John Graves Simcoe*, although not consulted on his appointment, described Small as "a *Gentleman* who possesses and is entitled to my highest confidence." Small received few other compliments. His work was soon badly in arrears, and the next lieutenant governor, Peter Hunter*, was sharply critical of his inefficiency. Small nevertheless held his post until his death, adding to it a justiceship

of the peace at York (1796), the lieutenant-colonelcy of the York militia (1798), and the office of clerk of the crown and pleas (12 March 1806 to 10 Aug. 1825).

Small is best known for the duel on 3 Jan. 1800 in which he mortally wounded John White*, the attorney general. Mrs Small had publicly snubbed the notoriously quarrelsome Mrs White. White reacted by questioning the legality of Small's marriage and the morals of his wife in a letter to David William Smith*, which was communicated to Chief Justice John Elmsley* and received credence in York society. Small insisted upon immediate satisfaction, without determining how much of the gossip had actually come from White. He was acquitted on a charge of murder after a brief trial, despite the hostility of the presiding judge, Henry Allcock*.

The affair ruined both Mrs Small's reputation and the connection that Small had formed with the Russells, Macaulays, and Macdonells of Collachie. Peter Russell*, who at Newark in May 1795 had defended Small against an anonymous libel, was White's friend and executor. When Small sought election to the House of Assembly in July 1800 he was defeated; and in a second attempt at a by-election a year later he was crushed, 112 votes to 32, by Angus Macdonell* (Collachie). Of his former friends, Joseph Willcocks* and the elder Robert Baldwin voted for him. On New Year's Day 1806 Elizabeth RUSSELL would still acknowledge him only by "a distant curtsey." Two years later, Mrs Small's invitation to a governor's levee occasioned resentment.

As clerk of the council, Small was paid £100 a year – less than an unskilled labourer and only slightly more than the senior of his two clerks – besides being entitled to about one-fifteenth of land fees. He had inherited property in Gloucestershire which he disposed of some time before the end of 1795. Forbidden in 1797 to collect fees from loyalists and unsuccessful in petitions for a higher stipend, he was able to establish his family by speculating in land at York. One of the first officials to buy a house there, in August 1795, he had accumulated over 2,500 acres before beginning to sell lots in 1797 and he continued to acquire and sell land. By the 1820s the rise in York land prices had made him prosperous.

He also regained a position in York society. An active churchman (his brother was prebendary of Gloucester Cathedral), he was a trustee of the York District grammar school by 1811 and soon after found a patron in John Strachan*. Small even achieved some political influence under Administrator Samuel SMITH, to whom Strachan thought him "a considerable Adviser." He launched one son, James Edward*, on a successful career as a lawyer and reform politician; the youngest, Charles Coxwell, succeeded him in the clerkship of the crown and pleas as well as

Smith

in his militia commission. His house at York, handsomely rebuilt by Charles Coxwell, stood until 1925.

S. R. MEALING

[The most informative references to Small are in the William Dummer Powell papers (at the AO, MTL, and PAC), the Russell papers (AO and MTL), the various collections of Simcoe papers (see the bibliography accompanying his biography, *DCB*, vol.5), and Strachan's *Letter book* (Spragge). The Gloucestershire County Record Office (Gloucester, Eng.) holds his uncle John's will as well as the baptismal, marriage, and land tax records of the family. See also E. S. Caswell, "A sketch of Major John Small," York Pioneer and Hist. Soc., *Report* (Toronto), 1933: 22–23; W. R. Riddell, "The duel in early Upper Canada," *Canadian Law Times* (Toronto), 35 (1915): 726–38; and *Robertson's landmarks of Toronto*, vol.1. s.R.M.]

SMITH, PETER, businessman, JP, and office holder; b. 1752; m. *c.* 1794 Ann Cook, and they had three sons and five daughters; d. 15 Aug. 1826 in Kingston, Upper Canada.

At the outbreak of the American revolution Peter Smith lived in Burlington, Vt, and during the conflict he served as a sergeant in Butler's Rangers. By 16 Oct. 1784 he had settled in Township No.1 (Cataraqui) of western Quebec. Two years later, with Richard Beasley* as a partner, he was involved in the Indian trade; their major supplier was the partnership of Hamilton and Cartwright. In April 1786 Richard Cartwright* urged Beasley and Smith to take Robert DICKSON as a partner but Smith did not "relish" the idea. In August 1789 Smith and Beasley were each granted 200 acres in the area of Toronto and present-day Port Hope.

By 1791 Smith was established in Kingston as one of the small group of merchants in the forwarding trade. At the first meeting of the Executive Council of Upper Canada, on 20 July 1792, he received permission to erect a wharf and build a storehouse and quay at Kingston. A major aspect of his trade was supply of the British army posts. By 1792 Smith and several others, including Cartwright and Joseph Forsyth*, had accumulated almost 4,000 barrels of flour in anticipation of high demand. When their expectations proved false, they petitioned Lieutenant Governor John Graves Simcoe* to purchase the flour for government stores. Although their request was refused (officials called them monopolists), from 1796 Smith appears frequently, either by himself or with partners, on the victualling accounts of the army commissariat. When in 1800 Upper Canadian merchants began to export flour to Lower Canada, Smith was among them. The following year he capitalized further on the new market, shipping large amounts of flour, cheese, potash, and peas to Montreal. One of the difficulties faced by merchants was the scarcity of river craft. Cartwright reported that Smith "has even

sent to bring up empty Boats [from Montreal] with three men in each to carry down his Flour."

During his career Smith had several partners. About 1796 he went into business with another Kingston merchant, John Cumming; this partnership was dissolved in 1803 when they divided their holdings. In 1811 Smith and other Kingston merchants including Cartwright purchased the *Kingston Gazette*, then sold it to Stephen Miles*. He was also among the group of businessmen who had by 1818 invested almost £16,000 in the steamboat *Frontenac* [*see* Henry Gildersleeve*]. Banking was another of Smith's interests and his name appears on the lists of Kingstonians who petitioned the House of Assembly in 1817 and again two years later for authorization to incorporate a bank of Upper Canada [*see* Thomas Dalton*].

Like other successful merchants, Smith was involved in most aspects of community life. He was appointed to the magistracy, the land board, and the school board. He subscribed to a host of local philanthropic societies and, as befitted a man with eligible daughters, was manager of the Kingston Assembly and the first subscription ball. A benefactor of the Church of England, he served twice as churchwarden of St George's Church. A contemporary later remembered him as "highly respected, upright in all his dealings, and free from any moral or political reproach," a "fine specimen of an English gentleman" who "carried with him evidence that he was no stranger to good dinners, and understood the qualities of good wine."

MARGARET ANGUS

AO, MU 500, letter-book, January–July 1786. PAC, RG 8, I (C ser.), 115B: 70, 348; 115C: 179. QUA, Richard Cartwright papers, letter-book, 14 May 1801. "Journals of Legislative Assembly of U.C.," AO *Report*, 1913: 47–48. *Kingston before War of 1812* (Preston). *Parish reg. of Kingston* (Young). "Settlements and surveys," PAC *Report*, 1891, note A: 6–7. *Kingston Chronicle*, 4 Jan., 19 March, 23 July 1819; 18 Aug. 1820; 23 Nov. 1821; 18 Aug. 1826. *Kingston Gazette*, 4 May 1814; 13 Oct., 18 Nov. 1815; 28 Sept. 1816; 29 March, 15 July 1817; 30 June 1818. Canniff, *Hist. of the settlement of U.C.*, 437. Wilson, *Enterprises of Robert Hamilton*, 61.

SMITH, SAMUEL, army officer, politician, and colonial administrator; b. 27 Dec. 1756 in Hempstead, N.Y., son of James Smith, a Scottish immigrant; m. 21 Oct. 1799 Jane Isabella Clarke at Newark (Niagara-on-the-Lake), Upper Canada, and they had two sons and nine daughters; d. 20 Oct. 1826 in York (Toronto).

Samuel Smith joined the Queen's Rangers as an ensign in 1777, rose to captain in 1780, and was among those officers who surrendered at Yorktown, Va, in 1781. After the war he settled briefly in New

Brunswick, and in 1784 went to England. Commissioned a captain in the second Queen's Rangers on 20 Dec. 1791, he was first stationed at Niagara (Niagara-on-the-Lake). In August 1794 he led the detachment sent to York. He commanded the regiment from 1799, was promoted lieutenant-colonel in 1801, but went on half pay when the Rangers were disbanded in November 1802.

He retired to the land he had taken up in 1796 in Etobicoke Township, where other disbanded Rangers joined him. It was a settlement that was to remain isolated from the town of York for another 20 years. Smith had 1,000 acres there, but could not afford the grand schemes that he entertained for their improvement. On his retirement his circumstances were modest enough to make his notably pretty sister Anne seem a poor match to the ambitious Joseph Willcocks*. Smith lived at Etobicoke without any public office for more than a decade until on 30 Nov. 1813 he was appointed to the Executive Council, on which he sat until the year before his death.

On 11 June 1817, as the senior councillor who was neither a Roman Catholic like James Baby nor the holder of another office like John McGill or William Dummer Powell, he was sworn in as administrator of the province, Lieutenant Governor Francis Gore* having left Upper Canada. He served until 13 Aug. 1818 and again, during the absence of Lieutenant Governor Sir Peregrine Maitland*, from 8 March to 30 June 1820.

As administrator he shelved the problem of granting land to American immigrants. His instructions were to administer the oath of allegiance to them (which Gore had raised a storm by refusing to do), but to require seven years' residence before granting them land and to dispossess those who did not qualify. Instead he accepted the advice of his Executive Council not to disturb the security of land titles by raising the question, which was not settled until the Naturalization Act of 1828 validated all grants up to 1820. His inaction was sensible, but it did leave the council "sleeping over an Office choked with applications," as Maitland put it.

Smith failed with the House of Assembly, which after its prorogation by Gore on 7 April 1817 was in no mood to be conciliatory. It quarrelled with the Legislative Council over the latter's amendment of money bills, refusing to vote supply except by an address directly to Smith, without the council's participation. It also demanded an accounting of civil expenditures and voted to repeal its original grant of 1816 when it found that, of £2,500 voted, £800 had gone to a pension for the former chief justice, Thomas Scott, and £400 to a salary for the speaker of the Legislative Council. After two months, despairing of any cooperation between the two houses, Smith prorogued the assembly on 1 April 1818.

Smith received most criticism for the ineptness of his attempt to cope with Robert Gourlay*. Gourlay wrote that "as a President he is nothing." John Strachan* thought him "feeble," and "without energy or talents." Yet it was Smith, without consulting either Powell or Strachan, who had decided in April 1818 that Gourlay must be arrested if there was a law to allow it; and, after Gourlay's acquittals for libel, Smith still sought advice on the possible illegality of Gourlay's York convention. Smith's tory abhorrence of sedition was restrained by the law, not by indecision. When Maitland arrived to take over Gourlay along with the other problems of government, there were expressions of relief in the province. It is likely that Smith, from his retirement in Etobicoke, shared them.

S. R. Mealing

[The published sketches of Smith in Chadwick, *Ontarian families*, and D. B. Read, *The lieutenant-governors of Upper Canada and Ontario, 1792–1899* (Toronto, 1900), are not very revealing. The basic sources for his public career are his official correspondence in PRO, CO 42, and the journals of the legislature. Contemporary comments are in *Statistical account of U.C.* (Gourlay), vol.2; Strachan's *Letter book* (Spragge); and in the papers of William Dummer Powell (at the AO, MTL, and PAC), Peter Russell (AO and MTL), and John Graves Simcoe (described in the bibliography accompanying his biography, *DCB*, vol.5). s.r.m.]

SMYTH, GEORGE STRACEY, army officer and colonial administrator; b. 4 April 1767, likely in Norwich, England, youngest son of the Reverend John Smyth and Sarah Gee, a cousin of the future 1st Marquess Camden; he and his wife, Amelia Anne, had two children, a daughter and a son; d. 27 March 1823 in Fredericton.

On 20 May 1779, at the age of 12, George Stracey Smyth was appointed an ensign in the East Norfolk Regiment of Militia. After joining the army the following year as an ensign in the 25th Foot, he rose through the ranks to become a major general on 1 Jan. 1812. In May 1791 he was a lieutenant and serving in Gibraltar as adjutant of the 7th Foot, under the command of Prince Edward* Augustus, the fourth son of George III. He shared with the prince an enthusiasm for music and made himself useful by accompanying Edward and Mme de Saint-Laurent [Montgenet] on the piano when they sang duets for the entertainment of the household. He served on the prince's staff for 12 years, in Gibraltar, Quebec, the West Indies, Nova Scotia, and Gibraltar a second time. "No Musick! The People No Souls in this Province," he lamented shortly after his arrival in Halifax, where he was fort major in the years 1794–99. He was promoted to the rank of major in September 1798. When Edward, now Duke of Kent, became commander-in-chief of the forces in British North America in 1799, he made Smyth his senior aide-de-camp and acting quartermaster general. He also named Smyth's elder brother, the Reverend John Gee Smyth, as his domestic chaplain. Four years later, on the duke's retirement to England, George Stracey Smyth was one of the grooms of his household. Subsequently, he served on the staff of the Duke of Cambridge, the youngest son of George III, who was in command of the Home District.

The association with royalty, backed up by the patronage of his politically powerful cousin Lord Camden, made it easy for Smyth to rise in his profession and accounts for his appointment as commander of the forces in New Brunswick soon after his promotion to major-general made him eligible for such a position. Under regulations instituted in 1808, the commander of the forces was responsible for the civil administration of the province, the lieutenant governor, Thomas Carleton*, being on permanent leave in England. Smyth served as president of the Council from 15 June 1812 to August 1813, when he fell ill, and from 2 July 1814 to June 1816, when he was called to Nova Scotia to administer that province and act as commander-in-chief until the arrival of Lord Dalhousie [Ramsay*] in October. He succeeded Carleton as lieutenant governor of New Brunswick in February 1817; after a brief visit to the province in June, he returned in July and remained there until his death.

In 1812 he took over his duties from Lieutenant-General Martin Hunter* shortly before word arrived of the American declaration of war. On receiving the news he met at once with his council to decide what action should be taken. Instructions were given that one-third of the militia should be ready for service at short notice but, since it was the planting season, it was decided that men would not immediately be called away from their farms. Smyth ordered the battalion commanders to retreat at first if there should be an invasion but to increase resistance when reinforcements were assembled. At Saint John, which was bound to be the objective of any serious attack, there was an enthusiastic response from the Common Council and the populace, who erected breastworks and batteries and prepared boats for the movement of troops.

After the declaration of war Americans on the border gave assurances of their peaceful intentions, and the Indians also expressed their desire for friendship. The pacifism of the New Englanders fitted in nicely with the policy of the British, who encouraged American shipowners and merchants to defy their government's efforts to prevent them engaging in international trade. Since 1807, when the embargo was imposed, illicit trade had flourished in Maritime ports, with the Americans selling food and supplies in exchange for British manufactures and for gypsum.

American ships, under licence from the British authorities, brought their cargoes openly into Saint John Harbour, while an extensive trade was carried on, somewhat less overtly, amid the islands and coastal waterways of Passamaquoddy Bay. On 10 July Smyth, following the example of Lieutenant Governor Sir John Coape SHERBROOKE in Nova Scotia, issued a proclamation forbidding British subjects to molest the inhabitants of the United States living on the shores near New Brunswick, or to interfere with their coasting or fishing vessels, so long as they abstained from molesting the inhabitants of Nova Scotia and New Brunswick.

Meanwhile, enterprising citizens of Saint John, remembering the profits that had been made from raiding enemy shipping in earlier wars, were being tempted by the opportunity for privateering. Supported by members of his council, who quoted precedents from the 1790s, Smyth naïvely responded to requests by issuing letters of marque and reprisal, the first, on July 27, to a Saint John privateer, renamed the *General Smyth*, authorizing it to seize American vessels as prizes of war. The activities of the privateers disrupted the licensed trade and he received a severe reprimand from Lord Bathurst, the secretary of state for War and the Colonies. A second initiative undertaken by Smyth was the purchase of a 70-ton sloop, the *Brunswicker*, on behalf of the colonial government. He fitted it up for the protection of the coastal trade, but Bathurst ordered him to rely on the navy and refused to pay the costs involved.

Apart from the threat to shipping in the Bay of Fundy, the situation remained quiet. Work proceeded on the building of a Martello tower and other coastal defences but the threat of invasion was so remote in January 1813 that Lieutenant-General Sir George Prevost*, the commander-in-chief in British North America, ordered the 104th Foot, the only significant body of regular soldiers in the province, to march to Upper Canada to reinforce the army there. There was a second exciting march on snowshoes that winter: some 200 Acadian militiamen from the Baie des Chaleurs appeared in Fredericton, having, in the words of Lieutenant-Colonel Joseph Gubbins, the inspecting field officer of militia, "without the aid of government passed through a wilderness of nearly 300 miles" to prove their readiness to assist in the defence of the frontier.

Smyth left the province on sick leave in 1813, having been stricken with "repeated attacks of pulmonice threatening Phthisis Pulmonia or Consumption." Though he had returned to duty by July 1814, he was not involved in the British occupation of the Maine towns of Eastport, on Moose Island in Passamaquoddy Bay, and Castine that year. However, Moose Island, which lies on the New Brunswick side of the channel the British then claimed as the boundary under the treaty of 1783, was placed under Smyth's command. In May 1815 Sherbrooke, as commander-in-chief in the region, stated in a letter that he had always considered Saint John to be the best military headquarters of the New Brunswick district and gave his approval to Smyth's residing there. Smyth preferred Saint John to Fredericton, the civil capital, which, however, was the only place where a quorum of Council could meet conveniently. He therefore wrote to Sherbrooke asking whether he should consider his letter a command, "as in that case it will be necessary for me to apply to the secy of state for a sufficient number of councillors to be appointed, who may be residents of St. John." Two years later Bathurst authorized the appointment of two wealthy merchants, William Pagan* and William Black*, thus providing Smyth with a counterweight to the dominant Fredericton bureaucrats on the Council. From then on, he held many of its meetings in Saint John.

The legislative session of 1816 was very different from that of 1813, which was the last that Smyth had presided over and which had been taken up mainly with routine measures, except for those designed to promote the conduct of the war. Provincial revenues were buoyant as the economy responded to the increased sale of timber under the protective system introduced in Britain over the previous decade. In 1815 New Brunswick sent to Britain 92,553 loads of fir or pine timber; for Nova Scotia and the Canadas in that year the figures were 19,382 and 11,676. In his speech at the opening of the session, Smyth stressed education, roads, and the need to improve navigation of the principal rivers. There was a great deal of housekeeping legislation, for no session had been held in the previous year and little attention had been paid to domestic affairs during the war years. Important acts were passed dealing with parish schools and grammar schools, including a provision to assess local districts for the support of schools which was removed two years later and not reintroduced for several decades. It is probable that Smyth was interested in this provision and that he was also responsible for a proposal to spend money systematically on the development of the "great roads"; the latter measure was adopted in principle but not implemented effectively.

Three months after the session ended Smyth was sent to Nova Scotia to act as administrator. Illness had continued to plague him and by 1816 his wife's health was also undermined. A year's absence failed to bring improvement and she died at Halifax on 1 July 1817. Four years earlier Edward Winslow*'s daughter Penelope had described her as "young, handsome, gay," "a thoughtless flirting little thing that is never at rest without a Beau at her elbow. . . . [She] is pleasant and good natured but has not one speck of dignity in her composition." Whatever her shortcomings as the chatelaine of Government House, she was dear to Smyth; their shared love of music and their two young children created a bond that had made his exile in New Brunswick tolerable. Her death came shortly before his return to the colony to take up his appointment as lieutenant governor. By then he had become a complete valetudinarian, spending a great deal of time with his personal physician, Dr Alexander Boyle*, and pining for England, for an income that would enable him to retire, or for a promotion that would take him back to Halifax where the climate suited him better.

Smyth's spirits seemed to rise only when he was engaged in musical activities or endeavouring to provide opportunities for education. He gave strong support to the efforts of the National Society for Promoting the Education of the Poor, which was encouraging the establishment in the Maritimes of schools using the monitorial system of teaching (called Madras schools). In England the organization was principally concerned with the poor, but in New Brunswick its schools were attended by students from all levels of society. Smyth encouraged this trend by sending his own son, George Brunswick, to the Central School in Saint John, the first to be established. He often instructed the boys there in singing and presided at the organ when the school was opened. In 1819 he granted a charter to its governor and trustees, giving them authority to establish schools wherever their funds permitted. He was not empowered by his instructions to issue such a charter but the Colonial Office later gave him the necessary powers and authorized the granting of money from crown revenues to the Madras School Board. The charter was approved by the legislature in 1820. Black children were not admitted to the Central School and Smyth, who in both his civil and his military capacities had responsibility for the black refugees settled in the province at the end of the war, was sympathetic to their plight. He himself paid the master's salary and other expenses of the "African School" in Saint John when he was unable to obtain support in either New Brunswick or England; the school was closed for a time after his death until new funding could be arranged.

In Smyth's time the denominational rivalries that were later to become such an affliction had not yet divided the provincial community. Although the Madras schools came under the supervision of the Society for the Propagation of the Gospel, they did not immediately take on an exclusively Anglican character and in the beginning received strong support from some nonconformists. A spirit of toleration was abroad in 1823 when Smyth and the Council agreed to a bill making provision for a large grant to the College of New Brunswick contingent upon the removal of religious tests for students. Land for the support of the college had been set aside in 1785 and a provincial

Smyth

charter granted in 1800. Teaching at the university level got under way in 1822, the Reverend James Somerville* having been appointed the institution's president and its only professor two years earlier. Smyth laboured to help clear up a serious problem that had arisen over land titles, in order to prepare the way for an application for a royal charter. He thus played an important role in the process leading up to the opening of King's College, Fredericton, in 1829, the only state-supported university to be successfully launched in the British empire in that decade. The spirit of compromise did not extend to the marriage law. In 1821 the Council rejected a bill passed by the assembly that would have granted authorization to solemnize marriages to all ministers of the gospel licensed to preach.

It was the great increase in income from the timber trade that made possible the advancement of education. The virtually uncontrolled cutting on crown lands had led Hunter to make representations to the British government in 1810, but he had received no response. In 1816 Smyth declared that unless conservation measures were taken quickly the timber in accessible stands would soon be totally destroyed. This time the response was vigorous and decisive. A new era had arrived in which the Colonial Office was determined to intervene in a positive way to give direction to the development of the colonies. Authority over the cutting of timber on the ungranted lands, which still made up nine-tenths of the province, was, in effect, taken away from Sir John Wentworth*, the surveyor general of the king's woods, in Halifax, and transferred to the lieutenant governor and Council. There then began the struggle over control of the public lands that was to be the central political issue in the province for the next 20 years.

Many New Brunswickers regarded the trees on ungranted land as a resource that was freely available to all, like the fish in the streams and the game in the forests. There was, therefore, widespread resentment in 1818 when Smyth and the Council instituted a system of timber licences and a levy of one shilling a ton on all timber taken from the crown lands; they justified the duty by the necessity for a fund from which to pay the costs of surveys. Although the sum demanded was only one-fourth of that exacted in neighbouring Maine, several leading timber merchants in the assembly, Hugh JOHNSTON and Robert PAGAN among them, rallied opposition there, arguing that a tax had been imposed without the consent of the lower house and a basic principle of the British constitution thus violated. When the assembly proceeded to challenge the crown's right to manage the royal domain, a furious Smyth dissolved the house. The policy of creating a timber fund went forward, the large sums that accumulated being expended in the province on the authority of the British government.

The effect of the fund was, as its opponents feared, to reduce the power of the assembly while enhancing the role of the governor and Council in provincial affairs. Smyth bore the opprobrium while his successor, Sir Howard Douglas*, enjoyed the advantages of the new system.

Smyth had already demonstrated his political ineptitude before he was challenged over the timber fund. In 1818, during the first session of the legislature after he became lieutenant governor, he bickered continually with the assembly and supported the Council, which needed little encouragement, in its rejection of a number of bills. Probably he was trying to re-establish the authority of his office, much attenuated during Carleton's long absence from the province. He revived memories of the earlier era by questioning the propriety of paying members of the assembly. He returned to this issue again in 1820 and 1822, to the considerable annoyance of Lord Bathurst, who wrote in June 1822: "I can neither approve of your having agitated the question without previously referring for my instructions, or in selecting a subject for discussion in which the Members of the Assembly were personally interested and consequently more likely to consider your recommendation as infringing on their Privileges." The reprimand was accompanied by an ambiguous set of instructions that would have allowed Smyth to bring the quarrel to an end without losing face, had he shown any inclination to compromise. He chose instead to imply in a message to the assembly that Lord Bathurst would not tolerate pay for members; the quarrel came to an end only when he became too ill to continue it.

Smyth belonged to the class of squire-parsons who provided the backbone of early 19th-century English high toryism; his grandfather, his father, a brother, and a nephew were all clergymen. He shared their fondness for horse-racing, and also their sense of the close identification of the state with religion, their dedication to the preservation of a hierarchical order in society, and their devotion to the politics of principle which made them so inflexible in their attitudes towards liberal movements in education and towards democratic political institutions, except when either would promote the interests of the church. He was completely out of place in a North American setting, the idea of politics as the art of the possible being foreign to his way of thinking. In New Brunswick he found few who shared his tastes and point of view, especially since he looked with disfavour on most of the old loyalist families and paid little heed to their claims that past services entitled them to receive special consideration from government.

Smyth's council was dominated by two justices of the Supreme Court, Ward CHIPMAN and John Murray BLISS, who were able, through extensive family connections and links to the Colonial Office, to exert great influence over the direction of affairs. Smyth resented the encouragement that they gave to his opponents in the assembly. In making appointments he passed over their young friends and relatives, the nadir being reached in 1822 when he appointed an inexperienced young lawyer, Edward James Jarvis*, to a vacancy on the Supreme Court. If it was his intention to build up a faction favourable to himself in Saint John, the move was a shrewd one, for Jarvis, the son of a loyalist merchant, had excellent connections there. But the appointment appears to have been mainly designed to spite William Botsford*, the solicitor general and speaker of the assembly. By the end of 1822 Smyth's standing at the Colonial Office was so low that the secretary of state refused to countenance the breach of the rule that the judgeship should have been offered to the solicitor general; the following spring he named Botsford to the vacancy on the New Brunswick bench and sent Jarvis to serve as king's assessor in Malta.

The Smyth years saw a number of innovations in New Brunswick life, as the community moved from pioneering agriculture into the commercial world of frontier lumbering and shipbuilding. The first steamboat service on the Saint John River was launched in the spring of 1816, with the vessel suitably named the *General Smyth*, the province's first steam sawmill was established in 1822, and the Bank of New Brunswick was incorporated in 1820. In 1816, "the year without a summer," the crops failed. This disaster and the arrival of numbers of immigrants from Britain in the following years drew attention to the condition of agriculture. In 1820 Smyth became president of the New Brunswick Central Society for Promoting the Rural Economy, one of whose objectives was to provide assistance to settlers.

Smyth was much criticized. Penelope Winslow, in 1812, described him as "a stiff pedantic old thing" and Ariana Margaretta Jekyll Saunders, whose husband, George Shore*, was to become Smyth's protégé and friend, wrote in June 1815: "The Smyths are more disliked here than ever. . . . They live in a mean niggardly stile disliking and disliked by every body." She was upset because the Smyths had not given a ball on the king's birthday. Unknown to the social world of Fredericton was the fact that Smyth's circumstances were particularly difficult that year, the failure of his agent in London having resulted in the loss of a significant part of his modest personal fortune. But people could not help noticing his stinginess and comparing it to the open-handed hospitality of Hunter. Even Sir James Kempt*, on a tour of inspection in 1822, made gentle fun of Smyth's saving himself the trouble and expense of entertaining by arranging for subscription dinners to be offered in St Andrews and Saint John. The following year Lord Dalhousie, now governor-in-chief of British North America, com-

mented on Smyth's failure to follow proper procedures, his selfishness, and his incompetence in handling the province's finances, noting that often money was not available for the payment of warrants, "a matter of public credit & importance which it was his duty to have communicated to the Governor in Cheif, in order to apply a remedy." Contrary to instructions, Smyth had even taken fees on grants of land to military settlers: "I have no hesitation in saying that this arose from motives of private interest, & is so considered by all who have represented the hardship and injustice of it."

Smyth's sense of his own penuriousness was shown in his selling of his wife's organ to the church at Fredericton in 1818 for the sum of £170 7s. 1½d., "as it will be the means of continuing the singing, which I have brought to some degree of perfection." Only in the final months of his life did he throw off the depression that had afflicted him from the time of his illness in 1813. He purchased a more elaborate new organ and presented it to the Fredericton church. He sent to England to have his teen-aged daughter join him, ordered great quantities of classical music, and authorized his agent to recruit two violinists and a cellist to come to Fredericton at his expense. His death at Fredericton on 27 March 1823 came, appropriately, on the final day of another unhappy session of the legislature, which was in fact prorogued because of his illness. Lord Dalhousie, writing in his journal shortly afterwards, noted that Smyth's death was spoken of publicly in New Brunswick as "a happy event," and added: "He gave encouragement to nothing but low schools and church Music; he made it his whole study to lay by money, kept no table, no servants, was fretful and ill tempered at all times, & utterly neglected the general machine of government." Smyth was the only lieutenant governor of the colonial period to die in the province and his funeral was conducted with great ceremony. His death occasioned a conflict over who was to succeed him as administrator, from which Ward Chipman ultimately emerged triumphant.

Smyth was a private person and a lover of music who seems to have been more at home with children than with adults. He lacked social grace and had no gift for conciliating divergent interests, though this failing was offset by a genuine Christian charity which he expressed through his concern for the souls and bodies of the poor and for outcasts such as the blacks in New Brunswick society. He was gentle and kind but so broken in health, so depressed by his circumstances, and so little a man of the world as to have been, in political matters, the most ineffective of all New Brunswick's lieutenant governors of the colonial era.

D. M. YOUNG

Smyth

PAC, MG 24, L6; MG 30, D1, 28. PANB, MC 211, MS4/5/2; RG 1, RS336; RG 2, RS7. PRO, CO 188/18–29; CO 189/11–12; CO 324/67; PROB 11/1673/441. Southampton City Record Office (Southampton, Eng.), Catalogue of Smyth family papers in private possession, comp. P. H. Mather (typescript, 1968; copy in National Reg. of Arch. (London), report no.13153). SRO, GD45/3 (mfm. at PAC). UNBL, MG H8; MG H11. Gubbins, *N.B. journals* (Temperley). N.B., House of Assembly, *Journal*, 1817–23; Legislative Council, *Journal* [1786–1830]. Ramsay, *Dalhousie journals* (Whitelaw), vol.2. *Winslow papers* (Raymond). *New-Brunswick Royal Gazette*, 1817–23. G.B., WO, *Army list*, 1780–1812. PANB, "A new calendar of the papers of the House of Assembly of New Brunswick," comp. R. P. Nason et al. (3v., typescript, Fredericton, 1975–77), 1–2. David Duff, *Edward of Kent: the life story of Queen Victoria's father* (London, 1938; repr. 1973). F. A. Firth, "King's College, Fredericton, 1829–1859," *The University of New Brunswick memorial volume . . .* , ed. A. G. Bailey (Fredericton, 1950), 22–32. Mollie Gillen, *The prince and his lady: the love story of the Duke of Kent and Madame de St Laurent* (London, 1970; repr. Halifax, 1985). Hannay, *Hist. of N.B.* K. F. C. MacNaughton, *The development of the theory and practice of education in New Brunswick, 1784–1900: a study in historical background*, ed. A. G. Bailey (Fredericton, 1947). MacNutt, *New Brunswick*. W. A. Spray, *The blacks in New Brunswick* ([Fredericton], 1972). W. A. Squires, *The 104th Regiment of Foot (the New Brunswick Regiment), 1803–1817* (Fredericton, 1962). D. M. Young, "The politics of higher education in the Maritimes in the 1820's: the New Brunswick experience" (paper delivered at the Atlantic Studies Conference, Halifax, April 1980).

SMYTH, WYLLYS, newspaperman; fl. 1832–33.

Wyllys Smyth played a minor role in the early development of Canadian literature. Little is known about his life, yet he must have been important to the cultural needs and aspirations of many people, particularly in the Hamilton area during the early 1830s. Smyth's *Canadian Garland*, which ran from 15 Sept. 1832 to 31 Aug. 1833, was the third attempt in Hamilton "to sustain *Canadian* Literature," as the *Garland* itself put it, in that decade. The first exclusively literary periodical in Hamilton was the *Canadian Casket*, published by A. Crosman from October 1831 to September 1832. On 3 Dec. 1831 the *Casket* acknowledged a competitor, the *Voyageur*. Two publications were also produced in York (Toronto): the *Canadian Magazine* (1833), published by Robert Stanton* and edited by William Sibbald, ceased after four numbers, and the *Canadian Literary Magazine* (1833), published by George Gurnett* and edited by John Kent, ceased after three. It is curious that the Hamilton publications, despite the smaller population base, were more successful. Their relatively greater success may be attributable to the large number of original contributions which Crosman and Smyth sought and obtained. The York publications depended chiefly on borrowed selections.

As both publisher and editor of the *Garland*, Smyth evidenced a pro-Canadian policy. His stance was apparent from the address to the patrons in the first number, which solicited contributions from local persons and claimed that "we have now arrived at that state of society, in which those faculties of the human mind that have beauty and elegance for their objects, begin to unfold themselves." Determined to encourage "the original talent of our country," Smyth supported other periodicals by giving notice of their publication. To promote the *Garland* itself, he enlisted agents in surrounding communities such as John Carey* in Springfield on the Credit (Erindale) and James Scott Howard* in York.

Smyth's success in obtaining contributors was quite remarkable, virtually all of the long prose pieces and the poetry in the *Garland* being by local residents. The poetry is chiefly of a sentimental nature, with occasional pieces on the political issues of the day or on the *Garland* itself. Much of it resembles work by popular poets such as Thomas Moore, Thomas Campbell, and Felicia Dorothea Hemans. The prose is far more interesting because, although it is marked by didacticism and excesses in emotive language, it possesses a degree of realism. Subjects are derived from local history and plots revolve around immigrant and pioneer experiences, events in the War of 1812, Indian legends, and natural phenomena.

By far the most prolific and interesting contributor to the *Garland* and the *Casket* was Charles Morrison Durand (son of James DURAND). A Dundas area resident who later moved to Toronto and practised law for many years, Durand signed his pieces C.M.D. and used the pseudonym of Briton. He contributed both prose and verse but the prose is much more varied and interesting; it includes exotic tales of didactic purpose as well as local history and lore, personal adventures, and natural history sketches. One of the most interesting pieces, "A sketch" (2 Feb. 1833), is an early defence of a Canadian way of seeing and a prediction of a distinctive Canadian literature. In this article Durand, reflecting on those who found their cultural inspiration in Scotland, noted: "I shall feel alike pleasure in anticipating a literary Fame in Canada; I shall feel content to praise fair Canada! she likewise has charms of her own." Durand celebrates the sights and sounds of his native land and claims a future for it when "Europe's laurels fade."

Smyth was fortunate in having a contributor such as Durand and he shared Durand's view of the Canadian future. In the closing numbers of the *Garland* and in his advertisements for the sale of the magazine, Smyth drew a parallel between the emergence of a mature civilization from savage Britain and the rapid transition in his own home from the Indian's America to the promise of mature literary culture: "We yet may become great in Literature and Fame. Who can presage to the contrary? Let us then improve the taste of our country." Smyth, therefore, acted as a catalyst of literary endeavour in the Hamilton area, but he chose the necessary fillers of wit and wisdom gleaned from American journals and occasionally from one of his Canadian competitors.

Apparently the first volume of the *Garland* was successful enough that Smyth planned a second, double the size of the first, which was eight pages per issue. That second volume was never published. Instead, beginning in October 1833 Smyth tried to sell the magazine because he had "other business to attend to." For eight months he advertised in the *Western Mercury* without finding a buyer. The advertisement indicates that he had a subscription list of 400 which he predicted could be increased to 1,000.

Whether Smyth remained in Hamilton is not known, but in October 1833 he was the defendant in a suit for rent owed, possibly for the printing office on the court-house square; the plaintiff feared that he might flee the province. The long period of advertising suggests that he did not.

CARL BALLSTADT

AO, RG 22, Hamilton (Wentworth), district court filings, 1831–33. *Canadian Casket* (Hamilton, [Ont.]), 15 Oct. 1831–29 Sept. 1832. *Canadian Garland* (Hamilton), 15 Sept. 1832–31 Aug. 1833 [the paper was published under the title *Garland* until February 1833]. *Western Mercury* (Hamilton), October 1833–May 1834. W. S. Wallace, "The periodical literature of Upper Canada," *CHR*, 12 (1931): 4–22.

SNEPPY. *See* ATKINSON, GEORGE

SNIPE. *See* NORTON, JOHN

SOVEREENE (Souvereene, Sovereign), HENRY, farmer, shingle weaver, and convicted murderer; b. *c.* 1788, probably in the vicinity of Schooley's Mountain, Morris County, N.J., eldest son of David Sovereen and Anne (Nancy) Culver; m. Mary (Polly) Beemer (Beamer); hanged 13 Aug. 1832 in London, Upper Canada.

Young Henry Sovereen was among a large party of Sovereen and Culver relatives who immigrated to Upper Canada in 1799. Travelling in some 20 wagons, together with 40 yoke of oxen, 300 sheep, and a large number of horses and cows, the group arrived about July at Long Point, where Jabez Collver* had settled a few years earlier. By 1802 David Sovereen's family was living at Round Plains in Townsend Township. Henry was a farmer in Windham Township and probably married, when in 1812 he purchased a 200-acre lot in that township from his uncle. Four years later he sold part of this lot.

In August 1819 he was tried and found guilty of "knowingly, wilfully, and maliciously shooting a horse" and was sentenced by Mr Justice William CAMPBELL to be hanged. Lieutenant Governor Sir Peregrine Maitland*, however, commuted the sentence and by 1821 Sovereene had resumed farming in Windham. Having sold the remainder of his land, he took up residence on the north part of lot 1, concession 5, owned by Ephraim Serles, his uncle by marriage, who lived close by. Although later described as industrious and a good provider – he made shingles as well as farmed – he had long been addicted to alcohol. Generally he got along well with his neighbours, many of whom were relatives. When sober he was "rather affectionate to his wife and children" but when drinking he could be abusive and had at times even threatened their lives.

Before sunrise on the morning of 23 Jan. 1832, Sovereene informed the Serles household that two men with blackened faces had broken into his house. He feared for the safety of his family as the men had stabbed him in the arm and on the chest. In his house neighbours found the bodies of two children; a third was fatally wounded, and a fourth was sleeping unharmed. Outside were discovered the bodies of four more children and the "perfectly cold" corpse of Sovereene's wife. When one of the murder weapons – a son's knife – was found by a constable, suspicion immediately turned to Henry. A blood-stained jack-knife, believed to have been used by Sovereene to inflict wounds on himself, was found in his vest pocket; another weapon, a beetle or maul used to split wood in the making of shingles, was discovered, gory and almost covered with human hair of different colours, concealed between the straw and feathers of a bed in the house. Following his arrest and an inquest, Sovereene was transported to the London jail.

Prior to the assizes, London had been ravaged by cholera and most of its residents had fled. Only nine grand jurors were present for the opening of the court and bystanders were recruited to fill out the jury. Sovereene was tried on 8 Aug. 1832. After retiring for less than an hour, the jury found him guilty. Mr Justice James Buchanan Macaulay* sentenced him, on the basis of extremely strong circumstantial evidence, to be hanged two days later. This date was subsequently postponed until 13 August.

Sovereene, who had always been extremely obstinate and self-willed, had shown no emotion during the trial, steadfastly and calmly maintaining his innocence. On the day of his execution he firmly and resolutely ascended the scaffold. After his death, witnessed by a crowd held to some 300 by fear of cholera, his body was handed over to surgeons for dissection. According to legend he was later interred in the Oakland Pioneer Cemetery. He was survived by three older children, away on the night of the murders, and by Anna, aged three, who had been found

Spilsbury

unharmed. No motive for the murders was ever established. When Sovereene called at the door of the Serles household that early January morning, he had "exhibited no signs of insanity" and "was perfectly sober."

DANIEL J. BROCK

Eva Brook Donly Museum (Simcoe, Ont.), Sovereign family file. *Dan Brock's Hist. Almanack of London*, comp. D. [J.] Brock (London, Ont.), summer 1975. *Christian Guardian*, 1 Feb. 1832.

SPILSBURY, FRANCIS BROCKELL, naval officer, colonist, and improver; b. 1784 in Plymouth, England, only son of Francis Brockell Spilsbury and Maria Taylor; m. 20 Dec. 1815 Fanny Bayly in Deptford (London), England, and they had six sons and three daughters; d. 6 Oct. 1830 near Colborne, Upper Canada.

When Francis Brockell Spilsbury followed his father, a naval surgeon, to sea he was not yet a teenager, but the Napoleonic Wars provided the circumstance for a rapid advance through the ranks of the Royal Navy. Between 1798 and 1812 he served in the Mediterranean fleet, first as a midshipman, during which service he was cited for "conspicuous bravery" at the siege of Acre ('Akko, Israel) in 1799. On 27 Dec. 1805 he was promoted lieutenant and during the battle of Málaga, in 1812, he led a party which captured French shore batteries and a privateer.

In the spring of 1813 he and his father were among those sent to North America to reinforce the British fleet on the Great Lakes. Following his arrival in Kingston, Upper Canada, Spilsbury Jr was promoted commander on 8 March 1813 and took command of the armed schooner *General Beresford*. In May he was part of Commodore Sir James Lucas Yeo*'s squadron on Lake Ontario which raided Sackets Harbor, N.Y., and in June Spilsbury's detachment captured the American shore batteries and stores at Forty Mile Creek, in the Niagara peninsula. On 11 September he commanded the brig *Lord Melville* during an engagement off the Genesee River and though his ship was hit below the water-line his skilful action allowed repairs to be made during the battle. He was also present at the actions off Burlington Bay (Hamilton Harbour) on 28 September and French Creek, N.Y., on 1 November. In the campaign of 1814 he commanded the ship *Niagara*; shortly after the successful attack on Oswego, N.Y., on 6 May, Spilsbury was taken prisoner during the bungled advance up nearby Sandy Creek and was later confined at Cheshire, Mass., until the end of hostilities.

Following the peace in 1815, Spilsbury was promoted post captain on 19 September and was soon retired on half pay. He returned to England, where he married, and settled at Newark (Newark-on-Trent). Though he was only 31 and possessed of a small pension, post-war England offered few prospects for naval officers with social pretensions but no landed estates. In 1818 he returned to Kingston, where his father had established a medical practice, and applied for and received 1,200 acres as a military claimant. Thereafter, he went back to England and organized a scheme for a colony in Upper Canada under the Colonial Office's £10 deposit plan [*see* Richard Talbot*]. When his party of 10 families arrived in 1819 Spilsbury sought to locate them in Otonabee Township, where he and a number of former officers, including his father and Charles Rubidge*, were drawing land. Although Spilsbury had set out an elaborate plan for a town on the Otonabee River and had proposed to provide a ferry across Rice Lake, the colony largely collapsed because delays in locating suitable property for the settlers, as well as deaths and illnesses in several families, had greatly demoralized the colonists. It was also evident that few were prepared to endure the rough isolation. Indeed, Spilsbury, who was later described by William Hamilton Merritt* as a "brave, determined fellow" who could "endure any hardship," chose to reside in the relative civility of the settlement at Cobourg, where other half-pay officers and genteel English immigrants had collected. Spilsbury nevertheless completed his settlement duties and received deeds for the lands granted him in Otonabee and Monaghan townships. In 1822 he bought land east of Cobourg near the village of Colborne; there he built Osmondthorpe Hall, the farm on which he remained until his death.

Like many of his class who had small incomes and pretensions to become gentry, Spilsbury indulged an interest in agricultural improvement and was vice president of the Northumberland Agricultural Society when it was organized in July 1829. The activities of these men bore little practical relation to the economic realities of the colony. When most farmers were struggling to clear land and develop a cash staple, improvers like Spilsbury were organizing agricultural libraries, competitions for prize farms, and ploughing contests. Spilsbury espoused high tory principles and ran unsuccessfully as the tory candidate for Northumberland in the general election of 1830. He died shortly afterwards, forcing his wife to support a young family by opening a boarding-school in Colborne in 1831.

PETER ENNALS

AO, Map coll., "Plan of the township of Otonabee . . . with the locations therein made at the Surveyor General's Office prior to the 6 Jan. 1820; surveyed by Richard Birdsall, Com^d, Dec. 8th 1819"; MS 787, memorandum no.1052; RG 1, A-I-6: 5750–51, 5817–18, 5857–58; C-I-3, 90: 59; 123: 4;

146: 12; C-I-4, 4: 12, 114, 117; RG 21, United Counties of Northumberland and Durham, Otonabee Township, census and assessment rolls, 1821; RG 22, ser.187, reg.1, 12 April 1831. Northumberland East Land Registry Office (Colborne, Ont.), Cramahe Township, deeds, 1 (mfm. at AO). PAC, RG 1, L3, 457A: S11/167; 460: S12/205–6, 276; RG 5, A1: 21177, 21259, 21261, 22307–8, 22487–88, 23369–70, 27372–75. PRO, CO 42/365: 143–46. *Select British docs. of War of 1812* (Wood), 3, pt.I: 61, 73; pt.II: 628, 639–40. *Church* (Cobourg, [Ont.]), 16 Feb. 1844, 8 May 1846. *Cobourg Star*, 25 Jan., 31 May 1831; 27 June 1838; 25 Jan. 1843. *Colonial Advocate*, 11 Nov. 1830. *Kingston Chronicle*, 16 July 1819, 17 Nov. 1820, 12 July 1822, 3 July 1830. G.B., ADM, *Navy list*, 1811, 1813, 1815, 1819. *Officers of British forces in Canada* (Irving), 225, 229. Joseph Allen, *Battles of the British navy* (rev. ed., 2v., London, 1898), 2: 389–90. William Canniff, *The medical profession in Upper Canada, 1783–1850* ... (Toronto, 1894; repr. 1980), 622–27. H. I. Cowan, *British emigration to British North America; the first hundred years* (rev. ed., Toronto, 1961), 44–46. T. W. Poole, *A sketch of the early settlement and subsequent progress of the town of Peterborough, and of each township in the county of Peterborough* (Peterborough, Ont., 1867; repub. 1941, 1967), 132. E. A. Cruikshank, "The contest for the command of Lake Ontario in 1814," *OH*, 21 (1924): 99–159.

STANSER, ROBERT, Church of England clergyman and bishop; b. 16 March 1760, probably in Harthill, Yorkshire, England (the place of his baptism), son of the Reverend Robert Stanser and Sarah Stanser; he and his wife Mary had at least eight children; d. 23 Dec. 1828 in Hampton, England.

Educated at St John's College, Cambridge, Robert Stanser was ordained deacon in 1783 and priest in 1784 and appointed his father's curate at Bulwell in Nottinghamshire. For several years before being recruited for service in Nova Scotia, he worked in the home department of the Society for the Propagation of the Gospel. In 1791 he was appointed by the SPG as clergyman at St Paul's Church in Halifax where the congregation had a reputation for acting independently, even in the choice of their rector. Fortunately for Stanser, the congregation was more interested in thwarting Lieutenant Governor John Parr*'s highly prized prerogative in church matters, especially his claim to the patronage of the parish, than in promoting a particular candidate for the position. In the autumn of 1791, a few months after arriving in Halifax, Stanser was inducted as the rector of St Paul's.

Stanser remained rector of St Paul's for the next 25 years, although he did return to England frequently on leaves of absence. As rector, he established a good rapport with the parishioners, his superiors, and the wider Halifax community. Despite later criticisms that he was a laborious and monotonous preacher, Stanser succeeded in satisfying his fastidious flock – known for its evangelical leanings and strong commitment to congregational independence – and impress-

ing Bishop Charles Inglis* with his diligence and engaging manners. He also maintained cordial relations with the non-Anglican ministers in the capital. He unabashedly sold to the clergy of dissenting denominations the marriage licences issued to him by the provincial secretary; this practice, which allowed dissenting clergy to perform nuptials for their own church members, was criticized in 1800 but quietly condoned thereafter. When in 1804 he engaged in a doctrinal disputation with Edmund Burke*, the Roman Catholic vicar general, his purpose was theological, not political. Since he had not been affected by the American revolution and lived through the period of the French revolution in the midst of a congenial multi-confessional society, he did not reach the conclusion favoured by Church of England extremists that non-Anglicans were disloyal subjects. As for Burke, he certainly held no grudges. Several years after the pamphlet debate, which had ranged Burke against Stanser and William COCHRAN's King's College, the Roman Catholic leader expressed his support for Stanser's elevation to the bishopric of Nova Scotia. Another example of Stanser's moderation was his approval of Walter Bromley*'s non-sectarian Royal Acadian School as a resort for the poor, especially the town's blacks who had until 1813 been taught correct religious principles and deferential social behaviour in the Bray charity school which Stanser supervised. Untypically, therefore, Stanser remained a non-controversial figure in a church and society poised on the brink of serious interdenominational disruption. His successful labours were recognized by the award of a Lambeth DD in 1806 during a visit to England.

Like other colonial clergy during the years of wartime inflation, Stanser was greatly concerned about his income. His small SPG stipend of £30 reflected the assumption that he would receive the same sufficiency of pew rents and local perquisites enjoyed by his predecessor, John Breynton*. But as a newcomer forced to compete for favours with grasping loyalist clergymen from the former American colonies, Stanser was unable to secure the same range of chaplaincies and deputy chaplaincies that had earlier belonged to the rector of the parish, although in 1793 he was made chaplain to Lieutenant Governor John Wentworth*'s new Royal Nova Scotia Regiment. No wonder, then, that he had to resort to the sale of marriage licences to his fellow clergymen. After 1800 his financial position improved as a result of an increase in his SPG stipend to £70 in 1799, the acquisition of chaplaincy appointments to the House of Assembly, Council, and two naval vessels between 1796 and 1802, and the sale in 1807 of his estate on the west side of Bedford Basin to Supreme Court judge Brenton Halliburton*.

As clergyman of the senior church in the diocese

Stevens

and as a popular local figure, Stanser became identified as the people's choice for the next bishop as early as 1812 when Inglis unsuccessfully petitioned the British government for the appointment of his son John* as suffragan. Learning of the campaign to promote Stanser's claim to the position, the bishop declared that "Stanser is a good parish priest, but his tameness, pliancy and want of firmness, to say nothing more, unfit him for the arduous office of a Bishop in this country at this most critical period." But in 1813 Stanser could demonstrate to Colonial Secretary Lord Bathurst that his candidacy was supported by an impressive cross-section of Halifax society, including the assembly, Council, and Halifax magistracy, the wardens and vestry of St Paul's, his colleague and former curate the Reverend George Wright* of St George's Church (with whom he had earlier quarrelled over chaplaincies and marriage licences), nearly 200 parishioners, and the leaders of the Roman Catholic, Church of Scotland, Methodist, Baptist, and Presbyterian secessionist churches in Halifax. The bishop, concerned about his son's future, continued to press John's claims to the bishopric, but to no avail. When Stanser was named bishop after Charles Inglis's death in February 1816, his success was interpreted as a triumph for broadly based colonial desires. The preferences of the people, however, were not the only consideration. Equally important were the objections of the British authorities to overt nepotism and the lack of any other acceptable candidates. Lieutenant Governor Sir John Coape SHERBROOKE concluded that Stanser "had the best claims and would be the most popular choice" only after he had strongly stated his preference for an outsider from England who would have enough "coolness, moderation and good sense to sooth and conciliate rather than irritate and disgust the dissenters which might disturb the peace of the country."

In the event the contest over the succession was rendered a pointless exercise. Stanser, consecrated bishop at Lambeth Palace on 19 May 1816, was back in Halifax by that August. For reasons of health, he returned to England late in 1817 and there he remained, keeping contact with his diocese through attendance at SPG meetings and occasional conferences with the new rector of St Paul's, John Inglis, on the latter's visits to England. Stanser held on to his sinecure until December 1824, when satisfactory financial arrangements were finally made for his retirement in the form of a £250 pension. In the mean time Inglis became, in his continuing position as ecclesiastical commissary, bishop in fact though not in name. His eventual appointment as bishop in 1825 was accompanied by another succession crisis at St Paul's, this one involving the Reverend John Thomas Twining*, against which the 1791 dispute paled in comparison. By the time of Stanser's death in 1828

non-Anglican Nova Scotians, as well as evangelical Anglican ones, had gained sufficient experience of John Inglis's heavy-handed, uncompromising character as a church leader to opine in their eulogies for Stanser: "Happy would it have been for the interests of all religious parties in Nova-Scotia, if Providence had prolonged his existence, and allowed him to continue his labours among us."

JUDITH FINGARD

Robert Stanser is the author of *A sermon, preached before the honorable House of Assembly, of the province of Nova-Scotia, in the parish church of St. Paul in Halifax, on Sunday, March 16th, 1800* (Halifax, [1800]) and *An examination of the Reverend Mr. Burke's "Letter of instruction, to the Catholic missionaries of Nova-Scotia, and its dependencies"; addressed to Christians of every denomination* (Halifax, 1804).

Lambeth Palace Library (London), SPG papers, XI, nos.41, 48–49, 50–53, 61, 63, 69–70. PAC, MG 24, A57, 1–2 (mfm.); B16. PANS, Biog., Charles Inglis, letter-books, 24–25 (mfm.); MG 1, 747, no.28; RG 1, 59, doc.88 (transcript); 63, doc.29. PRO, CO 217/89: 194; 217/90: 218–19; 217/91: 84–88; 217/92: 87–88, 135–36; 217/98: 10–15; 217/143: 79, 81–82, 333–34; CO 226/29: 96. St Paul's Anglican Church (Halifax), Reg. of baptisms, marriages, and burials, 1791–1816 (mfm. at PANS). SRO, GD45/3/552, no.46 (mfm. at PAC). USPG, C/CAN/NS, 2, nos.20–34; Dr. Bray's Associates, unbound papers, box 7; Journal of SPG, 25–35. *Acadian Recorder*, 5 Oct. 1816, 7 March 1829. *Colonial Patriot* (Pictou, N.S.), 18 March 1829. *Alumni Cantabrigienses . . .*, comp. John and J. A. Venn (2 pts. in 10v., Cambridge, Eng., 1922–54), pt.II, III. Susan Buggey, "Churchmen and dissenters: religious toleration in Nova Scotia, 1758–1835" (MA thesis, Dalhousie Univ., Halifax, 1981). Judith Fingard, *The Anglican design in loyalist Nova Scotia, 1783–1816* (London, 1972); "The Church of England in British North America, 1787–1825" (PHD thesis, Univ. of London, 1970). R. V. Harris, *The Church of Saint Paul in Halifax, Nova Scotia: 1749–1949* (Toronto, 1949). Pascoe, *S.P.G. J.* [E.] Tulloch, "Conservative opinion in Nova Scotia during an age of revolution, 1789–1815" (MA thesis, Dalhousie Univ., 1972). G. W. Hill, "History of St. Paul's Church," N.S. Hist. Soc., *Coll.*, 1 (1879): 35–58; 2 (1881): 63–99; 3 (1883): 13–70. C. E. Thomas, "Robert Stanser, 1760–1828," N.S. Hist. Soc., *Coll.*, 35 (1966): 1–27.

STEVENS, ABEL, colonizer and Baptist preacher; b. in Pittsford (Vt), son of Roger Stevens and Mary Doolittle; m. 1779 Eunice Buck of Pittsford, and they had at least ten children; d. in 1825 or 1826, probably in Steventown (near Delta), Upper Canada.

Abel Stevens's early life was closely intertwined with the exploits of his elder brother Roger. Shortly after the outbreak of the American revolution Roger Stevens, a large landowner in Pittsford, aroused the wrath of local rebels by refusing to renounce his allegiance to the crown – an act of defiance that led to his arrest and imprisonment and the confiscation of his property. Somehow managing to escape, Roger gained employment as a guide for a brigade of German troops serving under Major-General John Burgoyne*. Imprisoned again after Burgoyne's surrender at Saratoga (near Schuylerville, N.Y.) in October 1777, Roger engineered a second escape with the assistance of his brother Abel, then farming in the Pittsford area and known chiefly as a skilful hunter and courageous Indian-fighter. In 1781 Roger was a spy for British troops stationed in Vermont, and Abel frequently assisted him in the collection of military and political intelligence. From 1782 until the end of the war Abel, described by Roger as "a loyal Man and entirely unsuspected among the Rebels," travelled widely throughout the New England area gathering information that was later relayed to his brother at secret rendezvous points. Unfortunately, although Roger was satisfied with Abel's work, the British military was less than enthusiastic. One officer complained that Abel's reports were "not near Adequate to our expectations, nor the expence paid him and his brother in money and furrs, &c." He also claimed that Abel could not keep a secret and practised the "art of pretending to many important Secrets which had never any other foundation than in his own Brain."

Following the revolution Roger Stevens lived in Montreal for a few years before settling along the Rideau River in 1788. Abel, however, remained in Vermont until 1792, when he and a few other Pittsford residents conceived the idea of establishing a settlement in the new colony of Upper Canada. After journeying there in May 1793, he made a number of applications for land: one requested a township grant for himself and five associates; another asked for a grant of 30,000 acres along the Thames River for the purpose of creating a "Baptist society" under the British flag. Although neither application was accepted, Stevens received 200 acres for himself and for each of his children, along with a verbal promise of additional land for the families he might bring from Vermont. For some reason, however, he was dissatisfied and, with the encouragement of Lieutenant Governor John Graves Simcoe*, he began looking for a better site in the area to the east. Eventually he made his way to Leeds County, and there he applied to the local land board for a grant in Bastard Township. When his application was accepted he returned briefly to Vermont to recruit settlers. Shortly afterwards, in February 1794, he led six Baptist families back to Leeds County, where they immediately set to work laying the foundations of a community known, appropriately enough, as Steventown.

Stevens did useful work as a colonizer and promoter. By 1798, if his own testimony is to be believed, he had persuaded more than 200 Vermont Baptists to settle in the townships of Bastard and Kitley. As well,

in the late 1790s he played a leading role in the construction of an 18-mile road from Gananoque to Kingston, and from 1794 until the early 1800s he was closely connected with plans to build a foundry which would process the Gananoque area's rich resources of bog iron. The latter project was described in a detailed petition Stevens submitted to the Executive Council in February 1799. He informed the council that £3,000 in capital would be needed, and that once the project was completed 50 skilled workmen would be employed. He also claimed to have three American associates who would not come forward unless they received "suitable Apportionments of the Waste Lands of the Crown in the Vicinity of the manufactory." The council gave Stevens six months to reveal the names and identities of his associates as well as the amount of capital at their disposal, and also to "specify the progress which he will undertake to make annually in the business." In July 1799 Stevens provided the information. When the council was still unsatisfied, Stevens turned to Ruel Keith, the master workman of the proposed foundry. In the spring of 1800 Keith and an American entrepreneur by the name of Wallis Sunderlin came to Upper Canada with a large body of labourers to begin construction. Although Stevens himself no longer had a financial stake in the project, he assisted Sunderlin in his efforts to obtain a suitable land grant. At length, Stevens's lobbying paid dividends: in September 1800 the council ruled that Sunderlin would receive 12,000 acres upon construction of the foundry. By 1802 this foundry was completed, and it continued in operation until it was destroyed by fire in 1811.

Stevens was also a key figure in the province's early religious life. In 1796 he and four other Baptists from Bastard Township petitioned Simcoe to recognize the right of "regularly ordained Elders in any Baptist Church" to solemnize marriages. At about the same time Stevens and Daniel Derbyshire gathered a congregation of "baptized believers" in Steventown. In 1803 the members of this congregation, fearing that they had acted "in many respects not agreeable to gospel prudence," formed themselves into a church during a visit by two missionaries from the United States, Joseph Cornell and Peter Philanthropos Roots. Both missionaries returned the following spring to conduct the ordination of Stevens and Derbyshire. In an account of the ceremony written for the Massachusetts Baptist Missionary Society, Derbyshire wrote that "my poor unworthy soul never had a more solemn day than this. We left them offering up thanks to Heaven for the visit, and blessing you in the name of the Lord, for sending help among them who seemed ready to perish." From this time on Stevens preached frequently in neighbouring settlements, leaving the Steventown church in Derbyshire's care. In addition, he served as a delegate to the Thurlow Association, the first Baptist organization established in Upper Canada. He also assisted in forming Baptist churches in Gananoque, Augusta, and Crosby (North and South Crosby) townships, and in 1805 he participated in the ordination of Elijah Bentley* at a meeting held in Markham.

One of the many forgotten figures in early Upper Canadian history, Abel Stevens played a crucial part in the social and economic development of Leeds County. He was also one of a small band of preachers who succeeded in planting the Baptist faith throughout the eastern section of the province.

CURTIS FAHEY

Canadian Baptist Arch., McMaster Divinity College (Hamilton, Ont.), Phillipsville Baptist Church (Phillipsville, Ont.), minutes of Steventown Baptist Church. Leeds Land Registry Office (Brockville, Ont.), Liber K, no.124. PAC, RG 1, L3, 446a: S misc., 1793–1812/71, 175; 448: S1/64; 448a: S1/160, 162–63; S2/45; 450: S3/104; 451: S4/92, 136, 140; 452: S5/44. *Corr. of Lieut. Governor Simcoe* (Cruikshank), 4: 261. *Mass. Baptist Missionary Magazine* (Boston), 1 (1803–8), no.3: 65–77. S. [E. H.] Ivison and Fred Rosser, *The Baptists in Upper and Lower Canada before 1820* (Toronto, 1956), 88–89, 101, 127, 145, 147–48. E. A. Cruikshank, "The activity of Abel Stevens as a pioneer," *OH*, 31 (1936): 56–90; "The adventures of Roger Stevens, a forgotten loyalist pioneer in Upper Canada," *OH*, 33 (1939): 11–37. S. E. H. Ivison, "Noteworthy Canadian Baptists, 3: Abel Stevens, U.E.L.; an early Baptist preacher and colonizer," *Quest* (Toronto), 4 Dec. 1960: 784 (copy at Canadian Baptist Arch.).

STEVENS, BROOKE BRIDGES, Church of England clergyman and journalist; baptized 3 Aug. 1787 in Quorndon, Leicestershire, England, son of the Reverend Thomas Stevens and Sarah ——; m. 4 Sept. 1820 Elizabeth Nelles in Grimsby, Upper Canada, and they had six children, of whom two died in infancy; d. 13 May 1834 in Montreal and was buried 16 May in Lachine, Lower Canada.

Brooke Bridges Stevens was tutored by his father, who was rector of Panfield and Whitehall preacher to the king. Shortly after his father's death in 1809, Stevens entered the University of Cambridge, where he won two prizes for declamation and in 1813 obtained his BA. In the latter year he was made deacon by the bishop of Chester and served at Great Coggeshall as assistant to the Reverend Richard Mant, whom he soon succeeded. He was ordained a priest in 1814 by the bishop of London. The following year he resigned his parish on being appointed chaplain to the British forces in France under the command of the Duke of Wellington. In 1817 he received his MA from Cambridge and published *A series of discourses on the festivals and fasts . . . of the Church of England*.

In 1819 Stevens was ordered to Lower Canada. He arrived in July carrying a letter from the chaplain general to the Duke of Richmond [Lennox*] attesting to his respectability and to his having served "with the highest credit to himself." In the course of a short initial stay in Montreal, he visited the garrison at Chambly, where he organized many of the town's residents into a congregation and helped launch construction of a church, later named St Stephen's. For his initiative he received the first of several commendations from Bishop Jacob MOUNTAIN.

In 1820 Stevens was removed to Fort George (Niagara-on-the-Lake, Ont.). Besides exercising his duties as military chaplain there, he visited the surrounding area and encouraged the building of a small church at Queenston. On Mountain's recommendation, the Society for the Propagation of the Gospel accorded him a salary of £50 for his missionary services. In 1821 he was transferred back to Montreal, where on 23 June the *Montreal Herald* announced the imminent arrival of the man "with whose preaching the congregation of the Protestant Episcopal Church were so pleased during his short stay in this city."

Stevens soon became heavily involved in the religious life of Montreal and nearby districts. By 1823 he was performing his duties as garrison chaplain to the "great satisfaction" of the commanding officer and assisting the rector of Montreal, John Bethune*, to the extent that Mountain recommended again that he receive a salary of £50 from the SPG. In addition, he was organizing a congregation, named St Stephen's, at Lachine, serving in Montreal and Lachine as visitor to schools associated with the Royal Institution for the Advancement of Learning, of which another Anglican priest, Joseph Langley MILLS, was the secretary, and nurturing into existence a small school at Île-aux-Noix. At the same time he was making a name for himself as an eloquent and popular preacher through his evening lectures at Christ Church.

The scope of Stevens's activities continued to broaden. By 1824 he was grand chaplain to the recently formed United Masonic Lodge of Montreal and William Henry, deeply involved as librarian and secretary in the activities of the Montreal district committee of the Society for Promoting Christian Knowledge, and secretary to the committee of management of the large National School in Montreal, which was financed from Royal Institution funds. His involvement with schools of the Royal Institution became increasingly onerous as opposition to them from other denominations persisted, difficulties with teachers and shortages of funds developed, and competing schools came into existence. One of the most regular visitors to the schools, he also contributed substantial sums to their maintenance until, as he wrote to Mills in 1826, "common Prudence calls out, hold hard, and pull up!" He did not take his own advice.

As early as 1822 Bethune had raised with Stevens the possibility of editing a church magazine. This idea matured in 1827 when the office of editor of the *Christian Sentinel and Anglo-Canadian Churchman's Magazine* was, as he later put it, forced upon him "with gentle violence." During the year six numbers, one every second month, were issued under his editorship. The objectives of the magazine were to circulate "the genuine principles of the Catholic Church of Christ" and especially "to defend the Apostolic Constitution, Orthodox Doctrines, and Scriptural Ritual of the national Church of England." Stevens's approach – "*never* to act on the *offensive*, but, like a good sentinel, to defend one's own post, and to watch with vigilance the motions of an enemy from whatever quarter" – reflected the defensive attitude of the colonial church, whose claims to privileged status as the established church were being increasingly contested by Presbyterians, Methodists, and Roman Catholics. Providing an unofficial diocesan chronicle, Stevens's paper contained reports from religious societies, book reviews, ecclesiastical appointments, news of the colonial church, and biographies of important clergy. The experience of editorship was not a happy one for Stevens; at the end of 1827 he penned a "Valedictory Address" announcing his resignation because of fluctuating health and uneasiness about having found himself "surrounded by a host of *censors* and *counsellors*, whilst *fellow labourers* and *supporters* were rare and lukewarm." Bethune, as acting editor, and after him Samuel Simpson Wood* brought out nine more issues before the magazine folded in June 1829.

That year the additional responsibility of acting senior chaplain to the forces in the Canadas devolved upon Stevens when Joseph Langley Mills went to England. Stevens was obliged to handle all administrative tasks without assistance other than that he already had as chaplain at Montreal, and as part of his new work he was ordered in 1830 to carry out a tour of Upper Canada. Dissatisfaction with his situation was aggravated in May 1831 when, despite his objections, a change was made in the hour of divine service for the troops at Montreal, rendering more difficult his fulfilment of other duties. His mood was further darkened by cuts in financial support for the school at Lachine and deteriorating relations with Bethune, who undoubtedly felt the pressure of Stevens's eloquence and popularity and who had opposed him over the hour of divine service for the troops. To cap Stevens's frustrations, early in 1832 he received news that the office of chaplain at Montreal was to be discontinued and he himself put on half pay. He decided to present his case in England, and in July 1832 he left with the effusive good wishes of many groups in Montreal and Lachine ringing in his ears.

By late 1833, to the consternation of a few and the joy of many, Stevens was back in Montreal, restored to his duties as chaplain and to the position of evening lecturer, which he had resigned in England. A dismayed Bethune suggested to Archdeacon George Jehoshaphat Mountain* that Stevens's appointments be cancelled, adding: "The friends of horse racing, Theatres &c. (who are a majority) will prefer Stevens to any one who feels himself obliged to raise his voice against such things." But Bethune's discomfiture was short-lived. On his return, it was clear to his friends that Stevens was in declining health, and the resumption of his duties led to his death only eight months later. He was buried, according to his wish, in St Stephen's Church, Lachine. Admired and respected by those of other religions persuasions, Stevens was a compassionate and articulate priest, who gave himself to his vocation without reserve.

J. P. FRANCIS

Brooke Bridges Stevens is the author of *A series of discourses on the festivals and fasts (and other peculiar days) of the Church of England* . . . (London, 1817) and of *A masonic discourse delivered at the installation of the Hon. William McGillivray, as R.W.P.C.M. of the united districts of Montreal and William-Henry, Lower Canada* (Montreal, 1824). He was also editor of the *Christian Sentinel and Anglo-Canadian Churchman's Magazine* (Montreal) in 1827. A portrait of Stevens has been reproduced in F. D. Adams, *A history of Christ Church Cathedral, Montreal* (Montreal, 1941), and another in George Merchant, *The history of St. Stephen's Anglican Church, Lachine, Quebec, Canada, 1822–1956* (rev. ed., n.p., [1956]).

ACC, Diocese of Montreal Arch. (Montreal), G. J. Mountain papers; B. B. Stevens papers. ACC-Q, 103–5, 129, 314, 348. ANQ-M, CE1-65, 1821–34; CM1-2/4, 13 mai 1834; 1/17–18. McGill Univ. Arch., Royal Instit. for the Advancement of Learning, incoming corr., 1820–34. PAC, RG 8, I (C ser.), 65: 28B, 32B, 104–5, 170; 67: 139, 169–70, 194–96, 202–5, 226–52; 68: 2–4, 18–19, 122–23, 152–63. USPG, C/CAN/folder 480; C/CAN/Que., 1, no.17; Journal of SPG, 20: 391–93; 21: 384–88. "Early records of St. Mark's and St. Andrew's churches, Niagara," comp. Janet Carnochan, *OH*, 3 (1901): 79. "Masonic installation," *Canadian Magazine and Literary Repository* (Montreal), 1 (July–December 1823): 375. *Montreal Gazette*, 21–22 Oct. 1833; 13, 17 May 1834. *Montreal Herald*, 23 June 1821, 16 Oct. 1824, 16 Aug. 1826, 15 May 1834. *Quebec Gazette*, 19 July 1819. *Quebec Mercury*, 12 June 1832. Beaulieu et Hamelin, *La presse québécoise*, 1: 59. Millman, *Jacob Mountain*, 230, 248; *The life of the Right Reverend, the Honourable Charles James Stewart, D.D., Oxon., second Anglican bishop of Quebec* (London, Ont., 1953), 47, 68–69, 143, 219.

STEWART, JOHN, army officer, politician, office holder, and author; b. *c.* 1758 in Kintyre, Scotland, eldest son of Peter Stewart* and Helen MacKinnon; m. first 24 April 1780 Hannah Turner in Charlottetown; m. secondly 29 May 1817 Mary Ann James in

735

Stewart

St John's; m. thirdly 17 June 1832 Mary Rain; father of two sons and two daughters; d. 22 June 1834 at his estate, Mount Stewart, P.E.I.

John Stewart arrived on St John's (Prince Edward) Island in November 1775 with his father, recently appointed chief justice of the colony, his brother Charles*, and several other family members. The American revolution had broken out, and he soon obtained a lieutenancy in the military corps raised by Administrator Phillips Callbeck* for the defence of the Island. In the fall of 1779 a ship carrying part of a Hessian regiment was forced to land by a gale, and Stewart was appointed acting commissary to the troops.

He first came to political prominence as an opponent of Governor Walter Patterson*, with whom the Stewart family had fallen out. As chief justice, Peter Stewart sat on the Council, and during the 1784 election campaign for the House of Assembly, the Stewarts used their knowledge of an impending, but as yet unannounced, tax with great effectiveness. Patterson reported that John Stewart, "a very intemperate young man . . . by every artifice in his power infused into the people's minds the dread of a general tax." Almost two-thirds of the members elected were of the anti-Patterson party, and when the assembly met on 6 March John Stewart was chosen speaker. This first taste of office was brief, for Patterson shortly dissolved the house and called another election which, with the aid of an influx of loyalist voters, he won. Stewart lost his seat. When the new assembly met in 1785, it was discovered that the journals of the previous session were but copies of the originals and that "matters of the highest tendency" had been either totally omitted or mutilated to such a degree that they could scarcely be understood. An investigation revealed that the journals had been recopied under Stewart's direction, apparently "to prejudice the Governor in the minds of His Majesty's ministers."

In fact, Patterson was already in trouble with London for disobeying instructions and was doomed despite the discovery of Stewart's little conspiracy. He was dismissed in 1787 and replaced by Edmund Fanning*, who allied himself with the Stewarts and their friends. With their help, in 1790 he finally secured the election of an assembly subservient to his wishes. John Stewart, who had been successful in 1787 and again in 1790, was chosen speaker of this house in 1795 and held the position until 1801. Even more important was his appointment to the influential post of receiver general of quitrents in 1790. When he had solicited this post originally, he had found himself in competition with Robert GRAY, Fanning's private secretary, but he had succeeded in obtaining it through the interest of Lord Frederick Campbell in Britain.

The "Hellfire Jack" of Prince Edward Island politics, Stewart gave clear evidence of his turbulent disposition early on. During his voyage to the Island as a teen-age immigrant, he had been involved in a fight on board ship. Then, in 1784 he had accosted judge Thomas Wright* on his way to the court-house, castigating him relative to a case in which he, Stewart, was a party. He renewed the abuse on the judge's way home and physically attacked James Curtis* and another man who intervened. The Reverend Theophilus DESBRISAY narrowly escaped violence himself when he tried to pacify him. Stewart avoided prison on the intervention of his brother Charles, who successfully appealed to the injured parties' sense of chivalry by mentioning that the assailant's wife was "unwell and much alarmed." Having been made captain in one of the Island provincial companies in 1794, Stewart applied to the fort major, Charles Lyons, in the autumn of 1797 for permission to take two artificers from the public works to saw a threshing floor for his farm. Lyons refused and Stewart challenged him to a duel; when they met, however, they were prevented from fighting. As a result of this incident, Stewart's rank was temporarily reduced by sentence of a general court martial.

In 1789 Stewart had become the neighbour of another turbulent Islander, John MacDonald* of Glenaladale, by purchasing part of Lot 37. There, on a rising stretch of ground overlooking the Hillsborough River, he built his country home, Mount Stewart. The formidable Glenaladale, no friend of the Stewarts, was the proprietor of Lot 36. In 1797, as the movement for escheat of the lands on which proprietors had not fulfilled the terms of their grant gained fresh momentum, Glenaladale complained of a "Levelling Party" whose object was to prevent the settlement of the lands and thereby make them liable for escheat. When pressed to reveal the names of the members of the supposed party, he obliquely mentioned Stewart, among others. Stewart disclaimed all knowledge of a levelling party; however, he declared that he had noticed a recent revival of the subject of escheat. This, he felt, was due to the machinations of Glenaladale himself, who was endeavouring to gain the confidence of the proprietors in Britain for the furtherance of his views against the local government.

On one occasion in the winter of 1797–98, Stewart insulted Glenaladale in the streets of Charlottetown and Glenaladale attacked his tormentor with a small dirk. Bound up "in two heavy watch coats and loaded with other defenses from the cold, so as to be scarcely able to move," Glenaladale would have been unable to withstand the pressure from Stewart's "prodigious long cut-and-thrust sword," he later declared, had his opponent's sword arm not trembled. As it was, the combatants were parted before any injury was done. The feud, however, continued.

In 1802 Glenaladale, in London at the time, was horrified to learn that John Stewart, also in London, was to return to the Island with powers to prosecute for arrears of quitrents. He predicted that his own wife and children would shortly be "without a house to shelter them or a bed to lie upon . . . and without a bit of bread to eat." Events did not move that swiftly. Upon his arrival Stewart did commence proceedings against a number of the defaulters and, having obtained the requisite court judgements, eventually made his report to the Colonial Office. In the mean time, however, a change of administration had taken place in London, and he received no directions to proceed further. A compromise in 1803 on the matter of quitrents owing satisfied the Stewarts and began their turn away from the escheat movement.

In 1804, the year Joseph Frederick Wallet DES-BARRES was appointed to succeed Fanning, John Stewart left the Island to take up duties as paymaster general of the British forces in Newfoundland. He held this office until it was abolished in 1817. An important event of these years was the publication in 1806 of his book, *An account of Prince Edward Island*. This work won for its author the distinction of being the first Island historian. Its chief value today is the description it gives of the natural history of the colony at an early period. Of blueberries, Stewart notes: "A gallon of spirits resembling gin in flavour has been distilled from a bushel of them. In some districts they are in such pleanty as to furnish the swine with their chief food for several weeks." The work is intelligently written, gives evidence of keen powers of observation, and reveals genuine attachment to the Island and interest in its development.

Stewart earned a reputation for acquisitiveness regarding land. In 1795, alleging that the laying out of lots (done by Charles Morris*) almost 30 years before was in error, he had had the boundary between Lot 37 and Lot 38 resurveyed. The new survey, conducted by his brother-in-law, had assigned much additional territory to Stewart. The matter, however, became the subject of interminable litigation. On a visit to the Island Stewart gained fresh hope of a determination when he found that a bill had been proposed that would take the final settlement of boundaries out of the lieutenant governor's hands. DesBarres felt insulted by the bill because of his past career as a surveyor, and he managed to have the measure rejected by the assembly.

As early as 1807 Stewart was intriguing for Des-Barres's recall. He advised Colonial Secretary Lord Castlereagh that even a cursory consideration of the colony's affairs would lead his lordship to conclude that he ought "to provide the Island with a new Governor." The Stewarts were no longer in favour of escheat, having by this time acquired an interest in the *status quo*, and they no doubt feared that under the influence of the Loyal Electors DesBarres would support land reform. The proprietors in Britain se-

cured DesBarres's dismissal in 1812 and his successor, Charles Douglass Smith*, arrived the following year.

At this period the Colonial Office was engaged in preparing a new scale of quitrents for the Island, and in 1816 Smith, under instructions from London, summoned John Stewart from Newfoundland to prepare an account of his receipts and expenditures as receiver general of quitrents. Although ill, Stewart did as he was bidden. He was also forced to resign the post; declaring that he was in great pain, he said he was going away, "most probably never to see the Island again."

By 1823, however, Smith was advising the Colonial Office that "John Stewart, of political notoriety during the time of my two immediate predecessors, has chosen to resume his practice of agitating the public mind." It could not be said that Stewart's behaviour was unprovoked. In 1822 Smith had renewed his efforts to have arrears of quitrents collected. When requests failed, John Edward CARMICHAEL, who was Smith's son-in-law and the acting receiver general of quitrents, took a distress on the estates of Donald McDonald*, the son of Glenaladale, and John Stewart for non-payment. He then proceeded into the eastern district of Kings County, where the greatest number of small proprietors resided, with a demand for their respective arrears.

Stewart experienced no difficulty in obtaining signatures to a petition calling upon John MacGregor*, the high sheriff, to convene meetings to consider the lieutenant governor's behaviour. Although he dismissed MacGregor, Smith permitted the gatherings, the most important of which was held in Queen's Square, Charlottetown, in March 1823. There, a series of resolutions covering "upwards of thirty pages of foolscap paper" was moved by Stewart and seconded by McDonald. Highly critical of Smith's administration, the resolutions had been framed at numerous meetings presided over by Stewart. Petitions were subsequently prepared asking for Smith's recall and were circulated across the Island. It was intended that Stewart should be sent to England to work for the removal of the lieutenant governor.

On the pretext that some of the charges in the complaints were libellous, Smith moved to apprehend Stewart. On the night of 14 Oct. 1823 a search was made of his haunts in Charlottetown, but to no avail. A trip to Mount Stewart proved equally futile. Stewart had effected his escape, having been shipped from the Island, according to tradition, in a cask as produce.

On 21 Oct. 1824 Stewart, his popularity at its height, returned to Charlottetown accompanied by the new lieutenant governor, John Ready*. At a great victory celebration held at the Wellington Hotel, Stewart, who presided, spoke of "the general joy which His Excellency's arrival diffused throughout the Island." His words were reinforced by the "joyous acclamations" of the crowds who surrounded the building until a late hour.

His return to the Island being permanent, Stewart began collecting offices. Elected in 1824, he became speaker of the assembly in 1825 and in 1828 was reappointed receiver general of quitrents. He was speaker until 1830 and receiver until his death. The post of collector of customs eluded him. After a bitter struggle for it with his nephew Theophilus DesBrisay Jr, which he seemed to have won, a ruling of the customs department precluded him from receiving it because of his age. It went instead to John Stewart, son of Charles.

Stewart is associated with the founding of the Kirk of St James, the first Presbyterian church in Charlottetown. In June 1825 a meeting was held at the court-house with Stewart as chairman and it was resolved that a clergyman should be obtained, a suitable building erected, and a subscription opened to obtain funds. Stewart headed the subscription committee, and a considerable sum was contributed on the spot. The church was opened for worship in 1828.

Stewart is sometimes taxed with religious bigotry for his stand on the enfranchisement of Roman Catholics. Although they made up about half of the Island's population, they did not have the vote. When a bill to remove this civil disability was brought before the assembly in 1827, members were equally divided on the issue and Stewart, as speaker, cast his vote in the negative. Thus, until 1829, when the Island was ordered by Britain to give full political rights to members of that religion, it remained the only British North American colony to have an assembly for which Catholics could not vote. It is not known whether Stewart genuinely believed that the enfranchisement of Catholics was beyond the assembly's power or whether he was motivated by a fear that Catholics would strengthen the forces of the escheat movement.

After 1830 Stewart took little part in public affairs but "lived retired at his beautiful residence of Mount Stewart," according to Charlottetown's *Royal Gazette*. The house itself was destroyed by fire in the 19th century; however, the magnificent view of the Hillsborough and Pisquid rivers is probably not greatly altered. In the distance stood the Roman Catholic chapel at St Andrews, the seat of Bishop Angus Bernard MacEachern. According to tradition, Stewart sometimes invited that prelate to accompany him to Charlottetown in his large boat, rowed by retainers in Highland costume with a piper in the bow.

On 3 May 1834 an inquisition *de lunatico inquirendo* was held at Mount Stewart to ascertain Stewart's mental state. The investigation was the result of struggle between two individuals for the role of Stewart's attorney. The jury's verdict was that "John Stewart now is, and hath been for the last eight months

past, of unsound mind, and incapable of transacting business, and . . . during that time he did not enjoy lucid intervals." Stewart died at his home on 22 June, reportedly of a surfeit of fat meat.

It is unfortunate that much of the surviving record pertaining to this remarkable man consists of the violent diatribes of his enemies. The record reveals him to have been one of the most tempestuous figures ever to agitate the political life of Prince Edward Island. Yet, the same record, biased as it is, discloses one who had a genuine love for his adopted homeland and was prepared to go to extraordinary lengths to rid it of an unpopular administration. As he once said of himself, he was not a "good natured man by no means addicted to quarrelling." Neither was he one whose sole mission in life was the execution of mischief.

F. L. PIGOT

John Stewart is the author of *An account of Prince Edward Island, in the Gulph of St. Lawrence, North America . . .* (London, 1806; repr. [East Ardsley, Eng., and New York], 1967).

PANL, Vital statistics, vol.26A, 29 May 1817. PAPEI, Acc. 2320; RG 5, minutes, 15, 29 April, 9 May, 20 July 1797; 11 Aug. 1828; RG 16, land registry records, conveyance reg., liber 22: f.147. PRO, CO 226/8: 81–89, 171–77; 226/9: 71–73, 184–86, 188–90; 226/10: 31–32; 226/18: 99–101, 114–16, 137–38, 162–206, 211–22; 226/22: 140–42; 226/24: 52–92; 226/26: 165–75; 226/27: 49–52; 226/31: 142–48; 226/39: 11–14, 26–28, 416–23; 226/40: 130–31, 198–205, 232–34, 249–50, 254–56, 366–72 (mfm. at PAPEI); CO 228/2: 107. St Paul's Anglican Church (Charlottetown), Reg. of marriages (mfm. at PAPEI). Supreme Court of P.E.I. (Charlottetown), Estates Division, liber 3: f.39 (will of John Stewart) (mfm. at PAPEI). John MacGregor, *British America* (2v., Edinburgh and London, 1832), 1. P.E.I., House of Assembly, *Journal*, 28 March, 2 April 1785; 13 July 1801; 14 Jan. 1825. *Prince Edward Island Register*, 13 Sept., 1 Nov. 1823; 30 Oct. 1824; 1 July 1825; 17 April 1827. *Royal Gazette* (Charlottetown), 29 Oct. 1833; 11 March, 13 May, 24 June 1834. J. M. Bumsted, "'The only Island there is': the writing of Prince Edward Island history," *The Garden transformed: Prince Edward Island, 1945–1980*, ed. Verner Smitheram *et al.* (Charlottetown, 1982), 11–38. F. L. Pigot, *A history of Mount Stewart, Prince Edward Island* (Charlottetown, 1975). *Island Guardian and Christian Chronicle* (Charlottetown), 31 Oct. 1890. J. E. Rendle, "The phantom bell ringers; a story of the auld kirke," *Prince Edward Island Magazine* (Charlottetown), 1 (1899–1900): 361.

STONE, JOEL, businessman, JP, office holder, and militia officer; b. 7 Aug. 1749 in Guilford, Conn., son of Stephen Stone and Rebecca Bishop; m. first 23 March 1780 Leah Moore in New York City, and they had a son and a daughter who reached adulthood; m. secondly in the summer of 1799 Abigail Cogswell, widow of Abraham Dayton; d. 20 Nov. 1833 in Gananoque, Upper Canada.

Street

Joel Stone's early years were spent near Litchfield, Conn., where he helped on the family farm. In 1774 he entered partnership as a general merchant in Woodbury; he settled in the nearby parish of Judea and remained there until 1776, when his public profession of loyalist sentiments incurred the revolutionaries' wrath. His property was confiscated and he fled to New York. As a volunteer with the British forces, he was captured on Long Island, N.Y., in 1778 and imprisoned at Fairfield, Conn. Following his escape on 23 July, he gradually re-established himself as a merchant at New York and in 1780 became a captain in the city militia. In 1783 he left for England to seek compensation for the loss of personal effects and property in Connecticut, which he estimated to be worth about £1,500. He also hoped to be able to speed the settlement of a case in the Court of Chancery that involved a legacy to his wife. Bureaucratic and legal complications delayed his return to North America until October 1786, when he arrived at Quebec.

Impressed by the opportunities in the colony, Stone initially settled with his family at Cornwall (Ont.) in the spring of 1787 and established a small distillery. He applied for a grant of land at the mouth of the Gananoque River, but the geographical advantages of the situation also prompted a claim by Sir John JOHNSON. The ensuing dispute was not resolved for several years. Finally, in 1790, Stone was granted a 700-acre tract on the west side of the river.

Stone's resolve to recoup his losses through settlement in Upper Canada was no doubt weakened by the misfortunes that befell him between 1788 and 1790. Widespread grain shortages seriously affected his distillery and the resulting financial problems were exacerbated by the collapse of his marriage. By June 1789 he had begun steps to obtain a legal separation, and in October, hearing of his wife's proposed return to Cornwall from Montreal, he wrote to his brother: "If that RIB comes here . . . I shall endeavor to take my children with me directly to Connecticut." He did travel to Connecticut in 1791 and placed his son and daughter at school in Hartford under his sister's care "untill I can rid myself of Bad examples in my own family." He also made a final attempt to secure the return of his confiscated property in the state. Unsuccessful, he returned to Upper Canada after some months.

Once settled at Gananoque, the perennially ambitious Stone gradually established himself as its principal landowner and leading inhabitant. His development of a saw-milling operation in 1791 led to a further diversification of his business interests. By 1795 he was dealing with markets in Kingston and Montreal and had acquired a lease of property on Howe Island for lime kilns. His persistent petitioning led to the accumulation of a number of key positions in local government, including those of justice of the peace in 1796, customs collector in 1802, and roads commissioner in 1814. Access to the settlement was improved when in 1801 he began operating a ferry across the Gananoque River. Gradually he expanded his interests to include general merchandising.

The War of 1812 was in some ways the culmination of what Stone perceived as a series of misfortunes beginning with the death of his son in 1809. Located on the sole supply route for Upper Canada, Gananoque was the target for one of the first American incursions of the war, in September 1812, and considerable damage was inflicted on the settlement. Stone, who was colonel of the 2nd Leeds Militia, was absent at the time, but the invaders are reported to have fired into his home and wounded his wife, Abigail.

The post-war years witnessed a change in Stone's personality. Newly converted to Methodism through Abigail's influence, he showed an increasing preoccupation with religious and moral responsibility. In 1815 he officially turned almost all his business interests over to his son-in-law, Charles McDONALD, and he began to concentrate on his civic and judicial duties. His last years were spent in quiet introspection. His obituarist in the Kingston *Chronicle & Gazette* wrote of "a deeply lamented and truly loyal gentleman."

ELIZABETH M. MORGAN

AO, MS 519. Litchfield Hist. Museum (Litchfield, Conn.), Joel Stone papers. MTL, Joel Stone papers. PAC, MG 23, HII, 1. QUA, Joel Stone papers. *Loyalist narratives from Upper Canada*, ed. J. J. Talman (Toronto, 1946). *Chronicle & Gazette*, 29 June–30 Nov. 1833. *Kingston Chronicle*, 1819–33. *Kingston Gazette*, 1812–18. H. W. Hawke, *Historic Gananoque* (Belleville, Ont., 1974). Kenneth Donovan, "'Taking leave of an ungrateful country': the loyalist exile of Joel Stone," *Dalhousie Rev.*, 64 (1984–85): 125–45. H. S. McDonald, "Memoir of Colonel Joel Stone, a United Empire Loyalist and founder of Gananoque," *OH*, 18 (1920): 59–90.

STREET, SAMUEL DENNY, army officer, lawyer, politician, office holder, and poet; b. 16 May 1752 in Southwark (London), England, son of Thomas Street and Ann Lee; d. 11 Dec. 1830 in Fredericton.

Samuel Denny Street was apprenticed to a London attorney in 1766 and subsequently practised law briefly before joining the Royal Navy in the early 1770s. In 1775 he went to Boston on the *Merlin* and served under Lieutenant-General Thomas Gage*. After his discharge in Nova Scotia in 1776, he enlisted in Joseph Goreham*'s Royal Fencible Americans and arrived in Halifax with Captain Gilfred Studholme*. On 1 May 1776 he went with his regiment to garrison Fort Cumberland (near Sackville, N.B.), and the following year, when he was promoted lieutenant, he

Street

assisted Studholme in establishing Fort Howe at the mouth of the Saint John River. While stationed at Fort Cumberland, he married Abigail Freeman on 22 Feb. 1778. They were to have 12 children.

By 1780 Street had been transferred to Fort Howe, and in November of that year he set out by boat with six men on a secret mission to the rebel port of Machias (Maine) under orders from Brigadier Francis McLean*. His adventures among the rebels in 1780–81 are described by him in a remarkable and exciting narrative that at times seems more like fiction than fact. Yet there is no reason to doubt its veracity, judging from the carefulness of detail that characterizes the story. It begins on the return trip from Machias, when Street's vessel was chased by a rebel privateer in Passamaquoddy Bay. Finding their escape route was cut off at the narrows of Passamaquoddy, he and his men attempted to run in a small open boat but were forced to land on an island. They defended themselves for three hours and finally drove their pursuers back to their boats, capturing the rebel leader in the process. Street was highly commended for this action by Studholme and McLean.

When in April 1781 Street set out on a similar mission, the rebels had foreknowledge of his coming. Surrounded by superior numbers and taken, he was carried to Machias but, because local rebels feared him, he was quickly sent to Boston, where he was placed on board a prison ship. He immediately began to plot his escape. His plan, which involved the stealing of a boat, went awry, however, and Street and those who had accompanied him were recaptured the next day. They spent six weeks in the town jail before being returned to the prison ship.

At this point two relatively important rebel prisoners were offered in exchange for Street, but the exchange was refused. About the same time his next escape plan was betrayed by fellow prisoners who feared retaliation. Spurred by frustration, Street decided to act alone. He slipped away from the prison ship at night and swam ashore, where he was sheltered by loyalists with whom he had previously made contact. Disguised as a fisherman, he got out of Boston Harbour and boarded a ship sailing east to Fort George (Castine, Maine). From there he returned to Fort Howe. He had spent about five months in imprisonment, but managed to escape with his health and spirits intact. Street's exploits reveal a man of great courage, resourcefulness, and determination. Because McLean had died during his confinement, however, he never received the preferments that might have come his way, and the remainder of his war service was uneventful.

In 1783 Street retired on half pay and was employed in surveying and laying out Parrtown and Carleton (Saint John, N.B.). He applied to Governor John Parr* for a substantial grant on the Saint John River at Burton. He settled there and named his estate Elysian Fields. In February 1785 he was amongst the first to be admitted to the bar of the newly formed province of New Brunswick and he became one of the colony's leading lawyers.

Street's political career began inauspiciously with an unsuccessful attempt at winning an assembly seat in the general election of 1792. In 1795, however, he was elected, with James Glenie*, to represent Sunbury County, and he served in the assembly until defeated by Elijah Miles in 1802. Street and Glenie were leading figures in the extended struggle between the elected assembly and the appointed administration (Lieutenant Governor Thomas Carleton* and his council) over their respective rights and privileges in governing the province. It was a time when the political atmosphere was extremely volatile and tempers ran high. During this period Street was at the centre of two dramatic incidents, one private and one public.

On 16 Jan. 1800 Street challenged John Murray Bliss to a duel as a result of Bliss's implying that Street had lied to the jury in a case they had argued in court that day. The trial had been a test case, and a heated one, involving the ownership of slaves; Street and Ward Chipman had defended the slave, while J. M. Bliss, Thomas Wetmore, Charles Jeffery Peters*, William Botsford*, and Jonathan Bliss had represented the master, Caleb Jones*. The four judges of the Supreme Court split on the issue and no judgement was returned, but the resulting legal ambiguity was sufficient to undermine the value of slaves as property and stop the development of any trade in slaves. Shortly after eight o'clock in the evening on the day the trial ended, Street and Bliss met at the court-house in Fredericton with their seconds. They took up positions nine paces apart and, upon receiving the word, fired almost together. Both shots missed. Street was eager to reload and fire again, but the seconds were able to persuade Bliss to offer an apology, which Street finally accepted.

Street was again the centre of attention in 1802 when, upon the death of the clerk of the House of Assembly, he was elected to that position by a majority of the members. Lieutenant Governor Carleton refused to ratify the decision because he had his own candidate, Dugald Campbell*. The assembly refused to recognize the lieutenant governor's appointee and Street served out the session as clerk. In the appropriations bill of 1802 the assembly specified that Street be paid the clerk's salary to make sure it went to the right man. On 3 March, when the Council sent the bill back requesting that Street's name be deleted, most of the "opposition" clique absented themselves from the assembly in the expectation that the lack of a quorum would force the adjournment of the house for the year. However, the speaker, Amos Botsford*, called the house to order the next day and, in spite of the lack of a quorum, allowed the remaining members (mostly the "governor's friends") to change the money bill to suit the administration before adjournment. In May, Carleton called a general election and the campaign that followed was a lively one, highlighted by a pamphlet war, vitriolic letters in the newspapers, and a verse satire (entitled "Creon") by Street on the events of the last session. "Creon" was perhaps more effective as propaganda than as poetry, but none the less stands as one of the more interesting pieces of local narrative verse satire, a genre that occupied a significant place in the early literary culture of Maritime Canada. In the end, the election was won overwhelmingly by the "governor's friends." Street and most of the "opposition" members lost their seats.

In 1803 Street applied for a position in the Supreme Court, was turned down, so pursued his legal business. Six years later he was re-elected to the assembly for Sunbury, his fellow representative being James TAYLOR, and he served, uneventfully, until defeated in September 1816. That year he was again refused a Supreme Court positon, but in 1819 he was appointed to the Council by the lieutenant governor, George Stracey SMYTH. In 1821, after his son, George Frederick*, had killed George Ludlow WETMORE in a duel, Street went about Fredericton tearing down the hue-and-cry notices posted by the coroner, William TAYLOR. On 20 Dec. 1824 his wife died; six years later he himself died and was interred beside her in the Old Burying Ground, Fredericton.

Throughout his political life, in spite of the often partisan nature of his activities, Street appears to have had a clear and consistent political philosophy. At a time when many New Brunswickers were prepared to invest almost all political power in the governor and his council, Street agitated for a responsible role for the elected assembly, a role which would reflect the rights and privileges accorded parliament within the British constitution, in particular its control over appropriations. But in the wake of the American and French revolutions and in the face of the Napoleonic threat, New Brunswick opted in 1802 for the apparent security of a paternalistic, hierarchical form of authority with power clearly concentrated in the representatives of the crown. To most New Brunswickers, it was a question of loyalty, plain and simple; any distribution of authority smacked of republicanism. It would be another generation before Maritimers developed a desire for responsible government.

One of Street's greatest contributions to New Brunswick was his children. Of the 12, George Frederick became a judge of the Supreme Court of New Brunswick, William Henry and John Ambrose Sharman* were elected to the assembly, Samuel Denny Lee was Anglican rector of Woodstock for 40 years, and daughter Ann Frances married George

Duncan Berton, sheriff of York County. In addition to their own offspring, the Streets raised the three orphan children of Dr Ambrose Sharman, who had served with Street in the Royal Fencible Americans and who drowned at Burton in 1793. His daughter Ann married William Carman and was the grandmother of William Bliss Carman*, the poet.

THOMAS B. VINCENT

Samuel Denny Street's satirical poem "Creon" was published anonymously in the *Saint John Gazette and General Advertiser* (Saint John, N.B.), 23 Oct., 6–20 Nov. 1802. He also put out, under the pseudonym Creon, a pamphlet entitled *A statement of facts relative to the proceedings of the House of Assembly on Wednesday the third, and Thursday the fourth of March, 1802, at the close of the last session . . .* ([Saint John], 1802).

PANB, MC 1156, VIII. PANS, MG 1, 144, S. D. Street to Thomas ——, 2 Dec. 1781 (transcript); MG 100, 235, no.7. PRO, ADM 36/7909; IR 17/46. Sheffield City Libraries, Arch. Division (Sheffield, Eng.), WWM. BK. P. 1/3293 (transcript at PANS). N.B., House of Assembly, *Journal*, 1802. *Winslow papers* (Raymond). Hill, *Old Burying Ground. The old grave-yard, Fredericton, New Brunswick: epitaphs copied by the York-Sunbury Historical Society, Inc.*, comp. L. M. Beckwith Maxwell (Sackville, N.B., 1938). Beckwith Maxwell, *Hist. of central N.B.* Hannay, *Hist. of N.B.* Lawrence, *Judges of N.B.* (Stockton and Raymond). MacNutt, *New Brunswick.* D. R. Jack, "An affair of honor," *Acadiensis* (Saint John), 5 (1905): 173–77.

STROBRIDGE (Strowbridge), JAMES GORDON, civil engineer and contractor; b. 1788 in Solon, N.Y.; m. Nancy Mayberry, and they had six sons and two daughters; d. 10 March 1833 in Hamilton, Upper Canada.

An engineer, James Gordon Strobridge moved from the United States to Upper Canada in 1824 to become a contractor on the Burlington Bay Canal. This project, authorized and financed by the provincial government and under the supervision of canal commissioners, was to create a cut across Burlington Beach to provide the hinterland around Dundas with direct access to Lake Ontario. Although only a third of a mile long, the canal was to be of superior construction with piers on both Burlington Bay (Hamilton Harbour) and Lake Ontario.

Strobridge, in partnership with Captain John McKeen, began work on the cut during the summer of 1824. William Lyon Mackenzie* inspected their progress and was dismayed to find the "Goths and Vandals" despoiling the adjacent forests. In September Captain McKeen contracted typhus and died, leaving Strobridge solely responsible for the canal. Nevertheless, by October a cut had been made down to the level of the lake.

Throughout 1825 dredging machinery was used to dig the cut down to the specified 12 feet. It only remained to complete the two piers and install the decking and handrails. However, disquieting reports were surfacing about Strobridge's ability to complete the project. The superintendent engineer, Francis Hall, reported to the canal commissioners in February 1826 that the construction of the breakwater alone had already cost nearly one-half the original contract price for the whole project. According to Hall, the breakwater on Lake Ontario faced such strong currents and waves that its construction had proved "hazardous and expensive, beyond all calculations." Nevertheless, Strobridge had used the weather to his advantage and during the winter of 1825–26 he had had stone hauled across the frozen lake to the work site. Eventually, he overcame the engineering difficulties in constructing the piers and breakwater.

Financial difficulties were another matter. In February 1827 the provincial government authorized a further £8,000 for the project. But in the spring of that year the canal was abruptly taken out of Strobridge's hands, and he was required to give securities to the government before any additional monies were paid to him. Attorney General John Beverley Robinson* prepared the securities for Strobridge. It is a comment on the prevailing business morality that in March Strobridge sent him £4 in the hope of "more favours at your hands." Somewhat higher standards prevailed in the government; Robinson retained one pound for preparing the bond and returned the rest.

The valuation of the works became a continual matter of contention between Strobridge and the government. In 1828 arbitrators were appointed to determine the value of construction. They arrived at a figure of £3,000, which the canal commissioners proved reluctant to pay. After unsuccessfully invoking the courts in his behalf, Strobridge was sued by his own creditors and forced into debtors' jail by April 1829. From these unpleasant confines he petitioned Lieutenant Governor John Colborne*, who finally authorized the payment. In 1831 the legislature allowed him an additional £2,356.

During the course of his struggle for compensation, Strobridge had developed an interest in reform politics. In January 1829 he actively solicited names for a petition in favour of Francis COLLINS, a journalist who had been imprisoned for libel and an implacable foe of the provincial adminstration. He was called before the House of Assembly to explain his part in the so-called "Hamilton Outrage" of 29 Jan. 1829 – the hanging in effigy of the lieutenant governor allegedly over his refusal to release Collins. George Gurnett*'s progovernment *Gore Gazette*, in a reference to Strobridge, asked why "foreigners who came into the province, as it were, but yesterday" were allowed to undermine legitimate authority. Yet the government did not consider Strobridge dangerous and, in fact, welcomed debate on the canal. Robinson hoped it would "create a diversion from the Alien question and divide the interest during the session – a pleasing variety!"

Not satisfied with the 1831 settlement, Strobridge, with Collins's encouragement, went to York in 1833 to petition the legislature for interest on the unpaid amount. While there, he was seized by the sheriff for failing to pay outstanding debts and was once again cast into jail. Collins secured his release, but only two days later Strobridge succumbed to a fever contracted while in prison. His widow, Nancy, pursued the claims unsuccessfully, up to 1836.

The tenacity which James Strobridge brought to his crusade for just payment was also reflected in his work as an engineer. When in 1826 a hostile Lake Ontario threatened to smash the unfinished breakwater, Strobridge, watching grimly, saw that the caissons had been sunk deep enough to withstand the pounding. Francis Hall observed that "every part thereof, has been so severely tested, that the practicability of the measure and permanence of the works even in their unfinished state is now beyond doubt."

PATRICK BRODE

AO, RG 4, A-1, Strobridge to J. B. Robinson, 3 March 1827; RG 22, ser.204, no.177, 11 May 1833. PAC, RG 5, A1, J. G. Strobridge to Sir John Colborne, 10 April 1829; J. B. Robinson to ——, n.d. "Ancaster parish records, 1830–1838," comp. John Miller, *OH*, 5 (1904): 122–23. U.C., House of Assembly, *Journal*, 1829: 31; 1831–32, app.: 178; *Statutes*, 1827, c.19; 1828, c.12; 1831, c.21. *Colonial Advocate*, 27 May, 29 July, 27 Oct. 1824; 29 Dec. 1825; 2 March, 1 June 1826; 21 March 1833. *Gore Gazette, and Ancaster, Hamilton, Dundas and Flamborough Advertiser* (Ancaster, [Ont.]), 24 Jan. 1829. *Death notices of Ont.* (Reid), 258.

SURIA, TOMÁS DE, artist; b. May 1761 in Madrid, son of Francisco Suria and Feliciana Lozana; m. 15 Dec. 1788 Maria Josefa Dominguez de Mendoza; d. 1835 in Mexico City.

Tomás de Suria studied in Madrid at the San Fernando Royal Academy of Fine Arts. At age 17 he embarked for New Spain in the company of his mentor, Jerónimo Antonio Gil. In Mexico City he became an engraver at the viceregal mint and gained some measure of fame during his lifetime as a creator of medallions. With Gil in 1778 he was involved in the founding of the Royal Academy of San Carlos, where he served as artist and later as professor.

In 1791, married and with a family, Suria was selected to join the Spanish round-the-world expedition under Alejandro Malaspina*, for temporary duty on the northwest coast of North America as artist. Imbued with a spirit of adventure and uniting the qualifications desired by Malaspina, Suria was chosen by Viceroy Revilla Gigedo because he was the best available candidate in New Spain. Despite the strenuous protests of his wife, who fruitlessly carried her complaint to Revilla Gigedo, Suria determined to go, and with a substantial increase in salary and other emoluments he departed to join Malaspina in Acapulco, where Tadeo Haenke* and the other scientists attached to the expedition were making preparations for a visit to northern latitudes.

At his arrival in Acapulco on 16 February, Suria began a journal, a portion of which has survived. This diary, a private undertaking, contains information not available in the official accounts of the expedition, which began on 1 May, and has the unmistakable flavour of the landlubber. It also contains rough sketches of a number of his finished drawings done on the coast from Alaska to California.

The first artistic work done by Suria on the northwest coast was at Port Mulgrave (Yakutat Bay, Alaska), where he concentrated on the local Tlingit Indians. From here the expedition followed the coast southward and by mid August had reached Nootka Sound, B.C. There Suria made drawings of the Spanish settlement, the Indian leaders Muquinna*, Natsape, and Tlupananulg in their basket-weave whaling hats, and other Nootka Indians, as well as a small sketch of the internationally disputed anchorage in the sound [see Juan Francisco de la Bodega* y Quadra]. At the same time Suria recorded in his journal data of anthropological significance concerning local customs and the structure of Nootka society. Under Suria's tutelage, Manuel José Antonio Cardero*, a cabin-boy who had accompanied the expedition, drew zoological illustrations, depicted native customs, and sketched landscapes.

During the expedition's stay in Nootka Sound, Suria accompanied a party in two small boats up Tahsis Inlet. The results of this excursion, however, are little known since Suria's journal ends with their departure. Not so his art, for subsequently he drew Chief Tlupananulg commanding his great war canoe. A dance performed for the Spaniards on the beach by Tlupananulg was also captured by the artist.

The expedition was back in Acapulco by 16 October, and Suria resumed his employment at the mint and the academy, having left a copious artistic record of the voyage. His finished drawings bear the Latin inscription "Suria fecit." Malaspina, his commander for almost seven months, summed up Suria's effort: "Our collections for the Royal Museum have been numerous and very interesting, inasmuch as Don Tomás Suria has depicted with the greatest fidelity to nature all that merits the help of the engraver's art, so as to secure better understanding in the historical narrative of this voyage."

Suria spent the rest of his life as an engraver, a professor, a paymaster, and at times a minor government official. With dimmed eyesight, he completed his last artistic work in 1834 and died the following year in Mexico City at age 74.

DONALD C. CUTTER

Tomás de Suria's journal is held at the Yale Univ. Library, Beinecke Rare Book and MS Library (New Haven, Conn.), where it is identified as Western Americana MS no.464. Published as *Tomás de Suria y su viaje con Malaspina, 1791*, ed. Justino Fernández (Mexico City, 1939), it has also appeared in English: as "Journal of Tomás de Suria of his voyage with Malaspina to the northwest coast of America in 1791," ed. and trans. H. R. Wagner, *Pacific Coast Hist. Rev.* (Glendale, Calif.), 5 (1936): 234–76, and as a separate publication with this title, ed. D. C. Cutter (Fairfield, Wash., 1980). The Museo Naval and the Museo de America, both in Madrid, hold works by Suria.

D. C. Cutter, *Malaspina in California* ([San Francisco], 1960). J. F. Henry, *Early maritime artists of the Pacific northwest coast, 1741–1841* (Seattle, Wash., 1984). Carmen Sotos Serrano, *Los pintores de la expedición de Alejandro Malaspina* (2v., Madrid, 1982). D. C. Cutter, "Early Spanish artists on the northwest coast," *Pacific Northwest Quarterly* (Seattle), 54 (1963): 150–57. D. C. Cutter and Mercedes Palan de Iglesias, "Malaspina's artists," *El Palacio* (Santa Fe, N.Mex.), 84 (1976), no.4: 19–27.

SUTHERLAND, DANIEL, businessman, office holder, militia officer, and JP; b. *c.* 1756 in Ayrshire, Scotland; d. 19 Aug. 1832 at Quebec.

After receiving a mercantile education in Glasgow, Daniel Sutherland immigrated to the province of Quebec in 1776 and soon became involved in business in Montreal. By 1778 he was active in the fur trade, and the following year he was a partner in Porteous, Sutherland and Company; it was dissolved in October. From 1781 to 1786 he and James Grant* sent expeditions to Michilimackinac (Mackinac Island, Mich.) and to the Timiskaming area with cargoes valued at between £2,000 and £6,000; by 1789, however, their estate was in the hands of trustees. In addition, Sutherland stood security for other merchants. His marriage to Margaret Robertson in Montreal on 1 Sept. 1781 made him a son-in-law of the British officer Daniel Robertson*, who, as commander at Michilimackinac from 1782 to 1787, promoted Sutherland's business interests. In 1785 Sutherland made an exceptional investment in the fur trade, estimated at £20,500, almost as large as the investments of the leading merchants that year, James McGill* and Joseph Frobisher*. In December he bought a stone house and store on Rue Saint-Paul in Montreal's commercial district.

In 1790, apparently through a friendship with Simon McTavish*, Sutherland received a $\frac{1}{20}$th share in the North West Company and was sent to Grand Portage (near Grand Portage, Minn.) as a delegate of the Montreal partners at the annual meeting with the

Sutherland

wintering partners. When the company was reorganized in 1792 to bring in potential competitors [see Isaac Todd*], Sutherland was given 2 of the 46 shares in the new arrangement. The following year he was suspected of showing interest in a projected rival firm to the NWC, and in 1794 at Grand Portage he was spokesman, in opposition to the delegates representing McTavish, Frobisher and Company, of the firms brought into the NWC in 1792. In October 1795, desperate for cash after losses in the fur trade and the purchase of Frobisher's home in Montreal, and convinced that Frobisher and McTavish were responsible for his plight, Sutherland sold his interest in the NWC to McTavish, Frobisher and Company. Three years later he signed the articles of agreement that created the New North West Company (sometimes called the XY Company), to compete with the NWC [see John RICHARDSON], and he subsequently acted as its Montreal agent. In May 1806, after the union of the rivals, Sutherland withdrew, having obtained a settlement that cut his losses.

Like many of his business colleagues, Sutherland diversified his activities. He was a trustee or executor of estates and acquired landed property. In 1793 he had purchased another stone house on Rue Saint-Paul, and three years later he and Robert Griffin leased land from Thomas McCORD in the Nazareth sub-fief in the city. By 1810 he held land in Chatham Township originally granted in part to Robertson. In 1800 he had joined John GRAY and three others in establishing the Company of Proprietors of the Montreal Water Works, incorporated the following year.

No doubt as insurance against the vagaries of a business career, in October 1807 Sutherland obtained appointment as postmaster of Montreal, replacing Edward Edwards*. At the beginning of the War of 1812 he was appointed military postmaster "in consideration of the extra duty of the Postmaster of Montreal in forwarding letters to the Troops," but, finding the position over burdensome for the salary, he resigned it in 1814. As postmaster of Montreal he was conscientious, the deputy postmaster general for Upper and Lower Canada, George Heriot*, describing him in 1815 as "the most correct accountant of any Postmaster in the Department Here." The business community also appreciated Sutherland's work, and a number of London merchants trading to the Canadas successfully recommended him to succeed Heriot in 1816; the appointment was made in April, and Sutherland moved to Quebec.

Throughout his tenure as deputy postmaster general, Sutherland was obliged to walk a tightrope between the demands by colonists for expansion of what they considered an imperial service and those of the British government for restraint of expenditures on what it considered an instrument of taxation. From 1816 to 1827 Sutherland increased the number of post offices in Lower Canada from 10 to 49 and in Upper Canada from 9 to 65. Nevertheless, the Upper Canadian House of Assembly in particular complained that the number and distribution of post offices was inadequate. It also accused Sutherland of charging rates in excess of those laid down by an imperial statute in 1765. Dissatisfaction with the postal service led the assemblies of the two provinces to contest the deposit of postal revenues from the colonies in the British exchequer and to agitate for provincial control of the mails. Sutherland, who was more tactful in his personal relations with the governors than Heriot had been, and who supported them in their struggles with the provincial assemblies, obtained their backing for himself and the post office in his own battles with the legislatures.

A merchant himself, Sutherland endorsed complaints by the mercantile community about the postal service to Britain and to the United States, and a public expression of his sympathy nearly provoked his dismissal in 1819–20. The Lower Canadian merchants complained bitterly that the British system obliged them as senders to prepay postage while the American system forced them as receivers to pay postage on mail from the United States. Since Sutherland took a commission of 20 per cent on all postal revenues he collected for the American post office (a practice the legality of which was strongly contested by the British Post Office Department), he preferred the American system. After failing to persuade the British Post Office to adopt that system, he turned a blind eye to the illegal use by Lower Canadian merchants of private courier services that took correspondence for American recipients to the nearest American town for mailing; by evading prepayment of postage in this manner, the merchants deprived the British Post Office of revenues. He was less tolerant of the informal use of steamboat captains rather than official mail carriers for the conveyance of mails within the British colonies, and in England in 1819 he sought authority to impose penalties for the practice. However, fear that sanctions would furnish the colonial assemblies with yet another complaint against the imperial government induced the colonial secretary, Lord Bathurst, and the governor-in-chief, Lord Dalhousie [Ramsay*], to restrain Sutherland's ardour.

With a salary of £500, commissions, and fees, Sutherland was one of the best-remunerated officials in the colony. However, he was responsible for the accounts of his deputies, and he suffered personal losses totalling £3,000 when on two occasions deputies failed to regulate their accounts. Indeed, financial difficulties obliged him to go to England, probably in 1826, to plead his case with the Post Office. He found that a 35-year absence had left him "without either friends or acquaintants" in the country to help him, and on 19 Nov. 1827 he resigned his post in favour of his son-in-law Thomas Allen Stayner*; he was apparently not released from his financial obligations until 1828.

Sutherland's reputation in the business community possibly accounts for his appointment on 28 Nov. 1817 as Quebec agent for the newly formed Bank of Montreal, in which two former associates, John Gray and Robert Griffin, were active. He was undoubtedly expected to exploit his cordial relations with colonial officials in order to obtain the government account for the bank. Six weeks after the Bank of Montreal opened its doors in Montreal on 3 Nov. 1817, Sutherland opened his Quebec agency. As a commission, and to cover expenses, he was allowed two-eighths of one per cent on all transactions, which soon became numerous. In view of the demand for banking services at Quebec, and probably in an effort to forestall the establishment of a bank there, the Quebec agency was transformed in 1818 into a branch office – called an office of discount and deposit – which eventually provided nearly all the services offered at Montreal. Three hundred shares of Bank of Montreal stock were reserved for Quebec subscribers to encourage participation by Quebec businessmen in the branch's management, but only 184 were subscribed, a project for an independent Quebec bank being mooted at the time. Nevertheless, on 20 July 1818, with a board of directors, a staff of three, and an operating fund of £50,000, Sutherland, who had acquired the title of cashier and a salary of £300, opened his branch establishment on Rue Saint-Pierre in the heart of Quebec's business community. By the early 1820s the Quebec Bank, founded by Quebec businessmen in 1818, was contesting the presence of a branch of the Bank of Montreal in the city, particularly since Sutherland had succeeded in obtaining the government account, and in 1823–24 Sutherland was obliged to defend his institution before a committee of the Lower Canadian assembly inquiring into the state of banking. Nothing came of the inquiry, but Sutherland resigned his position on 17 June 1824.

Sutherland also engaged in real-estate ventures in Stoneham Township, near Quebec, in 1823 and sold properties in the city. In addition to his business and government occupations he took on public functions without remuneration. A captain in Montreal's 1st Militia Battalion by 1807, he was promoted major in April 1812 and lieutenant-colonel three years later. Following his move to Quebec he was active in the social life of the capital. In December 1818 he wrote to William Bent Berczy*, who with his brother Charles Albert* had become Sutherland's protégé after the death of William Berczy*, their father and Sutherland's friend: "Our winter Amusements are begun, the first Assembly took place last night & was well attended. His Grace [Charles Lennox*, 4th Duke of Richmond and Lennox] and Lady Mary were of the number – they also regularly visit our Amateur Theatre ... so that you see we are in a fair way of beguiling along a dreary winter, unless the news of the death of the old Queen should be received & put a stop to our Gaiety. " A subscriber to funds for the relief of destitute immigrants and to the Fire Society, the Quebec Emigrants' Society (for which he was a fund raiser), and the Agriculture Society, Sutherland was commissioned a justice of the peace in June 1821 and a trustee of the Royal Institution for the Advancement of Learning [see Joseph Langley MILLS] two years later. In 1831, inspired by the example of his friend William Dummer POWELL, Sutherland had a gold medal struck to celebrate 50 years of happy marriage with Margaret Robertson, during which they had had three children. He presented the medal the following year (the idea having come late); silver impressions were given to relatives and bronze ones to guests who had attended a gala anniversary celebration.

Sutherland died just a few months later during a cholera epidemic; he had been one of the few remaining members of the first generation of British merchants to arrive in the colony. Through their quest for personal gain they had expanded the frontiers of British North America, and, as in Sutherland's case, had helped to establish and develop the economic, administrative, and social infrastructure of the colony.

MYRON MOMRYK

ANQ-M, CE1-63, 1er sept. 1781, 28 juill. 1782, 6 juill. 1783, 3 mars 1786. ANQ-Q, CE1-66, 19 août 1832. AUM, P 58, U, Sutherland to McTavish, Frobisher and Company, 4 Oct. 1795; Sutherland to James Reid, 23 Aug. 1798; Sutherland to Mme de Lavaltrie, 11 March 1811; Sutherland to W. B. Berczy, 3 Oct., 19 Dec. 1818; 4, 16 Aug., 11, 14 Sept. 1819; 9 Nov. 1822; 3 May 1823. PAC, MG 19, A7, 1; MG 24, I26, 49; MG 28, II2, Resolve book, no. 1; MG 40, L; RG 1, L3ᴸ: 573, 1567, 2146–47, 31519–29, 81361–79, 81452–685, 90433–59; RG 4, A1: 32920; 331: 138; 337, 2 Oct. 1830; B28, 115; RG 8, I (C ser.), 284; II, 8–10; RG 68, General index, 1651–1841: 347, 683. William Berczy, "William von Moll Berczy," ANQ Rapport, 1940–41: 52, 80. Docs. relating to NWC (Wallace). L.C., House of Assembly, Journals, 1800: 48; 1823–24: 284–85. Quebec Gazette, 13 Sept. 1781; 6 June 1782; 9 Jan., 26 March 1783; 5 Jan. 1786; 14 Nov. 1793; 8 June 1797; 8 Oct. 1807; 14 April, 12 July 1808; 16 Nov. 1809; 22 March, 15 Nov. 1810; 5 Sept. 1811; 5 March, 30 April 1812; 18 May 1815; 3 July, 26 Aug. 1817; 12 March, 16 July, 9 Dec. 1818; 23 April, 17, 27 May, 9 June, 29 Nov. 1819; 6 March, 27 April, 23 Oct. 1820; 5 July, 5 Aug. 1821; 7 Aug., 18 Sept., 6 Nov., 8 Dec. 1823; 1 Jan., 12, 15 Feb., 1, 8, 15 April 1824. Quebec Mercury, 21 Aug. 1832. Officers of British forces in Canada (Irving). Denison, Canada's first bank. Miquelon, "Baby family," 189, 191. R. A. Pendergast, "The XY Company, 1798–1804" (PHD thesis, Univ. of Ottawa, 1957), 15, 63. William Smith, The history of the Post Office in British North America, 1639–1870 (Cambridge, Eng., 1920; repr. New York, 1973). H. A. Innis, "The North West Company,"

Swayze

CHR, 8 (1927): 308–21. R. W. McLachlan, "Two Canadian golden wedding medals," *Canadian Antiquarian and Numismatic Journal* (Montreal), 3rd ser., 3 (1901): 168–80. E. A. Mitchell, "The North West Company agreement of 1795," *CHR*, 36 (1955): 127, 130.

SWAYZE (Swayzie, Sweezey), ISAAC, politician, JP, office holder, and militia officer; b. 1751 in Morris County, N.J., son of Caleb Swayze and Miriam Drake; m. first Bethia Luce; m. secondly Sarah Secord; m. thirdly 18 Sept. 1806 Lena Ferris, a widow; d. 11 Feb. 1828 near Niagara (Niagara-on-the-Lake), Upper Canada.

The Swayze family emigrated from Germany in the early 17th century and settled in Salem, Mass. Isaac Swayze's forebears moved to Long Island, N.Y., and then to Morris County where he was living at the outbreak of the American revolution. He claimed early participation by his family in the royal cause and he himself was employed on secret service, twice made prisoner, and badly wounded during the course of the conflict. Tradition has it that during one incarceration he was sentenced to death. Apparently his wife visited him on the day of the execution and exchanged clothes with him; he escaped, never seeing her again. What is known for certain is that he broke out of jail on 4 Sept. 1780 in Morristown and a $5,000 reward was put on his head. He was described as 5 feet 8 or 9 inches, with a sandy complexion, and a bullet scar on one temple. In June 1783 Swayze was thrown into prison by the British authorities in New York on suspicion of having committed a robbery on Long Island. He was freed the following month, but ordered to leave the city immediately. Suspicions of criminality swirled around him for the rest of his life.

In 1784 Swayze removed to the Niagara peninsula, where he eventually settled at St Davids. His fellow settlers there had doubts about his allegiance during the revolution; it was not until he had produced proof of misrepresentation of character that he was allowed his loyalist grant of land. Despite his neighbours' suspicions, Swayze was elected for the riding of 3rd Lincoln to Upper Canada's first parliament in 1792. Initially he was something of a populist leader and was considered by the more established elements in society to be a demagogue. He later contended that he had been elected by the "farmers and genral classes" who had "more confidence in my attachment to their interests, than they had in the nobles." Because of his "integrity" in that anti-commercial House of Assembly, Swayze claimed, he was a victim of "shafts of malice incessantly hurled from some who ranked themselves high." In 1795 he shocked provincial officials by assuming leadership of a popular agitation against the form of wording in which deeds were made out. There were widespread fears that the deeds would prohibit the sale of land. To put a stop to the discontent, the government charged Swayze with sedition. On 5 April 1795 Peter Russell* noted in a letter to Lieutenant Governor Simcoe*, "I am told too that Mr. Swazey is to be informed against to the next Grand Jury as an Exciter of Sedition." He was tried, convicted, and forced to find sureties for good behaviour for two years. On 1 July 1796 he was commissioned a justice of the peace.

If Swayze ran for the second parliament, he was not re-elected. By 1799 he was campaigning in earnest for the election of 1800. The focus of public concern was the proposal by Robert Hamilton* and his associates to finance improvements of the Niagara portage by higher charges. Swayze emerged as a leader of the coalition of interests that challenged the commercial élite. He soon became the centre of a controversy. Accusations were made that he had been a horse thief in Pennsylvania. His supporters asserted that the story had been inspired by the "Caledonian Friends" of the *Canada Constellation*'s editor, Silvester Tiffany*. The reference was to the major Scots merchants of the peninsula led by Hamilton. When the voting took place, Swayze and Ralfe CLENCH defeated the merchant candidates Samuel Street* and William Dickson*.

In spite of his election, the allegations of horse theft against Swayze continued in the columns of Tiffany's new paper, the *Niagara Herald*. Swayze declared that the "attachment of the community to me did not decrease with the increase of the enmity of the few" and promised to return to the House of Assembly "unawed." He finally quashed the rumours with a legal suit against a voter who had accused him before three political gatherings of horse theft. The consequences of this action were sufficient to cause Tiffany to let the matter die. Within the assembly Swayze and Clench worked closely on legislation favourable to small merchants, farmers, loyalists, and local office holders; nothing of importance, however, was passed. In 1803 Swayze's erstwhile opponents found he could be influenced: he was persuaded to support an assessment act favouring large land speculators in exchange for aid in securing a local appointment at Niagara.

Swayze was returned for the riding of 2nd, 3rd and 4th Lincoln in 1804. His politics, however, had become notably more conservative since 1803 and he gradually earned a reputation as a rabid anti-republican. The rise of a parliamentary and extra-parliamentary opposition, with a strong base in the Niagara peninsula, ended the antagonisms between the large merchants and their local opponents led by Swayze and Clench.

Swayze's admission into local circles of power did not diminish his capacity for generating controversy or alter the aura of illegality that hung over his career. Some time before 1806 he was appointed inspector of shop, still, and tavern licences for the Niagara

District. In January 1806 he reported that three men with blackened faces had broken into his house and stolen £500 in licence and land fees. Doubts were cast on his story and he later withdrew his petition to the assembly in which he asked to be excused from restoring the money.

Unscrupulous in his methods, Swayze curried favour by tackling the dirty work of politics, apparently with relish. In 1808 he chaired the committee of the assembly which resolved that Joseph Willcocks*'s language had been "false, slanderous and highly derogatory to the dignity of this house"; as a result, Willcocks was later jailed. In 1810 Willcocks urged Lieutenant Governor Francis Gore* to prosecute Swayze for circulating counterfeit banknotes.

Although he appears not to have previously held a militia commission, Swayze was appointed captain of a troop he raised at the outbreak of the War of 1812 known as the Provincial Royal Artillery Drivers. William Hamilton Merritt* commented, in his memoir of the war, that Swayze deserved "the greatest credit for his indefatigable exertions." He was mentioned in dispatches after the battle of Queenston Heights. When the retreating American army burned Niagara in December 1813, Swayze lost his house and barn, which he valued at £200.

In January 1816 Swayze was briefly involved with Timothy Street and Richard COCKRELL in their attempt to establish a newspaper at St Davids. That same year he was elected in 4th Lincoln. He became a vociferous opponent of Robert Gourlay* and acted as the eyes and ears of civil authorities in the Niagara peninsula. He was, for instance, sent to the Credit River during the summer of 1818 to investigate rumours of preparations for an armed insurrection. In December 1818 he provided the information that led to Bartemas FERGUSON, editor of the *Niagara Spectator*, being charged with seditious libel for printing Gourlay's article, "Gagg'd-Gagg'd, by Jingo!" More important, he swore an affidavit that Gourlay was not an inhabitant of Upper Canada, thereby opening the way for charges against him under the Sedition Act of 1804. Gourlay's attempt to prosecute Swayze for defamation of character proved abortive.

Gourlay once posed the question, "How could such a man as Isaac Swayze be elected, and repeatedly elected?" His answer was that Swayze "could cover all the stains upon his character, before my time, with hypocrisy." The old tactic, however, failed abjectly in the election of 1820. His opponent, Robert RANDAL, portrayed him as a stooge of executive government and won an easy victory. The defeat in 1820 was Swayze's last political campaign. A member of the Presbyterian church and a proprietor of the Niagara Library, he appears to have spent his last years quietly.

BRUCE G. WILSON

AO, RG 22, ser.134, 5, civil assize, Niagara District, 25 Aug. 1819; ser.138, box 1, *R.* v. *Isaac Swayze*, 1795, affidavits of John Young *et al.*, 16 March 1795. MTL, W. D. Powell papers, B85: 16–21. PAC, MG 23, HI, 1, ser.3, 6: 3; ser.4, vol.5, packet A7: 65–66 (transcripts); MG 24, K5, 1: 1–3; RG 5, A1: 2888–89, 18717–18; RG 8, I (C ser.), 1203½G: 37; 1717: 74; RG 68, General index, 1651– 1841: 403. PRO, AO 13, bundle 83: 677–78; PRO 30/55, nos.7897, 8078, 8392. QUA, Richard Cartwright papers, letter-books, Cartwright to Elmsley, 6 June 1803 (transcripts at AO). *Corr. of Lieut. Governor Simcoe* (Cruikshank), 3: 342. *Documents relating to the revolutionary history of the state of New Jersey*, ed. W. S. Stryker *et al.* (5v., Trenton, N.J., 1901–17), 4: 648–49. "Early churches in the Niagara Peninsula, Stamford and Chippewa, with marriage records of Thomas Cummings, and extracts from the Cummings' papers," ed. Janet Carnochan, *OH*, 8 (1907): 149–225. R. F. Gourlay, *The banished Briton and Neptunian: being a record of the life, writings, principles and projects of Robert Gourlay . . .* (Boston, 1843), 153. "Journals of Legislative Assembly of U.C.," *AO Report*, 1911: 199. *Select British docs. of War of 1812* (Wood), 3, pt.II: 546–47. "The settlement of the township of Fort Erie, now known as the township of Bertie: an attempt at a Domesday Book," comp. E. A. Cruikshank, Welland County Hist. Soc., *Papers and Records* (Welland, Ont.), 5 (1938): 75. *Statistical account of U.C.* (Gourlay; ed. Mealing; 1974), 294–96.

Canada Constellation (Niagara [Niagara-on-the-Lake, Ont.]), 23 Aug., 6 Sept. 1799. *Gleaner, and Niagara Newspaper*, 18 Feb. 1828. *Niagara Herald*, 13 May 1801. *Niagara Spectator*, 17 Dec. 1818. *Upper Canada Guardian; or, Freeman's Journal* (Niagara), 10 Jan. 1810. Armstrong, *Handbook of Upper Canadian chronology* (1967). "Loyalist and pioneer families of West Lincoln, 1783–1833," comp. R. J. Powell, *Annals of the Forty* (Grimsby, Ont.), no.8 (1957): 86–88. *Quebec almanac*, 1806. Carnochan, *Hist. of Niagara*, 247. Charles Durand, *Reminiscences of Charles Durand of Toronto, barrister* (Toronto, 1897), 507. W. R. Riddell, "The information ex-officio in Upper Canada," in *Upper Canada sketches; incidents in the early times of the province*, ed. W. R. Riddell (Toronto, 1922), 86–89. Wilson, *Enterprises of Robert Hamilton*.

SYLVESTER, JOSEPH. *See* JOE, SYLVESTER

T

TABEAU, PIERRE-ANTOINE, Roman Catholic priest and vicar general; b. 11 Oct. 1782 in Montreal, son of Jean-Baptiste Tabeau, a voyageur and militia captain, and Françoise Prou; d. there 18 May 1835.

Tabeau

After studying at the Collège Saint-Raphaël in Montreal, Pierre-Antoine Tabeau received the tonsure on 23 Sept. 1800, and then did his theology at the Séminaire de Québec. He was ordained sub-deacon on 30 Oct. 1803 and deacon on 14 October of the following year; he also served as secretary to Bishop Joseph-Octave PLESSIS. On 13 Oct. 1805 he was ordained priest in Montreal. Vicar general Jean-Henry-Auguste ROUX, to whom young Tabeau had sometimes appeared "a little undisciplined," remarked that day, "This young man has talent, good health, virtue, and there is reason to think he will render service to the church."

Tabeau was curate at the cathedral of Notre-Dame in Quebec from 1805 until 1810, and then was entrusted with various responsibilities. He was parish priest of Sainte-Anne at Sainte-Anne-des-Plaines from 1810 until 1813, parish priest of Saint-Jean-Port-Joli from September 1813 until 1814, and curate of the parish of Notre-Dame in Quebec from October 1814 until 1815. From October 1815 to 1817 he was chaplain to the nuns of the Hôpital Général of Quebec and was also responsible for ministering to the mission chapels of Notre-Dame-des-Anges and Notre-Dame-de-Foy at Sainte-Foy. During those two years he was organist at the cathedral as well. Between September 1817 and the end of September 1831 he served as parish priest of Sainte-Famille at Boucherville. Liked by his flock despite his thoroughly military way of running the parish, Tabeau had a genuine concern for education. In 1821 he set up a Latin class which lasted some ten years.

In May 1816 Bishop Plessis delegated Tabeau to accompany the governor of Assiniboia, Miles MACDONELL, to that remote region in order to study the prospects for a permanent mission there. On learning of the skirmish at Seven Oaks (Winnipeg), during which the governor of the Hudson's Bay Company territories, Robert Semple*, was killed, Tabeau decided to venture no farther west than Rainy Lake. In his report to Plessis in 1818 he recommended against establishing a mission at Red River while there was still conflict between the HBC and the North West Company [see William McGILLIVRAY]. The bishop had nevertheless taken the decision to set up two missions, one at Red River, the other to serve Sault-Ste-Marie (Ont.) and Fort William (Thunder Bay), and in April 1818 he urged Tabeau to accept one of them. He chose the second, which he visited periodically.

Tabeau always inspired great confidence in his superiors. In the spring of 1829, for example, the archbishop of Quebec, Bernard-Claude PANET, delegated him to accompany Abbé Thomas Maguire*, the principal of the Collège de Saint-Hyacinthe, to Rome and London. Their mission had several aims. They were to support a petition to the king from the Lower Canadian clergy which had been transmitted by

Governor Sir James Kempt* in February and which requested that the Sulpicians be left in possession of their estates. They were also to obtain letters patent for the Collège de Saint-Hyacinthe [see Antoine GIROUARD], and to support a petition to the king from Archbishop Panet and his coadjutor, Joseph Signay*, dated 18 May 1829, for a bishopric in Montreal. Moreover, Jean-Jacques Lartigue*, the auxiliary bishop in Montreal to the archbishop of Quebec, who strongly favoured this last measure, had made them his personal representatives. Tabeau and Maguire reached London on 7 July 1829, but they made little progress in their initiatives. In the autumn, they left for Rome where they were to remain three months. The reports and petitions they brought to the authorities in Rome, among them the petition they presented to the pope on 16 December concerning Bishop Lartigue's differences with the Séminaire de Saint-Sulpice [see Jean-Charles BÉDARD; Augustin CHABOILLEZ], had meagre results. However, at their meeting on 1 March 1830 the cardinals of the Sacred Congregation of Propaganda temporarily suspended the permission they had previously given the Sulpicians to alienate their seigneurial holdings, such a permission being necessary since the holdings belonged in the first instance to the church [see Jean-Henry-Auguste Roux].

Tabeau returned to Montreal in the summer of 1830, and on 27 Sept. 1831 he was named vicar general to the archbishop of Quebec. At the same time he left Boucherville to become Lartigue's assistant at the Séminaire Saint-Jacques in Montreal. Bishop Lartigue was thinking of making him his successor one day. In November 1830 Lartigue had advised Nicholas Patrick Wiseman, the Canadian bishops' agent in Rome, to promote both the creation of a separate Montreal diocese and Tabeau's appointment to replace him. In January 1832 Archbishop Panet also put Tabeau's name forward to Rome as successor to Lartigue; so too did the new archbishop of Quebec, Signay, in May 1834. On the following 2 October, as a result of pressure from Maguire, who was again on a mission in Rome, Pope Gregory XVI approved the choice of Tabeau, leaving it to Signay to consecrate him at the right moment.

The news of his appointment in December 1834 as bishop of Spiga and auxiliary to Lartigue filled Pierre-Antoine Tabeau with dismay. He at first refused, then let himself be persuaded by Lartigue. But he was soon to fall ill, and late in January 1835 his condition began to cause concern. Shortly afterwards he was hospitalized. He grew steadily worse and on 11 May received the last sacraments. He died a week later, without having been consecrated bishop, just before the papal order of 7 March 1835 constraining him to accept the episcopate reached Quebec. His death was a terrible blow for Lartigue, whose every plan was upset. Tabeau was buried a few days later in the church at Boucherville. He was remembered as an affable man, full of gentleness despite his quick temper, and genuinely humble.

GILLES CHAUSSÉ

AAQ, 1 CB. ACAM, 901.017; 901.030. ANQ-M, CE1-22, 20 mai 1835; CE1-51, 11 oct. 1782. Arch. du diocèse de Saint-Jean-de-Québec (Longueuil, Qué.), 5A/17–18, 20–23, 25–31, 33–47, 49–50, 52–53, 61–64; 6A/136, 141; 13A/78. ASSM, 21, 27. Le Canadien, 24 juill. 1835. Allaire, Dictionnaire, 1: 505. F.-M. Bibaud, Le Panthéon canadien (A. et V. Bibaud; 1891). Caron, "Inv. de la corr. de Mgr Denaut," ANQ Rapport, 1931–32: 171, 205; "Inv. de la corr. de Mgr Panet," ANQ Rapport, 1935–36: 198, 221; "Inv. de la corr. de Mgr Plessis," ANQ Rapport, 1927–28: 277, 296, 310–11; ANQ Rapport, 1932–33: 17–18, 103; "Inv. de la corr. de Mgr Signay," ANQ Rapport, 1936–37: 257. Desrosiers, "Inv. de la corr. de Mgr Lartigue," ANQ Rapport, 1943–44: 224, 288, 299. Le Jeune, Dictionnaire, 2: 684–85. Chaussé, Jean-Jacques Lartigue, 105, 111. Lemieux, L'établissement de la première prov. eccl., 102–3, 284–87, 291–97, 367–71. A.-G. Morice, Histoire de l'Église catholique dans l'Ouest canadien, du lac Supérieur au Pacifique (1659–1905) (3v., Winnipeg et Montréal, 1912), 1: 114–15, 138–39. É.-Z. Massicotte, "Notes sur la famille Tabeau," BRH, 43 (1937): 367–70. Léon Pouliot, "L'abbé Pierre Tabeau," BRH, 44 (1938): 198–200.

TACHÉ, PASCAL (baptized **Paschal-Jacques**), seigneur, JP, politician, and militia officer; b. 30 Aug. 1757 at Quebec, son of Jean Taché* and Marie-Anne Jolliet de Mingan; m. 25 Sept. 1785 Marie-Louise Decharnay, a widow, in Kamouraska, Que., and they had one son; d. there 5 June 1830.

After a career of some ten years as a clerk in the company that leased the king's posts [see Thomas Dunn*], Pascal Taché settled down at Kamouraska in 1785, the year he married Marie-Louise Decharnay, the co-seigneur of this locality. Five years later his mother-in-law gave him her share in the seigneury. Like many Canadian seigneurs at the time, Taché displayed loyalty to the British crown and this is probably what earned him in 1794 the commission as a justice of the peace for the district of Quebec which was renewed periodically.

In March 1798 Taché ran for the House of Assembly in Cornwallis riding, to replace the late Pascal Sirois-Duplessis. He was elected, but the voting had taken place in bad weather and under an English-speaking electoral officer who was ill informed about voters' rights. Consequently some of the constituents petitioned the assembly to have the election annulled, but their request was rejected. Taché held his seat until June 1800 and, although he normally lived in his seigneurial manor-house, for the period he served in the assembly he took up residence on Rue Sainte-Anne at Quebec. He was often absent from the house, and played little part in its deliberations, confining himself to voting. He served on a single committee,

which was responsible for drawing up a bill on the production of maple sugar.

After this brief entry into Lower Canadian political life Taché devoted himself almost exclusively to managing the seigneury of Kamouraska, which was then developing at an extraordinary pace. In 1813, according to surveyor Joseph Bouchette*'s observations, it had about 5,500 inhabitants, who made their livelihood primarily from farming. Besides the church and the presbytery, the village contained some 60 houses, and it was much appreciated as a summer vacation centre. Two schools, one supported by the *fabrique*, the other by the Royal Institution for the Advancement of Learning, provided education for the children. In administering his fief, Taché took advantage of the rights attached to the seigneurial régime. He made land grants, claimed *cens et rentes* and *lods et ventes*, and protested when one *censitaire* showed his desire to build a grist-mill. He made money from renting out the communal mill and the lands that he owned, but especially from the fisheries, which were exploited on a large scale. For example, he rented, most often to residents, waterfront lots on the St Lawrence or on the approaches to Île aux Corneilles, Île aux Patins, Île de la Providence, and Île aux Harengs.

In 1813 Mme Taché died, leaving her share in the seigneury to their son Paschal, who from then on co-signed with his father all transactions concerning the fief. He too lived in the seigneurial manor-house and practised his profession of notary, albeit infrequently. Both father and son served in the Rivière-Ouelle battalion of militia during the War of 1812, the former as lieutenant-colonel and the latter as adjutant. Again following his father's example, he belonged to the Agriculture Society and together they attended its meetings, which were held at Rivière-du-Loup or Kamouraska.

Although they were not rich, the Taché seigneurs lived comfortably, surrounded by servants. They gave sumptuous dinners, receptions, and picnics on the islands, and for many years Kamouraska was the undisputed centre of social life in the region. The salon of the parish priest, Jacques Varin, was frequented by some of the élite – the seigneurs, merchants Jean-Charles Chapais and Amable Dionne*, notaries Thomas Casault, François Letellier de Saint-Just, and Jean-Baptiste Taché, as well as lawyer Charles-Eusèbe Casgrain*.

Pascal Taché died on 5 June 1830, and his son did not live long after him, dying on 3 Jan. 1833. They were both buried at Kamouraska under the seigneurs' pew in the church of Saint-Louis parish. On 14 May 1810 Taché's son had married Julie Larue at Quebec, and they had had four children. In his will Paschal Taché bequeathed the usufruct and enjoyment of the seigneurial property to his wife. His two daughters each inherited £1,000, and his son Jacques-Vinceslas

Taschereau

received the part of the fief that lay within the boundaries of Saint-Pascal parish. The elder son, Louis-Pascal-Achille*, received a piece of land at Kamouraska and the part of the fief that makes up Saint-Louis parish.

In collaboration with ÉVELINE BOSSÉ

ANQ-Q, CE1-1, 31 août 1757, 14 mai 1810; CE3-3, 26 sept. 1785, 7 juin 1830; CN3-10, 25, 28 avril, 7 nov., 5 déc. 1814; 14 janv., 23 févr., 4, 8 mars, 22 déc. 1815; 19 févr., 15 juill., 28 nov. 1816; 17 août 1818; 6 mars 1827; CN3-13, 25 sept. 1785; CN3-17, 23 juill., 29 août 1797; CN3-19, 9 août 1802; 8, 10 mars, 25 juill. 1804; 14 avril 1808; CN3-30, 15 nov. 1832. PAC, RG 68, General index, 1651–1841. "Les dénombrements de Québec" (Plessis), ANQ *Rapport*, 1948–49: 120. L.C., House of Assembly, *Journals*, 1798–1800. *Quebec Gazette*, 3 July 1794; 29 March 1798; 28 Sept. 1809; 8 April, 2, 16 Aug. 1819; 7 Sept. 1820. F.-J. Audet, "Les législateurs du Bas-Canada." Desjardins, *Guide parl. Officers of British forces in Canada* (Irving). Alexandre Paradis, *Kamouraska (1674–1948)* (Québec, 1948). P.-G. Roy, *La famille Taché* (Lévis, Qué., 1904).

TASCHEREAU, JEAN-THOMAS, office holder, politician, lawyer, businessman, militia officer, seigneur, JP, and judge; b. 26 Nov. 1778 in Sainte-Marie-de-la-Nouvelle-Beauce (Sainte-Marie), Que., son of Gabriel-Elzéar Taschereau* and Marie-Louise-Élizabeth Bazin; d. 14 June 1832 at Quebec.

Jean-Thomas Taschereau was admitted to the Petit Séminaire de Québec in 1789. Because of his intellectual ability he skipped grades with ease and thus completed the course of study in less than six years. In November 1799 his father, who was then *grand voyer* (chief road commissioner) for the district of Quebec, took him on as his assistant. He studied law with Jonathan Sewell* at the same time and was authorized to practise as a lawyer on 9 Nov. 1801.

Taschereau had been elected for Dorchester to the House of Assembly of Lower Canada on 28 July 1800. During his first term he split his votes between the English party and the Canadian party, but during his second he basically supported only the latter. His defeat at the polls in May 1808 was partly engineered by the political scheming of judge Pierre-Amable De Bonne* and his allies in the English party. The following month the governor, Sir James Henry Craig*, stripped him of his rank as militia captain because he was involved in publishing the newspaper *Le Canadien*. In the 1809 contest he was elected for Dorchester and Leinster ridings. However, a month after the session opened Craig prorogued the house. Taschereau used the pages of *Le Canadien* to keep up the fight against the governor's arbitrary conduct. But the issue of 17 March 1810 was suppressed and the presses and type seized. Pierre-Stanislas BÉDARD, François BLANCHET, and Taschereau, as well as the printer Charles LEFRANÇOIS, were arrested for sedi-

tious conduct and imprisoned. Taschereau protested to the Executive Council against the vague accusation of treason and demanded a trial. Although he was in prison when elections were held that year, he was nominated in Dorchester riding, where he was beaten by John Caldwell*. He was finally released at the end of June without having been brought before the courts.

War with the United States provided a distraction from the war of ideas in Lower Canada. In April 1812 Taschereau was commissioned major in the Sainte-Marie-de-la-Nouvelle-Beauce battalion of militia and in this capacity he was engaged in the early part of the campaign. On 27 March 1813 he replaced Xavier-Roch Tarieu* de Lanaudière as deputy adjutant general of the Lower Canadian militia.

Taschereau's duties did not prevent him from serving as a justice of the peace in the district of Quebec from May 1812; nor did they keep him from running in Dorchester riding, where he was elected in August. In the house he brought forward a motion to study ways and means of establishing schools in the rural parishes. The assembly pronounced itself in favour of granting a sum not exceeding £60 to pay a schoolteacher in any parish that asked for one, but the bill never became law. Taschereau did not give up his interest in education, and on 11 March 1814 he became a commissioner for setting up a school in Sainte-Marie-de-la-Nouvelle-Beauce under the aegis of the Royal Institution for the Advancement of Learning [*see* Joseph-Antoine PHILIPPON].

In June 1815 Taschereau was appointed commissioner for the district of Quebec to carry out the act to improve inland communications within the province. Four years later, with George Waters Allsopp*, Michel-Louis Juchereau* Duchesnay, and Robert Christie*, he became a member of a commission to inquire into title-deeds in the district of Gaspé, settle land-claim disputes, and investigate the needs of the inhabitants of the Gaspé peninsula. The commission held sittings in 1819 and 1820; its first report suggested that agriculture be encouraged, roads be laid out, and the facilities of the port of Gaspé be improved. The commissioners visited the Gaspé in 1819, 1820, and 1823 before their mandate expired in April 1825.

Taschereau had been appointed a justice of the peace for the district of Gaspé on 15 June 1819. In the elections the following year he was defeated in Dorchester by a newcomer, lawyer Louis LAGUEUX, but was elected in Gaspé riding. In 1821 he was appointed to serve on the Commissioners Court, a body authorized to hear small causes, in Sainte-Marie-de-la-Nouvelle-Beauce. On 6 June of that year he obtained a similar post on the Quebec Court of General Sessions. A few days later his commission as justice of the peace for the district of Quebec was renewed. In July and October of the same year he also received similar commissions for the districts of Montreal and Saint-François; he became a justice of the peace for the district of Gaspé in 1824, and for Trois-Rivières in 1828.

Taschereau was made a king's counsel on 9 Oct. 1821. The following year he became a member of the board of directors of the Royal Institution for the Advancement of Learning. In 1825 he received a commission to hear and judge criminal cases. Two years later he replaced his brother-in-law, Olivier PERRAULT, as judge of the Court of King's Bench for the district of Quebec. He held this office until he was appointed to the Legislative Council in May 1828.

Even before his father's death in 1809 Taschereau had prepared to take advantage of the division of the paternal seigneurial domain by beginning to build a huge manor-house, and he had encouraged the establishment of light industry in Sainte-Marie-de-la-Nouvelle-Beauce. In 1808, in partnership with his brother THOMAS-PIERRE-JOSEPH he had a distillery built. When his father died he inherited a part of the estate. He set up a potash factory in 1813, and a tannery and sawmill the following year. In 1820 Taschereau began work on a grist-mill with two sets of grinding machinery. With a brickyard already in place, Sainte-Marie-de-la-Nouvelle-Beauce had become a real industrial centre. Since he was detained at Quebec by his numerous duties, Taschereau from 1814 entrusted the management of his properties to Alexander Miller.

Taschereau caught cholera while attending the burial of a friend who had succumbed in the epidemic at Quebec. He died on 14 June 1832 and was buried there the same day. On 19 May 1806 he had married Marie Panet, daughter of Jean-Antoine Panet*, at Quebec. They had had seven children, six of whom reached adulthood: Marie-Louise and Élisabeth-Suzanne, who married respectively Randolph Isham Routh* and Elzéar-Henri Juchereau* Duchesnay; Jean-Thomas*; Claire-Caroline; Elzéar-Alexandre*; and Agnès. Mme Taschereau lived at Sainte-Marie-de-la-Nouvelle-Beauce until her death on 14 Sept. 1866.

HONORIUS PROVOST

Jean-Thomas Taschereau is the author of *Procédés d'un comité spécial, nommé mercredi, le 15e janvier, 1823, sur le bill pour mieux régler les pêches dans le district inférieur de Gaspé, avec une instruction de considérer, s'il n'est pas expédient d'étendre les dispositions du dit bill aux comtés de Cornwallis et Northumberland* (Québec, 1823).

ANQ-Q, CE1-1, 19 mai 1806, 14 juin 1832; CN1-178, 19 août 1813; CN1-230, 24, 29 nov. 1810; 1er, 22 mars 1811; ZQ6-45, 26 nov. 1778. ASQ, Fichier des anciens. *Docs. relating to constitutional hist., 1791–1818* (Doughty and McArthur), 427. F.-J. Audet, "Les législateurs du Bas-Canada." *Officers of British forces in Canada* (Irving). "Papiers d'État – Bas-Canada," PAC *Rapport*, 1893: 12, 19, 39. Turcotte, *Le Conseil législatif*, 103–5. Provost, *Sainte-Marie; hist. civile; Sainte-Marie; hist. religieuse.* J.-E. Roy, *Hist. de Lauzon*, 3: 381–96; 5: 254–60. P.-G. Roy, *La*

famille Panet (Lévis, Qué., 1906); *La famille Taschereau* (Lévis, 1901).

TASCHEREAU, MARIE-ANNE-LOUISE, named de Saint-François-Xavier, Ursuline, teacher, and superior; b. 18 Oct. 1743 at Quebec, daughter of Thomas-Jacques Taschereau* and Marie-Claire de Fleury de La Gorgendière, and sister of Gabriel-Elzéar Taschereau*; d. there 16 March 1825.

Marie-Anne-Louise Taschereau descended on her father's side from a family that had been ennobled around 1492 and was settled in Tours, France. Her father, who had come to New France in 1726, was agent of the treasurers general of the Marine and a member of the Conseil Supérieur. His prestigious offices and his marriage with Marie-Claire de Fleury de La Gorgendière, who came from a wealthy family [see Joseph de Fleury* de La Gorgendière], linked him closely with the Canadian nobility.

By the time Marie-Anne-Louise was born, her father had been the owner of Sainte-Marie seigneury for seven years and was busy developing it. He was, however, to die at Quebec on 25 Sept. 1749, leaving a young widow with eight children, albeit well provided for. Marie-Anne-Louise was immediately sent to the Ursuline school. A child with the best of dispositions and a quick, bright mind, she was the joy of her family and her instructors. At ten she entered the boarding-school, where her excellent qualities blossomed, but at that time she showed no inclination for the cloister. On the contrary, her lively imagination made her look forward to the pleasures of restored freedom when she left school.

Quebec was returning to its usual tempo after the disruptions of the conquest. The brilliant and animated social round, with innumerable receptions and balls, was well suited to make wealthy young people completely happy. Although she was deeply pious, the attraction of the world and its pleasures held Marie-Anne-Louise until she was 20. During Lent in 1764 Father Marin-Louis Le Franc, a French Jesuit who had come back from Michilimackinac (Mackinaw City, Mich.), preached the great novena to St Francis Xavier from 4 to 12 March, probably in the Ursuline chapel, which was still being used as the parish church. An eloquent preacher, he urged the faithful to choose between the good life and the better one. It was at this time that Marie-Anne-Louise felt strongly drawn to serve God and her fellows. Struck by the futility of the hours given to worldly pleasures, she went to seek the preacher's counsel, and finally decided to devote herself to discipleship. Since it was not in her nature to let matters drag, within a few weeks of taking her decision and informing her family, she bravely entered the Ursuline convent on 13 May 1764 as a postulant. In August she took the religious habit as Sister Marie-

Taschereau

Anne-Louise de Saint-François-Xavier, adopting the name of a saint whose zeal and devotion she longed to imitate. She was one of the first novices since the conquest and she took her religious vows on 12 Aug. 1766 in the presence of Bishop Jean-Olivier Briand*.

The new sister applied herself to overcoming her high-spirited nature and impetuous character through the efficacious practice of self-denial. Faithful in everything, she soon became known as "a living rule." She was inclined above all to fill herself with the spirit of the older nuns, admiring their gracious austerity, their edifying simplicity of manner, their devotion to prayer and work.

The boarding-school had been re-established in 1761–62, and Marie-Anne-Louise de Saint-François-Xavier devoted herself to teaching. She soon became mistress in charge of studies, an office she held for six years, to the great satisfaction of all. At the same time she served as vestry nun. Her particular talent for business affairs was recognized and the authorities took her out of teaching, appointing her bursar in 1787. Frightened at the magnitude of the temporal responsibilities and at the requirements for good bookkeeping as well as for sound administration, she unburdened herself to her brother, Gabriel-Elzéar, who reassured her. Although as seigneur he lived at Sainte-Marie, personal matters and the tasks entrusted to him frequently brought him to Quebec. In the winter of 1788 he set about reorganizing the Ursulines' affairs. During the time that his sister held successive appointments as either bursar or superior, he kept an eye on the community's property.

Elected superior of the community in 1793, Marie-Anne-Louise de Saint-François-Xavier held this office until 1799. Six years later she was chosen for another term, which was renewed in 1808 for three years. She held the office again from 1815 till 1818. Nevertheless it was not all smooth sailing. In 1807 there was a lawsuit against George Waters Allsopp* over crossing rights in the barony of Portneuf, which the Ursulines owned, and the case was lost. The question of the amount of the nuns' dowries had to be discussed, as well as the deposit of donations received. Then again, the superior and her council had to deal with the repairs and extensions needed for the classrooms. In 1807 Marie-Anne-Louise de Saint-François-Xavier had the church, house, and vestments insured against fire, in order to have a little money to rebuild if necessary.

With the death in 1809 of the seigneur Taschereau, the Ursulines lost a great benefactor who, in their view, had truly put their temporal affairs in order. Subsequently his son-in-law, judge Olivier PERRAULT, took a deep interest in the management of the community's assets, and he too rendered great services. Another good friend of the Ursulines, Philippe-Jean-Louis DESJARDINS, had left Lower Canada in 1802. For more than 30 years this priest's correspondence strengthened the bonds between the nuns and their relatives in France. The pious Desjardins got in touch with Marie-Anne-Louise de Saint-François-Xavier's brother, Charles-Antoine Taschereau, who had been taken prisoner at Montreal in 1760 and sent to France and who maintained a close correspondence with his sister. Charles-Antoine advised the Ursulines to bring their annuities back from France and to that end requested a power of attorney for Desjardins. As the years went by, there was an exchange of gifts ranging from reliquaries to handcrafted articles.

Open to consultation, disciplined, highly intelligent, Marie-Anne-Louise de Saint-François-Xavier adhered firmly to decisions once they had been taken. The administrative talent that she showed did not diminish her fervour or attentiveness to religious duties. In 1815 she was the third superior to celebrate her golden jubilee while in office. Over the course of her years as superior she presided with her council over the admission of 30 novices; only 3 of them did not persevere in the community. The desired replacements were thus assured. After 1818 she held the offices of zelatrice and assistant superior, continuing to serve the community with her experience and good advice. She passed away at 81 years of age on 16 March 1825 after catching a cold. Her death was deeply mourned by her family and her numerous friends.

SUZANNE PRINCE

ANQ-Q, CE1-1, 18 oct. 1743. Arch. du monastère des ursulines (Québec), Actes d'élections des supérieures; Actes des assemblées capitulaires, 1; Annales, II: 37–39; Cahiers des charges; Conclusions des assemblées des discrètes, 1; Terrier de la seigneurie de Portneuf; Terrier de la seigneurie de Sainte-Croix. Allaire, *Dictionnaire*, vol.1. Le Jeune, *Dictionnaire*, 2: 697–98. Tanguay, *Dictionnaire*, 7: 263. [Catherine Burke, dite de Saint-Thomas], *Les ursulines de Québec, depuis leur établissement jusqu'à nos jours* (4v., Québec, 1863–66), 4: 648–54. [Joséphine Holmes, named de Sainte-Croix], *Glimpses of the monastery, scenes from the history of the Ursulines of Quebec during two hundred years, 1639–1839* . . . (2nd ed., Quebec, 1897), 166–72. Provost, *Sainte-Marie; hist. civile*, 33–57. P.-G. Roy, *La famille Taschereau* (Lévis, Qué., 1901).

TASCHEREAU, THOMAS-PIERRE-JOSEPH, army and militia officer, businessman, seigneur, politician, judge, and office holder; b. 19 April 1775 at Quebec, son of Gabriel-Elzéar Taschereau* and Marie-Louise-Élizabeth Bazin; m. 29 Jan. 1805 Françoise Boucher de La Bruère de Montarville at Boucherville, Lower Canada; d. 8 Oct. 1826 at Quebec and was buried four days later in the church of Sainte-Marie-de-la-Nouvelle-Beauce (Sainte-Marie), Lower Canada.

Thomas-Pierre-Joseph Taschereau was admitted to the Petit Séminaire de Québec as a boarder in 1784.

Tattannoeuck

After spending eight years there, three of them in a preparatory form, he gave up his studies at the end of the fourth form (Versification) in 1792. His father eventually secured him a place in the Royal Canadian Volunteer Regiment. Taschereau was more successful in military life; by 1797 he was serving as a lieutenant at Niagara (Niagara-on-the-Lake), Upper Canada. The regiment was disbanded in 1802.

Taschereau rejoined his family at Sainte-Marie-de-la-Nouvelle-Beauce. He had a house built for himself near the church, and on 1 Dec. 1804 he formed a partnership with his brother JEAN-THOMAS to engage in retail trade and to build a distillery on the family's seigneurial domain. The partnership was dissolved on 6 Aug. 1808. The death of Taschereau's father on 18 Sept. 1809 initiated a long process to reach agreement on the division of his estate between the widow and seven surviving descendants from two marriages, three of whom were still minors. Gabriel-Elzéar, who had been ordained priest in 1796, renounced his share and his rights as the eldest in return for a life annuity. Thomas-Pierre-Joseph then became the titular seigneur of Sainte-Marie and the owner of the manorhouse. The movables and real estate, less the widow's and minors' rights, were apportioned amicably by drawing lots after being duly valued and divided by survey. Taschereau thenceforth gave his attention to his share of the estate. He made the house near the church over to Gabriel-Elzéar in 1813 and moved into a dwelling that he had recently built across from it, on the banks of the Rivière Chaudière.

By this juncture the War of 1812 had broken out and Taschereau had been recalled to military service. Lieutenant-colonel of the Sainte-Marie-de-la-Nouvelle-Beauce battalion of militia, he held that rank in the 4th Select Embodied Militia Battalion from 25 May 1812 and then in its 1st Battalion from 24 October. He went through the entire 1812–13 campaign with the last named battalion, and apparently used his own funds to pay several men who had not actually been called up but who had enlisted out of sheer patriotism. Not present at any pitched battle, the battalion did take part in a skirmish.

On 28 Jan. 1818 Taschereau became a member of the Legislative Council. Three years later he was appointed judge of the Commissioners Court of Sainte-Marie-de-la-Nouvelle-Beauce, a court authorized to hear small causes which was set up there that year. In 1823 he succeeded Jean-Baptiste-Philippe-Charles d'ESTIMAUVILLE as *grand voyer* (chief road commissioner) for the District of Quebec. Because of his duties he was frequently absent from Sainte-Marie. Consequently he bought a house on Rue Saint-François in Quebec and it was there that on Sunday 8 Oct. 1826 he died. A messenger was immediately dispatched on horseback and managed to reach Sainte-Marie before high mass was over to announce the news to the assembled people.

In his will Thomas-Pierre-Joseph Taschereau had bequeathed the usufruct of all his movables and real estate to his wife. His son Pierre-Elzéar inherited the seigneuries on condition that he pay his brothers and sisters annually half of the income from the real property. His widow returned to live at Sainte-Marie-de-la-Nouvelle-Beauce, where she died on 30 Sept. 1834. Five of his ten children, including Joseph-André*, survived him.

HONORIUS PROVOST

ANQ-Q, CE1-1, 19 avril 1775; CN1-230, 24, 29 nov. 1810; 1er, 22 mars 1811; ZQ6-45, 12 oct. 1826. *Quebec Gazette*, 29 April 1812, 14 Jan. 1813, 30 Nov. 1815, 13 Jan. 1819, 9 July 1821, 22 May 1823. F.-J. Audet, "Les législateurs du Bas-Canada." *Officers of British forces in Canada* (Irving). P.-G. Roy, *Fils de Québec*, 2: 177–79. Turcotte, *Le Conseil législatif*, 85–87. Provost, *Sainte-Marie; hist. civile*; *Sainte-Marie; hist. religieuse*. P.-G. Roy, *La famille Taschereau* (Lévis, Qué., 1901).

TATTANNOEUCK (meaning "it is full," also known as **Augustus**), Inuk interpreter; d. in late February or early March 1834 near Fort Resolution (N.W.T.).

Tattannoeuck was born and raised on the west coast of Hudson Bay, some 200 miles north of Fort Churchill (Churchill, Man.). He had at least one brother, to whom he was very attached. In the early 19th century the Hudson's Bay Company hired young natives to winter at its posts, where they could be trained as interpreters, and Tattannoeuck was thus employed at Fort Churchill from 1812 to 1814 and in 1815–16. In the summer of 1816 he returned to his people. He was married by 1818, and he would have at least three sons.

In 1820 Tattannoeuck and another Inuk, Hoeootoerock (also known as Junius), were engaged as interpreters for Sir John Franklin*'s first expedition to the Arctic. They arrived at Fort Enterprise (N.W.T.) in January 1821. Franklin's group departed for the Arctic coast on 14 June, and in the course of its explorations Tattannoeuck and Hoeootoerock demonstrated intrepidity and unflagging cheerfulness while providing an invaluable service. Franklin's was the first expedition to venture down the Coppermine River since Indian guides with Samuel Hearne* had massacred a band of Inuit at Bloody Falls 50 years earlier. Rightly worried that the Inuit would be nervous on seeing Europeans and Indians again, Franklin sent Tattannoeuck and Hoeootoerock ahead to reassure them. The interpreters made contact, but on the sudden appearance of others from the expedition, the Inuit fled. The next band encountered also took flight. Tattannoeuck was nevertheless able to obtain information on the inhabitants, the resources they exploited, and the Arctic coastline from an old man too frail to escape.

Tattannoeuck

The expedition explored along the coast and then turned back. The return to Fort Enterprise proved disastrous, however, more than half of the party dying, the majority from exposure or starvation [see Robert Hood]. Hoeootoerock disappeared on a hunting trip, and Tattannoeuck's search for his friend was in vain. Later, starving but still energetic, Tattannoeuck impatiently moved ahead of Franklin's struggling party and got lost. His eventual arrival at Fort Enterprise prompted an overjoyed Franklin to remark that "his having found his way through a . . . country he had never been in before, must be considered a remarkable proof of sagacity."

In 1822 Tattannoeuck returned to Fort Churchill, where he was employed by the HBC. In the summer of 1823 the missionary John West* used him as an interpreter, and he converted to Christianity. The following spring, after visiting his family, he was hired as an interpreter on Franklin's second expedition to the Arctic. Starting out on foot, he and a companion, Ooligbuck*, reached Franklin's party at Methy Portage (Portage La Loche, Sask.) on 25 June 1825. In August, as the expedition descended the Mackenzie River, it surprised an encampment of Indians, who immediately sprang to arms. Franklin recorded that a "brave youth," on perceiving Tattannoeuck's Inuit face, "threw up his hands for joy and desired every one of [his] party to embark at once . . . and a friendly intercourse followed." Tattannoeuck was "the centre of attraction," Franklin continued, "notwithstanding Mr Kendall [Edward Nicolas Kendall*] and myself were dressed in uniform, and were distributing presents. . . . We could not help admiring the demeanour of our excellent little companion under such unusual and extravagant marks of attention. He received every burst of applause . . . with modesty and affability, but would not allow them [the Indians] to interrupt him in the preparation of our breakfast, a task he always delighted to perform."

After wintering at Fort Franklin, the expedition continued down the Mackenzie in the summer of 1826, dividing into two groups at its mouth. Tattannoeuck accompanied Franklin's party, which on 7 July encountered several hundred Inuit. Circumstances led to the Inuits' pillaging Franklin's two boats, and they were driven off only by threatening gun muzzles, the butts having proved no deterrent. That night Tattannoeuck, alone, met with 40 Inuit and boldly warned them to change their behaviour or forgo trading in the future. "My tribe were in the same unhappy state in which you now are, before the white people came to Churchill," he told them, "but at present they are supplied with everything they need, and you see that I am well clothed." He concluded by announcing that "if a white man had fallen [during the pillaging] I would have been the first to have revenged his death." His efforts were unavailing; the Inuit

planned to massacre Franklin's party, including Tattannoeuck, the following day, but they did not get the chance.

The expedition's arrival at Norway House (Man.) in June 1827 signalled the end of Tattannoeuck's employment, and he wept at the separation. He spent much of the next three years at Fort Churchill, occasionally travelling north to visit his family. From 1830 to 1833 he and Ooligbuck worked for Nicol Finlayson* as interpreters and hunters at Fort Chimo (Que.). In the latter year Tattannoeuck learned that George Back*, a member of the two Franklin expeditions, was mounting one of his own to search for the explorer Captain John Ross*, presumed lost in the Arctic. Tattannoeuck hurried to Fort Churchill, where he bought a pound of gunpowder, two pounds of ball shot, and one-half pound of tobacco; with these meagre supplies he set out on foot, despite a lame leg, for Fort Resolution. He arrived several months later to discover that Back had moved on to Fort Reliance, 200 miles to the northeast. He pushed on but, losing his way, attempted to return and perished in bad weather on the Rivière à Jean (Jean River), only 20 miles from Fort Resolution.

Tattannoeuck was thought of with affection by the officers of Franklin's expeditions. Informed of his death, a grieving Back wrote: "Such was the miserable end of poor Augustus! – a faithful, disinterested, kind-hearted creature, who had won the regard not of myself only, but I may add of Sir John Franklin and Dr. Richardson [Sir John Richardson*] also, by qualities, which, wherever found, in the lowest as in the highest forms of social life, are the ornament and charm of humanity." Governor George Simpson* of the HBC described Tattannoeuck as "faithful attached intelligent." Finlayson's is the lone dissenting voice; he acknowledged that Tattannoeuck was a "good interpreter" but considered him a "bad hunter" and a "drunken sot." Tattannoeuck's attachment to the men he worked for was strong. During the return trip of Franklin's second expedition he had detoured to visit Richardson (Franklin's second officer and a member of the first expedition), then at Cumberland House (Sask.). On leaving Franklin's men at Norway House he had assured them that they could count on him should he ever be needed, and in fact he sacrificed his life in a courageous effort to fulfil his promise.

In recognition of Tattannoeuck's services to Franklin, a species of butterfly first collected at Cumberland House in 1827 was named – probably by Richardson – *Theta augustus* (now classified as *Incisalia augustus*), and a lake in the Northwest Territories was later named Augustus for him.

SUSAN ROWLEY

PAM, HBCA, B.42/a/138, 140–42, 144–45, 149, 151, 155–57; B.42/e/1/4, B.42/e/6/2. George Back, *Narrative of* the Arctic land expedition to the mouth of the Great Fish River, and along the shores of the Arctic Ocean in the years 1833, 1834, and 1835 (London, 1836), 241–43, 253. John Franklin, Narrative of a journey to the shores of the polar sea in the years 1819, 20, 21 and 22 . . . (London, 1823); Narrative of a second expedition to the shores of the polar sea, in the years 1825, 1826, and 1827 (London, 1828). HBRS, 24 (Davies and Johnson). Robert Hood, To the Arctic by canoe, 1819–1821: the journal and paintings of Robert Hood, midshipman with Franklin, ed. C. S. Houston (Montreal and London, 1974). John Richardson, Arctic ordeal: the journal of John Richardson, surgeon-naturalist with Franklin, 1820–1822, ed. C. S. Houston (Kingston, Ont., and Montreal, 1984). John West, The substance of a journal during a residence at the Red River colony, British North America; and frequent excursions among the North West American Indians, in the years 1820, 1821, 1822, 1823 (London, 1824; repr. New York, 1966). M. S. Flint, Operation Canon; a short account of the life and witness of the Reverend John Hudspith Turner . . . (London, 1949), 17. David Meyer, "Eskimos of west Hudson Bay, 1619–1820," Napao (Saskatoon), 6 (1976), nos. 1–2: 41–58.

TAYLOR, JAMES, businessman, farmer, and politician; b. February 1761 in Truro, N.S., son of Captain Matthew Taylor, a Londonderry Irishman who had emigrated to New Hampshire and then to Nova Scotia, and Elizabeth Archibald; m. Margaret Bartlett, daughter of Richard Bartlett, and they had at least four sons and two daughters; d. 27 Jan. 1834 in Maugerville, N.B.

James Taylor went to the Saint John valley some time in the 1780s to join the Bartletts, who, having arrived from Truro around 1779, had settled in Burton, Sunbury County. He set himself up as a lumber merchant in the parish of Maugerville, a few miles below Fredericton. In 1811, in addition to lumbering operations, he was farming 105 acres of meadow- and plough-land with 4 horses, 4 oxen, 28 cows, and 40 sheep; two of his sons, James and Richard, were farming independently. Taylor's assessed valuation was more than twice that of any other person in the parish and he was rivalled in worth by only four or five other landowners in the county. He also accumulated a large number of mortgages on properties of his neighbours. His sons became known in the countryside for their rough, intimidating ways; each of them appeared before the magistrates one or more times on charges of assault.

Local historians have confused James Taylor with a Fredericton resident by the same name, the father of William TAYLOR. Often it is impossible to determine which one is referred to in contemporary documents. Each was described as a merchant, each was engaged in lumbering and shipping, each was involved in many property transactions, and each had a son named James. They lived on the banks of the Saint John River less than ten miles apart. Both died in 1834. The picture is further confused by the presence of a third

James Taylor (1755–1841) who lived only two or three miles away at Taylortown, in the neighbouring parish of Sheffield; Sheffield James was a supporter of the Church of England in Maugerville, while Maugerville James was associated with the Congregational Church in Sheffield. Fredericton James was a Presbyterian, but in the absence of a Church of Scotland in Fredericton he was a pew holder for several years in the Anglican church there and in 1816 purchased a pew in the Sheffield Congregational Church.

Although the Sheffield church in 1816 was no longer associated with radical politics, in earlier years it had been a rallying point for dissenters in their opposition to Anglican domination of the institutions of government. Dissenters provided most of the votes to send the radical James Glenie* to the House of Assembly from 1789 until he left the province in the winter of 1804–5. Hostility between supporters and opponents of the government reached a climax following the election of 1802. A series of court cases ensued between members of the contending parties, ranging from petty lawsuits, through charges of intimidation, to allegations of criminal behaviour. Party rancour continued for several years and in 1805 two yokes of Taylor's oxen were seized by the county authorities, who threatened to auction them off to pay a tax bill amounting to a few shillings. Far more serious, though its origins may not have been political, was a case brought by Abijah Palmer about the same time accusing two of Taylor's daughters of the murder of an illegitimate child. They were acquitted and in 1806 Taylor successfully sued Palmer for damages. During the trial one of the daughters stated that she considered Palmer "the greatest enemy of her father and family."

In the general election of 1809 Taylor replaced Glenie as the candidate of the dissenters and was returned along with Samuel Denny STREET. He was defeated in the next election, in 1816, by Elijah MILES and by a popular lay preacher, William Wilmot, the spokesman for the Baptists, who were emerging as a prominent group in the community. The solidarity forged by the dissenters in the 1790s no longer existed. When Taylor ran once again in 1819, there were three dissenting candidates. He was elected and took his seat, but one of his rivals, Amos Perley, protested; after a 39-day inquiry in the assembly Taylor was unseated in March 1820 by a vote of 16 to 4, his only support coming from one Fredericton and three Saint John merchants. Defeated when he again stood for election in 1820, he retired from public life. Soon afterwards he became a resident of Saint John, where he probably had been spending part of each year.

Information on Taylor's business activities is both sparse and difficult to interpret. He was commonly referred to as "Captain," but it is not known whether

Taylor

this title derived from a militia appointment or was connected with the sea. John Hazen, a neighbour who lived across the river and often dined at "Taylor's," mentions in his diary his attendance at a number of "launchings" in the vicinity, usually of brigs or smaller vessels, but the entries of 25 and 26 July 1811 record the launching of a "ship" at "Captain Taylor's." Later, in 1825, Benjamin Taylor, who was to sign the inventory of James's estate and with whom he had business dealings, had a role in the building of the schooner *Sheffield*. In 1816 James Taylor's wharf was the stopping place at Maugerville for the *General Smyth*, the first steamboat on the Saint John River. James's business affairs may possibly have taken him to England: a draft application of the Sheffield congregation to the London Missionary Society, dated 24 Oct. 1814, states in a postscript, "Mr. Taylor who we expect to be the bearer of this will provide a passage for a missionary without any expense to the society"; however, the reference is more likely to Fredericton James, who chartered a vessel to bring immigrants to the province in 1816.

In 1812, with the backing of Hugh JOHNSTON, Taylor purchased a sawmill and a thousand acres of land on Swan Creek. The transfer to the New Brunswick Council in 1816 of responsibility for regulating the cutting of timber on crown lands brought an end to the freedom that he and his fellow lumbermen had enjoyed during Sir John Wentworth*'s lax administration as surveyor of the king's woods. In 1820, with his political influence also at an end, Taylor was denied a renewal of a lease on a tract of land along "Schoodewopscook" (Kellys) Creek in York County, despite his claim to have a house and barn there, as well as the mill irons from a saw- and grist-mill which had been destroyed by fire in 1818 and which only the depressed state of the market had prevented him from rebuilding.

At the height of his fortune, around 1816, Taylor had an estate of more than 2,000 acres with an extensive frontage of intervale land; he also owned timber land and held additional tracts on lease. By 1824 title to his main farm had passed to his son Gain Bartlett Taylor. James lost almost everything else, including a house in Saint John, around 1830. His mill at Swan Creek and some other properties went to Johnston. At his death in 1834, his estate was valued at less than £300, and consisted mainly of household effects and farm animals, as well as "2 pews in the Presbeterian meting in Sheffield." When his widow died the following year, she left only a gig and harness, two "collers," two "Brichens," and one "neck yoak."

Taylor's seven years in the assembly came during a quiescent period in provincial politics between the conflicts that had characterized the administration of Lieutenant Governor Thomas Carleton* and those of

Lieutenant Governor George Stracey SMYTH's régime. His attendance in 1820 was too brief to be significant, but clearly marked him as identified with the Saint John merchant group. While perhaps somewhat more rough-hewn than most, he appears to have been typical of the merchant-farmer-lumberman politicians of the early 19th century.

D. M. YOUNG

N.B. Museum, G. J. Dibblee papers, James Taylor to G. S. Smyth, 9 Dec. 1820; Hubbard family papers, F14, no.1; Jarvis family papers, box 18, no.2. PANB, MC 1156, VIII (copy at UNBL); RG 4, RS24, S16, S28; RG 5, RS35, C5, 1806; RG 7, RS72, 1835, Margaret Taylor; A, 1834, James Taylor; RG 10, RS108, 1783–1820; RG 18, RS157, J2/1. UNBL, MG H9, including John Hazen diary, 1800–15 (typescript). "Documents of the Congregational Church at Maugerville," N.B. Hist. Soc., *Coll.*, 1 (1894–97), no.1: 134, 148, 151. N.B., House of Assembly, *Journal*, 1803–20. "Sunbury County documents," N.B. Hist. Soc., *Coll.*, 1, no.1: 106. *Royal Gazette* (Fredericton), 1809–34. *The New Brunswick militia: commissioned officers' list, 1787–1867*, comp. D. R. Facey-Crowther ([Fredericton], 1984). Beckwith Maxwell, *Hist. of central N.B.* Esther Clark Wright, *Planters and pioneers* (rev. ed., Hantsport, N.S., 1982). MacNutt, *New Brunswick*. W. D. Moore, "Sunbury County, 1760–1830" (MA thesis, Univ. of N.B., Fredericton, 1977). D. F. Taylor, *The early steamboats of the St. John River* (Saint John, 1980).

TAYLOR, WILLIAM, businessman, office holder, and politician; b. *c.* 1789 in Fredericton, eldest son of James Taylor "the Elder" and Jane ——; m. first 27 Nov. 1816, in Fredericton, Ann Cameron, daughter of Stephen Cameron, a merchant; m. secondly 25 Aug. 1819, in Saint John, Sally Hatfield, daughter of merchant David Hatfield; d. 27 March 1834 in Fredericton, survived by his second wife and four children.

William Taylor's father, James (1756–1834), born in Port Glasgow, Scotland, was described as a man of undeviating integrity. He moved to New York early in life and served in the British forces during the American revolution. He was one of the first loyalist settlers at St Anne's Point (Fredericton) in 1783, building the third house in the town. An enterprising merchant, he erected the first public market there in 1814. Two years later he chartered a Saint John–built ship, the *Favorite*, to bring Scots settlers to New Brunswick on a government contract; his exceptionally well-organized arrangements for them suggest that he had excellent contacts in Scotland. Taylor Sr rented quarters in his market-house to the Court of General Sessions, of which he was a member, and in 1817 the magistrates purchased the building, which served until the mid 1850s both as a market and as the York County court-house. Taylor was named a director and first treasurer of the Fredericton Savings Bank in

Taylor

1824, was active in the Fredericton Emigrant Society, became a charter member and vice-president of the St Andrew's Society in 1825, and donated the site for building a church, St Paul's, when a Church of Scotland congregation was organized in 1828. His designation, "the Elder," to distinguish him from other James Taylors in the neighbourhood [*see* James TAYLOR], marked his status in the family rather than in the church.

William Taylor was educated at the Fredericton Academy and entered the family business while still very young. In 1816 he advertised as the proprietor of the Jerusalem Coffee-House, but he sold it two years later with the intention of leaving Fredericton. In 1821, as the coroner responsible for investigating the death of George Ludlow WETMORE, a young lawyer who had been killed in a duel with George Frederick Street*, Taylor issued a hue and cry against Street and the two seconds involved.

Taylor entered into a formal partnership with his father and his younger brothers, James* and John F., in 1821, under the name of James Taylor Senior and Company. Its main business was the supplying of provisions to lumbermen and the forwarding of timber and lumber to Saint John, but it also became extensively involved in property transactions and had mills on the Tobique River. In July 1826 the company, along with the firm of Cross and Murray of Saint John, signed a contract for the erection of a stone building to house the College of New Brunswick in Fredericton. The estimated cost of the structure, which was to be built on a site acquired from George BEST according to designs by John Elliott Woolford*, was £10,300. In the following summers Scottish stonemasons were brought to Fredericton to finish the work. The building has been in continuous use by the college, now the University of New Brunswick, since its completion in 1829.

In 1822 Taylor was a member of a five-man committee authorized to raise money, from among the citizens most likely to benefit, for the creation of a reservoir for the fighting of fires; a well was dug and a tank-house erected over it to prevent the water freezing, a civic building that was a forerunner of the city hall established when Fredericton was incorporated in 1848. Later Taylor was the auctioneer in most of the important public auctions in York County, a member (along with Alexander Rankin* and others) of the central committee to relieve victims of the Miramichi fire of 1825, and, beginning in January 1829, treasurer of the central board of the New-Brunswick Agricultural and Emigrant Society, adding the duties of secretary in February 1830. Devoutly religious, Taylor became a member of the Sheffield Congregational Church in 1825, and was a member of the committee to build St Paul's in Fredericton and one of the trustees when it was incorporated in 1832.

Taylor was elected to the House of Assembly in a by-election in 1822, following the death of Stair AGNEW. His three opponents had retired when the sheriff refused to move the poll to communities outside Fredericton, thus effectively denying the vote to upriver people, some of whom lived more than 150 miles from the capital. He was re-elected in the general elections of 1827 and 1830. Scotsmen usually occupied at least two of the four seats for York County and in 1833 he was joined in the assembly by his brother James. When William died after a lingering illness a year later, however, his place in the house was taken by a Methodist of American ancestry, Lemuel Allan Wilmot*.

Both Fredericton newspapers produced unusually long, laudatory obituaries of Taylor. "His manners were conciliatory," said one, "his benevolence was extensive; his charity free from ostentation, and his piety at once fervent and unobtrusive." Taylor's father died nine months later. His brother James, who had married a sister of William's wife Sally (another of her sisters married Charles Fisher*), carried on with a varied career in business, politics, and public service. The youngest brother, John F., was a much quieter person. A bachelor, he maintained the family home for William's widow and children, and ran the family store for many years. It was one of his close friends who provided the epitaph on the family tombstone: "This monument is erected by a Scotsman who from his first acquaintance with the family in 1822 never ceased to admire and appreciate their probity of character, their friendliness and general goodness of heart."

D. M. YOUNG

N.B. Museum, G. J. Dibblee papers, packets 125, 252, 270; F85, no.19; W. F. Ganong coll., box 8, packet 5. PAC, MG 24, L6, 1, 3. PANB, RG 2, RS6, B, 24 Nov. 1815; RG 4, RS24, 1817, "Number, names and descriptions of settlers brought into the province by Mr. James Taylor"; RG 7, RS75, 1834–35, James Taylor "the Elder." UNBL, UA, "Minute-book of the governor and trustees of the College of New Brunswick," 17 July 1826. Wilmot United Church (Fredericton), Reg. of baptisms, marriages, and burials, 29 July 1797 (mfm. at PANB). "Documents of the Congregational Church at Maugerville," N.B. Hist. Soc., *Coll.*, 1 (1894–97), no.1: 148, 151. John Mann, *Travels in North America* ... (Glasgow, 1824; repr. Fredericton, 1978). N.B., House of Assembly, *Journal*, 1822–33. *City Gazette* (Saint John, N.B.), 3 April 1834. *New-Brunswick Courier*, 5 April 1834. *Royal Gazette* (Fredericton), 1814–34. Hill, *Old Burying Ground.* W. T. Baird, *Seventy years of New Brunswick life* ... (Saint John, 1890; repr. Fredericton, 1978). Beckwith Maxwell, *Hist. of central N.B.* Lawrence, *Judges of N.B.* (Stockton and Raymond). *Official centennial book: the story of Fredericton; Fredericton's one hundred years*, ed. Frank Baird ([Fredericton, 1948]). W. A. Squires, *History of Fredericton: the last 200 years*, ed. J. K. Chapman (Fredericton, 1980).

Tehowagherengaraghkwen

TEHOWAGHERENGARAGHKWEN (Tehon-wawenkaragwen, **Thowaghwenkarakwen**; he wrote both Tehowagherengaraghkwen and **Thomas Davis**), Mohawk war chief; b. *c.* 1755, probably in what is now New York State; m. and had at least one son; fl. 1776–1834.

Thomas Davis, a member of the wolf clan and cousin of Joseph Brant [Thayendanegea*], fought as an ally of the British throughout the American revolution and rose to the rank of war chief. After their defeat he accompanied Brant to the lands granted the Six Nations on the Grand River (Ont.), where he lived for the next half-century. During the War of 1812 he again served the crown. Having fought alongside the British and lived for years on the Grand River near white settlers, he knew how to speak English.

Physically, Davis was an impressive-looking man. The Reverend Alvin Torry remembered him as "tall, well-formed, and as straight as one of his own forest pines." He was also a fine orator, a person with a natural dignity and presence and one who "prided himself on his stoical indifference in all minor matters, which moved the mass around him." As an older man he was preoccupied with one subject alone, religion.

In the early 1820s religious questions tormented Thomas Davis until he had no peace. He had been baptized an Anglican, but there was no resident Anglican missionary at the Grand River in these years. The Reverend Ralph Leeming* of Ancaster visited, and catechists such as Henry Aaron Hill [KENWEN-DESHON] conducted church services in his absence. Davis felt alcohol was ruining his people. About 1820 he gave up drinking and began holding prayer-meetings at his farmhouse on the Grand River about five miles north of the Mohawk village (present-day Brantford). Daily he blew a horn calling his Mohawk neighbours, a number like him being nominal Anglicans, to prayer. Then he read to them portions of the Bible and the Church of England prayers in Mohawk. One day a white settler passed by the farmhouse and heard the horn. After learning why it was blown, the settler, who was a Methodist, asked if the Indians wanted a Methodist preacher to call. As they did indeed, Edmund Stoney, a local Methodist preacher, began his visits. Alvin Torry, an ordained Methodist Episcopal minister, also preached there regularly, beginning in the late spring of 1823.

At Davis's invitation, a small, but growing, Methodist Indian community settled on and around his farm, which became known as Davisville or Davis's Hamlet. Through Peter Jones*, a Mississauga Ojibwa convert, many Mississaugas joined the faith as well as Mohawks. By the fall of 1824 the one room in Davis's home used for meetings proved insufficient for the approximately 30 native Methodists. At this point the pious chief gave over his entire house for religious meetings and a Methodist day-school, and retired to a log cabin in the woods until a new mission house was completed in the spring.

After the Mississauga converts left for their new mission station on the Credit River early in 1826, the Indian Methodist movement on the Grand River became completely Iroquois. Within ten years the number of adherents had swelled to some 150 out of a total population of less than 2,000 on the reserve. A decade after Torry first preached at his home Davis remained an enthusiastic church member. When the Reverend William Case* met him in March 1834 he found the aged chief in excellent health, "reading in the Gospel of Matthew without glasses" and still "much in the habit of reading and expounding the Scriptures to his people."

Davis's zeal for Methodism stemmed from several sources. As a nominal Anglican he apparently genuinely believed in the Christian message. To him the reformed Longhouse religion expounded by the Seneca prophet Skanyadariyoh (Handsome Lake) had little appeal. Secondly, as he clearly stated at a Methodist camp meeting in 1825, he had material expectations of the faith. If the Indians remained true Christians, the chief believed that "when their moccasins were worn out, God would send them more; that if their corn was poor, He would provide; and that, after toil and hunting were over, He would take them to heaven." Thirdly, the temperance aspect of Methodism appealed to him. He knew that Methodists must renounce alcohol, which he regarded as the greatest scourge of reservation life.

Thomas Davis, as an older man, had sought the regeneration of his society. To a certain extent he succeeded among his nominally Christianized neighbours. John Brant [TEKARIHOGEN], an Anglican, recognized as much when he wrote on 27 May 1826 of the "good effects" of Davis's efforts. Davis probably died in the late 1830s; a letter of November 1840 refers to him as "the late Chief."

DONALD B. SMITH

PAC, MG 19, F6, 1: 78; RG 10, D3, 104, file 1834. UCC, Central Arch. (Toronto), Credit Mission, record-book. Victoria Univ. Library (Toronto), Peter Jones coll., Eliza Jones Carey papers, diary, 25 Aug. 1834. J. [S.] Carroll, *My boy life, presented in a succession of true stories* (Toronto, 1882), 42–43. William Case, "River Credit, U.C., March 20, 1834," *Christian Advocate and Journal* (New York), 16 May 1834: 151; reprinted in *Christian Guardian*, 28 May 1834: 114. John Douse, "Earliest missionary letters of Rev. John Douse, written from the Salt Springs mission on the Grand River in 1834 and 1836," ed. A. J. Clark, *OH*, 28 (1932): 41–46. Methodist Episcopal Church, Canada Conference Missionary Soc., *Annual report* (n.p.), 1825. Alvin Torry, *Autobiography of Rev. Alvin Torry, first missionary to the Six Nations and the northwestern tribes of British North*

America, ed. William Hosmer (Auburn, N.Y., 1864), 77–78. *Valley of Six Nations* (Johnston). John West, *A journal of a mission to the Indians of the British provinces, of New Brunswick, and Nova Scotia, and the Mohawks, on the Ouse, or Grand River, Upper Canada* (London, 1827), 279–81. G. F. Playter, *The history of Methodism in Canada* . . . (Toronto, 1862).

TEKARIHOGEN (Decarrihoga, Dekarihokenh, Karrahogle, Tekarihogea, Tokarihogea, Tyhorihoga, Henry, Hendrick; in a modern Mohawk orthography, Tekarihó:ken), Mohawk chief; b. *c.* 1750 in the Mohawk valley, N.Y., a member of the turtle clan and probably the son or grandson of Sarah, who appears to have been the clan matron, and her husband, Karaghtadie*; m. Catharine, a Mohawk of the wolf clan; d. mid August 1830 at the Grand River, Upper Canada.

Through his mother, Henry belonged to the family in which the title Tekarihogen was hereditary, and the name was bestowed on him as a young man. In the council of the Six Nations Confederacy the chief who bore it served as the titular head of the Mohawks, the first in rank of that tribe's nine sachems. Since the Mohawks headed the roll listing the council's 49 or 50 chiefs, his name took precedence over all others. The position was thus one of great influence and dignity.

During the American revolution Henry Tekarihogen, as he was often known, fought in alliance with the British. His grandson even claimed that the Mohawks' decision to support them was the result of his grandfather's leadership. The fact that he participated in the war suggests that he became Tekarihogen after its conclusion, for customarily sachems could not go out on the warpath and still retain their titles as civil chiefs. After the American victory, the British made lands available for the loyal Iroquois in what was to become Upper Canada [*see* Thayendanegea* (Joseph Brant)]. On the large Six Nations reserve along the Grand River, Tekarihogen exercised considerable power, not only among the Mohawks but also among other members of the Confederacy who had settled there. In a letter of 28 Nov. 1808 Alexander McDonell* (Collachie), who was in the process of buying a portion of the Grand River lands on behalf of Lord Selkirk [Douglas*], remarked on his role. "Even during Brant's life time," he wrote, "Tyhorihoga was acknowledged the first Chief & Sachem, tho' the former from his education & knowledge of European manners, had the management of all their land concerns." In accounts of the Six Nations on the Grand River, historians, guided (or misguided) by the availability of the written word, have possibly exaggerated the power and influence of Joseph Brant, a mere war chief whose letters survive in relative abundance, and have ignored Tekarihogen who, although he could speak a little English, could not write it.

Much of Brant's influence on the reserve undoubtedly came from his close ties with Tekarihogen. About 1779 he had married Catharine [Ohtowaʔkéhson*], whom Tekarihogen called sister although she may have been just a close relative. Then, in 1798, Brant's friend Augustus Jones*, a white surveyor, married Tekarihogen's daughter Sarah. Together Tekarihogen and Brant, with Jones a trusted adviser, came to symbolize the "progressive" faction, as it would have been called in the later 19th century. Staunch Christians, and thus determined opponents of the Longhouse religion, they sought accommodation with the dominant society around them. They welcomed white farmers to their midst and leased or sold extensive portions of the large reserve to them. They justified this action by arguing that the monies obtained served as a trust fund with which Iroquois farmers could purchase seed and new equipment, and that the whites benefited the native community by introducing new farming techniques.

The "traditionalists," again to use the later terminology, fought Tekarihogen and Brant over the land question, particularly the large grants totalling nearly ten square miles that were made to Jones. On 1 July 1811 a Mohawk spokesman announced that Tekarihogen had been dismissed from office. "In old times," he said, "when any Chief did wrong we took their horns off, my nephew Tekarihoga has done very wrong. Our Tribe (the Turtle) met & from his conduct have considered him not a proper person to be at our Treaty we communicated this to our Nation, the Mohawk, and then to the six Nations who agreed with us, . . . we have taken his horns from his head and he is only to take care of the Church." Tekarihogen did not accept his dismissal, nor, apparently, did a substantial portion of his people. His name heads the list of 230 Six Nations warriors fighting for the British at Beaver Dams (Thorold) on 24 June 1813 and appears at the top of petitions prepared by the Six Nations chiefs on 22 Feb. 1815 and 6 Sept. 1823. His continuance in office underlines the fierce factionalism existing on the reserve between progressives and traditionalists.

After the War of 1812 Tekarihogen lost much of his sight, "not from old age," according to his granddaughter, but from "sickness settling in his eyes." At his death he was totally blind. In his later years he became greatly concerned with religion. John "Smoke" Johnson* recalled how Tekarihogen "used to read the Church service at the Indian chapel, and was a religious & good man." The right to appoint a successor after his death in 1830 (or shortly before, when complete blindness fell on him) belonged to Catharine Brant, who inherited it through her mother. With the consent of her maternal family she chose her son John [Tekarihogen].

George Henry Martin Johnson*, the son of John "Smoke" Johnson, once translated Tekarihogen as

Tekarihogen

"two statements together." This, Henry Tekarihogen – sachem and Christian – truly was. The descendants of his daughter Sarah and her husband Augustus Jones are today divided between those who remain on the Six Nations tribal roll and those who, several generations later, have chosen the other "statement," becoming members of the larger, non-Indian society.

DONALD B. SMITH

[The spelling of the name Tekarihogen is the one used by John Brant. Seth Newhouse, an Onondaga who spoke Mohawk fluently, wrote Dekarihokenh. Other versions abound, some of them more successful than others in representing the word. The opening paragraph of this entry gives a selection of the various forms. D.B.S.]
    PAC, RG 10, B3, 1974, file 5620/1. UCC, Central Arch. (Toronto), William Case, journal, 1806–9 (transcript at AO). Wis., State Hist. Soc. (Madison), Draper MSS, ser.F. *The Iroquois Book of Rites*, ed. H. [E.] Hale, intro. W. N. Fenton (Toronto, 1963). *Valley of Six Nations* (Johnston), 56, 67–68, 174, 176–77, 197, 203, 219, 281–82, 284, 296. *Handbook of North American Indians* (Sturtevant et al.), vol.15. Barbara Graymont, *The Iroquois in the American revolution* (Syracuse, N.Y., 1972). Isabel Thompson Kelsay, *Joseph Brant, 1743–1807: man of two worlds* (Syracuse, 1984).

TEKARIHOGEN (Dekarihokenh, Ahyonwaeghs, Ahyouwaeghs, John Brant), Mohawk chief and Indian Department official; b. 27 Sept. 1794 near present-day Brantford, Ont., a member of the turtle clan and youngest son of Joseph Brant [Thayendanegea*] and his wife Catharine [Ohtowaʔkéhson*]; d. there 27 Aug. 1832 and was buried the same day.

John Brant probably received some early education in the school for Indian children at the Mohawk village where he was born. Following his parents' move in 1802 to the vicinity of Burlington Bay (Hamilton Harbour), his education was completed at nearby Ancaster and then at Niagara (Niagara-on-the-Lake); one of his teachers was Richard COCKRELL, a number of whose pupils went on to prominence in Upper Canadian life. Brant must have learned well, for engineer John MACTAGGART remarked after making his acquaintance years later, "I have not met a more polite gentleman or a better scholar in all Canada."

As the War of 1812 approached, many Mohawks, influenced by Red Jacket [SHAKÓYE:WA:THAʔ] and others as well as by unhappy memories of the American revolution, hesitated to commit themselves to a fray. John Brant betrayed no such hesitation and with John NORTON and a party of like-minded Indians helped stop an invading American force at Queenston Heights on 13 Oct. 1812. In April 1813 he was made a lieutenant in the Indian Department and he took part in the defeat of the Americans at Beaver Dams on 24 June, a victory that British officer James FitzGibbon*

later credited entirely to the Indian contingent. Brant served in most of the subsequent skirmishes on the Niagara frontier and in the battles of Chippawa, Lundy's Lane, and Fort Erie. On 9 Jan. 1814, disgusted with those of his compatriots who refused to fight, he joined his uncle Henry TEKARIHOGEN, George Martin*, and others in signing a petition that begged the government to withhold the usual annual presents from such disloyal Indians.

Some time after his father's death in 1807, Brant's mother had returned to the Grand River, taking the younger children with her. At the war's end, Brant and his sister Elizabeth went back to the family house at Burlington Bay, where they lived in the English style. Their mother, who preferred Mohawk ways, remained at the Grand River.

Brant must still have been quite young when it became clear that he had the qualities that would fit him for the position of Tekarihogen, the primary chieftainship of the Six Nations Confederacy, which was hereditary in his mother's family. He could look forward to considerable influence, since to the prestige of that office he would add the knowledge of white ways that had been a major source of his father's power. As early as 1819 he was assisting Henry Tekarihogen, who was growing old and blind, in the Six Nations' dispute with white authorities over the nature and extent of their land grant on the Grand River. Governor Frederick Haldimand* had in 1784 bestowed lands "Six Miles deep from each Side of the River beginning at Lake Erie, & extending in that Proportion to the Head of the said River," and the Indians had been struggling for years to get the grant confirmed by formal deed in fee simple. They were especially anxious about the northern half of their property which had a flaw in its title, this part of the tract not having been bought from its original Mississauga Ojibwa owners before Governor Haldimand made his grant – an error easily explained by the lack of proper surveys and by the general ignorance of the country in 1784. The Six Nations had always expected and hoped that a legal purchase would eventually be made for them which would set this error straight. But when a purchase was finally made in 1819, Lieutenant Governor Sir Peregrine Maitland* informed the Indians in no uncertain terms that the land had been bought for white settlers, not for them.

In 1821 John Brant and Robert Johnson Kerr finally went to England to lobby on behalf of the Six Nations. The two delegates argued that the transfer of the valley from the Mississaugas to the Six Nations had actually been made by an agreement between those groups prior to Haldimand's proclamation and that the parties to this agreement had understood that the entire valley was being transferred. Brant and Kerr also remarked that it was absurd to maintain that titles were invalid because the king had not purchased the lands from the original proprietors. "The principle is undoubtedly just towards those proprietors," they observed, "but Europeans have derived their title to the greatest part of America from other sources." They proposed that their case be submitted to the law officers of the crown. The Colonial Office countered by suggesting that the Indians relinquish their claim to the disputed lands in return for a deed in a fee simple to the undisputed ones. Brant and Kerr offered to accept the deed and leave compensation for the disputed lands to arbitration, but the Colonial Office insisted on its own suggestion and by the end of April 1822 they had given in.

Once the delegates were back in Upper Canada, further difficulties arose. As in the time of Joseph Brant, the provincial government was opposed to any arrangement that would allow Indians to sell their own lands, and it was announced to the Six Nations at a council in February 1823 that if they were to receive their lands in fee simple, they would no longer be entitled to presents. Despite this threat, at a full council on the Grand River in September Brant managed to get the assent of a majority of chiefs to the agreement made in England, and seven chiefs were named as trustees for the lands. The government countered the following spring, when William CLAUS, the deputy superintendent general of Indian affairs in Upper Canada, told a council that in the opinion of the attorney general the Indians would, as a consequence of the grant in fee simple, become entirely subject to all the laws in force in Upper Canada. A number of chiefs who had supported Brant in September thereupon withdrew their approval and he was left in a minority. Through John Galt* he protested to the Colonial Office in the autumn of 1825, but the vigorous opposition from Upper Canada had won the day and formal control over the sale of Indian lands remained with the colony's government until 1841. In that year the problem of the alienation of the Grand River lands was finally settled, when the Indians surrendered them to the crown to be managed on their behalf.

Brant was involved in many other activities aimed at improving the lot of his people. In London he had been in contact with the New England Company, a non-sectarian missionary society, and on his return home he worked closely with that organization, welcoming missionaries of all Protestant faiths and encouraging the construction of schools. In 1829 he received a silver cup from the society in recognition of his work.

On 25 June 1828 Brant was officially appointed resident superintendent of the Six Nations of the Grand River, a position which involved close supervision of their affairs and which he held until his death. In practice, he looked after not only the Six Nations but also other Indian groups who had settled alongside

them. One of his first challenges was to fight the damming of the river by the Welland Canal Company. The welfare of Indians counted little with the government when weighed against canals, and despite forceful protests made as soon as he read of the scheme, he lost. "I am very anxious to receive His Excellency's commands as to the Nature of the Explanation to be made to the Six Nations," he rather pointedly remarked to Lieutenant Governor Sir John Colborne* in June 1829. In December he wrote, "I have the honor to report . . . that the dam thrown a cross the Grand River by the Welland Canal Company has overflowed the Indian Corn fields their Crops laid waste and their winters provision destroyed."

Brant also led the Six Nations in their dispute with John Claus, who on the death of his father, William, in 1826 had become trustee for funds belonging to the Indians. The Indians wanted to invalidate an enormous land grant obtained from them by the elder Claus shortly before his death; in retaliation, John Claus withheld the interest on the money of which he was trustee. In this controversy Brant succeeded to the extent that in 1830 Claus was dismissed.

Either with the death of Henry Tekarihogen in 1830 or perhaps shortly before, Brant officially assumed the ancient office and title. Moreover, he ran for the Upper Canadian House of Assembly in the riding of Haldimand in 1830. He took his seat in January 1831 but his election was challenged on the grounds that some of those who voted for him were leaseholders rather than the freeholders required by law, and in February his opponent John Warren was declared elected. Both men died in the cholera epidemic of 1832. In Brant's case it is not clear whether he succumbed to the disease itself or to the ministrations of the white doctors who were called in to treat him. He was not yet 38.

Many years later, a resident of the Burlington Bay area remembered John Brant at the time he had lived there. He had been a young man fond of dancing who had regularly attended neighbourhood parties and who had "so entirely given up the manner of the Indians that it would not be discovered that he was of the original inhabitants of the Country unless attention was called to it." Other evidence suggests that, although Brant had adopted an English gentleman's style of living, he was capable of Mohawk behaviour when dealing with other Mohawks. Yet in personal terms he paid a price for his accomplishments. He never married, and he is said to have commented rather wistfully on the subject to missionary Richard Phelps: "I might have married a fine English lady. I was thought something of there, even by the nobility. I was considered almost a king. But to . . . bring her here and let her see the degraded state of the people that I ruled, would have broken her heart." He was proud of his heritage, however, and went out of his way to defend his father's name, taking indignant exception to an article in John Strachan*'s *Christian Recorder* that portrayed him in an unfavourable manner. He apparently secured an apology from Strachan. When he was in England he undertook to demonstrate to poet Thomas Campbell, who had maligned the elder Brant as "the Monster" chiefly responsible for the "Wyoming massacre" of 1778, that his father was not even present. Campbell later apologized in print to the memory of Joseph Brant.

A portrait of John Brant, reproduced in William Leete Stone's biography of Joseph, reveals an amiable countenance but little of his Indian heritage. He was broad shouldered and about six feet three inches tall – an impressive height for the time. What struck people, however, was his bearing. Jurist Marshall Spring Bidwell* remembered his "dignity and composure," and Phelps was awed by "the dignity, the authority, the power there was in [his] look, gesture and emphasis."

ISABEL T. KELSAY

AO, MS 148, sect.I, Brant family. Hamilton Public Library, Special Coll. Dept. (Hamilton, Ont.), Arch. file, John Brant, copies of letters to the Indian Department, 1828–30, and proceedings of council meeting of Six Nations Indians. PAC, RG 1, L3, 43: B12/282; RG 5, A1: 50501–2; RG 8, I (C ser.), 268: 157. PRO, CO 42/369: 220–29; 42/370: 261; 42/374: 352–66; 42/376: 214–19. James Buchanan, *Sketches of the history, manners, and customs of the North American Indians, with a plan for their melioration* (2v., New York, 1824), 1: 32–37. Thomas Campbell, "Letter to the Mohawk Chief Ahyonwaeghs, commonly called John Brant, Esq., of the Grand River, Upper Canada," *New Monthly Magazine and Literary Journal* (London), [new ser.], 4 (1822, pt.I): 97–101. "Life of Capt. Brant," *Christian Recorder* (York [Toronto]), 1 (1819–20): 106–12, 145–51. John Mactaggart, *Three years in Canada: an account of the actual state of the country in 1826-7-8 . . .* (2v., London, 1829), 1: 45. B. B. Thatcher, *Indian biography . . .* (2v., New York, 1832; repr. Glorieta, N.Mex., 1973), 2: 314. U.C., House of Assembly, *Journal*, January–February 1831. *Valley of Six Nations* (Johnston). "Calendar of state papers," PAC *Report*, 1935: 248. *Death notices of Ont.* (Reid). J. [S.] Carroll, *Case and his cotemporaries . . .* (5v., Toronto, 1867–77). W. L. Stone, *Life of Joseph Brant – Thayendanegea . . .* (2v., New York, 1838; repr. New York, 1969, and St Clair Shores, Mich., 1970), 2: 500–19, 523–25, 527–34. Isabel Thompson Kelsay, *Joseph Brant, 1743–1807: man of two worlds* (Syracuse, N.Y., 1984), chaps.25–28; epilogue. G. F. G. Stanley, "The significance of the Six Nations participation in the War of 1812," *OH*, 55 (1963): 215–31.

TESSIER, FRANÇOIS-XAVIER, doctor, apothecary, militia officer, publisher, editor, translator, office holder, politician, and teacher; b. 15 Sept. 1799 at Quebec, son of Michel Tessier, a master saddler and merchant, and Josephte Huot Saint-Laurent; d. unmarried 24 Dec. 1835 at Quebec.

François-Xavier Tessier began studying medicine when he was about 16. In March 1820, after a four-year apprenticeship, he sought permission from the medical examiners for the district of Quebec to practise as a surgeon, and they considered that he had the required abilities. But a year and a half later, although they recognized he had made substantial progress, the same examiners recommended that for admission as a doctor he continue his studies at a university. Since there were no such establishments in Lower Canada, Tessier went to New York, where he spent nearly two years furthering his education.

On his return to the province Tessier qualified as a doctor. In April 1823 he became apothecary of the Emigrant Hospital at Quebec, a position that gave him responsibility for the institution and provided during the navigation season board, lodging, and a salary of £50. The young graduate proved a firm administrator. He even rebuked the esteemed physicians François BLANCHET and Joseph Parant* for not respecting hospital regulations. He dismissed the director and his wife, who were discovered drunk. Perhaps because of this severity, which some thought excessive, his appointment was not renewed the following season. He was then made assistant surgeon to Quebec's 1st Militia Battalion.

In January 1826 Tessier brought out at Quebec the first issue of the *Quebec Medical Journal/Journal de médecine de Québec*. An enterprising young man, he hoped to make his bimonthly periodical the strongest bond for the medical profession in Lower Canada. He also wanted to provide his colleagues with a means of "communicating with masters of the art" in both America and Europe. A further goal was to eradicate the popular prejudices "that constantly frustrate the Canadian doctor's zeal." But the journal ceased publication in October 1827 for lack of support.

The following year Tessier went back to New York, where he remained until the spring of 1830. There he contributed to a New York newspaper and published an English translation of Louis-Jacques Bégin's impressive *Thérapeutique*, to which he added numerous notes. During the same period he published a prospectus for a forthcoming "Journal des sciences naturelles de l'Amérique du Nord," which he described as a continuation of the *Quebec Medical Journal*. A periodical covering botany, natural history, chemistry, mineralogy, pharmacy, and of course medicine and surgery, it was to be published in New York and to be addressed to "the immense French population scattered all over America." Unlike the *Quebec Medical Journal*, which was bilingual, it would be entirely in French; "since that language is, among modern languages, the only one that is appropriate to all the sciences," he averred, "it is obvious that none of them, certainly [not] the English language, is suitable to serve as its interpreter." Tessier was quite certain his project would succeed and therefore was not afraid to announce that a 300-page issue would appear quarterly. His success did not, however, match his rashness, for the journal never saw the light of day. But the initiative was proof of his determination, especially after the failure of his earlier venture into medical journalism.

Tessier returned to Lower Canada, and on 7 July 1830 he was appointed health officer for the port of Quebec by the governor, on Louis-Joseph Papineau*'s recommendation, some said later. That summer he became administrator of a new hospital for "fever patients" which had been established at Pointe-Lévy (Lauzon and Lévis). He carried out the duties of the two offices under the extremely difficult conditions caused by the arrival of tens of thousands of immigrants suffering from hunger and contagious diseases. In October 1831, when a cholera epidemic was feared, Tessier returned to New York at the request of the House of Assembly to obtain information on the organization of a health and quarantine service in a big port.

Despite the measures taken, cholera broke out at Quebec in June 1832 and spread rapidly through the country. The dreadful scourge was soon beyond the resources of the board of health. There was a flood of recrimination. The board cast the blame on Tessier, who was alleged to have ignored the instructions given him. In October he was suspended and finally removed from his post as health officer. But the grounds that the board advanced for its action were dubious and, as two inquiries initiated by the assembly revealed, of a partisan nature. The board in fact found it difficult to conceal its motives. At the time, Tessier was seriously considering running for election to the assembly under the banner of the Patriote party. Several members of the board supported the opposing party and used the situation to settle political accounts. According to the painter Joseph Légaré*, the board had already closed the hospital at Pointe-Lévy "to persecute" Tessier.

In July 1832 elections had been called in Dorchester riding following the death of Louis LAGUEUX from cholera. Tessier had announced his candidacy but soon withdrew from the contest. In August, Thomas Lee's death left the Lower Town Quebec riding open, and Tessier entered the lists. He even published an address to the constituents in Le Canadien. As before, he withdrew. He later claimed that the hostility of the members of the board of health, who were "also my political adversaries," had put him in an awkward position and this was "one of the chief reasons that prompted me to retire from a contest in which I had every prospect of success." But his withdrawal may have been largely brought about by the attitude of several Patriote members of the assembly who held it against him that he had a highly paid government post.

Consequently his presence as a candidate would have split the Patriote vote. A year later things had changed. Tessier, who had lost his job because of his political friendships, was now considered a victim of the governor and his entourage. Therefore, when Saguenay riding fell vacant, Le Canadien supported his candidacy with alacrity, portraying him as an honest and enlightened Patriote. On 24 Oct. 1833 he was elected with a comfortable majority.

Tessier played an important role in the field of medicine. When a new medical act was passed in 1831 altering the method of appointment to the boards of medical examiners in Lower Canada, he was elected to the Quebec board, of which he became an active member. He shared with four leading doctors of the town the responsibility for drawing up the board's own regulations, was named its secretary after Charles-Norbert PERRAULT's death, also from cholera, and served on most of the committees it set up, including one that studied the havoc created by quack doctors and another that was responsible for inspecting apothecaries' shops. In July 1834 the municipal council of Quebec chose him, on the board's recommendation, as physician to the Marine and Emigrant Hospital. In addition Tessier had played a part in the founding of the Quebec Medical Society in 1826. He became the secretary, and then president, and presented several papers before it, including one on the relationship between pulmonary illnesses and premature puberty. The following year he helped found the Société pour l'Encouragement des Sciences et des Arts en Canada. He became the secretary general and one of its most ardent promoters.

Despite his many activities Tessier found time to teach medicine. During the cholera epidemic in 1832 he offered, with the aid of his students, to tend half the patients at the temporary cholera hospital. One of his major concerns was the founding of a society to encourage smallpox vaccination among the poor. Disappointed in his hopes, in November 1833 he organized a vaccination clinic in his home on Rue Saint-Joseph with the assistance of medical students.

It is difficult to define the theories and principles that guided Tessier in his practice. However, the catalogue of his library, the articles he published in the Quebec Medical Journal, and the notes appended to his translation of Bégin's work indicate who his mentors were and what he was concerned about. In his library the principal medical journals of England and the United States were side by side with the works of the famous French doctors of the period: Marie-François-Xavier Bichat, Jacques-Mathieu Delpech, and François Broussais, a trio who in Tessier's view had revitalized medical science, and Philippe Pinel, who had humanized the treatment of the mentally ill. Tessier deplored the conditions in which such patients lived in the Canadas. His journal adds the names of

Teyoninhokarawen

Guillaume Dupuytren and François Magendie to the list of illustrious Frenchmen. He considered the American Benjamin Rush, who greatly influenced contemporary medicine, one of the most knowledgeable doctors of his epoch. He never tired of urging his colleagues to forget "the theoretical approach" and to observe nature. He fought against the prejudices and "the old habits" that were deeply rooted among rural people particularly, constituting obstacles to the advance of medicine and fertile ground for quackery.

In the controversy among doctors in Europe and North America over whether cholera was contagious, Tessier sided with those who believed it was not. They held that it appeared suddenly as a result of "a particular condition of the atmosphere," as did measles and the plague. Tessier did admit the contagious nature of smallpox and syphilis. Like most of his colleagues, however, he theorized that fevers came from miasmas.

Tessier admired Jean-Jacques Rousseau and believed in the original goodness of man. He read Rabelais, Voltaire, and Diderot. Like many Patriote members of the assembly he apparently admired the neighbouring republic, inspired as it was "by the genius of liberty." With a few friends he had great confidence in the progress of humanity and distrusted intervention by the state in social concerns.

An energetic and ambitious man, François-Xavier Tessier would probably have achieved an enviable status if death had not cut short his brilliant career. He died at the age of 36 after a long illness. Papineau, who attended his funeral, regretted the loss of this "man of genius [and] incomparable zeal."

GILLES JANSON

François-Xavier Tessier translated a work by Louis-Jacques Bégin as *The French practice of medicine* . . . (New York, 1829). He is the author of *Précis d'un discours . . . le 4 janvier 1832 . . . contenant l'éloge historique de feu J. Labrie, écuïer, médecin et membre du Parlement provinciale, etc.* (Québec, 1832).

ANQ-M, P-26. ANQ-Q, CE1-1, 15 sept. 1799, 28 déc. 1835; P-68. Arch. de la ville de Québec, XI, A, 26 mars–24 sept. 1823; B, 12 mars–17 nov. 1832. ASQ, Fonds Viger–Verreau, carton 62, no.139; Univ., sér.U, U-18, 11 juill. 1831–6 oct. 1834. PAC, RG 4, B28, 49: 816–21. L.C., House of Assembly, *Journals*, 1831–33; *Statutes*, 1831–32, c.47. *La Bibliothèque canadienne* (Montréal), 6 (1827–28). *Le Canadien*, 26 oct., 2, 19 nov. 1831; 18, 30 mai, 4, 25 juill., 31 août, 7, 10, 12, 14, 17, 19 sept., 17 oct. 1832; 11, 15, 22, 27 févr., 26 avril, 24 mai, 17 juill., 20, 25 sept., 11, 18, 30 oct., 4, 8, 11 nov. 1833; 27 janv., 10, 14 mars, 18 avril 1834; 25 déc. 1835; 15 févr. 1836. *La Minerve*, 4 juin 1827; 23, 27 juill. 1829; 18, 22 oct. 1832. *L'Observateur* (Montréal), 25 déc. 1830, 2 juill. 1831. *Quebec Gazette*, 18 Jan., 28 June 1821; 15 April, 6 May 1824; 5 Jan. 1826. *Quebec Mercury*, 27, 29 Oct. 1831; 8, 18 Sept. 1832. F.-J. Audet, "Les législateurs du Bas-Canada."

Abbott, *Hist. of medicine*. M.-J. et G. Ahern, *Notes pour l'hist. de la médecine*. Antonio Drolet, "Un hôpital municipal à Québec en 1834," *Trois siècles de médecine québécoise* (Québec, 1970), 66–74. J. J. Heagerty, *Four centuries of medical history in Canada and a sketch of the medical history of Newfoundland* (2v., Toronto, 1928). C.-M. Boissonnault, "Histoire de la faculté de médecine de Laval," *Laval médical* (Québec), 17 (1952): 968–1008. Sylvio Leblond, "L'hôpital de la Marine de Québec," *Laval médical*, 16 (1951): 1082–97.

TEYONINHOKARAWEN. *See* NORTON, JOHN

THAIN, THOMAS, fur trader, militia officer, businessman, office holder, and politician; b. in Scotland; d. unmarried 26 Jan. 1832 in Aberdeen, Scotland.

Not much is known about Thomas Thain's origins; he is said to have been a nephew of John RICHARDSON and John Forsyth*, and thus a relative of the Phyns and Ellices. These family connections probably opened the doors to the fur trade for him. In 1803 he was a clerk with the New North West Company (sometimes called the XY Company), for which the firm of Forsyth, Richardson and Company, one of its copartners, acted as agent. On 5 Nov. 1804, when the North West Company and the New North West Company amalgamated, Thain was made the agent of the latter firm (then renamed Sir Alexander Mackenzie and Company) for a period of five years, and four days later he became a partner. In his capacity of agent, he received a share in the reorganized NWC as well as additional compensation of £200.

In each of the first five years following the amalgamation Thain, who was located in Montreal, went to the "depot" on the shores of Lake Superior. Indeed, he wrote up the minutes of the annual meetings there in 1808 and 1809. At this period the NWC was concerned with reducing expenses, and Thain was largely instrumental in instituting measures to that end. In 1808, as agent, he participated in a committee studying how to reduce certain fur-trading costs considered excessive, such as advances made to the Indians. He does not seem to have gone to Fort William (Thunder Bay, Ont.) in the period 1810–14.

When McTavish, McGillivrays and Company was reorganized on 1 Nov. 1814, Thain became a partner. He received 2 of the 19 shares and, "in consideration of the benefit expected to be derived by the Concern from the services and experience of the said Thomas Thain," he was accorded additional remuneration in proportion to profits made; he even continued to act as agent of Sir Alexander Mackenzie and Company. From 1818 Thain held a still more important position in McTavish, McGillivrays and Company: he replaced John McTavish in the accounting and bookkeeping departments. He was active in defending the NWC's interests. In September 1817 he had tried unsuccessfully to secure the arrest in Montreal of

Colin Robertson*, the agent of the Hudson's Bay Company who was already being prosecuted for having attacked the NWC's Fort Gibraltar (Winnipeg, Man.), and he played a somewhat shady role in the lawsuits resulting from the legal disputes between the NWC and the HBC.

The amalgamation of the two giants of the fur trade marked the beginning of the end for McTavish, McGillivrays and Company. The 1821 agreement made it the Montreal representative of the HBC and left it to run the Montreal department, which included the Ottawa River posts and, until the lease expired, the king's posts. This arrangement meant an obvious loss of authority for the firm, previously in supreme control of the NWC's operations. In 1823 Thain had to submit to the governor of the HBC the matter of concluding the sale to the government of company buildings at Sault Ste Marie (Ont.). In the period 1822–24 Thain and his firm were reprimanded several times by the London committee for the losses suffered at posts under their jurisdiction, their costly way of resolving the problem of competition, and their neglect of systematic reporting on trade at the posts.

In the autumn of 1821, when the brothers WILLIAM and Simon* McGillivray left for England, they had put Thain at the head of the firm. The agreement under which the firm operated expired in November 1822 and the three of them set up, though without a partnership contract, the firm of McGillivrays, Thain and Company, to serve as agents for the HBC and to liquidate McTavish, McGillivrays and Company. A partner of the latter firm, Henry McKENZIE, who disputed his partners' earlier decisions and who had vainly asked to examine the books, was persuaded to entrust management of the firm to Thain until November 1825, when he would have to give an accounting. During those years Thain settled some of the firm's debts with former partners and employees. The financial situation of the two companies kept deteriorating, to the point that in December 1825 Simon McGillivray had to suspend payments and declare them insolvent, and then in February 1826 hand over their assets and his own to trustees.

Thain seems to have been the person most responsible for this deterioration. If McGillivray is to be believed, Thain's numerous other activities harmed his main work. He had helped revitalize the Beaver Club, which he had joined in 1807. On 20 Feb. 1811 he was commissioned a lieutenant in Montreal's 1st Militia Battalion. One of the original shareholders of the Bank of Montreal, in 1819 or 1820 he was appointed a director, and from 1822 to 1825 he was vice-president. He held other offices at the same time: commissioner for building the Lachine Canal in 1819 and member of the House of Assembly for the riding of Montreal East from 1820 to 1824. He was also a shareholder in the Bank of Canada, and in March 1824 he transferred 100 shares to Charles Grant. He was likewise one of the promoters of the Theatre Royal in Montreal, founded in 1825.

On 5 Aug. 1825 Thain left Montreal for England "with a view," as he said, "of obtaining medical advice . . . , to visit my relatives in Scotland, and also to adjust accounts connected with the late firm of Sir Alex. Mackenzie & Co." He left his books and papers, along with those of the companies that he managed, in total disorder in his living quarters. He was never to return to Lower Canada; on arriving in England he suffered an attack of brain-fever and from the spring of 1826 till his death he was confined in an asylum in Scotland. John Richardson was appointed trustee of his real and personal estate on 5 Dec. 1826.

Thomas Thain is a controversial figure. One fur trader, John McLean*, considered that he was rather eccentric but that he had "a heart that glowed with the best feelings of humanity." Another, John Siveright*, also spoke highly of his kindness and generosity. Simon McGillivray, however, thought he had too much confidence in his own abilities, which led him "to undertake too much and to trust too much to the labour of his own hands." Henry McKenzie accused him, in effect, of embezzlement: according to McKenzie, the assets of McTavish, McGillivrays and Company had been used to liquidate McGillivrays, Thain and Company's debts, and Thain's personal debt to various companies amounted to some £96,000. Thain was caricatured as Hurlo-thrumbo, Lord Goddamnhim, in the *Scribbler*, a newspaper issued by Samuel Hull WILCOCKE, formerly a publicist for the NWC.

GRATIEN ALLAIRE

ANQ-M, CC1, 10 juin 1831, 17 avril 1832; CN1-16, 19 déc. 1822; CN1-29, 18, 29 avril, 6 nov. 1816; CN1-68, 27 juin 1815; CN1-187, 9 nov. 1816; 29 juin 1820; 3 déc. 1821; 26 févr., 18 mai, 10 juin 1822; 1er, 5 févr., 18 oct. 1823; 7 juin, 4 oct., 28, 31 déc. 1824; 29 juill., 4, 31 oct. 1825; 2 févr., 1er juin 1826; P1000-5-537. AUM, P 58, U, Inglis, Ellice & Co. to Thain, 15 April 1819; Thain to J. Mackenzie, 10 Aug. 1815; Thain to Alexander Mackenzie & Co., 17 April 1816; Thain to Inglis, Ellice & Co., 25 Oct. 1816; Thain to James Grant, 2 April 1821; Thain to Charles Grant, 4, 6 March 1824; Thain to John McDonald, 15 May 1829. McCord Museum, Beaver Club minute-book. PAC, MG 30, D1. *Les bourgeois de la Compagnie du Nord-Ouest* (Masson). *Docs. relating to NWC* (Wallace). [James] Hargrave, *The Hargrave correspondence, 1821–1843*, ed. G. P. de T. Glazebrook (Toronto, 1938). *HBRS*, 2 (Rich and Fleming); *HBRS*, 3 (Fleming). John McLean, *John McLean's notes of a twenty-five year's service in the Hudson's Bay territory*, ed. W. S. Wallace (Toronto, 1932). F.-J. Audet, *Les députés de Montréal*. "Calendar of the Dalhousie papers," PAC *Report*, 1938: 46. Desrosiers, "Inv. de la corr. de Mgr Lartigue," ANQ *Rapport*, 1941–42: 417. *The centenary of the Bank of Montreal, 1817–1917* (Montreal, 1917). G. C. Davidson,

Thomas

The North West Company (Berkeley, Calif., 1918; repr. New York, 1967). Denison, *Canada's first bank*, 1: 162, 171, 225. M. L. MacDonald, "The literary life of English and French Montreal from 1817 to 1830 as seen through the periodicals of the time" (MA thesis, Carleton Univ., Ottawa, 1976), 55. Rich, *Hist. of HBC* (1958–59), vol.2. W. S. Wallace, *The pedlars from Quebec and other papers on the Nor'Westers* (Toronto, 1954). M. [E.] Wilkins Campbell, *McGillivray, lord of the northwest* (Toronto, 1962); *NWC* (1957). C. F. Klinck, "The world of *The Scribbler*," *Journal of Canadian Fiction* (Montreal), 4 (1975), no.4: 123–48. "Question," *BRH*, 39 (1933): 48.

THOMAS. *See* TOMAH

THOMAS, JOHN, fur trader; b. *c.* 1751 apparently in London; m. first Margaret (d. 1813), an Indian or mixed-blood woman, and they had nine children; m. secondly Meenish; d. 9 June 1822 and was buried 12 June in Christ Church cemetery, Montreal.

Following the surrender of New France in 1760, the Hudson's Bay Company factories on Hudson and James bays found themselves subjected to increasing pressure inland by independent traders from Quebec, whom the HBC men scornfully called pedlars. In 1770 the HBC's London committee, convinced that the company must establish posts to meet the competition, ordered its officers to explore the interior with a view to setting up posts. As a result, Cumberland House (Sask.) was built in 1774 by men from York Factory (Man.), and that same year the Moose Factory (Ont.) council sent John Thomas, who had joined the service as a writer in 1769, with three Indians to survey a route to Lake Abitibi. Thomas thus became the first company officer to visit the pedlars at Fort Abitibi (near La Sarre, Que.) and his journal contains a detailed description of the house and its occupants. In 1775 he journeyed east from Moose Factory across Hannah Bay (Ont.) and then up the Rivière Nottaway (Que.), and in the following year he travelled west up the Moose River (Ont.). All these explorations were preliminary steps toward the settlement of posts in Moose Factory's hinterland.

In 1777 the HBC built Wapiscogamy House (near the junction of the Opasatika and Missinaibi rivers) as a "Halfway House" towards Lake Superior, and in the same year Thomas was instructed to establish a post at Michipicoten (Michipicoten River). The navigational hazards of the Michipicoten River, however, led him to settle instead on Missinaibi Lake, at the head of the Missinaibi River. Unfortunately provisions proved difficult to find locally, and in January 1778 Thomas retired to Wapiscogamy House, of which he assumed command. From then until Missinaibi House was abandoned in 1780 Thomas spent most of his time at Wapiscogamy, leaving Missinaibi to servants. Although appointed in 1779 second to Edward Jarvis*, chief at Moose Factory, he soon returned to Wapis-

cogamy House, remaining there until he succeeded Jarvis in 1782. In 1795 McTavish, Frobisher and Company, which held a controlling interest in the North West Company, bought the Timiskaming posts from Grant, Campion and Company of Montreal with a view to extending the NWC's trade to James Bay. Alarmed at the threat to Moose Factory, and apparently on his own initiative, Thomas instituted negotiations with the Nor'Westers for dividing the area's trade between the two companies, even travelling as far as Michipicoten in 1799 in the hope of meeting William McGILLIVRAY. Although his efforts failed and the Nor'Westers settled at Moose Factory and elsewhere in the James Bay region in 1800, entering it by sea three years later, Thomas nevertheless successfully defended his posts and in 1806 his opponents abandoned all their stations there.

In 1810 the HBC adopted its "retrenching system," which called for financial moderation and instituted profit sharing for men in senior trading positions. Under this scheme, which also reorganized the posts into Northern and Southern departments, Thomas stayed on as chief at Moose Factory, serving under Thomas THOMAS, superintendent of the Southern Department. Three years later he was dismissed for "mismanagement, negligence and disobedience," apparently in connection with his failure to develop agriculture at Moose. The retrenching system demanded the raising of grain and cattle at the post to reduce the need for European provisions, and Thomas can have had little faith in the policy. Perhaps, too, he found it difficult to take second place. Instead of returning to England, however, he travelled to Lower Canada by the Ottawa River with members of his family, including his daughter Charlotte and her husband, Peter Spence. He settled at Vaudreuil, where some of his collateral descendants still live.

In 1815 Thomas apparently applied to return to the service but the London committee refused his request, although agreeing to employ his sons at Moose Factory and offering him land in the Red River colony (Man.). There is no evidence of his accepting the offer and he apparently remained in Vaudreuil until his death in 1822. In 1824 the Prerogative Court of Canterbury in England granted administration of his effects to his widow Meenish, who by that time had remarried. About £1,600 of his estate was in the hands of Maitland, Garden, and Auldjo, the former Montreal agents of the HBC, when that firm failed in 1826.

One of Thomas's daughters, Ann, married Alexander Christie*, later governor of Assiniboia, and a son, Charles, was a well-known company trader along the Ottawa River and at nearby Golden Lake (Ont.).

ELAINE ALLAN MITCHELL

ACC, Diocese of Moosonee Arch. (Schumacher, Ont.),

Moose Factory and its dependencies, reg. of baptisms, marriages, and burials (mfm. at AO). ANQ-M, CE1-63, 12 juin 1822; CN1-187, 19 janv. 1822. PAM, HBCA, A.11/46: f.2; B.1/a; B.59/a; B.75/a; B.77/a; B.129/a; B.135/a/55; B.135/c/2; B.142/a; B.143/a; B.186/a; E.41 (mfm. at AO). St James' (Anglican) Church (Hudson Heights, Que.), Reg. of baptisms, marriages, and burials, 16 Feb. 1824. St Mary's (Anglican) Church (Como, Que.), Reg. of baptisms, marriages, and burials. *HBRS*, 17 (Rich). C. C. Kennedy, *The upper Ottawa valley* (Pembroke, Ont., 1970). Rich, *Hist. of HBC* (1958–59), vol.2.

THOMAS, MOLLY ANN. *See* GELL

THOMAS, THOMAS, surgeon, fur trader, JP, and politician; b. *c.* 1766, probably in Wales; m. according to the custom of the country, and formally on 30 March 1821, Sarah, a Cree, and they had two sons and six daughters; d. 24 Nov. 1828 in the Red River settlement (Man.).

Thomas Thomas joined the Hudson's Bay Company as a surgeon on 25 March 1789. He was described then as from the parish of St Andrew, Holborn (London), but later as coming from Carmarthen, Wales, no doubt his birthplace. He arrived at York Factory (Man.) on 27 August. In the HBC records he was usually designated as Thomas Sr to distinguish him from another surgeon of the same name, based at York Factory from 1791 to 1794, who was referred to as Thomas Thomas the 2nd. The post journal for York Factory contains passing references to Thomas Sr's hunting: in the spring of 1791 he and a companion supplemented the post fare by shooting 630 geese. A surgeon had little to do, since the company servants were mostly young and healthy, although in the spring of 1793 Thomas treated many suffering from scurvy.

On 14 July 1794 Thomas Sr went inland despite complaints voiced by company officials over the expenses incurred during Thomas the 2nd's two winters inland. Joseph Colen*, the chief at York Factory, explained that "I should not have permitted a Surgeon to have returned Inland – had it not been for the great attachment Mr. Thomas Senᵣ has for this country." The following summer Thomas sailed to England. Since he had seemingly enjoyed his years at York Factory, it is not surprising that the next summer he returned to Hudson Bay, this time as master of Severn House (Fort Severn, Ont.). He arrived at the post on 16 Sept. 1796 and remained in charge until 1810.

In 1810 Andrew Wedderburn, brother-in-law of Lord Selkirk [Douglas*], joined the London committee of the HBC, bringing new vigour to the company. His plan for the management of the trade, known as the "retrenching system," called for the elimination of extravagance, a profit-sharing scheme for company officers, and the division of trading posts into Northern and Southern departments. The posts around

James Bay, namely Fort Albany (Ont.), Moose Factory (Ont.), and Eastmain Factory (Eastmain, Que.), with their outposts, formed the Southern Department; Thomas was appointed superintendent with a salary of £150 a year and the guarantee of at least £250 as his "Share of Profits." In November 1811 he was appointed a justice of the peace for the Indian Territory and held this office until 1816.

Thomas's first winter as superintendent was spent at Eastmain Factory, no doubt at the request of the London committee, which had heard that there were "jealousies among the officers." He was to investigate the disagreements which had occurred between George ATKINSON and his colleagues. The committee attributed to friction the post's disappointingly small shipments of whale oil, which brought high prices in wartime Britain. In 1813 the committee decried the mismanagement of Moose Factory under John THOMAS and instructed Thomas Thomas to dismiss him even though he had many years of service.

From 1810 to 1814 Thomas made his headquarters at Fort Albany, and during this time, in 1813, his official designation was changed from superintendent to governor. The London committee in 1812 had declared itself "highly gratified to find that Mr. Thomas & all the factors & officers in his department are sensible to the propriety of the new regulations and are aware of their own interest being so closely combined with the prosperity of the Company."

In 1810 William AULD had been appointed superintendent of the larger and more complex Northern Department, which consisted of the posts of York Factory and Fort Churchill (Churchill, Man.), as well as the Saskatchewan and Winnipeg districts, that is, all the posts south and west of Hudson Bay. Unfortunately, Auld was unable to adapt to the retrenching system and resigned in 1814. Thomas succeeded him as governor of the Northern Department, accepting the command for one year only. He took up residence at York Factory. The London committee wanted to encourage its officers to exercise initiative; Thomas was informed at the conclusion of his instructions that "having thus given our Ideas on these points we leave the arrangements entirely to your discretion as the Governor."

During Thomas's winter of command he arranged for the supply of pemmican needed to sustain an expedition being mounted in Montreal to challenge the North West Company in the Athabasca country. Colin Robertson*, the organizer, recognizing defects of character in John Clarke*, who was to take command of the expedition, sought the opinion of James Bird* and Thomas at Lake Winnipeg in the summer of 1815. Since they approved of Clarke, they must share the blame for the disaster which befell the venture. During that summer the NWC succeeded in forcing the governor of Assiniboia, Miles MACDON-

Thompson

ELL, to resign, and in dispersing the settlers of the Red River colony. Some of them sought refuge at the end of Lake Winnipeg; there, Thomas persuaded Robertson to lead them back to re-establish the colony. Thomas's year in the Northern Department had been one of strain and anxiety. On 30 August, probably in recognition of his efforts, Robert Semple*, governor of the HBC territories, appointed him a councillor of Assiniboia.

After the death of Semple at Seven Oaks (Winnipeg) in June 1816 [see Cuthbert Grant*], the HBC asked Thomas to serve as governor-in-chief locum tenens, but he declined. With his family Thomas had spent the winter of 1815–16 at Jack River House and in 1818–19 he wintered at Cumberland House (Sask.), before finally settling in the Red River colony. There, on 30 March 1821, he formally married Sarah, the mother of his children. Later she and seven of the children received baptism.

On 24 Dec. 1822 Andrew H. Bulger*, governor locum tenens of Assiniboia, again appointed Thomas a member of the Council of Assiniboia. Later, George Simpson*, governor of the HBC's Northern Department, described the council as ineffective, and characterized Thomas as "timid and weak as a child." Robertson's appraisal of Thomas was that his knowledge of the fur trade was limited to what occurred on the bay, that he was a "rigid economist," and that, "like the tanner's blind horse," he was afraid of stepping out of his circular path. Nevertheless, the London committee seemed to consider him one of the best men available to direct their affairs in Rupert's Land.

Thomas's will provided an annuity of £25 for his wife Sarah, later described by Letitia Hargrave [Mactavish*] as "the most notorious drunkard at Red River." To each of his two sons he left £3,850, and to each of his six daughters £1,000 in three per cent Bank of England consols. Thomas was regarded as an influential citizen of the colony; his sons followed in their father's footsteps and several of his daughters married prominent men. Sophia*, the youngest daughter, played a role in translating the Bible into Cree.

BRUCE PEEL

PAC, RG 68, General index, 1651–1841. PAM, HBCA, A.6/18; A.30/4, 7; A.32/3: f.222; A.36/13; A.44/2; B.59/b/30; B.198/b/4, 6; B.239/a/89, 96–97; B.239/b; C.1/392, 400; E.4/1. HBRS, 2 (Rich and Fleming); HBRS, 24 (Davies and Johnson). Letitia [Mactavish] Hargrave, The letters of Letitia Hargrave, ed. Margaret Arnett MacLeod (Toronto, 1947). Morton, Hist. of Canadian west (1939). Rich, Hist. of HBC (1958–59), vol.2.

THOMPSON, JAMES, soldier and office holder; b. 1733 in Tain, Scotland, son of James Thompson; d. 25 Aug. 1830 at Quebec.

James Thompson probably came from a Jacobite family subjected to repression by the English after the battle of Culloden in 1746. He must have studied civil engineering, since he later put his knowledge in that field at the service of the British army. Like many young men from war-impoverished Scotland who were attracted by the promise of land grants, he enlisted in 1757 in the 78th Foot, known as Fraser's Highlanders, which had been raised to fight in North America. He chose the company commanded by his cousin, Captain Charles Baillie, who made him a sergeant and promised him an officer's commission in the event of an opening. Baillie's death the following year put an end to his chances of promotion.

In 1758 Thompson participated with his regiment in the siege of Louisbourg, Île Royale (Cape Breton Island), during which he learned how to make fascines. He took part in the capture of Quebec in 1759, and in the surrender of Montreal the following year. In the autumn of 1760 he was quartered at Saint-Pierre-de-la-Rivière-du-Sud and became friends with the family of Michel Blais*, a prominent farmer. Returning to Quebec for the winter, he was temporarily assigned to the military engineering service and was in charge of 200 soldiers building fascines near the Rivière Saint-Charles.

When the war ended in 1763, the 78th Foot was demobilized. Thompson remained at Quebec, as a clerk of works with the engineering corps. He was under the orders of Captain John Marr until 1772, but he does not seem to have had steady employment. In July 1770 Marr noted that Thompson had been paid only sporadically since March 1769 and it had been necessary to stop projects after the commander-in-chief refused to approve a pay-roll signed by Thompson. Thompson had married, probably shortly after the war, but his wife and their six children died before the American invasion in 1775–76.

When Marr went to Scotland on leave in 1772, military authorities decided to put Thompson, a civilian, at the head of the military engineering service, rather than appoint an infantry or artillery officer, the usual practice when there was no officer available from the Royal Engineers. Promoted overseer of works at double his former salary, Thompson carried out his duties for three and a half years with no assistant. He supervised repairs to military and government buildings and fortifications, made up pay-rolls, prepared estimates, bought construction materials, and negotiated contracts. His engineering office at Quebec being the only one for the whole colony, in 1773, for example, he dealt with the contract to build supply depots for the troops at Trois-Rivières.

When the Americans invaded, Thompson was responsible for readying the fortifications of Quebec for a siege. He put up stockades where the fortifications were not high and barricades at the edges of

Thompson

Lower Town and at the top of the rise leading to Upper Town. After the enemy's unsuccessful attack during the night of 30–31 Dec. 1775, Thompson saw to the burial in the Saint-Louis bastion of Richard Montgomery*, the American general killed in the fighting, and kept his sword as a souvenir.

In June 1776, when reinforcements arrived, Thompson was confirmed in his duties by William Twiss, the officer of the Royal Engineers who took command of the military engineering service. The state of war led to a multiplication of defensive works. In addition to supervising the personnel at Quebec, Thompson carried out special missions in the countryside. In 1780 he went to La Malbaie, which was on Major John Nairne*'s seigneury, to organize the construction of barracks for American prisoners. Then he negotiated contracts for putting up military buildings in Saint-Thomas parish (at Montmagny), where German troops were quartered.

After the war, in 1784, Thompson investigated a claim by James Cuthbert*, the seigneur of Berthier, for £10,000 for damages caused by the British army. He proved it was unjustified. The commander-in-chief, Frederick Haldimand*, was satisfied with Thompson's services and recommended to his successors that he be retained in his post despite the cuts that came with the return of peace. Thompson was worried, however, since in 1785 he had to ask the Board of Ordnance to confirm his appointment. He noted his activities in his diary in order to be able to justify his job and in the end he was successful.

On 6 Dec. 1780 Thompson married Frances (Fanny) Cooper in the Anglican church at Quebec. They had nine children, three of whom died in infancy. All but the eldest were baptized in St Andrew's Presbyterian Church. The family lived in the former episcopal palace, where the military engineers had offices, until 1788. Having received a living allowance that year, Thompson took up residence on Rue Saint-Louis, and then on Rue Sainte-Angèle. He bought a lot at the corner of Rue Sainte-Ursule and Ruette des Ursulines in 1791 and had a house built in 1793; his descendants would live there until 1957. Thompson, however, considered his income insufficient. In 1799 he asked for and obtained a 50 per cent increase in salary in consideration of his long service record and his large family. He had hoped for careers as engineering officers for his sons. Through Edward* Augustus, Duke of Kent and Strathearn, he made efforts to have them admitted to the Royal Military Academy in Woolwich (London). But candidates had to be between 14 and 16 years of age, and his three eldest sons had passed the maximum age before his plans could be carried out. Only the youngest, George, was admitted, in 1804, thanks to the support of Robert Mathews*, Haldimand's former military secretary, and Colonel Twiss. He became an officer in the Royal Regiment of Artillery in 1808, while James and William Alexander went into the commissariat service and John Gawler became a lawyer and later a judge. One of Thompson's daughters married a merchant and the other a schoolteacher.

Thompson belonged to the middle class. In addition to his house, from 1795 he owned a property in Armagh Township, a land grant that he had applied for jointly with Michel Blais as early as 1767. He earned £174 a year, a sum including the living allowance, a daily food allowance, and a supply of firewood, which was the equivalent of an army lieutenant's income. In 1821 his house was in a dangerous state of disrepair, and in recognition of his years of work the engineering service repaired it for him. Despite his advanced age, Thompson carried out his duties as overseer of works until 1825. He was then granted a pension equal to his full salary. In 1828 he asked for and received £188 a year.

Towards the end of his life Thompson became celebrated for his wealth of memories. Upon arriving at Quebec in 1818, the new governor, the Duke of Richmond [Lennox*], sent for him to ask about James Wolfe*, the siege of Quebec, and Fraser's Highlanders. Later Thompson was invited on several occasions to the home of Governor Lord Dalhousie [Ramsay*]. In 1828, as the last survivor of the battle on the Plains of Abraham and as deputy grand master of the freemasons, he had the honour of helping lay the foundation-stone of the monument to Wolfe and Montcalm* in the garden of the Château Saint-Louis. That year he dictated reminiscences and anecdotes from the two sieges of Quebec and that of Louisbourg to one of his sons.

James Thompson died in 1830, aged 97. The *Quebec Mercury* described him as an intrepid soldier, a faithful servant of the king, the father of a large and respectable family, and a practising Presbyterian. A Scottish immigrant who had lived at Quebec for 70 years, he had taken part in the capture of the town in 1759, its defence in 1775–76, and the construction of works such as the Hope and Prescott gates and the citadel. His memoirs and diary bear witness to his time.

Christian Rioux

[James Thompson's home remained in the family until 1957 when it was sold to Pietre Farago, probably because there were no more male heirs. Willy Côté bought it the following year and sold it in 1961 to the Ministère des Affaires Culturelles, which declared it a historic monument. But for Michel Gaumond's research, it would have been called Maison Côté instead of Maison Thompson-Côté. C.R.]

ANQ-Q, CE1-61, 6 déc. 1780; CE1-66, 10 avril 1784, 5 juill. 1789, 5 févr. 1792, 22 juill. 1793, 18 avril 1797, 17 juin 1798, 27 août 1830; CN1-284, 22 sept. 1791; P-254. BL, Add. mss 21885: ff.203–5, 266–73, 276. PAC, MG 24,

769

Thompson

A12, sect.3, nos.366, 422 (transcripts); vol.16, 1828; vol.17, 31 July 1828; RG 1, L3^L: 139, 144, 168, 184, 283, 1758, 21884, 91519–58; RG 8, I (C ser.), 223: 131–32, 135; 1208: 246. PRO, CO 42/192: 137; WO 55/1224: 186; 55/1820: 30–32. Québec, Ministère des Affaires culturelles, direction régionale de Québec, Dossiers hist. semi-actifs, maison Thompson-Côté. "Les dénombrements de Québec" (Plessis), ANQ Rapport, 1948–49: 17, 119, 169. James Thompson, "The journal of Sergeant James Thompson, 1758–1830," Literary and Hist. Soc. of Quebec, Trans. (Quebec), new ser., 22 (1892–98): 53–56. Quebec Mercury, 28 Aug. 1830. "Les Presbytériens à Québec en 1802," BRH, 42: 728. Quebec almanac, 1792–1801. Quebec directory, 1790–91. J. R. Harper, The Fraser Highlanders (Montreal, 1979). "À propos de Montgomery," BRH, 42 (1936): 85–86. "L'épée du général Montgomery," BRH, 20 (1914): 162; BRH, 33 (1927): 529–30. "L'honorable John-Gawler Thompson," BRH, 32 (1926): 125. "An interesting reminiscence," Quebec Gazette, 19 March 1862: 2. "Les jumeaux Thompson," BRH, 44 (1938): 356. J. M. LeMoine, "Les sièges de 1759 et 1775," BRH, 1 (1895): 157. Gérard Morin, "Trésors historiques accumulés par une famille écossaise de notre ville remis aux autorités," Le Soleil (Québec), 9 juin 1950: 3, 13. "Portrait de James Thompson," BRH, 61 (1955): 185. J.-E. Roy, "Armagh," BRH, 1: 125. P.-G. Roy, "Les amours du sergent James Thompson," BRH, 42: 573–76. "Wolfe est-il bien mort sur les plaines d'Abraham," BRH, 45 (1939): 91–92.

THOMPSON, MARY, servant and convicted criminal; b. 1801 in Upper Canada, daughter of Alexander Thomson; fl. 1823–24 in Upper Canada.

The veil of obscurity that cloaked Mary Thompson's life was lifted on 15 Aug. 1823 when she was charged with murdering her new-born infant. An illiterate young woman, Thompson was a member of a poor, landless family resident in the York (Toronto) area. At the time of her arrest she was single and had been a domestic servant for but a few months. The evidence for Thompson's trial is scanty, and so a detailed reconstruction of the crime or much insight into her personal life is precluded. Although her case has therefore less inherent interest than that of Angelique Pilotte* in 1817, it is of greater importance because of its impact upon Upper Canadian legal history.

For a time after her arrest Thompson "steadily denied" knowledge of the crime with which she was charged. At length, however, a confession was obtained and she led the authorities to the child's grave. Her incarceration was noted in Charles Fothergill*'s Weekly Register under the heading "Horrid Murder." He commented that she had "evinced but little concern" during the investigation. Indicted under a statute of 1624 (21 Jac.I, c.27), she was tried before Chief Justice William Dummer POWELL on 17 Oct. 1823. Attorney General John Beverley Robinson* prosecuted; the defence counsel was probably George Ridout*. After considering the testimony of seven witnesses, a petit jury, including John Doel*, found her guilty but recommended mercy. Powell, however, in spite of his obvious sympathy for Thompson, lacked legal cause to refer the case to Lieutenant Governor Sir Peregrine Maitland*. He sentenced her to be hanged on 20 October but he wrote to Maitland's secretary, Major George Hillier*, offering an opportunity for gubernatorial intervention. For his part, Maitland would not absolve the judge from signifying legal cause for review.

On 18 October Thompson petitioned Maitland for clemency. Unlike Pilotte, she did not plead innocence. She admitted that she had been "fairly and patiently tried with every Opportunity of Defence." However, she claimed that she had failed to present the "real situation" to the jury. She now declared that her labour had been "unexpected" and that "in the pains and anguish of child-birth . . . her unfortunate Offspring met it's untimely end, and that it's death was not the consequence of any premeditated design to conceal her shame, any predisposition to commit a Deed so foul, any felonious violence by the arm of an unnatural Mother." She appealed to Maitland's "known clemency" to "save her from that pending death she is so little prepared to meet." Two days later her father, who had spoken to Powell personally on the night of the conviction, uttered a plea for his "wretched Child . . . so lately the hope of an affectionate parents future happiness, [who] by one false step productive of Shame is doomed to die an ignominious death." Making no claim for her innocence, he simply urged that "the spirit of holy feeling and charity" be extended to his daughter as it had been to others.

By now Powell had decided to respite the execution because of new information. Under the statute of 1624 three key areas of evidence had to be established: that the pregnancy and birth were concealed, that the child was a bastard, and that it was born alive. After the trial, a "medical Person" had informed him that evidence admitted which had been taken as conclusive proof that the child was born alive had been "for many years disallowed" by English judges. This information threw doubt upon Powell's ruling in the last area, and by respiting the sentence, he was able to confer with justices William CAMPBELL and D'Arcy BOULTON. They agreed that he had erred in accepting the medical evidence as conclusive, but they added that the jury had convicted on the whole body of evidence and thus there were no grounds for overturning the verdict. On 25 October Powell reported their conclusions to Maitland, but he was still personally convinced that "the verdict might have been other wise had the Evidence been stated as hypothetical." He urged a further respite and royal review. Maitland concurred and directed him to prepare a report on the case to be forwarded to Colonial Secretary Lord Bathurst.

On 28 November the report was ready. In it Powell reviewed the statute and outlined the evidence bearing upon the verdict. He expressed the view that a major weakness in the crown case had been the failure to produce conclusive evidence consistent with English judicial precedents that the child was born alive. During the trial Powell had admitted the evidence of "two medical witnesses" who had immersed the child's lungs in water "and found them to float." At the time he had believed that there was "no question" but that the child was born alive and the compelling and gruesome circumstantial evidence of "a fracture of the skull, braine and extravagate blood," which the defendant had attributed to her falling with the baby while "crossing astride, a rail fence," had convinced both judge and jury of the prisoner's guilt. In his report, however, Powell indicated that English judges now regarded such evidence as either inadmissible or hypothetical, and that it was a principle of English law to require tangible and positive proof and to "admit no Inference from Circumstances." He also noted the disparity between the reformed English statute of 1803, which had reduced concealment to a misdemeanour, and the unreformed Canadian law.

On 30 July 1824 Powell granted his last respite. Finally, on 6 August, "in consideration of some favorable circumstances," Thompson was granted an unconditional pardon. Her name appears, for the last time, on the jail return of 30 Sept. 1824. After her release she returned to the obscurity from which she had come. But her disappearance from official notice in no way detracted from the parliamentary and legal ramifications of her case.

The most striking effect of Thompson's case was the nine years of parliamentary effort to repeal the unusual act by which she had been convicted. Interestingly, the initiative came from, and was sustained by, some of the most powerful political figures in the province: John Strachan*, John Beverley Robinson, George Herchmer Markland*, and Jonas Jones*. The difficult and chequered course of their efforts began shortly after Thompson's trial when, on 27 Nov. 1823, Markland gave notice in the Legislative Council of a repeal bill. It passed quickly through the council, but died in a House of Assembly committee. In 1825 the bill reappeared as part of Robinson's wider attempt at reform of criminal law; it was introduced in council by Strachan and steered through the assembly by Jones and Robinson. However, it was disallowed by the imperial government in 1827 for reasons which are not clear. For the next few years no action was taken but the bill was not forgotten. In 1830 Robinson introduced it in the council, but it died on the assembly's order paper. Finally, the next year, again on Robinson's initiative, it was passed by the assembly and council and received royal assent. The act, 2 Wm.IV, c.1, voided the authority of the old act

because of "doubts . . . respecting the true meaning" and specified that trials for the murder of bastard children were to proceed like other murder trials. Concealment was reduced to a misdemeanour punishable by a maximum prison term of two years. Juries were empowered upon acquittal of child murder to find concealment and the court would then sentence on that ground.

Judicial handling of the Thompson and Pilotte cases suggests, as the court records bear out, that cases of infanticide rarely reached the court. On 18 Aug. 1825 Fothergill commented on yet another young servant "who, after repeatedly denying her state of pregnancy, was privately delivered of a fine male child, which was discovered in a Privy, on the following morning." In this instance the woman escaped custody and fled. Fothergill feared that it was "not an uncommon offence" and noted that it was usually restricted to the "lower classes." Harsh winters and periods of economic distress, to say nothing of the shame of having a child out of wedlock, contributed to the incidence of infanticide.

Dead babies, whether found in shallow graves, privies, or under the ice of a frozen bay, were, and are, grim reminders of a brutal side of Upper Canadian life. So disturbing and contemptible a crime as infanticide elicited pity for, rather than outrage against, its perpetrators. In Mary Thompson's case, however, it was not her pathetic circumstances which occasioned the intermittent efforts of some of the most powerful men in the province, especially Robinson, to repeal the statute. It was rather the determination, in spite of uncooperative assemblies, indifference, and imperial disallowance, to rid the law of an act unusual in its presumption of guilt and difficult to enforce because of doubts as to its true meaning.

ROBERT LOCHIEL FRASER

[A thorough search of land records – deeds, petitions, and grants – quarter session records, wills, lists of inhabitants, and relevant secondary sources has failed to yield any information about Mary Thompson or her family. There were several Alexander Thompsons (Thomsons) in the York area at this time; none, however, seems to be Mary's father. R.L.F.]

AO, MS 537, 30 July, 6 Aug. 1824; RG 18, ser.C-I-2, 24, 40; RG 22, ser.134, vol.5, 17 Oct. 1823. PAC, RG 5, A1: 32947–66, 40609–10, 44978–81; B27, 1, Home District, 31 Dec. 1823; 31 March, 30 Sept. 1824. "Journals of Legislative Assembly of U.C.," AO *Report*, 1914: 531–32, 548, 551–52, 557–58. "The journals of the Legislative Council of Upper Canada . . . [1821–24]," AO *Report*, 1915: 196–97, 199–200, 211, 213, 216–17, 219. U.C., House of Assembly, *Journal*, 1825: 17; app.A: 36, 41, 43; 1826–27: 25–26, 47, 49; 1831: 49; Legislative Council, *Journal*, 1825; 8–9, 11 Feb., 23–25, 28–29 Nov., 1, 23 Dec. 1831; *The statutes of Upper Canada, to the time of the union* (2v., Toronto, [1843]), 1: 440, 539–40. *Weekly*

Thomson

Register (York [Toronto]), 21 Aug. 1823, 18 Aug. 1825. Patrick Brode, Sir John Beverley Robinson: bone and sinew of the compact ([Toronto], 1984), 106–7. Leon Radzinowicz, A history of English criminal law and its administration from 1750 (4v., London, 1948–68), 1: 86, 251. R. B. Splane, Social welfare in Ontario, 1791–1893; a study of public welfare administration (Toronto, 1965), 218–19.

THOMSON, HUGH CHRISTOPHER, businessman, printer, journalist, politician, office holder, JP, and militia officer; b. 1791 in Kingston (Ont.), son of Archibald Thomson and Elizabeth McKay; d. there 23 April 1834.

Hugh Christopher Thomson's father emigrated from Scotland to Tryon County, N.Y., in 1773 and during the American revolution served under Joseph Brant [Thayendanegea*]. By the late 1780s the family had settled in Kingston, where Archibald, a master carpenter, contracted to build a house for Sir John JOHNSON and also undertook the construction of the first St George's (Anglican) Church. The Thomsons moved to Newark (Niagara-on-the-Lake) in 1794 or 1795 and thence to York. Around 1807 young Hugh became a clerk in the general store of Laurent QUETTON St George in York. Soon afterwards he assumed responsibility for the Niagara branch of the business, and in 1810 he was transferred to Kingston. His correspondence with his employer from 1808 to 1815 throws light on the business methods of the time and reveals his integrity of character. When St George returned to France in 1815, Thomson bought the Kingston store and soon afterwards formed a partnership with George H. Detlor. Two years earlier, he had been involved with Joseph Forsyth*, John Kirby*, and other merchants in the creation of a Kingston banking association.

On 18 Sept. 1813 Thomson married Elizabeth Spafford, who died of a "lingering illness" less than a year later at the age of 22. His own poor health kept him from active service during the War of 1812. He married as his second wife Elizabeth Ruttan of Adolphustown on 18 March 1816. They were to have ten children, only three of whom would survive infancy or early childhood. A man of many interests, Thomson was active in the community. He was a justice of the peace, a militia officer, a warden of St George's Church, secretary of the Midland District Agricultural Society, and deputy crown clerk and commissioner of the Court of Requests for the district. He was also a freemason, an officer of the Kingston Emigration Society, treasurer of the Midland District School Society, and a generous subscriber to the Kingston Auxiliary Bible and Common Prayer Book Society.

In 1819 Thomson wound up his mercantile business to become proprietor and editor of the *Upper Canada Herald*, a weekly journal which began publication that September as a rival of the *Kingston Chronicle*, published by John Macaulay* and Alexander Pringle. By the mid 1820s the *Herald* had the largest circulation of any Upper Canadian newspaper, and in 1826 William Lyon Mackenzie* described it as "perhaps the most consistent, temperate, and useful periodical work in the Province." In addition to producing his newspaper, Thomson did job printing and published a score or more of pamphlets, annual reports, and tracts, as well as two slim volumes of verse and some full-length books, including *St. Ursula's convent, or the nun of Canada, containing scenes from real life* (2v., 1824) by Julia Catherine Hart [Beckwith*], the first novel written by a native Canadian and the first to be published in what is now Canada. In 1828 there appeared *A manual of parliamentary practice . . .*, compiled, edited, and published by Thomson. In point of fact it was a plagiarized reprint of Thomas Jefferson's volume of the same title (1801) omitting references to American law and history, and, where practice differed, substituting Canadian for American legislative procedures. Jointly with James MacFarlane*, who took over the *Chronicle* in 1824, Thomson also published *The statutes of the province of Upper Canada . . .* (1831), a compendium of all statutes passed in the province since 1793.

Although the *Herald* was independent politically – Thomson described it as being "loyal and patriotic, open to all parties, but under the control of none" – it did support moderate reform measures. The *Herald* gave its backing to the reform agitation of Robert Gourlay* and in the 1820s it supported the two leading reformers in the eastern section of the province, Barnabas BIDWELL and his son Marshall Spring Bidwell*. Thomson's first brush with authority came in 1823 as a result of publishing a letter to the editor (probably written by Thomas Dalton*) which criticized a report of a legislative committee on settling the affairs of the "pretended" Bank of Upper Canada, or, as the writer said, on unsettling its affairs. This article was held to be in contempt of the privileges of the House of Assembly, and Thomson, as publisher, was summoned to appear before the bar of the house, where he was sternly reprimanded by Speaker Levius Peters Sherwood* for printing a "false, scandalous, and malicious libel."

This rebuke by a member of the tory élite may have influenced Thomson's decision to stand as a moderate reformer in the general election of 1824. In this contest he headed the polls as one of the two members for Frontenac County, and he repeated the performance in the elections of 1828 and 1830. Sherwood's reprimand may also explain why Thomson rushed to champion liberty of the press in a special issue of the *Herald* when, in 1826, Mackenzie's printing-office was raided by a gang of young tories led by Samuel Peters Jarvis*. Similarly, in 1828 he protested the severity of the sentence accorded Francis COLLINS of the *Canadian Freeman* for his alleged libels on John Beverley Robinson* and Christopher Alexander Hagerman*. But Thomson drew a fine line between liberty and licence, and when Mackenzie overstepped the mark he lost Thomson's support.

During his ten years in the legislature Thomson won a reputation as a fair-minded and judicious committeeman, but he was neither a fluent nor a frequent debater on the floor of the house. Probably because of his experience in business and his grasp of financial issues, he was appointed to many committees dealing with money matters. When investigating pork imports in 1826 he found Lieutenant Governor Sir Peregrine Maitland* guilty of exceeding his authority in allowing the importation of American pork by two prominent tories, James Gray Bethune* and Peter Robinson*. For making this accusation public in the *Herald*, he was indicted at Maitland's insistence as "a malicious and evil-disposed person" who sought to bring the lieutenant governor into "great and public hatred, contempt, and disgrace." The case was quietly dropped by Attorney General Robinson when Maitland left the province.

From 1824 to 1830 Thomson sided with the forces of moderate reform in the assembly, opposing the Church of England's monopoly of the clergy reserves and attacking the government's stand in the alien controversy [*see* John Rolph*]. In the autumn of 1827 he became a friend of John Walpole Willis*, sent out from England to fill a vacancy on the Court of King's Bench. When Maitland dismissed Willis for declaring that the court could not sit in the absence of Chief Justice William CAMPBELL, reformers of every stripe protested. Thomson published Willis's lengthy defence *in toto* and deplored the action of the executive as "a fatal blow to the judicial independence of our Provincial Courts." The *Chronicle* retorted that Willis was "wrong headed" and "weak-minded" in trying to halt the judicial process on a "dubious technicality." The affair blew over when Willis returned to England, but it helped to ensure a reform majority in the general election of 1828.

After 1830 Thomson abandoned his reform allies and became a consistent supporter of the administration. The change in his political allegiance reflected the admiration of many reformers for Maitland's successor, Sir John Colborne*. It also reflected the strains imposed on the reform movement by the election of Mackenzie in 1828. After taking his seat in the house Mackenzie tended to dominate the debates, and his radicalism combined with his incivility quickly antagonized some of the more moderate reform members, including Thomson. Openly critical of his colleague, Thomson voted with the tories against some of Mackenzie's measures, an action for which he was denounced by Mackenzie in the *Colonial Advocate* but applauded by the *Chronicle*; the latter paper offered him the olive branch and welcomed him back "within the pale of civilized society." In December 1831 Thomson seconded a motion by James Hunter Samson* to expel Mackenzie for a double libel on the executive branch and the assembly. With biting sarcasm, Mackenzie railed at him for ranging himself "among the persecutors of the Press." Yet Thomson's opposition to Mackenzie was not a volte-face on his part; he was exercising the same independent judgement for which, in 1825, he had been presented in Kingston with a silver cup by "the friends of free discussion" (one of whom was the engraver of the cup, Samuel Oliver Tazewell*).

Thomson's greatest political achievement was the establishment of the provincial penitentiary in Kingston. He moved the first resolution on this subject in 1826, but no action was taken until Colborne adverted to the matter in his address to parliament in 1830. Thomson was then made chairman of a new committee, whose preliminary report was unanimously adopted. In 1832 he and John Macaulay were appointed commissioners to visit American penal institutions, procure plans, and submit an estimate of costs. Early in 1833 their detailed report was adopted and £12,500 was voted over a period of three years to buy land and erect a building. Having made himself an expert on penitentiary theory and operation, Thomson supervised the first stages of construction and drew up a comprehensive act for the administration and maintenance of the institution. Had his life not been cut short, he probably would have become the first warden of the penitentiary.

Never a man of robust health, Thomson was in York for a sitting of the assembly in late December 1833 when he suffered a haemorrhage of the lungs. His wife's brother-in-law Robert Stanton* sat up with him one night during his illness, explaining to their common friend John Macaulay that "he seems low spirited & dejected unless some old acquaintance is near him." Treated by doctors John Rolph and John King, Thomson managed to rally, and when navigation opened in April he was taken to Kingston. There he suffered a relapse and died on St George's Day. His brother Edward William*, who was with him at the end, wrote that "he died the death of a Christian without moving a finger and praising God to the last." In writing his obituary, James MacFarlane, his onetime antagonist at the *Chronicle*, extolled his devotion to public duty, deplored the calumnies he had had to endure, and said that in private life he was "universally esteemed." He was, MacFarlane noted, "a warm and faithful friend; an obliging and kind neighbour, and a most affectionate husband and father." His widow, Elizabeth, applied for and received from the provincial government a grant of £100 in recognition of his services. In 1824 she had managed the *Herald*

Thowaghwenkarakwen

during her husband's absence in York, thus becoming the first woman in the province to publish a newspaper, and upon his death she again took over the paper and carried it on until 1837.

H. P. GUNDY

[G. [H.] Patterson, in "An enduring Canadian myth: responsible government and the family compact," *Journal of Canadian Studies* (Peterborough, Ont.), 12 (1977), no.2: 3–16, assumes without any substantiation that the views expressed by A Plough-Jogger in the 7 June 1825 issue of the *Upper Canada Herald* were identical to Thomson's own views and were derived from Lord Bolingbroke and David Hume; he also claims that the phrases "Court influence" and "court party" can be found in letters to the *Herald* from One of the People and Hampden on 26 April and 17 May 1825 respectively, whereas they actually appeared in the communication by A Plough-Jogger. As well, Thomson himself never used the term "court party," nor did he enter into a controversy with the editor of the *Kingston Chronicle* over the assembly's withholding of supplies. H.P.G.]

AO, MS 78, Stanton to Macaulay, 26 Dec. 1833, 1 May 1834; MS 88, Thomson to St George, 1808, 1815; MU 631, no.99 (*Upper Canada Herald*, ledger, 1829–33). MTL, Laurent Quetton de St George papers, 1810–13. PAC, RG 1, L3, 497: T10/35, T11/5; 498: T12/10; RG 5, A1: 51867–68; RG 68, General index, 1651–1841: 469. *A manual of parliamentary practice, with an appendix, containing the rules of the Legislative Council and House of Assembly of Upper Canada*, comp. H. C. Thomson (Kingston, 1828). U.C., House of Assembly, *Journal*, 1824–33. *Colonial Advocate*, 2 March, 6 April 1826; 26 May, 22 Dec. 1831. *Gleaner, and Niagara Newspaper*, 27 Dec. 1823. *Kingston Chronicle*, 1819–33. *Upper Canada Herald*, 1819–34. H. P. Gundy, "Hugh C. Thomson: editor, publisher, and politician, 1791–1834," *To preserve & defend: essays on Kingston in the nineteenth century*, ed. G. [J. J.] Tulchinsky (Montreal and London, 1976), 203–22; "Liberty and licence of the press in Upper Canada," *His own man: essays in honour of Arthur Reginald Marsden Lower*, ed. W. H. Heick and Roger Graham (Montreal and London, 1974), 71–92. R. B. Splane, *Social welfare in Ontario, 1791–1893: a study of public welfare administration* (Toronto, 1965). M. A. Banks, "An undetected case of plagiarism," *Parliamentary Journal* (Chicago), 20 (1979), no.2: 1–11. H. P. Gundy, "The business career of Hugh C. Thomson of Kingston," *Historic Kingston*, no.21 (1973): 62–75, and "Publishing and bookselling in Kingston since 1810," no.10 (1962): 22–36.

THOWAGHWENKARAKWEN. *See* TEHOWA-GHERENGARAGHKWEN

TOKARIHOGEA. *See* TEKARIHOGEN (Henry)

TOMAH (Toma, Tomer, Tomma), JOSEPH. *See* SAINT-AUBIN, JOSEPH-THOMAS

TOMAH (Toma, Thomas), PIERRE, known as **Governor Tomah** (the name also appears as **Toma Pierre**), Malecite chief; b. *c.* 1734, possibly at Aukpaque (near Fredericton, N.B.), son of Pierre Tomah*, supreme sachem of the Malecites; m. 5 June 1768 Marie-Joseph of Aukpaque before Abbé Charles-François Bailly* de Messein; d. in or after 1827, likely at Meductic (near present-day Meductic), N.B.

Pierre Tomah had a long and distinguished career. In 1759 he fought with Montcalm*'s forces on the Plains of Abraham, where he lost an arm and an eye. His activities during the American revolution are not well documented, but on 28 July 1780 he is listed on the return of American agent John Allan* as being "Encamped at Passamaquoddy," accompanied by his wife and three children. On 2 Oct. 1781, through a skilful manœuvre of Nova Scotia's superintendent of Indians, Michael Francklin*, at a conference held at Burton (N.B.), Pierre Tomah became "governor" (roughly the equivalent of supreme sachem) of the Malecites, thereby succeeding his father. That Francklin considered intervention necessary may suggest that patrilineal succession was not unquestioningly accepted by all Malecites at this time.

In 1788 or 1789, Tomah, his wife, and four children were reported by Frederick DIBBLEE, founder of the New England Company's school at Meductic, to have stopped there. Since the quantity of goods that Tomah and his children received was far below average, it is likely that their participation at the school was only peripheral. It was probably the same Pierre Tomah who in 1790 was reported living with 29 other families at Becaguimec (Hartland), N.B., where he was tilling a large corn patch.

In the latter years of Tomah's life the Malecites began to experience the effects of loyalist expansion into the upper Saint John River region. It was a time of particular difficulty as they faced the need to adjust their way of life to a social environment increasingly moulded by whites. The younger generations were the ones to suffer the full consequences of greater contact with the English-speaking colonists [*see* Molly Ann GELL; Francis Tomah*].

The election of Francis Tomah as chief at Kingsclear in 1813 may indicate that Pierre Tomah had relinquished his leadership or that because of his age, infirmity, or some other reason the old chief was unable to maintain authority over the entire Malecite population of the Saint John valley. If Pierre Tomah still laid claims to be the major chief in the 1820s, and if he still had any support from his people, he had largely been forgotten by the New Brunswick authorities. Lieutenant Governor Sir Howard Douglas*, who visited Meductic in 1827, seems to have been surprised to find him still alive, a destitute man of 93 years. A contemporary account reported: "His Excellency, deeming him to be a very proper object of Charity, caused him to come down to Fredericton, and immediately directed the Commissioners for superintending Indian Affairs to have him decently clothed, and relieve his present wants, and also to adopt measures for his relief and sustenance. It is worthy of remark that while putting on his new Apparel he seemed to manifest the most sincere joy and gratitude." Nothing more is known of Pierre Tomah.

VINCENT O. ERICKSON

N.B. Museum, Webster MS coll., packet 31, [Walter Bromley], "Report of the state of the Indians in New Brunswick under the patronage of the New England Company, 14th August 1822." *Military operations in eastern Maine and Nova Scotia during the revolution, chiefly compiled from the journals and letters of Colonel John Allan . . .* , ed. Frederic Kidder (Albany, N.Y., 1867). *New-Brunswick Courier,* 18 Aug. 1827. W. O. Raymond, *The River St. John: its physical features, legends and history from 1604 to 1784* ([2nd ed.], ed. J. C. Webster, Sackville, N.B., 1943; repr. 1950); "The Indians after the coming of the English: continued," *Saint Croix Courier* (St Stephen, N.B.), 16 June 1892: 1; "The old Meductic fort," N.B. Hist. Soc., *Coll.*, 1 (1894–97), no.2: 221–72.

TOMISON, WILLIAM, fur trader; b. *c.* 1739 on South Ronaldsay, Scotland; d. there unmarried 26 March 1829.

Throughout a career spanning half a century William Tomison typified the strengths and weaknesses of the men who represented the Hudson's Bay Company as it expanded westward from the shores of Hudson Bay in competition with enterprising traders from Montreal. His successes and his failures were those of the company as it attempted to adapt to the new conditions it faced once it abandoned its "sleep by the frozen sea."

Little is known of Tomison's early years in the Orkney Islands except that his origins were humble and that he received no formal education. In 1760, at age 20, he signed on as a labourer with the HBC. For the next seven years he was stationed at York Factory (Man.) or its subsidiary post Severn House (Fort Severn, Ont.), where he caught the eye of Severn's master, Andrew Graham*. It was doubtless with Graham's encouragement and assistance that the young Orcadian acquired a basic but serviceable education; by 1767 he had been promoted Graham's steward.

In 1767 and again in 1769 Tomison was sent inland to winter with the Indians. On his first voyage he stayed near the eastern shore of Lake Winnipeg (Man.) and was humiliated to find that he could do little to dissuade the Indians from selling their best furs to Montreal-based traders already well established in the area. During his second winter he travelled beyond Lake Winnipeg into the parklands south and west of Lake Manitoba. His reports of these two voyages constitute the earliest coherent accounts documenting the rapid expansion of Canadian traders into what is now southern Manitoba. His experiences gave him a knowledge of Indian customs and languages which few of his fellow employees could match, and he came to the attention of the governor and London committee of the HBC as a valuable man who knew the ways of the fur trade and was "greatly beloved by the Natives."

For the next six years Tomison remained at Severn House as steward. In 1776 he was sent by the council at York Factory to assist Matthew Cocking*, master at Cumberland House (Sask.). Promoted inland master in 1778, Tomison began to implement the council's new policy of establishing company posts close to those of the Canadian traders. Robert Longmoor* was sent out that September, but poor conditions forced him to winter at the Canadian settlement on the North Saskatchewan River. The following year he and Tomison established Hudson House (near Brightholme, Sask.), the first in a series of posts built by the HBC under the new expansionist policy. Returns from the inland posts soared and Tomison received almost universal praise from his superiors. HBC surveyor Philip Turnor* reported to London that without Tomison the inland activity of the company "would intirely loose its present spirit." But Tomison's character and quality as a leader were severely tested by two crises. In the winter of 1781–82 the native tribes of the plains were decimated by smallpox. Although Tomison and other traders did their best to bury the dead and care for the survivors, they could do little to stem the progress of the disease. Tomison's account of the epidemic and its effects is the most detailed record of the first catastrophic epidemic known to have affected the native populations of the plains. Many of the trading Indians had perished and both the HBC and its Canadian rivals experienced a severe drop in furs collected. Prospects for a recovery by the HBC were seriously damaged with the capture of York Factory by the Comte de Lapérouse [Galaup*] in August 1782. When Tomison and his men arrived there in the summer of 1783 they found the fort destroyed and the plantation abandoned. Forced to return inland without supplies, they faced a difficult winter made even harder to bear by the necessity of begging for supplies from Canadian rivals such as William Holmes*.

Despite these set-backs Tomison achieved some notable successes in the early 1780s. Adversity and the need to be more self-reliant helped him to transform an inexperienced body of Orcadian workmen into a cadre of skilled canoemen and winterers with a strong *esprit de corps* and with new forms of social organization and discipline which were less rigid and more egalitarian than those at posts on Hudson Bay. The death of the traditional trading

Tomison

partners of the HBC facilitated the opening of direct trade with Indians farther to the west, an opportunity which Tomison was not slow to grasp. By 1786 he had acquired a lucrative and virtually exclusive trade with the Bloods and Peigans.

In that year Tomison was promoted chief at York Factory with the unusual proviso that he should continue to reside inland where he would be able to supervise personally operations against the Canadians. Doggedly maintaining pace with the North West Company in the establishment of new posts while continuing the policy of sending promising young men such as David Thompson* and Peter FIDLER to winter with the Peigans in order to learn their customs and language and to cement trading ties, Tomison continued to show solid trading results. When he returned on leave to London in 1789 he appeared to be at the peak of his reputation and influence within the company.

The seeds of the strife and bitterness which marred the later years of Tomison's long career, however, had already been sown. The comparative isolation of the inland posts had tended to solidify his natural preference for a solitary and Spartan existence. He showed little interest in social intercourse with his fellow officers and they in turn grew to dislike and then to resent deeply his parsimonious ways and his growing rigidity. When Tomison returned to York Factory in 1790 his powers had been reduced to extend over the inland posts only. In addition, the company had asked Turnor to lead an expedition, which included Fidler and Malchom Ross*, to the Athabasca country in a major attempt to break the Canadian monopoly there. As a result of this divided authority in the field, the coordination of inland activities broke down and relations between senior officers were embittered as they competed for a limited supply of men, canoes, trade goods, and supplies. Because of his tenacious defence of his interests in the Saskatchewan country and his unwillingness to support the projects of his fellow officers, Tomison came under increasing criticism. He reacted by withdrawing further from the company of his fellow officers. In the mean time the Athabasca project started by Turnor was continued by Ross and Thompson, but their attempts to find a shorter, more direct route to Lake Athabasca were obstructed by Tomison and finally came to an end in the maze of lakes and rivers northwest of Reindeer Lake. When Tomison returned to London in 1796 it appeared to his peers that he had finally lost the confidence of the governor and London committee and that his long career had come to an end.

One can imagine his colleagues' consternation when Tomison returned in 1797 to his position as inland chief. George Sutherland*, who had taken Tomison's place on the Saskatchewan, was publicly humiliated by Tomison in 1798 and left the company's service. In that year Joseph Colen*, chief factor of York Factory, was recalled by the London committee to account for his management of affairs at the bay. The responsibility for trade in the Athabasca was transferred to Fort Churchill (Churchill, Man.), and once again Tomison's beloved Saskatchewan country, with posts stretching from Cumberland House to Edmonton House (near Fort Saskatchewan, Alta), assumed pre-eminence in the trade directed from York Factory. It proved to be a somewhat hollow victory. Trade returns began to decline after 1797 now that the competing posts had tapped the resources as far as the Rockies, and a new and even more bitter phase in fur trade rivalry was beginning with the entry of new Canadian-based companies such as the New North West Company (sometimes called the XY Company). Increasingly rigid and petty and in deteriorating health, Tomison expended more energy in pointless disputes than in effective competition for the declining trade. In 1799 he returned to England once again.

After a visit to the Orkney Islands, however, he appears to have found the thought of retirement less appealing and he persuaded the governor and committee to send him out for one further term with instructions to make another attempt to break into the Athabasca using Cumberland House as an advanced base. Wartime conditions did not favour a rapid or effective prosecution of this policy, although sufficient resources were assembled to send Fidler north to Lake Athabasca in 1802. Tomison himself stayed at Cumberland House, where he was shunned more and more by a new generation of officers and by the Indians who regarded his growing reluctance to dispense brandy as the mark of an ungenerous man. In 1803 Tomison retired; but once again he soon wearied of playing the role of the retired "governor" in his native land. In 1806 he induced the company to allow him to mount an expedition to the Athabasca on their behalf, asking only to be granted a percentage of the returns. The proposal was a departure from established company procedures, but it was not to get a fair trial. With the renewal of hostilities between Britain and France, Tomison was unable to recruit enough men for an effective expedition. Despite that, he came out to Hudson Bay, in hopes of enjoying better health, and for the next four years he occupied a succession of minor posts northeast of Cumberland House. Once again he was avoided by officers of the company and most of the Indians. Finally, in 1810, he returned home to stay.

Tomison's final years were spent in Dundas House, an imposing residence he had built for himself in his home parish. Since 1793 he had been providing money to support a school and other charities in the parish but his relations with his neighbours appear to have been characterized mainly by aloofness and disputes. Nevertheless, lacking a direct heir, he bequeathed a major portion of the considerable fortune he had accumulated in years of frugal living to support the establishment of a free school for the poor of his native land.

JOHN NICKS

Orkney Arch., Orkney Library (Kirkwall, Scot.), 346Y. PAM, HBCA, A.5/1–3; A.6/10–15; A.11/116–17; B.49/a/13–22; B.198/a/1–18; B.239/a/48–95; B.239/b/36–58. *HBRS*, 14 (Rich and Johnson); *HBRS*, 15 (Rich and Johnson); *HBRS*, 26 (Johnson); *HBRS*, 27 (Williams). *Journals of Samuel Hearne and Philip Turnor*, ed. J. B. Tyrrell (Toronto, 1934; repr. New York, 1968). J. S. Nicks, "The Pine Island posts, 1786–1794: a study of competition in the fur trade" (MA thesis, Univ. of Alberta, Edmonton, 1975). Rich, *Hist. of HBC* (1958–59), vol.2. J. S. Clouston, "Orkney and the Hudson's Bay Company," *Beaver*, outfit 267 (December 1936): 4–8; (March 1937): 39–43; outfit 268 (September 1937): 37–39. E. W. Marwick, "William Tomison, pioneer of the fur trade," *Alberta Hist. Rev.* (Edmonton), 10 (1962): 1–8. J. S. Nicks, "William Tomison, a quintessential Orcadian servant? An analysis of his leadership style" (paper delivered to the Scottish Studies Conference, Saskatoon, Sask., 1979).

TONGE, GRIZELDA ELIZABETH COTTNAM,

poetess; b. *c.* 1803 in Windsor, N.S., third child of William Cottnam TONGE and Elizabeth Bonnell; d. 19 May 1825 in Demerara (Guyana).

Few details are known about the life of Grizelda Elizabeth Cottnam Tonge, but some general conclusions may be drawn from the kind of social and cultural environment in which she grew up. She was born and spent most of her brief life at Windsor, the rural retreat of a number of distinguished Nova Scotian families and the site of King's College, the first provincial university. After Halifax, Windsor afforded the most refined and sophisticated society in the province. In addition, there was a strong tradition of intellectual and literary activity within Grizelda's own family: her father, William Cottnam Tonge, was a noted orator; and both her grandmother, Martha Grace Cottnam (Tonge), and her great-grandmother, Deborah How* (Cottnam), wrote respectable poetry. Although her formal education was probably negligible, there is no doubt that she was raised in a genteel atmosphere which fostered intellectual perceptiveness and artistic sensitivity while promoting the social proprieties and the domestic duties of a gentlewoman. Of her personal appearance, all that we know comes from the reports of people writing after her death. According to Joseph Howe*, who based his comments on the testimony of one who had known her, she "was about the middle height, with dark hair and eyes, a figure singularly elegant and graceful, and features beaming with sweetness and intellectual expression."

In the spring of 1825 Grizelda sailed from Nova Scotia to join her father in the West Indies. He had gone there in 1808 with Lieutenant Governor Sir George Prevost*'s expedition against Martinique and had subsequently settled at Demerara. Shortly after arriving she died of a tropical fever, leaving behind a few short poems as her literary legacy. Her importance to Nova Scotian literature, however, lies not in her poetry, but in what she came to symbolize to a generation of Nova Scotian writers concerned with creating a native literary culture. Following her premature death, Grizelda Tonge emerged as the epitome of the young, beautiful, gifted poet tragically struck down just as her talent had begun to bloom. She thus symbolized both the promise of a Nova Scotian literature and the tragic fragility of such genius amid the harsh realities of 19th-century colonial life. This perception of her was based partly on her poem "Lines composed at midnight . . . occasioned by the recollection of my sisters," which she wrote during her passage to the West Indies. Her description of her feelings at being separated from her sisters appears to be almost a premonition of her unexpected but imminent death.

I'm borne along the mighty sea,
With dangers all around;
Sweet Sister blossoms, where are ye?
Still clinging to the parent tree,
Upon your native ground.

Long may you thus together grow –
And still Contentment's sunshine know,
While you expanding rise;
And she – the graceful bending bough –
When God sees fit to lay her low,
He'll raise her fallen flowers, I know,
And train them to the skies.

The apparent sensitivity of mind revealed in this poem caught the imaginations of young writers who, in their concern for the quality of life in Nova Scotia, sought to establish a native literature as an integral part of their social and cultural environment.

Grizelda Tonge's special status as the "highly-gifted songstress of Acadia" was initiated by Maria Morris in an elegiac poem published shortly after the news of Grizelda's death reached Halifax: "Acadia, o'er thine early tomb / Shall hover and deplore the doom, / That tore her songstress far away / To mingle with a foreign clay." But her imaginative significance was best expressed by Joseph Howe. In his "Western Rambles," published in the *Novascotian, or Colonial Herald* in 1828, Howe became lyrical when reflecting upon Grizelda, ignorant of the fate that awaited her, sailing to the West Indies: "Oh! God, that a thing so lovely and exquisite, so full of high and pure thoughts, so radiant with maidenly bloom and beauty, should be hurrying away to the grave. . . . But . . . *she shall not*

Tonge

die, while Acadia's lyre has a string – or a kindred spirit to mingle her memory with its silver tones." Many years later – in a *Novascotian* article of 1845 entitled "Nights with the muses" – Howe underlined Grizelda's symbolic importance to the cultural life of the province. "There is one," he wrote, ". . . who has left to her native land little more than the tradition of a gentle spirit and high poetic imagination, shrined in a form of exquisite loveliness. For twenty years GRIZEL-DA TONGE, has, in our moments of literary liberty and poetic *abandon*, stood before us again and again, as if to tempt us to embody, in language, the impressions made in 1825, by the publication of one or two of her productions, and by all that, in answer to our anxious enquiries, we could then learn from those to whom she was known."

THOMAS B. VINCENT

[A few poems by Grizelda Tonge were published in Nova Scotia newspapers and magazines, in most cases after her death, although an ode addressed "To my dear grandmother, on her 80th birth day" appeared in the *Acadian Recorder* on 5 March 1825. The poem is unsigned, but a letter preceding it describes it as the work of "a young lady of Windsor"; it was subsequently reprinted in the fourth instalment of Joseph Howe's "Nights with the Muses . . . ," *Novascotian*, 16 June 1845, and in another tribute to her in the uncredited series "Half hours with our poets," *Provincial: or Halifax Monthly Magazine*, 1 (1852): 45–49, 273. Tonge's "Lines composed at midnight, on my passage to the West Indies, occasioned by the recollection of my sisters" has likewise been printed under various titles in several articles including "Half hours with our poets" and the fifth instalment of Howe's "Nights with the Muses . . . ," *Novascotian*, 23 June 1845. A broadside version of this poem with no date or place of publication was also issued after her death; a copy of this is preserved in PANS, MG 100, 204: 3s.

Howe's article of 23 June 1845 also prints a number of her manuscript poems, including "A hymn of praise" and two elegies, "Lines . . . composed in the church yard of Windsor, N.S., . . ." and "Extempore lines, occasioned by seeing the corpse of Mary, youngest daughter of the Hon. James Fraser. . . ." Manuscripts of some of Tonge's poems, including the "Hymn of praise" and "Lines composed at midnight," are among the Joseph Howe papers at Harvard College Library, Houghton Library, Harvard Univ. (Cambridge, Mass.), MS Can. 58 (mfm. at PANS).

Comments on Grizelda Tonge after her death include those of Maria Morris, whose elegy "Verses occasioned by the death of a young lady" appeared under the pseudonym M in the *Acadian Recorder* for 9 July 1825 (pre-dating the paper's formal obituary, which appeared in the issue of the 16th); Peter & Paul, "Characteristics of Nova Scotia, no.1," *Acadian Magazine* (Halifax), 1 (1826–27): 433–35; [Joseph Howe], "Western rambles," *Novascotian, or Colonial Herald*, 14 Aug. 1828, and the fourth and fifth instalments of his "Nights with the Muses . . ."; and "Half hours with our poets."

Further details concerning the Tonge family were obtained from the Anglican church records of Trinity parish (Digby, N.S.) in PANS, MG 4, 23, and from Judith Tulloch of Halifax, whose sharing of genealogical information from the Tonge family correspondence is gratefully acknowledged. T.B.V.]

TONGE, WILLIAM COTTNAM, office holder, JP, judge, militia officer, and politician; b. 29 April 1764 in Windsor, N.S., eldest son of Winckworth Tonge* and Martha Grace Cottnam; m. 18 Feb. 1793 Elizabeth Bonnell in Digby, N.S., and they had two sons and three daughters; d. 6 Aug. 1832 in Georgetown (Guyana).

Although little known today, William Cottnam Tonge was a dominant figure in the struggle between the House of Assembly and the lieutenant governor in early 19th-century Nova Scotia and was remembered for decades as the "tribune of the people." Tonge was descended from a prominent and long-established Nova Scotia family. His father had come to the province as a British army officer in 1746 and had become a major landowner, imperial office holder, and influential member of the assembly. His mother was a granddaughter of Edward How*, a prosperous merchant and member of the council at Annapolis Royal that governed the province before the founding of Halifax. Tonge himself, naval officer for Nova Scotia, justice of the peace, and judge of the Inferior Court of Common Pleas for Hants County, was indisputably part of colonial officialdom. His social standing ensured that even during his quarrel with Lieutenant Governor Sir John Wentworth* he remained on good terms with civil and mercantile leaders throughout the province.

Little is known of Tonge's early life, probably spent on his father's large estate near Windsor. Antiquarians of the late 19th century claimed that he had been educated in Dublin, but there is no corroboration for this assertion. Later references suggest that he was trained as an attorney, although he was not a member of the bar in Nova Scotia. Tonge began his public career as deputy to his father, the provincial naval officer, and in 1790 he appeared before the assembly to answer complaints against the older man's management of the office. On his father's death two years later, Tonge was appointed to the post by Richard Bulkeley*, the provincial administrator. Wentworth, the newly appointed lieutenant governor, still in London, proposed instead a fellow loyalist, perhaps with the hope of settling the problems of the naval office with a new broom. Tonge was able to call on support within the British establishment, however, most probably from his distant relative the Earl of Macclesfield, who in 1772 had pushed for Winckworth Tonge's appointment in Nova Scotia. Wentworth's first attempt to use patronage as he had in New Hampshire to create an administration of supporters failed. Moreover, Tonge's English patrons gave him an independence from Wentworth's control that the new lieutenant governor distrusted.

By the late 1790s, Tonge was in serious financial difficulty. His extensive estate had been heavily indebted before his father's death and the younger man's attempts to develop it in the English manner with tenant farmers proved as unsuccessful as his father's earlier efforts had been. Much of the family land near Windsor was for sale by 1795. In 1799 Tonge moved his household to Halifax, where he had obtained a contract for military supplies, probably through the support of his friend the Duke of Kent [Edward* Augustus], commander-in-chief of the forces in British North America.

The quarrel between Tonge and Wentworth that was to dominate public life for nearly a decade appears to have had its roots in events of the late 1790s. Wentworth successfully blocked several attempts by Tonge to recoup his finances by participation in government projects, and the lieutenant governor's refusal to support his claims for patronage seems to have earned him Tonge's enmity. One source of conflict was the proposed settlement of the maroons, Jamaican rebels deported to Nova Scotia in 1796. Wentworth identified Tonge as one of the anonymous correspondents who criticized the lieutenant governor's attempt to establish the Jamaicans on farms near Halifax, and he claimed that Tonge had encouraged them in their demands to be sent to a warmer climate. Tonge, however, volunteered to employ some of the maroons on his estates where they could be provisioned by his tenants and friends. The proposal would have served the two-fold purpose of relieving Tonge's financial distress while embarrassing Wentworth, who had been ordered to limit government expenditure for the maroons. Wentworth was determined to pursue his plans for their settlement at Preston and refused to approve Tonge's scheme, arguing that it was aimed solely at alleviating his near-bankruptcy, which itself made the proposal impracticable. Disappointed in this bid to relieve his debts, Tonge tried to obtain an additional government post, apparently as a revenue collector. His opposition to Wentworth's handling of the maroons probably cost him the appointment. By refusing him the post, the lieutenant governor exacerbated the ill feeling between them.

Patronage was also the issue in 1797 when Tonge was passed over for promotion as major in the Hants County militia. Ignoring his precedence as senior captain, Wentworth appointed John McMonagle, an influential Windsor assemblyman. Tonge, who had earlier been recommended as a battalion commander by Edward Augustus, urged his fellow officers to resign their commissions over this breach of military custom and indeed over the way in which Wentworth had embodied the militia for work on the Halifax defences. When no support was forthcoming, Tonge resigned from the militia in February 1798. His actions were especially disquieting to Wentworth, with his memories of the disloyalty of the colonial militia during the American revolution. The lieutenant governor's reports on the incident emphasized what was to become a dominant theme in his denunciations of Tonge: the dangers to the peace and security of Nova Scotia posed by the naval officer's conduct. In time of war, Wentworth concluded, firm measures were required to deal with such agitators, "otherwise what is now the violence of one may *in these* times become the error & misfortune of many."

The personal dislike between Tonge and Wentworth found expression in a broader constitutional struggle in the Nova Scotian legislature. The legislative sessions of the 1790s had been generally harmonious as executive and assembly cooperated to eliminate the heavy provincial debt. By 1796 their economy measures had achieved success. Provincial revenues increased, swelled by the prosperous wartime economy, and assemblymen began to urge greater expenditure on public works, especially roads. Road construction not only benefited the rural areas by improving access to markets and opening land for settlement, but it also represented a reliable source of cash for country residents. On the other hand, revenue came primarily from customs duties which fell most heavily on the Halifax merchant community, whose members dominated the Council. As provincial revenues increased, the Council began to urge reductions in customs duties, and conflict between the two branches of the legislature became inevitable. The assembly tried to gain greater expenditure on road-works by delaying passage of the revenue bills, while the Council in turn delayed or amended the appropriations. The solution was usually a compromise but the assembly gradually strengthened its claim to financial supremacy. Wentworth was closely allied with the Council, many of whose members he had appointed and which, in its executive capacity, served as his adviser. Tonge had entered the assembly in 1792 for Newport Township and took a leading role in the campaign for greater financial control. In 1799 he incurred the lieutenant governor's wrath by directing the opposition to appropriations for construction of Wentworth's long-sought Government House, and he continued his attacks on the lieutenant governor's projects in subsequent years.

Wentworth's distrust of Tonge was greatly enhanced during the 1799 election campaign. Sure of return in his home constituency in Hants County, Tonge challenged the lieutenant governor directly by also contesting one of the Halifax County seats, all four of which had been held by Wentworth's supporters. In a mocking allusion to the latter's joint election card, Tonge noted that he himself ran "singly . . . without family connections, particular interest, or any

Tonge

influence but that arising from public opinion." In fact, Tonge formed his own coalition by persuading two prominent country residents, James FULTON of Londonderry Township and Edward Mortimer* of Pictou, to join him as candidates for the county. Tonge promised the backing of his friends in the Halifax merchant community in exchange for Mortimer's and Fulton's help in the rural districts. The three candidates were aided by well-organized committees which held meetings throughout the riding in their support. The election was hard fought, with turbulent campaign meetings and copious amounts of rum for all. When the last poll closed, Tonge stood first, followed by Mortimer and Fulton. Only Charles MORRIS of the former members was re-elected. The affront to the lieutenant governor and his coterie was reflected in the vehemence of Wentworth's denunciations of Tonge's campaign to "disturb the Peace and Harmony of the Country, by the tricks, falsehoods and follys used in popular elections." Wentworth may well have exaggerated Tonge's influence, however, since Mortimer's organizer in Pictou concluded that he had failed to deliver the promised support from Halifax.

Tonge possessed no property qualification in Halifax County and at the first session of the new assembly Michael WALLACE, who had stood fifth in the poll, petitioned against his election. Wallace won the subsequent by-election overwhelmingly. Still, Tonge's "country party" had succeeded in its deliberate challenge to the lieutenant governor and his supporters, whom Fulton, using the language of English political history, termed the "court party." Although their success brought to the eighth assembly more of an organized opposition to the executive than was to be seen for decades, this opposition was by no means that of disciplined political parties. These were still far in the future. Instead, loose combinations of assemblymen came together to oppose specific issues, and allies on one day could easily find themselves voting on opposite sides on the next.

Elected in Hants County, Tonge was nominated as speaker when the assembly met in February 1800. Although defeated by the previous speaker, Richard John UNIACKE Sr, his influence remained dominant throughout the sessions. The issue of financial control preoccupied the eighth assembly. Control of appropriations and appointments of road commissioners represented a basic issue of patronage for both assembly and executive. For Wentworth, this control was an opportunity of extending his influence throughout the province. For the assemblymen, it was equally a matter of political survival, providing means to reward friends with ready cash. In 1804 the conflict reached a peak when Wentworth took the unprecedented steps of specifying road expenditure and of proposing road commissioners accountable only to him. Convinced of its right to control road monies, the

assembly ignored Wentworth's specifications and drew up its own appropriations, which were in turn rejected by the Council. Wentworth then prorogued the session with the supply vote unpassed.

Faced with this stalemate, the lieutenant governor delayed calling the legislature until late November 1805, shortly before the annual revenue bills were due to expire. The new session opened with Tonge elected as speaker, replacing Uniacke, who had resigned. Tonge acknowledged that he had long sought the office, which made its holder the effective leader of the assembly in the days before firm party discipline, and he promised to uphold the assembly's established rights. Such sentiments may have rung hollowly in Wentworth's ears, but the session proved peaceful, with the assembly passing the previous year's appropriations with little discussion and accepting the lieutenant governor's suggestions for road expenditures without change. Controversy arose only at the end of the session over a delay in passage of the revenue bill. In the two weeks between expiry of the old law and passage of the new in January 1806, eight ships were unloaded and their cargoes sold duty free, a major loss to the province's annual revenue. Tonge appears to have deliberately withheld the revenue bill for an extra day so that Wentworth could not sign it before one of the speaker's friends could dispose of a cargo. This obvious violation of parliamentary procedure prompted the assembly to send Tonge, accompanied by three assemblymen, to explain the lapse to Wentworth.

Tonge's questionable conduct and his apparent loss of support led Wentworth to dissolve the assembly in May, one year before the end of its normal term. Tonge was returned for Hants County, and when the new assembly met in November he was re-elected speaker. Wentworth had now embarked on a more aggressive course and rejected Tonge as speaker because of his record of obstruction and his narrow win by a margin of only one vote. Obsolete in England, this aspect of royal prerogative had never been employed in Nova Scotia. In colonial American politics, however, from which Wentworth drew his precedents, the governor's refusal of a speaker was less exceptionable. Assembly members argued the issue for two days and went so far as to draft a report on the parliamentary precedents against Wentworth's action. Tonge could not muster enough supporters to pursue the constitutional point, however, and on 20 November the assembly presented a new speaker, Lewis Morris Wilkins*, for Wentworth's approval.

The events of the 1806 session suggest that Tonge's influence had indeed declined. Not only did the assembly accept Wentworth's rejection of its choice as speaker but a majority of members appears to have made concerted efforts to avoid conflict with lieutenant governor and Council. Only some of Tonge's steadfast supporters such as Mortimer, William Lawson*, and William Hersey Otis HALIBURTON voted with him on proposals for increasing the amount of road money and for presenting supply votes as one bill, measures which in past sessions had been the touchstones of the assembly's campaign for financial control. Tonge continued to serve on numerous committees but the session concluded without major controversy.

Wentworth's letters to officials in London had long been filled with accusations against Tonge. He exploited the rhetoric of the conservative response to the French revolution to emphasize aspects of Tonge's activities that would have the greatest impact on British authorities. In the 1790s Wentworth had styled him the "miniature of Abbe Sieyes" and the "United Nova Scotian" (implying his affinity with the Society of United Irishmen). He insinuated that Tonge's opposition to the executive might foment widespread disaffection, even among members of the army and navy, many of whom were friendly with Tonge and frequented assembly debates. Tonge's opposition was especially reprehensible, Wentworth contended, since as an office holder he ought instead to support the actions of government, particularly during the crisis of war. Wentworth concluded that such conduct was detrimental to the maintenance of British authority in Nova Scotia.

The lieutenant governor's remedy for the problem was simple: Tonge must be publicly chastised by dismissal from his naval office. Wentworth first hinted at this course of action in 1799 and frequently returned to it in his fulminations against Tonge. The silence of officials in London for many years suggests that they interpreted the struggle as one of local politics and personalities, an attitude Tonge was later to encourage. By 1806, however, the vehemence of Wentworth's arguments and the evident disruption in public affairs in the province seem to have had some effect, and in May British officials acknowledged Wentworth's authority to dismiss Tonge. Late in February 1807, shortly after the legislature rose for the year, the naval officer returned from a trip to eastern Nova Scotia to read of his expulsion from office in the newspapers.

Despite the years of conflict, Tonge seems never to have considered that Wentworth might dismiss him, and over the coming months he mounted a spirited campaign for reinstatement. A group of prominent Halifax shipowners submitted a petition to London in his favour, affirming him a "loyal subject and man of Integrity." In Annapolis and Hants counties, where his family had close ties with leading citizens, public meetings were called to prepare petitions to the king against Wentworth's actions. The lieutenant governor promptly quashed the meetings, declaring them illegal and provocative. Tonge employed all the techniques of 18th-century patronage and influence to present his case to the highest British authorities. He turned to personal acquaintants in England, including the Duke of Kent, asking for assistance in securing an official investigation of the charges against him. Another prominent London ally was the last royal governor of New Jersey, William Franklin, a close friend of Tonge's loyalist father-in-law. Franklin forwarded Tonge's petition to the colonial secretary, Viscount Castlereagh, for submission to the king, recommending him as an influential public figure. Such prestigious supporters proved ineffectual. Although no specific charges were made against Tonge, he was not reinstated. The need to uphold the authority of the executive branch militated against any intervention by the British government.

Tonge continued nevertheless to be a prominent figure in Halifax public life. By October 1807 he had become an acknowledged adviser to the new commander-in-chief, Major-General John Skerrett*, providing a detailed analysis of the defensive state of Nova Scotia which included accusations that Wentworth had neglected the militia. Skerrett's own doubts about the efficiency of the militia moved him to forward Tonge's memorandum to Castlereagh while praising his public-spirited action in preparing it. Tonge as well was probably the author of an anonymous letter to Castlereagh which vehemently condemned Wentworth's administration as marked by nepotism and financial speculation. Tonge was also friendly with Vice-Admiral George Cranfield Berkeley* and it was likely he who instigated the assembly resolution for a complimentary address and a presentation of silver plate to the admiral on his departure from Nova Scotia in 1807. Certainly Wentworth, who distrusted Berkeley's bellicose attitudes towards the United States, blamed Tonge for the resolution and refused to authorize expenditure for the plate.

The continuing conflict between Wentworth and the assembly and increasing tensions between Britain and the United States led the imperial government to replace the ageing Wentworth with a new lieutenant governor, Lieutenant-General Sir George Prevost*. Prevost landed at Halifax early in April 1808 before official notice of his appointment had reached Wentworth. Tradition states that Tonge was among the first to learn of Prevost's arrival and immediately rode out to Wentworth's country home to inform his old adversary that he "had the pleasure of announcing the arrival of a new governor." The last dispute involving Wentworth and Tonge occurred during the 1808 legislative session when Tonge conducted a day-long filibuster to strike complimentary references to Wentworth's administration from the assembly's address to the retiring lieutenant governor.

Tonge's affinity with military men stood him in good stead with Prevost. He advised him on the

Tonge

defence of the province and Prevost interested himself in Tonge's struggle for reinstatement. Tonge claimed that the lieutenant governor planned to send him on a secret mission to the United States, but the only recorded Nova Scotian commissioned by Prevost to observe conditions there was John Howe. Late in 1808 Prevost appointed Tonge deputy commissary general for his military expedition to the West Indies. Tonge never returned to Nova Scotia.

His career in the West Indies spanned nearly two decades and echoed many of his Nova Scotian activities. He served as a searcher in the custom-house in Martinique for several years but was dismissed after he quarrelled with Vice-Admiral Sir Alexander Forrester Inglis Cochrane. By late 1815 he was established at Georgetown, under the patronage of Lieutenant Governor John Murray, an old military friend. Murray appointed Tonge assistant government secretary, superintendent of pilots, and drossard (a type of sheriff). In 1821, despite Murray's support, Tonge lost these posts when he led a campaign against an unpopular judge accused of charging excessive fees.

Little is known of Tonge's last years. Following his departure from Nova Scotia, his children had been brought up by his mother: his wife had died, probably in childbirth, in May 1805. The eldest, Bonnell, apprenticed with Tonge's brother, a prominent Jamaican lawyer, and by 1820 was settled with his father. In 1825 Tonge's daughter GRIZELDA ELIZABETH COTTNAM, the "songstress of Acadia," died while visiting her Georgetown connections. The account of her death provides the last reference to Tonge in Nova Scotian records.

Lack of personal papers hinders detailed analysis of Tonge's motivation and character. The most complete portrayal of his activities occurs in Wentworth's correspondence, clearly a biased source. A campaign letter written in 1799 provides a rare glimpse of Tonge's political philosophy and might have served as the platform for the "country party" with which he was associated. "On my first Outset in Life," he declared, "I was firmly impressed with the Belief that the welfare of the Province would be best promoted by those who were most interested in it (Though perhaps of inferior abilities), & that the most suitable & trusty Representatives for the people were those who being resident among them were connected with them in Interests, & were acquainted with their Situations, their Difficulties, their objects & Sentiments." Tonge's debating skills and bitter feud with Wentworth made him the natural focus for the varied elements that composed the "country party," whose chief common interest was distrust of Halifax and its domination of Nova Scotia's economic and political life. Both loyalist and non-loyalist supported him when issues of concern to them and their constituents were at stake. As in the other North American colonies

in these early years, however, opposition to executive government continued to be motivated more by self-interest and personality than by coherent political philosophy.

Despite Wentworth's accusations, there is little evidence to suggest that Tonge sought essential changes in the Nova Scotian constitution. Indeed, the lieutenant governor's claim that Tonge advocated an elective legislative council represents the sole mention of genuine political innovation and the proposal, natural during conflict beween elected and appointed bodies, never became a major issue. The political strife in Nova Scotia was a manifestation of the not uncommon dissension between an elected assembly seeking to assert its role in government and a conservative supporter of the colonial *status quo*. The antipathy between Tonge and Wentworth intensified this discord and the waning of acrimony after their departure from Nova Scotian politics confirms that much of the constitutional struggle had been rooted in their mutual dislike. None the less, Tonge's adroit use of parliamentary tactics to pursue his feud and his tenacious support of the rights of the assembly earned him an enduring place in the legislative history of the province.

Tonge's personality remains an enigma. His consistent electoral successes indicate an effective and popular campaigner: only twice during his career did he face an opponent. Although by all accounts a charming, congenial man, he abandoned his young children, and for years they heard of him only through chance reports from the West Indies. Later generations remembered his brilliant oratory, his improvidence, and his indiscretions. Joseph Howe*'s conclusion to his account of Tonge's career serves as a final summation: "I have often wished I could have seen Tonge and all those whoever attempted to describe him to me concurred in the opinion that he was well worth seeing."

JUDITH TULLOCH

[I am indebted to Dr Brian C. Cuthbertson for his assistance in unravelling the sequence of events in the militia conflict and for his comments on the relationship between Tonge and Wentworth, and to Seepersaud Singh of Georgetown, Guyana, for locating Tonge's death record. J.T.]

Harvard College Library, Houghton Library, Harvard Univ. (Cambridge, Mass.), MS Can. 58 (Joseph Howe papers) (mfm. at PANS). PAC, MG 24, F1, 4. PANS, MG 1, 472–74A, 731A, 950; MG 20, 675, no.11; RG 1, 33, 50–54, 58, 60–63, 137–41, 171–72, 224–27, 287–88, 302–5, 525; RG 5, A, 13; RG 22, 27, pt.2. PRO, CO 111/29–39; CO 217/35–37; 217/62–98. Royal Arch., Windsor Castle (Windsor, Eng.), Add 7/356: 372 (copy at Can., Parks Canada, Halifax Defence Complex, Halifax). UCC-M, James MacGregor papers. N.S., House of Assembly, *Journal and proc.*, 1790–1809. *Weekly Chronicle*, 23 Oct. 1799.

Directory of N.S. MLAs. J. M. Beck, *The government of Nova Scotia* (Toronto, 1957). J. G. Marshall, *A brief history of public proceedings and events, legal, – parliamentary, – and miscellaneous, in the province of Nova Scotia, during the earliest years of the present century* (Halifax, [1878?]). Murdoch, *Hist. of N.S.*, vol.3. [A. G.] Archibald, "Life of Sir John Wentworth, governor of Nova Scotia, 1792–1808," N.S. Hist. Soc., *Coll.*, 20 (1921): 43–109. Margaret Ells, "Governor Wentworth's patronage," N.S. Hist. Soc., *Coll.*, 25 (1942): 49–73. Israel Longworth, "Hon. Simon Bradstreet Robie: a biography," N.S. Hist. Soc., *Coll.*, 20: 1–15. W. L. Morton, "The local executive in the British Empire, 1763–1828," *English Hist. Rev.* (London), 78 (1963): 436–57.

TONNANCOUR, JOSEPH-MARIE GODEFROY DE. *See* GODEFROY

TRACEY, DANIEL, physician, newspaper proprietor, editor, and politician; b. probably in 1794 in King's (Offaly) County (Republic of Ireland), son of Denis Tracey, a merchant, and —— Mainfold; d. unmarried 18 July 1832 in Montreal.

Little is known of Daniel Tracey's childhood. Born into a Catholic family, he lost his parents when he was very young and was taken in, with his brother John and sister Ann, by a paternal uncle. After studying at a school run by a man named Morris, he entered Trinity College, University of Dublin, on 5 Dec. 1814, at the age of 20. He is not known to have received a degree there, but is believed to have enrolled subsequently in the Royal College of Surgeons in Ireland. Upon being admitted to the practice of medicine and surgery, he began his career in Dublin, where his abilities were quickly recognized. However, he was adamant in his hostility to the British government, which ruled the Catholic population with an iron hand, and in the end preferred to leave his country.

Tracey landed in Montreal with his brother and sister in 1825. His hatred of the British government did not diminish while he lived there. Indeed, it led him to approve of the Patriote party's demands and aroused his interest in politics. With his launching on 12 Dec. 1828 of a bi-weekly paper, the *Irish Vindicator and Canada General Advertiser* (later the *Vindicator and Canadian Advertiser*), Tracey found a vehicle for his ideas. In its pages he displayed great admiration for Louis-Joseph Papineau*, whom he put on a level with Daniel O'Connell. As a defender of both the Irish and the Canadian causes, Tracey was in reality continuing the tradition of editorial writing begun by Jocelyn WALLER in the *Canadian Spectator* of Montreal.

Since the articles in the *Vindicator* were as fiery as those in *La Minerve*, if not more so, and since the members of the Legislative Council were sensitive to scrutiny, Tracey was charged with libel and imprisoned in 1832. The offending article, which was dated

3 January, had made an appeal for the "total annihilation" of the Legislative Council because it had rejected certain bills passed by the House of Assembly. Ludger Duvernay* of *La Minerve* met with the same fate as Tracey for an editorial published on 9 January in which he too demanded the "abolition" of the council. The two journalists were kept in jail at Quebec from 17 January until the close of the session on 25 February. Their imprisonment made them heroes in the eyes of the Patriotes, and as a result Tracey was chosen as a candidate for a by-election shortly afterwards.

The election was held to replace the member for Montreal West, John Fisher, who had resigned. It had been set for 25 April 1832 and the poll was to remain open according to legal regulations for six days a week until one hour had passed without any vote being cast. It ended on 22 May after 23 days of polling marred by numerous acts of violence. There were 691 votes for Tracey and 687 for Stanley Bagg, his opponent from the English party. Among Tracey's supporters were Louis-Hippolyte La Fontaine*, Côme-Séraphin Cherrier*, Jacob De Witt*, and most of the craftsmen, farmers, carters, and day-labourers in the riding. Almost all were Canadian or Irish. Bagg had mustered the businessmen and office holders, only a few of whom, for example Pierre-Édouard Leclère*, were Irish or Canadian.

Tracey won but at a heavy cost since bloodshed had occurred on the 22nd day of the election. According to members of the English party, it resulted from a "riot" instigated by Tracey's followers. To the Patriotes, on the other hand, it was clear that there had been an attempted "massacre." The day had been quiet until about 2:00 P.M. when two people came to blows. Soon scuffling was going on all over the Place d'Armes, and an emissary from Bagg's party went to get men from the 15th Foot. By the time they arrived everything had returned to order. Tracey was then 3 votes ahead. Shortly after, he and a group of friends proceeding to his home were attacked by some of Bagg's followers, who resented Tracey's lead. The soldiers, who had remained on the square, also began to pursue Tracey. After stones were thrown by both sides, some magistrates who wanted Bagg to win asked the commanding officer to give the order to open fire on the crowd and end the riot. Lieutenant-Colonel Alexander Fisher MacIntosh took it upon himself to do so, and three Canadians were killed. The following day Tracey received another vote and was declared elected.

The intervention by the armed forces against Canadians, which was upheld by the British authorities in the province and in London, demonstrated that the ethnic, social, and political problems facing Lower Canada had reached a serious stage. It also presaged new disturbances. The gulf between the Patriotes and the members of the English party would

Tremlett

from then on become deeper and the conflict intensify, leading finally to the events of 1837.

Less than two months after the by-election, a cholera epidemic hit the province, and especially Montreal. Daniel Tracey caught the disease while attending patients. He died on 18 July 1832, before he could take his seat in the House of Assembly. He was survived by his sister Ann, who married Charles Wilson* in 1835, and his brother John, who went to live in Albany, N.Y., in 1837. His newspspaper was bought by Édouard-Raymond Fabre*, who handed management over to Edmund Bailey O'Callaghan*.

FRANCE GALARNEAU

[The author would like to thank Mr Raymond Refaussé, archivist at Trinity College, Dublin, for information he provided regarding Daniel Tracey. F.G.]

ANQ-M, CE1-51, 18 juill. 1832. *La Minerve*, 9 janv., 26 mars–24 mai 1832. *Vindicator and Canadian Advertiser* (Montreal), 3 Jan. 1832, 26 Feb. 1833. F.-J. Audet, *Les députés de Montréal*. Beaulieu and Hamelin, *La presse québécoise*, vol.1. France Galarneau, "L'élection pour le Quartier-Ouest de Montréal en 1832: analyse politico-sociale" (thèse de MA, univ. de Montréal, 1977). P.-G. Roy, *Toutes petites choses du Régime anglais* (2 sér., Québec, 1946), 1: 270–72. Robert Rumilly, *Papineau et son temps* (2v., Montréal, 1977), 1. Taft Manning, *Revolt of French Canada*. Léon Trépanier, *On veut savoir* (4v., Montréal, 1960–62), 4: 69–71. [Hervé Biron], "Ceux qui firent notre pays: Daniel Tracey (1795–1832)," *Le Nouvelliste* (Trois-Rivières, Qué.), 2 mai 1946: 2. "Le docteur Daniel Tracey," Ovide Lapalice, édit., *BRH*, 33 (1927): 492–93. "MM. Duvernay et Tracey à la prison de Québec," *BRH*, 43 (1937): 86. E. J. Mullaly, "Dr. Daniel Tracey, a pioneer worker for responsible government in Canada," CCHA *Report*, 2 (1934–35): 33–45.

TREMLETT (Trimlett), THOMAS, merchant, office holder, and judge; baptized 5 Jan. 1770 in St Saviour's parish, Dartmouth, England, son of Thomas Tremlett and Hannah Stapeldon; d. unmarried August 1830 in Stoke Fleming, England.

The Tremletts were an old, established, south Devon family. The grandfather of Thomas Tremlett was the collector of customs for the port of Dartmouth, and an uncle was an Anglican clergyman in the same area. Tremlett's father succeeded to the post of collector of customs in 1767, but during the American Revolutionary War quit to go into trade. He sold American-built vessels, olive oil, ship stores, and sundries. After the Treaty of Paris in 1783, the Newfoundland fishery entered a period of feverish expansion, and the Tremletts were among many "new adventurers" who expected great and rapid profits from the trade. They opened stores in St John's and at Little Bay, in the newly settled Fortune Bay. In 1786 they claimed to be supplying 500 people in the neighbourhood and a year later owned eight vessels engaged in the trade between the west of England and Newfoundland. Like many others the Tremletts were caught with over-extended credit in the great crash of 1789 [*see* Peter Ougier*] and in October of that year they were declared insolvent. Their business in Little Bay was liquidated, but young Thomas went to St John's as a small-scale commission merchant. By 1798 the family's business had recovered to some degree: they owned one foreign-trading vessel in that year. By then, however, Thomas's brother Robert had come of age, and the enterprise was probably too small to support all the family.

In 1801, the last year of Benjamin Lester*'s life, control of patronage in Newfoundland seems to have passed from the town of Poole, in Dorset, to Dartmouth. Amongst other appointments Thomas Tremlett secured those of registrar of the Vice-Admiralty Court and deputy naval officer and, in October, the position of chief surrogate for the island of Newfoundland. The post of chief surrogate is easily confused with that of chief justice, but the two were separate. The chief surrogate was basically a justice of the peace, although he had an official salary and powers to hear cases all over the territory within the jurisdiction of the government of Newfoundland. No legal training was expected; indeed, there were no trained lawyers in Newfoundland at this time.

Few new positions were being created in the public administration of England and the same held true for Newfoundland. Vacancies generally depended on the death or retirement of the incumbent, and appointments required the extensive use of political patrons. Newfoundland's climate and situation provided vacancies fairly often. The second chief justice, D'Ewes Coke, chose to resign in 1798 rather than live on the island year-round. His successor, Richard Routh*, was lost at sea on a voyage from England to Newfoundland in 1801 and was succeeded by surgeon Jonathan Ogden. Within a few months Ogden was incapacitated by a stroke. Tremlett happened to be on the spot in the spring of 1803 and as chief surrogate had the best claim to promotion. He was accordingly appointed chief justice on 23 May by Governor James GAMBIER.

Like earlier magistrates, Tremlett was careful to keep the esteem of successive governors, writing lengthy and fulsome letters which combined flattery and assurances that Newfoundland was loyal and law-abiding. However, he was also reluctant to surrender some of his other paid appointments after becoming chief justice, and in 1804 and 1805 he had to be firmly instructed to do so.

By 1809 relations between Tremlett and the merchants of St John's had become strained; indeed, in October the merchants' society petitioned Governor John HOLLOWAY for his removal on grounds of incompetence, partiality, and venality. The charges against him were complex and, as time went on and the conflict deepened, became ever more so. There seems little doubt that Tremlett was technically incompetent: he, like his predecessors, had no legal training whatsoever. He also appears to have been heavily influenced by the officers of the court; however, he does not seem to have been venal. Many of the charges against him stemmed from the fact that his interpretations of law did not favour the mercantile élite, but on at least one point his accusers seem to have been correct: Tremlett had a tendency to interpret his will as the law. For example, in one celebrated case of debt he ordered all charges relating to the purchase of liquor and tobacco to be struck out on the grounds that "such things might do harm." Above all, Tremlett was hostile to creditors in cases of debt and insolvency. This attitude may well have been due to the Tremletts' own earlier insolvency.

In 1810 and 1811 Tremlett's case continued to simmer. The Privy Council committee for trade apparently found no legal grounds on which to remove him. After a full inquiry into three complaints by the merchants against him (which Tremlett had answered by writing: "To the first charge . . . I answer that it is a lie, to the second charge, I say, that it is a damned lie, and to the third charge it is a damned infernal lie"), the committee reported that he had not behaved unjustly or with partiality, but was at worst guilty of an "ungracious manner." However, given his continuing unpopularity in St John's and his evident want of judgement, something had to be done. In 1813 the British government thought that a solution had been found. On Prince Edward Island, Chief Justice Cæsar COLCLOUGH was similarly unpopular, and it was decided that Newfoundland could have Colclough, and Prince Edward Island, Tremlett, in fair exchange.

Colclough had become unpopular with a faction of the Prince Edward Island House of Assembly connected with Lieutenant Governor Joseph Frederick Wallet DESBARRES, chiefly as a result of his opposition to the Loyal Electors, a nascent political party. But he had many friends and supporters on the Island. Tremlett, who was appointed on 6 April 1813, rapidly succeeded in alienating virtually everyone of importance, first the new lieutenant governor, Charles Douglass Smith*, and soon the leading proprietors, much of the legal profession, and even ordinary freeholders called to jury duty at the only site of the Supreme Court, Charlottetown. His problems were both political and judicial.

Tremlett exasperated Smith, who was ever fearful of continuation of the levelling "demagoguery" of the Loyal Electors, led by James Bardin PALMER. From the lieutenant governor's perspective, the chief justice was entirely too sympathetic to the lawyer Palmer; Tremlett even adjourned his session of the court in 1814 from day to day to permit Palmer to pursue his

practice in Nova Scotia. Smith's immediate response was to protest privately to timber merchant John Hill* that it "would not be safe to suffer any question of Property to be tried in the Supreme Court against Palmer" with Tremlett on the bench. Palmer, admittedly the most proficient and learned lawyer on the Island, was in Smith's judgement too overwhelming for a chief justice who was "at a loss as to the Practice of Courts." Attorney General William JOHNSTON added that Tremlett was incredibly slow in trials, "which I suppose must arise from his never having practised or presided in a court of common law – Points of practice are to him matters of greater difficulty than even points of law." The chief justice was, moreover, accused of refusing to accept crown challenges of jurors regarded as sympathetic towards the Loyal Electors and of treating offenders too leniently. Part of Tremlett's difficulty was his tendency to approach cases as informally as he had in Newfoundland. He personally transcribed the testimony of each witness, and on at least one occasion had the temerity to suggest that the litigants settle their differences amicably by shaking hands and forgetting about their petty grievances.

By the summer of 1815 Smith was complaining to the Colonial Office itself about Tremlett. He denied any personal differences but added, "*I never can feel safe with him in my Council*, he universally hangs back about every thing, his sympathies are all with the lower orders, & Palmer can make him do any thing, except absolutely commit himself with me." Tremlett and George Wright* were regarded as Palmer's agents on the Council; assistant judge James Curtis* usually sided with Tremlett on the court, to the point where assistant judge Robert GRAY refused to attend. When Smith attempted to regularize (and reduce) the fee schedule for lawyers, Tremlett refused to make the lieutenant governor's proclamation of fees retroactive. This action should have pleased the Island's legal fraternity, but most members were too upset with the chief justice's wholesale rejection of "the most weighty authorities" in their pleading. John Hill added a complaint that Tremlett had been involved in an attempt to seize and condemn one of his vessels which the customs people claimed had been engaged in transporting timber illegally obtained. Tremlett further incurred the wrath of the Island administration by refusing to back attempts to enforce militia service through the courts. Correspondence to the Colonial Office became a constant litany of criticism of Tremlett and insistence on his removal. Smith even argued in 1817 that he could not convene the House of Assembly while both Palmer and Tremlett were on the Island; by this time Palmer was openly talking about Catholic emancipation and free land for tenants. Palmer's departure from the Island produced a satisfactory legislative session in 1817, although Smith subsequently dissolved this relatively friendly assembly.

The assembly that met in November of 1818 was hardly one sympathetic to Smith, much of the electorate having been worked up over his efforts to impose escheat and collect quitrent arrearages, especially from resident proprietors. In these endeavours Smith now had the support of Palmer. Not surprisingly, the legislators also turned against Chief Justice Tremlett, passing a series of 13 resolutions critical of his administration of justice. Smith's reply was to label the charges "as unjust as they were intemperate" and to refuse demands for Tremlett's suspension. Privately, the lieutenant governor admitted that complaints about the slowness of proceedings in the Supreme Court, which kept jurors and litigants for months in Charlottetown away from their farms, were legitimate points. But Tremlett had enforced the collection of quitrents in conformity to the law, and Smith had no complaints on this score. He supported Tremlett again in 1820.

Between 1818 and 1824 Smith, Tremlett, and Palmer appear to have reached some understanding. Smith ceased demanding Tremlett's removal and the chief justice appeared ready to enforce the law, especially regarding the quitrents. When Island unrest with Smith's administration, led by John STEWART and John Hill, finally reached the breaking point in 1823 and 1824, Tremlett was included in the condemnations. Petitions from each county in the Island complained of the long maladministration of justice by Tremlett; the one from Queens County observed that the chief justice "certainly enjoys less of the consideration and respect of his fellow-subjects than any other person that ever yet held his important office in the Colony." Tremlett was swiftly removed from his post in the clean sweep of 1824 made by the Colonial Office. Samuel George William Archibald* was named to replace him.

The expressions of popular discontent with Tremlett ought not to be exaggerated. The complaints that produced his dismissal were carefully orchestrated and came mainly from the professional and propertied classes of the Island. The length of court sittings was perhaps the most serious legitimate grievance, but objectionable too was the fact that the court sat only in Charlottetown, and this arrangement was not entirely Tremlett's responsibility. He had attempted to administer justice instead of law, and in the process he alienated most elements of Island society that mattered. As Smith himself put it, Tremlett's errors were "of the head" rather than of the heart.

Tremlett remained in Charlottetown through 1825 memorializing the government for back salary, but eventually retired to Devon, where he died in 1830 at the age of 62. He was buried in St Saviour's parish cemetery on 10 August.

J. M. BUMSTED and K. MATTHEWS

Much of the information concerning Tremlett's family in Devon and his Newfoundland career was drawn from the Tremlett name file and other copies of records relating to the trade and fisheries of Newfoundland available at the Maritime Hist. Arch., Memorial Univ. of Nfld. (St John's).

Devon Record Office (Exeter, Eng.), 2992 A (St Saviour, Dartmouth), reg. of baptisms, marriages, and burials, 22 April 1767, 5 Jan. 1770, August 1830. Hunt, Roope & Co. (London), Robert Newman & Co., ledgers and letter-books (mfm. at PANL). PANL, GN 2/1, 1801–13; GN 5/2/A/1, 1803–13. PAPEI, Acc. 2810/171. PRO, ADM 7; BT 6; CO 194/43–54 (copies at Maritime Hist. Arch.); CO 226/30–32; 226/41–42 (mfm. at PAPEI); CUST 65/33; E 190 (copies at Maritime Hist. Arch.). P.E.I., House of Assembly, *Journal*, 8 Dec. 1818. *Royal Gazette* (Charlottetown), 16 Nov. 1830. *Royal Gazette and Newfoundland Advertiser*, 1807–13. *Sherborne Mercury or the Weekly Magazine* (Sherborne, Eng.). *Trewman's Exeter Flying Post, or Plymouth and Cornish Advertiser* (Exeter). *The register of shipping* (London). Warburton, *Hist. of P.E.I.*, 324–25, 435.

TROTTIER DESRIVIÈRES, FRANÇOIS. *See* DESRIVIÈRES

TRULLIER, *dit* **Lacombe, JACQUES,** businessman, JP, militia officer, and politician; b. *c.* 1763, probably in Boucherville, Que., son of Jacques Trullier, *dit* Lacombe, and Marie-Anne Levasseur; m. 28 July 1788 Angélique Laurent, daughter of merchant Silvain Laurent, *dit* Bérichon, in Montreal, and they had four children; d. 5 Dec. 1821 in L'Assomption, Lower Canada.

Little is known about the youth of Jacques Trullier, *dit* Lacombe. He apparently studied and lived in Montreal, since in 1785 he was one of those who signed a petition aimed at exposing the misuse of statute labour in that town. Some time between 1788 and 1794 he settled in L'Assomption as a merchant. Around 1798 he bought a two-storey warehouse and from it carried on a trade in grain, which he shipped to Montreal via the Rivière L'Assomption, and an enterprise producing potash. In addition he and Laurent Leroux* had jointly received from the North West Company a monopoly on the manufacture and sale of sashes with an arrow design, a major activity in the region around L'Assomption. As a sideline to trading, he had ten or so houses built after 1815 and ran an inn. When he died, his enterprises were taken over by Urgel Archambault.

Trullier, *dit* Lacombe, had been named a justice of the peace for the District of Montreal in 1810, and during the War of 1812 he held the rank of major in the Lavaltrie battalion of militia. Having already shown his acceptance of the 1791 constitution and his sympathies for the Canadian party, he decided to go into politics; his career in this field was a highly chequered one. Although he received a majority in Leinster riding in 1814, his election was contested by Barthélemy Joliette*, who had also been a candidate;

Joliette accused him of having threatened to sue his debtors if they did not vote for him and of having bought some votes. The complaint was brought before the House of Assembly, which decided to have an investigation. On 15 Feb. 1815 a commission chaired by Louis-René CHAUSSEGROS de Léry, and including Jean-Marie Mondelet* and Jean-Philippe Leprohon, heard the witnesses at the presbytery in the parish of Saint-Pierre-du-Portage (Assomption-de-la-Sainte-Vierge) at L'Assomption. On 21 March the commissioners "satisfactorily proved to the House, that Jacques Lacombe, Esquire, did at his own cost and expense open and keep up, and did cause to be opened and kept up a House of Public Entertainment" during the elections. On that account he was declared disqualified to sit in the assembly and had to pay Joliette 181 *livres* expenses. His seat was taken by Michel Prévost on 10 June 1815. He returned to political life, however, securing election in the same riding in 1816, and he remained a member until his death. Even though elections were frequently contested at the time, Lacombe was the first Lower Canadian politician to lose his seat on such a charge.

Jacques Trullier, *dit* Lacombe, who was considered by his contemporaries to be a rich merchant, understood how to turn to account the economic and geographical advantages of his region, which was experiencing the stimulus of the intense trading activity going on in Montreal. He was active in his own milieu and he promoted the growth of L'Assomption by building houses. On three occasions, in 1806, 1811, and 1812, he petitioned for the construction of a toll-bridge over the Rivière L'Assomption. It would be interesting to pursue study of his career to bring out the relations that could develop between the Canadian merchants in an outlying region and the Montreal firms involved in trade with Great Britain, and then to judge the means open to these merchants of attaining freedom from their narrow local beginnings.

MARTIN ROCHEFORT

ANQ-M, CE1-51, 27 juill. 1788; CE5-14, 7 déc. 1821; CN1-158, 28 juill. 1788. L.C., House of Assembly, *Journals*, 1807, 1815–22. *Quebec Gazette*, 19 May 1785, 22 Jan. 1789, 19 June 1794, 9 May 1811, 26 March 1812. F.-J. Audet, "Les législateurs du Bas-Canada." *Officers of British forces in Canada* (Irving). Raymond Boyer, *Les crimes et les châtiments au Canada français du XVIIe au XXe siècle* (Montréal, 1966), 383. Marcel Fournier, *La représentation parlementaire de la région de Joliette* (Joliette, Qué., 1977). Pierre Poulin, *Légendes du portage*, Réjean Olivier, édit. (L'Assomption, Qué., 1975). Christian Roy, *Histoire de L'Assomption* (L'Assomption, 1967).

TURGEON, LOUIS, notary, JP, politician, militia officer, and seigneur; b. 10 April 1762 in Beaumont, Que., son of Louis Turgeon, a merchant, and Marie-Françoise Couillard; m. there 23 Nov. 1796 his cousin Geneviève Turgeon, and they had four children; d. 26 Sept. 1827 in Saint-Charles, Lower Canada.

Louis Turgeon belonged to the fourth generation of a family living at Beaumont since the late 17th century. Shortly after he was born his father moved to Quebec. Louis attended the Petit Séminaire de Québec, as did his half-brother Pierre-Flavien* subsequently. He studied there from 1772 till 1782, and then articled to become a notary. Licensed to practise on 25 Sept. 1792, he opened an office near Quebec, at Saint-Charles, the place from which he would draw most of his clients, who were largely farmers.

Even during his years of notarial training Turgeon had taken an interest in the political life of the province. In 1790, for example, he had signed a petition for a non-sectarian university [*see* Jean-François Hubert*], and in 1791 he had come out against a plan to replace seigneurial tenure with free and common socage [*see* Thomas-Laurent Bédard*]. In 1804 he was elected to the Lower Canadian House of Assembly for Hertford, along with Étienne-Féréol Roy. Turgeon was an assiduous member and took part in most crucial debates in the fourth parliament, which lasted from 1804 to 1808. As a general rule he supported the Canadian party. In addition he participated, often as chairman, in committees dealing with such varied matters as the organization of the militia, navigation on the St Lawrence, assembly accounts, fisheries in the district of Gaspé, road works, the administration of justice, and weights and measures. In 1805 he introduced a bill that was passed prohibiting the sale of goods and alcoholic beverages on Sundays.

Turgeon ran again in Hertford in the 1809 election but was defeated by physician François BLANCHET. His retirement from political life was temporary, since he was returned for that riding in the 1816 election. His parliamentary activity was, however, limited to sitting on a few unimportant committees. He quit the assembly in 1818 on his appointment to the Legislative Council.

In the uneasy year of 1794 Turgeon had signed a declaration of loyalty to the crown. He had received a commission as justice of the peace for the district of Quebec that year, and obtained similar commissions for the districts of Montreal, Trois-Rivières, and Saint-François in 1821, and for Gaspé in 1824. On 8 April 1812 he attained the rank of major in the Saint-Vallier battalion of militia. He served in the War of 1812 and in 1821 became lieutenant-colonel of the 1st Saint-Vallier battalion.

Turgeon had inherited part of the seigneury of Beaumont through his mother, who had died in 1768, and as a result of various transactions between 1816 and 1819 he became the principal seigneur. He personally managed his fief, which, by the time he took possession, had been almost entirely granted out, and he saw to it that the domain reserved to him as

Twiss

seigneur made a profit. In 1819 he was the agent in the parish of Saint-Charles for the Quebec District Agriculture Society.

Louis Turgeon had four children. His sons, Louis, who died in 1826, and Hubert, became notaries. One of his daughters, Geneviève, died in 1818; the other, Marie-Ermine, married the Patriote Louis-Michel Viger*. When he died in 1827, Turgeon, who was by then a widower, left the seigneury of Beaumont to his son Hubert's first male heir. Hubert, however, had the right of possession and also inherited Turgeon's other real and personal property, but he died the following year. Marie-Ermine received £3,000.

CÉLINE CYR

Louis Turgeon's minute-book, which contains 5,426 instruments notarized between 1792 and 1826, is kept at ANQ-Q, CN2-46.

AC, Québec, Holograph will of Louis Turgeon, 22 déc. 1827 (see P.-G. Roy, Inv. testaments, 3: 148). ANQ-Q, CE1-4, 10 avril 1762, 23 nov. 1796; CE2-4, 4 mars 1818, 13 juill. 1826, 29 sept. 1827, 18 juill. 1828; CN1-230, 25 juill. 1793, 27 mars 1795, 4 juill. 1816. ASQ, Fichier des anciens. PAC, RG 68, General index, 1651–1841. L.C., House of Assembly, Journals, 1805–9, 1817. Quebec Gazette, 4 Nov. 1790; 24 March 1791; 27 Sept. 1792; 3, 10 July 1794; 27 Dec. 1804; 2 June 1808; 20 April 1809; 22 Feb. 1810; 27 April 1812; 23 Feb. 1815; 16 May 1816; 5 March 1818; 8 April 1819; 7 Sept. 1820; 7 June 1821. F.-J. Audet, "Les législateurs du Bas-Canada." Desjardins, Guide parl., 129–30. Officers of British forces in Canada (Irving), 147–48. Turcotte, Le Conseil législatif, 93. P.-G. Roy, À travers l'histoire de Beaumont (Lévis, Qué., 1943), 35–38. "L'honorable Louis Turgeon," BRH, 34 (1928): 255.

TWISS, WILLIAM, army officer and military engineer; b. 1745; m. and had one daughter; d. 14 March 1827 at his residence, Harden Grange (West Yorkshire), England.

William Twiss entered the Ordnance department in 1760, and two years later was appointed overseer of works at Gibraltar. At the end of the Seven Years' War he was commissioned ensign in the engineers; on promotion to lieutenant in 1771, he returned to England and was employed on the fortifications for the Portsmouth dockyards from 1772 to 1775.

In early June 1776 31-year-old Twiss arrived at Quebec and was named aide-de-camp to Colonel William Phillips, under the command of Major-General John Burgoyne*. He spent most of that month in the campaign to force the Americans out of the province of Quebec. Shortly afterwards, Guy Carleton*, commander-in-chief of the British forces in the colony, appointed him controller of works for the building of a British fleet for Lake Champlain. Although John SCHANK was named superintendent of the dockyards at St Johns (Saint-Jean-sur-Richelieu), Twiss was responsible for their preparation; he also supervised the construction of 12 single-gun artillery boats and the building of launching slips for the large vessels that were brought overland. In October the fleet engaged and defeated an American flotilla under the command of Benedict Arnold*, thus securing the major north-south invasion route. Carleton noted that several junior officers, including Twiss, deserved "particular distinction" for the success of the operation.

In the spring of 1777 Burgoyne began his march from Quebec towards Albany, N.Y. Twiss was the senior and commanding engineer for the expedition; he took an important part in the capture of Fort Ticonderoga (near Ticonderoga, N.Y.) and was with Burgoyne's army when it surrendered in October 1777. Exchanged within a few days, he returned to Quebec. A year later he was promoted captain.

Carleton's successor as commander-in-chief, Frederick Haldimand*, held a high opinion of Twiss's "zeal" and "activity." In 1778 he explained to the master general of Ordnance, Lord Townshend*, that Carleton had stationed the senior engineer in the province, the aged and infirm John Marr, at Quebec and had placed all other military works under Twiss's direction. Haldimand was not attentive to Marr's protests and asked that Twiss be appointed chief engineer, a request which was only fulfilled on Marr's departure in 1781. Also in 1778 the commander-in-chief advised Lord George Germain, secretary of state for the American colonies, that work under Twiss's direction "is performed with great judgement and economy," and that he had "confidence in his [Twiss's] abilities and integrity." The comment in 1781 by Major-General Friedrich Adolph von Riedesel, commander of the German troops, that Twiss "has solved questions which seemed impossible" also suggests the growing trust senior officers had in his talents.

In August 1778 Haldimand instructed Twiss to select a site for, and oversee the construction of, a naval establishment in the vicinity of Cataraqui (Kingston, Ont.). With the assistance of Schank, Twiss chose Buck Island (N.Y.), which he renamed Carleton Island, as the site for a fort to be called Fort Haldimand. On Haldimand's orders, he returned to Montreal and left James Glenie* to oversee construction. The post, established to protect the supply routes to the west, was one of the most vital sites in the province between 1778 and 1783. In 1779 Haldimand called on Twiss to superintend a major work of military construction, a small fortified canal at Coteau-du-Lac, Que., to circumvent the rough water of the St Lawrence between Montreal and Point Maligne (Cornwall, Ont.) and thus improve communications with the interior. By the end of the year Twiss had completed the task. He wrote to Haldimand in 1780 that "it will be formed into Locks as useful to navigation as any in the world." From 1781 to 1783 he periodically inspected further improvements to navigation on the St Lawrence such as the canals at Les Cèdres and the Cascades (near Île des Cascades).

During the years 1777–83 Twiss was also engaged in a wide variety of works at important points (among them, Quebec, Sorel, Île aux Noix, St Johns, and Montreal) involving hospitals, windmills, storehouses, barracks, fortifications, roads, bridges, prisons, ironworks, dams, and bakeries; he was involved as well in plans for various posts throughout the province. In 1778 he reported to Haldimand on proposals for a permanent citadel at Quebec, but advised that it could not be completed in less than 12 to 15 years because of many problems, including the climate and the attitude of the local labour force. He explained that, "as every Canadian has his own House and Farm, it cannot be expected that he will attend the Publick Works with the same constancy, as Artificers, and Labourers do, who have only their Labour to depend on." Nevertheless, acting on orders from London, Haldimand asked Twiss to supervise the erection of a temporary citadel, construction of which began in 1779.

In October 1783, after the signing of the Treaty of Paris, William Twiss sailed for England. He had been 23 years in the service of the engineers, seven of which had been in North America during the swirl of the American revolution. From 1794 to 1810 he served as lieutenant governor of the Royal Military Academy at Woolwich (London). He was ordered to Holland in 1799 as the commanding engineer under the Duke of York, until the British evacuation was completed. In 1802 he became a colonel in the corps

and was sent to report on the defences of Ireland. He spent the greater part of the next few years engaged on more defence works, especially along the English coast. He was appointed colonel commandant of the Royal Engineers in 1809. The following year, after a service of 50 years, he retired from active duty. Not yet ready to seek complete retirement, he acted in 1811 as a member of a committee on major defence works then in progress. Promoted lieutenant-general in 1812 and general in 1825, he died in 1827, aged 82. At his death there was only one officer in the Royal Engineers with greater seniority, his successor as commanding engineer in Quebec, Gother MANN.

JOHN C. KENDALL

BL, Add. MSS 21674; 21814: ff.2–475. J. M. Hadden, *Hadden's journal and orderly books: a journal kept in Canada and upon Burgoyne's campaign in 1776 and 1777, by Lieut. James M. Hadden* . . . , ed. Horatio Rogers (Albany, N.Y., 1884; repr. Freeport, N.Y., [1970]). *Kingston before War of 1812* (Preston). [F. A. von] Riedesel, *Memoirs, and letters and journals of Major General Riedesel, during his residence in America*, ed. Max von Eelking, trans. W. L. Stone (2v., Albany, 1868). *DNB*. Harrison Bird, *Navies in the mountains: the battles on the waters of Lake Champlain and Lake George, 1609–1814* (New York, 1962). Whitworth Porter *et al.*, *History of the Corps of Royal Engineers* (9v. to date, London and Chatham, Eng., 1889– ; repr. vols.1–3, Chatham, 1951–54), 1. C. C. J. Bond, "The British base at Carleton Island," *OH*, 52 (1960): 1–30. J. C. Kendall, "William Twiss: royal engineer," *Duquesne Rev.* (Pittsburgh, Pa.), 15 (1970), no.1: 175–91.

TYHORIHOGA. *See* TEKARIHOGEN (Henry)

U

UNIACKE, RICHARD JOHN, lawyer, office holder, and politician; b. 22 Nov. 1753 in Castletownroche (Republic of Ireland), fourth son of Norman Uniacke and Alicia Purdon; m. first 3 May 1775 Martha Maria Delesdernier in Hopewell Township (N.B.), and they had six sons, including Norman Fitzgerald*, RICHARD JOHN, Robert Fitzgerald*, and James Boyle*, and six daughters; m. secondly 14 Jan. 1808 Eliza Newton in Halifax, and they had one son; d. 11 Oct. 1830 in Mount Uniacke, N.S.

As Roman Catholics, the Uniackes had suffered much repression during the periods of Tudor and Cromwellian rule in Ireland, but by the early 1700s they had become staunch Protestants and adherents to the British crown with powerful patrons. After going to school at Lismore, Richard John was articled to a

Dublin attorney, since his father had become alarmed by his son's increasing preference for the teachings of the local Catholic priest. In Dublin Uniacke seems to have taken part in political agitation probably related to the cause of Catholic relief, and so crossed his father that the young man "in passion" left home "to seek his fortune in the New World." First going to the West Indies, he arrived in Philadelphia in the summer of 1774 and formed a partnership with Moses Delesdernier*, a trader from Nova Scotia. After a dangerous voyage they arrived at Hopewell Township on the Petitcodiac River (N.B.), where Delesdernier became agent for the proprietors. In May 1775 Uniacke married Delesdernier's 12-year-old daughter, Martha Maria. He was to remain devoted to her until her death in 1803.

Uniacke

The extent of Uniacke's involvement on the rebel side of the uprising led by Jonathan Eddy* on the Chignecto Isthmus during the autumn of 1776 is difficult to determine. He was certainly initially sympathetic but seems to have supported the rebels out of fear of reprisals. Late in the year he was arrested and sent to Halifax to be tried for treason but was released, probably through the influence of Irish officers in the garrison and local officials who knew his family. In 1777 he embarked for Ireland to finish his legal studies. On 22 June 1779 he was admitted as attorney of King's Inns, Dublin, and after his return to Nova Scotia he was admitted to the bar on 3 April 1781. His Irish connections had secured him an interview in 1780 with Lord George Germain, secretary of state for the American colonies, who promised him the attorney generalship of Nova Scotia upon the first vacancy. One occurred in late 1781, but the position went to the more senior Richard Gibbons*, and Uniacke was appointed solicitor general on 27 Dec. 1781. He was elected to the House of Assembly in 1783 for Sackville Township.

Uniacke's prospects looked excellent, but the arrival of the loyalists forced him to fight for his professional survival. The attorney generalship became vacant in 1784, but he was again passed over, this time in favour of the loyalist Sampson Salter Blowers*. However, thanks to his friend and patron, Governor John Parr*, he was made advocate general of the Vice-Admiralty Court the same year. In the assembly Uniacke became the leader of the pre-loyalists in their struggle with the loyalists to obtain patronage, and he became speaker in 1789. Parr died two years later, and a loyalist, John Wentworth*, became lieutenant governor. Wentworth's appointment, the antipathy of the chief justice, Thomas Andrew Lumisden Strange*, and the enmity of prominent loyalists such as Blowers and Thomas Henry BARCLAY combined to exclude Uniacke from government and influence, and he declined to run in the 1793 elections. During the 1790s Uniacke clashed with Wentworth on several issues, once in connection with arrangements to defend Halifax against a threatened French attack. Wentworth responded by using his private correspondence with British officials to describe Uniacke's conduct as "dark and insidious secretly connected with seditious purposes."

When Strange resigned in 1797 it was accepted that Attorney General Blowers would succeed him. The loyalists were determined that Uniacke should never become attorney general, and Wentworth recommended that Jonathan Sterns, another loyalist and Blowers's protégé, receive the position. Uniacke appealed to the home secretary, the Duke of Portland, claiming that he should succeed by seniority and citing his family's patrons, one of whom was Portland's brother-in-law. Portland appointed Uniacke attorney general on 9 September (the date on which Blowers became chief justice) and administered to Wentworth one of the sharpest rebukes to a Nova Scotian governor on record. The bitterness between Uniacke and Sterns was deep, and after Uniacke had severely beaten Sterns in a street fight Blowers challenged Uniacke to a duel. Blowers and Uniacke were bound over to keep the peace but the enmity between them was to last until Uniacke's death.

Now more secure in his position, Uniacke reentered the assembly in 1798 for Queens County and the next year became speaker, a position he held until he retired in 1805. In that year he published a compilation of Nova Scotian statutes between 1758 and 1804, commonly known as Uniacke's laws and the standard reference work until 1851. While speaker he resisted Wentworth's attempts to challenge the assembly's right to supervise the provincial finances, and he worked to bring about Wentworth's downfall by castigating the lieutenant governor and his appointments in communications with Lord Castlereagh, the colonial secretary. Although Wentworth had recommended him, Uniacke refused to become a member of Wentworth's Council, and he was not appointed until 1808, after Wentworth had been replaced by Sir George Prevost*. For two decades after that date he was to occupy an extremely influential position in the government of Nova Scotia.

Uniacke's constitutional thinking had been moulded by his study of Sir William Blackstone's *Commentaries on the laws of England*, and it was rooted firmly in the 18th century. He wanted provincial governments to follow the model envisaged by the 18th-century British constitution, in which the fundamental principle was the balance of powers between the crown, lords, and commons and in which, he believed, the executive and legislature each had their own clear-cut functions. Uniacke ignored the changes in his lifetime which led to the executive becoming responsible to parliament; according to him, all public officials answered only to the king. His attitude was also much influenced by the excesses of the French revolutionaries, who he believed had attempted to "destroy the principles of true religion and . . . subvert the rules of civil government." In the 1820s he expressed fears that the revolutionary "heresies" of atheism and democracy spreading to the "hoards of semi-barbarians" in the south and west of the United States would engulf New England and then British North America.

To avert such a catastrophe, Uniacke advocated unions of the Maritime colonies and of the Canadas, beginning in 1806 when he presented a memoir on British North America at the Colonial Office. By 1821, however, he had concluded that only a general union would save the colonies from republicanism, atheism, and democracy, and in 1822 the introduction in the British parliament of a bill to bring about the union of the Canadas spurred him to propose a general union to Frederick John Robinson, president of the Privy Council committee for trade. Others in British North America such as Jonathan Sewell*, John Beverley Robinson*, and John Strachan* were also interested in a general union, although not always for the same reasons, and several such proposals arrived in London about this time. In 1826 Uniacke brought his "Observations on the British colonies in North America with a proposal for the confederation of the whole under one government" to the Colonial Office. The "Observations" read in parts like the British North America Act of 40 years later, and were at once the most persuasive of the various schemes and the last attempt to bring about new intercolonial arrangements until the 1839 report of Lord Durham [Lambton*]. By 1826 proposals for any sort of union were not regarded with much favour in Britain, and the "Observations" were never printed, although Uniacke's son James Boyle gave a copy to Durham.

Uniacke understood with greater prescience than any other British North American of his day that the British government would have to accept a substantial increase in colonial self-government if it allowed the colonies the commercial freedom he considered essential. For more than 30 years he struggled for what he called "the grand principle of free trade," by which he meant the removal of those laws that prevented the colonies from trading wherever and in whatever they wished. From the early 1790s he wanted free ports opened in Nova Scotia so that the province could become an entrepôt for British, West Indian, and American goods. His relationship with the Halifax merchants was close and on several occasions they turned to him as the Nova Scotian most capable of putting their case to the British government. The joint report of the assembly and Council which criticized the Convention of 1818 between Britain and the United States was mostly drafted by him and comes alive with his pungent and forceful language. In it he stated that Britain "must strengthen her colonies in North America . . . to enable them to stand by her side with effect, when the struggle for which the United States are manifestly preparing shall take place."

The least edifying aspect of Uniacke's public career was his opposition to any diminution of the role of the Church of England as the established church in Nova Scotia. As a youth he was attracted to the Anglican ministry, but rebelled against the "insatiable rapacity" of its servants. In the 1780s and 1790s he was a member of Mather's (St Matthew's), the dissenting church in Halifax, and it was not until 1801, for reasons still unknown, that he began to pay pew rents at St Paul's Anglican Church. After that date, however, he became a leading member of the extreme wing of the church and state party. Convinced that an established church was a necessity if Christian civilization was to triumph in its struggle against what he considered the revolutionary heresies of his day, he was utterly intransigent in his opinion that the Church of England was a bulwark of the British constitution. No one fought as hard as Uniacke to stop the secessionist Presbyterians led by Thomas McCulloch* from turning Pictou Academy into a college, and as principal law officer he drafted the restrictive charter of the academy in 1820. His opposition in 1819 to the otherwise almost unanimous consent of the assembly and Council to a bill granting dissenting ministers the right to marry by licence was most clearly expressed when he declared that "no good government can long exist without an established religion . . . and if such a bill should pass into law the final overthrow of the church must soon follow and with it the constitution of our fathers must perish."

Despite these extreme opinions, Uniacke was not intolerant of other religious beliefs, and in the 1820s he was one of the foremost leaders in the struggle for Catholic emancipation in Nova Scotia. At the same time, he was sometimes conciliatory in matters which affected the established church. It was Uniacke who, during a visit to England in 1806, was able to influence the archbishop of Canterbury and the British government to require subscription to the Thirty-Nine Articles from students at King's College only upon graduation and not on entrance. However, other members of the board of governors of the college conspired to enforce subscription upon entrance.

Uniacke made a substantial fortune, amassed mainly from his fees as advocate general of the Vice-Admiralty Court during the Napoleonic Wars and the War of 1812. This wealth he spent on the education of his 12 surviving children, a large town house in Halifax, and his country home, Mount Uniacke. The Mount, completed by 1815, was built 25 miles northwest of Halifax on an estate of 11,000 acres. It symbolized his triumph over the vicissitudes of life in the New World and his faith in Nova Scotia as the home for his children. Later generations remembered as grand and remarkable the sight of Uniacke and his six sons, all of whom were over six feet tall, walking through the streets of Halifax.

Uniacke's politics may best be described as those of a moderate tory in his constitutional views and an extreme tory when it came to church and state. His was not, however, a conservatism that simply defended the status quo. The fetters that bound colonial trading had to be removed, the colonial constitutions changed radically, and a great colonial union created; only with the adoption of these measures could British North America survive the onslaught he long feared.

Contemporaries remembered Uniacke mostly for the sheer force of his character and his exuberance. He loved life, and family and friendships were essential to his existence. His was a personality of exaggerations and his judgements of men and events were sometimes clouded by raw emotion. He was ambitious for himself and his children, and although his ambitions

Uniacke

were never entirely fulfilled, he achieved more than most men. Mount Uniacke is today a historic house open to the public, where the personality of a "remarkable and extraordinary man" still lives.

B. C. CUTHBERTSON

PAC, MG 11, [CO 217] Nova Scotia A, 96–171; MG 23, C6. PANS, MG 1, 926–27; 1769, no.42; RG 1, 192–95, 218W–XX, 222–36, 286–91. PRO, CO 217/59–160; CO 218/7–30 (mfm. at PANS). SRO, GD45 (mfm. at PAC). N.S., House of Assembly, *Journal and proc.*, 1781–1830. B. [C. U.] Cuthbertson, *The old attorney general; a biography of Richard John Uniacke* (Halifax, [1980]). "Trials for treason in 1776–7," ed. J. T. Bulmer, N.S. Hist. Soc., *Coll.*, 1 (1879): 110–18. R. G. Fitzgerald-Uniacke, "Some old County Cork families: the Uniackes of Youghal," Cork Hist. & Archaeological Soc., *Journal* (Cork, [Republic of Ire.]), 3 (1894), nos.30–31, 33–36. Murdoch, *Hist. of N.S.*, vol.3. L. G. Power, "Richard John Uniacke," N.S. Hist. Soc., *Coll.*, 9 (1895): 73–118.

UNIACKE, RICHARD JOHN, lawyer, politician, office holder, and judge; b. 6 June 1789 in Halifax, third son of Richard John UNIACKE and Martha Maria Delesdernier; m. there 29 Dec. 1821 Mary Ann Hill, daughter of Charles HILL, and they had two sons and two daughters; d. there 21 Feb. 1834.

After graduating from King's College, Windsor, Richard John Uniacke studied law and was admitted to the Nova Scotia bar on 25 July 1810. Hoping to improve his prospects, in 1813 he went to Cape Breton. That colony's administrator, Major-General Hugh Swayne*, had fallen out with his attorney general, Richard Collier Bernard DesBarres Marshall Gibbons, and being acquainted with the Uniacke family he readily accepted the recommendation of Uniacke by the lieutenant governor of Nova Scotia, Sir John Coape SHERBROOKE. Uniacke was appointed to the Executive Council on 6 December, made acting attorney general (confirmed in March 1814), and became Swayne's private secretary. From January 1815 to September 1816 he was acting chief justice, but the reinstatement of Archibald Charles DODD precluded his confirmation in this post. The fees and salary of the attorney generalship did not meet his expectations, and even his father's influence could not obtain him another appointment. He therefore returned to Halifax to practise law, having resigned his council seat on 18 Oct. 1816 and the attorney generalship in September 1817. On 22 Oct. 1819 he succeeded his father as advocate general of the Vice-Admiralty Court in Halifax.

Three months earlier Uniacke had fought the last fatal duel on record in Nova Scotia with merchant William Bowie. The quarrel had begun during a court case in which Uniacke apparently imputed smuggling to Bowie. Much of the blame for the outcome has been attributed to Uniacke's second, Edward McSweeny, who apparently insisted that the duellists fire a second time after neither had been hit during the first exchange. In the second round Bowie was mortally wounded. Uniacke and McSweeny were charged with murder but were acquitted.

Uniacke was elected to the House of Assembly as one of the two members for Cape Breton in 1820 after it was reunited to Nova Scotia. The other was Laurence KAVANAGH, a Roman Catholic, and Uniacke was active in the successful attempt to allow Kavanagh to take his seat without making a declaration against transubstantiation as required in the state oath. Although a leader for Catholic emancipation, Uniacke was less accommodating towards the Presbyterians. While on a visit to Pictou Academy in 1826 [*see* Thomas McCulloch*] he apparently left the impression that he supported a permanent annual grant to the institution. However, in the 1828 session of the assembly he opposed a bill for that purpose, claiming that the academy's charter had not been fulfilled and that such a grant would bring similar demands from other parts of the province. His stand drew the wrath of the Pictou *Colonial Patriot*, which described him as "interlarding his insipid harangues with . . . undeserved [insults]."

While a member of the assembly, Uniacke generally supported the Council in disputes over customs fees and bank bills. During the "Brandy Dispute" of 1830 [*see* Enos Collins*] he was one of three assemblymen to uphold the right of the Council to reject money bills. He did, however, side with the majority in the assembly in opposing a proposal for a bank in 1825, and in 1827 he supported the right of dissenters to be married by licence according to their own rites.

Made a KC on 17 March 1824, Uniacke became on 13 April 1830 the first native Nova Scotian to be appointed a puisne judge of the Supreme Court, after the more senior Samuel George William Archibald* had refused the post. In 1833 he tried two men and a woman for the murder of the woman's husband and sentenced them to be hanged. He supposedly became very melancholy, perhaps remembering his own involvement with a charge of murder, and after a short illness he died the next year at the age of 44.

B. C. CUTHBERTSON

PAC, MG 11, [CO 217] Nova Scotia A, 152, 155, 172; MG 24, A5. PANS, MG 1, 926; MG 20, 65; RG 1, 62, 114, 173, 215, 289, 322. N.S., House of Assembly, *Journal and proc.*, 1820–30. *Acadian Recorder. Colonial Patriot* (Pictou, N.S.). *Novascotian, or Colonial Herald.* B. [C. U.] Cuthbertson, *The old attorney general: a biography of Richard John Uniacke* (Halifax, [1980]). John Garner, "The enfranchisement of Roman Catholics in the Maritimes," *CHR*, 34 (1953): 203–18.

V

VAN BUSKIRK, JACOB, merchant, office holder, JP, judge, militia officer, and politician; b. 1760 in Bergen County, N.J., son of Dr Abraham Van Buskirk and Sophia Van Dam; m. 22 Feb. 1790 Sarah Breen in Shelburne, N.S., and they had one son and two daughters; d. 27 Nov. 1834 in Yarmouth, N.S.

Jacob Van Buskirk followed his father's example of loyalism during the American Revolutionary War, and in 1777 he was commissioned lieutenant in the 4th battalion of the New Jersey Volunteers. On 27 November of the same year he and three fellow officers were captured by the rebels in a raid on Staten Island, N.Y., and charged with high treason. General George Washington considered that this proceeding "may prove a dangerous expedient . . . [for] by the same rule that we try them, may not the Enemy try any natural born subject of Great Britain, taken in Arms in our Service." The trial never occurred. After his release Van Buskirk rejoined his regiment, and on 24 Feb. 1780 he was commissioned captain in the 4th battalion, transferring to the 3rd battalion on 13 May. On 8 Sept. 1781 he was wounded at the battle of Eutaw Springs while serving in the Provincial Light Infantry.

When the New Jersey Volunteers were disbanded in the fall of 1783 at Parrtown (Saint John, N.B.), Van Buskirk went to the Shelburne region, where his father and other family members also settled. He received half pay and was granted 200 acres on the west side of Shelburne Harbour at Gunning Cove, and an additional 300 acres at Tusket River in what is now Yarmouth County. He first lived on his property at Gunning Cove, where he cleared land for a farm he called Parr's Grove, but about the time of his marriage he went to Shelburne to live and in 1792 was established as a merchant there. As a resident of Shelburne he was appointed a grand juror of the Court of Quarter Sessions in 1791 and 1793, and in 1800 he served as one of the fire wardens for the town. In June 1802 he was appointed by Lieutenant Governor Sir John Wentworth* a justice of the peace, and eight years later he was commissioned a justice of the Inferior Court of Common Pleas, a position he held until his death. On the departure of the customs officer from Shelburne in 1816, Van Buskirk became deputy collector, and was later collector of the provincial duties of impost and excise for the district of Shelburne.

During these years Van Buskirk was commissioned major of the volunteer company of the Shelburne County Militia Regiment (1794), and in 1808 he was lieutenant-colonel commandant of the 22nd (Shelburne) Battalion of Militia. On the decease of James Cox, member for Shelburne County in the House of Assembly, in 1805, Van Buskirk was returned in a by-election, and also the next year in the general election. He served in the assembly until 1818. In that year he and the other owners of the privateer *Nelson* were arrested by the deputy marshal of the Vice-Admiralty Court for "contumacy and contempt" in having ignored a ruling to pay to the registry of the High Court of Appeals the proceeds from the sale of a prize vessel. Following the procedure of the House of Commons, a committee of the assembly requested Lieutenant Governor Lord Dalhousie [Ramsay*] to obtain from the Court of Chancery a writ in favour of the release of Van Buskirk "by virtue of his privilege" as an assemblyman.

Following his release, Van Buskirk continued to serve on the Court of Common Pleas and as collector of impost and excise until, after his wife's death in 1832, he moved to Yarmouth to live with his son-in-law, John Bingay, who had succeeded him in the assembly. There he died on 27 Nov. 1834. He left an estate in Shelburne valued at £292 which he willed to Bingay and to his grandchildren, Thomas, Jacob, and Mary Bingay. The sturdy house that was Jacob Van Buskirk's home for many years still stands and is marked as one of Shelburne's historic houses.

MARION ROBERTSON

PAC, RG 16, A2, 547, pt.2, 27 June 1816 (mfm. at Dalhousie Univ. Arch., Halifax). PANS, MG 1, 953, doc.1085; MG 4, 140 (photocopy); 141, Christ Church (Shelburne, N.S.), reg. of baptisms, marriages, and burials (typescript); Places, Shelburne County, Court of General Sessions records, 8 July 1791, 14 Jan. 1793, 7 May 1800, 9 July 1802 (mfm.); RG 1, 171: 132; 444, no.57; RG 46, 3, no.471. Private arch., Marion Robertson (Shelburne), Kurney papers, bond binding G. H. Deinstadt and James Bower to Van Buskirk, 9 May 1829; Van Buskirk, appointment of Jacob Weiser as captain, 22nd Battalion, Shelburne Militia, 6 July 1808 (transcripts). Shelburne County Registry of Deeds (Shelburne), Deeds, 2: f.517 (mfm. at PANS). Yarmouth County Court of Probate (Yarmouth, N.S.), Wills, 2: 128 (mfm. at PANS). N.S., House of Assembly, *Journal and proc.*, 12, 26 Feb. 1818. George Washington, *The writings of George Washington, from the original sources, 1745–1799*, ed. J. C. Fitzpatrick (39v., Washington, 1931–44), 10: 149. *Yarmouth Herald and Western Advertiser*, 28 Nov. 1834. *Directory of N.S. MLAs*. E. A. Jones, *The loyalists of New Jersey: their memorials, petitions, claims, etc., from English records* (Newark, N.J., 1927; repr. Boston, 1972), 226. *Loyalists in N.S.* (Gilroy), 103. R. M. Keesey, "Loyalty and reprisal: the loyalists of Bergen County, New Jersey, and their estates" (PHD thesis, Columbia Univ., New York, 1957), 122, 166–67. Robin May and G. A. Embleton, *The British army in North*

Vieth

America, 1775–1783 (Reading, Eng., 1974), 23. Murdoch, *Hist. of N.S.*, 3: 245, 254. Marion Robertson, *King's bounty: a history of early Shelburne, Nova Scotia . . .* (Halifax, 1983), 115, 145.

VIETH (Veith), ADOLPHUS CHRISTOPH, army and militia officer and office holder; b. 12 June 1754 in Niedergandern (Federal Republic of Germany), youngest son of Johann Ludwig Vieth, a local official, and his second wife, Anna Christina Vormitter, a pastor's daughter; m. 18 Jan. 1782 in Halifax, Anna Dorothea Brehm, daughter of Georg Philipp Brehm of that town, and they had 12 children; d. there 25 Aug. 1835.

Adolphus Christoph Vieth first appears in North American records in April 1777, when he was appointed ensign in the Hessian garrison regiment of von Stein, then in New York. The following year Vieth was promoted second lieutenant in the unit, now renamed Regiment von Seitz and stationed in Halifax, and he became a lieutenant in 1781. For marrying without permission, Vieth was arrested and demoted in 1782. The regiment left Nova Scotia in June 1783, but he remained behind and retired from the army two months later. In recognition of his wartime service he received a grant of 600 acres on the Halifax–Lunenburg road.

Although Halifax had been the home of several dozen German families since the 1750s, the arrival of Hessian officers and loyalists sparked the formation of the High German Society in February 1786. Vieth was secretary of this body in 1791, when it apparently was discontinued because of the departure of many of its key members. Thereafter Vieth channelled his energies into a masonic lodge, of which he was grand secretary in 1815.

Vieth's principal employment in Halifax was as a commissariat official. He began in 1796 as first clerk in the army accounts department, then in December 1811 was promoted deputy assistant commissary general, and in July 1821 assistant commissary general, before retiring in 1830. He also served as a first lieutenant and adjutant, then as a captain, in the 1st Halifax Militia Regiment. In his later years, his half pay and the income from his considerable local property supported him and his large family. Between 1819 and 1835, Vieth's Halifax property had appreciated in assessed value from £400 to £1,100, a substantial amount for that era.

Vieth was active in St George's Anglican Church, the successor to the German congregation of the so-called little Dutch church in Halifax [*see* George Wright*]. In 1800 he was deputized to accept tenders to construct St George's Round Church, and was receiver of the pew rentals in 1811 and 1812. In 1827 Vieth was one of a group which petitioned successfully to have St Paul's parish divided in two, the northern half to belong to St George's.

What makes Vieth unique in Nova Scotia was his enjoyment of feudal rights or fiefs in Germany. He held certain privileges in the Hanoverian lands of Calenberg which allowed him to receive taxes collected there on corn and grain. Moreover, he was invested several times (the last being in 1824) in the Hessian fief of von Bodenhausen, which had only a nominal annual value but did bestow a claim to minor German nobility. Despite repeated urgings from Europe, his sons allowed these rights to lapse after his death.

Vieth's claim to attention is that he typifies the more prominent members of the Halifax German community about the turn of the 19th century. He continued a Germanic presence among the vestry and wardens of St George's when the Lutheran and German character of that congregation was becoming Anglican and English. He belonged to a civil service family of Hesse and Hanover, and exemplified the honourable and competent aspects of such people in Nova Scotia. In short, Vieth is not exciting for what he did, but for what he was.

TERRENCE M. PUNCH

Halifax County Registry of Deeds (Halifax), Deeds, 29: ff.298, 302, 310, 321, 325, 329, 333. PANS, MG 100, 242, no.29H; RG 1, 140: 309; 172: 147; 223, doc.37. Pfarrant, Reckershausen/Niedergandern (Friedland, Federal Republic of Germany), Lutheran church records of the parishes of Reckershausen and Niedergandern. "Nova Scotia state papers," PAC *Report*, 1946: 136. *Novascotian, or Colonial Herald*, 27 Aug. 1835. *Nova-Scotia Royal Gazette*, 7 Jan. 1800. *Hessische Truppen im amerikanischen Unabhängigkeitskrieg (HETRINA): Index nach Familiennamen*, comp. E. G. Franz *et al.* (5v., Marburg, Federal Republic of Germany, 1972–76), 4. Joachim Lampe, *Aristokratie, Hofadel und Staatspatriziat in Kurhessen; die Lebenskreise der hæheren Beamten an den kurhannoverschen Zentral- und Hofbehærden, 1714–1760* (2v., Göttingen, Federal Republic of Germany, 1963). N.S., Provincial Museum, *Report* (Halifax), 1923: 25.

VINCENT, THOMAS, fur trader; b. *c.* 1776; d. 30 March 1832 in England.

Thomas Vincent was said to be of Edmonton (London), England, but he was evidently of a County Durham family, since he had numerous ties with that region. On 5 May 1790 he entered the Hudson's Bay Company as a writer. His first year of service was spent at Fort Albany (Ont.) and his second at Henley House (near the junction of the Albany and Kenogami rivers) under John HODGSON. Following several more years at Albany, he assumed charge of the post at Martin Falls in the summer of 1797. The next winter he was appointed master of Pointe-au-Foutre House (Man.) at the mouth of the Winnipeg River, a position he held until the summer of 1801. Competition with the North West Company and the New North West Company (sometimes called the XY Company) was lively there. In the fall of 1802 he was sent to re-establish the HBC post at Red Lake (Ont.); he found numerous traders in the area. The most immediate opposition came from Nor'Wester Jacques Adhémar and four men who arrived in September, but during his first year Vincent managed to trade 27 bundles of furs to their 8. The Nor'Westers burned Vincent's house following his departure in May 1804, doubtless being glad to see him and his 15 men depart.

After two seasons at Fort Albany and a summer at Martin Falls, Vincent took charge of Brandon House (Man.) for the season of 1806–7, replacing John McKay*. His rival there was Nor'Wester François-Antoine Larocque* He was sent to Fort Albany as second officer for the next two seasons and then spent a year in England, returning in 1810 as chief factor at Albany. When his superior, Thomas THOMAS, governor of the Southern Department, was made governor of the Northern Department in 1814 to succeed William AULD, Vincent became governor locum tenens of the Southern Department. One of his first acts in this position was to arrange, in accordance with instructions from London, for George ATKINSON to begin to explore systematically the interior of the Eastmain, the eastern coast of James and Hudson bays. Vincent himself explored a route linking Henley House and New Brunswick House (on Brunswick Lake, Ont.), and hence the drainages of the upper Albany and Moose rivers. At Moose Factory in the summer of 1815 Vincent received a formal appointment as governor of the Southern Department. From October 1815 to the summer of 1819, with the exceptions of a stay at Moose Factory between January and September 1816 and a visit to the Eastmain, Vincent made New Brunswick House his base, it being a useful post from which to watch NWC activities. While there, in 1817, he instructed Atkinson to carry out further explorations. Although the London committee censured his personal behaviour during this period, he retained his position owing to a shortage of officers. In 1819 and 1820 his headquarters were at Moose Factory.

At the merger of the HBC and the NWC in 1821, Vincent became a chief factor in the new concern and presided over the council held at Moose Factory that year. From 1822 to 1824 he had the charge of the Moose district; from 1824 until his retirement on 1 June 1826 he directed the trade of the Albany district. He returned to England that autumn.

Between the mid 1790s and 1810, three sons and three daughters were born to Vincent and Jane Renton, a native-born daughter of a company employee. Their eldest son, John, became a clerk in the company in 1816, and was the father of Anglican archdeacon Thomas Vincent. Their eldest daughter, Harriet, married HBC chief trader George Gladman*. According to Harriet Gladman's account, Jane Renton left Vincent when he took a second wife, Jane, daughter of the late James Sutherland*. Vincent described Jane Sutherland as his wife in his will of 1826. She apparently predeceased him, however, for his final will, dated Hartlepool, County Durham, 24 March 1832, made no reference to her but left legacies to his children and stepchildren and to Jane Renton, who was later described as his widow. Jane Renton lived for many years with George Gladman's widowed mother at Moose Factory, where James Hargrave* in 1837 described them as "without flattery two of the most respectable Ladies I have met in this land." She died there in September 1858 at age 76 and was buried as Mrs Jane Vincent. The considerable correspondence regarding Vincent's estate, legatees, and finances gives a vivid picture of his Hudson Bay ties, and of the varied problems facing mixed-blood offspring – his and others – in the early to mid 1800s.

JENNIFER S. H. BROWN

ACC, Diocese of Moosonee Arch. (Schumacher, Ont.), Moose Factory and its dependencies, reg. of baptisms (mfm. at AO). PAM, HBCA, A.36/14: ff.54–307; B.3/a/112: f.5; B.4/a/2–4; B.86/a/46; B.107/a/1; B.177/a/1, 6, 8. *HBRS*, 2 (Rich and Fleming); *HBRS*, 24 (Davies and Johnson); *HBRS*, 30 (Williams). Letitia [Mactavish] Hargrave, *The letters of Letitia Hargrave*, ed. Margaret Arnett MacLeod (Toronto, 1947). Morton, *Hist. of Canadian west* (1939). T. C. B. Boon, "Thomas Vincent, evangelist, builder, and traveller," *Winnipeg Free Press*, 15 April 1961: 34. N. J. Williamson, "Historic Bas de la Rivière," *Manitoba Pageant* (Winnipeg), 23 (1977), no.1: 8–17.

W

WAGEEZHEGOME **(Wakeshogomy).** *See* OGIMAUH-BINAESSIH

WALDEGRAVE, WILLIAM, 1st Baron RADSTOCK, naval officer and governor of Newfoundland; b. 9 July 1753, second son of John Waldegrave, 3rd Earl Waldegrave, and Lady Elizabeth Gower; m. 28 Dec. 1785 Cornelia van Lennap in Smyrna (3Izmir, Turkey), and they had two sons; d. 20 Aug. 1825 in England.

William Waldegrave entered the British navy in 1766, was promoted lieutenant in 1772, and by 1775

Waldegrave

had command of his own ship. He served with distinction, rising to rear-admiral in 1794, and to vice-admiral a year later. In the fleet under Sir John Jervis, Waldegrave, as third in command, took part in the battle of Cape St Vincent off the Portuguese coast on 14 Feb. 1797, and was offered a baronetcy for his role in the victory. He declined, apparently thinking this honour inferior to his rank as an earl's son. The patent appointing him governor and commander-in-chief of the island of Newfoundland "and the Islands adjacent, including the Islands of Saint Pierre and Miquelon," was dated 16 May 1797.

Waldegrave's administration occurred in wartime in an exposed corner of the British empire. In September 1796 a French squadron had attacked and burned Bay Bulls, a settlement just south of St John's, and the constant French menace ensured that military concerns remained paramount in Waldegrave's government. The topics of much of his correspondence are convoys, batteries, recruiting, and deserters – this last a serious problem in view of the inhabitants' tendency to shelter runaways. Nor were the French the only threat. Soon after his arrival in the summer of 1797, the governor found that a mutiny in the British fleet had spread to Newfoundland, and a dangerous uprising among seamen on the *Latona* had to be put down. Though "the most perfect tranquility" prevailed among the 5,000 or so inhabitants of St John's, Waldegrave thought it necessary to have an apparent onshore sympathizer, one Sergeant James Dayley, take the oath of allegiance in public before the magistrates. The mutineers had, he thought, tried to sow sedition among the soldiers in the garrison, many of whom were Irish Roman Catholics. Later events would show that his fears were not unfounded [*see* James Louis O'Donel*].

Waldegrave was governor for the usual triennium, but he stayed in Newfoundland for only about three months per year, departing for England in late October. This was the traditional system of British rule in Newfoundland, a system implying that government was needed only during the fishing season. John REEVES in 1791 had already pointed out to authorities in London the preposterousness of the arrangement. The island, he stated, "is no longer a place resorted to only by mere Fishermen"; and further, "there are many Merchants who do not engage at all in the Fishery." He added that the population had "encreased so much in number, as to Compose a Society," and that a local "legislative power" would be of benefit. Some recognition was given to these changed conditions during Waldegrave's term as governor, when it was decided (in 1798) to have the chief justice reside year-round in St John's. Yet official reluctance to concede that Newfoundland was becoming a colony *comme les autres* persisted, and Waldegrave maintained the age-old restrictions against building houses and issued proclamations against dieters (as servants

who stayed over the winter were termed). When the four St John's magistrates, acting as a sort of unofficial legislature, protested that "circumstances [were] so changed" in Newfoundland during wartime that these regulations no longer made sense, he replied that there were indeed reasons "for not pushing [dieters] too closely," and that "it never was my intention" to bring proclamations against buildings "into full force." As with most governors in the period 1770–1820, Waldegrave's imperial bark was worse than his bite. Yet he occasionally used his authority to forbid the erection of houses and to order others taken down.

Despite the pretence that no year-round government was needed, one in fact already existed, an informal and to some extent voluntarist structure comprising magistrates, resident surrogates, sheriff, and other officials. The population of Newfoundland had increased to around 30,000, and changes taking place in the local economy and society demanded attention. The south coast fishery, especially the herring fishery, was expanding, and with it the number of settlers in Fortune Bay and Bay d'Espoir. The gang rape of a woman by five men near Harbour Breton brought forcibly home to Waldegrave the need for protection of settlers on what was a lawless frontier. Another new factor in the economy was the seal fishery, carried out in ocean-going vessels in early spring and hence requiring a work-force that was permanently resident on the island. It was not possible, especially in wartime, to bring servants out annually from Britain to man this fishery. The war also compelled the issuing of licences to permit the importation of provisions from the United States, and with the growth of trade, emigration to that country reached a level that worried the governor. He also found reason to be concerned about the rising influence of Methodists and Roman Catholics, and he fretted about the number and condition of the poor. A decent and humane man, Waldegrave took steps to have established a "Committee for the Relief of the Poor" to collect money from residents of St John's. Over the winter of 1797–98, close to 300 people, more than half of them children, were given assistance from this source. The governor himself contributed generously to the fund, put pressure on the garrison and squadron to do likewise, and urged, with some success, that similar funds be set up in the outports.

The class of inhabitants that created the greatest uneasiness for Waldegrave were the merchants, now a strong and organized interest group in local society. "The power of the Merchants in the Out Harbors," he told the Home secretary, "is so great, that they rule as perfect despots, being the sole possessors of the meat, drink and clothing by which their wretched subjects are supported." Waldegrave recommended to London that magistrates be paid salaries, from a tax on rum and dieters, to remove them from the merchants' influence. On being asked for their views on a tax on rum by Chief Justice Richard Routh* – an action for which he was angrily rebuked by Waldegrave – the St John's merchants expressed vehement opposition, and in the event the proposal for a salaried magistracy was dropped. In their letter to Routh late in 1798, the merchants expressed concern that "we are not even allowed to build or repair our Houses except for the express purpose of carrying on the Fishery," and argued that the poor should be allowed to cultivate parts of the island. These would be themes taken up by reformers in the next century [see William Carson*]. Though he was obliged to have dealings with the merchants, Waldegrave thought them upstarts. Towards the end of his term as governor he wrote dispatches denouncing their "insolent idea of independence" and warning of their influence on the population. The island, he wrote, is "of all Places in His Majesty's Dominions, the one most prone to adopt the doctrines of Liberty & Equality." In comments such as these, Waldegrave seems to have been overreacting to minor stirrings of discontent.

Waldegrave was succeeded as governor by Charles Morice Pole, whose patent was dated 3 June 1800. Later in that year Waldegrave was created an Irish peer, with the title Baron Radstock, and in 1802 he was made an admiral. In effect, the governorship of Newfoundland was his last employment in the service of his country.

Waldegrave was a cautious, conservative, and perhaps hypersensitive governor. He defended with firmness, though not with great skill or patience, the interests of the mother country, and responded with compassion to the distressed members of the local community.

PATRICK O'FLAHERTY

NMM, WYN (mfm. at PANL). PANL, GN 2/1/A, 12–15. PRO, CO 194/38–42; CO 195/15. *DNB.* James Ralfe, *The naval biography of Great Britain . . .* (4v., London, 1828), 2: 27–31. W. L. Clowes, *The Royal Navy; a history from the earliest times to the present* (7v., London, 1897–1903). Prowse, *Hist. of Nfld* (1895).

WALKER, ALEXANDER, explorer and author; b. 12 May 1764 in Collessie, Scotland, eldest son of William Walker, Church of Scotland minister, and Margaret Manderston; m. 12 July 1812 Barbara Montgomery in Scotland; d. 5 March 1831 in Edinburgh.

Alexander Walker's father died when Alexander was seven. Although educated in St Andrews at the grammar school and the university, Walker later recorded that "poverty was vouchsafed . . . as a Counter balance to Family Pride," adding that "younger Branches had to seek their fortunes in distant lands." Like many young Scots, he turned to India, and was appointed an East India Company cadet in 1780. He sailed to Bombay in 1781; the following year he became an ensign. During the siege of Mangalore by the Indian leader Tipu Sahib, Walker served with distinction and, upon surrender of the fortress by the British in 1784, he offered himself a hostage as security for the conditions of the truce.

A bright and ambitious young man, eager to see what he could of the world, Walker jumped at the opportunity in 1785 to accompany merchant James Charles Stuart Strange* on a voyage to the northwest coast of America. The Bombay Council of the East India Company, hoping eventually to gain control for the company of the fur trade in that region, gave leave of absence to Walker and a small party of soldiers to accompany the expedition; Walker received command of the detachment, which was to be left in America as a garrison and factory. Leaving India late that year, the 350-ton brig *Captain Cook* and the 140-ton snow *Experiment* sailed via Goa, Borneo, and the Philippines for North America, arriving on the northwest coast in late June 1786. The expedition spent until 16 September trading and exploring from Woody Point (probably Cape Cook, B.C.) to Prince William Sound (Alaska), with extended stops at Friendly Harbour (Friendly Cove, B.C.) in Nootka Sound and in Prince William Sound. Especially at Friendly Harbour, Walker spent time ashore observing the natives and their way of life. Soon after the expedition's arrival Strange decided for reasons of economy not to leave a garrison. Walker regarded this decision as wrong-headed, the result of a failure of nerve on Strange's part.

Not involved in the trading activities of the expedition and having lost the *raison d'être* for his coming, Walker consoled himself by engaging in what was to be a lifelong interest: the observation and study of native peoples. The description he wrote of the customs, traditions, and habits of the Indians of Nootka and Prince William sounds was the first detailed account based upon extensive onshore study. After his return to India in 1787, Walker added other first-hand material, including the results of a lengthy interview, apparently in 1788, with John Mackay*, the only man Strange had left behind. Subsequently he revised his journal on several occasions in the light of new information and a growing ethnological literature.

Walker had a sharp eye and a willingness to speculate intelligently about what he observed. In addition, he was prepared to revise his views on the basis of superior evidence from other witnesses. Having studied Captain James Cook*'s Nootka vocabulary before his trip, Walker enjoyed some familiarity with that language, and he greatly enhanced it as his studies progressed. He was struck by the sharpness of the natives' trading practices and by their general good health, important observations in these early days of culture contact. Originally convinced that the Nootkas were cannibals, he revised this judgement as a result of Mackay's experiences. Despite a tendency to view the Indians as savages in a state of nature, Walker manifested a healthy relativism and functionalism in his assessments of their accomplishments and behaviour. "The Savage is the prototype of the Civilized Man," he wrote. "His faculties are less cultivated, his mind is stored with fewer ideas, and his Character possesses less variety. In many of the useful and necessary Arts of Life however, and in that knowledge which is necessary for his safety, the Savage is almost on a level with those who are instructed in the arts of regular Life." The struggle for survival accounted for "so many unfavorable features" in the Indian's character, Walker surmised. "He becomes suspicious, deceitful and treacherous. The mere Savage is therefore scarcely capable of generosity: gratitude and humanity are not among the list of his virtues. Their exercise would be useless to him, and dangerous to the safety of his Person." The same instinct for self-preservation also accounted for the virtues of the Indians, however. They were "alive to the feelings of nature and affection . . . [and] eminently faithful to each other[, for] their safety depends on the strength of their mutual attachment." Walker acknowledged that the Indian perceived life differently than did "civilized Man"; for the Indian, "the attachment to nature and liberty is more powerful than the temptations of voluptious pleasures." Walker was also prepared to admit that Europeans were not free from inhumane practices and often treated the Indians with neither justice nor understanding.

After his return to India from the Pacific coast Walker enjoyed a distinguished military and administrative career in the service of the East India Company. He was promoted lieutenant in 1788 and subsequently served in a number of campaigns. In 1802 he was political resident at Baroda, and five years later he led an expedition into Kattywar (Kathiawar) for which he received "the highest approbation and applause" from the governor general. In Kattywar he succeeded in suppressing the local practice of infanticide. He became a lieutenant-colonel in 1808. Walker also continued his intellectual activities, accumulating a valuable collection of Arabic, Persian, and Sanskrit manuscripts. In 1810 he left for England, and he retired in 1812 to Scotland. Ten years later he was reactivated with the rank of brigadier-general to govern St Helena, which was then under the jurisdiction of the East India Company. Both in retirement and on St Helena he continued his ethnographic studies and revisions to the manuscript of his North American visit. He died in March 1831 shortly after retiring a second time.

J. M. BUMSTED

[The manuscript of Alexander Walker's journal, ready for publication, is in the NLS, Dept. of MSS, MS 13780, among the vast Walker of Bowland papers, just a small fraction of which concerns North America. Only recently discovered, the journal was edited by Robin Fisher and J. M. Bumsted and published as *An account of a voyage to the north west coast of America in 1785 & 1786* (Vancouver and Toronto, n.d.). Along with rough drafts (MS 13776–79 and 13781) and autobiographical notes (MS 13735) in the same collection, it constitutes the most interesting source for a study of Walker's voyage. J.M.B.]

PABC, AA10, G79B, 6a (transcripts). *Gentleman's Magazine*, January–June 1831: 466–68. James Strange, *James Strange's journal and narrative of the commercial expedition from Bombay to the north-west coast of America . . .* (Madras, India, 1928; repr. 1929). *DNB*.

WALLACE, MICHAEL, merchant, politician, JP, judge, office holder, and colonial administrator; b. *c.* 1744 in Lanarkshire, Scotland; d. 8 Oct. 1831 in Halifax.

Michael Wallace, the central figure in the oligarchy of early 19th-century Nova Scotia, came from obscure origins in the rural environs of Glasgow. His possession of an education and his early entry into trade suggest that, although not prominent, his family had at least lower middle class social status and affluence. Michael and several of his brothers became minor merchants in Glasgow, which was then emerging as a major commercial metropolis. Attracted to the profits to be made from dealing in such staples as tobacco, the brothers set up branch operations in the southern American colonies. Michael located at Norfolk, Va, in 1771. As a recent arrival and one with continuing family and business connections in Britain, he naturally opposed the revolution. Driven out of Norfolk after suffering considerable loss of property, he moved about 1779 to Halifax, a garrison port where war had generated commercial bustle. He resumed business as a retailer and wholesaler, dealing primarily in British manufactures, along with fish and lumber received in barter exchanges. A portion of his imports came from Glasgow but Wallace also received shipments from other British ports, a pattern which suggests that he no longer functioned as agent for a Glasgow-based family enterprise. He appears to have operated on a relatively small-scale basis and did not rank as a leading figure within the Halifax merchant community. On 4 Jan. 1781 Wallace married Mary Kerby, the daughter of a recently deceased local trader with only marginal status and wealth.

The triumph of the American revolution had a decisive impact on Wallace's career. The British decision to enforce mercantilist trade regulations against the new United States created the prospect that Halifax might emerge in the post-war period as an entrepôt commanding a large share of the British Caribbean carrying trade. Thus Wallace had cause, as a trader, to remain in Nova Scotia. His persistence was also associated with the large-scale influx of loyalists into the colony during the early 1780s. Their presence and their rapid penetration of the local oligarchy gave him valuable connections, which soon brought him place and preferment.

Wallace's rise to prominence began in 1785 with his election to the House of Assembly as a representative for Halifax County. During the next decade and a half he secured a number of complementary honours such as a magisterial appointment, a place on the bench of the Inferior Court of Common Pleas, and membership on the commissions responsible for Halifax's streets and Sable Island's life-saving station [see James Rainstorpe Morris*]. Wallace also began to acquire lucrative government patronage. In 1791, for example, Lieutenant Governor John Parr* selected him as agent responsible for providing the shipping required to transport black loyalists to Sierra Leone [see Thomas Peters*; David George*]. "My motive," Parr explained, "was to give you a little employment, and put a little cash [£1,000] in your Pocket." The following year Wallace was chosen to purchase and distribute supplies to needy settlers in the Pictou district. In addition, military contracts began to come his way once war erupted with revolutionary France in 1793.

Wallace's good fortune appears to have derived primarily from his ability to ingratiate himself with loyalists prominent in the local administration. Bishop Charles Inglis*, for example, was writing to London in the 1780s to praise Wallace as "a very worthy, honest man." Wallace's enthusiasm for both tory politics and commercial expansion made him a natural ally of John Wentworth*, who became lieutenant governor in 1792. Wentworth's official correspondence soon began to carry references to Wallace as "my worthy friend," a man with "long experience in business, of unimpeachable integrity, and indefatigable diligence." Wallace received his major reward from this association in 1797, when he was appointed provincial treasurer. The office carried an income of £450 and the influence associated with supervision of the numerous excise officers stationed in outport communities. Equally decisive for Wallace's prospects was his appointment in 1802 to the Nova Scotia Council. No income was attached to the position, but it placed Wallace at the centre of decision-making within the colonial oligarchy. Not surprisingly, other rewards followed. In 1808 he became commissioner of escheats; in 1810 he was appointed deputy to Wentworth, no longer lieutenant governor but still surveyor general of the king's woods, succeeding Wentworth on his death in 1820. Wallace also served briefly after the War of 1812 as judge of the Vice-Admiralty Court. The chief value of these appointments was to provide Wallace with an ever-expanding degree of influence in the distribution of government patronage. His correspondence suggests that people applied to him for everything from land grants to relief supplies. For perhaps a decade after being named treasurer, Wallace continued in trade, but on a shrinking scale as the duties of office increasingly

made him a full-time public servant. By 1811 he was appealing to the assembly for an increase in salary, on the grounds that he had become completely dependent on the public purse. Wallace's total income, including miscellaneous fees and emoluments, cannot be determined; suffice it to say that he died leaving an estate in excess of £6,000. Critics alleged that much of his wealth had been obtained through speculation with public funds, behaviour made possible by lax accounting procedures.

As a major office holder and man of property, Wallace embraced the manners and style of the colonial urban gentry. His residence on Hollis Street, assessed at £2,000, made him a neighbour to the lieutenant governor, leading merchants, and other chief officials of government. Emulating his peers, he maintained a summer estate at Preston, east of Halifax. Wallace employed several servants, including a footman and a coachman, and ran up annual domestic accounts of at least £300. While maintaining a link with the Church of Scotland, he owned pews in the Anglican churches in Halifax and Dartmouth. His sons were sent to the exclusive and Anglican-dominated King's College at Windsor. Following the fashion set by Lieutenant Governor Lord Dalhousie [Ramsay*], Wallace served as a director of the provincial agricultural society. He was also twice president of the prestigious North British Society and helped found the select Halifax Library. Philanthropy directed towards the urban poor and immigrants did not, however, attract his interest.

Family affairs occupied much of Wallace's time. His correspondence reveals a chronic concern for the welfare of brothers, sons, and daughters. Acquisition of public offices and advantageous marriages were his favoured methods of obtaining security. The post of British consul in Savannah, Ga, came to be regarded as a family sinecure. Son John, admitted by his father to have "no turn, or application to business," was provided with a custom-house position paying a salary of £500. John also had the good fortune to marry the daughter of Christopher Billopp, a member of the New Brunswick Council. Sons Edward and William were set up in business on the Halifax waterfront, while their brother Charles Wentworth secured a medical training in Edinburgh and returned to serve as port medical officer in Halifax. Among the six daughters, Eleanor proved the most successful, marrying Charles Porter*, president of King's College.

Wallace stood out among his fellows, largely by virtue of the vehemence he employed in espousing a loyalist, counter-revolutionary design for Nova Scotia's economic and political development. He always claimed that British North America could be transformed into the commercial successor to New England, provided that Americans were excluded from the northern colonial fisheries and the ports of the British Caribbean. The British drift away from mer-

Wallace

cantilist orthodoxy after 1815 roused Wallace's ire, and in 1819 he played a leading role in drafting the Nova Scotian protest against British concessions on the fisheries in the Convention of 1818. Moreover, in his private correspondence Wallace persistently urged confrontation with the United States in economic affairs. Arguing that trade with the republic always worked to the disadvantage of Nova Scotia, he advocated closer commercial relations with the St Lawrence colonies. At the end of his life, he was still railing about the "disastrous consequences" of giving in to the "*Rebels*" with respect to trade. Here Wallace's attitude reflected not so much lingering memories of the revolution as the expansionist ambitions of Halifax's early 19th-century business community [*see* William SABATIER].

That Wallace shared the opinions of the merchants was natural since he cooperated with them in various investment ventures. He had stock in such enterprises as the Halifax-Dartmouth Steamboat Company, the Annapolis Iron Mining Company, and the Shubenacadie Canal Company. As an entrepreneur, he is best remembered as president of the canal company, although this is something of a false honour since he appears to have been essentially a corporate figurehead. In one important area Wallace clashed with many local investors. In 1819 he was largely responsible for the legislature's refusal to incorporate a public bank. Wallace claimed that the proposal, put forward by "a few designing monied Characters, supported by the ignorant & unwary," would introduce irresponsible American banking practices into Nova Scotia. His opponents replied that the treasurer wanted to protect his monopoly over the issuance of paper currency, bills popularly referred to as "Michael Wallaces." When an unincorporated bank was established in 1825, Wallace allegedly placed its president, Henry Hezekiah Cogswell*, among his leading enemies.

The bank dispute, which Wallace admitted had made him "extremely unpopular," was not an isolated episode. Wallace's temperament, described by a contemporary as being "impetuous and irritable," made him prone to controversy. While serving as a judge, he frequently erupted in outbursts of profanity. The agent for the Sierra Leone Company, John Clarkson, reported that on one occasion, when crossed, Wallace had flown into a temper, which "caused him to make use of language, highly unbecoming, but too contemptible . . . to take any notice of." The Pictou *Colonial Patriot* summed up Wallace's volatility by saying that he had "a mind perpetually boiling with effervescence of irritation." As a rule, Wallace reserved his spleen for those he viewed as posing a threat to the political order.

From his earliest days in Nova Scotia, Wallace had espoused an uncompromising toryism. As an assemblyman, he refused to join the loyalist-led attempt in the 1780s to purge the administration of allegedly incompe-

tent office holders [*see* Thomas Henry BARCLAY]. During the 1790s Wallace championed the interests of the Halifax-based oligarchy of merchants and officials on such issues as tariffs, public works, and education. Popular resentment of Wallace's role expressed itself in the 1799 election, in which he lost his seat to William Cottnam TONGE. Although successful in regaining it on a technicality, Wallace bore a chronic grudge against those who had crossed him, especially the secessionist Presbyterians of the Pictou area. Over the next three decades, Wallace and his allies within the Church of Scotland persistently sought to destroy the attempts of Thomas McCulloch* and liberal Presbyterians such as Edward Mortimer* to promote Pictou Academy as a rival to King's College.

Wallace's relations with the assembly remained antagonistic. In 1802 the house censured him for "highly reprehensible" behaviour as a commissioner in charge of construction of a new official residence for Lieutenant Governor Wentworth. Costs had been allowed to run ahead of estimates in the erection of a building "on a scale far beyond the wants or circumstances" of Nova Scotia. Subsequently, the assembly conducted inquisitorial investigations of the treasury accounts and refused to increase Wallace's salary. In return, on being appointed to the Council in 1802, Wallace sought to minimize assembly control over the public purse, taking the extreme view that expenditures could continue even if the legislature had failed to pass the annual appropriations bill. When the assembly sought to assert itself in 1809, Wallace, as acting president of the Council, ordered the members away after haranguing them "in a turbulent and violent manner." Old age did not mellow Wallace. A year before his death he was complaining about the assembly "faction" which disrupted public order by resisting the Council's claim to amend money bills.

The extent of Wallace's influence within government is difficult to assess, but after 1800, during the last half of Wentworth's administration, Wallace undoubtedly emerged as a dominant personality. Noting the age of the lieutenant governor and the "imbecility" of certain other officials, Wallace told his brother in 1807 that "almost the whole weight of this Government has rested upon my shoulders for years." Hostile critics agreed with this observation. Wallace's ascendancy probably persisted through the war years, when military affairs distracted the various successors to Wentworth. By the 1820s, however, Wallace may have become less influential as younger men emerged within the administration. Contemporaries began to observe that the treasurer was "very old and very unwieldy. Neither his mind nor his body will last much longer." Adherence to 18th-century modes of dress, including the wearing of his hair in a queue, enhanced the impression that Wallace had become an anachronism. Nevertheless, he retained considerable power, in part because as senior councillor he became administrator during the absence of the lieutenant governor. On five occasions between 1818 and 1830 Wallace assumed this position, one which allowed him to dispense considerable patronage on a unilateral basis. Commenting on Wallace's last term as administrator in 1829–30, a contemporary observed, "The Treasurer is again our *King* and Chest, and the province, and the people, he seems to consider as his own."

Attention to public business, which began at the treasurer's office every morning before breakfast, became integral to Wallace's existence. Thus he ignored initial hints that retirement would be appropriate. Finally, in 1830, he yielded to pressure on condition that the legislature petition the crown for the appointment of his son Charles Wentworth as his successor. Surprisingly, the assembly agreed, thanks to Wallace's friendship with such influential members as John Young*. Charles eventually got the post, although he was dismissed 16 years later amidst accusations of fraud and incompetence.

Michael Wallace continued as a member of the Council until his death in 1831. He died intestate, perhaps because he believed his boast that he would "live forever." The funeral became a public ceremony, attended by the Council, magistrates, garrison staff, naval officers, and "a long train of inhabitants." Their presence reflected not Wallace's personal popularity so much as his success in becoming the embodiment of oligarchy in Nova Scotia. A figure parallel in many ways to John Strachan* of Upper Canada, Wallace emerged from a Lowland Presbyterian, middle-class background and rose to prominence within the British North American gentry by virtue of an aggressive personality and a convert's zeal in advocating tory and Anglican social ideals.

D. A. SUTHERLAND

Some of Michael Wallace's correspondence has been published under the title "Halifax to Savannah; letters of Michael Wallace," ed. W. C. Hartridge, *Ga. Hist. Quarterly* (Savannah), 45 (1961): 73–91, 171–86.

Halifax County Court of Probate (Halifax), Estate papers, W13 (Michael Wallace). Halifax County Registry of Deeds (Halifax), Deeds, 54: f.224; 63: f.393 (mfm. at PANS). PANS, MG 1, 219, journal, 264–65; 479: f.136 (transcripts); 793, Robie to Halliburton, 28 Jan. 1831; 980, James Stewart to Peleg Wiswall, 3 May 1824, 17 Aug. 1828, 18 Dec. 1829; MG 2, 729, no.814; MG 4, 55, 10 Jan. 1787; RG 1, 52, Wentworth to Richard Molesworthy, 15 Jan. 1800; 54: f.129; 224, nos.77–78; 241, no.68; 291, nos.21, 25–26; RG 5, A, 17, 2 March 1811; RG 31-104, 1–6, 1780–1800; RG 31-117, 1–2, 1826–41; RG 35A, 2, 1830. PRO, CO 217/59: 31; 217/63: 196, 373; 217/66: 30; 217/68: 5–6; 217/81: 354; 217/85: 90; 217/99: 157, 167; 217/102: 59; 217/148: 85; 217/149: 86; 217/150: 4, 150. N.S., House of Assembly, *Journal and proc.*, 1785–1809. Perkins, *Diary, 1766–80* (Innis). "United Empire Loyalists: enquiry into losses and services," AO *Report*, 1904. *Acadian Recorder*, 19 Dec. 1818, 22 Nov. 1823, 11 March 1825, 15 Oct. 1831, 8 Feb. 1834. *Colonial Patriot* (Pictou, N.S.), 12 Nov. 1828; 21 Jan. 1829; 3 April, 22 May 1830; 6 Aug. 1831. *Novascotian*, 10 Aug. 1842. *Weekly Chronicle*, 12 April 1816. *Annals, North British Society, Halifax, Nova Scotia, with portraits and biographical notes, 1768–1903*, comp. J. S. Macdonald ([3rd ed.], Halifax, 1905). *Directory of N.S. MLAs*. *N.-S. calendar*, 1791–99. Sabine, *Biog. sketches of loyalists*. Akins, *Hist. of Halifax City*. R. V. Harris, *The Church of Saint Paul in Halifax, Nova Scotia: 1749–1949* (Toronto, 1949). Murdoch, *Hist. of N.S.* George Patterson, *A history of the county of Pictou, Nova Scotia* (Montreal, 1877). J. S. Martell, "A documentary study of provincial finance and currency, 1812–36," PANS *Bull.* (Halifax), 2 (1939–41), no.4. J. H. Soltow, "Scottish traders in Virginia, 1750–1775," *Economic Hist. Rev.* (London), 2nd ser., 12 (1959–60): 83–98.

WALLER, JOCELYN (also known as **Jocelyn Macartney Waller**), office holder, JP, publisher, and editor; b. *c.* 1772 in Newport, County Tipperary (Republic of Ireland), fourth son of Robert Waller and Catherine Moore; m. Elizabeth Willis, widow of Dr Cullen, and they had eight children; d. 2 Dec. 1828 in Montreal.

Jocelyn Waller, an able, well-educated man, was connected with influential families in Ireland. His father, created baronet in 1780, had been an MP. Waller was resident in Lower Canada in December 1817 when he was commissioned clerk of the crown. The following month he became clerk of the Court of Oyer and Terminer but he did not hold either post for long. The colonial secretary, Lord Bathurst, on learning that Waller, who was well known in Britain for his reformist views, had been nominated clerk of the crown, instructed Governor Sir John Coape SHERBROOKE to remove him from the post and reassign it to its former occupant, Gilbert Ainslie. Sherbrooke was reluctant to dismiss Waller, noting that he and his "large" family were in "distress" after having lost all their belongings in a shipwreck on their voyage to British North America, but Bathurst's instructions prevailed. Waller retired to a country home, probably at Saint-Gilles, near Quebec, living on an inherited income of about £200 per year. In June 1821 he was named a justice of the peace for the district of Quebec and commissioner for the summary trial of small causes in Saint-Gilles.

In 1822 Waller was asked to become a writer for the *Montreal Gazette*. His independent views and outspoken articles are said to have brought him into disfavour with the owners of the newspaper, with the result that he left journalism and returned to his country home. In that same year Edward Ellice* persuaded the British government to introduce a bill in parliament to unite Upper and Lower Canada. Opposition to the bill developed rapidly among French Canadians and Waller was asked to present the arguments against union to the English-speaking population of Lower Canada. *Le Spectateur canadien* was transformed into the *Canadian Spectator* in

Waltermeyer

October 1822 and Waller probably became its editor at that time. In 1824 the reform paper, aimed especially at the Irish inhabitants of Montreal, displayed his name as editor and in January 1825 he became its publisher. Late in 1826 Ludger Duvernay* would become the *Spectator*'s printer.

Although the bill for the union of the Canadas had been temporarily abandoned in 1823 as a result of opposition in the House of Commons, by 1825 the proposals for union were being urged more strongly than ever and Waller renewed his journalistic campaign against it. As a friend of Denis-Benjamin Viger*, Louis-Joseph Papineau*, Amable Berthelot*, and Augustin Cuvillier*, Waller was aware of the reasons for French Canadian opposition to union but his own editorial stand derived from the British tradition of self-determination and from opposition to changes in the Constitutional Act of 1791 made without the colonists' knowledge or consent. Waller's editorial writing, witty, learned, and energetic, was based on logic and example rather than on personal attack or prejudice. His articles were admired and republished in Upper Canada, the United States, and England. They aroused the hostility of the governor, Lord Dalhousie [Ramsay*], of the tory faction, and in particular of James Stuart*, attorney general of Lower Canada.

The *Canadian Spectator* was one of a group of newspapers opposed to union. Like others such as the *Canadian Freeman*, published in York (Toronto) by Francis COLLINS, and the *British Colonist and St. Francis Gazette*, published by Silas Horton Dickerson* in Stanstead, Lower Canada, it deplored the alien bill of 1826 [*see* John Rolph*] and the sudden prorogation of the House of Assembly by Dalhousie on 7 March 1827. The editors of these papers would all be charged at one time or another with libel or contempt of court and would serve time in prison during their battles for political reform.

In the *Canadian Spectator* Waller supported the efforts of the lieutenant governor, Sir Francis Nathaniel BURTON, to reach an agreement with the assembly over its control of colonial revenues. He attacked the official government organ, the *Quebec Gazette, Published by Authority* [*see* John Charlton Fisher*], and criticized Dalhousie's refusal on 21 Nov. 1827 to sanction the election of Papineau as speaker of the House of Assembly. He also approved of judge John Walpole Willis*'s conduct during the trial for libel of Francis Collins in the spring of 1828. In addition, he wrote general editorials on the essential right of British subjects to meet and discuss public affairs and on the necessary balance between executive and legislative powers.

After the paper called Dalhousie's prorogation speech of 22 Nov. 1827 "extraordinary, unsuitable, unwarrantable; [it] ... ought never to have been issued," Waller and Duvernay were arrested on 18 December for libel against the government by order of the attorney general. Waller had been on his way to address a constitutional meeting convened to prepare for the colonial secretary a list of complaints against the government. Bail was instantly procured. Waller's arrest was said to have given greater impetus to the protest movement, and he read with "active and excited feelings ... the various charges brought by the country, against the infamous government of the day." A true bill was found against him, but the special jury assembled for his trial in September 1828 was declared to have been illegally constituted and was dismissed. The case was held over until March 1829. But Waller, overcome by "sickness, weariness, hostility and worries," died on 2 Dec. 1828, while charges were still pending and the questions of colonists' rights and of union were far from settled. After his death, his ideas were perpetuated in *La Minerve* by Duvernay and in the *Irish Vindicator and Canada General Advertiser*, founded on 12 Dec. 1828 by fellow Irishman Daniel TRACEY.

Jocelyn Waller's death was followed within a year by the deaths of his two older brothers in Ireland; his eldest son, Edmund, succeeded to the baronetcy and to a considerable fortune of £6–7,000 a year. Waller's death was mourned by both French- and English-speaking inhabitants of Lower Canada. A committee to erect a monument was chaired by young Augustin-Norbert Morin*, who had been among the law students participating in the journalist's funeral rites. Waller had been much admired as a firm advocate of liberalism, a spokesman for French Canadians, and "an able and talented political writer" with an "amiable and virtuous character."

ELIZABETH WATERSTON

ANQ-M, CE1-63, 4 déc. 1828. ANQ-Q, P1000-41-757. PAC, RG 68, General index, 1651–1841. PRO, CO 42/178: 66, 322 (copies at PAC). *British Colonist and St. Francis Gazette* (Stanstead, Que.), 23 Aug. 1827. *Canadian Spectator* (Montreal), October 1822–December 1828. *Quebec Gazette*, 15 Jan. 1818; 5, 9 July 1821; 19 Sept. 1822. Beaulieu et Hamelin, *La presse québécoise*, vol.1. *Burke's peerage* (1826). H. J. Morgan, *Bibliotheca Canadensis; Sketches of celebrated Canadians*. J.-G. Barthe, *Souvenirs d'un demi-siècle ou mémoires pour servir à l'histoire contemporaine* (Montréal, 1885). Ægidius Fauteux, "Jocelyn Waller," *BRH*, 26 (1920): 307–10.

WALTERMEYER, HANS (Johannes Waltermyer). *See* MEYERS, JOHN WALDEN

WARREN, Sir JOHN BORLASE, naval officer; b. 2 Sept. 1753 in Stapleford (Nottinghamshire), England, fourth son of John Borlase Warren and Bridget Rossell; m. 13 Dec. 1780 Caroline Clavering in London, and they had three daughters and two sons; d. 27 Feb. 1822 in Greenwich Hospital (London), England, while visiting Sir Richard Goodwin KEATS.

John Borlase Warren was entered as an able seaman on the books of the *Marlborough* on 24 April 1771, although he had been admitted to Emmanuel College, Cambridge, in 1769. His college and naval careers were intermingled, and he graduated with a BA in 1773 and an MA in 1776. In 1774 Warren had been elected to parliament for Marlow in Buckinghamshire (he sat for several constituencies between then and 1807), and on 1 June 1775 he assumed the baronetcy that had been extinct since the death of his great-grandfather.

Warren served on the North American station during the American Revolutionary War, mainly aboard frigates and sloops, and was promoted lieutenant in July 1778 and captain in April 1781. In the French revolutionary wars he commanded a frigate squadron which captured most of a similar French force on 23 April 1794, and for this action was made a knight of the Bath. Warren was unleashed on the French coast with another frigate squadron in 1796 and captured 220 sail, including 37 naval vessels. With three sail of the line and five frigates, he caught a French squadron with 5,000 troops off the west coast of Ireland on 10 Oct. 1798, captured four ships, and scattered the rest. He received the thanks of the British and Irish parliaments and a gold medal. Warren served in the Mediterranean in 1801, and in 1802 undertook a special mission to St Petersburg (Leningrad, U.S.S.R.) to congratulate Emperor Alexander I on his accession. Promoted rear-admiral on 14 Feb. 1799, he became vice-admiral on 9 Nov. 1805 and an admiral on 31 July 1810. Between November 1807 and July 1810 he was commander-in-chief of the Halifax station.

Warren's major North American service came during the War of 1812. As admiral of the blue he was appointed on 3 Aug. 1812 to the Halifax, Leeward Islands, and Jamaica stations, the Admiralty having unified the three commands to allow him to direct the overall naval strategy of the war. Warren's initial task upon his arrival at Halifax in September was to negotiate an end to the conflict with the American secretary of state, James Monroe. After this attempt failed, he laid out his strategy of fighting a defensive war off the North American coast to protect trade, while keeping up limited blockades of American waters with forces operating from the two main bases of Halifax and Bermuda. Writing privately in December to Lord Melville, his patron at the Admiralty, Warren argued that a series of raids on the enemy coast, and selective blockades until reinforcements were sent, would keep American military forces tied down and relieve pressure on British North America. To strengthen inland naval defences, Warren advised the Admiralty to send a force to the Canadian lakes, a recommendation which was followed in March 1813 with the ordering out of seamen under Sir James Lucas Yeo*. Warren also urged Sir George Prevost*, the military commander in North America, to build more ships on the lakes, and dispatched three of his lieutenants, Robert Heriot Barclay*, Daniel Pring*, and Robert Finnis, there.

Unfortunately for Warren, the force at his disposal always lacked ships, seamen, provisions, and stores, even after reinforcements arrived. His incessant requests probably irritated the Admiralty, and he was reprimanded for them by its secretary, John Wilson Croker. Yet Warren's vessels had to blockade the main American ports from New York City south, watch and restrain scores of privateers, be alert for forays by the American frigates and sloops, guard the convoys from Jamaica to Quebec, protect Halifax and Bermuda, and carry out raids on the coasts of Chesapeake and Delaware bays. He was relieved in March 1814, when the Admiralty re-established independent stations and appointed Sir Alexander Forrester Inglis Cochrane to the North American one. Warren was embittered enough to protest to Lord Melville and to hold up transfer of the command to Cochrane until 1 April. Apart from the blow to his prestige, Warren was concerned that the loss of command would exclude him from receiving prize money. The station commander was allowed a percentage of the proceeds from the sale of every captured vessel, and Warren kept a secretary just to record captured vessels and his potential earnings.

Writers on the War of 1812 such as William James, Alfred Thayer Mahan, Cecil Scott Forester, and John K. Mahon have considerably undervalued Warren's achievements. But his earlier career reveals that he was at times a dashing and successful tactician. His conduct of the naval war, while not marked with spectacular successes, nevertheless helped to relieve the pressure on the Canadas and meshed well with Prevost's land strategy. The defeat of Napoleon in the spring of 1814 allowed a rapid buildup of men and material, and permitted the Admiralty to consider a more aggressive strategy than Warren's defensive approach with limited resources. By that time, however, Warren had returned to England, and he retired with a GCB in 1815.

FREDERICK C. DRAKE

A portrait of Warren by John Opie has descended in the Warren family; a reproduction of a lithograph is in W. L. Clowes, *The Royal Navy; a history from the earliest times to the present* (7v., London, 1897–1903), 4: 253.

NMM, HUL/1–47; LBK/2. PRO, ADM 1/502–3, 1/505; ADM 2/162, 2/933, 2/1375. *Annual reg.* (London), 1822: 272–73. William James, *The naval history of Great Britain, from the declaration of war by France in 1793, to the accession of George IV . . .* (new ed., 6v., London, 1837), 6. U.S., Congress, *American state papers: documents, legislative and executive, of the Congress of the United States . . .* , ed. Walter Lowrie *et al.* (38 vols. in 10 classes, Washington, 1832–61), class 1. *DNB*. C. S. Forester, *The age of fighting sail: the story of the naval War of 1812* (Garden City, N.Y., 1956), 78–80, 88–89, 91, 132–34, 140–42. A. T. Mahan, *Sea power in its relations to the War of 1812* (2v., London,

Washburn

1905), 1: 389–92, 401–4, 2: 155–69, 209–11. J. K. Mahon, *The War of 1812* (Gainesville, Fla., 1972), 54–55, 109–11, 115–17, 119–22.

WASHBURN, EBENEZER, merchant, politician, JP, and office holder; b. 8 April 1756 in Attleborough (Attleboro), Mass., son of Simeon Washburn and Jemimah Gary; m. first Sarah De Forest, and they had nine children; m. secondly 24 Jan. 1803 Hannah McBride, a widow, in York (Toronto); d. 12 Nov. 1826 in Hallowell (Picton), Upper Canada.

At the outbreak of the American revolution Ebenezer Washburn was a small farmer living in Rutland, which was then in the colony of New York but soon after became part of Vermont. Although his father had declared for the rebels, in July 1777 Washburn left his home and joined the army of Major-General John Burgoyne*. He was soon captured and kept "in Irons" for several months before being released. Early in October local revolutionary authorities in New York allowed him to visit his father in Keene, N.H., where Ebenezer spent a good part of the ensuing months. He left Keene on 18 April 1778, ostensibly to get his sister, and did not return. His land in Rutland was confiscated on 23 April. Meanwhile Washburn escaped to Quebec and enlisted in Edward Jessup*'s corps on 16 May, remaining with this unit for the duration of the conflict. He rose to the rank of sergeant and served as an assistant commissary for three years. After the war he started a new life on 200 acres of land in Township No.2 (Ernestown), in what was to become the province of Upper Canada.

During the 1780s the horizons of his life were family and farm. Washburn, however, was a man with ambitions, both for himself and for his children. By 1796 he had moved to Fredericksburgh Township, but a few years later he settled at Hallowell Bridge (Picton) in Prince Edward County. He was soon one of the largest landowners in Hallowell Township, owning 1,190 acres by 1808. He also took advantage of the opportunities provided by his location at Hallowell Bridge, which, with its good natural harbour, became the major shipping and mercantile centre of the county. By 1799 he was well established as a general merchant and forwarder and from 1800 was involved in the export of flour to Lower Canada. Between 1809 and 1811 he seems to have had minor problems paying bills, and he suffered heavily in the depression that hit the province in the late 1810s. By 1819, however, business seems to have improved, if only slightly.

Contemporaries regarded Washburn as a "man of wealth and influence" and stories illustrating his supposed riches were common. Yet to the extent that he is remembered by historians, it is as a politician. In 1800, and again four years later, he was elected to the House of Assembly for the riding of Prince Edward. There was nothing unusual about his activities during the third parliament (1801–4). He supported and often introduced legislation reflecting his regional and mercantile interests. He was concerned with the state of commerce, the condition of local roads, the revenue-sharing agreement with Lower Canada, and legislation to effect the speedy recovery of small debts. A matter of continuing interest was, as his critic Richard Cartwright* put it, "Mr. Washburn's extravagant project for making Quebec a free port" – a project inspired by his belief that the Navigation Acts, by closing the ports of Montreal and Quebec to non-British ships, allowed a few Lower Canadian merchants to dominate Upper Canada's import and export trade. On constitutional matters, he supported attempts to defend the prerogatives and increase the powers of the assembly.

Washburn's importance as an assemblyman derives from his association with the parliamentary opposition which originated in the fourth parliament (1805–8). Early in the first session he indicated his willingness to support, on certain issues, a small group usually consisting of William Weekes*, Benajah Mallory*, Thomas DORLAND, and David McGregor ROGERS. He voted with the minority on the motion of 1 March 1805 by Weekes and Rogers to take into consideration "the disquietude which prevails in the Province by reason of the administration of Public Offices." In subsequent sessions of this parliament, the loose association of opposition assemblymen evolved into a more cohesive group under the leadership of Weekes, Robert Thorpe*, and Joseph Willcocks*. One of the issues raised by this group was the widely unpopular reforms introduced in the land-granting system by Lieutenant Governor Peter Hunter*. Washburn had suffered temporarily at least under the new regulations and he seconded Thorpe's motion of 4 March 1807 to address Lieutenant Governor Francis Gore* on the changes in policy. For Cartwright, Washburn was on this occasion no more than Thorpe's cat's-paw. Cartwright insisted that on another occasion Thorpe had prepared a speech for Washburn to deliver: "But Washburn being as you know no scholar and having taken rather too deep a drink in order to animate himself . . . so mangled the Judge's horrid language that . . . he was obliged to break off abruptly and sit down to the no small confusion of his friend." A further instance of close cooperation with Thorpe occurred on 7 March. Washburn had been on Weekes's committee on public accounts which had pressured President Alexander Grant* in 1806 about a sum spent by Hunter without prior authorization by the assembly. After the money was restored to the house, a conciliatory motion was put forward to relinquish the funds "as we are convinced that the same was expended for the public use, and for the benefit of this Province." Having won its point, the assembly was disposed to accept this concession. Only Washburn and Thorpe opposed the compromise and voted against it.

As the main mover of the District School Act of 1807, which laid the foundation of the public school system, Washburn made his most lasting and significant contribution. He shepherded the bill through the house in the face of strong opposition, including Thorpe's. Because of his initiatives and continuing support for the principle of public support for education, he may be considered as one of the fathers of the Ontario educational system. In 1808 the schools established by the act came under a stinging attack in the Bay of Quinte region. The assault in the assembly was led by Rogers and Dorland. Rogers criticized Washburn for supporting a bill that had been "universally condemned" by the inhabitants of Prince Edward. Washburn replied that, although the act was opposed initially, the settlers were now "satisfied it was a good measure," adding, moreover, that "if every man in the County . . . was against the Bill he would vote for it!" His commitment was one of personal conviction, and it kept him either from siding with his old associates or from bowing to popular complaints. In his view schools were essential to the progress and development of society and of an individual. As for his own youngest sons, Daniel and Simon Ebenezer*, he "thought proper to Put them to School, in the best we had established in the Province."

Cartwright was wrong about Washburn; he was undoubtedly influenced by Thorpe on certain issues but, as his leadership on the school bill proved, he was not a dupe. Nor was he an unthinking member of the opposition. In fact, his record shows him to have been an independent who supported the principle of collective opposition but departed from his allies whenever his and their views collided. In spite of officialdom's uncomprehending and oft-times hysterical reaction to the perceived republicanism of the opposition, Washburn's political views were simply whiggish without a tinge of radicalism. Throughout his life he remained strongly committed to British institutions and especially to a functioning constitutional system of checks and balances and separation of powers – hence the importance, nay the necessity, of opposition. It was his very loyalism that led him to become a critic of executive government.

It is not known whether Washburn ran in the election of 1808. On 10 March of that year he was appointed a justice of the peace; he served continuously until his death. He was named a commissioner to check sedition in 1812 and appointed a high treason commissioner in 1814, but attended to both duties irregularly. He continued to take an interest in politics. On 25 Jan. 1810 he had signed the petition protesting the election to the assembly of John Roblin and James Wilson on the grounds that they were Methodist "public Preachers and Teachers." The protest was upheld and two months later their seats were declared vacant. He chaired a meeting in Hallowell on 14 Feb. 1818 to discuss Robert Gourlay*'s address to landowners; the meeting concluded that Gourlay's proposals "would be of general benefit to this Province." His son Daniel, a legal colleague of Barnabas BIDWELL, was elected for the district to Gourlay's Upper Canadian Convention of Friends to Enquiry. Washburn himself ran for election for the last time in the summer of 1820 but, receiving only marginal support, withdrew from the poll on the third day.

A steadfast Presbyterian (his daughter married the Reverend Robert McDowall*), Washburn was also an officer of the Midland District Agricultural Society. During the last ten years of his life he was plagued by edema, or dropsy as contemporaries knew it. Near the end his condition worsened and he "underwent the operation of tapping ten times." Upon his death he was eulogized as a loyalist and early settler who had served in political life "to the honour of himself and the benefit and satisfaction of the public."

ROBERT LOCHIEL FRASER

AO, MS 88, Hannah Washburn to St George, 28 Jan., 3 May 1815; MS 522, memoranda respecting the District School Bill, 5 March 1808; MS 788, Washburn to David Young, 3 Jan. 1818; MU 588, certificates, 15 Jan. 1818; MU 3104–5; RG 1, A-I-6: 2837, 2904, 3772; RG 22, ser.04, vol.6, 9 Jan. 1793; ser.54, 2; ser.131, 1: ff.53, 112, 249–51; ser.159, Ebenezer Washburn; RG 53, ser.2, 2: ff.255–57. BL, Add. mss 21826: 245; 21827: 317b; 21828: 7 (mfm. at PAC). Lennox and Addington County Museum (Napanee, Ont.), Lennox and Addington Hist. Soc. Coll., William Bell papers, pp.353–56; T. W. Casey papers, pp.11726–27. PAC, RG 1, E14, 12: 253–54; L3, 522: W2/48; 523: W3/147; 525: W8/87–88; 525a: W9/59; 527: W11/47, 54; 545: W leases/40; RG 5, A1: 2952–53, 4600–1, 7788–93, 8574–75, 11316–17; RG 8, I (C ser.), 20: 142a–44; RG 68, General index, 1651–1841: 242, 244, 419–20, 432, 435, 441, 452. PRO, AO 12/38: 331–33. QUA, Richard Cartwright papers, letter-books (transcripts at AO, 140, 214–19, 252–57, 262–67).

"Assessment of the township of Hallowell for the year 1808," OH, 6 (1905): 168–70. "District of Mecklenburg (Kingston): Court of Common Pleas," AO Report, 1917: 241. "Early municipal records of the Midland District," Ont., Bureau of Industries, App. to the report (Toronto), 1897: 76. "Grants of crown lands in U.C.," AO Report, 1928. "Journals of Legislative Assembly of U.C.," AO Report, 1909, 1911, 1914. "McDowall marriage register," comp. [Robert] McDowall, OH, 1 (1899): 73. Town of York, 1793–1815 (Firth), 89, 99. "United Empire Loyalists: enquiry into losses and services," AO Report, 1904: 1014. "U.C. land book B," AO Report, 1930. "U.C. land book C," AO Report, 1931. "U.C. land book D," AO Report, 1931. Vt., Secretary of State, Sequestration, confiscation and sale of estates, ed. Mary Greene Nye ([Montpelier, Vt.?, 1941]), 15, 17, 345. Vital records of Attleborough, Massachusetts, to the end of the year 1849 (Salem, Mass., 1934), 279. Vital statistics of the town of Keene, New Hampshire . . . , comp. F. H. Whitcomb (Keene, 1905), 238. Kingston

Waugh

Chronicle, 5 May, 14–21 July 1820; 24 Nov. 1826; 19 March 1831. *Kingston Gazette*, 4 May 1814; 6 July 1816; 17–24 Feb., 21 July 1818. *Upper Canada Gazette*, 5 March 1812. W. D. Reid, *The loyalists in Ontario: the sons and daughters of the American loyalists of Upper Canada* (Lambertville, N.J., 1973). *Rolls of the Provincial (Loyalist) Corps, Canadian command, American revolutionary period*, comp. Mary Beacock Fryer and W. A. Smy (Toronto, 1981), 89. Canniff, *Hist. of the settlement of U.C.* Cowdell Gates, *Land policies of U.C.*, 277. F. B. Kingsbury, *History of the town of Surry, Cheshire County, New Hampshire . . .* (Surry, 1925), 915–16. Richard and Janet Lunn, *The county: the first hundred years in loyalist Prince Edward* (Picton, Ont., 1967), 89, 131. Patterson, "Studies in elections in U.C.," 313.

WAUGH, WELLWOOD (Welwood), joiner, miller, farmer, estate manager, and JP; b. 15 Feb. 1741 in Lockerbie, Scotland, son of Alexander Waugh and Catherine Colven; m. 28 March 1760 Helen Henderson in Wallastown (probably in the Annandale valley), Scotland, and they had nine children; d. 3 June 1824 at Waughs River, N.S.

Wellwood Waugh's career is obscure until 1774, when he and his family emigrated with a group of fellow Lowland Scots on the *Lovely Nelly*, bound for Georgetown, St John's (Prince Edward) Island. Although the failure to "earn bread sufficient to support . . . his family" was cited as the reason for leaving, tradition claims that Waugh received a considerable inheritance upon his father's death and, with one John Smith, was largely responsible for financially underwriting the venture. Whatever the case, the lures of property ownership and religious independence, rather than simple poverty, were the likely determinants in prompting these persecuted, rent-weary Covenanters to leave their homeland for the New World.

The sojourn at Georgetown was brief and unhappy. In 1775 American raiders carried off all the supplies and the settlers were left starving. Desperation drove them in the spring of 1776 to Pictou, N.S., where they were welcomed into a struggling community of fellow Scots. Waugh was soon well established as a stavemaker and grist-mill operator, but his strict covenanter conscience prevented him from taking the oath of allegiance, and in a community endeavouring to maintain neutrality his loyalty was questioned. According to tradition, William Lowden, captain of the ship *Molly*, was detained at Waugh's home in November 1776, and afterwards both master and vessel were taken to Baie Verte (N.B.) by a gang of pro-Americans. Documentary evidence has since absolved Waugh, but in Pictou at the time his sympathies remained suspect.

In the summer of 1781, after fire had destroyed his home and belongings, Waugh was invited by Mary CANNON, agent and attorney for Joseph Frederick Wallet DESBARRES, to assume the short-term lease of the manor-farm on DesBarres's Tatamagouche property. She no doubt saw in Waugh the conscientious, hard-working individual needed to oversee the troublesome estate. Waugh, in turn, temporarily submerged his innate distaste for leasehold property in anticipation of a responsible position for himself and an atmosphere of religious tolerance among DesBarres's Montbéliard-French tenants. He was soon appointed local estate agent and in 1785 DesBarres granted him power of attorney to arrange leases, inducing the Scotsman to remain with what Waugh later termed "repeated assurances . . . that he [Waugh] should be liberally rewarded for his trouble."

The Tatamagouche estate was attached for debt three times in 1787, and to secure the property Waugh collected all outstanding rent and removed DesBarres's livestock to safety. Many tenants, fearing eviction by new landlords, bought security by also paying rent to the creditors, and then harangued Waugh for his earlier collection. There was an unfortunate incident in which Waugh's cattle, as well as some belonging to tenants, were seized and sold at ruinously low prices to satisfy the creditors. Confusion reigned, and Mary Cannon, desperate to raise funds, eventually offered Waugh, in return for £250, a lucrative 999-year lease on the manor-farm at £15 annual rent. The agent leapt at what amounted to outright ownership and, when he subsequently informed DesBarres of his actions, the latter "appeared much pleased and fully satisfied with and made no Objections whatever to the same."

At DesBarres's request Captain John MacDonald* of Glenaladale, a St John's Island landholder, toured the property in 1795. Afterwards MacDonald expressed regret over Waugh's management of affairs in 1787, fearing that the agent had seriously endangered the estate by alienating both tenants and prospective settlers. He did, however, support Waugh over the complaints of several disgruntled tenants, and reported that the agent and his family were "very active[,] industrious, and as fit for any business by sea or Land as any. . . . [They] excite all the life or stirr that appears to be in the place . . . [and] without them it would be dead to all intents."

MacDonald's fears were groundless, and Tatamagouche prospered under the direction of Waugh and his sons. They did their own ironwork, raised surplus cattle for sale, and, with DesBarres's financial aid, built a grist-mill and sawmill, the latter cutting 200,000 board feet annually. Two additional sawmills were built as well and the export of lumber became an important local industry. Waugh served as estate manager, as local magistrate, and also as government courier, carrying dispatches from Tatamagouche to Truro. Some time after his wife's death in 1795, he returned to Scotland and studied watchmaking for several years, writing to Tatamagouche in 1802 that he was "the oldest tradesman and the youngest apprentice." While overseas, he persuaded several of his countrymen to come out to Tatamagouche, thus augmenting the strong Scottish principles and new ethnic balance of the area.

The exact date of Waugh's return to Tatamagouche is not known, but he was certainly back in the settlement by 1806. As the immigrant families settled in, Waugh became a guiding force in local religious life, offering financial assistance and the use of his barn for summer services to the Reverend John Mitchell, who had arrived at River John in 1808. The planned construction of a meeting-house in Tatamagouche split the community, and Waugh lamented that by "incoherently dividing in their opinions, concerning matters of small importance, [they] soon desisted from their imaginary ideas [of having a church?], – ideas which seemed rather to frustrate, than to propagate the gospel among them." When a second attempt ended in failure, Waugh and his sons built the meeting-house themselves and Willow Church was opened in August 1820.

Waugh's last years were marred by conflict with DesBarres who, bitter over the failure of his colonial property ventures, took both Waugh and Mary Cannon to the Court of Chancery in 1809. Waugh was charged with collusion in accepting the 1787 farm lease, which DesBarres now denied knowledge of, calling it "not less remarkable for its preposterous illegality and subdolous futility, than for its glaring Depravity and arrogant Impudence." DesBarres also accused Waugh of granting to settlers long leases, at low rents, of prime Tatamagouche land without his permission, and contended that the family had been removing timber from his personal property. Waugh, with Samuel George William Archibald* acting as his counsel, made his innocence abundantly clear in reply; during some 25 years of local management, his actions had never been seriously questioned and, although he had fully advised DesBarres of his work, he had rarely received acknowledgement or instructions in return. Other than an order to cease cutting timber, no legal judgement was issued in the case, which dragged on until DesBarres's death in October 1824. Waugh had died four months previously, upset at the stain on an otherwise spotless career. He had worked long and hard in Tatamagouche, imbuing it with his Scottish vigour and moral probity, but receiving no recompense other than his sense of duty done. Sir John Wentworth* had called him "an upright, active, loyal subject . . . deriving therefrom a good property, [and] considerable influence in that Country." After his death Tatamagouche was never the same.

LOIS KERNAGHAN

PAC, MG 11, [CO 229] Prince Edward Island B, 1: 150–68

(transcripts); MG 23, F1, ser.2: 4–5, 28–38, 45–46; ser.5: 4580–87. PANS, Biog., Waugh family papers (mfm.); MG 5, 2, no.10: 87–88; RG 1, 174–76; RG 20A, 32; RG 36, no.179, *DesBarres v. Cannon, Waugh et al. Emigrants from Scotland to America, 1774–1775; copied from a loose bundle of Treasury papers in the Public Record Office, London, England*, comp. V. R. Cameron ([New York?], 1930; repr. Baltimore, Md., 1965). D. C. Mackay, *Silversmiths and related craftsmen of the Atlantic provinces* (Halifax, 1973). F. H. Patterson, *The days of the ships, Tatamagouche, N.S.* (Truro, N.S., 1970); *History of Tatamagouche, Nova Scotia* (Halifax, 1917; repr. Belleville, Ont., 1973); *Tatamagouche, N.S., 1771–1824* (Truro, 1971). George Patterson, *A history of the county of Pictou, Nova Scotia* (Montreal, 1877).

WEGGISHGOMIN. *See* OGIMAUH-BINAESSIH

WENGER, JOHANNES (later known as **John Winger**), Tunker bishop; b. in Lancaster County, Pa, son of Christian Wenger; m. 24 Aug. 1777 Elizabeth Eschlemann, and they had 10 children; d. 1827 at Black Creek, Bertie Township, Upper Canada.

Johannes Wenger grew up in Lancaster County among German and Swiss settlers who had emigrated in search of religious freedom. Family tradition told that his grandmother had left Switzerland to avoid having to attend the Roman Catholic church on the occasions required by law. Wenger became one of the leaders of the Brethren in Christ, known in Canada also as Tunkers, a pietistic group which emerged in Pennsylvania during the 1770s. He shared the Mennonite background of some of the early Brethren ministers, including the founder, Jacob Engel. The new church, however, also adopted many practices of the German Baptists of the area, particularly baptism by trine immersion.

The majority of the Brethren in Christ remained in Pennsylvania after the American Revolutionary War. Those who did emigrate considered themselves to be loyalist in spirit, although their pacifist principles had prevented them from bearing arms. In 1788 Wenger led a group of family and neighbours to the Niagara Peninsula. They first settled at the Short Hills, reminiscent of their hilly homeland in Pennsylvania. Here they experienced the hardships of 1788–89, known as the "hungry year," and in 1792 a violent storm laid waste their crops and buildings. Some time between 1792 and 1797 Wenger and his family relocated in Bertie Township.

Wenger appears to have held the offices of elder and overseer (bishop) on his arrival in the Niagara Peninsula. Under his leadership a small congregation was established at Short Hills, and on his removal to Bertie Township the largest Upper Canadian congregation was formed. As meetings were held in homes or barns, church buildings were not immediately required. Wenger did set aside a plot on his farm, on

Westbrook

the banks of Black Creek, for a cemetery. He also supervised the formation of congregations in York County and what was later to be Waterloo County.

Wenger must have been involved in prompting legislation affecting his co-religionists. By the Militia Act of 1793 Quakers, Mennonites, and Tunkers could be exempted from military service upon an annual payment of £1 in peace-time or £5 in time of invasion or insurrection. The exemption depended on presentation of a certificate of membership in one of those sects, and since adult baptism was practised, many young men would reach military age before attaining church membership. An act of 1810 remedied that difficulty. On a different front, in 1794 Mennonites, Tunkers, and others petitioned that their ministers be permitted to solemnize marriages. Action was postponed until after Lieutenant Governor Simcoe*'s departure. At the end of 1798 a marriage act came into force allowing Church of Scotland, Lutheran, and Calvinist ministers the right to celebrate matrimony, and Tunkers were presumed to be included under the rubric of Calvinist. Tunker tradition credits Wenger with being the first non-Anglican clergyman to be so authorized.

Wenger would have grown a beard (perhaps without moustache), kept his hair long and parted in the middle, and worn the coat of home-made cloth and the low, broad-rimmed hat of Tunker fashion. The image of patriarch is appropriate for one who combined the roles of pioneer farmer and church leader. As for the political developments in which he undoubtedly played a part, the legal concessions that allowed Tunkers to retain their pacifist principles, acknowledged their practice of adult baptism, and recognized marriages performed by their clergy contributed to the development of religious pluralism in Upper Canada.

RICHARD E. RUGGLE

PAC, RG 1, L3, 522: W2/100 (mfm. at AO). *Corr. of Lieut. Governor Simcoe* (Cruikshank), 3: 4. "U.C. land book B," AO *Report*, 1930. A. W. Climenhaga, *History of the Brethren in Christ Church* (Nappanee, Ind., 1942). George Cober, *A historical sketch of the Brethren in Christ Church, known as Tunkers in Canada*, with *Supplement . . .* (Gormley, Ont., [1953?]), 5–6, 43. *The history of the county of Welland, Ontario . . .* ([Welland], 1889; repr. with intro. by John Burtniak, Belleville, Ont., 1972). *Origin and history of the Tunker Church in Canada as gathered from authentic and reliable sources*, comp. Asa Bearss and Wellington Duxbury (Ridgeway, Ont., 1918). G. E. Reaman, *The trail of the black walnut* (Toronto, 1957). E. M. Sider, "History of the Brethren in Christ (Tunker) Church in Canada" (MA thesis, Univ. of Western Ont., London, 1955); "The early years of the Tunkers in Upper Canada," *OH*, 51 (1959): 121–29.

WESTBROOK, ANDREW, businessman and office holder; b. 1771 in Massachusetts, son of Anthony Westbrook and Sarah Decker; m. four times, to Sally Hull, Nancy Thorn, Margaret Ann Crawford, and a woman whose name has not been determined; he had at least 14 children; d. 1835 in St Clair County, Mich.

Shortly before the American Revolutionary War, Anthony Westbrook moved with his family from the Minisink (Port Jervis) region of New York state to Massachusetts. During the war Anthony, alone of his family, took the loyalist side. He fought under Joseph Brant [Thayendanegea*] and for this service received two tracts of land along the La Tranche (Thames) River in Upper Canada. Although the story is confusing, it appears that Anthony brought his family to Upper Canada at the close of the war and settled, not on his lands along the La Tranche, but on the banks of the Grand River. Andrew inherited his father's land by the Thames, and he seems to have moved there after Ebenezer Allan* established the Delaware settlement in 1794. Adding to this land through government grants and business arrangements, Andrew owned more than 4,000 acres at the outbreak of the War of 1812. On a tract in Delaware Township he had built a comfortable house as well as a distillery, barn, storehouse, sawmill, and grist-mill. His status in the community was reflected in his appointment as township constable in 1805.

Westbrook's life in Upper Canada was not without its problems, however. As a merchant he suffered from the commercial depression which began with a severe fall in prices in 1810. As a land speculator, he quarrelled with the government's restrictive immigration policy, and, in particular, with the despotic powers wielded by the government's chief representative in the area, Colonel Thomas Talbot*. It is likely that the frustrations Westbrook encountered were the determining factors in his decision to change sides during the War of 1812. In mid July 1812 an American army under Brigadier-General William Hull crossed the Detroit River into Upper Canada. Daniel Springer of Delaware, who had been appointed a magistrate by Talbot, reported to Major-General Isaac Brock* that Westbrook had helped circulate Hull's proclamation urging the local inhabitants to surrender. Springer also noted that Ebenezer Allan and Simon Zelotes Watson, two of Westbrook's friends and, like him, enemies of Talbot, were actively supporting the American cause.

Disaffection was rife in the southwestern part of the province and, in the atmosphere of alarm felt by the civil and military authorities, dissidents were easily suspected and arbitrarily imprisoned. The evidence is inconclusive as to whether Westbrook distributed Hull's proclamation or was just suspected of doing so. However, he certainly helped draw up a petition to Hull in which the signatories promised not to resist the invaders if their properties were spared. He met with Hull at Fort Detroit in early August and returned to Delaware to spy for the Americans. Captured by the militia in October, he escaped to join the American forces under Lieutenant-Colonel George Croghan as a spy. After the defeat of the British at the battle of Moraviantown in October 1813, he served as a guide to parties of Michigan Rangers who raided the vulnerable settlements along the Thames River and Lake Erie.

Powerfully built, 6 feet 2 inches tall, and red-haired, Westbrook struck terror into the hearts of Canadian settlers in 1814 when only the militia was available to defend them against marauders. On 31 Jan. 1814 Westbrook's band raided Delaware and captured officers and men of the Middlesex County militia, including Daniel Springer and Colonel François Baby*. Westbrook then burned his own house, buildings, and corn and guided his family to the American border. On another raid in the spring of 1814, this time on the village of Oxford (Oxford Centre), Westbrook captured an old rival, Sikes Tousley. He took Tousley from his bed at gunpoint and led him to the American lines, although not before Tousley had bayoneted him in the thigh in an unguarded moment.

The raids on Port Talbot were particularly damaging. On 16 August Westbrook just missed seizing Colonel Talbot, who escaped through a back window of his home. His practice of carrying off high-ranking officers made trouble for his Upper Canadian pursuers who, on one occasion, mistakenly shot a prisoner mounted on Westbrook's horse. He destroyed mills and plunged the areas he burned and pillaged into great hardship.

In 1815 Westbrook purchased a farm and lands on the St Clair River above Marine City in St Clair County, Mich. Governor Lewis Cass appointed him the first supervisor of highways in 1817 and one of the first three county commissioners in 1821. In 1828 the American Congress, in recognition of his war services, granted him two tracts of land, the larger being in Clay Township, Mich. A good description of Westbrook during his years in Michigan is provided by one American government official who wrote: "He has a quick-moving, and intelligent eye. . . . He has no education, yet he talks well, and is precise, and graphic in his descriptions. . . . If he once resolves upon the accomplishment of any object, he is sure to realize it. The means are mere materials to be judged of by his conceptions of Right; and these are generally made to obey the impulses of the moment, come from what quarter, or involve what consequences they may."

In Upper Canada, Westbrook had been indicted for treason at Ancaster in May 1814. The Court of Quarter Sessions of the Niagara District declared him an outlaw in 1816. A crown commission of Thomas Talbot and Robert NICHOL, charged to look into the extent of Westbrook's lands in the province, deter-

mined that he owned about 4,040 acres. Petitions to buy the land came in from former neighbours. In 1823 a sale of Westbrook's "land, premises and appurtenances" in Delaware Township was made to Daniel Springer.

Westbrook is the hero of John Richardson*'s novel *Westbrook, the outlaw; or, the avenging wolf*. Richardson skilfully draws a connection between Westbrook's status as a "yeoman" – a term that is used in the 1823 registration of sale of his lands – and the fictional character's resentment of government favours shown to Captain Stringer, a member of the landed gentry. In Michigan, the real Westbrook found no hindrance to his progress, social as well as material. He liked to be referred to as Baron Steuben, a role that he played with "certain amiable eccentricities."

D. R. BEASLEY

AO, MU 1368; MU 2389, file 29. Middlesex West Land Registry Office (Glencoe, Ont.), Deeds, liber B: f.542; Delaware, Ekfrid, and Metcalfe townships, patents, 1797–1870 (mfm. at AO). MTL, W. D. Powell papers, B85: 70–71. PAC, RG 1, L3, 522: W2/14. Wentworth Land Registry Office (Hamilton, Ont.), Abstract index to deeds, Ancaster Township (mfm. at AO). *Documents relating to the invasion of Canada and the surrender of Detroit, 1812*, ed. E. A. Cruikshank (Ottawa, 1912). *John Askin papers* (Quaife), 2: 713. T. L. McKenney, *Sketches of a tour to the lakes, of the character and customs of the Chippeway Indians, and of the incidents connected with the Treaty of Fond du Lac* (Baltimore, Md., 1827; repr. Minneapolis, Minn., 1959). "Minutes of the Court of General Quarter Sessions of the Peace for the London District . . . ," AO *Report*, 1933: 23, 31, 74, 85–86. John Richardson, *Westbrook, the outlaw; or, the avenging wolf* (New York, 1853; repr. with preface by D. R. Beasley, Montreal, 1973). *Select British docs. of War of 1812* (Wood), vols.1–2. U.S., House of Representatives report 58, Committee on private land claims, 19th Congress, 2nd session, 26 Jan. 1827; report 20, 20th Congress, 1st session, 19 Dec. 1827.

Ancaster's heritage: a history of Ancaster Township (Ancaster, Ont., 1973). D. R. Beasley, *The Canadian Don Quixote: the life and works of Major John Richardson, Canada's first novelist* (Erin, Ont., 1977). *The defended border: Upper Canada and the War of 1812 . . .*, ed. Morris Zaslow and W. B. Turner (Toronto, 1964). C. O. [Z.] Ermatinger, *The Talbot regime; or the first half century of the Talbot settlement* (St Thomas, Ont., 1904). F. C. Hamil, *The valley of the lower Thames, 1640 to 1850* (Toronto, 1951; repr. Toronto and Buffalo, N.Y., 1973). Hitsman, *Incredible War of 1812*. W. L. Jenks, *St. Clair County, Michigan, its history and its people; a narrative account of its historical progress and its principal interests* (2v., Chicago and New York, 1912). D. M. Mitts, *That noble country; the romance of the St. Clair River region* (Philadelphia, 1968), 217–20. *Westbrook–Gage miscellany: a souvenir of the Westbrook–Gage reunion, Stoney Creek, Ontario, July 1, 1909* ([Thamesville, Ont.], 1911), 5. M. E. Cropp, "A history of Beachville," *Western Ontario Hist. Nuggets* (London), 14

Wetmore

(1949). E. A. Cruikshank, "The early history of the London District," *OH*, 24 (1927): 199–201; "General Hull's invasion of Canada in 1812" and "A study of disaffection in Upper Canada in 1812–15," RSC *Trans.*, 3rd ser., 1 (1907), sect.II: 211–90, and 6 (1912), sect.II: 11–65. J. K. Elliott, "Crime and punishment in early Upper Canada," *OH*, 27 (1931): 335–40. Carl Wittke, "Canadian refugees in the American revolution," *CHR*, 3 (1922): 333.

WETMORE, GEORGE LUDLOW, lawyer and office holder; b. 26 Dec. 1795 in Gagetown, N.B., eldest son of Thomas WETMORE and Sarah Peters; m. 26 Dec. 1816 Harriet Rainsford, and they had four children, including Andrew Rainsford Wetmore*; d. 2 Oct. 1821 on Maryland Hill (Fredericton), N.B.

As the eldest son of the attorney general of New Brunswick, George Ludlow Wetmore had a promising future. He studied law with his father, was admitted to the Supreme Court as an attorney, and on 18 June 1816 was appointed clerk of the House of Assembly. After becoming a barrister on 2 March 1819, he entered into a partnership with his father in Fredericton. Their major competitors at the bar were Samuel Denny STREET and his son George Frederick Street*. Samuel Denny Street had long resented his exclusion from the inner circle of American-born loyalists who monopolized government patronage and in 1800 had fought a duel with John Murray BLISS, whose son, George Pidgeon Bliss, was to marry George Ludlow Wetmore's sister Sarah in 1819. The animosity between Street and the loyalist élite was passed on to the second generation. During the trial of the sheriff of York County for false arrest in 1821, George Frederick Street, who was counsel for the sheriff, and George Ludlow Wetmore, who was acting for the plaintiff, nearly came to blows outside the courtroom and Wetmore challenged Street to a duel.

In great secrecy, since duelling was illegal, the two men met early in the morning on 2 Oct. 1821 at Maryland Hill, four miles outside Fredericton. They exchanged a round of shots. According to his considerably less than impartial account, Street deliberately fired at the ground and was prepared for a reconciliation, but Wetmore insisted on another exchange. Street's second bullet hit Wetmore above the wrist, passed through his elbow, and struck him in the head. Doctors were summoned but by the time they arrived Wetmore was dead. He was not quite 26 and he left behind a pregnant wife and three children. The fourth child of the marriage was a daughter who would be named George. Wetmore's wife lived to be 94 but never spoke to a Street again.

Among the first generation of loyalists, many of whom had seen active service during the American revolution, duels had been common, particularly among members of the legal fraternity who were concerned to establish their status as gentlemen. But during the early 19th century duelling became less acceptable to public opinion. When Richard John UNIACKE Jr killed William Bowie in a duel in 1819, there was a public outcry both in Nova Scotia and in neighbouring New Brunswick. Street and the two seconds, Richard Davies and John Francis Wentworth Winslow, both of whom had a military background, were sufficiently frightened by what they had done to flee to Maine and during their absence the coroner, William TAYLOR, raised the "Hue and Cry" and the sheriff issued a warrant for their arrest for murder. In February 1822 they returned to stand trial. Trials for murder arising from duelling were rare in British North America, although more common in Britain, and no one had ever been convicted unless foul play was involved (Uniacke, for example, had been acquitted). Street's trial was a farce. A string of witnesses drawn from the loyalist élite testified to his "humane" character; the seconds refused to admit that they had seen Street kill Wetmore; the counsels for the defence, Ward Chipman* Jr and Henry Bliss*, attacked the circumstantial evidence produced by William Botsford*, the prosecutor, and attempted to cast doubts upon Street's very presence at the event; and the presiding judge, John SAUNDERS, directed the jury to acquit Street, which it did. As in similar cases elsewhere, one has the impression that the witnesses, the judges, and the prosecuting officers were united in a conspiracy to prevent the law against duelling from being enforced. These were, of course, the same men who enforced the criminal law with such vigour against those who were not members of the gentry.

In later years Street expressed his remorse about Wetmore but in 1834 to defend his honour he challenged Henry George Clopper* to a duel, a challenge that Clopper dismissed with scorn. Clearly a change in attitude to duelling had taken place even among the colonial élite and by contributing to that change Wetmore's death may not have been entirely in vain.

PHILLIP BUCKNER

PANB, MC 1, Wetmore file, "Thomas Wetmore . . . from England to America, 1635"; MC 300, RS160, L4a, no.77. UNBL, MG H11, legal papers, 21 Feb. [1822]. *New-Brunswick Royal Gazette*, 2 June 1816; 7 April, 10 Aug. 1818; 2 March 1819; 2, 9 Oct. 1821. Lawrence, *Judges of N.B.* (Stockton and Raymond). Lorenzo Sabine, *Notes on duels and duelling* . . . (Boston, 1855). Mary Barker, "The duel," *Atlantic Advocate* (Fredericton), 49 (1958–59), no.3: 49–55.

WETMORE, THOMAS, lawyer, office holder, militia officer, politician, and JP; b. 20 Sept. 1767 in Rye, N.Y., fifth of the eight children of Timothy Wetmore and Jane Haviland; m. 17 March 1793 Sarah

Peters in Gagetown, N.B., and they had 12 children; d. 22 March 1828 on his estate, called Kingswood, at Kingsclear (near Fredericton), N.B.

Thomas Wetmore came to New Brunswick "with the loyal Emigrants" in 1783 and settled with his father, Timothy Wetmore, first in Carleton (Saint John) and then in Gagetown. He studied law in the office of Ward CHIPMAN, became an attorney in 1788, and was admitted to the bar in 1790. Entering into partnership with his father, he was appointed deputy surrogate, clerk of the Inferior Court of Common Pleas, and registrar of deeds and wills for Queens County. In 1793 he married Sarah Peters, the daughter of judge James Peters. This union and the subsequent marriages of his children linked Wetmore to a wide network of prominent families, but for many years his influence with the leading members of the provincial élite was tenuous and he was unable to acquire "the favours of Government." Because of the limited opportunities in Gagetown, Timothy Wetmore eventually returned to the United States and Thomas relocated in Saint John. In 1796 he was selected as clerk of the Supreme Court; however, the chief justice, George Duncan Ludlow*, decided that the post should not be held by a practising lawyer. Two years later Thomas sought to become clerk of the Common Council of Saint John, replacing Elias Hardy*, but he did not possess sufficient influence.

In 1808, when the provincial militia was embodied during a temporary crisis in Anglo-American relations, Wetmore served as a lieutenant-colonel in charge of the militia units stationed in Saint John. By his exertions he won the support of Lieutenant-Colonel George Johnstone, who was shortly to become administrator of the colony, and judge John SAUNDERS, the commander of the militia around Fredericton; through their influence he became recorder of the city of Saint John and also attorney general, succeeding Jonathan BLISS, in July 1809. The former position Wetmore found "burthensome" and he relinquished it in 1811, but he remained attorney general until his death. In 1809 Wetmore had also been elected to the House of Assembly for Saint John County and City. He took his seat in January 1810 and played an active part in the deliberations of the assembly. In 1813, as attorney general, he was ordered by the lieutenant governor to move to the seat of government in Fredericton, and he did not reoffer himself as a candidate for Saint John County and City in the elections of 1816. In 1817 he was given a seat on the provincial council and was sworn in on 22 December, but he was never one of the inner circle of government advisers under either Major-General George Stracey SMYTH or Sir Howard Douglas*.

A strong supporter of the established church, Wetmore served on the board of the College of New Brunswick and for a time as president of the Frederic-

ton branch of the Society for Promoting Christian Knowledge. He also served as one of the justices of the peace for York County and as chairman of the York County Agricultural and Emigrant Society. His primary interest, however, was his legal business. Since his extensive private practice necessitated his going on circuit, he conducted all crown prosecutions himself, even after it was determined that the attorney general had no legal right to monopolize them. His income, especially from fees on land grants, was sufficiently large that he declined the offer of a judgeship in 1815, although he became a candidate for the post of chief justice in 1822, losing out to Saunders. His last years were not happy ones. In 1821 his eldest son, George Ludlow WETMORE, was killed in a duel and his wife died in 1827. Wetmore withdrew from political activity. His expenses exceeded his income and when he died in 1828 he was virtually insolvent. He was succeeded as attorney general by Robert Parker*.

In 1809 Administrator Martin Hunter* described Wetmore as "unquestionably the ablest and best qualified Barrister" in New Brunswick. In fact, Wetmore was a competent lawyer but not an outstanding one, and he does not appear to have made any significant contribution to the evolution of the law or the legal profession in the colony. He was also of marginal importance as a politician. As with many second-generation loyalists his primary claim to preference was that his family had been "ever firm in their loyalty."

PHILLIP BUCKNER

[There is a small collection of Wetmore letters in the Saunders papers, UNBL, MG H11, and an even smaller collection in the Winslow papers, UNBL, MG H2. A number of letters written by Wetmore while he was attorney general can be found in PANB, RG 2, RS8, attorney-general, 1/1, and there is scattered correspondence in PRO, CO 188 files, and in PANB, RG 10, RS108. Also useful are N.B., House of Assembly, *Journal*, 1810–15 and 1836, app.I, and the Executive Council minutes for 1817–28, PANB, RG 2, RS6, A2–3. The only secondary source of any value is Lawrence, *Judges of N.B.* (Stockton and Raymond), although there is a useful genealogy in J. C. Wetmore, *The Wetmore family of America, and its collateral branches: with genealogical, biographical, and historical notices* (Albany, N.Y., 1861). P.B.]

WHITE, ANDREW, artisan, businessman, and militiaman; b. c. 1783; d. 11 July 1832 in Montreal.

Andrew White was living in Montreal by 1805 when he acquired a plot in the Nazareth sub-fief. A carpenter and joiner who was occasionally described as a cabinet-maker, in 1807 he established a short-lived partnership with another carpenter and joiner, Samuel Fox. The following year he was sufficiently

White

prosperous to take on three apprentices and to get married, in Montreal on 18 February. His wife, Mary Telfer, was the daughter of a stonemason; the couple would have five children. It was possibly his marriage that prompted White in 1809 to purchase property – a lot and two wooden houses on Rue Saint-Charles-Borromée – and to acquire a pew in the Scotch Presbyterian Church, later known as St Gabriel Street Church.

In 1810 White formed a partnership with the cabinet-maker William Shand that would last until 1815. During this period White was involved in the construction of a number of houses in and around Montreal. Thus in 1813 he did wood and iron work on three houses erected by Joseph Courselle, dit Chevallier, and Thomas Phillips*. White had probably met Phillips earlier since both served in the Montreal Incorporated Volunteers, raised to assist in garrison duty during the War of 1812. White worked with Chevallier and Phillips again in 1816 when he did the carpentry work on a store they were building for the firm of Gerrard, Yeoward, Gillespie and Company [see Samuel Gerrard*]. He also undertook a number of projects as principal contractor, notably the Bank of Montreal on Rue Saint-Jacques in 1818–19 and a three-storey stone store for James Leslie and Company [see James Leslie*] in 1820–21. As well he may have engaged in property development. In 1817 he bought four contiguous lots on the corner of Rue Vitré and Rue Chêneville, and the two wooden dwellings on Saint-Charles-Borromée eventually gave way to five large stone houses.

Though he continued in private building construction, after 1819 White became increasingly active in public works. About 1820 he and others were hired by Thomas PORTEOUS, owner of the Company of Proprietors of the Montreal Water Works, to build supports for the utility's reservoir, which threatened to collapse after the military undermined it while levelling Citadel Hill, on which it stood. In 1821, in partnership with Thomas Phillips and the merchants Oliver Wait and Stanley Bagg, White undertook the excavation of the Lachine Canal, one of the most important public works of the time in Lower Canada. Construction work began on 17 July but was slowed by the inexperience of the contractors and their labourers, disagreements with the canal commissioners over the cost of extra excavation when it was decided to extend the project from the Windmills to Montreal Harbour, and rain, which flooded the site. The work as specified in the original contract was finished and the canal opened to traffic in 1824. When the commissioners decided to undertake the extension themselves, they hired White in January 1825 to superintend the job because he was "the most experienced" of the original contractors.

In March 1827 White joined in partnership three contractors on the Rideau Canal in Upper Canada, Thomas Phillips, Thomas McKay*, and John Redpath*. In May he left the Lachine Canal to join Phillips in undertaking the locks and other construction at Long Island and Black Rapids on the Rideau project. White took charge at Long Island, Phillips at Black Rapids. The quality of their work was highly praised by Lieutenant-Colonel John By*, who supervised the building of the canal. His contract completed and the partnership with Phillips, McKay, and Redpath dissolved in 1831, White returned to Montreal.

White had business interests besides construction. He was involved with the Montreal Savings Bank, and while in partnership with Wait and Bagg had speculated in lumber. Undoubtedly his work on canals generated his strong interest in the development of transportation. He held a share in the steamboat *William Annesly*, a ferry which operated between Montreal and Laprairie from 1824 to 1826, and he served for a time as secretary and treasurer of the company that owned it. He also had stock in another steamboat, the *John By*, built at Kingston, Upper Canada, in 1831 by Robert DRUMMOND, a contractor on the Rideau Canal. That year White purchased land in Fitzroy Township by the Chats Falls rapids on the Ottawa River, apparently with the intention of building a steamer and operating it between the rapids and Bytown. Late the same year he was a member of a group that proposed widening the Lachine Canal to at least the dimensions of the Rideau, but the project was not begun until 1843. In 1831 he seems once again to have taken up property development. That April he purchased a lot and three-storey brick dwelling on the corner of the extensions of Rue Saint-Jacques and Rue Saint-Pierre and began construction of two additional three-storey houses there. In August he acquired two more lots on Saint-Jacques, on one of which stood another large three-storey stone dwelling.

In the midst of this frenetic activity White was cut down by cholera "after a few hours of illness" at age 49. His wife Mary had died in November 1821, and he had married Margaret Logan in the Scotch Presbyterian Church on 18 Feb. 1823; they had a daughter. White had been elected an elder of the church in 1819 and had served on its temporal committee in 1825–26. A charitable man, he had readily contributed from his growing fortune, estimated at some £30,000 at the time of his death, to subscriptions for public improvements and the needy. He had been an original subscriber to the Montreal General Hospital and, shortly before his death, had been elected to its board of governors. The comfort of his social position is reflected in his ownership of a cottage on the Rivière Saint-Pierre at Montreal.

Andrew White, like his former partners McKay and Redpath, successfully made the occupational transition from skilled artisan to businessman at a time when strong expansion in the construction industry in Montreal and the transportation sector of the colonial economy offered excellent opportunities to men of technical skill, initiative, and business acumen. White's rise in social rank, which accompanied the occupational shift, was consolidated in the next generation; for his son, Andrew, became a merchant in Montreal and his daughter Mary married the engineer Nicol Hugh Baird*. White does not stand out for any single achievement. Rather, he is significant as a member of a group of aggressive Montreal business-men who, through their technical knowledge and skills, advanced significantly the early development of Canada's transportation network.

JOHN WITHAM

ANQ-M, CE1-126, 18 févr. 1808, 18 févr. 1823, 12 juill. 1832; CN1-185, 5 mars, 20 juill., 12 déc. 1807; 29 janv., 12 nov. 1808; 31 juill. 1810; 1er juin 1811; CN1-187, 27 févr. 1815; 18 sept. 1816; 3 janv. 1818; 15 févr., 29 août 1821; 27 juill. 1832. AO, MS 393. McCord Museum, Bagg papers; Redpath papers. PAC, MG 24, D93; RG 43, CIII, 2, vols.2454–55. Theodore Davis, *Reply to remarks on the Lachine Canal* (Montreal, 1822). E. F. Bush, *The builders of the Rideau Canal, 1826–32* (Can., National Hist. Parks and Sites Branch, *Manuscript report*, no.185, Ottawa, 1976). R. Campbell, *Hist. of Scotch Presbyterian Church*, 319–20. Denison, *Canada's first bank*. R. W. Passfield, *Building the Rideau Canal: a pictorial history* (Don Mills [Toronto], 1982). G. J. J. Tulchinsky, "The construction of the first Lachine Canal, 1815–1826" (MA thesis, McGill Univ., Montreal, 1960).

WHITE, GIDEON, JP, merchant, office holder, politician, militia officer, and judge; b. March 1753 in Plymouth, Mass., son of Captain Gideon White, yeoman, and Joanna Howland, both descendants of Pilgrim Fathers; cousin of Edward Winslow*; m. 17 April 1787 Deborah Whitworth, daughter of Dr Miles Whitworth of Boston, in Shelburne, N.S., and they had nine children, all of whom lived to adulthood; d. there 30 Sept. 1833.

Ten days after the battle of Bunker Hill in June 1775 Gideon White was relating his eyewitness account of that engagement to Simeon Perkins* in Liverpool, N.S. White, a Plymouth merchant, had just arrived from Boston on a trading voyage to Nova Scotian ports including Port Roseway (Shelburne). Because his movements during the next several months are unknown it is not certain whether he was the Gideon White who joined the evacuation of Boston in March 1776. By the summer, however, White was in Nova Scotia once more, and that September was captured by an American privateer off Barrington and taken to Massachusetts. Imprisoned and then placed under house arrest in Plymouth, in October 1777 he returned to Nova Scotia where he spent the winter of 1777–78

in Liverpool. By September 1779 he was in New York, and as master of the schooner *Apollo* traded in the Caribbean for a year. White then set up business as a merchant in Charleston, S.C., where he also served as a captain in the local militia prior to returning to New York in July 1782. By now a captain in the Duke of Cumberland's Regiment, he went to Jamaica to recruit, but with the end of hostilities in sight the recruits were not needed, and he returned to New York in the late fall to await evacuation.

At this time a group of refugees in New York formed an association to organize a settlement at Port Roseway. Since White was one of those familiar with the intended destination he was able to provide helpful advice and information. He became a member of the Port Roseway Associates, as the group was known, but because of ill health could not go with them when they left for Nova Scotia in the spring of 1783. Instead, that summer White returned to Jamaica to help gather his disbanded regiment and remove it to Nova Scotia, where its members were to receive land. He arrived at Halifax in February 1784 and that spring came to Shelburne with some of his regiment. The Duke of Cumberland's Regiment was granted land in the Chedabucto Bay region but White never saw his 850 acres there.

White's letter of introduction to John Wentworth*, surveyor general of the king's woods, reaped results with his appointment by Governor John Parr* as justice of the peace for Halifax County in May 1784. Joseph Tinkham of Liverpool, an old business associate, sent a house frame to Shelburne, where White was granted a 50-acre lot and a town lot. He seems to have been quite optimistic about the future of the town, stating, "It is dam'd hard' tho in the Course of a few years it will be very Eligible. . . . And business will soon be sprightly. the Whale and Cod fish^{ys} are now attended too." In spite of the area's rocky terrain White managed to produce an income from a surplus of farm produce with the help of eight black families who worked as tenant farmers. He also did some trading, but not on a large scale, and he employed Ward CHIPMAN of New Brunswick to collect his debts. White's main source of capital, however, was his half pay as a British officer, which he received until his death.

Once established on his land, White procured numerous appointments. As a former ship's master he fulfilled the duties of deputy registrar of the Vice-Admiralty Court. For a great many years he was a justice of the peace for Shelburne County, and also served as *custos rotulorum*. In 1790 he was elected to the House of Assembly for Barrington Township and served until 1793, when he was succeeded by John SARGENT, although his political career was not particularly significant. Similarly, he sought the position of deputy naval officer, and was finally appointed in

Wilcocke

April 1795. In subsequent years he was seizing officer of ships, vessels, and goods liable for forfeiture, searcher and examiner of ships and vessels for Shelburne and Queens counties, customs collector, and deputy protonotary. He was also sheriff, major of the 22nd (Shelburne) Battalion of Militia, commissioner of bridges and roads, and justice of the Inferior Court of Common Pleas.

Throughout his life White kept in constant touch with his family and friends in Massachusetts, which he visited in 1787 and 1791. As his brother-in-law's executor, White spent nearly a year in England attempting to settle the estate so that his son Nathaniel Whitworth could afford to attend Harvard. Although always disdainful of the rebellious colony, his hostility may have diminished somewhat at the time of his mother's death in 1811, when he offered to move to the United States to be with his sister. But just after the War of 1812 his old loyalties resurfaced when he wrote to his son, who had recently returned from the United States, asking, "Do the Yankees look kindly toward us British Nova Scotians? They have Escaped the *Rod* I had hoped would have made them smart to the *quick* – but so it is!" In 1821 he was honoured by his old friends by being made an honorary member of the Pilgrim Society, composed of descendants of the first white child born in New England. This society was the successor to the Old Colony Club, of which his elder brother, Cornelius, had been a founding member.

Gideon White made a significant contribution to Shelburne as a devoted public servant. He persevered under the difficult conditions in the late 1780s when Shelburne declined rapidly in importance; in the aftermath of the great fire of 1792, in which he lost much property, he remained in the town when many others were defeated and left. Perhaps his greatest contribution to early Nova Scotia history is his collection of personal papers, which describe his success in agriculture, his attempts to establish a school, the local efforts at fire-fighting, and the general social and cultural conditions of his lifetime.

MARY M. HARVEY

PAC, MG 9, B9-14; 1: 3–22. PANS, MG 1, 947–60; RG 1, 169, 172, 223, 444, 446. PRO, CO 137/84. Perkins, *Diary, 1766–80* (Innis). "Records of the Old Colony Club," Mass. Hist. Soc., *Proc.* (Boston), 2nd ser., 3 (1886–87): 382–444. *A calendar of the White collection of manuscripts in the Public Archives of Nova Scotia*, comp. Margaret Ells (Halifax, 1940). Jones, *Loyalists of Mass. Loyalists in N.S.* (Gilroy). *Mayflower families through five generations: descendants of the Pilgrims who landed at Plymouth, Mass., December 1620*, ed. L. M. Kellogg (1v. to date, Plymouth, Mass., 1975–). [Thomas and Samual White], *Ancestral chronological record of the William White family, from 1607–8 to 1895* (Concord, [N.H.?], 1895).

WILCOCKE, SAMUEL HULL, author and journalist; b. *c.* 1766 in Reigate, England, son of the Reverend Samuel Wilcocke; d. 3 July 1833 at Quebec.

Samuel Hull Wilcocke's father was a clergyman of the Church of England for a considerable time at Middelburg (Netherlands). He returned to England with his family when the French forces invaded in 1794. Samuel had evidently acquired most of his education in Europe; his writings have a continental scholastic flavour, with special emphasis on linguistics and enrichment from extensive reading in classical and English literature. Shortly after his return, he began to contribute to British literary periodicals and to prepare translations from Dutch, German, and French. His pursuits, however, soon "flowed in the channel of commerce," as he brought his erudition and research to the translation and editing of volumes on the East Indies and on Buenos Aires, works useful for the expansive mercantile interests of Liverpool. By 1800 he was "established in a promising mercantile concern" in that city. During his residence there of approximately 20 years, Wilcocke participated in civic, literary, and theatrical activities which he was later to recommend as examples for Montreal.

Although by 1800 Wilcocke was married, the name of his wife is not known. Domestic troubles are mentioned as one of his reasons for leaving England. In 1817 he came to the Canadas, probably with some of his children and their families, to serve as a publicist for the North West Company during its dispute with the Hudson's Bay Company over the attempts of Lord Selkirk [Douglas*] to establish a colony on the Red River. He published *A narrative of occurrences in the Indian countries of North America* in 1817, in reply to John Halkett*'s *Statement respecting the Earl of Selkirk's settlement of Kildonan, upon the Red River* (London, 1817), and in 1818 and 1819 three accounts of trials held during those years.

In 1820 Wilcocke came into conflict with the NWC. Warned that he was to be arrested because it was alleged that he possessed documents and secrets prejudicial to the interests of the company, he fled to Burlington, Vt, in October. NWC agents captured him in the United States and brought him back to Montreal before the end of the month, accusing him of having absconded with £1,500 in company funds. He was jailed for a year before being tried and acquitted of forgery and grand larceny. Immediately reimprisoned on charges of debt, he was held until pressure from the United States – where he had been illegally seized – accomplished his release. These events led him into a new form of literary expression; a newspaper, the *Scribbler*, was founded on 28 June 1821, while he was still in prison. When he gained his freedom on 8 May of the following year, the price was exile, but he

Wilcocke

continued to edit the *Scribbler*, which was always printed in Montreal, from the haven of Burlington and other places in the United States. His talents at last found a focus in a journal of defence for himself and of offence for many people in Montreal.

The *Scribbler* was initially conducted with the circumspection and restraint appropriate to its position as the first critical journal of its kind in Lower Canada and the first to be bound, volume by volume. When Wilcocke was released from prison, he introduced more of himself into his weekly paper. The journal's reputation for "scurrility" increased as did Wilcocke's attacks on the agents and officials of the NWC and on the respectability of prominent English-speaking Montrealers. He introduced scandal, so-called "news," innuendo, thinly disguised nicknames for his victims (such as Mr Reaper for Nahum Mower, Tommy Changling for Thomas Andrew Turner, Horatio Bigdoors for Horatio Gates, and Lord Goddamnhim for Thomas Thain), *double entendre*, and some obscenity. By giving an air of fiction and imagery to his pleasantries, he shared with his colonial readers, except his victims, a literary experience current in contemporary British journalism. Hundreds of persons were given literary life against the vividly described background of early provincial Montreal.

A series of articles in the journal entitled "Letters from Pulo Penang" gave his barely fictitious version of the persecution which he, and especially his wife, Ann, had suffered. Ann Lewis of South Lambeth (London) had joined him in Lower Canada in 1819. According to Wilcocke, their marriage was performed in Montreal in 1821, secretly for "prudential reasons connected with lawsuits instituted for recovery of property." On 22 Aug. 1825 they were remarried in Rouses Point, N.Y. His dedication in the first volume of the *Scribbler* celebrated the love and devotion of Ann: every day she had appeared at the prison gate and she had been the manager and distributor of the weekly journal. She had probably also been the city reporter and pseudonymous "correspondent." The journal may, indeed, have been written largely by this couple under dozens of pseudonyms. The *Scribbler* may find its niche in Canadian literature because it is largely "confessional," a strange and rare type of autobiography. It is the record of one of Canada's most intriguing love stories.

The paper included original poems by Wilcocke and "new" local poets, reviews of Canadian books, controversies with rival journalists, descriptions of life among the English-speaking inhabitants of Montreal, and constructive advice regarding civic institutions. Wilcocke prided himself on promoting the use of standard English among writers in Montreal and its environs. He printed many of his early and fugitive poems and stories. Notable among the exhibitions of his scholarship was a series of textual studies, largely linguistic, on the plays of Philip Massinger, the Caroline dramatist.

On several occasions Wilcocke attempted to publish other newspapers. In order to avoid political discussions in the *Scribbler*, he started a journal to oppose the bill to unite Lower and Upper Canada. The *Free Press*, although bearing a Montreal imprint, was published mainly in Burlington and ran from 10 Oct. 1822 to 4 Sept. 1823. Wilcocke then moved to Rouses Point, where he began another newspaper. The *Harbinger* was a disastrous excursion into American politics because of the misunderstandings which arose between Wilcocke and his Republican supporters. An advertisement for the *Colonial Magazine*, a monthly intended for general readers, appeared in a late number of the *Scribbler*, on 1 March 1827. One issue was available for review in October 1827, but there is no record of a second.

By 1828 Wilcocke had returned to Montreal. During the last five years of his life, he reported on the debates in the House of Assembly at Quebec for the province's newspapers and, from his shorthand notes, he compiled *The history of the session of the provincial parliament of Lower Canada for 1828–29*, which William Stewart Wallace* was to recognize as "the first approach in Canada to Hansard." In a petition to the governor general, Lord Aylmer [Whitworth-Aylmer*], in 1831, Wilcocke described the *History* as "daily and faithful reports of the proceedings, arguments and sentiments of the Representatives of the people," and asked for a grant of £100 to complete publication. Even though the *Quebec Gazette* and the *Quebec Mercury* had given him some financial compensation for his writings, by 1831 he was old, poor, and suffering "from a painful disorder." After several weeks of severe illness he died at Quebec on 3 July 1833.

Carl F. Klinck

Samuel Hull Wilcocke is the author of *A narrative of occurrences in the Indian countries of North America ...* (London, 1817; repr. 1818; repr. East Ardsley, Eng., and New York, 1968), a work which has sometimes been attributed to Edward Ellice* or Simon McGillivray*. Wilcocke's other works include *Report of the trials of Charles de Reinhard and Archibald M'Lellan, for murder ...* (Montreal, 1818); *Report of the proceedings connected with the disputes between the Earl of Selkirk and the North-West Company, at the assizes, held at York in Upper Canada, October 1818* (Montreal, 1819); *A letter to the sollicitor general on the seizure of papers* (Montreal, 1821); *The history of the session of the provincial parliament of Lower Canada for 1828–29* (n.p., n.d.); and "Narrative of circumstances attending the death of the late Benjamin Frobisher, Esq., a partner of the North-West Company," *Les bourgeois de la Compagnie du Nord-Ouest* (Masson), 2: 179–226. He edited the *Scribbler* (Montreal), 28 June 1821–March 1827; the *Free Press* (Montreal), 10 Oct. 1822–4 Sept. 1823;

815

Willard

the *Harbinger* (Rouses Point, N.Y.), November 1823–November 1824; and the prospectus for the *Colonial Magazine* (Montreal), 11 April 1827. For a complete list of the works Wilcocke wrote and translated, *see* the *National union catalog*.

ANQ-Q, P-68; P-1000-1-18. *Canadian Courant and Montreal Advertiser*, 28 Oct., 1, 18 Nov. 1820. *Montreal Gazette*, 5, 19 Dec. 1821; 2, 16 Jan. 1822. Beaulieu et Hamelin, *La presse québécoise*, 1: 41, 43, 60. Wallace, *Macmillan dict.* M. L. MacDonald, "The literary life of English and French Montreal from 1817 to 1830 as seen through the periodicals of the time" (MA thesis, Carleton Univ., Ottawa, 1976). A. H. U. Colquhoun, "A victim of Scottish Canadians," *Dalhousie Rev.*, 3 (1923–24): 286–90. C. F. Klinck, "Samuel Hull Wilcocke," *Journal of Canadian Fiction* (Montreal), 2 (1973), no.3: 13–21; "The world of *The Scribbler*," 4 (1975), no.3: 123–48. W. S. Wallace, "The literature relating to the Selkirk controversy," *CHR*, 13 (1932): 45–50.

WILLARD, SAMUEL, land agent, JP, office holder, militia officer, and merchant; b. 1 Dec. 1766 in Petersham, Mass., fourth child of Major Joshua Willard, a doctor, and Lucretia Ward; m. first 24 Feb. 1791 Lucinda Knowlton in Newfane, Vt, and they had two daughters; m. secondly in 1802 Elizabeth Patterson, and they had seven children; d. 28 Oct. 1833 in Stukely, Lower Canada, and was buried there three days later on his own land.

Samuel Willard's forefathers, who came from the county of Kent in England, emigrated to North America in 1634 and made a respectable place for themselves in Massachusetts, notably in Boston. During the American revolution several of the family remained loyal to the crown and distinguished themselves in the army; still a boy, Samuel was even given certain secret missions.

Around 1784 he moved to Newfane and went into partnership with a general merchant for a few years; from there he went to live at Sheldon. When Lieutenant Governor Alured CLARKE issued a proclamation on 7 Feb. 1792 offering land in Lower Canada, Joshua Willard, with six partners, applied for lands in Stukely and Orford townships. The whole family had great hopes, but upon Joshua's death in 1794 the estate he left proved to be precarious. Samuel had visited Quebec in 1790 and explored the territory they sought. But like other applicants for lands, he was obliged to put up with delays and assume expenditures as a result of the uncertainty about regulations and the quarrelling between Governor Robert Prescott* and the Executive Council. He went back to Quebec and repeated his requests, but in vain. At the invitation of Elmer Cushing and Gilbert HYATT, on 28 Nov. 1797 he participated in a meeting called at Missisquoi Bay to prepare a protest to Prescott about the situation. Willard was one of the five members of the committee that drafted the statement and the following day he

signed the text, which after being passed by the meeting was taken by Jesse PENNOYER to Quebec. A few dissatisfied people eventually commissioned Samuel GALE to present their case in London in 1800; Willard assumed responsibility for a large share of the mission's expenses.

On 3 Nov. 1800 Willard and his partners received half of Stukely Township. He settled there immediately and was soon recognized as the most prominent figure in the area. In 1803 he obtained a commission as a justice of the peace for the district of Montreal, which was renewed in 1810, 1821, and 1828. He transacted numerous land deals for himself and for others. As a commissioner and inspector of roads and bridges, he had an active interest in road works. He was in favour of roads being laid out to Montreal through the seigneury of Saint-Hyacinthe. His energies were to be concentrated on the construction of a vital road from Magog to Montreal.

From 1812 Willard was constantly harassed by claims, attachments, and sheriff's sales. When war broke out, he sent Governor Sir George Prevost* a loyal address from the committee for the security of the Eastern Townships, and he requested a lieutenant-colonelcy for himself. Since he had already turned down the rank when Sir John JOHNSON offered it to him in 1806, he had to wait for a vacancy, and it was not until 1814 that he was appointed lieutenant-colonel of the 3rd battalion of the Eastern Townships Militia. The following year he was promoted colonel of the 2nd battalion.

With the return of peace, Willard busied himself improving local conditions. He supported the creation of a judicial district and he sought in particular to set up schools. Appointed commissioner to erect two schoolhouses in Stukely Township in 1815, Willard, with the incentive of the House of Assembly's ambitious plans, finally in 1823 obtained a salary of £80 for each of the teachers in the two schools. In the mean time, he had hired a private teacher to hold classes in his home, and he lent the books from his library to local young people. In 1827 he enrolled his son and one of his grandsons in the Collège de Saint-Hyacinthe.

In contrast, a general store that Willard had set up at Frost Village was a failure, as was a contract for carrying the mail. His creditors, chief among them Henry LeMesurier* of Quebec, sued him successfully and in January 1828 his assets were sold by the sheriff. He managed to save his farm at Stukely, and his friends bought his possessions at ridiculously low prices in order to sell them back to him.

Despite his financial setbacks, Willard retained the confidence of the authorities. He had been appointed commissioner to hear small causes on 18 July 1826, and he became commissioner to improve the road between Lac Massawippi and Saint-Hyacinthe on 30

May 1831, and census commissioner on 15 June. He declined a commission as justice of the peace in 1830, however. Having remained active till a few weeks before the end, he died at 66 years of age on the farm at Stukely which had caused him so much trouble.

Samuel Willard was remembered as an honourable man completely devoted to his family and to those who entrusted him with responsibilities. He was rather modest by nature, and his gentlemanly conduct revealed his great qualities of heart and mind. Even though he met with adversity in personal undertakings, his civic sense and his devotion to the community earned him a place among the builders of his country.

MARIE-PAULE R. LABRÈQUE

ANQ-E, CE2-42, 28 oct. 1833; CN1-24; CN1-27; CN2-21; CN2-26. Brome County Hist. Soc. Arch. (Knowlton, Que.), Samuel Gale papers; Misc. family papers, LeMesurier file; Personal notes of Marion Phelps; Township papers; Samuel Willard papers. PAC, RG 1, L3ᴸ: 2487; RG 4, A1; RG 9, I, A1; RG 68, General index, 1651–1841. *Docs. relating to constitutional hist., 1759–1791* (Shortt and Doughty; 1918); *1791–1818* (Doughty and McArthur). *British Colonist and St. Francis Gazette* (Stanstead, Que.), 5 June 1823. *Quebec Gazette*, 18 Sept. 1817. Bouchette, *Topographical description of L.C. Illustrated atlas of Eastern Townships.* Langelier, *Liste des terrains concédés. Officers of British forces in Canada* (Irving). L.-P. Audet, *Le système scolaire*, vol.3. Boulianne, "Royal Instit. for the Advancement of Learning." Caron, *La colonisation de la prov. de Québec.* C.-P. Choquette, *Histoire de la ville de Saint-Hyacinthe* (Saint-Hyacinthe, Qué., 1930); *Histoire du séminaire de Saint-Hyacinthe depuis sa fondation jusqu'à nos jours* (2v., Montréal, 1911–12). Day, *Hist. of Eastern Townships; Pioneers of the Eastern Townships . . .* (Montreal, 1863). Albert Gravel, *Les Cantons de l'Est* ([Sherbrooke, Qué.], 1938); *Pages d'histoire régionale* (24 cahiers, Sherbrooke, 1960–67), 16; 19–20. G. F. McGuigan, "Land policy and land disposal under tenure of free and common socage, Quebec and Lower Canada, 1763–1809 . . ." (PHD thesis, univ. Laval, Québec, 1962). Jules Martel, "Histoire du système routier des Cantons de l'Est avant 1855" (MA thesis, univ. d'Ottawa, 1960). G. H. Montgomery, *Missisquoi Bay (Philipsburg, Que.)* (Granby, Que., 1950). H. B. Shufelt, *Nicholas Austin the Quaker and the township of Bolton* (Knowlton, 1971). C. W. Smith, *Brome County scenic and historical tours* (Knowlton, 1973). *The storied province of Quebec; past and present*, ed. William Wood et al. (5v., Toronto, 1931–32), 2. Cyrus Thomas, *Histoire de Shefford*, Ovila Fournier, trad. (Île-Perrot, Qué., 1973). Joseph Willard, *Willard genealogy, sequel to Willard memoir . . .* (Boston, 1915). J. P. Noyes, "The Canadian loyalists and early settlers in the district of Bedford," Missisquoi County Hist. Soc., *Report* (Saint-Jean-sur-Richelieu, Que.), 3 (1907–8): 90–107.

WILLSON (Wilson), SARAH. *See* AINSE

WINGER, JOHN. *See* WENGER, JOHANNES

WORSLEY, MILLER, naval officer; b. 8 July 1791 in Gatcombe, England, fifth of seven sons of the Reverend Henry Worsley and Mary Dickonson; m. 3 Oct. 1820 Johanna Evered Harris in London, and they had at least two sons and one daughter; d. 2 May 1835 in England.

Miller Worsley, who belonged to a junior branch of an old and wealthy Isle of Wight family, went to sea as a first class volunteer on 29 June 1803, became a midshipman on 19 March 1805, and passed his examination for lieutenant on 3 Oct. 1810. On 12 July 1813 he was promoted lieutenant, after being sent from Bermuda with Robert Heriot Barclay*, Daniel Pring*, and six other officers to serve on the lakes of the Canadas during the War of 1812. Already the veteran of several great naval engagements, he had served in the *Decade* (36 guns), *Swiftsure* (74 guns), *Pylades* (16 guns), *Glatton* (56 guns), and *Valiant* (74 guns). While in the *Swiftsure* he had, like Barclay, participated in the battle of Trafalgar. On Lake Ontario he served as first lieutenant of the *Princess Charlotte* (42 guns), and he performed well during the successful attack of 6 May 1814 on Oswego, N.Y.

Worsley earned distinction from an episode on Lake Huron later that year. Given the unenviable duty of replacing Lieutenant Newdigate Poyntz, the commander of a naval reinforcement for Michilimackinac (Mackinac Island, Mich.) who had made himself objectionable to the post's commanding officer, Lieutenant-Colonel Robert McDouall*, Worsley, accompanied by 20 seamen, made his way by the difficult overland route from York (Toronto) to Nottawasaga Bay in July 1814, and there took over the requisitioned North West Company schooner *Nancy*. The same month an American force of five vessels and more than a thousand troops sailed against Michilimackinac, and after the expedition's failure to capture the fort on 4 August its naval commander, Captain Arthur Sinclair, turned his attention to the *Nancy*, hoping to cut off the garrison's last remaining source of supplies.

Worsley had in fact sailed for Michilimackinac with supplies on the 1st, but he received warning from McDouall in time to return to Nottawasaga Bay and erect a temporary blockhouse. Three ships (the *Niagara*, *Tigress*, and *Scorpion*) and about 300 troops attacked on 14 August. Worsley, with only 50 seamen and Indians and a few small cannon, resisted as long as possible, then spiked his guns and prepared to destroy the *Nancy* before withdrawing into the woods. A shell which exploded the blockhouse magazine hastened the end by starting a fire that rapidly spread to the ship and burned it to the waterline. The Americans then blockaded the mouth of the Nottawasaga River in order to cut off all communications between York and Michilimackinac, but late-summer storms forced them to lift the blockade. Worsley loaded two bateaux

Wright

and a canoe with stores from an intact depot and slipped out of the river on 18 August. He made his way 360 miles along the shore of the lake, "exposed to great hardships and privations of every description having only what we could shoot or catch by fishing to subsist on," until he reached the vicinity of St Joseph Island on the 24th. There on the 29th he had to hide the bateaux from the *Tigress* and *Scorpion*, the only ships now on the lake, and slip past them in the canoe. The next day he reached Michilimackinac. He then persuaded McDouall that an attack on the two vessels, which were some distance apart, would be successful. On 3 September Worsley, with four boats and 90 men including some soldiers of the Royal Newfoundland Regiment under Lieutenant Andrew H. Bulger*, captured the *Tigress* by a *coup de main*, and on the 6th he took the *Scorpion*. The capture of the two ships gave control of Lake Huron to the British and ensured the survival of their presence in the old northwest for the remainder of the war.

Worsley was greatly praised for his exploits by his superiors, including McDouall, Lieutenant-General Gordon Drummond*, and Commodore Sir James Lucas Yeo*, but his merits were recognized by the Admiralty only on 13 July 1815, when he was promoted commander. He remained on Lake Huron, but in October 1814 fell victim to the sickness rife among naval personnel in Upper Canada and spent the winter in sick quarters on Lake Erie, reverting to half pay. He then returned to the Isle of Wight and had no further employment until 1832 when, possibly in response to his petition to King William IV the previous year, he became an inspecting commander of the coastguard. That duty came to an end in 1834 and he died the following year.

This "able, active and intelligent officer . . . of conciliatory manner," as Drummond described him, inspired universal admiration, but the War of 1812 was not one that Englishmen cared to recall, and there is little to remember him by. Canadians honoured his feat of arms in the mid 1920s, when they discovered the remains of the *Nancy*, around which an island had formed in the Nottawasaga River. The only tangible memorial to Miller Worsley is the museum on that island, which houses the skeleton of the ship he so resolutely defended.

W. A. B. DOUGLAS

PAC, RG 8, I (C ser.), 683–85, 1219–20. PRO, ADM 1/2719–20, 1/2728, 1/2738; ADM 6/108; ADM 12/174/85a; ADM 107/42, no.33. *Leaves from the war log of the "Nancy," eighteen hundred and thirteen*, ed. C. H. J. Snider (Toronto, 1936). *Select British docs. of War of 1812* (Wood). G.B., Admiralty, *The commissioned sea officers of the Royal Navy, 1660–1815*, [ed. D. B. Smith *et al.*] (3v., n.p., [1954]). *The Trafalgar roll, containing the names and services of all officers of the Royal Navy and the Royal Marines who participated in the glorious victory of the 21st October 1805, together with a history of the ships engaged in the battle*, comp. R. H. Mackenzie (London, 1913). C. H. J. Snider, *The story of the "Nancy" and other eighteen-twelvers* (Toronto, 1926). E. [A.] Cruikshank, "An episode of the War of 1812: the story of the schooner 'Nancy,'" *OH*, 9 (1910): 75–126. Elsie McLeod Jury, "U.S.S. *Tigress* – H.M.S. *Confiance*, 1813–1831," *Inland Seas* (Cleveland, Ohio), 28 (1972): 3–16.

WRIGHT, CHARLES, surveyor and office holder; b. 21 July 1782 on St John's (Prince Edward) Island, third son of Surveyor General Thomas Wright* and Susanna Turner; m. 16 April 1815 Lydia Cambridge, daughter of John CAMBRIDGE and Mary Winchester, and they had one son; d. 1 April 1828 in Charlottetown.

Charles Wright was trained by his father as a surveyor and, with his older brother George*, assisted him in that profession. George later became involved with the Cambridge family in its business interests but Charles continued as assistant surveyor, replacing his father from 1803 during periods of absence or illness. By 1812 Thomas Wright was in failing health and Charles petitioned Administrator William Townshend* for a recommendation to succeed him. The request was supported by Thomas who was anxious to retire after some 40 years in the post. Charles went to England in 1812 to press his claim but his request was refused. Although absent from the colony on his father's death that December, he was named to the post by Townshend. He secured official confirmation of the appointment from the Treasury before leaving for the Island the following spring.

While in England Charles complained about the activities of the Loyal Electors and especially James Bardin PALMER, and his protests should have won him the support of the newly appointed lieutenant governor, Charles Douglass Smith*; however, Smith, who learned of Wright's appointment after arriving on the Island in July 1813, was quick to protest "such Hereditary Successions" and expressed a wish that the appointment had been delayed for his opinion.

Charles appears to have achieved little notoriety under Smith. The major township surveys had been completed and Wright's chief activity was to provide surveys for the expanding road network and the few areas available for grants to settlers. The surveyor general had ceased to be an important official in a colony where there was almost no crown land to control.

After 1820 Wright became even less active. An increasing number of surveys were done by assistants and a later petition by one of them notes his work during the periods of Wright's "afflictions." In 1824, after a presentment by the grand jury as to the poor state of the roads and bridges, Wright resigned his position as chief overseer of roads, a post he had held for at least five years. The arrival that October of Lieutenant Governor John Ready* to replace Smith brought improvements in the colony's administration, including the removal of incompetent officials. There are indications that irregularities in land grants and surveys surfaced during the next three years and the lieutenant governor was forced to complain to the Council in 1825 of Wright's failure to supply requested information. Finally, in 1827, Ready wrote to the Colonial Office complaining of Wright's inability to perform his tasks owing to his "constant and habitual Intoxication" and asked that his appointment be revoked. The request was complied with in February 1828 but it is doubtful that the news reached the Island before Wright's death. Over the objections of others who had served as assistant surveyors Ready appointed Charles's brother George to succeed him as surveyor general. George was to achieve a reputation as an able administrator and official; the legacy Charles left was one of incompetence and drunkenness.

H. T. HOLMAN

PAPEI, Acc. 2702/373, 375–78, 380; Acc. 2810/85–86; RG 1, commission books, 1: 83, 90; RG 3, petitions, 1817–20; RG 5, minutes, 1800–27; petitions, 1817–27; RG 8, warrant books, 1819–24. Private arch., Mrs J. T. McIntyre (Calgary), Charles Wright papers (photocopies at PAC, MG 24, B133). PRO, CO 226/26: 54, 195; 226/27: 36–39, 74–75; 226/39: 7; 226/44: 106; 226/45: 277. St Paul's Anglican Church (Charlottetown), Reg. of baptisms, marriages, and burials, 1782–1828 (mfm. at PAPEI). Supreme Court of P.E.I. (Charlottetown), Estates Division, liber 2: f.121 (will of Charles Wright) (mfm. at PAPEI). *Prince Edward Island Register*, 1 April 1828.

WURTELE, JOSIAS, merchant, landowner, and seigneur; b. 11 April 1760 at Strümpfelbach (Federal Republic of Germany), son of Jacob and Elisabetha Wurtele; m. first Catherine Andrews, and they had ten children; m. secondly 30 April 1814 Eleonor Ramsay at Quebec, and they had at least two children; d. 30 May 1831 in Montreal.

Several members of the Wurtele family immigrated to the province of Quebec in the 1780s. Some chose to settle in Montreal but Josias, like his brother John, picked Quebec where his uncle Jonathan Eckart, who sold tobacco and sundries, was living. Eckart owned a house and retail business on Rue Buade which Josias inherited in 1795. The next year Wurtele added to his property by buying a house on Rue Saint-Louis and obtaining the grant of a lot on that street from the Ursulines. In 1799 he paid £500 for his brother's house, which was also on Rue Buade. Later Wurtele purchased two lots in the *faubourg* Saint-Jean, one

stone house at the corner of Rue Saint-Stanislas and Rue Sainte-Anne, and another in the *faubourg* Saint-Vallier. He also acquired two stone houses in the *faubourg* Saint-Laurent in Montreal.

In 1800 Wurtele began buying land in the Eastern Townships. He sought out chiefly militia veterans who had each received a 400-acre lot there from the government for their service in the War of American Independence. In this race for land Wurtele joined forces with John SAVAGE, whose task was to explore the townships and advise Wurtele on the quality of the land as well as the price of lots. The two men split profits and losses. Over a ten-year period Wurtele bought 50,245 acres in this way, mainly in the townships of Windsor, Granby, Somerset, and Milton, but also in those of Chester, Auckland, Stoke, Nelson, Halifax, and Grantham. As well, in 1830 he owned five lots totalling 860 acres in Gloucester and Hawkesbury townships, Upper Canada.

In addition, Wurtele had his eye on seigneurial properties. On 5 Oct. 1808 he paid the sheriff of the district of Trois-Rivières £1,300 for the seigneury of Deguire, which had been seized from the estate of William Grant*. Then on 28 Oct. 1822 he paid a similar amount for the adjoining seigneury of Bourg-Marie-Est, with its manor-house, sawmills, and flourmills.

Wurtele made sure that his real estate investments returned a profit. Thus, in January 1809 he sued some residents of Bourg-Marie-Est seigneury and Upton Township for cutting wood on his lands. That month he hired a habitant to fell pine and spruce trees suitable for masts on the Deguire domain and deliver them to him at Quebec. In February he started construction of a flour-mill on the domain. He built a spacious manor-house on it in 1812, and a sawmill some years later. On his land in Windsor Township he erected a house and sawmill which he rented out. Wurtele left the management of his property in the hands of his estate agents, who looked after the collection of various dues, *lods et ventes*, *cens et rentes*, rental fees, or other moneys owing.

Wurtele lived on Rue Buade at Quebec, where he attended to his retail business. From 1815 till 1819 he was in partnership with Pierre Rochette, a merchant in the *faubourg* Saint-Jean. Wurtele had also opened a general store on the Deguire seigneury with an inventory valued at £925 0s. 9d. in 1814. He retired from business in 1819, handing his store on Rue Buade over to his eldest son, Jonathan. He went to live on the seigneury and from there continued to advise his son. Later he moved to one of his properties in the *faubourg* Saint-Laurent in Montreal, where he died.

In his will Josias Wurtele bequeathed all his possessions to his wife, the children born of his two marriages, and his grandchildren. By its terms the

Yore

estate was to be managed by certain members of the family in the interests of the others. The seigneuries of Deguire and Bourg-Marie-Est, the core of the estate, went to Jonathan with the proviso that he was under no circumstances to let them go to anyone outside the family. Wurtele's three other sons received the lots in the townships, a total of 46,929 acres. His daughters, the grandchildren, and Mme Wurtele shared the money and the other landed properties. Only his direct descendants were beneficiaries since Wurtele made no charitable bequests.

CÉLINE CYR

ANQ-M, CE1-63, 1er juin 1831; CN1-187, 12 avril 1830; 14–15, 19–24 juill. 1831. ANQ-Q, CE1-61, 30 avril 1814; CN1-178, 18 avril 1795; 9 juill., 8 août 1799; 29 mars, 18 juill., 27 août 1800; 10, 12 janv., 13, 16 févr., 20, 23–24, 28, 30–31 mars, 5 avril, 14 sept. 1801; 20 nov. 1802; 21 janv., 5, 28 févr. 1803; 12 mars, 12 juin 1804; 31 juill. 1805; 26 sept. 1807; 13, 16 sept. 1815; CN1-230, 18 août, 1er sept. 1796; 14 août 1801; 29 oct. 1802; 14 avril, 1er oct. 1803; 26 janv., 30 avril, 8 juin 1804; 17 janv., 18 févr., 9 oct. 1805; 11, 15 févr. 1806; 11, 22, 27 juin 1808; 27 janv., 9 févr. 1809; 5 nov. 1810; 17 mai 1811; 10, 28 févr., 10 juill. 1812; 25–29 avril, 5 mai 1814; 13 nov. 1815; 24 févr. 1816; 30 mars 1818; P-279. *Quebec Gazette*, 20 March 1806; 24 March, 29 April, 13 May 1819.

Y

YORE. *See* EWER

YOUNG, Sir ARETAS WILLIAM, colonial administrator; probably b. 1777; m. Sarah Cox of County Wexford (Republic of Ireland), and they had at least 12 children; d. 1 Dec. 1835 in Charlottetown.

Although Aretas William Young's origins are obscure, he must have come from a respectable background, since after entering the army as an ensign on 3 Sept. 1795 he was able to purchase a lieutenant's commission on 28 Oct. 1795 and a captaincy on 15 Sept. 1796. He served in Ireland during the rebellion of 1798 and in Egypt in 1801, and he was aide-de-camp to General Henry Edward Fox in Gibraltar and Sicily between 1804 and 1806. On 17 Dec. 1807 he became a major and until 1812 was engaged in the campaigns in Spain and Portugal against the French, winning a medal at the battle of Talavera. On 25 Jan. 1813 he was made lieutenant-colonel of the 3rd West India Regiment stationed in Trinidad and from 1815 until 1820, when the regiment was disbanded and he was placed on half pay, he commanded the garrison on Tobago. He sufficiently impressed the governor of Trinidad, Sir Ralph James Woodford, that he was placed in charge of the government during Woodford's leaves of absence from April to July 1820 and from May 1821 to February 1823. Upon his return to office in 1820 Woodford praised Young's "judicious conduct" and selected him for a seat on the council. In 1820 and again in 1823, the local equivalent of an assembly publicly expressed its satisfaction. In 1826 Young was appointed to the newly created post of protector of the slaves for Demerara (now part of Guyana). He sold his commission in the army and assumed office on 5 June 1826.

Young's responsibility was to enforce the policy of ameliorating the condition of slaves which the British government had recently adopted to ward off criticism from the anti-slavery lobby in parliament. This policy was viewed unenthusiastically by the owners and nowhere more so than in Demerara, which had one of the largest concentrations of slaves in the British West Indies and had been the scene of a serious insurrection in 1823. Since the protector was supposed to win the confidence of the slaves while securing the cooperation of the local assembly and courts, which were controlled by the white colonists, his position was bound to be an uncomfortable one. Yet Young quickly impressed the governor, Sir Benjamin D'Urban, by his diligence and above all by his "discretion." In particularly acute cases of abuse, Young was prepared to enforce the law stringently, even if doing so meant incurring the enmity of the white population, but for the most part he was content to act as a mediator between the slaves and their masters rather than as a defender of the slaves. Since it was extremely difficult for slaves to establish proof of maltreatment, Young's approach effectively meant that conditions on the plantations improved only modestly, if at all. His limited effectiveness was masked to a considerable degree by the inadequacy of his reports to London, for which he was rebuked in 1827 and again in 1829. Moreover, by 1829 the imperial government was shifting away from a policy of exhorting the West Indian colonists to ameliorate the lot of the slaves and towards a program of compulsion. Implicit in this shift was a new and more aggressive role for the protectors of the slaves. Unfortunately, Young was insensitive to the changing mood of his superiors and in November 1830 the Colonial Office decided to suspend him. In February 1831 Young hastily departed for London to defend himself. Although unable to persuade the secretary of state, Lord Goderich, that he ought to be reinstated, Young made a convincing case that his conduct had resulted from a misunderstanding of his instructions and his lack of education in the law rather than from wilful disobedience. He was compensated with the post of lieutenant governor of Prince Edward Island, which fell vacant while he was in London.

Young took control of his government on 3 Oct. 1831 at a critical time in the history of Prince Edward Island. The election of William Cooper* to the assembly in a by-election that July had signalled a renewed effort to dispossess the absentee landlords of their vast and frequently neglected estates in the colony. In April 1832 the assembly passed a resolution asking the lieutenant governor to establish a court of escheat. Young had learned from his experience in Demerara the folly of misinterpreting the wishes of his superiors, and his cautious response to the assembly's petition was to request instructions from London. When Lord Goderich indicated his opposition to the measure, Young hoped that this would put an end to the agitation. Yet Young recognized that the absentee proprietors had contributed comparatively little to the development of the colony and, when the assembly passed a land assessment bill in April 1833 imposing a substantial tax on land, he tried, unsuccessfully, to persuade the Colonial Office to approve the measure because it would encourage the landlords to develop their estates. Although acutely aware of the influence of the proprietors' lobby in London, Young was also prepared to resist their efforts to use that influence in ways detrimental to the public interest. When several proprietors protested against an act forcing them to contribute to the building of roads across their estates, Young defended the act. When David Stewart, a prominent absentee landlord, persuaded Goderich that he should be allowed to purchase the fishing reserves adjacent to his lot, Young convinced the secretary of state that this purchase would hinder the long-term development of the fisheries.

Although Young sympathized with the assembly's efforts to develop the colony, the claim made by historian Francis William Pius Bolger that he showed "a deep concern for the plight of the tenantry" is exaggerated. In Demerara his desire to improve the condition of the slaves had been tempered by his commitment to the *status quo* and on Prince Edward Island his concern for the tenants was similarly circumscribed, as he again tried to mediate between two groups very unequal in power and influence. Thus, although he dismissed as unfounded the reports circulated by the proprietors in London of widespread civil disobedience to the law on the Island, he was willing to assist the landlords in the collection of rents. While Young was absent on a leave of absence between 18 May and 29 Sept. 1834, a minor incident took place at Naufrage when a body of tenants prevented the sheriff from performing his duties. Upon his return Young acted promptly to reassert the authority of the government. Yet he also insisted that the incident had only occurred because of the sheriff's "want of energy and tact" and dealt with the offenders leniently.

Commenting on Young's governorship, Thomas Frederick Elliot, the clerk in charge of the North American department at the Colonial Office, warmly praised him for acting "the part of a judicious moderator; restraining any signs of insubordination on the part of the people, and at the same time resisting all attempts of the Proprietors to create unfounded alarm or establish a belief in fictitious grievances." For this achievement Young had been knighted on 9 July 1834 while he was on leave in London. Yet his success in maintaining harmony on the Island was inevitably transitory. In the elections of December 1834 the escheat movement, led by Cooper, grew in strength and in April 1835 the assembly reiterated its demand for a court of escheat. Resistance to the payment of rents would become more common during the later 1830s. This increasing tension between the tenants and the landlords was reflected in the relationship between the assembly and the Council from the beginning of Young's term. In the session of 1832 the Council angered the assembly by rejecting a bill imposing a new tax on land, but during the legislative sessions of 1833 and 1834 Young did manage to maintain an uneasy peace between the two houses, partly through the appointment to the Council of men such as John Brecken*, who were not associated with the absentee proprietors. During the 1835 session, however, the assembly and Council disagreed over a wide range of measures and Young was compelled to prorogue the legislature on 10 April even though no supply bill had been passed. He reconvened it on 29 April and after a short session a supply bill was agreed to by both houses, but little else. By this time Young had fallen seriously ill and he authorized a commission consisting of Edward James Jarvis*, Ambrose Lane*, and Thomas Heath Haviland* to prorogue the legislature on 6 May. Despite a modest recovery later in the year, Young died on 1 Dec. 1835.

Sir Benjamin D'Urban described Young as "an Honest and an Honorable Man" and there is no denying that verdict. He was rigidly correct and conscientious in the performance of his assigned duties, with an "affability of manner" which the Charlottetown *Royal Gazette* praised as "peculiarly pleasing and unconstrained." But, badly frightened after his dismissal from Demerara, he made it his primary concern to follow his instructions to the letter. He had neither the intelligence nor the influence at home of his immediate successors, Sir John Harvey* and Sir Charles Augustus FitzRoy*, and so took few positive steps to redress the grievances of which the tenants of Prince Edward Island justly complained. That Young was appointed at all is a clear indication of the limited interest of the Colonial Office in the affairs of Prince Edward Island. That his accomplishments were meagre is therefore not surprising.

PHILLIP BUCKNER

Young

The major sources for this study were the Colonial Office records in the PRO for Trinidad (CO 295/50–59), British Guiana (CO 111/54–72 and CO 112/6–7, 112/15), and Prince Edward Island (CO 226/49–52 and CO 227/7–8). The journals of the House of Assembly and Legislative Council of P.E.I. can also be found in CO 229/7–8. Details about Young's military career have been taken from G.B., WO, *Army list*, and from the *DNB*. There is a brief obituary on 22 Dec. 1835 in the Charlottetown *Royal Gazette* and many references to Young during the years 1832–35. Duncan Campbell's *History of Prince Edward Island* (Charlottetown, 1875; repr. Belleville, Ont., 1972), 78–82, contains a brief sketch of Young's career there, and *Canada's smallest prov.* (Bolger), 98–105, a rather more substantial one.

YOUNG, JOHN, Presbyterian clergyman and schoolmaster; b. *c.* 1759 in Beith, Scotland, only son of James Young, schoolmaster; d. 10 March 1825 in Sheet Harbour, N.S.

John Young was educated at the University of Glasgow, and on 29 Nov. 1785 he was licensed to preach by the Presbytery of Irvine. Vacancies being rare in Scotland, he chose to emigrate with his wife, Mary Kerr, and an infant daughter, and in 1787 he was accepted as probationer by the Presbytery of New York, which sent him to visit vacancies north and west of Albany. He quickly received a call, and the following year he was ordained and installed as pastor of the United Congregations of Schenectady and Currie's Bush. In October 1790 the Presbytery of New York divided its membership; Young and his congregation fell within the newly formed Presbytery of Albany. Almost immediately Young asked that his pastoral relations with his congregation be dissolved. A serious charge, probably of drunkenness, had been levelled against him. At this critical juncture, and without the knowledge of his congregation, he visited Montreal, where the Presbyterians were without a minister. In December 1790 a presbyterial inquiry into Young's conduct took place, and although he was readmitted to his charge, it was only as "stated supply," that is, on probation until presbytery met again the following March.

In Montreal the Presbyterians had been worshipping with the Anglicans until March 1786, when the Reverend John Bethune* had established a small, separate congregation. Following Bethune's departure in 1787 the Presbyterians seem to have returned to the Protestant Congregation, an Anglican body that later became Christ Church, under David Chabrand* Delisle. Since they were looking for another minister, and Young for another congregation, when the Presbytery of Albany met in March 1791 Young declined a call from two churches under its jurisdiction in order to be available for Montreal, where Duncan Fisher* and others were organizing a congregation for him. In September Young reported to the Presbytery of

Albany that he was preaching in Montreal and requested an appointment there as stated supply, a request supported by the congregation, which also asked that it be taken under presbytery's wing. Albany merchants had been in contact for years with the mercantile community in Montreal, and it was no doubt because of this tie that the request was granted.

Young's was probably the only official connection to exist between an American presbytery and a Lower Canadian church until the American Presbyterian Church was formed in Montreal in 1822. However, the union was sterile and short-lived. In 1792 presbytery received no account of Young or his congregation, even though they had built, and on 7 October opened, a new church on Rue Saint-Philippe, later Saint-Gabriel. The following year the new Scotch Presbyterian Church, subsequently known as the St Gabriel Street Church, obtained dismissal from the Presbytery of Albany in order to join the Presbytery of Montreal, formed by Young, Bethune, and Alexander Spark* of Quebec. The new body quickly dissolved, however, apparently as a result of an altercation between Young and Spark.

Besides ministering to his own congregation, Young made occasional missionary trips as far away as the seigneuries of Saint-Armand and Caldwell's Manor, or Foucault, on Missisquoi Bay. In Montreal he sometimes took services for the Anglicans, whose clergyman, James Marmaduke Tunstall*, was subject to fits of derangement, and he entertained excellent relations with Tunstall's successor, Jehosaphat Mountain*, whom he assisted on occasion. As well he was chaplain to the Presbyterian soldiers in garrison, for which function he received a government salary of £50 per annum. The salary must have been welcome, since Young's stipend from the congregation was small and, having no manse, he was obliged to rent lodgings. His meagre income, barely equal to the support of his family, had also to finance his alcoholism and possibly a penchant for gambling; the load appears to have been too heavy, and he was continually in financial difficulty.

Despite his personal problems, Young gave general satisfaction to his congregation until at least 1800, when his position was challenged during a struggle for power between the temporal committee, until then dormant, and session, which had filled the void and was managing all aspects of the congregation's life. Young was necessarily identified with session and its perennial clerk, Duncan Fisher, was his close collaborator. In the elections to session of 1800 a clean sweep was made, Fisher himself being among the defeated. In November some members of the church, including the prominent merchants Isaac Todd* and Alexander HENRY, proposed Young's dismissal, but their motion was soundly defeated by the congregation. The following year the temporal committee began lodging formal complaints with session about Young's personal conduct, and session barred him from administering the sacraments until he had cleared himself. Young refused to accept the ban, and in August 1802 session, of which Fisher had again become clerk, locked him out of the church. This time the congregation overwhelmingly voted for his dismissal; Fisher abstained. Young was replaced temporarily by Robert Forrest, and then definitively by James Somerville*, but the call to Somerville revealed a profound division of the congregation along socio-ethnic lines [see Robert EASTON], which may earlier have played a role in Young's downfall.

After his dismissal Young went to Niagara (Niagara-on-the-Lake), Upper Canada, but he soon resigned his ministry there because of alcoholism. He then moved to Stamford (Niagara Falls), where until about 1804 he preached on Sundays and taught during the week. About 1813 he ministered for a short time to a congregation near Lake Champlain, and then, possibly the following year, moved to Lunenburg, N.S. He settled finally in Sheet Harbour in 1821, again taking up his round of preaching and teaching; the schoolhouse was also the church and his home. His alcoholism notwithstanding, he was universally esteemed in the infant village. This rotund giant of 6 feet 6 inches (his wife was of corresponding proportions), with "an eye in his head like a hawk," was, according

to the Presbyterian minister John Sprott*, "a searching and close preacher." However, within five years of his arrival, Young was dead. His grave was made, Sprott observed, "on the sea beaten shore within a few yards of the water, and within a few yards of the forest." The *Acadian Recorder*, which noted in Young "the infirmities of human nature," also commented that "few persons have experienced greater vicissitudes of fortune in their passage through life." Four of his eight children had died in infancy; two others had been left in Montreal in 1802 and a third possibly somewhere else; and at his death, the *Acadian Recorder* remarked, Young left in Sheet Harbour, "an aged widow and one daughter both deaf and dumb."

ELIZABETH ANN KERR McDOUGALL

ANQ-M, CE1-126, 1791–1802. *Acadian Recorder*, 19 March 1825. R. Campbell, *Hist. of Scotch Presbyterian Church*. William Gregg, *History of the Presbyterian Church in the dominion of Canada* . . . (Toronto, 1885). H. S. M'Collum, "Canadian Presbyterian history, no.II," *Canada Presbyterian* (Toronto), new ser., 1 (1877–78): 434–35. E. A. [Kerr] McDougall, "The American element in the early Presbyterian Church in Montreal (1786–1824)" (MA thesis, McGill Univ., Montreal, 1965), 37–38, 59–73, 170. J. S. Moir, *Enduring witness; a history of the Presbyterian Church in Canada* ([Hamilton, Ont., 1974]). J. E. Rutledge, *Sheet Harbour, a local history* (Halifax, 1954), 80.

GENERAL BIBLIOGRAPHY AND
LIST OF ABBREVIATIONS

List of Abbreviations

AAQ	Archives de l'archidiocèse de Québec	MAC-CD	Ministère des Affaires culturelles, Centre de documentation
AC	Archives civiles	MTL	Metropolitan Toronto Library
ACAM	Archives de la chancellerie de l'archevêché de Montréal	NLS	National Library of Scotland
		NMM	National Maritime Museum
ACC	Anglican Church of Canada	NWC	North West Company
AD	Archives départementales	*OH*	*Ontario History*
ADB	*Australian dictionary of biography*	PABC	Provincial Archives of British Columbia
ANQ	Archives nationales du Québec		
AO	Archives of Ontario	PAC	Public Archives of Canada
AP	Archives paroissiales	PAM	Provincial Archives of Manitoba
ASQ	Archives du séminaire de Québec	PANB	Provincial Archives of New Brunswick
ASSH	Archives du séminaire de Saint-Hyacinthe	PANL	Provincial Archives of Newfoundland and Labrador
ASSM	Archives du séminaire de Saint-Sulpice, Montréal	PANS	Public Archives of Nova Scotia
		PAPEI	Public Archives of Prince Edward Island
AUM	Archives de l'université de Montréal		
BCHQ	*British Columbia Historical Quarterly*	PRO	Public Record Office
BE	Bureau d'enregistrement	QUA	Queen's University Archives
BL	British Library	*RHAF*	*Revue d'histoire de l'Amérique française*
BRH	*Le Bulletin des recherches historiques*		
CCHA	Canadian Catholic Historical Association	RSC	Royal Society of Canada
		SGCF	Société généalogique canadienne-française
CHA	Canadian Historical Association		
CHR	*Canadian Historical Review*	*SH*	*Social History*
DAB	*Dictionary of American biography*	SPG	Society for the Propagation of the Gospel in Foreign Parts
DCB	*Dictionary of Canadian biography*		
DNB	*Dictionary of national biography*	SRO	Scottish Record Office
DOLQ	*Dictionnaire des œuvres littéraires du Québec*	UCC	United Church of Canada
		UNBL	University of New Brunswick Library
HBC	Hudson's Bay Company	USPG	United Society for the Propagation of the Gospel
HBCA	Hudson's Bay Company Archives		
HBRS	Hudson's Bay Record Society, *Publications*	UWOL	University of Western Ontario Library

General Bibliography

The General Bibliography is based on the sources most frequently cited in the individual bibliographies of volume VI. It should not be regarded as providing a complete list of background materials for the history of Canada in the 19th century.

Section I describes the principal archival sources and is arranged by country. Section II is divided into two parts: part A contains printed primary sources including documents published by the various colonial governments; part B provides a listing of the contemporary newspapers most frequently cited by contributors to the volume. Section III includes dictionaries, indexes, inventories, almanacs, and directories. Section IV contains secondary works of the 19th and 20th centuries, including a number of general histories and theses. Section V describes the principal journals and the publications of various societies consulted.

I. ARCHIVAL SOURCES

CANADA

ANGLICAN CHURCH OF CANADA, DIOCESE OF QUEBEC ARCHIVES, Lennoxville, Que. For a description of this archives, *see* A. R. Kelley, "The Quebec Diocesan Archives; a description of the collection of historical records of the Church of England in the Diocese of Quebec," ANQ *Rapport*, 1946–47: 181–298, and [A.] M. Awcock, "Catalogue of the Quebec Diocesan Archives" (typescript, Shawinigan, Que., 1973; copy available at the archives).

The following materials are cited in volume VI:

1: Letters patent declaring Jacob Mountain bishop of Quebec
2: Letters granting coat of arms to diocese of Quebec
16: Letters patent erecting diocese of Quebec with Jacob Mountain as bishop
17: Mandamus from George III authorizing bishop of Quebec to be lord bishop of Quebec
18: Letters patent to Jacob Mountain creating the bishop of Quebec to be lord bishop of Quebec
19: Writ of summons of bishop of Quebec to Legislative Council of Upper Canada
20: Letters patent creating J. Mountain lord bishop of Quebec at Newark, U.C.
21: Presentation of S. J. Mountain to be minister of church of Quebec
22: Commission appointing five commissioners for erection of a metropolitan church of Quebec

23: Letters patent erecting cathedral church at Quebec
24: Grant of George IV to establish two archdeaconries Quebec and York
26: Letters patent erecting parish of (Charleston) (Hatley) and T. Johnston as rector
27: Letters patent erecting parish of Drummondville, Quebec, and S. S. Wood as rector
28: Letters patent setting apart burying ground in St John's suburbs, Quebec
29: Letters patent appointing C. J. Stewart to be bishop of Quebec
30b: Letters patent erecting parish of Three Rivers, Quebec, and R. Q. Short as rector
47–71: Parish reports, correspondence, and other material relating to the parishes
  53: Hatley
  69: St Johns, Stoneham, St Francis (Indian) (Pierreville), Shigawake, Shefford, Sherrington
  70: Three Rivers
72–80: Correspondence of Jacob Mountain
  81: Correspondence of Jacob Mountain, [C.] J. Stewart, and G. J. Mountain
82–102: Copies of letters and papers referring to diocese of Quebec
103–4: Letters from C. J. Stewart to J. Reid
  105: Stewart letters
  106: H. C. Stewart, "Episcopate of Jacob Mountain"
107–8: Correspondence between bishops of Quebec and SPG
  109: Correspondence between bishops of

Quebec and Society for the Promotion of Christian Knowledge
110: Clergy reserves and erection of parishes
118: Education: McGill, Bishop's, Bishop's College School, etc.
123–25: Unbound manuscripts
129: Copies of correspondence of C. J. Stewart
314: *Christian Sentinel and Anglo-Canadian Churchman Magazine*
348: Society for Promoting Christian Knowledge, committee reports

ARCHIVES CIVILES. *See* Québec, Ministère de la Justice

ARCHIVES DE LA CHANCELLERIE DE L'ARCHEVÊCHÉ DE MONTRÉAL. A detailed inventory of many of the registers and files in this depository can be found in *RHAF*, 19 (1965–66): 652–64; 20 (1966–67): 146–66, 324–41, 669–700; 24 (1970–71): 111–42.
The following series are cited in volume VI:
Dossiers
465: Communautés d'hommes en particulier
.101: Compagnie de Saint-Sulpice
780: Associations et divers
.034: Journaux
901: Fonds Lartigue–Bourget
.013: Notice biographique de Mgr Plessis; érection du diocèse de Montréal
.016: Mgr Lartigue: lettres personnelles
.017: Messieurs Maguire et Tabeau, prêtres; division de Québec et biens de Saint-Sulpice; missions à Rome; projet de journal ecclésiastique
.029: Lettres: messieurs Viau, Terrasse, Duclaux, Roux
.030: P.-A. Tabeau: ses troubles et ses hésitations
.036: Mgr Lartigue: journal de voyage en Europe
.136: Notre-Dame: division de la paroisse
.137: Notre-Dame et Saint-Sulpice
RC: Registres de la chancellerie
RCD: Registres et cahiers divers
XXXVIII: Essai de tarif avec instructions sur le mariage de Mgr Plessis
RL: Registres de lettres
RLL: Registres des lettres de Mgr Lartigue. An inventory of the correspondence of Mgr Jean-Jacques Lartigue* from 1819 to 1840, compiled by L.-A. Desrosiers, appears in ANQ *Rapport*, 1941–42 [section III].

ARCHIVES DE L'ARCHIDIOCÈSE DE QUÉBEC. A guide to the collection is available in CCHA *Rapport*, 2 (1934–35): 65–73.
Series cited in volume VI:
A: Évêques et archevêques de Québec
12 A: Registres des insinuations ecclésiastiques
20 A: Lettres manuscrites des évêques de Québec
210 A: Registres des lettres expédiées. Inventories of the correspondence of a number of the bishops of Quebec, compiled by Ivanhoë Caron*, are available in ANQ *Rapport* [section III].
22 A: Copies de lettres expédiées
31-11 A: Papiers privés de J.-O. Plessis
C: Secrétairerie et chancellerie
CB: Structures de direction
1 CB: Vicaires généraux
CD: Discipline diocésaine
303 CD: Titres cléricaux
515 CD: Séminaire de Nicolet
61 CD: Paroisses
69 CD: Visites pastorales
71-31 CD: Sulpiciens
Diocèse de Québec (being reclassified)
CE: Rapports avec les organismes administratifs
6 CE: Société ecclésiastique Saint-Joseph
CM: Église universelle
10 CM: Correspondance de Rome
7 CM: États-Unis
90 CM: Angleterre
CN: Église canadienne
30 CN: Terre-Neuve
310 CN: Île-du-Prince-Édouard
311 CN: Nouveau-Brunswick
312 CN: Nouvelle-Écosse
320 CN: Haut-Canada
60 CN: Gouvernement du Canada
CP: Église du Québec
24 CP: Diocèse de Labrador
26 CP: Diocèse de Montréal
T: Papiers privés
TC: Ivanhoë Caron
TF: J.-B.-A. Ferland

ARCHIVES DE L'UNIVERSITÉ DE MONTRÉAL. The Service des archives de l'université de Montréal has prepared an important series of publications relating to its collections; a list of these can be found in *Bibliographie des publications du Service des archives* (3ᵉ éd., Montréal, 1980), compiled by Jacques Ducharme and Denis Plante.
The following collections are cited in volume VI:
P 58: Collection Baby. The *Catalogue de la collec-*

tion *François-Louis-Georges Baby*, compiled by Camille Bertrand, with preface by Paul Baby and introduction by Lucien Campeau (2v., Montréal, 1971), provides useful information to researchers. Transcripts of the bulk of this collection, which is being classified at present, are located in PAC, MG 24, L3.

G: Commerce et finance
G2: Commerce, finance, affaires
P: Documents militaires
P2: Papiers militaires
Q1: Documents hors-série
U: Correspondance générale

ARCHIVES DU SÉMINAIRE DE QUÉBEC.
    Series cited in volume VI:
C: Livres de comptes du séminaire
Fichier des anciens
Fonds H.-R. Casgrain
    Série O: Cahiers manuscrits
        0521: Compagnie du Nord-Ouest, livre de comptes, 1799–1804
Fonds Viger–Verreau
    Cartons: Papiers de H.-A.-J.-B. Verreau; Jacques Viger
    Série O: Cahiers manuscrits
        081: Notices sur la vie de plusieurs prêtres du Canada par Jacques Viger
        095–125: Ma saberdache de Jacques Viger
        0139–52: Ma saberdache de Jacques Viger
        0297: Album Gaspé
Lettres
MSS: Cahiers manuscrits divers
        7: H.-F. Gravé, Application des fondations
        12: Grand livre du séminaire
        13: Plumitif du Conseil du séminaire commencé en 1678
        20: Badelard, Observations sur la maladie de la baie Saint-Paul
        74: Louis Labadie, Journal
        205: Asselin, Abrégé d'histoire et de chronologie; Charles Bédard, Réponse de M. Chaboillez sur les affaires ecclésiastiques et déclarations à M. Roux sur le même sujet; C.-F. Painchaud, Mémoire sur le même sujet
    218–19: J.-F. Boucher, Lettres dogmatiques, pièces diverses
        257: Affaires ecclésiastiques de Montréal
    431–32: A.-E. Gosselin, Liste d'élèves, d'ordinations du grand séminaire
MSS-M: Cahiers de cours manuscrits
        102: J.-O. Plessis, Cours de rhétorique par H. Hudon
        134: P.-J. Bossu, Cours de géométrie par Antoine Robert

        148: Cordes
        151: Joseph Deguire, Cours de philosophie par Antoine Robert
        185: Cours de philosophie abrégé par Antoine Robert
        241: Pierre Bédard, Notes de philosophie, mathématiques, chimie, physique, grammaire, politique et journal
        978: F.-C. Gagnon, Cours d'histoire ancienne par Joseph Signay
Polygraphie: Affaires surtout extérieures
S: Seigneuries du séminaire
    S-184a: Aveu et dénombrement
Séminaire: Affaires diverses
Université
    Série U
        U-17: Procès-verbaux du Quebec Medical Board
        U-18: Procès-verbaux du Bureau de médecine

ARCHIVES DU SÉMINAIRE DE SAINT-HYACINTHE, Saint-Hyacinthe, Qué.
    Series cited in volume VI:
Section A: Archives du séminaire
    Série A: Fondation
Section F: Fonds particuliers
    Fg-4: Saint-Pierre, P.-A.
        A-64: Dessaules, Jean
        B: Liste des coupures de journaux

ARCHIVES DU SÉMINAIRE DE SAINT-SULPICE, Montréal.
    Sections cited in volume VI:
Section 1 bis: Démêlés relatifs aux biens
Section 9: Bornages et plans
Section 10: Baux et marchés
Section 11: Enseignement
Section 14: Successions
Section 16: Émigration, immigration, colonisation
Section 17: Finance, banque, monnaie
Section 18: Sociétés diverses
Section 21: Correspondance générale
Section 24: Histoire et géographie, biographies, divers
    Dossier 2: Biographies
    Dossier 3: Histoire et divers
    Dossier 6: Cahiers Faillon
Section 25: Séminaire de Saint-Sulpice
    Dossier 2: Emplois
Section 27: Séminaire, évêchés et paroisses
Section 28: Ordinations, juridictions, nominations
Section 36: Missions
    No.13: "Portrait d'un missionnaire apostolique"
Section 49: Prédication
    Dossier 23: Ciquard, F.-R.
    Dossier 25: Bédard, J.-B.-C.

ARCHIVES NATIONALES DU QUÉBEC. In 1980 the archives undertook to establish a new uniform classification for its regional centres. Inventories, catalogues, guides, conversion tables, and useful finding aids on microfiche are available in all the regional centres of the ANQ.

CENTRE RÉGIONAL DE L'ESTRIE (ANQ-E), Sherbrooke
    Series cited in volume VI:
C: Pouvoir judiciaire, archives civiles
    CE: État civil
      1: Sherbrooke
        41: Hatley Anglican Church
      2: Bedford
        42: Shefford Anglican Church (Waterloo)
    CN: Notaires
      1: Sherbrooke
        24: Ritchie, William
        27: Thomas, Daniel
      2: Bedford
        21: Gale, Samuel
        26: Lalanne, Léon
T: Justice
    11: Cour supérieure
      501: Saint-François

CENTRE RÉGIONAL DE MONTRÉAL (ANQ-M)
    The following were cited in volume VI:
C: Pouvoir judiciaire, archives civiles
    CC: Tutelles et curatelles
      1: Montréal
    CE: État civil
      1: Montréal
        2: La-Nativité-de-la-Très-Sainte-Vierge (Laprairie)
        4: La Visitation (Sault-aux-Récollets)
        10: Sainte-Anne (Varennes)
        12: Saint-Antoine (Longueuil)
        22: Sainte-Famille (Boucherville)
        23: Saint-François-d'Assise (Montréal)
        26: Saint-François-Xavier (Verchères)
        39: Saint-Joseph (Chambly)
        50: Saint-Michel (Vaudreuil)
        51: Notre-Dame de Montréal
        54: Saint-Philippe (Laprairie)
        59: Saint-Vincent-de-Paul (Laval)
        63: Christ Church Anglican (Montreal)
        65: Garrison Anglican Church (Montreal)
        125: St Andrew's Presbyterian Church (Montreal)
        126: St Gabriel's Presbyterian Church (Montreal)
      2: Saint-Hyacinthe
        5: Notre-Dame-du-Rosaire (Saint-Hyacinthe)
        12: Saint-Denis (Saint-Denis, sur le Richelieu)
      3: Sorel
        1: Christ Church (Sorel)
        5: Saint-Michel (Yamaska)
        6: Immaculée-Conception (Saint-Ours)
        8: Saint-François-du-Lac
      5: Joliette
        6: Saint-Antoine (Lavaltrie)
        14: Saint-Pierre-du-Portage (L'Assomption)
      6: Saint-Jérôme
        11: Saint-Eustache
        24: Saint-Louis (Terrebonne)
    CL: Licitations, adjudications, ventes par shérifs
    CM: Testaments
    1: Montréal
    CN: Notaires
    1: Montréal
        7: Arnoldi, G.-D.
        16: Barron, Thomas
        29: Beek, J. G.
        33: Lefebvre de Bellefeuille, H.-N.
        43: Boileau, René
        47: Bourassa, I.-G.
        68: Cadieux, J.-M.
        74: Chaboillez, Louis
        96: Constantin, J.-B.
        98: Coron, C.-F.
        107: Dandurand, R.-F.
        108: Danré de Blanzy, L.-C.
        117: Deguire, J.-B.
        120: De Lisle, Jean
        121: De Lisle, J.-G.
        123: Demers, Joseph
        126: Desautels, Joseph
        128: Desève, J.-B.
        134: Doucet, N.-B.
        136: Dubois, A.-A.
        158: Foucher, Antoine
        167: Gauthier, J.-P.
        168: Gauthier, P.-A.
        185: Gray, J. A.
        187: Griffin, Henry
        189: Grisé, Antoine
        194: Guy, Louis
        200: Henry, Edme
        229: Lalanne, Pierre
        243: Latour, Louis Huguet
        255: Leguay, François (fils)

269: Lukin, Peter (père)
273: Manthet, Nicolas
290: Mézières, Pierre
295: Mondelet, J.-M.
313: Papineau, Joseph
317: Payment, Joseph
327: Pinsonnault, P.-P.
334: Prévost, Charles
348: Ritchot, Pierre
383: Thibaudault, Louis
391: Vallée, Paul
2: Saint-Hyacinthe
  11: Bourdages, Louis
  19: Delagrave, L.-B.
  27: Dutalmé, P.-P.
  56: Michaud, Christophe
  57: Mignault, J.-E.
3: Sorel
  2: Berthelot, J.-A.
  7: Dufault, Jacques
  11: Gagnier, P.-R.
6: Saint-Jérôme
  13: Laforce, Pierre
  17: Limoges, Toussaint
  24: Prévost, J.-B.-L.-L.
  27: Séguin, F.-H.
  29: Turgeon, Joseph
P: Fonds et collections privées
  26: Trudeau, Romuald
  35: Neilson, John
  68: Duvernay, fonds
  P1000: Petits fonds
    4-461: Salaberry, Louis de
    5-537: Compagnie du Nord-Ouest
    32-774: Girouard, collection
    44-877: Salaberry, famille
    45-889: Duvernay, collection
T: Pouvoir judiciaire
  10: Cour du banc du roi

Centre régional de la Mauricie–Bois-Francs (ANQ-MBF), Trois-Rivières
The following materials were cited in volume VI:
C: Pouvoir judiciaire, archives civiles
  CE: État civil
  1: Trois-Rivières
    7: La Visitation (Champlain)
    15: Saint-Antoine-de-la-Rivière-du-Loup (Louiseville)
    48: Immaculée-Conception (Trois-Rivières)
    50: St James Protestant Congregation Church (Trois-Rivières)
  CN: Notaires
  1: Trois-Rivières
    4: Badeaux, A.-I.

5: Badeaux, J.-B.
6: Badeaux, Joseph
8: Bazin, Pierre
19: Craig, L.-D.
31: Dumoulin, F.-L.
32: Dumoulin, J.-E.
35: Duvernay, J.-M. Crevier
38: Gagnon, Antoine
56: Leblanc, A.-Z.
64: Maillet, C.-L.
77: Pratte, Charles
79: Ranvoyzé, Étienne
87: Saupin, J.-J.

Centre d'archives de Québec (ANQ-Q)
The following sources were consulted in the preparation of volume VI:
C: Pouvoir judiciaire, archives civiles
  CA: Arpenteurs
  1: Québec
    45: McCarthy, Jeremiah
  CC: Tutelles et curatelles
  CE: État civil
  1: Québec
    1: Notre-Dame de Québec
    2: Notre-Dame de l'Annonciation (L'Ancienne-Lorette)
    4: Saint-Étienne (Beaumont)
    5: Notre-Dame de Miséricorde (Beauport)
    7: Saint-Charles-Borromée (Charlesbourg)
    8: Sainte-Famille (Cap-Santé)
    10: Saint-Laurent (Île d'Orléans)
    11: Sainte-Famille (Île d'Orléans)
    12: Saint-Pierre (Île d'Orléans)
    15: Saint-François-de-Sales (Neuville)
    20: Notre-Dame-de-Foy (Sainte-Foy)
    25: Saint-Joseph (Deschambault)
    28: Saint-Ambroise (Loretteville)
    61: Holy Trinity Cathedral (Quebec)
    66: St Andrew's Presbyterian Church (Quebec)
    93: Hôpital Général de Québec
    94: Saint-Antoine-de-Tilly
  2: Montmagny
    3: Notre-Dame-de-Bon-Secours (L'Islet)
    4: Saint-Charles (Bellechasse)
    6: Saint-Pierre-de-la-Rivière-du-Sud (Montmagny)
    7: Saint-Thomas-de-la-Pointe-à-la-Caille (Montmagny)
    18: Saint-Jean-Port-Joli
    25: Saint-Roch-des-Aulnaies

3: Kamouraska
  1: Notre-Dame-de-Liesse
    (Rivière-Ouelle)
  3: Saint-Louis (Kamouraska)
  12: Sainte-Anne-de-la-Pocatière
    (La Pocatière)
4: Saguenay
  1: Saint-Pierre et Saint-Paul
    (Baie-Saint-Paul)
  2: Saint-Louis (Île aux Coudres)
  4: L'Assomption-de-la-Sainte-
    Vierge (Les Éboulements)
CN: Notaires
1: Québec
  16: Bélanger, Jean
  25: Berthelot Dartigny, M.-A.
  26: Berthelot, Michel
  28: Bigué, Paul
  49: Campbell, Archibald
  80: DeFoy, C.-M.
  81: De Léry, William
  83: Deschenaux, P.-L.
  92: Dumas, Alexandre
  99: Faribault, Barthélemy
  116: Glackmeyer, Edward
  134: Hébert, J.-B.-C.
  145: Jones, John
  147: Laforce, Pierre
  157: Larue, F.-X.
  171: Lee, Thomas
  178: Lelièvre, Roger
  188: Lindsay, E. B.
  197: McPherson, L. T.
  205: Panet, J.-A.
  207: Panet, J.-C.
  208: Panet, Louis
  212: Parent, A.-Archange
  219: Petitclerc, Joseph
  224: Pinguet, J.-N.
  230: Planté, J.-B.
  248: Saillant, J.-A.
  251: Sanguinet, Simon
  253: Scott, W. F.
  255: Sirois-Duplessis, A.-B.
  256: Stewart, Charles
  262: Têtu, Félix
  284: Voyer, Charles
  285: Voyer, Jacques
2: Montmagny
  7: Boisseau, N.-G.
  12: Fraser, Simon
  46: Turgeon, Louis
  48: Verreau, G.-A.
3: Kamouraska
  10: Casault, Thomas
  11: Cazes, Louis
  13: Colin, Jacques

  17: Dionne, Augustin
  19: Duberger, Bernard
  30: Garon, Pierre
  55: Taché, J.-B.
4: Saguenay
  16: Néron, Jean
E: Pouvoir exécutif
  18: Registraire
  21: Terres et forêts
    12: Fois et hommages
    77: Biens des jésuites, administration
      générale, 1800–13
    81: Biens des jésuites, administration
      générale, 1821–26
    96–97: Biens des jésuites, administra-
      tion des seigneuries, Trois-
      Rivières
    110: Biens des jésuites, administration
      des seigneuries, Cap-de-la-
      Madeleine
    357: Correspondance, rapports de
      Joseph Bouchette
  39: Syndicat national du rachat des rentes
    seigneuriales
P: Fonds et collections privées
  40: Chaussegros de Léry, famille
  44: Chartier de Lotbinière, famille
  163: Chartier de Lotbinière, M.-E.-G.-A.
  193: Neilson, imprimerie
  197: Panet, Jacques
  219: Quebec Board of Trade
  222: Quesnel, Jules
  232: Robitaille, Olivier
  239: Roy, P.-G.
  254: Thompson, John
  267: Moorehead, famille
  279: Papiers Wurtele
  289: Salaberry, famille de
  351: Joly de Lotbinière, famille
  398: Baillairgé, François
  417: Papineau, famille
  597: Morisset, Gérard
P1000: Petits fonds
  1-18: Ainslie, Gilbert
  21-378: Chartier de Lotbinière,
    M.-E.-G.-A.
  32-592: Drapeau, Joseph
  41-757: Waller, Jocelyn
  54-1047: Juchereau, famille
  81-1672: Plamondon, Louis
  93-1906: Salaberry, I.-M.-L.-A. de
T: Pouvoir judiciaire
  6-1: Cour de justice, Régime britannique
  11-1: Cour supérieure
Z: Copies de documents conservés en dehors des
ANQ
  C: Canada (en dehors du Québec)

I. ARCHIVAL SOURCES

2: Conseil exécutif
3: Comité des terres
Q: Québec (en dehors des ANQ)
6-45: État civil, Catholiques, Sainte-Marie-de-la-Nouvelle-Beauce
6-52: État civil, Catholiques, Saint-Édouard (Frampton)

ARCHIVES OF ONTARIO, Toronto. *A guide to the holdings of the Archives of Ontario*, ed. B. L. Craig and R. W. Ramsey (2v., Toronto, 1985), is supplemented by unpublished inventories, calendars, catalogue entries, guides, and other finding aids available in the archives. Some finding aids are also available on microfiche.

Materials used in volume VI include:
Hiram Walker Historical Museum collection
Historical plaque descriptions
MS: Microfilm Series
4: Robinson, Sir John Beverley
6: Crookshank–Lambert letters
35: Strachan, John
74: Merritt, William Hamilton
75: Russell family
78: Macaulay family
87: Playter, Eli, diary
88: Baldwin family
94: Norton, John
107: Church records, St Andrew's Presbyterian Church (Williamstown, Ont.)
148: Flamborough West manuscript collection
198: Reive, W. G., collection
393: Baird papers
444: Macdonald, Ewen, collection
451: Cemetery records collection
497: Gilkison family papers
498: Baby, Jacques Duperon, papers
500: Street, Samuel and Thomas
516: Mackenzie–Lindsey papers, Mackenzie correspondence
517: Simcoe, John Graves, Canadian section
519: Stone, Joel
520, 816: Jones, Solomon
521: Jessup, Edward, family
522: Rogers family
524: Robinson, Peter
525: Boulton, Henry John
533: Rolph, John
537: Ridout papers
606: Stuart, John, family
768: Canniff, William
787: Jarvis–Powell papers
788: Young, Henry
MU: Manuscript Units

275: Blanchard, Harry D., collection
500–15: Cartwright family
571: Clark, John, memoirs
588: Colquhoun, William
593–692: Commercial records collection
1063–103: Fraser, Alexander
1116–39: Genealogies collection
1368: High treason register
1760: McDonald, Colin and John
1780: Macdonell, John "LePretre"
1817–910: Mackenzie–Lindsey papers, Mackenzie newspaper clipping collection
1915–17: Mackenzie–Lindsey papers, Robert Randal records
2095–147: Miscellaneous collection
2196–205: Northwest Company collection
2316: Peters, Samuel
2388–89: Riddell family
2554–55: Rousseau family
3027: Tupper, Ferdinand Brock
3104–7: Washburn family
3705: Osgoode, William, letters
RG 1: Ministry of Natural Resources
A: Offices of surveyor general and commissioner of crown lands
I: Correspondence
1: Letters received, surveyor general
4: Commissioner's letter-books
6: Letters received, surveyor general and commissioner
II: Reports and statements
1: Surveyor general's reports
2: Commissioner's reports
5: Heir and Devisee Commission reports
IV: Schedules and land rolls
C: Lands Branch
I: Free grants
1: Petitions and applications
3: Fiats and warrants
4: Locations
IV: Township papers
RG 4: Ministry of Attorney General
A: Attorney general
1: Pre-confederation records
RG 18: Commissions and committees
C-I: Select committees of the Legislative Council, pre-confederation select committees
RG 20: Ministry of Correctional Services
F: Records of jails and detention centres
15: Hamilton Jail
RG 21: Municipal records
RG 22: Court records
Court of Common Pleas
ser.04: Mecklenburg District, Minutes

Court of General Quarter Sessions of the Peace
  Brockville
    ser.16: Accounts
  Cornwall
    ser.47: Minutes
  Kingston
    ser.54: Minutes
  London
    ser.61: Minutes
Court of King's Bench
  ser.125: Term-books
  ser.126: Term-books (rough)
  ser.131: Judgement docket-books
  ser.133: Ejectment books
  ser.134: Assize minute-books
  ser.138: Criminal filings
Court of Probate
  ser.155: Estate files
Surrogate courts
  Brockville
    ser.176: Registers
    ser.179: Estate files
  Cobourg
    ser.187: Registers
  Hamilton
    ser.204: Registers
  Kingston
    ser.156: Registers
    ser.159: Estate files
RG 40: Heir and Devisee Commission
  D: Claims case files
      1: Second commission
RG 53: Recording Office
  Records of land
      ser.2: Index to land patents by district
      ser.55: Index to land patents by township

ARCHIVES PAROISSIALES. The most noteworthy holdings of parish archives in Quebec are the registers of baptisms, marriages, and burials, copies of which are deposited at the Archives civiles of the judicial district in which the parish is located [see Québec, Ministère de la Justice]. Parish archives usually contain many other documents, including parish account-books, records of the *fabriques*, registers of parish confraternities, notebooks of sermons, and sometimes correspondence.

BUREAUX D'ENREGISTREMENT. *See* Québec, Ministère de la Justice

McCORD MUSEUM, Montreal. For information on this and other archival collections at McGill University, see *Guide to archival resources at McGill University*, ed. Marcel Caya *et al*. (3v., Montreal, 1985).

Collections cited in volume VI include the following:
Beaver Club minute-book
McCord family papers
War of 1812 collection

McGILL UNIVERSITY ARCHIVES, Montreal. Information on the various archival collections at McGill University is available in *Guide to archival resources at McGill University*, ed. Marcel Caya *et al*. (3v., Montreal, 1985).
    Material from the following collections is cited in volume VI:
Private archives
  MG 1007: James McGill papers
            James and Andrew McGill journal
  MG 2046: William Edmond Logan papers
Archival records of McGill University
  RG 4: Secretariat of the Royal Institution for
            the Advancement of Learning and the
            Board of Governors
            Royal Institution for the Advancement
            of Learning
  RG 38: Faculty of Medicine
            Montreal Medical Institution and
            McGill College Medical Faculty
  RG 96: Montreal General Hospital
            Board of Governors, visiting
            governors' book

McGILL UNIVERSITY LIBRARIES, DEPARTMENT OF RARE BOOKS AND SPECIAL COLLECTIONS, Montreal. For information on archival collections at McGill University, see *Guide to archival resources at McGill University*, ed. Marcel Caya *et al*. (3v., Montreal, 1985).
    The following materials are cited in volume VI:
    CH10.S46: Ryland, H. M.
    CH100.S118: Griffin, Frederick
    CH104.S122: Johnson, Sir John
      CH138.59: Blackwood, Thomas
    CH143.S13: McGill, James
    CH145.S15: Frobisher, Joseph
    CH308.S268: Griffin, Frederick
    CH334.S294: Clark, Festus
    CH341.S301: Griffin, Frederick
    CH344.S304: Griffin, Frederick
    CH356.S1316: Griffin, Frederick
    CH378.S338: Griffin, Frederick
CH379.S339–41: Griffin, Frederick
    CH389.S353: Griffin, Frederick
    CH395.OLS: Griffin, Frederick
    CH423.OLS: Griffin, Frederick

METROPOLITAN TORONTO LIBRARY. For information on the library's manuscript holdings, see *Guide to the manuscript collection in the Toronto Public Libraries* (Toronto, 1954).

Manuscripts consulted for volume VI include:
Robert Baldwin papers
William Warren Baldwin papers
Samuel Peters Jarvis papers
William Dummer Powell papers
Laurent Quetton de St George papers
Sir David William Smith papers
John Strachan papers

MINISTÈRE DES AFFAIRES CULTURELLES, CENTRE DE DOCUMENTATION. *See* Québec, Ministère des Affaires culturelles

NEW BRUNSWICK MUSEUM, Saint John, N.B. For a description of its holdings *see* New Brunswick Museum, *Inventory of manuscripts, 1967* ([Saint John, 1967]).

In addition to miscellaneous original and photo-copied documents relating to New Brunswick in the CB DOC (vertical files) and F (folders) groupings, the following are the principal collections used in volume VI:
George Jarvis Dibblee papers
William Francis Ganong collection
Jarvis family papers
Saint John, register of voters, 1785–1869
Sussex Indian Academy papers
Webster MS collection

PROVINCIAL ARCHIVES OF BRITISH COLUMBIA, Victoria. Manuscript collections received or catalogued since 1975 are listed in PABC, *Manuscript inventory*, ed. Frances Gundry (3v. to date, [Victoria], 1976–).

Series cited in volume VI:
AA10, G79B: G.B., India Office, East India Company, Bombay records (transcripts)
AA20, H76: Robert Hood, "Narrative of the proceedings of an expedition of discovery in North America under the command of Lieut. Franklin, R.N."
AA20.5, H12B: Journal of the proceedings of the brig *Halcyon* and log of the *Princess Frederica*
AA20.5, L92: Journal of the proceedings on board of the brig *Halcyon* and journal of proceedings on board of the *Loudoun*
AA20.5, L92W: J. T. Walbran, "The cruise of the *Imperial Eagle*"
AB20, L2: Archibald McDonald, Fort Langley journal
Add. MSS 623: Sabine, Edward

PROVINCIAL ARCHIVES OF MANITOBA, Winnipeg.
Materials used in the preparation of volume VI:
MG 2: Red River settlement
  C: Individuals and settlement
    21: Rhodes, G. A.
    23: Logan, Robert
MG 7: Church records and religious figures
  B: Church of England
    7: St John's Cathedral
  D: Roman Catholic
    8: Saint-Boniface

Hudson's Bay Company Archives. The PRO and the PAC hold microfilm copies of the archives' records for the years 1670 to 1870. For more information concerning the copies held at the PAC and the finding aids available, see *General inventory, manuscripts, 3*. The articles by R. H. G. Leveson Gower, "The archives of the Hudson's Bay Company," *Beaver*, outfit 264 (Dec. 1933): 40–42, 64, and Joan Craig, "Three hundred years of records," *Beaver*, outfit 301 (autumn 1970): 65–70, provide useful information to researchers. For series of HBCA documents published by the HBRS, *see* section II.

Section A: London office records
  A.1/: London minute-books
  A.5/: London correspondence books outward – general
  A.6/: London correspondence books outward – HBC official
  A.11/: London inward correspondence from HBC posts
  A.30/: Lists of servants
  A.32/: Servants' contracts
  A.36/: Officers' and servants' wills
  A.44/: Register book of wills and administrations of proprietors, etc.
  A.92/: Private correspondence
Section B: North America trading post records
  B.1/a: Abitibi journals
  B.3/a: Albany journals
  B.3/b: Albany correspondence books
  B.4/a: Fort Alexander journals
  B.22/a: Brandon House journals
  B.39/a: Fort Chipewyan journals
  B.42/a: Fort Churchill journals
  B.42/b: Fort Churchill correspondence books
  B.42/e: Fort Churchill reports on district
  B.49/a: Cumberland House journals
  B.59/a: Eastmain journals
  B.59/b: Eastmain correspondence
  B.75/a: Frederick House journals
  B.77/a: Fort George journals
  B.86/a: Henley House journals
  B.105/a: Rainy Lake journals
  B.107/a: Lac Seul journals
  B.121/a: Manchester House journals
  B.129/a: Michipicoten journals

B.134/c: Montreal correspondence inward
B.135/a: Moose Factory journals
B.135/b: Moose Factory correspondence books
B.142/a: Nemiskau journals
B.143/a: Neoskweskau journals
B.155/a: Osnaburgh House journals
B.177/a: Red Lake journals
B.186/a: Rupert House journals
B.198/b: Severn House correspondence books
B.224/c: Fort Vermilion correspondence inward
B.239/a: York Factory journals
B.239/b: York Factory correspondence books
Section C: Records of ships owned or chartered by the HBC
  C.1: Ships' logs
Section D: Governors' papers
  D.4/: George Simpson outward correspondence books
  D.5/: George Simpson correspondence inward
Section E: Miscellaneous records
  E.3/: Miscellaneous records, Peter Fidler
  E.4/: Red River settlement, register of baptisms, marriages, and burials
  E.5/: Red River settlement, census returns
  E.8/: Red River settlement, papers relating to the disturbances
  E.24/: John Stuart records
  E.41/: Angus Cameron records
Section F: Records of allied and subsidiary companies
  F.2/: North West Company post journals
  F.4/: North West Company account-books
Section G: Maps, plans, charts
  G.1/: Manuscript maps, plans

PROVINCIAL ARCHIVES OF NEW BRUNSWICK, Fredericton. For information on the manuscript holdings, *A guide to the manuscript collections in the Provincial Archives of New Brunswick*, comp. A. C. Rigby (Fredericton, 1977), is useful, although the classification system used when it was published has since been revised.

Materials used in the preparation of volume VI include:
MC 1: Family history collection
  211: Raymond Paddock Gorham collection
  216: Kathleen Williston collection
  256: Kirk-McColl Church papers
  300: York-Sunbury Historical Society collection
  315: Nashwaak Bicentennial Association collection
  1156: Graves papers
RG 1: Records of the lieutenant-governors and administrators
  RS336: Records of George Stracey Smyth
  RS558: Records of the regular military

RS559: Records of the New Brunswick militia
RG 2: Records of the central executive
  RS6: Minutes and orders-in-council of the Executive Council
  RS7: Executive Council records, Ottawa series
  RS8: Executive Council records, New Brunswick series
RG 4: Records of the New Brunswick General Assembly
  RS24: Legislative Assembly sessional records. The PANB has prepared a calendar for the years 1786 to 1832: "A new calendar of the papers of the House of Assembly of New Brunswick," comp. R. P. Nason *et al*. (3v., typescript, Fredericton, 1975–77).
RG 5: Records of the superior courts
  RS35: Supreme Court records: miscellaneous
RG 7: Records of the probate courts
  RS63: Charlotte County
  RS71: Saint John County
  RS72: Sunbury County
  RS75: York County
RG 10: Records of the Department of Natural Resources
  RS107: Crown Lands and Lands Branch records
  RS108: Land petitions
RG 11: Records of the Department of Education
  RS113: Board of Education records
RG 18: Records of the Department of Municipal Affairs
  RS148: Charlotte County Council records
  RS153: Northumberland County Council records
  RS157: Sunbury County Council records

PROVINCIAL ARCHIVES OF NEWFOUNDLAND AND LABRADOR, St John's. For information on the collections see *Preliminary inventory of the holdings . . . and Supplement . . .* (2 nos., St John's, 1970–74).

The following materials are cited in volume VI:
GN: Government records – Newfoundland
  GN 1: Governor's office
    13: Miscellaneous records
  GN 2: Department of the Colonial Secretary
    1: Letter-books, outgoing correspondence
    2: Incoming correspondence
    39: Census records
  GN 5: Court records
    1: Surrogate Court
    2: Supreme Court
  P: Private records
    P1: Governors' private papers
      5: Duckworth papers
    P3: Pre-1855 papers
      B: Mercantile
        22: MacBraire papers

P5: Miscellaneous groups
  25: Peyton papers
P7: Businesses
  A: Fishing related
    6: Slade & Sons, Fogo, ledgers
    18: Ryan & Morris collection, Burin
    48: George Welch Ledgard collection, Carbonear
    53: Munn & Co. Ltd., Harbour Grace, records

PUBLIC ARCHIVES OF CANADA, Ottawa. The PAC has published guides to its holdings in the various divisions, including *General guide series 1983, Federal Archives Division*, comp. Terry Cook and Glenn T. Wright (1983), and *General guide series 1983, Manuscript Division*, comp. [E.] Grace [Maurice] Hyam and Jean-Marie LeBlanc (1984).

The following inventories to materials in the Manuscript and the Federal Archives divisions which were used in the preparation of volume VI have been published:

General inventory, manuscripts, volume 1, MG 1–MG 10 (1971)
General inventory, manuscripts, volume 2, MG 11–MG 16 (1976)
General inventory, manuscripts, volume 3, MG 17–MG 21 (1974)
General inventory, manuscripts, volume 4, MG 22–MG 25 (1972)
General inventory, manuscripts, volume 7, MG 29 (1975)
General inventory, manuscripts, volume 8, MG 30 (1977)
General inventory series, no.1: records relating to Indian affairs (RG 10), comp. Peter Gillis *et al.* (1975)
General inventory series, no.6: records of Statistics Canada (RG 31), comp. Sandra G. Wright and Thomas A. Hillman (1977)
General inventory series: records of the Department of Railways and Canals (RG 43), comp. Glenn T. Wright (1986)

An older series of inventories has been essentially superseded by unpublished inventories available at the PAC, but the following are still of some limited use:

Record group 1, Executive Council, Canada, 1764–1867 (1953)
Record group 4, Civil and Provincial secretaries' offices, Canada East, 1760–1867; Record group 5, Civil and Provincial secretaries' offices, Canada West, 1788–1867 (1953)
Record group 7, Governor General's Office (1953)
Record group 8, British military and naval records (1954)
Record group 9, Department of Militia and Defence, 1776–1922 ([1957])

Also useful are *Census returns, 1666–1881, Public Archives of Canada* (1982) and *Checklist of parish registers* (3rd ed., 1981). The holdings of the National Map Collection are listed in *Catalogue of the National Map Collection, Public Archives of Canada, Ottawa, Ontario* (16v., Boston, 1976).

The PAC publishes the *Union list of MSS* [*see* section III], which lists holdings of the Federal Archives and Manuscript divisions. It has also issued a *Guide to Canadian photographic archives*, ed. Christopher Seifried (1984).

Material from the following collections is cited in volume VI:

MG 8: Documents relatifs à la Nouvelle-France et au Québec (XVIIᵉ–XXᵉ siècles)
  F: Documents relatifs aux seigneuries et autres lieux
    131: Les Éboulements
  G: Archives paroissiales
    8: Détroit (église catholique)
MG 9: Provincial, local, and territorial records
  B: Nova Scotia
    9: Local records
      14: Shelburne
  D: Ontario
    4: Department of Lands and Forests
MG 11: Public Record Office, London, Colonial Office papers
  [CO 42]. Q series. The Q transcripts were prepared by the PAC before the PRO reorganization of 1908–10 and include most of what is now in CO 42 up to the year 1841, plus material now found in CO 43, as well as items from other series. Documents for the period covered by volume VI are calendared in PAC *Report*, 1890–93, 1896, 1898, 1900.
  [CO 217]. Nova Scotia A; Cape Breton A. For the period up to 1801 these series are composites of transcripts from various sources in Great Britain, especially the PRO. By the time the work of transcription reached 1802 the PRO had established the CO 217 series; from 1802 the transcripts are from CO 217 only. Documents of Nova Scotia A for the period covered by volume VI have been calendared in PAC *Report*, 1894, 1946–47, and those of Cape Breton A in *Report*, 1895.
  [CO 220]. Cape Breton B (minutes of the Executive Council, 1785–1807). A composite series taken principally from sources now part of PRO, CO 220.
  [CO 229]. Prince Edward Island B. This is a composite and artificial series of transcripts derived primarily from material

now in PRO, CO 229; it includes
Executive Council minutes for 1770–98
and 1805–6.

MG 17: Ecclesiastical archives
  B: Church of England (Anglican)
    1: Society for the Propagation of the
      Gospel in Foreign Parts

MG 19: Fur trade and Indians
  A: Fur trade, general
    2: Ermatinger estate
    4: Henry, Alexander (the elder)
    7: Mackenzie, Sir Alexander
    12: La Mothe, famille
    31: Mackintosh, Angus
  B: Fur trade, companies and associations
    2: American Fur Company
  C: Fur trade, collections
    1: Masson collection
  E: Red River settlement
    1: Selkirk, Thomas Douglas, 5th Earl of
    2: Red River settlement
    4: Macdonell, Miles
    5: Bulger, Andrew
    11: McDonell, Alexander
  F: Indians
    1: Claus family
    2: Johnson family
    6: Brant, Joseph, and family
    10: Walsh, Edward
    16: McKee, Alexander
    29: McKay, William

MG 22: Autographs
  A: Canadian autographs
    9: Sandham, Alfred, collection

MG 23: Late eighteenth-century papers
  A: British statesmen
    1: Dartmouth, William Legge, 2nd
      Earl of
    6: Germain, George Sackville, 1st
      Viscount Sackville
  C: Nova Scotia
    6: Inglis family
  D: New Brunswick
    1: Chipman, Ward, Sr and Jr
    4: Botsford, Amos
  E: Prince Edward Island
    5: Fanning, Edmund
  F: Cape Breton
    1: DesBarres, Joseph Frederick Wallet
  GII: Quebec and Lower Canada: political figures
    3: Gray, Edward William
    10: Sewell, Jonathan, and family
    14: Smith, William
    17: Prescott, Robert
    18: Hale, John, and family
    27: Holland, Samuel

GIII: Quebec and Lower Canada: merchants and
  settlers
    1: Allsopp, George, and family
    6: St-Ours, famille de
    7: Porteous, John
    8: Birnie, Samuel
    12: Savage, John
    13: Cull, Henry
    15: Janvrin, Francis and Philip
    24: Robin, Charles
    26: Ainsse, Louis-Joseph
    30: Richardson, Richardson and
      Company

GIV: Quebec and Lower Canada: religious and
  fraternal
    7: Desjardins, Philippe-Jean-Louis

HI: Upper Canada: political figures
    1: Simcoe, John Graves
    3: Jarvis, William, and family
    4: Powell, William Dummer, and
      family
    5: White, John

HII: Upper Canada: merchants and settlers
    1: McDonald–Stone family
    6: Berczy, William von Moll
    7: Farmar, Hugh Hovell

J: Exploration and travel
    10: Mann, Gother

K: Military documents
    7: Individual service, records of
    10: Saumarez, Durell
    16: Clarke, Thomas

MG 24: Nineteenth-century pre-confederation papers
  A: British officials and political figures
    3: Douglas, Sir Howard, and family
    5: Swayne, Hugh
    6: Hunter, Peter
    12: Dalhousie, George Ramsay, 9th
      Earl of
    19: Roebuck, John Arthur
    57: Sherbrooke, Sir John Coape
    64: Burton, Sir Francis Nathaniel
  B: North American political figures and events
    1: Neilson collection
    2: Papineau, famille
    3: Ryland, Herman Witsius, and family
    4: Young, John
    6: Viger, Denis-Benjamin
    7: Jones, Charles
    10: Dunn, Thomas
    16: Cochran, Andrew Wilson
    18: Mackenzie, William Lyon
    25: Bellingham, Sydney Robert
    34: Nelson, Wolfred
    69: Markle, Abraham
    75: Buell, William

130: Clark(e) family
133: Wright, Charles
169: Sewell, Stephen
C: Correspondents of political figures
    1: Willcocks, Joseph
    43: Dawkins, Ann (née Douglas)
D: Industry, commerce, and finance
    1: Woolsey, John William, and family
    8: Wright, Philemon, and family
    9: Carteret, Priaulx and Company
    43: Auldjo, John
    93: *William Annesly* (steam vessel),
       Montreal
F: Military and naval figures
    1: Bowyer, Henry J.
    78: Rottenburg, Francis, Baron de
    86: O'Hara, Edward
G: Militia
    5: Vassal de Monviel, François
    8: War of 1812 medals
    9: Juchereau Duchesnay, Jean-Baptiste
    45: Salaberry, famille de
I: Immigration, land, and settlement
    8: Macdonell of Collachie family
    9: Hill collection
    11: Pennoyer, Jesse
    25: Gilkison, William, and family
    26: Hamilton, Alexander
    38: Perrault, Charles-N.
    61: Joseph, Abraham
    97: Tonnancour, Joseph-Marie-Godefroy
       de
    137: Street family, Upper Canada
    183: McMillan, Archibald, and family
J: Religious figures
    4: Plessis, Joseph-Octave
K: Education and cultural development
    2: Coventry, George
    5: McKenny, Amos
    61: Montreal Assembly
L: Miscellaneous
    3: Baby collection
    5: Bertrand, Camille
    6: Delancy–Robinson collection
MG 25: Genealogy
    G62: Kipling, Clarence
    G235: Birch family
MG 26: Papers of the prime ministers
A: Macdonald, Sir John Alexander
MG 28: Records of post-confederation corporate
    bodies
II: Financial institutions
    2: Bank of Montreal
III: Business establishments
    18: Robin, Jones and Whitman Limited
    44: Montreal Board of Trade

MG 29: Nineteenth-century post-confederation
    manuscripts
A: Economic
    24: Drummond, Andrew
C: Social
    89: LaRoque, famille
MG 30: Manuscripts of the first half of the twentieth
    century
D: Cultural
    1: Audet, Francis-Joseph
    11: Johnson, George
MG 40: Records and manuscripts from British
    repositories
L: General Post Office
MG 53: Lawrence M. Lande Collection
    191: Monk, Ethel
    215: Ryland, Herman Witsius
    246: Bédard, Joseph-Isidore
    B37: Kuhn, Jacobs
MG 55: Miscellaneous documents
RG 1: Executive Council: Quebec, Lower Canada,
    Upper Canada, Canada, 1764–1867
E: State records
    1: Quebec, Lower Canada, Upper
       Canada, Canada: Executive Council,
       minute-books (state matters)
    2: Quebec, Lower Canada, Upper
       Canada, Canada: Executive Com-
       mittee, draft minutes and reports
    3: Upper Canada: Executive Council,
       submissions on state matters
    14: Quebec, Lower Canada, Upper
       Canada, Canada: clerk of the
       Executive Council Office, records of
       the clerk
    15: Board of Audit of the provincial
       public accounts
       A: Quebec and Lower Canada
L: Land records
    1: Quebec, Lower Canada, Upper
       Canada, Canada: Executive Council,
       minute-books (on land matters)
    3: Upper Canada and Canada: Land
       Committee, petitions for land grants
       and leases
    3L: Quebec and Lower Canada: Land
       Committee, land petitions and related
       records
    4: Upper Canada: land boards, minutes
       and records
    7: Quebec, Lower Canada, Upper
       Canada, Canada: miscellaneous
       records
RG 4: Provincial and Civil secretaries' offices:
    Quebec, Lower Canada, and Canada East
    A1: Quebec and Lower Canada: S series

(correspondence received)

A2: Lower Canada: civil secretary, draft correspondence

A3: Quebec, Lower Canada, Canada: civil secretary, registers and entry-books

B8: Quebec and Lower Canada: applications for commissions to act as notaries and advocates

B17: Quebec and Lower Canada: lawsuits

B21: Lower Canada and Canada East: prison returns

B28: Quebec, Lower Canada, Canada East: applications for licences, bonds, and certificates

B33: Quebec, Lower Canada, Upper Canada, Canada: civil service records

B43: Quebec: Executive Council, committee of inquiry into accounts of Dr James Bowman and the St Paul's Bay disease

B46: Miscellaneous records relating to Lord Selkirk's colony and the Red River disturbances

B47: Canada Company miscellaneous records

B49: Gaspé: Returns, land surrenders, and petitions relating to Gaspé

RG 5: Provincial and Civil secretaries' offices: Upper Canada, Canada West

A1: Upper Canada sundries

B1: Upper Canada: district treasurers, accounts and returns

B6: Upper Canada: statistical returns

B9: Upper Canada and Canada West: bonds, licences, and certificates

B27: Upper Canada and Canada West: prison returns

D: Gazettes

1: *Upper Canada Gazette*

RG 7: Governor General's Office

G1: Dispatches from the Colonial Office

G15A: Quebec and Lower Canada: governor's internal letter-books

G15C: Quebec and Lower Canada: civil secretary's letter-books

G16C: Upper Canada: civil secretary's letter-books

RG 8: British military and naval records

I: C series (British military records)

II: Ordnance records

RG 9: Department of Militia and Defence

I: Pre-confederation records

A: Adjutant General's Office, Lower Canada

1: Correspondence

5: Registers of officers

6: Officers' commissions

B: Adjutant General's Office, Upper Canada

1: Correspondence

4: Pensions and land grants

7: Nominal rolls and paylists

II: Post-confederation records

A: Deputy Minister's Office

4: Pensions, gratuities, and compensation

5: Medals

RG 10: Indian affairs

A: Administrative records of the imperial government

1: Records of the governor general and lieutenant governors

1–7: Upper Canada, civil control

486–87: Lower Canada, civil control

789–92: General administration records

2: Records of the Superintendent's Office

8–21: Superintendent General's Office

26–46: Deputy Superintendent General's Office, correspondence

3: Records of the military

488–97: Military Secretary's Office, Montreal

4: Records of the Chief Superintendent's Office, Upper Canada

47–77: Correspondence

6: General office files

474–85: Accounts

B: Ministerial administration records

3: Central registry system

1855–3554: Red (Eastern) series

4376–5836: Departmental letter-books

D: Indian land records

3: Six Nations (Grand River) Superintendency

103–13: Grand River claims

10017–31: Blue books

RG 16: Department of National Revenue

A: Customs, excise, and inland revenue

1: Correspondence and returns

2: Port records

RG 19: Department of Finance

E: Departmental correspondence

5(a): Board of claims for War of 1812 losses

RG 31: Statistics Canada

C: Census field

1: Census returns

RG 42: Marine Branch

E: Ship registration

1: Shipping registers

RG 43: Department of Railways and Canals
    C: Canal records
        III: Lachine Canal
           1: Lachine Navigation Company,
             minutes and correspondence
           2: Lachine Canal Commission
RG 68: Registrar general

PUBLIC ARCHIVES OF NOVA SCOTIA, Halifax. For a description of the collections see *Inventory of manuscripts in the Public Archives of Nova Scotia* (Halifax, 1976).

Materials used in the preparation of volume VI include:

MG   1: Papers of families and individuals
       106: Baker family documents
       164C: Chamberlain and Chipman families, genealogical notes
       181–218: Chipman family documents
       219: John Clarkson documents
       223: William Cochran documents
       249–50A: Cunningham family documents
       258: Isaac Deschamps documents
       262B: Dodd family documents
       263A: Archibald C. Dodd, commission as justice of the peace, 1810
       332B: Hugh Graham, letters
       469C: Hill family documents
       472–74A: Edward How documents
       479–80: Charles Inglis documents
       544: T. H. Lodge collection
       574B: William Minns documents
       731A–B: O'Brien family documents
       742–44: George Patterson documents
       747: W. L. Payzant documents
       793: Simon B. Robie documents
       794–95: Ross family documents
       797B: Sargent family documents
       817–63: Thomas B. Smith, genealogy
       926–27: Uniacke family documents
       939–41: Sir John Wentworth documents
       947–62: White family documents
       979–80: Peleg Wiswall documents
       1184B: Theophilus Chamberlain documents
       1185–89A: Payzant family papers
       1206: Charles Morris II and III, correspondence
       1595–613: Bliss family papers
       1619A: Theophilus Chamberlain letters
       1769: Crofton James Uniacke papers
       1845: Fergusson papers
MG   2: Political papers
       562–665: Edgar Nelson Rhodes papers
       726–30: John Young papers
MG   3: Business papers

       150–51: William Forsyth (Halifax), sales- and letter-book
       154: Halifax Fire Insurance Company documents
       164–65: Charles Hill and nephew, Halifax, documents
MG   4: Churches and communities
       23: Trinity Anglican Church (Digby), records
       46–47A, 55, 68: St Matthew's Church (Halifax), records
       77–80: Liverpool Township documents
       94–105: Lunenburg County genealogies, comp. E. A. Harris
       109: Guysborough and Manchester Township, township book
       140: Shelburne County assessments
       141: Various Shelburne County documents
       166: Yarmouth County genealogies, comp. G. S. Brown
MG   5: Cemeteries
MG   9: Scrap-books
MG 20: Societies and special collections
       61–70: Charitable Irish Society, Halifax
       211–25: Nova Scotia Historical Society
       675: Nova Scotia Historical Society MSS
MG 100: Documents, newspaper clippings, and miscellaneous items
RG   1: Bound volumes of Nova Scotia records for the period 1624–1867
       29–185: Documents relating to the government of Nova Scotia: dispatches, letter-books, and commission books
       186–214½H: Council, minutes
       215–18DDD: Legislative Council, journals
       219–85: Miscellaneous documents
       286–300: Legislative Council, selections from the files
       301–14: Legislative Assembly, selections from the files
       318–25: Minutes of the Executive Council of Cape Breton
       364: Transcripts from the Massachusetts public records concerning American invasion of Nova Scotia, 1775–77
       368–69: Transcripts from the Dorchester papers concerning loyalists
       394–96B: Letter-books of Surveyor General Charles Morris II
       410–17: Papers of the settlement of Halifax
       419–22: Papers of negro and maroon immigrations and settlements
       443–54: Census and poll tax
       458–65½: Mines and minerals
       499–501: Letters of agency of the Vice-Admiralty Court of Nova Scotia

525: Annotated copy of Beamish, *Hist. of N.S.* [*see* section IV]

RG   4: Records of the Legislative Council of Nova Scotia
        LC: Petitions, reports, resolutions, and miscellaneous papers

RG   5: Records of the Legislative Assembly of Nova Scotia
        A: Assembly papers
        O: Orders of the day
        P: Petitions

RG   20: Lands and Forests
        A: Land grants and petitions
        B: Cape Breton land papers
        C: Crown lands

RG   22: Nova Scotia, military records

RG   24: Post Office records of Nova Scotia

RG   31: Treasury
        102–20: Impost, excise, and revenue

RG   32: Vital statistics
        132–69: Marriage bonds

RG   34: Court of General Sessions of the Peace
        309: Cumberland County
        311: Guysborough County
        312: Halifax County

RG 35A: Halifax city and county assessments
        1–4: Halifax city assessments

RG   36: Court of Chancery

RG   39: Supreme Court
        C: Civil and criminal cases
        J: Judgement books

RG   46: Commissions, oaths, and bonds

PUBLIC ARCHIVES OF PRINCE EDWARD ISLAND, Charlottetown.

Materials used in the preparation of volume VI include:

Acc. 2277: Benjamin Chappell, diary
      2320: George Leard files
      2367: Joseph Alexander McMillan papers
      2534: Miscellaneous documents
      2575: Miscellaneous documents
      2702: Smith–Alley collection
      2810: Ira Brown papers
      2849: Palmer family papers
      2984: John Cambridge, letter-book, 1793–1801
      3209: East River Baptist Church records
      3355: Robert Gray, military commissions

RG   1: Lieutenant Governor
RG   3: House of Assembly
RG   5: Executive Council
RG   6: Courts
RG   8: Warrant books
RG   9: Customs records
RG 16: Registry Office, land registry records

QUÉBEC, MINISTÈRE DE LA JUSTICE. The Archives civiles and the Archives judiciaires du Québec, which are under the joint jurisdiction of the courts and the Ministère de la Justice, are now separate repositories as a result of the reclassification of the former Archives judiciaires. They are deposited at the court-houses in the administrative centres of the 34 judicial districts of Quebec.

ARCHIVES CIVILES. These archives retain documents for the last 100 years, including registers of births, marriages, and deaths, notaries' *minutiers* (minute-books), and records of surveyors active in the district. Earlier documents are held by the ANQ.

BUREAUX D'ENREGISTREMENT. The registry offices hold all property titles and contracts affecting real estate: sales, marriages, wills and estates, mortgages, conveyances, assignments, gifts, guardian- and trusteeships. At present there are 82 registry offices in Quebec.

A list of the judicial districts and registry offices can be found in *The Quebec legal directory*, ed. Andrée Frenette-Lecoq (Montreal, 1980).

QUÉBEC, MINISTÈRE DES AFFAIRES CULTURELLES, CENTRE DE DOCUMENTATION, Québec. The Ministère des Affaires culturelles has consolidated into one documentation centre the collections of all its previously existing centres, including that of the Inventaire des biens culturels.

Series cited in volume VI:
Fonds Ministère des Affaires culturelles
Fonds Morisset
    2: Dossiers des artistes et artisans
    6: Dossiers des églises

QUEEN'S UNIVERSITY ARCHIVES, Kingston, Ont. For information on the collection see *A guide to the holdings of Queen's University Archives*, ed. Anne MacDermaid and G. F. Henderson (2nd ed., Kingston, 1986).

Various materials were used in the preparation of volume VI, in particular the following:
Richard Cartwright papers, letter-books

UNITED CHURCH OF CANADA. The present-day archives of the United Church of Canada are descended from 19th- and 20th-century archival collections of various Canadian Methodist, Presbyterian, Congregational, and Evangelical/United Brethren in Christ bodies. The Central Archives at Victoria University, Toronto, is national in scope. Material of local interest, including the official records of the conferences concerned, is housed in regional conference archives.

MARITIME CONFERENCE ARCHIVES, Halifax.
Various materials were used in the preparation of volume VI, in particular the following:
James MacGregor papers

UNIVERSITY OF NEW BRUNSWICK LIBRARY, Archives and Special Collections Department, Fredericton.
Materials used in volume VI include:
MG H: Historical
    H 2: Winslow family papers
    H 8: Edward Augustus, Duke of Kent and Strathern, papers
    H 9: Lilian Mary Beckwith Maxwell papers
    H 11: Saunders papers
    H 54: Indian Affairs – New Brunswick
  UA: University archives
    "Minute-book of the governors and trustees of the College of New Brunswick," 1800–28

UNIVERSITY OF WESTERN ONTARIO LIBRARY, Regional Collection, London, Ont. A description of the municipal record and personal manuscript collections is available on microfiche in *Regional Collection: the D. B. Weldon Library catalogue*, ed. S. L. Sykes (4 fiches, London, 1977).
Various municipal record and personal manuscript collections proved useful in the preparation of volume VI, in particular the following:
London District, Surrogate Court, estate files, 1800–39

FRANCE

ARCHIVES DÉPARTEMENTALES. For a list of analytical inventories, *see* France, Direction des archives, *État des inventaires des archives nationales, départementales, communales et hospitalières au 1er janvier 1937* (Paris, 1938); *Supplément, 1937–1954*, [by R.-H. Bautier] (Paris, 1955); and *Catalogue des inventaires, répertoires, guides de recherche et autres instruments de travail des archives départementales, communales et hospitalières . . . à la date du 31 décembre 1961* (Paris, 1962). For copies of documents held by the PAC, see *General inventory, manuscripts, 1*: 87–99. There is a uniform system of classification for all departmental archives. A list of the various series may be found in *DCB*, 2: 683–84.

GREAT BRITAIN

BRITISH LIBRARY, London. For a brief guide to catalogues and indexes of the manuscript collections, *see* M. A. E. Nickson, *The British Library: guide to the catalogues and indexes of the Department of Manuscripts* (2nd ed., London, 1982). The *Index of manuscripts in the British Library* (10v., Cambridge, Eng., 1984–86) provides person and place entries for all collections acquired up to 1950. For copies of documents from the British Library in the PAC see *General inventory, manuscripts, 3*.
Used in the preparation of volume VI were the following Additional manuscripts and Loans collections:
Add. MSS 7972–8090: Puisaye (Joseph de), Count, correspondence and papers relating to the affairs of the French royalists
Add. MSS 19069–70: Letters and papers of Jean-Paul Mascarene, commander-in-chief of Nova Scotia
Add. MSS 19071–73, 19075–76: Papers relating to Nova Scotia collected by Dr Andrew Brown
Add. MSS 21661–892: Official correspondence and papers of Lieutenant Governor Sir Frederick Haldimand
Add. MSS 35349–6278: Hardwicke papers
Add. MSS 38190–489: Liverpool papers
Add. MSS 38734–70: Huskisson papers
Loan 57: Bathurst papers

NATIONAL LIBRARY OF SCOTLAND, Department of Manuscripts, Edinburgh. Information on the manuscript collections is available in *Catalogue of manuscripts acquired since 1925* (5v. to date [1–4, 6], Edinburgh, 1938–).
Materials used in the preparation of volume VI include:
Manuscripts
    3847–51: Melville papers
    15001–195: Ellice papers
    13735, 13776–81: Walker of Bowland papers

NATIONAL MARITIME MUSEUM, London. For information on the manuscript collections see *Guide to the manuscripts in the National Maritime Museum*, ed. R. J. B. Knight (2v., London, 1977–80).
The following materials have been used in the preparation of volume VI:
Artificial collections
  PNS: Phillips Naval Collection
  RUSI: Royal United Services Institution
Personal collections
  HUL: Hulbert papers
  MID: Middleton papers
  WYN: Pole papers
Public records
  HAL: Halifax Dockyard records
Volumes acquired singly
  LBK: Letter-books

PUBLIC RECORD OFFICE, London. For an introduction to the holdings and arrangement of this archives see

Guide to the contents of the Public Record Office (3v., London, 1963–68). For copies of PRO documents available at the PAC see *General inventory, manuscripts, 2*.

The following series were used in the preparation of volume VI:

Admiralty
  Accounting departments. [*See* N. A. M. Rodger, *Naval records for genealogists* (London, 1984).]
    ADM 36: Ships' musters, ser.I
    ADM 37: Ships' musters, ser.II
  Admiralty and Secretariat
    ADM 1: Papers
    ADM 2: Out-letters
    ADM 6: Various
    ADM 7: Miscellanea
    ADM 9: Returns of officers' services
    ADM 11: Indexes and compilations, ser.II
    ADM 12: Indexes and compilations, ser.III
    ADM 50: Admirals' journals
  Greenwich Hospital
    ADM 80: Miscellanea, various
  Navy Board
    ADM 106: Navy Board records
    ADM 107: Passing certificates
Board of Customs and Excise
    CUST 65: Outport records, Dartmouth, England
Board of Inland Revenue
    IR 17: Index to apprenticeship records
Board of Trade
  General
    BT 1: In-letters and files, general
    BT 6: Miscellanea
  Registrar general of shipping and seamen
    BT 107: Ships' registers
Colonial Office. [*See* R. B. Pugh, *The records of the Colonial and Dominions offices* (London, 1964).]
  Barbados
    CO 33: Miscellaneous
  Canada
    CO 42: Original correspondence
    CO 43: Entry books
  Guiana, British
    CO 111: Original correspondence
    CO 112: Entry books
  Jamaica
    CO 137: Original correspondence
  New Brunswick
    CO 188: Original correspondence
    CO 189: Entry books
  Newfoundland
    CO 194: Original correspondence
    CO 195: Entry books
    CO 199: Miscellaneous
  Nova Scotia and Cape Breton
    CO 217: Original correspondence
    CO 218: Entry books
    CO 220: Sessional papers
  Prince Edward Island
    CO 226: Original correspondence
    CO 227: Entry books
    CO 228: Acts
    CO 229: Sessional papers
  Trinidad
    CO 295: Original correspondence
  Colonies, General
    CO 323: Original correspondence
    CO 324: Entry books, series I
  Board of Trade (Commercial)
    CO 388: Original correspondence
Exchequer and Audit Department
    AO 1: Declared accounts (in rolls)
    AO 2: Declared and passed accounts (in books)
    AO 12: Claims, American loyalists, series I
    AO 13: Claims, American loyalists, series II
Exchequer, King's Remembrancer
    E 190: Port books
Home Office
  Various
    HO 76: Naval officers' returns
Prerogative Court of Canterbury (formerly held at Somerset House)
    PROB 11: Registered copy wills
Privy Council Office
    PC 1: Papers, mainly unbound
Public Record Office
  Documents acquired by gift, deposit, or purchase
    PRO 30/11: Cornwallis papers
    PRO 30/55: Carleton papers
Treasury
  In-letters and files
    T 1: Treasury Board papers
  Out-letters
    T 28: Various
War Office
  Correspondence
    WO 7: Out-letters, departmental
  Returns
    WO 12: General
    WO 13: Muster-books and pay lists: militia and volunteers
    WO 17: Monthly returns
    WO 27: Inspection returns
    WO 42: Certificates of birth, etc.
    WO 76: Officers' services, records of
  Miscellanea
    WO 28: Headquarters papers
  Ordnance office
    WO 44: In-letters
    WO 55: Miscellanea

Judge Advocate General's office
>WO 71: Courts martial, proceedings
>WO 91: General courts martial: confirmed
>>at home

SCOTTISH RECORD OFFICE, Edinburgh. A comprehensive listing of materials relating to Canada is provided by the SRO's "List of Canadian documents" (typescript, 1977, with updates to 1983), available at major Canadian archives. An appendix records Canadian documents in private archives as surveyed by the National Reg. of Arch. (Scotland).
The following are cited in volume VI:
GD: Gifts and deposits
>GD1: Miscellaneous gifts and deposits
>>151: James Dunlop, letter-book
>GD45: Dalhousie muniments
>GD293: Montgomery estate papers in the muniments of Messrs. Blackwood and Smith, W.S., Peebles, estate papers
RS: Registers of sasines
>RS54: Particular register of sasines for Renfrew, 1660–1868

UNITED SOCIETY FOR THE PROPAGATION OF THE GOSPEL, London. In 1985 the society's archives were closed and its holdings were being transferred to Rhodes House Library at the University of Oxford. For information about materials relating to Canada, *see* William Westfall and Ian Pearson, "The archives of the United Society for the Propagation of the Gospel and Canadian history," Canadian Church Hist. Soc., *Journal* (Toronto), 25 (1983): 16–24. For copies of USPG documents available at the PAC, see *General inventory, manuscripts, 3.*
Some materials, particularly in the C/CAN series, were reorganized and reclassified by the USPG after having been microfilmed; thus classifications used by the PAC and other Canadian archives holding microfilm copies of USPG records do not always correspond to those of the archives itself. Individual references to microfilm copies in the reclassified groupings are cited under PAC, MG 17, B1.
The following collections were consulted:
C/CAN: Unbound letters from Canada, 1752–1860. Letters from the New Brunswick, Newfoundland, Nova Scotia, and Quebec groupings were used.
Dr Bray's Associates, unbound papers
Journal of proceedings of the Society for the Propagation of the Gospel. Comprises bound and indexed volumes of the proceedings of the general meetings held in London from 1701, and four appendices, A, B, C, D (1701–1860).
X: Miscellaneous volumes and papers, 18th–20th centuries

UNITED STATES

DETROIT PUBLIC LIBRARY, Burton Historical Collection.
Various materials were used in the preparation of volume VI, in particular the following:
John Askin papers

WILLIAM L. CLEMENTS LIBRARY, University of Michigan, Ann Arbor. Descriptions of the library's holdings appear in the *Guide to the manuscript collections in the William L. Clements Library*, comp. A. P. Shy assisted by B. A. Mitchell (3rd ed., Boston, 1978).
Materials cited in volume VI include:
Thomas Gage papers, American series

II. PRINTED PRIMARY SOURCES

A. OFFICIAL PUBLICATIONS AND CONTEMPORARY WORKS

American archives: consisting of a collection of authentick records, state papers, debates, and letters and other notices of publick affairs, the whole forming a documentary history of the origin and progress of the North American colonies. . . . Compiled by Matthew St Clair Clarke and Peter Force. 2 ser. in 9 vols. Washington, 1837–53; reprinted [New York, 1972]. Six series covering the years up to 1787 were projected but only the 4th and part of the 5th series appeared, covering the years 1774–76.

ARCHIVES NATIONALES DU QUÉBEC, Québec
>PUBLICATIONS [*see also* section III]
>*Rapport.* 54 vols. 1920/21–1976/77. There is an index to the contents of the first 42 volumes: *Table des matières des rapports des Archives du Québec, tomes 1 à 42 (1920–1964)* ([Québec], 1965).
ARCHIVES OF ONTARIO, Toronto
>PUBLICATIONS
>*Report.* 22 vols. 1903–33.
>"Board of land office for the District of Hesse, 1789–1794; minutes of meetings, etc." AO *Report*, 1905: 1–268.
>*Les bourgeois de la Compagnie du Nord-Ouest: récits*

de voyages, lettres et rapports inédits relatifs au Nord-Ouest canadien. Louis-[François-]Rodrigue Masson, éditeur. 2 vols. Québec, 1889–90; réimprimé New York, 1960.

CAMPBELL, PATRICK. *Travels in the interior inhabited parts of North America in the years 1791 and 1792.* . . . Edinburgh, 1793. [New edition.] Edited by Hugh Hornby Langton and William Francis Ganong. (Champlain Society publications, 23.) Toronto, 1937.

CANADA, PROVINCE OF
LEGISLATIVE ASSEMBLY/ASSEMBLÉE LÉGISLATIVE
   Appendix to the . . . journals of the Legislative Assembly of the Province of Canada/ Appendice . . . des journaux de la province du Canada, 1841–59. See also *The Legislative Assembly of the Province of Canada: an index to journal appendices and sessional papers, 1841–1866,* comp. P. A. Damphouse (London, Ont., 1974).

CHAMPLAIN SOCIETY, Toronto
   PUBLICATIONS
   54 vols. to date, exclusive of the Hudson's Bay Company series [see *HBRS*], the Ontario series, and the unnumbered series. Issued only to elected members of the society who are limited in numbers.
   13–15, 17: *Select British docs. of War of 1812* (Wood).
   22: *Docs. relating to NWC* (Wallace).
   23: P. Campbell, *Travels in North America* (Langton and Ganong).
   29: Perkins, *Diary, 1766–80* (Innis).
   35: Douglas, *Lord Selkirk's diary* (White).
   36: Perkins, *Diary, 1780–89* (Harvey and Fergusson).
   39: Perkins, *Diary, 1790–96* (Fergusson).
   43: Perkins, *Diary, 1797–1803* (Fergusson).
   46: Norton, *Journal* (Klinck and Talman).
   50: Perkins, *Diary, 1804–12* (Fergusson).
   ONTARIO SERIES
   12 vols. to date. Available for sale to the general public.
   3: *Kingston before War of 1812* (Preston).
   4: *Windsor border region* (Lajeunesse).
   5: *Town of York, 1793–1815* (Firth).
   7: *Valley of Six Nations* (Johnston).
   8: *Town of York, 1815–34* (Firth).

The correspondence of Lieut. Governor John Graves Simcoe, with allied documents relating to his administration of the government of Upper Canada. Edited by Ernest Alexander Cruikshank. (Ontario Historical Society publication.) 5 vols. Toronto, 1923–31.

The correspondence of the Honourable Peter Russell, with allied documents relating to his administration of the government of Upper Canada during the official term of Lieut.-Governor J. G. Simcoe, while on leave of absence. Edited by Ernest Alexander Cruikshank and Andrew Frederick Hunter. (Ontario Historical Society publication.) 3 vols. Toronto, 1932–36.

"Les dénombrements de Québec faits en 1792, 1795, 1798 et 1805." Joseph-Octave Plessis, compilateur. ANQ *Rapport,* 1948–49: 1–250.

The documentary history of the campaign upon the Niagara frontier. . . . Edited by Ernest [Alexander] Cruikshank. (Lundy's Lane Historical Society publication.) 9 vols. Welland, Ont., [1896]–1908.

Documents relating to the constitutional history of Canada. . . . Edited by Adam Shortt *et al.* (PAC publication.) 3 vols. Ottawa, 1907–35.
   [1]: *1759–1791.* Edited by Adam Shortt and Arthur George Doughty. 2nd edition. (PAC, Board of Historical Publications.) 2 parts. 1918.
   [2]: *1791–1818.* Edited by Arthur George Doughty and Duncan A. McArthur.
   [3]: *1819–1828.* Edited by Arthur George Doughty and Norah Story.

Documents relating to the North West Company. Edited by William Stewart Wallace. (Champlain Society publications, 22.) Toronto, 1934.

[DOUGLAS, THOMAS, 5TH EARL OF] SELKIRK. *Lord Selkirk's diary, 1803–1804; a journal of his travels in British North America and the northeastern United States.* Edited by Patrick Cecil Telfer White (Champlain Society publications, 35.) Toronto, 1958; reprinted New York, 1969.

Gentleman's Magazine. London, 1731–1907. Monthly.

"Grants of crown lands in Upper Canada, [1787–1796]." AO *Report,* 1928: 7–228; 1929: 1–177.

GUBBINS, JOSEPH. *Lieutenant Colonel Joseph Gubbins, inspecting field officer of militia: New Brunswick journals of 1811 & 1813.* Edited with an introduction and notes by Howard Temperley. (New Brunswick heritage publications, 1.) Fredericton, 1980.

[GWILLIM, ELIZABETH POSTHUMA] SIMCOE, MRS JOHN GRAVES. *The diary of Mrs. John Graves Simcoe, wife of the first lieutenant-governor of the province of Upper Canada, 1792–6.* Edited by John Ross Robertson. Toronto, 1911; reprinted [1973]. [Revised edition.] 1934.

HUDSON'S BAY RECORD SOCIETY, Winnipeg
   PUBLICATIONS
   33 vols. General editor for vols.1–22, Edwin Ernest Rich; vols.23–25, Kenneth Gordon Davies; vols.26–30, Glyndwr Williams; vols. 31–33, Hartwell Bowsfield. Vols.1–12 were issued in association with the Champlain Society [*q.v.*] and reprinted in 1968 in Nendeln, Liechtenstein; vol.13 was reprinted in Nendeln in 1979.

1: Simpson, George. *Journal of occurrences in the Athabasca Department by George Simpson, 1820 and 1821, and report.* Edited by Edwin Ernest Rich, with an introduction by Chester [Bailey] Martin. Toronto, 1938.

2: Robertson, Colin. *Colin Robertson's correspondence book, September 1817 to September 1822.* Edited with an introduction by Edwin Ernest Rich, assisted by Robert Harvey Fleming. Toronto, 1939.

3: *Minutes of Council, Northern Department of Rupert Land, 1821–31.* Edited by Robert Harvey Fleming, with an introduction by Harold Adams Innis. Toronto, 1940.

4: McLoughlin, John. *The letters of John McLoughlin from Fort Vancouver to the governor and committee, first series, 1825–38.* Edited by Edwin Ernest Rich, with an introduction by William Kaye Lamb. London, 1941.

13: Ogden, Peter Skene. *Peter Skene Ogden's Snake country journals, 1824–25 and 1825–26.* Edited by Edwin Ernest Rich, assisted by Alice Margaret Johnson, with an introduction by Burt Brown Barker. London, 1950.

14–15: *Cumberland House journals and inland journals, 1775–82. . . .* Edited by Edwin Ernest Rich, assisted by Alice Margaret Johnson, with an introduction by Richard [Gilchrist] Glover. 2 ser. London, 1951–52.
14: *First series, 1775–79.*
15: *Second series, 1779–82.*

17: *Moose Fort journals, 1783–85.* Edited by Edwin Ernest Rich, assisted by Alice Margaret Johnson, with an introduction by George Parkin de Twenebrokes Glazebrook. London, 1954.

21–22: Rich, *Hist. of HBC* [*see* section IV].

24: *Northern Quebec and Labrador journals and correspondence, 1819–35.* Edited by Kenneth Gordon Davies, assisted by Alice Margaret Johnson, with an introduction by Glyndwr Williams. London, 1963.

26: *Saskatchewan journals and correspondence; Edmonton House, 1795–1800, Chesterfield House, 1800–1802.* Edited with an introduction by Alice Margaret Johnson. London, 1967.

27: Graham, Andrew. *Andrew Graham's observations on Hudson's Bay, 1767–91.* Edited by Glyndwr Williams, with an introduction by Richard [Gilchrist] Glover. London, 1969.

30: *Hudson's Bay miscellany, 1670–1870.* Edited with introductions by Glyndwr Williams. Winnipeg, 1975.

The John Askin papers. Edited by Milo Milton Quaife. (DPL, Burton historical records, 1–2.) 2 vols. Detroit, 1928–31.

"The journals of the Legislative Assembly of Upper Canada . . . [1792–1824]." AO *Report*, 1909,

1911–14. The journals for part of 1794 and for 1795–97, 1809, 1813, and 1815 are missing.

Kingston before the War of 1812: a collection of documents. Edited by Richard Arthur Preston. (Champlain Society publications, Ontario series, 3.) Toronto, 1959.

LITERARY AND HISTORICAL SOCIETY OF QUEBEC/SOCIÉTÉ LITTÉRAIRE ET HISTORIQUE DE QUÉBEC, Quebec
PUBLICATIONS
Transactions. [1st series]. 1 (1824–29)–5 (1861–62). New series. 1 (1862–63)–30 (1924).

LOWER CANADA/BAS-CANADA
HOUSE OF ASSEMBLY/CHAMBRE D'ASSEMBLÉE
Journals/Journaux. Quebec, 1792/93–1837.
LEGISLATIVE COUNCIL/CONSEIL LÉGISLATIF
Journals/Journaux. Quebec, 1792/93–1837.
Provincial statutes/Les statuts provinciaux. Quebec, 1792/93–1837.
For further information *see* Thériault, *Les pub. parl.* [section III].

MACKENZIE, ALEXANDER. *The journals and letters of Sir Alexander Mackenzie.* Edited by William Kaye Lamb. (Hakluyt Society, [Works], extra series, 41.) Cambridge, Eng., 1970; Toronto, 1970.

Michigan Pioneer Collections. Lansing. 40 vols. 1874/76–1929. To avoid confusion the Michigan Historical Commission, Department of State, Lansing, has standardized the citation for these volumes, which were originally published by various historical agencies and under various titles. Volumes are traditionally cited by their spine dates.

NEW BRUNSWICK
HOUSE OF ASSEMBLY
Journal. Saint John, 1786–1814; Fredericton, 1816–40. Title varies: *Journal of the votes and proceedings*; *Journal and votes*; *Journals.*
LEGISLATIVE COUNCIL
Journal of the Legislative Council of the province of New Brunswick . . . [1786–1830]. 2 vols. Fredericton, 1831.

NEW BRUNSWICK HISTORICAL SOCIETY, Saint John
PUBLICATIONS
Collections. 12 nos. in 4 vols. and 22 additional nos. to date. 1894/97– . Used primarily for the documents reproduced.

NORTON, JOHN. *The journal of Major John Norton, 1816.* Edited by Carl Frederick Klinck and James John Talman. (Champlain Society publications, 46.) Toronto, 1970.

NOVA SCOTIA
Acts at the General Assembly. Halifax, 1798–1838.
HOUSE OF ASSEMBLY
Journal and proceedings. Halifax, 1761–1835. Title varies; *see* Bishop, *Pubs. of governments of N.S., P.E.I., N.B.* [section III].

ONTARIO HISTORICAL SOCIETY, Toronto
PUBLICATIONS
Corr. of Hon. Peter Russell (Cruikshank and Hunter).
Corr. of Lieut. Governor Simcoe (Cruikshank).
OH [*see* section v].
Strachan, *Letter book* (Spragge).
The parish register of Kingston, Upper Canada, 1785–1811. Edited by Archibald Hope Young. (Kingston Historical Society publication.) Kingston, Ont., 1921.
PERKINS, SIMEON. *The diary of Simeon Perkins. . . .* Edited by Harold Adams Innis *et al.* (Champlain Society publications, 29, 36, 39, 43, 50.) 5 vols. Toronto, 1948–78.
  [1]: *1766–1780.* Edited by Harold Adams Innis.
  [2]: *1780–1789.* Edited by Daniel Cobb Harvey with notes by Charles Bruce Fergusson.
  [3]: *1790–1796;* [4]: *1797–1803;* [5]: *1804–1812.* Edited by Charles Bruce Fergusson.
"Political state of Upper Canada in 1806–7." PAC *Report*, 1892: 32–135.
PRINCE EDWARD ISLAND
HOUSE OF ASSEMBLY
Journal. Charlottetown, 1788–1835. Title varies; *see* Bishop, *Pubs. of governments of N.S., P.E.I., N.B.* [section III].
PUBLIC ARCHIVES OF CANADA, Ottawa
BOARD OF HISTORICAL PUBLICATIONS
Docs. relating to constitutional hist., 1759–91 (Shortt and Doughty; 1918).
NUMBERED PUBLICATIONS [*see* section III]
OTHER PUBLICATIONS [*see also* section III]
Docs. relating to constitutional hist., 1791–1818 (Doughty and McArthur).
Docs. relating to constitutional hist., 1819–28 (Doughty and Story).
Report/Rapport. 1881–19 . Annually, with some omissions, until 1952; irregularly thereafter. For indexes, *see* section III.
QUEBEC/QUÉBEC
LEGISLATIVE COUNCIL/CONSEIL LÉGISLATIF
Ordinances/Ordonnances. Quebec, 1777–92.
[RAMSAY, GEORGE, 9TH EARL OF] DALHOUSIE. *The Dalhousie journals.* Edited by Marjory Whitelaw. 3 vols. [Ottawa], 1978–82.
Recensement de la ville de Québec en 1818 par le curé Joseph Signaÿ. Honorius Provost, édit. Québec, 1976.
Select British documents of the Canadian War of 1812. Edited with an introduction by William [Charles Henry] Wood. (Champlain Society publications, 13–15, 17.) 3 vols. in 4. Toronto, 1920–28; reprinted New York, 1968.
Statistical acccount of Upper Canada, compiled with a view to a grand system of emigration. Compiled by Robert [Fleming] Gourlay. 2 vols. London, 1822; reprinted East Ardsley, Eng., and New York, 1966. Abridged and with an introduction by Stanley Robert Mealing. 1 vol. Toronto, 1974.
STRACHAN, JOHN. *The John Strachan letter book: 1812–1834.* Edited with an introduction by George Warburton Spragge. (Ontario Historical Society publication.) Toronto, 1946.
The town of York, 1793–1815: a collection of documents of early Toronto. Edited by Edith Grace Firth. (Champlain Society publications, Ontario series, 5.) Toronto, 1962.
The town of York, 1815–1834: a further collection of documents of early Toronto. Edited by Edith Grace Firth. (Champlain Society publications, Ontario series, 8.) Toronto, 1966.
"United Empire Loyalists: enquiry into the losses and services in consequence of their loyalty; evidence in the Canadian claims." AO *Report*, 1904.
UPPER CANADA
HOUSE OF ASSEMBLY
Appendix to the journal, 1835–1839/40.
Journal, 1821, 1825–1839/40. For the period from 1792 to 1824, *see* "Journals of Legislative Assembly of U.C.," AO *Report*, 1909, 1911–14.
LEGISLATIVE COUNCIL
Journal, 1828–1839/40. The earlier journals are available in "The journals of the Legislative Council of Upper Canada . . . [1792–1824]," AO *Report*, 1910, 1915.
Statutes, 1793–1840.
"Upper Canada land book B, 19th August, 1796, to 7th April, 1797." AO *Report*, 1930: xi–126.
"Upper Canada land book C, 29th June, 1796, to 4th July, 1796; 1st July, 1797, to 20th December, 1797." AO *Report*, 1931: ix–98.
"Upper Canada land book C, 11th April, 1797, to 30th June, 1797." AO *Report*, 1930: 127–74.
"Upper Canada land book D, 22nd December, 1797, to 13th July, 1798." AO *Report*, 1931: 99–194.
The valley of the Six Nations; a collection of documents on the Indian lands of the Grand River. Edited by Charles Murray Johnston. (Champlain Society publications, Ontario series, 7.) Toronto, 1964.
The Windsor border region, Canada's southernmost frontier; a collection of documents. Edited by Ernest Joseph Lajeunesse. (Champlain Society publications, Ontario series, 4.) Toronto, 1960.
Winslow papers, A.D. 1776–1826. Edited by William Odber Raymond. Saint John, N.B., 1901.
WISCONSIN, STATE HISTORICAL SOCIETY, Madison
PUBLICATIONS
Collections. 31 vols. 1854–1931.

B. NEWSPAPERS

The following newspapers were particularly useful in the preparation of volume VI. Numerous sources have been used to determine their various titles and their dates of publication. These include, for all areas of the country: Canadian Library Assoc., *Canadian newspapers on microfilm, catalogue* (2 pts. in 3, Ottawa, 1959–69), *Union list of Canadian newspapers held by Canadian libraries* (Ottawa, 1977), and for pre-1800 newspapers, Tremaine, *Biblio. of Canadian imprints* [*see* section III]; for New Brunswick: J. R. Harper, *Historical directory of New Brunswick newspapers and periodicals* (Fredericton, 1961); for Newfoundland: "Chronological list of Newfoundland newspapers in the public collections at the Gosling Memorial Library and Provincial Archives," comp. Ian McDonald (typescript; copy in Nfld. Public Library Services, Provincial Reference and Resource Library, St John's), and *Serials holdings in the libraries of Memorial University of Newfoundland and St. John's Public Library: alphabetical list*, comp. C. D. Evans (8th ed., 2v., St John's, 1973); for Nova Scotia: G. E. N. Tratt, *A survey and listing of Nova Scotia newspapers, 1752–1957, with particular reference to the period before 1867* (Halifax, 1979) and *An historical directory of Nova Scotia newspapers and journals before confederation*, comp. T. B. Vincent (Kingston, Ont., 1977); for Ontario: *Catalogue of Canadian newspapers in the Douglas Library, Queen's University*, comp. L. C. Ellison *et al.* (Kingston, 1969), *Early Toronto newspapers* (Firth) [*see* section III], and W. S. Wallace, "The periodical literature of Upper Canada," *CHR*, 12 (1931): 4–22; for Prince Edward Island: W. L. Cotton, "The press in Prince Edward Island," *Past and present of Prince Edward Island . . .* , ed. D. A. MacKinnon and A. B. Warburton (Charlottetown, [1906]), 112–21; and for Quebec: Beaulieu et Hamelin, *La presse québécoise*, vol.1 [*see* section III]. Bishop, *Pubs. of governments of N.S., P.E.I., N.B.* [*see* section III], gives information on official government gazettes in the Maritime provinces.

Acadian Recorder. Halifax. Published from 16 Jan. 1813 until May 1930.

Canadian Courant and Montreal Advertiser. Montreal. Published from 11 May 1807 to 22 March 1834. In May 1830 it became the *Canadian Courant.*

Canadian Freeman. Toronto. Published from about June 1825 until August 1834.

Le Canadien. Québec; Montréal. The paper appeared at Quebec from 22 Nov. 1806 until 4 Dec. 1891, and then moved to Montreal, where it was published until 11 Feb. 1893 and from 22 Dec. 1906 to 11 Dec. 1909.

Christian Guardian. Toronto. Published from 21 Nov. 1829 until 3 June 1925. A general index for the years 1829–67 is available at the UCC, Central Arch. (Toronto).

Chronicle & Gazette. Kingston, [Ont.]. See *Kingston Chronicle*

Colonial Advocate. Queenston, [Ont.]; Toronto. Published in Queenston from 18 May until 18 Nov. 1824, when it moved to York [Toronto]. Its full title was *Colonial Advocate and Journal of Agriculture, Manufactures and Commerce* until 7 Oct. 1824 when it became the *Colonial Advocate*; on 5 Dec. 1833 it became the *Advocate*, and on 4 Nov. 1834 it amalgamated with the *Canadian Correspondent* to form the *Correspondent and Advocate.*

La Gazette de Québec. See *Quebec Gazette*

Gleaner, and Niagara Newspaper. Niagara [Niagara-on-the-Lake, Ont.]. Published from 4 Dec. 1817 until 1837. At some time between February and April 1830 it became the *Niagara Gleaner.*

Kingston Chronicle. Kingston, [Ont.]. A continuation of the *Kingston Gazette* (25 Sept. 1810–29 Dec. 1818), it appeared under this title from 1 Jan. 1819 to 22 June 1833, and then continued as the *Chronicle & Gazette* until around October 1847 when it became the *Chronicle and News*. From 29 June 1833 to 3 Jan. 1835 its full title was the *Chronicle & Gazette, and Weekly Commercial Advertiser*, and from 7 Jan. 1835 until 1847 it was the *Chronicle & Gazette, and Kingston Commercial Advertiser*, except for a brief period in 1840 when the subtitle was dropped.

Kingston Gazette. Kingston, [Ont.]. See *Kingston Chronicle*

La Minerve. Montréal. Published from 9 Nov. 1826 to 27 May 1899.

Montreal Gazette/La Gazette de Montréal. A bilingual continuation of the *Gazette littéraire, pour la ville & district de Montréal* (1778–79), the paper began publication on 25 Aug. 1785. From August 1822 to the present it has appeared only in English, with several changes in title.

Montreal Herald. Published from 19 Oct. 1811 to 18 Oct. 1957.

New-Brunswick Courier. Saint John, N.B. Published from 2 May 1811 until 1865.

New-Brunswick Royal Gazette. Saint John; Fredericton. See *Royal Gazette*

Newfoundland Mercantile Journal. St John's. Published from 1816 to 1827.

Novascotian, or Colonial Herald. Halifax. Published under various titles from 29 Dec. 1824 until some time in 1926, although no issues after 25 Dec. 1925 appear to have survived. Its title was the *Nova-*

scotian, or Colonial Herald until 2 Jan. 1840 when it became the *Novascotian.*

Nova-Scotia Royal Gazette. Halifax. Published under this title from 3 Jan. 1801 to 9 Feb. 1843. It began as the *Halifax Gazette* on 23 March 1752 and continued under various titles, including the *Nova-Scotia Gazette, and the Weekly Chronicle* (4 Sept. 1770–31 March 1789) and the *Royal Gazette and the Nova-Scotia Advertiser* (7 April 1789–30 Dec. 1800). On 16 Feb. 1843 the paper became the *Royal Gazette,* which continues to the present.

La Presse. Montréal. Began publication on 20 Oct. 1884 and continues to the present.

Prince Edward Island Register. Charlottetown. See *Royal Gazette*

Public Ledger. St John's. Published under various titles from about 1820 to 1882. Its full title was the *Public Ledger, and Newfoundland General Advertiser* until 17 July 1860 when the subtitle was dropped.

Quebec Gazette/La Gazette de Québec. Begun on 21 June 1764, the paper remained bilingual from 2 May 1832 until 30 April 1842, but the French and English editions were published separately. From 29 Oct. 1842 to 30 Oct. 1874 only the English edition appeared.

Quebec Mercury. Published under this title from 5 Jan. 1805 until 8 Jan. 1863; it continued under various other titles until 17 Oct. 1903.

Royal Gazette. Charlottetown. Published from 24 Aug. 1830 to the present, becoming an official government gazette in July 1851. Its predecessors include: *Royal Gazette and Miscellany of the Island of Saint John* (1791 to at least June 1794); *Royal Herald* (apparently 5 Jan. 1805 to at least October 1806); *Weekly Recorder of Prince Edward Island* (September 1810 to at least 25 November 1813); *Prince Edward Island Gazette* (February 1814 to at least 11 May 1822); and the *Prince Edward Island Register* (26 July 1823–17 Aug. 1830).

Royal Gazette. Saint John, N.B.; Fredericton. Published from 11 Oct. 1785 to the present, first in Saint John and then, from 10 March 1815, in Fredericton. It appeared originally as the *Royal Gazette, and the New-Brunswick Advertiser*; since 1 Dec. 1802 it has been called simply the *Royal*

Gazette, except from 1808 to 1814 when it was the *Royal Gazette, and New-Brunswick Advertiser* and from 18 April 1814 to 12 May 1828 when it was the *New-Brunswick Royal Gazette.*

Royal Gazette and Newfoundland Advertiser. St John's. Published from 27 Aug. 1807 until October 1924 when it was superseded by the *Newfoundland Gazette,* the official government gazette which continues to the present.

Royal Gazette and the Nova-Scotia Advertiser. Halifax. See *Nova-Scotia Royal Gazette*

Scribbler. Montreal. Published from 28 June 1821 until March 1827.

Upper Canada Gazette. Newark, later Niagara [Niagara-on-the-Lake, Ont.]; Toronto. Began 18 April 1793 and moved to York [Toronto] after the issue of 25 Aug. 1798. Its full title to 28 March 1807 was the *Upper Canadian Gazette; or, American Oracle,* from 15 April 1807 until the end of 1816 the *York Gazette,* and from 2 Jan. 1817 the *Upper Canada Gazette.* From 1821 to 1828 it was issued in two parts, with official announcements appearing as *Upper Canada Gazette* and the newspaper portion under the following titles: *York Weekly Post* (1821); *Weekly Register* (18 April 1822 until at least the end of 1825); and *U.E. Loyalist* (3 June 1826–24 May 1828). The paper appears to have been published until some time in 1849, although the latest extant issue is 9 March 1848.

Upper Canada Herald. Kingston, [Ont.]. Published under this title from 9 March 1819 until 19 July 1836; on 26 July 1836 it became the *Upper Canada Herald, a Political, Agricultural & Commercial Journal,* and on 16 Feb. 1841 continued as the *Kingston Herald; a Canadian Journal, Political, Agricultural & Commercial.* It ceased publication in 1851.

Weekly Chronicle. Halifax. Published from 28 May 1786 until 1826. On 5 Jan. 1827 it was superseded by the *Acadian, and General Advertiser.*

Weekly Register. York [Toronto]. See *Upper Canada Gazette*

York Gazette. York [Toronto]. See *Upper Canada Gazette*

III. REFERENCE WORKS

ALLAIRE, JEAN-BAPTISTE-ARTHUR. *Dictionnaire biographique du clergé canadien-français.* 6 vols. Montréal et Saint-Hyacinthe, Qué., 1908–34. [1]: *Les anciens.* Montréal, 1910.

[2]: *Les contemporains.* Saint-Hyacinthe, 1908.
[3]: [*Suppléments.*] 6 parts in 1 vol. Montréal, 1910–19.
[4]: *Le clergé canadien-français: revue mensuelle*

([Montréal]), 1 (1919–20). Only one volume of this journal was published.

[5]: *Compléments.* 6 parts in 1 vol. Montréal, 1928–32.

6: Untitled. Saint-Hyacinthe, 1934.

ALMANACS. The almanacs have been listed under this heading to facilitate their identification. Because titles within series vary and publishers often change, the almanacs have in the main been listed under a general title, with the specifics found on title pages following.

Almanach de Québec. See *Quebec almanac*

Halifax almanac. Published in Halifax from 1790 to at least 1821. Its actual title was *An almanack . . . calculated for the meridian of Halifax, in Nova-Scotia.* . . . Publishers: John Howe, 1790–1815; David Howe, 1816; unknown, 1817–20; John Munro, 1821.

Montreal almanack, or Lower Canada register. . . . Published in Montreal from 1829 to 1831 by Robert Armour.

New-Brunswick almanack. Saint John. Published by Henry Chubb, and later by his firm, from 1812 to 1864. Its title varies; from 1812 to 1830 it was *An almanack.* . . .

Nova-Scotia calendar. Published in Halifax from 1769 to 1801 as *The Nova-Scotia calender, or an almanack . . .*, and from 1814 to 1832 as *The Nova-Scotia calendar, for town and country.* . . . Publishers: Anthony Henry, 1769–1801; A. H. Holland, 1814–20; Holland and Company, 1821–24; P. J. Holland, 1825–32.

Quebec almanac/Almanach de Québec. Quebec, 1780–1841 (except for 1781, 1790, and 1793). Published by William Brown from 1780 to 1789, and continued by the Neilson family from 1791 until 1841. The spelling and language of the title vary, but from 1780 to 1789 it appeared solely in French as the *Almanach de Québec*, and from 1813 to 1841 it was published in English only as *The Quebec almanack; and British American royal kalendar.* . . .

York almanac. Published at York [Toronto] from 1821 to 1826. The issues for 1821 and 1822 appeared as *The York almanac, and provincial calendar . . .* [printed by R. C. Horne], and from 1823 to 1826 it was published by Charles Fothergill as *The York almanac and royal calendar, of Upper Canada.* . . .

ARCHIVES NATIONALES DU QUÉBEC, Québec PUBLICATIONS [*see also* section II]

P.-G. Roy, *Inv. concessions.*

—— *Inv. testaments.*

—— *Les juges de la prov. de Québec.*

ARMSTRONG, FREDERICK HENRY. *Handbook of Upper Canadian chronology and territorial legislation.*

(University of Western Ontario, Lawson Memorial Library publication.) London, 1967. Revised edition. Toronto and London, 1985.

AUDET, FRANCIS-JOSEPH. *Les députés de Montréal (ville et comtés), 1792–1867.* . . . Montréal, 1943.

—— *Les députés des Trois-Rivières (1808–1838).* Trois-Rivières, Qué., 1934.

—— "Les législateurs du Bas-Canada, 1760–1867." Manuscript held by the Morisset Library, University of Ottawa. 3 vols. 1940.

—— ET ÉDOUARD FABRE SURVEYER. *Les députés au premier Parlement du Bas-Canada, [1792–1796].* . . . Montréal, 1946.

Australian dictionary of biography. Edited by Douglas Pike *et al.* 10 vols. to date. Melbourne, 1966– .

BEAULIEU, ANDRÉ, ET JEAN HAMELIN. *La presse québécoise, des origines à nos jours.* [2ᵉ édition.] 7 vols. to date [1764–1944]. Québec, 1973– .

BIBAUD, [FRANÇOIS-]MAXIMILIEN. *Le Panthéon canadien; choix de biographies.* Nouvelle édition, revue, augmentée et complétée par Adèle et Victoria Bibaud. Montréal, 1891.

A bibliography of Canadiana, being items in the Public Library of Toronto, Canada, relating to the early history and development of Canada. Edited by Frances Maria Staton and Marie Tremaine. Toronto, 1934; reprinted 1965. 2 supplements to date. 1959– .

1: Edited by Gertrude Mabel Boyle with Marjorie Maud Colbeck. 1959; reprinted 1969.

2: Edited by Sandra Alston with Karen Evans. 1 part to date. 1985.

Biographie universelle (Michaud), ancienne et moderne. . . . Nouvelle édition. [Louis-Gabriel Michaud et Eugène-Ernest Desplaces, éditeurs.] 45 vols. Paris, [1854–65]; réimprimé Graz, Autriche, 1966–70.

BISHOP, OLGA BERNICE. *Publications of the government of the Province of Canada, 1841–1867.* (National Library of Canada publication.) Ottawa, 1963 [i.e. 1964].

—— *Publications of the governments of Nova Scotia, Prince Edward Island, New Brunswick, 1758–1952.* (National Library of Canada publication.) Ottawa, 1957.

BOUCHETTE, JOSEPH. *A topographical description of the province of Lower Canada, with remarks upon Upper Canada, and on the relative connexion of both provinces with the United States of America.* London, 1815; reprinted Saint-Lambert, Que., 1973. Published in French as *Description topographique de la province du Bas Canada . . .* (Londres, 1815; réimpr., J. E. Hare, édit., [Montréal, 1978]).

BRITISH MUSEUM. *General catalogue of printed*

books. Photolithographic edition to 1955. 263 vols. London, 1959–66. A new catalogue is being issued under the title *The British Library general catalogue of printed books to 1975* (326v. to date, 1979–).

BURKE, JOHN. *General and heraldic dictionary of the peerage and baronetage of the United Kingdom*. . . . London, 1826. 105th edition. Edited by Peter Townend. 1970.

"Calendar of state papers, addressed by the secretaries of state for the colonies to the lieutenant governors or officers administering the government of the province of Upper Canada, 1821–1835." PAC *Report*, 1935: 171–398.

The Canadian encyclopedia. Edited by James H. Marsh. 3 vols. Edmonton, 1985.

CARON, IVANHOË. "Inventaire de la correspondance de Mgr Bernard-Claude Panet, archevêque de Québec." ANQ *Rapport*, 1933–34: 235–421; 1934–35: 321–420; 1935–36: 157–272.

—— "Inventaire de la correspondance de Mgr Jean-François Hubert, évêque de Québec, et de Mgr Charles-François Bailly de Messein, son coadjuteur." ANQ *Rapport*, 1930–31: 199–351.

—— "Inventaire de la correspondance de Mgr Jean-Olivier Briand, évêque de Québec." ANQ *Rapport*, 1929–30: 47–136.

—— "Inventaire de la correspondance de Mgr Joseph-Octave Plessis, archevêque de Québec, 1797 à [1825]." ANQ *Rapport*, 1927–28: 215–316; 1928–29: 89–208; 1932–33: 3–244.

—— "Inventaire de la correspondance de Monseigneur Joseph Signay, archevêque de Québec – 1825–1835." ANQ *Rapport*, 1936–37: 125–330.

—— "Inventaire de la correspondance de Mgr Pierre Denaut, évêque de Québec." ANQ *Rapport*, 1931–32: 129–242.

CHADWICK, EDWARD MARION. *Ontarian families: genealogies of United-Empire-Loyalist and other pioneer families of Upper Canada*. 2 vols. Toronto, 1894–98; reprinted 2 vols. in 1, Lambertville, N.J., [1970]. Vol.1 reprinted with an introduction by William Felix Edmund Morley, Belleville, Ont., 1972.

Death notices of Ontario. Compiled by William D. Reid. Lambertville, N.J., 1980.

DESJARDINS, JOSEPH. *Guide parlementaire historique de la province de Québec, 1792 à 1902*. Québec, 1902.

DESROSIERS, LOUIS-ADÉLARD. "Inventaire de la correspondance de Mgr J.-J. Lartigue." ANQ *Rapport*, 1941–42: 347–496; 1942–43: 3–174; 1943–44: 212–334; 1944–45: 175–266; 1945–46: 45–134.

Dictionary of American biography. Edited by Allen Johnson *et al*. 20 vols., index, and 2 supplements [to 1940]. New York, 1928–58; reprinted, 22 vols.

in 11 and index, [1946?]–58. 5 additional supplements to date [to 1965]. Edited by Edward Topping James *et al*. 1973– . *Concise DAB*. 3rd edition. 1980.

Dictionary of national biography. Edited by Leslie Stephen and Sidney Lee. 63 vols., 3 supplements, and index and epitome [to 1900]. London, 1885–1903; reissued without index, 22 vols., 1908–9. 7 additional supplements to date [to 1970]. Edited by Sidney Lee *et al*. 1912– . *Concise DNB*. 2 vols. [1953]–61. *Corrections and additions to the "Dictionary of national biography"*. Boston, 1966.

Dictionnaire des œuvres littéraires du Québec. Maurice Lemire *et al*., éditeurs. 4 vols. Montréal, 1978–84.

DIRECTORIES. Issued initially as single works, these frequently became regular, usually annual, publications in the 19th century. Because titles within series varied greatly and editors or compilers frequently changed, the directories used in the preparation of volume VI have been listed below by region and under a general title, with the dates of relevant years following. Details of various titles and publishers given on title pages, as well as of the places of publication of these directories, can be found in Ryder, *Checklist of Canadian directories* [*see* below].

Montreal directory. Montreal. Issues cited in vol. VI are *An alphabetical list of the merchants, traders, and housekeepers, residing in Montreal* . . . , comp. Thomas Doige (1819; repr. 1899; 2nd ed., 1820); and *The Montreal directory, for 1842–3* . . . , comp. R. W. S. Mackay ([1842]).

Nova Scotia directory. Halifax. Cited in vol. VI are *Hutchinson's Nova Scotia directory, for 1864–65* . . . ([1864]), and *1866–67* . . . ([1866]), comp. Thomas Hutchinson, and *McAlpine's Nova Scotia directory, for 1868–69* . . . ([1868]).

Quebec directory. Quebec. Used in vol. VI are *The directory for the city and suburbs of Quebec* . . . (1790) and *Number II of the directory* . . . (1791), comp. Hugh MacKay; *The Quebec directory, for 1822* . . . , comp. T. H. Gleason (1822); and *The Quebec directory, or strangers' guide in the city, for 1826* . . . , comp. John Smith (1826).

Directory of the members of the Legislative Assembly of Nova Scotia, 1758–1958. Introduction by Charles Bruce Fergusson. (PANS publications, Nova Scotia series, 2.) Halifax, 1958. A revised edition has been issued as *The Legislative Assembly of Nova Scotia, 1758–1983: a biographical directory*, ed. S. B. Elliott ([Halifax], 1984).

Early Toronto newspapers, 1793–1867: a catalogue of newspapers published in the town of York and the city of Toronto from the beginning to confedera-

tion. Edited by Edith Grace Firth, with an introduction by Henry Cummings Campbell. Toronto, 1961.

Elections in New Brunswick, 1784–1984/Les élections au Nouveau-Brunswick, 1784–1984. (New Brunswick Legislative Library publication.) Fredericton, 1984.

Encyclopædia Britannica; a new survey of universal knowledge. [14th edition.] Edited by Warren E. Preece *et al.* 23 vols. and index. Chicago, 1966. *The new Encyclopædia Britannica.* 15th edition. 30 vols. 1977.

Encyclopedia Canadiana. Edited by John Everett Robbins *et al.* 10 vols. Ottawa, 1957–58. [Revised edition.] Edited by Kenneth H. Pearson *et al.* Toronto, 1975.

GAUTHIER, [JOSEPH-]HENRI. *Sulpitiana.* [2ᵉ édition.] Montréal, 1926.

GIROUX, ANDRÉ, *et al. Inventaire des marchés de construction des Archives nationales du Québec, à Montréal, 1800–1830.* (Canada, Parks Canada, National Historic Parks and Sites Branch, History and archaeology series, 49.) 2 vols. Ottawa, 1981.

Grand Larousse encyclopédique. 10 vols. Paris, 1960–64. 2 suppléments. 1969–75. *Grand dictionnaire encyclopédique Larousse.* 10 vols. 1982–85.

GREAT BRITAIN, ADMIRALTY. *A list of the flag-officers of his majesty's fleet. . . .* London, 1777–1840.

——— *The navy list. . . .* London, 1815– .

GREAT BRITAIN, WAR OFFICE. *A list of the general and field-officers, as they rank in the army. . . .* London, 1754–1868.

Guide to the reports of the Public Archives of Canada, 1872–1972. Compiled by Françoise Caron-Houle. (PAC publication.) Ottawa, 1975.

Halifax almanac. See ALMANACS

Handbook of Indians of Canada. Edited by Frederick Webb Hodge. Published as an appendix to the tenth report of the Geographic Board of Canada. Ottawa, 1913; reprinted New York, 1969. A republication of the Canadian material in *Handbook of American Indians north of Mexico,* ed. F. W. Hodge (2 pts., Washington, 1907–10; repr. New York, 1971).

Handbook of North American Indians. Edited by William C. Sturtevant *et al.* (Smithsonian Institution publications.) 6 vols. to date [5–6, 8–10, 15]. Washington, 1978– .

HARE, JOHN [ELLIS], ET JEAN-PIERRE WALLOT. *Les imprimés dans le Bas-Canada, 1801–1840: bibliographie analytique.* Montréal, 1967. Only one volume, *1801–1810,* was published.

HILL, ISABEL LOUISE. *The Old Burying Ground, Fredericton, N.B.* 2 vols. in 1. Fredericton, 1981.

Illustrated atlas of the Eastern Townships and south western Quebec. Edited by Ross Cumming. Port

Elgin, Ont., 1972. Originally published as *Illustrated atlas of the Dominion of Canada . . . ; Eastern Townships and southwestern Quebec supplement* (Toronto, 1881).

Index to reports of Canadian archives from 1872 to 1908. (PAC publications, 1.) Ottawa, 1909.

JONES, EDWARD ALFRED. *The loyalists of Massachusetts: their memorials, petitions and claims.* London, 1930; reprinted Baltimore, Md., 1969.

[LANGELIER, JEAN-CHRYSOSTOME.] *Liste des terrains concédés par la couronne dans la province de Québec, de 1763 au 31 décembre 1890.* Québec, 1891. Also published in English as *List of lands granted by the crown in the province of Quebec from 1763 to 31st December 1890* (1891).

LEBŒUF, JOSEPH-[AIMÉ-]ARTHUR. *Complément au dictionnaire généalogique Tanguay.* (SGCF publications, 2, 4, 6.) 3 séries. Montréal, 1957–64. *See also* Tanguay, *Dictionnaire.*

LE JEUNE, LOUIS[-MARIE]. *Dictionnaire général de biographie, histoire, littérature, agriculture, commerce, industrie et des arts, sciences, mœurs, coutumes, institutions politiques et religieuses du Canada.* 2 vols. Ottawa, [1931].

Loyalists and land settlement in Nova Scotia. Compiled by Marion Gilroy under the direction of Daniel Cobb Harvey. (PANS publications, 4.) Halifax, 1937.

MASSICOTTE, ÉDOUARD-ZOTIQUE. "Répertoire des engagements pour l'Ouest conservés dans les Archives judiciaires de Montréal, [1798–1821]." *ANQ Rapport,* 1943–44: 335–444; 1944–45: 309–401; 1945–46: 227–340.

Montreal almanac. See ALMANACS

Montreal directory. See DIRECTORIES

MORGAN, HENRY JAMES. *Bibliotheca Canadensis: or a manual of Canadian literature.* Ottawa, 1867; reprinted Detroit, 1968.

——— *Sketches of celebrated Canadians, and persons connected with Canada, from the earliest period in the history of the province down to the present time.* Quebec and London, 1862; reprinted Montreal, 1865.

NATIONAL LIBRARY OF CANADA, Ottawa
PUBLICATIONS
Bishop, *Pubs. of government of Prov. of Canada.*
——— *Pubs. of governments of N.S., P.E.I., N.B.*
Ryder, *Checklist of Canadian directories.*

The national union catalog, pre-1956 imprints. . . . 754 vols. London and Chicago, 1968–81.

New-Brunswick almanack. See ALMANACS

New Brunswick vital statistics from newspapers. . . . Compiled by Daniel F. Johnson *et al.* (New Brunswick Genealogical Society publication.) 5 vols. [1784–1834]. Fredericton, 1982–84. Continued as *Vital statistics from New Brunswick newspapers. . . .* Compiled by Daniel F. Johnson.

8 vols. to date [1835–52]. Saint John, N.B., 1985– .

Nova-Scotia calendar. See ALMANACS

Nova Scotia directory. See DIRECTORIES

Nova Scotia vital statistics from newspapers. . . . Compiled by Terrence M. Punch *et al.* (Royal Nova Scotia Historical Society, Genealogical Committee publications, 1, 3, 5–6, 8.) 5 vols. to date [1769–1839]. Halifax, 1978– .

Officers of the British forces in Canada during the War of 1812–15. Compiled by L. Homfray Irving. (Canadian Military Institute publication.) [Welland, Ont.], 1908.

"Papiers d'État, [1761–99]." PAC *Rapport,* 1890: 1–340. *See also* "State papers."

"Papiers d'État – Bas-Canada, [1791–1818]." PAC *Rapport,* 1891: 1–206; 1892: 155–293; 1893: 1–123; 1896: 1–256. *See also* "State papers – L.C."

Place-names and places of Nova Scotia. Introduction by Charles Bruce Fergusson. (PANS publications, Nova Scotia series, 3.) Halifax, 1967; reprinted Belleville, Ont., 1976.

Places in Ontario: their name origins and history. Compiled by Nick and Helma Mika. 3 parts. Belleville, Ont., 1977–83.

PUBLIC ARCHIVES OF CANADA, Ottawa

    NUMBERED PUBLICATIONS

    1: *Index to reports of PAC.*

    OTHER PUBLICATIONS [*see also* section II]

    Guide to reports of PAC (Caron-Houle).

    Inventories of holdings in the manuscript division [*see* section I].

    Union list of MSS (Gordon *et al.*; Maurice Hyam).

    Union list of MSS, supp. (Maurice Hyam *et al.*).

PUBLIC ARCHIVES OF NOVA SCOTIA, Halifax

    NOVA SCOTIA SERIES

    2: *Directory of N.S. MLAs.*

    3: *Place-names of N.S.*

    OTHER PUBLICATIONS

    4: *Loyalists in N.S.* (Gilroy).

Quebec almanac. See ALMANACS

Quebec directory. See DIRECTORIES

RAYBURN, ALAN. *Geographical names of New Brunswick.* (Canadian Permanent Committee on Geographical Names, Toponymy study, 2.) Ottawa, 1975.

——— *Geographical names of Prince Edward Island.* (Canadian Permanent Committee on Geographical Names, Toponymy study, 1.) Ottawa, 1973.

READ, DAVID BREAKENRIDGE. *The lives of the judges of Upper Canada and Ontario, from 1791 to the present time.* Toronto, 1888.

ROY, PIERRE-GEORGES. *Les avocats de la région de Québec.* Lévis, 1936 [i.e. 1937].

——— *Fils de Québec.* 4 séries. Lévis, 1933.

——— *Inventaire des concessions en fief et seigneurie, fois et hommages et aveux et dénombrements, conservés aux Archives de la province de Québec.* (ANQ publication.) 6 vols. Beauceville, Qué., 1927–29.

——— *Inventaire des testaments, donations et inventaires du Régime français conservés aux Archives judiciaires de Québec.* (ANQ publication.) 3 vols. Québec, 1941.

——— *Les juges de la province de Québec.* (ANQ publication.) Québec, 1933.

RYDER, DOROTHY EDITH. *Checklist of Canadian directories, 1750–1950/Répertoire des annuaires canadiens, 1790–1950.* (National Library of Canada publication.) Ottawa, 1979.

SABINE, LORENZO. *Biographical sketches of loyalists of the American revolution, with an historical essay.* [2nd edition.] 2 vols. Boston, 1864; reprinted Port Washington, N.Y., 1966. First published as *The American loyalists, or biographical sketches of adherents to the British crown in the war of the revolution . . .* (Boston, 1847).

SCOTT, HEW, *et al. Fasti ecclesiæ scoticanæ: the succession of ministers in the Church of Scotland from the Reformation.* 3 vols. in 6. Edinburgh, 1866–71. New edition. 9 vols. to date. 1915– .

SHIPTON, CLIFFORD KENYON. *Sibley's Harvard graduates. . . .* (Massachusetts Historical Society publication.) 17 vols. to date [1690–1771]. Cambridge and Boston, Mass., 1933– . A continuation of J. L. Sibley, *Biographical sketches of graduates of Harvard University, in Cambridge, Massachusetts* [1642–89] (3v., Cambridge, 1873–85), the volumes are numbered consecutively from it.

STARK, JAMES HENRY. *The loyalists of Massachusetts and the other side of the American revolution.* Boston, [1907]. Another edition. 1910.

"State papers, [1761–99]." PAC *Report,* 1890: 1–325. *See also* "Papiers d'État."

"State papers – Lower Canada, [1795–1807]." PAC *Report,* 1891: 1–200; 1892: 153–185. *See also* "Papiers d'État – Bas-Canada."

"State papers – Upper Canada, [1792–1807]." PAC *Report,* 1891: 1–177; 1892: 286–399.

TANGUAY, CYPRIEN. *Dictionnaire généalogique des familles canadiennes depuis la fondation de la colonie jusqu'à nos jours.* 7 vols. Montréal, 1871–90; réimprimé Baltimore, Md., 1967, and New York, 1969. *See also* Lebœuf, *Complément.*

——— *Répertoire général du clergé canadien par ordre chronologique depuis la fondation de la colonie jusqu'à nos jours.* [2ᵉ édition.] Montréal, 1893.

THÉRIAULT, YVON. *Les publications parlementaires*

d'hier et d'aujourd'hui. [2ᵉ édition.] Québec, 1982. Also published in English as *The parliamentary publications, past and present* (1983).

TREMAINE, MARIE. *A bibliography of Canadian imprints, 1751–1800*. Toronto, 1952.

TURCOTTE, GUSTAVE. *Le Conseil législatif de Québec, 1774–1933*. Beauceville, Qué., 1933.

Union list of manuscripts in Canadian repositories/ Catalogue collectif des manuscrits des archives canadiennes. Edited by Robert Stanyslaw Gordon et al. (PAC publication.) Ottawa, 1968. Revised edition. Edited by E. Grace Maurice [Hyam]. 2 vols. 1975. *Supplement/Supplément*. Edited by E. Grace Maurice Hyam et al. 4 vols. to date. 1976–

WALBRAN, JOHN THOMAS. *British Columbia coast names, 1592–1906, to which are added a few names in adjacent United States territory: their origin and history. . . .* (Geographic Board of Canada publication.) Ottawa, 1909; reprinted with an introduction by George Phillip Vernon Akrigg. Vancouver, 1971; reprinted Seattle, Wash., and London, 1972.

WALLACE, WILLIAM STEWART. *The Macmillan dictionary of Canadian biography*. Edited by William Angus McKay. 4th edition. Toronto, 1978. First published as *The dictionary of Canadian biography* (1926).

York almanac. See ALMANACS

IV. STUDIES (BOOKS AND THESES)

ABBOTT, MAUDE ELIZABETH [SEYMOUR]. *History of medicine in the province of Quebec*. Toronto, 1931; Montreal, 1931.

AHERN, MICHAEL-JOSEPH ET GEORGE. *Notes pour servir à l'histoire de la médecine dans le Bas-Canada depuis la fondation de Québec jusqu'au commencement du XIXᵉ siècle*. Québec, 1923.

AKINS, THOMAS BEAMISH. *History of Halifax City*. Belleville, Ont., 1973. First published as N.S. Hist. Soc., *Coll.*, 8 (1892–94) [*see* section v].

AUBERT DE GASPÉ, PHILIPPE[-JOSEPH]. *Mémoires*. Ottawa, 1866; réimprimé East Ardsley, Angl., 1966, et Montréal, 1971. Autres éditions: Québec, 1885; 2 vols. Montréal et Tours, France, [1930].

AUDET, LOUIS-PHILIPPE. *Le système scolaire de la province de Québec* [1635–1840]. 6 vols. Québec, 1950–56.

BECKWITH MAXWELL, LILIAN MARY. *An outline of the history of central New Brunswick to the time of confederation*. (York-Sunbury Historical Society publication.) Sackville, N.B., 1937; reprinted Fredericton, 1984.

BOULIANNE, RÉAL G. "The Royal Institution for the Advancement of Learning: the correspondence, 1820–1829; a historical and analytical study." PHD thesis, McGill University, Montreal, 1970.

CAMPBELL, ROBERT. *A history of the Scotch Presbyterian Church, St. Gabriel Street, Montreal*. Montreal, 1887.

Canada's smallest province: a history of P.E.I. Edited by Francis William Pius Bolger. [Charlottetown, 1973.]

CANNIFF, WILLIAM. *History of the settlement of Upper Canada (Ontario), with special reference to the Bay Quinte*. Toronto, 1869; reprinted as *The settlement of Upper Canada*, with an introduction by Donald Swainson. Belleville, Ont., 1971.

CARNOCHAN, JANET. *History of Niagara (in part)*. Toronto, 1914; reprinted Belleville, Ont., 1973.

CARON, IVANHOË. *La colonisation de la province de Québec*. 2 vols. Québec, 1923–27.
[1]: *Débuts du Régime anglais, 1760–1791*.
[2]: *Les cantons de l'Est, 1791–1815*.

CHAUSSÉE, GILLES. *Jean-Jacques Lartigue, premier évêque de Montréal*. Montréal, 1980.

CHRISTIE, ROBERT. *A history of the late province of Lower Canada, parliamentary and political, from the commencement to the close of its existence as a separate province. . . .* 6 vols. Quebec and Montreal, 1848–55. [2nd edition.] Montreal, 1866.

[COWDELL] GATES, LILLIAN FRANCIS. *Land policies of Upper Canada*. Toronto, 1968.

CRAIG, GERALD MARQUIS. *Upper Canada: the formative years, 1784–1841*. [Toronto], 1963.

DAY, CATHERINE MATILDA [TOWNSEND]. *History of the Eastern Townships, province of Quebec, Dominion of Canada, civil and descriptive, in three parts*. Montreal, 1869.

DENISON, MERRILL. *Canada's first bank: a history of the Bank of Montreal*. 2 vols. Toronto and Montreal, 1966–67. Translated by Paul A. Horguelin and Jean-Paul Vinay as *La première banque au Canada: histoire de la Banque de Montréal* (2v., Toronto et Montréal, 1966–67).

DIONNE, NARCISSE-EUTROPE. *Les ecclésiastiques et les royalistes français réfugiés au Canada à l'époque de la révolution – 1791–1802*. Québec, 1905.

GALARNEAU, CLAUDE. *La France devant l'opinion canadienne (1760–1815).* (Université Laval, Institut d'histoire, Cahiers, 16.) Québec et Paris, 1970.

GORMAN CONDON, ANN. "'The envy of the American states': the settlement of the loyalists in New Brunswick: goals and achievements." PHD thesis, Harvard University, Cambridge, Mass., 1975. Published as *The envy of the American states: the loyalist dream for New Brunswick* (Fredericton, 1984).

GRAHAM, JOHN HAMILTON. *Outlines of the history of freemasonry in the province of Quebec.* Montreal, 1892.

GREGG, WILLIAM. *History of the Presbyterian Church in the Dominion of Canada, from the earliest times to 1834; with a chronological table of events to the present time, and map.* Toronto, 1885.

HANNAY, JAMES. *History of New Brunswick.* 2 vols. Saint John, N.B., 1909.

HITSMAN, JOHN MACKAY. *The incredible War of 1812: a military history.* Toronto, 1965.

HOWLEY, JAMES PATRICK. *The Beothucks or Red Indians: the aboriginal inhabitants of Newfoundland.* Cambridge, Eng., 1915; reprinted Toronto, 1974, and New York, 1979.

INNIS, HAROLD ADAMS. *The fur trade in Canada: an introduction to Canadian economic history.* New Haven, Conn., and London, 1930. Revised edition. [Edited by Mary Quayle Innis *et al.*] Toronto, 1956. [Abridged edition] based on the revised edition of 1956, foreword by Robin William Winks. 1962. Revised edition (reprint of 1956 edition with revised foreword from the 1962 edition). 1970.

JOHNSTON, ANGUS ANTHONY. *A history of the Catholic Church in eastern Nova Scotia.* 2 vols. Antigonish, N.S., 1960–71.
1: *1611–1827.*
2: *1827–1880; with a brief appendix surveying the years 1880–1969.*

JOLOIS, JEAN-JACQUES. *Joseph-François Perrault (1753–1844), et les origines de l'enseignement laïque au Bas-Canada.* Montréal, 1969.

LAMBERT, JAMES HAROLD. "Monseigneur, the Catholic bishop: Joseph-Octave Plessis; church, state, and society in Lower Canada: historiography and analysis." D. ès L. thesis, Université Laval, Quebec, 1981.

LANCTOT, GUSTAVE. *Le Canada et la Révolution américaine.* Montréal, 1965. Translated by Margaret M. Cameron as *Canada & the American revolution, 1774–1783* (Toronto and Vancouver, 1967).

LAWRENCE, JOSEPH WILSON. *The judges of New Brunswick and their times.* Edited and annotated by Alfred Augustus Stockton [and William Odber Raymond]. [Saint John, N.B., 1907]; reprinted with an introduction by David Graham Bell. Fredericton, 1983 [i.e. 1985].

LEMIEUX, LUCIEN. *L'établissement de la première province ecclésiastique au Canada, 1783–1844.* Montréal et Paris, 1968.

MACMILLAN, DAVID STIRLING. "The 'new men' in action: Scottish mercantile and shipping operations in the North American colonies, 1760–1825." In *Canadian business history; selected studies, 1497–1971,* edited by David Stirling Macmillan, 44–103. Toronto, 1972.

MACNUTT, WILLIAM STEWART. *New Brunswick, a history: 1784–1867.* Toronto, 1963.

MAURAULT, OLIVIER. *Le collège de Montréal, 1767–1967.* 2ᵉ édition. Antonio Dansereau, éditeur. Montréal, 1967. The first edition was published as *Le petit séminaire de Montréal* (Montréal, 1918).

MILLMAN, THOMAS REAGH. *Jacob Mountain, first lord bishop of Quebec; a study in chuch and state, 1793–1825.* (University of Toronto studies, History and economics series, 10.) Toronto, 1947.

MIQUELON, DALE BERNARD. "The Baby family in the trade of Canada, 1750–1820." MA thesis, Carleton University, Ottawa, [1966].

MORGAN, ROBERT J. "Orphan outpost: Cape Breton colony, 1784–1820." PHD thesis, University of Ottawa, 1972.

MORTON, ARTHUR SILVER. *A history of the Canadian west to 1870–71, being a history of Rupert's Land (the Hudson's Bay Company's territory) and of the North-West Territory (including the Pacific slope).* London, [1939]. 2nd edition. Edited by Lewis Gwynne Thomas. Toronto and Buffalo, N.Y., 1973.

MURDOCH, BEAMISH. *A history of Nova-Scotia, or Acadie.* 3 vols. Halifax, 1865–67.

NEATBY, HILDA [MARION]. *Quebec: the revolutionary age, 1760–1791.* [Toronto], 1966.

OUELLET, FERNAND. *Le Bas-Canada, 1791–1840: changements structuraux et crise.* (Université d'Ottawa, Cahiers d'histoire, 6.) Ottawa, 1976. Translated and adapted by Patricia Claxton as *Lower Canada, 1791–1840: social change and nationalism* (Toronto, 1980).

—— *Histoire économique et sociale du Québec, 1760–1850: structures et conjoncture.* Montréal et Paris, 1966; réimprimé en 2 vols., Montréal, 1971. Translated as *Economic and social history of Quebec, 1760–1850: "structures" and "conjonctures"* ([Toronto], 1980).

PAQUET, GILLES, ET JEAN-PIERRE WALLOT. *Patronage et pouvoir dans le Bas-Canada (1794–1812); un essai d'économie historique.* Montréal, 1973.

PASCOE, CHARLES FREDERICK. *Two hundred years of the S.P.G.: an historical account of the Society for* the Propagation of the Gospel in Foreign Parts, 1701–1900 (based on a digest of the society's records). 2 vols. London, 1901.

PATTERSON, GRAEME HAZLEWOOD. "Studies in elections and public opinion in Upper Canada." PHD thesis, University of Toronto, 1969.

PROVOST, HONORIUS. Sainte-Marie de la Nouvelle-Beauce; histoire civile. Québec, 1970.

—— Sainte-Marie de la Nouvelle-Beauce; histoire religieuse. Québec, 1967.

PROWSE, DANIEL WOODLEY. A history of Newfoundland from the English, colonial, and foreign records. London and New York, 1895; reprinted Belleville, Ont., 1972. 2nd edition. London, 1896. 3rd edition. With additions by James Raymond Thoms and Frank Burnham Gill. St John's, 1971.

RICH, EDWIN ERNEST. The history of the Hudson's Bay Company, 1670–1870. (HBRS, 21–22.) 2 vols. London, 1958–59. [Trade edition.] 3 vols. Toronto, 1960. A copy of this work available at the PAC contains notes and bibliographical material omitted from the printed version.

RIDDELL, WILLIAM RENWICK. The bar and the courts of the province of Upper Canada, or Ontario. Toronto, 1928.

Robertson's landmarks of Toronto: a collection of historical sketches of the old town of York from 1792 until 1833, and of Toronto from 1834 to [1914]. . . . Edited by John Ross Robertson. 6 vols. Toronto, 1894–1914. Vols. 1 and 3 reprinted Belleville, Ont., 1976, 1974.

ROY, JOSEPH-EDMOND. Histoire de la seigneurie de Lauzon [1608–1840]. 5 vols. Lévis, Qué., 1897–1904; réimprimé, 1984 [i.e. 1985].

—— Histoire du notariat au Canada depuis la fondation de la colonie jusqu'à nos jours. 4 vols. Lévis, Qué., 1899–1902.

ROY, PIERRE-GEORGES. Toutes petites choses du Régime anglais. 2 séries. Québec, 1946.

SCADDING, HENRY. Toronto of old: collections and recollections illustrative of the early settlement and social life of the capital of Ontario. Toronto, 1873. Abridged edition, entitled Toronto of old. Edited by Frederick Henry Armstrong. Toronto, 1966.

TAFT MANNING, HELEN. The revolt of French Canada, 1800–1835; a chapter in the history of the British Commonwealth. Toronto, 1962.

Three history theses. (Ontario, Department of Records and Archives publication.) [Toronto], 1961.

TULCHINSKY, GERALD JACOB JOSEPH. "The construction of the first Lachine Canal, 1815–1826." MA thesis, McGill University, Montreal, 1960.

Les ursulines des Trois-Rivières depuis leur établissement jusqu'à nos jours. 4 vols. Trois-Rivières, Qué., 1888–1911.

WALLOT, JEAN-PIERRE. Un Québec qui bougeait: trame socio-politique du Québec au tournant du XIXᵉ siècle. Québec, 1973.

WARBURTON, ALEXANDER BANNERMAN. A history of Prince Edward Island from its discovery in 1534 until the departure of Lieutenant-Governor Ready in A.D. 1831. Saint John, N.B., 1923.

WILKINS CAMPBELL, MARJORIE [ELLIOTT]. The North West Company. Toronto, 1957. Revised edition. 1973.

WILSON, BRUCE GORDON. The enterprises of Robert Hamilton: a study of wealth and influence in early Upper Canada, 1776–1812. Ottawa, 1983.

V. JOURNALS AND STUDIES (ARTICLES)

Acadiensis: a Quarterly Devoted to the Interests of the Maritime Provinces of Canada. Saint John, N.B. 1 (1901)–8 (1908). An index to "Acadiensis," 1901–1908, comp. Dorothy Cooke (Dalhousie University Libraries and School of Library Service, Occasional papers, 33), has been published (Halifax, 1983).

Acadiensis: Journal of the History of the Atlantic Region/Revue de l'histoire de la région atlantique. Fredericton. Published by the Department of History of the University of New Brunswick. 1 (1971–72)– . The Acadiensis index, vols.I–XII (autumn 1971 to spring 1983), comp. E. L. Swanick with the assistance of David Frank, was published in 1985.

ALLEN, ROBERT S. "The British Indian Department and the frontier in North America, 1755–1830." Canadian Hist. Sites, no.14 (1975): 5–125.

Beaver: Magazine of the North. Winnipeg. Published by the HBC. 1 (1920–21)– . Index: 1–outfit 284 (June 1953–March 1954). Title varies.

British Columbia Historical Quarterly. Victoria. Published by the PABC in cooperation with the British Columbia Historical Association. 1 (1937)–21 (1957–58). Author/title and subject indexes are provided by A two-part index to the "British Columbia Historical Quarterly," volumes I–XXI . . . , published by Camosun College ([Victoria], 1977).

Le Bulletin des recherches historiques. Published usually in Lévis, Qué. Originally the organ of the Société des études historiques, it became in March

1923 the journal of the Archives de la province de Québec (now the ANQ). 1 (1895)–70 (1968). *Index*: 1–31 (1925) (4v., Beauceville, Qué., 1925–26). For subsequent years there is an index on microfiche at the ANQ-Q.

Les Cahiers des Dix. Montréal et Québec. Published by "Les Dix." 1 (1936)– .

CANADIAN CATHOLIC HISTORICAL ASSOCIATION/ SOCIÉTÉ CANADIENNE D'HISTOIRE DE L'ÉGLISE CATHOLIQUE, Ottawa. Publishes simultaneously a *Report* in English and a *Rapport* in French, of which the contents are entirely different. 1 (1933–34)– . *Index*: 1–25 (1958). Title varies: *Study sessions/Sessions d'étude*, 1966–83; in 1984 the English title became *Canadian Catholic Historical Studies*.

CANADIAN HISTORICAL ASSOCIATION/SOCIÉTÉ HISTORIQUE DU CANADA, Ottawa. *Annual report*. 1922– . *Index*: 1922–51; 1952–68. Title varies: *Historical papers/Communications historiques* from 1966.

Canadian Historical Review. Toronto. 1 (1920)– . *Index*: 1–10 (1929); 11 (1930)–20 (1939); 21 (1940)–30 (1949); 31 (1950)–51 (1970). Université Laval has also published an index: *"Canadian Historical Review," 1950–1964: index des articles et des comptes rendus de volumes*, René Hardy, compil. (Québec, 1969). A continuation of the *Review of Historical Publications relating to Canada*: 1 (1895–96)–22 (1917–18); *Index*: 1–10 (1905); 11 (1906)–20 (1915).

Canadian Historic Sites: Occasional Papers in Archaeology and History/Lieux historiques canadiens: cahiers d'archéologie et d'histoire. Ottawa. Published by Canada, National Historic Parks and Sites Branch. No.1 (1970)– .

Dalhousie Review. Halifax. Published by Dalhousie University. 1 (1921–22)– .

HARE, JOHN [ELLIS]. "L'Assemblée législative du Bas-Canada, 1792–1814: députation et polarisation politique." *RHAF*, 27 (1973–74): 361–95.

Historic Kingston. Kingston, Ont. Published by the Kingston Historical Society. No.1 (1952)– ; nos.1–10 reprinted in 1 vol., Belleville, Ont., 1972. *Index*: nos.1–20 (1972).

Island Magazine. Charlottetown. Published by the P.E.I. Heritage Foundation. No.1 (fall–winter 1976)– .

NIAGARA HISTORICAL SOCIETY, Niagara-on-the-Lake, Ont. [*Publications*.] Nos.1 (1896)–44 (1939). The first number is called *Transactions*; nos.2 (1897)–44 list titles of articles included but have no main title; nos.38 (1927)–44 are all called "Records of Niagara."

Nova Scotia Historical Quarterly. Halifax. 1 (1971)–10 (1980). Volume 10, nos.3–4 were issued by the PANS, which then continued the publication as the *Nova Scotia Historical Review*, 1 (1981)– .

NOVA SCOTIA HISTORICAL SOCIETY, Halifax. *See* Royal Nova Scotia Historical Society

Ontario History. Toronto. Published by the Ontario Historical Society. 1 (1899)– ; vols.1–49 (1957) reprinted Millwood, N.Y., 1975. An index to volumes 1 to 64 (1972) appears in *Index to the publications of the Ontario Historical Society, 1899–1972* (1974). Title varies: *Papers and Records* to 1946.

Revue d'histoire de l'Amérique française. Montréal. Published by the Institut d'histoire de l'Amérique française. 1 (1947–48)– . *Index*: 1–10 (1956–57); 11 (1957–58)–20 (1966–67); 21 (1967–68)–30 (1976–77).

ROYAL NOVA SCOTIA HISTORICAL SOCIETY, Halifax

GENEALOGICAL COMMITTEE PUBLICATIONS

1, 3, 5–6, 8: *N.S. vital statistics* (Punch *et al.*) [*see* section III].

OTHER PUBLICATIONS

Collections. 1 (1878)– ; vols.1–8 (1892/94) reprinted in 2 vols., Belleville, Ont., 1976–77. Index: 1–32 (1959) in 33 (1961). Vols.1–40 (1980) issued under the society's original name, the Nova Scotia Historical Society.

ROYAL SOCIETY OF CANADA/SOCIÉTÉ ROYALE DU CANADA, Ottawa. *Proceedings and Transactions/ Mémoires et comptes rendus*. 1st ser., 1 (1882–83)–12 (1894); 2nd ser., 1 (1895)–12 (1906); 3rd ser., 1 (1907)–56 (1962); 4th ser., 1 (1963)– . *General index*: 1st ser.–2nd ser.; *Author index*: 3rd ser., 1–35 (1941). The Canadian Library Association has published *A subject index to the Royal Society of Canada "Proceedings and Transactions": third series, vols. I–XXXI, 1907–1937*, comp. M. A. Martin (Ottawa, 1947).

Social History, a Canadian Review/Histoire sociale, revue canadienne. Ottawa. Published under the direction of an interdisciplinary committee from various Canadian universities. No.1 (April 1968)– .

SOCIÉTÉ GÉNÉALOGIQUE CANADIENNE-FRANÇAISE, Montréal

NUMBERED PUBLICATIONS

2, 4, 6: Lebœuf, *Complément* [*see* section III].

OTHER PUBLICATIONS

Mémoires. 1 (1944–45)– . An index to volumes 1–25 (1975) has been issued as *Index onomastique des "Mémoires" de la Société généalogique canadienne-française, 1944–1975*, R.-J. Auger compil. (2v., Lac-Beauport, Qué., 1975).

CONTRIBUTORS

Contributors

ABBOTT-GIBBS, ELIZABETH. Research director, Centre d'étude du Québec, Concordia University, Montreal, Quebec.
William Kain.

ABLER, THOMAS S. Associate professor of anthropology, University of Waterloo, Ontario.
Shakóye:wa:thaʔ.

ACHESON, THOMAS WILLIAM. Professor of history, University of New Brunswick, Fredericton, New Brunswick.
Hugh Johnston. Duncan M'Coll. John Robinson. James Simonds.

ALLAIRE, GRATIEN. Professeur agrégé d'histoire, University of Alberta, Edmonton, Alberta.
Angus Shaw. Thomas Thain.

ALLEN, ROBERT S. Deputy chief, Treaties and Historical Research Centre, Indian and Northern Affairs Canada, Ottawa, Ontario.
William Claus. Robert Dickson. David Fanning. Peter Fidler. William McKay.

ANDREAE, CHRISTOPHER. President, Historica Research Limited, London, Ontario.
Eleakim Field.

ANGUS, MARGARET SHARP. Writer, Kingston, Ontario.
Peter Smith.

ARCHER, CHRISTON I. Professor of history, University of Calgary, Alberta.
Francisco de Eliza y Reventa.

ARMOUR, DAVID ARTHUR. Assistant director, Mackinac Island State Park Commission, Michigan, U.S.A.
Josiah Bleakley. Arent Schuyler DePeyster. Alexander Henry. John Johnston. David Mitchell.

ARTHUR, ELIZABETH. Professor emeritus of history, Lakehead University, Thunder Bay, Ontario.
Francis Maseres.

†BABIN, BASILE J., C.J.M. Ex-archiviste, Maison provinciale des Pères eudistes, Charlesbourg, Québec.
François-Gabriel Le Courtois.

BAILLARGEON, NOËL. Historien, Séminaire de Québec, Québec.
Antoine-Bernardin Robert.

BALLSTADT, CARL P. A. Professor of English, McMaster University, Hamilton, Ontario.
Wyllys Smyth.

BARRETTE, ROGER. Chef de service, Ministère de la Main-d'œuvre du Québec, Québec.
Jean-Baptiste-Philippe-Charles d'Estimauville.

BEASLEY, DAVID R. Research librarian, The Research Libraries, New York Public Library, New York, U.S.A.
Andrew Westbrook.

BEAUREGARD, YVES. Étudiant au doctorat en histoire, Université Laval, Québec, Québec.
Étienne Ranvoyzé.

BECK, J. MURRAY. Professor emeritus of political science, Dalhousie University, Halifax, Nova Scotia.
William Hersey Otis Haliburton. John Howe.

BENSLEY, EDWARD HORTON. Honorary Osler librarian and honorary lecturer in the history of medicine, McGill University, Montreal, Quebec.
William Caldwell (1782–1833).

BERGERON, ADRIEN, S.S.S. Ex-professeur d'histoire de l'Église, Scholasticat du T. S. Sacrement, Montréal, Québec.
Étienne Hébert.

BERNARD, JEAN-PAUL. Professeur d'histoire, Université du Québec à Montréal, Québec.
Jean Dessaulles. Antoine Girouard.

BERNATCHEZ, GINETTE. Historienne, Charny, Québec.
William Green (1787–1832). James Irvine. Antoine-Louis Juchereau Duchesnay.

BERNIER, JACQUES. Professeur agrégé d'histoire, Université Laval, Québec, Québec.
François Blanchet.

BERVIN, GEORGE. Historien et chercheur, Sillery, Québec.
William Burns [in collaboration with D. Roberts]. *Louis Gauvreau.*

BILSON, GEOFFREY. Professor of history, University of Saskatchewan, Saskatoon, Saskatchewan.
James Macaulay.

BIRD, MICHAEL S. Associate professor of religious studies, University of Waterloo, Ontario.
Abraham Erb.

†BLAKELEY, PHYLLIS R. Formerly archivist emeritus, Public Archives of Nova Scotia, Halifax, Nova Scotia.
Charles Baker.

†BLAKEY SMITH, DOROTHY. Formerly archivist, Provincial Archives of British Columbia, Victoria, British Columbia.
Æmilius Simpson.

BOSSÉ, ÉVELINE. Professeure à la retraite, Québec, Québec.
Pascal Taché [in collaboration].

BOULIANNE, RÉAL G. Associate professor of education, McGill University, Montreal, Quebec.
Joseph Langley Mills.

BROCK, DANIEL J. Teacher, Catholic Central High School, London, Ontario.
Thomas Hornor. Henry Sovereene.

BRODE, PATRICK. Lawyer, Windsor, Ontario.
Anne Powell. James Gordon Strobridge.

BROWN, JENNIFER STACEY HARCOURT. Associate professor of history, University of Winnipeg, Manitoba.
John Hodgson. John McDonald. Thomas Vincent.

BROWN, WALLACE. Professor of history, University of New Brunswick, Fredericton, New Brunswick.
William Cobbett.

BRUN, RÉGIS S. Recherchiste, Musée acadien, Université de

Moncton, Nouveau-Brunswick.
Joseph Gueguen.

BUCKNER, PHILLIP. Professor of history, University of New Brunswick, Fredericton, New Brunswick.
John Murray Bliss. Jonathan Bliss. John Edward Carmichael. Ward Chipman. George Ludlow Wetmore. Thomas Wetmore. Sir Aretas William Young.

BUGGEY, SUSAN. Chief, Historical Services, Parks Canada, Winnipeg, Manitoba.
James Drummond MacGregor. John Merrick.

BUMSTED, J. M. Professor of history, University of Manitoba, Winnipeg, Manitoba.
Benjamin Chappell. Cæsar Colclough. Alexander Crawford. Robert Gray. Walter Johnstone. Angus Macaulay. Alexander Macdonell (Greenfield). William Roubel. Thomas Tremlett [in collaboration with K. Matthews]. *Alexander Walker.*

BURANT, JIM. Chief, Collections management section, Picture Division, Public Archives of Canada, Ottawa, Ontario.
Robert Hood.

BURGESS, JOANNE. Professeure d'histoire, Université du Québec à Montréal, Québec.
Benaiah Gibb.

BURLEY, EDITH I. Graduate student in history, University of Manitoba, Winnipeg, Manitoba.
Alexander MacDonell.

BURNS, ROBERT J. Historian, Parks Canada, Ottawa, Ontario.
Thomas Ridout.

BURNS, ROBIN B. Associate professor of history, Bishop's University, Lennoxville, Quebec.
Robert Quirk Short.

BURROUGHS, PETER. Professor of history, Dalhousie University, Halifax, Nova Scotia.
Sir Francis Nathaniel Burton. Sir Alured Clarke. Sir John Coape Sherbrooke.

BUSH, EDWARD F. Formerly historian, Parks Canada, Ottawa, Ontario.
Robert Drummond.

BUTLER, DARREL N. Curator, Kings Landing Historical Settlement, Fredericton, New Brunswick.
Frederick Dibblee. Daniel Morehouse.

CAHILL, J. B. Manuscripts archivist, Public Archives of Nova Scotia, Halifax, Nova Scotia.
Alexander Brymer. Sir Andrew Snape Hamond. Charles Hill.

CAMERON, CHRISTINA. Chief, Architectural History Division, Parks Canada, Ottawa, Ontario.
John Cannon.

CAMERON, WENDY. Partner, Wordforce, Toronto, Ontario.
Roswell Mount.

CANDOW, JAMES E. Project historian, Parks Canada, Halifax, Nova Scotia.
Hugh Graham.

CARTER-EDWARDS, DENNIS. Research historian, Parks Canada, Cornwall, Ontario.
George Ironside. Solomon Jones. Shawanakiskie.

CASTONGUAY, JACQUES. Doyen des études collégiales, Collège militaire royal de Saint-Jean, Saint-Jean-sur-Richelieu, Québec.
Pierre-Ignace Aubert de Gaspé.

CHABOT, RICHARD. Chercheur libre, Laval, Québec.

Charles-Jean-Baptiste Bouc. Louis Bourdages. Jean-François Hébert.

CHAPUT, DONALD. Curator of history, Natural History Museum, Los Angeles, California, U.S.A.
Joseph Bailly. Jean-Baptiste Nolin.

CHARD, DONALD F. Historic parks planner, Parks Canada, Halifax, Nova Scotia.
Charles Morris.

CHASSÉ, BÉATRICE. Historienne, Ministère des Affaires culturelles du Québec, Québec.
Jacques Labrie.

CHASSÉ, SONIA. Étudiante au doctorat en histoire, Université Laval, Québec, Québec.
Étienne Le Blanc.

CHAUSSÉ, GILLES, s.J. Professeur d'histoire de l'Église, Université de Montréal, Québec.
Jean-Charles Bédard. Augustin Chaboillez. Jean-Henry-Auguste Roux. Pierre-Antoine Tabeau.

CHIASSON, PAULETTE M. Rédactrice-historienne, *Dictionnaire biographique du Canada/Dictionary of Canadian biography*, Les Presses de l'université Laval, Québec, Québec.
Patrick Campbell. André Doucet.

CHRISTIE, CARL A. Historian, Directorate of History, National Defence, Ottawa, Ontario.
Joseph Wanton Morrison. Robert Pilkington.

CLARKE, JOHN. Professor of geography, Carleton University, Ottawa, Ontario.
Sarah Ainse (Montour; Maxwell; Willson). James Baby.

CLOUTIER, NICOLE. Conservatrice de l'art canadien ancien, Musée des beaux-arts de Montréal, Québec.
Louis Quévillon.

CONDON, ANN GORMAN. Associate professor of history, University of New Brunswick, Saint John, New Brunswick.
George Leonard.

COOKE, W. MARTHA E. Consulting curator of Canadian historical art, Winnipeg, Manitoba.
Sir George Bulteel Fisher.

COURVILLE, SERGE. Professeur agrégé de géographie, Université Laval, Québec, Québec.
Charles de Saint-Ours.

CRATHORNE, ETHEL A. Formerly administrative secretary, Nova Scotia Civil Service Commission, Halifax, Nova Scotia.
John Crosskill.

CUTHBERTSON, BRIAN C. Head, Heritage Unit, Department of Culture, Recreation and Fitness, Halifax, Nova Scotia.
John Payzant. Richard John Uniacke (1753–1830). Richard John Uniacke (1789–1834).

CUTTER, DONALD C. O'Connor professor of Spanish colonial history of Texas and the Southwest, St Mary's University, San Antonio, Texas, U.S.A.
Tomás de Suria.

CYR, CÉLINE. Rédactrice-historienne, *Dictionnaire biographique du Canada/Dictionary of Canadian biography*, Les Presses de l'université Laval, Québec, Québec.
Ignace-Michel-Louis-Antoine d'Irumberry de Salaberry. Jean-Baptiste Juchereau Duchesnay. [Biographies written in collaboration with M. Guitard.] *Nicolas-François Mailhot. Marie-Geneviève Noël (Drapeau). Louis Pla-*

mondon. *Louis Turgeon. Josias Wurtele.*

DALTON, ROY C. Formerly professor of history, Bethel College, St Paul, Minnesota, U.S.A.
William Bacheler Coltman [in collaboration].

DAVIES, GWENDOLYN. Head, Department of English, and associate, Centre for Canadian Studies, Mount Allison University, Sackville, New Brunswick.
William Green (fl. 1783–1833).

DAY, RÉGINALD. Directeur de la correspondance et de la rédaction, Cabinet du premier ministre du Québec, Québec.
Edward O'Hara.

DEROME, ROBERT. Professeur d'histoire de l'art, Université du Québec à Montréal, Québec.
Marie-Catherine Delezenne (Pélissier; Sales Laterrière).
Charles Duval [in collaboration with M. Henshaw].
Salomon Marion [in collaboration with J. Ménard].
Dominique Rousseau.

DESBARATS, AILEEN. Bibliothécaire de cartes, Bibliothèque Morisset, Université d'Ottawa, Ontario.
Pierre-Édouard Desbarats [in collaboration with J.-M. Lebel].

DÉSILETS, ANDRÉE. Professeure d'histoire, Université de Sherbrooke, Québec.
Henry Cull.

DESJARDINS, MARC. Chercheur, Institut québécois de recherche sur la culture, Québec, Québec.
John Janvrin.

DESLAURIERS, PETER. Teacher of history, Dawson College, and doctoral student in history, Concordia University, Montreal, Quebec.
John Fleming.

DEVEAU, J. ALPHONSE. Directeur, Centre acadien, Université Sainte-Anne, Church Point, Nouvelle-Écosse.
Joseph Dugas.

DEVER, ALAN. Television reporter, Canadian Broadcasting Corporation, Laval, Quebec.
Pierre Guerout. Jean-Baptiste Raymond.

DOUGLAS, W. A. B. Director, Directorate of History, National Defence, Ottawa, Ontario.
John Schank. Miller Worsley.

DRAKE, FREDERICK C. Professor of history, Brock University, St Catharines, Ontario.
Sir John Borlase Warren.

DUCHESNE, RAYMOND. Professeur d'histoire et de sociologie, Télé-Université, Université du Québec, Québec.
Thomas Delvecchio.

DUCLOS, LAURETTE, S.G.M. Archiviste, Archives des Sœurs Grises, Montréal, Québec.
Thérèse-Geneviève Coutlée.

DUFOUR, PIERRE. Historien, Québec, Québec.
Joseph Dufour, dit Bona. Pierre-Jean de Sales Laterrière.

DUNLOP, ALLAN C. Associate provincial archivist, Public Archives of Nova Scotia, Halifax, Nova Scotia.
Duncan Ross.

DUQUEMIN, COLIN KEATES. Consultant in outdoor studies, Niagara South Board of Education, Fonthill, Ontario.
John Darling.

EDWARDS, MARY JANE. Professor of English, and general editor at the Centre for Editing Early Canadian Texts, Carleton University, Ottawa, Ontario.
Adam Kidd.

EMMERSON, GEORGE S. Professor of engineering science,

University of Western Ontario, London, Ontario.
John Mactaggart.

ENNALS, PETER. Associate professor of geography, Mount Allison University, Sackville, New Brunswick.
Francis Brockell Spilsbury.

ERICKSON, VINCENT O. Professor of anthropology, University of New Brunswick, Fredericton, New Brunswick.
Joseph-Thomas Saint-Aubin. Pierre Tomah, known as Governor Tomah.

FAHEY, CURTIS. Editor, James Lorimer & Company Ltd, Publishers, Toronto, Ontario.
Abel Stevens.

FINGARD, JUDITH. Professor of history, Dalhousie University, Halifax, Nova Scotia.
Oliver Arnold. Robert Stanser.

FIRTH, EDITH G. Formerly head, Canadian History Department, Metropolitan Toronto Library, Ontario.
William Birdseye Peters. Elizabeth Russell.

FITZPATRICK, DIANE E. Librarian, Reference and Collections Development Department, University of Waterloo, Ontario.
William Gilkison.

FORTIER, MARIE-FRANCE. Historienne, Québec, Québec.
Zachary Macaulay. David Monro.

FOSTER, JOHN E. Professor of history, University of Alberta, Edmonton, Alberta.
William Auld.

FRANCIS, JACK P. Registrar and archivist, Anglican Church of Canada, Diocese of Ottawa, Ontario.
Brooke Bridges Stevens.

FRASER, ROBERT LOCHIEL. Hamilton, Ontario.
John Barclay. Cornelius Albertson Burley. John Burns. Sir William Campbell [in collaboration with R. J. Morgan]. *Peter Desjardins. Thomas Dorland. Bartemas Ferguson. Henry Floyd, known as Black Harry. Charles French. James Owen McCarthy. Abraham Markle. Robert Nichol. David McGregor Rogers. Mary Thompson. Ebenezer Washburn.*

FRENCH, GOLDWIN S. President, Victoria University, Toronto, Ontario.
William Black. Henry Ryan.

FRENETTE, YVES. Historien, Seattle, Washington, États-Unis.
Charles Desroches.

FROST, STANLEY BRICE. Director, History of McGill Project, McGill University, Montreal, Quebec.
François Desrivières.

GAGNON, SERGE. Professeur d'histoire, Université du Québec à Trois-Rivières, Québec.
Pierre Casgrain. Louis Labadie. Jacques Panet.

GALARNEAU, CLAUDE. Professeur titulaire d'histoire, Université Laval, Québec, Québec.
Jean-Antoine Bouthillier. Charles-Joseph Brassard Deschenaux. Jacques-Ladislas-Joseph de Calonne. Philippe-Jean-Louis Desjardins.

GALARNEAU, FRANCE. Rédactrice-historienne, *Dictionnaire biographique du Canada/Dictionary of Canadian biography*, Les Presses de l'université Laval, Québec, Québec.
Daniel Tracey.

GATES, LILLIAN FRANCIS. Ithaca, New York, U.S.A.
Asa Danforth.

GAUTHIER, RAYMONDE. Professeure d'histoire de l'art,

Université du Québec à Montréal, Québec.
Charles Jourdain.

GAUVIN, DANIEL. Bibliothécaire, Centre d'orientation et de réadaptation de Montréal, Québec.
Thomas Cary.

GILLEN, MOLLIE. Biographer, Toronto, Ontario.
Thérèse-Bernardine Montgenet, Comtesse de Montgenet, known as Mme de Saint-Laurent.

GOUGH, BARRY MORTON. Professor of history, Wilfrid Laurier University, Waterloo, Ontario.
Charles William Barkley.

GRANT, JOHN WEBSTER. Professor emeritus of church history, Victoria University, Toronto, Ontario.
Elkanah Holmes. Hester Ann Hubbard (Case).

GREENWOOD, F. MURRAY. Associate professor of history, University of British Columbia, Vancouver, British Columbia.
John Richardson. Stephen Sewell.

GUITARD, MICHELLE. Historienne-conseil, Québec, Québec.
Charles-Michel d'Irumberry de Salaberry. Ignace-Michel-Louis-Antoine d'Irumberry de Salaberry [in collaboration with C. Cyr]. Jean-Baptiste Juchereau Duchesnay [in collaboration with C. Cyr].

GUNDY, H. PEARSON. Professor emeritus of English language and literature, Queen's University, Kingston, Ontario.
Francis Collins. Hugh Christopher Thomson.

HAINES, CEDRIC L. Solicitor, Mouth of Keswick, New Brunswick.
Otho Robichaux.

HAMELIN, MARCEL. Professeur titulaire d'histoire et doyen de la faculté des arts, Université d'Ottawa, Ontario.
Michel-Eustache-Gaspard-Alain Chartier de Lotbinière.

HANDCOCK, W. GORDON. Associate professor of geography, Memorial University of Newfoundland, St John's, Newfoundland.
John Bland. William Cull. George Garland. John Peyton.

HAREL, BRUNO, P.S.S. Archiviste, Séminaire de Saint-Sulpice, Montréal, Québec.
François Ciquard. Antoine-Jacques Houdet. Jean-Baptiste Marchand.

†HARPER, J. RUSSELL. South Lancaster, Ontario.
Peter Rindisbacher [in collaboration].

HARVEY, MARY M. Formerly curatorial assistant, History Section, Nova Scotia Museum, Halifax, Nova Scotia.
Gideon White.

HEADON, CHRISTOPHER FERGUS. Historian, West Wickham, Kent, England.
Richard Pollard.

HÉBERT, PIERRE-MAURICE, O.F.M. CAP. Archiviste, Archives des Capucins, Montréal, Québec.
Jean-Baptiste Bro.

†HENSHAW, MARY. Montreal, Quebec.
Charles Duval [in collaboration with R. Derome].

HEWSON, JOHN. Professor of linguistics, Memorial University of Newfoundland, St John's, Newfoundland.
Sylvester Joe. John Leigh.

HOENIGER, JUDITH F. M. Associate professor of microbiology, University of Toronto, Ontario.
Thomas Drummond.

HOLLAND, CLIVE. Historian, Scott Polar Research Institute, Cambridge, England.

Henry Parkyns Hoppner.

HOLMAN, HARRY TINSON. Consulting archivist, Ottawa, Ontario.
John Cambridge. James Bardin Palmer. Charles Wright.

HOLMGREN, ERIC J. Historical consultant, Edmonton, Alberta.
Jacques-Raphaël Finlay.

HOSKINS, RONALD GERALD. Associate professor of history, University of Windsor, Ontario.
Angus Mackintosh of Mackintosh, 26th Chief of Clan Chattan and 25th Chief of Clan Mackintosh.

HOWELL, COLIN D. Professor of history, Saint Mary's University, Halifax, Nova Scotia.
Joseph Norman Bond.

HYATT, A. M. J. Professor of history, University of Western Ontario, London, Ontario.
Henry Procter.

INGERSOLL, L. K. Director emeritus of museology, Fredericton, New Brunswick.
Moses Gerrish. David Owen.

JACKSON, JOHN C. Independent scholar, Portland, Oregon, U.S.A.
Donald Mackay.

JANSON, GILLES. Archiviste, Université du Québec à Montréal, Québec.
James Fisher. Henry Nicholas Christopher Loedel. François-Xavier Tessier.

JANZEN, CAROL ANNE. Businesswoman, Kentville, Nova Scotia.
William Paine.

JEAN, MARGUERITE, S.C.I.M. Coordonnatrice, *la Revue internationale de l'Union internationale des supérieures générales*, Rome, Italie.
Marie-Anne Paquet, named de Saint-Olivier.

JONES, ELWOOD H. Professor of history, Trent University, Peterborough, Ontario.
Duncan McCall.

JONES, FREDERICK. Senior lecturer in business and professional studies, Dorset Institute of Higher Education, Bournemouth, England.
Lewis Amadeus Anspach [in collaboration with G. M. Story].

KALLMANN, HELMUT. Chief, Music Division, National Library of Canada, Ottawa, Ontario.
John Chrisostomus Brauneis. Guillaume-Joseph Mechtler.

KAREL, DAVID. Professeur agrégé d'histoire, Université Laval, Québec, Québec.
François Baillairgé [in collaboration with L. Noppen and M. Paradis].

KELSAY, ISABEL T. Free-lance historian, Media, Pennsylvania, U.S.A.
Tekarihogen (John Brant).

KENDALL, JOHN C. Professor and chairman, Department of History, California State University, Fresno, California, U.S.A.
Gother Mann. William Twiss.

KERNAGHAN, LOIS KATHLEEN. Historical researcher and editor, Boutilier's Point, Nova Scotia.
Mary Cannon. Wellwood Waugh.

KLINCK, CARL F. Professor emeritus of English, University of Western Ontario, London, Ontario.
John Norton. Samuel Hull Wilcocke.

864

c:no

KULISEK, LARRY L. Associate professor and head, Department of History, University of Windsor, Ontario.
William Caldwell (d. 1822).

LABERGE, ANDRÉ. Étudiant au doctorat en histoire de l'art, Université Laval, Québec, Québec.
Olivier Dugal.

LABRÈQUE, MARIE-PAULE R. Présidente, Société d'histoire des Six-Cantons, Acton-Vale, Québec.
Avery Denison. Gilbert Hyatt. Charles Kilborn. Ralph Merry. Jesse Pennoyer. John Savage. Samuel Willard.

LAHEY, RAYMOND J. Bishop, Diocese of St George's, Corner Brook, Newfoundland.
Thomas Anthony Ewer. John Power. Thomas Scallan.

LAMB, J. WILLIAM. Psychotherapist, United Church minister, and president, Canadian Methodist Historical Society, Toronto, Ontario.
William Losee.

LAMBERT, JAMES H. Rédacteur-historien, *Dictionnaire biographique du Canada/Dictionary of Canadian biography*, Les Presses de l'université Laval, Québec, Québec.
David David [in collaboration with E. K. Senior]. *James McCallum. Archibald McMillan* [in collaboration with D. S. Macmillan]. *Sir James Monk. Joseph-Octave Plessis.*

LANDRY, PIERRE B. Conservateur adjoint de l'art canadien, Musée des beaux-arts du Canada, Ottawa, Ontario.
Elizabeth Frances Amherst (Hale).

LANGELIER, GILLES. Archiviste, Collection nationale de cartes et plans, Archives publiques du Canada, Ottawa, Ontario.
Jeremiah McCarthy.

LAUZIER, ROCH. Travailleur autonome, Matane, Québec.
Augustin-Jérôme Raby.

LEBEL, JEAN-MARIE. Chargé de recherche, Groupe de recherche sur la production des catéchismes, Université Laval, Québec, Québec.
Pierre-Édouard Desbarats [in collaboration with A. Desbarats]. *Charles Lefrançois.*

LEE, DAVID. Historian, Parks Canada, Ottawa, Ontario.
Charles Robin.

LEFEBVRE, JEAN-JACQUES. Ex-archiviste en chef, Cour supérieure, Montréal, Québec.
Paul-Théophile Pinsonaut. Jacques-Philippe Saveuse de Beaujeu.

LEGAULT, ROCH. Étudiant à la maîtrise en histoire, Université de Montréal, Québec.
Louis-René Chaussegros de Léry.

LEIGHTON, J. DOUGLAS. Associate professor of history, University of Western Ontario, London, Ontario.
Joseph-Maurice Lamothe. Claude-Nicolas-Guillaume de Lorimier.

LEMON, DONALD P. Assistant head, Library and Archives Department, New Brunswick Museum, Saint John, New Brunswick.
Alexander McDonald.

LESSARD, RENALD. Archiviste de référence, Archives nationales du Québec, Québec.
Joseph Badeaux [in collaboration with J. Prince]. *Edmond-Victor de Koenig, Baron von Koenig. Charles-Norbert Perrault. Louis Picotte. George Selby.*

LEWIS, WALTER. Assistant chief librarian, Halton Hills Public Library, Georgetown, Ontario.
James McKenzie. James Richardson.

L'HEUREUX, JACQUES. Professeur titulaire de droit, Université Laval, Québec, Québec.
Sir William Grant. Olivier Perrault.

LITTLE, JOHN I. Associate professor of history, Simon Fraser University, Burnaby, British Columbia.
Samuel Gale.

LORTIE, JEANNE D'ARC, s.c.o. Professeure à la retraite, Ottawa, Ontario.
Joseph-Isidore Bédard.

LOWNSBROUGH, JOHN. Writer, Toronto, Ontario.
D'Arcy Boulton.

McCALLA, DOUGLAS. Professor of history, Trent University, Peterborough, Ontario.
Laurent Quetton St George.

MACDONALD, ALLAN J. Supervisor, Private Manuscripts, Archives of Ontario, Toronto, Ontario.
Hugh McDonell (Aberchalder). Neil McLean.

MACDONALD, G. EDWARD. Editor, *Island Magazine*, Prince Edward Island Museum and Heritage Foundation, Charlottetown, Prince Edward Island.
Angus Bernard MacEachern.

McDOUGALL, ELIZABETH ANN KERR. Research historian, Westmount, Quebec.
Robert Easton. John Young.

†MACKAY, DONALD C. Halifax, Nova Scotia.
Joseph Brown Comingo [in collaboration with S. R. Paikowsky]. *Benjamin Etter.*

MACLEAN, RAYMOND A. Professor of history, St Francis Xavier University, Antigonish, Nova Scotia.
François Lejamtel.

MACMILLAN, DAVID S. Professor of history, Trent University, Peterborough, Ontario.
John Black. John McKindlay. Archibald McMillan [in collaboration with J. H. Lambert]. *Robert Pagan* [in collaboration with R. Nason]. *Christopher Scott.*

MACPHERSON, IAN. Professor of history, University of Victoria, British Columbia.
William Buell.

MANNION, JOHN. Associate professor of geography, Memorial University of Newfoundland, St John's, Newfoundland.
Henry Shea.

MARCIL, EILEEN. Historian, Charlesbourg, Quebec.
John Goudie.

†MATTHEWS, KEITH. Formerly professor of history, and chairman of the Maritime History Group, Memorial University of Newfoundland, St John's, Newfoundland.
Marmaduke Hart. James MacBraire. Thomas Tremlett [in collaboration with J. M. Bumsted].

MAYS, HERBERT J. Associate professor and chairman, Department of History, University of Winnipeg, Manitoba.
Miles Macdonell.

MEALING, S. R. Professor of history, Carleton University, Ottawa, Ontario.
John McGill. William Osgoode. William Dummer Powell. John Small. Samuel Smith.

MÉNARD, JOSÉ. Montréal, Québec.
Salomon Marion [in collaboration with R. Derome].

MICHAUD, NELSON. Adjoint législatif, Cabinet de la secrétaire parlementaire à l'Expansion industrielle régionale,

Chambre des communes, Ottawa, Ontario.
François Malherbe.

MILLER, CARMAN. Associate professor of history, McGill University, Montreal, Quebec.
John Gray. Thomas Porteous.

MILLMAN, THOMAS R. Formerly archivist, Anglican Church of Canada, Toronto, Ontario.
Jacob Mountain.

MIMEAULT, MARIO. Professeur, École secondaire Antoine Roy, Gaspé, Québec.
Benjamin Hobson. Azariah Pritchard.

MITCHELL, ELAINE ALLAN. Toronto, Ontario.
Æneas Cameron. Alexander McDougall. John Thomas.

MOMRYK, MYRON. Archivist, Manuscript Division, Public Archives of Canada, Ottawa, Ontario.
Charles Oakes Ermatinger. Frederick William Ermatinger. Daniel Sutherland.

MOOGK, PETER N. Associate professor of history, University of British Columbia, Vancouver, British Columbia.
Edward William McBride. Joseph-Geneviève de Puisaye, Comte de Puisaye.

MORGAN, ELIZABETH M. Historian, Eden Mills, Ontario.
Joel Stone.

MORGAN, ROBERT J. Director, Beaton Institute, University College of Cape Breton, Sydney, Nova Scotia.
Sir William Campbell [in collaboration with R. L. Fraser]. *Joseph Frederick Wallet DesBarres. John Despard. Archibald Charles Dodd. Laurence Kavanagh. John Murray. Nicholas Nepean.*

MORRIS, JULIE. Archivist, Public Archives of Nova Scotia, Halifax, Nova Scotia.
Sarah Deblois (Deblois) [in collaboration with W. L. Thorpe].

NASON, ROGER. Historical research consultant, Fredericton, New Brunswick.
John Jones. Robert Pagan [in collaboration with D. S. Macmillan].

NEARY, PETER. Professor of history, University of Western Ontario, London, Ontario.
John Reeves.

NICKS, JOHN. Associate, Lord Cultural Resources Planning and Management Inc., Toronto, Ontario.
William Tomison.

NOPPEN, LUC. Professeur titulaire d'histoire de l'art, Université Laval, Québec, Québec.
François Baillairgé [in collaboration with D. Karel and M. Paradis].

O'FLAHERTY, PATRICK. Professor of English, Memorial University of Newfoundland, St John's, Newfoundland.
Sir Richard Goodwin Keats. James Lundrigan. William Waldegrave, 1st Baron Radstock.

OUELLET, FERNAND. Professeur d'histoire, York University, Downsview, Ontario.
Pierre-Stanislas Bédard. Benjamin Joseph Frobisher. William McGillivray. Henry McKenzie.

PAIKOWSKY, SANDRA ROSLYN. Associate professor of art history, and curator of Concordia Art Gallery, Concordia University, Montreal, Quebec.
Joseph Brown Comingo [in collaboration with D. C. Mackay].

PARADIS, MAGELLA. Conservateur, Musée du séminaire de Québec, Québec.

François Baillairgé [in collaboration with D. Karel and L. Noppen].

PARKER, BRUCE A. Teacher, Port Hope High School, Ontario.
Thomas Clark [in collaboration with B. G. Wilson].

PARKER, GEORGE L. Professor of English, Royal Military College of Canada, Kingston, Ontario.
William Minns.

PASTORE, RALPH T. Associate professor of history, Memorial University of Newfoundland, St John's, Newfoundland.
Shawnadithit [in collaboration with G. M. Story].

PATTERSON, GRAEME H. Associate professor of history, University of Toronto, Ontario.
Barnabas Bidwell. Asahel Bradley Lewis.

PAYMENT, DIANE PAULETTE. Historienne, Parcs Canada, Winnipeg, Manitoba.
Jean-Baptiste Letendre, dit Batoche.

PEEL, BRUCE. Librarian emeritus, University of Alberta, Edmonton, Alberta.
Thomas Thomas.

PIGOT, F. L. Reference librarian, Robertson Library, University of Prince Edward Island, Charlottetown, Prince Edward Island.
John Stewart.

†PLANTE, HERMANN. Ex-archiviste, Archives du séminaire Saint-Joseph, Trois-Rivières, Québec.
Phebe Arnoldi, named de Sainte-Angèle (Diehl).

POTHIER, BERNARD. Curator of historical resources, Canadian War Museum, Ottawa, Ontario.
Jean-Baptiste Duberger.

POULIN, PIERRE. Assistant de recherche, Institut québécois de recherche sur la culture, Québec, Québec.
François Huot.

PRINCE, JEAN. Généalogiste professionnel, Trois-Rivières, Québec.
Joseph Badeaux [in collaboration with R. Lessard].

PRINCE, SUZANNE. Professeure de lettres françaises, Collège Mérici, Québec, Québec.
Marie-Anne-Louise Taschereau, named de Saint-François-Xavier.

PROSS, CATHERINE. Free-lance librarian, Halifax, Nova Scotia.
Joseph Barss.

PROVOST, HONORIUS, PTRE. Archiviste à la retraite, Séminaire de Québec, et président, Société historique de Québec, Québec.
Joseph-Antoine Philippon. Jean-Thomas Taschereau. Thomas-Pierre-Joseph Taschereau.

PRYKE, KENNETH G. Professor of history, University of Windsor, Ontario.
George Benson Hall. John McGregor.

PUNCH, TERRENCE M. Vice-president, Royal Nova Scotia Historical Society, and president, Genealogical Institute of the Maritimes, Halifax, Nova Scotia.
Thomas Grace, named Father James. John M'Alpine. Adolphus Christoph Vieth.

RAUDZENS, GEORGE KARL. Senior lecturer in history, Macquarie University, North Ryde, New South Wales, Australia.
Friedrich DeGaugreben.

RAWLYK, GEORGE A. Professor of history, Queen's University, Kingston, Ontario.

Freeborn Garrettson.

READ, COLIN FREDERICK. Associate professor of history, University of Western Ontario, London, Ontario.
John Dennis.

REID, W. STANFORD. Professor emeritus of history, University of Guelph, Ontario.
Hubert-Joseph Lacroix. Nicolas-Eustache Lambert Dumont [in collaboration].

RICHARDSON, ARTHUR JOHN HAMPSON. Formerly assistant chief, Research Division, National Historic Parks and Sites Branch, Indian and Northern Affairs Canada, Ottawa, Ontario.
William Finlay.

RIOUX, CHRISTIAN. Archiviste, Archives publiques du Canada, Ottawa, Ontario.
James Thompson.

ROBB, ANDREW. Associate professor of history and Canadian studies, University of Prince Edward Island, Charlottetown, Prince Edward Island.
John George Pyke.

ROBERT, JEAN-CLAUDE. Professeur d'histoire, Université du Québec à Montréal, Québec.
Pierre Berthelet. Horatio Gates.

ROBERTS, DAVID. Manuscript editor, *Dictionary of Canadian biography/Dictionnaire biographique du Canada*, University of Toronto Press, Ontario.
François Bellet. William Burns [in collaboration with G. Bervin]. *Samuel Chaffey. Martin Chenneque. John Mure.*

ROBERTSON, MARION. Writer, Shelburne, Nova Scotia.
William Greenwood. John Sargent. Jacob Van Buskirk.

ROCHEFORT, MARTIN. Agent de recherche, Québec, Québec.
Joseph-Marie Godefroy de Tonnancour. Jacques Trullier, dit Lacombe.

ROLAND, CHARLES G. Jason A. Hannah professor of the history of medicine, McMaster University, Hamilton, Ontario.
Robert Kerr. John Mervin Nooth.

ROMNEY, PAUL. Historian, Baltimore, Maryland, U.S.A.
John Matthews. Robert Randal.

ROUSSEAU, LOUIS. Professeur de sciences religieuses, Université du Québec à Montréal, Québec.
Candide-Michel Le Saulnier.

ROWLEY, SUSAN D. M. Research fellow, Department of Anthropology, National Museum of Natural History, Smithsonian Institution, Washington, District of Columbia, U.S.A.
Tattannoeuck.

RUGGLE, RICHARD E. Rector, St Paul's Anglican Church, Norval, Ontario.
Kenwendeshon. Johannes Wenger.

SAUNDERS, ROBERT E. Education officer, Planning and Implementation Commission, Ontario Ministry of Education, Toronto, Ontario.
Elisha Beman.

SAUTTER, UDO. Professor of history, University of Windsor, Ontario.
John Frederick Traugott Gschwind.

SCOLLARD, ROBERT JOSEPH. Formerly archivist, University of St Michael's College, Toronto, Ontario.
Marie-Clotilde Raizenne, named *Marie de l'Incarnation.*

SENIOR, ELINOR KYTE. Assistant professor of history,

Acadia University, Wolfville, Nova Scotia.
Louis-Nicolas-Emmanuel de Bigault d'Aubreville. David David [in collaboration with J. H. Lambert]. *Thomas McCord.*

SHEPARD, CATHERINE J. Archivist, Archives of Ontario, Toronto, Ontario.
Thomas Fraser. Charles McDonald.

SHEPPERSON, GEORGE A. William Robertson professor of Commonwealth and American history, University of Edinburgh, Scotland.
Andrew Brown.

SHIPLEY, ROBERT J. M. Executive administrator, Welland Canals Preservation Association, St Catharines, Ontario.
John Walden Meyers.

SIROIS, FRANCE BOUTIN. Archiviste, Archives de la ville de Québec, Québec.
James Shepherd.

SLOAN, W. A. Part-time instructor, Department of Social Sciences, Selkirk College, Castlegar, British Columbia.
Aw-gee-nah.

SMITH, DONALD B. Associate professor of history, University of Calgary, Alberta.
Ogimauh-binaessih. Tehowagherengaraghkwen. Tekarihogen (Henry).

SPRAY, WILLIAM A. Vice-president (academic), St Thomas University, Fredericton, New Brunswick.
Stair Agnew. James Fraser. John Saunders.

STAGG, RONALD J. Professor of history, Ryerson Polytechnical Institute, Toronto, Ontario.
Peter Lossing.

STANLEY, LAURIE C. C. Doctoral student in history, Queen's University, Kingston, Ontario.
Donald Macpherson.

STEPPLER, GLENN A. Baie d'Urfé, Quebec.
Sir Thomas Sydney Beckwith. James Green.

STORY, G. M. Professor of English, Memorial University of Newfoundland, St John's, Newfoundland.
Lewis Amadeus Anspach [in collaboration with F. Jones]. *Shawnadithit* [in collaboration with R. T. Pastore].

SUTHERLAND, D. A. Associate professor of history, Dalhousie University, Halifax, Nova Scotia.
John Butler Butler (Dight). Lawrence Hartshorne. William Sabatier. Michael Wallace.

SUTHERLAND, STUART R. J. Toronto, Ontario.
Adam Charles Muir.

TAYLOR, M. BROOK. Historian, Willowdale, Ontario.
William Johnston.

TEATERO, BARBARA. Curator, Special Collections, Douglas Library, Queen's University, Kingston, Ontario.
Robert-Anne d'Estimauville.

TEATERO, WILLIAM. Policy analyst, Ontario Ministry of Health, Kingston, Ontario.
George Mackenzie.

THÉRIAULT, YVON. Chef, Division d'indexation, Bibliothèque de l'Assemblée nationale du Québec, Québec.
Louis Lagueux. William Lindsay. François Romain.

THOMAS, EARLE. Free-lance historian and writer, Kingston, Ontario.
Sir John Johnson.

THOMPSON, FREDERIC FRASER. Professor emeritus of history, Royal Military College of Canada, Kingston,

Ontario.
James Gambier, 1st Baron Gambier. John Holloway.
THOMPSON, JOHN BESWARICK. Writer and historian, Low, Quebec.
William Nelson.
THORPE, WENDY LISBETH. Manuscript archivist, Public Archives of Nova Scotia, Halifax, Nova Scotia.
Sarah Deblois (Deblois) [in collaboration with J. Morris].
TRATT, GERTRUDE E. N. Teacher, Halifax, Nova Scotia.
Theophilus Chamberlain. Anthony Henry Holland.
TREMBLAY, ROBERT. Étudiant au doctorat en histoire, Université du Québec à Montréal, Québec.
James O'Donnell.
TUCK, ROBERT CRITCHLOW. Anglican clergyman, Georgetown, Prince Edward Island.
Theophilus Desbrisay.
TULCHINSKY, GERALD J. J. Professor of history, Queen's University, Kingston, Ontario.
Alexander Auldjo. George Garden.
TULLOCH, JUDITH. Historian, Parks Canada, Halifax, Nova Scotia.
Thomas Henry Barclay. James Fulton. Phineas Lovett. William Cottnam Tonge.
TUNIS, BARBARA R. Research historian, writer, and editor, Ottawa, Ontario.
William Holmes.
TURNER, H. E. Associate professor of history, McMaster University, Hamilton, Ontario.
Robert Addison.
TURNER, LARRY. Historical researcher and writer, Peterborough, and associate, Cardinal Research and Design, Manotick, Ontario.
Robert Clark.
TURNER, WESLEY B. Associate professor of history, Brock University, St Catharines, Ontario.
Francis de Rottenburg, Baron de Rottenburg.
TYRWHITT-DRAKE, MONTAGUE L. Judge, County Court of Vancouver Island, Victoria, British Columbia.
David Douglas [in collaboration].
†UPTON, L. F. S. Formerly professor of history, University of British Columbia, Vancouver, British Columbia.
Molly Ann Gell (Thomas).
VEILLEUX, CHRISTINE. Étudiante au doctorat en histoire, Université Laval, Québec, Québec.
Sir George Pownall.
VERRETTE, MICHEL. Professeur d'histoire, Collège Laflèche, Trois-Rivières, Québec.
Joseph-Bernard Planté.
VILLENEUVE, RENÉ. Étudiant au doctorat en histoire de l'art, Université Laval, Québec, Québec.
James Orkney.
VINCENT, THOMAS B. Professor of English, Royal Military College of Canada, Kingston, Ontario.
Thomas Daniel Cowdell. Samuel Denny Street. Grizelda Elizabeth Cottnam Tonge.

VOISINE, NIVE. Professeur à la retraite, Pointe-au-Père, Québec.
Bernard-Claude Panet.
WALLACE, CARL M. Professor and chairman, Department of History, Laurentian University, Sudbury, Ontario.
Munson Jarvis. George Kilman Lugrin.
WATERSTON, ELIZABETH. Professor of English, University of Guelph, Ontario.
Jocelyn Waller.
WEAVER, JOHN C. Professor of history, McMaster University, Hamilton, Ontario.
James Durand.
WEBSTER, T. STEWART. Professor emeritus of history, Queen's University, Kingston, Ontario.
François-Alexandre-Frédéric de La Rochefoucauld, Duc de La Rochefoucauld-Liancourt, Duc d'Estissac.
WHITE, BRUCE MCCANN. Historian, St Paul, Minnesota, U.S.A.
Joseph Cadotte.
WILLIAMS, GLYNDWR. Professor of history, University of London, England.
George Atkinson.
WILSON, BRUCE G. Liaison officer, Public Programs Branch, Public Archives of Canada, Ottawa, Ontario.
Thomas Clark [in collaboration with B. A. Parker]. *Ralfe Clench. Thomas Dickson. Isaac Swayze.*
WILSON, J. DONALD. Professor of the history of education, University of British Columbia, Vancouver, British Columbia.
Thomas Appleton. Richard Cockrell.
WITHAM, JOHN. Head, Historical Research, Parks Canada, Cornwall, Ontario.
Andrew White.
WOLFF, ANNETTE R. Writer and historian, Montreal, Quebec.
Henry Joseph.
WOODCOCK, GEORGE. Man of letters, and founder and former editor, *Canadian Literature*, Vancouver, British Columbia.
John Rodgers Jewitt. Alexander McKenzie.
WRIGHT, C. P. Wolfville, Nova Scotia.
William Cochran.
WYLIE, WILLIAM N. T. Historian, Parks Canada, Ottawa, Ontario.
Archibald Macdonell. Thomas Scott.
YOUNG, CAROLYN A. Doctoral student in the history of art, University of Toronto, Ontario.
George Best.
YOUNG, D. MURRAY. Professor of history, University of New Brunswick, Fredericton, New Brunswick.
Archibald McLean. Elijah Miles. George Stracey Smyth. James Taylor. William Taylor.

INDEX OF IDENTIFICATIONS

CATEGORIES

Agriculture

Architects

Armed forces

Artisans

Arts

Authors

Blacks

Business

Criminals

Education

Engineers

Explorers

Fur traders

Indigenous peoples

Interpreters and
translators

Inventors

Journalists

Labourers and labour
organizers

Legal professions

Mariners

Medicine

Miscellaneous

Office holders

Politicians

Religious

Scientists

Surveyors

Women

Index of Identifications

Like the network of cross-references within biographies, this index is designed to assist readers in following their interests through the volume. Most of the groupings are by occupations carried on either by persons within Canada or by native-born Canadians in other countries, but some have been established to help readers who approach the past from other perspectives. Thus WOMEN appear in one grouping, as do BLACKS, a reflection of the interest in their history; however, they may also be found under the occupations in which they engaged. The category INDIGENOUS PEOPLES includes Indians, listed by tribe, and Inuit. Readers interested in immigration or in the history of ethnic groups in Canada should consult the first part of the Geographical Index, where subjects are listed by their place of birth.

Some of the occupational categories require explanation so that users will be better able to find biographies of particular interest. Under AGRICULTURE is to be found a variety of people: "seigneurs" form a readily identifiable sub-group; the sub-division "developers" includes improvers, land agents, and those responsible for colonization; listed as "settlers" are individuals who pioneered in new territories; "farmers" comprise only those for whom farming was the prime occupation. Major landowners and individuals who speculated in seigneuries or other lands are to be found under "real estate" in the BUSINESS grouping. The category ARTS includes both fine and performing arts.

While some of the engineers and doctors in this volume are military officers and so appear under ARMED FORCES, they also appear separately as ENGINEERS or under MEDICINE. Surveyors, hydrographers, and cartographers are found under SURVEYORS. Although FUR TRADERS might have appeared under BUSINESS, they are given a separate listing for the benefit of readers interested in this aspect of the economy. Under MARINERS are included civilian captains, pilots, navigators, and fishermen; naval officers appear as a sub-group of ARMED FORCES. Within OFFICE HOLDERS, the sub-division "administrators" includes high-ranking officials: governors, lieutenant governors, and administrators. Individuals who escape easy classification are grouped under MISCELLANEOUS.

Readers following a particular interest may need to consult more than one grouping. Those interested, for example, in the history of education and medicine should consult, as well as EDUCATION and MEDICINE, the category RELIGIOUS. Biographies relevant to the history of town planning, architecture, and the building trades may be listed under ENGINEERS, ARCHITECTS, ARTISANS (masons, carpenters, etc.), and BUSINESS (contractors). Readers pursuing legal history should turn to both LEGAL PROFESSIONS and CRIMINALS.

The DCB/DBC attempts by its assignments to encourage research in new areas as well as familiar ones, but its selection of individuals to receive biographies reflects the survival of documentation and the areas historians have chosen to investigate. The index should not, therefore, be used for quantitative judgements; it is merely a guide to what is contained in volume VI.

AGRICULTURE

Developers

Cambridge, John
Cannon, Mary
Danforth, Asa
DesBarres, Joseph Frederick Wallet
Dessaulles, Jean
Dufour, *dit* Bona, Joseph
Fraser, Thomas

Gale, Samuel
Hornor, Thomas
Hyatt, Gilbert
Leonard, George
Lossing, Peter
McCord, Thomas
McKenzie, Henry
McKindlay, John
McMillan, Archibald

Palmer, James Bardin
Pritchard, Azariah
Puisaye, Joseph-Geneviève de, Comte de Puisaye
Savage, John
Spilsbury, Francis Brockell
Stevens, Abel
Waugh, Wellwood
Willard, Samuel

ARCHITECTS

ARMED FORCES

873

BLACKS

BUSINESS

878

INTERPRETERS AND TRANSLATORS

Bouthillier, Jean-Antoine
Cadotte, Joseph
Desbarats, Pierre-Édouard

Finlay, Jacques-Raphaël
Gueguen, Joseph
Kenwendeshon

Norton, John
Tattannoeuck
Tessier, François-Xavier

INVENTORS

Cull, Henry

JOURNALISTS

Bédard, Pierre-Stanislas
Bouthillier, Jean-Antoine
Cary, Thomas
Cochran, William
Cockrell, Richard
Collins, Francis
Estimauville, Robert-Anne d'

Ferguson, Bartemas
Holland, Anthony Henry
Howe, John
Labrie, Jacques
Lewis, Asahel Bradley
Peters, William Birdseye
Smyth, Wyllys

Stevens, Brooke Bridges
Tessier, François-Xavier
Thomson, Hugh Christopher
Tracey, Daniel
Waller, Jocelyn
Wilcocke, Samuel Hull

LABOURERS AND LABOUR ORGANIZERS

Gell, Molly Ann (Thomas)
Gueguen, Joseph

Kain, William
Lundrigan, James

Peyton, John
Thompson, Mary

LEGAL PROFESSIONS

Judges

Agnew, Stair
Baby, James
Baker, Charles
Bédard, Pierre-Stanislas
Bland, John
Bliss, John Murray
Bliss, Jonathan
Bond, Joseph Norman
Boulton, D'Arcy
Campbell, Sir William
Chipman, Ward

Clench, Ralfe
Colclough, Cæsar
Dodd, Archibald Charles
Fraser, James
Fulton, James
Gray, Robert
Haliburton, William Hersey Otis
Hill, Charles
Jones, Solomon
Kavanagh, Laurence
Kerr, Robert
Lambert Dumont, Nicolas-Eustache
Lovett, Phineas

McLean, Neil
Miles, Elijah
Monk, Sir James
Nichol, Robert
Osgoode, William
Owen, David
Pagan, Robert
Perrault, Olivier
Pollard, Richard
Powell, William Dummer
Reeves, John
Robin, Charles
Sargent, John

POLITICIANS

Colonial and territorial

Appointed

Aubert de Gaspé, Pierre-Ignace
Baby, James
Barclay, Thomas Henry
Black, John
Bliss, John Murray
Bliss, Jonathan
Brymer, Alexander
Burns, William
Butler (Dight), John Butler
Campbell, Sir William
Chartier de Lotbinière, Michel-
   Eustache-Gaspard-Alain
Chaussegros de Léry, Louis-René
Chipman, Ward
Clark, Thomas
Claus, William
Coltman, William Bacheler
Desbrisay, Theophilus
Dessaulles, Jean
Dodd, Archibald Charles
Fraser, James
Fraser, Thomas
Gates, Horatio
Gray, Robert
Hartshorne, Lawrence
Hill, Charles
Irumberry de Salaberry, Charles-
   Michel d'
Irumberry de Salaberry, Ignace-
   Michel-Louis-Antoine d'
Irvine, James
Janvrin, John
Johnson, Sir John
Johnston, William
Juchereau Duchesnay, Antoine-Louis
Juchereau Duchesnay, Jean-Baptiste
Leonard, George
MacDonell, Alexander
McGill, John
McGillivray, William
Mackintosh of Mackintosh, Angus,
   26th Chief of Clan Chattan and 25th
   Chief of Clan Mackintosh
McLean, Neil
Monk, Sir James
Morris, Charles
Mountain, Jacob
Mure, John
Osgoode, William
Palmer, James Bardin
Perrault, Olivier
Plessis, Joseph-Octave
Powell, William Dummer
Pownall, Sir George
Richardson, John

Ridout, Thomas
Robinson, John
Saint-Ours, Charles de
Saunders, John
Saveuse de Beaujeu, Jacques-Philippe
Scott, Thomas
Smith, Samuel
Street, Samuel Denny
Taschereau, Jean-Thomas
Taschereau, Thomas-Pierre-Joseph
Thomas, Thomas
Turgeon, Louis
Uniacke, Richard John (1753–1830)
Uniacke, Richard John (1789–1834)
Wallace, Michael
Wetmore, Thomas

Elected

Agnew, Stair
Auldjo, Alexander
Badeaux, Joseph
Barclay, Thomas Henry
Bédard, Joseph-Isidore
Bédard, Pierre-Stanislas
Bellet, François
Bidwell, Barnabas
Black, John
Blanchet, François
Bliss, John Murray
Bliss, Jonathan
Bouc, Charles-Jean-Baptiste
Boulton, D'Arcy
Bourdages, Louis
Buell, William
Butler (Dight), John Butler
Campbell, Sir William
Cannon, John
Chappell, Benjamin
Chartier de Lotbinière, Michel-
   Eustache-Gaspard-Alain
Chipman, Ward
Clench, Ralfe
Dessaulles, Jean
Dickson, Thomas
Dorland, Thomas
Dufour, *dit* Bona, Joseph
Durand, James
Fanning, David
Fisher, James
Fraser, James
Fraser, Thomas
Frobisher, Benjamin Joseph
Fulton, James
Garden, George
Gauvreau, Louis
Godefroy de Tonnancour, Joseph-
   Marie
Guerout, Pierre

Haliburton, William Hersey Otis
Hall, George Benson
Hartshorne, Lawrence
Hill, Charles
Hornor, Thomas
Huot, François
Irumberry de Salaberry, Ignace-
   Michel-Louis-Antoine d'
Irvine, James
Jarvis, Munson
Johnston, Hugh
Johnston, William
Jones, Solomon
Juchereau Duchesnay, Antoine-Louis
Kavanagh, Laurence
Labrie, Jacques
Lacroix, Hubert-Joseph
Lagueux, Louis
Lambert Dumont, Nicolas-Eustache
Le Blanc, Étienne
Lorimier, Claude-Nicolas-Guillaume
   de
Lovett, Phineas
Macaulay, Angus
McBride, Edward William
McCall, Duncan
McCallum, James
McCord, Thomas
McDonell (Aberchalder), Hugh
Macdonell (Greenfield), Alexander
McGillivray, William
McGregor, John
McLean, Archibald
Markle, Abraham
Matthews, John
Miles, Elijah
Monk, Sir James
Monro, David
Morris, Charles
Mount, Roswell
Mure, John
Nichol, Robert
O'Hara, Edward
Owen, David
Pagan, Robert
Paine, William
Palmer, James Bardin
Picotte, Louis
Planté, Joseph-Bernard
Porteous, Thomas
Pyke, John George
Raby, Augustin-Jérôme
Randal, Robert
Ranvoyzé, Étienne
Raymond, Jean-Baptiste
Richardson, John
Ridout, Thomas
Robinson, John
Rogers, David McGregor

RELIGIOUS

SCIENTISTS

SURVEYORS

WOMEN

885

GEOGRAPHICAL INDEX

CANADA

Alberta

British Columbia
  Mainland
  Vancouver Island

Manitoba

New Brunswick

Newfoundland and Labrador
  Labrador
  Newfoundland

Northwest Territories

Nova Scotia
  Cape Breton Island
  Mainland

Ontario
  Centre
  East
  Niagara
  North
  Southwest

Prince Edward Island

Quebec
  Bas-Saint-Laurent–Gaspésie/
    Côte-Nord
  Montréal/Outaouais
  Nord-Ouest/Saguenay–Lac-Saint-Jean/
    Nouveau-Québec
  Québec
  Trois-Rivières/Cantons-de-l'Est

Saskatchewan

OTHER COUNTRIES

PLACE OF BIRTH

Africa
Bahamas
Belgium
Channel Islands
Federal Republic of Germany
France
German Democratic Republic
Germany
Gibraltar
Ireland
Italy
Poland
Republic of Ireland
Spain
Sweden

Switzerland
United Kingdom
United States of America
Windward Islands

CAREER

Guyana
India
Italy
Martinique
Netherlands
Republic of Ireland
United Kingdom
United States of America
West Indies

ONTARIO

I East
II Centre
III Niagara
IV Southwest
V North

QUEBEC

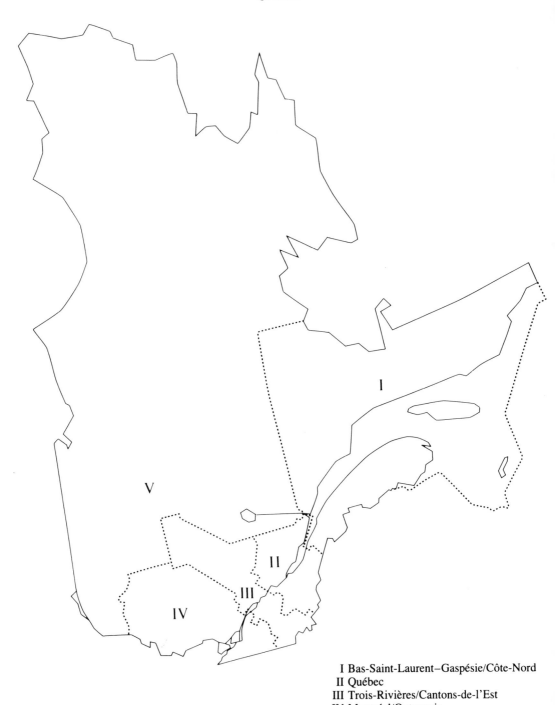

I Bas-Saint-Laurent–Gaspésie/Côte-Nord
II Québec
III Trois-Rivières/Cantons-de-l'Est
IV Montréal/Outaouais
V Nord-Ouest/Saguenay–Lac-Saint-Jean/
  Nouveau-Québec

Geographical Index

The Geographical Index, in two parts, provides a regional breakdown of subjects of biographies according to place of birth and according to career. Each part has two sub-sections: Canada and Other Countries.

For the purposes of this index, Canada is represented by the present provinces and territories, listed alphabetically. (The Yukon Territory does not appear here, however, since no one in volume VI lived in or visited the region.) Five provinces are further subdivided. British Columbia, Newfoundland and Labrador, and Nova Scotia each have two subdivisions. Ontario and Quebec appear in five subdivisions as shown on the maps; those for Quebec are based on the administrative regions defined by the Direction général du domaine territorial. The section Other Countries is based for the most part on modern political divisions, but overseas territories of European countries are listed separately. Only the United Kingdom is subdivided.

Place of Birth. This part of the index lists subjects of biographies by their birthplace, whether in Canada or elsewhere. Where only a strong probability of birth in a particular region exists, the name of the subject is followed by a question mark; where no such probability exists, names have not been included. It should be noted that the use of modern political divisions produces some anachronisms; a person born in Saxony, for example, appears under "German Democratic Republic." To accommodate those individuals whose place of birth is known only in general terms, additional listings – e.g. Ireland – have been provided; readers interested in Irish personalities or in immigration from Ireland should consult also "Republic of Ireland" and "United Kingdom: Northern Ireland."

Career. Subjects appear here on the basis of their activity as adults. Places of education, retirement, and death have not been considered. Persons whose functions gave them jurisdiction over several regions, such as a bishop or governor, are listed according to their seat of office, but their activities as described in the biographies have also been taken into consideration. Merchants appear only in the area of the primary location of their business, unless the biographies indicate active personal involvement in other regions. Explorers are found in the areas they discovered or visited. Only individuals who were born in the territory of present-day Canada and whose lives took them elsewhere are listed in the section Other Countries; they are listed under the country or countries in which they had a career or were active. "West Indies" has been used as a convenient grouping of careers in the Caribbean.

PLACE OF BIRTH

Canada

NEW BRUNSWICK

Gell, Molly Ann (Thomas) (?)
Lugrin, George Kilman
Taylor, William

Tomah, Pierre, known as Governor Tomah (?)

Wetmore, George Ludlow

NEWFOUNDLAND AND LABRADOR

Newfoundland

Cannon, John

Lundrigan, James

Shawnadithit

891

NORTHWEST TERRITORIES

Aw-gee-nah (?)

NOVA SCOTIA

Cape Breton Island

Estimauville, Jean-Baptiste-Philippe-
   Charles d'
Estimauville, Robert-Anne d'
Kavanagh, Laurence

Mainland

Barss, Joseph
Bro, Jean-Baptiste
Cannon, Mary (?)
Comingo, Joseph Brown
Dugas, Joseph
Haliburton, William Hersey Otis

Hébert, Étienne
Holland, Anthony Henry
Merrick, John
Robichaux, Otho
Taylor, James
Tonge, Grizelda Elizabeth Cottnam
Tonge, William Cottnam
Uniacke, Richard John (1789–1834)

ONTARIO

Centre

Ogimauh-binaessih
Thompson, Mary

East

Thomson, Hugh Christopher

Niagara

Burley, Cornelius Albertson (?)
McBride, Edward William

Southwest

Mount, Roswell
Tekarihogen (John Brant)

PRINCE EDWARD ISLAND

Wright, Charles

QUEBEC

Bas-Saint-Laurent–Gaspésie/
Côte-Nord

O'Hara, Edward

Montréal/Outaouais

Arnoldi, Phebe, named de Sainte-
   Angèle (Diehl)
Bailly, Joseph
Berthelet, Pierre
Bouc, Charles-Jean-Baptiste
Bouthillier, Jean-Antoine

Chaboillez, Augustin
Coutlée, Thérèse-Geneviève
David, David
Desrivières, François
Ermatinger, Charles Oakes
Frobisher, Benjamin Joseph
Girouard, Antoine
Jourdain, Charles
Lamothe, Joseph-Maurice
Letendre, dit Batoche, Jean-Baptiste
Lorimier, Claude-Nicolas-Guillaume
   de
Marchand, Jean-Baptiste

Marion, Salomon
Perrault, Charles-Norbert
Pinsonaut, Paul-Théophile
Plessis, Joseph-Octave
Powell, Anne
Quévillon, Louis
Raizenne, Marie-Clotilde, named
   Marie de l'Incarnation
Robert, Antoine-Bernardin
Tabeau, Pierre-Antoine
Trullier, dit Lacombe, Jacques

GEOGRAPHICAL INDEX

Nord-Ouest/Saguenay–Lac-Saint-Jean/Nouveau-Québec

Atkinson, George

Québec

Aubert de Gaspé, Pierre-Ignace
Baillairgé, François
Bédard, Jean-Charles
Bédard, Joseph-Isidore
Bédard, Pierre-Stanislas
Bellet, François
Blanchet, François
Bourdages, Louis
Brassard Deschenaux, Charles-Joseph
Casgrain, Pierre
Chartier de Lotbinière, Michel-Eustache-Gaspard-Alain
Delezenne, Marie-Catherine (Pélissier; Sales Laterrière)
Dufour, *dit* Bona, Joseph
Dugal, Olivier
Duval, Charles
Gauvreau, Louis
Green, William (1787–1832)

Hébert, Jean-François
Huot, François
Irumberry de Salaberry, Charles-Michel d'
Irumberry de Salaberry, Ignace-Michel-Louis-Antoine d'
Juchereau Duchesnay, Antoine-Louis
Juchereau Duchesnay, Jean-Baptiste
Labadie, Louis
Labrie, Jacques
Lacroix, Hubert-Joseph
Lagueux, Louis
Lefrançois, Charles
Mailhot, Nicolas-François
Malherbe, François
Noël, Marie-Geneviève (Drapeau)
Panet, Bernard-Claude
Panet, Jacques
Paquet, Marie-Anne, named de Saint-Olivier
Perrault, Olivier
Philippon, Joseph-Antoine
Plamondon, Louis
Planté, Joseph-Bernard
Raby, Augustin-Jérôme
Ranvoyzé, Étienne

Raymond, Jean-Baptiste
Romain, François
Rousseau, Dominique
Saint-Ours, Charles de
Saveuse de Beaujeu, Jacques-Philippe
Taché, Pascal
Taschereau, Jean-Thomas
Taschereau, Marie-Anne-Louise, named de Saint-François-Xavier
Taschereau, Thomas-Pierre-Joseph
Tessier, François-Xavier
Turgeon, Louis

Trois-Rivières/Cantons-de-l'Est

Badeaux, Joseph
Dessaulles, Jean
Doucet, André
Godefroy de Tonnancour, Joseph-Marie
Lambert Dumont, Nicolas-Eustache
Le Blanc, Étienne
Picotte, Louis
Sales Laterrière, Pierre-Jean de

SASKATCHEWAN

Finlay, Jacques-Raphaël (?)

Other Countries

AFRICA

Floyd, Henry, known as Black Harry

BAHAMAS

Gambier, James, 1st Baron Gambier

BELGIUM

Mechtler, Guillaume-Joseph

893

CHANNEL ISLANDS

Janvrin, John

Payzant, John

Robin, Charles

FEDERAL REPUBLIC OF GERMANY

Brauneis, John Chrisostomus
Loedel, Henry Nicholas Christopher (?)

Vieth, Adolphus Christoph

Wurtele, Josias

FRANCE

Calonne, Jacques-Ladislas-Joseph de
Chaussegros de Léry, Louis-René
Chenneque, Martin
Ciquard, François
Desjardins, Peter
Desjardins, Philippe-Jean-Louis
Desroches, Charles
Gueguen, Joseph

Guerout, Pierre
Houdet, Antoine-Jacques
La Rochefoucauld, François-
  Alexandre-Frédéric de, Duc de La
  Rochefoucauld-Liancourt, Duc
  d'Estissac
Le Courtois, François-Gabriel
Lejamtel, François

Le Saulnier, Candide-Michel
Montgenet, Thérèse-Bernardine,
  Comtesse de Montgenet, known as
  Mme de Saint-Laurent
Puisaye, Joseph-Geneviève de, Comte
  de Puisaye
Quetton St George, Laurent
Roux, Jean-Henry-Auguste

GERMAN DEMOCRATIC REPUBLIC

Gschwind, John Frederick Traugott

Koenig, Edmond-Victor de, Baron von
  Koenig

GERMANY

DeGaugreben, Friedrich (?)

GIBRALTAR

Russell, Elizabeth

IRELAND

Despard, John
French, Charles
Hall, George Benson

McCarthy, James Owen
Murray, John

Procter, Henry
Savage, John

UNITED STATES OF AMERICA

Agnew, Stair
Ainse, Sarah (Montour; Maxwell; Willson)
Arnold, Oliver
Baby, James
Baker, Charles
Barclay, Thomas Henry
Beman, Elisha
Bidwell, Barnabas
Bliss, John Murray
Bliss, Jonathan
Buell, William
Chamberlain, Theophilus
Chipman, Ward
Clark, Robert
Claus, William
Clench, Ralfe
Danforth, Asa
Darling, John
Deblois, Sarah (Deblois)
Denison, Avery
Dennis, John
DePeyster, Arent Schuyler
Dibblee, Frederick
Dorland, Thomas
Duberger, Jean-Baptiste
Erb, Abraham
Etter, Benjamin
Fanning, David
Ferguson, Bartemas

Field, Eleakim
Garrettson, Freeborn
Gates, Horatio
Gerrish, Moses
Greenwood, William
Hartshorne, Lawrence
Holmes, Elkanah
Hornor, Thomas
Howe, John
Hubbard, Hester Ann (Case)
Hyatt, Gilbert
Jarvis, Munson
Johnson, Sir John
Jones, Solomon
Kilborn, Charles
Leonard, George
Lewis, Asahel Bradley
Losee, William
Lossing, Peter
Lovett, Phineas (?)
McCall, Duncan
McKay, William
Markle, Abraham
Merry, Ralph
Meyers, John Walden
Miles, Elijah
Minns, William
Monk, Sir James
Morehouse, Daniel
Morris, Charles

Morrison, Joseph Wanton
Paine, William
Pennoyer, Jesse
Peters, William Birdseye
Powell, William Dummer
Pritchard, Azariah
Randal, Robert
Robinson, John
Rogers, David McGregor
Ryan, Henry
Sargent, John
Saunders, John
Sewell, Stephen
Shakóye:wa:tha?
Simonds, James
Smith, Samuel
Sovereene, Henry
Stevens, Abel
Stone, Joel
Strobridge, James Gordon
Swayze, Isaac
Tehowagherengaraghkwen
Tekarihogen (Henry)
Van Buskirk, Jacob
Washburn, Ebenezer
Wenger, Johannes
Westbrook, Andrew
Wetmore, Thomas
White, Gideon
Willard, Samuel

WINDWARD ISLANDS

Kain, William

CAREER

Canada

ALBERTA

Aw-gee-nah
Douglas, David
Drummond, Thomas
Fidler, Peter

Finlay, Jacques-Raphaël
Frobisher, Benjamin Joseph
Hood, Robert
Lamothe, Joseph-Maurice

Letendre, *dit* Batoche, Jean-Baptiste
McKenzie, Alexander
Shaw, Angus

897

BRITISH COLUMBIA

Mainland

Douglas, David
Drummond, Thomas
Finlay, Jacques-Raphaël
Lamothe, Joseph-Maurice

Simpson, Æmilius
Walker, Alexander

Vancouver Island

Barkley, Charles William

Eliza y Reventa, Francisco de
Jewitt, John Rodgers
Suria, Tomás de

MANITOBA

Auld, William
Aw-gee-nah
Cadotte, Joseph
Coltman, William Bacheler
Douglas, David
Ermatinger, Charles Oakes
Fidler, Peter
Frobisher, Benjamin Joseph
Hood, Robert

Letendre, *dit* Batoche, Jean-Baptiste
McDonald, John
MacDonell, Alexander
Macdonell, Miles
Macdonell (Greenfield), Alexander
McGillivray, William
Mackay, Donald
McKay, William
McKenzie, Alexander

Nolin, Jean-Baptiste
Rindisbacher, Peter
Shaw, Angus
Simpson, Æmilius
Tattannoeuck
Thomas, Thomas
Tomison, William
Vincent, Thomas

NEW BRUNSWICK

Agnew, Stair
Arnold, Oliver
Baker, Charles
Best, George
Black, John
Bliss, John Murray
Bliss, Jonathan
Calonne, Jacques-Ladislas-Joseph de
Campbell, Patrick
Chipman, Ward
Ciquard, François
Cobbett, William
Comingo, Joseph Brown
Dibblee, Frederick
Fanning, David
Fraser, James
Gell, Molly Ann (Thomas)

Gerrish, Moses
Girouard, Antoine
Grace, Thomas, named Father James
Green, William (fl. 1783–1833)
Gueguen, Joseph
Jarvis, Munson
Johnston, Hugh
Jones, John
Leonard, George
Lugrin, George Kilman
M'Coll, Duncan
McDonald, Alexander
McLean, Archibald
Miles, Elijah
Morehouse, Daniel
Owen, David
Pagan, Robert

Paine, William
Robichaux, Otho
Robinson, John
Saint-Aubin, Joseph-Thomas
Saunders, John
Scott, Christopher
Sewell, Stephen
Simonds, James
Smyth, George Stracey
Street, Samuel Denny
Taylor, James
Taylor, William
Tomah, Pierre, known as Governor
Tomah
Uniacke, Richard John (1753–1830)
Wetmore, George Ludlow
Wetmore, Thomas

NEWFOUNDLAND AND LABRADOR

Labrador

Power, John

Newfoundland

Anspach, Lewis Amadeus

Bland, John
Colclough, Cæsar
Cull, William

ONTARIO

901

SASKATCHEWAN

Other Countries

GUYANA

INDIA

ITALY

Tabeau, Pierre-Antoine

MARTINIQUE

Tonge, William Cottnam

NETHERLANDS

Irumberry de Salaberry, Charles-
Michel d'

REPUBLIC OF IRELAND

Irumberry de Salaberry, Charles-
Michel d'

UNITED KINGDOM

England

Irumberry de Salaberry, Charles-
Michel d'

Sales Laterrière, Pierre-Jean de
Tabeau, Pierre-Antoine

UNITED STATES OF AMERICA

Bailly, Joseph
Barss, Joseph
Berthelet, Pierre
Cadotte, Joseph
Chartier de Lotbinière, Michel-
Eustache-Gaspard-Alain

Ermatinger, Charles Oakes
Finlay, Jacques-Raphaël
Holland, Anthony Henry
Irumberry de Salaberry, Ignace-
Michel-Louis-Antoine d'

Lorimier, Claude-Nicolas-Guillaume
de
Marchand, Jean-Baptiste
Nolin, Jean-Baptiste
Rousseau, Dominique
Tessier, François-Xavier

WEST INDIES

Barss, Joseph

Irumberry de Salaberry, Charles-
Michel d'

O'Hara, Edward

904

NOMINAL INDEX

VOLUME I	1000–1700
VOLUME II	1701–1740
VOLUME III	1741–1770
VOLUME IV	1771–1800
VOLUME V	1801–1820
VOLUME VI	1821–1835
VOLUME VII	1836–1850
VOLUME VIII	1851–1860
VOLUME IX	1861–1870
VOLUME X	1871–1880
VOLUME XI	1881–1890
VOLUME XII	1891–1900

As of 1987 the following volumes have been published, volumes I–VI, VIII–XI, and an *Index, volumes I to IV*.

Nominal Index

Included in this index are the names of persons mentioned in volume VI. They are listed by their family names, with titles and first names following. Wives are entered under their maiden names with their married names in parenthesis. An asterisk indicates that the person has received a biography in a volume already published, or will probably receive one in a subsequent volume. The death date or last floruit date refers the reader to the volume in which the biography will be found. Numerals in bold face indicate the pages on which a biography appears. Titles, variants, and married and religious names are fully cross-referenced.

937

939

941

947